CHILTON'S

TOTAL CAR CARE REPAIR MANUAL

CHEVY/GMC FULL SIZE TRUCKS 1988-90 REPAIR MANUAL

CHILTON BOOK COMPANY
Chilton Way, Radnor, PA 19089
*ONE OF THE **ABC PUBLISHING COMPANIES**,*
*A PART OF **CAPITAL CITIES/ABC, INC.***

Manufactured in USA

Chilton Way, Radnor, PA 19089
ISBN 0–8019–8055–0
Library of Congress Catalog Card No. 90–055432
1234567890 9876543210

Contents

Contents

SAFETY NOTICE

Proper service and repair procedures are vital to the safe, reliable operation of all motor vehicles, as well as the personal safety of those performing repairs. This manual outlines procedures for servicing and repairing vehicles using safe, effective methods. The procedures contain many NOTES, CAUTIONS and WARNINGS which should be followed along with standard safety procedures to eliminate the possibility of personal injury or improper service which could damage the vehicle or compromise its safety.

It is important to note that the repair procedures and techniques, tools and parts for servicing motor vehicles, as well as the skill and experience of the individual performing the work vary widely. It is not possible to anticipate all of the conceivable ways or conditions under which vehicles may be serviced, or to provide cautions as to all of the possible hazards that may result. Standard and accepted safety precautions and equipment should be used when handling toxic or flammable fluids, and safety goggles or other protection should be used during cutting, grinding, chiseling, prying, or any other process that can cause material removal or projectiles.

Some procedures require the use of tools specially designed for a specific purpose. Before substituting another tool or procedure, you must be completely satisfied that neither your personal safety, nor the performance of the vehicle will be endangered

Although information in this manual is based on industry sources and is complete as possible at the time of publication, the possibility exists that some car manufacturers made later changes which could not be included here. While striving for total accuracy, Chilton Book Company cannot assume responsibility for any errors, changes or omissions that may occur in the compilation of this data.

PART NUMBERS

Part numbers listed in this reference are not recommendations by Chilton for any product by brand name. They are references that can be used with interchange manuals and aftermarket supplier catalogs to locate each brand supplier's discrete part number.

SPECIAL TOOLS

Special tools are recommended by the vehicle manufacturer to perform their specific job. Use has been kept to a minimum, but where absolutely necessary, they are referred to in the text by the part number of the tool manufacturer. These tools can be purchased under the appropriate part number, from your Chevrolet or GMC dealer or regional distributor or an equivalent tool can be purchased locally from a tool supplier or parts outlet. Before substituting any tool for the recommended one, read the SAFETY NOTICE at the top of this page.

ACKNOWLEDGMENTS

The Chilton Book Company expresses its appreciation to Chevrolet Motor Division, General Motors Corporation, Detroit, Michigan for their generous assistance.

1 General Information and Maintenance

QUICK REFERENCE INDEX

GENERAL INDEX

1 GENERAL INFORMATION AND MAINTENANCE

HOW TO USE THIS BOOK

Chilton's Repair Manual for ½, ¾ and 1 ton Chevrolet and GMC pick-ups, Blazers, Jimmys and Suburbans from 1988 to 1990, is intended to help you learn more about the inner workings of your vehicle and save you money on its upkeep and operation. All of the operations apply to both Chevrolet and GMC trucks unless specified otherwise.

The first two sections will be the most used, since they contain maintenance and tune-up information and procedures. Studies have shown that a properly tuned and maintained truck can get at least 10% better gas mileage (which translates into lower operating costs) and periodic maintenance will catch minor problems before they turn into major repair bills. The other sections deal with the more complex systems of your truck. Operating systems from engine through brakes are covered to the extent that the average do-it-yourselfer becomes mechanically involved. This book will not explain such things as rebuilding the differential for the simple reason that the expertise required and the investment in special tools make this task impractical and uneconomical. It will give you the detailed instructions to help you change your own brake pads and shoes, tune-up the engine, replace spark plugs and filters, and do many more jobs that will save you money, give you personal satisfaction and help you avoid expensive problems.

A secondary purpose of this book is a reference guide for owners who want to understand their truck and/or their mechanics better. In this case, no tools at all are required. Knowing just what a particular repair job requires in parts and labor time will allow you to evaluate whether or not you're getting a fair price quote and help decipher itemized bills from a repair shop.

Before attempting any repairs or service on your truck, read through the entire procedure outlined in the appropriate chapter. This will give you the overall view of what tools and supplies will be required. There is nothing more frustrating than having to walk to the bus stop on Monday morning because you were short one gasket on Sunday afternoon. So read ahead and plan ahead. Each operation should be approached logically and all procedures thoroughly understood before attempting any work. Some special tools that may be required can often be rented from local automotive jobbers or places specializing in renting tools and equipment. Check the yellow pages of your phone book.

All sections contain adjustments, maintenance, removal and installation procedures, and overhaul procedures. When overhaul is not considered practical, we tell you how to remove the failed part and then how to install the new or rebuilt replacement. In this way, you at least save the labor costs. Backyard overhaul of some components (such as the alternator or water pump) is just not practical, but the removal and installation procedure is often simple and well within the capabilities of the average truck owner.

Two basic mechanic's rules should be mentioned here. First, whenever the LEFT side of the truck or engine is referred to, it is meant to specify the DRIVER'S side of the truck. Conversely, the RIGHT side of the truck means the PASSENGER'S side. Second, all screws and bolts are removed by turning counterclockwise, and tightened by turning clockwise, unless otherwise noted.

Safety is always the most important rule. Constantly be aware of the dangers involved in working on or around an automobile and take proper precautions to avoid the risk of personal injury or damage to the vehicle. See the section in this section, Servicing Your Vehicle Safely, and the SAFETY NOTICE on the acknowledgment page before attempting any service procedures and pay attention to the instructions provided. There are 3 common mistakes in mechanical work:

1. Incorrect order of assembly, disassembly or adjustment. When taking something apart or putting it together, doing things in the wrong order usually just costs you extra time; however it CAN break something. Read the entire procedure before beginning disassembly. Do everything in the order in which the instructions say you should do it, even if you can't immediately see a reason for it. When you're taking apart something that is very intricate (for example, a carburetor), you might want to draw a picture of how it looks when assembled at one point in order to make sure you get everything back in its proper position. We will supply exploded views whenever possible, but sometimes the job requires more attention to detail than an illustration provides. When making adjustments (especially tune-up adjustments), do them in order. One adjustment often affects another and you cannot expect satisfactory results unless each adjustment is made only when it cannot be changed by any other.

2. Overtorquing (or undertorquing) nuts and bolts. While it is more common for overtorquing to cause damage, undertorquing can cause a fastener to vibrate loose and cause serious damage, especially when dealing with aluminum parts. Pay attention to torque specifications and utilize a torque wrench in assembly. If a torque figure is not available remember that, if you are using the right tool to do the job, you will probably not have to strain yourself to get a fastener tight enough. The pitch of most threads is so slight that the tension you put on the wrench will be multiplied many times in actual force on what you are tightening. A good example of how critical torque is can be seen in the case of spark plug installation, especially where you are putting the plug into an aluminum cylinder head. Too little torque can fail to crush the gasket, causing leakage of combustion gases and consequent overheating of the plug and engine parts. Too much torque can damage the threads or distort the plug, which changes the spark gap at the electrode. Since more and more manufacturers are using aluminum in their engine and chassis parts to save weight, a torque wrench should be in any serious do-it-yourselfer's tool box.

There are many commercial chemical products available for ensuring that fasteners won't come loose, even if they are not torqued just right (a very common brand is Loctite®). If you're worried about getting something together tight enough to hold, but loose enough to avoid mechanical damage during assembly, one of these products might offer substantial insurance. Read the label on the package and make sure the product is compatible with the materials, fluids, etc. involved before choosing one.

3. Crossthreading. This occurs when a part such as a bolt is screwed into a nut or casting at the wrong angle and forced, causing the threads to become damaged. Crossthreading is more likely to occur if access is difficult. It helps to clean and lubricate fasteners, and to start threading with the part to be installed going straight in, using your fingers. If you encounter resistance, unscrew the part and start over again at a different angle until it can be inserted and turned several times without much effort. Keep in mind that many parts, especially spark plugs, use tapered threads so that gentle turning will automatically bring the part you're threading to the proper angle if you don't force it or resist a change in angle. Don't put a wrench on the part until it's been turned in a couple of times by hand. If you suddenly encounter resistance and the part has not seated fully, don't force it. Pull it back out and make sure it's clean and threading properly.

Always take your time and be patient; once you have some experience, working on your truck will become an enjoyable hobby.

TOOLS AND EQUIPMENT

Naturally, without the proper tools and equipment it is impossible to properly service your vehicle. It would be impossible to catalog each tool that you would need to perform each or every operation in this book. It would also be unwise for the amateur to rush out and buy an expensive set of tools an the theory that he may need one or more of them at sometime.

The best approach is to proceed slowly, gathering together a good quality set of those tools that are used most frequently. Don't be misled by the low cost of bargain tools. It is far better to spend a little more for better quality. Forged wrenches, 6- or 12-point sockets and fine tooth ratchets are by far preferable to their less expensive counterparts. As any good mechanic can tell you, there are few worse experiences than trying to work on a truck with bad tools. Your monetary savings will be far outweighed by frustration and mangled knuckles.

Certain tools, plus a basic ability to handle tools, are required to get started. A basic mechanics tool set, a torque wrench, and, a Torx® bits set. Torx® bits are hexlobular drivers which fit both inside and outside on special Torx® head fasteners used in various places.

A special wheel bearing nut socket would be helpful when removing the front wheel bearings on 4x4 models.

Begin accumulating those tools that are used most frequently; those associated with routine maintenance and tune-up.

In addition to the normal assortment of screwdrivers and pliers you should have the following tools for routine maintenance jobs (your truck uses both SAE and metric fasteners):

1. SAE/Metric wrenches, sockets and combination open end/box end wrenches in sizes from 1/8 in. (3mm) to 3/4 in. (19mm); and a spark plug socket (13/16 in.) If possible, buy various length socket drive extensions. One break in this department is that the metric sockets available in the U.S. will all fit the ratchet handles and extensions you may already have (1/4 in., 3/8 in., and 1/2 in. drive).
2. One set each of metric and S.A.E. combination (one end open and one end box) wrenches.
3. Wire-type spark plug feeler gauge.
4. Blade-type feeler gauges.
5. Slot and Phillips head screwdrivers in various sizes.
6. Oil filter strap wrench, necessary for removing oil filters (never used, though, for installing the filters).
7. Funnel, for pouring fresh oil or automatic transmision fluid from quart oil bottles.
8. Pair of slip-lock pliers.
9. Pair of vise-type pliers.
10. Adjustable wrench.
11. A hydraulic floor jack of at least 1½ ton capacity. If you are serious about maintaining your own truck, then a floor jack is as necessary as a spark plug socket. The greatly increased utility, strength, and safety of a hydraulic floor jack makes it pay for itself many times over through the years.
12. At least 4 sturdy jackstands for working underneath the truck. Any other type of support (bricks, wood and especially cinderblocks) is just plain dangerous.
13. An inductive timing light.

In addition to the above items there are several others that are not absolutely necessary, but handy to have around. These include oil-dry (cat box litter works just as well and may be cheaper), a transmission funnel and the usual supply of lubricants, antifreeze and fluids, although these can be purchased as needed. This is a basic list for routine maintenance, but only your personal needs and desires can accurately determine your list of necessary tools.

This is an adequate set of tools, and the more work you do yourself on your truck, the larger you'll find the set growing—a pair of pliers here, a wrench or two there. It makes more sense to have a comprehensive set of basic tools as listed above, and then to acquire more along the line as you need them, than to go out and plunk down big money for a professional size set you may never use. In addition to these basic tools, there are several other tools and gauges you may find useful.

1. A compression gauge. The screw-in type is slower to use but it eliminates the possibility of a faulty reading due to escaping pressure.
2. A manifold vacuum gauge, very useful in troubleshooting ignition and emissions problems.
3. A drop light, to light up the work area (make sure yours is Underwriter's approved, and has a shielded bulb).
4. A volt/ohm meter, used for determining whether or not there is current in a wire. These are handy for use if a wire is broken somewhere and are especially necessary for working on today's electronics-laden vehicles.

As a final note, you will probably find a torque wrench necessary for all but the most basic work. The beam type models are perfectly adequate, although the newer click (breakaway) type are more precise, and you don't have to crane your neck to see a torque reading in awkward situations. The breakaway torque wrenches are more expensive and should be recalibrated periodically.

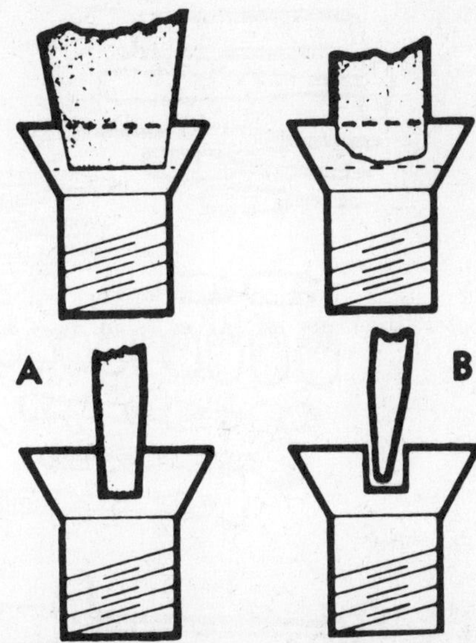

Keep screwdriver tips in good shape. They should fit in the screw head slots in the manner shown in "A". If they look like the tip shown in "B", they need grinding or replacing

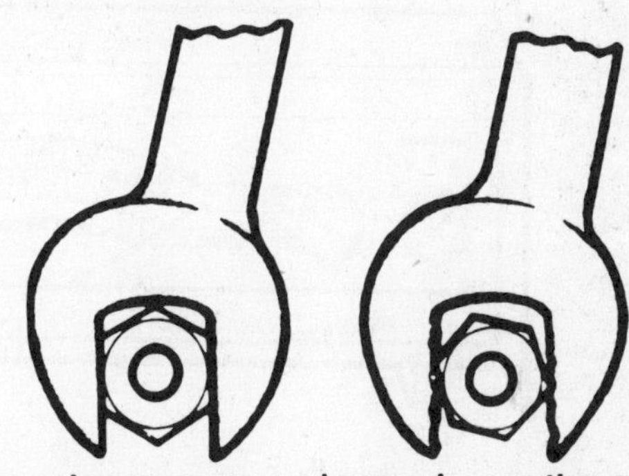
When using an open-end wrench, use the exact size needed and position it squarely on the flats of the bolt or nut

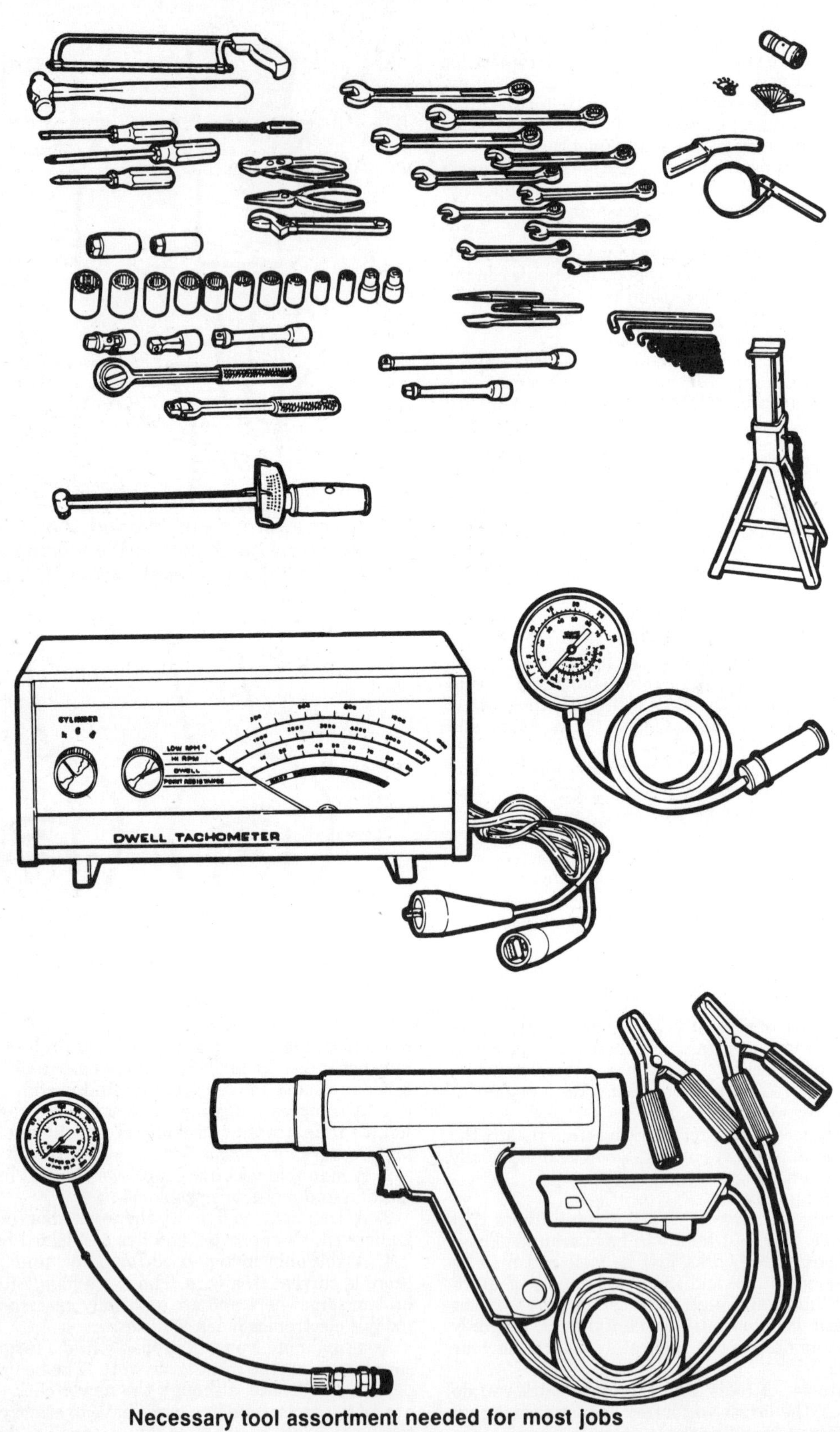

Necessary tool assortment needed for most jobs

Torque specification for each fastener will be given in the procedure in any case that a specific torque value is required. If no torque specifications are given, use the following values as a guide, based upon fastener size:

Bolts marked 6T
6mm bolt/nut – 5–7 ft. lbs.
8mm bolt/nut – 12–17 ft. lbs.
10mm bolt/nut – 23–34 ft. lbs.
12mm bolt/nut – 41–59 ft. lbs.
14mm bolt/nut – 56–76 ft. lbs.

Bolts marked 8T
6mm bolt/nut – 6–9 ft. lbs.
8mm bolt/nut – 13–20 ft. lbs.
10mm bolt/nut – 27–40 ft. lbs.
12mm bolt/nut – 46–69 ft. lbs.
14mm bolt/nut – 75–101 ft. lbs.

Special Tools

Normally, the use of special factory tools is avoided for repair procedures, since these are not readily available for the do-it-yourself mechanic. When it is possible to perform the job with more commonly available tools, it will be pointed out, but occasionally, a special tool was designed to perform a specific function and should be used. Before substituting another tool, you should be convinced that neither your safety nor the performance of the vehicle will be compromised.

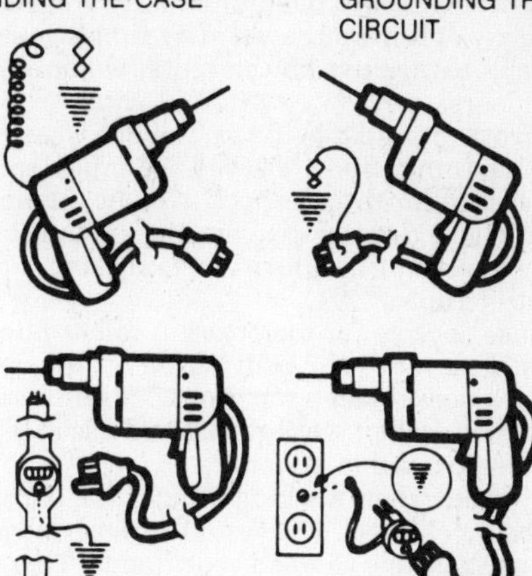

When using electric tools, make sure that they are properly grounded

Some special tools are available commercially from major tool manufacturers. Others can be purchased through your Chevy or GMC dealer.

SERVICING YOUR TRUCK SAFELY

It is virtually impossible to anticipate all of the hazards involved with automotive maintenance and service but care and common sense will prevent most accidents.

The rules of safety for mechanics range from "don't smoke around gasoline," to "use the proper tool for the job." The trick to avoiding injuries is to develop safe work habits and take every possible precaution.

Do's

- Do keep a fire extinguisher and first aid kit within easy reach.
- Do wear safety glasses or goggles when cutting, drilling, grinding or prying.
- Do shield your eyes whenever you work around the battery. Batteries contain sulphuric acid. In case of contact with the eyes or skin, flush the area with water or a mixture of water and baking soda and get medical attention immediately.
- Do use safety stands for any undercar service. Jacks are for raising vehicles; safety stands are for making sure the vehicle stays raised until you want it to come down. Whenever the vehicle is raised, block the wheels remaining on the ground and set the parking brake.
- Do disconnect the negative battery cable when working on the electrical system. The primary ignition system can contain up to 40,000 volts.
- Do properly maintain your tools. Loose hammerheads, mushroomed punches and chisels, frayed or poorly grounded electrical cords, excessively worn screwdrivers, spread wrenches (open end), cracked sockets, slipping ratchets, or faulty drop-light sockets can cause accidents and injuries.
- Do use the proper size and type of tool for the job being done.
- Do, when possible, pull on a wrench handle rather than push on it, and adjust your stance to prevent a fall.
- Do be sure that adjustable wrenches are tightly adjusted on the nut or bolt and pulled so that the face is on the side of the fixed jaw.
- Do select a wrench or socket that fits the nut or bolt. The wrench or socket should sit straight, not cocked.
- Do strike squarely with a hammer – avoid glancing blows.
- Do set the parking brake and block the drive wheels if the work requires that the engine be running.

Don'ts

- Don't run an engine in a garage or anywhere else without

proper ventilation – EVER! Carbon monoxide is poisonous. It takes a long time to leave the human body and you can build up a deadly supply of it in your system by simply breathing in a little every day. Always use power vents, windows, fans or open the garage doors.

- Don't work around moving parts while wearing a necktie or other loose clothing. Short sleeves are much safer than long, loose sleeves and hard toed shoes with neoprene soles protect your toes and give a better grip on slippery surfaces. Jewelry is not safe when working around a car. Long hair should be hidden under a hat or cap.
- Don't use pockets for toolboxes. A fall or bump can drive a screwdriver deep into your body. Even a wiping cloth hanging from the back pocket can wrap around a spinning shaft or fan.
- Don't smoke when working around gasoline, cleaning solvent or other flammable material.
- Don't smoke when working around the battery. When the battery is being charged, it gives off explosive hydrogen gas.
- Don't use gasoline to wash your hands. There are excellent soaps available. Gasoline may contain lead, and lead can enter the body through a cut, accumulating in the body until you are very ill. Gasoline also removes all the natural oils from the skin so that bone dry hands will absorb oil and grease.
- Don't service the air conditioning system unless you are equipped with the necessary tools and training. The refrigerant, R-12, is extremely cold and when exposed to the air, will instantly freeze any surface it comes in contact with, including your eyes. Although the refrigerant is normally non-toxic, R-12 becomes a deadly poisonous gas in the presence of an open flame. One good whiff of the vapors from burning refrigerant can be fatal.

Always us jackstands when working under your van

SERIAL NUMBER IDENTIFICATION

Vehicle

The V.I.N. plate is mounted on the driver's side of the instrument panel, and is visible through the windshield.

A 17 digit code is used:

- The 1st digit is the country of origin:
  1 = United States
  2 = Canada
  3 = Mexico
- The 2nd digit indicates the manufacturer. G = General Motors
- The 3rd digit indicates the make. Chevrolet (C) or GMC (T).
- The 4th character is the Gross Vehicle Weight range in pounds:
  B = 3,001–4,000
  C = 4,001–5,000
  D = 5,001–6,000
  E = 6,001–7,000
  F = 7,001–8,000
  G = 8,001–9,000
  H = 9,001–10,000
  J = 10,001–14,000
  K = 14,001–16,000
- The 5th digit is vehicle line and chassis type: C and R are 2-wheel drive conventional cabs; V and K are 4-wheel drive conventional cabs.
- The 6th digit is the weight code rating:
  1 = ½ ton
  2 = ¾ ton
  3 = 1 ton
- The 7th digit is the body type:
  0 = chassis only
  1 = cutaway van
  2 = forward control
  3 = 4-door cab
  4 = 2-door cab

VIN label location

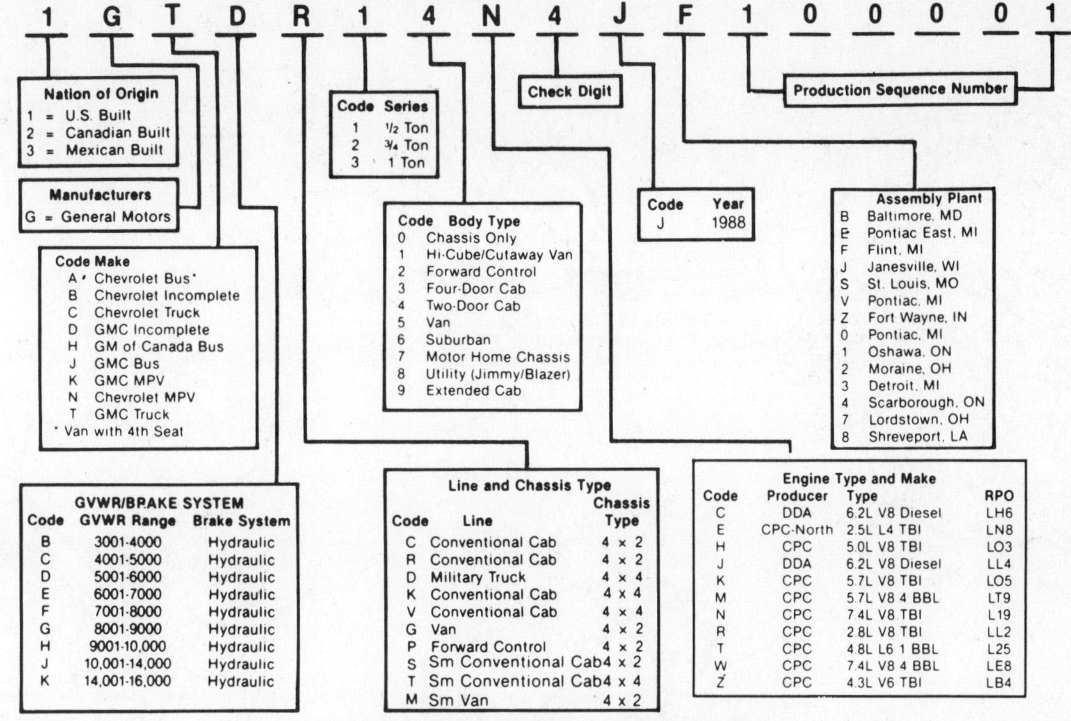

Vehicle Identification Label decoding

5 = van
6 = Suburban
7 = motor home chassis
8 = Blazer/Jimmy
9 = extended cab

- The 8th digit is the engine code:
  C = 8–6.2L (379) diesel
  H = 8–5.0L (305)
  J = 8–6.2L (379) diesel
  K = 8–5.7L (350) w/TBI
  M = 8–5.7L (350) w/4–bbl
  N = 8–7.4L (454) w/TBI
  T = 6–4.8L (292)
  W = 8–7.4L (454) w/4–bbl
  Z = 6–4.3L (262)
- The 9th digit is a check digit.
- The 10th digit is the year code. J = 1988; K= 1989; L = 1990.
- The 11th digit denotes the assembly plant:
  B = Baltimore, MD
  E = Pontiac East, MI
  F = Flint, MI
  J = Janesville, WI
  S = St. Louis, MO
  V = Pontiac, MI
  Z = Fort Wayne, IN
  0 = Pontiac, MI
  1 = Oshawa, ON
  2 = Moraine, OH
  3 = Detroit, MI
  4 = Scarborough, ON
  7 = Lordstown, OH
  8 = Shreveport, LA
- The last six numbers make up the consecutive serial number.

Engine

On the 4.8L, inline 6-cylinder engine, the engine idnetification number is found on a machined pad on the left side of the block, just rear of center, below the engine side cover.

On the 4.3L V6 engine, the engine identification number is found on a machined pad on the block, at the front just below the right side cylinder head.

On V8 gasoline engines, the engine identification number is found on a machined pad on the left, rear upper side of the block, where the engine mates with the bellhousing.

On V8 diesel engines, the engine identification number is found on a machined pad on the front of the block, between the left cylinder head and the thermostat housing, and/or on a machined pad on the left rear of the block, just behind the left cylinder head.

The engine number is broken down as follows:

Example – F1210TFA

- F – Manufacturing Plant. F-Flint and T-Tonawanda
- 12 – Month of Manufacture (December)
- 10 – Day of Manufacturer (Tenth)
- T – Truck engine
- FA – Transmission and Engine Combination

Transmission

The Muncie 117mm 4-speed transmission is numbered on the rear of the case, above the output shaft.

The 4-Speed 85mm and 5-Speed 85mm transmissions are numbered on the right rear of the case.

The Turbo Hydra-Matic is identified by a plate attached to the right side, which is stamped with the serial number.

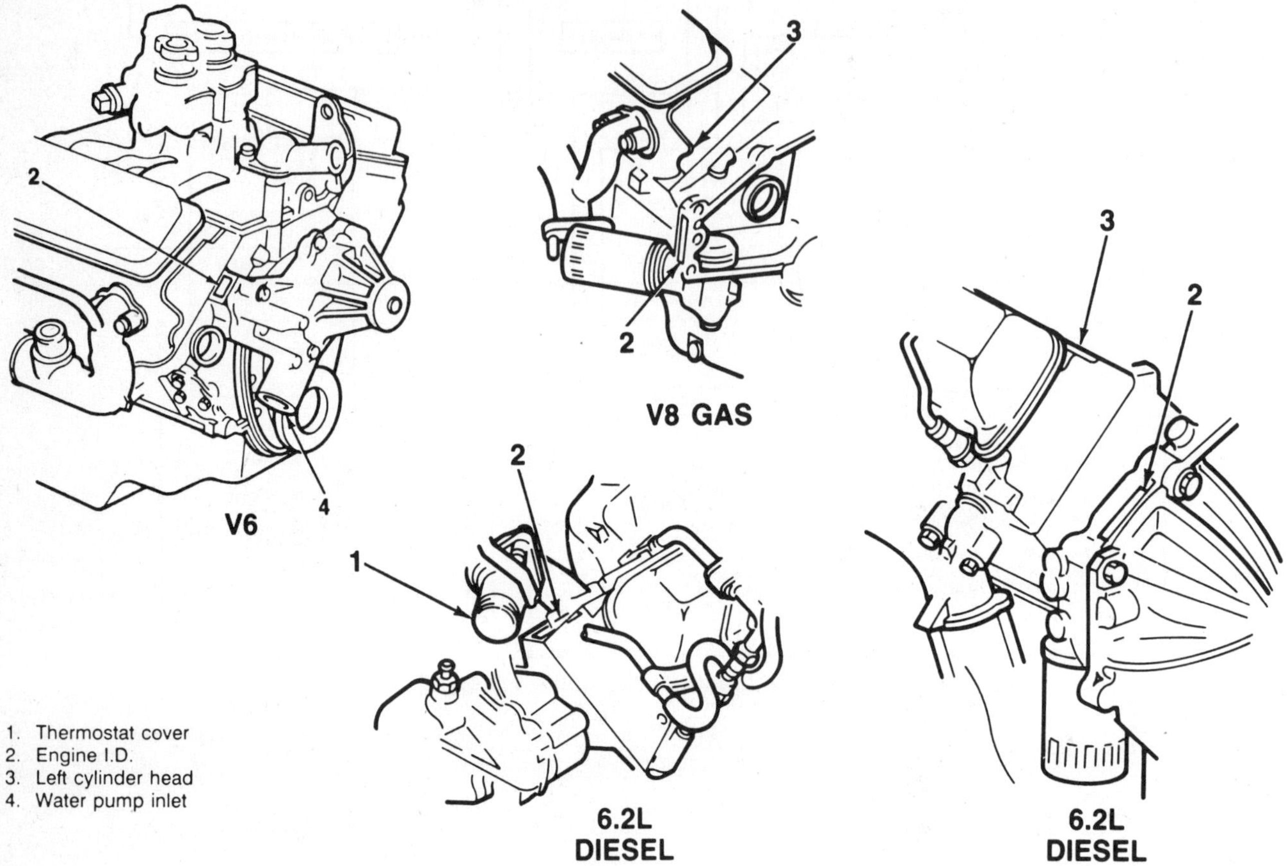

V6

V8 GAS

6.2L DIESEL

6.2L DIESEL

1. Thermostat cover
2. Engine I.D.
3. Left cylinder head
4. Water pump inlet

Engine I.D. locations

Transfer Case

The transfer cases have a build date tag attached to the front of the case.

Drive Axle

The drive axle serial number is stamped on the axle shaft housing, where it connects to the differential housing.

Front axles on 4 × 4s are marked on the front of the left axle tube.

Service Parts Identification Plate

The service parts identification plate, commonly known as the option list, is usually located on the inside of the glove compartment door. On some trucks, you may have to look for it on an inner fender panel. The plate lists the vehicle serial number, wheelbase, all regular production options (RPOs) and all special equipment. Probably, the most valuable piece of information on this plate is the paint code, a useful item when you have occasion to need paint.

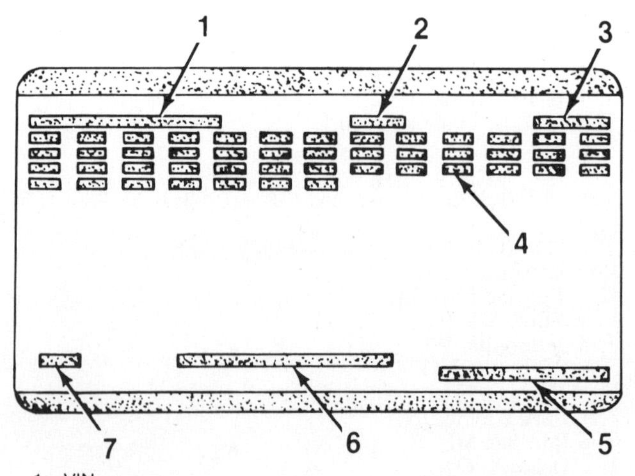

1. VIN
2. Wheel base
3. Model designation
4. RPO and/or SEO options
5. Order number
6. Exterior color
7. Paint technology

Service Parts Identification Label

ENGINE APPLICATION CHART

Engine	Actual Displacement Cu. In.	CC	Liters	Type	VIN	Fuel System	Mgf. by	Years
6–4.3	262.4	4299.7	4.3	OHV	Z	TBI	Chevrolet	1988–90
8–4.8	291.7	4779.8	4.8	OHV	T	1-bbl	Chevrolet	1989–90
8–5.0	305.2	5001.2	5.0	OHV	H	TBI	Chevrolet	1988–90
8–5.7	349.8	5732.9	5.7	OHV	M	4-bbl	Chevrolet	1988
					K	TBI	Chevrolet	1988–90
8–6.2	378.2	6197.7	6.2	OHV	C,J	Diesel	DDAD	1988–90
8–7.4	453.9	7439.0	7.4	OHV	N	TBI	Chevrolet	1988–90

TBI: Throttle Body Injection
DDAD: Detroit Diesel Allison Division

MANUAL TRANSMISSION APPLICATION CHART

Transmission Types	Years	Models
Muncie 117mm 4-speed	1988–90	R and V Series C and K 1 ton
Getrag 85mm 4-speed	1988–90	C and K $^1/_2$ and $^3/_4$ ton
Getrag 85mm 5-speed	1988–90	C and K $^1/_2$ and $^3/_4$ ton

AUTOMATIC TRANSMISSION APPLICATION CHART

Transmission Type	Years	Models
Turbo Hydra-Matic 400 3-speed	1988–90	All
Turbo Hydra-Matic 700-R4 4-speed	1988–90	All

TRANSFER CASE APPLICATION CHART

Transfer Case Type	Years	Models
New Process 205	1988–90	V 30/3500
New Process 208	1988	V 10/15, 20/25
New Process 241	1988	All K Series
	1989–90	V 10/15, 20/25
	1989–90	All K Series, exc. K 30 with DRW
Borg-Warner 1370	1989–90	K Series with DRW

DRW: Dual Rear Wheels

REAR AXLE APPLICATION CHART

Axle Type	Years	Models
GM $8^1/_2$ in. Ring Gear Semi-floating	1988–90	R, C Series $^1/_2$ ton
GM $9^1/_2$ in. Ring Gear Semi-Floating	1988–90	R, V, C, K Series $^1/_2$ ton
GM $10^1/_2$ in. Ring Gear Full-floating	1988–90	R, V Series $^3/_4$ and 1 ton
Dana $9^3/_4$ in. Ring Gear Full-floating	1988–90	R, V Series $^3/_4$ ton
Dana $10^1/_2$ in. Ring Gear Full-floating	1988–90	R, V, C, K Series $^3/_4$ and 1 ton

FRONT DRIVE AXLE APPLICATION CHART

Axle Type	Years	Models
GMC $8^1/_2$ in. Ring Gear	1988–90	V 10/15 and 20/25 Series
Dana 60 Series $9^3/_4$ in. Ring Gear	1988–90	V 30/35 Series
GMC $8^1/_4$ in. Ring Gear Independent Front Axle	1988–90	K 15/25 Series
GMC $9^1/_4$ in. Ring Gear Independent Front Axle	1988–90	K 35 Series

ROUTINE MAINTENANCE

Routine maintenance is preventive medicine. It is the key to extending the life of any truck. By getting into the habit of doing some quick and simple checks once a week, you'll be surprised how easy it is to keep your truck in tiptop shape. It will also give you a greater awareness of the workings of your truck.

By taking the time to check the engine oil, transmission fluid, battery and coolant level and the brake fluid regularly, you'll find yourself with a meticulously maintained truck. You'll also be able to spot any developing problems (like a slow leak in the radiator) before they become expensive repairs. Try to check all the hinges and keep them well lubricated, too. Routine maintenance really does pay off.

The Maintenance Intervals chart gives the maintenance intervals recommended by the manufacturer.

Air Cleaner

REMOVAL AND INSTALLATION

Paper Element Type

Loosen the wing nut on top of the cover and remove the cover. The element should be replaced when it has become oil saturated or filled with dirt. If the filter is equipped with a foam wrapper, remove the wrapper and wash it in kerosene or similar sol-

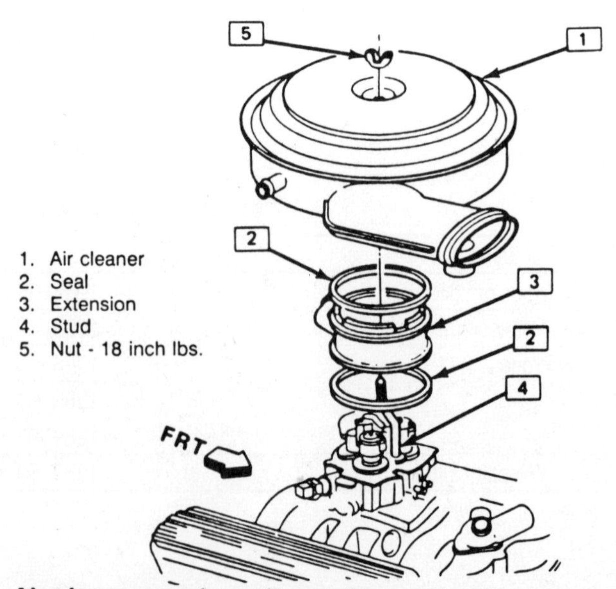

Air cleaner used on all gasoline engines except the 7.4L

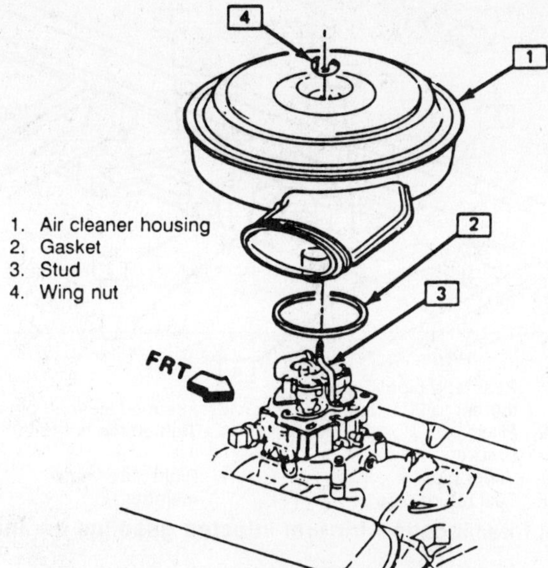

Air cleaner used on the 7.4L engine

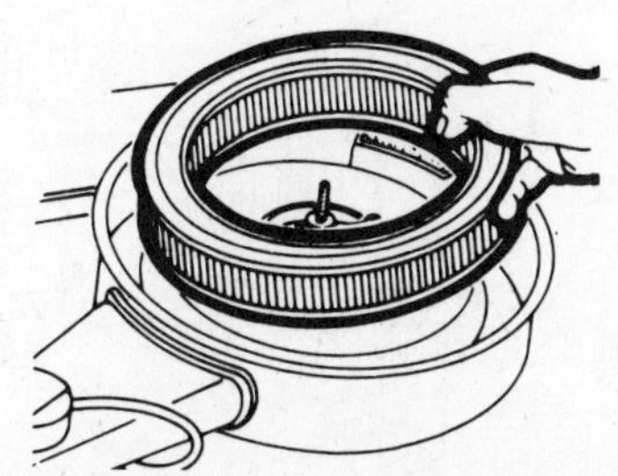

Removing the air cleaner paper element

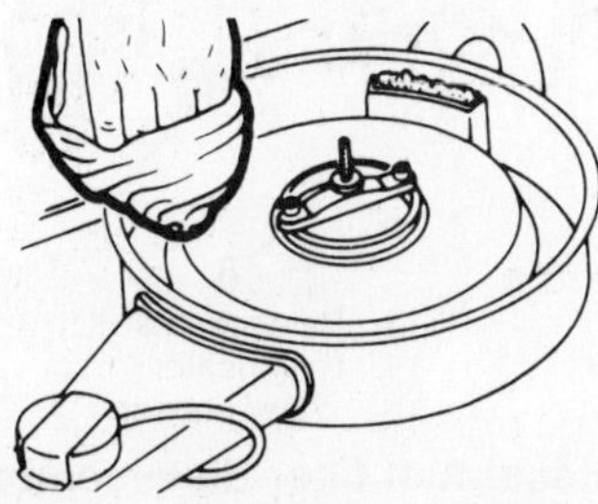

Clean out the housing before installing the new element

vent. Shake or blot dry. Saturate the wrapper in engine oil and squeeze it tightly in an absorbent towel to remove the excess oil.

Leave the wrapper moist. Clean the dirt from the filter by lightly tapping it against a workbench to dislodge the dirt particles. Wash the top of the air cleaner housing and wipe it dry. If equipped, replace the crankcase ventilation filter, located in the air filter housing if it appears excessively dirty. Replace the oiled wrapper on the air cleaner element and reinstall the element in the housing, repositioning it 180° from its original position.

NOTE: Inverting the air cleaner cover for increased intake air volume is not recommended. This causes an increase in intake noise, faster dirt buildup in both the air cleaner element and the crankcase ventilation filter, and poor cold weather driveability.

Fuel Filter

REMOVAL AND INSTALLATION

Carbureted Gasoline Engines

FILTER IN CARBURETOR

The fuel filter should be serviced at the interval given on the Maintenance Interval chart. Two types of fuel filters are used, a bronze type and a paper element type. Filter replacement should be attempted only when the engine is cold. Additionally, it is a good idea to place some absorbent rags under the fuel fittings to catch the gasoline which will spill out when the lines are loosened.

To replace the filter:

1. Disconnect the fuel line connecting at the intake fuel filter nut. Plug the opening to prevent loss of fuel.
2. Remove the intake fuel filter nut from the carburetor with a 1 in. wrench.
3. Remove the filter element and spring.
4. Check the element for restrictions by blowing on the cone end. Air should pass freely.
5. Clean or replace the element, as necessary.
6. Install the element spring, then the filter element in the carburetor. Bronze filters should have the small section of the cone facing out.
7. Install a new gasket on the intake fuel nut. Install the nut in the carburetor body and tighten securely.
8. Install the fuel line and tighten the connector.

INLINE FILTER

Some trucks may have an inline filter. This is a can shaped device located in the fuel line between the pump and the carburetor. It may be made of either plastic or metal. To replace the filter:

1. Place some absorbent rags under the filter. Remember, it will be full of gasoline when removed.
2. Use a pair of pliers to expand the clamp on one end of the filter, then slide the clamp down past the point to which the filter pipe extends in the rubber hose. Do the same with the other clamp.
3. Gently twist and pull the hoses free of the filter pipes. Remove and discard the old filter.

NOTE: Most replacement filters come with new hoses that should be installed with a new filter.

4. Install the new filter into the hoses, slide the clamps back into place, and check for leaks with the engine idling.

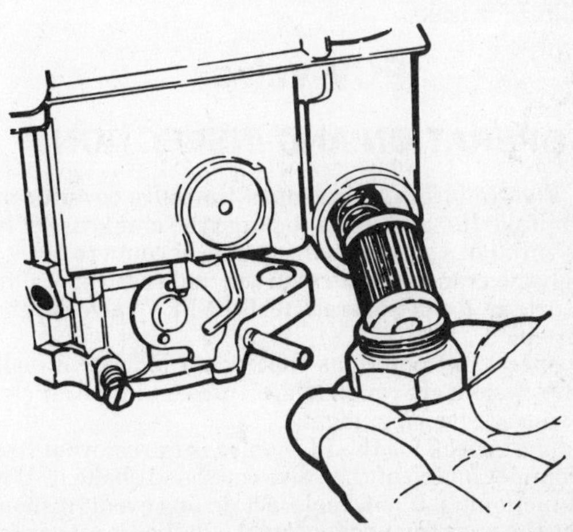

In-carburetor fuel filter

Fuel Injected Gasoline Engines

The inline filter on the fuel injected models is found along the frame rail.

1. Release the fuel system pressure.

CAUTION

The 220 TBI unit used on the V6 and V8 engines contains a constant bleed feature in the pressure regulator that relieves pressure any time the engine is turned off. Therefore, no special relieve procedure is required, however, a small amount of fuel may be released when the fuel line is disconnected.

To reduce the chance of personal injury, cover the fuel line with cloth to collect the fuel and then place the cloth in an approved container.

2. Disconnect the fuel lines.
3. Remove the fuel filter from the retainer or mounting bolt.
4. To install, reverse the removal procedures. Start the engine and check for leaks.

NOTE: The filter has an arrow (fuel flow direction) on the side of the case, be sure to install it correctly in the system, the with arrow facing away from the fuel tank.

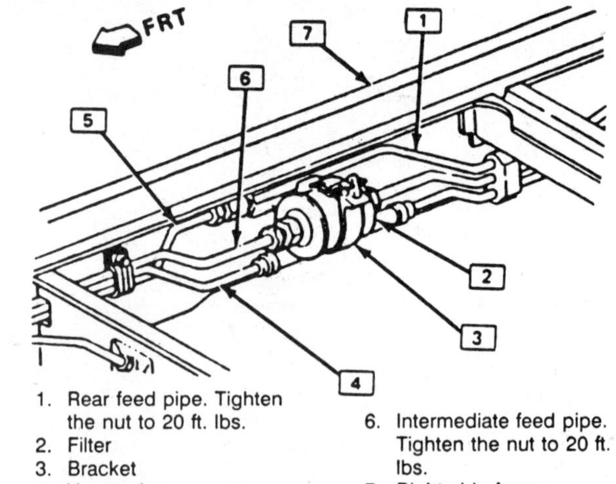

1. Rear feed pipe. Tighten the nut to 20 ft. lbs.
2. Filter
3. Bracket
4. Vapor pipe
5. Fuel return pipe
6. Intermediate feed pipe. Tighten the nut to 20 ft. lbs.
7. Right side frame member

Fuel filter location for fuel injected gasoline engines

Diesel Engines

1. Drain the fuel from the fuel filter by opening both the air bleed and the water drain valve allowing the fuel to drain out into an appropriate container.
2. Remove the fuel tank cap to release any pressure or vacuum in the tank.
3. Unstrap both bail wires with a screwdriver and remove the filter.
4. Before installing the new filter, insure that both filter mounting plate fittings are clear of dirt.
5. Install the new filter, snap into place with the bail wires.
6. Close the water drain valve and open the air bleed valve. Connect a 1/8 in. (3mm) I.D. hose to the air bleed port and place the other end into a suitable container.
7. Disconnect the fuel injection pump shut off solenoid wire.
8. Crank the engine for 10–15 seconds, then wait one minute for the starter motor to cool. Repeat until clear fuel is observed coming from the air bleed.

NOTE: If the engine is to be cranked, or starting attempted with the air cleaner removed, care must be taken to prevent dirt from being pulled into the air inlet manifold which could result in engine damage.

9. Close the air bleed valve, reconnect the injection pump solenoid wire and replace the fuel tank cap.
10. Start the engine, allow it to idle for 5 minutes and check the fuel filter for leaks.

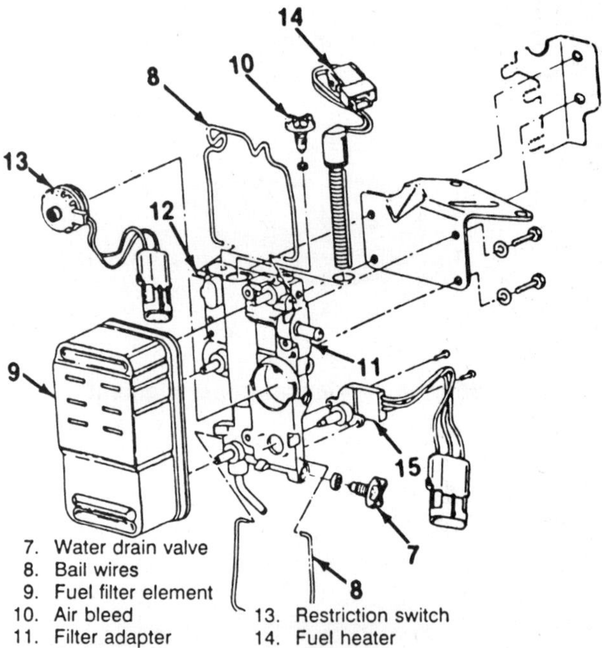

7. Water drain valve
8. Bail wires
9. Fuel filter element
10. Air bleed
11. Filter adapter
12. Air bleed port
13. Restriction switch
14. Fuel heater
15. Water sensor

Diesel fuel filter disassembled

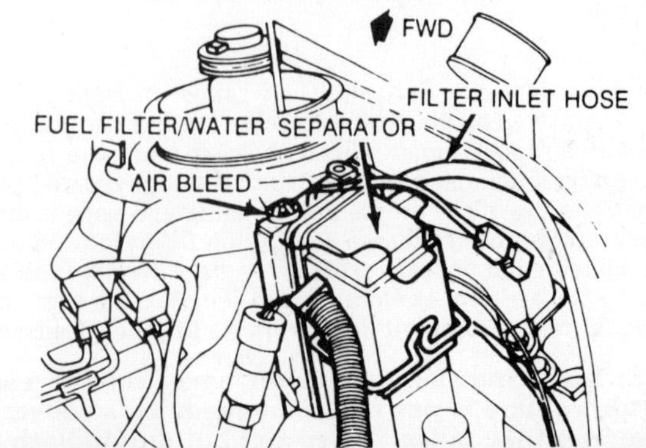

Combination fuel filter/water separator used on the diesel engine

PCV Valve

OPERATION AND INSPECTION

The PCV valve is located on top of the valve cover or on the intake manifold. Its function is to purge the crankcase of harmful vapors through a system using engine vacuum to draw fresh air through the crankcase. It reburns crankcase vapors, rather than exhausting. Proper operation of the PCV valve depends on a sealed engine.

Engine operating conditions that would indicate a malfunctioning PCV system are rough idle, oil present in the air cleaner, oil leaks or excessive oil sludging.

The simplest check for the PCV valve is to remove it from its rubber grommet on top of the valve cover and shake it. If it rattles, it is functioning. If not, replace it. In any event, it should be replaced at the recommended interval whether it rattles or not. While you are about it, check the PCV hoses for breaks or restrictions. As necessary, the hoses should also be replaced.

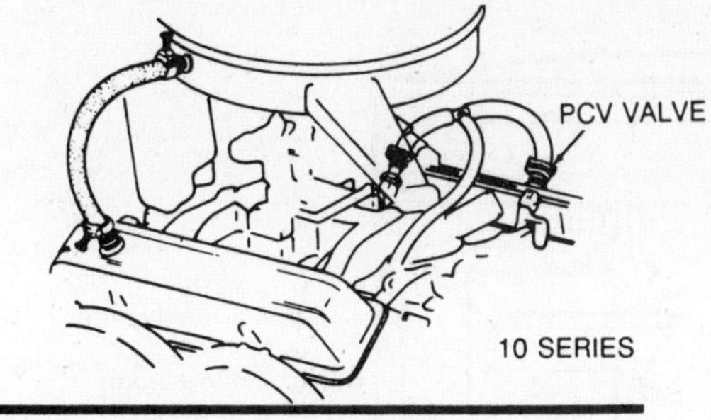

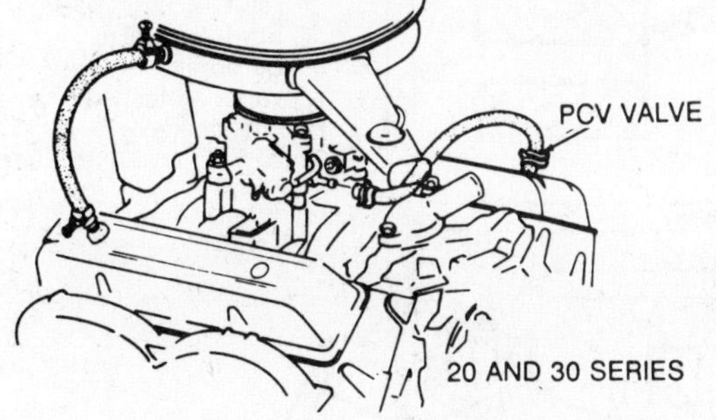

Typical PCV valve location

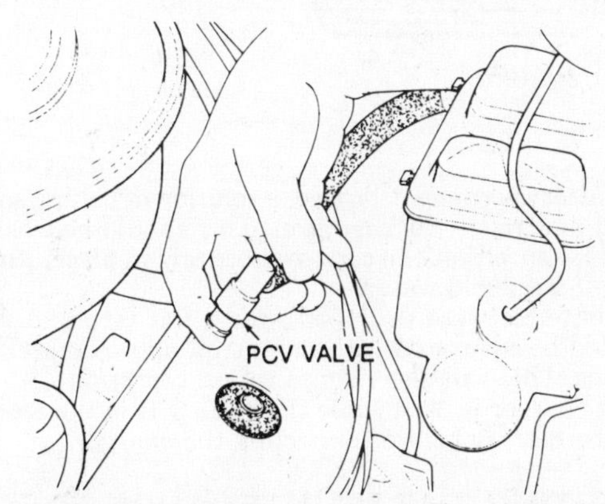

Checking the vacuum at the PCV valve

REMOVAL AND INSTALLATION

1. Pull the valve, with the hose still attached to the valve, from the rubber grommet in the rocker cover.
2. Use a pair of pliers to release the hose clamp, remove the PCV valve from the hose.
3. Install the new valve into the hose, slide the clamp into position, and install the valve into the rubber grommet.

Crankcase Depression Regulator and Flow Control Valve

SERVICING

Diesel Engines

The Crankcase Depression Regulator (CDR) is designed to scavenge crankcase vapors in basically the same manner as the PVC valve on gasoline engines. The valves are located either on the left rear corner of the intake manifold (CDR). On this system there are two ventilation filters, one per valve cover.

The filter assemblies should be cleaned every 15,000 miles by simply prying them carefully from the valve covers (be aware of the grommets underneath), and washing them out in solvent. The ventilation pipes and tubes should also be cleaned. The CDR valve should also be cleaned every 30,000 miles (the cover can be removed from the CDR). Dry each valve, filter, and hose with compressed air before installation.

NOTE: Do not attempt to test the crankcase controls on these diesels. Instead, clean the valve cover filter assembly and vent pipes and check the vent pipes. Replace the breather cap assembly every 30,000 miles. Replace all rubber fittings as required every 15,000 miles.

Evaporative Canister

SERVICING

The only regular maintenance that need be performed on the evaporative emission canister is to regularly change the filter and check the condition of the hoses. If any hoses need replacement, use only hoses which are marked EVAP. No other type should be used. Whenever the vapor vent hose is replaced, the restrictor adjacent to the canister should also be replaced.

The evaporative emission canister is located on the left side of the engine compartment, with a filter located in its bottom. Not all trucks have one.

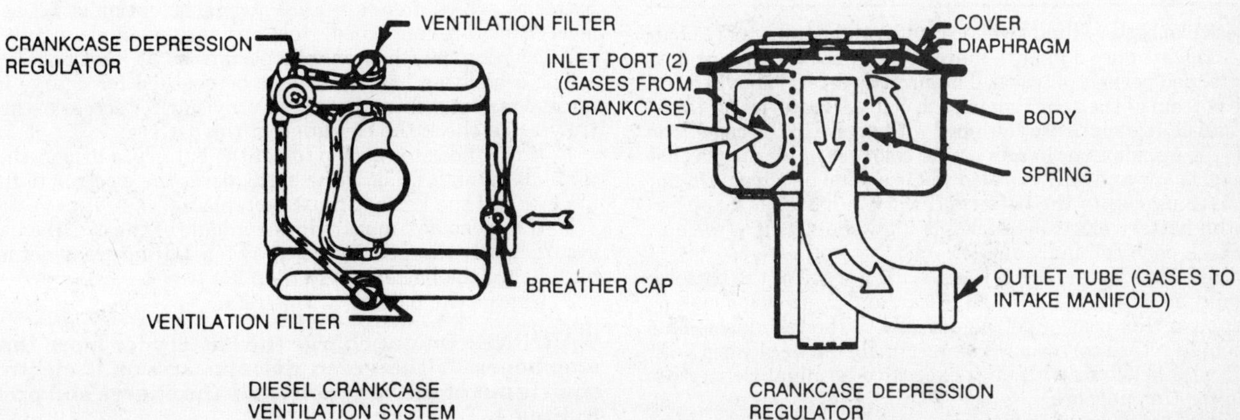

Diesel crankcase flow and depression regulator

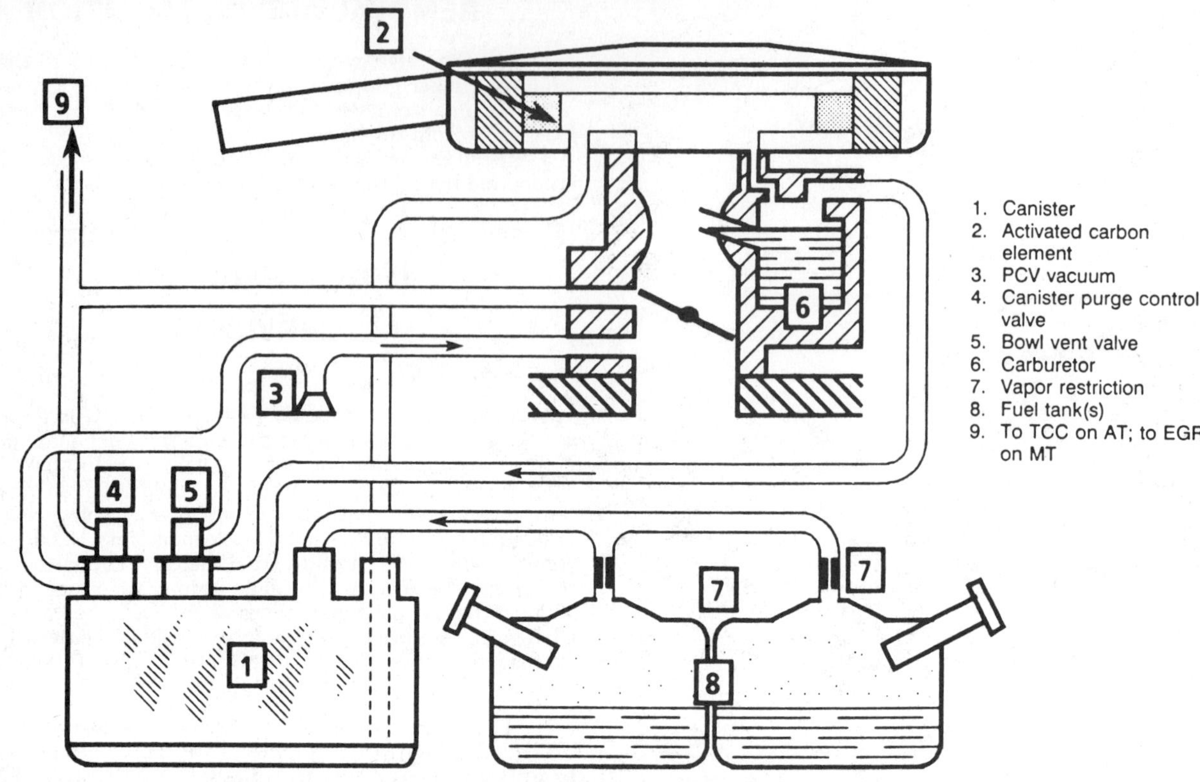

Typical evaporative canister system

To service the canister filter:

1. Note the installed positions of the hoses, tagging them as necessary, in case any have to be removed.
2. Loosen the clamps and remove the canister.
3. Pull the filter out and throw it away.
4. Install a new canister filter.
5. Install the canister and tighten the clamps.
6. Check the hoses.

Battery

CAUTION

Keep flame or sparks away from the battery! It gives off explosive hydrogen gas, while it is being charged.

Check the battery fluid level (except in Maintenance Free batteries) at least once a month, more often in hot weather or during extended periods of travel. The electrolyte level should be up to the bottom of the split ring in each cell. All batteries on Chevrolet and GMC trucks are equipped with an eye in the cap of one cell. If the eye glows or has an amber color to it, this means that the level is low and only distilled water should be added. Do not add anything else to the battery. If the eye has a dark appearance the battery electrolyte level is high enough. It is wise to also check each cell individually.

At least once a year, check the specific gravity of the battery. It should be between 1.20–1.26. Clean and tighten the clamps and apply a thin coat of petroleum jelly to the terminals. This will help to retard corrosion. The terminals can be cleaned with a staff wire brush or with an inexpensive terminal cleaner designed for this purpose.

If water is added during freezing weather, the truck should be driven several miles to allow the electrolyte and water to mix. Otherwise the battery could freeze.

If the battery becomes corroded, a solution of baking soda and water will neutralize the corrosion. This should be washed off after making sure that the caps are securely in place. Rinse the solution off with cold water.

Some batteries were equipped with a felt terminal washer. This should be saturated with engine oil approximately every 6,000 miles. This will also help to retard corrosion.

If a fast charger is used while the battery is in the truck, disconnect the battery before connecting the charger.

TESTING THE MAINTENANCE-FREE BATTERY

All later model trucks are equipped with maintenance-free batteries, which do not require normal attention as far as fluid level checks are concerned. However, the terminals require periodic cleaning, which should be performed at least once a year.

The sealed top battery cannot be checked for charge in the normal manner, since there is no provision for access to the electrolyte. To check the condition of the battery:

1. If the indicator eye on top of the battery is bright, the battery has enough fluid. If the eye is dark, the electrolyte fluid is too low and the battery must be replaced.
2. If a green dot appears in the middle of the eye, the battery is sufficiently charged. Proceed to Step 4. If no green dot is visible, charge the battery as in Step 3.
3. Charge the battery at this rate:

WARNING: Do not charge the battery for more than 50 amp/hours! If the green dot appears, or if electrolyte squirts out of the vent hole, stop the charge and proceed to Step 4.

It may be necessary to tip the battery from side to side to get the green dot to appear after charging.

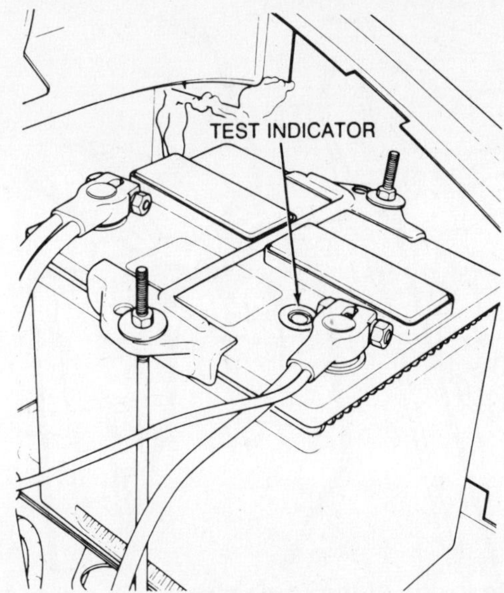

Indicator eye

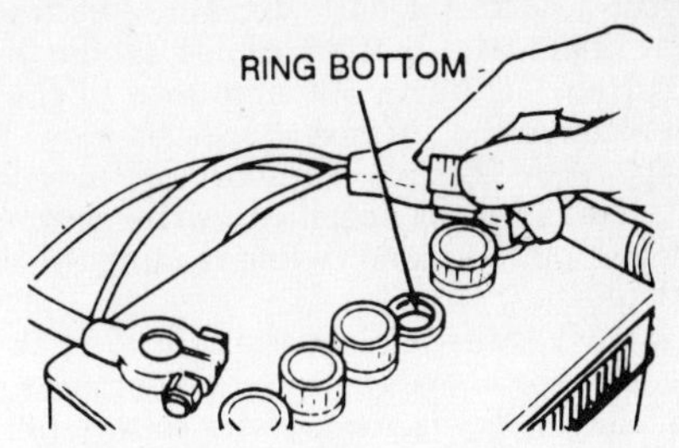

Fill each cell to the bottom of the split ring

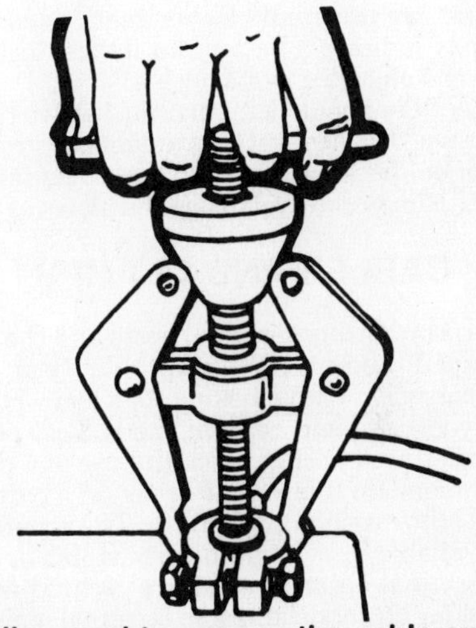

Special puller used to remove the cable end from the battery post

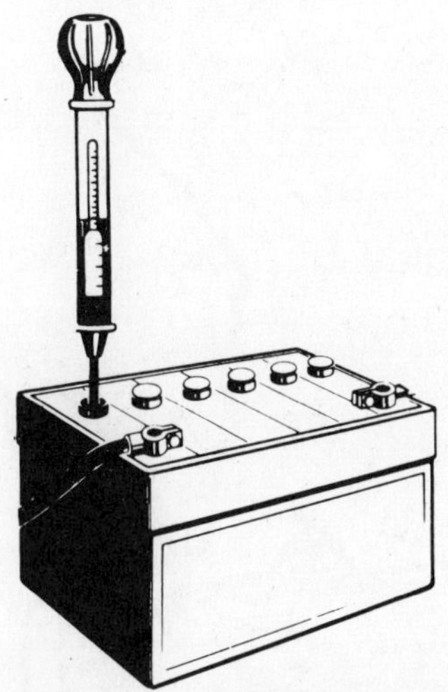

Using a hydrometer to check specific gravity

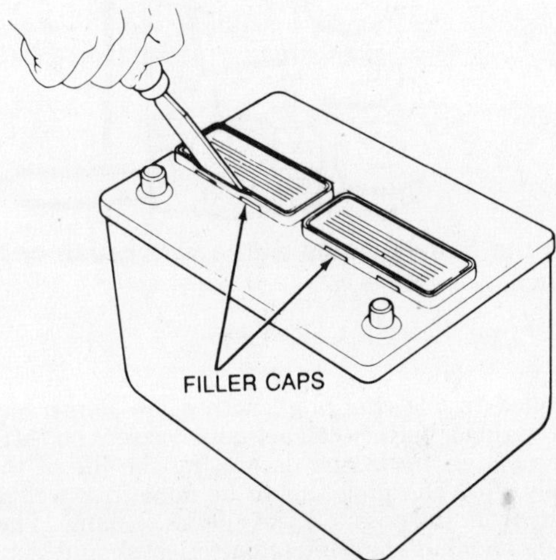

Prying off the filler caps

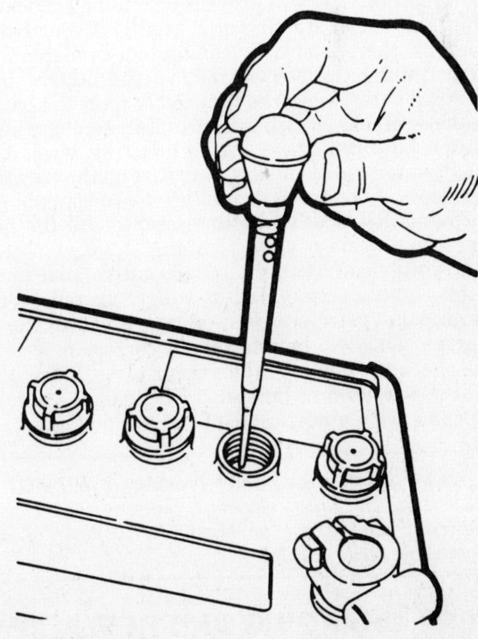

Testing the specific gravity of the battery

4. Connect a battery load tester and a voltmeter across the battery terminals (the battery cables should be disconnected from the battery). Apply a 300 amp load to the battery for 15 seconds to remove the surface charge. Remove the load.
5. Wait 15 seconds to allow the battery to recover. Apply the appropriate test load, as specified in the accompanying chart. Apply the load for 15 seconds while reading the voltage. Disconnect the load.
6. Check the results against the following chart. If the battery voltage is at or above the specified voltage for the temperature listed, the battery is good. If the voltage falls below what's listed, the battery should be replaced.

FILLING THE BATTERY

Batteries should be checked for proper electrolyte level at least once a month or more frequently. Keep a close eye on any cell or cells that are unusually low or seem to constantly need water—this may indicate a battery on its last legs, a leak, or a problem with the charging system.

Top up each cell to about 3/8 in. (9.5mm) above the tops of the plates. Always use distilled water (available in supermarkets or auto parts stores), because most tap water contains chemicals and minerals that may slowly damage the plates of your battery.

Clean the inside of the cable clamp with a wire brush

CABLES AND CLAMPS

Twice a year, the battery terminal posts and the cable clamps should be cleaned. Loosen the clamp bolts (you may have to brush off any corrosion with a baking soda and water solution if they are really messy) and remove the cables, negative cable first. On batteries with posts on top, the use of a battery clamp puller is recommended. It is easy to break off a battery terminal if a clamp gets stuck without the puller. These pullers are inexpensive and available in most auto parts stores or auto departments. Side terminal battery cables are secured with a bolt.

The best tool for battery clamp and terminal maintenance is a battery terminal brush. This inexpensive tool has a female ended wire brush for cleaning terminals, and a male ended wire brush inside for cleaning the insides of battery clamps. When using this tool, make sure you get both the terminal posts and the insides of the clamps nice and shiny. Any oxidation, corrosion or foreign material will prevent a sound electrical connection and inhibit either starting or charging. If your battery has side terminals, there is also a cleaning tool available for these.

Before installing the cables, remove the battery holddown clamp or strap and remove the battery. Inspect the battery casing for leaks or cracks (which unfortunately can only be fixed by buying a new battery). Check the battery tray, wash it off with warm soapy water, rinse and dry. Any rust on the tray should be sanded away, and the tray given at least two coats of a quality anti-rust paint. Replace the battery, and install the holddown clamp or strap, but do not overtighten.

Reinstall your clean battery cables, negative cable last. Tighten the cables on the terminal posts snugly; do not overtighten. Wipe a thin coat of petroleum jelly or grease all over the outsides of the clamps. This will help to inhibit corrosion.

Finally, check the battery cables themselves. If the insulation of the cables is cracked or broken, or if the ends are frayed, replace the cable with a new cable of the same length or gauge.

CAUTION

Batteries give off hydrogen gas, which is explosive. DO NOT SMOKE around the battery! The battery electrolyte contains sulfuric acid. If you should splash any into your eyes or skin, flush with plenty of clear water and get immediate medical help.

Clean the battery posts with a wire brush or the tool shown

BATTERY CHARGING AND REPLACEMENT

Charging a battery is best done by the slow charging method (often called trickle charging), with a low amperage charger. Quick charging a battery can actually "cook" the battery, damaging the plates inside and decreasing the life of the battery drastically. Any charging should be done in a well ventilated area away from the possibility of sparks or flame. The cell caps (not found on maintenance-free batteries) should be unscrewed from their cells, but not removed.

If the battery must be quick-charged, check the cell voltages and the color of the electrolyte a few minutes after the charge is started. If cell voltages are not uniform or if the electrolyte is discolored with brown sediment, stop the quick charging in favor of a trickle charge. A common indicator of an overcharged battery is the frequent need to add water to the battery.

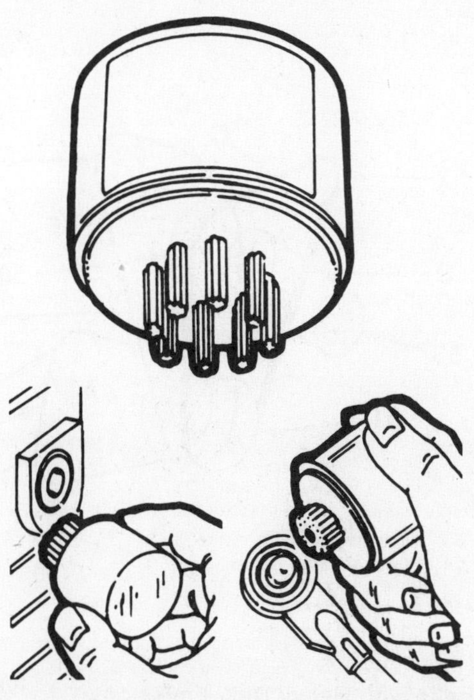

Special tools are available for cleaning the cables and terminals of side terminal batteries

Drive Belts

INSPECTION

At the interval specified in the Maintenance Intervals chart, check the water pump, alternator, power steering pump (if equipped), air conditioning compressor (if equipped) and air pump (if equipped) drive belts for proper tension. Also look for signs of wear, fraying, separation, glazing, and so on, and replace the belts as required.

BELT TENSION

Belt tension should be checked with a gauge made for the purpose. If a tension gauge is not available, tension can be checked with moderate thumb pressure applied to the belt at its longest span midway between pulleys. If the belt has a free span less than 12 in. (305mm), it should deflect approximately 1/8–1/4 in. (3–6mm). If the span is longer than 12 in. (305mm), deflection can range between 1/8 in. (3mm) and 3/8 in. (9.5mm).

If a tension gauge is available use the following procedure:

1. Place a belt tension gauge at the center of the greatest span of a warm not hot drive belt and measure the tension.
2. If the belt is below the specification, loosen the component mounting bracket and adjust to specification.
3. Run the engine at idle for 15 minutes to allow the belt to reseat itself in the pulleys.
4. Allow the drive belt to cool and re-measure the tension. Adjust as necessary to meet the following specifications:

- V6, V8 gasoline engines: used – 90 ft. lbs.; new – 135 ft. lbs.
- 6–4.8L: used – 90 ft. lbs.; new – 169 ft. lbs.
- 8–6.2L diesel: used – 67 ft. lbs.; new – 146 ft. lbs.

NOTE: A belt is considered "used" after 15 minutes of operation.

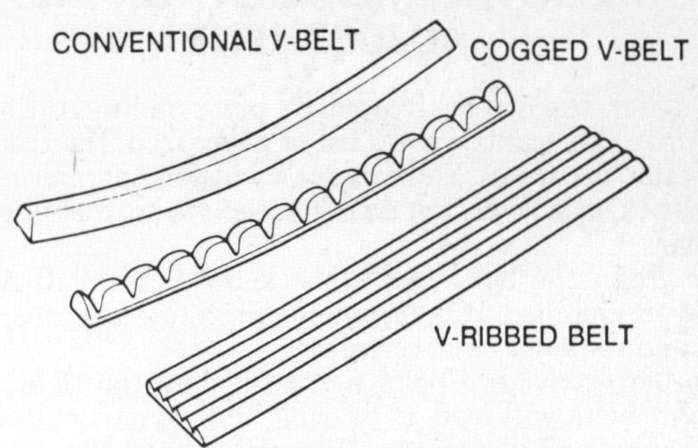

Different types of drive belts

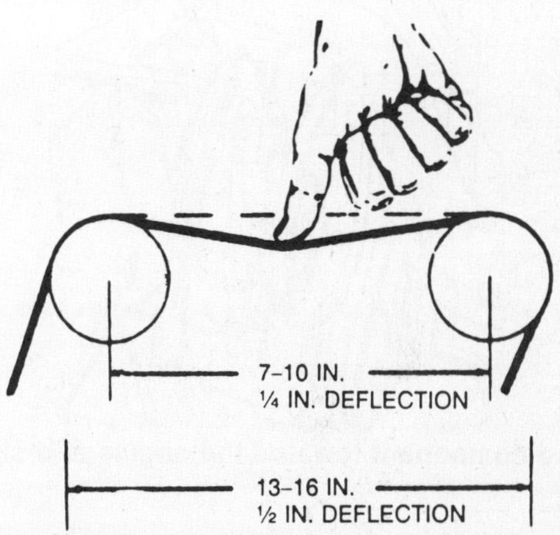

A tension gauge is the most precise way to measure belt tension, but you can check it using the deflection method shown

To adjust or replace a belt, first loosen the adjusting and mounting bolts

REMOVAL, INSTALLATION AND ADJUSTMENT

1. Loosen the driven accessory's pivot and mounting bolts.
2. Move the accessory toward or away from the engine until the tension is correct. You can use a wooden hammer handle, or broomstick, as a lever, but do not use anything metallic, such as a prybar.
3. Tighten the bolts and recheck the tension. If new belts have been installed, run the engine for a few minutes, then re-check and readjust as necessary.

It is better to have belts too loose than too tight, because overtight belts will lead to bearing failure, particularly in the water pump and alternator. However, loose belts place an extremely high impact load on the driven component due to the whipping action of the belt.

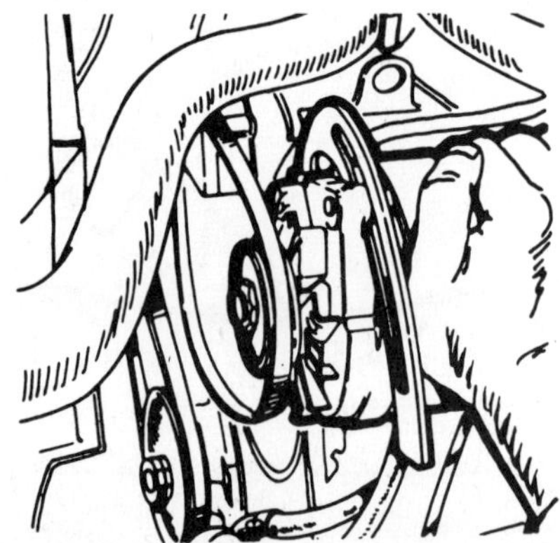

Push the component towards the engine and slip off the belt

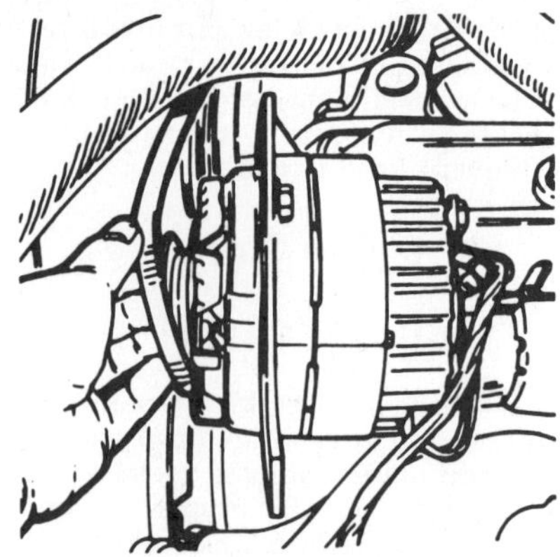

Slip the new belt over the pulley

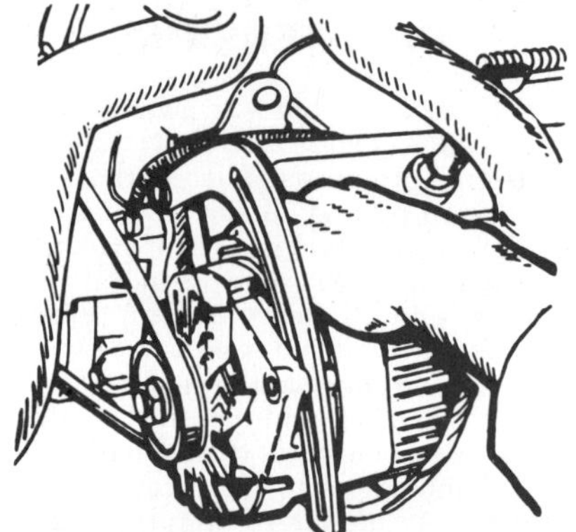

Pull outward on the component and tighten the adjusting and mounting bolts.

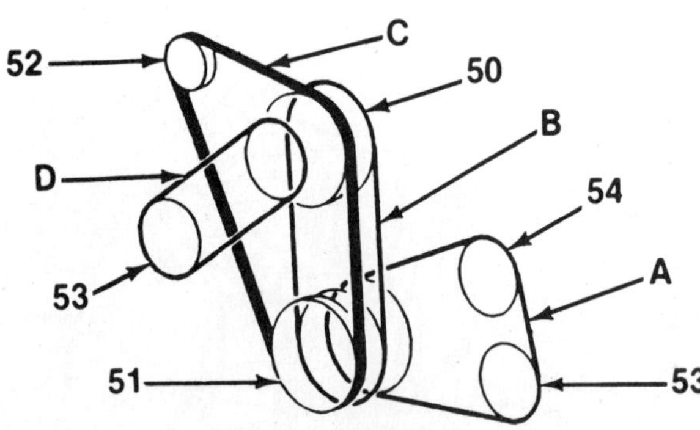

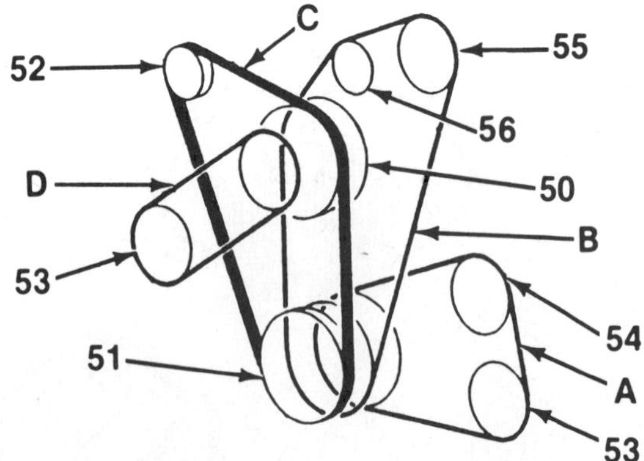

A. 1st track
B. 2nd track
C. 3rd track
D. 4th track
50. Water pump pulley
51. Crankshaft pulley
52. Alternator pulley
53. AIR pump pulley
54. Power steering pump pulley
55. Air conditioning compressor pulley
56. Idler pulley

Engine accessory drive belts for the 8-5.7L V-belts with Heavy Duty Emissions

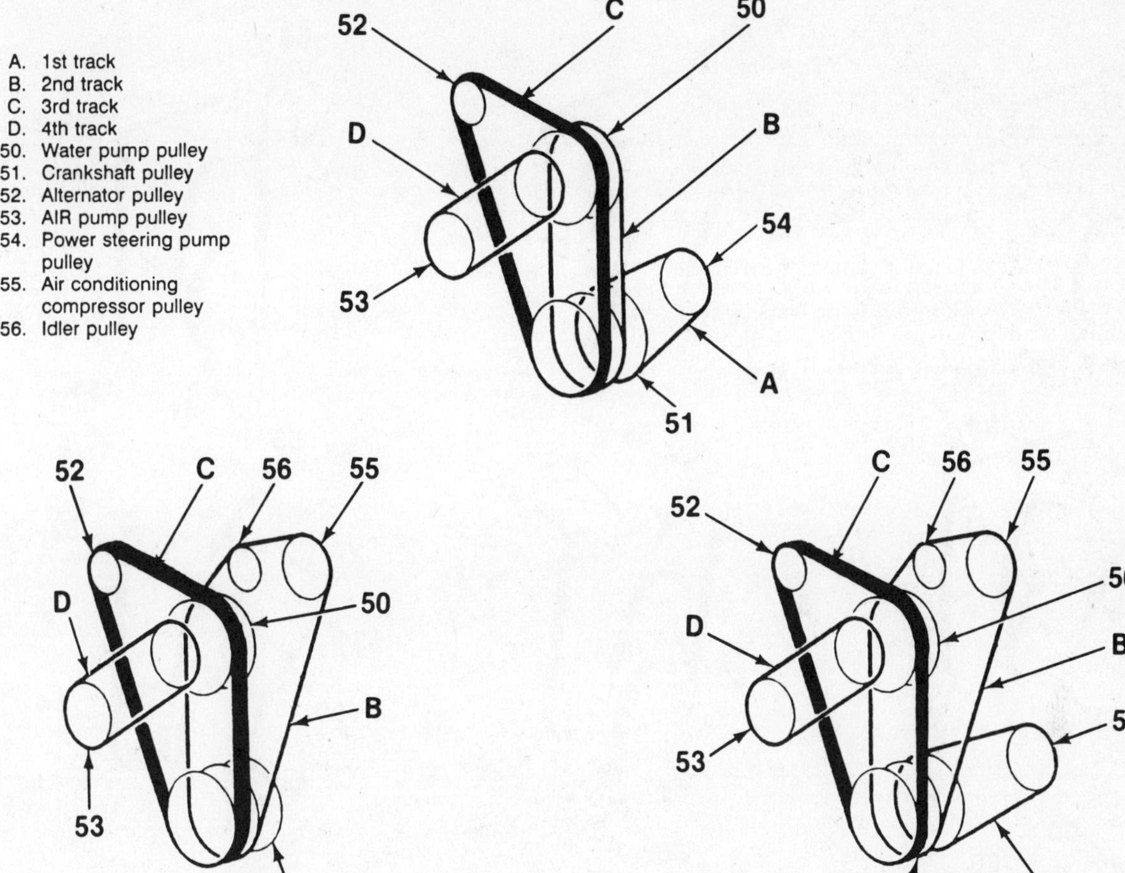

Engine accessory drive belts for the 8-5.7L and 8-6.2L engines

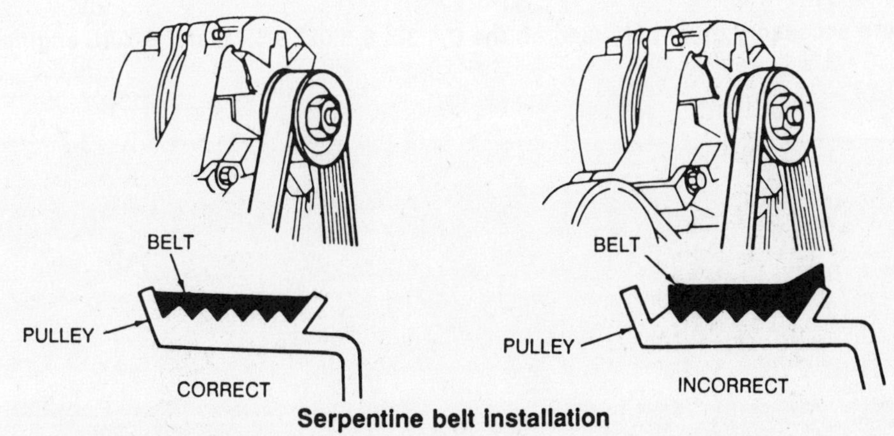

Serpentine belt installation

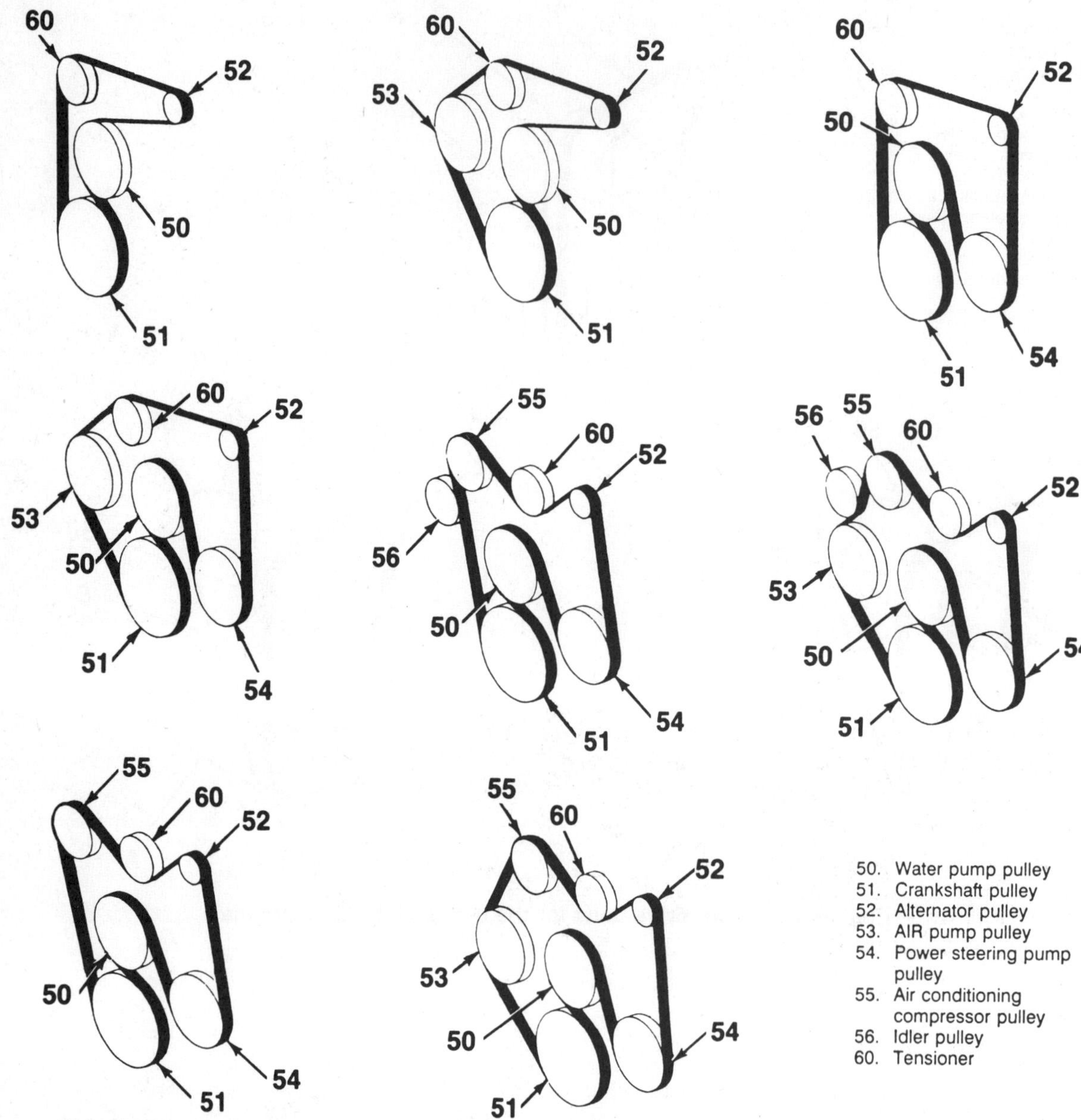

Serpentine accessory drive belt used on the 6-4.3L, 8-5.0L, 8-5.7L and 8-7.4L engines

HOW TO SPOT WORN V-BELTS

V–Belts are vital to efficient engine operation – they drive the fan, water pump and other accessories. They require little maintenance (occasional tightening) but they will not last forever. Slipping or failure of the V–belt will lead to overheating. If your V–belt looks like any of these, it should be replaced.

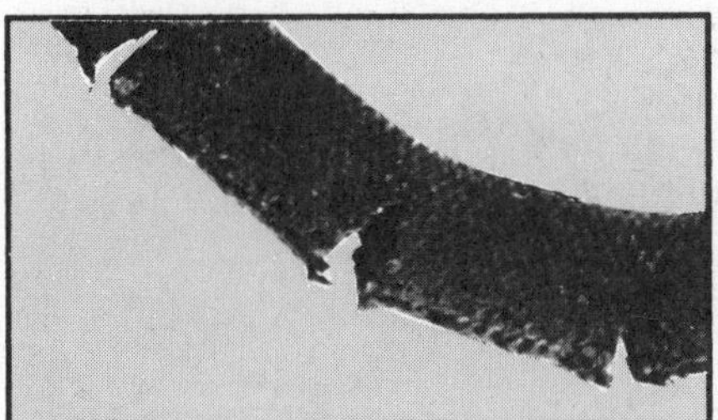

Cracking or Weathering

This belt has deep cracks, which cause it to flex. Too much flexing leads to heat build–up and premature failure. These cracks can be caused by using the belt on a pulley that is too small. Notched belts are available for small diameter pulleys.

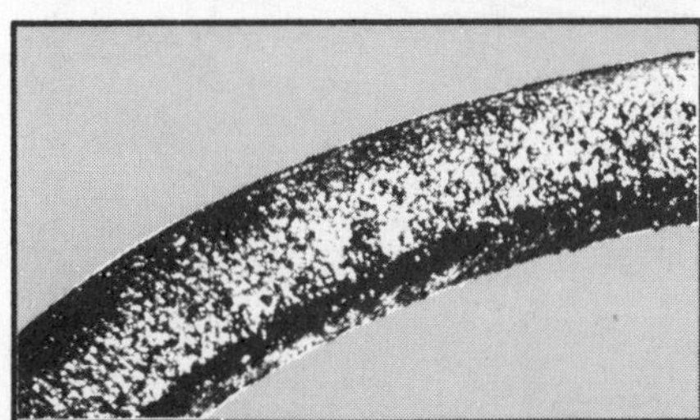

Softening (Grease and Oil)

Oil and grease on a belt can cause the belt's rubber compounds to soften and separate from the reinforcing cords that hold the belt together. The belt will first slip, then finally fail altogether.

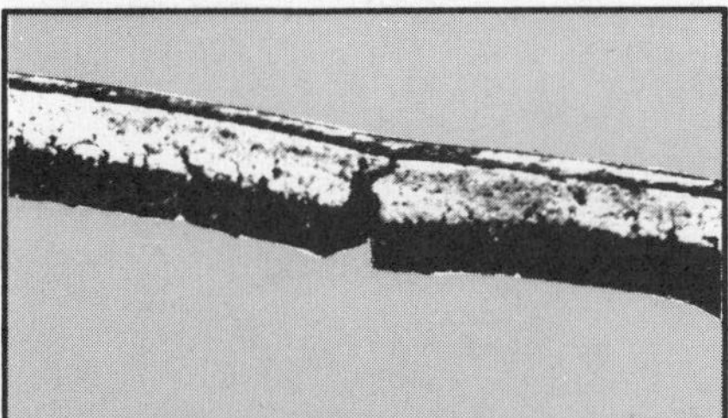

Glazing

Glazing is caused by a belt that is slipping. A slipping belt can cause a run-down battery, erratic power steering, overheating or poor accessory performance. The more the belt slips, the more glazing will be built up on the surface of the belt. The more the belt is glazed, the more it will slip. If the glazing is light, tighten the belt.

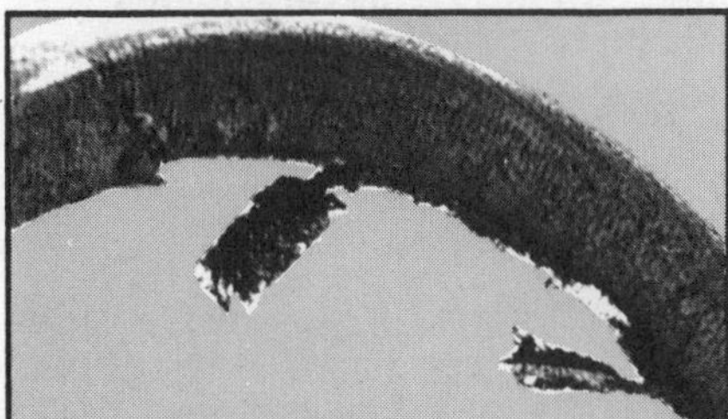

Worn Cover

The cover of this belt is worn off and is peeling away. The reinforcing cords will begin to wear and the belt will shortly break. When the belt cover wears in spots or has a rough jagged appearance, check the pulley grooves for roughness.

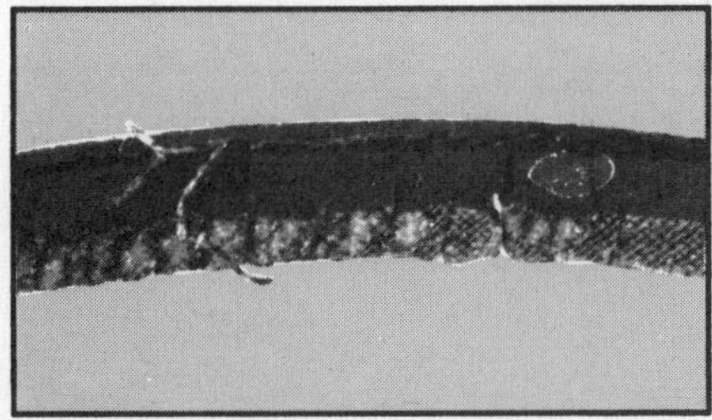

Separation

This belt is on the verge of breaking and leaving you stranded. The layers of the belt are separating and the reinforcing cords are exposed. It's just a matter of time before it breaks completely.

Hoses

Radiator hoses are generally of two constructions, the preformed (molded) type, which is custom made for a particular application, and the spring-loaded type, which is made to fit several different applications. Heater hoses are all of the same general construction.

INSPECTION

Inspect the condition of the radiator and heater hoses periodically. Early spring and at the beginning of the fall or winter, when you are performing other maintenance, are good times. Make sure the engine and cooling system are cold. Visually inspect for cracking, rotting or collapsed hoses, replace as necessary. Run your hand along the length of the hose. If a weak or swollen spot is noted when squeezing the hose wall, replace the hose.

1. Drain the cooling system into a suitable container (if the coolant is to be reused).

CAUTION

When draining the coolant, keep in mind that cats and dogs are attracted by the ethylene glycol antifreeze, and are quite likely to drink any that is left in an uncovered container or in puddles on the ground. This will prove fatal in sufficient quantity. Always drain the coolant into a sealable container. Coolant should be reused unless it is contaminated or several years old.

2. Loosen the hose clamps at each end of the hose that requires replacement.
3. Twist, pull and slide the hose off the radiator, water pump, thermostat or heater connection.
4. Clean the hose mounting connections. Position the hose clamps on the new hose.
5. Coat the connection surfaces with a water resistant sealer and slide the hose into position. Make sure the hose clamps are located beyond the raised bead of the connector (if equipped) and centered in the clamping area of the connection.
6. Tighten the clamps to 20–30 inch lbs. Do not overtighten.
7. Fill the cooling system.
8. Start the engine and allow it to reach normal operating temperature. Check for leaks.

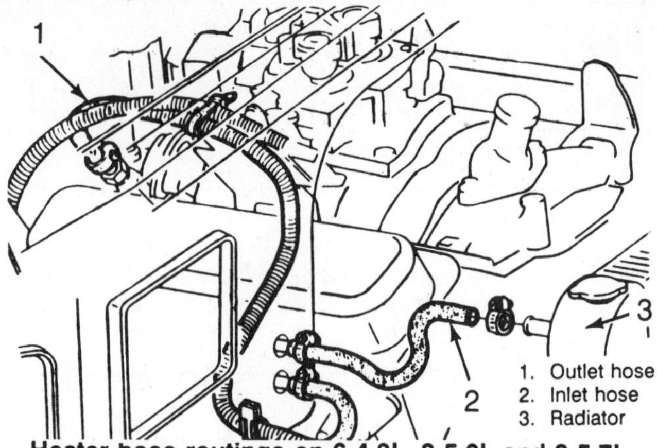

Heater hose routings on 6-4.3L, 8-5.0L and 8-5.7L engines with fuel injection

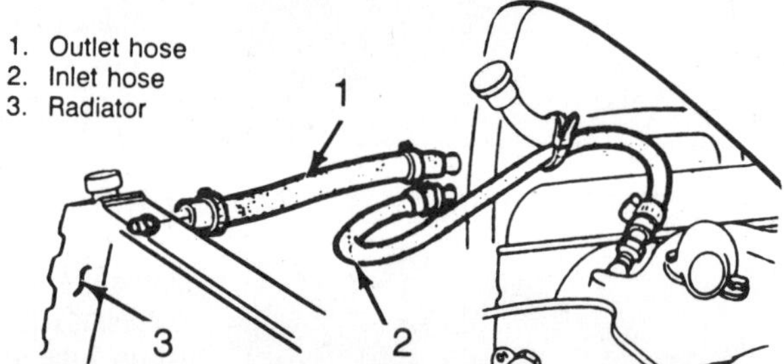

Heater hose routings on 8-5.7L engines with a carburetor

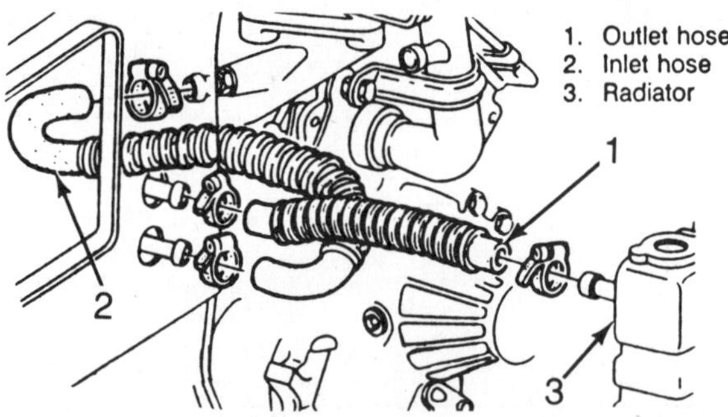

Heater hose routings on 8-6.2L diesel engines

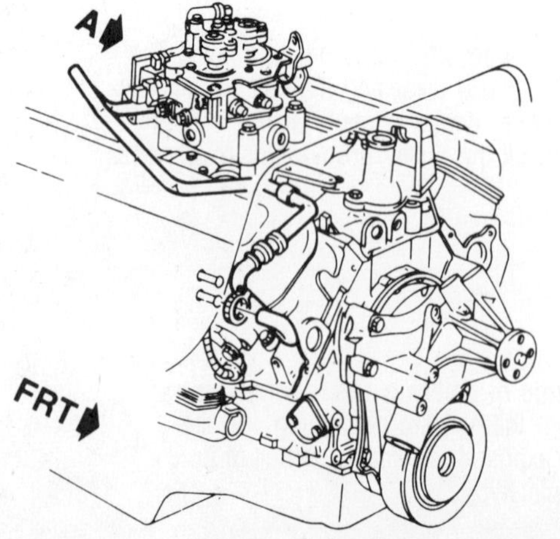

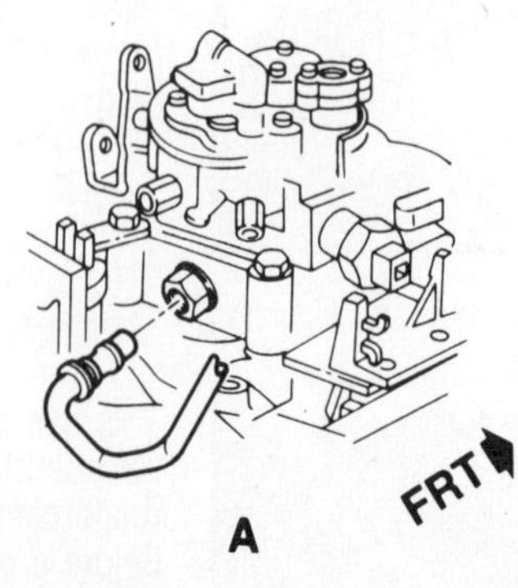

Heater inlet hose routings on 8-7.4L engines

HOW TO SPOT BAD HOSES

Both the upper and lower radiator hoses are called upon to perform difficult jobs in an inhospitable environment. They are subject to nearly 18 psi at under hood temperatures often over 280°F, and must circulate nearly 7500 gallons of coolant an hour – 3 good reasons to have good hoses.

Swollen Hose

A good test for any hose is to feel it for soft or spongy spots. Frequently these will appear as swollen areas of the hose. The most likely cause is oil soaking. This hose could burst at any time, when hot or under pressure.

Cracked Hose

Cracked hoses can usually be seen but feel the hoses to be sure they have not hardened; a prime cause of cracking. This hose has cracked down to the reinforcing cords and could split at any of the cracks.

Frayed Hose End (Due to Weak Clamp)

Weakened clamps frequently are the cause of hose and cooling system failure. The connection between the pipe and hose has deteriorated enough to allow coolant to escape when the engine is hot.

Debris in Cooling System

Debris, rust and scale in the cooling system can cause the inside of a hose to weaken. This can usually be felt on the outside of the hose as soft or thinner areas.

Air Conditioning

GENERAL SERVICING PROCEDURES

The most important aspect of air conditioning service is the maintenance of a pure and adequate charge of refrigerant in the system. A refrigeration system cannot function properly if a significant percentage of the charge is lost. Leaks are common because the severe vibration encountered in an automobile can easily cause a sufficient cracking or loosening of the air conditioning fittings; as a result, the extreme operating pressures of the system force refrigerant out.

The problem can be understood by considering what happens to the system as it is operated with a continuous leak. Because the expansion valve regulates the flow of refrigerant to the evaporator, the level of refrigerant there is fairly constant. The receiver/drier stores any excess of refrigerant, and so a loss will first appear there as a reduction in the level of liquid. As this level nears the bottom of the vessel, some refrigerant vapor bubbles will begin to appear in the stream of liquid supplied to the expansion valve. This vapor decreases the capacity of the expansion valve very little as the valve opens to compensate for its presence. As the quantity of liquid in the condenser decreases, the operating pressure will drop there and throughout the high side of the system. As the R-12 continues to be expelled, the pressure available to force the liquid through the expansion valve will continue to decrease, and, eventually, the valve's orifice will prove to be too much of a restriction for adequate flow even with the needle fully withdrawn.

At this point, low side pressure will start to drop, and severe reduction in cooling capacity, marked by freeze-up of the evaporator coil, will result. Eventually, the operating pressure of the evaporator will be lower than the pressure of the atmosphere surrounding it, and air will be drawn into the system wherever there are leaks in the low side.

Because all atmospheric air contains at least some moisture, water will enter the system and mix with the R-12 and the oil. Trace amounts of moisture will cause sludging of the oil, and corrosion of the system. Saturation and clogging of the filter/drier, and freezing of the expansion valve orifice will eventually result. As air fills the system to a greater and greater extent, it will interfere more and more with the normal flows of refrigerant and heat.

From this description, it should be obvious that much of the repairman's time will be spent detecting leaks, repairing them, and then restoring the purity and quantity of the refrigerant charge. A list of general precautions that should be observed while doing this follows:

1. Keep all tools as clean and dry as possible.
2. Thoroughly purge the service gauges and hoses of air and moisture before connecting them to the system. Keep them capped when not in use.
3. Thoroughly clean any refrigerant fitting before disconnecting it, in order to minimize the entrance of dirt into the system.
4. Plan any operation that requires opening the system beforehand, in order to minimize the length of time it will be exposed to open air. Cap or seal the open ends to minimize the entrance of foreign material.
5. When adding oil, pour it through an extremely clean and dry tube or funnel. Keep the oil capped whenever possible. Do not use oil that has not been kept tightly sealed.
6. Use only refrigerant 12. Purchase refrigerant intended for use in only automatic air conditioning systems. Avoid the use of refrigerant 12 that may be packaged for another use, such as cleaning, or powering a horn, as it is impure.
7. Completely evacuate any system that has been opened to replace a component, or that has leaked sufficiently to draw in moisture and air. This requires evacuating air and moisture with a good vacuum pump for at least one hour.

   If a system has been open for a considerable length of time it may be advisable to evacuate the system for up to 12 hours (overnight).
8. Use a wrench on both halves of a fitting that is to be disconnected, so as to avoid placing torque on any of the refrigerant lines.
9. When overhauling a compressor, pour some of the oil into a clean glass and inspect it. If there is evidence of dirt or metal particles, or both, flush all refrigerant components with clean refrigerant before evacuating and recharging the system. In addition, if metal particles are present, the compressor should be replaced.
10. Schrader valves may leak only when under full operating pressure. Therefore, if leakage is suspected but cannot be located, operate the system with a full charge of refrigerant and look for leaks from all Schrader valves. Replace any faulty valves.

Additional Preventive Maintenance Checks

ANTIFREEZE

In order to prevent heater core freeze-up during air condition-

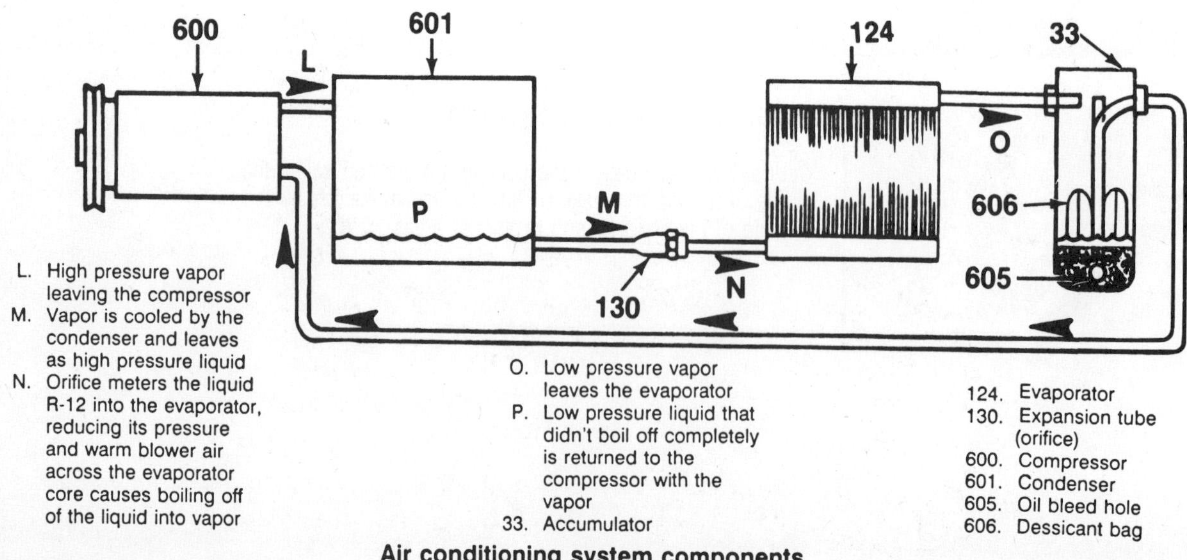
600
601
L
P
M
124
33
O
606
605
130
N
L. High pressure vapor leaving the compressor
M. Vapor is cooled by the condenser and leaves as high pressure liquid
N. Orifice meters the liquid R-12 into the evaporator, reducing its pressure and warm blower air across the evaporator core causes boiling off of the liquid into vapor
O. Low pressure vapor leaves the evaporator
P. Low pressure liquid that didn't boil off completely is returned to the compressor with the vapor
33. Accumulator
124. Evaporator
130. Expansion tube (orifice)
600. Compressor
601. Condenser
605. Oil bleed hole
606. Dessicant bag

Air conditioning system components

ing operation, it is necessary to maintain permanent type antifreeze protection of +15°F (−9°C), or lower. A reading of −15°F (−26°C) is ideal since this protection also supplies sufficient corrosion inhibitors for the protection of the engine cooling system.

NOTE: The same antifreeze should not be used longer than the manufacturer specifies.

RADIATOR CAP

For efficient operation of an air conditioned truck's cooling system, the radiator cap should have a holding pressure which meets manufacturer's specifications. A cap which fails to hold these pressures should be replaced.

CONDENSER

Any obstruction of or damage to the condenser configuration will restrict the air flow which is essential to its efficient operation. It is therefore a good rule to keep this unit clean and in proper physical shape.

NOTE: Bug screens are regarded as obstructions.

CONDENSATION DRAIN TUBE

This single molded drain tube expels the condensation, which accumulates on the bottom of the evaporator housing, into the engine compartment. If this tube is obstructed, the air conditioning performance can be restricted and condensation buildup can spill over onto the vehicle's floor.

SAFETY PRECAUTIONS

Because of the importance of the necessary safety precautions that must be exercised when working with air conditioning systems and R-12 refrigerant, a recap of the safety precautions are outlined.

1. Avoid contact with a charged refrigeration system, even when working on another part of the air conditioning system or vehicle. If a heavy tool comes into contact with a section of copper tubing or a heat exchanger, it can easily cause the relatively soft material to rupture.
2. When it is necessary to apply force to a fitting which contains refrigerant, as when checking that all system couplings are securely tightened, use a wrench on both parts of the fitting involved, if possible. This will avoid putting torque on refrigerant tubing. (It is advisable, when possible, to use tube or line wrenches when tightening these flare nut fittings.)
3. Do not attempt to discharge the system by merely loosening a fitting, or removing the service valve caps and cracking these valves. Precise control is possible only when using the service gauges. Place a rag under the open end of the center charging hose while discharging the system to catch any drops of liquid that might escape. Wear protective gloves when connecting or disconnecting service gauge hoses.
4. Discharge the system only in a well ventilated area, as high concentrations of the gas can exclude oxygen and act as an anaesthetic. When leak testing or soldering, this is particularly important, as toxic gas is formed when R-12 contacts any flame.
5. Never start a system without first verifying that both service valves are back-seated, if equipped, and that all fittings throughout the system are snugly connected.
6. Avoid applying heat to any refrigerant line or storage vessel. Charging may be aided by using water heated to less than 125° (52°C) to warm the refrigerant container. Never allow a refrigerant storage container to sit out in the sun, or near any other source of heat, such as a radiator.
7. Always wear goggles when working on a system to protect the eyes. If refrigerant contacts the eyes, it is advisable in all cases to see a physician as soon as possible.
8. Frostbite from liquid refrigerant should be treated by first gradually warming the area with cool water, and then gently applying petroleum jelly. A physician should be consulted.
9. Always keep refrigerant drum fittings capped when not in use. Avoid sudden shock to the drum, which might occur from dropping it, or from banging a heavy tool against it. Never carry a drum in the passenger compartment of a truck.
10. Always completely discharge the system before painting the vehicle (if the paint is to be baked on), or before welding anywhere near refrigerant lines.

Troubleshooting Basic Air Conditioning Problems

Problem	Cause	Solution
There's little or no air coming from the vents (and you're sure it's on)	• The A/C fuse is blown • Broken or loose wires or connections • The on/off switch is defective	• Check and/or replace fuse • Check and/or repair connections • Replace switch
The air coming from the vents is not cool enough	• Windows and air vent wings open • The compressor belt is slipping • Heater is on • Condenser is clogged with debris • Refrigerant has escaped through a leak in the system • Receiver/drier is plugged	• Close windows and vent wings • Tighten or replace compressor belt • Shut heater off • Clean the condenser • Check system • Service system
The air has an odor	• Vacuum system is disrupted • Odor producing substances on the evaporator case • Condensation has collected in the bottom of the evaporator housing	• Have the system checked/repaired • Clean the evaporator case • Clean the evaporator housing drains

Troubleshooting Basic Air Conditioning Problems (cont.)

Problem	Cause	Solution
System is noisy or vibrating	· Compressor belt or mountings loose · Air in the system	· Tighten or replace belt; tighten mounting bolts · Have the system serviced
Sight glass condition Constant bubbles, foam or oil streaks Clear sight glass, but no cold air Clear sight glass, but air is cold Clouded with milky fluid	· Undercharged system · No refrigerant at all · System is OK · Receiver drier is leaking dessicant	· Charge the system · Check and charge the system · Have system checked
Large difference in temperature of lines	· System undercharged	· Charge and leak test the system
Compressor noise	· Broken valves · Overcharged · Incorrect oil level · Piston slap · Broken rings · Drive belt pulley bolts are loose	· Replace the valve plate · Discharge, evacuate and install the correct charge · Isolate the compressor and check the oil level. Correct as necessary. · Replace the compressor · Replace the compressor · Tighten with the correct torque specification
Excessive vibration	· Incorrect belt tension · Clutch loose · Overcharged · Pulley is misaligned	· Adjust the belt tension · Tighten the clutch · Discharge, evacuate and install the correct charge · Align the pulley
Condensation dripping in the passenger compartment	· Drain hose plugged or improperly positioned · Insulation removed or improperly installed	· Clean the drain hose and check for proper installation · Replace the insulation on the expansion valve and hoses
Frozen evaporator coil	· Faulty thermostat · Thermostat capillary tube improperly installed · Thermostat not adjusted properly	· Replace the thermostat · Install the capillary tube correctly · Adjust the thermostat
Low side low—high side low	· System refrigerant is low · Expansion valve is restricted	· Evacuate, leak test and charge the system · Replace the expansion valve
Low side high—high side low	· Internal leak in the compressor—worn	· Remove the compressor cylinder head and inspect the compressor. Replace the valve plate assembly if necessary. If the compressor pistons, rings or

Troubleshooting Basic Air Conditioning Problems (cont.)

Problem	Cause	Solution
Low side high—high side low (cont.)		cylinders are excessively worn or scored replace the compressor
	• Cylinder head gasket is leaking	• Install a replacement cylinder head gasket
	• Expansion valve is defective	• Replace the expansion valve
	• Drive belt slipping	• Adjust the belt tension
Low side high—high side high	• Condenser fins obstructed	• Clean the condenser fins
	• Air in the system	• Evacuate, leak test and charge the system
	• Expansion valve is defective	• Replace the expansion valve
	• Loose or worn fan belts	• Adjust or replace the belts as necessary
Low side low—high side high	• Expansion valve is defective	• Replace the expansion valve
	• Restriction in the refrigerant hose	• Check the hose for kinks—replace if necessary
	• Restriction in the receiver/drier	• Replace the receiver/drier
	• Restriction in the condenser	• Replace the condenser
Low side and high normal (inadequate cooling)	**• Air in the system**	**• Evacuate, leak test and charge the system**
	• Moisture in the system	**• Evacuate, leak test and charge the system**

Air Conditioning Tools and Gauges

Test Gauges

Most of the service work performed in air conditioning requires the use of a set of two gauges, one for the high (head) pressure side of the system, the other for the low (suction) side.

The low side gauge records both pressure and vacuum. Vacuum readings are calibrated from 0 to 30 inches and the pressure graduations read from 0 to no less than 60 psi.

The high side gauge measures pressure from 0 to at least 600 psi.

Both gauges are threaded into a manifold that contains two hand shut-off valves. Proper manipulation of these valves and the use of the attached test hoses allow the user to perform the following services:

1. Test high and low side pressures.
2. Remove air, moisture, and contaminated refrigerant.
3. Purge the system (of refrigerant).
4. Charge the system (with refrigerant).

The manifold valves are designed so they have no direct effect on gauge readings, but serve only to provide for, or cut off, flow of refrigerant through the manifold. During all testing and hook-up operations, the valves are kept in a closed position to avoid disturbing the refrigeration system. The valves are opened only to purge the system of refrigerant or to charge it.

When purging the system, the center hose is uncapped at the lower end, and both valves are cracked open slightly. This allows refrigerant pressure to force the entire contents of the system out through the center hose. During charging, the valve on the high side of the manifold is closed, and the valve on the low side is cracked open. Under these conditions, the low pressure in the evaporator will draw refrigerant from the relatively warm refrigerant storage container into the system.

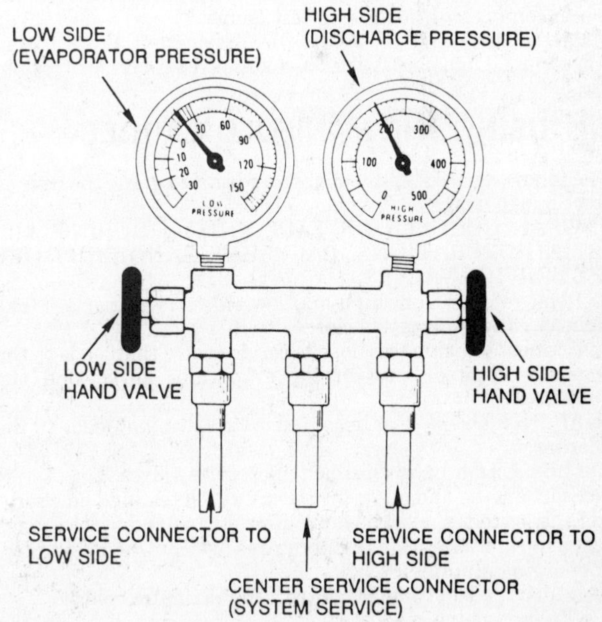

Manifold gauge set

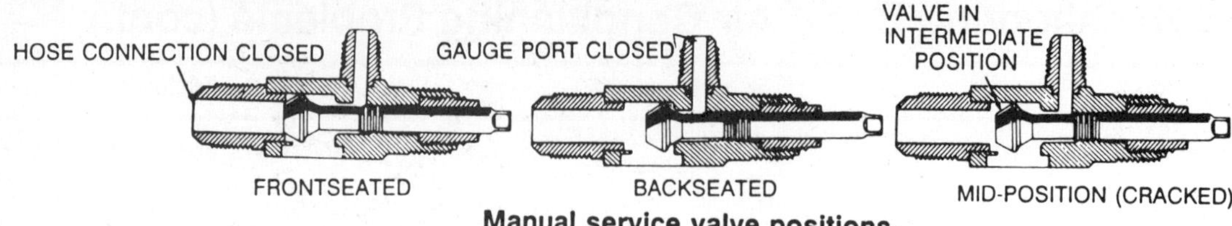

Manual service valve positions

Service Valves

For the user to diagnose an air conditioning system he or she must gain "entrance" to the system in order to observe the pressures. There are two types of terminals for this purpose, the hand shut off type and the familiar Schrader valve.

The Schrader valve is similar to a tire valve stem and the process of connecting the test hoses is the same as threading a hand pump outlet hose to a bicycle tire. As the test hose is threaded to the service port the valve core is depressed, allowing the refrigerant to enter the test hose outlet. Removal of the test hose automatically closes the system.

Extreme caution must be observed when removing test hoses from the Schrader valves as some refrigerant will normally escape, usually under high pressure. (Observe safety precautions.)

Some systems have hand shut-off valves (the stem can be rotated with a special ratcheting box wrench) that can be positioned in the following three ways:

1. FRONT SEATED – Rotated to full clockwise position.
   a. Refrigerant will not flow to compressor, but will reach test gauge port. COMPRESSOR WILL BE DAMAGED IF SYSTEM IS TURNED ON IN THIS POSITION.
   b. The compressor is now isolated and ready for service. However, care must be exercised when removing service valves from the compressor as a residue of refrigerant may still be present within the compressor. Therefore, remove service valves slowly observing all safety precautions.
2. BACK SEATED – Rotated to full counter clockwise position. Normal position for system while in operation. Refrigerant flows to compressor but not to test gauge.
3. MID-POSITION (CRACKED) – Refrigerant flows to entire system. Gauge port (with hose connected) open for testing.

USING THE MANIFOLD GAUGES

The following are step-by-step procedures to guide the user to correct gauge usage.

1. WEAR GOGGLES OR FACE SHIELD DURING ALL TESTING OPERATIONS. BACKSEAT HAND SHUT-OFF TYPE SERVICE VALVES.
2. Remove caps from high and low side service ports. Make sure both gauge valves are closed.
3. Connect low side test hose to service valve that leads to the evaporator (located between the evaporator outlet and the compressor).
4. Attach high side test hose to service valve that leads to the condenser.
5. Mid-position hand shutoff type service valves.
6. Start engine and allow for warm-up. All testing and charging of the system should be done after engine and system have reached normal operation temperatures (except when using certain charging stations).
7. Adjust air conditioner controls to maximum cold.
8. Observe gauge readings.

When the gauges are not being used it is a good idea to:

a. Keep both hand valves in the closed position.

b. Attach both ends of the high and low service hoses to the manifold, if extra outlets are present on the manifold, or plug them if not. Also, keep the center charging hose attached to an empty refrigerant can. This extra precaution will reduce the possibility of moisture entering the gauges. If air and moisture have gotten into the gauges, purge the hoses by supplying refrigerant under pressure to the center hose with both gauge valves open and all openings unplugged.

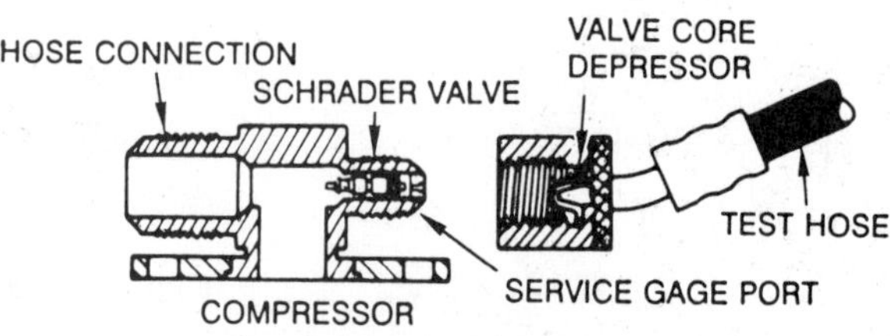

Typical Schraeder valve

SYSTEM CHECKS

CAUTION

Do not attempt to charge or discharge the refrigerant system unless you are thoroughly familiar with its operation and the hazards involved. The compressed refrigerant used in the air conditioning system expands and evaporates (boils) into the atmosphere at a temperature of −21.7°F (−29.8°C) or less. This will freeze any surface that it comes in contact with, including your eyes. In addition, the refrigerant decomposes into a poisonous gas in the presence of flame.

These air conditioning systems have no sight glass for checking.

1. Warm the engine to normal operating temperature.
2. Open the hood and doors.
3. Set the selector lever at A/C.
4. Set the temperature lever at the first detent to the right of COLD (outside air).
5. Set the blower on HI.
6. Idle the engine at 1,000 rpm.
7. Feel the temperature of the evaporator inlet and the accumulator outlet with the compressor engaged.

Both lines should be cold. If the inlet pipe is colder than the outlet pipe the system is low on charge.

DISCHARGING THE SYSTEM

CAUTION

Perform operation in a well ventilated area.

When it is necessary to remove (purge) the refrigerant pressurized in the system, follow this procedure:

1. Operate air conditioner for at least 10 minutes.
2. Attach gauges, shut off engine and air conditioner.
3. Place a container or rag at the outlet of the center charging hose on the gauge. The refrigerant will be discharged there and this precaution will avoid its uncontrolled exposure.
4. Open low side hand valve on gauge slightly.
5. Open high side hand valve slightly.

NOTE: Too rapid a purging process will be identified by the appearance of an oily foam. If this occurs, close the hand valves a little more until this condition stops.

6. Close both hand valves on the gauge set when the pressures read 0 and all the refrigerant has left the system.

EVACUATING THE SYSTEM

Before charging any system it is necessary to purge the refrigerant and draw out the trapped moisture with a suitable vacuum pump. Failure to do so will result in ineffective charging and possible damage to the system.

Use this hook-up for the proper evacuation procedure:

1. Connect both service gauge hoses to the high and low service outlets.
2. Open high and low side hand valves on gauge manifold.
3. Open both service valves a slight amount (from back seated position), allow refrigerant to discharge from system.
4. Install center charging hose of gauge set to vacuum pump.
5. Operate vacuum pump for at least one hour. (If the system has been subjected to open conditions for a prolonged period of time it may be necessary to "pump the system down" overnight. Refer to "System Sweep" procedure.)

NOTE: If low pressure gauge does not show at least 28 in.Hg within 5 minutes, check the system for a leak or loose gauge connectors.

6. Close hand valves on gauge manifold.
7. Shut off pump.
8. Observe low pressure gauge to determine if vacuum is holding. A vacuum drop may indicate a leak.

SYSTEM SWEEP

An efficient vacuum pump can remove all the air contained in a contaminated air conditioning system very quickly, because of its vapor state. Moisture, however, is far more difficult to remove because the vacuum must force the liquid to evaporate before it will be able to remove it from the system. If a system has become severely contaminated, as, for example, it might become after all the charge was lost in conjunction with vehicle accident damage, moisture removal is extremely time consuming. A vacuum pump could remove all of the moisture only if it were operated for 12 hours or more.

Under these conditions, sweeping the system with refrigerant will speed the process of moisture removal considerably. To sweep, follow the following procedure:

1. Connect vacuum pump to gauges, operate it until vacuum ceases to increase, then continue operation for ten more minutes.
2. Charge system with 50% of its rated refrigerant capacity.
3. Operate system at fast idle for ten minutes.
4. Discharge the system.
5. Repeat twice the process of charging to 50% capacity, running the system for ten minutes, and discharging it, for a total of three sweeps.
6. Replace drier.
7. Pump system down as in Step 1.
8. Charge system.

CHARGING THE SYSTEM

CAUTION

Never attempt to charge the system by opening the high pressure gauge control while the compressor is operating. The compressor accumulating pressure can burst the refrigerant container, causing sever personal injuries.

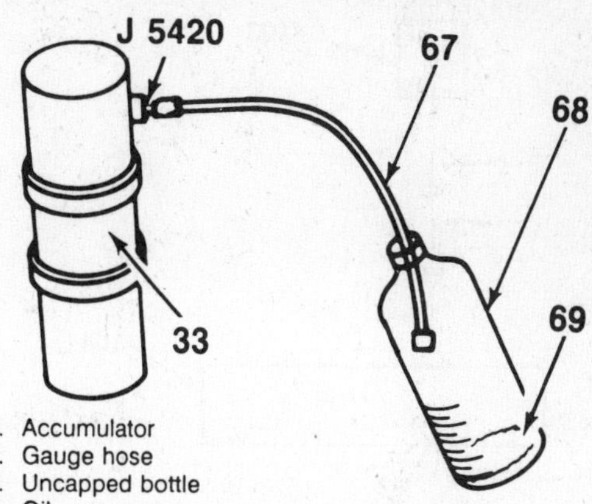

33. Accumulator
67. Gauge hose
68. Uncapped bottle
69. Oil

Discharging the system

Basic System

In this procedure the refrigerant enters the suction side of the system as a vapor while the compressor is running. Before proceeding, the system should be in a partial vacuum after adequate evacuation. Both hand valves on the gauge manifold should be closed.

1. Attach both test hoses to their respective service valve ports. Mid-position manually operated service valves, if present.
2. Install dispensing valve (closed position) on the refrigerant container. (Single and multiple refrigerant manifolds are available to accommodate one to four 15 oz. cans.)
3. Attach center charging hose to the refrigerant container valve.
4. Open dispensing valve on the refrigerant can.
5. Loosen the center charging hose coupler where it connects to the gauge manifold to allow the escaping refrigerant to purge the hose of contaminants.
6. Tighten center charging hose connection.
7. Purge the low pressure test hose at the gauge manifold.
8. Start the truck's engine, roll down the windows and adjust the air conditioner to maximum cooling. The engine should be at normal operating temperature before proceeding. The heated environment helps the liquid vaporize more efficiently.
9. Crack open the low side hand valve on the manifold. Manipulate the valve so that the refrigerant that enters the system does not cause the low side pressure to exceed 40 psi. Too sudden a surge may permit the entrance of unwanted liquid to the compressor. Since liquids cannot be compressed, the compressor will suffer damage if compelled to attempt it. If the suction

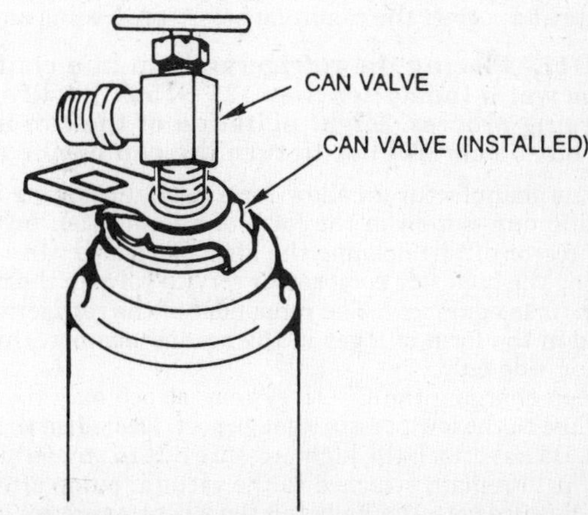

1 lb. R-12 can with opener/valve connected

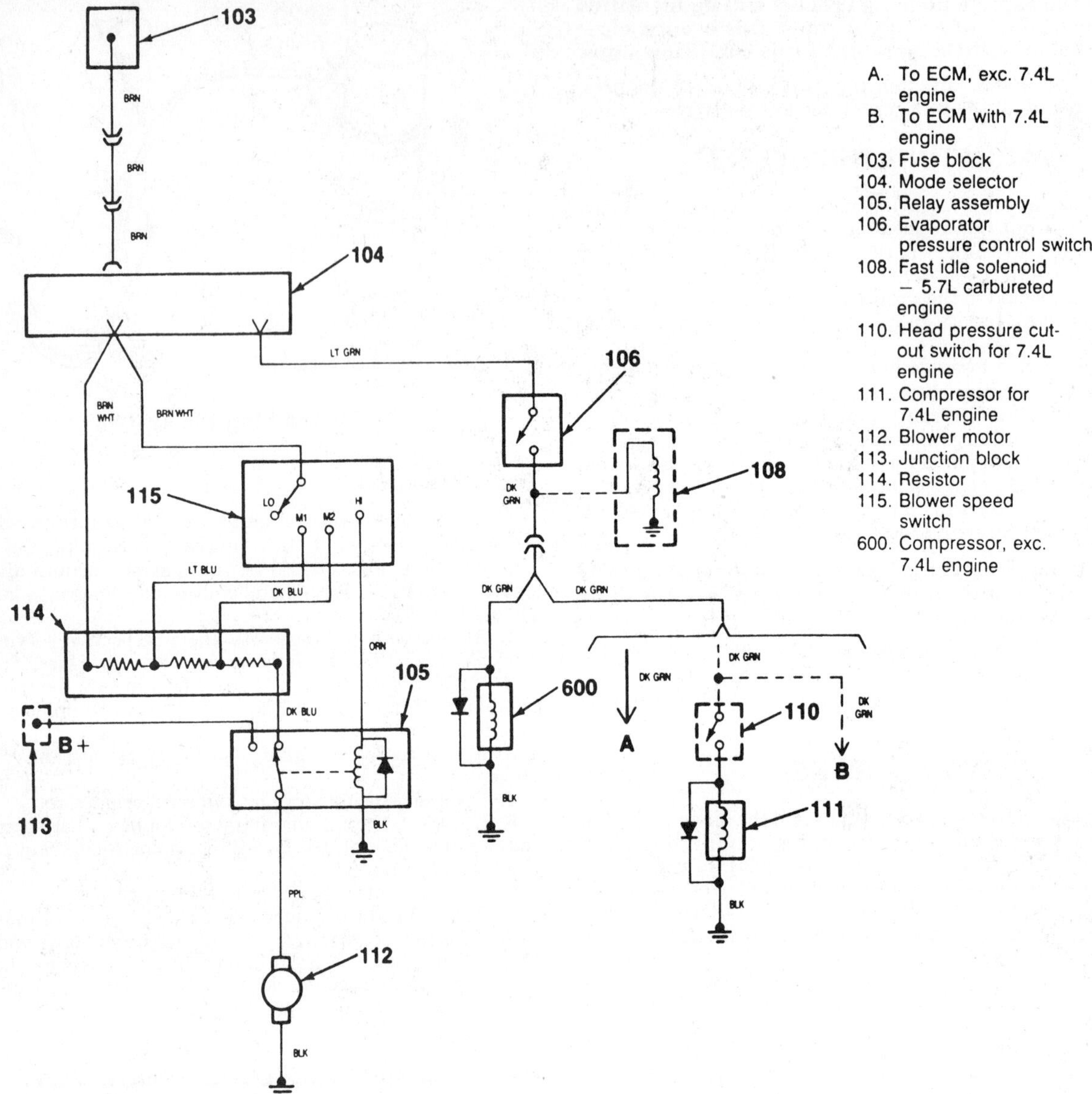

Air conditioning system wiring diagram

side of the system remains in a vacuum the system is blocked. Locate and correct the condition before proceeding any further.

NOTE: Placing the refrigerant can in a container of warm water (no hotter than 125°F [52°C]) will speed the charging process. Slight agitation of the can is helpful too, but be careful not to turn the can upside down.

Some manufacturers allow for a partial charging of the air conditioning system in the form of a liquid (can inverted and compressor off) by opening the high side gauge valve only, and putting the high side compressor service valve in the middle position (if so equipped). The remainder of the refrigerant is then added in the form of a gas in the normal manner, through the suction side only.

When charging the CCOT system, attach only the low pressure line to the low pressure gauge port, located on the accumulator. Do not attach the high pressure line to any service port or allow it to remain attached to the vacuum pump after evacuation. Be sure both the high and the low pressure control valves are closed on the gauge set. To complete the charging of the system, follow the outline supplied.

1. Start the engine and allow to run at idle, with the cooling system at normal operating temperature.
2. Attach the center gauge hose to a single or multi-can dispenser.
3. With the multi-can dispenser inverted, allow one pound or the contents of one or two 14 oz. cans to enter the system through the low pressure side by opening the gauge low pressure control valve.
4. Close the low pressure gauge control valve and turn the air conditioning system on to engage the compressor. Place the blower motor in its high mode.
5. Open the low pressure gauge control valve and draw the remaining charge into the system. Refer to the capacity chart at the end of this section for the individual vehicle or system capacity.
6. Close the low pressure gauge control valve and the refrigerant source valve, on the multi-can dispenser. Remove the low pressure hose from the accumulator quickly to avoid loss of refrigerant through the Schrader valve.

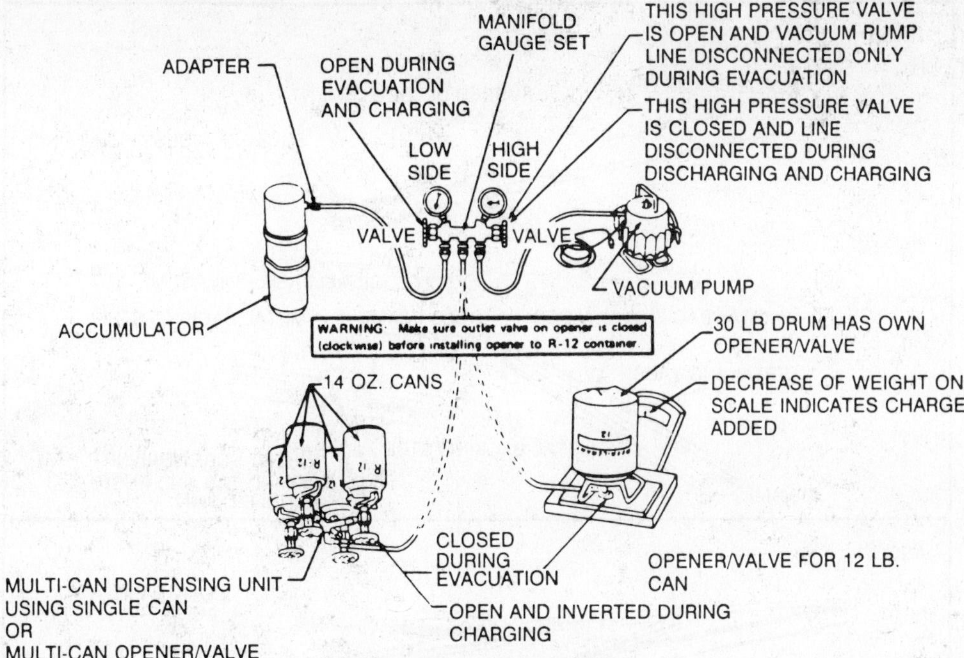
MANIFOLD
GAUGE SET
THIS HIGH PRESSURE VALVE
IS OPEN AND VACUUM PUMP
LINE DISCONNECTED ONLY
DURING EVACUATION
ADAPTER
OPEN DURING
EVACUATION
AND CHARGING
THIS HIGH PRESSURE VALVE
IS CLOSED AND LINE
DISCONNECTED DURING
DISCHARGING AND CHARGING
LOW
SIDE
HIGH
SIDE
VALVE
VALVE
VACUUM PUMP
ACCUMULATOR
WARNING: Make sure outlet valve on opener is closed (clockwise) before installing opener to R-12 container.
30 LB DRUM HAS OWN
OPENER/VALVE
14 OZ. CANS
DECREASE OF WEIGHT ON
SCALE INDICATES CHARGE
ADDED
CLOSED
DURING
EVACUATION
OPENER/VALVE FOR 12 LB.
CAN
MULTI-CAN DISPENSING UNIT
USING SINGLE CAN
OR
MULTI-CAN OPENER/VALVE
OPEN AND INVERTED DURING
CHARGING

Typical gauge connections

7. Install the protective cap on the gauge port and check the system for leakage.
8. Test the system for proper operation.

Refrigerant Capacities

- 1988–89 R/V Models, Front Only: 3 lb. 4 oz.
- 1988–89 R/V Models, Rear: 5 lb. 4 oz.
- 1988–90 C/K Models: 2 lb. 8 oz.
- 1990 R/V Models, Front Only: 3 lb. 2 oz.
- 1990 R/V Models, Rear: 5 lb. 2 oz.

Leak Testing the System

There are several methods of detecting leaks in an air conditioning system; among them, the two most popular are (1) halide leak-detection or the "open flame method," and (2) electronic leak-detection.

The halide leak detection is a torch like device which produces a yellow-green color when refrigerant is introduced into the flame at the burner. A purple or violet color indicates the presence of large amounts of refrigerant at the burner.

An electronic leak detector is a small portable electronic device with an extended probe. With the unit activated the probe is passed along those components of the system which contain refrigerant. If a leak is detected, the unit will sound an alarm signal or activate a display signal depending on the manufacturer's design. It is advisable to follow the manufacturer's instructions as the design and function of the detection may vary significantly.

CAUTION

Care should be taken to operate either type of detector in well ventilated areas, so as to reduce the chance of personal injury, which may result from coming in contact with poisonous gases produced when R-12 is exposed to flame or electric spark.

Windshield Wipers

Intense heat from the sun, snow and ice, road oils and the chemicals used in windshield washer solvents combine to deteriorate the rubber wiper refills.

For maximum effectiveness and longest element life, the windshield and wiper blades should be kept clean. Dirt, tree sap, road tar and so on will cause streaking, smearing and blade deterioration if left on the windshield. It is advisable to wash the windshield carefully with a commercial glass cleaner at least once a month. Wipe off the rubber blades with a wet rag afterwards. Do not attempt to move the wipers back and forth by hand! Damage to the motor and drive mechanism will result.

If the blades are found to be cracked, broken or torn they should be replaced immediately. Replacement intervals will vary with usage, although ozone deterioration usually limits blade lift to about one year. If the wiper pattern is smeared or streaked, or if the blade chatters across the glass, the blades should be replaced. It is easiest and most sensible to replace them in pairs.

WIPER REFILL REPLACEMENT

Normally, if the wipers are not cleaning the windshield properly, only the refill has to be replaced. The blade and arm usually require replacement only in the event of damage. It is not necessary to remove the arm or the blade to replace the refill (rubber part), though you may have to position the arm higher on the glass. You can do this by turning the key on and operating the wipers. When they are positioned where they are accessible, turn the key off.

There are several types of refills and your vehicle could have any kind, since aftermarket blades and arms may not use exactly the same type refill as the original equipment.

Most Trico® styles use a release button that is pushed down to allow the refill to slide out of the yoke jaws. The new refill slides in an locks in place. Some Trico® refills are removed by locating where the metal backing strip or the refill is wider and inserting a small screwdriver blade between the frame and metal backing strip. Press down to release the refill from the retaining tab.

The Anco® style is unlocked at one end by squeezing the metal tabs, and the refill is slid out of the frame jaws. When the new refill is installed, the tabs will click into place, locking the refill.

The polycarbonate type is held in place by a locking lever that is pushed downward out of the groove in the arm to free the re-

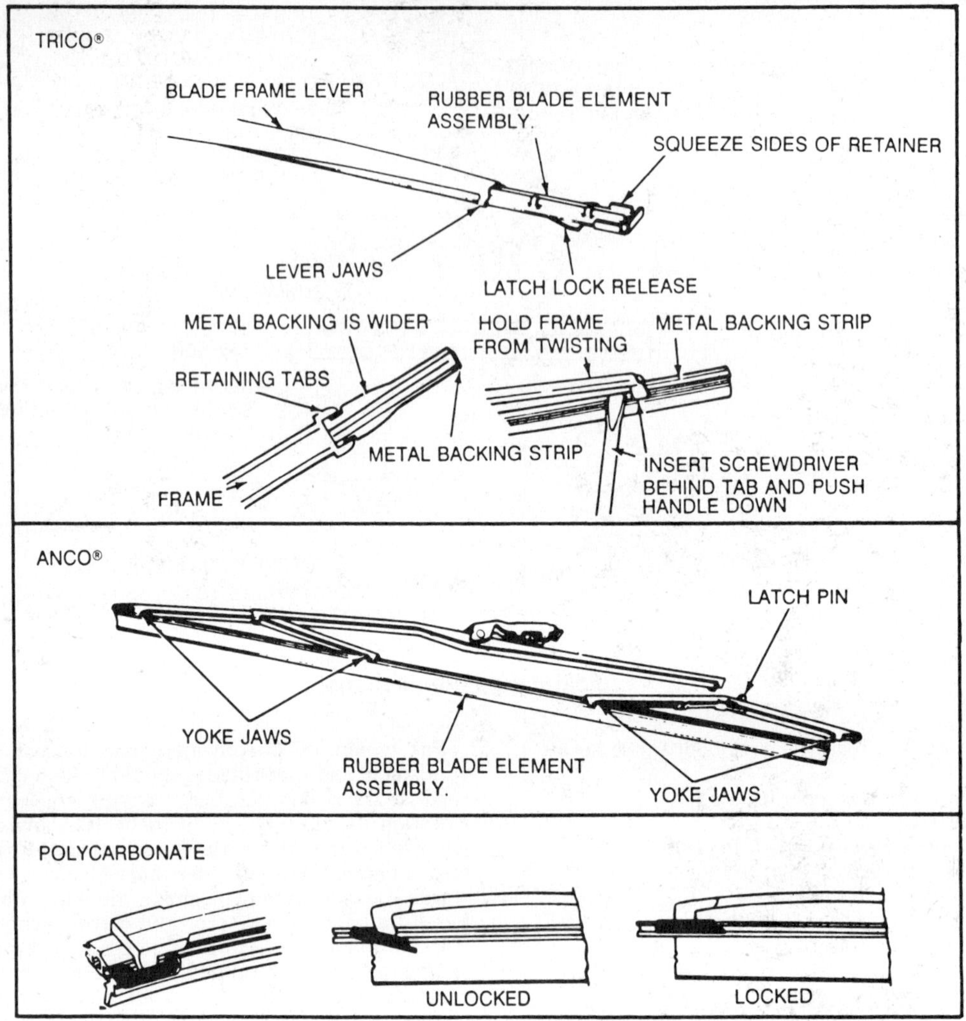

Windshield wiper blade refills

fill. When the new refill is installed, it will lock in place automatically.

No matter which type of refill you use, be sure that all of the frame claws engage the refill. Before operating the wipers, be sure that no part of the metal frame is contacting the windshield.

Tires and Wheels

INSPECTION

The tires on your truck should have built-in tread wear indicators, which appear as ½ in. (12.7mm) bands when the tread depth gets as low as $^1/_{16}$ in. (1.6mm). When the indicators appear in 2 or more adjacent grooves, it's time for new tires.

For optimum tire life, you should keep the tires properly inflated, rotate them often and have the wheel alignment checked periodically.

Some models have the maximum load pressures listed in the V.I.N. plate on the left door frame. In general, pressure of 28–32 psi would be suitable for highway use with moderate loads and passenger car type tires (load range B, non-flotation) of original equipment size. Pressures should be checked before driving, since pressure can increase as much as 6 psi due to heat. It is a good idea to have an accurate gauge and to check pressures weekly. Not all gauges on service station air pumps are to be trusted. In general, truck type tires require higher pressures and flotation type tires, lower pressures.

TIRE ROTATION

It is recommended that you have the tires rotated every 6,000 miles. There is no way to give a tire rotation diagram for every combination of tires and vehicles, but the accompanying diagrams are a general rule to follow. Radial tires should not be cross-switched. They last longer if their direction of rotation is not changed. Truck tires sometimes have directional tread, indicated by arrows on the sidewalls. The arrow shows the direction of rotation. They will wear very rapidly if reversed. Studded snow tires will lose their studs if their direction of rotation is reversed.

NOTE: Mark the wheel position or direction of rotation on radial tires or studded snow tires before removing them.

If your truck is equipped with tires having different load ratings on the front and the rear, the tires should not be rotated front to rear. Rotating these tires could affect tire life (the tires with the lower rating will wear faster, and could become overloaded), and upset the handling of the truck.

TIRE USAGE

The tires on your truck were selected to provide the best all around performance for normal operation when inflated as specified. Oversize tires (Load Range D) will not increase the maximum carrying capacity of the vehicle, although they will provide an extra margin of tread life. Be sure to check overall height before using larger size tires which may cause interference with suspension components or wheel wells. When replacing conventional tire sizes with other tire size designations, be sure to check the manufacturer's recommendations. Interchangeability is not always possible because of differences in load ratings, tire dimensions, wheel well clearances, and rim size. Also due to differences in handling characteristics, 70 Series and 60 Series tires should be used only in pairs on the same axle. Radial tires should be used only in sets of four.

The wheels must be the correct width for the tire. Tire dealers have charts of tire and rim compatibility. A mismatch can cause sloppy handling and rapid tread wear. The old rule of thumb is that the tread width should match the rim width (inside bead to inside bead) within 1 in. (25.4mm). For radial tires, the rim width should be 80% or less of the tire (not tread) width.

The height (mounted diameter) of the new tires can greatly change speedometer accuracy, engine speed at a given road speed, fuel mileage, acceleration, and ground clearance. Tire manufacturers furnish full measurement specifications. Speedometer drive gears are available for correction.

NOTE: Dimensions of tires marked the same size may vary significantly, even among tires from the same manufacturer.

The spare tire should be usable, at least for low speed operation, with the new tires.

TIRE DESIGN

For maximum satisfaction, tires should be used in sets of five. Mixing or different types (radial, bias/belted, fiberglass belted) should be avoided. Conventional bias tires are constructed so that the cords run bead-to-bead at an angle. Alternate plies run at an opposite angle. This type of construction gives rigidity to both tread and sidewall. Bias/belted tires are similar in construction to conventional bias ply tires. Belts run at an angle and also at a 90° angle to the bead, as in the radial tire. Tread life is improved considerably over the conventional bias tire. The radial tire differs in construction, but instead of the carcass plies running at an angle of 90° to each other, they run at an angle of 90° to the bead. This gives the tread a great deal of rigidity and the sidewall a great deal of flexibility and accounts for the characteristic bulge associated with radial tires.

Chevrolet and GMC trucks are capable of using radial tires and they are recommended in some years. If they are used, tire sizes and wheel diameters should be selected to maintain ground clearance and tire load capacity equivalent to the minimum specified tire. Radial tires should always be used in sets of five, but in an emergency radial tires can be used with caution on the rear axle only. If this is done, both tires on the rear should be of radial design.

NOTE: Radial tires should never be used on only the front axle.

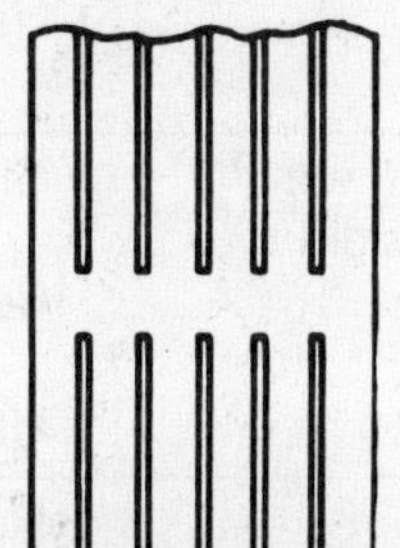

Tread wear indicators appear as solid bands when the tread is worn

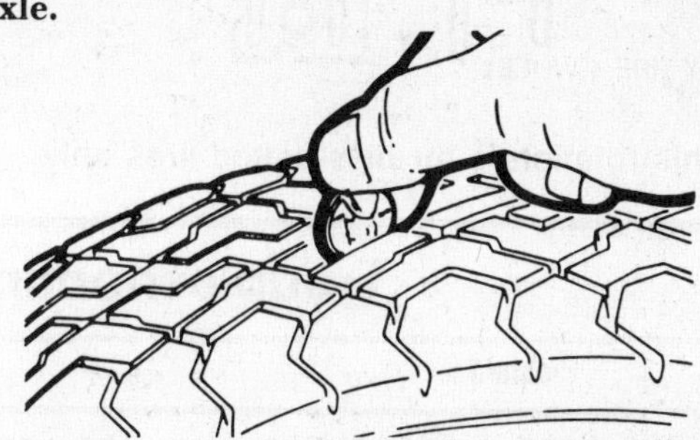

Tread depth can be checked with a penny; when the top of Lincoln's head is visible, it's time for new tires

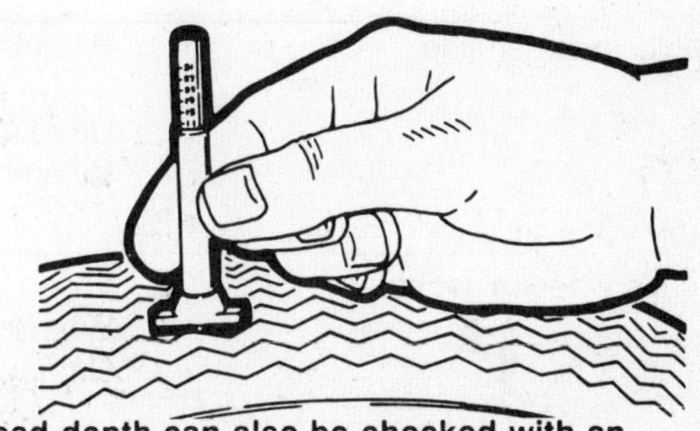

Tread depth can also be checked with an inexpensive gauge made for the purpose

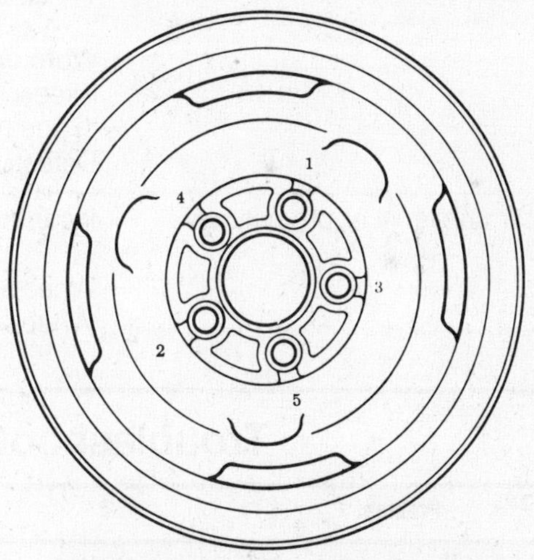

Wheel lug tightening sequence

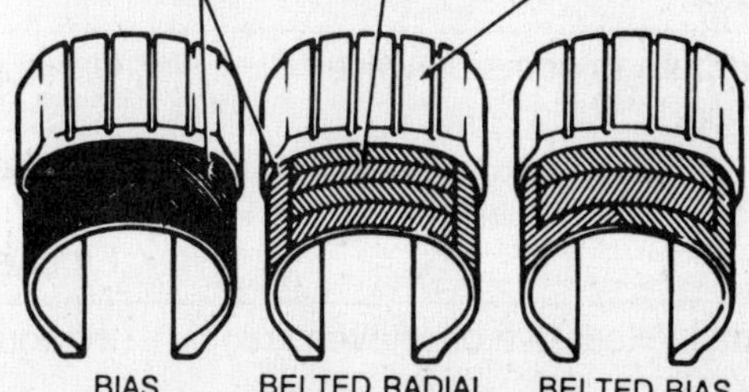

Types of tire construction

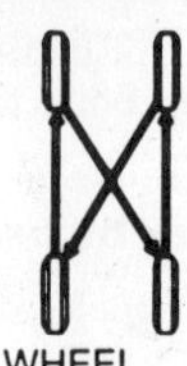

BIAS PLY TIRE 4 WHEEL ROTATION

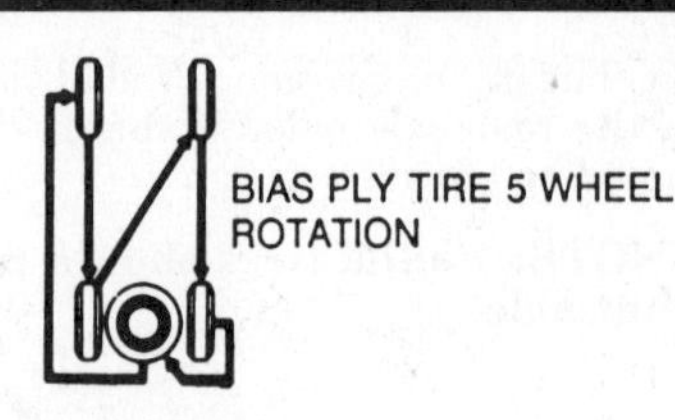

BIAS PLY TIRE 5 WHEEL ROTATION

This rotation is for bias-belted tires only

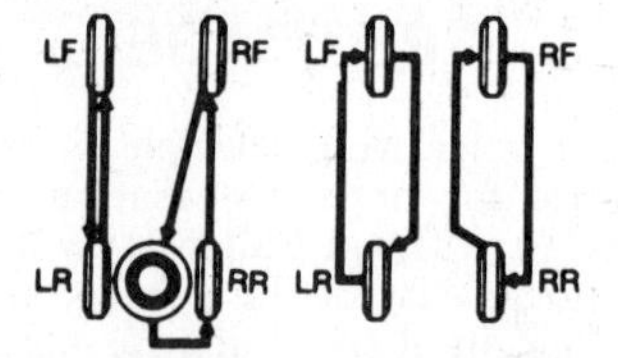

5 WHEEL ROTATION 4 WHEEL ROTATION

This rotation is for radial tires

Troubleshooting Basic Wheel Problems

Problem	Cause	Solution
The car's front end vibrates at high speed	• The wheels are out of balance • Wheels are out of alignment	• Have wheels balanced • Have wheel alignment checked/adjusted
Car pulls to either side	• Wheels are out of alignment • Unequal tire pressure • Different size tires or wheels	• Have wheel alignment checked/adjusted • Check/adjust tire pressure • Change tires or wheels to same size
The car's wheel(s) wobbles	• Loose wheel lug nuts • Wheels out of balance • Damaged wheel • Wheels are out of alignment • Worn or damaged ball joint • Excessive play in the steering linkage (usually due to worn parts) • Defective shock absorber	• Tighten wheel lug nuts • Have tires balanced • Raise car and spin the wheel. If the wheel is bent, it should be replaced • Have wheel alignment checked/adjusted • Check ball joints • Check steering linkage • Check shock absorbers
Tires wear unevenly or prematurely	• Incorrect wheel size • Wheels are out of balance • Wheels are out of alignment	• Check if wheel and tire size are compatible • Have wheels balanced • Have wheel alignment checked/adjusted

Troubleshooting Basic Tire Problems

Problem	Cause	Solution
The car's front end vibrates at high speeds and the steering wheel shakes	• Wheels out of balance • Front end needs aligning	• Have wheels balanced • Have front end alignment checked
The car pulls to one side while cruising	• Unequal tire pressure (car will usually pull to the low side) • Mismatched tires • Front end needs aligning	• Check/adjust tire pressure • Be sure tires are of the same type and size • Have front end alignment checked
Abnormal, excessive or uneven tire wear	• Infrequent tire rotation • Improper tire pressure	• Rotate tires more frequently to equalize wear • Check/adjust pressure

Troubleshooting Basic Tire Problems

Problem	Cause	Solution
See "How to Read Tire Wear"	· Sudden stops/starts or high speed on curves	· Correct driving habits
Tire squeals	· Improper tire pressure · Front end needs aligning	· Check/adjust tire pressure · Have front end alignment checked

Tire Size Comparison Chart

"Letter" sizes			Inch Sizes	Metric-inch Sizes		
"60 Series"	"70 Series"	"78 Series"	1965–77	"60 Series"	"70 Series"	"80 Series"
			5.50-12, 5.60-12	165/60-12	165/70-12	155-12
		Y78-12	6.00-12			
		W78-13	5.20-13	165/60-13	145/70-13	135-13
		Y78-13	5.60-13	175/60-13	155/70-13	145-13
			6.15-13	185/60-13	165/70-13	155-13, P155/80-13
A60-13	A70-13	A78-13	6.40-13	195/60-13	175/70-13	165-13
B60-13	B70-13	B78-13	6.70-13	205/60-13	185/70-13	175-13
			6.90-13			
C60-13	C70-13	C78-13	7.00-13	215/60-13	195/70-13	185-13
D60-13	D70-13	D78-13	7.25-13			
E60-13	E70-13	E78-13	7.75-13			195-13
			5.20-14	165/60-14	145/70-14	135-14
			5.60-14	175/60-14	155/70-14	145-14
			5.90-14			
A60-14	A70-14	A78-14	6.15-14	185/60-14	165/70-14	155-14
	B70-14	B78-14	6.45-14	195/60-14	175/70-14	165-14
	C70-14	C78-14	6.95-14	205/60-14	185/70-14	175-14
D60-14	D70-14	D78-14				
E60-14	E70-14	E78-14	7.35-14	215/60-14	195/70-14	185-14
F60-14	F70-14	F78-14, F83-14	7.75-14	225/60-14	200/70-14	195-14
G60-14	G70-14	G77-14, G78-14	8.25-14	235/60-14	205/70-14	205-14
H60-14	H70-14	H78-14	8.55-14	245/60-14	215/70-14	215-14
J60-14	J70-14	J78-14	8.85-14	255/60-14	225/70-14	225-14
L60-14	L70-14		9.15-14	265/60-14	235/70-14	
	A70-15	A78-15	5.60-15	185/60-15	165/70-15	155-15
B60-15	B70-15	B78-15	6.35-15	195/60-15	175/70-15	165-15
C60-15	C70-15	C78-15	6.85-15	205/60-15	185/70-15	175-15
	D70-15	D78-15				
E60-15	E70-15	E78-15	7.35-15	215/60-15	195/70-15	185-15
F60-15	F70-15	F78-15	7.75-15	225/60-15	205/70-15	195-15
G60-15	G70-15	G78-15	8.15-15/8.25-15	235/60-15	215/70-15	205-15
H60-15	H70-15	H78-15	8.45-15/8.55-15	245/60-15	225/70-15	215-15
J60-15	J70-15	J78-15	8.85-15/8.90-15	255/60-15	235/70-15	225-15
	K70-15		9.00-15	265/60-15	245/70-15	230-15
L60-15	L70-15	L78-15, L84-15	9.15-15			235-15
	M70-15	M78-15				255-15
		N78-15				

NOTE: Every size tire is not listed and many size comaprisons are approximate, based on load ratings. Wider tires than those supplied new with the vehicle should always be checked for clearance

HOW TO READ TIRE WEAR

The way your tires wear is a good indicator of other parts of your car. Abnormal wear patterns are often caused by the need for simple tire maintenance, or for front end alignment.

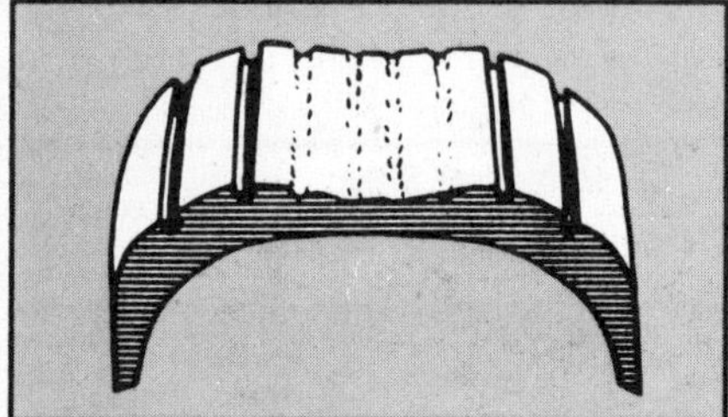

Over-Inflation

Excessive wear at the center of the tread indicates that the air pressure in the tire is consistently too high. The tire is riding on the center of the tread and wearing it prematurely. Occasionally, this wear pattern can result from outrageously wide tires on narrow rims. The cure for this is to replace either the tires or the wheels.

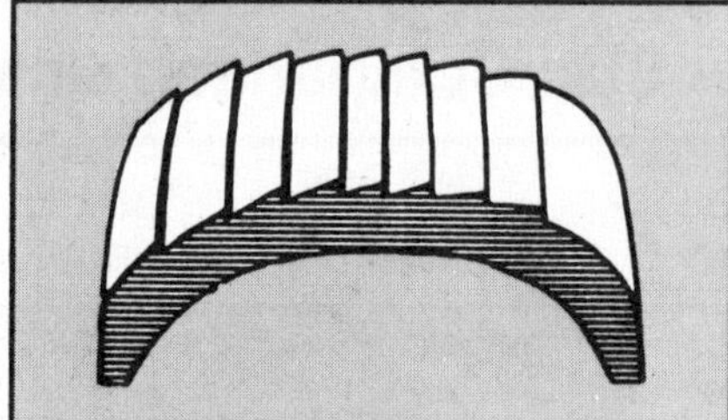

Feathering

Feathering is a condition when the edge of each tread rib develops a slightly rounded edge on one side and a sharp edge on the other. By running your hand over the tire, you can usually feel the sharper edges before you'll be able to see them. The most common causes of feathering are incorrect toe-in setting or deteriorated bushings in the front suspension.

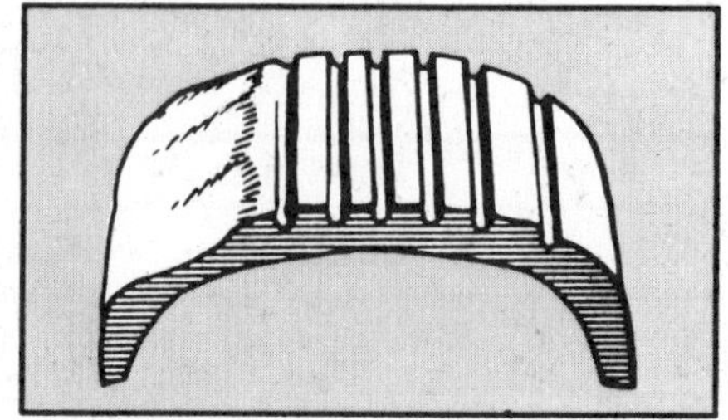

Cupping

Cups or scalloped dips appearing around the edge of the tread almost always indicate worn (sometimes bent) suspension parts. Adjustment of wheel alignment alone will seldom cure the problem. Any worn component that connects the wheel to the vehicle can cause this type of wear. Occasionally, wheels that are out of balance will wear like this, but wheel imbalance usually shows up as bald spots between the outside edges and center of the tread.

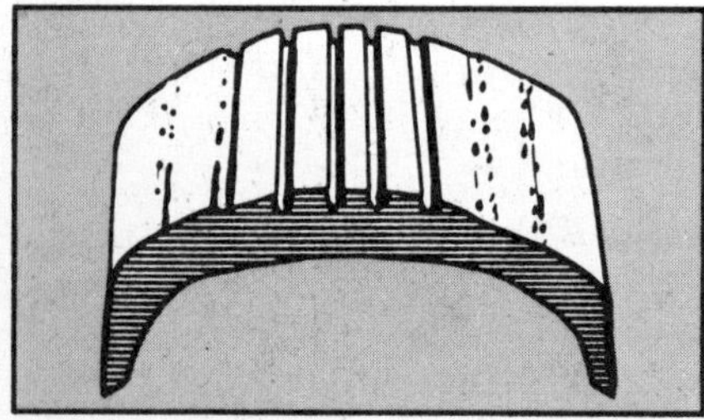

Under-Inflation

This type of wear usually results from consistent under–inflation. When a tire is under inflated, there is too much contact with the road by the outer threads, which wear prematurely. When this type of wear occurs, and the tire pressure is known to be consistenly correct, a bent or worn steering component or the need for wheel alignment could be indicated.

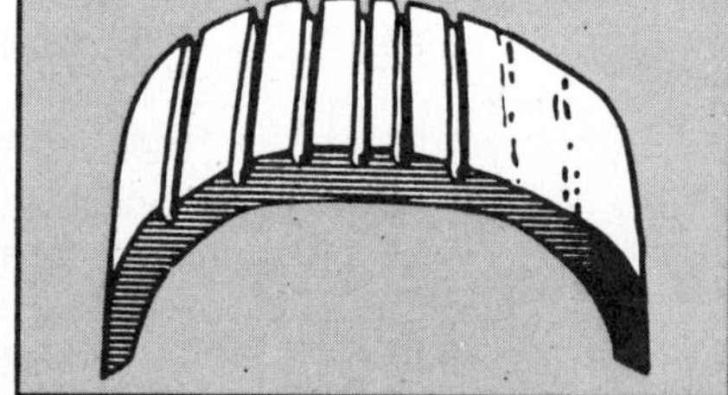

One Side Wear

When an inner or outer rib wears faster than the rest of the tire, the need for wheel alignment is indicated. There is excessive camber in the front suspension, causing the wheel to lean too much, putting excessive load on one side of the tire. Misalignment could also be due to sagging springs, worn ball joints, or worn control arm bushings. Be sure the vehicle is loaded the way it's normally driven when you have the wheels aligned.

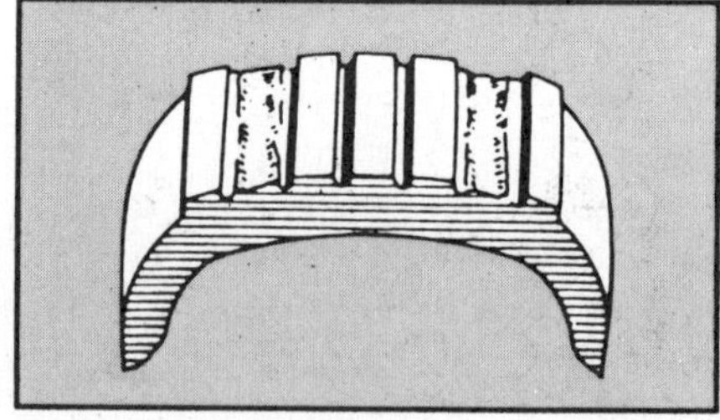

Second-Rib Wear

Second-rib wear is normally found only in radial tires, and appears where the steel belts end in relation to the tread. Normally, it can be kept to a minimum by paying careful attention to tire pressure and frequently rotation the tires. This is often considered normal wear but excessive amounts indicate that the tires are too wide for the wheels.

FLUIDS AND LUBRICANTS

Fuel Recommendations

GASOLINE ENGINES

Chevrolet and GMC trucks with Gross Vehicle Weight Ratings (GVWR) which place them in the heavy duty emissions class do not require a catalytic converter. However, the light duty classification applies to all trucks with GVWR's under 8,600 lbs.

The catalytic converter is a muffler shaped device installed in the exhaust system. It contains platinum and palladium coated pellets which, through catalytic action, oxidize hydrocarbon and carbon monoxide gases into hydrogen, oxygen, and carbon dioxide.

The design of the converter requires the exclusive use of unleaded fuel. Leaded fuel renders the converter inoperative, raising exhaust emissions to legal levels. In addition, the lead in the gasoline coats the pellets in the converter, blocking the flow of exhaust gases. This raises exhaust back pressure and severely reduces engine performance. In extreme cases, the exhaust system becomes so clocked that the engine will not run.

Converter equipped trucks are delivered with the label "Unleaded Fuel Only" placed next to the fuel gauge on the instrument panel and next to the gas tank filler opening. In general, any unleaded fuel is suitable for use in these trucks as long as the gas has an octane rating or 87 or more. Octane ratings are posted on the gas pumps. However, in some cases, knocking may occur even though the recommended fuel is being used. The only practical solution for this is to switch to a slightly higher grade of unleaded fuel, or to switch brands of unleaded gasoline.

DIESEL ENGINES

Diesel engined trucks require the use of diesel fuel. Two grades of diesel fuel are manufactured, #1 and #2, although #2 grade is generally the only grade available. Better fuel economy results from the use of #2 grade fuel. In some northern parts of the U.S., and in most parts of Canada, #1 grade fuel is available in winter, or a winterized blend of #2 grade is supplied in winter months. If #1 grade is available, it should be used whenever temperatures fall below +20°F (−7°C). Winterized #2 grade may also be used at these temperatures. However, unwinterized #2 grade should not be used below +20°F (−7°C). Cold temperatures cause unwinterized #2 grade to thicken (it actually gels), blocking the fuel lines and preventing the engine from running.

WARNING: Do not use home heating oil or gasoline in the diesel engine. Do not attempt to thin unwinterized #2 diesel fuel with gasoline. Gasoline line or home heating oil will damage the engine and void the manufacturer's warranty.

ENGINE OIL RECOMMENDATIONS

The SAE grade number indicates the viscosity of the engine oil, or its ability to lubricate under a given temperature. The lower the SAE grade number, the lighter the oil; the lower the viscosity, the easier it is to crank the engine in cold weather.

The API (American Petroleum Institute) designation indicates the classification of engine oil for use under given operating conditions. Only oils designated for "Service SF or SG" should be used. These oils provide maximum engine protection. Both the SAE grade number and the API designation can be found on the top of a can of oil.

NOTE: Non-detergent oils should not be used.

Oil viscosities should be chosen from those oils recommended for the lowest anticipated temperatures during the oil change interval.

The multi-viscosity oils offer the important advantage of being adaptable to temperature extremes. They allow easy starting at low temperatures, yet give good protection at high speeds and engine temperatures. This is a decided advantage in changeable climates or in long distance driving.

Diesel engines also require SF or SG engine oil. In addition, the oil must qualify for a CC and/or CD rating. The API has a number of different diesel engine ratings, including CB, CC, and CD.

For recommended oil viscosities, refer to the chart. 10W-30 grade oils are not recommended for sustained high speed driving.

Single viscosity oil (SAE 30) is recommended for sustained high speed driving.

SYNTHETIC OIL

There are excellent synthetic and fuel-efficient oils available that, under the right circumstances, can help provide better fuel mileage and better engine protection. However, these advantages come at a price, which can be three or four times the price per quart of conventional motor oils.

Before pouring any synthetic oils into your truck's engine, you should consider the condition of the engine and the type of driving you do. Also, check the truck's warranty conditions regarding the use of synthetics.

Generally, it is best to avoid the use of synthetic oil in both brand new and older, high mileage engines. New engines require a proper break-in, and the synthetics are so slippery that they can prevent this. Most manufacturers recommend that you

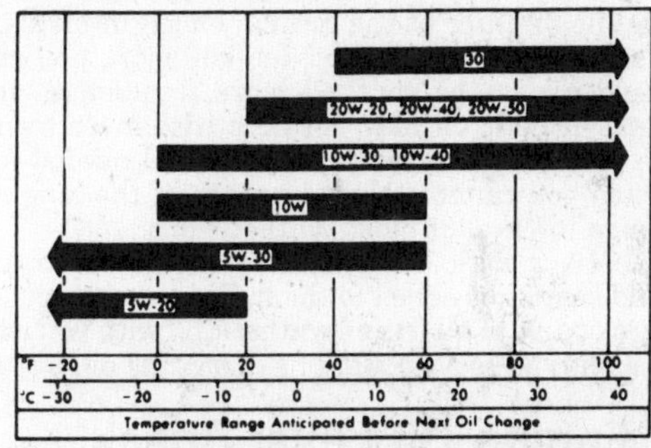

NOTES: 1. SAE 5W and 5W-20 are not recommended for sustained high speed driving.
2. SAE 5W-30 is recommended for all seasons in Canada

Gasoline engine oil viscosity chart

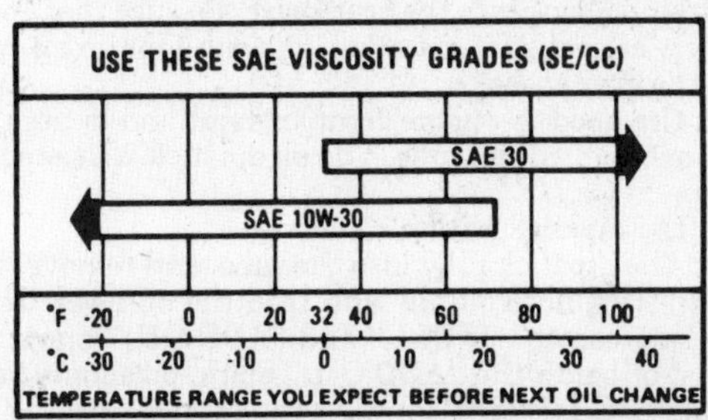

Diesel engine oil viscosity chart

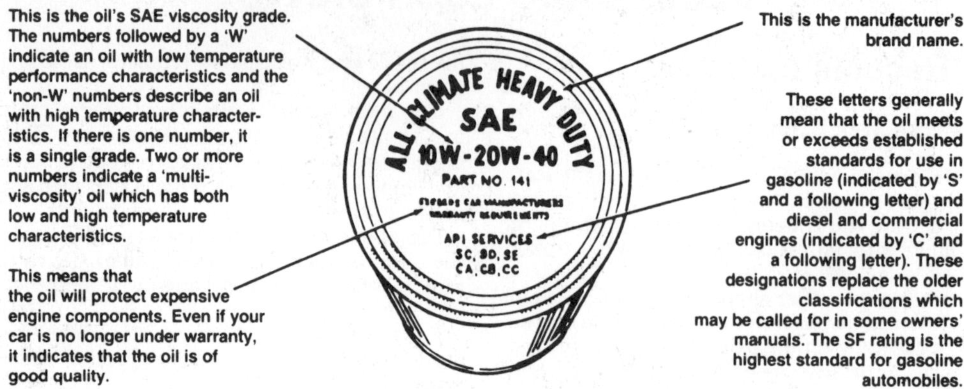

This is the oil's SAE viscosity grade. The numbers followed by a 'W' indicate an oil with low temperature performance characteristics and the 'non-W' numbers describe an oil with high temperature characteristics. If there is one number, it is a single grade. Two or more numbers indicate a 'multi-viscosity' oil which has both low and high temperature characteristics.
This means that the oil will protect expensive engine components. Even if your car is no longer under warranty, it indicates that the oil is of good quality.
ALL-CLIMATE HEAVY DUTY
SAE
10W-20W-40
PART NO. 141
API SERVICES
SC, SD, SE
CA, CB, CC
This is the manufacturer's brand name.
These letters generally mean that the oil meets or exceeds established standards for use in gasoline (indicated by 'S' and a following letter) and diesel and commercial engines (indicated by 'C' and a following letter). These designations replace the older classifications which may be called for in some owners' manuals. The SF rating is the highest standard for gasoline automobiles.

The oil can or bottle will tell you all you need to know about engine oil

wait at least 5,000 miles before switching to a synthetic oil. Conversely, older engines are looser and tend to use more oil. Synthetics will slip past worn pats more readily than regular oil, and will be used up faster. If your truck already leaks and/or uses oil (due to worn parts and bad seals or gaskets), it will leak and use more with a slippery synthetic inside.

Consider your type of driving. If most of your accumulated mileage is on the highway at higher, steadier speeds, a synthetic oil will reduce friction and probably help deliver fuel mileage. Under such ideal highway conditions, the oil change interval can be extended, as long as the oil filter will operate effectively for the extended life of the oil. If the filter can't do its job for this extended period, dirt and sludge will build up in your engine's crankcase, sump, oil pump and lines, no matter what type of oil is used. If using synthetic oil in this manner, you should continue to change the oil filter at the recommended intervals.

Trucks used under harder, stop-and-go, short hop circumstances should always be serviced more frequently, and for these trucks, synthetic oil may not be a wise investment. Because of the necessary shorter change interval needed for this type of driving, you cannot take advantage of the long recommended change interval of most synthetic oils.

Finally, most synthetic oil are not compatible with conventional oils and cannot be added to them. This means you should always carry a couple of quarts of synthetic oil with you while on a long trip, as not all service stations carry this oil.

Engine Oil Level Check

The engine oil should be checked on a regular basis, ideally at each fuel stop. If the truck is used for trailer towing or for heavy duty use, it would be safer to check it more often.

When checking the oil level it is best that the oil be at operating temperature, although checking the level immediately after stopping will give a false reading because all of the oil will not yet have drained back into the crankcase. Be sure that the truck is resting on a level surface, allowing time for the oil to drain back into the crankcase.

1. Open the hood or engine compartment and locate the dipstick. Remove it from the tube. The oil dipstick is located on the driver's side.
2. Wipe the dipstick with a clean rag.
3. Insert the dipstick fully into the tube, and remove it again. Hold the dipstick horizontally and read the oil level. The level should be between the "FULL" and "ADD OIL" marks. If the oil level is at or below the "ADD OIL" mark, oil should be added as necessary. Oil is added through the capped opening on the valve cover(s). See Oil and Fuel Recommendations for proper viscosity and oil to use.
4. Replace the dipstick and check the level after adding oil. Be careful not to overfill the crankcase. There is about 1 quart between the marks.

Check the engine oil level with the dipstick

The oil level should be between the ADD and FULL marks

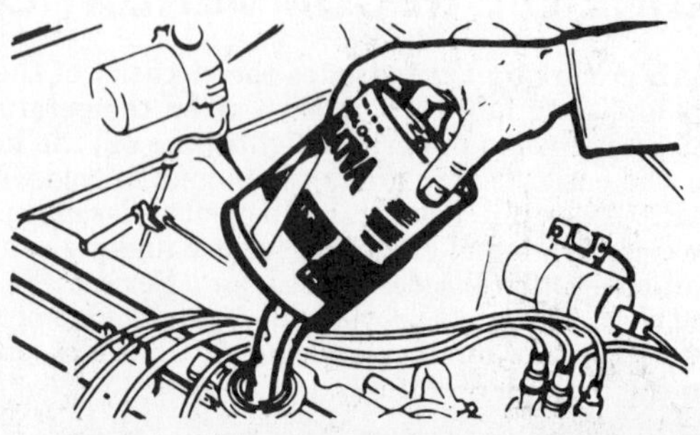

Add oil through the opening in the valve cover

Engine Oil and Filter Change

Engine oil should be changed according to the schedule in the Maintenance Interval Chart. Under conditions such as:

- Driving in dusty conditions
- Continuous trailer pulling or RV use
- Extensive or prolonged idling
- Extensive short trip operation in freezing temperatures (when the engine is not thoroughly warmed up)
- Frequent long runs at high speeds and high ambient temperatures
- Stop-and-go service such as delivery trucks, the oil change interval and filter replacement interval should be cut in half. Operation of the engine in severe conditions such as a dust storm may require an immediate oil and filter change.

Chevrolet and GMC recommended changing both the oil and filter during the first oil change and the filter every other oil change thereafter. HOWEVER, For the small price of an oil filter, it's cheap insurance to replace the filter at every oil change. One of the larger filter manufacturers points out in its advertisements that not changing the filter leaves one quart of dirty oil in the engine. This claim is true and should be kept in mind when changing your oil.

NOTE: The oil filter on the diesel engines must be changed every oil change.

To change the oil, the truck should be on a level surface, and the engine should be at operating temperature. This is to ensure that the foreign matter will be drained away along with the oil, and not left in the engine to form sludge. You should have available a container that will hold a minimum of 8 quarts of liquid, a wrench to fit the old drain plug, a spout for pouring in new oil, and a rag or two, which you will always need. If the filter is being replaced, you will also need a band wrench or filter wrench to fit the end of the filter.

NOTE: If the engine is equipped with an oil cooler, this will also have to be drained, using the drain plug. Be sure to add enough oil to fill the cooler in addition to the engine.

1. Position the truck on a level surface and set the parking brake or block the wheels. Slide a drain pan under the oil drain plug.
2. From under the truck, loosen, but do not remove the oil drain plug. Cover your hand with a rag or glove and slowly unscrew the drain plug.

CAUTION

The engine oil will be HOT! Keep your arms, face and hands clear of the oil as it drains out!

3. Remove the plug and let the oil drain into the pan.

NOTE: Do not drop the plug into the drain pan.

4. When all of the oil has drained, clean off the drain plug and put it back into the hole. Remember to tighten the plug 20 ft. lbs. (30 ft. lbs. for diesel engines).
5. Loosen the filter with a band wrench or special oil filter cap wrench. On most Chevrolet engines, especially the V8s, the oil filter is next to the exhaust pipes. Stay clear of these, since even a passing contact will result in a painful burn.

CAUTION

On trucks equipped with catalytic converters stay clear of the converter. The outside temperature of a hot catalytic converter can approach 1,200°F (650°C)!

6. Cover your hand with a rag, and spin the filter off by hand.
7. Coat the rubber gasket on a new filter with a light film of clean engine oil. Screw the filter onto the mounting stud and

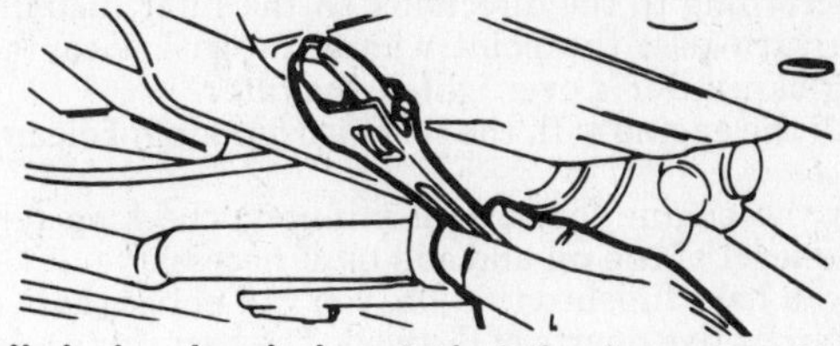

The oil drain plug is located at the lowest point of the oil pan

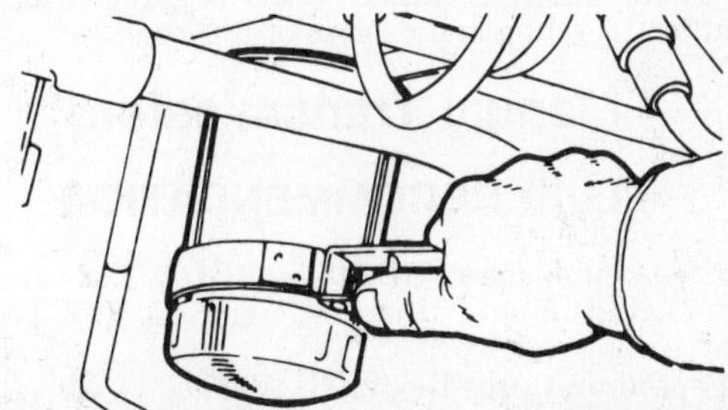

Use a strap wrench to loosen the oil filter, but, tighten it by hand

Coat the gasket on the new oil filter with clean engine oil

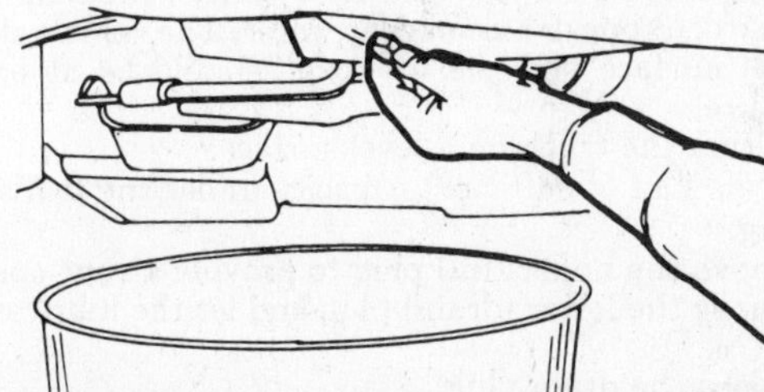

After loosening the plug with a wrench, unscrew the plug by hand, keeping an inward pressure on the plug, so that the hot oil won't escape until you pull the plug away

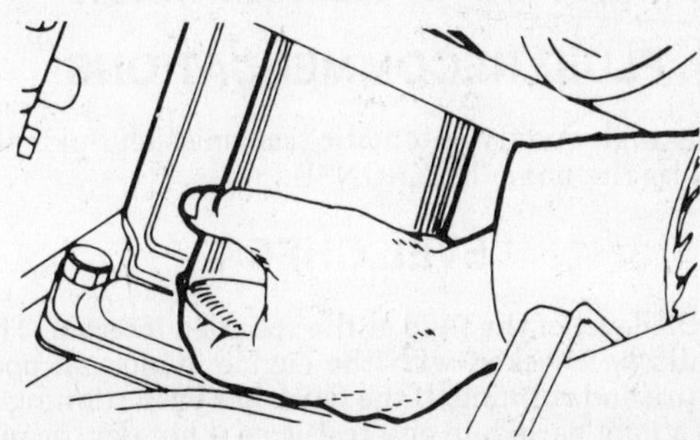

Install the filter by hand only! Do not use a strap wrench!

tighten according to the directions on the filter (usually hand tight one turn past the point where the gasket contacts the mounting base). Don't overtighten the filter.

8. Refill the engine with the specified amount of clean engine oil.

9. Run the engine for several minutes, checking for leaks. Check the level of the oil and add oil if necessary.

When you have finished this job, you will notice that you now possess four or five quarts of dirty oil. The best thing to do with it is to pour it into plastic jugs, such as milk or antifreeze containers. Then, find a gas station or service garage which accepts waste oil for recycling and dispose of it there.

Manual Transmission

FLUID RECOMMENDATION

The 3-speed unit uses SAE 80W-90 GL-5. For vehicles normally operated in cold climates, use SAE 80W GL-5 gear lubricant.

The 4-speed unit uses Dexron®II ATF.

FLUID LEVEL CHECK

Check the lubricant level at the interval specified in the maintenance chart.

1. With the truck parked on a level surface, remove the filler plug from the side of the transmission case. Be careful not to take out the drain plug at the bottom.
2. If lubricant begins to trickle out of the hole, there is enough. If not, carefully insert a finger (watch out for sharp threads) and check that the level is up to the edge of the hole.
3. If not, add sufficient lubricant with a funnel and tube, or a squeeze bulb to bring it to the proper level.
4. Replace the plug and check for leaks.

DRAIN AND REFILL

No intervals are specified for changing the transmission lubricant, but it is a good idea on a used vehicle, one that has been worked hard, or one driven in deep water. The vehicle should be on a level surface and the lubricant should be at operating temperature.

1. Position the truck on a level surface.
2. Place a pan of sufficient capacity under the transmission drain plug.
3. Remove the upper (fill) plug to provide a vent opening.
4. Remove the lower (drain) plug and let the lubricant drain out.
5. Replace the drain plug.
6. Add lubricant with a suction gun or squeeze bulb.
7. Reinstall the filler plug. Run the engine and check for leaks.

Automatic Transmission

FLUID RECOMMENDATIONS

Use only high quality automatic transmission fluids that are identified by the name DEXRON®II.

LEVEL CHECK

Check the level of the fluid at the specified interval. The fluid level should be checked with the engine at normal operating temperature and running. If the truck has been running at high speed for a long period, in city traffic on a hot day, or pulling a trailer, let it cool down for about thirty minutes before checking the level.

1. Park on the level with the engine running and the shift lever in Park.
2. Remove the dipstick at the rear of the engine compartment. Cautiously feel the end of the dipstick with your fingers. Wipe it off and replace it, then pull it again and check the level of the fluid on the dipstick.
3. If the fluid felt cool, the level should be between the two dimples below ADD. If it was too hot to hold, the level should be between the ADD and FULL marks.
4. If the fluid is at or below the ADD mark, add fluid through the dipstick tube. One pint raises the level from ADD to FULL when the fluid is hot. The correct fluid to use is DEXRON®II. Be certain that the transmission is not overfilled, this will cause foaming, fluid loss, and slippage.

PAN AND FILTER SERVICE/DRAIN AND REFILL

The fluid should be drained with the transmission warm. It is easier to change the fluid if the truck is raised somewhat from the ground, but this is not always easy without a lift. The transmission must be level for it to drain properly.

1. Place a shallow pan underneath to catch the transmission fluid (about 5 pints). Loosen all the pan bolts, then pull one corner down to drain most of the fluid. If it sticks, VERY CAREFULLY pry the pan loose. You can buy aftermarket drain plug kits that makes this operation a bit less messy, once installed.

NOTE: If the fluid removed smells burnt, serious transmission troubles, probably due to overheating, should be suspected.

2. Remove the pan bolts and empty out the pan. On some models, there may not be much room to get at the screws at the front of the pan.
3. Clean the pan with solvent and allow it to air dry. If you use a rag to wipe it out, you risk leaving bits of lint and threads in the transmission.
4. Remove the filter or strainer retaining bolts. On the Turbo Hydra-Matic 400, there are two screws securing the filter or screen to the valve body. A reusable strainer may be found on some models. The strainer may be cleaned in solvent and air dried thoroughly. The filter and gasket must be replaced.
5. Install a new gasket and filter.
6. Install a new gasket on the pan, and tighten the bolts evenly to 12 foot pounds in a criss-cross pattern.
7. Add DEXRON®II transmission fluid through the dipstick tube. The correct amount is in the Capacities Chart. Do not overfill.
8. With the gearshift lever in PARK, start the engine and let it idle. Do not race the engine.
9. Move the gearshift lever through each position, holding the brakes. Return the lever to PARK, and check the fluid level with the engine idling. The level should be between the two dimples on the dipstick, about 1/4 in. (6mm) below the ADD mark. Add fluid, if necessary.
10. Check the fluid level after the truck has been driven enough to thoroughly warm up the transmission. If the transmission is overfilled, the excess must be drained off. Overfilling causes aerated fluid, resulting in transmission slippage and probable damage.

Transfer Case

FLUID RECOMMENDATIONS

Transfer cases require SAE 80W or SAE 80W-90 GL-5 gear lubricant.

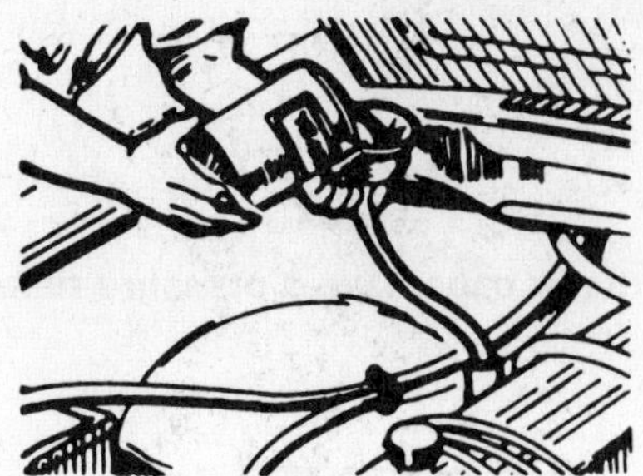

Add automatic transmission fluid through the dipstick tube

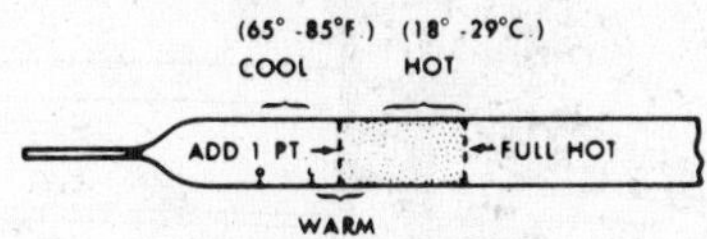

Automatic transmission dipstick markings

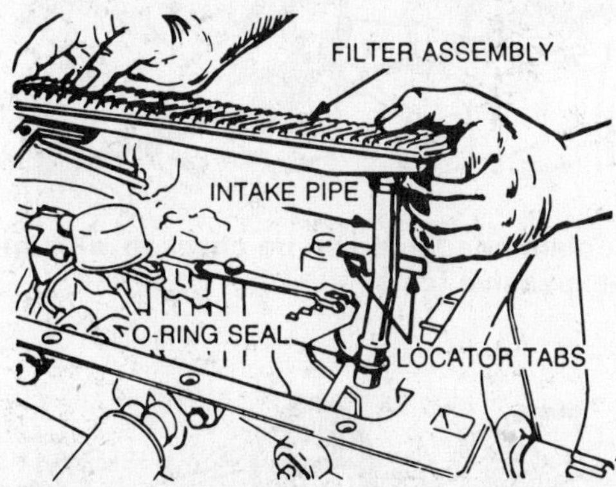

The Turbo Hydra-Matic 400 has an O-ring on the intake pipe. Check the condition of this O-ring and replace it as necessary

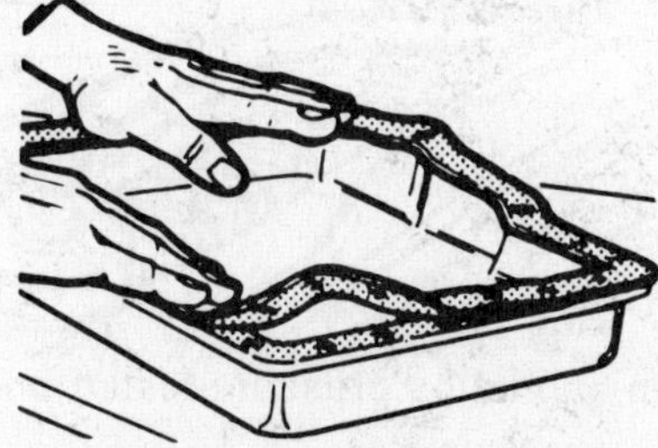

Install a new gasket on the pan

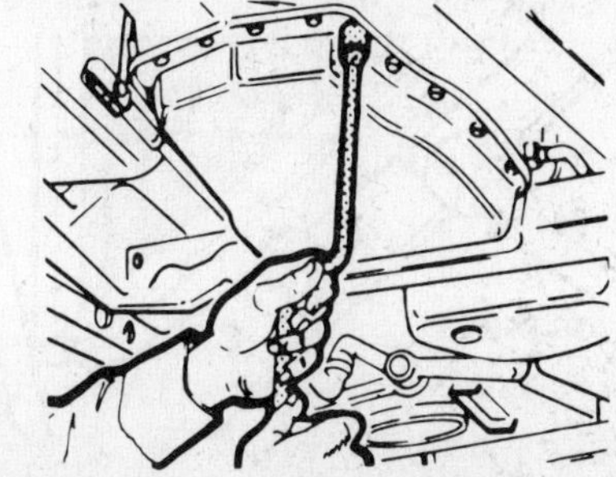

Removing the transmission drain pan

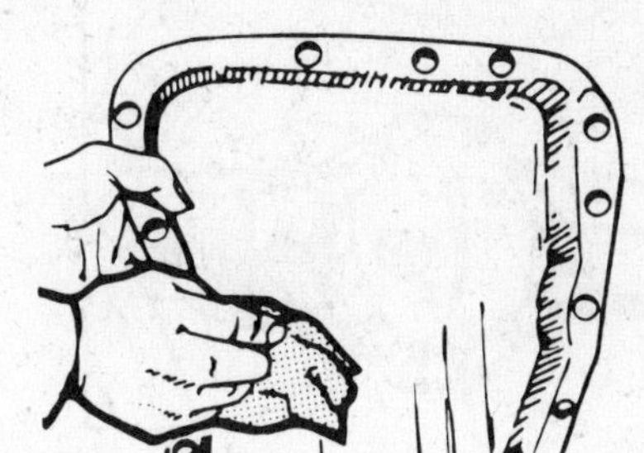

Clean the pan with a non-flammable solvent and dry it thoroughly

LEVEL CHECKS

Check the four wheel drive transfer case lubricant level every 4 months or 6,000 miles.

1. With the truck parked on a level surface, remove the filler plug from the rear of the transfer case (behind the transmission). Be careful not to take out the drain plug at the bottom.
2. If lubricant trickles out, there is enough. If not, carefully insert a finger and check that the level is up to the edge of the hole, EXCEPT in full time four wheel drive cases should be ½ in. (13mm) below the hole.

Lubricant may be added, if necessary, with a funnel and tube, or a squeeze bulb.

DRAIN AND REFILL

1. With the transfer case warmed up, park on a level surface.
2. Slide a pan of a least 6 pts. capacity under the case drain plug.
3. Remove the filler plug from the rear of the transfer case (behind the transmission). Remove the drain plug from the bottom.
4. Wipe the area clean and replace the drain plug.
5. Add lubricant with a suction gun or squeeze bulb. Conventional transfer cases require SAE 80W-90 GL-5 Gear Lubricant.
6. When the lubricant level is up to the bottom of the filler hole, replace the plug.

Drive Axle (Rear and/or Front)

FLUID RECOMMENDATIONS

Front axles use SAE 80W-90, GL-5 Gear Lubricant. Rear axles use SAE 80W-90 gear oil. Positraction axles must use special lubricant available from dealers. If the special fluid is not used, noise, uneven operation, and damage will result. There is also a Positraction additive used to cure noise and slippage. Positraction axles have an identifying tag, as well as a warning sticker near the jack or on the rear wheel well.

LEVEL CHECK

The fluid level in the front axle should be ½ in. (13mm) below the filler plug opening. The fluid level in the rear axle should be up to the bottom of the filler plug opening. Lubricant may be added with a suction gun or squeeze bulb.

1. Park on level ground.
2. Remove the filler plug from the differential housing cover.
3. If lubricant trickles out there is enough. If not, carefully insert a finger and check that the level is up to the bottom of the hole. Locking front hubs should be run in the LOCK position for at least 10 miles each month to assure proper lubrication to the front axle.

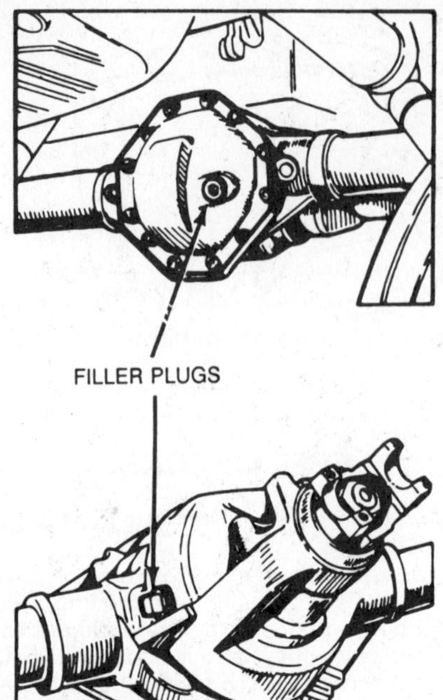

The rear axle filler plug may be in either of these two locations

Some radiator caps have a pressure relief lever

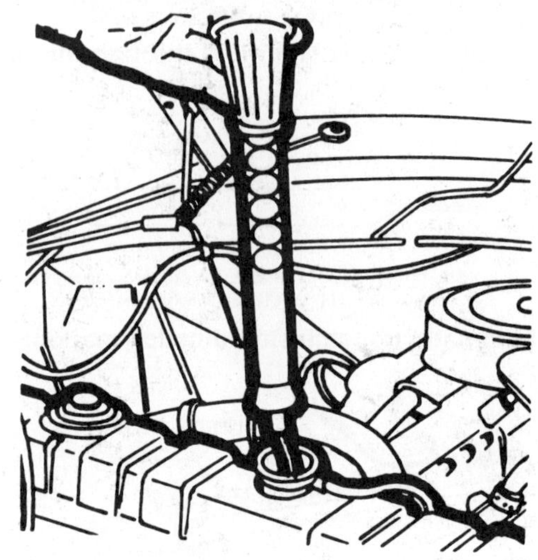

Coolant condition can be checked with an inexpensive tester

DRAIN AND REFILL

No intervals are specified for changing axle lubricant, but it is a good idea, especially if you have driven in water over the axle vents.

1. Park the vehicle on the level with the axles at normal operating temperature.
2. Place a pan of at least 6 pints capacity under the differential housing.
3. Remove the filler plug.
4. If you have a drain plug, remove it. If not, unbolt and remove the differential cover.
5. Replace the drain plug, or differential cover. Use a new gasket if the differential cover has been removed.

Cooling System

The coolant level should be checked at each fuel stop, ideally, to prevent the possibility of overheating and serious engine damage. If not, it should at least be checked once each month.

The cooling system was filled at the factory with a high quality coolant solution that is good for year around operation and protects the system from freezing down to −20°F (−29°C) (−32°F [−36°C] in Canada). It is good for two full calendar years or 24,000 miles, whichever occurs first, provided that the proper concentration of coolant is maintained.

The hot coolant level should be at the FULL HOT mark on the expansion tank and the cold coolant level should be at the FULL COLD mark on the tank. Do not remove the radiator cap to check the coolant level.

FLUID RECOMMENDATION

Coolant mixture in Chevy/GMC trucks is 50/50 ethylene glycol and water for year round use. Use a good quality antifreeze with water pump lubricants, rust inhibitors and other corrosion inhibitors along with acid neutralizers.

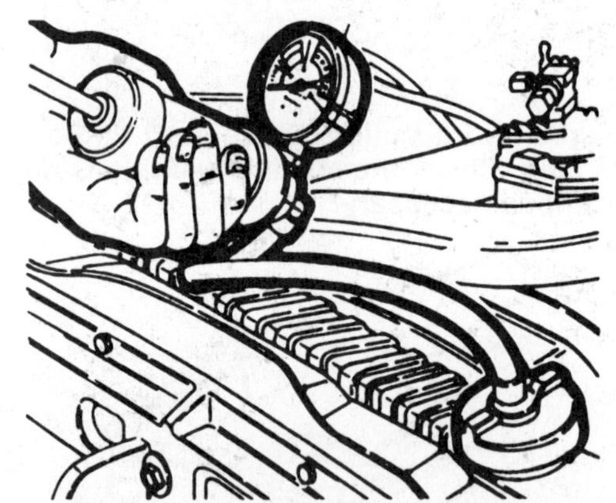

The system should be pressure-tested once a year

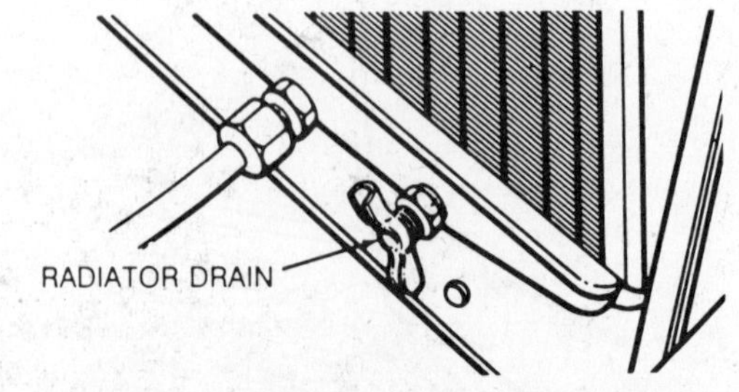

Radiator drain cock

LEVEL CHECK

1. Check the level on the see-through expansion tank.

CAUTION

The radiator coolant is under pressure when hot. To avoid the danger of physical harm, coolant level should be checked or replenished only when the engine is cold. To remove the radiator cap when the engine is hot, first cover the cap with a thick rag, or wear a heavy glove for protection. Press down on the cap slightly and slowly turn it counterclockwise until it reaches the first stop. Allow all the pressure to vent (indicated when the hissing sound stops). When the pressure is released, press down on the cap and continue to rotate it counterclockwise. Some radiator caps have a lever for venting the pressure, but you should still exercise extreme caution when removing the cap.

2. Check the level and, if necessary, add coolant to the proper level. Use a 50/50 mix of ethylene glycol antifreeze and water. Alcohol or methanol base coolants are not recommended. Antifreeze solutions should be used, even in summer, to prevent rust and to take advantage of the solution's higher boiling point compared to plain water. This is imperative on air conditioned trucks; the heater core can freeze if it isn't protected. Coolant should be added through the coolant recovery tank, not the radiator filler neck.

WARNING: Never add large quantities of cold coolant to a hot engine! A cracked engine block may result!

3. Replace the plug.

Each year the cooling system should be serviced as follows:

- Wash the radiator cap and filler neck with clean water.
- Check the coolant for proper level and freeze protection.
- Have the system pressure tested (15 psi). If a replacement cap is installed, be sure that it conforms to the original specifications.
- Tighten the hose clamps and inspect all hoses. Replace hoses that are swollen, cracked or otherwise deteriorated.
- Clean the frontal area of the radiator core and the air conditioning condenser, if so equipped.

DRAINING, FLUSHING AND TESTING THE COOLING SYSTEM AND COOLANT

The cooling system in you truck accumulates some internal rust and corrosion in its normal operation. A simple method of keeping the system clean is known as flushing the system. It is performed by circulating a can of radiator flush through the system, and then draining and refilling the system with the normal coolant. Radiator flush is marketed by several different manufacturers, and is available in cans at auto departments, parts stores, and many hardware stores. This operation should be performed every 30,000 miles or once a year.

To flush the cooling system:

CAUTION

When draining the coolant, keep in mind that cats and dogs are attracted by the ethylene glycol antifreeze, and are quite likely to drink any that is left in an uncovered container or in puddles on the ground. This will prove fatal in sufficient quantity. Always drain the coolant into a sealable container. Coolant should be reused unless it is contaminated or several years old.

1. Drain the existing antifreeze and coolant. Open the radiator and engine drain petcocks (located near the bottom of the radiator and engine block, respectively), or disconnect the bottom radiator hose at the radiator outlet.

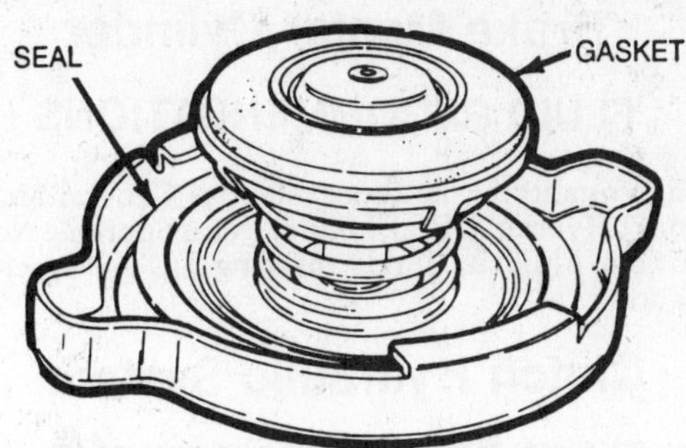

Check the condition of the radiator cap gasket and seal

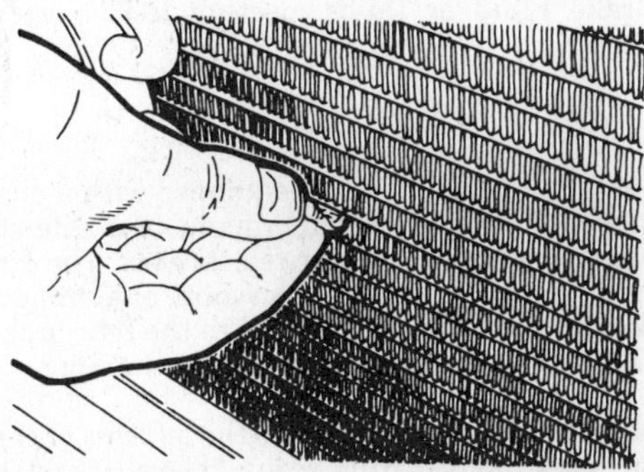

Remove any debris from the radiator's cooling fins

NOTE: Before opening the radiator petcock, spray it with some penetrating oil. Be aware that if the engine has been run up to operating temperature, the coolant emptied will be HOT.

2. Close the petcock or reconnect the lower hose and fill the system with water—hot water if the system has just been run.
3. Add a can of quality radiator flush to the radiator or recovery tank, following any special instructions on the can.
4. Idle the engine as long as specified on the can of flush, or until the upper radiator hose gets hot.
5. Drain the system again. There should be quite a bit of scale and rust in the drained water.
6. Repeat this process until the drained water is mostly clear.
7. Close all petcocks and connect all hoses.
8. Flush the coolant recovery reservoir with water and leave empty.
9. Determine the capacity of your truck's cooling system (see Capacities specifications in this guide. Add a 50/50 mix of ethylene glycol antifreeze and water to provide the desired protection.
10. Run the engine to operating temperature, then stop the engine and check for leaks. Check the coolant level and top up if necessary.
11. Check the protection level of your antifreeze mix with an antifreeze tester (a small, inexpensive syringe type device available at any auto parts store). The tester has five or six small colored balls inside, each of which signify a certain temperature rating. Insert the tester in the recovery tank and suck just enough coolant into the syringe to float as many individual balls as you can (without sucking in too much coolant and floating all the balls at once). A table supplied with the tester will explain how many floating balls equal protection down to a certain temperature (three floating balls might mean the coolant will protect your engine down to +5°F (−15°C), for example.

Brake Master Cylinder

FLUID RECOMMENDATIONS

Only high quality brake fluids, such as General Motors Supreme No. 11 Hydraulic Brake Fluid, Delco Supreme No. 11 Hydraulic Brake Fluid or fluids meeting DOT-3 specifications should be used.

Clutch Hydraulic System

FLUID RECOMMENDATIONS

Only high quality brake fluids, such as General Motors Supreme No. 11 Hydraulic Brake Fluid, Delco Supreme No. 11 Hydraulic Brake Fluid or fluids meeting DOT-3 specifications should be used.

LEVEL CHECK

Chevrolet and GMC trucks are equipped with a dual braking system, allowing a vehicle to be brought to a safe stop in the event of failure in either front or rear brakes. The dual master cylinder has 2 entirely separate reservoirs, one connected to the front brakes and the other connected to the rear brakes. In the event of failure in either portion, the remaining part is not affected.

The master cylinder is mounted to the left side of the firewall.

1. Clean all of the dirt from around the cover of the master cylinder.
2. Be sure that the vehicle is resting on a level surface.
3. Carefully pry the clip from the top of the master cylinder to release the cover.
4. The fluid level should be approximately ¼ in. (6mm) from the top of the master cylinder. If not, add fluid until the level is correct. Replacement fluid should be Delco Supreme No. 11, DOT 3, or its equivalent. It is normal for the fluid level to fall as the disc brake ads wear.

WARNING: Brake fluid dissolves paint! It also absorbs moisture from the air. Never leave a container or the master cylinder uncovered any longer than necessary!

5. Install the cover of the master cylinder. On most models there is a rubber gasket under the cover, which fits into 2 slots on the cover. Be sure that this is seated properly.
6. Push the clip back into place and be sure that it seats in the groove on the top of the cover.
7. As necessary, replace the access cover and floor mat.

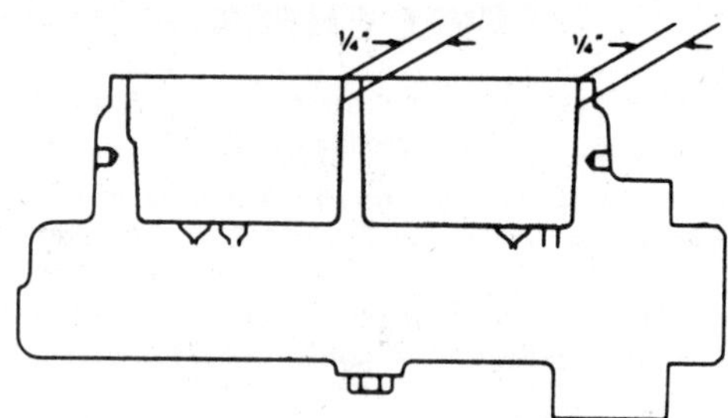

Master cylinder fluid level

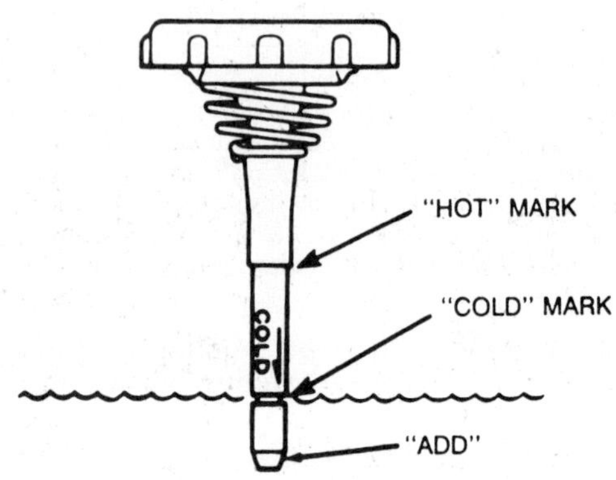

Power steering reservoir dipstick

Power Steering Pump

FLUID RECOMMENDATION

The power steering reservoir should be filled with GM Power Steering fluid, or its equivalent. Automatic Transmission Fluid DEXRON®II is also satisfactory.

POWER STEERING RESERVOIR LEVEL CHECK

Check the dipstick in the pump reservoir when the fluid is at operating temperature. The fluid should be between the HOT and COLD marks. If the fluid is at room temperature, the fluid should be between the ADD and COLD marks. The fluid does not require periodic changing.

On systems with a remote reservoir, the level should be maintained approximately ½–1 in. (13–25mm) from the top with the wheels in the full left turn position.

Steering Gear

FLUID RECOMMENDATION

No lubrication is needed for the life of the gear, except in the event of seal replacement or overhaul, when the gear should be refilled with a 13 oz. container of Steering Gear Lubricant (Part No. 1051052) which meets GM Specification GM 4673M, or its equivalent.

NOTE: On these models do not use EP Chassis Lubricant.

FLUID LEVEL CHECK

The steering gear is factory filled with a lubricant which does not require seasonal change. The housing should not be drained. No lubricant is required for the life of the gear.

The gear should be inspected for seal leakage. Look for solid grease, not an oily film. If a seal is replaced or the gear overhauled, the gear should be filled with Part No. 1051052, which is a 13 oz. container of Steering Gear lubricant which meets GM Specifications. Do not use EP Chassis Lube to lubricate the gear and do not overfill.

Chassis Greasing

Refer to the diagrams for chassis points to be lubricated. Not all vehicles have all the fittings illustrated. Water resistant EP chassis lubricant (grease) conforming to GM specification 6031–M should be used for all chassis grease points.

Every year or 7,500 miles the front suspension ball points, both upper and lower on each side of the truck, must be greased. Most trucks covered in this guide should be equipped with grease nipples on the ball joints, although some may have plugs which must be removed and nipples fitted.

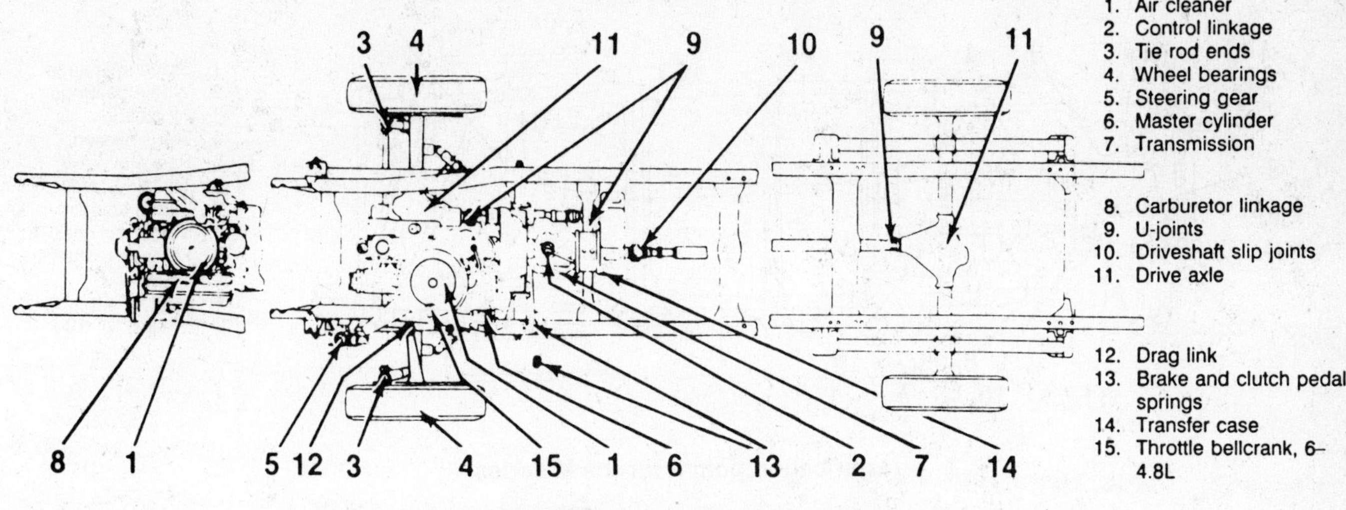

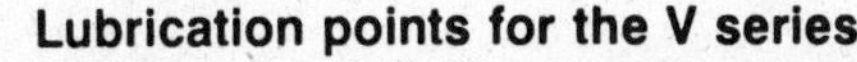
Lubrication points for the V series

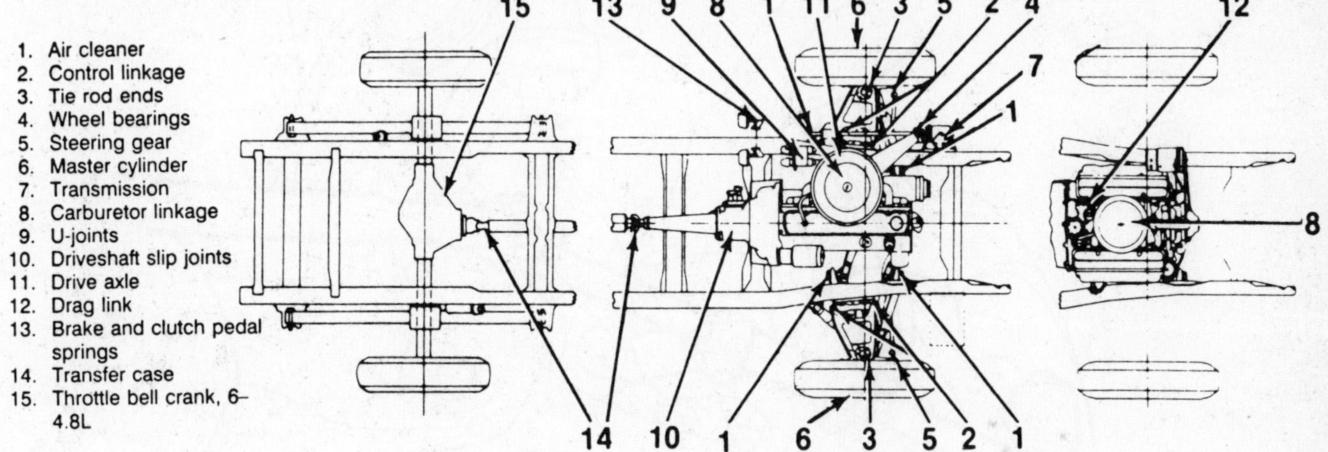

Lubrication points for the R series

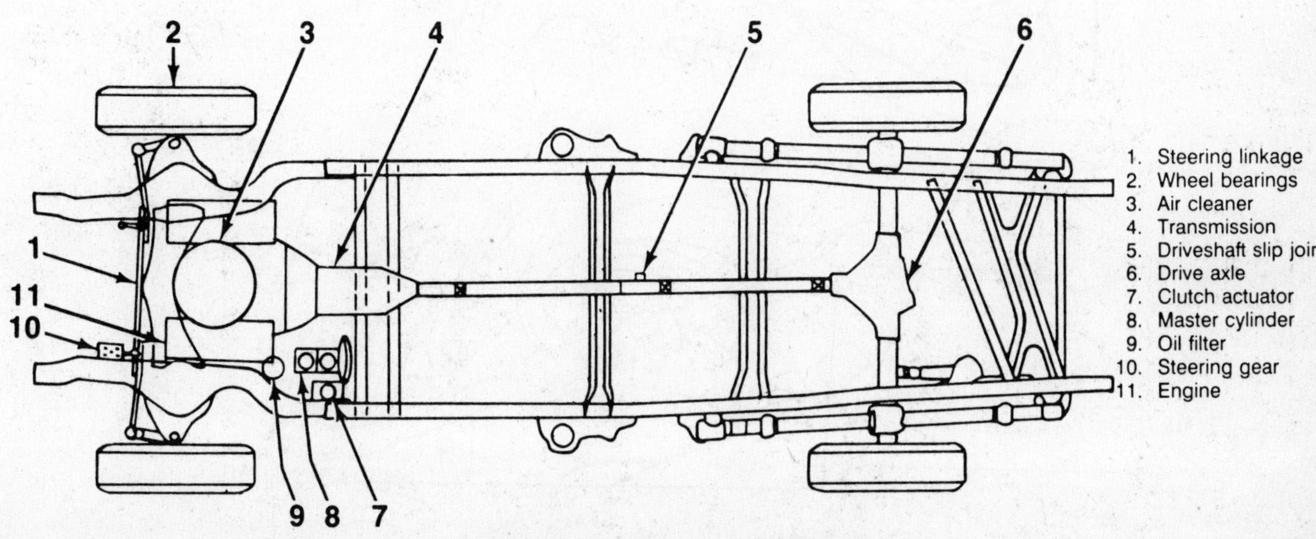

Lubrication points for the C series

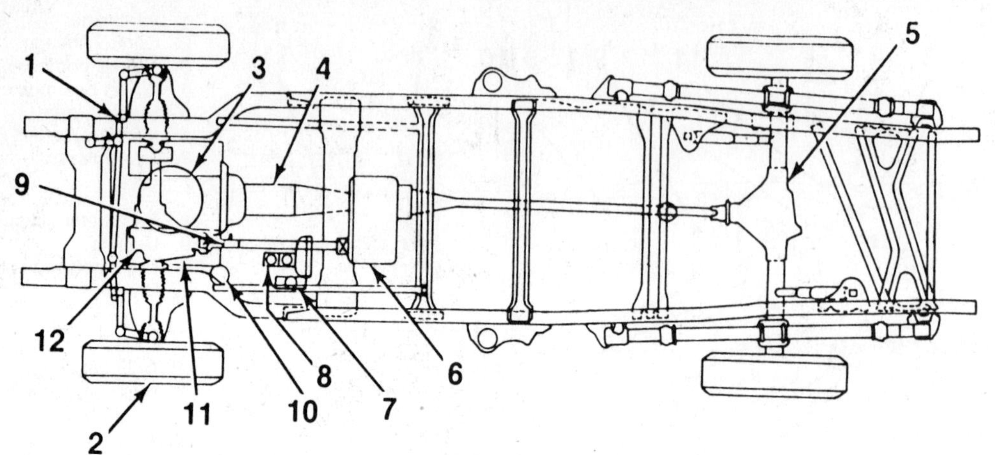

1. Steering linkage
2. Wheel bearings
3. Air cleaner
4. Transmission
5. Rear Drive axle
6. Transfer case
7. Clutch actuator
8. Master cylinder
9. Front driveshaft
10. Oil filter
11. Engine
12. Front drive axle

Lubrication points for the K series

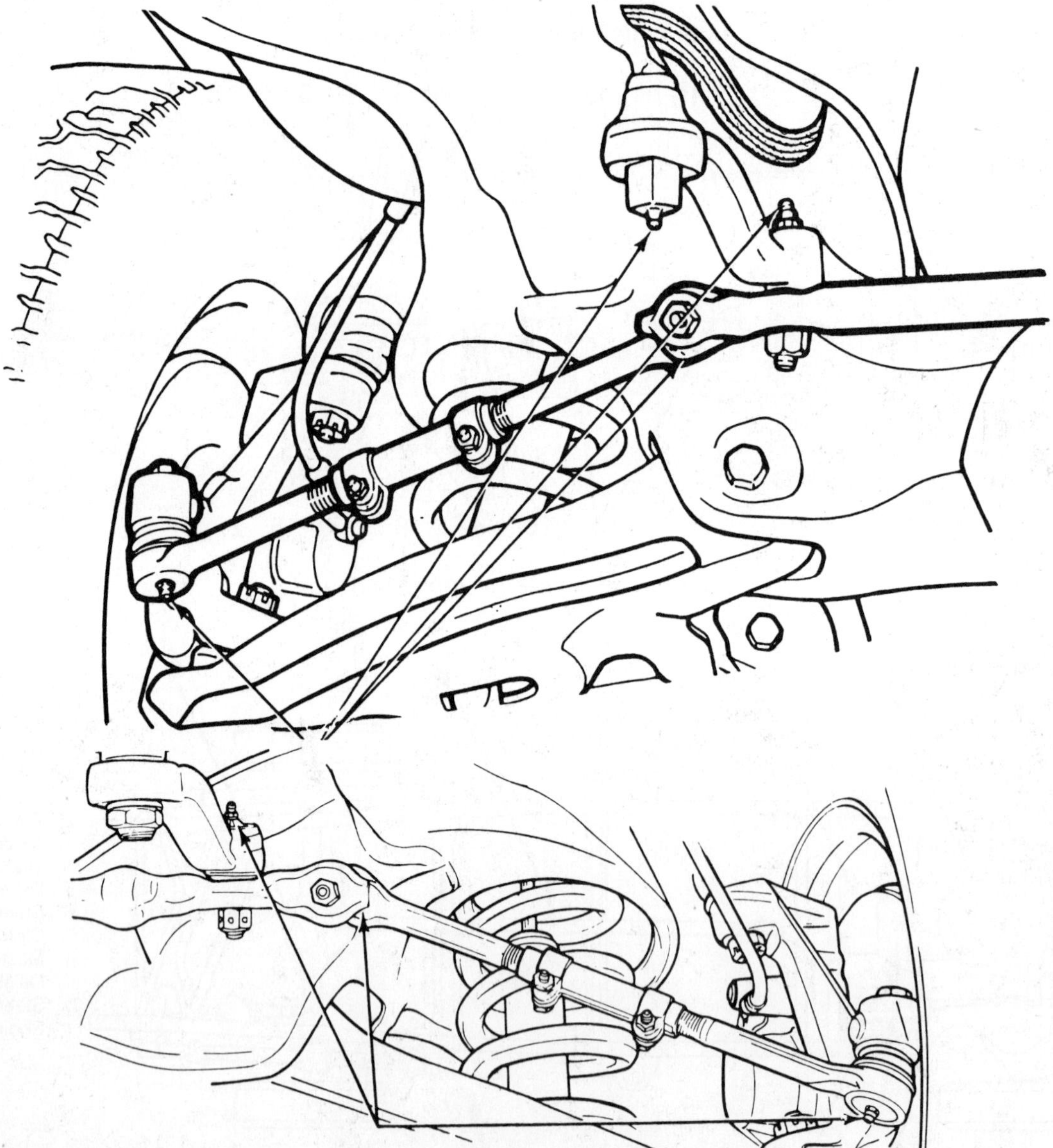

C and K series lubrication fittings

WARNING: Do not pump so much grease into the ball joint that excess grease squeezes out of the rubber boot. This destroys the watertight seal.

Jack up the front end of the truck and safely support it with jackstands. Block the rear wheels and firmly apply the parking brake. If the truck has been parked in temperatures below 20°F (−7°C)for any length of time, park it in a heated garage for an hour or so until the ball joints loosen up enough to accept the grease.

Depending on which front wheel you work on first, turn the wheel and tire outward, either full-lock right or full-lock left. You now have the ends of the upper and lower suspension control arms in front of you; the grease nipples are visible pointing up (top ball joint) and down (lower ball joint) through the end of each control arm. If the nipples are not accessible enough, remove the wheel and tire. Wipe all dirt and crud from the nipples or from around the plugs (if installed). If plugs are on the truck, remove them and install grease nipples in the holes (nipples are available in various thread sizes at most auto parts stores). Using a hand operated, low pressure grease gun loaded with a quality chassis grease, grease the ball joint only until the rubber joint boot begins to swell out.

Steering Linkage

The steering linkage should be greased at the same interval as the ball joints. Grease nipples are installed on the steering tie rod ends on most models. Wipe all dirt and crud from around the nipples at each tie rod end. Using a hand operated, low pressure grease gun loaded with a suitable chassis grease, grease the linkage until the old grease begins to squeeze out around the tie rod ends. Wipe off the nipples and any excess grease. Also grease the nipples on the steering idler arms.

Parking Brake Linkage

Use chassis grease on the parking brake cable where it contacts the cable guides, levers and linkage.

Automatic Transmission Linkage

Apply a small amount of clean engine oil to the kickdown and shift linkage points at 7,500 mile intervals.

OUTSIDE VEHICLE MAINTENANCE

Lock Cylinders

Apply graphite lubricant sparingly through the key slot. Insert the key and operate the lock several times to be sure that the lubricant is worked into the lock cylinder.

Hood Latch and Hinges

Clean the latch surfaces and apply clean engine oil to the latch pilot bolts and the spring anchor. Also lubricate the hood hinges with engine oil. Use a chassis grease to lubricate all the pivot points in the latch release mechanism.

Door Hinges

The gas tank filler door and truck doors should be wiped clean and lubricated with clean engine oil once a year. The door lock cylinders and latch mechanisms should be lubricated periodically with a few drops of graphite lock lubricant or a few shots of silicone spray.

Body Drain Holes

Be sure that the drain holes in the doors and rocker panels are cleared of obstruction. A small punch, screwdriver or unbent wire coat hanger can be used to clear them of any debris.

FRONT WHEEL BEARINGS

Only the front wheel bearings require periodic maintenance. A premium high melting point grease meeting GM specification 6031-M must be used. Long fiber type greases must not be used. This service is recommended at the intervals in the Maintenance Intervals Chart or whenever the truck has been driven in water up to the hubs.

Before handling the bearings, there are a few things that you should remember to do and not to do.

Remember to DO the following:

- Remove all outside dirt from the housing before exposing the bearing.
- Treat a used bearing as gently as you would a new one.
- Work with clean tools in clean surroundings.
- Use clean, dry canvas gloves, or at least clean, dry hands.
- Clean solvents and flushing fluids are a must.
- Use clean paper when laying out the bearings to dry.
- Protect disassembled bearings from rust and dirt. Cover them up.
- Use clean rags to wipe bearings.
- Keep the bearings in oil-proof paper when they are to be stored or are not in use.
- Clean the inside of the housing before replacing the bearing.

Do NOT do the following:

- Don't work in dirty surroundings.
- Don't use dirty, chipped or damaged tools.
- Try not to work on wooden work benches or use wooden mallets.
- Don't handle bearings with dirty or moist hands.
- Do not use gasoline for cleaning; use a safe solvent.
- Do not spin-dry bearings with compressed air. They will be damaged.
- Do not spin dirty bearings.
- Avoid using cotton waste or dirty cloths to wipe bearings.
- Try not to scratch or nick bearing surfaces.
- Do not allow the bearing to come in contact with dirt or rust at any time.

2-Wheel Drive

1. Raise and support the front end on jackstands.
2. Remove the wheel.
3. Dismount the caliper and wire it out of the way.
4. Pry out the grease cap, remove the cotter pin, spindle nut, and washer, then remove the hub. Do not drop the wheel bearings.
5. Remove the outer roller bearing assembly from the hub. The inner bearing assembly will remain in the hub and may be removed after prying out the inner seal. Discard the seal.
6. Clean all parts in a non-flammable solvent and let them air dry. Never spin-dry a bearing with compressed air! Check for excessive wear and damage.
7. Using a hammer and drift, remove the bearing races from the hub. They are driven out from the inside out. When installing new races, make sure that they are not cocked and that they are fully seated against the hub shoulder.
8. Pack both wheel bearings using high melting point wheel bearing grease for disc brakes. Ordinary grease will melt and ooze out ruining the pads. Bearings should be packed using a cone-type wheel bearing greaser tool. If one is not available they may be packed by hand. Place a healthy glob of grease in the palm of one hand and force the edge of the bearing into it so that the grease fills the bearing. Do this until the whole bearing is packed.
9. Place the inner bearing in the hub and install a new inner seal, making sure that the seal flange faces the bearing race.
10. Carefully install the wheel hub over the spindle.
11. Using your hands, firmly press the outer bearing into the hub. Install the spindle washer and nut.
12. Spin the wheel hub by hand and tighten the nut until it is just snug (12 ft. lbs.). Back off the nut until it is loose, then tighten it finger tight. Loosen the nut until either hole in the spindle lines up with a slot in the nut and insert a new cotter pin. There should be 0.001–0.005 in. (0.025–0.127mm) endplay. This can be measured with a dial indicator, if you wish.
13. Replace the dust cap, wheel and tire.

V Series 4-Wheel Drive

NOTE: Sodium-based grease is not compatible with lithium-based grease. Read the package labels and be careful not to mix the two types. If there is any doubt as to the type of grease used, completely clean the old grease from the bearing and hub before replacing.

Before handling the bearings, there are a few things that you should remember to do and not to do.

Remember to DO the following:

- Remove all outside dirt from the housing before exposing the bearing.
- Treat a used bearing as gently as you would a new one.

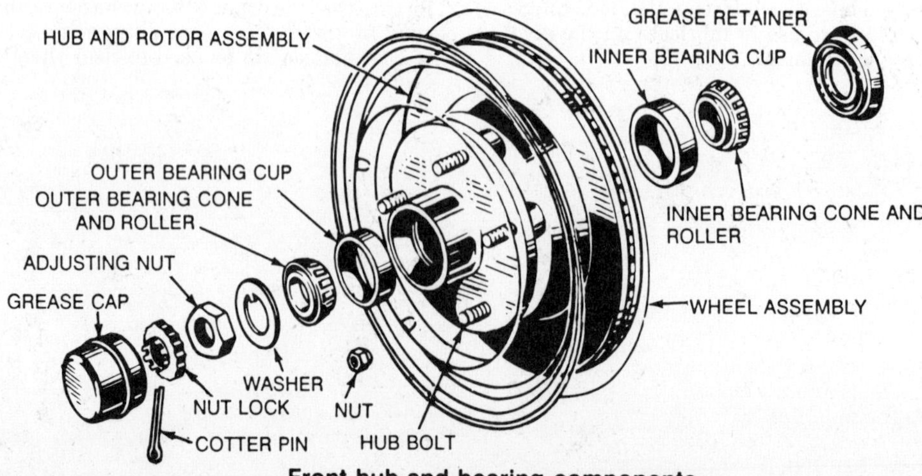

Front hub and bearing components

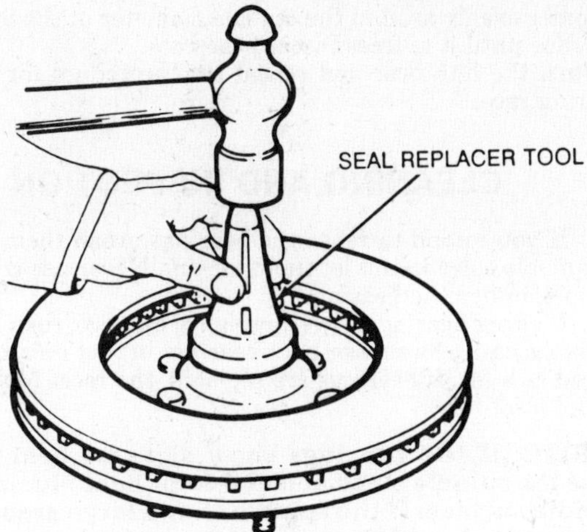

Install the inner seal

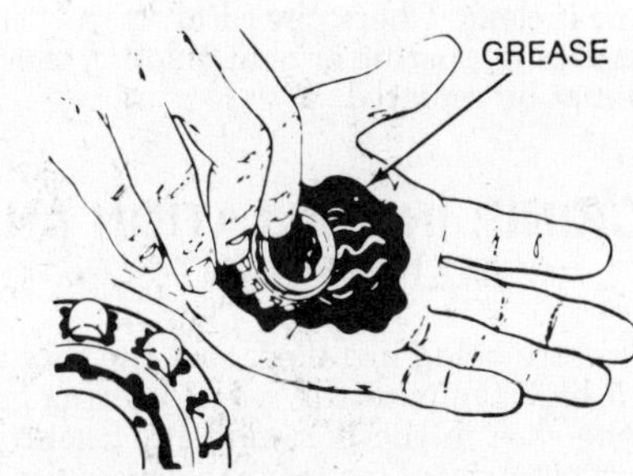

Packing the wheel bearing by hand

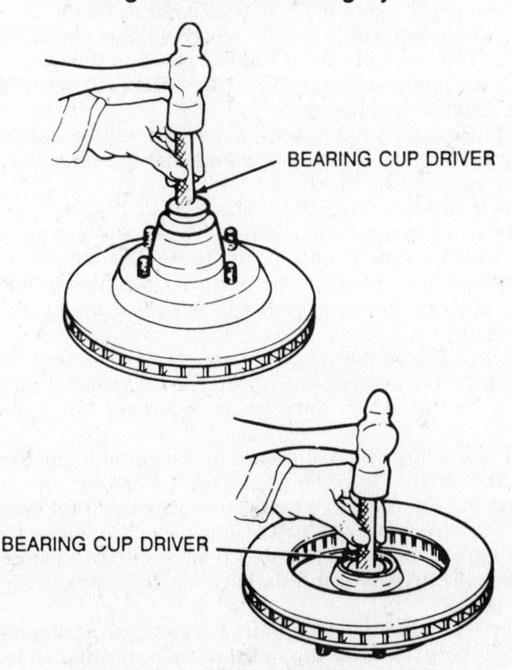

Install front wheel bearing races

- Work with clean tools in clean surroundings.
- Use clean, dry canvas gloves, or at least clean, dry hands.
- Clean solvents and flushing fluids are a must.
- Use clean paper when laying out the bearings to dry.
- Protect disassembled bearings from rust and dirt. Cover them up.
- Use clean rags to wipe bearings.
- Keep the bearings in oil-proof paper when they are to be stored or are not in use.
- Clean the inside of the housing before replacing the bearing.

Do NOT do the following:

- Don't work in dirty surroundings.
- Don't use dirty, chipped or damaged tools.
- Try not to work on wooden work benches or use wooden mallets.
- Don't handle bearings with dirty or moist hands.
- Do not use gasoline for cleaning. Use a safe solvent.
- Do not spin-dry bearings with compressed air. They will be damaged.
- Do not spin dirty bearings.
- Avoid using cotton waste or dirty cloths to wipe bearings.
- Try not to scratch or nick bearing surfaces.
- Do not allow the bearing to come in contact with dirt or rust at any time.

REMOVAL

NOTE: Before starting:
a. You'll need a special wheel bearing nut socket for your ½ inch drive ratchet. These sockets are available through auto parts stores and catalogs. You can't do this job properly without it!
b. You'll need a ½ inch drive torque wrench.
c. Have a clean container, like a shoe box, for the parts as you remove them.
d. Have PLENTY of paper towels handy.

1. Raise and support the front end on jackstands.
2. Remove the wheels.
3. Remove the hubs. See the Section 7.
4. Wipe the inside of the hub to remove as much grease as possible.
5. Using your bearing nut socket, remove the locknut from the spindle.
6. With the locknut off you'll be able to see the locking ring on the adjusting nut. Remove the locking ring. A tool such as a dental pick will make this easier.
7. Using the special socket, remove the bearing adjusting nut.

NOTE: You'll notice that the adjusting nut and the locknut are almost identical. The difference is, the adjusting nut has a small pin on one side which indexes with a hole in the locking ring. DO NOT CONFUSE THE TWO NUTS!

8. Dismount the brake caliper and suspend it out of the way, without disconnecting the brake line. See Section 9.
9. Pull the hub off of the spindle. The outer bearing will tend to fall out as soon as it clears the spindle, so have a hand ready to catch it.

DISASSEMBLY

1. If you are going to reuse the outer bearing, place it on a clean surface.
2. Position the hub, face up, on 2 wood blocks placed under opposite sides of the rotor. Have a paper towel positioned under the hub.
3. Using a hardened wood dowel or a hammer handle, drive out the inner bearing and seal. If your are going to reuse the inner bearing, move it to a clean area. Discard the seal.
4. If the bearings are being replaced, you'll have to replace the races. The races are pressed into the hub, but you can drive them out.

With the hub in position on the blocks, use a long drift and

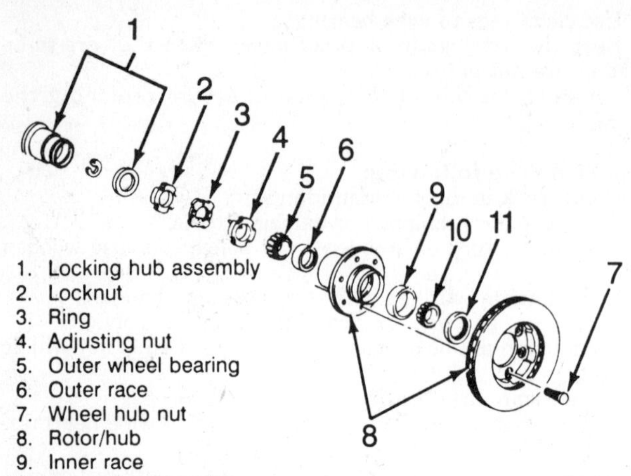

V10/1500 and 20/2500 series front hub/bearing components

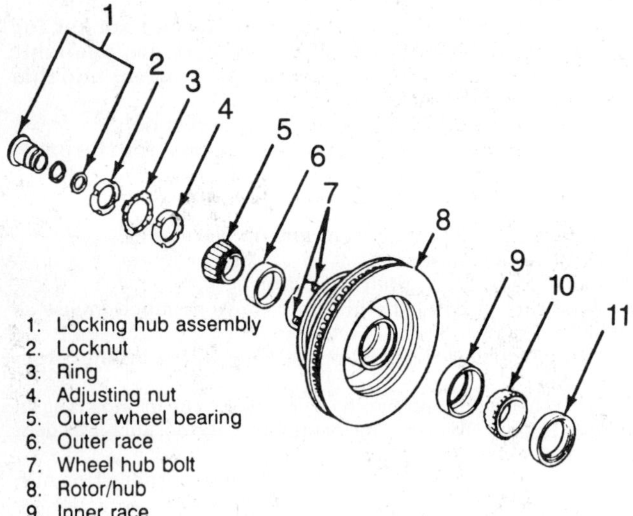

V30/3500 series front hub/bearing components

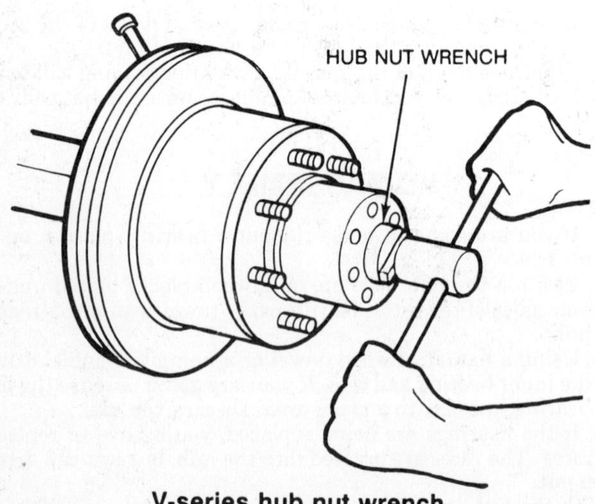

V-series hub nut wrench

hammer evenly around the outside diameter of the inner bearing race until it is free. Discard the race.

Turn the hub over and repeat this procedure for the outer bearing race.

CLEANING AND INSPECTION

1. If you intend to reuse the bearings, wash them in a non-flammable solvent and let them air-dry. Never use compressed air to spin-dry the bearings!
2. If either bearing shows any sign of damage, rust, heat blueing or excessive looseness, both bearings in that hub must be replaced as a set. If bearings are replaced, the races MUST be replaced also!

NOTE: If the bearings show signs of heat blueing, wipe the spindle clean and check for heat blueing on the spindle surface. If the spindle shows large areas of heat blueing, it should be replaced.

3. If you intend to reuse the bearings, wash out the hub with solvent and wipe it clean. Check the races. If they show signs of wear, pitting, cracking, rusting or heat blueing, they, along with the bearings, must be replaced.

PACKING, INSTALLATION AND ADJUSTMENT

1. If new races are being installed, coat the race and its bore in the hub with high temperature wheel bearing grease.
2. Position the race in the bore and start gently tapping it into place. There are drivers made for this purpose, but you can do it with a blunt rift and hammer. Just tap evenly around the race as you drive it into place so that it doesn't cock in the bore. Drive the race in until it is fully seated against the shoulder in the bore. You can tell that it's fully seated in 2 ways:
   a. Your hammer blows will sound differently when the race seats against the shoulder.
   b. The grease you applied to the bore will be squeezed out below the race as the race seats against the shoulder.
   Either race can be installed first.
3. Pack the bearings thoroughly with high temperature wheel bearing grease. An inexpensive wheel bearing packing tool is available at most auto parts stores. The tool has a grease fitting which utilizes a grease gun and completely packs the bearing. You can, however, pack a bearing reasonably well without the tool:
   a. Open the container of grease.
   b. Force the bearing down into the container, first on one side, then the other, until grease squeezes out among the rollers.
   c. Place a large blob of grease in the palm of one hand and force the bearing into the grease to squeeze out any air cavities among the rollers. When you're satisfied that each bearing is *completely* packed, place them on a clean paper towel, in a clean area, and cover them with another clean paper towel.
4. Pack the area of the hub, between the races, with wheel bearing grease.
5. Place the inner bearing in its race and position a new seal in the hub bore. Gentlty tap around the outer diameter of the seal with a plastic mallet until the seal is flush with the end of the bore.
6. Carefully place the hub assembly on the spindle. Take care to avoid damaging the seal on the spindle threads. Make sure the hub is all the way on the spindle.
7. Place the outer bearing on the spindle and slide it into place in its race.
8. Thread the adjusting nut on the spindle until it contacts the outer bearing.

WARNING: Make sure you are using the adjusting nut. Remember, it has a small pin on one side. That pin must face outwards, towards you!

9. Using the special socket and the torque wrench:
   a. Tighten the adjusting nut to 50 ft. lbs. while rotating the hub.
   b. Back off the adjusting nut until it is loose.
   c. While rotating the hub, tighten the adjusting nut to 35 ft. lbs. for automatic locking hubs or 50 ft. lbs. for manual locking hubs.
   d. Back off the adjusting nut 1/4 to 3/8 of a turn for automatic hubs or 1/6 to 1/4 turn for manual hubs.
10. Coat the locking ring with wheel bearing grease. Place the locking rin on the spindle. There is a tab on the inner diameter of the ring which must fit in the slot on the top of the spindle. Slide the locking ring in until it contacts the adjusting nut. The pin on the adjusting nut must enter one of the holes in the locking ring. You can tell that the locking ring is seated properly when you see the grease on the ring get pushed out of one of the holes by the pin, *and* the ring does not rock from side-to-side when you press on either side with your finger.

   If the locking ring and pin don't index, take note of how far off they are, pull the ring off the spindle and turn the nut, either by hand or with the socket, just enough for a goo fit. Try the locking ring again.
11. When the locking ring engages the adjusting nut pin properly, your bearing adjustment is set. Thread the locknut onto the spindle until it contacts the locking ring.
12. Tighten the locknut to *at least* 160 ft. lbs. This locknut ensures that the locking ring and adjusting nut don't move. Overtightening the locknut has no effect on the bearing adjustment.
13. Install the locking hub. See Section 7.
14. Install the caliper. See Section 9.
15. Install the wheel.

K Series 4-Wheel Drive

These axles have integral hub/bearing assemblies. No periodic service is required. See Section 7 for disassembly details.

TRAILER TOWING

Chevrolet and GMC trucks have long been popular as trailer towing vehicles. Their strong construction, and wide range of engine/transmission combinations make them ideal for towing campers, boat trailers and utility trailers.

Factory trailer towing packages are available on most Chevrolet and GMC trucks, if you are installing a trailer hitch and wiring on your truck, there are a few thing that you ought to know.

Trailer Weight

Trailer weight is the first, and most important, factor in determining whether or not your vehicle is suitable for towing the trailer you have in mind. The horsepower-to-weight ratio should be calculated. The basic standard is a ratio of 35:1. That is, 35 pounds of GVW for every horsepower.

To calculate this ratio, multiply you engine's rated horsepower by 35, then subtract the weight of the vehicle, including passengers and luggage. The resulting figure is the ideal maximum trailer weight that you can tow. One point to consider: a numerically higher axle ratio can offset what appears to be a low trailer weight. If the weight of the trailer that you have in mind is somewhat higher than the weight you just calculated, you might consider changing your rear axle ratio to compensate.

Hitch Weight

There are three kinds of hitches: bumper mounted, frame mounted, and load equalizing.

Bumper mounted hitches are those which attach solely to the vehicle's bumper. Many states prohibit towing with this type of hitch, when it attaches to the vehicle's stock bumper, since it subjects the bumper to stresses for which it was not designed. Aftermarket rear step bumpers, designed for trailer towing, are acceptable for use with bumper mounted hitches.

Frame mounted hitches can be of the type which bolts to two or more points on the frame, plus the bumper, or just to several points on the frame. Frame mounted hitches can also be of the tongue type, for Class I towing, or, of the receiver type, for classes II and III.

Load equalizing hitches are usually used for large trailers. Most equalizing hitches are welded in place and use equalizing bars and chains to level the vehicle after the trailer is hooked up.

The bolt-on hitches are the most common, since they are relatively easy to install.

Check the gross weight rating of your trailer. Tongue weight is usually figured as 10% of gross trailer weight. Therefore, a trailer with a maximum gross weight of 2,000 lb. will have a maximum tongue weight of 200 lb. Class I trailers fall into this category. Class II trailers are those with a gross weight rating of 2,000–3,500 lb., while Class III trailers fall into the 3,500–6,000 lb. category. Class IV trailers are those over 6,000 lb. and are for use with fifth wheel trucks, only.

When you've determined the hitch that you'll need, follow the manufacturer's installation instructions, exactly, especially when it comes to fastener torques. The hitch will subjected to a lot of stress and good hitches come with hardened bolts. Never substitute an inferior bolt for a hardened bolt.

Wiring

Wiring the truck for towing is fairly easy. There are a number of good wiring kits available and these should be used, rather than trying to design your own. All trailers will need brake lights and turn signals as well as tail lights and side marker lights. Most states require extra marker lights for overly wide trailers. Also, most states have recently required back-up lights

Recommended Equipment Checklist

Equipment	Class I Trailers Under 2,000 pounds	Class II Trailers 2,000-3,500 pounds	Class III Trailers 3,500-6,000 pounds	Class IV Trailers 6,000 pounds and up
Hitch	Frame or Equalizing	Equalizing	Equalizing	Fifth wheel Pick-up truck only
Tongue Load Limit**	Up to 200 pounds	200-350 pounds	350-600 pounds	600 pounds and up
Trailer Brakes	Not Required	Required	Required	Required
Safety Chain	3/16" diameter links	1/4" diameter links	5/16" diameter links	—
Fender Mounted Mirrors	Useful, but not necessary	Recommended	Recommended	Recommended
Turn Signal Flasher	Standard	Constant Rate or heavy duty	Constant Rate or heavy duty	Constant Rate or heavy duty
Coolant Recovery System	Recommended	Required	Required	Required
Transmission Oil Cooler	Recommended	Recommended	Recommended	Recommended
Engine Oil Cooler	Recommended	Recommended	Recommended	Recommended
Air Adjustable Shock Absorbers	Recommended	Recommended	Recommended	Recommended
Flex or Clutch Fan	Recommended	Recommended	Recommended	Recommended
Tires	***	***	***	***

NOTE The information in this chart is a guide. Check the manufacturer's recommendations for your car if in doubt.

*Local laws may require specific equipment such as trailer brakes or fender mounted mirrors. Check your local laws. Hitch weight is usually 10-15% of trailer gross weight and should be measured with trailer loaded.

**Most manufacturer's do not recommend towing trailers of over 1,000 pounds with compacts. Some intermediates cannot tow Class III trailers.

***Check manufacturer's recommendations for your specific car trailer combination.

—Does not apply

for trailers, and most trailer manufacturers have been building trailers with back-up lights for several years.

Additionally, some Class I, most Class II and just about all Class III trailers will have electric brakes.

Add to this number an accessories wire, to operate trailer internal equipment or to charge the trailer's battery, and you can have as many as seven wires in the harness.

Determine the equipment on your trailer and buy the wiring kit necessary. The kit will contain all the wires needed, plus a plug adapter set which included the female plug, mounted on the bumper or hitch, and the male plug, wired into, or plugged into the trailer harness.

When installing the kit, follow the manufacturer's instructions. The color coding of the wires is standard throughout the industry.

One point to note: some domestic vehicles, and most imported vehicles, have separate turn signals. On most domestic vehicles, the brake lights and rear turn signals operate with the same bulb. For those vehicles with separate turn signals, you can purchase an isolation unit so that the brake lights won't blink whenever the turn signals are operated, or, you can go to your local electronics supply house and buy four diodes to wire in series with the brake and turn signal bulbs. Diodes will isolate the brake and turn signals. The choice is yours. The isolation units are simple and quick to install, but far more expensive than the diodes. The diodes, however, require more work to install properly, since they require the cutting of each bulb's wire and soldering in place of the diode.

One, final point, the best kits are those with a spring loaded cover on the vehicle mounted socket. This cover prevent dirt and moisture from corroding the terminals. Never let the vehicle socket hang loosely. Always mount it securely to the bumper or hitch.

Cooling

ENGINE

One of the most common, if not THE most common, problem associated with trailer towing is engine overheating.

With factory installed trailer towing packages, a heavy duty cooling system is usually included. Heavy duty cooling systems are available as optional equipment on most GM vehicles, with or without a trailer package. If you have one of these extra capacity systems, you shouldn't have any overheating problems.

If you have a standard cooling system, without an expansion tank, you'll definitely need to get an aftermarket expansion tank kit, preferably one with at least a 2 quart capacity. These kits are easily installed on the radiator's overflow hose, and come with a pressure cap designed for expansion tanks.

Another helpful accessory is a Flex Fan. These fan are large diameter units are designed to provide more airflow at low speeds, with blades that have deeply cupped surfaces. The blades then flex, or flatten out, at high speed, when less cooling air is needed. These fans are far lighter in weight than stock fans, requiring less horsepower to drive them. Also, they are far quieter than stock fans.

If you do decide to replace your stock fan with a flex fan, note that if your truck has a fan clutch, a spacer between the flex fan and water pump hub will be needed.

Aftermarket engine oil coolers are helpful for prolonging engine oil life and reducing overall engine temperatures. Both of these factors increase engine life.

While not absolutely necessary in towing Class I and some Class II trailers, they are recommended for heavier Class II and all Class III towing.

Engine oil cooler systems consist of an adapter, screwed on in place of the oil filter, a remote filter mounting and a multi-tube, finned heat exchanger, which is mounted in front of the radiator or air conditioning condenser.

TRANSMISSION

An automatic transmission is usually recommended for trailer towing. Modern automatics have proven reliable and, of course, easy to operate, in trailer towing.

The increased load of a trailer, however, causes an increase in the temperature of the automatic transmission fluid. Heat is the worst enemy of an automatic transmission. As the temperature of the fluid increases, the life of the fluid decreases.

It is essential, therefore, that you install an automatic transmission cooler. The cooler, which consists of a multi-tube, finned heat exchanger, is usually installed in front of the radiator or air conditioning compressor, and hooked inline with the transmission cooler tank inlet line. Follow the cooler manufacturer's installation instructions.

Select a cooler of at least adequate capacity, based upon the combined gross weights of the truck and trailer.

Cooler manufacturers recommend that you use an aftermarket cooler in addition to, and not instead of, the present cooling tank in your truck's radiator. If you do want to use it in place of the radiator cooling tank, get a cooler at least two sizes larger than normally necessary.

One note: transmission cooler can, sometimes, cause slow or harsh shifting in the transmission during cold weather, until the fluid has a chance to come up to normal operating temperature. Some coolers can be purchased with or retrofitted with a temperature bypass valve which will allow fluid flow through the cooler only when the fluid has reached operating temperature, or above.

PUSHING

Chevrolet and GMC trucks with manual transmissions can be push started, but this is not recommended if you value the appearance of your truck.

To push start, make sure that both bumpers are in reasonable alignment. Bent sheet metal and inflamed tempers are both common results from misaligned bumpers when push starting. Turn the ignition key to ON and engage High gear. Depress the clutch pedal. When a speed of about 10 mph is reached, slightly depress the gas pedal and slowly release the clutch. The engine should start.

WARNING: Never get an assist by having your vehicle towed! Automatic transmission equipped trucks cannot be started by pushing.

Towing

2-Wheel Drive

Chevrolet and GMC trucks can be towed on all four wheels (flat towed) at speeds of less than 35 mph for distances less than 50 miles, providing that the axle, driveline and engine/transmis-

Four Wheel Drive Towing Chart

FRONT WHEELS OFF THE GROUND	
FULL TIME (4 X 4) AUTOMATIC TRANSMISSION	PART TIME (4 X 4) MANUAL TRANSMISSION
1. TRANSFER CASE IN NEUTRAL 2. TRANSMISSION IN PARK 3. MAXIMUM SPEED 35 MPH 4. MAXIMUM DISTANCE 50 MILES NOTE: For distances over 50 miles, disconnect rear propshaft at rear axle carrier and secure in safe position.	1. TRANSFER CASE IN 2 H 2. TRANSMISSION IN NEUTRAL 3. MAXIMUM SPEED 35 MPH 4. MAXIMUM DISTANCE 50 MILES NOTE: For distances over 50 miles, disconnect the rear propshaft at rear axle carrier and secure in safe position.
REAR WHEELS OFF THE GROUND CAUTION: When towing a vehicle in this position, the steering wheel should be secured to keep the front wheels in a straight ahead position.	
FULL TIME (4 X 4)	PART TIME (4 X 4)
1. TRANSFER CASE IN NEUTRAL 2. TRANSMISSION IN PARK 3. MAXIMUM SPEED 35 MPH 4. MAXIMUM DISTANCE 50 MILES NOTE: For distances over 50 miles, disconnect front propshaft at front axle carrier and secure in safe position.	1. TRANSFER CASE IN 2 H 2. TRANSMISSION IN NEUTRAL 3. MAXIMUM SPEED 35 MPH 4. MAXIMUM DISTANCE 50 MILES NOTE: For distances over 50 miles, disconnect the front propshaft at front axle carrier and secure in safe position.
ALL FOUR WHEELS ON GROUND	
FULL TIME (4 X 4)	PART TIME (4 X 4)
1. TRANSFER CASE IN NEUTRAL 2. TRANSMISSION IN PARK NOTE: Do not exceed speed as per State laws for towing vehicles.	1. TRANSFER CASE IN 2 H 2. TRANSMISSION IN NEUTRAL 3. MAXIMUM SPEED 35 MPH 1. MAXIMUM DISTANCE 50 MILES NOTE: For speeds or distances greater than above, both propshafts must be disconnected at the axle carrier end and secured in a safe position. It is recommended that both propshafts be removed and stored in the vehicle. NOTE: Do not exceed speeds as per State laws for towing vehicles.

sion are normally operable. The transmission should be in Neutral, the engine off, the steering unlocked, and the parking brake released.

The rear wheels must be raised off the ground or the driveshaft disconnected when the transmission if not operating properly, or when speeds of over 35 mph will be used or when towing more than 50 miles.

Do not attach chains to the bumpers or bracketing. All attachments must be made to the structural members. Safety chains should be used. It should also be remembered that power steering and brake assists will not be working with the engine off.

4–Wheel Drive

Details for towing procedures are given in the Towing Four Wheel Drive Chart.

Remember that the power steering and power brakes will not have their power assist with the engine off. The only safe way to tow is with a tow bar. The steering column must be unlocked and the parking brake released. Attachments should be made to the frame and to the bumper or its brackets. Safety chains are also required.

JUMP STARTING A DUAL BATTERY DIESEL

All GM V8 diesels are equipped with two 12 volt batteries. The batteries are connected in parallel circuit (positive terminal to positive terminal, negative terminal to negative terminal). Hooking the batteries up in parallel circuit increases battery cranking power without increasing total battery voltage output (12 volts). On the other hand, hooking two 12 volt batteries up in a series circuit (positive terminal to negative terminal, positive terminal to negative terminal) increases total battery output to 24 volts (12 volts + 12 volts).

CAUTION

NEVER hook the batteries up in a series circuit or the entire electrical system will go up in smoke.

In the event that a dual battery diesel must be jump started, use the following procedure.

1. Open the hood and locate the batteries. On GM diesels, the manufacturer usually suggests using the battery on the driver's side of the truck to make the correction.
2. Position the donor vehicle so that the jumper cables will reach from its battery (must be 12 volt, negative ground) to the appropriate battery in the diesel. Do not allow the vehicles to touch.
3. Shut off all electrical equipment on both vehicles. Turn off the engine of the donor vehicle, set the parking brakes on both vehicles and block the wheels. Also, make sure both vehicles are in Neutral (manual transmission models) or Park (automatic transmission models).
4. Using the jumper cables, connect the positive (+) terminal of the donor vehicle's battery to the positive terminal of one (not both) of the diesel batteries.
5. Using the second jumper cable, connect the negative (–) terminal of the donor battery to a solid, stationary, metallic point on the diesel (alternator bracket, engine block, etc.). Be very careful to keep the jumper cables away from moving parts (cooling fan, alternator belt, etc.) on both vehicles.
6. Start the engine of the donor can and run it at moderate speed.
7. Start the engine of the diesel.
8. When the diesel starts, disconnect the battery cables in the reverse order of attachment.

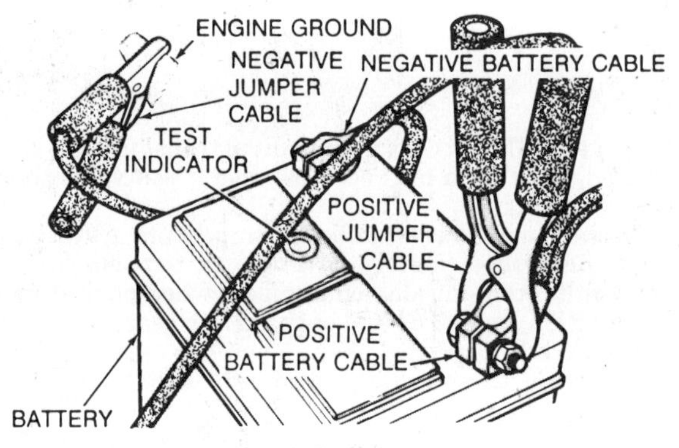

Jumper cable installation

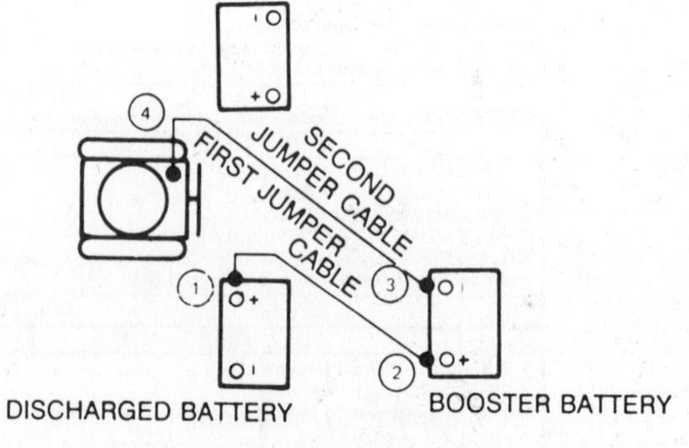

Dual battery jump-starting diagram

JUMP STARTING A DEAD BATTERY

The chemical reaction in a battery produces explosive hydrogen gas. This is the safe way to jump start a dead battery, reducing the chances of an accidental spark that could cause an explosion.

Jump Starting Precautions

1. Be sure both batteries are of the same voltage.
2. Be sure both batteries are of the same polarity (have the same grounded terminal).
3. Be sure the vehicles are not touching.
4. Be sure the vent cap holes are not obstructed.
5. Do not smoke or allow sparks around the battery.
6. In cold weather, check for frozen electrolyte in the battery. Do not jump start a frozen battery.
7. Do not allow electrolyte on your skin or clothing.
8. Be sure the electrolyte is not frozen.

CAUTION: Make certin that the ignition key, in the vehicle with the dead battery, is in the OFF position. Connecting cables to vehicles with on-board computers will result in computer destruction if the key is not in the OFF position.

Jump Starting Procedure

1. Determine voltages of the two batteries; they must be the same.
2. Bring the starting vehicle close (they must not touch) so that the batteries can be reached easily.
3. Turn off all accessories and both engines. Put both vehicles in Neutral or Park and set the handbrake.
4. Cover the cell caps with a rag—do not cover terminals.
5. If the terminals on the run-down battery are heavily corroded, clean them.
6. Identify the positive and negative posts on both batteries and connect the cables in the order shown.
7. Start the engine of the starting vehicle and run it at fast idle. Try to start the car with the dead battery. Crank it for no more than 10 seconds at a time and let it cool for 20 seconds in between tries.
8. If it doesn't start in 3 tries, there is something else wrong.
9. Disconnect the cables in the reverse order.
10. Replace the cell covers and dispose of the rags.

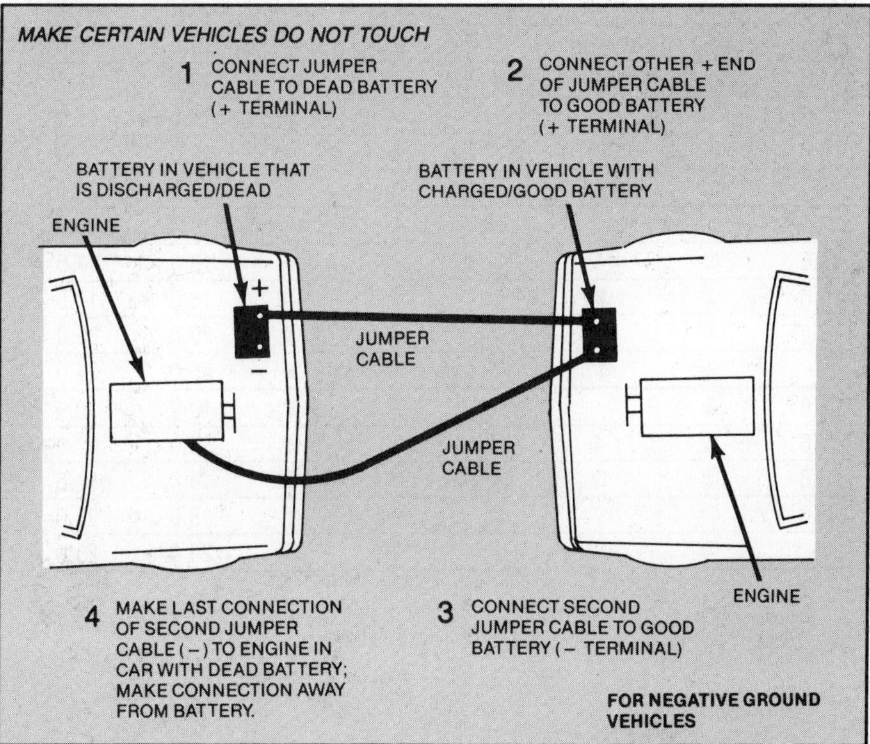
MAKE CERTAIN VEHICLES DO NOT TOUCH
1 CONNECT JUMPER CABLE TO DEAD BATTERY (+ TERMINAL)
2 CONNECT OTHER + END OF JUMPER CABLE TO GOOD BATTERY (+ TERMINAL)
BATTERY IN VEHICLE THAT IS DISCHARGED/DEAD
BATTERY IN VEHICLE WITH CHARGED/GOOD BATTERY
ENGINE
+
−
JUMPER CABLE
JUMPER CABLE
ENGINE
4 MAKE LAST CONNECTION OF SECOND JUMPER CABLE (−) TO ENGINE IN CAR WITH DEAD BATTERY; MAKE CONNECTION AWAY FROM BATTERY.
3 CONNECT SECOND JUMPER CABLE TO GOOD BATTERY (− TERMINAL)
FOR NEGATIVE GROUND VEHICLES

Side terminal batteries occasionally pose a problem when connecting jumper cables. There frequently isn't enough room to clamp the cables without touching sheet metal. Side terminal adaptors are available to alleviate this problem and should be removed after use

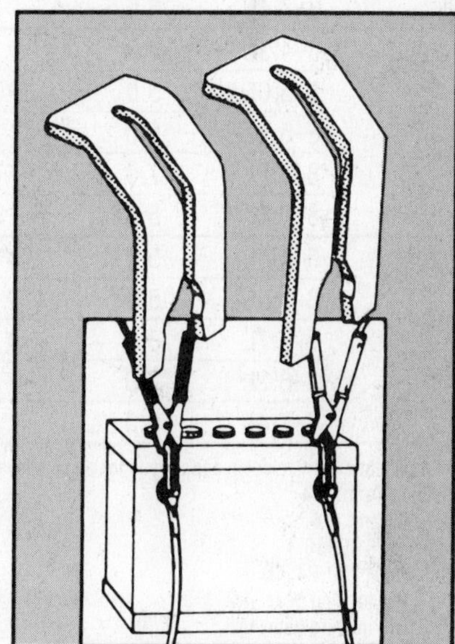

JACKING

The jack supplied with the truck was meant for changing tires. It was not meant to support a truck while you crawl under it and work. Whenever it is necessary to get under a truck to perform service operations, always be sure that it is adequately supported, preferably by jackstands at the proper points.

If your truck is equipped with a Positraction® or locking rear axle, do not run the engine for any reason with one rear wheel off the ground. Power will be transmitted through the rear wheel remaining on the ground, possibly causing the vehicle to drive itself off the jack.

LOWER CONTROL ARM
JACK
BALL JOINT
JACK HANDLE
6.00
FRONT
POSITION JACK AS CLOSE TO WHEEL AS POSSIBLE
AXLE ASSEMBLY
JACK
JACK HANDLE
REAR

Jacking points for 20, 30, 2500 and 3500 Series

LOWER CONTROL ARM PIVOT BAR
JACK
JACK HANDLE
FRONT
POSITION JACK UNDER AXLE HOUSING BETWEEN U-BOLTS

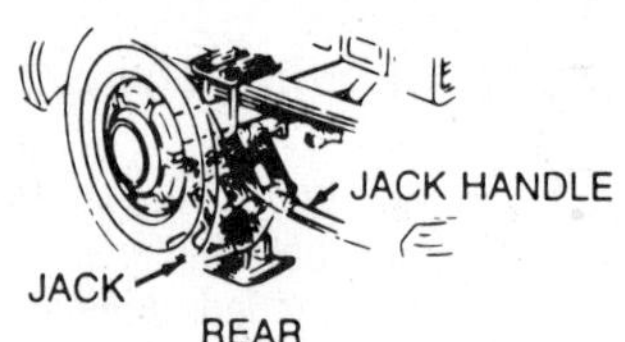

Jacking points for 10 and 1500 Series

CAPACITIES CHART
C and K Series Pickup

Years	Engines	Crank-case Incl. Filter (qt.)	Transmission (pt.)*			Trans-fer Case (qt.)	Rear Drive Axle (pt.)	Front Drive Axle (pt.)	Fuel Tank (gal.)	Cooling System (qt.)	
			4-sp	5-sp	Auto.					w/AC	wo/AC
1988	6-4.3L	5.0	①	3.6	②	—	③	—	⑤	10.9	10.9
	8-5.0L	5.0	①	3.6	②	1.4	③	1.75	⑤	18.0	17.5
	8-5.7L	5.0	①	3.6	②	⑥	③	④	⑤	18.0	17.5
	8-6.2L	7.0	—	3.6	②	⑥	③	④	⑤	25.0	25.0
	8-7.4L	6.0	—	—	②	⑥	③	④	⑤	25.0	23.0
1989	6-4.3L	5.0	①	3.6	②	—	③	—	⑤	10.9	10.9
	8-5.0L	5.0	①	3.6	②	1.4	③	1.75	⑤	18.0	17.5
	8-5.7L	5.0	①	3.6	②	⑥	③	④	⑤	18.0	17.5
	8-6.2L	7.0	—	3.6	②	⑥	③	④	⑤	25.0	25.0
	8-7.4L	6.0	—	—	②	⑥	③	④	⑤	25.0	23.0
1990	6-4.3L	5.0	①	3.6	②	—	③	—	⑧	10.9	10.9
	8-5.0L	5.0	①	3.6	②	1.4	③	1.75	⑧	18.0	17.5
	8-5.7L	5.0	①	3.6	②	⑦	③	④	⑧	18.0	17.5
	8-6.2L	7.0	—	3.6	②	⑦	③	④	⑧	25.0	25.0
	8-7.4L	6.0	—	—	②	⑦	③	④	⑧	25.0	23.0

*Automatic Transmission capacity is for pan removal only

① 117mm: 8.4
85mm: 3.6

② THM 400: 8.4
THM 700-R4: 10.0

③ 8.5 in. ring gear: 4.2
9.5 in. ring gear: 6.5
9.75 in. ring gear: 6.0
10.5 in. ring gear: 6.5

④ 15/25 series: 3.5
35 series: 4.4

⑤ Standard: 26
Optional: 34

⑥ 15/25 series: 1.4
35 series: 2.75

⑦ 15/25 series: 2.3
35 series, exc. w/dual rear wheels: 2.75
35 series w/dual rear wheels: 1.5

⑧ Pickup: standard 25; optional 34
Chassis/cab: standard 22; optional 30

CAPACITIES CHART
R and V Series Pickup

Years	Engines	Crank-case Incl. Filter (qt.)	Transmission (pt.)*			Trans-fer Case (qt.)	Rear Drive Axle (pt.)	Front Drive Axle (pt.)	Fuel Tank (gal.)	Cooling System (qt.)	
			4-sp	5-sp	Auto.					w/AC	wo/AC
1988	6–4.3L	5.0	8.4	—	③	—	②	—	①	10.9	10.9
	8–5.7L	5.0	8.4	—	③	⑤	②	④	①	18.0	17.5
	8–6.2L	7.0	—	8.0	③	⑤	②	④	①	25.5	25.5
	8–7.4L	6.0	—	—	③	⑤	②	④	①	23.0	23.0
1989	6–4.8L	6.0	8.4	—	—	—	②	—	⑦	16.5	15.5
	8–5.7L	5.0	—	—	③	⑥	②	④	⑦	17.0	17.0
	8–6.2L	7.0	—	8.0	③	⑥	②	④	⑦	25.5	25.5
	8–7.4L	6.0	—	—	③	⑥	②	④	⑦	23.0	23.0
1990	6–4.8L	6.0	8.4	—	—	—	②	—	⑦	16.5	15.5
	8–5.7L	5.0	—	—	③	⑥	②	④	⑦	17.5	18.0
	8–6.2L	7.0	—	8.0	③	⑥	②	④	⑦	25.0	25.0
	8–7.4L	6.0	—	—	③	⑥	②	④	⑦	23.0	25.0

*Drain and refill only

① Standard: 20.0
Dual Tanks w/gasoline engine: 16 gal. each
Dual Tanks w/diesel engine: 20 gal each

② 8.5 in. ring gear: 4.2
9.75 in. ring gear: 6.0
Dana 10.5 in. ring gear: 7.2
Chevrolet 10.5 in. Ring Gear: 6.5

③ Turbo Hydra-Matic 400: 9.0
Turbo Hydra-Matic 700–R4: 10.0

④ GMC axle: 10.4
Dana 60: 5.0

⑤ 10/15 and 20/25 series: 5.0
30/35 series: 2.5

⑥ 10/15 and 20/25 series: 1.4
30/35 series: 2.5

⑦ Single Tank: 20 gal.
Dual Tanks: 20 gal. each

CAPACITIES CHART
Blazer and Suburban

Years	Engines	Crank-case Incl. Filter (qt.)	Transmission (pt.)*			Trans-fer Case (qt.)	Rear Drive Axle (pt.)	Front Drive Axle (pt.)	Fuel Tank (gal.)	Cooling System (qt.)	
			4-sp	5-sp	Auto.					w/AC	wo/AC
1988	8–5.7L	5.0	8.4	—	③	⑤	②	④	①	18.0	17.5
	8–6.2L	7.0	—	8.0	③	⑤	②	④	①	25.5	25.5
	8–7.4L	6.0	—	—	③	⑤	②	④	①	23.0	23.0
1989	6–4.8L	6.0	8.4	—	—	⑤	②	—	①	16.5	15.5
	8–5.7L	5.0	—	—	③	⑤	②	④	①	17.0	17.0
	8–6.2L	7.0	—	8.0	③	⑤	②	④	①	25.5	25.5
	8–7.4L	6.0	—	—	③	⑤	②	④	①	23.0	23.0
1990	8–5.7L	5.0	—	—	③	⑤	②	④	①	17.5	18.0
	8–6.2L	7.0	—	8.0	③	⑤	②	④	①	25.0	25.0
	8–7.4L	6.0	—	—	③	⑤	②	④	①	23.0	25.0

*Drain and refill only

① Standard: 25.0
Optional: 31.0
Optional, Suburban only: 40

② 8.5 in. ring gear: 4.2
9.75 in. ring gear: 6.0
Dana 10.5 in. ring gear: 7.2
Chevrolet 10.5 in. ring gear: 6.5

③ Turbo Hydra-Matic 400: 9.0
Turbo Hydra-Matic 700-R4: 10.0

④ GMC axle: 10.4
Dana 60: 5.0

⑤ 10/15 and 20/25 series: 5.2
30/35 series: 2.5

MAINTENANCE INTERVAL CHART

Maintenance Item	Interval
Air cleaner element	Replace every 30,000 miles
Automatic transmission fluid and filter	Check once a month. Change every 30,000 miles
Battery	Check fluid level twice a month. Clean terminals as necessary
Brake fluid	Check once a month. Add as necessary
Chassis lubrication	Every 6 months
Coolant level	Check once a week. Add as necessary
Drive belts	Check every month. Adjust as necessary
Engine oil	Check at every fuel stop. Change every 3,000 miles
Engine oil filter	Change every oil change
Evaporative canister filter	Replace every 24 mos/30,000 miles
Front drive axle	Check twice a year. Add as necessary
Front wheel bearings	Clean and repack every 30,000 miles
Fuel filter	Replace every 6,000 miles
Manual transmission fluid	Check twice a year. Add as necessary
PCV valve	Replace every 12 mos./15,000 miles
Power steering reservoir	Check once a month. Add as necessary
Rear axle	Check twice a year. Add as necessary
Tires	Check pressure once a week. Rotate every 6,000 miles
Transfer case	Check twice a year. Add as necessary

2 Engine Performance and Tune-Up

QUICK REFERENCE INDEX

GENERAL INDEX

TUNE-UP PROCEDURES

Troubleshooting Engine Performance

Problem	Cause	Solution
Hard starting (engine cranks normally)	• Binding linkage, choke valve or choke piston	• Repair as necessary
	• Restricted choke vacuum diaphragm	• Clean passages
	• Improper fuel level	• Adjust float level
	• Dirty, worn or faulty needle valve and seat	• Repair as necessary
	• Float sticking	• Repair as necessary
	• Faulty fuel pump	• Replace fuel pump
	• Incorrect choke cover adjustment	• Adjust choke cover
	• Inadequate choke unloader adjustment	• Adjust choke unloader
	• Faulty ignition coil	• Test and replace as necessary
	• Improper spark plug gap	• Adjust gap
	• Incorrect ignition timing	• Adjust timing
	• Incorrect valve timing	• Check valve timing; repair as necessary
Rough idle or stalling	• Incorrect curb or fast idle speed	• Adjust curb or fast idle speed
	• Incorrect ignition timing	• Adjust timing to specification
	• Improper feedback system operation	• Refer to Chapter 4
	• Improper fast idle cam adjustment	• Adjust fast idle cam
	• Faulty EGR valve operation	• Test EGR system and replace as necessary
	• Faulty PCV valve air flow	• Test PCV valve and replace as necessary
	• Choke binding	• Locate and eliminate binding condition
	• Faulty TAC vacuum motor or valve	• Repair as necessary
	• Air leak into manifold vacuum	• Inspect manifold vacuum connections and repair as necessary
	• Improper fuel level	• Adjust fuel level
	• Faulty distributor rotor or cap	• Replace rotor or cap
	• Improperly seated valves	• Test cylinder compression, repair as necessary
	• Incorrect ignition wiring	• Inspect wiring and correct as necessary
	• Faulty ignition coil	• Test coil and replace as necessary
	• Restricted air vent or idle passages	• Clean passages
	• Restricted air cleaner	• Clean or replace air cleaner filler element
	• Faulty choke vacuum diaphragm	• Repair as necessary
Faulty low-speed operation	• Restricted idle transfer slots	• Clean transfer slots
	• Restricted idle air vents and passages	• Clean air vents and passages
	• Restricted air cleaner	• Clean or replace air cleaner filter element

Troubleshooting Engine Performance

Problem	Cause	Solution
Faulty low-speed operation (cont.)	• Improper fuel level	• Adjust fuel level
	• Faulty spark plugs	• Clean or replace spark plugs
	• Dirty, corroded, or loose ignition secondary circuit wire connections	• Clean or tighten secondary circuit wire connections
	• Improper feedback system operation	• Refer to Chapter 4
	• Faulty ignition coil high voltage wire	• Replace ignition coil high voltage wire
	• Faulty distributor cap	• Replace cap
Faulty acceleration	• Improper accelerator pump stroke	• Adjust accelerator pump stroke
	• Incorrect ignition timing	• Adjust timing
	• Inoperative pump discharge check ball or needle	• Clean or replace as necessary
	• Worn or damaged pump diaphragm or piston	• Replace diaphragm or piston
	• Leaking carburetor main body cover gasket	• Replace gasket
	• Engine cold and choke set too lean	• Adjust choke cover
	• Improper metering rod adjustment (BBD Model carburetor)	• Adjust metering rod
	• Faulty spark plug(s)	• Clean or replace spark plug(s)
	• Improperly seated valves	• Test cylinder compression, repair as necessary
	• Faulty ignition coil	• Test coil and replace as necessary
	• Improper feedback system operation	• Refer to Chapter 4
Faulty high speed operation	• Incorrect ignition timing	• Adjust timing
	• Faulty distributor centrifugal advance mechanism	• Check centrifugal advance mechanism and repair as necessary
	• Faulty distributor vacuum advance mechanism	• Check vacuum advance mechanism and repair as necessary
	• Low fuel pump volume	• Replace fuel pump
	• Wrong spark plug air gap or wrong plug	• Adjust air gap or install correct plug
	• Faulty choke operation	• Adjust choke cover
	• Partially restricted exhaust manifold, exhaust pipe, catalytic converter, muffler, or tailpipe	• Eliminate restriction
	• Restricted vacuum passages	• Clean passages
	• Improper size or restricted main jet	• Clean or replace as necessary
	• Restricted air cleaner	• Clean or replace filter element as necessary
	• Faulty distributor rotor or cap	• Replace rotor or cap
	• Faulty ignition coil	• Test coil and replace as necessary
	• Improperly seated valve(s)	• Test cylinder compression, repair as necessary

Troubleshooting Engine Performance (cont.)

Problem	Cause	Solution
Faulty high speed operation (cont.)	• Faulty valve spring(s)	• Inspect and test valve spring tension, replace as necessary
	• Incorrect valve timing	• Check valve timing and repair as necessary
	• Intake manifold restricted	• Remove restriction or replace manifold
	• Worn distributor shaft	• Replace shaft
	• Improper feedback system operation	• Refer to Chapter 4
Misfire at all speeds	• Faulty spark plug(s)	• Clean or replace spark plug(s)
	• Faulty spark plug wire(s)	• Replace as necessary
	• Faulty distributor cap or rotor	• Replace cap or rotor
	• Faulty ignition coil	• Test coil and replace as necessary
	• Primary ignition circuit shorted or open intermittently	• Troubleshoot primary circuit and repair as necessary
	• Improperly seated valve(s)	• Test cylinder compression, repair as necessary
	• Faulty hydraulic tappet(s)	• Clean or replace tappet(s)
	• Improper feedback system operation	• Refer to Chapter 4
	• Faulty valve spring(s)	• Inspect and test valve spring tension, repair as necessary
	• Worn camshaft lobes	• Replace camshaft
	• Air leak into manifold	• Check manifold vacuum and repair as necessary
	• Improper carburetor adjustment	• Adjust carburetor
	• Fuel pump volume or pressure low	• Replace fuel pump
	• Blown cylinder head gasket	• Replace gasket
	• Intake or exhaust manifold passage(s) restricted	• Pass chain through passage(s) and repair as necessary
	• Incorrect trigger wheel installed in distributor	• Install correct trigger wheel
Power not up to normal	• Incorrect ignition timing	• Adjust timing
	• Faulty distributor rotor	• Replace rotor
	• Trigger wheel loose on shaft	• Reposition or replace trigger wheel
	• Incorrect spark plug gap	• Adjust gap
	• Faulty fuel pump	• Replace fuel pump
	• Incorrect valve timing	• Check valve timing and repair as necessary
	• Faulty ignition coil	• Test coil and replace as necessary
	• Faulty ignition wires	• Test wires and replace as necessary
	• Improperly seated valves	• Test cylinder compression and repair as necessary
	• Blown cylinder head gasket	• Replace gasket
	• Leaking piston rings	• Test compression and repair as necessary
	• Worn distributor shaft	• Replace shaft
	• Improper feedback system operation	• Refer to Chapter 4

Troubleshooting Engine Performance (cont.)

Problem	Cause	Solution
Intake backfire	• Improper ignition timing • Faulty accelerator pump discharge • Defective EGR CTO valve • Defective TAC vacuum motor or valve • Lean air/fuel mixture	• Adjust timing • Repair as necessary • Replace EGR CTO valve • Repair as necessary • Check float level or manifold vacuum for air leak. Remove sediment from bowl
Exhaust backfire	• Air leak into manifold vacuum • Faulty air injection diverter valve • Exhaust leak	• Check manifold vacuum and repair as necessary • Test diverter valve and replace as necessary • Locate and eliminate leak
Ping or spark knock	• Incorrect ignition timing • Distributor centrifugal or vacuum advance malfunction • Excessive combustion chamber deposits • Air leak into manifold vacuum • Excessively high compression • Fuel octane rating excessively low • Sharp edges in combustion chamber • EGR valve not functioning properly	• Adjust timing • Inspect advance mechanism and repair as necessary • Remove with combustion chamber cleaner • Check manifold vacuum and repair as necessary • Test compression and repair as necessary • Try alternate fuel source • Grind smooth • Test EGR system and replace as necessary
Surging (at cruising to top speeds)	• Low carburetor fuel level • Low fuel pump pressure or volume • Metering rod(s) not adjusted properly (BBD Model Carburetor) • Improper PCV valve air flow • Air leak into manifold vacuum • Incorrect spark advance • Restricted main jet(s) • Undersize main jet(s) • Restricted air vents • Restricted fuel filter • Restricted air cleaner • EGR valve not functioning properly • Improper feedback system operation	• Adjust fuel level • Replace fuel pump • Adjust metering rod • Test PCV valve and replace as necessary • Check manifold vacuum and repair as necessary • Test and replace as necessary • Clean main jet(s) • Replace main jet(s) • Clean air vents • Replace fuel filter • Clean or replace air cleaner filter element • Test EGR system and replace as necessary • Refer to Chapter 4

GASOLINE ENGINE TUNE-UP SPECIFICATIONS

Years	Engine	Spark Plugs Type	Spark Plugs Gap (in.)	Ignition Timing (deg.) Man. Trans.	Ignition Timing (deg.) Auto. Trans.	Fuel Pump Pressure (psi.)	Idle Speed Man. Trans.	Idle Speed Auto. Trans.
1988	6-4.3L	R43TS	0.045	①	①	4.5–6.0	Not Adjustable	
	8-5.0L	R43TS	0.045	①	①	7.5–9.0	Not Adjustable	
	8-5.7L	R44T	0.045	①	①	7.5–9.0	①	①
	8-7.4L	CR43TS	0.045	①	①	7.5–9.0	Not Adjustable	
1989	6-4.3L	CR43TS	0.045	①	①	4.5–6.0	Not Adjustable	
	6-4.8L	R44T	0.035	①	①	4.5–5.5	700	—
	8-5.0L	CR43TS	0.045	①	①	7.5–9.0	Not Adjustable	
	8-5.7L	CR43TS	0.045	①	①	7.5–9.0	①	①
	8-7.4L	CR43TS	0.045	①	①	7.5–9.0	Not Adjustable	
1990	6-4.3L	CR43TS	0.045	①	①	4.5–6.0	Not Adjustable	
	6-4.8L	R44T	0.035	①	①	4.5–5.5	700	—
	8-5.0L	CR43TS	0.045	①	①	7.5–9.0	Not Adjustable	
	8-5.7L	CR43TS	0.045	①	①	7.5–9.0	①	①
	8-7.4L	CR43TS	0.045	①	①	7.5–9.0	Not Adjustable	

① See underhood sticker

DIESEL ENGINE TUNE-UP SPECIFICATIONS

Engine	Years	Injection Timing	Nozzle Opening Pressure (psi)	Idle Speed (rpm) MT	Idle Speed (rpm) AT
8-6.2L	1988–90	scribe mark	1,500	575	550

In order to extract the full measure of performance and economy from your engine it is essential that it be properly tuned at regular intervals. A regular tune-up will keep your vehicle's engine running smoothly and will prevent the annoying minor breakdowns and poor performance associated with an untuned engine.

Neither tune-up nor troubleshooting can be considered independently since each has a direct relationship with the other.

It is advisable to follow a definite and thorough tune-up procedure. Tune-up consists of three separate steps: Analysis, the process of determining whether normal wear is responsible for performance loss, and whether parts require replacement or service; parts replacement or service; and adjustment, where engine adjustments are performed.

The manufacturer's recommended interval for tune-ups is every 22,500 miles or 18 months, except for heavy duty emission models, which use the 12 mo/12,000 miles schedule in all years. These intervals should be shortened if the truck is subjected to severe operating conditions such as trailer pulling, or if starting and running problems are noticed. It is assumed that the routine maintenance described in Section 1 has been kept up, as this will have an effect on the results of the tune-up. All the applicable tune-up steps should be followed, as each adjustment complements the effects of the others. If the tune-up (emission control) sticker in the engine compartment disagrees with the information presented in the Tune-up Specifications chart in this section, the sticker figures must be followed. The sticker information reflects running changes made by the manufacturer during production. The light duty sticker is usually found on the underhood sheet metal above the grille. The heavy duty sticker is usually on top of the air cleaner.

Diesel engines do not require tune-ups per say, as there is no ignition system.

Troubleshooting is a logical sequence of procedures designed to locate a particular cause of trouble.

It is advisable to read the entire section before beginning a tune-up, although those who are more familiar with tune-up procedures may wish to go directly to the instructions.

Spark Plugs

A typical spark plug consists of a metal shell surrounding a ceramic insulator. A metal electrode extends downward through the center of the insulator and protrudes a small distance. Located at the end of the plug and attached to the side of the outer metal shell is the side electrode. The side electrode bends in at a 90° angle so that its tip is even with, and parallel to, the tip of the center electrode. The distance between these two electrodes (measured in thousandths of an inch) is called the spark plug

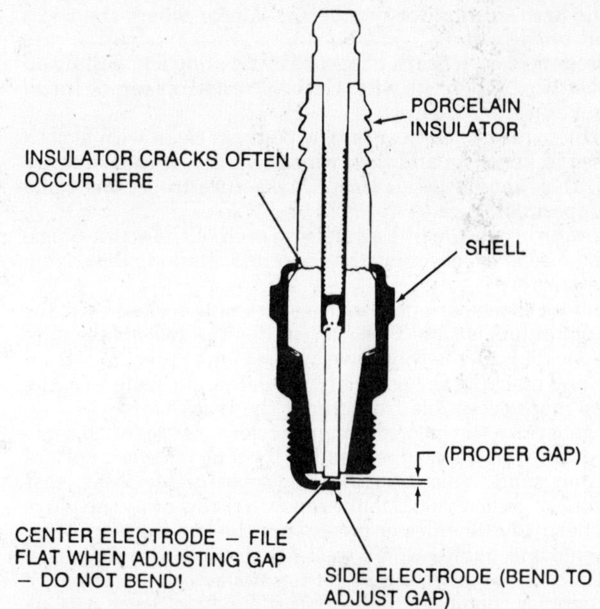

Cutaway of a spark plug

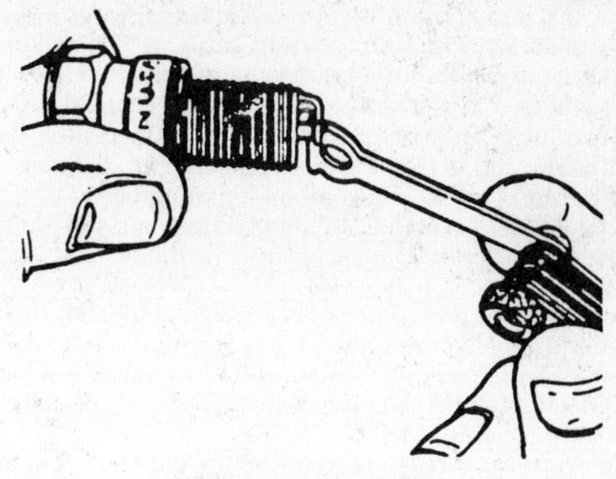

Adjusting the gap

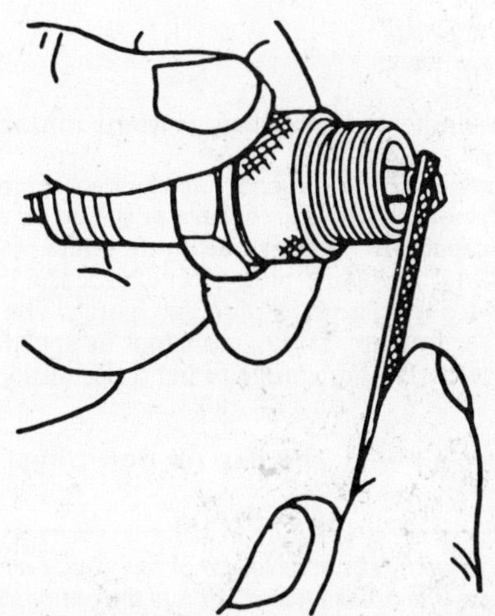

Filing the electrodes on a used plug

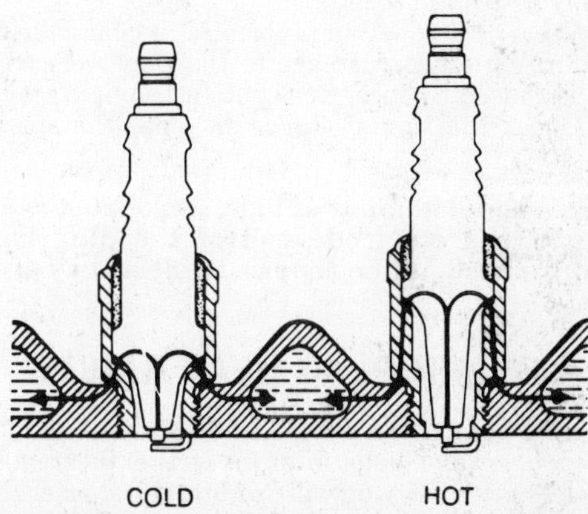

Spark plug heat range. The plug with the higher heat range is on the right. It has a longer heat flow path and thus operates at a higher tip temperature. It should be used for low speed driving and light load conditions

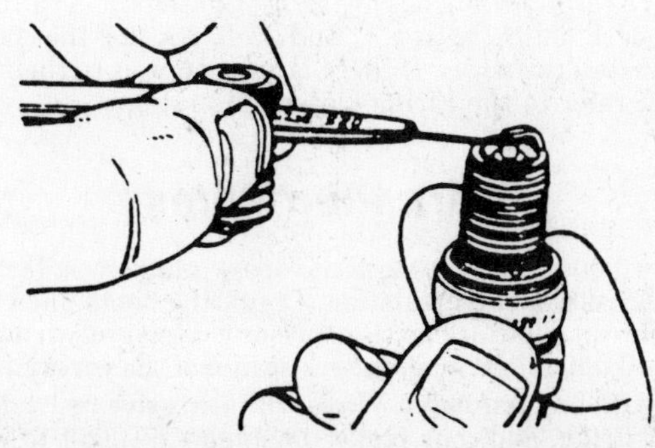

Use a wire gauge to check the plug's electrode gap

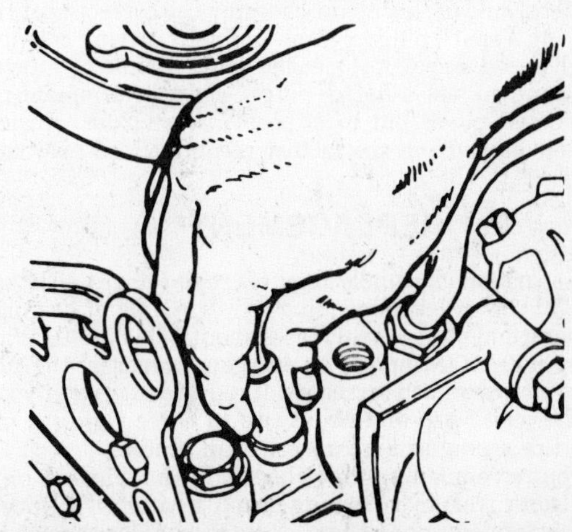

Twis and pull the boot to remove a spark plug wire

gap. The spark plug in no way produces a spark but merely provides a gap across which the current can arc. The coil produces anywhere from 20,000 to 40,000 volts which travels to the distributor where it is distributed through the spark plug wires to the spark plugs. The current passes along the center electrode and jumps the gap to the side electrode, and, in do doing, ignites the air/fuel mixture in the combustion chamber.

Rough idle, hard starting, frequent engine miss at high speeds and physical deterioration are all indications that the plugs should be replaced.

The electrode end of a spark plug is a good indicator of the internal condition of your engine. If a spark plug is fouled, causing the engine to misfire, the problem will have to be found and corrected. Often, reading the plugs will lead you to the cause of the problem.

There are several reasons why a spark plug will foul and you can learn which reason by just looking at the plug. The two most common problems are oil fouling and pre-ignition/detonation.

Oil fouling is easily noticed as dark, wet oily deposits on the plug's electrodes. Oil fouling is caused by internal engine problems, the most common of which are worn valve seals or guides and worn or damaged piston rings. These problems can be corrected only by engine repairs.

Pre-ignition or detonation problems are characterized by extensive burning and/or damage to the plug's electrodes. The problem is caused by incorrect ignition timing or faulty spark control. Check the timing and/or diagnose the spark control system.

NOTE: A small amount of light tan or rust red colored deposits at the electrode end of the plug is normal. These plugs need not be renewed unless they are severely worn.

SPARK PLUG HEAT RANGE

Spark plug heat range is the ability of the plug to dissipate heat. The longer the insulator (or the farther it extends into the engine), the hotter the plug will operate; the shorter the insulator the cooler it will operate. A plug that absorbs little heat and remains too cool will quickly accumulate deposits of oil and carbon since it is not hot enough to burn them off. This leads to plug fouling and consequently to misfiring. A plug that absorbs too much heat will have no deposits, but, due to the excessive heat, the electrodes will burn away quickly and in some instances, pre-ignition may result. Pre-ignition takes place when plug tips get so hot that they glow sufficiently to ignite the fuel/air mixture before the actual spark occurs. This early ignition will usually cause a pinging during low speeds and heavy loads.

The general rule of thumb for choosing the correct heat range when picking a spark plug is: if most of your driving is long distance, high speed travel, use a colder plug; if most of your driving is stop and go, use a hotter plug. Original equipment plugs are compromise plugs, but most people never have occasion to change their plugs from the factory recommended heat range.

REPLACEMENT

A set of spark plugs usually requires replacement after about 20,000 to 30,000 miles, depending on your style of driving. In normal operation, plug gap increases about 0.001 in. (0.025mm) for every 1,000–2,500 miles. As the gap increases, the plug's voltage requirement also increases. It requires a greater voltage to jump the wider gap and about two to three times as much voltage to fire a plug at high speeds than at idle.

When you're removing spark plugs, you should work on one at a time. Don't start by removing the plug wires all at once, because unless you number them, they may become mixed up. Take a minute before you begin and number the wires with tape. The best location for numbering is near where the wires come out of the cap.

1. Disconnect each spark plug wire by twisting and pulling on the rubber cap, not on the wire. Carbon core wires can be internally broken rather easily.
2. If the wires are dirty or oily, wipe them clean with a cloth dampened in kerosene and then wipe them dry. If the wires are cracked, they should be replaced. Make sure to get the radio noise suppression type.
3. Blow or brush the dirt away from each of the spark plugs. This can be done by loosening the plugs and cranking the engine with the starter.
4. Remove each spark plug with a spark plug socket; $5/8$ in. for plug designations with a **T** or $^{13}/_{16}$ in. for the rest. Make sure that the socket is all the way down on the plug to prevent it from slipping and cracking the porcelain insulator. On some V8s, the plugs are more accessible from under the truck.
5. In general, a tan or medium gray color (rust red with some unleaded fuels) on the business end of the plug indicates normal combustion conditions. A spark plug's useful life is at least 12,000 miles. Thus it would make sense to throw away the plugs if it has been 12,000 miles or more since the last tune-up. Most professional mechanics won't waste their time cleaning used plugs. There is too much chance of unsatisfactory performance and a customer comeback. Refer to the Tune-Up Specifications chart for the proper spark plug type.

The letter codes on the General Motors original equipment type plus are read this way:

- R – resistor
- S – extended tip
- T – tapered seat
- X – wide gap

The numbers indicate heat range. Hotter running plugs have higher numbers.

6. If the plugs are to be reused, file the center and side electrodes flat with a small, fine file. Heavy or baked on deposits can be carefully scraped off with a small knife blade or the scraper tool on a combination spark plug tool. Check the gap between the two electrodes with a spark plug gap gauge. The round wire type is the most accurate. If the gap is not as specified, use the adjusting device on the gap gauge to bend the outside electrode to correct.

NOTE: Always check the gap on new plugs.

CAUTION

Be careful not to bend the electrode too far or too often, because excessive bending may cause it to break off and fall into the combustion chamber. This would require cylinder head removal to reach the broken piece, and could result in cylinder wall, ring, or valve damage.

7. Clean the plug threads with a wire brush. If you choose to lubricate the threads, use only one drop of engine oil.
8. Screw the plugs in finger tight. Tighten them with the plug socket. If a torque wrench is available, tighten them to 15 ft. lbs. for plug designation with a T, and 25 ft. lbs. for the rest.
9. Reinstall the wires. If there is any doubt as to their proper locations, refer to the Firing Order illustrations.

Spark Plug Wires

Every 10,000 miles, inspect the spark plug wires for burns, cuts, or breaks in the insulation. Check the boots and the nipples on the distributor cap. Replace any damaged wiring.

Every 30,000 miles or so, the resistance of the wires should be checked with an ohmmeter. Wires with excessive resistance will cause misfiring, and may make the engine difficult to start in damp weather. Generally, the useful life of the cables is 45,000–60,000 miles.

Diagnosis of Spark Plugs

Problem	Possible Cause	Correction
Brown to grayish-tan deposits and slight electrode wear.	• Normal wear.	• Clean, regap, reinstall.
Dry, fluffy black carbon deposits.	• Poor ignition output.	• Check distributor to coil connections.
Wet, oily deposits with very little electrode wear.	• "Break-in" of new or recently overhauled engine. • Excessive valve stem guide clearances. • Worn intake valve seals.	• Degrease, clean and reinstall the plugs. • Refer to Section 3. • Replace the seals.
Red, brown, yellow and white colored coatings on the insulator. Engine misses intermittently under severe operating conditions.	• By-products of combustion.	• Clean, regap, and reinstall. If heavily coated, replace.
Colored coatings heavily deposited on the portion of the plug projecting into the chamber and on the side facing the intake valve.	• Leaking seals if condition is found in only one or two cylinders.	• Check the seals. Replace if necessary. Clean, regap, and reinstall the plugs.
Shiny yellow glaze coating on the insulator.	• Melted by-products of combustion.	• Avoid sudden acceleration with wide-open throttle after long periods of low speed driving. Replace the plugs.
Burned or blistered insulator tips and badly eroded electrodes.	• Overheating.	• Check the cooling system. • Check for sticking heat riser valves. Refer to Section 1. • Lean air-fuel mixture. • Check the heat range of the plugs. May be too hot. • Check ignition timing. May be over-advanced. • Check the torque value of the plugs to ensure good plug-engine seat contact.
Broken or cracked insulator tips.	• Heat shock from sudden rise in tip temperature under severe operating conditions. Improper gapping of plugs.	• Replace the plugs. Gap correctly.

To check resistance, remove the distributor cap, leaving the wires in place. Connect one lead of an ohmmeter to an electrode within the cap. Connect the other lead to the corresponding spark plug terminal (remove it from the spark plug for this test). Replace any wire which shows a resistance over 30,000Ω. Generally speaking, however, resistance should not be over 25,000Ω, and 30,000Ω must be considered the outer limit of acceptability.

It should be remembered that resistance is also a function of length. The longer the wire, the greater the resistance. Thus, if the wires on your truck are longer than the factory originals, the resistance will be higher, possibly outside these limits.

When installing new wires, replace them one at a time to avoid mixups. Start by replacing the longest one first. Install the boot firmly over the spark plug. Route the wire over the same path as the original. Insert the nipple firmly onto the tower on the distributor cap, then install the cap cover and latches to secure the wires.

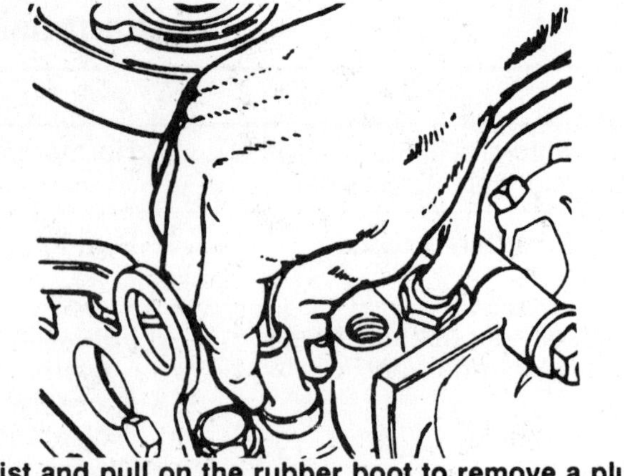

Twist and pull on the rubber boot to remove a plug wire; never pull on the wire itself!

FIRING ORDERS

Before removing any sparl plug wire, label it for installation purposes!

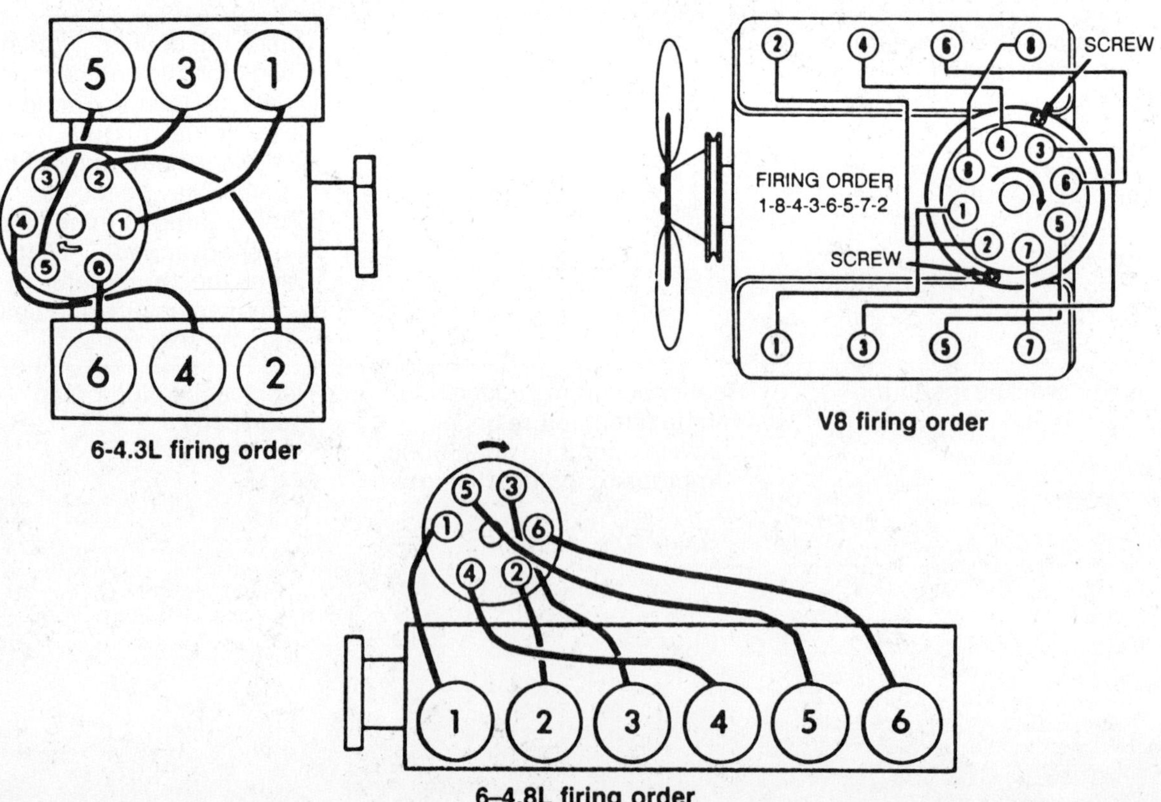

6-4.3L firing order

V8 firing order

6–4.8L firing order

ELECTRONIC IGNITION SYSTEM

All engines use the breakerless HEI (High Energy Ignition) system. Since there is no mechanical contact, there is no wear or need for periodic service. There is an item in the distributor that resembles a condenser. It is a radio interference suppression capacitor which requires no service.

Description

The General Motors HEI system is a pulse-triggered, transistorized controlled, inductive discharge ignition system. The entire HEI system is contained within the distributor cap.

The distributor, in addition to housing the mechanical and vacuum advance mechanisms, contains the ignition coil, the electronic control module, and the magnetic triggering device. The magnetic pickup assembly contains a permanent magnet, a pole piece with internal teeth, and a pickup coil (not to be confused with the ignition coil).

In the HEI system, as in other electronic ignition systems, the breaker points have been replaced with an electronic switch—a transistor—which is located within the control module. This switching transistor performs the same function the points did in a conventional ignition system. It simply turns coil primary current on and off at the correct time. Essentially then, electronic and conventional ignition systems operate on the same principle.

The module which houses the switching transistor is controlled (turned on and off) by a magnetically generated impulse induced in the pickup coil. When the teeth of the rotating timer align with the teeth of the pole piece, the induced voltage in the pickup coil signals the electronic module to open the coil primary circuit. The primary current then decreases, and a high voltage is induced in the ignition coil secondary windings which is then directed through the rotor and high voltage leads (spark plug wires) to fire the spark plugs.

In essence then, the pickup coil module system simply replaces the conventional breaker points and condenser. The condenser found within the distributor is for radio suppression purposes only and had nothing to do with the ignition process. The module automatically controls the dwell period, increasing it with increasing engine speed. Since dwell is automatically controlled, it cannot be adjusted. The module itself is non-adjustable and non-repairable and must be replaced if found defective.

HEI SYSTEM PRECAUTIONS

Before going on to troubleshooting, it might be a good idea to take note of the following precautions:

Timing Light Use

Inductive pickup timing lights are the best kind to use if your truck is equipped with HEI. Timing lights which connect between the spark plug and the spark plug wire occasionally (not always) give false readings.

Spark Plug Wires

The plug wires used with HEI systems are of a different construction than conventional wires. When replacing them, make sure you get the correct wires, since conventional wires won't carry the voltage. Also, handle them carefully to avoid cracking or splitting them and never pierce them.

Tachometer Use

Not all tachometers will operate or indicate correctly when used on a HEI system. While some tachometers may give a reading, this does not necessarily mean the reading is correct. In addition, some tachometers hook up differently from others. If you can't figure out whether or not your tachometer will work on your truck, check with the tachometer manufacturer. Dwell readings, of course, have no significance at all.

HEI Systems Testers

Instruments designed specifically for testing HEI systems are available from several tool manufacturers. Some of these will even test the module itself. However, the tests given in the following section will require only a ohmmeter and a voltmeter.

TROUBLESHOOTING THE HEI SYSTEM

The symptoms of a defective component within the HEI system are exactly the same as those you would encounter in a conventional system.

Some of these symptoms are:

- Hard or no Starting
- Rough Idle
- Fuel Poor Economy
- Engine misses under load or while accelerating

If you suspect a problem in the ignition system, there are certain preliminary checks which you should carry out before you begin to check the electronic portions of the system. First, it is extremely important to make sure the vehicle battery is in a good state of charge. A defective or poorly charged battery will cause the various components of the ignition system to read incorrectly when they are being tested. Second, make sure all wiring connections are clean and tight, not only at the battery, but also at the distributor cap, ignition coil, and at the electronic control module.

Since the only change between electronic and conventional ignition systems is in the distributor component area, it is imperative to check the secondary ignition circuit first. If the secondary circuit checks out properly, then the engine condition is probably not the fault of the ignition system. To check the secondary ignition system, perform a simple spark test. Remove one of the plug wires and insert some sort of extension in the plug socket. An old spark plug with the ground electrode removed makes a good extension. Hold the wire and extension about ¼" away from the block and crank the engine. If a normal spark occurs, then the problem is most likely not in the ignition system. Check for fuel system problems, or fouled spark plugs.

If, however, there is no spark or a weak spark, then further ignition system testing will have to be done. Troubleshooting techniques fall into two categories, depending on the nature of the problem. The categories are (1) Engine cranks, but won't start or (2) Engine runs, but runs rough or cuts out.

Engine Fails to Start

If the engine won't start, perform a spark test as described earlier. If no spark occurs, check for the presence of normal battery voltage at the battery (BAT) terminal in the distributor cap. The ignition switch must be in the **on** position for this test. Either a voltmeter or a test light may be used for this test. Connect the test light wire to ground and the probe end to the BAT terminal at the distributor. If the light comes on, you have voltage to the distributor. If the light fails to come on, this indicates an open circuit in the ignition primary wiring leading to the distributor. In this case, you will have to check wiring continuity back to the ignition switch using a test light. If there is battery voltage at the BAT terminal, but no spark at the plugs, then the problem lies within the distributor assembly. Go on to the distributor components test section.

Engine Runs, but Runs Roughly or Cuts Out

1. Make sure the plug wires are in good shape first. There

should be no obvious cracks or breaks. You can check the plug wires with an ohmmeter, but do not pierce the wires with a probe. Check the chart for the correct plug wire resistance.

2. If the plug wires are OK, remove the cap assembly, and check for moisture, cracks, chips, or carbon tracks, or any other high voltage leaks or failures. Replace the cap if you find any defects. Make sure the timer wheel rotates when the engine is cranked. If everything is all right so far, go on to the distributor components test section.

Distributor Components Testing

If the trouble has been narrowed down to the units within the distributor, the following tests can help pinpoint the defective component. An ohmmeter with both high and low ranges should be used. These tests are made with the cap assembly removed and the battery wire disconnected.

1. Connect an ohmmeter between the TACH and BAT terminals in the distributor cap. The primary coil resistance should be less than one ohm (zero or nearly zero).
2. To check the coil secondary resistance, connect an ohmmeter between the rotor button and the BAT terminal. Then connect the ohmmeter between the ground terminal and the rotor button. The resistance in both cases should be between 6,000 and 30,000 ohms.
3. Replace the coil only if the readings in step one and two are infinite.

NOTE: These resistance checks will not disclose shorted coil windings. This condition can be detected only with scope analysis or a suitably designed coil tester. If these instruments are unavailable, replace the coil with a known good coil as a final coil test.

4. To test the pickup coil, first disconnect the white and green module leads. Set the ohmmeter on the high scale and connect it between a ground and either the white or green lead. Any resistance measurement less than infinity requires replacement of the pickup coil.
5. pickup coil continuity is tested by connecting the ohmmeter (on low range) between the white and green leads. Normal resistance is between 500 and 1500 ohms. Move the vacuum advance arm while performing this test. This will detect any break in coil continuity. Such a condition can cause intermittent misfiring. Replace the pickup coil if the reading is outside the specified limits.
6. If no defects have been found at this time, and you still have a problem, then the module will have to be checked. If you do not have access to a module tester, the only possible alternative is a substitution test. If the module fails the substitution test, replace it.

COMPONENT REPLACEMENT

Ignition Coil

1. Disconnect the feel and module wire terminal connectors from the distributor cap.
2. Remove the ignition set retainer.
3. Remove the 4 coil cover-to-distributor cap screws and coil cover.
4. Remove the 4 coil-to-distributor cap screws.
5. Using a blunt drift, press the coil wire spade terminals up out of distributor cap.
6. Lift the coil up out of the distributor cap.
7. Remove and clean the coil spring, rubber seal washer and coil cavity of the distributor cap.
8. Coat the rubber seal with a dielectric lubricant furnished in the replacement ignition coil package.
9. Reverse the above procedures to install.

Distributor Cap

1. Remove the feel and module wire terminal connectors from the distributor cap.
2. Remove the retainer and spark plug wires from the cap.
3. Depress and release the 4 distributor cap-to-housing retainers and lift off the cap assembly.
4. Remove the 4 coil cover screws and cover.
5. Using a finger or a blunt drift, push the spade terminals up out of the distributor cap.
6. Remove all 4 coil screws and lift the coil, coil spring and rubber seal washer out of the cap coil cavity.
7. Using a new distributor cap, reverse the above procedures to assemble, being sure to clean and lubricate the rubber seal washer with dielectric lubricant.

Rotor

1. Disconnect the feel and module wire connectors from the distributor.

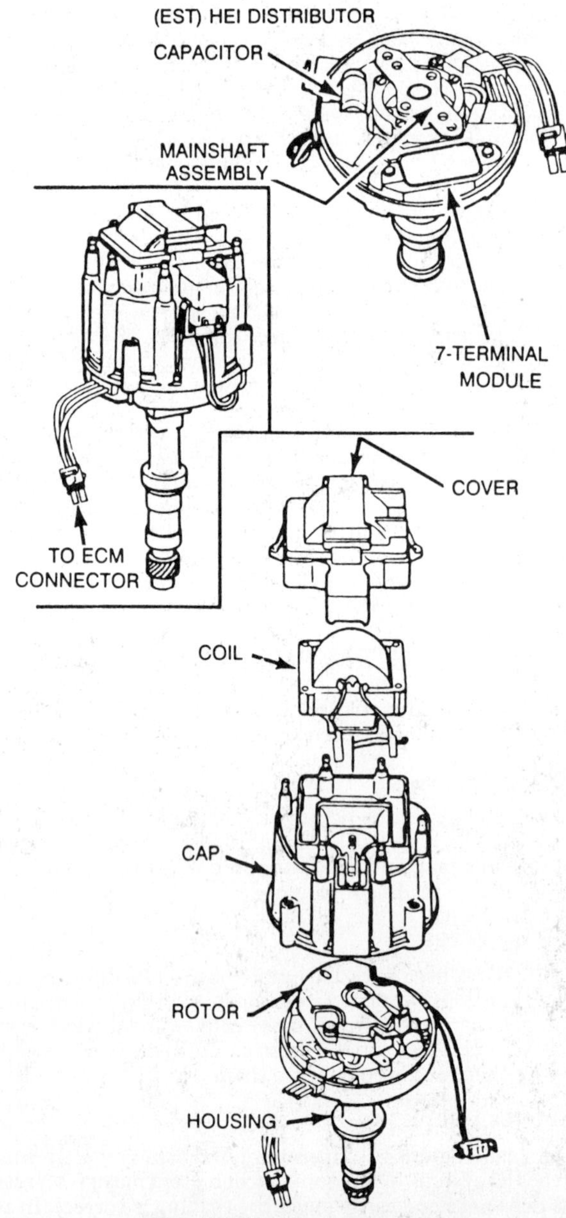

HEI distributor components

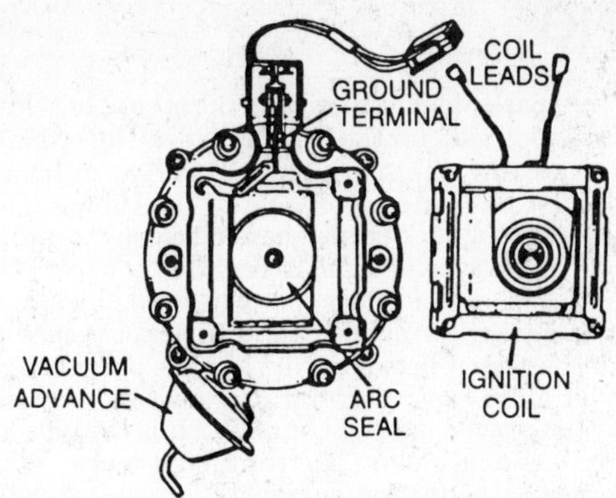

Check the condition of the arc seal under the coil

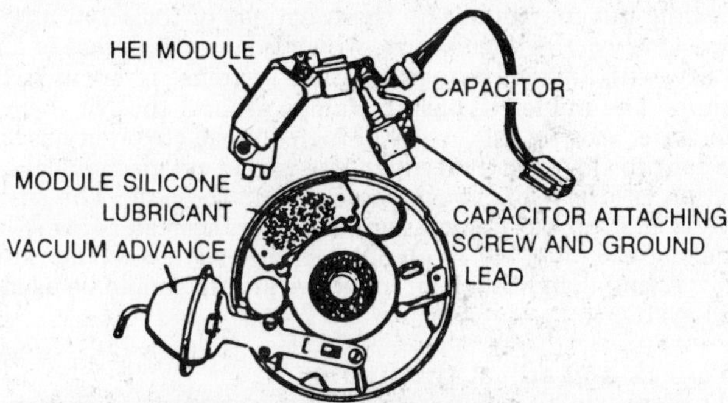

Module replacement. Be sure to coat the mating surfaces with silicone lubricant

A. Ground
B. Diagnostic terminal
C. A.I.R. (if used)
D. Serial data (see special tools)
E. T.C.C. (if used)

Terminal identification of the ALCL connector

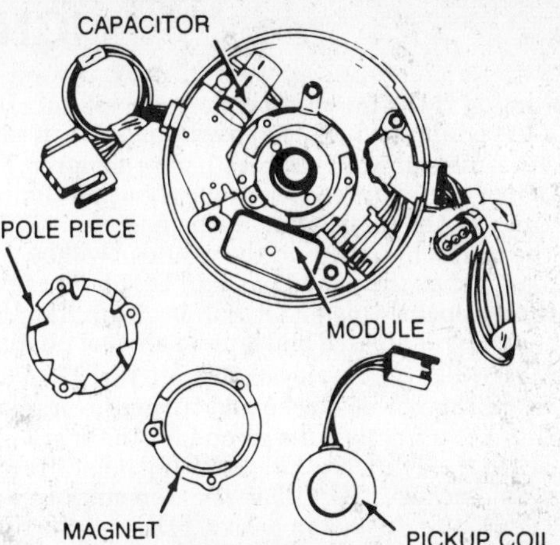

Pickup coil removed and disassembled

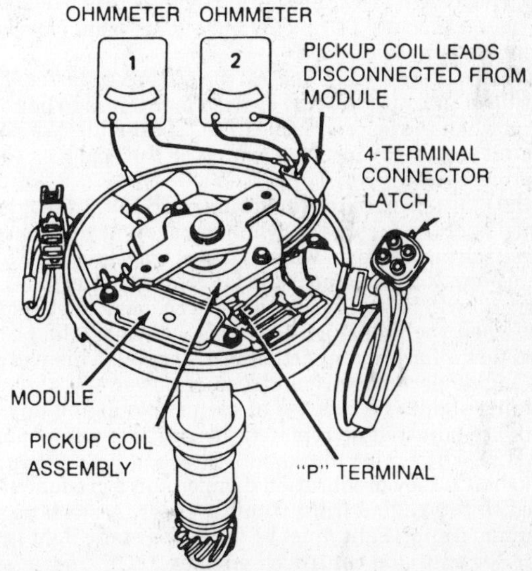

Ohmmeter 1 shows the connections for testing the pickup coil. Ohmmeter 2 shows the connections for testing the pickup coil continuity

2. Depress and release the 4 distributor cap to housing retainers and lift off the cap assembly.
3. Remove the two rotor attaching screws and rotor.
4. Reverse the above procedure to install.

Vacuum Advance

1. Remove the distributor cap and rotor as previously described.
2. Disconnect the vacuum hose from the vacuum advance unit.
3. Remove the two vacuum advance retaining screws, pull the advance unit outward, rotate and disengage the operating rod from its tang.
4. Reverse the above procedure to install.

Module

1. Remove the distributor cap and rotor as previously described.
2. Disconnect the harness connector and pickup coil spade connectors from the module. Be careful not to damage the wires when removing the connector.
3. Remove the two screws and module from the distributor housing.
4. Coat the bottom of the new module with dielectric lubricant supplies with the new module. Reverse the above procedure to install.

IGNITION TIMING

Ignition timing is the measurement, in degrees of crankshaft rotation, of the point at which the spark plugs fire in each of the cylinders. It is measured in degrees before or after Top Dead Center (TDC) of the compression stroke. Ignition timing is controlled by turning the distributor in the engine.

Ideally, the air/fuel mixture in the cylinder will be ignited by the spark plug just as the piston passes TDC of the compression stroke. If this happens, this piston will be beginning the power stroke just as the compressed and ignited air/fuel mixture starts to expand. The expansion of the air/fuel mixture then forces the piston down on the power stroke and turns the crankshaft.

Because it takes a fraction of a second for the spark plug to ignite the gases in the cylinder, the spark plug must fire a little before the piston reaches TDC. Otherwise, the mixture will not be completely ignited as the piston passes TDC and the full benefit of the explosion will not be used by the engine. The timing measurement is given in degrees of crankshaft rotation before the piston reaches TDC (BTDC). If the setting for the ignition timing is 5 degrees BTDC, the spark plug must fire 5 degrees before that piston reaches TDC. This only holds true, however, when the engine is at idle speed.

As the engine speed increases, the pistons go faster. The spark plugs have to ignite the fuel even sooner if it is to be completely ignited when the piston reaches TDC. To do this, the distributor has a means to advance the timing of the spark as the engine speed increases.

If the ignition is set too far advanced (BTDC), the ignition and expansion of the fuel in the cylinder will occur too soon and tend to force the piston down while it is still traveling up. This causes engine ping. If the engine is too far retarded after TDC (ATDC), the piston will have already passed TDC and started on its way down when the fuel is ignited. This will cause the piston to be forced down for only a portion of its travel. This will result in poor engine performance and lack of power.

Timing should be checked at each tune-up and any time the points are adjusted or replaced. It isn't likely to change much with HEI. The timing marks consist of a notch on the rim of the crankshaft pulley or vibration damper and a graduated scale attached to the engine front (timing) cover. A stroboscopic flash (dynamic) timing light must be used, as a static light is too inaccurate for emission controlled engines.

There are three basic types of timing light available. The first is a simple neon bulb with two wire connections. One wire connects to the spark plug terminal and the other plugs into the end of the spark plug wire for the No. 1 cylinder, thus connecting the light in series with the spark plug. This type of light is pretty dim and must be held very closely to the timing marks to be seen. Sometimes a dark corner has to be sought out to see the flash at all. This type of light is very inexpensive. The second type operates from the vehicle battery – two alligator clips connect to the battery terminals, while an adapter enables a third clip to be connected between No. 1 spark plug and wire. This type is a bit more expensive, but it provides a nice bright flash that you can see even in bright sunlight. It is the type most often seen in professional shops. The third type replaces the battery power source with 100 volt current.

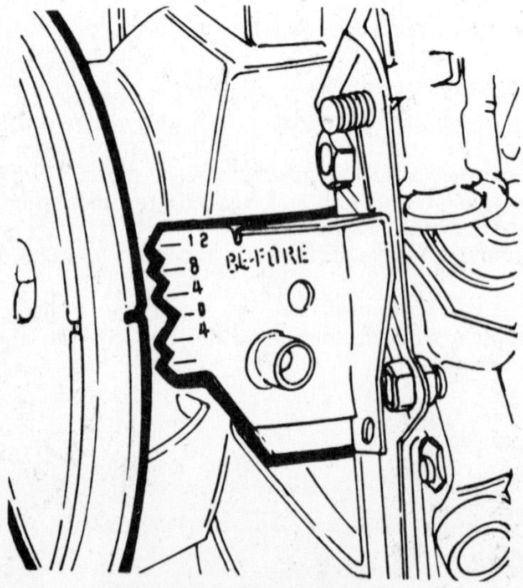

Typical timing marks

Some timing lights have other features built into them, such as dwell meters, or tachometers. These are convenient, in that they reduce the tangle of wires under the hood when you're working, but may duplicate the functions of tools you already have. One worthwhile feature, which is becoming more of a necessity with higher voltage ignition systems, is an inductive pickup. The inductive pickup clamps around the No. 1 spark plug wire, sensing the surges of high voltage electricity as they are sent to the plug. The advantage is that no mechanical connection is inserted between the wire and the plug. The advantage is that no mechanical connection is inserted between the wire and the plug, which eliminates false signals to the timing light. A timing light with an inductive pickup should be used on HEI systems.

To check and adjust the timing:

1. Warm up the engine to normal operating temperature. Stop the engine and connect the timing light to the No. 1 (left front) spark plug wire, at the plug or at the distributor cap. You can also use the No. 6 wire, if it is more convenient. Numbering is illustrated earlier in this section.

NOTE: Do not pierce the plug wire insulation with HEI; it will cause a miss. The best method is an inductive pickup timing light.

Clean off the timing marks and mark the pulley or damper notch and timing scale with white chalk.

2. Disconnect and plug the vacuum line at the distributor. This is done to prevent any distributor vacuum advance. Check the underhood emission sticker for any other hoses or wires which may need to be disconnected.
3. Start the engine and adjust the idle speed to that specified in the Tune-up Specifications chart. With automatic transmission, set the specified idle speed in Park. It will be too high, since it is normally (in most cases) adjusted in Drive. You can disconnect the idle solenoid, if any, to get the speed down. Otherwise, adjust the idle speed screw. This is done to prevent any centrifugal (mechanical) advance.

The tachometer connects to the TACH terminal on the distributor and to a ground. Some tachometers must connect to the TACH terminal and to the positive battery terminal. Some tachometers won't work with HEI.

WARNING: Never ground the HEI TACH terminal; serious system damage will result.

4. Aim the timing light at the pointer marks. Be careful not to touch the fan, because it may appear to be standing still. If the pulley or damper notch isn't aligned with the proper timing mark (see the Tune-up Specifications chart), the timing will have to be adjusted.

NOTE: TDC or Top Dead Center corresponds to 0°B, or BTDC, or Before Top Dead Center may be shown as BEFORE. A, or ATDC, or After Top Dead Center may be shown as AFTER.

5. Loosen the distributor base clamp locknut. You can buy trick wrenches which make this task a lot easier on V8s. Turn the distributor slowly to adjust the timing, holding it by the body and not the cap. Turn the distributor in the direction of rotor rotation (found in the Firing Order illustration) to retard, and against the direction of rotation to advance.

6. Tighten the locknut. Check the timing again, in case the distributor moved slightly as you tightened it.

7. Replace the distributor vacuum line. Correct the idle speed.

8. Stop the engine and disconnect the timing light.

DIESEL INJECTION TIMING

For the engine to be properly timed, the marks on the top of the engine front cover must be aligned with the marks on the injection pump flange. The engine must be OFF when the timing is reset.

NOTE: On 49-state engines, the marks are scribe lines. On California engines, the marks are half circles.

1. Loosen the three pump retaining nuts. If the marks are not aligned, adjustment is necessary.
2. Loosen the three pump retaining nuts.
3. Align the mark on the injection pump with the mark on the front cover. Tighten the nuts to 30 ft. lbs.

NOTE: Use a ¾ in. open end wrench on the nut at the front of the injection pump to aid in rotating the pump to align the marks.

4. Adjust the throttle linkage if necessary.

Diesel injection timing marks

VALVE LASH

All engines covered in this guide are equipped with hydraulic valve lifters. Engines so equipped operate with zero clearance in the valve train. Because of this the rocker arms are non-adjustable. The hydraulic lifters themselves do not require any adjustment as part of the normal tune-up, although they occasionally become noisy (especially on high mileage engines) and need to be replaced. In the event of cylinder head removal or any operation that requires disturbing or removing the rocker arms, the rocker arms have to be adjusted. Please refer to Section 3. Hydraulic lifter service is also covered in Section 3.

FUEL SYSTEM

Idle Speed and Mixture Adjustments

In most cases, the mixture screws have limiter caps, but in later years the mixture screws are concealed under staked-in plugs. Idle mixture is adjustable only during carburetor overhaul, and requires the addition of propane as an artificial mixture enrichener. For these reasons, mixture adjustments are not covered here for affected models.

See the emission control label in the engine compartment for procedures and specifications not supplied here.

NOTE: See Carburetor Identification in Section 5 for carburetor I.D. specifics.

These procedures require the use of a tachometer. Tachometer hookup was explained earlier under Ignition Timing, Step 3. In some cases, the degree of accuracy required is greater than that available on a hand-held unit; a shop tachometer would be required to follow the instructions exactly. If the idle speed screws have plastic limiter caps, it is not recommended that they be removed unless a satisfactory idle cannot be obtained with them in place. If the caps are removed, exhaust emissions may go beyond the specified legal limits. This can be checked on an exhaust gas analyzer.

NOTE: Most 4-bbl carburetors have an internal fuel passage restriction. Beyond a certain limited point, turning the idle mixture screws out has no further richening effect.

Idle speed and mixture are set with the engine at normal running temperature. The automatic transmission should be in Drive, except when specified otherwise. The air conditioner should be off for adjusting mixture and off unless otherwise specified in the text or specifications chart for setting idle speed.

CAUTION

Block the wheels, set the parking brake, and don't stand in front of the truck.

Idle Speed Adjustment

6–4.8L

CURB IDLE SPEED

With the idle speed solenoid energized, turn the solenoid body to establish the curb idle speed shown on your underhood sticker.

BASE IDLE SPEED

With the solenoid wire disconnected, turn the ⅛ in. hex head solenoid plunger adjusting screw to establish the base idle speed shown on your underhood sticker.

8–5.7L

1. All adjustments should be made with the engine at normal operating temperature, air cleaner on, choke open, and air conditioning off, unless otherwise noted. Set the parking brake and block the rear wheels. Automatic transmissions should be set in Drive, manuals in Neutral, unless otherwise noted in the procedures or on the emission control label.
2. Refer to the underhood emission sticker and prepare the vehicle for adjustment as specified on the sticker. On models without a solenoid, turn the idle speed to obtain the idle speed listed in the Tune-Up chart. On models with a solenoid, turn the idle speed screw to obtain the idle speed listed in the Tune-Up chart. Disconnect the wire at the air conditioning compressor and turn the air conditioning On. Rev the engine momentarily to fully extend the solenoid plunger. Turn the solenoid screw to obtain the solenoid idle speed listed on the underhood emission sticker. Reconnect the air conditioning wire at the compressor.

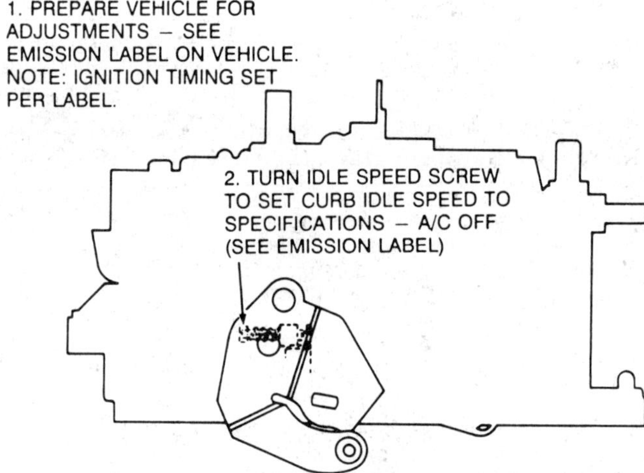

1. PREPARE VEHICLE FOR ADJUSTMENTS – SEE EMISSION LABEL ON VEHICLE. NOTE: IGNITION TIMING SET PER LABEL.
2. TURN IDLE SPEED SCREW TO SET CURB IDLE SPEED TO SPECIFICATIONS – A/C OFF (SEE EMISSION LABEL)

Idle speed adjustment points on the 4-bbl without a solenoid

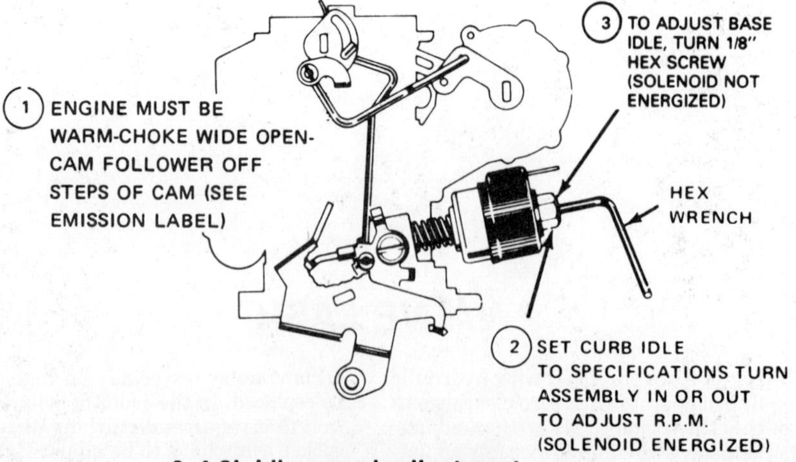

6–4.8L idle speed adjustment

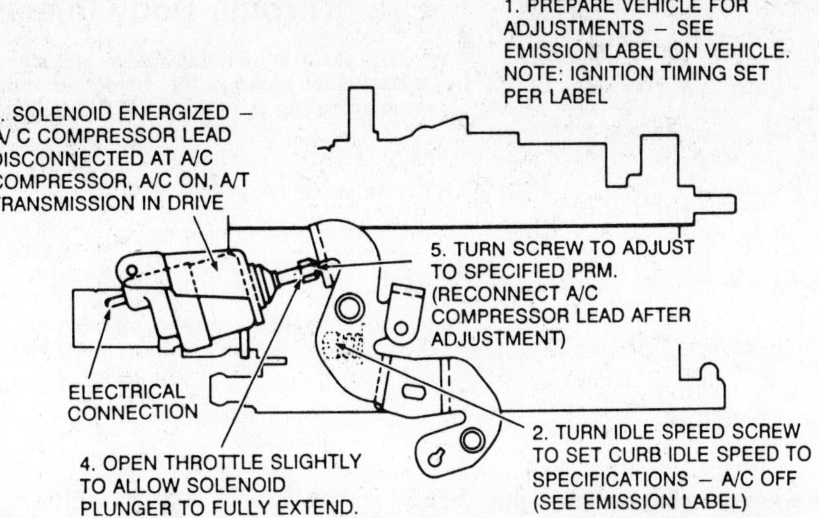
1. PREPARE VEHICLE FOR ADJUSTMENTS – SEE EMISSION LABEL ON VEHICLE. NOTE: IGNITION TIMING SET PER LABEL
3. SOLENOID ENERGIZED – A/C COMPRESSOR LEAD DISCONNECTED AT A/C COMPRESSOR, A/C ON, A/T TRANSMISSION IN DRIVE
5. TURN SCREW TO ADJUST TO SPECIFIED PRM. (RECONNECT A/C COMPRESSOR LEAD AFTER ADJUSTMENT)
ELECTRICAL CONNECTION
2. TURN IDLE SPEED SCREW TO SET CURB IDLE SPEED TO SPECIFICATIONS – A/C OFF (SEE EMISSION LABEL)
4. OPEN THROTTLE SLIGHTLY TO ALLOW SOLENOID PLUNGER TO FULLY EXTEND.

Idle speed adjustment points on the 4-bbl with a solenoid

MIXTURE ADJUSTMENTS

6–4.8L

1. Set the parking brake and block the drive wheels.
2. Remove the carburetor from the engine.
3. Drain the fuel from the the carburetor into a container. Dispose of the fuel in an approved container.
4. Remove the idle mixture needle plug as follows:
   a. Invert the carburetor and support it to avoid damaging external components.
   b. Make two parallel hacksaw cuts in the throttle body, between the locator points near one idle mixture needle plug. The distance between the cuts depends on the size of the punch to be used.
   c. Cut down to the plug, but not more than 1/8 in. (3mm) beyond the locator point.
   d. Place a flat punch at a point near the ends of the saw marks. Hold the punch at a 45° angle and drive it into the throttle body until the casting breaks away, exposing the steel plug.
   e. Use a center punch to break the plug apart, uncover idle mixture needle. Remove all loose pieces of plug.
   f. Repeat the previous steps for the other needle plug.
5. Use idle mixture needle socket J-29030-B or equivalent to lightly seat the idle mixture needle, then back it out 3 full turns.
6. Reinstall the carburetor on the engine.
7. Reinstall the air cleaner.
8. Place the transmission in Park (automatic transmission) or Neutral (manual transmission).
9. Start the engine and bring it to a normal operating temperature, choke valve open, and air conditioning off.
10. Connect a known, accurate tachometer to the engine.
11. Check ignition timing, and adjust if necessary, by following the procedure described on the Emission Control Information Label located under the hood on the vehicle.
12. Use idle mixture needle socket J-29030-B or equivalent to turn the mixture needle (1/8 turn at a time), in or out, to obtain the highest rpm (best idle).
13. Adjust the idle speed solenoid to obtain the curb idle speed specified on the underhood emission control information label.
14. Again try to readjust mixture needle to obtain the highest idle rpm. The adjustment is correct when the highest rpm (best idle) is reached with the minimum number of mixture needle turns from the seated position.

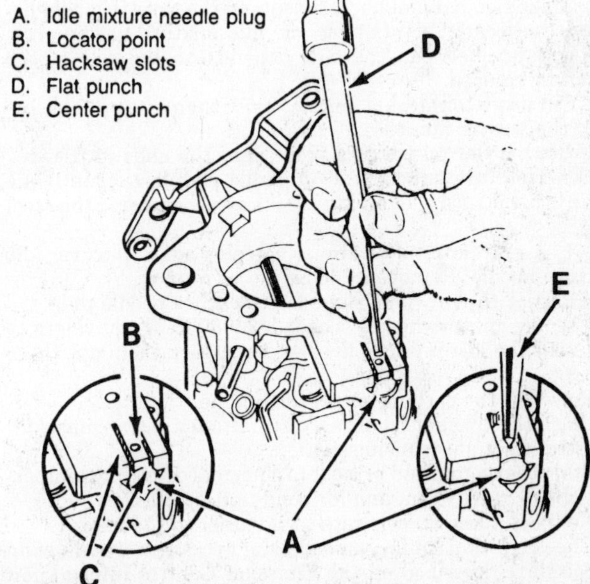
A. Idle mixture needle plug
B. Locator point
C. Hacksaw slots
D. Flat punch
E. Center punch
D
E
B
A
C

Removing the idle mixture needle plug on the 1-bbl carburetor

15. If necessary, readjust the idle stop solenoid to obtain the specified curb idle speed.
16. Check (and if necessary adjust) the base idle speed and fast idle speed. Refer to the underhood emission control information label.
17. Turn off the engine, remove all test equipment and remove the block from the drive wheels.

8–5.7L

1. Set the parking brake and block the drive wheels.
2. Remove the carburetor from the engine.
3. Drain the fuel from the the carburetor into a container. Dispose of the fuel in an approved container.

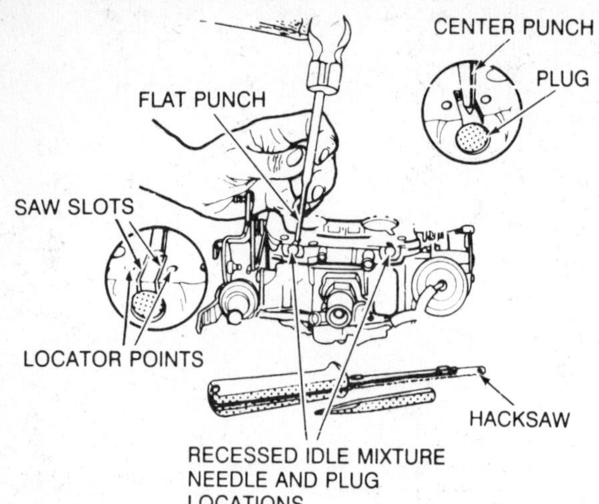

Removing the idle mixture needle plug on the 4-bbl carburetor

4. Remove the idle mixture needle plugs as follows:

a. Invert the carburetor and support it to avoid damaging external components.

b. Make two parallel hacksaw cuts in the throttle body, between the locator points near one idle mixture needle plug. The distance between the cuts depends on the size of the punch to be used.

c. Cut down to the plug, but not more than ⅛ in. (3mm) beyond the locator point.

d. Place a flat punch at a point near the ends of the saw marks. Hold the punch at a 45° angle and drive it into the throttle body until the casting breaks away, exposing the steel plug.

e. Use a center punch to break the plug apart, uncover idle mixture needle. Remove all loose pieces of plug.

f. Repeat the previous steps for the other needle plug.

5. Use idle mixture needle socket J-29030-B or equivalent to lightly seat the idle mixture needles, then back them out three turns.

6. Reinstall the carburetor on the engine.

7. Place the transmission in Park (automatic transmission) or Neutral (manual transmission).

8. Start the engine and bring it to a normal operating temperature, choke valve open, and air conditioning off.

9. Connect a known accurate tachometer to the engine.

10. Check ignition timing, and adjust if necessary, by following the procedure described on the Emission Control Information Label located under the hood on the vehicle.

11. Use idle mixture needle socket J-29030-B or equivalent to turn the mixture needles equally (⅛ turn at a time), in or out, to obtain the highest rpm (best idle).

12. Adjust the idle speed screw (throttle stop) to obtain the base idle speed specified on the underhood emission control information label.

13. Again try to readjust mixture needles to obtain the highest idle rpm. The adjustment is correct when the highest rpm (best idle) is reached with the minimum number of mixture needle turns from the seated position.

14. If necessary, readjust the idle speed screw (throttle stop) to obtain the specified base idle speed.

15. Check (and if necessary adjust) the idle speed solenoid activated speed and fast idle speed. Refer to the underhood emission control information label.

16. Check the throttle kicker and adjust if necessary.

17. Turn off the engine, remove all test equipment and remove the block from the drive wheels.

Throttle Body Injection (TBI)

The throttle body injected vehicles are controlled by a computer which supplies the correct amount of fuel during all engine operating conditions; no adjustment is necessary.

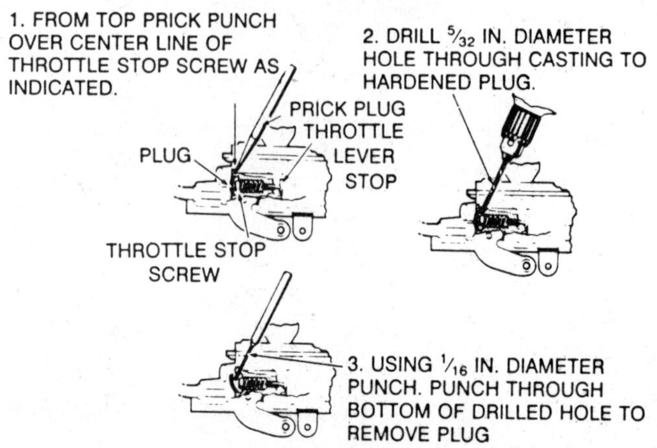

Removing the throttle stop screw from the throttle body

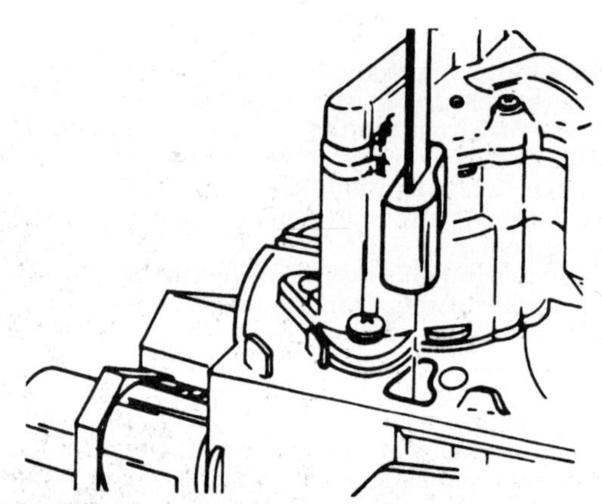

Using GM tool J-33047 to plug the idle air passage of the throttle body

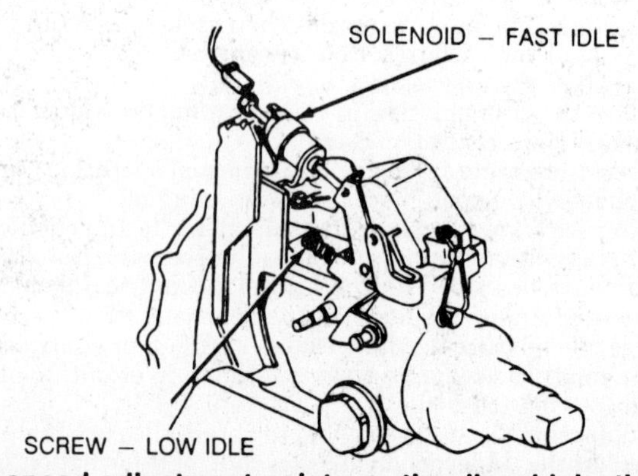

Idle speed adjustment points on the diesel injection pump

Diesel Fuel Injection

IDLE SPEED ADJUSTMENT

NOTE: A special tachometer suitable for diesel engines must be used. A gasoline engine type tach will not work with the diesel engine.

1. Set the parking brake and block the drive wheels.
2. Run the engine up to normal operating temperature. The air cleaner must be mounted and all accessories turned off.
3. Install the diesel tachometer as per the manufacturer's instructions.
4. Adjust the low idle speed screw on the fuel injection pump to 650 rpm in Neutral or Park for both manual and automatic transmissions.

NOTE: All idle speeds are to be set within 25 rpm of the specified values.

5. Adjust the fast idle speed as follows:
   a. Remove the connector from the fast idle solenoid. Use an insulated jumper wire from the battery positive terminal to the solenoid terminal to energize the solenoid.
   b. Open the throttle momentarily to ensure that the fast idle solenoid plunger is energized and fully extended.
   c. Adjust the extended plunger by turning the hex-head screw to an engine sped of 800 rpm in Neutral.
   d. Remove the jumper wire and reinstall the connector to the fast idle solenoid.
6. Disconnect and remove the tachometer.

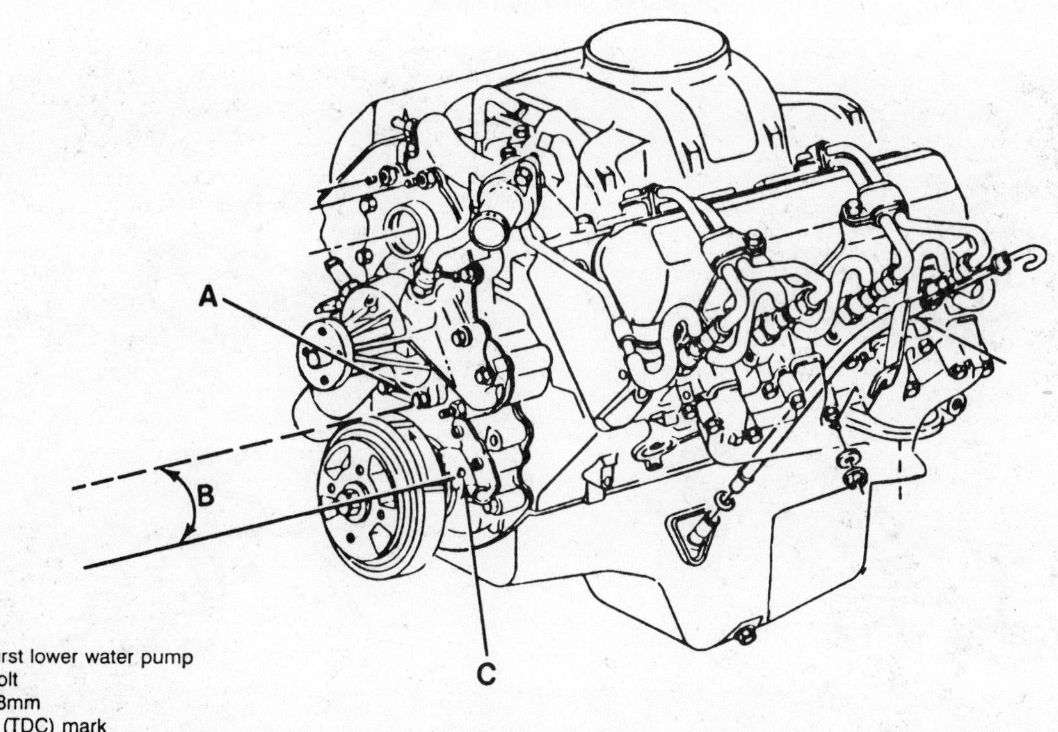

A. First lower water pump bolt
B. 88mm
C. 0 (TDC) mark

Diesel injection timing mark alignment

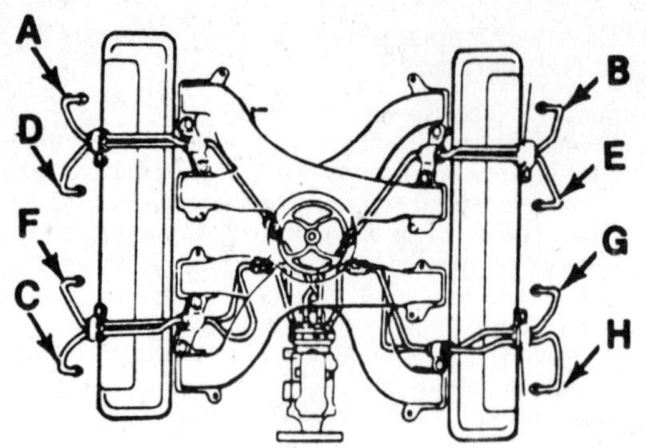

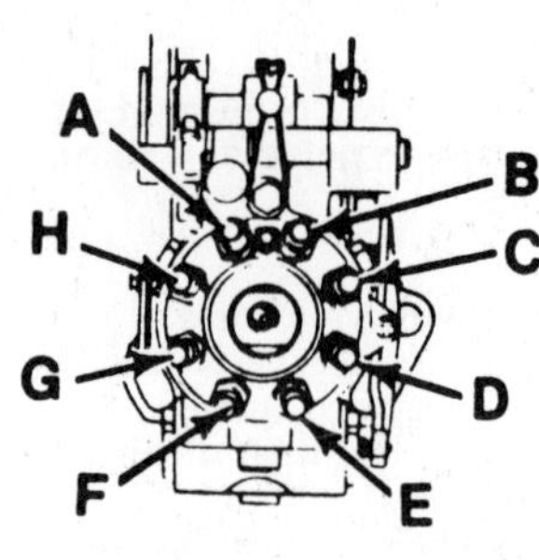

A. Cylinder number 8
B. Cylinder number 7
C. Cylinder number 2
D. Cylinder number 6
E. Cylinder number 5
F. Cylinder number 4
G. Cylinder number 3
H. Cylinder number 1

Diesel injection lines

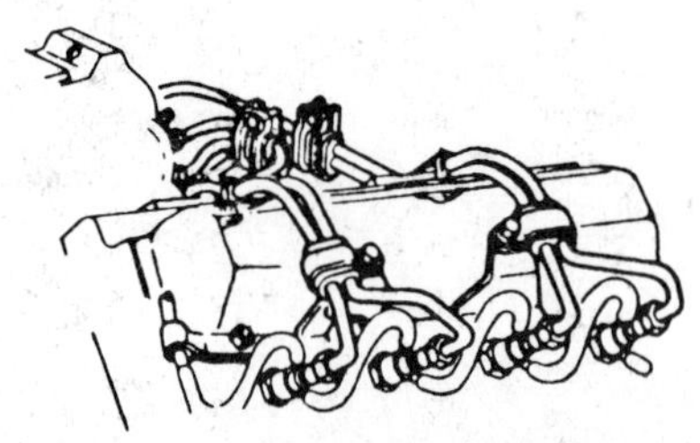

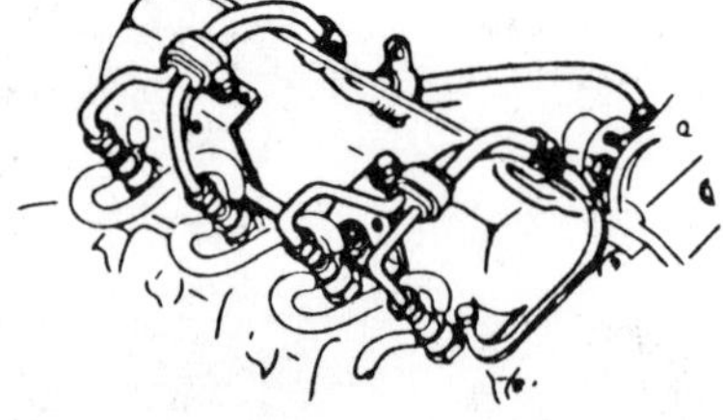

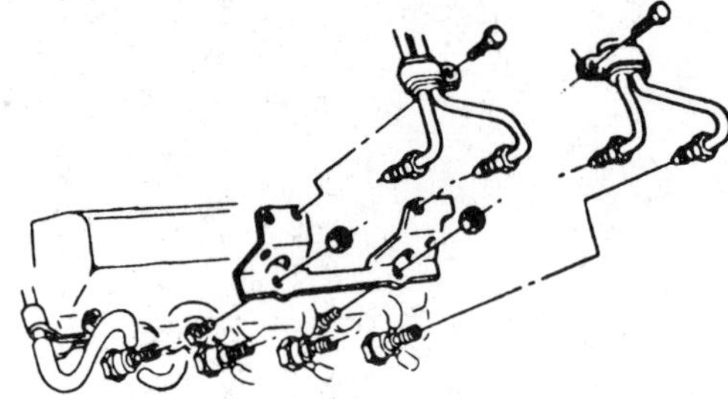

LEFT BANK

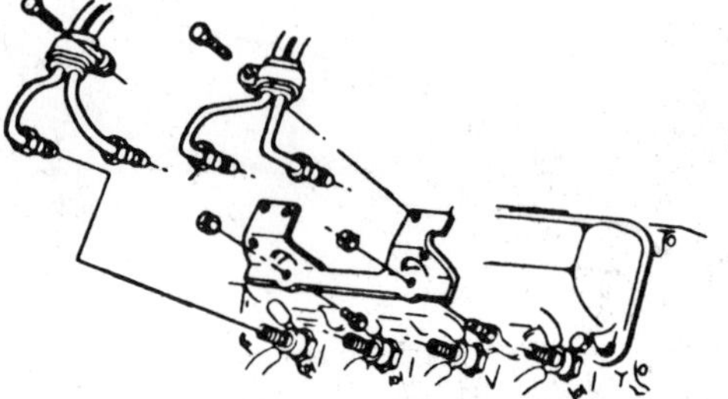

RIGHT BANK

Diesel injection line routing

3 Engine and Engine Overhaul

QUICK REFERENCE INDEX

GENERAL INDEX

ENGINE ELECTRICAL

GENERAL ENGINE SPECIFICATIONS

Years	Engine	Fuel System Type	SAE net Horsepower @ rpm	SAE net Torque ft. lb. @ rpm	Bore × Stroke	Comp. Ratio	Oil Press. (psi.) @ 2000 rpm
1988	6-4.3L	TBI	155 @ 4000	235 @ 2400	4.000 × 3.480	9.3:1	50
	8-5.0L	TBI	170 @ 4000	250 @ 2400	3.736 × 3.480	8.5:1	40
	8-5.7L	4-bbl	165 @ 3800	275 @ 1600	4.000 × 3.480	8.2:1	40
	8-5.7L	TBI	185 @ 4000	285 @ 2400	4.000 × 3.480	8.2:1	40
	8-6.2L	Diesel	140 @ 3600	240 @ 2000	3.980 × 3.800	21.5:1	45
	8-7.4L	TBI	240 @ 3800	375 @ 3200	4.250 × 4.000	8.0:1	45
1989	6-4.3L	TBI	155 @ 4000	235 @ 2400	4.000 × 3.480	9.3:1	50
	6-4.8L	1-bbl	115 @ 3400	215 @ 1600	3.876 × 4.120	8.0:1	45
	8-5.0L	TBI	170 @ 4400	250 @ 2400	3.736 × 3.480	8.5:1	40
	8-5.7L	4-bbl	165 @ 3800	275 @ 1600	4.000 × 3.480	8.2:1	40
	8-5.7L	TBI	185 @ 4000	285 @ 2400	4.000 × 3.480	8.2:1	40
	8-6.2L	Diesel	140 @ 3600	240 @ 2000	3.980 × 3.800	21.5:1	45
	8-7.4L	TBI	240 @ 3800	375 @ 3200	4.250 × 4.000	8.0:1	45
1990	6-4.3L	TBI	155 @ 4000	235 @ 2400	4.000 × 3.480	9.3:1	50
	6-4.8L	1-bbl	115 @ 3400	215 @ 1600	3.876 × 4.120	8.0:1	45
	8-5.0L	TBI	170 @ 4400	250 @ 2400	3.736 × 3.480	8.5:1	40
	8-5.7L	4-bbl	165 @ 3800	275 @ 1600	4.000 × 3.480	8.2:1	40
	8-5.7L	TBI	185 @ 4000	285 @ 2400	4.000 × 3.480	8.2:1	40
	8-6.2L	Diesel	140 @ 3600	240 @ 2000	3.980 × 3.800	21.5:1	45
	8-7.4L	TBI	240 @ 3800	375 @ 3200	4.250 × 4.000	8.0:1	45

TBI: Throttle Body Injection

VALVE SPECIFICATIONS

Engine	Years	Seat Angle (deg)	Face Angle (deg)	Spring Test Pressure (lbs. @ in.)	Spring Installed Height (in.)	Stem-to-Guide Clearance (in.)		Stem Diameter (in.)	
						Intake	Exhaust	Intake	Exhaust
6-4.3L	1988–90	46	45	200 @ 1.25	1.72	0.0010–0.0027	0.0010–0.0027	0.3414	0.3414
6-4.8L	1989–90	46	46	175 @ 1.26	1.66	0.0010–0.0027	0.0015–0.0032	0.3414	0.3414
8-5.0L	1988–90	46	45	200 @ 1.25	1.71	0.0010–0.0027	0.0010–0.0027	0.3414	0.3414
8-5.7L	1988–90	46	45	200 @ 1.25	1.71	0.0010–0.0027	0.0010–0.0027	0.3414	0.3414
8-6.2L	1988–90	46	45	230 @ 1.39	1.81	0.0010–0.0027	0.0010–0.0027	NA	NA
8-7.4L	1988–90	46	45	205 @ 1.40	1.80	0.0010–0.0027	0.0012–0.0029	0.3719	0.3719

NA: Information Not Available

CAMSHAFT SPECIFICATIONS

(All specifications in inches)

Engine	Years	Journal Diameter	Lobe Lift Int.	Lobe Lift Exh.	End Play
6-4.3L	1988–90	1.8682–1.8692	0.3570	0.3900	0.004–0.012
6-4.8L	1989–90	1.8677–1.8697	0.2315	0.2315	0.003–0.008
8-5.0L	1988–90	1.8682–1.8692	0.2336	0.2565	0.004–0.012
8-5.7L	1988–90	1.8682–1.8692	0.2565	0.2690	0.004–0.012
8-6.2L	1988–90	①	0.2808	0.2808	0.002–0.012
8-7.4L	1988–90	1.9482–1.9492	0.2343	0.2530	0

① Nos. 1, 2, 3, 4: 2.1642–2.1663
No. 5: 2.0067–2.0089

CRANKSHAFT AND CONNECTING ROD SPECIFICATIONS

(All specifications in inches)

Engine	Years	Crankshaft Main Bearing Journal Dia.	Crankshaft Main Bearing Oil Clearance	Crankshaft Shaft End Play	Thrust on No.	Connecting Rod Journal Dia.	Connecting Rod Oil Clearance	Connecting Rod Side Clearance
6-4.3L	1988–90	①	②	0.002–0.006	3	2.2487–2.2497	0.0013–0.0035	0.006–0.014
6-4.8L	1989–90	2.2979–2.2994	⑨	0.002–0.006	7	2.0990–2.1000	0.0010–0.0026	0.006–0.017
8-5.0L	1988–90	③	④	0.002–0.006	5	2.0988–2.0998	0.0013–0.0035	0.006–0.014
8-5.7L	1988–90	③	④	0.002–0.006	5	2.0988–2.0998	0.0013–0.0035	0.006–0.014
8-6.2L	1988	⑤	⑥	0.002–0.007	5	2.3980–2.3990	0.0018–0.0039	0.007–0.024
	1989–90	⑤	⑥	0.004–0.010	5	2.3981–2.3992	0.0018–0.0039	0.006–0.025
8-7.4L	1988–90	⑦	⑧	0.006–0.010	5	2.1990–2.2000	0.0009–0.0025	0.013–0.023

① No. 1: 2.4484–2.4493
Nos. 2 and 3: 2.4481–2.4990
No. 4: 2.4479–2.4488
② No. 1: 0.0008–0.0020
Nos. 2 and 3: 0.0011–0.0023
No. 3: 0.0017–0.0032
③ No. 1: 2.4484–2.4493
Nos. 2, 3, 4: 2.4481–2.4490
No. 5: 2.4479–2.4488
④ No. 1: 0.0008–0.0020
Nos. 2, 3, 4: 0.0011–0.0023
No. 5: 0.0017–0.0033
⑤ Nos. 1, 2, 3, 4: 2.9495–2,9504
No. 5: 2.9493–2.9502
⑥ Nos. 1, 2, 3, 4: 0.0018–0.0032
No. 5: 0.0022–0.0037
⑦ Nos. 1, 2, 3, 4: 2.7481–2.7490
No. 5: 2.7476–2.7486
⑧ Nos. 1, 2, 3, 4: 0.0013–0.0025
No. 5: 0.0024–0.0040
⑨ Nos. 1, 2, 3, 4, 5, 6: 0.0010–0.0025
No. 7: 0.0016–0.0035

PISTON AND RING SPECIFICATIONS

(All specifications in inches)

Engine	Years	Ring Gap #1 Compr.	Ring Gap #2 Compr.	Ring Gap Oil Control	Ring Side Clearance #1 Compr.	Ring Side Clearance #2 Compr.	Ring Side Clearance Oil Control	Piston-to-Bore Clearance
6-4.3L	1988–90	0.010–0.020	0.010–0.025	0.015–0.055	0.0012–0.0032	0.0012–0.0032	0.0020–0.0070	0.0007–0.0017
6-4.8L	1989–90	0.010–0.020	0.010–0.020	0.015–0.055	0.0020–0.0040	0.0020–0.0040	0.0050–0.0055	0.0026–0.0036
8-5.0L	1988–90	0.010–0.020	0.010–0.025	0.015–0.055	0.0012–0.0032	0.0012–0.0032	0.0020–0.0070	0.0007–0.0017

PISTON AND RING SPECIFICATIONS

(All specifications in inches)

Engine	Years	Ring Gap #1 Compr.	Ring Gap #2 Compr.	Ring Gap Oil Control	Ring Side Clearance #1 Compr.	Ring Side Clearance #2 Compr.	Ring Side Clearance Oil Control	Piston-to-Bore Clearance
8-5.7L	1988–90	0.010–0.020	0.010–0.025	0.015–0.055	0.0012–0.0032	0.0012–0.0032	0.0020–0.0070	0.0007–0.0017
8-6.2L	1988–90	0.012–0.022	0.030–0.040	0.010–0.020	0.0030–0.0070	0.0015–0.0031	0.0016–0.0038	①
8-7.4L	1988–90	0.010–0.020	0.010–0.020	0.015–0.055	0.0017–0.0032	0.0017–0.0032	0.0050–0.0065	0.0030–0.0040

① Bohn pistons
Bores 1, 2, 3, 4, 5, 6: 0.0035–0.0045
Bores 6 & 7: 0.0040–0.0050
Zollner pistons
Bores 1, 2, 3, 4, 5, 6: 0.0044–0.0054
Bores 6 & 7: 0.0049–0.0059

TORQUE SPECIFICATIONS

(All specifications in ft. lbs.)

Engine	Years	Cyl. Head	Conn. Rod	Main Bearing	Crankshaft Damper	Flywheel	Manifold Intake	Manifold Exhaust
6-4.3L	1988–90	65	45	80	70	75	35	②
6-4.8L	1989–90	⑥	44	65	50	110	⑦	⑦
8-5.0L	1988–90	65	45	③	70	75	35	④
8-5.7L	1988–90	65	45	③	70	75	35	④
8-6.2L	1988–90	⑤	48	①	200	65	30	26
8-7.4L	1988	80	48	110	85	65	30	40
	1989–90	80	48	100	85	65	30	40

① Inner: 111
Outer: 100
② Center two bolts: 26
All others: 20
③ Outer bolts on Nos. 2, 3, 4: 70
All others: 80
④ Cast iron manifold
Center two bolts: 26
All others: 20
Stainless steel manifold: 26
⑤ Tighten bolts in sequence to
Step 1: 20
Step 2: 50
Step 3: ¼ turn (90 degrees) more
⑥ Front left bolt: 85
All others: 95
⑦ Manifold-to-head: 38
Manifold-to-manifold: 44

Understanding the Engine Electrical System

The engine electrical system can be broken down into three separate and distinct systems:

1. The starting system.
2. The charging system.
3. The ignition system.

BATTERY AND STARTING SYSTEM

Basic Operating Principles

The battery is the first link in the chain of mechanisms which work together to provide cranking of the automobile engine. In most modern trucks, the battery is a lead/acid electrochemical device consisting of six 2v subsections connected in series so the unit is capable of producing approximately 12v of electrical pressure. Each subsection, or cell, consists of a series of positive and negative plates held a short distance apart in a solution of sulfuric acid and water. The two types of plates are of dissimilar metals. This causes a chemical reaction to be set up, and it is this reaction which produces current flow from the battery when its positive and negative terminals are connected to an electrical appliance such as a lamp or motor. The continued transfer of electrons would eventually convert the sulfuric acid in the electrolyte to water, and make the two plates identical in chemical composition. As electrical energy is removed from the battery, its voltage output tends to drop. Thus, measuring battery voltage and battery electrolyte composition are two ways of checking the ability of the unit to supply power. During the starting of the engine, electrical energy is removed from the battery. However, if the charging circuit is in good condition and the operating conditions are normal, the power removed from the battery will be replaced by the generator (or alternator) which will force electrons back through the battery, reversing the normal flow, and restoring the battery to its original chemical state.

The battery and starting motor are linked by very heavy electrical cables designed to minimize resistance to the flow of current. Generally, the major power supply cable that leaves the battery goes directly to the starter, while other electrical system needs are supplied by a smaller cable. During starter operation, power flows from the battery to the starter and is grounded through the truck's frame and the battery's negative ground strap.

The starting motor is a specially designed, direct current electric motor capable of producing a very great amount of power for its size. One thing that allows the motor to produce a great deal of power is its tremendous rotating speed. It drives the engine through a tiny pinion gear (attached to the starter's armature), which drives the very large flywheel ring gear at a greatly reduced speed. Another factor allowing it to produce so much power is that only intermittent operation is required of it. This, little allowance for air circulation is required, and the windings can be built into a very small space.

The starter solenoid is a magnetic device which employs the small current supplied by the starting switch circuit of the ignition switch. This magnetic action moves a plunger which mechanically engages the starter and electrically closes the heavy switch which connects it to the battery. The starting switch circuit consists of the starting switch contained within the ignition switch, a transmission neutral safety switch or clutch pedal switch, and the wiring necessary to connect these in series with the starter solenoid or relay.

A pinion, which is a small gear, is mounted to a one-way drive clutch. This clutch is splined to the starter armature shaft. When the ignition switch is moved to the **start** position, the solenoid plunger slides the pinion toward the flywheel ring gear via a collar and spring. If the teeth on the pinion and flywheel match properly, the pinion will engage the flywheel immediately. If the gear teeth butt one another, the spring will be compressed and will force the gears to mesh as soon as the starter turns far enough to allow them to do so. As the solenoid plunger reaches the end of its travel, it closes the contacts that connect the battery and starter and then the engine is cranked.

As soon as the engine starts, the flywheel ring gear begins turning fast enough to drive the pinion at an extremely high rate of speed. At this point, the one-way clutch begins allowing the pinion to spin faster than the starter shaft so that the starter will not operate at excessive speed. When the ignition switch is released from the starter position, the solenoid is de-energized, and a spring contained within the solenoid assembly pulls the gear out of mesh and interrupts the current flow to the starter.

Some starter employ a separate relay, mounted away from the starter, to switch the motor and solenoid current on and off. The relay thus replaces the solenoid electrical switch, buy does not eliminate the need for a solenoid mounted on the starter used to mechanically engage the starter drive gears. The relay is used to reduce the amount of current the starting switch must carry.

THE CHARGING SYSTEM

Basic Operating Principles

The automobile charging system provides electrical power for operation of the vehicle's ignition and starting systems and all the electrical accessories. The battery services as an electrical surge or storage tank, storing (in chemical form) the energy originally produced by the engine driven generator. The system also provides a means of regulating generator output to protect the battery from being overcharged and to avoid excessive voltage to the accessories.

The storage battery is a chemical device incorporating parallel lead plates in a tank containing a sulfuric acid/water solution. Adjacent plates are slightly dissimilar, and the chemical reaction of the two dissimilar plates produces electrical energy when the battery is connected to a load such as the starter motor. The chemical reaction is reversible, so that when the generator is producing a voltage (electrical pressure) greater than that produced by the battery, electricity is forced into the battery, and the battery is returned to its fully charged state.

The vehicle's generator is driven mechanically, through V-belts, by the engine crankshaft. It consists of two coils of fine wire, one stationary (the stator), and one movable (the rotor). The rotor may also be known as the armature, and consists of fine wire wrapped around an iron core which is mounted on a shaft. The electricity which flows through the two coils of wire (provided initially by the battery in some cases) creates an intense magnetic field around both rotor and stator, and the interaction between the two fields creates voltage, allowing the generator to power the accessories and charge the battery.

There are two types of generators: the earlier is the direct current (DC) type. The current produced by the DC generator is generated in the armature and carried off the spinning armature by stationary brushes contacting the commutator. The commutator is a series of smooth metal contact plates on the end of the armature. The commutator is a series of smooth metal contact plates on the end of the armature. The commutator plates, which are separated from one another by a very short gap, are connected to the armature circuits so that current will flow in one directions only in the wires carrying the generator output. The generator stator consists of two stationary coils of wire which draw some of the output current of the generator to form a powerful magnetic field and create the interaction of fields which generates the voltage. The generator field is wired in series with the regulator.

Newer automobiles use alternating current generators or alternators, because they are more efficient, can be rotated at higher speeds, and have fewer brush problems. In an alternator, the field rotates while all the current produced passes only through the stator winding. The brushes bear against continuous slip rings rather than a commutator. This causes the current produced to periodically reverse the direction of its flow. Diodes (electrical one-way switches) block the flow of current from traveling in the wrong direction. A series of diodes is wired together to permit the alternating flow of the stator to be converted to a pulsating, but unidirectional flow at the alternator output. The alternator's field is wired in series with the voltage regulator.

The regulator consists of several circuits. Each circuit has a core, or magnetic coil of wire, which operates a switch. Each switch is connected to ground through one or more resistors. The coil of wire responds directly to system voltage. When the voltage reaches the required level, the magnetic field created by the winding of wire closes the switch and inserts a resistance into the generator field circuit, thus reducing the output. The contacts of the switch cycle open and close many times each second to precisely control voltage.

While alternators are self-limiting as far as maximum current is concerned, DC generators employ a current regulating circuit which responds directly to the total amount of current flowing through the generator circuit rather than to the output voltage. The current regulator is similar to the voltage regulator except that all system current must flow through the energizing coil on its way to the various accessories.

HIGH ENERGY IGNITION (HEI) SYSTEM

The HEI system operates in basically the same manner as the conventional ignition system, with the exception of the type of switching device used. A toothed iron timer core is mounted on the distributor shaft which rotates inside of an electronic pole piece. The pole piece has internal teeth (corresponding to those on the timer core) which contains a permanent magnet and pick-up coil (not to be confused with the ignition coil). The pole piece senses the magnetic field of the timer core teeth and sends a signal to the ignition module which electronically controls the primary coil voltage. The ignition coil operates in basically the same manner as a conventional ignition coil (though the ignition coils DO NOT interchange).

NOTE: The HEI systems uses a capacitor within the distributor which is primarily used for radio interference purposes.

None of the electrical components used in the HEI systems are adjustable. If a component is found to be defective, it must be replaced.

Timing Light Use

Inductive pick-up timing lights are the best kind to use. Timing lights which connect between the spark plug and the spark plug wire occasionally give false readings.

Some engines incorporate a magnetic timing probe terminal (at the damper pulley) for use of special electronic timing equipment. Refer to the manufacturer's instructions when using this equipment.

Spark Plug Wires

The plug wires are of a different construction than conventional wires. When replacing them, make sure to use the correct wires, since conventional wires won't carry the higher voltage. Also, handle them carefully to avoid cracking or splitting them and never pierce them.

Tachometer Use

Not all tachometers will operate or indicate correctly. While some tachometers may give a reading, this does not necessarily mean the reading is correct. In addition, some tachometers connect differently than others. If you can't figure out whether or not your tachometer will work on your vehicle, check with the tachometer manufacturer.

System Testers

Instruments designed specifically for testing the HEI system are available from several tool manufacturers. Some of these will even test the module.

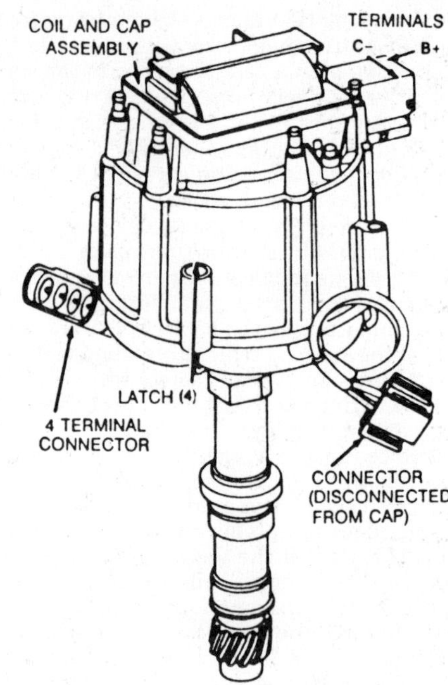

Coil-in-cap distributor used on carbureted V8 engines

Ignition Coil

TESTING, REMOVAL AND INSTALLATION

1. Detach the wiring connector from the distributor cap.
2. Turn the four latches and remove the cap and coil assembly from the lower housing.
3. Connect an ohmmeter. Test 1.
4. Reading should be zero, or nearly zero. If not replace the coil.
5. Connect the ohmmeter both ways. Test 2. Use the high scale. Replace the coil only if both readings are infinite.
6. If the coil is good, go to step 13.
7. Remove the coil cover attaching screws and lift off the cover.
8. Remove the ignition coil attaching screws and lift the coil, with the leads, from the cap.
9. Remove the ignition coil arc seal.
10. Clean with a soft cloth and inspect the cap for defects. Replace if necessary.
11. Assemble the new coil and cover to the cap.
12. On all distributors, including distributors with a Hall Effect Switch identified in step 27, remove the rotor and pick-up coil leads from the module.
13. Connect the ohmmeter Test 1 and then Test 2.
14. If a vacuum unit is used, connect a vacuum source to the vacuum unit. Replace the vacuum unit if inoperative. Observe the ohmmeter throughout the vacuum range; flex the leads by hand without vacuum to check for intermittent opens.
15. Test 1 should read infinite at all times. Test 2 should read steady at one value within 500–1,500Ω range.

NOTE: Ohmmeter may deflect if operating vacuum unit causes teeth to align. This is not a defect.

16. If the pickup coil is defective go to step 17. If the coil is okay, go to step 22.
17. Mark the distributor shaft and gear so they can be reassembled in the same position.
18. Drive out the roll pin.

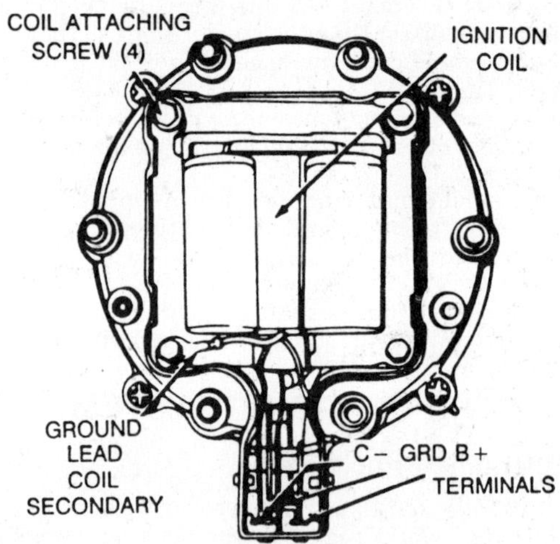

Coil attaching screws

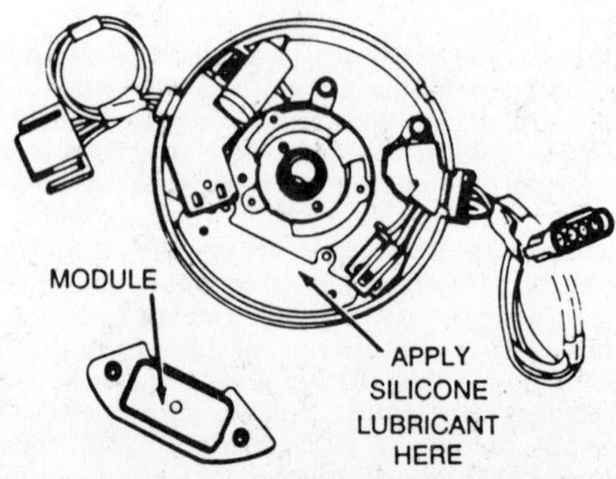

Module removal

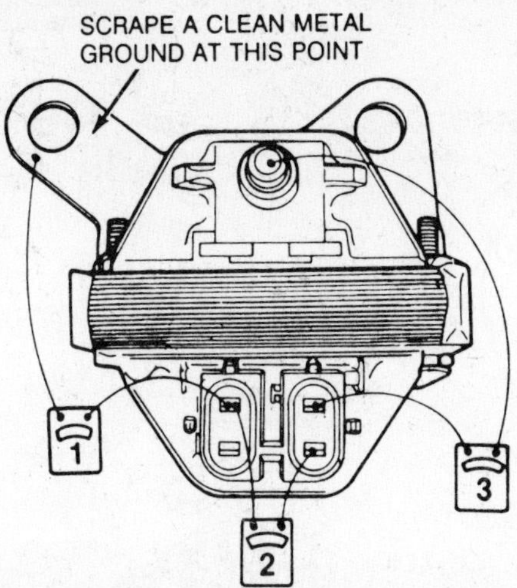

Coil test connections on engines with TBI

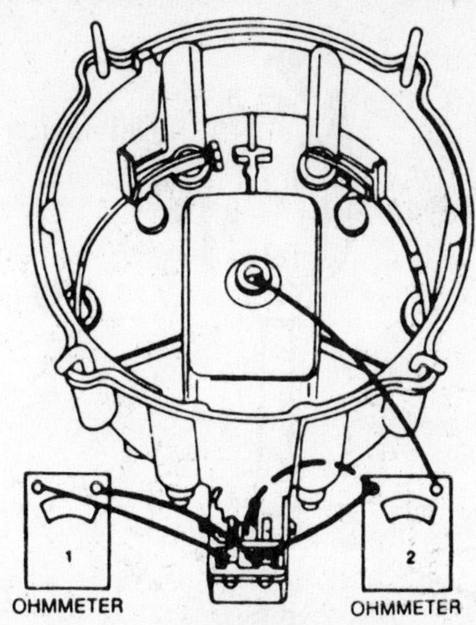

Testing the coil

19. Remove the gear and pull the shaft assembly from the distributor.
20. Remove the three attaching screws and remove the magnetic shield.
21. Remove the retaining ring and remove the pickup coil, magnet and pole piece.
22. Remove the two module attaching screws, and the capacitor attaching screw. Lift the module, capacitor and harness assembly from the base.
23. Disconnect the wiring harness from the module.
24. Check the module with an approved module tester.
25. Install the module, wiring harness, and capacitor assembly. Use silicone lubricant on the housing under the module.
26. The procedures previously covered, Steps 1–25, also apply to distributors with Hall Effect Switches.

Ignition Module

REMOVAL AND INSTALLATION

1. Remove the distributor cap and rotor.
2. Remove the two module attaching screws, and capacitor attaching screw. Lift the module, capacitor and harness assembly from the base.
3. Disconnect the wiring harness from the module.

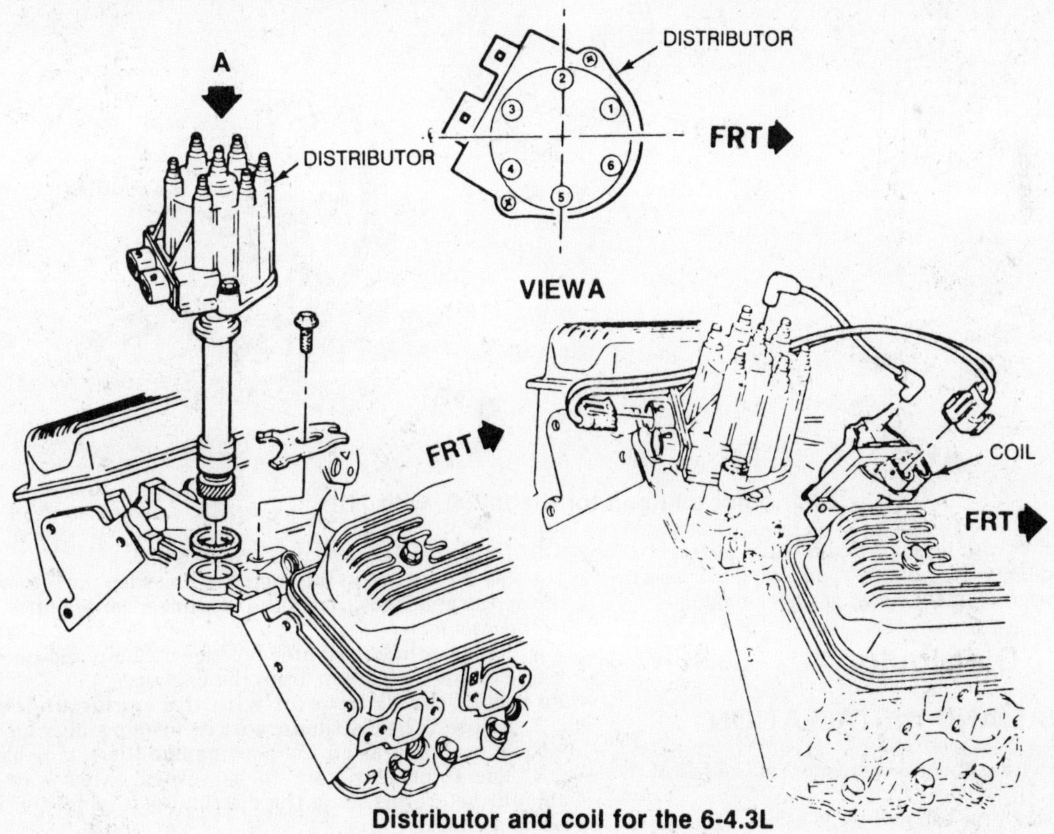

Distributor and coil for the 6-4.3L

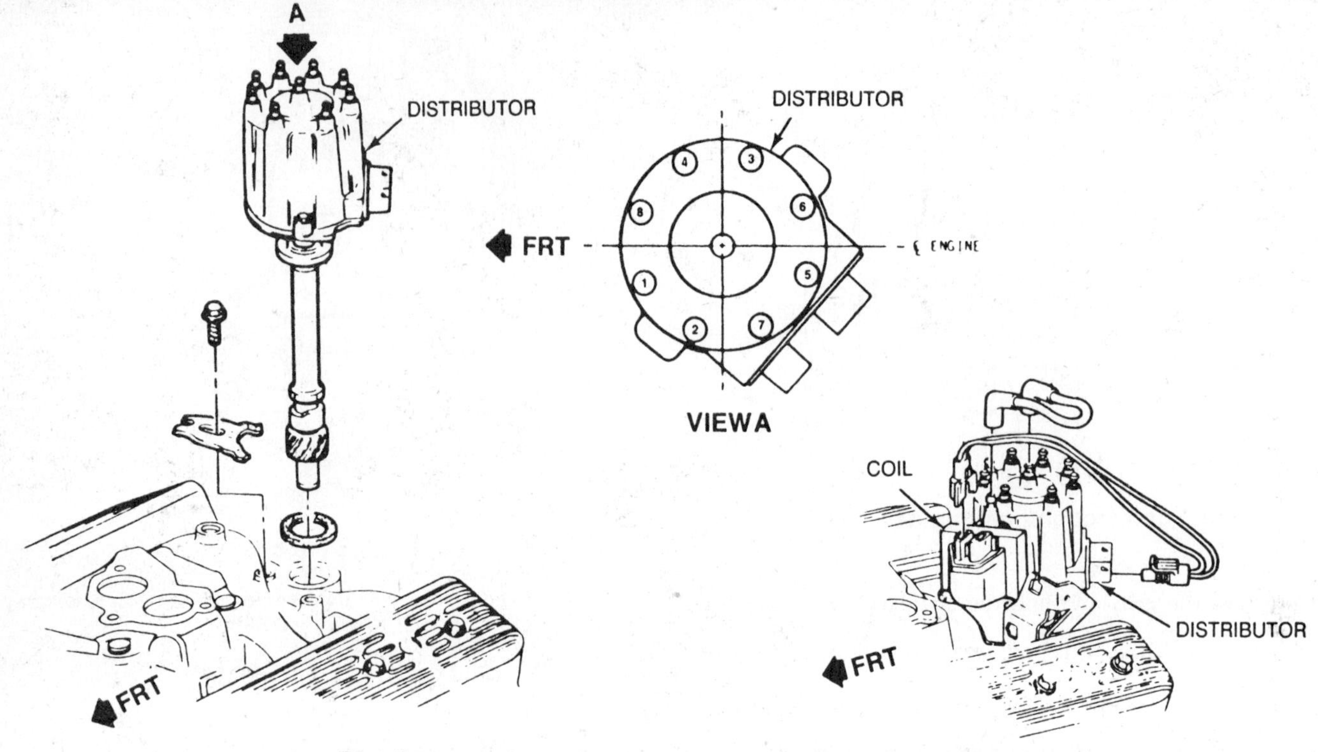

Distributor and coil for the 8-5.0L and 8-5.7L with TBI

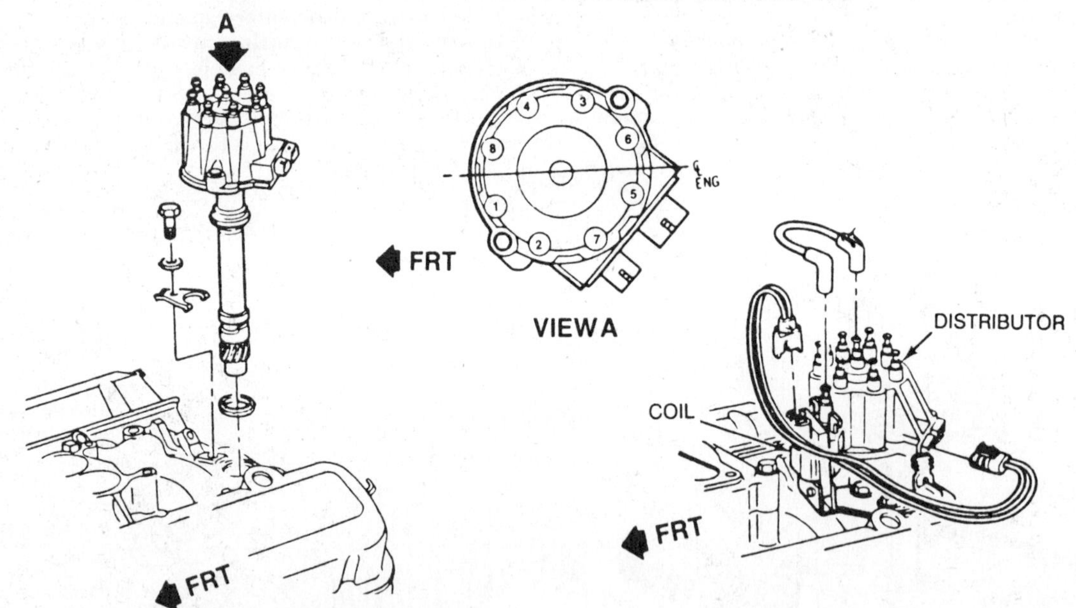

Distributor and coil for the 8-7.4L with TBI

4. Check the module with an approved module tester.
5. Install the module, wiring harness, and capacitor assembly. Use silicone lubricant on the housing under module.

Distributor

REMOVAL AND INSTALLATION

1. Disconnect the wiring harness connectors at the side of the distributor cap.
2. Remove the distributor cap and set it aside.
3. Disconnect the vacuum advance line.
4. Scribe a mark on the engine in line with the rotor and note the approximate position of the vacuum advance unit in relation to the engine.
5. Remove the distributor holddown clamp and nut.
6. Lift the distributor from the engine.

To install the distributor with the engine undisturbed:

7. Reinsert the distributor into its opening, aligning the previously made marks on the housing and the engine block.
8. The rotor may have to be turned either way a slight amount before inserting the distributor to align the rotor-to-housing marks.

9. Install the retaining clamp and bolt. Install the distributor cap, primary wire, and the vacuum hose.

10. Start the engine and check the ignition timing.

To install the distributor with the engine disturbed (the engine was turned while the distributor was out) or to install a new distributor:

11. Turn the engine to bring the No. 1 piston to the top of its compression stroke. This may be determined by covering the No. 1 spark plug hole with your thumb and slowly turning the engine over. When the timing mark on the crankshaft pulley aligns with the 0 on the timing scale and your thumb is pushed out by compression, No. 1 piston is at top dead center (TDC). If you don't feel compression, you've No. 6 at TDC.

12. Install the distributor to the engine block so that the vacuum advance unit points in the correct direction.

13. Turn the rotor so that it will point to the No. 1 terminal in the cap. Some distributors have a punch mark on the gear facing the same way as the rotor tip.

14. Install the distributor into the engine block. It may be necessary to turn the rotor a little in either direction in order to engage the gears.

15. Tap the starter switch a few times to ensure that the oil pump shaft is mated to the distributor shaft.

16. Bring the engine to No. 1 TDC again and check to see that the rotor is indeed pointing toward the No. 1 terminal of the cap.

17. After correct positioning is assured, turn the distributor housing so that the points are just opening. Tighten the retaining clamp.

18. Install the cap and primary wire. Check the ignition timing. Install the vacuum hose.

Alternator

APPLICATION

Three basic alternators are used: the 5.5 in. (140mm) Series 1D Delcotron, the 6.2 in. (158mm) Series 150 Delcotron and the integral regulator 10 SI Delcotron.

OPERATION

The alternator charging system is a negative (−) ground system which consists of an alternator, a regulator, a charge indica-

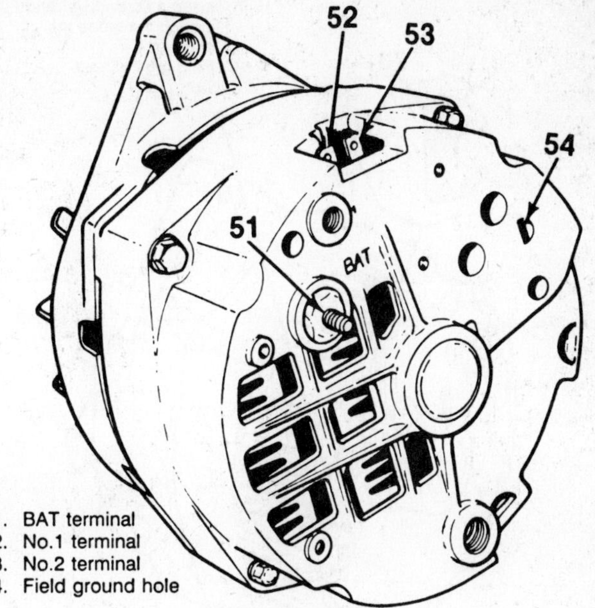

17–SI alternator

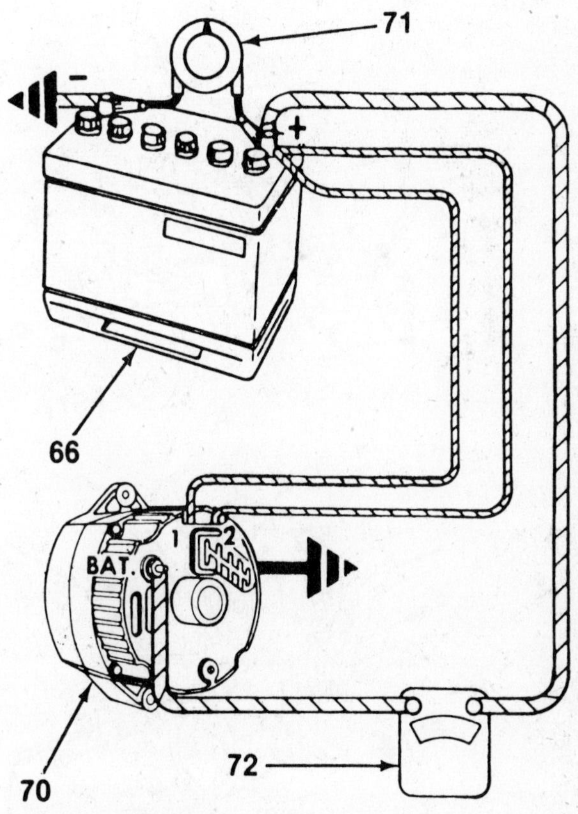

Connectors for the alternator output test

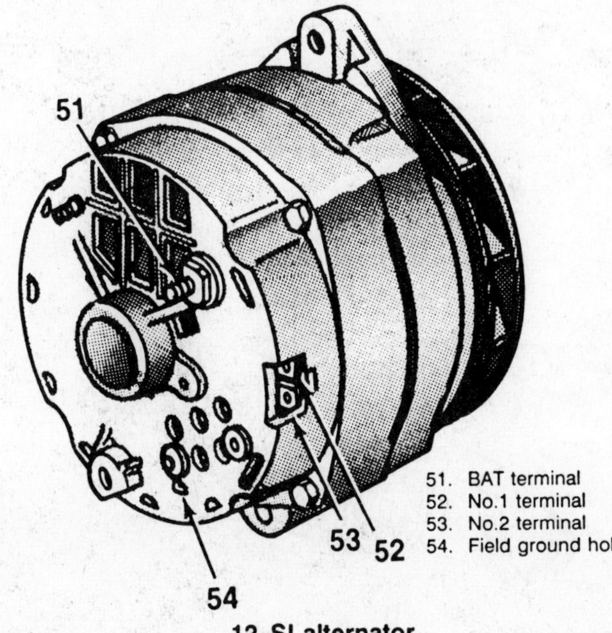

12–SI alternator

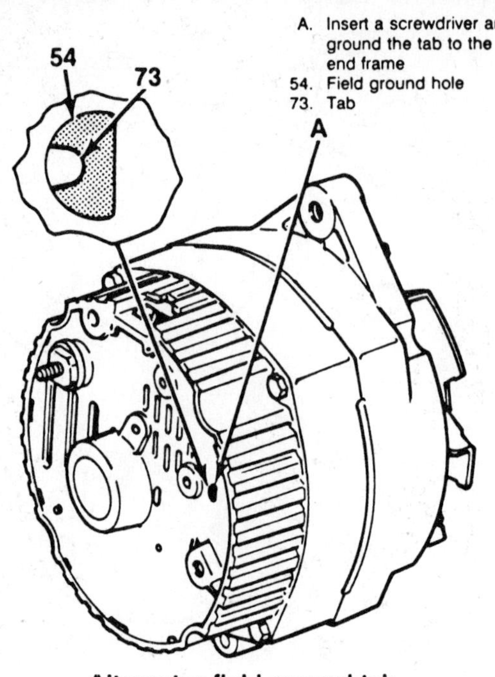

Alternator field ground tab

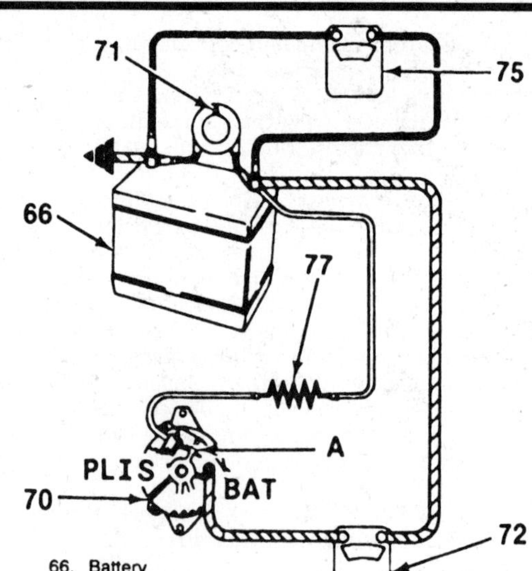

Connections for a bench test

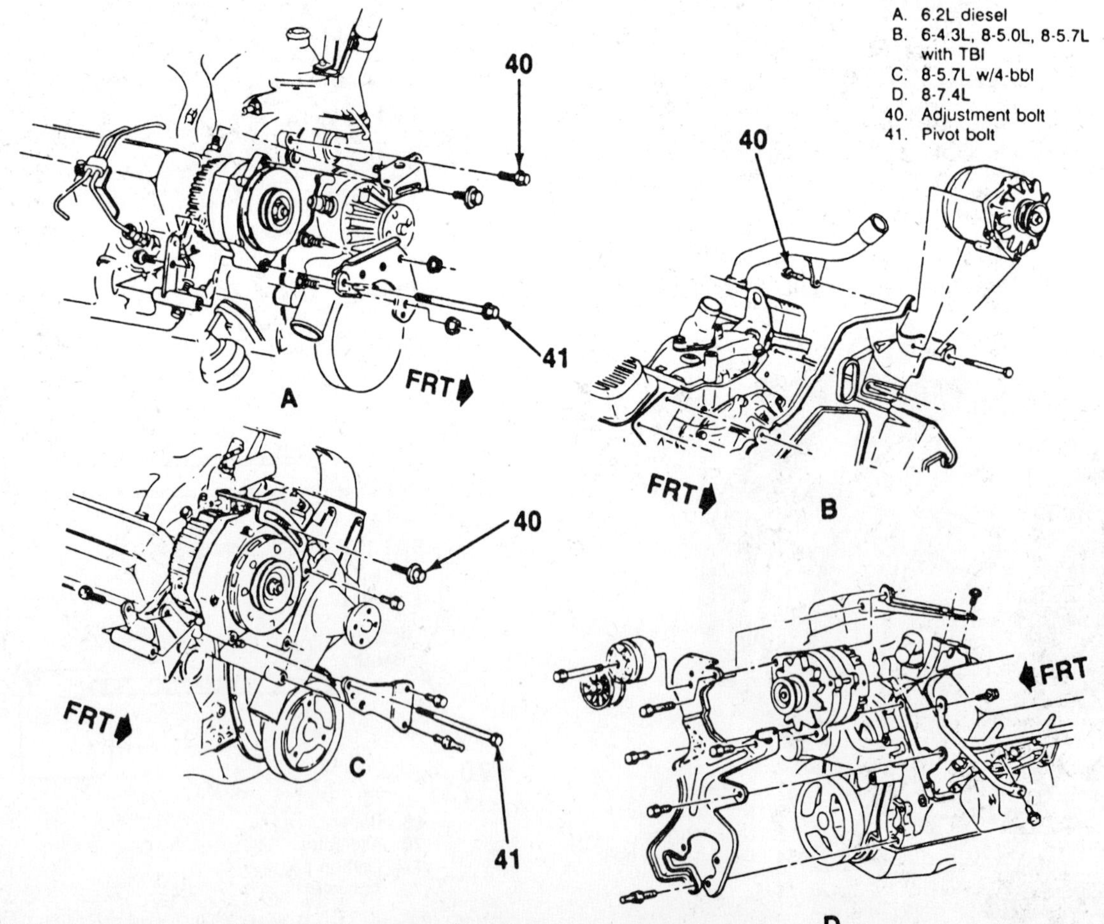

Alternator mounting positions

Troubleshooting Basic Charging System Problems

Problem	Cause	Solution
Noisy alternator	· Loose mountings · Loose drive pulley · Worn bearings · Brush noise · Internal circuits shorted (High pitched whine)	· Tighten mounting bolts · Tighten pulley · Replace alternator · Replace alternator · Replace alternator
Squeal when starting engine or accelerating	· Glazed or loose belt	· Replace or adjust belt
Indicator light remains on or ammeter indicates discharge (engine running)	· Broken fan belt · Broken or disconnected wires · Internal alternator problems · Defective voltage regulator	· Install belt · Repair or connect wiring · Replace alternator · Replace voltage regulator
Car light bulbs continually burn out—battery needs water continually	· Alternator/regulator overcharging	· Replace voltage regulator/alternator
Car lights flare on acceleration	· Battery low · Internal alternator/regulator problems	· Charge or replace battery · Replace alternator/regulator
Low voltage output (alternator light flickers continually or ammeter needle wanders)	· Loose or worn belt · Dirty or corroded connections · Internal alternator/regulator problems	· Replace or adjust belt · Clean or replace connections · Replace alternator or regulator

tor, a storage battery and wiring connecting the components, and fuse link wire.

The alternator is belt-driven from the engine. Energy is supplied from the alternator/regulator system to the rotating field through two brushes to two slip-rings. The slip-rings are mounted on the rotor shaft and are connected to the field coil. This energy supplied to the rotating field from the battery is called excitation current and is used to initially energize the field to begin the generation of electricity. Once the alternator starts to generate electricity, the excitation current comes from its own output rather than the battery.

The alternator produces power in the form of alternating current. The alternating current is rectified by 6 diodes into direct current. The direct current is used to charge the battery and power the rest of the electrical system.

When the ignition key is turned on, current flows from the battery, through the charging system indicator light on the instrument panel, to the voltage regulator, and to the alternator. Since the alternator is not producing any current, the alternator warning light comes on. When the engine is started, the alternator begins to produce current and turns the alternator light off. As the alternator turns and produces current, the current is divided in two ways: part to the battery to charge the battery and power the electrical components of the vehicle, and part is returned to the alternator to enable it to increase its output. In this situation, the alternator is receiving current from the battery and from itself. A voltage regulator is wired into the current supply to the alternator to prevent it from receiving too much current which would cause it to put out too much current. Conversely, if the voltage regulator does not allow the alternator to receive enough current, the battery will not be fully charged and will eventually go dead.

The battery is connected to the alternator at all times, whether the ignition key is turned on or not. If the battery were shorted to ground, the alternator would also be shorted. This would damage the alternator. To prevent this, a fuse link is installed in the wiring between the battery and the alternator. If the battery is shorted, the fuse link is melted, protecting the alternator.

ALTERNATOR PRECAUTIONS

Some precautions should be taken when working on this, or any other, AC charging system.

1. Never switch battery polarity.
2. When installing a battery, always connect the grounded terminal first.
3. Never disconnect the battery while the engine is running.
4. If the molded connector is disconnected from the alternator, never ground the hot wire.
5. Never run the alternator with the main output cable disconnected.
6. Never electric weld around the truck without disconnecting the alternator.
7. Never apply any voltage in excess of battery voltage while testing.
8. Never jump a battery for starting purposes with more than 12v.

CHARGING SYSTEM TROUBLESHOOTING

There are many possible ways in which the charging system can malfunction. Often the source of a problem is difficult to diagnose, requiring special equipment and a good deal of experience. This is usually not the case, however, where the charging system fails completely and causes the dash board warning light to come on or the battery to become dead. To troubleshoot a complete system failure only two pieces of equipment are needed: a test light, to determine that current is reaching a certain point; and a current indicator (ammeter), to determine the direction of the current flow and its measurement in amps.

This test works under three assumptions:

1. The battery is known to be good and fully charged.
2. The alternator belt is in good condition and adjusted to the proper tension.
3. All connections in the system are clean and tight.

NOTE: In order for the current indicator to give a valid reading, the truck must be equipped with battery cables which are of the same gauge size and quality as original equipment battery cables.

1. Turn off all electrical components on the truck.
2. Make sure the doors of the truck are closed.
3. If the truck is equipped with a clock, disconnect the clock by removing the lead wire from the rear of the clock.
4. Disconnect the positive battery cable from the battery and connect the ground wire on a test light to the disconnected positive battery cable.
5. Touch the probe end of the test light to the positive battery post. The test light should not light. If the test light does light, there is a short or open circuit on the truck.
6. Disconnect the voltage regulator wiring harness connector at the voltage regulator.
7. Turn on the ignition key.
8. Connect the wire on a test light to a good ground (engine bolt).
9. Touch the probe end of a test light to the ignition wire connector into the voltage regulator wiring connector. This wire corresponds to the **I** terminal on the regulator. If the test light goes on, the charging system warning light circuit is complete. If the test light does not come on and the warning light on the instrument panel is on, either the resistor wire, which is parallel with the warning light, or the wiring to the voltage regulator, is defective. If the test light does not come on and the warning light is not on, either the bulb is defective or the power supply wire form the battery through the ignition switch to the bulb has an open circuit. Connect the wiring harness to the regulator.
10. Examine the fuse link wire in the wiring harness from the starter relay to the alternator. If the insulation on the wire is cracked or split, the fuse link may be melted.
11. Connect a test light to the fuse link by attaching the ground wire on the test light to an engine bolt and touching the probe end of the light to the bottom of the fuse link wire where it splices into the alternator output wire. If the bulb in the test light does not light, the fuse link is melted.
12. Start the engine and place a current indicator on the positive battery cable.
13. Turn off all electrical accessories and make sure the doors are closed. If the charging system is working properly, the gauge will show a draw of less than 5 amps. If the system is not working properly, the gauge will show a draw of more than 5 amps. A charge moves the needle toward the battery, a draw moves the needle away from the battery. Turn the engine off.
14. Disconnect the wiring harness from the voltage regulator at the regulator at the regulator connector.
15. Connect a male spade terminal (solderless connector) to each end of a jumper wire.
16. Insert one end of the wire into the wiring harness connector which corresponds to the **A** terminal on the regulator.
17. Insert the other end of the wire into the wiring harness connector which corresponds to the **F** terminal on the regulator.
18. Position the connector with the jumper wire installed so that it cannot contact any metal surface under the hood.
19. Position a current indicator gauge on the positive battery cable. Have an assistant start the engine. Observe the reading on the current indicator. Have your assistant slowly raise the speed of the engine to about 2,000 rpm or until the current indicator needle stops moving, whichever comes first. Do not run the engine for more than a short period of time in this condition. If the wiring harness connector or jumper wire becomes excessively hot during this test, turn off the engine and check for a grounded wire in the regulator wiring harness. If the current indicator shows a charge of about three amps less than the output of the alternator, the alternator is working properly. If the previous tests showed a draw, the voltage regulator is defective. If the gauge does not show the proper charging rate, the alternator is defective.

PRELIMINARY CHARGING SYSTEM TESTS

1. If you suspect a defect in your charging system, first perform these general checks before going on to more specific tests.
2. Check the condition of the alternator belt and tighten it if necessary.
3. Clean the battery cable connections at the battery. Make sure the connections between the battery wires and the battery clamps are good. Reconnect the negative terminal only and proceed to the next step.
4. With the key off, insert a test light between the positive terminal on the battery and the disconnected positive battery terminal clamp. If the test light comes on, there is a short in the electrical system of the truck. The short must be repaired before proceeding. If the light does not come on, proceed to the next step.

NOTE: If the truck is equipped with an electric shock, the clock must be disconnected.

5. Check the charging system wiring for any obvious breaks or shorts.
6. Check the battery to make sure it is fully charged and in good condition.

CHARGING SYSTEM OPERATIONAL TEST

NOTE: You will need a current indicator to perform this test. If the current indicator is to give an accurate reading, the battery cables must be the same gauge and length as the original equipment.

1. With the engine running and all electrical systems turned off, place a current indicator over the positive battery cable.
2. If a charge of roughly five amps is recorded, the charging system is working. If a draw of about five amps is recorded, the system is not working. The needle moves toward the battery when a charge condition is indicated, and away from the battery when a draw condition is indicated.
3. If a draw is indicated, proceed with further testing. If an excessive charge (10–15 amps) is indicated, the regulator may be at fault.

OUTPUT TEST

1. You will need an ammeter for this test.
2. Disconnect the battery ground cable.
3. Disconnect the wire from the battery terminal on the alternator.
4. Connect the ammeter negative lead to the battery terminal wire removed in step three, and connect the ammeter positive lead to the battery terminal on the alternator.
5. Reconnect the battery ground cable and turn on all electrical accessories. If the battery is fully charged, disconnect the coil wire and bump the starter a few times to partially discharge it.
6. Start the engine and run it until you obtain a maximum current reading on the ammeter.
7. If the current is not within ten amps of the rated output of the alternator, the alternator is working properly. If the current is not within ten amps, insert a screwdriver in the test hole in the end frame of the alternator and ground the tab in the test hole against the side of the hole.
8. If the current is now within ten amps of the rated output,

remove the alternator and have the voltage regulator replaced. If it is still below ten amps of rated output, have the alternator repaired.

REMOVAL AND INSTALLATION

1. Disconnect the battery ground cable to prevent diode damage.
2. Disconnect and tag all wiring to the alternator.
3. Remove the alternator brace bolt.
4. Remove the drive belt.
5. Support the alternator and remove the mounting bolts. Remove the alternator.
6. Install the unit using the reverse procedure of removal. Adjust the belt to have ½ in. (13mm) depression under thumb pressure on its longest run.

Regulator

REMOVAL AND INSTALLATION

The regulator on these models is an integral part of the alternator. Alternator disassembly is required to replace it.

Battery

REMOVAL AND INSTALLATION

1. Disconnect the negative (ground) cable terminal and then the positive cable terminal. Special pullers are available to remove clamp type battery terminals.

NOTE: To avoid sparks, always disconnect the battery ground cable first, and connect it last.

2. Remove the holddown clamp.
3. Remove the battery, being careful not to spill the acid.

NOTE: Spilled acid can be neutralized with a backing soda/water solution. If you somehow get acid in your eyes, flush with lots of water and visit a doctor.

4. Clean the cable terminals of any corrosion, using a wire brush tool or an old jackknife inside and out.
5. Install the battery. Replace the hold down clamp.
6. Connect the positive and then the negative cable terminal. Do not hammer them in place. The terminals should be coated lightly (externally) with grease or petroleum jelly to prevent corrosion.

WARNING: Make absolutely sure that the battery is connected properly before you start the engine! Reversed polarity can destroy your alternator and regulator in a matter of seconds!

Starter

DIAGNOSIS

Starter Won't Crank The Engine

1. Dead battery.
2. Open starter circuit, such as:
   a. Broken or loose battery cables.
   b. Inoperative starter motor solenoid.
   c. Broken or loose wire from ignition switch to solenoid.
   d. Poor solenoid or starter ground.
   e. Bad ignition switch.
3. Defective starter internal circuit, such as:
   a. Dirty or burnt commutator.
   b. Stuck, worn or broken brushes.
   c. Open or shorted armature.
   d. Open or grounded fields.
4. Starter motor mechanical faults, such as:
   a. Jammed armature end bearings.
   b. Bad bearings, allowing armature to rub fields.
   c. Bent shaft.
   d. Broken starter housing.
   e. Bad starter drive mechanism.
   f. Bad starter drive or flywheel-driven gear.
5. Engine hard or impossible to crank, such as:
   a. Hydrostatic lock, water in combustion chamber.
   b. Crankshaft seizing in bearings.
   c. Piston or ring seizing.
   d. Bent or broken connecting rod.
   e. Seizing of connecting rod bearings.
   f. Flywheel jammed or broken.

Starter Spins Freely, Won't Engage

1. Sticking or broken drive mechanism.
2. Damaged ring gear.

SHIMMING THE STARTER

Starter noise during cranking and after the engine fires is often a result of too much or too little distance between the starter pinion gear and the flywheel. A high pitched whine during cranking (before the engine fires) can be caused by the pinion and flywheel being too far apart. Likewise, a whine after the engine starts (as the key is released) is often a result of the pinion-flywheel relationship being too close. In both cases flywheel damage can occur. Shims are available in 0.015 in. sizes to properly adjust the starter on its mount. You will also need a flywheel turning tool, available at most auto parts stores or from any auto tool store or salesperson.

If your truck's starter emits the above noises, follow the shimming procedure below:

1. Disconnect the negative battery cable.
2. Remove the flywheel inspection cover on the bottom of the bellhousing.
3. Using the flywheel turning tool, turn the flywheel and examine the flywheel teeth. If damage is evident, the flywheel should be replaced.
4. Insert a screwdriver into the small hole in the bottom of the starter and move the starter pinion and clutch assembly so the pinion and flywheel teeth mesh. If necessary, rotate the flywheel so that a pinion tooth is directly in the center of the two flywheel teeth and on the centerline of the two gears, as shown in the accompanying illustration.
5. Check the pinion-to-flywheel clearance by using a 0.020 in. (0.5mm)wire gauge (a spark plug wire gauge may work here, or you can make your own). Make sure you center the pinion tooth between the flywheel teeth and the gauge—NOT in the corners, as you may get a false reading. If the clearance is under this minimum, shim the starter away from the flywheel by adding shim(s) one at a time to the starter mount. Check clearance after adding each shim.
6. If the clearance is a good deal over 0.020 in. (0.5mm) – in the vicinity of 0.050 in. (1.3mm) plus, shim the starter towards the flywheel. Broken or severely mangled flywheel teeth are also a good indicator that the clearance here is too great. Shimming the starter towards the flywheel is done by adding shims to the outboard starter mounting pad only. Check the clearance after each shim is added. A shim of 0.015 in. at this location will decrease the clearance about 0.010 in.

Troubleshooting Basic Starting System Problems

Problem	Cause	Solution
Starter motor rotates engine slowly	• Battery charge low or battery defective	• Charge or replace battery
	• Defective circuit between battery and starter motor	• Clean and tighten, or replace cables
	• Low load current	• Bench-test starter motor. Inspect for worn brushes and weak brush springs.
	• High load current	• Bench-test starter motor. Check engine for friction, drag or coolant in cylinders. Check ring gear-to-pinion gear clearance.
Starter motor will not rotate engine	• Battery charge low or battery defective	• Charge or replace battery
	• Faulty solenoid	• Check solenoid ground. Repair or replace as necessary.
	• Damage drive pinion gear or ring gear	• Replace damaged gear(s)
	• Starter motor engagement weak	• Bench-test starter motor
	• Starter motor rotates slowly with high load current	• Inspect drive yoke pull-down and point gap, check for worn end bushings, check ring gear clearance
	• Engine seized	• Repair engine
Starter motor drive will not engage (solenoid known to be good)	• Defective contact point assembly	• Repair or replace contact point assembly
	• Inadequate contact point assembly ground	• Repair connection at ground screw
	• Defective hold-in coil	• Replace field winding assembly
Starter motor drive will not disengage	• Starter motor loose on flywheel housing	• Tighten mounting bolts
	• Worn drive end busing	• Replace bushing
	• Damaged ring gear teeth	• Replace ring gear or driveplate
	• Drive yoke return spring broken or missing	• Replace spring
Starter motor drive disengages prematurely	• Weak drive assembly thrust spring	• Replace drive mechanism
	• Hold-in coil defective	• Replace field winding assembly
Low load current	• Worn brushes	• Replace brushes
	• Weak brush springs	• Replace springs

REMOVAL AND INSTALLATION

The following is a general procedure for all trucks, and may vary slightly depending on model and series.

1. Disconnect the battery ground cable at the battery.
2. Raise and support the vehicle.
3. Disconnect and tag all wires at the solenoid terminal.
4. Reinstall all nuts as soon as they are removed, since the thread sizes are different.
5. Remove the front bracket from the starter and the two mounting bolts. On engines with a solenoid heat shield, remove the front bracket upper bolt and detach the bracket from the starter.
6. Remove the front bracket bolt or nut. Lower the starter front end first, and then remove the unit from the truck.
7. Reverse the removal procedures to install the starter. Torque the two mounting bolts to 25–35 ft. lbs.

STARTER OVERHAUL

Solenoid Replacement

1. Remove the screw and washer from the field strap terminal.

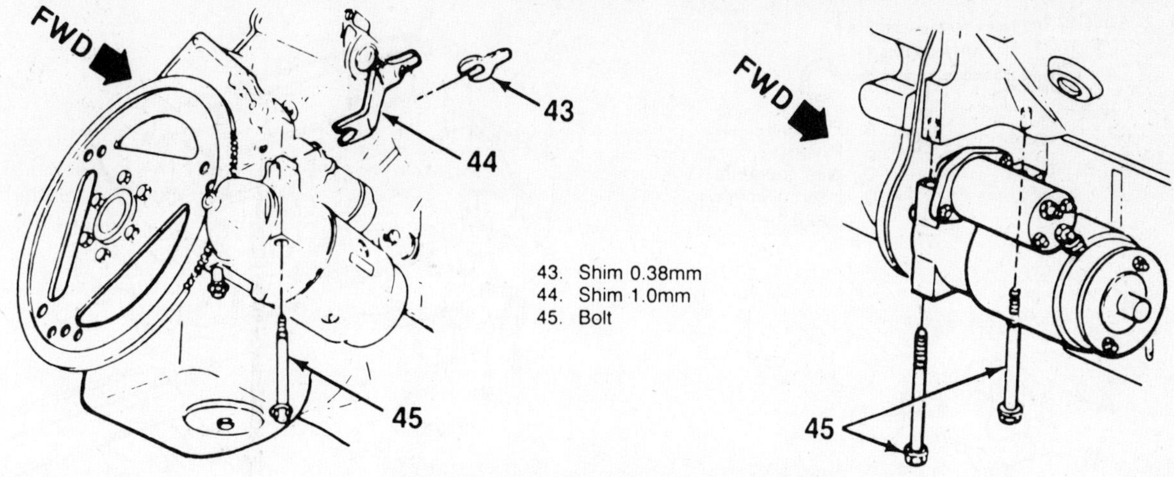

Simming the gasoline engine starter

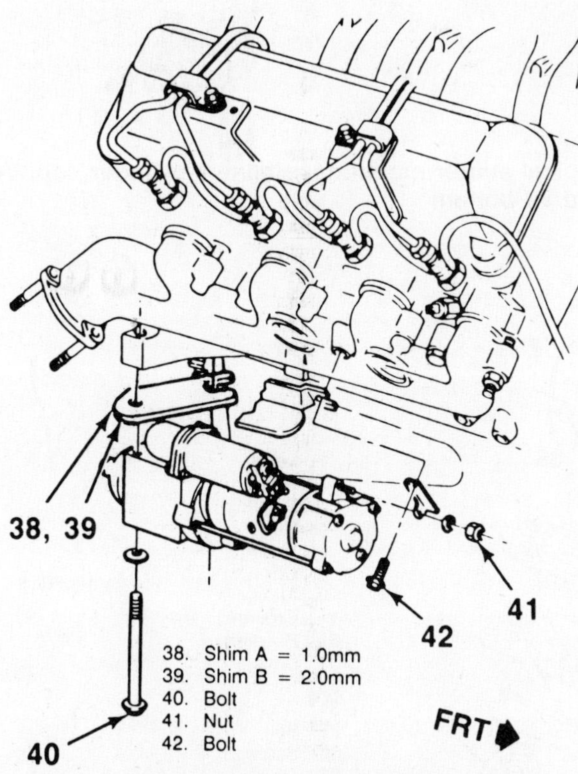

Shimming the diesel starter

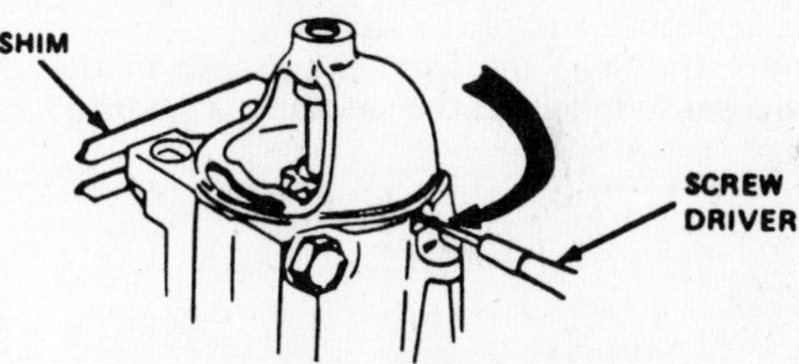

Meshing the starter teeth

2. Remove the two solenoid-to-housing retaining screws and the motor terminal bolt.
3. Remove the solenoid by twisting the unit 90 degrees.
4. To replace the solenoid, reverse the above procedure. Make sure the return spring is on the plunger, and rotate the solenoid unit into place on the starter.

Brush Replacement

1. Disconnect the field coil connectors from the starter motor solenoid terminal.
2. Remove the through bolts.
3. Remove the end frame and the field frame from the drive housing.
4. Disassemble the brush assembly from the field frame by releasing the spring and removing the supporting pin. Pull the brushes and the brush holders out and disconnect the wiring.
5. Install the new brushes into the holders.
6. Assemble the brush holder using the spring and position the unit on the supporting pin.
7. Install the unit in the starter motor and attach the wiring.
8. Position the field frame over the armature.
9. Install the through bolts.
10. Connect the field coil connectors to the solenoid.

Starter Drive Replacement

1. Disconnect the field coil straps from the solenoid.
2. Remove the through-bolts (usually 2), and separate the commutator end frame, field frame assembly, drive housing, and armature assembly from each other.

NOTE: On the diesel starters, remove the insulator from the end frame. The armature on the diesel starter remains in the drive end frame.

3. On diesel starters, remove the shift lever pivot bolt. On the diesel 25 MT starter only, remove the center bearing screws and remove the drive gear housing from the armature shaft. The shift lever and plunger assembly will now fall away from the starter clutch.
4. Slide the two-piece thrust collar off the end of the armature shaft.
5. Slide a ⅝ in. deep socket, piece of pipe or an old pinion onto the shaft so that the end of the pipe, socket, or pinion butts up against the edge of the pinion retainer.

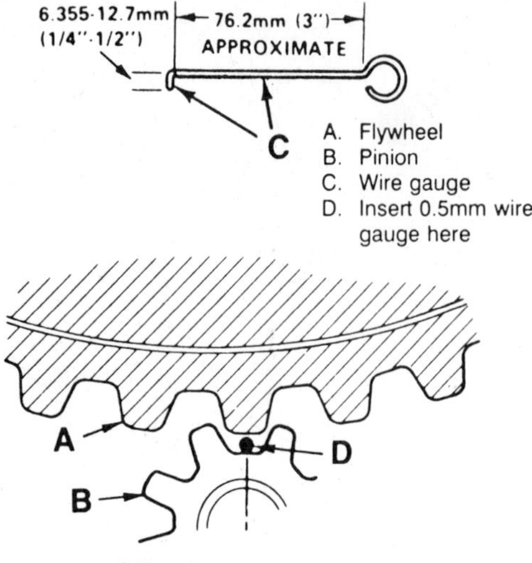

Pinion-to-flywheel clearance

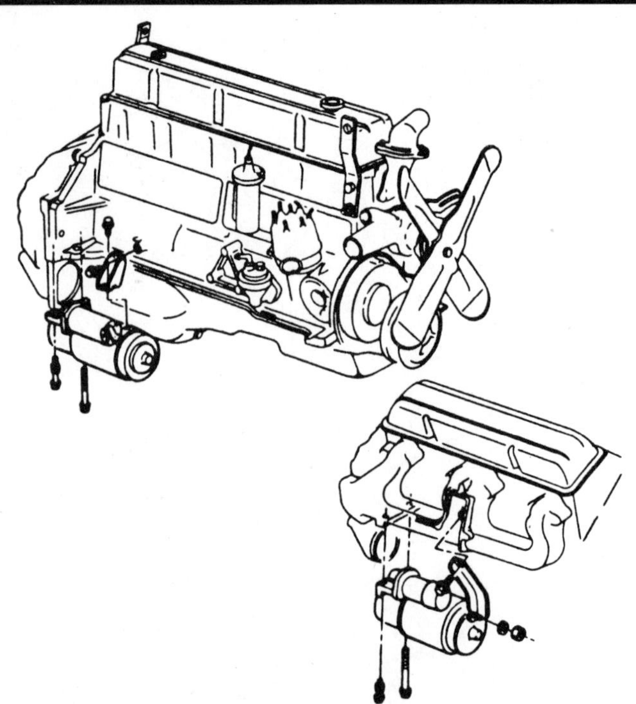

Typical starter mountings: inline 6-cylinder, top; V6 and V8 bottom

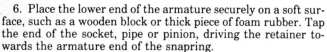

6. Place the lower end of the armature securely on a soft surface, such as a wooden block or thick piece of foam rubber. Tap the end of the socket, pipe or pinion, driving the retainer towards the armature end of the snapring.

7. Remove the snapring from the groove in the armature shaft with a pair of pliers. If the snapring is distorted, replace it

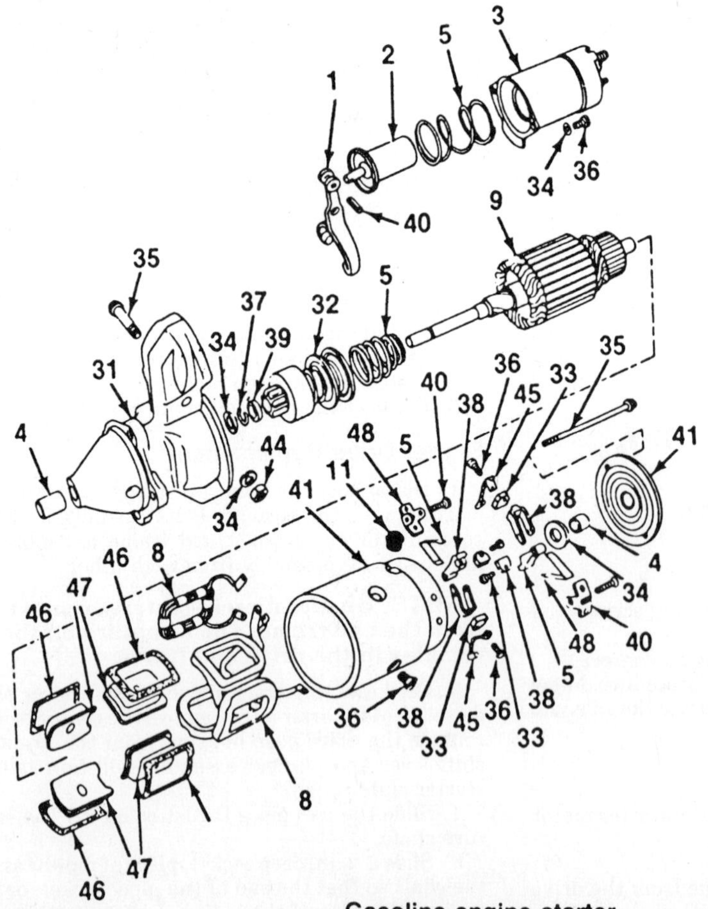

Gasoline engine starter

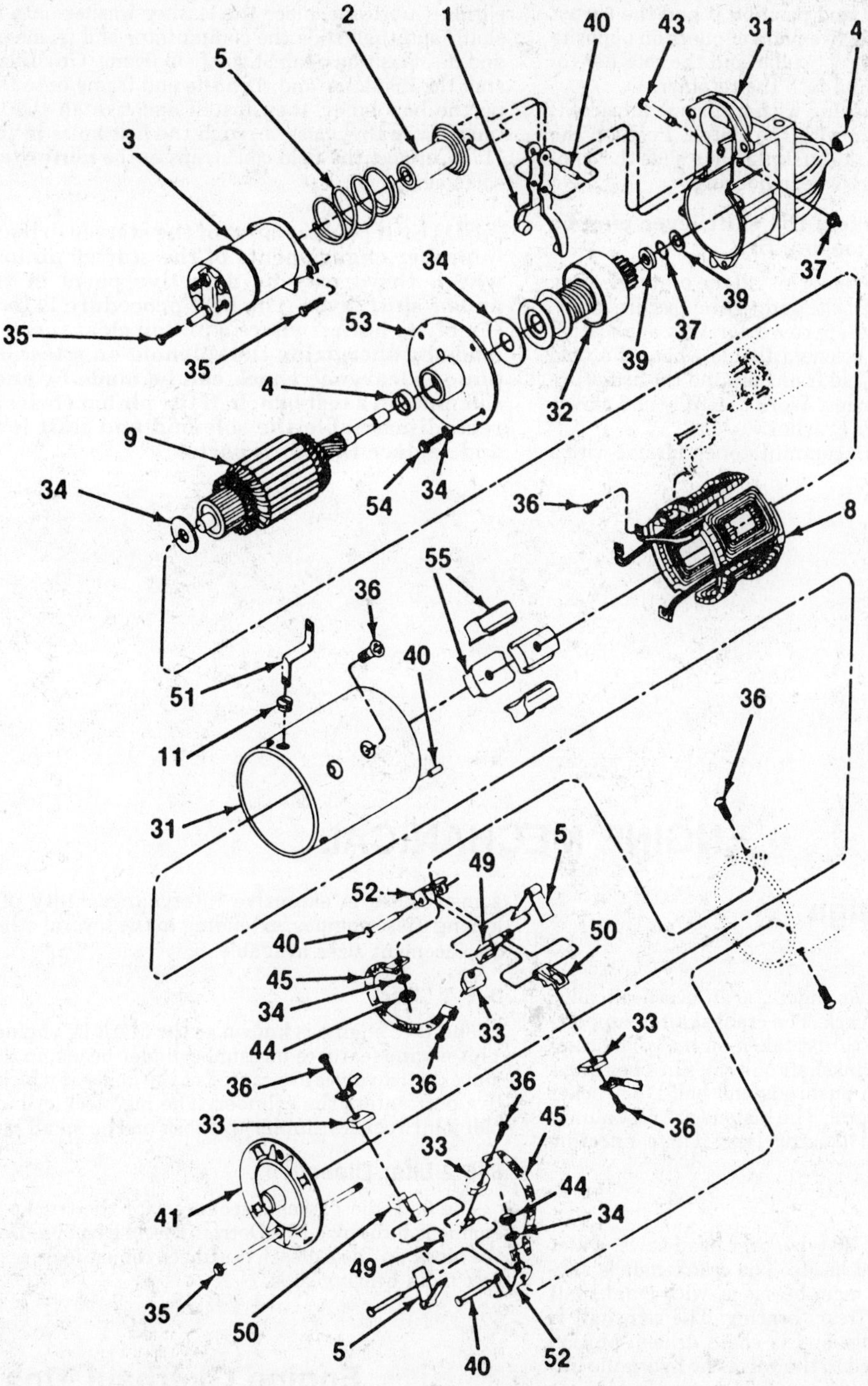

1. Lever
2. Plunger
3. Solenoid
4. Bushing
5. Spring
8. Coil
9. Armature
11. Grommet
31. Housing
32. Drive
33. Brushes
34. Washers
35. Bolt
36. Screw
37. Ring
39. Collar
40. Pin
41. Frame
43. Shaft
44. Nut
45. Lead
49. Grounded brush holder
50. Insulated brush holder
51. Field coil connection
52. Support
53. Center bearing
54. Retaining screw
55. Shoe pole

Diesel engine starter

with a new one during reassembly. Slide the retainer and starter drive from the shaft; on diesel starters, remove the fiber washer and the center bearing from the armature shaft. On gasoline engine starters, the shift lever and plunger may be disassembled at this time (if necessary) by removing the roll pin.

8. To reassemble, lubricate the drive end of the armature shaft with silicone lubricant. On diesel starters, install the center bearing with the bearing toward the armature winding, then install the fiber washer on the armature shaft.

9. Slide the starter drive onto the armature shaft with the pinion facing outward (away from the armature). Slide the retainer onto the shaft with the cupped surace facing outward.

10. Again support the armature on a soft surface, with the pinion on the upper end. Center the snapring on the top of the shaft (use a new ring if the old one was misshapen or damaged). Gently place a block of wood on top of the snapring so as not to move it from a centered position. Tap the wooden block with a hammer in order to force the snapring around the shaft. Slide the ring down into the snap groove.

11. Lay the armature down flat on your work surface. Slide the

retainer close up onto the shaft and position it and the thrust collar next to the snapring. Using two pairs of pliers on opposite ends of the shaft, squeeze the thrust collar and the retainer together until the snapring is forced into the retainer.

12. Lube the drive housing bushing with a silicone lubricant.
13. Engage the shift lever yoke with the clutch. Position the front of the armature shaft into the bushing, then slide the complete drive assembly into the drive gear housing.

NOTE: On non-diesel starters the shift lever may be installed in the drive gear housing first.

14. On the 25 MT diesel starter only, install the center bearing screws and the shift lever pivot bolt, and tighten securely.
15. Apply a sealing compound approved for this application onto the drive housing, to the solenoid flange where the field frame contacts it. Position the field frame around the armature shaft and against the drive housing. Work carefully and slowly to prevent damaging the starter brushes.
16. Lubricate the bushing in the commutator end frame with a silicone lubricant, place the leather washer onto the armature shaft, and then slide the commutator end frame over the shaft and into position against the field frame. On diesel starters, install the insulator and then the end frame onto the shaft. Line up the bolt holes, then install and tighten the through-bolts (make sure they pass through the bolt holes in the insulator).
17. Connect the field coil straps to the **motor** terminal of the solenoid.

NOTE: If replacement of the starter drive fails to cure improper engagements of the starter pinion to the flywheel, there may be defective parts in the solenoid and/or shift lever. The best procedure is to take the assembly to a shop where a pinion clearance check can be made by energizing the solenoid on a test bench. If the pinion clearance check can be made by energizing the solenoid on a test bench. If the pinion clearance is incorrect, disassemble the solenoid and shift lever, inspect, and replace the worn parts.

ENGINE MECHANICAL

Design

6–4.8 Liter

The 4.8 Liter, inline 6–cylinder engine, is an overhead valve design with cast iron head and block. The crankshaft is supported by 7 main bearings with the thrust taken on no.7. The camshaft is driven directly by the crankshaft and rides in 4 bearings. Hydraulic lifters are used with pushrods and ball-type rocker arms. The valve guides are integral. The pistons are cast aluminum and the pins are press-fit floating type. The connecting rods are forged steel.

6–4.3 Liter

The 4.3 Liter engines are 90° V6 type, over head valve, water cooled, with cast iron block and heads. The crankshaft is supported by four precision insert main bearings, with crankshaft thrust taken at the number 4 (rear) bearing. The camshaft is supported by four plain bearings and is chain driven. Motion from the camshaft is transmitted to the valves by hydraulic lifters, pushrods, and ball type rocker arms. The valve guides are integral in the cylinder head. The connecting rods are forged steel, with precision insert type crankpin bearings. The piston pins are a press fit in the connecting rods. The pistons are cast aluminum alloy and the piston pins are a floating fit in the piston.

8–5.0 Liter
8–5.7 Liter

The small block family of V8 engines, 5.0L and 5.7L, are derived from the innovative design of the original 1955 265 cu in. Chevrolet V8. This engine introduced the ball mounted rocker arm design, replacing the once standard shaft mounted rocker arms. There is extensive interchangeability of components among these engines, extending to the several other small block displacement sizes available.

8–7.4 Liter

The 7.4L engine is known as the Mark IV engine or big block. This engine features unusual cylinder heads, in that the intake and exhaust valves are canted at the angle at which their respective port enters the cylinder. The big block cylinder heads use ball joint rockers similar to those on the small block engines.

8–6.2 Liter Diesel

The 6.2L diesel was introduced for the trucks in 1983. This engine is built by GM's Detroit Diesel Division. Designed "from the block up" as a diesel, it utilizes robust features such as four-bolt main bearing caps.

Engine Overhaul Tips

Most engine overhaul procedures are fairly standard. In addition to specific parts replacement procedures and complete specifications for your individual engine, this section also is a guide to accept rebuilding procedures. Examples of standard rebuilding practice are shown and should be used along with specific details concerning your particular engine.

Competent and accurate machine shop services will ensure maximum performance, reliability and engine life.

In most instances it is more profitable for the do-it-yourself mechanic to remove, clean and inspect the component, buy the necessary parts and deliver these to a shop for actual machine work.

On the other hand, much of the rebuilding work (crankshaft, block, bearings, piston rods, and other components) is well within the scope of the do-it-yourself mechanic.

TOOLS

The tools required for an engine overhaul or parts replacement will depend on the depth of your involvement. With a few exceptions, they will be the tools found in a mechanic's tool kit (see Section 1). More in-depth work will require any or all of the following:

- a dial indicator (reading in thousandths) mounted on a universal base
- micrometers and telescope gauges
- jaw and screw type pullers
- scraper
- valve spring compressor
- ring groove cleaner
- piston ring expander and compressor
- ridge reamer
- cylinder hone or glaze breaker
- Plastigage®
- engine stand

Use of most of these tools is illustrated in this section. Many can be rented for a one time use from a local parts jobber or tool supply house specializing in automotive work.

Occasionally, the use of special tools is called for. See the information on Special Tools and Safety Notice in the front of this book before substituting another tool.

INSPECTION TECHNIQUES

Procedures and specifications are given in this section for inspecting, cleaning and assessing the wear limits of most major components. Other procedures such as Magnaflux® and Zyglo® can be used to locate material flaws and stress cracks. Magnaflux® is a magnetic process applicable only to ferrous materials. The Zyglo® process coats the material with a fluorescent dye penetrant and can be used on any material Check for suspected surface cracks can be more readily made using spot check dye. The dye is sprayed onto the suspected area, wiped off and the area sprayed with a developer. Cracks will show up brightly.

OVERHAUL TIPS

Aluminum has become extremely popular for use in engines, due to its low weight. Observe the following precautions when handling aluminum parts:

- Never hot tank aluminum parts (the caustic hot tank solution will eat the aluminum.
- Remove all aluminum parts (identification tag, etc.) from engine parts prior to the tanking.
- Always coat threads lightly with engine oil or anti-seize compounds before installation, to prevent seizure.
- Never over torque bolts or spark plugs especially in aluminum threads.

Stripped threads in any component can be repaired using any of several commercial repair kits (Heli-Coil®, Microdot®, Keenserts®, etc.).

When assembling the engine, any parts that will be frictional contact must be prelubed to provide lubrication at initial start-up. Any product specifically formulated for this purpose can be used, but engine oil is not recommended as a prelube.

When semi-permanent (locked, but removable) installation of bolts or nuts is desired, threads should be cleaned and coated with Loctite® or other similar, commercial non-hardening sealant.

REPAIRING DAMAGED THREADS

Several methods of repairing damaged threads are available. Heli-Coil®, Keenserts® and Microdot® are among the most widely used. All involve basically the same principle—drilling out stripped threads, tapping the hole and installing a prewound insert—making welding, plugging and oversize fasteners unnecessary.

Two types of thread repair inserts are usually supplied—a standard type for most Inch Coarse, Inch Fine, Metric Course and Metric Fine thread sizes and a spark lug type to fit most spark plug port sizes. Consult the individual manufacturer's catalog to determine exact applications. Typical thread repair kits will contain a selection of prewound threaded inserts, a tap

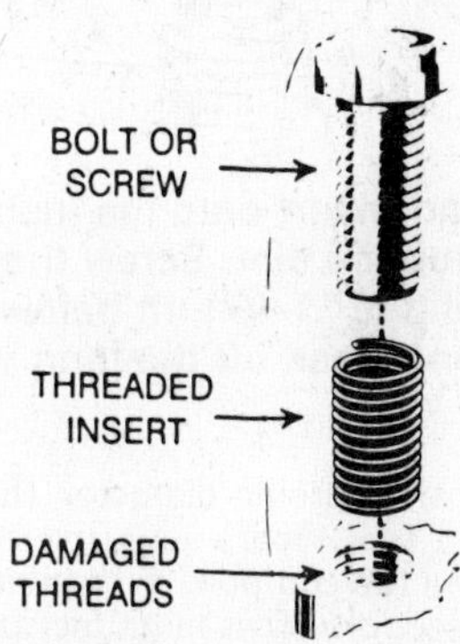

Damaged bolt holes can be repair with thread inserts

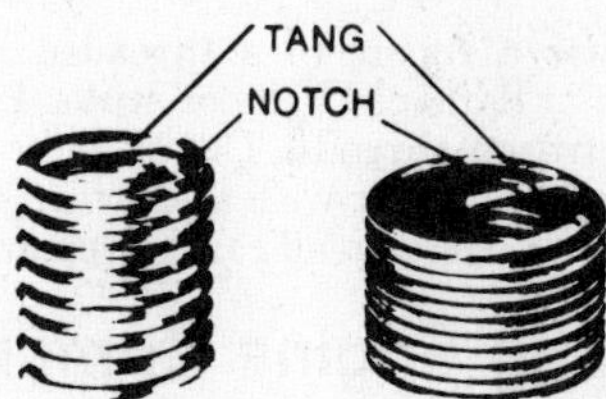

Standard thread insert (left) and spark plug insert

Drill out the damaged threads with the specified bit. Drill completely through an open hole, or to the bottom of a blind hole

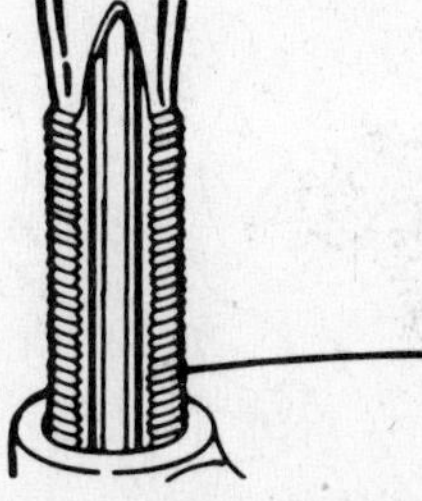

With the tap supplied, tap the hole to receive the thread insert. Keep the tap well oiled and back it out frequently to avoid clogging the threads

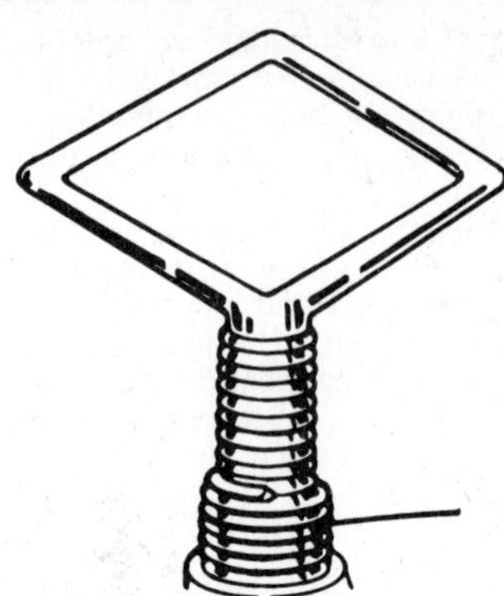

Screw the thread insert onto the installation tool until the tang engages the slot. Screw the insert into the taped hole until it is ¼–½ turn below the top surface. After installation, break off the tang with a hammer and punch

(corresponding to the outside diameter threads of the insert) and an installation tool. Spark plug inserts usually differ because they require a tap equipped with pilot threads and a combined reamer/tap section. Most manufacturers also supply blister-packed thread repair inserts separately in addition to a master kit containing a variety of taps and inserts plus installation tools.

Before effecting a repair to a threaded hole, remove any snapped, broken or damaged bolts or studs. Penetrating oil can be used to free frozen threads. The offending item can be removed with locking pliers or with a screw or stud extractor. After the hole is clear, the thread can be repaired, as follows:

Checking Engine Compression

A noticeable lack of engine power, excessive oil consumption and/or poor fuel mileage measured over an extended period are all indicators of internal engine war. Worn piston rings, scored or worn cylinder bores, blown head gaskets, sticking or burnt valves and worn valve seats are all possible culprits here. A check of each cylinder's compression will help you locate the problems.

As mentioned in the Tools and Equipment section of Section 1, a screw-in type compression gauge is more accurate that the type you simply hold against the spark plug hole, although it takes slightly longer to use. It's worth it to obtain a more accurate reading. Follow the procedures below for gasoline and diesel engined trucks.

GASOLINE ENGINES

1. Warm up the engine to normal operating temperature.
2. Remove all spark plugs.

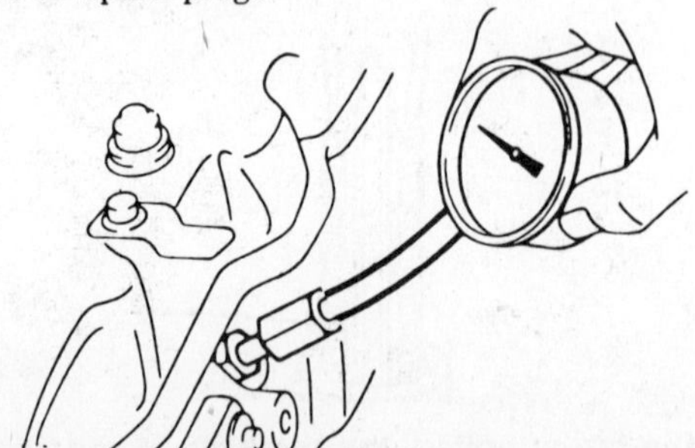

The screw-in type of compression gauge is mush more accurate than the push-in type

3. Disconnect the high tension lead from the ignition coil.
4. On fully open the throttle either by operating the throttle linkage by hand or by having an assistant floor the accelerator pedal.
5. Screw the compression gauge into the no.1 spark plug hole until the fitting is snug.

NOTE: Be careful not to crossthread the plug hole. On aluminum cylinder heads use extra care, as the threads in these heads are easily ruined.

6. Ask an assistant to depress the accelerator pedal fully on both carbureted and fuel injected trucks. Then, while you read the compression gauge, ask the assistant to crank the engine two or three times in short bursts using the ignition switch.
7. Read the compression gauge at the end of each series of cranks, and record the highest of these readings. Repeat this procedure for each of the engine's cylinders. Compare the highest reading of each cylinder to the compression pressure specification in the Tune-Up Specifications chart in Section 2. The specs in this chart are maximum values.

A cylinder's compression pressure is usually acceptable if it is not less than 80% of maximum. The difference between each cylinder should be no more than 12–14 pounds.

8. If a cylinder is unusually low, pour a tablespoon of clean engine oil into the cylinder through the spark plug hole and repeat the compression test. If the compression comes up after adding the oil, it appears that the cylinder's piston rings or bore are damaged or worn. If the pressure remains low, the valves may not be seating properly (a valve job is needed), or the head gasket may be blown near that cylinder. If compression in any two adjacent cylinders is low, and if the addition of oil doesn't help the compression, there is leakage past the head gasket. Oil and coolant water in the combustion chamber can result from this problem. There may be evidence of water droplets on the engine dipstick when a head gasket has blown.

DIESEL ENGINES

Checking cylinder compression on diesel engines is basically the same procedure as on gasoline engines except for the following:

1. A special compression gauge adaptor suitable for diesel engines (because these engines have much greater compression pressures) must be used.
2. Remove the injector tubes and remove the injectors from each cylinder.

NOTE: Don't forget to remove the washer underneath each injector; otherwise, it may get lost when the engine is cranked.

3. When fitting the compression gauge adaptor to the cylinder head, make sure the bleeder of the gauge (if equipped) is closed.
4. When reinstalling the injector assemblies, install new washers underneath each injector.

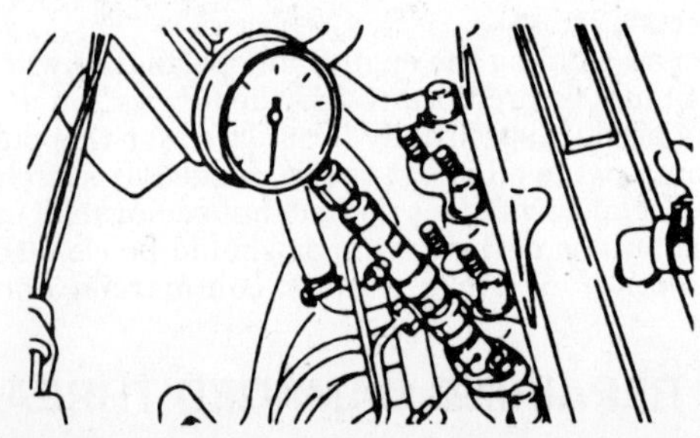

Diesel engines require a special gauge adapter

Standard Torque Specifications and Fastener Markings

In the absence of specific torques, the following chart can be used as a guide to the maximum safe torque of a particular size/grade of fastener.

- There is no torque difference for fine or coarse threads.
- Torque values are based on clean, dry threads. Reduce the value by 10% if threads are oiled prior to assembly.
- The torque required for aluminum components or fasteners is considerably less.

U.S. Bolts

SAE Grade Number	1 or 2			5			6 or 7		
Number of lines always 2 less than the grade number.									
Bolt Size (Inches)—(Thread)	Maximum Torque			Maximum Torque			Maximum Torque		
	Ft./Lbs.	Kgm	Nm	Ft./Lbs.	Kgm	Nm	Ft./Lbs.	Kgm	Nm
¼—20	5	0.7	6.8	8	1.1	10.8	10	1.4	13.5
—28	6	0.8	8.1	10	1.4	13.6			
5/16—18	11	1.5	14.9	17	2.3	23.0	19	2.6	25.8
—24	13	1.8	17.6	19	2.6	25.7			
⅜—16	18	2.5	24.4	31	4.3	42.0	34	4.7	46.0
—24	20	2.75	27.1	35	4.8	47.5			
7/16—14	28	3.8	37.0	49	6.8	66.4	55	7.6	74.5
—20	30	4.2	40.7	55	7.6	74.5			
½—13	39	5.4	52.8	75	10.4	101.7	85	11.75	115.2
—20	41	5.7	55.6	85	11.7	115.2			
9/16—12	51	7.0	69.2	110	15.2	149.1	120	16.6	162.7
—18	55	7.6	74.5	120	16.6	162.7			
⅝—11	83	11.5	112.5	150	20.7	203.3	167	23.0	226.5
—18	95	13.1	128.8	170	23.5	230.5			
¾—10	105	14.5	142.3	270	37.3	366.0	280	38.7	379.6
—16	115	15.9	155.9	295	40.8	400.0			
⅞—9	160	22.1	216.9	395	54.6	535.5	440	60.9	596.5
—14	175	24.2	237.2	435	60.1	589.7			
1—8	236	32.5	318.6	590	81.6	799.9	660	91.3	894.8
—14	250	34.6	338.9	660	91.3	849.8			

Metric Bolts

Relative Strength Marking	4.6, 4.8			8.8		
Bolt Markings						
Bolt Size Thread Size x Pitch (mm)	Maximum Torque			Maximum Torque		
	Ft./Lbs.	Kgm	Nm	Ft./Lbs.	Kgm	Nm
6 x 1.0	2-3	.2-.4	3-4	3-6	.4-.8	5-8
8 x 1.25	6-8	.8-1	8-12	9-14	1.2-1.9	13-19
10 x 1.25	12-17	1.5-2.3	16-23	20-29	2.7-4.0	27-39
12 x 1.25	21-32	2.9-4.4	29-43	35-53	4.8-7.3	47-72
14 x 1.5	35-52	4.8-7.1	48-70	57-85	7.8-11.7	77-110
16 x 1.5	51-77	7.0-10.6	67-100	90-120	12.4-16.5	130-160
18 x 1.5	74-110	10.2-15.1	100-150	130-170	17.9-23.4	180-230
20 x 1.5	110-140	15.1-19.3	150-190	190-240	26.2-46.9	160-320
22 x 1.5	150-190	22.0-26.2	200-260	250-320	34.5-44.1	340-430
24 x 1.5	190-240	26.2-46.9	260-320	310-410	42.7-56.5	420-550

Troubleshooting Engine Mechanical Problems

Problem	Cause	Solution
External oil leaks	• Fuel pump gasket broken or improperly seated	• Replace gasket
	• Cylinder head cover RTV sealant broken or improperly seated	• Replace sealant; inspect cylinder head cover sealant flange and cylinder head sealant surface for distortion and cracks
	• Oil filler cap leaking or missing	• Replace cap
	• Oil filter gasket broken or improperly seated	• Replace oil filter
	• Oil pan side gasket broken, improperly seated or opening in RTV sealant	• Replace gasket or repair opening in sealant; inspect oil pan gasket flange for distortion
	• Oil pan front oil seal broken or improperly seated	• Replace seal; inspect timing case cover and oil pan seal flange for distortion
	• Oil pan rear oil seal broken or improperly seated	• Replace seal; inspect oil pan rear oil seal flange; inspect rear main bearing cap for cracks, plugged oil return channels, or distortion in seal groove
	• Timing case cover oil seal broken or improperly seated	• Replace seal
	• Excess oil pressure because of restricted PCV valve	• Replace PCV valve
	• Oil pan drain plug loose or has stripped threads	• Repair as necessary and tighten
	• Rear oil gallery plug loose	• Use appropriate sealant on gallery plug and tighten
	• Rear camshaft plug loose or improperly seated	• Seat camshaft plug or replace and seal, as necessary
	• Distributor base gasket damaged	• Replace gasket
Excessive oil consumption	• Oil level too high	• Drain oil to specified level
	• Oil with wrong viscosity being used	• Replace with specified oil
	• PCV valve stuck closed	• Replace PCV valve
	• Valve stem oil deflectors (or seals) are damaged, missing, or incorrect type	• Replace valve stem oil deflectors
	• Valve stems or valve guides worn	• Measure stem-to-guide clearance and repair as necessary
	• Poorly fitted or missing valve cover baffles	• Replace valve cover
	• Piston rings broken or missing	• Replace broken or missing rings
	• Scuffed piston	• Replace piston
	• Incorrect piston ring gap	• Measure ring gap, repair as necessary
	• Piston rings sticking or excessively loose in grooves	• Measure ring side clearance, repair as necessary
	• Compression rings installed upside down	• Repair as necessary
	• Cylinder walls worn, scored, or glazed	• Repair as necessary

Troubleshooting Engine Mechanical Problems (cont.)

Problem	Cause	Solution
	• Piston ring gaps not properly staggered	• Repair as necessary
	• Excessive main or connecting rod bearing clearance	• Measure bearing clearance, repair as necessary
No oil pressure	• Low oil level	• Add oil to correct level
	• Oil pressure gauge, warning lamp or sending unit inaccurate	• Replace oil pressure gauge or warning lamp
	• Oil pump malfunction	• Replace oil pump
	• Oil pressure relief valve sticking	• Remove and inspect oil pressure relief valve assembly
	• Oil passages on pressure side of pump obstructed	• Inspect oil passages for obstruction
	• Oil pickup screen or tube obstructed	• Inspect oil pickup for obstruction
	• Loose oil inlet tube	• Tighten or seal inlet tube
Low oil pressure	• Low oil level	• Add oil to correct level
	• Inaccurate gauge, warning lamp or sending unit	• Replace oil pressure gauge or warning lamp
	• Oil excessively thin because of dilution, poor quality, or improper grade	• Drain and refill crankcase with recommended oil
	• Excessive oil temperature	• Correct cause of overheating engine
	• Oil pressure relief spring weak or sticking	• Remove and inspect oil pressure relief valve assembly
	• Oil inlet tube and screen assembly has restriction or air leak	• Remove and inspect oil inlet tube and screen assembly. (Fill inlet tube with lacquer thinner to locate leaks.)
	• Excessive oil pump clearance	• Measure clearances
	• Excessive main, rod, or camshaft bearing clearance	• Measure bearing clearances, repair as necessary
High oil pressure	• Improper oil viscosity	• Drain and refill crankcase with correct viscosity oil
	• Oil pressure gauge or sending unit inaccurate	• Replace oil pressure gauge
	• Oil pressure relief valve sticking closed	• Remove and inspect oil pressure relief valve assembly
Main bearing noise	• Insufficient oil supply	• Inspect for low oil level and low oil pressure
	• Main bearing clearance excessive	• Measure main bearing clearance, repair as necessary
	• Bearing insert missing	• Replace missing insert
	• Crankshaft end play excessive	• Measure end play, repair as necessary
	• Improperly tightened main bearing cap bolts	• Tighten bolts with specified torque
	• Loose flywheel or drive plate	• Tighten flywheel or drive plate attaching bolts
	• Loose or damaged vibration damper	• Repair as necessary

Troubleshooting Engine Mechanical Problems (cont.)

Problem	Cause	Solution
Connecting rod bearing noise	• Insufficient oil supply	• Inspect for low oil level and low oil pressure
	• Carbon build-up on piston	• Remove carbon from piston crown
	• Bearing clearance excessive or bearing missing	• Measure clearance, repair as necessary
	• Crankshaft connecting rod journal out-of-round	• Measure journal dimensions, repair or replace as necessary
	• Misaligned connecting rod or cap	• Repair as necessary
	• Connecting rod bolts tightened improperly	• Tighten bolts with specified torque
Piston noise	• Piston-to-cylinder wall clearance excessive (scuffed piston)	• Measure clearance and examine piston
	• Cylinder walls excessively tapered or out-of-round	• Measure cylinder wall dimensions, rebore cylinder
	• Piston ring broken	• Replace all rings on piston
	• Loose or seized piston pin	• Measure piston-to-pin clearance, repair as necessary
	• Connecting rods misaligned	• Measure rod alignment, straighten or replace
	• Piston ring side clearance excessively loose or tight	• Measure ring side clearance, repair as necessary
	• Carbon build-up on piston is excessive	• Remove carbon from piston
Valve actuating component noise	• Insufficient oil supply	• Check for: (a) Low oil level (b) Low oil pressure (c) Plugged push rods (d) Wrong hydraulic tappets (e) Restricted oil gallery (f) Excessive tappet to bore clearance
	• Push rods worn or bent	• Replace worn or bent push rods
	• Rocker arms or pivots worn	• Replace worn rocker arms or pivots
	• Foreign objects or chips in hydraulic tappets	• Clean tappets
	• Excessive tappet leak-down	• Replace valve tappet
	• Tappet face worn	• Replace tappet; inspect corresponding cam lobe for wear
	• Broken or cocked valve springs	• Properly seat cocked springs; replace broken springs
	• Stem-to-guide clearance excessive	• Measure stem-to-guide clearance, repair as required
	• Valve bent	• Replace valve
	• Loose rocker arms	• Tighten bolts with specified torque
	• Valve seat runout excessive	• Regrind valve seat/valves
	• Missing valve lock	• Install valve lock
	• Push rod rubbing or contacting cylinder head	• Remove cylinder head and remove obstruction in head
	• Excessive engine oil (four-cylinder engine)	• Correct oil level

Troubleshooting the Cooling System

Problem	Cause	Solution
High temperature gauge indication—overheating	• Coolant level low • Fan belt loose • Radiator hose(s) collapsed • Radiator airflow blocked • Faulty radiator cap • Ignition timing incorrect • Idle speed low • Air trapped in cooling system • Heavy traffic driving • Incorrect cooling system component(s) installed • Faulty thermostat • Water pump shaft broken or impeller loose • Radiator tubes clogged • Cooling system clogged • Casting flash in cooling passages • Brakes dragging • Excessive engine friction • Antifreeze concentration over 68% • Missing air seals • Faulty gauge or sending unit • Loss of coolant flow caused by leakage or foaming • Viscous fan drive failed	• Replenish coolant • Adjust fan belt tension • Replace hose(s) • Remove restriction (bug screen, fog lamps, etc.) • Replace radiator cap • Adjust ignition timing • Adjust idle speed • Purge air • Operate at fast idle in neutral intermittently to cool engine • Install proper component(s) • Replace thermostat • Replace water pump • Flush radiator • Flush system • Repair or replace as necessary. Flash may be visible by removing cooling system components or removing core plugs. • Repair brakes • Repair engine • Lower antifreeze concentration percentage • Replace air seals • Repair or replace faulty component • Repair or replace leaking component, replace coolant • Replace unit
Low temperature indication—undercooling	• Thermostat stuck open • Faulty gauge or sending unit	• Replace thermostat • Repair or replace faulty component
Coolant loss—boilover	• Overfilled cooling system • Quick shutdown after hard (hot) run • Air in system resulting in occasional "burping" of coolant • Insufficient antifreeze allowing coolant boiling point to be too low • Antifreeze deteriorated because of age or contamination • Leaks due to loose hose clamps, loose nuts, bolts, drain plugs, faulty hoses, or defective radiator	• Reduce coolant level to proper specification • Allow engine to run at fast idle prior to shutdown • Purge system • Add antifreeze to raise boiling point • Replace coolant • Pressure test system to locate source of leak(s) then repair as necessary

Troubleshooting the Cooling System (cont.)

Problem	Cause	Solution
Coolant loss—boilover	• Faulty head gasket • Cracked head, manifold, or block • Faulty radiator cap	• Replace head gasket • Replace as necessary • Replace cap
Coolant entry into crankcase or cylinder(s)	• Faulty head gasket • Crack in head, manifold or block	• Replace head gasket • Replace as necessary
Coolant recovery system inoperative	• Coolant level low • Leak in system • Pressure cap not tight or seal missing, or leaking • Pressure cap defective • Overflow tube clogged or leaking • Recovery bottle vent restricted	• Replenish coolant to FULL mark • Pressure test to isolate leak and repair as necessary • Repair as necessary • Replace cap • Repair as necessary • Remove restriction
Noise	• Fan contacting shroud • Loose water pump impeller • Glazed fan belt • Loose fan belt • Rough surface on drive pulley • Water pump bearing worn • Belt alignment	• Reposition shroud and inspect engine mounts • Replace pump • Apply silicone or replace belt • Adjust fan belt tension • Replace pulley • Remove belt to isolate. Replace pump. • Check pulley alignment. Repair as necessary.
No coolant flow through heater core	• Restricted return inlet in water pump • Heater hose collapsed or restricted • Restricted heater core • Restricted outlet in thermostat housing • Intake manifold bypass hole in cylinder head restricted • Faulty heater control valve • Intake manifold coolant passage restricted	• Remove restriction • Remove restriction or replace hose • Remove restriction or replace core • Remove flash or restriction • Remove restriction • Replace valve • Remove restriction or replace intake manifold

NOTE: *Immediately after shutdown, the engine enters a condition known as heat soak. This is caused by the cooling system being inoperative while engine temperature is still high. If coolant temperature rises above boiling point, expansion and pressure may push some coolant out of the radiator overflow tube. If this does not occur frequently it is considered normal.*

Troubleshooting the Serpentine Drive Belt

Problem	Cause	Solution
Tension sheeting fabric failure (woven fabric on outside circumference of belt has cracked or separated from body of belt)	• Grooved or backside idler pulley diameters are less than minimum recommended	• Replace pulley(s) not conforming to specification
	• Tension sheeting contacting (rubbing) stationary object	• Correct rubbing condition
	• Excessive heat causing woven fabric to age	• Replace belt
	• Tension sheeting splice has fractured	• Replace belt
Noise (objectional squeal, squeak, or rumble is heard or felt while drive belt is in operation)	• Belt slippage	• Adjust belt
	• Bearing noise	• Locate and repair
	• Belt misalignment	• Align belt/pulley(s)
	• Belt-to-pulley mismatch	• Install correct belt
	• Driven component inducing vibration	• Locate defective driven component and repair
	• System resonant frequency inducing vibration	• Vary belt tension within specifications. Replace belt.
Rib chunking (one or more ribs has separated from belt body)	• Foreign objects imbedded in pulley grooves	• Remove foreign objects from pulley grooves
	• Installation damage	• Replace belt
	• Drive loads in excess of design specifications	• Adjust belt tension
	• Insufficient internal belt adhesion	• Replace belt
Rib or belt wear (belt ribs contact bottom of pulley grooves)	• Pulley(s) misaligned	• Align pulley(s)
	• Mismatch of belt and pulley groove widths	• Replace belt
	• Abrasive environment	• Replace belt
	• Rusted pulley(s)	• Clean rust from pulley(s)
	• Sharp or jagged pulley groove tips	• Replace pulley
	• Rubber deteriorated	• Replace belt
Longitudinal belt cracking (cracks between two ribs)	• Belt has mistracked from pulley groove	• Replace belt
	• Pulley groove tip has worn away rubber-to-tensile member	• Replace belt
Belt slips	• Belt slipping because of insufficient tension	• Adjust tension
	• Belt or pulley subjected to substance (belt dressing, oil, ethylene glycol) that has reduced friction	• Replace belt and clean pulleys
	• Driven component bearing failure	• Replace faulty component bearing
	• Belt glazed and hardened from heat and excessive slippage	• Replace belt
"Groove jumping" (belt does not maintain correct position on pulley, or turns over and/or runs off pulleys)	• Insufficient belt tension	• Adjust belt tension
	• Pulley(s) not within design tolerance	• Replace pulley(s)
	• Foreign object(s) in grooves	• Remove foreign objects from grooves

Troubleshooting the Serpentine Drive Belt (cont.)

Problem	Cause	Solution
"Groove jumping" (belt does not maintain correct position on pulley, or turns over and/or runs off pulleys)	• Excessive belt speed • Pulley misalignment • Belt-to-pulley profile mismatched • Belt cordline is distorted	• Avoid excessive engine acceleration • Align pulley(s) • Install correct belt • Replace belt
Belt broken (Note: identify and correct problem before replacement belt is installed)	• Excessive tension • Tensile members damaged during belt installation • Belt turnover • Severe pulley misalignment • Bracket, pulley, or bearing failure	• Replace belt and adjust tension to specification • Replace belt • Replace belt • Align pulley(s) • Replace defective component and belt
Cord edge failure (tensile member exposed at edges of belt or separated from belt body)	• Excessive tension • Drive pulley misalignment • Belt contacting stationary object • Pulley irregularities • Improper pulley construction • Insufficient adhesion between tensile member and rubber matrix	• Adjust belt tension • Align pulley • Correct as necessary • Replace pulley • Replace pulley • Replace belt and adjust tension to specifications
Sporadic rib cracking (multiple cracks in belt ribs at random intervals)	• Ribbed pulley(s) diameter less than minimum specification • Backside bend flat pulley(s) diameter less than minimum • Excessive heat condition causing rubber to harden • Excessive belt thickness • Belt overcured • Excessive tension	• Replace pulley(s) • Replace pulley(s) • Correct heat condition as necessary • Replace belt • Replace belt • Adjust belt tension

Engine

REMOVAL AND INSTALLATION

6–4.8L

1. Matchmark and remove the hood.
2. Disconnect the negative battery cable.
3. Remove the battery.
4. Drain the cooling system.

CAUTION

When draining the coolant, keep in mind that cats and dogs are attracted by the ethylene glycol antifreeze, and are quite likely to drink any that is left in an uncovered container or in puddles on the ground. This will prove fatal in sufficient quantity. Always drain the coolant into a sealable container. Coolant should be reused unless it is contaminated or several years old.

6. Disconnect the accelerator cable from the carburetor throttle lever.
7. On trucks with automatic tranmission, remove the detent cable from the throttle lever.
8. Remove air cleaner assembly.
9. Mark and disconnect all necessary electrical wiring from the engine.
10. Mark and disconnect all necessary vacuum hoses from the engine.
11. Disconnect the radiator hoses at the radiator.
12. Disconnect the heater hoses at the engine.
13. Remove the radiator.
14. On trucks with air conditioning, discharge the system. See Section 1.
15. Remove the air conditioning condenser.
16. Remove the fan assembly and water pump pulley.
17. Disconnect and plug the fuel line at the fuel pump.
18. Raise and support the truck on jackstands.
19. Drain the engine oil.
20. Remove the starter.
21. Remove the flywheel cover.
22. Disconnect the exhaust pipe from the exhaust manifold.
23. Support the weight of the engine with a shop crane and remove the engine mount through bolts.
24. If equipped with an automatic transmission, remove the torque converter-to-flex plate bolts.
25. If equipped with 4WD, unbolt the strut rods at the engine mounts.
26. Remove the bellhousing-to-engine retaining bolts.
27. Support the transmission with a floor jack.
28. Using the shop crane, carefully remove the engine from the vehicle.

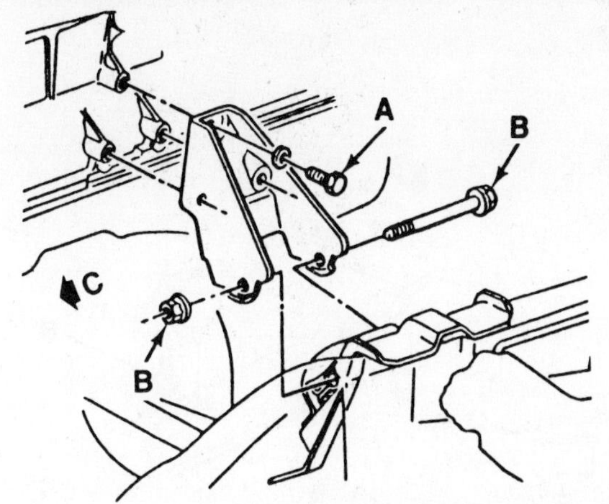

A. 36 ft. lbs.
B. Torque the nut to 54 ft. lbs. or torque the bolt to 85 ft. lbs.
C. Forward
D. 30 ft. lbs.
E. Lower bolt must be installed pointing up

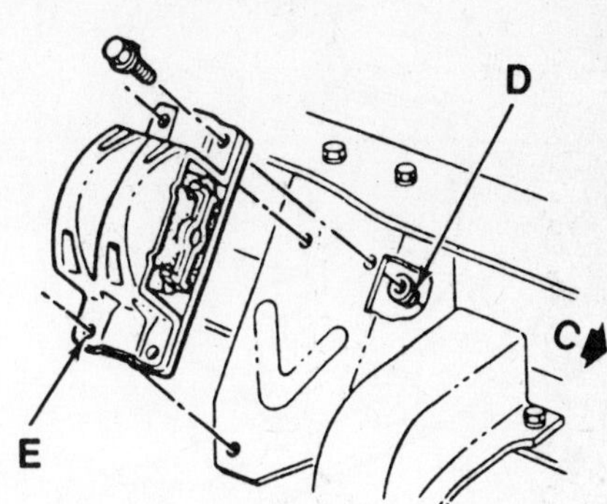

Front engine mounts for the 6-4.8L in the 10/1500 series

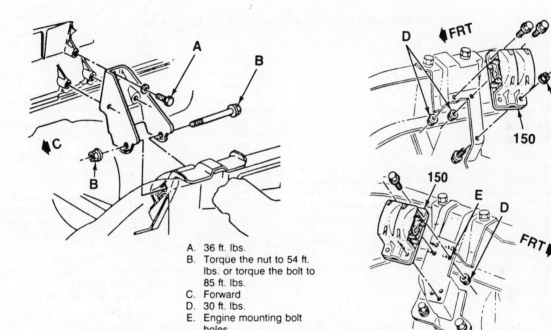

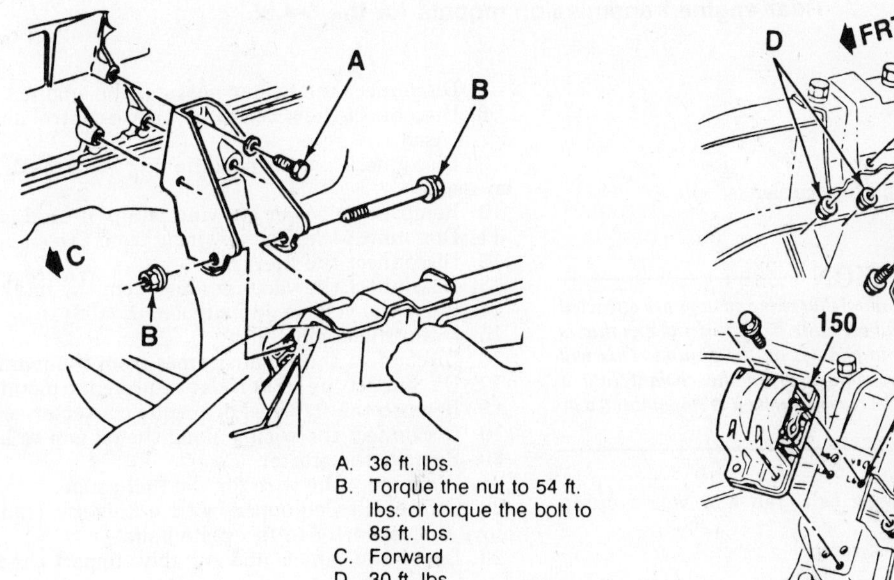

D FRT
D
150
150
E
D
FRT

A. 36 ft. lbs.
B. Torque the nut to 54 ft. lbs. or torque the bolt to 85 ft. lbs.
C. Forward
D. 30 ft. lbs.
E. Engine mounting bolt holes

Front engine mounts for the 6-4.8L in the 20/2500 and 30/3500 series

To install:

29. Using the shop crane, carefully lower the engine into the truck.
30. Install the bellhousing-to-engine retaining bolts. Torque the bolts to 30 ft. lbs.
31. Remove the floor jack.
32. If equipped with 4WD, bolt the strut rods to the engine mounts. Torque the bolts to 45 ft. lbs.
33. If equipped with an automatic transmission, install the torque converter-to-flex plate bolts. Torque the bolts to 40 ft. lbs.
34. Install the engine mount through bolts. Torque them to 60 ft. lbs. Remove the shop crane.
35. Connect the exhaust pipe at the exhaust manifold. Torque the nuts to 20 ft. lbs.
36. Install the flywheel cover.
37. Install the starter.
38. Lower the truck.
39. Connect the fuel line at the fuel pump.
40. Install the fan assembly and water pump pulley.
41. Install the air conditioning condenser.
42. Install the radiator.
43. Connect the heater hoses at the engine.
44. Connect the radiator hoses at the radiator.
45. Connect all vacuum hoses.
46. Connect all electrical wiring.
47. On trucks with automatic tranmission, connect the detent cable at the throttle lever.
48. Connect the accelerator cable at the carburetor throttle lever.
49. Fill the cooling system.
50. Fill the engine crankcase with oil.
51. Install the battery.
52. Connect the negative battery cable.
53. Charge the air conditioning system. See Section 1.
54. Install air cleaner assembly.
55. Install the hood.

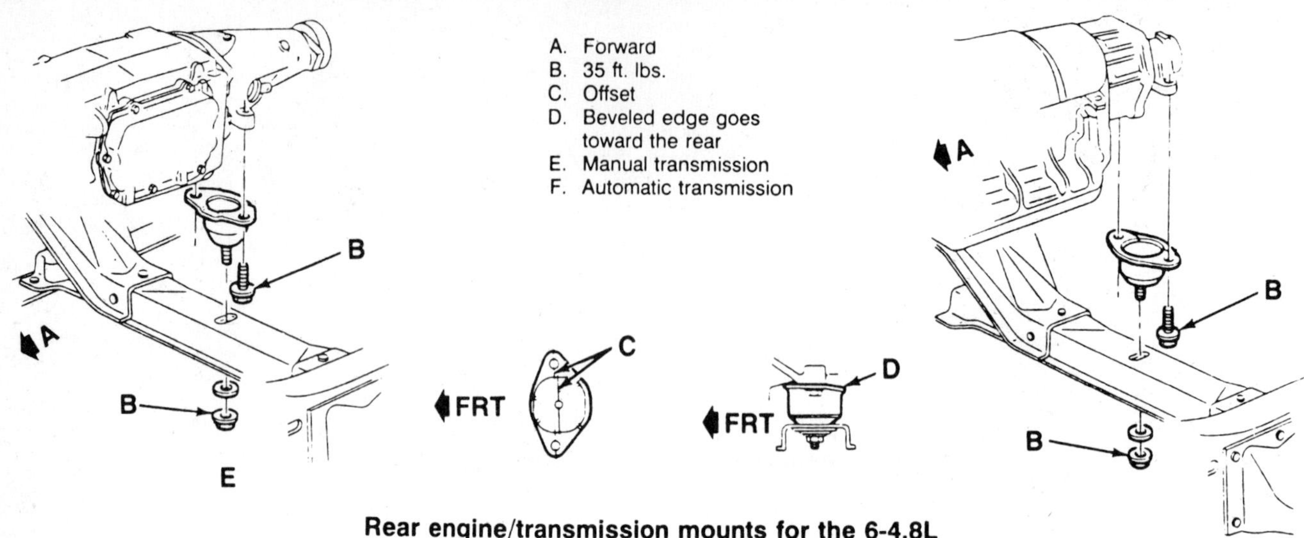

Rear engine/transmission mounts for the 6-4.8L

6-4.3L
8-5.0L
8-5.7L

1. Disconnect the negative battery cable.
2. Remove the hood.
3. Drain the cooling system.

CAUTION

When draining the coolant, keep in mind that cats and dogs are attracted by the ethylene glycol antifreeze, and are quite likely to drink any that is left in an uncovered container or in puddles on the ground. This will prove fatal in sufficient quantity. Always drain the coolant into a sealable container. Coolant should be reused unless it is contaminated or several years old.

4. Remove the air cleaner.
5. Remove the accessory drive belt, fan and water pump pulley.
6. Remove the radiator and shroud.
7. Disconnect the heater hoses at the engine.
8. Disconnect the accelerator, cruise control and detent linkage if used.
9. Disconnect the air conditioning compressor, if used, and lay aside.
10. Remove the power steering pump, if used, and lay aside.
11. Disconnect the engine wiring from the engine.
12. Disconnect the fuel line.
13. Disconnect the vacuum lines from the intake manifold.
14. Raise the vehicle and support it safely.
15. Drain the engine oil.
16. Disconnect the exhaust pipes from the manifold.
17. Disconnect the strut rods at the engine mountings, if used.
18. Remove the flywheel or torque converter cover.
19. Disconnect the wiring along the oil pan rail.
20. Remove the starter.
21. Disconnect the wire for the fuel gauge.
22. On vehicles equipped with automatic transmission, remove the converter to flex plate bolts.
23. Lower the vehicle and suitably support the transmission.

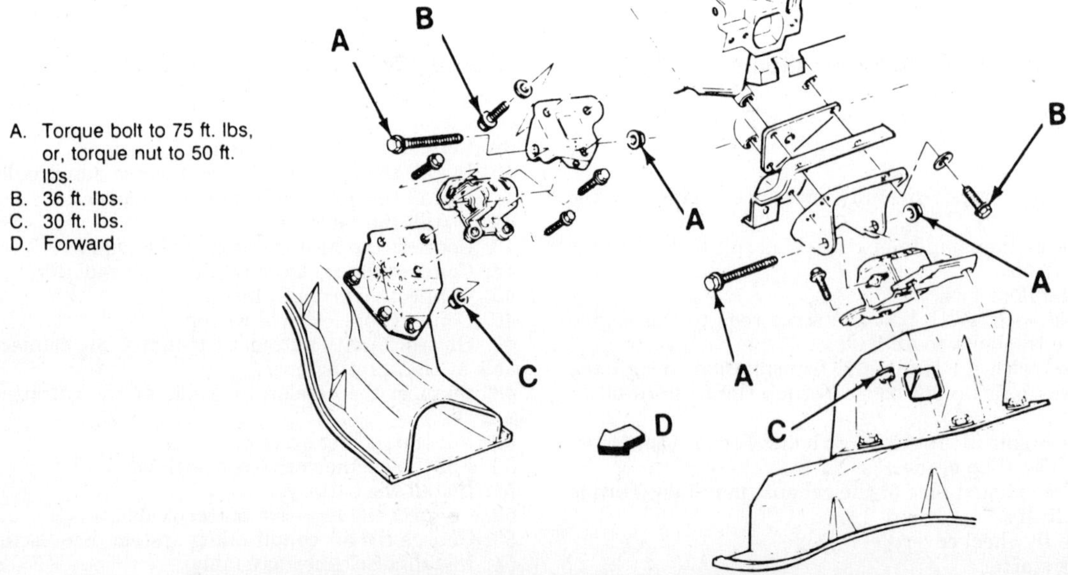

Front engine mounts for the 6-4.3L in R and V series trucks

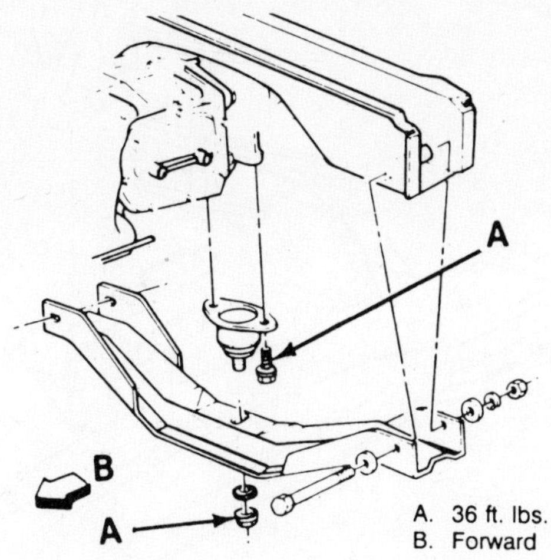

Rear engine mounts for the 6-4.3L in R and V series trucks

Attach a suitable lifting fixture to the engine.

24. Remove the bell housing to engine bolts.
25. Remove the rear engine mounting to frame bolts and the front through bolts and remove the engine.

To install:

26. Raise the vehicle and support it safely.
27. Lower the engine and install the engine mounting bolts. Torque the rear engine mounting to frame bolts or nuts to 45 ft. lbs., the front through-bolts to 70 ft. lbs. and the front nuts to 50 ft. lbs.
28. Install the bell housing to engine bolts and torque to 35 ft. lbs.
29. Remove the transmission support.
30. Install the converter to flex bolts and torque to 35 ft. lbs.
31. Install the fuel gauge wiring and starter.
32. Install the flywheel or torque converter cover.
33. Connect the strut rods at the engine mountings, if used.
34. Install the exhaust pipes at the manifold.
35. Lower the vehicle.
36. Connect the vacuum lines to the intake manifold.
37. Install the fuel line.
38. Connect the engine wiring harness.
39. Install the power steering pump, if used.
40. Connect the air conditioning compressor, if used.
41. Connect the accelerator, cruise control and detent linkage.
42. Conncet the heater hoses.
43. Install the radiator and shroud.
44. Install the accessory drive belts.
45. Install the hood.
46. Install the proper quantity and grade of coolant and engine oil.
47. Connect the negative battery cable.

8-7.4L

1. Remove the hood.

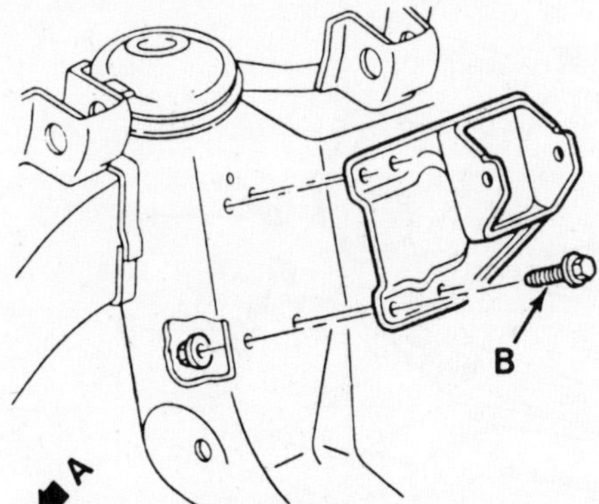

A. Forward
B. 65 ft. lbs.
C. Torque bolts to 70 ft. lbs. or torque nuts to 50 ft. lbs.
D. Bracket used with C15 only

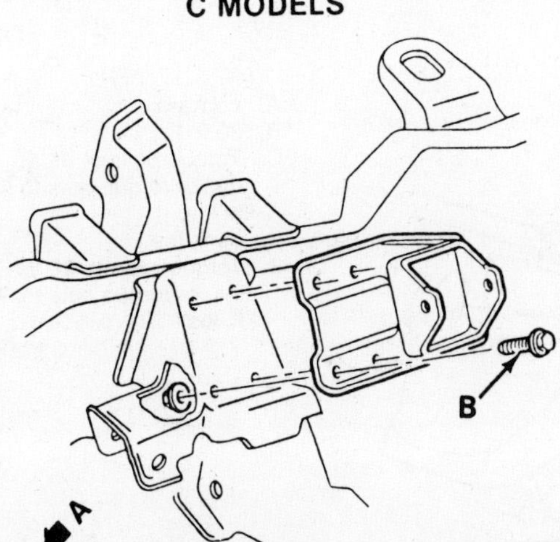

150
B
C
C

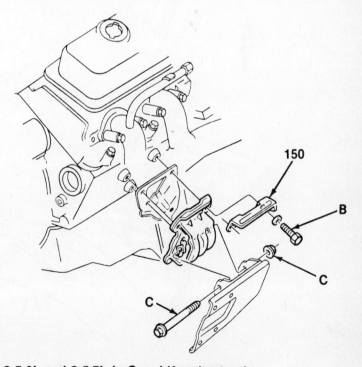

Front engine mounts for the 6-4.3L, 8-5.0L and 8-5.7L in C and K series trucks

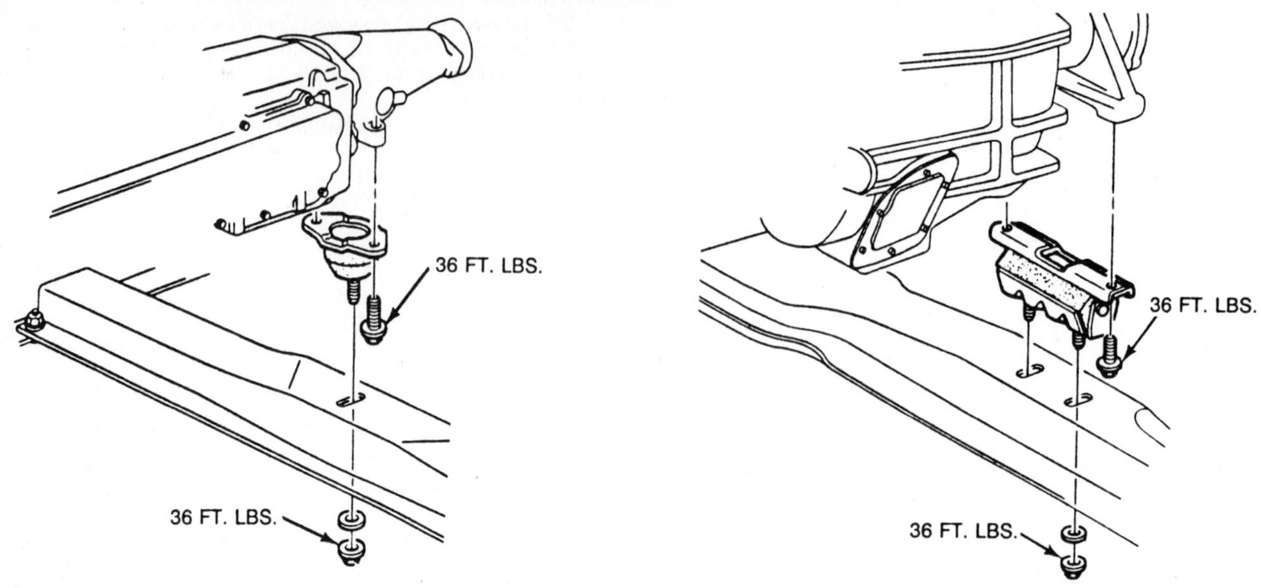

Rear engine mounts for the 6-4.3L, 8-5.0L and 8-5.7L in C series trucks

Rear engine mounts for the 6-4.3L, 8-5.0L and 8-5.7L in K series trucks

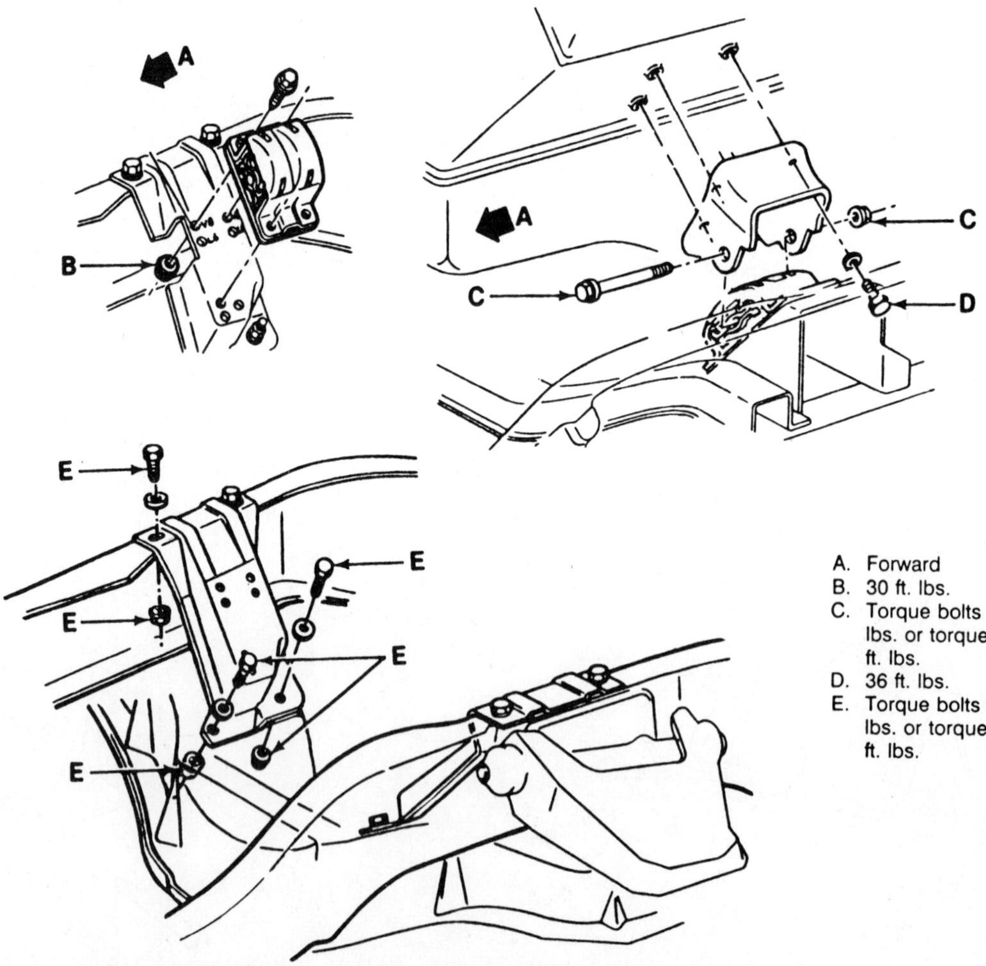

A. Forward
B. 30 ft. lbs.
C. Torque bolts to 85 ft. lbs. or torque nuts to 55 ft. lbs.
D. 36 ft. lbs.
E. Torque bolts to 36 ft. lbs. or torque nuts to 30 ft. lbs.

Front engine mounts for the 8-5.0L and 8-5.7L in R and V series trucks

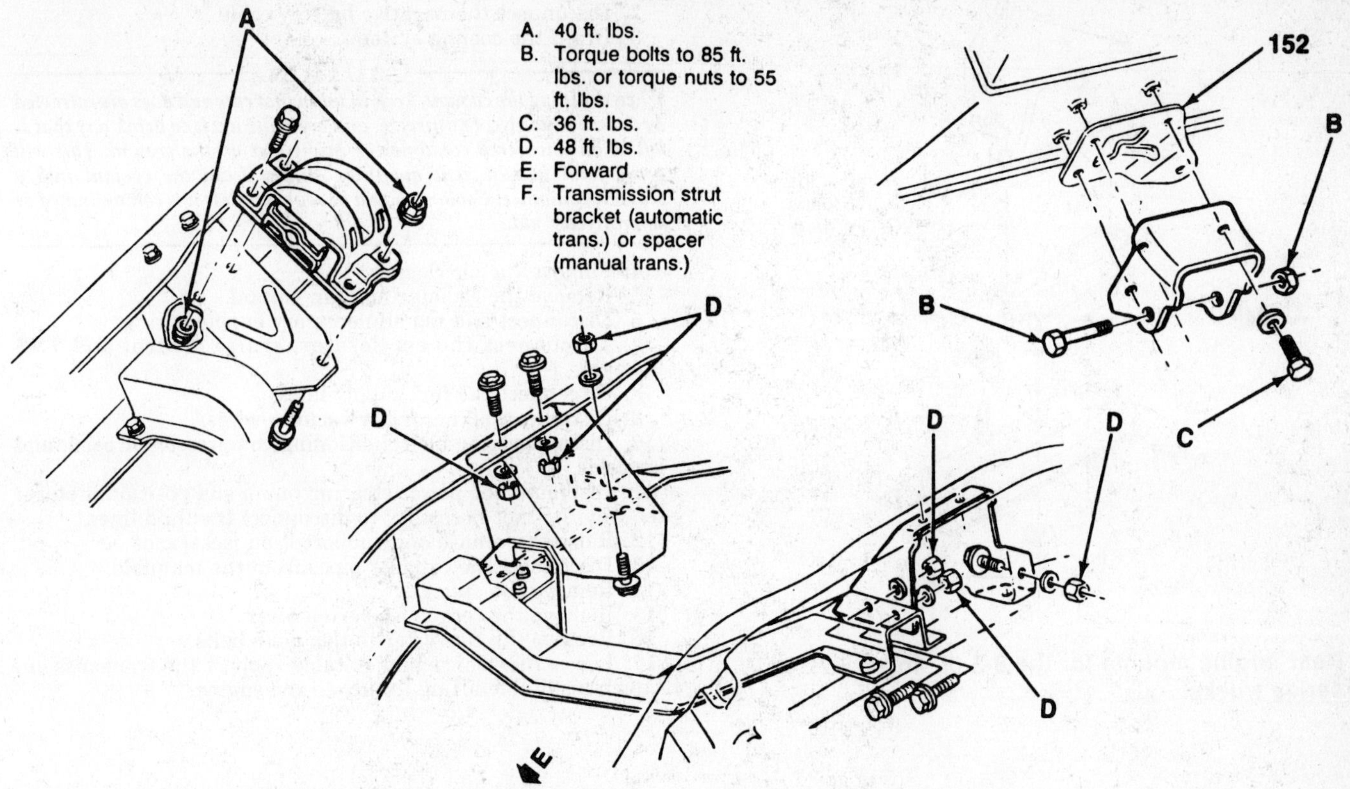

Front engine mounts for the 8-5.0L and 8-5.7L in V series trucks

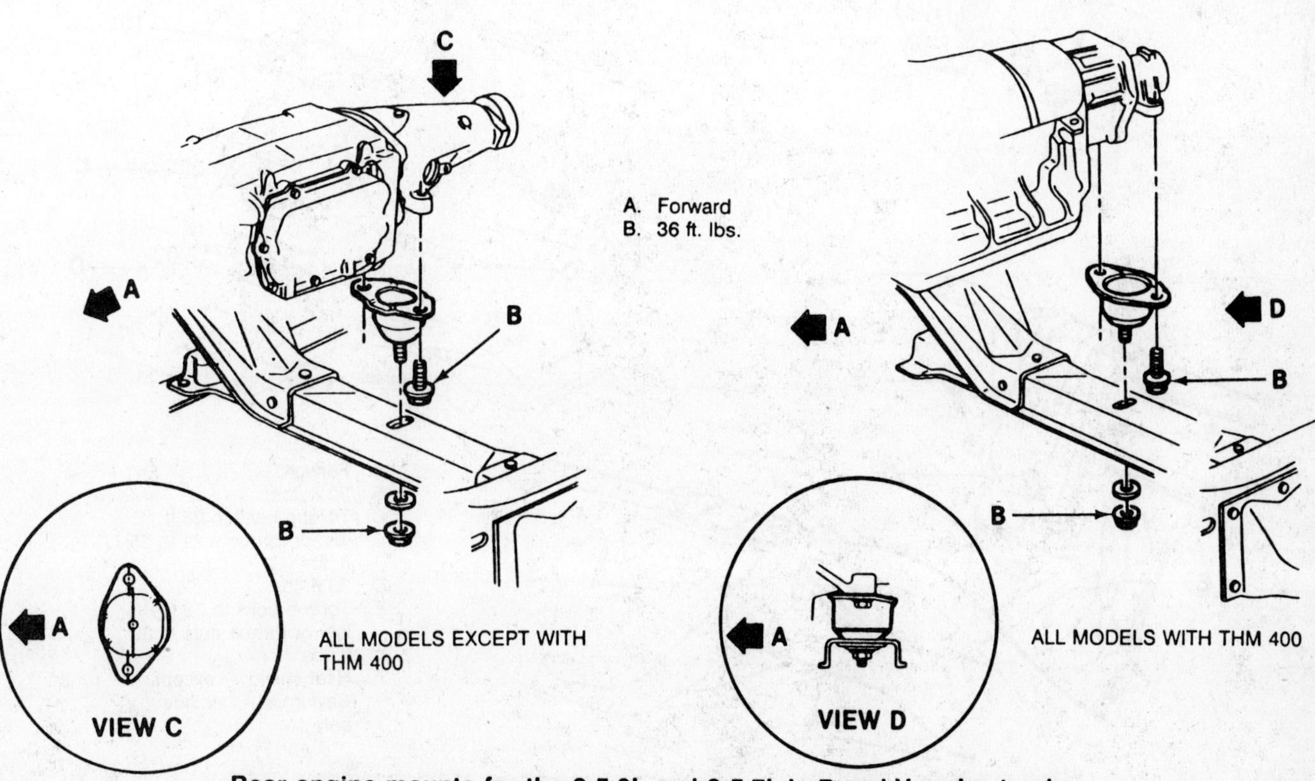

Rear engine mounts for the 8-5.0L and 8-5.7L in R and V series trucks

A. 40 ft. lbs.
B. 36 ft. lbs.
C. Forward
C
A
B

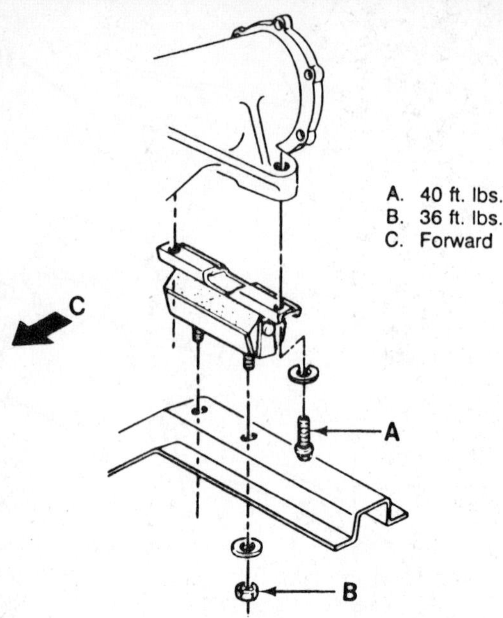

Rear engine mounts for the 8-5.0L and 8-5.7L in V series trucks

2. Disconnect the negative battery cable.
3. Drain the cooling system.

CAUTION

When draining the coolant, keep in mind that cats and dogs are attracted by the ethylene glycol antifreeze, and are quite likely to drink any that is left in an uncovered container or in puddles on the ground. This will prove fatal in sufficient quantity. Always drain the coolant into a sealable container. Coolant should be reused unless it is contaminated or several years old.

4. Remove the air cleaner.
5. Remove the radiator and fan shroud.
6. Disconnect and tag all necessary engine wiring.
7. Disconnect the accelerator, cruise control and TVS linkage.
8. Disconnect the fuel supply lines.
9. Disconnect all necessary vacuum wires.
10. Disconnect the air conditioning compressor, if used, and lay aside.
11. Dismount the power steering pump and position it out of the way. It's not necessary to disconnect the fluid lines.
12. Raise the vehicle and support it on jackstands.
13. Disconnect the exhaust pipes from the manifold.
14. Remove the starter.
15. Remove the torque converter cover.
16. Remove the converter-to-flex plate bolts.
17. Lower the vehicle and suitably support the transmission. Attach a suitable lifting fixture to the engine.

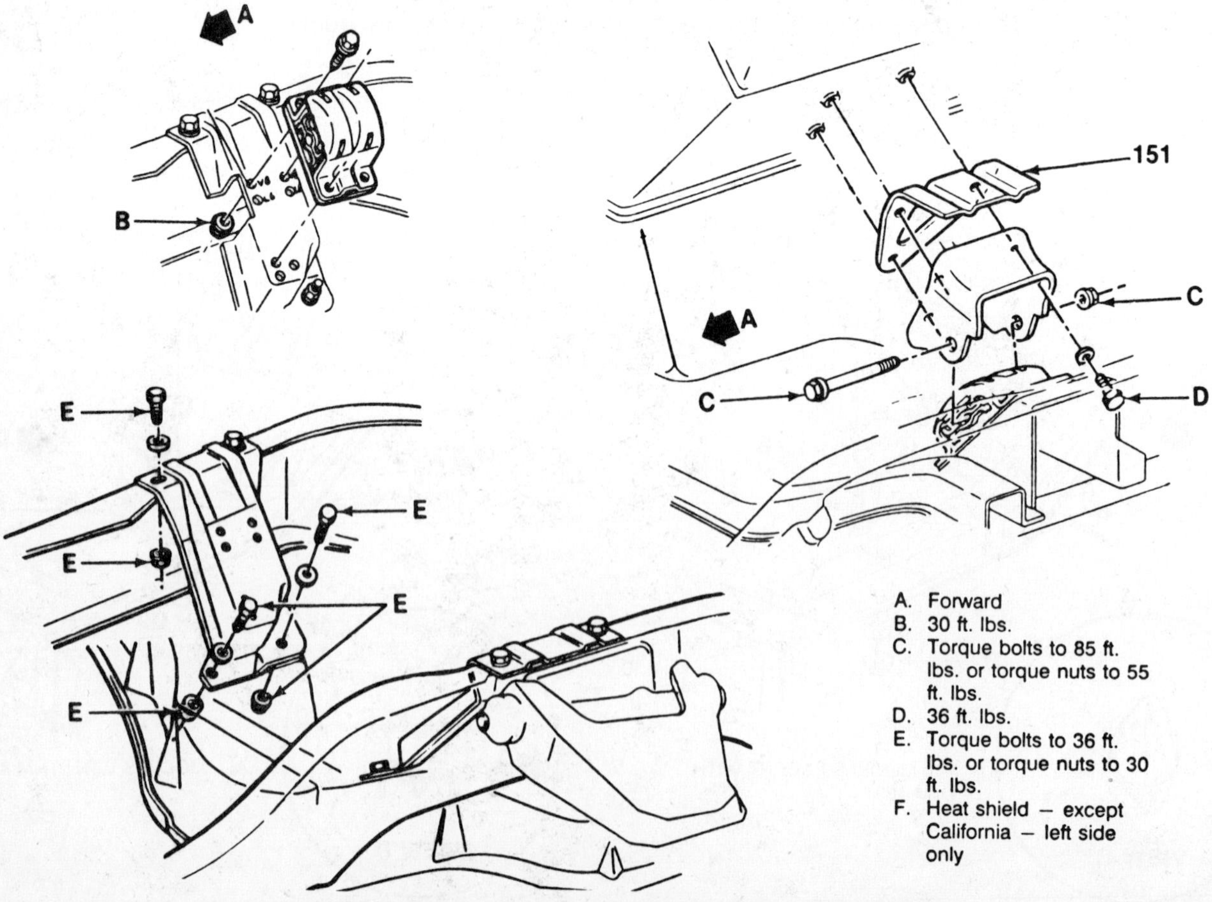

A
B
151
A
C
C
D
E
E
E
E
E
A. Forward
B. 30 ft. lbs.
C. Torque bolts to 85 ft. lbs. or torque nuts to 55 ft. lbs.
D. 36 ft. lbs.
E. Torque bolts to 36 ft. lbs. or torque nuts to 30 ft. lbs.
F. Heat shield – except California – left side only

Front engine mounts for the 8-7.4L in R series trucks

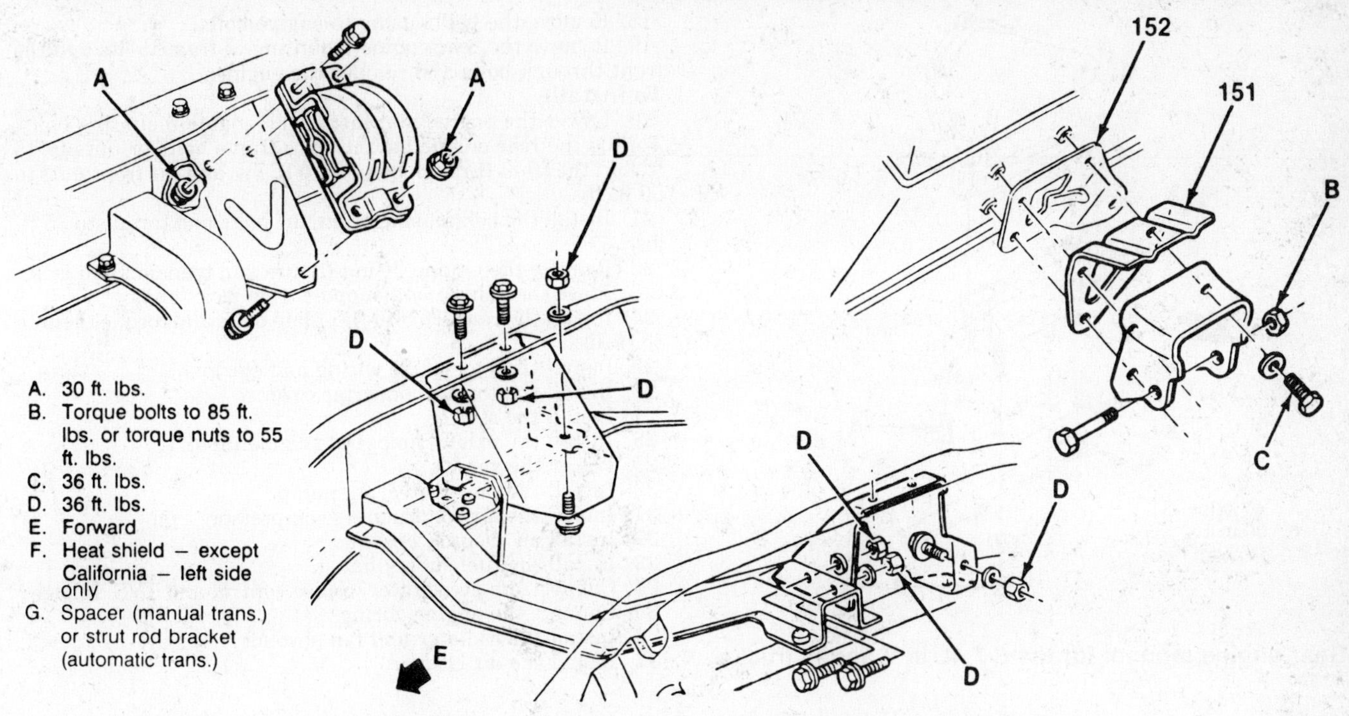

Front engine mounts for the 8-7.4L in V series trucks

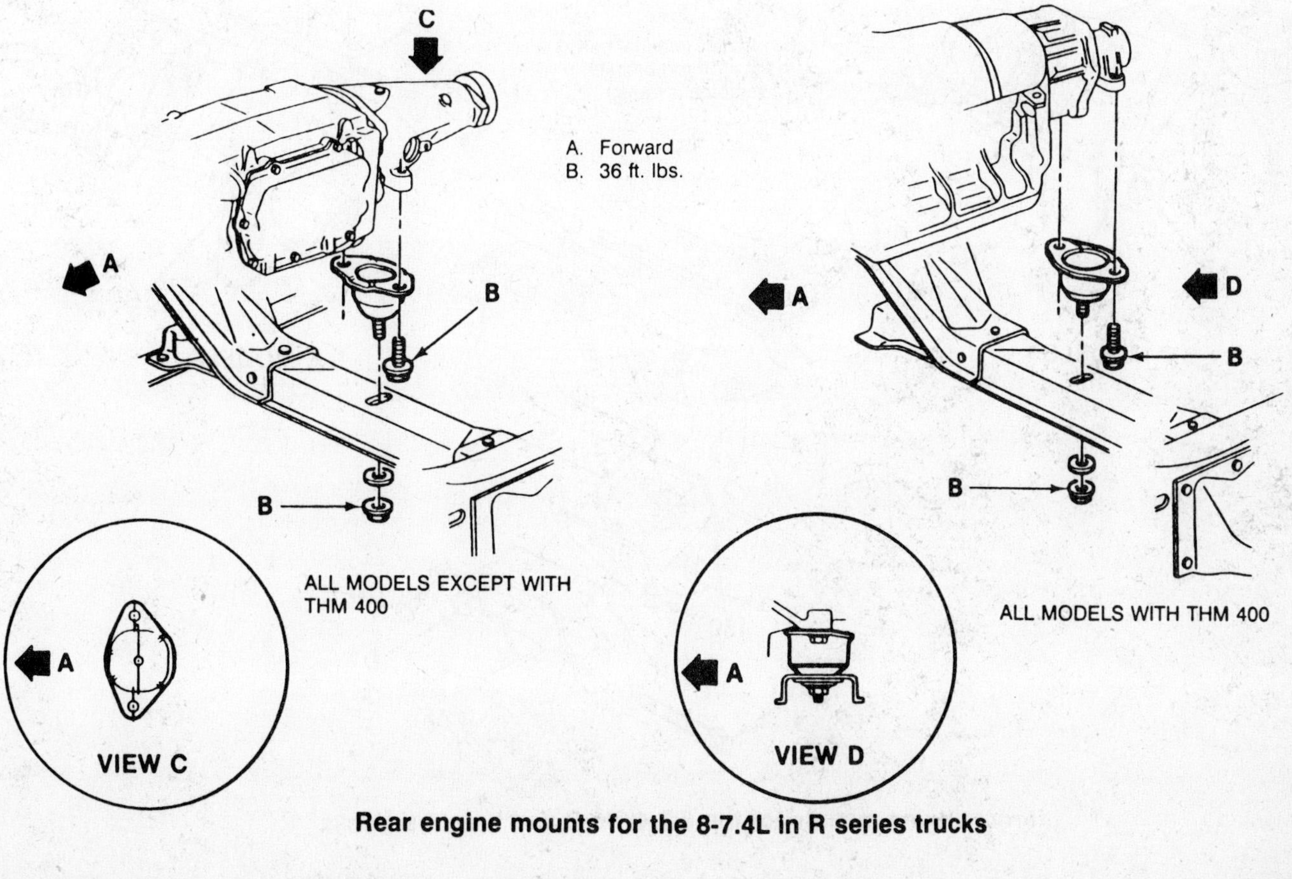

A. Forward
B. 36 ft. lbs.

ALL MODELS EXCEPT WITH THM 400

ALL MODELS WITH THM 400

VIEW C

VIEW D

Rear engine mounts for the 8-7.4L in R series trucks

C
A
B
A. 40 ft. lbs.
B. 36 ft. lbs.
C. Forward

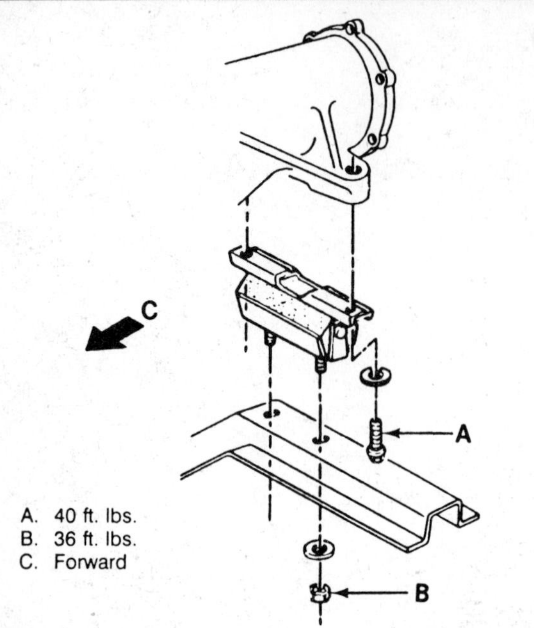

Rear engine mounts for the 8-7.4L in V series trucks

18. Remove the bellhousing-to-engine bolts.
19. Remove the rear engine mounting-to-frame bolts and the front through bolts and remove the engine.

To install:

20. Lower the engine and install the engine mounting bolts. Torque the rear engine mounting-to-frame bolts or nuts to 45 ft. lbs., the front through bolts to 70 ft. lbs. and the front nuts to 50 ft. lbs.
21. Install the bellhousing-to-engine bolts and torque to 35 ft. lbs.
22. Remove the engine lifting fixture and transmission jack.
23. Raise the vehicle and support it on jackstands.
24. Install the converter-to-flex plate bolts and torque them to 35 ft. lbs.
25. Install the fuel gauge wiring and starter.
26. Install the torque converter cover.
27. Install the starter.
28. Install the exhaust pipes at the manifold.
29. Lower the vehicle.
30. Install the power steering pump.
31. Install the air conditioning compressor.
32. Install all vacuum hoses.
33. Install the fuel supply line.
34. Connect the accelerator, cruise control and TVS linkage.
35. Connect the engine wiring.
36. Install the radiator and fan shroud.
37. Install the air cleaner.

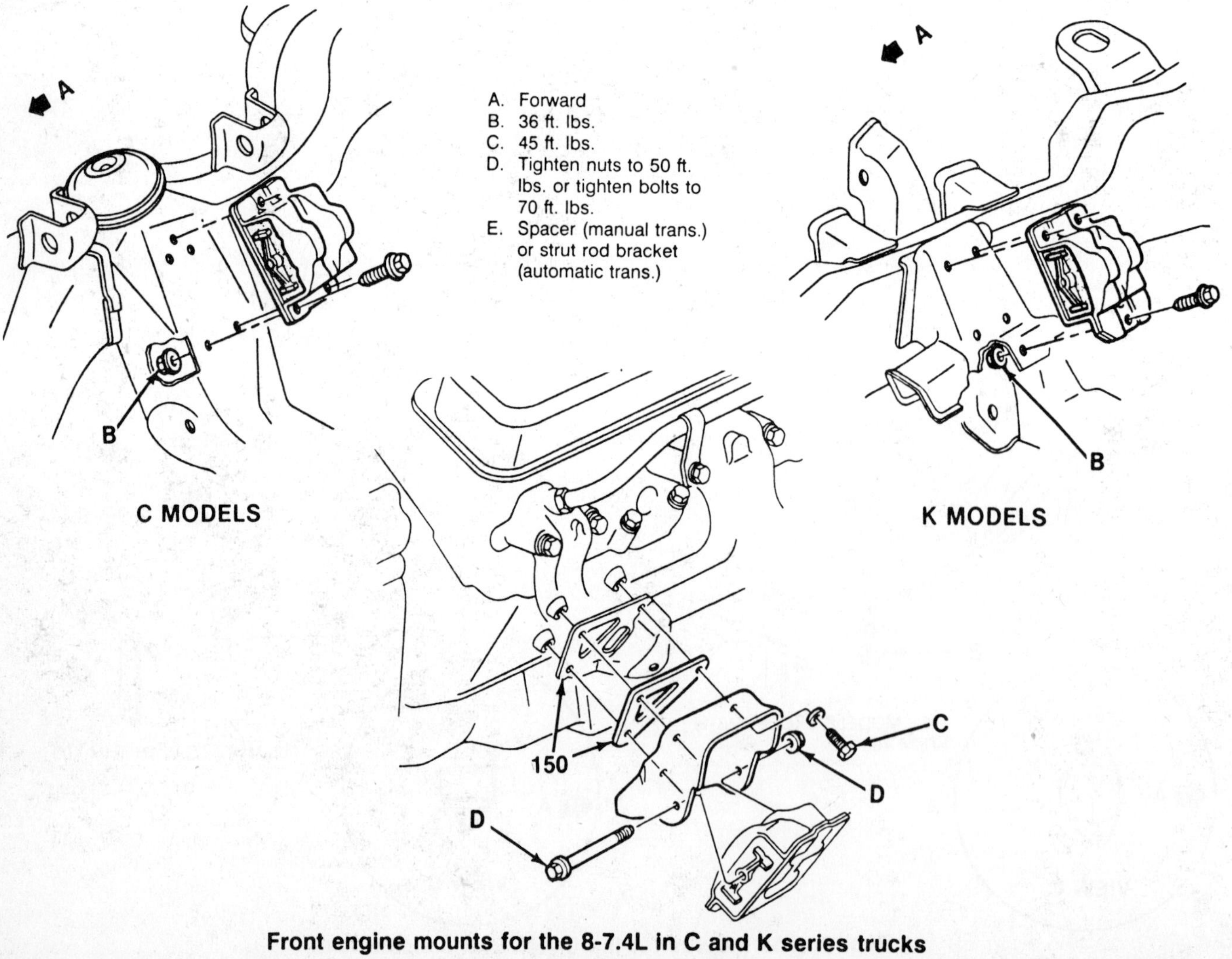

A
B
C MODELS
A. Forward
B. 36 ft. lbs.
C. 45 ft. lbs.
D. Tighten nuts to 50 ft. lbs. or tighten bolts to 70 ft. lbs.
E. Spacer (manual trans.) or strut rod bracket (automatic trans.)
A
B
K MODELS
150
C
D
D

Front engine mounts for the 8-7.4L in C and K series trucks

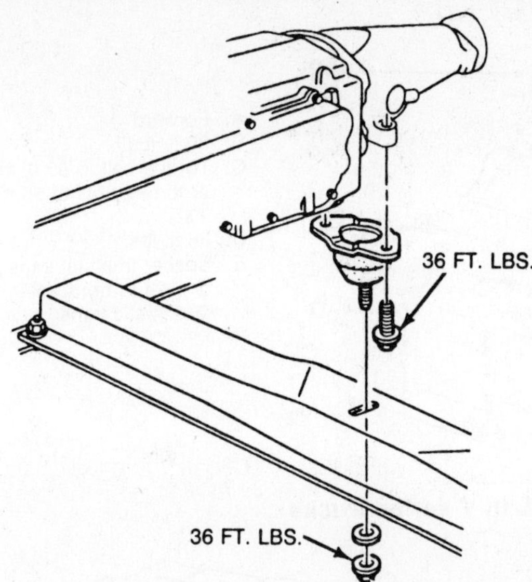

Rear engine mounts for the 8-7.4L in C series trucks

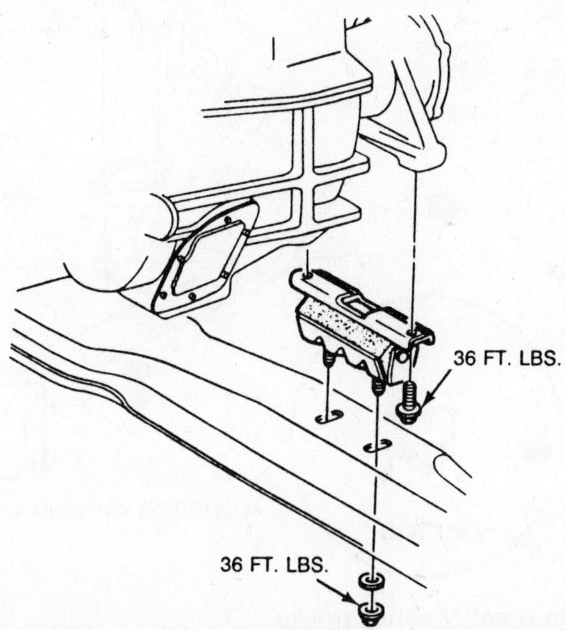

Rear engine mounts for the 8-7.4L in K series trucks

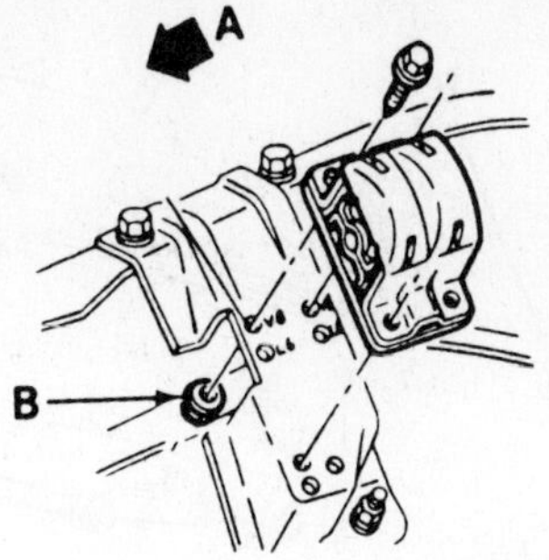

A. Forward
B. 30 ft. lbs.
C. Torque bolt to 85 ft. lbs. or torque nuts to 55 ft. lbs.
D. 36 ft. lbs.
E. Torque bolts to 36 ft. lbs. or torque nuts to 30 ft.lbs.

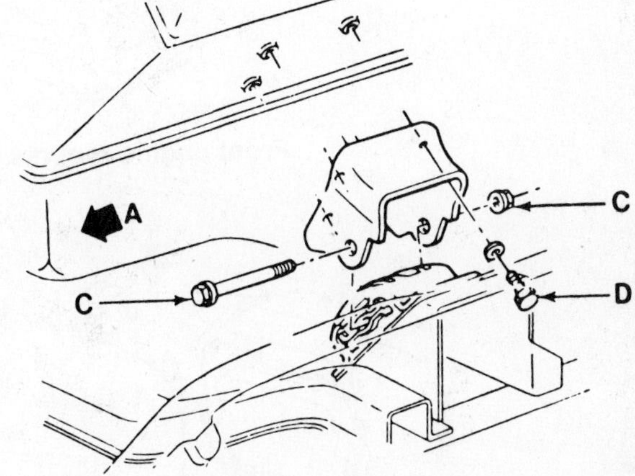

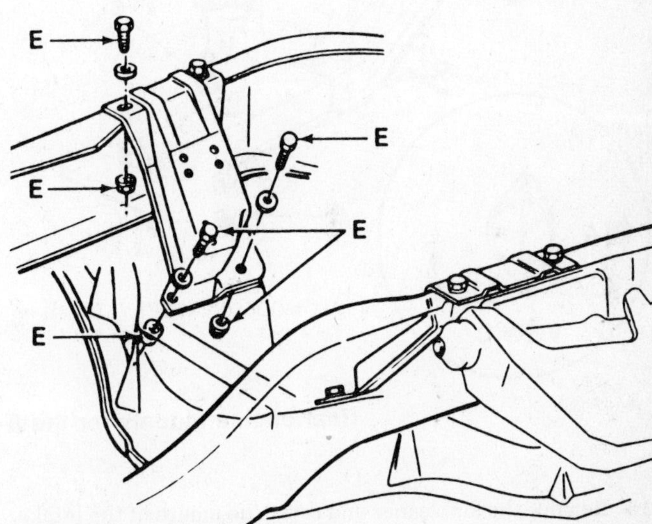

Front engine mounts for the 8-6.2L in R series trucks

38. Install the hood.
39. Connect the negative battery cable.
40. Install the proper quantity and grade of coolant.

8–6.2L

1. Disconnect the negative battery cable.
2. Raise the vehicle and support it safely.
3. Remove the flywheel or torque converter cover.
4. On vehicles equipped with automatic transmission, remove the converter-to-flex plate bolts.
5. Disconnect the exhaust pipes from the manifold.
6. Remove the starter.
7. Remove the bellhousing bolts.
8. Remove the engine mounting through bolts.
9. Disconnect the block heater wiring.
10. Disconnect the wiring harness, transmission cooler lines, and a battery cable clamp at the oil pan.
11. Disconnect the fuel return lines at the engine.
12. Disconnect the oil cooler lines at the engine.
13. Lower the vehicle.
14. Remove the hood.
15. Drain the cooling system.

CAUTION

When draining the coolant, keep in mind that cats and dogs are attracted by the ethylene glycol antifreeze, and are quite likely to drink any that is left in an uncovered container or in puddles on the ground. This will prove fatal in sufficient quantity. Always drain the coolant into a sealable container. Coolant should be reused unless it is contaminated or several years old.

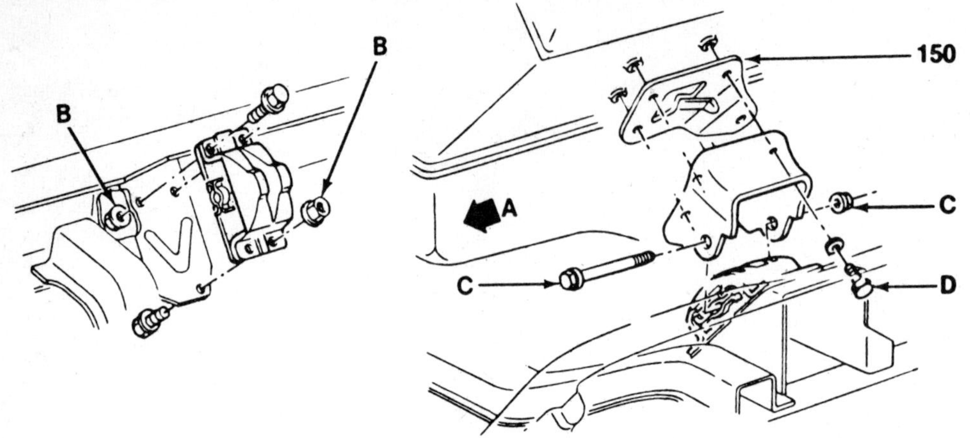

Front engine mounts for the 8-6.2L in V series trucks

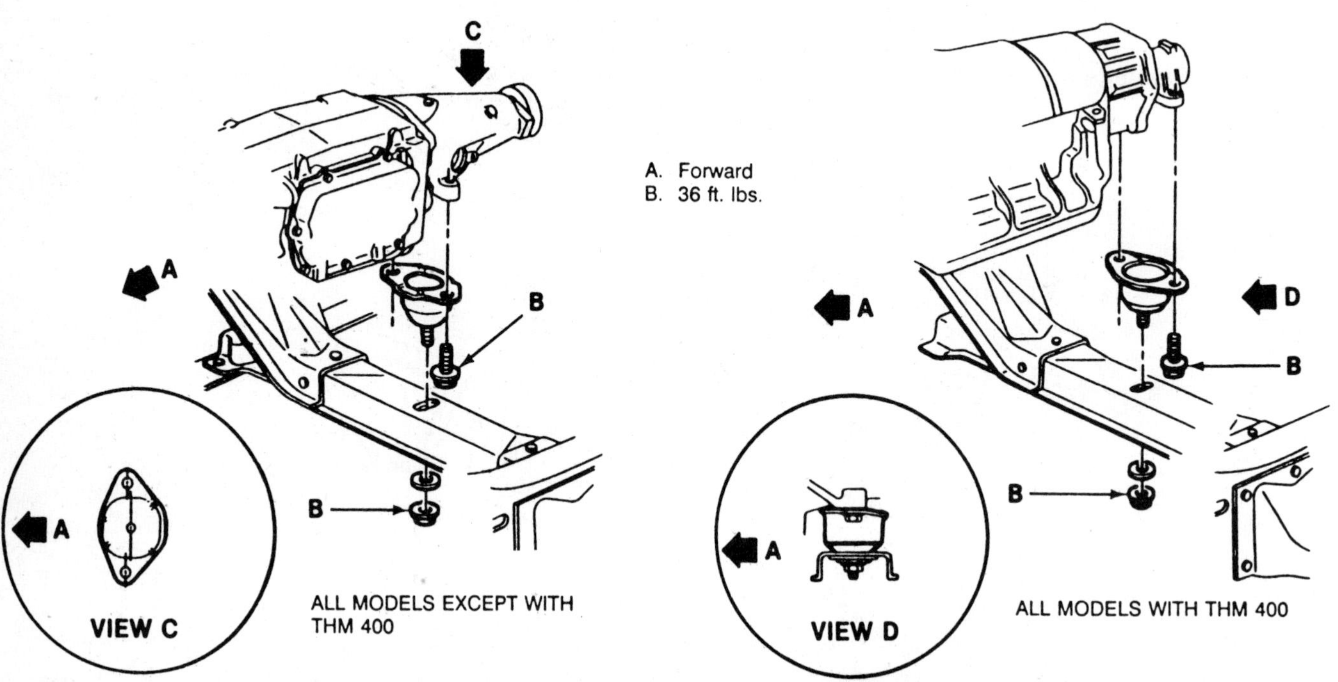

Rear engine mounts for the 8-6.2L in R and V series trucks

16. Remove the air cleaner and cover the mouth of the intake manifold.
17. Remove the alternator wires and clips.
18. Disconnect the wiring at the injector pump.
19. Disconnect the wiring from the rocker cover including the glow plug wires.
20. Disconnect the EGR-EPR solenoids, glow plug controller and temperature solenoid and move the harness aside.
21. Disconnect the left or right ground strap.
22. Remove the upper fan shroud and fan.
23. Disconnect the power steering pump and reservoir and lay to one side.
24. Disconnect the accelerator, cruise control and detent cables at the injection pump.
25. Disconnect the heater hose at the engine.
26. Remove the radiator.
27. Support the transmission with a suitable jack.
28. Remove the engine.

To install:

29. Lower the engine and install the engine mounting bolts. Torque the rear engine mounting to frame bolts or nuts to 45 ft. lbs., the front through bolts to 70 ft. lbs. and the front nuts to 50 ft. lbs.
30. Install the bellhousing-to-engine bolts and torque to 30 ft. lbs.
31. Remove the engine lifting fixture and transmission jack.
32. Raise the vehicle and support it on jackstands.
33. Install the converter-to-flex plate bolts and torque to 35 ft. lbs.
34. Install the fuel gauge wiring and starter.
35. Install the flywheel or torque converter cover.
36. Install the starter.
37. Install the exhaust pipes at the manifold.
38. Connect the wiring harness, transmission cooler lines, and a battery cable clamp at the oil pan.
40. Connect the fuel return lines at the engine.

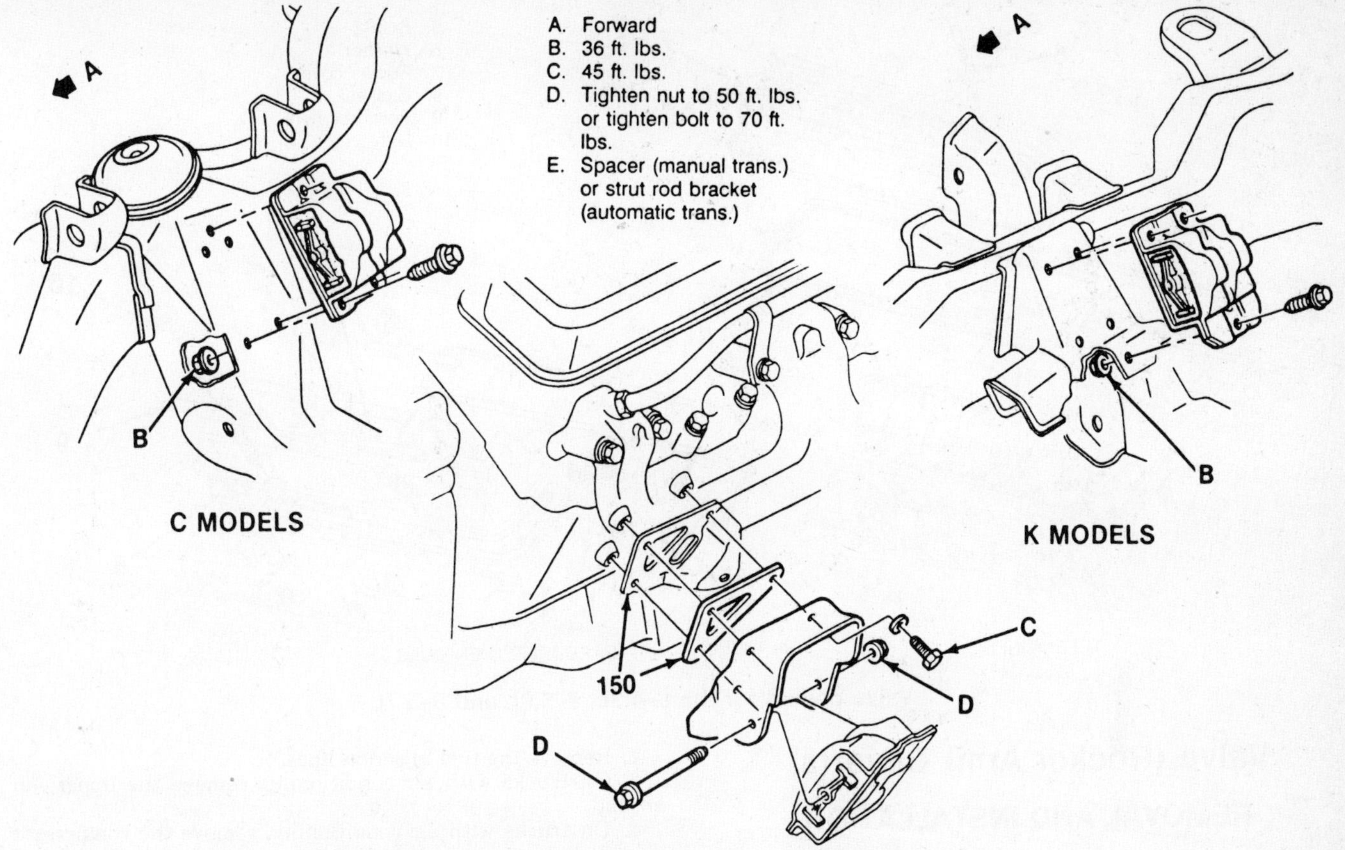

A. Forward
B. 36 ft. lbs.
C. 45 ft. lbs.
D. Tighten nut to 50 ft. lbs. or tighten bolt to 70 ft. lbs.
E. Spacer (manual trans.) or strut rod bracket (automatic trans.)
A
B
C MODELS
150
C
D
D
A
B
K MODELS

Front engine mounts for the 8-6.2L in C and K series trucks

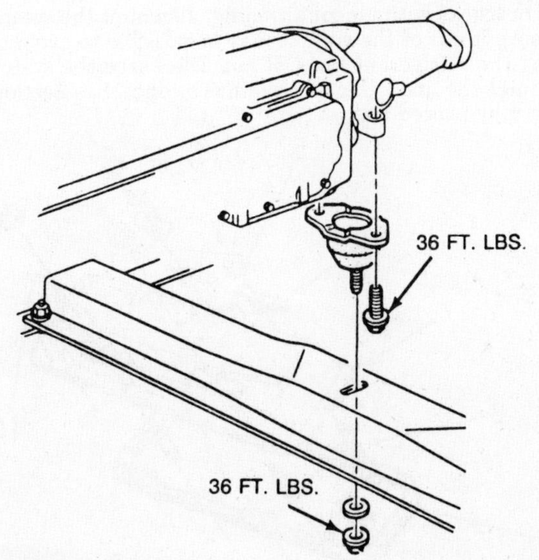

36 FT. LBS.
36 FT. LBS.

Rear engine mounts for the 8-6.2L in C series trucks

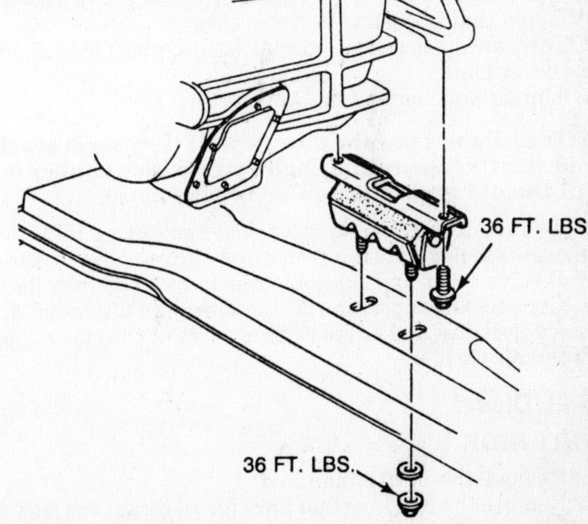

36 FT. LBS.
36 FT. LBS.

Rear engine mounts for the 8-6.2L in K series trucks

42. Connect the oil cooler lines at the engine.
38. Lower the vehicle.
40. Install the radiator.
41. Install the heater hose to the engine.
42. Connect the accelerator, cruise control and detent cables at the injection pump.
43. Connect the power steering pump and reservoir.
44. Install the fan and the upper fan shroud.
45. Install the ground strap.
46. Connect the wiring to the rocker cover including the glow plug wires.
47. Connect the EGR-EPR solenoids, glow plug controller and temperature solenoid harness.
48. Connect the alternator wires and clips.
49. Connect the wiring at the injector pump.
50. Install the air cleaner.
51. Install the hood.
52. Connect the negative battery cable.
53. Install the proper quantity and grade of coolant.

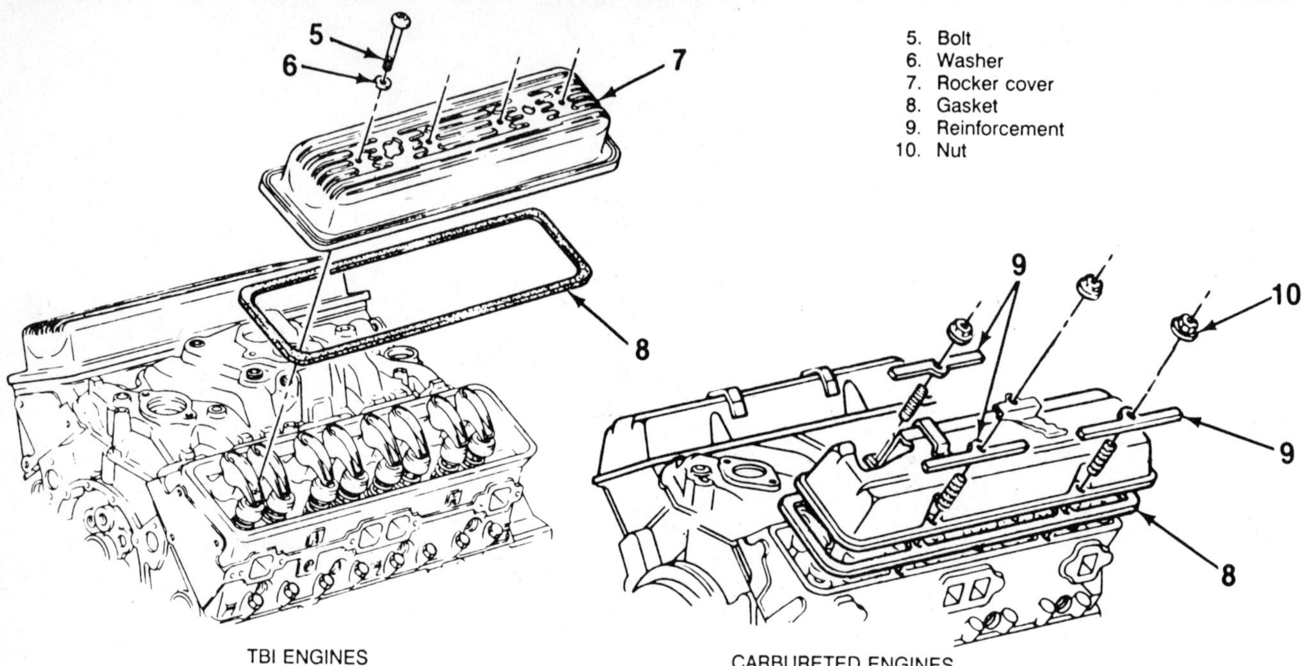

Valve covers for the 6–4.3L, 8–5.0L and 8–5.7L

Valve (Rocker Arm) Cover(s)

REMOVAL AND INSTALLATION

All Gasoline Engines

1. Remove air cleaner.
2. Disconnect and reposition as necessary any vacuum or PCV hoses that obstruct the valve covers.
3. Disconnect electrical wire(s) (spark plug, etc.) from the valve cover clips.
4. Unbolt and remove the valve cover(s).

NOTE: Do not pry the covers off if they seem stuck. Instead, gently tap around each cover with a rubber mallet until the old gasket or sealer breaks loose.

5. To install, use a new valve cover gasket or RTV (or any equivalent) sealer. If using sealer, follow directions on the tube. Install valve cover and tighten cover bolts to 36 inch lbs.
6. Connect and reposition all vacuum and PCV hoses, and reconnect electrical and/or spark plug wires at the cover clips. Install the air cleaner.

8–6.2L Diesel

RIGHT SIDE

1. Remove the intake manifold.
2. Remove the fuel injection lines for all except the Nos. 5 and 7 injectors.
3. Disconnect the glow plug wires.
4. Remove the wiring harness from the clip.
5. Remove the cover bolts.
6. Remove the cover. If the cover sticks, jar it loose with a plastic or rubber mallet. NEVER pry it loose!
7. Installation is the reverse of removal. Clean all old RTV gasket material from the mating surfaces. Apply a $^{5}/_{16}$ in. (8mm) bead of sealer to the head mating surfaces. Tighten the cover bolts to 16 ft. lbs.

LEFT SIDE

1. Remove the intake manifold.
2. Remove the fuel injection lines.
3. On trucks with air conditioning, remove the upper fan shroud.
4. On trucks with air conditioning, remove the compressor drive belt.
5. On trucks with air conditioning, remove the left exhaust manifold.
6. On trucks with air conditioning, dismount the compressor and move it out of the way. It may be possible to avoid disconnecting the refrigerant lines. If not, Discharge the system and disconnect the lines. Cap all openings at once. See Section 1 for discharging procedures.

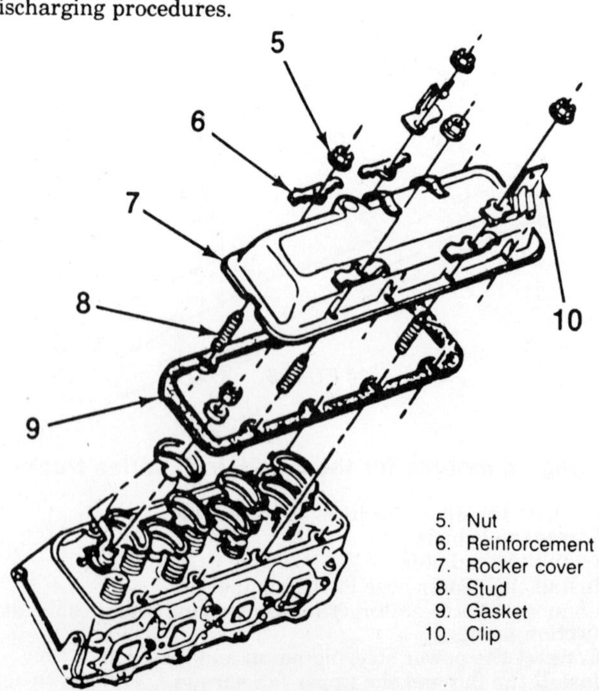

Valve cover for the 8–7.4L

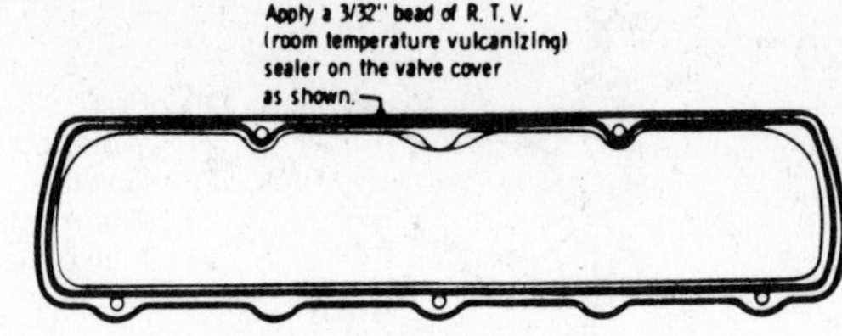

Correct RTV application on the rocker cover

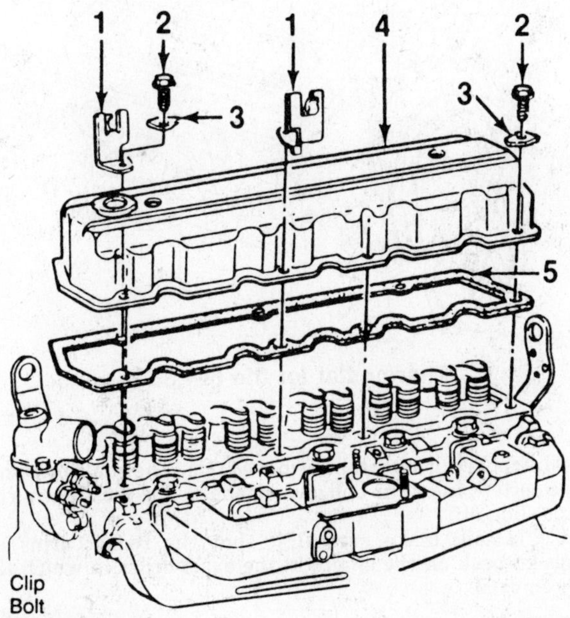

1. Clip
2. Bolt
3. Reinforcement
4. Rocker arm cover
5. Gasket

6–4.8L rocker arm cover installation

7. Remove the dipstick tube front bracket from the stud.
8. Remove the wiring harness brackets.
9. Remove the rocker arm cover bolts and fuel return bracket.
10. Remove the cover. If the cover sticks, jar it loose with a plastic or rubber mallet. NEVER pry it loose!
11. Installation is the reverse of removal. Clean all old RTV gasket material from the mating surfaces. Apply a $^5/_{16}$ in. (8mm) bead of sealer to the head mating surfaces. Tighten the cover bolts to 16 ft. lbs.

Pushrod (Engine Side) Cover

REMOVAL AND INSTALLATION

6–4.8L

1. Disconnect the batteru ground cable.
2. Remove the oil dipstick tube.
3. Remove the distributor.
4. Remove the side cover bolts.
5. Carefully pry off the side cover.
6. Remove all traces of the old gasket.
7. Installation is the reverse of removal. Use sealer on both sides of the gasket. Torque the bolts to 80 inch lbs.

Rocker Arms

REMOVAL AND INSTALLATION

6–4.8L

1. Remove the rocker arm cover.
2. Remove the rocker arm nut.
3. Remove the rocker arm and ball.
4. Coat the replacement rocker arm with Molycoat® or its equvalent, and the rocker arm and pivot with SAE 90 gear oil, and install the pivots.
5. Install the nut. See the valve adjustment procedure later in this section.
6. Install the cover.

8–5.0L
8–5.7L

1. Remove the valve cover.
2. Remove the rocker arm flanged bolts, and remove the rocker pivots.
3. Remove the rocker arms.

NOTE: Remove each set of rocker arms (one set per cylinder) as a unit.

4. To install, position a set of rocker arms (for one cylinder) in the proper location.

NOTE: Install the rocker arms for each cylinder only when the lifters are off the cam lobe and both valves are closed.

5. Coat the replacement rocker arm with Molycoat® or its equvalent, and the rocker arm and pivot with SAE 90 gear oil, and install the pivots.
6. Install the flange bolts and tighten alternately. See the valve adjustment procedure later in this section.

6–4.3L and 8–7.4L

1. Remove the valve cover.
2. Remove the rocker arm flanged bolts, and remove the rocker pivots.

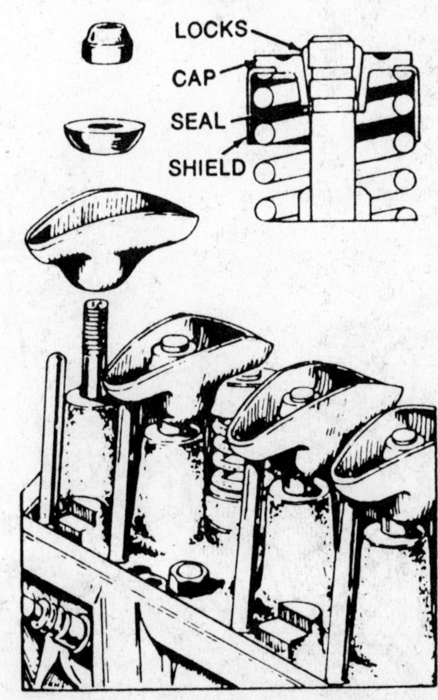

Typical gasoline engine rocker arm components

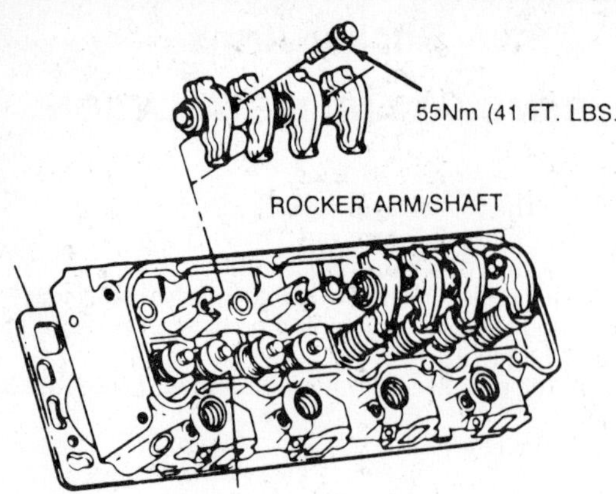

8–6.2L diesel rocker shaft assembly

3. Remove the rocker arms and the balls.

NOTE: Remove each set of rocker arms and balls (one set per cylinder) as a unit.

4. To install, position a set of rocker arms, and balls (for one cylinder) in the proper location.

NOTE: Install the rocker arms for each cylinder only when the lifters are off the cam lobe and both valves are closed.

5. Coat the replacement rocker arms and balls with Molycoat® or its equvalent, and install the pivots.
6. Install the flange bolts and tighten alternately. See the valve adjustment procedure later in this section.

8–6.2L Diesel

1. Remove the valve cover as previously explained.
2. The rocker assemblies are mounted on two short rocker shafts per cylinder head, with each shaft operating four rockers. Remove the two bolts which secure each rocker shaft assembly, and remove the shaft.

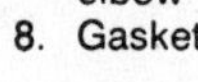

1. Bolt
2. Water outlet elbow
3. Gasket
4. Thermostat
5. Bolt
6. Stud
7. Thermostat adapter elbow
8. Gasket

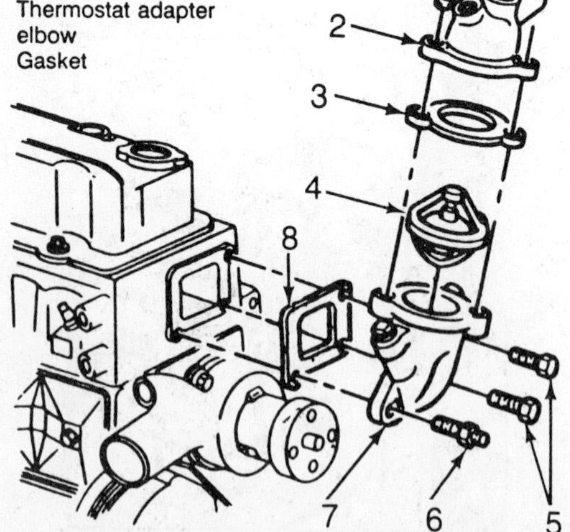

6–4.8L thermostat replacement

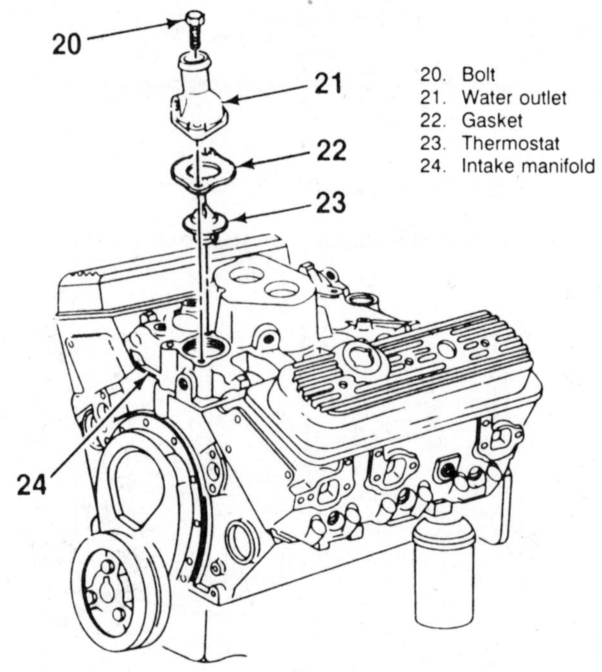

Thermostat for the 6–4.3L

3. The rocker arms can be removed from the shaft by removing the cotter pin on the end of each shaft. The rocker arms and springs slide off.
4. To install, make sure first that the rocker arms and springs go back on the shafts in the exact order in which they were removed.

NOTE: Always install new cotter pins on the rocker shaft ends.

5. Install the rocker shaft assemblies, torquing the bolts to 41 ft. lbs.

Thermostat

REMOVAL AND INSTALLATION

All Gasoline Engines

1. Drain the radiator until the level is below the thermostat level (below the level of the intake manifold).

CAUTION

When draining the coolant, keep in mind that cats and dogs are attracted by the ethylene glycol antifreeze, and are quite likely to drink any that is left in an uncovered container or in puddles on the ground. This will prove fatal in sufficient quantity. Always drain the coolant into a sealable container. Coolant should be reused unless it is contaminated or several years old.

2. Remove the water outlet elbow assembly from the engine. Remove the thermostat from the engine, or, on the 6–4.8L, from inside the adapter elbow.
3. Install new thermostat in the reverse order of removal, making sure the spring side is inserted into the engine, or, on the 6-4.8L, downward into the thermostat housing. Clean the gasket surfaces on the water outlet elbow and the intake manifold. Use a new gasket when installing the elbow to the mani-

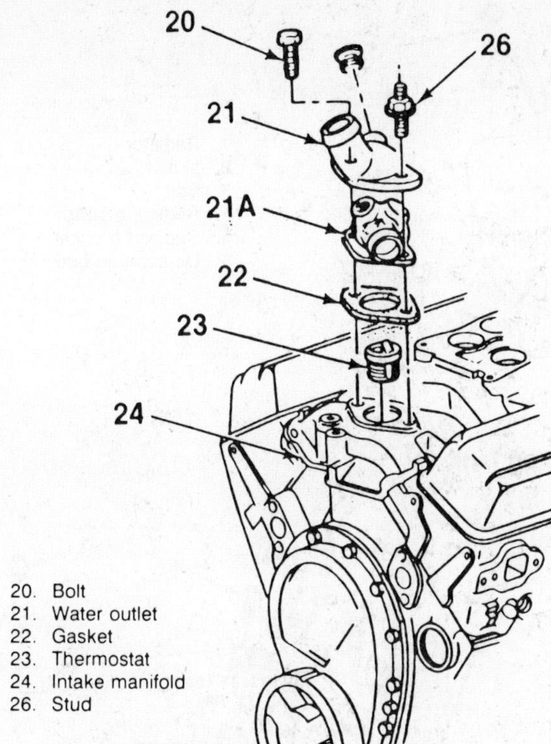

Thermostat for the 8–5.0L and 8–5.7L

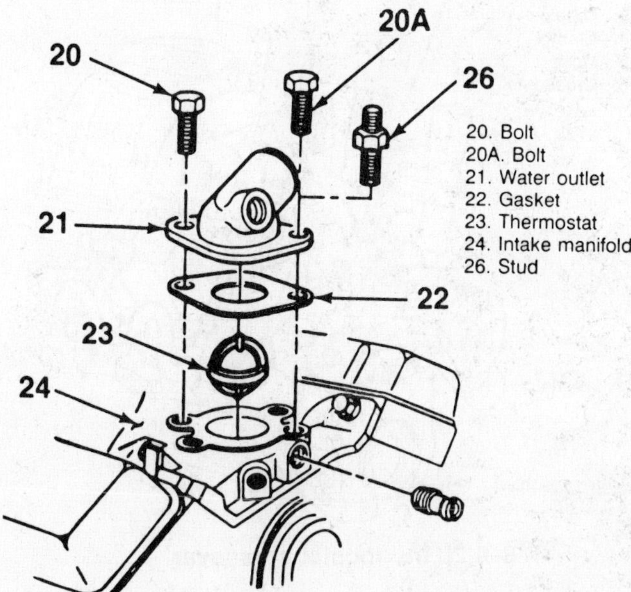

Thermostat for the 8–7.4L

fold. Torque the thermostat housing bolts to 20 ft. lbs. on all except the 6–4.8L. On that engine, torque the bolts to 28 ft. lbs.

4. Refill the cooling system.

8–6.2L Diesel

1. Remove the upper fan shroud.
2. Drain the cooling system to a point below the thermostat.

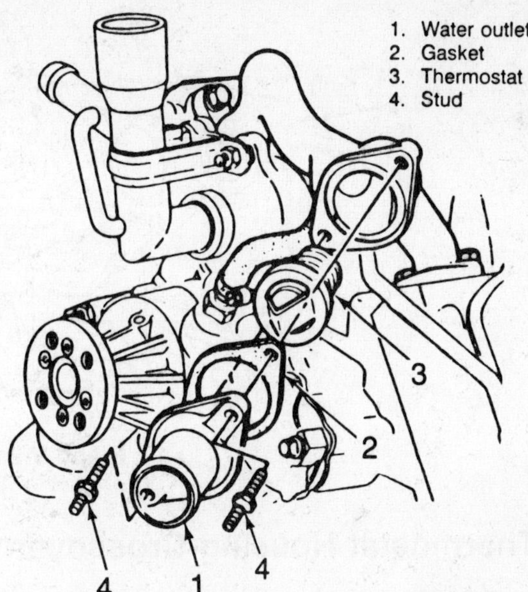

8–6.2L diesel thermostat replacement

CAUTION

When draining the coolant, keep in mind that cats and dogs are attracted by the ethylene glycol antifreeze, and are quite likely to drink any that is left in an uncovered container or in puddles on the ground. This will prove fatal in sufficient quantity. Always drain the coolant into a sealable container. Coolant should be reused unless it is contaminated or several years old.

3. Remove the engine oil dipstick tube brace and the oil fill brace.
4. Remove the upper radiator hose.
5. Remove the water outlet.
6. Remove the thermostat and gasket.
7. Installation is the reverse of removal. Use a new gasket coated with sealer, Make sure that the spring end of the thermostat is in the engine. Torque the bolts to 35 ft. lbs.

De–Aeration Tank

REMOVAL AND INSTALLATION

R and V Series

1. Drain the cooling system to a point below the level of the tank.

CAUTION

When draining the coolant, keep in mind that cats and dogs are attracted by the ethylene glycol antifreeze, and are quite likely to drink any that is left in an uncovered container or in puddles on the ground. This will prove fatal in sufficient quantity. Always drain the coolant into a sealable container. Coolant should be reused unless it is contaminated or several years old.

2. Disconnect the overflow hose from the radiator.
3. Disconnect the return hose from the tank.
4. Remove the tank's mounting screw and bolt and lift the tank from the truck.
5. Installation is the reverse of removal.
6. Fill the cooling system.

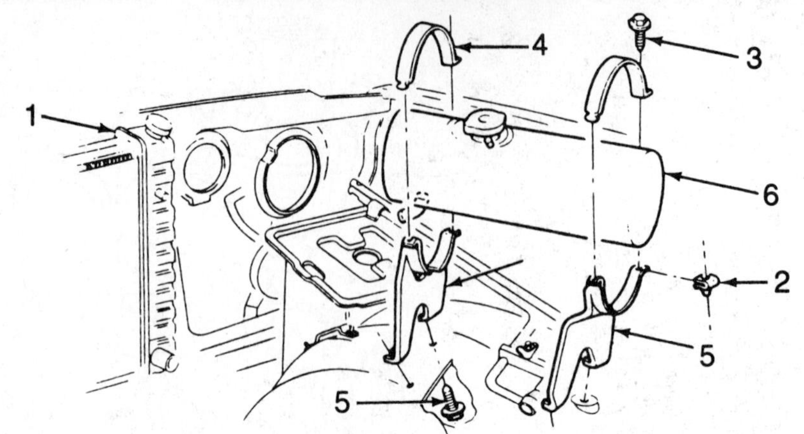

R and V series de-aeration tank

Thermostat Housing Crossover

REMOVAL AND INSTALLATION

Diesel Engine

1. Drain the cooling system.

CAUTION

When draining the coolant, keep in mind that cats and dogs are attracted by the ethylene glycol antifreeze, and are quite likely to drink any that is left in an uncovered container or in puddles on the ground. This will prove fatal in sufficient quantity. Always drain the coolant into a sealable container. Coolant should be reused unless it is contaminated or several years old.

2. Remove the engine cover.
3. Remove the air cleaner.
4. Remove the air cleaner resonator and bracket.
5. Remove the upper fan shroud.
6. Remove the upper alternator bracket.
7. Remove the bypass hose.
8. Remove the upper radiator hose.
9. Disconnect the heater hose.
10. Remove the attaching bolts and lift out the crossover.

To install:

11. Thoroughly clean the mating surfaces.
12. Position the crossover, using new gaskets coated with sealer.
13. Install the attaching bolts and torque them to 35 ft. lbs.
14. Connect the heater hose.
15. Install the upper radiator hose.
16. Install the bypass hose.
17. Install the upper alternator bracket.
18. Install the upper fan shroud.
19. Install the air cleaner resonator and bracket.
20. Install the air cleaner.
21. Install the engine cover.
22. Fill the cooling system.

Intake Manifold

NOTE: For the 6–4.8L, see Combination Manifold, below.

REMOVAL AND INSTALLATION

6–4.3L

1. Drain the cooling system.

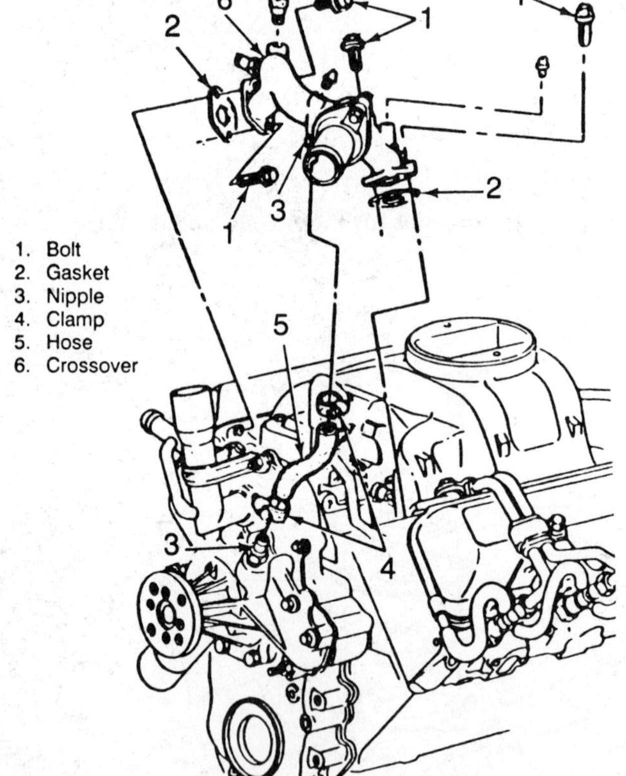

8–6.2L thermostat crossover

CAUTION

When draining the coolant, keep in mind that cats and dogs are attracted by the ethylene glycol antifreeze, and are quite likely to drink any that is left in an uncovered container or in puddles on the ground. This will prove fatal in sufficient quantity. Always drain the coolant into a sealable container. Coolant should be reused unless it is contaminated or several years old.

2. Remove the air cleaner assembly.
3. Remove the thermostat housing and the bypass hose. It is not necessary to remove the top radiator hose from the thermostat housing.

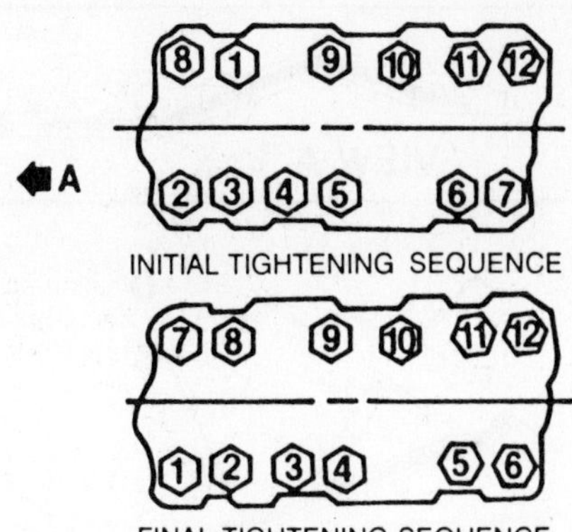

A. Front of Engine

Intake manifold bolt tightening sequence for the 6–4.3L

4. Disconnect the heater hose at the rear of the manifold.
5. Disconnect all electrical connections and vacuum lines from the manifold. Remove the EGR valve if necessary.
6. On vehicles equipped with power brakes remove the vacuum line from the vacuum booster to the manifold.
7. Remove the distributor (if necessary).
8. Remove the fuel line at the TBI unit.
9. Remove the accelerator linkage.
10. Remove the TBI unit.
11. Remove the intake manifold bolts. Remove the manifold and the gaskets. Remember to reinstall the O-ring between the intake manifold and timing chain cover during assembly, if so equipped.

To install:

NOTE: Before installing the intake manifold, be sure that the gasket surfaces are thoroughly clean.

13. Use plastic gasket retainers to prevent the manifold gasket from slipping out of place, if so equipped.
14. Install the manifold and the gaskets. Remember to reinstall the O-ring between the intake manifold and timing chain cover, if so equipped.
15. Install the intake manifold bolts.
16. Install the TBI unit.
17. Install the TBI linkage.
18. Install the fuel line.
19. Install the distributor (if necessary).
20. On vehicles equipped with power brakes install the vacuum line between the vacuum booster and manifold.
21. Connect all electrical connections and vacuum lines at the manifold. Install the EGR valve if necessary.
22. Connect the heater hose at the rear of the manifold.
23. Install the thermostat housing and the bypass hose.
24. Install the air cleaner assembly.
25. Fill the cooling system.

8–5.0L

8–5.7L

1. Drain the cooling system.

CAUTION

When draining the coolant, keep in mind that cats and dogs are attracted by the ethylene glycol antifreeze, and are quite likely to drink any that is left in an uncovered container or in puddles on the ground. This will prove fatal in sufficient quantity. Always drain the coolant into a sealable container. Coolant should be reused unless it is contaminated or several years old.

2. Remove the air cleaner assembly.
3. Remove the thermostat housing and the bypass hose. It is not necessary to remove the top radiator hose from the thermostat housing.
4. Disconnect the heater hose at the rear of the manifold.
5. Disconnect all electrical connections and vacuum lines from the manifold. Remove the EGR valve if necessary.

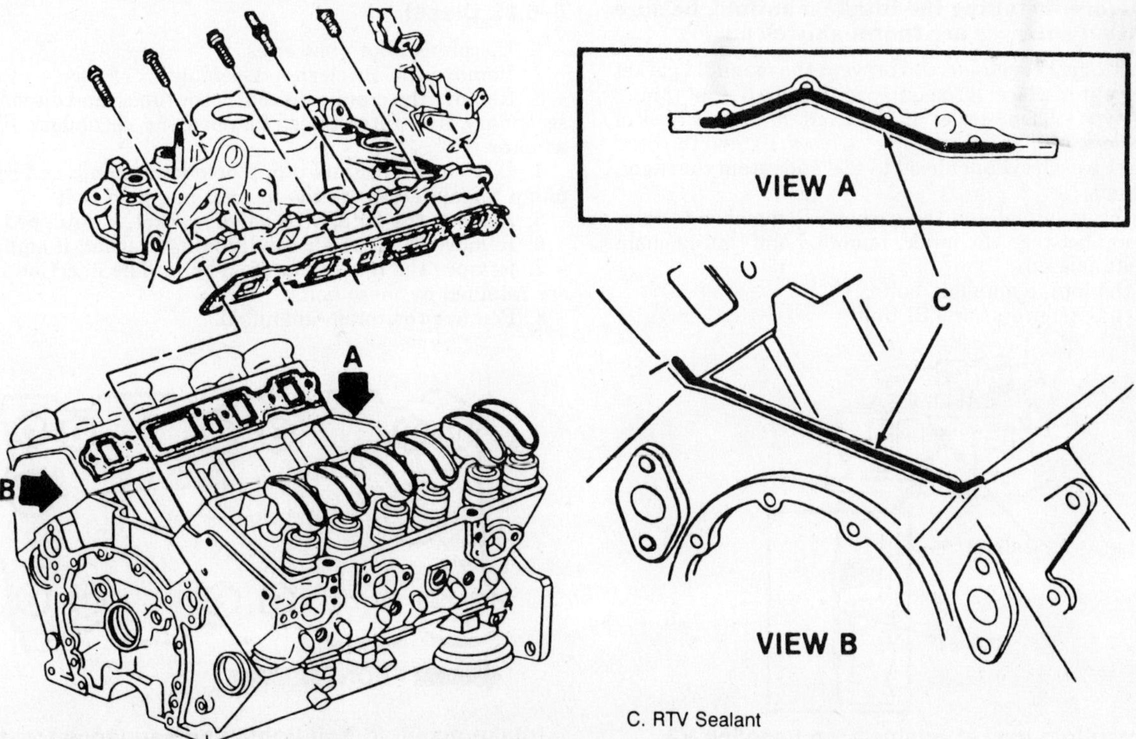

C. RTV Sealant

6–4.3L intake manifold

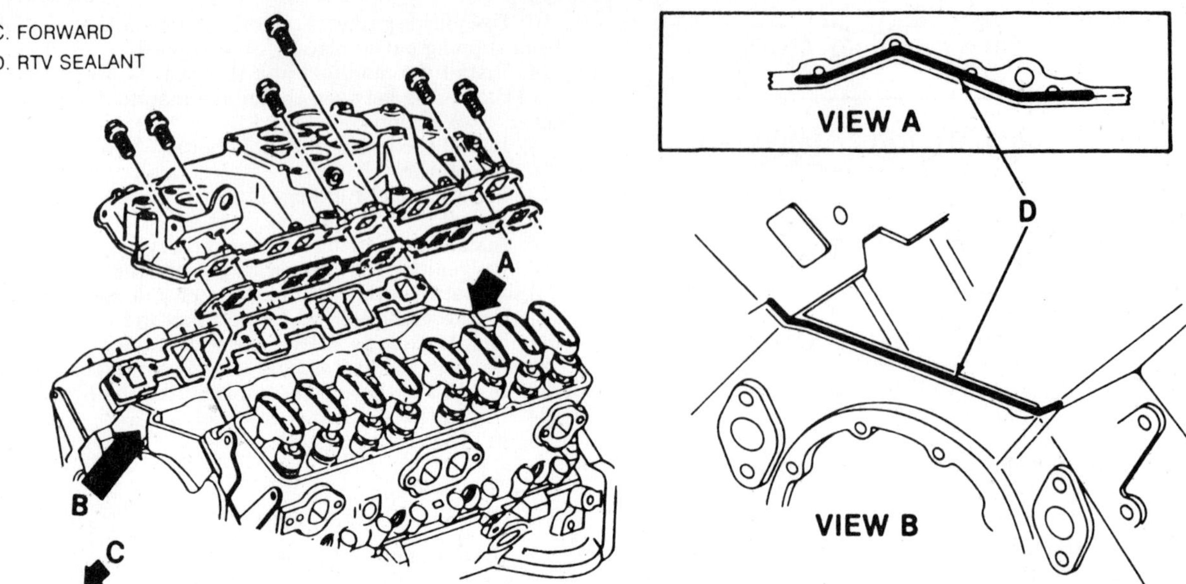

Intake manifold for the 8–5.0L or 8–5.7L

6. On vehicles equipped with power brakes remove the vacuum line from the vacuum booster to the manifold.
7. Remove the distributor (if necessary).
8. Remove the fuel line at the carburetor or TBI unit.
9. Remove the accelerator linkage.
10. Remove the carburetor or TBI unit.
11. Remove the intake manifold bolts. Remove the manifold and the gaskets. Remember to reinstall the O-ring between the intake manifold and timing chain cover during assembly, if so equipped.

To install:

NOTE: Before installing the intake manifold, be sure that the gasket surfaces are thoroughly clean.

13. Use plastic gasket retainers to prevent the manifold gasket from slipping out of place, if so equipped. Place a $^3/_{16}$ in. (5mm) bead of RTV type silicone sealer on the front and rear ridges of the cylinder block-to-manifold mating surfaces. Extend the bead ½ in. (13mm) up each cylinder head to seal and retain the manifold side gaskets.
14. Install the manifold and the gaskets. Remember to reinstall the O-ring between the intake manifold and timing chain cover, if so equipped.
15. Install the intake manifold bolts.
16. Install the carburetor or TBI unit.
17. Install the carburetor or TBI linkage.
18. Install the fuel line.
19. Install the distributor (if necessary).
20. On vehicles equipped with power brakes install the vacuum line between the vacuum booster and manifold.
21. Connect all electrical connections and vacuum lines at the manifold. Install the EGR valve if necessary.
22. Connect the heater hose at the rear of the manifold.
23. Install the thermostat housing and the bypass hose.
24. Install the air cleaner assembly.
25. Fill the cooling system.

8–6.2L Diesel

1. Disconnect both batteries.
2. Remove the air cleaner assembly.
3. Remove the crankcase ventilator tubes, and disconnect the secondary fuel filter lines. Remove the secondary filter and adaptor.
4. Loosen the vacuum pump holddown clamp and rotate the pump to gain access to the nearest manifold bolt.
5. Remove the EPR/EGR valve bracket, if equipped.
6. Remove the rear air conditioning bracket, if equipped.
7. Remove the intake manifold bolts. The injection line clips are retained by these bolts.
8. Remove the intake manifold.

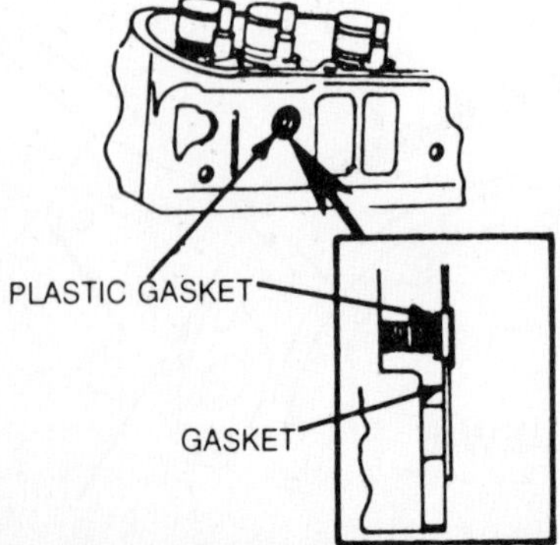

Plastic manifold gasket retainers on gasoline V8 engines

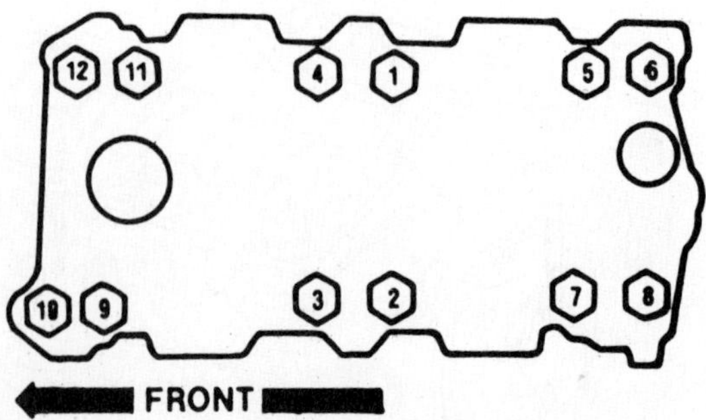

Intake manifold bolt tightening sequence for the 8–5.0L or 8–5.7L

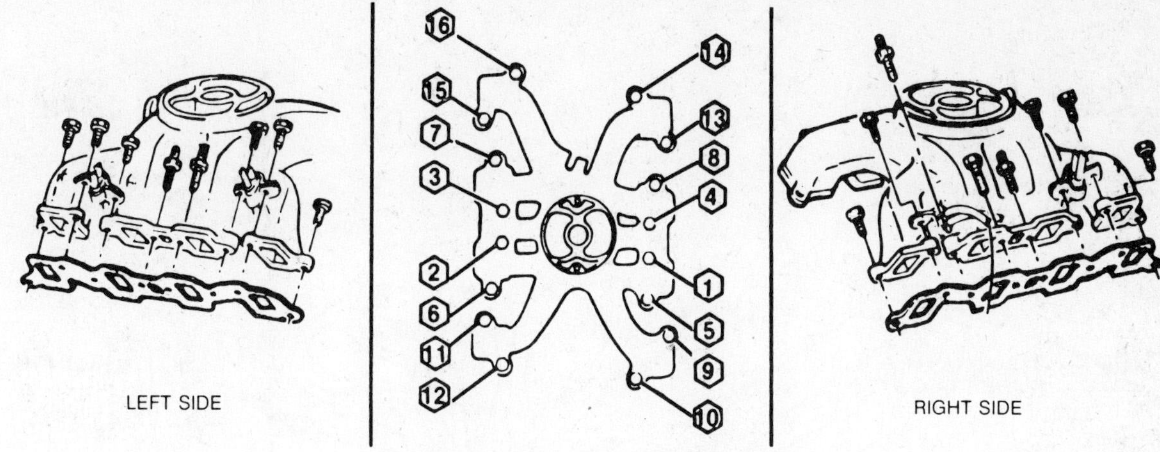

Intake manifold for the 6.2L diesel

NOTE: If the engine is to be further serviced with the manifold removed, install protective covers over the intake ports.

To install:

9. Clean the manifold gasket surfaces on the cylinder heads and install new gaskets before installing the manifold.

NOTE: The gaskets have an opening for the EGR valve on light duty installations. An insert covers this opening on heavy duty installations.

10. Install the manifold. Torque the bolts in the sequence illustrated.
11. The secondary filter must be filled with clean diesel fuel before it is reinstalled.
12. Install the rear air conditioning bracket, if equipped.
13. Install the EPR/EGR valve bracket, if equipped.
14. Tighten the vacuum pump holddown clamp.
15. Install the secondary filter and adaptor.
16. Connect the secondary fuel filter lines.
17. Install the crankcase ventilator tubes.
18. Install the air cleaner assembly.
19. Connect both batteries.

8–7.4L

1. Disconnect the battery.
2. Drain the cooling system.

CAUTION

When draining the coolant, keep in mind that cats and dogs are attracted by the ethylene glycol antifreeze, and are quite likely to drink any that is left in an uncovered container or in puddles on the ground. This will prove fatal in sufficient quantity. Always drain the coolant into a sealable container. Coolant should be reused unless it is contaminated or several years old.

3. Remove the air cleaner assembly.
4. Remove the upper radiator hose, thermostat housing and the bypass hose.
5. Disconnect the heater hose and pipe.
6. Tag and disconnect all electrical connections and vacuum lines from the manifold.
7. Disconnect the accelerator linkage.
8. Disconnect the cruise control cable.
9. Disconnect the TVS cable.
10. Remove the fuel line at the TBI unit.
11. Remove the TBI unit.
12. Remove the distributor.
13. Remove the cruise control transducer.
14. Disconnect the ignition coil wires.
15. Remove the EGR solenoid and bracket.
16. Remove the MAP sensor and bracket.
17. Remove the air conditioning compressor rear bracket.
18. Remove the front alternator/AIR pump bracket.
19. Remove the intake manifold bolts.
20. Remove the manifold and the gaskets and seals.

NOTE: Remember to reinstall the O-ring between the intake manifold and timing chain cover during assembly, if so equipped.

To install:

NOTE: Before installing the intake manifold, be sure that the gasket surfaces are thoroughly clean.

21. Install the manifold and the gaskets and seals.
22. Install the intake manifold bolts. Torque the bolts to 30 ft. lbs.
23. Install the front alternator/AIR pump bracket.
24. Install the air conditioning compressor rear bracket.
25. Install the MAP sensor and bracket.
26. Install the EGR solenoid and bracket.
27. Connect the ignition coil wires.
28. Install the cruise control transducer.
29. Install the distributor.
30. Install the TBI unit.
31. Install the fuel line at the TBI unit.
32. Connect the TVS cable.
33. Connect the cruise control cable.
34. Connect the accelerator linkage.
35. Connect all electrical connections and vacuum lines at the manifold.

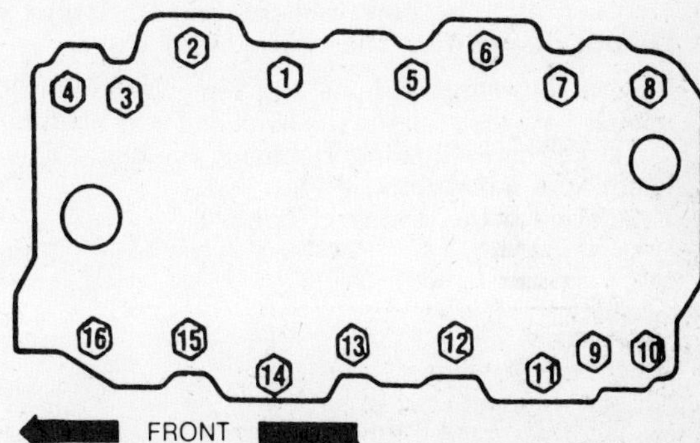

8–7.4L intake manifold bolt tightening sequence

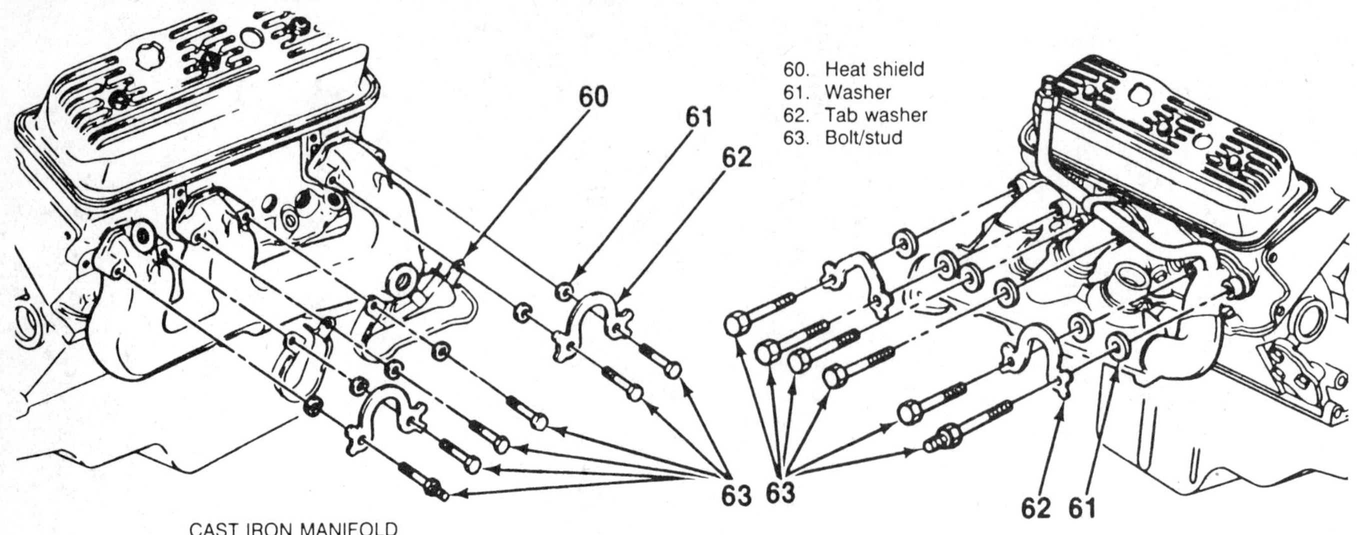

6–4.3L exhaust manifold

36. Connect the heater hose and pipe.
37. Install the upper radiator hose, thermostat housing and the bypass hose.
38. Install the air cleaner assembly.
39. Fill the cooling system.
40. Connect the battery.

Exhaust Manifold

NOTE: For the 6–4.8L, see Combination Manifold, below.

REMOVAL AND INSTALLATION

6–4.3L

8–5.0L

8–5.7L

Tab locks are used on the front and rear pairs of bolts on each exhaust manifold. When removing the bolts, straighten the tabs from beneath the truck using a suitable tool. When installing the tab locks, bend the tabs against the sides of the bolt, not over the top of the bolt.

1. Remove the air cleaner.
2. Remove the hot air shroud, (if so equipped).
3. Loosen the alternator and remove its lower bracket.
4. Jack up your truck and support it with jackstands.
5. Disconnect the crossover pipe from both manifolds.

NOTE: On models with air conditioning it may be necessary to remove the compressor, and tie it out of the way. Do not disconnect the compressor lines.

6. Remove the manifold bolts and remove the manifold(s). Some models have lock tabs on the front and rear manifold bolts which must be removed before removing the bolts. These tabs can be bent with a drift pin.
7. Installation is the reverse of removal.

8–7.4L

RIGHT SIDE

1. Disconnect the battery.
2. Remove the heat stove pipe.
3. Remove the dipstick tube.
4. Disconnect the AIR hose at the check valve.
5. Remove the park plugs.
6. Disconnect the exhaust pipe at the manifold.
7. Remove the manifold bolts and spark plug heat shields.
8. Remove the manifold.

To install:

9. Clean the mating surfaces.
10. Clean the stud threads.
11. Install the manifold and bolts. Tighten the bolts to 40 ft. lbs. starting from the center bolts and working towards the outside.
12. Connect the exhaust pipe at the manifold.
13. Install the park plugs.
14. Connect the AIR hose at the check valve.
15. Install the dipstick tube.
16. Install the heat stove pipe.
17. Connect the battery.

LEFT SIDE

1. Disconnect the battery.
2. Disconnect the oxygen sensor wire.
3. Disconnect the AIR hose at the check valve.
4. Remove the park plugs.
5. Disconnect the exhaust pipe at the manifold.
6. Remove the manifold bolts and spark plug heat shields.
7. Remove the manifold.

To install:

8. Clean the mating surfaces.
9. Clean the stud threads.

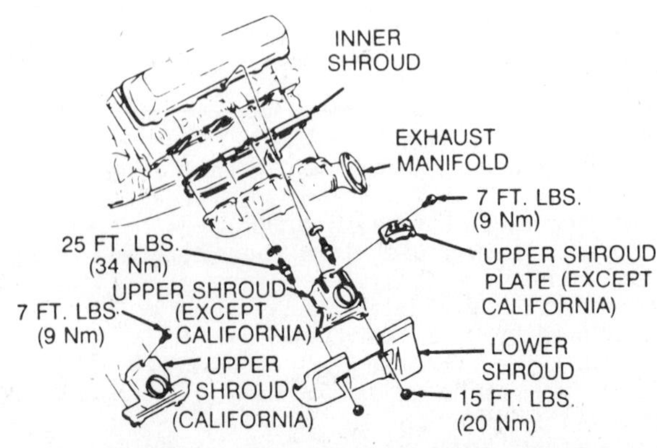

8–5.0L and 8–5.7L exhaust manifold

10. Install the manifold and bolts. Tighten the bolts to 40 ft. lbs. starting from the center bolts and working towards the outside.
11. Connect the exhaust pipe at the manifold.
12. Install the park plugs.
13. Connect the AIR hose at the check valve.
14. Connect the oxygen sensor wire.
15. Connect the battery.

8–6.2L Diesel

RIGHT SIDE

1. Disconnect the batteries.
2. Jack up the truck and safely support it with jackstands.
3. Disconnect the exhaust pipe from the manifold flange and lower the truck.
4. Disconnect the glow plug wires.
5. Remove the air cleaner duct bracket.
6. Remove the glow plug wires.
7. Remove the manifold bolts and remove the manifold.
8. To install, reverse the above procedure and torque the bolts to 25 ft. lbs.

LEFT SIDE

1. Disconnect the batteries.
2. Remove the dipstick tube nut, and remove the dipstick tube.
3. Disconnect the glow plug wires.
4. Jack up the truck and safely support it with jackstands.
5. Disconnect the exhaust pipe at the manifold flange.
6. Remove the manifold bolts. Remove the manifold from underneath the truck.
7. Reverse the above procedure to install. Start the manifold bolts while the truck is jacked up first. Torque the bolts to 25 ft. lbs.

Combination Manifold

REMOVAL AND INSTALLATION

6–4.8L

1. Disconnect the negative battery cable.
2. Remove the air cleaner.
3. Disconnect the throttle controls at the bellcrank.
4. Remove the carburetor.
5. Disconnect the fuel and vacuum lines from the manifold.
6. Remove the AIR pump and bracket.
7. Disconnect the PCV hose.
8. Disconnect the exhaust pipe.
9. Remove the manifold heat stove.
10. Remove the clamps, bolts and washers and remove the combination manifold.
11. Separate the manifolds by removing the bolts and nuts.

To install:

12. Clean the mating surfaces.
13. Clean the stud threads.
14. Assemble the manifolds with a new gasket and leave the nuts finger tight.
15. Install a new gasket over the manifold studs on the cylinder head and install the manifold assembly.
16. Install the bolts, clamps and nuts.

NOTE: Always tighten the manifold to cylinder head bolts and nuts (38 ft. lbs.) before tightening the manifold center bolts and nuts (44 ft. lbs.).

17. Install the manifold heat stove.
18. Connect the exhaust pipe.
19. Connect the PCV hose.
20. Install the AIR pump and bracket.
21. Connect the fuel and vacuum lines from the manifold.
22. Install the carburetor.
23. Connect the throttle controls at the bellcrank.
24. Install the air cleaner.
25. Connect the negative battery cable.

Vacuum Pump

REMOVAL AND INSTALLATION

Diesel Engine

1. Remove the air cleaner. Cover the intake with a cloth.
2. Disconnect the vacuum hose at the pump inlet.
3. Unplug the speed sensor connector.
4. Unbolt and remove the bracket holding the pump drive to the block.
5. Pull the pump and drive assembly from the block.

WARNING: Never operate the engine without the vacuum pump installed! The oil pump is driven by the vacuum pump drive gear. Without the vacuum pump in position, no oil would circulate through the engine.

6. Check the gasket on the pump. If it appears damaged in any way, replace it.

To install:

7. Place the pump in the block. Make sure that the gears mesh.
8. Rotate the pump so that the inlet tube faces front. The pump should be on a 20° angle.
9. Install the bracket and bolt. Torque the bolt to 20 ft. lbs.
10. Connect the vacuum hose.
11. Connect the speed sensor.
12. Install the air cleaner.

Air Conditioning Compressor

REMOVAL AND INSTALLATION

1. Disconnect the negative battery cable.

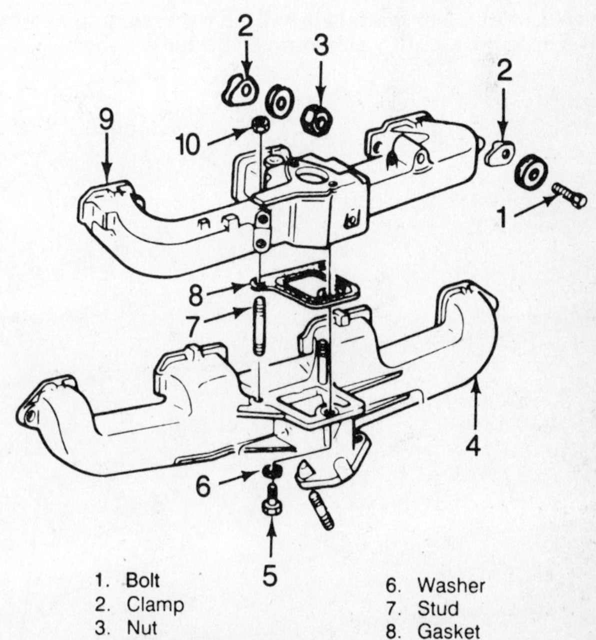

6-4.8L combination manifold and related parts

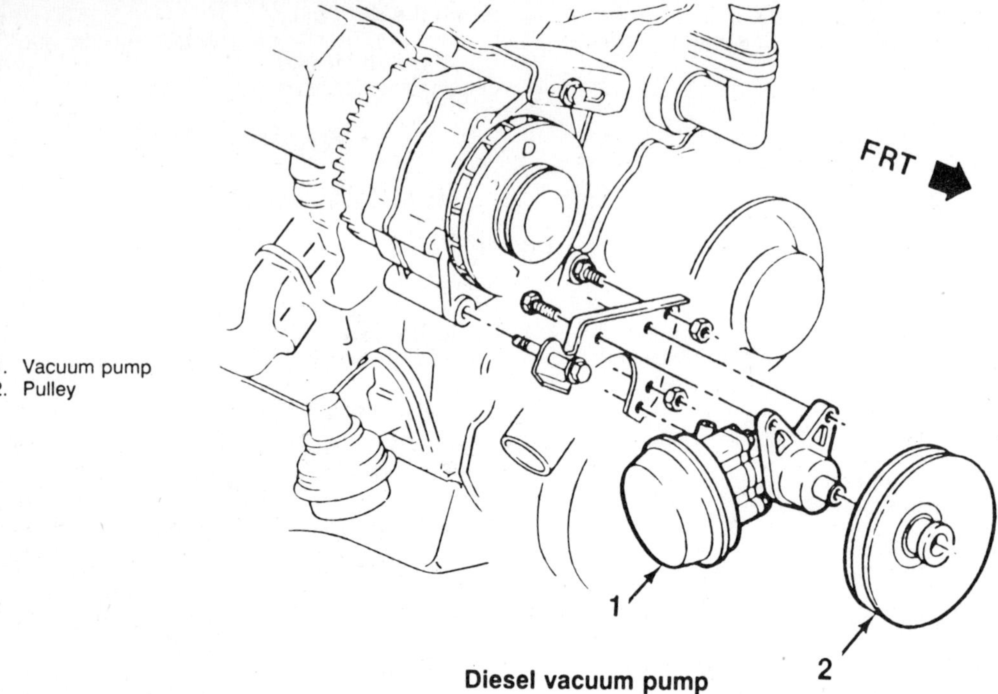

Diesel vacuum pump

2. Disconnect the compressor clutch connector.
3. Purge the system of refrigerant.

CAUTION

Discharging the air conditioning refrigerant should only be attempted by those who have the proper tools and training to do so, as serious personal injury may result. The refrigerant will instantly freeze any surface it comes in contact with, including your eyes.

4. Remove the belt by releasing the belt tension at the idler pulley.

NOTE: On some models it will be necessary to remove the crankshaft pulley to remove the belt.

5. Remove the engine cover (if necessary).
6. Remove the air cleaner.
7. Remove the fitting and muffler assembly. Cap and plug all open connections.
8. Remove the compressor bracket.
9. Remove the engine oil tube support bracket bolt and nut.
10. Disconnect the clutch ground lead.
11. Remove the compressor.
12. Drain and measure the oil in the compressor and check for contamination.

To install:

13. Install the compressor.
14. Install the measured amount of oil in the compressor.

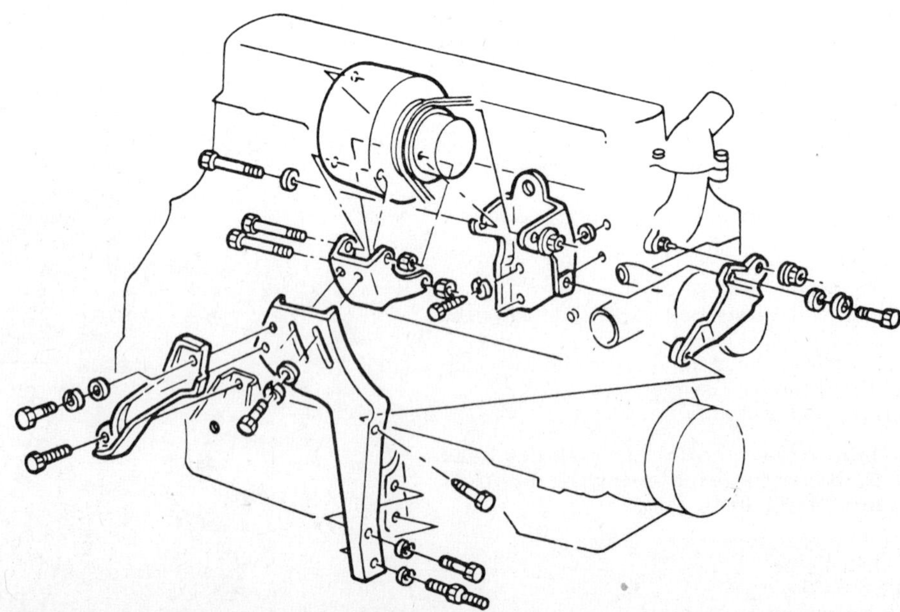

Compressor installation on the 6-4.8L engine in R and V series trucks

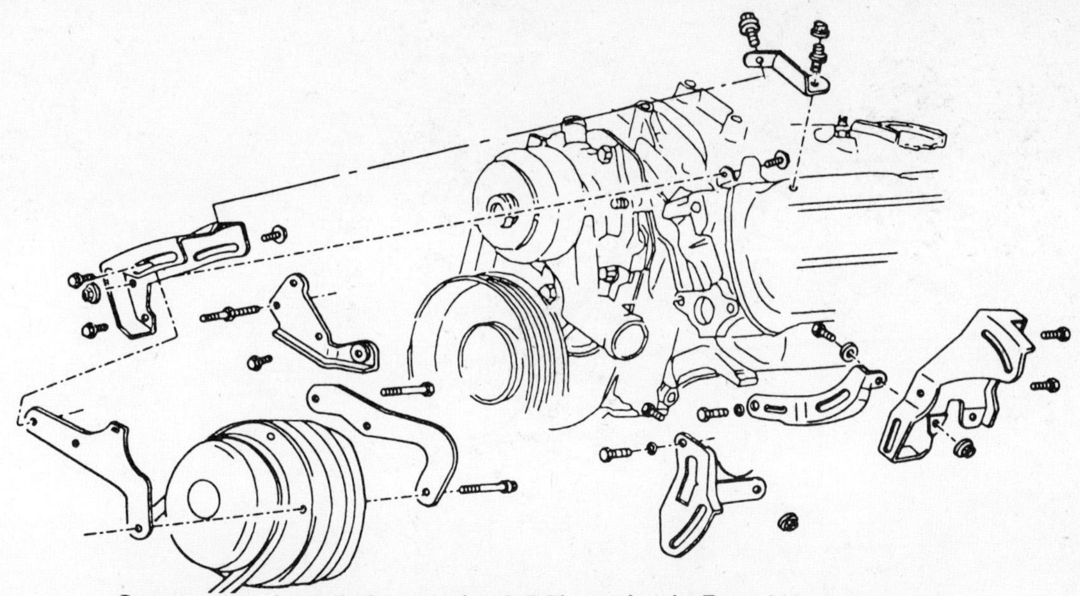

Compressor installation on the 8-5.7L engine in R and V series trucks

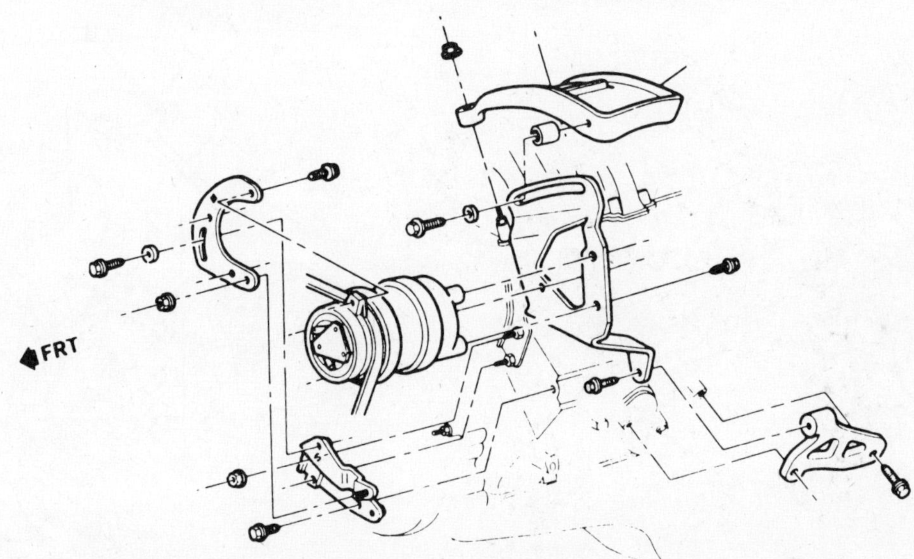

Compressor installation on the 8-6.2L engine in R and V series trucks

15. Connect the clutch ground lead.
16. Install the engine oil tube support bracket bolt and nut.
17. Install the compressor bracket.
18. Install the fitting and muffler assembly.
19. Install the air cleaner.
20. Install the engine cover (if necessary).
21. Install the crankshaft pulley.
22. Install the belt.
23. Charge refrigerant system. See Section 1.
24. Connect the compressor clutch connector.
25. Connect the negative battery cable.

Radiator

REMOVAL AND INSTALLATION

Gasoline Engines

1. Drain the cooling system.

CAUTION

When draining the coolant, keep in mind that cats and dogs are attracted by the ethylene glycol antifreeze, and are quite likely to drink any that is left in an uncovered container or in puddles on the ground. This will prove fatal in sufficient quantity. Always drain the coolant into a sealable container. Coolant should be reused unless it is contaminated or several years old.

2. Disconnect the radiator upper and lower hoses and, if applicable, the transmission coolant lines. Remove the coolant recovery system line, if so equipped.
3. Remove the radiator upper panel if so equipped.
4. If there is a radiator shroud in front of the radiator, the radiator and shroud are removed as an assembly.
5. If there is a fan shroud, remove the shroud attaching screws and let the shroud hang on the fan.
6. Remove the radiator attaching bolts and remove the radiator.
7. Installation is the reverse of the removal procedure.

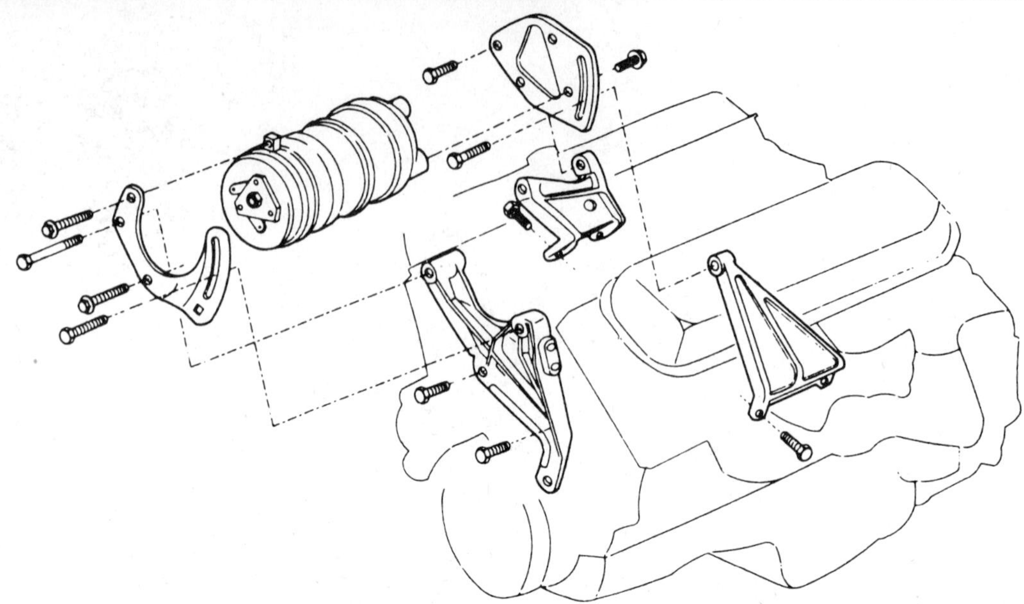
Compressor installation on the 8-7.4L engine in R and V series trucks

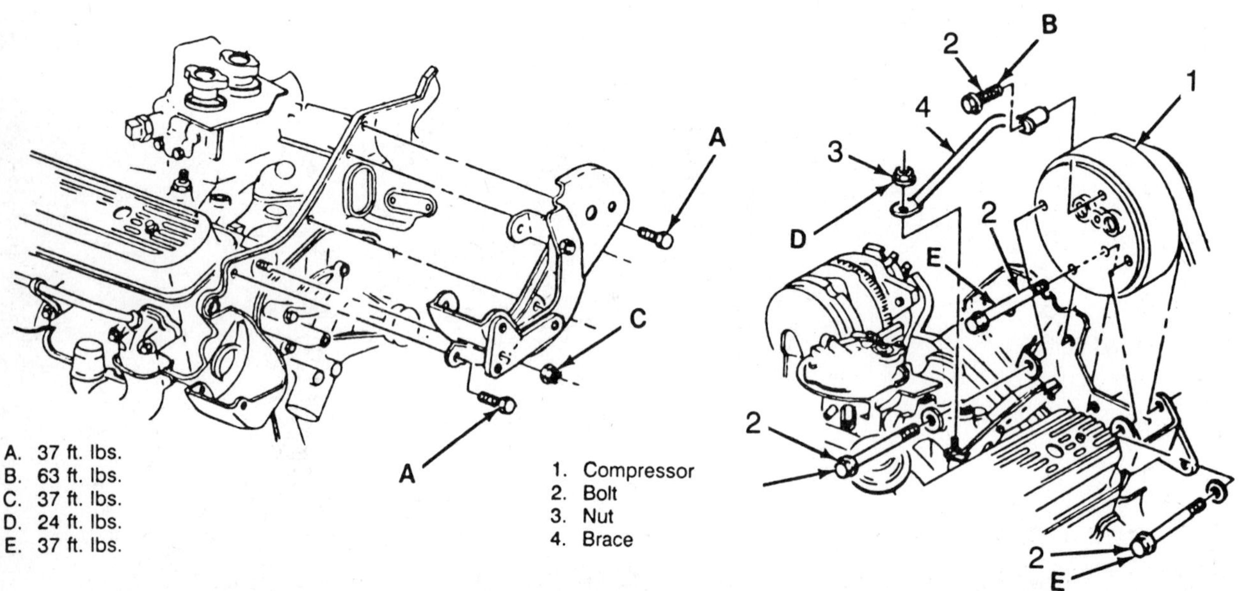

Compressor installation on the 6-4.3L, 8-5.0L and 8- 5.7L engines in C and K series trucks

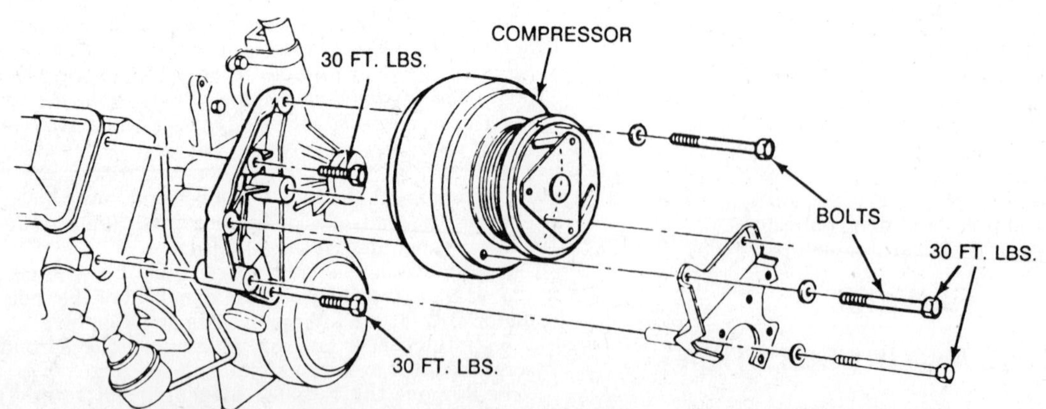

Compressor installation on the 8-6.2L engine in C and K series trucks

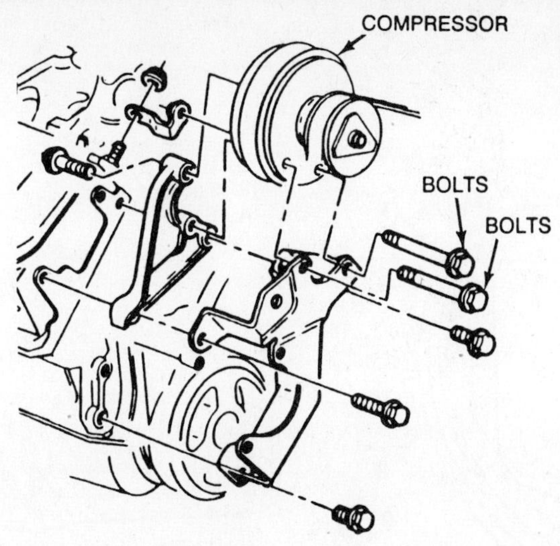

Compressor installation on the 8-7.4L engine in C and K series trucks

Diesel Engine

1. Drain the cooling system.

CAUTION

When draining the coolant, keep in mind that cats and dogs are attracted by the ethylene glycol antifreeze, and are quite likely to drink any that is left in an uncovered container or in puddles on the ground. This will prove fatal in sufficient quantity. Always drain the coolant into a sealable container. Coolant should be reused unless it is contaminated or several years old.

2. Remove the air intake snorkel.
3. Remove the windshield washer bottle.
4. Remove the hood relase cable.
5. Remove the upper fan shroud.
6. Disconnect the upper radiator hose.
7. Disconnect the transmission cooler lines.
8. Disconnect the low coolant sensor wire.
9. Disconnect the overflow hose.
10. Disconnect the engine oil cooler lines.
11. Disconnect the lower radiator hose.
12. Remove the brake master cylinder. See Section 9.
13. Unbolt and remove the radiator.

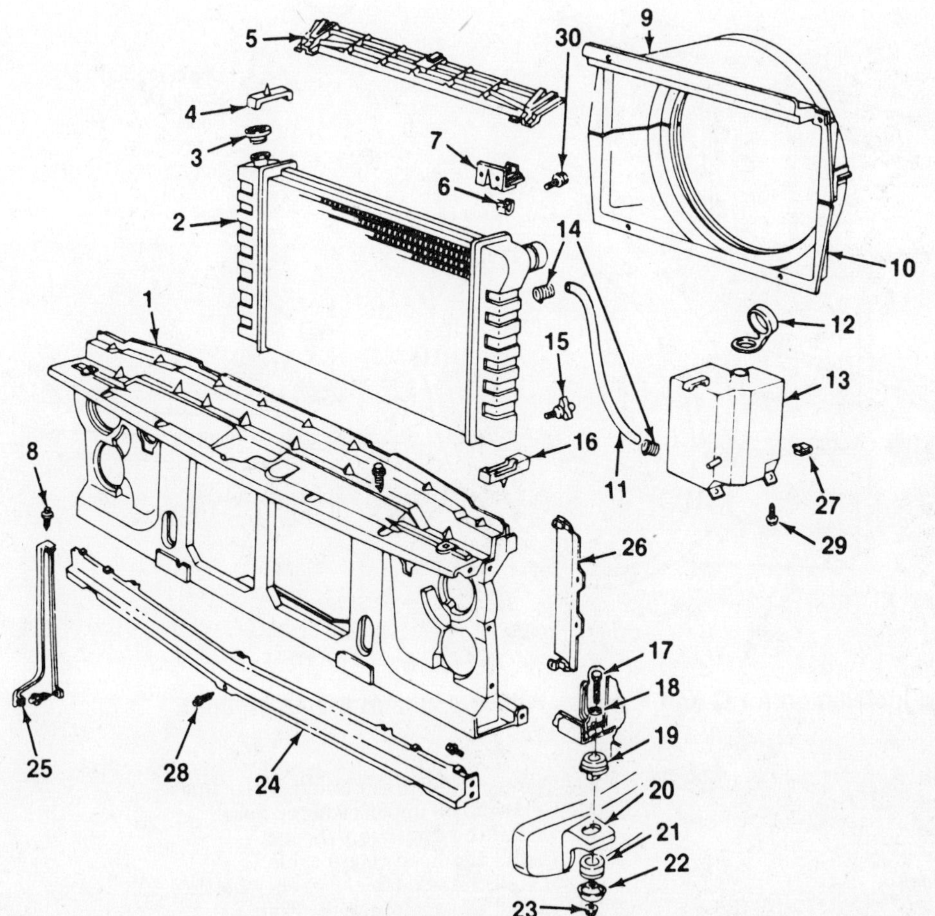

1. Support
2. Radiator
3. Filler cap
4. Upper insulator
5. Upper panel
6. U-nut
7. Shroud bracket
8. Screw
9. Upper shroud
10. Lower shroud
11. Hose
12. Reservoir cap
13. Reservoir
14. Worm clamp
15. Drain cock
16. Lower insulator
17. Bolt
18. Washer
19. Upper cushion
20. Support bracket
21. Lower cushion
22. Cushion retainer
23. Nut
24. End panel
25. Support
26. Left baffle
27. Nut
28. Screw
29. Screw
30. Screw

Radiator and related parts for R and V series

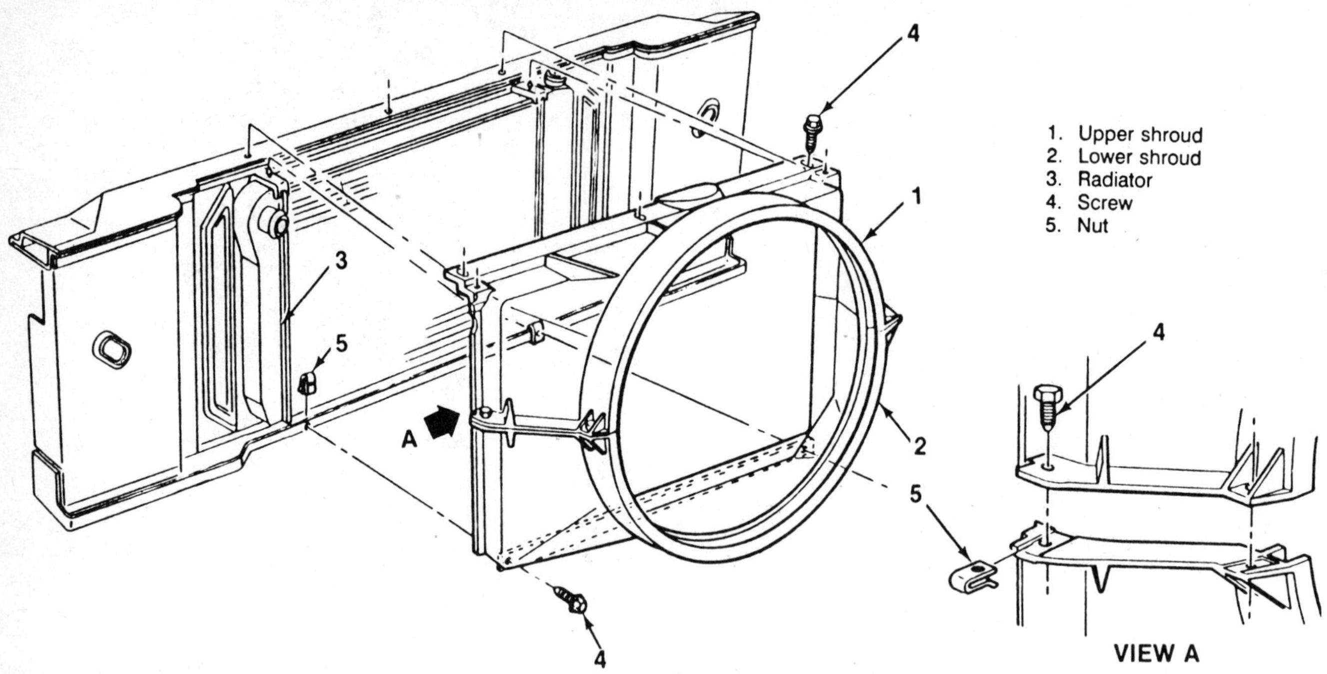

Radiator shroud installation for C and K series with 8-5.0L and 8-5.7L engines

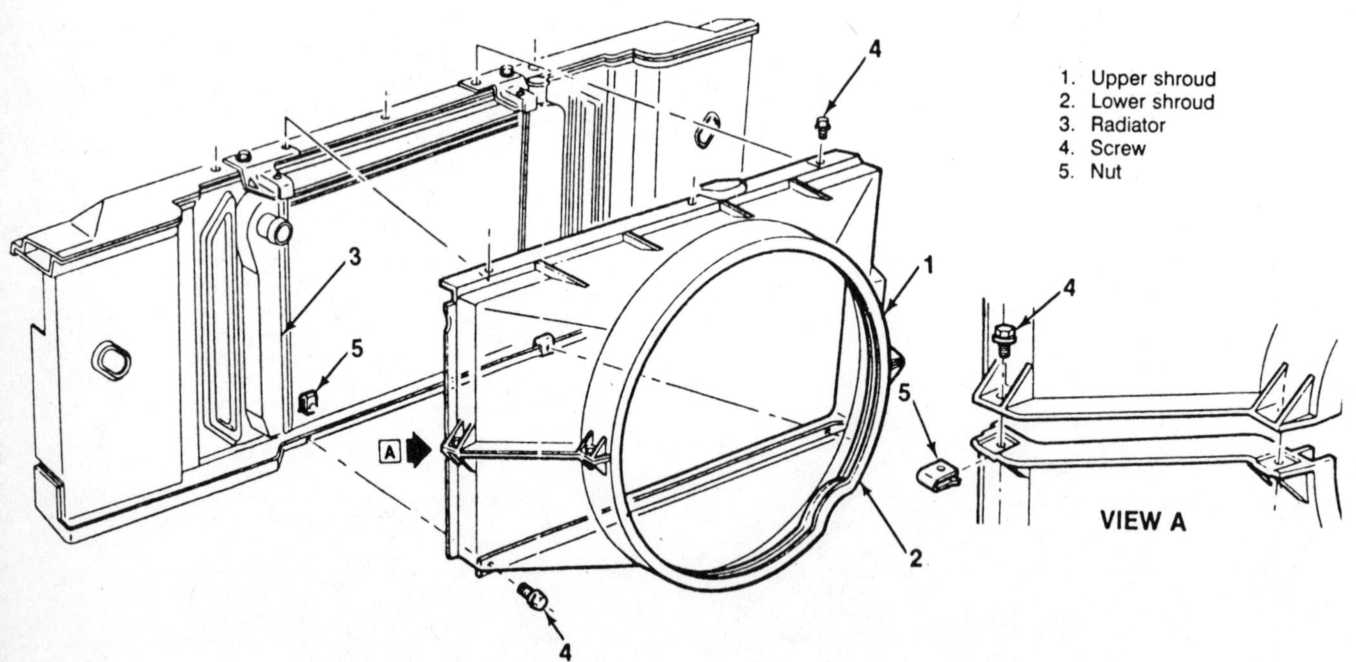

Radiator shroud installation for C and K series with 8-6.2L and 8-7.4L engines

To install:

14. Install the radiator.
15. Install the brake master cylinder.
16. Connect the lower radiator hose.
17. Connect the engine oil cooler lines.
18. Connect the overflow hose.
19. Connect the low coolant sensor wire.
20. Connect the transmission cooler lines.
21. Connect the upper radiator hose.
22. Install the upper fan shroud.
23. Install the hood relase cable.
24. Install the windshield washer bottle.
25. Install the air intake snorkel.
26. Fill the cooling system.

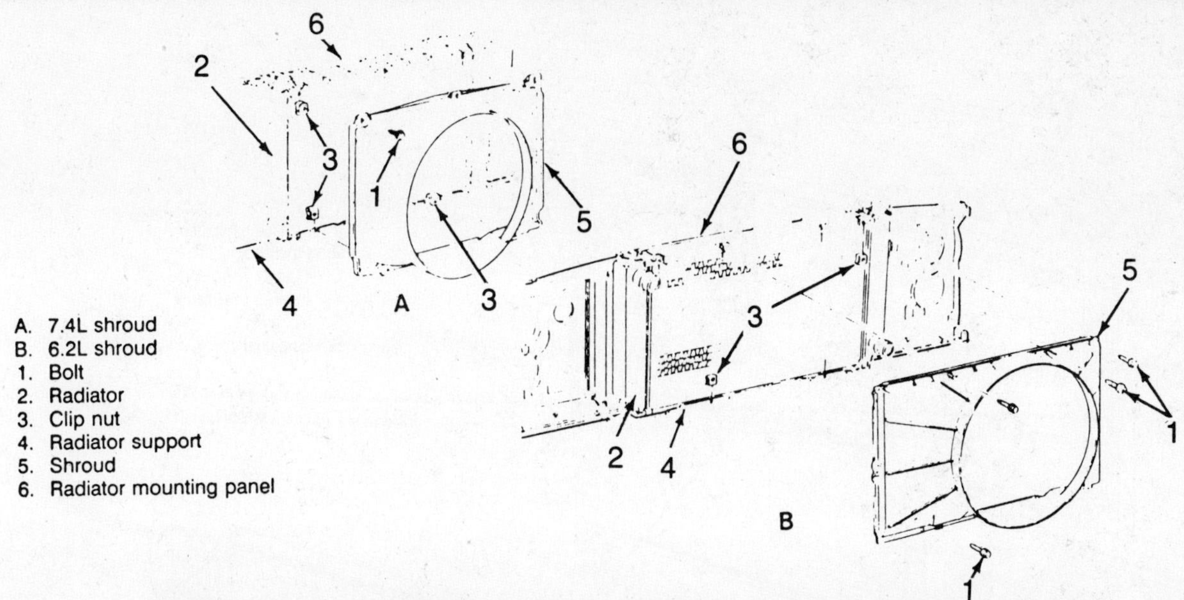

Radiator shroud installation for R and V series with 8-6.2L and 8-7.4L engines

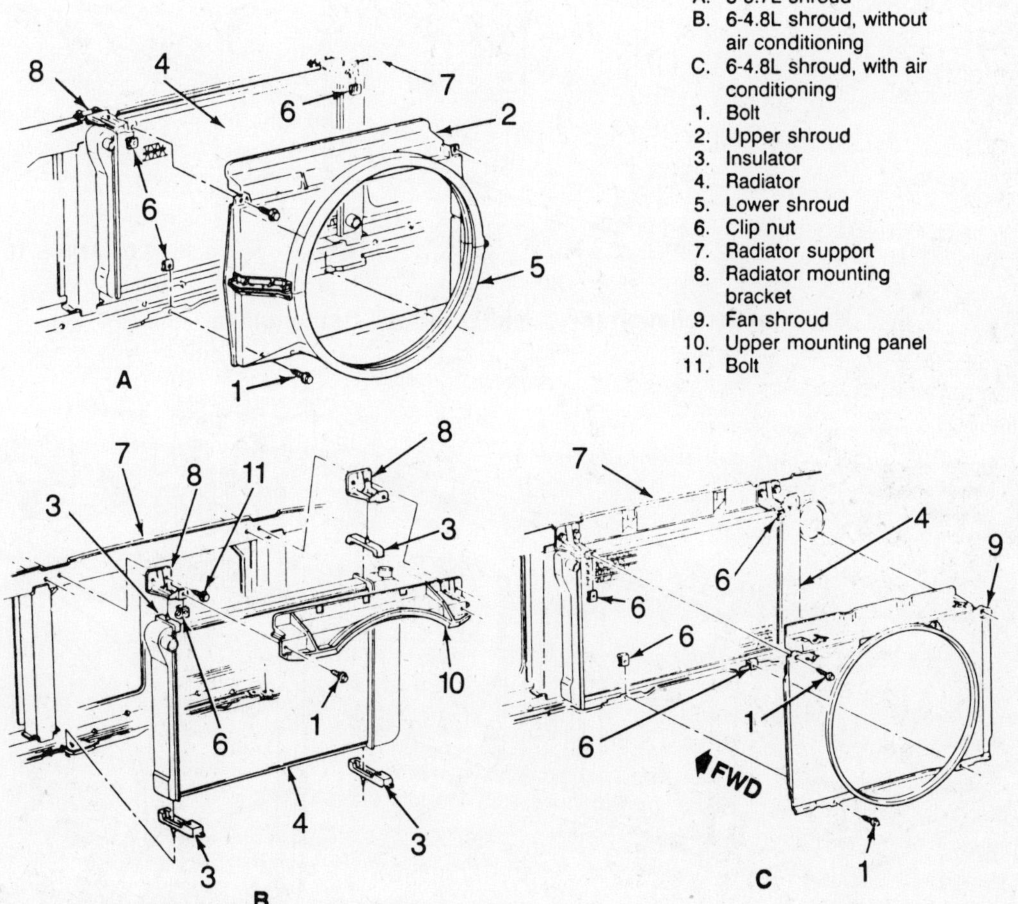

Radiator shroud installation for R and V series with 6-4.8L and 8-5.7L engines

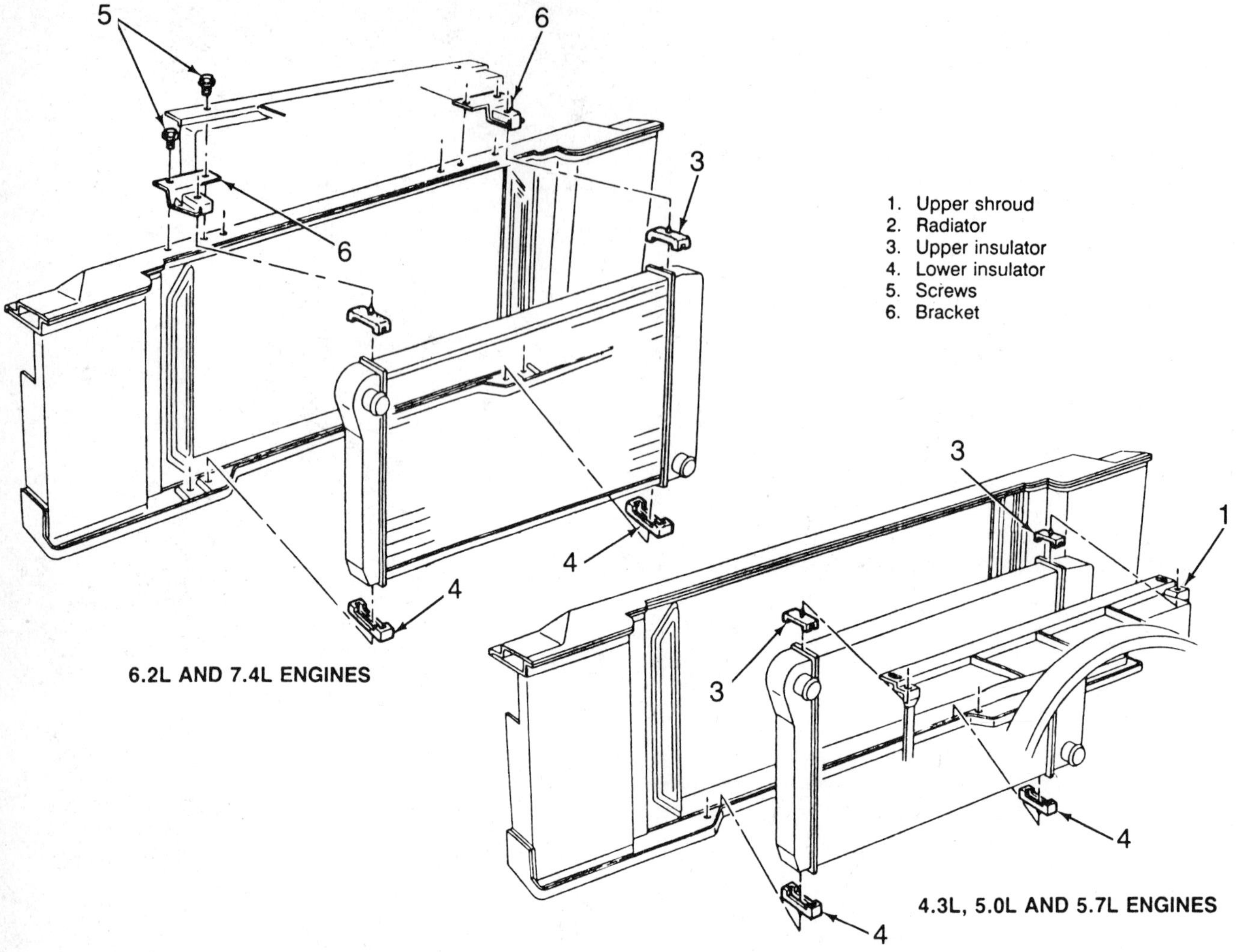

5
6
3
6
1. Upper shroud
2. Radiator
3. Upper insulator
4. Lower insulator
5. Screws
6. Bracket
3
1
4
4
6.2L AND 7.4L ENGINES
3
4
4
4.3L, 5.0L AND 5.7L ENGINES

Radiator installation for C and L series – all engines

4
1. Upper shroud
2. Lower shroud
3. Radiator
4. Screw
5. Nut
1
4
3
5
5
5
2
4

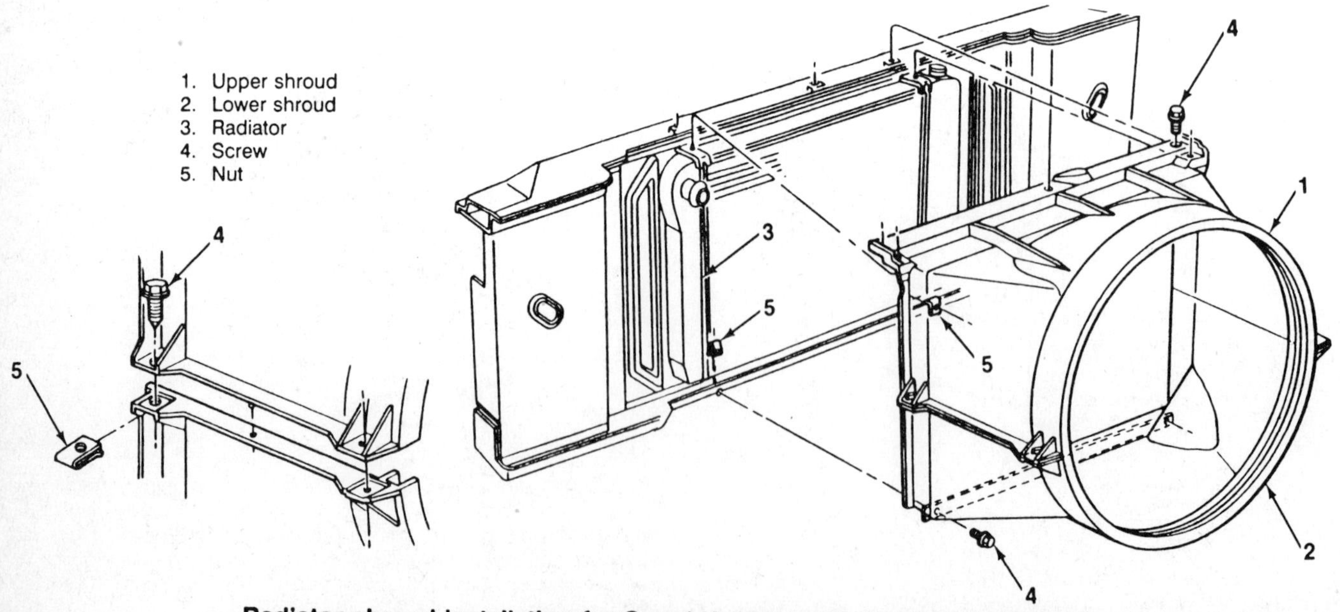

Radiator shroud installation for C and K series with the 6-4.3L engine

Air Conditioning Condenser

REMOVAL AND INSTALLATION

All Series

1. Disconnect the battery ground cable.
2. Discharge the system. See Section 1.
3. Remove the grille. See Section 10.
4. Remove the radiator grille center support. See Section 10.
5. Remove the left grille support-to-upper fender support bolts.
6. Using a back-up wrench, disconnect the refrigerant lines at the condenser. Cap all openings at once!
7. Remove the condenser mounting bolts and lower the condenser out of the truck.
8. Installation is the reverse of removal. Evacuate, charge and leak-test the system. Use new O-rings, coated with clean refrigerant oil, at the refrigerant line connections. When install a new condenser, add 1 oz. of clean refrigerant oil.

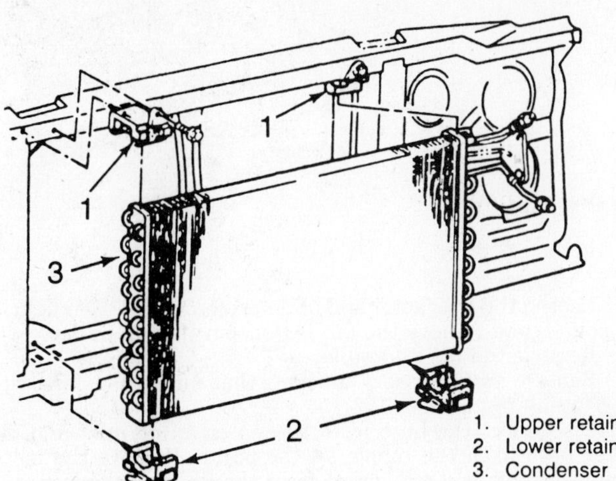

Condenser installation for R and V series trucks

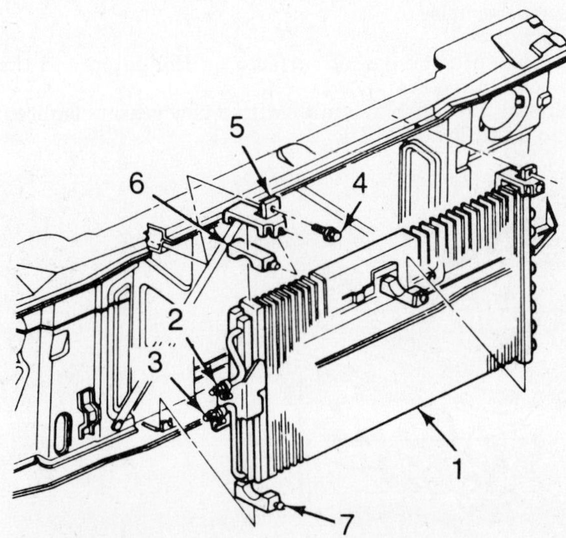

Condenser installation for C and K series trucks

Auxiliary Cooling Fan

REMOVAL AND INSTALLATION

1. Remove the grille.
2. Unplug the fan harness connector.
3. Remove the fan-to-brace bolts and lift out the fan.
4. Installation is the reverse of removal. Torque the bolts to 53 ft. lbs.

Water Pump

REMOVAL AND INSTALLATION

6–4.8L

1. Disconnect the negative battery cable.
2. Drain the radiator.

CAUTION

When draining the coolant, keep in mind that cats and dogs are attracted by the ethylene glycol antifreeze, and are quite likely to drink any that is left in an uncovered container or in puddles on the ground. This will prove fatal in sufficient quantity. Always drain the coolant into a sealable container. Coolant should be reused unless it is contaminated or several years old.

3. Loosen the alternator and other accessories at their adjusting points, and remove the fan belts from the fan pulley.
4. Remove the fan, fan clutch and pulley.
5. Remove any accessory brackets that might interfere with water pump removal.
6. Disconnect the hose from the water pump inlet and the heater hose from the nipple on the pump. Remove the bolts, pump assembly and old gasket from the timing chain cover.
7. Check the pump shaft bearings for endplay or roughness in operation. Water pump bearings usually emit a squealing sound with the engine running when the bearings need to be replaced. Replace the pump if the bearings are not in good shape or have been noisy.

To install:

8. Make sure the gasket surfaces on the pump and engine block are clean.
9. Install the pump assembly with a new gasket. Tighten the bolts to 15 ft. lbs.
10. Connect the hose between the water pump inlet and the nipple on the pump.
11. Install any accessory brackets.
12. Install the fan and pulley.
13. Install and adjust the alternator and other accessories.
14. Install the fan belts from the fan pulley.
15. Fill the cooling system.
16. Connect the battery.

6–4.3L
8–5.0L, 5.7L, 7.4L

1. Disconnect the battery.
2. Drain the radiator.

CAUTION

When draining the coolant, keep in mind that cats and dogs are attracted by the ethylene glycol antifreeze, and are quite likely to drink any that is left in an uncovered container or in puddles on the ground. This will prove fatal in sufficient quantity. Always drain the coolant into a sealable container. Coolant should be reused unless it is contaminated or several years old.

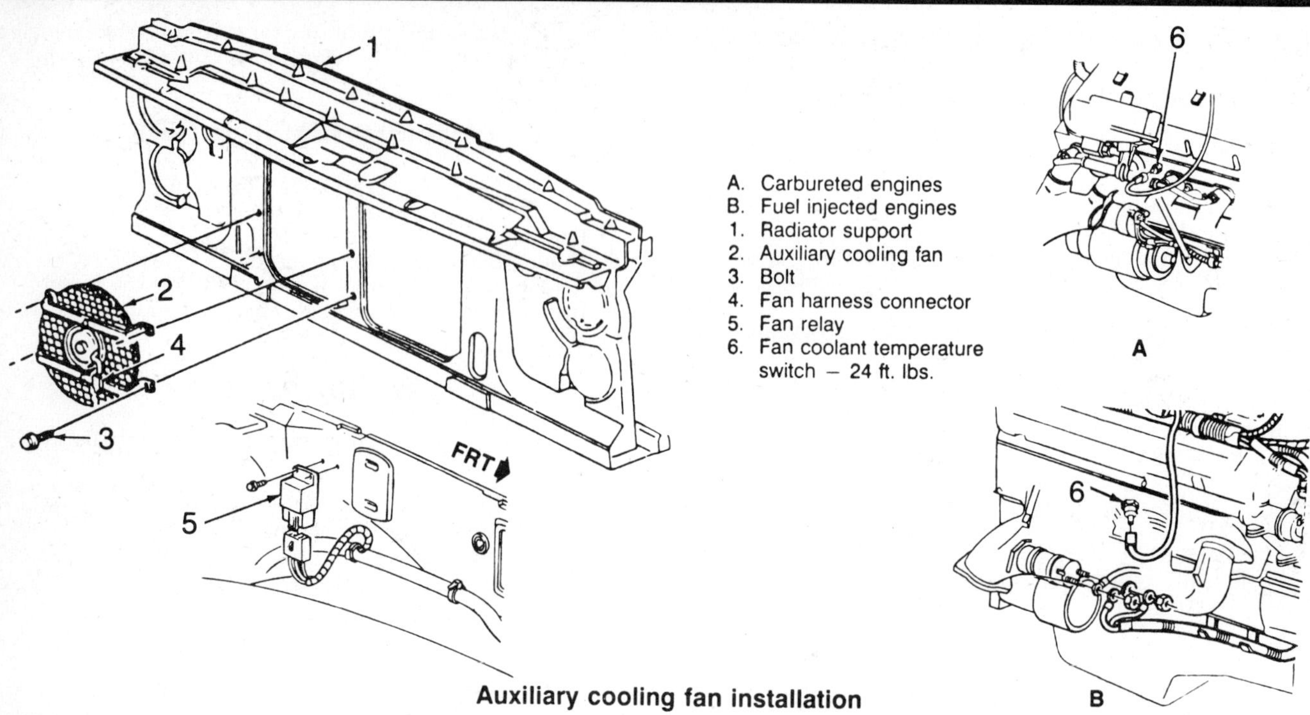

Auxiliary cooling fan installation

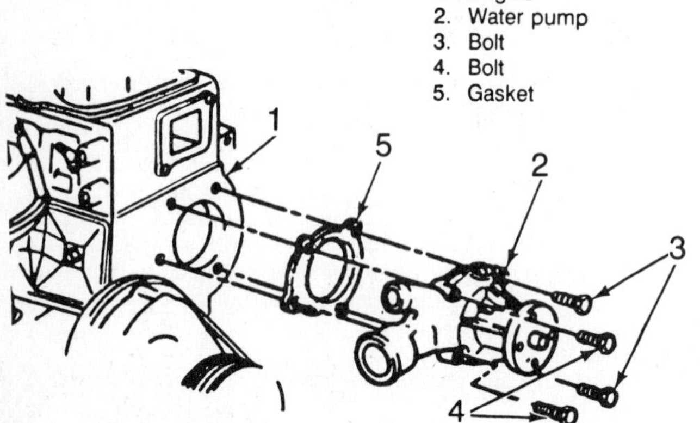

Water pump replacement for the 6-4.8L

3. Loosen the alternator and other accessories at their adjusting points, and remove the fan belts from the fan pulley.

4. Remove the fan and pulley.

5. Remove any accessory brackets that might interfere with water pump removal.

6. Disconnect the hose from the water pump inlet and the heater hose from the nipple on the pump. Remove the bolts, pump assembly and old gasket from the timing chain cover.

7. Check the pump shaft bearings for end play or roughness in operation. Water pump bearings usually emit a squealing sound with the engine running when the bearings need to be replaced. Replace the pump if the bearings are not in good shape or have been noisy.

To install:

8. Make sure the gasket surfaces on the pump and timing chain cover are clean.

9. Install the pump assembly with a new gasket. Tighten the bolts to 30 ft. lbs.

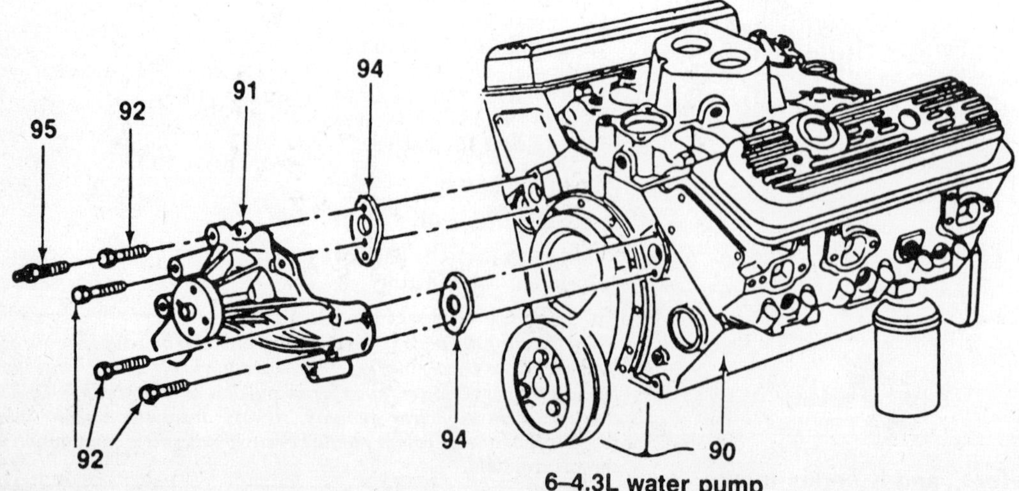

6–4.3L water pump

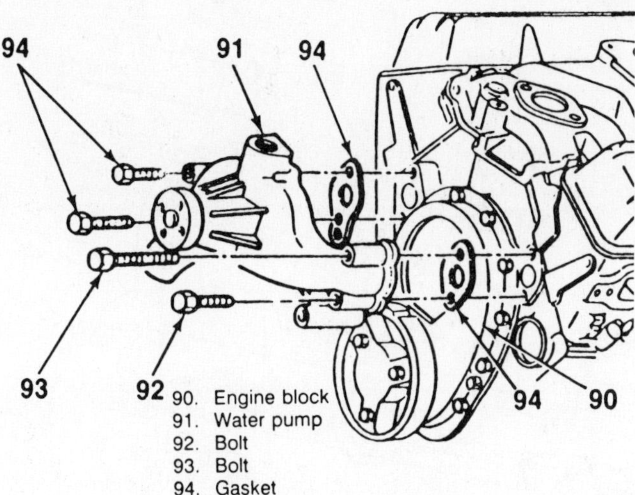

8–5.0L/5.7L water pump

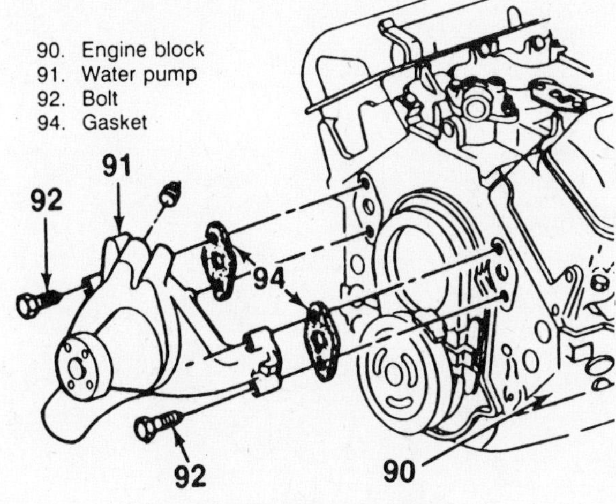

8–7.4L water pump

10. Connect the hose bewteen the water pump inlet and the nipple on the pump.
11. Install any accessory brackets.
12. Install the fan and pulley.
13. Install and adjust the alternator and other accessories.
14. Install the fan belts from the fan pulley.
15. Fill the cooling system.
16. Connect the battery.

8–6.2L Diesel

1. Disconnect the batteries.
2. Remove the fan and fan shroud.
3. Drain the radiator.

CAUTION

When draining the coolant, keep in mind that cats and dogs are attracted by the ethylene glycol antifreeze, and are quite likely to drink any that is left in an uncovered container or in puddles on the ground. This will prove fatal in sufficient quantity. Always drain the coolant into a sealable container. Coolant should be reused unless it is contaminated or several years old.

4. If the truck is equipped with air conditioning, remove the air conditioning hose bracket nuts.
5. Remove the oil filler tube.
6. Remove the generator pivot bolt and remove the generator belt.
7. Remove the generator lower bracket.
8. Remove the power steering belt and secure it out of the way.
9. Remove the air conditioning belt if equipped.
10. Disconnect the by-pass hose and the lower radiator hose.
11. Remove the water pump bolts. Remove the water pump plate and gasket and water pump. If the pump gasket is to be replaced, remove the plate attaching bolts to the water pump and remove (and replace) the gasket.

To install:

12. When installing the pump, the flanges must be free of oil. Apply an anaerobic sealer (GM part #1052357 or equvalent) as shown in the accompanying illustration.

NOTE: The sealer must be wet to the touch when the bolts are torqued.

13. Attach the water pump and plate assembly. Torque the bolts to 35 ft. lbs.
14. Connect the by-pass hose and the lower radiator hose.
15. Install the air conditioning belt if equipped.
16. Install the power steering belt.
17. Install the generator lower bracket.
18. Install the generator pivot bolt.
19. Install the generator belt.
20. Install the oil filler tube.
21. If the truck is equipped with air conditioning, install the air conditioning hose bracket nuts.
22. Fill the radiator.
23. Install the fan and fan shroud.
24. Connect the batteries.

Hydraulic Lifters

REMOVAL AND INSTALLATION

6–4.8L

1. Remove the rocker cover.
2. Remove the engine side cover.
3. Back off the rocker arm adjusting nuts and remove the pushrods. Keep them in order for installation.
4. Reaching through the side cover opening, lift out the hydraulic lifters. If your are going to re-use the lifters, remove them one at a time and mark each one for installation. They *must* be re-installed in the same locations.

   If a lifter is stuck, it can be removed with a grasping-type lifter tool, available form most auto parts stores.
5. Inspect each lifter thoroughly. If any of them shows any signs of wear, heat bluing or damage, replace the whole set.
6. Installation is the reverse of removal. Coat each lifter with engine oil supplement prior to installation. Adjust the valves as described below.

6–4.3L

1. Remove the rocker cover.
2. Remove the intake manifold.
3. Back off the rocker arm adjusting nuts and remove the pushrods. Keep them in order for installation.
4. Remove the lifter retainer bolts, retainer and restrictor.
5. Remove the lifters. If your are going to re-use the lifters, remove them one at a time and mark each one for installation. They *must* be re-installed in the same locations.

   If a lifter is stuck, it can be removed with a grasping-type lifter tool, available form most auto parts stores.
6. Inspect each lifter thoroughly. If any of them shows any signs of wear, heat bluing or damage, replace the whole set.

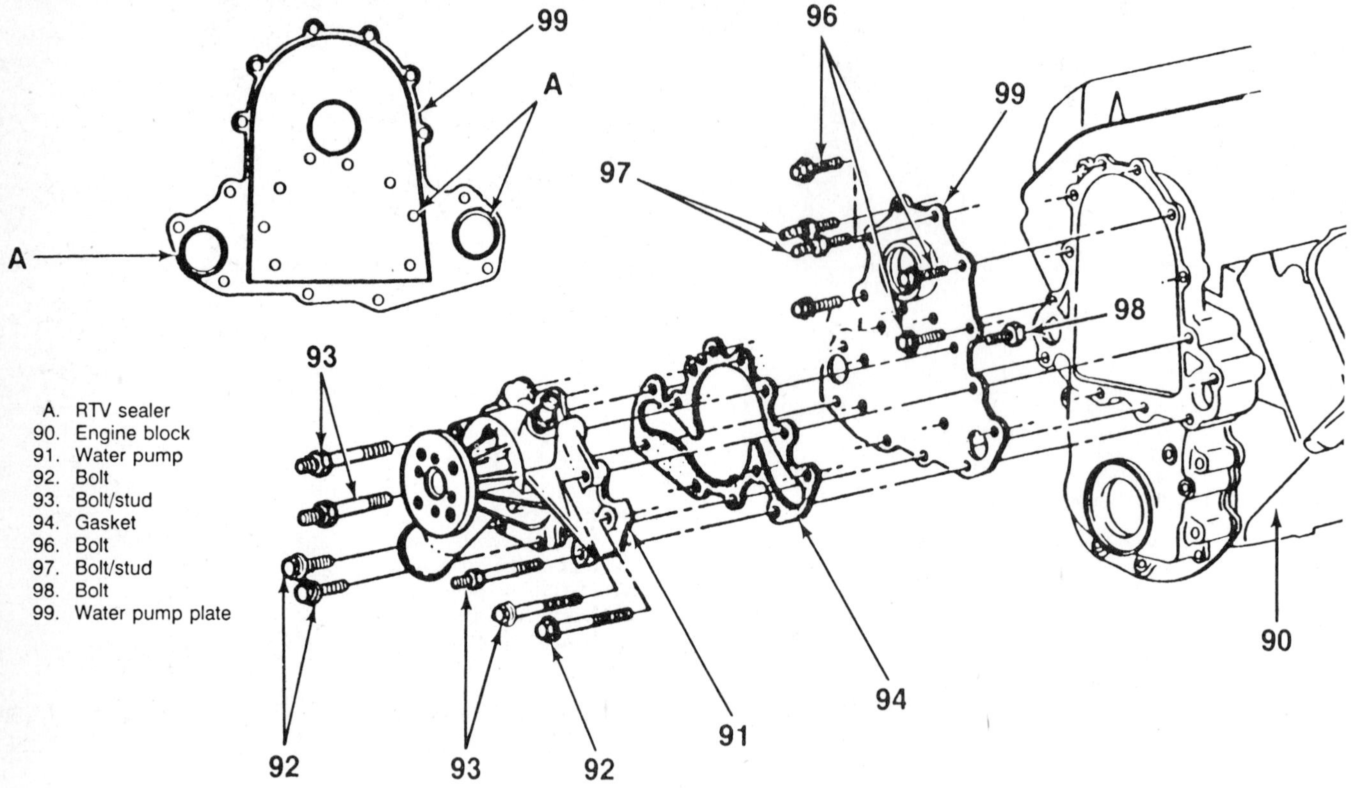

99
A
96
99
97
A
98
93
A. RTV sealer
90. Engine block
91. Water pump
92. Bolt
93. Bolt/stud
94. Gasket
96. Bolt
97. Bolt/stud
98. Bolt
99. Water pump plate
90
94
91
92
93
92

8–6.2L diesel water pump

J 3049

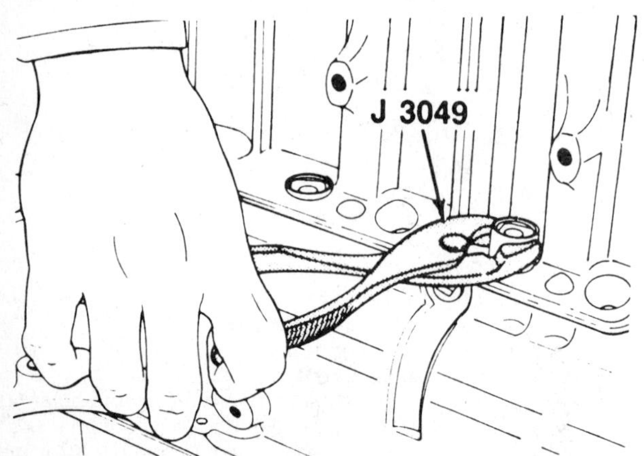

Removing the lifters from a 6-4.8L engine

J 9290-01

Removing a stuck lifter from a 6-4.8L engine

7. Installation is the reverse of removal. Coat each lifter with engine oil supplement prior to installation. Torque the retainer bolts to 12 ft. lbs. Adjust the valves as described below.

8–5.0L
8–5.7L
8–7.4L

1. Remove the rocker cover.
2. Remove the intake manifold.
3. Back off the rocker arm adjusting nuts and remove the pushrods. Keep them in order for installation.

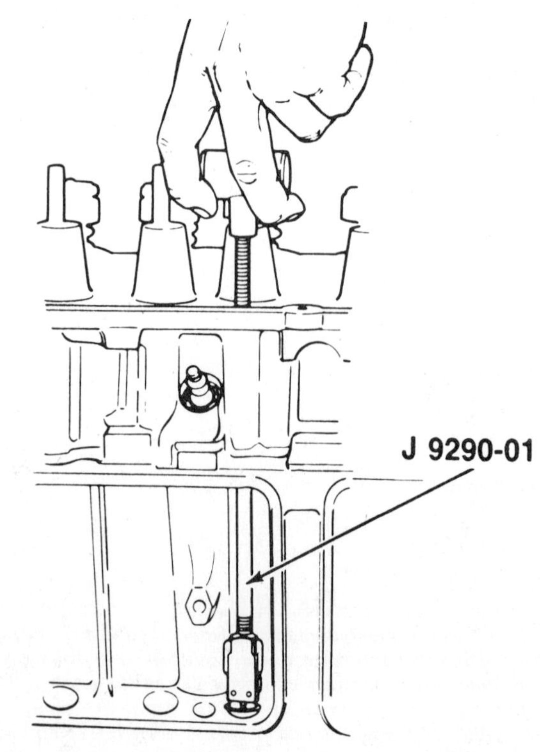

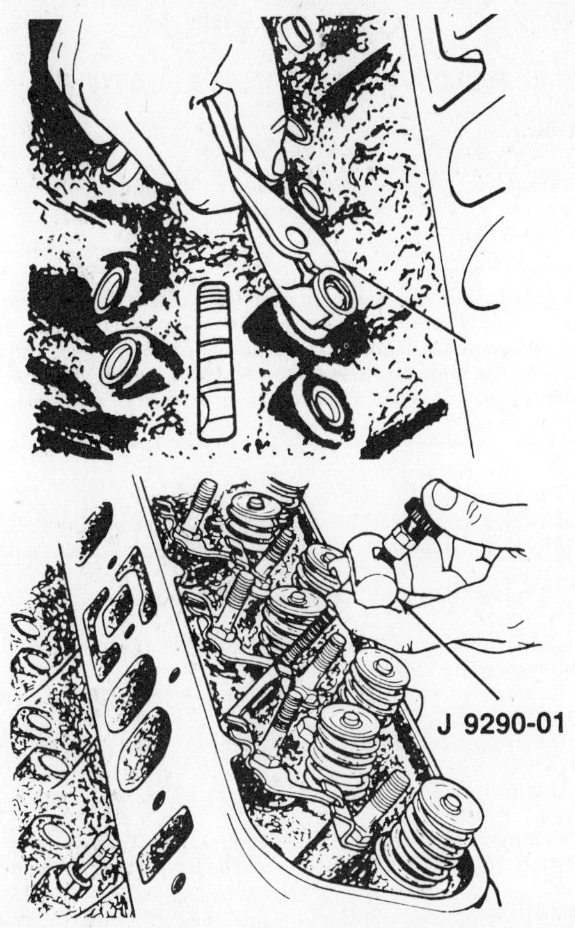

Removing hydraulic lifters from V6 or V8 engines

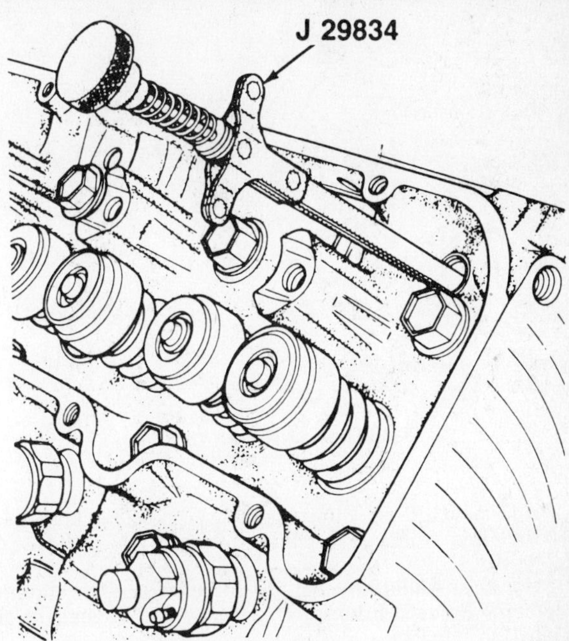

Removing the hydraulic liftersfrom the diesel engine

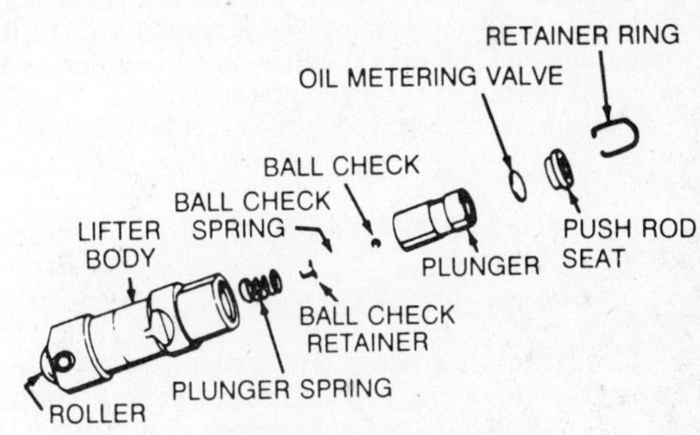

Diesel engine lifter

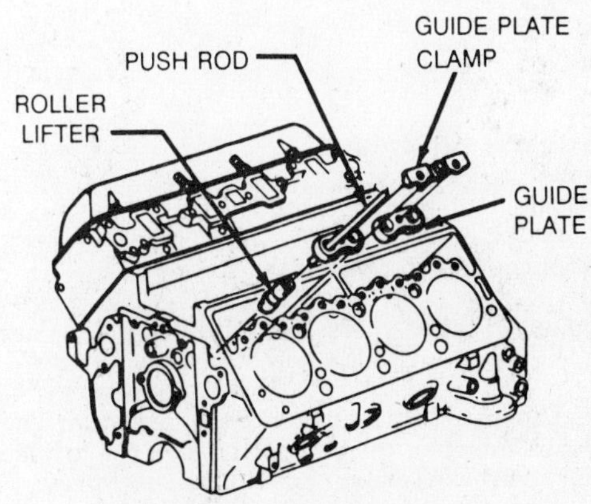

Diesel lifter retaining parts

4. Remove the lifters. If your are going to re-use the lifters, remove them one at a time and mark each one for installation. They *must* be re-installed in the same locations.

If a lifter is stuck, it can be removed with a grasping-type lifter tool, available form most auto parts stores.

5. Inspect each lifter thoroughly. If any of them shows any signs of wear, heat bluing or damage, replace the whole set.
6. Installation is the reverse of removal. Coat each lifter with engine oil supplement prior to installation. Adjust the valves as described below.

8–6.2L Diesel

1. Remove the rocker cover.
2. Remove the rocker arm shaft, rocker arms and pushrods. Keep all parts in order and properly identified for installation.
3. Remove the clamps and lifter guide plates.
4. Remove the lifters by reaching through the access holes in the cylinder head with a magnetic lifter tool. If your are going to re-use the lifters, remove them one at a time and mark each one for installation. They *must* be re-installed in the same locations.

If a lifter is stuck, it can be removed with a grasping-type lifter tool, available form most auto parts stores.

5. Inspect each lifter thoroughly. If any of them shows any signs of wear, heat bluing or damage, replace the whole set.

NOTE: Some engines will have both standard and 0.010 in. oversize lifters. The oversized lifters will have "10" etched into the side. The block will be stamped "OS" on the cast pad next to the lifter bore. and on the top rail of the crankcase above the lifter bore.

To install:

WARNING: New lifters must be primed before installation. Damage to the lifters and engine will result if new lifters are installed dry!

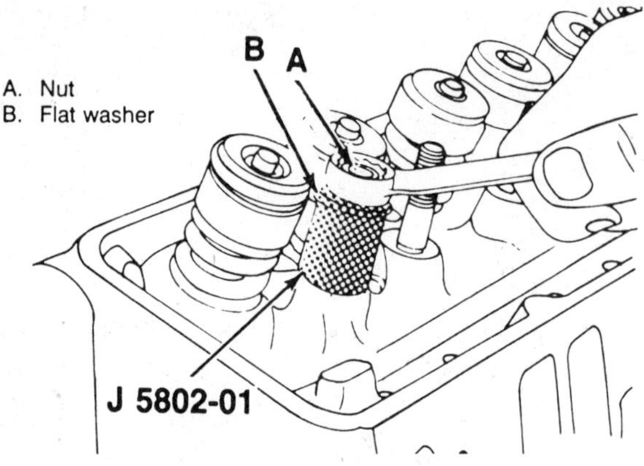

Rocker stud removal

6. Prime new lifters by immersing them in clean kerosene or diesel fuel and working the lifter plunger while the unit is submerged.
7. Prior to installation, coat the lifter roller with engine oil supplement. Re-used lifters must be installed in their original positions!
8. Install the lifters.
9. Install the guide plates and clamps. Torque the clamp bolts to 18 ft. lbs.
10. After all the clamps are installed, turn the crankshaft by hand, 2 full turns (720°) to ensure free movement of the lifters in the guide plates. If the crankshaft won't turn, one or more lifters may be jamming in the gude plates.
11. The remainder of assembly the the reverse of disassembly.

Rocker Stud

REPLACEMENT

NOTE: The following tools will be necessary for this procedure: Rocker stud replacement tool J-5802-01, Reamer J-5715 (0.003 in. os) or Reamer J-6036 (0.013 in. os) and Installer J-6880, or their equivalents.

6–4.3L
6–4.8L
8–5.0L
8–5.7L

1. Remove the rocker cover.
2. Remove the rocker arm.
3. Place the tool over the stud. Install the nut and flat washer.
4. Tighten the nut to remove the stud.

To install:

5. Using one of the reamers, ream the stud hole as necessary.
6. Coat the lower end of the new stud with SAE 80W-90 gear oil.
7. Using the installing tool, install the new stud. The stud is properly installed when the tool bottoms on the cylinder head.
8. Install the rocker arm(s) and adjust the valves.
9. Install the cover.

8–7.4L

1. Remove the rocker cover.
2. Remove the rocker arm.
3. Using a deep socket, unscrew the stud.
4. Installation is the reverse of removal. Tighten the stud to 50 ft. lbs. Adjust the valves.

Cylinder Head

REMOVAL AND INSTALLATION

6–4.8L

1. Disconnect the negative battery cable and unbolt it at the engine.
2. Drain the cooling system.

CAUTION

When draining the coolant, keep in mind that cats and dogs are attracted by the ethylene glycol antifreeze, and are quite likely to drink any that is left in an uncovered container or in puddles on the ground. This will prove fatal in sufficient quantity. Always drain the coolant into a sealable container. Coolant should be reused unless it is contaminated or several years old.

3. Remove the air cleaner assembly.
4. Disconnect the fuel line at the carburetor.
5. Disconnect the accelerator and transmission linkages.
6. Mark and disconnect all required electrical and vacuum lines.
7. Remove the combination manifold assembly retaining bolts.
8. Remove the combination manifold from the engine.
9. Remove the valve cover.
10. Remove the rocker arms and pushrods. Keep them in order for re-installation.
11. If equipped, disconnect the AIR injection hose at the check valve.
12. Disconnect the upper radiator hose at the thermostat housing.
13. Remove the cylinder head retaining bolts.
14. With the aid of an assistant, lift the cylinder head from the engine.

To install:

15. Thoroughly clean both the head and block surfaces. See the paragraphs below on Cylinder Head Inspection.
16. Install a new head gasket on the block. If an all steel gasket is used, coat both sides with sealer. If a composition gasket is used, do not use sealer. Position the gasket on the block with the bead up.
17. With the aid of an assistant, lower the cylinder head onto the engine.
18. Coat the threads of the head bolts with sealer and install them. Torque the bolts, in 3 equal steps, in the sequence shown, to 95 ft. lbs. for all but the left front (no.12) bolt. Torque that one to 85 ft. lbs.
19. Connect the upper radiator hose at the thermostat housing.
20. Connect the AIR injection hose at the check valve.
21. Install the rocker arms and pushrods. Adjust the valves.
22. Install the valve cover.
23. Install the combination manifold.
24. Connect all electrical and vacuum lines.
25. Connect the accelerator and transmission linkages.
26. Connect the fuel line at the carburetor.

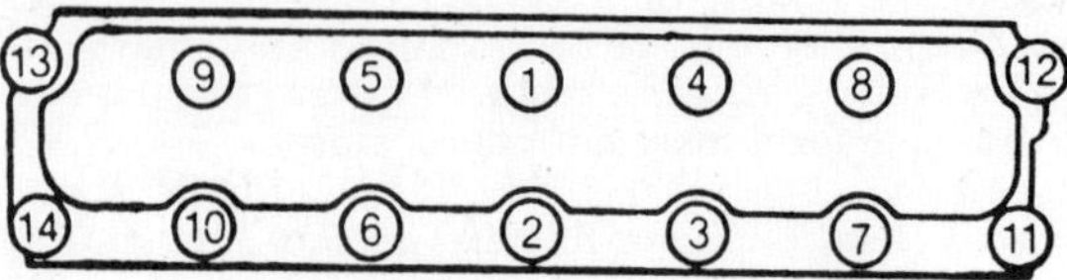

6-4.8L cylinder head bolt torque sequence

27. Install air cleaner assembly.
28. Fill the cooling system.
29. Install the negative battery cable.

6–4.3L

1. Disconnect the negative battery cable.
2. Remove the engine cover.
3. Remove the intake manifold as described later.
4. Remove the exhaust manifold as describer later.
5. Remove the air pipe at the rear of the head (right cylinder head).
6. Remove the generator mounting bolt at the cylinder head (right cylinder head).
7. Remove the power steering pump and brackets from the cylinder head, and lay them aside (left cylinder head).
8. Remove the air conditioner compressor, and lay it aside (left cylinder head).
9. Remove the rocker arm cover as outlined previously.
10. Remove the spark plugs.
11. Remove the pushrods, as outlined previously.
12. Remove the cylinder head bolts.
13. Remove the cylinder head.

To install:

14. Clean all gasket mating surfaces, install a new gasket and reinstall the cylinder head.
15. Install the cylinder heads using new gaskets. Install the gaskets with the head up.

NOTE: Coat a steel gasket on both sides with sealer. If a composition gasket is used, do not use sealer.

16. Clean the bolts, apply sealer to the threads, and install them hand tight.
17. Tighten the head bolts a little at a time in the sequence shown. Head bolt torque is listed in the Torque Specifications chart.
18. Install the intake and exhaust manifolds.
19. Adjust the rocker arms.
20. Install the pushrods.
21. Install the spark plugs.
22. Install the rocker arm cover.
23. Install the air conditioner compressor.
24. Install the power steering pump and brackets.
25. Install the generator mounting bolt at the cylinder head.
26. Install the air pipe at the rear of the head.
27. Install the exhaust manifold.
28. Install the intake manifold.
29. Install the engine cover.
30. Connect the negative battery cable.

8–5.0L
8–5.7L

1. Remove the intake manifold.
2. Remove the exhaust manifolds as described later and tie out of the way.
3. If the truck is equipped with air conditioning, remove the air conditioning compressor and the forward mounting bracket and lay the compressor aside. Do not disconnect any of the refrigerant lines.
4. Back off the rocker arm nuts and pivot the rocker arms out of the way so that the pushrods can be removed. Identify the pushrods so that they can be installed in their original positions.
5. Remove the cylinder head bolts and remove the heads.
6. Install the cylinder heads using new gaskets. Install the gaskets with the word **HEAD** up.

NOTE: Coat a steel gasket on both sides with sealer. If a composition gasket is used, do not use sealer.

7. Clean the bolts, apply sealer to the threads, and install them hand tight.
8. Tighten the head bolts a little at a time in the sequence shown. Head bolt torque is listed in the Torque Specifications chart.
9. Install the intake and exhaust manifolds.
10. Adjust the rocker arms as explained later.

8–6.2L Diesel

RIGHT SIDE

1. Remove the intake manifold.
2. Remove the fuel injection lines. See Section 5.
3. Remove the cruise control transducer.
4. Remove the upper fan shroud.
5. Remove the air conditioning compressor belt.
6. Remove the exhaust manifold.
7. Disconnect and label the glow plug wiring.
8. Remove the oil dipsticke tube.
9. Remove the oil fill tube upper bracket.
10. Remove the rocker arm cover(s), after removing any accessory brackets which interfere with cover removal.
11. Remove the rocker arm assemblies. It is a good practice to number or mark the parts to avoid interchanging them.
12. Remove the pushrods. Keep them in order.
13. Remove the air cleaner resonator and bracket.
14. Remove the automatic transmission dipstick and tube.
15. Drain the cooling system.

CAUTION

When draining the coolant, keep in mind that cats and dogs are attracted by the ethylene glycol antifreeze, and are quite likely to drink any that is left in an uncovered container or in puddles on the ground. This will prove fatal in sufficient quantity. Always drain the coolant into a sealable container. Coolant should be reused unless it is contaminated or several years old.

16. Disconnect the heater hoses at the head.
17. Disconnect the upper radiator hose.
18. Disconnect the bypass hose.
19. Remove the alternator upper bracket.
20. Remove the coolant crossover pipe and thermostat.
21. Remove the head bolts.
22. Remove the cylinder head.

To install:

23. Clean the mating surfaces of the head and block thoroughly.
24. Install a new head gasket on the engine block. Do NOT coat the gaskets with any sealer on either engine. The gaskets have a special coating that eliminates the need for sealer. The use of sealer will interfere with this coating and cause leaks. In-

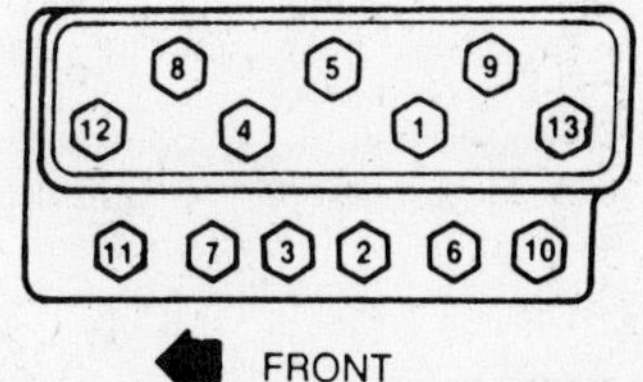

6–4.3L head bolt torque sequence

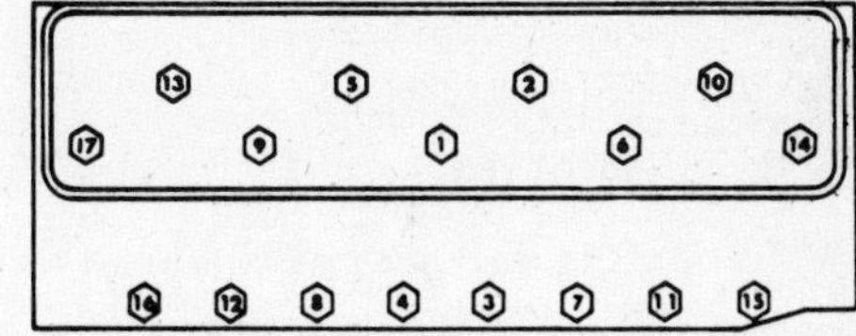

8–5.0L and 8–5.7L head bolt torque sequence

stall the cylinder head onto the block.
25. Clean the head bolts thoroughly. The left rear head bolt must be installed into the head prior to head installation. Coat the threads and heads of the head bolts with sealing compound (GM part #1052080 or equivalent) before installation. Tighten the head bolts as explained in the Torque Specifications Chart.
26. Install the coolant crossover pipe and thermostat.
27. Install the alternator upper bracket.
28. Connect the bypass hose.
29. Connect the upper radiator hose.
30. Connect the heater hoses at the head.
31. Install the automatic transmission dipstick and tube.
32. Install the air cleaner resonator and bracket.
33. Install the pushrods.
34. Install the rocker arm assemblies.
35. Adjust the valves.
36. Install the rocker arm cover(s).
37. Install the oil fill tube upper bracket.
38. Install the oil dipsticke tube.
39. Connect the glow plug wiring.
40. Install the exhaust manifold.
41. Install the air conditioning compressor belt.
42. Install the upper fan shroud.
43. Install the cruise control transducer.
44. Install the fuel injection lines. See Section 5.
45. Install the intake manifold.
46. Fill the cooling system.

LEFT SIDE

1. Remove the intake manifold.
2. Remove the fuel injection lines. See Section 5.
3. Remove the cruise control transducer.
4. Remove the upper fan shroud.
5. Remove the air conditioning compressor belt.
6. Remove the exhaust manifold.
7. Remove the power steering pump lower adjusting bolts.
8. Disconnect and label the glow plug wiring.
9. Remove the air conditioning compressor and position it out of the way. DO NOT DISCONNECT ANY REFRIGERANT LINES!
10. Remove the power steering pump and position it out of the way. DO NOT DISCONNECT THE FLUID LINES!
11. Remove the oil dipsticke tube.
12. Disconnect the transmission detent cable.
13. Remove the glow plug controller and bracket.
14. Remove the rocker arm cover(s), after removing any accessory brackets which interfere with cover removal.
15. Remove the rocker arm assemblies. It is a good practice to number or mark the parts to avoid interchanging them.
16. Remove the pushrods. Keep them in order.
17. Remove the air cleaner resonator and bracket.
18. Remove the automatic transmission dipstick and tube.
19. Drain the cooling system.

CAUTION

When draining the coolant, keep in mind that cats and dogs are attracted by the ethylene glycol antifreeze, and are quite likely to drink any that is left in an uncovered container or in puddles on the ground. This will prove fatal in sufficient quantity. Always drain the coolant into a sealable container. Coolant should be reused unless it is contaminated or several years old.

20. Remove the alternator upper bracket.
21. Remove the coolant crossover pipe and thermostat.
22. Remove the head bolts.
23. Remove the cylinder head.

To install:

24. Clean the mating surfaces of the head and block thoroughly.
25. Install a new head gasket on the engine block. Do NOT coat the gaskets with any sealer on either engine. The gaskets have a special coating that eliminates the need for sealer. The use of sealer will interfere with this coating and cause leaks. Install the cylinder head onto the block.
26. Clean the head bolts thoroughly. The left rear head bolt must be installed into the head prior to head installation. Coat the threads and heads of the head bolts with sealing compound (GM part #1052080 or equivalent) before installation. Tighten the head bolts as explained in the Torque Specifications Chart.
27. Install the coolant crossover pipe and thermostat.
28. Install the alternator upper bracket.
29. Install the automatic transmission dipstick and tube.
30. Install the air cleaner resonator and bracket.
31. Install the pushrods.
32. Install the rocker arm assemblies.
33. Adjust the valves.
34. Install the rocker arm cover(s).
35. Install the oil fill tube upper bracket.
36. Install the oil dipsticke tube.
37. Connect the glow plug wiring.
38. Install the compressor.
39. Install the power steering pump.
40. Install the glow plug controller.
41. Install the exhaust manifold.
42. Connect the detent cable.
43. Install the air conditioning compressor belt.
44. Install the upper fan shroud.
45. Install the cruise control transducer.
46. Install the fuel injection lines. See Section 5.
47. Install the intake manifold.
48. Fill the cooling system.

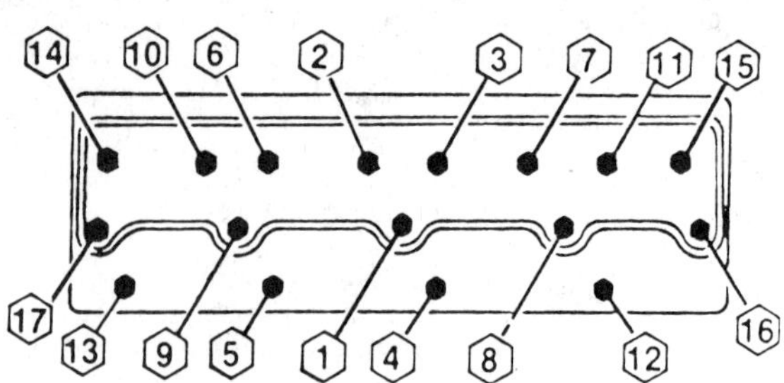

8–6.2L diesel head bolt torque sequence

8–7.4L

RIGHT SIDE

1. Remove the intake manifold.
2. Remove the exhaust manifolds.
3. Remove the alternator.
4. Remove the AIR pump.
5. If the truck is equipped with air conditioning, remove the air conditioning compressor and the forward mounting bracket and lay the compressor aside. Do not disconnect any of the refrigerant lines.
6. Remove the rocker arm cover.
7. Remove the spark plugs.
8. Remove the AIR pipes at the rear of the head.
9. Disconnect the ground strap at the rear of the head.
10. Disconnect the sensor wire.
11. Back off the rocker arm nuts and pivot the rocker arms out of the way so that the pushrods can be removed. Identify the pushrods so that they can be installed in their original positions.
12. Remove the cylinder head bolts and remove the heads.

To install:

13. Thoroughly clean the mating surfaces of the head and block. Clean the bolt holes thoroughly.
14. Install the cylinder heads using new gaskets. Install the

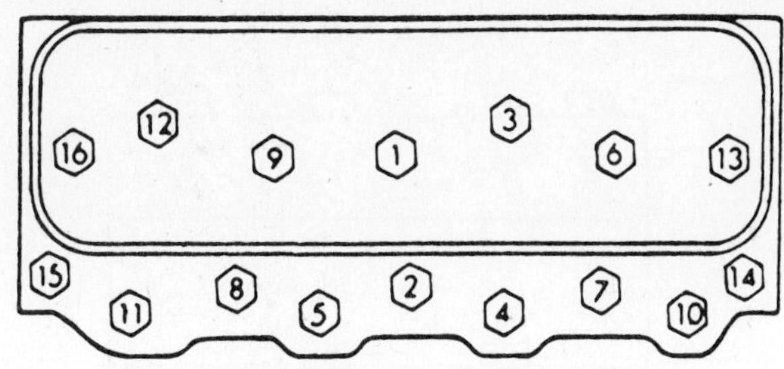

8–7.4L head bolt torque sequence

gaskets with the word **HEAD** up.

NOTE: Coat a steel gasket on both sides with sealer. If a composition gasket is used, do not use sealer.

15. Clean the bolts, apply sealer to the threads, and install them hand tight.
16. Tighten the head bolts a little at a time in the sequence shown. Head bolt torque is listed in the Torque Specifications chart.
17. Install the intake and exhaust manifolds.
18. Install the pushrods.
19. Install the rocker arms and adjust them as described in this Section.
20. Connect the sensor wire.
21. Connect the ground strap at the rear of the head.
22. Install the AIR pipes at the rear of the head.
23. Install the spark plugs.
24. Install the rocker arm cover.
25. Install the air conditioning compressor and the forward mounting bracket.
26. Install the AIR pump.
27. Install the alternator.

LEFT SIDE

1. Remove the intake manifold.
2. Remove the exhaust manifolds.
3. Remove the alternator.
4. If the truck is equipped with air conditioning, remove the air conditioning compressor and the forward mounting bracket and lay the compressor aside. Do not disconnect any of the refrigerant lines.
5. Remove the rocker arm cover.
6. Remove the spark plugs.
7. Remove the AIR pipes at the rear of the head.
8. Disconnect the ground strap at the rear of the head.
9. Disconnect the sensor wire.
10. Back off the rocker arm nuts and pivot the rocker arms out of the way so that the pushrods can be removed. Identify the pushrods so that they can be installed in their original positions.
11. Remove the cylinder head bolts and remove the heads.

To install:

12. Thoroughly clean the mating surfaces of the head and block. Clean the bolt holes thoroughly.
13. Install the cylinder heads using new gaskets. Install the gaskets with the word **HEAD** up.

NOTE: Coat a steel gasket on both sides with sealer. If a composition gasket is used, do not use sealer.

14. Clean the bolts, apply sealer to the threads, and install them hand tight.
15. Tighten the head bolts a little at a time in the sequence shown. Head bolt torque is listed in the Torque Specifications chart.
16. Install the intake and exhaust manifolds.
17. Install the pushrods.
18. Install the rocker arms and adjust them as described in this Section.
19. Connect the sensor wire.
20. Connect the ground strap at the rear of the head.
21. Install the AIR pipes at the rear of the head.
22. Install the spark plugs.
23. Install the rocker arm cover.
24. Install the air conditioning compressor and the forward mounting bracket.
25. Install the alternator.

CLEANING AND INSPECTION

Gasoline Engines

NOTE: Any diesel cylinder head work should be handled by a reputable machine shop familiar with diesel engines. Disassembly, valve lapping, and assembly can be completed by the following engine procedures.

One the complete valve train has been removed from the cylinder head(s), the head itself can be inspected, cleaned and machined (if necessary). Set the head(s) on a clean work space, so the combustion chambers are facing up. Begin cleaning the chambers and ports with a hardwood chisel or other non-metallic tool (to avoid nicking or gouging the chamber, ports, and especially the valve seats). Chip away the major carbon deposits, then remove the remainder of carbon with a wire brush fitted to an electric drill.

NOTE: Be sure that the carbon is actually removed, rather than just burnished.

After decarbonizing is completed, take the head(s) to a machine shop and have the head hot tanked. In this process, the head is lowered into a hot chemical bath that very effectively cleans all grease, corrosion, and scale from all internal and external head surfaces. Also have the machinist check the valve seats and recut them if necessary. When you bring the clean head(s) home, place them on a clean surface. Completely clean the entire valve train with solvent.

CHECKING FOR HEAD WARPAGE

Lay the head down with the combustion chambers facing up. Place a straight edge across the gasket surface of the head, both diagonally and straight across the center. Using a flat feeler gauge, determine the clearance at the center of the straight edge. If warpage exceeds 0.003 in. (0.0762mm) in a 6 in. (152mm) span, or 0.006 in. (0.152mm) over the total length, the cylinder head must be resurfaced (which is akin to planing a piece of wood). Resurfacing can be performed at most machine shops.

NOTE: When resurfacing the cylinder head(s) of V8 engines, the intake manifold mounting position is altered, and must be corrected by machining a proportionate amount from the intake manifold flange.

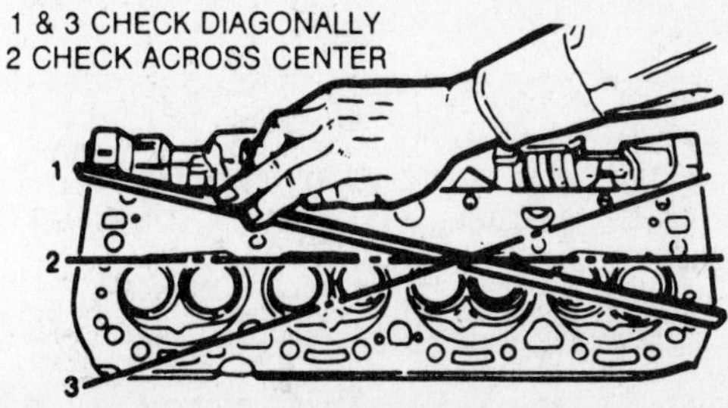

Check the cylinder head mating surface for warpage with a machinist's straightedge

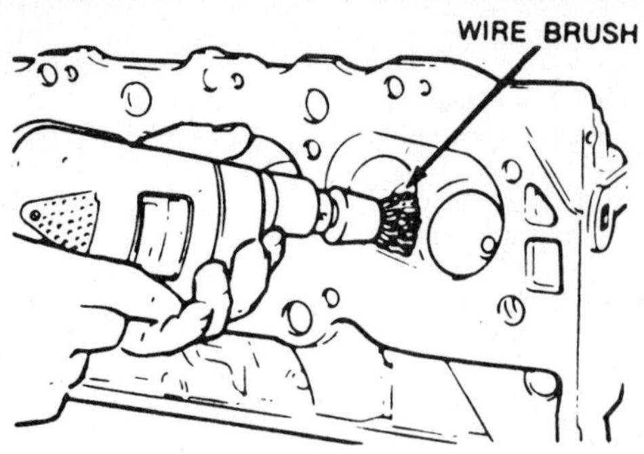

Using a drill-mounted wire brush to de-carbon the cylinder head

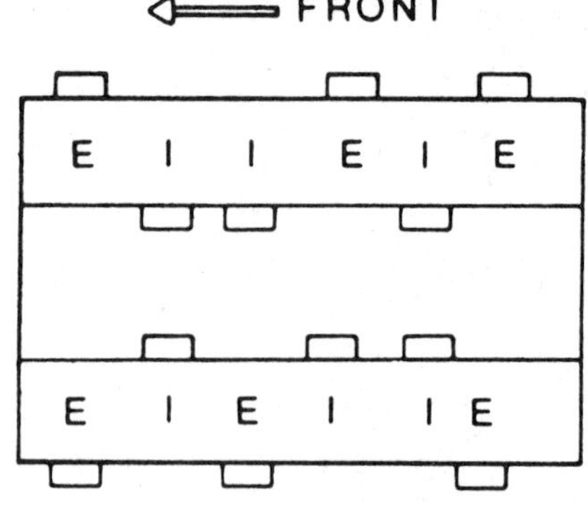

6-4.3L valve arrangement

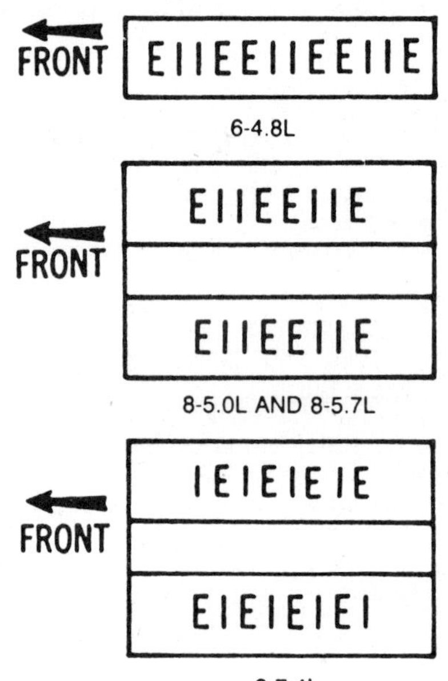

Valve arrangement for gasoline engines, exc. the 6-4.3L

RESURFACING

Cylinder head resurfacing should be done by a qualified machine shop.

Valves and Springs

REMOVAL AND INSTALLATION

Cylinder Heads Removed

1. Remove the head(s), and place on a clean surface.
2. Using a suitable spring compressor (for pushrod type overhead valve engines), compress the valve spring and remove the valve spring cap key. Release the spring compressor and remove the valve spring and cap (and valve rotator on some engines).

NOTE: Use care in removing the keys. They are easily lost.

3. Remove the valve seals from the intake valve guides. Throw these old seals away, as you'll be installing new seals during reassembly.
4. Slide the valves out of the head from the combustion chamber side.
5. Make a holder for the valves out of a piece of wood or cardboard, as outlined for the pushrods in gasoline engine Cylinder Head Removal. Make sure you number each hole in the cardboard to keep the valves in proper order. Slide the valves out of the head from the combustion chamber side. They MUST be installed as they were removed.

Cylinder Head(s) Installed

Special tool J-23590, or its equivalent, will be necessary for this job.

It is often not necessary to remove the cylinder head(s) in order to service the valve train. Such is the case when valve seals need to be replaced. Valve seals can be easily replaced with the head(s) on the engine. The only special equipment needed for this job are an air line adapter (sold in most auto parts stores), which screws a compressed air line into the spark plug hole of the cylinder on which you are working, and a valve spring compressor. A source of compressed air is needed, of course.

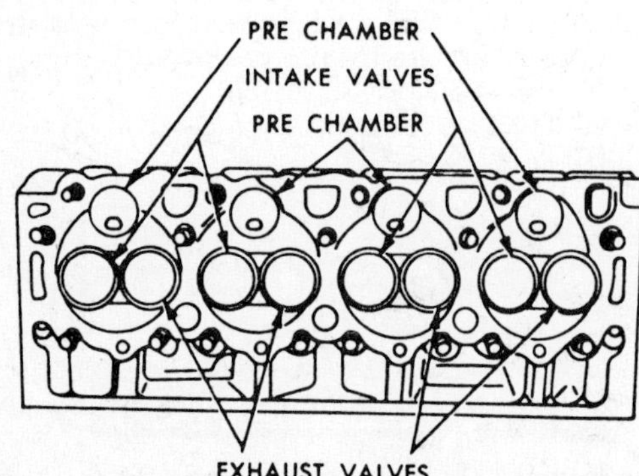

Diesel valve arrangement

1. Remove the valve cover as previously detailed.
2. Remove the spark plug, rocker arm and pushrod on the cylinder(s) to be serviced.
3. Install the air line adapter (GM tool No. J-23590 or equivalent) into the spark plug hole. Turn on the air compressor to apply compressed air into the cylinder. This keeps the valves up in place.

NOTE: Set the regulator of the air compressor at least 50 pounds to ensure adequate pressure.

4. Using the valve spring compressor, compress the valve spring and remove the valve keys and keepers, the valve spring and damper.
5. Remove the valve stem seal.
6. To reassemble, oil the valve stem and new seal. Install a new seal over the valve stem. Set the spring, damper and keeper in place. Compress the spring. Coat the keys with grease to hold

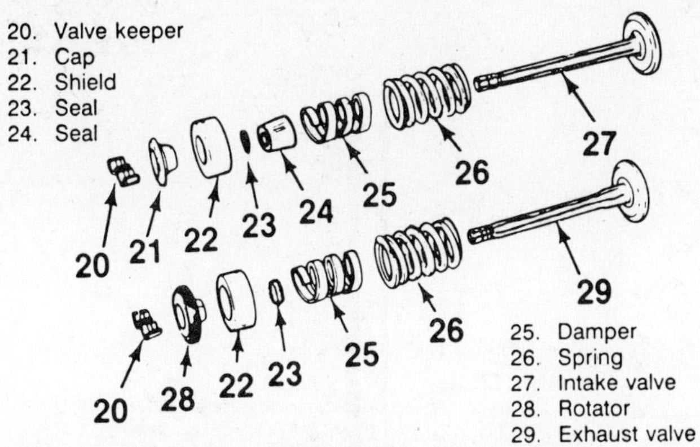

Valves and related components for the 6-4.3L, 6-4.8L, 8-5.0L and 8-5.7L engines

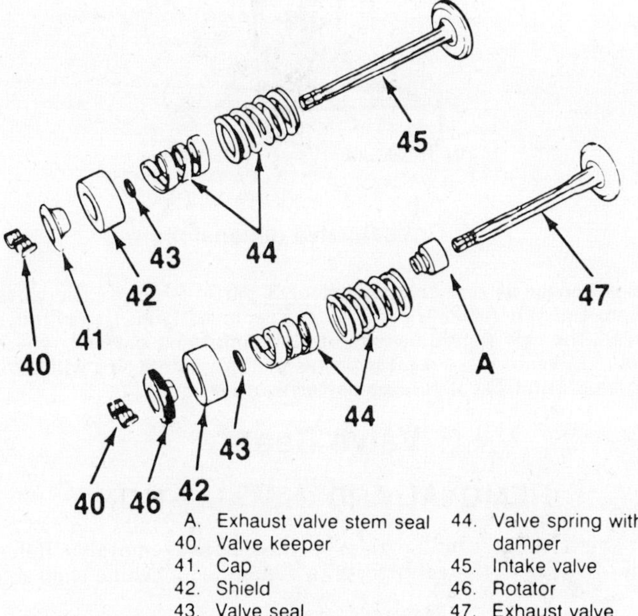

Valves and components for the 6.2L diesel engine

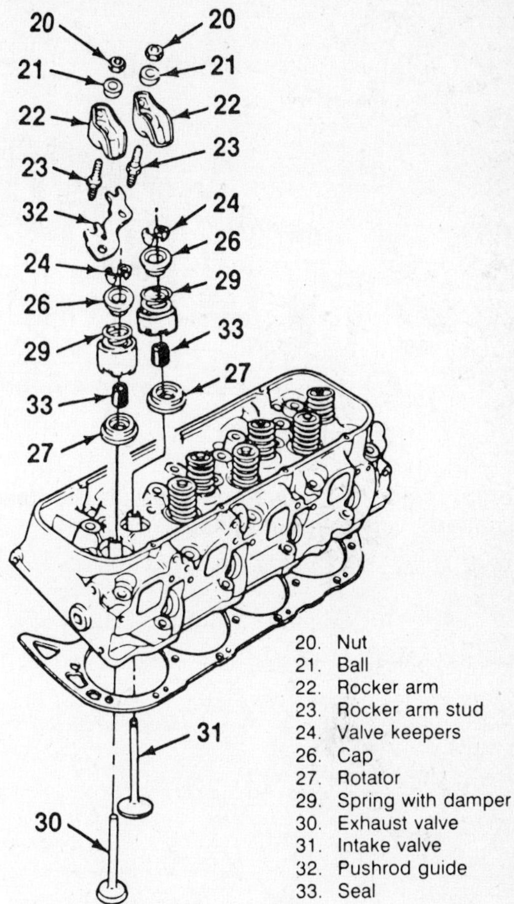

Valves and components for the 7.4L engine

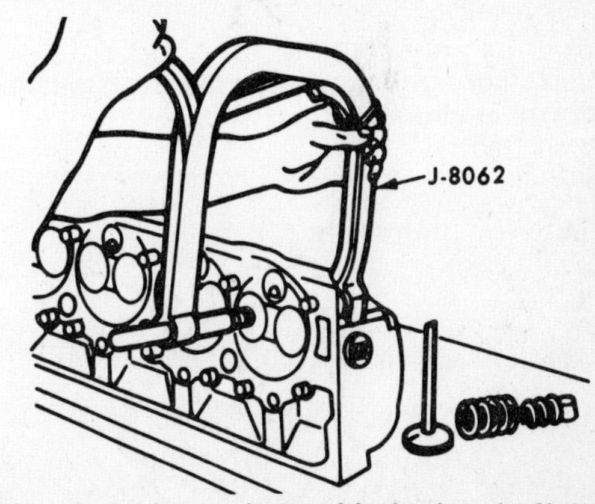

Removing the valve springs with the head off the engine

them onto the valve stem and install the keys, making sure they are seated fully in the keeper. Reinstall the valve cover after adjusting the valves, as outlined in this Section.

INSPECTION

Inspect the valve faces and seats (in the head) for pits, burned spots and other evidence of poor seating. If a valve face is in such bad shape that the head of the valve must be ground in order to true up the face, discard the valve because the sharp edge will run too hot. The correct angle for valve faces is 45°. We recommend the refacing be done at a reputable machine shop.

Check the valve stem for scoring and burned spots. If not noticeably scored or damaged, clean the valve stem with solvent to remove all gum and varnish. Clean the valve guides using solvent an an expanding wire type valve guide cleaner. If you have access to a dial indicator for measuring valve stem-to-guide clearance, mount it so that the stem of the indicator is at 90° to the valve stem, and as close to the valve guide as possible. Move the valve off its seat, and measure the valve guide-to-stem clearance by rocking the stem back and forth to actuate the dial indicator. Measure the valve stems using a micrometer, and compare to specifications to determine whether stem or guide wear is responsible for the excess clearance. If a dial indicator and micrometer are not available to you, take your cylinder head and valves to a reputable machine shop for inspection.

Some of the engines covered in this guide are equipped with valve rotators, which double as valve spring caps. In normal operation the rotators put a certain degree of wear on the tip of the valve stem. This wear appears as concentric rings on the stem tip. However, if the rotator is not working properly, the wear

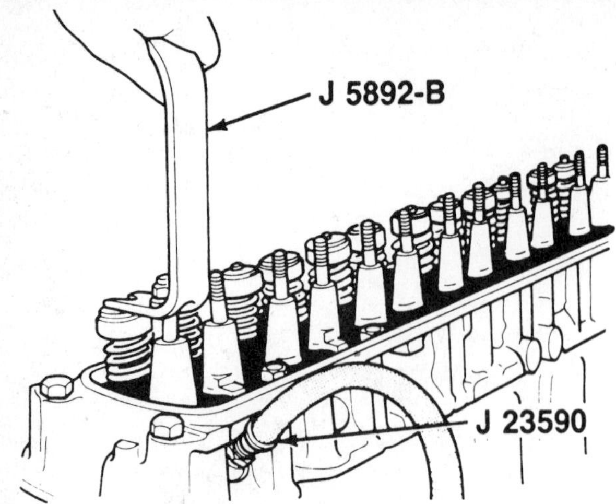

Compressing the valve springs with the head installed – gasoline engines

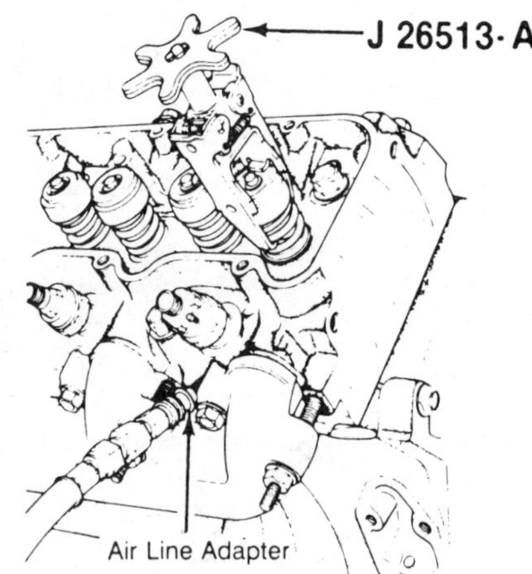

Valve spring removal with the head installed, on diesel engines

Checking the valve seat concentricity

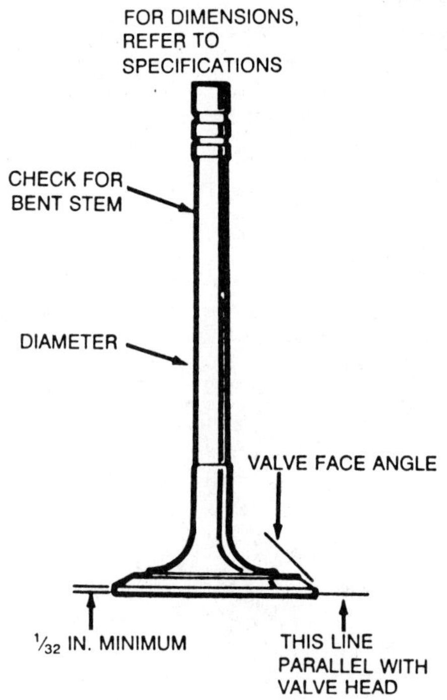

Critical valve dimensions

may appear as straight notches or **X** patterns across the valve stem tip. Whenever the valves are removed from the cylinder head, the tips should be inspected for improper pattern, which could indicate valve rotator problems. Valve stem tips will have to be ground flat if rotator patterns are severe.

Valve Seats

REMOVAL AND INSTALLATION

The valve seats in Chevrolet engines are not removable. Refer all servicing of the valve seats to a qualified machine shop.

Valve Guides

The engines covered in this guide use integral valve guides. That is, they are a part of the cylinder head and cannot be replaced. The guides can, however, be reamed oversize if they are found to be worn past an acceptable limit. Occasionally, a valve guide bore will be oversize as manufactured. These are marked on the inboard side of the cylinder heads on the machined surface just above the intake manifold.

If the guides must be reamed (this service is available at most machine shops), then valves with oversize stems must be fitted. Valves are usually available in 0.001 in., 0.003 in., and 0.005 in. stem oversizes. Valve guides which are not excessively worn or distorted may, in some cases, be knurled rather than reamed. Knurling is a process in which the metal on the valve guide bore is displaced and raised, thereby reducing clearance. Knurling also provides excellent oil control. The option of knurling rather than reaming valve guides should be discussed with a reputable machinist or engine specialist.

LAPPING THE VALVES

When valve faces and seats have been refaced and recut, or if they are determined to be in good condition, the valves must be lapped in to ensure efficient sealing when the valve closes against the seat.

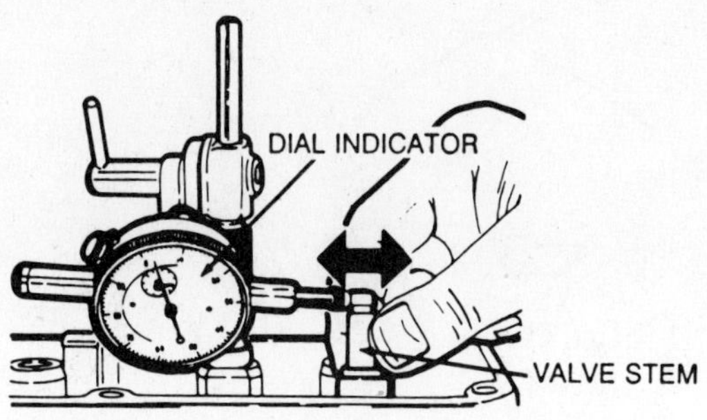

Check the stem-to-guide clearance

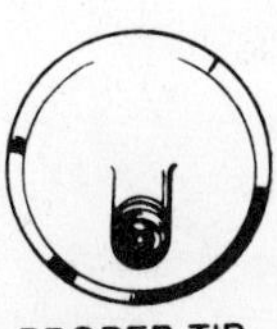

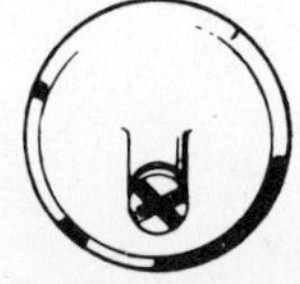
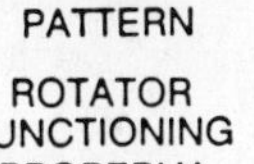

Valve stem wear

Lapping the valves by hand

1. Invert the cylinder head so that the combustion chambers are facing up.
2. Lightly lubricate the valve stems with clean oil, and coat the valve seats with valve grinding compound. Install the valves in the head as numbered.
3. Attach the suction cup of a valve lapping tool to a valve head. You'll probably have to moisten the cup to securely attach the tool to the valve.
4. Rotate the tool between the palms. changing position and lifting the tool often to prevent grooving. Lap the valve until a smooth, polished seat is evident (you may have to add a bit more compound after some lapping is done).
5. Remove the valve and tool, and remove ALL traces of grinding compound with solvent soaked rag, or rinse the head with solvent.

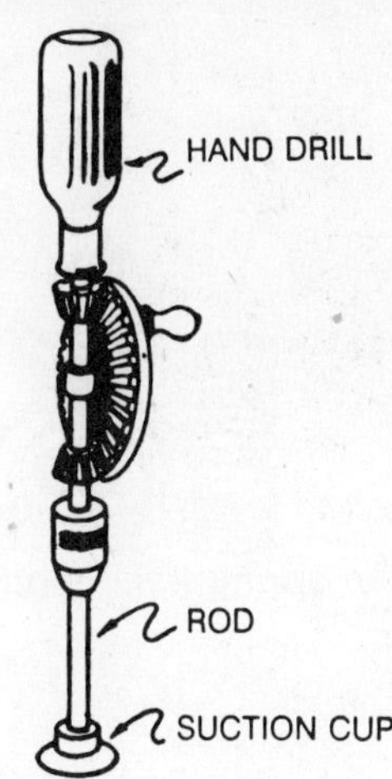

Homemade lapping tool

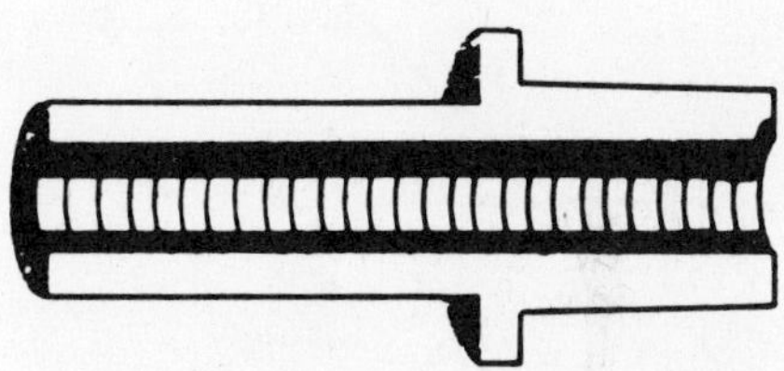

Cutaway view of a knurled guide

NOTE: Valve lapping can also be done by fastening a suction cup to a piece of drill rod in a hand eggbeater type drill. Proceed as above, using the drill as a lapping tool. Due to the higher speeds involved when using the hand drill, care must be exercised to avoid grooving the seat. Lift the tool and change direction of rotation often.

Valve Springs

HEIGHT AND PRESSURE CHECK

1. Place the valve spring on a flat, clean surface next to a square.
2. Measure the height of the spring, and rotate it against the edge of the square to measure distortion (out-of-roundness). If spring height varies between springs by more than $^1/_{16}$ in. (1.6mm) replace the spring.

A valve spring tester is needed to test spring test pressure, so the valve springs must usually be taken to a professional machine shop for this test. Spring pressure at the installed and compressed heights is checked, and a tolerance of plus or minus 5 lbs. is permissible on the springs covered in this guide.

VALVE INSTALLATION

NOTE: For installing new valve stem seals without removing the cylinder head(s), see the procedure under Valves and Springs – Cylinder Head(s) Installed earlier in this Section.

New valve seals must be installed when the valve train is put back together. Certain seals slip over the valve stem and guide boss, while others require that the boss be machined. Teflon® guide seals are available. Check with a machinist and/or automotive parts store for a suggestion on the proper seals to use.

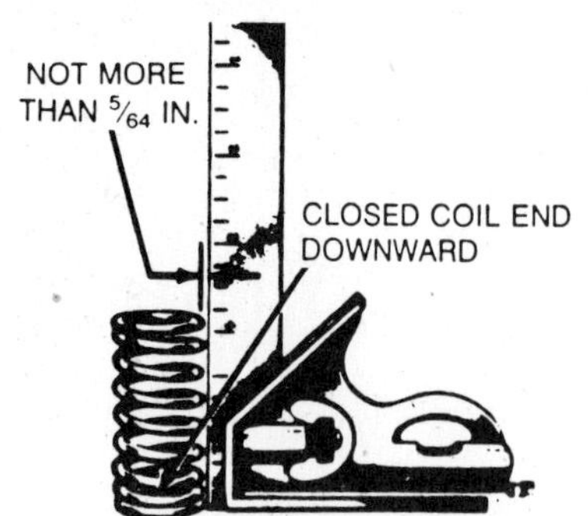

Checking valve spring free length and squareness

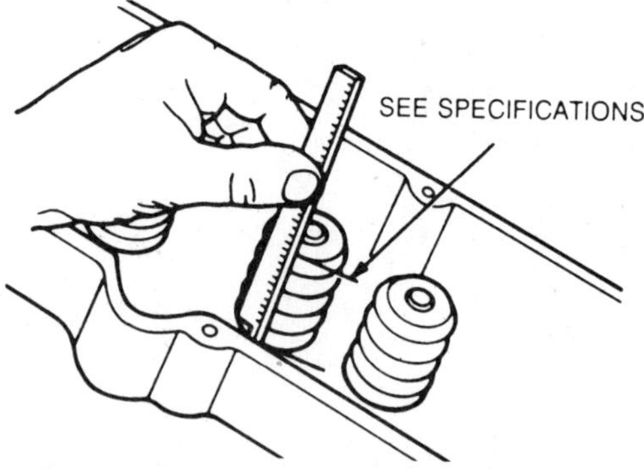

Checking valve spring installed height

Checking valve spring pressure

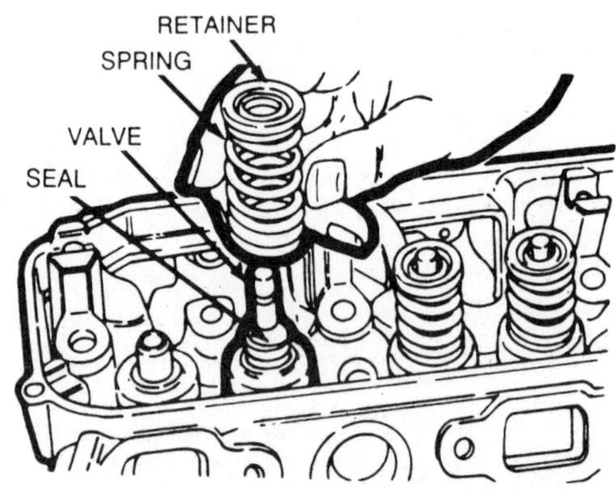

Installing valve stem seal

NOTE: Remember that when installing valve seals, a small amount of oil must be able to pass the seal to lubricate the valve guides; otherwise, excessive wear will result.

To install the valves and rocker assembly:

1. Lubricate the valve stems with clean engine oil.
2. Install the valves in the cylinder head, one at a time, as numbered.
3. Lubricate and position the seals and valve springs, again a valve at a time.
4. Install the spring retainers, and compress the springs.
5. With the valve key groove exposed above the compressed valve spring, wipe some wheel bearing grease around the groove. This will retain the keys as you release the spring compressor.
6. Using needlenose pliers (or your fingers), place the keys in the key grooves. The grease should hold the keys in place. Slowly release the spring compressor. The valve cap or rotator will raise up as the compressor is released, retaining the keys.
7. Install the rocker assembly, and install the cylinder head(s).

VALVE LASH ADJUSTMENT

All engines described in this book use hydraulic lifters, which require no periodic adjustment. In the event of cylinder head removal or any operation that requires disturbing the rocker arms, the rocker arms will have to be adjusted.

Inline 6–4.8L Engine

1. Remove the rocker arm cover.
2. Mark the distributor housing at the no.1 and no.6 wire positions and remove the cap.
3. Turn the crankshaft until the rotor points to the no.1 position. The following valves can be adjusted:
   - no.1 exhaust and intake
   - no.2 intake
   - no.3 exhaust
   - no.4 intake
   - no.5 exhaust

To adjust a valve, back off the adjusting nut untillash (play) is felt at the pushrod. Tighten the nut just until all lash is removed. This can be determined by rotating the pushrod with your fingers. When all lash is removed, the pushrod will stop rotating. When all play is removed, tighten the nut 1 full turn (360°).

4. Rotate the crankshaft until the rotor points to the no.6 position. The following valves can be adjusted:
   - no.2 exhaust
   - no.3 intake
   - no.4 exhaust
   - no.5 intake
   - no.6 intake and exhaust
5. Install the distributor cap.
6. Install the rocker cover.

V6 and V8 Engines

1. Remove the rocker covers and gaskets.

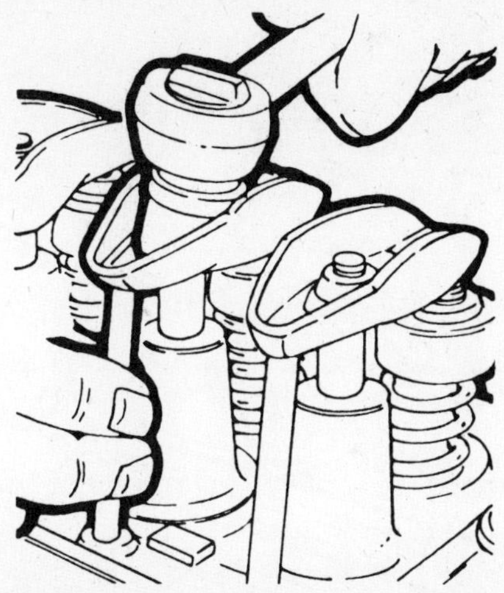

Adjusting the valves on gasoline engines

2. Crank the engine until the mark on the damper aligns with the **TDC** or **0** mark on the timing tab and the engine is in No. 1 firing position. This can be determined by placing the fingers on the No. 1 cylinder valves as the marks align. If the valves do not move, it is in No. 1 firing position. If the valves move, it is in No. 6 firing position (No. 4 on the V6) and the crankshaft should be rotated 1 more revolution to the No. 1 firing position.

To adjust a valve, back off the adjusting nut untillash (play) is felt at the pushrod. Tighten the nut just until all lash is removed. This can be determined by rotating the pushrod with your fingers. When all lash is removed, the pushrod will stop rotating. When all play is removed, tighten the nut 1 full turn (360°).

3. The adjustment is made in the same manner as 6 cylinder engines.

4. With the engine in No. 1 firing position, the following valves can be adjusted:

V6 Engines

- Exhaust – 1, 5, 6,
- Intake – 1, 2, 3,

V8 Engines

- Exhaust – 1,3,4,8
- Intake – 1,2,5,7

5. Crank the engine 1 full revolution until the marks are again in alignment. This is No. 6 firing position (No. 4 on the V6). The following valves can now be adjusted:

V6 Engines

- Exhaust – 2, 3, 4
- Intake – 4, 5, 6

V8 Engines

- Exhaust – 2,5,6,7
- Intake – 3,4,6,8

6. Reinstall the rocker arm covers using new gaskets.
7. Install the distributor cap and wire assembly.

Oil Pan

REMOVAL AND INSTALLATION

6–4.3L

A one piece type oil pan gasket is used.

1. Disconnect the negative battery cable. Raise the vehicle, support it safely, and drain the engine oil.
2. Remove the exhaust crossover pipe.
3. Remove the torque converter cover (on models with automatic transmission).
4. Remove the strut rods at the flywheel cover. On 4wd vehicles with automatic transmission, remove the strut rods at the engine mounts.

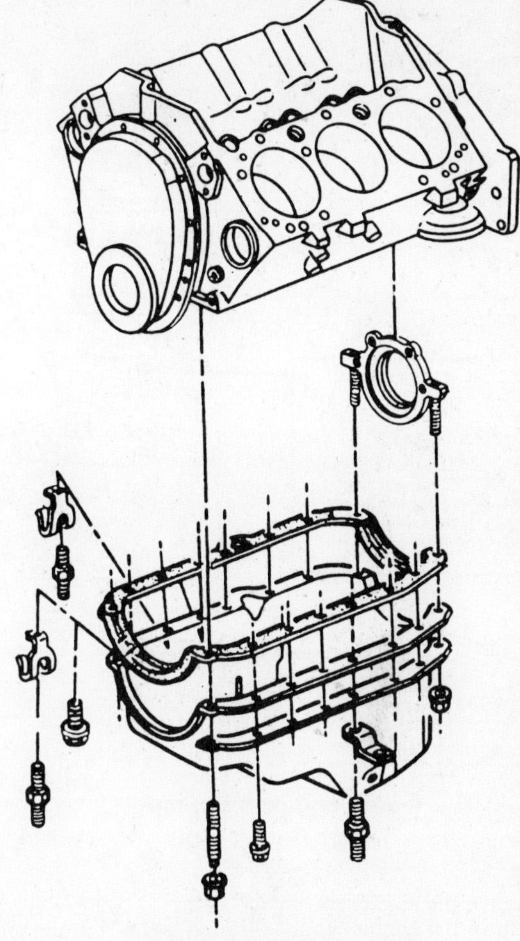

6-4.3L engine oil pump

5. Remove the strut rod brackets at the front engine mountings.
6. Remove the starter.
7. Remove the oil pan bolts, nuts and reinforcements.
8. Remove the oil pan and gaskets.

To install:

9. Thoroughly clean all gasket surfaces and install a new gasket, using only a small amount of sealer at the front and rear corners of the oil pan.
10. Install the oil pan and new gaskets.
11. Install the oil pan bolts, nuts and reinforcements. Torque the pan bolts to 100 inch lbs.
12. Install the starter.
13. Install the strut rod brackets at the front engine mountings.
14. Install the strut rods at the flywheel cover.
15. Install the torque converter cover (on models with automatic transmission).
16. Install the exhaust crossover pipe.
17. Connect the negative battery cable.
18. Fill the crankcase.

6–4.8L

1. Disconnect the negative battery cable.
2. Raise and support the truck on jackstands.
3. Drain the engine oil.
4. Remove the flywheel cover.

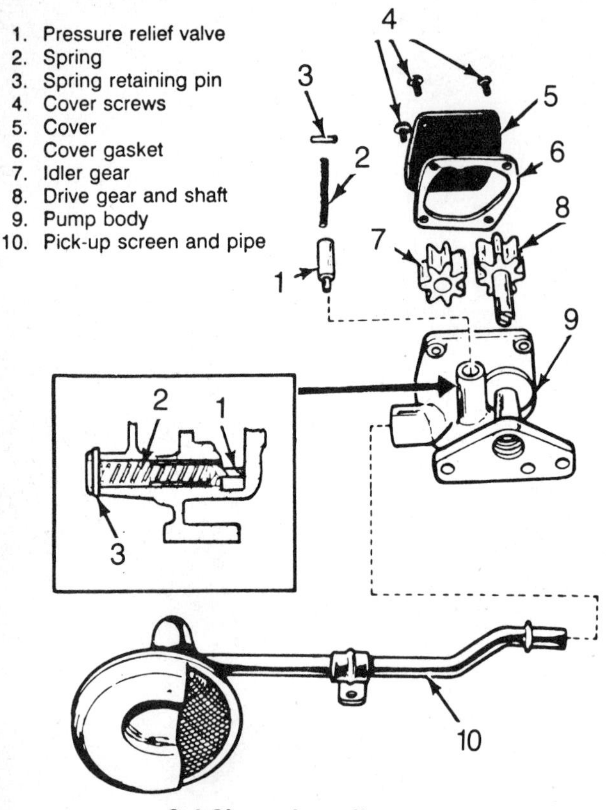

6-4.8L engine oil pump

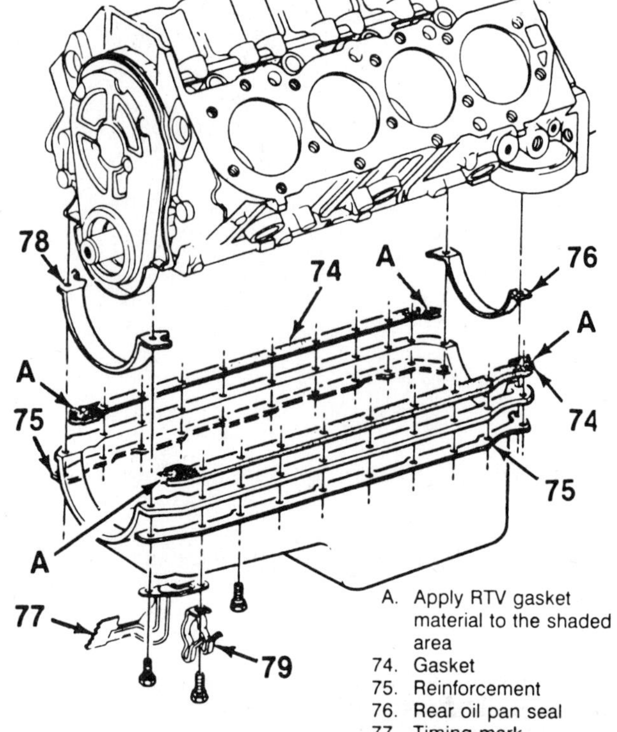

7.4L engine oil pan

5. Remove the starter assembly.
6. Remove the engine mount through bolts from the engine front mounts.
7. Using a floor jack under the damper, raise the engine enough to remove the oil pan.
8. Remove the oil pan retaining bolts. Remove the oil pan from the engine. You may have to break loose the pan with a soft mallet.
9. Thoroughly clean the mating surfaces of the pan and block. If the lips of the pan are bent, straighten them.
10. Installation is the reverse of the removal procedure. Use new gaskets and seals. Torque the pan-to-front cover bolts to 45 inch lbs. Torque the ¼ in. pan-to-block bolts to 80 in. lbs. and the $^{5}/_{16}$ in. bolts to 14 ft. lbs.

8-5.0L
8-5.7L

1. Drain the engine oil.
2. Remove the oil dipstick and tube.
3. If necessary remove the exhaust pipe crossover.
4. If equipped with automatic transmission, remove the converter housing pan.
5. Remove the starter brace and bolt and swing the starter aside. On 4wd vehicles with automatic transmission, remove the strut rods at the engine mounts.
6. Remove the oil pan and discard the gaskets.
7. Installation is the reverse of removal. Clean all gasket surfaces and use new gaskets to assemble. Use gasket sealer to retain side gaskets to the cylinder block. Install a new oil pan rear seal in the rear main bearing cap slot with the ends butting the side gaskets. Install a new front seal in the crankcase front cover with the ends butting the side gaskets. Torque the pan bolts to 65 inch lbs. Fill the engine with oil and check for leaks.

8-7.4L

1. Disconnect the battery.
2. Remove the fan shroud.
3. Remove the air cleaner.
4. Remove the distributor cap.
5. Raise and support the front end on jackstands.
6. Drain the engine oil.
7. Remove the converter housing pan. On 4wd vehicles with automatic transmission, remove the strut rods at the engine mounts.
8. Remove the oil filter.
9. Remove the oil pressure line.
10. Support the engine with a floor jack.

WARNING: Do not place the jack under the pan, sheet metal or pulley!

11. Remove the engine mount through-bolts.
12. Raise the engine just enough to remove the pan.
13. Remove the oil pan and discard the gaskets.

To install:

14. Clean all mating surfaces thoroughly.
15. Apply RTV gasket material to the front and rear corners of the gaskets.
16. Coat the gaskets with adhesive sealer and position them on the block.
17. Install the rear pan seal in the pan with the seal ends mating with the gaskets.
18. Install the front seal on the bottom of the front cover, pressing the locating tabs into the holes in the cover.
19. Install the oil pan.
20. Install the pan bolts, clips and reinforcements. Torque the pan-to-cover bolts to 70 inch lbs.; the pan-to-block bolts to 13 ft. lbs.

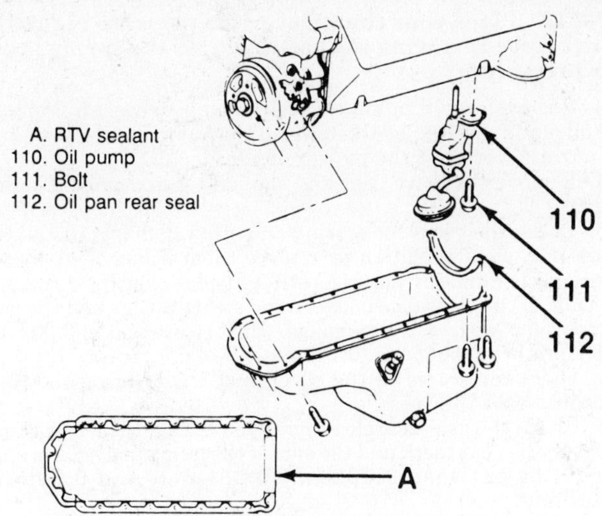

6.2L diesel engine oil pan

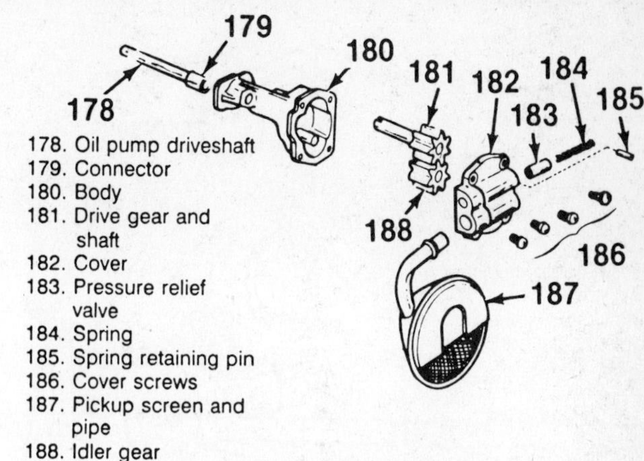

5.0L/5.7L oil pump

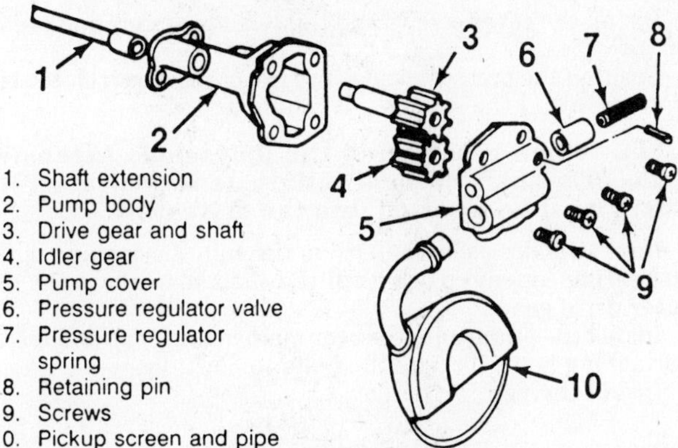

4.3L engine oil pump

21. Lower the engine onto the mounts.
22. Install the engine mount through-bolts.
23. Install the oil pressure line.
24. Install the oil filter.
25. Install the converter housing pan.
26. Install the distributor cap.
27. Install the air cleaner.
28. Install the fan shroud.
29. Connect the battery.
30. Fill the crankcase.

8–6.2L Diesel

1. Remove the vacuum pump and drive (with air conditioning or the oil pump drive (without air conditioning).
2. Disconnect the batteries and remove the dipstick.
3. Remove the upper radiator support and fan shroud.
4. Raise and support the truck. Drain the oil.
5. Remove the flywheel cover. On 4wd vehicles with automatic transmission, remove the strut rods at the engine mounts.
6. Disconnect the exhaust and crossover pipes.
7. Remove the oil cooler lines at the filter base.
8. Remove the starter assembly. Support the engine with a jack.
9. Remove the engine mounts from the block.
10. Raise the front of the engine and remove the oil pan.

To install:

11. Using new gaskets coated with sealer, position the oil pan on the block and install the bolts. Torque the bolts to 84 inch lbs., except for the two rear bolts. Torque them to 17 ft. lbs.
12. Install the engine mounts.
13. Remove the jack.
14. Install the starter assembly.
15. Install the oil cooler lines at the filter base.
16. Connect the exhaust and crossover pipes.
17. Install the flywheel cover.
18. Install the upper radiator support and fan shroud.
19. Connect the batteries.
20. Install the dipstick.
21. Install the vacuum pump and drive (with air conditioning or the oil pump drive (without air conditioning).
22. Fill the crankcase.

Oil Pump

REMOVAL AND INSTALLATION

6–4.3L

1. Remove the oil pan.
2. Remove the bolt attaching the pump to the rear main bearing cap. Remove the pump and the extension shaft, which will come out behind it.
3. If the pump has been disassembled, is being replaced, or for any reason oil has been removed from it, it must be primed. It can either be filled with oil before installing the cover plate (and oil kept within the pump during handling), or the entire pump cavity can be filled with petroleum jelly. IF THE PUMP IS NOT PRIMED, THE ENGINE COULD BE DAMAGED BEFORE IT RECEIVES ADEQUATE LUBRICATION WHEN YOU START IT!
4. Engage the extension shaft with the oil pump shaft. Align the slot on the top of the extension shaft with the drive tang on the lower end of the distributor driveshaft, and then position the pump at the rear main bearing cap so the mounting bolt can be installed. Install the bolt, torquing to 65 ft. lbs.
5. Install the oil pan.

6–4.8L

1. Raise and support the truck on jackstands.
2. Remove the oil pan.
3. Remove the oil pump tube bracket main bearing cap nut.
4. Remove the oil pump bolts and the oil pump.

To install:

5. Position the oil pump to he engine and align the slot in the oil pump shaft with the tang on the distributor shaft. The oil pump should slide easily in place.

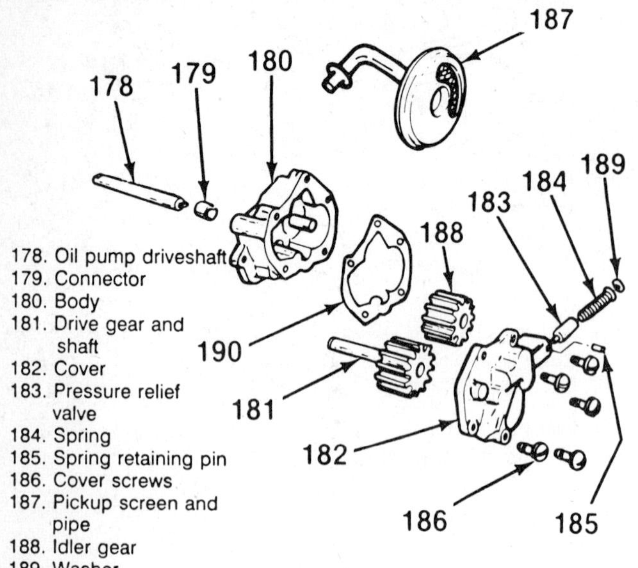

7.4L oil pump

6. Install the oil pump bolts and tighten to 115 inch lbs.
7. Install the oil pump pick-up tube to the main bearing cap nut and tighten to 25 ft. lbs.
8. Install the oil pan.

8–5.0L
8–5.7L
8–7.4L

1. Drain the oil and remove the oil pan.
2. Remove the bolt holding the pump to the rear main bearing cap.
3. Remove the pump and extension shaft.
4. To install, assemble the pump and extension shaft to the rear main bearing cap aligning the slot on the top of the extension shaft with the drive tang on the distributor driveshaft. The installed position of the oil pump screen is with the bottom edge parallel to the oil pan rails. Further installation is the reverse of removal.

8–6.2L Diesel

1. Drain the oil.
2. Lower the oil pan enough to gain access to the pump.
2. Rotate the crankshaft so that the forward crankshaft throw and Nos. 1 and 2 connecting rod journals are up.
3. Remove the bolt retaining the pump to the main bearing cap. Let the pump and extension shaft fall into the pan.

To install:

4. Maneuver the pan, pump and extension shaft into position.
5. Position the pump on the bearing cap.
6. Align the extension shaft with the oil pump drive or vacuum pump. The pump should push easily into place. Install the pump and tighten the bolt to 65 ft. lbs.
7. Install the pan as described above.

OVERHAUL

6–4.3L

1. Remove the oil pump driveshaft extension.
2. Remove the cotter pin, spring and the pressure regulator valve.

NOTE: Place your thumb over the pressure regulator bore before removing the cotter pin, as the spring is under pressure.

3. Remove the oil pump cover attaching screws and remove the oil pump cover and gasket. Clean the pump in solvent or kerosene, and wash out the pickup screen.
4. Remove the drive gear and the idler gear from the pump body.
5. Check the gears for scoring and other damage. Install the gears if in good condition or replace them if damaged. Check gear end clearance by placing a straight edge over the gears and measuring the clearance between the straight edge and the gasket surface with a feeler gauge. End clearance is 0.002 in. (0.051mm) to 0.0065 in. (0.165mm). If end clearance is excessive, check for scores in the cover that would bring the total clearance over the specs.
6. Check the gear side clearance by inserting the feeler gauge between the gear teeth and the side of the pump body. Clearance should be between 0.002 in. (0.051mm) and 0.005 in. (0.127mm).
7. Pack the inside of the pump completely with petroleum jelly. DO NOT USE ENGINE OIL. The pump MUST be primed this way or it will not produce any oil pressure when the engine is started.
8. Install the cover screws and tighten alternately and evenly to 96 inch lbs.
9. Position the pressure valve into the pump cover, closed end first, then install the spring and retaining pin.

NOTE: When assembling the driveshaft extension into the driveshaft, the end of the extension nearest the washers must be inserted into the driveshaft.

10. Insert the driveshaft extension through the opening in the main bearing cap and block until the shaft mates into the distributor drive gear.
11. Install the pump onto the rear main bearing cap and install the attaching bolts. Torque the bolts to 35 ft. lbs.
12. Install the pan.

6–4.8L

1. Remove the cover screws and lift off the cover. Discard the gasket.
2. Matchmark the gear teeth for installation purposes.
3. Remove the drive gear and shaft.
4. Remove the idler gear.
5. Remove the spring retaining pin.
6. Remove the spring.
7. Remove the pressure relief valve.
8. If replacement is necessary, remove the pickup screen and pipe. The pipe is a press-fit.
9. Check all parts for wear and/or damage. Check the gears for looseness and wear. Check the drive gear and shaft for looseness and wear. If any parts are suspect, replace them. The gears, cover and body are not serviced separately. The regulator valve should slide freely in its bore without sticking or binding.

To assemble:

10. Install the pressure relief valve.
11. Install the spring.
12. Install the spring retaining pin.
13. Install the drive gear and shaft.
14. Install the idler gear with the smooth side of the gear towards the cover opening. Align the matchmarks.
15. Install a new gasket with the cover. Torque the cover screws to 70 inch lbs.

8–5.0L
8–5.7L
8–7.4L

1. Remove the oil pump driveshaft extension.

2. Remove the cotter pin, spring and the pressure regulator valve.

NOTE: Place your thumb over the pressure regulator bore before removing the cotter pin, as the spring is under pressure.

3. Remove the oil pump cover attaching screws and remove the oil pump cover and gasket. Clean the pump in solvent or kerosene, and wash out the pickup screen.
4. Remove the drive gear and the idler gear from the pump body.
5. Check the gears for scoring and other damage. Install the gears if in good condition or replace them if damaged. Check gear end clearance by placing a straight edge over the gears and measuring the clearance between the straight edge and the gasket surface with a feeler gauge. End clearance is 0.002 in. (0.051mm) to 0.0065 in. (0.165mm). If end clearance is excessive, check for scores in the cover that would bring the total clearance over the specs.
6. Check the gear side clearance by inserting the feeler gauge between the gear teeth and the side of the pump body. Clearance should be between 0.002 in. (0.051mm) and 0.005 in. (0.127mm).
7. Pack the inside of the pump completely with petroleum jelly. DO NOT USE ENGINE OIL. The pump MUST be primed this way or it will not produce any oil pressure when the engine is started.
8. Install the cover screws and tighten alternately and evenly to 8 ft. lbs.
9. Position the pressure valve into the pump cover, closed end first, then install the spring and retaining pin.

NOTE: When assembling the driveshaft extension into the driveshaft, the end of the extension nearest the washers must be inserted into the driveshaft.

10. Insert the driveshaft extension through the opening in the main bearing cap and block until the shaft mates into the distributor drive gear.
11. Install the pump onto the rear main bearing cap and install the attaching bolts. Torque the bolts to 35 ft. lbs.
12. Install the pan.

8–6.2L Diesel

1. Remove the oil pump driveshaft extension.
2. Remove the cotter pin, spring and the pressure regulator valve.

NOTE: Place your thumb over the pressure regulator bore before removing the cotter pin, as the spring is under pressure.

3. Remove the oil pump cover attaching screws and remove the oil pump cover and gasket. Clean the pump in solvent or kerosene, and wash out the pickup screen.
4. Remove the drive gear and the idler gear from the pump body.
5. Check the gears for scoring and other damage. Install the gears if in good condition or replace them if damaged. Check gear end clearance by placing a straight edge over the gears and measuring the clearance between the straight edge and the gasket surface with a feeler gauge. End clearance is 0.002 in. (0.051mm) to 0.0065 in. (0.165mm). If end clearance is excessive, check for scores in the cover that would bring the total clearance over the specs.
6. Check the gear side clearance by inserting the feeler gauge between the gear teeth and the side of the pump body. Clearance should be between 0.002 in. (0.051mm) and 0.005 in. (0.127mm).
7. Pack the inside of the pump completely with petroleum jelly. DO NOT USE ENGINE OIL. The pump MUST be primed this way or it will not produce any oil pressure when the engine is started.
8. Install the cover screws and tighten alternately and evenly to 96 inch lbs.
9. Position the pressure valve into the pump cover, closed end first, then install the spring and retaining pin.

NOTE: When assembling the driveshaft extension into the driveshaft, the end of the extension nearest the washers must be inserted into the driveshaft.

10. Insert the driveshaft extension through the opening in the main bearing cap and block until the shaft mates into the distributor drive gear.
11. Install the pump onto the rear main bearing cap and install the attaching bolts. Torque the bolts to 35 ft. lbs.
12. Install the pan.

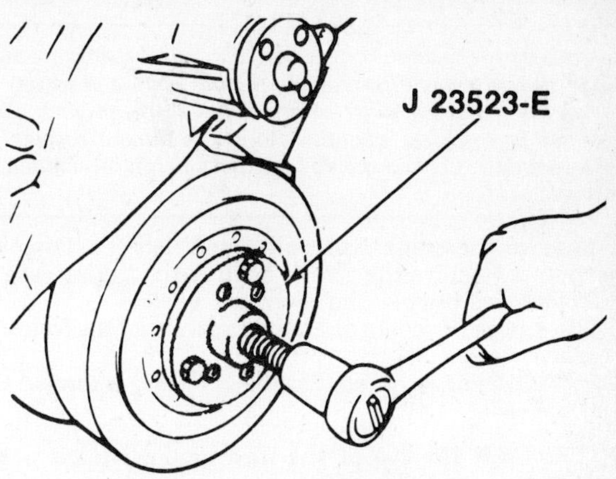

Removing the crankshaft damper

Crankshaft Damper

REMOVAL AND INSTALLATION

Torsional damper puller tool No. J–23523–E is required to perform this procedure.

1. Remove the fan belts, fan and pulley.
2. Remove the fan shroud assembly.
3. If necessary, remove the radiator.
4. Remove the accessory drive pulley.
5. Remove the torsional damper bolt.
6. Remove the torsional damper using tool # J–23523–E.

NOTE: Make sure you do not loose the crankshaft key, if it has been removed.

To install:

7. Coat the crankshaft stub with engine oil.
8. Position the damper on the shaft and tap it into place with a plastic mallet. Make sure the key is in place.
9. Make sure the damper is all the way on, then install the bolt. Torque the bolt to the figure given in the Torque Specifications Chart.

Timing Chain Cover and Front Oil Seal

REMOVAL AND INSTALLATION

6–4.3L

1. Drain the cooling system.

CAUTION

When draining the coolant, keep in mind that cats and dogs are attracted by the ethylene glycol antifreeze, and are quite likely to drink any that is left in an uncovered container or in puddles on the ground. This will prove fatal in sufficient quantity. Always drain the coolant into a sealable container. Coolant should be reused unless it is contaminated or several years old.

2. Remove the crankshaft pulley and damper. Remove the water pump. Remove the screws holding the timing case cover to the block and remove the cover and gaskets.
3. Use a suitable tool to pry the old seal out of the front face of the cover.
4. Install the new seal so that the open end is toward the inside of the cover.

NOTE: Coat the lip of the new seal with oil prior to installation.

5. Check that the timing chain oil slinger is in place against the crankshaft sprocket.
6. Apply sealer to the front cover as shown in the accompanying illustration. Install the cover carefully onto the locating dowels.
7. Tighten the attaching screws to 72–96 inch lbs.

8–5.0L
8–5.7L

1. Drain the cooling system.

CAUTION

When draining the coolant, keep in mind that cats and dogs are attracted by the ethylene glycol antifreeze, and are quite likely to drink any that is left in an uncovered container or in puddles on the ground. This will prove fatal in sufficient quantity. Always drain the coolant into a sealable container. Coolant should be reused unless it is contaminated or several years old.

2. Remove the crankshaft pulley and damper. Remove the water pump. Remove the screws holding the timing case cover to the block and remove the cover and gaskets.
3. Use a suitable tool to pry the old seal out of the front face of the cover.
4. Install the new seal so that the open end is toward the inside of the cover.

NOTE: Coat the lip of the new seal with oil prior to installation.

5. Check that the timing chain oil slinger is in place against the crankshaft sprocket.
6. Apply sealer to the front cover as shown in the accompanying illustration. Install the cover carefully onto the locating dowels.
7. Tighten the attaching screws to 72–96 inch lbs.

Seal installation with the cover removed

8–7.4L

Special tool J-22102, or its equivalent, will be necessary for this job.

1. Disconnect the battery.
2. Drain the cooling system.

CAUTION

When draining the coolant, keep in mind that cats and dogs are attracted by the ethylene glycol antifreeze, and are quite likely to drink any that is left in an uncovered container or in puddles on the ground. This will prove fatal in sufficient quantity. Always drain the coolant into a sealable container. Coolant should be reused unless it is contaminated or several years old.

3. Remove the water pump.
4. Remove the crankshaft pulley and damper.
5. Remove the oil pan-to-front cover bolts.
6. Remove the screws holding the timing case cover to the block, pull the cover forward enough to cut the front oil pan seal. Cut the seal flush with the block on both sides.
7. Pull off the cover and gaskets.

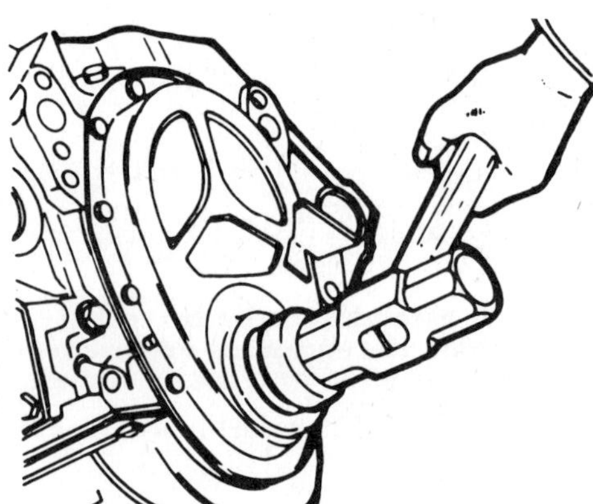

Seal installation with the cover installed

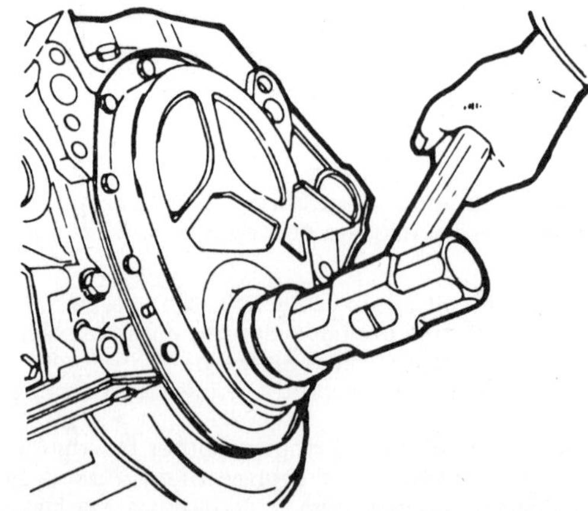

Seal installation with cover installed, on V8 engines

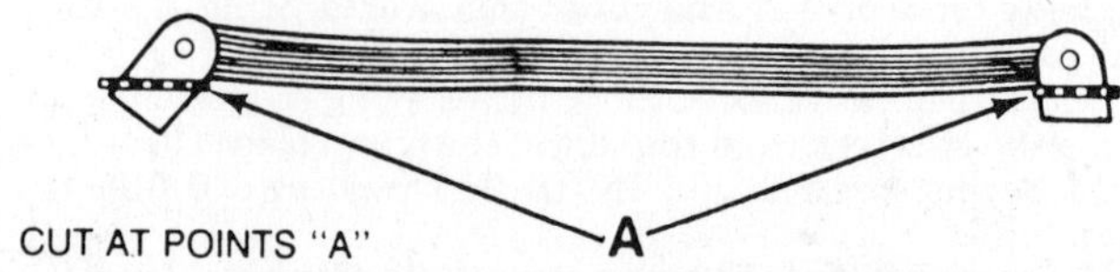

Front oil pan seal modification

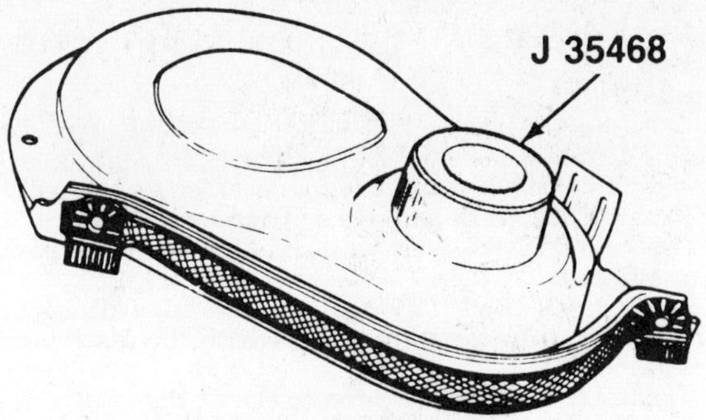

Front seal installed

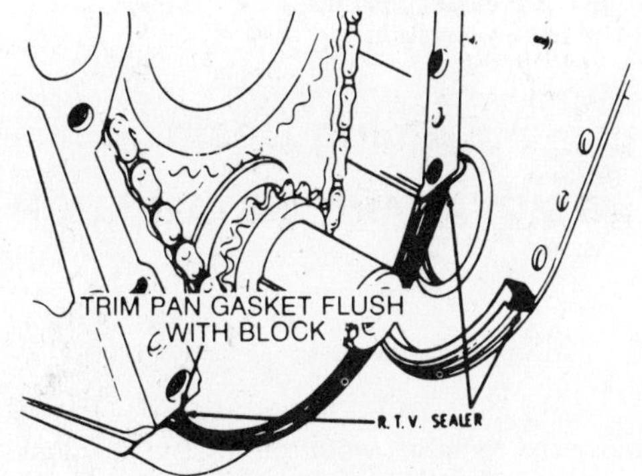

Sealer application

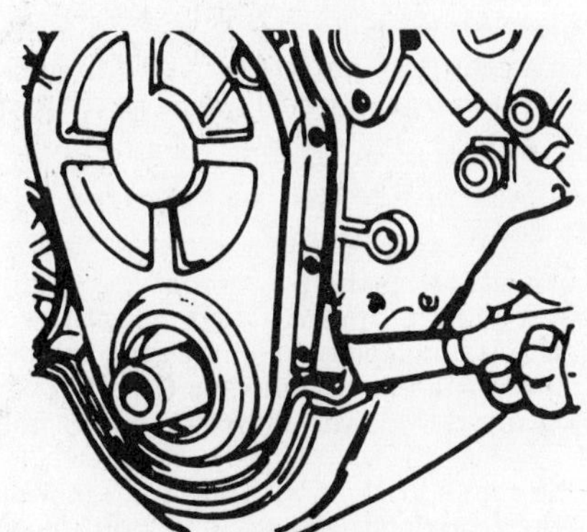

Cutting the seal

8. Use a suitable tool to pry the old seal out of the front face of the cover.

To install:

9. Using seal driver J–22102, or equivalent, install the new seal so that the open end is toward the inside of the cover.

NOTE: Coat the lip of the new seal with oil prior to installation.

10. Install a new front pan seal, cutting the tabs off.
11. Coat a new cover gasket with adhesive sealer and position it on the block.
12. Apply a ⅛ in. bead of RTV gasket material to the front cover. Install the cover carefully onto the locating dowels.
13. Tighten the attaching screws to 96 inch lbs.
14. Tighten the cover-to-pan bolts to 70 inch lbs.
15. Install the damper.
16. Install the water pump.

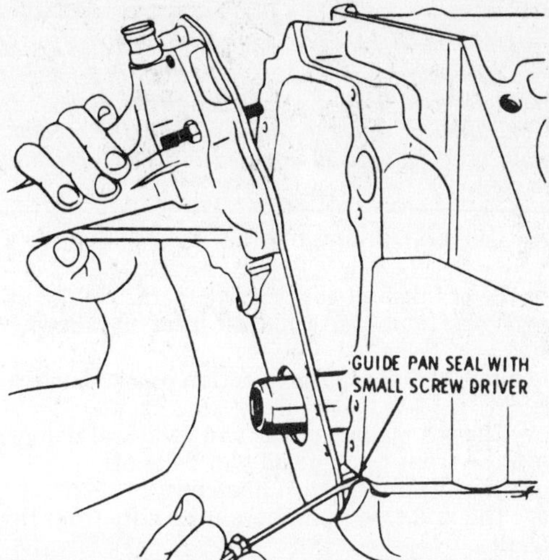

Guiding the cover into place. Make sure the seal remains undisturbed

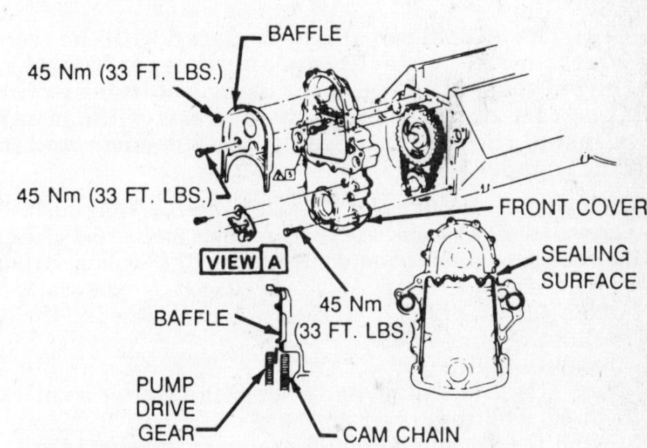

Diesel front cover installation showing sealer application

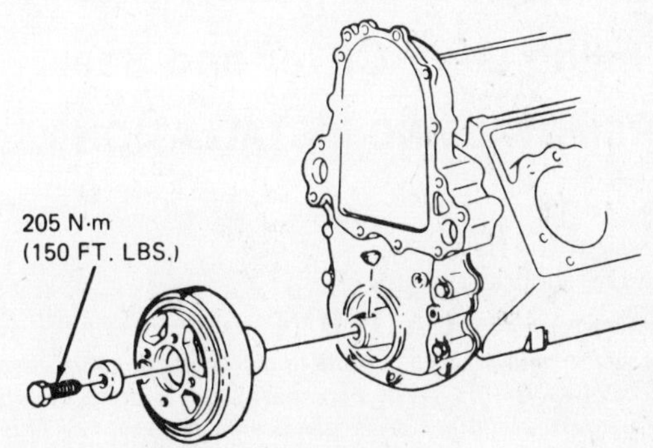

Diesel torsional damper removal

17. Connect the battery cables.
18. Fill the cooling system.

8–6.2L Diesel

1. Drain the cooling system.

CAUTION

When draining the coolant, keep in mind that cats and dogs are attracted by the ethylene glycol antifreeze, and are quite likely to drink any that is left in an uncovered container or in puddles on the ground. This will prove fatal in sufficient quantity. Always drain the coolant into a sealable container. Coolant should be reused unless it is contaminated or several years old.

2. Remove the water pump as outlined elsewhere in this Section.
3. Rotate the crankshaft to align the marks on the injection pump driven gear and the camshaft gear as shown in the illustration.
4. Scribe a mark aligning the injection pump flange and the front cover.
5. Remove the crankshaft pulley and torsional damper.
6. Remove the front cover-to-oil pan bolts (4).
7. Remove the two fuel return line clips.
8. Remove the injection pump retaining nuts from the front cover.
9. Remove the baffle. Remove the remaining cover bolts, and remove the front cover.
10. If the front cover oil seal is to be replaced, it can now be pried out of the cover with a suitable prying tool. Press the new seal into the cover evenly.

NOTE: The oil seal can also be replaced with the front cover installed. Remove the torsional damper first, then pry the old seal out of the cover using a suitable prying tool. Use care not to damage the surface of the crankshaft. Install the new seal evenly into the cover and install the damper.

11. To install the front cover, first clean both sealing surfaces until all traces of old sealer are gone. Apply a 2mm bead of sealant (GM sealant #1052357 or equivalent) to the sealing surface as shown in the illustration. Apply a bead of RTV type sealer to the bottom portion of the front cover which attached to the oil pan. Install the front cover.
12. Install the baffle.
13. Install the injection pump, making sure the scribe marks on the pump and front cover are aligned.
14. Install the injection pump driven gear, making sure the marks on the cam gear and pump are aligned. Be sure the dowel pin and the three holes on the pump flange are also aligned.
15. Install the fuel line clips, the front cover-to-oil bolts, and the torsional damper and crankshaft pulley. Torque the pan bolts to 4–7 ft. lbs., and the damper bolt to 140–162 ft. lbs.

Timing Gear Cover and Seal

REMOVAL AND INSTALLATION

6–4.8L

1. Disconnect the battery.
2. Drain the cooling system.

CAUTION

When draining the coolant, keep in mind that cats and dogs are attracted by the ethylene glycol antifreeze, and are quite likely to drink any that is left in an uncovered container or in puddles on the ground. This will prove fatal in sufficient quantity. Always drain the coolant into a sealable container. Coolant should be reused unless it is contaminated or several years old.

3. Remove the water pump.
4. Remove the crankshaft pulley and damper.
5. Remove the oil pan-to-front cover bolts.
6. Remove the screws holding the timing case cover to the block, pull the cover forward enough to cut the front oil pan seal. Cut the seal flush with the block on both sides.
7. Pull off the cover and gaskets.
8. Use a suitable tool to pry the old seal out of the front face of the cover.

To install:

9. Lubricate the new seal lip with engine oil and using a seal centering tool and installer J–23042, or equivalent, press the new seal into place. Leave the tool in position on the seal.
10. Install a new front pan seal, cutting the tabs off.
11. Coat a new cover gasket with adhesive sealer and position it on the block.
12. Apply a ⅛ in. bead of RTV gasket material to the front cover. Install the cover carefully in place with the centering tool still atttached.
13. Tighten the timing gear cover to block bolts to 80 inch lbs.
14. Tighten the cover-to-pan bolts to 45 inch lbs.
15. Install the damper.
16. Install the water pump.
17. Connect the battery cables.
18. Fill the cooling system.

Timing Chain

REMOVAL AND INSTALLATION

6–4.3L
8–5.0L
8–5.7L
8–7.4L

1. Remove the radiator, water pump, the harmonic balancer and the crankcase front cover. This will allow access to the timing chain.
2. Crank the engine until the timing marks on both sprockets are nearest each other and in line between the shaft centers.
3. Take out the three bolts that hold the camshaft gear to the camshaft. This gear is a light press fit on the camshaft and will come off easily. It is located by a dowel. The chain comes off with the camshaft gear.

NOTE: A gear puller will be required to remove the crankshaft gear.

4. Without disturbing the position of the engine, mount the new crankshaft gear on the shaft, and mount the chain over the camshaft gear. Arrange the camshaft gear in such a way that the timing marks will line up between the shaft centers and the camshaft locating dowel will enter the dowel hole in the cam sprocket.
5. Place the cam sprocket, with its chain mounted over it, in position on the front of the truck and pull up with the three bolts that hold it to the camshaft.
6. After the gears are in place, turn the engine two full revolutions to make certain that the timing marks are in correct alignment between the shaft centers.

End play of the camshaft is zero.

8–6.2L Diesel

1. Remove the front cover as previously detailed.
2. Remove the bolt and washer attaching the camshaft gear. Remove the injection pump gear.
3. Remove the camshaft sprocket, timing chain and crankshaft sprocket as a unit.

To install:

4. Install the cam sprocket, timing chain and crankshaft sprocket as a unit, aligning the timing marks on the sprockets as shown in the illustration.
5. Rotate the crankshaft 360° so that the camshaft gear and the injection pump gear are aligned as shown in the illustration (accompanying the 6.2L Diesel Front Cover Removal Procedure).

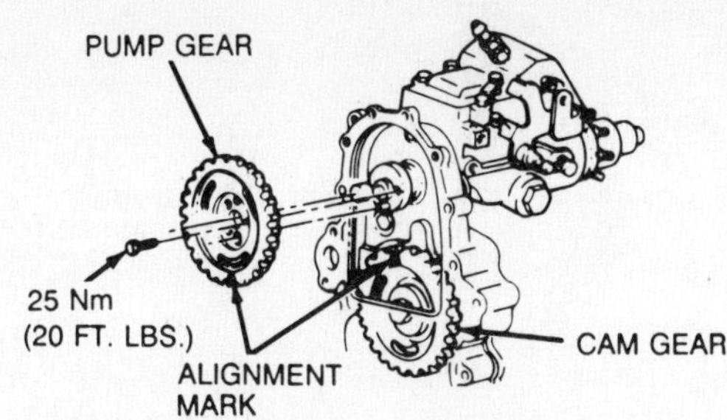

Injection pump and cam gear alignment

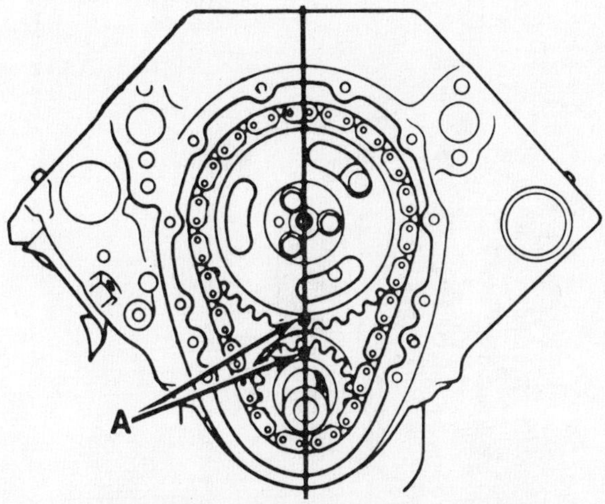

Timing mark alignment for all engines

6. Install the front cover as previously detailed. The injection pump must be retimed since the timing chain assembly was removed. See Section 5 for this procedure.

Timing Gears

REMOVAL AND INSTALLATION

6–4.8L

The camshaft on these engines is gear driven, unlike the chain driven V6 and V8 engines. The camshaft must be removed to replace the gear.

1. Disconnect the negative battery cable. Remove the camshaft and place in an arbor press.

NOTE: Support the camshaft gear not the thrust plate.

2. Press the gear off of the camshaft and remove the thrust plate and the spacer.

To install:

3. Support the camshaft at the front journal with tool J-22912–01 or equivalent, and mount the camshaft in a press.
4. Lubricate the thrust plate with engine oil.
5. Install the key if removed.
6. Install the spacer making sure the chamfer in the spacer faces toward the journal radius.
7. Install the thrust plate.
8. Install the camshaft gear on with the timing mark to the outside and press the gear on until it bottoms on the spacer.
9. Remove the camshaft from the press.

NOTE: The clearance between the camshaft and thrust plate should be 0.003–0.008 in.

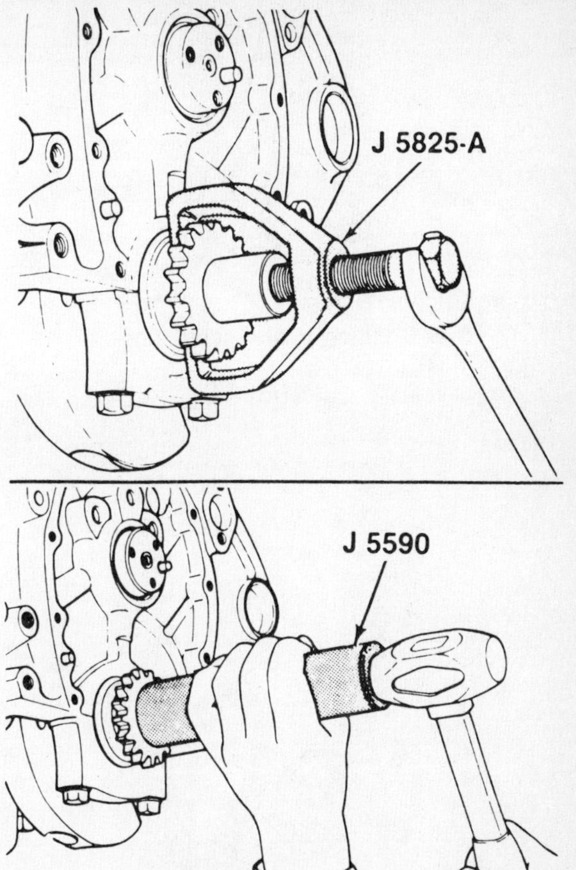

Removing and installing the crankshaft sprocket on the 4.3, 5.0 and 5.7L engines

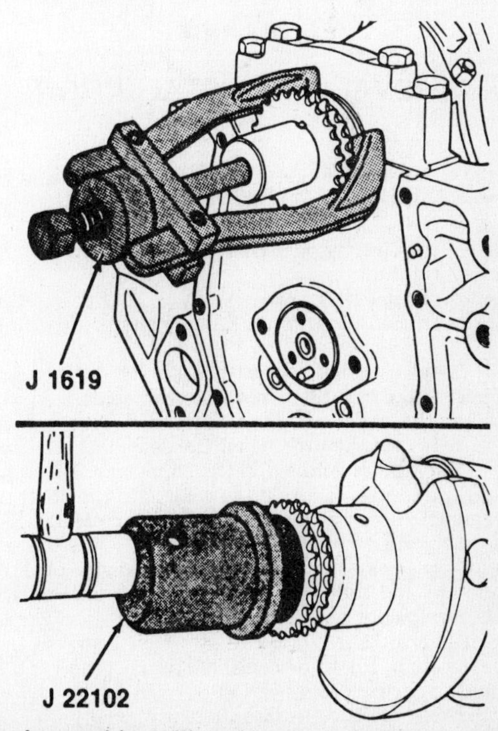

Removing and installing the crankshaft sprocket on the 7.4L engines

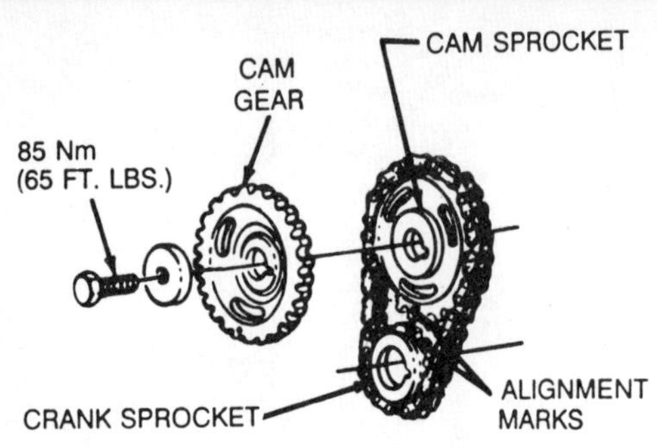

Diesel timing chain installation

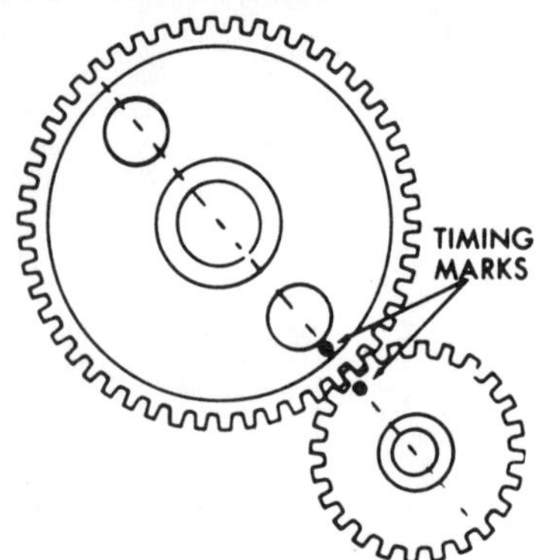

6-4.8L timing gear alignment

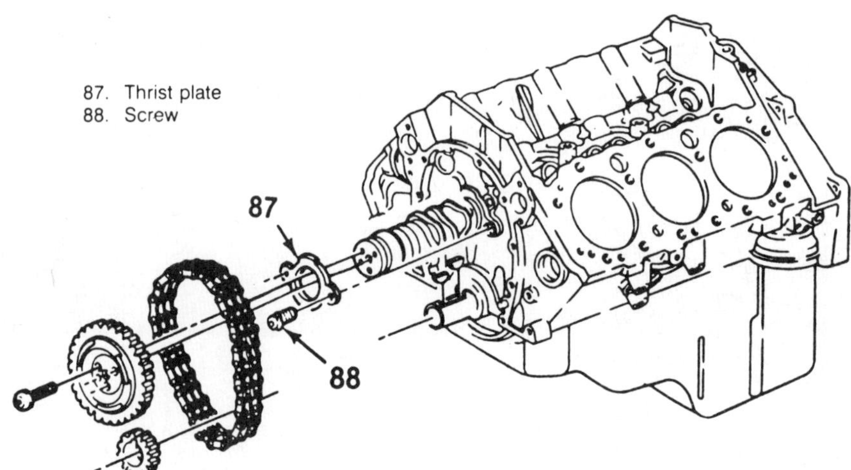

6–4.3L camshaft and timing chain

Camshaft

REMOVAL AND INSTALLATION

6–4.8L

1. Remove the grille. Remove the radiator hoses and remove the radiator.
2. Remove the hydraulic lifters.
3. Remove the timimg gear cover.
4. Remove the fuel pump.
5. Remove the distributor.
6. Align the timing marks on the camshaft and crankshaft gears.
7. Remove the camshaft thrust plate bolts.
8. Support and carefully remove the camshaft.
9. If either the camshaft or the camshaft gear is being renewed, the gear must be pressed off the camshaft. The replacement parts must be assembled in the same way. When placing the gear on the camshaft, press the gear onto the shaft until it bottoms against the gear spacer ring. The end clearance of the thrust plate should be 0.003–0.008 in.
10. Pre-lube the camshaft lobes with clean engine oil or engine oil supplement, and then install the camshaft assembly in the engine. Be careful not to damage the bearings.
11. Turn the crankshaft and the camshaft gears so that the timing marks align. Push the camshaft into position and install and torque the thrust plate bolts to 80 inch lbs.
12. Check camshaft and crankshaft gear runout with a dial indicator. Camshaft gear runout should not exceed 0.004 in. and crankshaft gear run-out should not be above 0.003 in.
13. Using a dial indicator, check the backlash at several points between the camshaft and crankshaft gear teeth. Backlash should be 0.004–0.006 inches.
14. Install the timing gear cover.
15. Install the distributor.
16. Install the fuel pump.
17. Install the valve lifters and the pushrods.
18. Install the engine.

6–4.3L

1. Disconnect the battery.
2. Drain and remove the radiator.

CAUTION

When draining the coolant, keep in mind that cats and dogs are attracted by the ethylene glycol antifreeze, and are quite likely to drink any that is left in an uncovered container or in puddles on the ground. This will prove fatal in sufficient quantity. Always drain the coolant into a sealable container. Coolant should be reused unless it is contaminated or several years old.

3. Remove the fuel pump.
4. Disconnect the throttle cable and the air cleaner.
5. Remove the alternator belt, loosen the alternator bolts and move the alternator to one side.
6. Remove the power steering pump from its brackets and move it out of the way.
7. Remove the air conditioning compressor from its brackets and move the compressor out of the way without disconnecting the lines.
8. Disconnect the hoses from the water pump.

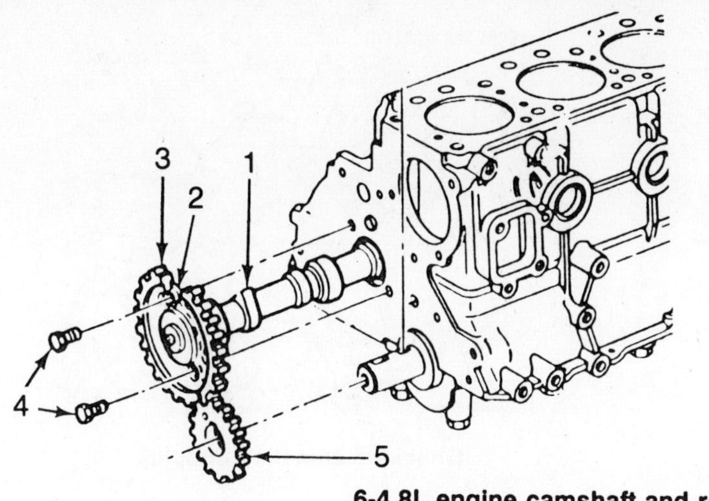

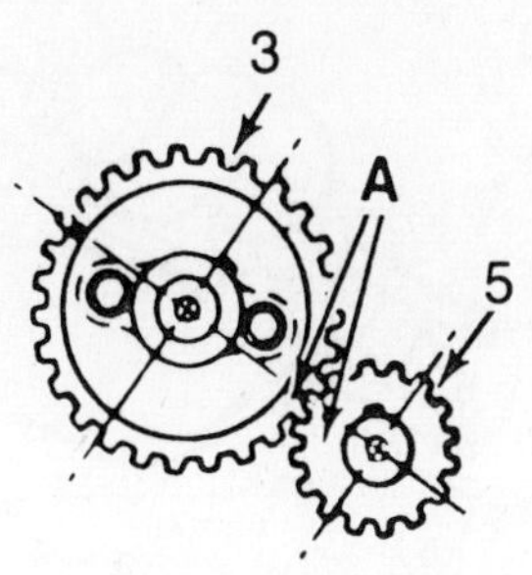

6-4.8L engine camshaft and related components

Removing the camshaft thrust plate bolts

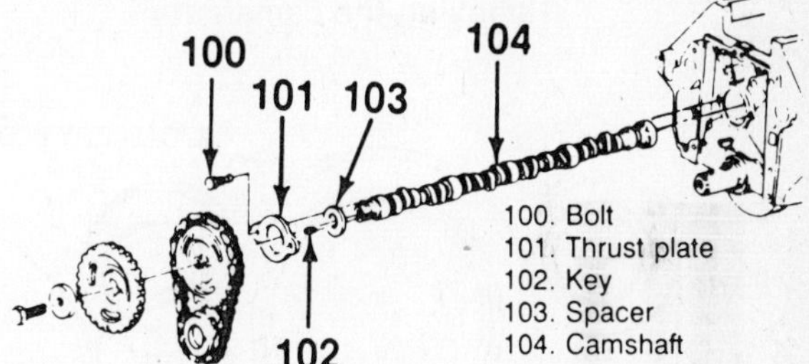

V8 gasoline engine camshaft and related parts

9. Disconnect the electrical and vacuum connections.
10. Mark the distributor as to location in the block. Remove the distributor.
11. Raise the truck and drain the oil pan.
12. Remove the exhaust crossover pipe and starter motor.
13. Disconnect the exhaust pipe at the manifold.
14. Remove the harmonic balancer and pulley.
15. Support the engine and remove the front motor mounts.
16. Remove the flywheel inspection cover.
17. Remove the engine oil pan.
18. Support the engine by placing wooden blocks between the exhaust manifolds and the front crossmember.
19. Remove the engine front cover.
20. Remove the valve covers.
21. Remove the intake manifold, oil filler pipe, and temperature sending switch.
22. Mark the lifters, pushrods, and rocker arms as to location so that they may be installed in the same position. Remove these parts.
23. If the truck is equipped with air conditioning, discharge the air conditioning system and remove the condenser.
24. Remove the fuel pump eccentric, camshaft gear, oil slinger, and timing chain.
25. Remove the camshaft thrust plate (on front of camshaft) if equipped.
26. Carefully remove the camshaft from the engine.
27. Inspect the shaft for signs of excessive wear or damage.

To install:

28. Liberally coat camshaft and bearing with heavy engine oil, engine assembly lubricant or engine oil supplement, and carefully insert the cam into the engine.
29. Align the timing marks on the camshaft and crankshaft gears. See Timing Chain Replacement for details.
30. Install the distributor using the locating marks made during removal. If any problems are encountered, see Distributor Installation.
31. Install the camshaft thrust plate (on front of camshaft) if equipped.
32. Install the timing chain, oil slinger, camshaft gear, and fuel pump eccentric.
33. Install the condenser. If the truck is equipped with air conditioning, charge the air conditioning system. See Section 1.
34. Install the lifters, pushrods, and rocker arms.
35. Install the temperature sending switch.
36. Install the oil filler pipe.
37. Install the intake manifold.
38. Install the valve covers.
39. Install the engine front cover.
40. Install the engine oil pan.
41. Install the front motor mounts.
42. Remove the wood blocks.
43. Install the flywheel inspection cover.
44. Install the harmonic balancer and pulley.
45. Connect the exhaust pipe at the manifold.
46. Install the exhaust crossover pipe.
47. Install the starter motor.
48. Install the flywheel inspection cover.
49. Install the distributor.
50. Connect the electrical wiring.
51. Connect all vacuum connections.
52. Connect the hoses at the water pump.
53. Install the air conditioning compressor.

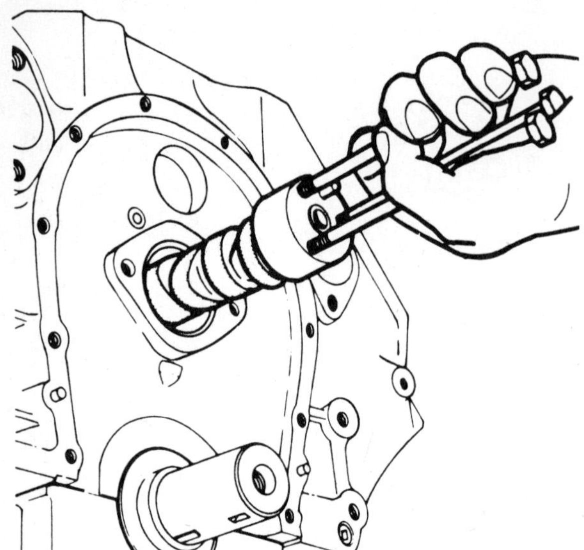

Removing the camshaft

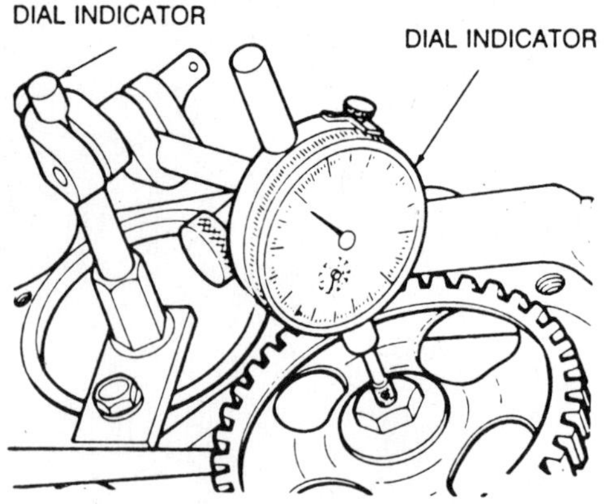

Checking camshaft endplay

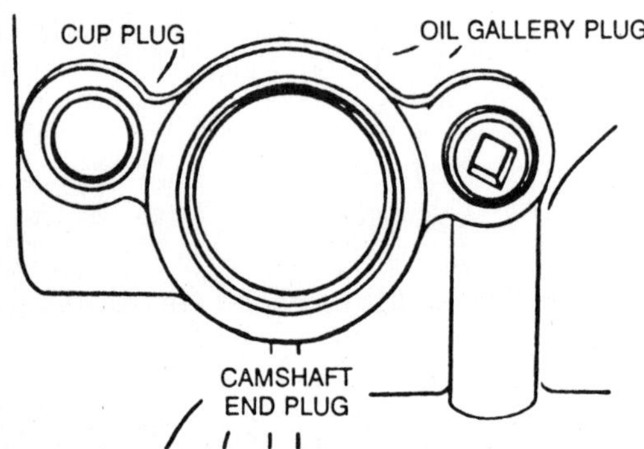

Camshaft oil gallery plugs at the rear of the block.

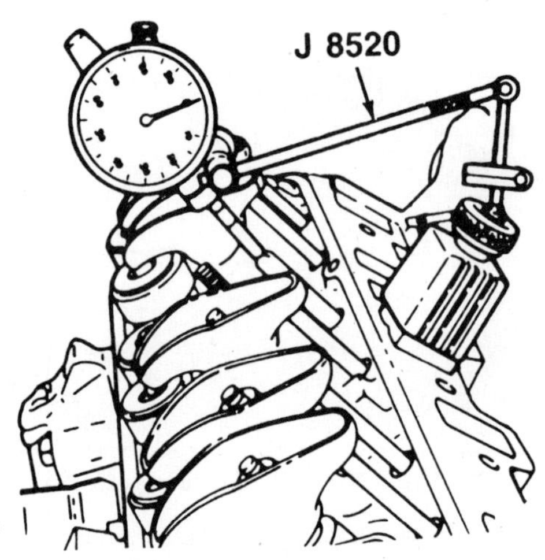

Measuring camshaft lobe lift

54. Install the timing indicator.
55. Install the power steering pump.
56. Install the alternator and belt.
57. Connect the throttle cable.
58. Install the air cleaner.
59. Install the fuel pump.
60. Install the radiator.
61. Connect the battery.
62. Fill the crankcase.
63. Fill the cooling system.

8–5.0L
8–5.7L

1. Disconnect the battery.
2. Drain and remove the radiator.

CAUTION

When draining the coolant, keep in mind that cats and dogs are attracted by the ethylene glycol antifreeze, and are quite likely to drink any that is left in an uncovered container or in puddles on the ground. This will prove fatal in sufficient quantity. Always drain the coolant into a sealable container. Coolant should be reused unless it is contaminated or several years old.

3. Disconnect the fuel line at the fuel pump. Remove the pump.
4. Disconnect the throttle cable and the air cleaner.
5. Remove the alternator belt, loosen the alternator bolts and move the alternator to one side.
6. Remove the power steering pump from its brackets and move it out of the way.
7. Remove the air conditioning compressor from its brackets and move the compressor out of the way without disconnecting the lines.
8. Disconnect the hoses from the water pump.
9. Disconnect the electrical and vacuum connections.
10. Mark the distributor as to location in the block. Remove the distributor.
11. Raise the truck and drain the oil pan.
12. Remove the exhaust crossover pipe and starter motor.
13. Disconnect the exhaust pipe at the manifold.
14. Remove the harmonic balancer and pulley.
15. Support the engine and remove the front motor mounts.
16. Remove the flywheel inspection cover.
17. Remove the engine oil pan.
18. Support the engine by placing wooden blocks between the exhaust manifolds and the front crossmember.
19. Remove the engine front cover.
20. Remove the valve covers.
21. Remove the intake manifold, oil filler pipe, and temperature sending switch.
22. Mark the lifters, pushrods, and rocker arms as to location

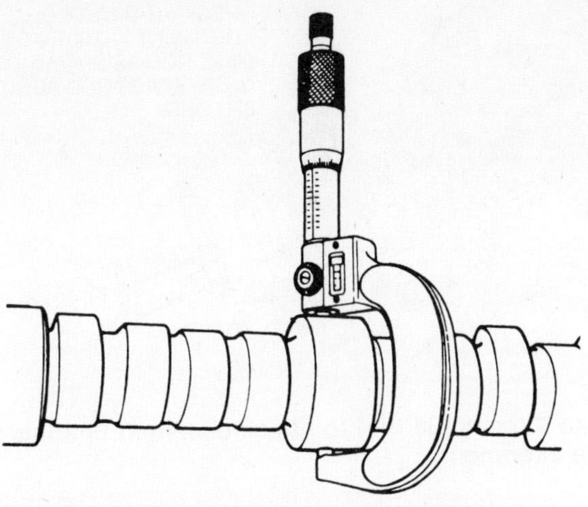

Checking camshaft journal diameter

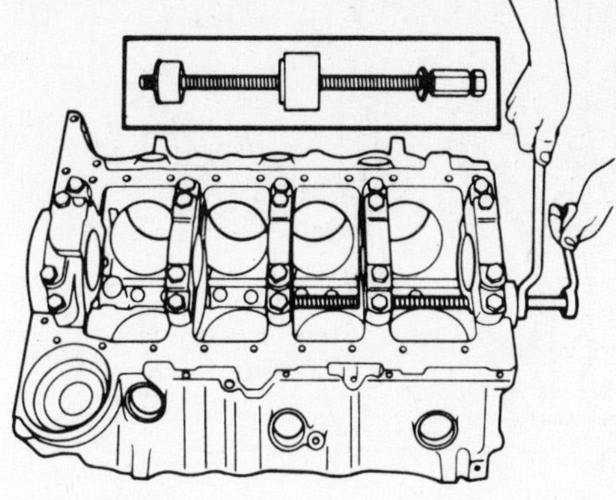

Removing camshaft bearings

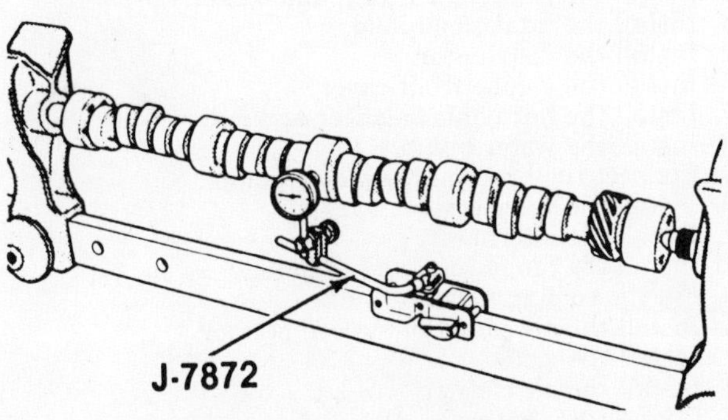

Measuring camshaft runout

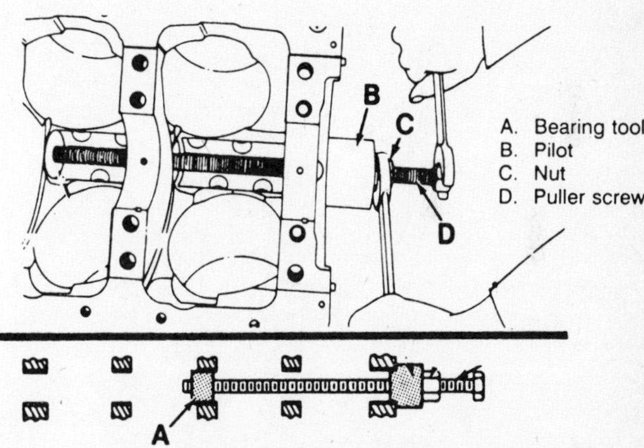

Replacing the inner camshaft bearings

so that they may be installed in the same position. Remove these parts.

23. If the truck is equipped with air conditioning, discharge the air conditioning system and remove the condenser.
24. Remove the fuel pump eccentric, camshaft gear, oil slinger, and timing chain. Remove the camshaft thrust plate (on front of camshaft) if equipped.
25. Carefully remove the camshaft from the engine.
26. Inspect the shaft for signs of excessive wear or damage.

To install:

27. Liberally coat camshaft and bearing with heavy engine oil or engine assembly lubricant and insert the cam into the engine.
28. Align the timing marks on the camshaft and crankshaft gears. See Timing Chain Replacement for details.
29. Install the distributor using the locating marks made during removal. If any problems are encountered, see Distributor Installation.
30. Install the camshaft thrust plate (on front of camshaft) if equipped.
31. Install the timing chain, oil slinger,, camshaft gear, and fuel pump eccentric.
32. Install the condenser. If the truck is equipped with air conditioning, charge the air conditioning system. See Section 1.
33. Install the lifters, pushrods, and rocker arms.
34. Install the temperature sending switch.
35. Install the oil filler pipe.
36. Install the intake manifold.
37. Install the valve covers.
38. Install the engine front cover.
39. Install the engine oil pan.
40. Install the front motor mounts.
41. Remove the wood blocks.
42. Install the flywheel inspection cover.
43. Install the harmonic balancer and pulley.
44. Connect the exhaust pipe at the manifold.
45. Install the exhaust crossover pipe.
46. Install the starter motor.
47. Install the flywheel inspection cover.
48. Install the distributor.
49. Connect the electrical wiring.
50. Connect all vacuum connections.
51. Connect the hoses at the water pump.
52. Install the air conditioning compressor.
53. Install the timing indicator.
54. Install the power steering pump.
55. Install the alternator and belt.
56. Connect the throttle cable.
57. Install the air cleaner.
58. Connect the fuel line at the fuel pump. Install the pump.
59. Install the radiator.
60. Connect the battery.
61. Fill the crankcase.
62. Fill the cooling system.

8–7.4L

1. Disconnect the battery.
2. Remove the air cleaner.
3. Remove the grille.

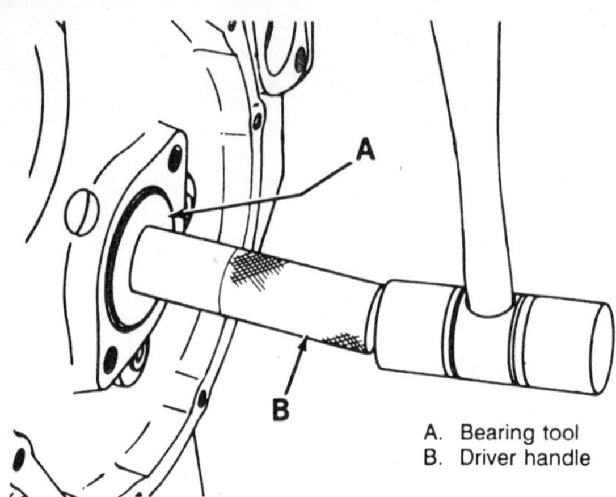

Install outer camshaft bearings

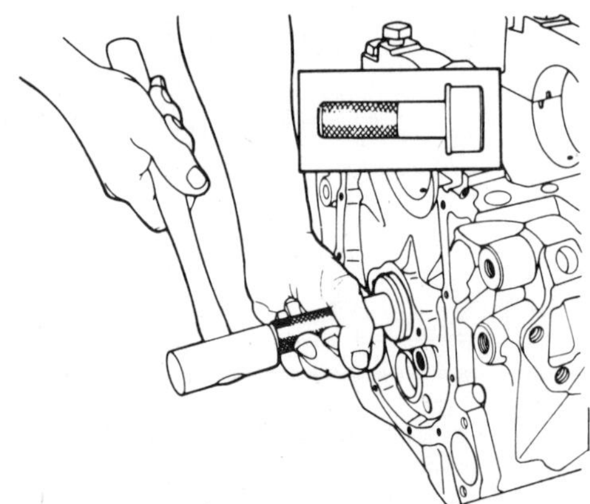

Installing the front camshaft bearing on the diesel. The bearing tool is illustrated in the inset

4. Remove the air conditioning compressor from its brackets and move the compressor out of the way without disconnecting the lines.
5. Drain the cooling system.
6. Remove the fan shroud and radiator.
7. Remove the alternator belt, loosen the alternator bolts and move the alternator to one side.
8. Remove the valve covers.
9. Disconnect the hoses from the water pump.
10. Remove the water pump.
11. Remove the harmonic balancer and pulley.
12. Remove the engine front cover.
13. Mark the distributor as to location in the block. Remove the distributor.
14. Remove the intake manifold.
15. Mark the lifters, pushrods, and rocker arms as to location so that they may be installed in the same position. Remove these parts.
16. Rotate the camshaft so that the timing marks align.
17. Remove the camshaft sprocket bolts.
18. Pull the camshaft sprocket and timing chain off. The sprocket is a tight fit, so you'll have to tap it loose with a plastic mallet.
19. Install two $^5/_{16}$ in.–18 bolts in the holes in the front of the camshaft and carefully pull the camshaft from the block.

To install:

20. Liberally coat camshaft and bearing with heavy engine oil or engine assembly lubricant and insert the cam into the engine.

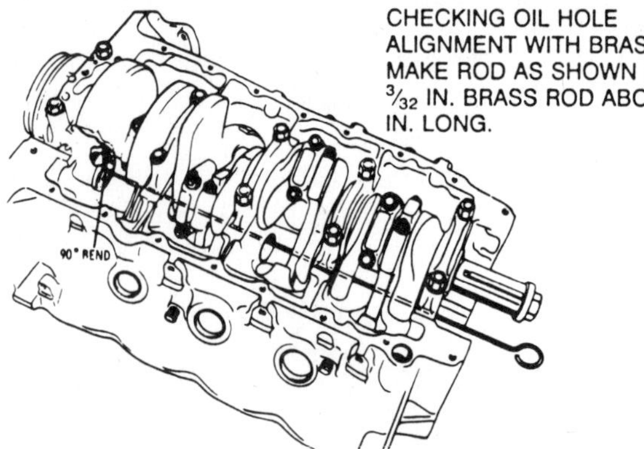

Make this simple tool to check camshaft bearing oil hole alignment

21. Install the distributor using the locating marks made during removal. If any problems are encountered, see Distributor Installation.
22. Install the camshaft sprocket bolts.
23. Install the lifters, pushrods, and rocker.
24. Install the intake manifold.
25. Install the distributor.
26. Install the engine front cover.
27. Install the harmonic balancer and pulley.
28. Install the water pump.
29. Connect the hoses at the water pump.
30. Install the valve covers.
31. Install the alternator.
32. Install the fan shroud and radiator.
33. Fill the cooling system.
34. Install the air conditioning compressor.
35. Install the grille.
36. Install the air cleaner.
37. Connect the battery.

8–6.2L Diesel

1. Disconnect the battery.
2. Jack up the truck and safely support it with jackstands.
3. Drain the cooling system, including the block.

CAUTION

When draining the coolant, keep in mind that cats and dogs are attracted by the ethylene glycol antifreeze, and are quite likely to drink any that is left in an uncovered container or in puddles on the ground. This will prove fatal in sufficient quantity. Always drain the coolant into a sealable container. Coolant should be reused unless it is contaminated or several years old.

4. Disconnect the exhaust pipes at the manifolds. Remove the fan shroud.
5. Lower the truck.
6. Remove the radiator and fan.
7. Remove the vacuum pump, and remove the intake manifolds as previously detailed.
8. Remove the injection pump and lines as outlined in Chapter 5. Make sure you cap all injection lines to prevent dirt from entering the system, and tag the lines for later installation.
9. Remove the water pump.
10. Remove the injection pump drive gear.
11. Scribe a mark aligning the line on the injection pump flange to the front cover.
12. Remove the injection pump from the cover.
13. Remove the power steering pump and the generator and lay them aside.
14. If the truck is equipped with air conditioning, remove the compressor (with the lines attached) and position it out of the way.

CAUTION

DO NOT disconnect the air conditioning lines unless you are familiar with this procedure.

15. Remove the valve covers.
16. Remove the rocker shaft assemblies and pushrods. Place the pushrods in order in a rack (easily by punching holes in a piece of heavy cardboard and numbering the holes) so that they can be installed in correct order.
17. Remove the thermostat housing and the crossover from the cylinder heads.
18. Remove the cylinder heads as previously detailed, with the exhaust manifolds attached.
19. Remove the valve lifter clamps, guide plates and valve lifters. Place these parts in a rack so they can be installed in the correct order.
20. Remove the front cover.
21. Remove the timing chain assembly.
22. Remove the fuel pump.
23. Remove the camshaft retainer plate.
24. If the truck is equipped with air conditioning, remove the air conditioning condenser mounting bolts. Have an assistant help in lifting the condenser out of the way.
15. Remove the camshaft by carefully sliding it out of the block.

NOTE: Whenever a new camshaft installed, GM recommends replacing all the valve lifters, as well as the oil filter. The engine oil must be changed. These measures will help ensure proper wear characteristics of the new camshaft.

To install:

16. Coat the camshaft lobes with Molykote® or an equivalent lube. Liberally tube the camshaft journals with clean engine oil and install the camshaft carefully.
17. Install the camshaft retainer plate and torque the bolts to 20 ft. lbs.
18. Install the fuel pump.
19. Install the timing chain assembly as previously detailed.
20. Install the front cover as previously detailed.
21. Install the valve lifters, guide plates and clamps, and rotate the crankshaft as previously outlined so that the lifters are free to travel.
22. Install the cylinder heads.
23. Install the pushrods in their original order. Install the rocker shaft assemblies, then install the valve covers.
24. Install the injection pump to the front cover, making sure the lines on the pump and the scribe line on the front cover are aligned.
25. Install the injection pump driven gear, making sure the gears are aligned. Retime the injection pump.
26. Install the air conditioning condenser. Charge the system. See Section 1.
27. Install the thermostat housing and the crossover.
28. Install the compressor.
29. Install the power steering pump.
30. Install the alternator.
31. Install the water pump.
32. Install the vacuum pump.
33. Install the intake manifolds.
34. Install the radiator and fan.
35. Install the fan shroud.
36. Connect the exhaust pipes at the manifolds.
37. Fill the cooling system.
38. Connect the battery.

CAMSHAFT INSPECTION

Completely clean the camshaft with solvent, paying special attention to cleaning the oil holes. Visually inspect the cam lobes and bearing journals for excessive wear. If a lobe is questionable, have the cam checked at a reputable machine shop. If a journal or lobe is worn, the camshaft must be reground or replaced. Also have the camshaft checked for straightness on a dial indicator.

NOTE: If a cam journal is worn, there is a good chance that the bushings are worn.

Camshaft Bearings

REMOVAL AND INSTALLATION

If excessive camshaft wear is found, or if the engine is completely rebuilt, the camshaft bearings should be replaced.

NOTE: The front and rear bearings should be removed last, and installed first. Those bearings act as guides for the other bearings and pilot.

1. Drive the camshaft rear plug from the block.
2. Assemble the removal puller with its shoulder on the bearing to be removed. Gradually tighten the puller nut until the bearing is removed.
3. Remove the remaining bearings, leaving the front and rear for last. To remove these, reverse the position of the puller, so as to pull the bearings towards the center of the block. Leave the tool in this position, pilot the new front and rear bearings on the installer, and pull them into position.
4. Return the puller to its original position and pull the remaining bearings into position.

NOTE: You must make sure that the oil holes of the bearings and block align when installing the bearings. If they don't align, the camshaft will not get proper lubrication and may seize or at least be seriously damaged. To check for correct oil hole alignment, use a piece of brass rod with a 90° bend in the end as shown in the illustration. Check all oil hole openings. The wire must enter each hole, or the hole is not properly aligned.

5. Replace the camshaft rear plug, and stake it into position. On the 8–6.2L diesel, coat the outer diameter of the new plug with GM sealant #1052080 or equivalent, and install it flush to $^1/_{32}$ in. (0.794mm) deep.

Pistons and Connecting Rods

REMOVAL AND INSTALLATION

Before removing the pistons, the top of the cylinder bore must be examined for a ridge. A ridge at the top of the bore is the result of normal cylinder wear, caused by the piston rings only traveling so far up the bore in the course of the piston stroke. The ridge can be felt by hand. It must be removed before the pistons are removed.

A ridge reamer is necessary for this operation. Place the piston at the bottom of its stroke, and cover it with a rag. Cut the ridge away with the ridge reamer, using extreme care to avoid cutting too deeply. Remove the rag, and remove the cuttings that remain on the piston with a magnet and a rag soaked in clean oil. Make sure the piston top and cylinder bore are absolutely clean before moving the piston.

1. Remove intake manifold and cylinder head or heads.
2. Remove oil pan.
3. Remove oil pump assembly if necessary.
4. Matchmark the connecting rod cap to the connecting rod with a scribe. Each cap must be reinstalled on its proper rod in the proper direction. Remove the connecting rod bearing cap and the rod bearing. Number the top of each piston with silver paint or a felt tip pen for later assembly.

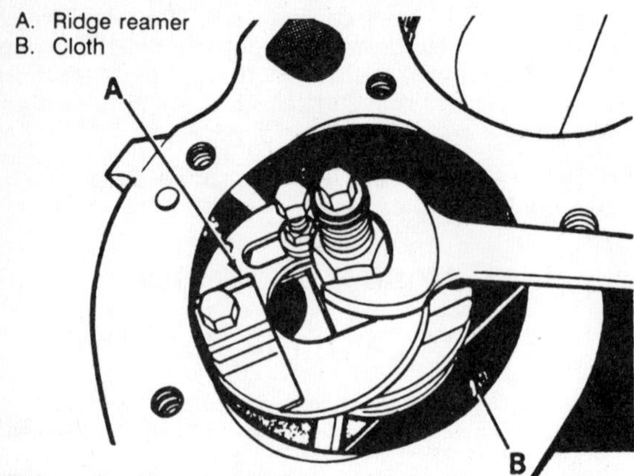

Removing the ridge at the top of the cylinder

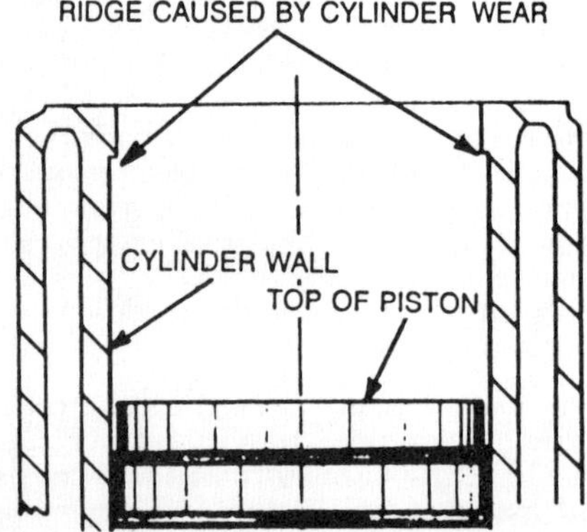

Ridge formed by pistons at the top of their travel

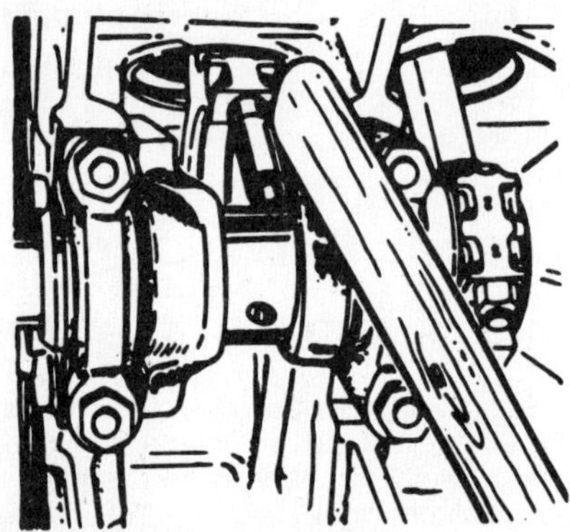
Push the piston and rod assembly out with a hammer handle

5. Cut lengths of 3/8 in. (9.53mm) diameter hose to use as rod bolt guides. Install the hose over the threads of the rod bolts, to prevent the bolt threads from damaging the crankshaft journals and cylinder walls when the piston is removed.

6. Squirt some clean engine oil onto the cylinder wall from above, until the wall is coated. Carefully push the piston and rod assembly up and out of the cylinder by tapping on the bottom of the connecting rod with a wooden hammer handle.

7. Place the rod bearing and cap back on the connecting rod, and install the nuts temporarily. Using a number stamp or punch, stamp the cylinder number on the side of the connecting rod and cap. This will help keep the proper piston and rod assembly on the proper cylinder.

NOTE: On all V8s, starting at the front the right bank cylinders are 2-4-6-8 and the left bank 1-3-5-7. On the V6 engine even number cylinders 2-4-6 are in the right bank, odd number cylinders 1-3-5 are in the left bank, when viewed from the rear of the engine. The inline 6-cylinder is numbered from front to back.

8. Remove remaining pistons in similar manner.

On all gasoline engines, the notch on the piston will face the front of the engine for assembly. The chamfered corners of the bearing caps should face toward the front of the left bank and toward the rear of the right bank, and the boss on the connecting rod should face toward the front of the engine for the right bank and to the rear of the engine on the left bank.

On the 6.2L diesel, install the piston and rod assemblies with the rod bearing tang slots on the side opposite the camshaft.

On various engines, the piston compression rings are marked with a dimple, a letter **T**, a letter **O**, **GM** or the word **TOP** to identify the side of the ring which must face toward the top of the piston.

Piston Ring and Wrist Pin

REMOVAL

Some of the engines covered in this guide utilize pistons with pressed in wrist pins. These must be removed by a special press designed for this purpose. Other pistons have their wrist pins secured by snaprings, which are easily removed with snapring pliers. Separate the piston from the connecting rod.

A piston ring expander is necessary for removing piston rings without damaging them. Any other method (screwdriver blades, pliers. etc.) usually results in the rings being bent, scratched or distorted, or the piston itself being damaged. When the rings are removed, clean the ring grooves using an appropriate ring groove cleaning tool, using care not to cut too deeply. Thoroughly clean all carbon and varnish from the piston with solvent.

Do not use a wire brush or caustic solvent (acids, etc.) on pistons.

Inspect the pistons for scuffing, scoring, cracks, pitting, or excessive ring groove wear. If these are evident, the piston must be replaced.

The piston should also be checked in relation to the cylinder diameter. Using a telescoping gauge and micrometer, or a dial gauge, measure the cylinder bore diameter perpendicular (90°) to the piston pin, 2½ in. (63.5mm) below the cylinder block deck (surface where the block mates with the heads). Then, with the micrometer, measure the piston perpendicular to its wrist pin on the shirt. The difference between the two measurements is the piston clearance. If the clearance is within specifications or slightly below (after the cylinders have been bored or honed), finish honing is all that is necessary. If the clearance is excessive, try to obtain a slightly larger piston to bring clearance to within specifications. If this is not possible, obtain the first oversize piston and hone (if necessary, bore) the cylinder to size. Generally, if the cylinder bore is tapered 0.005 in. (0.127mm) or more or is out-of-round 0.003 in. (0.0762mm) or more, it is advisable to rebore for the smallest possible oversize piston and rings.

After measuring, mark pistons with a felt tip pen for reference and for assembly.

NOTE: Cylinder honing and/or boring should be performed by a reputable, professional mechanic with the proper equipment. In some cases, cleanup honing can be done with the cylinder block in the car, but most excessive honing and all cylinder boring must be done with the block stripped and removed from the car.

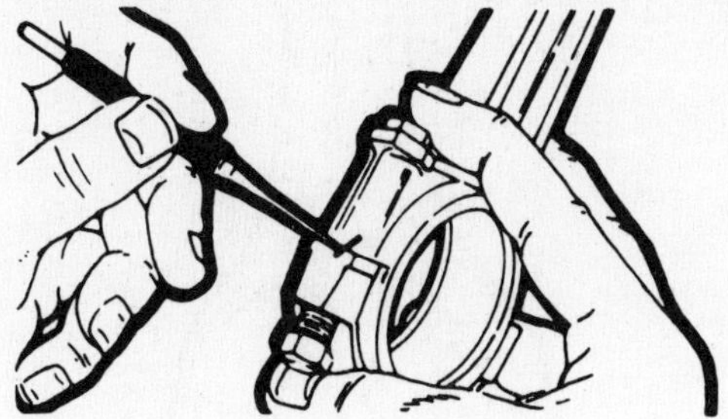

Match the connecting rods to their caps with a scribe mark

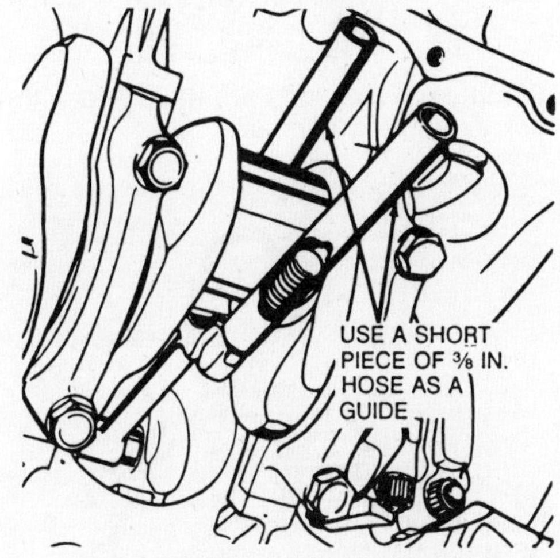

Connecting rod bolt guide

Using a hammer handle, tap the piston down, through the ring compressor, and into the cylinder

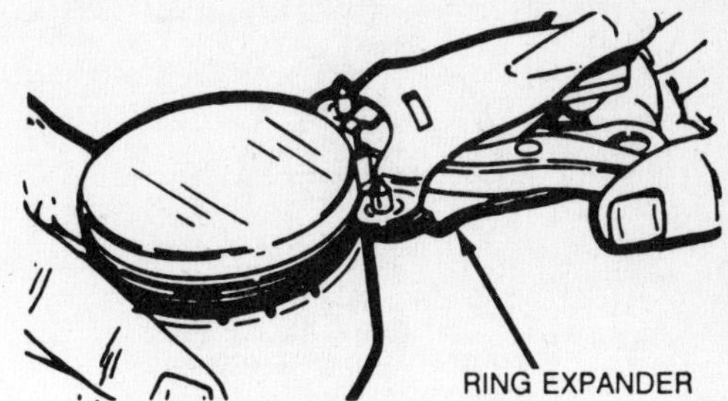

Removing the piston rings

Installing the piston pin lock rings

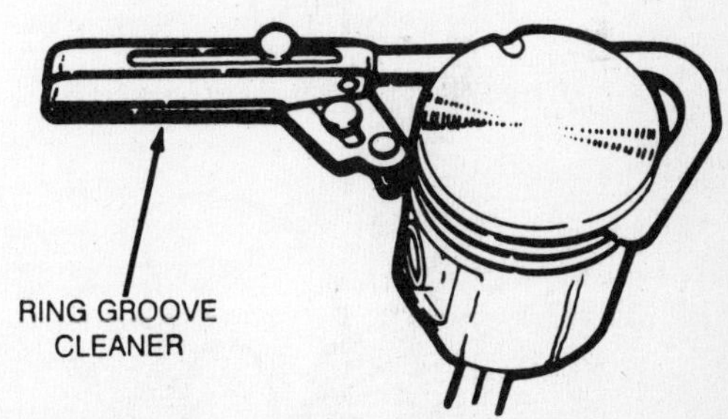

Cleaning the piston ring grooves with a ring groove cleaner

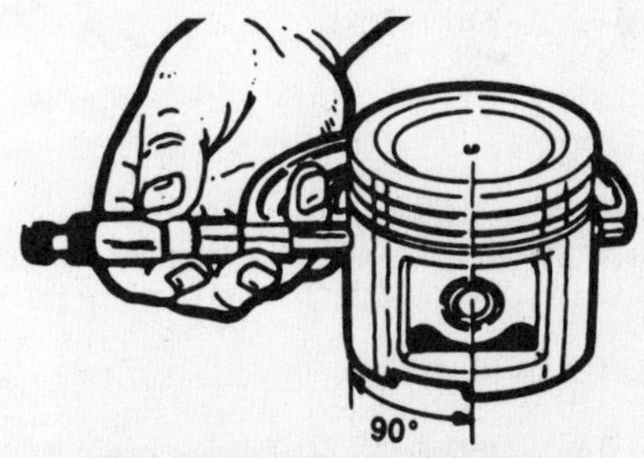

Measuring piston diameter

PISTON RING END GAP

Piston ring end gap should be checked while the rings are removed from the pistons. Incorrect end gap indicates that the wrong size rings are being used; ring breakage could occur.

Compress the piston rings to be used in a cylinder, one at a time, into that cylinder. Squirt clean oil into the cylinder, so that the rings and the top 2 in. (51mm) of cylinder wall are coated. Using an inverted piston, press the rings approximately 1 in. (25.4mm) below the deck of the block (on diesels, measure ring gap clearance with the ring positioned at the bottom of ring travel in the bore). Measure the ring end gap with a feeler gauge, and compare to the Ring Gap chart in this Section. Carefully pull the ring out of the cylinder and file the ends squarely with a fine file to obtain the proper clearance.

PISTON RING SIDE CLEARANCE CHECK AND INSTALLATION

Check the piston to see that the ring grooves and oil return holes have been properly cleaned. Slide a piston ring into its groove, and check the side clearance with a feeler gauge. On gasoline engines, make sure you insert the gauge between the ring and its lower land (lower edge of the groove), because any wear that occurs forms a step at the inner portion of the lower land. On diesels, insert the gauge between the ring and the upper land. If the piston grooves have worn to the extent that relatively high steps exist on the lower land, the piston should be re-

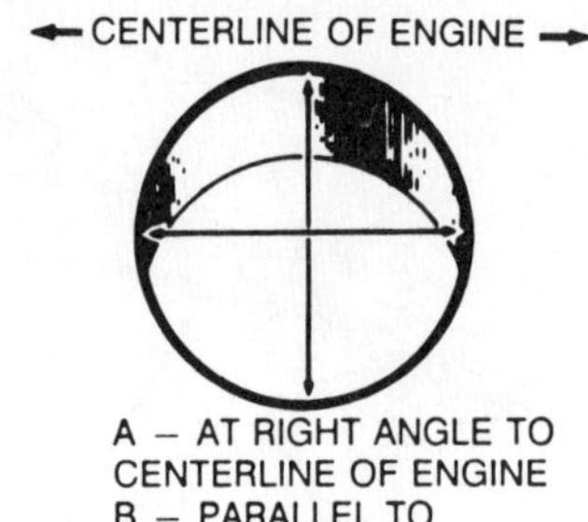

Cylinder bore measuring points

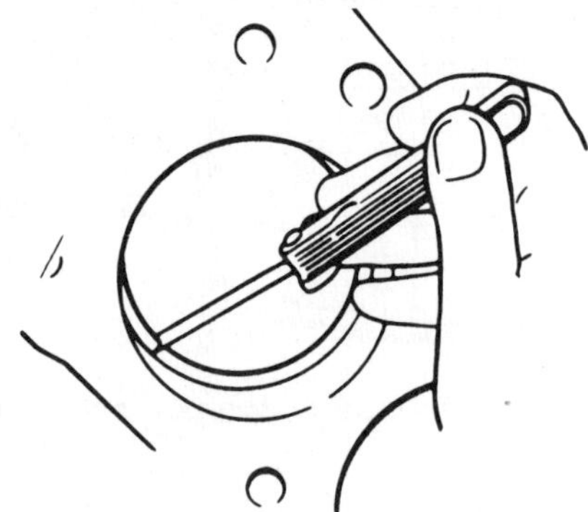

Checking piston ring end gap

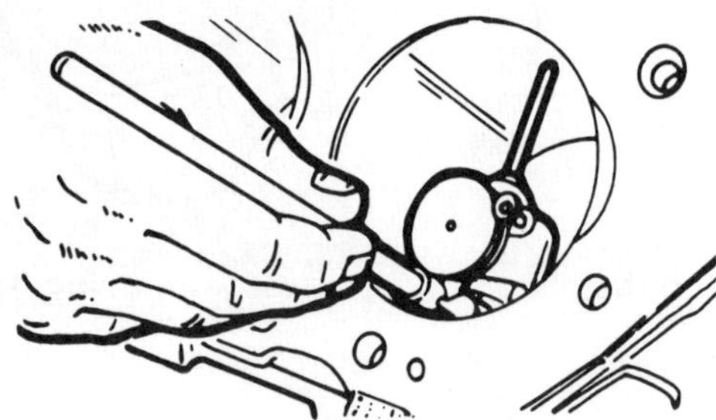

Measuring cylinder bore with a dial gauge

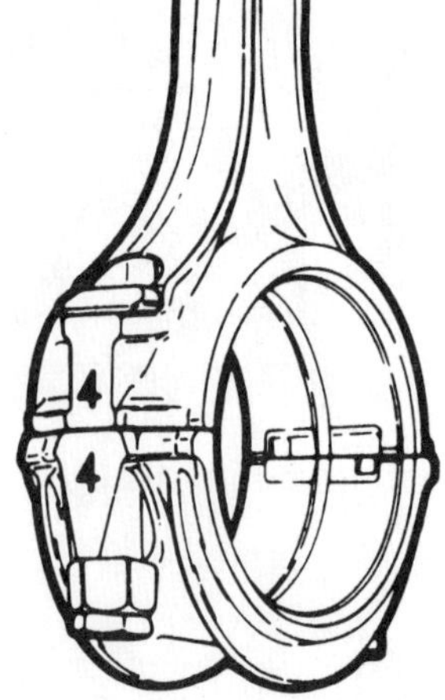

Some caps and rods are identified with corresponding numbers

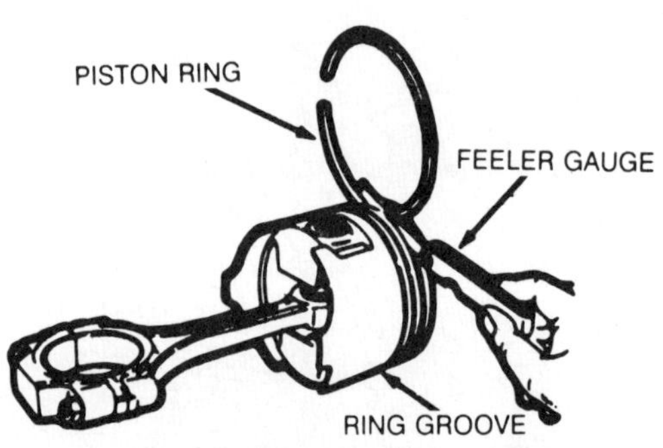

Checking piston ring side clearance

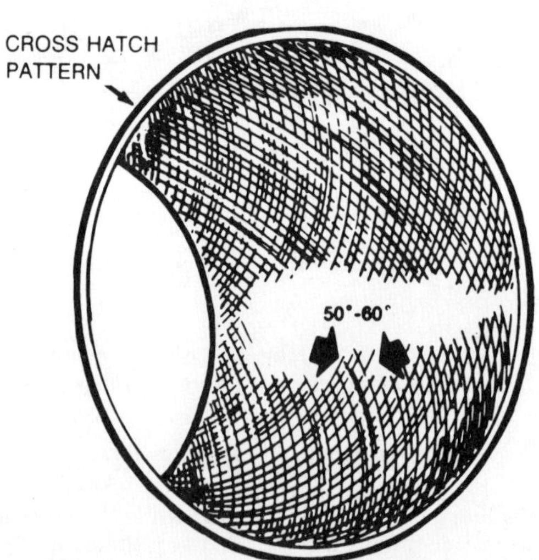

A properly honed cylinder bore

placed, because these will interfere with the operation of the new rings and ring clearances will be excessive. Pistons rings are not furnished in oversize widths to compensate for ring groove wear.

Install the rings on the piston, lowest ring first, using a piston ring expander. There is a high risk of breaking or distorting the rings, or scratching the piston, if the rings are installed by hand or other means.

Position the rings on the piston as illustrated. Spacing of the various piston ring gaps is crucial to proper oil retention and even cylinder wear. When installing new rings, refer to the illustration diagram furnished with the new parts.

Connecting Rod Bearings

Connecting rod bearings for the engine covered in this guide consist of two halves or shells which are interchangable in the rod and cap. When the shells are placed in position, the ends extend slightly beyond the rod and cap surfaces so that when the rod bolts are torqued the shells will be capped tightly in place to insure positive seating and to prevent turning. A tang holds the shells in place.

NOTE: The ends of the bearing shell must never be filed flush with the mating surface of the rod and cap.

If a rod bearing becomes noisy or is worn so that its clearance on the crank journal is sloppy, a new bearing of the correct undersize must be selected and installed since there is a provision for adjustment.

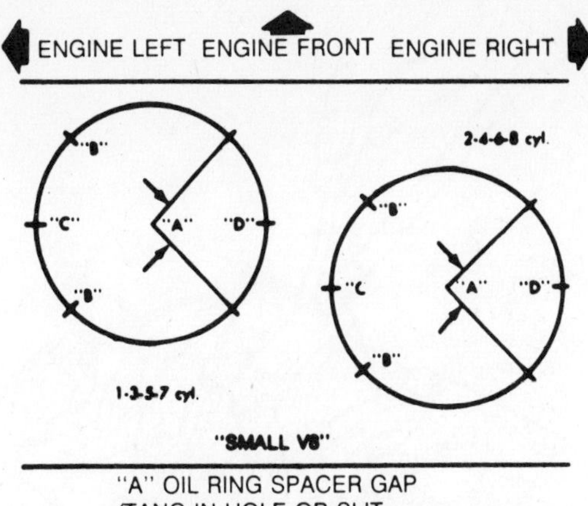

Ring gap locations for all gasoline engines

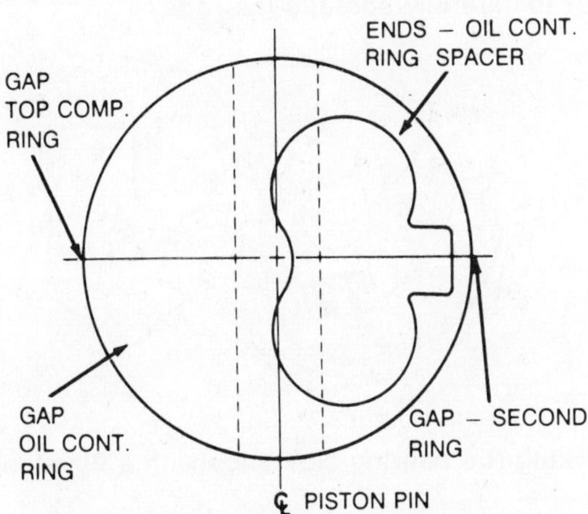

Ring gap positioning for diesel engines

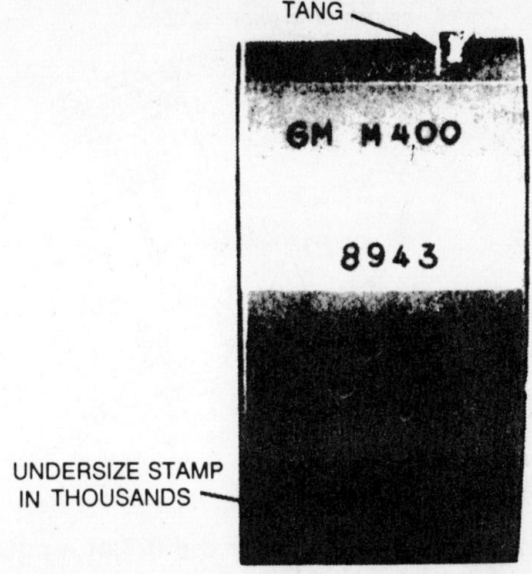

Undersize marks are stamped on the bearing shells. The tang fits in the notches in the rod and cap

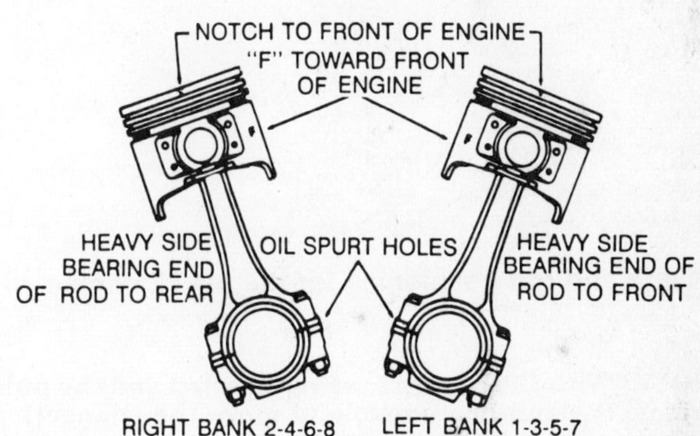

Piston and rod positioning for the 6-4.3L, 8-5.0L and 8-5.7L engines

Under no circumstances should the rod end or cap be filed to adjust the bearing clearance, nor should shims of any kind be used.

Inspect the rod bearings while the rod assemblies are out of the engine. If the shells are scored or show flaking, they should be replaced. If they are in good shape check for proper clearance on the crank journal (see below). Any scoring or ridges on the crank journal means the crankshaft must be replaced, or reground and fitted with undersized bearings.

CHECKING BEARING CLEARANCE AND REPLACING BEARINGS

NOTE: Make sure connecting rods and their caps are kept together, and that the caps are installed in the proper direction.

Replacement bearings are available in standard size, and in undersizes for reground crankshafts. Connecting rod-to-crankshaft bearing clearance is checked using Plastigage® at either the top or bottom of each crank journal. The Plastigage® has a range of 0.001–0.003 in. (0.0254–0.0762mm).

1. Remove the rod cap with the bearing shell. Completely clean the bearing shell and the crank journal, and blow any oil from the oil hole in the crankshaft; Plastigage® is soluble in oil.
2. Place a piece of Plastigage® lengthwise along the bottom center of the lower bearing shell, then install the cap with shell and torque the bolt or nuts to specification. DO NOT turn the crankshaft with Plastigage® in the bearing.
3. Remove the bearing cap with the shell. The flattened Plastigage® will be found sticking to either the bearing shell or crank journal. Do not remove it yet.
4. Use the scale printed on the Plastigage® envelope to measure the flattened material at its widest point. The number within the scale which most closely corresponds to the width of the Plastigage® indicates bearing clearance in thousandths of an inch.
5. Check the specifications chart in this Section for the desired clearance. It is advisable to install a new bearing if clearance exceeds 0.003 in. (0.0762mm). However, if the bearing is in good condition and is not being checked because of bearing noise, bearing replacement is not necessary.
6. If you are installing new bearings, try a standard size, then each undersize in order until one is found that is within the specified limits when checked for clearance with Plastigage®. Each undersize shell has its size stamped on it.
7. When the proper size shell is found, clean off the Plastigage®, oil the bearing thoroughly, reinstall the cap with its shell and torque the rod bolt nuts to specification.

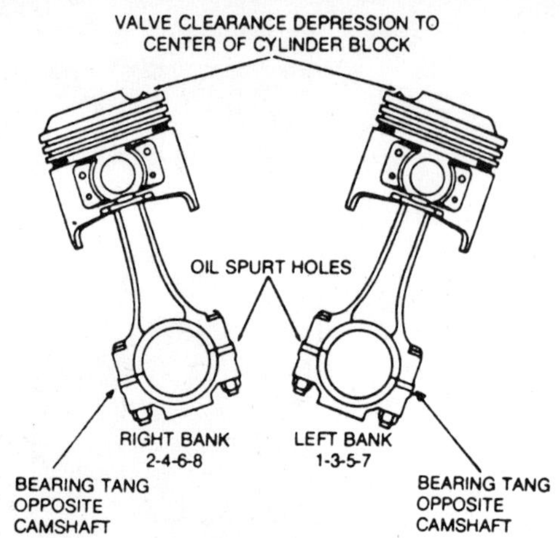

Piston and rod positioning for the 8-7.4L engine

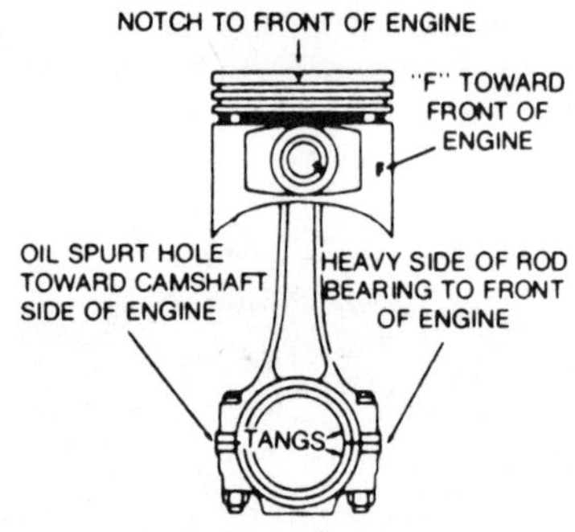

Piston and rod positioning for the 6-4.8L engine

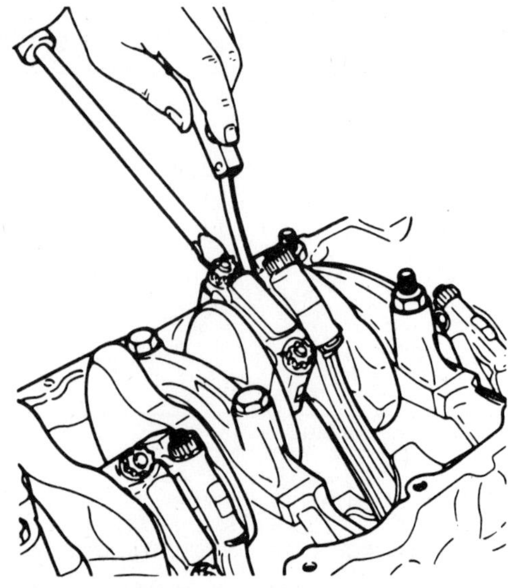

Checking connecting rod side clearance. Use a small prybar to carefully spreads the rods

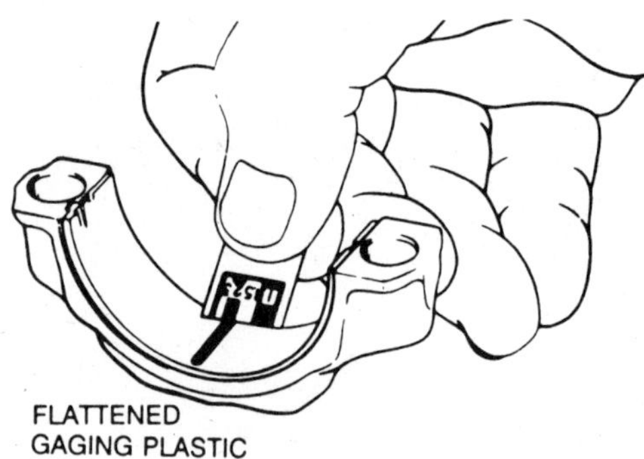

Checking rod bearing clearance with a Plastigage®

NOTE: With the proper bearing selected and the nuts torqued, it should be possible to move the connecting rod back and forth freely on the crank journal as allowed by the specified connecting rod and clearance. If the rod cannot be moved, either the rod bearing is too far undersize or the rod is misaligned.

PISTON AND CONNECTING ROD ASSEMBLY AND INSTALLATION

NOTE: Most engines are equipped with silicone coated pistons. If your engine has these pistons, if replaced, they must be replaced with silicone coated pistons. Substituting another type of piston could reduce the life of the engine.

Install the connecting rod to the piston, making sure piston installation notches and any marks on the rod are in proper relation to one another. Lubricate the wrist pin with clean engine oil, and install the pin into the rod and piston assembly, either by hand or by using a wrist pin press as required. Install snaprings if equipped, and rotate them in their grooves to make sure they are seated. To install the piston and connecting rod assembly:

1. Make sure connecting rod big end bearings (including end cap) are of the correct size and properly installed.
2. Fit rubber hoses over the connecting rod bolts to protect the crankshaft journals, as in the Piston Removal procedure. Coat the rod bearings with clean oil.
3. Using the proper ring compressor, insert the piston assembly into the cylinder so that the notch in the top of the piston faces the front of the engine (this assumes that the dimple(s) or other markings on the connecting rods are in correct relation to the piston notch(es).
4. From beneath the engine, coat each crank journal with clean oil. Pull the connecting rod, with the bearing shell in place, into position against the crank journal.
5. Remove the rubber hoses. Install the bearing cap and cap nuts and torque to specification.

NOTE: When more than one rod and piston assembly is being installed, the connecting rod cap attaching nuts should only be tightened enough to keep each rod in position until all have been installed. This will ease the installation of the remaining piston assemblies.

6. Check the clearance between the sides of the connecting rods and the crankshaft using a feeler gauge. Spread the rods slightly with a screwdriver to insert the gauge. If clearance is below the minimum tolerance, the rod may be machined to provide adequate clearance. If clearance is excessive, substitute an unworn rod, and recheck. If clearance is still outside specifications, the crankshaft must be welded and reground or replaced.
7. Replace the oil pump if removed and the oil pan.
8. Install the cylinder head(s) and intake manifold.

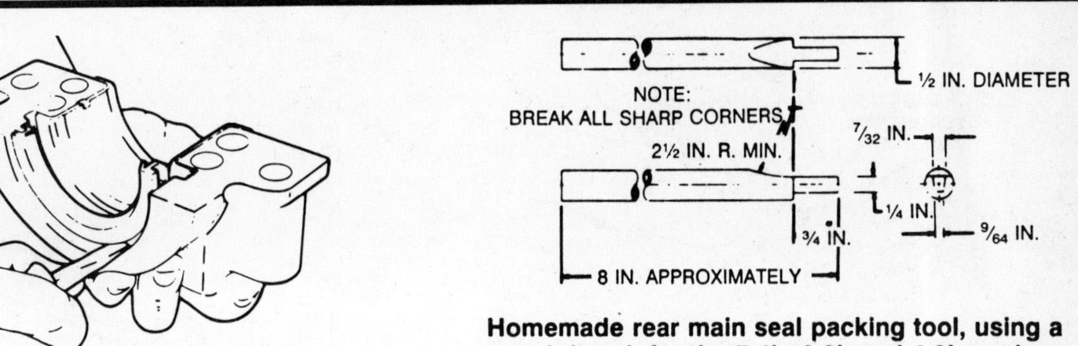

Removing the rear seal half from the bearing cap on the 7.4L, 6.2L and 4.8L engine

Homemade rear main seal packing tool, using a wood dowel, for the 7.4L, 6.2L and 4.8L engine

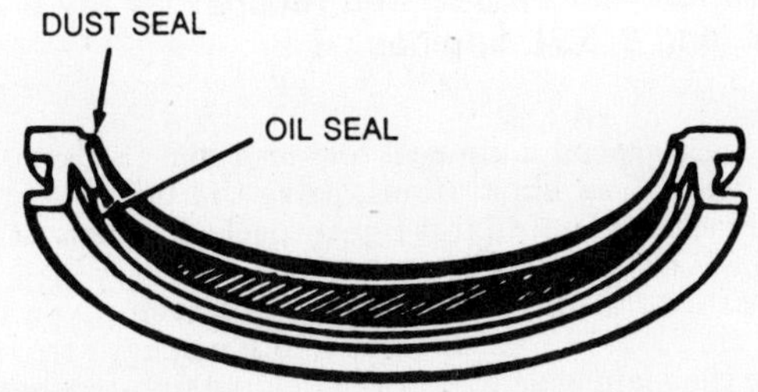

7.4L, 6.2L and 4.8L engine rear main seal half – bearing cap side

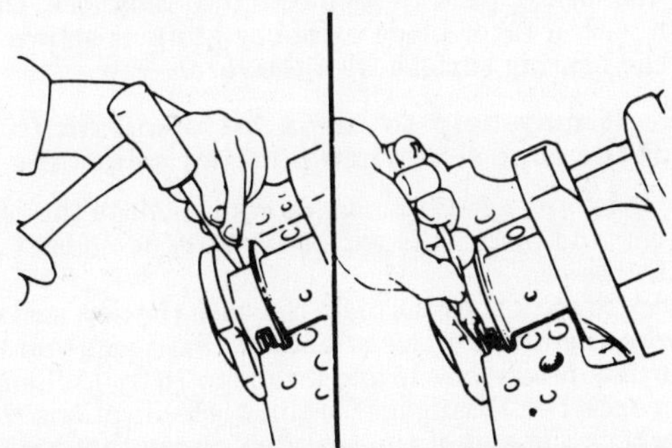

Removing the upper rear seal half from the 7.4L and 6.2L engine

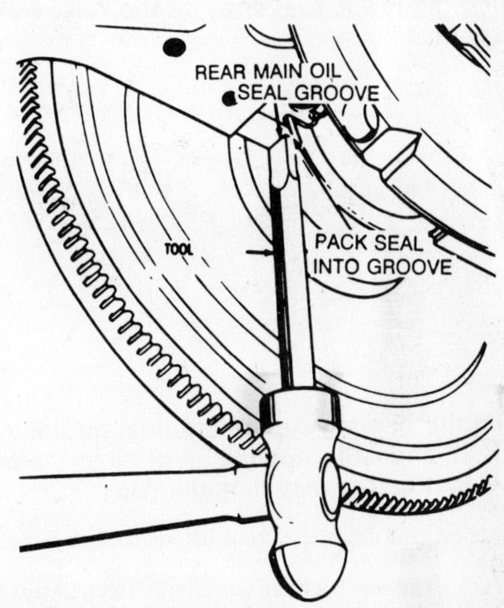

Packing the upper rear seal on the 7.4L, 6.2L and 4.8L engine

Rear Main Oil Seal

REMOVAL AND INSTALLATION

6-4.8L

The rear main bearing oil seal, both halves, can be removed without removal of the crankshaft. Always replace the upper and lower halves together.

1. Raise and support the truck on jackstands.
2. Drain the oil.
3. Remove the oil pan.
4. Remove the rear main bearing cap.
5. Remove the old oil seal from its groove in the cap, prying from the bottom using a suitable tool.
6. Coat a new seal half completely with clean engine oil, and insert it into the bearing cap groove. Keep the oil off of the parting line surface, as this surface is treated with glue. Gradually push the seal with a hammer handle until the seal is rolled into place.
7. To remove the upper half of the old seal, use a small hammer and a soft, blunt punch to tap one end of the oil seal out until it protrudes far enough to be removed with needlenosed pliers.
8. Push the new seal into place with the lip toward the front of the engine.
9. Install the bearing cap and torque the bolts to a loose fit; do not final-torque.
10. With the cap fitted loosely, move the crankshaft first to the rear and then to the front with a rubber mallet. This will properly position the thrust bearing.
11. Torque the bearing cap to a final torque of 65 ft. lbs.
12. Install the oil pan.

8-7.4L

1. Remove the oil pan, oil pump and rear main bearing cap.
2. Remove the oil seal from the bearing cap by prying it out with a suitable tool.
3. Remove the upper half of the seal with a small punch. Drive it around far enough to be gripped with pliers.

To install:

4. Clean the crankshaft and bearing cap.
5. Coat the lips and bead of the seal with light engine oil, keeping oil from the ends of the seal.

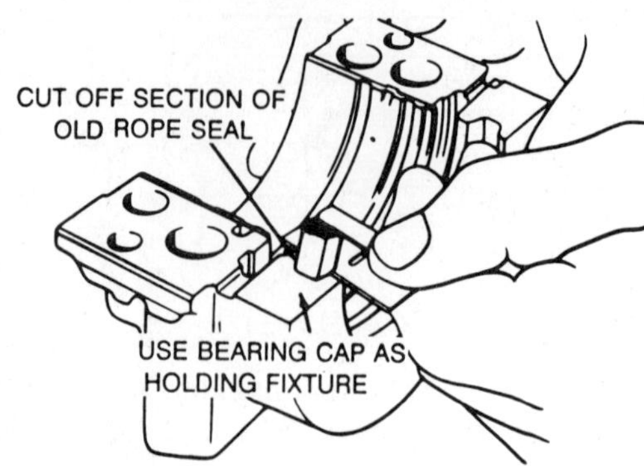

Cutting the lower seal ends on the 7.4L, 6.2L and 4.8L engine

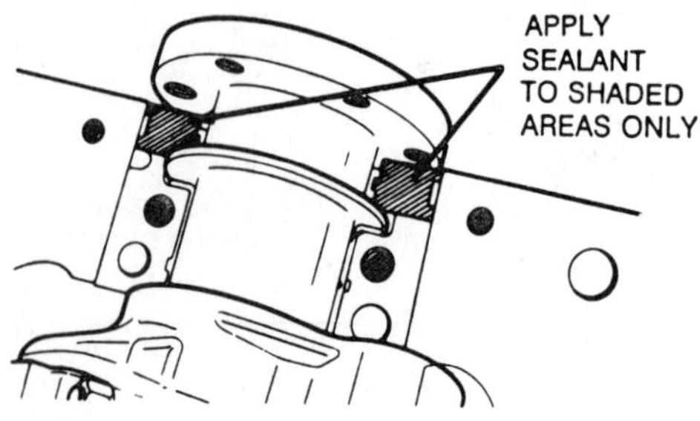

Sealing the bearing cap before final torquing, on the 7.4L, 6.2L and 4.8L. Apply a bit of oil to the crank journal just before installing the cap

6. Position the fabricated tool between the crankshaft and seal seat.
7. Position the seal between the crankshaft and tip of the tool so that the seal bead contacts the tip of the tool. The oil seal lip should face forward.
8. Roll the seal around the crankshaft using the tool to protect the seal bead from the sharp corners of the crankcase.
9. The installation tool should be left installed until the seal is properly positioned with both ends flush with the block.
10. Remove the tool.
11. Install the other half of the seal in the bearing cap using the tool in the same manner as before. Light thumb pressure should install the seal.
12. Install the bearing cap with sealant applied to the mating areas of the cap and block. Keep sealant from the ends of the seal.
13. Torque the main bearing cap retaining bolts to 10–12 ft. lbs. Tap the end of the crankshaft first rearward, then forward with a lead hammer. This will line up the rear main bearing and the crankshaft thrust surfaces. Tighten the main bearing cap to specification.
14. Install the oil pump.
15. Install the oil pan.

8–6.2L Diesel

The crankshaft need not be removed to replace the rear main bearing upper oil seal. The lower seal is installed in the bearing cap.

NOTE: Engines are originally equipped with a rope-type seal. This should be replaced with the lip-type seal available as a service replacement.

1. Drain the crankcase oil and remove the oil pan and rear main bearing cap.

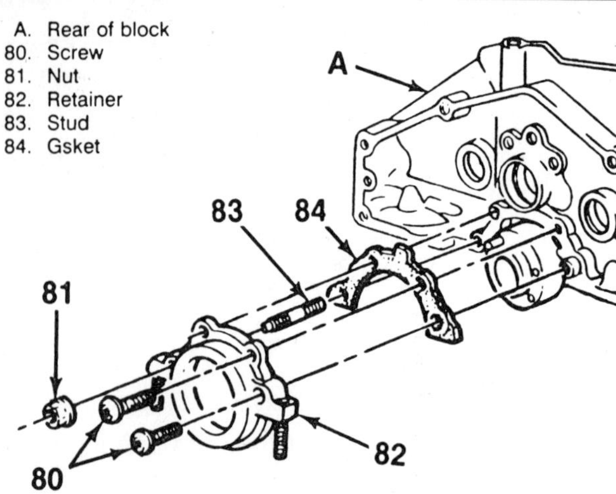

Crankshaft rear oil seal and retainer for the 6–4.3L, 8–5.0L and 8–5.7L engines

2. Using a special main seal tool or a tool that can be made from a dowel (see illustration), drive the upper seal into its groove on each side until it is tightly packed. This is usually $^1/_4$–$^3/_4$ in. (6.35–19.05mm).
3. Measure the amount the seal was driven up on one side. Add $^1/_{16}$ in. (1.5875mm) and cut another length from the old seal. Use the main bearing cap as a holding fixture when cutting the seal as illustrated. Carefully trim protruding seal.
4. Work these two pieces of seal up into the cylinder block on each side with two nailsets or small screwdrivers. Using the packing tool again, pack these pieces into the block, then trim the flush with a razor blade or hobby knife as shown. Do not scratch the bearing surface with the razor.

NOTE: It may help to use a bit of oil on the short pieces of the rope seal when packing it into the block.

5. Apply Loctite® # 496 sealer or equivalent to the rear main bearing cap and install the rope seal. Cut the ends of the seal flush with the cap.
6. Check to see if the rear main cap with the new seal will seat properly on the block. Place a piece of Plastigage® on the rear main journal, install the cap and torque to 70 ft. lbs. Remove the cap and check the Plastigage® against specifications. If out of specs, recheck the end of the seal for fraying that may be preventing the cap from seating properly.
7. Make sure all traces of Plastigage® are removed from the crankshaft journal. Apply a thin film of sealer (GM part # 1052357 or equvalent) to the bearing cap. Keep the sealant off of both the seal and the bearing.
8. Just before assembly, apply a light coat of clean engine oil on the crankshaft surface that will contact the seal.
9. Install the bearing cap and torque to specification.
10. Install the oil pump and oil pan.

6–4.3L
8–5.0L
8–5.7L

Special tool J-35621, or its equivalent, will be necessary for this job.

1. Remove the transmission.
2. With manual transmission, remove the clutch.
3. Remove the flywheel or flexplate.
4. Insert a small prying tool in the notches provided in the seal retainer and pry out the old seal. Be VERY CAREFUL to avoid nicking or scratching the sealing surfaces of the crankshaft.

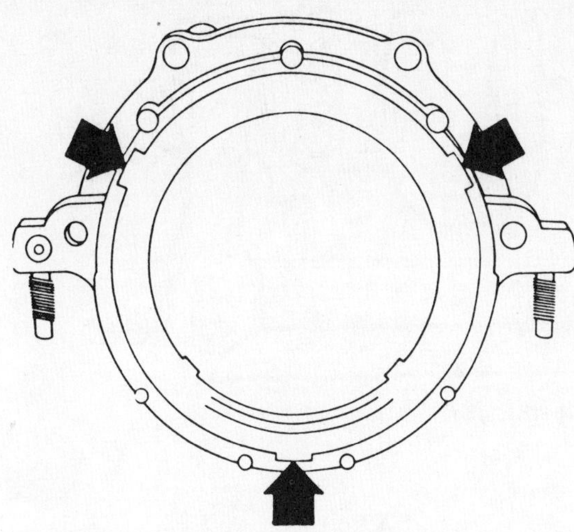

Seal removal notches

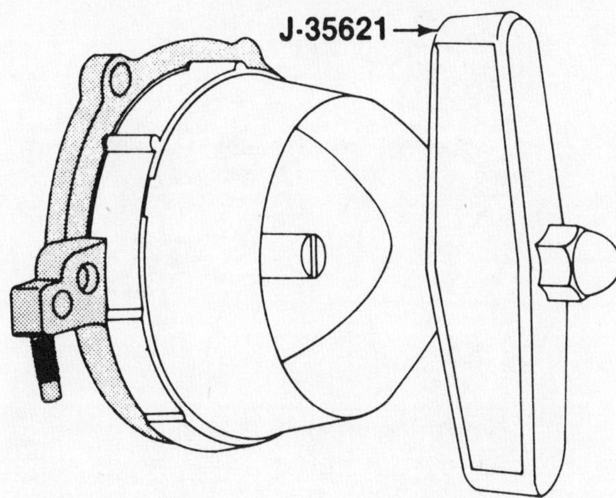

Installing the rear oil seal on the 6–4.3L, 8–5.0L and 8–5.7L engines

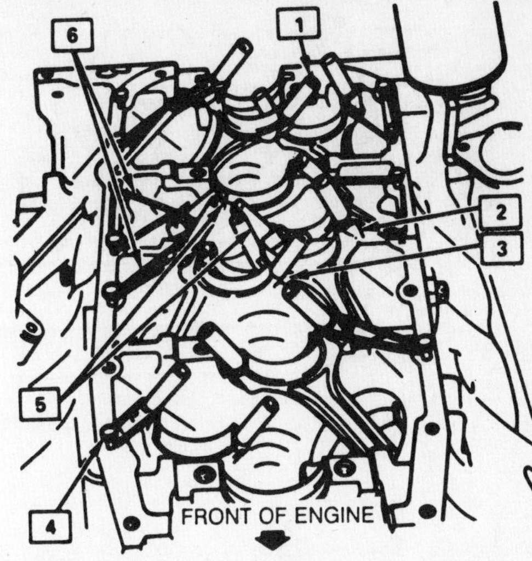

1. Rubber hose
2. #4 rod
3. #3 rod
4. Oil pan bolt
5. Note overlap of adjacent rods
6. Rubber bands

Crankshaft removal, showing hose lengths on the rod bolts

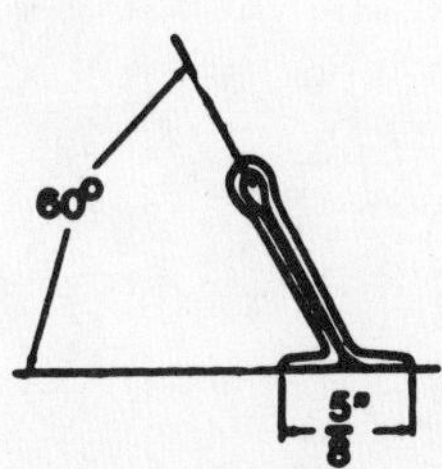

Homemade bearing roll-out pin

To install:

5. Coat the inner and outer diameters of the new seal with clean engine oil.
6. Using seal tool J–35621, or equivalent, position the seal on the tool.
7. Thread the attaching screws into the holes in the crankshaft end and tighten them securely with a screwdriver.
8. Turn the installer handle until it bottoms.
9. Remove the tool.
10. Install the flywheel/flexplate, clutch and transmission.

Crankshaft and Main Bearings

CRANKSHAFT REMOVAL

1. Drain the engine oil and remove the engine from the car. Mount the engine on a work stand in a suitable working area. Invert the engine, so the oil pan is facing up.
2. Remove the engine front (timing) cover.
3. Remove the timing chain and gars.
4. Remove the oil pan.
5. Remove the oil pump.
6. Stamp the cylinder number on the machined surfaces of the bolt bosses of the connecting rods and caps for identification when reinstalling. If the pistons are to be removed eventually from the connecting rod, mark the cylinder number on the pistons with silver paint or felt tip pen for proper cylinder identification and cap-to-rod location.
7. Remove the connecting rod caps. Install lengths of rubber hose on each of the connecting rod bolts, to protect the crank journals when the crank is removed.
8. Mark the main bearing caps with a number punch or punch so that they can be reinstalled in their original positions.
9. Remove all main bearing caps.
10. Note the position of the keyway in the crankshaft so it can be installed in the same position.
11. Install rubber bands between a bolt on each connecting rod and oil pan bolts that have been reinstalled in the block (see illustration). This will keep the rods from banging on the block when the crank is removed.
12. Carefully lift the crankshaft out of the block. The rods will pivot to the center of the engine when the crank is removed.

MAIN BEARING INSPECTION

Like connecting rod big end bearings, the crankshaft main bearings are shell type inserts that do not utilize shims and cannot be adjusted. The bearings are available in various standard and undersizes. If main bearing clearance is found to be too sloppy, a new bearing (both upper and lower halves) is required.

Measuring crankshaft runout

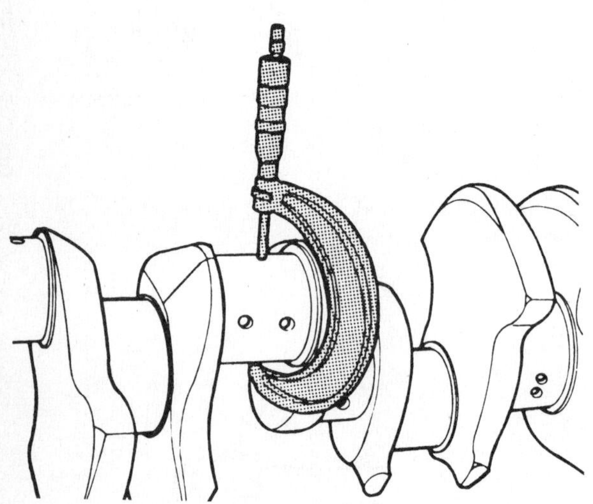

Measuring crankshaft bearing journals

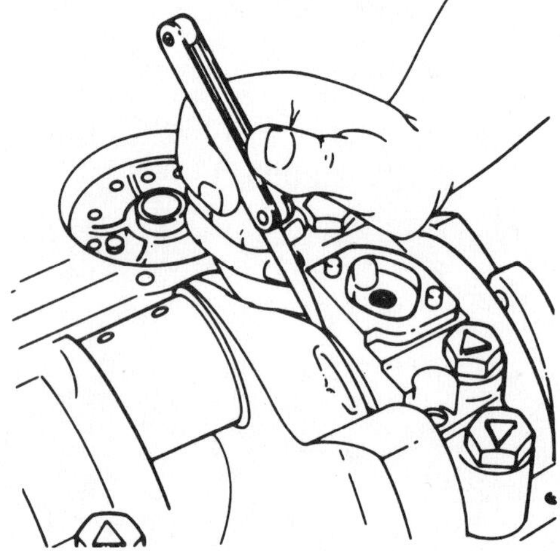

Measuring crankshaft endplay

NOTE: Factory undersized crankshafts are marked, sometimes with a 9 and/or a large spot of light green paint. The bearing caps also will have the paint on each side of the undersized journal.

Generally, the lower half of the bearing shell (except No. 1 bearing) shows greater wear and fatigue. If the lower half only shows the effects of normal wear (no heavy scoring or discoloration), it can usually be assumed that the upper half is also in good shape. Conversely, if the lower half is heavily worn or damaged, both halves should be replaced. Never replace one bearing half without replacing the other.

CHECKING CLEARANCE

Main bearing clearance can be checked both with the crankshaft in the truck and with the engine out of the car. If the engine block is still in the car, the crankshaft should be supported both front and rear (by the damper and to remove clearance from the upper bearing. Total clearance can then be measured between the lower bearing and journal. If the block has been removed from the car, and is inverted, the crank will rest on the upper bearings and the total clearance can be measured between the lower bearing and journal. Clearance is checked in the same manner as the connecting rod bearings, with Plastigage®.

NOTE: Crankshaft bearing caps and bearing shells should NEVER be filed flush with the cap-to-block mating surface to adjust for wear in the old bearings. Always install new bearings.

1. If the crankshaft has been removed, install it (block removed from car). If the block is still in the car, remove the oil pan and oil pump. Starting with the rear bearing cap, remove the cap and wipe all oil from the crank journal and bearing cap.
2. Place a strip of Plastigage® the full width of the bearing, (parallel to the crankshaft), on the journal.

WARNING: Do not rotate the crankshaft while the gaging material is between the bearing and the journal!

3. Install the bearing cap and evenly torque the cap bolts to specification.
4. Remove the bearing cap. The flattened Plastigage® will be sticking to either the bearing shell or the crank journal.
5. Use the graduated scale on the Plastigage® envelope to measure the material at its widest point.

NOTE: If the flattened Plastigage® tapers toward the middle or ends, there is a difference in clearance indicating the bearing or journal has a taper, low spot or other irregularity. If this is indicated, measure the crank journal with a micrometer.

6. If bearing clearance is within specifications, the bearing insert is in good shape. Replace the insert if the clearance is not

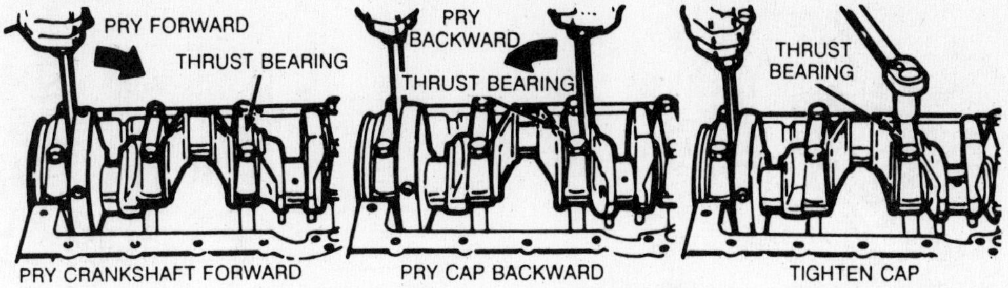

Aligning the crankshaft thrust bearing

within specifications. Always replace both upper and lower inserts as a unit.

7. Standard, 0.001 in. (0.0254mm) or 0.002 in. (0.051mm) undersize bearings should produce the proper clearance. If these sizes still produce too sloppy a fit, the crankshaft must be reground for use with the next undersize bearing. Recheck all clearances after installing new bearings.

8. Replace the rest of the bearings in the same manner. After all bearings have been checked, rotate the crankshaft to make sure there is no excessive drag. When checking the No. 1 main bearing, loosen the accessory drive belts (engine in car) to prevent a tapered reading with the Plastigage®.

MAIN BEARING REPLACEMENT

Engine Out of Truck

1. Remove and inspect the crankshaft.
2. Remove the main bearings from the bearing saddles in the cylinder block and main bearing caps.
3. Coat the bearing surfaces of the new, correct size main bearings with clean engine oil and install them in the bearing saddles in the block and in the main bearing caps.
4. Install the crankshaft. See Crankshaft Installation.

Engine in Truck

1. With the oil pan, oil pump and spark plugs removed, remove the cap from the main bearing needing replacement and remove the bearing from the cap.
2. Make a bearing roll out pin, using a bent cotter pin as shown in the illustration. Install the end of the pin in the oil hole in the crankshaft journal.
3. Rotate the crankshaft clockwise as viewed from the front of the engine. This will roll the upper bearing out of the block.
4. Lube the new upper bearing with clean engine oil and insert the plain (unnotched) end between the crankshaft and the indented or notched side of the block. Roll the bearing into place, making sure that the oil holes are aligned. Remove the roll pin from the oil hole.
5. Lube the new lower bearing and install the main bearing cap. Install the main bearing cap, making sure it is positioned in proper direction with the matchmarks in alignment.
6. Torque the main bearing cap bolts to specification.

NOTE: See Crankshaft Installation for thrust bearing alignment.

CRANKSHAFT END PLAY AND INSTALLATION

When main bearing clearance has been checked, bearings examined and/or replaced, the crankshaft can be installed. Thoroughly clean the upper and lower bearing surfaces, and lube them with clean engine oil. Install the crankshaft and main bearing caps.

Dip all main bearing cap bolts in clean oil, and torque all main bearing caps, excluding the thrust bearing cap, to specifications (see the Crankshaft and Connecting Rod chart in this Section to determine which bearing is the thrust bearing). Tighten the thrust bearing bolts finger tight. To align the thrust bearing, pry the crankshaft the extent of its axial travel several times, holding the last movement toward the front of the engine. Add thrust washers if required for proper alignment. Torque the thrust bearing cap to specifications.

To check crankshaft end play, pry the crankshaft to the extreme rear of its axial travel, then to the extreme front of its travel. Using a feeler gauge, measure the end plat at the front of the rear main bearing. End play may also be measured at the thrust bearing. Install a new rear main bearing oil seal in the cylinder block and main bearing cap. Continue to reassemble the engine.

Engine Block Heater and Freeze Plugs

REMOVAL AND INSTALLATION

CAUTION

Removing the block heater or freeze plug may cause personal injury if the engine is not completely cooled down. Even after the radiator has been drained, there will be engine coolant still in the block. Use care when removing assembly from the block.

To remove an engine freeze plug or block heater, accessories may have to be removed, such as the starter motor, motor mount, etc. Remove an obstruction before attempting to remove the freeze plug.

1. Disconnect the negative (−) battery cable.
2. **To remove the block heater, drian the engine coolant, disconnect the electrical connector, loosen the retaining screw and remove the heater from the block.**

CAUTION

When draining the coolant, keep in mind that cats and dogs are attracted by the ethylene glycol antifreeze, and are quite likely to drink any that is left in an uncovered container or in puddles on the ground. This will prove fatal in sufficient quantity. Always drain the coolant into a sealable container. Coolant should be reused unless it is contaminated or several years old.

3. **To remove the freeze plug,** drain the engine coolant, drive chisel through the plug and pry outward. Or drill an 1/8 in.

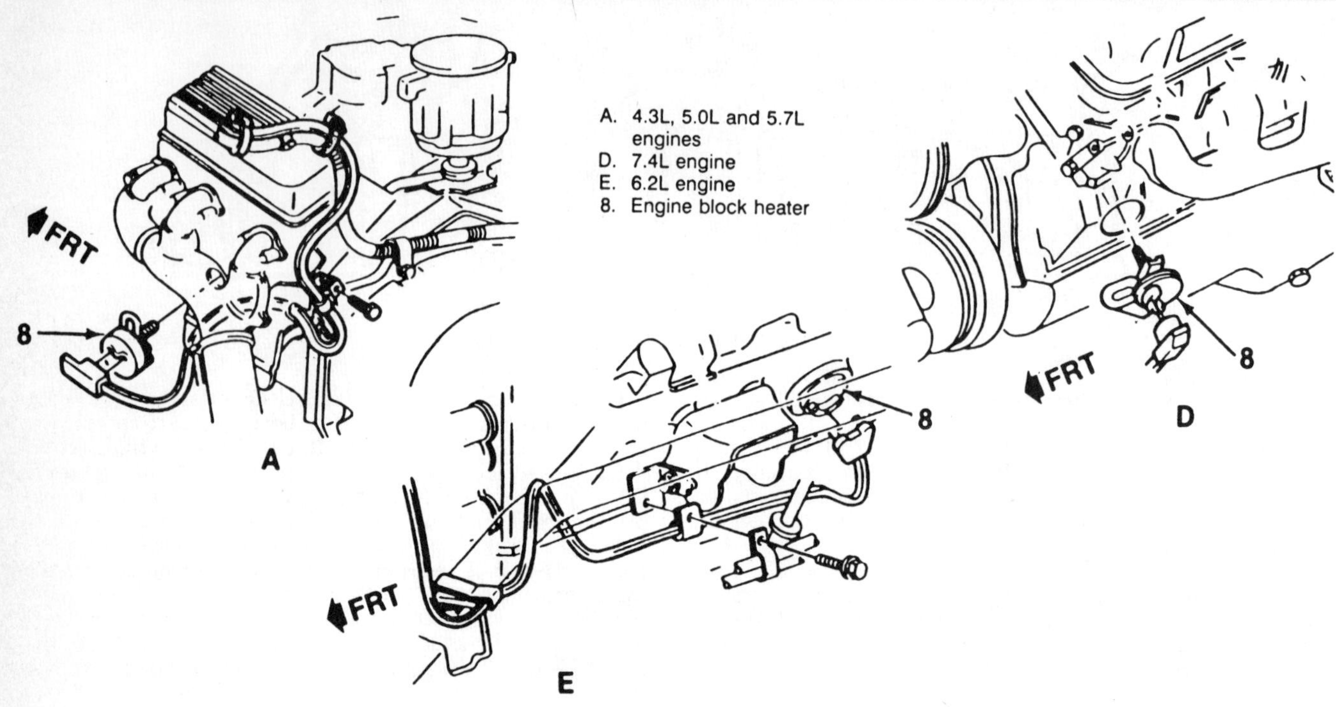

Engine block heater locations

hole into the plug and use a dent puller to remove the freeze plug.

To install:

1. **To install the block heater,** coat the O-ring with engine oil and clean the block mating surface free of rust and corrosion. Install the heater and tighten the retaining screw. Connect the electrical and negative battery cable.

2. **To install the freeze plug,** coat the new plug with silicone sealer and clean the block mating surface free of rust and corrosion. Using a deep socket the size of the interior of the plug, drive the plug into the block until the plug lip is flush with the cylinder block. Run silicone sealer around the mating area.
3. Fill the engine with coolant and check for leaks.

Flywheel and Ring Gear

REMOVAL AND INSTALLATION

The ring gear is an integral part of the flywheel and is not replaceable.

1. Remove the transmission.
2. Remove the six bolts attaching the flywheel to the crankshaft flange. Remove the flywheel.
3. Inspect the flywheel for cracks, and inspect the ring gear for burrs or worn teeth. Replace the flywheel if any damage is apparent. Remove burrs with a mill file.
4. Install the flywheel. The flywheel will only attach to the crankshaft in one position, as the bolt holes are unevenly spaced. Install the bolts and torque to specification.

EXHAUST SYSTEM

Safety Precautions

For a number of reasons, exhaust system work can be the most dangerous type of work you can do on your truck. Always observe the following precautions:

1. Support the truck extra securely. Not only will you often be working directly under it, but you'll frequently be using a lot of force, say, heavy hammer blows, to dislodge rusted parts. This can cause a truck that's improperly supported to shift and possibly fall.
2. Wear goggles. Exhaust system parts are always rusty. Metal chips can be dislodged, even when you're only turning rusted bolts. Attempting to pry pipes apart with a chisel makes the chips fly even more frequently.

3. If you're using a cutting torch, keep it a great distance from either the fuel tank or lines. Stop what you're doing and feel the temperature of the fuel bearing pipes on the tank frequently. Even slight heat can expand and/or vaporize fuel, resulting in accumulated vapor, or even a liquid leak, near your torch.

4. Watch where your hammer blows fall. You could easily tap a brake or fuel line when you hit an exhaust system part with a glancing blow. Inspect all lines and hoses in the area where you've been working.

Special Tools

A number of special exhaust system tools can be rented from auto supply houses or local stores that rent special equipment. A common one is a tail pipe expander, designed to enable you to join pipes of identical diameter.

It may also be quite helpful to use solvents designed to loosen rusted bolts or flanges. Soaking rusted parts the night before you do the job can speed the work of freeing rusted parts considerably. Remember that these solvents are are often flammable. Apply only to parts after they are cool!

Crossover Pipe

REMOVAL AND REPLACEMENT

The crossover pipe (used on V-type engines only) is typically connected to the manifolds by flanged connections or collars. In some cases, bolts that are unthreaded for part of their length are used in conjunction with springs. Make sure you install the springs and that they are in good mechanical condition (no broken coils) when installing the new pipe. Replace ring type seals, also.

Headpipe

REMOVAL AND REPLACEMENT

The headpipe is typically attached to the rear of one exhaust manifold with a flange or collar type connector and flagged to the front of the catalytic converter. Remove nuts and bolts and, if springs are used to maintain the seal, the springs. The pipe may then be separated from the rest of the system at both flanges.

Replace ring seals; inspect springs and replace them if any coils are broken.

Catalytic Converter

REMOVAL AND REPLACEMENT

CAUTION

Be very careful when working on or near the converter! External temperatures can reach +1,500°F (+816°C) and more, causing severe burns! Removal or installation should only be performed on a cold exhaust system.

Remove bolts at the flange at the rear end. Then, loosen nuts and remove U-clamp to remove the catalyst. Slide the catalyst out of the outlet pipe. Replace all ring seals. In some cases, you'll have to disconnect an air line coming from the engine compartment before catalyst removal. In some cases, a hanger supports the converter via one of the flange bolts. Make sure the hanger gets properly reconnected. Also, be careful to retain all parts used to heat shield the converter and reinstall them. Make sure the converter is replaced for proper direction of flow and air supply connections.

Muffler and Tailpipes

REMOVAL AND INSTALLATION

These units are typically connected by flanges at the rear of the converter and at either end of mufflers either by an original weld or by U-clamps working over a pipe connection in which one side of the connection is slightly larger than the other. You may have to cut the original connection and use the pipe expander to allow the original equipment exhaust pipe to be fitted over the new muffler. In this case, you'll have to purchase new U-clamps to fasten the joints. GM recommends that whenever you replace a muffler, all parts to the rear of the muffler in the

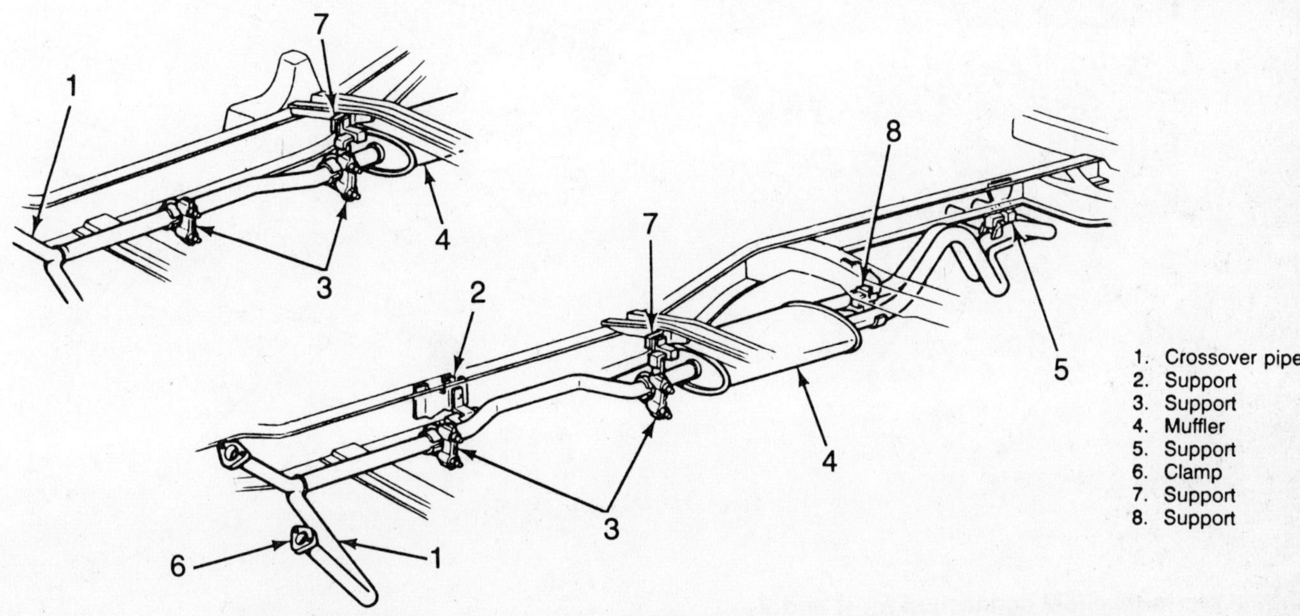

Exhaust system for C and K trucks with light duty emissions 8-6.2L diesel

exhaust system must be replaced. Also, all slip joints rearward of the converter should be coated with sealer before they are assembled.

Be careful to connect all U-clamps or other hanger arrangements so the exhaust system will not flex. Assemble all parts loosely and rotate parts inside one another or clamps on the pipes to ensure proper routing of all exhaust system parts to avoid excessive heating of the floorpan, fuel lines and tank, etc. Also, make sure there is clearance to prevent the system from rattling against spring shackles, the differential, etc. You may be able to bend long pipes slightly by hand to help get enough clearance, if necessary.

While disassembling the system, keep your eye open for any leaks or for excessively close clearance to any brake system parts. Inspect the brake system for any sort of heat damage and repair as necessary.

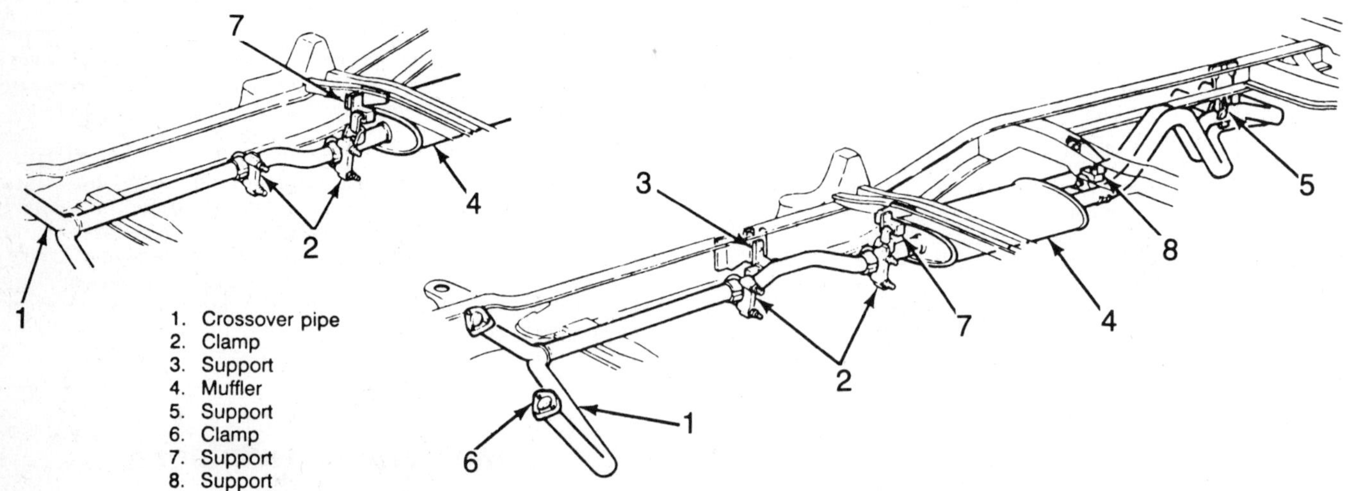

Exhaust system for C and K trucks with heavy duty emissions 8-6.2L diesel

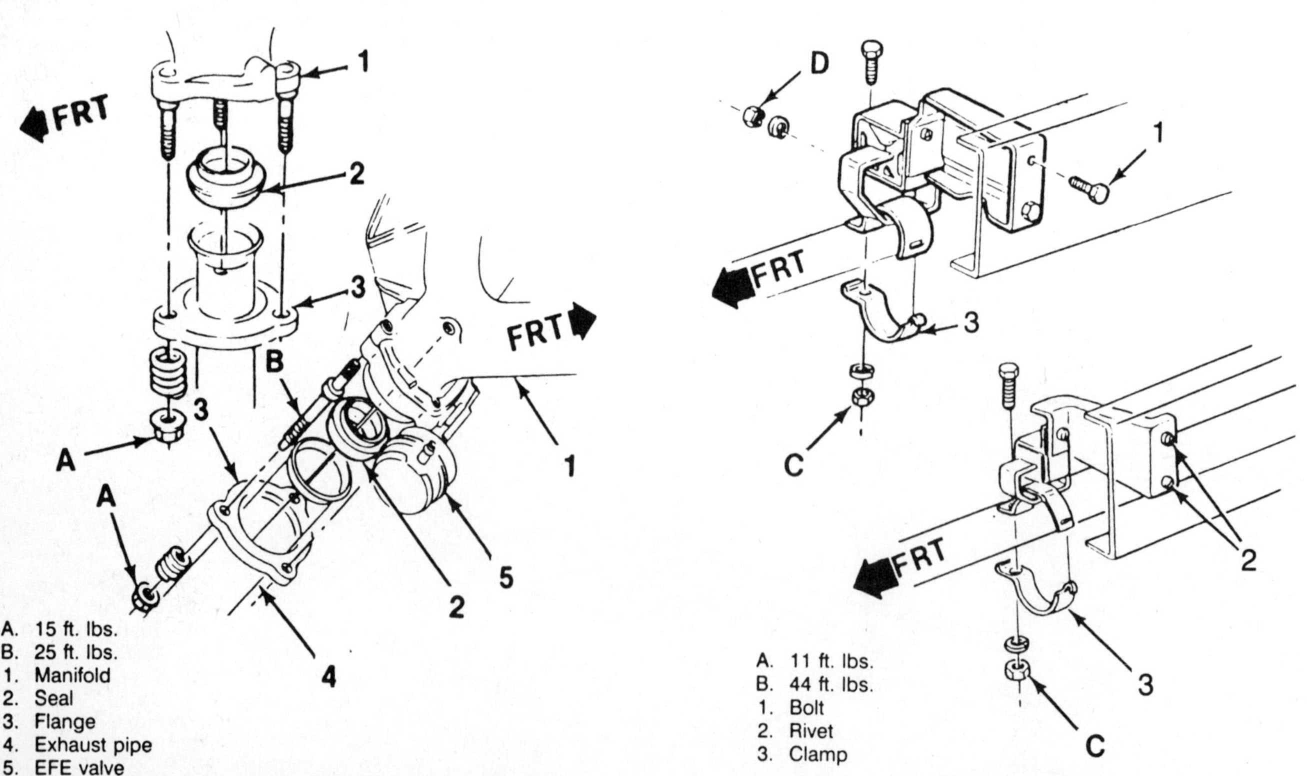

Exhaust pip-to-manifold connection for R and V series

R and V series exhaust pipe hangers

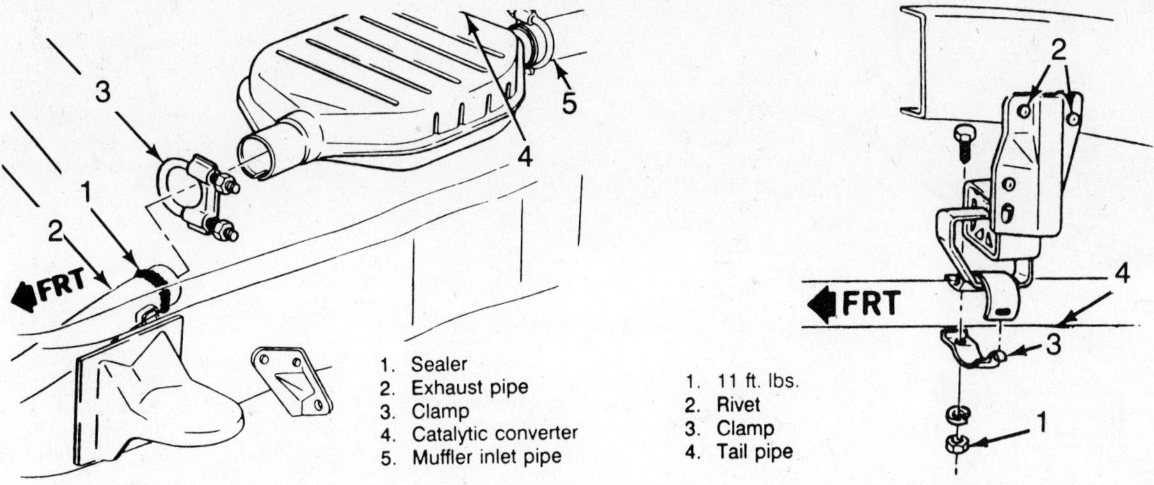

Catalytic converter clamping for R and V series

R and V series tail pipe hanger

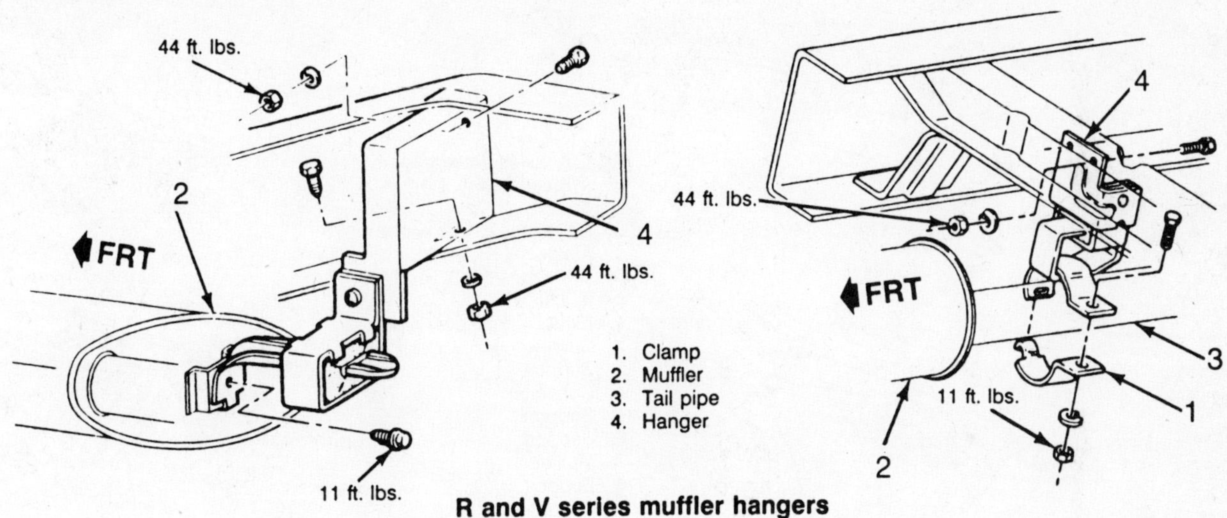

R and V series muffler hangers

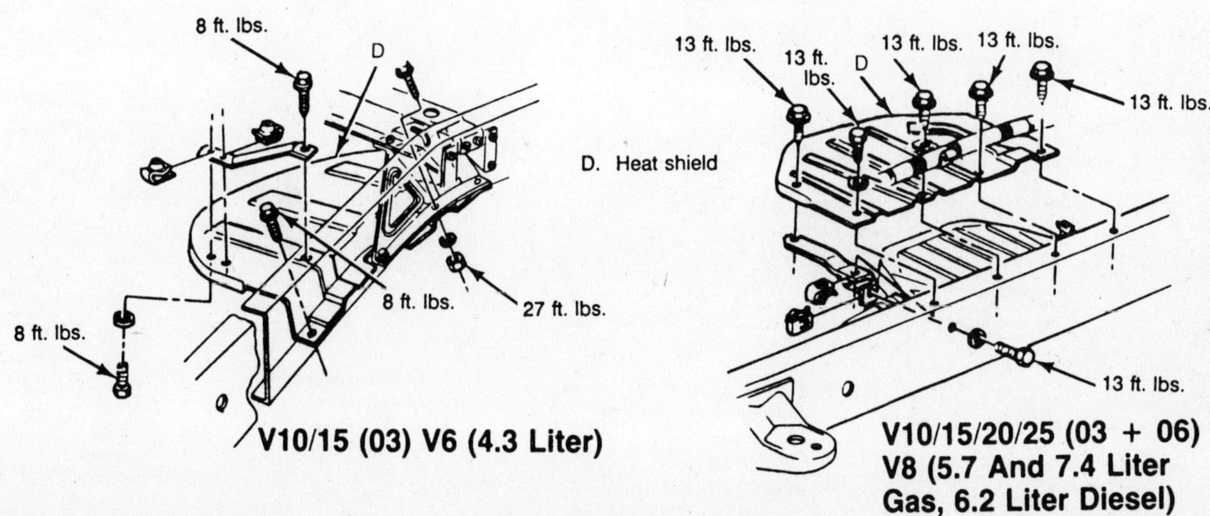

V series converter heat shield

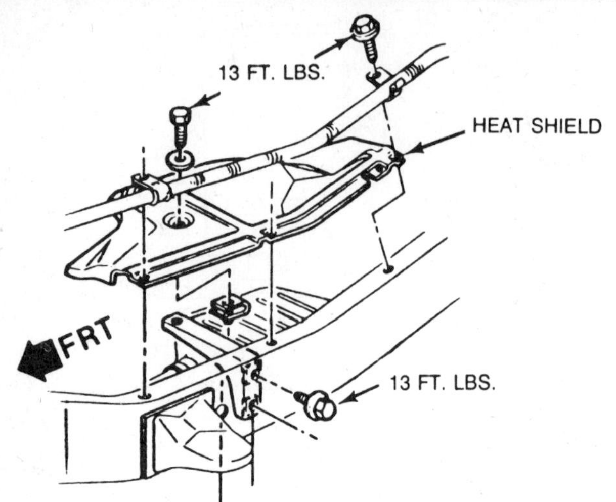

R series converter heat shield

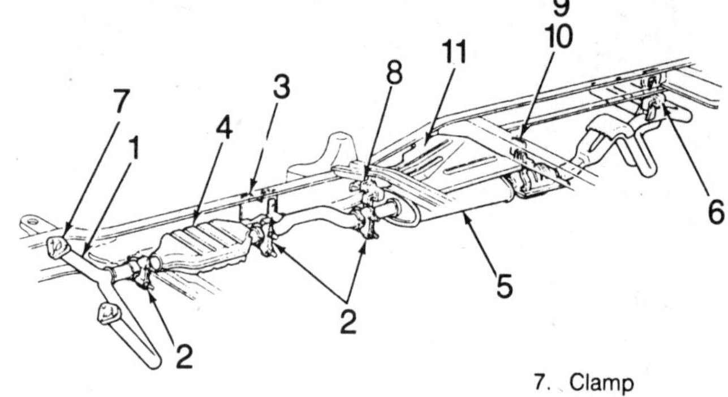

1. Crossover pipe
2. Clamp
3. Support
4. Converter
5. Muffler
6. Support
7. Clamp
8. Support
9. Support
10. Support
11. Heat shield

Exhaust system for C and K series with 8-7.4L engine

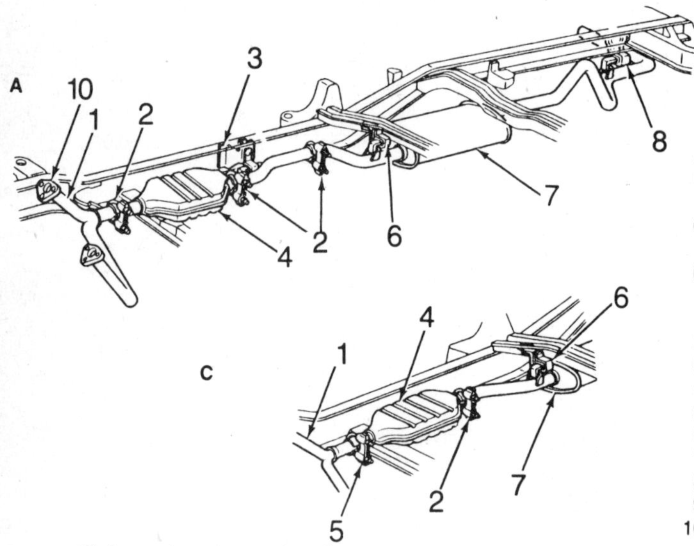

A. C/K series entire system
B. C/K series with 6½ ft. box
C. C/K series 8-5.0L with 8 ft. box
D. C/K seires 6-4.3L with 8 ft. lbs.

1. Exhaust crossover pipe
2. Clamp
3. Support
4. Converter
5. Support
6. Support
7. Muffler
8. Support
9. Oxygen sensor
10. Clamp

B

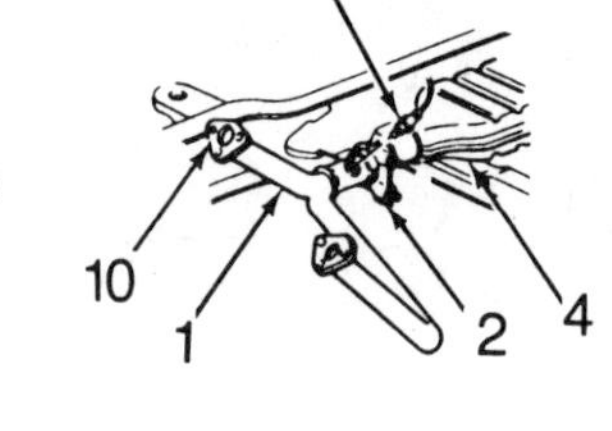

Exhaust system for C and K series, extended cab, 6½ ft. and 8 ft. box, with 6-4.3L or 8-5.0L engine

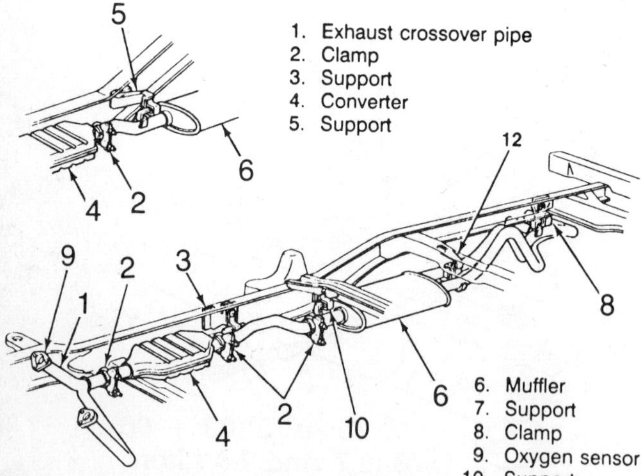

1. Exhaust crossover pipe
2. Clamp
3. Support
4. Converter
5. Support
6. Muffler
7. Support
8. Clamp
9. Oxygen sensor
10. Support

Exhaust system for C and K series, extended cab, 6½ ft. and 8 ft. box, with 8-5.7L engine

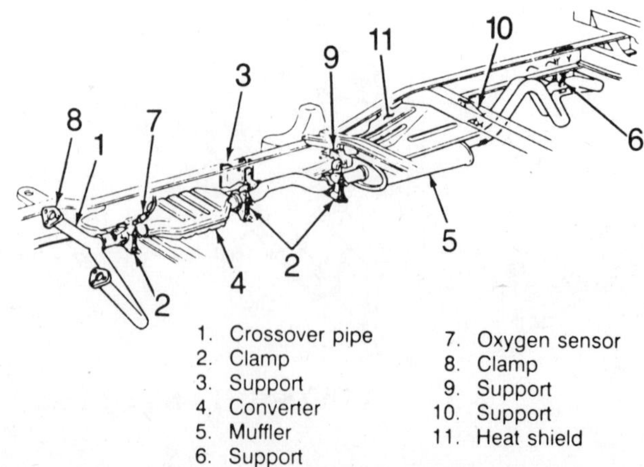

1. Crossover pipe
2. Clamp
3. Support
4. Converter
5. Muffler
6. Support
7. Oxygen sensor
8. Clamp
9. Support
10. Support
11. Heat shield

Exhaust system for C and K 35 series with 8-5.7L engine

4 Emission Controls

QUICK REFERENCE INDEX

GENERAL INDEX

EMISSION CONTROLS

Positive Crankcase Ventilation

PCV is the earliest form of emission control. Prior to its use, crankcase vapors were vented into the atmosphere through a road draft tube or crankcase breather. The PCV system first appeared in 1955.

This system draws crankcase vapors that are formed through normal combustion into the intake manifold and subsequently into the combustion chambers to be burned. Fresh air is introduced to the crankcase by way of a hose connected to the carburetor air cleaner or a vented oil filler cap or older models. Manifold vacuum is used to draw the vapors from the crankcase through a PCV valve and into the intake manifold. Non-vented filler caps are used on all models.

SERVICE

Other than checking and replacing the PCV valve and associated hoses, there is not service required. Engine operating conditions that would direct suspicion to the PCV system are rough idle, oil present in the air cleaner, oil leaks and excessive oil sludging or dilution. If any of the above conditions exist, remove the PCV valve and shake it. A clicking sound indicates that the valve is free. If no clicking sound is heard, replace the valve. Inspect the PCV breather in the air cleaner. Replace the breather if it is so dirty that it will not allow gases to pass through. Check all the PCV hoses for condition and tight connections. Replace any hoses that have deteriorated.

Air Injector Reactor (Air Pump)

The AIR system injects compressed air into the exhaust system, near enough to the exhaust valves to continue the burning of the normally unburned segment of the exhaust gases. To do this it employs an air injection pump and a system of hoses, valves, tubes, etc., necessary to carry the compressed air from the pump to the exhaust manifolds.

A diverter valve is used to prevent backfiring. The valve senses sudden increases in manifold vacuum and ceases the injection of air during dual rich periods. During coasting, this valve diverts the entire air flow through a muffler and during high engine speeds, expels it through a relief valve. Check valves in the system prevent exhaust gases from entering the pump.

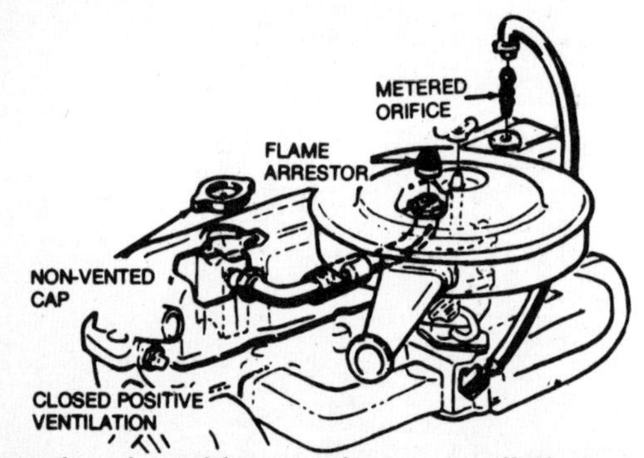

Closed and positive crankcase ventilation systems

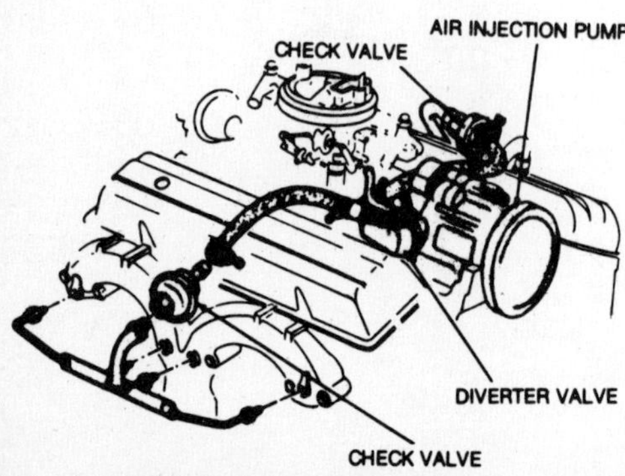

AIR system components

TESTING

Check Valve

To test the check valve, disconnect the hose at the diverter valve. Blow into the hose and suck on it. Air should flow only into the engine.

Diverter Valve

Pull off the vacuum line to the top of the valve with the engine running. There should be vacuum in the line. Replace the line. No air should be escaping with the engine running at a steady idle. Open and quickly close the throttle. A blast of air should come out of the valve muffler for at least one second.

Air Pump

Disconnect the hose from the diverter valve. Start the engine and accelerate it to about 1,500 rpm. The air flow should increase as the engine is accelerated. If no air flow is noted or it remains constant, check the following:

1. Drive belt tension.
2. Listen for a leaking pressure relief valve. If it is defective, replace the whole relief/diverter valve.
3. Foreign matter in pump filter openings. If the pump is defective or excessively noisy, it must be replaced.

SERVICE

All hoses and fittings should be inspected for condition and tightness of connections. Check the drive belt for wear and tension periodically.

NOTE: The A.I.R. system is not completely silent under normal conditions. Noises will rise in pitch as engine speed increases. If the noise is excessive, eliminate the air pump itself by disconnecting the drive belt. If the noise disappears, the air pump is not at fault.

Air Pump

REMOVAL AND INSTALLATION

1. Disconnect the output hose.
2. Hold the pump from turning by squeezing the drive belt.
3. Loosen the pulley bolts.
4. Loosen the alternator so the belt can be removed.
5. Remove the pulley.
6. Remove the pump mounting bolts and the pump.
7. Install the pump with the mounting bolts loose.
8. Install the pulley and tighten the bolts finger tight.
9. Install and adjust the drive belt.
10. Squeeze the drive belt to prevent the pump from turning.
11. Torque the pulley bolts to 25 ft. lbs. Tighten the pump mountings.
12. Check and adjust the belt tension again, if necessary.
13. Connect the hose.
14. If any hose leaks are suspected, pour soapy water over the

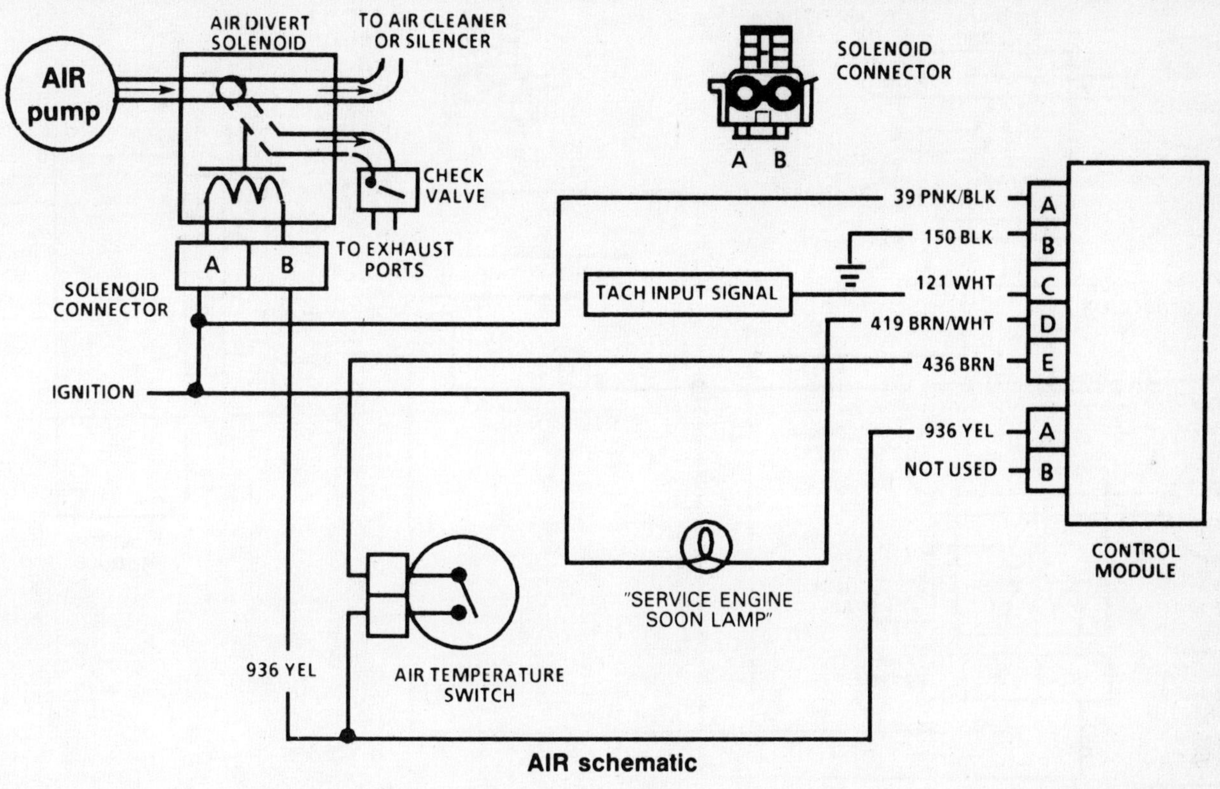

AIR schematic

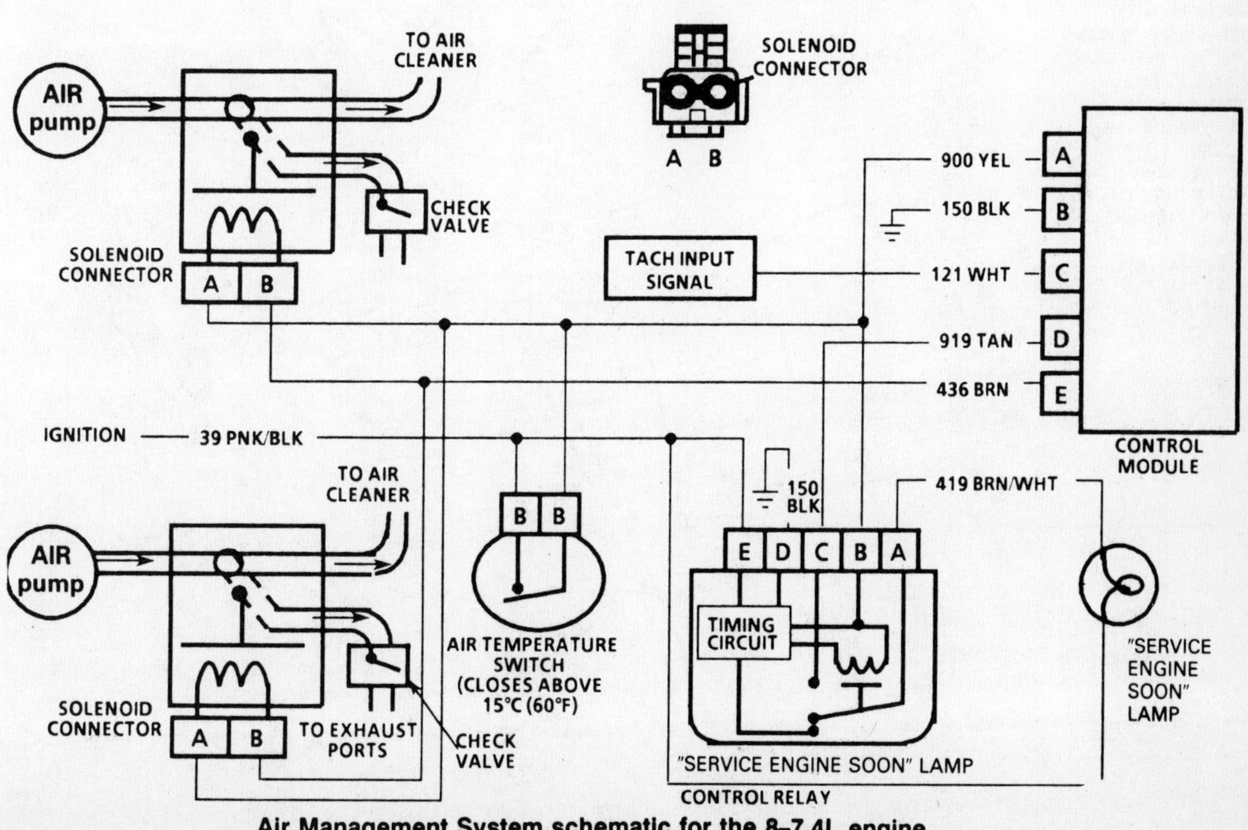

Air Management System schematic for the 8–7.4L engine

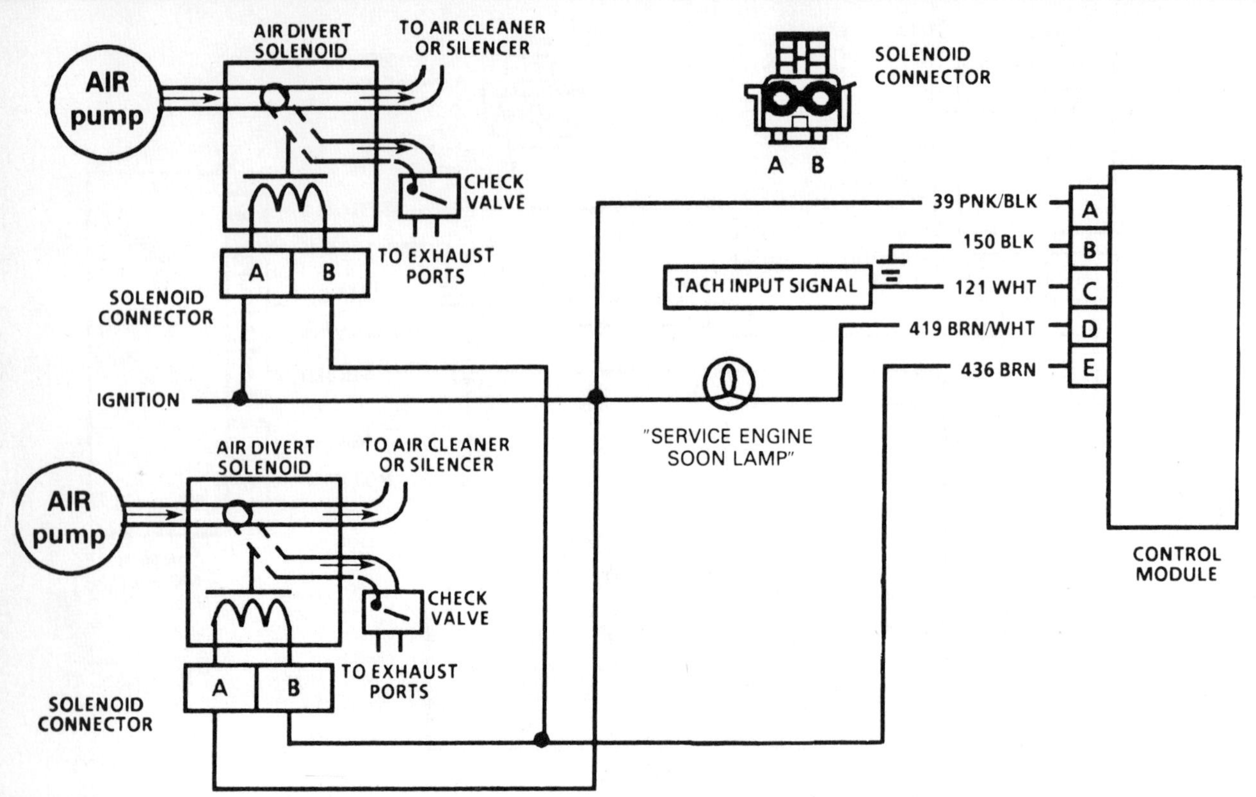

Air Management System schematic for the 8–5.7L engine

1. Check valve – tighten to 74 ft. lbs.
2. Hose – valve-to-check valve
3. Air control valve – tighten mounting screws to 98 inch lbs.
4. Air pump – tighten mounting screws to 24 ft. lbs.
5. Hose – valve-to-air cleaner
6. Air injection pipe – tighten nuts to 44 ft. lbs. – right side is similar

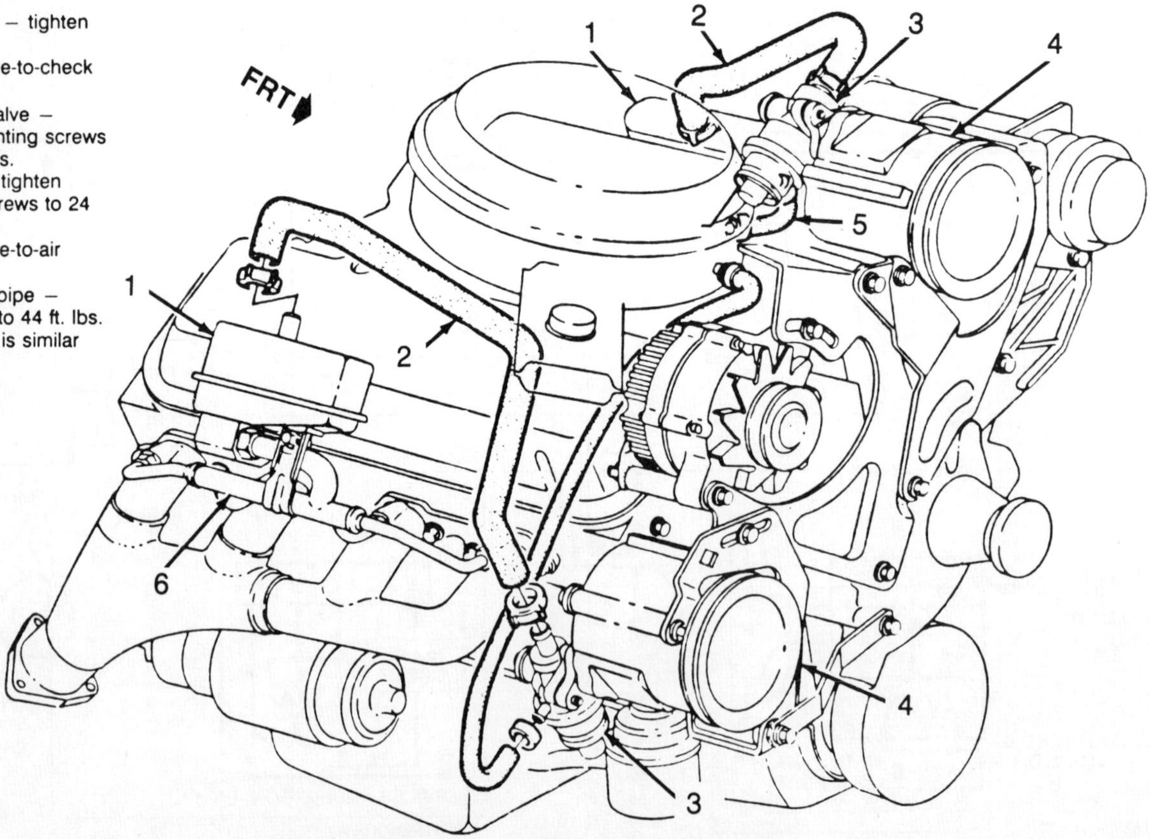

FRT

AIR system components for the 8–7.4L engine

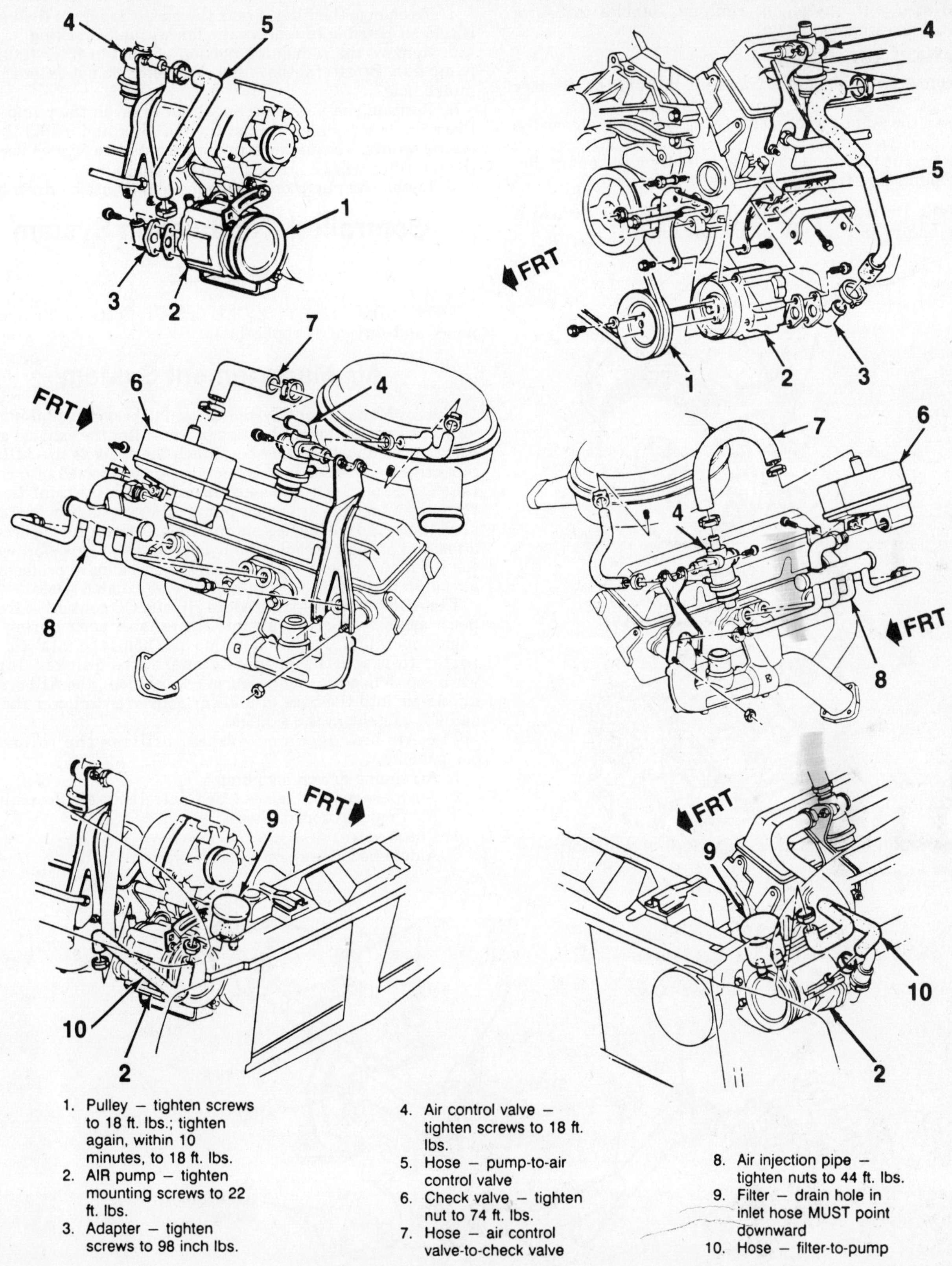

1. Pulley – tighten screws to 18 ft. lbs.; tighten again, within 10 minutes, to 18 ft. lbs.
2. AIR pump – tighten mounting screws to 22 ft. lbs.
3. Adapter – tighten screws to 98 inch lbs.
4. Air control valve – tighten screws to 18 ft. lbs.
5. Hose – pump-to-air control valve
6. Check valve – tighten nut to 74 ft. lbs.
7. Hose – air control valve-to-check valve
8. Air injection pipe – tighten nuts to 44 ft. lbs.
9. Filter – drain hole in inlet hose MUST point downward
10. Hose – filter-to-pump

AIR system components for the 8–5.7L engine

suspected area with the engine running. Bubbles will form wherever air is escaping.

FILTER REPLACEMENT

1. Disconnect the air and vacuum hoses from the diverter valve.
2. Loosen the pump pivot and adjusting bolts and remove the drive belt.
3. Remove the pivot and adjusting bolts from the pump. Remove the pump and the diverter valve as an assembly.

WARNING: Do not clamp the pump in a vise or use a hammer or pry bar on the pump housing!

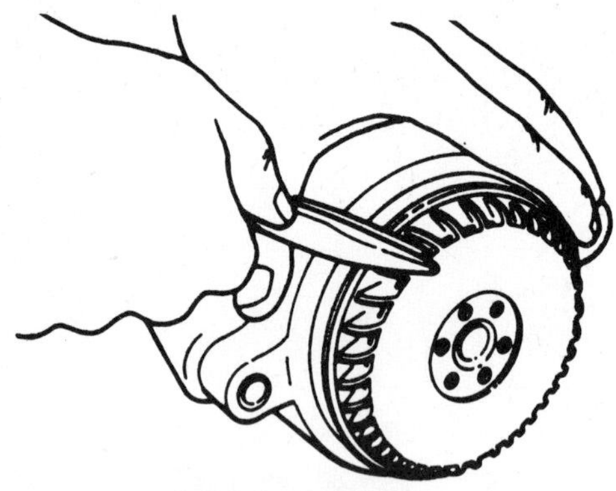

AIR filter removal

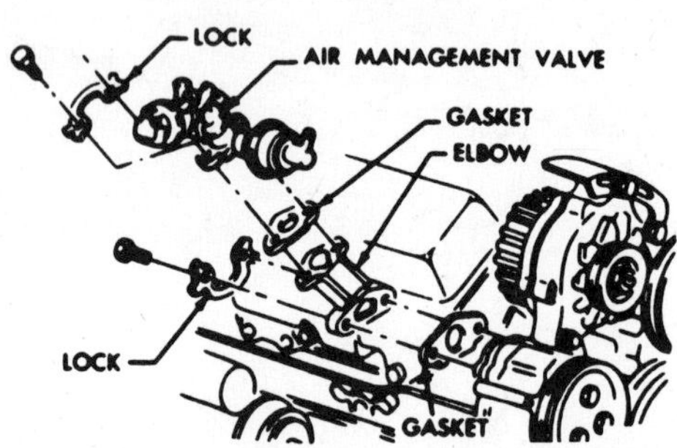

Air management system component installation — typical

4. To change the filter, break the plastic fan from the hub. It is seldom possible to remove the fan without breaking it.
5. Remove the remaining portion of the fan filter from the pump hub. Be careful that filter fragments do not enter the air intake hole.
6. Position the new centrifugal fan filter on the pump hub. Place the pump pulley against the fan filter and install the securing screws. Torque the screws alternately to 95 inch lbs. and the fan filter will be pressed onto the pump hub.
7. Install the pump on the engine and adjust its drive belt.

Controlled Combustion System

SERVICE

Refer to the CHA, TCS, CEC or EGR Sections for maintenance and service (if applicable).

Air Management System

The Air Management System is used to provide additional oxygen to continue the combustion process after the exhaust gases leave the combustion chamber; much the same as the AIR system described earlier in this Section. Air is injected into either the exhaust port(s), the exhaust manifold(s) or the catalytic converter by an engine driven air pump. The system is in operating at all times and will bypass air only momentarily during deceleration and at high speeds. The bypass function is performed by the Air Management Valve, which the check valve protects the air pump by preventing any backflow of exhaust gases.

The AIR system helps to reduce HC and CO content in the exhaust gases by injecting air into the exhaust ports during cold engine operation. This air injection also helps the catalytic converter to reach the proper temperature quicker during warm-up. When the engine warm (closed loop), the AIR system injects air into the beds of a 3-way converter to lower the HC and CO content in the exhaust.

The Air Management System utilizes the following components:

1. An engine driven air pump.
2. Air management valves (Air Control and Air Switching)
3. Air flow and control hoses
4. Check valves
5. A dual bed, 3-way catalytic converter

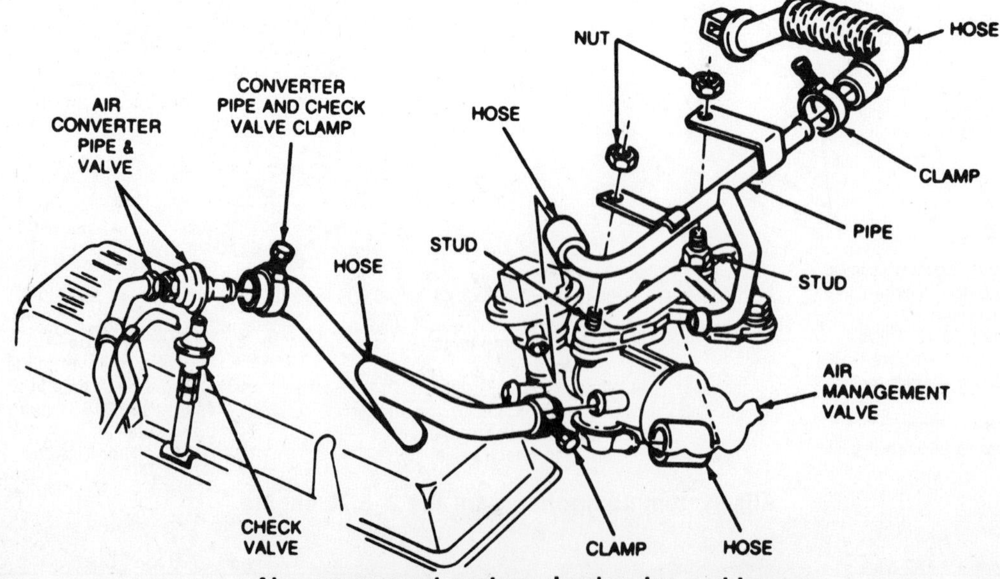

Air management system check valve and hoses

The belt driven, vane type air pump is located at the front of the engine and supplies clean air to the system for purposes already stated. When the engine is cold, the Electronic Control Module (ECM) energizes an air control solenoid. This allows air to flow to the air switching valve. The air switching valve is then energized to direct air into the exhaust ports.

When the engine is warm, the ECM de-energizes the air switching valve, thus directing the air between the beds of the catalytic converter. This then provides additional oxygen for the oxidizing catalyst in the second bed to decrease HC and CO levels, while at the same time keeping oxygen levels low in the first bed, enabling the reducing catalyst to effectively decrease the levels of NOx.

If the air control valve detects a rapid increase in manifold vacuum (deceleration), certain operating modes (wide open throttle, etc.) or if the ECM self diagnostic system detects any problems in the system, air is diverted to the air cleaner or directly into the atmosphere.

The primary purpose of the ECM's divert mode is to prevent backfiring. Throttle closure at the beginning of deceleration will temporarily create air/fuel mixtures which are too rich to burn completely. These mixtures will be come burnable when they reach the exhaust if they are combined with injection air. The next firing of the engine will ignite the mixture causing an exhaust backfire. Momentary diverting of the injection air from the exhaust prevents this.

The Air Management System check valves and hoses should be checked periodically for any leaks, cracks or deterioration.

REMOVAL AND INSTALLATION

Air Pump

1. Remove the valves and/or adapter at the air pump.
2. Loosen the air pump adjustment bolt and remove the drive belt.
3. Unscrew the three mounting bolts and then remove the pump pulley.
4. Unscrew the pump mounting bolts and then remove the pump.
5. Installation is in the reverse order of removal. Be sure to adjust the drive bolt tension after installing it.

Check Valve

1. Release the clamp and disconnect the air hoses from the valve.
2. Unscrew the check valve from the air injection pipe.
3. Installation is in the reverse order of removal.

Air Management Valve

1. Disconnect the negative battery cable.
2. Remove the air cleaner.
3. Tag and disconnect the vacuum hose from the valve.
4. Tag and disconnect the air outlet hoses from the valve.
5. Bend back the lock tabs and then remove the bolts holding the elbow to the valve.
6. Tag and disconnect any electrical connections at the valve and then remove the valve from the elbow.
7. Installation is in the reverse order of removal.

Thermostatic Air Cleaner

This system is designed to warm the air entering the carburetor when underhood temperatures are low. This allows more precise calibration of the carburetor.

The thermostatically controlled air cleaner is composed of the air cleaner body, a filter, sensor unit, vacuum diaphragm, damper door and associated hoses and connections. Heat radiating from the exhaust manifold is trapped by a heat stove and is

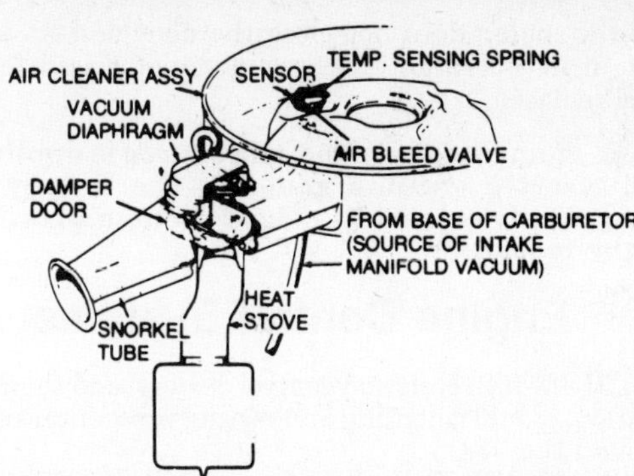

Thermostatically controlled air cleaner

ducted to the air cleaner to supply heated air to the carburetor. A movable door in the air cleaner snorkel allows air to be drawn in from the heat stove (cold operation) or from the underhood air (warm operation). Periods of extended idling, climbing a grade or high speed operation are followed by a considerable increase in engine compartment temperature. Excessive fuel vapors enter the intake manifold causing an over-rich mixture, resulting in a rough idle. To overcome this, some engines may be equipped with a hot idle compensator.

SERVICE

1. Either start with a cold engine or remove the air cleaner from the engine for at least half an hour. While cooling the air cleaner, leave the engine compartment hood open.
2. Tape a thermometer, of known accuracy, to the inside of the air cleaner so that it is near the temperature sensor unit. Install the air cleaner on the engine but do not fasten its securing nut.
3. Start the engine. With the engine cold and the outside temperature less than +90°F (+32°C), the door should be in the HEAT ON position (closed to outside air).

NOTE: Due to the position of the air cleaner on some trucks, a mirror may be necessary when observing the position of the air door.

4. Operate the throttle lever rapidly to ½–¾ of its opening and release it. The air door should open to allow outside air to enter and then close again.
5. Allow the engine to warm up to normal temperature. Watch the door. When it opens to the outside air, remove the cover from the air cleaner. The temperature should be over +90°F (+32°C) and no more than +130°F (+54°C); +115°F (+46°C) is about normal. If the door does not work within these temperature ranges, or fails to work at all, check for linkage or door binding.

If binding is not present and the air door is not working, proceed with the vacuum tests, given below. If these indicate no faults in the vacuum motor and the door is not working, the temperature sensor is defective and must be replaced.

Vacuum Motor Test

NOTE: Be sure that the vacuum hose which runs between the temperature switch and the vacuum motor is not pinched by the retaining clip under the air cleaner. This could prevent the air door from closing.

1. Check all of the vacuum lines and fittings for leaks. Correct any leaks. If none are found, proceed with the test.
2. Remove the hose which runs from the sensor to the vacuum motor. Run a hose directly from the manifold vacuum source to the vacuum motor.
3. If the motor closes the air door, it is functioning properly and the temperature sensor is defective.

4. If the motor does not close the door and no binding is present in its operation, the vacuum motor is defective and must be replaced.

NOTE: If an alternate vacuum source is applied to the motor, insert a vacuum gauge in the line by using a T-fitting. Apply at least 9 in.Hg of vacuum in order to operate the motor.

Engine Control Systems

The 4.3L (6–262) emission control devices, and their removal, installation, troubleshooting and testing procedures are similar to those on the V8s.

The 4.3L (6–262), 5.0L (8–305), and 5.7L (8–350) engines in California have a Computer Command Control system which controls:

- Fuel control system.
- Air injection reaction (AIR).
- Exhaust gas recirculation (EGR).
- Evaporative Emission Control System (EECS).
- Electronic Spark Timing (EST).
- Electronic Spark Control (ESC) (4.3L CAL.).
- Transmission Converter Clutch (TCC).

An Electronic Control Module (ECM) is the heart of the Computer Command Control System. The ECM uses sensors to get information about engine operation which it uses to vary systems it controls.

The ECM has the ability to do some diagnosis of itself. When it recognizes a problem, it lights a "Service Engine Soon" lamp on the instrument panel. When this occurs, the cause of the light coming on should be checked as soon as reasonably possible, and the malfunction corrected.

All diagnosis and repair of the Computer Command Control system, the Electronic Control Module, and the components they control, should be referred to a qualified technician possessing the proper diagnostic equipment.

TESTING

If there is a TCS system malfunction, first connect a vacuum gauge in the hose between the solenoid valve and the distributor vacuum unit. Drive the vehicle or raise it on a frame lift and observe the vacuum gauge. If full vacuum is available in all gears, check for the following:

1. Blown fuse.
2. Disconnected wire at solenoid operated vacuum valve.
3. Disconnected wire at transmission switch.
4. Temperature override switch energized due to low engine temperature.
5. Solenoid failure.

If no vacuum is available in any gear, check the following:

1. Solenoid valve vacuum lines switched.
2. Clogged solenoid vacuum valve.
3. Distributor or manifold vacuum lines leaking or disconnected.
4. Transmission switch or wire grounded.

Tests for individual components are as follows:

Idle Stop Solenoid

This unit may be checked simply by observing it while an assistant switches the ignition on and off. It should extend further with the current switched on. The unit is not repairable.

Solenoid Vacuum Valve

Check that proper manifold vacuum is available. Connect the vacuum gauge in the line between the solenoid valve and the distributor. Apply 12 volts to the solenoid. If vacuum is still not

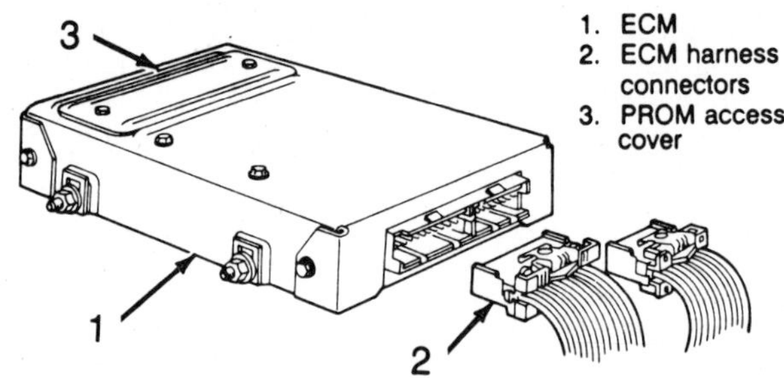

Electronic control module for V6 and V8 engines

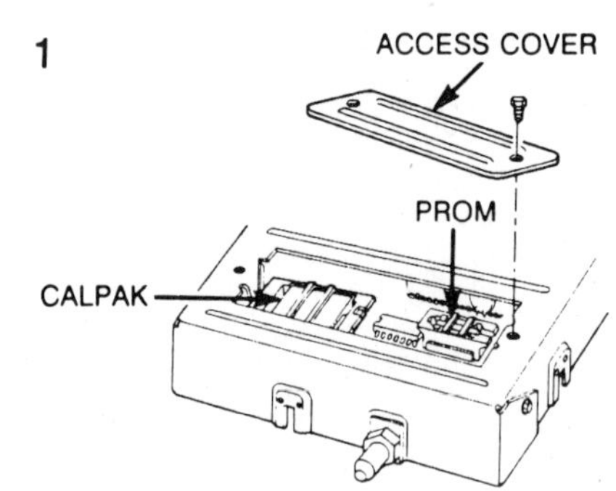

Access cover removal

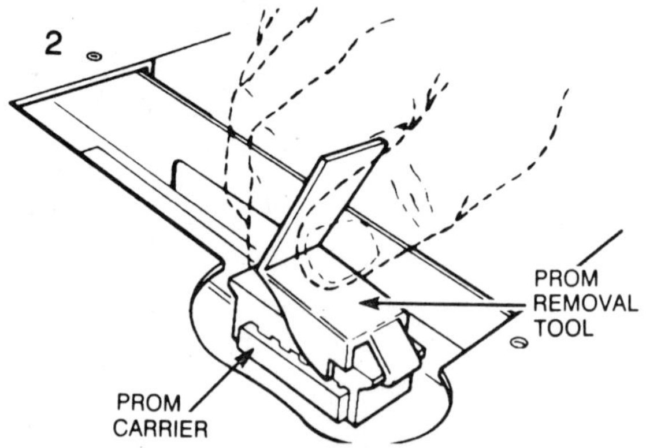

Removing PROM carrier

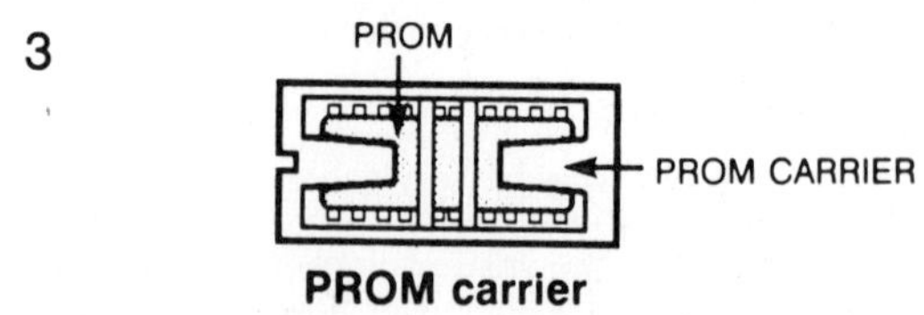

PROM carrier

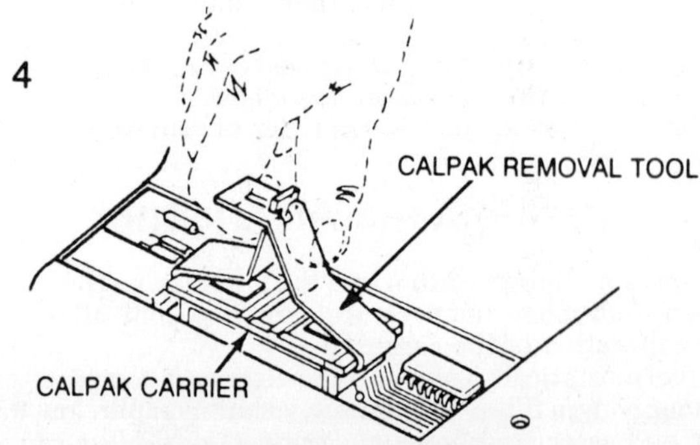

Removing the CALPAK

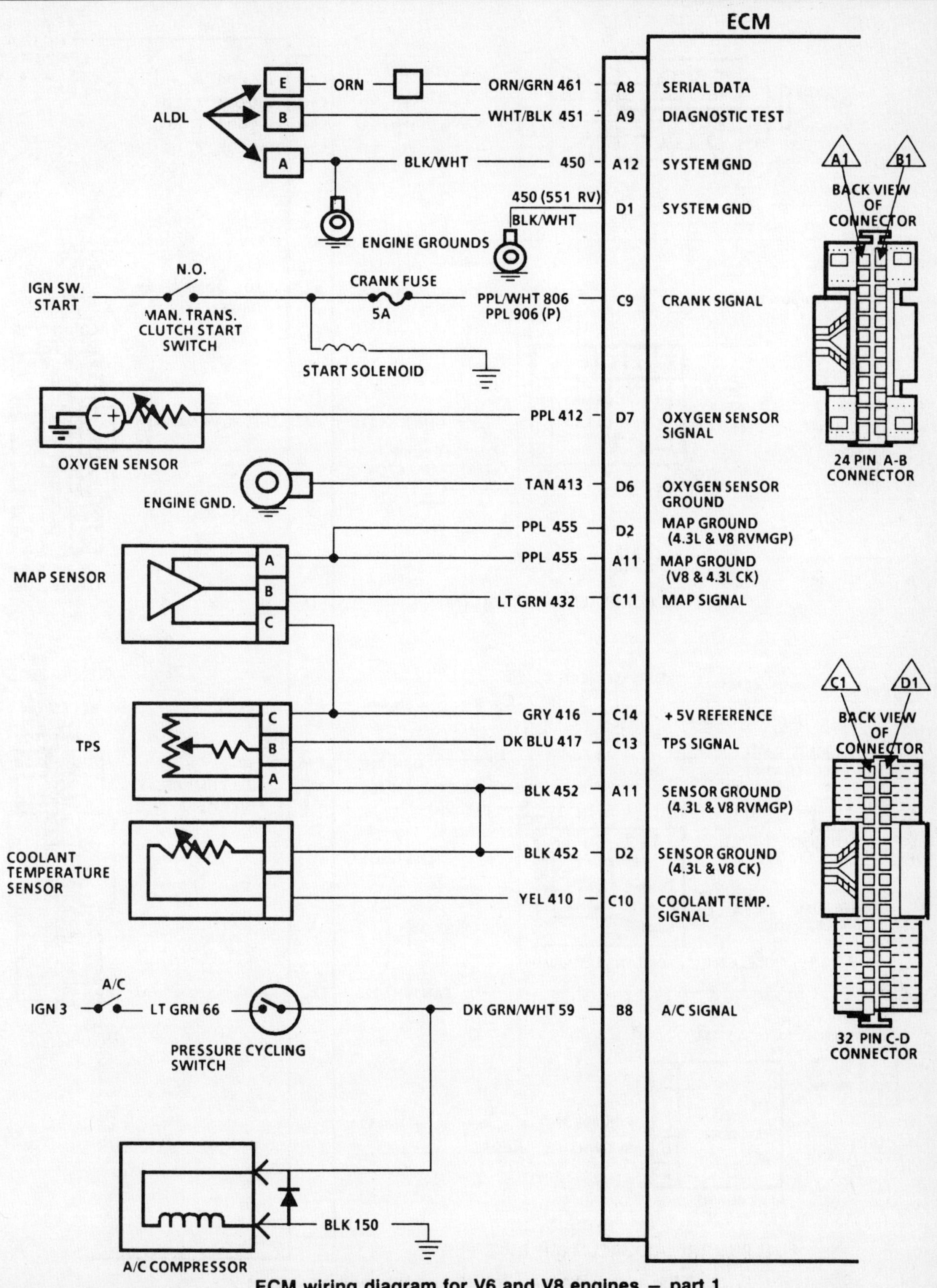

ECM wiring diagram for V6 and V8 engines – part 1

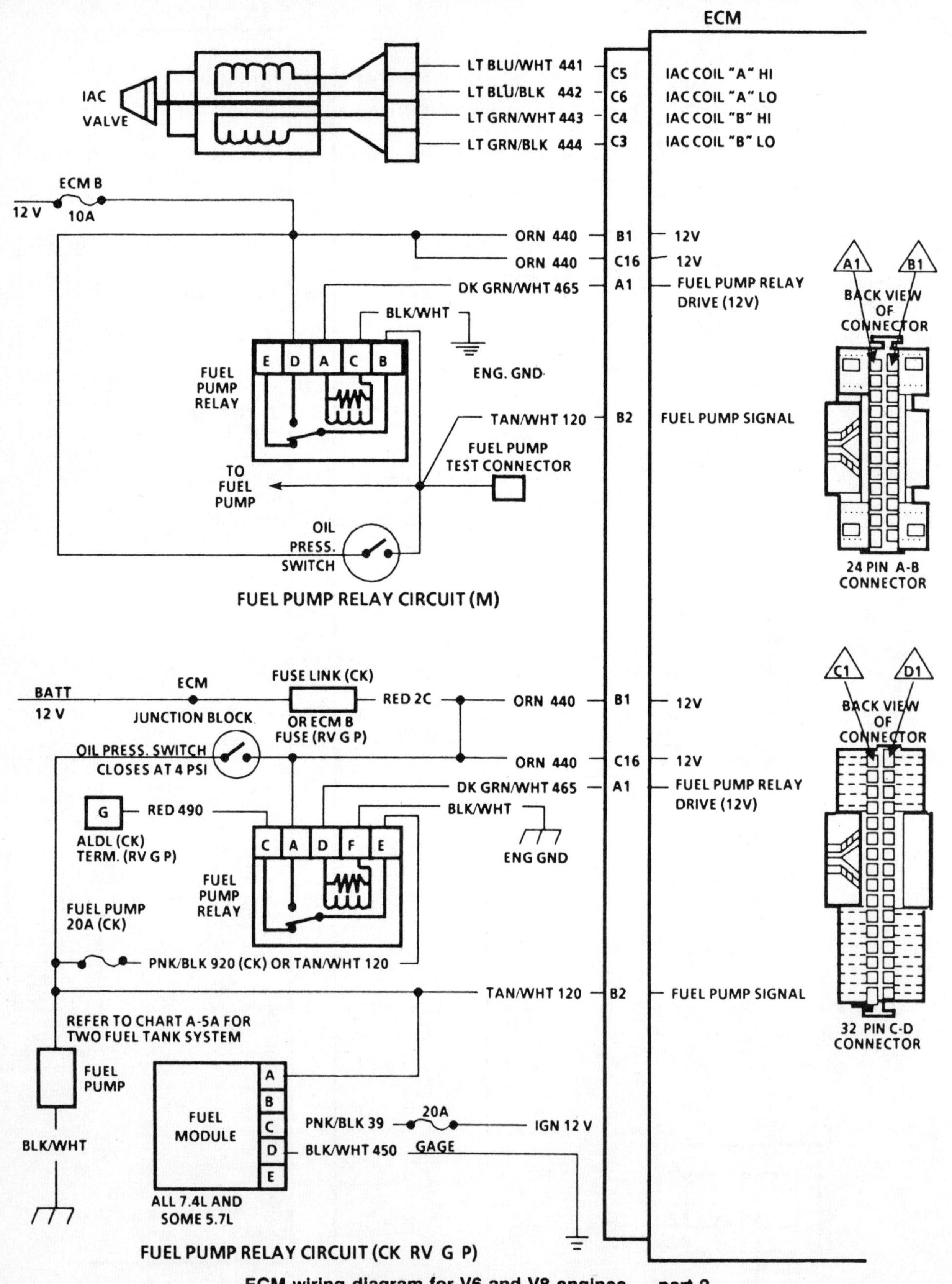
ECM
IAC VALVE
LT BLU/WHT 441
LT BLU/BLK 442
LT GRN/WHT 443
LT GRN/BLK 444
C5
C6
C4
C3
IAC COIL "A" HI
IAC COIL "A" LO
IAC COIL "B" HI
IAC COIL "B" LO
ECM B
12 V
10A
ORN 440
ORN 440
B1
C16
12V
12V
DK GRN/WHT 465
A1
FUEL PUMP RELAY DRIVE (12V)
BLK/WHT
ENG. GND
E D A C B
FUEL PUMP RELAY
TAN/WHT 120
B2
FUEL PUMP SIGNAL
FUEL PUMP TEST CONNECTOR
TO FUEL PUMP
OIL PRESS. SWITCH
FUEL PUMP RELAY CIRCUIT (M)
A1
B1
BACK VIEW OF CONNECTOR
24 PIN A-B CONNECTOR
BATT 12 V
ECM JUNCTION BLOCK
FUSE LINK (CK)
OR ECM B FUSE (RV G P)
RED 2C
ORN 440
B1
12V
OIL PRESS. SWITCH CLOSES AT 4 PSI
ORN 440
C16
12V
DK GRN/WHT 465
A1
FUEL PUMP RELAY DRIVE (12V)
G
RED 490
BLK/WHT
ALDL (CK) TERM. (RV G P)
ENG GND
C A D F E
FUEL PUMP RELAY
FUEL PUMP 20A (CK)
PNK/BLK 920 (CK) OR TAN/WHT 120
TAN/WHT 120
B2
FUEL PUMP SIGNAL
REFER TO CHART A-5A FOR TWO FUEL TANK SYSTEM
FUEL PUMP
BLK/WHT
FUEL MODULE
A
B
C
D
E
PNK/BLK 39
20A
IGN 12 V
BLK/WHT 450
GAGE
ALL 7.4L AND SOME 5.7L
FUEL PUMP RELAY CIRCUIT (CK RV G P)
C1
D1
BACK VIEW OF CONNECTOR
32 PIN C-D CONNECTOR

ECM wiring diagram for V6 and V8 engines – part 2

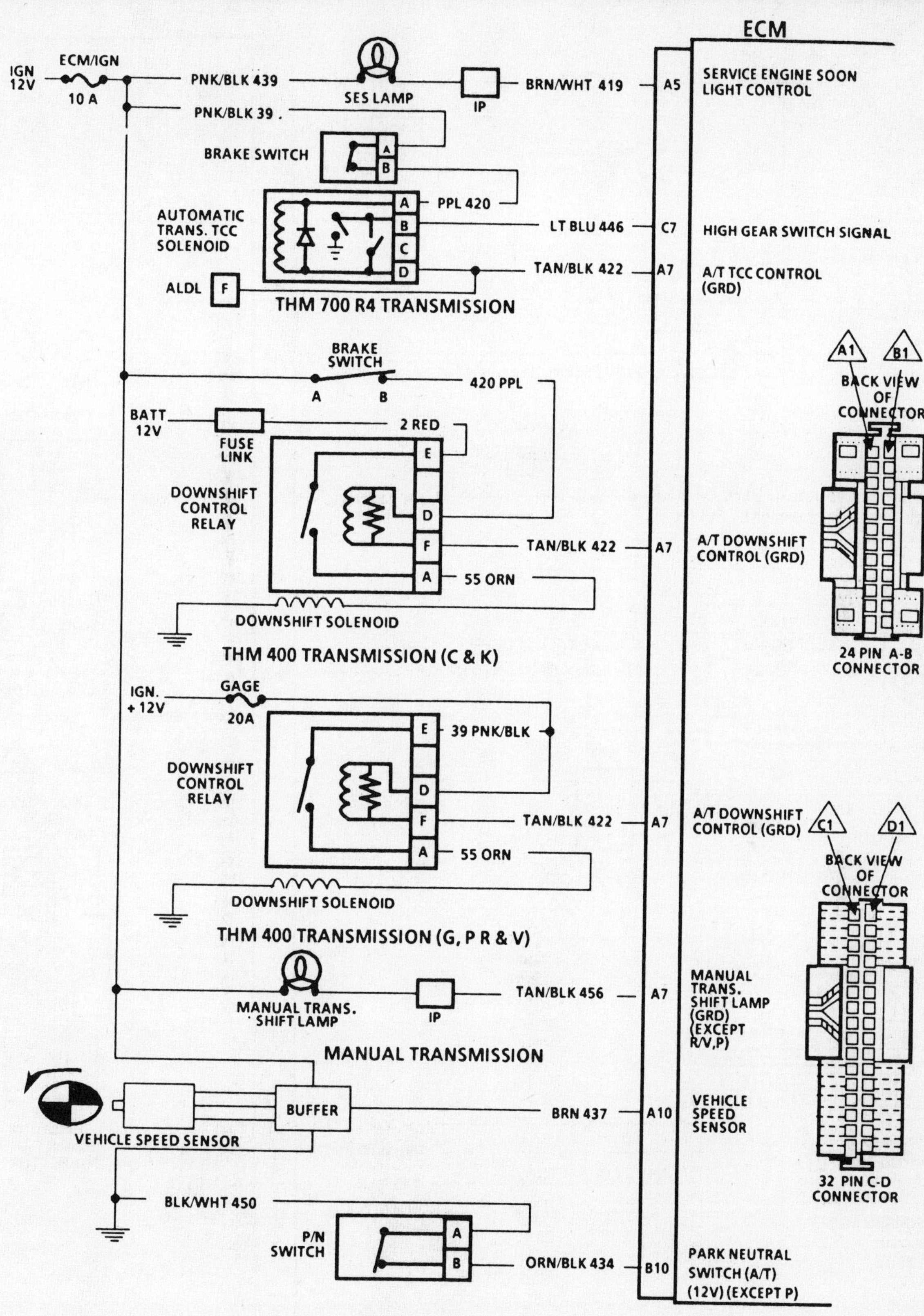

ECM wiring diagram for V6 and V8 engines – part 3

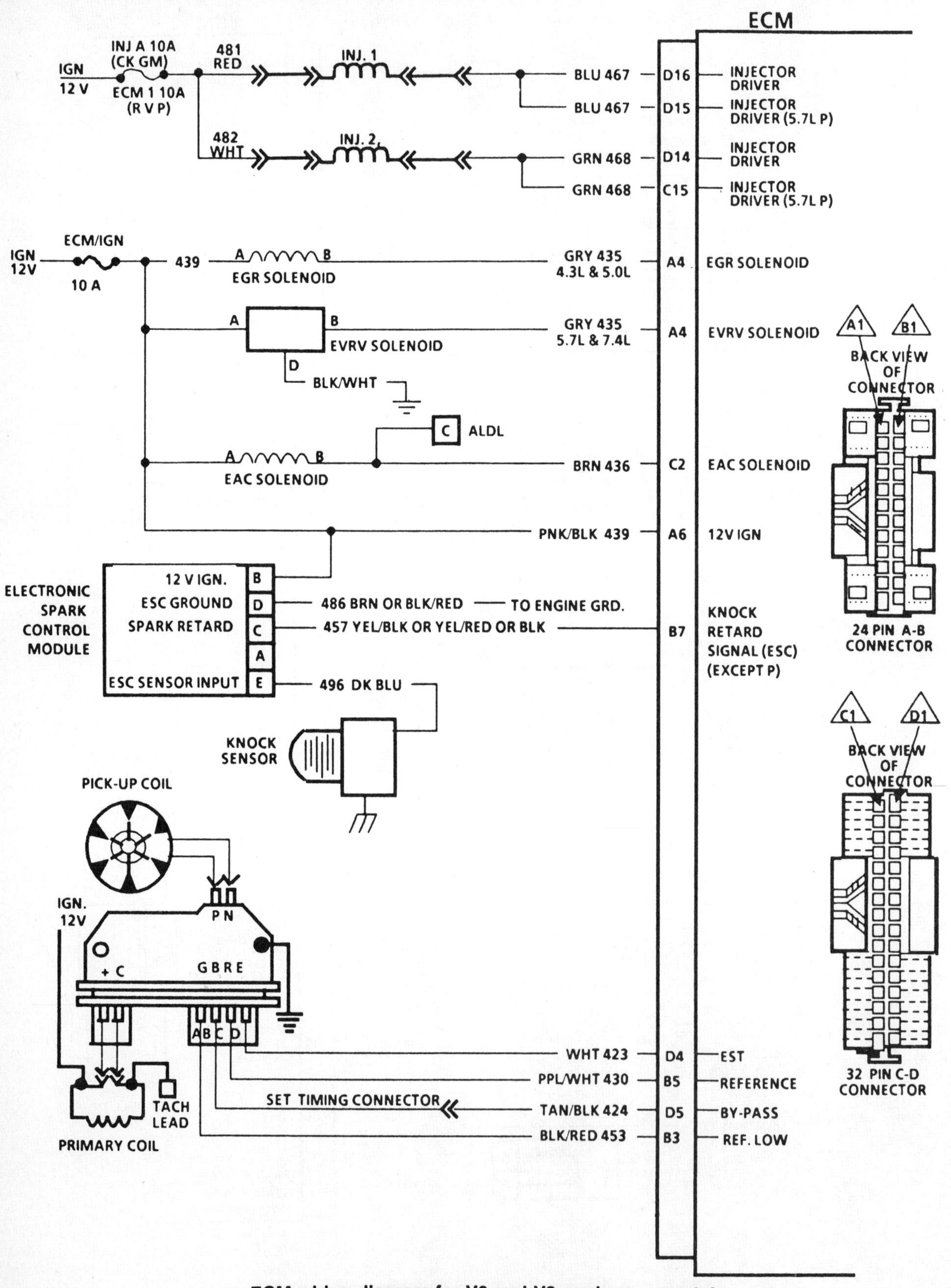

ECM wiring diagram for V6 and V8 engines – part 4

available, the valve is defective, either mechanically or electrically. The unit is not repairable. If the valve is satisfactory, check the relay next.

Relay

1. With the engine at normal operating temperature and the ignition on, ground the solenoid vacuum valve terminal with the black lead. The solenoid should energize (no vacuum) if the relay is satisfactory.

2. With the solenoid energized as in Step 1, connect a jumper from the relay terminal with the green/white stripe lead to ground. The solenoid should de-energize (vacuum available) if the relay is satisfactory.

3. If the relay worked properly in Steps 1 and 2, check the temperature switch. The relay unit is not repairable.

Temperature Switch

The vacuum valve solenoid should be de-energized (vacuum available) with the engine cold. If it is not, ground the green/white stripe wire from the switch. If the solenoid now de-energizes, replace the switch. If the switch was satisfactory, check the transmission switch.

Transmission Switch

With the engine at normal operating temperature and the transmission in one of the no vacuum gears, the vacuum valve solenoid should be energized (no vacuum). If not, remove and ground the switch electrical lead. If the solenoid energizes, replace the switch.

Exhaust Gas Recirculation

The EGR system's purpose is to control oxides of nitrogen which are formed during the peak combustion temperatures. The end products of combustion are relatively inert gases derived from the exhaust gases which are directed into the EGR valve to help lower peak combustion temperatures.

The EGR valve contains a vacuum diaphragm operated by manifold vacuum. The vacuum signal port is located in the carburetor body and is exposed to engine vacuum in the off/idle and part throttle operation. In 1974, a thermal delay switch was added to delay operation of the valve during engine warmup, when NOx levels are already at a minimum.

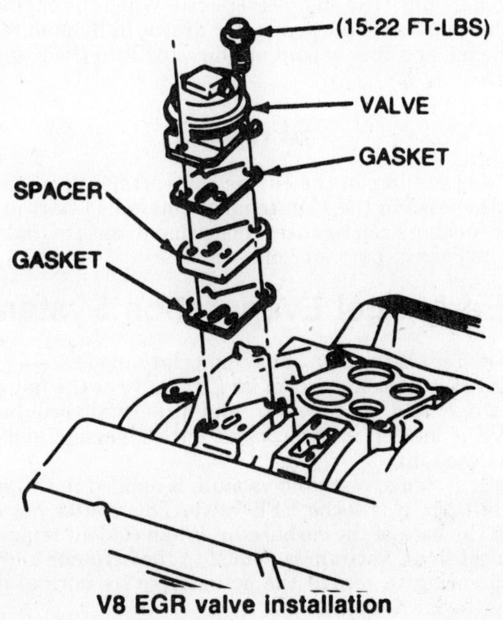

V8 EGR valve installation

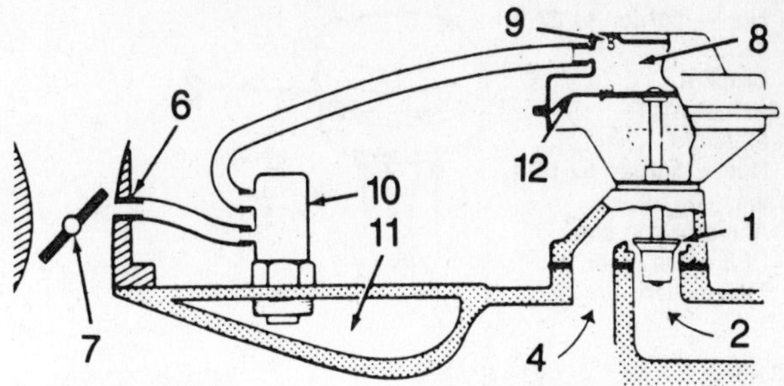

1. EGR valve
2. Exhaust gas
4. Intake flow
6. Vacuum port
7. Throttle valve
8. Vacuum chamber
9. Valve return spring
10. Thermal vacuum switch
11. Coolant
12. Diaphragm

EGR system with TVS

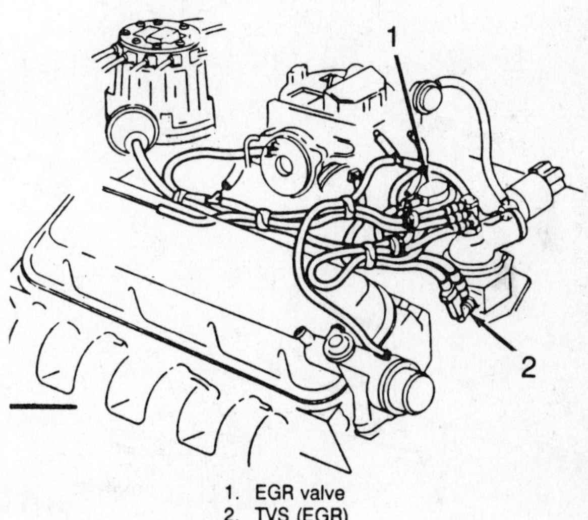

1. EGR valve
2. TVS (EGR)

TVS location on the 8–7.4L engine

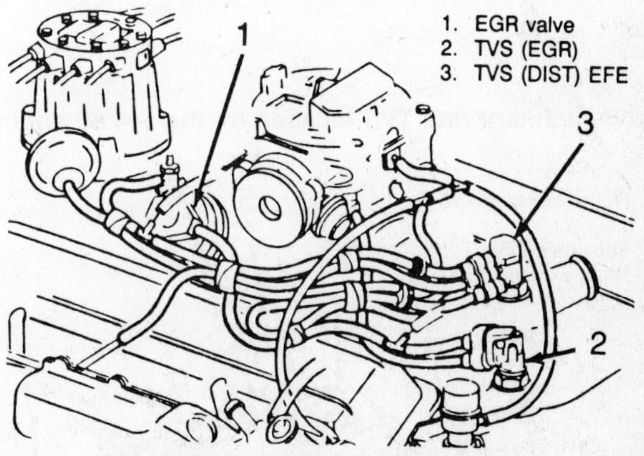

1. EGR valve
2. TVS (EGR)
3. TVS (DIST) EFE

TVS location on the 8–5.7L engine

On 4.8L (6–292) engines, the EGR valve is located on the intake manifold adjacent to the carburetor.

On the 4.3L (6–262), 5.0L (8–305) and 5.7L (8–350) engines, the valve is located on the right rear side of the intake manifold adjacent to the rocker arm cover.

On the 7.4L (8–454), the EGR valve is located in the left front corner of the intake manifold in front of the carburetor.

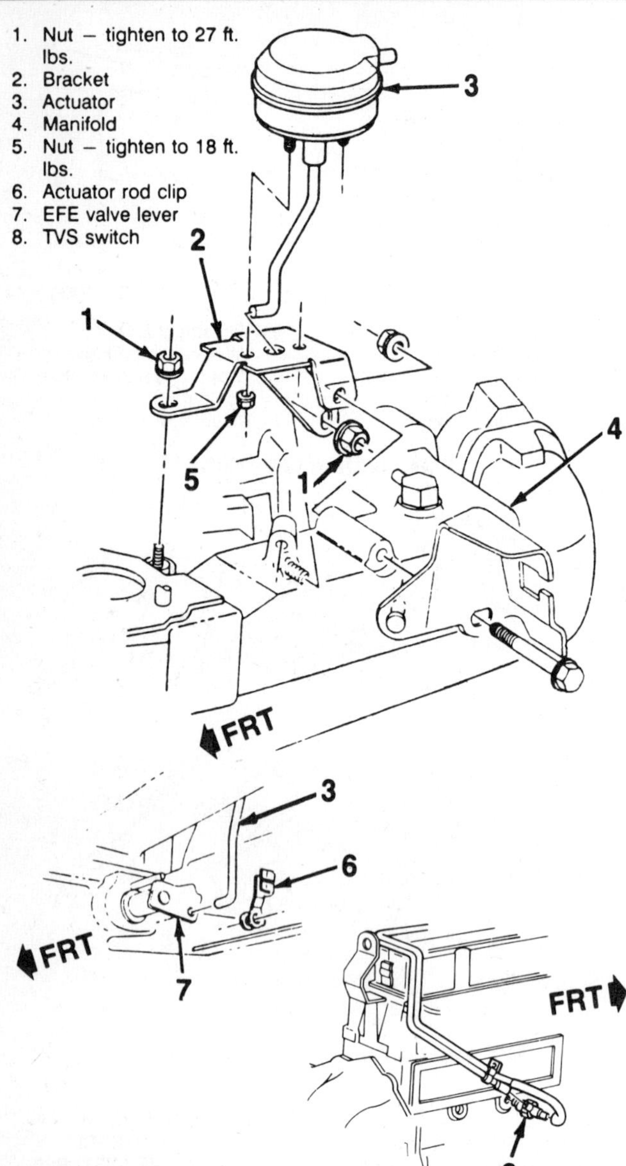

Valve, actuator and TVS location on the 6–4.8L engine

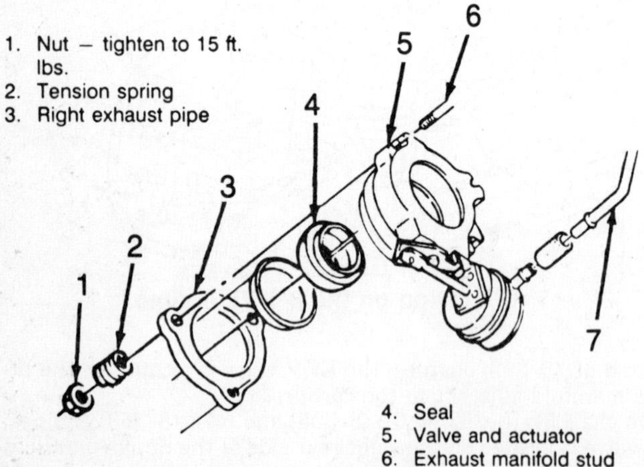

Valve and actuator on the 8–5.7L engine

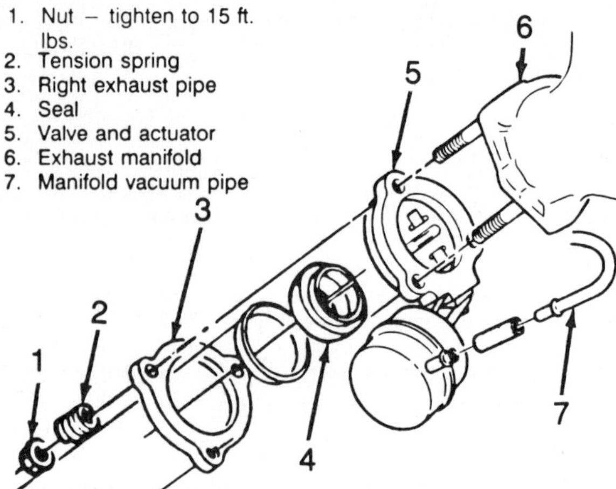

Valve and actuator on the 8–7.4L engine

SERVICE

The EGR valve is not serivceable, except for replacement. To check the valve, proceed as follows:

1. Connect a tachometer to the engine.
2. With the engine running at normal operating temperature, with the choke valve fully open, set the engine rpm at 2000. The transmission should be in Park (automatic) or Neutral (manual) with the parking brake On and the wheels blocked.
3. Disconnect the vacuum hose at the valve. Make sure that vacuum is available at the valve and look at the tachometer to see if the engine speed increases. If it does, a malfunction of the valve is indicated.
4. If necessary, replace the valve.

Evaporation Control System

This system reduces the amount of escaping gasoline vapors. The venting of fuel tank vapors into the air has been stopped. Fuel vapors are now directed through lines to a canister containing an activated charcoal filter. Unburned vapors are trapped here until the engine is started. When the engine is running, the canister is purged by air drawn in by manifold vacuum. The air and fuel vapors are directed into the engine to be burned.

SERVICE

Replace the filter in the engine compartment canister at the intervals shown in the Maintenance Intervals Chart in Section 1. If the fuel tank cap requires replacement, ensure that the new cap is the correct part for your truck.

Early Fuel Evaporation System

This system is used on some light duty models.

The EFE system consists of an EFE valve at the flange of the exhaust manifold, an actuator, and a thermal vacuum switch. The TVS is located in the coolant outlet housing and directly controls vacuum.

In both systems, manifold vacuum is applied to the actuator, which in turn, closes the EFE valve. This routes hot exhaust gases to the base of the carburetor. When coolant temperatures reach a set limit, vacuum is denied to the actuator allowing an internal spring to return the actuator to its normal position, opening the EFE valve.

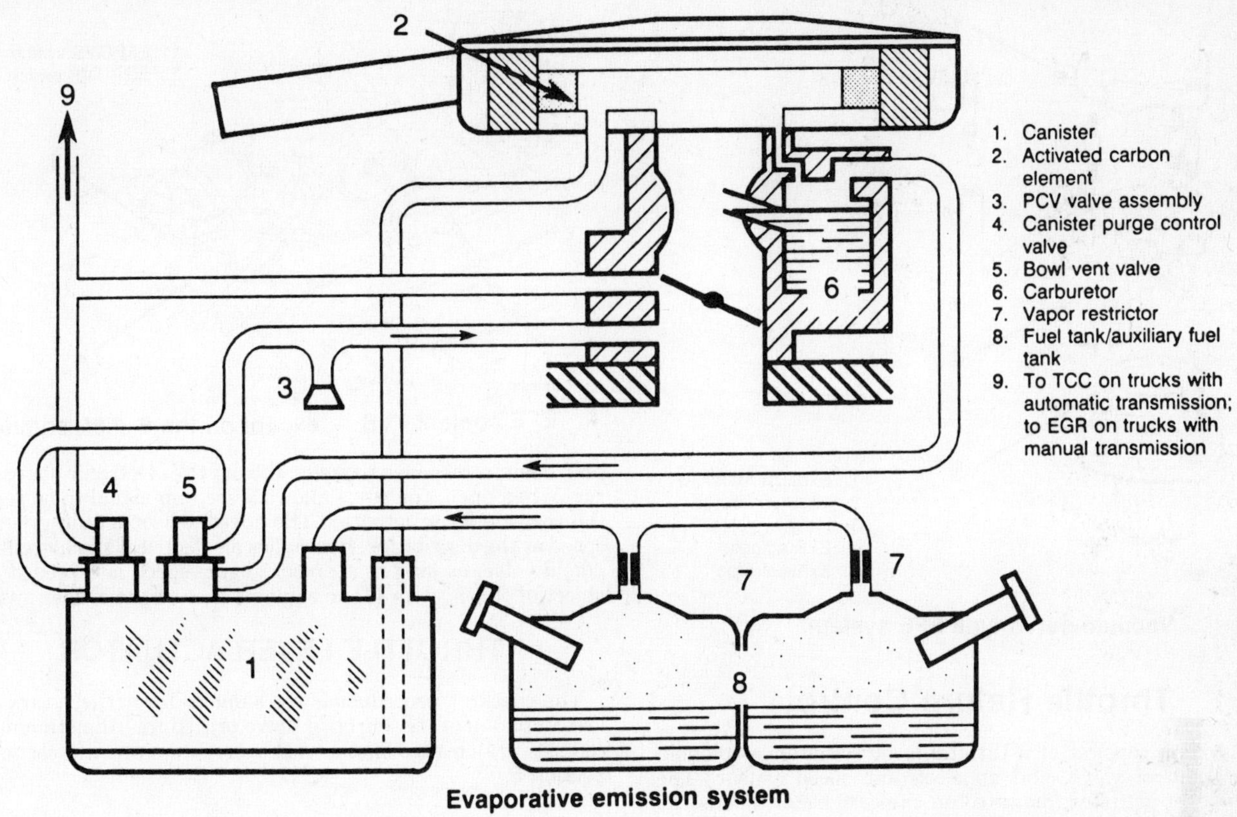
1. Canister
2. Activated carbon element
3. PCV valve assembly
4. Canister purge control valve
5. Bowl vent valve
6. Carburetor
7. Vapor restrictor
8. Fuel tank/auxiliary fuel tank
9. To TCC on trucks with automatic transmission; to EGR on trucks with manual transmission

Evaporative emission system

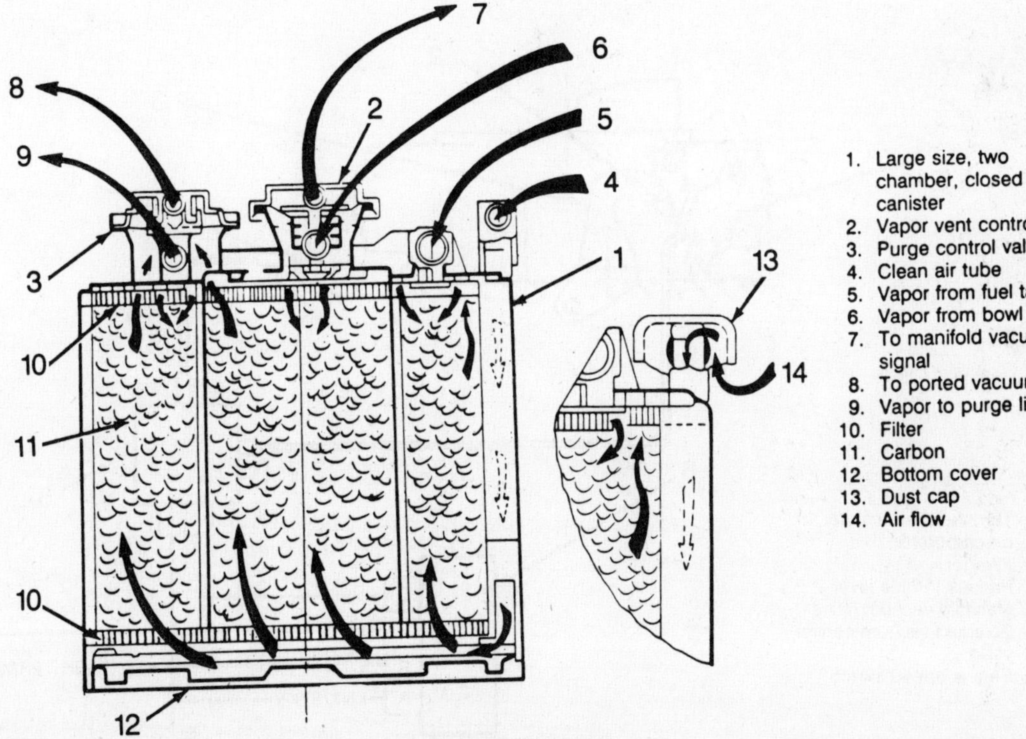
1. Large size, two chamber, closed bottom canister
2. Vapor vent control valve
3. Purge control valve
4. Clean air tube
5. Vapor from fuel tank
6. Vapor from bowl vent
7. To manifold vacuum signal
8. To ported vacuum
9. Vapor to purge line
10. Filter
11. Carbon
12. Bottom cover
13. Dust cap
14. Air flow

Fuel vapor canister

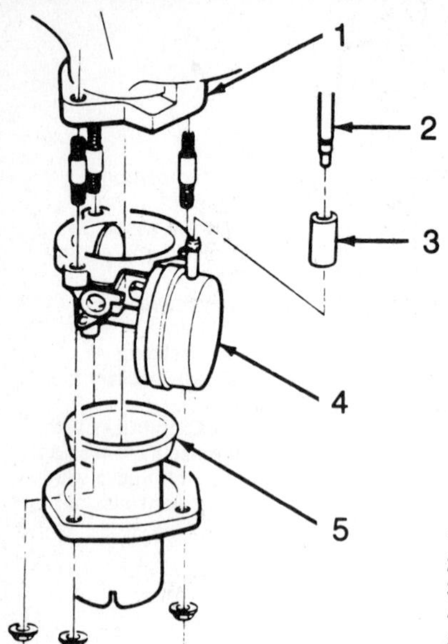

Vacuum servo type EFE system

Throttle Return Control

The system consists of a throttle lever actuator, a solenoid vacuum control valve, and an electronic speed sensor. The throttle lever actuator, mounted on the carburetor, opens the primary throttle plates a present amount, above normal engine idle speed, in response to a signal from the solenoid vacuum control valve. The valve is mounted at the left rear of the engine above the intake manifold on the 4.8L (6–292), or on the thermostat housing mounting stud on the 5.7L (8–350) 4–bbl. It is

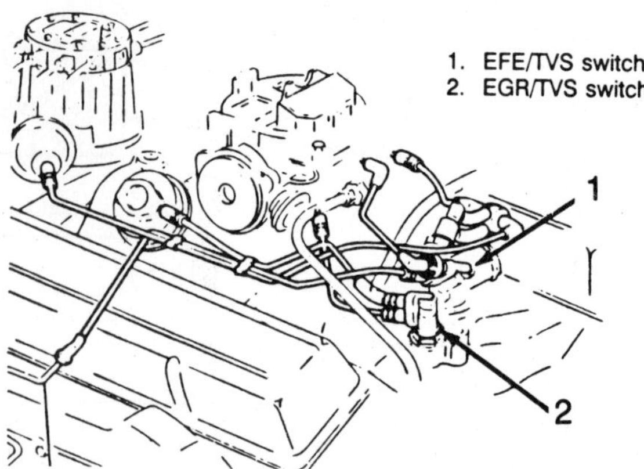

EFE coolant TVS – except on the 6–4.8L engine

held open in response to a signal from the electronic speed sensor. When open, the valve allows a vacuum signal to be sent to the throttle lever actuator. The speed sensor monitors engine speed at the distributor. It supplies an electrical signal to the solenoid valve, as long as a preset engine speed is exceeded. The object of this system is the same as that of the earlier system.

THROTTLE LEVER ACTUATOR

The checking procedure is the same as for earlier years. Follow Steps 1–9 of the Throttle Valve procedure. Adjustment procedures are covered in the carburetor adjustments section in Section 5.

TRC SYSTEM CHECK

1. Connect a tachometer to the distributor TACH terminal. Start the engine and raise the engine speed to 1890 rpm. The throttle lever actuator on the carburetor should extend.

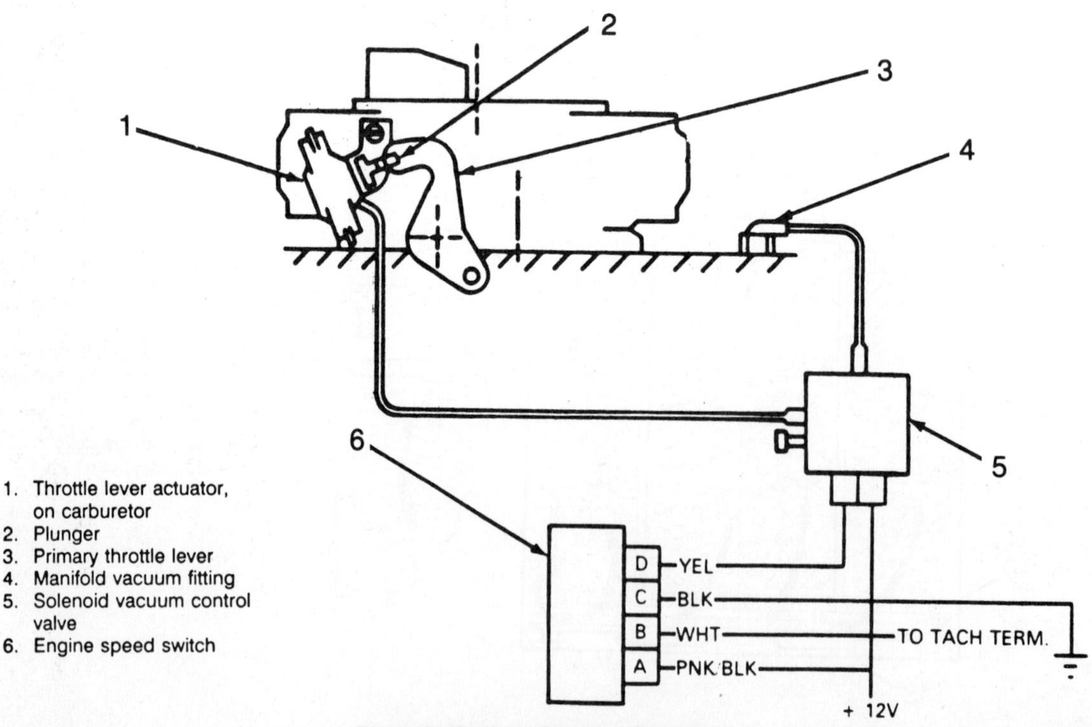

Throttle Return Control System

2. Reduce the engine speed to 1700 rpm. The lever actuator should retract.

3. If the actuator operates outside of the speed limits, the speed switch is faulty and must be replaced. It cannot be adjusted.

4. If the actuator does not operate at all:

a. Check the voltage at the vacuum solenoid and the speed switch with a voltmeter. Connect the negative probe of the voltmeter to the engine ground and the positive probe to the voltage source wire on the component. The positive probe can be inserted on the connector body at the wire side; it is not necessary to unplug the connector. Voltage should be 12 to 14 volts in both cases.

b. If the correct voltage is present at one component but not the other, the engine wiring harness is faulty.

c. If the voltage is not present at all, check the engine harness connections at the distributor and the bulkhead connector and repair as necessary.

d. If the correct voltage is present at both components, check the solenoid operation: ground the solenoid-to-speed switch connecting wire terminal at the solenoid connector with a jumper wire. This should cause the throttle lever actuator to extend, with the engine running.

e. If the lever actuator does not extend, remove the hose from the solenoid side port which connects the actuator hose. Check the port for obstructions or blockage. If the port is not plugged, replace the solenoid.

f. If the actuator extends in Step d, ground the solenoid-to-speed switch wire terminal at the switch. If the actuator does not extend, the wire between the speed switch and the solenoid is open and must be repaired. If the actuator does extend, check the speed switch ground wire for a ground; it should read zero volts with the engine running. Check the speed switch-to-distributor wire for a proper connection. If the ground and distributor wires are properly connected and the actuator still does not extend when the engine speed is above 1890 rpm, replace the speed switch.

5. If the actuator is extended at all speeds:

a. Remove the connector from the vacuum solenoid.

b. If the actuator remains extended, check the solenoid side port orifice for blockage. If plugged, clear and reconnect the system and recheck. If the actuator is still extended, remove the solenoid connector; if the actuator does not retreat, replace the vacuum solenoid.

c. If the actuator retracts with the solenoid connector off, reconnect it and remove the speed switch connector. If the actuator retracts, the problem is in the speed switch, which should be replaced. If the actuator does not retract, the solenoid-to-speed switch wire is shorted to ground in the wiring harness. Repair the short.

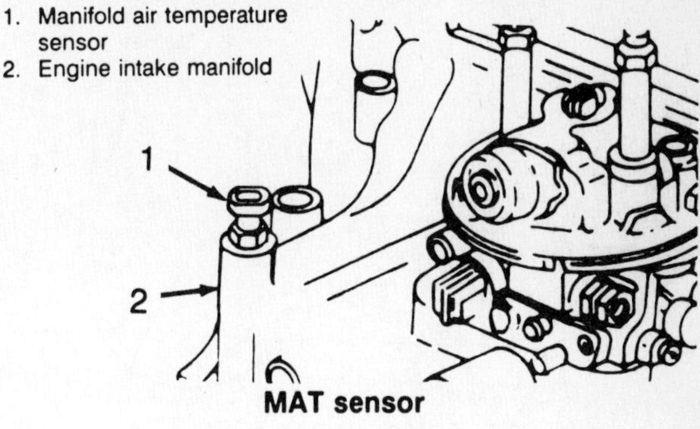

MAT sensor

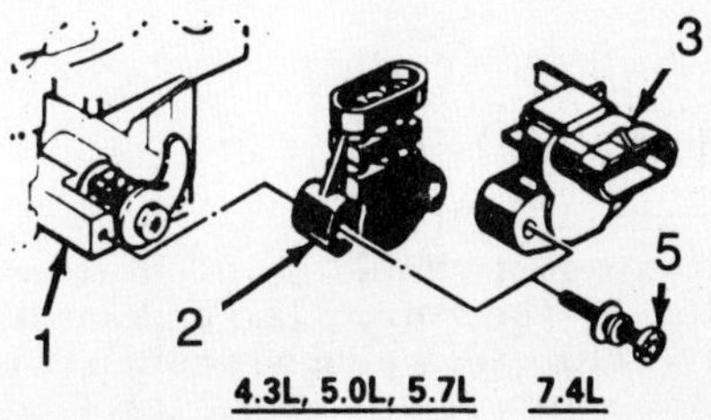

Throttle position sensor

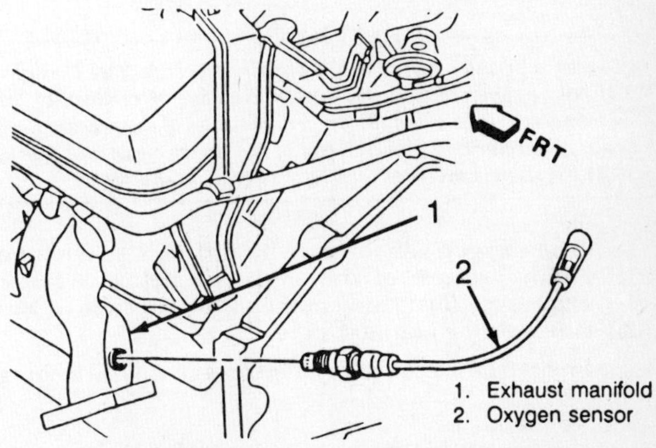

Oxygen sensor on the 8–7.4L engine

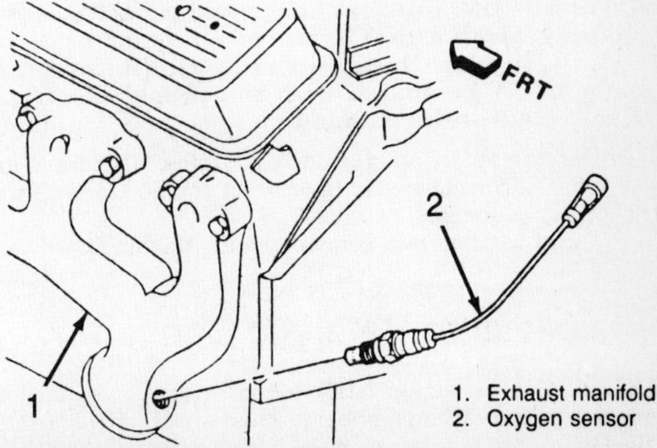

Oxygen sensor on the 8–5.0L and 8–5.7L engines

Oxygen Sensor

The oxygen sensor is a spark plug shaped device that is screwed into the exhaust manifold on V6 and V8 engines, and into the exhaust pipe on the 4.8L (6–292). It monitors the oxygen content of the exhaust gases and sends a voltage signal to the Electronic Control Module (ECM). The ECM monitors this voltage and, depending on the value of the received signal, issues a command to the mixture control solenoid on the carburetor to adjust for rich or lean conditions.

The proper operation of the oxygen sensor depends upon four basic conditions:

1. Good electrical connections. Since the sensor generates low currents, good clean electrical connections at the sensor are a must.

2. Outside air supply. Air must circulate to the internal portion of the sensor. When servicing the sensor, do not restrict the air passages.

3. Proper operating temperatures. The ECM will not recog-

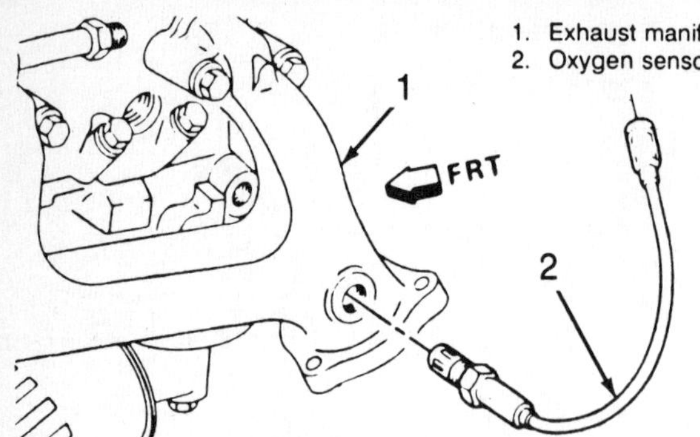

Oxygen sensor on the 6–4.3L

nize the sensor's signals until the sensor reaches approximately +600°F (+316°C).

4. Non-leaded fuel. The use of leaded gasoline will damage the sensor very quickly.

NOTE: No attempt should be made to measure the output voltage of the sensor. The current drain of any conventional voltmeter would be enough to permanently damage the sensor. No jumpers, test leads, or other electrical connections should ever be made to the sensor. Use these tool ONLY on the ECM side of the harness connector AFTER the oxygen sensor has been disconnected.

REMOVAL AND INSTALLATION

CAUTION

The sensor uses a permanently attached pigtail and connector. This pigtail should not be removed from the sensor. Damage or removal of the pigtail or connector could affect the proper operation of the sensor. Keep the electrical connector and louvered end of the sensor clean and free of grease. NEVER use cleaning solvents of any type on the sensor!

NOTE: The oxygen sensor may be difficult to remove when the temperature of the engine is below +120°F (+49°C). Excessive force may damage the threads in the exhaust manifold or exhaust pipe.

1. Disconnect the electrical connector and any attaching hardware.
2. Remove the sensor.
3. Coat the threads of the sensor with a GM anti-seize compound, part number 5613695, or its equivalent, before installation. New sensors are precoated with this compound.

NOTE: The GM antiseize compound is NOT a conventional anti-seize paste. The use of a regular paste may electrically insulate the sensor, rendering it useless. The threads MUST be coated with the proper electrically conductive anti-seize compound.

4. Install the sensor and torque to 30 ft. lbs. Use care in making sure the silicone boot is in the correct position to avoid melting it during operation.
5. Connect the electrical connector and attaching hardware if used.

Oxidizing Catalytic Converter

An underfloor oxidizing catalytic converter is used to control hydrocarbon and carbon monoxide emissions. Control is accomplished by placing a catalyst in the exhaust system to enable all exhaust gas flow to pass through it and undergo a chemical reaction before passing into the atmosphere. The chemical reaction involved is the oxidizing of hydrocarbons and carbon monoxide into water vapor and carbon dioxide.

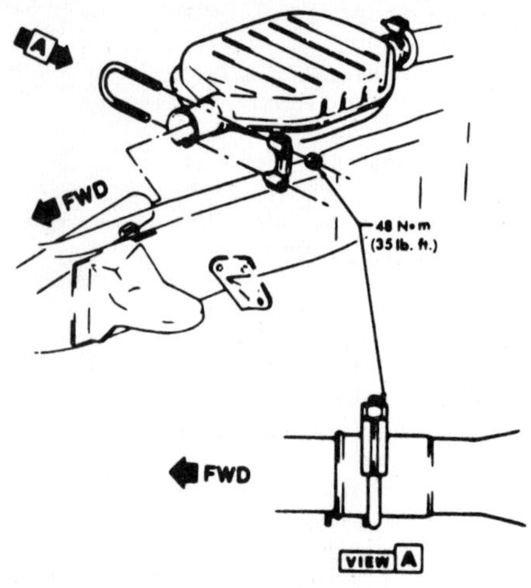

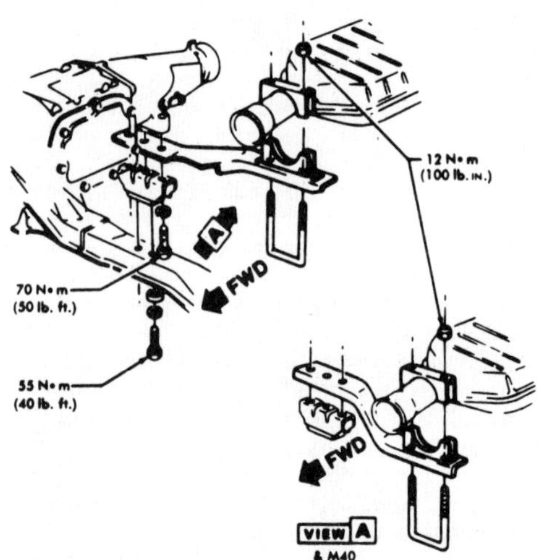

Typical catalytic converter installation

REMOVAL AND INSTALLATION

CAUTION

Catalytic converter operating temperatures are extremely high. Outside converter temperatures can go well over +1,000°F (+538°C). Use extreme care when working on or around the catalytic converter.

1. Raise and support the truck.
2. Remove the clamps at the front and rear of the converter.
3. Cut the converter pipes at the front and rear of the converter and remove it.
4. Remove the support from the transmission.
5. Remove the converter pipe-to-exhaust pipe and the converter pipe-to-tailpipe.

To install the converter:

6. Install the exhaust pipe and tailpipe into the converter with sealer.
7. Loosely install the support on the transmission.
8. Install new U-bolts and clamps, check all clearances and tighten the clamps.
9. Lower the truck.

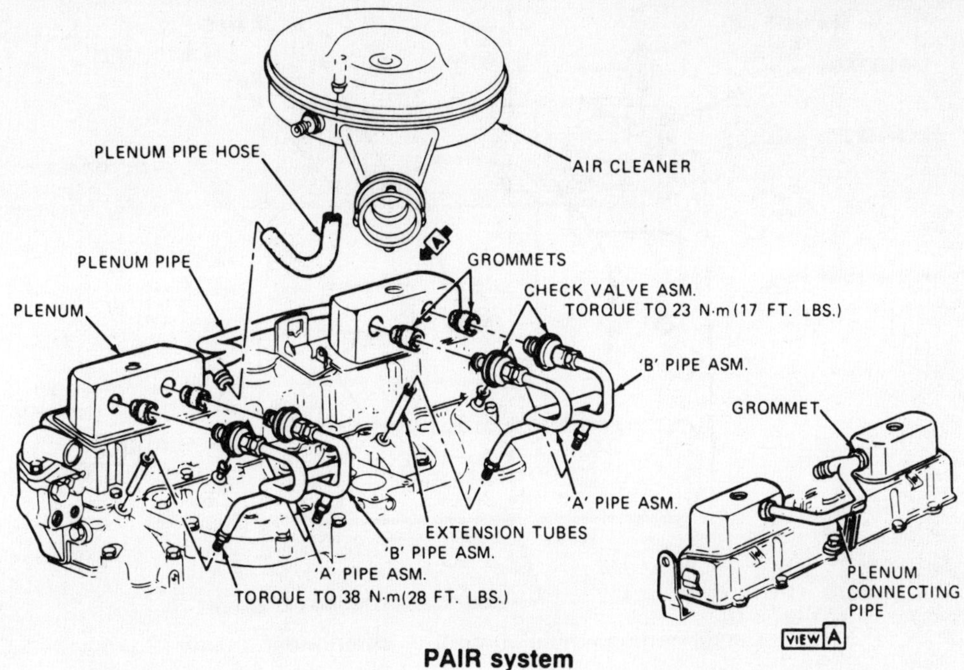

PAIR system

NOTE: Dealers have equipment to remove and replace the converter contents (pellets) without removing the converter from the exhaust system.

Pulse Air Injection Reactor System

This system consists of four air valves which inject fresh air into the exhaust system in order to further the combustion process of the exhaust gases. The firing of the engine creates a pulsating flow of exhaust gases, which are of either positive or negative pressure. Negative pressure at the pulse air valve will result in air being injected into the exhaust system. Positive pressure will force the check valve closed and no exhaust gases will flow into the fresh air supply.

Regularly inspect the pulse air valves, pipes, grommets and hose for cracks and leaks. Replace the necessary part if any are found. If a check valve fails, exhaust gases will get into the carburetor through the air cleaner and cause the engine to surge and perform poorly.

If exhaust gases pass through a pulse air valve, the paint will be burned off the rocker arm cover plenum as a result of the excessive heat. The rubber grommets and hose will also deteriorate. Failure of the pulse air valve can also be indicated by a hissing sound.

REMOVAL AND INSTALLATION

1. Remove the air cleaner. Disconnect the rubber hose from the plenum connecting pipe. (See illustration).
2. Disconnect the four check valve fittings at the cylinder head and remove the check valve pipes from the plenum grommets.
3. Disconnect the check valve from the check valve pipe.
4. Assemble the replacement check valve to the check valve pipe.
5. Attach the check valve assembly to the cylinder head as illustrated. Hand tighten the fittings.
6. Using a 1 in. open end wrench as a lever, align the check valve on pipe A with the plenum grommet. Using the palm of your left hand, press the check valve into the grommet. Using a silicone lubricant on the grommet will make thing a little easier. Repeat this procedure for pipe **B** using your left hand for the tool and your right hand for installing the valve in the grommet.

DIESEL ENGINE EMISSIONS CONTROLS

Crankcase Ventilation

A Crankcase Depression Regulator Valve (CDRV) is used to regulate (meter) the flow of crankcase gases back into the engine to be burned. The CDRV is designed to limit vacuum in the crankcase as the gases are drawn from the valve covers through the CDRV and into the intake manifold (air crossover).

Fresh air enters the engine through the combination filter, check valve and oil fill cap. The fresh air mixes with blow-by gases and enters both valve covers. The gases pass through a filter

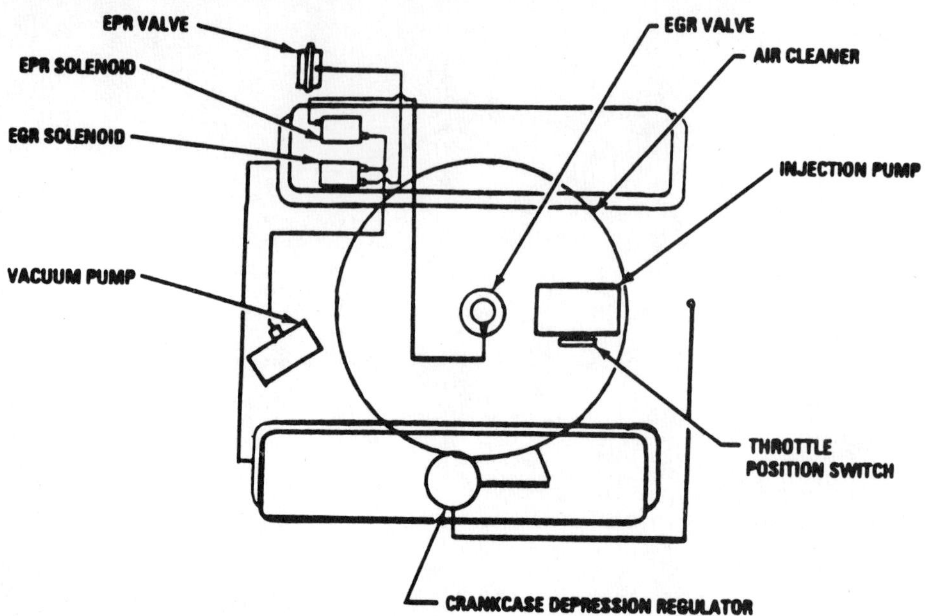

Diesel engine emission control component locator

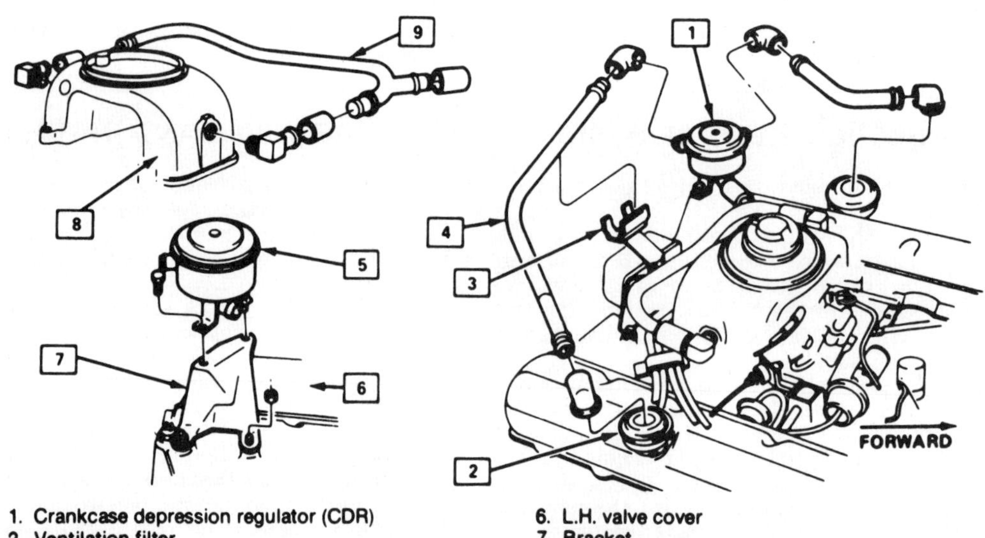

1. Crankcase depression regulator (CDR)
2. Ventilation filter
3. Brace clip
4. Ventilation pipes
5. Crankcase depression regulator (CDR)
6. L.H. valve cover
7. Bracket
8. Air crossover
9. Air crossover to regulator valve pipe

Diesel engine crankcase ventilation system

installed on the valve covers and are drawn into connecting tubing.

Intake manifold vacuum acts against a spring loaded diaphragm to control the flow of crankcase gases. Higher intake vacuum levels pull the diaphragm closer to the top of the outlet tube. This reduces the amount of gases being drawn from the crankcase and decreases the vacuum level in the crankcase. As the intake vacuum decreases, the spring pushes the diaphragm away from the top of the outlet tube allowing more gases to flow to the intake manifold.

NOTE: Do not allow any solvent to come in contact with the diaphragm of the Crankcase Depression Regulator Valve because the diaphragm will fail.

Exhaust Gas Recirculation (EGR)

To lower the formation of nitrogen oxides (NOx) in the exhaust, it is necessary to reduce combustion temperatures. This is done in the diesel, as in the gasoline engine, by introducing exhaust gases into the cylinders through the EGR valve.

On the 6.2L diesel, and Exhaust Pressure Regulator (EPR) valve and solenoid operate in conjunction with the EGR valve. The EPR valve's job is to increase exhaust backpressure in order to increase EGR flow (to reduce nitrous oxide emissions). The EPR valve is usually open, and the solenoid is normally closed. When energized by the **B+** wire from the Throttle Position Switch (TPS), the solenoid opens, allowing vacuum to the

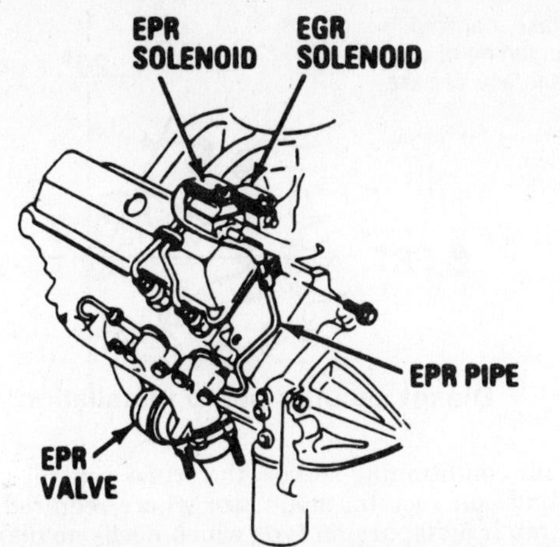

Exhaust pressure regulator valve and solenoid

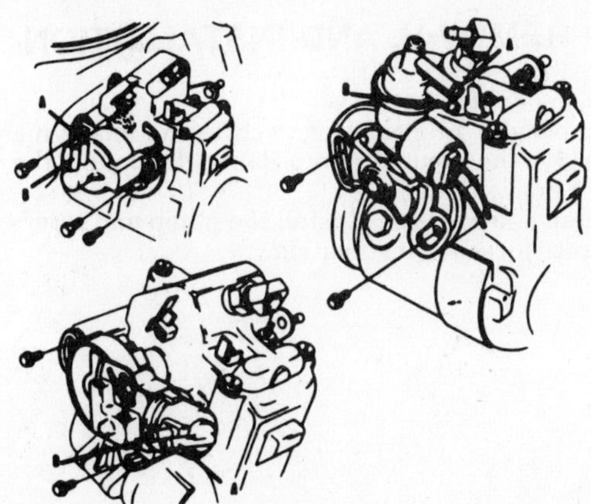
Diesel vacuum regulator valve, mounted on the injection pump

EPR valve, closing it. This occurs at idle. As the throttle is opened, at a calibrated throttle angle, the TPS de-energizes the EPR solenoid, cutting off vacuum to the EPR valve, closing the valve.

FUNCTIONAL TESTS OF COMPONENTS

Vacuum Regulator Valve (VRV)

The Vacuum Regulator Valve is attached to the side of the injection pump and regulates vacuum in proportion to throttle angle. Vacuum from the vacuum pump is supplied to port **A** and vacuum at port **B** is reduced as the throttle is opened. At closed throttle, the vacuum is 15 in.Hg; at half throttle, 6 in.Hg; at wide open throttle there is zero vacuum.

Exhaust Gas Recirculation (EGR) Valve

Apply vacuum to vacuum port. The valve should be fully open at 10.5 in.Hg and closed below 6 in.Hg.

Response Vacuum Reducer (RVR)

Connect a vacuum gauge to the port marked **To EGR** valve to T.C.C. solenoid. Connect a hand operated vacuum pump to the VRV port. Draw a 50.66 kPa (15 in.Hg) vacuum on the pump and the reading on the vacuum gauge should be lower than the vacuum pump reading as follows:

- 0.75 in.Hg Except High Altitude
- 2.5 in.Hg High Altitude

Torque Converter Clutch Operated Solenoid

When the torque converter clutch is engaged, an electrical signal energizes the solenoid allowing ports 1 and 2 to be interconnected. When the solenoid is not energized, port 1 is closed and ports 2 and 3 are interconnected.

Solenoid Energized

- Ports 1 and 3 are connected.

Solenoid De-Energized

- Ports 2 and 3 are connected.

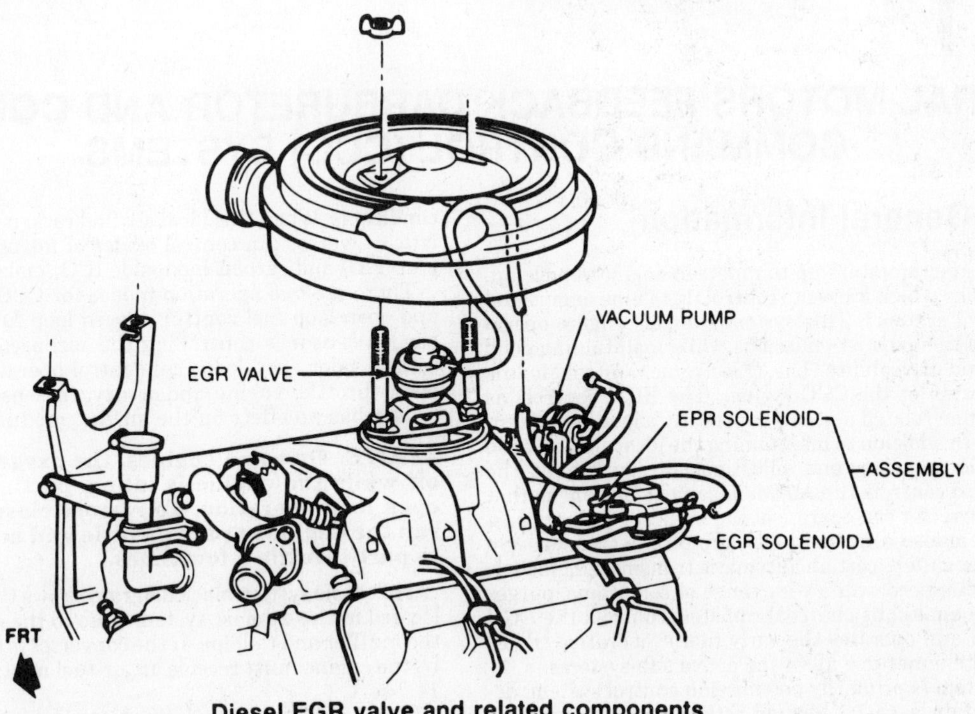

Diesel EGR valve and related components

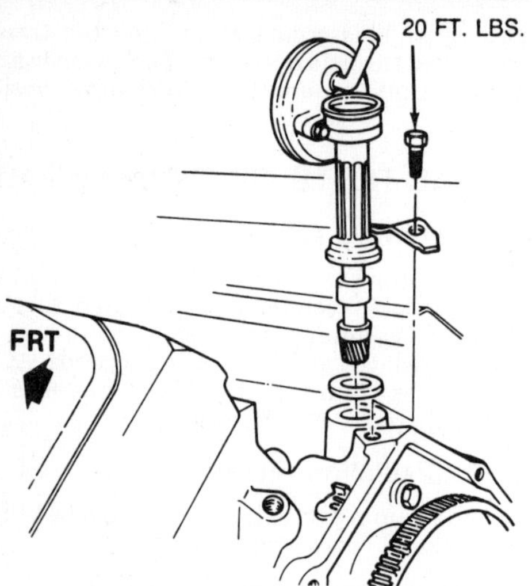

Diesel vacuum pump removal

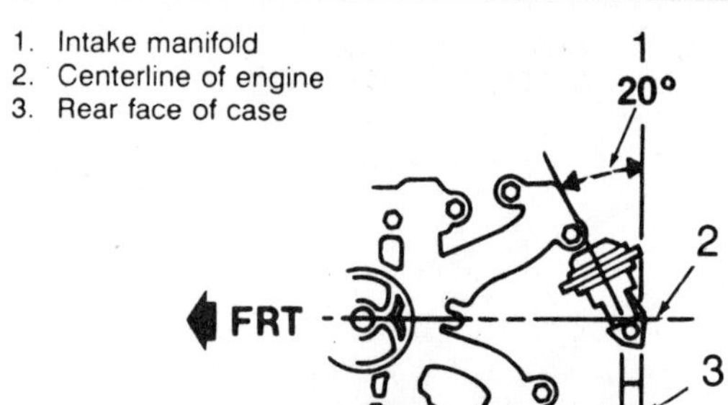

Diesel vacuum pump installation

Vacuum Pump

Since the air crossover and intake manifold in a diesel engine is unrestricted (unlike a gasoline engine which has throttle plates creating a venturi effect) there is no vacuum source. To provide vacuum, a vacuum pump is mounted in the location occupied by the distributor in a gasoline engine. This pump supplies the air conditioning servos, the cruise control servos, and the transmission vacuum modulator where required.

The pump is a diaphragm type which needs no maintenance. It is driven by a drive gear on its lower end which meshes with gear teeth on the end of the engine's camshaft.

REMOVAL AND INSTALLATION

1. Disconnect the batteries.
2. Remove the air cleaner, and cover the intake manifold.
3. Remove the vacuum pump clamp, disconnect the vacuum line and remove the pump.
4. Install a new gasket. Install the pump and reverse the removal procedures for installation.

GENERAL MOTORS FEEDBACK CARBURETOR AND COMPUTER COMMAND CONTROL (CCC) SYSTEMS

General Information

The CCC System monitors up to nineteen engine/vehicle operating conditions which it uses to control up to nine engine and emission control systems. This system controls engine operation and lowers the exhaust emissions while maintaining good fuel economy and driveability. The "Electronic Control Module (ECM) is the brain of the CCC system. The ECM controls as many as 12 engine related systems constantly adjusting the engine operation. In addition to maintaining the ideal air/fuel ratio for the catalytic converter and adjusting ignition timing, the CCC System also controls the Air Management System so that the catalytic converter can operate at the highest efficiency possible. The system also controls the lockup on the transmission torque converter clutch (certain automatic transmission models only), adjusts idle speed over a wide range of conditions, purges the evaporative emissions charcoal canister, controls the EGR valve operation and operates the early fuel evaporative (EFE) system. Not all engines use all of the above sub-systems.

The CCC system is primarily an emission control system, designed to maintain a 14.7:1 air/fuel ratio under all operating conditions. When this ideal air/fuel ratio is maintained the catalytic converter can control oxides of nitrogen (NOx), hydrocarbon (HC) and carbon monoxide (CO) emissions.

There are two operation modes for CCC System: closed loop and open loop fuel control. Closed loop fuel control means the oxygen sensor is controlling the carburetor's air/fuel mixture ratio. Under open loop fuel control operating conditions (wide open throttle, engine and/or oxygen sensor cold), the oxygen sensor has no effect on the air/fuel mixture.

NOTE: On some engines, the oxygen sensor will cool off while the engine is idling, putting the system into open loop operation. To restore closed loop operation, run the engine at part throttle and accelerate from idle to part throttle a few times.

This basic system block diagram shows the catalytic converter located in the exhaust system close to the engine. It is ahead of the muffler and tailpipe. If the converter is to do its job effectively, the engine must receive an air-fuel mixture of approximately 14.7 to 1.

The carburetor mixes air and gasoline into a combustible mixture before delivering it to the engine. However, carburetors have reached a point where they can no longer control the air-fuel mixture sufficiently close to the ideal 14.7 too 1 ratio for most operating conditions. Therefore, a different type of control must be used on the carburetor, something that has never been used before.

An electric solenoid in the carburetor controls the air-fuel ratio. The solenoid is connected to an electronic module (ECM) which is an on board computer. The ECM provides a controlling signal to the solenoid. The solenoid controls the metering rod(s) and an idle air bleed valve to closely control the air-fuel ration throughout the operating range of the engine. However, since the engine operates under a wide variety of conditions, the computer must be told what those conditions are. This is so that it will know what to tell the carburetor solenoid to do.

A sensor is located in the exhaust stream close to the engine. It's known as an oxygen sensor or simply an O_2 sensor. This sensor functions when the engine's exhaust temperature rises above 600°F (316°C). There is a direct relationship between the mixture delivered by the carburetor and the amount of oxygen left in the exhaust gases. The O_2 sensor can determine whether the exhaust is too rich or too lean. It sends a varying voltage signal to the ECM.

The ECM will then signal the mixture control solenoid to deliver richer or leaner mixture for the current engine operating conditions. As the carburetor makes a change, the O_2 sensor will sense that change and signal the ECM whether or not it's too rich or too lean. The ECM will then make a correction, if necessary. This goes on continually and is what we refer to as Closed Loop operation. Closed loop conditions deliver a 14.7 to 1 air/fuel mixture to the engine. This makes it possible for the converter to act upon all three of the major pollutants in an efficient and effective manner. consider, however, what happens in the morning when it's cold and the car is started. If the system where to keep the air/fuel mixture to the 14.7 to 1 air/fuel ratio when it's cold the chances are that the engine wouldn't run very well. When the engine is cold, it has to have a richer mixture. An automatic choke is used to give the engine a richer mixture until it is up to normal operating temperature. during this time, the O_2 sensor signals are ignored by the ECM.

A temperature sensor is located in the water jacket of the engine and connected to the electronic control module. When the engine is cold, the temperature sensor will tell the ECM to ignore the oxygen sensor signal, since the sensor is too cold to operate. The electronic control module then tells the carburetor to deliver a richer mixture based upon what has already been programmed into the ECM. The ECM will also use information from other sensors during cold start operation.

After the engine has been running for some time and has reached normal operating temperature, the temperature sensor will signal the ECM that the engine is warm, and it can accept the oxygen sensor signal. If other system requirements are met, closed loop operations begins. The oxygen sensor will then influence the ECM as to what mixture it should deliver to the engine. In addition to these two conditions, there are three other conditions which affect the air/fuel mixture delivered to the engine. First is the load that is placed upon the engine. When an engine is working hard, such as pulling a heavy load up a long grade, it requires a richer air/fuel mixture. This is different from a vehicle that is operating in a cruise condition on a level highway at a constant rate of speed.

Manifold vacuum is used to determine engine load. A manifold pressure sensor is located in the intake manifold. It detects changes in the manifold pressure which are signaled to the ECM. As changes occur, the load placed upon the engine varies. The ECM takes this varying signal into account when determining what mixture the carburetor should be delivering to the engine. The next condition in determining what air/fuel mixture should be is the amount of throttle opening. The more throttle opening at any given time, the richer the mixture required by the engine. On most applications a TPS (throttle position sensor) in the carburetor sends a signal to the ECM. It tells the ECM the position of the throttle, whether it it at idle, part throttle, wide open or whatever condition that exists in between.

The last condition, which has a bearing on the mixture that the engine would require, is the speed the engine is running. Certainly when an engine is operating at 600 rpm, it doesn't need as much gasoline as it does when it is operating at 4000 rpm. Therefore, a tachometer signal from the distributor is delivered to the electronic control module. This tells the ECM how fast the engine is running. This signal will also be taken into consideration when the ECM decides what mixture the carburetor should be delivering to the engine. In the typical CCC system, the ECM will use various inputs to make decisions that will best control the operation of the mixture control solenoid for maximum system efficiency.

SYSTEM COMPONENTS

Electronic Control Module (ECM)

The ECM is a reliable solid state computer, protected in a metal box. It is used to monitor and control all the functions of the CCC System and is located in one of several places in the passenger compartment. The ECM can perform several on-car functions at the same time and has the ability to diagnose itself as well as other CCC System circuits.

The ECM performs the functions of an on and off switch. It can send a voltage signal to a circuit or connect a circuit to ground at a precise time. Programmed into the ECM's memory are voltage and time values. These valves will differ from one engine to another. As an example then, if the ECM "sees" a proper voltage value for the correct length of time it will perform a certain function. This could be turning the EGR system on as the engine warms up. If however, the voltage or the time interval is not correct, the ECM will also recognize this. It will not perform its function and in most cases turn the CHECK ENGINE or SERVICE ENGINE SOON Light ON.

The other CCC components include the oxygen sensor, an electronically controlled variable-mixture carburetor, a three-way catalytic converter, throttle position and coolant sensors, a barometric pressure (BARO) sensor, a manifold absolute pressure (MAP) sensor, a "Check Engine" light on the instrument cluster, and an Electronic Spark Timing (EST), which is linked to an Electronic Spark Control system for all engines except the 7.4L (8–454).

Other components used by the CCC System include the Air Injection Reaction (AIR) Management System, charcoal canister purge solenoid, EGR valve control, vehicle speed sensor (located in the instrument cluster), transmission torque converter clutch solenoid (automatic transmission models only), idle speed control, and early fuel evaporative (EFE) system.

The CCC System ECM, in addition to monitoring sensors and sending a control signal to the carburetor, also controls the charcoal canister purge, AIR Management System,fuel control, idle speed control, idle air control, automatic transmission converter clutch lockup, distributor ignition timing, EGR valve control, EFE control, air conditioner compressor clutch operation, electric fuel pump and the CHECK ENGINE light.

- The AIR Management System is an emission control which provides additional oxygen either to the catalyst or the cylinder head ports (in some cases exhaust manifold). An AIR Management System, composed of an air switching valve and/or an air control valve, controls the air pump flow and is itself controlled by the ECM. A complete description of the AIR system is given towards the front of this unit repair section. The major difference between the CCC AIR System and the systems used on other cars is that the flow of air from the air pump is controlled electrically by the ECM, rather than by vacuum signal.

NOTE: On some models the Air Management System may not be controlled by the ECM.

• The charcoal canister purge control is an electrically operated solenoid valve controlled by the ECM. When energized, the purge control solenoid blocks vacuum from reaching the canister purge valve. When the ECM de-energizes the purge control solenoid, vacuum is allowed to reach the canister and operate the purge valve. This releases the fuel vapors collected in the canister into the induction system.

• The EGR valve control solenoid is activated by the ECM in similar fashion to the canister purge solenoid. When the engine is cold, the ECM energizes the solenoid, which blocks the vacuum signal to the EGR valve. When the engine is warm, the ECM de-energizes the solenoid and the vacuum signal is allowed to reach and activate the EGR valve.

• The Transmission Converter Clutch (TCC) lock is controlled by the ECM through an electrical solenoid in the automatic transmission. When the vehicle speed sensor in the instrument panel signals the ECM that the vehicle has reached the correct speed, the ECM energizes the solenoid which allows the torque converter to mechanically couple the engine to the transmission. When the brake pedal is pushed or during deceleration, passing, etc., the ECM returns the transmission to fluid drive.

• The idle speed control adjusts the idle speed to load conditions, and will lower the idle speed under no-load or low-load conditions to conserve gasoline.

• The Early Fuel Evaporative (EFE) system is used on most engines to provide rapid heat to the engine induction system to promote smooth start-up and operation. There are two types of system: vacuum servo and electrically heated. They use different means to achieve the same end, which is to pre-heat the incoming air/fuel mixture. They may or may not be controlled by the ECM.

• A/C Wide Open Throttle (WOT) Control, on this system the ECM controls the A/C compressor clutch to disengage the clutch during hard acceleration. On some engines, the ECM disengages the clutch during the engine start-up on a warm engine. The WOT control is not installed on all engines.

• Electronic Spark Control (ESC) system controls the spark timing on certain engines to allow the engine to have maximum spark advance without spark knock. This improves the driveability and fuel ecomomy. This system is not used on the 7.4L (8–454) engine.

• Shift Light Control: the ECM controls the shift light on the manual transmission to indicate the best shift point for maximum fuel economy. This control is not used on all engines.

• Electric Cooling Fan Control, under certain conditions, the ECM may control the electric cooling fan to cool the engine and the A/C condenser. At cruising speed, the ECM may turn the fan off for better fuel economy. This control is on most transverse engine front wheel drive vehicles.

Basic Troubleshooting

NOTE: The following explains how to activate the Trouble Code signal light in the instrument cluster and gives an explanation of what each code means. This is not a full CCC System troubleshooting and isolation procedure.

Before suspecting the CCC System or any of its components as faulty, check the ignition system including distributor, timing, spark plugs and wires. Check the engine compression, air cleaner, and emission control components not controlled by the ECM. Also check the intake manifold, vacuum hoses and hose connectors for leaks and the carburetor bolts for tightness.

The following symptoms could indicate a possible problem with the CCC System.

1. Detonation
2. Stalls or rough idle-cold
3. Stalls or rough idle-hot
4. Missing
5. Hesitation
6. Surges
7. Poor gasoline mileage
8. Sluggish or spongy performance
9. Hard starting-cold
10. Objectionable exhaust odors (that "rotten egg" smell)
11. Cuts out
12. Improper idle speed

As a bulb and system check, the CHECK ENGINE light will come on when the ignition switch is turned to the ON position but the engine is not started. The CHECK ENGINE light will also produce the trouble code or codes by a series of flashes which translate as follows. When the diagnostic test terminal under the dash is grounded, with the ignition in the ON position and the engine not running, the CHECK ENGINE light will flash once, pause, then flash twice in rapid succession. This is a code 12, which indicates that the diagnostic system is working. After a long pause, the code 12 will repeat itself two more times. The cycle will then repeat itself until the engine is started or the ignition is turned off.

When the engine is started, the CHECK ENGINE light will remain on for a few seconds, then turn off. If the CHECK ENGINE light remains on, the self-diagnostic system has detected a problem. If the test terminal is then grounded, the trouble code will flash three times. If more than one problem is found, each trouble code will flash three times. Trouble codes will flash in numerical order (lowest code number to highest). The trouble codes series will repeat as long as the test terminal is grounded.

A trouble code indicates a problem with a given circuit. For example, trouble code 14 indicates a problem in the cooling sensor circuit. This includes the coolant sensor, its electrical harness, and the Electronic Control Module (ECM) Since the self-diagnostic system cannot diagnose every possible fault in the system, the absence of a trouble code does not mean the system is trouble-free. To determine problems within the system which do not activate a trouble code, a system performance check must be made.

In the case of an intermittant fault in the system, the CHECK ENGINE light will go out when the fault goes away, but the trouble code will remain in the memory of the ECM. Therefore, it a trouble code can be obtained even though the CHECK ENGINE light is not on, the trouble code must be evaluated. It must be determined if the fault is intermittant or if the engine must be at certain operating conditions (under load, etc.) before the CHECK ENGINE light will come on. Some trouble codes will not be recorded in the ECM until the engine has been operated at part throttle for about 5–18 minutes. On the CCC System, a trouble code will be stored until terminal **R** of the ECM has been disconnected from the battery for 10 seconds.

An easy way to erase the computer memory on the CCC System is to disconnect the battery terminals from the battery. If this method is used, don't forget to reset clocks and electronic preprogrammable radios. Another method is to remove the fuse marked ECM in the fuse panel. Not all models have such a fuse.

CCC SYSTEM CIRCUIT DIAGNOSIS

For in-depth diagnosis of the CCC system, refer to Chilton's Electronic Engine Controls Manual.

ELECTRONIC SPARK TIMING SYSTEM (EST)

General Description

The High Energy Ignition (HEI) system controls fuel combustion by providing the spark to ignite the compressed air/fuel mixture, in the combustiuon chamber, at the correct time. To provide improved engine performance, fuel economy and control of the exhaust emissions, the ECM controls distributor spark advance (timing) with the Electronic Spark Timing (EST) system.

The standard High Energy Ignition (HEI) system has a modified distributor module which is used in conjunction with the EST system. The module has seven terminals instead of the four used without EST. Two different terminal arrangements are used, depending upon the distributor used with a particular engine application.

To properly control ignition/combustion timing, the ECM needs to know the following information:

1. Crankshaft position.
2. Engine speed (rpm).
3. Engine load (manifold pressure or vacuum).
4. Atmospheric (barometric) pressure.
5. Engine temperature.
6. Transmission gear position (certain models)

The EST system consists of the distributor module, ECM and its connecting wires. The distributor has four wires from the HEI module connected to a four terminal connector, which mates with a four wire connector from the ECM.

These circuits perform the following functions:

1. Distributor reference at terminal B – This provides the ECM with rpm and crankshaft position information.
2. Reference ground at terminal D – This wire is grounded in the distributor and makes sure the ground circuit has no voltage drop, which could affect performance. If this circuit is open, it could cause poor performance.
3. By-pass at terminal C – At approximately 400 rpm, the ECM applies 5 volts to this circuit to switch the spark timing control from the HEI module to the ECM. An open or grounded bypass circuit will set a Code 42 and the engine will run at base timing, plus a small amount of advance built into the HEI module.
4. EST at terminal A – This triggers the HEI module. The ECM does not know what the actual timing is, but it does know when it gets its reference signal. It then advances or retards the spark timing from that point. Therefore, if the base timing is set incorrectly, the entire spark curve will be incorrect.

An open circuit in the EST circuit will set a Code 42 and cause the engine to run on the HEI module timing. This will cause poor performance and poor fuel economy. A ground may set a Code 42, but the engine will not run.

The ECM uses information from the MAP or VAC and coolant sensors, in addition to rpm, in order to calculate spark advance as follows:

1. Low MAP output voltage (high VAC sensor output voltage) would require MORE spark advance.
2. Cold engine would require MORE spark advance.
3. High MAP output voltage (low VAC sensor output voltage) would require LESS spark advance.
4. Hot engine would require LESS spark advance.

RESULTS OF INCORRECT EST OPERATION

Detonation could be caused by low MAP output (high VAC sensor output), or high resistance in the coolant sensor circuit.

Poor performance could be caused by high MAP output (low VAC sensor output) or low resistance in the coolant sensor circuit.

HOW CODE 42 IS DETERMINED

When the systems is operating on the HEI module with no voltage in the by-pass line, the HEI module grounds the EST signal. The ECM expects to sense no voltage on the EST line during this condition. If it senses voltage, it sets Code 42 and will not go into the EST mode.

When the rpm for EST is reached (approximately 400 rpm), the ECM applies 5 volts to the by-pass line and the EST should no longer be grounded in the HEI module, so the EST voltage should be varying.

If the by-pass line is open, the HEI module will not switch to the EST mode, so the EST voltage will be low and Code 42 will be set.

If the EST line is grounded, the HEI module will switch to the EST, but because the line is grounded, there will be no EST signal and the engine will not operate. A Code 42 may or may not be set.

NOTE: For in-depth diagnosis of the EST system, refer to Chilton's Electronic Engine Controls Manual.

ELECTRONIC SPARK CONTROL SYSTEM (ESC)

General Description

The Electronic Spark Control (ESC) operates in conjunction with the Electronic Spark Timing (EST) system and modifies (retards) the spark advance when detonation occurs. The retard mode is held for approximately 20 seconds after which the spark control will again revert to the Electronic Spark Timing (EST) system. There are three basic components of the Electronic Spark Control (ESC) system.

SENSOR

The Electronic Spark Control (ESC) sensor detects the presence (or absence) and intensity of the detonation by the vibration characteristics of the engine. The output is an electrical signal that goes to the controller. A sensor failure would allow no spark retard.

DISTRIBUTOR

The distributor is an HEI/EST unit with an electronic module, modified so it can respond to the ESC controller signal. This command is delayed when detonation is occurring, thus providing the level of spark retard required. The amount of spark retard is a function of the degree of detonation.

CONTROLLER

The Electronic Spark Control (ESC) controller processes the sensor signal into a command signal to the distributor, to adjust the spark timing. The process is continuous, so that the presence of detonation is monitored and controlled. The controller is a hard wired signal processor and amplifier which operates from 6-16 volts. Controller failure would be no ignition, no retard or full retard. The controller has no memory storage.

CODE 43

Should a Code 43 be set in the ECM memory, it would indicate that the ESC system retard signal has been sensed by the ECM for too long a period of time. When voltage at terminal **L** of the ECM is low, spark timing is retarded. Normal voltage in the non-retarded mode is approximately 7.5 volts or more.

BASIC IGNITION TIMING

Basic ignition timing is critical to the proper operation of the ESC system. Always follow the Vehicle Emission Control Information label procedures when adjusting ignition timing.

Some engines will incorporate a magnetic timing probe hole for use with special electronic timing equipment. Consult the manufacturer's instructions for the use of this electronic timing equipment.

NOTE: For indepth diagnosis of the ESC system, refer to Chilton's Electronic Engine Controls manual.

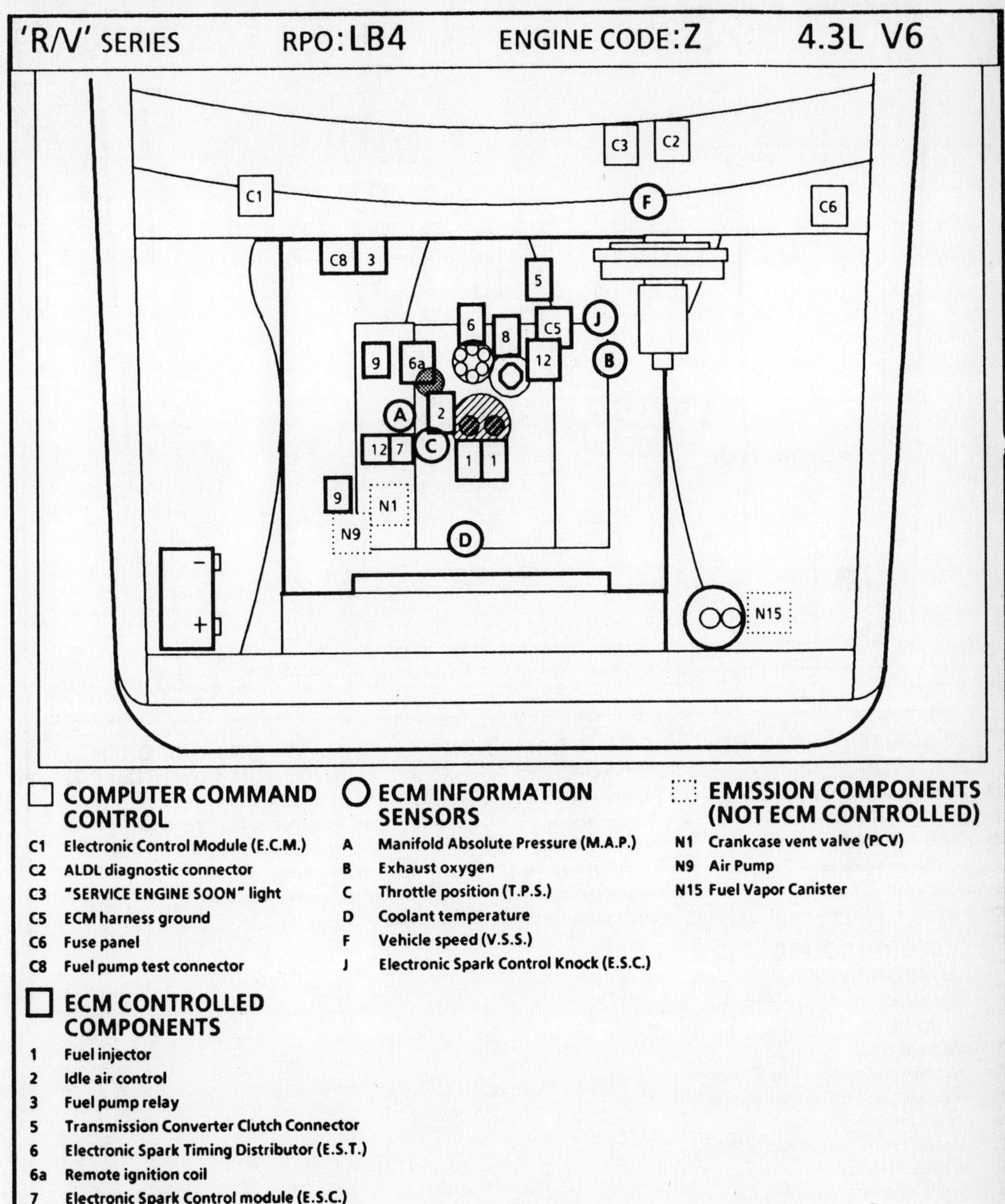
'R/V' SERIES
RPO: LB4
ENGINE CODE: Z
4.3L V6
C3
C2
C1
F
C6
C8
3
5
6
8
C5
J
9
6a
12
B
A
2
12
7
C
1
1
9
N1
N9
D
N15
COMPUTER COMMAND CONTROL
C1 Electronic Control Module (E.C.M.)
C2 ALDL diagnostic connector
C3 "SERVICE ENGINE SOON" light
C5 ECM harness ground
C6 Fuse panel
C8 Fuel pump test connector
ECM CONTROLLED COMPONENTS
1 Fuel injector
2 Idle air control
3 Fuel pump relay
5 Transmission Converter Clutch Connector
6 Electronic Spark Timing Distributor (E.S.T.)
6a Remote ignition coil
7 Electronic Spark Control module (E.S.C.)
8 Oil pressure switch
9 Electric Air Control solenoid (E.A.C.)
12 Exhaust Gas Recirculation Vacuum Solenoid
ECM INFORMATION SENSORS
A Manifold Absolute Pressure (M.A.P.)
B Exhaust oxygen
C Throttle position (T.P.S.)
D Coolant temperature
F Vehicle speed (V.S.S.)
J Electronic Spark Control Knock (E.S.C.)
EMISSION COMPONENTS (NOT ECM CONTROLLED)
N1 Crankcase vent valve (PCV)
N9 Air Pump
N15 Fuel Vapor Canister

Component locations for R and V series with the 6–4.3L engine

'C/K' SERIES RPO: L03/L05 ENGINE CODE: H/K 5.0/5.7L V8

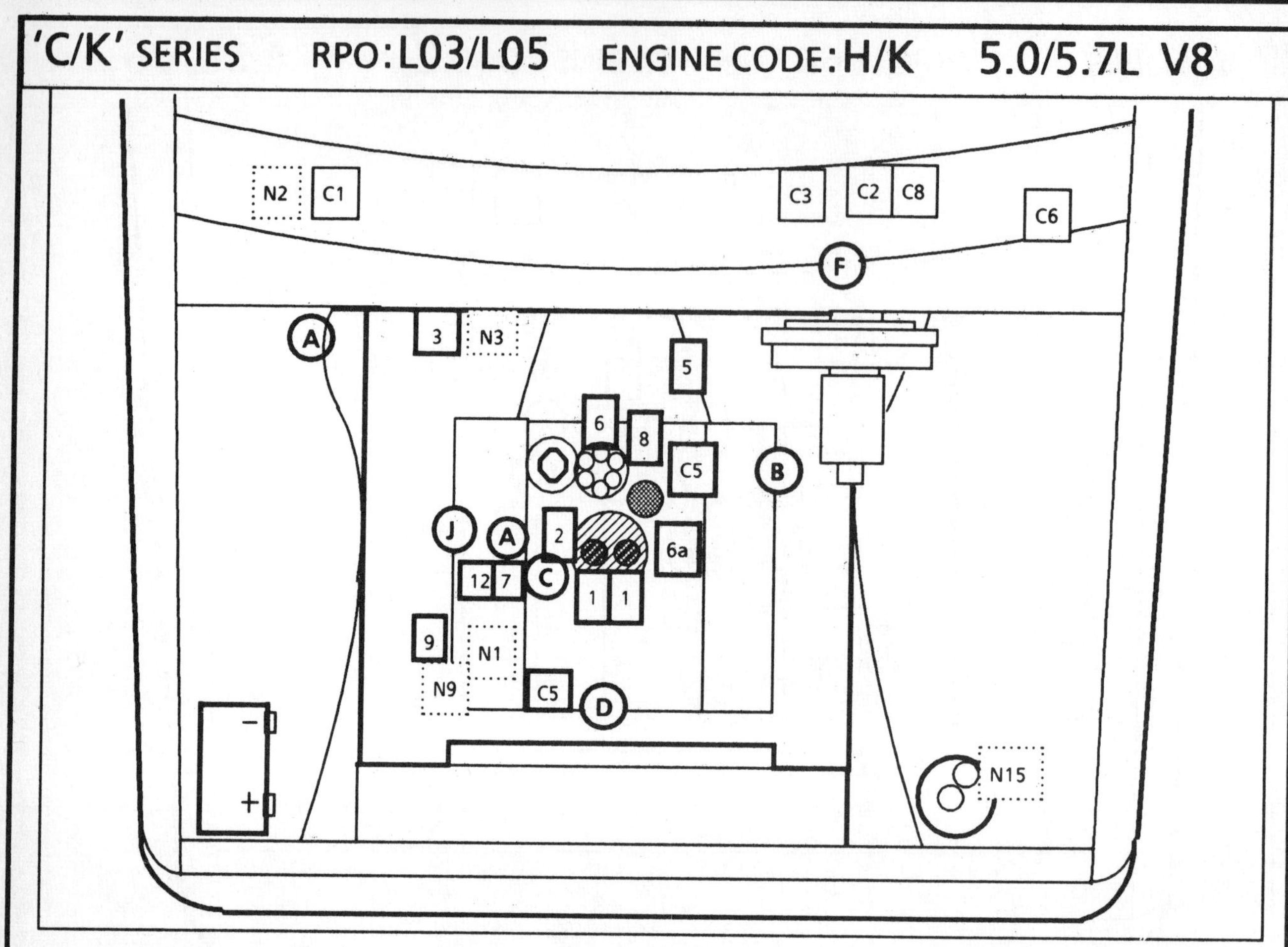

COMPUTER COMMAND CONTROL

- C1 Electronic Control Module (E.C.M.)
- C2 ALDL diagnostic connector
- C3 "SERVICE ENGINE SOON" light
- C5 ECM harness ground
- C6 Fuse panel
- C8 Fuel pump test connector

ECM CONTROLLED COMPONENTS

- 1 Fuel injector
- 2 Idle air control
- 3 Fuel pump relay
- 5 Transmission Converter Clutch Connector
- 6 Electronic Spark Timing Distributor (E.S.T.)
- 6a Remote ignition coil
- 7 Electronic Spark Control module (E.S.C.)
- 8 Oil pressure switch
- 9 Electric Air Control solenoid (E.A.C.)
- 12 Exhaust Gas Recirculation Vacuum Solenoid

ECM INFORMATION SENSORS

- A Manifold Absolute Pressure (M.A.P.)
- B Exhaust oxygen
- C Throttle position (T.P.S.)
- D Coolant temperature
- F Vehicle speed (V.S.S.)
- J Electronic Spark Control Knock (E.S.C.)

EMISSION COMPONENTS (NOT ECM CONTROLLED)

- N1 Crankcase vent valve (PCV)
- N2 Fuel Module (5.7L H.D. only)
- N3 Downshift Relay (THM 400 only)
- N9 Air Pump
- N15 Fuel Vapor Canister

Component locations for C and K series with the 8–5.0L and 8–5.7L engine

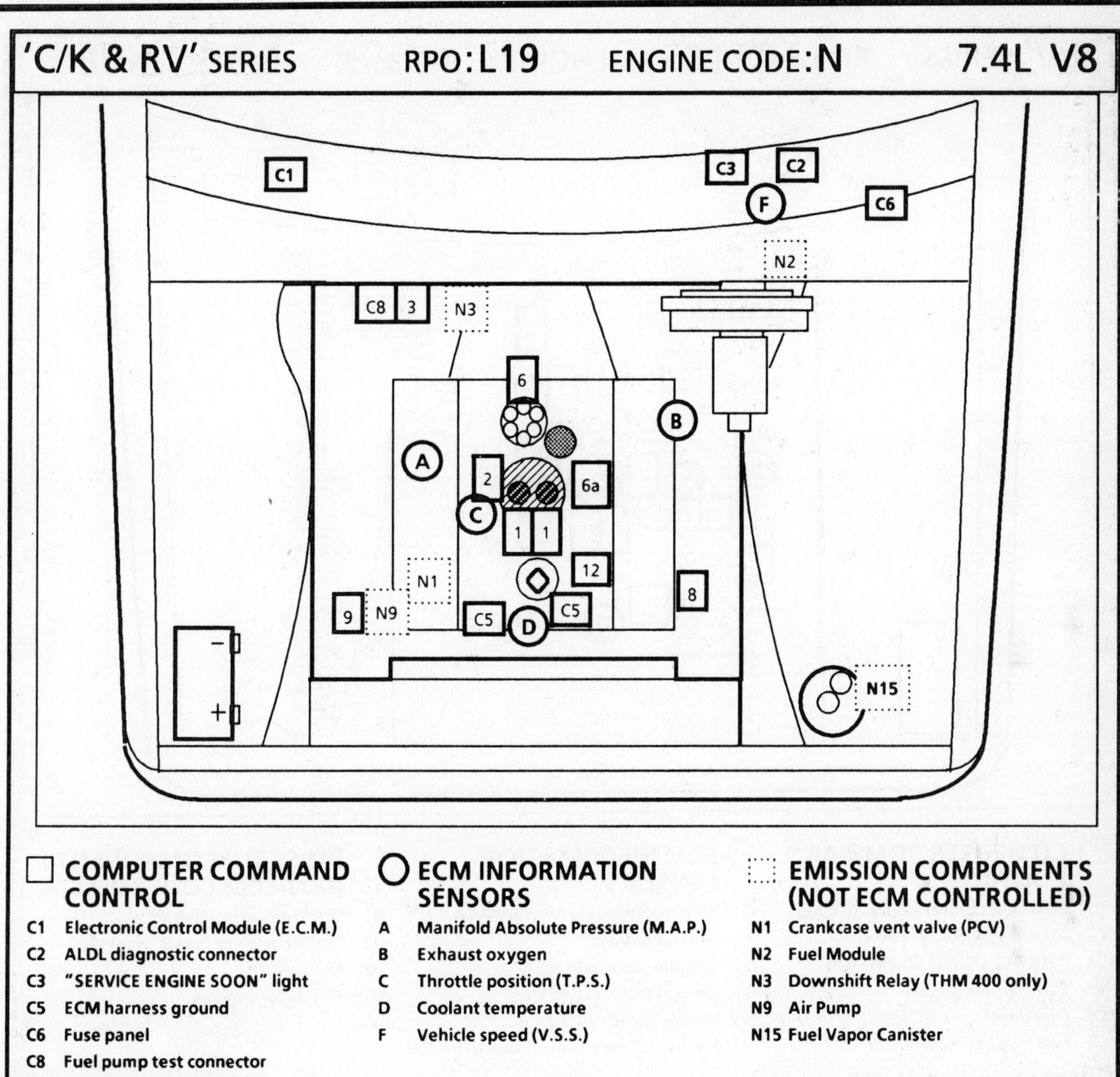

☐ **COMPUTER COMMAND CONTROL**

- C1 Electronic Control Module (E.C.M.)
- C2 ALDL diagnostic connector
- C3 "SERVICE ENGINE SOON" light
- C5 ECM harness ground
- C6 Fuse panel
- C8 Fuel pump test connector

☐ **ECM CONTROLLED COMPONENTS**

- 1 Fuel injector
- 2 Idle air control
- 3 Fuel pump relay
- 6 Electronic Spark Timing Distributor (E.S.T.)
- 6a Remote ignition coil
- 8 Oil pressure switch
- 9 Electric Air Control solenoid (E.A.C.)
- 12 Exhaust Gas Recirculation Vacuum Solenoid

○ **ECM INFORMATION SENSORS**

- A Manifold Absolute Pressure (M.A.P.)
- B Exhaust oxygen
- C Throttle position (T.P.S.)
- D Coolant temperature
- F Vehicle speed (V.S.S.)

⬚ **EMISSION COMPONENTS (NOT ECM CONTROLLED)**

- N1 Crankcase vent valve (PCV)
- N2 Fuel Module
- N3 Downshift Relay (THM 400 only)
- N9 Air Pump
- N15 Fuel Vapor Canister

Component locations for all series with the 8–7.4L engine

'R/V' SERIES RPO: L03/L05 ENGINE CODE: H/K 5.0/5.7L V8

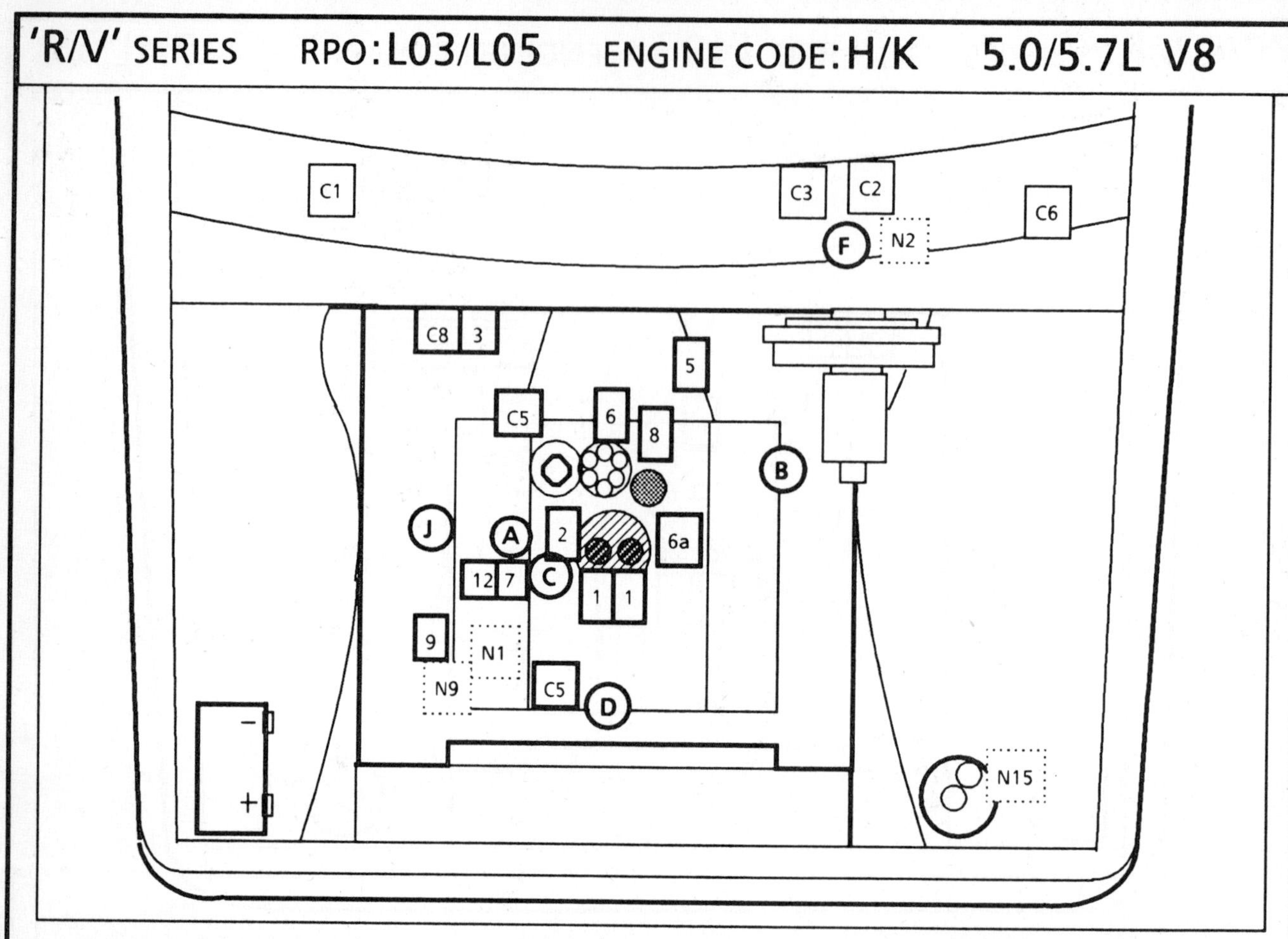

COMPUTER COMMAND CONTROL

- C1 Electronic Control Module (E.C.M.)
- C2 ALDL diagnostic connector
- C3 "SERVICE ENGINE SOON" light
- C5 ECM harness ground
- C6 Fuse panel
- C8 Fuel pump test connector

ECM CONTROLLED COMPONENTS

- 1 Fuel injector
- 2 Idle air control
- 3 Fuel pump relay
- 5 Transmission Converter Clutch Connector
- 6 Electronic Spark Timing Distributor (E.S.T.)
- 6a Remote ignition coil
- 7 Electronic Spark Control module (E.S.C.)
- 8 Oil pressure switch
- 9 Electric Air Control solenoid (E.A.C.)
- 12 Exhaust Gas Recirculation Vacuum Solenoid

ECM INFORMATION SENSORS

- A Manifold Absolute Pressure (M.A.P.)
- B Exhaust oxygen
- C Throttle position (T.P.S.)
- D Coolant temperature
- F Vehicle speed (V.S.S.)
- J Electronic Spark Control Knock (E.S.C.)

EMISSION COMPONENTS (NOT ECM CONTROLLED)

- N1 Crankcase vent valve (PCV)
- N2 Fuel Module (5.7L H.D. only)
- N9 Air Pump
- N15 Fuel Vapor Canister

Component locations for R and V series with the 8– 5.0L and 8–5.7L engine

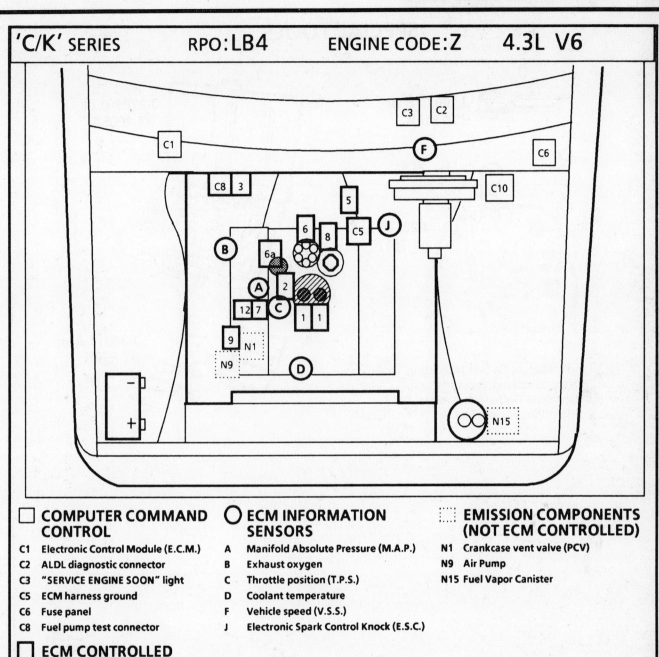

'C/K' SERIES RPO:LB4 ENGINE CODE:Z 4.3L V6

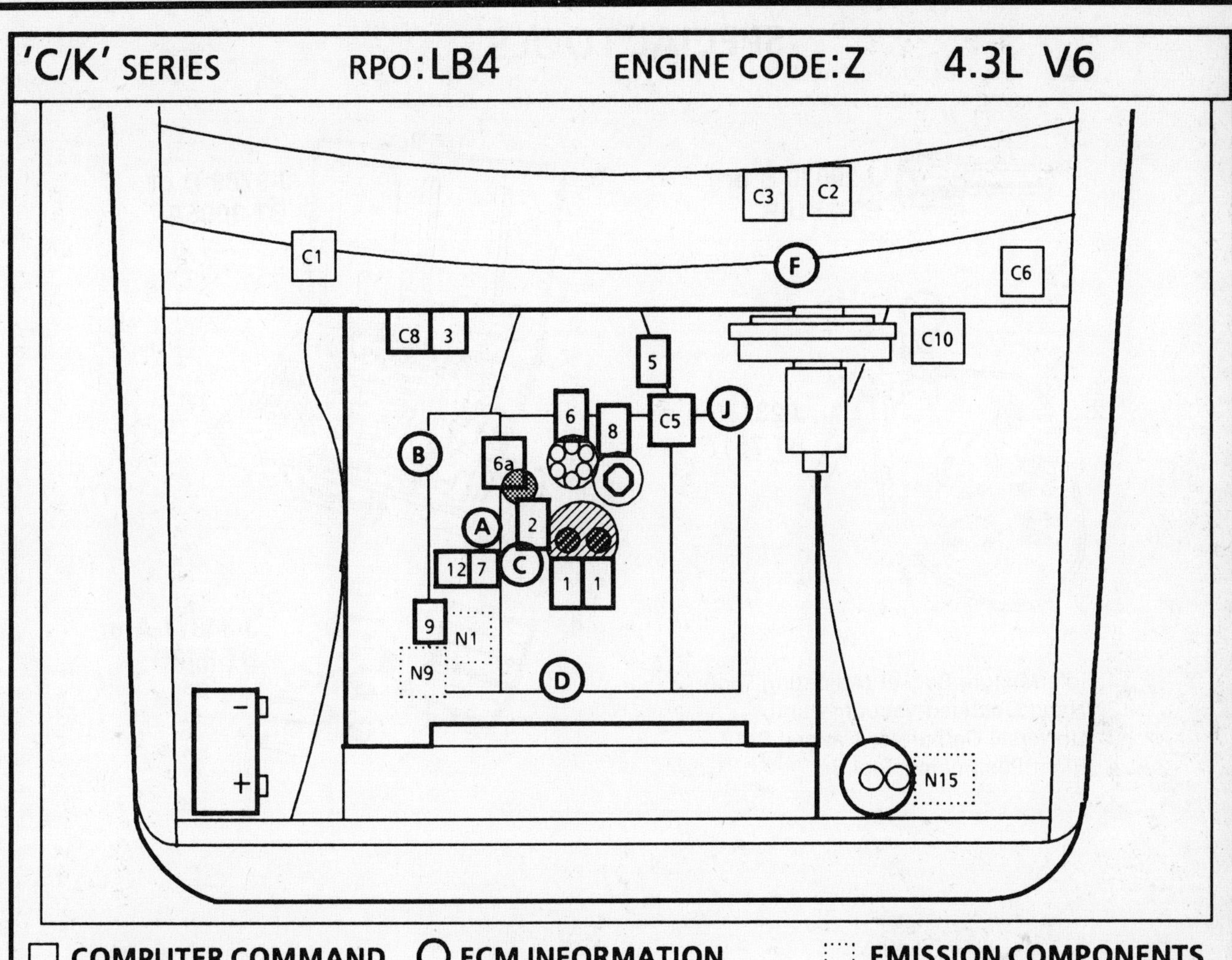

COMPUTER COMMAND CONTROL

- C1 Electronic Control Module (E.C.M.)
- C2 ALDL diagnostic connector
- C3 "SERVICE ENGINE SOON" light
- C5 ECM harness ground
- C6 Fuse panel
- C8 Fuel pump test connector

ECM CONTROLLED COMPONENTS

- 1 Fuel injector
- 2 Idle air control
- 3 Fuel pump relay
- 5 Transmission Converter Clutch Connector
- 6 Electronic Spark Timing Distributor (E.S.T.)
- 6a Remote ignition coil
- 7 Electronic Spark Control module (E.S.C.)
- 8 Oil pressure switch
- 9 Electric Air Control solenoid (E.A.C.)
- 12 Exhaust Gas Recirculation Vacuum Solenoid

ECM INFORMATION SENSORS

- A Manifold Absolute Pressure (M.A.P.)
- B Exhaust oxygen
- C Throttle position (T.P.S.)
- D Coolant temperature
- F Vehicle speed (V.S.S.)
- J Electronic Spark Control Knock (E.S.C.)

EMISSION COMPONENTS (NOT ECM CONTROLLED)

- N1 Crankcase vent valve (PCV)
- N9 Air Pump
- N15 Fuel Vapor Canister

Component locations for C and K series with the 6–4.3L engine

SPECIAL TOOLS

1. 

2. 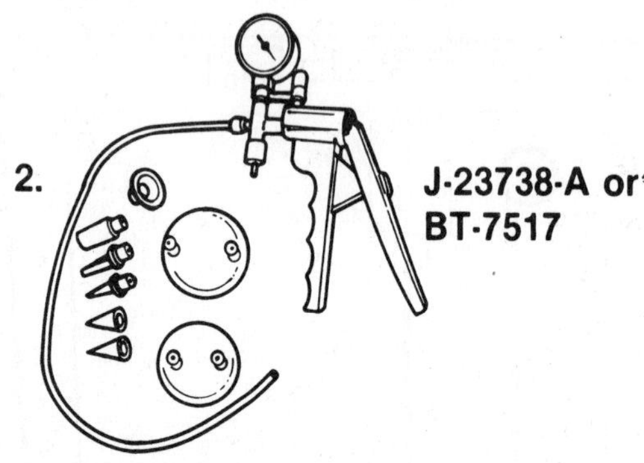

3. 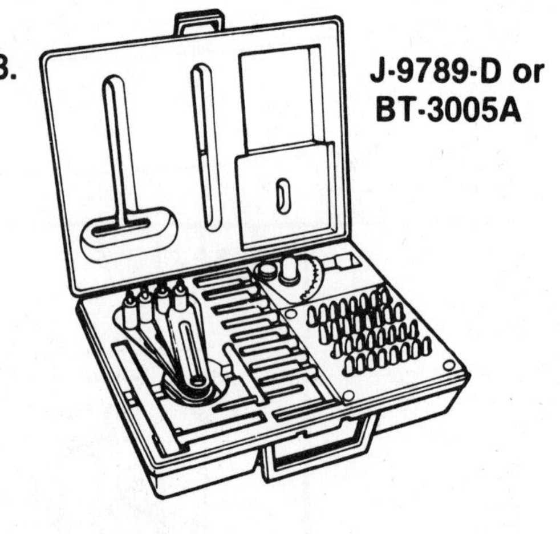

4. 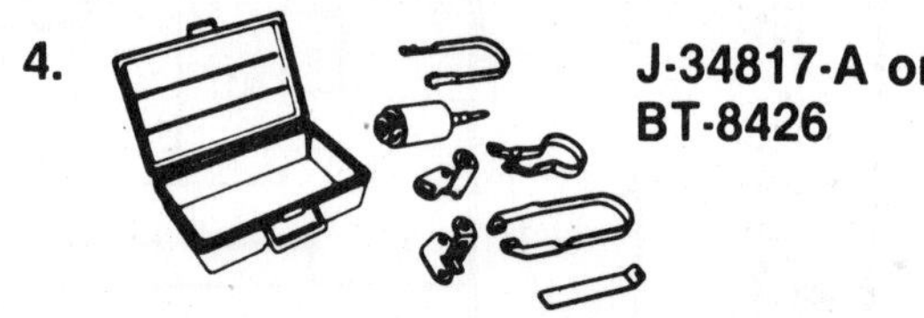

1. Idle Mixture Socket (Adjusting Tool)
2. Hand Operated Vacuum Pump
3. Universal Carburetor Gauged Set
4. Float Positioning Tool Set

5 Fuel System

QUICK REFERENCE INDEX

GENERAL INDEX

CARBURETED GASOLINE ENGINE FUEL SYSTEM

Troubleshooting Basic Fuel System Problems

Problem	Cause	Solution
Engine cranks, but won't start (or is hard to start) when cold	· Empty fuel tank · Incorrect starting procedure · Defective fuel pump · No fuel in carburetor · Clogged fuel filter · Engine flooded · Defective choke	· Check for fuel in tank · Follow correct procedure · Check pump output · Check for fuel in the carburetor · Replace fuel filter · Wait 15 minutes; try again · Check choke plate
Engine cranks, but is hard to start (or does not start) when hot—(presence of fuel is assumed)	· Defective choke	· Check choke plate
Rough idle or engine runs rough	· Dirt or moisture in fuel · Clogged air filter · Faulty fuel pump	· Replace fuel filter · Replace air filter · Check fuel pump output
Engine stalls or hesitates on acceleration	· Dirt or moisture in the fuel · Dirty carburetor · Defective fuel pump · Incorrect float level, defective accelerator pump	· Replace fuel filter · Clean the carburetor · Check fuel pump output · Check carburetor
Poor gas mileage	· Clogged air filter · Dirty carburetor · Defective choke, faulty carburetor adjustment	· Replace air filter · Clean carburetor · Check carburetor
Engine is flooded (won't start accompanied by smell of raw fuel)	· Improperly adjusted choke or carburetor	· Wait 15 minutes and try again, without pumping gas pedal · If it won't start, check carburetor

Only the 6–4.8L and 8–5.7L are equipped with a carburetor. The 6–4.8L uses a Rochester 1MEF 1-bbl; the 8–5.7L uses the Rochester M4MEF 4-bbl.

Mechanical Fuel Pump

The fuel pump is a single action AC diaphragm type. The pump is operated by an eccentric on the camshaft.

On the 6–4.8L, the eccentric acts directly on the pump rocker arm.

On the 8–5.7L, a pushrod between the camshaft eccentric and the fuel pump operates the pump rocker arm.

TESTING THE FUEL PUMP

Fuel pumps should always be tested on the vehicle. The larger line between the pump and tank is the suction side of the system and the smaller line, between the pump and carburetor, is the pressure side. A leak in the pressure side would be apparent because of dripping fuel. A leak in the suction side is usually only apparent because of a reduced volume of fuel delivered to the pressure side.

1. Tighten any loose line connections and look for any kinks or restrictions.

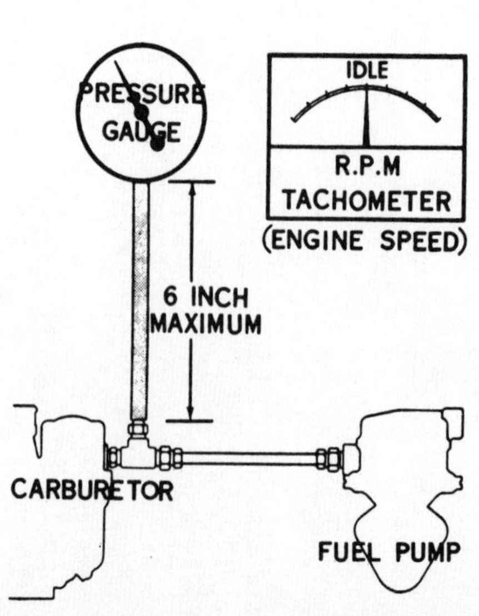

Pressure testing the mechanical fuel pump

2. Disconnect the fuel line at the carburetor. Disconnect the distributor-to-coil primary wire. Place a container at the end of the fuel line and crank the engine a few revolutions. If little or no fuel flows from the line, either the fuel pump is inoperative or the line is plugged. Blow through the lines with compressed air and try the test again. Reconnect the line.

3. If fuel flows in good volume, check the fuel pump pressure to be sure.

4. Attach a pressure gauge to the pressure side of the fuel line. On trucks equipped with a vapor return system, squeeze off the return hose.

5. Run the engine at idle and note the reading on the gauge. Stop the engine and compare the reading with the specifications listed in the Tune-Up Specifications chart. If the pump is operating properly, the pressure will be as specified and will be constant at idle speed. If pressure varies sporadically or is too high or low, the pump should be replaced.

6. Remove the pressure gauge.

The following flow test can also be performed:

1. Disconnect the fuel line from the carburetor. Run the fuel line into a suitable measuring container.

2. Run the engine at idle until there is one pint of fuel in the container. One pint should be pumped in 30 seconds or less.

3. If the flow is below minimum, check for a restriction in the line.

The only way to check fuel pump pressure is by connecting an accurate pressure gauge to the fuel line at the carburetor level. Never replace a fuel pump without performing this simple test. If the engine seems to be starving out, check the ignition system first. Also check for a plugged fuel filter or a restricted fuel line before replacing the pump.

REMOVAL AND INSTALLATION

CAUTION

Never smoke when working around gasoline! Avoid all sources of sparks or ignition. Gasoline vapors are EXTREMELY volatile!

NOTE: When you connect the fuel pump outlet fitting, always use 2 wrenches to avoid damaging the pump.

6–4.8L

1. Disconnect the fuel intake and outlet lines at the pump and plug the pump intake line.

2. Remove the two pump mounting bolts and lockwashers; remove the pump and its gasket.

3. Install the fuel pump with a new gasket reversing the removal procedure. Coat the mating surfaces with sealer.

4. Connect the fuel lines and check for leaks.

8–5.7L

1. Disconnect the fuel intake and outlet lines at the pump and plug the pump intake line.

2. You can remove the upper bolt from the right front engine mounting boss (on the front of the block) and insert a long bolt (3/8 in.–16 × 2 in.) to hold the fuel pump pushrod.

3. Remove the two pump mounting bolts and lockwashers; remove the pump and its gasket.

4. If the rocker arm pushrod is to be removed, remove the two adapter bolts and lockwashers and remove the adapter and its gasket.

5. Install the fuel pump with a new gasket reversing the removal procedure. Heavy grease can be used to hold the fuel pump pushrod up when installing the pump, if you didn't install the long bolt in Step 2. Coat the mating surfaces with sealer.

6. Connect the fuel lines an check for leaks.

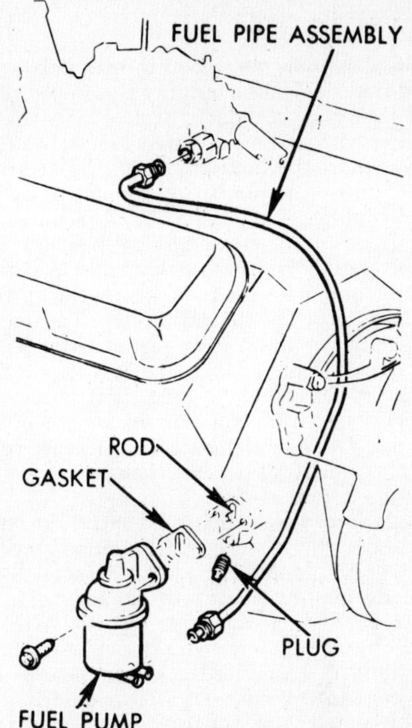

Typical mechanical fuel pump installation

Carburetor

DESCRIPTION AND OPERATING PRINCIPALS

6–4.8L

The carburetors are 1–barrel, single stage units. The "M" in the model identification number indicates that the carburetor is of a Modified primary metering "open loop" design. The "E" indicates that it has an inetgral, electric choke and the "F" indicates that it has an adjustable wide-open mixture control.

These models have three major assemblies: the air horn, float bowl, and throttle body. They have six basic operating systems:

1. Float
2. Idle
3. Main Metering
4. Power
5. Pump
6. Choke

8–5.7L

These Rochester models are four barrel, two stage carburetors with three major assemblies: the air horn, float bowl, and throttle body. They have six basic operating systems:

1. Float
2. Idle
3. Main Metering
4. Power
5. Pump
6. Choke

The first "M" in the model identification number indicates that the carburetor is of a Modified primary metering "open loop" design. The "4M" is the model designation, indicating it is a four barrel carburetor. The remaining letters designate specific features as follows:

- C – It has an integral Hot Air Choke.

• D – Dual capacity pump valve and a combined mixture control/dual capacity pump solenoid assembly.
• E – Has an electric choke.
• F – Has an adjustable wide open throttle mixture control.

The carburetor identification number is stamped vertically on the float bowl near the secondary throttle lever. Refer to this number before servicing the carburetor. If replacing the float bowl assembly, follow the instructions in the service package and stamp or engrave the number on the new float bowl.

A single float chamber supplies fuel to all carburetor bores. A float, float needle with pull clip and a float needle seat are used to control the level of fuel in the float chamber. A vacuum-operated power piston and metering rods control the air/fuel metering in the primary bores of the carburetor. Tapered metering rods are attached to the power valve piston assembly and move in fixed metering jets to provide the fuel flow for varying engine demands. A factory-set adjustable part throttle screw, used on all models, precisely positions the tapered portion of the metering rods in the jets. On M4MEF models, the factory-set rich stop adjusting bushing precisely positions the enrichment portion of the metering rods in the jets.

Air valves and tapered metering rods control the air/fuel mixture in the secondary bores during increased engine air flow at wide open throttle. On M4MEF models, the factory-set secondary well air bleed adjusting screw provides additional control of the air/fuel mixture during wide open throttle (WOT).

The accelerator pump system on all models uses a throttle actuated pump plunger, operating in the pump well. The pump provides extra fuel during quick throttle openings.

An electrically heated choke coil provides the choke valve closing force for cold startup and for correct opening time during warm-up. A vacuum break assembly(ies) controls initial choke valve opening at startup to provide sufficient air flow to the engine. An unloader tang on the throttle lever forces the choke valve to open to purge a flooded engine when the accelerator is pressed to the floor. The fast idle cam, following choke valve movement, acts as a graduated throttle stop to provide increased idle speed during warm-up.

The electric Idle Stop Solenoid (ISS) on Federal V8 engines with manual transmission provides the desired engine idle speed, and prevents dieseling when the ignition is switched off. A vacuum-operated Throttle Kicker assembly on California V8 engines retards throttle closing during deceleration to improve emission control. Vacuum to the kicker is controlled by the Throttle Return Control system.

1MEF 1-BBL FUNCTIONAL TESTS

Choke Checking Procedure (Engine Off)

1. Remove the air cleaner assembly.
2. Hold the throttle half way down.
3. Open and close the choke several times. Be sure all links are connected and not damaged. Choke valve, linkage, and fast idle cam must operate freely.
4. If the choke valve, linkage or fast idle cam is sticking due to varnish, clean with choke cleaner.
5. Do not lubricate linkage, as lubricant will collect dust and cause sticking.

Checking Vacuum Break

A hand-operated vacuum pump such as J-23738-A or equivalent will be needed for this procedure.

1. If the vacuum break has an air bleed hole, plug it during this checking procedure.
2. Apply 15 in.Hg vacuum to the vacuum break with the hand pump.
   a. Apply finger pressure to see if the plunger has moved through full travel. If not, replace the vacuum break.
   b. Observe the vacuum gauge. Vacuum should hold vacuum for at least twenty seconds. If not, replace the vacuum break.
3. Replace vacuum break hoses that are cracked, cut or hardened.

Checking Idle Stop Solenoid (ISS)

A non-functioning idle stop solenoid (if equipped) could cause stalling or rough idle.

1. Turn the ignition ON, but do not start the engine.
2. Open the throttle momentarily to allow the solenoid plunger to extend.
3. Disconnect the wire at the solenoid. The plunger should drop back from the throttle lever. If not, back out (counterclockwise) the ⅛ in. hex screw 1 full turn. Reconnect the wire and repeat this step.
4. Connect the solenoid wire. The plunger should move out and contact the throttle lever.
5. If the plunger does not move in and out as the wire is disconnected and connected, or, if the plunger can be pushed back and forth with light finger pressure when the wire is connected, check the voltage across the feed wire:
   a. If 12–15 volts are present in the feed wire, replace the solenoid.
   b. If the voltage is low, locate the cause of the open circuit in the solenoid feed wire and repair as necessary.

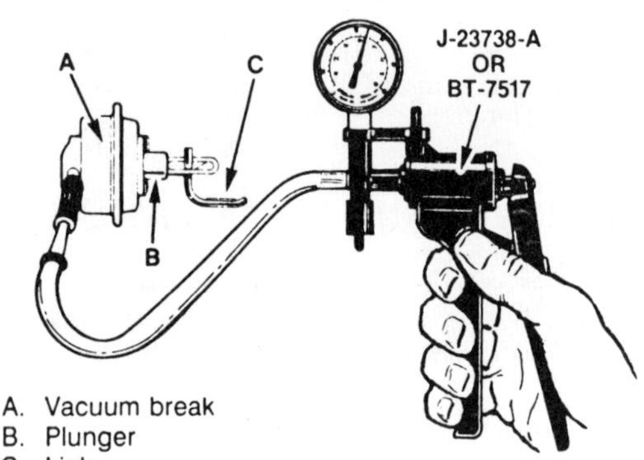

Vacuum break functional test – 1bbl

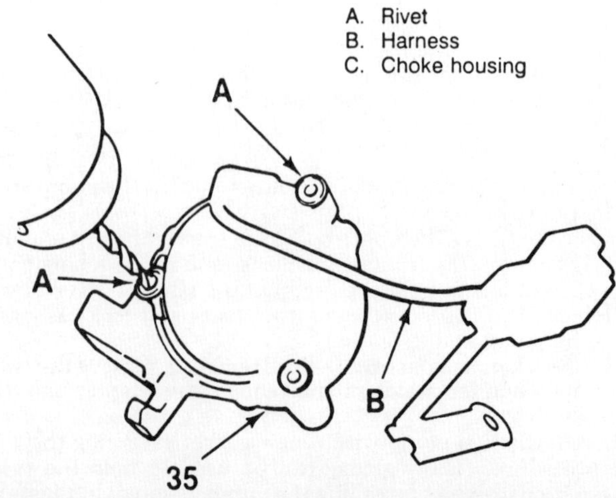

Removing the choke cap rivets

1MEF 1-BBL ADJUSTMENTS

Fast Idle

1. Check and adjust the idle speed.
2. With the engine at normal operating temperature, air cleaner ON, EGR valve signal line disconnected and plugged and the air conditioning OFF, connect a tachometer.
3. Disconnect the vacuum advance hose at the distributor and plug the line.
4. With the transmission in Neutral, start the engine and set the fast idle cam follower on the high step of the cam.
5. Bend the tank in or out to obtain the fast idle speed shown on your underhood sticker.

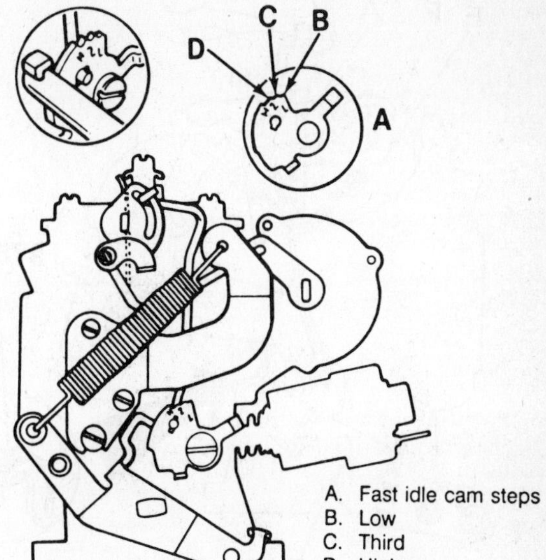

Fast idle speed adjustment – 1bbl

Fast Idle Cam

1. Check and adjust the fast idle speed.
2. Set the fast idle cam follower on the second step of the cam.
3. Apply force to the choke coil rod and hold the choke valve toward the closed position.
4. Measure the clearance between the lower edge of the choke valve and the inside of the air horn wall. The gap should be 7mm (0.275 in.).
5. Bend the fast idle cam link at the upper end, to obtain the correct clearance.

Choke Unloader

1. Hold the choke valve down by applying light force to the choke coil lever.
2. Open the throttle valve to wide open.
3. Measure the clearance between the lower edge of the choke valve and the air horn wall. The gap should be 13mm (0.52 in.).
4. If adjustment is necessary, bend the unloader tang on the throttle lever.

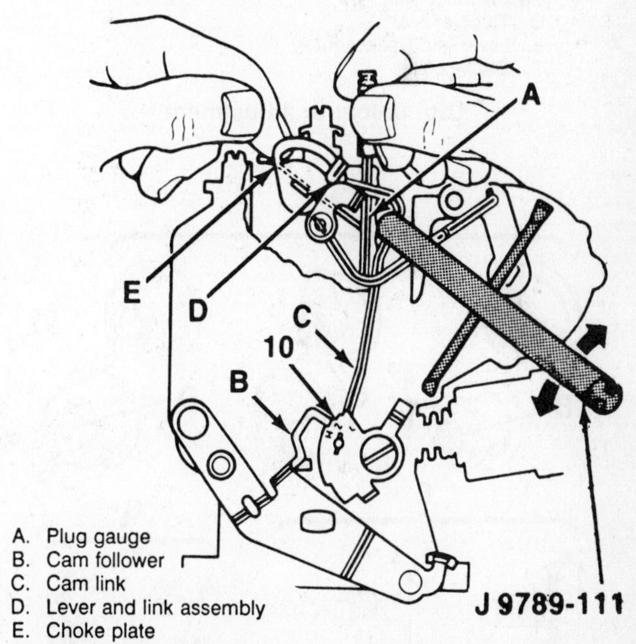

1bbl fast idle cam adjustment

Choke Coil Rod

1. Place the cam follower on the highest step of the fast idle cam.
2. Hold the choke valve completely closed.
3. A 3mm (0.120 in.) plug gauge must pass through the hole in the lever attached to the choke coil housing and enter the hole in the casting.
4. Bend the choke link to adjust.

Primary Vacuum Break

1. Place the fast idle cam follower on highest step of the fast idle cam.
2. Plug purge bleed hole in the vacuum break with masking tape. Not all models will have this hole.
3. Using an outside vacuum source, apply 15 in.Hg of vacuum to the primary vacuum break diaphragm. Push down on the choke valve. Make sure the plunger is fully extended.
4. Insert a 5mm (0.2 in.) gauge between the lower edge of the choke valve and the air horn wall.
5. Bend vacuum break rod for adjustment.
6. After adjustment, check for binding or interference. Remove tape.

Metering Rod Adjustment

1. Remove the air horn and gasket.
2. Remove metering rod by holding throttle valve wide open. Push downward on metering rod against spring tension, then slide metering rod out of slot in holder and remove from main metering jet.
3. Back out idle stop solenoid to allow the throttle valve to close completely. Hold throttle valve in the completely closed position.
4. Hold power piston down and swing metering rod holder over flat surface (gasket removed) of bowl casting next to carburetor bore.
5. Using a 2.3mm (0.09 in.) gauge, measure the distance between the end of the metering rod holder and the mating (gasket) surface of the float bowl.
6. Bend the hanger at the center point as necessary.
7. Hold the throttle wide open and position the metering rod in the main metering jet. Then, connect the rod to the power piston metering rod hanger with the metering rod spring on TOP of the hanger.

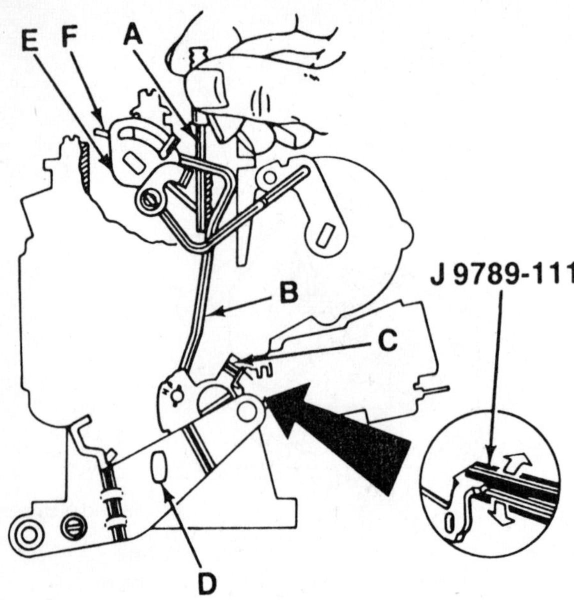

A. Plug gauge
B. Cam link
C. Unloader tang
D. Throttle lever
E. Lever and link assembly
F. Choke plate

1bbl unloader adjustment

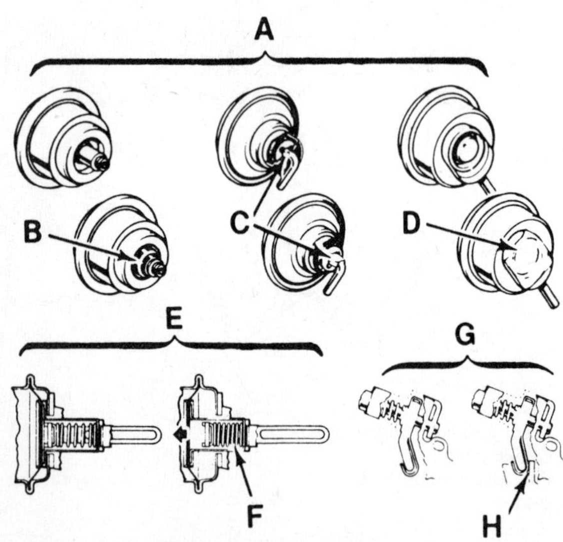

A. Plug the air bleed holes
B. Pump cup or valve stem seal
C. Tape hole in tube
D. Tape end of cover
E. Plunger bucking spring
F. Plunger stem extended
G. Leaf type bucking spring
H. Spring seated

Vacuum break adjustment preparation

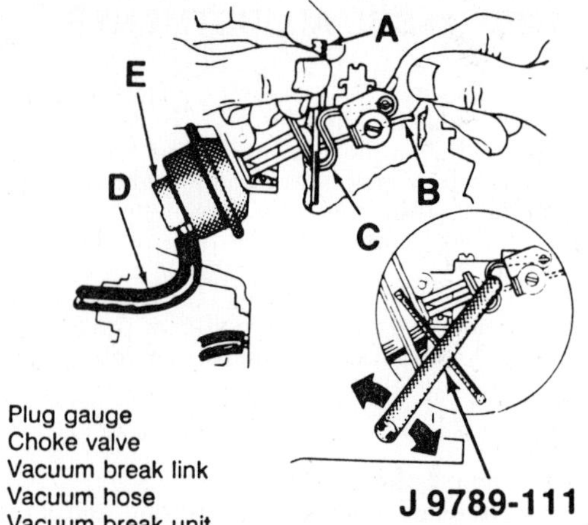

A. Plug gauge
B. Choke valve
C. Vacuum break link
D. Vacuum hose
E. Vacuum break unit

Vacuum break adjustment – 1bbl

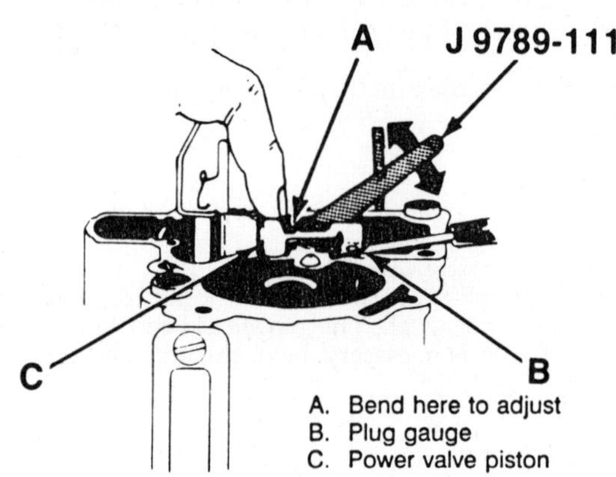

A. Bend here to adjust
B. Plug gauge
C. Power valve piston

Metering rod adjustment – 1bbl

Float Level

1. Remove the air horn and gasket.
2. Hold the float retainer in place, and hold the float arm against the top of the float needle by pushing down on the float arm at the outer end toward the float bowl casting.

NOTE: A special tool is available to make this job a little easier, but it's not absolutely necessary.

3. Using an adjustable T-scale, measure the distance from the toe of the float to the float bowl gasket surface. The distance should be 8.7mm ± 1.6mm ($^{11}/_{32}$ in. ± $^{1}/_{16}$ in.).

NOTE: The gauge should be held on the index point on the float for accurate measurement.

4. Adjust the float level by bending the float lever up or down at the float arm junction.

M4MEF 4-BBL FUNCTIONAL TESTS

Float Level External Test

This procedure requires the use of an external float level gauge tool No. J-34935-1 or equivalent.

1. With the engine idling and the choke valve wide open, insert tool J-34935-1 in the vent slot or vent hole. Allow the gauge to float freely.

NOTE: Do not press down on the gauge. Flooding or float damage could result.

2. Observe the mark on the gauge that lines up with the top

of the casting. The setting should be within $^1/_{16}$ in. (1.6mm) of the specified float level setting. Incorrect fuel pressure will adversely affect the fuel level.

3. If not within specification, remove the air horn and adjust the float.

Choke Checking Procedure (Engine Off)

1. Remove the air cleaner assembly.
2. Hold the throttle half way down.
3. Open and close the choke several times. Be sure all links are connected and not damaged. Choke valve, linkage, and fast idle cam must operate freely.
4. If the choke valve, linkage or fast idle cam is sticking due to varnish, clean with choke cleaner.
5. Do not lubricate linkage, as lubricant will collect dust and cause sticking.

Checking Electric Choke (On Vehicle)

1. Allow the choke thermostat to stabilize at about 70°F (21°C).
2. Open the throttle to allow the choke valve to close.
3. Start the engine and determine the length of time for the choke valve to reach full open position:
   a. If longer than five minutes, check the voltage at the choke stat connector, with the engine running.
   b. If voltage is between 12 and 15 volts, check for proper ground between choke cover and choke housing. If correct, replace choke cover assembly.
   c. If the voltage is low or zero, check all wires and connections.

Checking Vacuum Break

A hand-operated vacuum pump such as J-23738-A or equivalent will be needed for this procedure.

1. If the vacuum break has an air bleed hole, plug it during this checking procedure.
2. Apply 15 in.Hg vacuum to the vacuum break with the hand pump.
   a. Apply finger pressure to see if the plunger has moved through full travel. If not, replace the vacuum break.
   b. Observe the vacuum gauge. Vacuum should hold vacuum for at least twenty seconds. If not, replace the vacuum break.
3. Replace vacuum break hoses that are cracked, cut or hardened.

Checking Idle Stop Solenoid (ISS)

A non-functioning idle stop solenoid (if equipped) could cause stalling or rough idle.

1. Turn the ignition ON, but do not start the engine.
2. Open the throttle momentarily to allow the solenoid plunger to extend.
3. Disconnect the wire at the solenoid. The plunger should drop back from the throttle lever.
4. Connect the solenoid wire. The plunger should move out and contact the throttle lever.
5. If the plunger does not move in and out as the wire is disconnected and connected, check the voltage across the feed wire:
   a. If 12–15 volts are present in the feed wire, replace the solenoid.
   b. If the voltage is low, locate the cause of the open circuit in the solenoid feed wire and repair as necessary.

Checking Throttle Kicker

A hand-operated vacuum pump such as J-23738-A or equivalent will be needed for this procedure.

1. Hold the throttle half way open to allow the plunger to extend fully.
2. Apply 20 in.Hg vacuum to the throttle kicker with the hand vacuum pump.
   a. Apply finger pressure to the plunger to see if it has extended fully. If not, replace the throttle kicker.
   b. Observe the vacuum gauge. Vacuum should hold for at least twenty seconds. If not, replace the throttle kicker.
3. Release the vacuum to the throttle kicker.
4. If the plunger does not retract to its starting position, replace kicker.

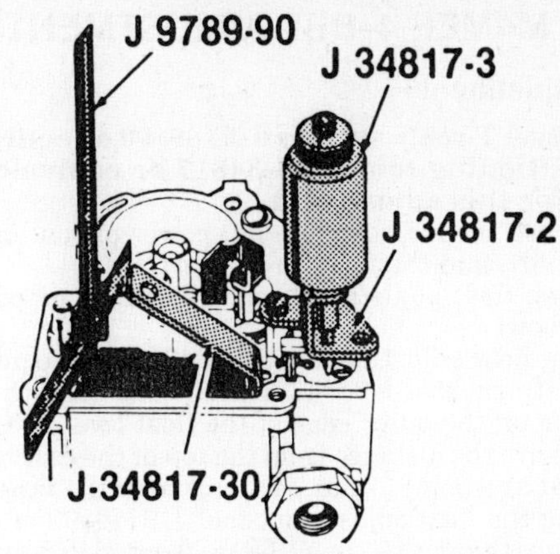

Float adjustment – 1bbl

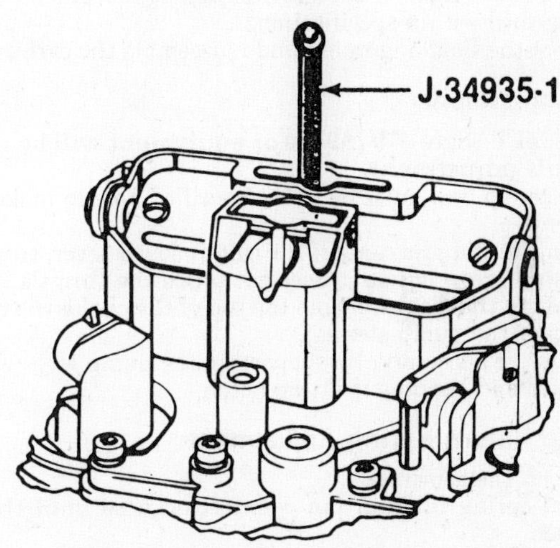

Float level external check – 4bbl

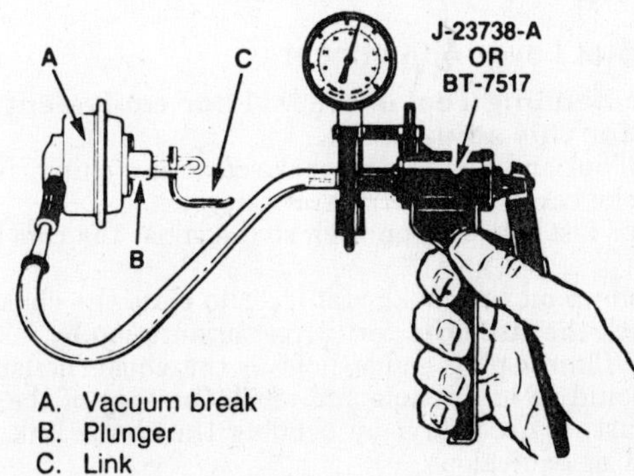

Vacuum break functional test – 4bbl

M4MEF 4-BBL ADJUSTMENTS

Float Adjustment

A float level T-scale such as J-9789-90 or equivalent and float positioning tool kit J-34817 or equivalent will be needed for this adjustment.

1. Remove the air horn, gasket, power piston and metering rod assembly, and the float bowl insert.
2. Attach float adjustment tool J-34817-1 or equivalent to the float bowl.
3. Place float adjustment tool J-34817-3 or equivalent into float adjustment tool J-34817-1 or equivalent, with the contact pin resting on the outer edge of the float lever.
4. Measure the distance from the top of the casting to the top of the float at a point $^3/_{16}$ in. (4.8mm) from the large end of the float using the float adjustment tool J-9789-90 or equivalent.
5. If more than $\pm$ $^1/_{16}$ in. (1.6mm) from specification, use the float gauge adjusting tool J-34817-25 or equivalent to bend the lever up or down. Remove the gauge adjusting tool and measure, repeating until within specifications.
6. Check the float alignment and reassemble the carburetor.

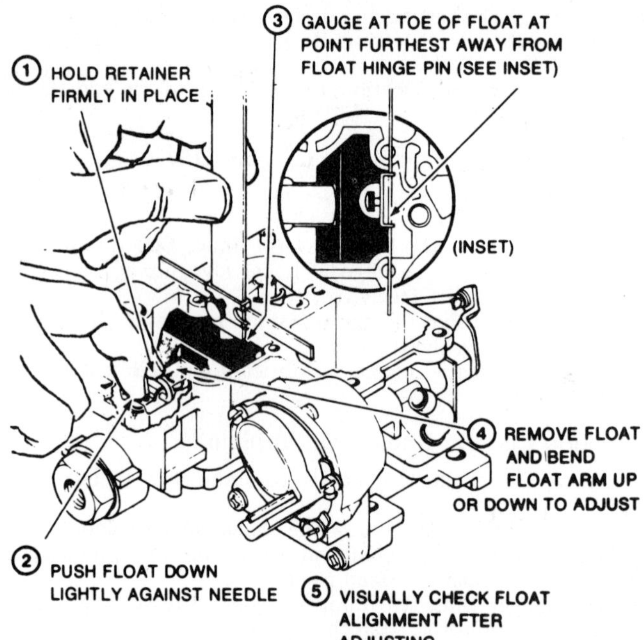

Float adjustment – 4bbl

Pump Adjustment

Float Level T-scale J-9789-90 or equivalent will be needed for this adjustment.

1. The pump link must be in the specified hole to make this adjustment.
2. With the fast idle cam off the cam follower lever, turn the throttle stop screw out so it does not touch the throttle lever.
3. Measure the distance from the top of the choke valve wall to the top of the pump stem.
4. Adjust, if necessary, by supporting the pump lever with a screwdriver and bending it at the notch.

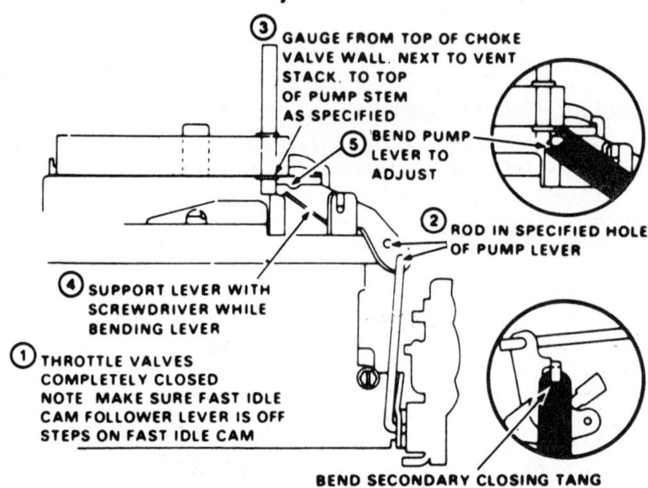

Pump adjustment – 4bbl

Air Valve Return Spring Adjustment

1. Loosen the setscrew.
2. Turn spring fulcrum pin counterclockwise until the air valves open.
3. Turn the pin clockwise until the air valves close, then the additional turns specified.
4. Tighten the setscrew. Apply lithium grease to the spring contact area.

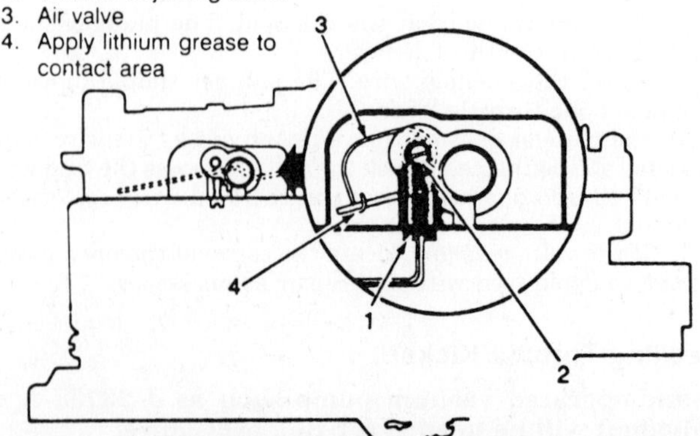

Air valve spring adjustment

Choke Stat Lever Adjustment

Linkage Bending Tool J-9789-111 or equivalent will be needed for this adjustment.

1. Drill out and remove the choke cover attaching rivets. Remove choke cover and thermostat assembly.
2. Place fast idle cam on high step against the cam follower lever.
3. Push up on the choke stat lever to close the choke valve.
4. Check the stat lever for correct orientation by inserting a 0.120 in. (3mm) plug gauge hole in the choke housing. The gauge should fit in the hole and touch the edge of the lever.
5. Adjust, if necessary, by bending the choke link with J-9789-111 or equivalent.

Choke Link and Fast Idle Cam Adjustment

Choke Valve Angle Gauge J-26701-A or equivalent will be needed for this adjustment.

1. Attach a rubber band to the vacuum break lever of the intermediate choke shaft.
2. Open the throttle to allow the choke valve to close.
3. Set up J-26701-A or equivalent and set the angle to specification as follows:
   a. Rotate the degree scale until zero is opposite the pointer.
   b. Center the leveling bubble.
   c. Rotate the scale to the specified angle.

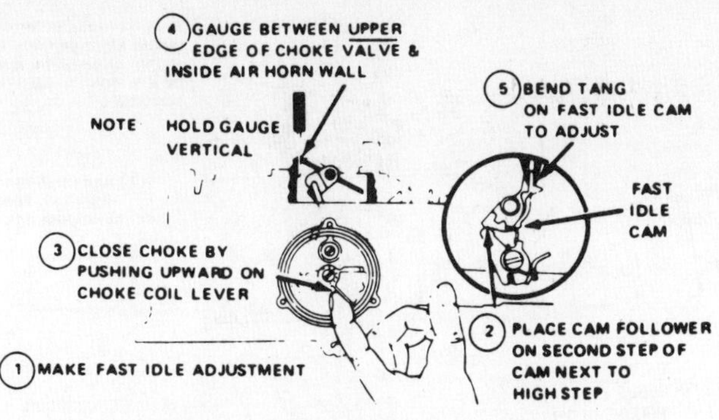

Choke rod adjustment – 4bbl

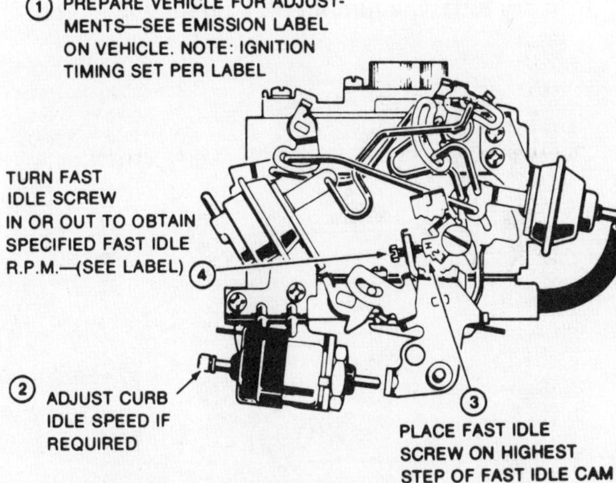

Fast idle adjustment, on vehicle – 4bbl

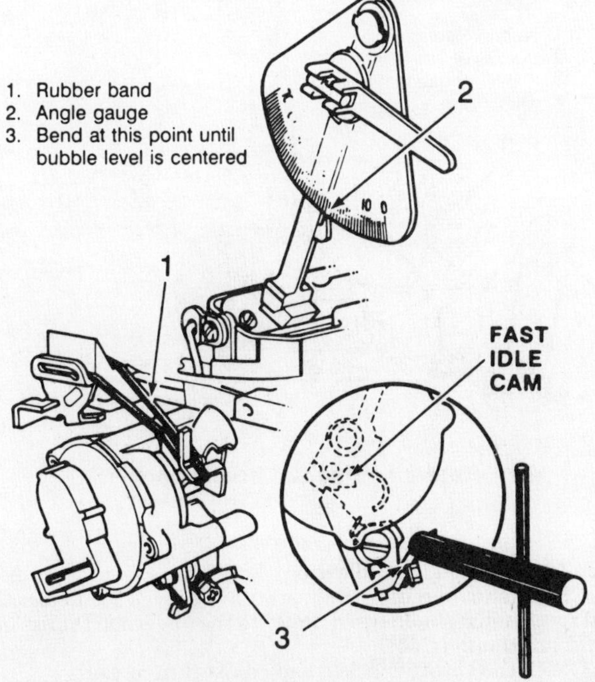

Fast idle adjustment, on vehicle

4. Place the fast idle cam on the second step against the cam follower lever, with the lever contacting the rise of the high step. If the lever does not contact the cam, turn the fast idle adjusting screw in additional turn(s).

NOTE: Final fast idle speed adjustment must be performed according to the underhood emission control information label.

5. Adjust, if bubble is not recentered, by bending the fast idle cam kick lever with pliers.

Primary Side Vacuum Break Adjustment

Choke Valve Angle Gauge J-26701-A and Hand Operated Vacuum Pump J-23738-A or equivalents, will be needed for this adjustment.

1. Attach rubber band to the vacuum break lever of the intermediate choke shaft.
2. Open the throttle to allow the choke valve to close.
3. Set up J-26701-A or equivalent and set angle to specifications.
4. Plug the vacuum break bleed holes, if applicable. Apply 15 in. Hg vacuum to seat the vacuum break plunger.
5. Seat the bucking spring, if so equipped. If necessary, bend the air valve link to permit full plunger travel, then re-apply vacuum to fully retract plunger.
6. Adjust, if bubble is not re-centered, by turning the vacuum break adjusting screw.

Secondary Side Vacuum Break Adjustment

Choke Valve Angle Gauge J-26701-A, Hand Operated Vacuum Pump J-23738-A and Linkage Bending Tool J-9789-111 or equivalents will be needed for this adjustment.

1. Attach a rubber band to the vacuum break lever of the intermediate choke shaft.
2. Open the throttle to allow the choke valve to close.
3. Set up J-26701-A or equivalent and set angle to specification.
4. Plug vacuum break bleed holes, if so equipped. Apply 15 in.Hg vacuum to seat the vacuum break plunger.
5. Compress the plunger bucking spring, if so equipped. If necessary, bend the air valve link to permit full plunger travel, then re-apply vacuum to fully retract the plunger.
6. Adjust, if bubble is not re-centered, by either supporting the link where shown and bending it with J-9789-111 or equivalent, or by turning the screw with a ⅛ in. hex wrench.

Air Valve Link Adjustment

Hand Operated Vacuum Pump J-23738-A and Linkage Bending Tool J-9789-111 or equivalents will be needed for this adjustment.

1. Plug vacuum break bleed holes, if applicable. With the air valves closed, apply 15 in.Hg vacuum to seat the vacuum break plunger.
2. Gauge the clearance between the air valve link and the end of the slot in the air valve lever. Clearance should be 0.025 in. (0.6mm).
3. Adjust, if necessary, by bending the link with J-9789-111 or equivalent.

Unloader Adjustment

Choke Valve Angle Gauge J-26701-A and Linkage Bending Tool J-9789-111 or equivalents will be needed for this adjustment.

1. Attach rubber band to the vacuum break lever of the intermediate choke shaft.
2. Open the throttle to allow the choke valve to close.
3. Set up J-26701-A or equivalent and set angle to specifications.

4. Hold the secondary lockout lever away from the pin.
5. Hold the throttle lever in wide open position.
6. Adjust, if bubble is not re-centered, by bending fast idle lever with J-9789-111 or equivalent.

Secondary Throttle Lockout Adjustment

1. Place the fast idle cam on the high step against the cam follower lever.
2. Hold the throttle lever closed.
3. Gauge the clearance between the lockout lever and pin. It must be 0.015 inch ± 0.005 in. (0.38mm ± 0.13mm).
4. Adjust, if necessary, by bending pin.
5. Push down on tail of fast idle cam to move lockout lever away from pin.
6. Rotate the throttle lever to bring the lockout pin to the position of minimum clearance with the lockout lever.
7. Gauge the clearance between the lockout lever and pin. The minimum must be 0.015 in. (0.38mm).
8. Adjust, if necessary, by filing the end of the pin.

Idle Speed and Mixture Adjustment

In case of a major carburetor overhual, throttle body replacement, or high idle CO (when indicated by an emissions inspection), the idle mixture may be adjusted. Adjusting the mixture by other than the following method may violate Federal and/or state laws. **Idle mixture needle socket J-29030-B or equivalent is required for this adjustment.**

1. Set the parking brake and block the drive wheels.
2. Remove the carburetor from the engine.
3. Drain the fuel from the the carburetor into a container. Dispose of the fuel in an approved container.
4. Remove the idle mixture needle plugs as follows:
   a. Invert the carburetor and support it to avoid damaging external components.
   b. Make two parallel hacksaw cuts in the throttle body, between the locator points near one idle mixture needle plug. The distance between the cuts depends on the size of the punch to be used.
   c. Cut down to the plug, but not more than ⅛ in. (3mm) beyond the locator point.
   d. Place a flat punch at a point near the ends of the saw marks. Hold the punch at a 45° angle and drive it into the throttle body until the casting breaks away, exposing the steel plug.
   e. Use a center punch to break the plug apart, uncover idle mixture needle. Remove all loose pieces of plug.
   f. Repeat the previous steps for the other needle plug.
5. Use idle mixture needle socket J-29030-B or equivalent to lightly seat the idle mixture needles, then back them out three turns.
6. Reinstall the carburetor on the engine.
7. Place the transmission in Park (automatic transmission) or Neutral (manual transmission).
8. Start the engine and bring it to a normal operating temperature, choke valve open, and air conditioning off.
9. Connect a known accurate tachometer to the engine.
10. Check ignition timing, and adjust if necessary, by following the procedure described on the Emission Control Information Label located under the hood on the vehicle.
11. Use idle mixture needle socket J-29030-B or equivalent to turn the mixture needles equally (⅛ turn at a time), in or out, to obtain the highest rpm (best idle).
12. Adjust the idle speed screw (throttle stop) to obtain the base idle speed specified on the underhood emission control information label.
13. Again try to readjust mixture needles to obtain the highest idle rpm. The adjustment is correct when the highest rpm (best idle) is reached with the minimum number of mixture needle turns from the seated position.
14. If necessary, readjust the idle speed screw (throttle stop) to obtain the specified base idle speed.
15. Check (and if necessary adjust) the idle speed solenoid activated speed and fast idle speed. Refer to the underhood emission control information label.
16. Check the throttle kicker and adjust if necessary.
17. Turn off the engine, remove all test equipment and remove the block from the drive wheels.

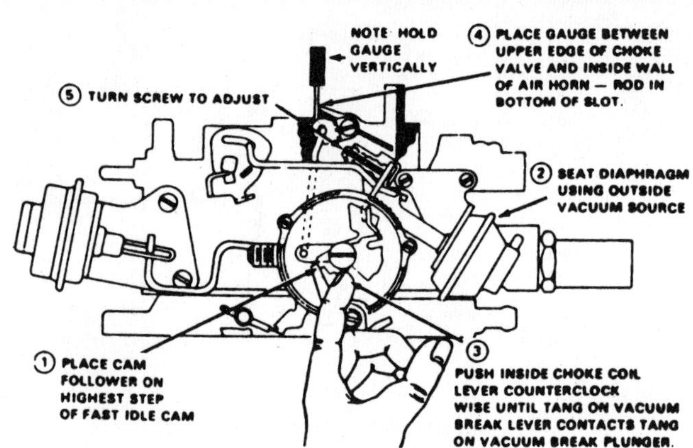

Primary side vacuum break adjustment — 4bbl

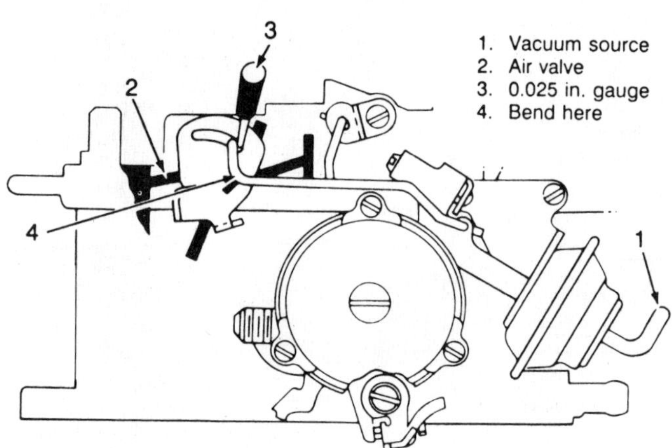

Front air valve rod adjustment

1. Vacuum source
2. Air valve
3. 0.025 in. gauge
4. Bend here

Rear air valve rod adjustment

Carburetor Removal and Installation

1MEF 1-bbl

1. Disconnect the negative battery terminal.
2. Remove the air cleaner assembly and gasket.
3. Disconnect the electrical connectors from the choke and idle stop solenoid.
4. Disconnect and tag the vacuum hoses.
5. Disconnect the accelerator linkage, downshift cable (automatic transmission only) and cruise control linkage (if equipped).
6. Disconnect the fuel line connection at the fuel inlet nut.
7. Remove the carburetor attaching nuts and the carburetor with the mounting insulator and gaskets.

CAUTION

Clean the sealing surfaces on the intake manifold and carburetor. Be sure to extinguish all open flames while filling and testing carburetor with gasoline to avoid the risk of fire.

8. Install the carburetor with a new flange gasket. It is good shop practice to fill the carburetor float bowl before installing the carburetor. This reduces the strain on starting motor and battery and reduces the possibility of backfiring while attempting to start the engine. Operate the throttle several times and check the discharge from pump jets before installing the carburetor.
9. Install the carburetor attaching bolts and torque them to 12 ft. lbs. (16 Nm). Be sure to torque the bolts in a criss-cross pattern.
10. Install the fuel line to the fuel inlet nut, cruise control cable (if equipped), downshift cable (automatic transmission only), accelerator linkage, vacuum hoses, electrical connectors to the choke and idle stop solenoid, air cleaner assembly with gasket and the negative battery terminal.

NOTE: After servicing the carburetor, tighten the mounting bolts in a clockwise direction to 12 ft. lbs. (16 Nm). When tightening the carburetor at recommended maintenance intervals, check the bolt torque. If less than 5 ft. lbs. (7 Nm), retighten to 8 ft. lbs. (11 Nm); but if greater than 5 ft. lbs. (7 Nm), do not retighten.

M4MEF 4-bbl

1. Disconnect the negative battery terminal. Remove the air cleaner assembly and gasket.
2. Disconnect the electrical connectors from the choke and idle stop solenoid.
3. Disconnect and tag the vacuum hoses.
4. Disconnect the accelerator linkage, downshift cable (automatic transmission only) and cruise control linkage (if equipped).
5. Disconnect the fuel line connection at the fuel inlet nut.
6. Remove the carburetor attaching bolts and the carburetor with the flange insulator.

CAUTION

Clean the sealing surfaces on the intake manifold and carburetor. Be sure to extinguish all open flames while filling and testing carburetor with gasoline to avoid the risk of fire.

7. Install the carburetor with a new flange gasket. It is good shop practice to fill the carburetor float bowl before installing the carburetor. This reduces the strain on starting motor and battery and reduces the possibility of backfiring while attempting to start the engine. Operate the throttle several times and check the discharge from pump jets before installing the carburetor.
8. Install the carburetor attaching bolts and torque them to 12 ft. lbs. (16 Nm). Be sure to torque the bolts in a criss-cross pattern.

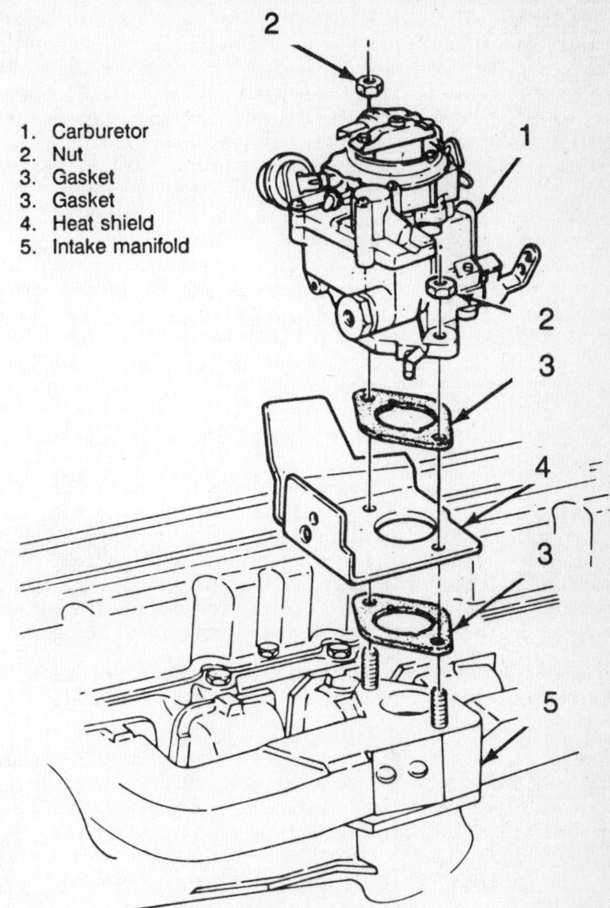

1bbl carburetor installation

9. Install the fuel line to the fuel inlet nut, cruise control cable (if equipped), downshift cable (automatic transmission only), accelerator linkage, vacuum hoses, electrical connectors to the choke and idle stop solenoid, air cleaner assembly with gasket and the negative battery terminal.

NOTE: After servicing the carburetor, tighten the mounting bolts in a clockwise direction to 12 ft. lbs. (16 Nm). When tightening the carburetor at recommended maintenance intervals, check the bolt torque. If less than 5 ft. lbs. (7 Nm), retighten to 8 ft. lbs. (11 Nm); but if greater than 5 ft. lbs. (7 Nm), do not retighten.

M4MEF 4-bbl Overhaul

Efficient carburetion depends greatly on careful cleaning and inspection during overhaul, since dirt, gum, water, or varnish in or on the carburetor parts are often responsible for poor performance.

Overhaul your carburetor in a clean, dustfree area. Carefully disassembly the carburetor, referring often to the exploded views and directions packaged with the rebuilding kit. Keep all similar and look alike parts segregated during disassembly and cleaning to avoid accidental interchange during assembly. Make a note of all jet sizes.

NOTE: Before performing any service on the carburetor, it is recommended that it be placed on a suitable holding fixture, such as Tool J-9789-118, BY-30-15 or equivalent. Without the use of the holding fixture, it is possible to damage throttle valves or other parts of the carburetor.

When the carburetor is disassembled, wash all parts (except diaphragms, electric choke units, pump plunger, and any other plastic, leather, fiber, or rubber parts) in clean carburetor solvent. Do not leave parts in the solvent any longer than is necessary to sufficiently loosen the deposits. Excessive cleaning may remove the special finish from the float bowl and choke valve bodies, leaving these parts unfit for service. Soak all parts in clean solvent and blow them dry with compressed air or allow them to air dry. Wipe clean all cork, plastic, leather, and fiber parts with a clean, lint free cloth.

Blow out all passages and jets with compressed air and be sure that there are no restrictions or blockages. Never use wire or similar tools to clean jets, fuel passages, or air bleeds. Clean all jets and valves separately to avoid accidental interchange.

Check all parts for wear or damage. If wear or damage is found, replace the defective parts.

Especially check the following:

1. Check the float needle and seat for wear. If wear is found, replace the complete assembly.
2. Check the float hinge pin for wear and the floats for dents or distortion. Replace the float if fuel has leaked into it.
3. Check the throttle and choke shaft bores for wear or an out-of-round condition. Damage or wear to the throttle arm, shaft, or shaft bore will often require replacement of the throttle body. These parts require a close tolerance of fit; wear may allow air leakage, which could affect starting and idling.

NOTE: Throttle shafts and bushings are not included in overhaul kits. They can be purchased separately.

4. Inspect the idle mixture adjusting needles for burrs or grooves. Any such condition requires replacement of the needle, since you will not be able to obtain a satisfactory idle.
5. Test the accelerator pump check valves. They should pass air one way but not the other. Test for proper seating by blowing and sucking on the valve. Replace the valve as necessary. If the valve is satisfactory, wash the valve again to remove breath moisture.
6. Check the bowl cover for warped surfaces with a straightedge.
7. Closely inspect the valves and seats for wear and damage, replacing as necessary.
8. After the carburetor is assembled, check the choke valve for freedom of operation.

Carburetor overhaul kits are recommended for each overhaul. These kits contain all gaskets and new parts to replace those which deteriorate most rapidly. Failure to replace all parts supplied with the kit (especially gaskets) can result in poor performance later.

Some carburetor manufacturers supply overhaul kits of three basic types: minor repair; major repair; and gasket kits.

Refer to exploded view for parts identification. Always replace internal gaskets that are removed. Base gasket should be inspected and replaced, only if damaged.

After cleaning and checking all components, reassemble the carburetor, using new parts and referring to the exploded view. When reassembling, make sure that all screws and jets are tight in their seats, buy do not overtighten as the tips will be distorted. Tighten all screws gradually, in rotation. Do not tighten needle valves into their seats; uneven jetting will result. Always use new gaskets. Be sure to adjust the float level when reassembling.

DISASSEMBLY

Idle Speed Solenoid Removal

Remove the attaching screws, then remove the Idle Speed Solenoid. The Idle Speed Solenoid should not be immersed in any carburetor cleaner, and should always be removed before complete carburetor overhaul, as carburetor cleaner will damage the internal components.

Idle Mixture Needle Plug Removal

1. Use hacksaw to make two parallel cuts in the throttle body, one on each side of the locator points near one idle mixture needle plug. The distance between the cuts will depend on the size of the punch to be used. Cuts should reach down to the steel plug, but should but extend more than ⅛ in. (3mm) beyond the locator points.
2. Place a flat punch at a point near the ends of the saw marks in the throttle body. Hold the punch at a 45° angle, and drive it into the throttle body until the casting breaks away, exposing the hardened steel plug. The plug will break, rather than remaining intact. Remove all the loose pieces.
3. Repeat the procedure for the other idle mixture needle plug.

Idle Air Bleed Valve Removal

1. Cover internal bowl vents and air inlets to the bleed valve with masking tape.
2. Carefully align a $^{7}/_{64}$ in. drill bit on rivet head. Drill only enough to remove head of each rivet holding the idle air bleed valve cover.
3. Use a suitably sized punch to drive out the remainder of the rivet from the castings. Repeat procedure with other rivet.

CAUTION

For the next operation, safety glasses must be worn to protect eyes from possible metal shaving damage.

4. Lift off cover and remove any pieces of rivet still inside tower. Use shop air to blow out any remaining chips.
5. Remove idle air bleed valve from the air horn.
6. Remove and discard O-ring seals from valve. New O-ring seals are required for reassembly. The idle air bleed valve is serviced as a complete assembly only.

Air Horn Removal

1. Remove upper choke lever from the end of choke shaft by removing retaining screw. Rotate upper choke lever to remove choke rod from slot in lever.
2. Remove choke rod from lower lever inside the float bowl casting. Remove rod by holding lower lever outward with small screwdriver and twisting rod counterclockwise.
3. Remove secondary metering rods by removing the small screw in the top of the metering rod hanger. Lift upward on the metering rod hanger until the secondary metering rods are completely out of the air horn. Metering rods may be disassembled from the hanger by rotating the ends out of the holes in the end of the hanger.
4. Remove pump link retainer and remove link from pump lever.

NOTE: Do not attempt to remove the lever, as damage to the air horn could result.

5. Remove front vacuum break hose from tube on float bowl.
6. Remove eleven air horn-to-bowl screws; then remove the two countersunk attaching screws located next to the venturi. If used, remove secondary air baffle deflector from beneath the two center air horn screws.
7. Remove air horn from float bowl by lifting it straight up. The air horn gasket should remain on the float bowl for removal later.

NOTE: When removing air horn from float bowl, use care to prevent damaging the mixture control solenoid connector, Throttle Position Sensor (TPS) adjustment lever, and the small tubes protruding from the air horn. These tubes are permanently pressed into the air horn casting. DO NOT remove them.

8. Remove front vacuum break bracket attaching screws. The vacuum break assembly may now be removed from the air valve

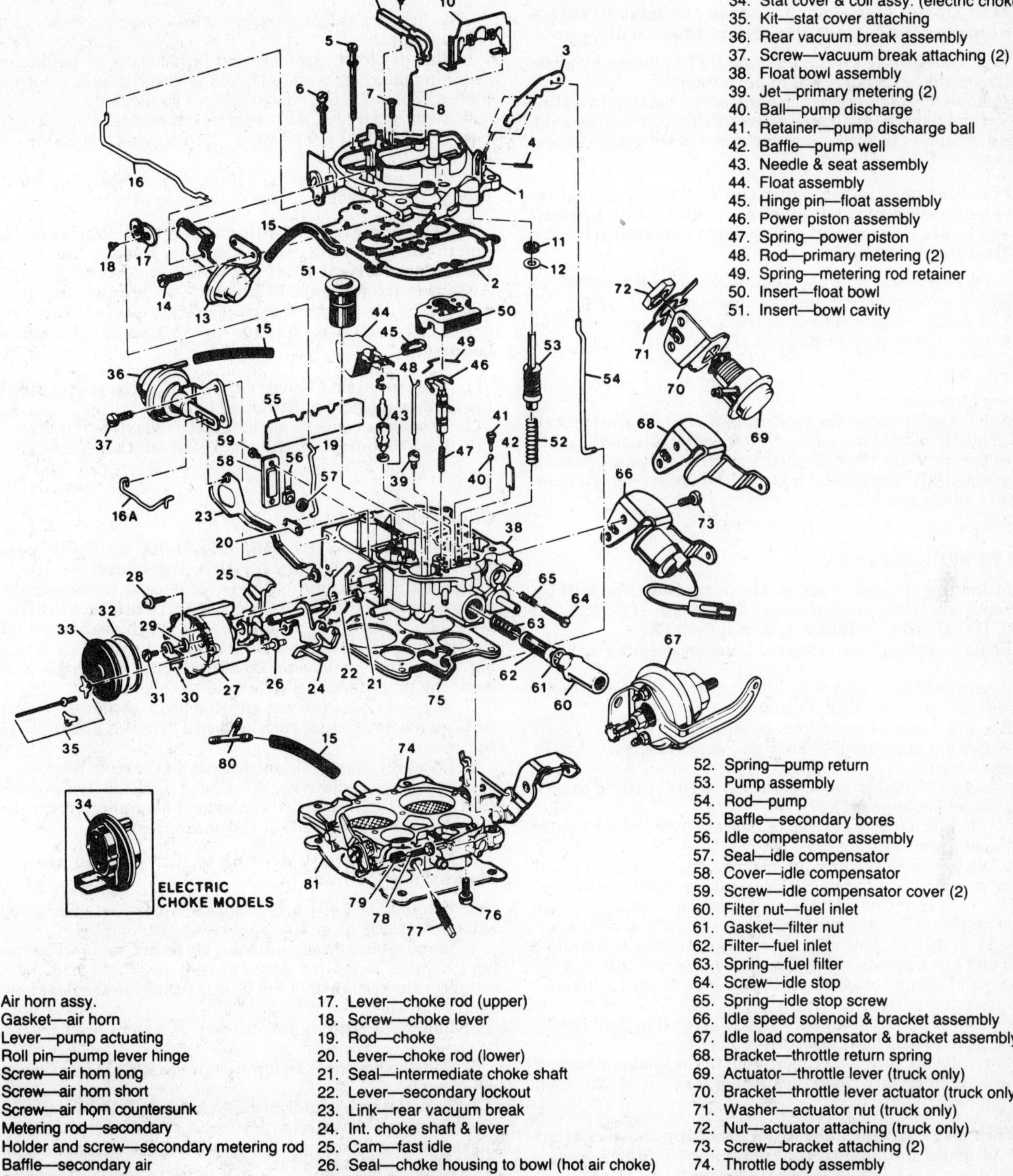

1. Air horn assy.
2. Gasket—air horn
3. Lever—pump actuating
4. Roll pin—pump lever hinge
5. Screw—air horn long
6. Screw—air horn short
7. Screw—air horn countersunk
8. Metering rod—secondary
9. Holder and screw—secondary metering rod
10. Baffle—secondary air
11. Seal—pump plunger
12. Retainer—pump seal
13. Vac. break control & bracket—front
14. Screw—control attaching
15. Hose—vacuum
16. Rod—air valve

16A. Rod—air valve (truck)

17. Lever—choke rod (upper)
18. Screw—choke lever
19. Rod—choke
20. Lever—choke rod (lower)
21. Seal—intermediate choke shaft
22. Lever—secondary lockout
23. Link—rear vacuum break
24. Int. choke shaft & lever
25. Cam—fast idle
26. Seal—choke housing to bowl (hot air choke)
27. Kit—choke housing
28. Screw—choke housing to bowl
29. Seal—intermediate choke shaft (hot air choke)
30. Lever—choke coil
31. Screw—choke coil lever
32. Gasket—stat cover (hot air choke)
33. Stat cover & coil assy. (hot air choke)
34. Stat cover & coil assy. (electric choke)
35. Kit—stat cover attaching
36. Rear vacuum break assembly
37. Screw—vacuum break attaching (2)
38. Float bowl assembly
39. Jet—primary metering (2)
40. Ball—pump discharge
41. Retainer—pump discharge ball
42. Baffle—pump well
43. Needle & seat assembly
44. Float assembly
45. Hinge pin—float assembly
46. Power piston assembly
47. Spring—power piston
48. Rod—primary metering (2)
49. Spring—metering rod retainer
50. Insert—float bowl
51. Insert—bowl cavity
52. Spring—pump return
53. Pump assembly
54. Rod—pump
55. Baffle—secondary bores
56. Idle compensator assembly
57. Seal—idle compensator
58. Cover—idle compensator
59. Screw—idle compensator cover (2)
60. Filter nut—fuel inlet
61. Gasket—filter nut
62. Filter—fuel inlet
63. Spring—fuel filter
64. Screw—idle stop
65. Spring—idle stop screw
66. Idle speed solenoid & bracket assembly
67. Idle load compensator & bracket assembly
68. Bracket—throttle return spring
69. Actuator—throttle lever (truck only)
70. Bracket—throttle lever actuator (truck only)
71. Washer—actuator nut (truck only)
72. Nut—actuator attaching (truck only)
73. Screw—bracket attaching (2)
74. Throttle body assembly
75. Gasket—throttle body
76. Screw—throttle body (3)
77. Idle mixture needle & spring assy. (2)
78. Screw—fast idle adjusting
79. Spring—fast idle screw
80. Tee—vacuum hose
81. Gasket—flange

M4ME/M4MEF exploded view

dashpot rod, and the dashpot rod from the air valve lever.

NOTE: Do not place vacuum break assembly in carburetor cleaner, as damage to vacuum break will occur.

9. Remove Throttle Position Sensor (TPS) plunger by pushing plunger down through seal in air horn.
10. Remove TPS seal and pump plunger stem seal by inverting air horn and using a small screwdriver to remove staking holding seal retainers in place. Remove and discard retainers and seals.

NOTE: Use care in removing the TPS plunger seal retainer and pump plunger stem seal retainer to prevent damage to air horn casting. New seals and retainers are required for reassembly.

11. Invert air horn, and use Tool J-28696-4, BT-7967A, or equivalent, to remove rich mixture stop screw and spring.
12. Use a suitable punch to drive the lean mixture screw plug and rich mixture stop screw plug out of the air horn. Discard the plugs.
13. Further disassembly of the air horn is not required for cleaning purposes.

The choke valve and choke valve screws, the air valves and air valve shaft should not be removed. However, if it is necessary to replace the air valve closing springs or center plastic eccentric cam, a repair kit is available. Instructions for assembly are included in the repair kit.

Float Bowl Disassembly

The following special tools, or their equivalents, will be necessary for this procedure: J-28696-10, BT-7928, J-22769, BT-3006M, J-28696-4, and BT-7928.

1. Remove solenoid metering rod plunger by lifting straight up.
2. Remove air horn gasket by lifting it from the dowel locating pins on float bowl. Discard gasket.
3. Remove pump plunger from pump well.
4. Remove staking holding Throttle Position Sensor (TPS) in bowl as follows:
   a. Lay a flat tool or metal piece across bowl casting to protect gasket sealing surface.
   b. Use a small screwdriver to depress TPS sensor lightly and hold against spring tension.
   c. Observing safety precautions, pry upward with a small chisel or equivalent to remove bowl staking, making sure prying force is exerted against the metal piece and not against the bowl casting. Use care not to damage the TPS sensor.
   d. Push up from bottom on electrical connector and remove TPS and connector assembly from bowl. Use care in removing sensor and connector assembly to prevent damage to this critical electrical part.
   e. Remove spring from bottom of TPS well in float bowl.
5. Remove plastic bowl insert from float bowl.
6. Carefully lift each metering rod out of the guided metering jet, checking to be sure the return spring is removed with each metering rod.

NOTE: Use extreme care when handling these critical parts to avoid damage to the metering rod and spring.

7. Remove the mixture control solenoid from the float bowl as follows:
   a. Remove screw attaching solenoid connector to float bowl. Do not remove solenoid connector from float bowl until called for in text.
   b. Use Tool J-28696-10, BT-7928, or equivalent, to remove lean mixture (solenoid) screw. Do not remove plunger return spring or connector and wires from the solenoid body. The mixture control solenoid, with plunger and connector, is only serviced as a complete assembly.
   c. Remove rubber gasket from top of solenoid connector and discard.
   d. Remove solenoid screw tension spring (next to float hanger pin).
8. Remove float assembly and float needle by pulling up on retaining pin. Remove needle and seat and gasket using set remover Tool J-22769, BT-3006M, or equivalent.
9. Remove large mixture control solenoid tension spring from boss on bottom of float bowl located between guided metering jets.
10. If necessary, remove the primary main metering jets using special Tool J-28696-4, BT-7928, or equivalent.

NOTE: Use care installing tool on jet, to prevent damage to the metering rod guide (upper area), and locating tool over vertical float sections on lower area of jet. Also, no attempt should be made to remove the secondary metering jets (metering orifice plates). These jets are fixed and, if damaged, entire bowl replacement is required.

11. Remove pump discharge check ball retainer and turn bowl upside down, catching discharge ball as if falls.
12. Remove secondary air baffle, if replaced is required.
13. Remove pump well fill slot baffle only if necessary.

Choke Disassembly

Special tools J-9789-118, BT-30-15, or their equivalents, will be necessary for this procedure.

The tamper-resistant choke cover is used to discourage unnecessary readjustment of the choke thermostatic cover and coil assembly. However, if it is necessary to remove the cover and coil assembly during normal carburetor disassembly for cleaning and normal carburetor disassembly for cleaning and overhaul, the procedures below should be followed.

1. Support float bowl and throttle body, as an assembly, on a suitable holding fixture such as Tool J-9789-118, BT-30-15, or equivalent.
2. Carefully align a $^5/_{32}$ in. drill bit on the rivet head and drill only enough to remove the rivet head. Drill the two remaining rivet heads, then use a drift and small hammer to drive the remainder of the rivets out of the choke housing.

NOTE: Use care in drilling to prevent damage to the choke cover or housing.

3. Remove the two conventional retainers, retainer with tab, and choke cover assembly from choke housing.
4. Remove choke housing assembly from float bowl by removing retaining screw and washer inside the choke housing. The complete choke assembly can be removed from the float bowl by sliding outward.
5. Remove secondary throttle valve lock-out lever from float bowl.
6. Remove lower choke lever from inside float bowl cavity by inverting bowl.
7. To disassemble intermediate choke shaft from choke housing, remove coil lever retaining screw at end of shaft inside the choke housing. Remove thermostatic coil lever from flats on intermediate choke shaft.
8. Remove intermediate choke shaft from the choke housing by sliding it outward. The fast idle cam can now be removed from the intermediate choke shaft. Remove the cup seal from the float bowl cleaning purposes. DO NOT ATTEMPT TO REMOVE THE INSERT!
9. Remove fuel inlet nut, gasket, check valve, filter assembly and spring. Discard Check valve filter assembly and gasket.
10. Remove three throttle body-to-bowl attaching screws and lockwashers and remove throttle body assembly.
11. Remove throttle body-to-bowl insulator gasket.

Throttle Body Disassembly

Special tools J-29030-B and BT-7610B, or their equivalents, will be necessary for this procedure.

Place throttle body assembly on carburetor holding fixture to avoid damage to throttle valves.

1. Remove pump rod from the throttle lever by rotating the rod until the tang on the rod aligns with the slot in the lever.
2. Use Tool J-29030-B, BT-7610B, or equivalent, to remove idle mixture needles for thorough throttle body cleaning.
3. Further disassembly of the throttle body is not required for cleaning purposes. The throttle valve screws are permanently staked in place and should not be removed. The throttle body is serviced as a complete assembly.

ASSEMBLY

The following special tools, or their equivalents, will be necessary for this procedure: J-29030-B, BT-7610B, J-9789-118, BT-30-15, J-23417, BT-6911, J-28696-4, J-22769, BT-3006M, J-33815-1, BT-8253-A, J-28696-10, and BT-7928.

1. Install the lower end of the pump rod in the throttle lever by aligning the tang on the rod with the slot in the lever. The end of the rod should point outward toward the throttle lever.
2. Install idle mixture needles and springs using Tool J-29030-B, BT-7610B, or equivalent. Lightly seat each needle and then turn counterclockwise the number of specified turns, the final idle mixture adjustment is made on the vehicle.
3. If a new float bowl assembly is used, stamp or engrave the model number on the new float bowl. Install new throttle body-to-bowl insulator gasket over two locating dowels on bowl.
4. Install throttle body making certain throttle body is properly located over dowels on float bowl. Install three throttle body-to-bowl screws and lockwashers and tighten evenly and securely.
5. Place carburetor on proper holding fixture such as J-9789-118, BT-30-15 or equivalent.
6. Install fuel inlet filter spring, a new check valve filter assembly, new gasket and inlet nut. Tighten nut to 18 ft. lbs. (24 Nm).

NOTE: When installing a service replacement filter, make sure the filter is the type that includes the check valve to meet government safety standard. New service replacement filters with check valve meet this requirement. When properly installed, the hole in the filter faces toward the inlet nut. Ribs on the closed end of the filter element prevent it from being installed incorrectly, unless forced. Tightening beyond the specified torque can damage the nylon gasket.

7. Install a new cup seal into the insert on the side of the float bowl for the intermediate choke shaft. The lip on the cup seal faces outward.
8. Install the secondary throttle valve lock-out lever on the boss of the float bowl, with the recess hole in the lever facing inward.
9. Install the fast idle cam on the intermediate choke shaft (steps on cam face downward).
10. Carefully install fast idle cam and intermediate choke shaft assembly in the choke housing. Install the thermostatic coil lever on the flats on the intermediate choke shaft. Inside thermostatic choke coil lever is properly aligned when both inside and outside levers face toward the fuel inlet. Install inside lever retaining screw into the end of the intermediate choke shaft.
11. Install lower choke rod (inner) lever into cavity in float bowl.
12. Install choke housing to bowl, sliding intermediate choke shaft into lower (inner) lever. Tool J-23417, BT-6911 or equivalent, can be used to hold the lower choke lever in correct position while installing the choke housing. The intermediate choke shaft lever and fast idle cam are in correct position when the tang on lever is beneath the fast idle cam.
13. Install choke housing retaining screws and washers. Check linkage for freedom of movement. Do not install choke cover and coil assembly until inside coil lever is adjusted.
14. If removed, install air baffle in secondary side of float bowl with notches toward the top. Top edge of baffle must be flush with bowl casting.
15. If removed, install baffle inside of the pump well with slot toward the bottom.
16. Install pump discharge check ball and retainer screw in the passage next to the pump well.
17. If removed, carefully install primary main metering jets in bottom of float bowl using or Tool J-28696-4, BT-7928, equivalent.

NOTE: Use care in installing jets to prevent damage to metering rod guide.

18. Install large mixture control solenoid tension spring over boss on bottom of float bowl.
19. Install needle seat assembly, with gasket, using seat installer J-22769, BT-3006M, or equivalent.
20. To make adjustment easier, carefully bend float arm before assembly.
21. Install float needle onto float arm by sliding float lever under needle pull clip. Proper installation of the needle pull clip is to hook the clip over the edge of the float on the float arm facing the float pontoon.
22. Install float hinge pin into float arm with end of loop of pin facing pump well. Install float assembly by aligning needle in the seat, and float hinge pin into locating channels in float bowl. DO NOT install float needle pull clip into holes in float arm.
23. Make a float level adjustment as necessary.
24. Install mixture control solenoid screw tension spring between raised bosses next to float hanger pin.
25. Install mixture control solenoid and connector assembly as follows:
    a. Install new rubber gasket on top of solenoid connector.
    b. Install solenoid carefully in the float chamber, aligning pin on end of solenoid with hole in raised boss at bottom of bowl. Align solenoid connector wires to fit in slot in bowl.
    c. Install lean mixture (solenoid) screw through hole in solenoid bracket and tension spring in bowl, engaging first six screw threads to assure proper thread engagement.
    d. Install mixture control solenoid gauging Tool J-33815-1, BT-8253-A, or equivalent over the throttle side metering jet rod guide, and temporarily install solenoid plunger.
    e. Holding the solenoid plunger against the Solenoid Stop, use Tool J-28696-10, BT-7928, or equivalent, to turn the lean mixture (solenoid) screw slowly clockwise, until the solenoid plunger just contacts the gauging tool. The adjustment is correct when the solenoid plunger is contacting BOTH the Solenoid Stop and the Gauging Tool.
    f. Remove solenoid plunger and gauging tool.
26. Install connector attaching screw, but DO NOT overtighten, as that could cause damage to the connector.
27. Install Throttle Position Sensor return spring in bottom of well in float bowl.
28. Install Throttle Position Sensor and connector assembly in float bowl by aligning groove in electrical connector with slot in float bowl casting. Push down on connector and sensor assembly so that connector and wires are located below bowl casting surface.
29. Install plastic bowl insert over float valve, pressing downward until properly seated (flush with bowl casting surface).
30. Slide metering rod return spring over metering rod tip until small end of spring stops against shoulder on rod. Carefully install metering rod and spring assembly through holding in

plastic bowl insert and gently lower the metering rod into the guided metering jet, until large end of spring seats on the recess on end of jet guide.

CAUTION

Do not force metering rod down in jet. Use extreme care when handling these critical parts to avoid damage to rod and spring. if service replacement metering rods, springs and jets are installed, they must be installed in matched sets.

31. Install pump return spring in pump well.
32. Install pump plunger assembly in pump well.
33. Holding down on pump plunger assembly against return spring tension, install air horn gasket by aligning pump plunger stem with hole in gasket, and aligning holes in gasket over TPS plunger, solenoid plunger return spring metering rods, solenoid attaching screw and electrical connector. Position gasket over the two dowel locating pins on the float bowl.
34. Holding down on air horn gasket and pump plunger assembly, install the solenoid–metering rod plunger in the solenoid, aligning slot in end of plunger with solenoid attaching screw. Be sure plunger arms engage top of each metering.
35. If a service replacement Mixture Control Solenoid package is installed, the solenoid and plunger MUST be installed as a matched set.

Air Horn Assembly

The following special tools, or their equivalents, will be necessary for this procdure: J-28696-10, J-2869-4, BT-7967A, J-34935-1, BT-8420A, BT-7928, J-33815-2, and BT-8353B.

1. If removed, install the TPS adjustment screw in the air horn using Tool J-28696-10, BT-7967A, or equivalent. Final adjustment of the Throttle Position Sensor is made on the vehicle.
2. Inspect the air valve shaft pin for lubrication. Apply a liberal quantity of lithium base grease to the air valve shaft pin, especially in the area contacted by the air valve spring.
3. Install new pump plunger and TPS plunger seals and retainers in air horn casting. The lip on the seal faces outward, away from the air horn mounting surface. Lightly stake seal retainer in three places, choosing locations different from the original stakings.
4. Install rich mixture stop screw and rich authority adjusting spring from bottom side of the air horn. Use Tool J-2869-4, BT-7967A, or equivalent, to bottom the stop screw lightly, then back out ¼ turn. Final adjustment procedure will be covered later in this section.
5. Install TPS actuator plunger in the seal.
6. Carefully lower the air horn assembly onto the float bowl while positioning the TPS Adjustment Lever over the TPS sensor and guiding pump plunger stem through the seal in the air horn casting. To ease installation, insert a thin screwdriver between the air horn gasket and float bowl to raise the TPS Adjustment Lever, positioning it over the TPS sensor.
7. Make sure that the bleed tubes and accelerating well tubes are positioned properly through the holes in the air horn gasket. Do not force the air horn assembly onto the bowl, but lower it lightly into place over the two dowel locating pins.
8. Install two long air horn screws and lockwashers, nine short screws and lockwashers and two countersunk screws located next to the carburetor venturi area. Install secondary air baffle beneath the No. 3 and 4 screws. Tighten all screws evenly and securely.
9. Install air valve rod into slot in the lever on the end of the air valve shaft. Install the other end of the rod in hole in front vacuum break plunger. Install front vacuum break and bracket assembly on the air horn, using two attaching screws. Tighten screw securely. Connect pump link to pump lever and install retainer.

NOTE: Use care installing the roll pin to prevent damage to the pump lever bearing surface and casting bosses.

10. Install two secondary metering rods into the secondary metering rod hanger (upper end of rods point toward each other). Install secondary metering rod holder, with rods, onto air valve cam follower. Install retaining screw and tighten securely. Work air valves up and down several times to make sure they remove freely in both directions.
11. Connect choke rod into lower choke lever inside bowl cavity. Install choke rod in slot in upper choke lever, and position lever on end of choke shaft, making sure flats on end of shaft align with flats in lever. Install attaching screw and tighten securely. When properly installed, the number on the lever will face outward.
12. Adjust the rich mixture stop screw:
    a. Insert external float gauging Tool J-34935-1, BT-8420A, or equivalent, in the vertical D-shaped vent hole in the air horn casting (next to the idle air bleed valve) and allow it to float freely.
    b. Read (at eye level) the mark on the gauge, in inches, that lines up with the tip of the air horn casting.
    c. Lightly press down on gauge, and again read and record the mark on the gauge that lines up with the top of the air horn casting.
    d. Subtract gauge UP dimension, found in Step b, from gauge DOWN dimension, found in Step c, and record the difference in inches. This difference in dimension is the total solenoid plunger travel.
    e. Insert Tool J-28696-10, BT-7928, or equivalent, in the access hole in the air horn, and adjust the rich mixture stop screw to obtain ⅛ in. (3mm) total solenoid plunger travel.
13. With the solenoid plunger travel correctly set, install the plugs supplied in the service kit into the air horn to retain the setting and prevent fuel vapor loss:
    a. Install the plug, hollow end down, into the access hole to the lean mixture (solenoid) screw and use a suitably sized punch to drive the plug into the air horn until top of plug is even with the lower edge of the hole chamber.
    b. In a similar manner, install the plug over the rich mixture screw access hole and drive the plug into place so that the tip of the plug is $^1/_{16}$ in. (1.6mm) below the surface of the air horn casting.
14. Install the Idle Air Bleed Valve as follows:
    a. Lightly coat two new O-ring seals with automatic transmission fluid, to aid in their installation on the idle air bleed valve body. The thick seal goes in the upper groove and the thin seal goes in the lower groove.
    b. Install the idle air bleed valve in the air horn, making sure that there is proper thread engagement.
    c. Insert idle air bleed valve gauging Tool J-33815-2, BT-8353B, or equivalent, in throttle side D-shaped vent hole of the air horn casting. The upper end of the tool should be positioned over the open cavity next to the idle air bleed valve.
    d. Hold the gauging tool down lightly so that the solenoid plunger is against the solenoid stop, then adjust the idle air bleed valve so that the gauging tool will pivot over and just contact the top of the valve.
    e. Remove the gauging tool.
    f. The final adjustment of the idle air bleed valve is made on the vehicle to obtain idle mixture control.
15. Perform the Air Valve Spring Adjustment and Choke coil Lever Adjustment as previously described.
16. Install the cover and coil assembly in the choke housing, as follows:
    a. Place the cam follower on the highest step of the fast idle cam.
    b. Install the thermostatic cover and coil assembly in the choke housing, making sure the coil tang engages the inside coil pickup lever. Ground contact for the electric choke is pro-

vided by a metal plate located at the rear of the choke cover assembly. DO NOT install a choke cover gasket between the electric choke assembly and the choke housing.

c. A choke cover retainer kit is required to attach the choke cover to the choke housing. Follow the instructions found in the kit and install the proper retainer and rivets using a suitable blind rivet tool.

d. It may be necessary to use an adapter (tube) if the installing tool interferes with the electrical connector tower on the choke cover.

17. Install the hose on the front vacuum brake and on the tube on the float bowl.

18. Position the idle speed solenoid and bracket assembly on the float bowl, retaining it with two large countersunk screws.

19. Perform the Choke Rod-Fast Idle Cam Adjustment, Primary (Front) Vacuum Break Adjustment, Air Valve Rod Adjustment - Front, Unloader Adjustment and the Secondary Lockout Adjustment as previously described.

20. Reinstall the carburetor on the vehicle with a new flange gasket.

1MEF 1-bbl Overhaul

Efficient carburetion depends greatly on careful cleaning and inspection during overhaul, since dirt, gum, water, or varnish in or on the carburetor parts are often responsible for poor performance.

Overhaul your carburetor in a clean, dustfree area. Carefully disassembly the carburetor, referring often to the exploded views and directions packaged with the rebuilding kit. Keep all similar and look alike parts segregated during disassembly and cleaning to avoid accidental interchange during assembly. Make a note of all jet sizes.

NOTE: Before performing any service on the carburetor, it is recommended that it be placed on a suitable holding fixture, such as Tool J-9789-118, BY-30-15 or equivalent. Without the use of the holding fixture, it is possible to damage throttle valves or other parts of the carburetor.

When the carburetor is disassembled, wash all parts (except diaphragms, electric choke units, pump plunger, and any other plastic, leather, fiber, or rubber parts) in clean carburetor solvent. Do not leave parts in the solvent any longer than is necessary to sufficiently loosen the deposits. Excessive cleaning may remove the special finish from the float bowl and choke valve bodies, leaving these parts unfit for service. Soak all parts in clean solvent and blow them dry with compressed air or allow them to air dry. Wipe clean all cork, plastic, leather, and fiber parts with a clean, lint free cloth.

Blow out all passages and jets with compressed air and be sure that there are no restrictions or blockages. Never use wire or similar tools to clean jets, fuel passages, or air bleeds. Clean all jets and valves separately to avoid accidental interchange.

Check all parts for wear or damage. If wear or damage is found, replace the defective parts.

Especially check the following:

1. Check the float needle and seat for wear. If wear is found, replace the complete assembly.
2. Check the float hinge pin for wear and the floats for dents or distortion. Replace the float if fuel has leaked into it.
3. Check the throttle and choke shaft bores for wear or an out-of-round condition. Damage or wear to the throttle arm, shaft, or shaft bore will often require replacement of the throttle body. These parts require a close tolerance of fit; wear may allow air leakage, which could affect starting and idling.

NOTE: Throttle shafts and bushings are not included in overhaul kits. They can be purchased separately.

4. Inspect the idle mixture adjusting needles for burrs or grooves. Any such condition requires replacement of the needle, since you will not be able to obtain a satisfactory idle.
5. Test the accelerator pump check valves. They should pass air one way but not the other. Test for proper seating by blowing and sucking on the valve. Replace the valve as necessary. If the valve is satisfactory, wash the valve again to remove breath moisture.
6. Check the bowl cover for warped surfaces with a straightedge.
7. Closely inspect the valves and seats for wear and damage, replacing as necessary.
8. After the carburetor is assembled, check the choke valve for freedom of operation.

Carburetor overhaul kits are recommended for each overhaul. These kits contain all gaskets and new parts to replace those which deteriorate most rapidly. Failure to replace all parts supplied with the kit (especially gaskets) can result in poor performance later.

Some carburetor manufacturers supply overhaul kits of three basic types: minor repair; major repair; and gasket kits.

Refer to exploded view for parts identification. Always replace internal gaskets that are removed. Base gasket should be inspected and replaced, only if damaged.

After cleaning and checking all components, reassemble the carburetor, using new parts and referring to the exploded view. When reassembling, make sure that all screws and jets are tight in their seats, buy do not overtighten as the tips will be distorted. Tighten all screws gradually, in rotation. Do not tighten needle valves into their seats; uneven jetting will result. Always use new gaskets. Be sure to adjust the float level when reassembling.

DISASSEMBLY

Idle Speed Solenoid Removal

Remove the attaching screws, then remove the Idle Speed Solenoid. The Idle Speed Solenoid should not be immersed in any carburetor cleaner, and should always be removed before complete carburetor overhaul, as carburetor cleaner will damage the internal components.

Idle Mixture Needle Plug Removal

1. Use hacksaw to make two parallel cuts in the throttle body, one on each side of the locator points near one idle mixture needle plug. The distance between the cuts will depend on the size of the punch to be used. Cuts should reach down to the steel plug, but should but extend more than 1/8 in. (3mm) beyond the locator points.
2. Place a flat punch at a point near the ends of the saw marks in the throttle body. Hold the punch at a 45° angle, and drive it into the throttle body until the casting breaks away, exposing the hardened steel plug. The plug will break, rather than remaining intact. Remove all the loose pieces.

DISASSEMBLY

1. Remove the fuel inlet nut, gasket, filter and spring.
2. Unscrew and remove the idle stop solenoid.
3. Remove the throttle return spring bracket.
4. Remove the vacuum break hose.
5. Remove the vacuum break attaching screws, disconnect the link and remove he vacuum break assembly. Allow the choke wire connector bracket to hang freely.
6. Remove the choke housing attaching screws and remove the housing and bearing.
7. Remove the fast idle cam attaching screw, cam and cam link.
8. Remove the air horn attaching screws and lift off the air horn. Discard the gasket.

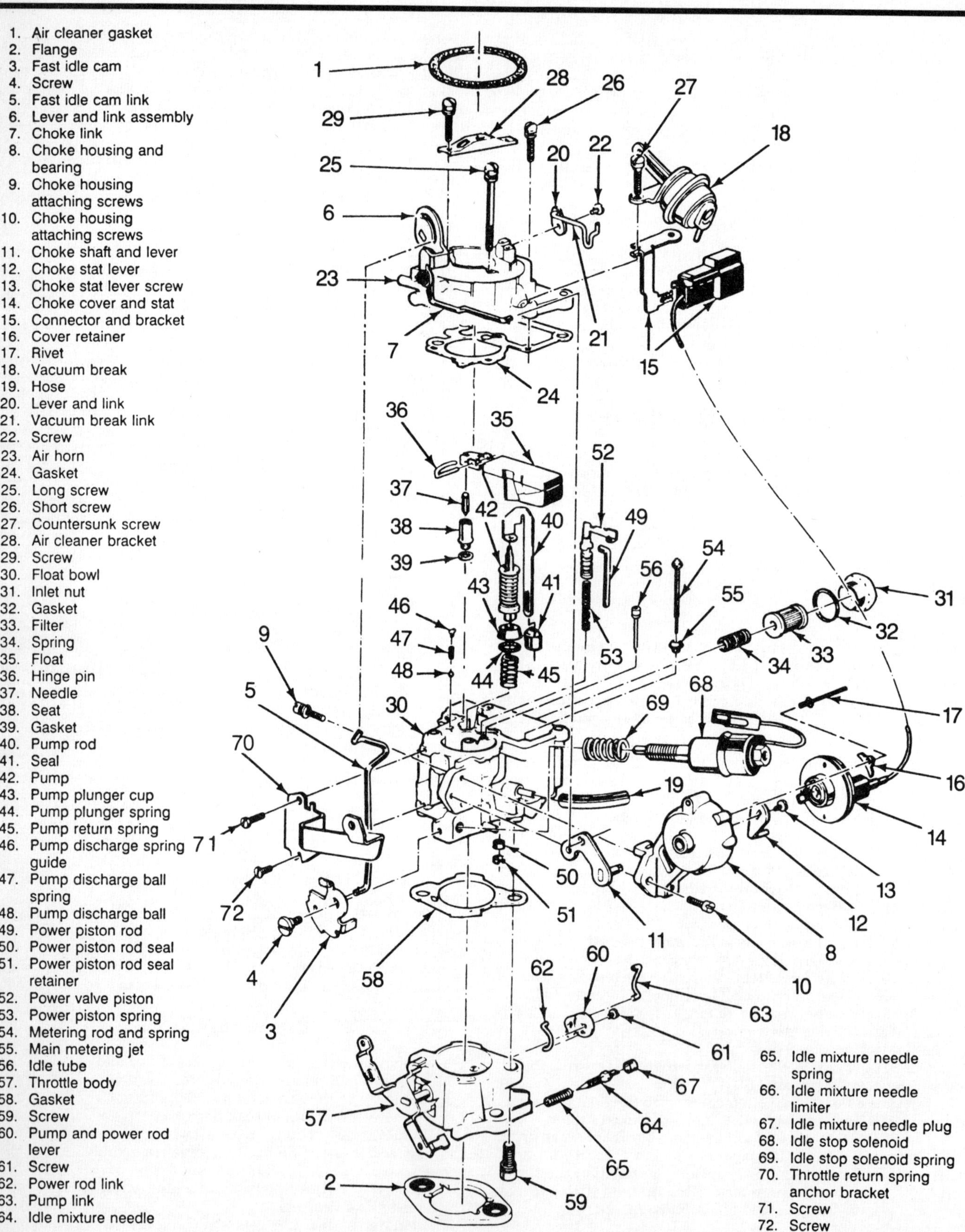
1. Air cleaner gasket
2. Flange
3. Fast idle cam
4. Screw
5. Fast idle cam link
6. Lever and link assembly
7. Choke link
8. Choke housing and bearing
9. Choke housing attaching screws
10. Choke housing attaching screws
11. Choke shaft and lever
12. Choke stat lever
13. Choke stat lever screw
14. Choke cover and stat
15. Connector and bracket
16. Cover retainer
17. Rivet
18. Vacuum break
19. Hose
20. Lever and link
21. Vacuum break link
22. Screw
23. Air horn
24. Gasket
25. Long screw
26. Short screw
27. Countersunk screw
28. Air cleaner bracket
29. Screw
30. Float bowl
31. Inlet nut
32. Gasket
33. Filter
34. Spring
35. Float
36. Hinge pin
37. Needle
38. Seat
39. Gasket
40. Pump rod
41. Seal
42. Pump
43. Pump plunger cup
44. Pump plunger spring
45. Pump return spring
46. Pump discharge spring guide
47. Pump discharge ball spring
48. Pump discharge ball
49. Power piston rod
50. Power piston rod seal
51. Power piston rod seal retainer
52. Power valve piston
53. Power piston spring
54. Metering rod and spring
55. Main metering jet
56. Idle tube
57. Throttle body
58. Gasket
59. Screw
60. Pump and power rod lever
61. Screw
62. Power rod link
63. Pump link
64. Idle mixture needle
65. Idle mixture needle spring
66. Idle mixture needle limiter
67. Idle mixture needle plug
68. Idle stop solenoid
69. Idle stop solenoid spring
70. Throttle return spring anchor bracket
71. Screw
72. Screw

1MEF carburetor exploded view

NOTE: No further disassembly of the air horn is permitted. Under no circumstances should you remove the metering rod adjusting screw. Any attempt to turn this screw will cause illegal emission levels.

9. Remove the float and hinge pin.
10. Remove the needle from the seat.
11. Remove the pump lever attaching screw.
12. Close the throttle plate.
13. Remove the pump and power rod lever from the end of the throttle shaft.
14. Press down on the power valve piston assembly and disconnect the power rod link from the power piston rod.
15. Press down on the pump rod and disconnect the pump link from the slot in the rod.
16. Remove the plunger spring and cup from the pump rod and pump.
17. Remove the pump rod seal from the boss on the float bowl.
18. Remove the return spring from the pump well.
19. Remove the power valve piston assembly, metering rod and spring assembly and the power piston rod.
20. Remove the metering rod and spring assembly from the metering rod hanger.
21. Remove the power piston spring from the float bowl.
22. Remove the float needle seat and gasket.
23. Remove the main metering jet.
24. Turn the carburetor over and catch the idle tube.
25. Using needle-nose pliers, remove the pump discharge spring guide.
26. Turn the carburetor over and catch the pump discharge spring and ball.
27. Turn the idle mixture needle clockwise, slowly, counting the number of turns until it seats. Record this number for assembly purposes.
28. Remove the idle mixture needle.
29. Remove the float bowl-to-throttle body screws, separate the two pieces and discard the gasket.

NOTE: No further disassembly of the throttle body is necessary. It is serviced as a unit.

30. Remove the power piston seal retainer from the float bowl with a small screwdriver.
31. Remove the power piston rod seal.

ASSEMBLY

1. Install a new power piston rod seal.
2. Install a new power piston seal retainer in the float bowl, flush with the casting surface.
3. Using a new gasket, assemble the float bowl and throttle body. Torque the screws to 15 ft. lbs.
4. Install the idle mixture needle. Turn the idle mixture needle clockwise, slowly, until it seats and back it out the number of turns recorde.
5. Install the pump discharge spring and ball.
6. Install the pump discharge spring guide flush with the casting surface.
7. Install the idle tube. The tube should be flush with the casting surface.
8. Install the main metering jet.
9. Install the float needle seat and new gasket.
10. Install the power piston spring in the float bowl.
11. Install the power piston rod with the drive end facing away from the piston cavity.
12. Install the power valve piston assembly, WITHOUT the metering rod.
13. Press down on the power valve piston assembly and connect the power rod link from the power piston rod.
14. Assemble the plunger spring and new cup to the pump rod and pump.
15. Install the return spring in the pump well.
16. Install a new pump rod seal on the boss in the float bowl.
17. Press down on the pump rod and connect the pump link with the slot in the rod.
18. Install the pump and power rod lever on the end of the throttle shaft.
19. Install the pump lever attaching screw.
20. Close the throttle plate.
21. Hold power piston down and swing metering rod holder over flat surface (gasket removed) of bowl casting next to carburetor bore.
22. Using a 2.3mm (0.09 in.) gauge, measure the distance between the end of the metering rod holder and the mating (gasket) surface of the float bowl.
23. Bend the hanger at the center point as necessary.
24. Hold the throttle wide open and position the metering rod in the main metering jet. Then, connect the rod to the power piston metering rod hanger with the metering rod spring on TOP of the hanger.
25. Install the float needle in the seat.
26. Install the float and hinge pin. Adjust the float as described earlier in this Section.
27. Install the air horn and new gasket. Finger tighten the bolts at this time.
28. Install the fast idle cam and cam link.
29. Install the choke housing and bearing.
30. Install the vacuum break assembly. Install the choke wire connector bracket to hang freely.
31. Install the vacuum break hose.
32. Tighten all the air horn-to-float bowl screws.
33. Install the throttle return spring bracket.
34. Install the idle stop solenoid.
35. Install the fuel inlet nut, gasket, filter and spring.
36. Perform all the carburetor adjustments lisetd earlier in this Section.

GASOLINE FUEL INJECTION SYSTEM

General Information

The electronic fuel injection system is a fuel metering system with the amount of fuel delivered by the throttle body injectors (TBI) determined by an electronic signal supplied by the Electronic Control Module (ECM). The ECM monitors various engine and vehicle conditions to calculate the fuel delivery time (pulse width) of the injectors. The fuel pulse may be modified by the ECM to account for special operating conditions, such as cranking, cold starting, altitude, acceleration, and deceleration.

The ECM controls the exhaust emissions by modifying fuel delivery to achieve, as near as possible, and air/fuel ratio of 14.7 to 1. The injector "ON" time is determined by various inputs to the ECM. By increasing the injector pulse, more fuel is delivered, enriching the air/fuel ratio. Decreasing the injector pulse, leans the air/fuel ratio. Pulses are sent to the injector in two different modes: synchronized and nonsynchronized.

Synchronized Mode

In synchronized mode operation, the injector is pulsed once for each distributor reference pulse.

Nonsynchronized Mode

In nonsynchronized mode operation, the injector is pulsed once every 12.5 milliseconds or 6.25 milliseconds depending on calibration. This pulse time is totally independent of distributor reference pulses.

Nonsynchronized mode results only under the following conditions.

1. The fuel pulse width is too small to be delivered accurately by the injector (approximately 1.5 milliseconds).
2. During the delivery of prime pulses (prime pulses charge the intake manifold with fuel during or just prior to engine starting).
3. During acceleration enrichment.
4. During deceleration leanout.

The basic TBI unit is made up of two major casting assemblies: (1) a throttle body with a valve to control airflow and (2) a fuel body assembly with an integral pressure regulator and fuel injector to supply the required fuel. An electronically operated device to control the idle speed and a device to provide information regarding throttle valve position are included as part of the TBI unit.

The fuel injector(s) is a solenoid-operated device controlled by the ECM. The incoming fuel is directed to the lower end of the injector assembly which has a fine screen filter surrounding the injector inlet. The ECM actuates the solenoid, which lifts a normally closed ball valve off a seat. The fuel under pressure is injected in a conical spray pattern at the walls of the throttle body bore above the throttle valve. The excess fuel passes through a pressure regulator before being returned to the vehicle fuel tank.

The pressure regulator is a diaphragm-operated relief valve with injector pressure on one side and air cleaner pressure on the other. The function of the regulator is to maintain a constant pressure drop across the injector throughout the operating load and speed range of the engine.

The throttle body portion of the TBI may contain ports located at, above, or below the throttle valve. These ports generate the vacuum signals for the EGR valve, MAP sensor, and the canister purge system.

The throttle position sensor (TPS) is a variable resistor used to convert the degree of throttle plate opening to an electrical signal to the ECM. The ECM uses this signal as a reference point of throttle valve position. In addition, an idle air control assembly (IAC), mounted in the throttle body is used to control idle speeds. A cone-shaped valve in the IAC assembly is located in an air passage in the throttle body that leads from the point beneath the air cleaner to below the throttle valve. The ECM monitors idle speeds and, depending on engine load, moves the IAC cone in the air passage to increase or decrease air bypassing the throttle valve to the intake manifold for control of idle speeds.

COMPONENTS AND OPERATION

The throttle body injection (TBI) system provides a means of fuel distribution for controlling exhaust emissions within legislated limits by precisely controlling the air/fuel mixture and under all operating conditions for, as near as possible, complete combustion.

This is accomplished by using an Electronic Control Module (ECM) - a small "on-board" microcomputer - that receives electrical inputs from various sensors about engine operating conditions. An oxygen sensor in the main exhaust stream functions to provide "feedback" information to the ECM as to the oxygen content, lean or rich, in the exhaust. The ECM uses this information from the oxygen sensor, and other sensors, to modify fuel delivery to achieve, as near as possible, an ideal air/fuel ratio of 14.7:1. This air/fuel ratio allows the three-way catalytic converter to be more efficient in the conversion process of reducing exhaust emissions while at the same time providing acceptable levels of driveability and fuel economy.

The ECM program electronically signals the fuel injector in the TBI assembly to provide the correct quantity of fuel for a wide range of operating conditions. Several sensors are used to determine existing operating conditions and the ECM then signals the injector to provide the precise amount of fuel required.

The ECM used on EFI vehicles has a "learning" capability. If the battery is disconnected to clear diagnostic codes, or for repair, the "learning" process has to begin all over again. A change may be noted in vehicle performance. To "teach" the vehicle, make sure the vehicle is at operating temperature and drive at part throttle, under moderate acceleration and idle conditions, until performance returns.

With the EFI system the TBI assembly is centrally located on the intake manifold where air and fuel are distributed through a single bore in the throttle body, similar to a carburated engine. Air for combustion is controlled by a single throttle valve which is connected to the accelerator pedal linkage by a throttle shaft and lever assembly. A special plate is located directly beneath the throttle valve to aid in mixture distribution.

Fuel for combustion is supplied by a single fuel injector, mounted on the TBI assembly, whose metering tip is located directly above the throttle valve. The injector is "pulsed" or "timed" open or closed by an electronic output signal received from the ECM. The ECM receives inputs concerning engine operating conditions from the various sensors (coolant temperature sensor, oxygen sensor, etc.). The ECM, using this information, performs highspeed calculations of engine fuel requirements and "pules" or "times" the injector , open or closed, thereby controlling fuel and air mixtures to achieve, as near as possible, ideal air/fuel mixture ratios.

When the ignition key is turned on, the ECM will initialize (start program running) and energize the fuel pump relay. The fuel pump pressurizes the system to approximately 10 psi. If the ECM does not receive a distributor reference pulse (telling the ECM the engine is turning) within two seconds, the ECM will then de-energize the fuel pump relay, turning off the fuel pump. If a distributor reference pulse is later received, the ECM will turn the fuel pump back on.

Cranking Mode

During engine crank, for each distributor reference pulse the ECM will deliver an injector pulse (synchronized). The crank air/fuel ratio will be used if the throttle position is less than 80% open. Crank air fuel is determined by the ECM and ranges from 1.5:1 at −33°F (−36°C) to 14.7:1 at 201°F (94°C).

The lower the coolant temperature, the longer the pulse width (injector on-time) or richer the air/fuel ratio. The higher the coolant temperature, the less pulse width (injector on-time) or the leaner the air/fuel ratio.

Clear Flood Mode

If for some reason the engine should become flooded, provisions have been made to clear this condition. To clear the flood, the driver must depress the accelerator pedal enough to open to wide-open throttle position. The ECM then issues injector pulses at a rate that would be equal to an air/fuel ratio of 20:1. The ECM maintains this injector rate as long as the throttle remains wide open and the engine RPM is below 600. If the throttle position becomes less than 80%, the ECM then would immediately start issuing crank pulses to the injector calculated by the ECM based on the coolant temperature.

Run Mode

There are two different run modes. When the engine RPM is above 600, the system goes into open loop operation. In open loop operation, the ECM will ignore the signal from the oxygen (O_2) sensor and calculate the injector on-time based upon inputs from the coolant and MAP sensors.

During open loop operation, the ECM analyzes the following items to determine when the system is ready to go to the closed loop mode.

1. The oxygen sensor varying voltage output. (This is dependent on temperature).
2. The coolant sensor must be above specified temperature.
3. A specific amount of time must elapse after starting the engine. These values are stored in the PROM.

When these conditions have been met, the system goes into closed loop operation In closed loop operation, the ECM will modify the pulse width (injector on-time) based upon the signal from the oxygen sensor. The ECM will decrease the on-time if the air/fuel ratio is too rich, and will increase the on-time if the air/fuel ratio is too lean.

The pulse width, thus the amount of enrichment, is determined by manifold pressure change, throttle angle change, and coolant temperature. The higher the manifold pressure and the wider the throttle opening, the wider the pulse width. The acceleration enrichment pulses are delivered nonsynchronized. Any reduction in throttle angle will cancel the enrichment pulses. This way, quick movements of the accelerator will not over-enrich the mixture.

Acceleration Enrichment

When the engine is required to accelerate, the opening of the throttle valve(s) causes a rapid increase in manifold absolute pressure (MAP). This rapid increase in MAP causes fuel to condense on the manifold walls. The ECM senses this increase in throttle angle and MAP, and supplies additional fuel for a short period of time. This prevents the engine from stumbling due to too lean a mixture.

Deceleration Leanout

Upon deceleration, a leaner fuel mixture is required to reduce emission of hydrocarbons (H) and carbon monoxide (CO). To adjust the injection on-time, the ECM uses the decrease in MAP and the decrease in throttle position to calculate a decrease in pulse width. To maintain an idle fuel ratio of 14.7:1, fuel output is momentarily reduced. This is done because of the fuel remaining in the intake manifold.

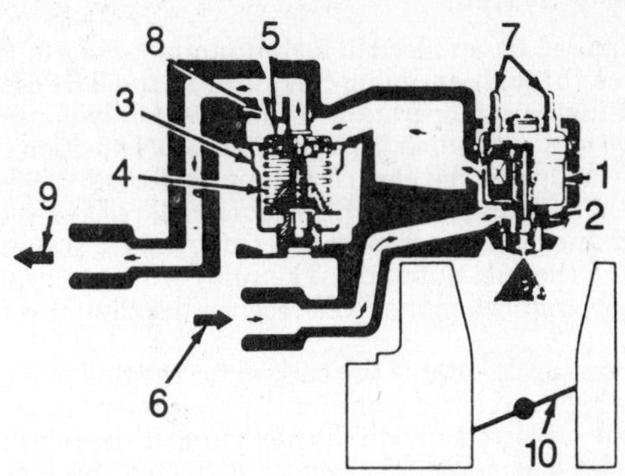

1. Fuel injector
2. Inlet filter
3. Pressure regulator
4. Spring
5. Diaphragm assembly
6. Fuel from pump
7. Injector electrical terminals
8. Constant bleed
9. Fuel return to tank
10. Throttle valve

Cross-sectional view of the TBI 220 unit

Deceleration Fuel Cut-Off

The purpose of deceleration fuel cut-off is to remove fuel from the engine during extreme deceleration conditions. Deceleration fuel cut-off is based on values of manifold pressure, throttle position, and engine RPM stored in the calibration PROM. Deceleration fuel cut-off overrides the deceleration enleanment mode.

Battery Voltage Correction

The purpose of battery voltage correction is to compensate for variations in battery voltage to fuel pump and injector response. The ECM modifies the pulse width by a correction factor in the PROM. When battery voltage decreases, pulse width increases.

Battery voltage correction takes place in all operating modes. When battery voltage is low, the spark delivered by the distributor may be low. To correct this low battery voltage problem, the ECM can do any or all of the following:

a. Increase injector pulse width (increase fuel).
b. Increase idle RPM.
c. Increase ignition dwell time.

Fuel Cut-Off

When the ignition is off, the ECM will not energize the injector. Fuel will also be cut off if the ECM does not receive a reference pulse from the distributor. To prevent dieseling, fuel delivery is completely stopped as soon as the engine is stopped. The ECM will not allow any fuel supply until it receives distributor reference pulses which prevents flooding.

ELECTRONIC FUEL INJECTION SUBSYSTEMS

Electronic fuel injection (EFI) is the name given to the entire fuel injection system. Various "subsystems" are combined to form the overall system. These subsystems are:

1. Fuel Supply System.
2. Throttle Body Injector Assembly (TBI).
3. Idle Air Control (IAC).
4. Electronic Control Module (ECM).
5. Data Sensors.
6. Electronic Spark Timing (EST).
7. Emission Controls.

Each subsystem is described in the following paragraphs.

Fuel Supply System

Fuel, supplied by an electric fuel pump mounted in the fuel tank, passes through an inline fuel filter to the TBI assembly. To control fuel pump operation, a fuel pump rely is used.

When the ignition switch is turned to the ON position the fuel pump relay activates the electric fuel pump for 1.5–2.0 seconds to prime the injector. If the ECM does not receive reference pulses from the distributor after this time, the ECM signals the relay to turn the fuel pump off. The relay will once again activate the fuel pump when the ECM receives distributor reference pulses.

The oil pressure sender is the backup for the fuel pump relay. The sender has two circuits, one for the instrument cluster light or gauge, the other to activate the fuel pump if the relay fails. If the fuse relay has failed, the sender activates the fuel pump when oil pressure reaches 4 psi. Thus a failed fuel pump relay would cause a longer crank, especially in cold weather. If the fuel pump fails, a no start condition exists.

Throttle Body Injector (TBI) Assembly

The basic TBI unit is made up of two major casting assemblies: (1) a throttle body with a valve to control airflow and (2) a fuel body assembly with an integral pressure regulator and fuel injector to supply the required fuel. A device to control idle speed (IAC) and a device to provide information about throttle valve position (TPS) are included as part of the TBI unit.

The throttle body portion of the TBI unit may contain ports located at, above, or below the throttle valve. These ports generate the vacuum signals for the EGR valve, MAP sensor, and the canister purge system.

The fuel injector is a solenoid-operated device controlled by the ECM. The incoming fuel is directed to the lower end of the injector assembly which has a fine screen filter surrounding the injector inlet. The ECM turns on the solenoid, which lifts a normally closed ball valve off a seat. The fuel, under pressure, is injected in a conical spray pattern at the walls of the throttle body bore above the throttle valve. The excess fuel passes through a pressure regulator before being returned to the vehicle fuel tank.

The pressure regulator is a diaphragm-operated relief valve with the injector pressure on one side, and the air cleaner pressure on the other. The function of the regulator is to maintain constant pressure (approximately 11 psi) to the injector throughout the operating loads and speed ranges of the engine. If the regulator pressure is too low, below 9 psi, it can cause poor performance. Too high a pressure could cause detonation and a strong fuel odor.

Idle Air Control (IAC)

The purpose of the idle air control (IAC) system is to control engine idle speeds while preventing stalls due to changes in engine load. The IAC assembly, mounted on the throttle body, controls bypass air around the throttle plate. By extending or retracting a conical valve, a controlled amount of air can move around the throttle plate. If RPM is too low, more air is diverted around the throttle plate to increase RPM.

During idle, the proper position of the IAC valve is calculated by the ECM based on battery voltage, coolant temperature, engine load, and engine RPM. If the RPM drops below a specified rate, the throttle plate is closed. The ECM will then calculate a new valve position.

Three different designs are used for the IAC conical valve. The first design used is single 35 taper while the second design used is a dual taper. The third design is a blunt valve. Care should be taken to insure use of the correct design when service replacement is required.

The IAC motor has 255 different positions or steps. The zero, or reference position, is the fully extended position at which the pintle is seated in the air bypass seat and no air is allowed to bypass the throttle plate. When the motor is fully retracted, maximum air is allowed to bypass the throttle plate. When the motor is fully retracted, maximum air is allowed to bypass the throttle plate.

The ECM always monitors how many steps it has extended or retracted the pintle from the zero or reference position; thus, it always calculates the exact position of the motor. Once the engine has started and the vehicle has reached approximately 40 MPH, the ECM will extend the motor 255 steps from whatever position it is in. This will bottom out the pintle against the seat. The ECM will call this position "0" and thus keep its zero reference updated.

The IAC only affects the engine's idle characteristics. If it is stuck fully open, idle speed is too high (too much air enters the throttle bore) If it is stuck closed, idle speed is too low (not enough air entering). If it is stuck somewhere in the middle, idle may be rough, and the engine won't respond to load changes.

Idle Speed Control

Incorrect diagnosis and/or misunderstanding of the idle speed control systems used on EFI engines may lead to unnecessary replacement of the IAC valve. Engine idle speed is controlled by the ECM which changes the idle speed by moving the IAC valve. The ECM adjusts idle speed in response to fluctuations in engine load (A/C, power steering, electrical loads, etc.) to maintain acceptable idle quality and proper exhaust emission performance.

The following is provided to assist the technician to better understand the system and correctly respond to the following customer concerns:

1. Rough Idle/Low Idle Speed.
2. High Idle Speed/Warm-up Idle Speed; No "Kickdown".

Rough Idle/Low Idle Speed

The ECM will respond to increases in engine load, which would cause a drop in idle speed, by moving the IAC valve to maintain proper idle speed. After the induced load is removed the ECM will return the idle speed to the proper level.

During A/C compressor operation. (MAX, BI-LEVEL, NORM or DEFROST mode) the ECM will increase idle speed in response to an "A/C-ON" signal, thereby compensating for any drop in idle speed due to compressor load. The ECM will also increase the idle speed models in response to high power steering loads.

During periods of especially heavy loads (A/C-ON plus parking maneuvers) significant effects on idle quality may be experienced. Abnormally low idle, rough idle and idle shake may occur if the ECM does not receive the proper signals from the monitored systems.

High Idle Speed/Warm-Up Idle Speed No "Kickdown"

Engine idle speeds as high as 2100 RPM may be experienced during cold starts to quickly raise the catalytic converter to operating temperature for proper exhaust emissions performance. The idle speed attained after a cold start is ECM-controlled and will not drop for 45 seconds regardless of diver attempts to "kickdown."

It is important to recognize the EFI engines have no accelerator pump or choke. Idle speed during warm-up is entirely ECM-controlled and cannot be changed by accelerator "kickdown" or "pumping".

DIAGNOSIS

Abnormally low idle speeds are usually caused by an ECM system-controlled or system-monitored irregularity, while the most common cause for abnormally high idle speed is an induction (intake air) leak. The idle air control valve may occasionally lose its memory function, and it has an ECM-programmed method of "relearning" the correct idle position. This reset, when required, will occur the next time the car exceeds 35 MPH. At this time the ECM seats the pintle of the IAC valve in the throttle body to determine a reference point. Then it backs out a fixed distance to maintain proper idle speed.

Electronic Control Module (ECM)

The ECM, located in the passenger compartment, is the control center of the fuel injection system. The ECM constantly monitors the input information, processes this information from various sensors, and generates output commands to the various systems that affect vehicle performance.

The ability of the ECM to recognize and adjust for vehicle variations (engine transmission, vehicle weight, axle ratio, etc.) is provided by a removable calibration unit (PROM) that is programmed to tailor the ECM for the particular vehicle. There is a specific ECM/PROM combination for each specific vehicle, and the combinations are not interchangeable with those of other vehicles.

The ECM also performs the diagnostic function of the system. It can recognize operational problems, alert the driver through the "CHECK ENGINE" light, and store a code or codes which identify the problem areas to aid the technician in making repairs.

DATA SENSORS

A variety of sensors provide information to the ECM regarding engine operating characteristics. These sensors and their functions are described below.

Engine Coolant Temperature

The coolant sensor is a thermister (a resistor which changes value based on temperature) mounted on the engine coolant stream. As the temperature of the engine coolant changes, the resistance of the coolant sensor changes. Low coolant temperature produces a high resistance (100,000 ohms at −40°C/−40°F), while high temperature causes low resistance (70 ohms at 130°C/266°F).

The ECM supplies a 5 volt signal to the coolant sensor and measures the voltage that returns. By measuring the voltage change, the ECM determines the engine coolant temperature. This information is used to control fuel management, IAC, spark timing, EGR, canister purge and other engine operating conditions.

Oxygen Sensor

The exhaust oxygen sensor is mounted in the exhaust system where it can monitor the oxygen content of the exhaust gas stream. The oxygen content in the exhaust reacts with the oxygen sensor to produce a voltage output. This voltage ranges from approximately 100 millivolts (high oxygen - lean mixture) to 900 millivolts (low oxygen - rich mixture).

By monitoring the voltage output of the oxygen sensor, the ECM will determine what fuel mixture command to give to the injector (lean mixture-low voltage-rich command, rich mixture-high voltage lean command).

Remember that oxygen sensor indicates to the ECM what is happening in the exhaust. It does not cause things to happen. It is a type of gauge: high oxygen content = lean mixture; low oxygen content = rich mixture. The ECM adjust fuel to keep the system working.

MAP Sensor

The manifold absolute pressure (MAP) sensor measures the changes in the intake manifold pressure which result from engine load and speed changes. The pressure measured by the MAP sensor is the difference between barometric pressure (outside air) and manifold pressure (vacuum). A closed throttle engine coastdown would produce a relatively low MAP value (approximately 20–35 kPa), while wide-open throttle would produce a high value (100 kPa). This high value is produced when the pressure inside the manifold is the same as outside the manifold, and 100% of outside air (or 100 kPa) is being measured. This MAP output is the opposite of what you would measure on a vacuum gauge. The use of this sensor also allows the ECM to adjust automatically for different altitude.

The ECM sends a 5 volt reference signal to the MAP sensor. As the MAP changes, the electrical resistance of the sensor also changes. By monitoring the sensor output voltage the ECM can determine the manifold pressure. A higher pressure, lower vacuum (high voltage) requires more fuel, while a lower pressure, higher vacuum (low voltage) requires less fuel.

Vehicle Speed Sensor (VSS)

NOTE: Vehicle should not be driven without a VSS as idle quality may be affected.

The vehicle speed sensor (VSS) is mounted behind the speedometer in the instrument cluster. It provides electrical pulses to the ECM from the speedometer head. The pulses indicate the road speed. The ECM uses this information to operate the IAC, canister purge, and TCC.

Some vehicles equipped with digital instrument clusters use a permanent magnet (PM) generator to provide the VSS signal. The PM generator is located in the transmission and replaces the speedometer cable. The signal from the PM generator drives a stepper motor which drives the odometer.

Throttle Position Sensor (TPS)

The throttle position sensor (TPS) is connected to the throttle shaft and is controlled by the throttle mechanism. A 5 volt reference signal is sent to the TPS from the ECM. As the throttle valve angle is changed (accelerator pedal moved), the resistance of the TPS also changes. At a closed throttle position, the resistance of the TPS is high, so the output voltage to the ECM will be low (approximately 0.5 volt). As the throttle plate opens, the resistance decreases so that, at wide open throttle, the output voltage should be approximately 5 volts.

By monitoring the output voltage from the TPS, the ECM can determine fuel delivery based on throttle valve angle (driver demand). The TPS can either be misadjusted, shorted, open or loose. Misadjustment might result in poor idle or poor wide-open throttle performance. An open TPS signals the ECM that the throttle is always closed, resulting in poor performance. This usually sets a Code 22. A shorted TPS gives the ECM a constant wide-open throttle signal and should set a Code 21. A loose TPS indicates to the ECM that the throttle is moving. This causes intermittent bursts of fuel from the injector and an unstable idle.

Park/Neutral Switch

NOTE: Vehicle should not be driven with the Park/Neutral switch disconnected as idle quality may be affected in Park or Neutral.

This switch indicates to the ECM when the transmission is in Park or Neutral.

A/C Compressor Clutch Engagement. This signal indicates to the ECM that the A/C compressor clutch is engaged.

CAUTION

The 220 TBI unit has a bleed in the pressure regulator to relieve pressure any time the engine is turned off, however a small amount of fuel may be released when the fuel line is disconnected. As a precaution, cover the fuel line with a cloth and dispose of properly.

Electric Fuel Pump

REMOVAL AND INSTALLATION

1. With the engine turned OFF, relieve the fuel pressure at the pressure regulator. See Warning above.
2. Disconnect the negative battery cable.
3. Raise and support the rear of the vehicle on jackstands.
4. Drain the fuel tank, then remove it.
5. Using a hammer and a drift punch, drive the fuel lever sending device and pump assembly locking ring (located on top of the fuel tank) counterclockwise, Lift the assembly from the tank and remove the pump from the fuel lever sending device.
6. Pull the pump up into the attaching hose while pulling it outward away from the bottom support. Be careful not to damage the rubber insulator and strainer during removal. After the pump assembly is clear of the bottom support, pull it out of the rubber connector.
7. To install, reverse the removal procedures.

Testing

Special tools J-29658-82 and J-29658, or their equivalents, will be necessary for this procedure.

1. Secure two sections of 3/8 in. × 10 in. (9.5mm × 254mm) steel tubing, with a double-flare on one end of each section.
2. Install a flare nut on each section of tubing, then connect each of the sections into the flare nut-to-flare nut adapter, while care included in the Gauge Adapter tool No. J-29658-82.
3. Attach the pipe and the adapter assembly to the Gauge tool No. J-29658.
4. Raise and support the vehicle on jackstands.
5. Remove the air cleaner and plug the THERMAC vacuum port on the TBI.
6. Disconnect the fuel feed hose between the fuel tank and the filter, then secure the other ends of the 3/8 in. (9.5mm) tubing into the fuel hoses with hose clamps.
7. Start the engine, check for leaks and observe the fuel pressure, it should be 9–13 psi.
8. Depressurize the fuel system, remove the testing tool, remove the plug from the THERMAC vacuum port, reconnect the fuel line, start the engine and check for fuel leaks.

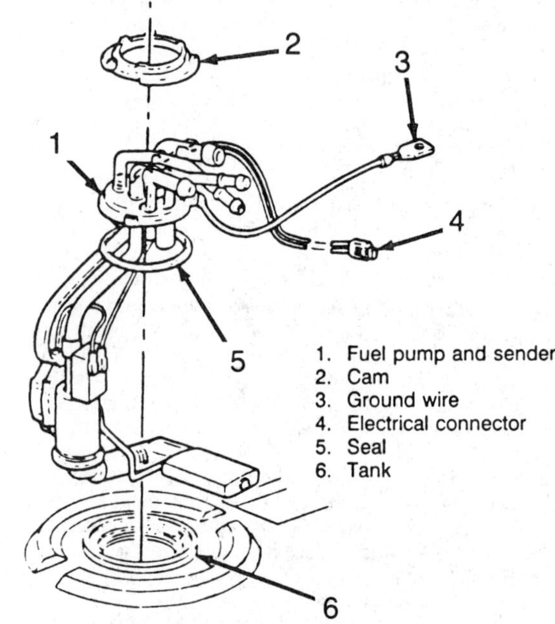

Electric fuel pump

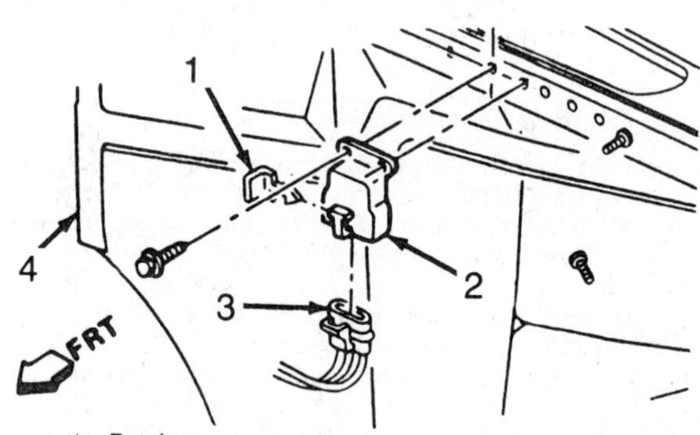

Fuel pump relay on C and K series

Throttle Body

REMOVAL AND INSTALLATION

1. Release the fuel pressure at the pressure regulator (see Warning above).
2. Disconnect the THERMAC hose from the engine fitting and remove the air cleaner.
3. Disconnect the electrical connectors at the idle air control, throttle position sensor and the injector.
4. Disconnect the throttle linkage, return spring and cruise control (if equipped).
5. Disconnect the throttle body vacuum hoses, the fuel supply and fuel return lines.
6. Disconnect the bolts securing the throttle body, then remove it.
7. To install, reverse the removal procedures. Replace the manifold gaskets and O-rings.

Injector

REPLACEMENT

WARNING: When removing the injectors, be careful not to damage the electrical connector pins (on top of the injector), the injector fuel filter and the nozzle. The fuel injector is serviced as a complete assembly ONLY. The

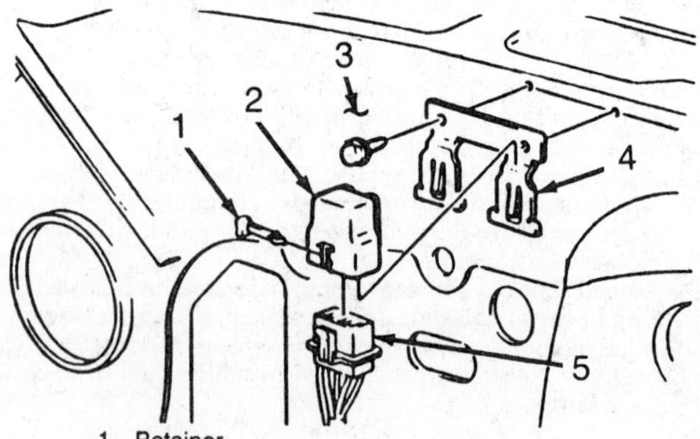

Fuel pump relay on R and V series

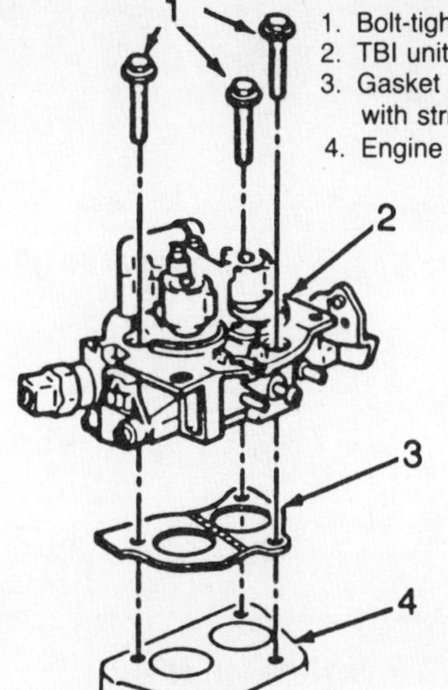

Throttle body installation on the V6

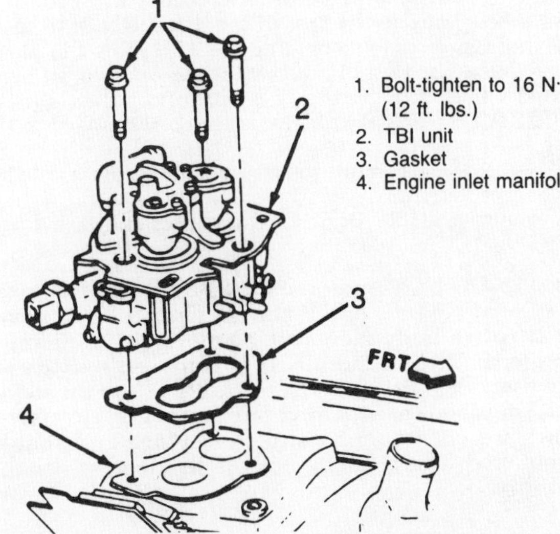

Throttle body installation on the 8–5.0L and 8–5.7L

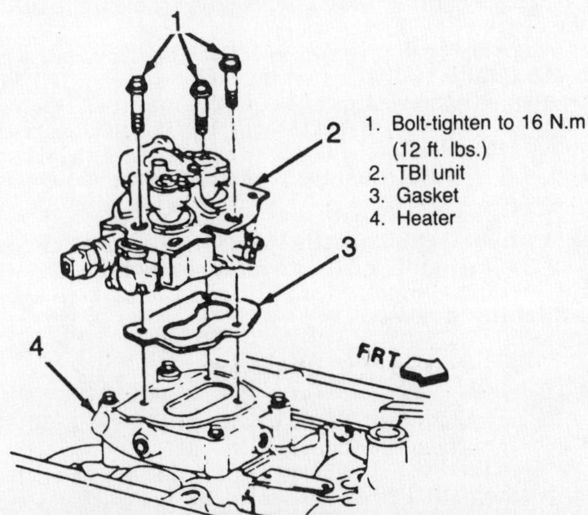

Throttle body installation on the 8–7.4L

injector is an electrical component and should not be immersed in any kind of cleaner.

1. Remove the air cleaner. Relieve the fuel pressure (see Warning above).
2. At the injector connector, squeeze the two tabs together and pull straight up.
3. Remove the fuel meter cover and leave the cover gasket in place.
4. Using a small pry bar or tool No. J–26868, carefully lift the injector until it is free from the fuel meter body.
5. Remove the small O-ring from the nozzle end of the injector. Carefully rotate the injector's fuel filter back and forth to remove it from the base of the injector.
6. Discard the fuel meter cover gasket.
7. Remove the large O-ring and back-up washer from the top of the counterbore of the fuel meter body injector cavity.
8. To install, lubricate the O-rings with automatic transmission fluid and reverse the removal procedures.

Fuel Meter Cover

REPLACEMENT

1. Depressurize the fuel system.
2. Raise the hood, install fender covers and remove the air cleaner assembly.
3. Disconnect the negative battery cable.
4. Disconnect electrical connector at the injector by squeezing the two tabs and pulling straight up.
5. Remove the five screws securing the fuel meter cover to the fuel meter body. Notice the location of the two short screws during removal.

CAUTION

Do not remove the four screws securing the pressure regulator to the fuel meter cover! The fuel pressure regulator includes a large spring under heavy tension which, if accidentally released, could cause personal injury! The fuel meter cover is serviced only as a complete assembly and includes the fuel pressure regulator preset and plugged at the factor.

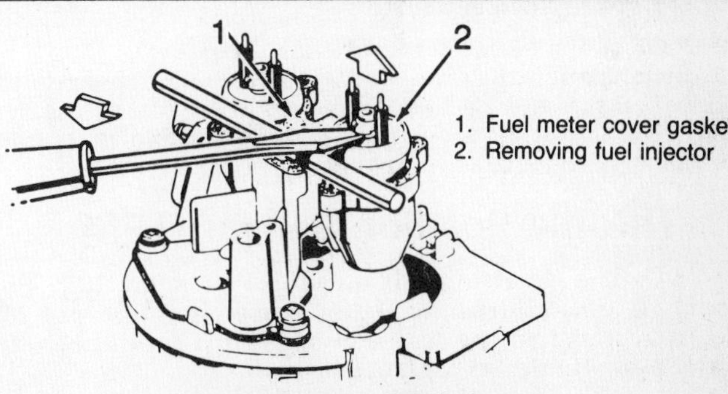

Removing the TBI injector

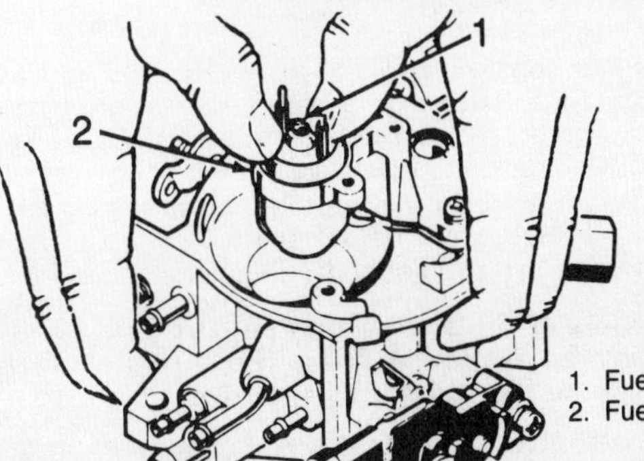

Installing the TBI injector

6. Remove the fuel meter cover assembly from the throttle body.

WARNING: DO NOT immerse the fuel meter cover (with pressure regulator) in any type of cleaner! Immersion of cleaner will damage the internal fuel pressure regulator diaphragms and gaskets.

7. Installation is the reverse of removal. Be sure to use new gaskets and torque the fuel meter cover attaching screws to 28 inch lbs.

NOTE: The service kits include a small vial of thread locking compound with directions for use. If the material is not available, use part number 1054.3L4, Loctite® 4.3L, or equivalent. Do not use a higher strength locking compound than recommended, as this may prevent attaching screw removal or breakage of the screwhead if removal is again required.

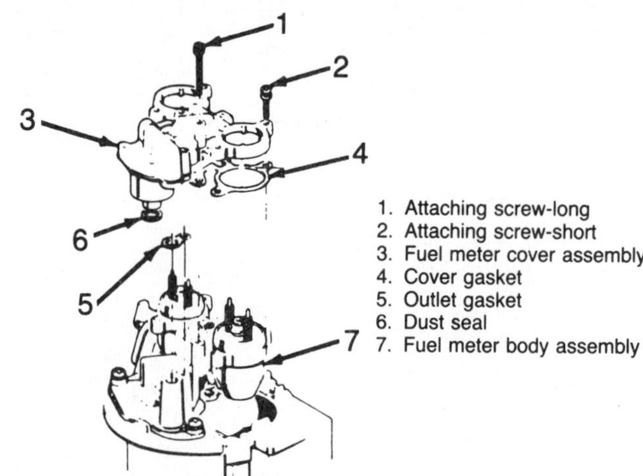

Replacing the fuel meter cover

Fuel Meter Body

REMOVAL AND INSTALLATION

1. Depressurize the fuel system.
2. Raise the hood, install fender covers and remove the air cleaner assembly.
3. Disconnect the negative battery cable.
4. Remove the fuel meter cover assembly.
5. Remove the fuel meter cover gasket, fuel meter outlet gasket and pressure regulator seal.
6. Remove the fuel injectors.
7. Remove the fuel inlet and fuel outlet nuts and gaskets from the fuel meter body.
8. Remove the three screws and lockwashers, then remove the fuel meter body from the throttle assembly.

NOTE: DO not remove the center screw and staking at each end holding the fuel distribution skirt in the throttle body. The skirt is an integral part of the throttle body and is not serviced separately.

9. Remove the fuel meter body insulator gasket.
10. Installation is the reverse order of the removal procedure. Be sure to install new gaskets and O-rings where ever necessary. Apply threadlocking compound, Threadlock Sealer 262 or equivalent to the fuel meter retaining screws.

Throttle Position Sensor (TPS)

NOTE: The throttle position sensor on some 1987–88 models is not adjustable. If the sensor is found out of specifications and the sensor is at fault it cannot be adjusted and should be replaced.

REMOVAL

The Throttle Position Sensor (TPS) is an electrical unit and must not be immersed in any type of liquid solvent or cleaner. The TPS is factory adjusted and the retaining screws are spot welded in place to retain the critical setting. With these considerations, it is possible to clean the throttle body assembly without removing the TPS if care is used. Should TPS replacement be required however, proceed using the following steps:

NOTE: On some of the earlier models, the TPS retaining screws may be removed from the outside of the throttle body, from the side of the sensor.

1. Remove the throttle body as previously outlined in this section. Invert the throttle body and place it on a clean, flat surface.
2. Using a $^5/_{16}$ in. drill bit, drill completely through the 2 TPS screw access holes in the base of the throttle body to be sure of removing the spot welds holding the TPS screws in place.
3. Remove the two TPS attaching screws, lockwashers, and retainers. Then, remove the TPS sensor from the throttle body. DISCARD THE SCREWS! New screws are supplied in the service kits.
4. If necessary, remove the screw holding the Throttle Position Sensor actuator lever to the end of the throttle shaft.
5. Remove the Idle Air Control assembly and gasket from the throttle body.

NOTE: DO NOT immerse the Idle Air Control motor in any type of cleaner and it should always be removed before throttle body cleaning. Immersion in cleaner will damage the IAC assembly. It is replaced only as a complete assembly. Further disassembly of the throttle body is not required for cleaning purposes. The throttle valve screws are permanently staked in place and should not be removed. The throttle body is serviced as a complete assembly.

INSTALLATION

1. Place the throttle body assembly on a holding fixture to avoid damaging the throttle valve.
2. Using a new sealing gasket, install the Idle Air Control motor in the throttle body. Tighten the motor securely. DO NOT overtighten it, to prevent damage to valve.
3. If it was removed, install the Throttle Position Sensor actuator lever by aligning the flats on the lever with the flats on the end of the shaft. Install the retaining screw and tighten it securely.

NOTE: Install the Throttle Position Sensor after completing the assembly of the throttle body unit. Use the thread locking compound supplied in the service kit on the attaching screws.

ADJUSTMENT

1. After installing the TPS on the throttle body, install the throttle body unit on the engine.
2. Remove the EGR valve and the heat shield from engine.
3. Disconnect the TPS harness from the TPS. Using 3, 6 in. (152mm)jumpers, connect the TPS harness to the TPS.
4. With the ignition ON and the engine stopped, use a digital

voltmeter to measure the voltage between the TPS terminals A and B.

5. Loosen the 2 TPS attaching screws and rotate the throttle position sensor to obtain a voltage reading of 0.525 ± 0.75 volts.

6. With the ignition OFF, remove the jumpers and reconnect the TPS harness to the TPS.

7. Install the EGR valve and heat shield on the engine, using a new gasket as necessary.

8. Install the air cleaner gasket and air cleaner on the throttle body unit.

Non-Adjustable TPS Output Check

This check should only be performed, when the throttle body or the TPS has been replaced or after the minimum idle speed has been adjusted.

1. Remove the air cleaner.
2. Disconnect the TPS harness from the TPS.
3. Using suitable jumper wires, connect a digital voltmeter J-29125-A or equivalent to TPS terminals A and B (a suitable ALDL scanner can also be used to read the TPS output voltage).
4. With the ignition ON and the engine running, the TPS voltage should be 0.450–1.25 volts at base idle to approximately 4.5 volts at wide open throttle.
5. If the reading on the TPS is out of specification, check the minimum idle speed before replacing the TPS.
6. If the voltage reading is correct, remove the voltmeter and jumper wires and reconnect the TPS connector to the sensor. Re-install the air cleaner.

Idle Air Control Valve

NOTE: All engines except the 8–7.4L use a thread type IAC valve. The 8–7.4L is equipped with a flange type IAC valve which is attached with screws.

REPLACEMENT

1. Remove the air cleaner.
2. Disconnect the electrical connector from the idle air control valve.
3. On the threaded type, use a 1¼ in. wrench or tool J-33031, remove the idle air control valve.
4. On the 8–7.4L engine, remove the retaining screws and remove the IAC valve.

WARNING: Before install a new idle air control valve, measure the distance that the valve extends (from the motor housing to the end of the cone); the distance should be no greater than 1⅛ in. (28.5mm). If it extends too far, damage will occur to the valve when it is installed.

5. To adjust the threaded type without a collar compress the valve retaining spring, while turning the valve **in**. On all others, exert firm pressure, with slight side to side movement, on the pintle to retract it.
6. To complete the installation, use a new gasket and reverse the removal procedures. Start the engine and allow it to reach operating temperature.

NOTE: The ECM will reset the idle speed when the vehicle is driven at 30 mph.

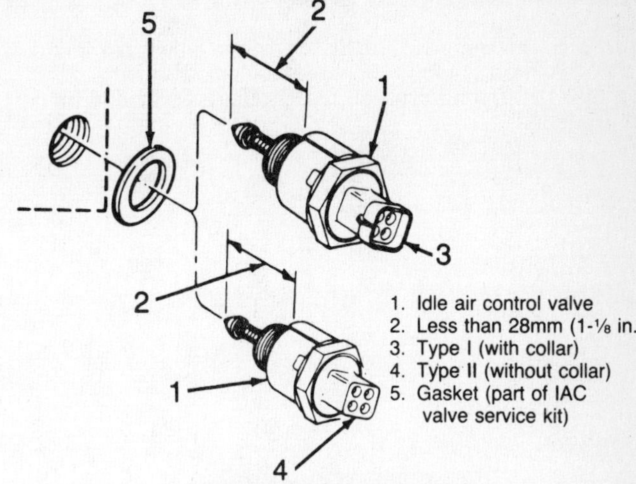

Threaded type IAC valve

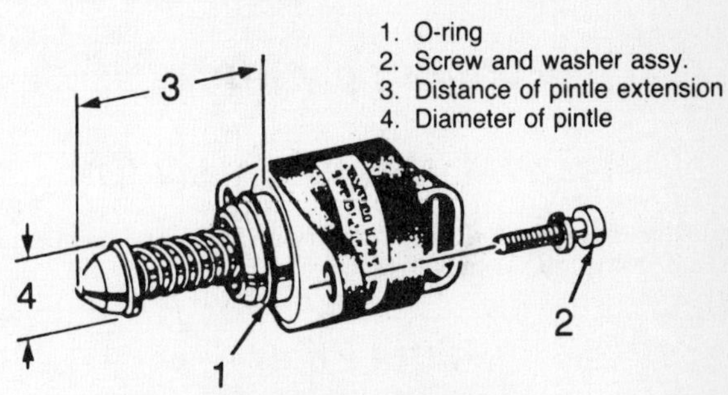

Flange type IAC valve

Fuel Pump Relay

REPLACEMENT

The fuel pump relay is located in the engine compartment. Other than checking for loose electrical connections, the only service necessary is to replace the relay.

Oil Pressure Switch

REPLACEMENT

The oil pressure switch is mounted to the top rear of the engine.

1. Remove the electrical connector from the switch.
2. Remove the oil pressure switch.
3. To install, reverse the removal procedures.

Minimum Idle Speed

ADJUSTMENT

Only if parts of the throttle body have been replaced should this procedure be performed; the engine should be at operating temperature.

1. Remove the air cleaner, adapter and gaskets. Discard the gaskets. Plug any vacuum line ports, as necessary.
2. Leave the idle air control (IAC) valve connected and ground the diagnostic terminal (ALDL connector).
3. Turn the ignition switch to the on position, do not start the engine. Wait for at least 30 seconds (this allows the IAC valve pintle to extend and seat in the throttle body).
4. With the ignition switch still in the on position, disconnect IAC electrical connector.
5. Remove the ground from the diagnostic terminal and start the engine. Let the engine reach normal operating temperature.
6. Apply the parking brake and block the drive wheels. Remove the plug from the idle stop screw by piercing it first with a

suitable tool, then applying leverage to the tool to lift the plug out.

7. With the engine in the drive position adjust the idle stop screw to obtain the following specifications:

- 500–550 rpm in drive on models equipped with automatic transmissions.
- 600–650 rpm in neutral on models equipped with manual transmissions.

8. Turn the ignition off and reconnect the IAC valve connector. Unplug any plugged vacuum line ports and install the air cleaner, adapter and new gaskets.

DIESEL ENGINE FUEL SYSTEM

Fuel Supply Pump

REMOVAL AND INSTALLATION

The diesel fuel supply pump is serviced in the same manner as the fuel pump on the gasoline engines.

Fuel Filter

See Diesel Fuel Filter in Section 1 for service procedures.

WATER IN FUEL

Water is the worst enemy of the diesel fuel injection system. The injection pump, which is designed and constructed to extremely close tolerances, and the injectors can be easily damaged if enough water if forced through them in the fuel. Engine performance will also be drastically affected, and engine damage can occur.

Diesel fuel is much more susceptible than gasoline to water contamination. Diesel engined trucks are equipped with an indicator lamp system that turns on an instrument panel lamp if water (1 to 2½ gallons) is detected in the fuel tank. The lamp will come on for 2 to 5 seconds each time the ignition is turned on, assuring the driver the lamp is working. If there is water in the fuel, the light will come back on after a 15 to 20 second off delay, and then remain on.

PURGING THE FUEL TANK

The 8–6.2L diesel equipped trucks also have a water-in-fuel warning system. The fuel tank is equipped with a filter which screens out the water and lets it lay in the bottom of the tank below the fuel pickup. When the water level reaches a point where it could be drawn into the system, a warning light flashes in the cab. A built-in siphoning system starting at the fuel tank and going to the rear spring hanger on some models, and at the midway point of the right frame rail on other models permits you to attach a hose at the shut-off and siphon out the water.

If it becomes necessary to drain water from the fuel tank, also check the primary fuel filter for water. This procedure is covered under Diesel Fuel Filter in Section 1.

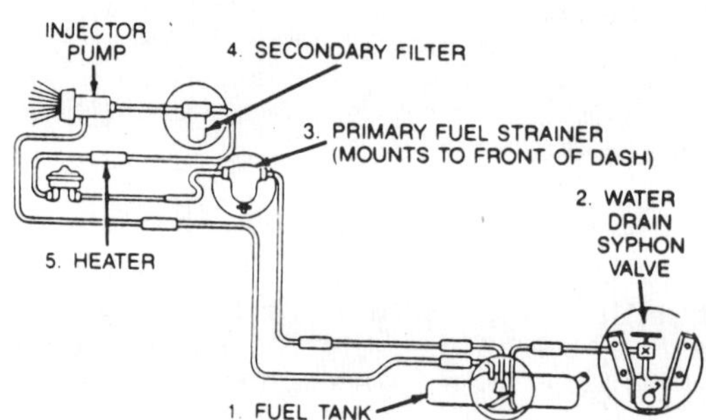

Anti-water system used on diesel engines

Fuel Injection Pump

REMOVAL AND INSTALLATION

1. Disconnect both batteries.
2. Remove the fan and fan shroud.
3. Remove the intake manifold as described in Section 3.
4. Remove the fuel lines as described in this Section.
5. Disconnect the alternator cable at the injection pump, and the detent cable (see illustration) where applicable.
6. Tag and disconnect the necessary wires and hoses at the injection pump.
7. Disconnect the fuel return line at the top of the injection pump.
8. Disconnect the fuel feed line at the injection pump.
9. Remove the air conditioning hose retainer bracket if equipped with A/C.
10. Remove the oil fill tube, including the crankcase depression valve vent hose assembly.
11. Remove the grommet.
12. Scribe or paint a match mark on the front cover and on the injection pump flange.
13. The crankshaft must be rotated in order to gain access to the injection pump drive gear bolts through the oil filler neck hole.
14. Remove the injection pump-to-front cover attaching nuts. Remove the pump and cap all open lines and nozzles.

To install:

15. Replace the gasket. This is important.
16. Align the locating pin on the pump hub with the slot in the

injection pump driven gear. At the same time, align the timing marks.

17. Attach the injection pump to the front cover, aligning the timing marks before torquing the nuts to 30 ft. lbs.

18. Install the drive gear to injection pump bolts, torquing the bolts to 20 ft. lbs.

19. Install the remaining components in the reverse order of removal. Torque the fuel feed line at the injection pump to 20 ft. lbs. Start the engine and check for leaks.

Injection Pump Fuel Lines

REMOVAL AND INSTALLATION

NOTE: When the fuel lines are to be removed, clean all fuel line fittings thoroughly before loosening. Immediately cap the lines, nozzles and pump fittings to maintain cleanliness.

1. Disconnect both batteries.
2. Disconnect the air cleaner bracket at the valve cover.
3. Remove the crankcase ventilator bracket and move it aside.
4. Disconnect the secondary filter lines.
5. Remove the secondary filter adapter.
6. Loosen the vacuum pump holddown clamp and rotate the pump in order to gain access to the intake manifold bolt. Remove the intake manifold bolts. The injection line clips are retained by the same bolts.
7. Remove the intake manifold. Install a protective cover (GM part no. J-29664-1 or equivalent) so no foreign material falls into the engine.
8. Remove the injection line clips at the loom brackets.
9. Remove the injection lines at the nozzles and cover the nozzles with protective caps.
10. Remove the injection lines at the pump and tag the lines for later installation.
11. Remove the fuel line from the injection pump.
12. Install all components in the reverse order of removal. Follow the illustrations for injection line connection.

Fuel Injectors

REMOVAL AND INSTALLATION

Special tool J-29873, or its equivalent, will be necessary for this procedure.

1. Disconnect the truck's batteries.
2. Disconnect the fuel line clip, and remove the fuel return hose.
3. Remove the fuel injection line as previously detailed.
4. Using GM special tool J-29873, remove the injector. Al-

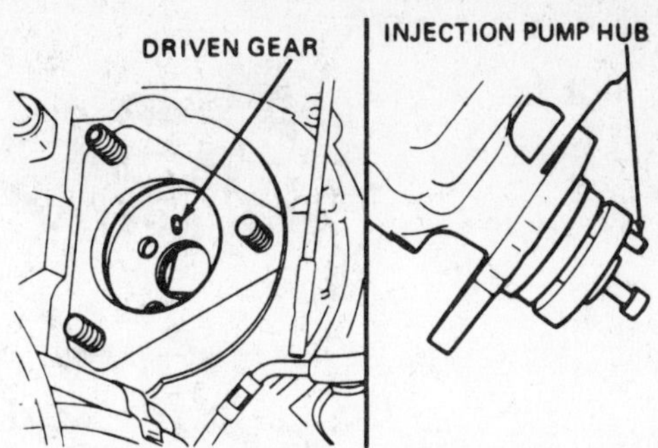

Injection pump locating pin

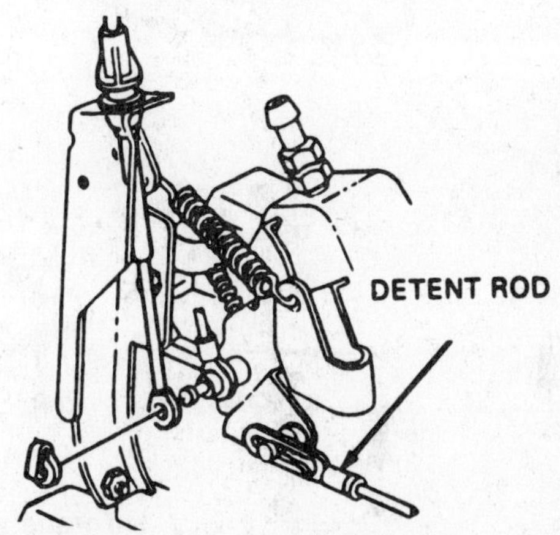

Diesel accelerator cable linkage

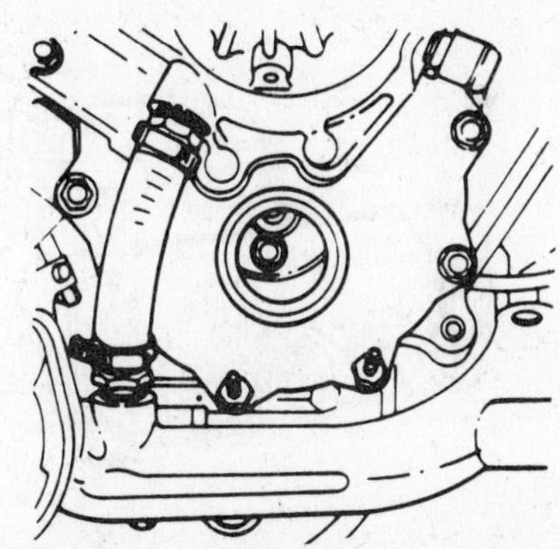
Rotate the crankshaft so that the injection pump drive gear bolts become accessible through the hole

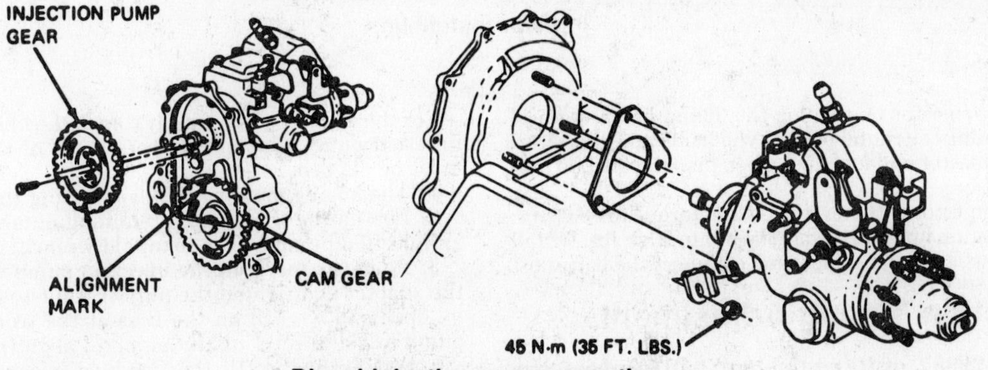

Diesel injection pump mounting

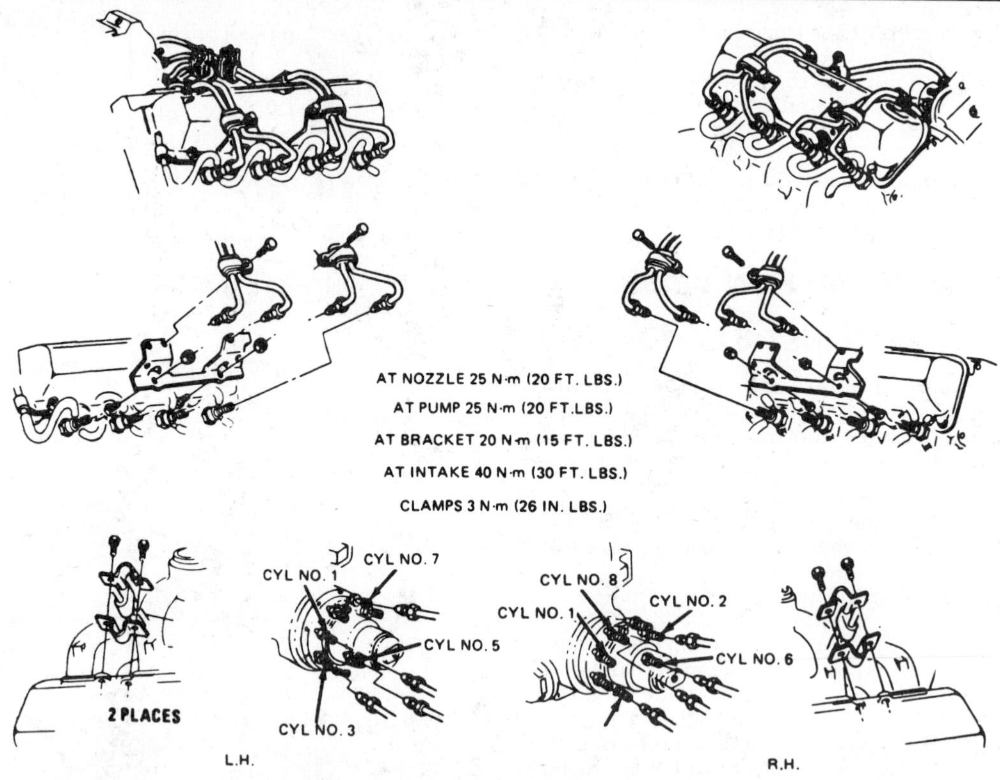

Torque specifications and fuel line routing

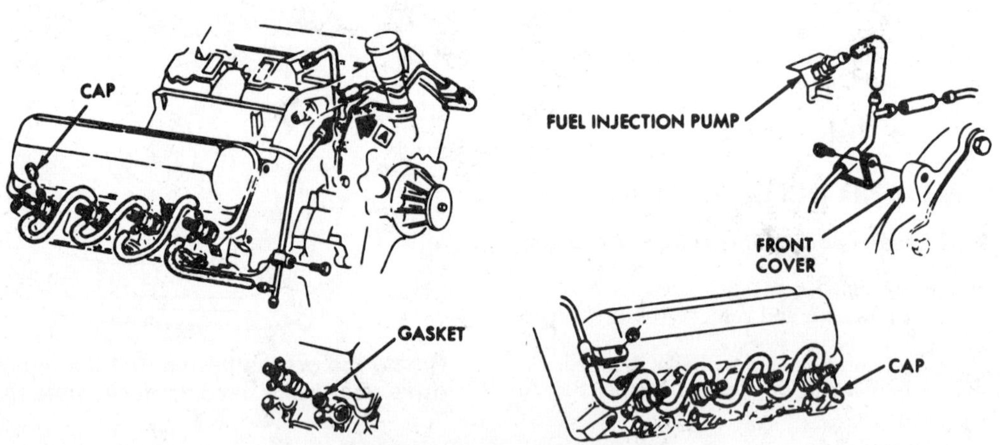

Injector installation

ways remove the injector by turning the 30mm hex protion of the injector; turning the round portion will damage the injector. Always cap the injector and fuel lines when disconnected, to prevent contamination.

5. Install the injector with new gasket and torque to 50 ft. lbs. Connect the injection line and torque the nut to 20 ft. lbs. Install the fuel return hose, fuel line clips, and connnect the batteries.

Injection Timing Adjustment

Special tool J-26987, or its equivalent, will be necessary for this procedure.

For the engine to be properly timed, the lines on the top of the injection pump adapter and the flange of the injection pump must be aligned.

1. The engine must be off for resetting the timing.
2. Loosen the three pump retaining nuts with tool J-26987, an injection pump intake manifold wrench, or its equivalent.
3. Align the mark on the injection pump with the marks on the adapter and tighten the nuts. Torque to 35 ft. lbs. Use a 3/4 in. open-end wrench on the boss at the front of the injection pump to aid in rotating the pump to align the marks.
4. Adjust the throttle rod. See Fuel Injection Pump Removal and Installation.

FUEL TANK

DRAINING

CAUTION

Disconnect the battery before beginning the draining operation.

If the vehicle is not equipped with a drain plug, use the following procedure to remove the fuel.

1. Using a 10 ft. (305cm) piece of ⅜ in. (9.5mm) hose cut a flap slit 18 in. (457mm) from one end.
2. Install a pipe nipple, of slightly larger diameter than the hose, into the opposite end of the hose.
3. Install the nipple end of the hose into the fuel tank with the natural curve of the hose pointing downward. Keep feeding the hose in until the nipple hits the bottom of the tank.
4. Place the other end of the hose in a suitable container and insert a air hose pointing it in the downward direction of the slit and inject air into the line.

NOTE: If the vehicle is to be stored, always drain the fuel from the complete fuel system including the carburetor or throttle body, fuel pump supply, fuel injection pump, fuel lines, and tank.

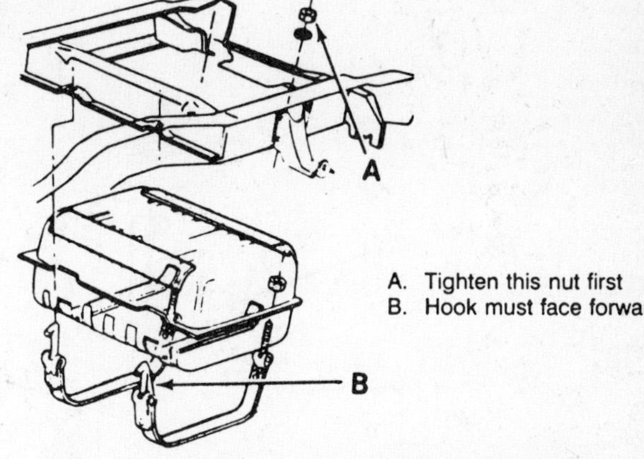

Blazer and Suburban fuel tank mounting

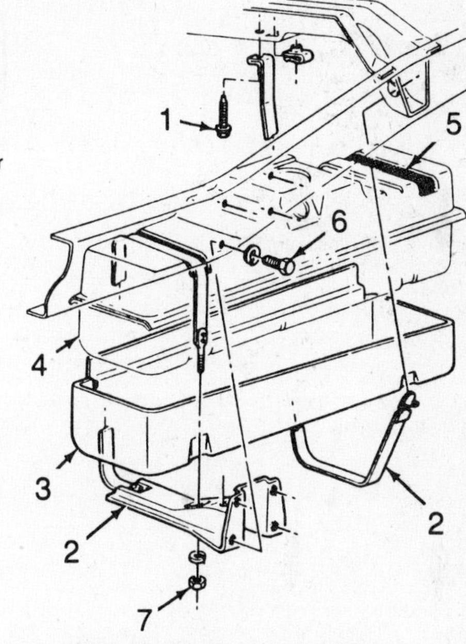

K series fuel tank mounting

REMOVAL AND INSTALLATION

1. Drain the tank.
2. Jack up your vehicle and support it with jackstands.
3. Remove the clamp on the filler neck and the vent tube hose.
4. Remove the gauge hose which is attached to the frame.
5. While supporting the tank securely, remove the support straps.
6. Lower the tank until the gauge wiring can be removed.
7. Remove the tank.
8. Install the unit by reversing the removal procedure. Make certain that the anti-squeak material is replaced during installation.
9. Lower the vehicle.

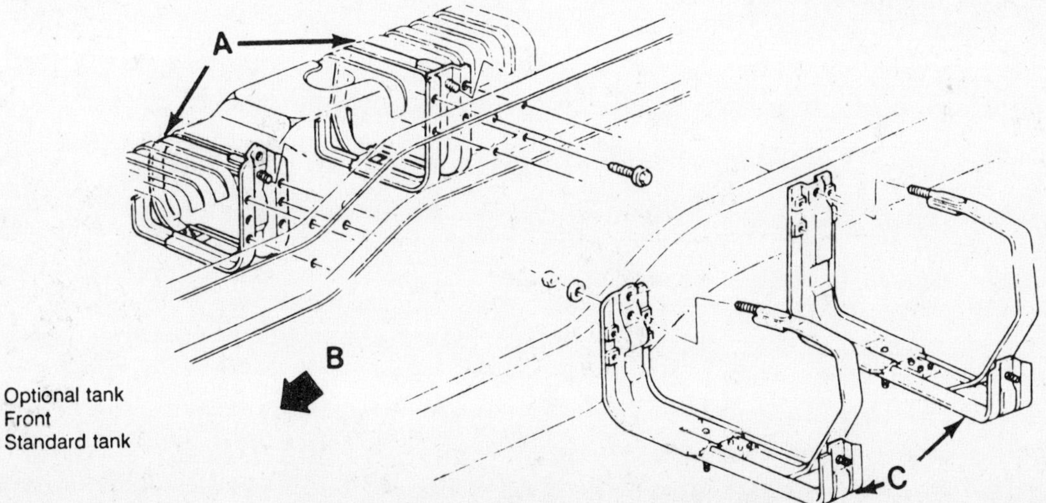

R and V series pickup fuel tank mounting

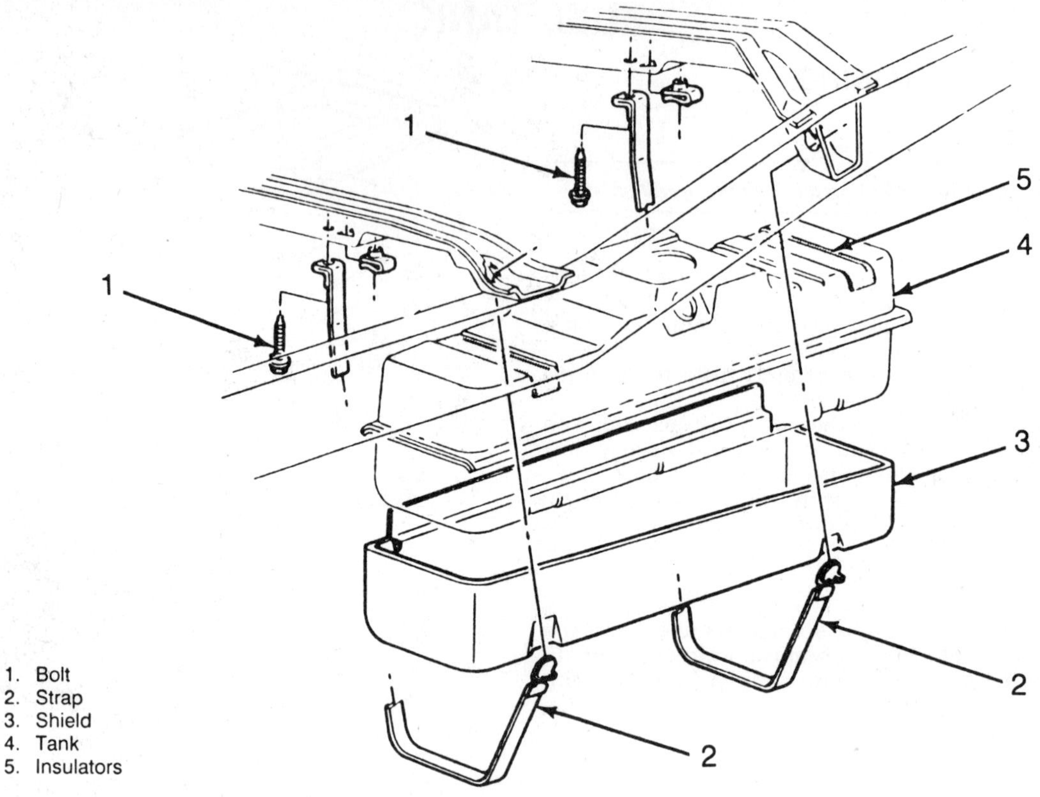

C series fuel tank mounting

6 Chassis Electrical

QUICK REFERENCE INDEX

GENERAL INDEX

UNDERSTANDING BASIC ELECTRICITY

At the rate which both import and domestic manufacturers are incorporating electronic control systems into their production lines, it won't be long before every new vehicle is equipped with one or more on-board computer. These electronic components (with no moving parts) should theoretically last the life of the vehicle, provided nothing external happens to damage the circuits or memory chips.

While it is true that electronic components should never wear out, in the real world malfunctions do occur. It is also true that any computer-based system is extremely sensitive to electrical voltages and cannot tolerate careless or haphazard testing or service procedures. An inexperienced individual can literally do major damage looking for a minor problem by using the wrong kind of test equipment or connecting test leads or connectors with the ignition switch ON. When selecting test equipment, make sure the manufacturers instructions state that the tester is compatible with whatever type of electronic control system is being serviced. Read all instructions carefully and double check all test points before installing probes or making any test connections.

The following section outlines basic diagnosis techniques for dealing with computerized automotive control systems. Along with a general explanation of the various types of test equipment available to aid in servicing modern electronic automotive systems, basic repair techniques for wiring harnesses and connectors is given. Read the basic information before attempting any repairs or testing on any computerized system, to provide the background of information necessary to avoid the most common and obvious mistakes that can cost both time and money. Although the replacement and testing procedures are simple in themselves, the systems are not, and unless one has a thorough understanding of all components and their function within a particular computerized control system, the logical test sequence these systems demand cannot be followed. Minor malfunctions can make a big difference, so it is important to know how each component affects the operation of the overall electronic system to find the ultimate cause of a problem without replacing good components unnecessarily. It is not enough to use the correct test equipment; the test equipment must be used correctly.

Safety Precautions

CAUTION

Whenever working on or around any computer based microprocessor control system, always observe these general precautions to prevent the possibility of personal injury or damage to electronic components.

- Never install or remove battery cables with the key ON or the engine running. Jumper cables should be connected with the key OFF to avoid power surges that can damage electronic control units. Engines equipped with computer controlled systems should avoid both giving and getting jump starts due to the possibility of serious damage to components from arcing in the engine compartment when connections are made with the ignition ON.
- Always remove the battery cables before charging the battery. Never use a high output charger on an installed battery or attempt to use any type of "hot shot" (24 volt) starting aid.
- Exercise care when inserting test probes into connectors to insure good connections without damaging the connector or spreading the pins. Always probe connectors from the rear (wire) side, NOT the pin side, to avoid accidental shorting of terminals during test procedures.
- Never remove or attach wiring harness connectors with the ignition switch ON, especially to an electronic control unit.
- Do not drop any components during service procedures and never apply 12 volts directly to any component (like a solenoid or relay) unless instructed specifically to do so. Some component electrical windings are designed to safely handle only 4 or 5 volts and can be destroyed in seconds if 12 volts are applied directly to the connector.
- Remove the electronic control unit if the vehicle is to be placed in an environment where temperatures exceed approximately 176°F (80°C), such as a paint spray booth or when arc or gas welding near the control unit location in the car.

ORGANIZED TROUBLESHOOTING

When diagnosing a specific problem, organized troubleshooting is a must. The complexity of a modern automobile demands that you approach any problem in a logical, organized manner. There are certain troubleshooting techniques that are standard:

1. Establish when the problem occurs. Does the problem appear only under certain conditions? Were there any noises, odors, or other unusual symptoms?
2. Isolate the problem area. To do this, make some simple tests and observations; then eliminate the systems that are working properly. Check for obvious problems such as broken wires, dirty connections or split or disconnected vacuum hoses. Always check the obvious before assuming something complicated is the cause.
3. Test for problems systematically to determine the cause once the problem area is isolated. Are all the components functioning properly? Is there power going to electrical switches and motors? Is there vacuum at vacuum switches and/or actuators? Is there a mechanical problem such as bent linkage or loose mounting screws? Doing careful, systematic checks will often turn up most causes on the first inspection without wasting time checking components that have little or no relationship to the problem.
4. Test all repairs after the work is done to make sure that the problem is fixed. Some causes can be traced to more than one component, so a careful verification of repair work is important to pick up additional malfunctions that may cause a problem to reappear or a different problem to arise. A blown fuse, for example, is a simple problem that may require more than another fuse to repair. If you don't look for a problem that caused a fuse to blow, for example, a shorted wire may go undetected.

Experience has shown that most problems tend to be the result of a fairly simple and obvious cause, such as loose or corroded connectors or air leaks in the intake system; making careful inspection of components during testing essential to quick and accurate troubleshooting. Special, hand held computerized testers designed specifically for diagnosing the Computer Command Control system are available from a variety of aftermarket sources, as well as from the vehicle manufacturer, but care should be taken that any test equipment being used is designed to diagnose that particular computer controlled system accurately without damaging the control module (ECM) or components being tested.

NOTE: Pinpointing the exact cause of trouble in an electrical system can sometimes only be accomplished by the use of special test equipment. The following describes commonly used test equipment and explains how to put it to best use in diagnosis. In addition to the information covered below, the manufacturer's instructions booklet provided with the tester should be read and clearly understood before attempting any test procedures.

TEST EQUIPMENT

Jumper Wires

Jumper wires are simple, yet extremely valuable, pieces of test equipment. Jumper wires are merely wires that are used to bypass sections of a circuit. The simplest type of jumper wire is merely a length of multistrand wire with an alligator clip at each end. Jumper wires are usually fabricated from lengths of standard automotive wire and whatever type of connector (alligator clip, spade connector or pin connector) that is required for the particular vehicle being tested. The well equipped tool box will have several different styles of jumper wires in several different lengths. Some jumper wires are made with three or more terminals coming from a common splice for special purpose testing. In cramped, hard-to-reach areas it is advisable to have insulated boots over the jumper wire terminals in order to prevent accidental grounding, sparks, and possible fire, especially when testing fuel system components.

Jumper wires are used primarily to locate open electrical circuits, on either the ground (−) side of the circuit or on the hot (+) side. If an electrical component fails to operate, connect the jumper wire between the component and a good ground. If the component operates only with the jumper installed, the ground circuit is open. If the ground circuit is good, but the component does not operate, the circuit between the power feed and component is open. You can sometimes connect the jumper wire directly from the battery to the hot terminal of the component, but first make sure the component uses 12 volts in operation. Some electrical components, such as fuel injectors, are designed to operate on about 4 volts and running 12 volts directly to the injector terminals can burn out the wiring. By inserting an inline fuseholder between a set of test leads, a fused jumper wire can be used for bypassing open circuits. Use a 5 amp fuse to provide protection against voltage spikes. When in doubt, use a voltmeter to check the voltage input to the component and measure how much voltage is being applied normally. By moving the jumper wire successively back from the lamp toward the power source, you can isolate the area of the circuit where the open is located. When the component stops functioning, or the power is cut off, the open is in the segment of wire between the jumper and the point previously tested.

CAUTION

Never use jumpers made from wire that is of lighter gauge than used in the circuit under test. If the jumper wire is of too small gauge, it may overheat and possibly melt. Never use jumpers to bypass high resistance loads (such as motors) in a circuit. Bypassing resistances, in effect, creates a short circuit which may, in turn, cause damage and fire. Never use a jumper for anything other than temporary bypassing of components in a circuit.

12 Volt Test Light

The 12 volt test light is used to check circuits and components while electrical current is flowing through them. It is used for voltage and ground tests. Twelve volt test lights come in different styles but all have three main parts; a ground clip, a probe, and a light. The most commonly used 12 volt test lights have pick-type probes. To use a 12 volt test light, connect the ground clip to a good ground and probe wherever necessary with the pick. The pick should be sharp so that it can penetrate wire insulation to make contact with the wire, without making a large hole in the insulation. The wrap-around light is handy in hard to reach areas or where it is difficult to support a wire to push a probe pick into it. To use the wrap around light, hook the wire to probed with the hook and pull the trigger. A small pick will be forced through the wire insulation into the wire core.

CAUTION

Do not use a test light to probe electronic ignition spark plug or coil wires. Never use a pick-type test light to probe wiring on computer controlled systems unless specifically instructed to do so. Any wire insulation that is pierced by the test light probe should be taped and sealed with silicone after testing.

Like the jumper wire, the 12 volt test light is used to isolate opens in circuits. But, whereas the jumper wire is used to bypass the open to operate the load, the 12 volt test light is used to locate the presence of voltage in a circuit. If the test light glows, you know that there is power up to that point; if the 12 volt test light does not glow when its probe is inserted into the wire or connector, you know that there is an open circuit (no power). Move the test light in successive steps back toward the power source until the light in the handle does glow. When it does glow, the open is between the probe and point previously probed.

NOTE: The test light does not detect that 12 volts (or any particular amount of voltage) is present; it only detects that some voltage is present. It is advisable before using the test light to touch its terminals across the battery posts to make sure the light is operating properly.

Self-Powered Test Light

The self-powered test light usually contains a 1.5 volt penlight battery. One type of self-powered test light is similar in design to the 12 volt test light. This type has both the battery and the light in the handle and pick-type probe tip. The second type has the light toward the open tip, so that the light illuminates the contact point. The self-powered test light is dual purpose piece of test equipment. It can be used to test for either open or short circuits when power is isolated from the circuit (continuity test). A powered test light should not be used on any computer controlled system or component unless specifically instructed to do so. Many engine sensors can be destroyed by even this small amount of voltage applied directly to the terminals.

Open Circuit Testing

To use the self-powered test light to check for open circuits, first isolate the circuit from the vehicle's 12 volt power source by disconnecting the battery or wiring harness connector. Connect the test light ground clip to a good ground and probe sections of the circuit sequentially with the test light. (start from either end of the circuit). If the light is out, the open is between the probe and the circuit ground. If the light is on, the open is between the probe and end of the circuit toward the power source.

Short Circuit Testing

By isolating the circuit both from power and from ground, and using a self-powered test light, you can check for shorts to ground in the circuit. Isolate the circuit from power and ground. Connect the test light ground clip to a good ground and probe any easy-to-reach test point in the circuit. If the light comes on, there is a short somewhere in the circuit. To isolate the short, probe a test point at either end of the isolated circuit (the light should be on). Leave the test light probe connected and open connectors, switches, remove parts, etc., sequentially, until the light goes out. When the light goes out, the short is between the last circuit component opened and the previous circuit opened.

NOTE: The 1.5 volt battery in the test light does not provide much current. A weak battery may not provide enough power to illuminate the test light even when a complete circuit is made (especially if there are high resistances in the circuit). Always make sure that the test battery is strong. To check the battery, briefly touch the ground clip to the probe; if the light glows brightly the battery is strong enough for testing. Never use a self-powered test light to perform checks for opens or shorts when power is applied to the electrical system under test. The 12 volt vehicle power will quickly burn out the 1.5 volt light bulb in the test light.

Voltmeter

A voltmeter is used to measure voltage at any point in a circuit, or to measure the voltage drop across any part of a circuit.

It can also be used to check continuity in a wire or circuit by indicating current flow from one end to the other. Voltmeters usually have various scales on the meter dial and a selector switch to allow the selection of different voltages. The voltmeter has a positive and a negative lead. To avoid damage to the meter, always connect the negative lead to the negative (–) side of circuit (to ground or nearest the ground side of the circuit) and connect the positive lead to the positive (+) side of the circuit (to the power source or the nearest power source). Note that the negative voltmeter lead will always be black and that the positive voltmeter will always be some color other than black (usually red). Depending on how the voltmeter is connected into the circuit, it has several uses.

A voltmeter can be connected either in parallel or in series with a circuit and it has a very high resistance to current flow. When connected in parallel, only a small amount of current will flow through the voltmeter current path; the rest will flow through the normal circuit current path and the circuit will work normally. When the voltmeter is connected in series with a circuit, only a small amount of current can flow through the circuit. The circuit will not work properly, but the voltmeter reading will show if the circuit is complete or not.

Available Voltage Measurement

Set the voltmeter selector switch to the 20V position and connect the meter negative lead to the negative post of the battery. Connect the positive meter lead to the positive post of the battery and turn the ignition switch ON to provide a load. Read the voltage on the meter or digital display. A well charged battery should register over 12 volts. If the meter reads below 11.5 volts, the battery power may be insufficient to operate the electrical system properly. This test determines voltage available from the battery and should be the first step in any electrical trouble diagnosis procedure. Many electrical problems, especially on computer controlled systems, can be caused by a low state of charge in the battery. Excessive corrosion at the battery cable terminals can cause a poor contact that will prevent proper charging and full battery current flow.

Normal battery voltage is 12 volts when fully charged. When the battery is supplying current to one or more circuits it is said to be "under load". When everything is off the electrical system is under a "no-load" condition. A fully charged battery may show about 12.5 volts at no load; will drop to 12 volts under medium load; and will drop even lower under heavy load. If the battery is partially discharged the voltage decrease under heavy load may be excessive, even though the battery shows 12 volts or more at no load. When allowed to discharge further, the battery's available voltage under load will decrease more severely. For this reason, it is important that the battery be fully charged during all testing procedures to avoid errors in diagnosis and incorrect test results.

Voltage Drop

When current flows through a resistance, the voltage beyond the resistance is reduced (the larger the current, the greater the reduction in voltage). When no current is flowing, there is no voltage drop because there is no current flow. All points in the circuit which are connected to the power source are at the same voltage as the power source. The total voltage drop always equals the total source voltage. In a long circuit with many connectors, a series of small, unwanted voltage drops due to corrosion at the connectors can add up to a total loss of voltage which impairs the operation of the normal loads in the circuit.

INDIRECT COMPUTATION OF VOLTAGE DROPS

1. Set the voltmeter selector switch to the 20 volt position.
2. Connect the meter negative lead to a good ground.
3. Probe all resistances in the circuit with the positive meter lead.
4. Operate the circuit in all modes and observe the voltage readings.

DIRECT MEASUREMENT OF VOLTAGE DROPS

1. Set the voltmeter switch to the 20 volt position.
2. Connect the voltmeter negative lead to the ground side of the resistance load to be measured.
3. Connect the positive lead to the positive side of the resistance or load to be measured.
4. Read the voltage drop directly on the 20 volt scale.

Too high a voltage indicates too high a resistance. If, for example, a blower motor runs too slowly, you can determine if there is too high a resistance in the resistor pack. By taking voltage drop readings in all parts of the circuit, you can isolate the problem. Too low a voltage drop indicates too low a resistance. If, for example, a blower motor runs too fast in the MED and/or LOW position, the problem can be isolated in the resistor pack by taking voltage drop readings in all parts of the circuit to locate a possibly shorted resistor. The maximum allowable voltage drop under load is critical, especially if there is more than one high resistance problem in a circuit because all voltage drops are cumulative. A small drop is normal due to the resistance of the conductors.

HIGH RESISTANCE TESTING

1. Set the voltmeter selector switch to the 4 volt position.
2. Connect the voltmeter positive lead to the positive post of the battery.
3. Turn on the headlights and heater blower to provide a load.
4. Probe various points in the circuit with the negative voltmeter lead.
5. Read the voltage drop on the 4 volt scale. Some average maximum allowable voltage drops are:

FUSE PANEL – 7 volts
IGNITION SWITCH – 5 volts
HEADLIGHT SWITCH – 7 volts
IGNITION COIL (+) – 5 volts
ANY OTHER LOAD – 1.3 volts

NOTE: Voltage drops are all measured while a load is operating; without current flow, there will be no voltage drop.

Ohmmeter

The ohmmeter is designed to read resistance (ohms) in a circuit or component. Although there are several different styles of ohmmeters, all will usually have a selector switch which permits the measurement of different ranges of resistance (usually the selector switch allows the multiplication of the meter reading by 10, 100, 1,000, and 10,000). A calibration knob allows the meter to be set at zero for accurate measurement. Since all ohmmeters are powered by an internal battery (usually 9 volts), the ohmmeter can be used as a self-powered test light. When the ohmmeter is connected, current from the ohmmeter flows through the circuit or component being tested. Since the ohmmeter's internal resistance and voltage are known values, the amount of current flow through the meter depends on the resistance of the circuit or component being tested.

The ohmmeter can be used to perform continuity test for opens or shorts (either by observation of the meter needle or as a self-powered test light), and to read actual resistance in a circuit. It should be noted that the ohmmeter is used to check the resistance of a component or wire while there is no voltage applied to the circuit. Current flow from an outside voltage source (such as the vehicle battery) can damage the ohmmeter, so the circuit or component should be isolated from the vehicle electrical system before any testing is done. Since the ohmmeter uses its own voltage source, either lead can be connected to any test point.

NOTE: When checking diodes or other solid state components, the ohmmeter leads can only be connected one way in order to measure current flow in a single direction. Make sure the positive (+) and negative (−) terminal connections are as described in the test procedures to verify the one-way diode operation.

In using the meter for making continuity checks, do not be concerned with the actual resistance readings. Zero resistance, or any resistance readings, indicate continuity in the circuit. Infinite resistance indicates an open in the circuit. A high resistance reading where there should be none indicates a problem in the circuit. Checks for short circuits are made in the same manner as checks for open circuits except that the circuit must be isolated from both power and normal ground. Infinite resistance indicates no continuity to ground, while zero resistance indicates a dead short to ground.

RESISTANCE MEASUREMENT

The batteries in an ohmmeter will weaken with age and temperature, so the ohmmeter must be calibrated or "zeroed" before taking measurements. To zero the meter, place the selector switch in its lowest range and touch the two ohmmeter leads together. Turn the calibration knob until the meter needle is exactly on zero.

NOTE: All analog (needle) type ohmmeters must be zeroed before use, but some digital ohmmeter models are automatically calibrated when the switch is turned on. Self-calibrating digital ohmmeters do not have an adjusting knob, but its a good idea to check for a zero readout before use by touching the leads together. All computer controlled systems require the use of a digital ohmmeter with at least 10 megohms impedance for testing. Before any test procedures are attempted, make sure the ohmmeter used is compatible with the electrical system or damage to the on-board computer could result.

To measure resistance, first isolate the circuit from the vehicle power source by disconnecting the battery cables or the harness connector. Make sure the key is OFF when disconnecting any components or the battery. Where necessary, also isolate at least one side of the circuit to be checked to avoid reading parallel resistances. Parallel circuit resistances will always give a lower reading than the actual resistance of either of the branches. When measuring the resistance of parallel circuits, the total resistance will always be lower than the smallest resistance in the circuit. Connect the meter leads to both sides of the circuit (wire or component) and read the actual measured ohms on the meter scale. Make sure the selector switch is set to the proper ohm scale for the circuit being tested to avoid misreading the ohmmeter test value.

WARNING: Never use an ohmmeter with power applied to the circuit. Like the self-powered test light, the ohmmeter is designed to operate on its own power supply. The normal 12 volt automotive electrical system current could damage the meter!

Ammeters

An ammeter measures the amount of current flowing through a circuit in units called amperes or amps. Amperes are units of electron flow which indicate how fast the electrons are flowing through the circuit. Since Ohms Law dictates that current flow in a circuit is equal to the circuit voltage divided by the total circuit resistance, increasing voltage also increases the current level (amps). Likewise, any decrease in resistance will increase the amount of amps in a circuit. At normal operating voltage, most circuits have a characteristic amount of amperes, called "current draw" which can be measured using an ammeter. By referring to a specified current draw rating, measuring the amperes, and comparing the two values, one can determine what is happening within the circuit to aid in diagnosis. An open circuit, for example, will not allow any current to flow so the ammeter reading will be zero. More current flows through a heavily loaded circuit or when the charging system is operating.

An ammeter is always connected in series with the circuit being tested. All of the current that normally flows through the circuit must also flow through the ammeter; if there is any other path for the current to follow, the ammeter reading will not be accurate. The ammeter itself has very little resistance to current flow and therefore will not affect the circuit, but it will measure current draw only when the circuit is closed and electricity is flowing. Excessive current draw can blow fuses and drain the battery, while a reduced current draw can cause motors to run slowly, lights to dim and other components to not operate properly. The ammeter can help diagnose these conditions by locating the cause of the high or low reading.

Multimeters

Different combinations of test meters can be built into a single unit designed for specific tests. Some of the more common combination test devices are known as Volt/Amp testers, Tach/Dwell meters, or Digital Multimeters. The Volt/Amp tester is used for charging system, starting system or battery tests and consists of a voltmeter, an ammeter and a variable resistance carbon pile. The voltmeter will usually have at least two ranges for use with 6, 12 and 24 volt systems. The ammeter also has more than one range for testing various levels of battery loads and starter current draw and the carbon pile can be adjusted to offer different amounts of resistance. The Volt/Amp tester has heavy leads to carry large amounts of current and many later models have an inductive ammeter pickup that clamps around the wire to simplify test connections. On some models, the ammeter also has a zero-center scale to allow testing of charging and starting systems without switching leads or polarity. A digital multimeter is a voltmeter, ammeter and ohmmeter combined in an instrument which gives a digital readout. These are often used when testing solid state circuits because of their high input impedance (usually 10 megohms or more).

The tach/dwell meter combines a tachometer and a dwell (cam angle) meter and is a specialized kind of voltmeter. The tachometer scale is marked to show engine speed in rpm and the dwell scale is marked to show degrees of distributor shaft rotation. In most electronic ignition systems, dwell is determined by the control unit, but the dwell meter can also be used to check the duty cycle (operation) of some electronic engine control systems. Some tach/dwell meters are powered by an internal battery, while others take their power from the car battery in use. The battery powered testers usually require calibration much like an ohmmeter before testing.

Special Test Equipment

A variety of diagnostic tools are available to help troubleshoot and repair computerized engine control systems. The most sophisticated of these devices are the console type engine analyzers that usually occupy a garage service bay, but there are several types of aftermarket electronic testers available that will allow quick circuit tests of the engine control system by plugging directly into a special connector located in the engine compartment or under the dashboard. Several tool and equipment manufacturers offer simple, hand held testers that measure various circuit voltage levels on command to check all system components for proper operation. Although these testers usually cost about $300–500, consider that the average computer control module (or ECM) can cost just as much and the money saved by not replacing perfectly good sensors or components in an attempt to correct a problem could justify the purchase price of a special diagnostic tester the first time it's used.

These computerized testers can allow quick and easy test measurements while the engine is operating or while the car is being driven. In addition, the on-board computer memory can be read to access any stored trouble codes; in effect allowing the computer to tell you where it hurts and aid trouble diagnosis by pinpointing exactly which circuit or component is malfunctioning. In the same manner, repairs can be tested to make sure the problem has been corrected. The biggest advantage these special testers have is their relatively easy hookups that minimize or eliminate the chances of making the wrong connections and getting false voltage readings or damaging the computer accidentally.

NOTE: It should be remembered that these testers check voltage levels in circuits; they don't detect mechanical problems or failed components if the circuit voltage falls within the preprogrammed limits stored in the tester PROM unit. Also, most of the hand held testes are designed to work only on one or two systems made by a specific manufacturer.

A variety of aftermarket testers are available to help diagnose different computerized control systems. Owatonna Tool Company (OTC), for example, markets a device called the OTC Monitor which plugs directly into the assembly line diagnostic link (ALDL). The OTC tester makes diagnosis a simple matter of pressing the correct buttons and, by changing the internal PROM or inserting a different diagnosis cartridge, it will work on any model from full size to subcompact, over a wide range of years. An adapter is supplied with the tester to allow connection to all types of ALDL links, regardless of the number of pin terminals used. By inserting an updated PROM into the OTC tester, it can be easily updated to diagnose any new modifications of computerized control systems.

Wiring Harnesses

The average automobile contains about ½ mile of wiring, with hundreds of individual connections. To protect the many wires from damage and to keep them from becoming a confusing tangle, they are organized into bundles, enclosed in plastic or taped together and called wire harnesses. Different wiring harnesses serve different parts of the vehicle. Individual wires are color coded to help trace them through a harness where sections are hidden from view.

A loose or corroded connection or a replacement wire that is too small for the circuit will add extra resistance and an additional voltage drop to the circuit. A ten percent voltage drop can result in slow or erratic motor operation, for example, even though the circuit is complete. Automotive wiring or circuit conductors can be in any one of three forms:

1. Single strand wire
2. Multistrand wire
3. Printed circuitry

Single strand wire has a solid metal core and is usually used inside such components as alternators, motors, relays and other devices. Multistrand wire has a core made of many small strands of wire twisted together into a single conductor. Most of the wiring in an automotive electrical system is made up of multistrand wire, either as a single conductor or grouped together in a harness. All wiring is color coded on the insulator, either as a solid color or as a colored wire with an identification stripe. A printed circuit is a thin film of copper or other conductor that is printed on an insulator backing. Occasionally, a printed circuit is sandwiched between two sheets of plastic for more protection and flexibility. A complete printed circuit, consisting of conductors, insulating material and connectors for lamps or other components is called a printed circuit board. Printed circuitry is used in place of individual wires or harnesses in places where space is limited, such as behind instrument panels.

Wire Gauge

Since computer controlled automotive electrical systems are very sensitive to changes in resistance, the selection of properly sized wires is critical when systems are repaired. The wire gauge number is an expression of the cross section area of the conductor. The most common system for expressing wire size is the American Wire Gauge (AWG) system.

Wire cross section area is measured in circular mils. A mil is $^{1}/_{1000}$ in. (0.001 in.); a circular mil is the area of a circle one mil in diameter. For example, a conductor ¼ in. in diameter is 0.250 in. or 250 mils. The circular mil cross section area of the wire is 250 squared (250^2) or 62,500 circular mils. Imported car models usually use metric wire gauge designations, which is simply the cross section area of the conductor in square millimeters (mm^2).

Gauge numbers are assigned to conductors of various cross section areas. As gauge number increases, area decreases and the conductor becomes smaller. A 5 gauge conductor is smaller than a 1 gauge conductor and a 10 gauge is smaller than a 5 gauge. As the cross section area of a conductor decreases, resistance increases and so does the gauge number. A conductor with a higher gauge number will carry less current than a conductor with a lower gauge number.

NOTE: Gauge wire size refers to the size of the conductor, not the size of the complete wire. It is possible to have two wires of the same gauge with different diameters because one may have thicker insulation than the other.

12 volt automotive electrical systems generally use 10, 12, 14, 16 and 18 gauge wire. Main power distribution circuits and larger accessories usually use 10 and 12 gauge wire. Battery cables are usually 4 or 6 gauge, although 1 and 2 gauge wires are occasionally used. Wire length must also be considered when making repairs to a circuit. As conductor length increases, so does resistance. An 18 gauge wire, for example, can carry a 10 amp load for 10 feet without excessive voltage drop; however if a 15 foot wire is required for the same 10 amp load, it must be a 16 gauge wire.

An electrical schematic shows the electrical current paths when a circuit is operating properly. It is essential to understand how a circuit works before trying to figure out why it does not. Schematics break the entire electrical system down into individual circuits and show only one particular circuit. In a schematic, no attempt is made to represent wiring and components as they physically appear on the vehicle; switches and other components are shown as simply as possible. Face views of harness connectors show the cavity or terminal locations in all multi-pin connectors to help locate test points.

If you need to backprobe a connector while it is on the component, the order of the terminals must be mentally reversed. The wire color code can help in this situation, as well as a keyway, lock tab or other reference mark.

NOTE: Some wiring diagrams are included in this book. As trucks have become more complex and available with longer option lists, wiring diagrams have grown in size and complexity. It has become almost impossible to provide a readable reproduction of a wiring diagram in a book this size.

WIRING REPAIR

Soldering is a quick, efficient method of joining metals permanently. Everyone who has the occasion to make wiring repairs should know how to solder. Electrical connections that are soldered are far less likely to come apart and will conduct electricity much better than connections that are only "pig-tailed" together. The most popular (and preferred) method of soldering is with an electrical soldering gun. Soldering irons are available in many sizes and wattage ratings. Irons with higher wattage ratings deliver higher temperatures and recover lost heat faster. A small soldering iron rated for no more than 50 watts is recommended, especially on electrical systems where excess heat can damage the components being soldered.

There are three ingredients necessary for successful soldering; proper flux, good solder and sufficient heat. A soldering flux is necessary to clean the metal of tarnish, prepare it for soldering and to enable the solder to spread into tiny crevices. When soldering, always use a resin flux or resin core solder which is non-corrosive and will not attract moisture once the job is finished. Other types of flux (acid core) will leave a residue that will attract moisture and cause the wires to corrode. Tin is a unique metal with a low melting point. In a molten state, it dissolves and alloys easily with many metals. Solder is made by mixing tin with lead. The most common proportions are 40/60, 50/50 and 60/40, with the percentage of tin listed first. Low priced solders usually contain less tin, making them very difficult for a beginner to use because more heat is required to melt the solder. A common solder is 40/60 which is well suited for all-around general use, but 60/40 melts easier, has more tin for a better joint and is preferred for electrical work.

Soldering Techniques

Successful soldering requires that the metals to be joined be heated to a temperature that will melt the solder – usually 360–460°F (182–238°C). Contrary to popular belief, the purpose of the soldering iron is not to melt the solder itself, but to heat the parts being soldered to a temperature high enough to melt the solder when it is touched to the work. Melting flux-cored solder on the soldering iron will usually destroy the effectiveness of the flux.

NOTE: Soldering tips are made of copper for good heat conductivity, but must be "tinned" regularly for quick transference of heat to the project and to prevent the solder from sticking to the iron. To "tin" the iron, simply heat it and touch the flux-cored solder to the tip; the solder will flow over the hot tip. Wipe the excess off with a clean rag, but be careful as the iron will be hot.

After some use, the tip may become pitted. If so, simply dress the tip smooth with a smooth file and "tin" the tip again. An old saying holds that "metals well cleaned are half soldered." Flux-cored solder will remove oxides but rust, bits of insulation and oil or grease must be removed with a wire brush or emery cloth. For maximum strength in soldered parts, the joint must start off clean and tight. Weak joints will result in gaps too wide for the solder to bridge.

If a separate soldering flux is used, it should be brushed or swabbed on only those areas that are to be soldered. Most solders contain a core of flux and separate fluxing is unnecessary. Hold the work to be soldered firmly. It is best to solder on a wooden board, because a metal vise will only rob the piece to be soldered of heat and make it difficult to melt the solder. Hold the soldering tip with the broadest face against the work to be soldered. Apply solder under the tip close to the work, using enough solder to give a heavy film between the iron and the piece being soldered, while moving slowly and making sure the solder melts properly. Keep the work level or the solder will run to the lowest part and favor the thicker parts, because these require more heat to melt the solder. If the soldering tip overheats (the solder coating on the face of the tip burns up), it should be retinned. Once the soldering is completed, let the soldered joint stand until cool. Tape and seal all soldered wire splices after the repair has cooled.

Wire Harness and Connectors

The on-board computer (ECM) wire harness electrically connects the control unit to the various solenoids, switches and sensors used by the control system. Most connectors in the engine compartment or otherwise exposed to the elements are protected against moisture and dirt which could create oxidation and deposits on the terminals. This protection is important because of the very low voltage and current levels used by the computer and sensors. All connectors have a lock which secures the male and female terminals together, with a secondary lock holding the seal and terminal into the connector. Both terminal locks must be released when disconnecting ECM connectors.

These special connectors are weather-proof and all repairs require the use of a special terminal and the tool required to service it. This tool is used to remove the pin and sleeve terminals. If removal is attempted with an ordinary pick, there is a good chance that the terminal will be bent or deformed. Unlike standard blade type terminals, these terminals cannot be straightened once they are bent. Make certain that the connectors are properly seated and all of the sealing rings in place when connecting leads. On some models, a hinge-type flap provides a backup or secondary locking feature for the terminals. Most secondary locks are used to improve the connector reliability by retaining the terminals if the small terminal lock tangs are not positioned properly.

Molded-on connectors require complete replacement of the connection. This means splicing a new connector assembly into the harness. All splices in on-board computer systems should be soldered to insure proper contact. Use care when probing the connections or replacing terminals in them as it is possible to short between opposite terminals. If this happens to the wrong terminal pair, it is possible to damage certain components. Always use jumper wires between connectors for circuit checking and never probe through weatherproof seals.

Open circuits are often difficult to locate by sight because corrosion or terminal misalignment are hidden by the connectors. Merely wiggling a connector on a sensor or in the wiring harness may correct the open circuit condition. This should always be considered when an open circuit or a failed sensor is indicated. Intermittent problems may also be caused by oxidized or loose connections. When using a circuit tester for diagnosis, always probe connections from the wire side. Be careful not to damage sealed connectors with test probes.

All wiring harnesses should be replaced with identical parts, using the same gauge wire and connectors. When signal wires are spliced into a harness, use wire with high temperature insulation only. With the low voltage and current levels found in the system, it is important that the best possible connection at all wire splices be made by soldering the splices together. It is seldom necessary to replace a complete harness. If replacement is necessary, pay close attention to insure proper harness routing. Secure the harness with suitable plastic wire clamps to prevent vibrations from causing the harness to wear in spots or contact any hot components.

NOTE: Weatherproof connectors cannot be replaced with standard connectors. Instructions are provided with replacement connector and terminal packages. Some wire harnesses have mounting indicators (usually pieces of colored tape) to mark where the harness is to be secured.

In making wiring repairs, it's important that you always replace damaged wires with wires that are the same gauge as the wire being replaced. The heavier the wire, the smaller the gauge number. Wires are color-coded to aid in identification and whenever possible the same color coded wire should be used for replacement. A wire stripping and crimping tool is necessary to install solderless terminal connectors. Test all crimps by pulling on the wires; it should not be possible to pull the wires out of a good crimp.

Wires which are open, exposed or otherwise damaged are repaired by simple splicing. Where possible, if the wiring harness is accessible and the damaged place in the wire can be located, it is best to open the harness and check for all possible damage. In an inaccessible harness, the wire must be bypassed with a new insert, usually taped to the outside of the old harness.

When replacing fusible links, be sure to use fusible link wire, NOT ordinary automotive wire. Make sure the fusible segment is of the same gauge and construction as the one being replaced and double the stripped end when crimping the terminal connector for a good contact. The melted (open) fusible link segment of the wiring harness should be cut off as close to the harness as possible, then a new segment spliced in as described. In the case of a damaged fusible link that feeds two harness wires, the harness connections should be replaced with two fusible link wires so that each circuit will have its own separate protection.

NOTE: Most of the problems caused in the wiring harness are due to bad ground connections. Always check all vehicle ground connections for corrosion or looseness before performing any power feed checks to eliminate the chance of a bad ground affecting the circuit.

Repairing Hard Shell Connectors

Unlike molded connectors, the terminal contacts in hard shell connectors can be replaced. Weatherproof hard-shell connectors with the leads molded into the shell have non-replaceable terminal ends. Replacement usually involves the use of a special terminal removal tool that depress the locking tangs (barbs) on the connector terminal and allow the connector to be removed from the rear of the shell. The connector shell should be replaced if it shows any evidence of burning, melting, cracks, or breaks. Replace individual terminals that are burnt, corroded, distorted or loose.

NOTE: The insulation crimp must be tight to prevent the insulation from sliding back on the wire when the wire is pulled. The insulation must be visibly compressed under the crimp tabs, and the ends of the crimp should be turned in for a firm grip on the insulation.

The wire crimp must be made with all wire strands inside the crimp. The terminal must be fully compressed on the wire strands with the ends of the crimp tabs turned in to make a firm grip on the wire. Check all connections with an ohmmeter to insure a good contact. There should be no measurable resistance between the wire and the terminal when connected.

Mechanical Test Equipment

Vacuum Gauge

Most gauges are graduated in inches of mercury (in.Hg), although a device called a manometer reads vacuum in inches of water (in. H_2O). The normal vacuum reading usually varies between 18 and 22 in.Hg at sea level. To test engine vacuum, the vacuum gauge must be connected to a source of manifold vacuum. Many engines have a plug in the intake manifold which can be removed and replaced with an adapter fitting. Connect the vacuum gauge to the fitting with a suitable rubber hose or, if no manifold plug is available, connect the vacuum gauge to any device using manifold vacuum, such as EGR valves, etc. The vacuum gauge can be used to determine if enough vacuum is reaching a component to allow its actuation.

Hand Vacuum Pump

Small, hand-held vacuum pumps come in a variety of designs. Most have a built-in vacuum gauge and allow the component to be tested without removing it from the vehicle. Operate the pump lever or plunger to apply the correct amount of vacuum required for the test specified in the diagnosis routines. The level of vacuum in inches of Mercury (in.Hg) is indicated on the pump gauge. For some testing, an additional vacuum gauge may be necessary.

Intake manifold vacuum is used to operate various systems and devices on late model vehicles. To correctly diagnose and solve problems in vacuum control systems, a vacuum source is necessary for testing. In some cases, vacuum can be taken from the intake manifold when the engine is running, but vacuum is normally provided by a hand vacuum pump. These hand vacuum pumps have a built-in vacuum gauge that allow testing while the device is still attached to the component. For some tests, an additional vacuum gauge may be necessary.

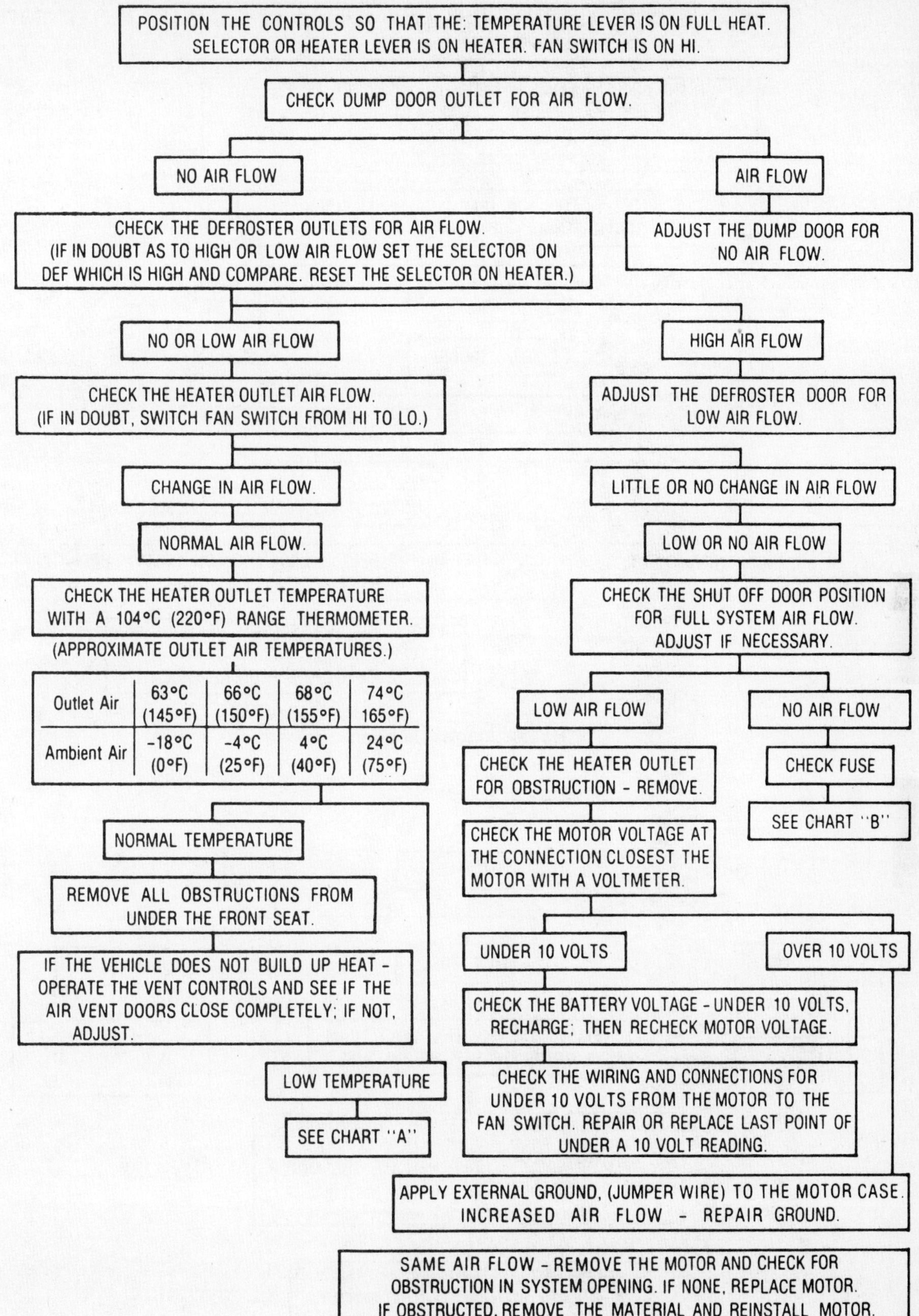

Heater diagnosis chart

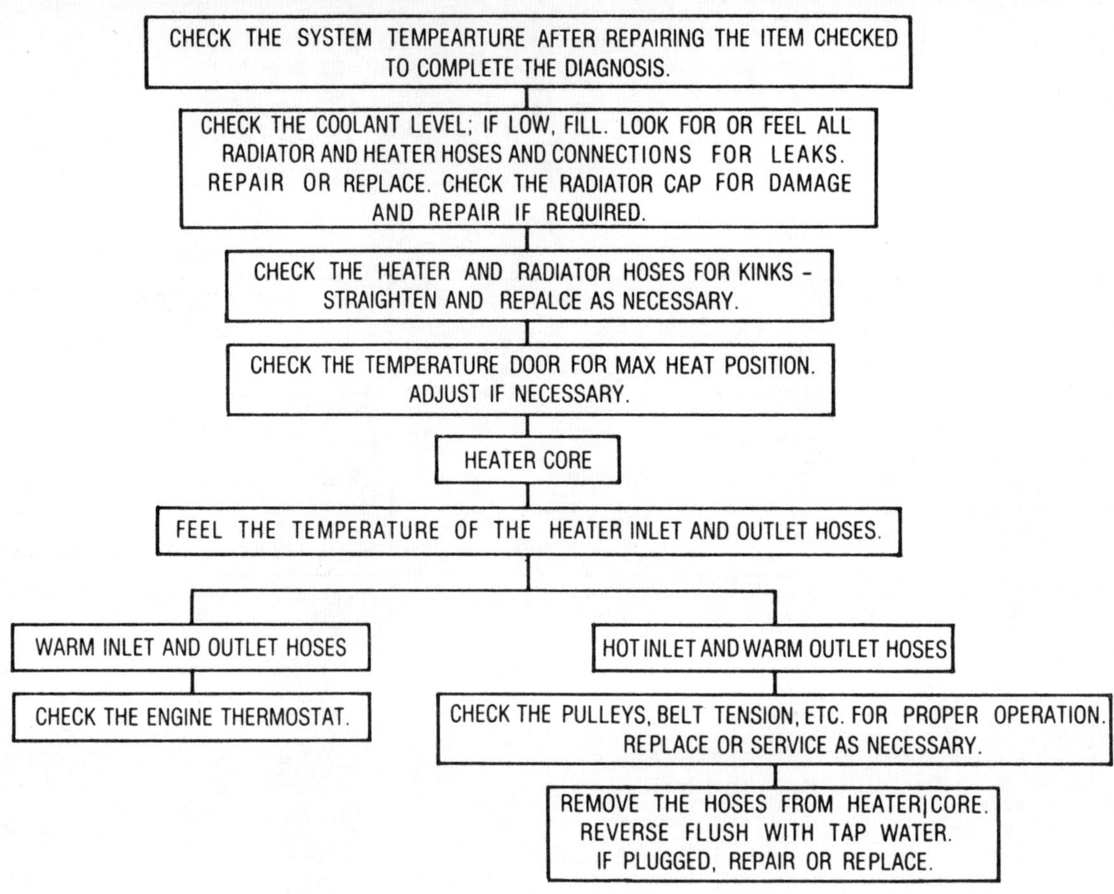
CHECK THE SYSTEM TEMPEARTURE AFTER REPAIRING THE ITEM CHECKED TO COMPLETE THE DIAGNOSIS.
CHECK THE COOLANT LEVEL; IF LOW, FILL. LOOK FOR OR FEEL ALL RADIATOR AND HEATER HOSES AND CONNECTIONS FOR LEAKS. REPAIR OR REPLACE. CHECK THE RADIATOR CAP FOR DAMAGE AND REPAIR IF REQUIRED.
CHECK THE HEATER AND RADIATOR HOSES FOR KINKS - STRAIGHTEN AND REPALCE AS NECESSARY.
CHECK THE TEMPERATURE DOOR FOR MAX HEAT POSITION. ADJUST IF NECESSARY.
HEATER CORE
FEEL THE TEMPERATURE OF THE HEATER INLET AND OUTLET HOSES.
WARM INLET AND OUTLET HOSES
CHECK THE ENGINE THERMOSTAT.
HOT INLET AND WARM OUTLET HOSES
CHECK THE PULLEYS, BELT TENSION, ETC. FOR PROPER OPERATION. REPLACE OR SERVICE AS NECESSARY.
REMOVE THE HOSES FROM HEATER CORE. REVERSE FLUSH WITH TAP WATER. IF PLUGGED, REPAIR OR REPLACE.

Heater diagnosis chart

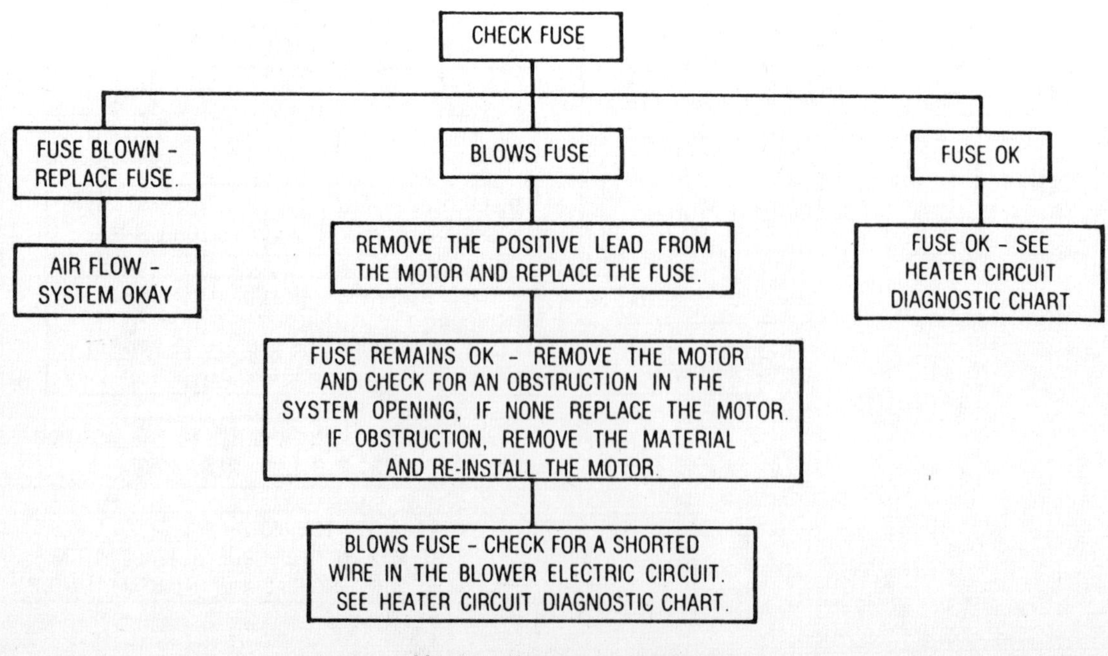
CHECK FUSE
FUSE BLOWN - REPLACE FUSE.
AIR FLOW - SYSTEM OKAY
BLOWS FUSE
REMOVE THE POSITIVE LEAD FROM THE MOTOR AND REPLACE THE FUSE.
FUSE REMAINS OK - REMOVE THE MOTOR AND CHECK FOR AN OBSTRUCTION IN THE SYSTEM OPENING, IF NONE REPLACE THE MOTOR. IF OBSTRUCTION, REMOVE THE MATERIAL AND RE-INSTALL THE MOTOR.
BLOWS FUSE - CHECK FOR A SHORTED WIRE IN THE BLOWER ELECTRIC CIRCUIT. SEE HEATER CIRCUIT DIAGNOSTIC CHART.
FUSE OK
FUSE OK - SEE HEATER CIRCUIT DIAGNOSTIC CHART

Heater diagnosis chart

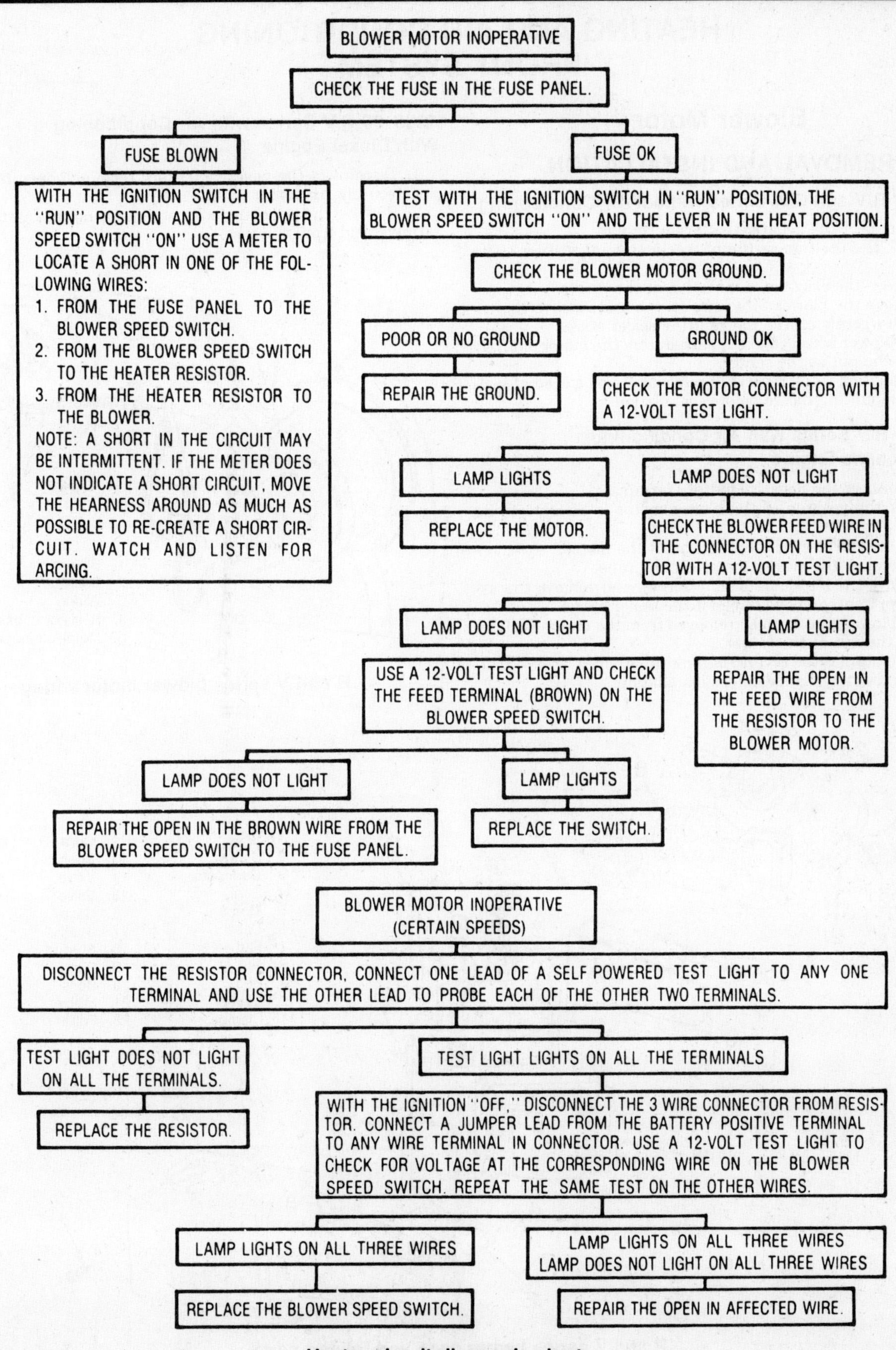

Heater circuit diagnosis chart

HEATING AND AIR CONDITIONING FRONT SYSTEM

Blower Motor

REMOVAL AND INSTALLATION

1988–90 R/V and C/K Series without Air Conditioning

1. Disconnect the negative battery terminal.
2. Mark the position of the blower motor in relation to its case.
3. Remove the electrical connection at the motor.
4. Remove the blower attaching screws and remove the assembly. Pry gently on the flange if the sealer sticks.
5. The blower wheel can be removed from the motor shaft by removing the nut at the center.
6. Installation is the reverse of removal. Apply a bead of sealer to the mounting flange before installation.

1988–90 R/V Series with Air Conditioning With Gasoline Engine

1. Disconnect the negative battery terminal.
2. Mark the position of the blower motor in relation to its case.
3. Remove the electrical connection at the motor.
4. Disconnect the blower motor cooling tube.
5. Remove the blower attaching screws and remove the assembly. Pry gently on the flange if the sealer sticks.
6. The blower wheel can be removed from the motor shaft by removing the nut at the center.
7. Installation is the reverse of removal. Apply a bead of sealer to the mounting flange before installation.

1988–90 R/V Series with Air Conditioning With Diesel Engine

1. Disconnect the negative battery terminal, open the hood, and securely support it.
2. Remove the attaching bolts and nuts and remove the insulating shield from the case.

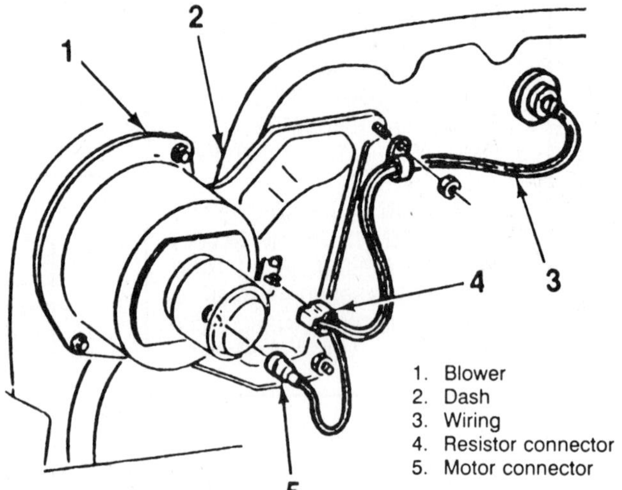

R and V series blower motor wiring

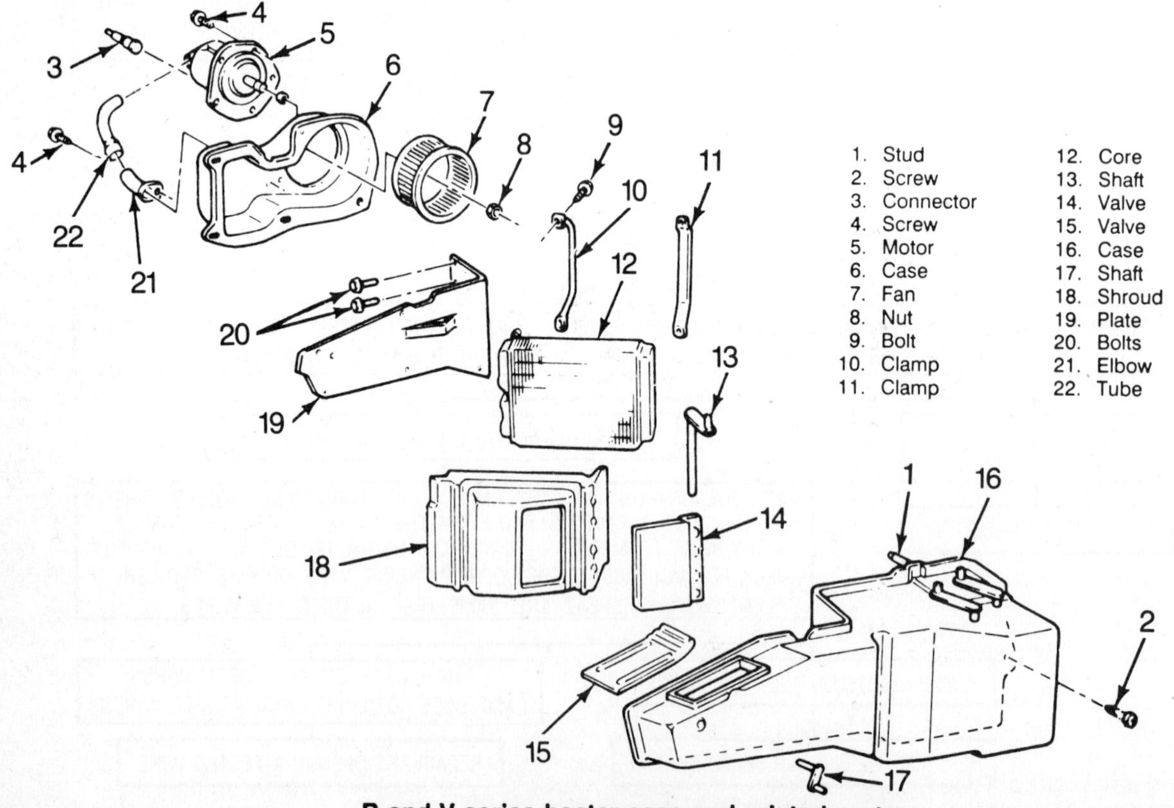

R and V series heater case and related parts

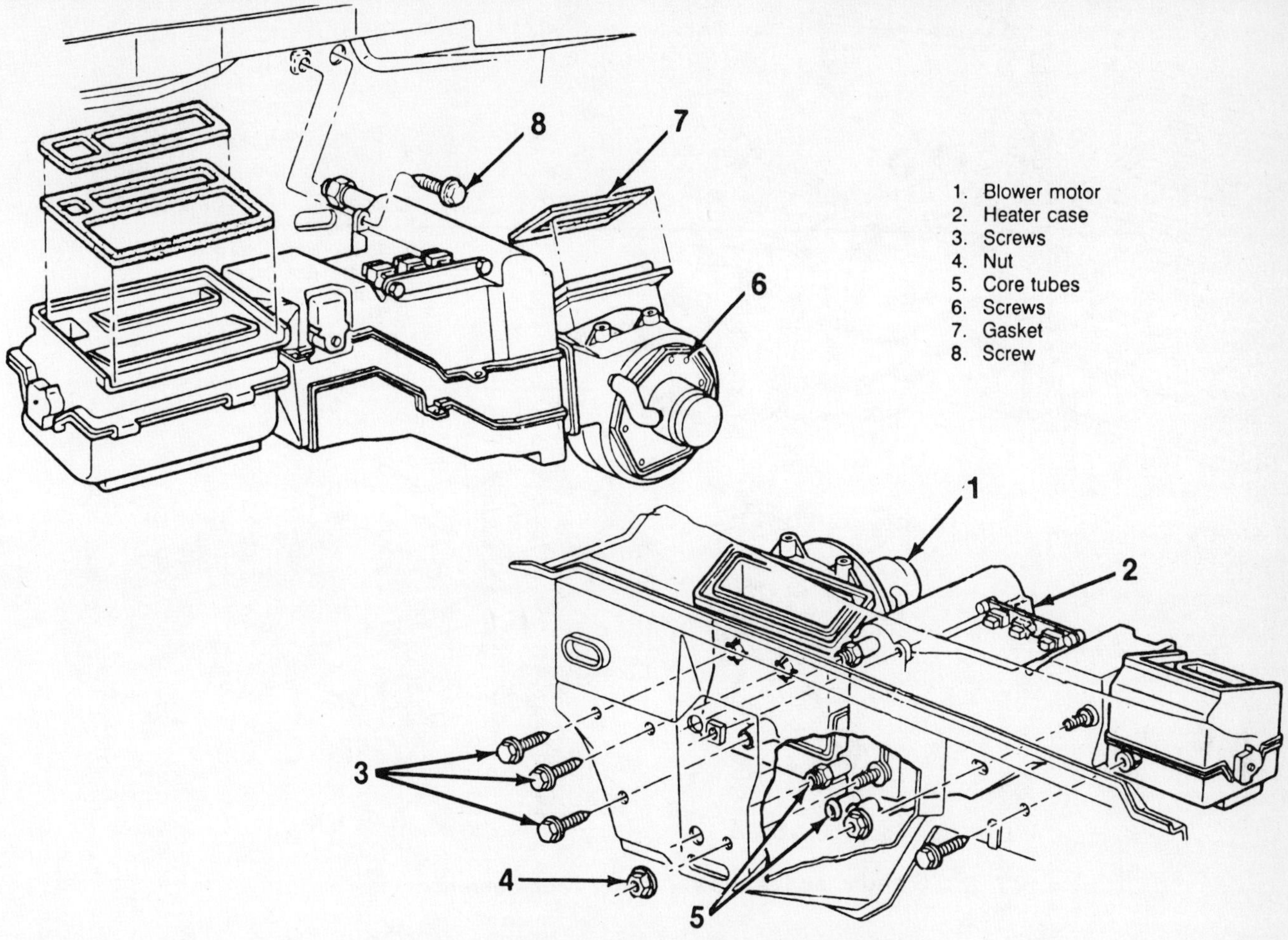

C and K series heater case components

3. Mark the position of the blower motor in relation to its case.
4. Remove the electrical connection at the motor.
5. Disconnect the blower motor cooling tube.
6. Remove the blower attaching screws and remove the assembly. Pry gently on the flange if the sealer sticks.
7. The blower wheel can be removed from the motor shaft by removing the nut at the center.
8. Installation is the reverse of removal. Apply a bead of sealer to the mounting flange before installation.

1988–90 C/K Series with Air Conditioning

1. Disconnect the negative battery terminal.
2. Remove the electrical connection at the motor.
3. Remove the blower attaching screws and remove the assembly. Pry gently on the flange if the sealer sticks.
4. The blower wheel can be removed from the motor shaft by removing the nut at the center.
5. Installation is the reverse of removal. Apply a bead of sealer to the mounting flange before installation.

Heater Core

REMOVAL AND INSTALLATION

1988–90 R/V Series without Air Conditioning

1. Disconnect the battery ground cable.
2. Disconnect the heater hoses at the core tubes and drain the engine coolant. Plug the core tubes to prevent spillage.

CAUTION

When draining the coolant, keep in mind that cats and dogs are attracted by the ethylene glycol antifreeze, and are quite likely to drink any that is left in an uncovered container or in puddles on the ground. This will prove fatal in sufficient quantity. Always drain the coolant into a sealable container. Coolant should be reused unless it is contaminated or several years old.

3. Remove the nuts from the distributor air ducts in the engine compartment.
4. Remove the glove compartment and door.
5. Disconnect the Air-Defrost and Temperature door cables.
6. Remove the floor outlet and remove the defroster duct-to-heater distributor screw.
7. Remove the heater distributor-to-instrument panel screws. Pull the assembly rearward to gain access to the wiring harness and disconnect the wires attached to the unit.
8. Remove the heater distributor from the truck.
9. Remove the heater core retaining straps and remove the core from the truck.
10. Installation is the reverse of removal. Be sure that the core-to-core and case-to-dash panel sealer is intact. Fill the cooling system and check for leaks.

1988–90 C/K without Air Conditioning

1. Disconnect the battery ground cable.

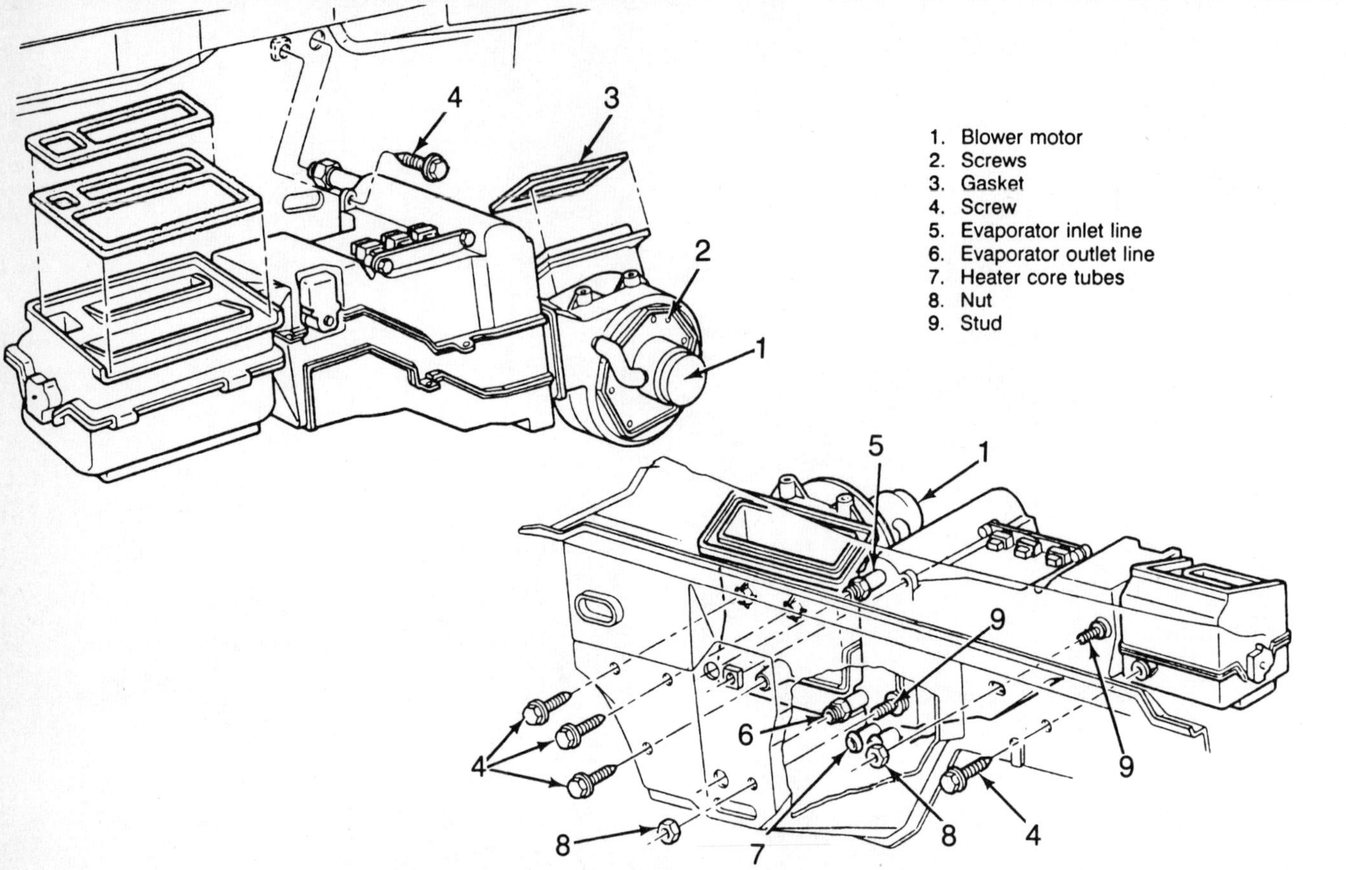

1. Blower motor
2. Screws
3. Gasket
4. Screw
5. Evaporator inlet line
6. Evaporator outlet line
7. Heater core tubes
8. Nut
9. Stud

C and K series blower motor replacement

1. Resistor
2. Accumulator
3. Blower
4. Relay
5. Screw
6. Grommet
7. Case
8. Grommet
9. Core
10. Clamp
11. Screw
12. Rivet
13. Bracket
14. Plate
15. Orifice
16. O-ring
17. Cooling tube
18. Wire
19. Switch
20. Case
21. Seal
22. Clamp
23. Switch

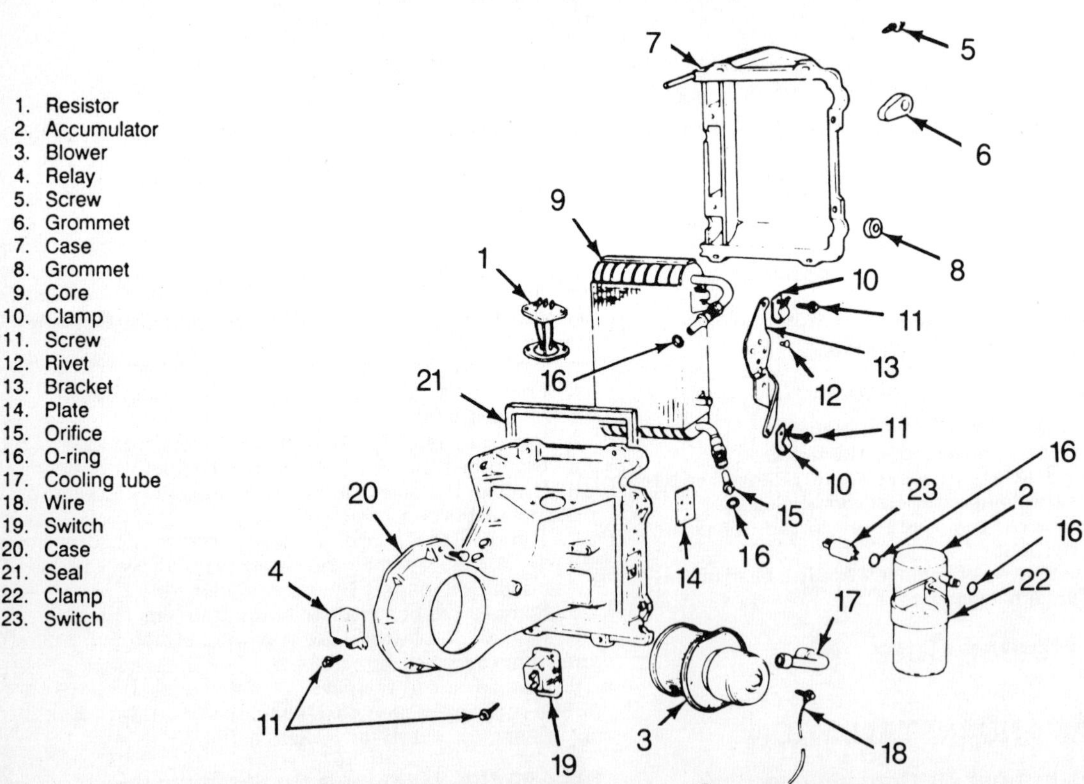

R and V series evaporator, blower and related parts

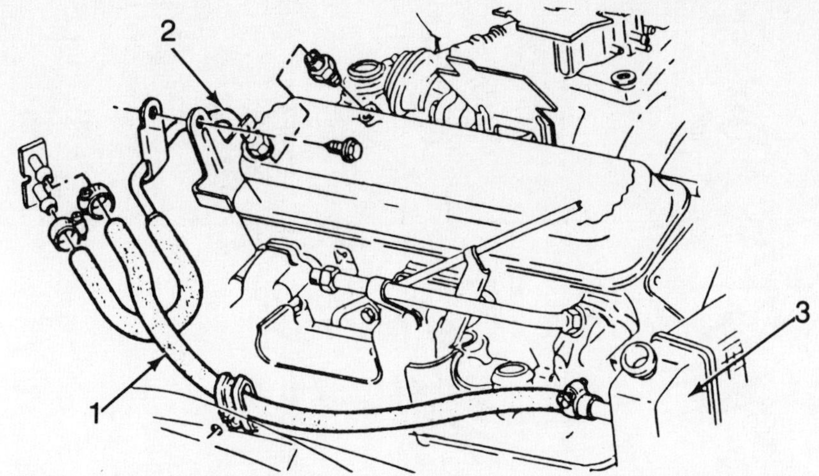

Heater hose routing for R and V series with the 6- 4.3L, 8-5.0L or 8-5.7L engine

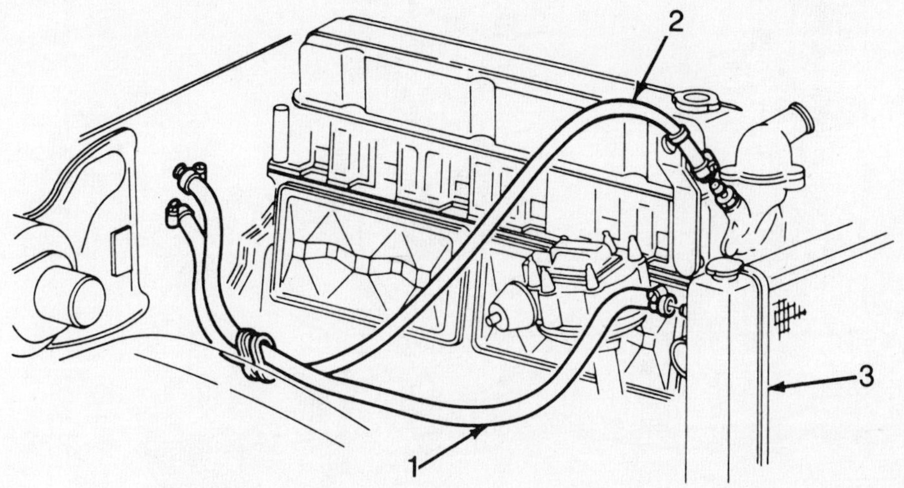

Heater hose routing for R and V series with the 6- 4.8L engine

2. Remove the coolant overflow bottle.
3. Drain the cooling system.

CAUTION

When draining the coolant, keep in mind that cats and dogs are attracted by the ethylene glycol antifreeze, and are quite likely to drink any that is left in an uncovered container or in puddles on the ground. This will prove fatal in sufficient quantity. Always drain the coolant into a sealable container. Coolant should be reused unless it is contaminated or several years old.

4. Disconnect the heater hoses at the core tubes.
5. In the engine compartment, remove the heater case-to-firewall screws.
6. Disconnect the antenna cable at the mast.
7. Remove the glove box.
8. Disconnect the wiring harness at the engine's Electronic Control Module (ECM).
9. Remove the ECM and bracket.
10. Remove the right side kick panel.
11. Remove the right side lower dash panel bolt and nut.
12. Remove the heater case mounting bolts.
13. While lifting the instrument panel slightly, remove the case assembly.
14. Lift the core from the case.

To install:

15. Lower the core into the case.
16. Position the case assembly against the firewall.
17. Install the heater case mounting bolts.
18. Install the right side lower dash panel bolt and nut.
19. Install the right side kick panel.
20. Install the ECM and bracket.
21. Connect the ECM wiring harness.
22. Install the glove box.
23. Connect the antenna cable at the mast.
24. Install the heater case-to-firewall screws.
25. Connect the heater hoses at the core tubes.
26. Fill the cooling system.
27. Install the coolant overflow bottle.
28. Connect the battery ground cable.

1988–90 R/V Series with Air Conditioning

1. Disconnect the battery ground cable.

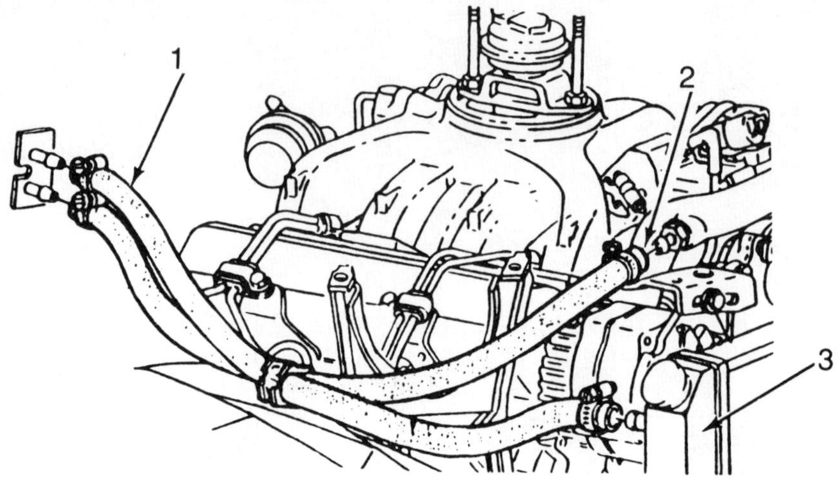

Heater hose routing for R and V series with the 8- 6.2L engine

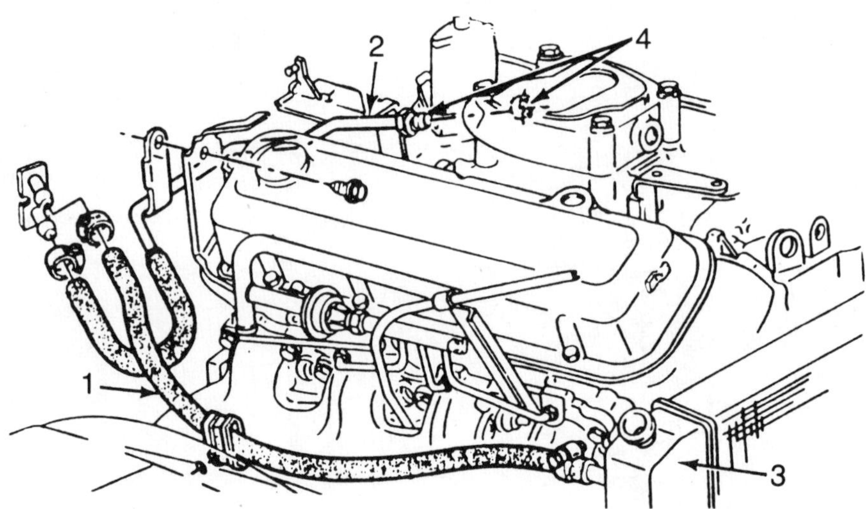

Heater hose routing for R and V series with the 8- 7.4L engine

2. Disconnect the heater hoses at the core tubes and drain the engine coolant. Plug the core tubes to prevent spillage.

CAUTION

When draining the coolant, keep in mind that cats and dogs are attracted by the ethylene glycol antifreeze, and are quite likely to drink any that is left in an uncovered container or in puddles on the ground. This will prove fatal in sufficient quantity. Always drain the coolant into a sealable container. Coolant should be reused unless it is contaminated or several years old.

3. Remove the glove compartment and door.
4. Disconnect the center duct from the defroster outlet duct.
5. Disconnect the center, lower air distributor and the center air outlet ducts.
6. Disconnect the temperature door cable.
7. Remove the nuts from the 3 selector duct studs that project into the engine compartment.
8. Remove the outlet duct-to-instrument panel screws. Pull the assembly rearward to gain access to the wiring harness and disconnect the wires and vacuum tubes attached to the unit.
9. Remove the heater distributor from the truck.
10. Remove the heater core retaining straps and remove the core from the case.
11. Installation is the reverse of removal. Be sure that the core-to-core and case-to-dash panel sealer is intact. Fill the cooling system and check for leaks.

1988–90 C/K with Air Conditioning

1. Disconnect the battery ground cable.
2. Drain the cooling system.

CAUTION

When draining the coolant, keep in mind that cats and dogs are attracted by the ethylene glycol antifreeze, and are quite likely to drink any that is left in an uncovered container or in puddles on the ground. This will prove fatal in sufficient quantity. Always drain the coolant into a sealable container. Coolant should be reused unless it is contaminated or several years old.

3. Discharge the system. See Section 1.
4. Remove the coolant overflow tank.
5. Disconnect the heater hoses at the core tubes.
6. Disconnect the refrigerant lines at the evaporator. Always use a back-up wrench! Cap all openings at once!
7. Unplug the electrical connector at the temperature actuator.

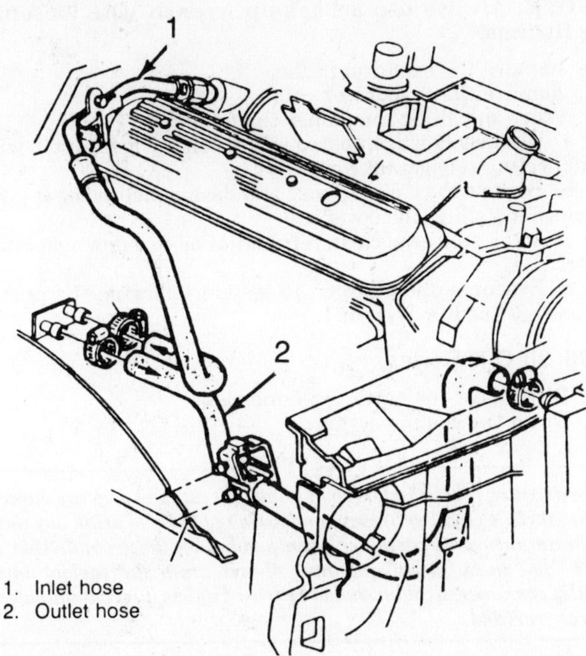

Heater hose routing for C and K series with the 6-4.3L, 8-5.0L or 8-5.7L engine

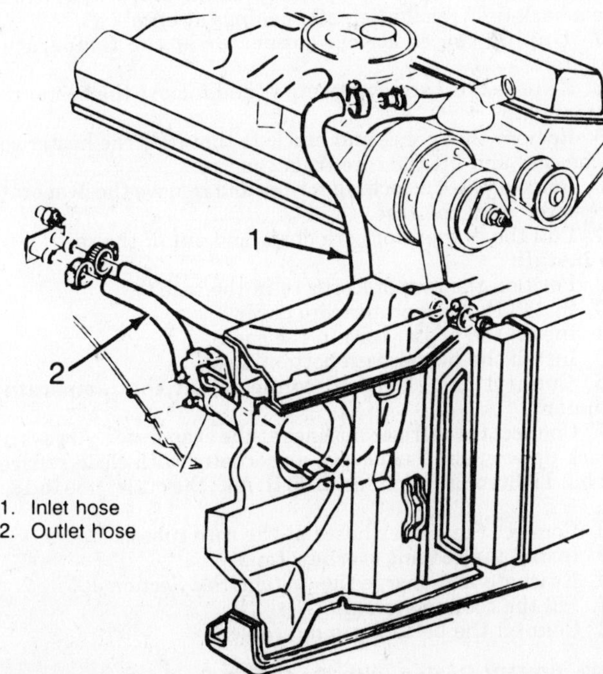

Heater hose routing for C and K series with the 8-6.2L engine

8. Remove the 7 attaching screws and remove the heater case bottom plate.
9. Remove the screws and brackets that hold the heater core to the case and lift the core from the case.

To install:

10. Install the heater core in the case.
11. Install the heater case bottom plate.

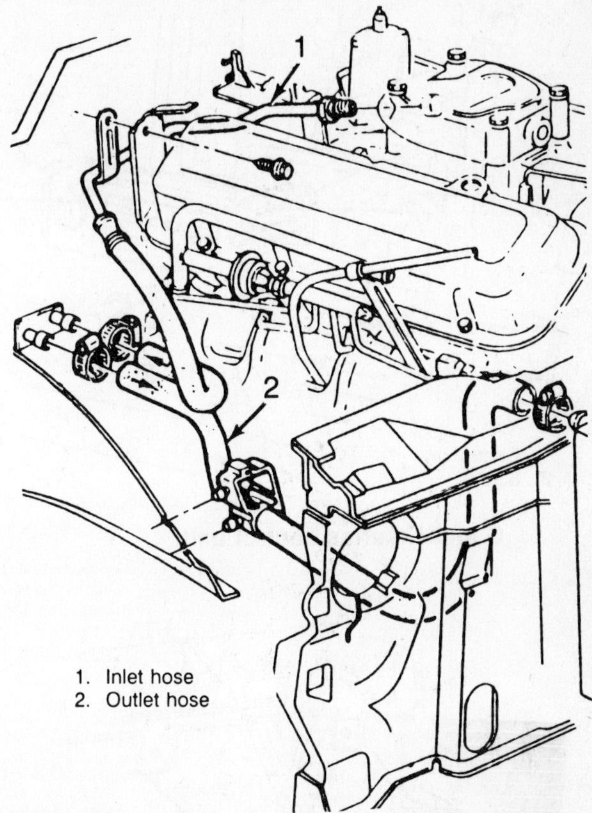

Heater hose routing for C and K series with the 8-7.4L engine

12. Connect the electrical connector at the temperature actuator.
13. Connect the refrigerant lines at the evaporator. Always use a back-up wrench! Use new O-rings coated with clean refrigerant oil. Tighten the inlet line to 30 ft. lbs.; the outlet line to 18 ft. lbs.
14. Connect the heater hoses at the core tubes.
15. Install the coolant overflow tank.
16. Evacuate and charge the system. See Section 1.
17. Fill the cooling system.
18. Connect the battery ground cable.

Control Assembly

REMOVAL AND INSTALLATION

1988 R/V Series with or without Air Conditioning

1. Disconnect the negative battery cable.
2. Remove the radio.
3. Remove the instrument panel bezel.
4. Remove the control head-to-dash screws.
5. Lower the control head from the dash, without kinking the cable, and disconnect the cable, vacuum harness and electrical harness.
6. Reverse the above to install.

1989–90 R/V Series with or without Air Conditioning

1. Disconnect the negative battery cable.
2. Remove the instrument panel bezel.
3. Disconnect the defroster and temperature cables at the control.

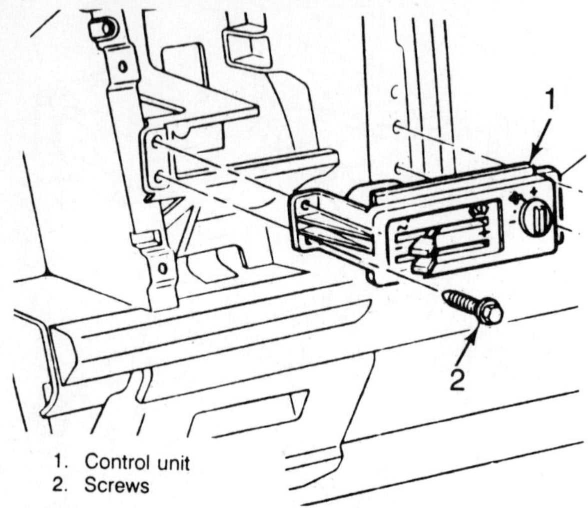

C and K series control unit

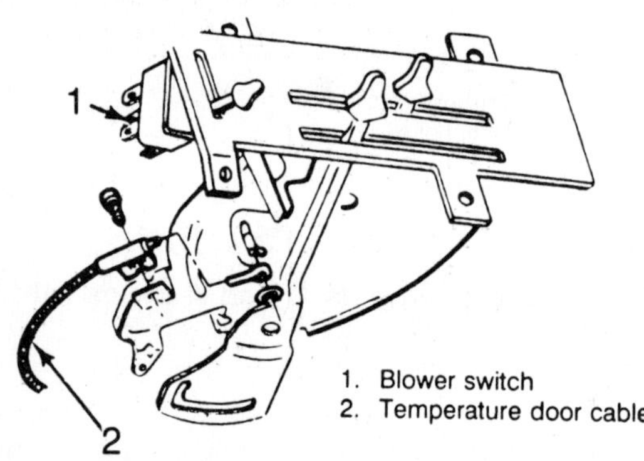

R and V series control unit

4. Disconnect the blower switch wiring connector.
5. Pull the control assembly through the opening above the control.

1988–90 C/K Series with or without Air Conditioning

1. Disconnect the negative battery cable.
2. Remove the instrument panel bezel.
3. Remove the control head-to-dash screws.
4. Lower the control head from the dash, without kinking the cable, and disconnect the cable, vacuum harness and electrical harness.
5. Reverse the above to install.

Evaporator Core

REMOVAL AND INSTALLATION

1988 R/V Series

1. Disconnect the battery ground cable.
2. Purge the system of refrigerant. See Section 1.
3. Remove the nuts from the selector duct studs projecting through the dash panel.
4. Remove the evaporator cover-to-dash and cover-to-case screws and remove the evaporator case cover.
5. Disconnect the evaporator core inlet and outlet lines and cap or plug all open connections at once.

NOTE: Always use a back-up wrench whe loosening the fittings!

6. Remove the expansion tube.
7. Remove the evaporator core.
8. When installing remember the following:
   a. Use new O-rings, coated with clean refrigerant oil, when connecting refrigerant lines.
   b. Be sure the cover to case and dash panel sealer is intact before installing the cover.
   c. Add 3 ounces of clean refrigerant oil to a new evaporator core.
   d. Evacuate and charge the system following the precautions outlined in Section 1.

1988–90 C/K Series

1. Disconnect the battery ground cable.
2. Drain the cooling system.

CAUTION

When draining the coolant, keep in mind that cats and dogs are attracted by the ethylene glycol antifreeze, and are quite likely to drink any that is left in an uncovered container or in puddles on the ground. This will prove fatal in sufficient quantity. Always drain the coolant into a sealable container. Coolant should be reused unless it is contaminated or several years old.

3. Discharge the system. See Section 1.
4. Remove the coolant overflow tank.
5. Disconnect the heater hoses at the core tubes.
6. Disconnect the refrigerant lines at the evaporator. Always use a back-up wrench! Cap all openings at once!
7. Unplug the electrical connector at the temperature actuator.
8. Remove the 7 attaching screws and remove the heater case bottom plate.
9. Remove the screws and brackets that hold the heater core to the case and lift the core from the case.
10. Remove the 4 attaching screws and remove the evaporator core cover from the case.
11. Pull the evaporator core down and out of the case.

To install:

12. Position the evaporator core in the case.
13. Install the evaporator core cover.
14. Install the heater core in the case.
15. Install the heater case bottom plate.
16. Connect the electrical connector at the temperature actuator.
17. Connect the refrigerant lines at the evaporator. Always use a back-up wrench! Use new O-rings coated with clean refrigerant oil. Tighten the inlet line to 30 ft. lbs.; the outlet line to 18 ft. lbs.
18. Connect the heater hoses at the core tubes.
19. Install the coolant overflow tank.
20. Evacuate and charge the system. See Section 1.
21. Fill the cooling system.
22. Connect the battery ground cable.

1989–90 R/V Series with Gasoline Engines

1. Disconnect the battery ground cable.
2. Discharge the system. See Section 1.
3. Unplug the wiring at the pressure switch.
4. Disconnect the refrigerant lines at the accumulator. Always use a back-up wrench! Cap all openings at once!
5. Remove the bracket screws and remove the accumulator and bracket. Drain the oil into a calibrated container and take note of the amount.
6. Remove the liquid line retaining screw.
7. Remove the liquid line from the evaporator. Cap all openings at once.

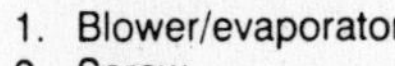

1. Blower/evaporator
2. Screw
3. Resistor
4. Screw
5. Auxiliary resistor
6. Hose connector
7. Compressor
8. Upper retainer
9. Screw
10. Lower retainer
11. Condenser
12. Seal
13. Accumulator
14. Refrigerant line
15. Cap
16. Relay
17. Bolt
18. Blower motor
19. Ground wire
20. Wiring harness
21. Evaporator inlet

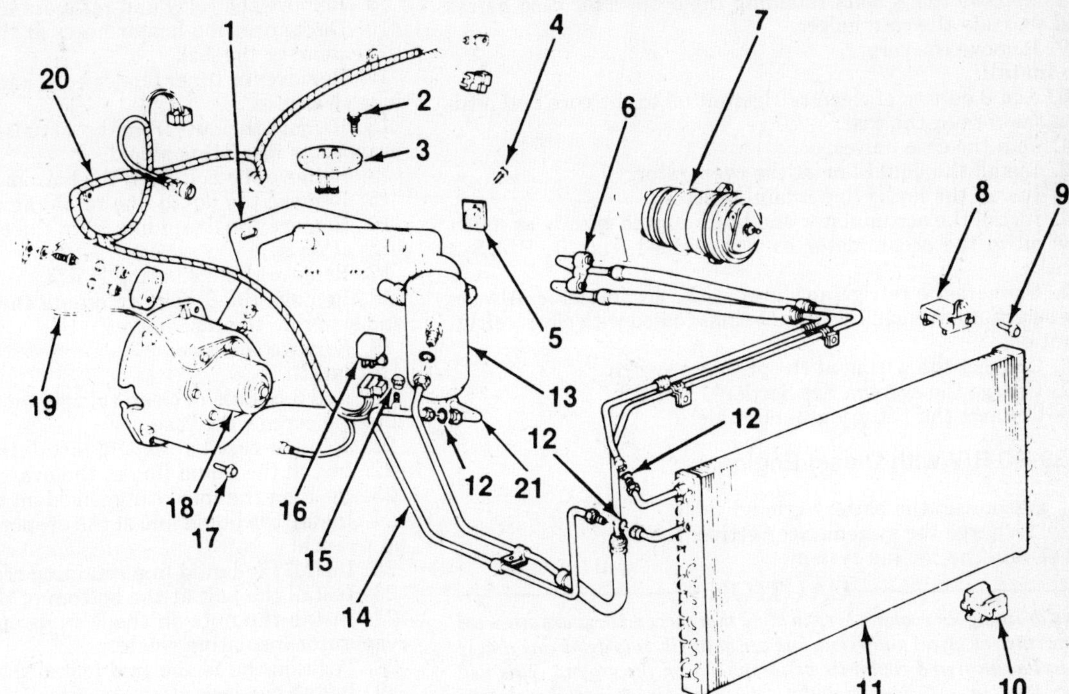

R and V series air conditioning components

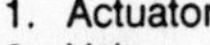

1. Actuator
2. Valve
3. Housing
4. Screw
5. Core
6. Strap
7. Screw
8. Clamp
9. Connector
10. Link
11. Connector
12. Screw
13. Bracket
14. Shaft
15. Spacer
16. Spring
17. Shaft
18. Bracket
19. Case
20. Valve
21. Nut
22. Valve
23. Screw
24. Link
25. Pin
26. Seal
27. Valve
28. Connector
29. Plate
30. Grommet
31. Hose
32. Screw
33. Yoke

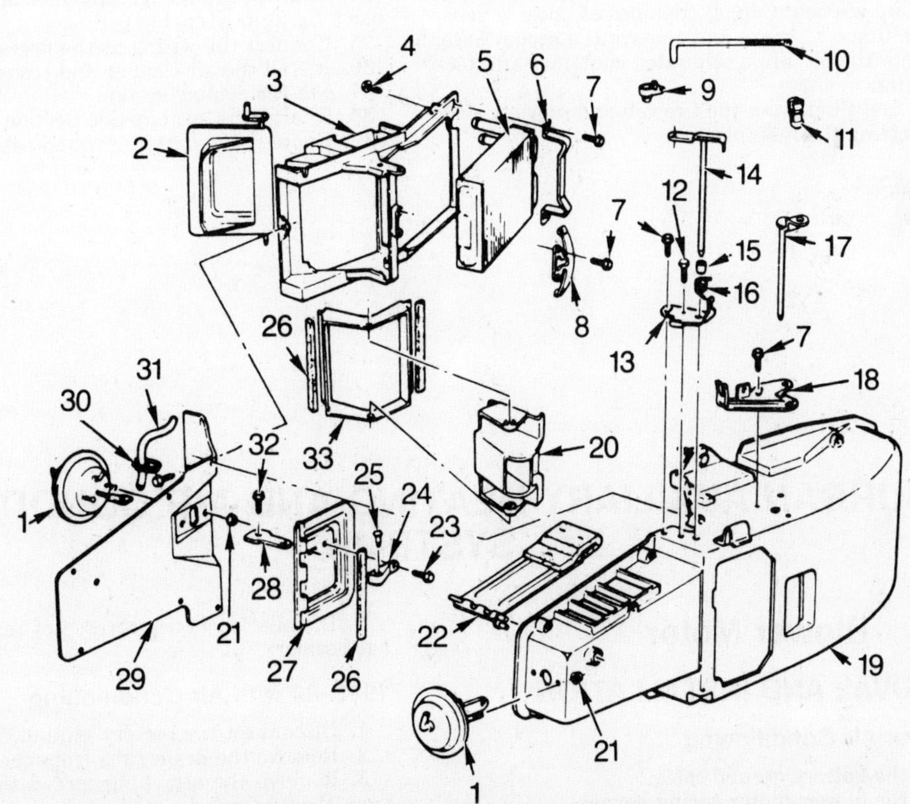

Heater/air conditioner components for the C and K series

8. Remove the 8 bolts retaining the evaporator case halves and separate the case halves.
9. Remove the core.

To install:

10. Add 3 ounces of clean refrigerant oil to the core and position the core in the case.
11. Join the case halves.
12. Install the liquid line at the evaporator.
13. Install the liquid line retaining screw.
14. Install the accumulator and bracket. Add exactly as much new oil to the accumulator as was drained from it, PLUS 2 ounces.
15. Connect the refrigerant lines at the accumulator. Always use a back-up wrench! Use new O-rings coated with clean refrigerant oil.
16. Connect the wiring at the pressure switch.
17. Charge the system. See Section 1.
18. Connect the battery ground cable.

1988–90 R/V with Diesel Engine

1. Disconnect the battery ground cable.
2. Discharge the system. See Section 1.
3. Drain the cooling system.

CAUTION

When draining the coolant, keep in mind that cats and dogs are attracted by the ethylene glycol antifreeze, and are quite likely to drink any that is left in an uncovered container or in puddles on the ground. This will prove fatal in sufficient quantity. Always drain the coolant into a sealable container. Coolant should be reused unless it is contaminated or several years old.

4. Remove the air cleaner and resonator.
5. Unplug the wiring at the pressure switch.
6. Disconnect the refrigerant lines at the accumulator. Always use a back-up wrench! Cap all openings at once!
7. Remove the bracket screws and remove the accumulator and bracket. Drain the oil into a calibrated container and take note of the amount.
8. Unbolt the fuel filter from the firewall and move it aside without disconnecting the fuel lines.
9. Remove the relay and resistors from the evaporator case.
10. Disconnect the heater hoses at the core tubes.
11. Remove the jack.
12. Remove the inner fender bolts and lower the fender to provide clearance.
13. Remove the nuts from the 2 studs on the firewall above the evaporator insulating shield.
14. Remove the bolt from the bottom of the insulating shield.
15. Remove the liquid line retaining screw.
16. Remove the liquid line from the evaporator. Cap all openings at once.
17. Remove the insulating shield.
18. Remove the 8 bolts retaining the evaporator case halves and separate the case halves.
19. Remove the core.

To install:

20. Add 3 ounces of clean refrigerant oil to the core and position the core in the case.
21. Join the case halves and install the bolts.
22. Install the liquid line at the evaporator.
23. Position the insulating shield on the case.
24. Install the liquid line at the evaporator. Always use a backup wrench!
25. Install the liquid line retaining screw.
26. Install the bolt at the bottom of the insulating shield.
27. Install the nuts on the 2 studs on the firewall above the evaporator insulating shield.
28. Position the fender and install the inner fender bolts.
29. Install the jack.
30. Connect the heater hoses at the core tubes.
31. Install the relay and resistors on the evaporator case.
32. Install the fuel filter on the firewall.
33. Add the same amount of refrigerant oil drained from the accumulator, PLUS 2 ounces. Install the accumulator and bracket.
34. Connect the refrigerant lines at the accumulator. Always use a back-up wrench!
35. Connect the wiring at the pressure switch.
36. Install the air cleaner and resonator.
37. Fill the cooling system.
38. Charge the system. See Section 1.
39. Connect the battery ground cable.

SUBURBAN AUXILIARY HEATING AND AIR CONDITIONING SYSTEMS

Blower Motor

REMOVAL AND INSTALLATION

1988–90 without Air Conditioning

1. Disconnect the battery ground cable.
2. Disconnect the blower motor wiring harness.
3. Remove the blower motor clamp.
4. Remove the motor attaching screws and lift out the motor.
5. Installation is the reverse of removal. Replace any damaged sealer.

1988–89 with Air Conditioning

1. Disconnect the battery ground cble.
2. Remove the drain tube from the rear duct.
3. Remove the attaching screws and remove the rear duct from the roof panel.
4. Disconnect the blower motor wiring and remove the ground strap and wire.

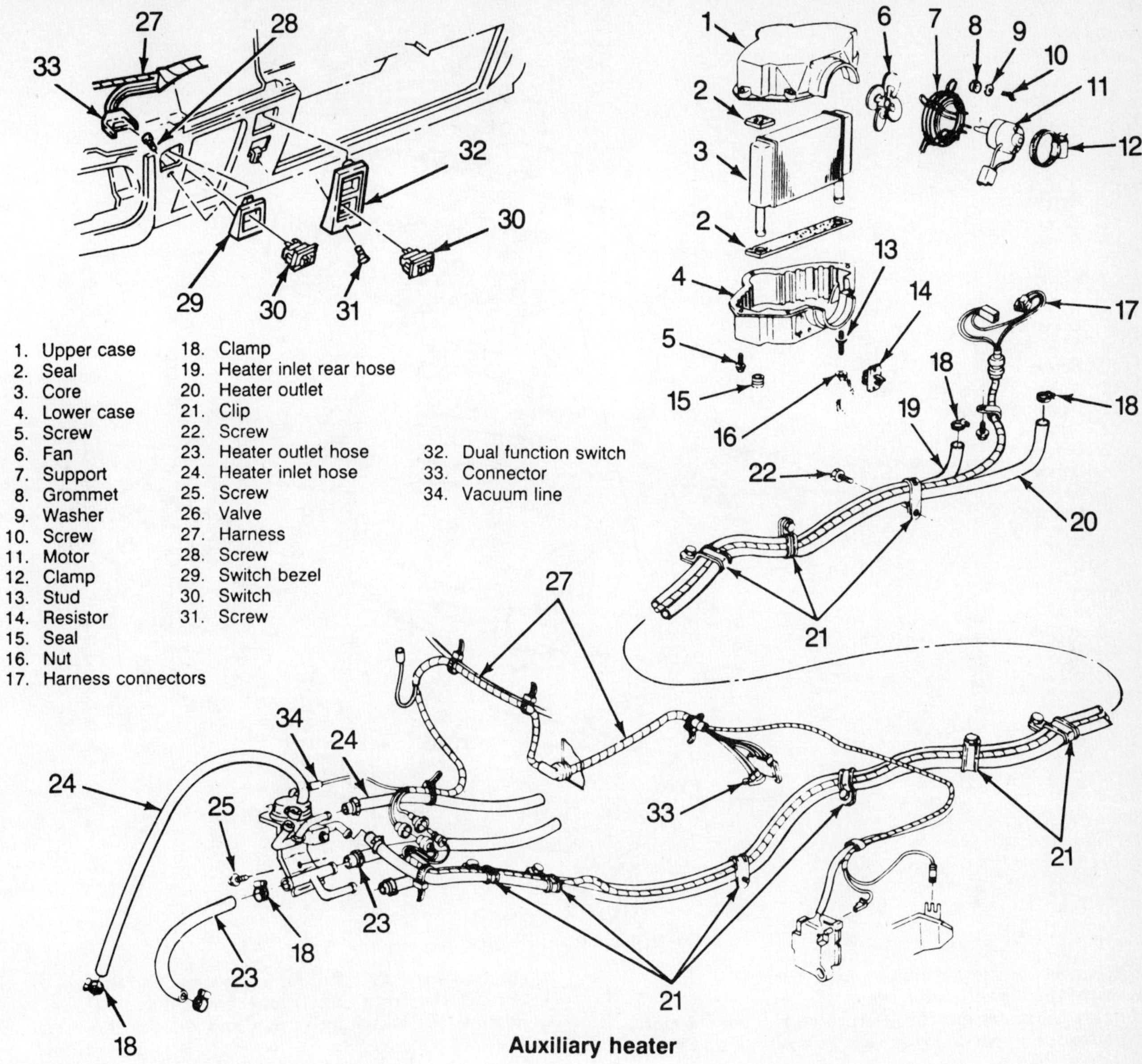

Auxiliary heater

5. Support the case and remove the lower-to-upper case half screws and lower the case and motor assemblies.
6. Remove the motor retaining strap and remove the motor and wheels.

To install:

7. Install the motor and wheels.
8. Install the motor retaining strap.
9. Raise the case and install the lower-to-upper case half screws.
10. Connect the blower motor wires.
11. Connect the blower motor ground straps at the center connector between the motors.
12. Install the duct.
13. Install the screws securing the duct to the roof and case.
14. Connect the drain tubes at the rear of the blower-evaporator duct.
15. Connect the battery ground cable.

Heater Core

REMOVAL AND INSTALLATION

1988–90

1. Disconnect the battery ground cable.
2. Drain the cooling system.

CAUTION

When draining the coolant, keep in mind that cats and dogs are attracted by the ethylene glycol antifreeze, and are quite likely to drink any that is left in an uncovered container or in puddles on the ground. This will prove fatal in sufficient quantity. Always drain the coolant into a sealable container. Coolant should be reused unless it is contaminated or several years old.

3. Disconnect the heater hoses at the core tubes.

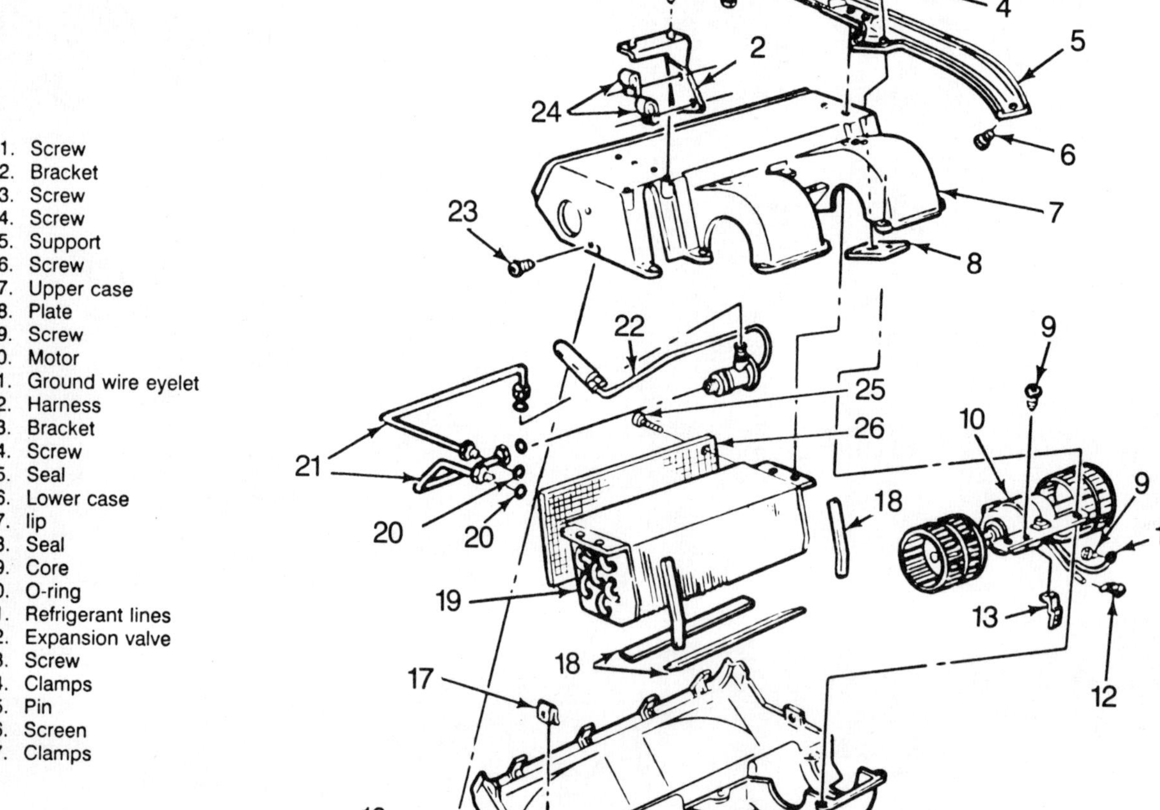

Auxiliary air conditioner

4. Disconnect the blower motor wiring harness.
5. Remove the blower motor clamp.
6. Remove the motor attaching screws and lift out the motor.
7. Remove the upper-to-lower case half screws and remove the upper case half.
8. Remove the core seal.
9. Lift out the core.
10. Installation is the reverse of removal. Replace any damaged sealer.

Blower Switch

REMOVAL AND INSTALLATION

1988–90

1. Disconnect the battery ground cable.
2. Unplug the wiring at the switch.
3. Remove the attaching screws and bezel.
4. Remove the switch.

Expansion Valve

REMOVAL AND INSTALLATION

1988–90

1. Disconnect the negative battery cable.
2. Discharge the air conditioning system. See Section 1.
3. Remove the drain tube from the rear duct.
4. Remove the attaching screws and remove the rear duct from the roof panel.
5. Disconnect the blower motor lead and ground wires.
6. Support the case assembly. Remove the lower to upper blower/evaporator case screws. Lower the case and motor assembly.
7. Remove the expansion valve sensing bulb clamps.
8. Disconnect the valve inlet and outlet lines. Always use a back-up wrench! Cap the openings immediately.
9. Remove the expansion valve assembly.
10. Installation is the reverse of the removal procedure. Evacuate, charge and check the system for proper operation. See Section 1.

Evaporator Core

REMOVAL AND INSTALLATION

1988–89

1. Disconnect the battery ground cable.
2. Discharge the system. See Section 1.
3. Disconnect the drain tubes at the rear of the blower-evaporator duct.
4. Remove the screws securing the duct to the roof and case.

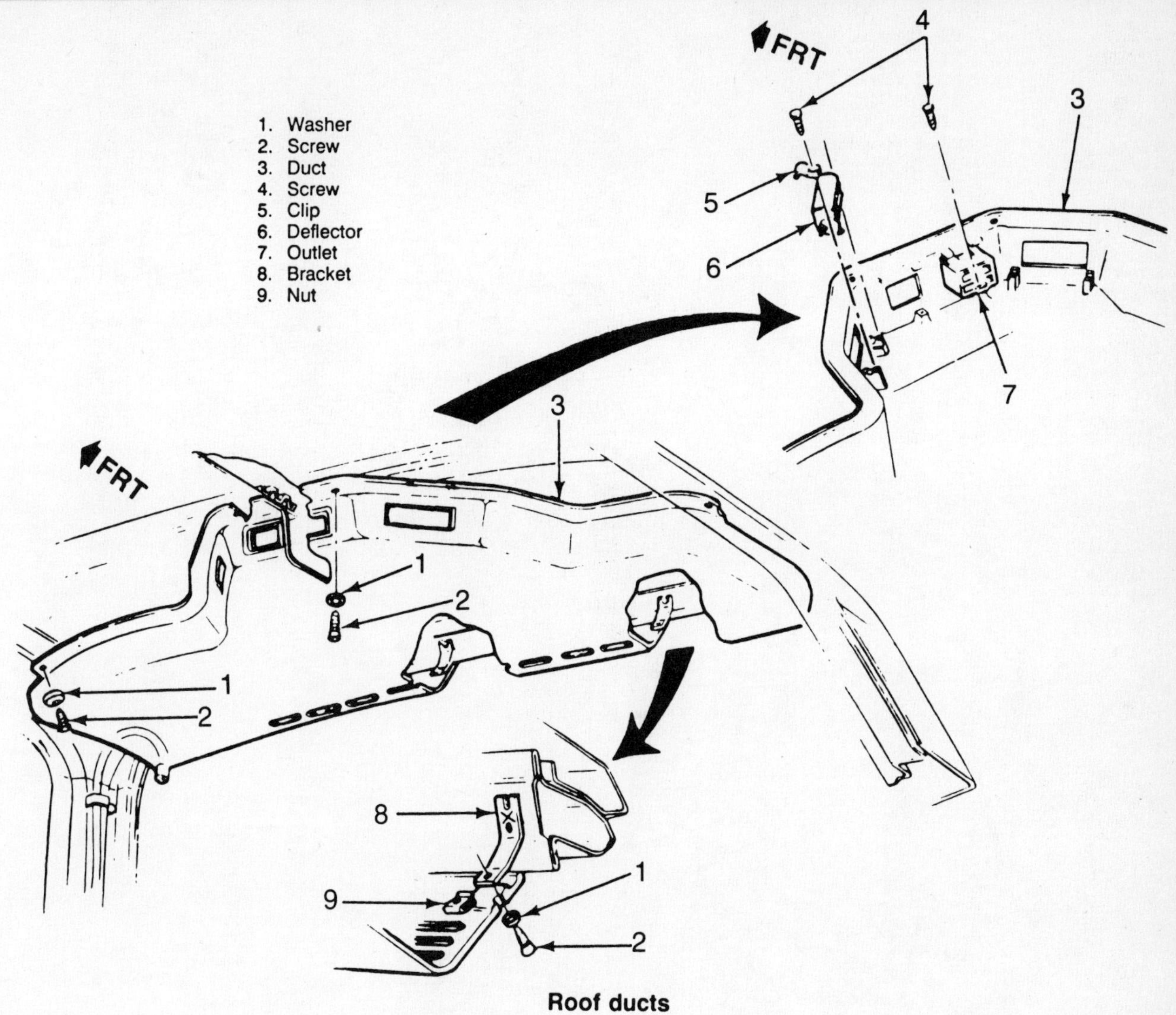

Roof ducts

5. Remove the duct.
6. Disconnect the blower motor ground straps at the center connector between the motors.
7. Disconnect the blower motor wires.
8. Disconnect the refrigerant lines at the case. Always use a back-up wrench! Cap all openings at once!
9. Support the case and remove the case-to-roof screws. Lower the case assembly.
10. Place the unit upside-down on a clean workbench.
11. Remove the screws and separate the case halves.
12. Remove the upper shroud and upper case from the evaporator core.
13. Disconnect the expansion valve lines. Always use a back-up wrench! Cap all openings at once!
14. Remove the expansion valve capillary bulbs from the evaporator outlet line and remove the valves.
15. Remove the screen from the core.

To install:

16. Always use new O-rings coated with clean refrigerant oil. Add 3 ounces of clean refrigerant oil to a new core.
17. Install the screen on the core.
18. Install the expansion valves.
19. Install the expansion valve capillary bulbs in the evaporator outlet line.
20. Connect the expansion valve lines.
21. Install the upper shroud and upper case.
22. Install the case screws.
23. Raise the case into position and install the case-to-roof screws.
24. Connect the refrigerant lines at the case.
25. Connect the blower motor wires.
26. Connect the blower motor ground straps at the center connector between the motors.
27. Install the shroud/duct.
28. Connect the drain tubes at the rear of the blower-evaporator shroud/duct.
29. Charge the system. See Section 1.
30. Connect the battery ground cable.

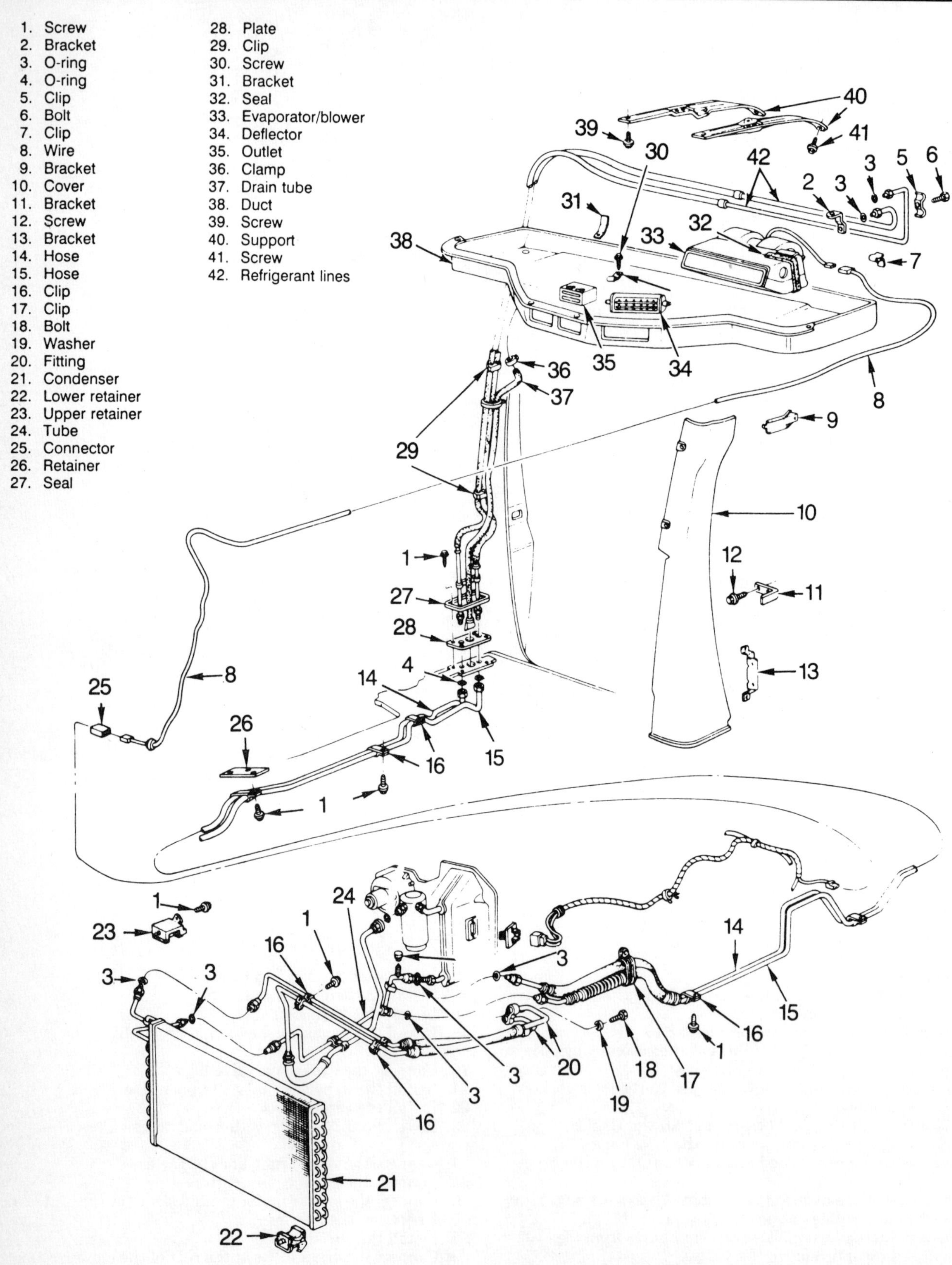
1. Screw
2. Bracket
3. O-ring
4. O-ring
5. Clip
6. Bolt
7. Clip
8. Wire
9. Bracket
10. Cover
11. Bracket
12. Screw
13. Bracket
14. Hose
15. Hose
16. Clip
17. Clip
18. Bolt
19. Washer
20. Fitting
21. Condenser
22. Lower retainer
23. Upper retainer
24. Tube
25. Connector
26. Retainer
27. Seal
28. Plate
29. Clip
30. Screw
31. Bracket
32. Seal
33. Evaporator/blower
34. Deflector
35. Outlet
36. Clamp
37. Drain tube
38. Duct
39. Screw
40. Support
41. Screw
42. Refrigerant lines

Roof mounted system refrigerant lines

RADIO

REMOVAL AND INSTALLATION

WARNING: Make certain that the speaker is attached to the radio before the unit is turned ON. If it is not, the output transistors will be damaged.

1988–90 R/V Series

1. Disconnect the negative battery cable.
2. Remove the control knobs and the bezels from the radio control shafts.
3. Remove the nuts from the support shafts.
4. Remove the support bracket retaining screws.
5. Lifting the rear edge of the radio, push the radio forward until the control shafts clear the instrument panel then lower the radio far enough so that the electrical connections can be disconnected.
6. Remove the power lead, speaker, and antenna wires and then pull out the unit.
7. Installation is the reverse of removal.

1988–90 C/K Series

RECEIVER

1. Working behind the instrument panel, disconnect the wiring and antenna from the receiver.
2. Remove the receiver bracket screws.
3. Remove the receiver and bracket from the dash.
4. Remove the receiver-to-bracket nuts.
5. Installation is the reverse of removal. Totque the nuts to 14 ft. lbs.

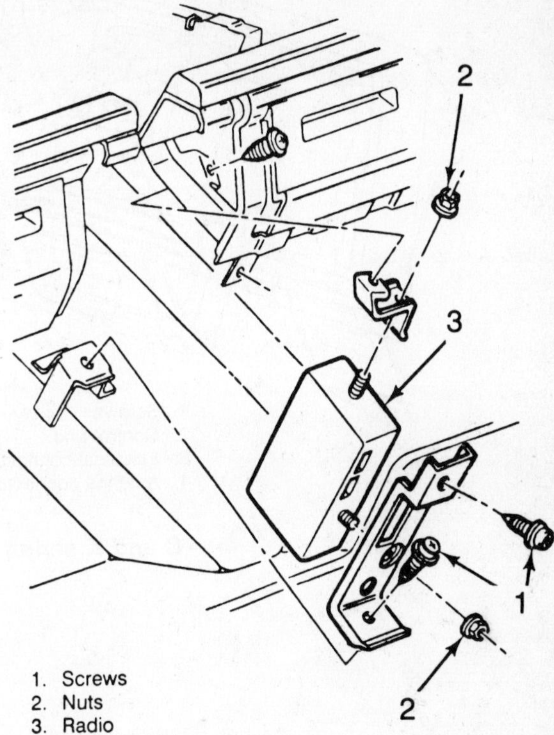

C and K series radio receiver installation

TAPE PLAYER

1. Remove the control knobs and trim plate.
2. Remove the tape player-to-instrument panel screws.
3. Pull the unit towards you just far enough to disconnect the wiring. Then, remove the unit.
4. Installation is the reverse of removal.

RADIO/TAPE PLAYER CONTROL HEAD

1. Remove the instrument cluster trim and bezel.
2. Remove the mounting screws.
3. Pull the unit towards you just far enough to disconnect the wiring. Then, remove the unit.
4. Installation is the reverse of removal.

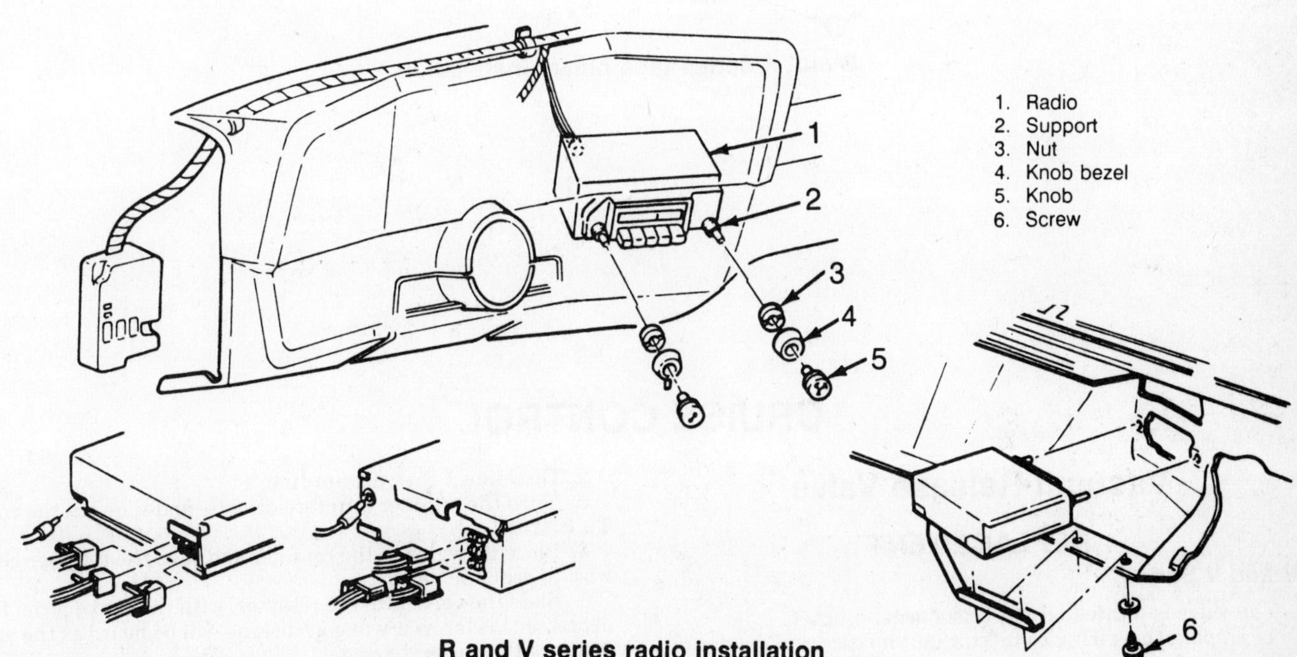

R and V series radio installation

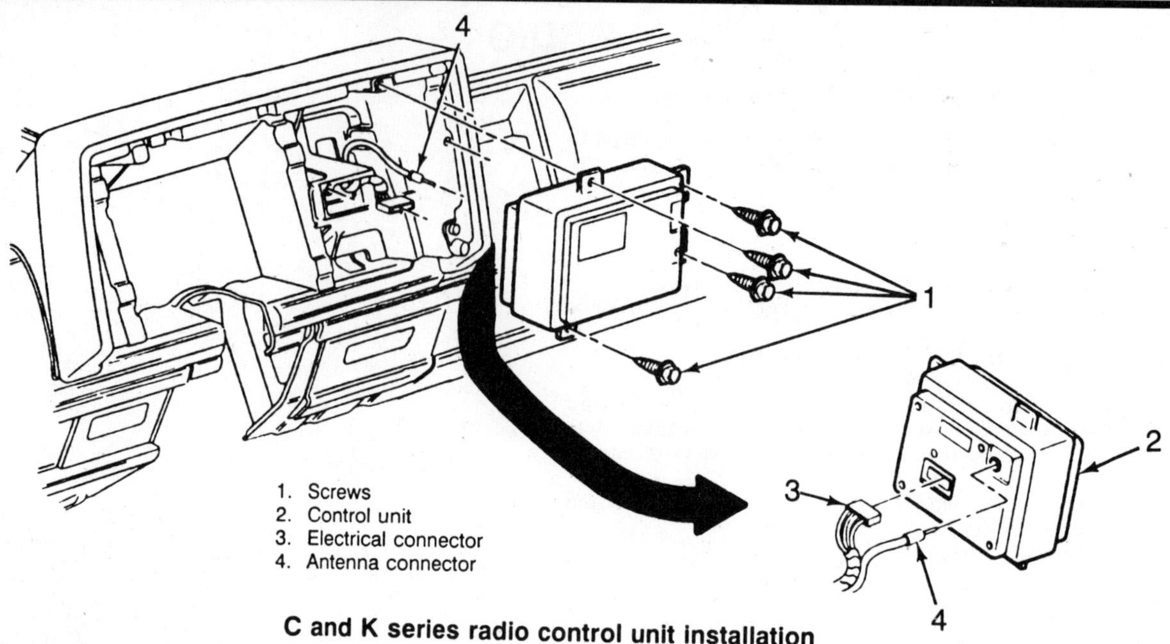

C and K series radio control unit installation

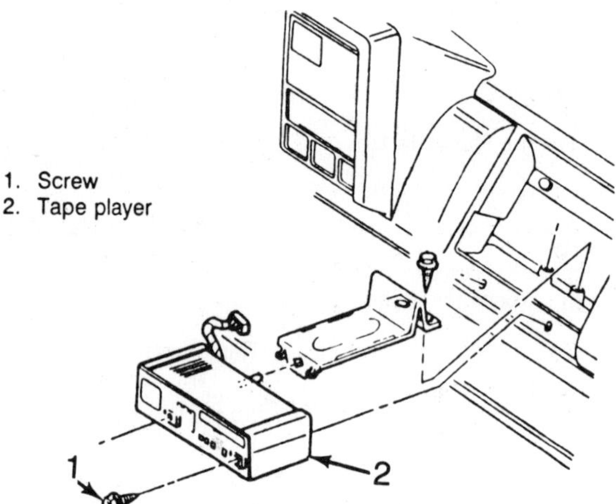

C and K series tape player installation

CRUISE CONTROL

Vacuum Release Valve

REPLACEMENT

R and V Series

The valve is located on the brake pedal bracket.

1. Unplug the wiring connector (automatic transmission).
2. Disconnect the vacuum line.
3. Turn the retainer counterclockwise and slide out the valve.

To install:

4. Place the valve in the retainer and turn the retainer clockwise to seat the valve.
5. Slide the valve into the retainer, with the brake pedal fully depressed, as far as it will go. Clicking will be heard as the valve is pushed towards the pedal.

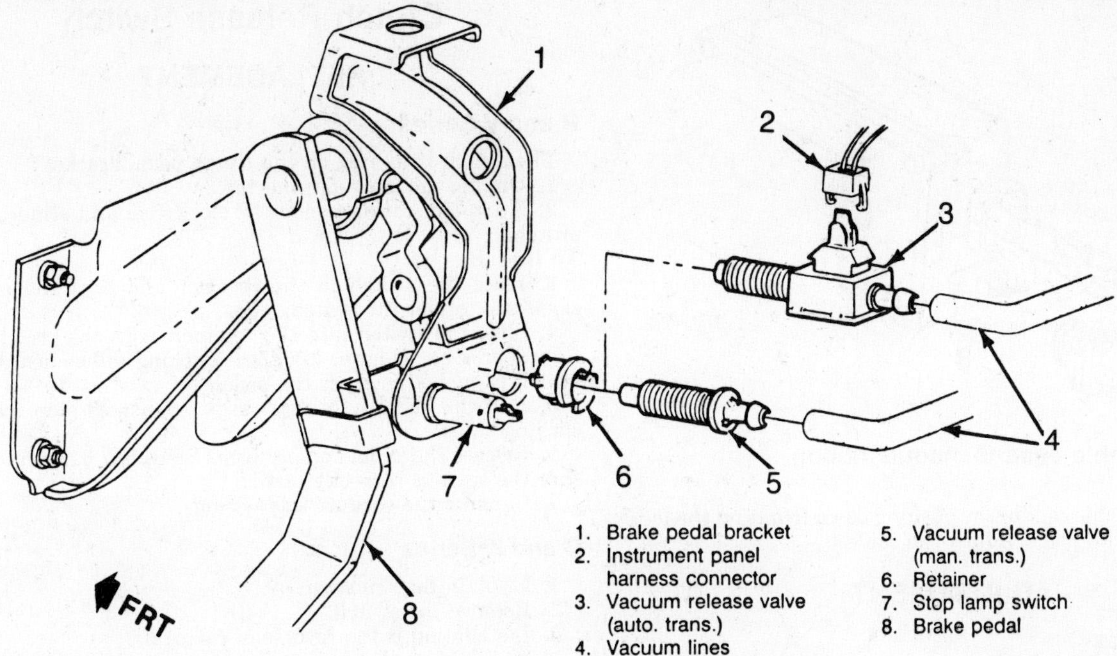

R and V series vacuum release valve

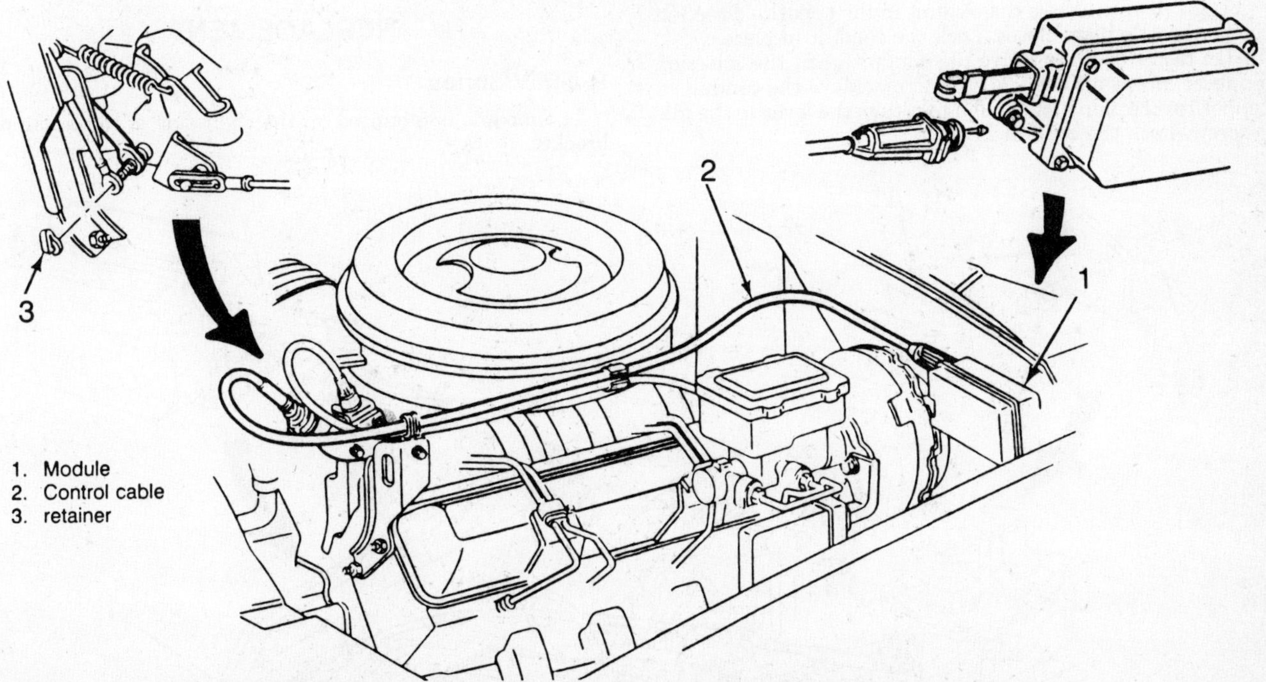

Cruise control module for C and K series with the diesel engine

6. Pull the pedal fully rearwards against its stop until the clicking stops.
7. Release the pedal and performs Steps 5 & 6 again to make sure the valve is correctly seated.
8. Connect the vacuum and wiring.

Control Cable

REPLACEMENT

C and K Series

1. Remove the retaining clip.
2. Remove the engine-end fitting from the lever stud.
3. Disconnect the cable conduit from the engine bracket.
4. Disconnect the cable conduit from the module housing.
5. Disconnect the cable bead from the end of the ribbon.

To install:

6. Connect the cable bead to the module ribbon fitting.
7. Pull the eng end of the cable until the cable is snug. Turn the engine end of the cable to starighten the ribbon, if necessary THE RIBBON MUST NOT BE TWISTED! Place the cable conduit over the ribbon and tangs, into the module housing.
8. Connect the end end of the conduit to the bracket.
9. Connect the engine end of the cable to the lever stud.

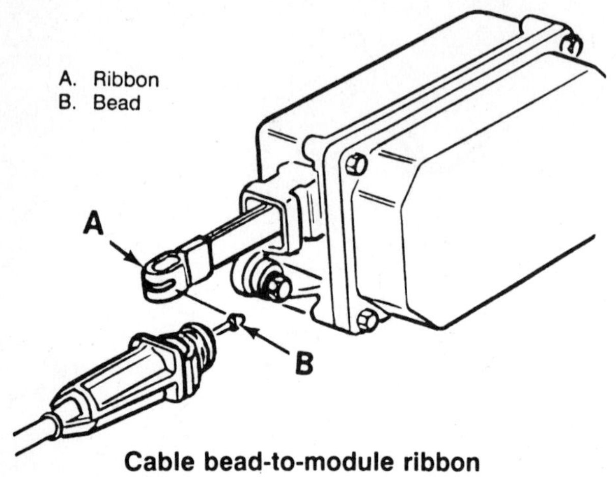

Cable bead-to-module ribbon

10. Lock the cable conduit by pushing down firmly on the lock until it snaps into place. Adjust the cable.

ADJUSTMENT

C and K Series

1. Unlock the cable conduit engine fitting.

2a. On gasoline engines: move the conduit until the throttle plate begins to open. Move the conduit in the opposite direction until the throttle plate closes. Lock the conduit in place.

2b. On diesel engines: move the conduit until the injection pump lever moves off the idle stop screw. Move the conduit in the opposite direction just enough to return the lever to the idle stop screw. Lock the conduit in place.

Clutch Release Switch

REPLACEMENT

R and V Series

The switch is located on the clutch pedal bracket.

1. Unplug the wiring connector.
2. Turn the retainer counterclockwise and slide out the switch.

To install:

3. Place the switch in the retainer and turn the retainer clockwise to seat the switch.
4. Slide the switch into the retainer, with the clutch pedal fully depressed, as far as it will go. Clicking will be heard as the switch is pushed towards the pedal.
5. Pull the pedal fully rearwards against its stop until the clicking stops.
6. Release the pedal and performs Steps 5 & 6 again to make sure the valve is correctly seated.
7. Connect the vacuum and wiring.

C and K Series

1. Unplug the connector.
2. Remove the switch.
3. Installation is the reverse of removal.

Control Module

REPLACEMENT

R and V Series

The module is mounted on the right side of the brake pedal bracket.

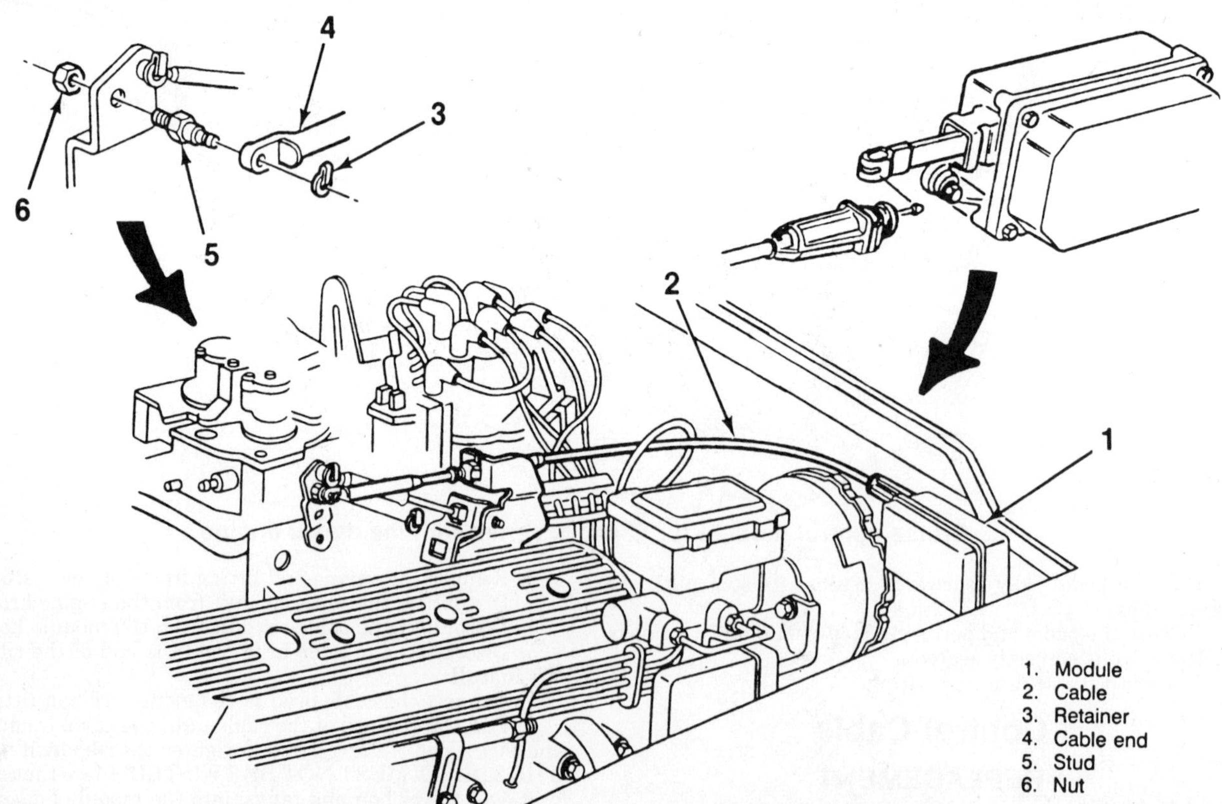

Cruise control module for C and K series with gasoline engines

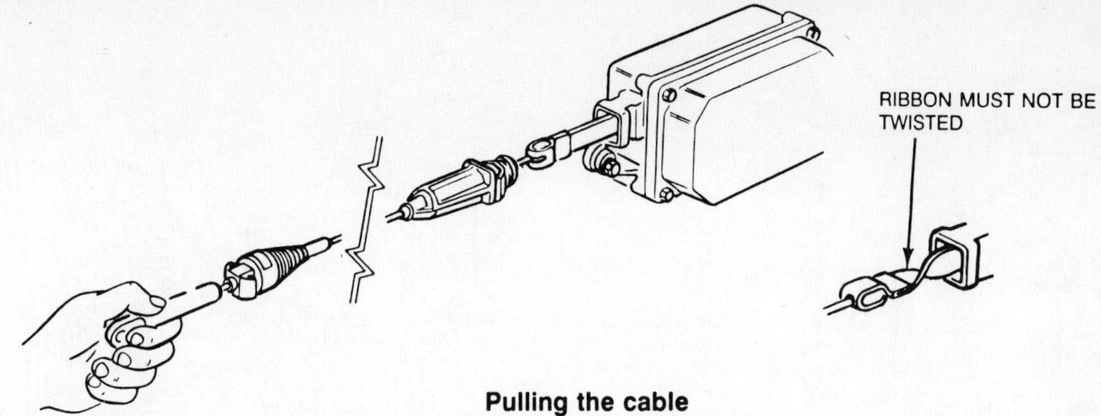

Pulling the cable

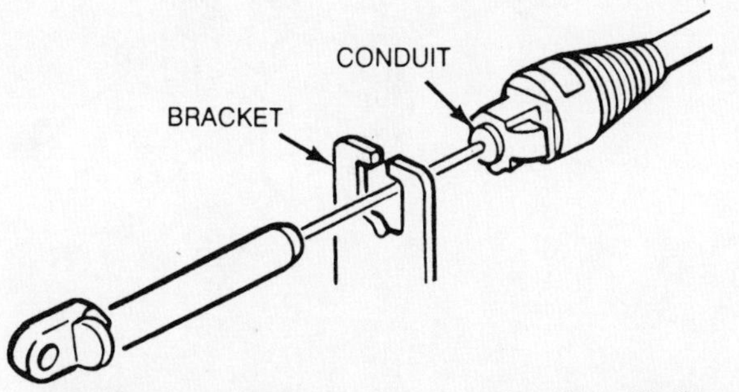

Cable conduit-to-engine bracket installation

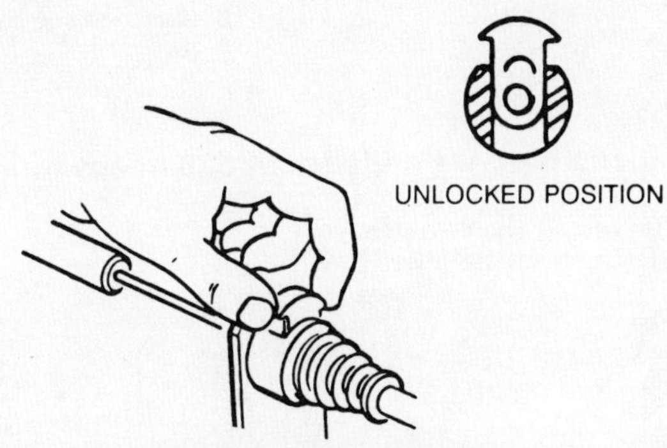

Unlocking the conduit

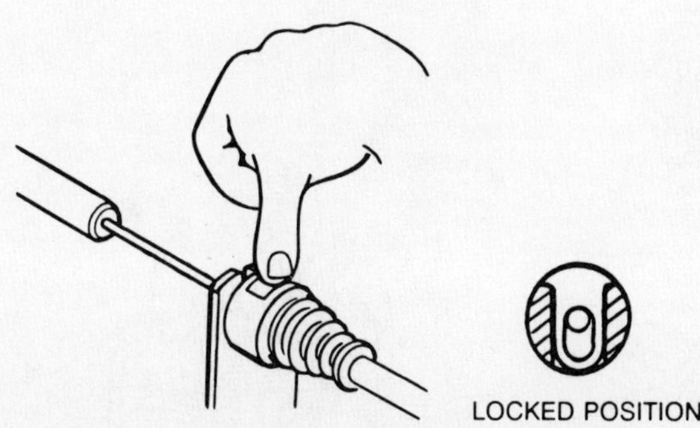

Locking the conduit

1. Unplug the harness connector.
2. Remove the module by prying back the retaining clip on the bracket and sliding off the module.
3. Installation is the reverse of removal.

C and K Series

The module is located on the driver's side of the firewall, in the engine compartment.

1. Disconnect the control cable from the module.
2. Remove the attaching screws, lift off the module and unplug the wiring.
3. Installation is the reverse of removal.

Servo

REPLACEMENT

R and V Series

The servo is mounted in the engine compartment. On gasoline engines, it is mounted on the driver's side, next to the distributor. On the diesel it is at the center, front of the engine.

1. Disconnect and tag the vacuum hoses.
2. Remove the actuator rod retainer and remove the rod.
3. Disconnect the control cable.
4. Remove the servo mounting bolts and lift off the servo.

To install:

5. Position the servo and tighten the bolts securely.
6. Connect the control cable.

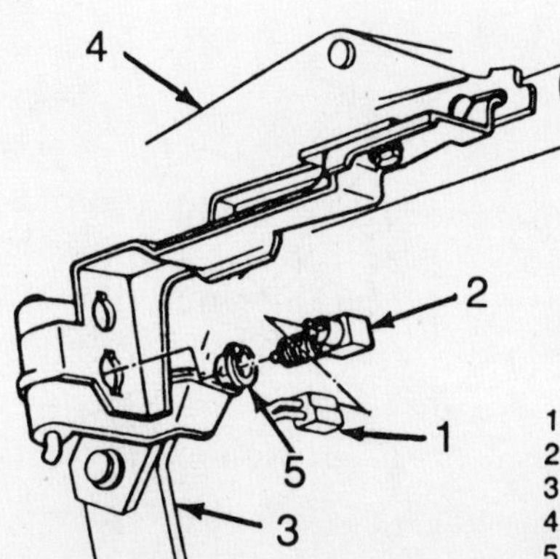

1. Connector
2. Release switch
3. Clutch
4. Brake pedal bracket
5. Retainer

Clutch release switch for R and V series

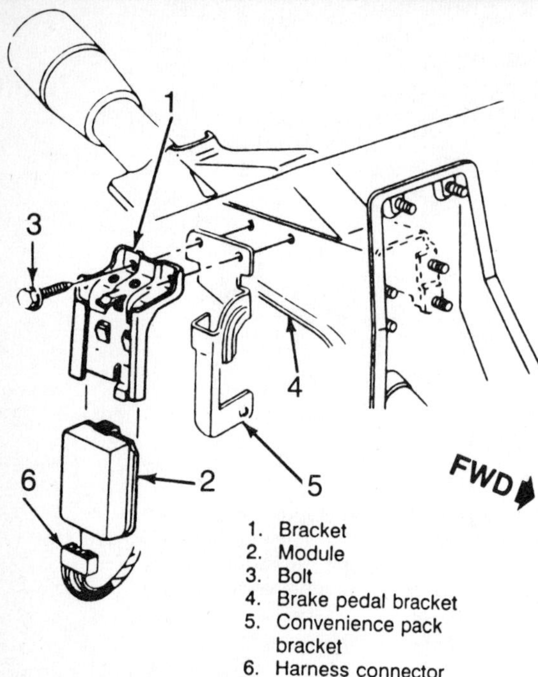

1. Bracket
2. Module
3. Bolt
4. Brake pedal bracket
5. Convenience pack bracket
6. Harness connector

R and V series control module

7a. Gasoline engines: With the ignition switch OFF and the fast idle cam not engaged, and the throttle fully closed, hook the rod in the servo and position over the stud. Position the rod so that there is a gap of 1-5mm between the stud and the outer end of the slot in the rod. Install the retainer.

7b. Hook the rod in the servo and position the pin on the rod in the hole closest to the servo that allows 1mm of play at the throttle cable.

8. Connect the cruise control cable on the 3rd ball of the servo chain.

9. Turn the locknut until the cable sleeve at the throttle lever is tight, but not holding the throttle open.

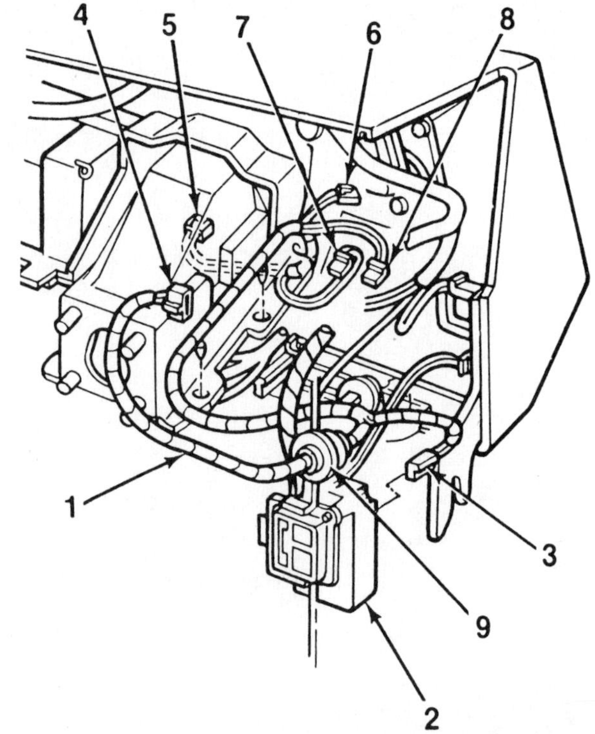

1. Harness
2. Convenience center
3. Convenience center connector
4. Module/motor connector
5. Steering column connector
6. Brake switch connector
7. Redundant brake switch connector
8. Clutch switch connector
9. Grommet

C and K series cruise control harness routing

10. Install the retainer.
11. Connect the hoses.

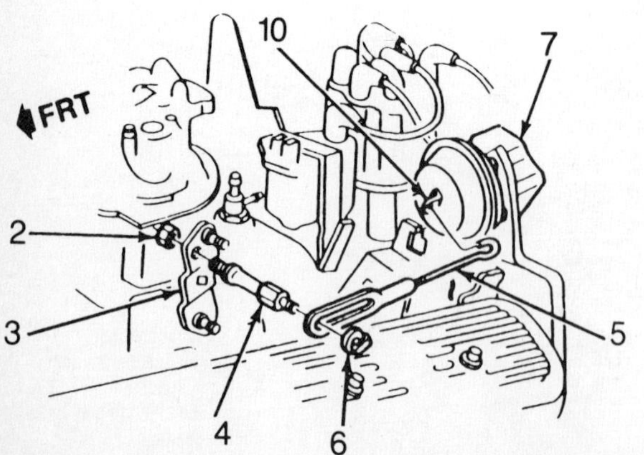

1. 1.0-5.0mm
2. Nut
3. Lever
4. Stud
5. Rod
6. Retainer
7. Servo
8. Bolt
9. Bracket
10. Tab

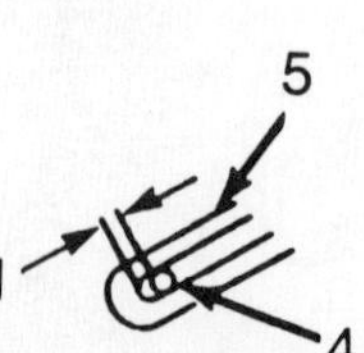

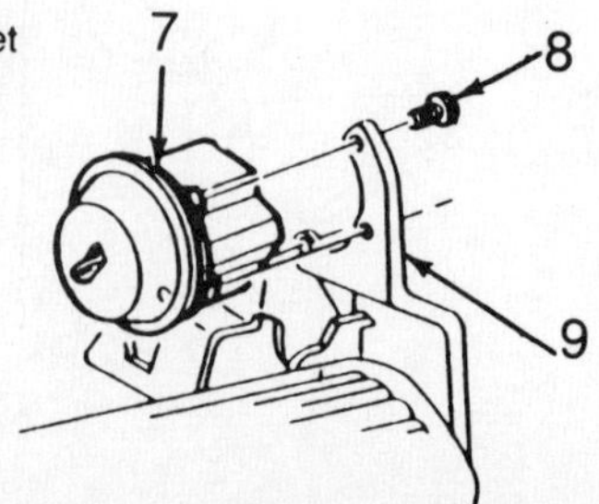

R and V series servo mounting with gasoline engines

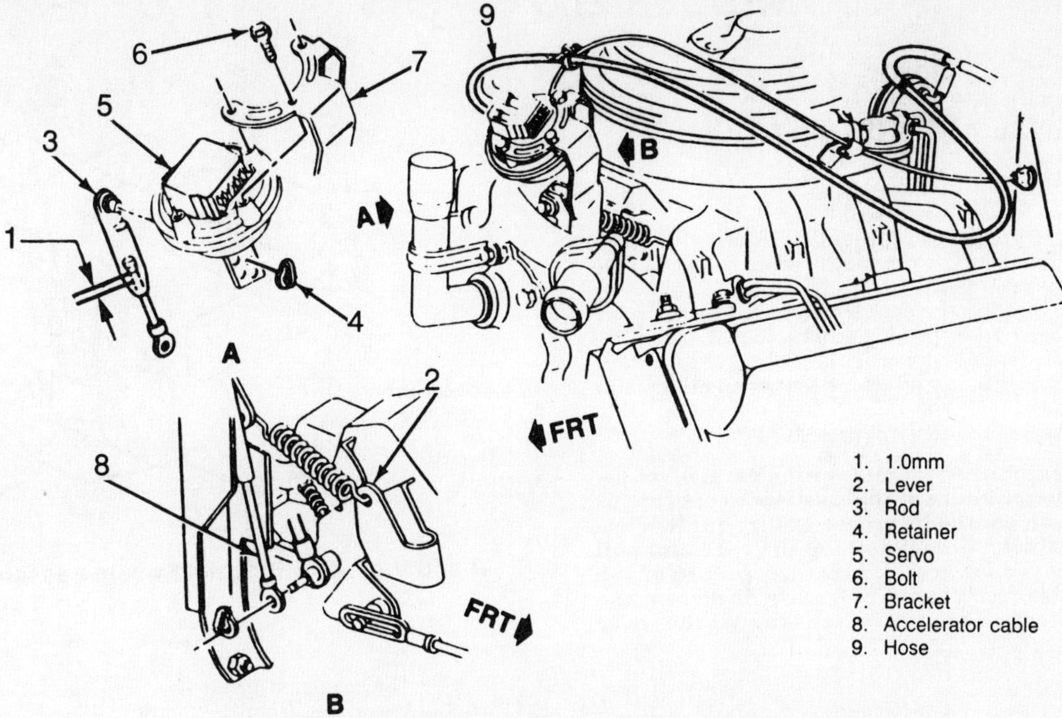

R and V series servo mounting with the diesel engines

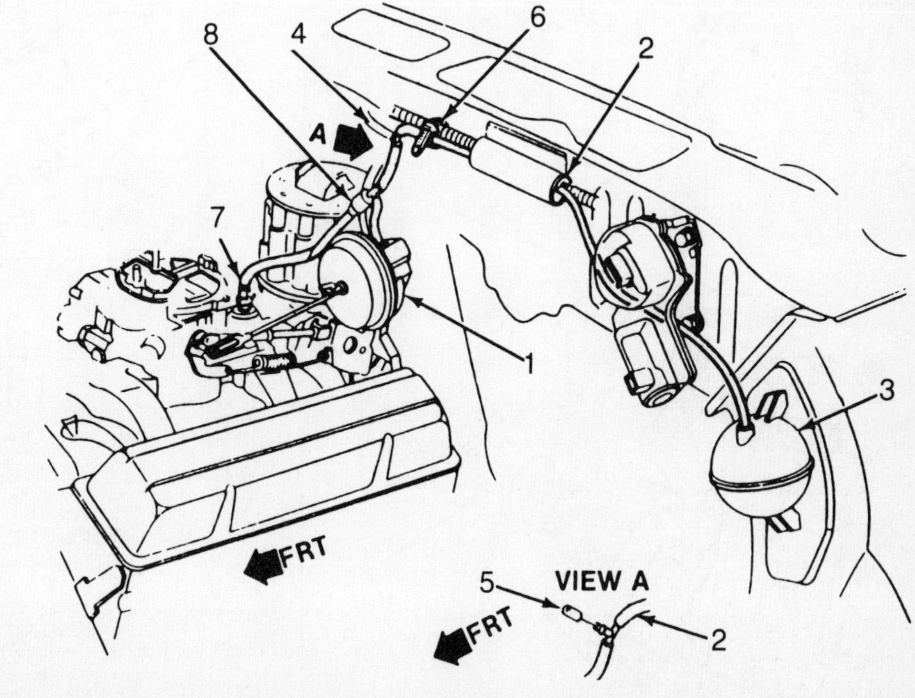

1. Servo
2. Vacuum hose
3. Vacuum tank
4. A/C vacuum hose
5. Cap
6. Strap
7. Vacuum fitting
8. Check valve

Vacuum hose routing for R and V series with V8 gasoline engines

WINDSHIELD WIPERS

Motor

REMOVAL AND INSTALLATION

1988–90 R/V Series

1. Make sure the wipers are parked.
2. Disconnect the ground cable from the battery.
3. Disconnect the wiring harness at the wiper motor and the hoses from the washer pump.
4. Reach down through the access hole in the plenum and loosen the wiper drive rod attaching screws. Remove the drive rod from the wiper motor crank arm.
5. Remove the wiper motor attaching screws and the motor assembly and linkage.
6. To install, reverse the removal procedure.

NOTE: Lubricate the wiper motor crank arm pivot before reinstallation. Failure of the washers to operate or to shut off is often caused by grease or dirt on the electromagnetic contacts. Simply unplug the wire and pull off the plastic cover for access. Likewise, failure of the wipers to park is often caused by grease or dirt on the park switch contacts. The park switch is under the cover behind the pump.

1988–90 C/K Series

1. Disconnect the battery ground cable.
2. Pivot the wiper arm away from the windshield, move the latch to the open position and lift the wiper arm off of the driveshaft.

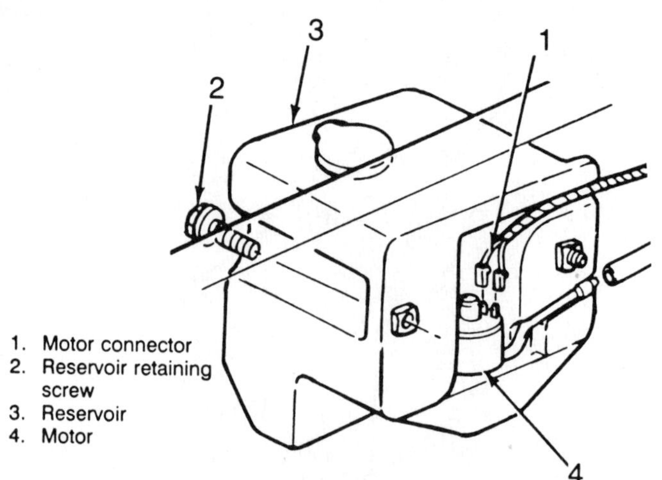

R and V series windshield washer assembly

3. Remove the cowl vent grille.
4. Unplug the wiring from the motor.
5. Remove the drive link-to-crank arm screws and slide the links from the arm.
6. Remove the motor mounting bolts and lift the motor out.
7. Installation is the reverse of removal.

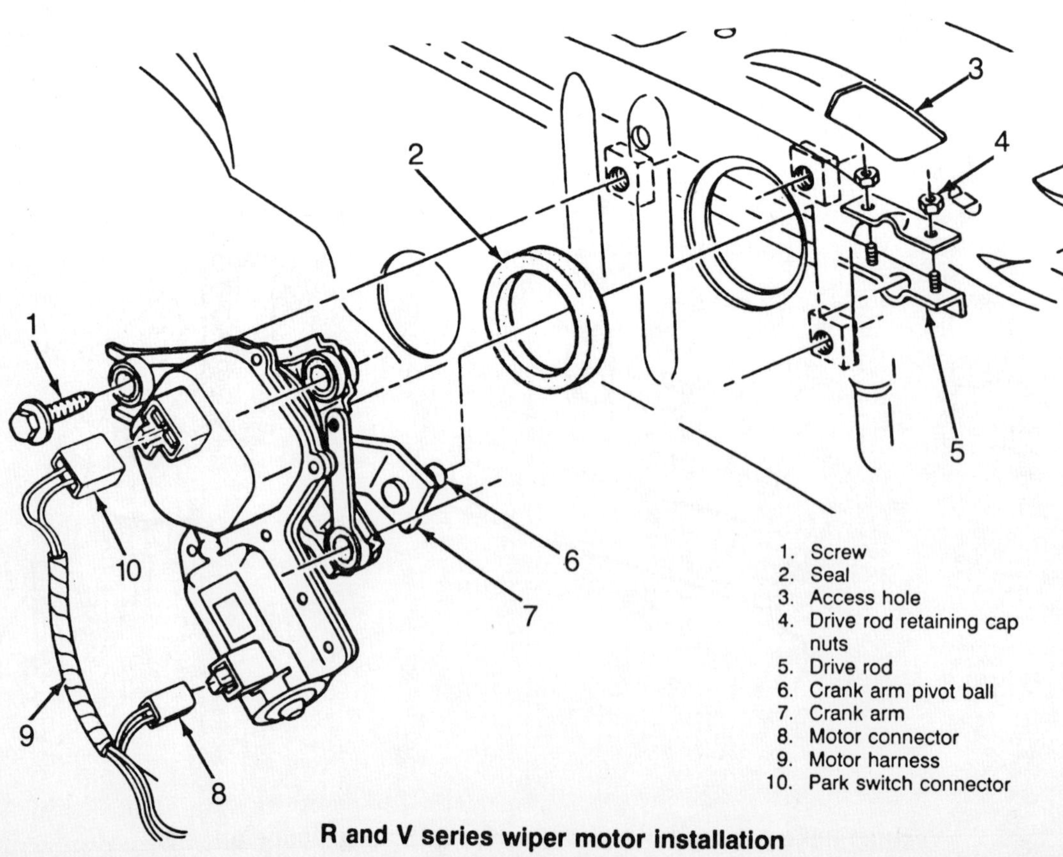

R and V series wiper motor installation

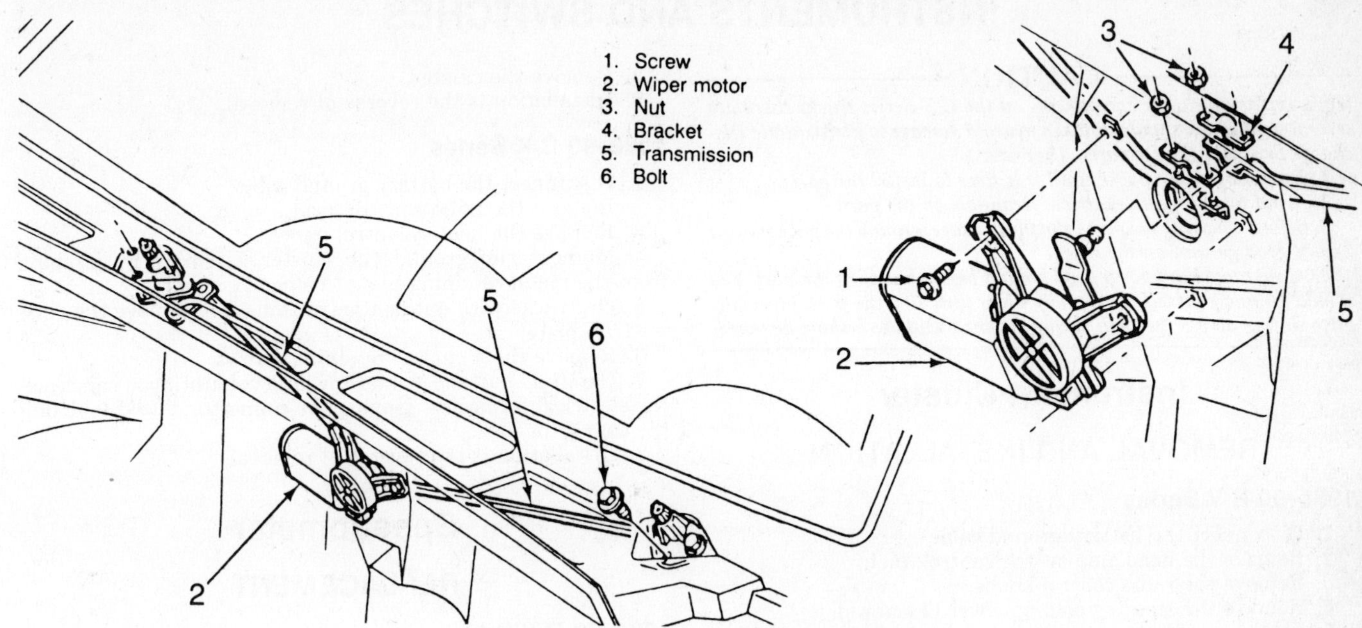

C and K series wiper motor installation

Delay Module

REPLACEMENT

R and V Series

1. Remove the steering column shrouds.
2. Unplug the harness connectors.
3. Slide the module off the bracket.
4. Installation is the reverse of removal.

C and K Series

1. Disconnect the battery ground cable.
2. Unplug the connector from the module.
3. Remove the module-to-motor screw.
4. Installation is the reverse of removal.

Windhshield Washer Motor

REPLACEMENT

R and V Series

1. Disconnect the battery ground cable.
2. Remove the 2 attaching screws and remove the reservoir.
3. Unplug the wiring at the motor.
4. Disconnect the fluid tube at the motor.
5. Remove the motor from the reservoir.
6. Installation is the reverse of removal.

C and K Series

1. Disconnect the battery ground cable.
2. Unplug the wiring harness from the pump.
3. Disconnect the hose from the pump.
4. Remove the attaching screws and lift off the reservoir.
5. Remove the pump from the reservoir.
6. Installation is the reverse of removal.

Linkage

REMOVAL AND INSTALLATION

1988–90 R/V Series

The linkage is removed with the motor.

1988–90 C/K Series

1. Disconnect the battery ground cable.
2. Pivot the wiper arm away from the windshield, move the latch to the open position and lift the wiper arm off of the driveshaft.
3. Remove the cowl vent grille.
4. Remove the drive link-to-crank arm screws and slide the links from the arm.
5. Remove the linkage mounting bolts and lift the linkage out.
6. Installation is the reverse of removal.

INSTRUMENTS AND SWITCHES

CAUTION

When replacing cluster components on the C/K Series trucks there are several steps which should be taken to avoid damage to Electrostatic Discharge Sensitive (ESD) parts. They are:

1. Do not open the packe until it is time to install the part.

2. Avoid touching the electrical terminals on the part.

3. Before removing the part from the package, ground the package to a known good gorund on the truck.

4. Always touch a known good ground before handling the part. You should ground yourself occasionaly while installing the part, especially after sliding across the seat, sitting down or walking a short distance.

Instrument Cluster

REMOVAL AND INSTALLATION

1988–90 R/V Series

1. Disconnect the battery ground cable.
2. Remove the headlamp switch control knob.
3. Remove the radio control knobs.
4. Remove the steering column cover (4 screws).
5. Remove eight screws and remove instrument bezel.
6. Reach under the dash, depress the speedometer cable tang, and remove the cable.
7. Pull instrument cluster out just far enough to disconnect all lines and wires.
8. Remove the cluster.
9. Installation is the reverse of removal.

1988–90 C/K Series

1. Disconnect the battery ground cable.
2. Remove the radio control head.
3. Remove the heater control panel.
4. Momentarily ground the cluster assembly by jumping from the metal retaining plate to a good ground.
5. On trucks with automatic transmission, remove the cluster trim plate.
6. Remove the 4 cluster retaining screws.
7. Carefully pull the cluster towards you until you can reach the electrical connector. Unplug the connector. Avoid touching the connector pins.
8. Installation is the reverse of removal.

Speedometer

REPLACEMENT

1988–90 R/V Series

1. Disconnect the battery ground cable.
2. Remove the headlamp switch control knob.
3. Remove the radio control knobs.
4. Remove the clock adjuster stem.

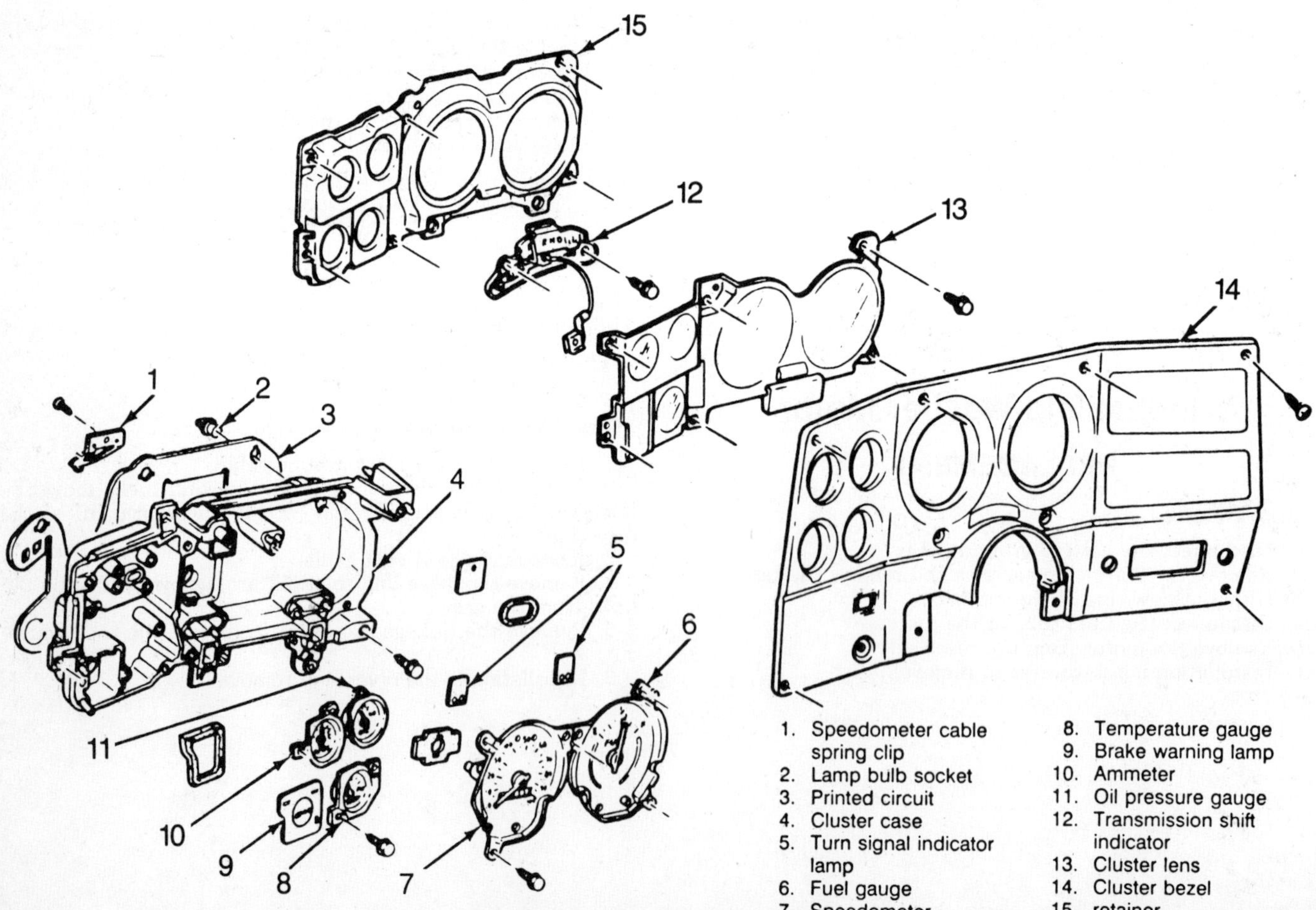

R and V series instrument panel

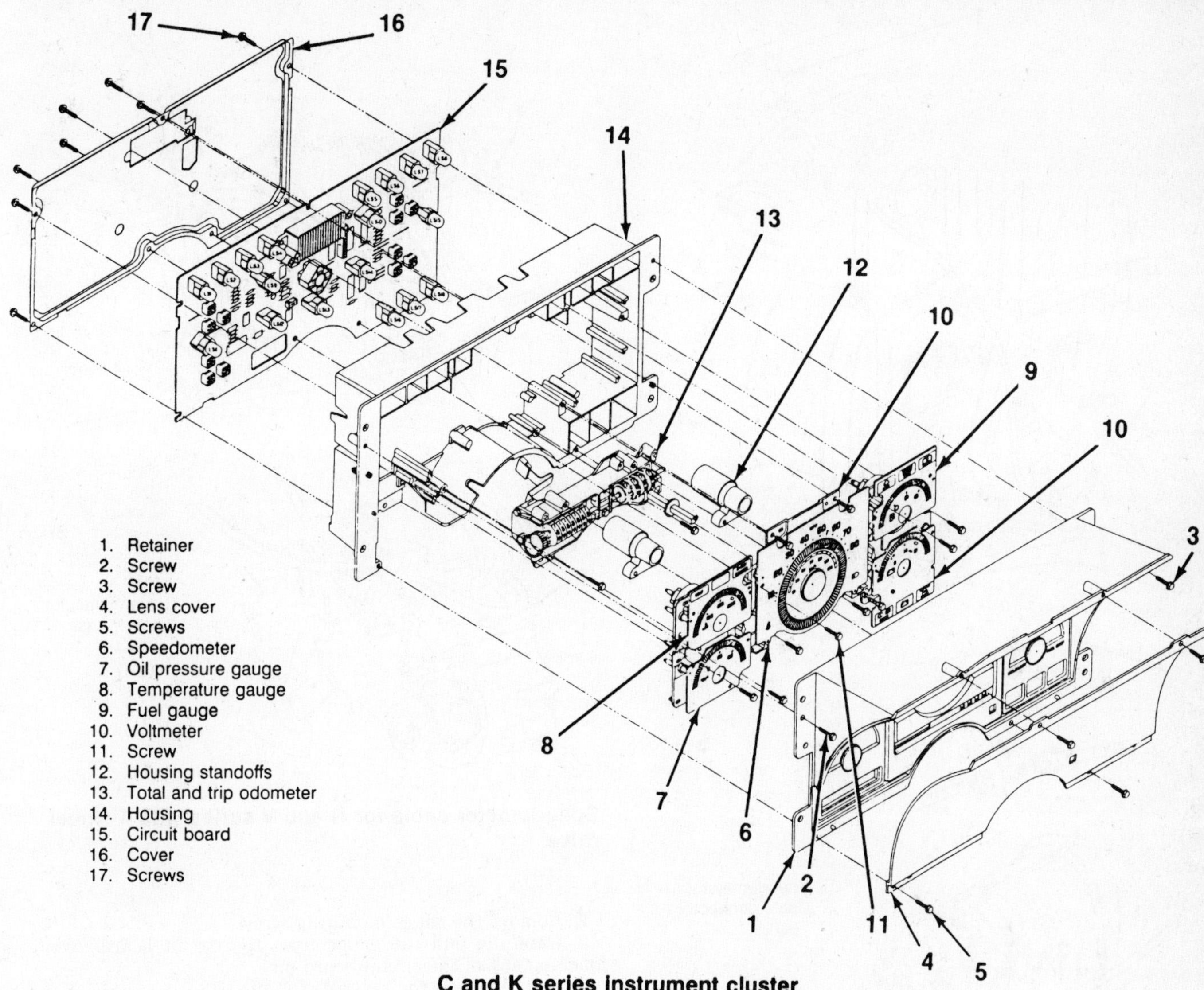

C and K series instrument cluster

5. Remove the steering column cover (4 screws).
6. Remove eight screws and remove instrument bezel.
7. Remove the cluster lens.
8. Remove the shift indicator.
9. Remove the gauge retainer plate.
10. Reach under the dash, depress the speedometer cable tang, and remove the cable.
11. Installation is the reverse of removal.

1988–90 C/K Series

1. Remove the cluster.
2. Remove the speedometer mounting screws.
3. Carefully pull the speedometer from the circuit board. Avoid touching any of the circuit board pins.
4. Installation is the reverse of removal.

Fuel Gauge

REPLACEMENT

1988–90 R/V Series

1. Disconnect the battery ground cable.
2. Remove the headlamp switch control knob.
3. Remove the radio control knobs.
4. Remove the clock adjuster stem.
5. Remove the steering column cover (4 screws).
6. Remove eight screws and remove instrument bezel.
7. Remove the cluster lens.
8. Remove the shift indicator.
9. Remove the gauge retainer plate.
10. Remove the gauge retaining screws and lift out the gauge.
11. Installation is the reverse of removal.

1988–90 C/K Series

1. Remove the cluster.
2. Remove the gauge mounting screws.
3. Carefully pull the gauge from the circuit board. Avoid touching any of the circuit board pins.
4. Installation is the reverse of removal.

Temperature Gauge

REPLACEMENT

1988–90 R/V Series

1. Disconnect the battery ground cable.

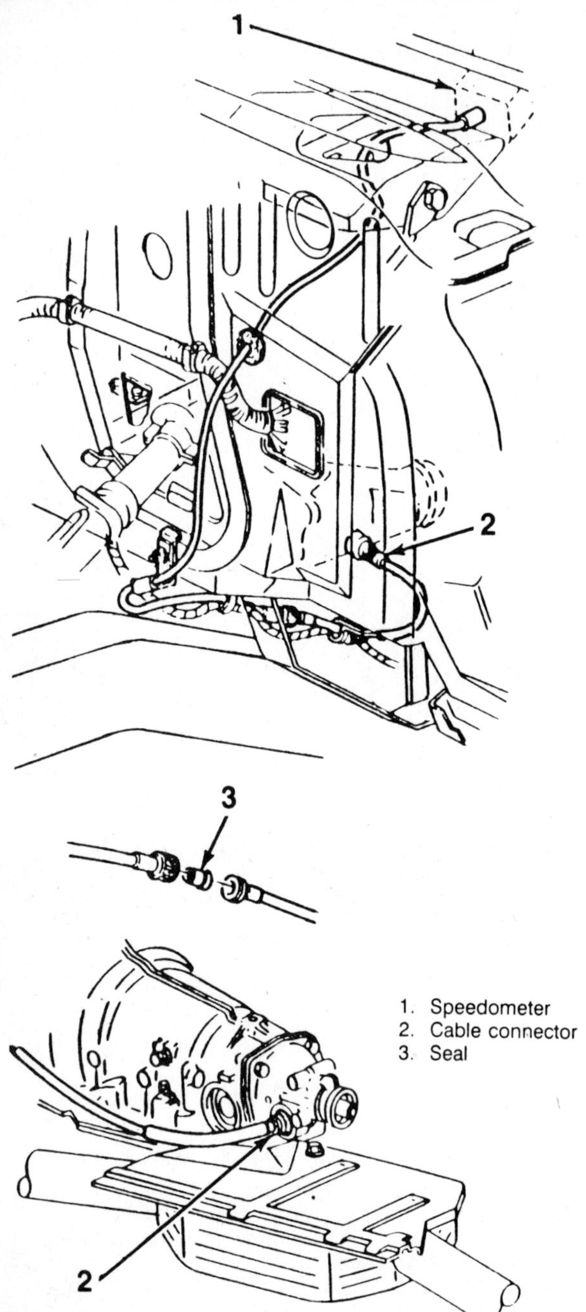

Speedometer cable for R and V series with 2-wheel drive

2. Remove the headlamp switch control knob.
3. Remove the radio control knobs.
4. Remove the clock adjuster stem.
5. Remove the steering column cover (4 screws).
6. Remove eight screws and remove instrument bezel.
7. Remove the cluster lens.
8. Remove the shift indicator.
9. Remove the gauge retainer plate.
10. Remove the gauge retaining screws and lift out the gauge.
11. Installation is the reverse of removal.

1988–90 C/K Series

1. Remove the cluster.

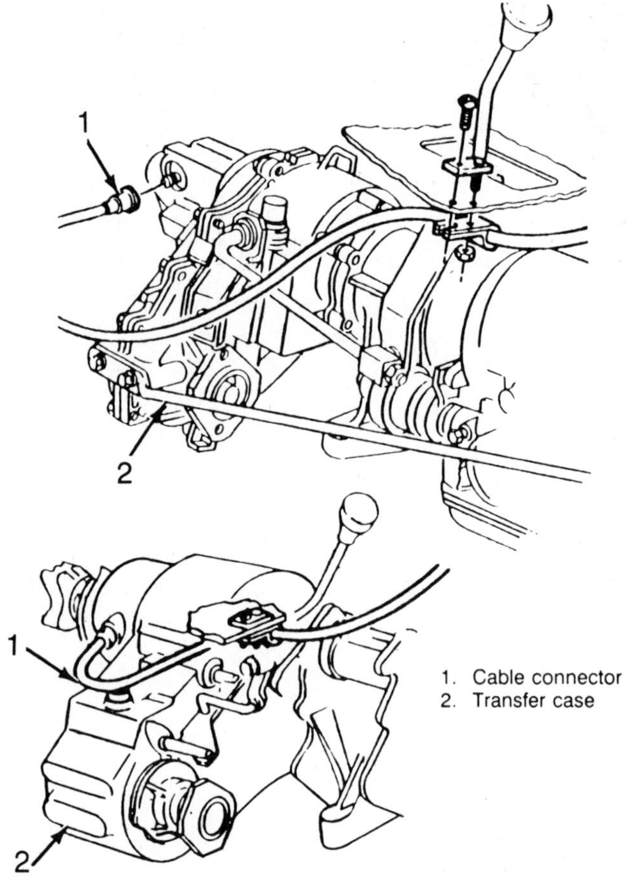

Speedometer cable for R and V series with 4-wheel drive

2. Remove the gauge mounting screws.
3. Carefully pull the gauge from the circuit board. Avoid touching any of the circuit board pins.
4. Installation is the reverse of removal.

Oil Pressure Gauge

REPLACEMENT

1988–90 R/V Series

1. Disconnect the battery ground cable.
2. Remove the headlamp switch control knob.
3. Remove the radio control knobs.
4. Remove the clock adjuster stem.
5. Remove the steering column cover (4 screws).
6. Remove eight screws and remove instrument bezel.
7. Remove the cluster lens.
8. Remove the shift indicator.
9. Remove the gauge retainer plate.
10. Remove the gauge retaining screws and lift out the gauge.
11. Installation is the reverse of removal.

1988–90 C/K Series

1. Remove the cluster.
2. Remove the gauge mounting screws.
3. Carefully pull the gauge from the circuit board. Avoid touching any of the circuit board pins.
4. Installation is the reverse of removal.

Voltmeter

REPLACEMENT

1988–90 R/V Series

1. Disconnect the battery ground cable.
2. Remove the headlamp switch control knob.
3. Remove the radio control knobs.
4. Remove the clock adjuster stem.
5. Remove the steering column cover (4 screws).
6. Remove eight screws and remove instrument bezel.
7. Remove the cluster lens.
8. Remove the shift indicator.
9. Remove the gauge retainer plate.
10. Remove the gauge retaining screws and lift out the gauge.
11. Installation is the reverse of removal.

1988–90 C/K Series

1. Remove the cluster.
2. Remove the gauge mounting screws.
3. Carefully pull the gauge from the circuit board. Avoid touching any of the circuit board pins.
4. Installation is the reverse of removal.

Printed Circuit Board

REPLACEMENT

1988–90 R/V Series

1. Disconnect the battery ground cable.
2. Remove the headlamp switch control knob.
3. Remove the radio control knobs.
4. Remove the steering column cover (4 screws).
5. Remove eight screws and remove instrument bezel.
6. Reach under the dash, depress the speedometer cable tang, and remove the cable.
7. Pull instrument cluster out just far enough to disconnect all lines and wires.
8. Remove the cluster.
9. Remove the cluster lamp bulbs.
10. Remove the circuit board retaining screws.
11. Carefully lift the circuit board from the cluster.
12. Installation is the reverse of removal.

Headlight Switch

REPLACEMENT

1988–90 R/V Series

1. Disconnect battery ground cable.
2. Reaching up behind instrument cluster, depress shaft retaining button and remove switch knob and rod.
3. Remove instrument cluster bezel screws on left end. Pull out on bezel and hold switch nut with a wrench.
4. Disconnect multiple wiring connectors at switch terminals.
5. Remove switch by rotating while holding switch nut.
6. Installation is thr reverse of removal.

1988–90 C/K Series

1. Remove the instrument cluster bezel.
2. Remove the headlamp switch retaining screws.
3. Pull the switch away from the bezel.
4. Installation is the reverse of removal.

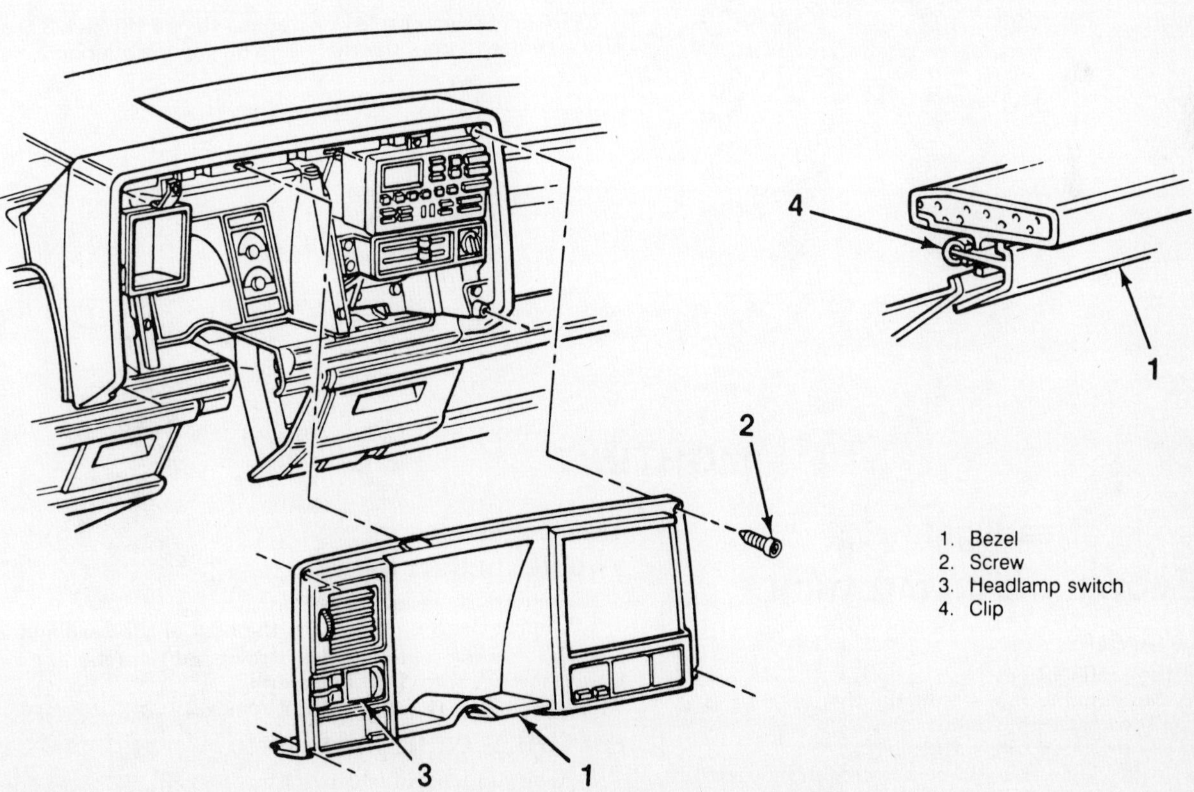

C and K series instrument panel bezel

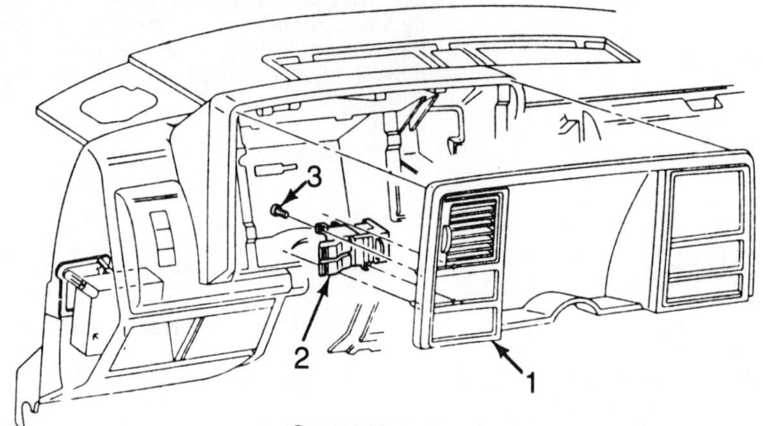

C and K series headlamp switch

Speedometer Cable

REMOVAL AND INSTALLATION

R/V Series

1. Disconnect the negative battery terminal.
2. Disconnect the cable from the back of the speedometer.
3. Remove the old core by pulling it out at the speedometer end. If the core is broken, it will be necessary to remove the broken half from the transmission end of the cable.
4. Lubricate the entire length of the core before installation.
5. Installation is the reverse of removal.

Speedometer Cable Core

REPLACEMENT

R/V Series

1. Disconnect the battery ground cable.
2. Disconnect the speedometer cable from the speedometer head by reaching up under the instrument panel, depressing the spring clip and pulling the cable from the head.
3. Remove the old core by pulling it out at the end of the speedometer cable casing. If the old cable core is broken it will be necessary to remove the lower piece from the transmission end of the casing. It is also important to replace both the casing and the core.
4. Lubricate the entire length of cable core with speedometer cable lubricant.
5. Install the new cable by reversing steps 1 through 3 above. Use care not to kink the cable core during installation.

LIGHTING

Headlights

REMOVAL AND INSTALLATION

1988–90 R/V Series

1. Remove the headlight bezel.
2. Remove the retaining ring screws and the retaining ring. Do not disturb the adjusting screws.
3. Remove the retaining ring spring.
4. Unplug the headlight from the electrical connector and remove it.
5. Installation is the reverse of removal.

1988 C/K Series

TWO HEADLIGHT SYSTEM

1. Remove the headlight bezel.
2. Unplug the connector from the back of the headlight.
3. Remove the retaining ring screws and the retaining ring. Do not disturb the adjusting screws.
4. Installation is the reverse of removal.

FOUR HEADLIGHT SYSTEM

1. Remove the headlight bezel.
2. Remove the retaining ring screws and the retaining ring. Do not disturb the adjusting screws.

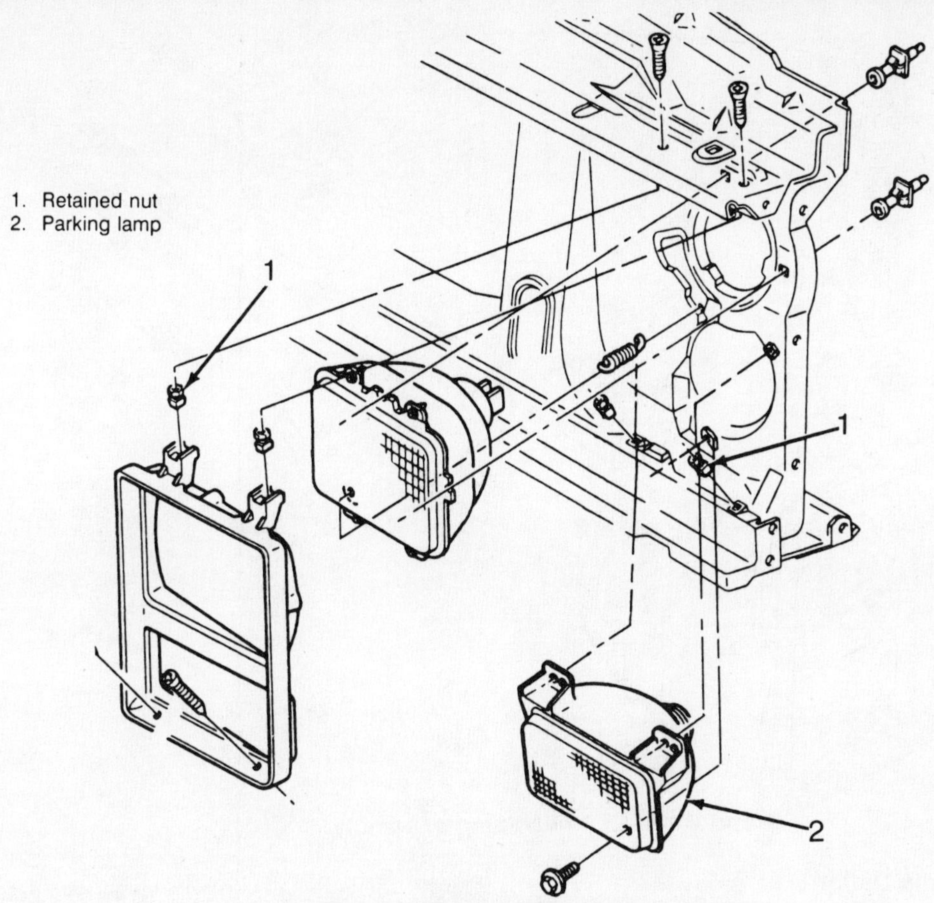

R and V series 2-headlamp assembly

3. Unplug the connector from the back of the headlight and remove the lamp.
4. Installation is the reverse of removal.

1989–90 C/K Series

TWO OR FOUR HEADLIGHT SYSTEM

1. Remove the retaining ring screws and the retaining ring. Do not disturb the adjusting screws.
2. Remove the headlamp from the mounting bracket.
3. Unplug the headlamp wiring connector.
4. Installation is the reverse of removal.

HEADLIGHT AIMING

The headlights must be properly aimed to provide the best, safest road illumination. The lights should be checked for proper aim, and adjusted if necessary, after installing a new sealed beam unit or if the front end sheet metal has been replaced. Certain state and local authorities have requirements for headlight aiming and you should check these before adjusting.

The truck's fuel tank should be about half full when adjusting the headlights. Tires should be properly inflated, and if a heavy load is carried in the pick-up bed, it should remain there.

Horizontal and vertical aiming of each sealed beam unit is provided by two adjusting screws, which move the mounting ring in the body against the tension of the coil spring. There is no adjustment for focus; this is done during headlight manufacturing.

Fog Lights

AIMING

1. Park the truck on level ground, facing, perpendicular to, and about 25 ft. from a flat wall.
2. Remove any stone shields and switch on the fog lights.
3. Loosen the mounting hardware of the lights so you can aim them as follows:
   a. The horizontal distance between the light beams on the wall should be the same as between the lights themselves.
   b. The vertical height of the light beams above the ground should be 4 inches less than the distance between the ground and the center of the lamp lenses.
4. Tighten the mounting hardware.

Front Parking Lamp Assembly

REMOVAL AND INSTALLATION

R/V Series With Two Lamp Option

1. Disconnect the negative battery cable.
2. Remove the four bezel retaining screws and remove the bezel.
3. Remove the three parking lamp retaining screws, disconnect the electrical connector and remove the parking lamp.
4. Reverse the above to replace.

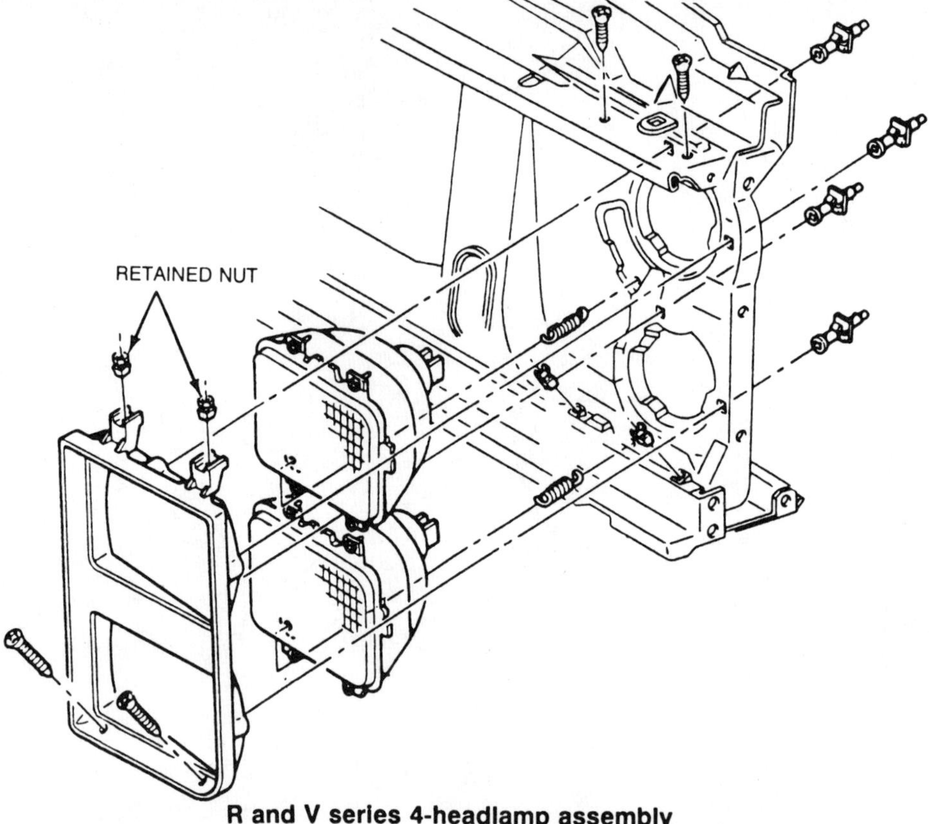

R and V series 4-headlamp assembly

R/V Series With Four Lamp Option

1. Remove the radiator grille.
2. Disconnect the electrical connector from the parking lamp assembly.
3. Remove the two nuts at the top of the housing and lift it up from the radiator grille.
4. Reverse the above to install.

C/K Series

1. Remove the 4 parking lamp assembly retaining screws.
2. Twist the bulb holder and pull the bulb and holder from the lamp.
3. Twist the bulb and remove it from the holder.
4. Installation is the reverse of removal.

Front Side Marker Lamp Bulb and/or Housing

REMOVAL AND REPLACEMENT

R/V Series

1. Remove the two screws and remove the side marker lamp.
2. Remove the bulb from the lamp.
3. Reverse the above to install.

Rear Side Marker Lamp Bulb and/or Housing

REMOVAL AND REPLACEMENT

R/V Series

1. Remove the lens-to-housing screws.
2. Replace the bulb and check its operation.
3. Position the lens and install the four attaching screws.

C/K Series

1. Remove the lamp attaching screws.
2. Pull the lamp from the fender.
3. Twist the bulb holder and remove the holder and bulb from the lamp.
4. Twist the bulb and remove it from the holder.
5. Installation is the reverse of removal.

Tail, Stop and Backup Lamp Bulbs

REMOVAL AND REPLACEMENT

R/V Series

1. Remove the lens-to-housing attaching screws.
2. Replace the bulb and check its operation.
3. Position the lens and install the attaching screws.

Tail, Stop and Backup Lamp Housing

REMOVAL AND REPLACEMENT

R/V Series

1. Remove the lens-to-housing attaching screws.
2. Remove the bulbs from the sockets.
3. Remove the housing attaching screws.
4. Rotate the wiring harness sockets counterclockwise and remove the housing.
5. To install, reverse Steps 1-4 above.

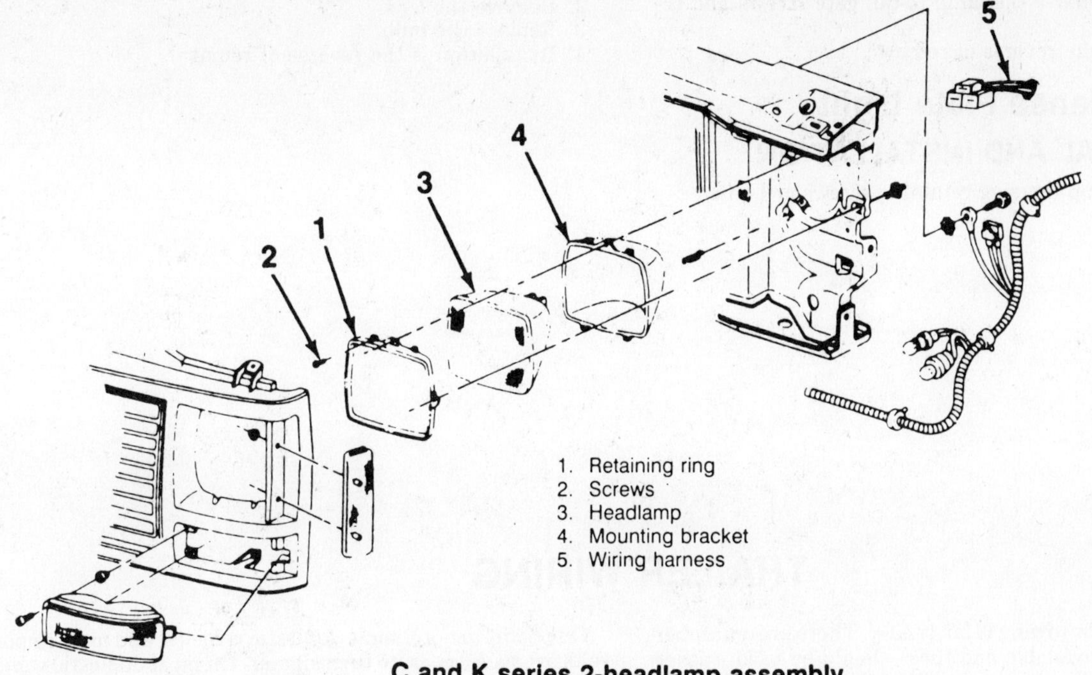

C and K series 2-headlamp assembly

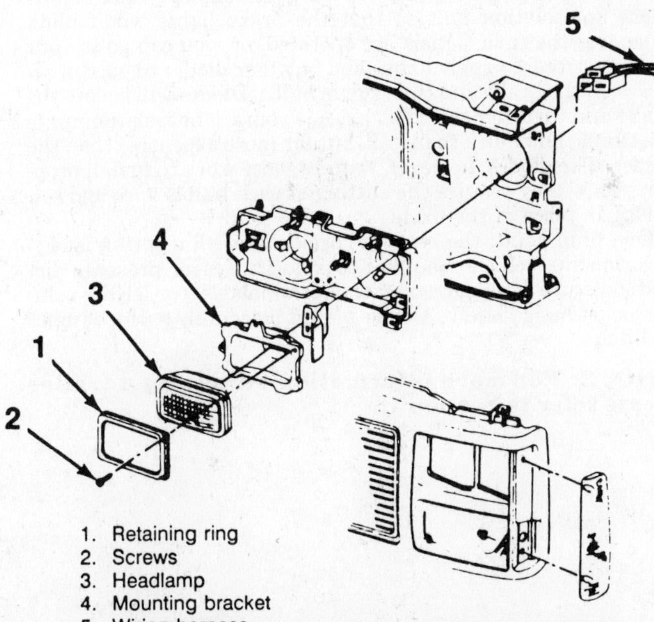

C and K series 4-headlamp assembly

Rear Lamp and Bulb Assembly

REMOVAL AND INSTALLATION

C/K Series

1. Lower the tailgate.
2. Remove the lamp assembly retaining screws.
3. Pull the lamp assembly from the truck and disconnect the wiring.
4. Remove the bulb(s) from the lamp.
5. Installation is the reverse of removal.

Roof Marker Lamps

REMOVAL AND INSTALLATION

1. Remove the lens screws.
2. Remove the lens.
3. Remove the insulator.
4. Remove the bulb.
5. Installation is the reverse of removal.

Dome Light

REMOVAL AND INSTALLATION

1. Remove the lens screws.
2. Remove the lens.
3. Remove the bulb.
4. Installation is the reverse of removal.

Cargo Lamp

REMOVAL AND INSTALLATION

1. Remove the lens screws.
2. Remove the lens.
3. Remove the bulb.
4. Installation is the reverse of removal.

Tail Gate Stop Light

REMOVAL AND INSTALLATION

1. Unsnap the lens from the lamp.
2. Remove the bulb.

3. If necessary, remove the lamp-to-tail gate screws and remove the lamp body.
4. Installation is the reverse of removal.

License Plate Light

REMOVAL AND INSTALLATION

1. Remove the lamp housing retaining screws or bolts.
2. Remove the lens.
3. Replace the bulb.
4. Installation is the reverse of removal.

TRAILER WIRING

Wiring the truck for towing is fairly easy. There are a number of good wiring kits available and these should be used, rather than trying to design your own. All trailers will need brake lights and turn signals as well as tail lights and side marker lights. Most states require extra marker lights for overly wide trailers. Also, most states have recently required back-up lights for trailers, and most trailer manufacturers have been building trailers with back-up lights for several years.

Additionally, some Class I, most Class II and just about all Class III trailers will have electric brakes.

Add to this number an accessories wire, to operate trailer internal equipment or to charge the trailer's battery, and you can have as many as seven wires in the harness.

Determine the equipment on your trailer and buy the wiring kit necessary. The kit will contain all the wires needed, plus a plug adapter set which included the female plug, mounted on the bumper or hitch, and the male plug, wired into, or plugged into the trailer harness.

When installing the kit, follow the manufacturer's instructions. The color coding of the wires is standard throughout the industry.

One point to note, some domestic vehicles, and most imported vehicles, have separate turn signals. On most domestic vehicles, the brake lights and rear turn signals operate with the same bulb. For those vehicles with separate turn signals, you can purchase an isolation unit so that the brake lights won't blink whenever the turn signals are operated, or, you can go to your local electronics supply house and buy four diodes to wire in series with the brake and turn signal bulbs. Diodes will isolate the brake and turn signals. The choice is yours. The isolation units are simple and quick to install, but far more expensive than the diodes. The diodes, however, require more work to install properly, since they require the cutting of each bulb's wire and soldering in place of the diode.

One final point, the best kits are those with a spring loaded cover on the vehicle mounted socket. This cover prevents dirt and moisture from corroding the terminals. Never let the vehicle socket hang loosely. Always mount it securely to the bumper or hitch.

NOTE: For more information on towing a trailer please refer to Section 1.

CIRCUIT PROTECTION

Fusible Links

In addition to circuit breakers and fuses, the wiring harness incorporates fusible links to protect the wiring. Links are used rather than a fuse, in wiring circuits that are not normally fused, such as the ignition circuit. Fusible links are color coded red in the charging and load circuits to match the color of the circuits they protect. Each link is four gauges smaller than the cable it protects, and is marked on the insulation with the gauge size because the insulation makes it appear heavier than it really is.

The engine compartment wiring harness has several fusible links. The same size wire with a special hypalon insulation must be used when replacing a fusible link.

The links are located in the following areas:

1. A molded splice at the starter solenoid **Bat** terminal, a 14 gauge red wire.
2. A 16 gauge red fusible link at the junction block to protect the unfused wiring of 12 gauge or larger wire. This link stops at the bulkhead connector.
3. The alternator warning light and field circuitry is protected by a 20 gauge red wire fusible link used in the battery feed to voltage regular #3 terminal. The link is installed as a molded splice in the circuit at the junction block.
4. The ammeter circuit is protected by two 20 gauge fusible links installed as molded splices in the circuit at the junction block and battery to starter circuit.

FUSIBLE LINK REPAIR

1. Determine which circuit is damaged, its location and the cause of the open fuse link. If the damaged fuse link is one of three fed by a common No. 10 or 12 gauge feed wire, determine the specific affected circuit.
2. Disconnect the negative battery cable.
3. Cut the damaged fuse link from the wiring harness and discard it. If the fuse link is one of three circuits fed by a single feed wire, cut it out of the harness at each splice end and discard it.
4. Identify and procure the proper fuse link and butt connectors for attaching the fuse link to the harness.
5. To repair any fuse link in a 3-link group with one feed:
   a. After cutting the open link out of the harness, cut each of the remaining undamaged fuse links close to the feed wire weld.
   b. Strip approximately ½ in. (13mm) of insulation from the detached ends of the two good fuse links. Then insert two wire ends into one end of a butt connector and carefully push one stripped end of the replacement fuse link into the same end of the butt connector and crimp all three firmly together.

NOTE: Care must be taken when fitting the three fuse links into the butt connector as the internal diameter is a snug it for three wires. Make sure to use a proper crimping tool. Pliers, side cutters, etc. will not apply the proper crimp to retain the wires and withstand a pull test.

   c. After crimping the butt connector to the three fuse links, cut the weld portion from the feed wire and strip approximately ½ in. (13mm) of insulation from the cut end. Insert the stripped end into the open end of the butt connector and crimp very firmly.
   d. To attach the remaining end of the replacement fuse link, strip approximately ½ in. (13mm) of insulation from the wire end of the circuit from which the blown fuse link was removed, and firmly crimp a butt connector or equivalent to the stripped wire. Then, insert the end of the replacement link into the other end of the butt connector and crimp firmly.
   e. Using rosin core solder with a consistency of 60 percent tin and 40 percent lead, solder the connectors and the wires at the repairs and insulate with electrical tape.
6. To replace any fuse link on a single circuit in a harness, cut out the damaged portion, strip approximately ½ in. (13mm) of insulation from the two wire ends and attach the appropriate replacement fuse link to the stripped wire ends with two proper size butt connectors. Solder the connectors and wires and insulate the tape.
7. To repair any fuse link which has an eyelet terminal on one end such as the charging circuit, cut off the open fuse link behind the weld, strip approximately ½ in. (13mm) of insulation from the cut end and attach the appropriate new eyelet fuse link to the cut stripped wire with an appropriate size butt connector. Solder the connectors and wires at the repair and insulate with tape.
8. Connect the negative battery cable to the battery and test the system for proper operation.

NOTE: Do not mistake a resistor wire for a fuse link. The resistor wire is generally longer and has print stating, "Resistor: don't cut or splice."

Circuit Breakers

A circuit breaker is an electrical switch which breaks the circuit in case of an overload. All models have a circuit breaker in the headlight switch to protect the headlight and parking light systems. An overload may cause the lamps to flicker or flash on and off, or in some cases, to remain off. 1974 and later windshield wiper motors are protected by a circuit breaker at the motor.

Fuses and Flashers

Fuses are located in the junction box below the instrument panel to the left of the steering column. The turn signal flasher and the hazard/warning flasher also plug into the fuse block. Each fuse receptacle is marked as to the circuit it protects and the correct amperage of the fuse. Inline fuses are also used on the underhood lamp and air conditioning.

NOTE: A special heavy duty turn signal flasher is required to properly operate the turn signals when a trailer's lights are connected to the system.

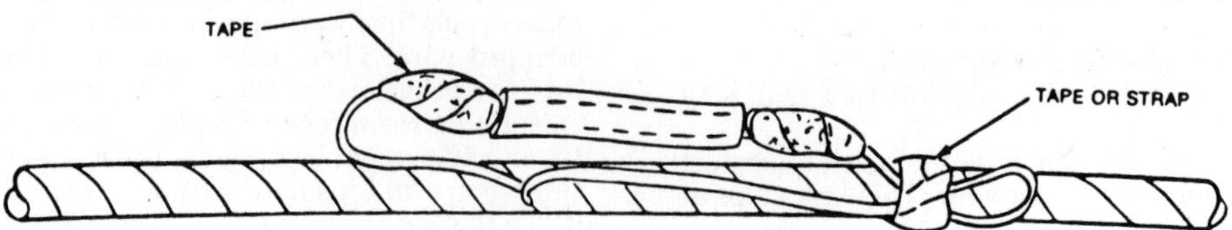

TYPICAL REPAIR USING THE SPECIAL #17 GA. (9.00" LONG-YELLOW) FUSE LINK REQUIRED FOR THE AIR/COND. CIRCUITS (2) #687E and #261A LOCATED IN THE ENGINE COMPARTMENT

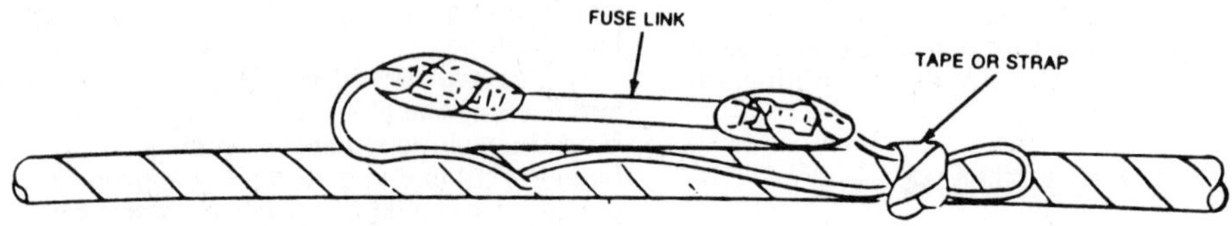

TYPICAL REPAIR FOR ANY IN-LINE FUSE LINK USING THE SPECIFIED GAUGE FUSE LINK FOR THE SPECIFIC CIRCUIT

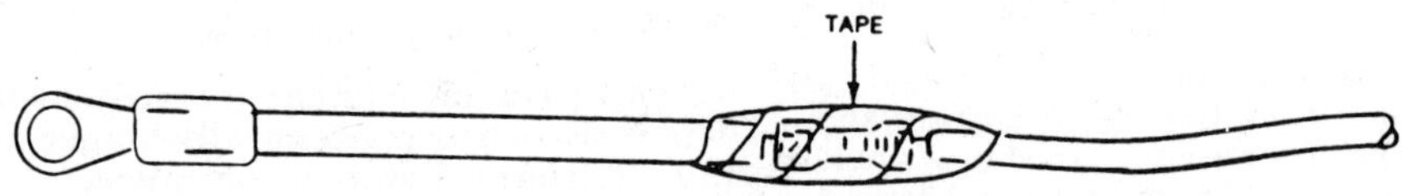

TYPICAL REPAIR USING THE EYELET TERMINAL FUSE LINK OF THE SPECIFIED GAUGE FOR ATTACHMENT TO A CIRCUIT WIRE END

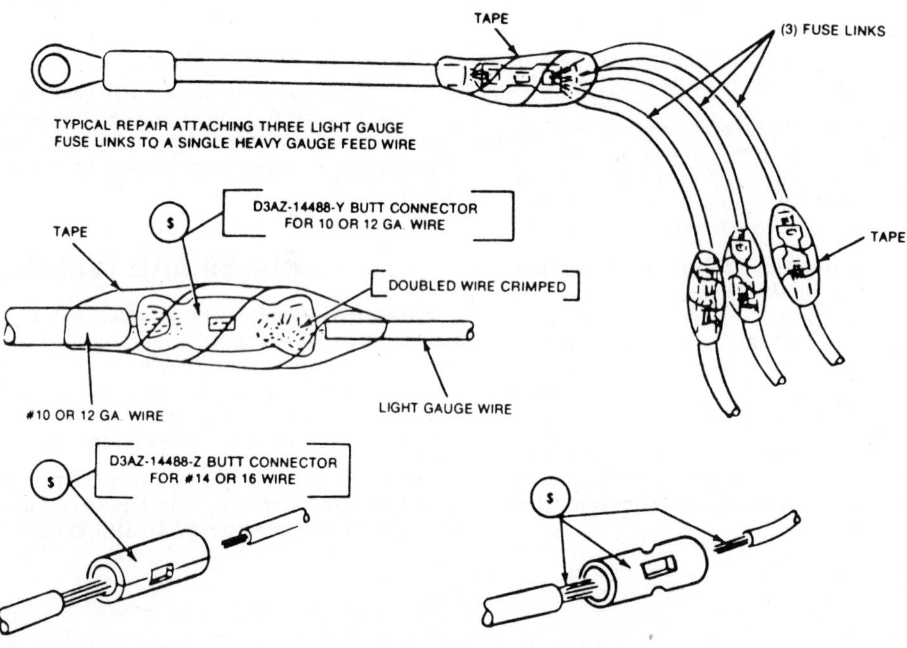

General fuse link repair procedure

7 Drive Train

QUICK REFERENCE INDEX

GENERAL INDEX

UNDERSTANDING THE MANUAL TRANSMISSION

Because of the way an internal combustion engine breathes, it can produce torque, or twisting force, only within a narrow speed range. Most modern, overhead valve engines must turn at about 2,500 rpm to produce their peak torque. By 4,500 rpm they are producing so little torque that continued increases in engine speed produce no power increases.

The manual transmission and clutch are employed to vary the relationship between engine speed and the speed of the wheels so that adequate engine power can be produced under all circumstances. The clutch allows engine torque to be applied to the transmission input shaft gradually, due to mechanical slippage. The car can, consequently, be started smoothly from a full stop.

The transmission changes the ratio between the rotating speeds of the engine and the wheels by the use of gears. 4-speed or 5-speed transmissions are most common. The lower gears allow full engine power to be applied to the rear wheels during acceleration at low speeds.

The clutch drive plate is a thin disc, the center of which is splined to the transmission input shaft. Both sides of the disc are covered with a layer of material which is similar to brake lining and which is capable of allowing slippage without roughness or excessive noise.

The clutch cover is bolted to the engine flywheel and incorporates a diaphragm spring which provides the pressure to engage the clutch. The cover also houses the pressure plate. The driven disc is sandwiched between the pressure plate and the smooth surface of the flywheel when the clutch pedal is released, thus forcing it to turn at the same speed as the engine crankshaft.

The transmission contains a mainshaft which passes all the way through the transmission, from the clutch to the driveshaft. This shaft is separated at one point, so that front and rear portions can turn at different speeds.

Power is transmitted by a countershaft in the lower gears and reverse. The gears of the countershaft mesh with gears on the mainshaft, allowing power to be carried from one to the other. All the countershaft gears are integral with that shaft, while several of the mainshaft gears can either rotate independently of the shaft or be locked to it. Shifting from one gear to the next causes one of the gears to be freed from rotating with the shaft and locks another to it. Gears are locked and unlocked by internal dog clutches which slide between the center of the gear and the shaft. The forward gears usually employ synchronizers; friction members which smoothly bring gear and shaft to the same speed before the toothed dog clutches are engaged.

MANUAL TRANSMISSION

Troubleshooting the Manual Transmission and Transfer Case

Problem	Cause	Solution
Transmission shifts hard	• Clutch adjustment incorrect	• Adjust clutch
	• Clutch linkage or cable binding	• Lubricate or repair as necessary
	• Shift rail binding	• Check for mispositioned selector arm roll pin, loose cover bolts, worn shift rail bores, worn shift rail, distorted oil seal, or extension housing not aligned with case. Repair as necessary.
	• Internal bind in transmission caused by shift forks, selector plates, or synchronizer assemblies	• Remove, dissemble and inspect transmission. Replace worn or damaged components as necessary.
	• Clutch housing misalignment	• Check runout at rear face of clutch housing
	• Incorrect lubricant	• Drain and refill transmission

Troubleshooting the Manual Transmission and Transfer Case (cont.)

Problem	Cause	Solution
Transmission shifts hard	• Block rings and/or cone seats worn	• Blocking ring to gear clutch tooth face clearance must be 0.030 inch or greater. If clearance is correct it may still be necessary to inspect blocking rings and cone seats for excessive wear. Repair as necessary.
Gear clash when shifting from one gear to another	• Clutch adjustment incorrect	• Adjust clutch
	• Clutch linkage or cable binding	• Lubricate or repair as necessary
	• Clutch housing misalignment	• Check runout at rear of clutch housing
	• Lubricant level low or incorrect lubricant	• Drain and refill transmission and check for lubricant leaks if level was low. Repair as necessary.
	• Gearshift components, or synchronizer assemblies worn or damaged	• Remove, disassemble and inspect transmission. Replace worn or damaged components as necessary.
Transmission noisy	• Lubricant level low or incorrect lubricant	• Drain and refill transmission. If lubricant level was low, check for leaks and repair as necessary.
	• Clutch housing-to-engine, or transmission-to-clutch housing bolts loose	• Check and correct bolt torque as necessary
	• Dirt, chips, foreign material in transmission	• Drain, flush, and refill transmission
	• Gearshift mechanism, transmission gears, or bearing components worn or damaged	• Remove, disassemble and inspect transmission. Replace worn or damaged components as necessary.
	• Clutch housing misalignment	• Check runout at rear face of clutch housing
Jumps out of gear	• Clutch housing misalignment	• Check runout at rear face of clutch housing
	• Gearshift lever loose	• Check lever for worn fork. Tighten loose attaching bolts.
	• Offset lever nylon insert worn or lever attaching nut loose	• Remove gearshift lever and check for loose offset lever nut or worn insert. Repair or replace as necessary.
	• Gearshift mechanism, shift forks, selector plates, interlock plate, selector arm, shift rail, detent plugs, springs or shift cover worn or damaged	• Remove, disassemble and inspect transmission cover assembly. Replace worn or damaged components as necessary.
	• Clutch shaft or roller bearings worn or damaged	• Replace clutch shaft or roller bearings as necessary

Troubleshooting the Manual Transmission and Transfer Case (cont.)

Problem	Cause	Solution
Jumps out of gear (cont.)	• Gear teeth worn or tapered, synchronizer assemblies worn or damaged, excessive end play caused by worn thrust washers or output shaft gears	• Remove, disassemble, and inspect transmission. Replace worn or damaged components as necessary.
	• Pilot bushing worn	• Replace pilot bushing
Will not shift into one gear	• Gearshift selector plates, interlock plate, or selector arm, worn, damaged, or incorrectly assembled	• Remove, disassemble, and inspect transmission cover assembly. Repair or replace components as necessary.
	• Shift rail detent plunger worn, spring broken, or plug loose	• Tighten plug or replace worn or damaged components as necessary
	• Gearshift lever worn or damaged	• Replace gearshift lever
	• Synchronizer sleeves or hubs, damaged or worn	• Remove, disassemble and inspect transmission. Replace worn or damaged components.
Locked in one gear—cannot be shifted out	• Shift rail(s) worn or broken, shifter fork bent, setscrew loose, center detent plug missing or worn	• Inspect and replace worn or damaged parts
	• Broken gear teeth on countershaft gear, clutch shaft, or reverse idler gear	• Inspect and replace damaged part
	Gearshift lever broken or worn, shift mechanism in cover incorrectly assembled or broken, worn damaged gear train components	• Disassemble transmission. Replace damaged parts or assemble correctly.
Transfer case difficult to shift or will not shift into desired range	• Vehicle speed too great to permit shifting	• Stop vehicle and shift into desired range. Or reduce speed to 3–4 km/h (2–3 mph) before attempting to shift.
	• If vehicle was operated for extended period in 4H mode on dry paved surface, driveline torque load may cause difficult shifting	• Stop vehicle, shift transmission to neutral, shift transfer case to 2H mode and operate vehicle in 2H on dry paved surfaces
	• Transfer case external shift linkage binding	• Lubricate or repair or replace linkage, or tighten loose components as necessary
	• Insufficient or incorrect lubricant	• Drain and refill to edge of fill hole with SAE 85W-90 gear lubricant only
	• Internal components binding, worn, or damaged	• Disassemble unit and replace worn or damaged components as necessary

Troubleshooting the Manual Transmission and Transfer Case

Problem	Cause	Solution
Transfer case noisy in all drive modes	• Insufficient or incorrect lubricant	• Drain and refill to edge of fill hole with SAE 85W-90 gear lubricant only. Check for leaks and repair if necessary. Note: If unit is still noisy after drain and refill, disassembly and inspection may be required to locate source of noise.
Noisy in—or jumps out of four wheel drive low range	• Transfer case not completely engaged in 4L position	• Stop vehicle, shift transfer case in Neutral, then shift back into 4L position
	• Shift linkage loose or binding	• Tighten, lubricate, or repair linkage as necessary
	• Shift fork cracked, inserts worn, or fork is binding on shift rail	• Disassemble unit and repair as necessary
Lubricant leaking from output shaft seals or from vent	• Transfer case overfilled • Vent closed or restricted	• Drain to correct level • Clear or replace vent if necessary
Lubricant leaking from output shaft seals or from vent (cont.)	• Output shaft seals damaged or installed incorrectly	• Replace seals. Be sure seal lip faces interior of case when installed. Also be sure yoke seal surfaces are not scored or nicked. Remove scores, nicks with fine sandpaper or replace yoke(s) if necessary.
Abnormal tire wear	• Extended operation on dry hard surface (paved) roads in 4H range	• Operate in 2H on hard surface (paved) roads

Back-Up Light

REMOVAL AND INSTALLATION

Transmission Mounted

1. Disconnect the negative battery cable.
2. Raise the vehicle and support it safely.
3. Disconnect the electrical connector at the switch.
4. Remove the retaining screws.
5. After installation, check the operation of the switch.

Vehicle Speed Sensor

REMOVAL AND INSTALLATION

C/K Series

1. Raise and support the truck on jackstands.
2. Unplug the harness connector at the sensor.
3. Remove the retaining screw, if used.
4. Remove the speed sensor.
5. Installation is the reverse of removal. Use a new seal coated with clean transmission oil.

Extension Housing Rear Seal

REPLACEMENT

85mm 4- and 5-Speed Transmission

1. Raise and support the truck end on jackstands.
2. Drain the transmission oil.
3. Matchmark and disconnect the driveshaft.
4. Deform the seal with a punch and pull it from the housing.
5. Installation is the reverse of removal. Coat the outside new seal with locking compound and fill the gap between the seal lips with chassis grease.

Rear Retainer Seal

REPLACEMENT

117mm 4-Speed Transmission

1. Raise and support the truck on jackstands.
2. Matchmark and remove the driveshaft.
3. Drain the transmission.
4. Disconnect the speedometer cable.
5. Remove the flange nut and washer.

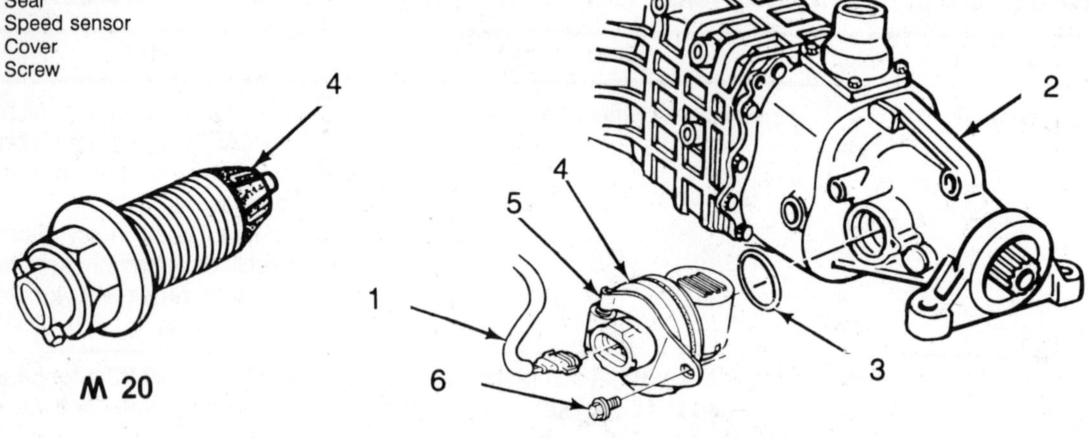

C and K series vehicle speed sensor

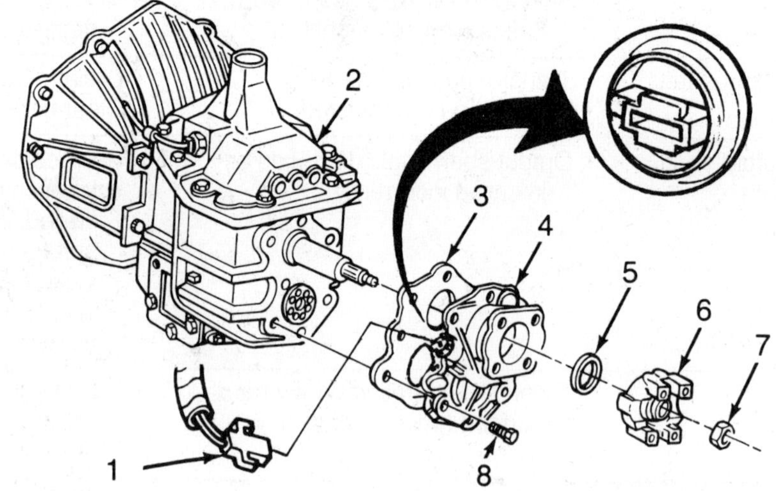

Rear retainer and seal for the 85mm 4-speed and 117mm 4-speed

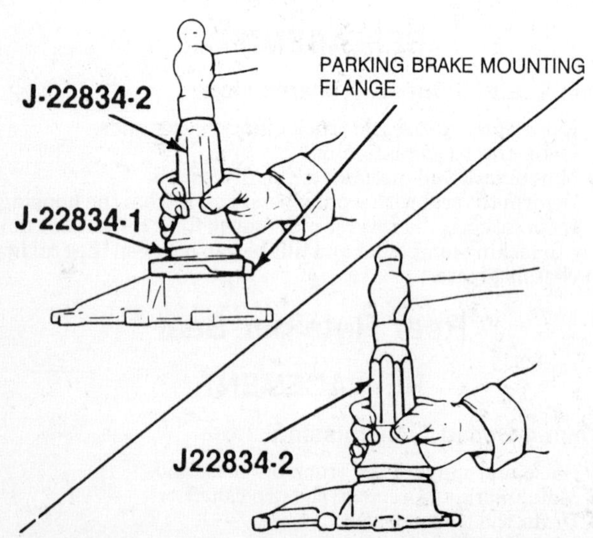

Installing the oil seal on the 85mm 4-speed

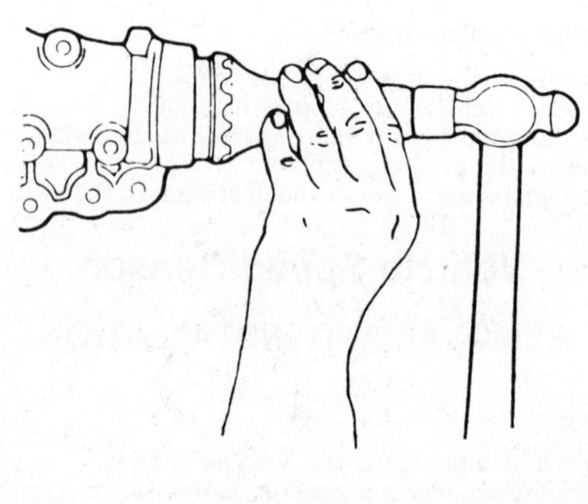

Installing the oil seal on the 85mm 5-speed

6. Pull the flange off the shaft.
7. Support the transmisison with a floor jack.
8. Remove the transmission mount.
9. Unbolt and remove the rear bearing retainer and gasket.
10. Drive out the seal.

To install:

11. Coat the outside rim of the new seal with sealer.
12. Fill the gap between the seal lips with chassis grease.
13. Install the retainer and new gasket. Torque the top bolts to 20 ft. lbs.; the bottom bolts to 30 ft. lbs.
14. Install the transmission mount. Torque the bolts to 40 ft. lbs.
15. Install the flange, washer and nut. Torque the nut to 100 ft. lbs.
16. Connect the speedometer cable.
17. Install the driveshaft.
18. Refill the transmission.

Floor Shift Lever

REMOVAL AND INSTALLATION

R/V and C/K Series with 117mm 4-Speed

1. On 4-wheel drive, remove the transfer case lever boot.
2. Remove the transmission lever boot retaining ring.
3. Remove the boot retaining screws.
4. Remove the boot.
5. Push downward on the cap at the bottom of the lever and turn it counterclockwise. Pull the lever from the transmission.
6. Installation is the reverse of removal.

C/K Series with 85mm 4- or 5-Speed

1. On 4-wheel drive, remove the transfer case lever boot.
2. Remove the shift boot retaining ring.
3. Remove the boot retaining screws and lift off the boot.
4. Loosen the jam nut and unscrew the lever.

Transmission

REMOVAL AND INSTALLATION

R/V Series 2-Wheel Drive

1. Jack up your vehicle and support it with jackstands.
2. Drain the transmission.
3. Disconnect the speedometer cable, and back-up lamp wire at transmission.
4. Remove the gearshift lever by pressing down firmly on the slotted collar plate with a pair of channel lock pliers and rotating counterclockwise. Plug the opening to keep out dirt.
5. Remove driveshaft after making the position of the shaft to the flange.
6. Position a transmission jack or its equivalent under the transmission to support it.
7. Remove the crossmember. Visually inspect to see if other equipment, brackets or lines, must be removed to permit removal of transmission.

NOTE: Mark position of crossmember when removing to prevent incorrect installation. The tapered surface should face the rear.

8. Remove the flywheel housing underpan.
9. Remove the top two transmission to housing bolts and insert two guide pins.

NOTE: The use of guide pins will not only support the transmission but will prevent damage to the clutch disc. Guide pins can be made by taking two bolts, the same as those just removed only longer, and cutting off the heads. Slot for a screwdriver. Be sure to support the clutch release bearing and support assembly during removal of the transmission. This will prevent the release from falling out of the flywheel housing.

10. Remove two remaining bolts and slide transmission straight back from engine. Use care to keep the transmission drive gear straight in line with clutch disc hub.
11. Remove the transmission from beneath your vehicle.

To install:

12. Place the transmission in 4th gear.
13. Coat the input shaft splines with high temperature grease.
14. Raise the transmission into position.
15. Install the guide pins in the top 2 bolt holes.
16. Roll the transmission forward and engage the clutch splines. Keep pushing the transmission forward until it mates with the engine.
17. Install the bolts, removing the guide pins. Torque the bolts to 75 ft. lbs.
18. Install the flywheel housing underpan.
19. Install the crossmember. Torque the crossmember-to-frame bolts to 55 ft. lbs.; the crossmember-to-transmission bolts to 40 ft. lbs.
20. Remove the transmission jack.
21. Install the driveshaft.
22. Install the gearshift lever.
23. Connect the speedometer cable, and back-up lamp wire at transmission.
24. Fill the transmission.

WARNING: Do not force the transmission into the clutch disc hub. Do not let the transmission hang unsupported in the splined portion of the clutch disc.

R/V Series 4-Wheel Drive

1. Jack up your vehicle and support it with jackstands.
2. Drain the transmission.
3. Disconnect the speedometer cable, and back-up lamp wire at transmission.
4. Remove the gearshift lever by pressing down firmly on the slotted collar plate with a pair of channel lock pliers and rotating counterclockwise. Plug the opening to keep out dirt.
5. Remove driveshaft after making the position of the shaft to the flange.
6. Remove the transfer case.
7. Remove the exhaust pipes.
8. Position a transmission jack or its equivalent under the transmission to support it.
9. Remove the crossmember. Visually inspect to see if other equipment, brackets or lines, must be removed to permit removal of transmission.

NOTE: Mark position of crossmember when removing to prevent incorrect installation. The tapered surface should face the rear.

10. Remove the flywheel housing underpan.
11. Remove the top two transmission to housing bolts and insert two guide pins.

NOTE: The use of guide pins will not only support the transmission but will prevent damage to the clutch disc. Guide pins can be made by taking two bolts, the same as those just removed only longer, and cutting off the heads. Slot for a screwdriver. Be sure to support the clutch release bearing and support assembly during removal of the transmission. This will prevent the release from falling out of the flywheel housing.

12. Remove two remaining bolts and slide transmission straight back from engine. Use care to keep the transmission drive gear straight in line with clutch disc hub.

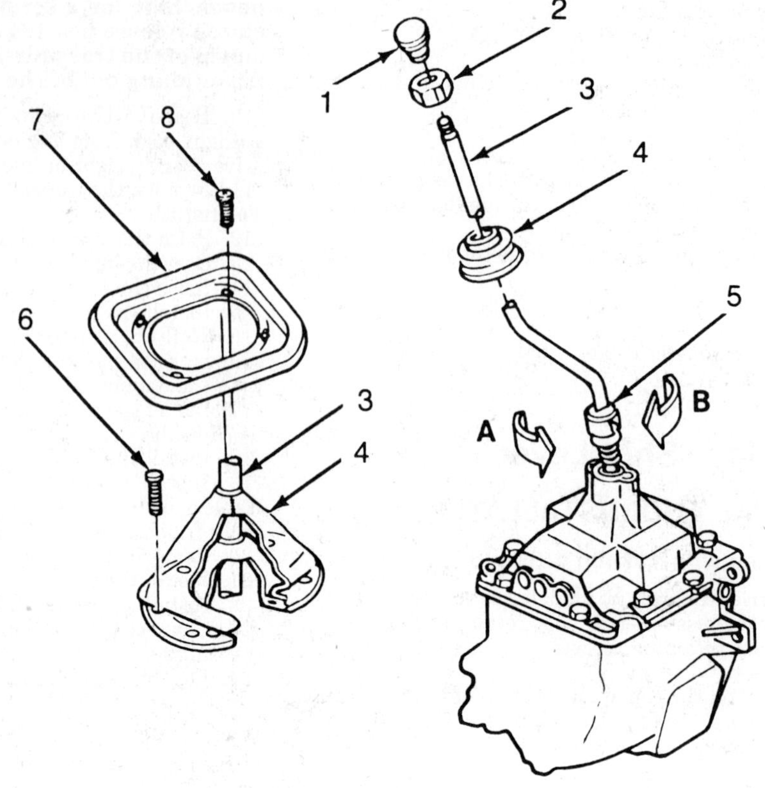

177mm 4-speed shift control lever

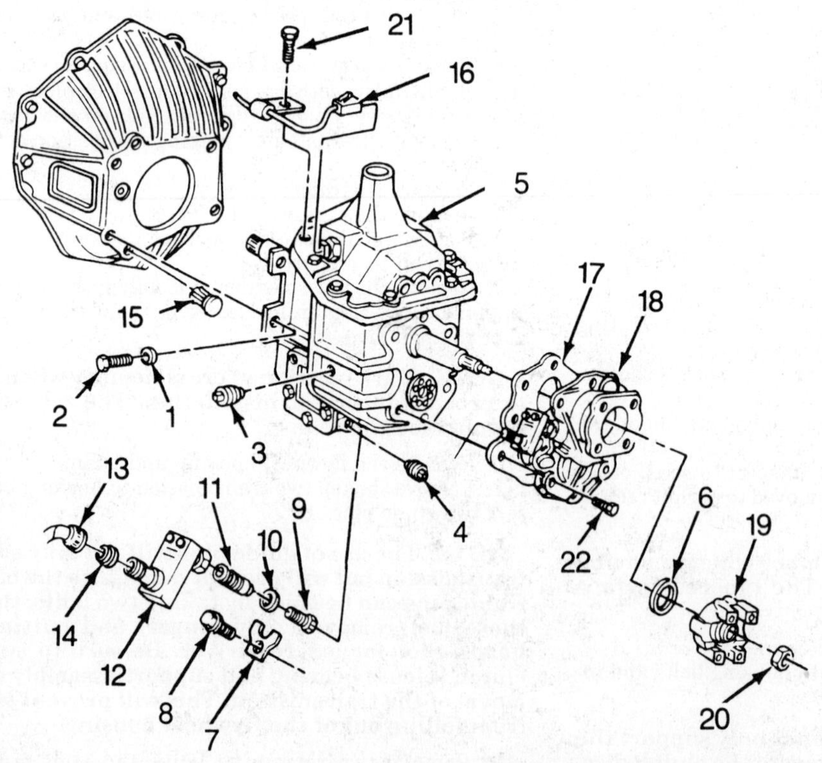

117mm 4-speed transmission installation details

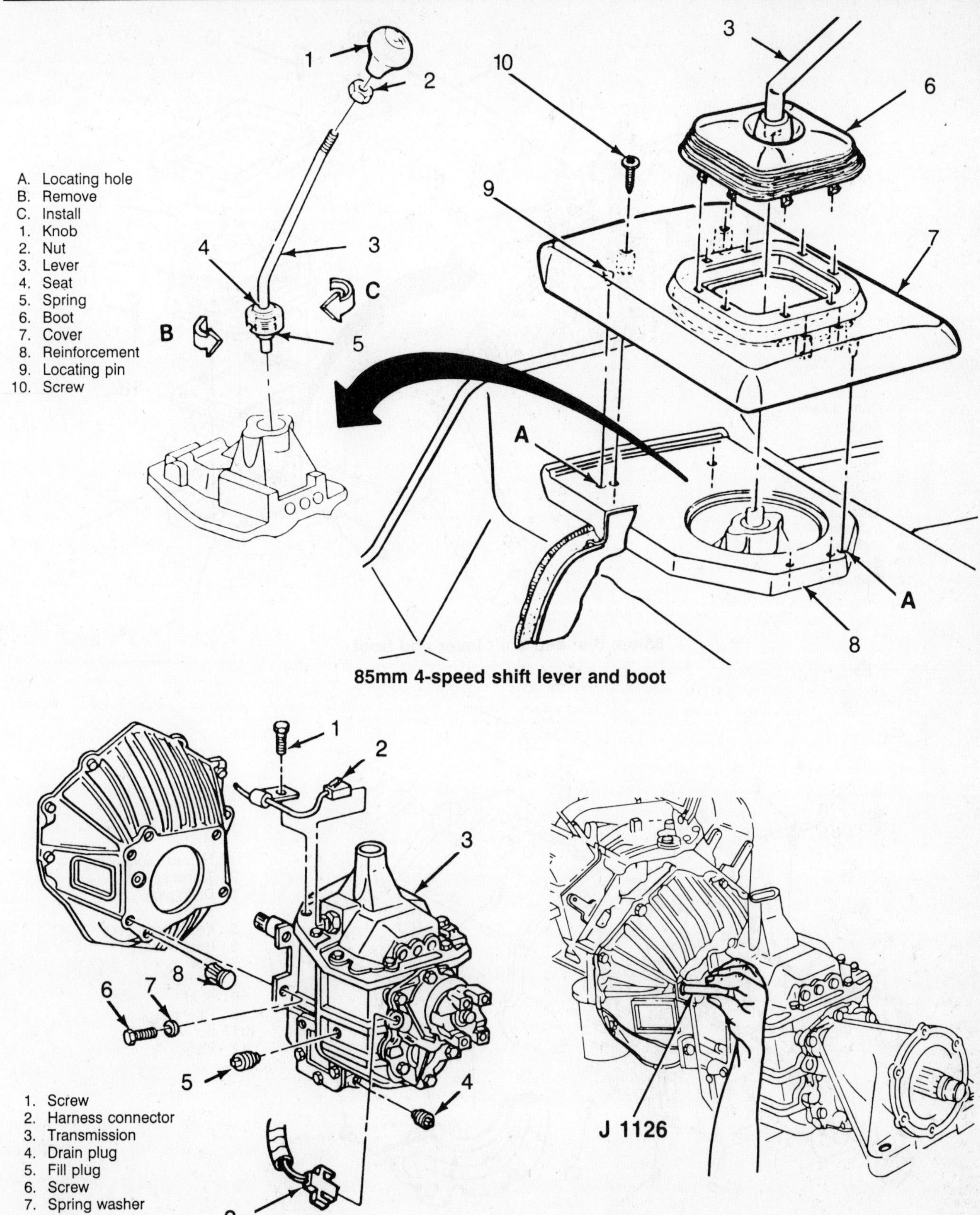

85mm 4-speed shift lever and boot

85mm 4-speed transmission installation details

Installing the guide pin on the 117mm

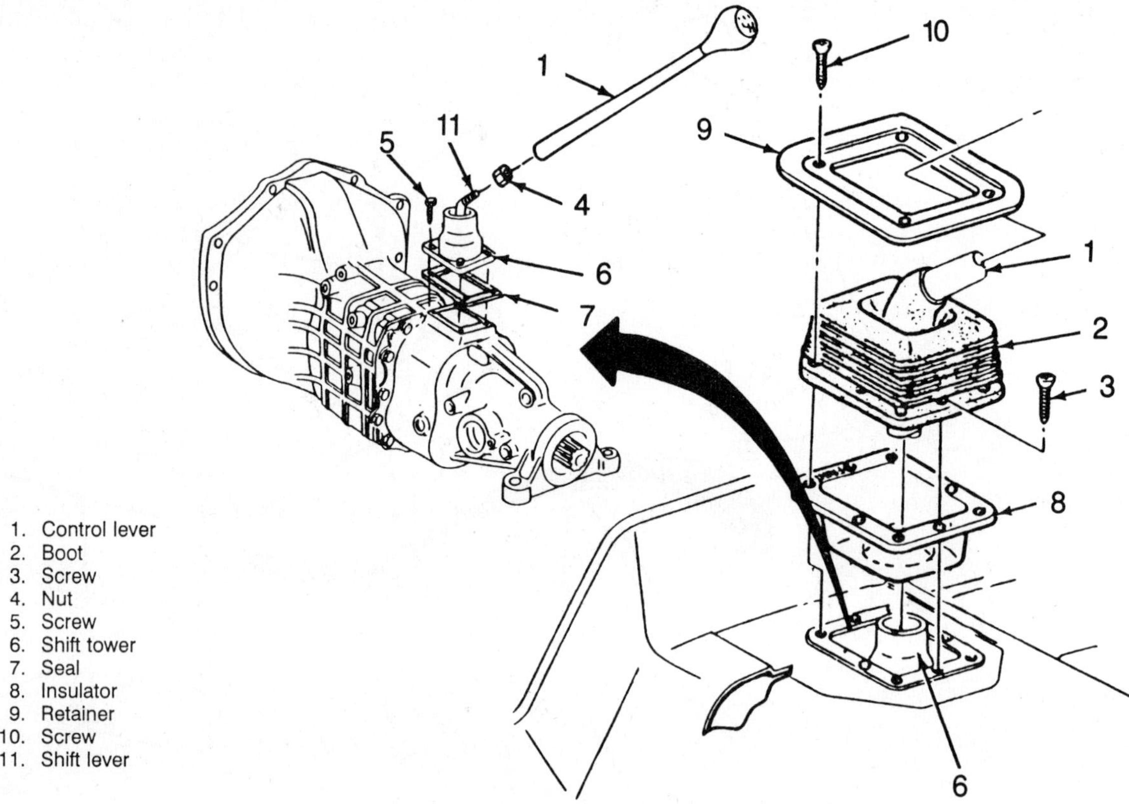

85mm 5-speed shift lever and boot

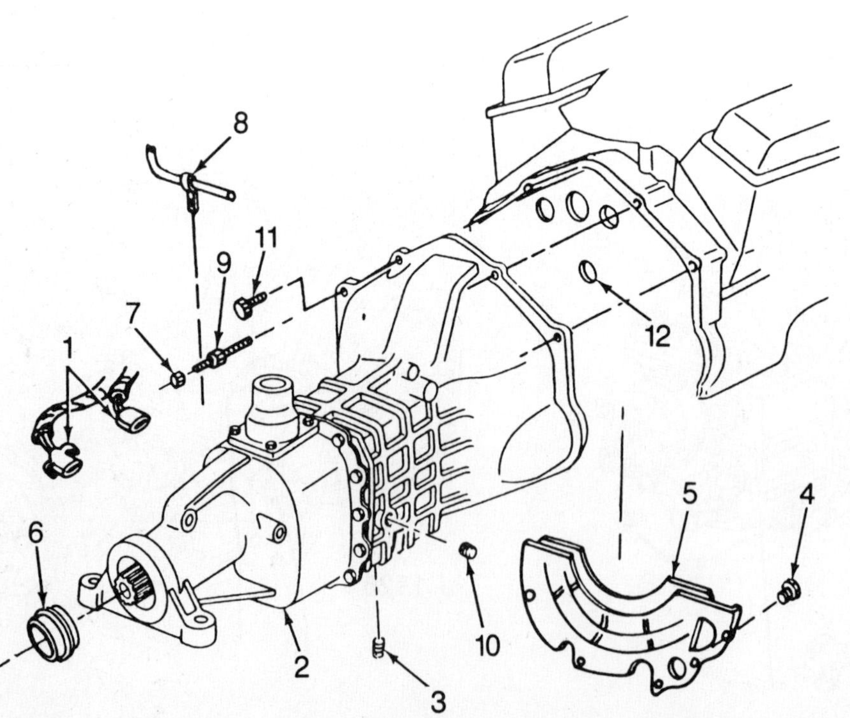

85mm 5-speed transmission installation details

13. Remove the transmission from beneath your vehicle.

To install:

14. Place the transmission in 4th gear.
15. Coat the input shaft splines with high temperature grease.
16. Raise the transmission into position.
17. Install the guide pins in the top 2 bolt holes.
18. Roll the transmission forward and engage the clutch splines. Keep pushing the transmission forward until it mates with the engine.
19. Install the bolts, removing the guide pins. Torque the bolts to 75 ft. lbs.
20. Install the flywheel housing underpan.
21. Install the crossmember. Torque the crossmember-to-frame bolts to 55 ft. lbs.; the crossmember-to-transmission bolts to 40 ft. lbs.
22. Install the transfer case.
23. Remove the transmission jack.
24. Install the exhaust system.
25. Install the driveshaft.
26. Install the gearshift lever.
27. Connect the speedometer cable, and back-up lamp wire at transmission.
28. Fill the transmission.

WARNING: Do not force the transmission into the clutch disc hub. Do not let the transmission hang unsupported in the splined portion of the clutch disc.

C-Series with 117mm 4-Speed

1. Raise and support the truck on jackstands.
2. Drain the transmission.
3. Remove driveshaft after making the position of the shaft to the flange.
4. Remove the exhaust pipes.
5. Disconnect the wiring harness at the transmission.
6. Remove the gearshift lever.
7. Remove the clutch slave cylinder and support it out of the way.
8. Position a transmission jack or its equivalent under the transmission to support it.
9. Remove the crossmember. Visually inspect to see if other equipment, brackets or lines, must be removed to permit removal of transmission.

NOTE: Mark position of crossmember when removing to prevent incorrect installation. The tapered surface should face the rear.

10. Remove the top two transmission to housing bolts and insert two guide pins.

NOTE: The use of guide pins will not only support the transmission but will prevent damage to the clutch disc. Guide pins can be made by taking two bolts, the same as those just removed only longer, and cutting off the heads. Slot for a screwdriver. Be sure to support the clutch release bearing and support assembly during removal of the transmission. This will prevent the release from falling out of the flywheel housing.

11. Remove the remaining bolts and slide transmission straight back from engine. Use care to keep the transmission drive gear straight in line with clutch disc hub.
12. Remove the transmission from beneath your vehicle.

To install:

13. Place the transmission in 4th gear.
14. Coat the input shaft splines with high temperature grease.
15. Raise the transmission into position.
16. Install the guide pins in the top 2 bolt holes.
17. Roll the transmission forward and engage the clutch splines. Keep pushing the transmission forward until it mates with the engine.
18. Install the bolts, removing the guide pins. Torque the bolts to 75 ft. lbs.
19. Install the crossmember. Torque the crossmember-to-frame bolts to 55 ft. lbs.; the crossmember-to-transmission bolts to 40 ft. lbs.
20. Remove the transmission jack.
21. Install the slave cylinder.
22. Install the driveshaft.
23. Install the exhaust system.
24. Install the gearshift lever.
25. Connect the wiring harness at the transmission.
26. Fill the transmission.

WARNING: Do not force the transmission into the clutch disc hub. Do not let the transmission hang unsupported in the splined portion of the clutch disc.

C-Series with 85mm 4- or 5-Speed

1. Raise and support the truck on jackstands.
2. Drain the transmission.
3. Remove driveshaft after making the position of the shaft to the flange.
4. Remove the exhaust pipes.
5. Disconnect the wiring harness at the transmission.
6. Remove the gearshift lever.
7. Remove the clutch slave cylinder and support it out of the way.
8. Remove the flywheel housing inspection cover.
9. Position a transmission jack or its equivalent under the transmission to support it.
10. Remove the crossmember. Visually inspect to see if other equipment, brackets or lines, must be removed to permit removal of transmission.

NOTE: Mark position of crossmember when removing to prevent incorrect installation. The tapered surface should face the rear.

11. Remove the top two transmission to housing bolts and insert two guide pins.

NOTE: The use of guide pins will not only support the transmission but will prevent damage to the clutch disc. Guide pins can be made by taking two bolts, the same as those just removed only longer, and cutting off the heads. Slot for a screwdriver. Be sure to support the clutch release bearing and support assembly during removal of the transmission. This will prevent the release from falling out of the flywheel housing.

12. Remove the remaining bolts and slide transmission straight back from engine. Use care to keep the transmission drive gear straight in line with clutch disc hub.
13. Remove the transmission from beneath your vehicle.

To install:

14. Place the transmission in 4th gear.
15. Coat the input shaft splines with high temperature grease.
16. Raise the transmission into position.
17. Install the guide pins in the top 2 bolt holes.
18. Roll the transmission forward and engage the clutch splines. Keep pushing the transmission forward until it mates with the engine.
19. Install the bolts, removing the guide pins. Torque the bolts to 37 ft. lbs.
20. Install the crossmember. Torque the crossmember-to-frame bolts to 55 ft. lbs.; the crossmember-to-transmission bolts to 40 ft. lbs.
21. Remove the transmission jack.
22. Install the slave cylinder.
23. Install the driveshaft.
24. Install the exhaust system.
25. Install the gearshift lever.

26. Install the inspection cover.
27. Connect the wiring harness at the transmission.
28. Fill the transmission.

WARNING: Do not force the transmission into the clutch disc hub. Do not let the transmission hang unsupported in the splined portion of the clutch disc.

K-Series

1. Raise and support the truck on jackstands.
2. Drain the transmission.
3. Remove driveshaft after making the position of the shaft to the flange.
4. Remove the transfer case.
5. Remove the exhaust pipes.
6. Disconnect the wiring harness at the transmission.
7. Remove the gearshift lever.
8. Remove the clutch slave cylinder and support it out of the way.
9. Remove the flywheel housing inspection cover.
10. Position a transmission jack or its equivalent under the transmission to support it.
11. Remove the crossmember. Visually inspect to see if other equipment, brackets or lines, must be removed to permit removal of transmission.

NOTE: Mark position of crossmember when removing to prevent incorrect installation. The tapered surface should face the rear.

12. Remove the top two transmission to housing bolts and insert two guide pins.

NOTE: The use of guide pins will not only support the transmission but will prevent damage to the clutch disc. Guide pins can be made by taking two bolts, the same as those just removed only longer, and cutting off the heads. Slot for a screwdriver. Be sure to support the clutch release bearing and support assembly during removal of the transmission. This will prevent the release from falling out of the flywheel housing.

13. Remove the remaining bolts and slide transmission straight back from engine. Use care to keep the transmission drive gear straight in line with clutch disc hub.
14. Remove the transmission from beneath your vehicle.

To install:

15. Place the transmission in 4th gear.
16. Coat the input shaft splines with high temperature grease.
17. Raise the transmission into position.
18. Install the guide pins in the top 2 bolt holes.
19. Roll the transmission forward and engage the clutch splines. Keep pushing the transmission forward until it mates with the engine.
20. Install the bolts, removing the guide pins. Torque the bolts to 37 ft. lbs.
21. Install the crossmember. Torque the crossmember-to-frame bolts to 55 ft. lbs.; the crossmember-to-transmission bolts to 40 ft. lbs.
22. Install the transfer case.
23. Remove the transmission jack.
24. Install the slave cylinder.
25. Install the driveshaft.
26. Install the exhaust system.
27. Install the gearshift lever.
28. Install the inspection cover.
29. Connect the wiring harness at the transmission.
30. Fill the transmission.

WARNING: Do not force the transmission into the clutch disc hub. Do not let the transmission hang unsupported in the splined portion of the clutch disc.

117mm 4-Speed Overhaul

TRANSMISSION UNIT DISASSEMBLY

1. Remove transmission cover assembly. Move reverse shifter fork so that reverse idler gear is partially engaged before attempting to remove cover. Forks must be positioned so rear edge of the slot in the reverse fork is in line with the front edge of the slot in the forward forks as viewed through tower opening.
2. Lock transmission into two gears. Remove the universal joint flange nut, universal joint front flange and brake drum assembly.

NOTE: On 4-wheel drive models, use a special tool to remove mainshaft rear lock nut.

3. Remove parking brake and brake flange plate assembly on those vehicles having a driveshaft parking brake.
4. Remove rear bearing retainer and gasket.
5. Slide speedometer drive gear off mainshaft.
6. Remove clutch gear bearing retainers and gasket.
7. Remove countergear front bearing cap and gasket.
8. Using a prybar, pry off countershaft front bearing.
9. Remove countergear rear bearing snaprings from shaft and bearing. Using special tool, remove countergear rear bearings.
10. Remove clutch gear bearing outer race to case retaining ring.
11. Remove clutch gear and bearing by tapping gently on bottom side of clutch gear shaft and prying directly opposite against the case and bearing snapring groove at the same time. Remove 4th gear synchronizer ring. Index cut out section of clutch gear in down position with countergear to obtain clearance for removing clutch gear.
12. Remove rear mainshaft bearing snapring and, using special tools, remove bearing from case. Slide 1st speed gear thrust washer off mainshaft.
13. Lift mainshaft assembly from case. Remove synchronizer cone from shaft.
14. Slide reverse idler gear rearward and move countergear rearward, then lift to remove from case.
15. To remove reverse idler gear, drive reverse idler gear shaft out of case from front to rear using a drift. Remove reverse idler gear from case.

TRANSMISSION COVER DISASSEMBLY

1. Remove shifter fork retaining pins and drive out expansion plugs. The 3rd and 4th shifter fork must be removed before the reverse shifter head pin can be removed.
2. With shifter shafts in neutral position, remove shafts. Care should be taken when removing the detent balls and springs since removal of the shifter shafts will cause these parts to be forcibly ejected.
3. Remove retaining pin and drive out reverse shifter shaft.

TRANSMISSION COVER ASSEMBLY

1. In reassembling the cover, care should be taken to install the shifter shafts in order, reverse, 3rd/4th and 1st/2nd.
2. Place fork detent ball springs and balls in cover.
3. Start shifter shafts into cover and, while depressing the detent balls, push the shafts over the balls. Push reverse shaft through the yoke.
4. With the 3rd/4th shaft in neutral, line up the retaining holes in the fork and shaft. Detent balls should line up with detents in shaft.
5. After 1st and 2nd fork is installed, place two interlock balls between the low speed shifter shaft and the high speed shifter

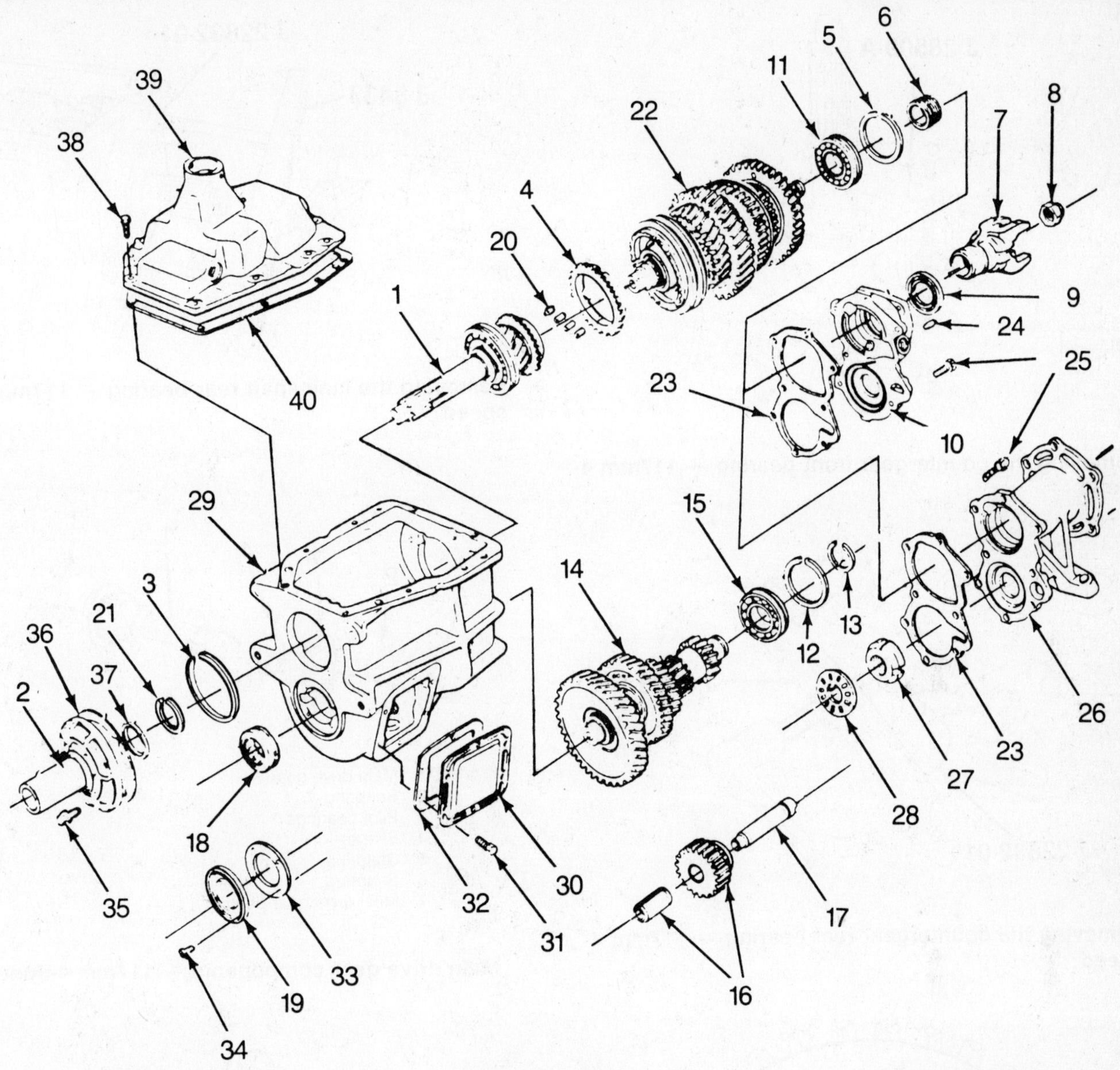

1. Main drive gear
2. Bearing retainer
3. Snapring
4. 4th gear blocker ring
5. Snapring
6. Speedometer drive gear
7. Output yoke
8. Flange nut
9. Oil seal
10. Rear bearing retainer
11. Snapring
12. Snapring
13. Snapring
14. Countergear
15. Countergear rear bearing
16. Reverse idler gear
17. Reverse idler gear shaft
18. Countergear front bearing
19. Countergear front cover
20. Pilot bearings
21. Snapring
22. Mainshaft
23. Gasket
24. Dowel pin
25. Screw
26. Transfer case adapter
27. Rear locknut
28. Lock washer
29. Case
30. Screw
31. Cover plate
32. Gasket
33. Gasket
34. Screw
35. Screw
36. Gasket
37. Oil seal
38. Screw
39. Shift cover
40. Gasket

117mm 4-speed transmission exploded view

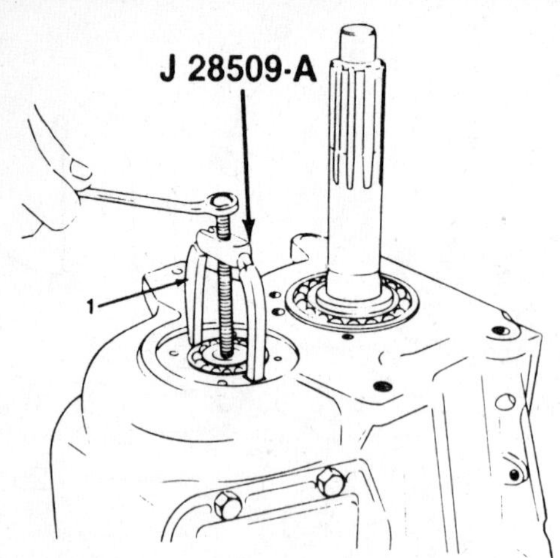

Removing the countergear front bearing — 117mm 4-speed

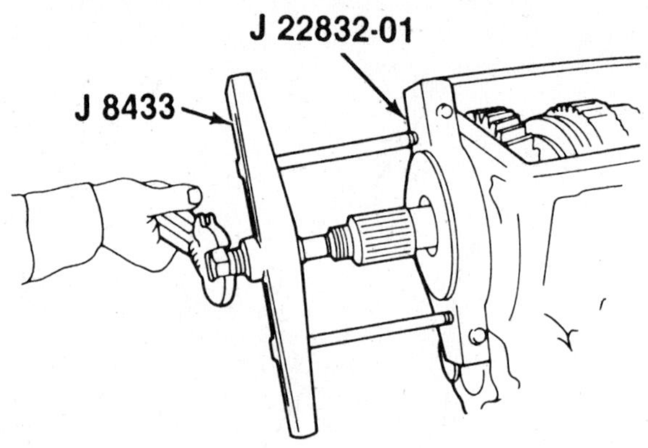

Removing the mainshaft rear bearing — 117mm 4-speed

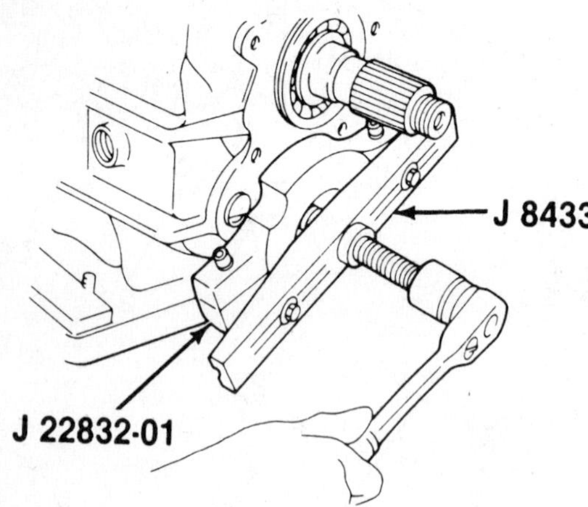

Removing the countergear rear bearing — 117mm 4-speed

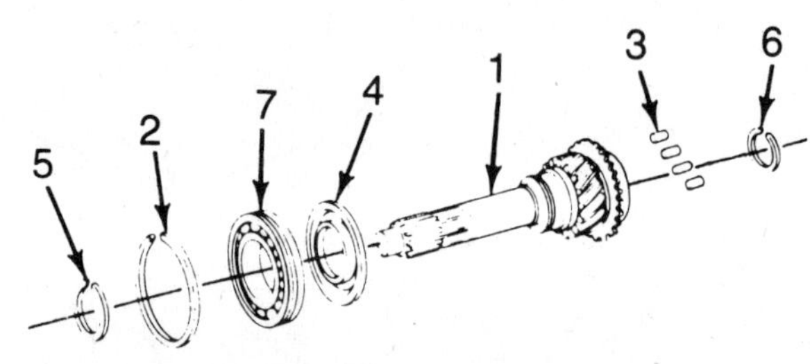

1. Main drive gear
2. Snapring
3. Pilot bearings
4. Slinger
5. Snapring
6. Snapring
7. Main drive gear bearing

Main drive gear components — 117mm 4-speed

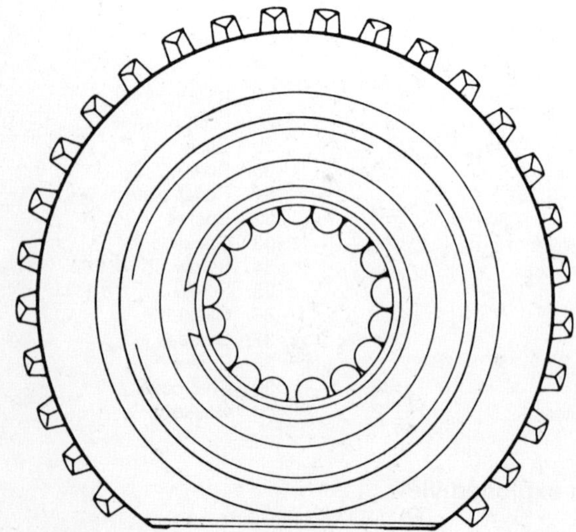

main drive gear cutout — 117mm 4-speed

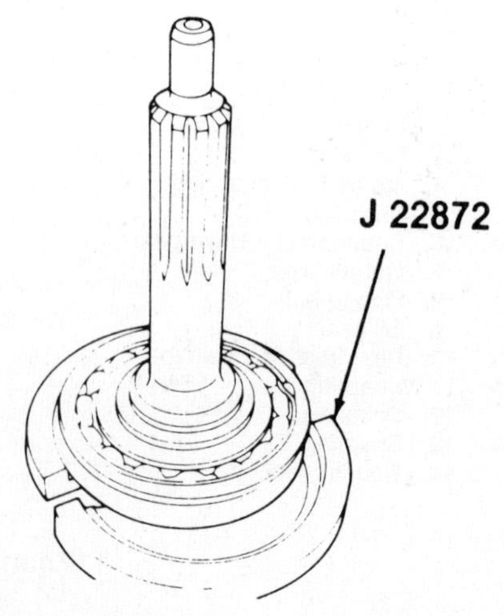

Tool installation — 117mm 4-speed

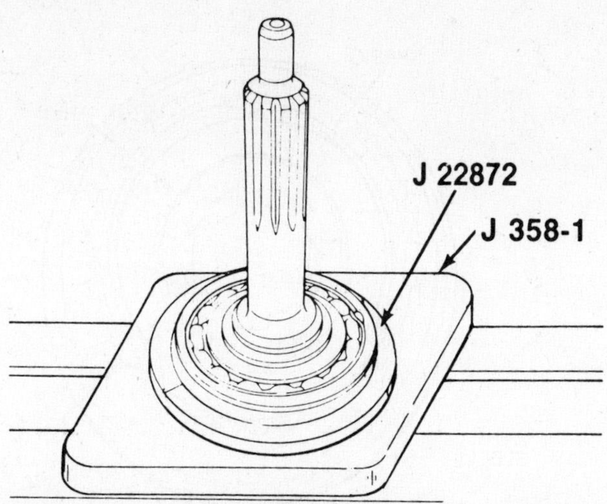

Removing the main drive gear bearing – 117mm 4-speed

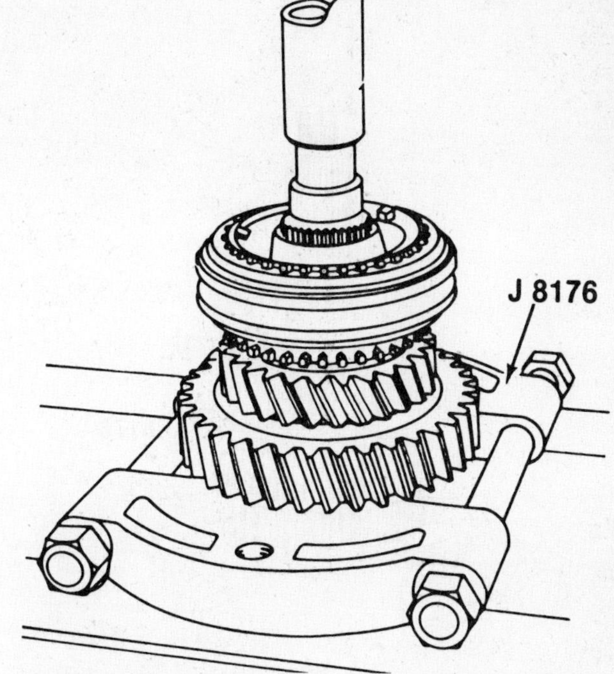

Removing the mainshaft from the 2nd and 3rd gears – 117mm 4-speed

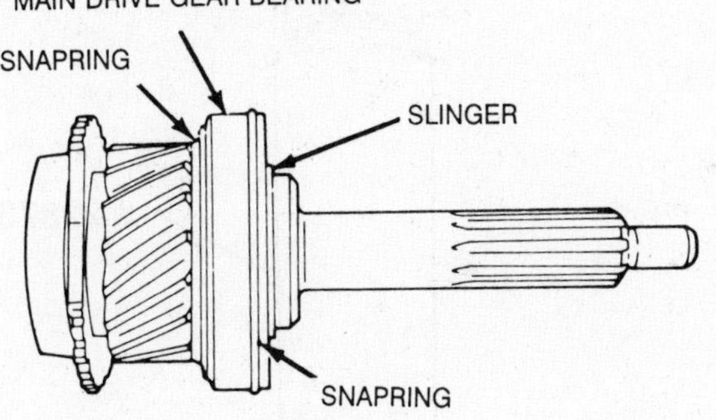

Main drive gear assembly – 117mm 4-speed

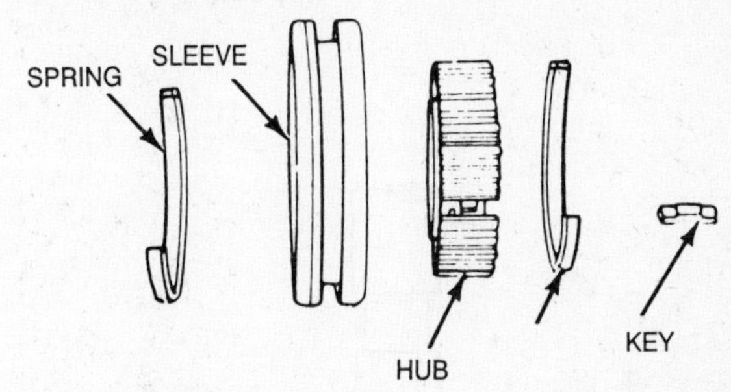

Synchronizer components – 117mm 4-speed

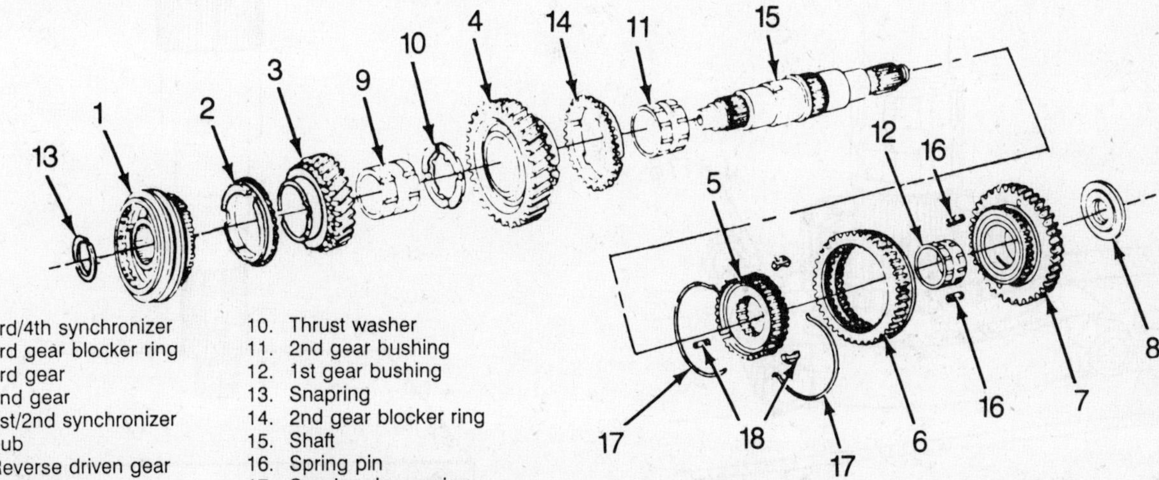

Mainshaft components – 117mm 4-speed

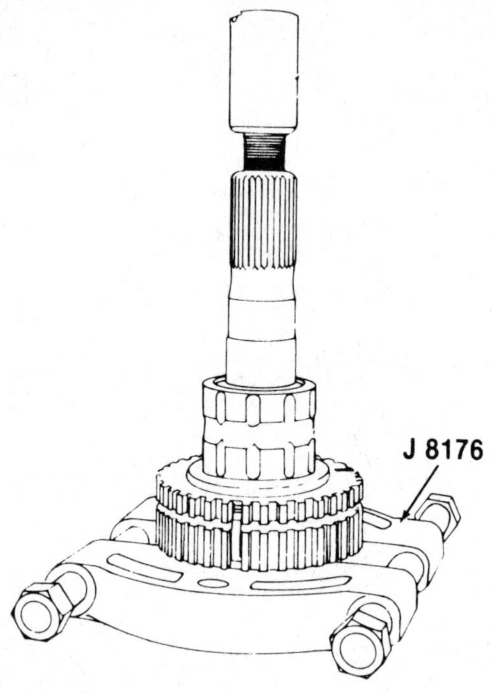

Removing the mainshaft from the 1st and 2nd gear synchronizer hub — 117mm 4-speed

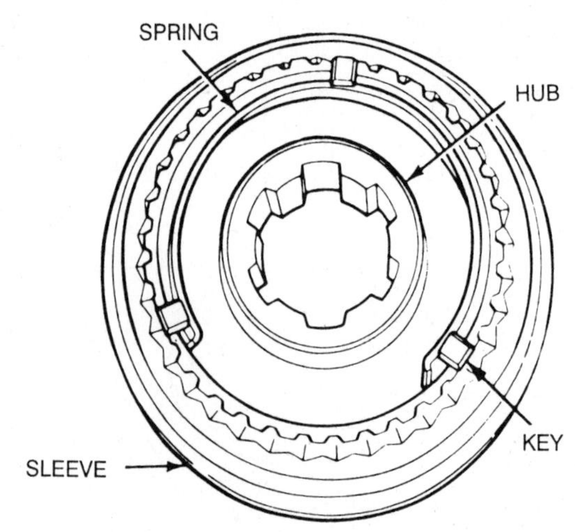

Synchronizer assembled — 117mm 4-speed

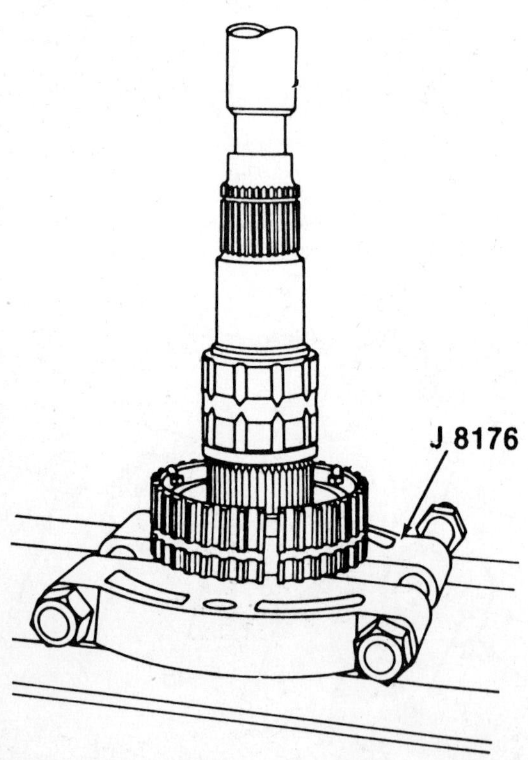

Installing the 1st/2nd synchronizer — 117mm 4-speed

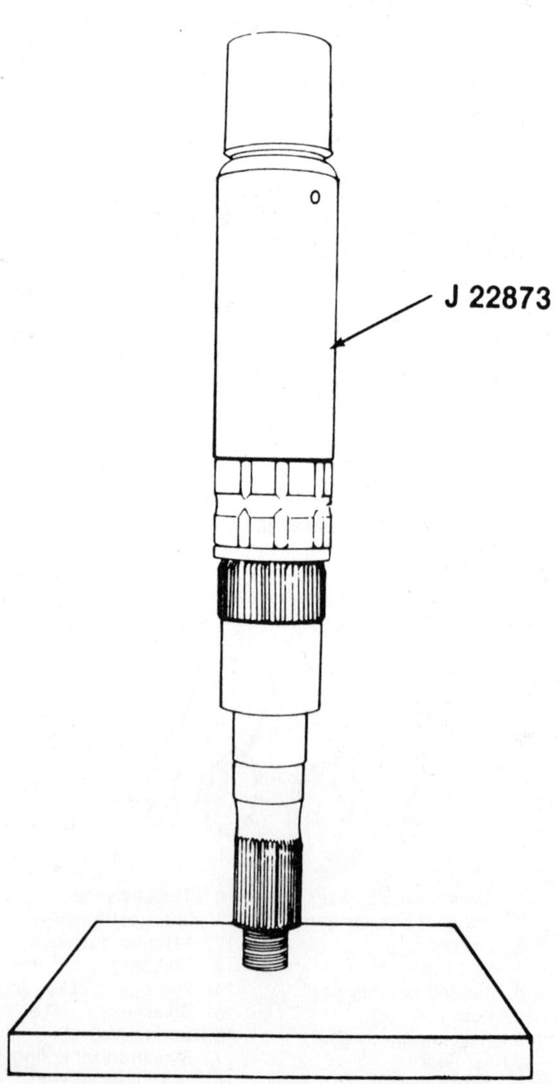

Installing the 2nd gear bushing — 117mm 4-speed

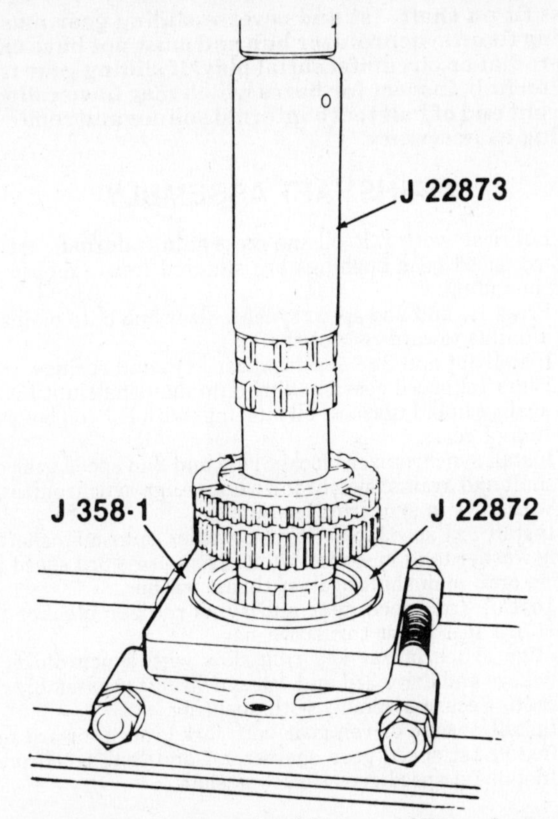

Installing the 1st gear bushing — 117mm 4-speed

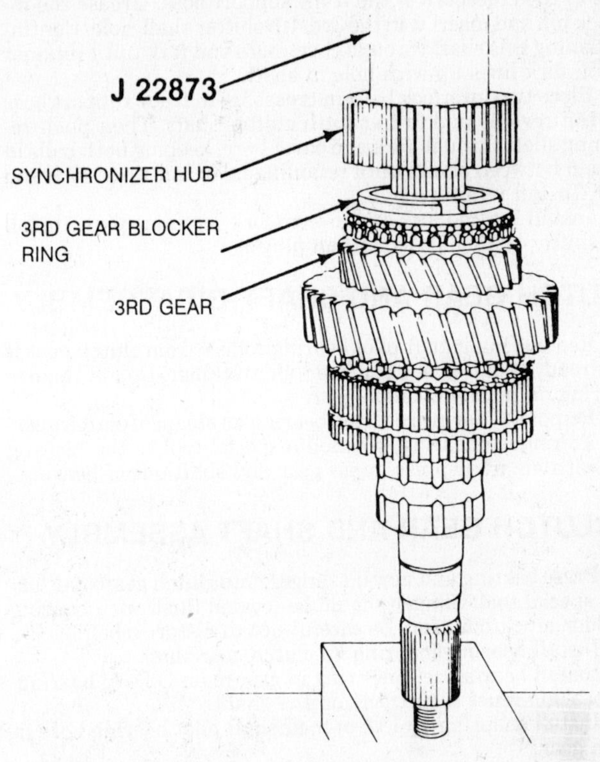

Installing the 3rd/4th synchronizer hub — 117mm 4-speed

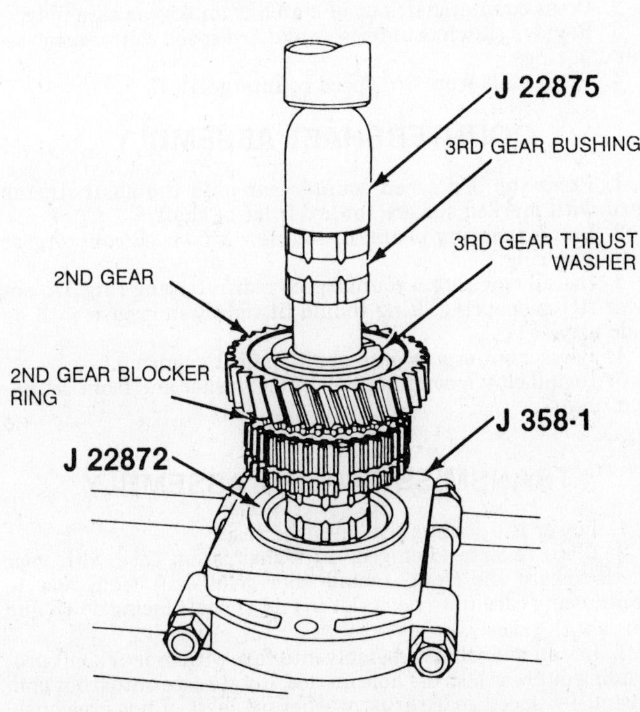

Installing the 3rd gear bushing — 117mm 4-speed

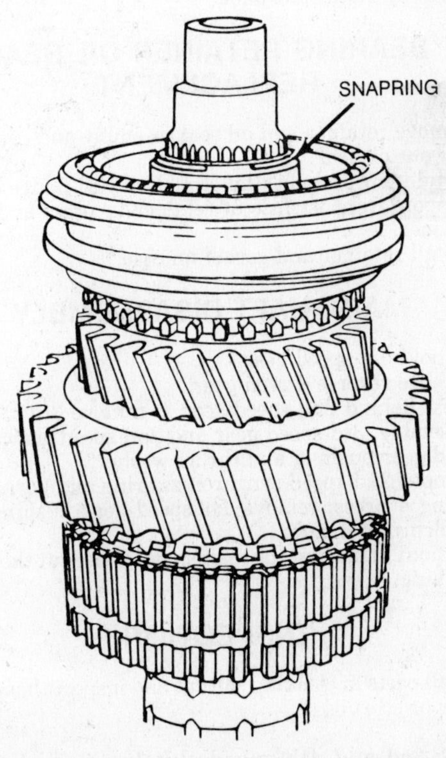

3rd/4th synchronizer hub snapring — 117mm 4-speed

shaft in the crossbore of the front support boss. Grease the interlock pin and insert it in the 3rd/4th shifter shaft hole. Continue pushing this shaft through cover bore and fork until retainer hole in fork lines up with hole in shaft.

6. Place two interlock balls in crossbore in front support boss between reverse and 3rd and 4th shifter shaft. Then push remaining shaft through fork and cover bore, keeping both balls in position between shafts until retaining holes line up in fork and shaft. Install retaining pin.

7. Install 1st/2nd fork and reverse fork retaining pins. Install new shifter shaft hole expansion plugs.

CLUTCH GEAR AND SHAFT DISASSEMBLY

1. Remove mainshaft pilot bearing rollers from clutch gear if not already removed and remove roller retainer. Do not remove snapring on inside of clutch gear.
2. Remove snapring securing bearing on steam of clutch gear.
3. To remove bearing, position a special tool to the bearing and, with an arbor press, press gear and shaft out of bearing.

CLUTCH GEAR AND SHAFT ASSEMBLY

1. Press bearing and new oil slinger onto clutch gear shaft using a special tool. Slinger should be located flush with bearing shoulder on clutch gear. Be careful not to distort oil slinger.
2. Install bearing snapring on clutch gear shaft.
3. Install bearing retainer ring in groove on O.D. of bearing. The bearing must turn freely on the shaft.
4. Install snapring on I.D. of mainshaft pilot bearing bore in clutch gear.
5. Lightly grease bearing surface in shaft recess, install transmission mainshaft pilot roller bearings and install roller bearing retainer. This roller bearing retainer holds bearings in position and, in final transmission assembly, is pushed forward into recess by mainshaft pilot.

BEARING RETAINER OIL SEAL REPLACEMENT

1. Remove retainer and oil seal assembly and gasket.
2. Pry out oil seal.
3. Install new seal with lip of seal toward flange of tool.
4. Support front surface of retainer in press and drive seal into retainer.
5. Install retainer and gasket on case.

MAINSHAFT DISASSEMBLY

1. Remove 1st speed gear.
2. Remove reverse driven gear.
3. Press behind 2nd speed gear to remove 3rd/4th synchronizer assembly, 3rd speed gear and 2nd speed gear along with 3rd speed gear bushing and thrust washer.
4. Remove 2nd speed synchronizer ring and keys.
5. Using a press, remove 1st speed gear bushing and 2nd speed synchronizer hub.
6. Without damaging the mainshaft, chisel out the 2nd speed gear bushing.

INSPECTION

Wash all parts in cleaning solvent and inspect them for excessive wear or scoring.

NOTE: 3rd and 4th speed clutch sleeve should slide freely on clutch hub but clutch hub should fit snugly on shaft splines. 3rd speed gear must be running fit on mainshaft bushing and mainshaft bushing should be press fit on shaft. 1st and reverse sliding gear must be sliding fit on synchronizer hub and must not have excessive radial or circumferential play. If sliding gear is not free on hub, inspect for burrs which may have rolled up on front end of half tooth internal splines and remove by honing as necessary.

MAINSHAFT ASSEMBLY

1. Lubricate with E.P. oil and press onto mainshaft. 1st, 2nd and 3rd speed gear bushings are sintered iron, exercise care when installing.
2. Press 1st and 2nd speed synchronizer hub onto mainshaft with annulus toward rear of shaft.
3. Install 1st and 2nd synchronizer keys and springs.
4. Press 1st speed gear bushing onto mainshaft until it bottoms against hub. Lubricate all bushings with E.P. oil before installation of gears.
5. Install synchronizer blocker ring and 2nd speed gear onto mainshaft and against synchronize hub. Align synchronizer key slots with keys in synchronizer hub.
6. Install 3rd speed gear thrust washer onto mainshaft inserting washer tang in slotted shaft. Then press 3rd speed gear bushing onto mainshaft against thrust washer.
7. Install 3rd speed gear and synchronizer blocker ring against 3rd speed gear thrust washer.
8. Align synchronizer key ring slots with synchronizer assembly keys and drive 3rd and 4th synchronizer assembly onto mainshaft. Secure assembly with snapring.
9. Install reverse driven gear with fork groove toward rear.
10. Install 1st speed gear against 1st and 2nd synchronizer hub. Install 1st speed gear thrust washer.

COUNTERSHAFT DISASSEMBLY

1. Remove front countergear retaining ring and thrust washer. Do not re-use this snapring or any others.
2. Press countershaft out of clutch countergear assembly.
3. Remove clutch countergear and 3rd speed countergear retaining rings.
4. Press shift from 3rd speed countergear.

COUNTERSHAFT ASSEMBLY

1. Press the 3rd speed countergear onto the shaft. Install gear with marked surface toward front of shaft.
2. Using snapring pliers, install new 3rd speed countergear retaining ring.
3. Install new clutch countergear rear retaining ring. Do not over stress snapring. Ring should fit tightly in groove with no side play.
4. Press countergear onto shaft against snapring.
5. Install clutch countergear thrust washer and front retaining ring.

TRANSMISSION UNIT ASSEMBLY

1. Lower the countergear into the case.
2. Place reverse idler gear in transmission case with gear teeth toward the front. Install idler gear shaft from rear to front, being careful to have slot in end of shaft facing down and flush with case.
3. Install mainshaft assembly into case with rear of shaft protruding out rear bearing hole in case. Rotate case onto front end. Install 1st speed gear thrust washer on shaft, if not previously installed.
4. Install snapring on bearing O.D. and place rear mainshaft bearing on shaft. Drive bearing onto shaft and into case.
5. Install synchronizer cone on mainshaft and slide rearward

to clutch hub. Make sure three cut out sections of 4th speed synchronizer cone align with three clutch keys in clutch assembly.

6. Install snapring on clutch gear bearing O.D. Index cut out portion of clutch gear teeth to obtain clearance over countershaft drive gear teeth and install into case.

7. Install clutch gear bearing retainer and gasket and torque 15–18 ft. lbs.

8. Rotate case onto front end.

9. Install snapring on countergear rear bearing O.D. and drive bearing into place. Install snapring on countershaft at rear bearing.

10. Tap countergear front bearing assembly into case.

11. Install countergear front bearing cap and new gasket and torque 20–30 inch lbs.

12. Slide speedometer drive gear over mainshaft to bearing.

13. Install rear bearing retainer with new gasket. Be sure snapring ends are in lube slot and cut out in bearing retainer. Install bolts and tighten 15–18 ft. lbs. Install brake backing plate assembly on those models having driveshaft brake.

NOTE: On models equipped with 4-wheel drive, install rear lock nut and washer and torque to 120 ft. lbs. and bend washer tangs to fit slots in nut.

14. Install parking brake drum and/or universal joint flange. Lightly oil seal surface.

15. Lock transmission in two gears at once. Install universal joint flange locknut and tighten 90–120 ft. lbs.

16. Move all transmission gears to neutral except the reverse idler gear which should be engaged approximately ⅜ in. (9.5mm) (leading edge of reverse idler gear taper lines up with the front edge of the 1st speed gear). Install cover assembly and gasket. Shifting forks must slide into their proper positions on clutch sleeves and reverse idler gear. Forks must be positioned as in removal.

17. Install cover attaching bolts and gearshift lever and check operation of transmission.

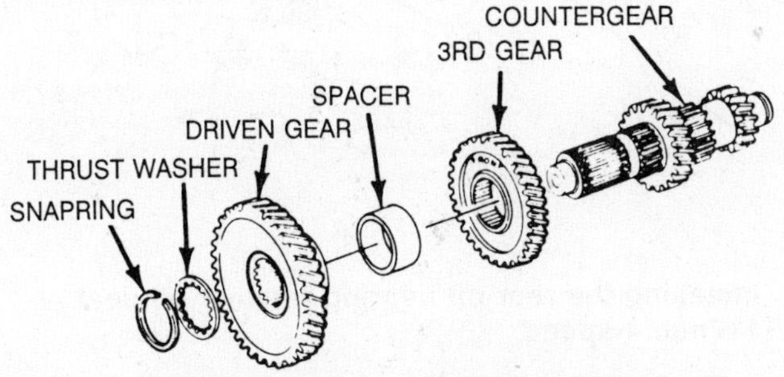

Countergear – 117mm 4-speed

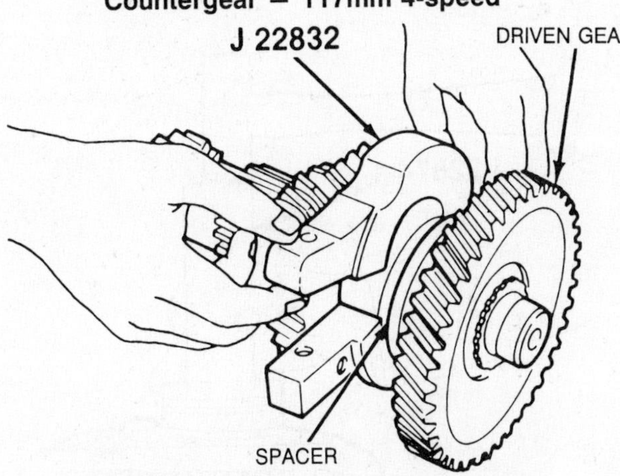

Installing the tool – 117mm 4-speed

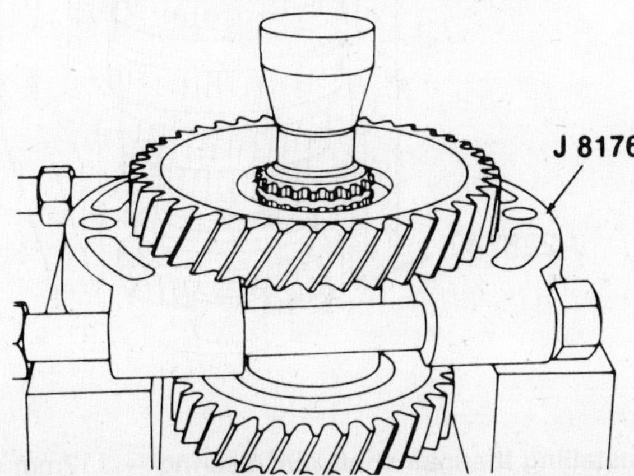

Removing the driven gear – 117mm 4-speed

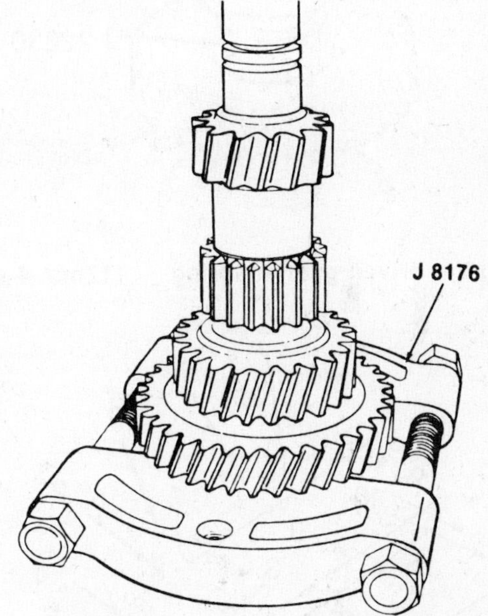

Installing 3rd gear – 117mm 4-speed

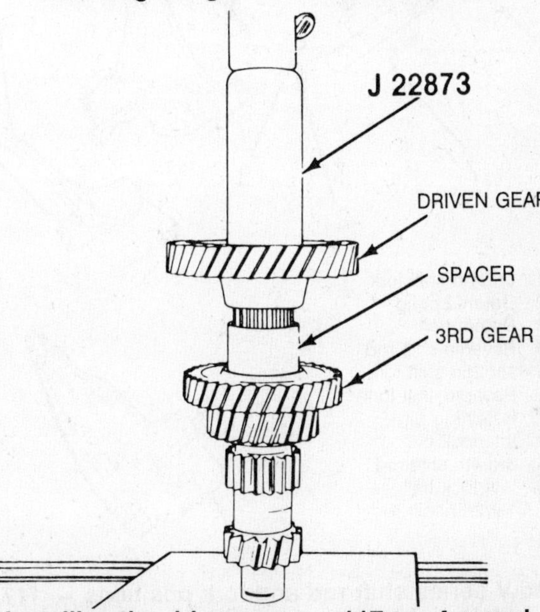

Installing the driven gear – 117mm 4-speed

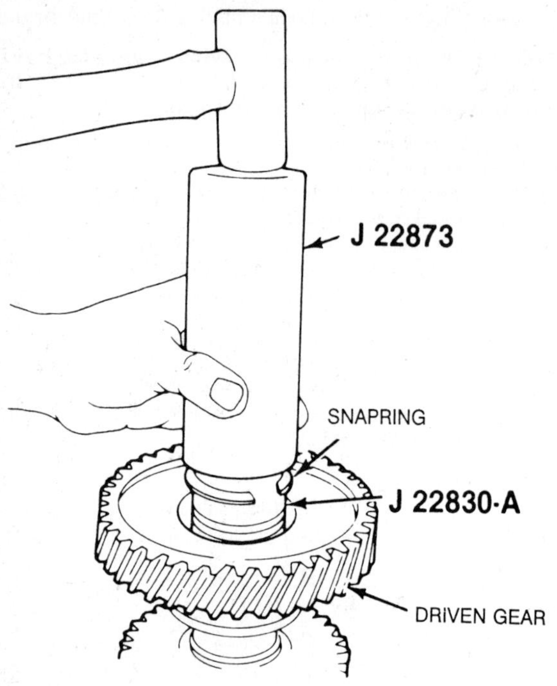

Installing the driven gear snapring — 117mm 4-speed

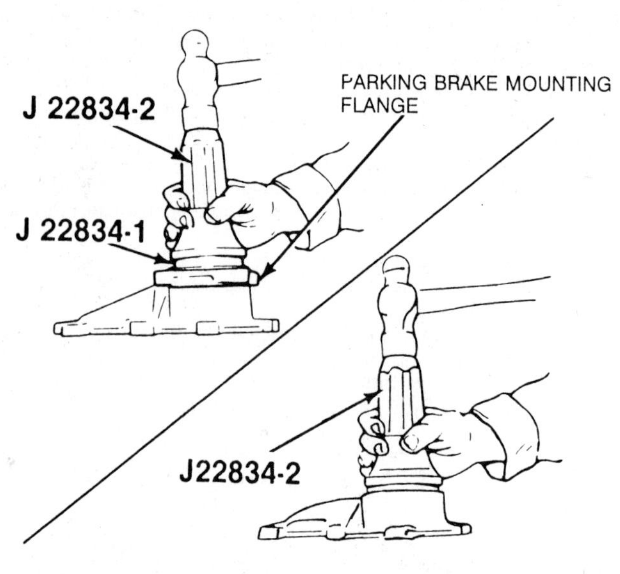

Installing the rear oil bearing retainer oil seal — 117mm 4-speed

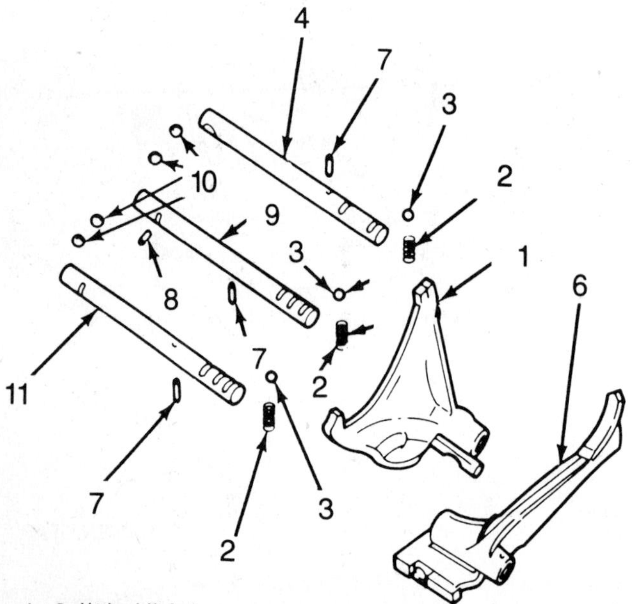

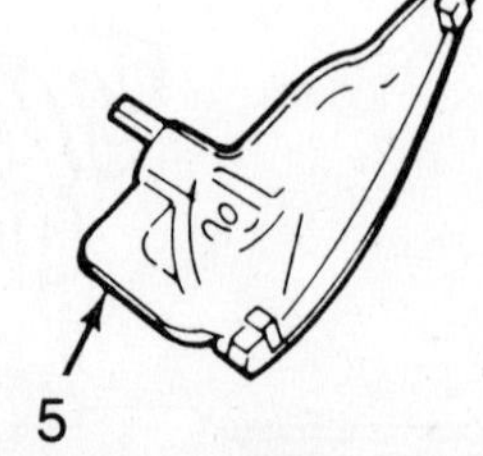

1. 3rd/4th shift fork
2. Detent spring
3. Detent ball
4. Reverse shift rod
5. 1st/2nd shift fork
6. Reverse shift fork
7. Retaining pin
8. Interlock pin
9. 3rd/4th shift rod
10. Interlock ball
11. 1st/2nd shift rod

R and V series shift rod and fork positions — 117mm 4-speed

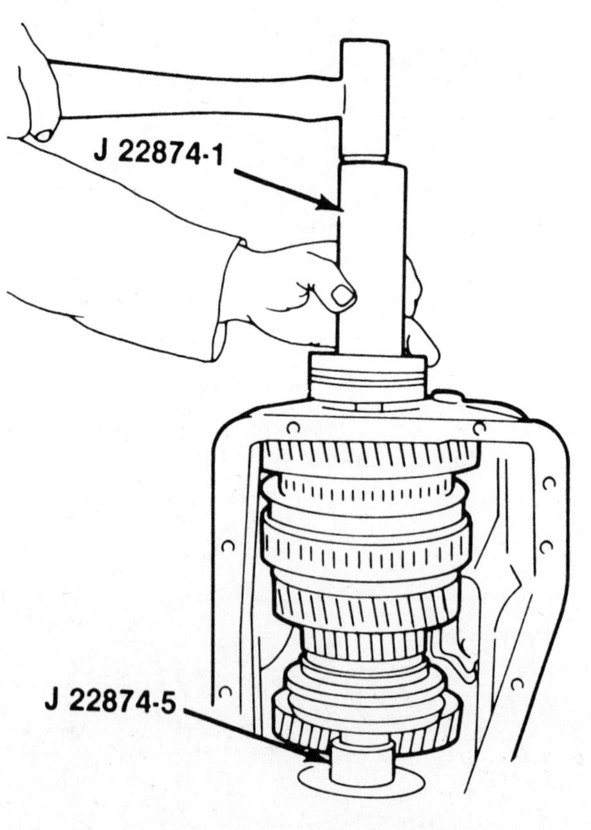

Installing the mainshaft rear bearing — 117mm 4-speed

1. 3rd/4th shift fork
2. 1st and 2nd/reverse detent spring
3. Detent pin
4. Reverse shift rod
5. 1st/2nd shift fork
6. Reverse shift fork
7. Retaining pin
8. Interlock pin
9. 3rd/4th shift rod
10. Interlock shuttle
11. 1st/2nd shift rod
12. 3rd/4th detent spring
13. 3rd/4th stop
14. 3rd/4th shift gate

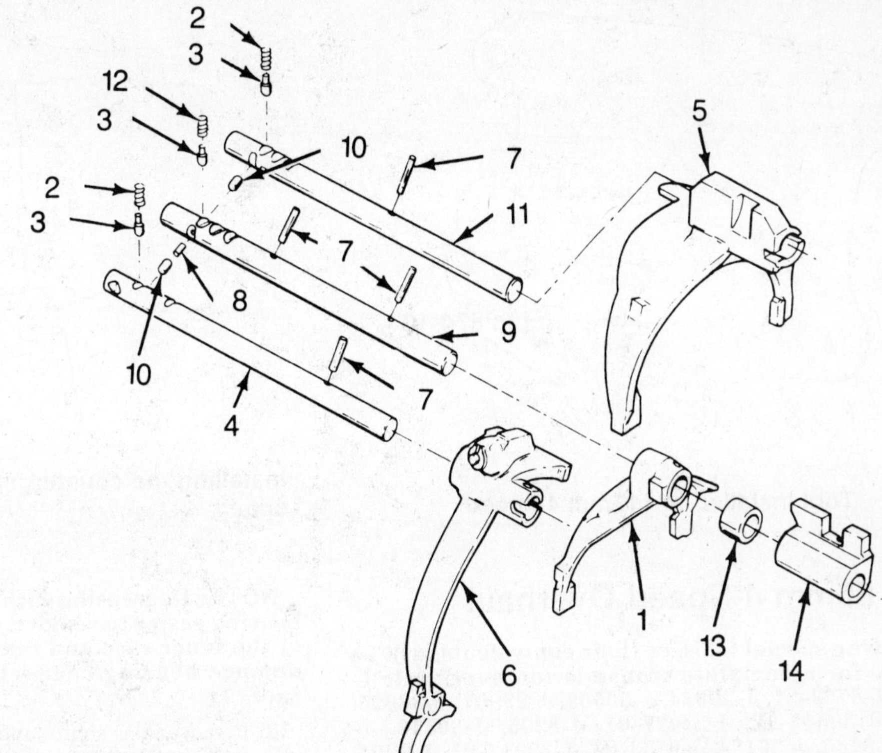

C and K series shift rod and fork positions – 117mm 4-speed

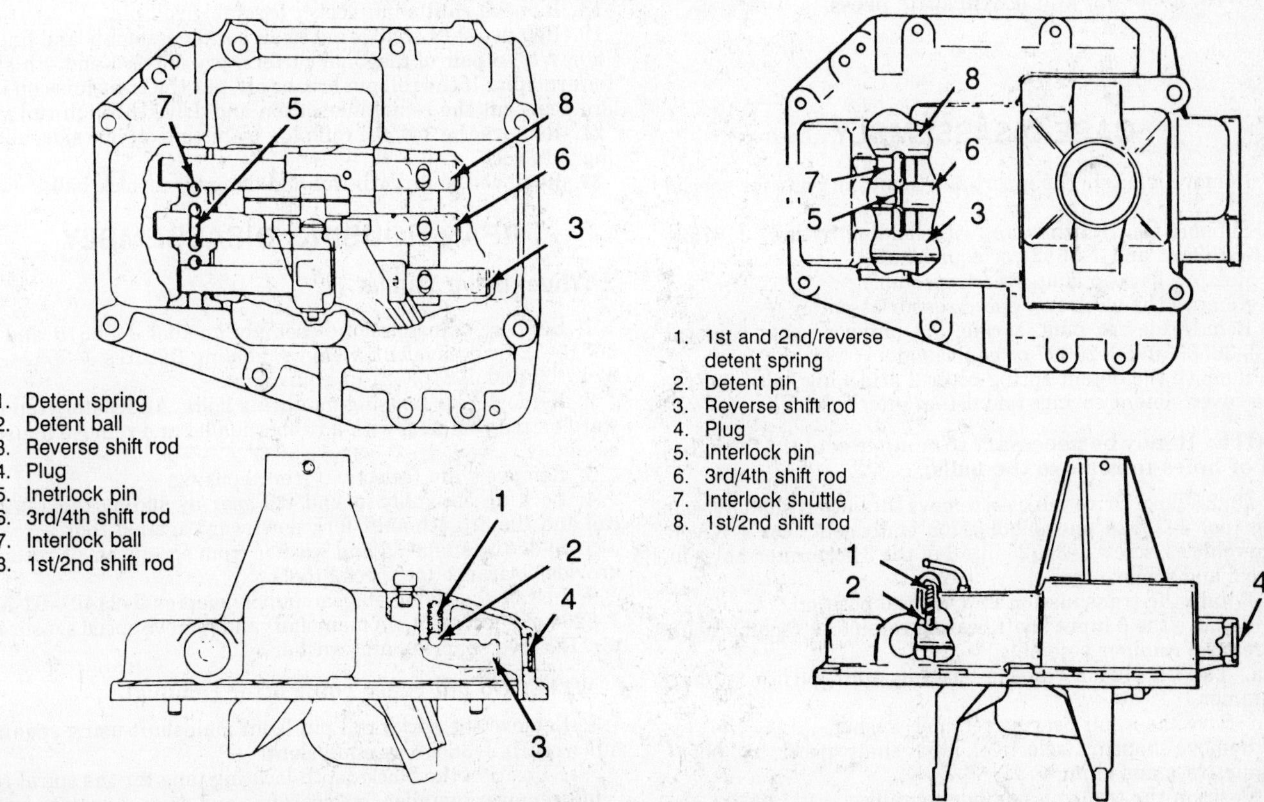

1. Detent spring
2. Detent ball
3. Reverse shift rod
4. Plug
5. Inetrlock pin
6. 3rd/4th shift rod
7. Interlock ball
8. 1st/2nd shift rod

R and V series interlock shuttles and pin – 117mm 4-speed

1. 1st and 2nd/reverse detent spring
2. Detent pin
3. Reverse shift rod
4. Plug
5. Interlock pin
6. 3rd/4th shift rod
7. Interlock shuttle
8. 1st/2nd shift rod

C and K series interlock shuttles and pin – 117mm 4-speed

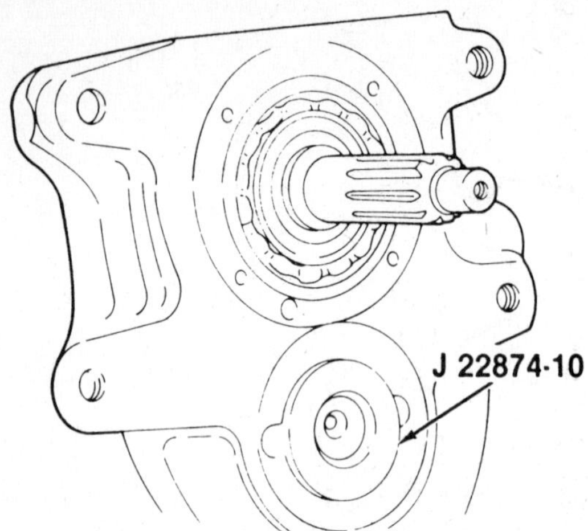

Tool installed — 117mm 4-speed

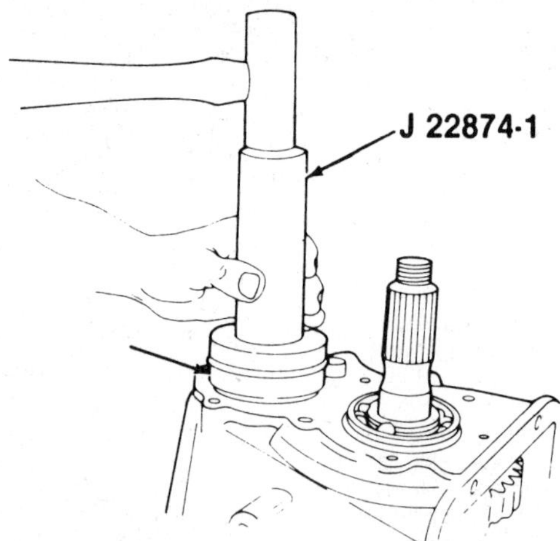

Installing the countergear rear bearing — 117mm 4-speed

85mm 4-Speed Overhaul

The following special tools, or their equivalents, will be necessary for a complete transmission overhaul: J–8763–02, J–8763–21, J–36824, J–36509, J–23907, J–36825, J–36515, J–36515–12, J–21427–01, J–8205, J–36516, J–36513, J–36183, J–36184, J–6133–01, J–22912–01, J–8001, J–25025–A, J–8092, J–36799, J–36800, J–36506, J–36507, J–36511, J–36798–1, J–36190, J–36798–2, J–36510, J–36515–10, J–36502, and a hydraulic press.

CASE DISASSEMBLY

1. Remove idler shaft support and 2 bottom bolts for special tools.
2. Support the transmission with holding fixtures J–8763–02, J–8763–21 and J–36824 or equivalent.
3. Remove backup lamp switch assembly.
4. Remove the electronic speed sensor assembly.
5. Remove detent plug, spring and plunger using removal tool J–36509 and J–23907 or equivalent.
6. Remove the detent spring cover 2 attaching bolts and remove cover, detent springs and detent/interlock balls.

NOTE: It may be necessary to remove sealant from inside of holes to remove the balls.

7. On 2-Wheel Drive vehicles, remove the output shaft oil seal using tool J–36825 and J–23907 or equivalent. On 4-Wheel Drive vehicles, screw J–36825 into 1 of the 3 perforated holes in the seal and remove seal.
8. Rotate the transmission in a vertical position.
9. Remove the 6 input shaft bearing retainer attaching bolts and remove retainer assembly.
   a. Tap on clutch release bearing pilot with a rubber hammer.
   b. Save the input bearing retainer washer.
10. Remove snapring (selective), input shaft spacer, ball bearing inner race and shim.
11. Position the transmission horizontally.
12. Remove front housing to rear housing attaching bolts.
13. Drive dowels into front housing and remove housing.
14. Remove the countershaft bearing.
15. Remove bearing inner race and roller bearing.

NOTE: Degreasing with a liquid cleaner will make the bearing easier to remove. Grab the outer diameter edge of the inner race and remove with large pliers. Do not damage bearing cage while removing bearing inner race.

16. Remove idler shaft support.
17. Remove 4 rollers. Pull shift shaft forward and cock to detent cover side and remove roll pin. Support the shift shaft end while driving out finger roll pin.
18. Remove shift shaft socket assembly roll pin.
19. Remove shift shaft, shift shaft socket assembly and finger.
20. With a pair of diagonal cutters, pry out 3rd and 4th shift fork roll pin. If the roll pin breaks off, put the transmission into 3rd gear, cut the remainder of pin and drive through rail.
21. Remove the 3rd/4th rail plug by hitting on one side, allowing it to cock.
22. Remove the 3rd/4th rail and detent/interlock balls.

REAR HOUSING DISASSEMBLY

2-Wheel Drive Trucks

1. Support transmission assembly on tool J–36515 and J–36515–12 or equivalent. Remove holding fixtures J–36824, J–8763–02 and J–8763–21 or equivalent.
2. Remove rear housing mounting bolts. Alternately tap upward on rear housing with a rubber mallet and remove housing assembly.
3. Remove shim (selective) from housing.
4. Lock up assembly in 2nd/4th gear by sliding the 1st/2nd rail and the 3rd/4th shift fork downward against tool.
5. Slide the snapring and washer from speed sensor rotor to provide clearance for special tools.
6. Install speedometer gear puller adapter J–21427–01 and J–8205 or equivalent, on mainshaft and remove speed sensor rotor. Remove snapring and washer.

NOTE: Do not reuse rotor after removal.

7. Remove the sprial roll pin from mainshaft using spanner nut wrench J–36516 or equivalent.
   a. Position the black depth locating tang for the spiral roll pin remover/installer for clearance and drive downward.
   b. Position the black depth locating tang back into place with the rod going through it.
   c. Rotate spanner nut wrench J–36516 or equivalent clockwise until it stops.

8. Remove the threaded thrust ring (inner), ball and threaded thrust ring (outer) from mainshaft.
 a. Hold the countershaft against the mainshaft.
 b. Rotate spanner nut wrench J–36516 or equivalent clockwise until both threaded thrust rings are completely apart.
9. Remove the reverse idler gear and countershaft.
10. Remove 1st/2nd shift rail assembly, reverse shift rail assembly and 3rd/4th shift fork. Remove the spacer block.
11. Remove the mainshaft assembly.

NOTE: Leave the synchronizer ring on the 3rd/4th synchronizer assembly to prevent the synchronizer detent balls from popping out.

12. Remove the input shaft gear and pilot bearing.

4-Wheel Drive Trucks

1. Lock up the transmission in 2nd/4th gear by sliding the 1st/2nd shift rail assembly and 3rd/4th shift fork downward against tool.
2. Remove the spiral roll pin using spanner nut wrench J–36516 or equivalent.
 a. Position the black depth locating tang for the spiral roll pin remover/installer for clearance and drive downward.
 b. Position the black depth locating tang back into place with the rod going through it.
 c. Rotate spanner nut wrench J–36516 or equivalent clockwise until it stops.
3. Remove the threaded thrust ring (inner), ball and threaded thrust ring (outer) from mainshaft. Rotate spanner nut wrench J–36516 or equivalent clockwise until both threaded thrust rings are completely apart.
4. Remove the rear housing by alternately tapping upward on rear housing with a rubber mallet and remove housing assembly.
5. Save the ball bearing outer race that will be left in the rear housing.
6. Remove the countershaft bearing, countershaft and reverse idler assembly.
7. Remove reverse shift rail assembly, 1st/2nd shift rail assembly and 3rd/4th shift fork.

NOTE: Leave the synchronizer ring on the 3rd/4th synchronizer assembly to prevent the synchronizer detent balls from popping out.

8. Remove the input shaft gear and pilot bearing.

MAINSHAFT DISASSEMBLY

1. Remove snapring (selective) from mainshaft.
2. Using bearing separator plate J–36513 or equivalent and a hydraulic press, remove 3rd/4th synchronizer assembly, synchronizer rings and 3rd speed gear.

NOTE: Mark the hub and sleeve so they can be installed in the same position. Also, leave the synchronizer rings to prevent the synchronizer detent balls from popping out.

3. Remove the 3rd gear bearing.
4. Remove the snapring (selective).
5. Using bearing separator plate J–36513 or equivalent and a hydraulic press, remove 2nd speed gear assembly and 2nd speed gear bearing race.
6. Remove the bearing assembly. Leave the synchronizer ring on the 1st/2nd synchronizer assembly to prevent the synchronizer detent balls from popping out.
7. Using bearing separator plate J–36513 or equivalent and a hydraulic press, remove the 1st speed gear and 1st/2nd synchronizer assembly.

NOTE: Mark the hub and sleeve so they can be installed in the same position. Also, leave the synchronizer rings on the 1st/2nd synchronizer assembly to prevent the synchronizer detent balls from popping out.

8. Remove the bearing assembly.
9. Remove snapring (selective).
10. Using bearing separator plate J–36513 and a hydraulic press, remove reverse speed gear assembly and 4th/reverse synchronizer assembly.

NOTE: Mark the hub and sleeve so they can be installed in the same position. Also, leave the synchronizer rings on the 4th/reverse synchronizer assembly to prevent the synchronizer detent balls from popping out.

12. Remove the bearing assembly.
13. Place the 1st/2nd and 3rd/4th speed synchronizers in separate shop towels, wrap assemblies and press against inner hub.

Inspection

1. Wash all parts in a suitable solvent and air dry.

NOTE: Do not spin dry the ball bearings.

2. Inspect all gears for cracks, chipped gear teeth, thrust face surfaces, bearing surface diameters and other damage.

NOTE: The black phosphate coating will develop wear patterns, this is a normal condition.

3. Inspect synchronizer sleeves for a sliding fit on synchronizer hubs and hubs to have a force fit on the mainshaft splines.
4. Inspect the synchronizer springs, keys and rings for wear or other damage.
5. Inspect the synchronizer clutching teeth for wear, scuffed, nicked, burred or broken teeth.
6. Inspect gear clutching cones for synchronizer ring metal transfer.
7. Inspect the bearings and bearing surfaces for nicks, burrs, bent cages and wear.
9. Lubricate all bearings with light engine oil and check for rough rotation.
 a. If scuffed, nicked, burred, scoring, or synchronizer ring metal transfer conditions cannot be removed with a soft cloth, replace the component and inspect mating parts.
 b. Lubricate all components with 5W–30 oil or equivalent.

MAINSHAFT ASSEMBLY

NOTE: Prior to installation, heat the roller bearing race, ball bearing inner race and the speed sensor rotor (2-Wheel Drive) for a period of 7–10 minutes at 250°F (121°C) and 2nd speed gear race for a period of 20 minutes minimum, at 250°F (121°C).

1. Install 1st/2nd gear synchronizer assembly and 3rd/4th gear synchronizer assembly.
2. Install 4th/reverse gear synchronizer assembly.
3. Install bearing assembly and reverse speed gear.

NOTE: When pressing the 4th/reverse synchronizer assembly, manually align and engage the splines. Press synchronizer until seated. Make certain all shavings are removed.

4. Using tools J–36183, J–36184, J–36513 or equivalents and a hydraulic press, install 4th/reverse synchronizer assembly with synchronizer ring.
 a. Aling marks made previously, for correct positions.
 b. Position the groove in the hub towards reverse speed gear.
5. Install a new selective snapring.

NOTE: Install the thickest snapring that will fit in the groove.

6. Using tool J-6133-01 and bearing separator plate J-36513 or equivalent and a hydraulic press, install the roller bearing race with the shoulder down towards reverse gear.
7. Using tool J-6133-01, J-36513 or equivalent and a hydraulic press, install roller bearing and inner ball bearing race.
   a. Apply grease to roller bearing.
   b. The smaller diameter of bearing cage should be up.
   c. The shoulder of the inner ball bearing race should face down towards the reverse gear.
8. Install bearing assembly and 1st speed gear.
   a. When pressing 1st/2nd synchronizer assembly, manually align and engage the splines.
   b. Start pressing and stop before tangs engage.
   c. Lift and rotate gear to engage synchronizer ring.
   d. Press until seated.
   e. Make certain all shavings are removed.
9. Using tools J-36183, J-36184, J-22912-01 and a hydraulic press, install 1st/2nd synchronizer assembly with both synchronizer rings.
   a. Align marks made previously, for correct positions.
   b. Groove on outside of sleeve must go toward the 2nd speed gear to prevent gear clash during 1st and 2nd gear shifts (teeth on sleeve have different angles).
10. Install bearing assembly and 2nd speed gear. Make sure bearing cage is together.
11. Using tools J-36183, J-36184, J-22912-01 and a hydraulic press, install 2nd gear race (Heated).
12. Install a new selective snapring. Install the thickest snapring that will fit in the groove.
13. Install bearing assembly and 3rd speed gear.
   a. When pressing 3rd/4th synchronizer assembly, manually align and engage the splines.
   b. Start pressing and stop before tangs engage.
   c. Lift and rotate gear to engage synchronizer ring.
   d. Press until seated.
   e. Make certain all shavings are removed.
14. Using tools J-36183, J-36184, J-22912-01 and a hydraulic press, install 3rd/4th synchronizer assembly with both synchronizer rings. Align marks made previously, for correct positions.
15. Install a new selective snapring. Install the thickest snapring that will fit in the groove.

REVERSE IDLER UNIT DISASSEMBLY

1. Remove snapring.
2. Remove thrust washer, ball, reverse gear, 3 bearing assemblies and O-ring.

Inspection

1. Wash all parts in a suitable solvent.
2. Inspect gear teeth for scuffed, nicked, burred or broken teeth.
3. Inspect bearing assemblies for roughness while rotating, burred or pitted condition and gage damage.
4. Inspect the shaft for scoring, wear or overheating.

NOTE: If scuffed, nicked, burred or scoring conditions cannot be removed with a soft stone or crocus cloth, replace the component.

REVERSE IDLER UNIT ASSEMBLY

1. Lubricate all components with 5W-30 oil or equivalent.
2. Install the 3 bearing assembly.
3. Install the reverse gear. The extended part of the hub faces the thrust washer.
4. Install the thrust washer and ball. Retain ball with petroleum jelly.
5. Install a new snapring and O-ring.

COUNTERSHAFT DISASSEMBLY

NOTE: If the 4th gear cannot be pressed off the countershaft, replace the complete assembly.

Inspection

1. Wash all parts in a suitable solvent.
2. Inspect countershaft for cracks.
3. Inspect bearings for roughness while rotating, burred or pitted condition.
4. Inspect bearing races for scoring, wear or overheating.
5. Inspect gear teeth for scuffed, nicked, burred or broken teeth.

NOTE: If scuffed, nicked, burred or scoring conditions cannot be removed with a soft stone or crocus cloth, replace the component.

COUNTERSHAFT ASSEMBLY

1. Install 4th gear on countershaft assembly or replace assembly, if necessary.
2. Lubricate assembly with 5W-30 oil or equivalent.

ENDPLAY ADJUSTMENT

NOTE: This procedure must be performed if the countershaft bearings, front housing countershaft bearing race or the front or rear housing was replaced. If a gear rattle noise complaint (not clutch disc related) is experienced, it is recommended the countershaft endplay be checked.

1. Remove bearing race using a brass drift.
2. Remove the countershaft bearing plug.
3. Remove the snapring, shims and oil fill plug.
4. Inspect bearing and countershaft.
   a. Smaller diameter of bearing cage into bearing race (202).
   b. Install bearings in bearing races prior to assembly and retain with petroleum jelly.
5. Install tools J-8001 and J-25025-A or equivalent, to front housing in one of the input shaft bearing retainer bolt holes.
   a. Use a pry bar, pry the countershaft upward, noting the dial indicator travel. Use the fill plug hole to reach the third gear part of the countershaft for prying.
   b. Measure off gear tooth.
   c. Make certain tool J-8001 stays on gear tooth while measuring endplay.
   d. Allow the countershaft to lower to its original position, noting the dial indicator travel. Total travel should be 0.005–0.009 in. (0.13–0.23mm).
6. Move bearing race with tool J-8092 and J-36799 or equivalent to achieve specified endplay.
7. Use the least number of shims to retain specified endplay and install snapring.
8. Seat the countershaft bearing race using tool J-8092 and J-36799 or equivalent.
9. Recheck Step 5a-7 to make sure endplay is still correct after seating countershaft bearing race.
10. Install oil fill plug.
11. Install a new countershaft bearing plug. Apply gasket maker GM part number 1052943 or equivalent to outer edge of plug.

NOTE: The countershaft bearing plug will require cooling for 20 minutes minimum, at 32°F (0°C) prior to installation during assembly.

FRONT HOUSING DISASSEMBLY

1. Using a brass drift, remove ball bearing assembly outer race.
2. Using tools J–36800 and J–23907 or equivalent, remove the 3 shift rail front housing bearings.
3. Using tools J–36509 and J–23907 or equivalent, remove clutch fork pivot assembly.
4. Use a punch and drive out shift shaft/rail plugs.
5. Remove countershaft bearing plug.
   a. Destake plug first.
   b. Screw a ⅜–16 bottom tap into the plug and remove with tool J–6725 or equivalent.
6. Using tools J–36799 and J–8092 or equivalent, remove snapring, shims and countershaft bearing race.
   a. Tap in countershaft bearing race before removing snapring.
   b. Check countershaft endplay adjustment, if countershaft bearing race is removed.
   c. Measure the countershaft bearing race bore in 2 locations diagonally, 0.157 in. (4mm) in from inside of transmission housing. If the housing bore is not within 2.045–2.046 in. (51.946–51.965mm), replace the housing.
7. Remove 4th/reverse detent hex head plug, 4th/reverse detent spring and 4th/reverse detent plunger assembly.
8. Remove detent cam bolt, washer, and reverse detent cam. Using a flat blade type tool, release tension of bias spring from end of shift lever pin.

CAUTION

The spring is under considerable tension. Take care to avoid personal injury!

9. Remove bias spring bolt, bias spring and sleeve seat, bias spring, bias spring sleeve, shift shaft lever assembly and detent roller.
10. Remove detent cam support bolt and remove detent cam support.
11. Using tool J–36506, remove the 2 4th/reverse detent bushings.
12. Using tool J–36507, remove the 2 detent bushings. Remove 1 bushing at a time.
13. Remove the breather assembly. Metal tube must remain in case.
14. Remove drain and fill plugs using tool J–36511 or equivalent.

Inspection

1. Clean all gasket material from case using liquid gasket remover.
2. Clean all parts in a suitable solvent and air dry.
3. Inspect the bearing race bore for wear, scratches or grooves. If countershaft bearing race is worn or damaged, the rear housing must be replaced.
4. Inspect bushings for scores, burrs, roundness or evidence of overheating.
5. Inspect the case for cracks, damaged threads, mounting surfaces for nicks, burrs, or scratches. If the case is crack, it must be replaced.
6. Using a straight edge, check machined surfaces for flatness.

NOTE: If scuffed, nicked, burred or scoring conditions cannot be removed with a soft stone or crocus cloth, replace the component. Clean-up damaged threads with the correct size tap.

FRONT HOUSING ASSEMBLY

NOTE: If the countershaft bearing plug was removed, it will require cooling for a period of 20 minutes minumum, at 32°F (0°C) before installation.

1. Using a brass driff, install the ball bearing outer race.
2. Using tools J–36798–1 and J–36190 or equivalent, install 3 shift rail front housing bearings. Install until flush and stake using tools J–36798–1, J–36798–2 and J–36190 or equivalent. Do not stake the tabs on the bushings.
3. Using tools J–36190 and J–36510 or equivalent, install the clutch fork pivot assembly. Grease assembly after installation through lube fitting.
4. Using tool J–36507 or equivalent, install 2 detent plunger bushings.
   a. Install 1 bushing at a time.
   b. Install the first bushing until the second scribe mark on the tool lines up with the housing.
   c. Install the second bushing until the first scribe mark on the tool lines up with the housing.
5. Using tools J–36799 and J–8092 or equivalent, install countershaft bearing race. Align lube slot in race with groove in the housing. Install shims and snapring.

NOTE: If the countershaft bearing races, countershaft bearings, countershaft or front or rear housing are replaced, the countershaft endplay must be checked.

6. Using tools J–36799 and J–8092 or equivalent, install a new countershaft bearing plug. Apply gasket maker GM part number 1052943 or equivalent, to the outside edge of the plug and stake in 3 places evenly apart.
7. Using tool J–36506, install both 4th/reverse detent bushings.
   a. Install 1 bushing at a time.
   b. Install the first bushing until the second scribe mark on the tool lines up with the housing.
   c. Install the second bushing until the first scribe mark on the tool lines up with the housing.
8. Install detent cam support and bolt. Torque bolt to 7 ft. lbs. (8.5 Nm).
9. Install reverse detent cam, bushing, washer and bolt. Torque bolt to 7 ft. lbs. (8.5 Nm).
10. Install detent roller on shift shaft lever assembly and install into housing.
11. Install bias spring sleeve, bias load torsional spring, bias spring and sleeve seat and bolt. Torque bolt to 7 ft. lbs. (8.5 Nm).
12. Install bias load torsional spring end back onto shift shaft lever pin.
13. Install 4th/reverse plunger assembly, 4th/reverse detent spring and hex head plug.
   a. Make certain slot in plunger is lined up with reverse cam.
   b. Use pipe sealant GM part number 1052080 or equivalent to threads.
   c. Torque hex head plug to 46 ft. lbs. (60 Nm).
14. Install breather assembly, oil fill plug and drain plug. Apply pipe sealant GM part number 1052080 or equivalent on threads and torque drain plug to 46 ft. lbs. (60 Nm).
15. Install shift shaft/rails plugs until flush. Apply gasket maker GM part number 1052943 or equivalent to the edge of plugs.

SHIFT SHAFT/RAIL AND FORK

Inspection

1. Wash all parts in a suitable solvent and air dry.
2. Inspect 1st/2nd shift rail, 3rd/4th rail, and shift shaft for wear or scoring.
3. Inspect 1st/2nd shift fork, 3rd/4th shift fork and reverse shift fork for wear, scoring or distortion. Black coloring on the edge of forks is a normal condition.
4. Inspect 1st/2nd shift yoke and finger for wear or

distortion.

5. Inspect both pins for wear or distortion.
6. Inspect shift shaft socket aassembly for wear or distortion.

NOTE: Wear, scoring or distortion requires replacement of assembly and inspection of mating parts.

SELECTIVE SHIMIMG PROCEDURE

Input Shaft Bearing Retainer

1. Measure the distance between the sealing flange of the retainer and the flanged part of the release guide. Record this measurement.
2. Measure the height of the input bearing outer race from the sealing surface of the front housing. Record this measurement.
3. Subtract the bearing race height from the retainer depth and select a shim the same (or next smaller) size as the difference in measurements.

Output Shaft Bearing

1. Measure the distance between the bearing retainer surface and the bottom of the bearing bore in the rear housing. Record this measurement.
2. Measure the width of the mainshaft rear bearing. Record this measurement.
3. Subtract the bearing width from the housing bore depth. Select a shim which is the same (or next smaller) size as the difference in measurements.

REAR HOUSING ASSEMBLY

2-Wheel Drive

1. Install the pilot bearing into input shaft with the smaller diameter of bearing cage toward input shaft. Retain with petroleum jelly.
2. Assemble the input shaft, pilot bearing, synchronizer ring and mainshaft assembly on fixture J-36515 or equivalent.
3. Assemble adapter J-36515-12 or equivalent on countershaft and install assembly onto fixture J-36515 or equivalent.
4. Install the reverse idler assembly using a new O-ring.
5. Install bearing assembly outer race and ball bearing outer race.
6. Install on the mainshaft assembly:
   a. 3rd/4th shift fork with taper on fork towards 3rd gear.
   b. 1st/2nd shift rail assembly and spacer block.
   c. Lock up the transmission by sliding the 3rd/4th shift fork and 1st/2nd shift rail assembly downward towards fixture J-36515 or equivalent.
7. Install ball to output shaft and retain with petroleum jelly.
8. Install the inner threaded thrust ring and outer threaded thrust ring. Make certain the old spiral roll pin is removed from the outer threaded thrust ring.
   a. Completely screw the rings together, then back off of rings until both identification slots for the ball line up.
   b. Slide the assembled rings over the ball that is retained on the output shaft.
   c. Slide the rod up on spanner nut wrench J-36516 or equivalent, turn the black depth locating tang over, slide the rod through so the roll pin will be installed to the correct depth.
   d. Allow clearance for the snapring by screwing the rings together counterclockwise with spanner nut wrench J-36516 or equivalent.
9. Install a new snapring.
10. Turn spanner nut wrench J-36516 or equivalent clockwise to obtain a torque of 12 ft. lbs. (15 Nm), then advance to the next sprial roll pin notch.
11. Install a new spiral roll pin into spanner nut wrench J-36516 or equivalent and retain with petroleum jelly. Lined up roll pin and drive pin into outer thrust ring.
12. Install the snapring and speedo gear thrust washer.
13. Install the speed sensor rotor. Rotor must be heated.
14. Install shim onto output shaft bearing assembly and retain with pertroleum jelly.

NOTE: The rear housing output shaft bearing assembly bore must be heated for 3–5 minutes before assembly.

15. Install retainer alignment cables J-36515-10 or equivalent, through bolt and holes in rear housing.
   a. Install the screw into the output shaft bearing retainer.
   b. The notch in the retainer faces the oil delivery tube.
16. Install bearing in bearing race of housing and retain with petroleum jelly. The smaller diameter of bearing cage into bearing race.

NOTE: Press each roller towards the race to secure them for easier assembly.

17. Install the rear housing assembly.
   a. Make certain the reverse idler shaft is lined up with the hole in the case.
   b. Rotate back and forth while pulling down.
   c. Pull up on retainer alignment cables J-36515-10 or equivalent, while installing rear housing.

NOTE: Bring the housing straight down. If resistance is felt at about ¼ in. (6mm), the rollers are cocked. Repeat procedure above. Do not force housing down.

18. Remove tool J-36515-10 or equivalent and install bolts. Apply pipe sealant GM part number 1052080 or equivalent to bolt holes of rear housing. Apply threadlocker GM part number 12345382 or equivalent to bolt threads. Torque bolts to 17 ft. lbs. (22 Nm).

4-Wheel Drive

1. Install the pilot bearing into input shaft with the smaller diameter of bearing cage toward input shaft. Retain with petroleum jelly.
2. Assemble the input shaft, pilot bearing, synchronizer ring and mainshaft assembly on fixture J-36515 or equivalent.
3. Assemble adapter J-36515-12 or equivalent on countershaft and install assembly onto fixture J-36515 or equivalent.
4. Install the reverse idler assembly using a new O-ring.
5. Install bearing assembly outer race and ball bearing outer race.
6. Install on the mainshaft assembly:
   a. 3rd/4th shift fork with taper on fork towards 3rd gear.
   b. 1st/2nd shift rail assembly and spacer block.
   c. Lock up the transmission by sliding the 3rd/4th shift fork and 1st/2nd shift rail assembly downward towards fixture J-36515 or equivalent.
7. Install bearing in bearing race of housing and retain with petroleum jelly. Smaller diameter of bearing cage into bearing race.

NOTE: Press each roller towards the race to secure them for easier assembly.

8. Install the rear housing assembly. Make certain the reverse idler shaft is lined up with hole in the case. Rotate back and forth while pulling down.

NOTE: Bring the housing straight down. If resistance is felt at about ¼ in. (6mm), the rollers are cocked. Repeat procedure above. Do not force housing down.

9. Install the outer bearing race and ball. Retain ball with petroleum jelly.
10. Install the inner threaded thrust ring and outer threaded

thrust ring. Make certain the old spiral roll pin is removed from the outer threaded thrust ring.

a. Completely screw the rings together, then back off of rings until both identification slots for the ball line up.

b. Slide the assembled rings over the ball that is retained on the output shaft.

c. Slide the rod up on spanner nut wrench J-36516 or equivalent, turn the black depth locating tang over, slide the rod through so the roll pin will be installed to the correct depth.

d. Allow clearance for the snapring by screwing the rings together counterclockwise with spanner nut wrench J-36516 or equivalent.

11. Install a new snapring.
12. Turn spanner nut wrench J-36516 or equivalent clockwise to obtain a torque of 12 ft. lbs. (15Nm), then advance to the next sprial roll pin notch.
13. Install a new spiral roll pin into spanner nut wrench J-36516 or equivalent and retain with petroleum jelly. Line up roll pin and drive pin into outer thrust ring.
14. Install seal protector onto output shaft. Fill the output shaft seal lips with chassis grease and install seal with seal installer J-36502 or equivalent.
15. Remove seal protector.

TRANSMISSION CASE

1. Install the idler shaft support. Line up bolt threads in idler shaft support with bolt hole.

NOTE: The machined surface on the face casting must be installed down into case because the bolt hole is slightly off center. Incorrect installation will cause incorrect reverse gear tooth pattern under load.

a. Apply pipe sealant GM part number 1052080 or equivalent to bolt holes of rear housing.

b. Apply threadlocker GM part number 12345382 or equivalent to bolt threads.

c. Hold reverse idler shaft against idler support while torqueing.

d. Torque bolts to 17 ft. lbs. (22 Nm).

2. Assemble transmission holding fixture J-36824 or equivalent to transmission case.
3. Place all forks in neutral position. Coat the 2 interlock check balls with petroleum jelly and insert balls through plug hole using a small magnetic. Push 1 ball into 1st/2nd shift rail side and the other into 3rd/4th shift rail side.
4. Install the 3rd/4th shift rail with interlock pin. Retain pin with petroleum jelly.

a. The detent slots in 3rd/4th shift rail faces up.

b. Install through 3rd/4th shift fork and into the rear housing shift rail bearing.

NOTE: The 1st/2nd and 4th/reverse shift rail must be in NEUTRAL position or the interlock system will not allow the 3rd/4th rail to engage.

5. Install the roll pin to a depth where a maximum of 12.5mm of the roll pin remains. Measure from the edge of the 3rd/4th rail to the top of the roll pin.

NOTE: If the roll pin is not installed to its proper depth, it may rub against the front housing and cause the 3rd or 4th gear to hop-out.

6. Test the interlock system to be certain the interlock balls are in place, by trying to move 2 shift rails.
7. Apply gasket maker GM part number 1052943 or equivalent to plug and install plug until flush.
8. Install the shift shaft, finger and shift shaft socket assembly. The detent slots must faces the idler support side of the transmission and the finger extension must be on the underside of the 4th/reverse shift rail.
9. Install roll pins.
10. Install the 3 detent/interlock balls and springs.
11. Apply gasket maker GM part number 1052943 or equivalent to the outside of bolt holes of the detent spring cover and install cover and attaching bolts. Torque bolts to 7 ft. lbs. (8.5 Nm).
12. Install the 4 rollers to shift shaft. Retain with petroleum jelly.
13. Install the countershaft bearing in bearing race of front housing. The smaller diameter of the bearing cage toward bearing race.
14. Install roller bearing and ball bearing outer race.
15. Apply gasket maker GM part number 1052943 or equivalent to the outside of bolt holes of the rear housing and install front housing.

NOTE: Bring the housing straight down. If resistance is felt at about 1/4 in. (6mm), the rollers are cocked. Repeat procedure above. Do not force housing down.

16. Install the dowel pins and attaching bolts. Do not tighten bolts at this time.
17. Install ball bearing outer race, input shaft spacer and a new selective snapring. Install the thickest snapring that fits into the groove. It may be necessary to pull out on the input shaft to install the selective snapring.
18. Apply gasket maker GM part number 1052943 or equivalent to the inside cover bolt hole pattern.

NOTE: Do not apply too much gasket maker around the oil drain back hole. It may clog the hole causing a low fluid flow through the bearing resulting in premature bearing failure.

19. Install the shim into the input shaft bearing retainer assembly. Make certain the input bearing retainer washer is in place. Retain with petroleum jelly.
20. Align the oil drain back hole of the input shaft bearing retainer assembly with the hole in the housing and install attaching bolts. Torque bolts to 7 ft. lbs. (8.5 Nm).
21. Install the shift shaft detent plunger, shift shaft detent spring and plug using a brass drift. Apply pipe sealant GM part number 1052080 or equivalent to the plug.
22. On 2WD vehicles, install a new O-ring on the electronic speed sensor and coat with a thin flim of transmission oil. Install the electronic speed sensor.
23. Install back-up lamp switch. Apply pipe sealant GM part number 1052080 or equivalent to the threads.
24. Tighten housing attaching bolts to 27 ft. lbs. (35 Nm).

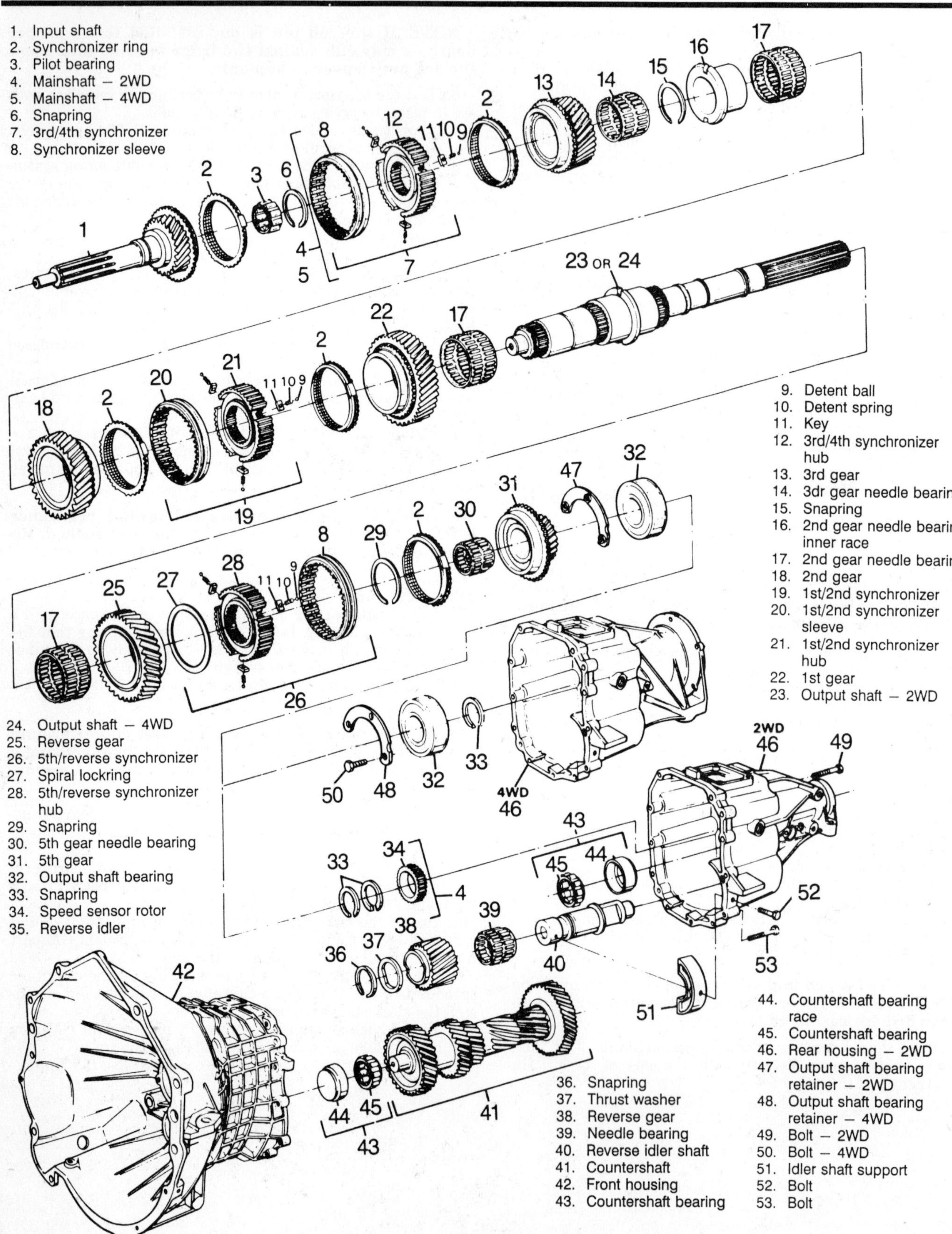
1. Input shaft
2. Synchronizer ring
3. Pilot bearing
4. Mainshaft – 2WD
5. Mainshaft – 4WD
6. Snapring
7. 3rd/4th synchronizer
8. Synchronizer sleeve
9. Detent ball
10. Detent spring
11. Key
12. 3rd/4th synchronizer hub
13. 3rd gear
14. 3dr gear needle bearing
15. Snapring
16. 2nd gear needle bearing inner race
17. 2nd gear needle bearing
18. 2nd gear
19. 1st/2nd synchronizer
20. 1st/2nd synchronizer sleeve
21. 1st/2nd synchronizer hub
22. 1st gear
23. Output shaft – 2WD
24. Output shaft – 4WD
25. Reverse gear
26. 5th/reverse synchronizer
27. Spiral lockring
28. 5th/reverse synchronizer hub
29. Snapring
30. 5th gear needle bearing
31. 5th gear
32. Output shaft bearing
33. Snapring
34. Speed sensor rotor
35. Reverse idler
36. Snapring
37. Thrust washer
38. Reverse gear
39. Needle bearing
40. Reverse idler shaft
41. Countershaft
42. Front housing
43. Countershaft bearing
44. Countershaft bearing race
45. Countershaft bearing
46. Rear housing – 2WD
47. Output shaft bearing retainer – 2WD
48. Output shaft bearing retainer – 4WD
49. Bolt – 2WD
50. Bolt – 4WD
51. Idler shaft support
52. Bolt
53. Bolt
23 OR 24
2WD 46
4WD 46

85mm 4- or 5-speed exploded view

1. 1st & 2nd shift rail assembly
2. 1st & 2nd shift rail
3. Roll pin
4. 1st & 2nd Shift yoke
5. Roll pin
6. Fork, 1st - 2nd Shift
7. Rail Assembly, 3rd & 4th Shift
8. Pin, Roll (3rd & 4th shift)
9. Fork, 3rd & 4th Shift
10. Rail, 3rd & 4th
11. Pin, 3rd & 4th Shift Interlock
12. Rail Assembly, 5th & Reverse Shift
13. Rail, 5th & Reverse
14. Pin, Roll
15. Fork, 5th & Reverse Shift
16. Shaft Assembly, Shift
17. Shaft, Shift
18. Roller, Shift Shaft
19. Pin, Roller
20. Pin, Roll (6 × 28mm)
21. Finger
22. Pin, Roll
23. Socket Assembly, Shift Shaft
24. Boot
25. Seal, Shift Lever Housing
26. Nut, Hex Jam
27. Housing Assembly, Shift Lever
28. Housing Front
29. Bolt, Hex Head (M6 × 25mm)
30. Retainer Assembly, Input Shaft Bearing
31. Retainer, Input Shaft Bearing
32. Washer, Input Bearing Retainer
33. Seal, Input Shaft Bearing Retainer Oil
34. Ring, Snap (selective)
35. Spacer, Input Shaft
36. Shim, (selective)
37. Ring, Input Shaft Bearing Assembly Snap
38. Bearing Assembly, Input Shaft
39. Race, Ball Bearing (outer)
40. Race, Bearing Assembly (outer)
41. Race, Ball Bearing (inner)
42. Bearing, Roller
43. Pivot Assembly, Clutch Fork
44. Fitting, Lube
45. Plug, Shift Shaft/Rails
46. Plug, Oil Fill
47. Breather Assembly
48. Adapter, Breather Hose
49. Plug, Oil Drain
50. Bolt, Hex Head (M10 × 24.4mm)
51. Nut, Lock
52. Bearing, Shift Rail Front Housing
53. Lever Assembly, Shift Shaft (230 & 231)
54. Lever, Shift Shaft
55. Pin, Shift Shaft Lever
56. Sleeve, Bias Spring
57. Spring, Bias Load Torsional
58. Seat, Bias Spring & Sleeve
59. Bolt, Hex Head (M6 × 16mm)
60. Support, 5th & Reverse Detent Cam
61. Cam, 5th & Reverse Detent

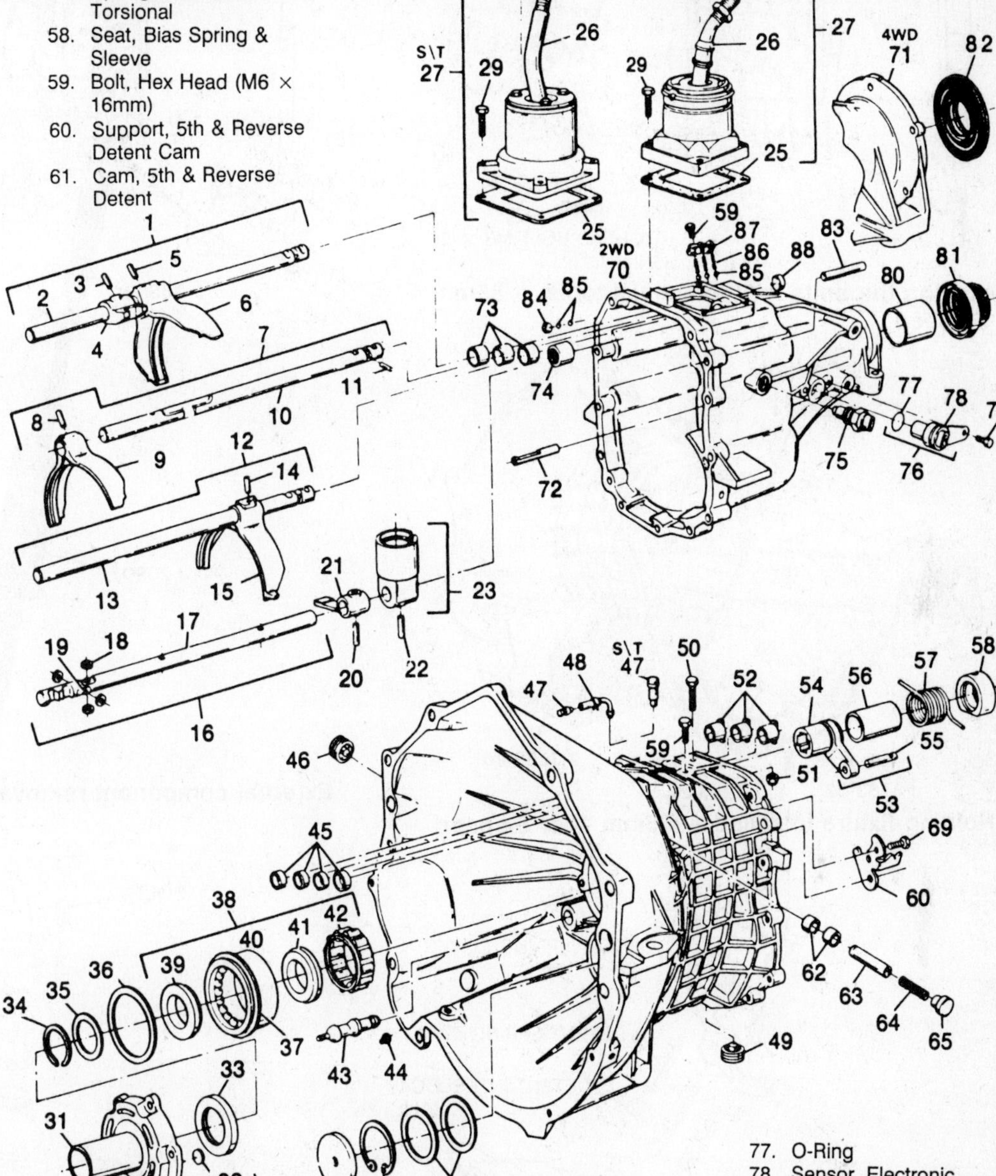

62. Bushing, Detent Plunger
63. Plunger, Shift Shaft Detent
64. Spring, Shift Shaft Detent Plunger
65. Plug
66. Plug, Countershaft Bearing
67. Ring, Snap
68. Shim(s)
69. Bolt, Pan Head (M6 × 18mm)
70. Housing, Rear (2wd)
71. Housing, Rear (4wd)
72. Tube Assembly, Oil Delivery
73. Bearing, Rear Housing Shift Rail
74. Bearing, Rear Housing Shift Shaft
75. Switch Assembly, Back-up Lamp
76. Sensor Assembly, Electronic Speed
77. O-Ring
78. Sensor, Electronic Speed
79. Bolt, Hex Head (M6 × 16)
80. Bearing, Rear Extension (2wd)
81. Seal, Slip Yoke Oil (4wd)
82. Seal, Output Shaft Oil (4wd)
83. Pin, Dowel
84. Plug
85. Ball, Detent/Interlock
86. Spring, Detent
87. Cover, Detent Spring
88. Plug

85mm 4- or 5-speed shift mechanism and case components

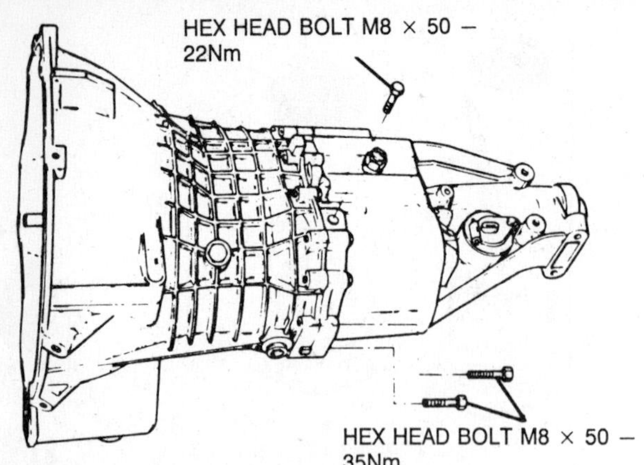

Removing the bolts for the special tools – 85mm 4- or 5-speed

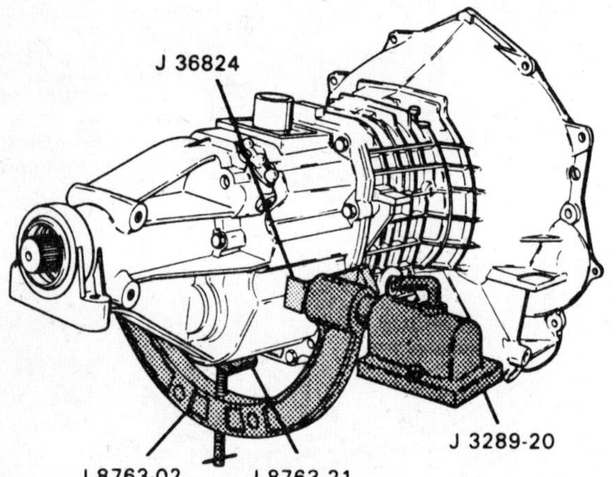

Holding fixture installed – 85mm 4- or 5-speed

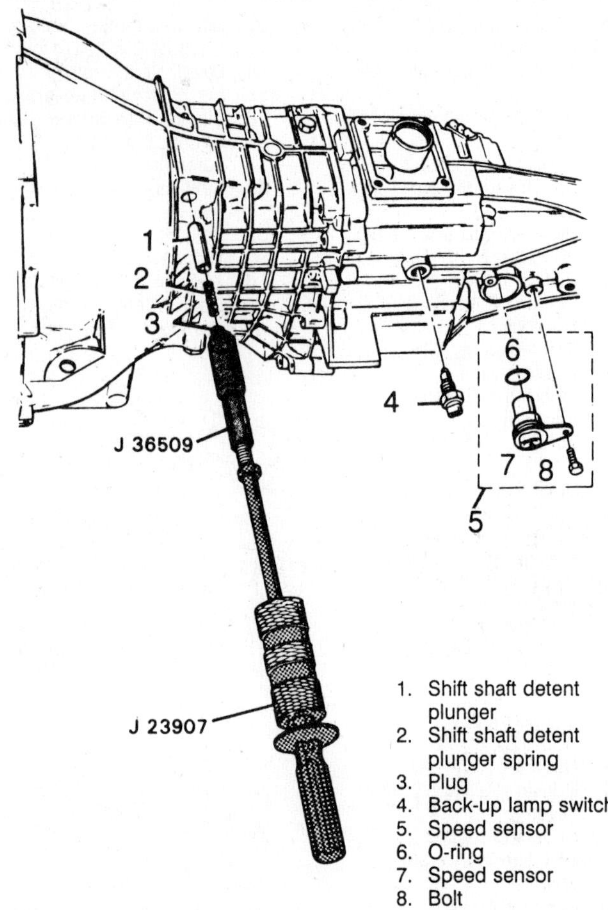

1. Shift shaft detent plunger
2. Shift shaft detent plunger spring
3. Plug
4. Back-up lamp switch
5. Speed sensor
6. O-ring
7. Speed sensor
8. Bolt

External component removal – 85mm 4- or 5-speed

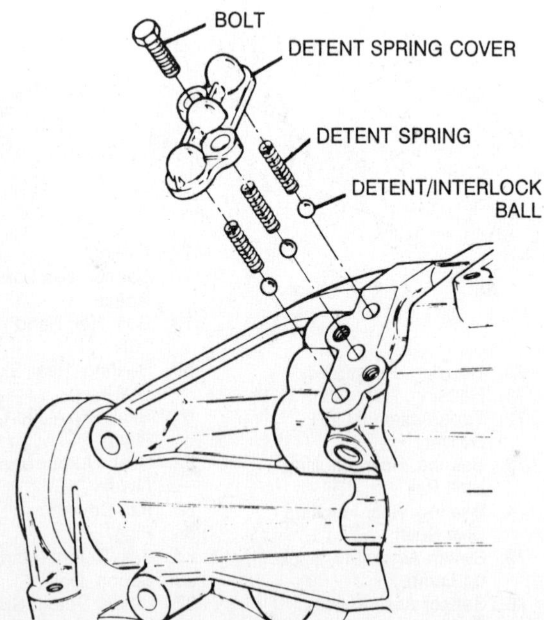

Removing shift rail detent – 85mm 4- or 5-speed

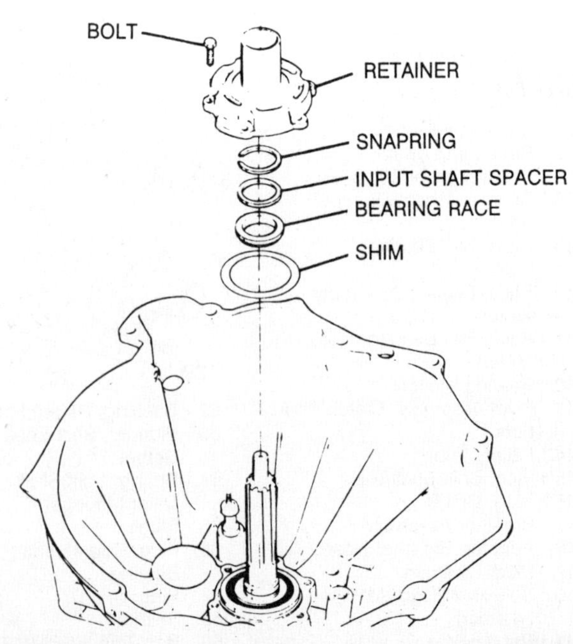

Removing the input shaft bearing retainer – 85mm 4- or 5-speed

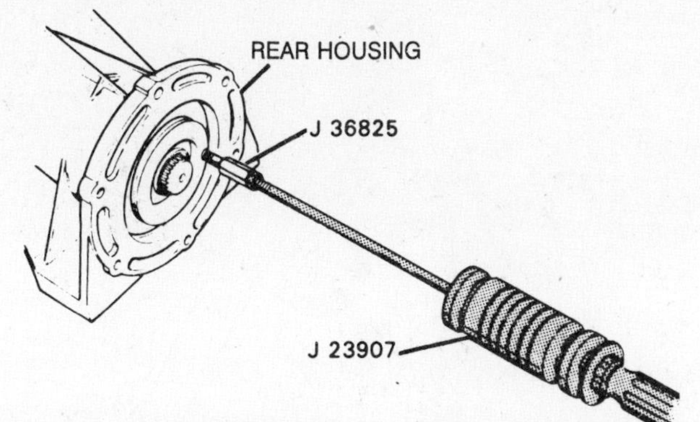

Removing the 4WD oil seal – 85mm 4- or 5-speed

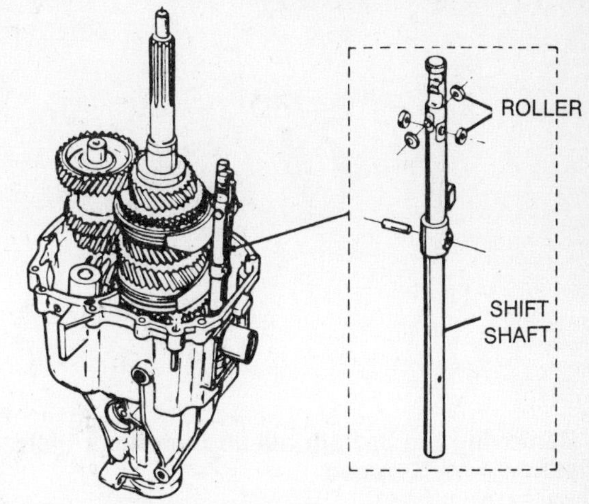

Removing the shift shaft rollers and fingers – 85mm 4- or 5-speed

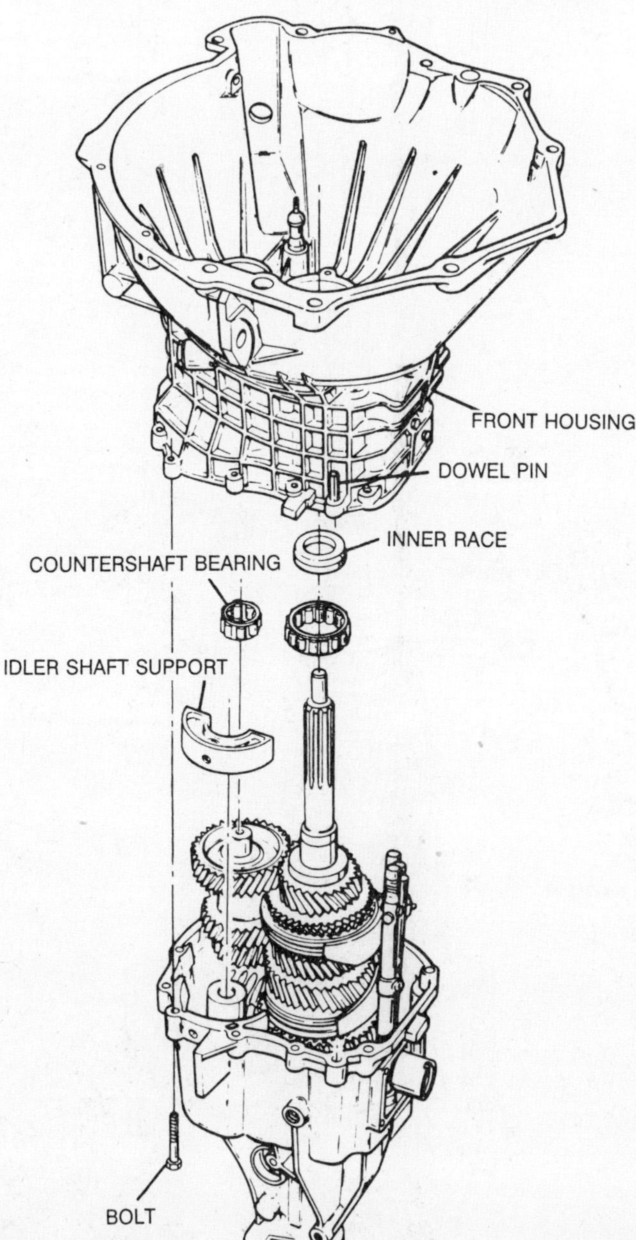

Removing the front housing – 85mm 4- or 5-speed

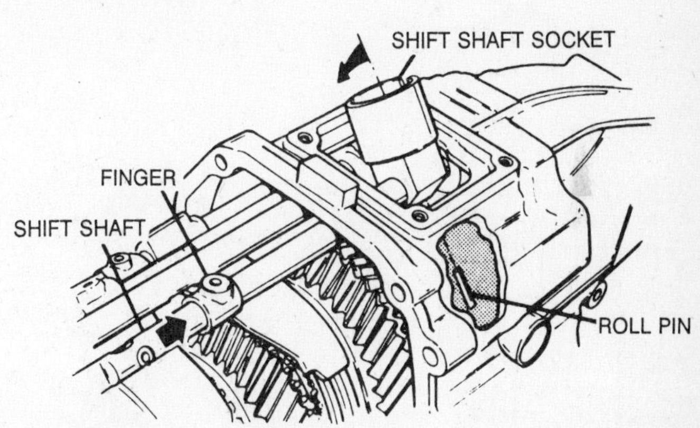

Removing the shift socket assembly roll pin – 85mm 4- or 5-speed

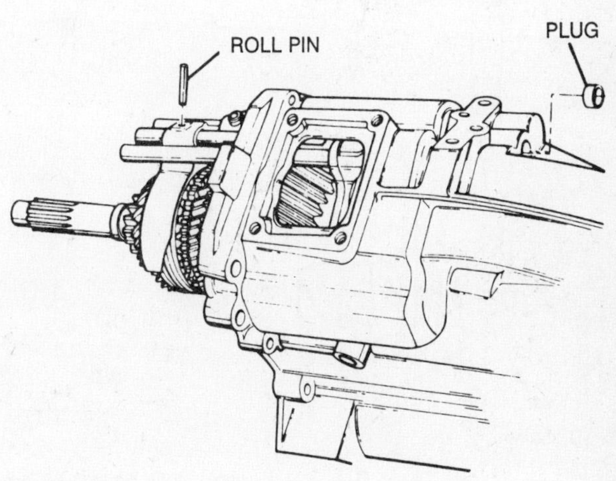

Removing the 3rd/4th rail plug and roll pin – 85mm 4- or 5-speed

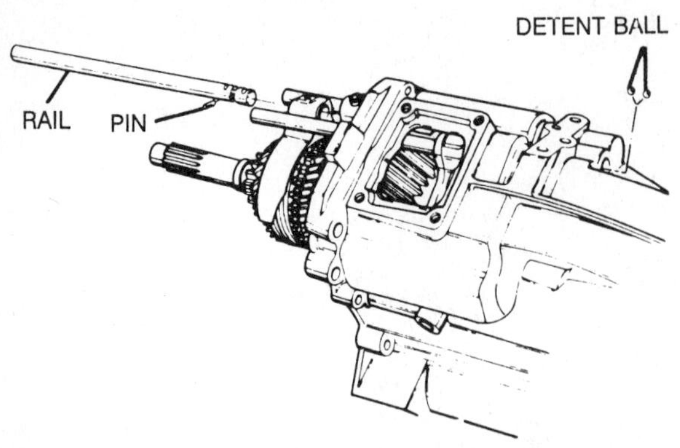

Removing the 3rd/4th rail and interlock balls – 85mm 4- or 5-speed

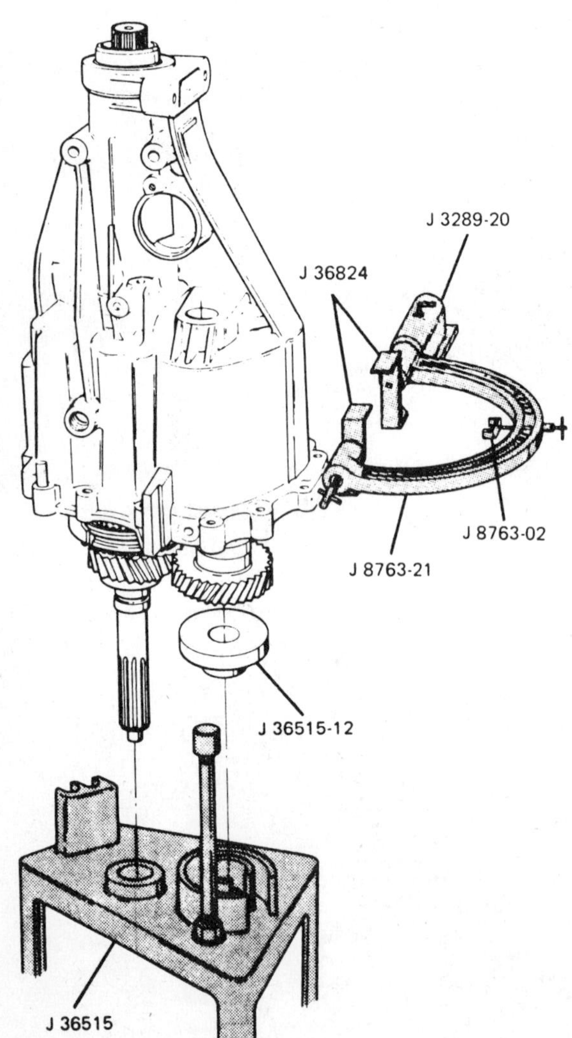

Special tool use – 85mm 4- or 5-speed

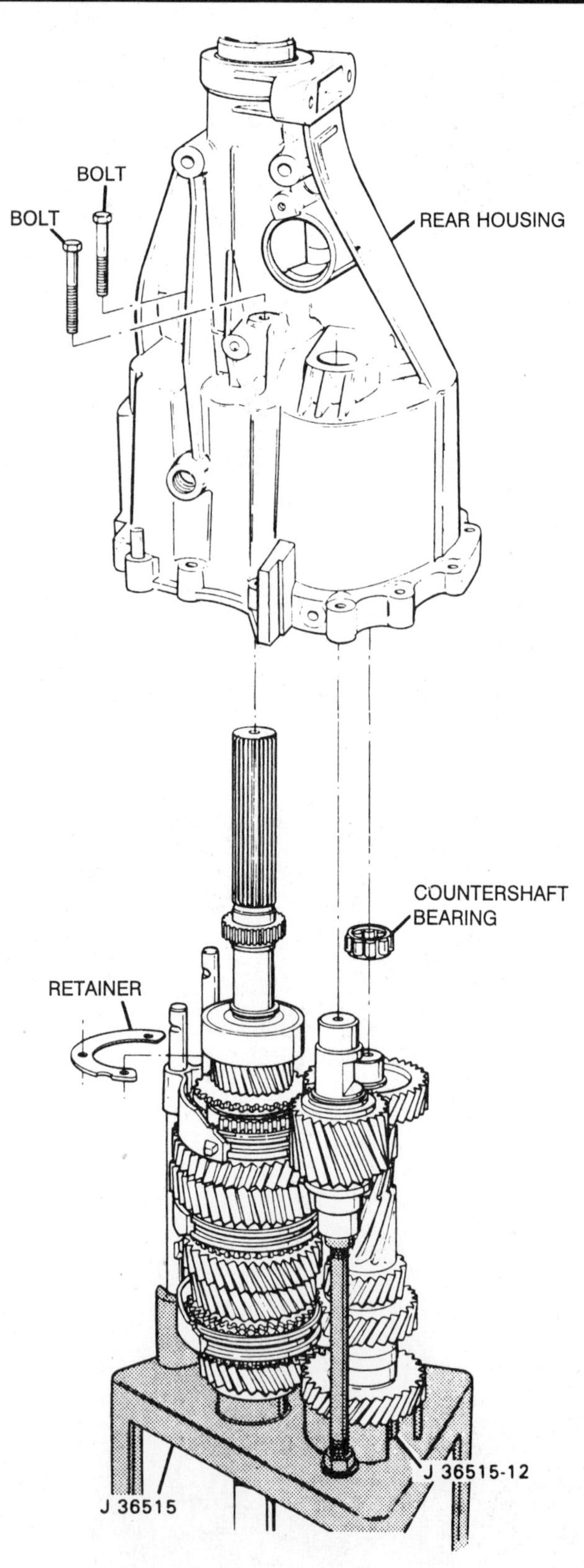

Removing the 2WD rear housing – 85mm 4- or 5-speed

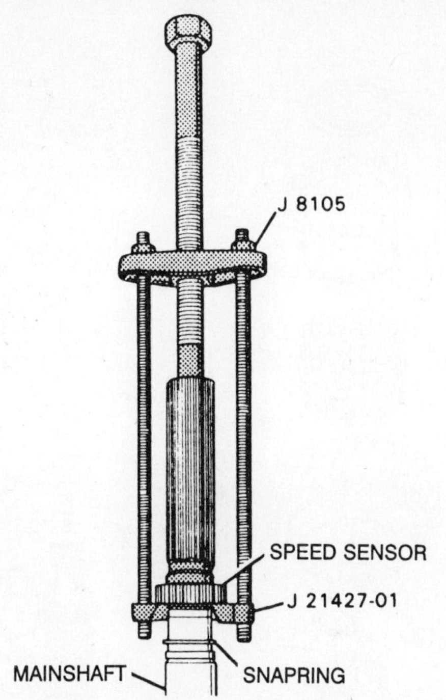

Removing the 2WD speed sensor rotor — 85mm 4- or 5-speed

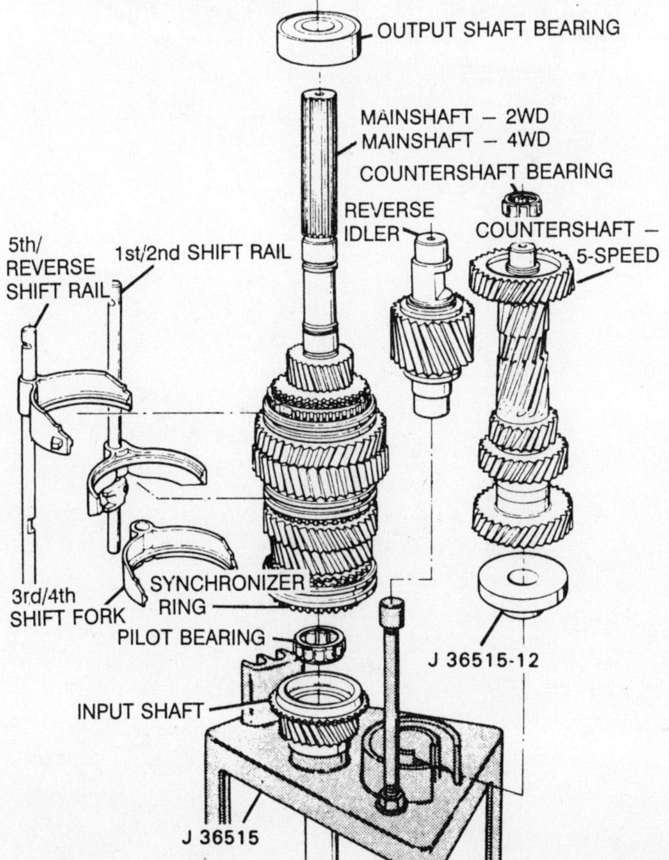

Removing the gears and shift rails — 85mm 4- or 5-speed

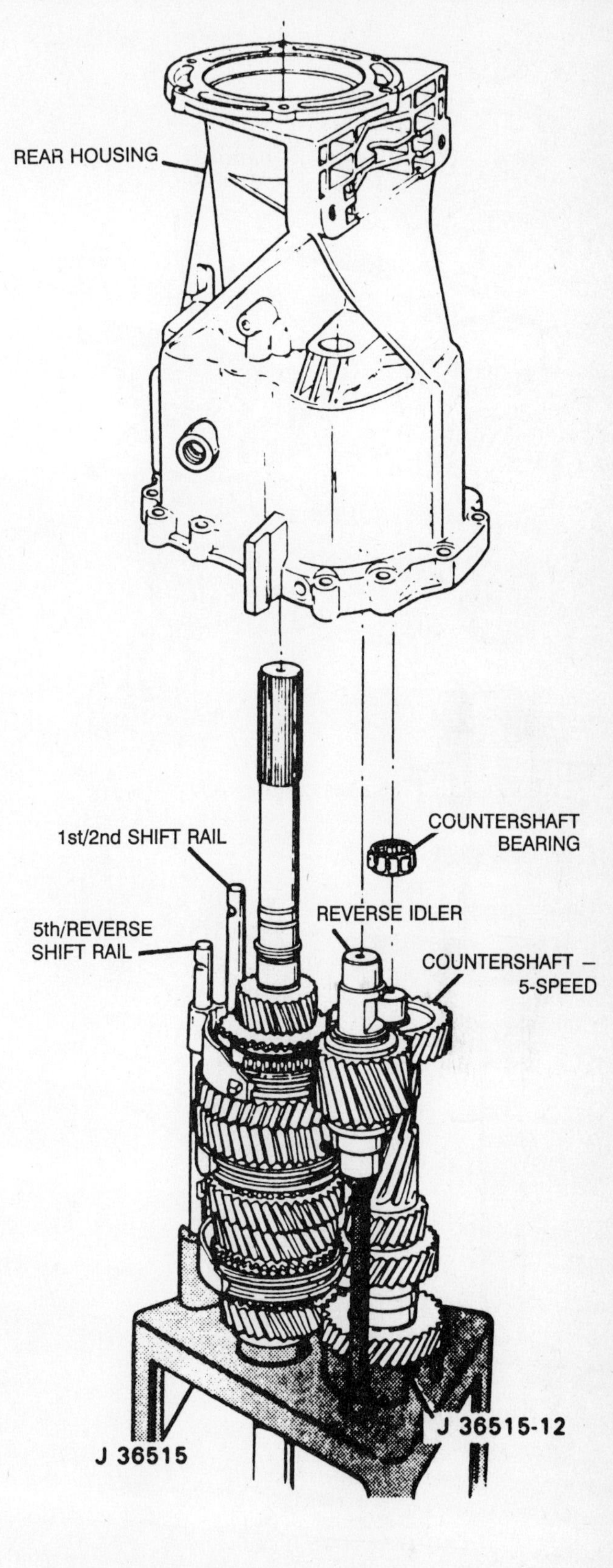

Removing the 4WD rear housing — 85mm 4- or 5-speed

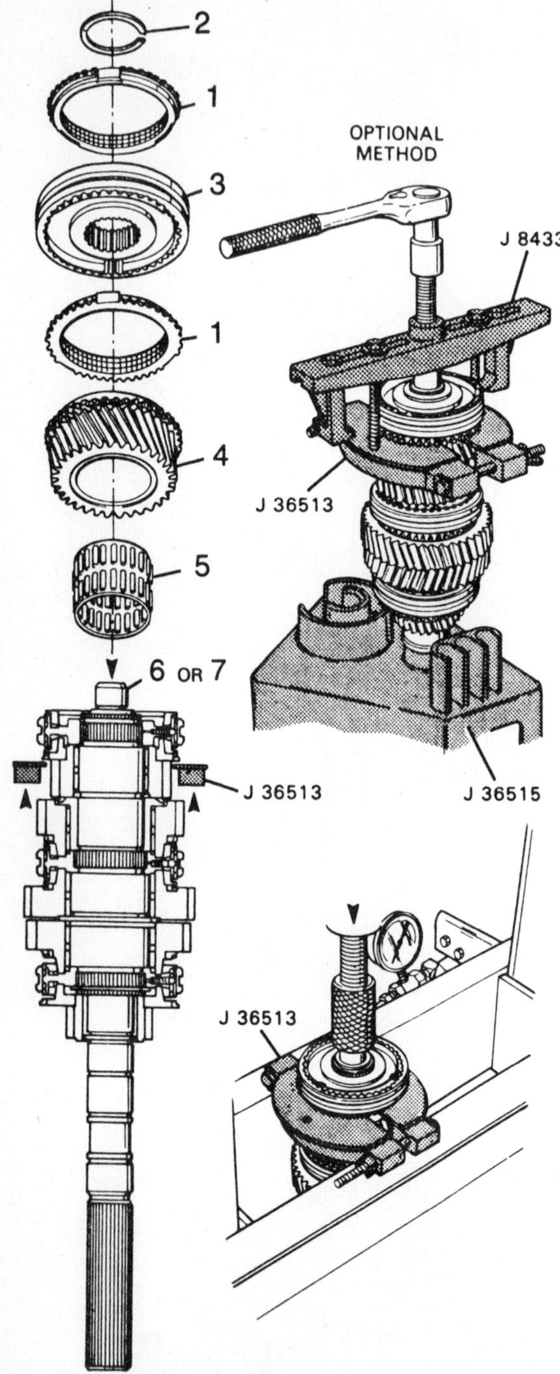

1. Synchronizer ring
2. Snapring
3. Synchronizer
4. 3rd gear
5. Needle bearing
6. Output shaft – 2wd
7. Output shaft – 4wd

Removing the 3rd/4th gear components – 85mm 4- or 5-speed

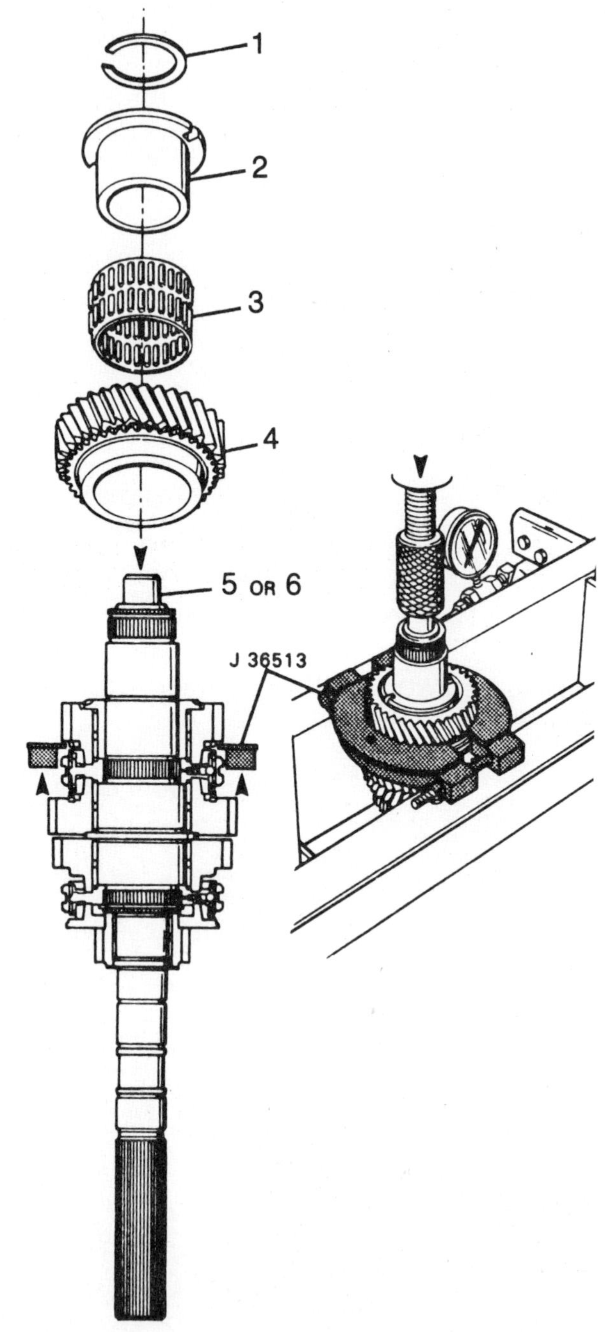

1. Snapring
2. Inner needle bearing race
3. Needle bearing
4. 2nd gear
5. Output shaft – 2wd
6. Output shaft – 4wd

Removing the 2nd gear components – 85mm 4- or 5-speed

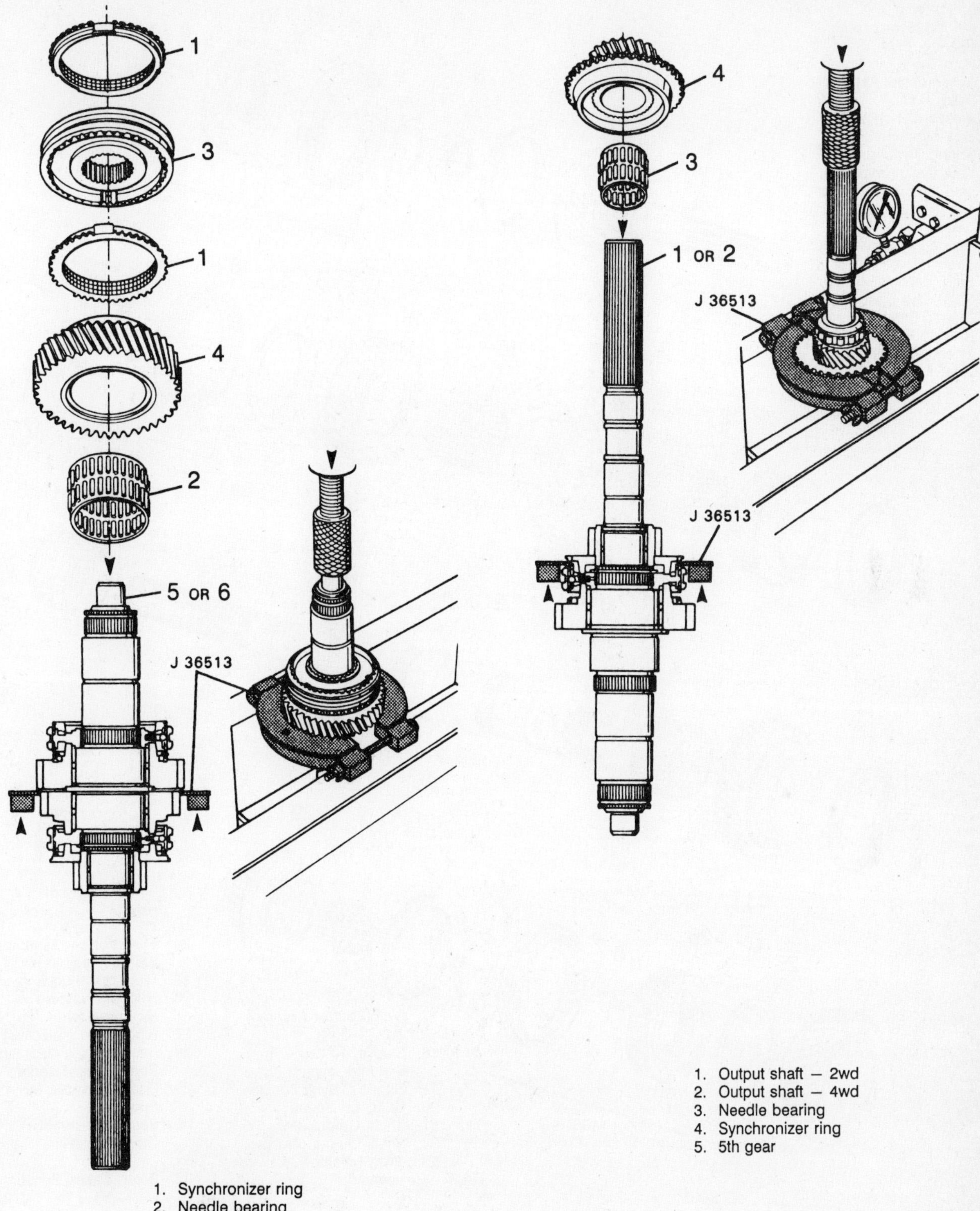

1. Synchronizer ring
2. Needle bearing
3. Synchronizer
4. 1st gear
5. Output shaft – 2wd
6. Output shaft – 4wd

Removing 1st gear components – 85mm 4- or 5-speed

1. Output shaft – 2wd
2. Output shaft – 4wd
3. Needle bearing
4. Synchronizer ring
5. 5th gear

Removing 5th gear components – 85mm 4- or 5-speed

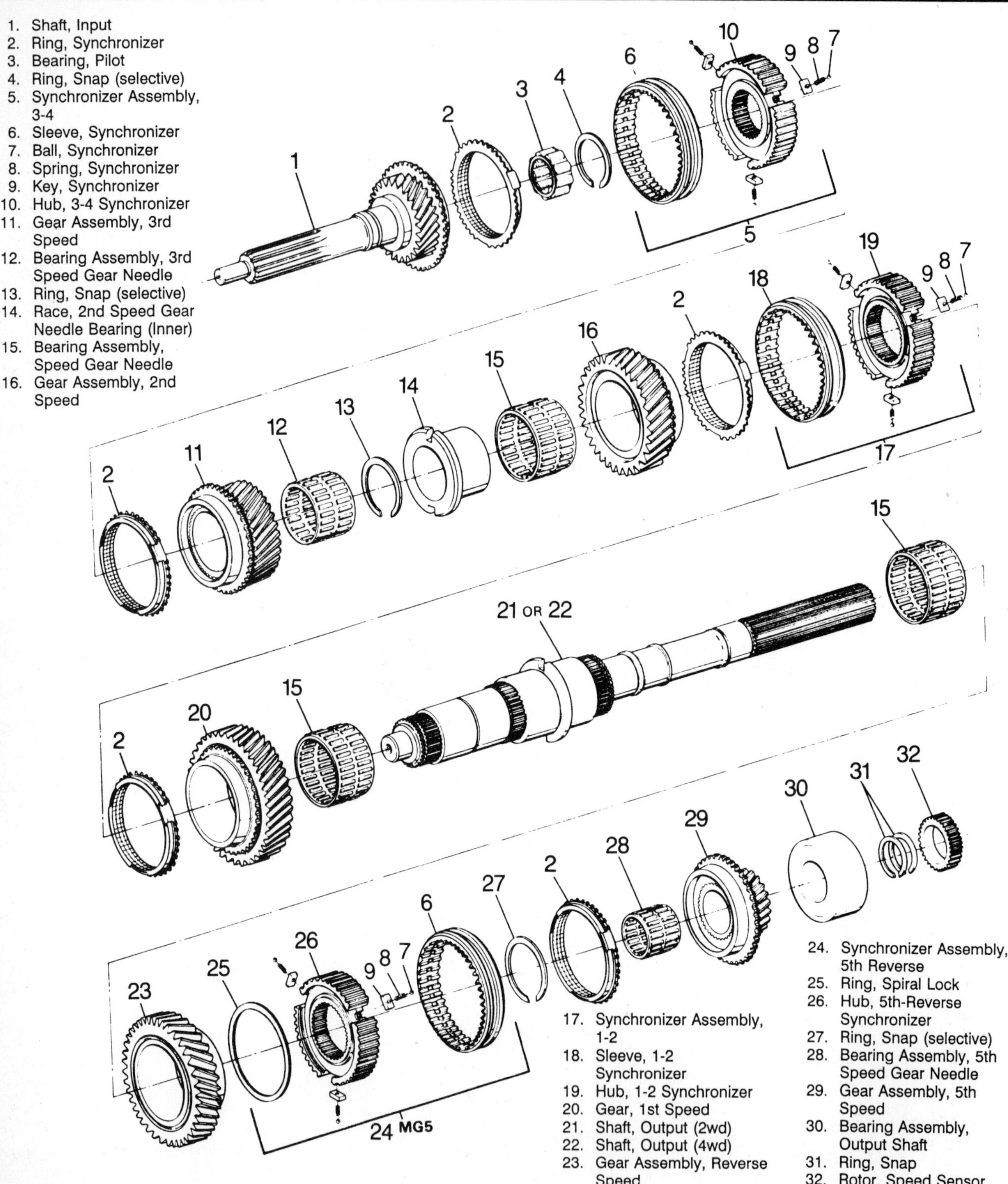
1. Shaft, Input
2. Ring, Synchronizer
3. Bearing, Pilot
4. Ring, Snap (selective)
5. Synchronizer Assembly, 3-4
6. Sleeve, Synchronizer
7. Ball, Synchronizer
8. Spring, Synchronizer
9. Key, Synchronizer
10. Hub, 3-4 Synchronizer
11. Gear Assembly, 3rd Speed
12. Bearing Assembly, 3rd Speed Gear Needle
13. Ring, Snap (selective)
14. Race, 2nd Speed Gear Needle Bearing (Inner)
15. Bearing Assembly, Speed Gear Needle
16. Gear Assembly, 2nd Speed
17. Synchronizer Assembly, 1-2
18. Sleeve, 1-2 Synchronizer
19. Hub, 1-2 Synchronizer
20. Gear, 1st Speed
21. Shaft, Output (2wd)
22. Shaft, Output (4wd)
23. Gear Assembly, Reverse Speed
24. Synchronizer Assembly, 5th Reverse
25. Ring, Spiral Lock
26. Hub, 5th-Reverse Synchronizer
27. Ring, Snap (selective)
28. Bearing Assembly, 5th Speed Gear Needle
29. Gear Assembly, 5th Speed
30. Bearing Assembly, Output Shaft
31. Ring, Snap
32. Rotor, Speed Sensor
21 OR 22
24 MG5

Maninshaft components — 85mm 4- or 5-speed

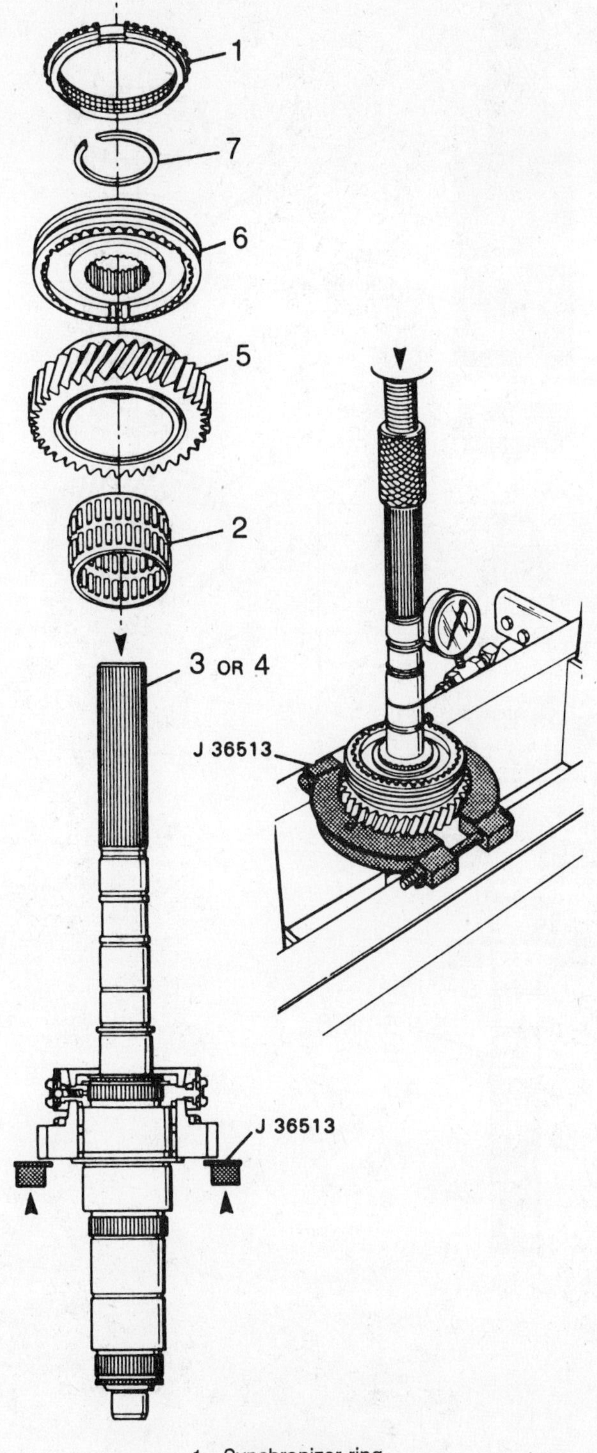

1. Synchronizer ring
2. Needle bearing
3. Output shaft – 2wd
4. Output shaft – 4wd
5. Reverse gear
6. Synchronizer
7. Snapring

Removing Reverse gear components – 85mm 4- or 5-speed

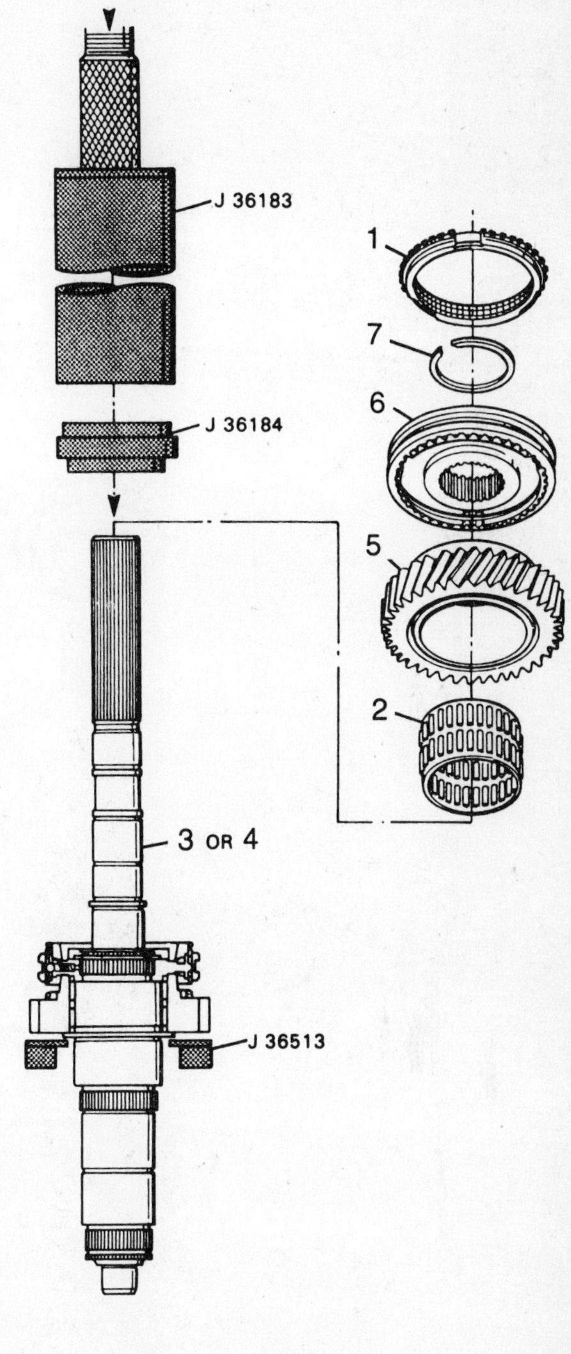

1. Synchronizer ring
2. Needle bearing
3. Output shaft – 2wd
4. Output shaft – 4wd
5. Reverse gear
6. Synchronizer
7. Snapring

Reverse gear installed – 85mm 4- or 5-speed

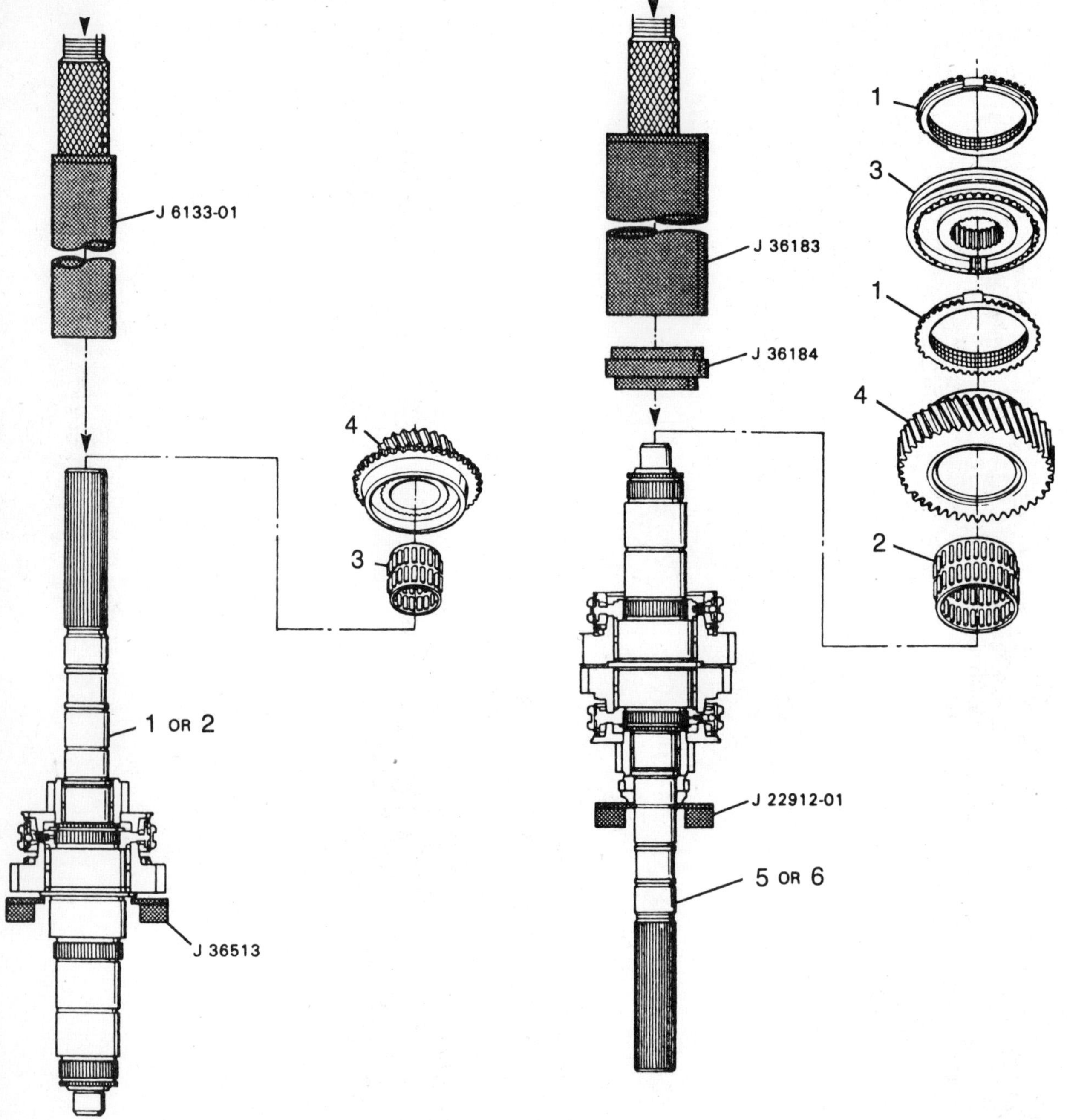

1. Output shaft – 2wd
2. Output shaft – 4wd
3. Needle bearing
4. 5th gear

5th gear installed – 85mm 4- or 5-speed

1. Synchronizer ring
2. Needle bearing
3. Synchronizer
4. 1st gear
5. Output shaft – 2wd
6. Output shaft – 4wd

1st gear installed – 85mm 4- or 5-speed

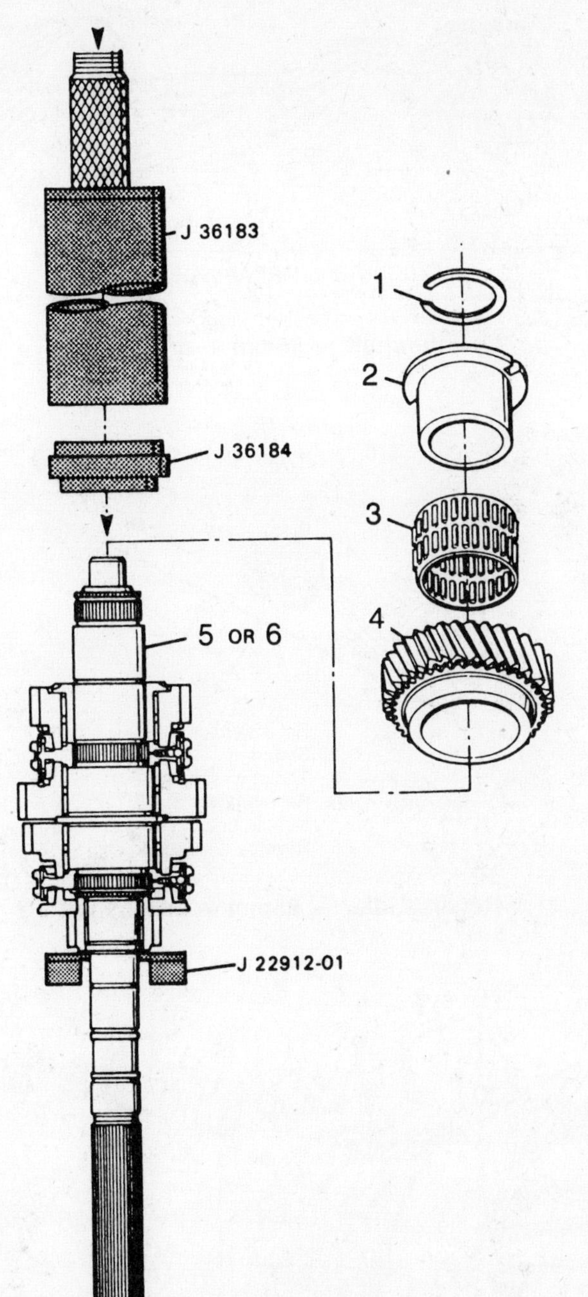

1. Snapring
2. Inner needle bearing race
3. Needle bearing
4. 2nd gear
5. Output shaft – 2wd
6. Output shaft – 4wd

2nd gear installed – 85mm 4- or 5-speed

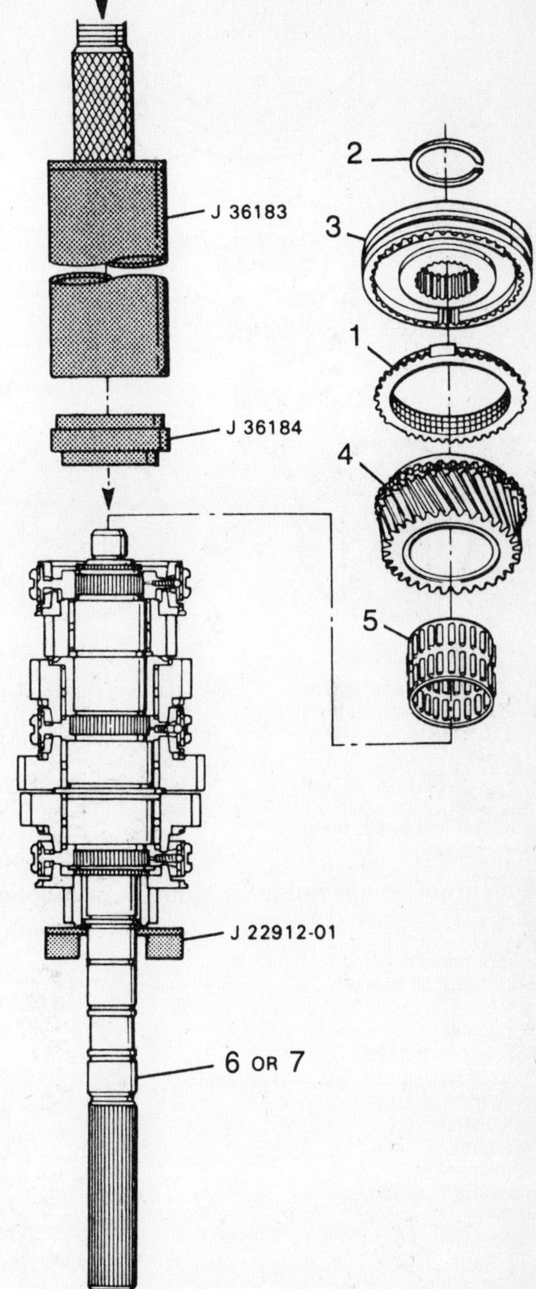

1. Synchronizer ring
2. Snapring
3. Synchronizer
4. 3rd gear
5. Needle bearing
6. Output shaft – 2wd
7. Output shaft – 4wd

3rd gear installed – 85mm 4- or 5-speed

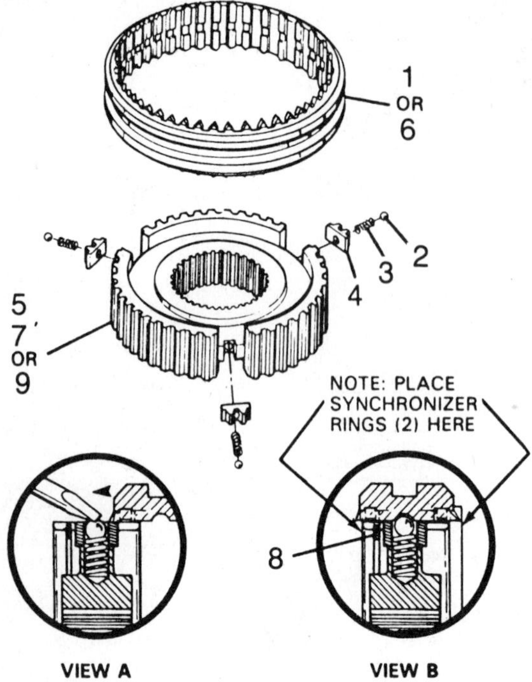

1. Synchronizer sleeve
2. Detent ball
3. Detent spring
4. Key
5. 3rd/4th synchronizer hub
6. 1st/2nd synchronizer sleeve
7. 1st/2nd synchronizer hub
8. 5th/reverse spiral lock ring
9. 5th/reverse synchronizer hub

Synchronizer assembly – 85mm 4- or 5-speed

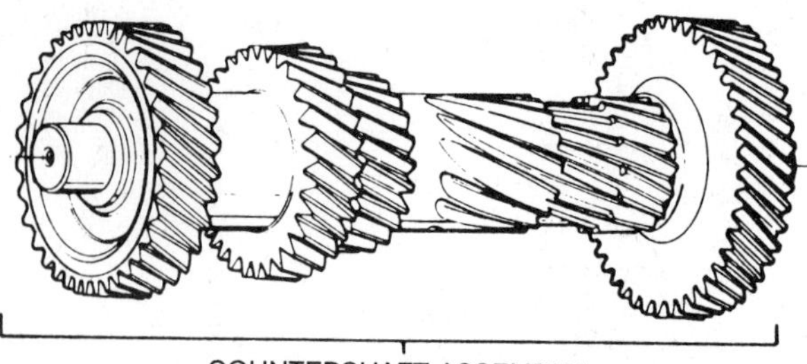

Countershaft – 85mm 4- or 5-speed

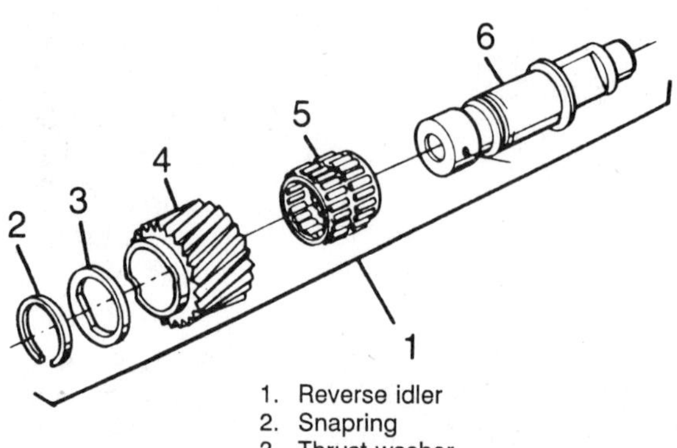

1. Reverse idler
2. Snapring
3. Thrust washer
4. Reverse gear
5. Needle bearing
6. Reverse idler shaft

Reverse idler – 85mm 4- or 5-speed

1. Front housing
2. Countershaft bearing race
3. Snapring
4. Outer bearing race
5. Clutch fork pivot
6. Lube fitting
7. Shift shaft plug
8. Fill plug
9. Breather
10. Breather hose adapter
11. Drain plug
12. Bolt
13. Locknut
14. Shift rail bearing
15. Shift shaft lever
16. Shift lever
17. Pin
18. Sleeve
19. Spring
20. Bias spring and sleeve seat
21. 5th/reverse detent cam support
22. Detent plunger bushing
23. Countershaft bearing plug
24. Snapring
25. Shims
26. Bolt

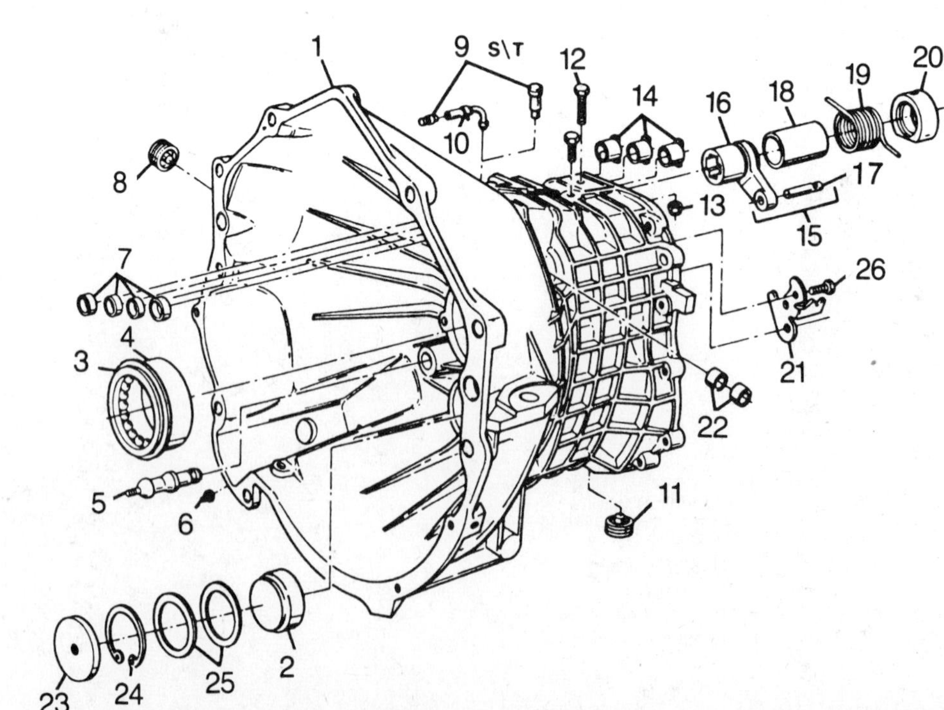

Front housing components – 85mm 4- or 5-speed

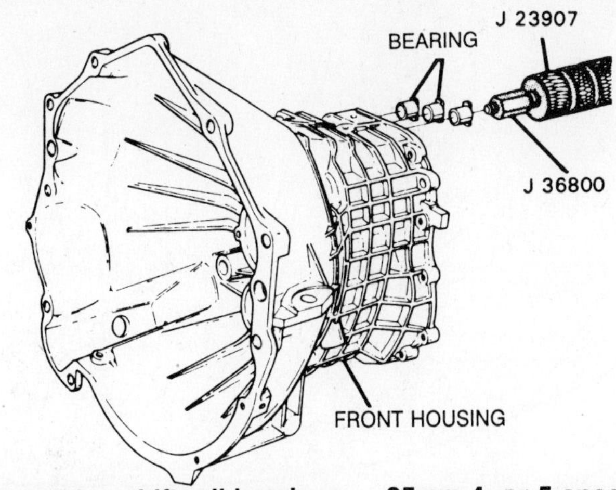

Removing shift rail bearings — 85mm 4- or 5-speed

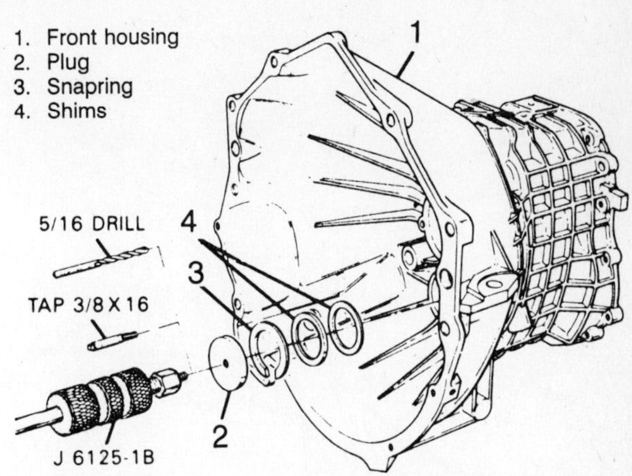

Removing the countershaft bearing plug — 85mm 4- or 5-speed

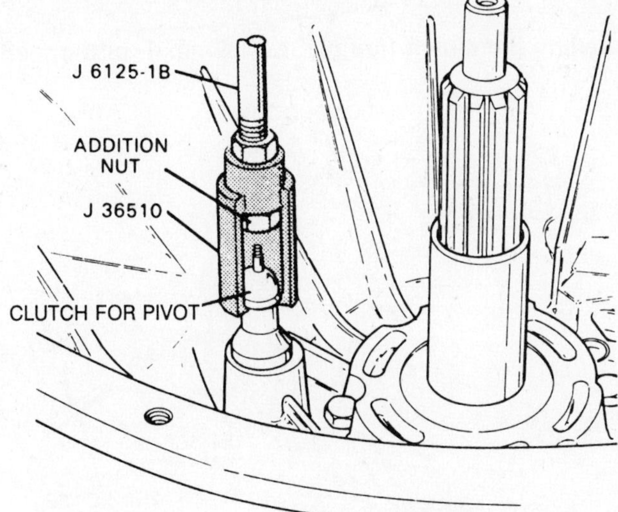

Removing clutch fork pivot — 85mm 4- or 5-speed

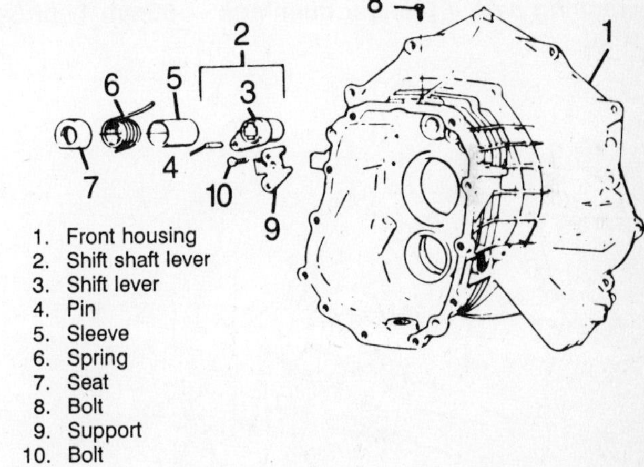

Removing bias spring components — 85mm 4- or 5-speed

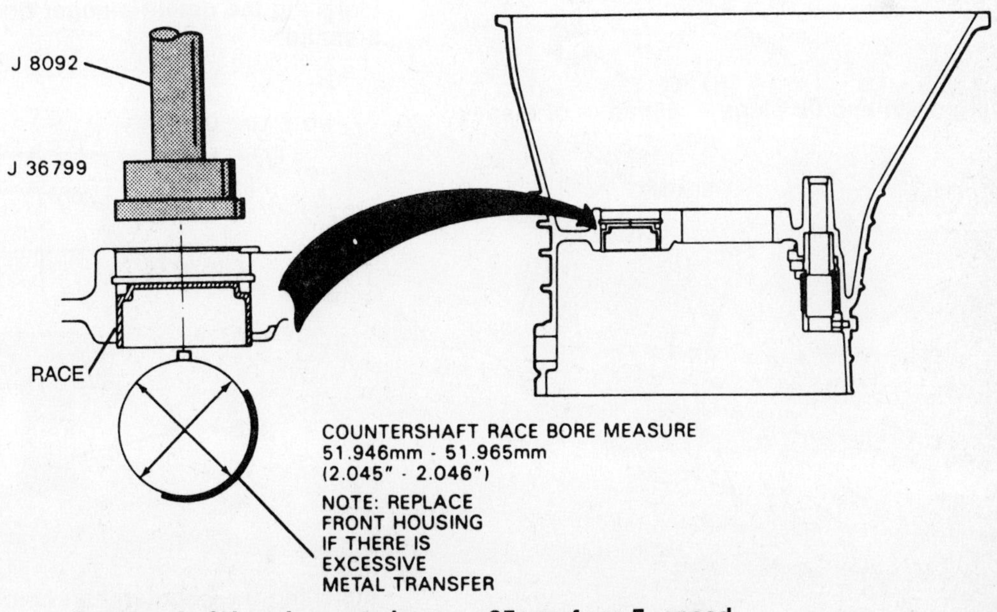

Countershaft bearing race bore — 85mm 4- or 5- speed

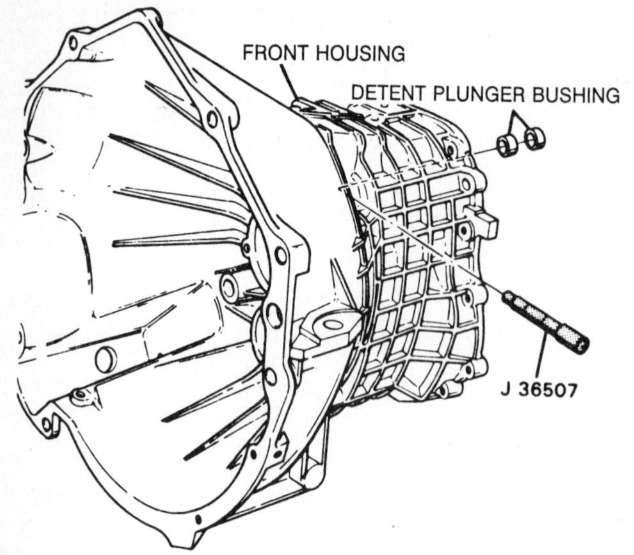

Removing detent plunger bushings – 85mm 4- or 5-speed

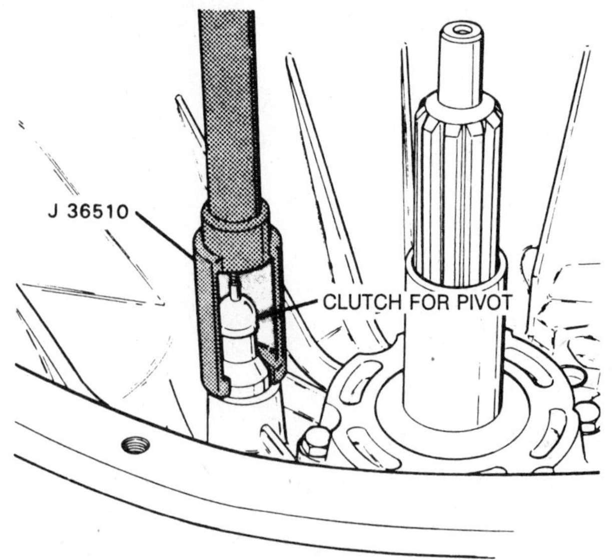

Installing the clutch fork pivot – 85mm 4- or 5-speed

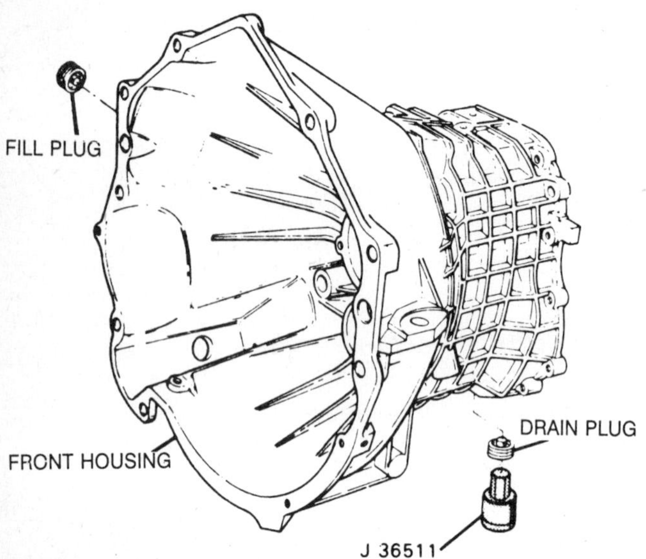

Removing drain and fill plugs – 85mm 4- or 5-speed

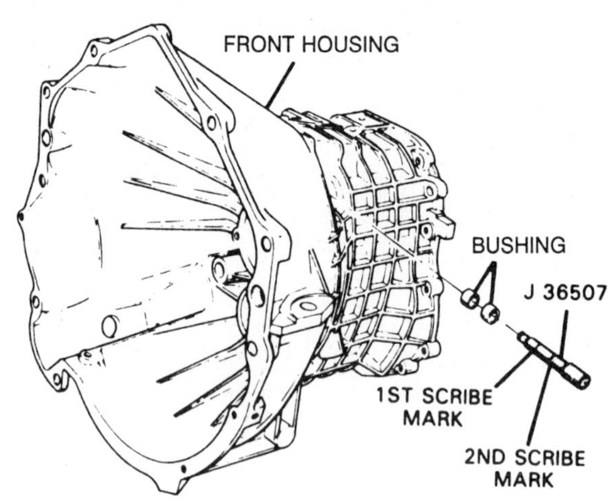

Installing the detent plunger bushings – 85mm 4- or 5-speed

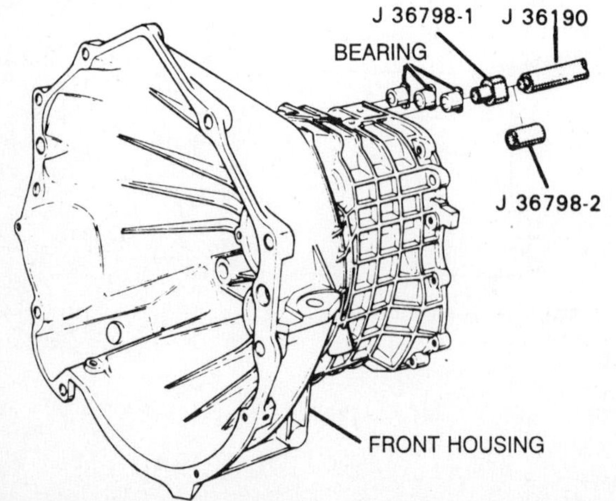

Installing shift rail bearings – 85mm 4- or 5-speed

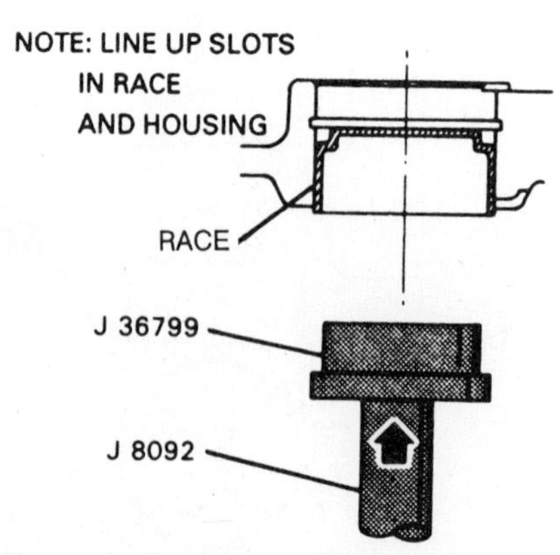

Installing the countershaft bearing race – 85mm 4- or 5-speed

85mm 5-Speed Overhaul

The following special tools, or their equivalents, will be necessary for a complete transmission overhaul: J-8763-02, J-8763-21, J-36824, J-36509, J-23907, J-36825, J-36515, J-36515-12, J-21427-01, J-8205, J-36516, J-36513, J-36183, J-36184, J-6133-01, J-22912-01, J-8001, J-25025-A, J-8092, J-36799, J-36800, J-36506, J-36507, J-36511, J-36798-1, J-36190, J-36798-2, J-36510, J-36515-10, J-36502, and a hydraulic press.

EXCEPT REAR HOUSING

1. Remove idler shaft support and 2 bottom bolts for special tools.
2. Support the transmission with holding fixtures J-8763-02, J-8763-21 and J-36824 or equivalent.
3. Remove backup lamp switch assembly.
4. Remove the electronic speed sensor assembly.
5. Remove detent plug, spring and plunger using removal tool J-36509 and J-23907 or equivalent.
6. Remove the detent spring cover 2 attaching bolts and remove cover, detent springs and 3 detent/interlock balls.

NOTE: It may be necessary to remove sealant from inside of holes to remove the balls.

7. On 2-Wheel Drive vehicles, remove the output shaft oil seal using tool J-36825 and J-23907 or equivalent. On 4-Wheel Drive vehicles, screw J-36825 into 1 of the 3 perforated holes in the seal and remove seal.
8. Rotate the transmission in a vertical position.
9. Remove the 6 input shaft bearing retainer attaching bolts and remove retainer assembly.
   a. Tap on clutch release bearing pilot with a rubber hammer.
   b. Save the input bearing retainer washer.
10. Remove snapring (selective), input shaft spacer, ball bearing inner race and shim.
11. Position the transmission horizontally.
12. Remove front housing to rear housing attaching bolts.
13. Drive dowels into front housing and remove housing.
14. Remove the countershaft bearing.
15. Remove bearing inner race and roller bearing.

NOTE: Degreasing with a liquid cleaner will make the bearing easier to remove. Grab the outer diameter edge of the inner race and remove with large pliers. Do not damage bearing cage while removing bearing inner race.

16. Remove idler shaft support.
17. Remove 4 rollers. Pull shift shaft forward and cock to detent cover side and remove roll pin. Support the shift shaft end while driving out finger roll pin.
18. Remove shift shaft socket assembly roll pin.
19. Remove shift shaft, shift shaft socket assembly and finger.
20. With a pair of diagonal cutters, pry out 3rd and 4th shift fork roll pin. If the roll pin breaks off, put the transmission into 3rd gear, cut the remainder of pin and drive through rail.
21. Remove the 3rd/4th rail plug by hitting on one side, allowing it to cock.
22. Remove the 3rd/4th rail and detent/interlock balls.

REAR HOUSING ASSEMBLY

2-Wheel Drive Trucks

1. Support transmission assembly on tool J-36515 and J-36515-12 or equivalent. Remove holding fixtures J-36824, J-8763-02 and J-8763-21 or equivalent.
2. Remove rear housing mounting bolts. Alternately tap upward on rear housing with a rubber mallet and remove housing assembly.
3. Remove shim (selective) from housing.
4. Lock up assembly in 2nd/4th gear by sliding the 1st/2nd rail and the 3rd/4th shift fork downward against tool.
5. Slide the snapring and washer from speed sensor rotor to provide clearance for special tools.
6. Install speedometer gear puller adapter J-21427-01 and J-8205 or equivalent, on mainshaft and remove speed sensor rotor. Remove snapring and washer.

NOTE: Do not reuse rotor after removal.

7. Remove the sprial roll pin from mainshaft using spanner nut wrench J-36516 or equivalent.
   a. Position the black depth locating tang for the spiral roll pin remover/installer for clearance and drive downward.
   b. Position the black depth locating tang back into place with the rod going through it.
   c. Rotate spanner nut wrench J-36516 or equivalent clockwise until it stops.
8. Remove the threaded thrust ring (inner), ball and threaded thrust ring (outer) from mainshaft.
   a. Hold the countershaft against the mainshaft.
   b. Rotate spanner nut wrench J-36516 or equivalent clockwise until both threaded thrust rings are completely apart.
9. Remove the reverse idler gear and countershaft.
10. Remove 1st/2nd shift rail assembly, 5th/reverse shift rail assembly and 3rd/4th shift fork.
11. Remove the mainshaft assembly.

NOTE: Leave the synchronizer ring on the 3rd/4th synchronizer assembly to prevent the synchronizer detent balls from popping out.

12. Remove the input shaft gear and pilot bearing.

4-Wheel Drive

1. Lock up the transmission in 2nd/4th gear by sliding the 1st/2nd shift rail assembly and 3rd/4th shift fork downward against tool.
2. Remove the spiral roll pin using spanner nut wrench J-36516 or equivalent.
   a. Position the black depth locating tang for the spiral roll pin remover/installer for clearance and drive downward.
   b. Position the black depth locating tang back into place with the rod going through it.
   c. Rotate spanner nut wrench J-36516 or equivalent clockwise until it stops.
3. Remove the threaded thrust ring (inner), ball and threaded thrust ring (outer) from mainshaft. Rotate spanner nut wrench J-36516 or equivalent clockwise until both threaded thrust rings are completely apart.
4. Remove the rear housing by alternately tapping upward on rear housing with a rubber mallet and remove housing assembly.
5. Save the ball bearing outer race that will be left in the rear housing.
6. Remove the countershaft bearing, countershaft and reverse idler assembly.
7. Remove 5th/reverse shift rail assembly, 1st/2nd shift rail assembly and 3rd/4th shift fork.

NOTE: Leave the synchronizer ring on the 3rd/4th synchronizer assembly to prevent the synchronizer detent balls from popping out.

8. Remove the input shaft gear and pilot bearing.

MAINSHAFT DISASSEMBLY

1. Remove snapring (selective) from mainshaft.

2. Using bearing separator plate J–36513 or equivalent and a hydraulic press, remove 3rd/4th synchronizer assembly, synchronizer rings and 3rd speed gear.

NOTE: Mark the hub and sleeve so they can be installed in the same position. Also, leave the synchronizer rings to prevent the synchronizer detent balls from popping out.

3. Remove the 3rd gear bearing.
4. Remove the snapring (selective).
5. Using bearing separator plate J–36513 or equivalent and a hydraulic press, remove 2nd speed gear assembly and 2nd speed gear bearing race.
6. Remove the bearing assembly. Leave the synchronizer ring on the 1st/2nd synchronizer assembly to prevent the synchronizer detent balls from popping out.
7. Using bearing separator plate J–36513 or equivalent and a hydraulic press, remove the 1st speed gear and 1st/2nd synchronizer assembly.

NOTE: Mark the hub and sleeve so they can be installed in the same position. Also, leave the synchronizer rings on the 1st/2nd synchronizer assembly to prevent the synchronizer detent balls from popping out.

8. Remove the bearing assembly.
9. Using bearing separator plate J–36513 and a hydraulic press, remove the inner ball bearing race, roller bearing, roller bearing race and 5th speed gear.
10. Remove the 5th speed gear bearing.
11. Remove snapring (selective).
12. Using bearing separator plate J–36513 and a hydraulic press, remove reverse speed gear assembly and 5th/reverse synchronizer asembly.

NOTE: Mark the hub and sleeve so they can be installed in the same position. Also, leave the synchronizer rings on the 5th/reverse synchronizer assembly to prevent the synchronizer detent balls from popping out.

13. Remove the bearing assembly.
14. Place the 1st/2nd, 3rd/4th and 5th speed synchronizers in separate shop towels, wrap assemblies and press against inner hub.

Inspection

1. Wash all parts in a suitable solvent and air dry.

NOTE: Do not spin dry the ball bearings.

2. Inspect all gears for cracks, chipped gear teeth, thrust face surfaces, bearing surface diameters and other damage.

NOTE: The black phosphate coating will develop wear patterns, this is a normal condition.

3. Inspect synchronizer sleeves for a sliding fit on synchronizer hubs and hubs to have a force fit on the mainshaft splines.
4. Inspect the synchronizer springs, keys and rings for wear or other damage.
5. Inspect the synchronizer clutching teeth for wear, scuffed, nicked, burred or broken teeth.
6. Inspect gear clutching cones for synchronizer ring metal transfer.
7. Inspect the bearings and bearing surfaces for nicks, burrs, bent cages and wear.
9. Lubricate all bearings with light engine oil and check for rough rotation.
   a. If scuffed, nicked, burred, scoring, or synchronizer ring metal transfer conditions cannot be removed with a soft cloth, replace the component and inspect mating parts.
   b. Lubricate all components with 5W–30 oil or equivalent.

MAINSHAFT ASSEMBLY

NOTE: Prior to installation, heat the roller bearing race, ball bearing inner race and the speed sensor rotor (2-Wheel Drive) for a period of 7–10 minutes at 250°F (121°C) and 2nd speed gear race for a period of 20 minutes minimum, at 250°F (121°C).

1. Install 1st/2nd gear synchronizer assembly and 3rd/4th gear synchronizer assembly.
2. Install 5th/reverse gear synchronizer assembly.
3. Install bearing assembly and reverse speed gear.

NOTE: When pressing the 5th/reverse synchronizer assembly, manually align and engage the splines. Press synchronizer until seated. Make certain all shavings are removed.

4. Using tools J–36183, J–36184, J–36513 or equivalents and a hydraulic press, install 5th/reverse synchronizer assembly with synchronizer ring.
   a. Align marks made previously, for correct positions.
   b. Install the unit with the spiral lock ring in the hub towards the reverse speed gear.
5. Install a new selective snapring.

NOTE: Install the thickest snapring that will fit in the groove.

6. Install bearing assembly and 5th speed gear.

NOTE: Press the bearing races onto the mainshaft until there is no clearance between roller bearing race and stop on mainshaft.

7. Using tool J–6133–01 and bearing separator plate J–36513 or equivalent and a hydraulic press, install the roller bearing race. Shoulder down towards reverse gear.
8. Using tool J–6133–01, J–36513 or equivalent and a hydraulic press, install roller bearing and inner ball bearing race.
   a. Apply grease to roller bearing.
   b. Smaller diameter of bearing cage up.
   c. Shoulder of inner ball bearing race down towards reverse gear.
9. Install bearing assembly and 1st speed gear.
   a. When pressing 1st/2nd synchronizer assembly, manually align and engage splines.
   b. Start pressing and stop before tangs engage.
   c. Lift and rotate gear to engage synchronizer ring.
   d. Press until seated.
   e. Make certain all shavings are removed.
10. Using tools J–36183, J–36184, J–22912–01 and a hydraulic press, install 1st/2nd synchronizer assembly with both synchronizer rings.
   a. Align marks made previously, for correct positions.
   b. Groove on outside of sleeve must go toward the 2nd speed gear to prevent gear clash during 1st and 2nd gear shifts (teeth on sleeve have different angles).
11. Install bearing assembly and 2nd speed gear. Make sure bearing cage is together.
12. Using tools J–36183, J–36184, J–22912–01 and a hydraulic press, install 2nd gear race (Heated).
13. Install a new selective snapring. Install the thickest snapring that will fit in the groove.
14. Install bearing assembly and 3rd speed gear.
   a. When pressing 3rd/4th synchronizer assembly, manually align and engage splines.
   b. Start pressing and stop before tangs engage.
   c. Lift and rotate gear to engage synchronizer ring.
   d. Press until seated.
   e. Make certain all shavings are removed.
15. Using tools J–36183, J–36184, J–22912–01 and a hydraulic press, install 3rd/4th synchronizer assembly with both syn-

chronizer rings. Align marks made previously, for correct positions.

16. Install a new selective snapring. Install the thickest snapring that will fit in the groove.

REVERSE IDLER UNIT DISASSEMBLY

1. Remove snapring.
2. Remove thrust washer, ball, reverse gear, 3 bearing assemblies and O-ring.

Inspection

1. Wash all parts in a suitable solvent.
2. Inspect gear teeth for scuffed, nicked, burred or broken teeth.
3. Inspect bearing assemblies for roughness while rotating, burred or pitted condition and gage damage.
4. Inspect the shaft for scoring, wear or overheating.

NOTE: If scuffed, nicked, burred or scoring conditions cannot be removed with a soft stone or crocus cloth, replace the component.

REVERSE IDLER UNIT ASSEMBLY

1. Lubricate all components with 5W–30 oil or equivalent.
2. Install the 3 bearing assembly.
3. Install the reverse gear. The extended part of the hub faces the thrust washer.
4. Install the thrust washer and ball. Retain ball with petroleum jelly.
5. Install a new snapring and O-ring.

COUNTERSHAFT DISASSEMBLY

NOTE: If the 5th gear cannot be pressed off the countershaft, replace the complete assembly.

Inspection

1. Wash all parts in a suitable solvent.
2. Inspect countershaft for cracks.
3. Inspect bearings for roughness while rotating, burred or pitted condition.
4. Inspect bearing races for scoring, wear or overheating.
5. Inspect gear teeth for scuffed, nicked, burred or broken teeth.

NOTE: If scuffed, nicked, burred or scoring conditions cannot be removed with a soft stone or crocus cloth, replace the component.

COUNTERSHAFT ASSEMBLY

1. Install 5th gear to countershaft assembly or replace assembly, if necessary.
2. Lubricate assembly with 5W–30 oil or equivalent.

ENDPLAY ADJUSTMENT

NOTE: This procedure must be performed if the countershaft bearings, front housing countershaft bearing race or the front or rear housing was replaced. If a gear rattle noise complaint (not clutch disc related) is experienced, it is recommended the countershaft endplay be checked.

1. Remove bearing race using a brass drift.
2. Remove the countershaft bearing plug.
3. Remove the snapring, shims and oil fill plug.
4. Inspect bearing and countershaft.
   a. Smaller diameter of bearing cage into bearing race.
   b. Install bearings in bearing races prior to assembly and retain with petroleum jelly.
5. Install tools J–8001 and J–25025–A or equivalent, to front housing in one of the input shaft bearing retainer bolt holes.
   a. Use a pry bar, pry the countershaft upward, noting the dial indicator travel. Use the fill plug hole to reach the third gear part of the countershaft for prying.
   b. Measure off gear tooth.
   c. Make certain tool J–8001 stays on gear tooth while measuring endplay.
   d. Allow the countershaft to lower to its original position, noting the dial indicator travel. Total travel should be 0.005–0.009 in. (0.13–0.23mm).
6. Move bearing race with tool J–8092 and J–36799 or equivalent to achieve specified endplay.
7. Use the least number of shims to retain specified endplay and install snapring.
8. Seat the countershaft bearing race using tool J–8092 and J–36799 or equivalent.
9. Recheck Step 5a–7 to make sure endplay is still correct after seating countershaft bearing race.
10. Install oil fill plug.
11. Install a new countershaft bearing plug. Apply gasket maker GM part number 1052943 or equivalent to outer edge of plug.

NOTE: The countershaft bearing plug will require cooling for 20 minutes minimum, at 32°F (0°C) prior to installation during assembly.

FRONT HOUSING DISASSEMBLY

1. Using a brass drift, remove ball bearing assembly outer race.
2. Using tools J–36800 and J–23907 or equivalent, remove the 3 shift rail front housing bearings.
3. Using tools J–36509 and J–23907 or equivalent, remove clutch fork pivot assembly.
4. Use a punch and drive out shift shaft/rail plugs.
5. Remove countershaft bearing plug.
   a. Destake plug first.
   b. Screw a ⅜–16 bottom tap into the plug and remove with tool J–6725 or equivalent.
6. Using tools J–36799 and J–8092 or equivalent, remove snapring, shims and countershaft bearing race.
   a. Tap in countershaft bearing race before removing snapring.
   b. Check countershaft endplay adjustment, if countershaft bearing race is removed.
   c. Measure the countershaft bearing race bore in 2 locations diagonally, 0.157 in. (4mm) in from inside of transmission housing. If the housing bore is not within 2.045–2.046 in. (51.946–51.965mm), replace the housing.
7. Remove 5th/reverse detent hex head plug, 5th/reverse detent spring and 5th/reverse detent plunger assembly.
8. Remove detent cam bolt, washer, 5th/reverse cam and bushing. Using a flat blade type tool, release tension of bias spring from end of shift lever pin.

CAUTION

The spring is under considerable tension. Be careful when removing it!

9. Remove bias spring bolt, bias spring and sleeve seat, bias spring, bias spring sleeve, shift shaft lever assembly and detent roller.
10. Remove detent cam support bolt and remove detent cam support.
11. Using tool J–36506, remove the 2 5th/reverse detent bushings.
12. Using tool J–36507, remove the 2 detent bushings. Remove 1 bushing at a time.

13. Remove the breather assembly. Metal tube must remain in case.
14. Remove drain and fill plugs using tool J-36511 or equivalent.

Inspection

1. Clean all gasket material from case using liquid gasket remover.
2. Clean all parts in a suitable solvent and air dry.
3. Inspect the bearing race bore for wear, scratches or grooves. If countershaft bearing race is worn or damaged, the rear housing must be replaced.
4. Inspect bushings for scores, burrs, roundness or evidence of overheating.
5. Inspect the case for cracks, damaged threads, mounting surfaces for nicks, burrs, or scratches. If the case is crack, it must be replaced.
6. Using a straight edge, check machined surfaces for flatness.

NOTE: If scuffed, nicked, burred or scoring conditions cannot be removed with a soft stone or crocus cloth, replace the component. Clean-up damaged threads with the correct size tap.

FRONT HOUSING ASSEMBLY

NOTE: If the countershaft bearing plug was removed, it will require cooling for a period of 20 minutes minumum, at 32°F (0°C) before installation.

1. Using a brass driff, install the ball bearing outer race.
2. Using tools J-36798–1 and J-36190 or equivalent, install 3 shift rail front housing bearings. Install until flush and stake using tools J-36798–1, J-36798–2 and J-36190 or equivalent. Do not stake the tabs on the bushings.
3. Using tools J-36190 and J-36510 or equivalent, install the clutch fork pivot assembly. Grease assembly after installation through lube fitting.
4. Using tool J-36507 or equivalent, install 2 detent plunger bushings.
   a. Install 1 bushing at a time.
   b. Install the first bushing until the second scribe mark on the tool lines up with the housing.
   c. Install the second bushing until the first scribe mark on the tool lines up with the housing.
5. Using tools J-36799 and J-8092 or equivalent, install countershaft bearing race. Align lube slot in race with groove in the housing. Install shims and snapring.

NOTE: If the countershaft bearing races, countershaft bearings, countershaft or front or rear housing are replaced, the countershaft endplay must be checked.

6. Using tools J-36799 and J-8092 or equivalent, install a new countershaft bearing plug. Apply gasket maker GM part number 1052943 or equivalent, to the outside edge of the plug and stake in 3 places evenly apart.
7. Using tool J-36506, install both 5th/reverse detent bushings.
   a. Install 1 bushing at a time.
   b. Install the first bushing until the second scribe mark on the tool lines up with the housing.
   c. Install the second bushing until the first scribe mark on the tool lines up with the housing.
8. Install detent cam support and bolt. Torque bolt to 7 ft. lbs. (8.5 Nm).
9. Install 5th/reverse cam, bushing, washer and bolt. Torque bolt to 7 ft. lbs. (8.5 Nm).
10. Install detent roller on shift shaft lever assembly and install into housing.
11. Install bias spring sleeve, bias load torsional spring, bias spring and sleeve seat and bolt. Torque bolt to 7 ft. lbs. (8.5 Nm).
12. Install bias load torsional spring end back onto shift shaft lever pin.
13. Install 5th/reverse plunger assembly, 5th/reverse detent spring and hex head plug.
    a. Make certain the slot in the plunger is lined up with the reverse cam.
    b. Use pipe sealant GM part number 1052080 or equivalent on the threads.
    c. Torque hex head plug to 46 ft. lbs. (60 Nm).
14. Install breather assembly, oil fill plug and drain plug. Apply pipe sealant GM part number 1052080 or equivalent on threads and torque drain plug to 46 ft. lbs. (60 Nm).
15. Install shift shaft/rails plugs until flush. Apply gasket maker GM part number 1052943 or equivalent to the edge of plugs.

SHIFT SHAFT/RAIL AND FORK

Inspection

1. Wash all parts in a suitable solvent and air dry.
2. Inspect 1st/2nd shift rail, 3rd/4th rail, 5th/reverse rail and shift shaft for wear or scoring.
3. Inspect 1st/2nd shift fork, 3rd/4th shift fork and 5th/reverse shift fork for wear, scoring or distortion. Black coloring on the edge of forks is a normal condition.
4. Inspect 1st/2nd shift yoke and finger for wear or distortion.
5. Inspect both pins for wear or distortion.
6. Inspect shift shaft socket aassembly for wear or distortion.

NOTE: Wear, scoring or distortion requires replacement of assembly and inspection of mating parts.

SELECTIVE SHIMIMG PROCEDURE

Input Shaft Bearing Retainer

1. Measure the distance between the sealing flange of the retainer and the flanged part of the release guide. Record this measurement.
2. Measure the height of the input bearing outer race from the sealing surface of the front housing. Record this measurement.
3. Subtract the bearing race height from the retainer depth and select a shim the same (or next smaller) size as the difference in measurements.

Output Shaft Bearing

1. Measure the distance between the bearing retainer surface and the bottom of the bearing bore in the rear housing. Record this measurement.
2. Measure the width of the mainshaft rear bearing. Record this measurement.
3. Subtract the bearing width from the housing bore depth. Select a shim which is the same (or next smaller) size as the difference in measurements.

REAR HOUSING ASSEMBLY

2-Wheel Drive

1. Install the pilot bearing into input shaft with the smaller diameter of bearing cage toward input shaft. Retain with petroleum jelly.
2. Assemble the input shaft, pilot bearing, synchronizer ring and mainshaft assembly on fixture J-36515 or equivalent.
3. Assemble adapter J-36515-12 or equivalent on countershaft and install assembly onto fixture J-36515 or equivalent.
4. Install the reverse idler assembly using a new O-ring.

5. Install bearing assembly outer race and ball bearing outer race.

6. Install on the mainshaft assembly:

a. 3rd/4th shift fork with taper on fork towards 3rd gear.

b. Lock up the transmission by sliding the 3rd/4th shift fork and 1st/2nd shift rail assembly downward towards fixture J-36515 or equivalent.

7. Install ball to output shaft and retain with petroleum jelly.

8. Install the inner threaded thrust ring and outer threaded thrust ring. Make certain the old spiral roll pin is removed from the outer threaded thrust ring.

a. Completely screw the rings together, then back off of rings until both identification slots for the ball line up.

b. Slide the assembled rings over the ball that is retained on the output shaft.

c. Slide the rod up on spanner nut wrench J-36516 or equivalent, turn the black depth locating tang over, slide the rod through so the roll pin will be installed to the correct depth.

d. Allow clearance for the snapring by screwing the rings together counterclockwise with spanner nut wrench J-36516 or equivalent.

9. Install a new snapring.

10. Turn spanner nut wrench J-36516 or equivalent clockwise to obtain a torque of 12 ft. lbs. (15 Nm), then advance to the next sprial roll pin notch.

11. Install a new spiral roll pin into spanner nut wrench J-36516 or equivalent and retain with petroleum jelly. Lined up roll pin and drive pin into outer thrust ring.

12. Install the snapring and speedo gear thrust washer.

13. Install the speed sensor rotor. Rotor must be heated.

14. Install shim onto output shaft bearing assembly and retain with pertroleum jelly.

NOTE: The rear housing output shaft bearing assembly bore must be heated for 3–5 minutes before assembly.

15. Install retainer alignment cables J-36515-10 or equivalent, through bolt and holes in rear housing.

a. Install the screw into the output shaft bearing retainer.

b. The notch in the retainer is installed towards the oil delivery tube.

16. Install bearing in bearing race of housing and retain with petroleum jelly. The smaller diameter of bearing cage into bearing race.

NOTE: Press each roller towards the race to secure them for easier assembly.

17. Install the rear housing assembly.

a. Make certain the reverse idler shaft is lined up with the hole in the case.

b. Rotate back and forth while pulling down.

c. Pull up on retainer alignment cables J-36515-10 or equivalent, while installing rear housing.

NOTE: Bring the housing straight down. If resistance is felt at about ¼ in. (6mm), the rollers are cocked. Repeat procedure above. Do not force housing down.

18. Remove tool J-36515-10 or equivalent and install bolts. Apply pipe sealant GM part number 1052080 or equivalent to bolt holes of rear housing. Apply threadlocker GM part number 12345382 or equivalent to bolt threads. Torque bolts to 17 ft. lbs. (22 Nm).

4-Wheel Drive

1. Install the pilot bearing into input shaft with the smaller diameter of bearing cage toward input shaft. Retain with petroleum jelly.

2. Assemble the input shaft, pilot bearing, synchronizer ring and mainshaft assembly on fixture J-36515 or equivalent.

3. Assemble adapter J-36515-12 or equivalent on countershaft and install assembly onto fixture J-36515 or equivalent.

4. Install the reverse idler assembly using a new O-ring.

5. Install bearing assembly outer race and ball bearing outer race.

6. Install on the mainshaft assembly:

a. 3rd/4th shift fork with taper on fork towards 3rd gear.

b. Lock up the transmission by sliding the 3rd/4th shift fork and 1st/2nd shift rail assembly downward towards fixture J-36515 or equivalent.

7. Install bearing in bearing race of housing and retain with petroleum jelly. Smaller diameter of bearing cage into bearing race.

NOTE: Press each roller towards the race to secure them for easier assembly.

8. Install the rear housing assembly. Make certain the reverse idler shaft is lined up with hole in the case. Rotate back and forth while pulling down.

NOTE: Bring the housing straight down. If resistance is felt at about ¼ in. (6mm), the rollers are cocked. Repeat procedure above. Do not force housing down.

9. Install the outer bearing race and ball. Retain ball with petroleum jelly.

10. Install the inner threaded thrust ring and outer threaded thrust ring. Make certain the old spiral roll pin is removed from the outer threaded thrust ring.

a. Completely screw the rings together, then back off of rings until both identification slots for the ball line up.

b. Slide the assembled rings over the ball that is retained on the output shaft.

c. Slide the rod up on spanner nut wrench J-36516 or equivalent, turn the black depth locating tang over, slide the rod through so the roll pin will be installed to the correct depth.

d. Allow clearance for the snapring by screwing the rings together counterclockwise with spanner nut wrench J-36516 or equivalent.

11. Install a new snapring.

12. Turn spanner nut wrench J-36516 or equivalent clockwise to obtain a torque of 12 ft. lbs. (15Nm), then advance to the next sprial roll pin notch.

13. Install a new spiral roll pin into spanner nut wrench J-36516 or equivalent and retain with petroleum jelly. Line up roll pin and drive pin into outer thrust ring.

14. Install seal protector onto output shaft. Fill the output shaft seal lips with chassis grease and install seal with seal installer J-36502 or equivalent.

15. Remove seal protector.

TRANSMISSION CASE

1. Install the idler shaft support. Line up bolt threads in idler shaft support with bolt hole.

NOTE: The machined surface on the face casting must be installed down into case because the bolt hole is slightly off center. Incorrect installation will cause incorrect reverse gear tooth pattern under load.

a. Apply pipe sealant GM part number 1052080 or equivalent to bolt holes of rear housing.

b. Apply threadlocker GM part number 12345382 or equivalent to bolt threads.

c. Hold reverse idler shaft against idler support while torqueing.

d. Torque bolts to 17 ft. lbs. (22 Nm).

2. Assemble transmission holding fixture J-36824 or equivalent to transmission case.

3. Place all forks in neutral position. Coat the 2 interlock

check balls with petroleum jelly and insert balls through plug hole using a small magnetic. Push 1 ball into 1st/2nd shift rail side and the other into 3rd/4th shift rail side.

4. Install the 3rd/4th shift rail with interlock pin. Retain pin with petroleum jelly.
   a. The detent slots in 3rd/4th shift rail faces up.
   b. Install through 3rd/4th shift fork and into the rear housing shift rail bearing.

NOTE: The 1st/2nd and 5th/reverse shift rail must be in NEUTRAL position or the interlock system will not allow the 3rd/4th rail to engage.

5. Install the roll pin to a depth where a maximum of 12.5mm of the roll pin remains. Measure from the edge of the 3rd/4th rail to the top of the roll pin.

NOTE: If the roll pin is not installed to its proper depth, it may rub against the front housing and cause the 3rd or 4th gear to hop-out.

   a. Test the interlock system to be certain the interlock balls are in place, by trying to move 2 shift rails.

6. Apply gasket maker GM part number 1052943 or equivalent to plug and install plug until flush.
7. Install the shift shaft, finger and shift shaft socket assembly. The detent slots must faces the idler support side of the transmission and the finger extension must be on the underside of the 5th/reverse shift rail.
8. Install roll pins.
9. Install the 3 detent/interlock balls and springs.
10. Apply gasket maker GM part number 1052943 or equivalent to the outside of bolt holes of the detent spring cover and install cover and attaching bolts. Torque bolts to 7 ft. lbs. (8.5 Nm).
11. Install the 4 rollers to shift shaft. Retain with petroleum jelly.
12. Install the countershaft bearing in bearing race of front housing. The smaller diameter of the bearing cage toward bearing race.
13. Install roller bearing and ball bearing outer race.
14. Apply gasket maker GM part number 1052943 or equivalent to the outside of bolt holes of the rear housing and install front housing.

NOTE: Bring the housing straight down. If resistance is felt at about ¼ in. (6mm), the rollers are cocked. Repeat procedure above. Do not force housing down.

15. Install the dowel pins and attaching bolts. Do not tighten bolts at this time.
16. Install ball bearing outer race, input shaft spacer and a new selective snapring.
   a. Install the thickest snapring that fits into the groove. It may be necessary to pull out on the input shaft to install the selective snapring.
17. Apply gasket maker GM part number 1052943 or equivalent to the inside cover bolt hole pattern.

NOTE: Do not apply too much gasket maker around the oil drain back hole. It may clog the hole causing a low fluid flow through the bearing resulting in premature bearing failure.

18. Install the shim into the input shaft bearing retainer assembly. Make certain the input bearing retainer washer is in place. Retain with petroleum jelly.
19. Align the oil drain back hole of the input shaft bearing retainer assembly with the hole in the housing and install attaching bolts. Torque bolts to 7 ft. lbs. (8.5 Nm).
20. Install the shift shaft detent plunger, shift shaft detent spring and plug using a brass drift. Apply pipe sealant GM part number 1052080 or equivalent to the plug.
21. On 2-Wheel Drive vehicles, install a new O-ring on the electronic speed sensor and coat with a thin flim of transmission oil. Install the electronic speed sensor.
22. Install back-up lamp switch. Apply pipe sealant GM part number 1052080 or equivalent to the threads.
23. Tighten housing attaching bolts to 27 ft. lbs. (35 Nm).

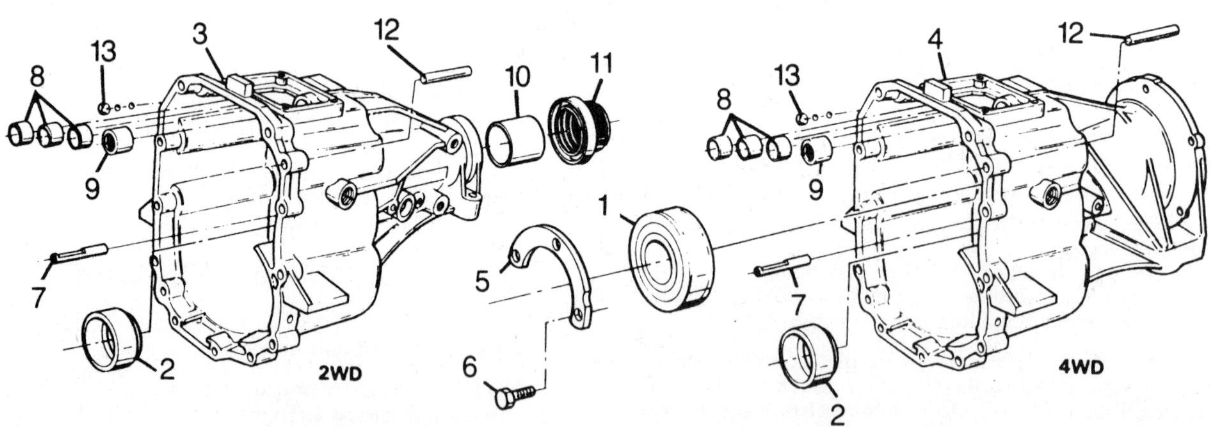

1. Output shaft bearing
2. Countershaft bearing race
3. Rear housing - 2WD
4. Rear housing - 4WD
5. Output shaft bearing retainer - 4WD
6. Bolt
7. Oil delivery tube
8. Rear housing shift rail bearing
9. Rear housing shift shaft bearing
10. Rear extension bearing - 2WD
11. Seal - 2WD
12. Dowel pin
13. Plug

Rear housing components — 85mm 4- or 5-speed

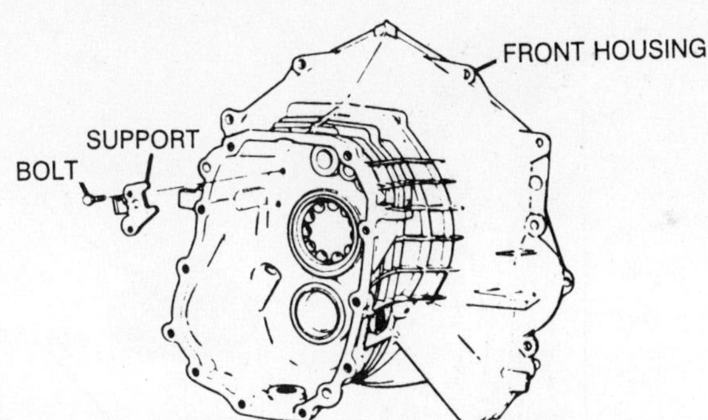

Installing the detent components – 85mm 4- or 5-speed

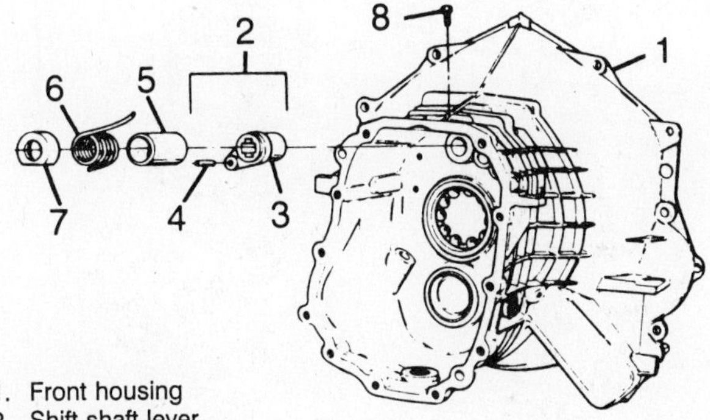

1. Front housing
2. Shift shaft lever
3. Shift lever
4. Shift shaft lever pin
5. Bias spring sleeve
6. Spring
7. Seat
8. Bolt

Installing the bias spring – 85mm 4- or 5-speed

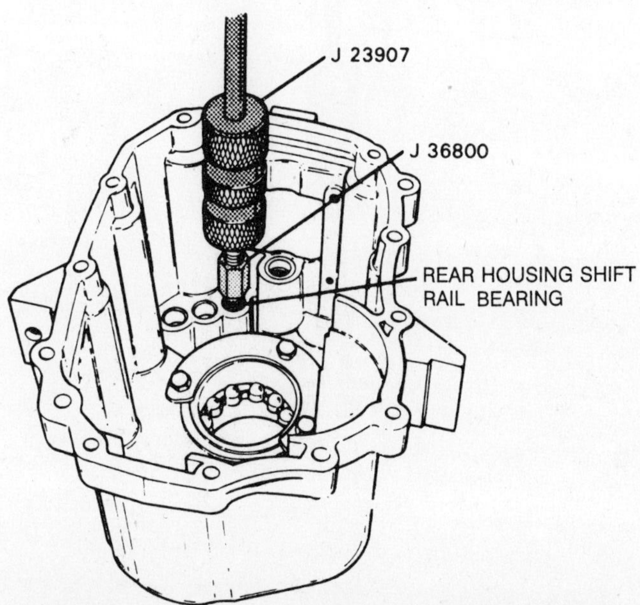

Removing the shift rail bearing – 85mm 4- or 5-speed

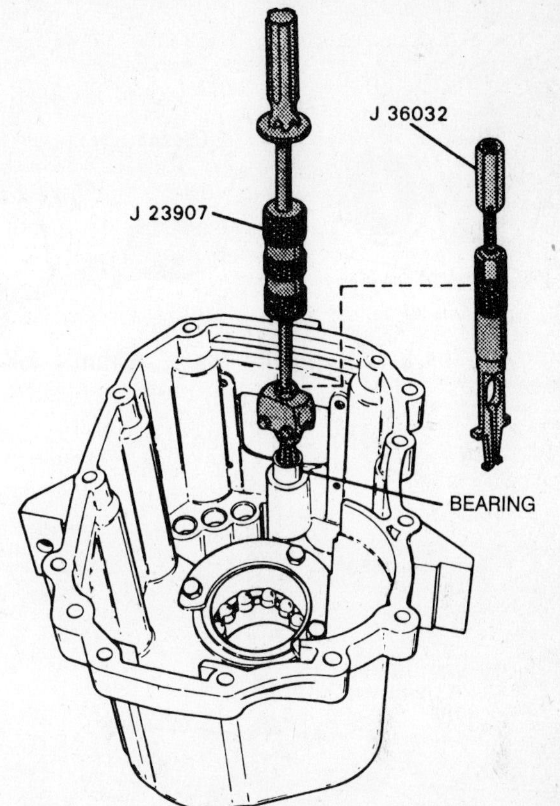

Removing the shift rail bearing – 85mm 4- or 5-speed

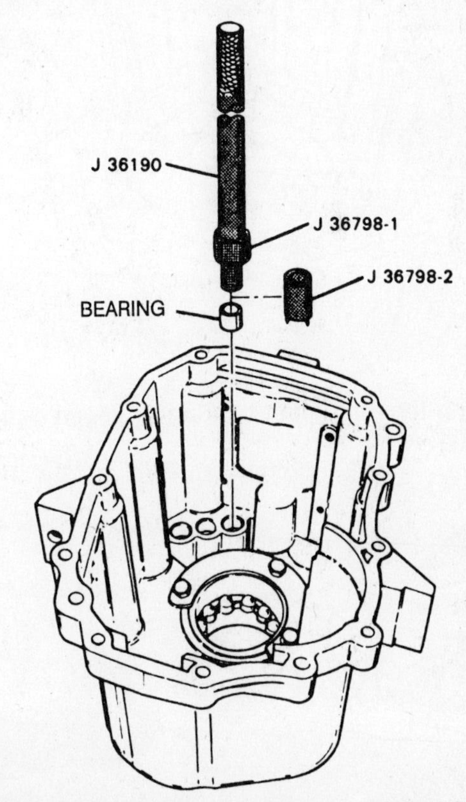

Installing the shift rail bearings – 85mm 4- or 5-speed

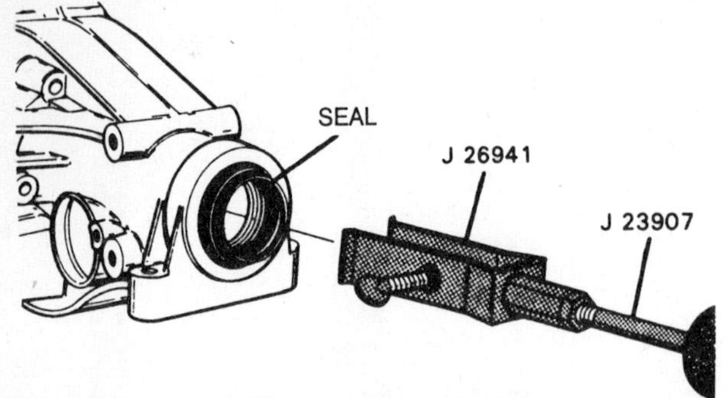

Removing the 2WD slip yoke seal — 85mm 4- or 5-speed

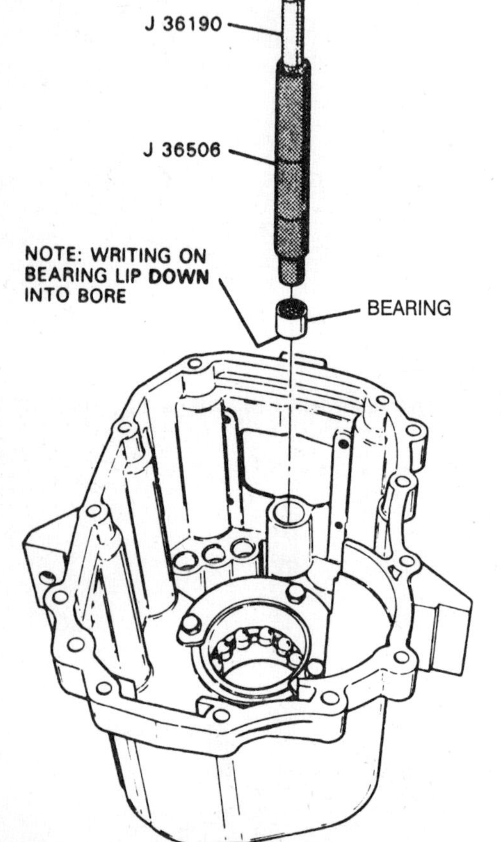

Installing the shift shaft bearing — 85mm 4- or 5-speed

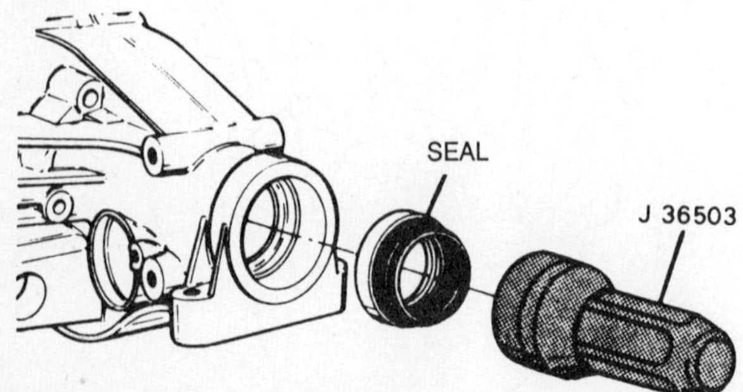

2WD slip yoke seal installation — 85mm 4- or 5-speed

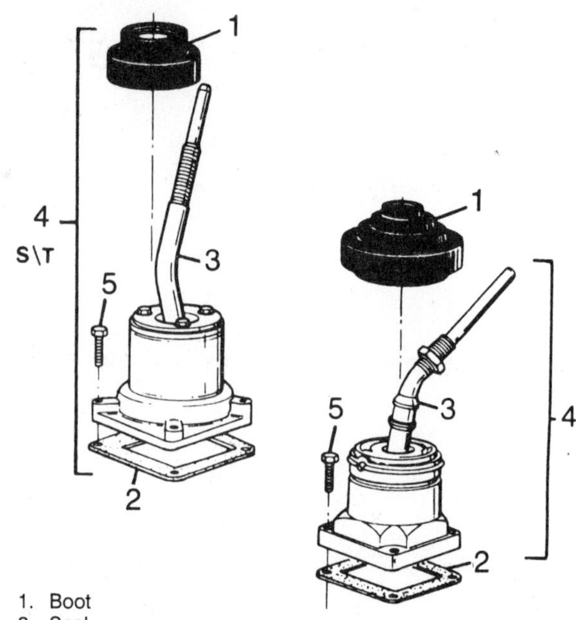

1. Boot
2. Seal
3. Nut
4. Housing
5. Bolt

Shift housing assembly — 85mm 4- or 5-speed

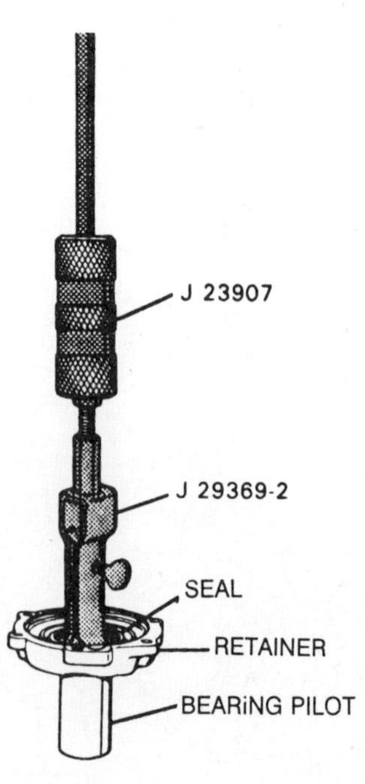

Removing the input shaft bearing retainer oil seal — 85mm 4- or 5-speed

1. Rail Assembly, 1st & 2nd Shift
2. Rail, 1st & 2nd Shift
3. Pin, Roll
4. Yoke, 1st & 2nd Shift
5. Pin, Roll
6. Fork, 1st - 2nd Shift
7. Rail Assembly, 3rd & 4th Shift
8. Pin, Roll (3rd & 4th shift)
9. Fork, 3rd & 4th Shift
10. Rail, 3rd & 4th
11. Pin, 3rd & 4th Shift Interlock
12. Rail Assembly, 5th & Reverse Shift
13. Rail, 5th & Reverse
14. Pin, Roll
15. Fork, 5th & Reverse Shift
16. Shaft Assembly, Shift
17. Shaft, Shift
18. Roller, Shift Shaft
19. Pin, Roller
20. Pin, Roll (6 × 28mm)
21. Finger
22. Pin, Roll
23. Socket Assembly, Shift Shaft

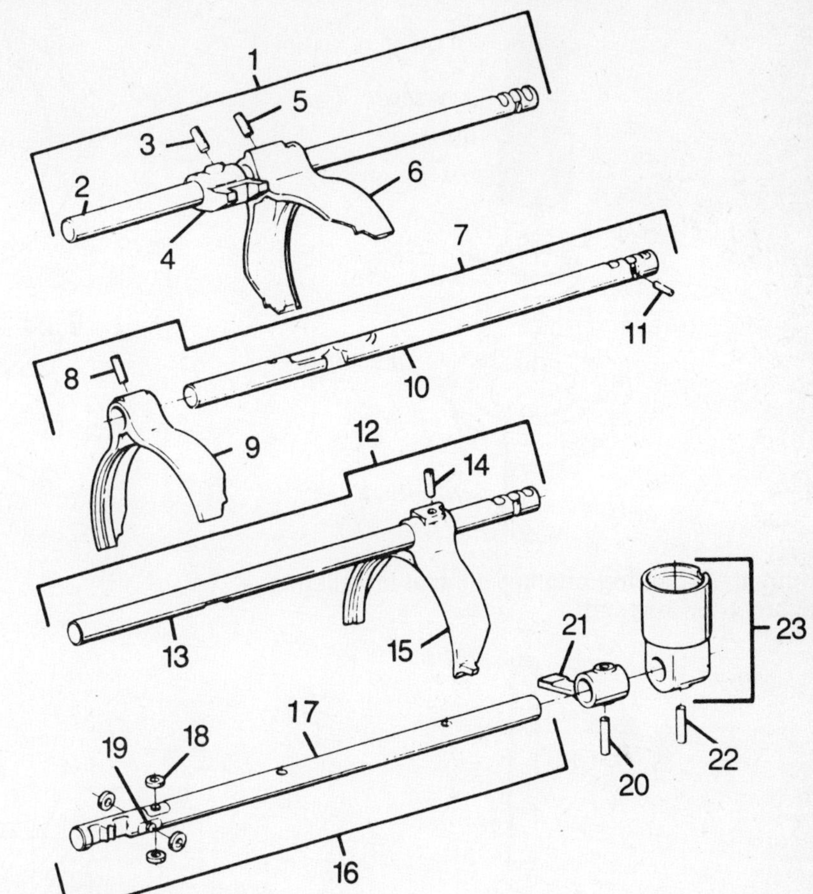

Shift/shaft rails — 85mm 4- or 5-speed

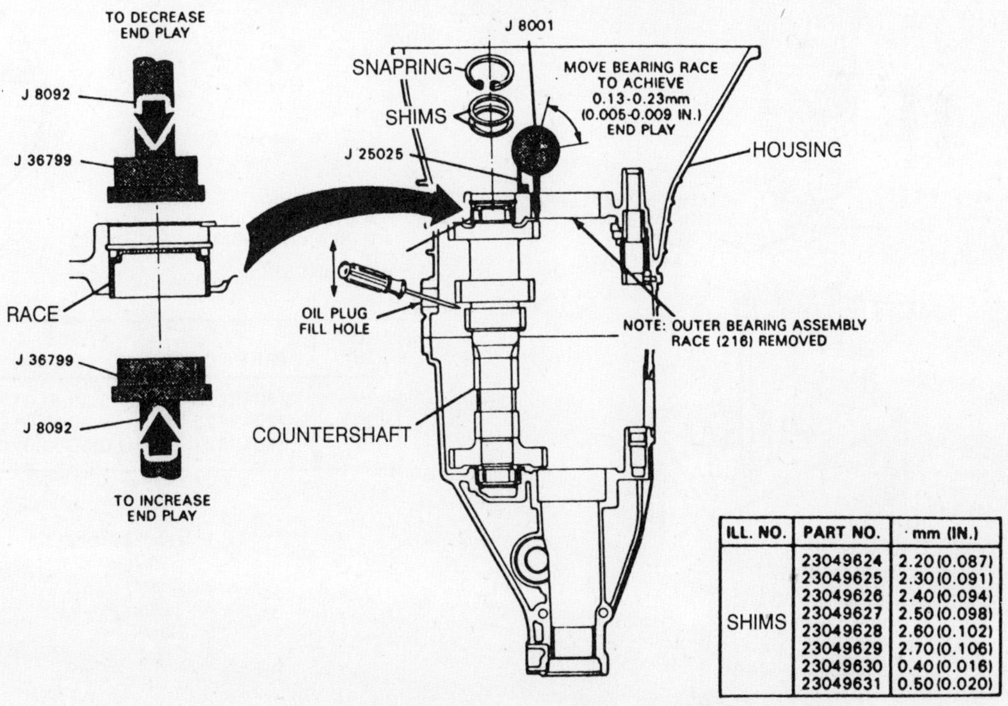

ILL. NO.	PART NO.	mm (IN.)
SHIMS	23049624	2.20 (0.087)
	23049625	2.30 (0.091)
	23049626	2.40 (0.094)
	23049627	2.50 (0.098)
	23049628	2.60 (0.102)
	23049629	2.70 (0.106)
	23049630	0.40 (0.016)
	23049631	0.50 (0.020)

Countershaft endplay adjustment — 85mm 4- or 5- speed

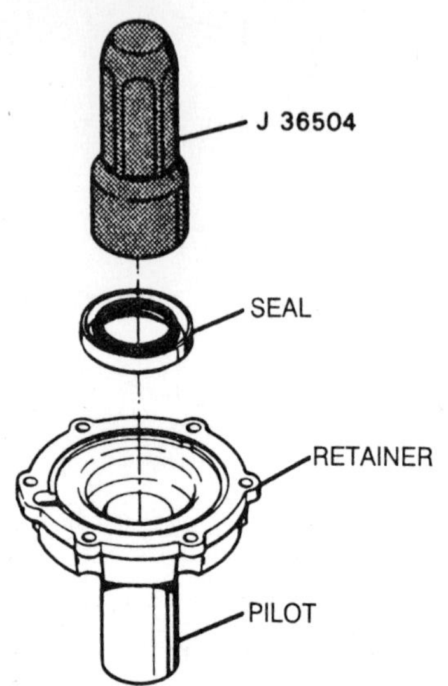

Input shaft bearing retainer oil seal installation – 85mm 4- or 5-speed

DIMENSION C

DIAL DEPTH GAUGE

3

2

DIMENSION A

1

4

6

A

B

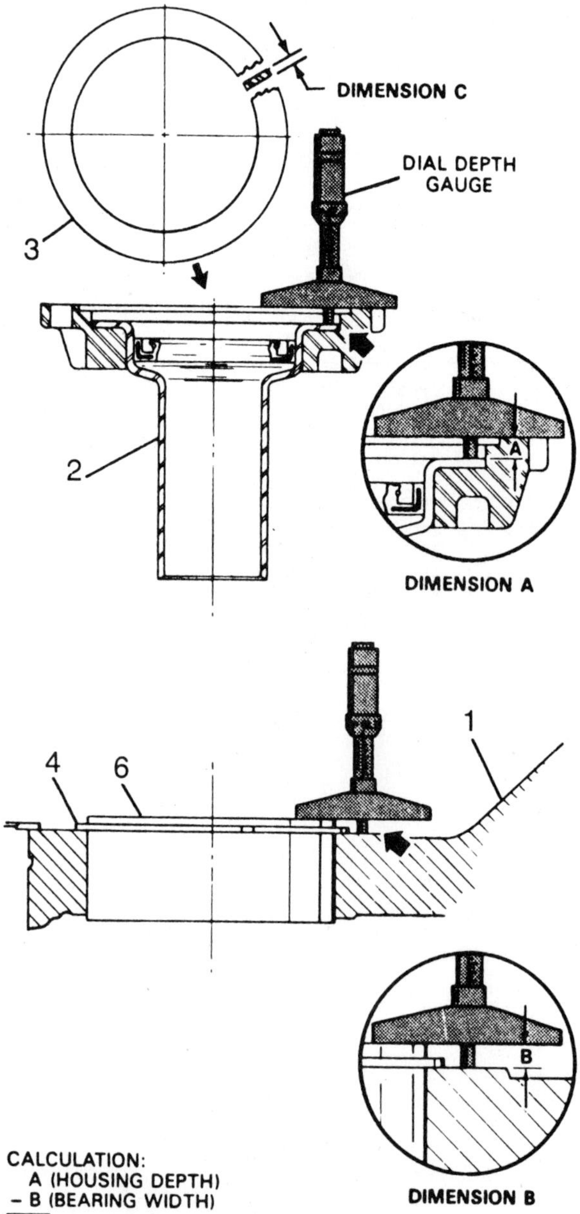

CALCULATION:
A (HOUSING DEPTH)
– B (BEARING WIDTH)
= C (SHIM SPACE)

DIMENSION B

ILL. NO.	PART NO.	DIM. C mm (IN.)
212	23049825 23049826 23049827	0.30 (0.012) 0.40 (0.016) 0.50 (0.020)

1. Front housing
2. Retainer
3. Shim
4. Bearing
5. Race
6. Shim

Input shaft bearing retainer selective shim procedure – 85mm 4- or 5-speed

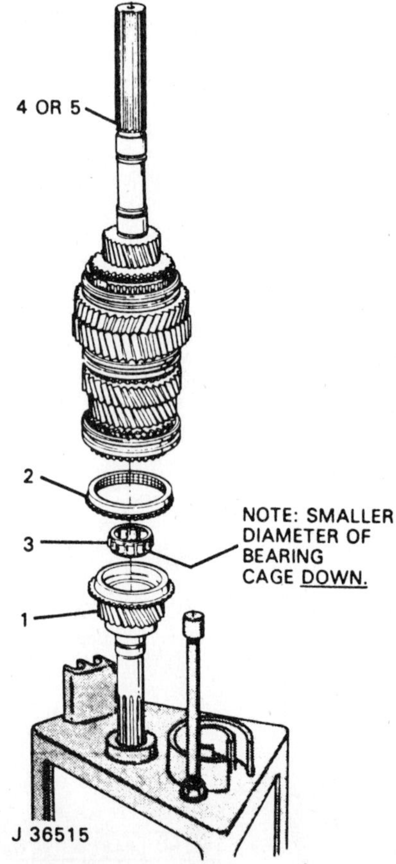

1. Input shaft
2. Synchronizer ring
3. Pilot bearing
4. Mainshaft – 2wd
5. Mainshaft – 4wd

Installing mainshaft components – 85mm 4- or 5-speed

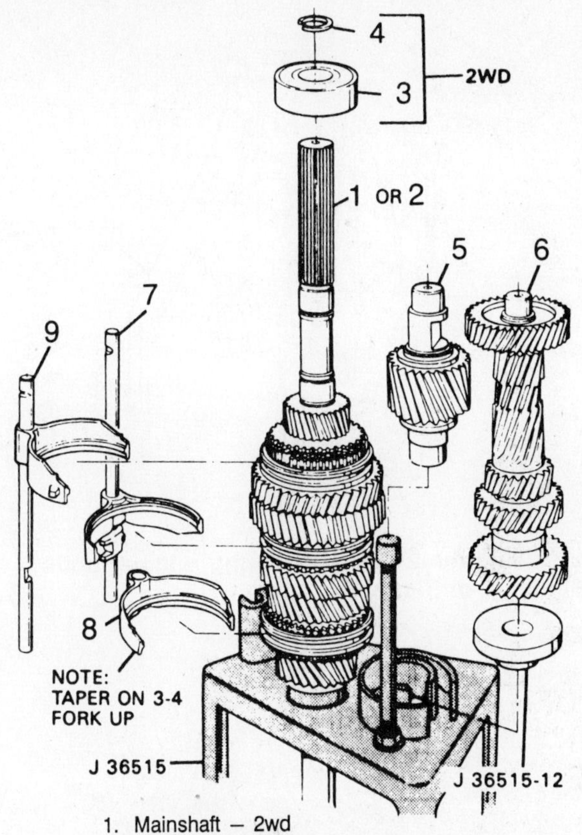

1. Mainshaft – 2wd
2. Mainshaft – 4wd
3. Output shaft bearing
4. Snapring
5. Reverse idler
6. Countershaft – 5-speed
7. 1st/2nd shift rail
8. 3rd/4th shift fork
9. 5th/reverse shift rail

Installing the countershaft and reverse idler assembly – 85mm 4- or 5-speed

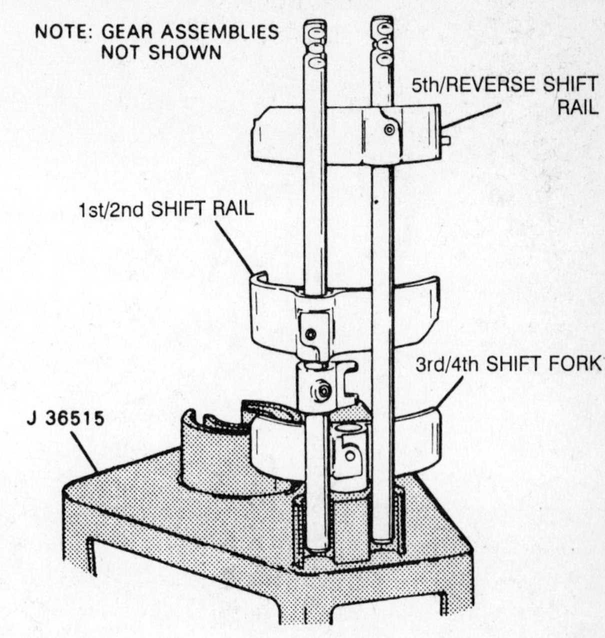

Positioning the shift forks and rails – 85mm 4- or 5-speed

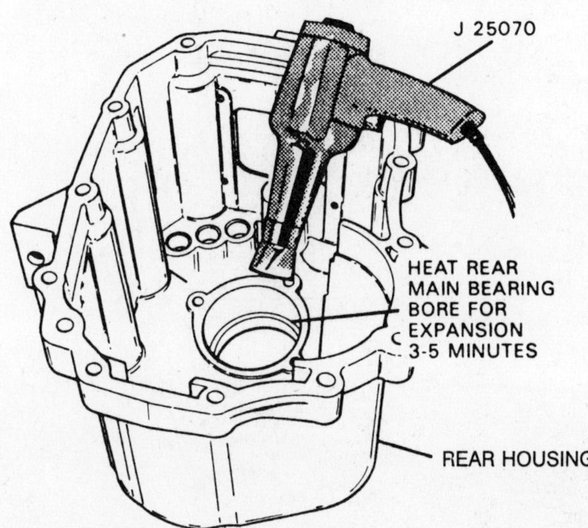

Heating the 2WD rear main bore – 85mm 4- or 5-speed

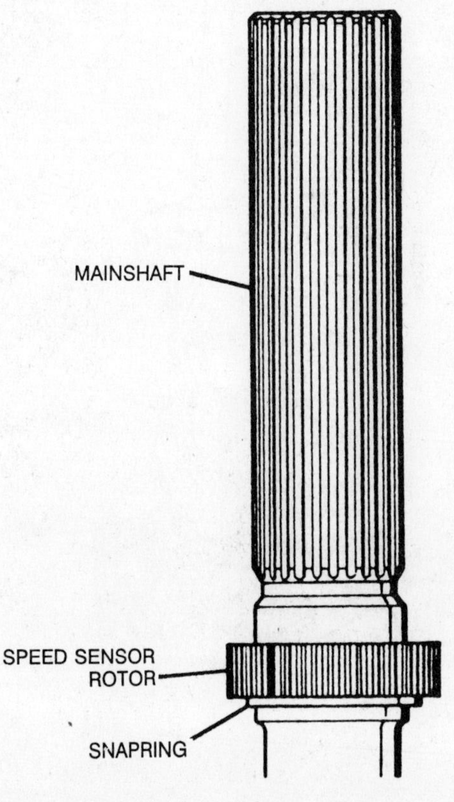

2WD speed sensor installation – 85mm 4- or 5-speed

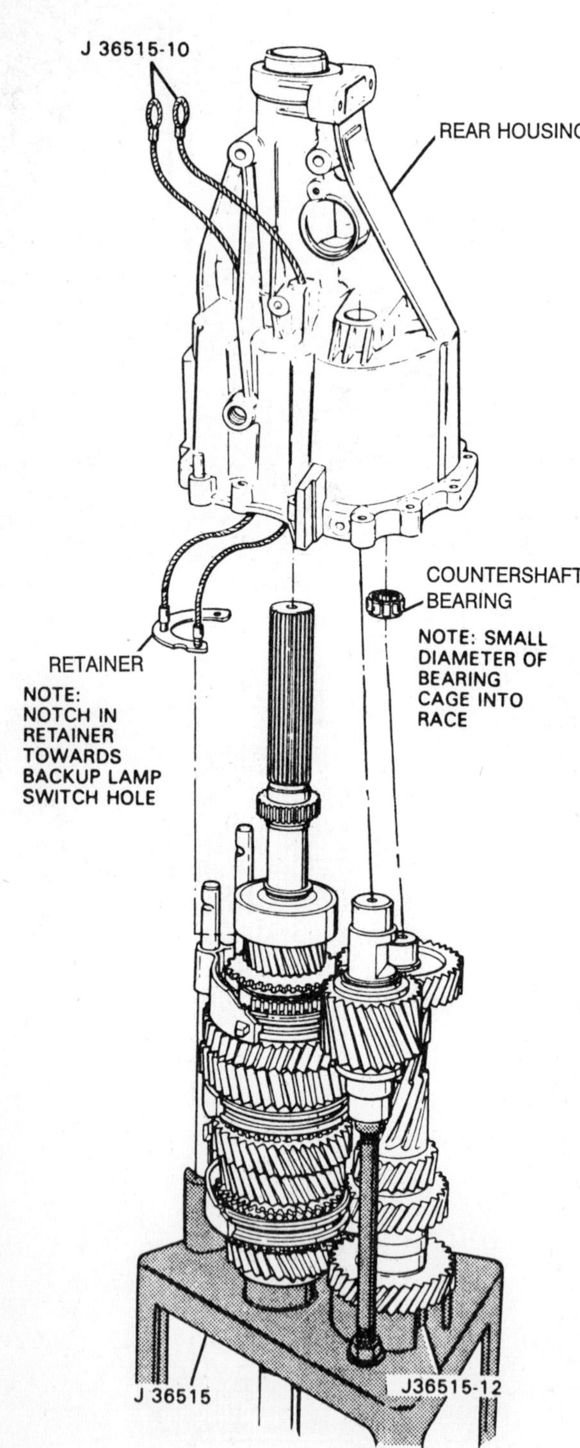

Installing the 2WD rear housing – 85mm 4- or 5-speed

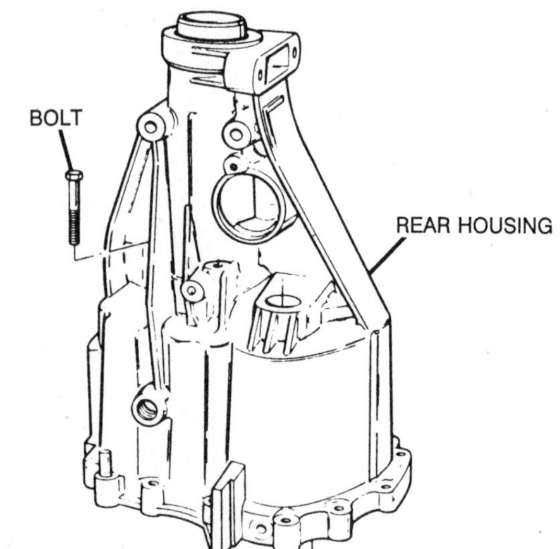

Installing the 2WD rear bearing retainer bolts – 85mm 4- or 5-speed

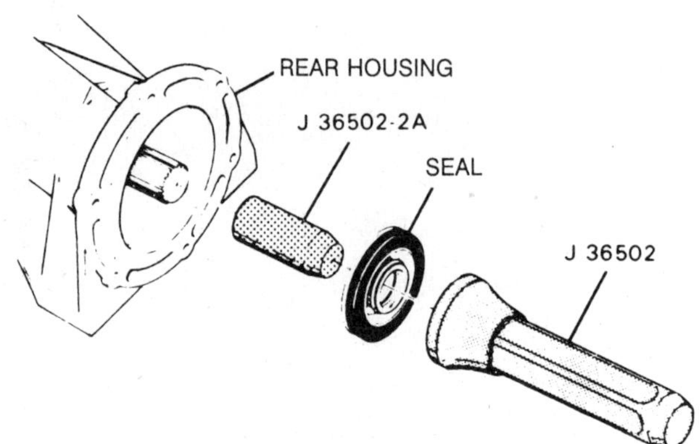

Installing the 4WD oil seal – 85mm 4- or 5-speed

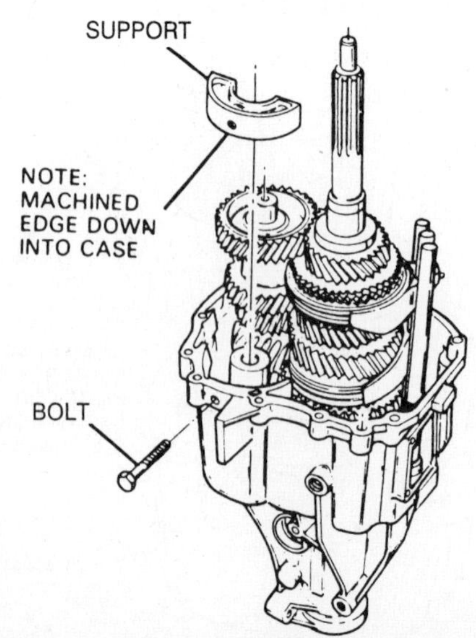

Installing the reverse idler support – 85mm 4- or 5-speed

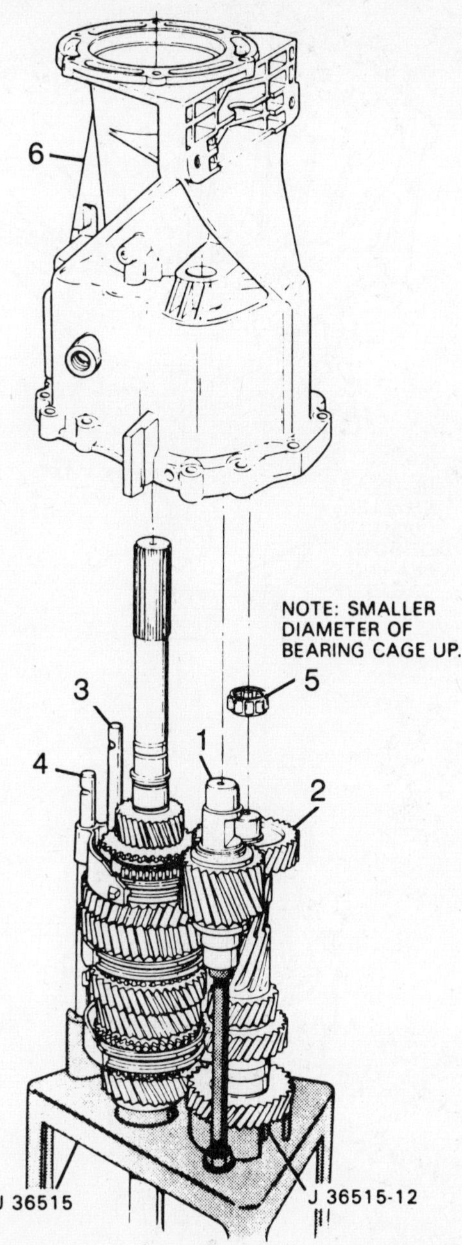

Installing the 4WD rear housing — 85mm 4- or 5-speed

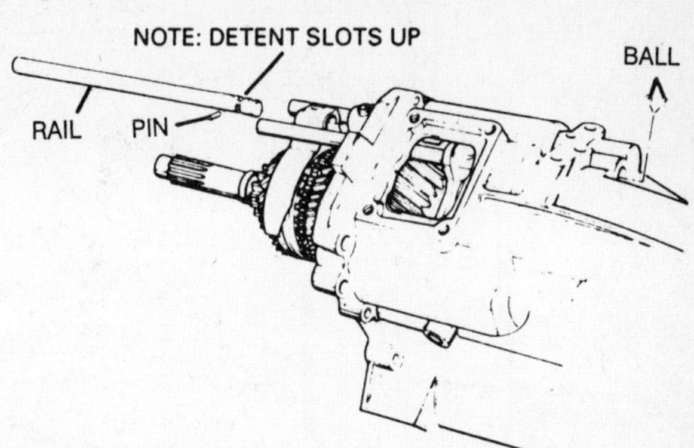

Installing the 3rd/4th interlock balls — 85mm 4- or 5-speed

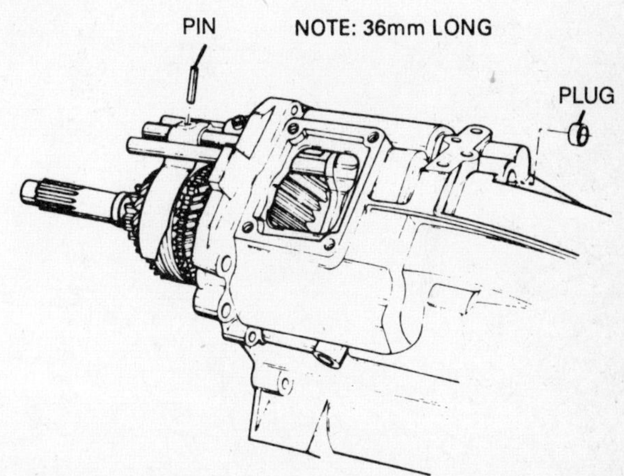

Installing the fork roll pin and plug — 85mm 4- or 5-speed

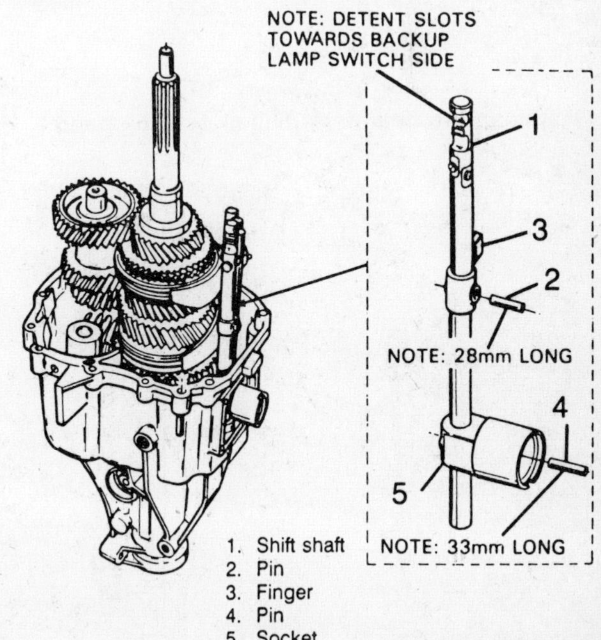

Installing the shift shaft — 85mm 4- or 5-speed

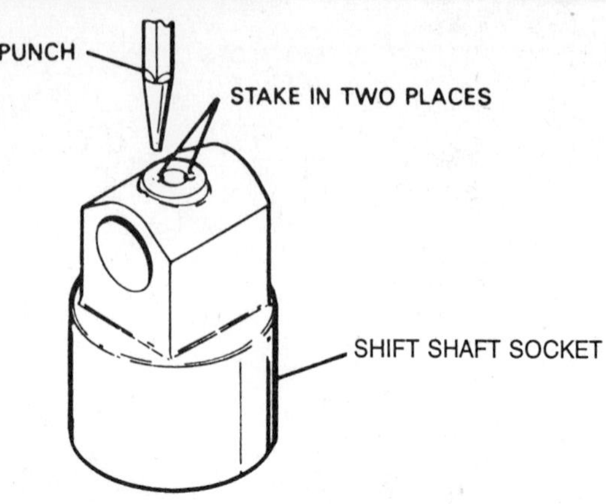

Staking the shift shaft socket — 85mm 4- or 5-speed

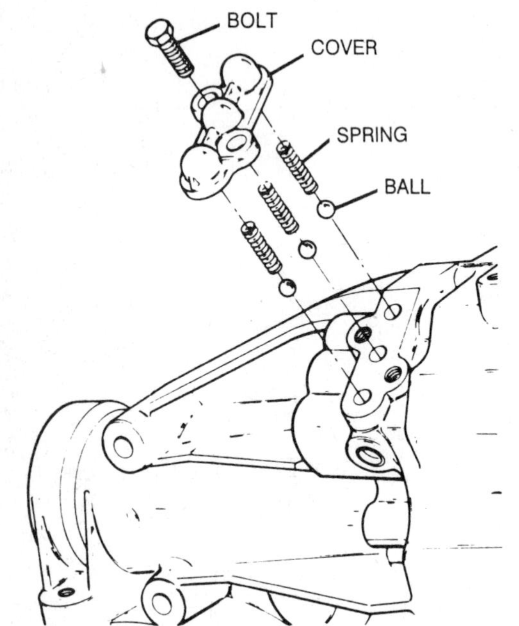

Installing the detents — 85mm 4- or 5-speed

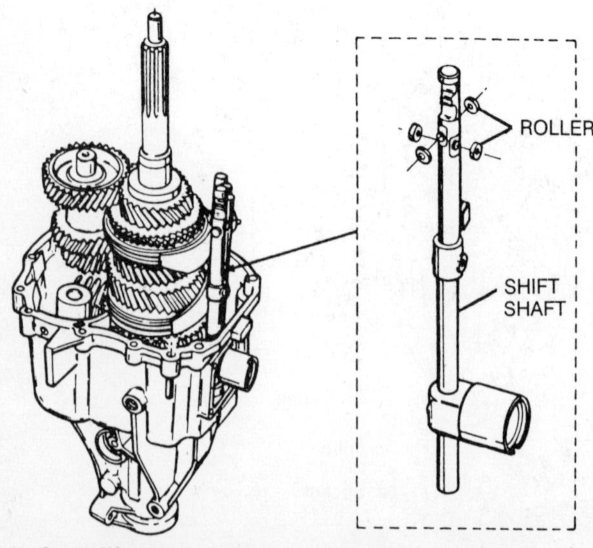

Installing the rollers — 85mm 4- or 5-speed

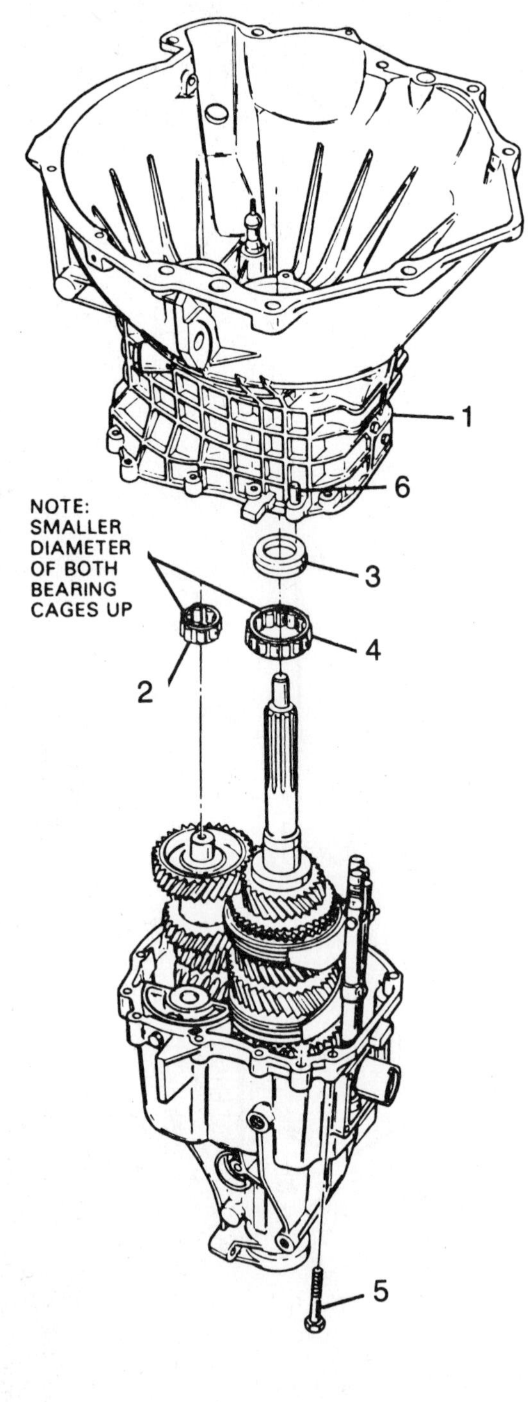

1. Housing
2. Countershaft bearing
3. Inner race
4. Roller bearing
5. Bolt
6. Dowel pin

Installing the front housing — 85mm 4- or 5-speed

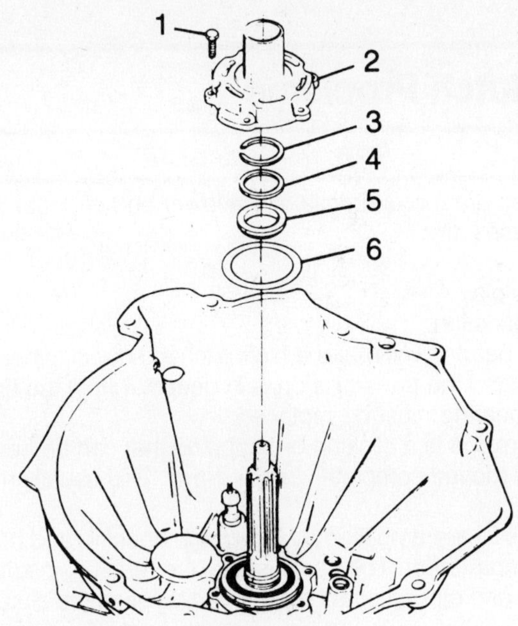

ILL. NO.	PART NO.	DIM. A mm (IN.)
210	23049935	2.00 (0.079)
	23049936	2.10 (0.083)
	23049937	2.20 (0.087)
	23049938	2.30 (0.090)

1. Bolt
2. Retainer
3. Snapring
4. Snapring
5. Spacer
6. Shim
7. Race

Input shaft bearing retainer assembly — 85mm 4- or 5-speed

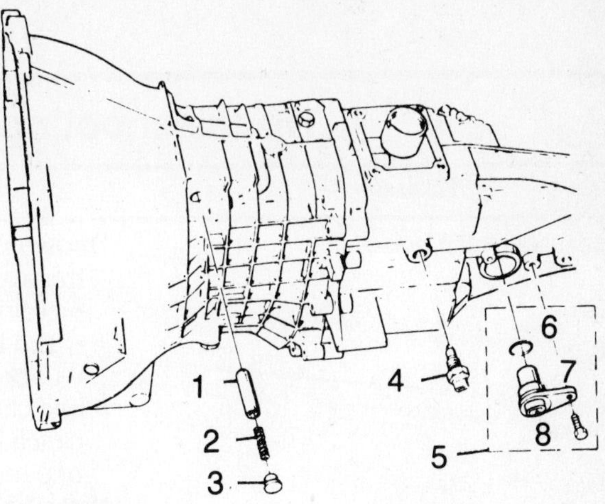

1. Plunger
2. Spring
3. Plug
4. Back-up switch
5. Speed sensor
6. O-ring
7. Speed sensor
8. Bolt

Installing the external components — 85mm 4- or 5-speed

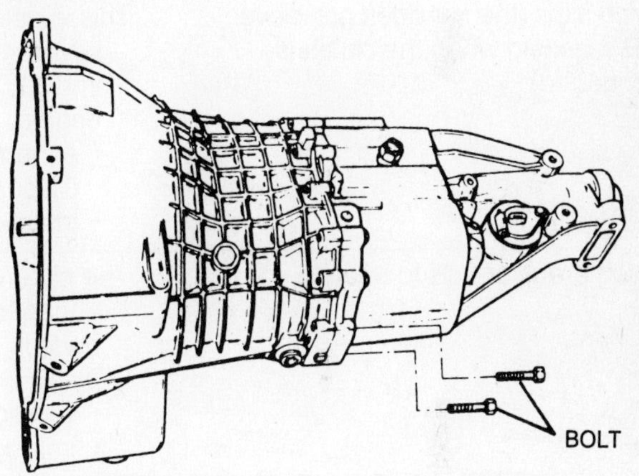

Bolt installation — 85mm 4- or 5-speed

CLUTCH

Troubleshooting Basic Clutch Problems

Problem	Cause
Excessive clutch noise	Throwout bearing noises are more audible at the lower end of pedal travel. The usual causes are: • Riding the clutch • Too little pedal free-play • Lack of bearing lubrication A bad clutch shaft pilot bearing will make a high pitched squeal, when the clutch is disengaged and the transmission is in gear or within the first 2" of pedal travel. The bearing must be replaced. Noise from the clutch linkage is a clicking or snapping that can be heard or felt as the pedal is moved completely up or down. This usually requires lubrication. Transmitted engine noises are amplified by the clutch housing and heard in the passenger compartment. They are usually the result of insufficient pedal free-play and can be changed by manipulating the clutch pedal.
Clutch slips (the car does not move as it should when the clutch is engaged)	This is usually most noticeable when pulling away from a standing start. A severe test is to start the engine, apply the brakes, shift into high gear and SLOWLY release the clutch pedal. A healthy clutch will stall the engine. If it slips it may be due to: • A worn pressure plate or clutch plate • Oil soaked clutch plate • Insufficient pedal free-play
Clutch drags or fails to release	The clutch disc and some transmission gears spin briefly after clutch disengagement. Under normal conditions in average temperatures, 3 seconds is maximum spin-time. Failure to release properly can be caused by: • Too light transmission lubricant or low lubricant level • Improperly adjusted clutch linkage
Low clutch life	Low clutch life is usually a result of poor driving habits or heavy duty use. Riding the clutch, pulling heavy loads, holding the car on a grade with the clutch instead of the brakes and rapid clutch engagement all contribute to low clutch life.

Understanding the Clutch

The purpose of the clutch is to disconnect and connect engine power from the transmission. A truck at rest requires a lot of engine torque to get all that weight moving. An internal combustion engine does not develop a high starting torque, so it must be allowed to operate without any load until it builds up enough torque to move the truck. Torque increases with engine rpm. The clutch allows the engine to build up torque by physically disconnecting the engine from the transmission, relieving the engine of any load or resistance. The transfer of engine power to the transmission (the load) must be smooth and gradual; if it weren't, driveline components would wear out or break quickly. This gradual power transfer is made possible by gradually releasing the clutch pedal. The clutch disc and pressure plate are the connecting link between the engine and transmission. When the clutch pedal is released, the disc and plate contact each other (clutch engagement), physically joining the engine and transmission. When the pedal is pushed in, the disc and plate separate (the clutch is disengaged), disconnecting the engine from the transmission.

The clutch assembly consists of the flywheel, the clutch disc, the clutch pressure plate, the throwout bearing and fork, the hydraulic system and the pedal. The flywheel and clutch pressure plate (driving members) are connected to the engine crankshaft and rotate with it. The clutch disc is located between the flywheel and pressure plate, and splined to the transmission shaft. A driving member is one that is attached to the engine and transfers engine power to a driven member (clutch disc) on the transmission shaft. A driving member (pressure plate) rotates (drives) a driven member (clutch disc) on contact and, in so doing, turns the transmission shaft. There is a circular diaphragm spring within the pressure plate cover (transmission side). In a relaxed state (when the clutch pedal is fully released), this spring is convex; that it, it is dished outward toward the transmission. Pushing in the clutch pedal actuates the master cylinder, applying pressure to the hydraulic fluid. The hydrualic fluid then exerts pressure in the system, extending the actuating rod in the slave cylinder. Connected to the other end of this rod is the throwout bearing fork. The throwout bearing is attached to the fork. When the clutch pedal is depressed, the clutch linkage pushes the fork and bearing forward to contact the diaphragm spring of the pressure plate. The outer edges of the spring are secured to the pressure plate and are pivoted on rings so that when the center of the spring is compressed by the throwout bearing, the outer edges bow outward and, by so doing, pull the pressure plate in the same direction – away from the clutch disc. This action separates the disc from the plate, disengaging the clutch and allowing the transmission to be shifted into another gear. A coil type clutch return spring attached to the clutch pedal arm permits full release of the pedal. Releasing the pedal pulls the throwout bearing away from the diaphragm spring resulting in a reversal of spring position. As bearing pressure is gradually released from the spring center, the outer edges of the spring bow outward, pushing the pressure plate into closer contact with the clutch disc. As the disc and plate move closer together, friction between the two increases and slippage is reduced until, when full spring pressure is applied (by fully releasing the pedal), The speed of the disc and plate are the same. This stops all slipping, creating a direct connection between the plate and disc which results in the transfer of power from the engine to the transmission. The clutch disc is now rotating with the pressure plate at engine speed and, because it is splined to the transmission shaft, the shaft now turns at the same engine speed. Understanding clutch operation can be rather difficult at first; if you're still confused after reading this, consider the following analogy. The action of the diaphragm spring can be compared to that of an oil can bottom. The bottom of an oil can is shaped very much like the clutch diaphragm spring and pushing in on the can bottom and then releasing it produces a similar effect. As mentioned earlier, the clutch pedal return spring permits full release of the pedal and reduces linkage slack due to wear. As the linkage wears, clutch free-pedal travel will increase and free-travel will decrease as the clutch wears. Free-travel is actually throwout bearing lash.

The diaphragm spring type clutches used are available in two different designs: flat diaphragm springs or bent spring. The bent fingers are bent back to create a centrifugal boost ensuring quick re-engagement at higher engine speeds. This design enables pressure plate load to increase as the clutch disc wears and makes low pedal effort possible even with a heavy duty clutch. The throwout bearing used with the bent finger design is 1¼ in. (32mm) long and is shorter than the bearing used with the flat finger design. These bearings are not interchangeable. If the longer bearing is used with the bent finger clutch, free-pedal travel will not exist. This results in clutch slippage and rapid wear.

The transmission varies the gear ratio between the engine and rear wheels. It can be shifted to change engine speed as driving conditions and loads change. The transmission allows disengaging and reversing power from the engine to the wheels.

The clutch operating controls are hydraulic, consisting of a master cylinder and a slave cylinder.

REMOVAL AND INSTALLATION

CAUTION

The clutch driven disc contains asbestos, which has been determined to be a cancer causing agent. Never clean clutch surfaces with compressed air! Avoid inhaling any dust from any clutch surface! When cleaning clutch surfaces, use a commercially available brake cleaning fluid.

NOTE: Before removing the bellhousing, the engine must be supported. This can be done by placing a hydraulic jack, with a board on top, under the oil pan.

1. Remove the transmission.
2. Remove the slave cylinder.
3. Remove the bellhousing cover.
4. Remove the bellhousing from the engine.
5. Remove the throwout spring and fork.
6. Remove the ballstud from the bellhousing.
7. Install a pilot tool (an old mainshaft makes a good pilot tool) to hold the clutch while you are removing it.

NOTE: Before removing the clutch from the flywheel, mark the flywheel, clutch cover and one pressure plate lug, so that these parts may be assembled in their same relative positions. They were balanced as an assembly.

8. Loosen the clutch attaching bolts one turn at a time to prevent distortion of the clutch cover until the tension is released.
9. Remove the clutch pilot tool and the clutch from the vehicle.
   Check the pressure plate and flywheel for signs of wear, scoring, overheating, etc. If the clutch plate, flywheel, or pressure plate is oil-soaked, inspect the engine rear main seal and the transmission input shaft seal, and correct leakage as required. Replace any damaged parts.

To install:

10. Install the pressure plate in the cover assembly, aligning the notch in the pressure plate with the notch in the cover flange. Install pressure plate retracting springs, lockwashers and drive strap-to-pressure plate bolts. Tighten to 11 ft. lbs. The clutch is now ready to be installed.

NOTE: The manufacturer recommends that new pressure plate bolts and washers be used.

11. Turn the flywheel until the **X** mark is at the bottom.
12. Install the clutch disc, pressure plate and cover, using an old mainshaft as an aligning tool.
13. Turn the clutch until the **X** mark or painted white letter on the clutch cover aligns with the **X** mark on the flywheel.
14. Install the attaching bolts and tighten them a little at a time in a crossing pattern until the spring pressure is taken up.
15. Remove the aligning tool.
16. Coat the rounded end of the ballstud with high temperature wheel bearing grease.
17. Install the ballstud in the bellhousing. Pack the ballstud from the lubrication fitting.
18. Pack the inside recess and the outside groove of the release bearing with high temperature wheel bearing grease and install the release bearing and fork.
19. Install the relase bearing seat and spring.
20. Install the clutch housing. Torque the bolts to 55 ft. lbs.
21. Install the cover.
22. Install the slave cylinder. Torque the bolt to 13 ft. lbs.
23. Install the transmission.
24. Bleed the hydraulic system.

Clutch Master Cylinder and Reservoir

REMOVAL AND INSTALLATION

R/V Series

1. Disconnect the negative battery cable.
2. Remove the lower steering column covers.
3. Remove the lower left side air conditioning duct, if so equipped.
4. Disconnect the pushrod from the clutch pedal.
5. Disconnect the reservoir hose.
6. Disconnect the secondary cylinder hydraulic line to the master cylinder.
7. Remove the master cylinder retaining nuts and remove the master cylinder.
8. Remove the retaining nuts and remove the reservoir from the firewall.

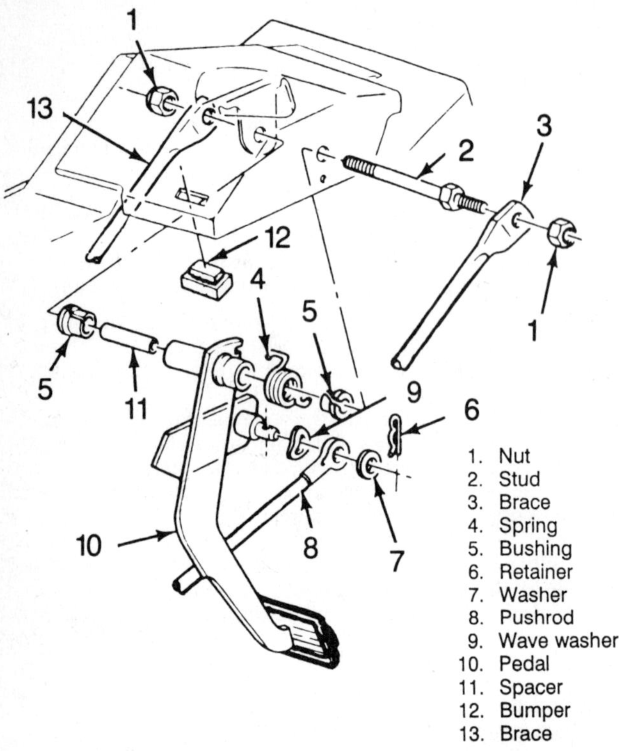

R and V series clutch pedal components

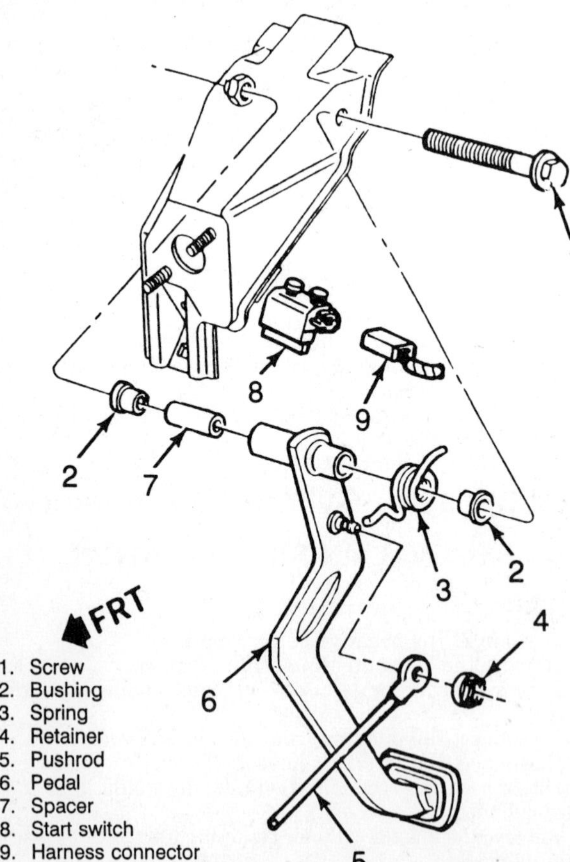

C and K series clutch pedal components

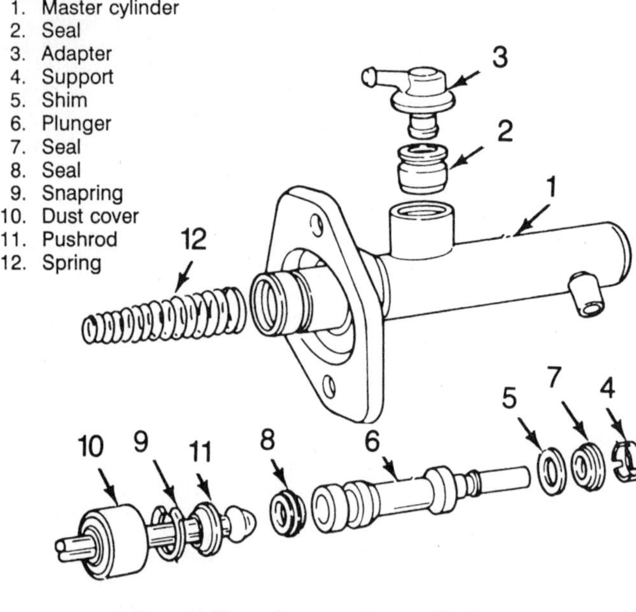

R and V series master cylinder

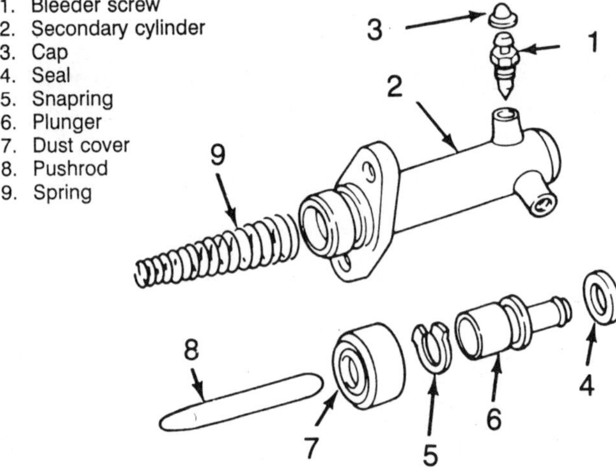

R and V series secondary cylinder

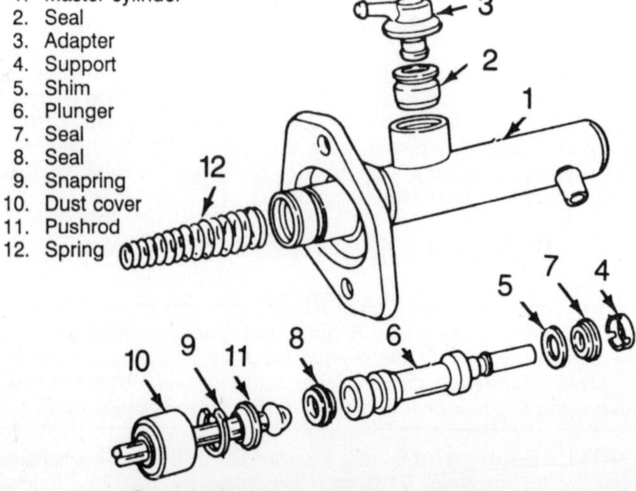

C and K seires master cylinder

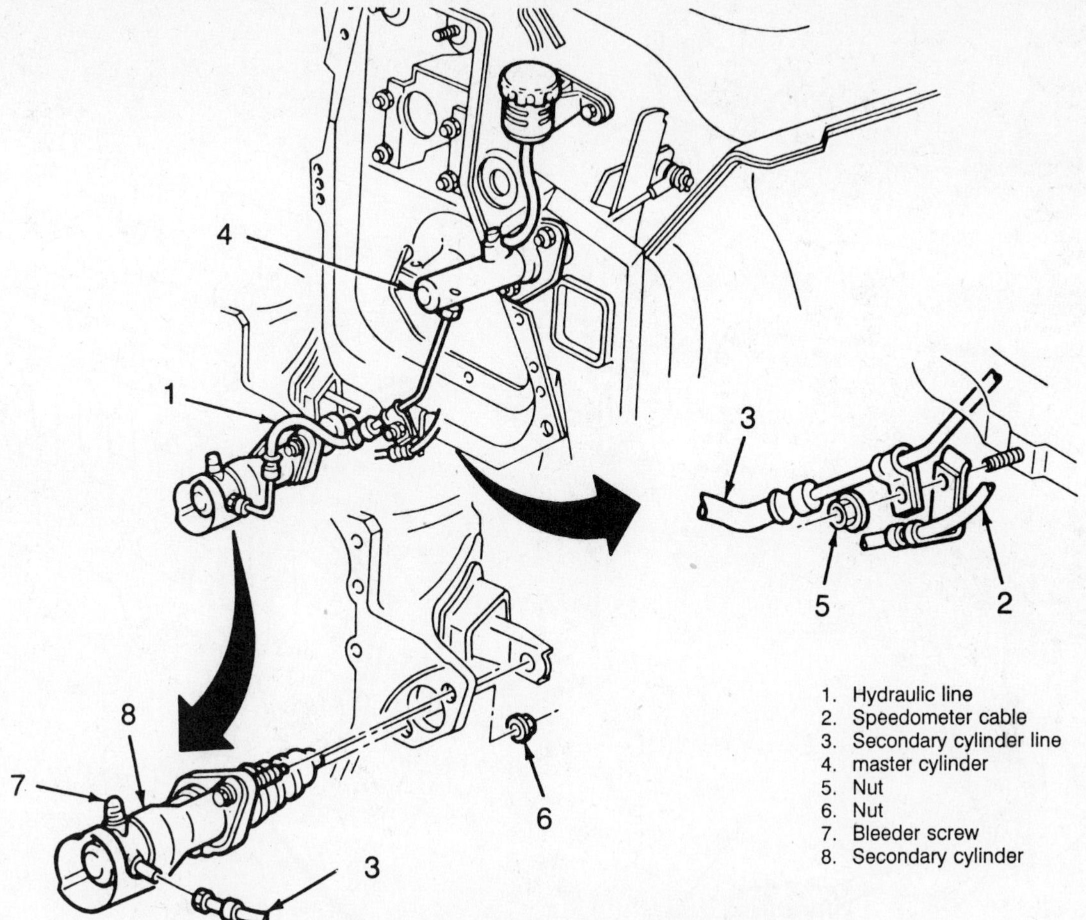

R and V series clutch hydraulic system

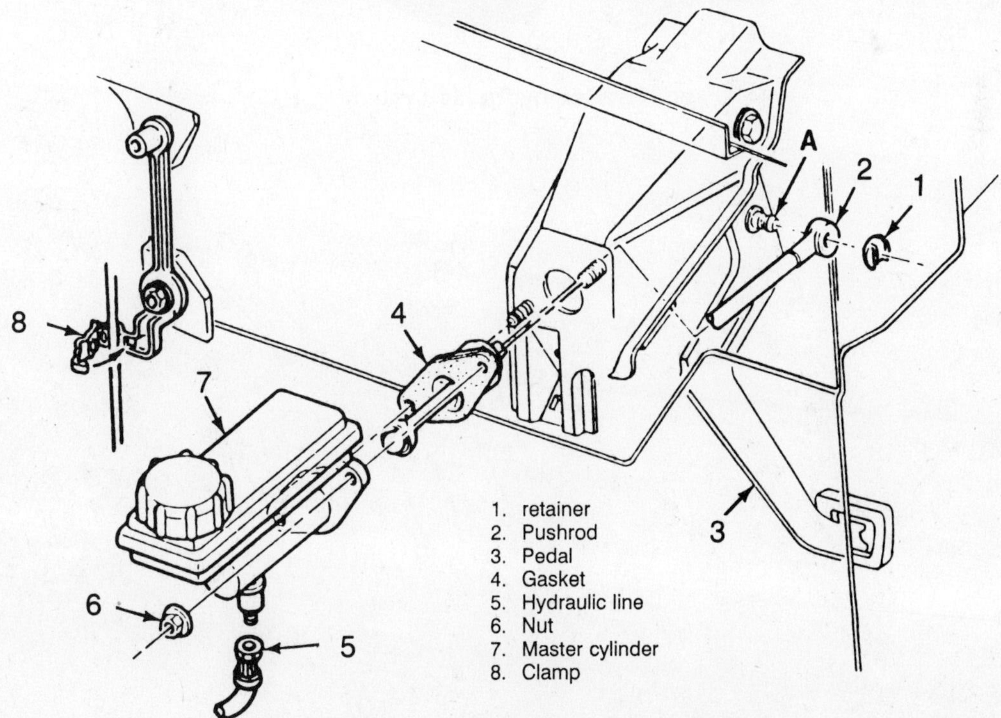

C and K series master cylinder installation

1. Hydraulic line
2. Master cylinder
3. Clip
4. Secondary cylinder
5. Plug
6. Nut
7. Nut
8. Washer
9. Bleeder screw

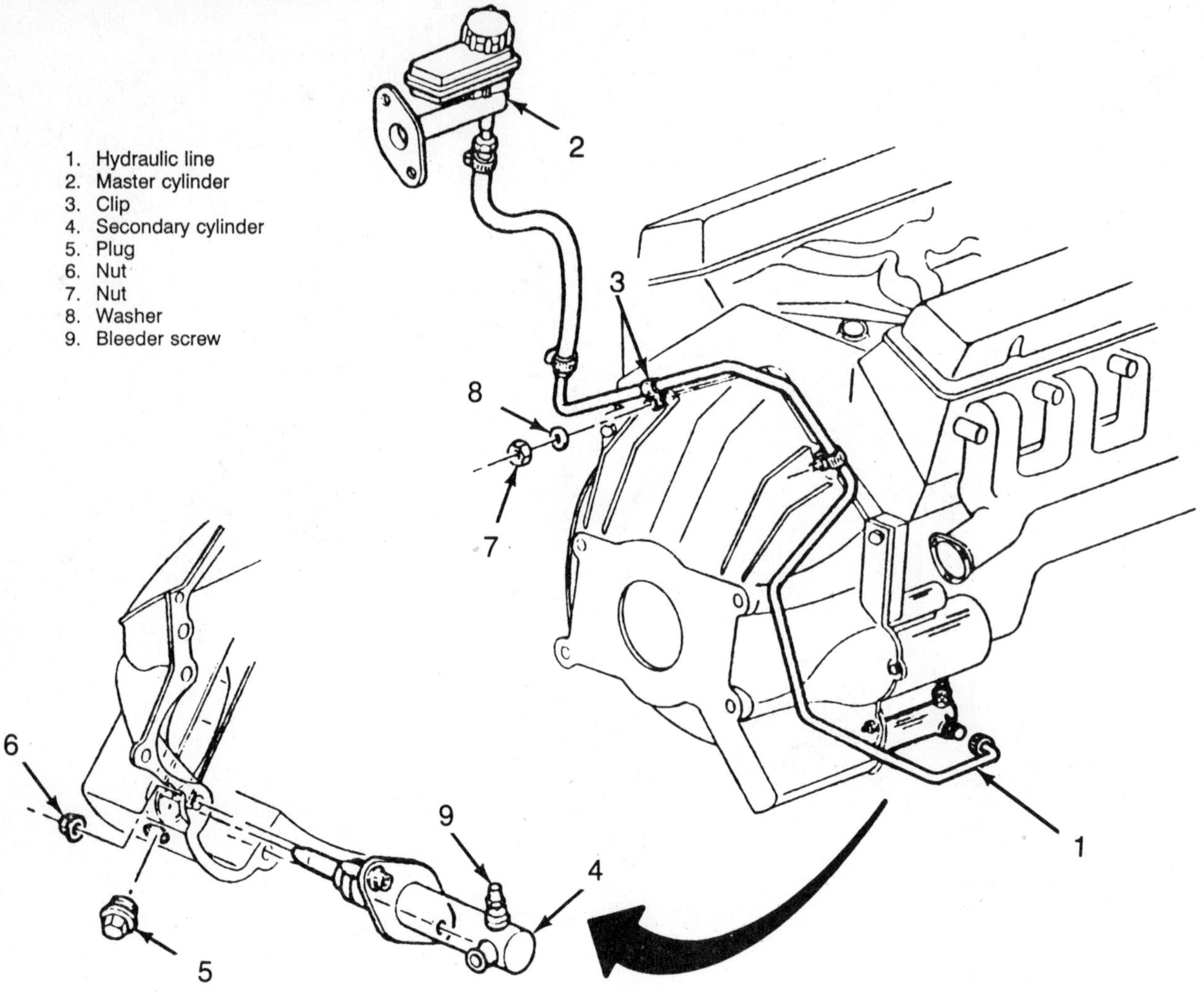

C and K series hydraulic system

1. Clutch fork
2. Spring washer
3. Screw
4. Flywheel housing
5. Screw
6. Ball stud
7. Boot
8. Retainer
9. Release bearing
10. Cover
11. Driven plate
12. Cover
13. Screw
14. Pilot bearing
15. Screw
16. Strap
17. Pressure plate

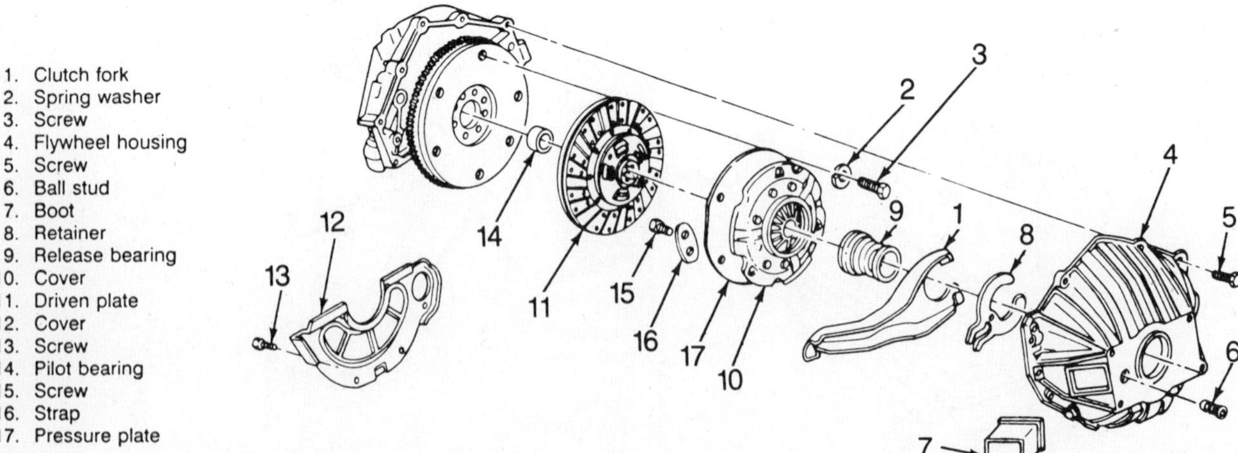

R and V series clutch components

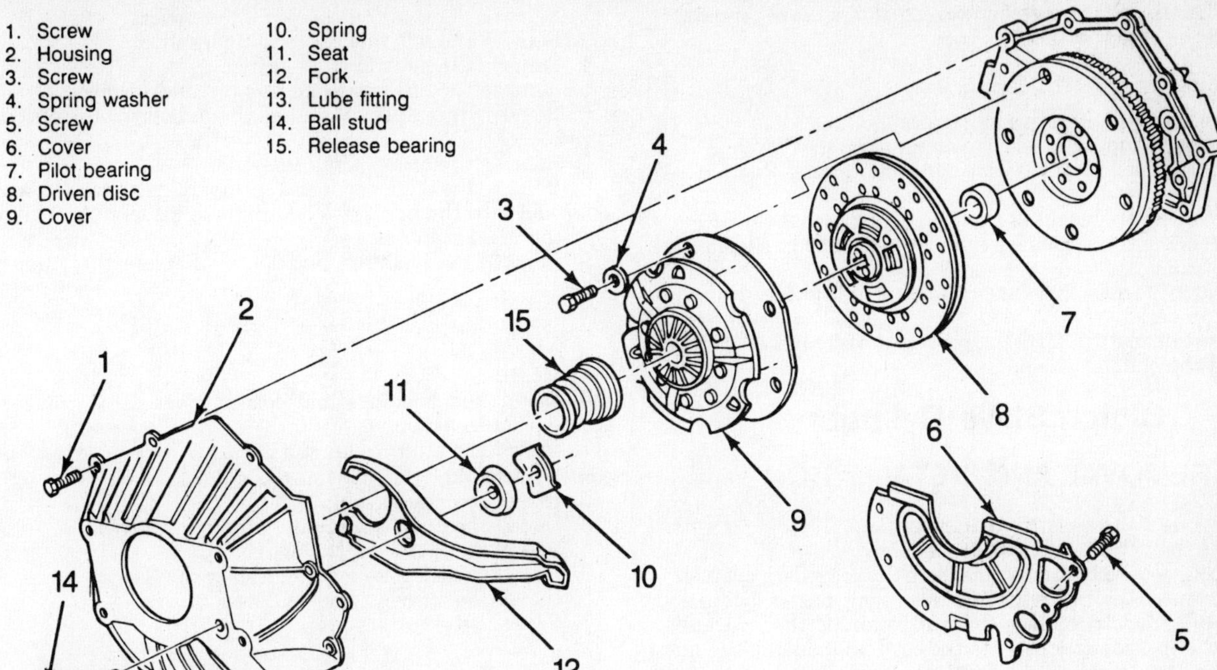

C and K series clutch components

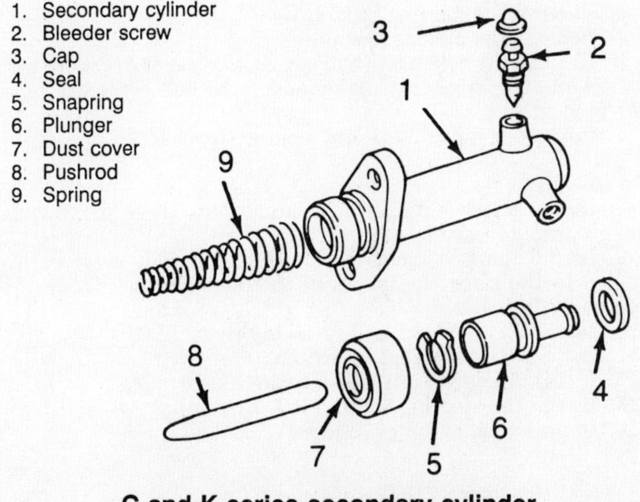

C and K series secondary cylinder

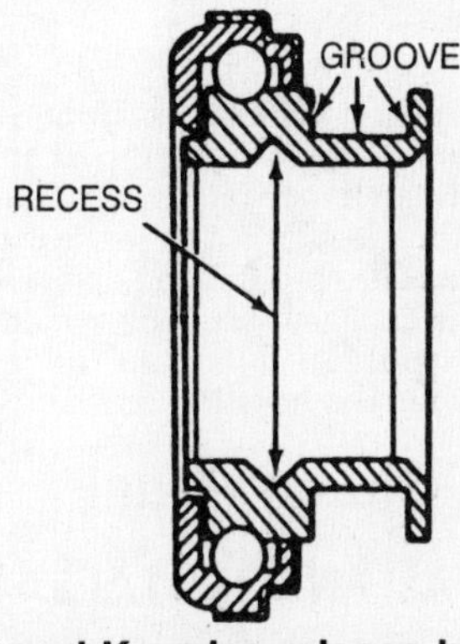

C and K series release bearing

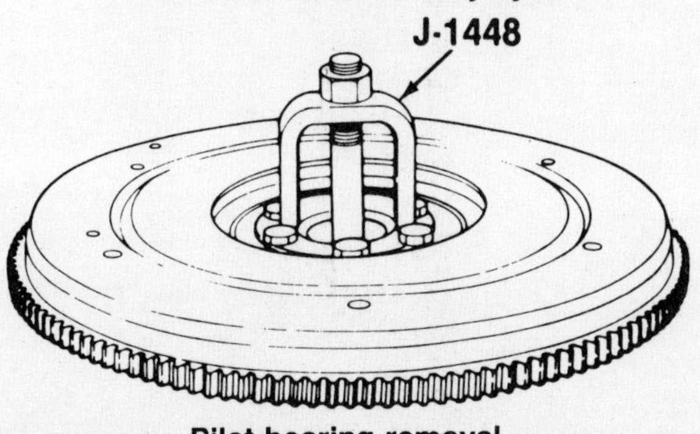

Pilot bearing removal

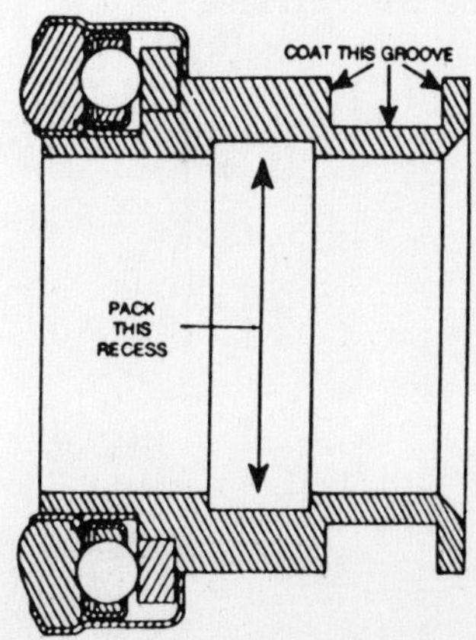

Lubrication points on the clutch throwout bearing

8. To install, use a new gasket, reverse the removal procedure and bleed the clutch system.

C/K Series

1. Disconnect the negative battery cable.
2. Remove the lower steering column covers.
3. Remove the lower left side air conditioning duct, if so equipped.
4. Disconnect the pushrod from the clutch pedal.
5. Disconnect the secondary cylinder hydraulic line from the master cylinder.
6. Remove the master cylinder retaining nuts and remove the master cylinder.
7. To install, use a new gasket, reverse the removal procedure and bleed the clutch system.

Clutch Slave Cylinder

REMOVAL AND INSTALLATION

1. Disconnect the negative battery cable.
2. Raise the vehicle and support it safely.
3. Disconnect the hydraulic line from the secondary cylinder.
4. Disconnect the hydraulic line from ther master cylinder.
5. On R/V models, remove the nut retaining the hydraulic line and the speedometer cable to the cowl, than install the nut to hold the speedometer cable in place.
6. Cover all hydraulic lines to prevent dirt and moisture from entering the system.
7. Installation is the reverse of removal. Bleed the clutch hydraulic system.

BLEEDING THE HYDRAULIC CLUTCH SYSTEM

1. Fill the clutch master cylinder with the proper grade and type fluid. See Section 1. Raise and support the vehicle safely.
2. Remove the slave cylinder retaining bolts. Hold the cylinder about 45° with the bleeder at the highest point.
3. Fully depress the clutch pedal and open the bleeder screw. Repeat until all air is expelled from the system.
4. Be sure that the fluid level remains full in the clutch master cylinder throughout the bleeding procedure.

Clutch Pedal

REMOVAL AND INSTALLATION

R/V Series

1. Disconnect the battery ground.
2. Remove the steering column lower covers.
3. Remove the left side air conditioner duct.
4. Remove the neutral start switch.
5. Remove the pushrod retaining pin and washer.
6. Remove the nuts retaining the inboard and outboard braces.
7. Remove the braces from the stud.
8. Remove the stud, pedal and spring. Slide a long screwdriver or rod into the bracket while removing the stud. This will hold the bracket in place.
9. Remove the bushings and spacer. Replace the bumper if it's worn.

To install:

10. Install the bushings and spacer. Coat these parts with grease prior to assembly.
11. Install the stud, pedal and spring. The stud must be installed in the direction shown in the illustration.
12. Install the braces.
13. Install the pushrod retaining pin and washer.
14. Install the neutral start switch.
15. Install the left side air conditioner duct.
16. Install the steering column lower covers.
17. Connect the battery ground.

C/K Series

1. Disconnect the battery ground.
2. Remove the steering column lower covers.
3. Remove the lower left side air conditioner duct.
4. Remove the neutral start switch.
5. Remove the pushrod retaining ring.
6. Remove the bolt, pedal and spring. Slide a long screwdriver or rod into the bracket while removing the bolt. This will hold the bracket in place.
7. Remove the bushings and spacer. Replace the bumper if it's worn.

To install:

8. Install the bushings and spacer. Coat these parts with grease prior to assembly.
9. Install the bolt, pedal and spring. The bolt must be installed in the direction shown in the illustration. Torque the bolt to 27 ft. lbs.
10. Install the pushrod and retaining ring.
11. Install the neutral start switch.
12. Install the lower left side air conditioner duct.
13. Install the steering column lower covers.
14. Connect the battery ground.

AUTOMATIC TRANSMISSION

Troubleshooting Basic Automatic Transmission Problems

Problem	Cause	Solution
Fluid leakage	• Defective pan gasket • Loose filler tube • Loose extension housing to transmission case • Converter housing area leakage	• Replace gasket or tighten pan bolts • Tighten tube nut • Tighten bolts • Have transmission checked professionally
Fluid flows out the oil filler tube	• High fluid level • Breather vent clogged • Clogged oil filter or screen • Internal fluid leakage	• Check and correct fluid level • Open breather vent • Replace filter or clean screen (change fluid also) • Have transmission checked professionally
Transmission overheats (this is usually accompanied by a strong burned odor to the fluid)	• Low fluid level • Fluid cooler lines clogged • Heavy pulling or hauling with insufficient cooling • Faulty oil pump, internal slippage	• Check and correct fluid level • Drain and refill transmission. If this doesn't cure the problem, have cooler lines cleared or replaced. • Install a transmission oil cooler • Have transmission checked professionally
Buzzing or whining noise	• Low fluid level • Defective torque converter, scored gears	• Check and correct fluid level • Have transmission checked professionally
No forward or reverse gears or slippage in one or more gears	• Low fluid level • Defective vacuum or linkage controls, internal clutch or band failure	• Check and correct fluid level • Have unit checked professionally
Delayed or erratic shift	• Low fluid level • Broken vacuum lines • Internal malfunction	• Check and correct fluid level • Repair or replace lines • Have transmission checked professionally

Lockup Torque Converter Service Diagnosis

Problem	Cause	Solution
No lockup	• Faulty oil pump • Sticking governor valve • Valve body malfunction (a) Stuck switch valve (b) Stuck lockup valve (c) Stuck fail-safe valve • Failed locking clutch • Leaking turbine hub seal • Faulty input shaft or seal ring	• Replace oil pump • Repair or replace as necessary • Repair or replace valve body or its internal components as necessary • Replace torque converter • Replace torque converter • Repair or replace as necessary
Will not unlock	• Sticking governor valve • Valve body malfunction (a) Stuck switch valve (b) Stuck lockup valve (c) Stuck fail-safe valve	• Repair or replace as necessary • Repair or replace valve body or its internal components as necessary
Stays locked up at too low a speed in direct	• Sticking governor valve • Valve body malfunction (a) Stuck switch valve (b) Stuck lockup valve (c) Stuck fail-safe valve	• Repair or replace as necessary • Repair or replace valve body or its internal components as necessary
Locks up or drags in low or second	• Faulty oil pump • Valve body malfunction (a) Stuck switch valve (b) Stuck fail-safe valve	• Replace oil pump • Repair or replace valve body or its internal components as necessary
Sluggish or stalls in reverse	• Faulty oil pump • Plugged cooler, cooler lines or fittings • Valve body malfunction (a) Stuck switch valve (b) Faulty input shaft or seal ring	• Replace oil pump as necessary • Flush or replace cooler and flush lines and fittings • Repair or replace valve body or its internal components as necessary
Loud chatter during lockup engagement (cold)	• Faulty torque converter • Failed locking clutch • Leaking turbine hub seal	• Replace torque converter • Replace torque converter • Replace torque converter
Vibration or shudder during lockup engagement	• Faulty oil pump • Valve body malfunction • Faulty torque converter • Engine needs tune-up	• Repair or replace oil pump as necessary • Repair or replace valve body or its internal components as necessary • Replace torque converter • Tune engine
Vibration after lockup engagement	• Faulty torque converter • Exhaust system strikes underbody • Engine needs tune-up • Throttle linkage misadjusted	• Replace torque converter • Align exhaust system • Tune engine • Adjust throttle linkage

Lockup Torque Converter Service Diagnosis

Problem	Cause	Solution
Vibration when revved in neutral	• Torque converter out of balance	• Replace torque converter
Overheating: oil blows out of dip stick tube or pump seal	• Plugged cooler, cooler lines or fittings • Stuck switch valve	• Flush or replace cooler and flush lines and fittings • Repair switch valve in valve body or replace valve body
Shudder after lockup engagement	• Faulty oil pump • Plugged cooler, cooler lines or fittings • Valve body malfunction • Faulty torque converter • Fail locking clutch • Exhaust system strikes underbody • Engine needs tune-up • Throttle linkage misadjusted	• Replace oil pump • Flush or replace cooler and flush lines and fittings • Repair or replace valve body or its internal components as necessary • Replace torque converter • Replace torque converter • Align exhaust system • Tune engine • Adjust throttle linkage

Transmission Fluid Indications

The appearance and odor of the transmission fluid can give valuable clues to the overall condition of the transmission. Always note the appearance of the fluid when you check the fluid level or change the fluid. Rub a small amount of fluid between your fingers to feel for grit and smell the fluid on the dipstick.

If the fluid appears:	It indicates:
Clear and red colored	• Normal operation
Discolored (extremely dark red or brownish) or smells burned	• Band or clutch pack failure, usually caused by an overheated transmission. Hauling very heavy loads with insufficient power or failure to change the fluid, often result in overheating. Do not confuse this appearance with newer fluids that have a darker red color and a strong odor (though not a burned odor).
Foamy or aerated (light in color and full of bubbles)	• The level is too high (gear train is churning oil) • An internal air leak (air is mixing with the fluid). Have the transmission checked professionally.
Solid residue in the fluid	• Defective bands, clutch pack or bearings. Bits of band material or metal abrasives are clinging to the dipstick. Have the transmission checked professionally.
Varnish coating on the dipstick	• The transmission fluid is overheating

Two transmission are available depending on selected drive-train combinations and GVW packages. They are the Turbo Hydra-Matic 400 3-speed and the Turbo Hydra-Matic 700R4 4-speed overdrive.

In 1990 the designations were changed, while the transmissions remained essentially the same. The THM 400 3-speed became the 3L80; the THM 700R4 became the 4L60.

Fluid Pan and Filter

REMOVAL AND INSTALLATION

The fluid should be drained with the transmission warm. It is easier to change the fluid if the truck is raised somewhat from the ground, but this is not always easy without a lift. The transmission must be level for it to drain properly.

1. Place a shallow pan underneath to catch the transmission fluid (about 5 pints). Loosen all the pan bolts, then pull one corner down to drain most of the fluid. If it sticks, VERY CAREFULLY pry the pan loose. You can buy aftermarket drain plug kits that makes this operation a bit less messy, once installed.

NOTE: If the fluid removed smells burnt, serious transmission troubles, probably due to overheating, should be suspected.

2. Remove the pan bolts and empty out the pan. On some models, there may not be much room to get at the screws at the front of the pan.
3. Clean the pan with solvent and allow it to air dry. If you use a rag to wipe it out, you risk leaving bits of lint and threads in the transmission.
4. Remove the filter or strainer retaining bolts. On the Turbo Hydra-Matic 400, there are two screws securing the filter or screen to the valve body. A reusable strainer may be found on some models. The strainer may be cleaned in solvent and air dried thoroughly. The filter and gasket must be replaced.
5. Install a new gasket and filter.
6. Install a new gasket on the pan, and tighten the bolts evenly to 12 foot pounds in a criss-cross pattern.
7. Add or DEXRON®II transmission fluid through the dipstick tube. The correct amount is in the Capacities Chart. Do not overfill.
8. With the gearshift lever in **PARK**, start the engine and let it idle. Do not race the engine.
9. Move the gearshift lever through each position, holding the brakes. Return the lever to **PARK**, and check the fluid level with the engine idling. The level should be between the two dimples on the dipstick, about ¼ in. (6mm) below the **ADD** mark. Add fluid, if necessary.
10. Check the fluid level after the truck has been driven enough to thoroughly warm up the transmission. Details are given under Fluid Level Checks earlier in Section 1. If the transmission is overfilled, the excess must be drained off. Overfilling causes aerated fluid, resulting in transmission slippage and probable damage.

Shift Linkage

ADJUSTMENT

All Models

1. Raise and support the front end on jackstands.
2. Loosen the shift lever bolt or nut at the transmission lever so that the lever is free to move on the rod.
3. Set the column shift lever to the Neutral gate notch, by rotating it until the shift lever drops into the Neutral gate. Do not use the indicator pointer as a reference to position the shift lever, as this will not be accurate.
4. Set the transmission lever in the neutral position by mov-

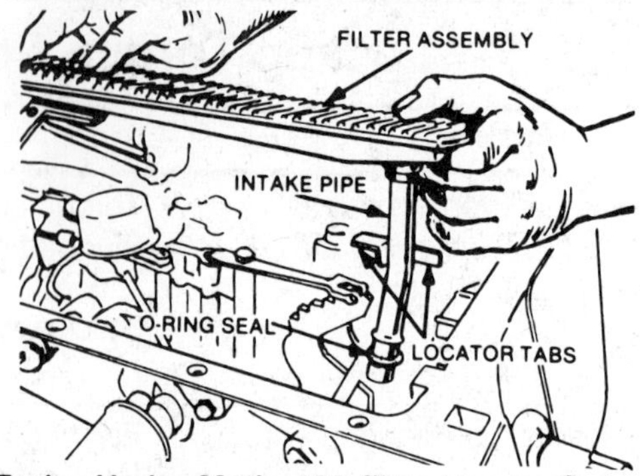

The Turbo Hydra-Matic 400 filter has an O-ring on the intake pipe; check the condition of this O-ring, and replace it as necessary

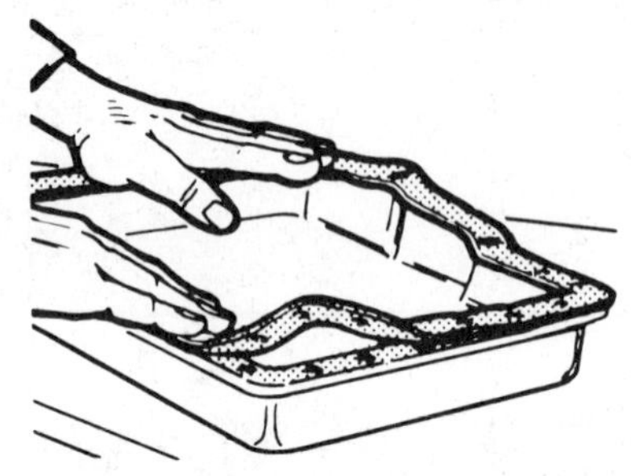

Install the new gasket on the pan

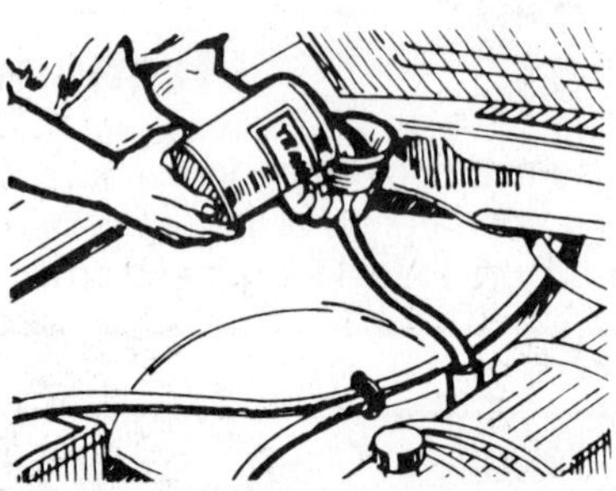

Transmission fluid is added through the dipstick tube

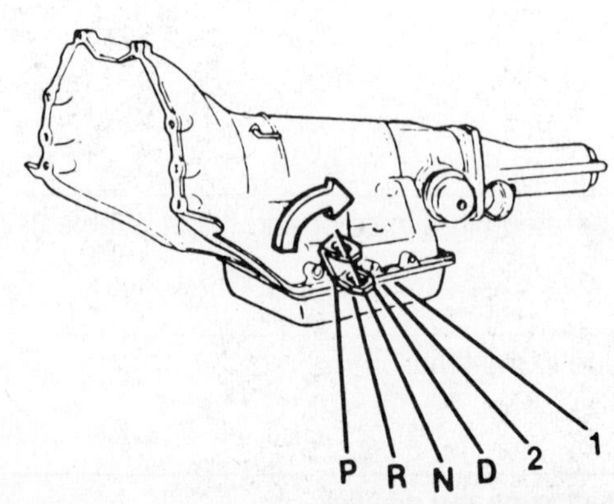

Shift positions

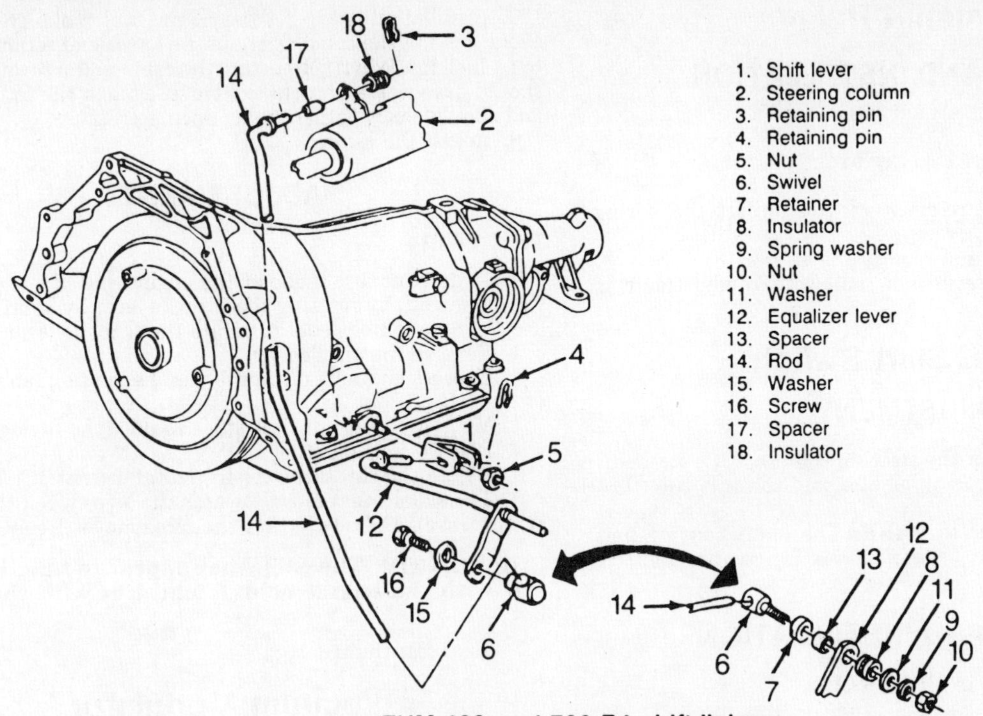

THM 400 and 700-R4 shift linkage

ing it clockwise to the Park detent, then counterclockwise 2 detents to Neutral.

5. Hold the rod tightly in the swivel and tighten the nut or bolt to 17 ft. lbs.

6. Move the column shifter to Park and check that the engine starts. Check the adjustment by moving the selector to each gear position.

REMOVAL AND INSTALLATION

THM 400

1. Remove the linakge rod-to-column bolt and washer.
2. Remove the rod and swivel from the column.
3. Remove the control rod-to-equalizer lever retaining pin and disconnect the rod from the lever.
4. Remove the intermediate rod-to-transmission lever retaining pin and remove the rod and equalizer lever assembly. Don't lose the spring and bushing.
5. Installation is the reverse of removal. Adjust the linkage as described above.

THM 700R4

1. Remove the linakge rod-to-column retaining pin.
2. Remove the rod, bushing and spring from the column. Note any washers and/or spacers and their location(s).
3. Remove the control rod-to-equalizer lever bolt and swivel and disconnect the rod from the lever.
4. Remove the intermediate rod-to-transmission lever retaining pin and remove the rod and equalizer lever assembly. Don't lose the spring and bushing.
5. Installation is the reverse of removal. Adjust the linkage as described above.

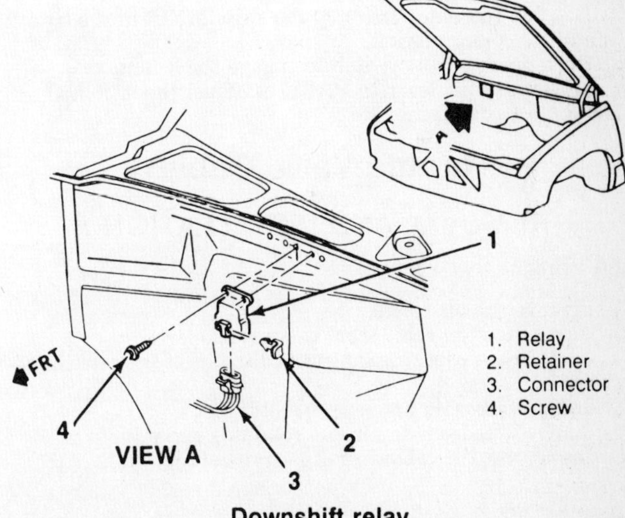

Downshift relay

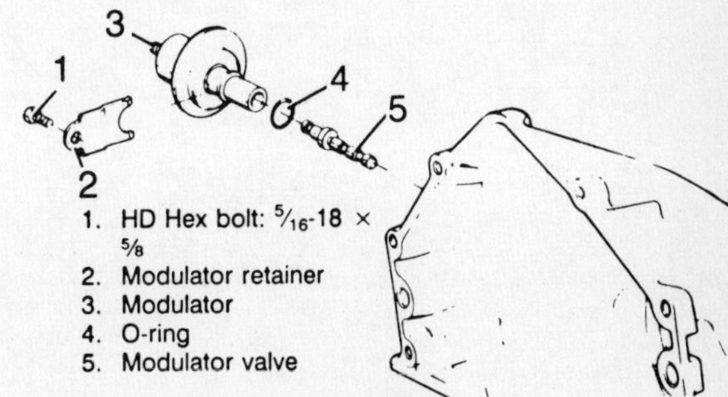

Vacuum modulator

Downshift Relay

REMOVAL AND INSTALLATION

THM 400

The relay is located just slightlty to the passemger's side of center on the firewall.

1. Remove the wiring retainer and disconnect the wiring from the switch.
2. Remove the screws and remove the switch.
3. Installation is the reverse of removal. No adjustment is necessary.

Neutral Start Switch

ADJUSTMENT

The switch is located on the steering column.

1. Move the switch housing all the way towards the "low gear" position.
2. Move the shift lever to **PARK**. The main housing and housing back should ratchet, providing proper switch adjustment.

REMOVAL AND INSTALLATION

1. Place the shift lever in **NEUTRAL**.
2. Disconnect the wiring at the switch.
3. Spread the tangs on the housing and pull the switch out.

To install:

4. Align the actuator on the switch with the hole in the shift tube.
5. Position the rear portion of the switch to fit in the cutout in the lower column jacket.
6. Push down on the switch to engage the 2 tangs.
7. Move the shift lever to **PARK** to adjust the switch.
8. Connect the wiring.

Throttle Valve Cable

REMOVAL AND INSTALLATION

THM 700R4

1. Remove the air cleaner.
2. Disconnect the cable from the throttle lever.
3. Compress the locking tangs and disconnect the cable housing from the bracket.
4. Remove all cable brackets and straps.
5. Remove the cable lower end retaining screw.
6. Disconnect the cable from the transmission link.
7. Installation is the reverse of removal. Take great care to avoid kinking the cable. Tighten the lower end retaining screw to 84 inch lbs. When connecting the cable to the throttle lever it should have a small amount of travel against the return spring and should easily return under spring pressure.
8. Adjust the cable.

ADJUSTMENT

THM 700R4

The adjustment is made at the engine end of the cable with the engine off, by rotating the throttle lever by hand. DO NOT use the accelerator pedal to rotate the throttle lever.

1. Remove the air cleaner.
2. Depress and hold down the metal adjusting tab at the end of the cable.
3. Move the slider until it stops against the fitting.
4. Release the adjusting tab.
5. Rotate the throttle lever to the full extent of it travel.
6. The slider must move towards the lever when the lever is at full travel. Make sure that the cable moves freely.

CHILTON TIP: The cable may appear to function properly with the engine cold. Recheck it with the engine hot.

7. Road test the truck.

Vacuum Modulator

REMOVAL AND INSTALLATION

THM 400

1. Raise and support the front end on jackstands.
2. Disconnect the vacuum line at the modulator.
3. Remove the screw and retaining clamp.
4. Remove the modulator. Be careful! Some fluid may run out.
5. Installation is the reverse of removal. Don't kink the vacuum line. Replace any lost fluid.

Vehicle Speed Sensor

REMOVAL AND INSTALLATION

THM 400

1. Raise and support the front end on jackstands.
2. Disconnect wiring harness at the sensor.
3. Remove the retaining screw and retainer.
4. Remove the speed sensor.

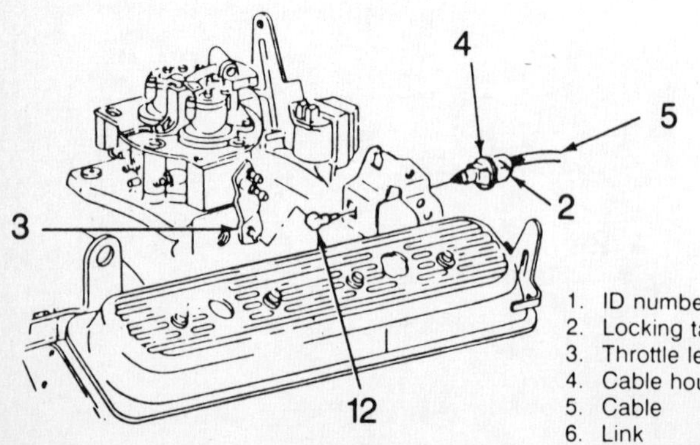

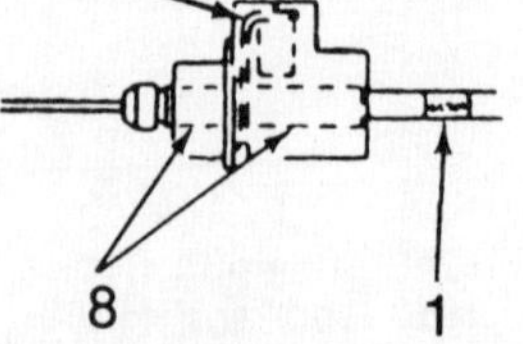

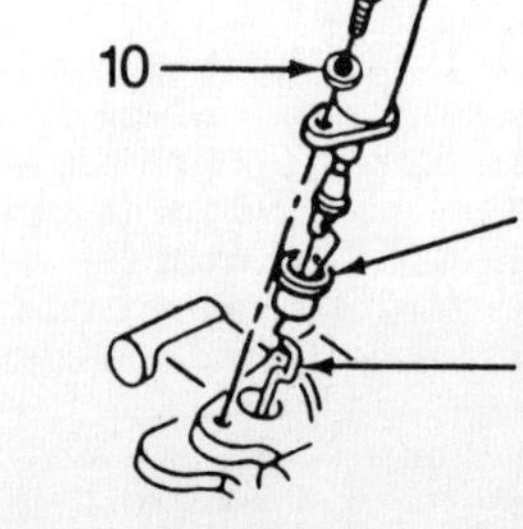

1. ID number
2. Locking tangs
3. Throttle lever
4. Cable housing
5. Cable
6. Link
7. Re-adjust tab
8. Slider
9. Screw
10. Washer
11. Seal
12. Terminal

TV cable replacement

5. Remove the seal.
6. Installation is the reverse of removal. Tighten the screw to 84 inch lbs.

Extension Housing Rear Seal

REPLACEMENT

1. Raise and support the truck on jackstands.
2. Matchmark and remove the driveshaft. Be careful! Some fluid may run out. You can avoid this by raising only the rear of the truck.
3. Centerpunch the seal to distort it and carefully pry it out.
4. Coat the outer edge of the new seal with non-hardening sealer.
5. Place the seal in the bore and carefully drive it into place. A seal installer makes this job easier.
6. Install the driveshaft. It's a good idea to coat the driveshaft end with grease to avoid damaging the seal.
7. Lower the truck and replace any lost fluid.

Transmission

REMOVAL AND INSTALLATION

NOTE: It would be best to drain the transmission before starting.

It may be necessary to disconnect and remove the exhaust crossover pipe on V8s, and to disconnect the catalytic converter and remove its support bracket.

R Series

1. Disconnect the battery ground cable.
2. Remove the air cleaner.
3. Disconnect the detent cable at the throttle lever.
4. Raise and support the truck on jackstands.
5. Drain the transmission fluid.
6. Remove the driveshaft, after matchmarking its flanges.
7. Disconnect the:
   a. speedometer cable

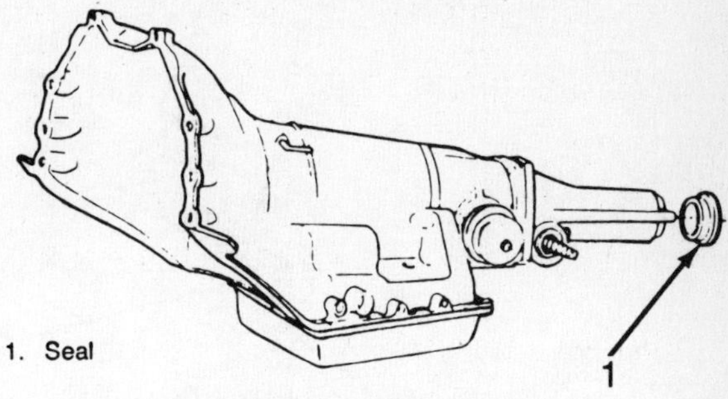

Extension housing seal

   b. downshift cable
   c. vacuum modulator line
   d. shift linkage
   e. throttle linkage
   f. fluid cooler lines
8. Remove the filler tube.
9. Disconnect the support bracket at the catalytic converter.
10. Look around to see if there is anything else in the way.
11. Support the transmission on a transmission jack and unbolt the rear mount from the crossmember.
12. Remove the crossmember.
13. Remove any tranmission support braces. Note their exact positions for installation.
14. Remove the torque converter underpan, matchmark the flywheel and converter, and remove the converter bolts.
15. Support the engine on a jack and lower the transmission slightly for access to the upper transmission to engine bolts.
16. Remove the transmission to engine bolts and pull the transmission back. Rig up a strap or keep the front of the transmission up so the converter doesn't fall out.

To install:

17. Raise the transmission into position.
18. Roll the unit forward and against the engine, engaging the locating dowels and aligning the torque converter marks. Install the transmission to engine bolts. Install all the bolts finger-

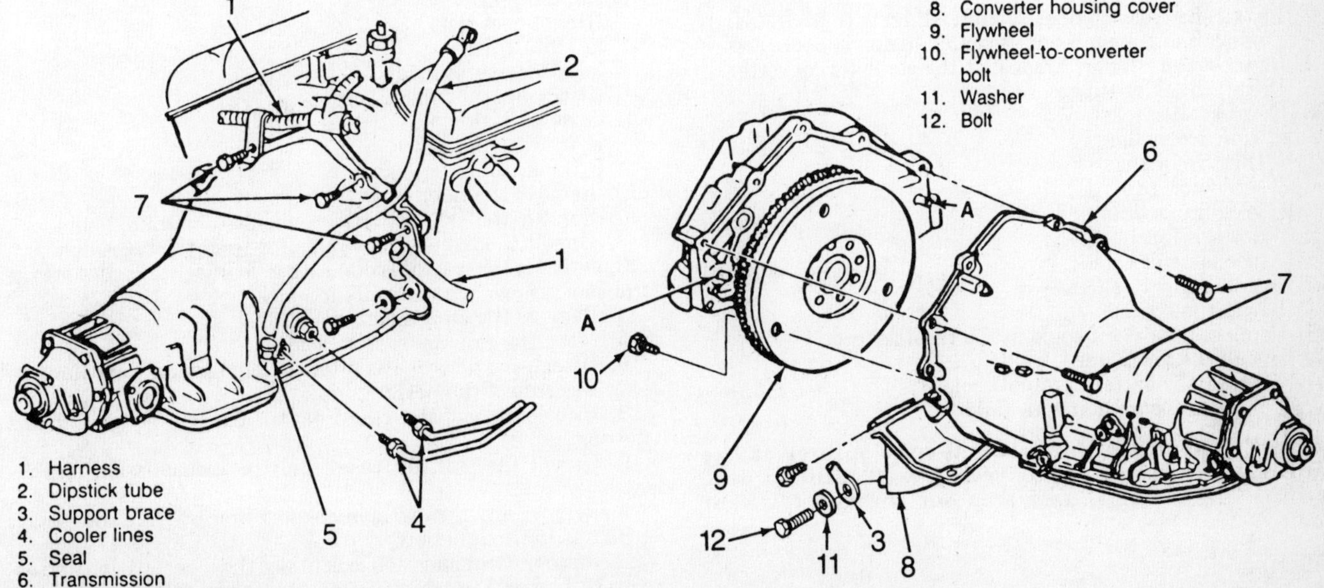

THM 400 transmission and related components

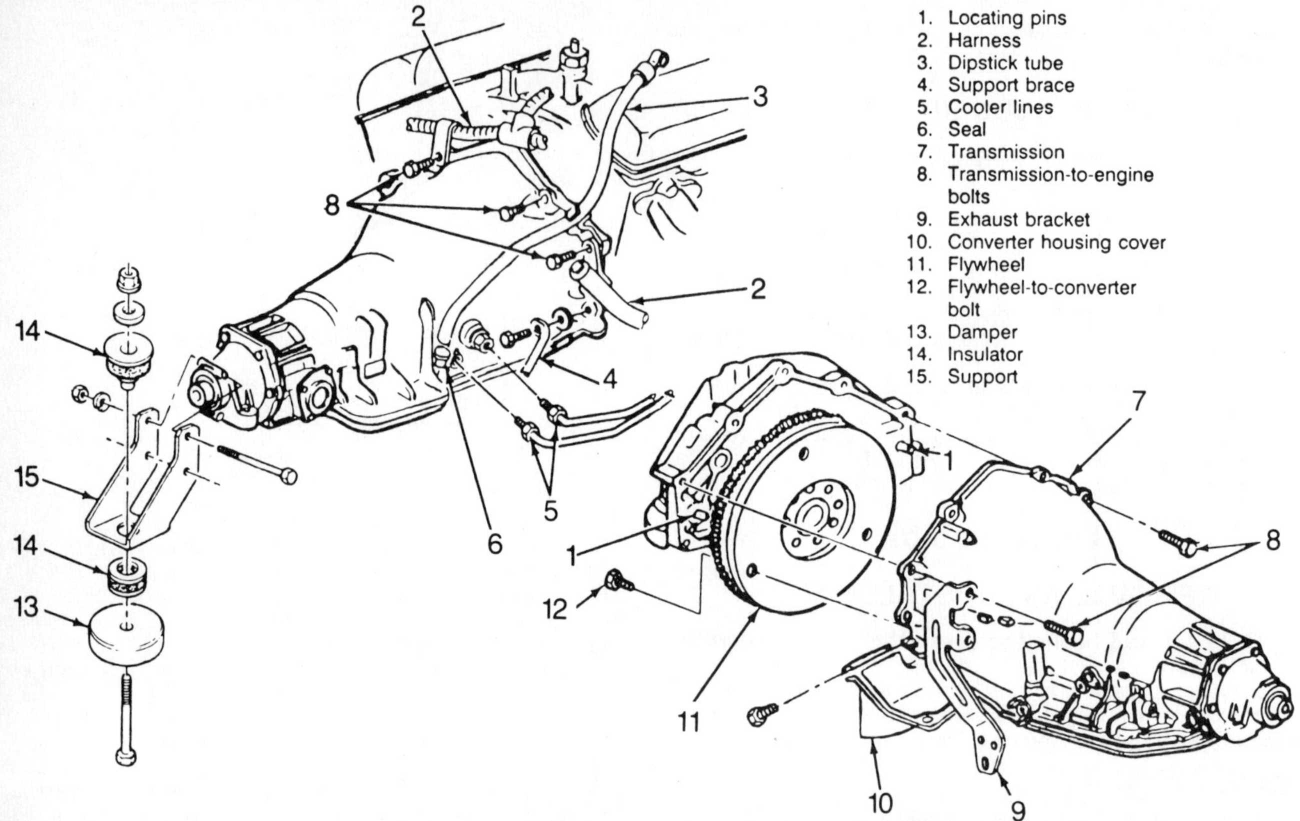

THM 700-R4 transmission and related components

tight, then torque them to 35 ft. lbs.

19. Install the converter bolts finger-tight. Then, torque the bolts to 50 ft. lbs.
20. Install the converter cover.
21. Install the tranmission support braces. The braces must be installed in the exact positions from which they were removed! Torque the bolts to 35 ft. lbs.
22. Install the crossmember. Torque all bolts to 35 ft. lbs.
23. Remove the transmission jack and engine support jack.
24. Connect the support bracket at the catalytic converter.
25. Install the filler tube.
26. Connect the:
    a. fluid cooler lines
    b. throttle linkage
    c. shift linkage
    d. vacuum modulator line
    e. downshift cable
    f. speedometer cable
27. Install the driveshaft.
28. Lower the truck.
29. Connect the detent cable at the throttle lever.
30. Install the air cleaner.
31. Connect the battery ground cable.
32. Fill the transmission with fluid.

NOTE: Lubricate the internal yoke splines at the transmission end of the driveshaft with lithium base grease. The grease should seep out through the vent hole.

V Series

1. Disconnect the battery ground cable.
2. Remove the transmission dipstick.
3. Detach the TV cable at the throttle linkage.
4. Remove the transfer case shift lever knob and boot.
5. Raise and support the truck on jackstands.
6. Remove the skid plate.
7. Remove the torque converter cover.
8. Matchmark the flywheel and torque converter, remove the bolts, and secure the converter so it doesn't fall out of the transmission.
9. Disconnect the:
    a. shift linkage
    b. speedometer cable
    c. vacuum modulator line
    d. downshift cable
    e. throttle linkage
    f. cooler times
10. Remove the filler tube.
11. Remove the exhaust crossover pipe-to-manifold bolts.
12. Unbolt the transfer case adapter from the crossmember.
13. Support the transmission with a floor jack and support the transfer case with a transmission jack.
14. Remove the crossmember.
15. Move the exhaust system aside.
16. Detach the driveshafts after matchmarking their flanges.
17. Disconnect the parking brake cable.
18. Unbolt the transfer case from the frame bracket. Support the engine.
19. Unbolt the transfer case from the transmission and remove it.
20. Remove any tranmission support braces. Note their exact positions for installation.
21. Place the transmission jack under the transmission and secure it. Unbolt the transmission from the engine, pull the assembly back, and remove it.

To install:

22. Raise the transmission into position and roll it forward to

engage the locating dowels on the engine. Make sure that the torque converter-to-flex plate matchmarks are aligned.

23. Install all engine-to-transmission bolts finger-tight. Then, torque them to 35 ft. lbs.
24. Install all the torque converter bolts finger-tight. Then, torque them to 50 ft. lbs.
25. Install the support braces in the same, excat position from which they were removed. Torque the bolts to 35 ft. lbs.
26. Raise the transfer case into position and mate it with the transmission. Torque the attaching bolts to 24 ft. lbs.
27. Install the crossmember. Torque the bolts to 35 ft. lbs.
26. Bolt the transfer case from the frame bracket. Torque the bolts to 35 ft. lbs.
28. Remove the jacks and engine support.
29. Connect the parking brake cable.
30. Install the driveshafts.
31. Install the exhaust crossover pipe-to-manifold bolts.
32. Install the filler tube.
33. Connect the:
    a. cooler lines
    b. throttle linkage
    c. downshift cable
    d. vacuum modulator line
    e. speedometer cable
    f. shift linkage
34. Install the torque converter cover.
35. Install the skid plate.
36. Lower the truck.
37. Install the transfer case shift lever knob and boot.
38. Connect the TV cable at the throttle linkage.
39. Install the transmission dipstick.
40. Connect the battery ground cable.
41. Fill the transmission.

C Series

1. Disconnect the battery ground cable.
2. Remove the air cleaner.
3. Disconnect the TV cable at the throttle lever.
4. Raise and support the truck on jackstands.
5. Drain the transmission fluid.
6. Remove the driveshaft, after matchmarking its flanges.
7. Disconnect the:
    a. wiring harness at the transmission
    b. vacuum modulator line
    c. shift linkage
    d. fluid cooler lines
8. Remove the filler tube.
9. Disconnect the support bracket at the catalytic converter.
10. Look around to see if there is anything else in the way.
11. Support the transmission on a transmission jack and unbolt the rear mount from the crossmember.
12. Remove the crossmember.
13. Remove any tranmission support braces. Note their exact positions for installation.
14. Remove the torque converter underpan, matchmark the flywheel and converter, and remove the converter bolts.
15. Support the engine on a jack and lower the transmission slightly for access to the upper transmission to engine bolts.
16. Remove the transmission to engine bolts and pull the transmission back. Rig up a strap or keep the front of the transmission up so the converter doesn't fall out.

To install:

17. Raise the transmission into position.
18. Roll the unit forward and against the engine, engaging the locating dowels and aligning the torque converter marks. Install the transmission to engine bolts. Install all the bolts finger-tight, then torque them to 35 ft. lbs.
19. Install the converter bolts finger-tight. Then, torque the bolts to 50 ft. lbs.
20. Install the converter cover.
21. Install the tranmission support braces. The braces must be installed in the exact positions from which they were removed! Torque the bolts to 35 ft. lbs.
22. Install the crossmember. Torque all bolts to 35 ft. lbs.
23. Remove the transmission jack and engine support jack.
24. Connect the support bracket at the catalytic converter.
25. Install the filler tube.
26. Connect the:
    a. fluid cooler lines
    b. wiring harness
    c. shift linkage
    d. vacuum modulator line
27. Install the driveshaft.
28. Lower the truck.
29. Connect the TV cable at the throttle lever.
30. Install the air cleaner.
31. Connect the battery ground cable.
32. Fill the transmission with fluid.

K Series

1. Disconnect the battery ground cable.
2. Remove the transmission dipstick.
3. Detach the TV cable at the throttle linkage.
4. Remove the transfer case shift lever knob and boot.
5. Raise and support the truck on jackstands.
6. Remove the skid plate.
7. Remove the torque converter cover.
8. Matchmark the flywheel and torque converter, remove the bolts, and secure the converter so it doesn't fall out of the transmission.
9. Disconnect the:
    a. shift linkage
    b. wiring harness at the transmission
    c. vacuum modulator line
    d. cooler lines
10. Remove the filler tube.
11. Remove the exhaust crossover pipe-to-manifold bolts.
12. Unbolt the transfer case adapter from the crossmember.
13. Support the transmission with a floor jack and support the transfer case with a transmission jack.
14. Remove the crossmember.
15. Move the exhaust system aside.
16. Detach the driveshafts after matchmarking their flanges.
17. Disconnect the parking brake cable.
18. Unbolt the transfer case from the frame bracket. Support the engine.
19. Unbolt the transfer case from the transmission and remove it.
20. Remove any tranmission support braces. Note their exact positions for installation.
21. Place the transmission jack under the transmission and secure it. Unbolt the transmission from the engine, pull the assembly back, and remove it.

To install:

22. Raise the transmission into position and roll it forward to engage the locating dowels on the engine. Make sure that the torque converter-to-flex plate matchmarks are aligned.
23. Install all engine-to-transmission bolts finger-tight. Then, torque them to 35 ft. lbs.
24. Install all the torque converter bolts finger-tight. Then, torque them to 50 ft. lbs.
25. Install the support braces in the same, excat position from which they were removed. Torque the bolts to 35 ft. lbs.
26. Raise the transfer case into position and mate it with the transmission. Torque the attaching bolts to 24 ft. lbs.
27. Install the crossmember. Torque the bolts to 35 ft. lbs.
26. Bolt the transfer case from the frame bracket. Torque the bolts to 35 ft. lbs.
28. Remove the jacks and engine support.
29. Connect the parking brake cable.

30. Install the driveshafts.
31. Install the exhaust crossover pipe-to-manifold bolts.
32. Install the filler tube.
33. Connect the:
    a. cooler lines
    b. wiring harness at the transmission
    d. vacuum modulator line
    f. shift linkage
34. Install the torque converter cover.
35. Install the skid plate.
36. Lower the truck.
37. Install the transfer case shift lever knob and boot.
38. Connect the TV cable at the throttle linkage.
39. Install the transmission dipstick.
40. Connect the battery ground cable.
41. Fill the transmission.

TRANSFER CASE

On 1988 V Series trucks, the New Process 205 and 208 units were used. The 208 is used on ½ and ¾ ton models; the 205 on all 1 ton models.

On 1989–90 V Series trucks the New Process 241 unit is used for all ½ and ¾ ton models; the 205 is still used on all 1 ton models.

On 1988 K Series trucks, the NP 241 is used on all models.

On 1989–90 K Series trucks the NP241 is used on all models except the 30 series with dual rear wheels; the Borg-Warner 1370 is used on the 30 series with dual rear wheels.

Linkage

ADJUSTMENTS

NP-208 and Early 241

1. Raise and support the front end on jackstands.
2. Disconnect the shift rod from the case lever.
3. Place the shift lever in the 4H position.
4. Move the case lever forward to the 4H position.
5. Push the swivel into the levr.
6. Hang a 0.20 in. (5mm) gauge over the rod behind the swivel on the threaded portion.
7. Thread the nut down against the gauge and remove the gauge.
8. Push the swivel against the nut and tighten the nut.

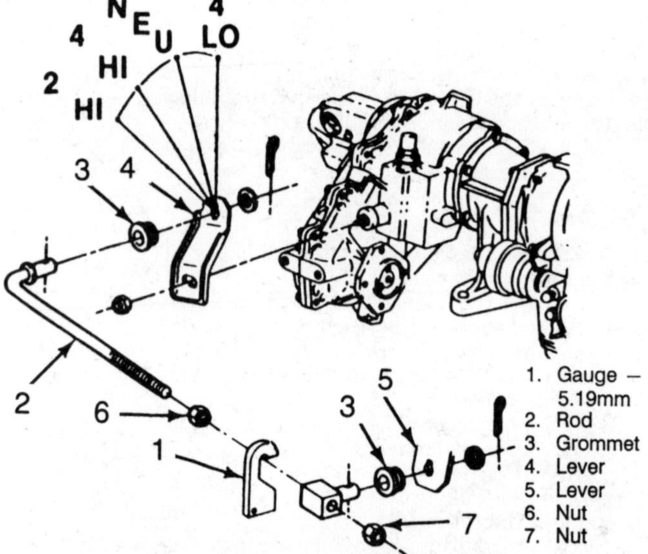

NP-208 linkage adjustment

Borg-Warner 1370

1. Raise and support the front end on jackstands.
2. Place the shift lever in the 4H position.
3. Disconnect the linkage rod from the shift lever.
4. Move the case lever all the way forward to the 4H position.
5. Adjust the swivel so that the swivel stud will drop in the hole in the case lever. Connect the rod.

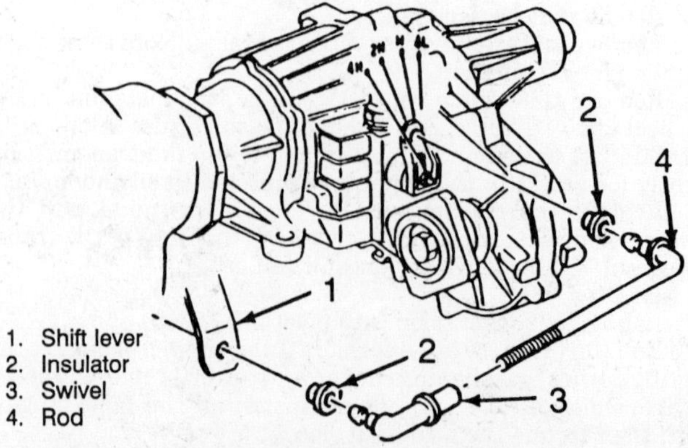

1370 linkage adjustment

Electronic Synchronizer

SYSTEM CHECK

Borg-Warner 1370

1. Turn the ignition switch to the **RUN** position with 4WD engaged.

NOTE: It may be necessary to rotate the front wheels slightly to engage the axle.

2. Raise and support the front end on jackstands.
3. Disconnect the wiring plug at the transfer case.
4. Connect a test light from the red wire of the connector to a good ground. The light should come on. If it does not, check the circuit for opens. If no opens are found, replace the relay.
5. If the test lamp does light, check the synchronizer coil for continuity with an ohmmeter. If the coil is open, replace it. If the coil has continuity, it's okay. Recheck fluid levels, linkage adjustment, etc., before assuming the synchronizer is faulty.

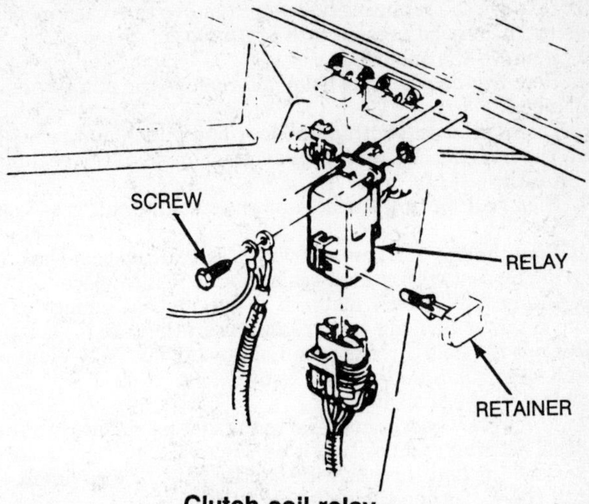

Clutch coil relay

Clutch Coil Relay

REPLACEMENT

Borg-Warner 1370

The relay is mounted on the firewall, in the engine comaprtment.

1. Remove the connector retainer.
2. Unplug the harness connector.
3. Remove the retaining screws.
4. Installation is the reverse of removal.

Front or Rear Output Shaft Seal

REPLACEMENT

All Models

1. Raise and support the truck on jackstands.
2. Remove the skid plate if necessary to gain access to the front seal.
3. Matchmark and remove the driveshaft.
4. Remove the nut, washer and yoke.

NOTE: Some models don't use a washer at the rear yoke nut.

5. Some models employ a shield around the seal. Remove it.
6. Using a hammer and a punch, carefully distort the seal so that you can pull it out with a pliers. Be careful to avoid damage to the seal bore!
7. Coat the seal lips with clean oil fluid. Coat the outer edge of the seal with gasket sealer.
8. Position the seal in the bore and drive it into place by carefully tapping around it with a hammer. If you have access to one, a seal installer will make the job a little easier.
9. Install the shield, if used.
10. Coat the outer surface of the yoke neck with clean oil and slide it into place.
11. Install the nut and washer. Torque the nut to:
    - NP-241: 110 ft. lbs.
    - NP-205: 150 ft. lbs.
    - NP-208: 120 ft. lbs.
    - BW-1370 front: 165 ft. lbs.
    - BW-1370 rear: 125 ft. lbs.
12. Install the driveshaft.
13. Install the skid plate.

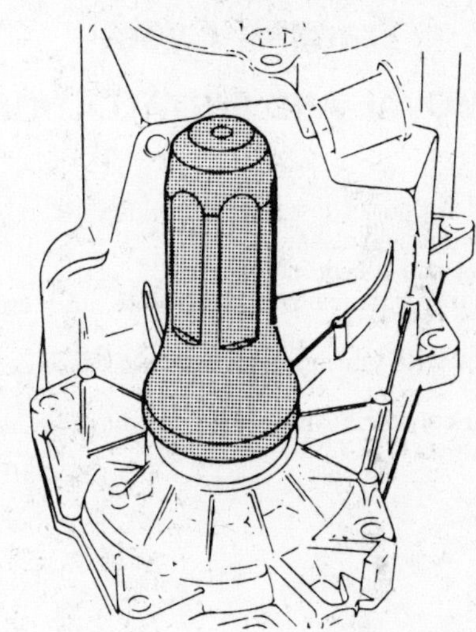
Installing the output shaft seal

Rear Extension Housing or Rear Pump Retainer Housing

REMOVAL AND INSTALLATION

NP-241

1. Raise and support the truck on jackstands.
2. Matchmark and remove the driveshaft and yoke.

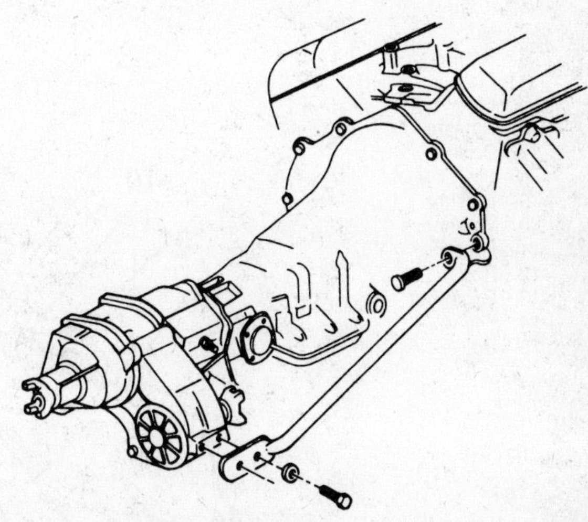
Strut rod support

3. Remove the retaining bolts and remove the rear extension housing. It may be necessary to tap it loose.
4. Remove the snapring.
5. Remove the retaining bolts and remove the pump retainer housing.
6. Distort the seal with a hammer and punch and remove it from the housing. Be careful to avoid damage to the seal bore!

To install:

7. Clean all mating surfaces of gasket material, grease and oil.
8. Coat the lips of a new seal with clean oil and coat the outer edge of the seal with gasket sealer. Drive it into place.
9. Apply RTV gasket material to the mating surface of the pump retainer housing and position it on the case.
10. Coat the bolt threads with Loctite 242® or equivalent and install them. Torque the bolts to 30 ft. lbs.
11. Install the snapring.
12. Apply RTV gasket material to the mating surface of the extension housing and position it on the case.
13. Coat the bolt threads with Loctite 242® or equivalent and install them. Torque the bolts to 23 ft. lbs.
14. Install the driveshaft and yoke.

Transfer Case

REMOVAL AND INSTALLATION

NP-205

1. Raise and support the truck on jackstands.
2. Drain the transfer case.
3. Disconnect the speedometer cable.
4. If necessary, remove the skid plate and crossmember support.
5. On trucks with automatic transmission, disconnect the strut rod.
6. Matchmark the driveshafts, disconnect them, and support them out of the way.
7. Disconnect the shift lever rod from the shift rail link.
8. Support the transfer case and remove the bolts attaching the transfer case to transmission adaptor.
9. Move the transfer case to the rear until the input shaft clears the adaptor and lower the transfer case from the truck.

To install:

10. Raise the transfer case into position and roll it forward until the input shaft engages the adapter.
11. Install the bolts attaching the transfer case to transmission adaptor. Torque them to 24 ft. lbs.
12. Connect the shift lever rod to the shift rail link.
13. Connect the driveshafts.
14. On trucks with automatic transmission, connect the strut rod. Torque the transmission end bolts to 129 ft. lbs.; the transfer case end bolts to 35 ft. lbs.
15. Install the skid plate and crossmember support.
16. Remove the jack.
17. Connect the speedometer cable.
18. Fill the transfer case.

NP-208

1. Raise and support the truck on jackstands.
2. Drain the transfer case.
3. Place the case in the 4H position.
4. Disconnect the speedometer cable.
5. Disconnect the shift lever rod at the swivel.
6. Disconnect the indicator light switch.
7. Matchmark the driveshafts, disconnect them, and support them out of the way.
8. Remove the parking brake cable guide from the pivot on the right frame rail.
9. On trucks with automatic transmission, disconnect the strut rod.
10. If necessary, remove the skid plate.
11. Support the transfer case on a transmission jack and remove the bolts attaching the transfer case to transmission adaptor.

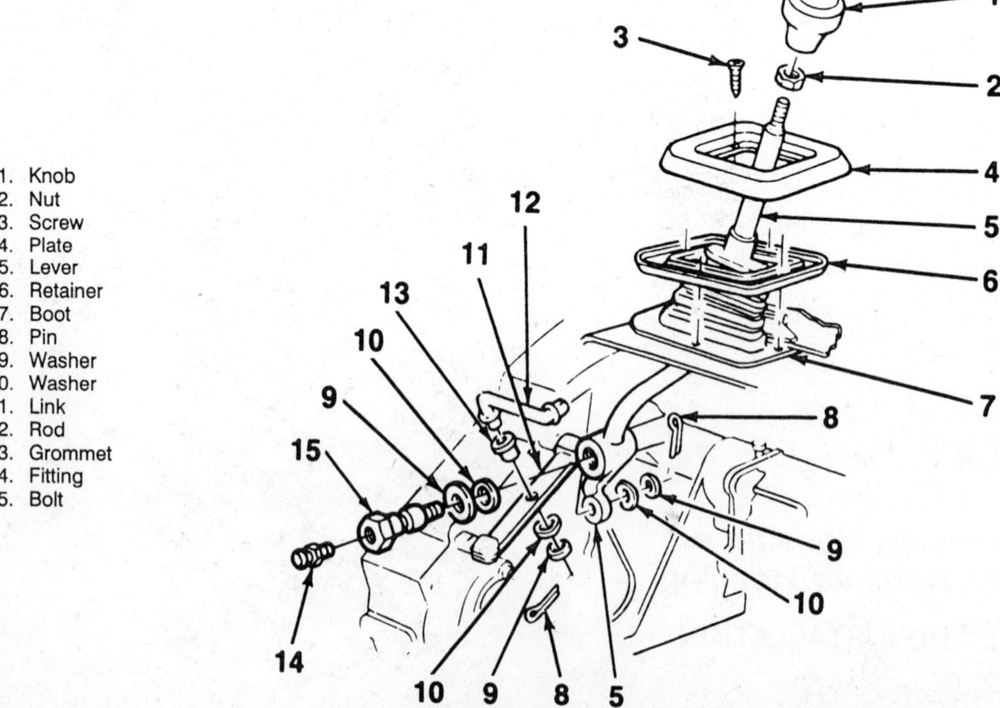

NP-205 shift control components

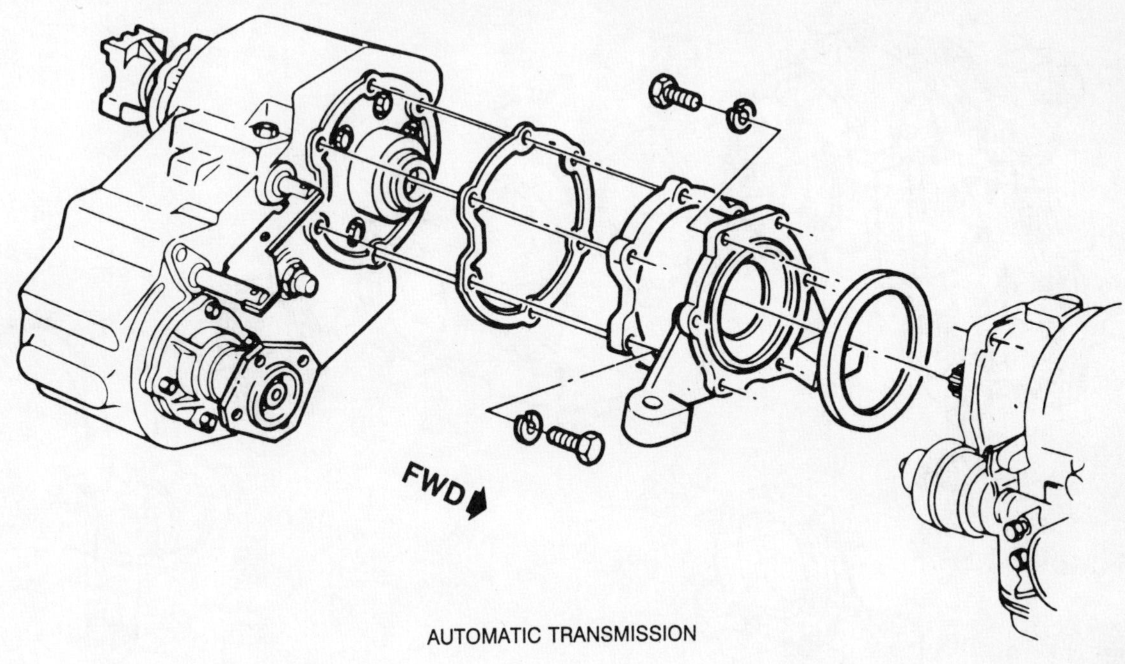

AUTOMATIC TRANSMISSION

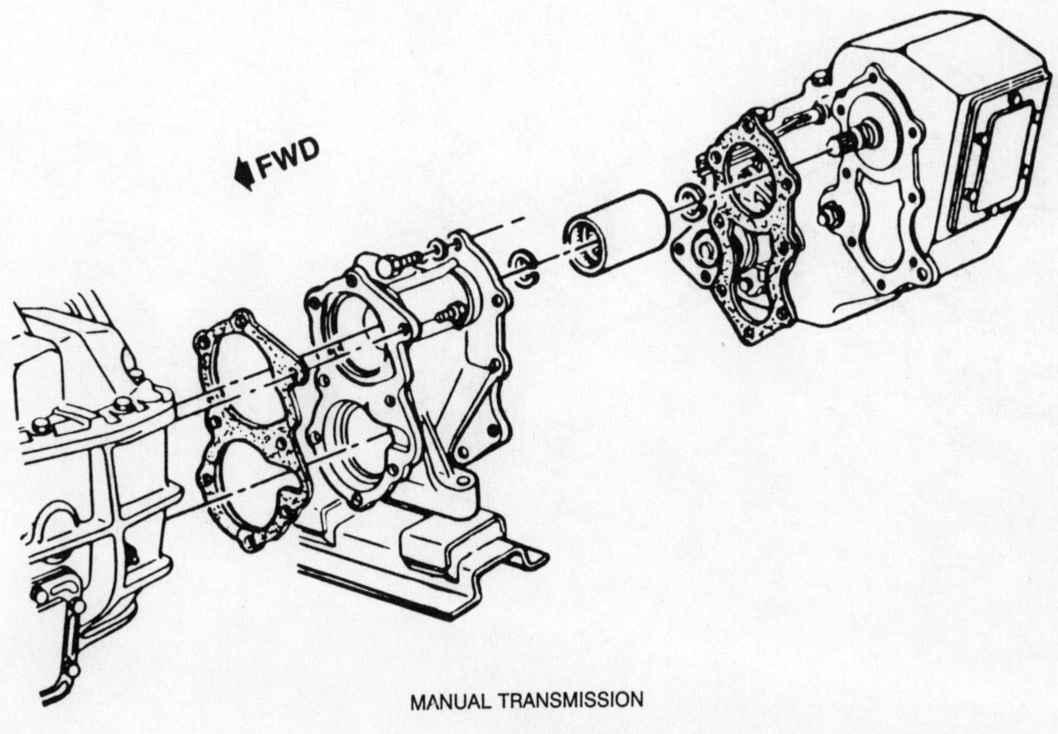

MANUAL TRANSMISSION

NP-205 transmission adapters

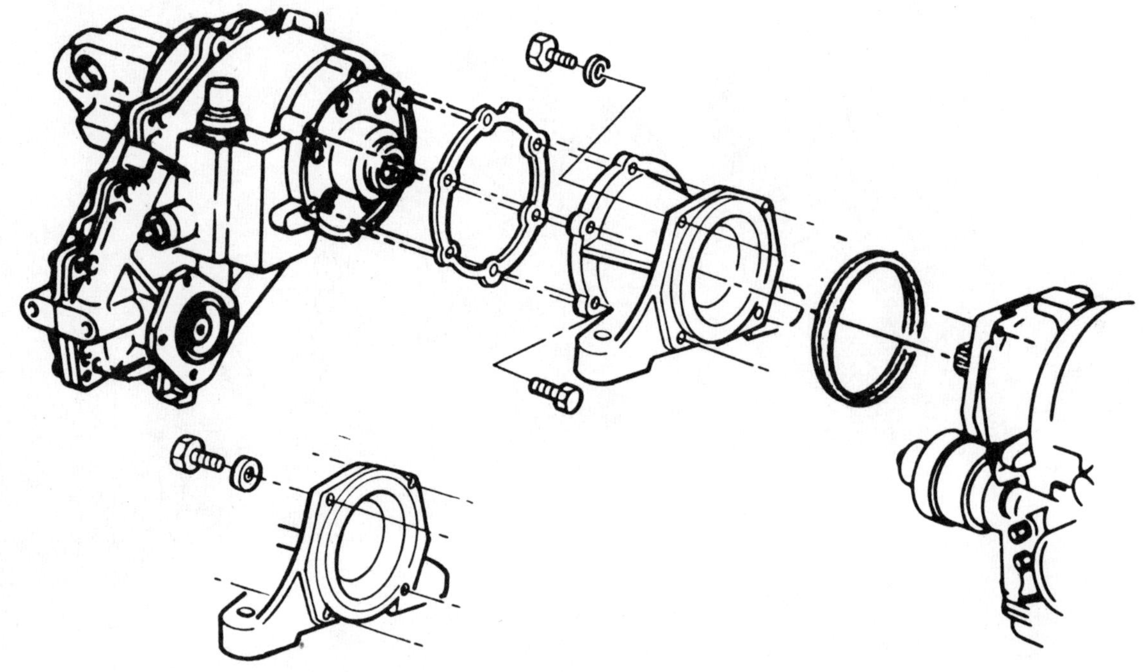

AUTOMATIC TRANSMISSION

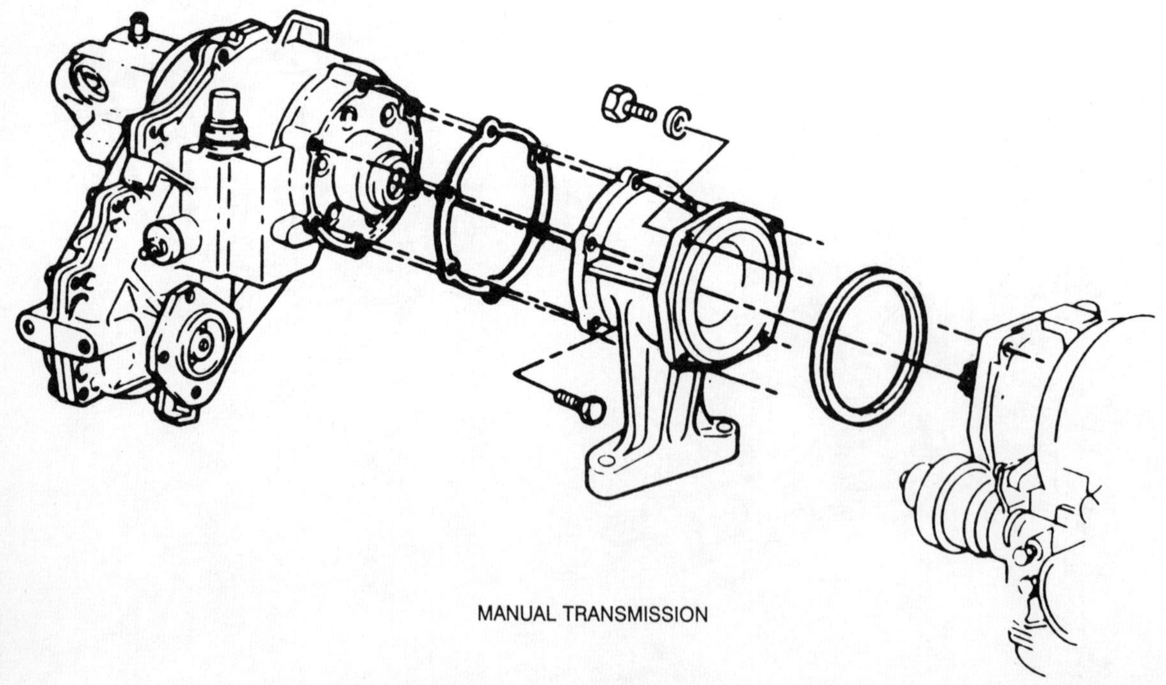

MANUAL TRANSMISSION

NP-208 transmission adapters

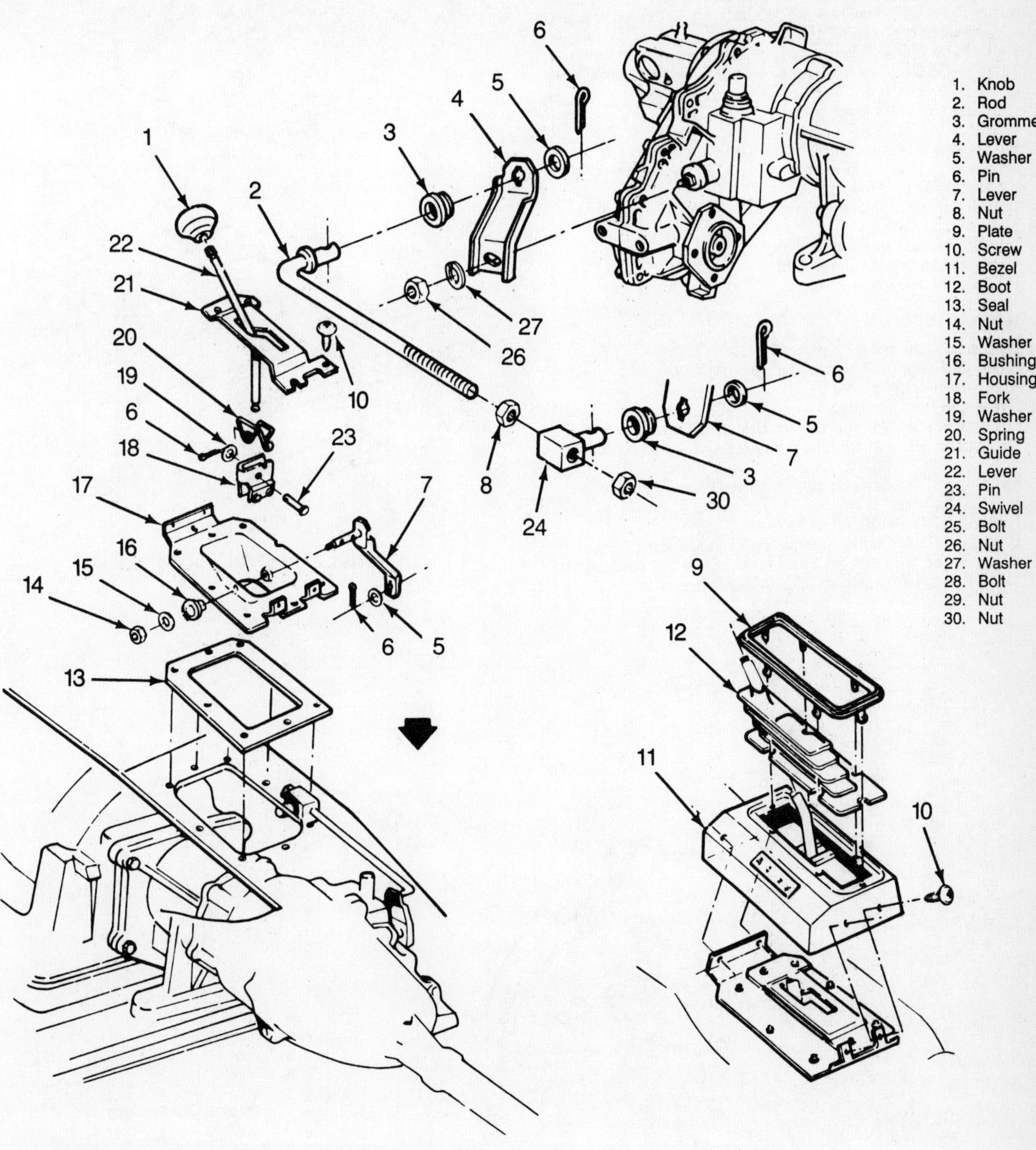

NP-208 console and shift controls

12. Move the transfer case to the rear until the input shaft clears the adaptor and lower the transfer case from the truck.

To install:

13. Using a new gasket, raise the transfer case into position and roll it forward until the input shaft engages the output shaft. Make sure it's still in 4H.
14. Install the bolts attaching the transfer case to transmission adaptor. Make sure the transfer case is flush against the adapter. Torque the bolts to 30 ft. lbs.
15. Connect the shift lever rod.
16. Connect the driveshafts.
17. On trucks with automatic transmission, connect the strut rod. Torque the transmission end bolts to 129 ft. lbs.; the transfer case end bolts to 35 ft. lbs.
18. Install the skid plate. Torque the bolts to 46 ft. lbs.
19. Remove the jack.
20. Install the parking brake cable.
21. Connect the speedometer cable.
22. Fill the transfer case.

NP-241

1. Disconnect the battery ground cable.
2. Raise and support the truck on jackstands.
3. Remove the skid plate.
4. Drain the transfer case.
5. On V series trucks, disconnect the speedometer cable.
6. On trucks with automatic transmission, disconnect the strut rod.
7. Matchmark the driveshafts, disconnect them, and support them out of the way.
8. Disconnect the shift lever linkage.
9. Disconnect the electrical connectors at the case.
10. Support the transfer case and remove the bolts attaching the transfer case to transmission adapter.

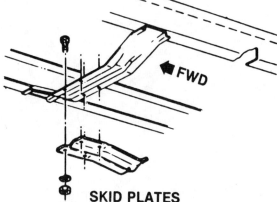

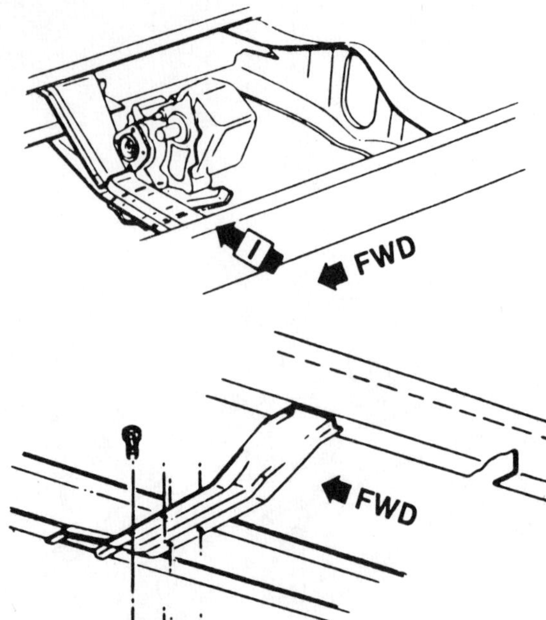

V series skid plate installation

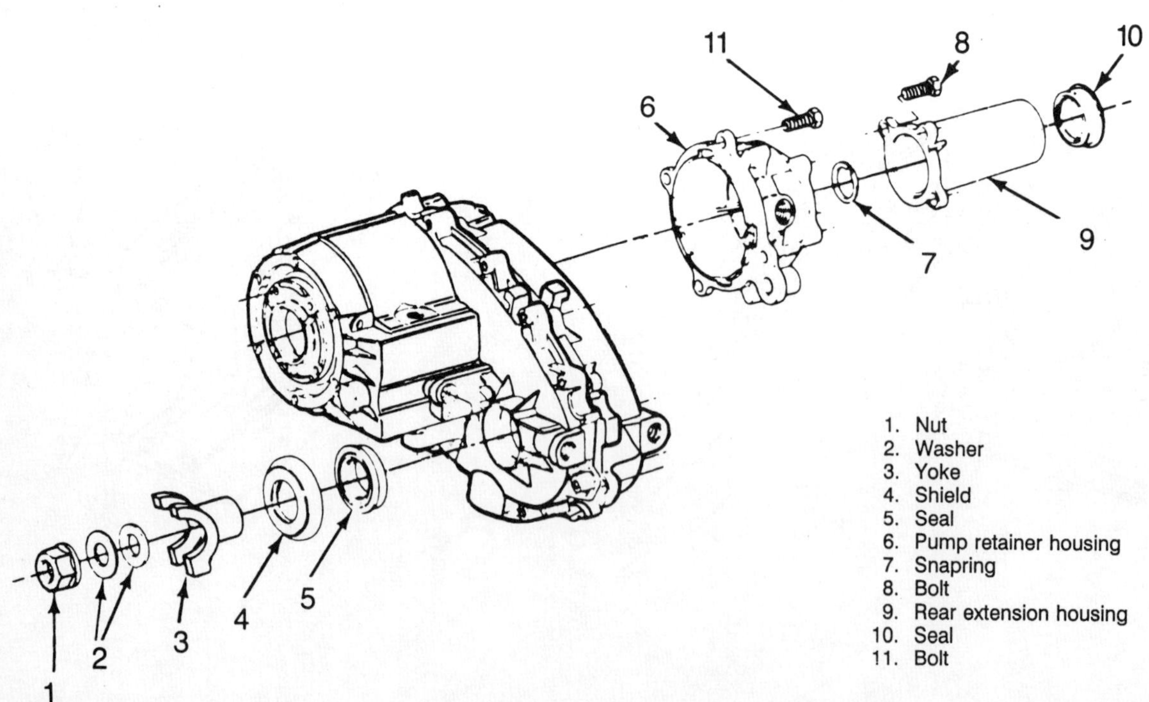

V series NP-241 main components

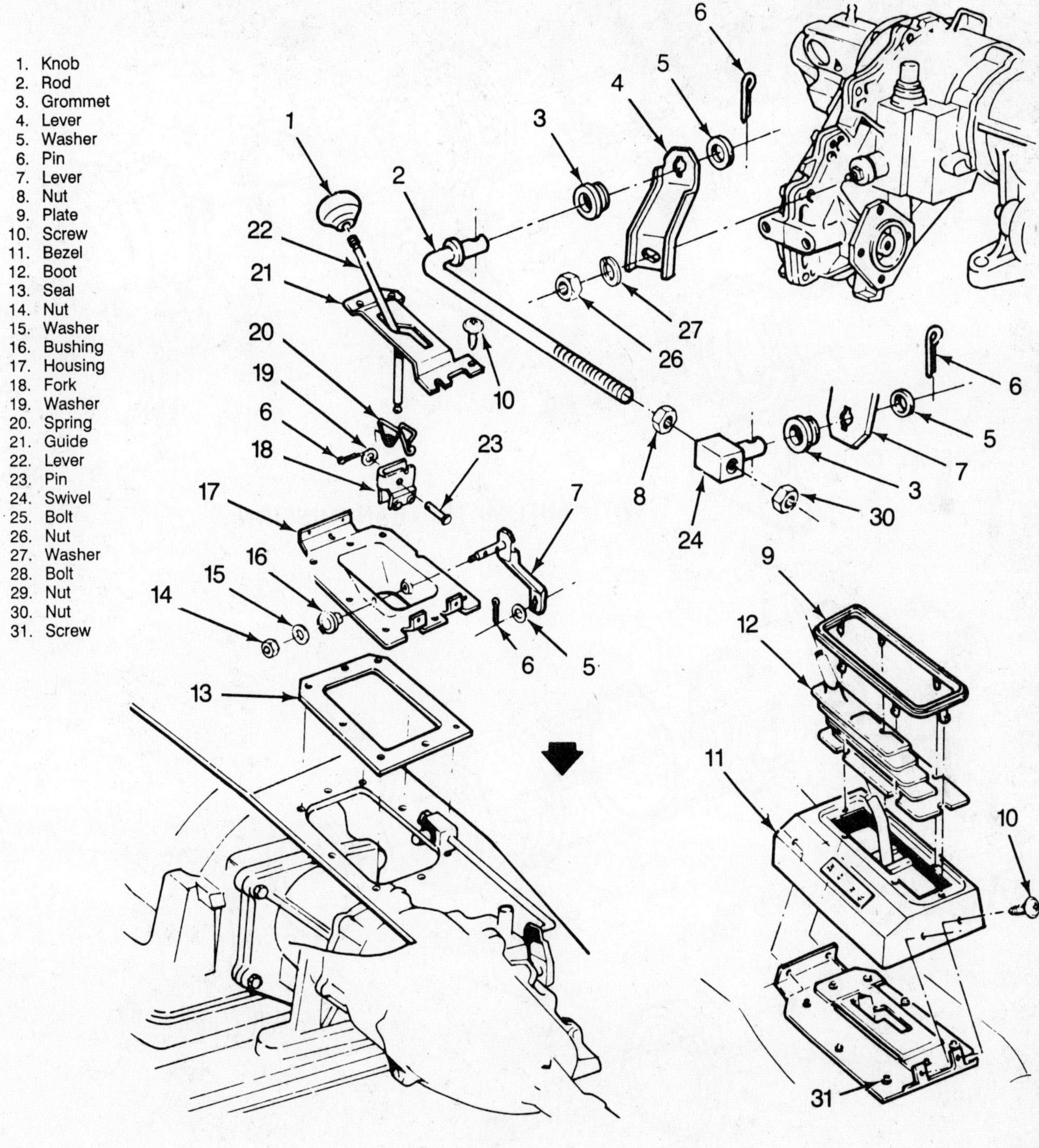
1. Knob
2. Rod
3. Grommet
4. Lever
5. Washer
6. Pin
7. Lever
8. Nut
9. Plate
10. Screw
11. Bezel
12. Boot
13. Seal
14. Nut
15. Washer
16. Bushing
17. Housing
18. Fork
19. Washer
20. Spring
21. Guide
22. Lever
23. Pin
24. Swivel
25. Bolt
26. Nut
27. Washer
28. Bolt
29. Nut
30. Nut
31. Screw

V series NP-241 linkage

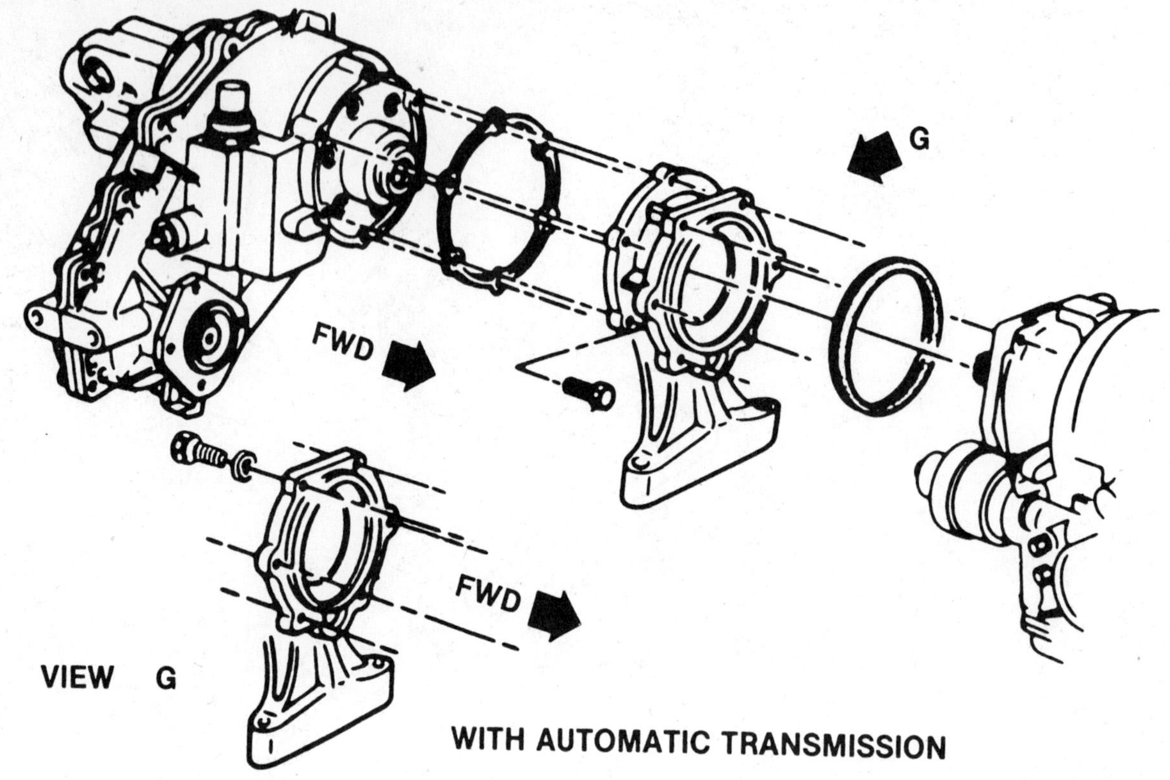

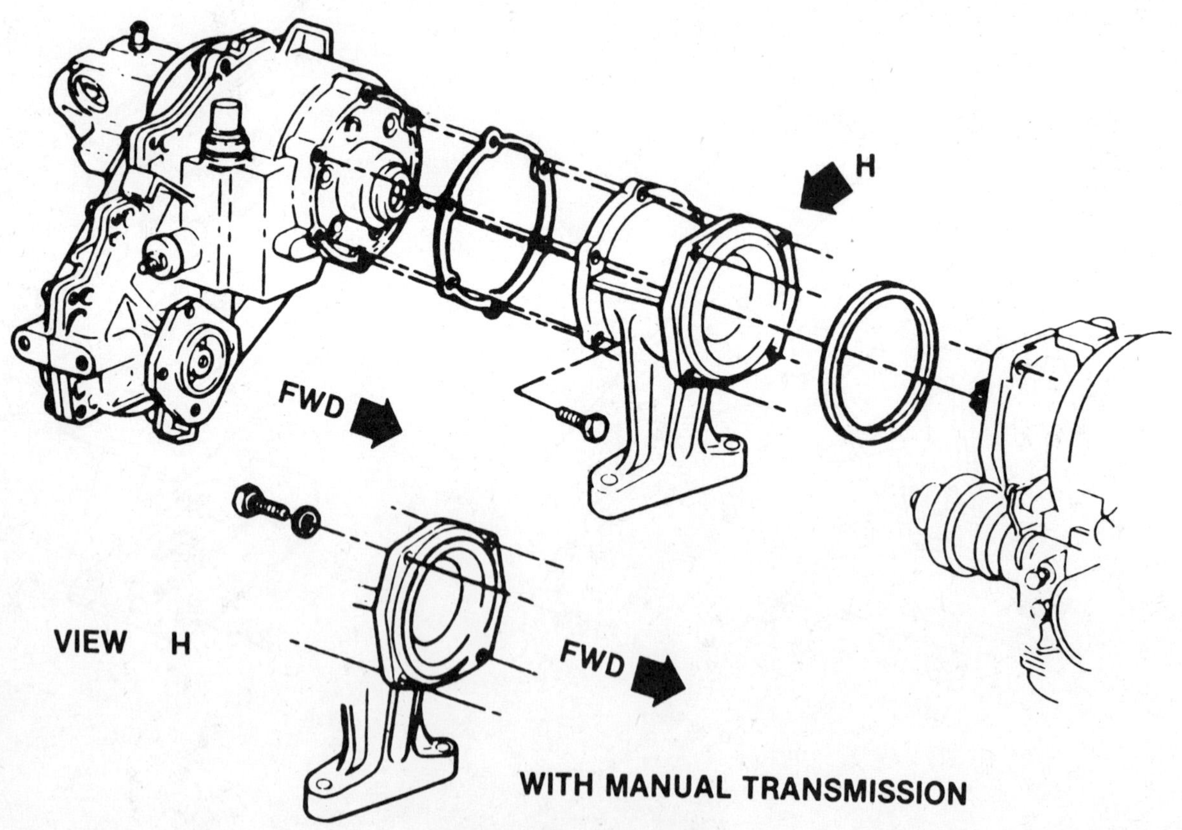

V series NP-241 adapters

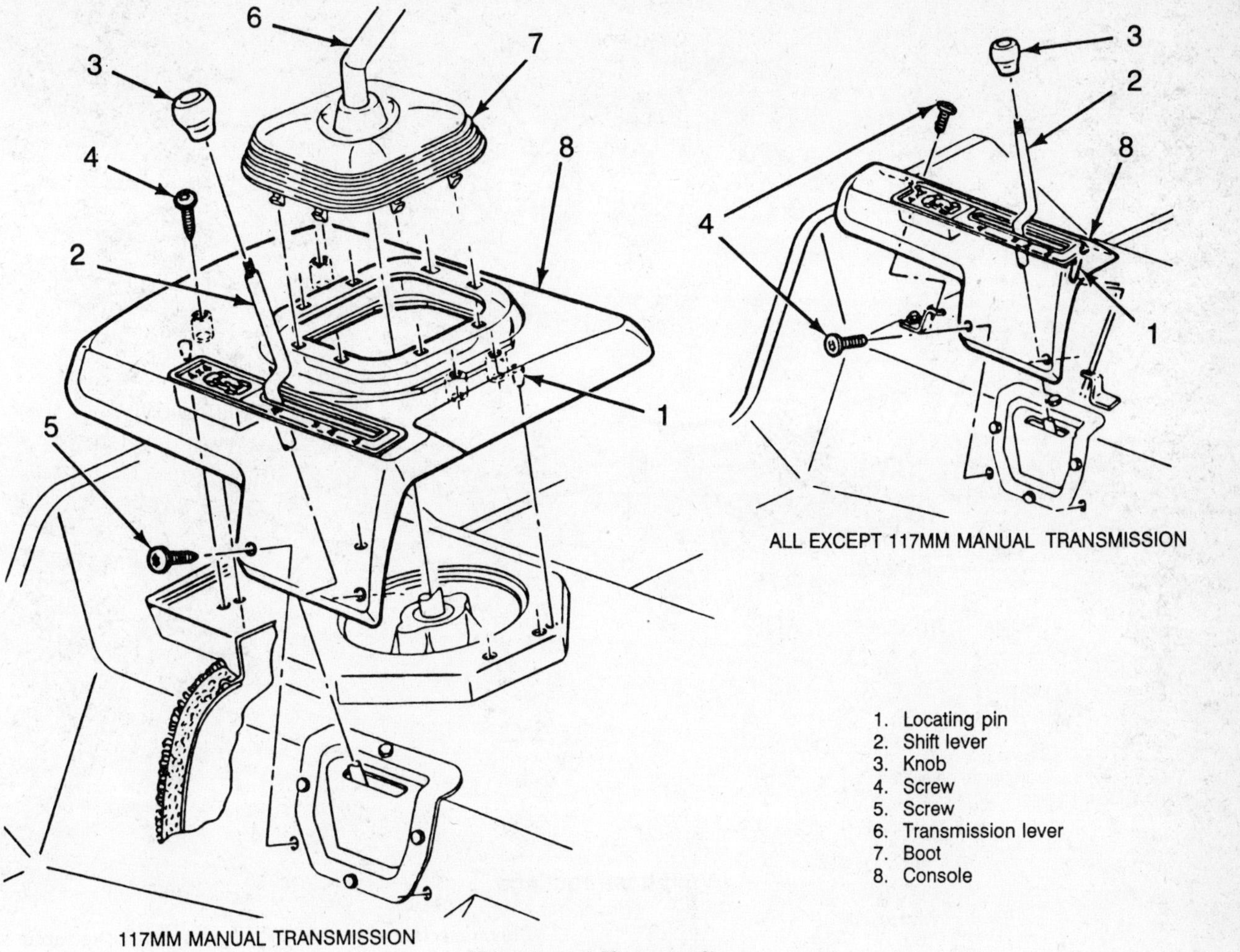

6
7
3
4
8
2
1
5
117MM MANUAL TRANSMISSION
3
2
8
4
1
ALL EXCEPT 117MM MANUAL TRANSMISSION
1. Locating pin
2. Shift lever
3. Knob
4. Screw
5. Screw
6. Transmission lever
7. Boot
8. Console

K series shift console

INDICATOR LAMP
FRONT AXLE SWITCH
IGNITION SWITCH
BATTERY
TRANSFER CASE SWITCH
CLUTCH COIL RELAY
CLUTCH COIL
FRONT AXLE ACTUATOR

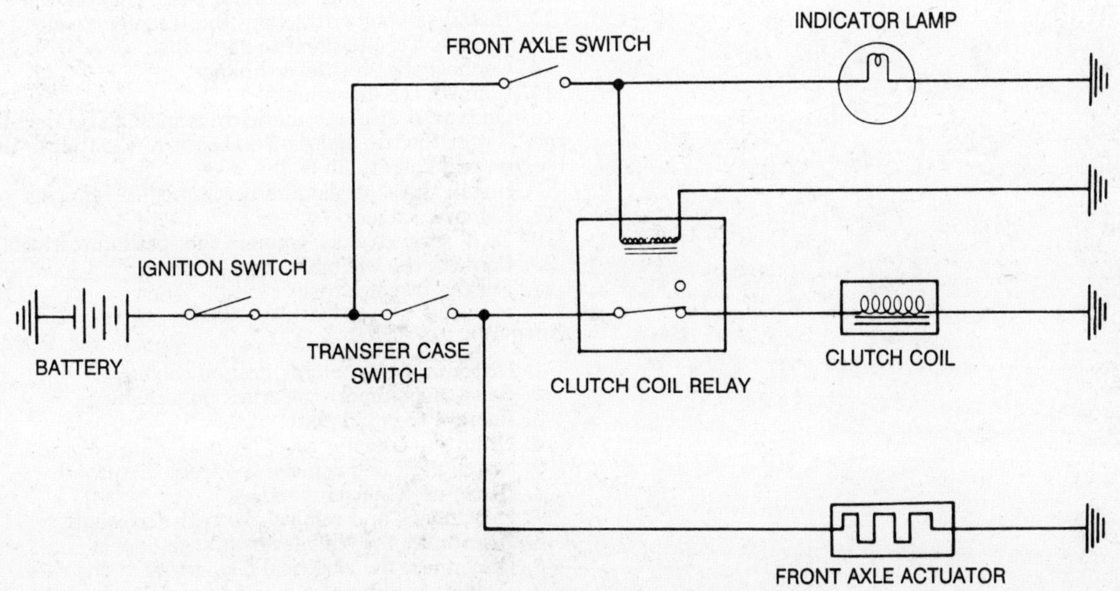

K series 4WD system wiring schematic

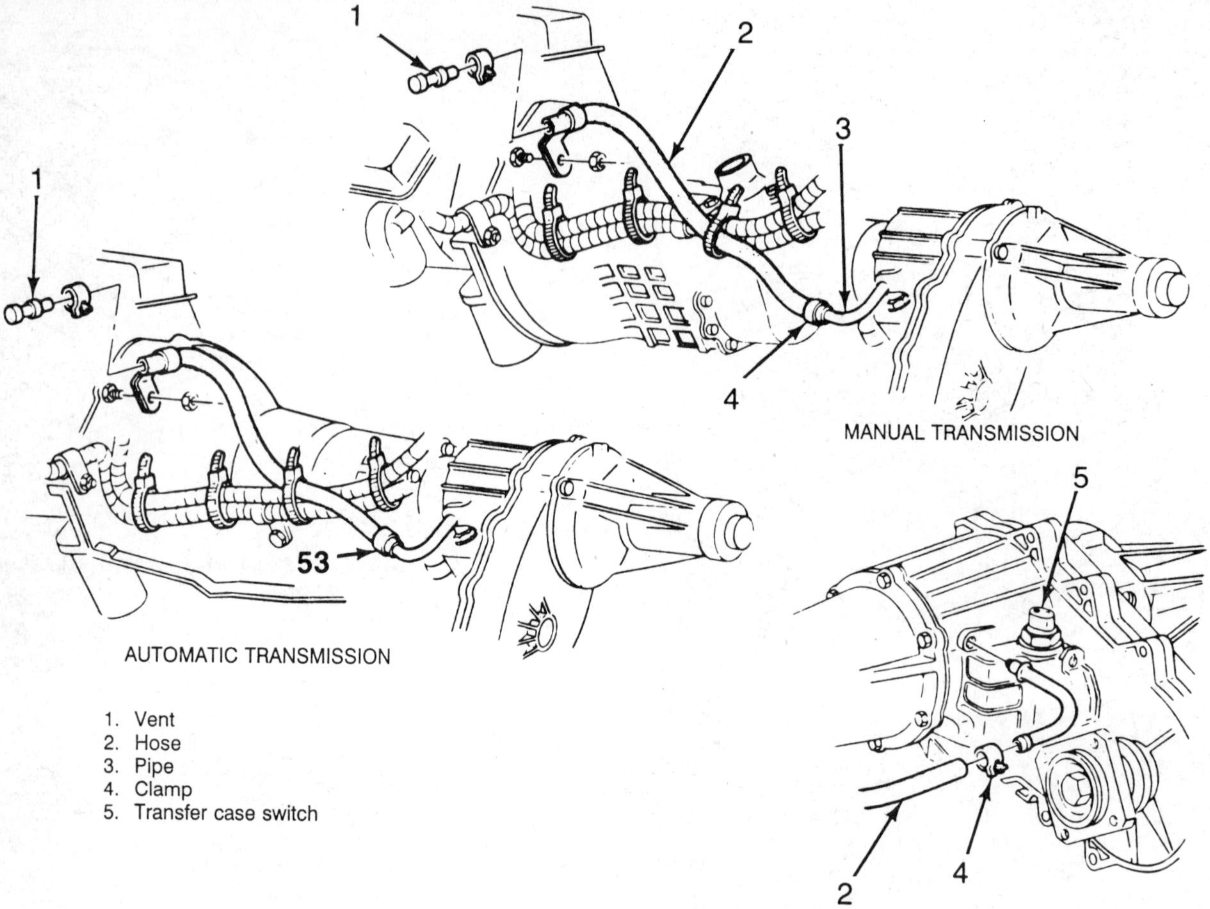

MANUAL TRANSMISSION

AUTOMATIC TRANSMISSION

1. Vent
2. Hose
3. Pipe
4. Clamp
5. Transfer case switch

Vent hose routings

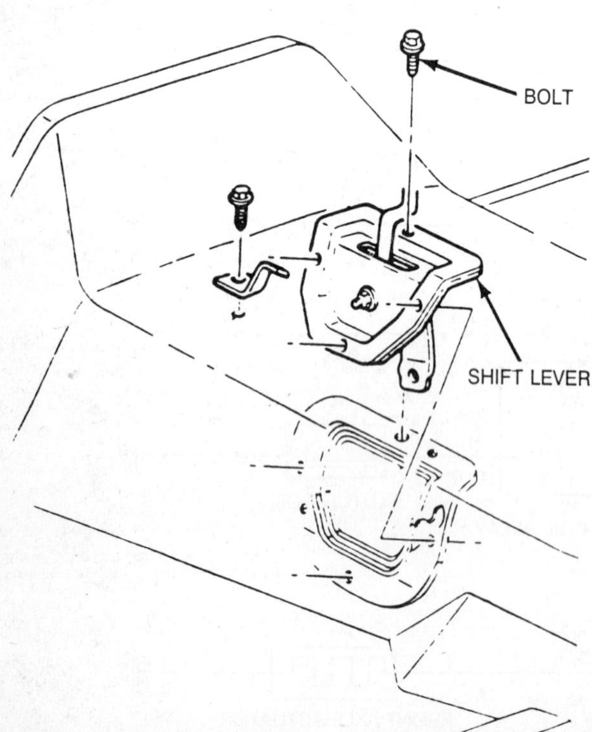

K series shift lever installation

11. Move the transfer case to the rear until the input shaft clears the adapter and lower the transfer case from the truck.

To install:

12. Using a new gasket, raise the transfer case into position and roll it forward until the input shaft engages the adapter.
13. Install the bolts attaching the transfer case to transmission adapter. Torque them to 24 ft. lbs.
14. Connect the shift lever linkage.
15. Connect the driveshafts.
16. On trucks with automatic transmission, connect the strut rod. Torque the transmission end bolts to 129 ft. lbs.; the transfer case end bolts to 35 ft. lbs.
17. Install the skid plate and crossmember support.
18. Remove the jack.
19. On V series trucks, connect the speedometer cable.
20. Connect the wiring.
21. Fill the transfer case.

Borg-Warner 1370

1. Disconnect the battery ground cable.
2. Raise and support the truck on jackstands.
3. Remove the skid plate.
4. Drain the transfer case.
5. Matchmark and remove the front driveshaft.
6. Disconnect the strut rod.
7. Matchmark and remove the rear driveshaft.
8. Disconnect the shift lever linkage.
9. Disconnect the electrical connectors at the case.
10. Support the transfer case and remove the bolts attaching the transfer case to transmission adapter.
11. Move the transfer case to the rear until the input shaft

clears the adapter and lower the transfer case from the truck.

To install:

12. Using a new gasket, raise the transfer case into position and roll it forward until the input shaft engages the adapter.
13. Install the bolts attaching the transfer case to transmission adapter. Torque them to 24 ft. lbs.
14. Connect the shift lever linkage.
15. Connect the rear driveshaft.
16. Connect the strut rod. Torque the transmission end bolts to 129 ft. lbs.; the transfer case end bolts to 35 ft. lbs.
17. Install the front driveshaft.
18. Install the skid plate.
19. Remove the jack.
20. Connect the wiring.
21. Fill the transfer case.

New Process Model 205 Transfer Case Overhaul

The New Process Model 205 transfer case is a 2-speed gearbox mounted between the main transmission and the rear axle. The gearbox transmits power from the transmission and engine to the front and rear driving axles.

CASE DISASSEMBLY

1. Clean the exterior of the case.
2. Remove the nuts from the universal joint flanges.
3. Remove the front output shaft rear bearing retainer, front bearing retainer and drive flange.
4. Tap the front output shaft assembly from the case with a soft hammer. Remove the sliding clutch, front output high gear, washer and bearing from the case.
5. Remove the rear output shaft housing attaching bolts and remove the housing, output shaft, bearing retainer and speedometer gear.
6. Slide the rear output shaft from the housing.

NOTE: Be careful not to lose the 15 needle bearings that will be loose when the rear output shaft is removed.

7. Drive the two ¼ in. (6mm) shift rail pin access hole plugs into the transfer case with a punch and hammer.
8. Remove the two shift rail detent nuts and springs from the case. Use a magnet to remove the two detent balls.
9. Position both shift rails in neutral and remove the shift fork retaining roll pins with a long punch.
10. Remove the clevis pin from one shift rail and rail link.
11. Remove the range shift rail first, then the 4WD shift rail.
12. Remove the shift forks and and sliding clutch from the case. Remove the input shaft bearing retainer, bearing and shaft.
13. Remove the cup plugs and rail pins, if they were driven out, from the case.
14. Remove the locknut from the idler gear shaft.
15. Remove the idler gear shaft rear cover.
16. Remove the idler gear shaft, using a soft hammer and a drift.
17. Roll the idler gear assembly to the front output shaft hole and remove the assembly from the case.

REAR OUTPUT SHAFT AND YOKE

1. Loosen rear output shaft yoke nut.
2. Remove shaft housing bolts, then remove the housing and retainer assembly.
3. Remove retaining nut and yoke from the shaft, then remove the shaft assembly.
4. Remove and discard snapring.
5. Remove thrust washer and pin.

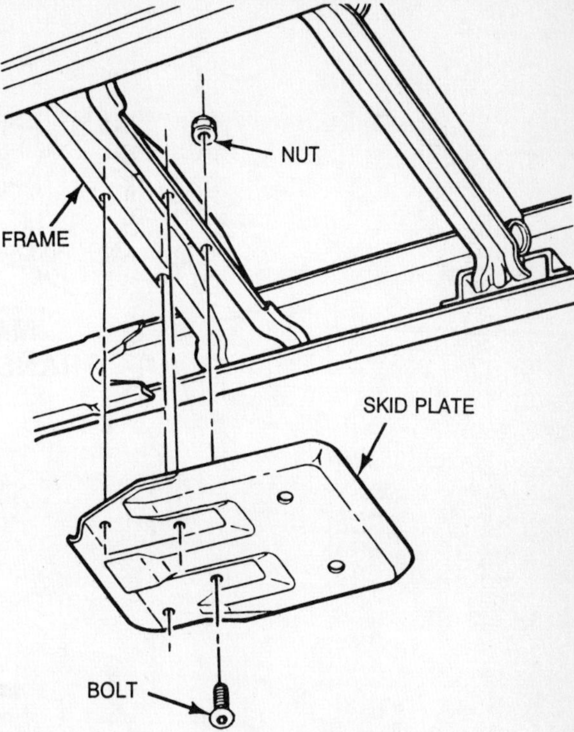

1370 skid plate

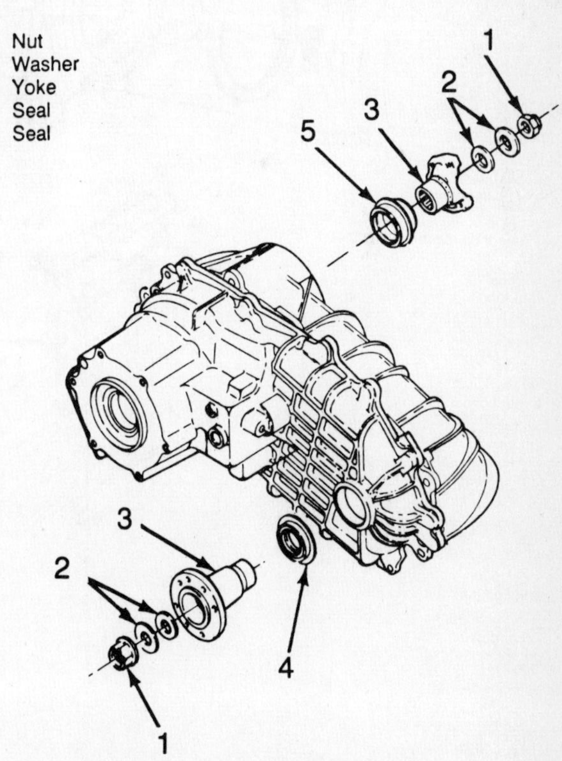

1370 main components

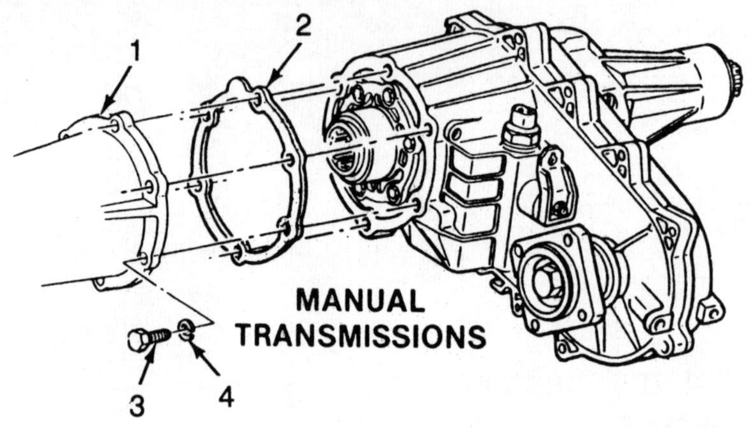

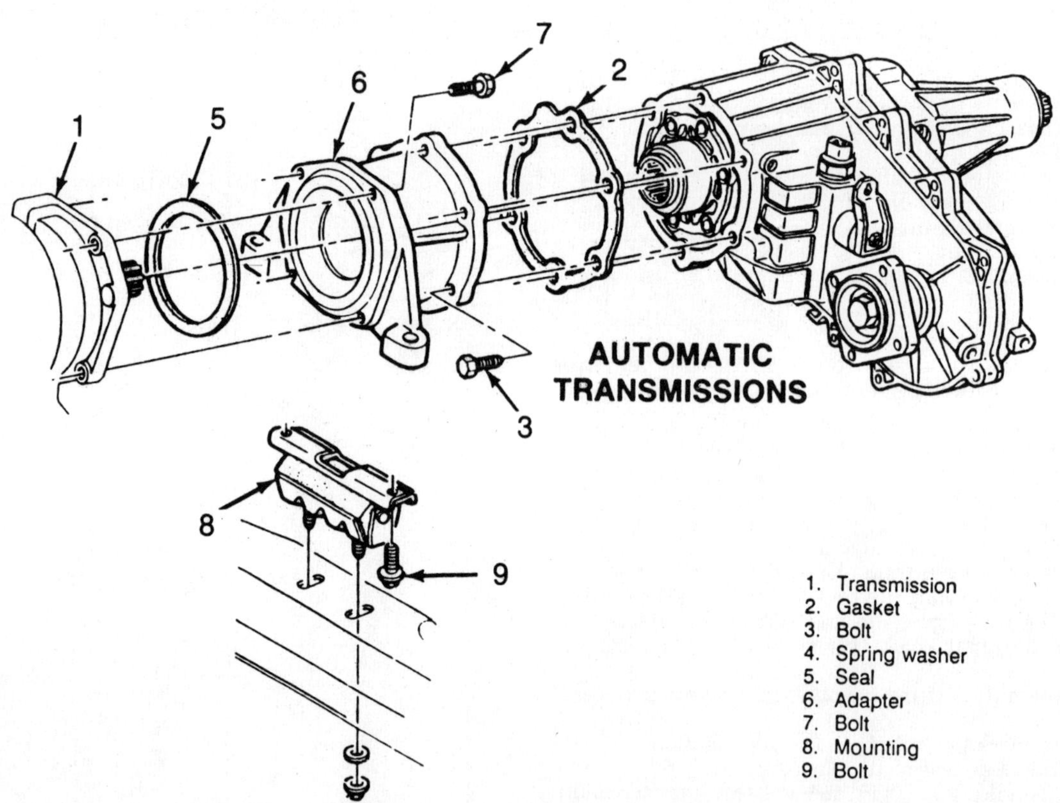

1. Transmission
2. Gasket
3. Bolt
4. Spring washer
5. Seal
6. Adapter
7. Bolt
8. Mounting
9. Bolt

1370 installation

6. Remove tanged bronze washer. Remove gear needle bearings, spacer and second row of needle bearings.
7. Remove tanged bronze thrust washer.
8. Remove pilot rollers, retainer ring and washer.
9. Remove oil seal retainer, ball bearing, speedometer gear and spacer. Discard gaskets.
10. Press out bearing.
11. Remove oil seal from the retainer.

FRONT OUTPUT SHAFT

1. Remove lock nut, washer and yoke.
2. Remove attaching bolts and front bearing retainer.
3. Remove rear bearing retainer attaching bolts.
4. Tap output shaft with a soft-faced hammer and remove shaft, gear assembly and rear bearing retainer.
5. Remove sliding clutch, gear, washer and bearing from output high gear.
6. Remove sliding clutch from the high output gear; then remove gear, washer and bearing.
7. Remove gear retaining snapring from the shaft, using large snapring picks. Discard ring.
8. Remove thrust washer and pin.
9. Remove gear, needle bearings and spacer.
10. Replace rear bearing, if necessary.

WARNING: Always replace the bearing and retainer as an assembly. Do not try to press a new bearing into an old retainer.

SHIFT RAILS AND FORKS

1. Remove the two poppet nuts, springs, and using a magnet, the poppet balls.
2. Remove cup plugs on top of case, using a ¼ in. (6mm) punch.
3. Position both shift rails in neutral, then remove fork pins with a long handled screw extractor.
4. Remove clevis pins and shift rail link.
5. Lower shift rails; upper rail first and then lower.
6. Remove shift forks and sliding clutch.
7. Remove the front output high gear, washer and bearing. Remove the shift rail cup plugs.

INPUT SHAFT

1. Remove snapring in front of bearing. Tap shaft out rear of case and bearing out front of case, using a soft-faced hammer or mallet.
2. Tilt case up on power take-off and remove the two interlock pins from inside.

IDLER GEAR

1. Remove idler gear shaft nut.
2. Remove rear cover.
3. Tap out idler gear shaft, using a soft-faced hammer and a drift approximately the same diameter as the shaft.
4. Remove idler gear through the front output shaft hole.
5. Remove two bearing cups from the idler gear.

CASE ASSEMBLY

1. Assemble the idler shaft gears, bearings, spacer and shims, and bearings on a dummy shaft tool and install the assembly into the case through the front output shaft bore, large end first.
2. Install the idler shaft from the large bore side, using a soft hammer to drive it through the bearings, spacer, gears, and shims.

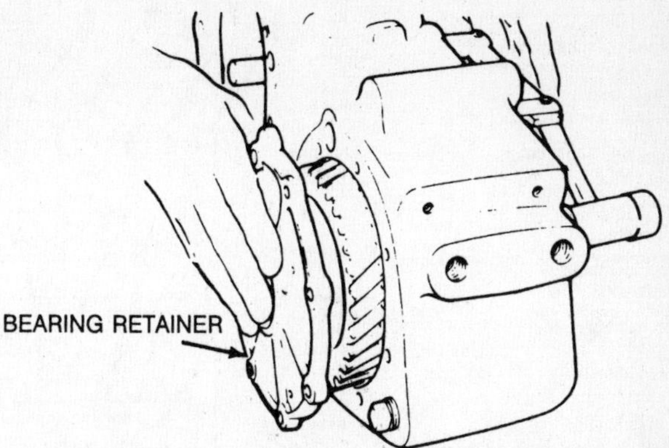

Removing the front output shaft bearing – NP-205

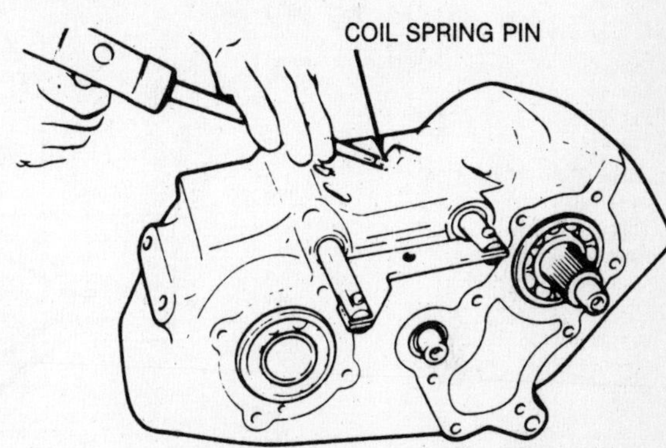

Removing the shift fork roll pin – NP-205

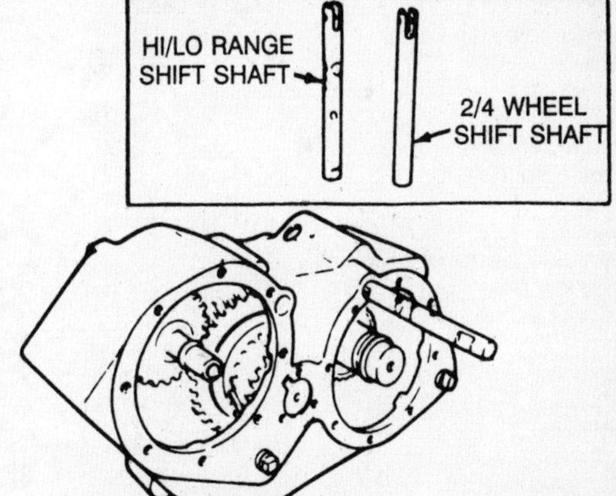

Removing the shift rail – NP-205

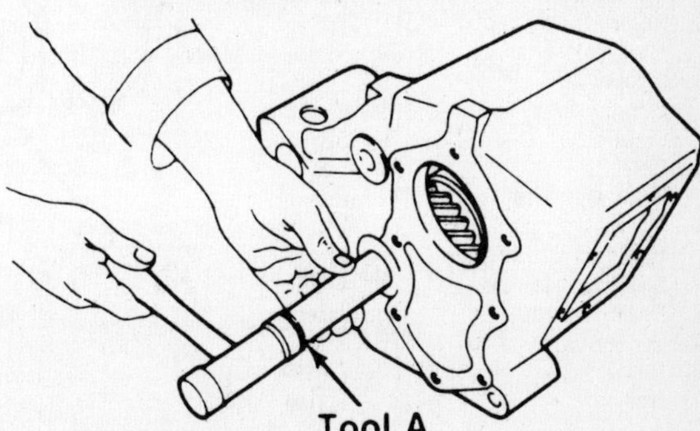

Removing the idler shaft – NP-205

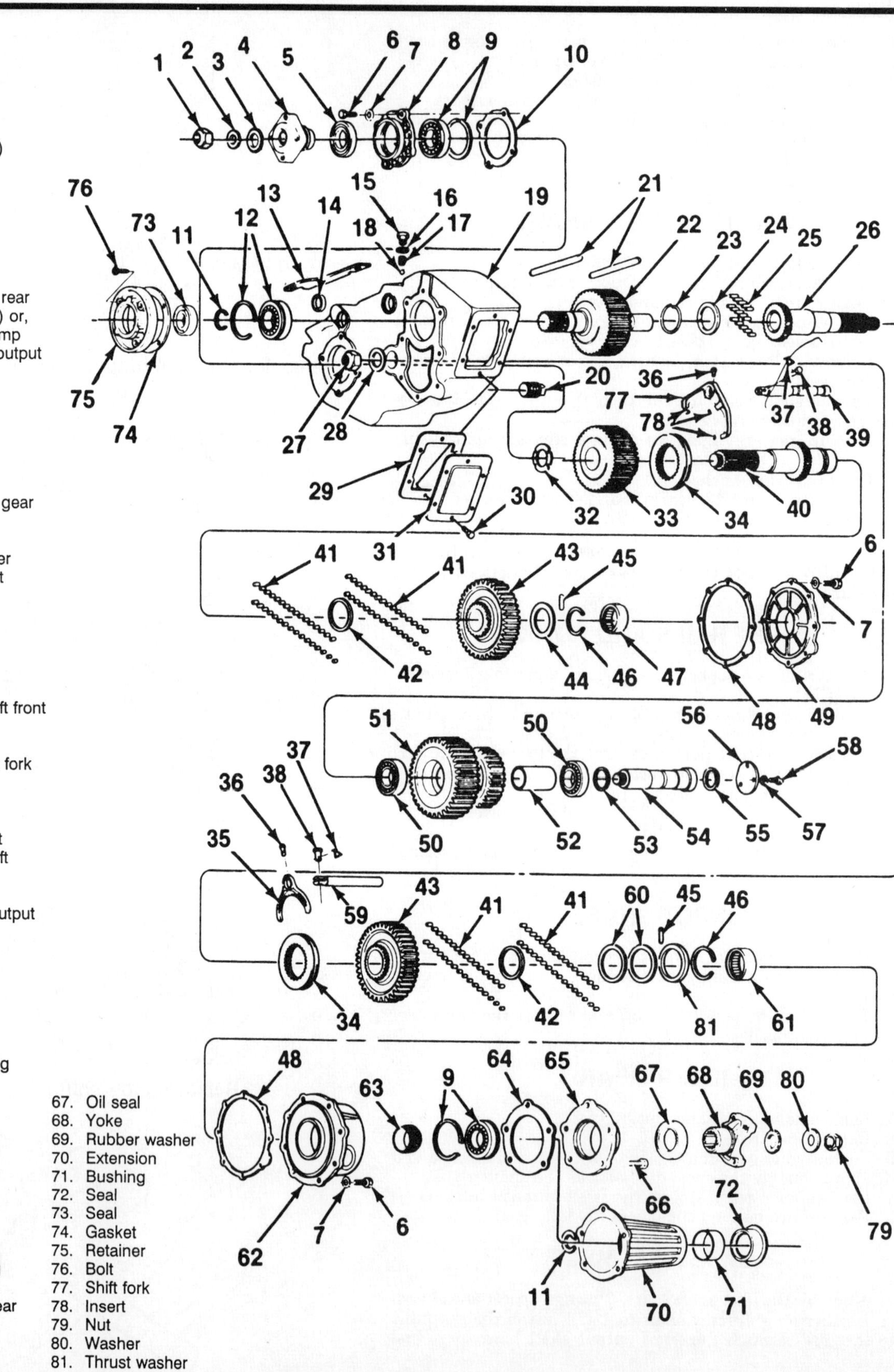

1. Nut
2. Washer
3. Washer (rubber)
4. Yoke
5. Seal
6. Bolt
7. Washer (toothed)
8. Retainer
9. Bearing
10. Gasket
11. Snapring
12. Bearing
13. Shift shaft link
14. Seal
15. Poppet plug (on rear output shift shaft) or, 4WD indicator lamp switch (on front output shift shaft)
16. Gasket
17. Spring
18. Ball
19. Case
20. Fill plug
21. Plunger
22. Input main drive gear
23. Retainer ring
24. Thrust washer
25. Pilot bearing roller
26. Rear output shaft
27. Nut
28. Washer
29. Gasket
30. Bolt
31. PTO Cover
32. Thrust washer
33. Front output shaft front gear
34. Clutch hub
35. Front wheel shift fork
36. Lock pin
37. Spring clip
38. Pin
39. 2/4WD shift shaft
40. Front output shaft
41. Roller
42. Spacer
43. Front and rear output shaft low gear
44. Thrust bearing
45. Pin
46. Snapring
47. Bearing
48. Gasket
49. Retainer
50. Idler gear bearing
51. Idler gear
52. Spacer
53. Shim
54. Idler gear shaft
55. Gasket
56. Cover
57. Washer
58. Bolt
59. Li/Lo shift shaft
60. Thrust washer
61. Retainer bearing
62. Bearing retainer
63. Speedometer gear
64. Gasket
65. Retainer
66. Bolt
67. Oil seal
68. Yoke
69. Rubber washer
70. Extension
71. Bushing
72. Seal
73. Seal
74. Gasket
75. Retainer
76. Bolt
77. Shift fork
78. Insert
79. Nut
80. Washer
81. Thrust washer

NP-205 exploded view

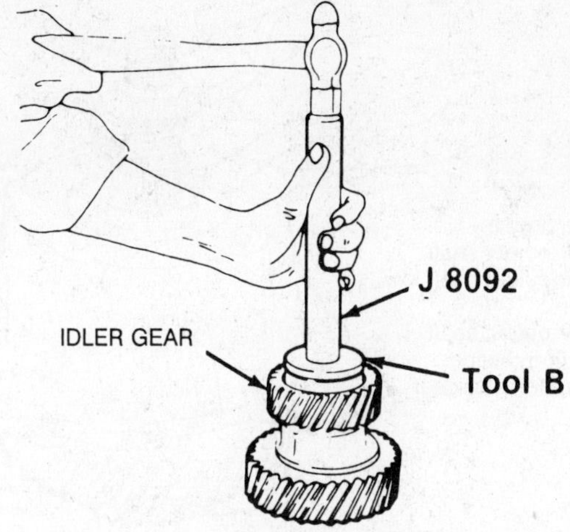

Installing the bearing cup – NP-205

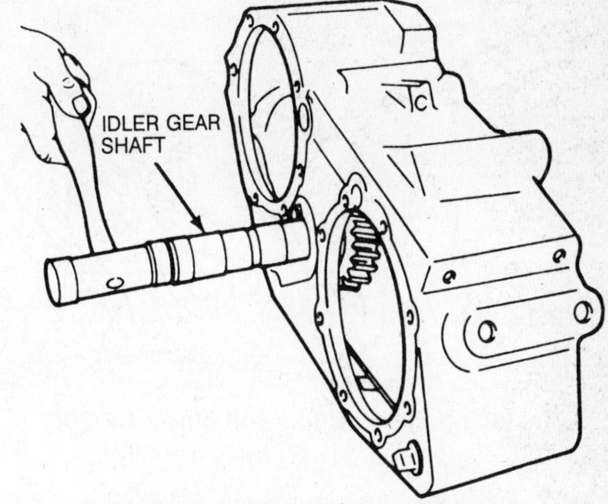

Installing the idler shaft – NP-205

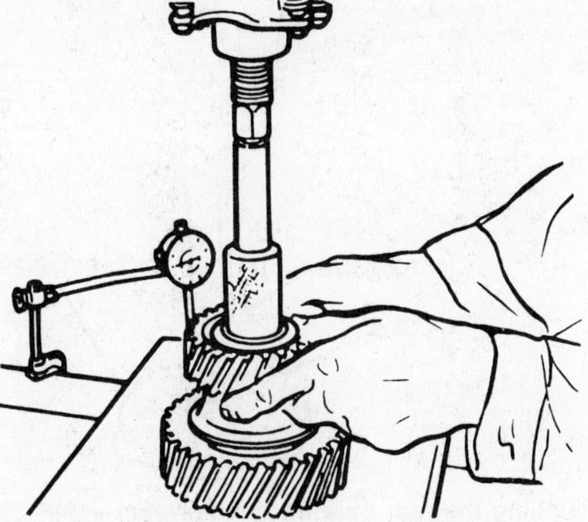

Idler gear endplay check – NP-205

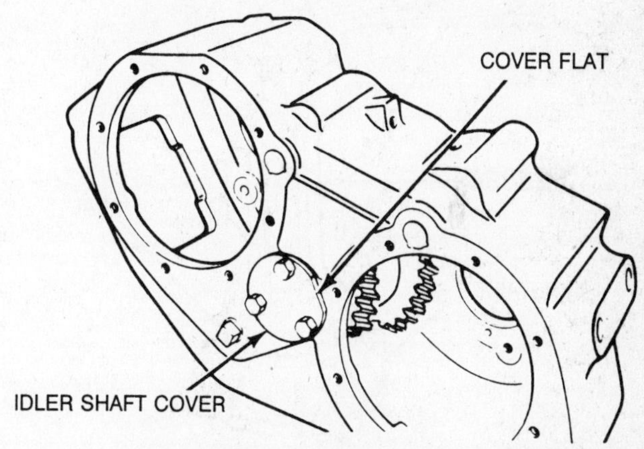

Idler shaft cover alignment – NP-205

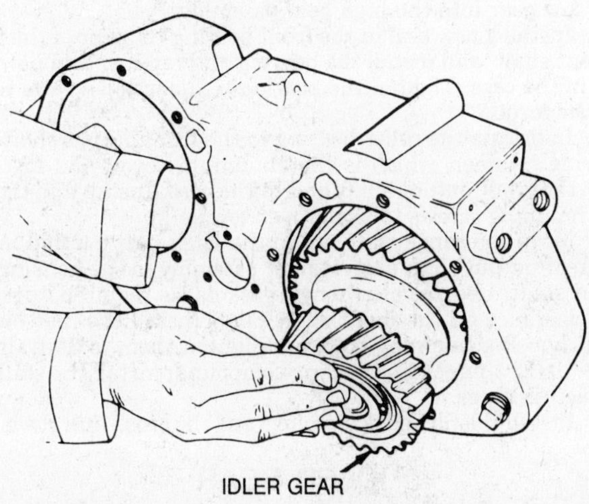

Installing the idler gear – NP-205

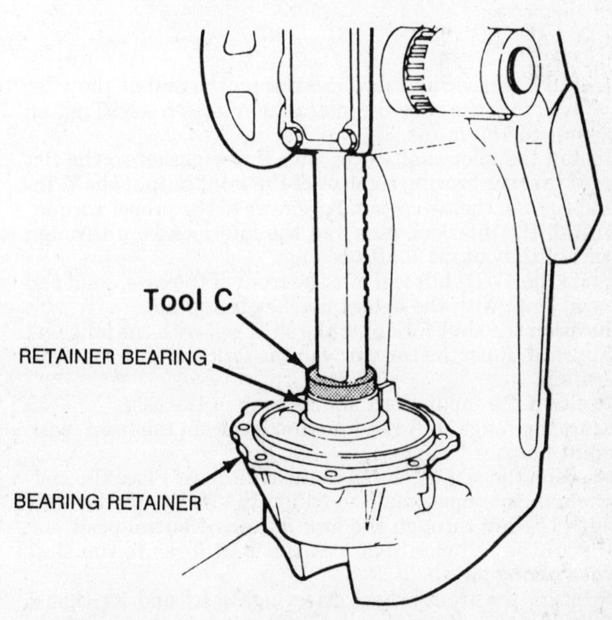

Installing the rear output shaft bearing retainer – NP-205

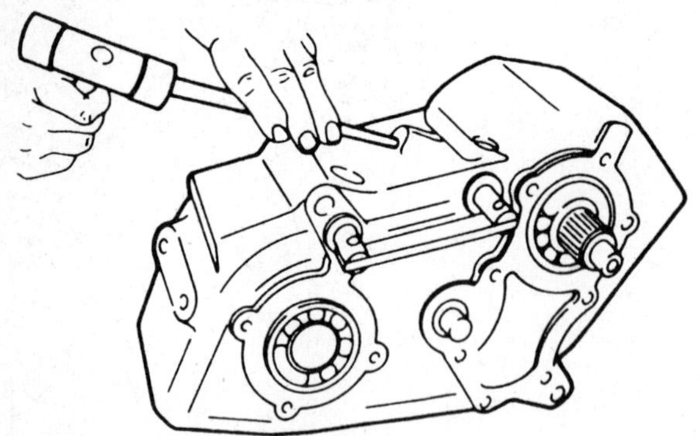

Installing the shift fork roll pin – NP-205

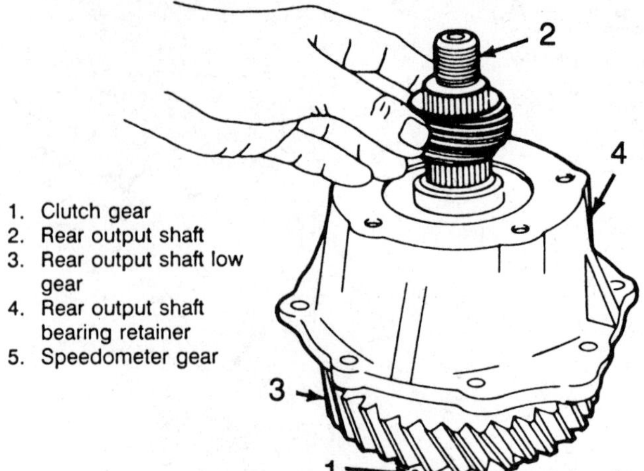

Installing the speedometer gear – NP-205

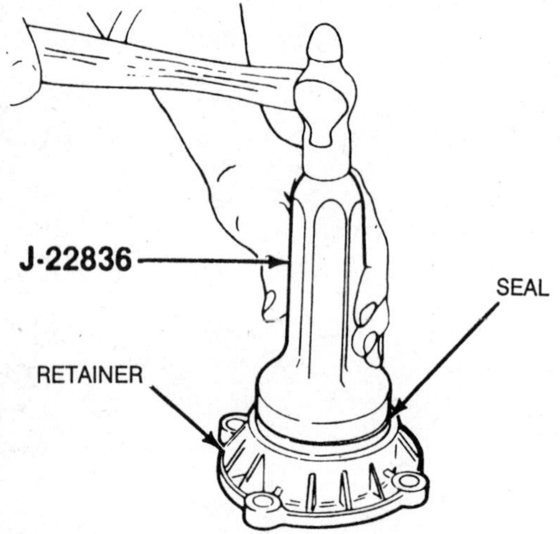

Installing the front output bearing retainer seal – NP-205

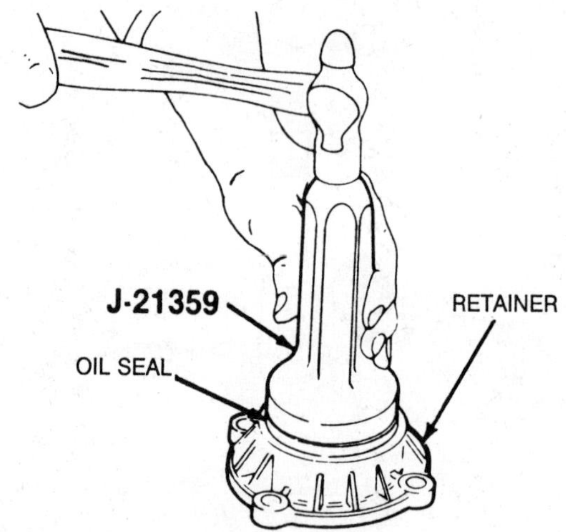

Installing the rear bearing retainer seal – NP-205

3. Install a washer and new locknut on the end of the idler shaft. Check to make sure the idler gear rotates freely. Tighten the locknut to 150 ft. lbs.
4. Install the idler shaft cover with a new gasket so the flat side faces the rear bearing retainer of the front output shaft. Install and tighten the two retaining screws to the proper torque.
5. Install the interlock pins into the interlock bore through the front of the output shaft opening.
6. Start the 4WD shift rail into the front of the case, solid end of the rail first, with the detent notches facing up.
7. Position the shift fork onto the shift rail with the long end facing inward. Push the rail through the fork and into the Neutral position.
8. Position the input shaft and bearing in the case.
9. Start the range shift rail into the case from the front, with the detent notches facing up.
10. Position the sliding clutch to the shift fork. Place the sliding clutch on the input shaft and align the fork with the shift rail. Push the rail through the fork into the Neutral position.
11. Install the roll pins that lock the shift forks to the shift rails with a long punch.
12. Position the front wheel drive high gear and its thrust washer in the case. Position the sliding clutch in the shift fork. Shift the rail and fork into the front wheel drive (4WD–Hi) position, while at the same time, meshing the clutch with the mating teeth on the front wheel drive high gear.
13. Align the thrust washer, high gear and sliding clutch with the bearing bore in the case and insert the front output shaft and low gear into the high gear assembly.
14. Install a new seal in the front bearing retainer of the front output shaft, and install the bearing and retainer and new gasket in the case. Tighten the bearing retainer cap screws to the proper torque.
15. Lubricate the roller bearing in the front output shaft rear bearing retainer, which is the aluminum cover, and install it over the front output shaft and to the case. Install and tighten the retaining screws to the proper torque.
16. Move the range shift rail to the High position and install the rear output shaft and retainer assembly to the housing and input shaft. Use one or two new gaskets, as required, to adjust the clearance on the input shaft pilot. Install the rear output shaft housing retaining bolts and tighten them to 35 ft. lbs.
17. Using a punch and sealing compound, install the shift rail pin access plugs.
18. Install the fill and drain plugs and the cross-link clevis pin.

IDLER GEAR

1. Press the two bearing cups in the idler gear.
2. Assemble the two bearing cones, spacer, shims and idler gear on a dummy shaft, with bore facing up. Check end-play.
3. Install idler gear assembly (with dummy shaft) into the

case, large end first, through the front output shaft bore.
4. Install idler shaft from large bore side, driving it through with a soft-faced hammer or mallet.
5. Install washer and new locknut. Check for free rotation and measure end-play. Endplay should be 0–0.002 in. (0–0.05mm). Torque the locknut to 150 ft. lbs.
6. Install idler shaft cover and new gasket. Torque cover bolts to 20 ft. lbs.

NOTE: Flat side of cover must be positioned towards front output shaft rear cover.

SHIFT RAILS AND FORKS

1. Press the two rail seals into the case.

NOTE: Install seals with metal lip outward.

2. Install interlock pins from inside case.
3. Insert slotted end of front output drive shift rail (with poppet notches up) into back of case.
4. While pushing rail through to neutral position, install shift fork (long end inward).
5. Install input shaft and bearing into case.
6. Install end of range rail (with poppet notches up) into front of case.
7. Install sliding clutch on fork, then place over input shaft in case.
8. Push range rail, while engaging sliding clutch and fork, through to neutral position.
9. Drive new lockpins into forks through holes at top of case.

NOTE: Tilt case on power take-off opening to install range rail lockpin.

FRONT OUTPUT SHAFT AND GEAR

1. Install two rows of needle bearings in the front low output gear and retain with grease.

NOTE: Each row consists of 32 needle bearings and the two rows are separated by a spacer.

2. Position front output shaft in a soft-jaw vise, with spline end down. Place front low gear over shaft with clutch gear facing down; then install thrust washer pin, thrust washer and new snapring.

NOTE: Position snapring gap opposite the thrust washer pin.

3. Place front drive high gear and washer in case. Install sliding clutch in the shift fork, then put fork and rail into 4–High position, meshing front drive high gear and clutch teeth.
4. Align washer, high gear and sliding clutch and bearing bore. Insert front output shaft and low gear assembly through the high gear assembly.
5. Install front output bearing and retainer with a new seal in the case.
6. Clean and grease rollers in front output rear bearing retainer. Install on case with one gasket and bolts coated with sealant. Torque bolts to 35 ft. lbs.
7. Install front output yoke, washer and locknut. Torque locknut to 150 ft. lbs.

REAR OUTPUT SHAFT

1. Install two rows of needle bearings into the output low gear, retaining them with grease.

NOTE: Each row consists of 32 needle bearings and the two rows are separated by a spacer.

2. Install thrust washer (with tang down in clutch gear groove) onto the rear output shaft.
3. Install output low gear onto shaft with clutch teeth facing downward.
4. Install thrust washer over gear with tab pointing up and away. Install washer pin.
5. Install large thrust washer over shaft and pin. Turn washer until tab fits into slot located approximately 90° away from pin.
6. Install snapring and measure shaft endplay. Endplay should be 0–0.027 in. (0–0.686mm).
7. Grease pilot bore and install needle bearings.

NOTE: There are 15 pilot needle bearings.

8. Install thrust washer and new snapring in pilot bore.
9. Press new bearing into retainer housing.
10. Install housing on output shaft assembly.
11. Install spacer and speedometer gear. Install rear bearing.
12. Install rear bearing retainer seal.
13. Install bearing retainer assembly on housing, using one or two gaskets to achieve specified clearance. Torque attaching bolts to 35 ft. lbs.
14. Install yoke, washer and locknut on output shaft.
15. Position range rail in high, then install output shaft and retainer assembly on case. Torque the yoke nut to 150 ft. lbs.

CASE ASSEMBLY

1. Install power take-off cover and gasket. Torque attaching bolts to 15 ft. lbs.
2. Install cup plugs at rail pin holes.

NOTE: After installing, seal the cup plugs.

3. Install drain and filler plugs. Torque to 30 ft. lbs.
4. Install shift rail cross link, clevis pins and lock pins.

New Process 208 Transfer Case Overhaul

The NP208 is a part-time unit with a two piece aluminum housing. On the front case half, the front output shaft, front input shaft, four wheel drive indicator switch and shift lever assembly are located. On the rear case half, the rear output shaft, bearing retainer and drain and fill plugs are located.

DISASSEMBLY

1. Drain the fluid from the case.
2. Remove the attaching nuts from the front and rear output yokes. Remove the yokes and sealing washers.
3. Remove the four bolts and separate the rear bearing retainer from the rear case half.
4. Remove the retaining ring, speedometer drive gear nylon oil pump housing, and oil pump gear from the rear output shaft.
5. Remove the eleven bolts and separate the case halves by inserting a screw driver in the pry slots on the case.
6. Remove the magnetic chip collector from the bottom of the rear case half.
7. Remove the thick thrust washer, thrust bearing and thin thrust washer from the front output shaft assembly.
8. Remove the drive chain by pushing the front input shaft inward and by angling the gear slightly to obtain adequate clearance to remove the chain.
9. Remove the output shaft from the front case half and slide the thick thrust washer, thrust bearing and thin thrust washer off the output side of the front output shaft.
10. Remove the screw, poppet spring and check ball from the front case half.
11. Remove the four wheel drive indicator switch and washer from the front case half.

1. Main driveshaft
2. Speedometer drive gear
3. Rear housing
4. Bolt
5. Pump seal
6. Pump housing
7. Pump gear
8. Mainshaft rear bearing
9. Mainshaft extension
10. Vent
11. Mainshaft extension bushing
12. Seal
13. Clip
14. Bolt
15. Fill plug
16. Dowel
17. Washer
18. Bolt
19. Low range lock plate
20. Planetary gear carrier
21. Planetary gear thrust washer
22. Annulus gear
23. Thrust washer
24. Range for center pad
25. Retainer ring
26. Retainer ring
27. Synchronizer
28. Synchronizer strut spring
29. Synchronizer shift strut
30. Stop ring
31. Roller spacer
32. Roller
33. Sprocket
34. Thrust washer
35. Retainer ring
36. Range fork
37. Shift pin
38. Mode fork and spring retainer
39. Spring
40. Spring cup
41. Shifter fork shaft
42. End pad
43. Center pad
44. Mode fork
45. Shifter pin
46. Thrust bearing
47. Pilot bearing
48. Plug
49. Input drive gear
50. Thrust bearing
51. Thrust washer
52. Range sector with shaft
53. Indicator lamp switch
54. Front housing
55. Bolt
56. Seal
57. Bearing
58. Plunger
59. Spring
60. Screw
61. Nut
62. Washer
63. Yoke
64. Deflector
65. Seal
66. Bearing

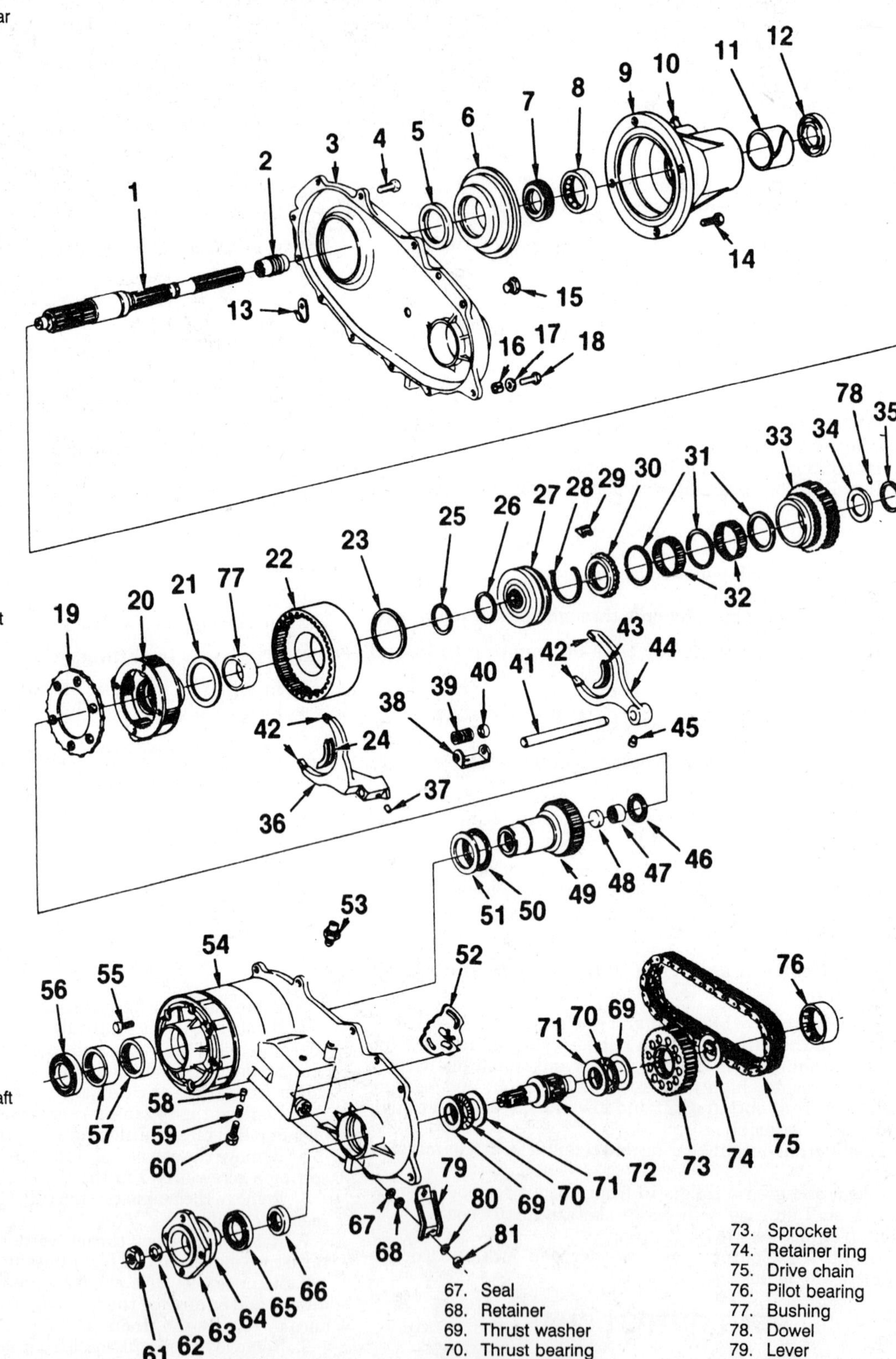

67. Seal
68. Retainer
69. Thrust washer
70. Thrust bearing
71. Thrust washer
72. Front output shaft
73. Sprocket
74. Retainer ring
75. Drive chain
76. Pilot bearing
77. Bushing
78. Dowel
79. Lever
80. Washer
81. Nut

NP-208 exploded view

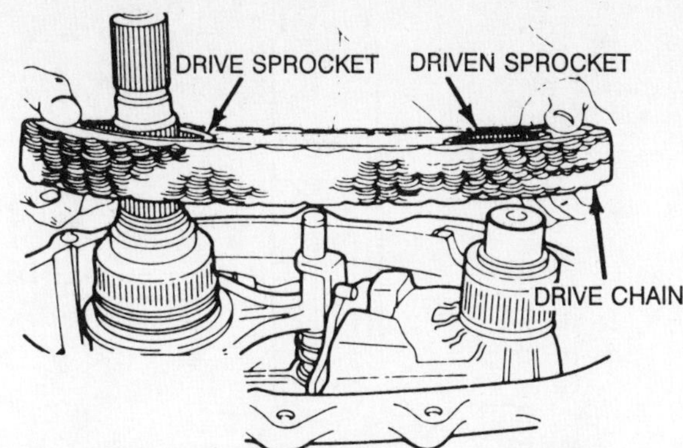

Sprocket and chain removal – NP-208

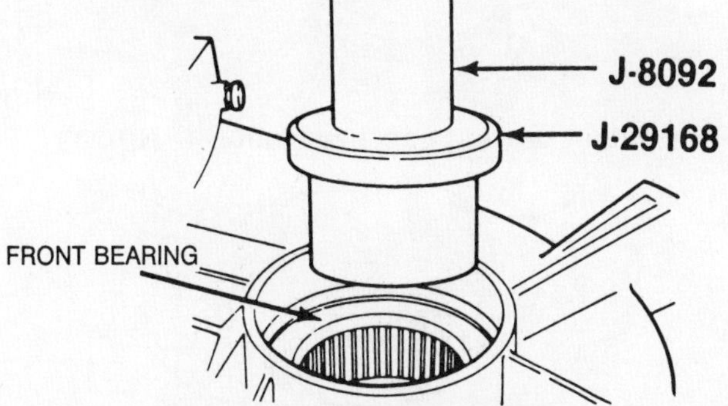

Front output shaft front bearing removal – NP-208

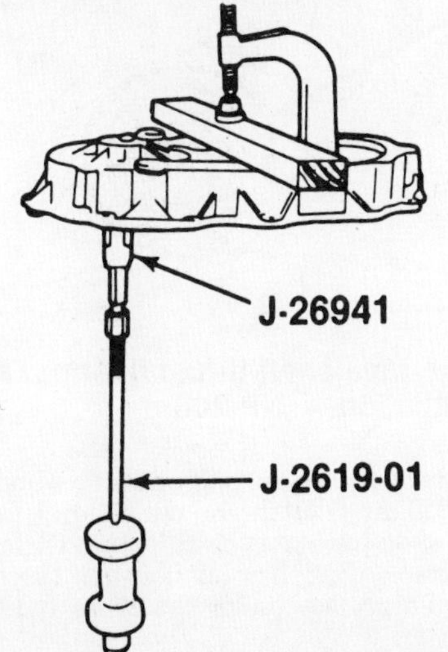

Front output shaft rear bearing removal – NP-208

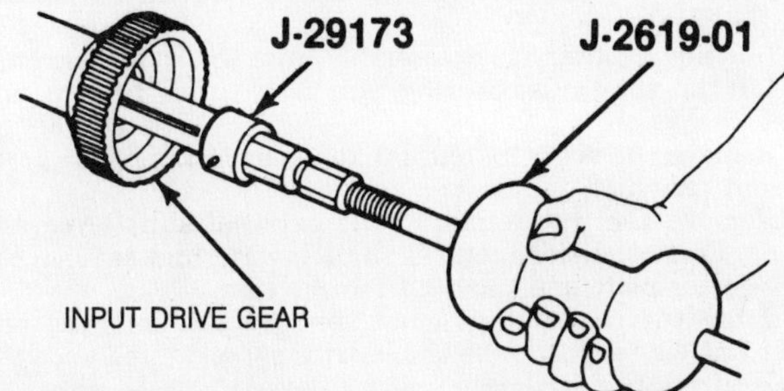

Mainshaft pilot bearing removal – NP-208

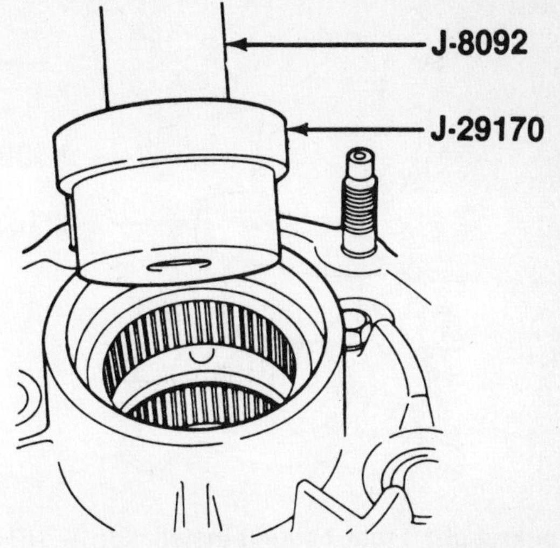

Input gear bearing removal – NP-208

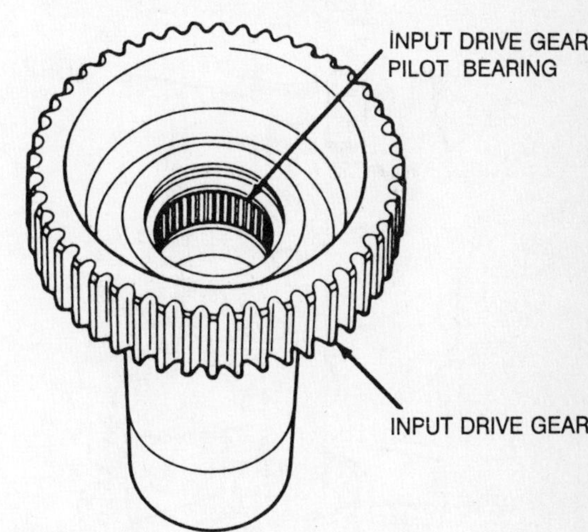

Mainshaft pilot bearing installation – NP-208

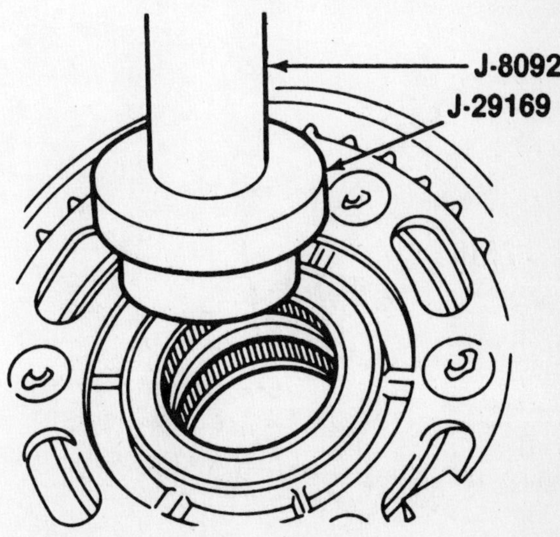

Input gear bearing installation – NP-208

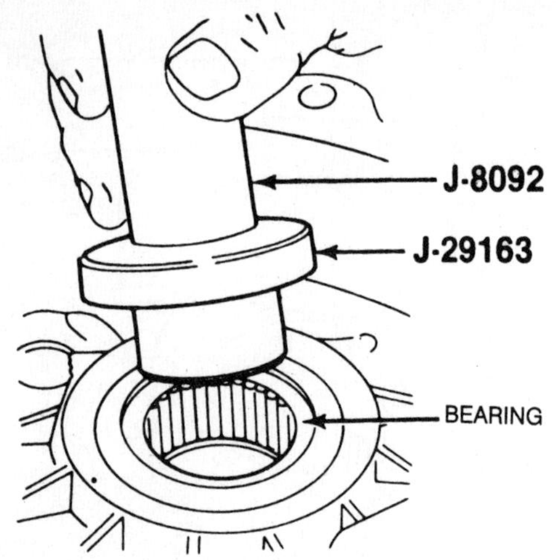

Front output shaft rear bearing installation — NP-208

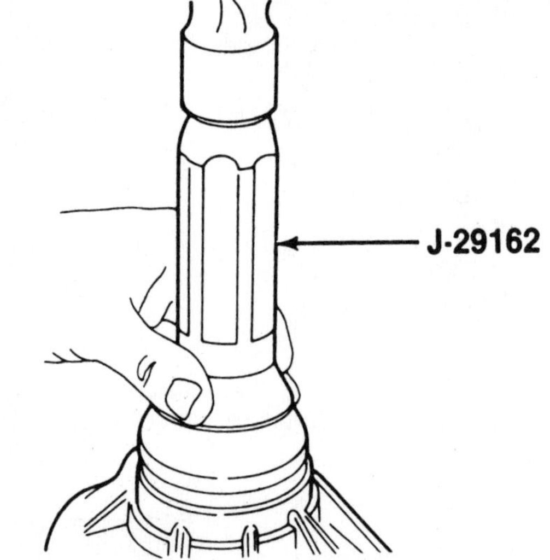

Rear output bearing seal installation — NP-208

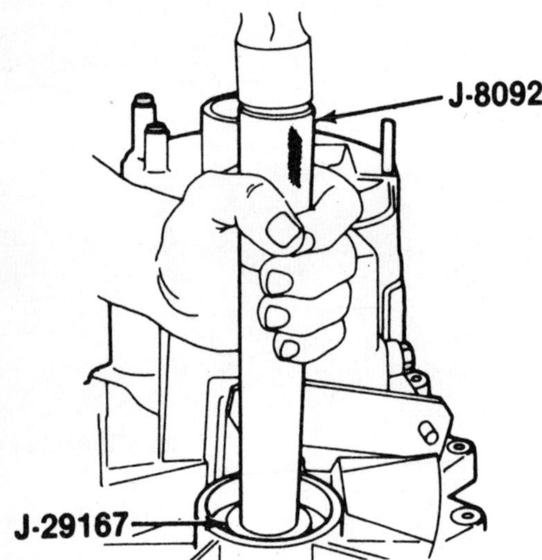

Front output shaft front bearing installation — NP-208

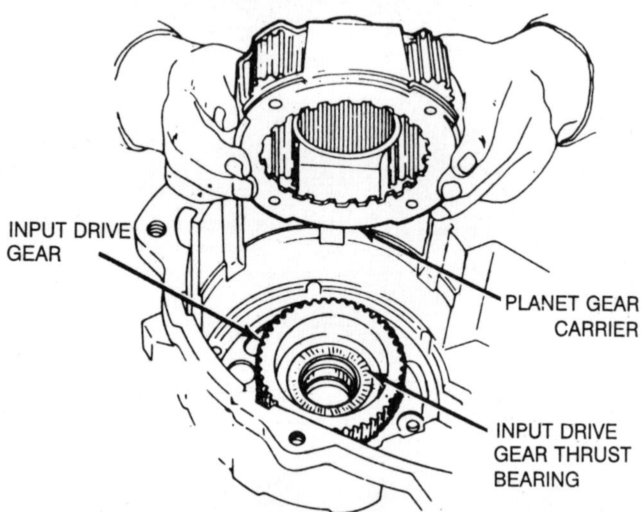

Input gear, mainshaft thrust bearing, and planetary gear installation — NP-208

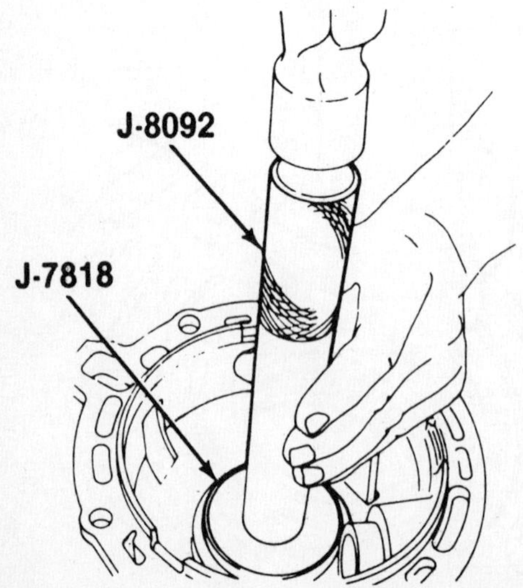

Rear output bearing installation — NP-208

12. Position the front case half on its face and lift out the rear output shaft, sliding clutch and clutch shift fork and spring.
13. Place a shop towel on the shift rail. Clamp the rail with a vise grip pliers so that they lay between the rail and the case edge. Position a pry bar under the pliers and pry out the shift rail.
14. Remove the snap ring and thrust washer from the planetary gear set assembly in the front case half.
15. Remove the annulus gear assembly and thrust washer from the front case half.
16. Lift the planetary gear assembly from the front case half.
17. Lift out the thrust bearing, sun gear, thrust bearing and thrust washer.
18. Remove the six bolts and lift the gear locking plate from the front case half.
19. Remove the nut retaining the external shift lever and washer. Press the shift control shaft inward and remove the shift selector plate and washer from the case.
20. From the rear output shaft, remove the snapring and thrust washer retaining the chain drive sprocket and slide the sprocket from the drive gear.
21. Remove the retaining ring from the sprocket carrier gear.
22. Carefully slide the sprocket carrier gear from the rear out-

put shaft. Remove the two rows of 60 loose needle bearings. Remove the three separator rings from the output shaft.

ASSEMBLY

1. Slide the thrust washer against the gear on the rear output shaft.
2. Place the three space rings in position on the rear output shaft. Liberally coat the shaft with petroleum jelly and install the two rows (60 each) of needle bearings in position on the rear output shaft.
3. Carefully slide the sprocket gear carrier over the needle bearings. Be careful not to dislodge any of the needles.
4. Install the retaining ring on the sprocket gear.
5. Slide the chain drive sprocket onto the sprocket carrier gear.
6. Install the thrust washer and snap ring on the rear output shaft.
7. Install the shift selector plate and washer through the front of the case.
8. Place the shift lever assembly on the shift control shaft and torque the nut to 14–20 ft. lbs.
9. Place the locking plate in the front case half and torque the bolts to 25–35 ft. lbs.
10. Place the thrust bearing and washer over the input shaft of the sun gear. Insert the input shaft through the front case half from the inside and insert the thrust bearing.
11. Install the planetary gear assembly so the fixed plate and planetary gears engage the sun gear.
12. Slide the annulus gear and clutch assembly with the shift fork assembly engaged, over the hub of the planetary gear assembly. The shift fork pin must engage the slot in the shift selector plate. Install the thrust washer and snap ring.
13. Position the shift rail through the shift fork hub in the front case. Tap lightly with a soft hammer to seat the rail in the hole.
14. Position the sliding clutch shift fork on the shift rail and place the sliding clutch and clutch shift spring into the front case half. Slide the rear output shaft into the case.
15. On the output side of the front output shaft, assemble the thin thrust washer, thrust bearing, and thick thrust washer and partially insert the front output shaft into the case.
16. Place the drive chain on the rear output shaft drive gear. Insert the rear output shaft into the front case half and engage the drive chain on the front output shaft drive gear. Push the front output shaft into position in the case.
17. Assemble the thin thrust washer, thrust bearing and thick thrust washer on the inside of the front output shaft drive gear.
18. Position the magnetic chip collector into position in the front case half.
19. Place a bead of RTV sealant completely around the face of the front case half and assemble the case halves being careful that the shift rail and forward output shafts are properly retained.
20. Alternately tighten the bolts to 20–25 ft. lbs.
21. Slide the oil pump gear over the input shaft and slide the spacer collar into position.
22. Engage the speedometer drive gear onto the rear output shaft and slide the retaining ring into position.
23. Use petroleum jelly to hold the nylon oil pump housing in position at the rear bearing retainer. Apply a bead of RTV sealant around the mounting surface of the retainer and carefully position the retainer assembly over the output shaft and onto the rear case half. The retainer must be installed so that the vent hole is vertical when the case is installed.
24. Torque the retainer bolts alternately to 20–25 ft. lbs.
25. Place a new thrust washer under each yoke and install the yokes on their respective shafts. Place the oil slinger under the front yoke. Torque the nuts to 90–130 ft. lbs.
26. Install the poppet ball, spring and screw in the front case half. Torque the screw to 20–25 ft. lbs.
27. Install the 4WD indicator switch and washer and tighten to 15–20 ft. lbs.
28. Fill the unit with 6 pints of DEXRON®II.

New Process 241 Transfer Case Overhaul

The NP241 is a part-time unit with a 2-piece aluminum housing. On the front case half, the front output shaft, front input shaft, four wheel drive indicator switch and shift lever assembly are located. On the rear case half, the rear output shaft, bearing retainer and drain and fill plugs are located.

The following Special Tools will be necessary for this procedure: J-22912-1, J-29369-1, J-29369-2, J-33832, J-8092, J-2619-5, J-36370, J-36372, J-36373, and J-36371.

DISASSEMBLY

1. Drain the fluid from the case, if not already drained.
2. Remove the attaching nuts from the front and rear output yokes. Remove the yokes and sealing washers.
3. Remove the indicator switch and seal, then, remove the speedometer switch and seal.
4. Remove the poppet screw, spring and the range selection plunger.
5. Remove the bolts and disconnect the mainshaft extension housing from the rear case half.
6. Remove the retaining ring, speedometer drive gear nylon, oil pump housing, and the oil pump gear from the rear output shaft.
7. Remove the case bolts and separate the case halves by inserting a small pry bar in the pry slots on the case.
8. Remove the fork shift spring.
9. Remove the oil pump pick–up tube and the magnetic chip collector.
10. Remove the retainer from the driven socket.
11. Remove the mainshaft, chain and driven sprocket as a unit from the front case half.
12. Remove the synchronizer assembly retainer, then remove the syncro. assembly, sleeve, thrust washer, hub and ring.
13. Remove the range fork, range selector, mode fork and range shift hub. Remove the shift lever nut, washer, and shift lever.
14. Remove the input shaft bearing retainer plate and seal.
15. Remove the input shaft bearing retainer, bearing, and the planetary assembly. Remove the bearing from the input gear with special tool J-22912-1.
16. Remove the retainer, lock ring and thrust washer from the annulus gear assembly.
17. Remove the needle bearing from the input gear as follows:
    a. Insert needle bearing tool J-29369-1 and adapter with J-2619-5 slide hammer.
    b. Using the tools mentioned above, hammer the bearing from the input gear.
18. Remove the drive sprocket from the main drive shaft.
19. Remove the needle bearings from the drive sprocket as follows:
    a. Insert needle bearing tool J-29369-2 and adapter with J-2619-5 slide hammer.
    b. Using the tools mentioned above, hammer the bearing from the drive sprocket.
20. Remove the retainer and bearing from the front output shaft. Use bearing remover tool J-33832 and driver J-8092 to drive the bearing from the case.
21. Remove the seal from the mainshaft extension housing and the seal from the front input bearing retainer.

1. Seal
2. Bushing
3. Bolts
4. Rear extension
5. Snapring
6. Front output bearing
7. Bolts
8. Pump retainer housing
9. Speedometer sensor
10. Snapring
11. Tone wheel
12. Oil pump
13. Seal
14. O-ring
15. Plug
16. Bolt
17. Rear case
18. Pickup
19. Mainshaft
20. Drive sprocket
21. Front output shaft
22. Driven sprocket
23. Snapring
24. Front output rear bearing
25. Magnet
26. Connector
27. Washer
28. Stop ring
29. Sleeve
30. Strut
31. Synchronizer hub
32. Retainer
33. Dowel
34. Range shift hub
35. Screen
36. Planetary carrier
37. Thrust washer
38. Input gear
39. Snapring
40. Input bearing
41. Snapring
42. Seal
43. Bolt
44. Retainer
45. Front case half
46. Indicator lamp switch
47. O-ring
48. Shift rail
49. Pads
50. Pads
51. Range shift fork
52. Spring
53. Pin
54. Shift fork
55. Sector with shaft
56. Bushing
57. Pin
58. Chain
59. Snapring
60. Snapring
61. Front output bearing
62. Annulus gear
63. Shift lever nut
64. Washer
65. Shift lever
66. Plastic washer
67. O-ring 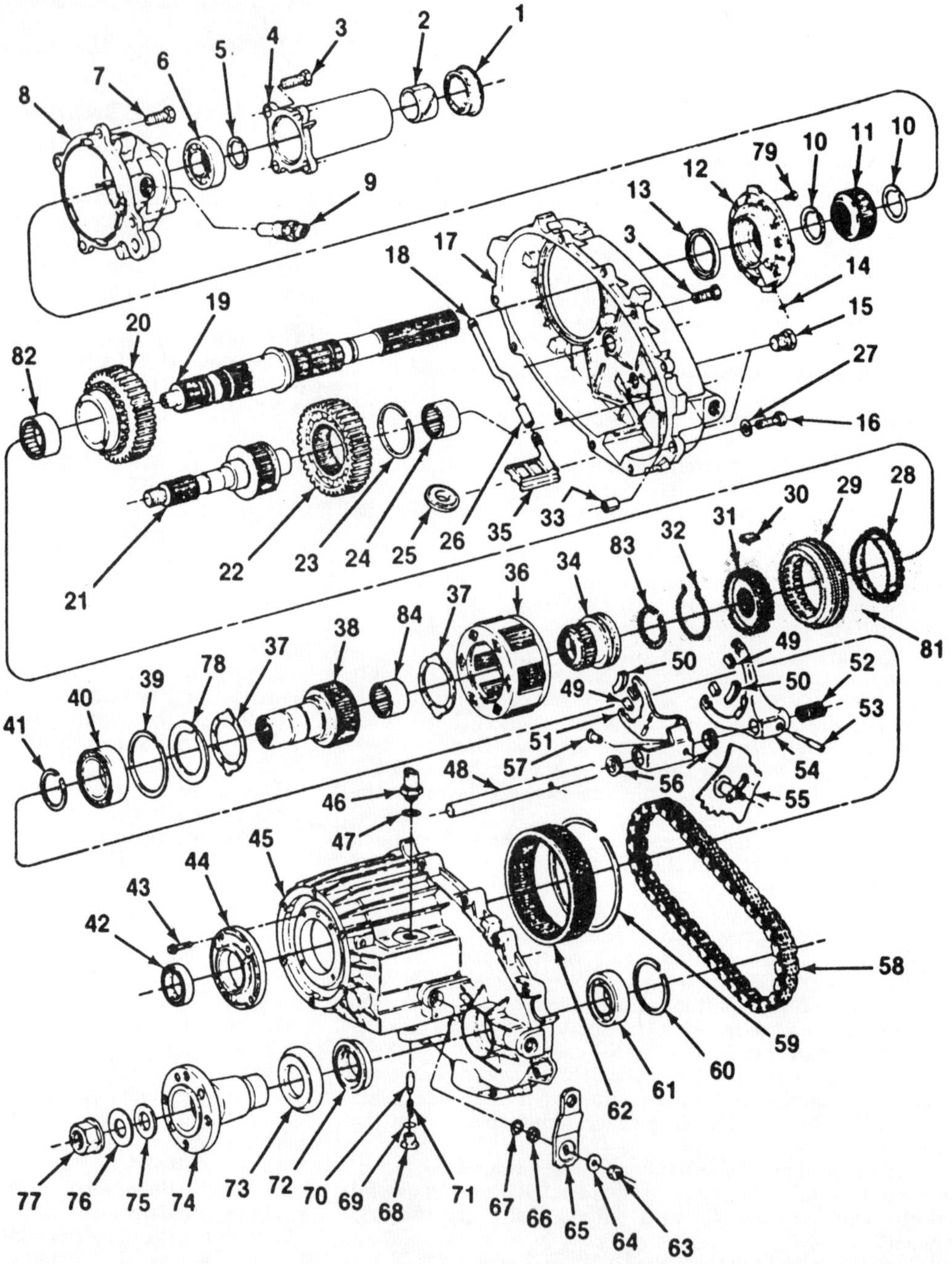
68. Screw
69. O-ring
70. Plunger
71. Spring
72. Seal
73. Deflector
74. Flange
75. Rubber washer
76. Washer
77. Nut
78. Lock ring
79. Screw
80. ID tag
81. Synchronizer
82. Drive sprocket bearing
83. Snapring
84. Pilot bearing

NP-241 exploded view

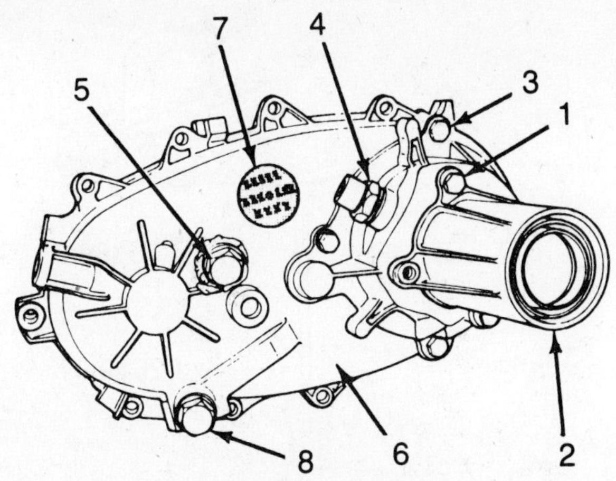

1. Mainshaft extension bolt
2. Mainshaft extension
3. Pump retainer housing bolt
4. Speedometer pick-up switch
5. Plug
6. Rear case
7. ID tag
8. Drain plug

NP-241 external components

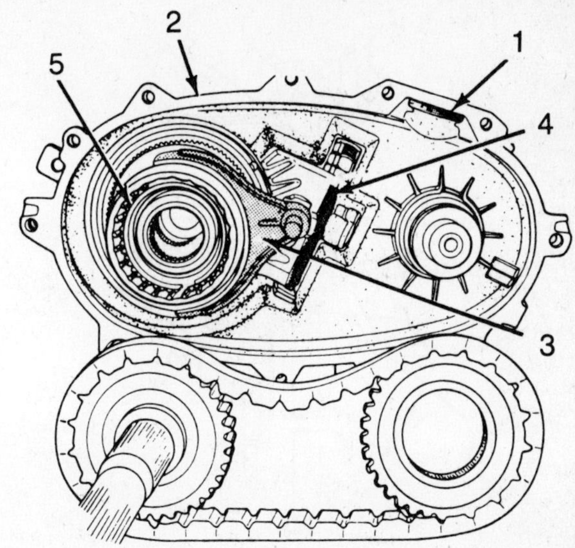

1. Magnet
2. Front case
3. Mode fork
4. Sector and shaft
5. Synchronizer

Mode for and shaft — NP-241

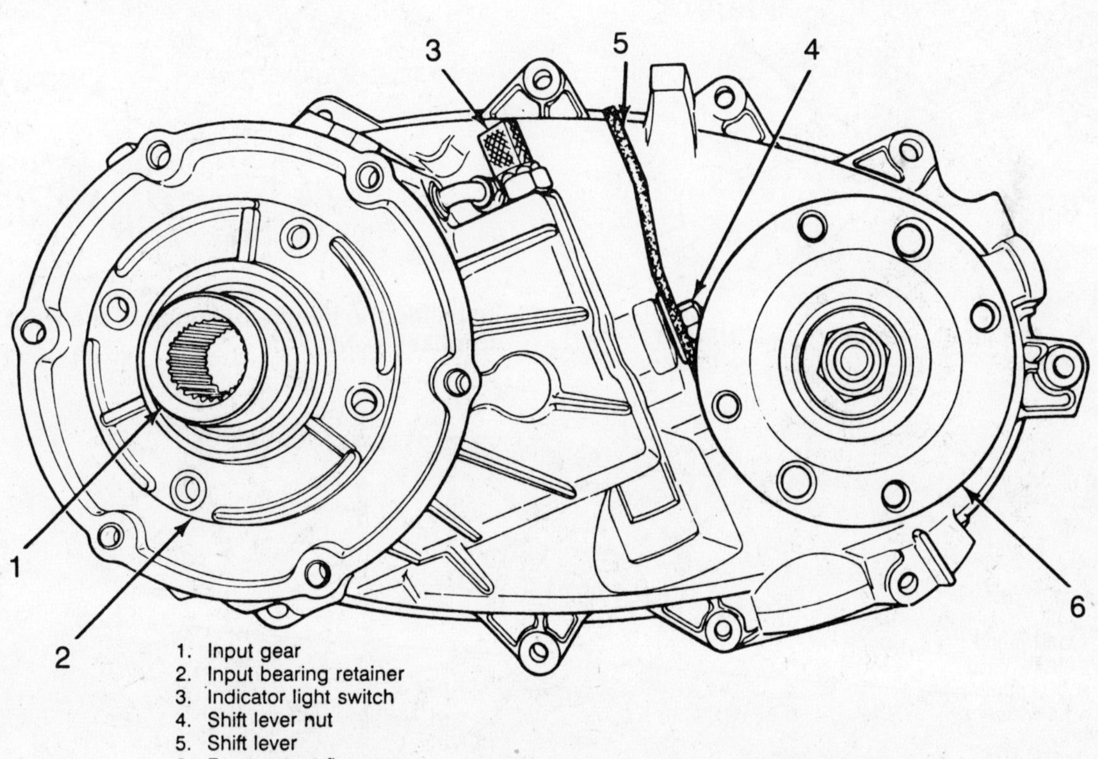

1. Input gear
2. Input bearing retainer
3. Indicator light switch
4. Shift lever nut
5. Shift lever
6. Front output flange

NP-241 front view

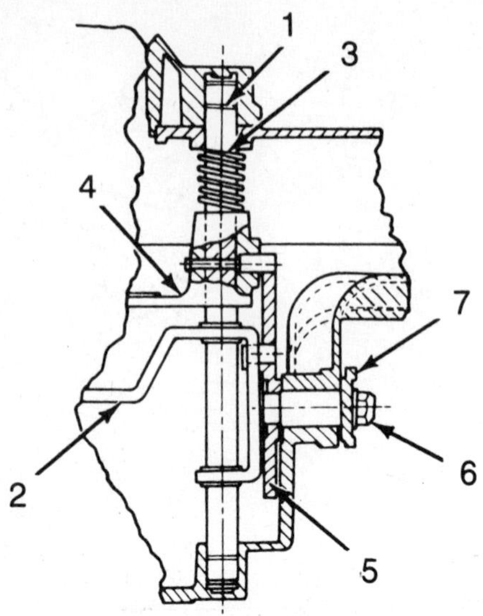

1. Shift rail
2. Range fork
3. Mode fork spring
4. Mode fork
5. Sector and shaft
6. Shift lever nut
7. Lever

Shift rail — NP-241

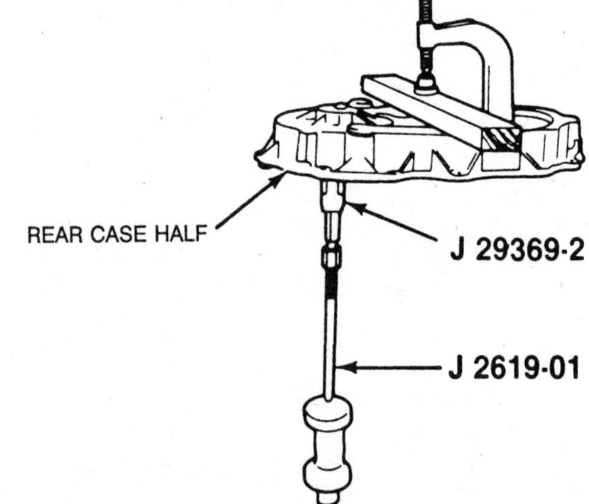

Removing the front output shaft rear bearing — NP-241

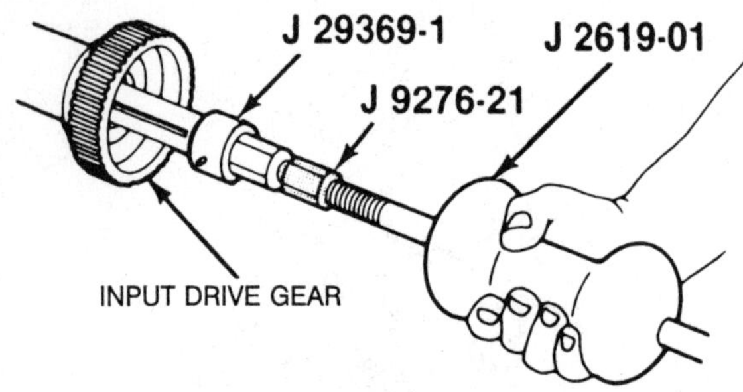

Removing the input gear bearing — NP-241

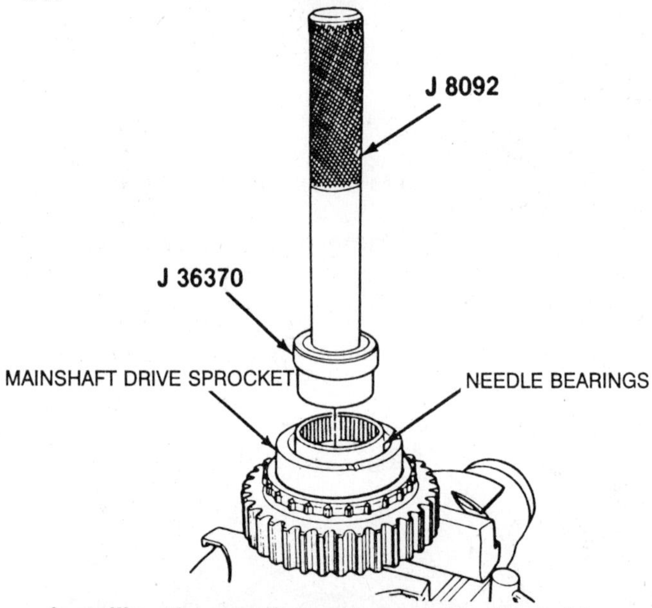

Installing the needle bearings in the front drive sprocket — NP-241

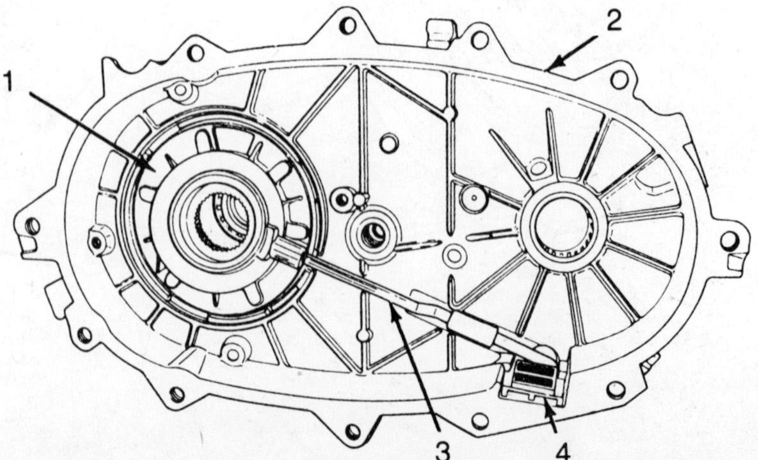

1. Oil pump
2. Rear case
3. Oil pump tube
4. Oil filter

Pump housing installation — NP-241

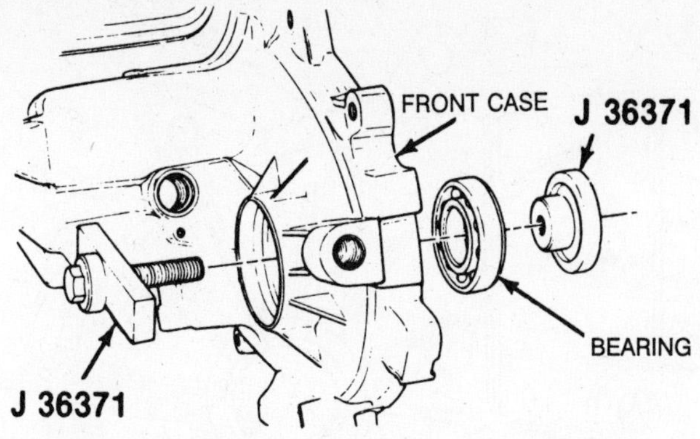

Installing the front output bearing – NP-241

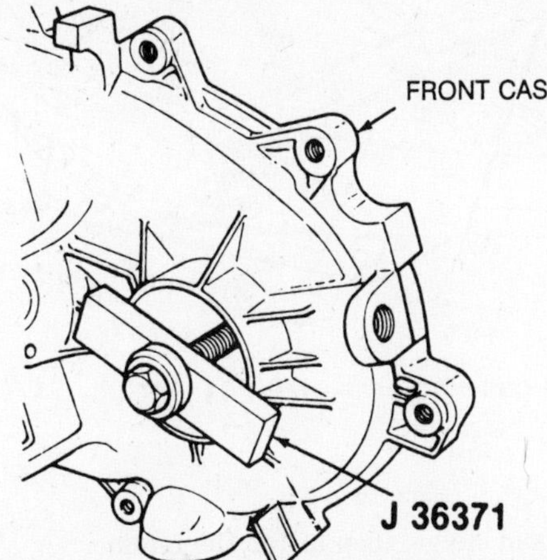

Pulling the bearing with the special tool – NP-241

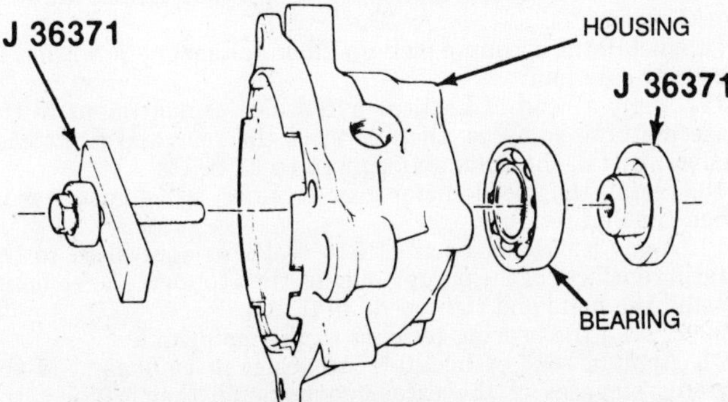

Installing the pump housing bearing – NP-241

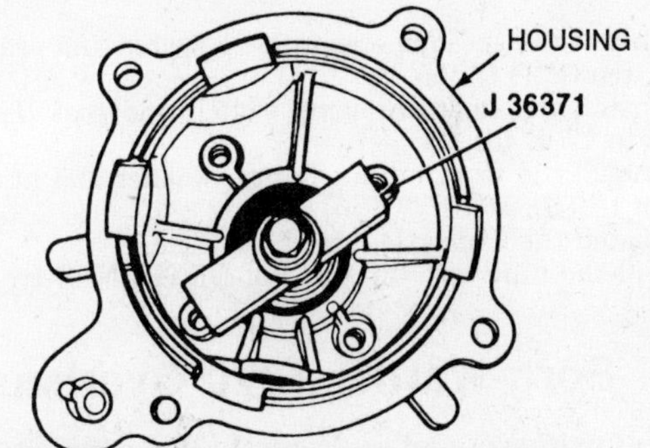

Bearing installation tool – NP-241

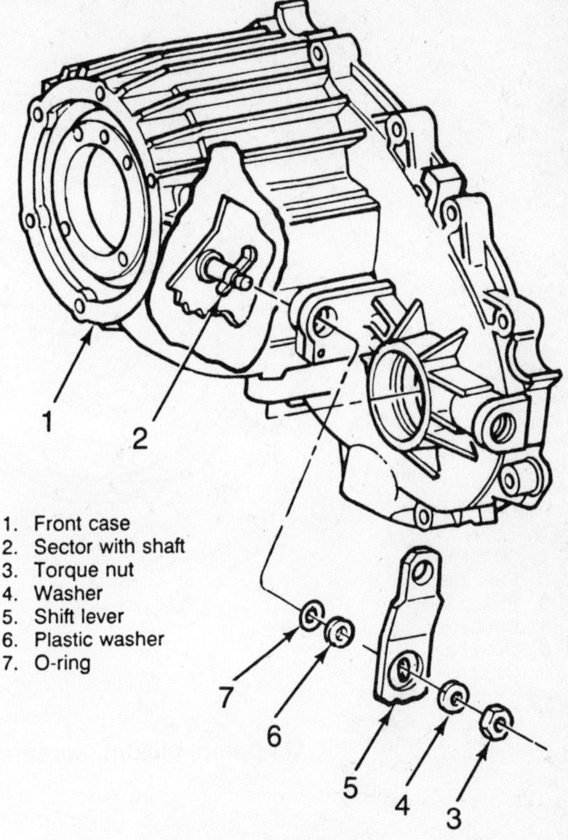

1. Front case
2. Sector with shaft
3. Torque nut
4. Washer
5. Shift lever
6. Plastic washer
7. O-ring

Sector with shaft installation – NP-241

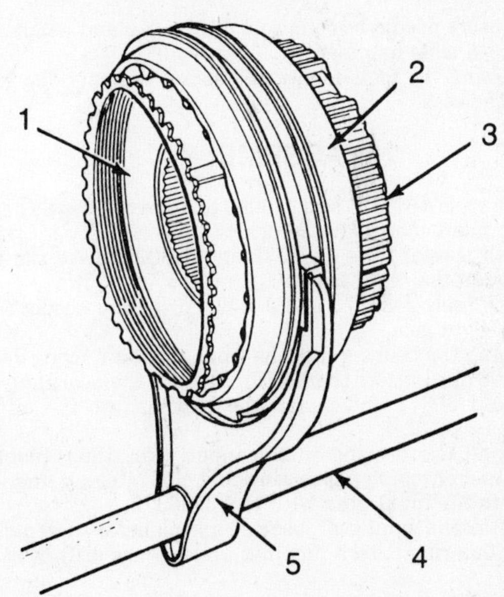

1. Synchronizer stop ring
2. Synchronizer sleeve
3. Synchronizer hub
4. Shift rail
5. Mode fork

Synchronizer hub and mode fork – NP-241

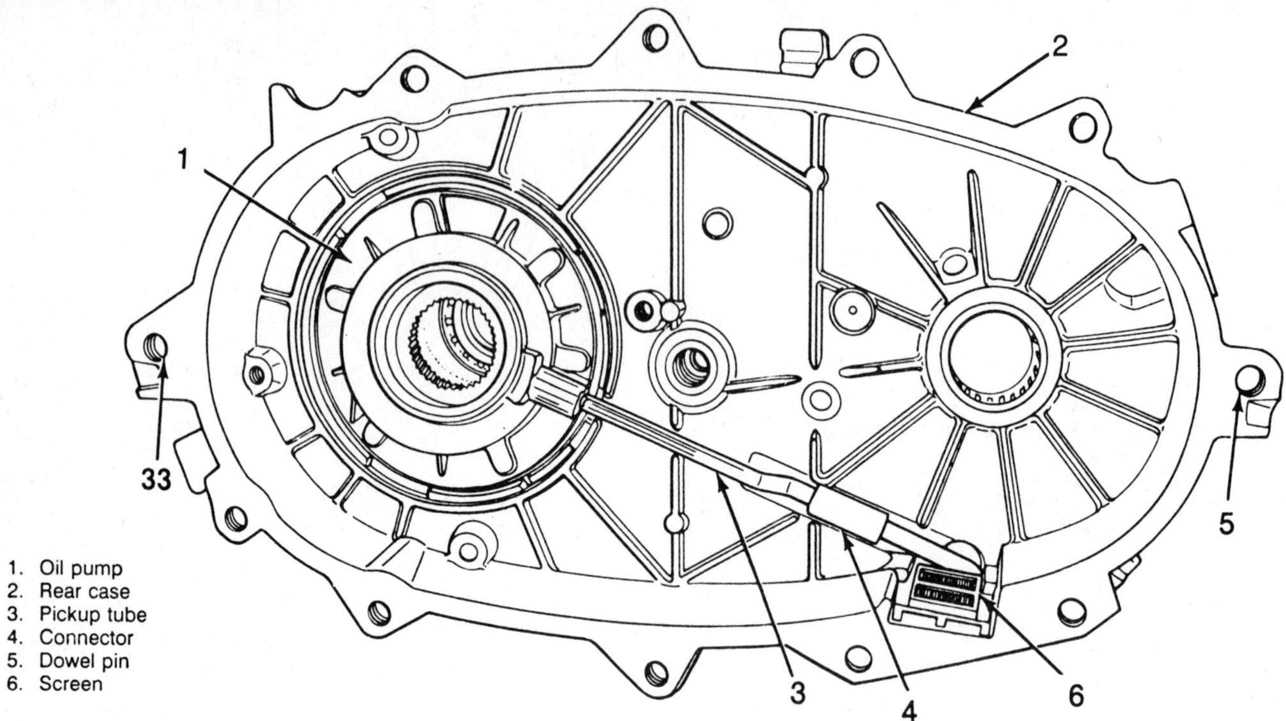

Oil pump, pickup, screen, and doweled case holes – NP-241

22. Remove the needle bearing from the rear case half as follows:

a. Insert needle bearing tool J–29369–2 and adapter with J–2619–5 slide hammer.

b. Using the tools mentioned above, hammer the bearing from the case.

ASSEMBLY

1. Use tools J–36370 and J–8092 to drive the needle bearings onto the main shaft drive sprocket.
2. With special tools J–36372 and J–8092, drive the needle bearing into the rear case half.
3. With tools J–36373 and J–8092, drive the needle bearing into the input gear.
4. Install the bearing into the front case half, using J–36371 and J–36373 to insert the bearing. Install the bearing.
5. Use J–36371 and install the bearing into the oil pump housing.
6. Install the bearing to the input gear, then, install the thrust washer, carrier lock ring and the retainer. Install the bearing to the input gear with tool J–36372.
7. Install the input gear, bearing and planetary assembly into the annulus ring. Use a hammer and a brass drift to seat the bearing.
8. Install the retainer to the input shaft bearing.
9. Install the retainer to the input gear.
10. Install the input shaft bearing retainer, seal and bolts. Tighten the bolts to 14 ft. lbs.
11. Install the range shift hub, mode fork, range selector and range fork. Install the shift lever, washer and nut and tighten to 20 ft. lbs.
12. Install the drive sprocket and needle bearings to the main drive shaft.
13. Assembly the synchronizer assembly; ring, hub, thrust washer and sleeve, then install the retainer.
14. Install the mainshaft, chain and driven sprocket as a unit into the front case half.
15. Install the retainer to the driven sprocket. Install the shift fork spring.
16. Install the oil pump pick-up, filler and magnetic washer to the rear case half.
17. Apply a bead of Loctite® 515 sealer or equivalent to the case matinng surfaces, then connect the rear and front case halves. Install the bolts and tighten to 23 ft. lbs.
18. Install the speedometer gear retainer, speedometer gear, then the 2nd retainer.
19. Apply a bead of Loctite® 515 sealer or equivalent to the mating surfaces of the pump housing, then connect the housing. Install the bolts and tighten to 30 ft. lbs.
20. Install the bearing retainer to the mainshaft.
21. Apply a bead of Loctite® 515 sealer or equivalent to the mating surfaces of the extension housing, then connect the housing. Install the bolts and tighten to 23 ft. lbs.
22. Install the range selector plunger, spring and poppet screw.
23. Install the speedometer pick-up switch and seal. Tighten the switch to 23 ft. lbs.
24. Install the indicator lamp switch and seal. Tighten the switch to 17 ft. lbs.
25. Install the front output flange, washer and nut. Tighten the nut to 110 ft. lbs.
26. Install the transaxle into the vehicle.
27. Fill the unit with 4.6 pints of DEXRON®II transmission fluid.

Borg-Warner 1370 Overhaul

The following special tools, or their equivalents, are required for this procedure: J–22912 and J–8433–4 J–5590.

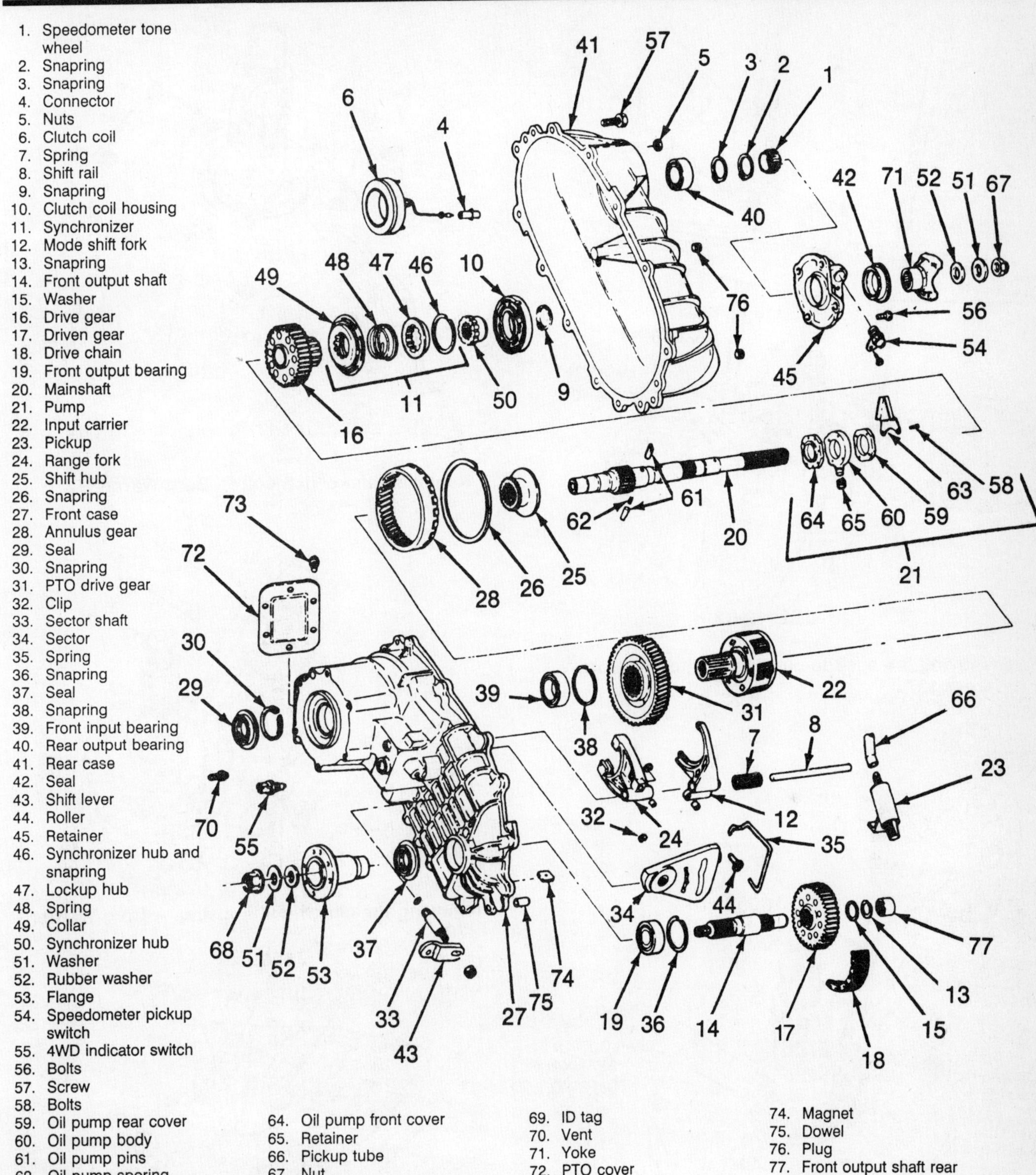

1. Speedometer tone wheel
2. Snapring
3. Snapring
4. Connector
5. Nuts
6. Clutch coil
7. Spring
8. Shift rail
9. Snapring
10. Clutch coil housing
11. Synchronizer
12. Mode shift fork
13. Snapring
14. Front output shaft
15. Washer
16. Drive gear
17. Driven gear
18. Drive chain
19. Front output bearing
20. Mainshaft
21. Pump
22. Input carrier
23. Pickup
24. Range fork
25. Shift hub
26. Snapring
27. Front case
28. Annulus gear
29. Seal
30. Snapring
31. PTO drive gear
32. Clip
33. Sector shaft
34. Sector
35. Spring
36. Snapring
37. Seal
38. Snapring
39. Front input bearing
40. Rear output bearing
41. Rear case
42. Seal
43. Shift lever
44. Roller
45. Retainer
46. Synchronizer hub and snapring
47. Lockup hub
48. Spring
49. Collar
50. Synchronizer hub
51. Washer
52. Rubber washer
53. Flange
54. Speedometer pickup switch
55. 4WD indicator switch
56. Bolts
57. Screw
58. Bolts
59. Oil pump rear cover
60. Oil pump body
61. Oil pump pins
62. Oil pump sporing
63. Retainer
64. Oil pump front cover
65. Retainer
66. Pickup tube
67. Nut
68. Nut
69. ID tag
70. Vent
71. Yoke
72. PTO cover
73. Bolt
74. Magnet
75. Dowel
76. Plug
77. Front output shaft rear bearing

Borg-Warner 1370 exploded view

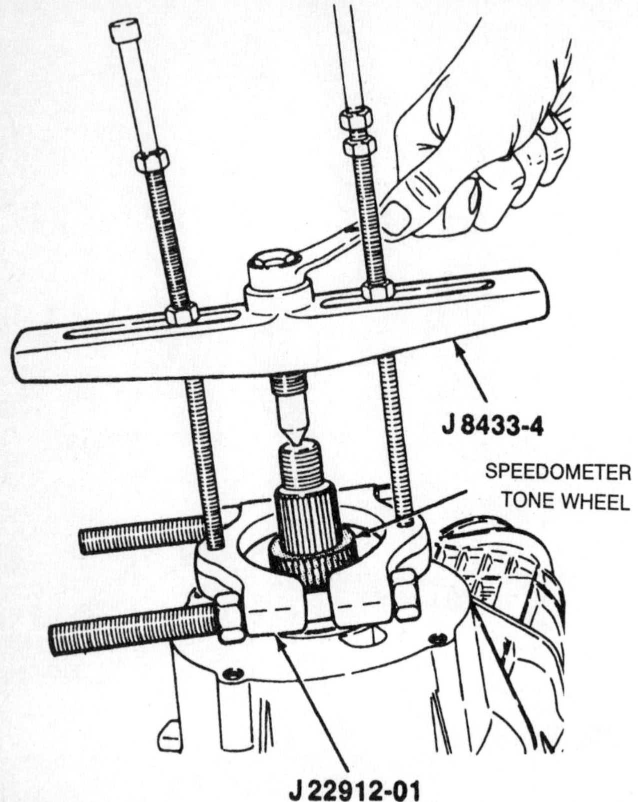

Removing the speedometer tone wheel — Borg-Warner 1370

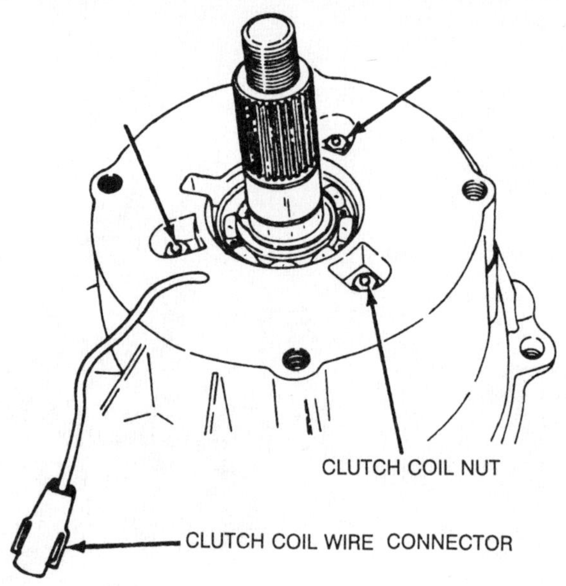

Removing the clutch coil — Borg-Warner 1370

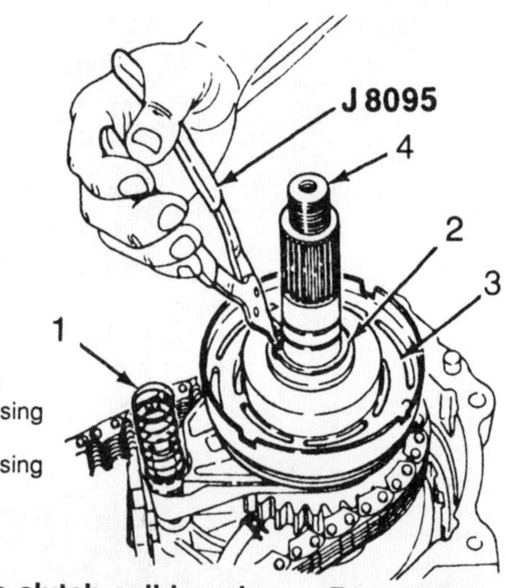

1. Shift rail spring
2. Clutch coil housing snapring
3. Clutch coil housing
4. Mainshaft

Removing the clutch coil housing — Borg-Warner 1370

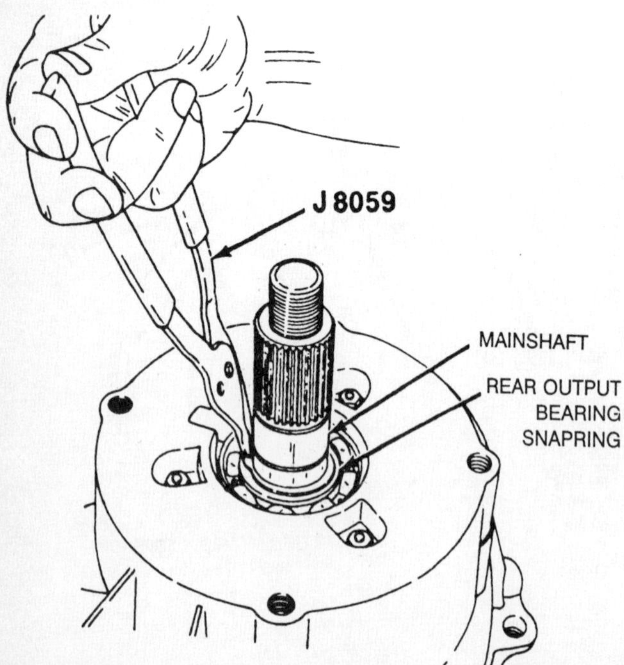

Removing the output bearing snapring — Borg-Warner 1370

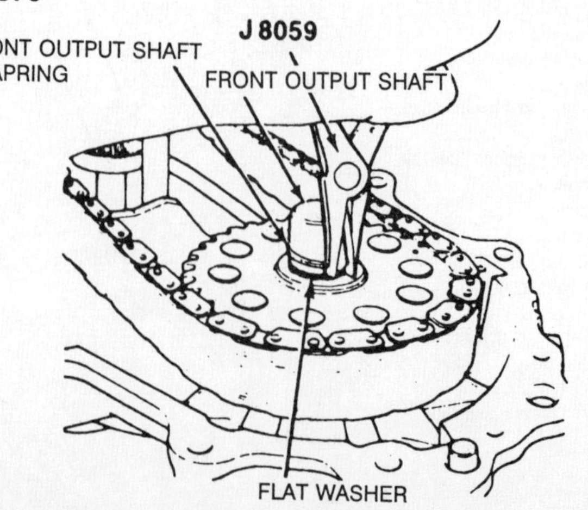

Removing the front output shaft snapring — Borg-Warner 1370

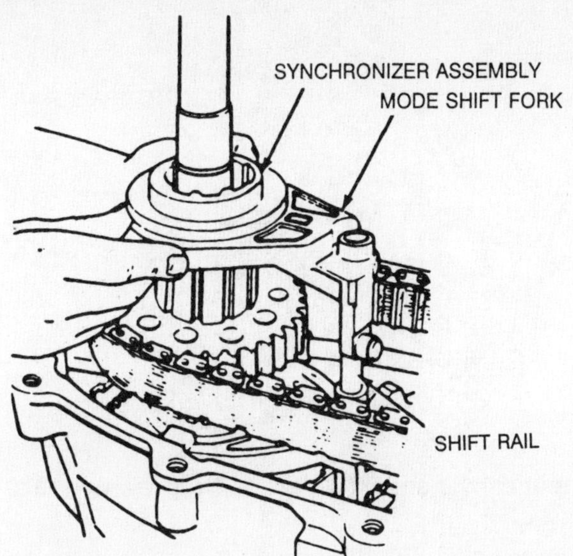

Removing the shift mode fork and synchronizer – Borg-Warner 1370

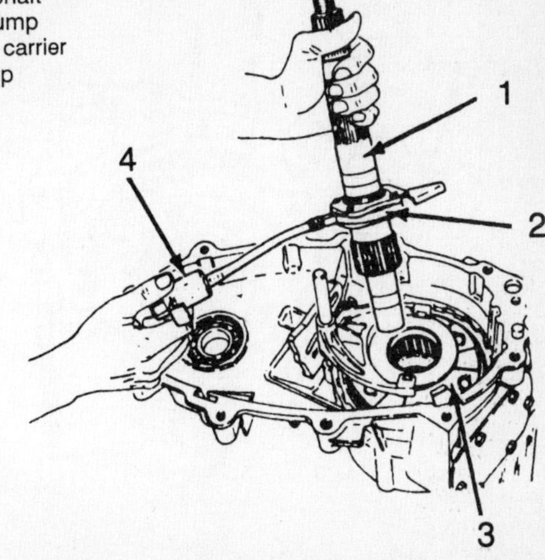

Removing the mainshaft and oil pump – Borg-Warner 1370

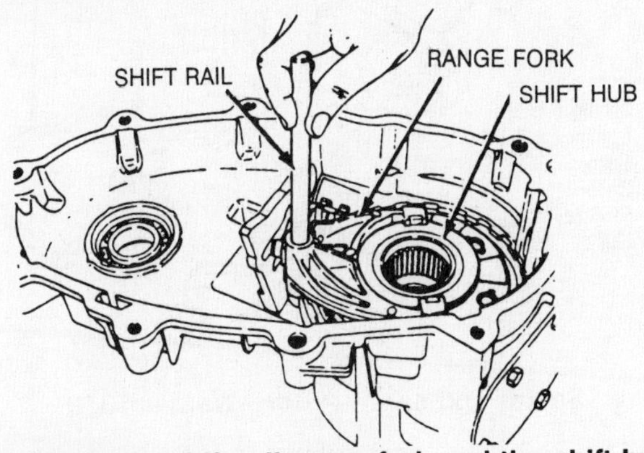

Removing the shift rail range fork and the shift hub – Borg-Warner 1370

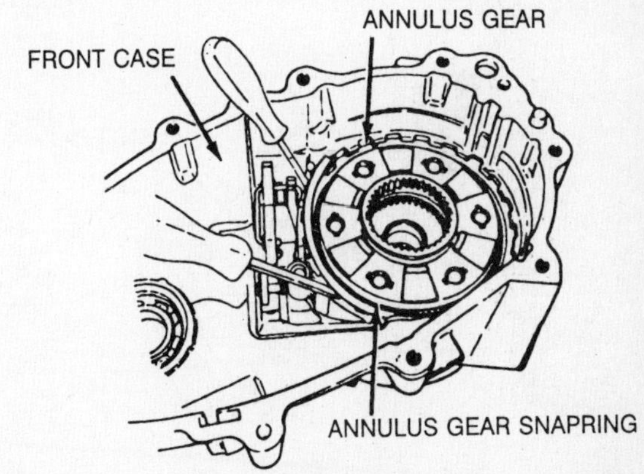

Removing the annulus gear snapring – Borg-Warner 1370

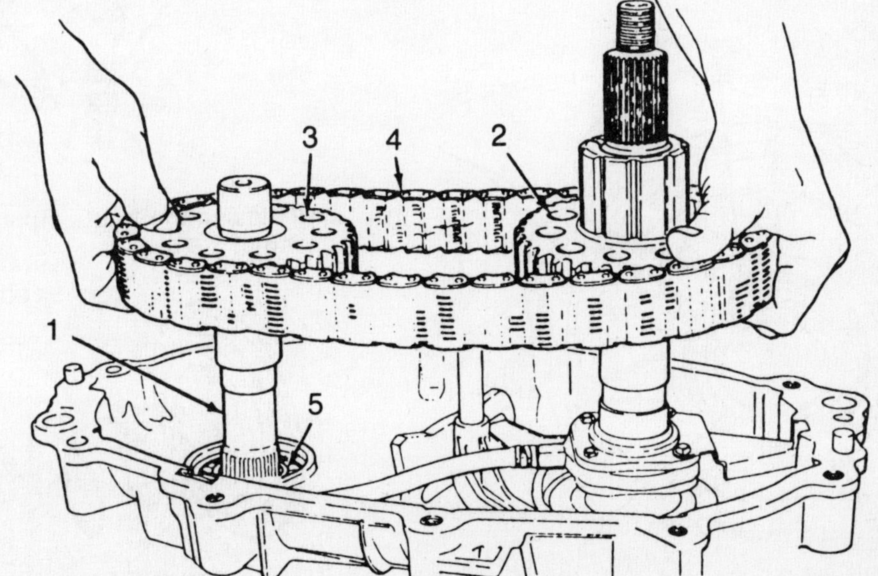

Removing the drive chain – Borg-Warner 1370

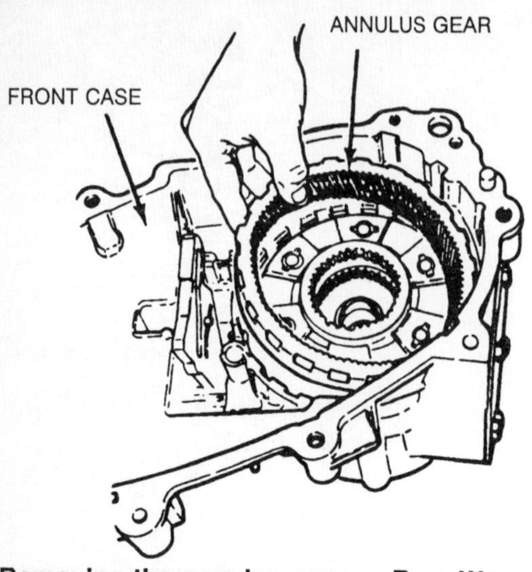

Removing the annulus gear – Borg-Warner 1370

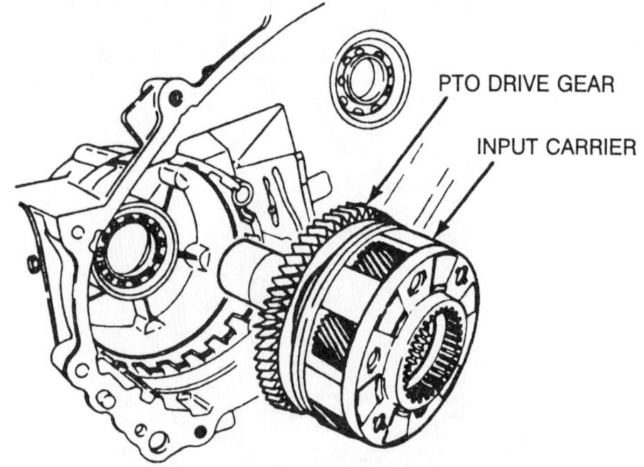

Input carrier and PTO gear – Borg-Warner 1370

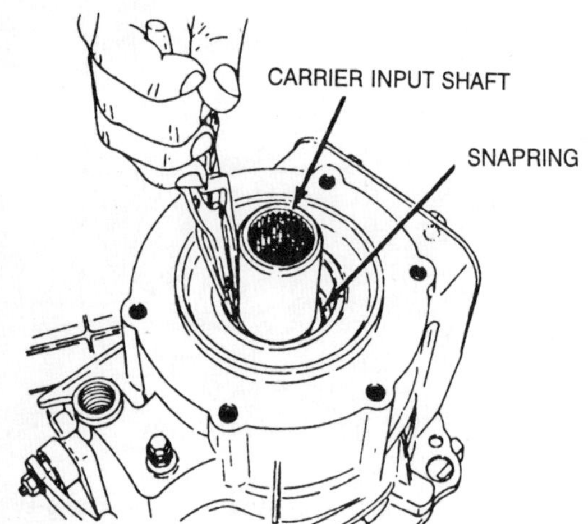

Removing the carrier assembly snapring – Borg-Warner 1370

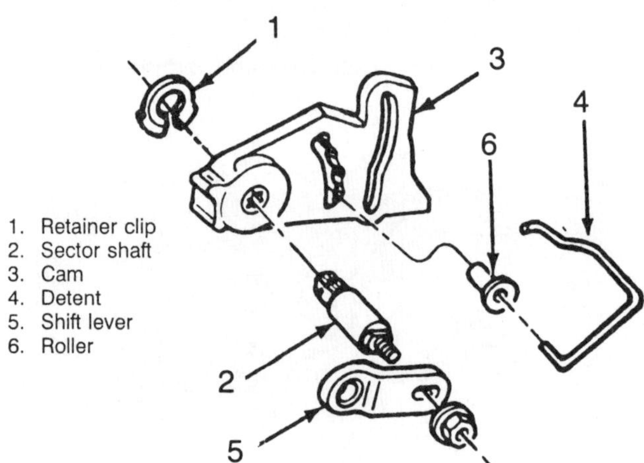

Sector and shaft – Borg-Warner 1370

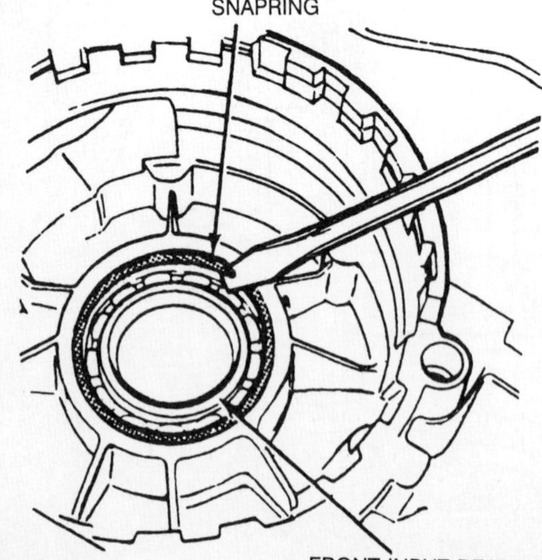

Removing the front input bearing snapring – Borg-Warner 1370

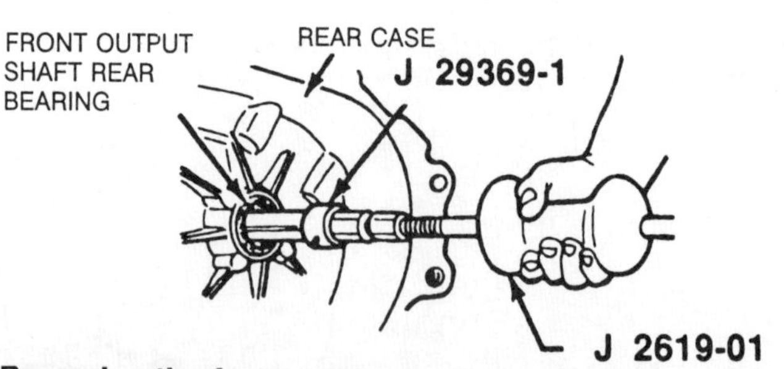

Removing the front output shaft rear bearing – Borg-Warner 1370

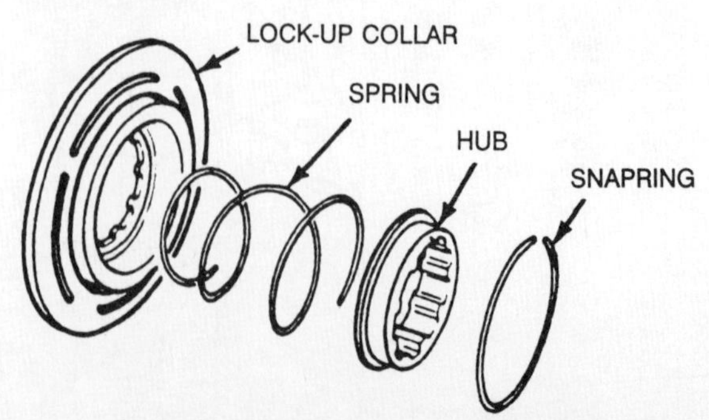

Synchronizer hub – Borg-Warner 1370

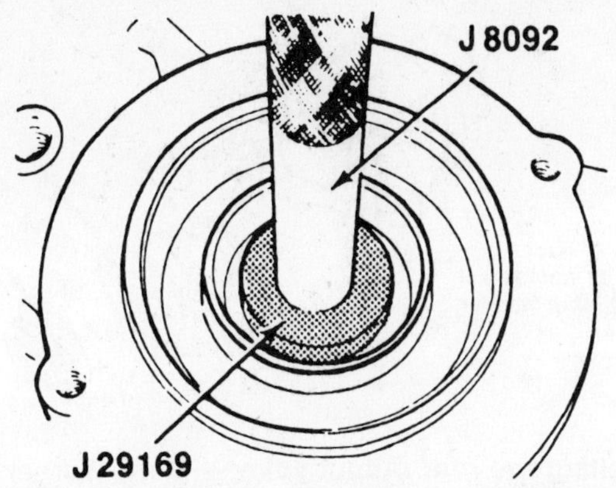

Removing the front input bearing – Borg-Warner 1370

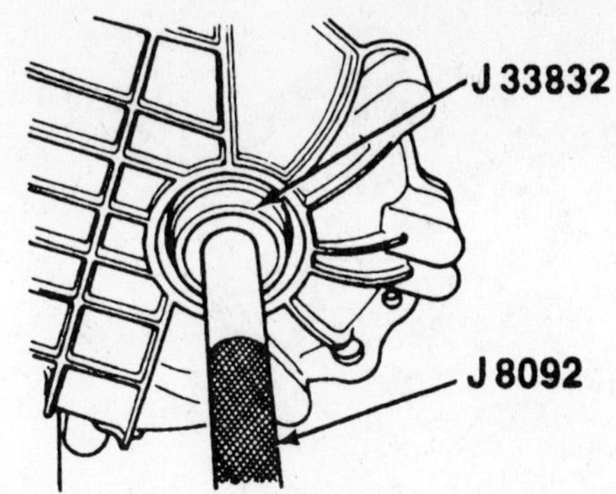

Removing the front output bearing – Borg-Warner 1370

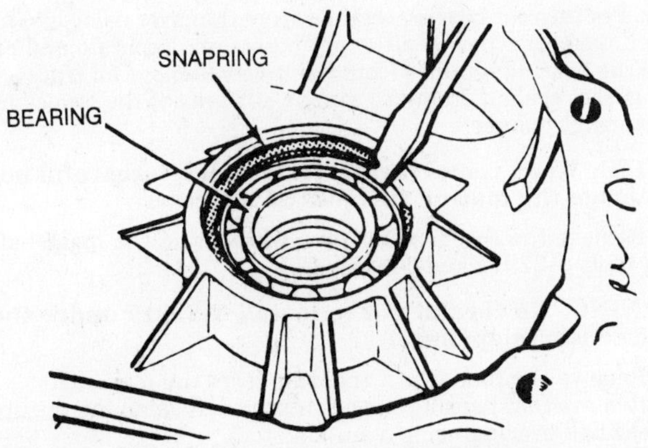

Removing the front output bearing snapring – Borg-Warner 1370

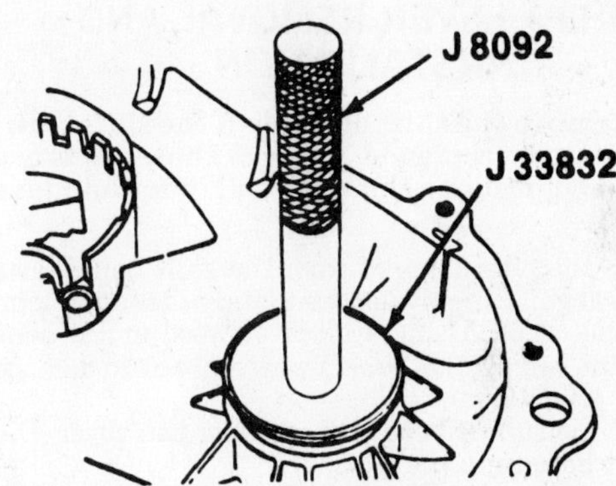

Installing the front output bearing – Borg-Warner 1370

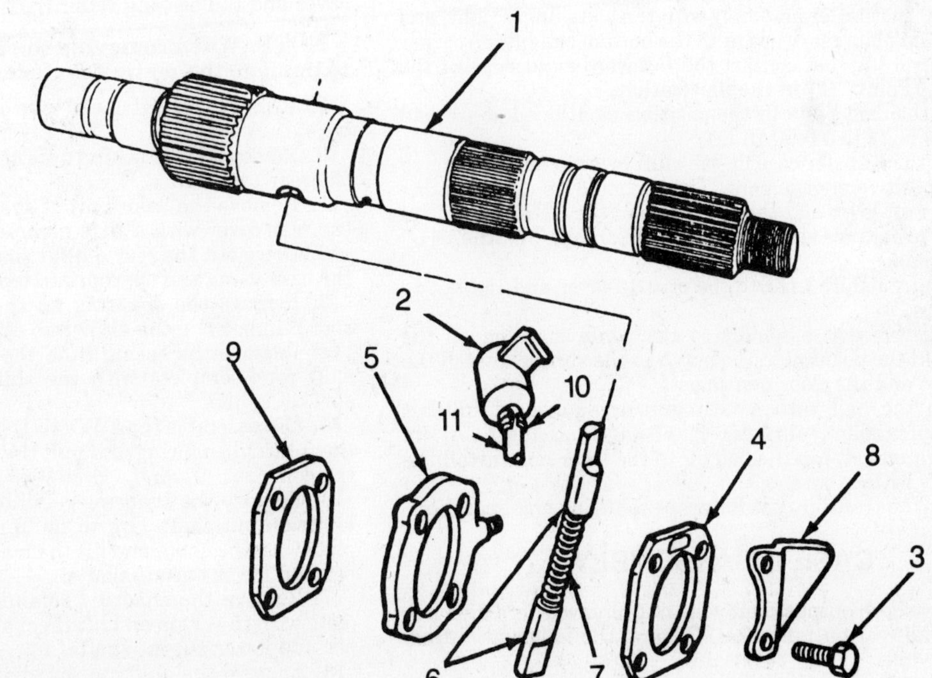

1. Mainshaft
2. Strainer
3. Bolts
4. Rear cover
5. Pump housing
6. Pins
7. Spring
8. Retainer
9. Front cover
10. Retainer clip
11. Pickup tube

Mainshaft and oil pump – Borg-Warner 1370

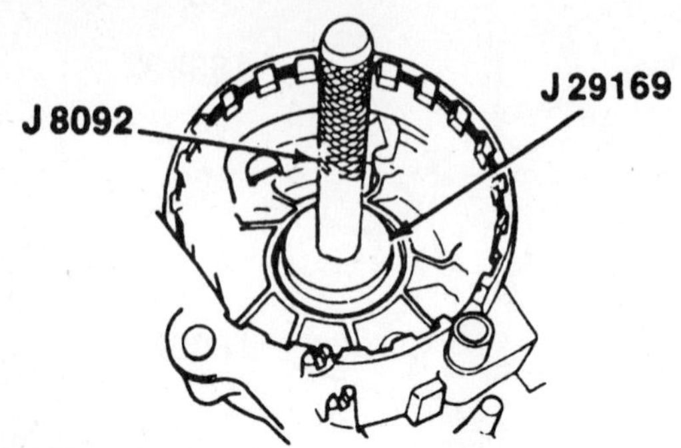

Installing the front input bearing – Borg-Warner 1370

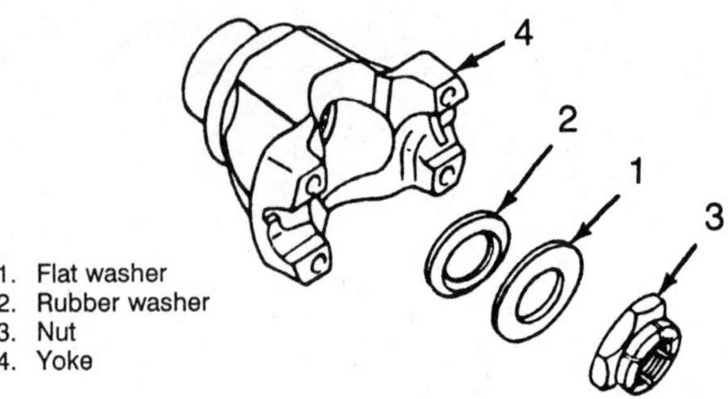

Installing the rear output yoke – Borg-Warner 1370

SHIFT LEVER REMOVAL AND INSTALLATION

NOTE: Remove the shift ball only if the shift ball, boot or lever have to be replaced. If any of these parts are not being replaced, remove the shift ball, boot and lever as an assembly.

1. Remove the plastic insert from the shift ball. Warm the ball with a heat gun or equivalent until it reaches approximately 140–180°F (60–80°C). Using a block of wood and a hammer, knock the shift ball off the lever. Be careful not to damage the finish on the shift lever.
2. Remove the rubber boot with the floor pan cover. Disconnect the vent hose from the shift lever.
3. Disconnect the transfer case shift rod from the shift lever. Remove the bolts holding the shift lever to transfer case. Remove the shift lever and bushings.

To install:

1. Before installing the shifter assembly, move the transfer case lever to the "4L" position.
2. Install the shifter assembly with the bolts finger tight, and move the cam plate rearward until the bottom chamfered corner of the neutral lug just contact the foreward right edge of the shift lever, (Point "C" in the illustration).
3. Hold the cam plate in the position mentioned above and tighten the bolts to 71–90 ft. lbs.
4. Move the transfer case in–cab shift lever to all positions to check for positive engagement. There should be clearance between the shift lever and the cam plate in the "2H" front, and "4H" rear (clearance should not exceed 2.0mm), and the "4L" shift positions.
5. Attach the shift lever to the control lever and tighten to 23–32 ft. lbs.
6. Install the vent assembly so the white marking on the housing is in the position in the notch in the shifter. Install the rubber boot and the floor pan cover
7. Warm the ball with a heat gun or equivalent until it reaches approximately 140–180°F (60–80°C). Using a $^{7}/_{16}$ in. socket and a mallet, tap the ball on to the lever and install the plastic shift pattern insert.
8. Check the transfer case for proper shifting and operation.

CASE DISASSEMBLY

1. Remove both output shaft yoke nuts and washers. Remove the front and rear output yokes. Remove the four-wheel drive indicator switch.
2. Remove the front and rear output shaft yoke seals.
3. Remove the input shaft seals.
4. Remove the bolts securing the rear bearing retainer to the cover. Pry the rear bearing retainer from the cover using a ½ in. drive breaker bar between the pry bosses and separate and remove the bearing retainer from the cover. Remove all traces of RTV gasket sealant from the mating surfaces of the cover and the bearing retainer.

NOTE: When removing the RTV sealer, be careful not to damage the mating surfaces of the cases.

5. Remove the speedometer tone wheel from the mainshaft using tools J–22912 and J–8433–4.

WARNING: Be careful not to install J–22912 under the speed sensor snapring.

6. Remove the tone wheel snapring from the mainshaft.
7. Remove the snapring on the output shaft retaining the upper rear ball bearing using a suitable tool.
8. Remove the bolts that retain the front case to the rear cover. Insert a ½ in. drive breaker bar between the pry bosses and separate. Lift the front case from the rear cover. Remove all traces of RTV gasket sealant from the mating surfaces of the cover and the bearing retainer.

NOTE: When removing the RTV sealer, be careful not to damage the mating surfaces of the magnesium cases.

9. Remove the clutch coil wire connector from the clutch coil wire.
10. Remove the attaching nuts and remove the clutch coil from the rear case half.
11. Remove the front output shaft inner needle bearing from the rear cover with a slide hammer, and collet.
12. Drive out the rear output shaft bearing from the inside of the case using the appropriate tools.
13. Remove the snapring on the output shaft securing the clutch hub. Slide the 4WD hub off of the output shaft.
14. Remove the spring from the shift rail and lift the mode shift fork complete with the shifting collar from the upper sproket spline.
15. Dissassemble the 2WD/4WD lockup assembly by removing the internal snapring and pull the lockup hub and spring from the collar.
16. Remove the snapring retaining the lower sprocket to the lower output shaft. Grasp the upper and lower sprocket complete with the chain and lift them at the same time from the upper and lower output shafts.
17. Remove the snapring retaining the lower sprocket complete with the chain and lift them at the same time from the upper and lower output shafts.
18. Remove the shift rail by sliding it straight out from the shift fork.
19. Remove the high and low shift fork by first rotating it until the roller is free from the cam then sliding out of the engage-

ment from the shift hub.
20. Remove the chip collecting magnet from its slot in the case.
21. Lift out the pump screen and remove the output shaft assembly with the pump assembled on it. If the pump is to be disassembled, remove the four bolts from the pump body. Note the position of the pump front body, pins, spring, rear cover and pump retainer as removed.
22. Remove the high low shift hub.
23. Remove the front output shaft from the case.
24. Turn the front case over and remove the front oil seal from the case.
25. Reaching through the front opening with a pair of snapring pliers, expand the snapring on the input shaft allowing it to drop out of the bearing. The carrier assembly, including the input shaft is serviced as an assembly only. If the bearing or bushing is to be replaced, drive out both of them through the input spline using suitable tools.
26. Remove the ring gear by prying out the internal snapring and lift out the gear.
27. Remove the internal snapring securing the input shaft bearing to the case and drive it out from the outside of the case.
28. Remove the internal snapring securing the front output shaft bearing in the magnesium housing and drive the bearing out from the front of the case.
29. Remove the shift cam by removing the retaining clip and sliding the shift shaft out of the case.
30. Remove the shift shaft seal by carefully prying it out of the case, being careful not to damage the case.
31. Remove the shift cam, assist spring, and the assist spring bushing from the case.

CASE ASSEMBLY

NOTE: Before starting the assembly procedure, lubricate all the internal parts, with DEXRON®II transmission fluid or equivalent.

1. Install the input shaft and the front output shaft bearings in the case using the appropriate tools. Install the internal snaprings retaining the bearings in the case.
2. Drive the front output shaft seal into the case unit until it is fully seated against the case.
3. Install the front output shaft through the lower bearing. The front output shaft is held in place in the case by the front output yoke and oil seal slinger assembly. Install the front yoke assembly onto the front output shaft then the rubber seal, flat washer and 30mm locknut. Torque the yoke locknut to 130–180 ft. lbs.
4. Press the power take-off drive gear onto the input shaft assembly if it was removed.
5. Press the needle bearing and bronze bushing into the input shaft with the appropriate tools.
6. Install the ring gear into the slots in the case and retain it with the large internal snapring making sure that it is fully seated.
7. Install the input shaft and carrier assembly in the case through the input shaft bearing being careful not to damage the gear teeth when aligning them with the ring gear teeth.
8. While supporting the carrier assembly in position, install a new spring on the front side of the input bearing making sure that it is fully seated in the snapring groove of the input shaft.
9. Install the upper input shaft oil seal into the case using an appropriate tool until it is fully seated against the case.
10. Install a new shifter shaft seal into the case using an appropriate tool.
11. Assemble the shift cam assembly into the case by sliding the shift shaft and lever assembly through the case and seal into engagement with the shift cam. Secure the shift cam with the retaining clip.
12. Install the shift cam assist spring in position in the bushing of the shift cam and in the recess in the case.
13. Assemble the pump and output shaft as follows: Place the oil pump cover with the word **TOP** facing the front of the front case. Install the two pins (with the flats facing upwards) with the spring between the pins and place the assembly in the oil pump bore in the output shaft. Place the oil pump body and the pick up tube over the shaft and make sure that the pins are riding against the inside of the pump body. Place the oil pump rear cover with the words **TOP REAR** facing the rear of the case. The word **TOP** on the front cover and the rear cover should be on the same side. Install the pump retainer with the tabs facing the front of the transfer case. Install the four retaining bolts and rotate the output shaft while tightening the bolts to prevent the pump from binding. Tighten the bolts to 36–40 inch lbs. Lubricate the assembly with automatic transmission fluid.

NOTE: The output shaft must turn freely within the oil pump. If binding occurs, loosen the four bolts and retighten again.

14. Install the high low shift hub. Install the high low shift fork by engaging it with the shift hub flange and rotating it until the roller is engaged with the lower groove of the cam.
15. Install the shift rail through the high low fork bore and into the rail bore in the case.
16. Install the output shaft and oil pump assembly in the input shaft. Make certain that the external splines of the output shaft engage the internal splines of the high low shift hub. Make sure that the oil pump retainer and oil filter leg are in the groove and notch of the front case. Install the collector magnet in the notch in the front case.
17. Assemble the upper and lower sprockets with the chain and place them as an assembly over the upper and lower output shafts. Install the washer and snapring which retain the lower sprocket to the front output shaft.
18. Assemble the 2WD/4WD lockup assembly by installing the tapered compression spring in the lockup collar with the small end installed first. Place the lockup hub over the spring and compress the spring while installing the internal snapring which holds the lockup assembly together.
19. Install the lockup assembly and its shift fork over the external splines of the upper sprocket and the shift rail with the long boss of the shift rail facing foreward.
20. Assemble the 4WD return spring over the shift rail and against the shift fork.
21. Place the 4WD hub over the external splines of the output shaft and secure with the appropriate snapring. Make sure that the snapring is fully seated in the snapring groove.
22. Press the lower output needle bearing in its bore in the rear cover using an appropriate tool.
23. Press the rear output shaft bearing into position in the cover. Install the bearing snapring retainer in the cover.
24. Install the rear output shaft oil seal in the bearing retainer using the appropriate tool making sure it is fully seated.
25. Coat the mating surface of the front case with a bead of RTV.
26. Place the cover on the case making sure that the lower output shaft, shift shaft and the shift rail are aligned. Install and torque the 12 No. 50-torx head case to cover bolts to 22–36 ft. lbs.
27. Install the bearing retainer snapring on the output shaft making sure that the snapring is fully seated in the groove on the shaft.
28. Assemble the clutch coil housing and snapring on the mainshaft.
29. Install the shift rail spring on the shift rail.
30. Install the clutch coil in the rear case half. Tighten the nuts to 84 inch lbs. Pass the wires through the case and install the connector.
31. Apply a bead of RTV to the face of the rear bearing retainer or to the rear slip yoke extension housing.
32. Place the rear bearing retainer or the rear slip yoke exten-

sion housing in its position and secure with the 4 torx head bolts.

33. Install the rear output shaft yoke and slinger assembly onto the rear splines of the output shaft. Install the rubber seal, flat steel washer and 30mm locknut on the output shaft and torque to 150–180 ft. lbs.

34. Install a new speedometer tone wheel on the mainshaft using tool J-5590.

35. Install the drain plug and tighten to 14–22 ft. lbs.

36. Install the 4WD indicator light switch and aluminum washer into the case.

37. Install the speedometer pickup switch. Tighten the bolt to 12 ft. lbs.

38. Place a ⅜ in. drive ratchet in the fill plug and remove the plug. Fill the transfer case with 64 oz. of Dexron®II transmission fluid.

39. Install the fill plug and tighten to 14–22 ft. lbs.

40. Install the transfer case as described below.

41. Start the engine, check the transfer case for proper operation. Stop the engine and check the fluid level. The fluid should drip out of the "LEVEL" hole. If the fluid flows out of the "LEVEL" hole, the oil pump may not be funtioning properly.

DRIVELINE

Troubleshooting Basic Driveshaft and Rear Axle Problems

When abnormal vibrations or noises are detected in the driveshaft area, this chart can be used to help diagnose possible causes. Remember that other components such as wheels, tires, rear axle and suspension can also produce similar conditions.

BASIC DRIVESHAFT PROBLEMS

Problem	Cause	Solution
Shudder as car accelerates from stop or low speed	• Loose U-joint • Defective center bearing	• Replace U-joint • Replace center bearing
Loud clunk in driveshaft when shifting gears	• Worn U-joints	• Replace U-joints
Roughness or vibration at any speed	• Out-of-balance, bent or dented driveshaft • Worn U-joints • U-joint clamp bolts loose	• Balance or replace driveshaft • Replace U-joints • Tighten U-joint clamp bolts
Squeaking noise at low speeds	• Lack of U-joint lubrication	• Lubricate U-joint; if problem persists, replace U-joint
Knock or clicking noise	• U-joint or driveshaft hitting frame tunnel • Worn CV joint	• Correct overloaded condition • Replace CV joint

BASIC REAR AXLE PROBLEMS

First, determine when the noise is most noticeable.

Drive Noise—Produced under vehicle acceleration.

Coast Noise—Produced while the car coast with a closed throttle.

Float Noise—Occurs while maintaining constant car speed (just enough to keep speed constant) on a level road.

Road Noise

Brick or rough surfaced concrete roads produce noises that seem to come from the rear axle. Road noise is usually identical in Drive or Coast and driving on a different type of road will tell whether the road is the problem.

Tire Noise

Tire noises are often mistaken for rear axle problems. Snow treads or unevenly worn tires produce vibrations seeming to originate elsewhere. Temporarily inflating the tire to 40 lbs will significantly alter tire noise, but will have no effect on rear axle noises (which normally cease below about 30 mph).

Engine/Transmission Noise

Determine at what speed the noise is more pronounced, then stop the car in a quiet place. With the transmission in Neutral, run the engine through speeds corresponding to road speeds where the noise was noticed. Noises produced with the car standing still are coming from the engine or transmission.

Front Wheel Bearings

While holding the car speed steady, lightly apply the foot brake; this will often decease bearing noise, as some of the load is taken from the bearing.

Rear Axle Noises

Eliminating other possible sources can narrow the cause to the rear axle, which normally produces noise from worn gears or bearings. Gear noises tend to peak in a narrow speed range, while bearing noises will usually vary in pitch with engine speeds.

NOISE DIAGNOSIS

The Noise Is	Most Probably Produced By
• Identical under Drive or Coast	• Road surface, tires or front wheel bearings
• Different depending on road surface	• Road surface or tires
• Lower as the car speed is lowered	• Tires
• Similar with car standing or moving	• Engine or transmission
• A vibration	• Unbalanced tires, rear wheel bearing, unbalanced driveshaft or worn U-joint
• A knock or click about every 2 tire revolutions	• Rear wheel bearing
• Most pronounced on turns	• Damaged differential gears
• A steady low-pitched whirring or scraping, starting at low speeds	• Damaged or worn pinion bearing
• A chattering vibration on turns	• Wrong differential lubricant or worn clutch plates (limited slip rear axle)
• Noticed only in Drive, Coast or Float conditions	• Worn ring gear and/or pinion gear

Tubular driveshafts are used on all models, incorporating needle bearing U-joints. An internally splined sleeve at the forward end compensates for variation in distance between the rear axle and the transmission.

The number of rear driveshafts used is determined by the length of the wheelbase. On trucks that use a two-piece rear driveshaft there is a center support incorporating a rubber cushioned ball bearing mounted in a bracket attached to the frame crossmember. The ball bearing is permanently sealed and lubricated.

4WD models use a front driveshaft with a constant velocity joint.

Extended life U-joints have been incorporated on most models and can be identified by the absence of a lubrication fitting.

Front Driveshaft

REMOVAL AND INSTALLATION

V Series

Chevrolet and GMC use U-bolts or straps to secure the driveshaft to the pinion flange. Use the following procedure to remove the driveshaft.

1. Jack up your vehicle and support it with jackstands.
2. Scribe aligning marks on the driveshaft and the pinion flange to aid in reassembly.
3. Remove the U-bolts or straps at the axle end of the shaft. Compress the shaft slightly and tape the bearings into place to avoid losing them.
4. Remove the U-bolts or flange bolts at the transfer case end of the shaft. Tape the bearings into place.
5. Remove the driveshaft.
6. Installation is the reverse of removal. Make certain that the marks made earlier line up correctly to prevent possible imbalances. Be sure that the constant velocity joint is at the transfer case end. Torque U-bolts to 15 ft. lbs.; flange bolts to 75 ft. lbs.

K Series

1. Jack up your vehicle and support it with jackstands.
2. Scribe aligning marks on the driveshaft and each flange to aid in reassembly.

3. Remove the flange bolts and retainers at each end of the shaft.

4. Push the driveshaft forward until it clears the transfer case flange and remove it. If the shaft is difficult to disengage from either flange, pry it loose; never hammer it loose!

5. Remove the driveshaft.

6. Installation is the reverse of removal. Make certain that the marks made earlier line up correctly to prevent possible imbalances. Be sure that the constant velocity joint is at the transfer case end. Torque the axle end flange bolts to 15 ft. lbs.; the transfer case end flange bolts to 75 ft. lbs.

Rear Driveshaft

REMOVAL AND INSTALLATION

All Models

1. Jack up your truck and support it with jackstands.

2. Scribe alignment marks on the driveshaft and flange of the rear axle, and transfer case or transmission. If the truck is equipped with a two piece driveshaft, be certain to also scribe marks at the center joint near the splined connection. When reinstalling driveshafts, it is necessary to place the shafts in the same position from which they were removed. Failure to reinstall the driveshaft properly will cause driveline vibrations and reduced component life.

3. Disconnect the rear universal joint by removing U-bolts or straps. Tape the bearings into place to avoid losing them.

4. If there are U-bolts or straps at the front end of the shaft, remove them. Tape the bearings into place. For trucks with two piece shafts, remove the bolts retaining the bearing support to the frame crossmember. Compress the shaft slightly and remove it.

5. If there are no fasteners at the front end of the transmission, there will only be a splined fitting. Slide the shaft forward slightly to disengage the axle flange, lower the rear end of the shaft, then pull it back out of the transmission. Most two wheel

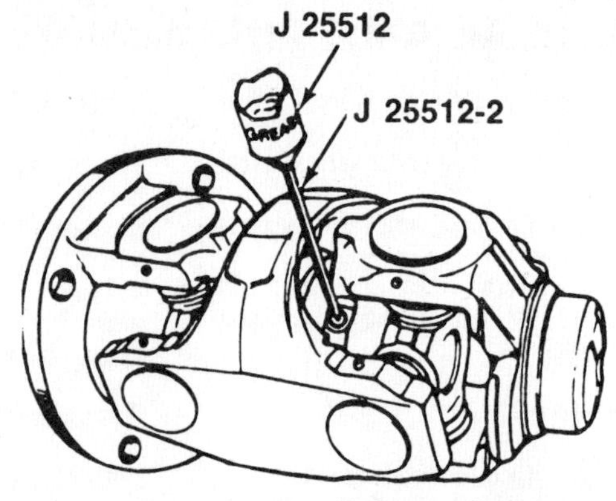

Lubricating the CV-joint fitting

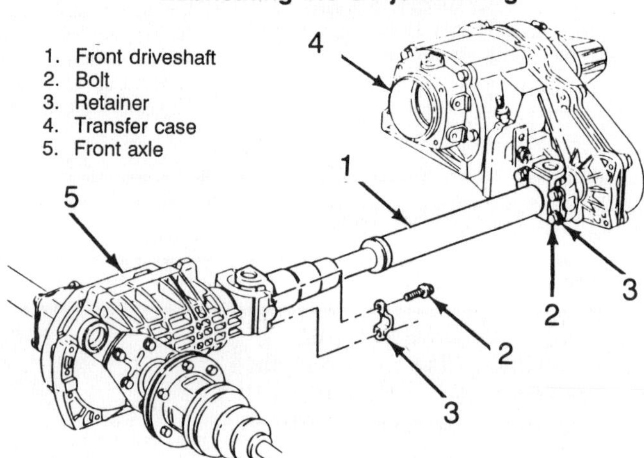

K series front driveshaft and related parts

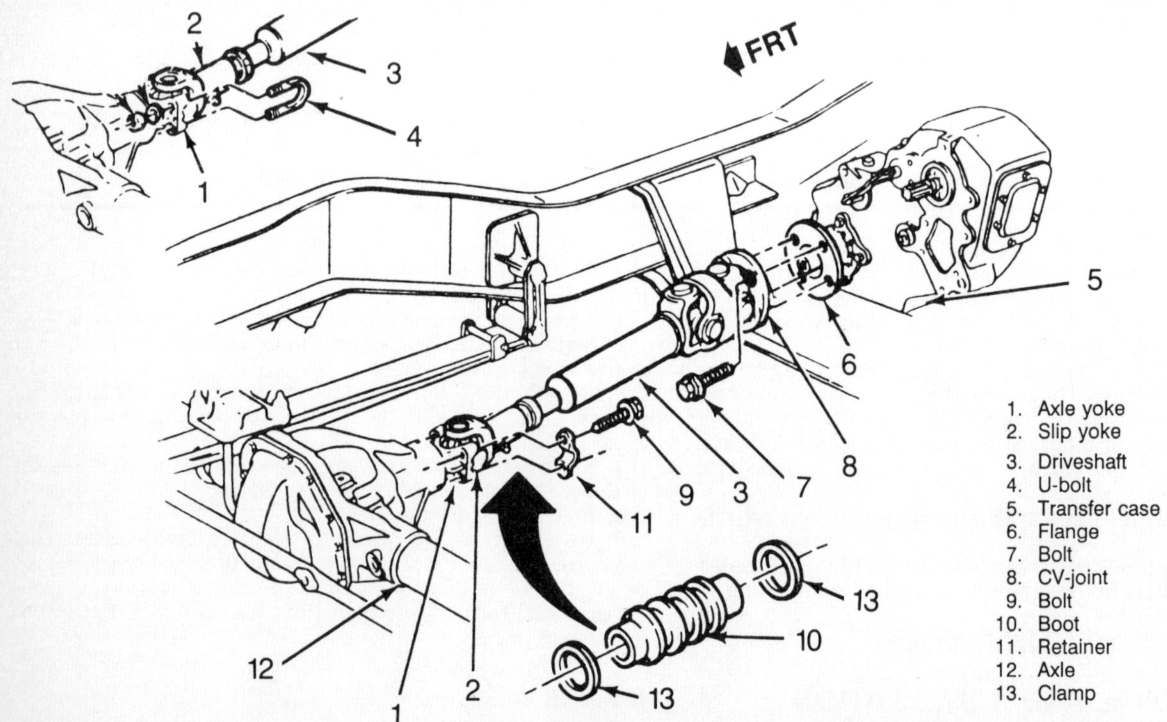

V series front driveshaft and related parts

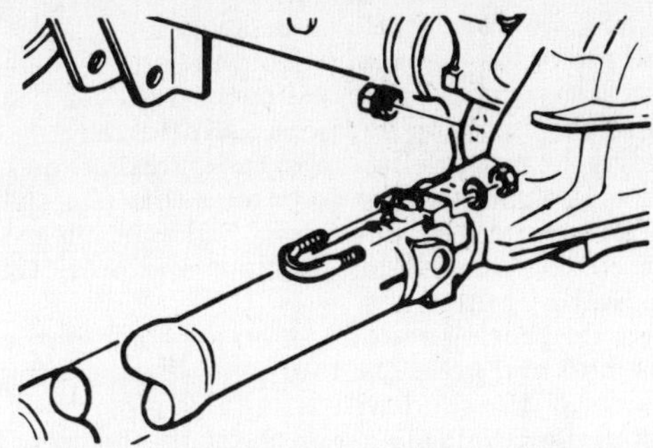
Rear driveshaft U-bolt attachment

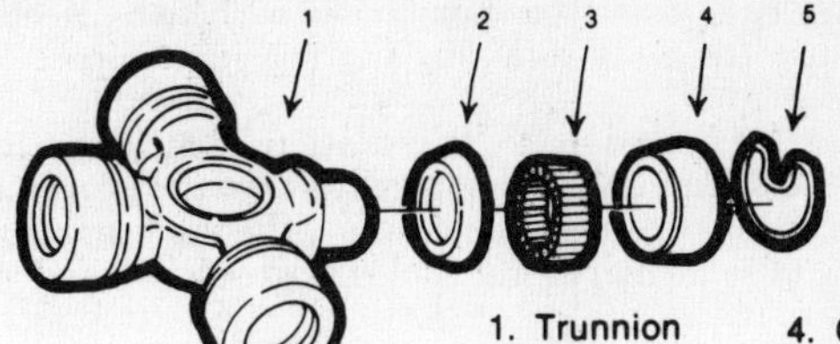

Snapring type U-joint

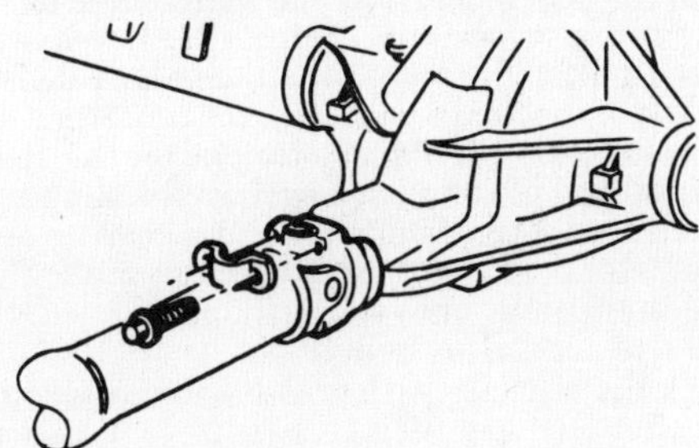
Rear driveshaft strap attachment

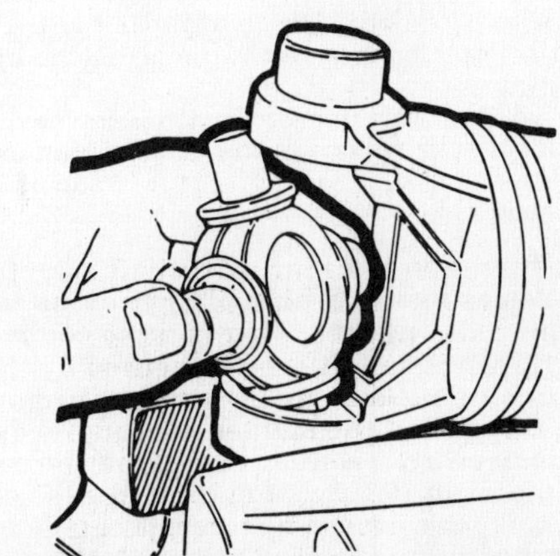
Installing the trunnion on the driveshaft yoke

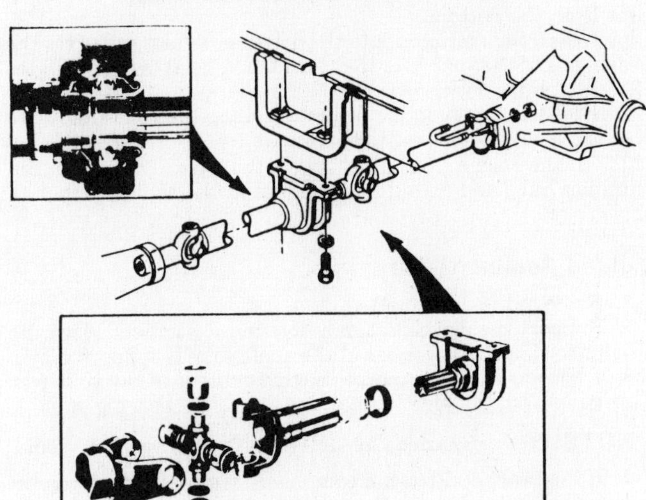
2-piece driveshaft

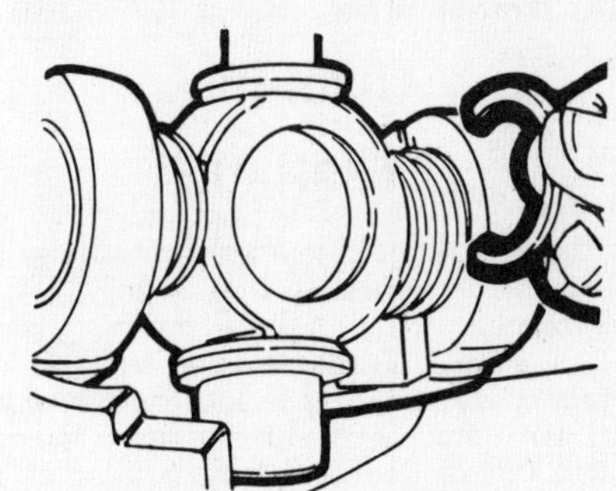
Installing the snapring

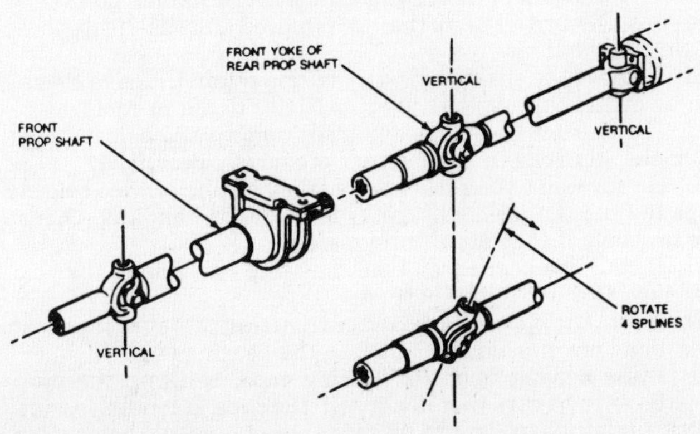

2-piece driveshaft alignment

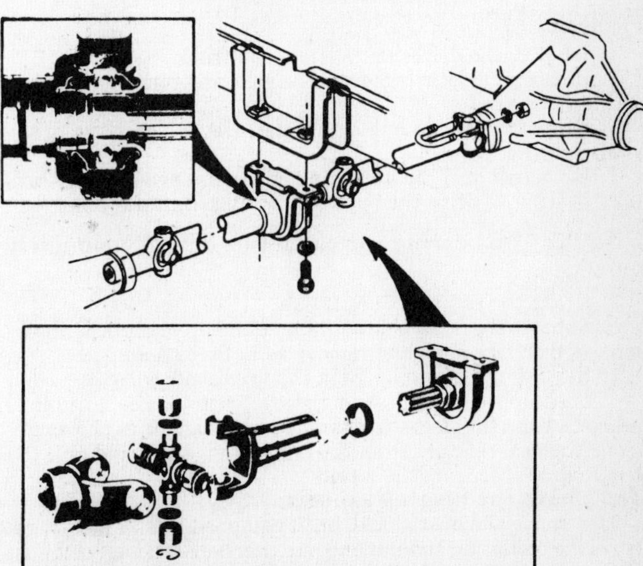
Driveshaft, U-joint and bearing support

drive trucks are of this type. For trucks with two piece driveshafts, remove the bolts retaining the bearing support to the frame crossmember.

6. Reverse the procedure for installation. It may be tricky to get the scribed alignment marks to match up on trucks with two piece driveshafts. For those models only, the following instructions may be of some help. First, slide the grease cap and gasket onto the rear splines.

- K models with 16 splines, after installing the front shaft to the transmission and bolting the support to the crossmember, arrange the front trunnion vertically and the second trunnion horizontally.
- Models with 32 splines have an alignment key. The driveshaft cannot be replaced incorrectly. Simply match up the key with the keyway.

7. On two wheel drive automatic transmission models, lubricate the internal yoke splines at the transmission end of the shaft with lithium base grease. The grease should seep out through the vent hole.

NOTE: A thump in the rear driveshaft sometimes occurs when releasing the brakes after braking to a stop, especially on a downgrade. This is most common with automatic transmission. It is often caused by the driveshaft splines binding and can be cured by removing the driveshaft, inspecting the splines for rough edges, and carefully lubricating. A similar thump may be caused by the clutch plates in Positraction limited slip rear axles binding. If this isn't caused by wear, it can be cured by draining and refilling the rear axle with the special lubricant and adding Positraction additive, both of which are available from dealers.

U-Joints

OVERHAUL

There are three types of U-joints used in these trucks. The first is held together by wire snaprings in the yokes. The second type is held together with injection molded plastic retainer rings. This type cannot be reassembled with the same parts, once disassembled. However, repair kits are available. The third type (4-wheel drive models only) is the large constant velocity joint which looks like a double U-joint, located at the transfer case end of the front driveshaft.

Snapring Type

1. Remove the driveshaft(s) from the truck.
2. Remove the lockrings from the yoke and remove the lubrication fitting.
3. Support the yoke in a bench vise. Never clamp the driveshaft tube.
4. Use a soft drift pin and hammer to drive against one trunnion bearing to drive the opposite bearing from the yoke.

NOTE: The bearing cap cannot be driven completely out.

5. Grasp the cap and work it out.
6. Support the other side of the yoke and drive the other bearing cap from the yoke and remove as in Steps 4 and 5.
7. Remove the trunnion from the driveshaft yoke.
8. If equipped with a sliding sleeve, remove the trunnions bearings from the sleeve yoke in the same manner as above. Remove the seal retainer from the end of the sleeve and pull the seal and washer from the retainer.

To remove the bearing support:

9. Remove the dust shield, or, if equipped with a flange, remove the cotter pin and nut and pull the flange and deflector assembly from the shaft.
10. Remove the support bracket from the rubber cushion and pull the cushion away from the bearing.
11. Pull the bearing assembly from the shaft. If equipped, remove the grease retainers and slingers from the bearing.

Assemble the bearing support as follows:

12. Install the inner deflector on the driveshaft and punch the deflector on 2 opposite sides to be sure that it is tight.
13. Pack the retainers with special high melting grease. Insert a slinger (if used) inside one retainer and press this retainer over the bearing outer race.
14. Start the bearing and slinger on the shaft journal. Support the driveshaft and press the bearing and inner slinger against the shoulder of the shaft with a suitable pipe.
15. Install the second slinger on the shaft and press the second retainer on the shaft.
16. Install the dust shield over the shaft (small diameter first) and depress it into position against the outer slinger or, if equipped with a flange, install the flange and deflector. Align the centerline of the flange yoke with the centerline of the driveshaft yoke and start the flange straight on the splines of the shaft with the end of the flange against the slinger.
17. Force the rubber cushion onto the bearing and coat the outside diameter of the cushion with clean brake fluid.
18. Force the bracket onto the cushion.

Assemble the trunnion bearings:

19. Repack the bearings with grease and replace the trunnion dust seals after any operation that requires disassembly of the U-joint. But be sure that the lubricant reservoir at the end of the trunnion is full of lubricant. Fill the reservoirs with lubricant from the bottom.
20. Install the trunnion into the driveshaft yoke and press the bearings into the yoke over the trunnion hubs as far as it will go.
21. Install the lockrings.
22. Hold the trunnion in one hand and tap the yoke slightly to seat the bearings against the lockrings.
23. On the rear driveshafts, install the sleeve yoke over the trunnion hubs and install the bearings in the same manner as above.

Molded Retainer Type

1. Remove the driveshaft.
2. Support the driveshaft in a horizontal position. Place the U-joint so that the lower ear of the shaft yoke is supported by a 1⅛ in. socket. Press the lower bearing cup out of the yoke ear. This will shear the plastic retaining the lower bearing cup.

NOTE: Never clamp the driveshaft tubing in a vise.

3. If the bearing cup is not completely removed, lift the cross, insert a spacer and press the cup completely out.
4. Rotate the driveshaft, shear the opposite plastic retainer, and press the other bearing cup out in the same manner.
5. Remove the cross from the yoke. Production U-joints cannot be reassembled. There are no bearing retainer grooves in the cups. Discard all parts that we removed and substitute those in the overhaul kit.
6. Remove the sheared plastic bearing retainer. Drive a small pin or punch through the injection holes to aid in removal.
7. If the front U-joint is serviced, remove the bearing cups from the slip yoke in the manner previously described.
8. Be sure that the seals are installed on the service bearing cups to hold the needle bearings in place for handling. Grease the bearings if they aren't pregreased.
9. Install one bearing cup partway into one side of the yoke and turn this ear to the bottom.
10. Insert the opposite bearing cup partway. Be sure that both trunnions are started straight into the bearing cups.
11. Press against opposite bearing cups, working the cross constantly to be sure that it is free in the cups. If binding occurs, check the needle rollers to be sure that one needle has not become lodged under an end of the trunnion.
12. As soon as one bearing retainer groove is exposed, stop

pressing and install the bearing retainer snapring.

13. Continue to press until the opposite bearing retainer can be installed. If difficulty installing the snaprings is encountered, rap the yoke with a hammer to spring the yoke ears slightly.

14. Assemble the other half of the U-joint in the same manner.

Constant Velocity (CV) Joint

OVERHAUL

4-Wheel Drive Models Only

1. Using a punch, mark the link yoke and the adjoining yokes before disassembly to ensure proper reassembly and driveshaft balance.

NOTE: It is easier to remove the universal joint bearings from the flange yoke first. The first pair of flange yoke universal joint bearings to be removed is the pair in the link yoke.

2. With the driveshaft in a horizontal position, solidly support the link yoke. A 1⅞ in. (48mm) pipe will do.

3. Apply force to the bearing cup on the opposite side with a 1⅛ in. pipe or a socket the size of the bearing cup. Use a vise or press to apply force. Force the cup inward as far as possible.

NOTE: In the absence of a press, a heavy vise may be used, but make sure that the universal to be removed is at a right angle to the jaws of the vise. Do not cock the bearing cups in their bores.

4. Remove the pieces of pipe and complete the removal of the protruding bearing cup by tapping around the circumference of the exposed portion of the bearing with a small hammer.

5. Reverse the position of the pieces of pipe and apply force to the exposed journal end. This will force the other bearing cup out of its bore and allow removal of the flange.

NOTE: There is a ball joint located between the two universals. The ball portion of this joint is on the inner end of the flange yoke. The ball, as well as the ball seat parts, is replaceable. Care must be taken not to damage the ball. The ball portion of this joint is on the driveshaft. To remove the seat, pry the seal out with a screwdriver.

6. To remove the journal from the flange, use steps two through five.

7. Remove the universal joint bearings from the driveshaft using the steps from two through five. The first pair of bearing caps that should be removed is the pair in the link yoke.

8. Examine the ball stud seat and ball stud for scores or wear. Worn seats can be replaced with a kit. A worn ball, however, requires the replacement of the entire shaft yoke and flange assembly. Clean the ball seat cavity and fill it with grease. Install the spring, washer, ball seats, and spacer, if removed.

9. Install the universal joints opposite the order in which they were disassembled.

10. Install a bearing ¼ of the way into one side of the yoke.

11. Insert the journal into the yoke so that an arm of the journal seats into the bearing.

12. Press the bearing in the remaining distance and install its snapring.

13. Install the opposite bearing. Do not allow the bearing rollers to jam. Continually check for free movement of the journal in the bearings as they are pressed into the yoke.

14. Install the rest of the bearings in the same manner.

NOTE: The flange yoke should snap over center to the right or left and up or down by the pressure of the ball seat spring.

REAR AXLE

Determining Axle Ratio

Axle ratios offered in these trucks vary from a heavy duty ratio of 4.57:1 to an economy ratio of 2.73:1.

The axle ratio is obtained by dividing the number of teeth on the drive pinion gear into the larger number of teeth on the ring gear. It is always expressed as a proportion and is a simple expression of gear speed reduction and torque multiplication.

To find a unknown axle ratio, make a chalk mark on a tire and on the driveshaft. Move the truck ahead (or back) slowly for one tire rotation and have an observer note the number of driveshaft rotations. The number of driveshaft rotations if the axle ratio. You can get more accuracy by going more than one tire rotation and dividing the result by the number of tire rotations. This can also be done by jacking up both rear wheels and turning them by hand.

The axle ration is also identified by the axle serial number prefix on Chevrolet (GMC) axles. See Section 1 for serial number locations; the prefixes are listed in parts books. Dana axles usually have a tag under one of the cover bolts, giving either the ratio or the number of pinion ring gear teeth.

Axle Shaft, Bearing, and Seal

REMOVAL AND INSTALLATION

All Semi-Floating Axles Except Locking Differential

1. Support the axle on jackstands.
2. Remove the wheels and brake drums.
3. Clean off the differential cover area, loosen the cover to drain the lubricant, and remove the cover.
4. Turn the differential until you can reach the differential pinion shaft lockscrew. Remove the lockscrew and the pinion shaft.

5. Push in on the axle end. Remove the C-lock from the inner (button) end of the shaft.
6. Remove the shaft, being careful of the oil seal.
7. You can pry the oil seal out of the housing by placing the inner end of the axle shaft behind the steel case of the seal, then prying it out carefully.
8. A puller or a slide hammer is required to remove the bearing from the housing.
9. Pack the new or reused bearing with wheel bearing grease and lubricate the cavity between the seal lips with the same grease.
10. The bearing has to be driven into the housing. Don't use a drift, you might cock the bearing in its bore. Use a piece of pipe or a large socket instead. Drive only on the outer bearing race. In a similar manner, drive the seal in flush with the end of the tube.
11. Slide the shaft into place, turning it slowly until the splines are engaged with the differential. Be careful of the oil seal.
12. Install the C-lock on the inner axle end. Pull the shaft out so that the C-lock seats in the counterbore of the differential side gear.
13. Position the differential pinion shaft through the case and the pinion gears, aligning the lockscrew hole. Install the lockscrew.
14. Install the cover with a new gasket and tighten the bolts evenly in a criss-cross pattern.
15. Fill the axle with lubricant as specified in Section 1.
16. Replace the brake drums and wheels.

Semi-Floating Locking Differential Axles

This axle uses a thrust block on the differential pinion shaft.

1. Follow Steps 1–3 of the preceding procedure.
2. Rotate the differential case so that you can remove the lockscrew and support the pinion shaft so it can't fall into the housing. Remove the differential pinion shaft lockscrew.
3. Carefully pull the pinion shaft partway out and rotate the differential case until the shaft touches the housing at the top.
4. Use a screwdriver to position the C-lock with its open end directly inward. You can't push in the axle shaft till you do this.
5. Push the axle shaft in and remove the C-lock.
6. Follow Steps 6–11 of the preceding procedure.
7. Keep the pinion shaft partway out of the differential case while installing the C-lock on the axle shaft. Put the C-lock on the axle shaft and carefully pull out on the axle shaft until the C-lock is clear of the thrust block.
8. Follow Steps 13–16 of the previous procedure.

Full-Floating Axles with 9¾ and 10½ in. Ring Gear

The procedures are the same for locking and non-locking axles.

The best way to remove the bearings from the wheel hub is with an arbor press. Use of a press reduces the chances of damaging the bearing races, cocking the bearing in its bore, or scoring the hub walls. A local machine shop is probably equipped with the tools to remove and install bearings and seals. However, if one is not available, the hammer and drift method outlined can be used.

1. Support the axles on jackstands.
2. Remove the wheels.
3. Remove the bolts and lock washers that attach the axle shaft flange to the hub.
4. Rap on the flange with a soft faced hammer to loosen the shaft. Grip the rib on the end of the flange with a pair of locking pliers and twist to start shaft removal. Remove the shaft from the axle tube.
5. The hub and drum assembly must be removed to remove the bearings and oil seals. You will need a large socket to remove and later adjust the bearing adjustment nut. There are also special tools available.

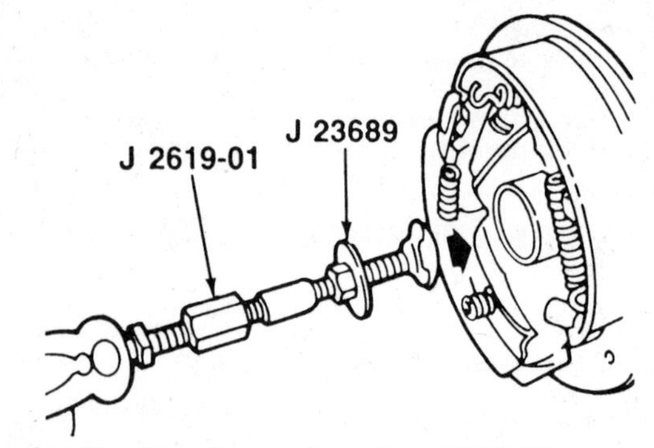

Removing the bearing and seal – GMC 8½ and 9½ in. axles

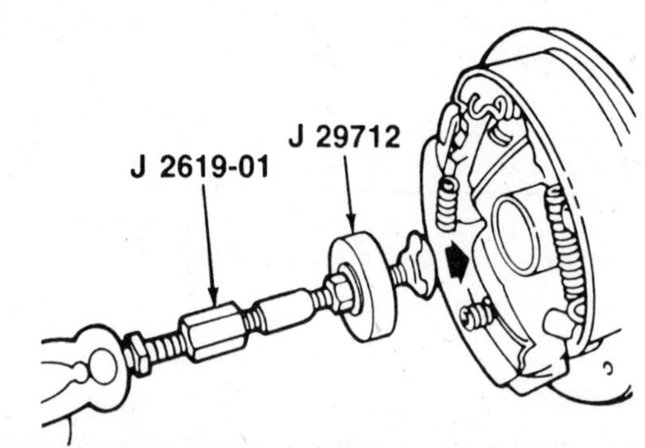

Removing the bearing – GMC 8½ and 9½ in. axles

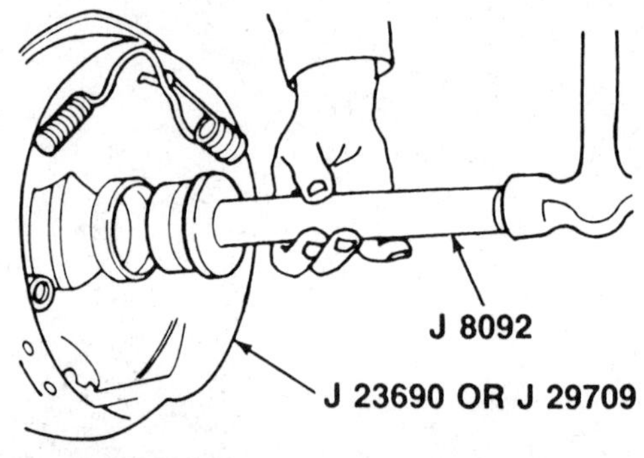

Installing the bearing – GMC 8½ and 9½ in. axles

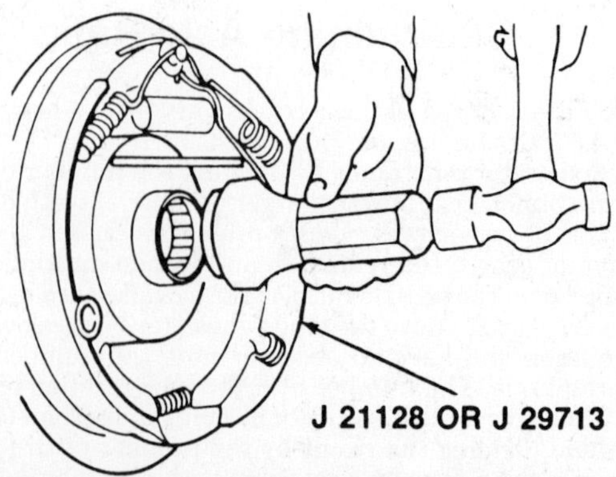

Installing the seal – GMC 8½ and 9½ in. axles

6. Disengage the tang of the locknut retainer from the slot or slat of the locknut, then remove the locknut from the housing tube.
7. Disengage the tang of the retainer from the slot or flat of the adjusting nut and remove the retainer from the housing tube.
8. Remove the adjusting nut from the housing tube.
9. Remove the thrust washer from the housing tube.
10. Pull the hub and drum straight off the axle housing.
11. Remove the oil seal and discard.
12. Use a hammer and a long drift to knock the inner bearing, cup, and oil seal from the hub assembly.
13. Remove the outer bearing snapring with a pair of pliers. It may be necessary to tap the bearing outer race away from the retaining ring slightly by tapping on the ring to remove the ring.
14. Drive the outer bearing from the hub with a hammer and drift.
15. To reinstall the bearings, place the outer bearing into the hub. The larger outside diameter of the bearing should face the outer end of the hub. Drive the bearing into the hub using a washer that will cover both the inner and outer races of the bearing. Place a socket on top of this washer, then drive the bearing into place with a series of light taps. If available, an arbor press should be used for this job.
16. Drive the bearing past the snapring groove, and install the snapring. Then, turning the hub assembly over, drive the bearing back against the snapring. Protect the bearing by placing a washer on top of it. You can use the thrust washer that fits between the bearing and the adjusting nut for the job.
17. Place the inner bearing into the hub. The thick edge should be toward the shoulder in the hub. Press the bearing into the hub until it seats against the shoulder, using a washer and socket as outlined earlier. Make certain that the bearing is not cocked and that it is fully seated on the shoulder.
18. Pack the cavity between the oil seal lips with wheel bearing grease, and position it in the hub bore. Carefully press it into place on top of the inner bearing.
19. Pack the wheel bearings with grease, and lightly coat the inside diameter of the hub bearing contact surface and the outside diameter of the axle housing tube.
20. Make sure that the inner bearing, oil seal, axle housing oil deflector, and outer bearing are properly positioned. Install the hub and drum assembly on the axle housing, being careful so as not to damage the oil seal or dislocate other internal components.
21. Install the thrust washer so that the tang on the inside diameter of the washer is in the keyway on the axle housing.
22. Install the adjusting nut. Tighten to 50 ft. lbs. while rotating the hub. Back off the nut and retighten to 35 ft. lbs., then back off 1/4 turn.
23. Install the tanged retainer against the inner adjusting nut. Align the adjusting nut so that the short tang of the retainer will engage the nearest slot on the adjusting nut.
24. Install the outer locknut and tighten to 65 ft. lbs. Bend the long tang of the retainer into the slot of the outer nut. This method of adjustment should provide 0.001–0.010 in. (0.0254–0.254mm) end play.
25. Place a new gasket over the axle shaft and position the axle shaft in the housing so that the shaft splines enter the differential side gear. Position the gasket so that the holes are in alignment, and install the flange-to-hub attaching bolts. Torque to 115 ft. lbs.

NOTE: To prevent lubricant from leaking through the flange holes, apply a non-hardening sealer to the bolt threads. Use the sealer sparingly.

26. Replace the wheels.

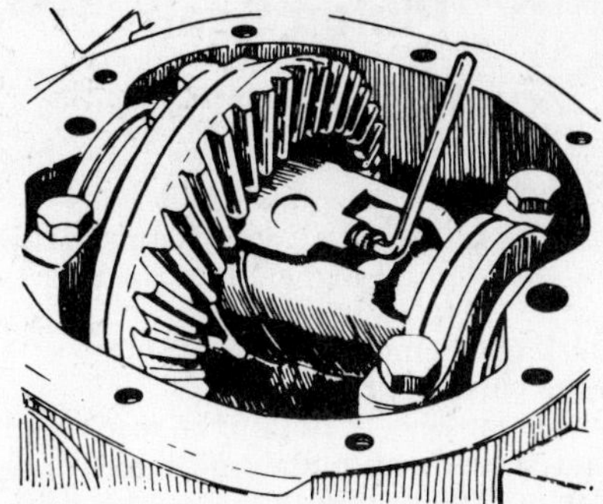

Removing the differential pinion lockscrew

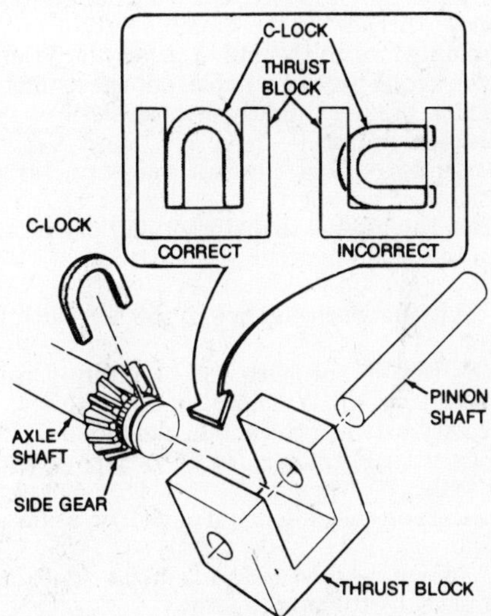

C-lock and thrust block installation

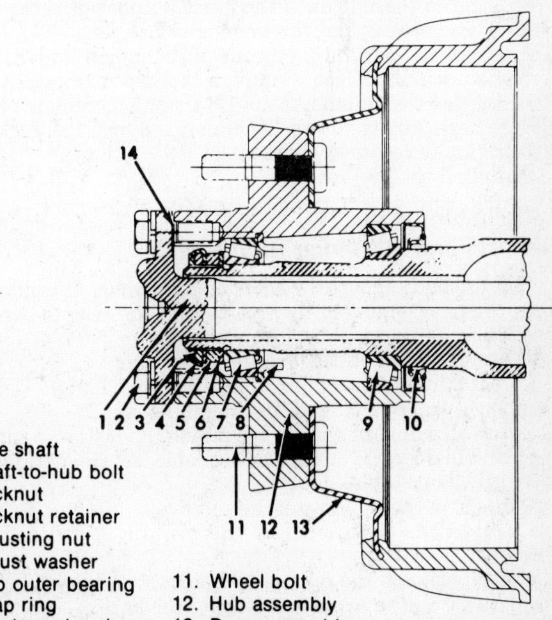

1. Axle shaft
2. Shaft-to-hub bolt
3. Locknut
4. Locknut retainer
5. Adjusting nut
6. Thrust washer
7. Hub outer bearing
8. Snap ring
9. Hub inner bearing
10. Oil seal
11. Wheel bolt
12. Hub assembly
13. Drum assembly
14. Gasket

Full-floating axle bearing and hub

Pinion Seal

REPLACEMENT

Semi-Floating Axles

1. Raise and support the truck on jackstands. It would help to have the front end slightly higher than the rear to avoid fluid loss.
2. Matchmark and remove the driveshaft.
3. Release the parking brake.
4. Remove the rear wheels. Rotate the rear wheels by hand to make sure that there is absolutely no brake drag. If there is brake drag, remove the drums.
5. Using a torque wrench on the pinion nut, record the force needed to rotate the pinion.
6. Matchmark the pinion shaft, nut and flange. Count the number of exposed threads on the pinion shaft.
7. Install a holding tool on the pinion. A very large adjustable wrench will do, or, if one is not available, put the drums back on and set the parking brake as tightly as possible.
8. Remove the pinion nut.
9. Slide the flange off of the pinion. A puller may be necessary.
10. Centerpunch the oil seal to distort it and pry it out of the bore. Be careful to avoid scrratching the bore.

To install:

11. Pack the cavity between the lips of the seal with lithium-based chassis lube.
12. Position the seal in the bore and carefully drive it into place. A seal installer is VERY helpful in doing this.
13. Pack the cavity between the end of the pinion splines and the pinion flange with Permatex No.2® sealer, or equivalent non-hardening sealer.
14. Place the flange on the pinion and push it on as far as it will go.
15. Install the pinion washer and nut on the shaft and force the pinion into place by turning the nut.

WARNING: Never hammer the flange into place!

16. Tighten the nut until the exact number of threads previously noted appear and the matchmarks align.
17. Measure the rotating torque of the pinion under the same circumstances as before. Compare the two readings. As necessary, tighten the pinion nut in VERY small increments until the torque necessary to rotate the pinion is 3 inch lbs. higher than the originally recorded torque.
18. Install the driveshaft.

Full Floating Axle with 9¾ and 10½ inch Ring Gear

1. Raise and support the truck on jackstands. It would help to have the front end slightly higher than the rear to avoid fluid loss.
2. Matchmark and remove the driveshaft.
3. Matchmark the pinion shaft, nut and flange. Count the number of exposed threads on the pinion shaft.
4. Install a holding tool on the pinion. A very large adjustable wrench will do, or, if one is not available, set the parking brake as tightly as possible.
5. Remove the pinion nut.
6. Slide the flange off of the pinion. A puller may be necessary.
7. Centerpunch the oil seal to distort it and pry it out of the bore. Be careful to avoid scrratching the bore.

To install:

8. Pack the cavity between the lips of the seal with lithium-based chassis lube.
9. Position the seal in the bore and carefully drive it into place. A seal installer is VERY helpful in doing this.
10. Place the flange on the pinion and push it on as far as it will go.
11. Install the pinion washer and nut on the shaft and force the pinion into place by turning the nut.

WARNING: Never hammer the flange into place!

12. Tighten the nut until the exact number of threads previously noted appear and the matchmarks align.
13. Install the driveshaft.

Axle Housing

REMOVAL AND INSTALLATION

1. Raise and support the rear end on jackstands.
2. For the 9¾ in. ring gear and the 10½ in. ring gear axles, place jackstands under the frame side rails for support.
3. Drain the lubricant from the axle housing and remove the driveshaft.
4. Remove the wheel, the brake drum or hub and the drum assembly.
5. Disconnect the parking brake cable from the lever and at the brake flange plate.
6. Disconnect the hydraulic brake lines from the connectors.
7. Disconnect the shock absorbers from the axle brackets.
8. Remove the vent hose from the axle vent fitting (if used).
9. Disconnect the height sensing and brake proportional valve linkage (if used).
10. Support the stabilizer shaft assembly with a hydraulic jack and remove (if used).
11. Remove the nuts and washers from the U-bolts.
12. Remove the U-bolts, spring plates and spacers from the axle assembly.
13. Lower the jack and remove the axle assembly.

To install:

14. Raise the axle assembly into position.
15. Install the U-bolts, spring plates and spacers.
16. Install the nuts and washers on the U-bolts. Torque the nuts to 130 ft. lbs. for 30/3500 series; 120 series for all other models.
17. Install the stabilizer shaft.
18. Connect the height sensing and brake proportional valve linkage.
19. Install the vent hose at the axle vent fitting.
20. Connect the shock absorbers at the axle brackets. Torque the nuts to 80 ft. lbs.
21. Connect the hydraulic brake lines.
22. Connect the parking brake cable.
23. Install the wheels.
24. Install the driveshaft.
25. Fill the axle housing.

GMC 8½ in. and 9½ in. Ring Gear Differential Overhaul

DISASSEMBLY

Differential Case

1. Remove the inspection cover from the axle housing and drain the gear lubricant into a pan.
2. Remove the screw or pin that holds the pinion shaft in place and remove the shaft.
3. Push the axle shaft(s) in a little and remove the C-locks from the ends of the shafts. Remove the axle shafts from the housing.
4. Measure and record the backlash; this will allow the old gears to be reassembled at the same amount of lash to avoid

changing the gear tooth pattern. It also helps to indicate if there is gear or bearing wear and if there is any error in the original backlash setting.

5. Remove the differential pinions, the side gears and thrust washers from the case; be sure to mark the pinions and side gears so they may be reassembled in their original position.

6. Mark the bearing caps and housing and loosen the retaining bolts. Tap the caps lightly to loosen them. When the caps are loose, remove the bolts and reinstall them, just a few turns; this will keep the case from falling out of the housing when it is pried loose.

7. Using a pry bar, carefully, pry the case assembly loose; be careful not to damage the gasket surface on the housing when prying. The case assembly may suddenly come free if the bearings were preloaded, so pry very slowly.

8. When the case assembly is loose, remove the bearing cap bolts and the caps. Place the caps so they may be reinstalled in the same position. Place any shims that were removed with the cap.

9. Using a bearing puller, pull the differential bearing from the case.

10. To remove the drive pinion bearing, perform the following procedures:

a. Depending on the bearing that is being replaced, remove the front or rear bearing cup from the carrier assembly.

b. With the pinion gear mounted in a press, press the rear bearing from the pinion shaft. Be sure to record the thicknesses of the shims that were removed from between the bearing and the gear.

Drive Pinion

1. With the differential removed, check the pinion preload. Do this by checking the amount of torque needed to turn the pinion gear. For a new bearing, it should be 20–25 inch lbs. and for a used bearing it should be 10–15 inch lbs. If there is no preload reading check the pinion for looseness. If there is any looseness, replace the bearing.

2. Using a holder assembly to secure the flange, remove the flange nut and washer.

3. Using a puller, press the flange from the pinion splines.

4. Thread the pinion nut, a few turns, onto the pinion shaft. Using a brass drift and hammer, lightly tap the end of the pinion shaft to remove the pinion from the carrier; be careful not to allow the pinion to fall out of the carrier.

5. With the pinion removed from the carrier, discard the old seal pinion nut and collapsible spacer; install new ones when reassembling.

Ring Gear

1. Remove the ring gear-to-differential case bolts and tap the ring gear from the case with a soft hammer.

NOTE: Do not try to pry the ring gear off the case. This will damage the machined surfaces.

2. Clean all dirt from the case assembly and lubricate the case with gear lube.

CLEANING AND INSPECTION

1. Clean all parts in solvent and blow dry.

2. Check all of the parts for any signs of wear, chips, cracks or distortion; replace any parts that are defective.

3. Check the fit of the differential side gears in the case and the fit of the side gear and axle shaft splines.

ASSEMBLY

Drive Pinion Bearing

1. Using a bearing driver, install a new bearing cup for each one that was removed; make sure the cups are seated fully against the shoulder in the housing.

2. The pinion depth must be checked to determine the nominal setting. This allows for machining variations in the housing and enables selection of the proper shim so the pinion depth can be set for the best bear tooth contact.

3. Clean the housing and carrier assemblies to insure accurate measurement of the pinion depth.

4. Lubricate the front and rear pinion bearings with gear lubricant and install them in their races in the carrier assembly.

5. Using a pinion setting gauge, select the proper clover leaf plate and install it on the preload stud.

6. Using the proper pilot, insert the stud through the rear bearing, with the proper size pilot on the stud and through the front bearing. Install the hex nut and tighten it until it is snug.

7. Using a wrench to hold the preload stud, torque the hex nut until 20 inch lbs. of torque are required to rotate the bearings.

8. Install the side bearing discs on the ends of the arbor assembly, using the step of the disc that fits the bore of the carrier.

9. Install the arbor and plunger assembly into the carrier; make sure the side bearing discs fit properly.

10. Install the bearing caps in the carrier assembly finger tight; make sure the discs do not move.

11. Mount a dial indicator on the mounting post of the arbor with the contact button resting on the top surface of the plunger.

13. Preload the dial indicator by turning it ½ revolution and tightening it in this position.

14. Use the button on the gauge plate that corresponds to the ring gear size and turn the plate so the plunger rests on top of it.

15. Rock the plunger rod back and forth across the top of the button until the dial indicator reads the greatest amount of variation. Set the dial indicator to zero at the point of most variation. Repeat the rocking of the plunger several times to check the setting.

16. Turn the plunger until it is removed from the gauge plate button. The dial indicator will now read the pinion shim thickness required to set the nominal pinion depth; record the reading.

17. Check for the pinion code number, located on the rear face of the pinion gear; the number will indicate the necessary change to the pinion shim thickness.

NOTE: If the pinion is marked with a plus (+) and a number, add that much to the reading of the dial indicator. If the pinion has no mark, use the reading from the dial indicator as the correct shim thickness. If the pinion is marked with a minus (−) and a number, subtract that amount from the reading on the dial indicator.

18. Remove the depth gauge tools from the carrier assembly and install the proper size shim on the pinion gear.

19. Lubricate the bearing with gear lubricant and use a shop press to press the bearing onto the pinion shaft.

Drive Pinion

1. Lubricate the front bearing and install it into the front cup.

2. Using a seal driver and a gauge plate, drive the pinion seal into the bore until the gauge plate is flush with the shoulder of the carrier.

3. Lubricate the seal lips and install a new bearing spacer on the pinion gear.

4. Install the pinion gear into the carrier assembly. Using a large washer and nut, draw the pinion gear through the front bearing, far enough to install the companion flange.

5. With the companion flange installed on the pinion shaft, use a holder assembly and tighten the pinion nut until all of the endplay is removed from the drive pinion.

6. When no more endplay exists, check the preload; the pre-

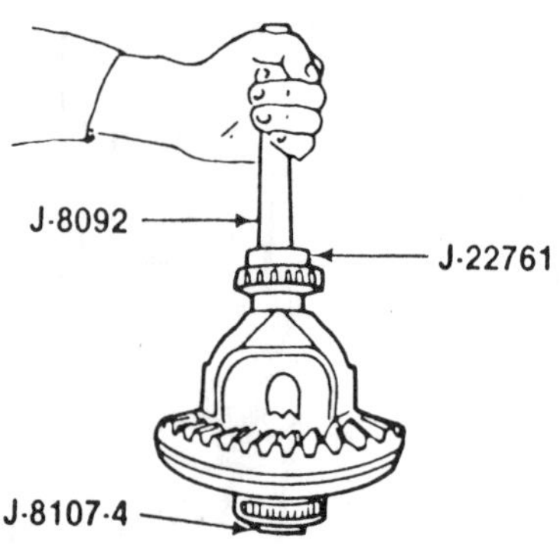

Installing the side bearing – GMC 8½ and 9½ in. axles

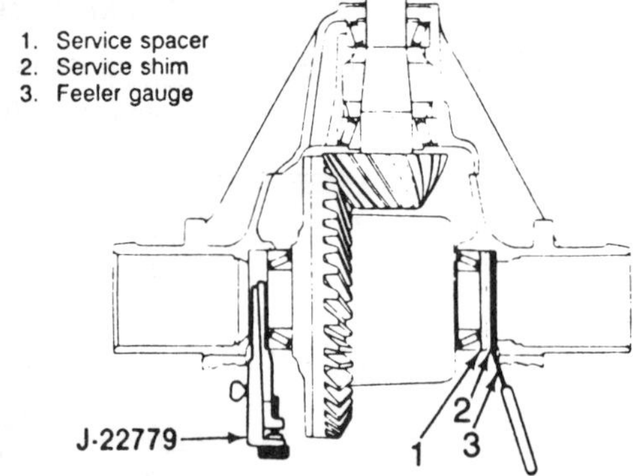

Measuring side bearing shim requirements – GMC 8½ and 9½ in. axles

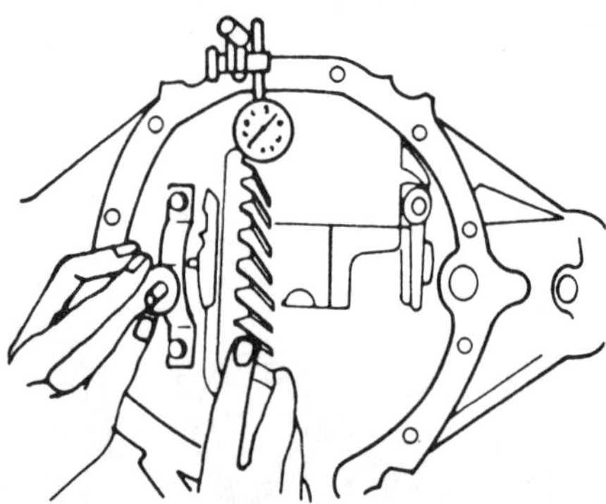

Installing the side bearing gauging tool – GMC 8½ and 9½ in. axles

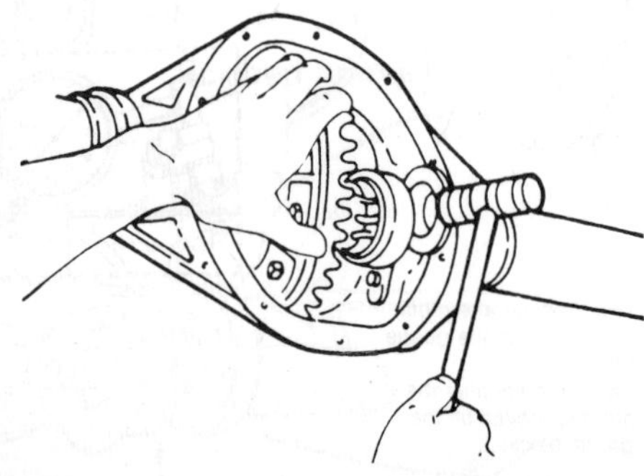

Installing the final preload shim – GMC 8½ and 9½ in. axles

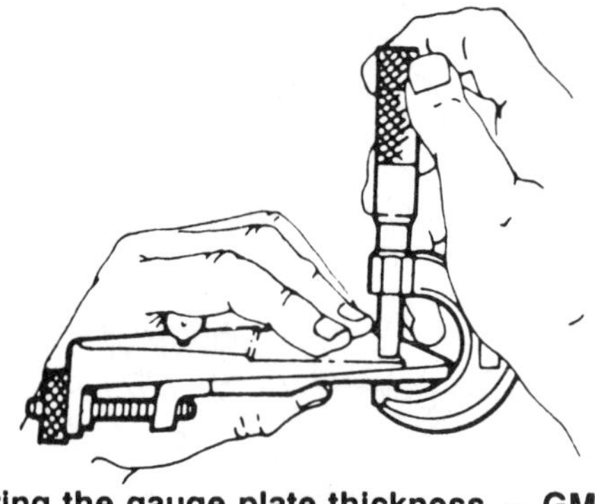

Measuring the gauge plate thickness – GMC 8½ and 9½ in. axles

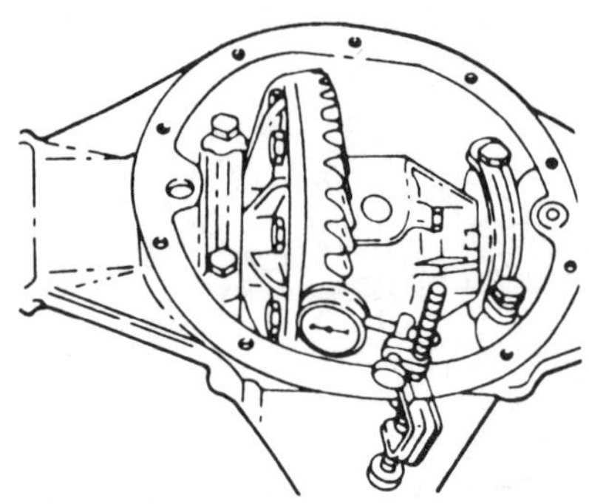

Checking ring gear backlash – GMC 8½ and 9½ in. axles

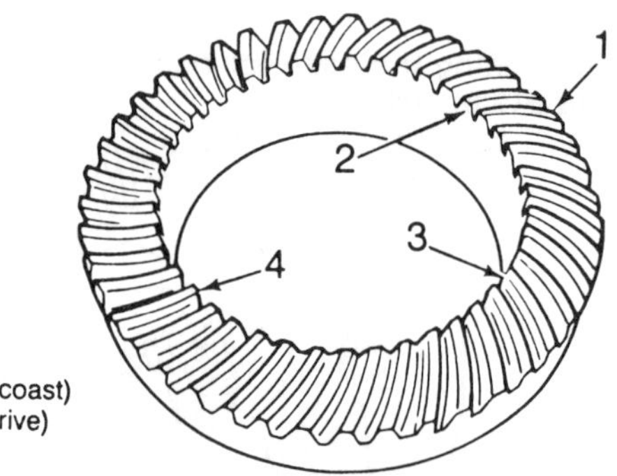

Gear tooth nomenclature – GMC 8½ and 9½ in. axles

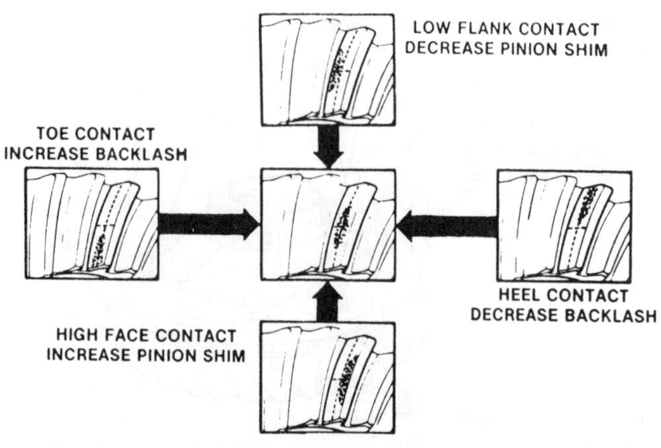

Gear tooth patterns – GMC 8½ and 9½ in. axles

load should be 20–25 inch lbs. on new bearings or 10–15 inch lbs. on used bearings. Tighten the pinion nut until these figures are reached; do not over tighten the pinion, for this will collapse the spacer too much and make it necessary to replace it.

7. Turn the pinion gear several times to make sure the bearings are seated and recheck the preload.

Ring Gear

1. Align the ring gear bolt holes with the carrier holes and lightly press the ring gear onto the case assembly.
2. Install the bolts and tighten them all evenly, using a crisscross pattern to avoid cocking the ring gear.
3. When the ring gear is firmly seated against the case, torque the bolts to 60 ft. lbs.

Differential Case

1. Place the new differential bearing onto the case hub with the thick side of the inner race toward the case. Using a bearing driver, drive the bearing onto the case until it seats against the shoulder on the case.
2. Install the thrust washers and side gears into the case assembly. If the original parts are being used, be sure to place them in their original position.
3. Place the pinions in the case so they are 180° apart as they engage the side gears.
4. Turn the pinion gears so the case holes align with the gear holes. When the holes are aligned, install the pinion shaft and lock screw; do not tighten the lock screw too tightly at this time.
5. Check the bearings, bearing cups, cup seat and carrier caps to make sure they are in good condition.
6. Lubricate the bearings with gear lube. Install the cups on the bearings and the differential assembly into the carrier. Support the carrier assembly to keep it from falling.
7. Install a support strap on the left side bearing and tighten the bearing bolts to an even, snug fit.
8. With the ring gear tight against the pinion gear, insert a gauge tool between the left side bearing cup and the carrier housing.
9. While lightly shaking the tool back and forth, turn the adjusting wheel until a slight drag is felt and tighten the locknut.
10. Between the right side bearing and carrier, install a 0.170 in. thick service spacer, a service shim and a feeler gauge. The feeler gauge must be thick enough so a light drag is felt when it is moved between the carrier and the shim.
11. Add the total of the service spacer, service shim and the feeler gauge. Remove the gauge tool from the left side of the carrier, then, using a micrometer, measure the thickness in at least 3 places. Average the readings and record the result.
12. Refer to the chart to determine the proper thickness of the shim packs.
13. Install the left side shim first, then, the right side shim between the bearing cup and spacer. Position the shim so the chamfered side is facing outward or next to the spacer.

NOTE: If there is not enough chamfer around the outside of the shim, file or grind the chamfer a little to allow for easy installation.

14. If there is difficulty in installing the shim, partially remove the case from the carrier and slide both the shim and case back into place.
15. Install the bearing caps and torque them to 60 ft. lbs. Tighten the pinion shaft lock screw.

NOTE: The differential side bearings are now preloaded. If any adjustments are made in later procedures, make sure not to change the preload. Do not change the total thickness of the shim packs.

16. Mount a dial indicator on the carrier assembly with the indicator button perpendicular to the tooth angle and aligned with the gear rotation.
17. Measure the amount of backlash between the ring and pinion gears; it should be between 0.005–0.008 in. (0.127–0.203mm). Take readings at 4 different spots on the gear; there should not be variations greater than 0.002 in. (0.05mm).
18. If there are variations greater than 0.002 in. (0.05mm) between the readings, check the runout between the case and ring gear; the gear runout should not be greater than 0.003 in. (0.076mm). If the runout exceeds 0.003 in. (0.076mm), check the case and ring gear for the deformation or dirt between the case and gear.
19. If the gear backlash exceeds 0.008 in. (0.20mm), increase the thickness of the shims on the ring gear side and decrease the thickness of the shims on the opposite side, an equal amount.
20. If the backlash is less than 0.005 in. (0.127mm), decrease the shim thickness on the ring gear side and increase the shim thickness on the opposite side an equal amount.

Gear Pattern Check

Before final assembly of the differential, a pattern check of the gear teeth must be made. This determines if the teeth of the ring and pinion gears are meshing properly, for low noise level and long life of the gear teeth. The most important thing to note is if the pattern is located centrally up and down on the face of the ring gear.

1. Wipe any oil from the carrier and all dirt and oil from the teeth of the ring gear.
2. Coat the teeth of the ring gear with a gear marking compound.
3. With the bearing caps torqued to 55 ft. lbs., expand the brake shoes until it takes 20–30 ft. lbs. of torque to turn the pinion gear.
4. Turn the companion flange so the ring gear makes a full rotation in 1 direction, then, turn it a full rotation in the opposite direction.
5. Check the pattern on the teeth and refer to the chart for any adjustments necessary.
6. With the gear tooth pattern checked and properly adjusted, install the axle housing cover gasket and cover and tighten securely. Refill the axle with gear lube to the correct level.
7. Road test the vehicle to check for any noise and proper operation of the rear.

GMC 10½ in. Ring Gear Differential Overhaul

DISASSEMBLY

Differential

1. Place the axle assembly in a vise or holding fixture.
2. Remove the cover bolts, the cover and allow the gear lubricant to drain into a pan.
3. Remove the axle shafts from the axle assembly.

NOTE: Measure and record the pinion backlash so if the same gears are reused they may be installed at the same backlash to avoid changing the gear tooth pattern.

4. From the bearing caps, remove the adjusting nut lock retainers.
5. Mark the bearing caps so they may be reinstalled in the same position and remove the bearing caps.
6. Loosen the side bearing adjusting nut and remove the differential carrier from the axle housing.

Pinion

1. Remove the differential assembly from the axle.

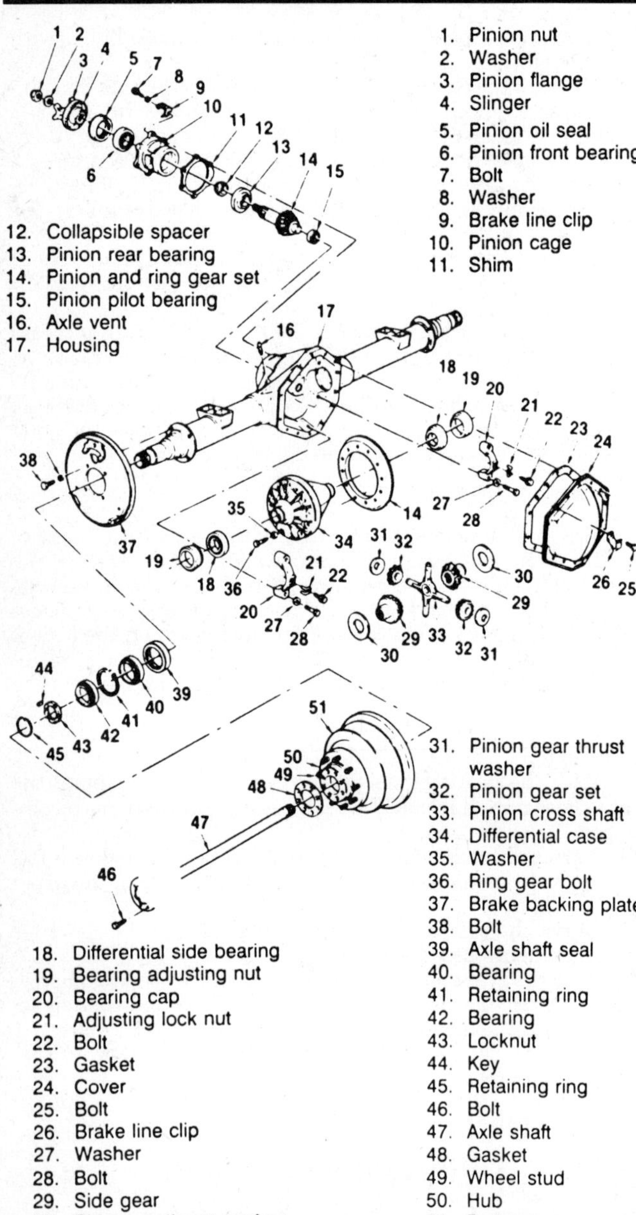

Exploded view – GMC 10½ in. axles

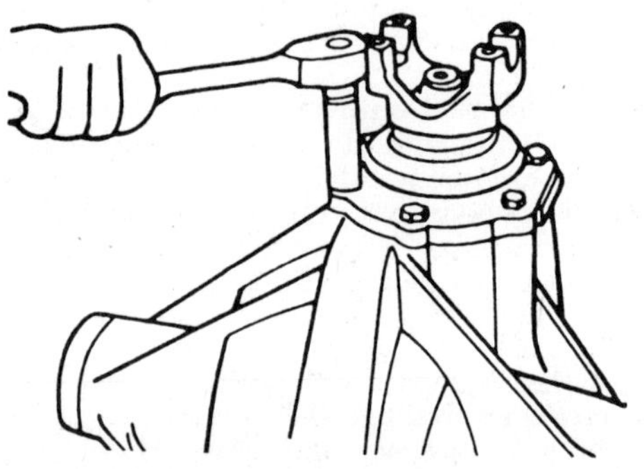

Checking the pinion preload – GMC 10½ in. axles

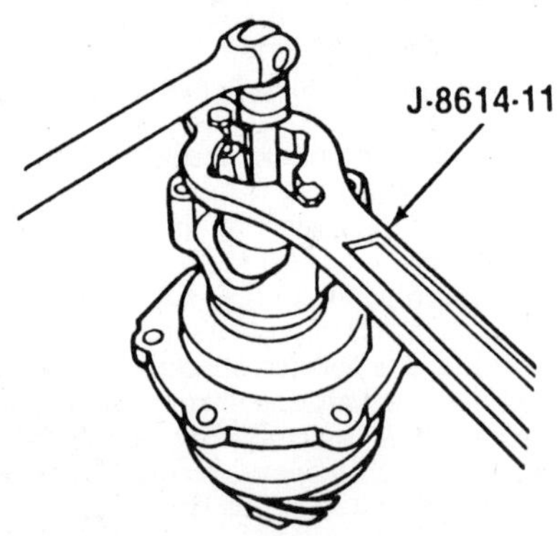

Removing the pinion cage – GMC 10½ in. axles

Removing the drive pinion nut – GMC 10½ in. axles

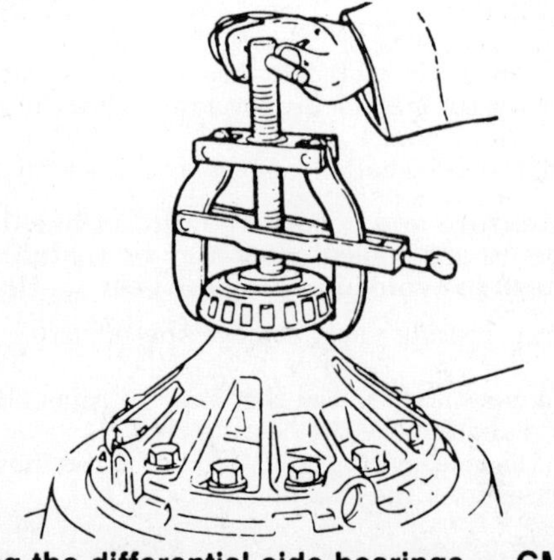

Removing the differential side bearings – GMC 10½ in. axles

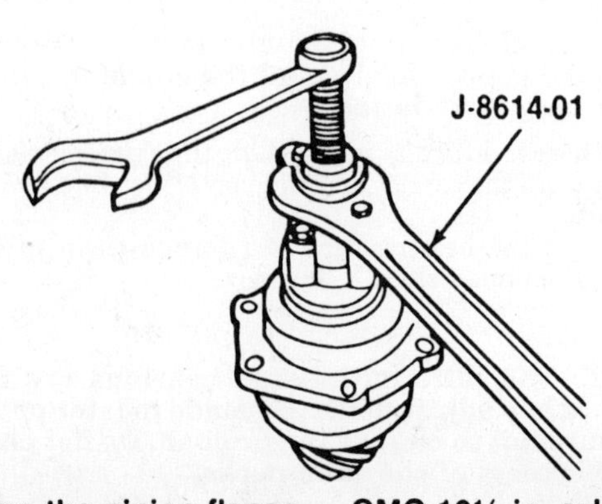

Removing the pinion flange – GMC 10½ in. axles

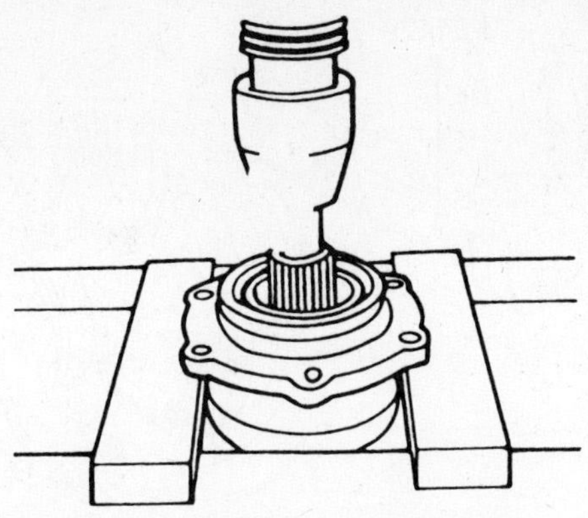
Pressing the drive pinion from the flange – GMC 10½ in. axles

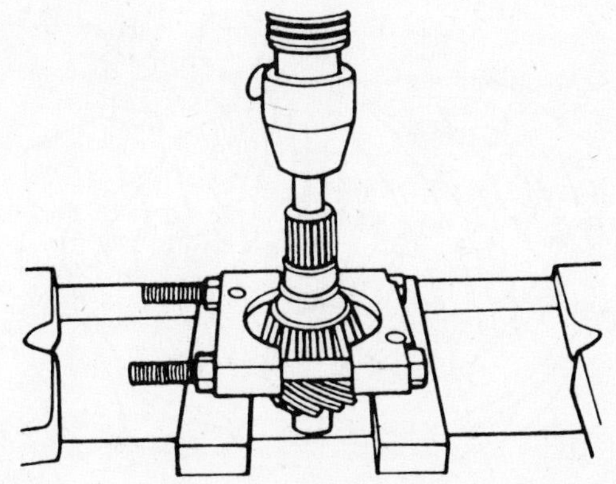
Removing the pinion inner bearing – GMC 10½ in. axles

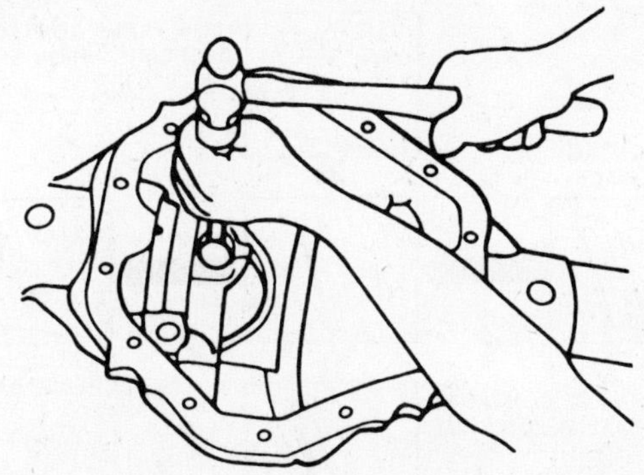
Removing the pilot bearing – GMC 10½ in. axles

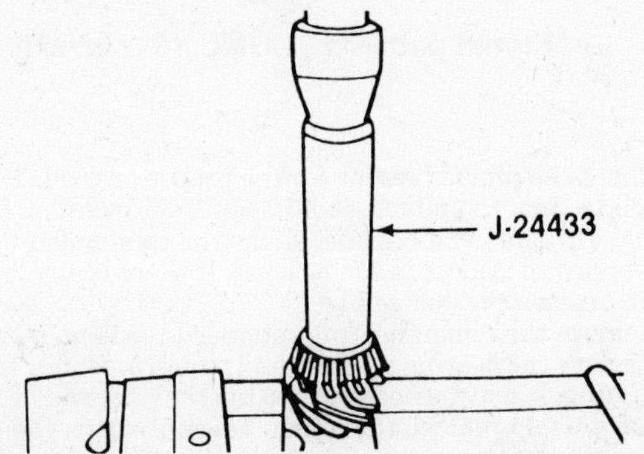

Installing the inner pinion bearing – GMC 10½ in. axles

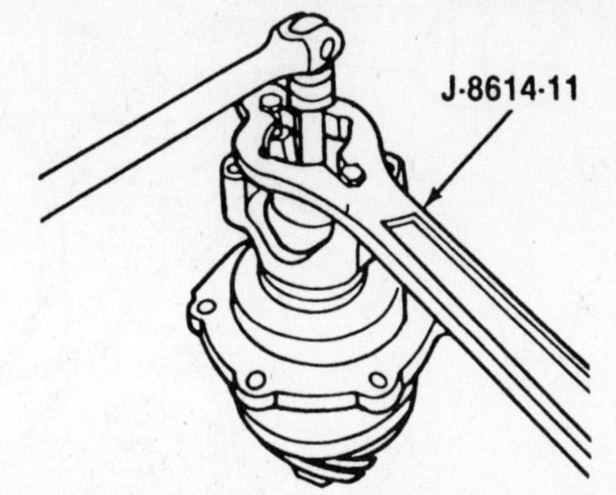

Installing the pinion nut – GMC 10½ in. axles

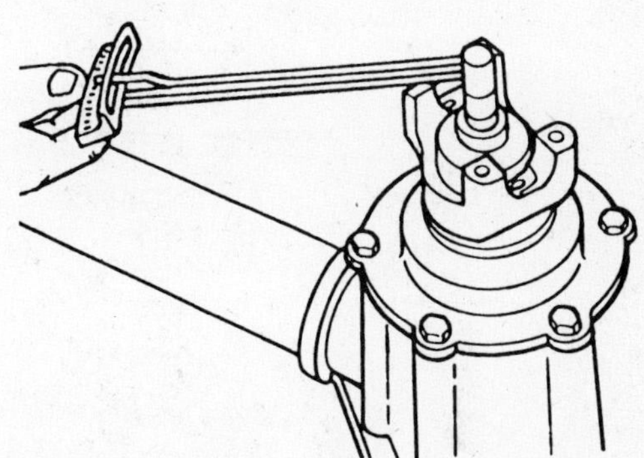
Checking preload – GMC 10½ in. axles

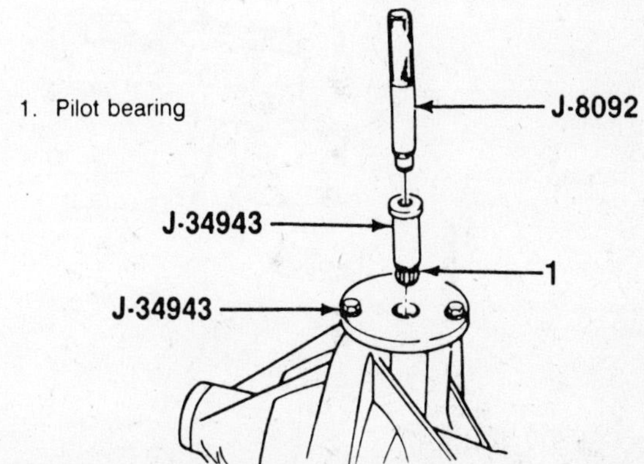

Installing the pilot bearing – GMC 10½ in. axles

		CODE NUMBER ON ORIGINAL PINION				
		+2	+1	0	-1	-2
Code Number On Service Pinion	+2	—	Add .001	Add .002	Add .003	Add .004
	+1	Subt. .001	—	Add .001	Add .002	Add .003
	0	Subt. .002	Subt. .001	—	Add .001	Add .002
	-1	Subt. .003	Subt. .002	Subt. .001	—	Add .001
	-2	Subt. .004	Subt. .003	Subt. .002	Subt. .001	—

Pinion depoth codes – GMC 10½ in. axles

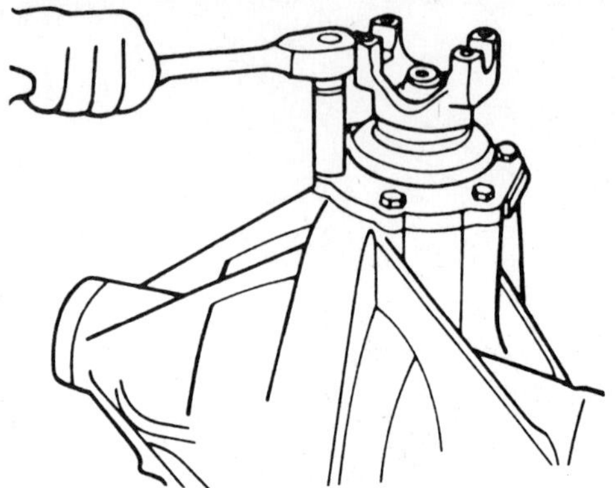
Installing the pinion cage – GMC 10½ in. axles

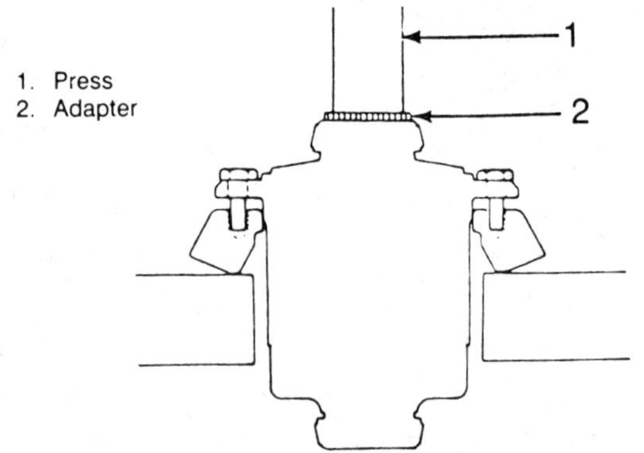

Installing the ring on the case – GMC 10½ in. axles

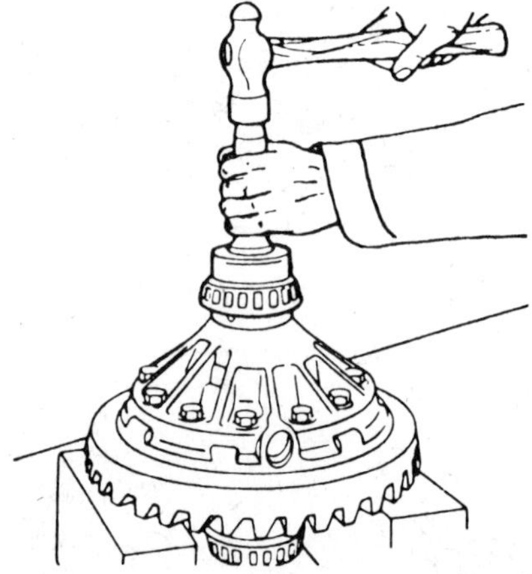
Installing the differential bearings – GMC 10½ in. axles

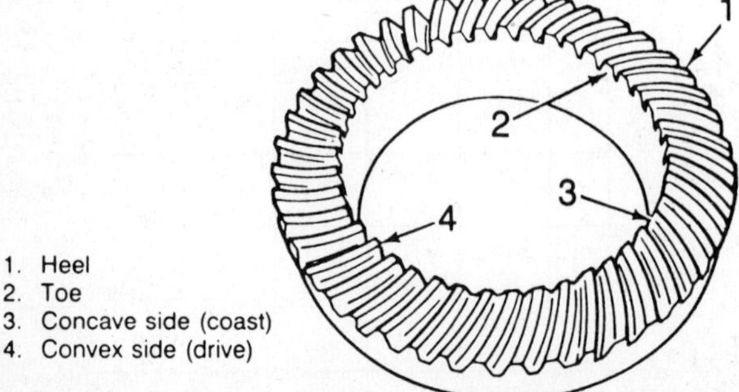

Gear tooth nomenclature – GMC 10½ in. axles

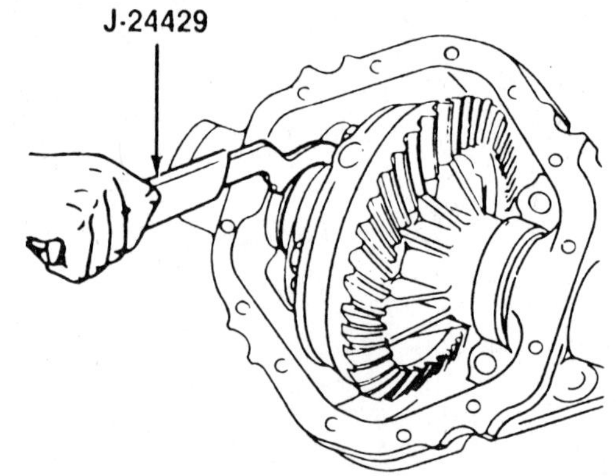

Adjusting the differential preload – GMC 10½ in. axles

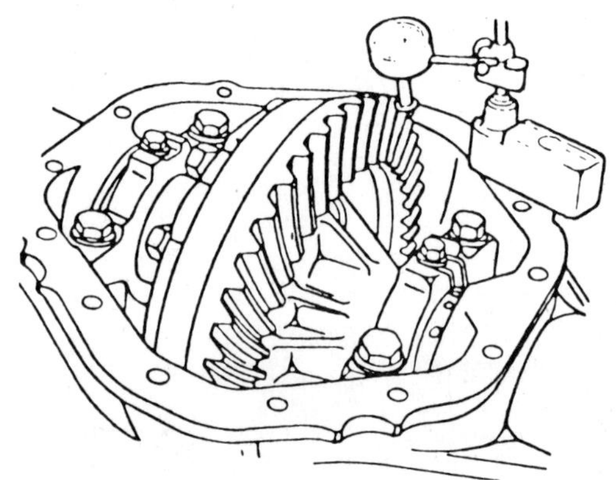
Measuring gear set backlash – GMC 10½ in. axles

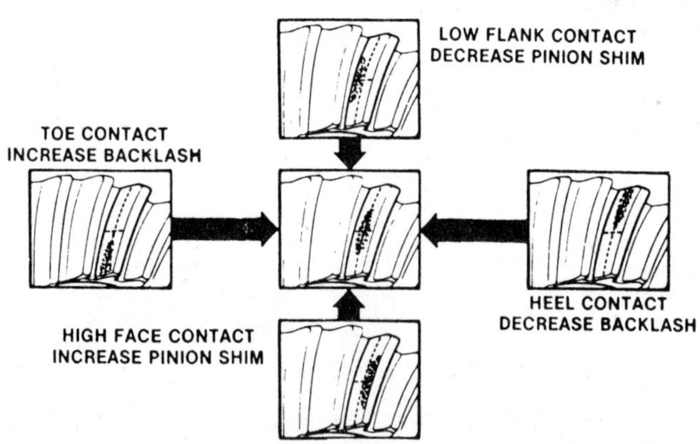

Gear tooth patterns – GMC 10½ in. axles

2. Check the pinion bearing for the proper preload. The force required to turn the pinion should be 25–35 inch lbs. for used bearings. If there is no reading, shake the companion flange to check for any looseness in the bearing. If there is any looseness present, replace the bearing.

3. Remove the pinion bearing retainer-to-axle housing bolts.

4. Remove the bearing retainer and pinion assembly from the axle housing. It may be necessary to tap the pilot end of the pinion shaft to help remove the pinion assembly from the carrier.

5. Record the thickness of the shims that are removed from between the carrier assembly and the bearing retainer assembly.

Drive Pinion

1. With the pinion assembly clamped in a vise, install a holder assembly on the flange.
2. Using the proper size socket, remove the pinion nut and washer from the pinion.

NOTE: When reassembling the pinion use a new nut and washer assembly.

3. With the holder assembly still in place, use a puller to remove the flange from the pinion.
4. With the bearing retainer supported in a shop press, press the pinion out of the retainer assembly; be careful not to allow the pinion gear to fall onto the floor because this can damage the gear.
5. Separate the pinion flange, the oil seal, the front bearing and the bearing retainer; if the oil seal needs to be replaced it may have to be driven from the retainer.
6. Using a drift, drive the front and rear bearing cups from the bearing retainer.
7. Support the pinion assembly in a press, with the bearing supported. Press the bearing from the pinion gear.
8. Using a drift, drive the straddle bearing from the carrier assembly.

Differential Case

1. Scribe a line across both halves of the differential case so they may be reassembled in the same position and with the ring gear removed, separate the halves.
2. Remove the ring gear bolts and washers; using a soft hammer tap the ring gear from the case.
3. Remove the internal parts from the case and set them aside in order so they may be reassembled in the same position.
4. If removing the side bearing, perform the following procedures:
   a. Install a bearing puller on the bearing and press the bearing assembly from the differential case.
   b. Check the bearings for any signs of wear on distortion.

CLEANING AND INSPECTION

1. Clean all of the parts in solvent and blow dry.
2. Check the differential gears, pinions, thrust washers and spider for any signs of unusual wear, chips, cracks or pitting.
3. Check the pinion gear for signs of wear, chips, cracks or any other imperfections. Check the splines for signs of wear or distortion.
4. Check all mating surfaces for signs of wear.
5. Check the bearings for signs of wear or pitting on the rollers and races and check the bearing cage for dents and bends. Check the bearing retainer for any cracks, pits, grooves or corrosion.
6. Check the pinion flange splines for any signs of wear or distortion.
7. Replace parts that show any of the signs mentioned above.

ASSEMBLY

Differential Case

1. If the side bearing was removed, perform the following procedures:
   a. Install a new bearing on the differential case.
   b. Using a bearing driver, drive the bearing onto the case assembly until it seats against the shoulder on the case.
2. Using a good quality gear lubricant coat all of the parts.
3. Assemble the differential pinions and thrust washers onto the spider and install the assembly into the differential case.
4. Align the scribe marks on both halves of the differential case and install the ring gear.
5. Install the ring gear washers and bolts and torque the bolts to approx. 10 ft. lbs.

Drive Pinion

1. Coat all of the parts with a good quality gear lubricant.
2. Position the pinion gear into a shop press and press the rear bearings onto the pinion assembly.
3. Using a bearing driver, install the front and rear bearing cups into the bearing retainer.
4. Using a bearing driver, install the straddle bearing assembly in the axle housing.
5. Install the bearing retainer, with the bearing cups, onto the pinion gear and install a new collapsible spacer.
6. Using a shop press, press the front bearing onto the pinion gear.
7. Lubricate the oil seal with a good quality high pressure grease and install the seal into the retainer bore; be sure to press the seal until it rests against the internal shoulder.
8. Install the pinion flange and oil deflector onto the pinion gear splines, then, install a new lock washer and pinion nut.
9. With the pinion flange clamped in a vise and a holder assembly installed on the flange, tighten the nut to obtain the proper preload; 25–35 inch lbs. for a new bearing or 5–15 inch lbs. for a used bearing. To preload the bearing, tighten the pinion nut to approx. 350 ft. lbs. and take a reading of the torque required to turn the pinion. Continue tightening the nut until the proper preload is obtained.

NOTE: Do not tighten the nut too tightly because it will collapse the spacer too much. This will make replacement necessary.

Pinion

1. If installing a new pinion gear, check the top of the new gear for the depth code number.
2. Compare the new number with the old number on top of the old pinion and check the pinion depth chart for preliminary setting of the pinion depth.
3. Check the thickness of the original shims removed from the pinion and either add or subtract from the shims according to the chart.
4. Place the shim on the carrier assembly and align the holes with those in the axle housing; make sure the surfaces are clean of all dirt and grease.
5. Install the retainer and pinion assembly in the housing making sure the holes align. Install the retaining bolts and torque to approx. 45 ft. lbs.

Differential Case

1. Place the bearing cups over the side bearings on the differential assembly and place the unit into the carrier in the axle housing.
2. Align the marks and install the bearing caps and the bolts. Tighten the bearing retaining bolts.
3. Loosen the right side nut and tighten the left side nut until the ring gear comes in contact with the pinion gear; do not force the gears together. This brings the gears to zero lash.
4. Back off the left side adjusting nut about 2 slots and install the lock fingers into the nut.
5. In this order, tighten the right side adjusting nut firmly to force the case assembly into tight contact with the left side adjusting nut, then, loosen the right side nut until it is free from the bearing.
6. Again, retighten the right side adjusting nut until it comes in contact with the bearing. Tighten the right adjusting nut about 2 slots for an old bearing or 3 slots for a new bearing.
7. Install the lock retainers into the slots and torque the bearing cap bolts to 100 ft. lbs.; this procedure now insures the bearings are preloaded properly. If more adjustments are made,

make sure the preload stays the same. To do this, 1 adjusting nut must be loosened the same amount the other nuts is tightened.

8. Install a dial indicator on the housing and measure the amount of backlash between the ring and pinion gear. The backlash should measure between 0.003–0.012 in. (0.076–0.305mm) with the best figure being between 0.005–0.008 in. (0.127–0.203mm).

9. If the backlash is more than 0.012 in. (0.305mm), loosen the right side adjusting nut 1 slot and tighten the left side 1 slot. If the backlash is less than 0.003 in. (0.076mm), loosen the left side nut 1 slot and tighten the right side 1 slot. These adjustments should bring the backlash measurement into an acceptable range.

Pattern Check

1. Clean all the oil from the ring gear. Using a gear marking compound, coat the teeth of the ring gear.

2. Make sure the bearing caps are torqued to 110 ft. lbs. and apply load to the gears while rotating the pinion. Rotate the ring gear a full turn in both directions.

NOTE: Load must be applied to the assembly while rotating or the pattern will not show completely.

3. Check the pattern on the ring gear, adjust the assembly to get the contact pattern located centrally on the face of the ring gear teeth.

Dana 9¾ in. Ring Gear Differential Overhaul

DISASSEMBLY

Differential Carrier

1. The axle assembly can be overhauled either in or out of the vehicle. Either way, the free-floating axle shafts must be removed.

2. Drain the lubricant and remove the rear cover and gasket.

3. Matchmark the bearing caps and the housing for reassembly in the same position. Remove the bearing caps and bolts.

4. Using a spreader tool mounted to the carrier housing, spread the housing a maximum of 0.015 in. (0.38mm).

NOTE: Do not exceed this measurement. The housing could be permanently damaged. The use of a dial indicator is recommended to prevent over-stretching the housing.

5. Using a pry bar, remove the differential case from the housing.

6. Remove the differential side bearing cups and tag to identify the side, if they are to be used again.

7. Remove the differential gear pinion shaft lock pin and remove the shaft. Rotate the side and pinion gears to remove them from the carrier. Remove the thrust bearings.

8. Remove the bearing cones and rollers from the carrier, marking and noting the shim locations.

9. Remove the ring gear bolts and tap the ring gear from the carrier housing.

10. Inspect the components.

Drive Pinion

1. Remove the pinion nut and flange from the pinion gear.

2. Remove the pinion gear assembly from the housing. It may be necessary to tap the pinion from the housing with a soft faced hammer. Catch the pinion so as not to allow it to drop on the floor.

3. With a long drift, remove the inner bearing cup, pinion seal, slinger, gasket, outer pinion bearing and the shim pack. Label the shim pack for reassembly.

4. Remove the rear pinion bearing cup and shim pack from the housing. Label the shims for reassembly.

5. Remove the rear pinion bearing from the pinion gear with an arbor press and special plates.

INSPECTION

1. Clean the gears, bearings and component parts with solvent and inspect for scoring, chipping or excessive wear.

2. Inspect the flanges and splines for excessive wear.

3. Replace the necessary parts as required.

Pinion Shim Selection

Ring gears and pinions are supplied in matched sets only. The matched numbers are etched on both gears for verification. On the rear face of the pinion, a plus (+) or a minus (−) number will be etched, indicating the best running position for each particular gear set. This dimension is controlled by the shimming behind the inner bearing cup. Whenever baffles or oil slingers are used, they become part of the adjusting shim pack. An example: If a pinion is etched +3, this pinion would require 0.003 in. (0.076mm) less shimming than a pinion etched 0. This means by removing shims, the mounting distance of the pinion is increased by 0.003 in. (0.076mm), which is just what a plus (+) etching indicates. If a pinion is etched −3, it would be necessary to add 0.003 in. (0.076mm) more shimming than would be required if the pinion was etched 0. By adding the 0.003 in. (0.076mm) shims, the mounting distance of the pinion is decreased 0.003 in. (0.076mm), which is just what the minus (−) etching indicates. Pinion adjusting shims are available in thicknesses of 0.003 in., 0.005 in. and 0.010 in. An example: If a new gear set is used and the old pinion reads +2 and the new pinion reads −2, add 0.004 in. shims to the original shim pack.

ASSEMBLY

Drive Pinion

1. Select the correct pinion depth shims and install in the rear pinion bearing cup bore.

2. Install the rear bearing cup in the axle housing.

3. Add or subtract an equal amount of shim thickness to or from the preload or outer shim pack, as was added or subtracted from the inner shim pack.

4. Install the front pinion bearing cup into its bore in the axle housing.

5. Press the rear pinion bearing onto the pinion gear shaft and install the pinion gear with bearing into the axle housing.

6. Install the preload shims and the front pinion bearing; do not install the oil seal at this time.

7. Install the flange with the holding bar tool attached, the washer and the nut on the pinion shaft end. Torque the nut to 255 ft. lbs.

8. Remove the holding bar from the flange and with an inch lb. torque wrench, measure the rotating torque of the pinion gear. The rotating torque should be 10–20 inch lbs. with the original bearings or 20–40 inch lbs. with new bearings. Disregard the torque reading necessary to start the shaft to turn.

9. If the preload torque is not in specifications, adjust the shim pack as required.

   a. To increase preload, decrease the thickness of the preload shim pack.

   b. To decrease preload, increase the thickness of the preload shim pack.

10. When the proper preload is obtained, remove the nut, washer and flange from the pinion shaft.

11. Install a new pinion seal into the housing and reinstall the

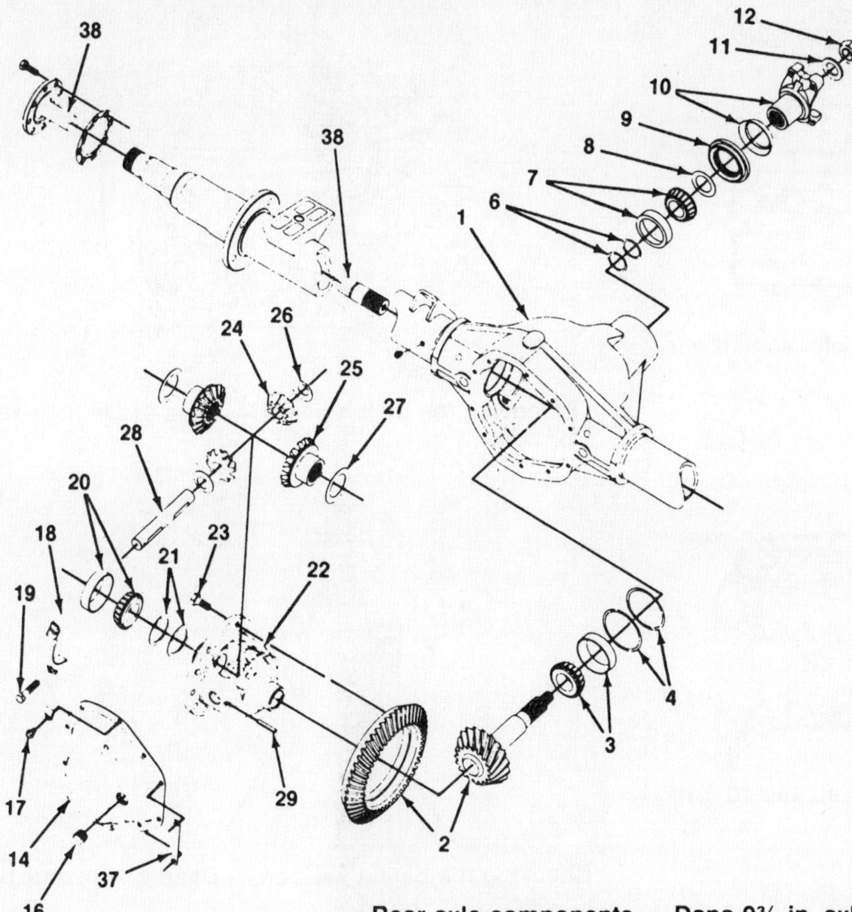

1. Axle housing
2. Ring and pinion set
3. Inner pinion bearing
4. Shims
5. Preload shims
6. Bearing
7. Slinger
8. Pinion oil seal
9. Pinion flange
10. Washer
11. Pinion nut
12. Cover
13. Plug
14. Bolt
15. Bearing cap
16. Bolt
17. Bearing
18. Shim
19. Differential case
20. Ring gear bolt
21. Pinion gear
22. Side gear
23. Pinion thrust washer
24. Side gear thrust washer
25. Pinion shaft
26. Roll pin
27. ID tag

Rear axle components – Dana 9¾ in. axles

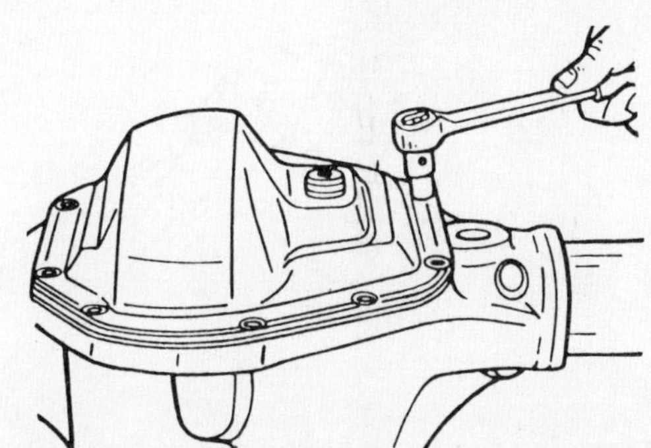

Removing the cover – Dana 9¾ in. and 10½ in. axles

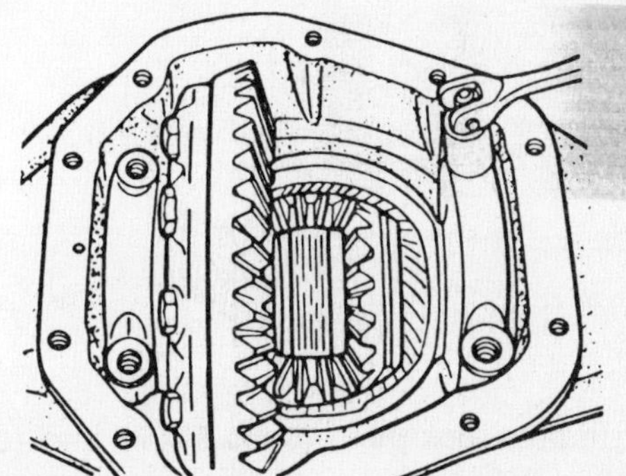

Removing the bearing cap – Dana 9¾ in. and 10½ in. axles

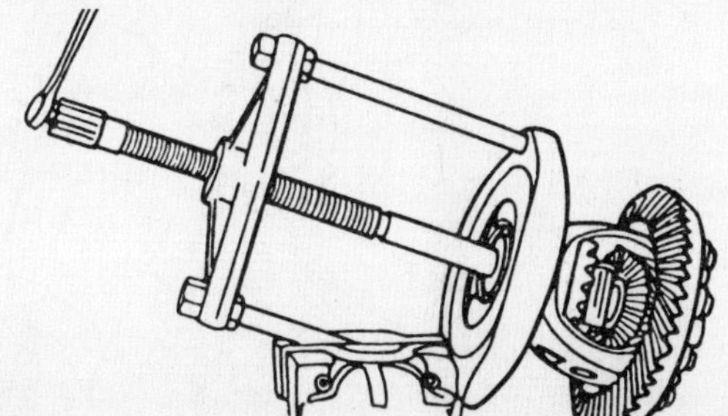

Removing the side bearings – Dana 9¾ in. and 10½ in. axles

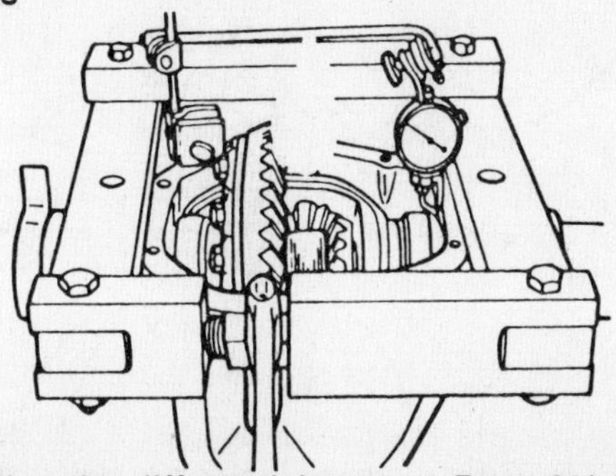

Spreading the differential case – Dana 9¾ in. and 10½ in. axles

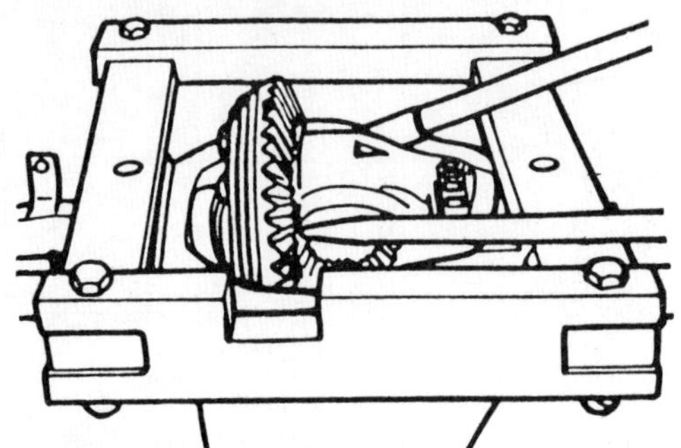
Removing the differential – Dana 9¾ in. and 10½ in. axles

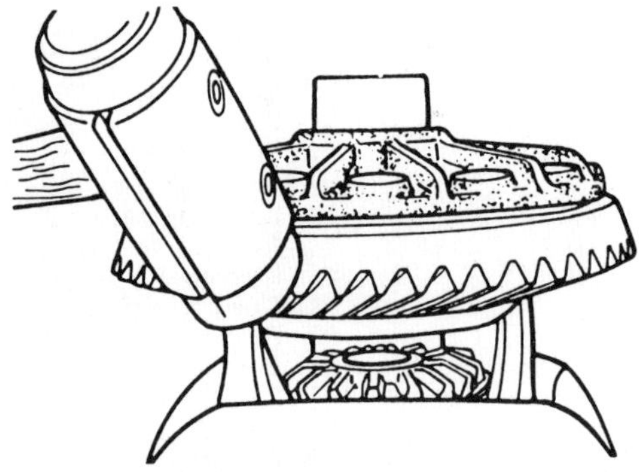
Removing the ring gear – Dana 9¾ in. and 10½ in. axles

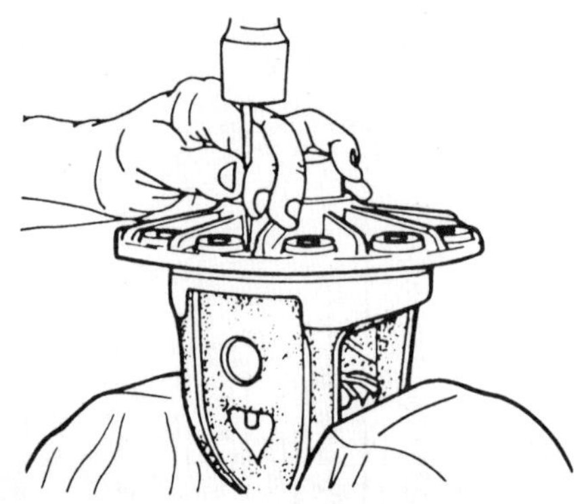
Removing the lock pin – Dana 9¾ in. and 10½ in. axles

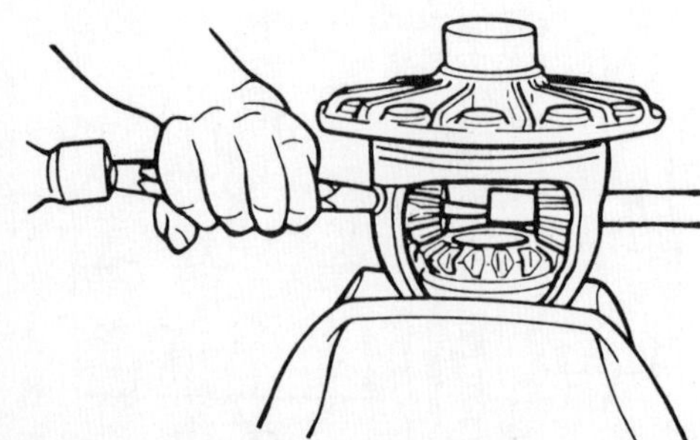
Removing the pinion shaft – Dana 9¾ in. and 10½ in. axles

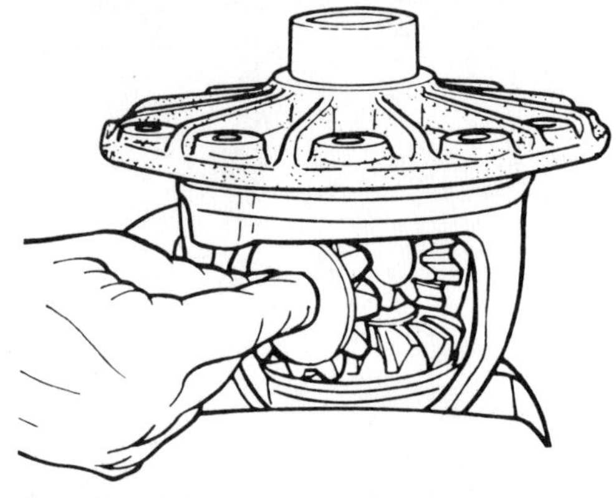
Removing the pinion gears – Dana 9¾ in. and 10½ in. axles

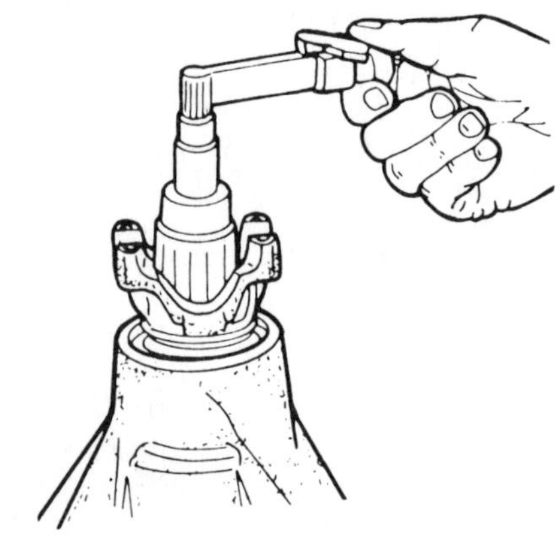
Checking the pinion preload – Dana 9¾ in. and 10½ in. axles

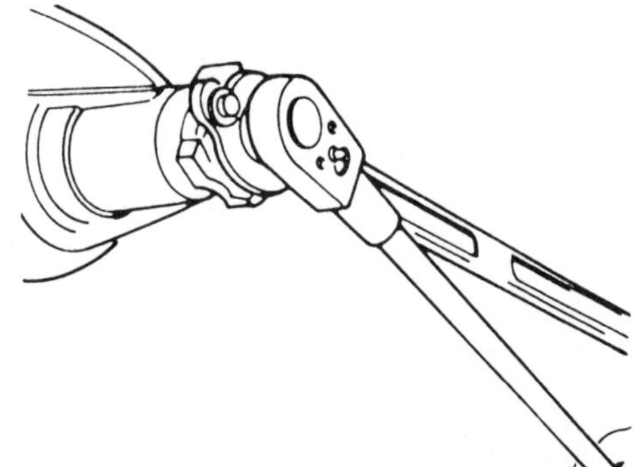
Removing the drive pinion nut – Dana 9¾ in. and 10½ in. axles

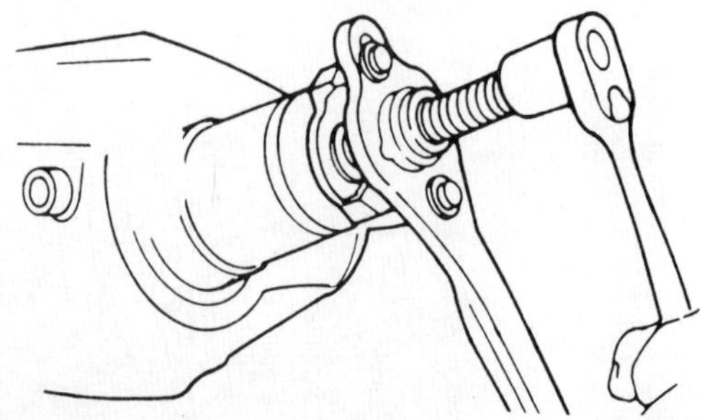
Removing the flange – Dana 9¾ in. and 10½ in. axles

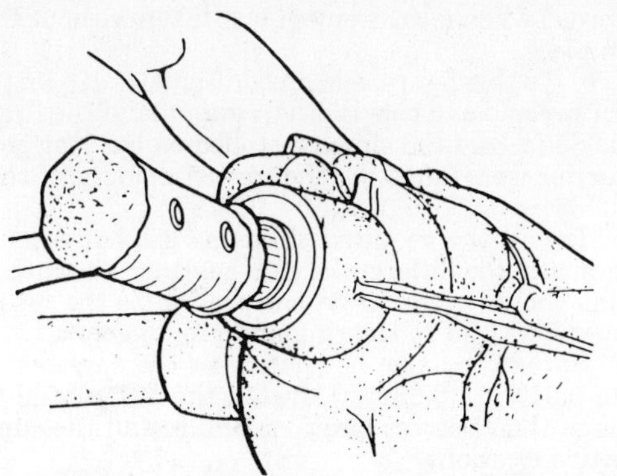
Removing the pinion – Dana 9¾ in. and 10½ in. axles

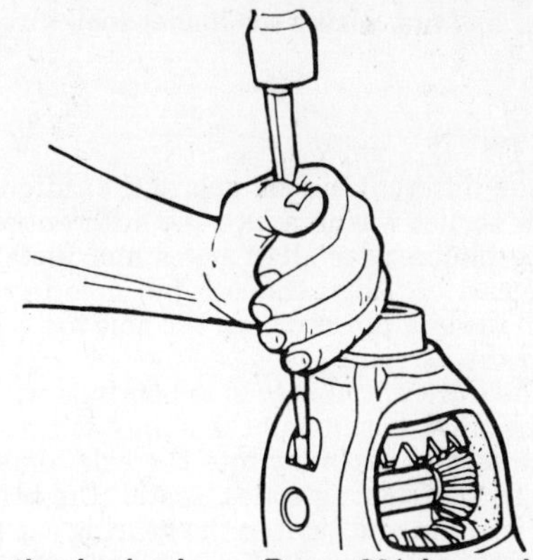
Installing the lock pin – Dana 9¾ in. and 10½ in. axles

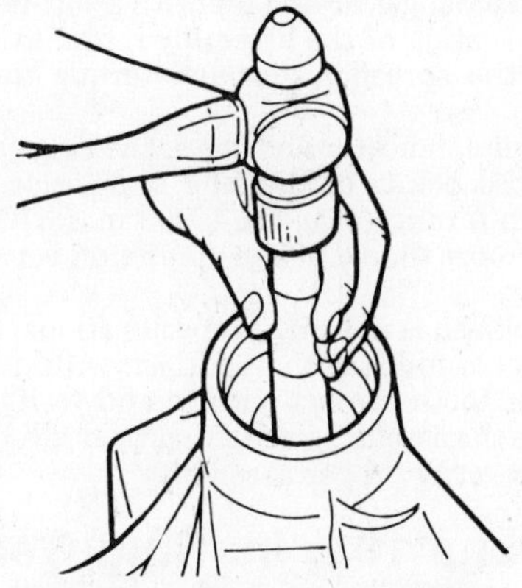
Removing the bearing cups – Dana 9¾ in. and 10½ in. axles

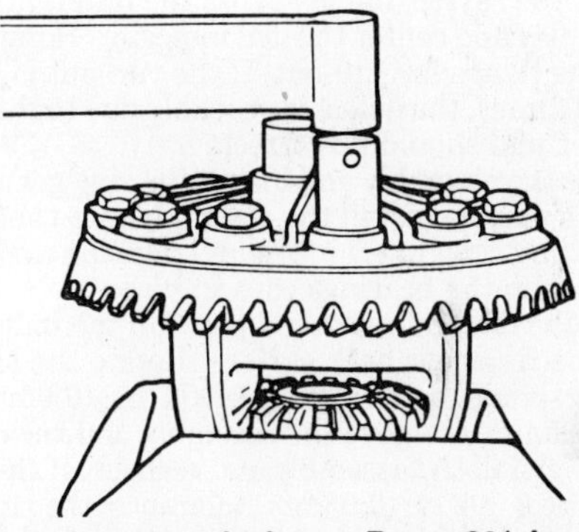
Installing the ring gear bolts – Dana 9¾ in. and 10½ in. axles

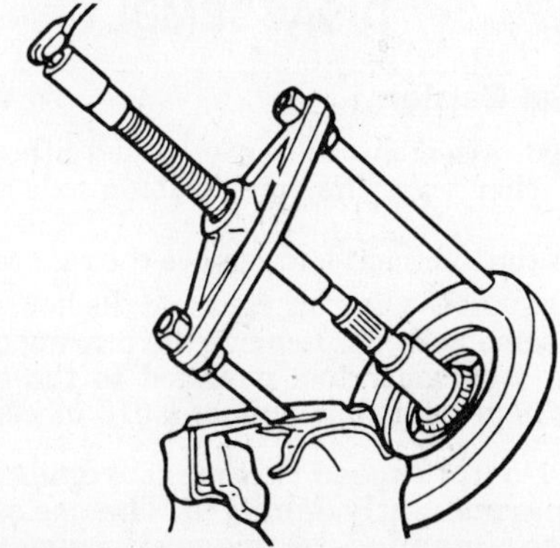
Removing the pinion inner bearing – Dana 9¾ in. and 10½ in. axles

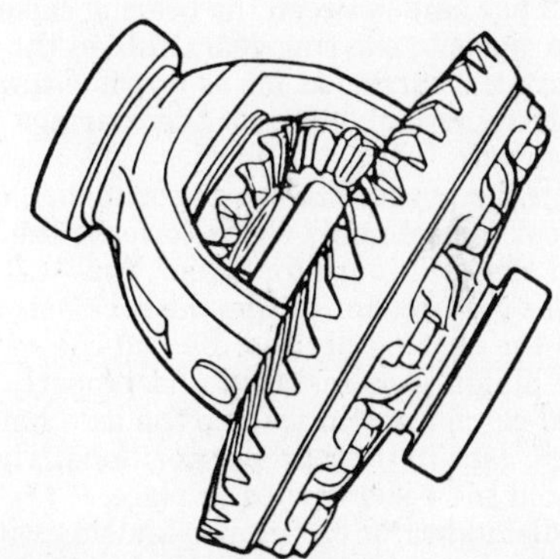
Differential with master bearings – Dana 9¾ in. and 10½ in. axles

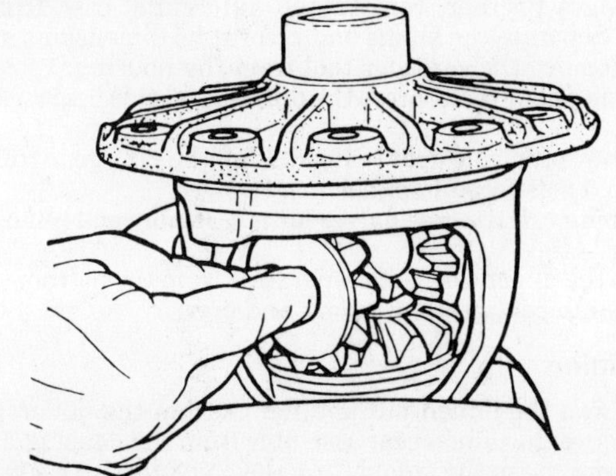
Installing the pinion gears – Dana 9¾ in. and 10½ in. axles

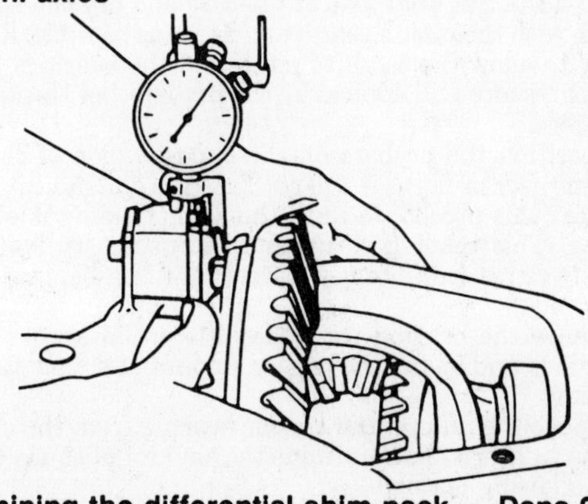
Determining the differential shim pack – Dana 9¾ in. and 10½ in. axles

flange, washer and nut. Using the holder tool, torque the nut to 255 ft. lbs.

Differential Carrier

1. Install the differential side gears, the differential pinion gears and new thrust washers into the differential carrier.
2. Align the pinion gear shaft holes and install the pinion shaft into the carrier. Align the lock pin hole in the shaft and carrier. Install the lock pin and peen the hole to avoid having the pin drop from the carrier.
3. Install the differential case side bearings with the proper installation tools. Do not install the shims at this time.
4. Place the carrier assembly into the axle housing with the bearing cups on the bearing cones. Install the bearing caps in their original position and tighten the bearing cap bolts enough to keep the bearing caps in place.
5. Install a dial indicator on the housing so the indicator button contacts the carrier flange. Press the differential carrier to prevent sideplay and center the dial indicator. Rotate the carrier and check the flange for run-out. If the run-out is greater than 0.002 in. (0.05mm), the defect is probably due to the bearings or to the carrier and should be corrected.
6. Remove the assembly and install the ring gear. Torque the retaining bolts and reinstall the assembly into the housing. Install the bearing caps in their original position and tighten the cap bolts to keep the bearings caps in place.
7. Install the dial indicator and position the indicator button to contact the ring gear back surface. Rotate the assembly and the run-out should be less than 0.002 in. (0.05mm). If over 0.002 in. (0.05mm), remove the assembly and relocate the ring gear 180°. Reinstall the assembly and recheck. If the run-out remains over the 0.002 in. (0.05mm) tolerance, the ring gear is defective. If the measurement is within tolerances, continue on with the assembly.
8. Position 2 pry bars between the bearing cap and the housing on the side opposite the ring gear. Pull on the pry bars and force the differential carrier as far as possible towards the dial indicator. Rock the assembly to seat the bearings and reset the dial indicator to zero.
9. Reposition the prybars to the opposite side of the carrier and force the carrier assembly as far towards the center of the housing. Read the dial indicator scale. This will be the total amount of shims required for setting the backlash during the reassembly, less the bearing preload. Record the measurement.
10. With the pinion gear installed and properly set, position the differential carrier assembly into the axle housing and install the bearing caps in their proper positions. Tighten the cap bolts just to hold the bearing cups in place.
11. Install a dial indicator on the axle housing with the indicator button contacting the back of the ring gear.
12. Position 2 prybars between the bearing cup and the axle housing on the ring gear side of the case and pry the ring gear into mesh with the pinion gear teeth, as far as possible. Rock the ring gear to allow the teeth to mesh and the bearings to seat. With the pressure still applied by the prybars, set the dial indicator to zero.
13. Reposition the prybars on the opposite side of ring gear and pry the gear as far as it will go. Take the dial indicator reading. Repeat this procedure until the same reading is obtained each time. This reading represents the necessary amount of shims between the differential carrier and the bearing on the ring gear side.
14. Remove the bearing from the differential carrier on the ring gear side and install the proper amount of shims. Reinstall the bearing.
15. Remove the differential carrier bearing from the opposite side of the ring gear. To determine the amount of shims needed, use the following method.
    a. Subtract the size of the shim pack just installed on the ring gear side of the carrier from the reading obtained and recorded when measurement was taken without the pinion gear in place.
    b. To this figure, add an additional 0.015 in. to compensate for preload and backlash. An example: If the first reading was 0.085 in. and the shims installed on the ring gear side of the carrier were 0.055 in., the correct amount of shims would be 0.085 − 0.055 + 0.015 = 0.045 in.
16. Install the required shims as determined under step 15 and install the differential side bearing. The installation of the shims should give the proper preload to the bearings and the proper backlash to the ring and pinion gears.
17. Spread the axle housing with the spreader tool no more than 0.015 in. (0.38mm). Install the differential bearing outer cups in their correct locations and install the cups in their respective locations.
18. Install the bolts and tighten finger-tight. Rotate the differential carrier and ring gear and tap with a soft-faced hammer to insure proper seating of the assembly in the axle housing.
19. Remove the spreader tool and torque the cap bolts to specifications.
20. Install a dial indicator and check the ring gear backlash at 4 equally spaced points of the ring gear circle. The backlash must be within a range of 0.004–0.009 in. (0.10–0.23mm) and must not vary more than 0.002 in. (0.05mm) between the points checked.
21. If the backlash is not within specifications, the shim packs must be corrected to bring the backlash within limits.
22. Check the tooth contact pattern and verify.
23. Complete the assembly, refill to proper level with lubricant and operate to verify proper assembly.

Dana 10½ in. Ring Gear Differential Overhaul

DISASSEMBLY

Differential Carrier

1. The axle assembly can be overhauled either in or out of the vehicle. Either way, the free-floating axle shafts must be removed.
2. Drain the lubricant and remove the rear cover and gasket.
3. Matchmark the bearing caps and the housing for reassembly in the same position. Remove the bearing caps and bolts.
4. Using a spreader tool mounted to the carrier housing, spread the housing a maximum of 0.015 in. (0.38mm).

NOTE: Do not exceed this measurement. The housing could be permanently damaged. The use of a dial indicator is recommended to prevent over-stretching the housing.

5. Using a pry bar, remove the differential case from the housing. Separate the shims and record the dimensions and location. Remove the spreader tool from the housing.
6. Using puller tools, press the differential side bearings from the case.
7. Remove the ring gear bolts and tap the ring gear from the case with a soft-faced hammer.
8. Matchmark the case halves for reassembly and remove the retaining bolts.
9. Tap the upper case ½ to separate it from the bottom ½. Remove the internal gears, washers and cross.

Drive Pinion

1. Remove the pinion nut and flange from the pinion gear.
2. Remove the pinion gear assembly from the housing. It may be necessary to tap the pinion from the housing with a soft faced hammer. Catch the pinion so as not to allow it to drop on the floor.

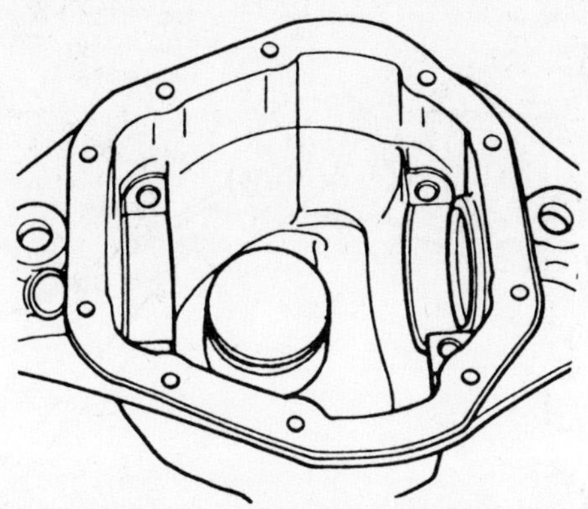
Master pinion block – Dana 9¾ in. and 10½ in. axles

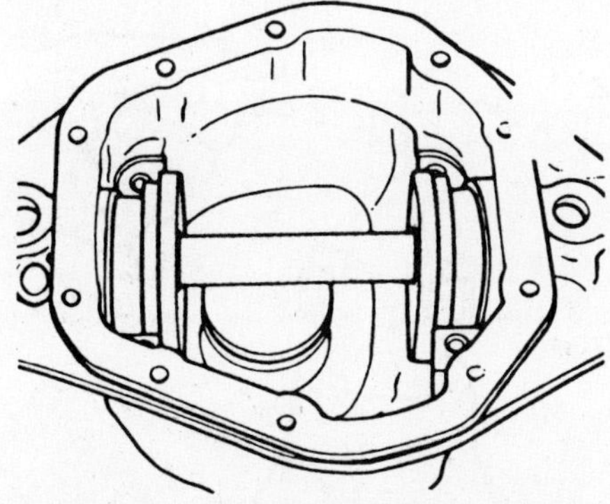
Arbor and discs – Dana 9¾ in. and 10½ in. axles

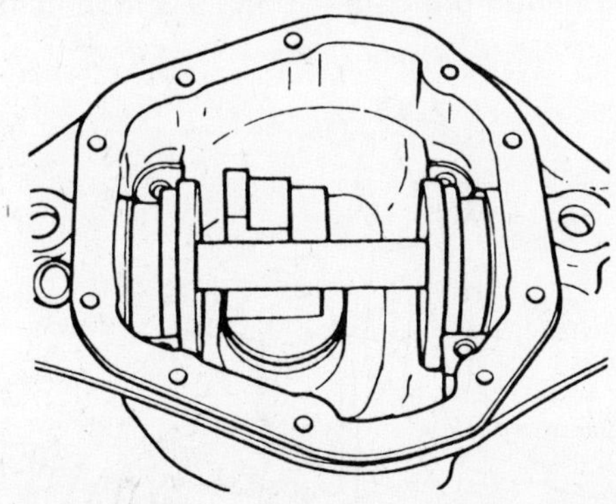
Pinion height block – Dana 9¾ in. and 10½ in. axles

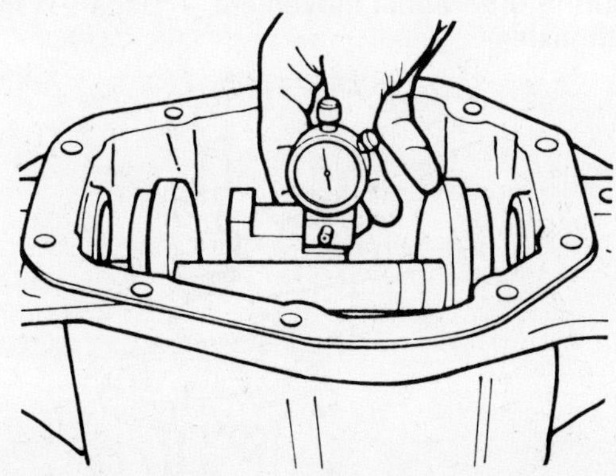
Scooter gauge on the height block – Dana 9¾ in. and 10½ in. axles

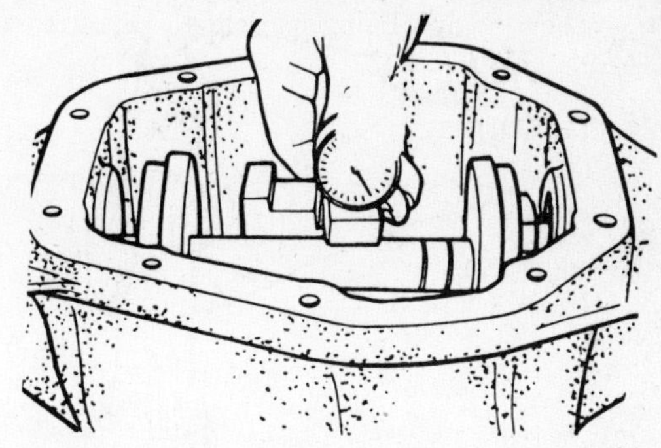
Scooter gauge on the arbor – Dana 9¾ in. and 10½ in. axles

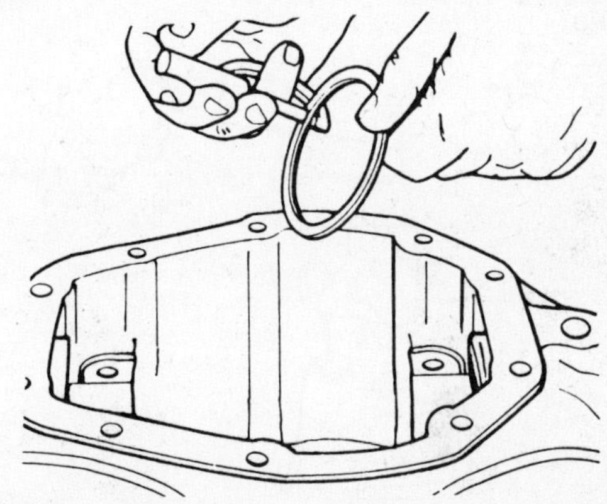
Measuring the shims – Dana 9¾ in. and 10½ in. axles

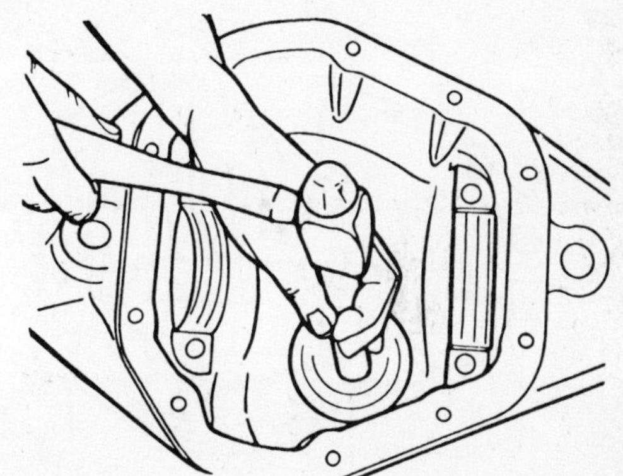
Installing the pinion inner cup – Dana 9¾ in. and 10½ in. axles

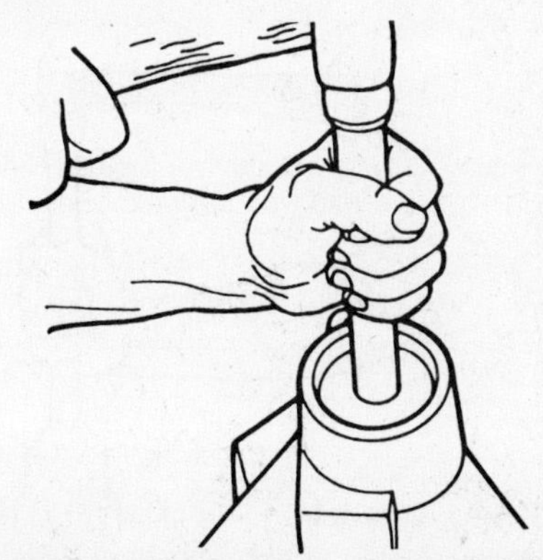
Installing the pinion front cup – Dana 9¾ in. and 10½ in. axles

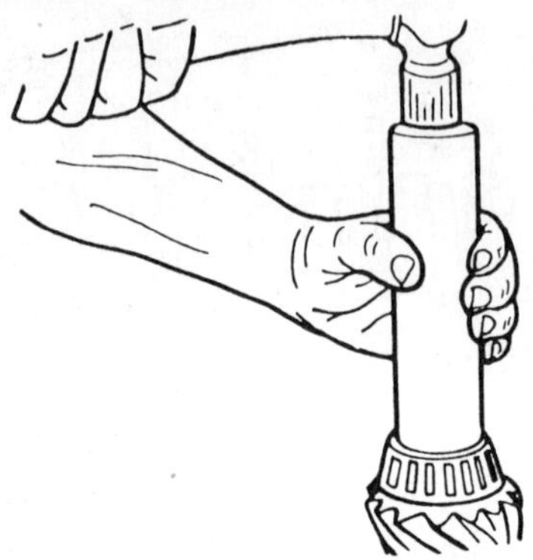

Installing the inner bearing – Dana 9¾ in. and 10½ in. axles

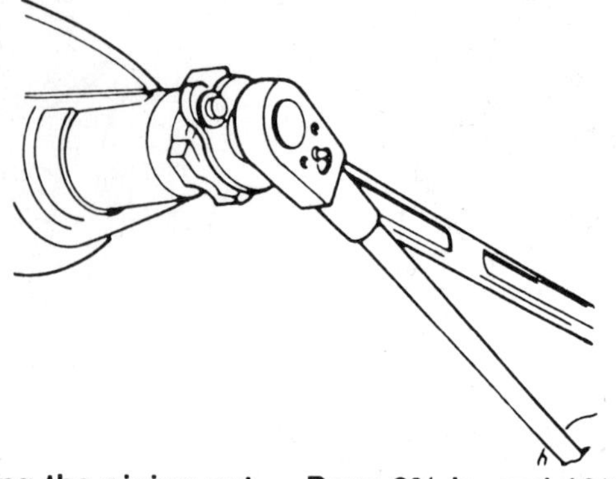

Tightening the pinion nut – Dana 9¾ in. and 10½ in. axles

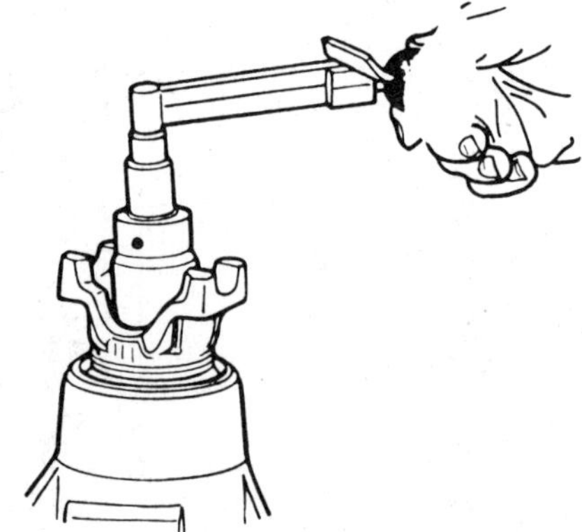

Checking the preload – Dana 9¾ in. and 10½ in. axles

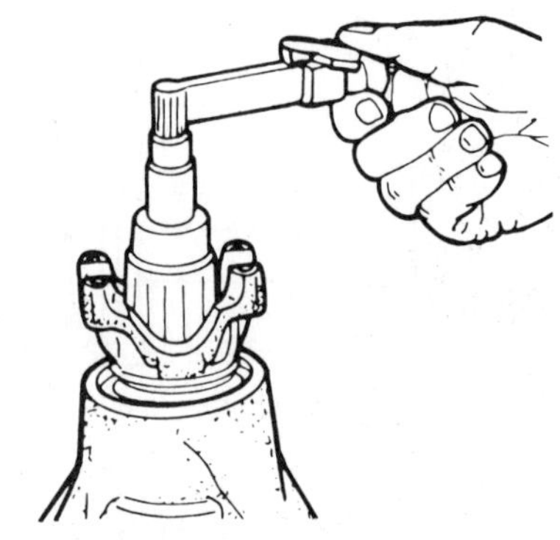

Checking pinion preload – Dana 9¾ in. and 10½ in. axles

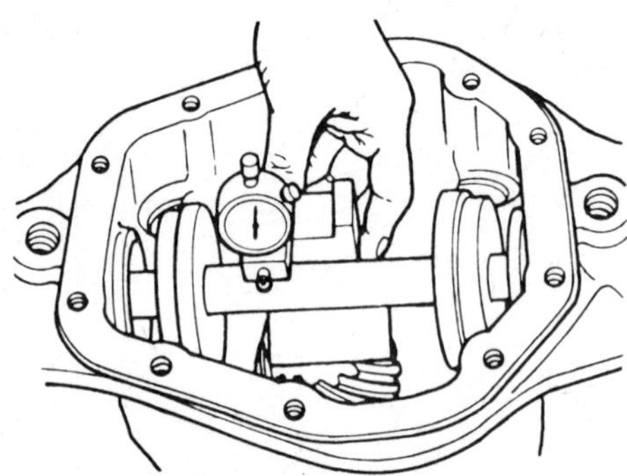

Checking the pinion depth setting – Dana 9¾ in. and 10½ in. axles

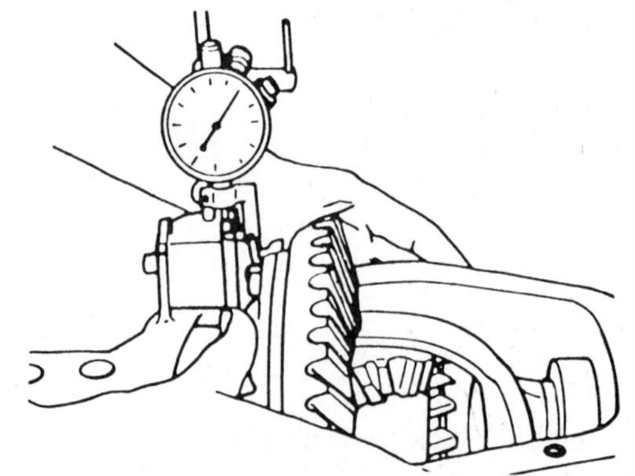

Measuring differential movement – Dana 9¾ in. and 10½ in. axles

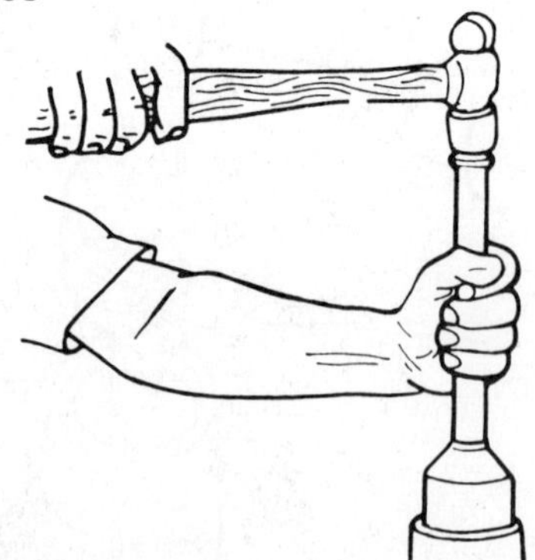

Installing the pinion seal – Dana 9¾ in. and 10½ in. axles

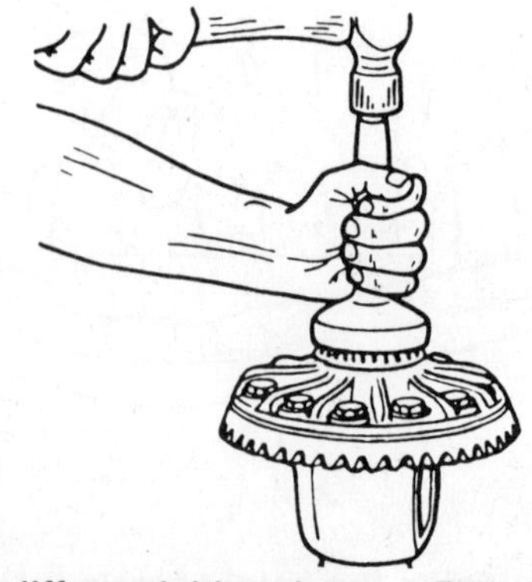

Installing the differential bearings – Dana 9¾ in. and 10½ in. axles

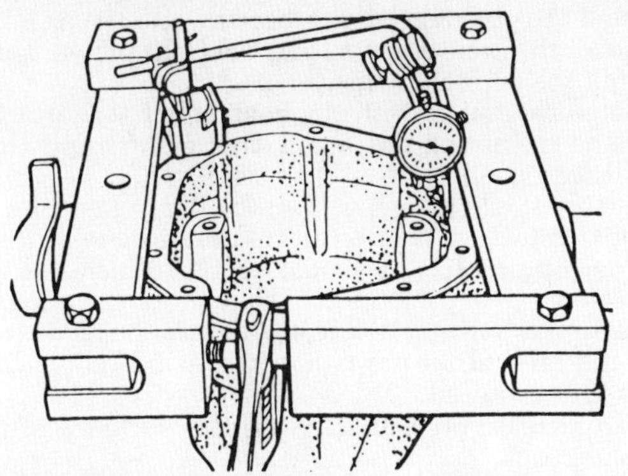
Mounting the carrier spreader – Dana 9¾ in. and 10½ in. axles

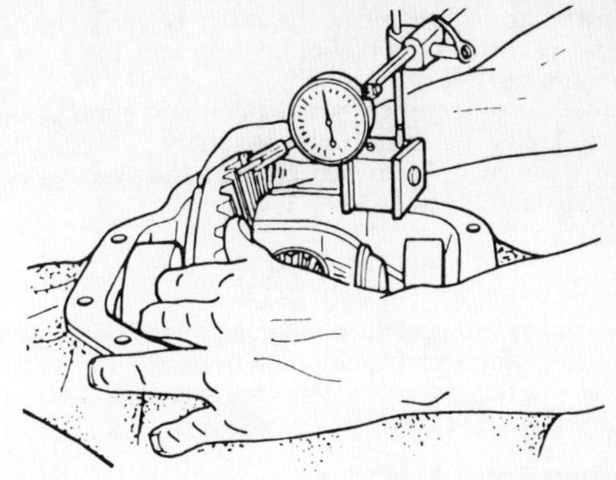
Measuring backlash – Dana 9¾ in. and 10½ in. axles

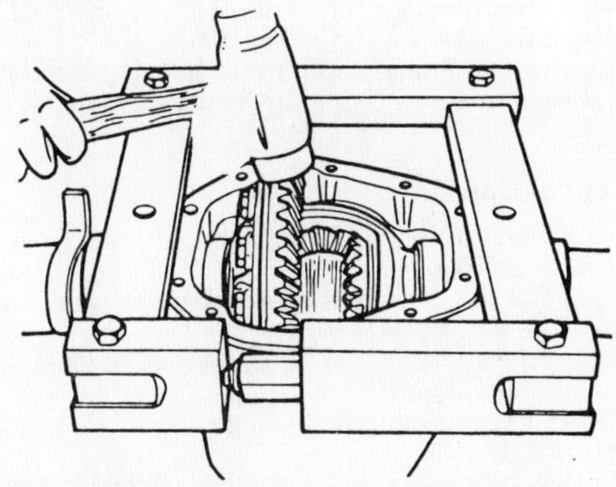
Installing the differential case – Dana 9¾ in. and 10½ in. axles

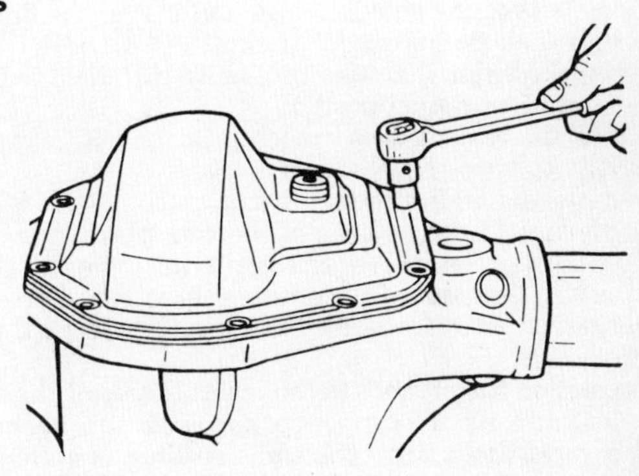
Installing the axle cover – Dana 9¾ in. and 10½ in. axles

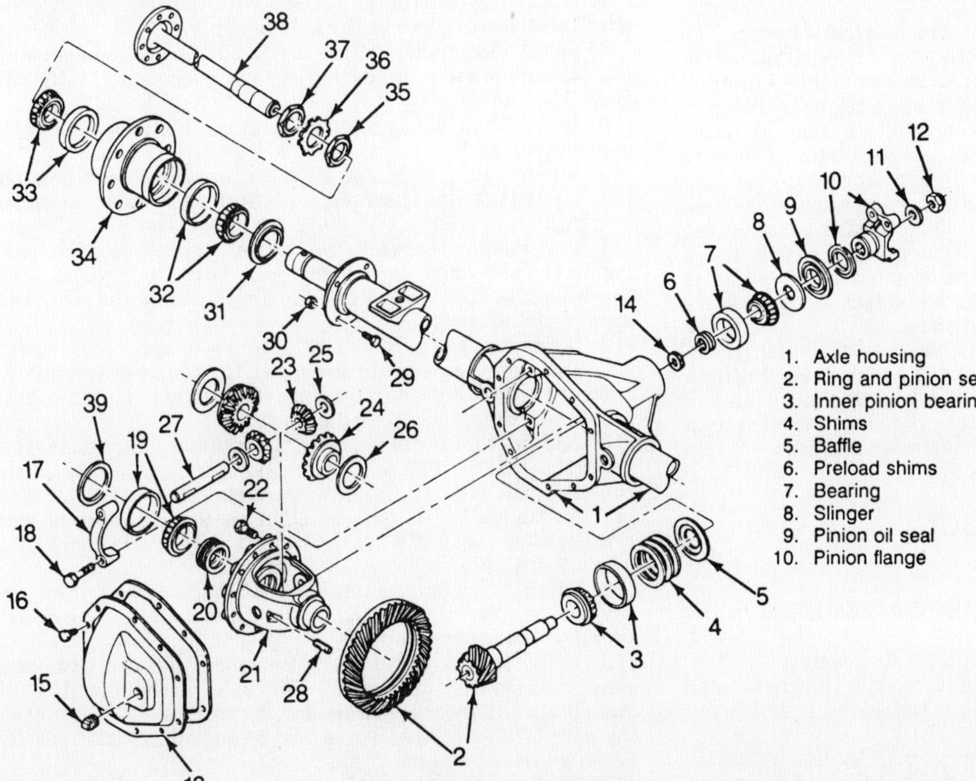

Rear axle components – Dana 10½ in. axles

3. With a long drift, remove the inner bearing cup, pinion seal, slinger, gasket, outer pinion bearing and the shim pack. Label the shim pack for reassembly.
4. Remove the rear pinion bearing cup and shim pack from the housing. Label the shims for reassembly.
5. Remove the rear pinion bearing from the pinion gear with an arbor press and special plates.

INSPECTION

1. Clean the gears, bearings and component parts with solvent and inspect for scoring, chipping or excessive wear.
2. Inspect the flanges and splines for excessive wear.
3. Replace the necessary parts as required.

Side Bearing Shim Selection

1. With the pinion gear not in the axle housing, place the bearing cups over the side bearings and install the differential carrier into the axle housing.
2. Place the shim that was originally installed on the ring gear side into its original position.
3. Install the bearing caps in their proper positions and tighten the bolts to keep the bearings in place.
4. Mount a dial indicator on the axle housing with the indicator button contacting the back of the ring gear.
5. Position 2 prybars between the bearing shim and the housing on the ring gear side of the differential carrier. Force the differential carrier away from the dial indicator and set the indicator to zero.
6. Reposition the prybars to the opposite side of the differential carrier and force the carrier back towards the dial indicator. Repeat several times until the same reading is obtained each time.
7. To the dial indicator reading, add the thickness of the shim and record the results to be used later in the assembly.

Pinion Shim Selection

Ring gears and pinions are supplied in matched sets only. The matched numbers are etched on both gears for verification. On the rear face of the pinion, a plus (+) or a minus (−) number will be etched, indicating the best running position for each particular gear set. This dimension is controlled by the shimming behind the inner bearing cup. Whenever baffles or oil slingers are used, they become part of the adjusting shim pack. An example: If a pinion is etched +3, this pinion would require 0.003 in. less shims than a pinion etched 0. This means by removing shims, the mounting distance of the pinion is increased by 0.003 in., which is just what a plus (+) etching indicates. If a pinion is etched −3, it would be necessary to add 0.003 in. more shims than would be required if the pinion was etched 0. By adding the 0.003 in. shims, the mounting distance of the pinion is decreased 0.003 in., which is just what the minus (−) etching indicates. Pinion adjusting shims are available in thicknesses of 0.003, 0.005 and 0.010 in. An example: If a new gear set is used and the old pinion reads +2 and the new pinion reads −2, add 0.004 in. shims to the original shim pack.

ASSEMBLY

Drive Pinion

1. Select the correct pinion depth shims and install in the rear pinion bearing cup bore.
2. Install the rear bearing cup in the axle housing.
3. Add or subtract an equal amount of shim thickness to or from the preload or outer shim pack, as was added or subtracted from the inner shim pack.
4. Install the front pinion bearing cup into its bore in the axle housing.
5. Press the rear pinion bearing onto the pinion gear shaft and install the pinion gear with bearing into the axle housing.
6. Install the preload shims and the front pinion bearing; do not install the oil seal at this time.
7. Install the flange with the holding bar tool attached, the washer and the nut on the pinion shaft end. Torque the nut to 250 ft. lbs.
8. Remove the holding bar from the flange and with an inch lb. torque wrench, measure the rotating torque of the pinion gear. The rotating torque should be 10–20 inch lbs. with the original bearings or 20–40 inch lbs. with new bearings. Disregard the torque reading necessary to start the shaft to turn.
9. If the preload torque is not in specifications, adjust the shim pack as required.
   a. To increase preload, decrease the thickness of the preload shim pack.
   b. To decrease preload, increase the thickness of the preload shim pack.
10. When the proper preload is obtained, remove the nut, washer and flange from the pinion shaft.
11. Install a new pinion seal into the housing and reinstall the flange, washer and nut. Using the holder tool, torque the nut to 250 ft. lbs.

Differential Carrier

1. Install new thrust washers to the side gears and lubricate the contact surfaces.
2. Assemble the side gears, pinion bears, washers and cross shaft into the flanged case ½.
3. Install the upper case ½ to the bottom ½, making sure the scribe marks are aligned.
4. Install the retaining bolts finger tight, then, torque the bolts alternately.
5. If a new ring gear is to be installed or the old one used, install it to the differential case and align the bolt holes and torque the bolts alternately.
6. Install the side carrier bearings.
7. Install the differential carrier, with the side bearings and cups installed, in place in the axle housing.
8. Select the smallest of the original shims as a gauge shim and place it between the bearing cup and the housing on the ring gear side.
9. Install the bearing caps and tighten the bolts to hold the cups in place.
10. Mount a dial indicator on the ring gear side of the axle housing and position the indicator button on the rear side of the ring gear.
11. Position 2 prybars between the bearing cup and the housing on the side opposite the ring gear. With the prybars, force the differential carrier towards the dial indicator and set the indicator dial to zero.
12. Reposition the prybars on the ring gear side of the carrier and force the ring gear into mesh with the pinion gear while observing the dial indicator reading. Repeat this operation until the same reading is obtained each time.
13. Add this indicator reading to the gauging shim thickness to determine the correct shim dimension for installation on the ring gear side of the differential carrier.
14. An example: If the gauging shim was 0.115 in. and the indicator reading was 0.017 in., the correct shim would be 0.115 + 0.017 = 0.172 in.
15. Remove the gauge shim and install the correct shim into position between the bearing cup and the axle housing on the ring gear side of the housing.
16. To determine the correct dimension for the remaining shim, refer to the side bearing shim selection for the 10½ in. and obtain the recorded shim size. From that figure, subtract the size of the shim installed in step 14 and add 0.006 in. for the bearing preload and backlash.
17. An example: If the reading of the shim just installed on the ring gear side of the carrier was 0.172 in. and the reading ob-

tained during the checking of clearance without the pinion installed was 0.329, the correct shim dimension would be as follows: 0.329 − 0.172 = 0.157 + 0.006 = 0.163 in.

18. Spread the axle housing with a spreader tool, no more than 0.015 in. The carrier assembly is in place in the housing.
19. Assemble the shim, as determined previously, into place between the bearing cup and the housing. Remove the spreader tool.
20. Install the bearing caps in their marked positions and torque the bolts to specifications.
21. Install a dial indicator and check the ring gear backlash at 4 equally spaced points around the ring gear.
22. The backlash must be within 0.004–0.009 in. and must not vary more than 0.002 in. between the positions checked.
23. Whenever the backlash is not within the allowable limits, it must be corrected. Changing of the shim packs is required.
    a. Low backlash is corrected by decreasing the shim on the ring gear side and increasing the opposite side shim an equal amount.
    b. High backlash is corrected by increasing the shim on the ring gear side and decreasing the opposite side shim an equal amount.
24. Check the tooth contact pattern and correct as required.
25. Complete the assembly, refill to the correct level and operate to verify correct repairs.

FRONT DRIVE AXLE V SERIES

10/15 series and 20/25 series trucks use a GMC 8½ in. ring gear axle.

30/35 series trucks use a Dana 60, 9¾ in. ring gear axle.

Manual Locking Hubs All Axles

The engagement and disengagement of the hubs is a manual operation which must be performed at each hub assembly. The hubs should be placed FULLY in either Lock or Free position or damage will result.

WARNING: Do not use place the transfer case in either 4-wheel mode unless the hubs are in the Lock position!

Locking hubs should be run in the Lock position periodically for a few miles to assure proper differential lubrication.

REMOVAL

NOTE: This procedure requires snapring pliers. It cannot be performed properly without them!

1. Raise and support the front end on jackstands.
2. Remove the wheels.
3. Lock the hubs. Remove the outer retaining plate Allen head bolts and take off the plate, O-ring, and knob assembly.

NOTE: These bolts may have washers. Don't lose them!

4. Remove the external snapring from the axle shaft.
5. Remove the compression spring.
6. Remove the clutch cup.
7. Remove the O-ring and dial screw.
8. Remove the clutch nut and seal.
9. Remove the large internal snapring from the wheel hub.
10. Remove the inner drive gear.
11. Remove the clutch ring and spring.

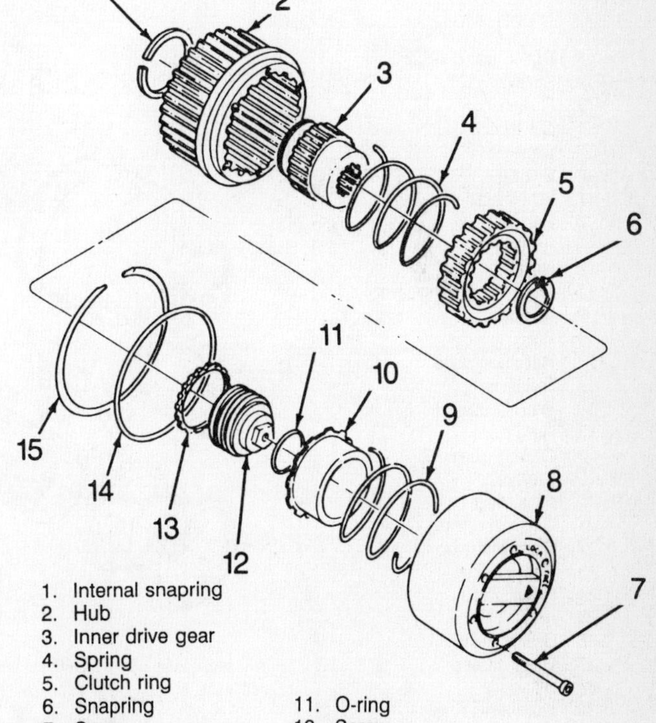

Manual locking hubs

12. Remove the smaller internal snapring from the clutch hub body and remove the hub body.

INSPECTION AND CLEANING

1. Clean all hub parts in a safe, non-flammable solvent and wipe them dry.
2. Inspect each component for wear or damage. Make sure that the springs are functional and stiff. Make sure that all gear teeth are intact, with no chips or burrs.
3. Make sure that the splines on the inside of the wheel hub are clean and free of dirt, chips and burrs.
4. Surface irregularities can be cleaned up with light filing or emery paper.
5. Prior to assembly, coat all parts with the same wheel bearing grease you've used on the wheel bearings.

INSTALLATION

1. Install the hub body. Install the smaller internal snapring in the clutch hub body.
2. Install the clutch ring and spring.
3. Install the inner drive gear.
4. Install the large internal snapring in the wheel hub.
5. Install the external snapring on the axle shaft. If the snapring groove is not completely visible, reach around, inside the knuckle and push the axle shaft outwards.
6. Install the clutch nut and seal.
7. Install the O-ring and dial screw.
8. Install the clutch cup.
9. Install the compression spring.
10. Place the hub dial in the Lock position.
11. Coat the hub dial assembly O-ring with wheel bearing grease and position the hub dial and retainer on the hub.
12. Install the allen head bolts. Make sure that you used any washers that were there originally. Tighten these bolts to 45 inch lbs.
13. Rotate the hub dial to the Free position and turn the wheel hubs to make sure that the axle is free.
14. Install the wheels.

Automatic Locking Hubs 10/15 and 20/25 Series Trucks

REMOVAL AND INSTALLATION

The following procedure covers removal and installation only, for the hub assembly. The hub should be disassembled ONLY if overhaul is necessary. In that event, an overhaul kit will be required. Follow the instructions in the overhaul kit to rebuild the hub.

1. Remove the capscrews and washer from the hub cap.
2. Remove the hub cap and spring.

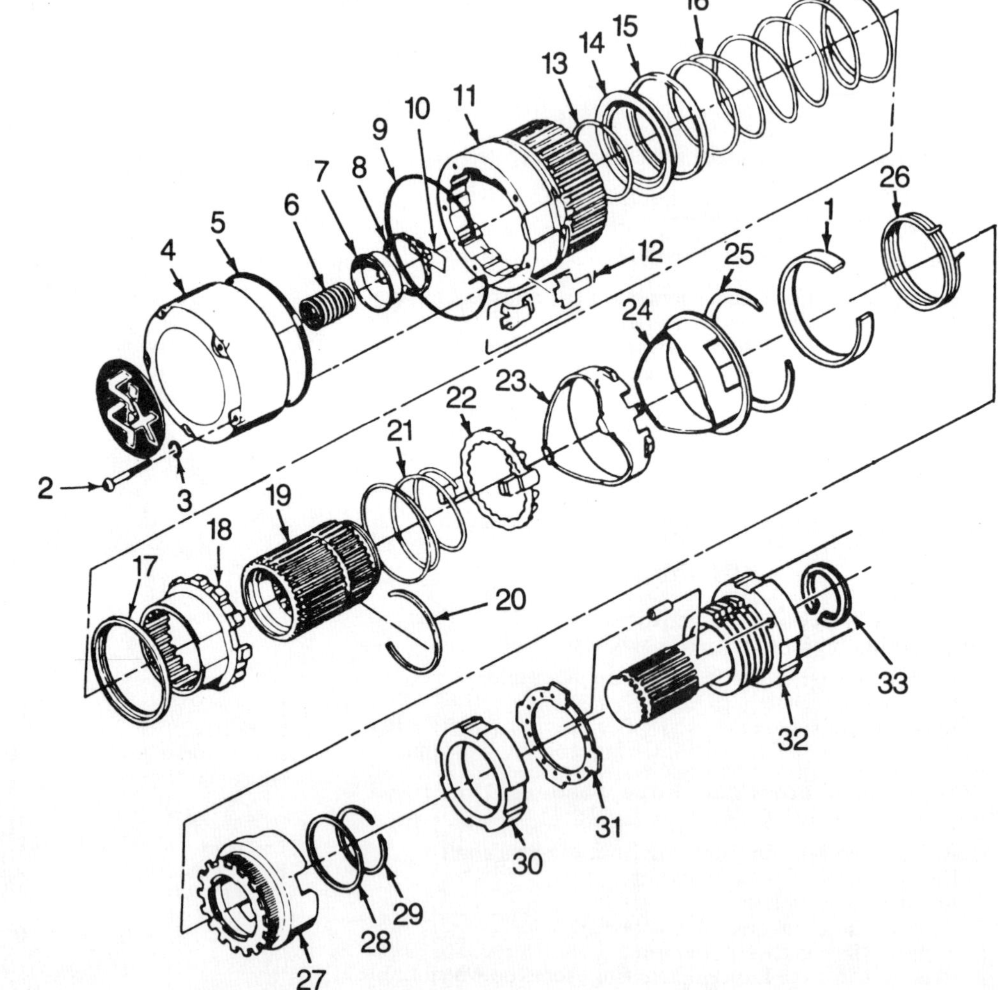

Automatic locking hub

3. Remove the bearing race, bearing and retainer.
4. Remove the keeper from the outer clutch housing.
5. Remove the large snapring to release the locking unit. The snapring is removed by squeezing the ears of the snapring with needle-nose pliers.
6. Remove the locking unit from the hub. You can make this job easier by threading 2 hub cap screws into the outer clutch housing and hold these to pull out the unit.

To install:

7. Wipe clean all parts and check for wear or damage.
8. Coat all parts with the same wheel bearing grease you've used on the bearings.
9. Position the locking unit in the hub and install the large snapring. Pull outward on the unit to make sure the snapring is fully seated in its groove.
10. Install the keepers.
11. Install the bearing retainer, bearing and race. Make sure that the bearing is fully pack with grease.
12. Coat the hub cap O-ring with wheel bearing grease and install the hub cap.
13. Install the capscrews and washers. Torque the screws to 45 inch lbs.

Wheel Bearings

NOTE: Sodium-based grease is not compatible with lithium-based grease. Read the package labels and be careful not to mix the two types. If there is any doubt as to the type of grease used, completely clean the old grease from the bearing and hub before replacing.

Before handling the bearings, there are a few things that you should remember to do and not to do.

Remember to DO the following:

- Remove all outside dirt from the housing before exposing the bearing.
- Treat a used bearing as gently as you would a new one.
- Work with clean tools in clean surroundings.
- Use clean, dry canvas gloves, or at least clean, dry hands.
- Clean solvents and flushing fluids are a must.
- Use clean paper when laying out the bearings to dry.
- Protect disassembled bearings from rust and dirt. Cover them up.
- Use clean rags to wipe bearings.
- Keep the bearings in oil-proof paper when they are to be stored or are not in use.
- Clean the inside of the housing before replacing the bearing.

Do NOT do the following:

- Don't work in dirty surroundings.
- Don't use dirty, chipped or damaged tools.
- Try not to work on wooden work benches or use wooden mallets.
- Don't handle bearings with dirty or moist hands.
- Do not use gasoline for cleaning. Use a safe solvent.
- Do not spin-dry bearings with compressed air. They will be damaged.
- Do not spin dirty bearings.
- Avoid using cotton waste or dirty cloths to wipe bearings.
- Try not to scratch or nick bearing surfaces.
- Do not allow the bearing to come in contact with dirt or rust at any time.

REMOVAL

NOTE: Before starting:
a. You'll need a special wheel bearing nut socket for your ½ inch drive ratchet. These sockets are available through auto parts stores and catalogs. You can't do this job properly without it!
b. You'll need a ½ inch drive torque wrench.
c. Have a clean container, like a shoe box, for the parts as you remove them.
d. Have PLENTY of paper towels handy.

1. Raise and support the front end on jackstands.
2. Remove the wheels.
3. Remove the hubs. See the procedures above.
4. Wipe the inside of the hub to remove as much grease as possible.
5. Using your bearing nut socket, remove the locknut from the spindle.
6. With the locknut off you'll be able to see the locking ring on the adjusting nut. Remove the locking ring. A tool such as a dental pick will make this easier.
7. Using the special socket, remove the bearing adjusting nut.

NOTE: You'll notice that the adjusting nut and the locknut are almost identical. The difference is, the adjusting nut has a small pin on one side which indexes with a hole in the locking ring. DO NOT CONFUSE THE TWO NUTS!

8. Dismount the brake caliper and suspend it out of the way, without disconnecting the brake line. See Section 9.
9. Pull the hub off of the spindle. The outer bearing will tend to fall out as soon as it clears the spindle, so have a hand ready to catch it.

DISASSEMBLY

1. If you are going to reuse the outer bearing, place it on a clean surface.
2. Position the hub, face up, on 2 wood blocks placed under opposite sides of the rotor. Have a paper towel positioned under the hub.
3. Using a hardened wood dowel or a hammer handle, drive out the inner bearing and seal. If your are going to reuse the inner bearing, move it to a clean area. Discard the seal.
4. If the bearings are being replaced, you'll have to replace the races. The races are pressed into the hub, but you can drive them out.

With the hub in position on the blocks, use a long drift and hammer evenly around the outside diameter of the inner bearing race until it is free. Discard the race.

Turn the hub over and repeat this procedure for the outer bearing race.

CLEANING AND INSPECTION

1. If you intend to reuse the bearings, wash them in a non-flammable solvent and let them air-dry. Never use compressed air to spin-dry the bearings!
2. If either bearing shows any sign of damage, rust, heat blueing or excessive looseness, both bearings in that hub must be replaced as a set. If bearings are replaced, the races MUST be replaced also!

NOTE: If the bearings show signs of heat blueing, wipe the spindle clean and check for heat blueing on the spindle surface. If the spindle shows large areas of heat blueing, it should be replaced.

3. If you intend to reuse the bearings, wash out the hub with solvent and wipe it clean. Check the races. If they show signs of wear, pitting, cracking, rusting or heat blueing, they, along with the bearings, must be replaced.

PACKING, INSTALLATION AND ADJUSTMENT

1. If new races are being installed, coat the race and its bore

in the hub with high temperature wheel bearing grease.

2. Position the race in the bore and start gently tapping it into place. There are drivers made for this purpose, but you can do it with a blunt rift and hammer. Just tap evenly around the race as you drive it into place so that it doesn't cock in the bore. Drive the race in until it is fully seated against the shoulder in the bore. You can tell that it's fully seated in 2 ways:

a. Your hammer blows will sound differently when the race seats against the shoulder.

b. The grease you applied to the bore will be squeezed out below the race as the race seats against the shoulder.

Either race can be installed first.

3. Pack the bearings thoroughly with high temperature wheel bearing grease. An inexpensive wheel bearing packing tool is available at most auto parts stores. The tool has a grease fitting which utilizes a grease gun and completely packs the bearing. You can, however, pack a bearing reasonably well without the tool:

a. Open the container of grease.

b. Force the bearing down into the container, first on one side, then the other, until grease squeezes out among the rollers.

c. Place a large blob of grease in the palm of one hand and force the bearing into the grease to squeeze out any air cavities among the rollers. When you're satisfied that each bearing is *completely* packed, place them on a clean paper towel, in a clean area, and cover them with another clean paper towel.

4. Pack the area of the hub, between the races, with wheel bearing grease.

5. Place the inner bearing in its race and position a new seal in the hub bore. Gentlty tap around the outer diameter of the seal with a plastic mallet until the seal is flush with the end of the bore.

6. Carefully place the hub assembly on the spindle. Take care to avoid damaging the seal on the spindle threads. Make sure the hub is all the way on the spindle.

7. Place the outer bearing on the spindle and slide it into place in its race.

8. Thread the adjusting nut on the spindle until it contacts the outer bearing.

WARNING: Make sure you are using the adjusting nut. Remember, it has a small pin on one side. That pin must face outwards, towards you!

9. Using the special socket and the torque wrench:

a. Tighten the adjusting nut to 50 ft. lbs. while rotating the hub.

b. Back off the adjusting nut until it is loose.

c. While rotating the hub, tighten the adjusting nut to 35 ft. lbs. for automatic locking hubs or 50 ft. lbs. for manual locking hubs.

d. Back off the adjusting nut ¼ to ⅜ of a turn for automatic hubs or ⅙ to ¼ turn for manual hubs.

10. Coat the locking ring with wheel bearing grease. Place the locking rin on the spindle. There is a tab on the inner diameter of the ring which must fit in the slot on the top of the spindle. Slide the locking ring in until it contacts the adjusting nut. The pin on the adjusting nut must enter one of the holes in the locking ring. You can tell that the locking ring is seated properly when you see the grease on the ring get pushed out of one of the holes by the pin, *and* the ring does not rock from side-to-side when you press on either side with your finger.

If the locking ring and pin don't index, take note of how far off they are, pull the ring off the spindle and turn the nut, either by hand or with the socket, just enough for a goo fit. Try the locking ring again.

11. When the locking ring engages the adjusting nut pin properly, your bearing adjustment is set. Thread the locknut onto the spindle until it contacts the locking ring.

12. Tighten the locknut to *at least* 160 ft. lbs. This locknut en-

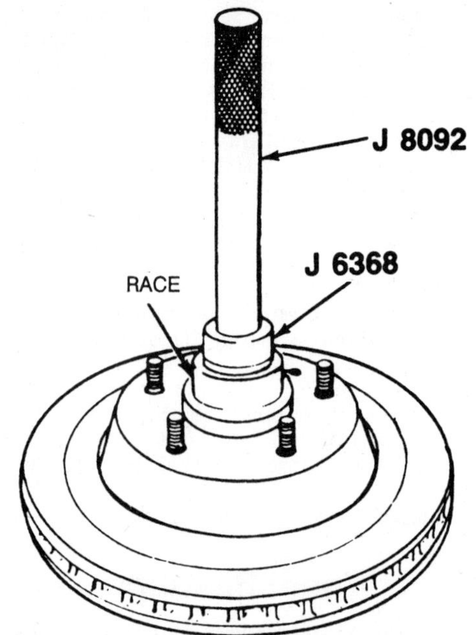

Installing the outer wheel bearing race — V series

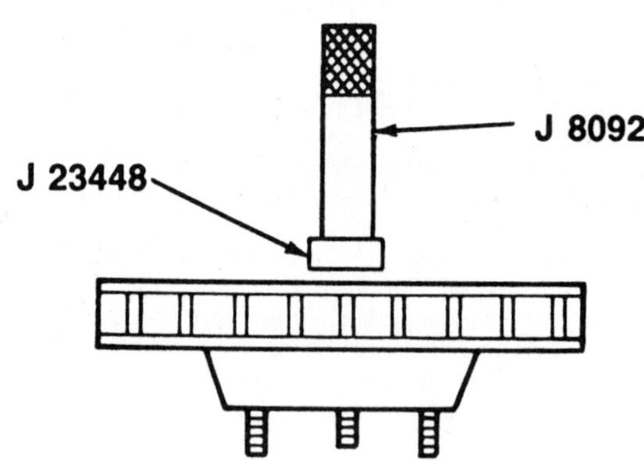

Installing the inner wheel bearing race — V series

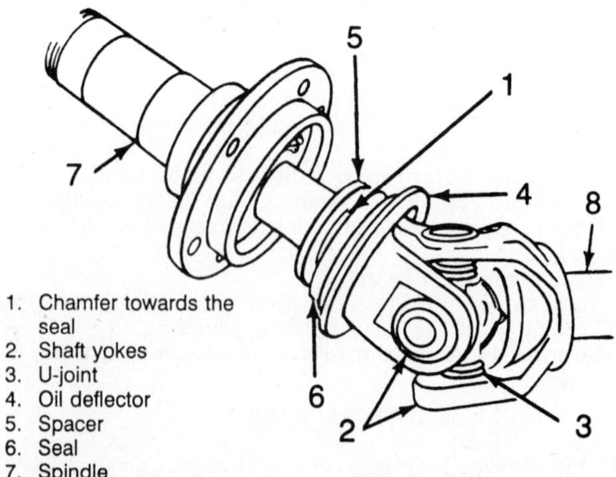

Axle shaft assembly

sures that the locking ring and adjusting nut don't move. Overtightening the locknut has no effect on the bearing adjustment.

13. Install the locking hub.
14. Install the caliper. See Section 9.
15. Install the wheel.

Axle Shaft

REMOVAL AND INSTALLATION

All Series

1. Raise and support the front end on jackstands.
2. Remove the wheel.
3. Remove the locking hub. See the procedures above.
4. Remove the hub and bearing assembly. See the procedures above.
5. Remove the nuts and remove the caliper mounting bracket and splash shield.
6. Tap the end of the spindle with a plastic mallet to break it loose from the knuckle. If tapping won't break it loose, you'll have to do the following:
   a. Thread the bearing locknut part way onto the spindle.
   b. Position a 2- or 3-jawed pull with the jaws grabbing the locknut and the screw bearing in the end of the axle shaft.
   c. Tighten the puller until the spindle breaks free. It will be very helpful to spray Liquid Wrench®, WD-40® or similar solvent around the spindle mating area and around the bolt holes. As the puller is tightened, tap the spindle with the plastic mallet. This often helps break the spindle loose.
7. Pull out the axle shaft assembly.

To install:

8. Place the spacer and a new seal on the axle shaft.

NOTE: The spacer's chamfer points towards the oil deflector.

9. Pack the spindle bearing with wheel bearing grease.
10. Slide the axle shaft into the housing. When installing the axle shaft, turn the shaft slowly to align the splines with the differential.
11. Place the spindle on the knuckle. Be sure the seal and oil deflector are in place.
12. Install the caliper bracket and splash shield.
13. Using new washers, install the nuts and torque them to 65 ft. lbs.
14. Install the hub and rotor assembly. Adjust the wheel bearings.
15. Install the locking hubs.
16. Install the caliper. See Section 9.
17. Install the wheel.

AXLE SHAFT U-JOINT OVERHAUL

1. Remove the axle shaft.
2. Squeeze the ends of the trunnion bearings in a vise to relieve the load on the snaprings. Remove the snaprings.
3. Support the yoke in a vise and drive on one end of the trunnion bearing with a brass drift enough to drive the opposite bearing from the yoke.
4. Support the other side of the yoke and drive the other bearing out.
5. Remove the trunnion.
6. Clean and check all parts. You can buy U-joint repair kits to replace all the worn parts.
7. Lubricate the bearings with wheel bearing grease.
8. Replace the trunnion and press the bearings into the yoke and over the trunnion hubs far enough to install the lock rings.
9. Hold the trunnion in one hand and tap the yoke lightly to seat the bearings against the lock rings.
10. The axle slingers can be pressed off the shaft.

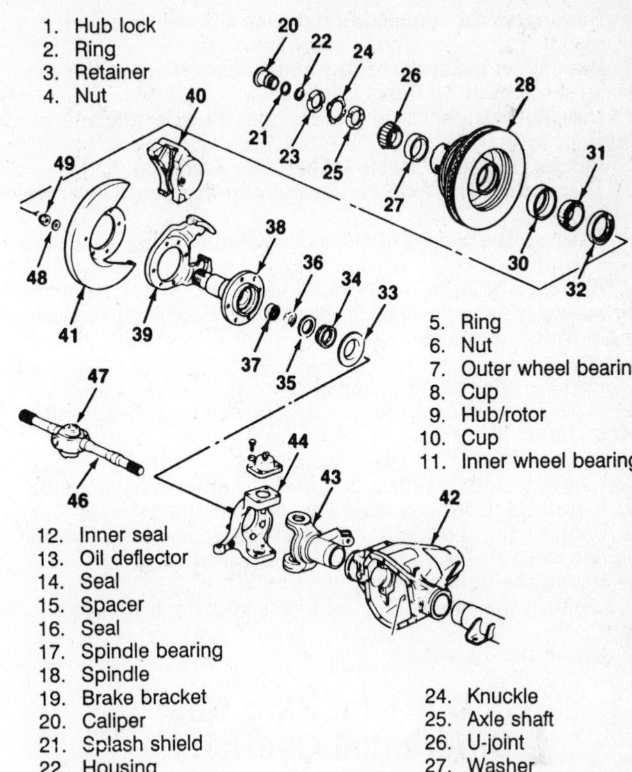

V series front axle components

NOTE: Always replace the slingers if the spindle seals are replaced.

11. Replace the shaft.

Pinion Seal

REMOVAL AND INSTALLATION

All Series

The following special tools, or their equivalents, are required for this procedure: J-8614-1, J-8614-2, J-8614-3, and J-22804.

1. Using a Holding Bar Tool J-8614-1, attached to the pinion shaft flange, remove the self locking nut and washer from the pinion shaft.
2. Install Tool J-8614-2, and 3 into the holding bar and remove the flange from the drive pinion. Remove the drive pinion from the carrier.
3. With a long drift, tap on the inner race of the outer pinion bearing to remove the seal.
4. Install the oil seal, gasket and using Tool J-22804 install the oil seal.
5. Install the flange, washer and nut and torque the nut to 270 ft. lbs. for the GMC axle; 255 ft. lbs. for the Dana axle

Axle Housing

REMOVAL AND INSTALLATION

All Series

1. Raise and support the vehicle safely.
2. Matchmark and remove the driveshaft.

3. Disconnect the connecting rod from the steering arm. See Section 8.
4. Disconnect the brake caliper and position it out of the way, without disconnecting the brake line.
5. Disconnect the shock absorbers from the axle brackets. See Section 8.
6. Remove the front stabilizer bar. See Section 8.
7. Disconnect the axle vent tube clip at the differential housing.
8. Take up the weight of the axle assembly using a suitable jack.
9. Remove the nuts, washers, U-bolts and plates from the axle and separate the axle from the springs. Remove the axle assembly from the vehicle.

To install:

10. Position the axle under the truck.
11. Install the plates, U-bolts, washers, and nuts. Tighten the nuts to 150 ft. lbs.
12. Remove the jack.
13. Connect the axle vent tube clip at the differential housing.
14. Install the front stabilizer bar. See Section 8.
15. Connect the shock absorbers at the axle brackets. Torque the bolts to 65 ft. lbs.; 88 ft. lbs. with quad shocks.
16. Install the brake caliper
17. Connect the connecting rod at the steering arm. See Section 8.
18. Install the driveshaft.

GMC 8½ in. Ring Gear Differential Overhaul

DISASSEMBLY

Differential Case

1. Remove the inspection cover from the axle housing and drain the gear lubricant into a pan.
2. Remove the screw or pin that holds the pinion shaft in place and remove the shaft.
3. Push the axle shaft(s) in a little and remove the C-locks from the ends of the shafts. Remove the axle shafts from the housing.
4. Measure and record the backlash; this will allow the old gears to be reassembled at the same amount of lash to avoid changing the gear tooth pattern. It also helps to indicate if there is gear or bearing wear and if there is any error in the original backlash setting.
5. Remove the differential pinions, the side gears and thrust washers from the case; be sure to mark the pinions and side gears so they may be reassembled in their original position.
6. Mark the bearing caps and housing and loosen the retaining bolts. Tap the caps lightly to loosen them. When the caps are loose, remove the bolts and reinstall them, just a few turns; this will keep the case from falling out of the housing when it is pried loose.
7. Using a pry bar, carefully, pry the case assembly loose; be careful not to damage the gasket surface on the housing when prying. The case assembly may suddenly come free if the bearings were preloaded, so pry very slowly.
8. When the case assembly is loose, remove the bearing cap bolts and the caps. Place the caps so they may be reinstalled in the same position. Place any shims that were removed with the cap.
9. Using a bearing puller, pull the differential bearing from the case.
10. To remove the drive pinion bearing, perform the following procedures:
    a. Depending on the bearing that is being replaced, remove the front or rear bearing cup from the carrier assembly.
    b. With the pinion gear mounted in a press, press the rear

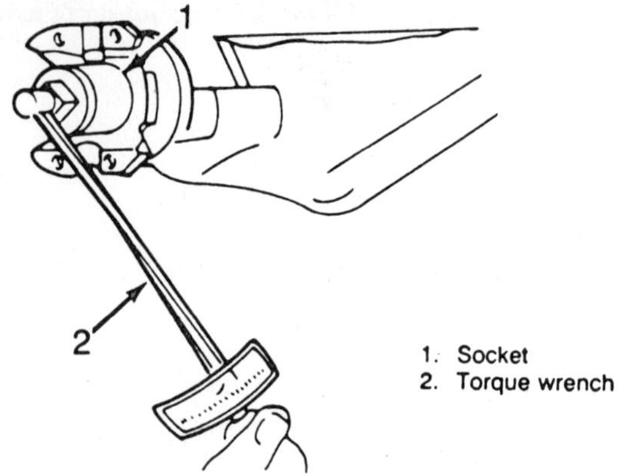

Measuring pinion rotating torque

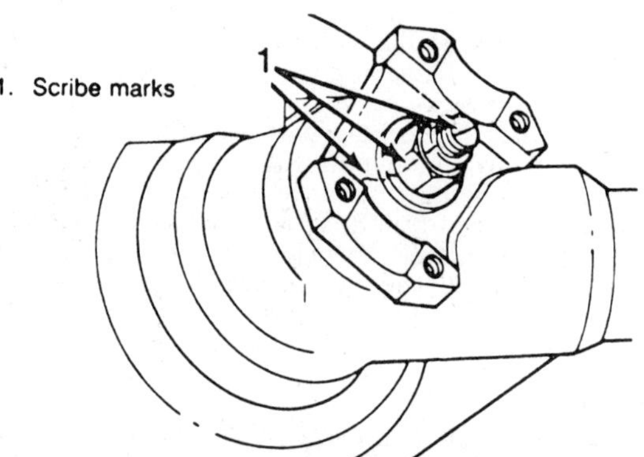

Scribed marks

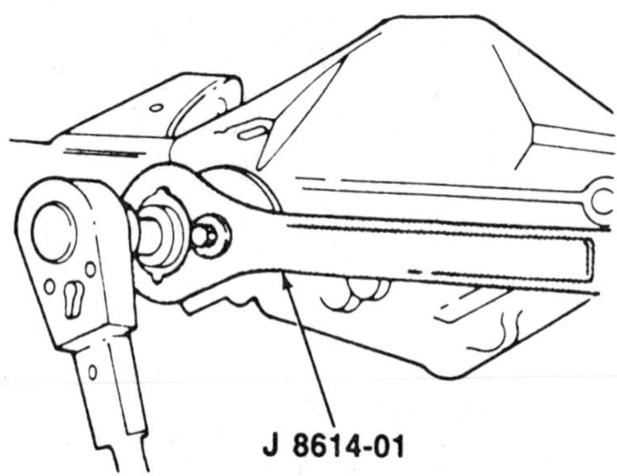

Removing or installing the pinion nut

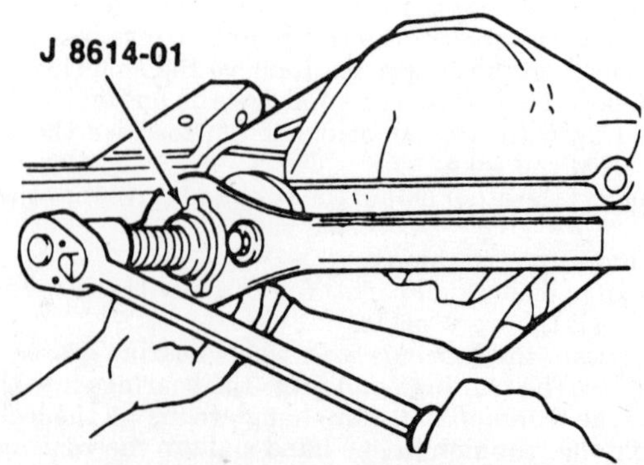

Removing the pinion flange

bearing from the pinion shaft. Be sure to record the thicknesses of the shims that were removed from between the bearing and the gear.

Drive Pinion

1. With the differential removed, check the pinion preload. Do this by checking the amount of torque needed to turn the pinion gear. For a new bearing, it should be 20–25 inch lbs. and for a used bearing it should be 10–15 inch lbs. If there is no preload reading check the pinion for looseness. If there is any looseness, replace the bearing.
2. Using a holder assembly to secure the flange, remove the flange nut and washer.
3. Using a puller, press the flange from the pinion splines.
4. Thread the pinion nut, a few turns, onto the pinion shaft. Using a brass drift and hammer, lightly tap the end of the pinion shaft to remove the pinion from the carrier; be careful not to allow the pinion to fall out of the carrier.
5. With the pinion removed from the carrier, discard the old seal pinion nut and collapsible spacer; install new ones when reassembling.

Ring Gear

1. Remove the ring gear-to-differential case bolts and tap the ring gear from the case with a soft hammer.

NOTE: Do not try to pry the ring gear off the case. This will damage the machined surfaces.

2. Clean all dirt from the case assembly and lubricate the case with gear lube.

CLEANING AND INSPECTION

1. Clean all parts in solvent and blow dry.
2. Check all of the parts for any signs of wear, chips, cracks or distortion; replace any parts that are defective.
3. Check the fit of the differential side gears in the case and the fit of the side gear and axle shaft splines.

ASSEMBLY

Drive Pinion Bearing

1. Using a bearing driver, install a new bearing cup for each one that was removed; make sure the cups are seated fully against the shoulder in the housing.
2. The pinion depth must be checked to determine the nominal setting. This allows for machining variations in the housing and enables selection of the proper shim so the pinion depth can be set for the best bear tooth contact.
3. Clean the housing and carrier assemblies to insure accurate measurement of the pinion depth.
4. Lubricate the front and rear pinion bearings with gear lubricant and install them in their races in the carrier assembly.
5. Using a pinion setting gauge, select the proper clover leaf plate and install it on the preload stud.
6. Using the proper pilot, insert the stud through the rear bearing, with the proper size pilot on the stud and through the front bearing. Install the hex nut and tighten it until it is snug.
7. Using a wrench to hold the preload stud, torque the hex nut until 20 inch lbs. of torque are required to rotate the bearings.
8. Install the side bearing discs on the ends of the arbor assembly, using the step of the disc that fits the bore of the carrier.
9. Install the arbor and plunger assembly into the carrier; make sure the side bearing discs fit properly.
10. Install the bearing caps in the carrier assembly finger tight; make sure the discs do not move.
11. Mount a dial indicator on the mounting post of the arbor

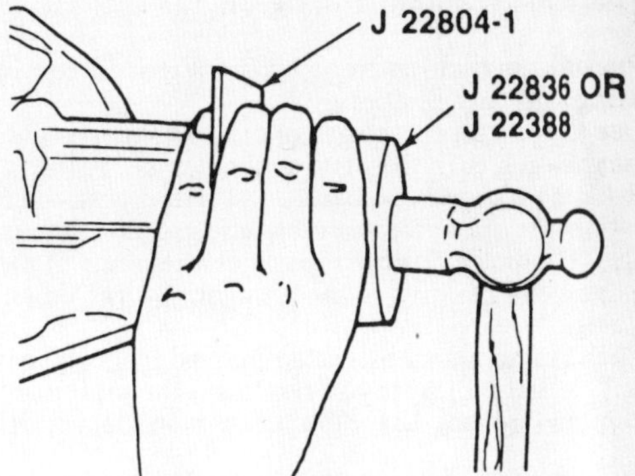

Installing the pinion seal

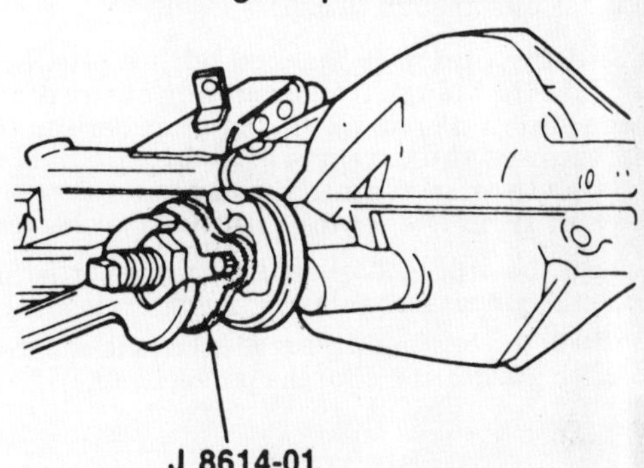

Installing the pinion flange

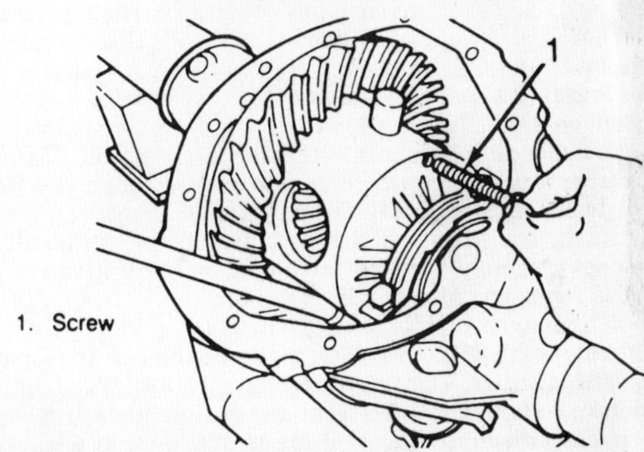

Removing the lockscrew – GMC 8½ and 9½ in. axles

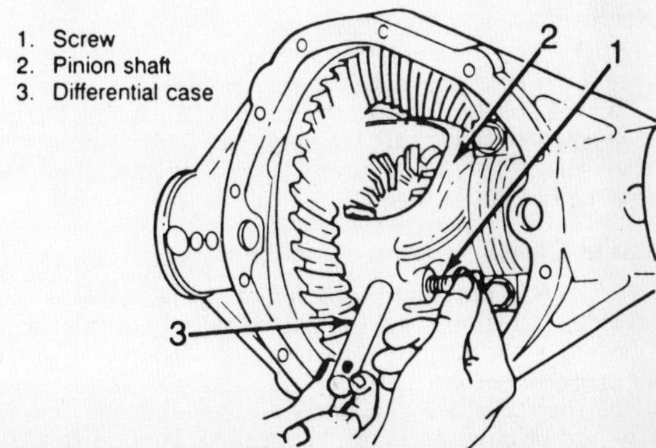

Removing or installing the differential pinion – GMC 8½ and 9½ in. axles

ntact button resting on the top surface of the

ad the dial indicator by turning it ½ revolution and it in this position.

the button on the gauge plate that corresponds to the size and turn the plate so the plunger rests on top of it.

ck the plunger rod back and forth across the top of the until the dial indicator reads the greatest amount of vari- Set the dial indicator to zero at the point of most varia- Repeat the rocking of the plunger several times to check setting.

. Turn the plunger until it is removed from the gauge plate tton. The dial indicator will now read the pinion shim thick- ess required to set the nominal pinion depth; record the reading.

17. Check for the pinion code number, located on the rear face of the pinion gear; the number will indicate the necessary change to the pinion shim thickness.

NOTE: If the pinion is marked with a plus (+) and a number, add that much to the reading of the dial indicator. If the pinion has no mark, use the reading from the dial indicator as the correct shim thickness. If the pinion is marked with a minus (−) and a number, subtract that amount from the reading on the dial indicator.

18. Remove the depth gauge tools from the carrier assembly and install the proper size shim on the pinion gear.

19. Lubricate the bearing with gear lubricant and use a shop press to press the bearing onto the pinion shaft.

Drive Pinion

1. Lubricate the front bearing and install it into the front cup.
2. Using a seal driver and a gauge plate, drive the pinion seal into the bore until the gauge plate is flush with the shoulder of the carrier.
3. Lubricate the seal lips and install a new bearing spacer on the pinion gear.
4. Install the pinion gear into the carrier assembly. Using a large washer and nut, draw the pinion gear through the front bearing, far enough to install the companion flange.
5. With the companion flange installed on the pinion shaft, use a holder assembly and tighten the pinion nut until all of the endplay is removed from the drive pinion.
6. When no more endplay exists, check the preload; the preload should be 20–25 inch lbs. on new bearings or 10–15 inch lbs. on used bearings. Tighten the pinion nut until these figures are reached; do not over tighten the pinion, for this will collapse the spacer too much and make it necessary to replace it.
7. Turn the pinion gear several times to make sure the bearings are seated and recheck the preload.

Ring Gear

1. Align the ring gear bolt holes with the carrier holes and lightly press the ring gear onto the case assembly.
2. Install the bolts and tighten them all evenly, using a criss-cross pattern to avoid cocking the ring gear.
3. When the ring gear is firmly seated against the case, torque the bolts to 60 ft. lbs.

Differential Case

1. Place the new differential bearing onto the case hub with the thick side of the inner race toward the case. Using a bearing driver, drive the bearing onto the case until it seats against the shoulder on the case.
2. Install the thrust washers and side gears into the case assembly. If the original parts are being used, be sure to place them in their original position.
3. Place the pinions in the case so they are 180 degrees apart

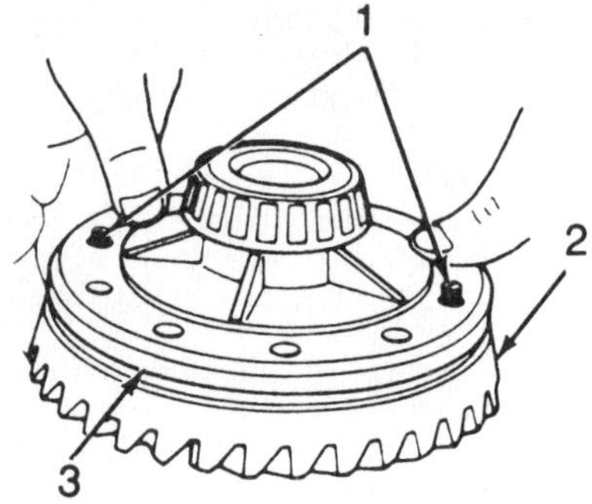

Aligning the ring gear studs – GMC 8½ axles

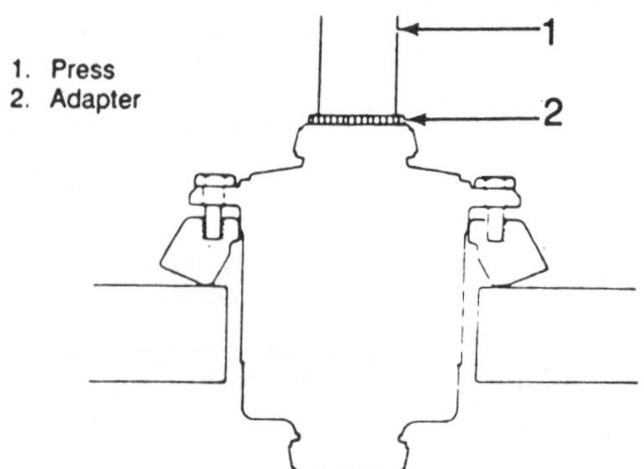

Installing the ring gear on the case – GMC 8½in. axles

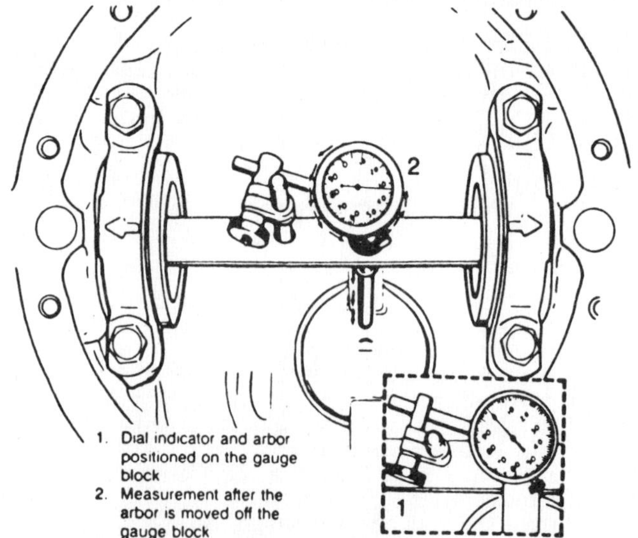

Checking pinion depth – GMC 8½ in. axles

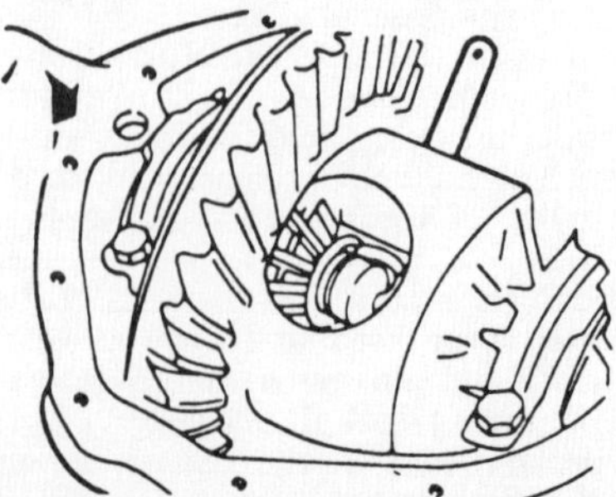

Pushing the axle shaft inward – GMC 8½ in. axles

as they engage the side gears.

4. Turn the pinion gears so the case holes align with the gear holes. When the holes are aligned, install the pinion shaft and lock screw; do not tighten the lock screw too tightly at this time.

5. Check the bearings, bearing cups, cup seat and carrier caps to make sure they are in good condition.

6. Lubricate the bearings with gear lube. Install the cups on the bearings and the differential assembly into the carrier. Support the carrier assembly to keep it from falling.

7. Install a support strap on the left side bearing and tighten the bearing bolts to an even, snug fit.

8. With the ring gear tight against the pinion gear, insert a gauge tool between the left side bearing cup and the carrier housing.

9. While lightly shaking the tool back and forth, turn the adjusting wheel until a slight drag is felt and tighten the locknut.

10. Between the right side bearing and carrier, install a 0.170 in. thick service spacer, a service shim and a feeler gauge. The feeler gauge must be thick enough so a light drag is felt when it is moved between the carrier and the shim.

11. Add the total of the service spacer, service shim and the feeler gauge. Remove the gauge tool from the left side of the carrier, then, using a micrometer, measure the thickness in at least 3 places. Average the readings and record the result.

12. Refer to the chart to determine the proper thickness of the shim packs.

13. Install the left side shim first, then, the right side shim between the bearing cup and spacer. Position the shim so the chamfered side is facing outward or next to the spacer.

NOTE: If there is not enough chamfer around the outside of the shim, file or grind the chamfer a little to allow for easy installation.

14. If there is difficulty in installing the shim, partially remove the case from the carrier and slide both the shim and case back into place.

15. Install the bearing caps and torque them to 60 ft. lbs. Tighten the pinion shaft lock screw.

NOTE: The differential side bearings are now preloaded. If any adjustments are made in later procedures, make sure not to change the preload. Do not change the total thickness of the shim packs.

16. Mount a dial indicator on the carrier assembly with the indicator button perpendicular to the tooth angle and aligned with the gear rotation.

17. Measure the amount of backlash between the ring and pinion gears; it should be between 0.005–0.008 in. Take readings at 4 different spots on the gear; there should not be variations greater than 0.002 in.

18. If there are variations greater than 0.002 in. between the readings, check the runout between the case and ring gear; the gear runout should not be greater than 0.003 in. If the runout exceeds 0.003 in., check the case and ring gear for the deformation or dirt between the case and gear.

19. If the gear backlash exceeds 0.008 in., increase the thickness of the shims on the ring gear side and decrease the thickness of the shims on the opposite side, an equal amount.

20. If the backlash is less than 0.005 in., decrease the shim thickness on the ring gear side and increase the shim thickness on the opposite side an equal amount.

Gear Pattern Check

Before final assembly of the differential, a pattern check of the gear teeth must be made. This determines if the teeth of the ring and pinion gears are meshing properly, for low noise level and long life of the gear teeth. The most important thing to note is if the pattern is located centrally up and down on the face of the ring gear.

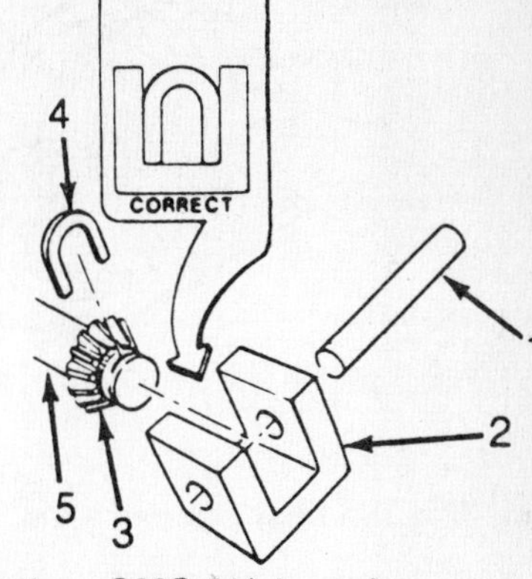

Aligning the lock – GMC 8½ in. axles

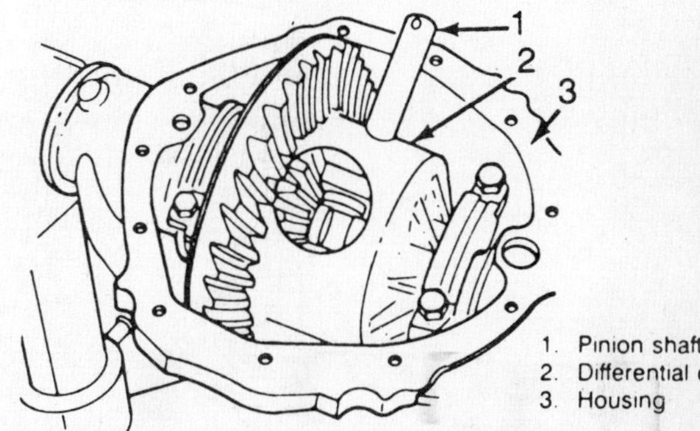

Positioning the case for best clearance – GMC 8½ in. axles

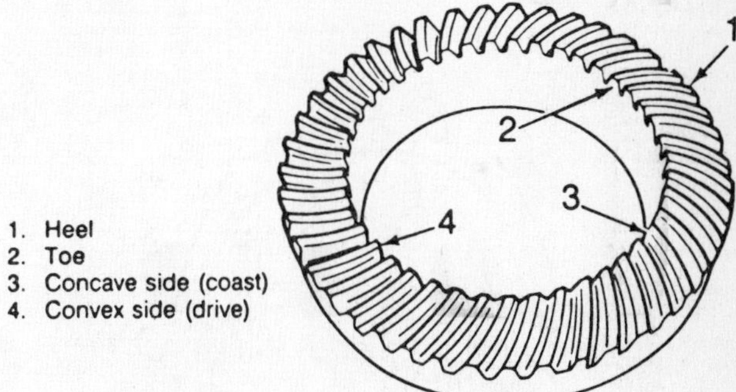

Gear tooth nomenclature – GMC 8½ axles

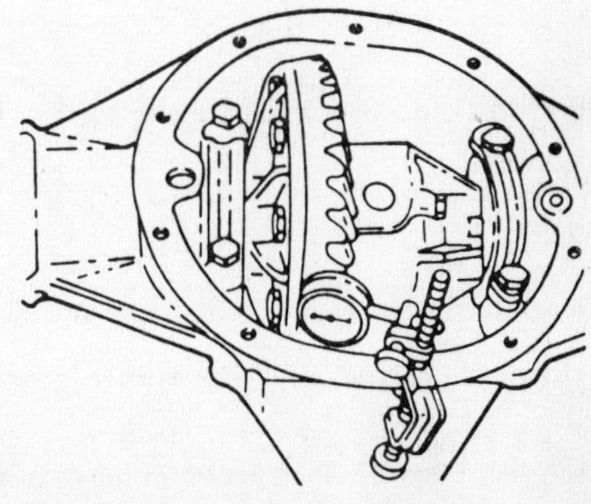

Checking ring gear backlash – GMC 8½ in. axles

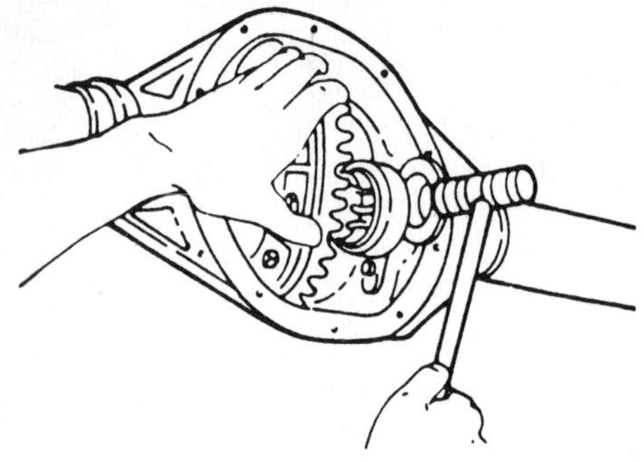

Installing the final preload shim – GMC 8½ in. axles

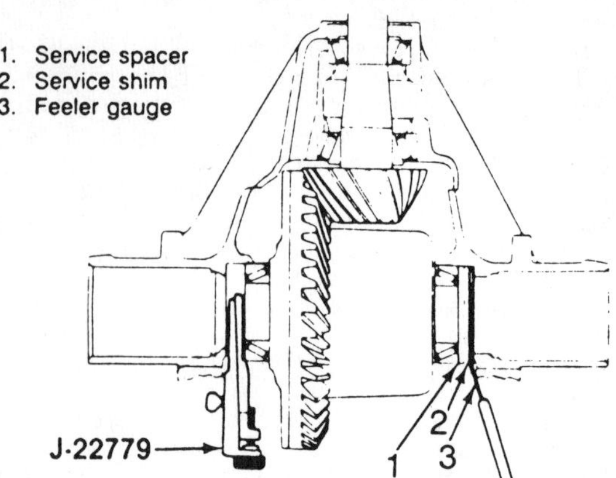

Measuring side bearing shim requirements – GMC 8½ in. axles

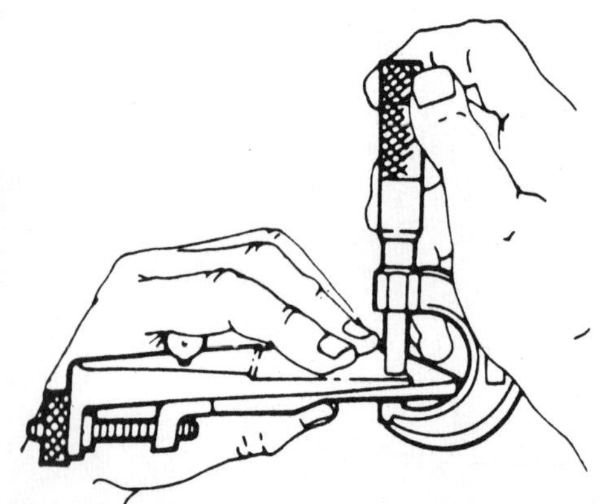

Measuring the gauge plate thickness – GMC 8½ in. axles

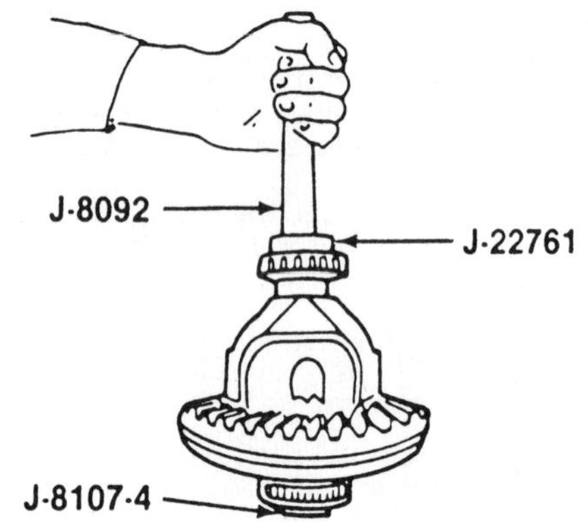

Installing the side bearing – GMC 8½ axles

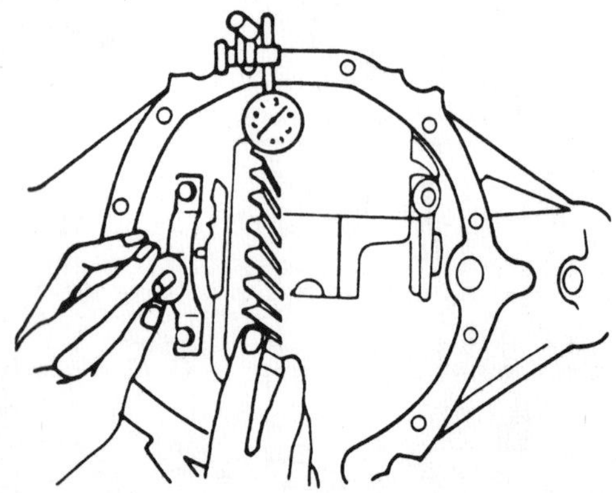

Installing the side bearing gauging tool – GMC 9½ in. axles

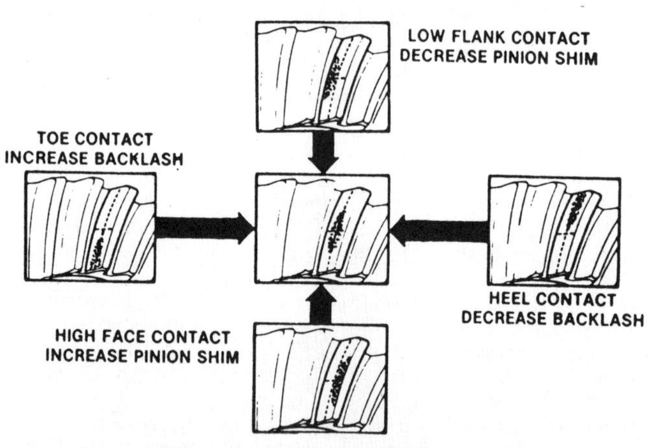

Gear tooth patterns – GMC 8½ in. axles

1. Wipe any oil from the carrier and all dirt and oil from the teeth of the ring gear.
2. Coat the teeth of the ring gear with a gear marking compound.
3. With the bearing caps torqued to 55 ft. lbs., expand the brake shoes until it takes 20–30 ft. lbs. of torque to turn the pinion gear.
4. Turn the companion flange so the ring gear makes a full rotation in 1 direction, then, turn it a full rotation in the opposite direction.
5. Check the pattern on the teeth and refer to the chart for any adjustments necessary.
6. With the gear tooth pattern checked and properly adjusted, install the axle housing cover gasket and cover and tighten securely. Refill the axle with gear lube to the correct level.
7. Road test the vehicle to check for any noise and proper operation of the rear.

Dana 60 9¾ in. Ring Gear Differential Overhaul

DISASSEMBLY

Differential Carrier

1. The axle assembly can be overhauled either in or out of the vehicle. Either way, the free-floating axle shafts must be removed.
2. Drain the lubricant and remove the rear cover and gasket.
3. Matchmark the bearing caps and the housing for reassembly in the same position. Remove the bearing caps and bolts.
4. Using a spreader tool mounted to the carrier housing, spread the housing a maximum of 0.015 in.

NOTE: Do not exceed this measurement. The housing could be permanently damaged. The use of a dial indicator is recommended to prevent over-stretching the housing.

5. Using a pry bar, remove the differential case from the housing. Remove the spreader tool from the housing.
6. Remove the differential side bearing cups and tag to identify the side, if they are to be used again.
7. Remove the differential gear pinion shaft lock pin and remove the shaft. Rotate the side and pinion gears to remove them from the carrier. Remove the thrust bearings.
8. Remove the bearing cones and rollers from the carrier, marking and noting the shim locations.
9. Remove the ring gear bolts and tap the ring gear from the carrier housing.
10. Inspect the components.

Drive Pinion

1. Remove the pinion nut and flange from the pinion gear.
2. Remove the pinion gear assembly from the housing. It may be necessary to tap the pinion from the housing with a soft faced hammer. Catch the pinion so as not to allow it to drop on the floor.
3. With a long drift, remove the inner bearing cup, pinion seal, slinger, gasket, outer pinion bearing and the shim pack. Label the shim pack for reassembly.
4. Remove the rear pinion bearing cup and shim pack from the housing. Label the shims for reassembly.
5. Remove the rear pinion bearing from the pinion gear with an arbor press and special plates.

INSPECTION

1. Clean the gears, bearings and component parts with solvent and inspect for scoring, chipping or excessive wear.
2. Inspect the flanges and splines for excessive wear.
3. Replace the necessary parts as required.

Pinion Shim Selection

Ring gears and pinions are supplied in matched sets only. The matched numbers are etched on both gears for verification. On the rear face of the pinion, a plus (+) or a minus (−) number will be etched, indicating the best running position for each particular gear set. This dimension is controlled by the shimming behind the inner bearing cup. Whenever baffles or oil slingers are used, they become part of the adjusting shim pack. An example: If a pinion is etched +3, this pinion would require 0.003 in. less shims than a pinion etched 0. This means by removing shims, the mounting distance of the pinion is increased by 0.003 in., which is just what a plus (+) etching indicates. If a pinion is etched −3, it would be necessary to add 0.003 in. more shims than would be required if the pinion was etched 0. By adding the 0.003 in. shims, the mounting distance of the pinion is decreased 0.003 in., which is just what the minus (−) etching indicates. Pinion adjusting shims are available in thicknesses of 0.003, 0.005 and 0.010 in. An example: If a new gear set is used and the old pinion reads +2 and the new pinion reads −2, add 0.004 in. shims to the original shim pack.

ASSEMBLY

Drive Pinion

1. Select the correct pinion depth shims and install in the rear pinion bearing cup bore.
2. Install the rear bearing cup in the axle housing.
3. Add or subtract an equal amount of shim thickness to or from the preload or outer shim pack, as was added or subtracted from the inner shim pack.
4. Install the front pinion bearing cup into its bore in the axle housing.
5. Press the rear pinion bearing onto the pinion gear shaft and install the pinion gear with bearing into the axle housing.
6. Install the preload shims and the front pinion bearing; do not install the oil seal at this time.
7. Install the flange with the holding bar tool attached, the washer and the nut on the pinion shaft end. Torque the nut to 255 ft. lbs.
8. Remove the holding bar from the flange and with an inch lb. torque wrench, measure the rotating torque of the pinion gear. The rotating torque should be 10–20 inch lbs. with the original bearings or 20–40 inch lbs. with new bearings. Disregard the torque reading necessary to start the shaft to turn.
9. If the preload torque is not in specifications, adjust the shim pack as required.
   a. To increase preload, decrease the thickness of the preload shim pack.
   b. To decrease preload, increase the thickness of the preload shim pack.
10. When the proper preload is obtained, remove the nut, washer and flange from the pinion shaft.
11. Install a new pinion seal into the housing and reinstall the flange, washer and nut. Using the holder tool, torque the nut to 255 ft. lbs.

Differential Carrier

1. Install the differential side gears, the differential pinion gears and new thrust washers into the differential carrier.
2. Align the pinion gear shaft holes and install the pinion shaft into the carrier. Align the lock pin hole in the shaft and carrier. Install the lock pin and peen the hole to avoid having the pin drop from the carrier.
3. Install the differential case side bearings with the proper installation tools. Do not install the shims at this time.
4. Place the carrier assembly into the axle housing with the bearing cups on the bearing cones. Install the bearing caps in their original position and tighten the bearing cap bolts enough to keep the bearing caps in place.
5. Install a dial indicator on the housing so the indicator button contacts the carrier flange. Press the differential carrier to prevent sideplay and center the dial indicator. Rotate the carrier and check the flange for run-out. If the run-out is greater than 0.002 in., the defect is probably due to the bearings or to the carrier and should be corrected.
6. Remove the assembly and install the ring gear. Torque the retaining bolts and reinstall the assembly into the housing. Install the bearing caps in their original position and tighten the cap bolts to keep the bearings caps in place.
7. Install the dial indicator and position the indicator button to contact the ring gear back surface. Rotate the assembly and the run-out should be less than 0.002 in. If over 0.002 in., remove the assembly and relocate the ring gear 180 degrees. Rein-

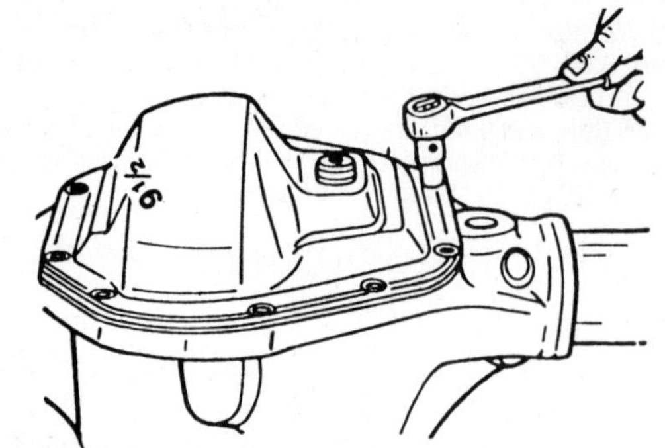

Removing the cover – Dana 9¾ in. axles

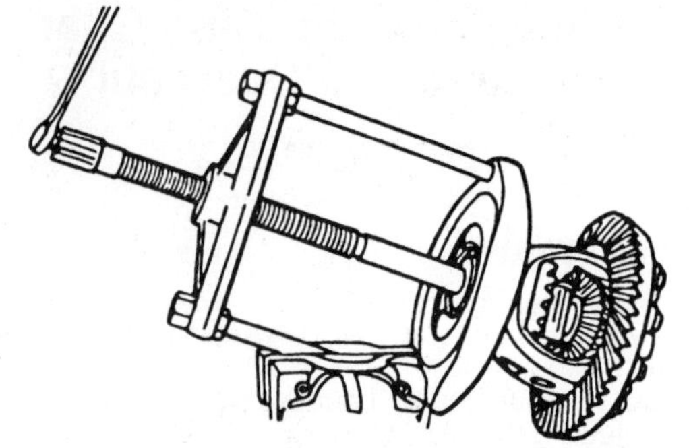

Removing the side bearings – Dana 9¾ in. axles

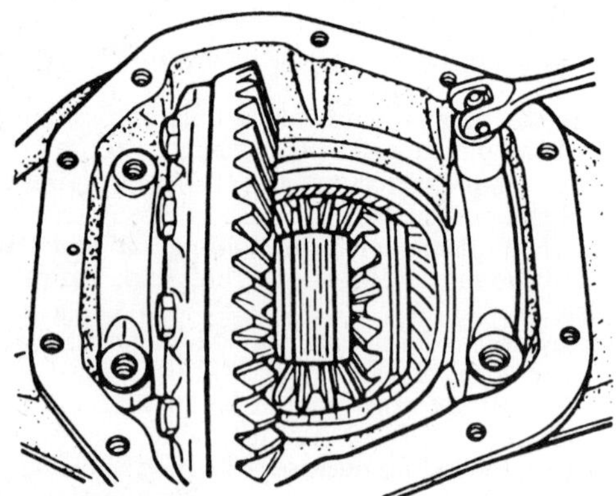

Removing the bearing cap – Dana 9¾ in. axles

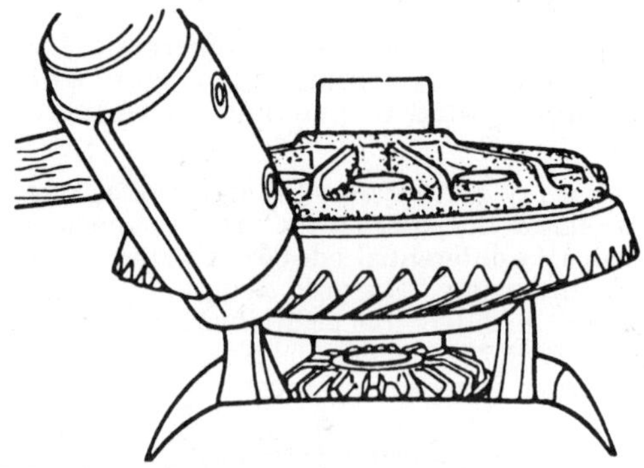

Removing the ring gear – Dana 9¾ in. and 10½ in. axles

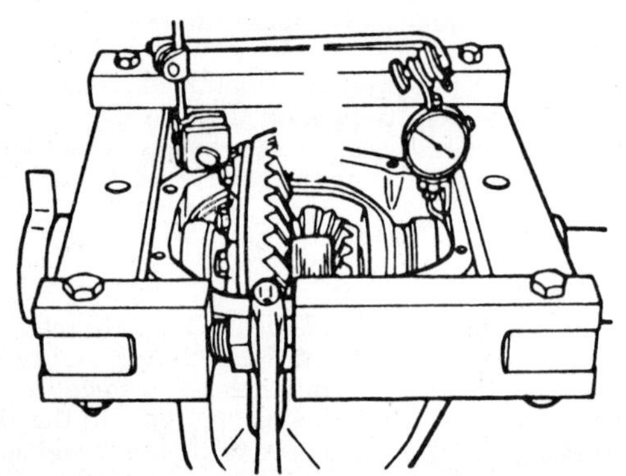

Spreading the differential case – Dana 9¾ in.axles

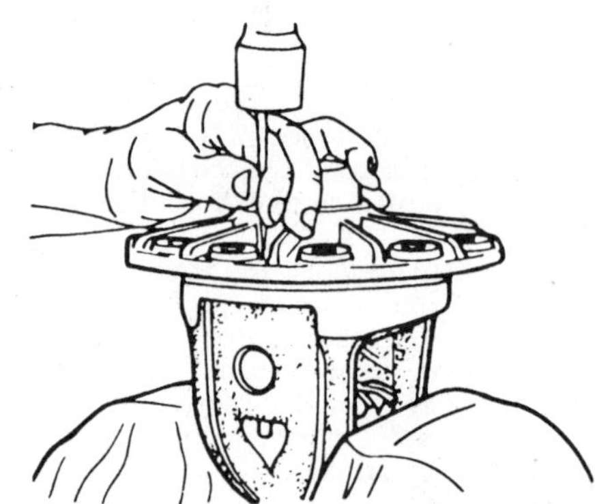

Removing the lock pin – Dana 9¾ in. axles

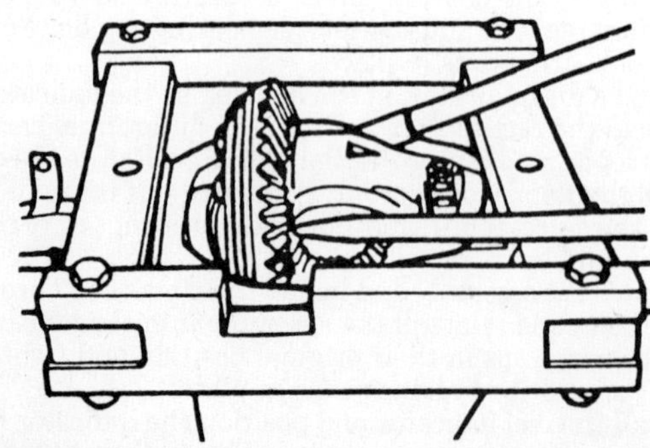

Removing the differential – Dana 9¾ in. axles

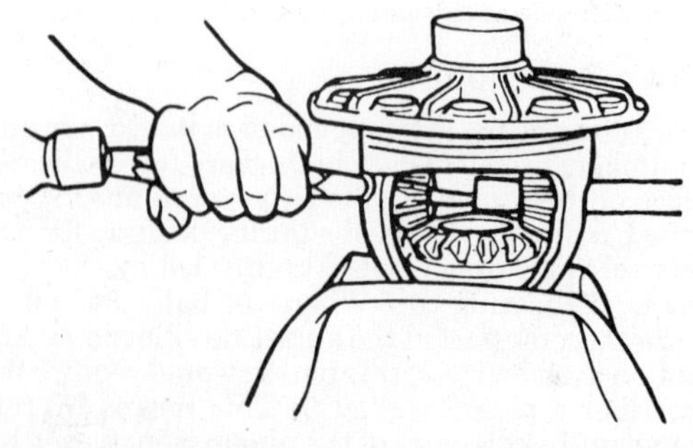

Removing the pinion shaft – Dana 9¾ in. axles

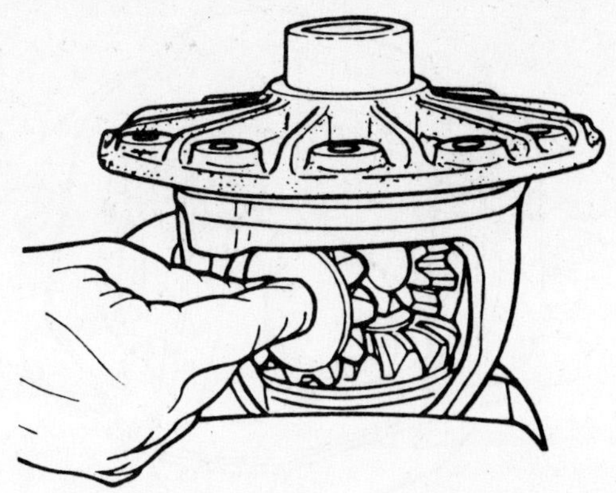
Removing the pinion gears – Dana 9¾ in. axles

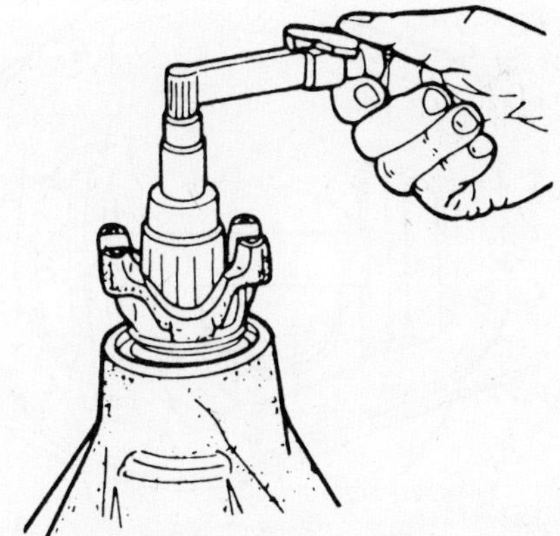
Checking the pinion preload – Dana 9¾ in. axles

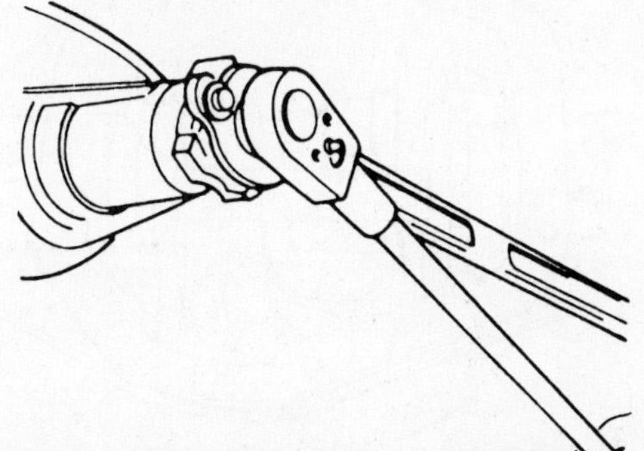
Removing the drive pinion nut – Dana 9¾ in. axles

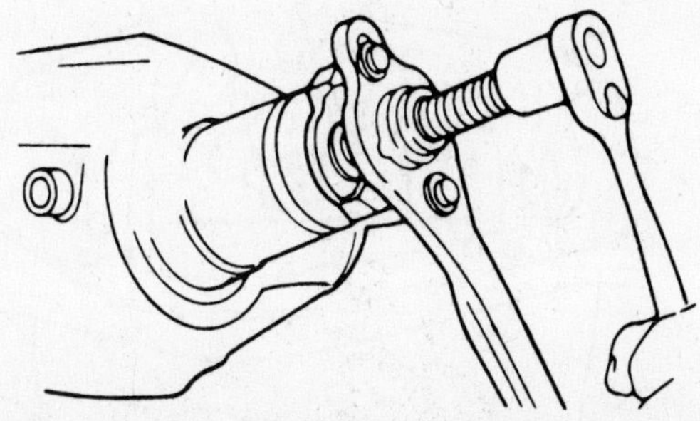
Removing the flange – Dana 9¾ in. axles

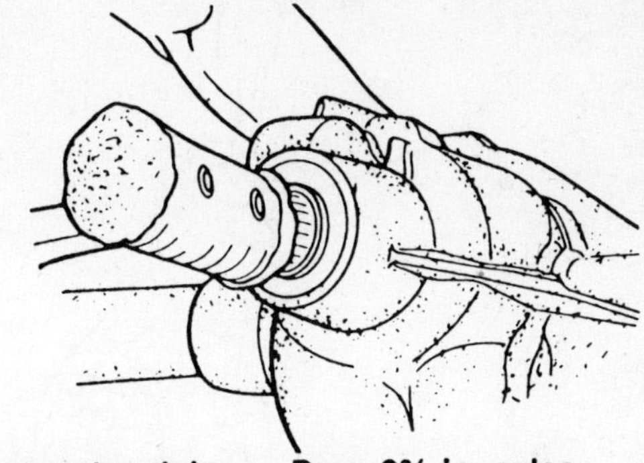
Removing the pinion – Dana 9¾ in. axles

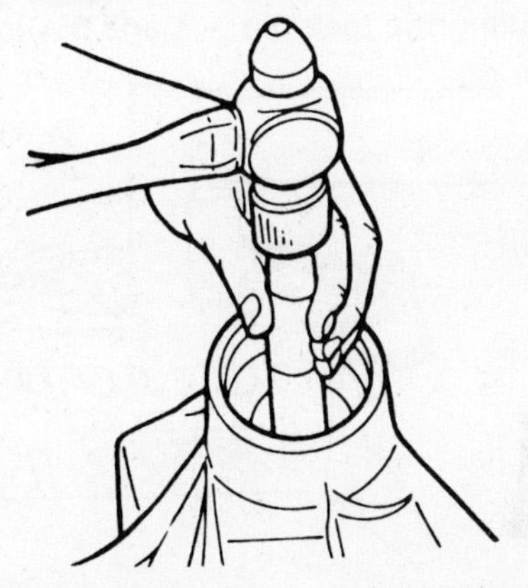
Removing the bearing cups – Dana 9¾ in. axles

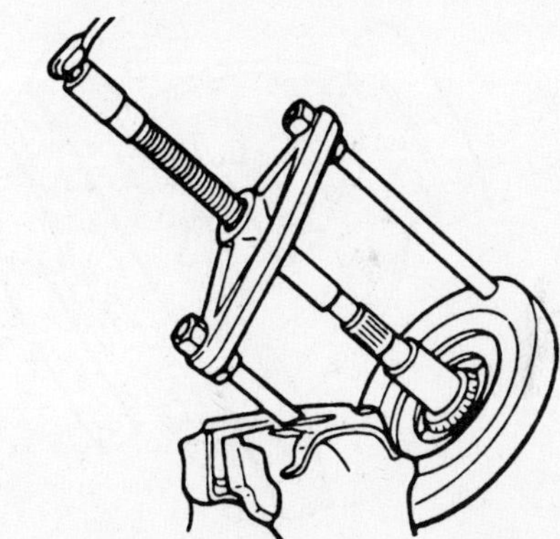
Removing the pinion inner bearing – Dana 9¾ in. axles

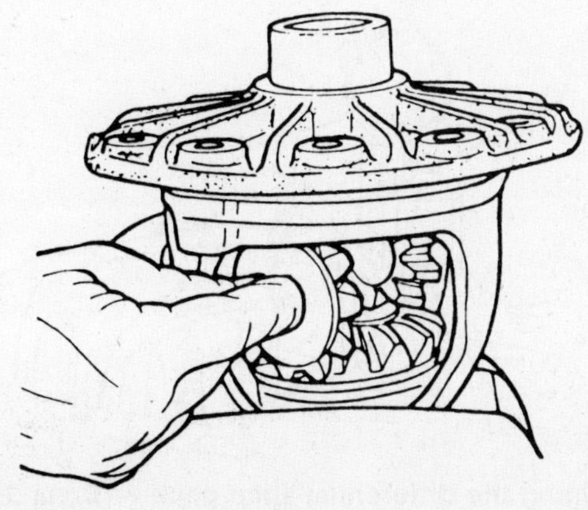
Installing the pinion gears – Dana 9¾ in. axles

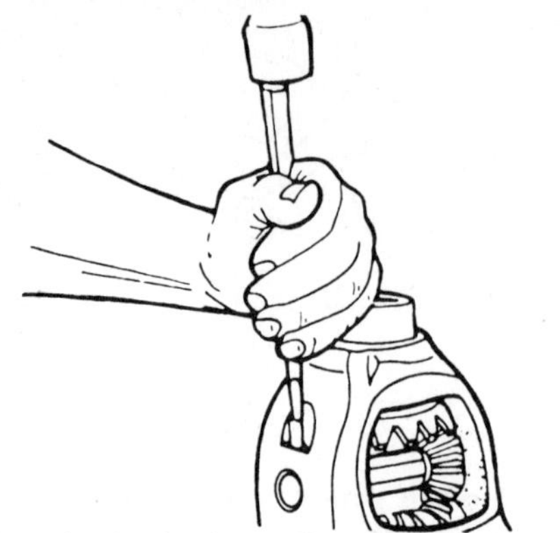
Installing the lock pin – Dana 9¾ in. axles

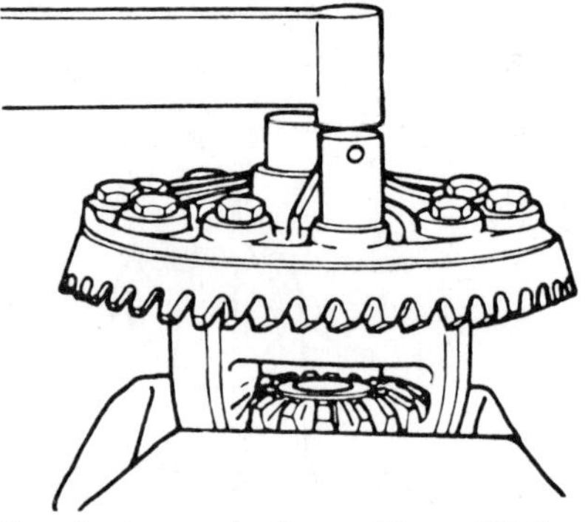
Installing the ring gear bolts – Dana 9¾ in. axles

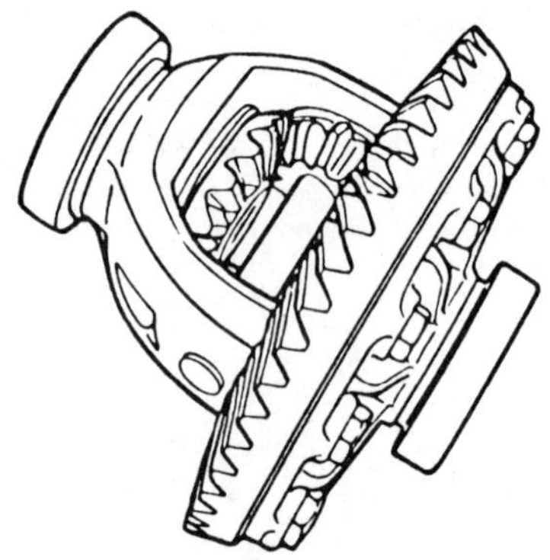
Differential with master bearings – Dana 9¾ in. axles

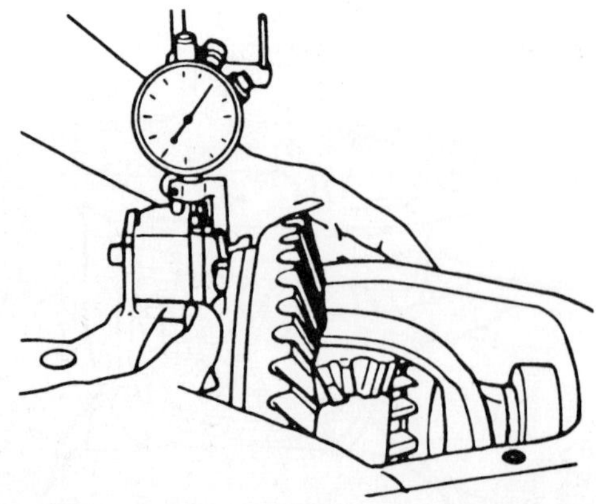
Determining the differential shim pack – Dana 9¾ in. axles

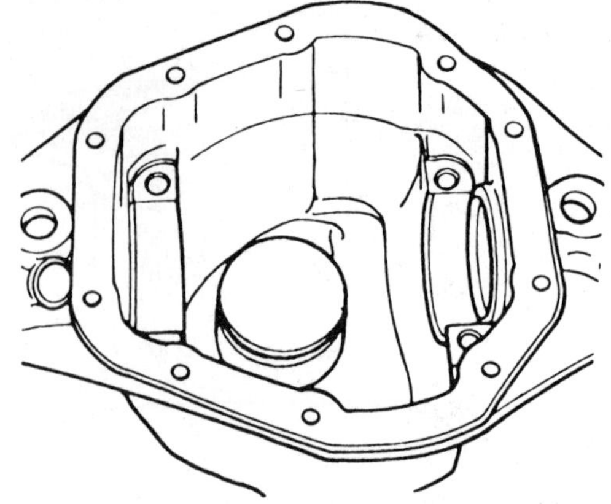
Master pinion block – Dana 9¾ in. axles

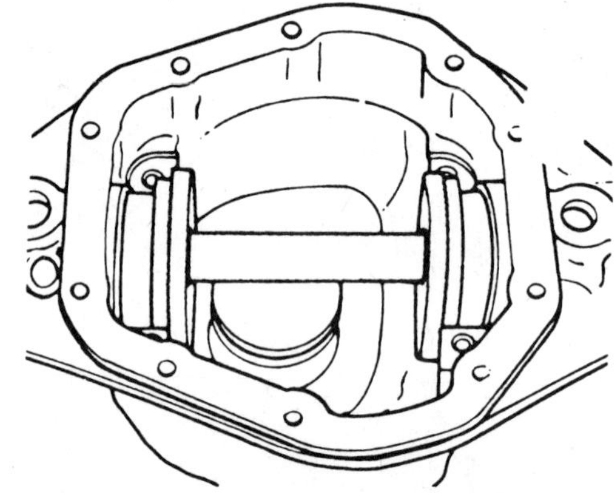
Arbor and discs – Dana 9¾ in. axles

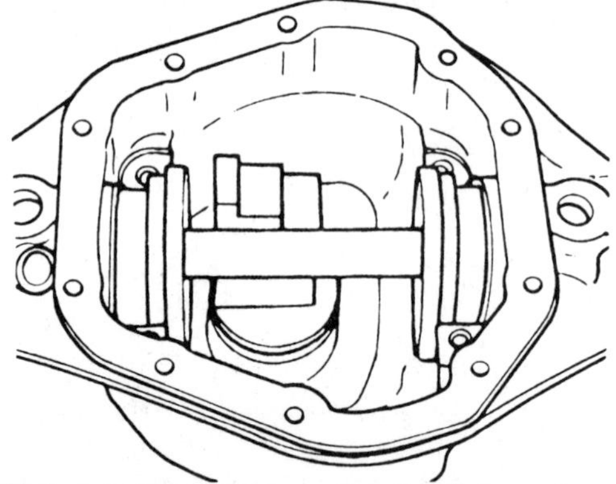
Pinion height block – Dana 9¾ in. axles

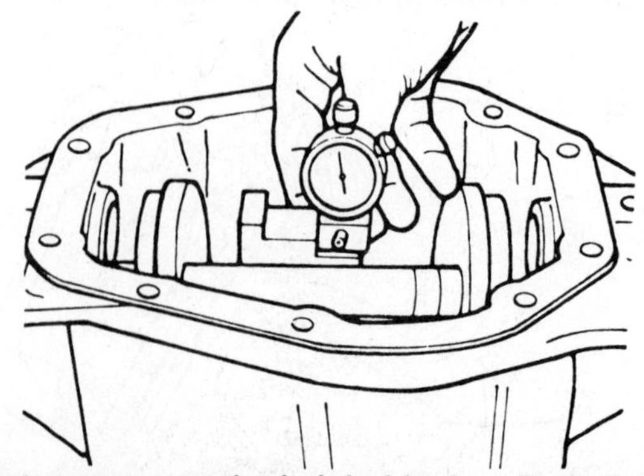
Scooter gauge on the height block – Dana 9¾ in. axles

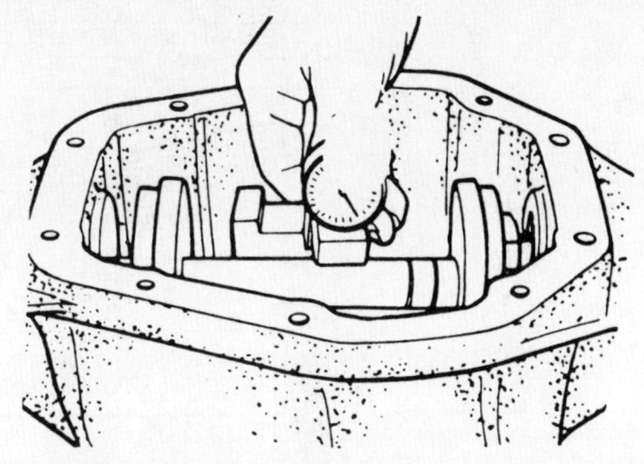
Scooter gauge on the arbor – Dana 9¾ in. axles

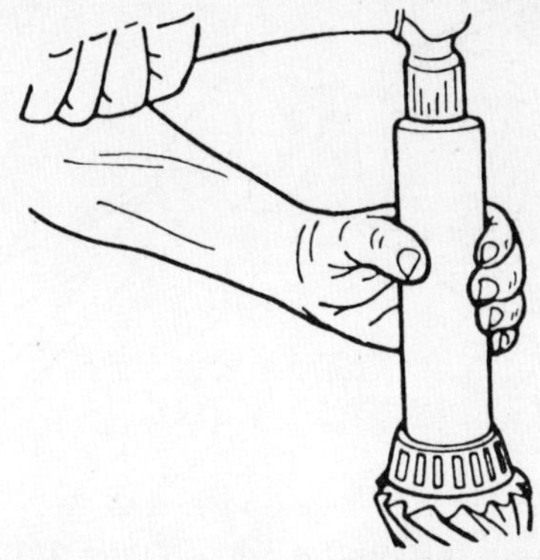
Installing the inner bearing – Dana 9¾ in. axles

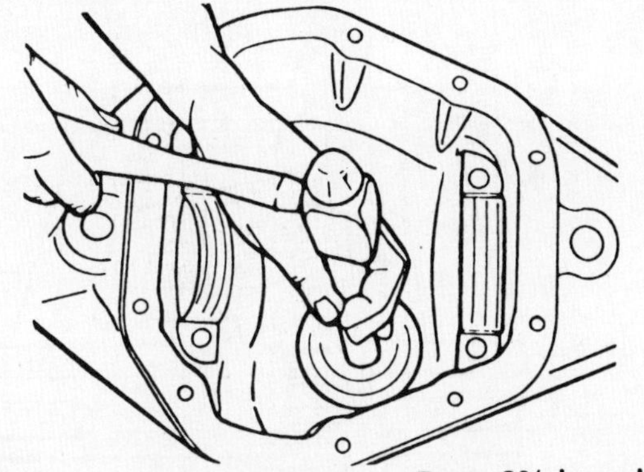
Installing the pinion inner cup – Dana 9¾ in. axles

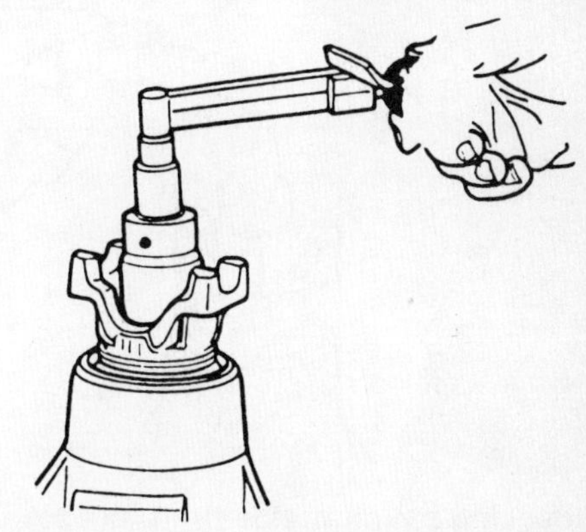
Checking the preload – Dana 9¾ in. axles

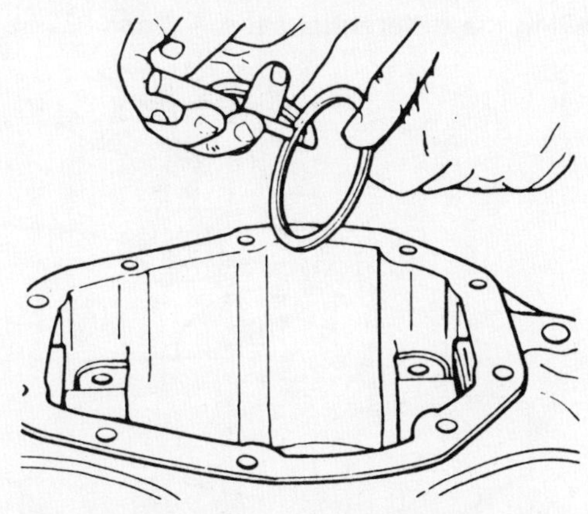
Measuring the shims – Dana 9¾ in. axles

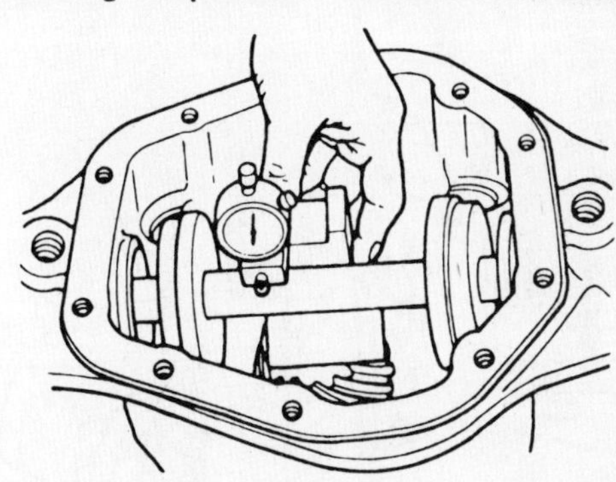
Checking the pinion depth setting – Dana 9¾ in. axles

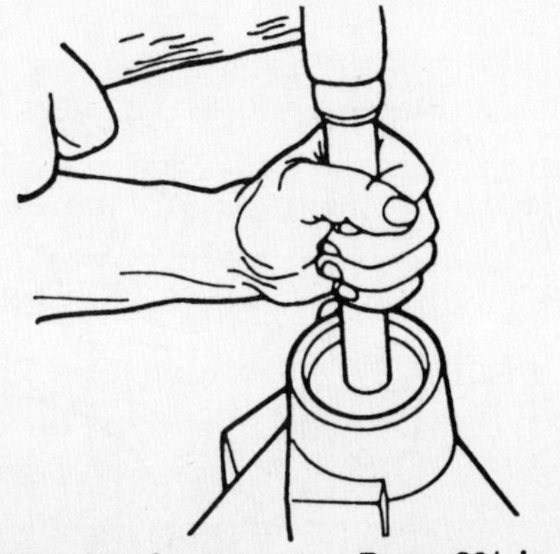
Installing the pinion front cup – Dana 9¾ in. axles

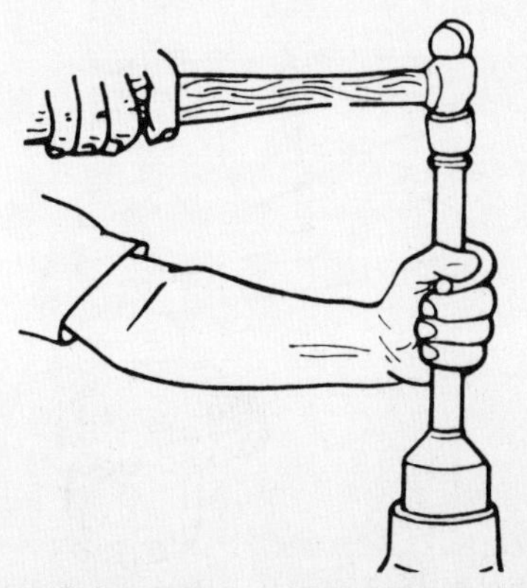
Installing the pinion seal – Dana 9¾ in. axles

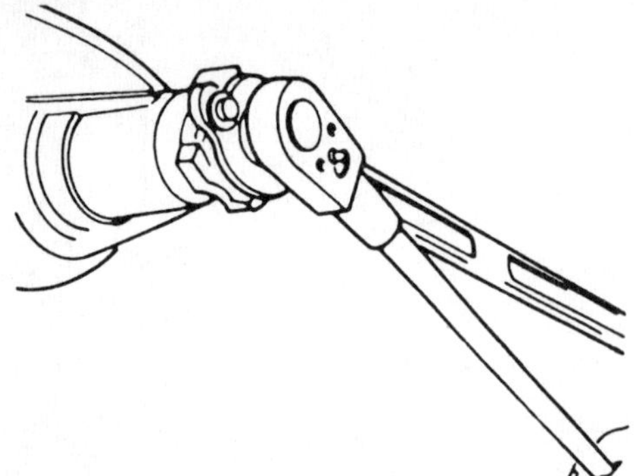
Tightening the pinion nut – Dana 9¾ in. axles

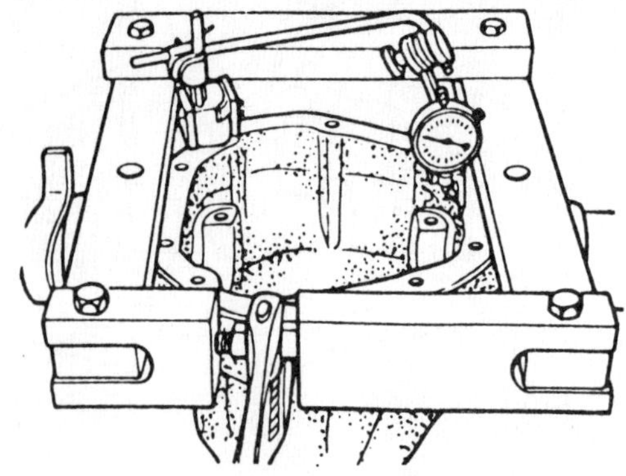
Mounting the carrier spreader – Dana 9¾ in. axles

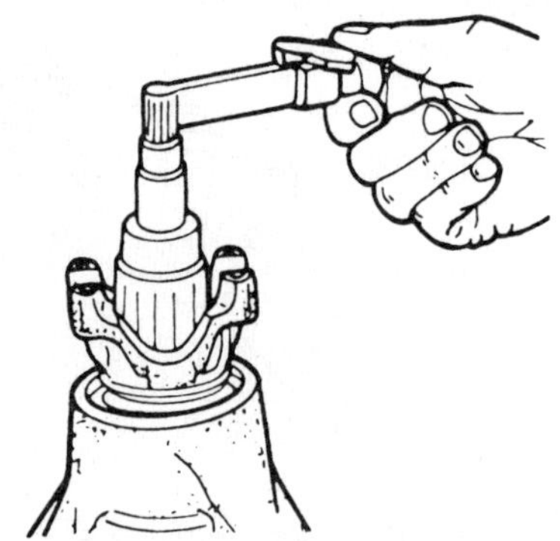
Checking pinion preload – Dana 9¾ in. axles

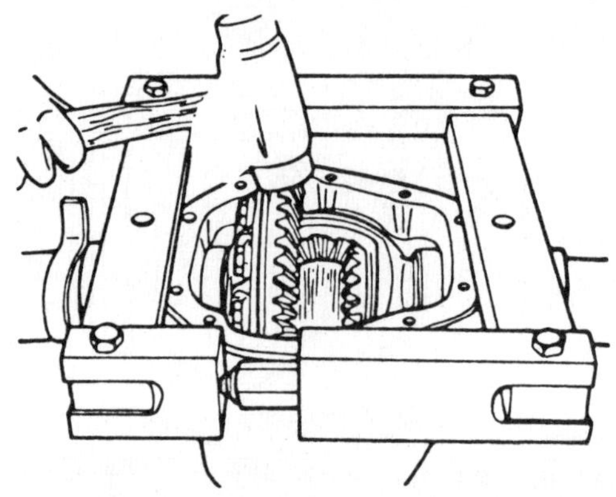
Installing the differential case – Dana 9¾ in. axles

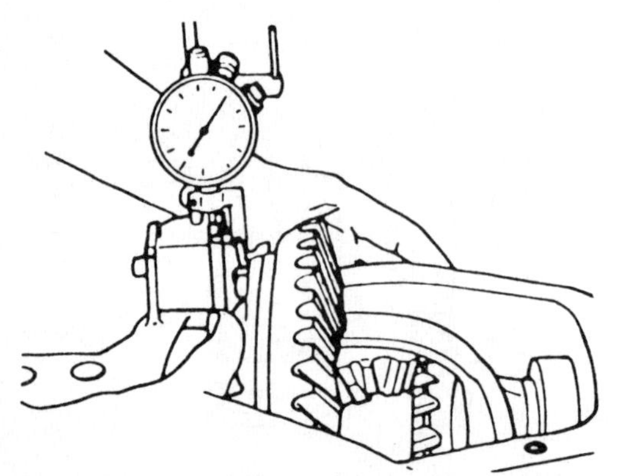
Measuring differential movement – Dana 9¾ in. axles

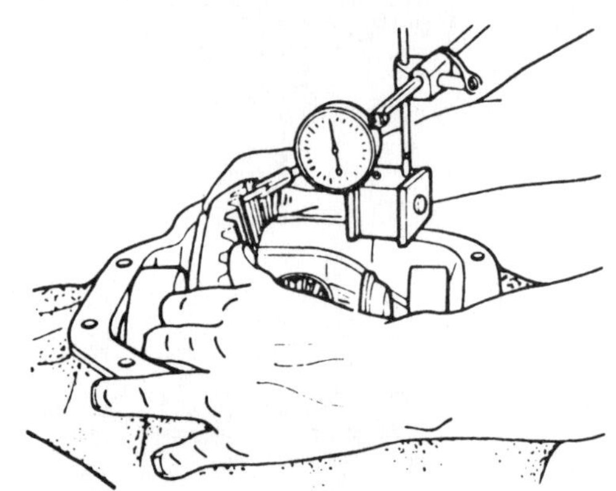
Measuring backlash – Dana 9¾ in. axles

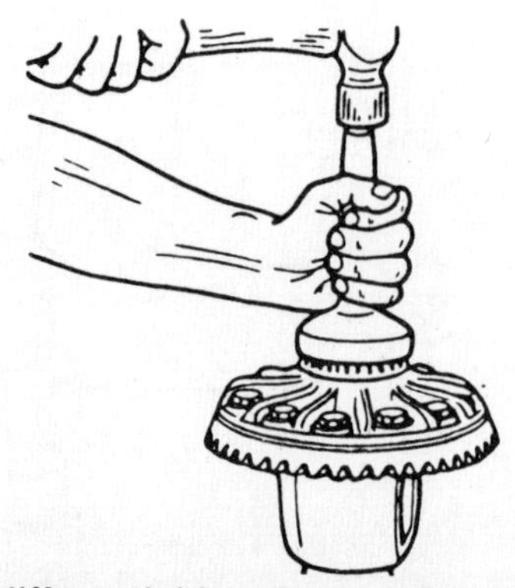
Installing the differential bearings – Dana 9¾ in. axles

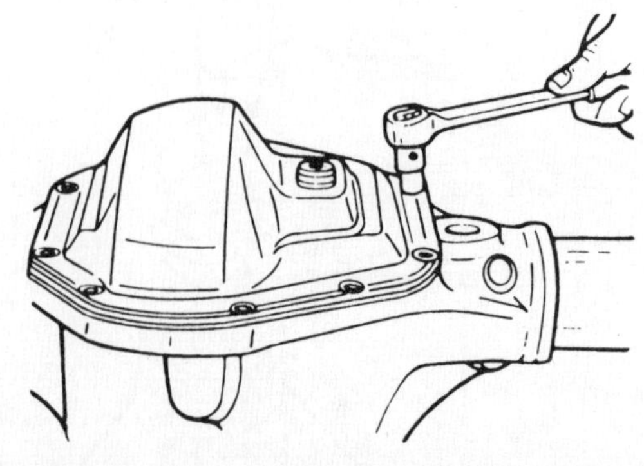
Installing the axle cover – Dana 9¾ in. axles

stall the assembly and recheck. If the run-out remains over the 0.002 in. tolerance, the ring gear is defective. If the measurement is within tolerances, continue on with the assembly.

8. Position 2 pry bars between the bearing cap and the housing on the side opposite the ring gear. Pull on the pry bars and force the differential carrier as far as possible towards the dial indicator. Rock the assembly to seat the bearings and reset the dial indicator to zero.

9. Reposition the prybars to the opposite side of the carrier and force the carrier assembly as far towards the center of the housing. Read the dial indicator scale. This will be the total amount of shims required for setting the backlash during the reassembly, less the bearing preload. Record the measurement.

10. With the pinion gear installed and properly set, position the differential carrier assembly into the axle housing and install the bearing caps in their proper positions. Tighten the cap bolts just to hold the bearing cups in place.

11. Install a dial indicator on the axle housing with the indicator button contacting the back of the ring gear.

12. Position 2 prybars between the bearing cup and the axle housing on the ring gear side of the case and pry the ring gear into mesh with the pinion gear teeth, as far as possible. Rock the ring gear to allow the teeth to mesh and the bearings to seat. With the pressure still applied by the prybars, set the dial indicator to zero.

13. Reposition the prybars on the opposite side of ring gear and pry the gear as far as it will go. Take the dial indicator reading. Repeat this procedure until the same reading is obtained each time. This reading represents the necessary amount of shims between the differential carrier and the bearing on the ring gear side.

14. Remove the bearing from the differential carrier on the ring gear side and install the proper amount of shims. Reinstall the bearing.

15. Remove the differential carrier bearing from the opposite side of the ring gear. To determine the amount of shims needed, use the following method.

a. Subtract the size of the shim pack just installed on the ring gear side of the carrier from the reading obtained and recorded when measurement was taken without the pinion gear in place.

b. To this figure, add an additional 0.015 in. to compensate for preload and backlash. An example: If the first reading was 0.085 in. and the shims installed on the ring gear side of the carrier were 0.055 in., the correct amount of shims would be 0.085 − 0.055 + 0.015 = 0.045 in.

16. Install the required shims as determined under step 15 and install the differential side bearing. The installation of the shims should give the proper preload to the bearings and the proper backlash to the ring and pinion gears.

17. Spread the axle housing with the spreader tool no more than 0.015 in. Install the differential bearing outer cups in their correct locations and install the cups in their respective locations.

18. Install the bolts and tighten finger-tight. Rotate the differential carrier and ring gear and tap with a soft-faced hammer to insure proper seating of the assembly in the axle housing.

19. Remove the spreader tool and torque the cap bolts to specifications.

20. Install a dial indicator and check the ring gear backlash at 4 equally spaced points of the ring gear circle. The backlash must be within a range of 0.004–0.009 in. and must not vary more than 0.002 in. between the points checked.

21. If the backlash is not within specifications, the shim packs must be corrected to bring the backlash within limits.

22. Check the tooth contact pattern and verify.

23. Complete the assembly, refill to proper level with lubricant and operate to verify proper assembly.

FRONT DRIVE AXLE K-SERIES

Skid Plate

REPLACEMENT

1. Support the skid plate.
2. Remove the 4 bolts.
3. Installation is the reverse of removal. Torque the bolts to 25 ft. lbs.

Indicator Switch

REPLACEMENT

1. Remove the skid plate.
2. Unplug the electrical connector.
3. Unscrew the switch.
4. Installation is the reverse of removal. Coat the threads of the switch with sealer. Torque the switch to 15 ft. lbs.

Thermal Actuator

REPLACEMENT

1. Remove the skid plate.
2. Unplug the electrical connector.
3. Unscrew the actuator.
4. Installation is the reverse of removal. Coat the threads of the actuator with sealer. Torque the actuator to 16 ft. lbs.

Left Side Axle Shaft, Hub and Bearing

REMOVAL AND INSTALLATION

1. Raise and support the front end on jackstands.

2. Remove the wheel.
3. Remove the skid plate.
4. Remove the left stabilizer bar clamp.
5. Remove the left stabilizer bar bolt, spacer and bushings at the lower control arm.
6. Disconnect the left inner tie rod end from the steering relay rod.
7. Remove the hub nut and washer. Insert a long drift or dowel through the vanes in the brake rotor to hold the rotor in place.
8. Remove the axle shaft inner flange bolts.
9. Using a puller, force the outer end of the axle shaft out of the hub. Remove the shaft.

WARNING: Never allow the vehicle to rest on the wheels with the axle shaft removed!

To install:

10. Position the shaft in the hub and install the washer and hub nut. Leave the drift in the rotor vanes and tighten the hub nut to 175 ft. lbs.
11. Install the flange bolts. Tighten them to 59 ft. lbs. Remove the drift.
12. Connect the left inner tie rod end at the steering relay rod. Torque the nut to 35 ft. lbs.
13. Install the left stabilizer bar bolt, spacer and bushings at the lower control arm. Torque the bolt to 24 ft. lbs.
14. Install the left stabilizer bar clamp. Torque the bolts to 12 ft. lbs.
15. Install the skid plate.

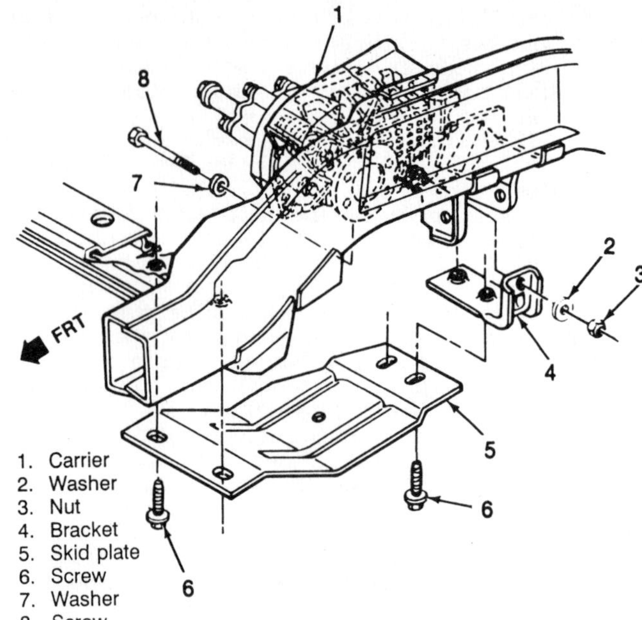

K series skid plate

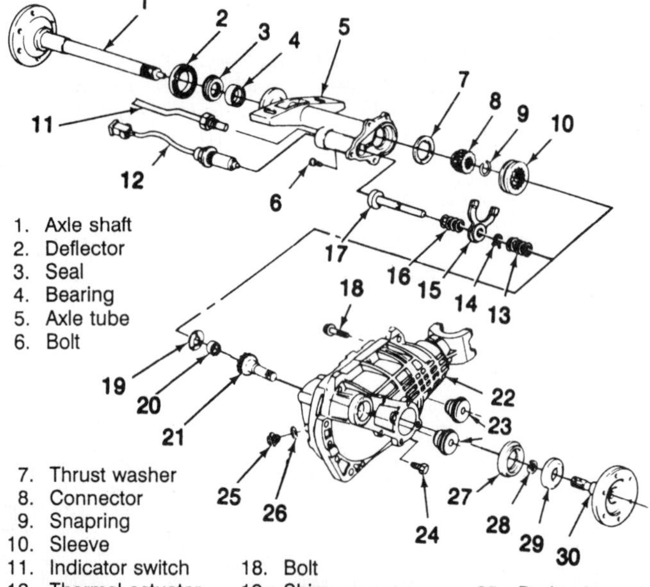

K series front axle – main components

Right Side Axle Shaft, Hub and Bearing

REMOVAL AND INSTALLATION

1. Raise and support the front end on jackstands.
2. Remove the wheel.
3. Remove the skid plate.
4. Remove the right stabilizer bar clamp.
5. Remove the right stabilizer bar bolt, spacer and bushings at the lower control arm.
6. Disconnect the right inner tie rod end from the steering relay rod.
7. Remove the hub nut and washer. Insert a long drift or dowel through the vanes in the brake rotor to hold the rotor in place.
8. Remove the axle shaft inner flange bolts.
9. Using a puller, force the outer end of the axle shaft out of the hub. Remove the shaft.

WARNING: Never allow the vehicle to rest on the wheels with the axle shaft removed!

To install:

10. Position the shaft in the hub and install the washer and hub nut. Leave the drift in the rotor vanes and tighten the hub nut to 175 ft. lbs.
11. Install the flange bolts. Tighten them to 59 ft. lbs. Remove the drift.
12. Connect the right inner tie rod end at the steering relay rod. Torque the nut to 35 ft. lbs.
13. Install the right stabilizer bar bolt, spacer and bushings at the lower control arm. Torque the bolt to 12 ft. lbs.
14. Install the right stabilizer bar clamp. Torque the bolts to 24 ft. lbs.
15. Install the skid plate.

Axle Tube Assembly

REMOVAL

1. Raise and support the front end on jackstands.
2. Remove the right wheel.
3. Position a drain pan under the axle.
4. Remove the stabilizer bar. See Section 8.

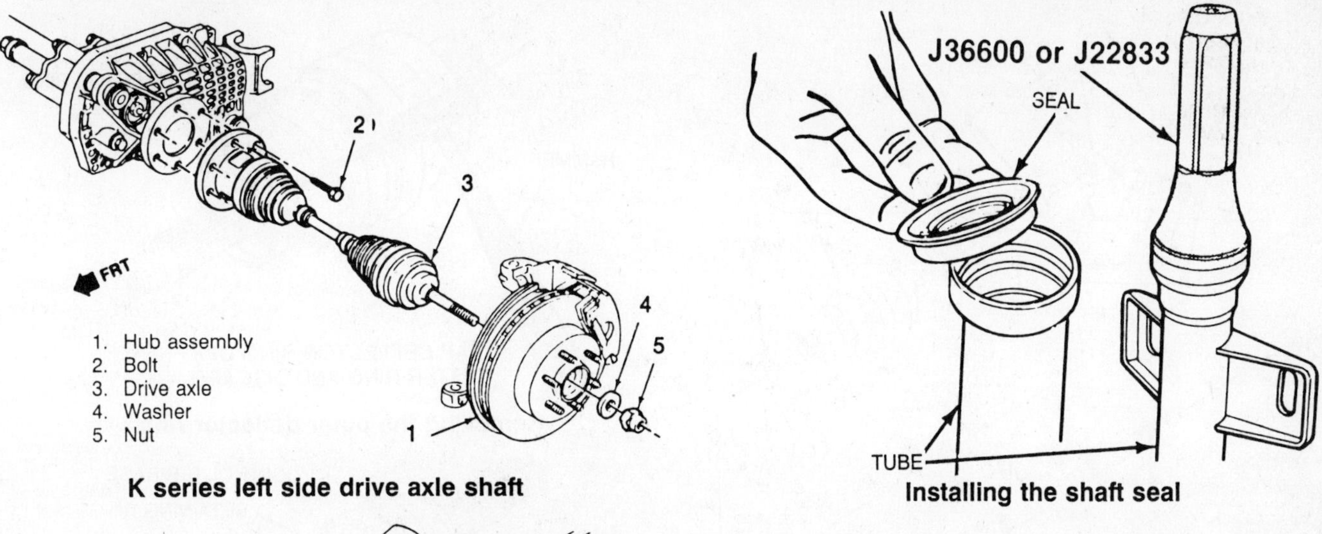

K series left side drive axle shaft

Installing the shaft seal

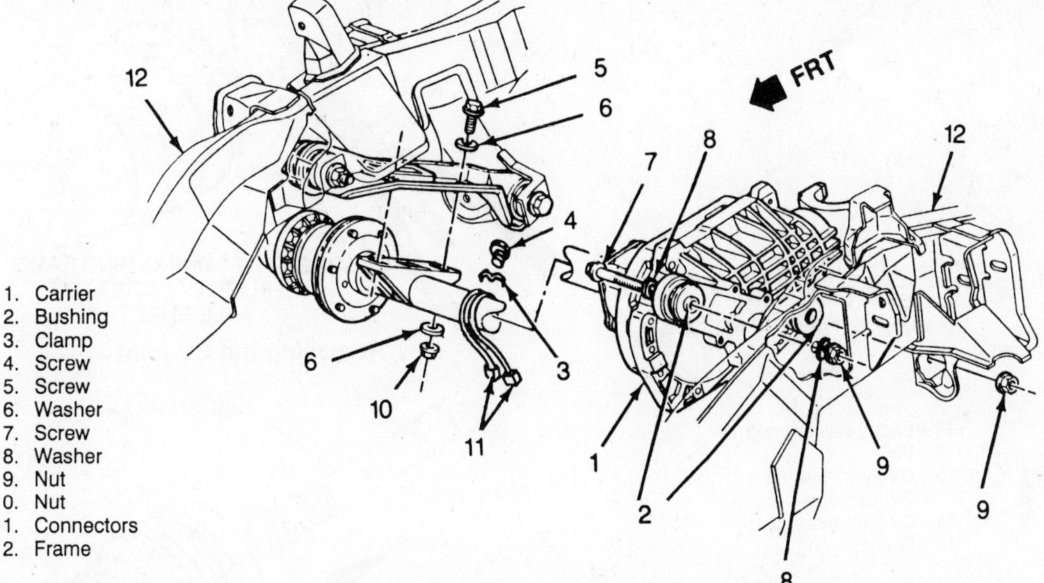

K series differential carrier installation

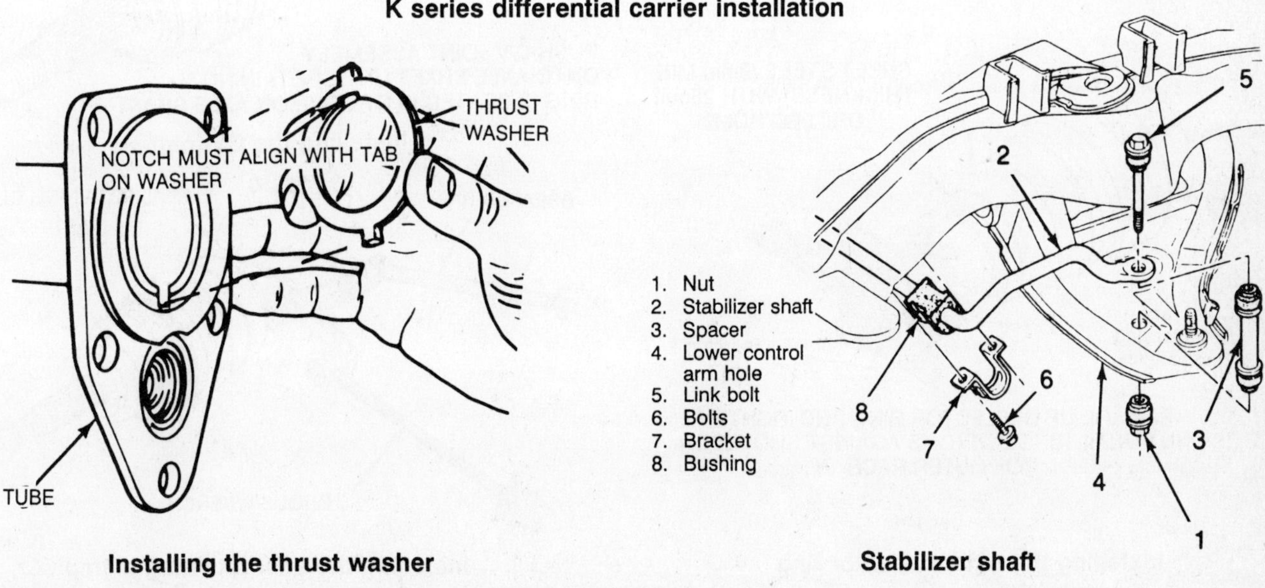

Installing the thrust washer

Stabilizer shaft

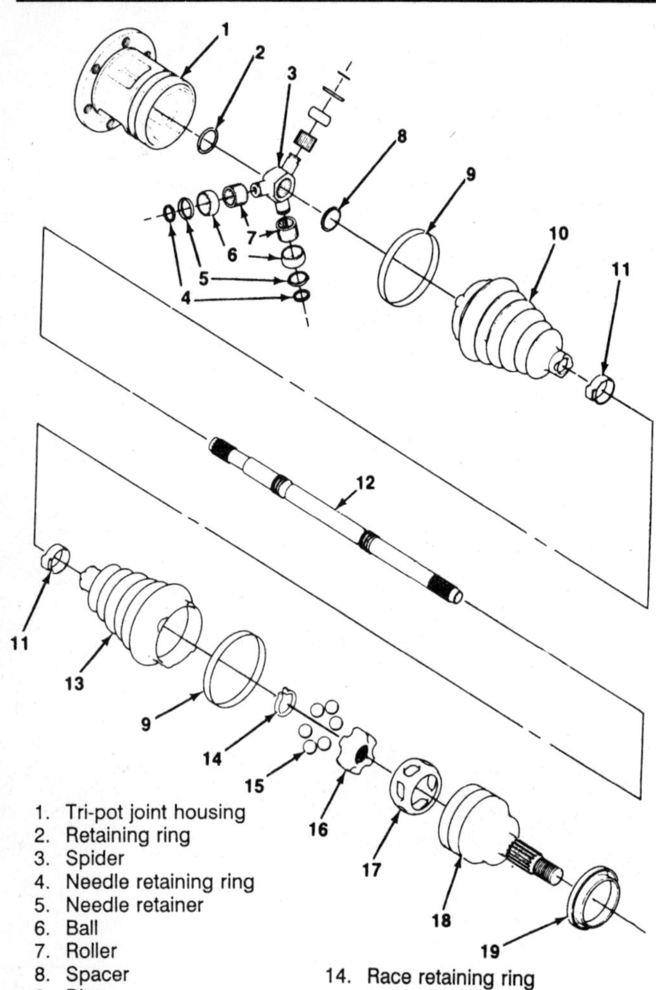

1. Tri-pot joint housing
2. Retaining ring
3. Spider
4. Needle retaining ring
5. Needle retainer
6. Ball
7. Roller
8. Spacer
9. Ring swage
10. Seal
11. Clamp
12. Axle shaft
13. CV-joint seal
14. Race retaining ring
15. Ball
16. CV-joint inner race
17. CV-joint cage
18. CV-joint outer race
19. Deflector ring

Front drive axle components

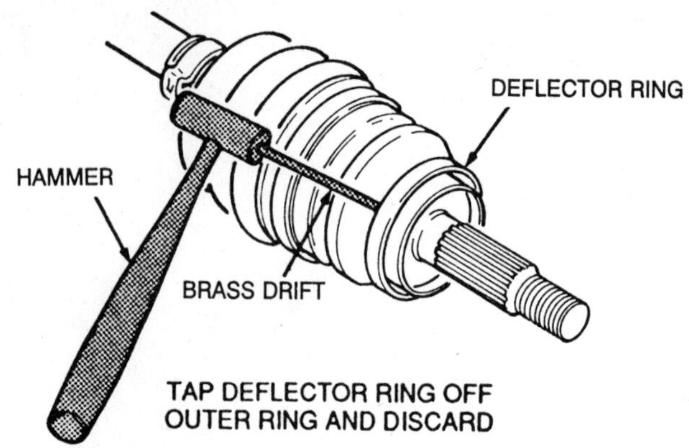

Removing the outer deflector ring

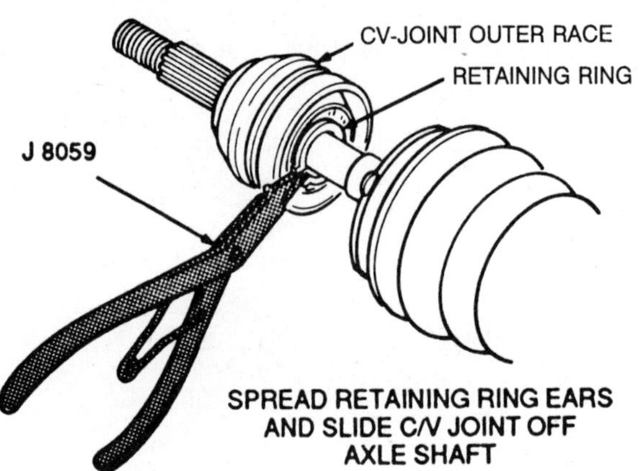

Removing the CV-joint

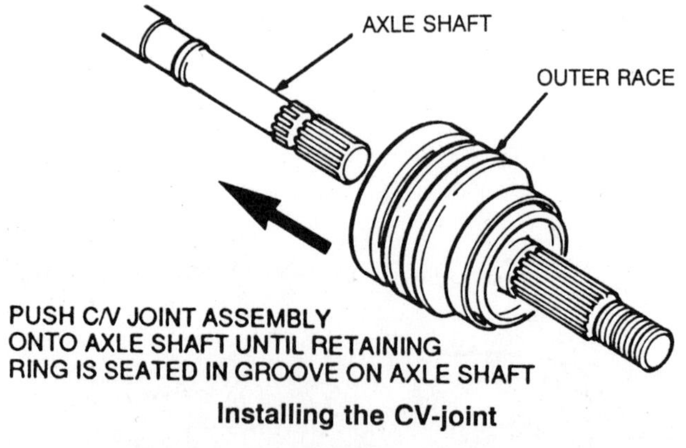

Installing the CV-joint

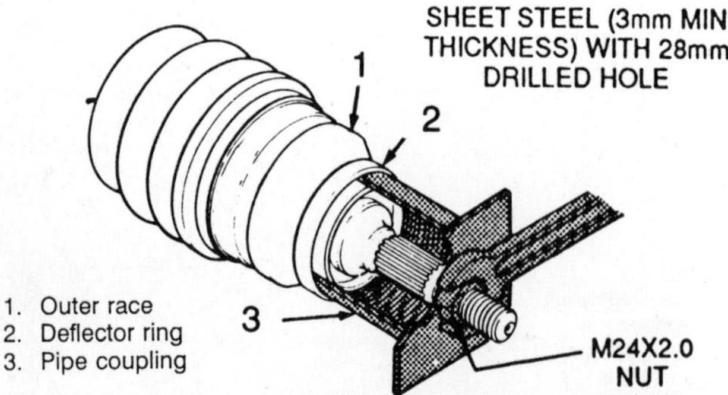

1. Outer race
2. Deflector ring
3. Pipe coupling

SQUARE UP DEFLECTOR RING AND TIGHTEN NUT UNTIL RING BOTTOMS AGAINST SHOULDER OF OUTER RACE

Installing the outer deflector ring

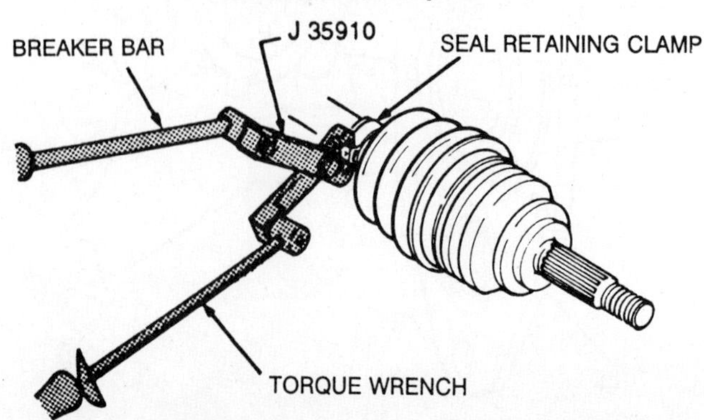

Installing the seal retaining clamp

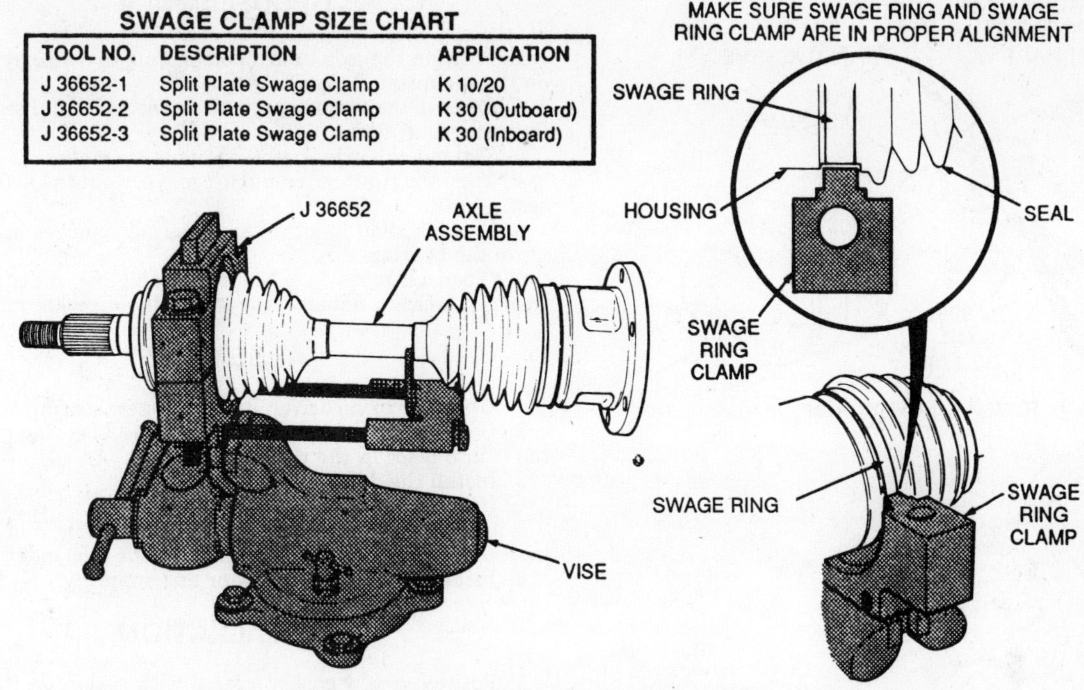

SWAGE CLAMP SIZE CHART

TOOL NO.	DESCRIPTION	APPLICATION
J 36652-1	Split Plate Swage Clamp	K 10/20
J 36652-2	Split Plate Swage Clamp	K 30 (Outboard)
J 36652-3	Split Plate Swage Clamp	K 30 (Inboard)

Installing the swage ring

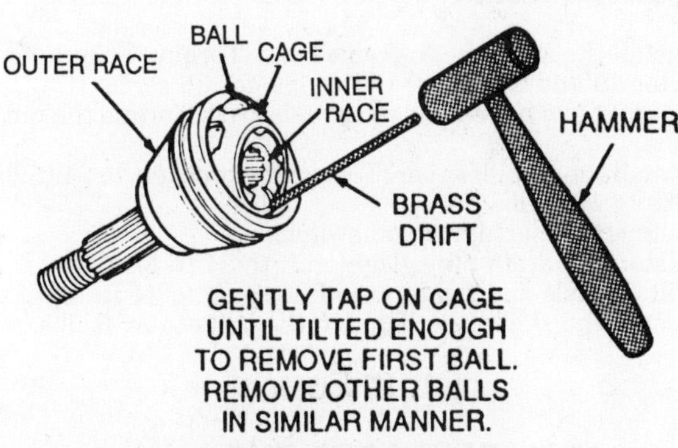

Removing the balls

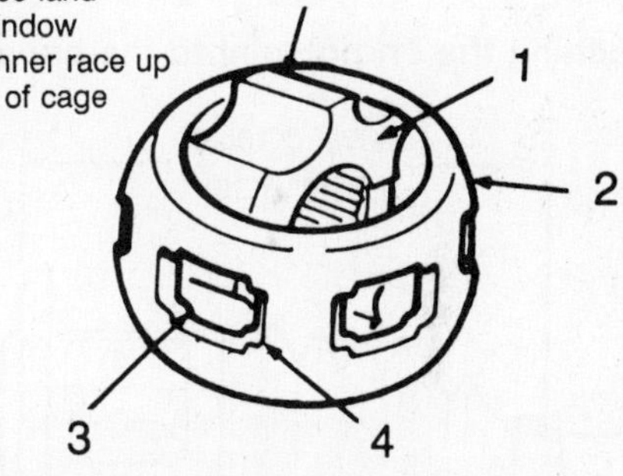

Separating inner race and cage

PIVOT CAGE AND INNER RACE AT 90° TO CENTER LINE OF OUTER RACE WITH CAGE WINDOWS ALIGNED WITH LANDS OF OUTER RACE. LIFT OUT CAGE AND INNER RACE.

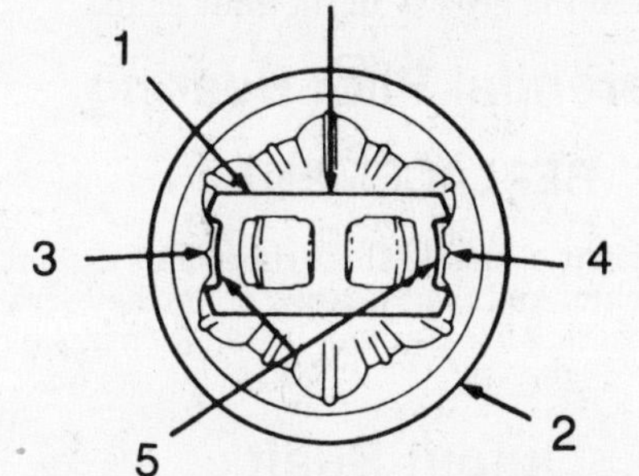

1. Cage
2. Outer race
3. Land
4. Land
5. Windows

Separating outer race and cage

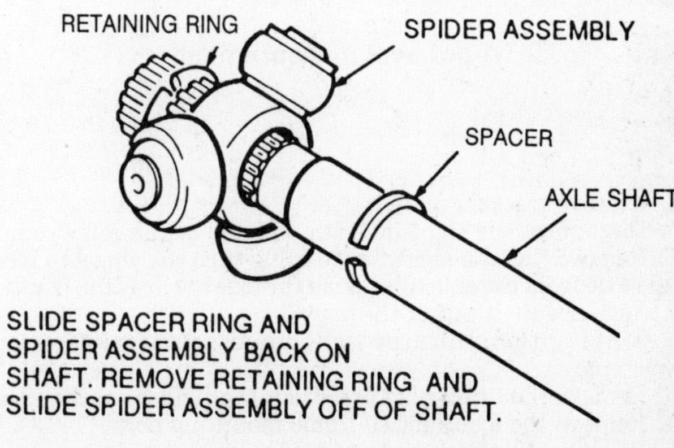

Removing the spider

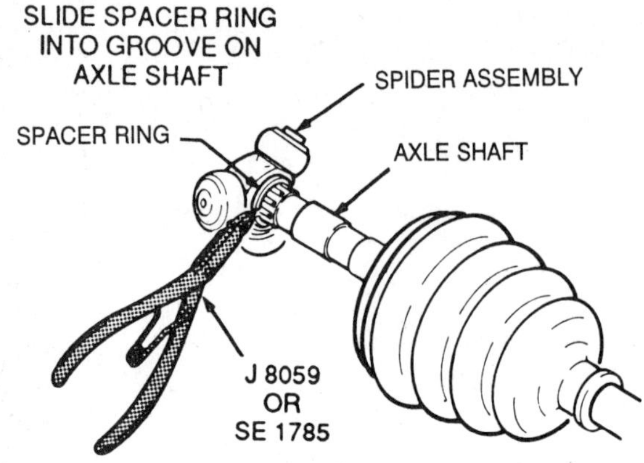

Installing the spider

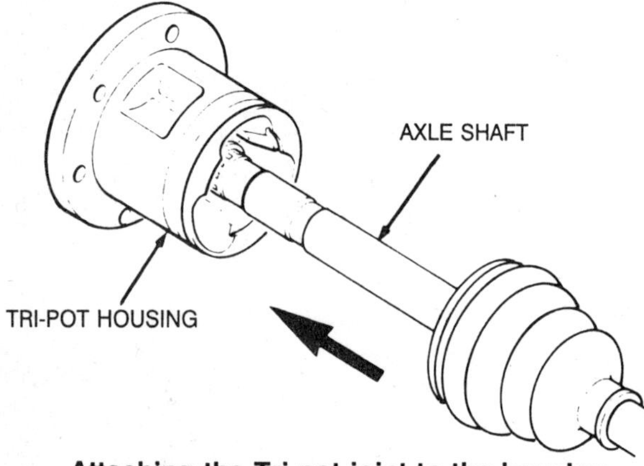

Attaching the Tri-pot joint to the housing

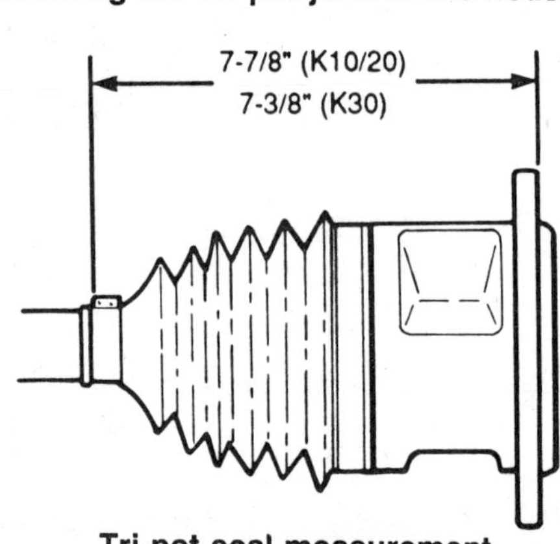

Tri-pot seal measurement

5. Remove the skid plate.
6. Disconnect the right inner tie rod end at the relay rod.
7. Remove the axle shaft flange bolts, turn the wheel to loosen the axle from the axle tube, push the axle towards the front of the truck and tie it out of the way.
8. Unplug the indicator switch and actuator electrical connectors.
9. Remove the drain plug and drain the fluid from the case.
10. Remove the axle tube-to-frame mounting bolts.
11. Remove the axle tube-to-carrier bolts.
12. Remove the axle tube/shaft assembly. Keep the open end up.

DISASSEMBLY

1. Position the axle tube, open end up, in a vise by clamping on the mounting flange.
2. Remove the snapring, sleeve, connector and thrust washer from the shaft end.
3. Tap out the axle shaft with a plastic mallet.
4. Turn the tube, outer end up, and pry out the deflector and seal.
5. Using a slide hammer and bearing remover adapter, remove the bearing.
6. Clean all parts in a non-flammable solvent and inspect them for wear or damage. Clean off all old gasket material.

ASSEMBLY

1. Using a bearing driver, install the new bearing in the tube.
2. Coat the lips of a new seal with wheel bearing grease and tap it into place in the tube.
3. Install the deflector.
4. Insert the axle shaft into the tube.
5. Coat the thrust washer with grease to hold it in place and position it on the tube end. Make sure the tabs index the slots.
6. Install the sleeve, connector and snapring.

INSTALLATION

1. Position a new gasket, coated with sealer, on the carrier. Raise the tube assembly into position and install the tube-to-carrier bolts. Torque the bolts to 30 ft. lbs.
2. Install the axle shaft flange bolts and torque them to 59 ft. lbs.
3. Install the axle tube-to-frame bolts. Torque the nuts to 75 ft. lbs. for 15 and 25 series; 107 ft. lbs. for 35 series.
4. Connect the tie rod end to the relay rod. Torque the nut to 35 ft. lbs.
5. Install the stabilizer bar. Torque the brackets to 24 ft. lbs.; the links to 12 ft. lbs.
6. Connect the actuator and switch.
7. Install the drain plug. Tighten it to 24 ft. lbs.
8. Fill the axle and tighten the filler plug to 24 ft. lbs.
9. Install the skid plate. Tighten the bolts to 25 ft. lbs.

Shift Fork

REPLACEMENT

1. Remove the right side axle tube/shaft assembly.
2. Remove the shift shaft, spring, fork and clip from the tube.
3. Remove the spring from the carrier. Be careful to avoid losing the shim!
4. Installation is the reverse of removal. Make sure that the clip is fully seated in the groove on the shift shaft.

Differential Pilot Bearing

REPLACEMENT

1. Remove the right side axle shaft tube/shaft assembly.
2. Remove the shim and pilot bearing from the carrier.
3. Dip the new bearing in axle fluid. Installation is the reverse of removal.

Output Shaft

REMOVAL AND INSTALLATION

1. Raise and support the front end on jackstands.

2. Drain the axle.
3. Remove the left side axle shaft.
4. Remove the lower carrier mounting bolt.
5. CAREFULLY pry against the lower part of the carrier to provide clearance for the output shaft removal. While prying, insert a prybar between the output shaft flange and the carrier case. Pry the output shaft free. BE CAREFUL! It's possible to damage the carrier if you pry too hard.
6. Remove the deflector and seal from the carrier.

To install:

1. Lubricate the lips of a new seal with wheel bearing grease and drive it into place.
2. Install the deflector.
3. Pry against the case and position the output shaft in the carrier. Tap it into place with a plastic mallet.
4. Install the lower carrier mounting bolt, washer and nut. Torque the bolt to 80 ft. lbs.
5. Install the left axle shaft.
6. Fill the axle.

Pinion Seal

REPLACEMENT

1. Raise and support the front end on jackstands.
2. Matchmark and disconnect the front driveshaft at the carrier.
3. Remove the wheels.
4. Dismount the calipers and wire them up, out of the way. See Section 9.
5. Position an inch pound torque wrench on the pinion nut. Measure the torque needed to rotate the pinion one full revolution. Record the figure.
6. Matchamrk the pinion flange, shaft and nut. Count and record the number of exposed threads on the pinion shaft.
7. Hold the flange and remove the nut and washer.
8. Using a puller, remove the flange.
9. Carefully pry the seal from its bore. Be careful to avoid scratching the seal bore.
10. Remove the deflector from the flange.

To install:

11. Clean the seal bore thoroughly.
12. Remove any burrs from the deflector staking on the flange.
13. Tap the deflector onto the flange and stake it in three places.
14. Position the new seal in the carrier bore and drive it into place until flush. Coat the seal lips with wheel bearing grease.
15. Coat the outer edge of the flange neck with wheel bearing grease and slide it onto the pinion shaft.
16. Place a new nut and washer onto the pinion shaft and tighten it to the position originally recorded. That is, the alignment marks are aligned, and the recorded number of threads are exposed on the pinion shaft.

WARNING: Never hammer the flange onto the pinion!

17. Measure the rotating torque of the pinion. Compare this to the original torque. Tighten the pinion nut, in small increments, until the rotating torque is 3 inch lbs. GREATER than the original torque.
18. Install the driveshaft.
19. Install the calipers.
20. Install the wheels.

Differential Carrier

REMOVAL AND INSTALLATION

1. Raise and support the front end on jackstands.
2. Remove the wheels.

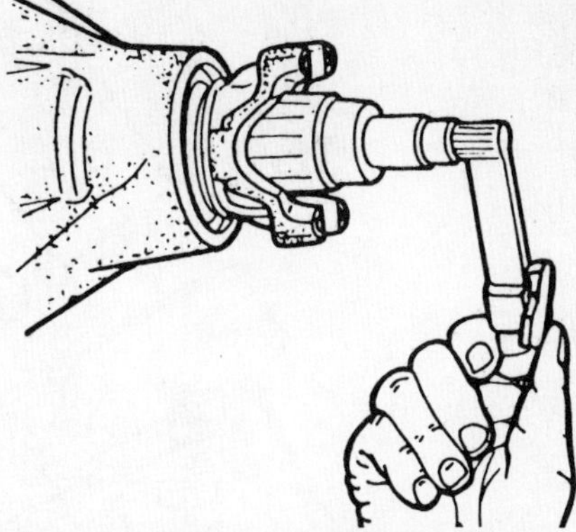
Measuring pinion rotating torque

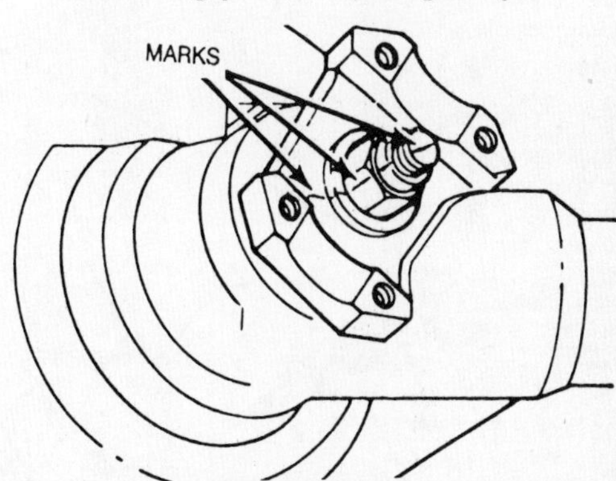

Scribed marks

Removing the pinion nut

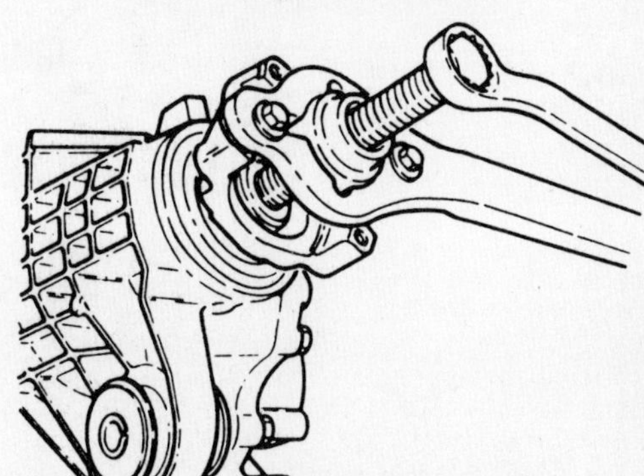
Removing the pinion flange

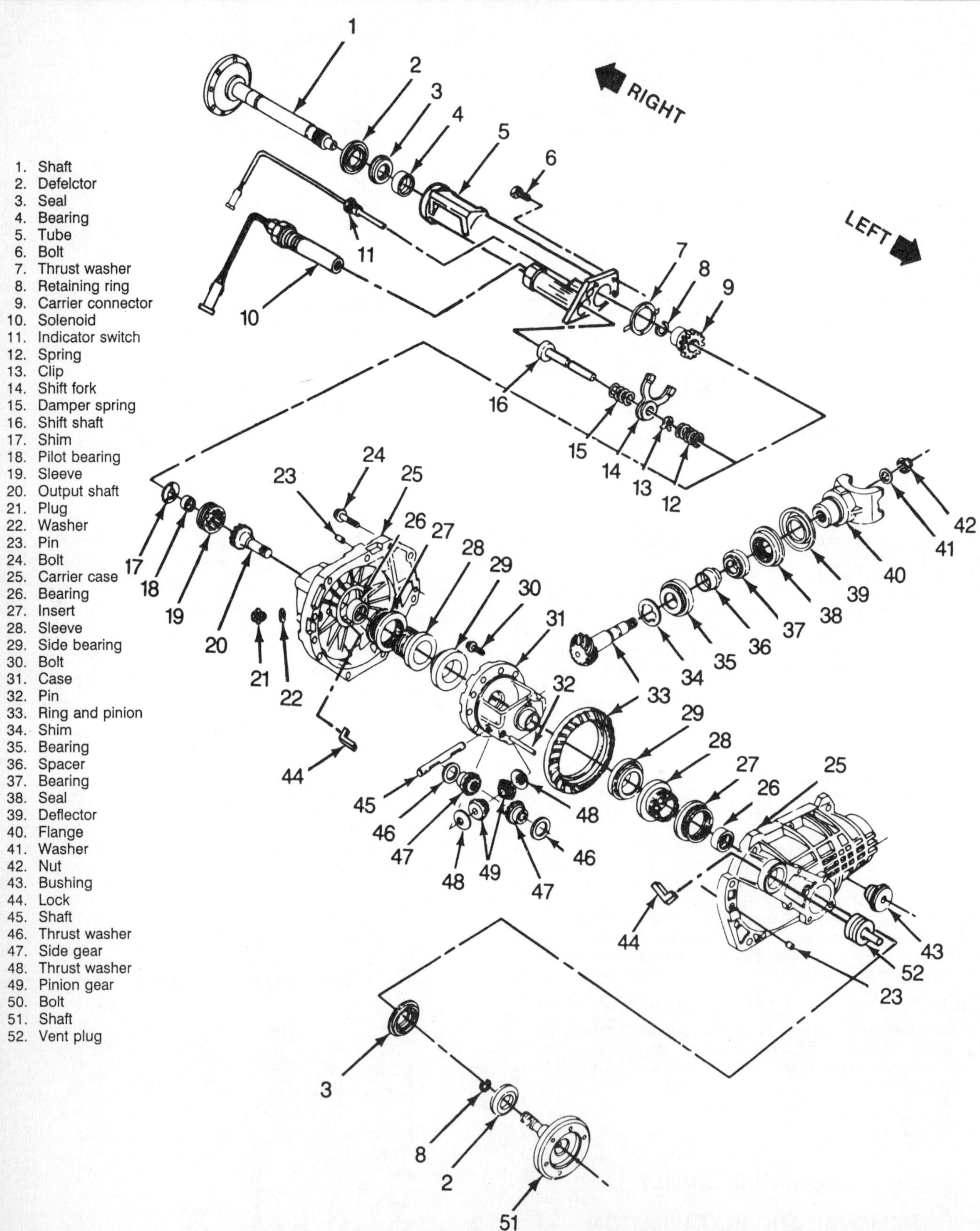
RIGHT
LEFT
1. Shaft
2. Defelctor
3. Seal
4. Bearing
5. Tube
6. Bolt
7. Thrust washer
8. Retaining ring
9. Carrier connector
10. Solenoid
11. Indicator switch
12. Spring
13. Clip
14. Shift fork
15. Damper spring
16. Shift shaft
17. Shim
18. Pilot bearing
19. Sleeve
20. Output shaft
21. Plug
22. Washer
23. Pin
24. Bolt
25. Carrier case
26. Bearing
27. Insert
28. Sleeve
29. Side bearing
30. Bolt
31. Case
32. Pin
33. Ring and pinion
34. Shim
35. Bearing
36. Spacer
37. Bearing
38. Seal
39. Deflector
40. Flange
41. Washer
42. Nut
43. Bushing
44. Lock
45. Shaft
46. Thrust washer
47. Side gear
48. Thrust washer
49. Pinion gear
50. Bolt
51. Shaft
52. Vent plug

K15/25 front axle exploded view

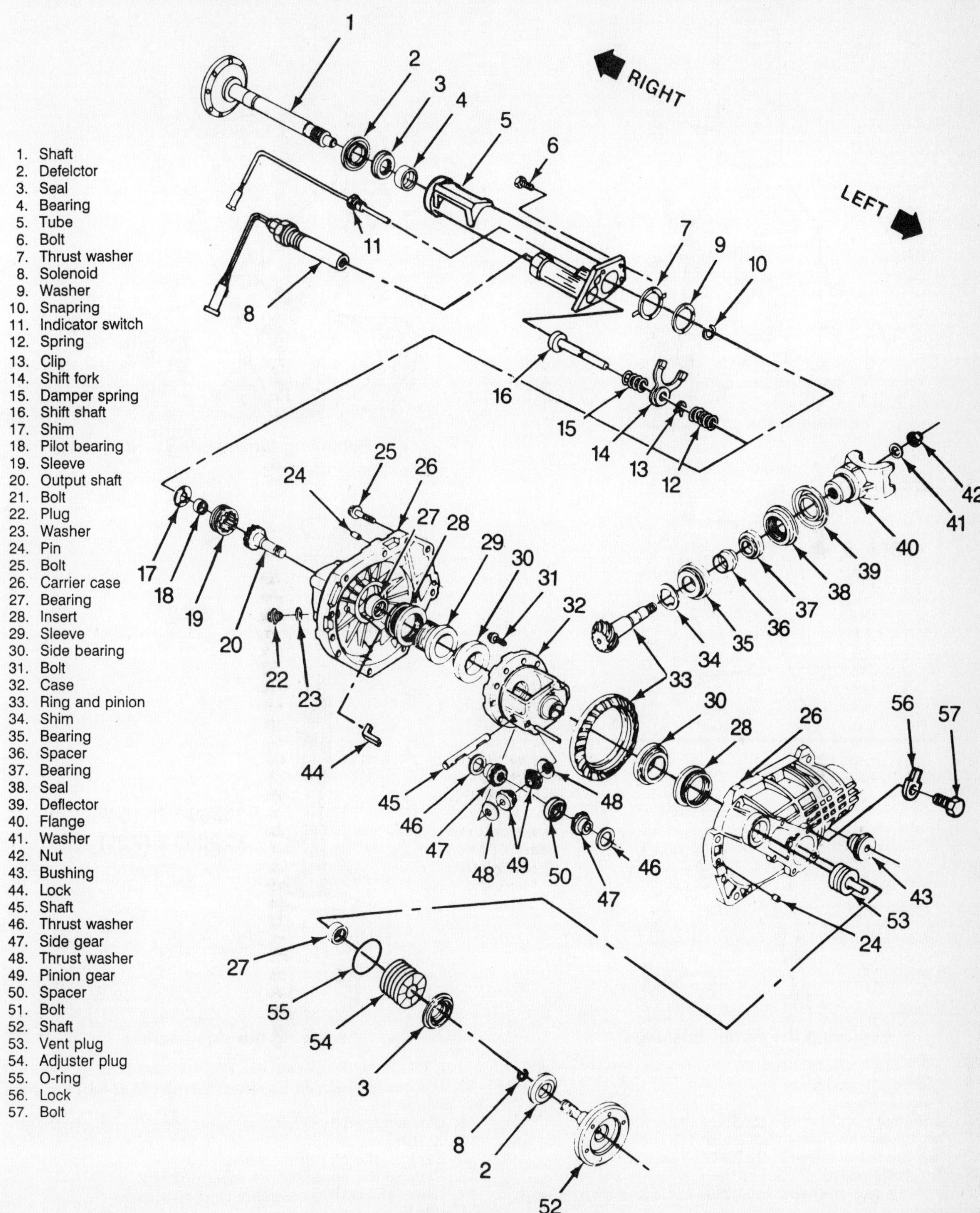

K35 front axle exploded view

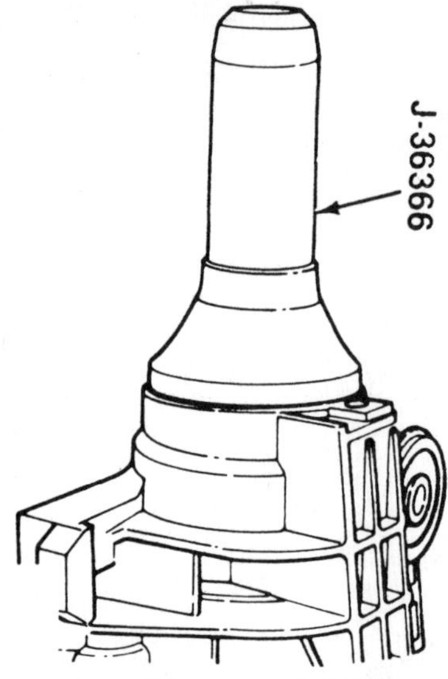

Installing the pinion seal

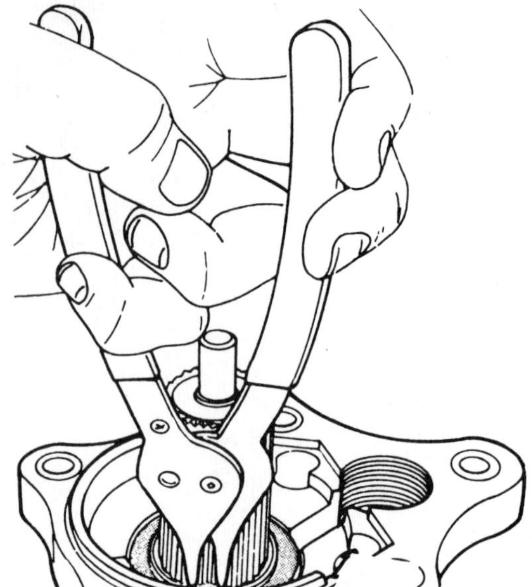
Removing the snapring – K35

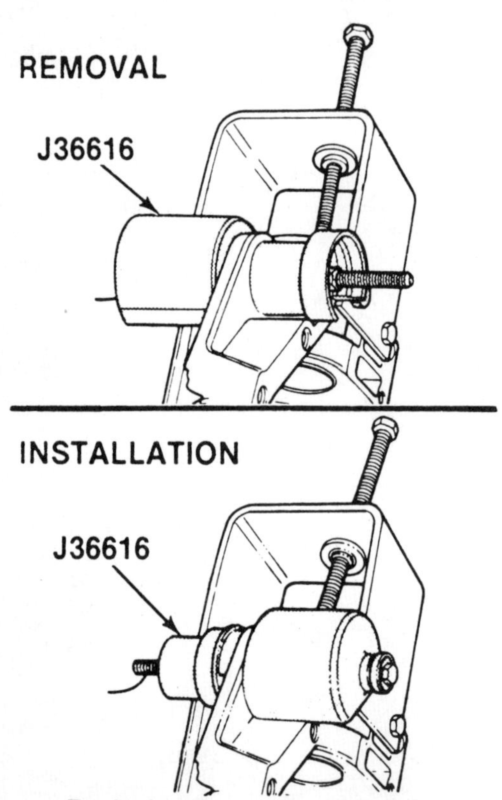

Replacing the carrier bushings

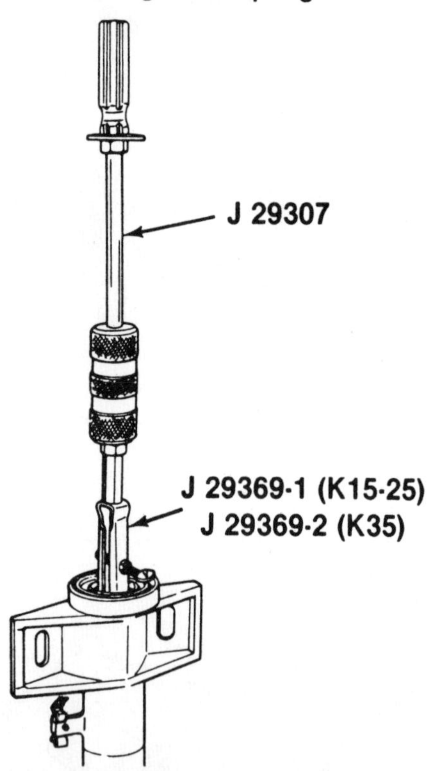

Removing the axle bearing

3. Remove the skid plate.
4. Drain the carrier.
5. Matchmark and remove the front driveshaft.
6. Disconnect the right axle shaft at the tube flange.
7. Disconnect the left axle shaft at the carrier flange.
8. Wire both axle shafts out of the way.
9. Unplug the connectors at the indicator switch and actuator.
10. Disconnect the carrier vent hose.
11. Remove the axle tube-to-frame bolts, washers and nuts.
12. Remove the lower carrier mounting bolt.
13. Disconnect the right side inner tie rod end at the relay rod. See Section 8.
14. Depending on model, it may be necessary to remove the engine oil filter.
15. Support the carrier on a floor jack
16. Remove the upper carrier mounting bolt.
17. Lower the carrier assembly from the truck.

To install:

18. Raise the carrier into position.
19. Install the upper carrier mounting bolt, washers and nut. Then, install the lower carrier mounting bolt, washers and nut.

Torque the bolts to 80 ft. lbs.
20. Remove the jack.
21. Install the oil filter.
22. Connect the tie rod end. Torque the nut to 35 ft. lbs.
23. Install the axle tube-to-frame bolts, washers and nuts. Torque the nuts to 75 ft. lbs. for 15 and 25 series; 107 ft. lbs. for 35 series.
24. Connect the vent hose.
25. Connect the wiring.
26. Connect the axle shafts at the flanges. Torque the bolts to 59 ft. lbs.
27. Connect the driveshaft. Torque the bolts to 15 ft. lbs.
28. Fill the carrier with SAE 85W-90 gear oil.
29. Install the wheels.
30. Add any engine oil lost when the filter was removed.

Differential Overhaul

The following special tools, or their equivalents, will be necessary for this job: J–8001–1, J–8092, J–8107–2, J–8614–01, J–22761, J–22888–D, J–29307, J–29362, J–29369–2, J–29710, J–29763, J–33842, J–34011, J–34047–1, J–34047–3, J–35512, J–36266, J–36597, J–36598, J–36598–3, J–36598–4, J–36598–6, J–36598–15, J–36599, J–36601–3, J–36601–4, J–36602, J–36612, J–36613, J–36614, J–36615, J–36616.

DISASSEMBLY

1. Remove the drain plug and drain the fluid from the axle. Remove the axle from the truck.
2. Measure and record the backlash for it may help to determine the cause of an axle problem.
3. Remove the solenoid and the indicator switch.
4. Remove the right axle tube-to-carrier case bolts and the tube with the shaft.
5. Remove the right output shaft sleeve, the shift shaft, damper spring, shift fork and clip assembly.
6. Remove the inner spring and shim.
7. Clamp the axle shaft tube in a vise, using the mounting flange. Strike the inside of the shaft flange to dislodge the carrier connector. Remove the carrier connector and the retaining ring.
8. On K35 Series, remove the snapring, the washer and the thrust washer from the right axle tube.
9. Remove the right side axle shaft with the deflector.
10. Using pullers J–29362 for 15/25 series or J–29369–2 for 35 series, along with J–29307, or their equivalents, remove the seal and bearing from the axle shaft tube.
11. Remove the output shaft.
12. Using a tool J–34011 or equivalent, press the differential pilot bearing.
13. Using a prybar and a soft faced hammer, remove the left side output shaft and delector.
14. Using a prybar, remove the seal from the axle tube.
15. Using pullers J–29362 for 15/25 series or J–29369–2 for 35 series, along with J–29307, or their equivalents, remove the left output shaft bearings from the case.
16. Remove the carrier case bolts, tap on the carrier case lugs and separate the right and left side carrier case halves.
17. Remove the differential assembly. On the right side of K35 series, you'll have to pry up the locks first.
18. On the K35 series, remove the bolt, the lock, the sleeves and the side bearing cups; turn the sleeves to push the cups from the bores.
19. On the K35 series, remove the adjuster plug with the side bearing cup and the O-ring, if equipped, using tool J–36615.
20. Using a holding tool such as J–8614–01, remove the pinion flange nut and washer.
21. Using a pinion flange removal tool, press the pinion flange from the differential.
22. Remove the pinion with the shim, the bearing cone and the spacer, using tool J–36598.
23. Press the spacer from the pinion.
24. Using a bearing removal tool such as J–36598, press the bearing from the pinion.
25. Remove the shim, the seal, the bearing cup and the cone.
26. Using the puller tool, press the bearing cup from the pinion.
27. Remove the side bearings, using tools J–22888–D and J–8107–2 (15/25 series) or J–36597 (35 series).

NOTE: The ring gear bolts are equipped with left handed threads.

28. Remove the ring gear bolts. Using a brass drift, drive the ring gear from the differential case.
29. Using a drift and a hammer, drive the roll pin from the differential case.
30. Remove the retaining bolt (35 series only) and pinion gear shaft.
31. Roll the pinion gears out of the case with their thrust washers.
32. Remove the side gears and their thrust washers.
33. Place identifying marks on the gears and differential case halves.
34. On K35 series, remove the spacer from the carrier.
35. Using a 6-point deep-well socket, remove the vent plug.
36. Drive the carrier bushings out using tool J–36616.

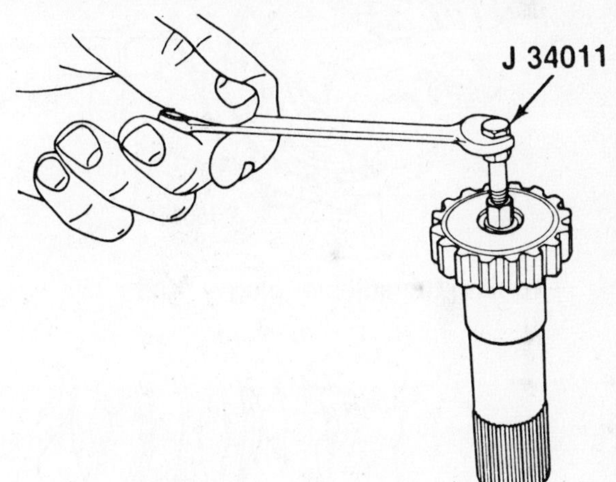

Removing the pilot bearing

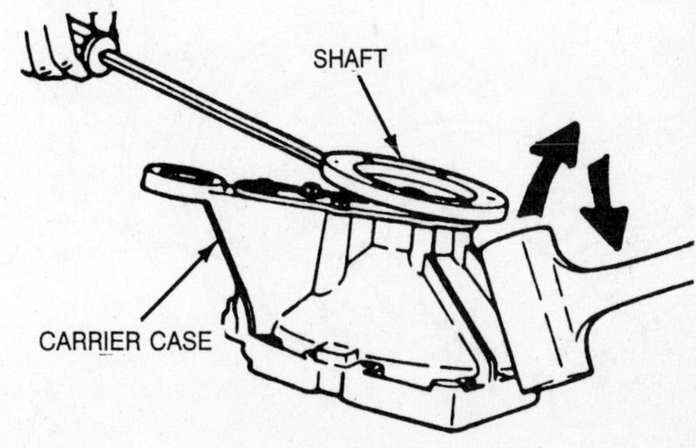

Removing the left shaft

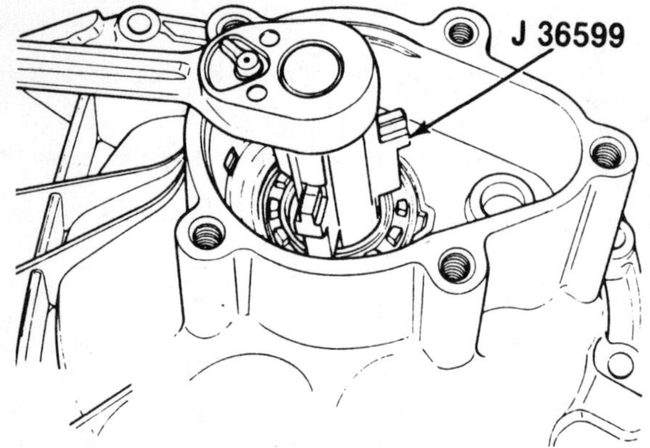

Turning the adjuster sleeve

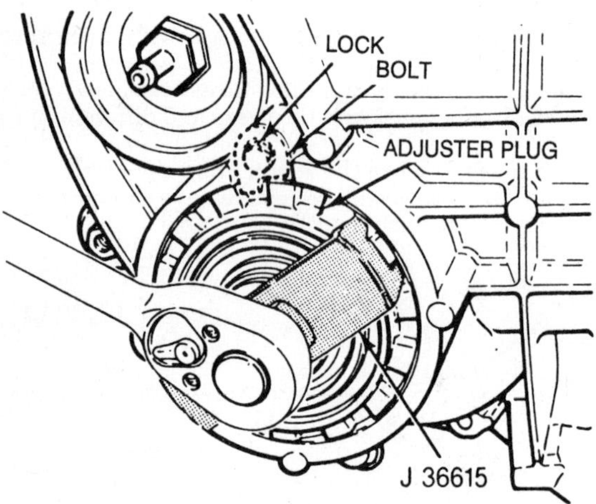

Turning the adjuster plug — K35

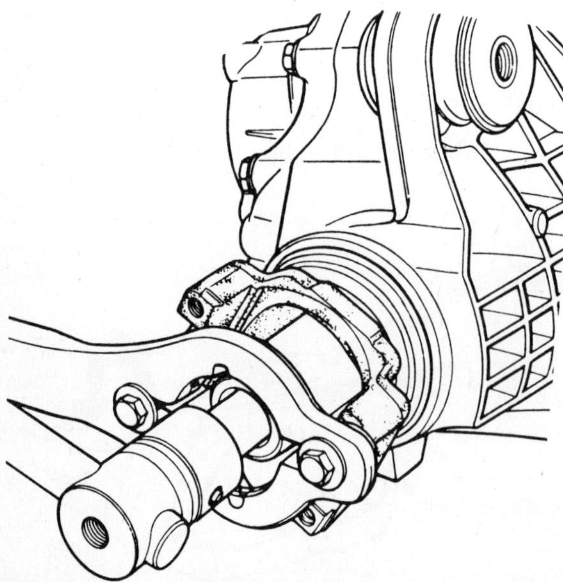
Removing the pinion nut

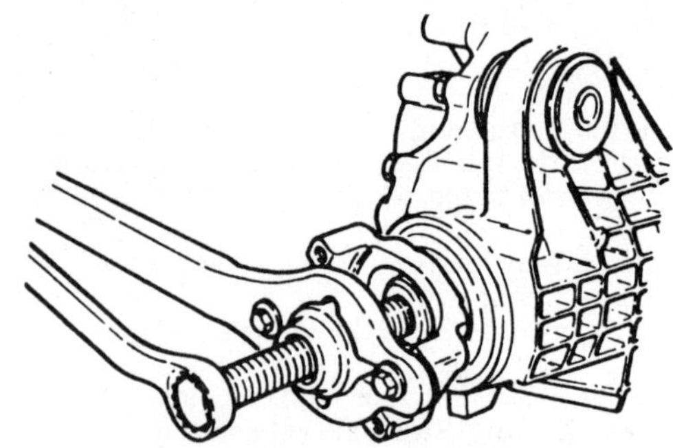
Removing the pinion flange

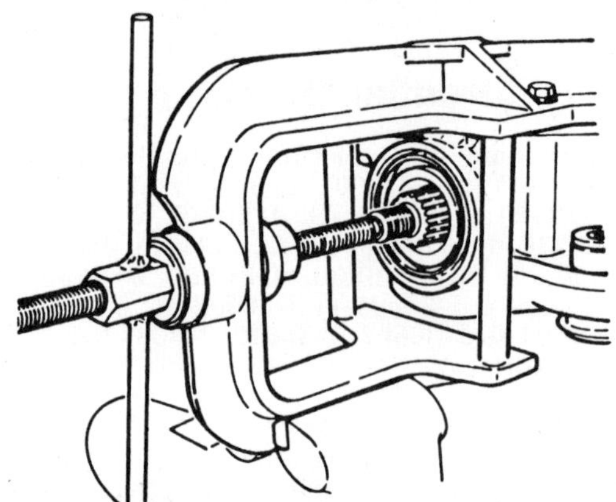
Removing the pinion

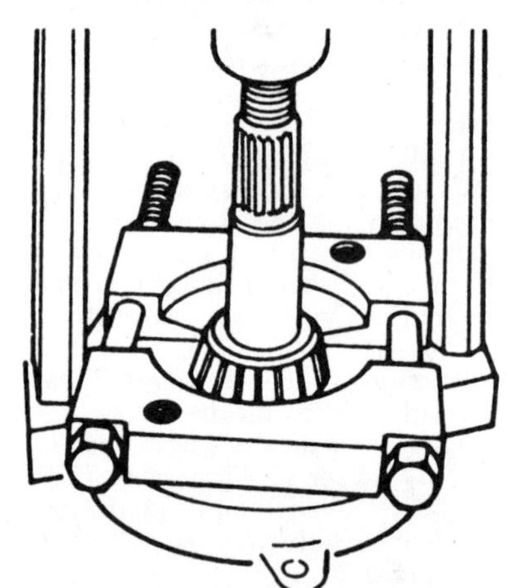
Removing the pinion bearing

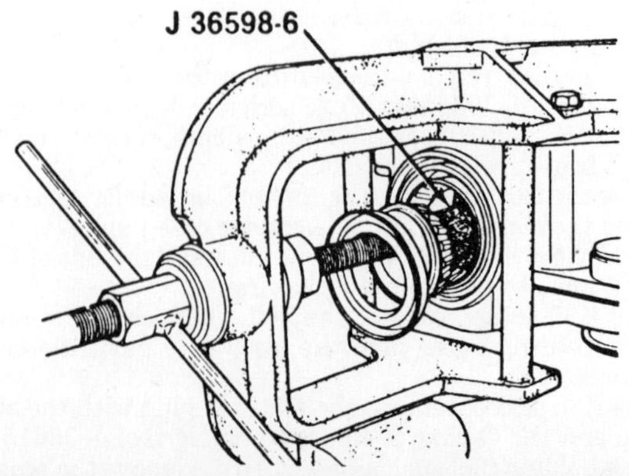

Removing the outer pinion bearing and seal

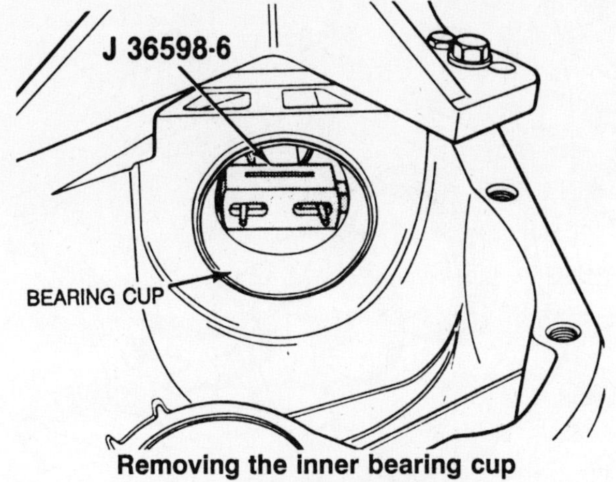

Removing the inner bearing cup

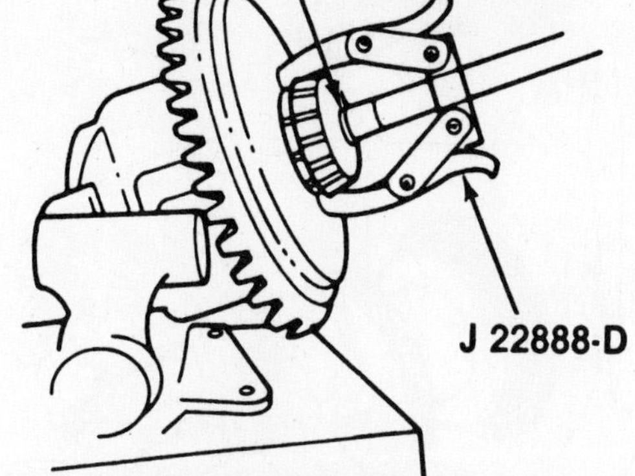

Removing the side bearings

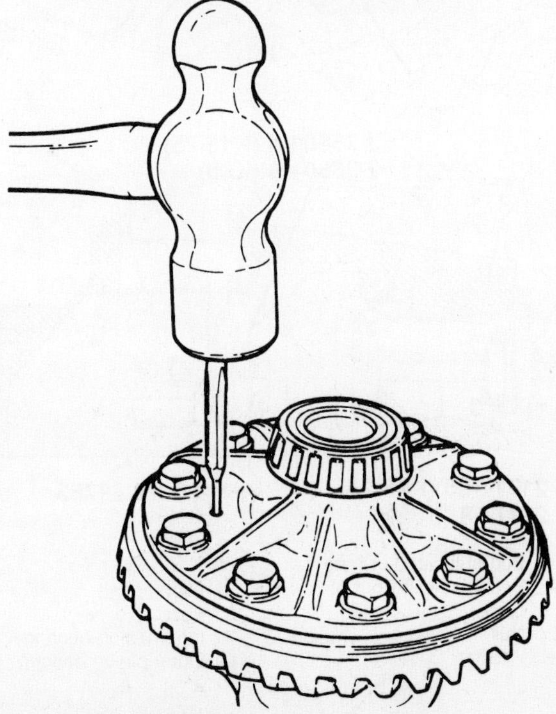
Removing the pin – K15/25

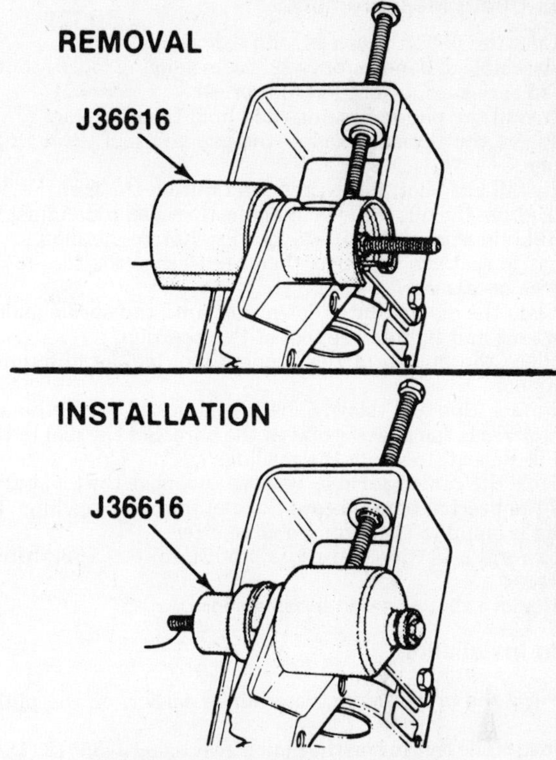

Replacing the carrier bushings

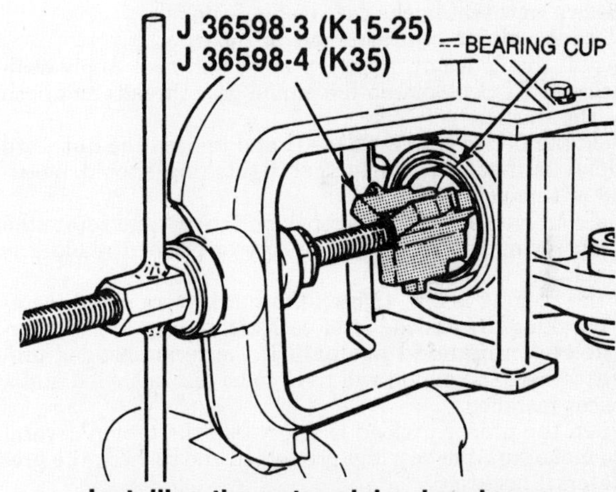

Installing the outer pinion bearing cup

ASSEMBLY

Pinion Bearing Cup

1. Mount the left case half in a holding fixture such as J-36598. For 15/25 series, use adapter J-36598-6. Tighten the fixture bolts securely.
2. Using J-36598-3 (15/25 series) or J-36598-4 (35 series), install the outer bearing cup.
3. Remove J-36598-3 (15/25 series) or J-36598-4 (35 series), and place J-36598-15 in the pinion seal bore. Extend the forcing screw through the bore.
4. Install J-36598-3 (15/25 series) or J-36598-4 (35 series) on the forcing screw. Turn the forcing screw until the installer is snug against the bearing cup. Rotate the tool several times to make sure it's not cocked in the bore.
5. Pull the inner bearing cup into place in the bore.

Pinion Depth Measurement

1. Coat the pinion bearings with axle fluid.
2. Assemble dial indicator J-29763 on gauging tool J-36601-4 (15/25 series) or J-36601-3 (35 series).
3. Install the pinion bearings and hold them in place.
4. Insert the threaded rod of the gauging tool through the bearings.
5. Install the pilot, flat washer and nut on the tool.
6. Tighten the nut while holding the threaded rod. Adjust the nut to obtain a preload of 10–15 inch lbs. Rotate the shaft several times to seat the bearings, then re-measure the torque and adjust as necessary.
7. Push the dial indicator downward until the needle make 3 revolutions and tighten the tool at this position.
8. Place the button of the gauging tool on the differential bearing bore.
9. Rotate the tool, slowly, back and forth, until the dial inidactor reads the lowest point in the bore. Set the dial indicator to **0**. Repeat, to verify the reading.
10. Hold the gauging arm by its flats and move the tool button out of the bearing bore. Record the dial indicator reading. The reading is equal to the required shim size.

    Example: if the reading is 0.508mm, a 0.508 shim is required.
11. Remove the tools and bearing cones.

Pinion Installation

1. Place the proper shim, determined earlier, on the pinion gear.
2. Install the bearing on the pinion gear using J-35512 (15/25 series) or J-36614 (35 series).
3. Place a new spacer on the pinion gear.
4. Place a new seal in the case using J-36266.
5. Place the pinion gear assembly in the case.
6. Install the deflector, flange, washer and nut. Apply sealant, such as PST Sealant® on the pinion gear threads and both sides of the washer.
7. Hold the flange with J-8614-01 and tighten the nut until no endplay is detected. No further tightening should be attempted at this point!
8. Place an inch lbs. torque wrench on the nut and rotate the pinion, observing the reading. The correct preload reading is 15–25 inch lbs.
9. If the reading is low, tighten the nut in very small increments, checking the preload after each tightening. **Do not exceed the recommended preload!** If the recommended preload is exceeded, the pinion will have to be disassembled and a new spacer installed.
10. When the proper preload is set, rotate the pinion several times to make sure the bearings are seated and recheck the preload. Reset, if necessary.

Differential Case

1. On 35 series, install the side gear spacer.
2. Install the thrust washers and side gears in the differential case. On the 35 series, the side gear spacer goes on the left shaft. If used gears and washers are being installed, they must be installed in the same places from which they were removed. Check your identifying marks.
3. Position one pinion gear between the side gears and rotate the gears until the pinion gear is directly opposite the opening in the case.
4. Place the other pinion gear between the side gears, making sure that the holes in the gears line up.
5. Install the thrust washers. Rotate the pinion gears as needed.
6. Install the shaft and pin (15/25 series) or bolt (35 series).
7. Install the ring gear using **new** bolts. Never reuse old bolts! Using an alternating sequence, torque the bolts in 3 pro-

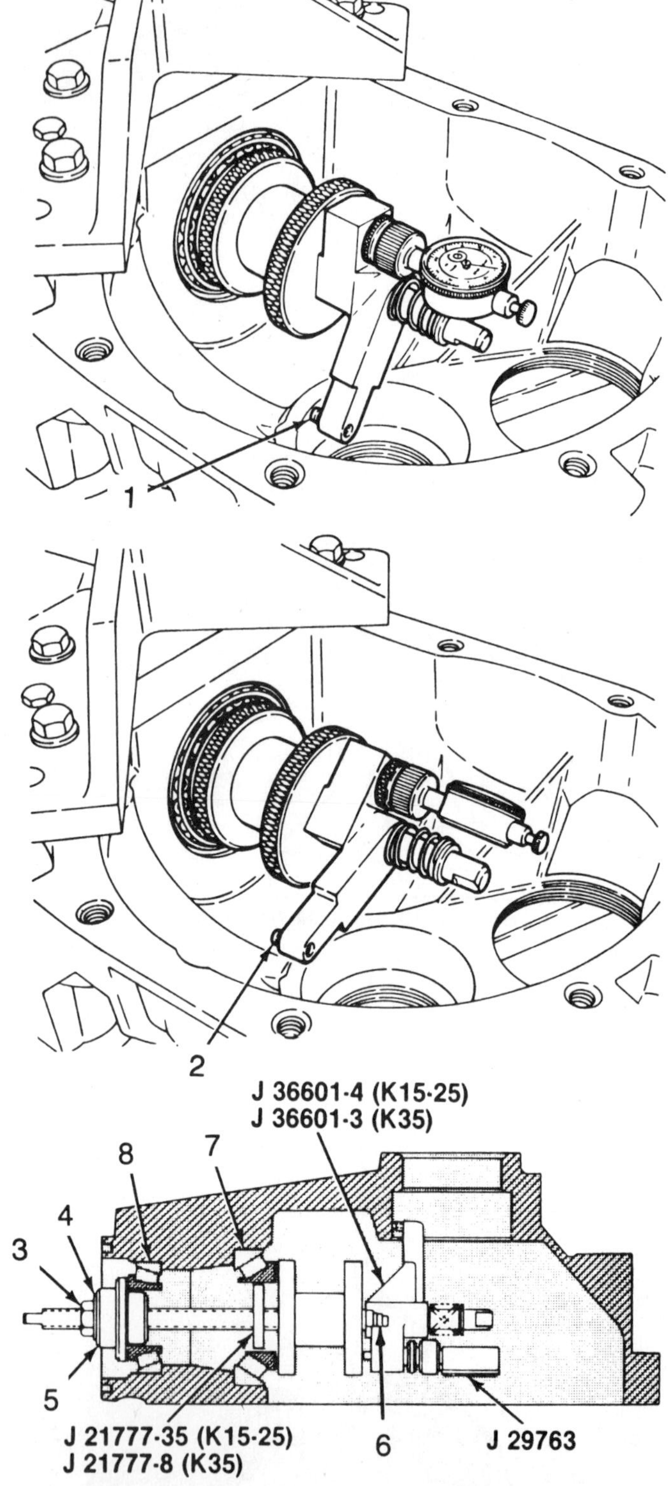

Measuring pinion depth

gressive steps, to a maximum torque of 88 ft. lbs.

8. Using tools J-22761 (15/25 series) or J-29710 (35 series), along with J-8092, install the side bearings.

9. Using tools J-8092 and J-36612 (15/25 series) or J-36613 (35 series) install the carrier bearings on the sleeves or adjuster plug (35 series).

10. On the 35 series, install a new O-ring on the adjuster plug.

11. On 15/25 series, install the sleeves in the carrier case using J-36599.

12. On 35 series, install the right sleeve using J-36599; install the adjuster plug using J-36615.

13. Using J-36602 and J-8092, install the side bearing cups.

14. Place the differential assembly in the carrier case half containing the pinion gear assembly.

Turn the left sleeve (15/25 series) or adjuster plug (35 series) inward until backlash is felt between the ring and pinion.

15. Remove the case from the holding fixture.

16. Join the case halves **without using sealer at this time**. If the case halves do not mate completely, back out the right sleeve until they do. Tighten the bolts to 35 ft. lbs.

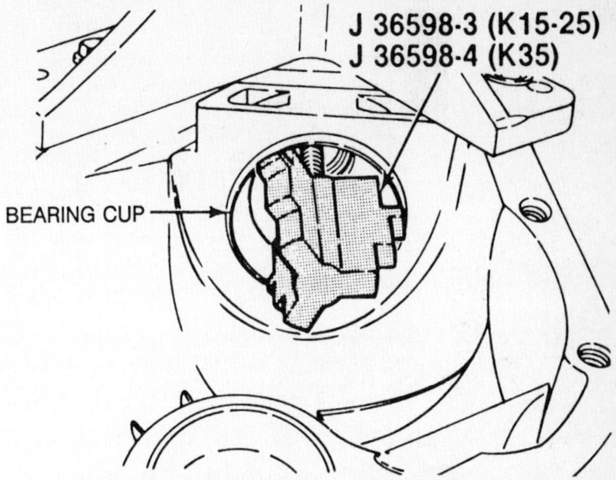

Installing the inner pinion bearing cup

Backlash Adjustment

1. Tighten the right sleeve to 100 ft. lbs.
2. Tighten the left sleeve (15/25 series) or adjuster plug (35 series) to 100 ft. lbs.
3. Matchmark the sleeves and/or plug and the case so that the notches can be counted when turned.
4. Turn the right sleeve **out** 2 notches.
5. Turn the left sleeve or adjuster plug **in** 1 notch.
6. Rotate the pinion several times to seat the bearings.
7. Install indicator and fixture J-34047-3, J-34047-1 and J-8001-1 in the filler plug hole so the stem of the indicator is at the heel end of a tooth.
8. Check and record the backlash at 3 or 4 points around the gear. The pinion must be held stationary while checking backlash. The backlash should be the same at each point ± 0.05mm. If the backlash varies more than ± 0.05mm, check for burrs, a distorted case flange, uneven bolt torques or foreign matter.

   Gear backlash should be 0.08–0.25mm with a preferred setting of 0.13–0.18mm.
9. If backlash is incorrect, adjust the sleeves and/or plug as necessary. Follow this example: If it is necessary to turn the right sleeve **in** 1 notch, turn the left sleeve or plug **out** 1 notch.

   To increase backlash, turn the left sleeve or plug **in** and the right sleeve **out** an identical amount.

   To decrease backlash turn the right sleeve **in** and the left sleeve or plug **out** an identical amount.

   A 1 notch change will cause an 0.08mm change in backlash.

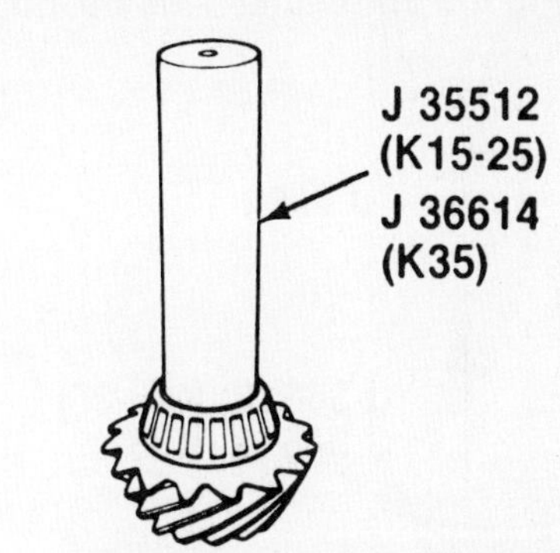

Installing the pinion bearing

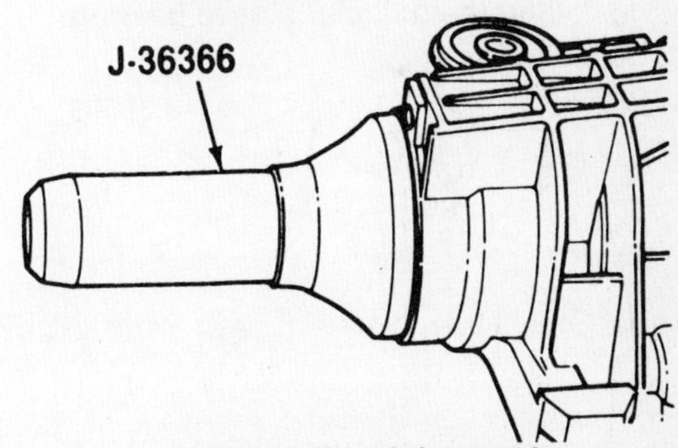

Installing the pinion seal

Gear Pattern Check

Before final assembly of the differential, a pattern check of the gear teeth must be made. This determines if the teeth of the ring and pinion gears are meshing properly, for low noise level and long life of the gear teeth. The most important thing to note is if the pattern is located centrally up and down on the face of the ring gear.

1. Wipe any oil from the carrier and all dirt and oil from the teeth of the ring gear.
2. Coat the teeth of the ring gear with a gear marking compound.
3. Apply a load until it takes 40–50 ft. lbs. of torque to turn the pinion gear.
4. Turn the companion flange so the ring gear makes a full rotation in 1 direction, then, turn it a full rotation in the opposite direction.
5. Check the pattern on the teeth and refer to the chart for any adjustments necessary. Contact pattern can be adjusted by either a change in the pinion depth or a change in backlash. Adjust the pattern as necessary.

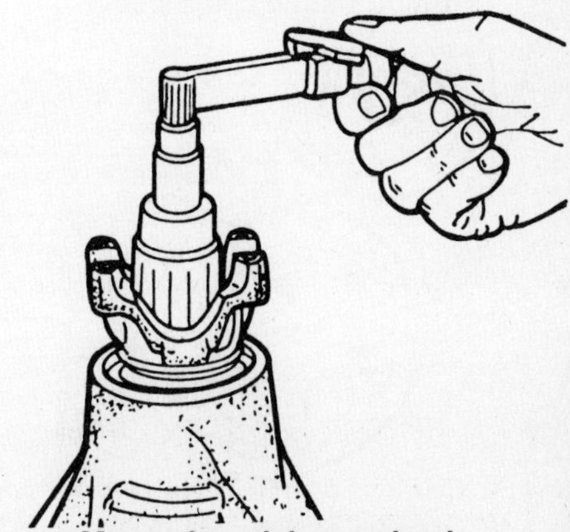

Measuring pinion preload

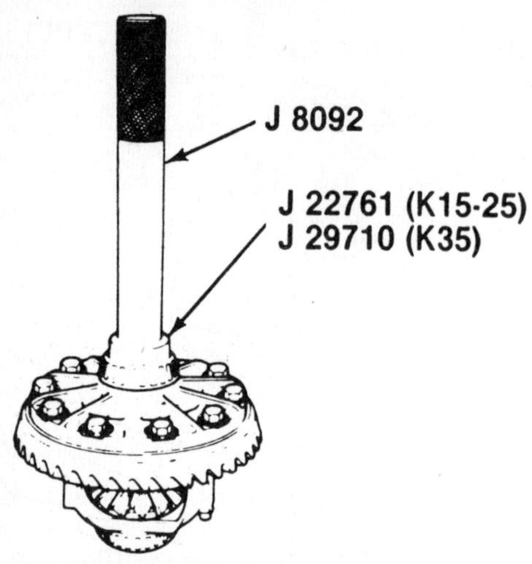

Installing the differential side bearing

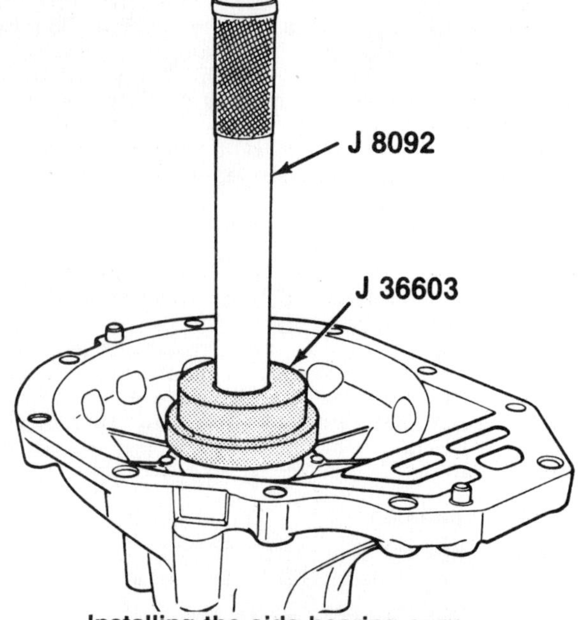

Installing the side bearing cups

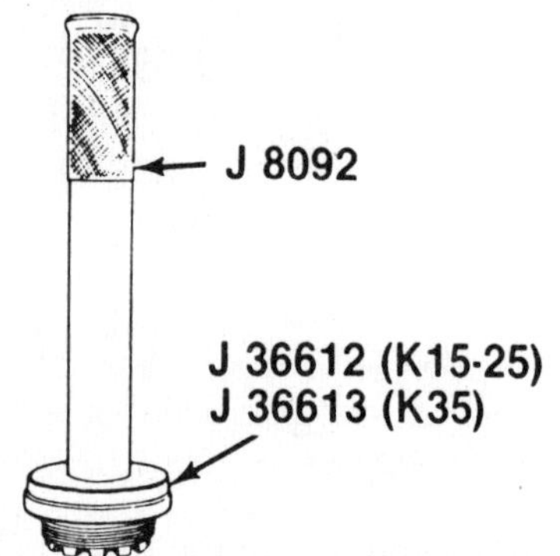

Installing the adjuster sleeve bearing

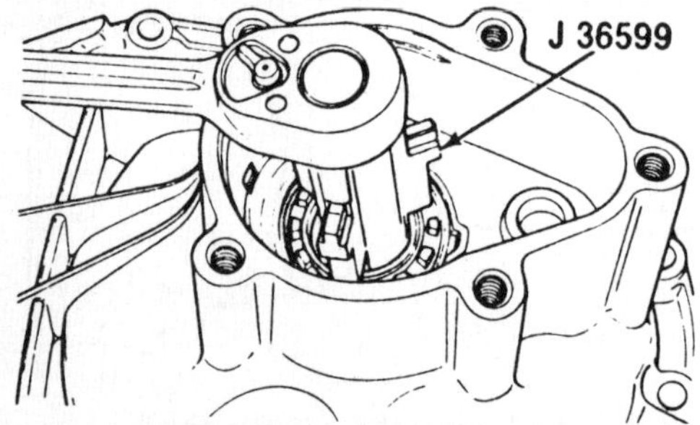

Turning the adjuster sleeve

J 8001-1
J 34047-3
J 34047

Measuring backlash at the ring gear

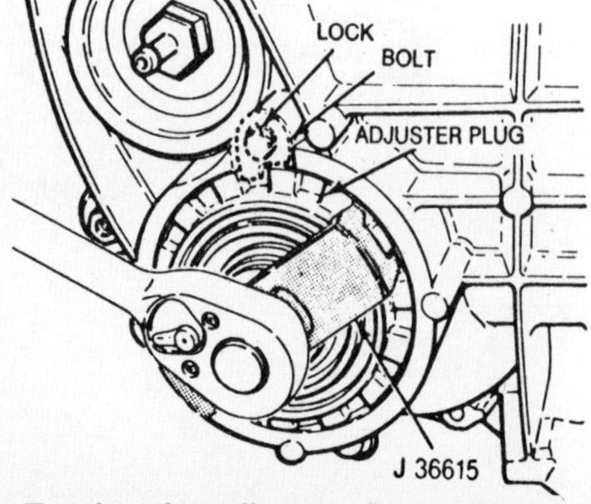

Turning the adjuster plug – K35

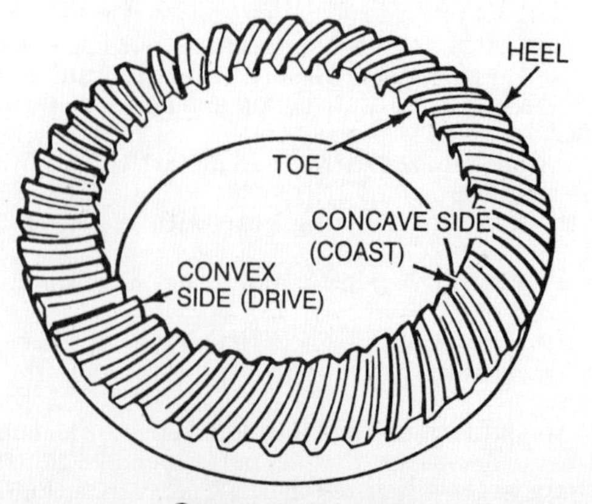

Gear tooth terms

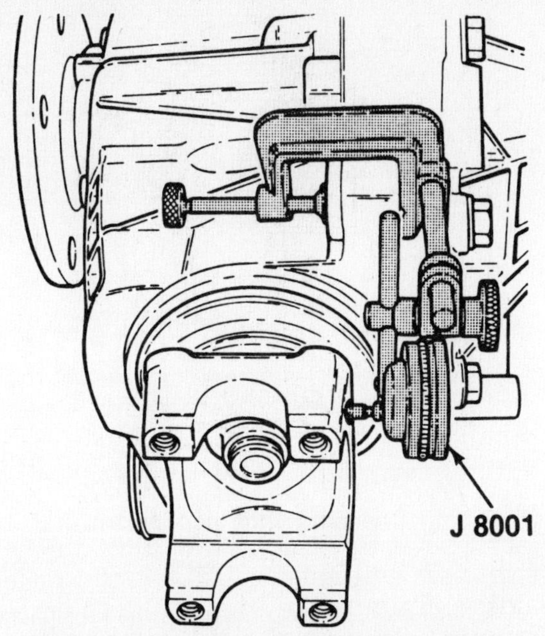

Measuring backlash at the pinion flange

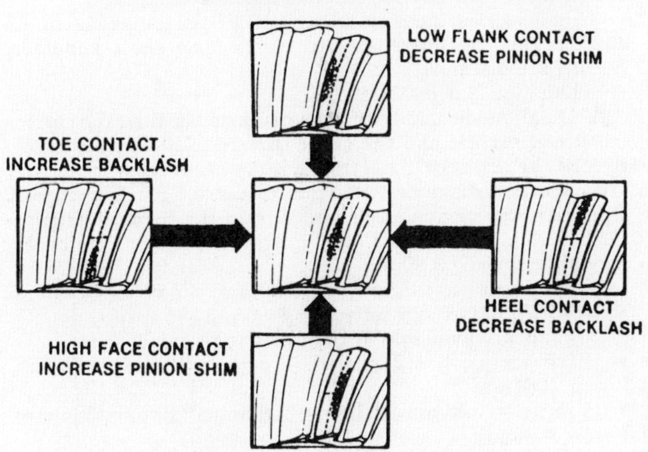

Gear tooth contact pattern

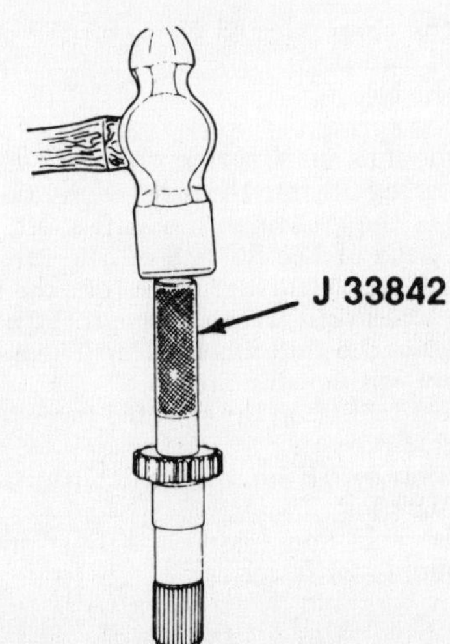

Installing the pilot bearing

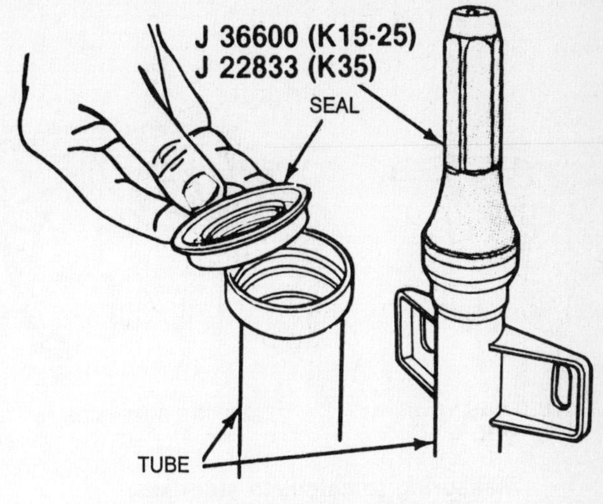

Installing the axle tube seal

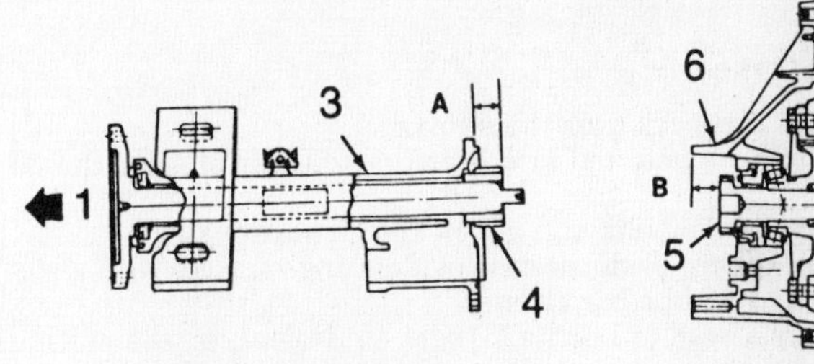

1. Measure with axle shaft forced outboard
2. Shaft
3. Tube
4. Carrier connector
5. Output shaft
6. Carrier case

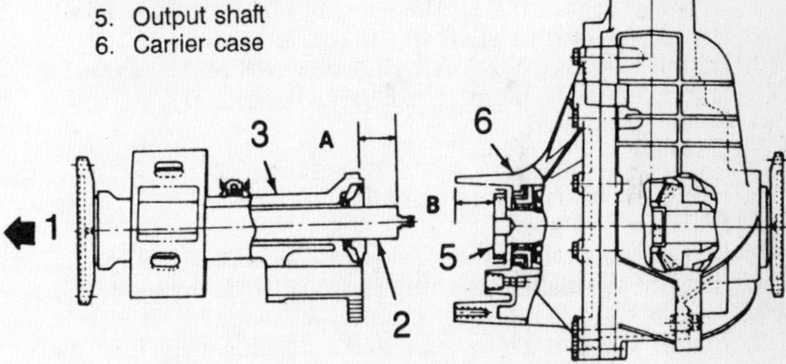

Measuring to calculate shim size

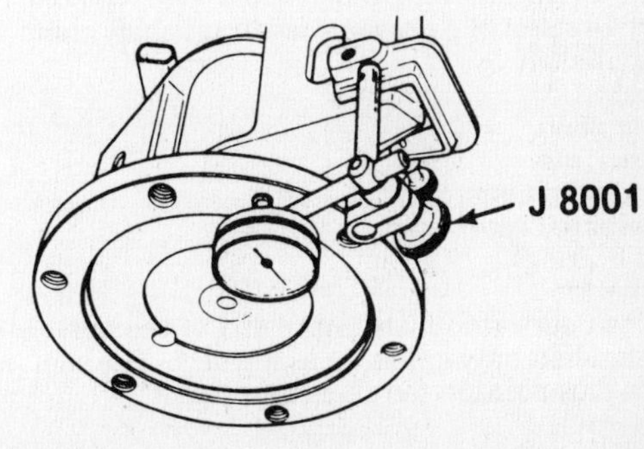

Measuring axle shaft end play

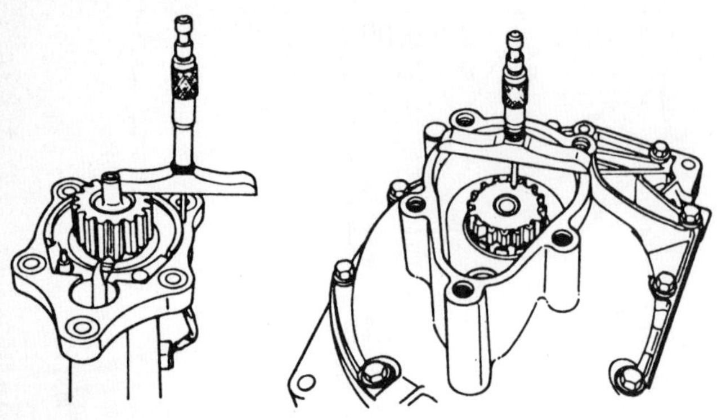

Measuring to calculate shim size

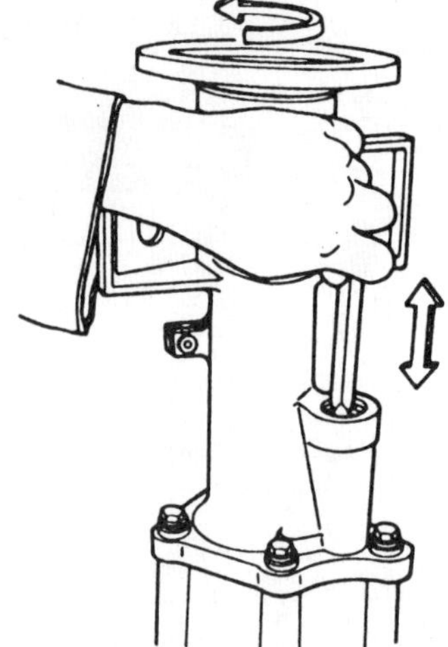
Checking shift mechanism

Carrier Case

1. Bend the locks over the sleeves.
2. Install the bolt and lock over the adjuster plug on the 35 series.
3. Remove the bolts and lift off the right case half.
4. Thoroughly clean the case half mating surfaces with a solvent such as carburetor cleaner.
5. Apply a bead of Loctite®518, or equivalent, on the mating surface of either carrier half. Install the right half and torque the bolts to 35 ft. lbs.
6. Install the left seal, driving it into place with a seal driver and hammer.
7. Drive the shaft and deflector into place.
8. Using J–33842, install the bearing on the output shaft.
9. Install the output shaft in the carrier.
10. Install the vent plug, using Loctite®518 on the threads.
11. Using J–36616, install the carrier bushings.

Axle Tube

1. Drive the bearing into the tube.
2. Install a new seal.
3. Install the shaft and deflector in the tube.
4. Install the washer, aligning the tabs with the slots in the tube.
5. Install the connector gear and retaining ring into place with a plastic mallet.
6. Install the washer and a new snapring (35 series). Make sure that the snapring is fully seated.
7. If any of the following components were replaced, it will be necessary to select the proper size output shaft shim:
   - Output shaft
   - Tube
   - Outer shaft
   - Carrier case
   - Ring and pinion
   - Differential case
   - Side bearings
   - Connector

   a. Push outward on the inner end of the outer shaft and move the shaft outward as far as it will go. The shaft must remain in this position for all measurements.

   b. On 15/25 series, measure between the tube flange machined end and the inner surface of the connector. Record the distance.

   On 35 series, measure between the tube flange machined surface and the inner surface of the axle shaft shoulder. Record the distance.

   This figure is distance "A".

   d. On all models, measure the distance between the carrier machined surface and the outer surface of the output shaft. Record the distance. This figure is distance "B".

   e. Subtract distance "A" from distance "B". The correct shim size will be one size smaller than the resultant figure. For example: If the resultant figure was 3.53mm, the necessary shim will be 3.30mm.

   If the resultant figure was 3.30mm, the necessary shim will be 2.70mm (15/25 series) or 2.80mm (35 series).

   Shims are available in the following sizes:

   - 15/25 series – 1.27mm, 1.78mm, 2.29mm, 2.70mm, 3.30mm, 3.81mm
   - 35 series – 1.80mm, 2.30mm, 2.80mm, 3.30mm, 3.80mm, 4.30mm, 4.80mm

Final Assembly

1. Install the shim selected above on the output shaft. Use grease to hold it in place.
2. Install the sleeve.
3. Install the spring.
4. Install the shift shaft, spring, shift fork and clip in the case. The damper spring fits into the fork indentation. Make sure the clip is seated in the groove on the shift shaft.
5. Apply a bead of Loctite®518 on the tube mating surface and assemble the tube and carrier. Torque the bolts to 30 ft. lbs.
6. Using a brass drift, reach through the actuator hole and manually operate the shift mechanism. The mechanism should move smoothly, without binding.
7. Apply Loctite®518 on the solenoid threads. Tighten the solenoid to 16 ft. lbs.
8. Apply Loctite®518 on the switch threads. Tighten the switch to 45 inch lbs.
9. Refill the axle and install the filler plug and washer. Torque the plug to 24 ft. lbs.

8 Suspension and Steering

QUICK REFERENCE INDEX

GENERAL INDEX

8 SUSPENSION AND STEERING

CAUTION

All suspension and steering fasteners are important attaching parts in that they could affect the performance of vital components and systems, and/or could result in major repair expense. They must be replaced with one of the same part number or with an equivalent part if replacement becomes necessary. Do not use a replacement part of lesser quality or substitute design. Torque values must be used as specified during reassembly to assure proper retention of these parts. Observe all nut and bolt torque specifications.

WHEELS

REMOVAL

1. Raise the truck on a jack just enough to take up the weight of the truck, leaving the tire on the ground.
2. Using a lug wrench or breaker bar and socket, break loose the lug nuts in a crisscross pattern.
3. Raise and safely support the truck, remove the lug nuts and remove the wheel(s).

To install:

Single Wheel

4. Lift the wheel onto the lugs. Snug down the topmost nut, then snug down the rest of the nuts in a crisscross pattern. When all nuts are snugged, torque them, in a crisscross pattern, to the specifications at the end of this procedure.

Dual Wheels

5. Install the inner and outer wheels, and clamp ring. Be sure that the pins on the clamp ring face outwards.
6. Install the nuts snugly, in a crisscross pattern. When all the lugs are snugged, tighten them in the sequence shown to the specifications at the end of this procedure.

Wheel tightening sequence

Trucks with single front and rear wheels

- R10/1500 w/5 studs and steel or aluminum wheels: 100 ft. lbs.
- V10/1500 w/6 studs and steel wheels: 88 ft. lbs.
- V10/1500 w/6 studs and aluminum wheels: 100 ft. lbs.
- All C and K Series: 105 ft. lbs.
- All R and V Series with 8 studs: 120 ft. lbs.

Trucks with single front and dual rear wheels

- R and V Series: 140 ft. lbs.
- C and K Series: 125 ft. lbs.

R SERIES 2-WHEEL DRIVE FRONT SUSPENSION

Coil Spring

CAUTION

Coil springs are under considerable tension. Be very careful when removing and installing them; they can exert enough force to cause serious injury. Always use spring compressors or a safety chain when removing a coil spring, or releasing spring tension!

REMOVAL AND INSTALLATION

1. Raise and support the truck under the frame rails. The control arms should hang freely.
2. Remove the wheel.
3. Disconnect the shock absorber at the lower end and move it aside.
4. Disconnect the stabilizer bar from the lower control arm.
5. Support the lower control arm and install a spring compressor on the spring, or chain the spring to the control arm as a safety precaution.

NOTE: On trucks with an air cylinder inside the spring, remove the valve core from the cylinder and expel the air by compressing the cylinder with a prybar. With the cylinder compressed, replace the valve core so that the cylinder will stay in the compressed position. Push the cylinder as far as possible towards the top of the spring.

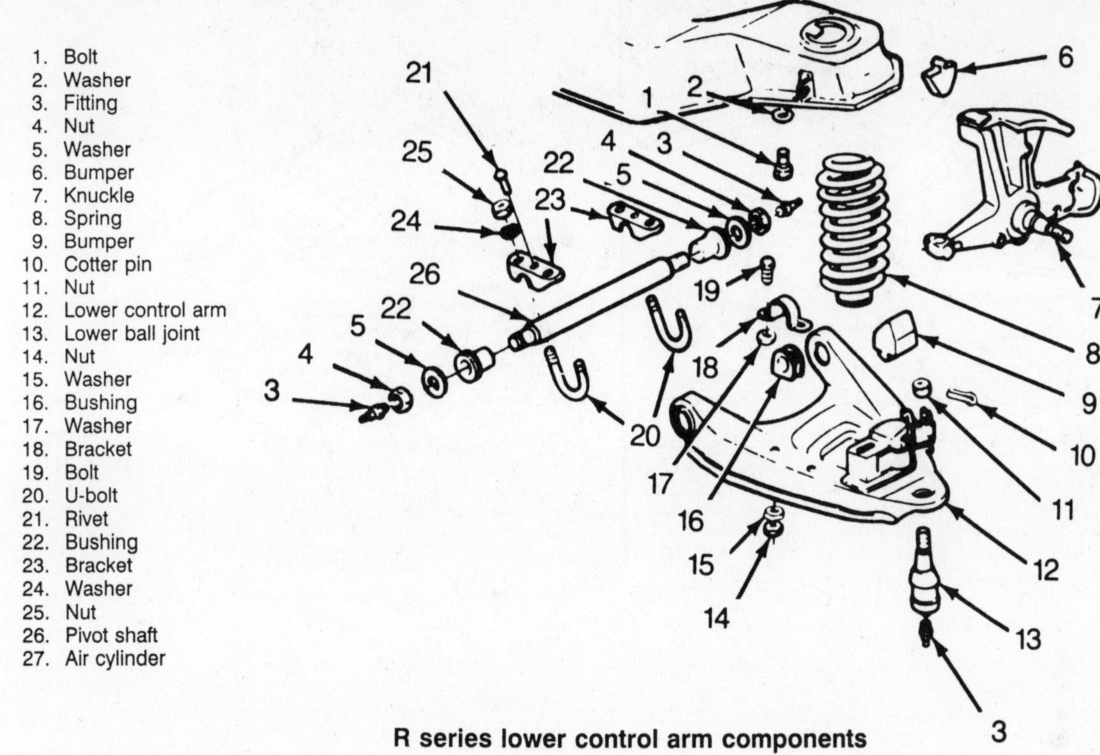

R series lower control arm components

6. Raise the jack to remove the tension from the lower control arm cross-shaft and remove the two U-bolts securing the cross-shaft to the crossember.

CAUTION

The cross-shaft and lower control arm keeps the coil spring compressed. Use care when you lower the assembly.

7. Slowly release the jack and lower the control arm until the spring can be removed. Be sure that all compression is relieved from the spring.
8. If the spring was chained, remove the chain and spring. If you used spring compressors, remove the spring and slowly release the compressors.
9. Remove the air cylinder, if so equipped.

To install:

CAUTION

All suspension and steering fasteners are important attaching parts in that they could affect the performance of vital components and systems, and/or could result in major repair expense. They must be replaced with one of the same part number or with an equivalent part if replacement becomes necessary. Do not use a replacement part of lesser quality or substitute design. Torque values must be used as specified during reassembly to assure proper retention of these parts. Observe all nut and bolt torque specifications.

10. Install the air cylinder so that the protector plate is towards the upper control arm. The schrader valve should protrude through the hole in the lower control arm.
11. Install the chain and spring. If you used spring compressors, install the spring and compressors.
12. Slowly raise the jack and lower the control arm. Line up the indexing hole in the shaft with the crossmember attaching studs.
13. Install the two U-bolts securing the cross-shaft to the crossember. Torque the nuts to 85 ft. lbs.
14. Remove the jack.
15. Connect the stabilizer bar to the lower control arm. Torque the nuts to 24 ft. lbs.
16. Connect the shock absorber at the lower end. Torque the bolt to 59 ft. lbs.
17. If equipped with air cylinders, inflate the cylinder to 60 psi.
18. Install the wheel.
19. Lower the truck. Once the weight of the truck is on the wheels, reduce the air cylinder pressure to 50 psi.
20. Have the alignment checked.

Shock Absorbers

REMOVAL AND INSTALLATION

1. Raise and support the front end on jackstands.
2. Remove the upper end nut and washer.
3. Remove the lower end nut, bolt and washer.

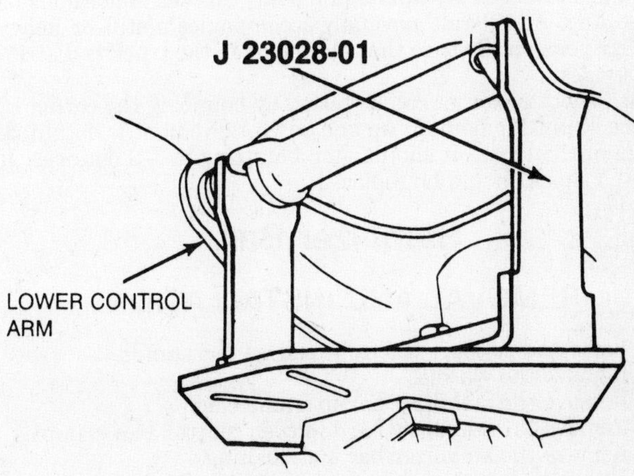

Removing the coil spring – R series

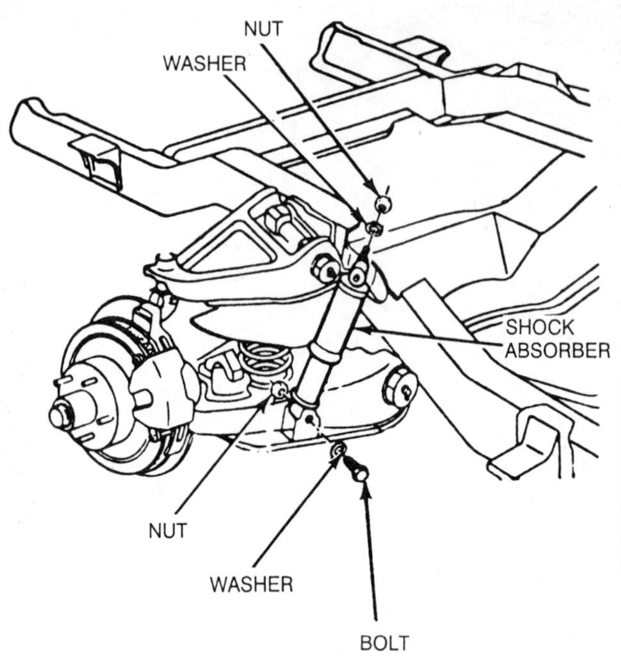

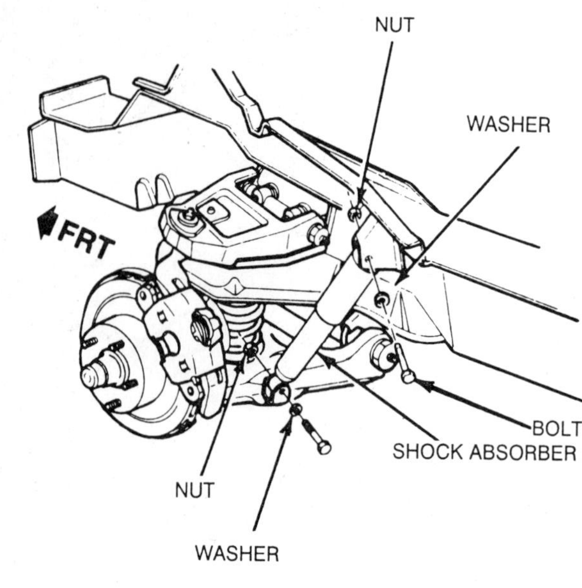

R series front shock absorbers

4. Remove the shock absorber and inspect the rubber bushings. If these are defective, replace the shock absorber assembly.
5. Installation is the reverse of removal. Torque the upper end nut to 140 ft. lbs.; the lower end bolt to 59 ft. lbs.

CAUTION

All suspension and steering fasteners are important attaching parts in that they could affect the performance of vital components and systems, and/or could result in major repair expense. They must be replaced with one of the same part number or with an equivalent part if replacement becomes necessary. Do not use a replacement part of lesser quality or substitute design. Torque values must be used as specified during reassembly to assure proper retention of these parts. Observe all nut and bolt torque specifications.

TESTING

Adjust the tire pressure before testing the shocks. If the truck is equipped with heavy duty equipment, this can sometimes be misleading. A stiff ride normally accompanies a stiff or heavy duty suspension. Be sure that all weight in the truck is distributed evenly.

Each shock absorber can be tested by bouncing the corner of the truck until maximum up and down movement is obtained. Let go of the truck. It should stop bouncing in 1-2 bounces. If not, the shock should be replaced.

Stabilizer Bar

REMOVAL AND INSTALLATION

1. Raise and support the front end on jackstands.
2. Remove the wheels.
3. Remove the stabilizer bar-to-frame clamps.
4. Remove the stabilizer bar-to-lower control arm clamps.
5. Remove the stabilizer bar and bushings.
6. Check the bushings for wear or splitting. Replace any damaged bushings.
7. Installation is the reverse of removal. Note, the split in the bushing faces forward. Coat the bushings with silicone grease prior to installation. Install all fasteners finger-tight. When all the fasteners are in place torque all of them to 24 ft. lbs.

CAUTION

All suspension and steering fasteners are important attaching parts in that they could affect the performance of vital components and systems, and/or could result in major repair expense. They must be replaced with one of the same part number or with an equivalent part if replacement becomes necessary. Do not use a replacement part of lesser quality or substitute design. Torque values must be used as specified during reassembly to assure proper retention of these parts. Observe all nut and bolt torque specifications.

Wheel Hub, Rotor and Bearings

Before handling the bearings, there are a few things that you should remember to do and not to do.

Remember to DO the following:

- Remove all outside dirt from the housing before exposing the bearing.
- Treat a used bearing as gently as you would a new one.
- Work with clean tools in clean surroundings.
- Use clean, dry canvas gloves, or at least clean, dry hands.
- Clean solvents and flushing fluids are a must.
- Use clean paper when laying out the bearings to dry.
- Protect disassembled bearings from rust and dirt. Cover them up.
- Use clean rags to wipe bearings.
- Keep the bearings in oil-proof paper when they are to be stored or are not in use.
- Clean the inside of the housing before replacing the bearing.

Do NOT do the following:

- Don't work in dirty surroundings.
- Don't use dirty, chipped or damaged tools.

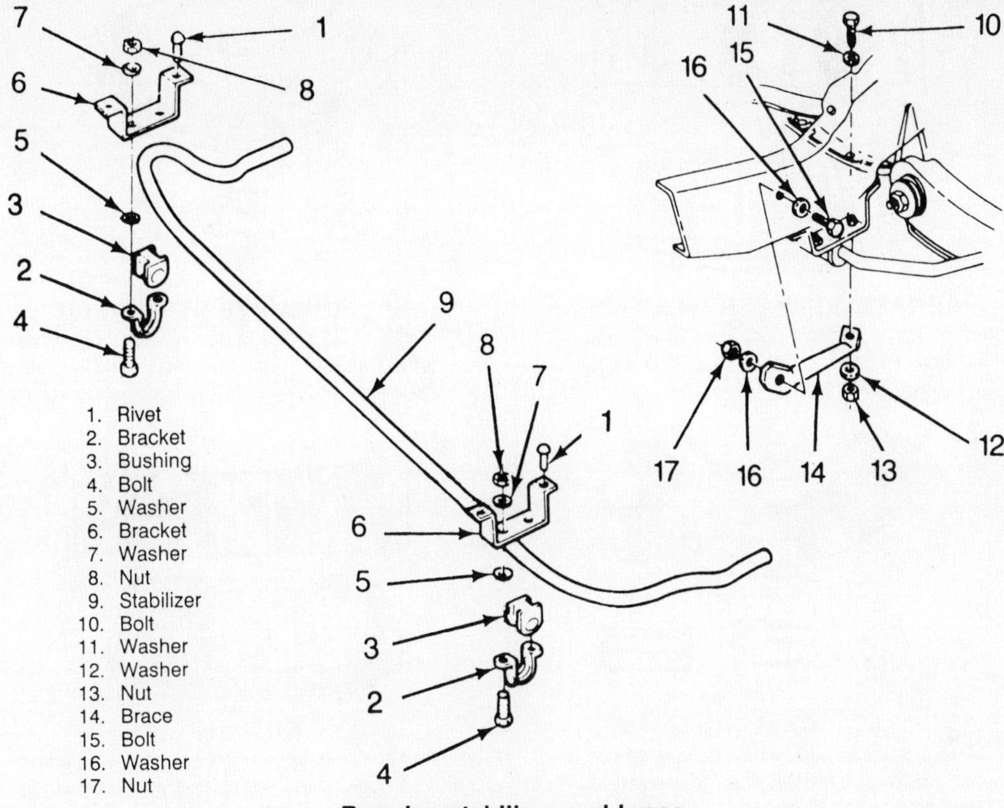

R series stabilizer and brace

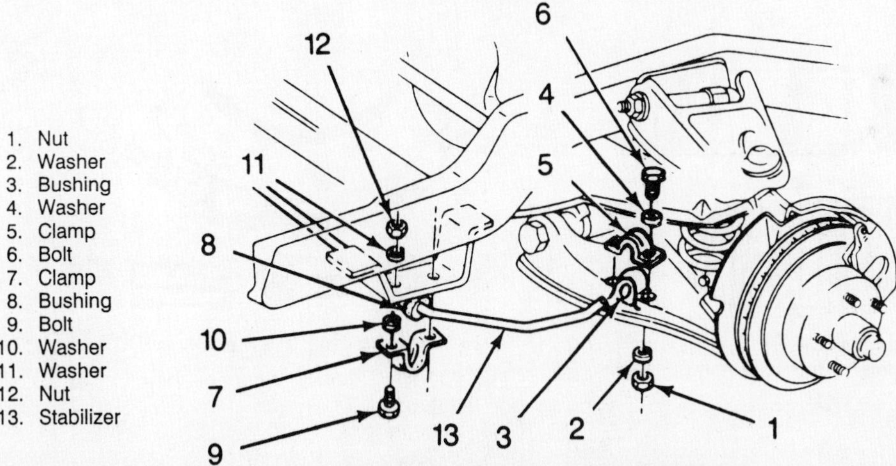

R series stabilizer bar installation

- Try not to work on wooden work benches or use wooden mallets.
- Don't handle bearings with dirty or moist hands.
- Do not use gasoline for cleaning; use a safe solvent.
- Do not spin-dry bearings with compressed air. They will be damaged.
- Do not spin dirty bearings.
- Avoid using cotton waste or dirty cloths to wipe bearings.
- Try not to scratch or nick bearing surfaces.
- Do not allow the bearing to come in contact with dirt or rust at any time.

1. Raise and support the front end on jackstands.
2. Remove the wheel.
3. Dismount the caliper and wire it out of the way.
4. Pry out the grease cap, remove the cotter pin, spindle nut, and washer, then remove the hub. Do not drop the wheel bearings.
5. Remove the outer roller bearing assembly from the hub. The inner bearing assembly will remain in the hub and may be removed after prying out the inner seal. Discard the seal.
6. Clean all parts in a non-flammable solvent and let them air dry. Never spin-dry a bearing with compressed air! Check for excessive wear and damage.
7. Using a hammer and drift, remove the bearing races from the hub. They are driven out from the inside out. When installing new races, make sure that they are not cocked and that they are fully seated against the hub shoulder.
8. Pack both wheel bearings using high melting point wheel

ABRASIVE ROLLER WEAR
Pattern on races and rollers caused by fine abrasives. Clean all parts and housings, check seals and bearings and replace if leaking, rough or noisy.

ABRASIVE STEP WEAR
Pattern on roller ends caused by fine abrasives. Clean all parts and housings, check seals and bearings and replace if leaking, rough or noisy.

GALLING
Metal smears on roller ends due to overheat, lubricant failure or overload. Replace bearing, check seals and check for proper lubrication.

ETCHING
Bearing surfaces appear gray or grayish black in color with related etching away of material usually at roller spacing. Replace bearings, check seals and check for proper lubrication.

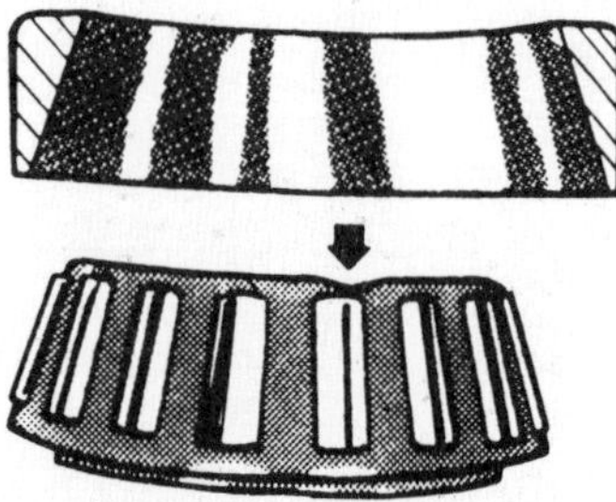

BENT CAGE
Cage damaged due to improper handling or tool usage.
Replace bearing.

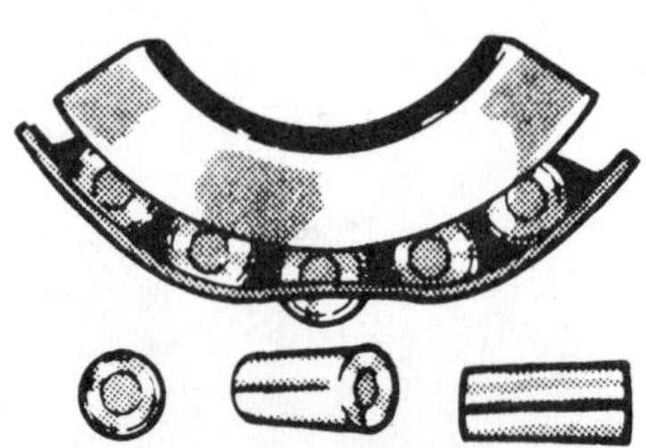

BENT CAGE
Cage damaged due to improper handling or tool usage.
Replace bearing.

CAGE WEAR
Wear around outside diameter of cage and roller pockets caused by abrasive material and inefficient lubrication.
Clean related parts and housings.
Check seals and replace bearings.

INDENTATIONS
Surface depressions on race and rollers caused by hard particles of foreign material.
Clean all parts and housings. Check seals and replace bearings if rough or noisy.

Diagnosis of front wheel bearings

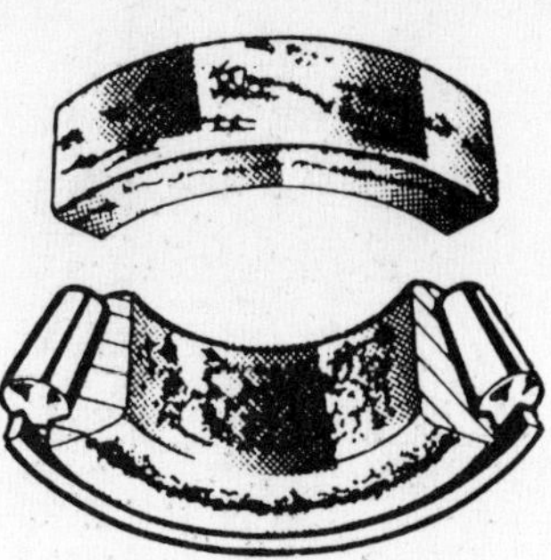

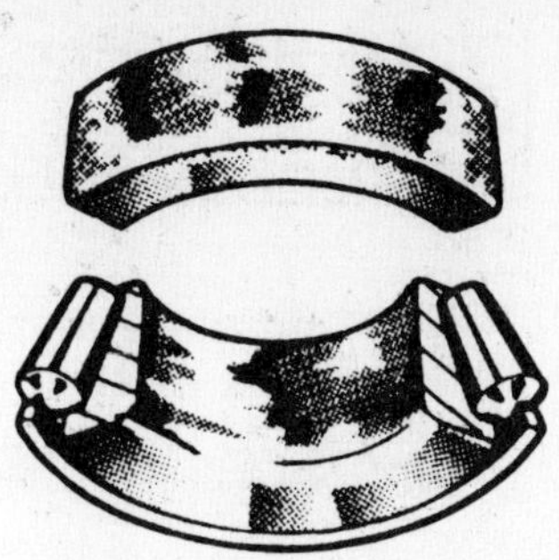

FRETTAGE

Corrosion set up by small relative movement of parts with no lubrication.

Replace bearing. Clean related parts. Check seals and check for proper lubrication.

SMEARS

Smearing of metal due to slippage. Slippage can be caused by poor fits, lubrication, overheating, overloads or handling damage. Replace bearings, clean related parts and check for proper fit and lubrication.

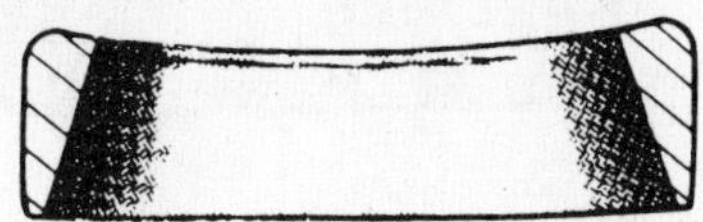

STAIN DISCOLORATION

Discoloration can range from light brown to black caused by incorrect lubricant or moisture.

Re-use bearings if stains can be removed by light polishing or if no evidence of overheating is observed.

Check seals and related parts for damage.

HEAT DISCOLORATION

Heat discoloration can range from faint yellow to dark blue resulting from overload or incorrect lubricant.

Excessive heat can cause softening of races or rollers. To check for loss of temper on races or rollers a simple file test may be made. A file drawn over a tempered part will grab and cut metal, whereas, a file drawn over a hard part will glide readily with no metal cutting.

Replace bearings if over heating damage is indicated. Check seals and other parts.

Diagnosis of front wheel bearings

bearing grease for disc brakes. Ordinary grease will melt and ooze out ruining the pads. Bearings should be packed using a cone-type wheel bearing greaser tool. If one is not available they may be packed by hand. Place a healthy glob of grease in the palm of one hand and force the edge of the bearing into it so that the grease fills the bearing. Do this until the whole bearing is packed.

9. Place the inner bearing in the hub and install a new inner seal, making sure that the seal flange faces the bearing race.
10. Carefully install the wheel hub over the spindle.
11. Using your hands, firmly press the outer bearing into the hub. Install the spindle washer and nut.
12. Spin the wheel hub by hand and tighten the nut until it is just snug (12 ft. lbs.). Back off the nut until it is loose, then tighten it finger tight. Loosen the nut until either hole in the spindle lines up with a slot in the nut and insert a new cotter pin. There should be 0.001–0.005 in. (0.025–0.127mm) endplay. This can be measured with a dial indicator, if you wish.
13. Replace the dust cap, wheel and tire.

Lower Ball Joint

INSPECTION

1. Support the weight of the control arm at the wheel hub.
2. Measure the distance between the tip of the ball joint stud and the grease fitting below the ball joint.
3. Move the support to the control arm and allow the hub to hang free. Measure the distance again. If the variation between the two measurements exceeds $^3/_{32}$ in. (2.4mm) the ball joint should be replaced.

REMOVAL AND INSTALLATION

1. Raise and support the front end on jackstands.
2. Support the lower control arm with a floor jack.
3. Remove the wheel.
4. Remove the lower stud cotter pin and loosen, but do not remove, the stud nut.

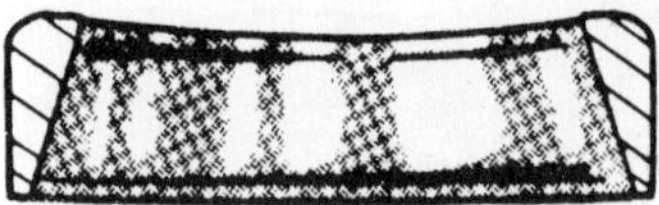

MISALIGNMENT
Outer race misalignment due to foreign object.
Clean related parts and replace bearing. Make sure races are properly seated.

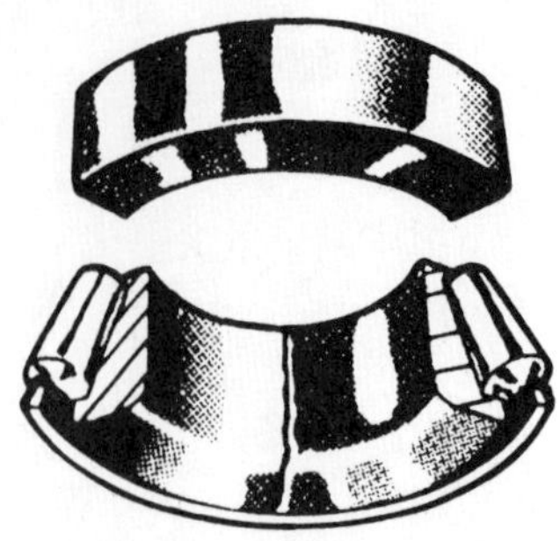

CRACKED INNER RACE
Race cracked due to improper fit, cocking, or poor bearing seats.
Replace bearing and correct bearing seats.

FATIGUE SPALLING
Flaking of surface metal resulting from fatigue.
Replace bearing, clean all related parts.

BRINELLING
Surface indentations in raceway caused by rollers either under impact loading or vibration while the bearing is not rotating.
Replace bearing if rough or noisy.

Diagnosis of front wheel bearings

5. Loosen the ball joint with a forcing-type ball joint tool. It may be necessary to remove the brake caliper and wire it to the frame to gain enough clearance.
6. When the stud is loose, remove the tool and ball stud nut.
7. Install a spring compressor on the coil spring for safety.
8. Pull the brake disc and knuckle assembly up and off the ball stud and support the upper arm with a block of wood.
9. Remove the ball joint from the control arm with a ball joint fork or another suitable tool.

To install:

CAUTION

All suspension and steering fasteners are important attaching parts in that they could affect the performance of vital components and systems, and/or could result in major repair expense. They must be replaced with one of the same part number or with an equivalent part if replacement becomes necessary. Do not use a replacement part of lesser quality or substitute design. Torque values must be used as specified during reassembly to assure proper retention of these parts. Observe all nut and bolt torque specifications.

10. Start the new ball joint into the control arm. Position the bleed vent in the rubber boot facing inward.
11. Turn the screw until the ball joint is seated in the control arm.
12. Lower the upper arm and match the steering knuckle to the lower ball stud.
13. Install the brake caliper, if removed.
14. Install the ball stud nut and torque it to 80–100 ft. lbs. plus the additional torque necessary to align the cotter pin hole. Do not exceed 130 ft. lbs. or back the nut off to align the holes with the pin.
15. Install a new lube fitting and lubricate the new joint.
16. Install the tire and wheel.
17. Lower the truck.

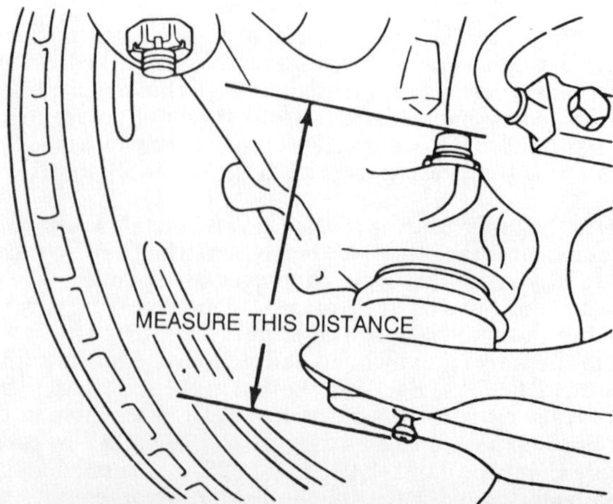

Inspecting the R series lower ball joint

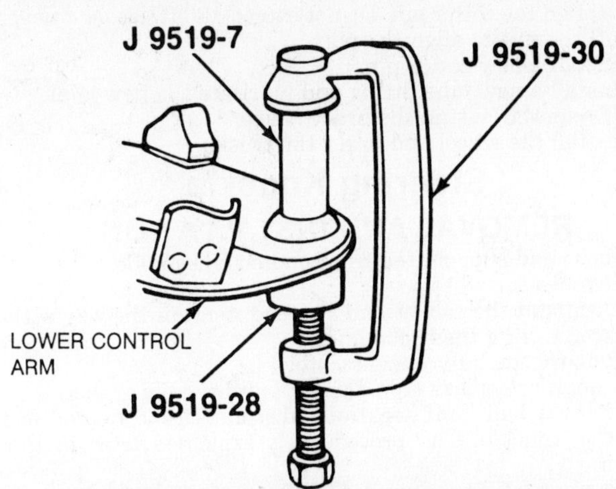

Removing the R series lower ball joint

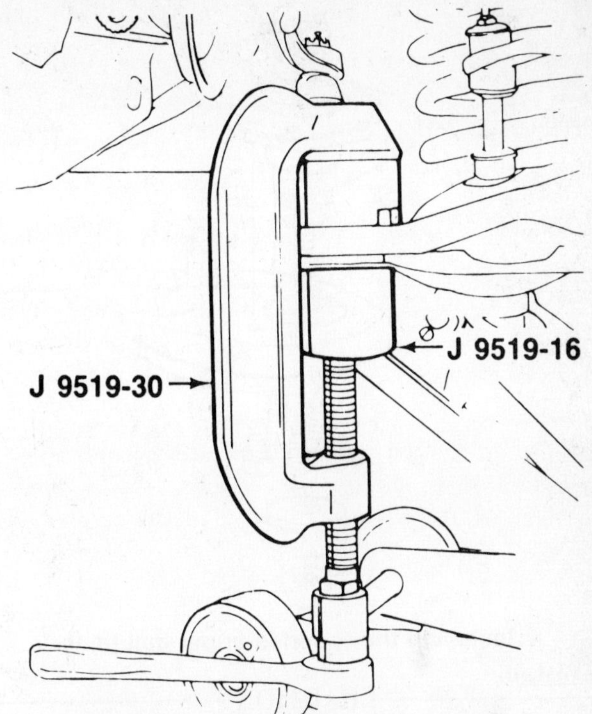

Installing the R series lower ball joint

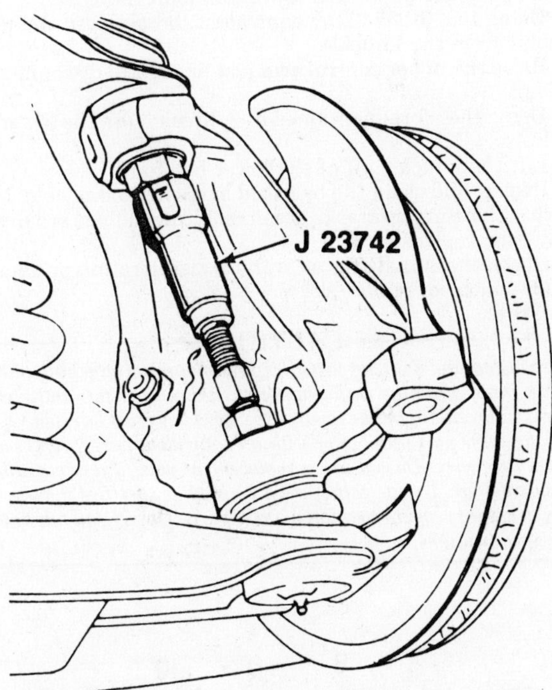

Disconnecting the R series lower ball joint

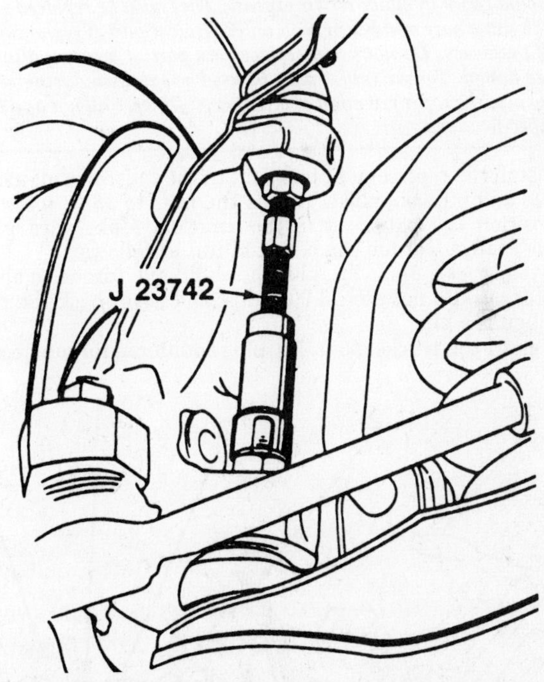

Disconnecting the R series upper ball joint

Upper Ball Joint

INSPECTION

1. Raise and support the front end on jackstands so that the control arms hang freely.
2. Remove the wheel.
3. The upper ball joint is spring-loaded. Replace the ball joint if the is any lateral movement or if it can be twisted in its socket with your fingers.

REMOVAL AND INSTALLATION

1. Raise and support the truck with jackstands. Remove wheel.
2. Support the lower control arm with a floor jack.
3. Remove the cotter pin from the upper ball stud and loosen, but do not remove the stud nut.
4. Using a forcing-type ball joint separator tool, loosen the ball stud in the steering knuckle. When the stud is loose, remove the tool and the stud nut. It may be necessary to remove the brake caliper and wire it to the frame to gain clearance.
5. Drill out the rivets using a 1/8 in. drill bit. Remove the ball joint assembly.

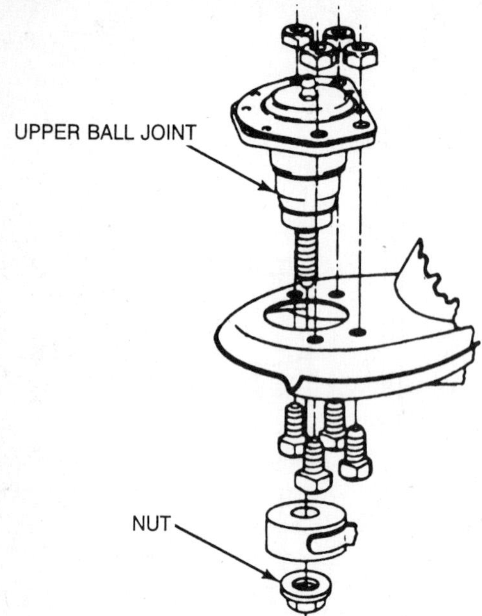

Installing the R series upper ball joint

To Install:

CAUTION

All suspension and steering fasteners are important attaching parts in that they could affect the performance of vital components and systems, and/or could result in major repair expense. They must be replaced with one of the same part number or with an equivalent part if replacement becomes necessary. Do not use a replacement part of lesser quality or substitute design. Torque values must be used as specified during reassembly to assure proper retention of these parts. Observe all nut and bolt torque specifications.

6. Install the replacement ball joint in the control arm, using the bolts and nuts supplied. Torque the nuts to 18 ft. lbs.
7. Position the ball stud in the knuckle. Make sure it is sqaurely seated. Torque the ball stud nut as follows:
   - ½ ton trucks: 50 ft. lbs. plus the additional torque to align the cotter pin. Do not exceed 90 ft. lbs. and never back the nut off to align the pin.
   - ¾ and 1 ton trucks: 90 ft. lbs. plus additional torque necessary to align the cotter pin. Do not exceed 130 ft. lbs. and never back off the nut to align the pin.
8. Install a new cotter pin.
9. Install a new lube fitting and lubricate the new joint.
10. If removed, install the brake caliper.
11. Install the wheel and lower the truck.

Steering Knuckle

REMOVAL AND INSTALLATION

1. Raise and support the front end on jackstands.
2. Remove the wheels.
3. Dismount the caliper and suspend it out of the way without disconnecting the brake lines.
4. Remove the hub/rotor assembly.
5. Unbolt the splash shield and discard the old gasket.
6. Using a ball joint separator, disconnect the tie rod end from the knuckle. The procedure is explained later in this Section.
7. Position a floor jack under the lower control arm, near the spring seat. Raise the jack until it *just* takes up the weight of the suspension, compressing the spring. Safety-chain the coil spring to the lower arm.
8. Remove the upper and lower ball joint nuts.
9. Using tool J-23742, or equivalent, break loose the upper ball joint from the knuckle.
10. Raise the upper control arm just enough to disconnect the ball joint.
11. Using the afore-mentioned tool, break loose the lower ball joint.
12. Lift the knuckle off of the lower ball joint.
13. Inspect and clean the ball stud bores in the knuckle. Make sure that there are no cracks or burrs. If the knuckle is damaged in any way, replace it.
14. Check the spindle for wear, heat discoloration or damage. If at all damaged, replace it.

To install:

CAUTION

All suspension and steering fasteners are important attaching parts in that they could affect the performance of vital components and systems, and/or could result in major repair expense. They must be replaced with one of the same part number or with an equivalent part if replacement becomes necessary. Do not use a replacement part of lesser quality or substitute design. Torque values must be used as specified during reassembly to assure proper retention of these parts. Observe all nut and bolt torque specifications.

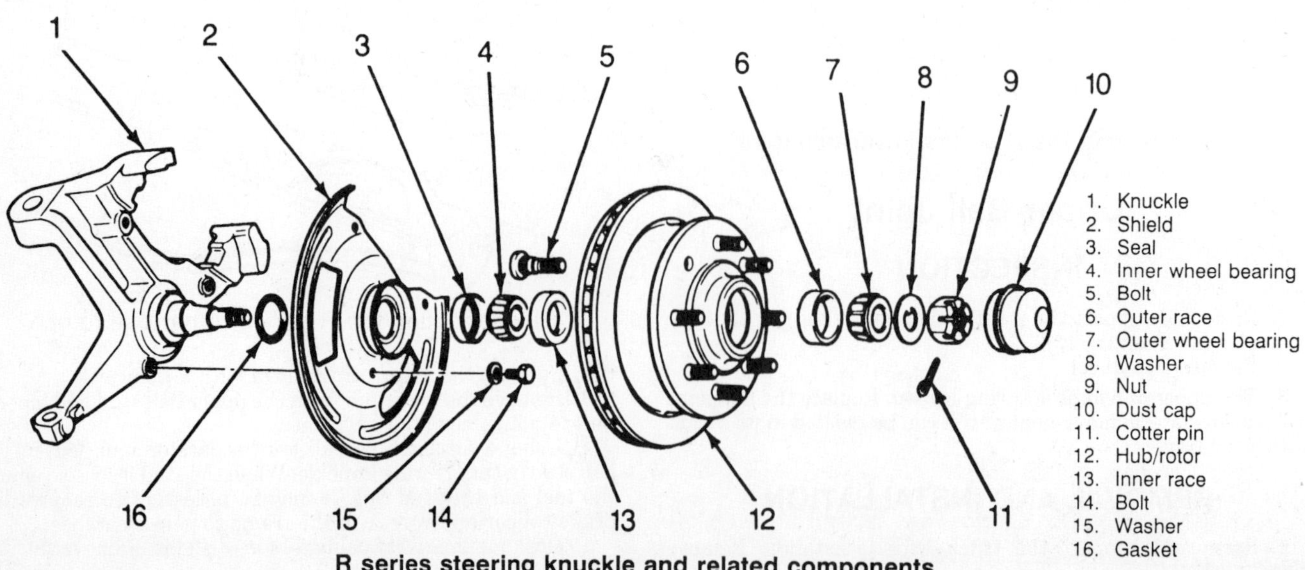

R series steering knuckle and related components

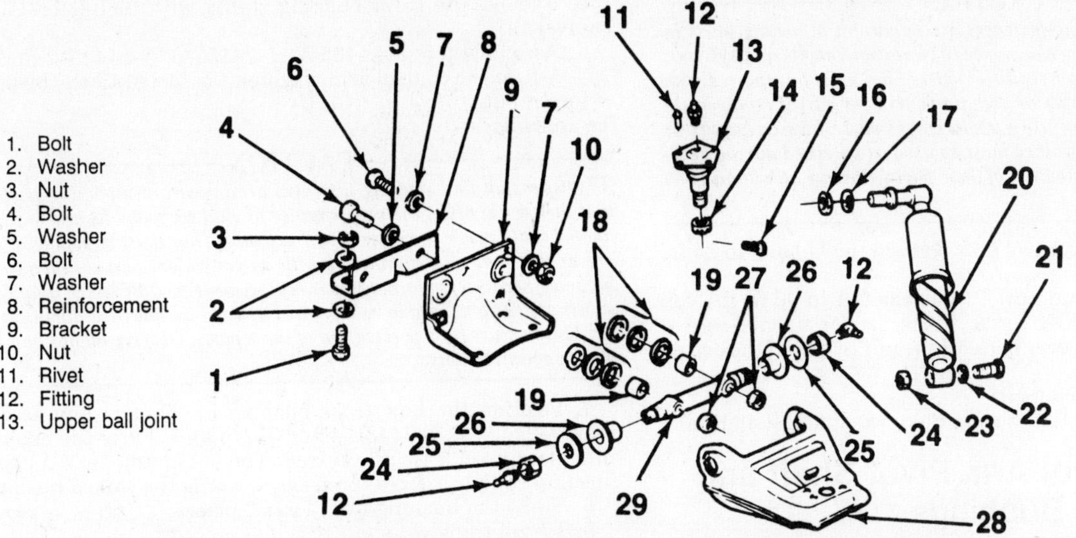

R series upper control arm and related components

15. Maneuver the knuckle onto both ball joints.
16. Install both nuts. On 10/1500 series and 20/2500 series, torque the upper nut to 50 ft. lbs. and the lower nut to 90 ft. lbs. On 30/3500 series, torque both nuts to 90 ft. lbs.
17. Install the cotter pins. Always advance the nut to align the cotter pin hole. NEVER back it off! On the upper nut which was originally torque to 50 ft. lbs., don't exceed 90 ft. lbs. when aligning the hole. On nuts torqued originally to 90 ft. lbs., don't exceed 130 ft. lbs. to align the hole.
18. Remove the floor jack.
19. Install a new gasket and the splash shield. Torque the bolts to 10 ft. lbs.
20. Connect the tie rod end.
21. Install the hub/rotor assembly.
22. Install the caliper.
23. Adjust the wheel bearings.
24. Install the wheels.
25. Have the alignment checked.

Upper Control Arm

REMOVAL AND INSTALLATION

1. Raise and support the truck on jackstands.
2. Support the lower control arm with a floor jack.
3. Remove the wheel.
4. Remove the cotter pin from the upper control arm ball stud and loosen the stud nut until the bottom surface of the nut is slightly below the end of the stud.
5. Install a spring compressor on the coil spring for safety.
6. Loosen the upper control arm ball stud in the steering knuckle using a ball joint stud removal tool. Remove the nut from the ball stud and raise the upper arm to clear the steering knuckle. It may be necessary to remove the brake caliper and wire it to the frame to gain clearance. Do not allow the caliper to hang by the brake hose.
7. Remove the nuts securing the control arm shaft studs to the crossmember bracket and remove the control arm.
8. Tape the shims and spacers together and tag for proper reassembly.

To install:

CAUTION

All suspension and steering fasteners are important attaching parts in that they could affect the performance of vital components and systems, and/or could result in major repair expense. They must be replaced with one of the same part number or with an equivalent part if replacement becomes necessary. Do not use a replacement part of lesser quality or substitute design. Torque values must be used as specified during reassembly to assure proper retention of these parts. Observe all nut and bolt torque specifications.

9. Place the control arm in position and install the nuts. Before tightening the nuts, insert the caster and camber shims in the same order as when installed.
10. Install the nuts securing the control arm shaft studs to the crossmember bracket. Tighten the nuts to 70 ft. lbs. for 10/1500 and 20/2500 series; 105 ft. lbs. for 30/3500 series.
11. Install the ball stud nut. Torque the nut to 90 ft. lbs. for 10/1500 series and 20/2500 series; 130 ft. lbs. for 30/3500 series. Install the cotter pin. Never back off the nut to install the cotter pin. Always advance it.
12. Install the brake caliper.
13. Remove the spring compressor.
14. Install the wheel and tire.
15. Have the front end alignment checked, and as necessary adjusted.

Lower Control Arm

REMOVAL AND INSTALLATION

1. Raise and support the truck on jackstands.
2. Remove the spring (see Spring Removal and Installation).
3. Support the inboard end of the control arm after spring removal.
4. Remove the cotter pin from the lower ball stud and loosen the nut.
5. Loosen the lower ball stud in the steering knuckle using a ball joint stud removal tool. When the stud is loose, remove the nut from the stud. It may be necessary to remove the brake caliper and wire it to the frame to gain clearance.
6. Remove the lower control arm.

To install:

CAUTION

All suspension and steering fasteners are important attaching parts in that they could affect the performance of vital components and systems, and/or could result in major repair expense. They must be replaced with one of the same part number or with an equivalent part if replacement becomes necessary. Do not use a replacement part of lesser quality or substitute design. Torque values must be used as specified during reassembly to assure proper retention of these parts. Observe all nut and bolt torque specifications.

7. Install the lower control arm. Torque the U-bolts to 85 ft. lbs.
8. Install the ball stud nut. Torque the nut to 90 ft. lbs. for 10/1500 series and 20/2500 series; 130 ft. lbs. for 30/3500 series. Install the cotter pin. Never back off the nut to install the cotter pin. Always advance it.
9. Install the brake caliper.
10. Install the spring (see Spring Removal and Installation).

Lower Control Arm Pivot Shaft and Bushings

REMOVAL AND INSTALLATION

10/1500 Series

The following special tools, or their equivalents, are necessary for this procedure: J-22717, J-24435-7, J-24435-3, J-24435-2, J-24435-6, J-24435-4.

1. Remove the lower control arm as explained earlier in this Section.
2. Remove the pivot shaft nuts and washers.
3. Place the control arm in a press and press on the front end of the pivot shaft to remove the rear bushing.
4. Remove the pivot shaft.

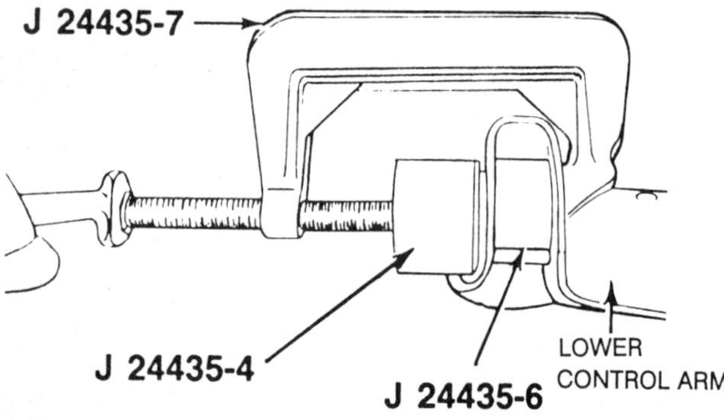

R10/1500 lower control arm bushing removal/installation

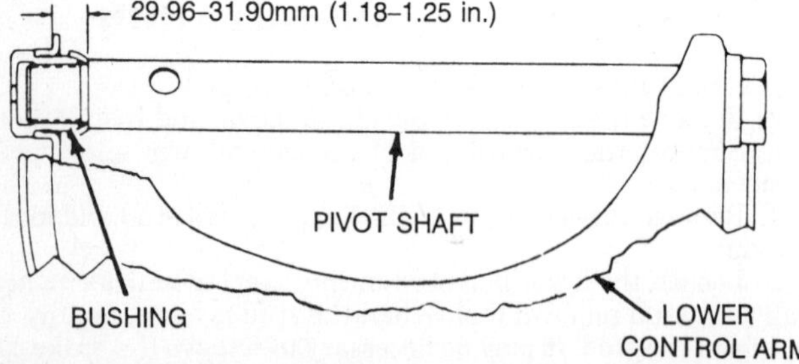

Centering the lower control arm shaft on the R20/2500 and 30/3500 series

5. Remove the front bushing stakes with tool J-22717, or equivalent.
6. Assemble tool J-24435-7. J-24435-3, J-24435-2 and J-24435-6 on the control arm. Tighten the tool until the bushing is forced out.

To install:

CAUTION

All suspension and steering fasteners are important attaching parts in that they could affect the performance of vital components and systems, and/or could result in major repair expense. They must be replaced with one of the same part number or with an equivalent part if replacement becomes necessary. Do not use a replacement part of lesser quality or substitute design. Torque values must be used as specified during reassembly to assure proper retention of these parts. Observe all nut and bolt torque specifications.

7. Position the new front bushing in the arm and asseble tools J-24435-6, J-24435-4 and J-24435-7. Force the bushing into place until it is fully seated. The outer tube hole must be lined up so that it faces the front, towards the staked bushing.
8. Stake the bushing in at least 2 places.
9. Install the pivot shaft.
10. Install the rear bushing.
11. Install the washers and pivot shaft nuts. Torque the nuts to 70 ft. lbs.
12. Install the lower control arm.

20/2500 and 30/3500 Series

1. Remove the lower control arm.
2. Remove the grease fittings and unscrew the bushings.
3. Slide out the pivot shaft.
4. Discard the old seals.

To install:

CAUTION

All suspension and steering fasteners are important attaching parts in that they could affect the performance of vital components and systems, and/or could result in major repair expense. They must be replaced with one of the same part number or with an equivalent part if replacement becomes necessary. Do not use a replacement part of lesser quality or substitute design. Torque values must be used as specified during reassembly to assure proper retention of these parts. Observe all nut and bolt torque specifications.

5. Install new seals on the pivot shaft.
6. Slide the shaft into the arm.
7. Start the bushings into the arm and center the shaft in the bushings. Hand tighten the bushings to make sure the shaft doesn't bind.
8. Tighten the bushings to 280 ft. lbs.
9. Check the pivot shaft for free rotation.
10. Install the grease fittings and lubricate the bushings.
11. Install the lower arm.

Upper Control Arm Pivot Shaft and Bushings

REMOVAL AND INSTALLATION

10/1500 Series

The following special tools, or their equivalents, are necessary for this procedure: J-24435-1, J-24435-3, J-24435-4, J-24435-5 and J-24435-7.

1. Remove the upper control arm as explained earlier in this Section.
2. Remove the pivot shaft nuts and washers.
3. Assemble tool J-24435-1. J-24435-3, and J-24435-7 on the control arm. Tighten the tool until the front bushing is forced out.

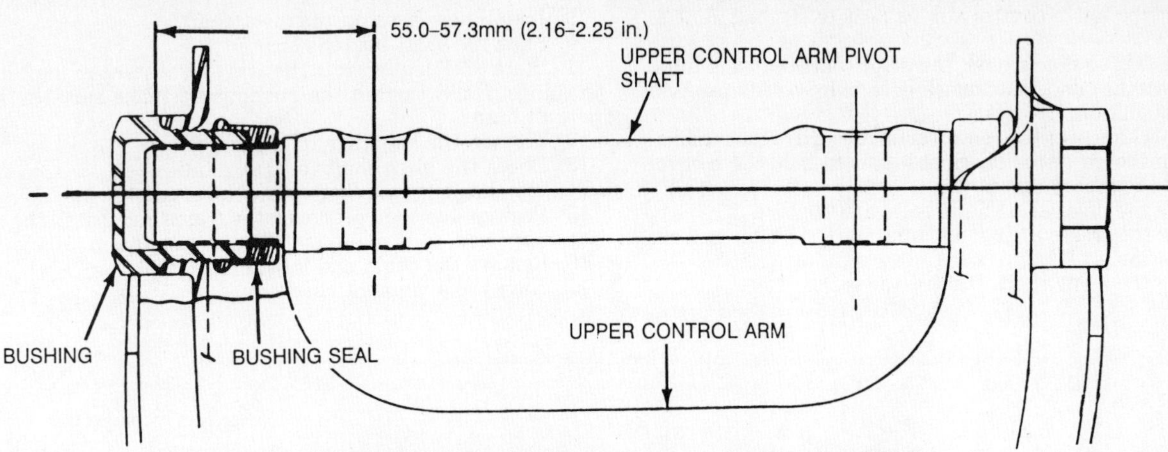

Centering the upper control arm shaft on the R20/2500 and 30/3500 series

4. Remove the pivot shaft.
5. Use the forcing procedure to remove the rear bushing.

To install:

CAUTION

All suspension and steering fasteners are important attaching parts in that they could affect the performance of vital components and systems, and/or could result in major repair expense. They must be replaced with one of the same part number or with an equivalent part if replacement becomes necessary. Do not use a replacement part of lesser quality or substitute design. Torque values must be used as specified during reassembly to assure proper retention of these parts. Observe all nut and bolt torque specifications.

6. Position the new front bushing in the arm and assemble tools J–24435–4, J–24435–5 and J–24435–7. Force the bushing into place until it is fully seated.
7. Install the pivot shaft.
8. Repeat the forcing procedure to install the rear bushing.
9. Install the lower control arm.
10. Install the nuts and washers. Torque the nuts to 115 ft. lbs.
11. Install the control arm.

20/2500 and 30/3500 Series

1. Raise and support the front end on jackstands.
2. Take up the weight of the suspension with a floor jack posi-

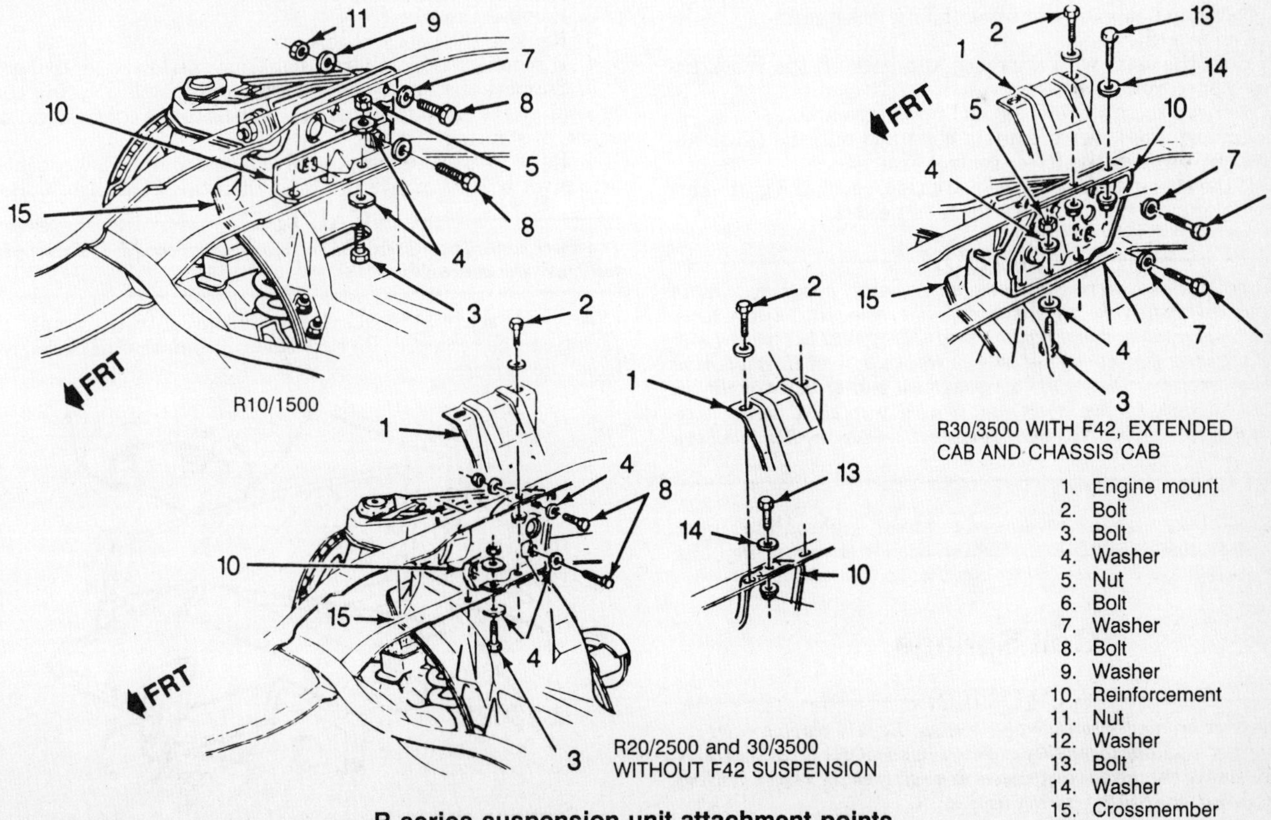

R series suspension unit attachment points

tioned under the lower control arm as near to the ball joint as possible.

3. Loosen, but do not remove, the pivot shaft-to-frame nuts.
4. Tape together and matchmark each shim pack's psoition for exact installation.
5. Install a chain over the control arm, inboard of the stabilizer bar and outboard of the shock absorber to hold the control arm close to the crossmember.
6. Remove the pivot shaft nuts, bolts and spacers.
7. Remove the grease fittings and unscrew the bushings from the control arm.
8. Remove the pivot shaft. Discard the seals.

To install:

9. Install new seals on the pivot shaft.
10. Slide the shaft into the arm.
11. Start the bushings into the arm and center the shaft in the bushings. Hand tighten the bushings to make sure the shaft doesn't bind.
12. Tighten the bushings to 190 ft. lbs.
13. Check the pivot shaft for free rotation.
14. Install the grease fittings and lubricate the bushings.
15. Position the control arm on the frame and install the shim packs, spacers, nuts and bolts. Torque the nuts to 105 ft. lbs.
16. Remove the chain and install the wheel.
17. Have the alignment checked.

C SERIES 2-WHEEL DRIVE FRONT SUSPENSION

Shock Absorbers

REMOVAL AND INSTALLATION

1. Raise and support the front end on jackstands.
2. Remove the wheel.
3. Hold the stem with a wrench and back off the shock absorber upper nut.
4. Remove the nut, retainer and upper grommet.
5. Remove the lower mounting bolts and pull the shock absorber out through the lower control arm.
6. If the shock absorber is being reused, check the grommets for wear and damage. Replace them as needed.

CAUTION

All suspension and steering fasteners are important attaching parts in that they could affect the performance of vital components and systems, and/or could result in major repair expense. They must be replaced with one of the same part number or with an equivalent part if replacement becomes necessary. Do not use a replacement part of lesser quality or substitute design. Torque values must be used as specified during reassembly to assure proper retention of these parts. Observe all nut and bolt torque specifications.

7. Installation is the reverse of removal. Tighten the upper nut to 8 ft. lbs. (96 inch lbs.); tighten the lower mounting bolts to 20 ft. lbs.

Coil Springs

CAUTION

Coil springs are under considerable tension. Be very careful when removing and installing them; they can exert enough force to cause serious injury. Always use spring compressors or a safety chain when removing a coil spring, or releasing spring tension!

REMOVAL AND INSTALLATION

1. Raise and support the truck under the frame rails. The control arms should hang freely.
2. Remove the wheel.
3. Remove the shock absorber.
4. Disconnect the stabilizer bar from the lower control arm.
5. Support the lower control arm and install a spring compressor on the spring, or chain the spring to the control arm as a safety precaution.
6. Raise the jack to remove the tension from the lower control arm pivot bolts. Remove the rear, then the front pivot bolts.

CAUTION

The lower control arm keeps the coil spring compressed. Use care when you lower the assembly.

7. Slowly release the jack and lower the control arm until the spring can be removed. Be sure that all compression is relieved from the spring.

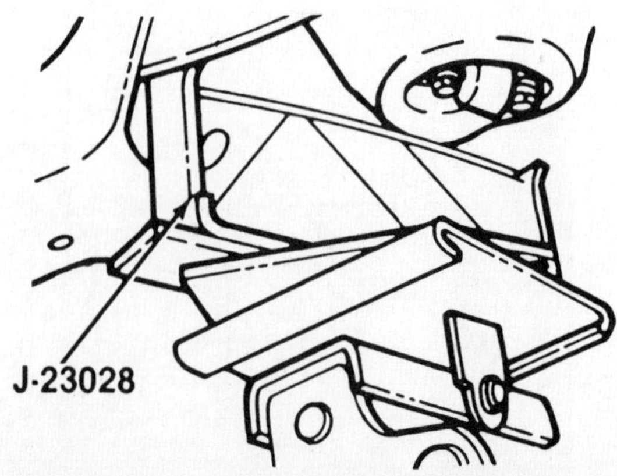

Cradling the lower control arm on C series

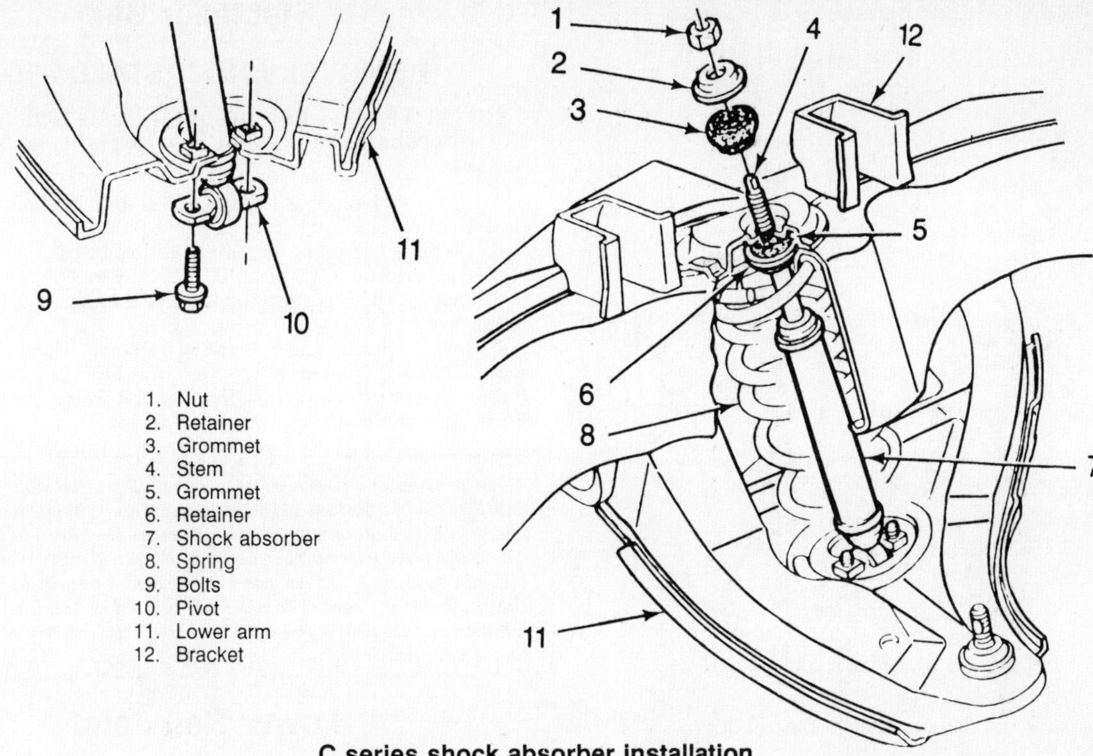

C series shock absorber installation

8. Place a piece of tape on one of the lower coil so you can tell the top from the bottom during installation. If the spring was chained, remove the chain and spring. If you used spring compressors, remove the spring and slowly release the compressors.

To install:

CAUTION

All suspension and steering fasteners are important attaching parts in that they could affect the performance of vital components and systems, and/or could result in major repair expense. They must be replaced with one of the same part number or with an equivalent part if replacement becomes necessary. Do not use a replacement part of lesser quality or substitute design. Torque values must be used as specified during reassembly to assure proper retention of these parts. Observe all nut and bolt torque specifications.

9. Install the chain and spring. If you used spring compressors, install the spring and compressors.
   - Make sure that the insulator is in place.
   - Make sure that the tape is at the lower end. New springs will have an identifying tape.
   - Make sure that the gripper notch on the top coil is in the frame bracket.
   - Make sure that on drain hole in the lower arm is covered by the bottom coil and the other is open.
10. Slowly raise the jack and lower the control arm. Guide the control arm into place with a prybar.
11. Install the pivot shaft bolts, front one first. The bolts *must* be installed with the heads towards the front of the truck! Remove the safety chain or spring compressors.

NOTE: Do not torque the bolts yet. The bolts must be torque with the truck at its proper ride height.

12. Remove the jack.
13. Connect the stabilizer bar to the lower control arm. Torque the nuts to 13 ft. lbs.
14. Install the shock absorber.
15. Install the wheel.
16. Lower the truck. Once the weight of the truck is on the wheels:
    a. Lift the front bumper about 38mm and let it drop.
    b. Repeat this procedure 2 or 3 more times.
    c. Draw a line on the side of the lower control arm from the centerline of the control arm pivot shaft, dead level to the outer end of the control arm.
    d. Measure the distance between the lowest corner of the steering knuckle and the line on the control arm. Record the figure.
    e. Push down about 38mm on the front bumper and let it return. Repeat the procedure 2 or 3 more times.

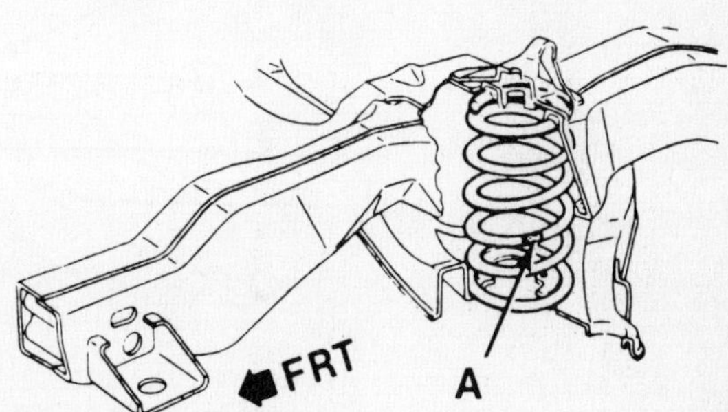

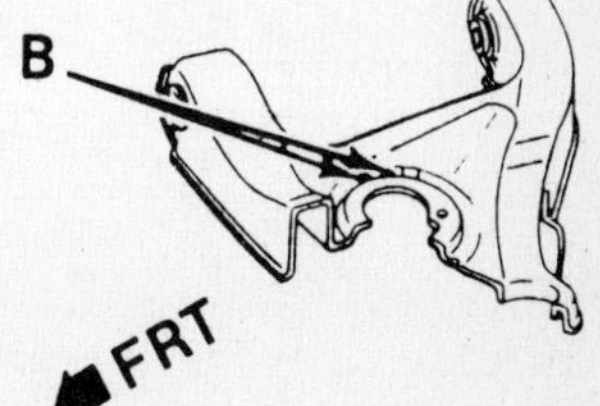

A. COIL SPRING SHOULD BE INSTALLED WITH THE TAPE AT THE LOWEST POSITION AND THE GRIPPER NOTCH AT THE TOP
B. INSPECTION DRAIN HOLES: ONE MUST BE COVERED BY THE END OF THE SPRING AND ONE MUST BE OPEN

Positioning the coil spring on C series

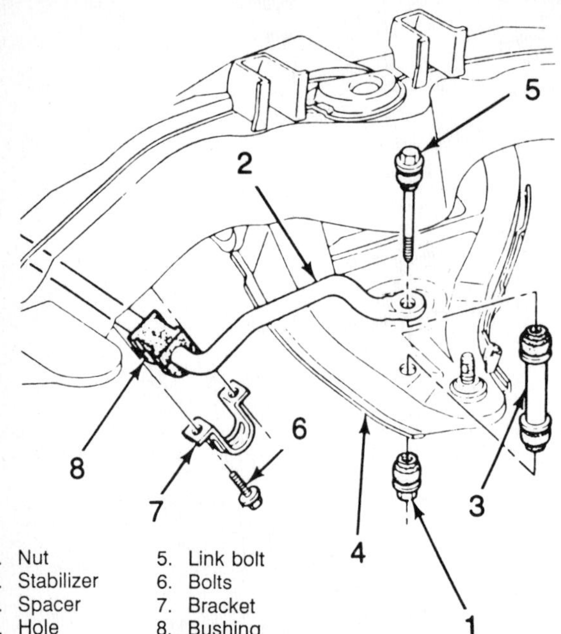

C series stabilizer bar

f. Re-measure the distance at the control arm.

g. Determine the average of the 2 measurements. The average distance should be 95.0mm ± 6mm.

h. If the figure is correct, tighten the control arm pivot nuts to 96 ft. lbs.

i. If the figure is not correct, tighten the pivot bolts to 96 ft. lbs. and have the front end alignment corrected.

Stabilizer Bar

REMOVAL AND INSTALLATION

NOTE: The end link bushings, bolts and spacers are not interchangeable from left to right, so keep them separate.

1. Raise and support the front end on jackstands.
2. Remove the nuts from the end link bolts.
3. Remove the bolts, bushings and spacers.
4. Remove the bracket bolts and remove the stabilizer bar.
5. Inspect the bushings for wear or damage. Replace them as necessary.
6. Installation is the reverse of removal. Coat the bushiogs with silicone grease prior to assembly. The slit in the bushings faces the front of the truck. Torque the frame bracket bolts to 24 ft. lbs.; the end link nuts to 13 ft. lbs.

CAUTION

All suspension and steering fasteners are important attaching parts in that they could affect the performance of vital components and systems, and/or could result in major repair expense. They must be replaced with one of the same part number or with an equivalent part if replacement becomes necessary. Do not use a replacement part of lesser quality or substitute design. Torque values must be used as specified during reassembly to assure proper retention of these parts. Observe all nut and bolt torque specifications.

Lower Ball Joint

INSPECTION

1. Support the weight of the control arm at the wheel hub.
2. Measure the distance between the tip of the ball joint stud and the grease fitting below the ball joint.

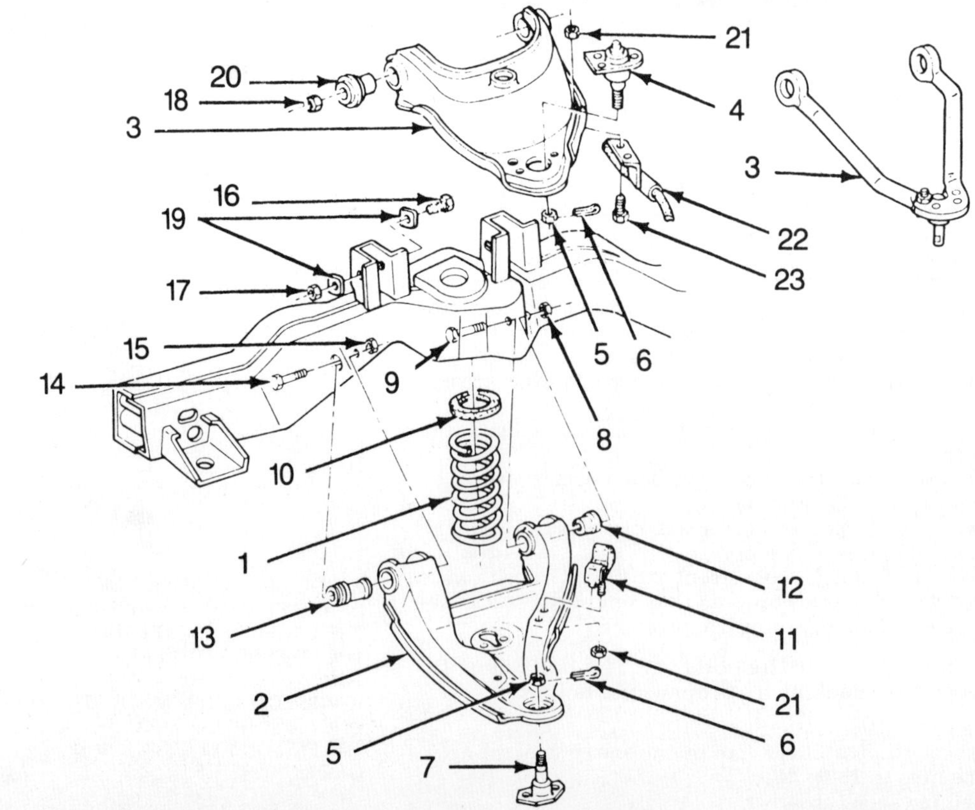

C series control arms and related components

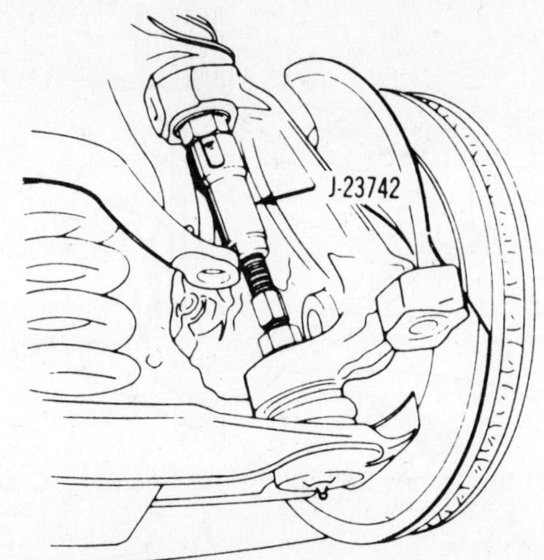

Disconnecting the lower ball joint on C series

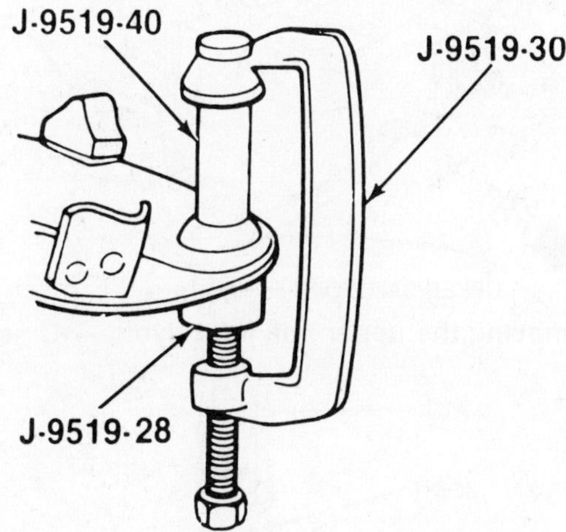

Removing the lower ball joint on C series

3. Move the support to the control arm and allow the hub to hang free. Measure the distance again. If the variation between the two measurements exceeds $^3/_{32}$ in. (2.4mm) the ball joint should be replaced.

REMOVAL AND INSTALLATION

1. Raise and support the front end on jackstands.
2. Support the lower control arm with a floor jack.
3. Remove the wheel.
4. Install a spring compressor on the coil spring for safety.
5. Remove the lower stud cotter pin and stud nut.
6. Loosen the ball joint with a forcing-type ball joint tool. It may be necessary to remove the brake caliper and wire it to the frame to gain enough clearance.
7. When the stud is loose, remove the tool and guide the control arm out of the splash shield with a prybar, while lifting the upper control arm with a prybar. Block the knuckle assembly out of the way by placing a wood block bewteen the frame and upper control arm.
8. Remove the ball joint from the control arm with a forcing-type ball joint remover.

To install:

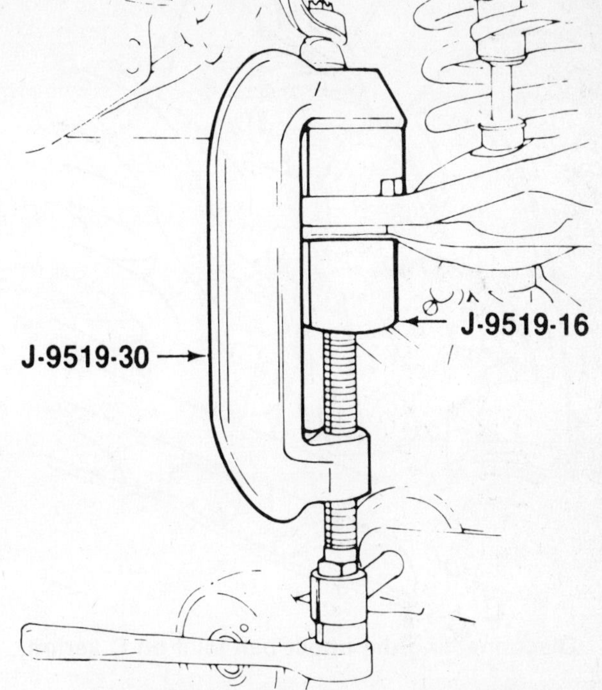

Installing the lower ball joint on C series

CAUTION

All suspension and steering fasteners are important attaching parts in that they could affect the performance of vital components and systems, and/or could result in major repair expense. They must be replaced with one of the same part number or with an equivalent part if replacement becomes necessary. Do not use a replacement part of lesser quality or substitute design. Torque values must be used as specified during reassembly to assure proper retention of these parts. Observe all nut and bolt torque specifications.

9. Start the new ball joint into the control arm.
10. Force the ball joint into position using a screw-type forcing tool. The ball joint will bottom in the control arm. The grease seal should face inboard.
11. Start ball stud into the knuckle. Install the nut and tighten it to 90 ft. lbs. Advance the nut to align the cotter pin hole and insert the new cotter pin. NEVER back off the nut to align the cotter pin hole; always advance it!
12. Install the brake caliper, if removed.
13. Install a new lube fitting and lubricate the new joint.
14. Install the wheel.
15. Lower the truck.
16. Check the front end alignment.

Upper Ball Joint

INSPECTION

1. Raise and support the front end on jackstands so that the control arms hang freely.
2. Remove the wheel.
3. The upper ball joint is spring-loaded. Replace the ball joint if the is any lateral movement or if it can be twisted in its socket with your fingers.

REMOVAL AND INSTALLATION

1. Raise and support the front end on jackstands.
2. Remove the wheel.

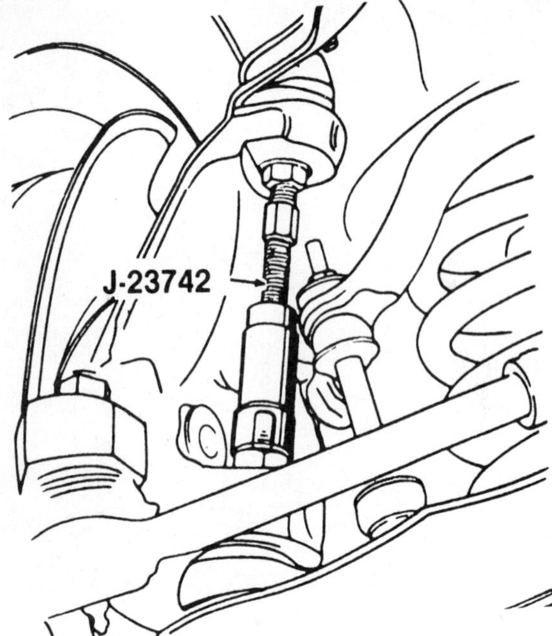

Disconnecting the upper ball joint on C series

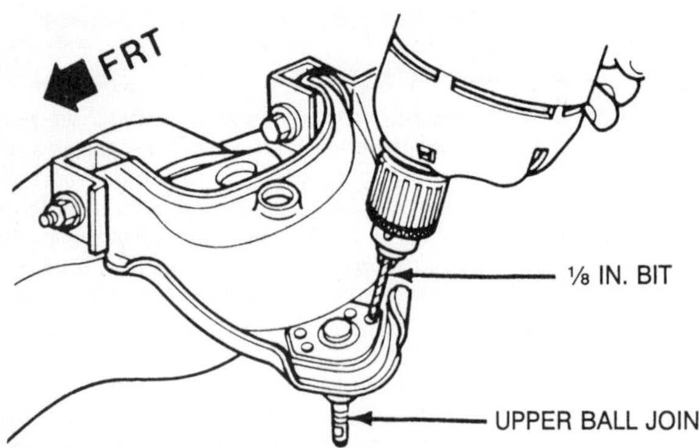

Drilling the upper ball joint rivets — C series

2. Support the lower control arm with a floor jack.
3. Remove the cotter pin from the upper ball stud and loosen, but do not remove the stud nut.
4. Using a forcing-type ball joint separator tool, loosen the ball stud in the steering knuckle. When the stud is loose, remove the tool and the stud nut. It may be necessary to remove the brake caliper and wire it to the frame to gain clearance.
5. Drill out the rivets using a 1/8 in. drill bit to start a pilot hole. Drill out the rivets with a 1/2 in. bit. Remove the ball joint assembly using a screw-type forcing tool.

To Install:

CAUTION

All suspension and steering fasteners are important attaching parts in that they could affect the performance of vital components and systems, and/or could result in major repair expense. They must be replaced with one of the same part number or with an equivalent part if replacement becomes necessary. Do not use a replacement part of lesser quality or substitute design. Torque values must be used as specified during reassembly to assure proper retention of these parts. Observe all nut and bolt torque specifications.

6. Install the replacement ball joint in the control arm, using the bolts and nuts supplied. Torque the nuts to 17 ft. lbs. for 15 and 25 Series; 52 ft. lbs. for 35 Series.

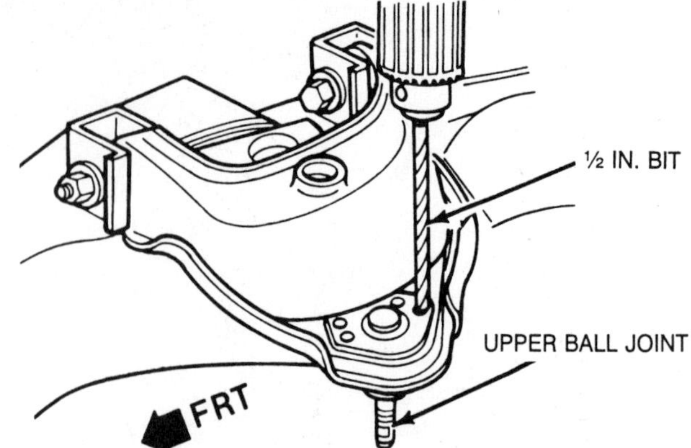

Drilling the upper ball joint rivet heads — C series

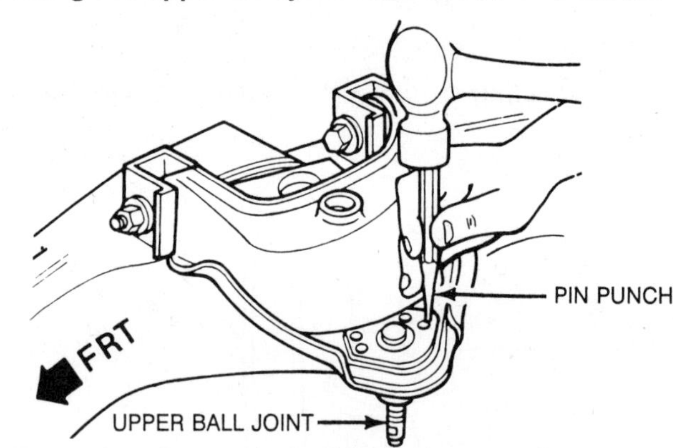

Removing the upper ball joint rivets — C series

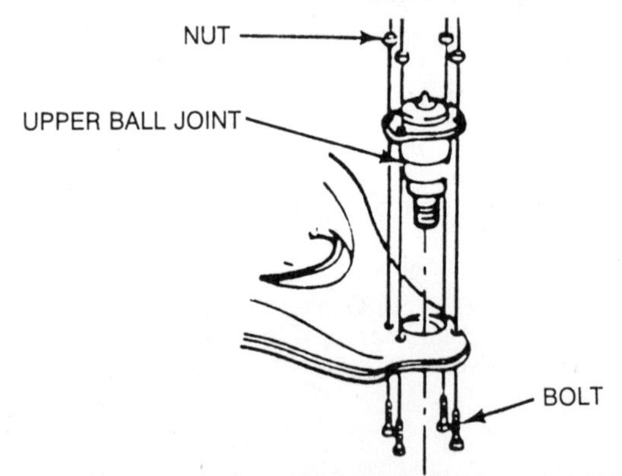

Installing the upper ball joint — C series

7. Position the ball stud in the knuckle. Make sure it is sqaurely seated. Torque the ball stud nut to 90 ft. lbs.
8. Install a new cotter pin.
9. Install a new lube fitting and lubricate the new joint.
10. If removed, install the brake caliper.
11. Install the wheel and lower the truck.

Steering Knuckle

REMOVAL AND INSTALLATION

1. Raise and support the front end on jackstands. Let the control arms hang freely.
2. Remove the wheels.
3. Disconnect the tie rod end from the knuckle.

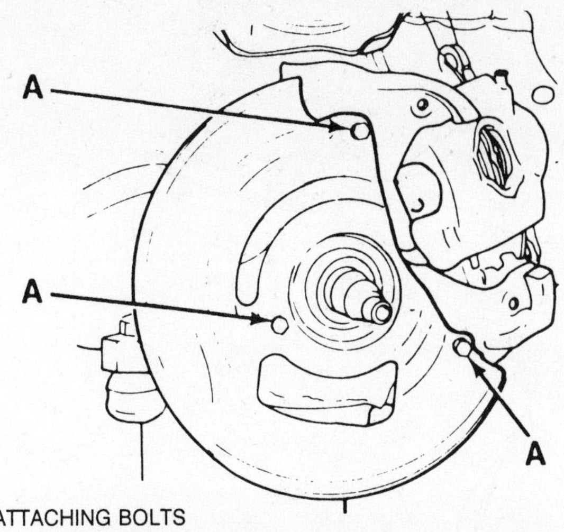

Splash shield installation — C series

4. Dismount the caliper and suspend it out of the way without disconnecting the brake lines.
5. Remove the hub/rotor assembly.
6. Unbolt the splash shield from the knuckle and discard the old gasket.
7. If a new knuckle is being installed, remove the knuckle seal carefully, without damaging it.
8. Position a floor jack under the lower control arm, near the spring seat. Raise the jack until it *just* takes up the weight of the suspension, compressing the spring. Safety-chain the coil spring to the lower arm.
9. Remove the upper and lower ball joint nuts.
10. Using tool J–23742, or equivalent, break loose the upper ball joint from the knuckle.
11. Raise the upper control arm just enough to disconnect the ball joint.
12. Using the afore-mentioned tool, break loose the lower ball joint.
13. Lift the knuckle off of the lower ball joint.
14. Inspect and clean the ball stud bores in the knuckle. Make sure that there are no cracks or burrs. If the knuckle is damaged in any way, replace it.
15. Check the spindle for wear, heat discoloration or damage. If at all damaged, replace it.

To install:

CAUTION

All suspension and steering fasteners are important attaching parts in that they could affect the performance of vital components and systems, and/or could result in major repair expense. They must be replaced with one of the same part number or with an equivalent part if replacement becomes necessary. Do not use a replacement part of lesser quality or substitute design. Torque values must be used as specified during reassembly to assure proper retention of these parts. Observe all nut and bolt torque specifications.

16. Maneuver the knuckle onto both ball joints.
17. Install both nuts. Torque the nuts to 90 ft. lbs.
18. Install new cotter pins. Always advance the nut to align the cotter pin hole. NEVER back it off!
19. Install the knuckle seal.
20. Remove the floor jack.

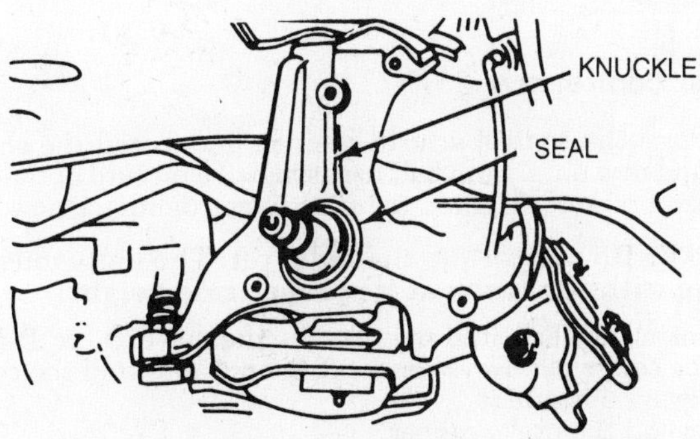

Locating the seal on the yoke — C series

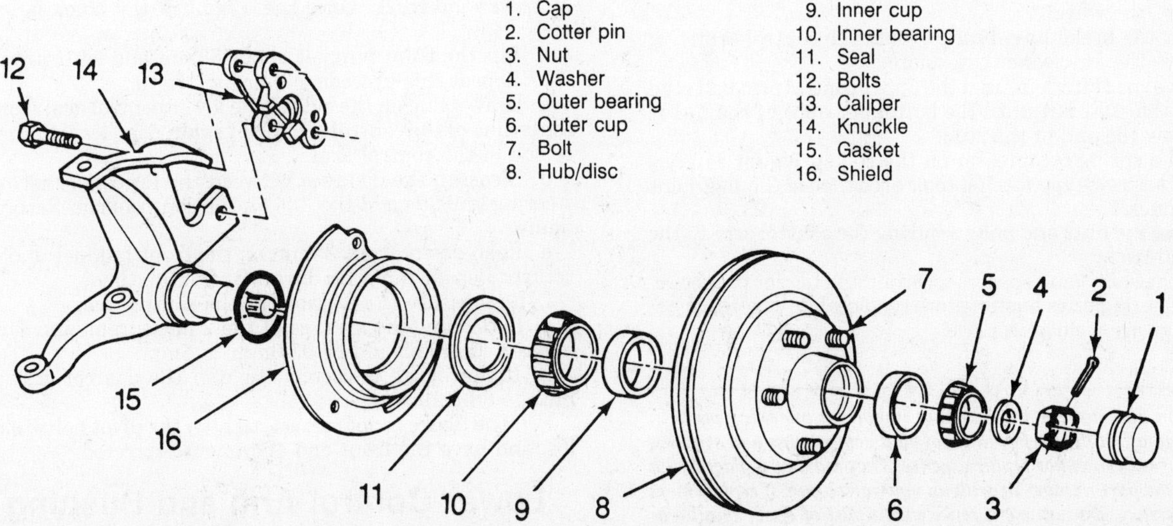

C series hub, knuckle and bearings

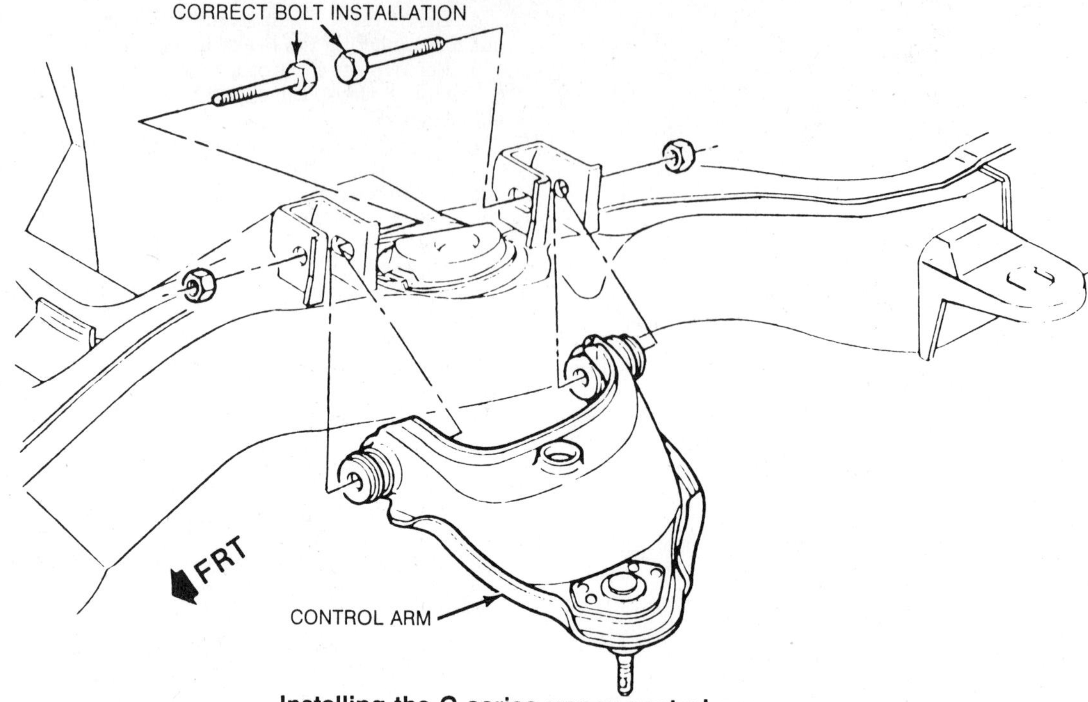

Installing the C series upper control arm

21. Install a new gasket and the splash shield. Torque the bolts to 12 ft. lbs.
22. Connect the tie rod end.
23. Install the hub/rotor assembly.
24. Install the caliper.
25. Adjust the wheel bearings.
26. Install the wheels.
27. Have the alignment checked.

Upper Control Arm and Bushings

REMOVAL AND INSTALLATION

1. Raise and support the truck on jackstands.
2. Support the lower control arm with a floor jack.
3. Remove the wheel.
4. Unbolt the brake hose bracket from the control arm.
5. Remove the air cleaner extension.
6. Remove the cotter pin from the upper control arm ball stud and loosen the stud nut until the bottom surface of the nut is slightly below the end of the stud.
7. Install a spring compressor on the coil spring for safety.
8. Using a screw-type forcing tool, break loose the ball joint from the knuckle.
9. Remove the nuts and bolts securing the control arm to the frame brackets.
10. Tape the shims and spacers together and tag for proper reassembly. The 35 Series bushings are replaceable. The 15/25 Series bushings are welded in place.

To install:

CAUTION

All suspension and steering fasteners are important attaching parts in that they could affect the performance of vital components and systems, and/or could result in major repair expense. They must be replaced with one of the same part number or with an equivalent part if replacement becomes necessary. Do not use a replacement part of lesser quality or substitute design. Torque values must be used as specified during reassembly to assure proper retention of these parts. Observe all nut and bolt torque specifications.

11. Place the control arm in position and install the shims, bolts and new nuts. Both bolt heads *must* be inboard of the control arm brackets. Tighten the nuts finger tighte for now.

NOTE: Do not torque the bolts yet. The bolts must be torque with the truck at its proper ride height.

12. Install the ball stud nut. Torque the nut to 90 ft. lbs. Install the cotter pin. Never back off the nut to install the cotter pin. Always advance it.
13. Install the brake caliper.
14. Remove the spring compressor or safety chain.
15. Install the wheel.
16. Install the brake hose.
17. Install the air cleaner extension.
18. Install the battery ground cable.
19. Lower the truck. Once the weight of the truck is on the wheels:
    a. Lift the front bumper about 38mm and let it drop.
    b. Repeat this procedure 2 or 3 more times.
    c. Draw a line on the side of the lower control arm from the centerline of the control arm pivot shaft, dead level to the outer end of the control arm.
    d. Measure the distance between the lowest corner of the steering knuckle and the line on the control arm. Record the figure.
    e. Push down about 38mm on the front bumper and let it return. Repeat the procedure 2 or 3 more times.
    f. Re-measure the distance at the control arm.
    g. Determine the average of the 2 measurements. The average distance should be 95.0mm ± 6mm.
    h. If the figure is correct, tighten the control arm pivot nuts to 88 ft. lbs.
    i. If the figure is not correct, tighten the pivot bolts to 88 ft. lbs. and have the front end alignment corrected.

Lower Control Arm and Bushing

REMOVAL AND INSTALLATION

1. Raise and support the truck on jackstands.

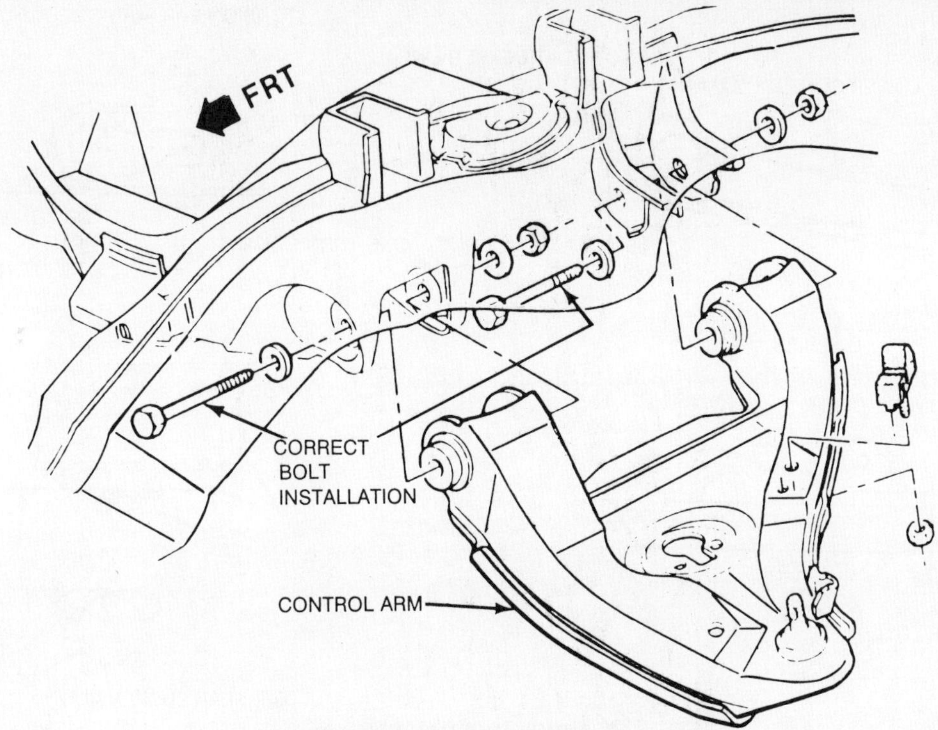

Installing the C series lower control arm

2. Remove the coil spring. See Coil Spring Removal and Installation.

3. Support the inboard end of the control arm after spring removal.

4. Remove the cotter pin from the lower ball stud and loosen the nut.

5. Loosen the lower ball stud in the steering knuckle using a ball joint stud removal tool. When the stud is loose, remove the nut from the stud. It may be necessary to remove the brake caliper and wire it to the frame to gain clearance.

6. Remove the lower control arm.

To install:

CAUTION

All suspension and steering fasteners are important attaching parts in that they could affect the performance of vital components and systems, and/or could result in major repair expense. They must be replaced with one of the same part number or with an equivalent part if replacement becomes necessary. Do not use a replacement part of lesser quality or substitute design. Torque values must be used as specified during reassembly to assure proper retention of these parts. Observe all nut and bolt torque specifications.

7. Slowly raise the jack and lower the control arm. Guide the control arm into place with a prybar.

8. Install the pivot shaft bolts, front one first. The bolts *must* be installed with the heads towards the front of the truck! Remove the safety chain or spring compressors.

NOTE: Do not torque the bolts yet. The bolts must be torque with the truck at its proper ride height.

9. Remove the jack.

10. Connect the stabilizer bar to the lower control arm. Torque the nuts to 13 ft. lbs.

11. Install the shock absorber.

12. Install the wheel.

13. Lower the truck. Once the weight of the truck is on the wheels:

a. Lift the front bumper about 38mm and let it drop.

b. Repeat this procedure 2 or 3 more times.

c. Draw a line on the side of the lower control arm from the centerline of the control arm pivot shaft, dead level to the outer end of the control arm.

d. Measure the distance between the lowest corner of the steering knuckle and the line on the control arm. Record the figure.

e. Push down about 38mm on the front bumper and let it return. Repeat the procedure 2 or 3 more times.

f. Re-measure the distance at the control arm.

g. Determine the average of the 2 measurements. The average distance should be 95.0mm ± 6mm.

h. If the figure is correct, tighten the control arm pivot nuts to 96 ft. lbs.

i. If the figure is not correct, tighten the pivot bolts to 96 ft. lbs. and have the front end alignment corrected.

Wheel Hub, Rotor and Bearings

Before handling the bearings, there are a few things that you should remember to do and not to do.

Remember to DO the following:

- Remove all outside dirt from the housing before exposing the bearing.
- Treat a used bearing as gently as you would a new one.
- Work with clean tools in clean surroundings.
- Use clean, dry canvas gloves, or at least clean, dry hands.
- Clean solvents and flushing fluids are a must.
- Use clean paper when laying out the bearings to dry.
- Protect disassembled bearings from rust and dirt. Cover them up.
- Use clean rags to wipe bearings.
- Keep the bearings in oil-proof paper when they are to be stored or are not in use.
- Clean the inside of the housing before replacing the bearing.

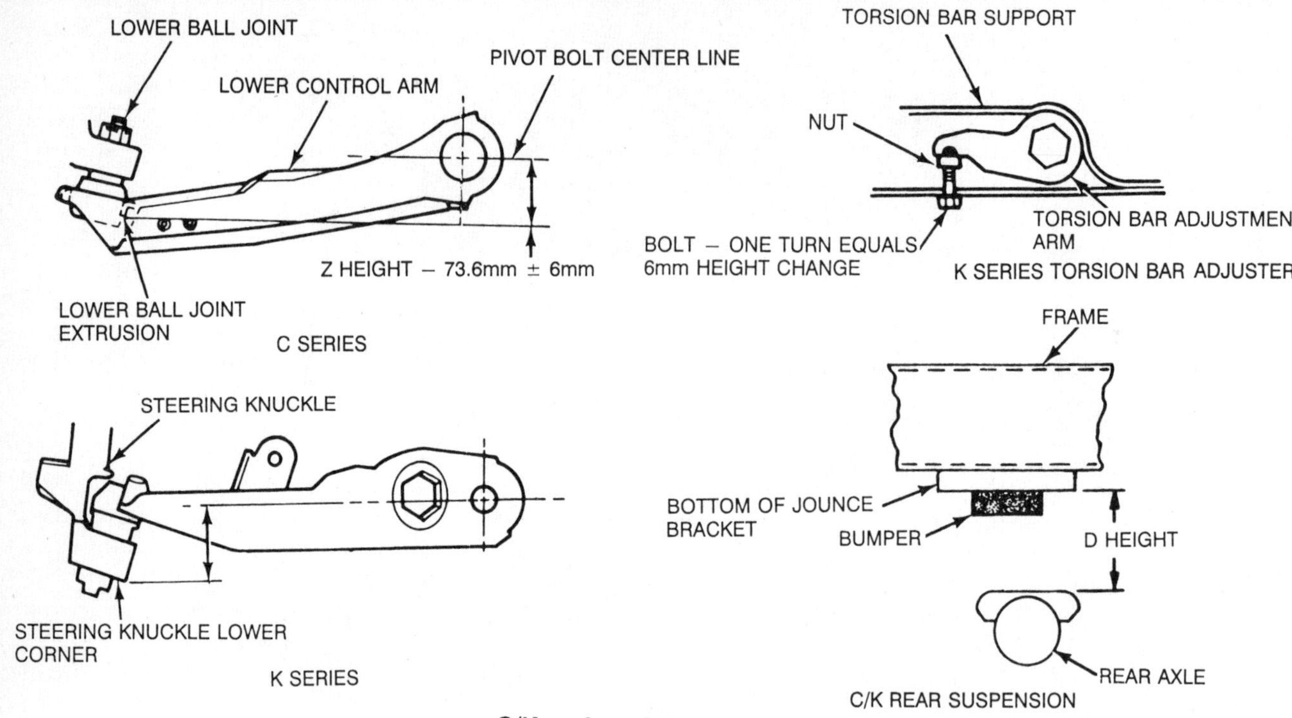

C/K series trim heights

Do NOT do the following:

- Don't work in dirty surroundings.
- Don't use dirty, chipped or damaged tools.
- Try not to work on wooden work benches or use wooden mallets.
- Don't handle bearings with dirty or moist hands.
- Do not use gasoline for cleaning; use a safe solvent.
- Do not spin-dry bearings with compressed air. They will be damaged.
- Do not spin dirty bearings.
- Avoid using cotton waste or dirty cloths to wipe bearings.
- Try not to scratch or nick bearing surfaces.
- Do not allow the bearing to come in contact with dirt or rust at any time.

1. Raise and support the front end on jackstands.
2. Remove the wheel.
3. Dismount the caliper and wire it out of the way.
4. Pry out the grease cap, remove the cotter pin, spindle nut, and washer, then remove the hub. Do not drop the wheel bearings.
5. Remove the outer roller bearing assembly from the hub. The inner bearing assembly will remain in the hub and may be removed after prying out the inner seal. Discard the seal.
6. Clean all parts in a non-flammable solvent and let them air dry. Never spin-dry a bearing with compressed air! Check for excessive wear and damage.
7. Using a hammer and drift, remove the bearing races from the hub. They are driven out from the inside out. When installing new races, make sure that they are not cocked and that they are fully seated against the hub shoulder.
8. Pack both wheel bearings using high melting point wheel bearing grease for disc brakes. Ordinary grease will melt and ooze out ruining the pads. Bearings should be packed using a cone-type wheel bearing greaser tool. If one is not available they may be packed by hand. Place a healthy glob of grease in the palm of one hand and force the edge of the bearing into it so that the grease fills the bearing. Do this until the whole bearing is packed.
9. Place the inner bearing in the hub and install a new inner seal, making sure that the seal flange faces the bearing race.
10. Carefully install the wheel hub over the spindle.
11. Using your hands, firmly press the outer bearing into the hub. Install the spindle washer and nut.
12. Spin the wheel hub by hand and tighten the nut until it is just snug (12 ft. lbs.). Back off the nut until it is loose, then tighten it finger tight. Loosen the nut until either hole in the spindle lines up with a slot in the nut and insert a new cotter pin. There should be 0.001–0.008 in. (0.025–0.200mm) endplay. This can be measured with a dial indicator, if you wish.
13. Replace the dust cap, wheel and tire.

V SERIES
4-WHEEL DRIVE FRONT SUSPENSION

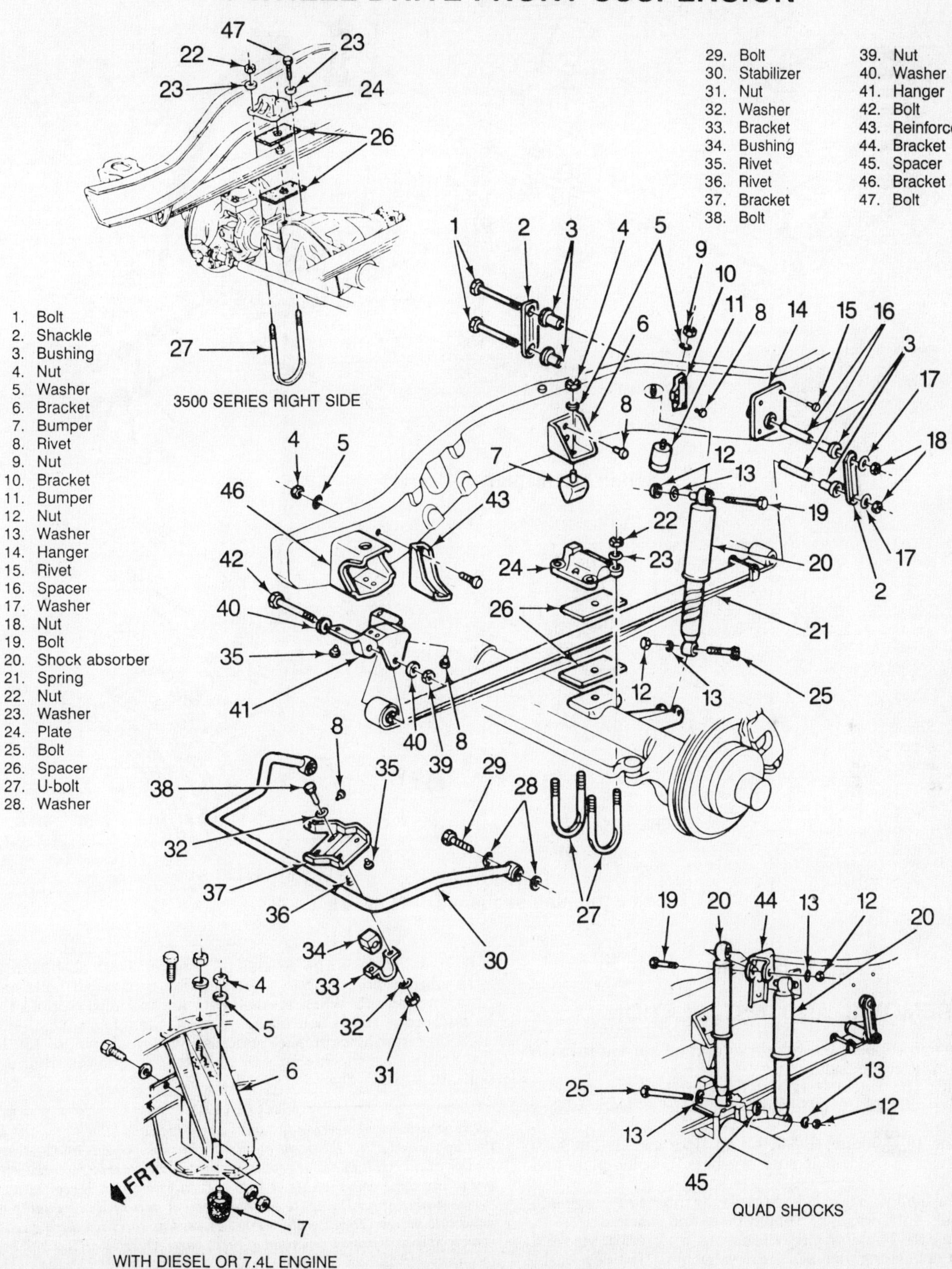

V series front suspension

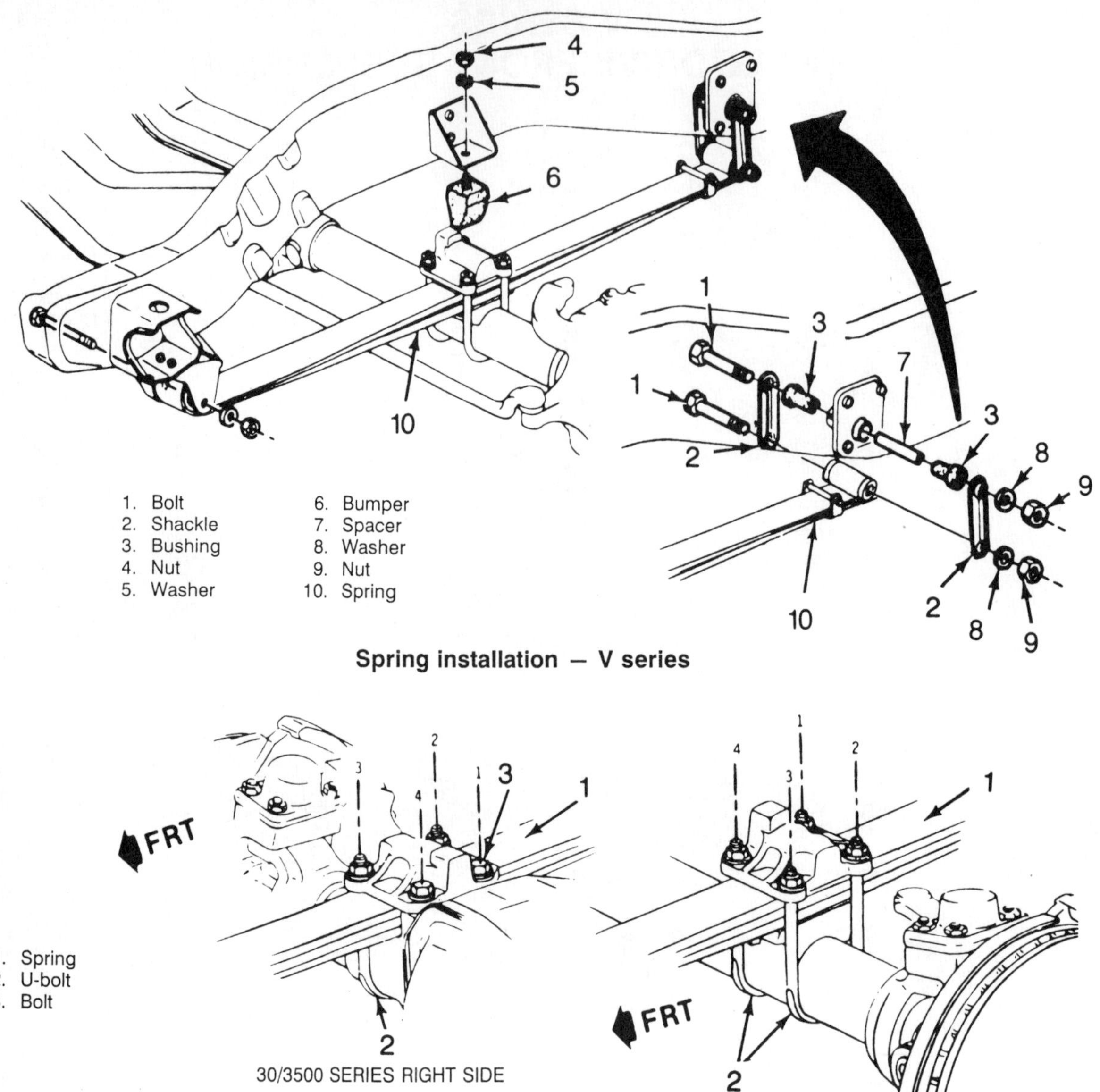

Spring installation — V series

U-bolt tightening sequence — V series

Leaf Spring

REMOVAL AND INSTALLATION

1. Raise and support the vehicle so that all tension is taken off of the front suspension.
2. Remove the shackle retaining bolts, nuts and spacers.
3. Remove the front spring-to-frame bracket bolt, washer and nut.
4. On the 10/1500 and 20/2500 both sides and the 30/3500 left side: remove the U-bolt nuts, washers, U-bolts, plate and spacers.
5. On the 30/3500 right side: remove the inboard spring plate bolts, U-bolt nuts, washers, U-bolt, plate and spacers.

To replace the bushing, place the spring in a press or vise and press out the bushing. Press in the new bushing. The new bushing should protrude evenly on both sides of the spring.

6. Installation is the reverse of removal. Coat all bushings with silicone grease prior to installation. Install all bolts and nuts finger-tight. When all fasteners are installed, torque the bolts. Torque the U-bolt nuts, inclusind the inboard right side 30/3500 series bolts, in the crisscross pattern shown, to 150 ft. lbs. Torque the shackle nuts to 50 ft. lbs. Torque the front eye bolt nut to 90 ft. lbs.

CAUTION

All suspension and steering fasteners are important attaching parts in that they could affect the performance of vital components and systems, and/or could result in major repair expense. They must be replaced with one of the same part number or with an equivalent part if replacement becomes necessary. Do not use a replacement part of lesser quality or substitute design. Torque values must be used as specified during reassembly to assure proper retention of these parts. Observe all nut and bolt torque specifications.

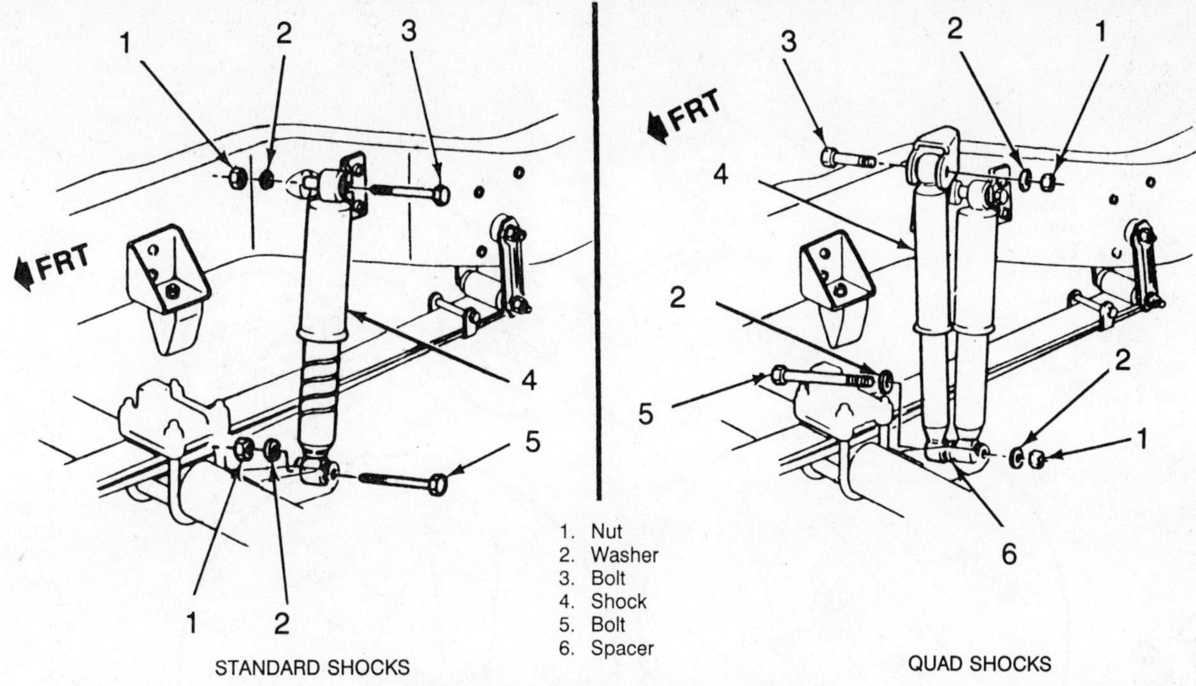

V series shock absorber installation

Shock Absorbers

REMOVAL AND INSTALLATION

Dual or Quad Shocks

1. Raise and support the front end on jackstands.
2. Remove the nuts and eye bolts securing the upper and lower shock absorber eyes. Quad shocks have a spacer between the lower end bushings.
3. Remove the shock absorber(s) and inspect the rubber eye bushings. If these are defective, replace the shock absorber assembly.
4. Installation is the reverse of removal. Make sure that the spacer is installed at the bottom end on quad shocks. Torque the upper end nut to 65 ft. lbs. On dual shocks, torque the lower end to 65 ft. lbs. On quad shocks, torque the lower end to 89 ft. lbs.

CAUTION

All suspension and steering fasteners are important attaching parts in that they could affect the performance of vital components and systems, and/or could result in major repair expense. They must be replaced with one of the same part number or with an equivalent part if replacement becomes necessary. Do not use a replacement part of lesser quality or substitute design. Torque values must be used as specified during reassembly to assure proper retention of these parts. Observe all nut and bolt torque specifications.

TESTING

Adjust the tire pressure before testing the shocks. If the truck is equipped with heavy duty equipment, this can sometimes be misleading. A stiff ride normally accompanies a stiff or heavy duty suspension. Be sure that all weight in the truck is distributed evenly.

Each shock absorber can be tested by bouncing the corner of the truck until maximum up and down movement is obtained. Let go of the truck. It should stop bouncing in 1–2 bounces. If not, the shock should be replaced.

Stabilizer Bar

REMOVAL AND INSTALLATION

1. Raise and support the front end on jackstands.
2. Remove the wheels.
3. Remove the stabilizer bar-to-frame clamps.
4. Remove the stabilizer bar-to-spring plate bolts.
5. Remove the stabilizer bar and bushings.
6. Check the bushings for wear or splitting. Replace any damaged bushings.
7. Installation is the reverse of removal. Note, the split in the bushing faces forward. Coat the bushings with silicone grease prior to installation. Install all fasteners finger-tight. When all the fasteners are in place torque the stabilizer bar-to-frame nuts to 52 ft. lbs. Torque the stabilizer bar-to-spring plate bolts to 133 ft. lbs.

CAUTION

All suspension and steering fasteners are important attaching parts in that they could affect the performance of vital components and systems, and/or could result in major repair expense. They must be replaced with one of the same part number or with an equivalent part if replacement becomes necessary. Do not use a replacement part of lesser quality or substitute design. Torque values must be used as specified during reassembly to assure proper retention of these parts. Observe all nut and bolt torque specifications.

Spindle

REMOVAL AND INSTALLATION

Special tools J-23445-A/J-8092, and J-21465-17, or their equivalents, are necessary for this procedure.

1. Raise and support the front end on jackstands.
2. Remove the wheel.
3. Remove the locking hub. See Section 7.
4. Remove the hub and bearing assembly. See Section 7.

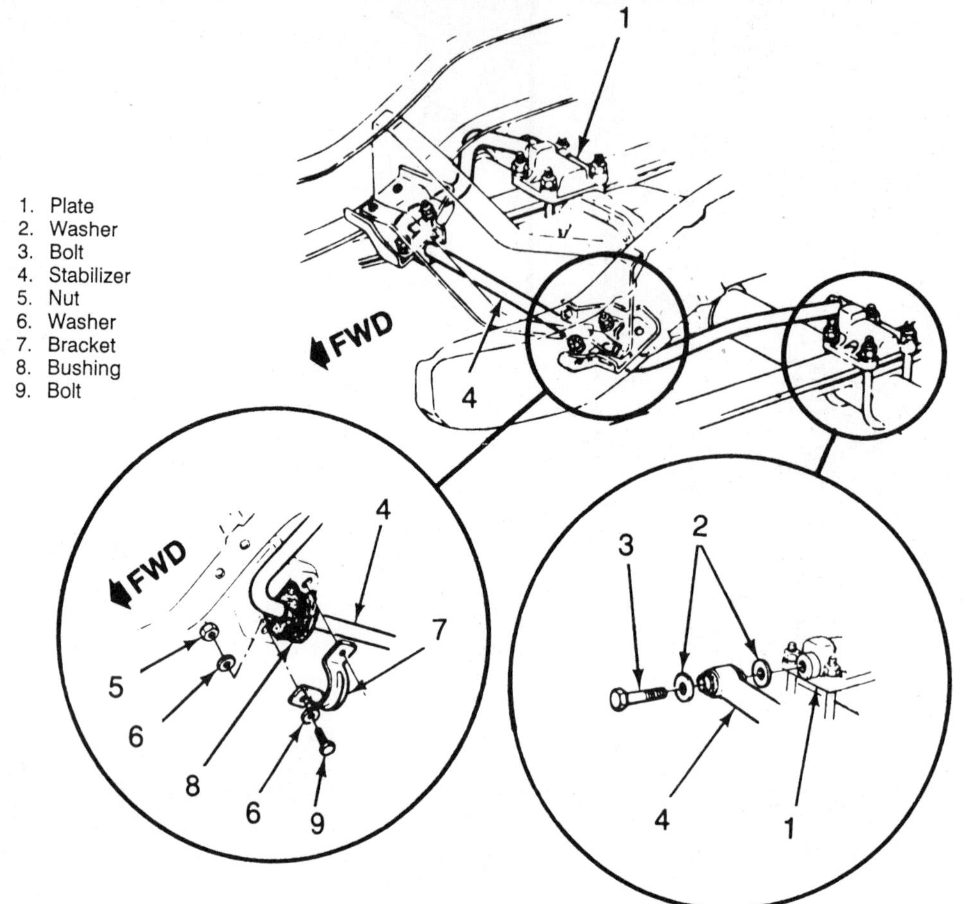

V series stabilizer bar installation

5. Remove the nuts and remove the caliper mounting bracket and splash shield.

6. Tap the end of the spindle with a plastic mallet to break it loose from the knuckle. If tapping won't break it loose, you'll have to do the following:

a. Thread the bearing locknut part way onto the spindle.

b. Position a 2- or 3-jawed pull with the jaws grabbing the locknut and the screw bearing in the end of the axle shaft.

c. Tighten the puller until the spindle breaks free. It will be very helpful to spray Liquid Wrench®, WD-40® or similar solvent around the spindle mating area and around the bolt holes. As the puller is tightened, tap the spindle with the plastic mallet. This often helps break the spindle loose.

7. Drive out the bearing and seal.

To install:

CAUTION

All suspension and steering fasteners are important attaching parts in that they could affect the performance of vital components and systems, and/or could result in major repair expense. They must be replaced with one of the same part number or with an equivalent part if replacement becomes necessary. Do not use a replacement part of lesser quality or substitute design. Torque values must be used as specified during reassembly to assure proper retention of these parts. Observe all nut and bolt torque specifications.

8. Drive in a new bearing using bearing installer J-23445-A/J-8092 for 10/1500 and 20/2500 Series or J-21465-17 for 30/3500 Series.

9. Pack the spindle bearing with wheel bearing grease.

10. Install a new seal.

11. Place the spindle on the knuckle. Be sure the seal and oil deflector are in place.

12. Install the caliper bracket and splash shield.

13. Using new washers (30/3500 Series), install new nuts and torque them to 65 ft. lbs.

14. Install the hub and rotor assembly. Adjust the wheel bearings.

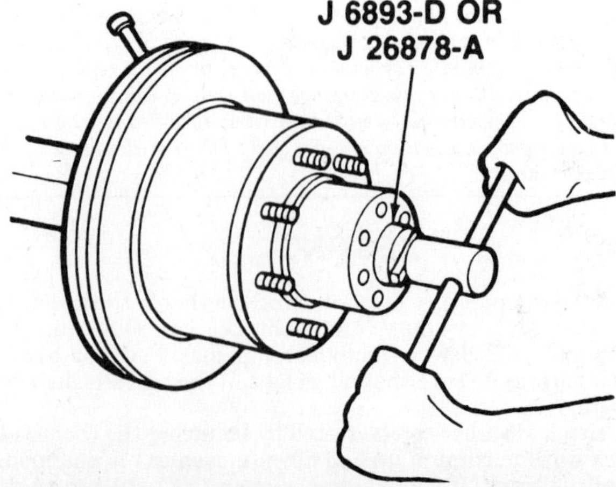

Removing the hub adjusting nut – V series

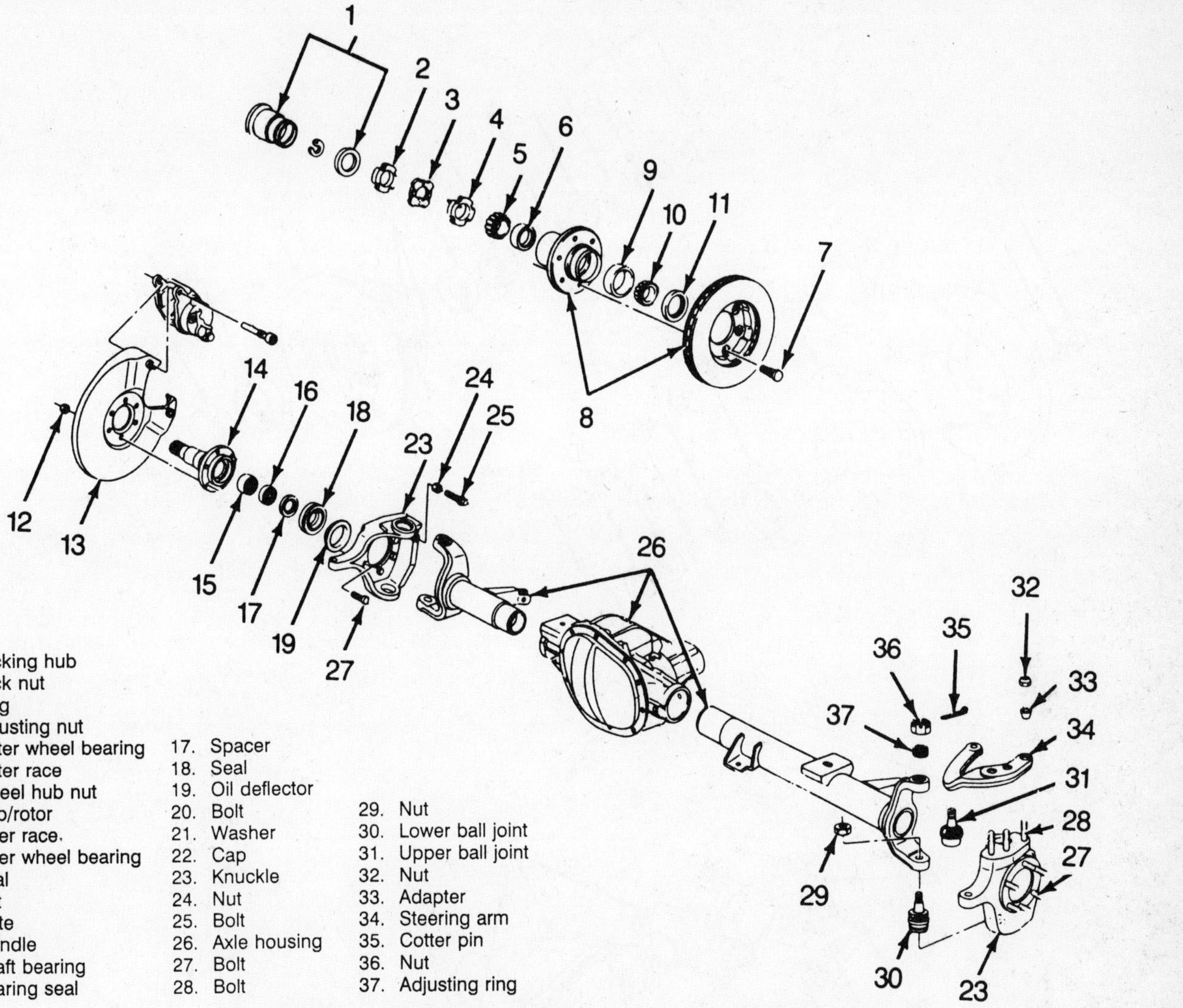

1. Locking hub
2. Lock nut
3. Ring
4. Adjusting nut
5. Outer wheel bearing
6. Outer race
7. Wheel hub nut
8. Hub/rotor
9. Inner race.
10. Inner wheel bearing
11. Seal
12. Nut
13. Plate
14. Spindle
15. Shaft bearing
16. Bearing seal
17. Spacer
18. Seal
19. Oil deflector
20. Bolt
21. Washer
22. Cap
23. Knuckle
24. Nut
25. Bolt
26. Axle housing
27. Bolt
28. Bolt
29. Nut
30. Lower ball joint
31. Upper ball joint
32. Nut
33. Adapter
34. Steering arm
35. Cotter pin
36. Nut
37. Adjusting ring

V10/1500 and 20/2500 knuckle, hub and rotor components

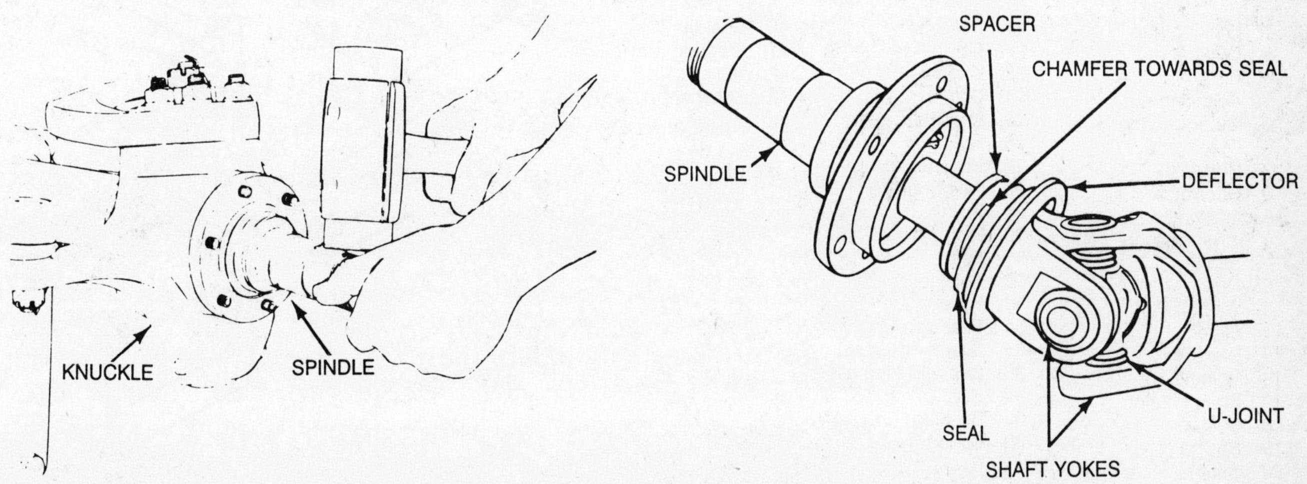

Removing the spindle – V series

Installing the spindle – V series

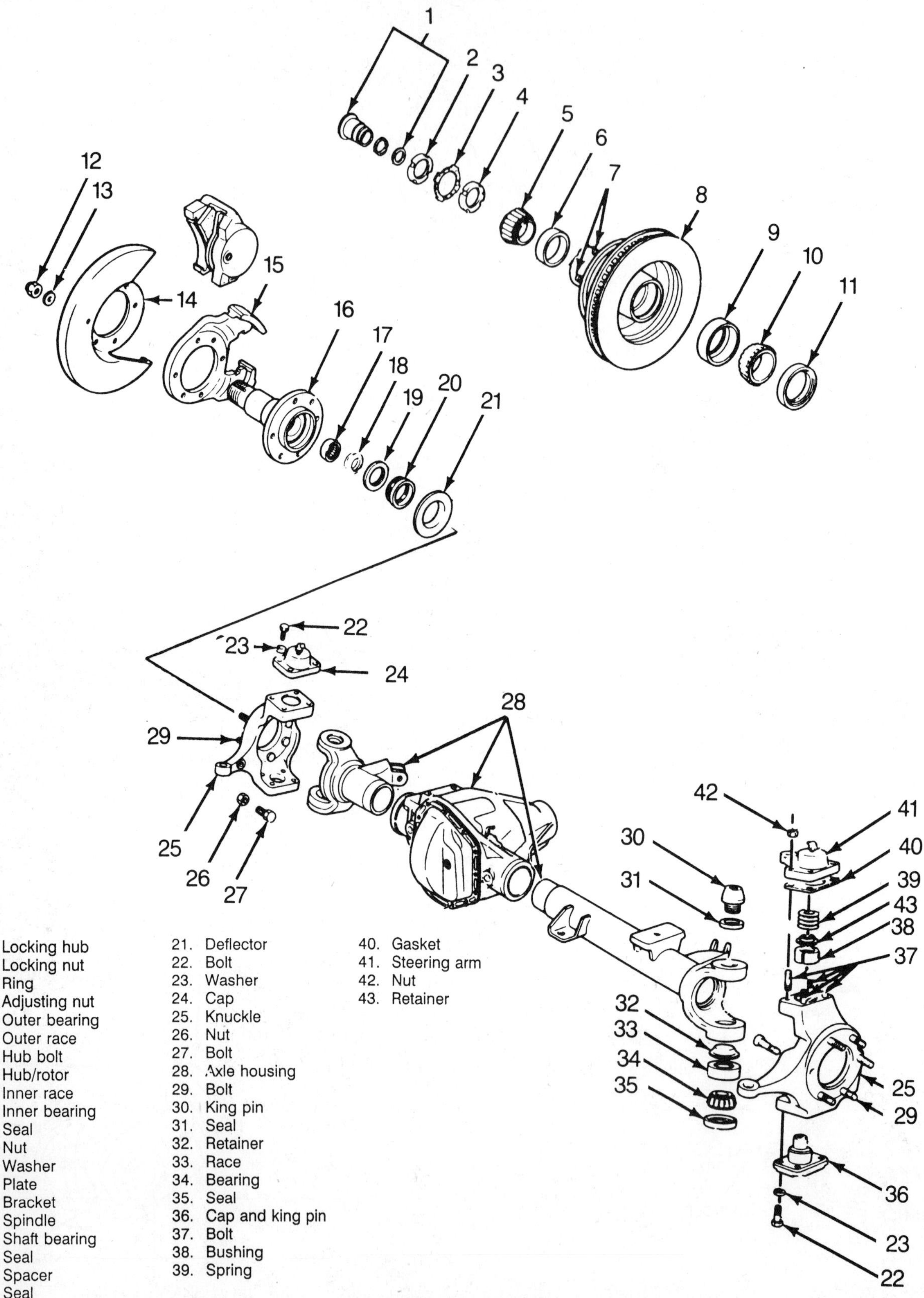
1. Locking hub
2. Locking nut
3. Ring
4. Adjusting nut
5. Outer bearing
6. Outer race
7. Hub bolt
8. Hub/rotor
9. Inner race
10. Inner bearing
11. Seal
12. Nut
13. Washer
14. Plate
15. Bracket
16. Spindle
17. Shaft bearing
18. Seal
19. Spacer
20. Seal
21. Deflector
22. Bolt
23. Washer
24. Cap
25. Knuckle
26. Nut
27. Bolt
28. Axle housing
29. Bolt
30. King pin
31. Seal
32. Retainer
33. Race
34. Bearing
35. Seal
36. Cap and king pin
37. Bolt
38. Bushing
39. Spring
40. Gasket
41. Steering arm
42. Nut
43. Retainer

V30/3500 knuckle, hub and rotor components

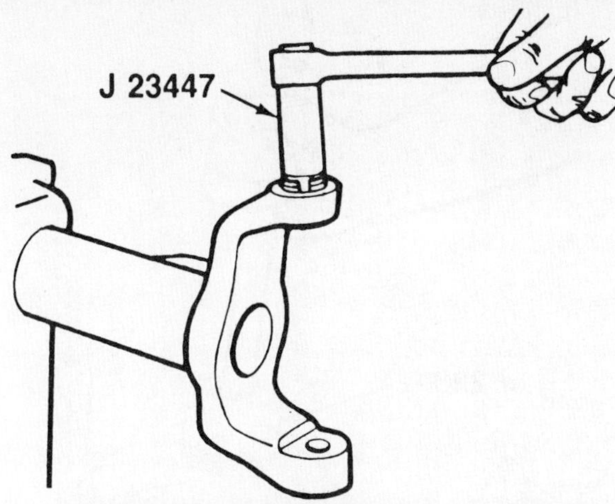

Tightening the adjusting ring – V series

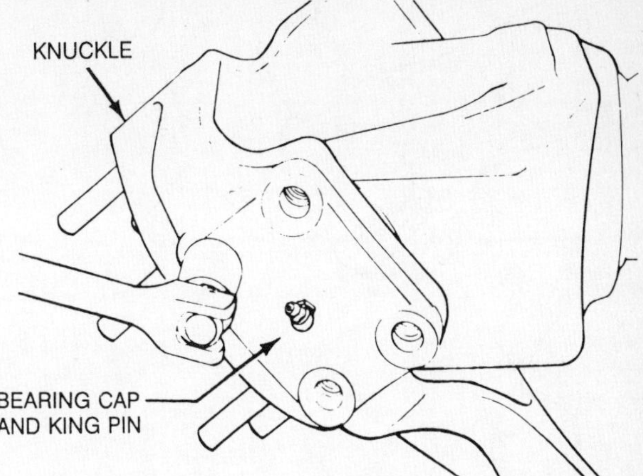

Removing the lower cap and king pin – V series

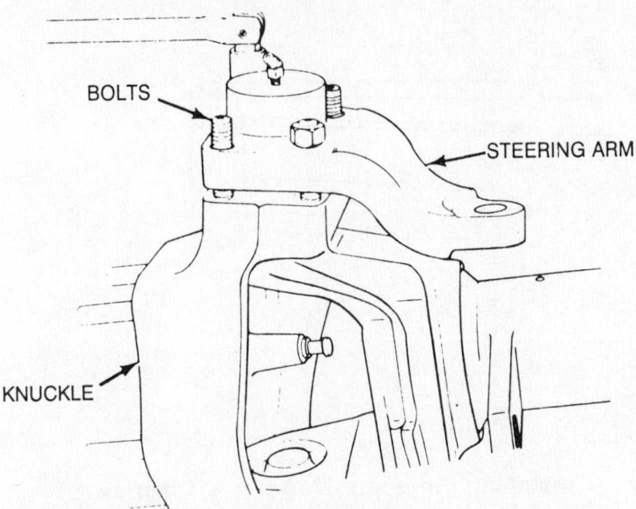

Removing the cap and steering arm – V series

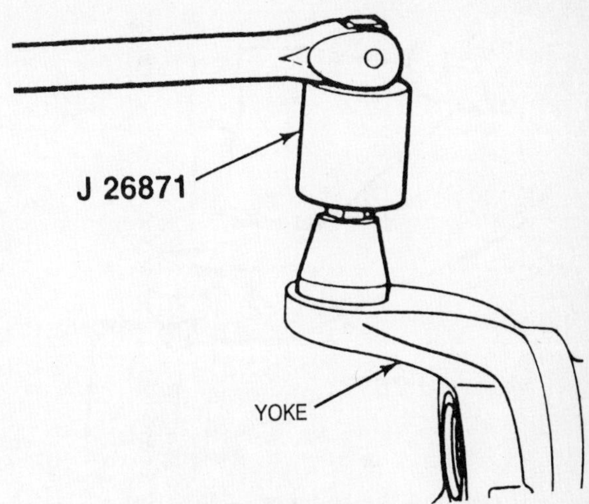

Removing the upper king pin – V series

15. Install the locking hubs.
16. Install the caliper. See Section 9.
17. Install the wheel.

Steering Knuckle

REMOVAL AND INSTALLATION

10/1500 and 20/2500 Series

Special tool J–23447, or its equivalent, is necessary for this procedure.

1. Raise and support the front end on jackstands.
2. Remove the wheels.
3. Remove the locking hubs. See Section 7.
4. Remove the spindle.
5. Disconnect the tie rod end from the knuckle.
6. Remove the knuckle-to-steering arm nuts and adapters.
7. Remove the steering arm from the knuckle.
8. Remove the cotter pins and nuts from the upper and lower ball joints.

NOTE: Do not remove the adjusting ring from the knuckle. If it is necessary to loosen the ring to remove the knuckle, don't loosen it more than 2 threads. The non-hardened threads in the yoke can be easily damaged by the hardened threads in the adjusting ring if caution is not used during knuckle removal!

9. Insert the wedge-shaped end of the heavy prybar, or wedge-type ball joint tool, between the lower ball joint and the yoke. Drive the prybar in to break the knuckle free.
10. Repeat the procedure at the upper ball joint.
11. Lift off the knuckle.

To install:

CAUTION

All suspension and steering fasteners are important attaching parts in that they could affect the performance of vital components and systems, and/or could result in major repair expense. They must be replaced with one of the same part number or with an equivalent part if replacement becomes necessary. Do not use a replacement part of lesser quality or substitute design. Torque values must be used as specified during reassembly to assure proper retention of these parts. Observe all nut and bolt torque specifications.

12. Position the knuckle on the yoke.
13. Start the ball joints into their sockets. Place the nuts onto the ball studs. The nut with the cotter pin slot is the upper nut. Tighten the lower nut to 30 ft. lbs., for now.
14. Using tool J–23447, tighten the adjusting ring to 50 ft. lbs.
15. Tighten the upper nut to 100 ft. lbs. Install a new cotter pin. NEVER loosen the nut to align the cotter pin hole; always tighten it.

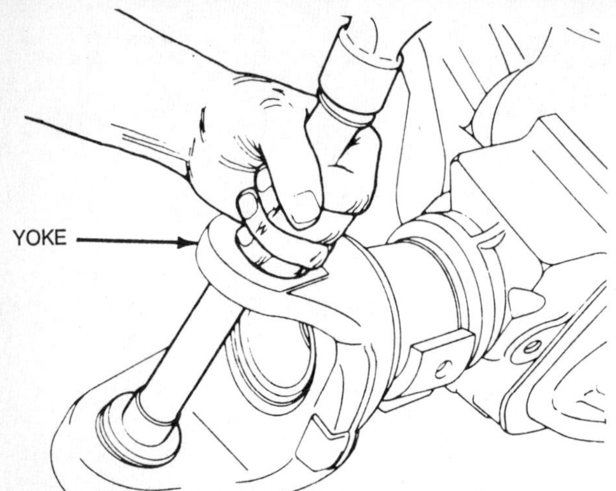

Removing the retainer, race, bearing and seal – V series

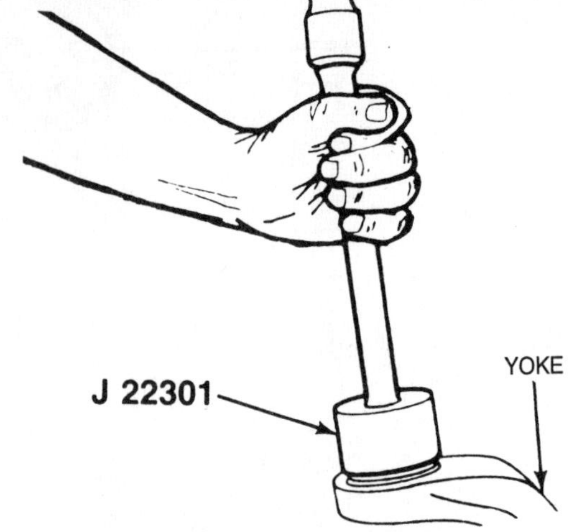

Installing the seal – V series

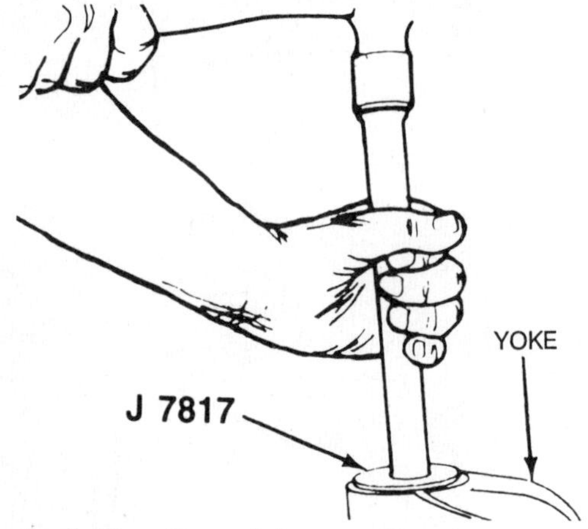

Installing the retainer – V series

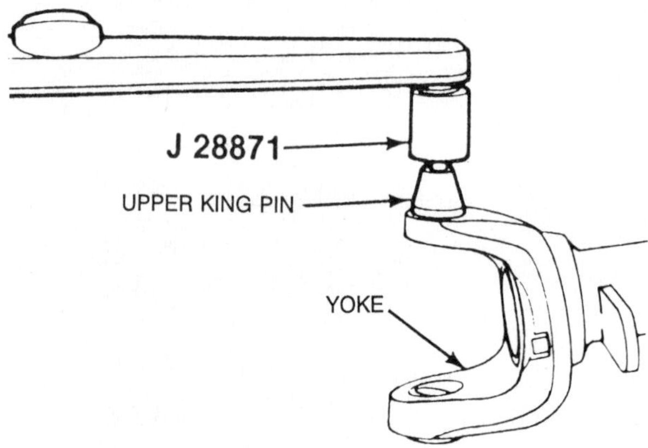

Installing the upper king pin – V series

16. Tighten the lower nut to 70 ft. lbs.
17. Attach the steering arm to the knuckle using adapters and NEW nuts. Torque the nuts to 90 ft. lbs.
18. Connect the tie rod end to the knuckle.
19. Install the spindle. See the procedure above.
20. Install the hub/rotor assembly and wheel bearings. Adjust the bearings. See section 7.
21. Install the locking hubs. See Section 7.
22. Install the wheel.

30/3500 Series

The following special tools, or their equivalents, are necessary for this procedure: J-26871, J-7817, and J-22301.

1. Raise and support the front end on jackstands.
2. Remove the wheel.
3. Remove the hub/rotor/bearings assembly. See Section 7.
4. Remove the locking hubs. See Section 7.
5. Remove the spindle. See the procedure above.
6. Remove the upper cap from the right side knuckle and/or steering arm from the left side knuckle, by loosening the bolts (right side) and/or nuts (left side) a little at a time in an alternating pattern. This will safely relieve spring pressure under the cap and/or arm. Once spring pressure is relieved, remove the bolts and/or nuts, washers and cap and/or steering arm.
7. Remove the gasket and compression spring.
8. Remove the bolts and washers and remove the lower bearing cap and the lower kingpin.
9. Remove the upper kingpin bushing by pulling it out through the knuckle.
10. Remove the knuckle from the axle yoke.
11. Remove the retainer from the knuckle.
12. Using a large breaker bar and adapter J-26871, remove the upper kingpin from the axle yoke by applying 500–600 ft. lbs. of torque to the kingpin to break it free.
13. Using a hammer and blunt drift, drive out the retainer, race bearing and seal from the axle yoke. These are driven out all at once.

To install:

CAUTION

All suspension and steering fasteners are important attaching parts in that they could affect the performance of vital components and systems, and/or could result in major repair expense. They must be replaced with one of the same part number or with an equivalent part if replacement becomes necessary. Do not use a replacement part of lesser quality or substitute design. Torque values must be used as specified during reassembly to assure proper retention of these parts. Observe all nut and bolt torque specifications.

14. Using tool J-7817, install a new retainer and race in the axle yoke.
15. Fill the recessed area in the retainer and race with the same grease used on the wheel bearings.
16. Completely pack the upper yoke roller bearing with wheel bearing grease. A cone-type bearing packer is preferable, but the bearing may be packed by hand. See the Wheel Bearing PAcking procedure.

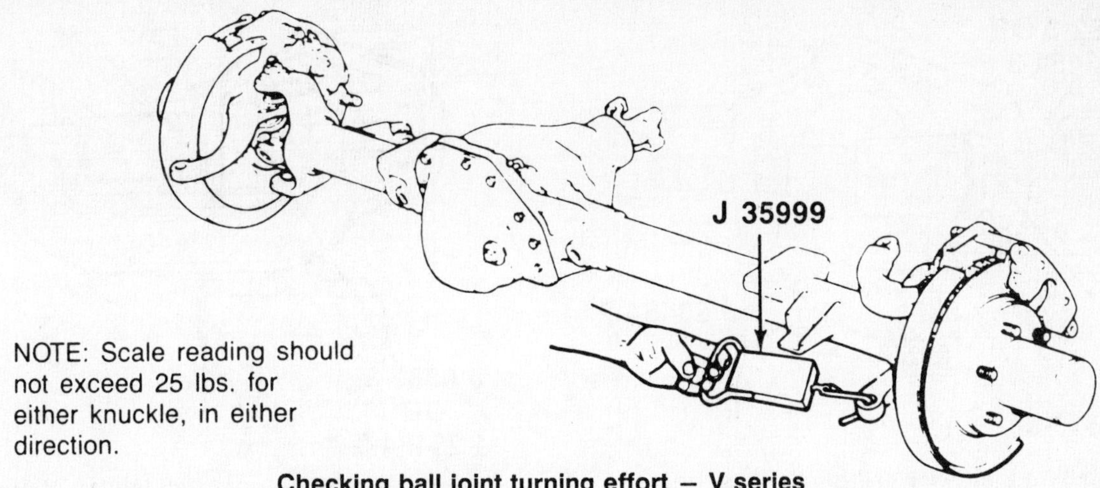

J 35999
NOTE: Scale reading should not exceed 25 lbs. for either knuckle, in either direction.

Checking ball joint turning effort – V series

17. Install the bearing and a new seal in the upper axle yoke, using a bearing driver such as J-22301. DON'T distort the seal. It should protrude slightly above the yoke when fully seated.

18. Using adapter tool J-28871, install the upper kingpin. The kingpin must be torque to 550 ft. lbs.

19. Position the knuckle in the yoke. Working through the knuckle, install a new felt seal over the kingpin and position the knuckle on the kingpin.

20. Install the bushing over the kingpin.

21. Install the compression spring, gasket, bearing cap and/or steering arm and bolts and/or nut and washer. Torque the bolts and/or nuts, in an alternating pattern, to 80 ft. lbs.

22. Install the lower bearing cap and kingpin. Torque the bolts to 80 ft. lbs. in an alternating pattern.

23. Thoroughly lube both kingpins through the grease fittings.

24. Install the spindle.

25. Install the hub/rotor/bearing assembly. Adjust the bearings. See Section 7.

27. Install the locking hubs. See Section 7.

28. Install the wheel.

29. Have the front end alignment checked and reset as necessary.

Ball Joints 10/1500 and 20/2500 Series

CHECKING THE TURNING EFFORT

1. Raise and support the front end on jackstands.
2. Remove the wheels.
3. Disconnect the connecting rod and tie rod at each knuckle.
4. Position the knuckle in the straight-ahead position and attach a spring scale to the tie rod hole of the knuckle. Pull at a right (90°) angle and determine the amount of pull necessary to keep the knuckle moving *after* initial break-away. The pull should not exceed 25 lbs. in either direction for each knuckle. If pull is excessive, the ball joint can be adjusted. See the procedure immediately following. If no adjustment is required, connect the connecting rod and tie rod.

ADJUSTMENT

Tool J-23447, or its equivalent, is necessary for this procedure.

1. Raise and support the front end on jackstands.
2. Remove the wheels.
3. Remove the cotter pin and nut from the upper ball joint.
4. Using tool J-23447, back off the adjusting ring no more than 2 threads, then, tighten the adjusting ring to 50 ft. lbs.
5. Install the upper nut. Tighten the upper nut to 100 ft. lbs. Install a new cotter pin. NEVER loosen the nut to align the cotter pin hole; always tighten it.
6. Install the wheel.

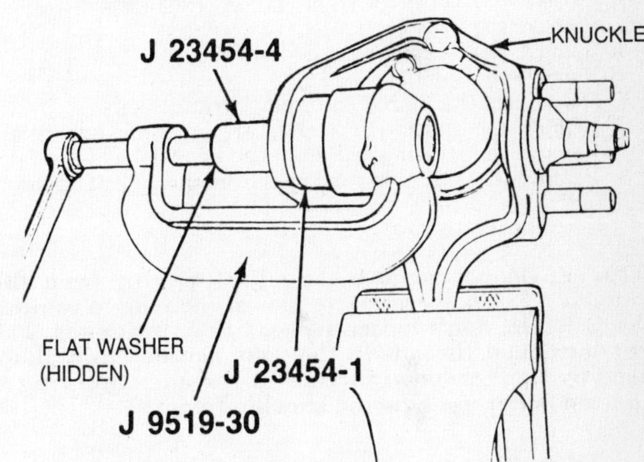

Removing the lower ball joint – V series

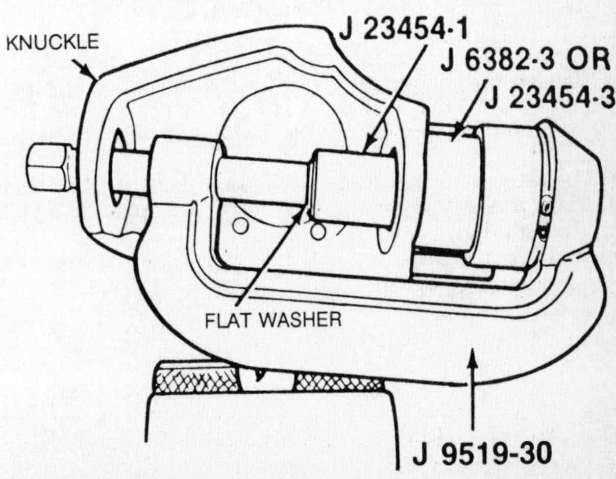

Removing the upper ball joint – V series

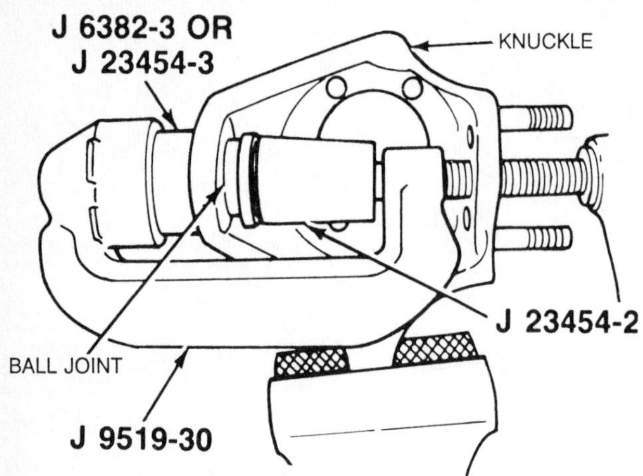

Installing the lower ball joint – V series

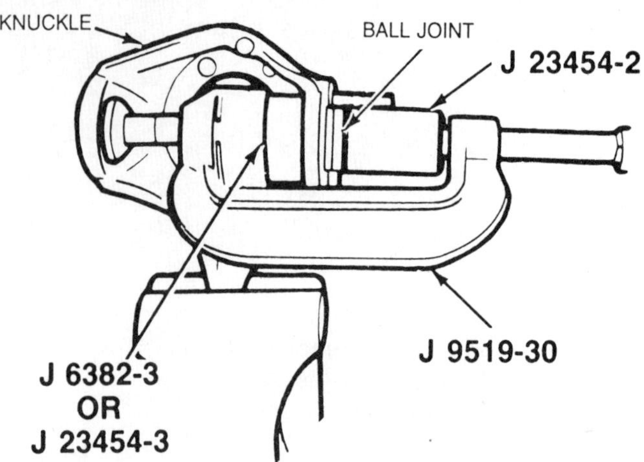

Installing the upper ball joint – V series

REMOVAL AND INSTALLATION

The following special tools, or their equivalents, are necessary for this procedure: J-9519-30, J-23454-1, J-23454-4, J-23454-3, J-23454-2, J-23447.

1. Raise and support the front end on jackstands.
2. Remove the wheels.
3. Remove the locking hubs. See Section 7.
4. Remove the spindle.
5. Disconnect the tie rod end from the knuckle.
6. Remove the knuckle-to-steering arm nuts and adapters.
7. Remove the steering arm from the knuckle.
8. Remove the cotter pins and nuts from the upper and lower ball joints.

NOTE: Do not remove the adjusting ring from the knuckle. If it is necessary to loosen the ring to remove the knuckle, don't loosen it more than 2 threads. The non-hardened threads in the yoke can be easily damaged by the hardened threads in the adjusting ring if caution is not used during knuckle removal!

9. Insert the wedge-shaped end of the heavy prybar, or wedge-type ball joint tool, between the lower ball joint and the yoke. Drive the prybar in to break the knuckle free.
10. Repeat the procedure at the upper ball joint.
11. Lift off the knuckle.
12. Secure the knuckle in a vise.
13. Remove the snapring from the lower ball joint. Using tools J-9519-30, J-23454-1 and J-23454-4, or their equivalent screw-type forcing tool, force the lower ball joint from the knuckle.
14. Using tools J-9519-30, J-23454-3 and J-23454-4, or their equivalent screw-type forcing tool, force the upper ball joint from the knuckle.

To install:

CAUTION

All suspension and steering fasteners are important attaching parts in that they could affect the performance of vital components and systems, and/or could result in major repair expense. They must be replaced with one of the same part number or with an equivalent part if replacement becomes necessary. Do not use a replacement part of lesser quality or substitute design. Torque values must be used as specified during reassembly to assure proper retention of these parts. Observe all nut and bolt torque specifications.

15. Position the lower ball joint (the one without the cotter pin hole) squarely in the knuckle. Using tools J-9519-30, J-23454-2 and J-23454-3, or their equivalent screw-type forcing tool, force the lower ball joint into the knuckle until it is fully seated.
16. Install the snapring.
17. Position the upper ball joint (the one with the cotter pin hole) squarely in the knuckle. Using tools J-9519-30, J-23454-2 and J-23454-3, or their equivalent screw-type forcing tool, force the upper ball joint into the knuckle until it is fully seated.
18. Position the knuckle on the yoke.
19. Start the ball joints into their sockets. Place the nuts onto the ball studs. The nut with the cotter pin slot is the upper nut. Tighten the lower nut to 30 ft. lbs., for now.
20. Using tool J-23447, tighten the adjusting ring to 50 ft. lbs.
21. Tighten the upper nut to 100 ft. lbs. Install a new cotter pin. NEVER loosen the nut to align the cotter pin hole; always tighten it.
22. Tighten the lower nut to 70 ft. lbs.
23. Attach the steering arm to the knuckle using adapters and NEW nuts. Torque the nuts to 90 ft. lbs.
24. Connect the tie rod end to the knuckle.
25. Install the spindle. See the procedure above.
26. Install the hub/rotor assembly and wheel bearings. Adjust the bearings. See section 7.
27. Install the locking hubs. See Section 7.
28. Install the wheel.
29. Have the front end alignment checked and adjusted as necessary.

K SERIES
4-WHEEL DRIVE FRONT SUSPENSION

Shock Absorbers

REMOVAL AND INSTALLATION

1. Raise and support the front end on jackstands.
2. Remove the upper end bolt, nut and washer.
3. Remove the lower end bolt, nut and washer.
4. Remove the shock absorber and inspect the rubber bushings. If these are defective, replace the shock absorber assembly.
5. Installation is the reverse of removal. Torque the both nuts to 48 ft. lbs. Make sure that the bolts are inserted in the proper direction. The bolt head on the upper end should be forward; the bottom end bolt head is rearward.

CAUTION

All suspension and steering fasteners are important attaching parts in that they could affect the performance of vital components and systems, and/or could result in major repair expense. They must be replaced with one of the same part number or with an equivalent part if replacement becomes necessary. Do not use a replacement part of lesser quality or substitute design. Torque values must be used as specified during reassembly to assure proper retention of these parts. Observe all nut and bolt torque specifications.

TESTING

Adjust the tire pressure before testing the shocks. If the truck is equipped with heavy duty equipment, this can sometimes be misleading. A stiff ride normally accompanies a stiff or heavy duty suspension. Be sure that all weight in the truck is distributed evenly.

Each shock absorber can be tested by bouncing the corner of the truck until maximum up and down movement is obtained. Let go of the truck. It should stop bouncing in 1-2 bounces. If not, the shock should be replaced.

Stabilizer Bar

REMOVAL AND INSTALLATION

Special tool J-36202, or its equivalent, is necessary for this procedure.

1. Raise and support the front end on jackstands.
2. Remove the wheels.
3. Remove the stabilizer bar-to-frame clamps.
4. Remove the stabilizer bar-to-lower control arm bolts, nut/grommet assemblies and spacers.

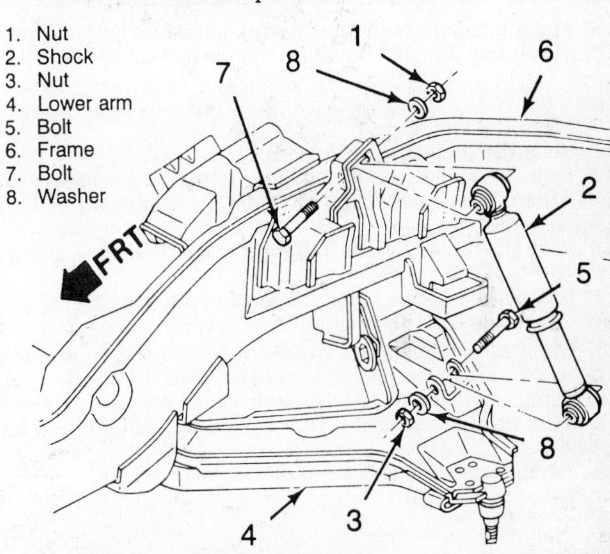

Shock absorber installation — K series

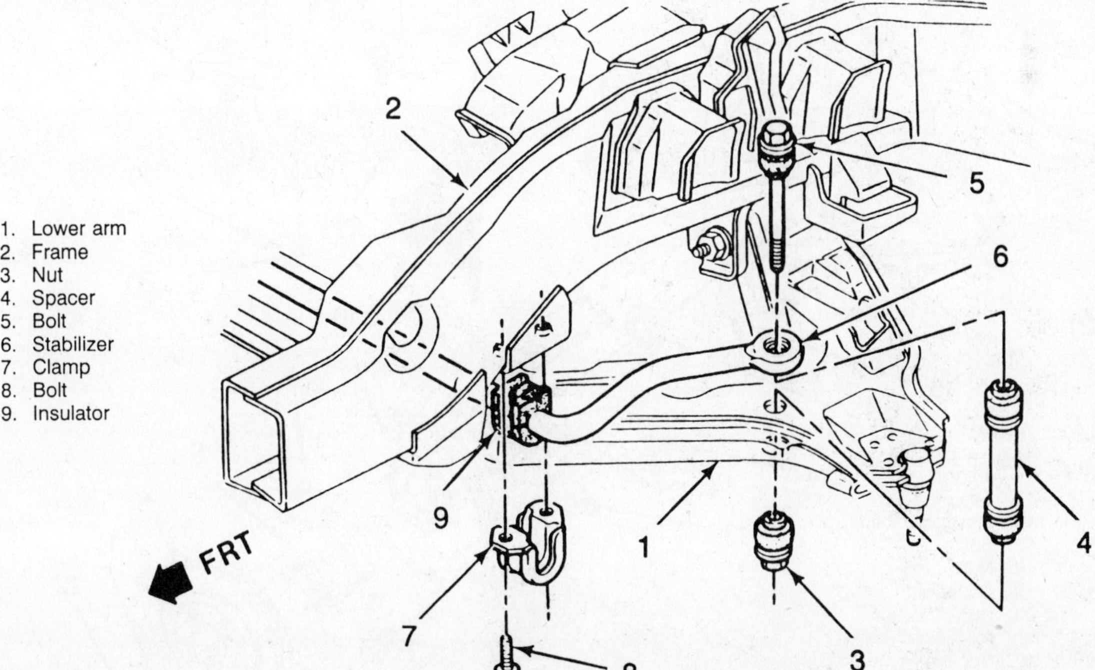

Stabilizer bar installation — K series

NOTE: The bolts, spacers and nuts are not interchangeable from side-to-side. Keep them separated.

5. Remove the stabilizer bar and bushings.
6. Check the bushings for wear or splitting. Replace any damaged bushings.

To install:

CAUTION

All suspension and steering fasteners are important attaching parts in that they could affect the performance of vital components and systems, and/or could result in major repair expense. They must be replaced with one of the same part number or with an equivalent part if replacement becomes necessary. Do not use a replacement part of lesser quality or substitute design. Torque values must be used as specified during reassembly to assure proper retention of these parts. Observe all nut and bolt torque specifications.

7. Matchmark the both torsion bar adjustment bolt positions.
8. Using tool J-36202, increase the tension on the adjusting arm.
9. Remove the adjustment bolt and retaining plate.
10. Move the tool aside.
11. Slide the torsion bars forward.
12. Coat the stabilizer bar bushings with silicone grease and install them on the stabilizer bar. Note, the split in the bushing faces forward.
13. Position the stabilizer bar and install the frame clamps. Make the bolts finger tight.
14. Install the end link bolts, spacers and nut/grommet assemblies. Make the bolts finger tight.
15. When all fasteners are installed, torque the frme clamp bolts to 24 ft. lbs.; the end link bolts to 12 ft. lbs.
16. Using tool J-36202, increase tension on both torsion bars.
17. Install the adjustment retainer plate and bolt on both torsion bars.
18. Set the adjustment bolt to the marked position.

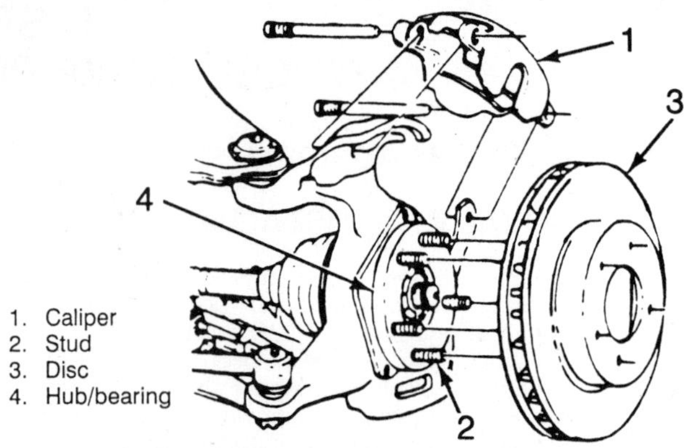

Removing the disc – K series

19. Release the tension on the torsion bar until the load is take up by the adjustment bolt.
20. Remove the tool.
21. Install the wheels.
22. Have the front end alignment checked and adjusted as necessary.

Left Side Knuckle and Seal

REMOVAL AND INSTALLATION

1. Raise and support the front end on jackstands.
2. Remove the wheel.
3. Remove the skid plate.
4. Remove the left stabilizer bar clamp.
5. Remove the left stabilizer bar bolt, spacer and bushings at the lower control arm.

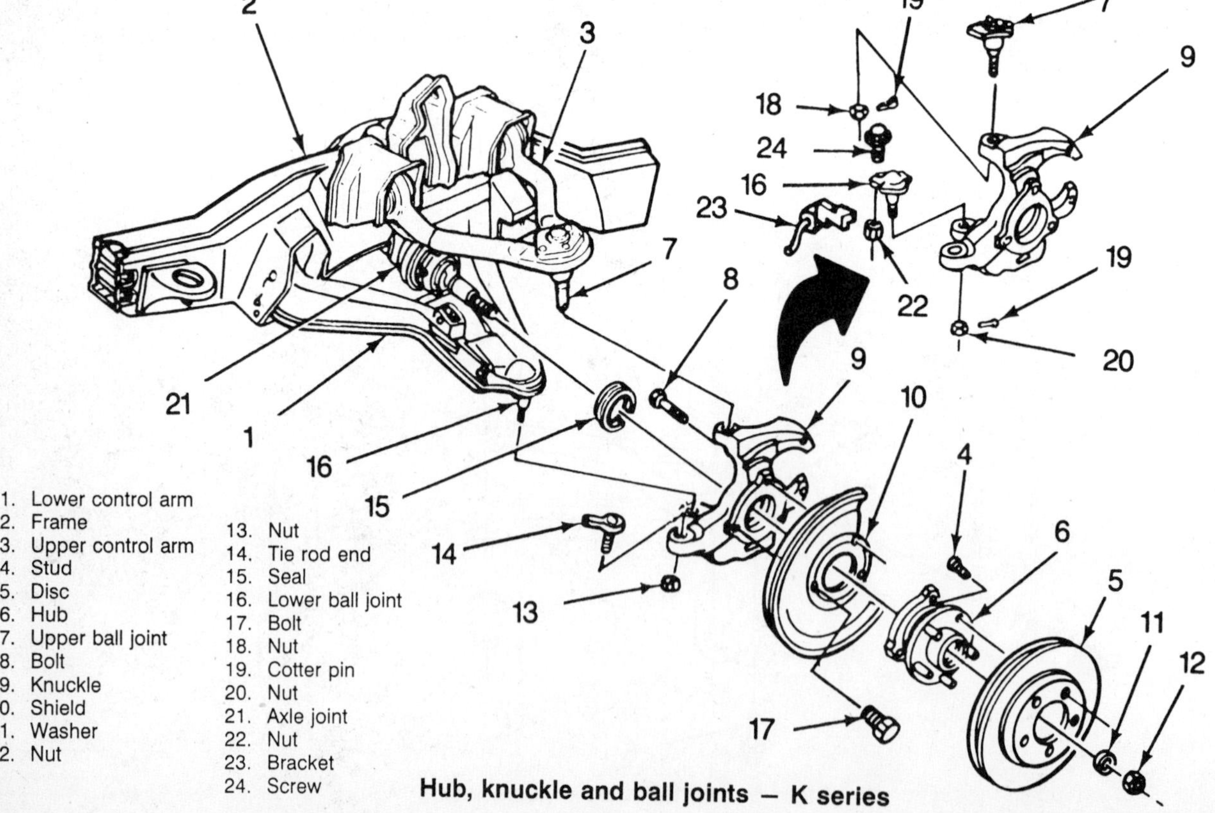

Hub, knuckle and ball joints – K series

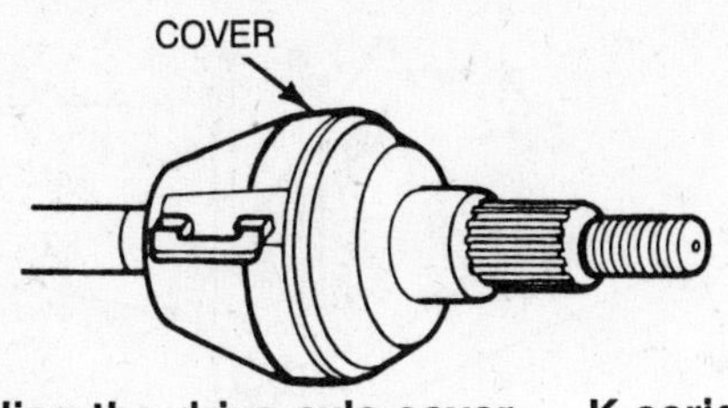

Installing the drive axle cover — K series

6. Disconnect the left inner tie rod end from the steering relay rod.
7. Remove the caliper and suspend it out of the way.
8. Remove the brake disc. See Section 9.
9. Remove the hub nut and washer.
10. Using a puller, force the outer end of the axle shaft out of the hub. Remove the hub/bearing assembly.
11. Remove the axle shaft inner flange bolts. Remove the shaft.
12. Support the lower control arm with a floor jack.
13. Unbolt and remove the splash shield.
14. Remove the upper and lower ball joint nuts and cotter pins. Using a screw-type forcing tool, separate the upper, then the lower, ball joint from the knuckle.
15. Remove the knuckle.
16. Pry the old seal from the knuckle.

To install:

CAUTION

All suspension and steering fasteners are important attaching parts in that they could affect the performance of vital components and systems, and/or could result in major repair expense. They must be replaced with one of the same part number or with an equivalent part if replacement becomes necessary. Do not use a replacement part of lesser quality or substitute design. Torque values must be used as specified during reassembly to assure proper retention of these parts. Observe all nut and bolt torque specifications.

17. Drive a new seal into the knuckle.
18. Position the knuckle on the ball joint studs and start the studs squarely into the knuckle. Install the nuts and torque them to 94 ft. lbs. Advance the nuts to align the cotter pin holes. NEVER back them off! When advancing the nuts, don't exceed $^{1}/_{6}$ turn.
19. Install new cotter pins. Bend the pins against the flats.
20. Position the splash shield on the knuckle. Make sure it is properly aligned and torque the bolts to 12 ft. lbs.
21. Position the axle shaft and install the flange bolts. Tighten them to 59 ft. lbs.
22. Position the shaft in the hub and install the washer and hub nut. Position a drift in the rotor vanes and tighten the hub nut to 175 ft. lbs.
23. Connect the left inner tie rod end at the steering relay rod. Torque the nut to 35 ft. lbs.
24. Install the left stabilizer bar bolt, spacer and bushings at the lower control arm. Torque the bolt to 24 ft. lbs.
25. Install the left stabilizer bar clamp. Torque the bolts to 12 ft. lbs.
26. Install the disc and caliper.
27. Install the skid plate.

Right Side Knuckle and Seal

REMOVAL AND INSTALLATION

1. Raise and support the front end on jackstands.
2. Remove the wheel.
3. Remove the skid plate.
4. Remove the right stabilizer bar clamp.
5. Remove the right stabilizer bar bolt, spacer and bushings at the lower control arm.
6. Disconnect the right inner tie rod end from the steering relay rod.
7. Remove the caliper and suspend it out of the way.
8. Remove the brake disc. See Section 9.
9. Remove the hub nut and washer.
10. Using a puller, force the outer end of the axle shaft out of the hub. Remove the hub/bearing assembly.
11. Remove the axle shaft inner flange bolts. Remove the shaft.
12. Support the lower control arm with a floor jack.
13. Unbolt and remove the splash shield.
14. Remove the upper and lower ball joint nuts and cotter pins. Using a screw-type forcing tool, separate the upper, then the lower, ball joint from the knuckle.
15. Remove the knuckle.
16. Pry the old seal from the knuckle.

To install:

CAUTION

All suspension and steering fasteners are important attaching parts in that they could affect the performance of vital components and systems, and/or could result in major repair expense. They must be replaced with one of the same part number or with an equivalent part if replacement becomes necessary. Do not use a replacement part of lesser quality or substitute design. Torque values must be used as specified during reassembly to assure proper retention of these parts. Observe all nut and bolt torque specifications.

17. Drive a new seal into the knuckle.
18. Position the knuckle on the ball joint studs and start the studs squarely into the knuckle. Install the nuts and torque them to 94 ft. lbs. Advance the nuts to align the cotter pin holes. NEVER back them off! When advancing the nuts, don't exceed $^{1}/_{6}$ turn.
19. Install new cotter pins. Bend the pins against the flats.
20. Position the splash shield on the knuckle. Make sure it is properly aligned and torque the bolts to 12 ft. lbs.
21. Position the axle shaft and install the flange bolts. Tighten them to 59 ft. lbs.
22. Position the shaft in the hub and install the washer and hub nut. Position a drift in the rotor vanes and tighten the hub nut to 175 ft. lbs.
23. Connect the right inner tie rod end at the steering relay rod. Torque the nut to 35 ft. lbs.
24. Install the right stabilizer bar bolt, spacer and bushings at the lower control arm. Torque the bolt to 24 ft. lbs.
25. Install the right stabilizer bar clamp. Torque the bolts to 12 ft. lbs.
26. Install the disc and caliper.
27. Install the skid plate.

Upper Ball Joint

REPLACEMENT

1. Raise and support the front end on jackstands.
2. Remove the wheel.
3. Unbolt the brake hose braket from the control arm.
4. Using a ⅛ in. drill bit, drill a pilot hole through each ball joint rivet.
5. Drill out the rivets with a ½ in. drill bit. Punch out any remaining rivet material.
6. Remove the cotter pin and nut from the ball stud.
7. Support the lower control arm with a floor jack.
8. Using a screw-type forcing tool, separate the ball joint from the knuckle.

To install:

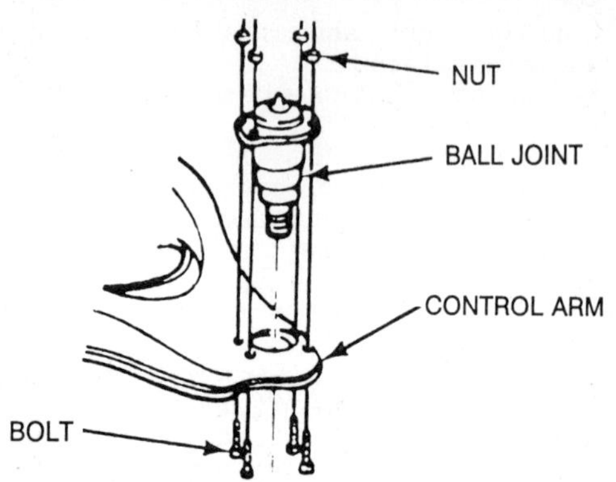

Installing the upper ball joint – K series

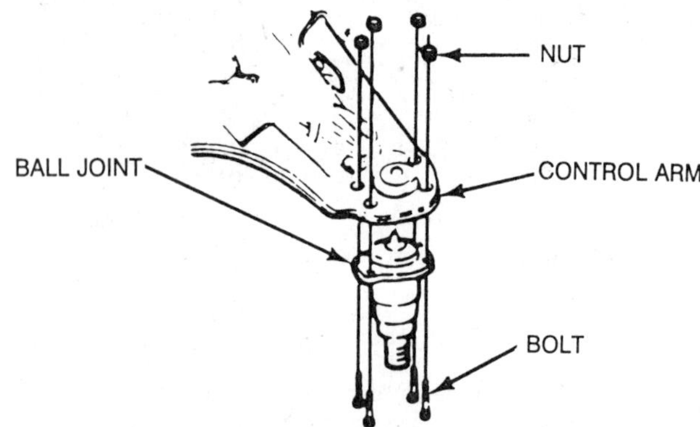

Installing the lower ball joint – K series

CAUTION

All suspension and steering fasteners are important attaching parts in that they could affect the performance of vital components and systems, and/or could result in major repair expense. They must be replaced with one of the same part number or with an equivalent part if replacement becomes necessary. Do not use a replacement part of lesser quality or substitute design. Torque values must be used as specified during reassembly to assure proper retention of these parts. Observe all nut and bolt torque specifications.

9. Position the new ball joint on the control arm.

NOTE: Service replacement ball joints come with nuts and bolts to replace the rivets.

10. Install the bolts and nuts. Tighten the nuts to 17 ft. lbs. for 15 and 25 Series; 52 ft. lbs. for 35 Series.

NOTE: The bolts are inserted from the bottom.

11. Start the ball stud into the knuckle. Make sure it is squarely seated. Install the ball stud nut and pull the ball stud into the knuckle with the nut. Don't final-torque the nut yet.
12. Install the wheel.
13. Lower the truck. Once the weight of the truck is on the wheels:
    a. Lift the front bumper about 38mm and let it drop.
    b. Repeat this procedure 2 or 3 more times.
    c. Draw a line on the side of the lower control arm from the centerline of the control arm pivot shaft, dead level to the outer end of the control arm.
    d. Measure the distance between the lowest corner of the steering knuckle and the line on the control arm. Record the figure.
    e. Push down about 38mm on the front bumper and let it return. Repeat the procedure 2 or 3 more times.
    f. Re-measure the distance at the control arm.
    g. Determine the average of the 2 measurements. The average distance should be:

- K15/25 without F60 option: 157.0mm ± 6.0mm
- K15/25 with F60 option: 183.0mm ± 6.0mm
- K35 without F60 option: 145.0mm ± 6.0mm
- K35 with F60 option: 173.0mm ± 6.0mm

    h. If the figure is correct, tighten the control arm pivot nuts to 94 ft. lbs.
    i. If the figure is not correct, tighten the pivot bolts to 94 ft. lbs. and have the front end alignment corrected.

Lower Ball Joint

REPLACEMENT

Special tool J-36202, or its equivalent, is necessary for this procedure.

1. Raise and support the front end on jackstands.
2. Remove the wheel.
3. Remove the splash shield from the knuckle.
4. Disconnect the the inner tie rod end from the relay rod using a ball joint separator.
5. Remove the hub nut and washer. Insert a long drift or dowel through the vanes in the brake rotor to hold the rotor in place.
6. Remove the axle shaft inner flange bolts.
7. Using a puller, force the outer end of the axle shaft out of the hub. Remove the shaft.
8. Using a ⅛ in. drill bit, drill a pilot hole through each ball joint rivet.
9. Drill out the rivets with a ½ in. drill bit. Punch out any remaining rivet material.
10. Remove the cotter pin and nut from the ball stud.
11. Support the lower control arm with a floor jack.
12. Matchmark the both torsion bar adjustment bolt positions.
13. Using tool J-36202, increase the tension on the adjusting arm.
14. Remove the adjustment bolt and retaining plate.
15. Move the tool aside.
16. Slide the torsion bars forward.
17. Using a screw-type forcing tool, separate the ball joint from the knuckle.

To install:

CAUTION

All suspension and steering fasteners are important attaching parts in that they could affect the performance of vital components and systems, and/or could result in major repair expense. They must be replaced with one of the same part number or with an equivalent part if replacement becomes necessary. Do not use a replacement part of lesser quality or substitute design. Torque values must be used as specified during reassembly to assure proper retention of these parts. Observe all nut and bolt torque specifications.

18. Position the new ball joint on the control arm.

NOTE: Service replacement ball joints come with nuts and bolts to replace the rivets.

19. Install the bolts and nuts. Tighten the nuts to 45 ft. lbs.

NOTE: The bolts are inserted from the bottom.

20. Start the ball stud into the knuckle. Make sure it is squarely seated. Install the ball stud nut and pull the ball stud into the knuckle with the nut. Don't final-torque the nut yet.
21. Using tool J-36202, increase tension on both torsion bars.
22. Install the adjustment retainer plate and bolt on both torsion bars.
23. Set the adjustment bolt to the marked position.
24. Release the tension on the torsion bar until the load is take up by the adjustment bolt.

25. Remove the tool.

26. Position the shaft in the hub and install the washer and hub nut. Leave the drift in the rotor vanes and tighten the hub nut to 175 ft. lbs.

27. Install the flange bolts. Tighten them to 59 ft. lbs. Remove the drift.

28. Connect the inner tie rod end at the steering relay rod. Torque the nut to 35 ft. lbs.

29. Install the splash shield.

30. Install the wheel.

31. Lower the truck. Once the weight of the truck is on the wheels:

a. Lift the front bumper about 38mm and let it drop.

b. Repeat this procedure 2 or 3 more times.

c. Draw a line on the side of the lower control arm from the centerline of the control arm pivot shaft, dead level to the outer end of the control arm.

d. Measure the distance between the lowest corner of the steering knuckle and the line on the control arm. Record the figure.

e. Push down about 38mm on the front bumper and let it return. Repeat the procedure 2 or 3 more times.

f. Re-measure the distance at the control arm.

g. Determine the average of the 2 measurements. The average distance should be:

- K15/25 without F60 option: 157.0mm ± 6.0mm
- K15/25 with F60 option: 183.0mm ± 6.0mm
- K35 without F60 option: 145.0mm ± 6.0mm
- K35 with F60 option: 173.0mm ± 6.0mm

h. If the figure is correct, tighten the control arm pivot nuts to 94 ft. lbs.

i. If the figure is not correct, tighten the pivot bolts to 94 ft. lbs. and have the front end alignment corrected.

Upper Control Arm and Bushings

REMOVAL AND INSTALLATION

1. Raise and support the truck on jackstands.

2. Support the lower control arm with a floor jack.

3. Remove the wheel.

4. Unbolt the brake hose bracket from the control arm.

5. Remove the air cleaner extension.

6. Remove the cotter pin from the upper control arm ball stud and loosen the stud nut until the bottom surface of the nut is slightly below the end of the stud.

7. Using a screw-type forcing tool, break loose the ball joint from the knuckle.

8. Remove the nuts and bolts securing the control arm to the frame brackets.

9. Tape the shims and spacers together and tag for proper reassembly.

To install:

CAUTION

All suspension and steering fasteners are important attaching parts in that they could affect the performance of vital components and systems, and/or could result in major repair expense. They must be replaced with one of the same part number or with an equivalent part if replacement becomes necessary. Do not use a replacement part of lesser quality or substitute design. Torque values must be used as specified during reassembly to assure proper retention of these parts. Observe all nut and bolt torque specifications.

10. Place the control arm in position and install the shims, bolts and new nuts. Both bolt heads *must* be inboard of the control arm brackets. Tighten the nuts finger tight for now.

NOTE: Do not torque the bolts yet. The bolts must be torque with the truck at its proper ride height.

11. Install the ball stud nut. Torque the nut to 90 ft. lbs. Install the cotter pin. Never back off the nut to install the cotter pin. Always advance it. Never advance it more than ⅙ turn.

12. Install the brake caliper.

13. Install the wheel.

14. Install the brake hose.

15. Install the air cleaner extension.

16. Lower the truck. Once the weight of the truck is on the wheels:

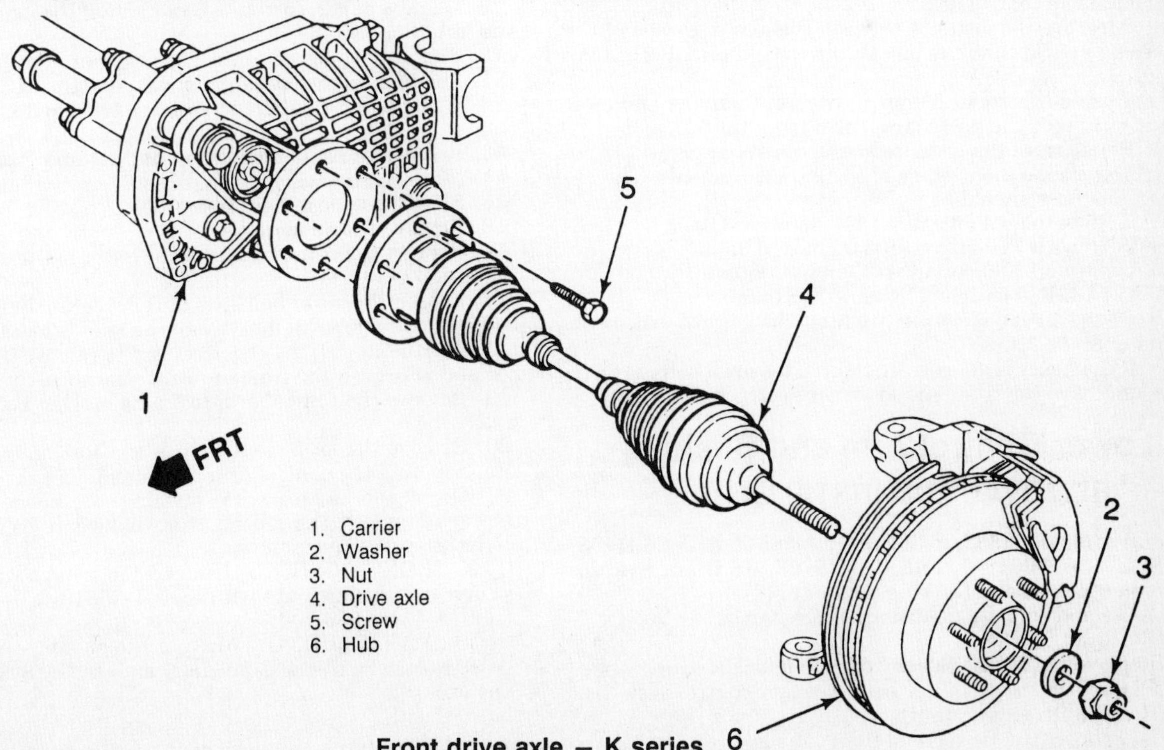

Front drive axle — K series

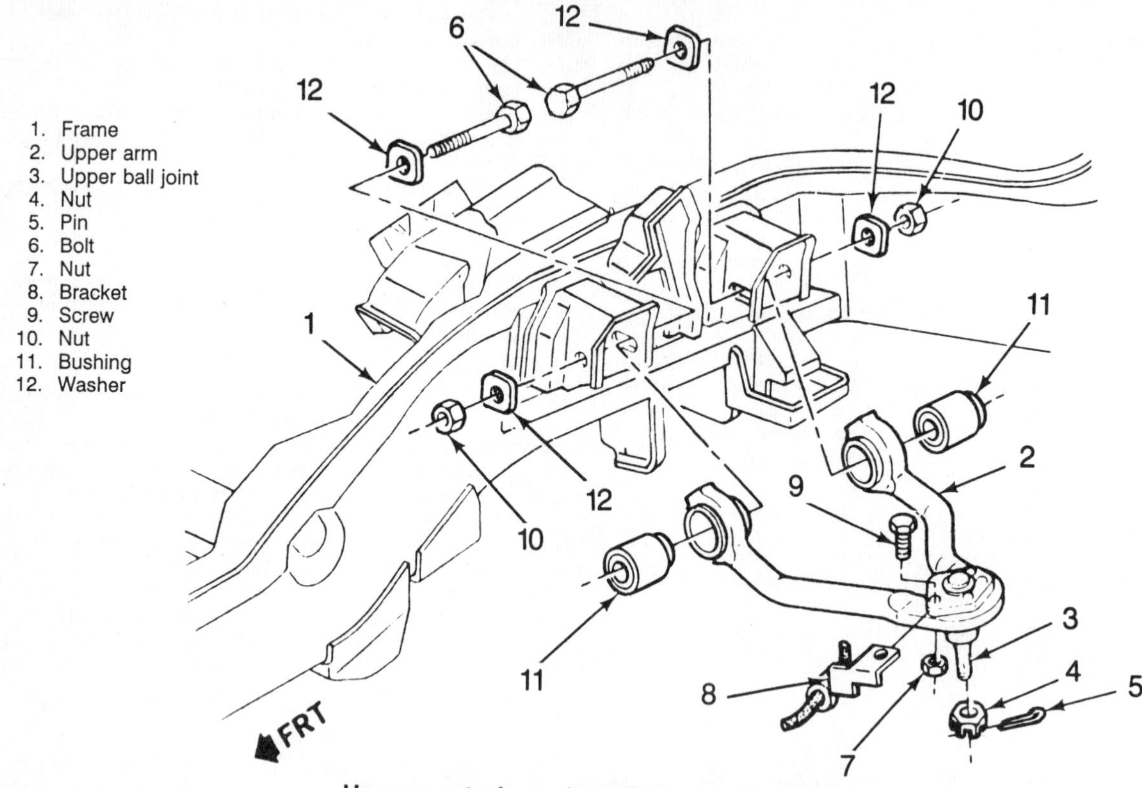

Upper control arm installation — K series

a. Lift the front bumper about 38mm and let it drop.

b. Repeat this procedure 2 or 3 more times.

c. Draw a line on the side of the lower control arm from the centerline of the control arm pivot shaft, dead level to the outer end of the control arm.

d. Measure the distance between the lowest corner of the steering knuckle and the line on the control arm. Record the figure.

e. Push down about 38mm on the front bumper and let it return. Repeat the procedure 2 or 3 more times.

f. Re-measure the distance at the control arm.

g. Determine the average of the 2 measurements. The average distance should be:

- K15/25 without F60 option: 157.0mm ± 6.0mm
- K15/25 with F60 option: 183.0mm ± 6.0mm
- K35 without F60 option: 145.0mm ± 6.0mm
- K35 with F60 option: 173.0mm ± 6.0mm

h. If the figure is correct, tighten the control arm pivot nuts to 88 ft. lbs.

i. If the figure is not correct, tighten the pivot bolts to 88 ft. lbs. and have the front end alignment corrected.

Lower Control Arm and Bushing

REMOVAL AND INSTALLATION

Special tools J-36202, J-36618-1, J-36618-2, J-36618-3, J-36618-4, J-36618-5, and J-9519-23, or their equivalents, are necessary for this procedure.

1. Raise and support the truck on jackstands.
2. Remove the wheel.
3. Remove the splash shield from the knuckle.
4. Disconnect the stabilizer bar from ther control arm.
5. Remove the shock absorber.
6. Disconnect the tie rod end from the relay rod.
7. Remove the hub nut and washer. Insert a long drift or dowel through the vanes in the brake rotor to hold the rotor in place.
8. Remove the axle shaft inner flange bolts.
9. Using a puller, force the outer end of the axle shaft out of the hub. Remove the shaft.
10. Support the lower control arm with a floor jack.
11. Matchmark the both torsion bar adjustment bolt positions.
12. Using tool J-36202, increase the tension on the adjusting arm.
13. Remove the adjustment bolt and retaining plate.
14. Move the tool aside.
15. Slide the torsion bars forward.
16. Remove the adjusting arm.
17. Remove the cotter pin from the lower ball stud and loosen the nut.
18. Loosen the lower ball stud in the steering knuckle using a ball joint stud removal tool. When the stud is loose, remove the nut from the stud. It may be necessary to remove the brake caliper and wire it to the frame to gain clearance.
19. Remove the control arm-to-frame bracket bolts, nuts and washers.
20. Remove the lower control arm and torsion bar as a unit.
21. Separate the control arm and torsion bar.
22. On 15 and 25 Series, the bushings are not replaceable. If they are damaged, the control arm will have to be replaced. On 35 Series, proceed as follows:

a. FRONT BUSHING: Unbend the crimps with a punch. Force out the bushings with tools J-36618-2, J-9519-23, J-36618-4 and 36618-1.

b. REAR BUSHING: Force out the bushings with tools J-36618-5, J-9519-23, J-36618-3 and J-36618-2. There are no crimps.

To install:

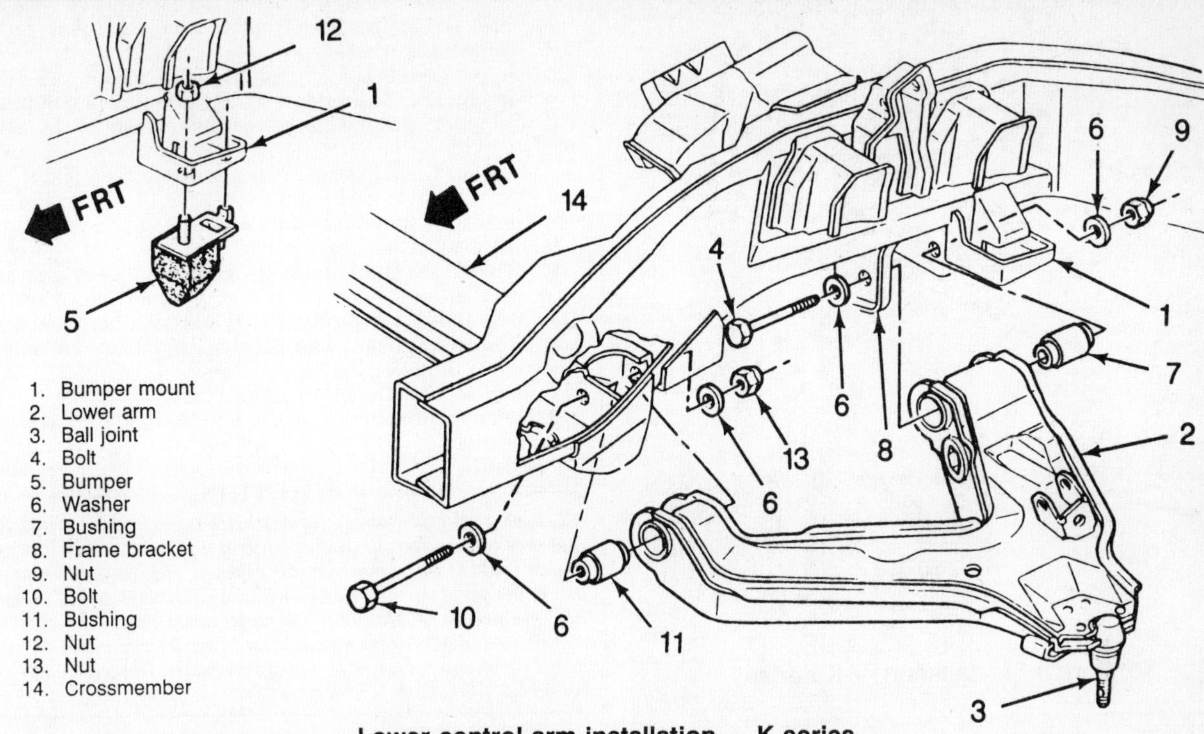

Lower control arm installation – K series

CAUTION

All suspension and steering fasteners are important attaching parts in that they could affect the performance of vital components and systems, and/or could result in major repair expense. They must be replaced with one of the same part number or with an equivalent part if replacement becomes necessary. Do not use a replacement part of lesser quality or substitute design. Torque values must be used as specified during reassembly to assure proper retention of these parts. Observe all nut and bolt torque specifications.

23. On 35 Series, install a new front bushings, then a new rear bushing using the removal tools.
24. Assemble the control arm and torsion bar.
25. Raise the control arm assembly into position. Insert the front leg of the control arm into the crossmember first, then the rear leg into the frame bracket.
26. Install the bolts, front one first. The bolts *must* be installed with the front bolt head heads towards the front of the truck and the rear bolt head towards the rear of the truck!

NOTE: Do not torque the bolts yet. The bolts must be torque with the truck at its proper ride height.

27. Start the ball joint into the knuckle. Make sure it is squarely seated. Tighten the nut to 96 ft. lbs. and install a new cotter pin. Always advance the nut to align the cotter pin hole. NEVER back it off!
28. Install the adjuster arm.
29. Using tool J–36202, increase tension on both torsion bars.
30. Install the adjustment retainer plate and bolt on both torsion bars.
31. Set the adjustment bolt to the marked position.
32. Release the tension on the torsion bar until the load is take up by the adjustment bolt.
33. Remove the tool.
34. Position the shaft in the hub and install the washer and hub nut. Leave the drift in the rotor vanes and tighten the hub nut to 175 ft. lbs.
35. Install the flange bolts. Tighten them to 59 ft. lbs. Remove the drift.
36. Connect the inner tie rod end at the steering relay rod. Torque the nut to 35 ft. lbs.
37. Install the splash shield.
38. Connect the stabilizer bar to the lower control arm. Torque the nuts to 13 ft. lbs.
39. Install the shock absorber.
40. Install the wheel.
41. Lower the truck. Once the weight of the truck is on the wheels:
   a. Lift the front bumper about 38mm and let it drop.
   b. Repeat this procedure 2 or 3 more times.
   c. Draw a line on the side of the lower control arm from the centerline of the control arm pivot shaft, dead level to the outer end of the control arm.
   d. Measure the distance between the lowest corner of the steering knuckle and the line on the control arm. Record the figure.
   e. Push down about 38mm on the front bumper and let it return. Repeat the procedure 2 or 3 more times.
   f. Re-measure the distance at the control arm.
   g. Determine the average of the 2 measurements. The average distance should be:
   - K15/25 without F60 option: 157.0mm ± 6.0mm
   - K15/25 with F60 option: 183.0mm ± 6.0mm
   - K35 without F60 option: 145.0mm ± 6.0mm
   - K35 with F60 option: 173.0mm ± 6.0mm

   h. If the figure is correct, tighten the control arm nuts to 135 ft. lbs.
   i. If the figure is not correct, tighten the pivot bolts to 135 ft. lbs. and have the front end alignment corrected.

Torsion Bars and Support Assembly

REMOVAL AND INSTALLATION

Special tool J-36202, or its equivalent, is necessary for this procedure.

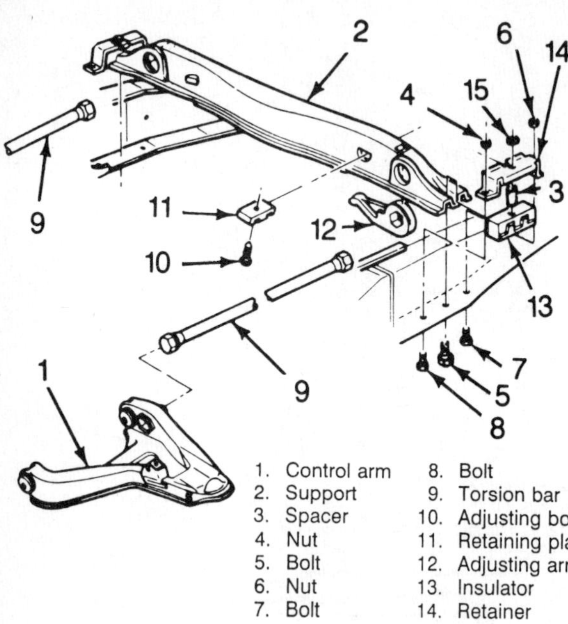

Torsion bar installation – K series

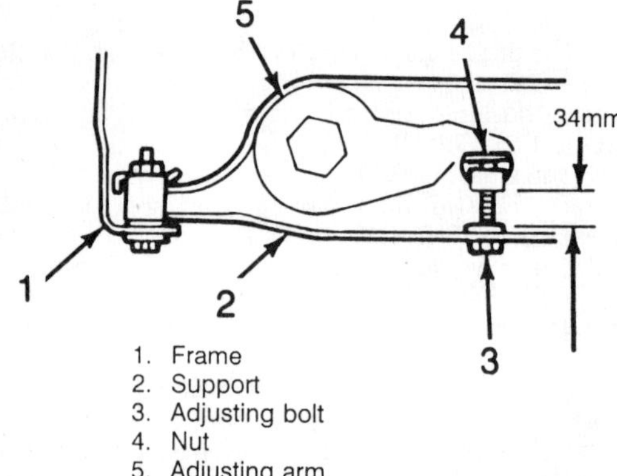

Torsion bar adjuster height – K series

1. Raise and support the front end on jackstands.
2. Remove the wheels.
3. Support the lower control arm with a floor jack.
4. Matchmark the both torsion bar adjustment bolt positions.
5. Using tool J–36202, increase the tension on the adjusting arm.
6. Remove the adjustment bolt and retaining plate.
7. Move the tool aside.
8. Slide the torsion bars forward.
9. Remove the adjusting arms.
10. Remove the nuts and bolts from the torsion bar support crossmember and slide the support crossmember rearwards.
11. Matchmark the position of the torsion bars and note the markings on the front end of each bar. They are not interchangeable. Remove the torsion bars.
12. Remove the support crossmember.
13. Remove the retainer, spacer and bushing from the support crossmember.

To install:

CAUTION

All suspension and steering fasteners are important attaching parts in that they could affect the performance of vital components and systems, and/or could result in major repair expense. They must be replaced with one of the same part number or with an equivalent part if replacement becomes necessary. Do not use a replacement part of lesser quality or substitute design. Torque values must be used as specified during reassembly to assure proper retention of these parts. Observe all nut and bolt torque specifications.

14. Assemble the retainer, spacer and bushing on the support.
15. Position the support assembly on the frame, out of the way.
16. Align the matchmarks and install the torsion bars, sliding them forward until they are supported.
17. Install the adjuster arms on the torsion bars.
18. Bolt the support crossmember into position. Torque the center nut to 18 ft. lbs.; the edge nuts to 46 ft. lbs.
19. Install the adjuster retaining plate and bolt on each torsion bar.
20. Using tool J–36202, increase tension on both torsion bars.
21. Install the adjustment retainer plate and bolt on both torsion bars.
22. Set the adjustment bolt to the marked position.
23. Release the tension on the torsion bar until the load is take up by the adjustment bolt.
24. Remove the tool.
25. Install the wheels.
26. Have the front end alignment checked.

FRONT END ALIGNMENT

Correct alignment of the front suspension is necessary to provide optimum tire life and for proper and safe handling of the vehicle. Caster and camber cannot be set or measured accurately without professional equipment. Toe-in can be adjusted with some degree of success without any special equipment.

Caster

Caster is the tilt of the front steering axis either forward or backward away from the vertical. A tilt toward the rear is said to be positive and a forward tilt is negative. Caster is calculated with a special instrument but one can see the caster angle by looking straight down from the top of the upper control arm. You will see that the ball joints are not aligned if the caster angle is more or less than 0 degrees. If the vehicle has positive caster, the lower ball joint would be ahead of the upper ball joint center line.

Caster is designed into the front axle on four wheel drive trucks and is not adjustable.

Camber

Camber is the slope of the front wheels from the vertical when viewed from the front of the vehicle. When the wheels tilt outward at the top, the camber is positive. When the wheels tilt inward at the top, the camber is negative. The amount of positive and negative camber is measured in degrees from the vertical and the measurement is called camber angle.

Camber is designed into the front axle of all four wheel drive vehicles and is not adjustable.

Toe-In

Toe-in is the amount, measured in a fraction of an inch, that the wheels are closer together in front than at the rear. Some vehicles are set with toe-out, that is, the wheels are closer together at the rear, than the front, to prevent excessive toe-in under power.

Ride Height

Before performing front end alignment on C/K Series trucks, the "trim height", or ride height must be determined. This measurement is taken at 2 different positions, known as "Z" height and "D" height.

"Z" Height

1. Lift the front bumper by hand, about 38mm. Remove your hands and let the truck settle under it own weight.
2. Repeat this procedure 2 more times.
3. Draw a line horizontally along the side of the lower control arm, parallel with the centerline of the control arm pivot bolt, outbaord to the outer end.
4. Using this line as a reference, measure between the line and the lowest point of the steering knuckle. Record the measurement.
5. Push down on the front bumper about 38mm and let it rise on its own.
6. Repeat this procedure 2 more times.
7. Remeasure the ride height. Add the 2 measurement together and divide by 2 to find the average. This is the "Z" height. The measurement should be:
   - All C Series: 95.0mm ± 6mm
   - K15/25 without F60 option: 157.0mm ± 6.0mm
   - K15/25 with F60 option: 183.0mm ± 6.0mm
   - K35 without F60 option: 145.0mm ± 6.0mm
   - K35 with F60 option: 173.0mm ± 6.0mm

"D" Height

"D" height is measured from the bottom surface of the rear axle rebound bumper to the contact point on the top of the rear axle.

Use the same procedure for settling the truck as you did when determining "Z" height.

"D" height should be 182.0mm ± 6mm for all trucks.

CASTER AND CAMBER ADJUSTMENTS

R Series Trucks

Caster and camber adjustments on R Series trucks are made by removing or adding shims between the upper control arm shaft and the mounting bracket which is attached to the suspension crossmember. All adjustments should be made with the truck in the normally loaded condition. Shims are available in adjustment kits.

A normal shim pack will leave at least 2 threads on the control arm bolt exposed beyond the nut. If at least 2 threads are not exposed, check the control arms and related parts for wear or damage.

The difference between the front and rear shim packs must not exceed 0.3 in. The front shim pack must be at least 0.10 in.

To gain access to the nut, support the truck under the frame and allow the wheels to drop as far as possible. On trucks with a ⅞ in. nut, you'll have to remove the upper control arm bumper.

C Series Trucks

Caster and camber adjustments are made by installing an adjustment kit which is comprised of adjusting cams installed on the upper control arm pivots. These kits are available at your Chevrolet or GMC dealer.

To install the kit:

1. Raise and support the front end on jackstands.
2. Support the lower control arm with a floor jack.
3. Remove the wheel.
4. Remove the front control arm bolt, nut and washer. You won't be re-using them.
5. Break off the large washer which is welded to the control arm bracket. Grind the area smooth, removing all traces of welding beads.
6. Using the parts from the kit, install an adjusting cam, bolt and nut. Don't tighten the nut yet.
7. Repeat the procedure for the aft control arm pivot.
8. Camber and caster are adjusted by rotating the bolt head.
9. Tighten the nuts to 75–90 ft. lbs.

TOE-IN

Toe-in must be checked after caster and camber have been adjusted, but it can be adjusted without disturbing the other two settings. You can make this adjustment without special equipment, if you make careful measurements. The adjustment is made at the tie rod sleeves. The wheels must be straight ahead.

Trucks that are consistantly operated with heavy loads should have the toe-in adjusted in the heavily loaded condition.

NOTE: Some alignment specialists set toe-in to the lower specified limit on vehicles with radial tires. The reason is that radial tires have less drag, and therefore a lesser tendency to toe-out at speed. By the same reasoning, off-road tires would require the upper limit of toe-in.

1. Toe-in can be determined by measuring the distance between the centers of the tire treads, front and rear. If the tread pattern of your tires makes this impossible, you can measure between the edges of the wheel rims, but make sure to move the truck forward and measure in a couple of places to avoid errors caused by bent rims or wheel runout.
2. Loosen the clamp bolts on the tie rod sleeves.
3. Rotate the sleeves equally (in opposite directions) to obtain the correct measurement. If the sleeves are not adjusted equally, the steering wheel will be crooked.

NOTE: If your steering wheel is already crooked, it can be straightened by turning the sleeves equally in the same direction.

4. When the adjustment is complete, tighten the clamps.

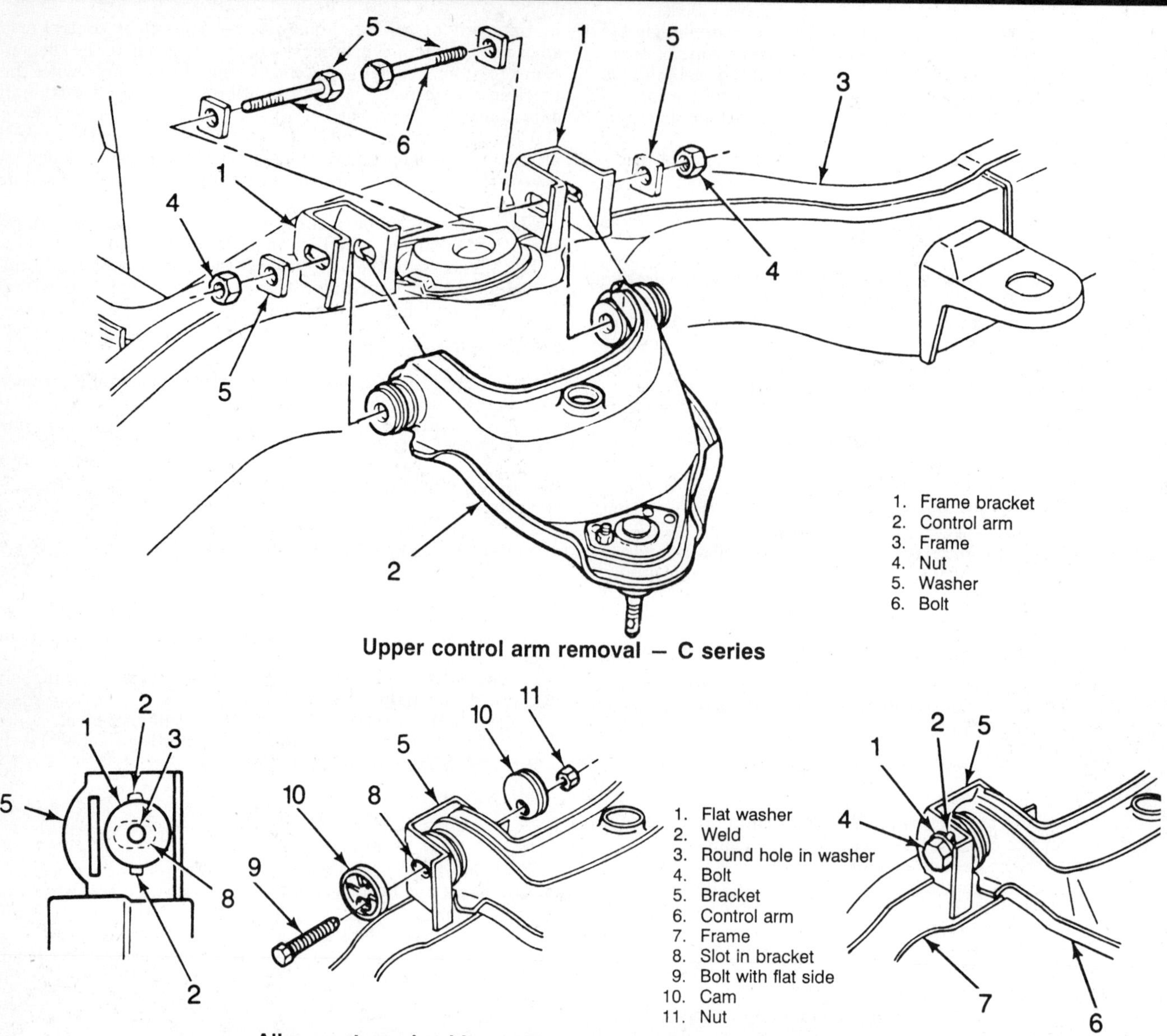

Upper control arm removal — C series

Alignment service kit #15538569 installation — C series

REAR SUSPENSION

Shock Absorbers

REMOVAL AND INSTALLATION

R and V Series

1. Raise and support the rear end on jackstands.
2. Support the rear axle with a floor jack.
3. If the truck is equipped with air lift shocks, bleed the air from the lines and disconnect the line from the shock absorber.
4. Disconnect the shock absorber at the top by removing the nut and washers.
5. Remove the nut, washers and bolt from the bottom mount.

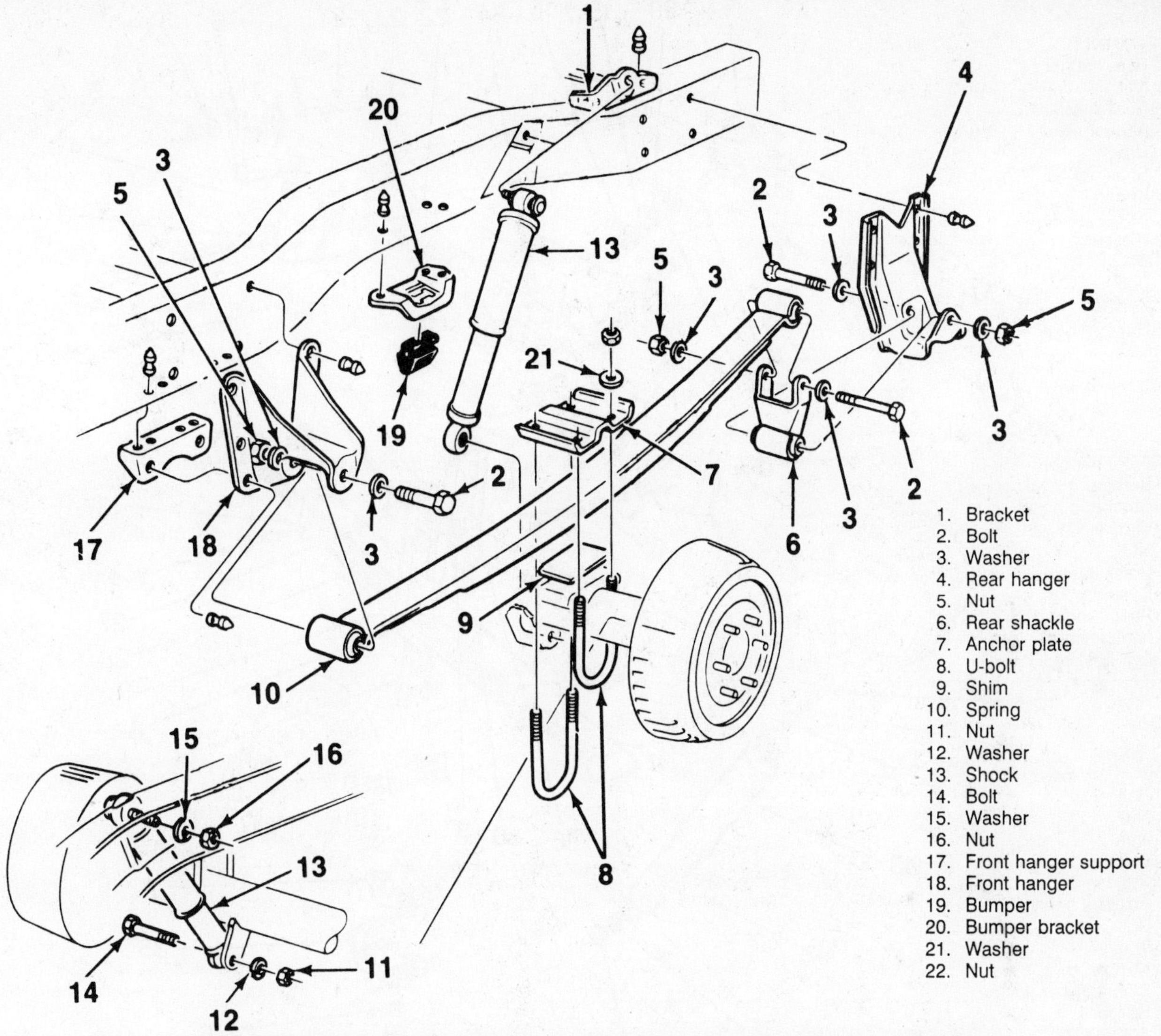

1. Bracket
2. Bolt
3. Washer
4. Rear hanger
5. Nut
6. Rear shackle
7. Anchor plate
8. U-bolt
9. Shim
10. Spring
11. Nut
12. Washer
13. Shock
14. Bolt
15. Washer
16. Nut
17. Front hanger support
18. Front hanger
19. Bumper
20. Bumper bracket
21. Washer
22. Nut

Rear suspension for R/V 10/1500, 20/2500 pickup, Suburban and Blazer

6. Remove the shock from the truck.
7. Installation is the reverse of removal. Torque the upper mount to 140 ft. lbs. on 10/15 and 20/25 Series, or 52 ft. lbs. on 30/35 Series; the lower to 115 ft. lbs. on all series.

CAUTION

All suspension and steering fasteners are important attaching parts in that they could affect the performance of vital components and systems, and/or could result in major repair expense. They must be replaced with one of the same part number or with an equivalent part if replacement becomes necessary. Do not use a replacement part of lesser quality or substitute design. Torque values must be used as specified during reassembly to assure proper retention of these parts. Observe all nut and bolt torque specifications.

C and K Series

1. Raise and support the rear end on jackstands.
2. Support the rear axle with a floor jack.
3. If the truck is equipped with air lift shocks, bleed the air from the lines and disconnect the line from the shock absorber.
4. Disconnect the shock absorber at the top by removing the 2 mounting bolts and nuts from the frame bracket.
5. Remove the nut, washers and bolt from the bottom mount.
6. Remove the shock from the truck.
7. Installation is the reverse of removal. Torque the upper mounting nuts to 17 ft. lbs.; the lower mounting nut to 52 ft. lbs.

CAUTION

All suspension and steering fasteners are important attaching parts in that they could affect the performance of vital components and systems, and/or could result in major repair expense. They must be replaced with one of the same part number or with an equivalent part if replacement becomes necessary. Do not use a replacement part of lesser quality or substitute design. Torque values must be used as specified during reassembly to assure proper retention of these parts. Observe all nut and bolt torque specifications.

TESTING

Adjust the tire pressure before testing the shocks. If the truck is equipped with heavy duty equipment, this can sometimes be misleading. A stiff ride normally accompanies a stiff or heavy duty suspension. Be sure that all weight in the truck is distributed evenly.

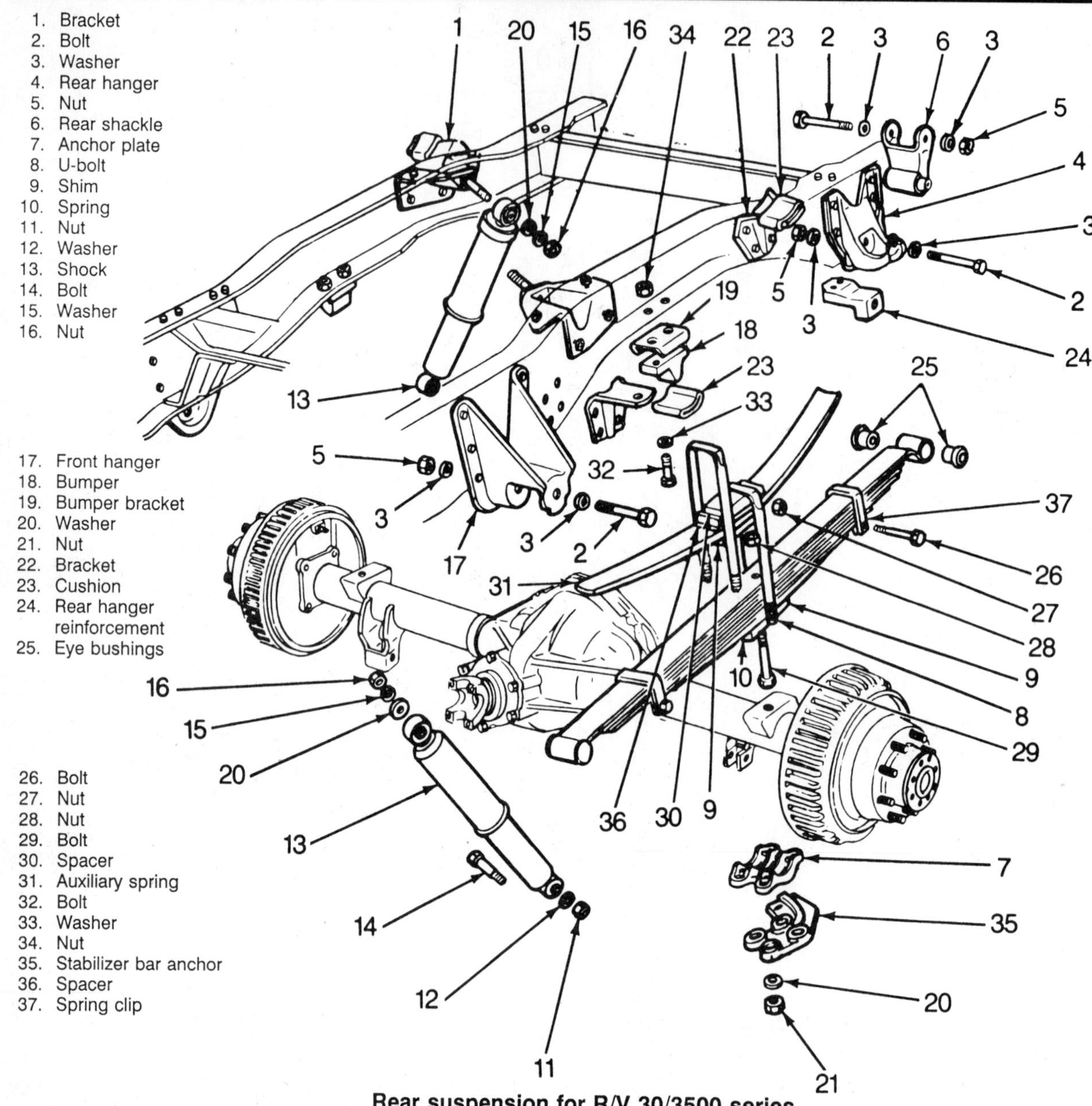

Rear suspension for R/V 30/3500 series

Each shock absorber can be tested by bouncing the corner of the truck until maximum up and down movement is obtained. Let go of the truck. It should stop bouncing in 1–2 bounces. If not, the shock should be replaced.

Stabilizer Bar

REMOVAL AND INSTALLATION

R and V Series

1. Raise and support the rear end on jackstands.
2. Remove the stabilizer bar end link nuts, bolts, washers, grommets and spacers. Take note of their respective positions for installation.
3. Remove the clamps securing the stabilizer bar to the anchor arms.
4. Remove the bar.
5. Remove the bushings from the clamps and check them for wear or damage. Replace them as necessary.

CAUTION

All suspension and steering fasteners are important attaching parts in that they could affect the performance of vital components and systems, and/or could result in major repair expense. They must be replaced with one of the same part number or with an equivalent part if replacement becomes necessary. Do not use a replacement part of lesser quality or substitute design. Torque values must be used as specified during reassembly to assure proper retention of these parts. Observe all nut and bolt torque specifications.

6. Installation is the reverse of removal. Coat the bushings and all rubber parts with silicone grease. Tighten the end link nuts just until they reach the unthreaded part of the bolt. Tighten the clamp-to-anchor bolts to 24 ft. lbs.

CAUTION

Make sure that the parking brake cable is routed over the stabilizer bar!

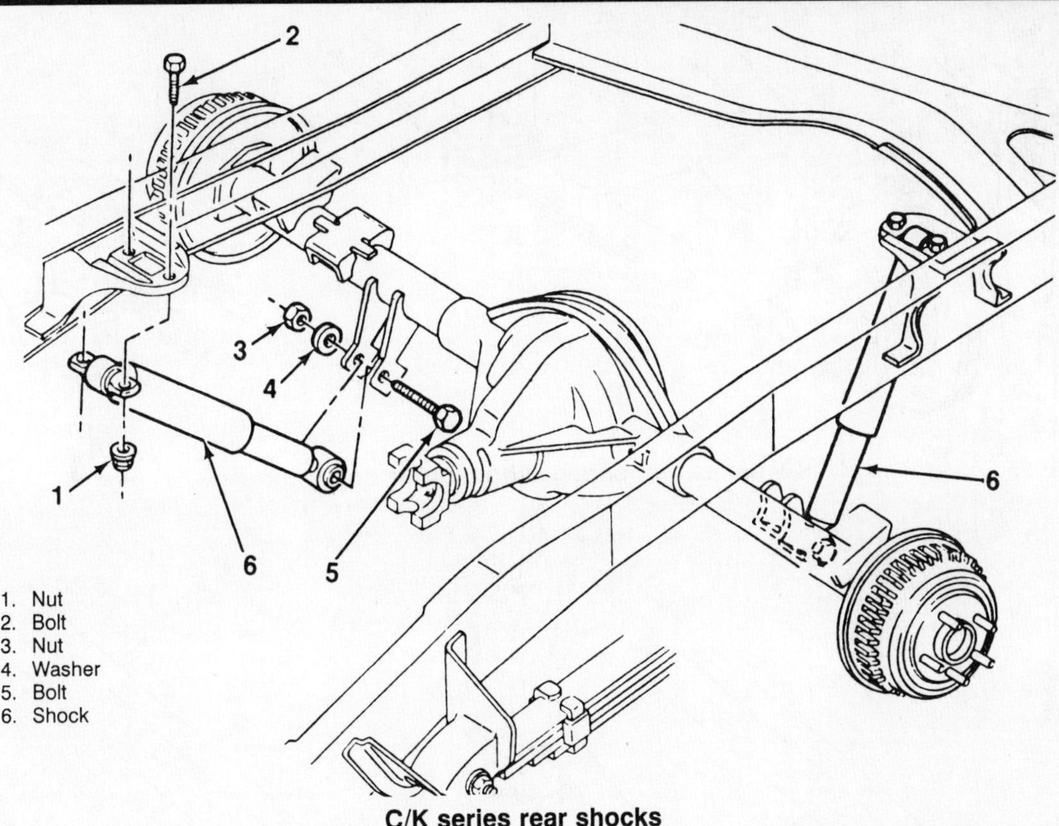

C/K series rear shocks

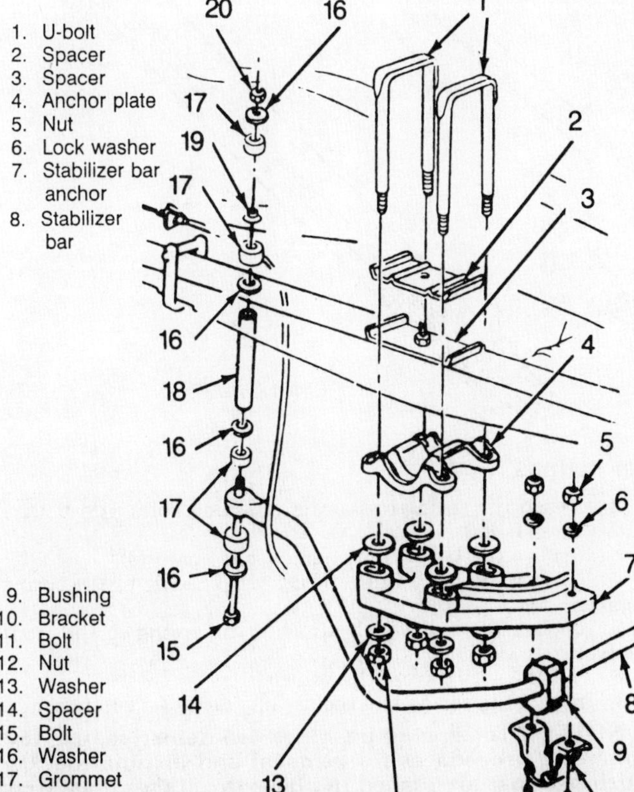

R 30/3500 rear stabilizer bar installation

Leaf Spring

REMOVAL AND INSTALLATION

R and V Series

1. Raise the vehicle and support it so that there is no tension on the leaf spring assembly.
2. Remove the stabilizer bar.
3. Loosen the spring-to-shackle retaining bolts. (Do not remove these bolts).
4. Remove the bolts which attach the shackle to the spring hanger.
5. Remove the nut and bolt which attach the spring to the front hanger.
6. Remove the U-bolt nuts.
7. Remove the stabilizer bar anchor plate, spacers, and shims. Take note of their positions.
8. If so equipped, remove the auxiliary spring.
9. Pull the spring from the vehicle.
10. Inspect the spring and replace any damaged components.

NOTE: If the spring bushings are defective, use the following procedures for removal and installation. ¾ ton and 1 ton trucks use bushings that are staked in place. The stakes must first be straightened. When a new bushing is installed stake it in 3 equally spaced locations. Using a press or vise, remove the bushing and install the new one.

To install:

11. Place the spring assembly onto the axle housing. Position the front and rear of the spring at the hangers. Raise the axle with a floor jack as necessary to make the alignments. Install the front and rear hanger bolts loosely.
12. Install the spacers, shims, auxiliary spring and anchor plate or spring plate.

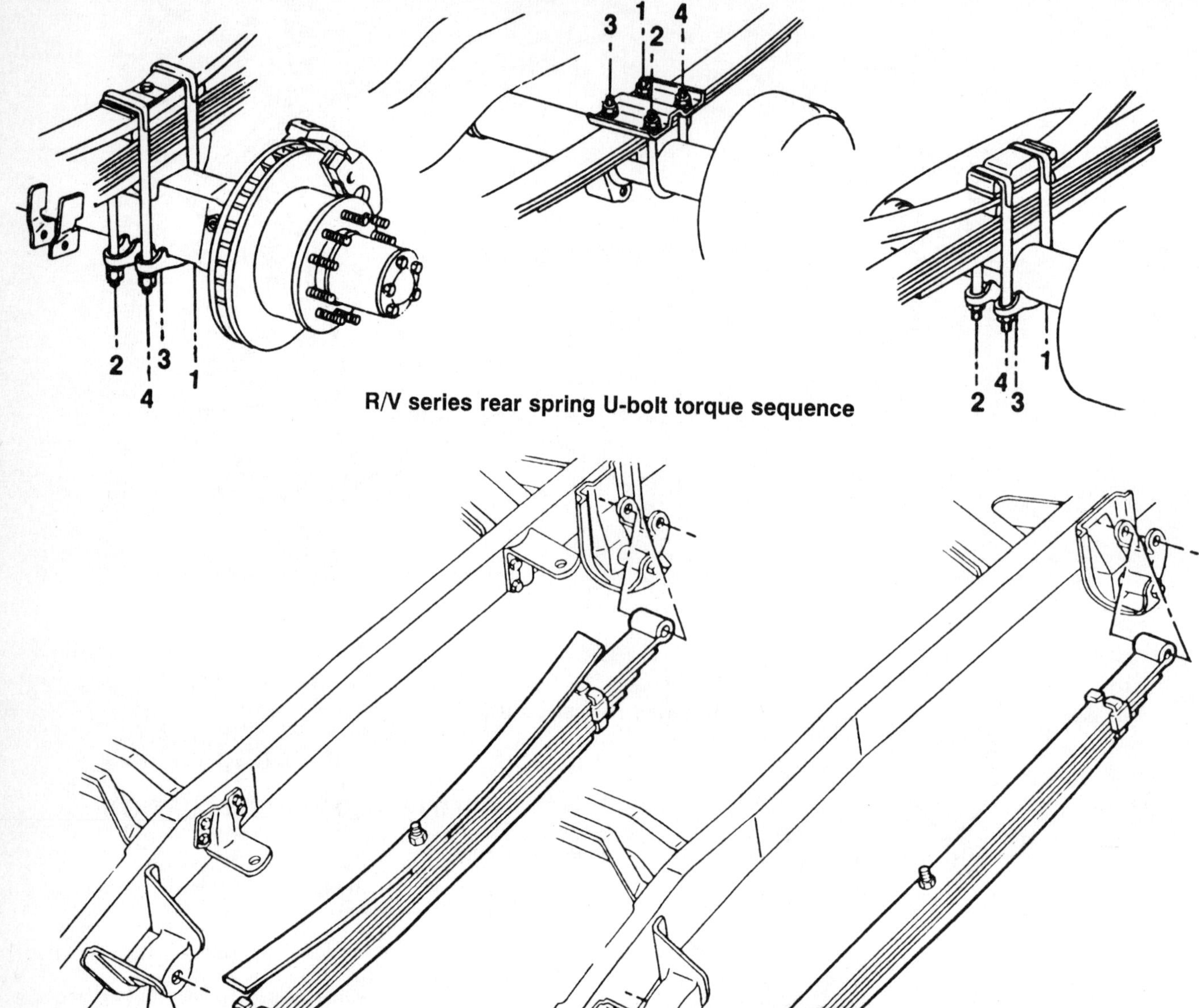

R/V series rear spring U-bolt torque sequence

C/K series rear springs

13. Install the U-bolts, washers and nuts.

14. Tighten the nuts, in a diagonal sequence, to 18 ft. lbs. When the spring is evenly seated, Torque the 10/15 and 20/25 Series nuts to 125 ft. lbs. Torque the 30/35 Series nuts to 147 ft. lbs. Use the same diagonal sequence.

15. Make sure that the hanger and shackle bolts are properly installed. The front hanger bolt head is outboard as is the rear spring-to-shackle bolt head. The shackle-to-hanger bolt head faces inboard. When all the bolts, washers and nuts are installed, torque them to 92 ft. lbs. if your are torquing on the nut; 110 ft. lbs. if your are torquing on the bolt head.

16. Install the stabilizer bar.

C and K Series

1. Raise the vehicle and support it so that there is no tension on the leaf spring assembly.

2. Loosen the spring-to-shackle retaining bolts. (Do not remove these bolts).

3. Remove the U-bolt nuts, plates, and spacer(s).

4. Remove the bolts which attach the shackle to the spring hanger.

5. Remove the bolt which attaches the spring to the front hanger.

6. Pull the spring from the vehicle.

7. Inspect the spring and replace any damaged components.

NOTE: If the spring bushings are defective, use the following procedures for removal and installation. On bushings that are staked in place, the stakes must first be straightened. Using a press or vise, remove the bushing and install the new one. When a new, previosuly staked bushing is installed, stake it in 3 equally spaced locations.

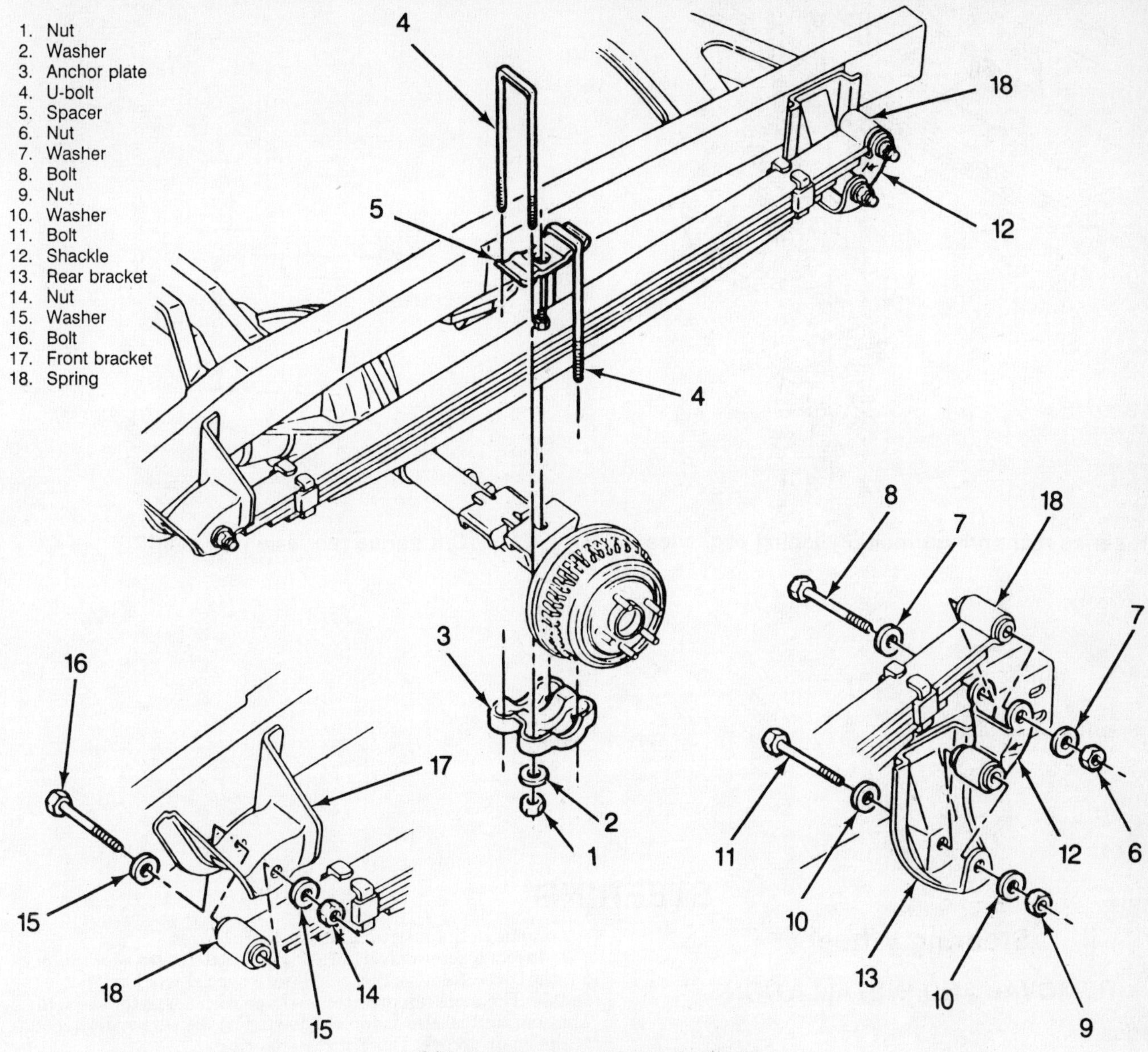

C/K series rear spring installation

To install:

CAUTION

All suspension and steering fasteners are important attaching parts in that they could affect the performance of vital components and systems, and/or could result in major repair expense. They must be replaced with one of the same part number or with an equivalent part if replacement becomes necessary. Do not use a replacement part of lesser quality or substitute design. Torque values must be used as specified during reassembly to assure proper retention of these parts. Observe all nut and bolt torque specifications.

8. Place the spring assembly onto the axle housing. Position the front and rear of the spring at the hangers. Raise the axle with a floor jack as necessary to make the alignments. Install the front and rear hanger bolts loosely.
9. Install the spacers and spring plate.
10. Install the U-bolts, washers and nuts.
11. Tighten the nuts, in a diagonal sequence, to 15 ft. lbs. When the spring is evenly seated, Torque the nuts as follows:
    - 15/25 Series: 81 ft. lbs.
    - 35 Series without dual wheels or 8–7.4L engine: 81 ft. lbs.
    - 35 Series with dual wheels: 110 ft. lbs.
    - 35 Series with 8-7.4L engine, without dual wheels: 110 ft. lbs.
12. Make sure that the hanger and shackle bolts are properly installed. All bolt heads should be inboard. Don't tighten them yet.
13. Using the floor jack, raise the axle until the distance between the bottom of the rebound bumper and its contact point on the axle is 182mm ± 6mm.
14. When the spring is properly positioned, torque all the hanger and shackle nuts to 81 ft. lbs.

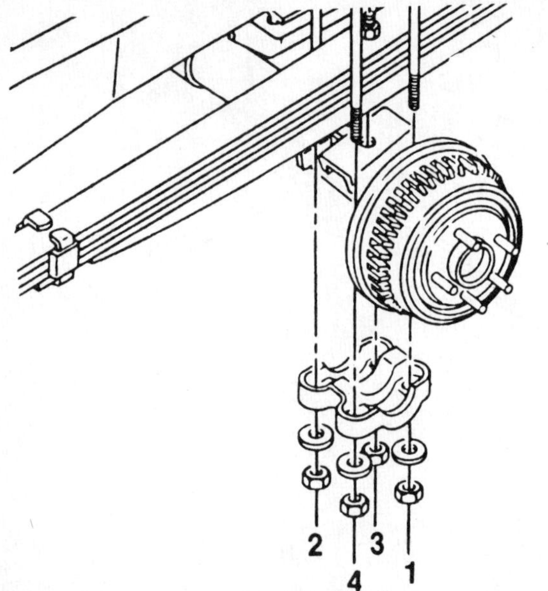

C/K series rear spring U-bolt tightening sequence

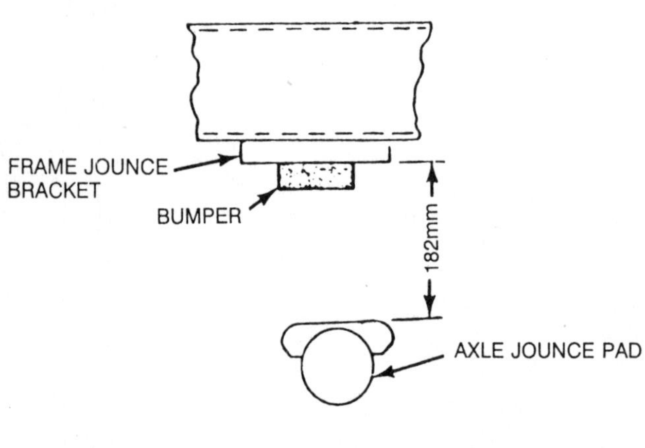

C/K series rear axle trim height

STEERING

Steering Wheel

REMOVAL AND INSTALLATION

All Series

1. Disconnect the battery ground cable.
2. Remove the horn button cap.
3. Mark the steering wheel-to-steering shaft relationship.
4. Remove the snapring from the steering shaft.
5. Remove the nut and washer from the steering shaft.
7. On some models, you'll have to disconnect the horn wires at this point.
8. Remove the steering wheel with a puller.

WARNING: Don't hammer on the steering shaft!

9. Installation is the reverse of removal. The turn signal control assembly must be in the Neutral position to prevent damaging the canceling cam and control assembly. Tighten the nut to 30 ft. lbs.

Turn Signal Switch

REPLACEMENT

All Series

1. Remove the steering wheel as previously outlined.
2. Remove the instrument panel trim cover.
3. Insert a screwdriver into the lockplate cover slot and pry out the cover. Remove the lockplate. A special tool is available to do this. The tool is an inverted U-shape with a hole for the shaft. The shaft nut is used to force it down. Pry the wire snapring out of the shaft groove. Discard the snapring.

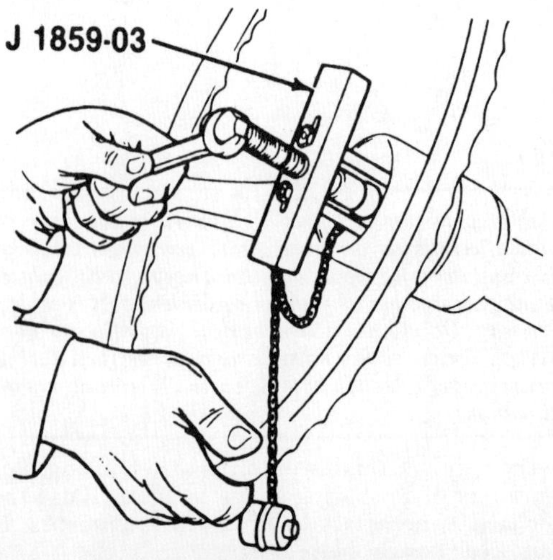

Steering wheel removal

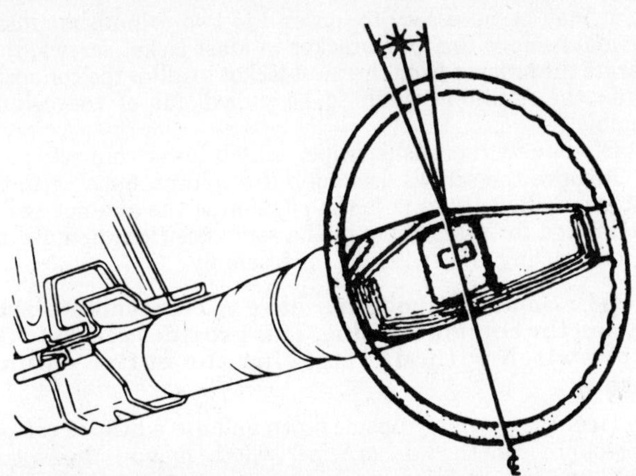

Steering wheel alignment. Dimension A is 1 inch to either side of the centerline

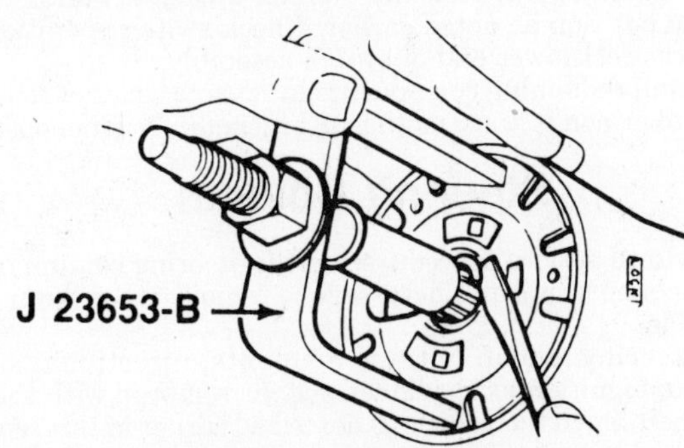

Retaining ring removal

4. Remove the tool and lift the lockplate off the shaft.
5. Remove the turn signal lever screw and lever.
6. Press the hazard button inward and unscrew it.
7. Pull the switch connector out of the mast jacket and feed the switch connector through the column support bracket.
8. Position the turn signal lever and shifter housing in the downward, or "low" position and pull downward on the lower end of the column using a pliers on the tab provided. Remove the wire protector.
9. Remove the switch mounting screws. Remove the switch by pulling it straight up while guiding the wiring harness cover through the column.
10. Install the replacement switch by working the connector and cover down through the housing and under the bracket.
11. Install the switch mounting screws and the connector on the mast jacket bracket. Install the column-to-dash trim plate.
12. Install the flasher knob and the turn signal lever.
13. With the turn signal lever in neutral and the flasher knob out, slide the thrust washer, upper bearing preload spring, and canceling cam into the shaft.
14. Position the lockplate on the shaft and press it down until a new snapring can be inserted in the shaft groove.
15. Install the cover and the steering wheel.

Lock Cylinder

REMOVAL AND INSTALLATION

All Series

1. Remove the steering wheel.
2. Remove the turn signal switch. It is not necessary to completely remove the switch from the column. Pull the switch rearward far enough to slip it over the end of the shaft, but do not pull the harness out of the column.
3. Turn the lock to Run.
4. Remove the lock retaining screw and remove the lock cylinder.

WARNING: If the retaining screw is dropped on removal, it may fall into the column, requiring complete disassembly of the column to retrieve the screw.

5. To install, rotate the key to the stop while holding onto the cylinder.
6. Push the lock all the way in.
7. Install the screw. Tighten the screw to 40 inch lbs. for regular columns, 22 inch lbs. for tilt columns.
8. Install the turn signal switch and the steering wheel.

Turn signal wire protector removal

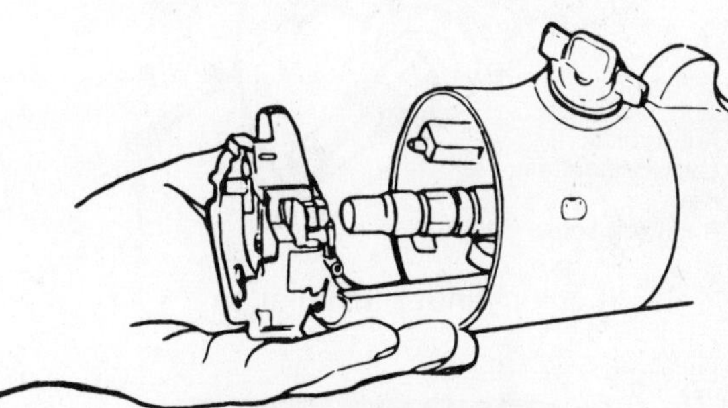

Turn signal switch removal

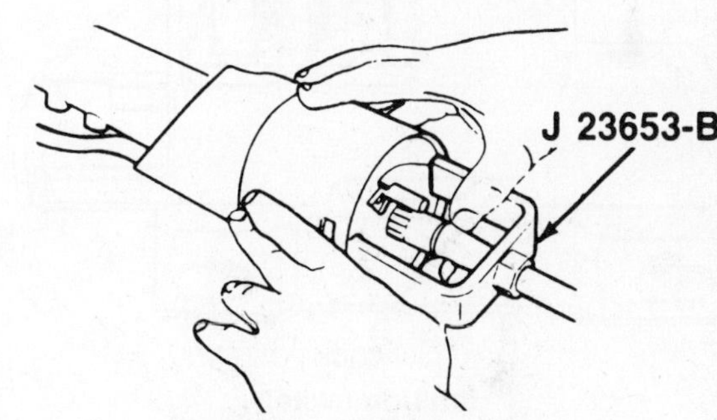

Retaining ring installation

Ignition Switch

REMOVAL AND INSTALLATION

All Series

1. Remove the column shroud halves.
2. Remove the column-to-dash attaching bolts and slowly lower the steering column, making sure that it is supported.

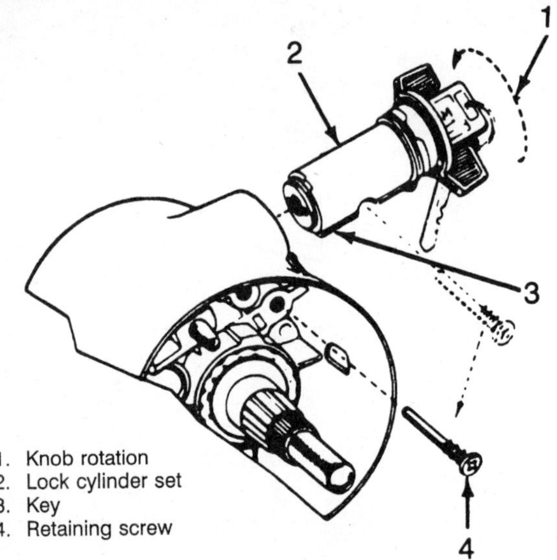

Lock cylinder installation

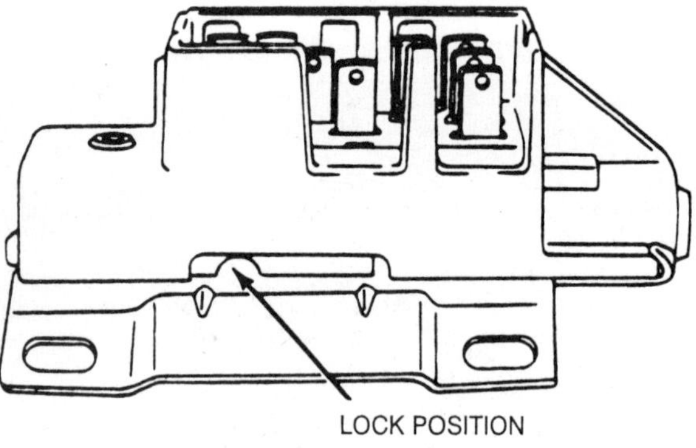

Ignition switch

WARNING: Extreme care is necessary to prevent damage to the collapsible column.

3. Make sure that the switch is in the Lock position. If the lock cylinder is out, pull the switch rod up to the stop, then go down one detent.
4. Remove the two screws and the switch.
5. Before installation, make sure the switch is in the Lock position.
6. Install the switch using the original screws.

CAUTION

Use of screws that are too long could prevent the column from collapsing on impact.

7. Replace the column. Torque the nuts to 22 ft. lbs.; the bolts to 20 ft. lbs.
8. Install the column shroud halves.

Windshield Washer/Wiper Switch

REPLACEMENT

All Series

1. Disconnect the negative battery cable. Remove the steering wheel. Remove the turn signal switch.
2. It may be necessary to loosen the two column mounting nuts and remove the four bracket to mast jacket screws, then separate the bracket from the mast jacket to allow the connector clip on the ignition switch to be pulled out of the column assembly.
3. Disconnect the washer/wiper switch lower connector.
4. Remove the screws attaching the column housing to the mast jacket. Be sure to note the position of the dimmer switch actuator rod for reassembly in the same position. Remove the column housing and switch as an assembly.

NOTE: Some tilt columns have a removable plastic cover on the column housing. This provides access to the wiper switch without removing the entire column housing.

5. Turn the assembly upside down and use a drift to remove the pivot pin from the washer/wiper switch. Remove the switch.
6. Place the switch into position in the housing, then install the pivot pin.
7. Position the housing onto the mast jacket and attach by installing the screws. Install the dimmer switch actuator rod in the same position as noted earlier. Check switch operation.
8. Reconnect lower end of switch assembly.
9. Install remaining components in reverse order of removal. Be sure to attach column mounting bracket in original position.

Steering Column

To perform service procedures on the steering column upper end components, it is not necessary to remove the column from the vehicle.

The steering wheel, horn components, directional signal switch, and ignition lock cylinder may be removed with the column remaining in the vehicle as described earlier in this section.

WARNING: The outer most jacket shift tube, steering shaft and instrument panel mounting bracket are designed as energy absorbing units. Because of the design of these components, it is absolutely necessary to handle the column with care when performing any service operation. Avoid hammering, jarring, dropping or leaning on any portion of the column. When reassembling the column components, use only the specified screws, nuts and bolts and tighten to specified torque. Care should be exercised in using over-length screws or bolts as they may prevent a portion of the column from compressing under impact.

INSPECTION

To determine if the energy absorbing steering column components are functioning as designed, or if repairs are required, a close inspection should be made. Inspection is called for in all cases where damage is evident or whenever the vehicle is being repaired due to a front end collision. Whenever a force has been exerted on the steering wheel or steering column, or its components, inspection should also be made. If damage is evident, the affected parts must be replaced.

The inspection procedure for the various steering column components is as follows:

Column Support Bracket

Damage in this area will be indicated by separation of the mounting capsules from the bracket. The bracket will have moved forward toward the engine compartment and will usually result in collapsing of the jacket section of the steering column.

Column Jacket

Inspect jacket section of column for looseness, and/or bends.

Shifter Shaft

Separation of the shifter shaft sections will be internal and cannot be visually identified. Hold lower end of the shifter shaft and move shift lever on column through its ranges and up and down. If there is little or no movement of the shifter shaft, the plastic joints are sheared.

Steering Shaft

If the steering shaft plastic pins have been sheared, the shaft will rattle when struck lightly from the side and some lash may be felt when rotating the steering wheel while holding the rag joint. It should be noted that if the steering shaft pins are sheared due to minor collision the vehicle can be safely steered; however, steering shaft replacement is recommended.

Because of the differences in the steering column types, be sure to refer to the set of instructions below which apply to the column being serviced.

COULMN REMOVAL AND INSTALLATION

R and V Series

1. Disconnect the battery ground cable.
2. Remove the steering wheel as outlined under Steering Wheel Removal.
3. Remove the nuts and washers securing the flanged end of the steering shaft to the flexible coupling.
4. Disconnect the transmission control linkage from the column shift tube levers.
5. Disconnect the steering column harness at the connector. Disconnect the neutral start switch and back-up lamp switch connectors if so equipped.
6. Remove the floor pan trim cover screws and remove the cover.
7. Remove the transmission indicator cable, if so equipped.

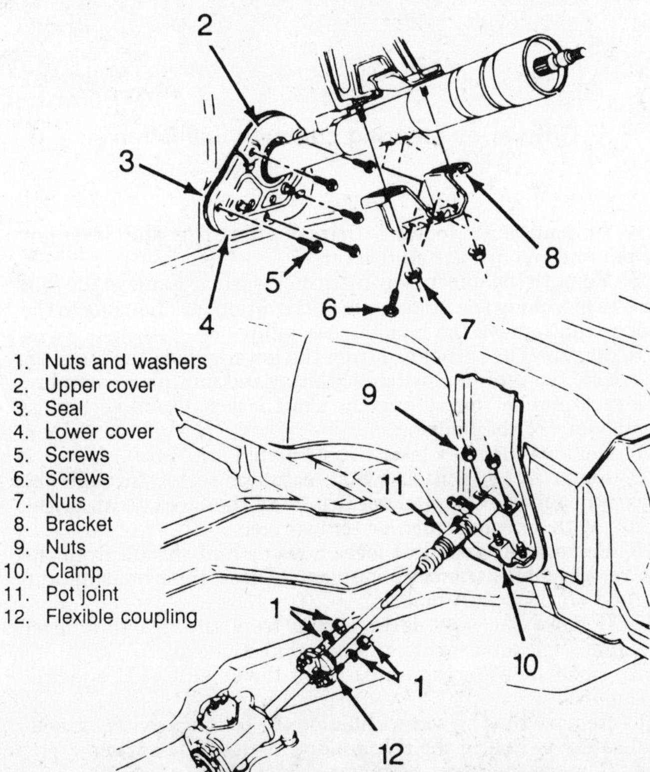

1. Nuts and washers
2. Upper cover
3. Seal
4. Lower cover
5. Screws
6. Screws
7. Nuts
8. Bracket
9. Nuts
10. Clamp
11. Pot joint
12. Flexible coupling

R/V series steering column installation

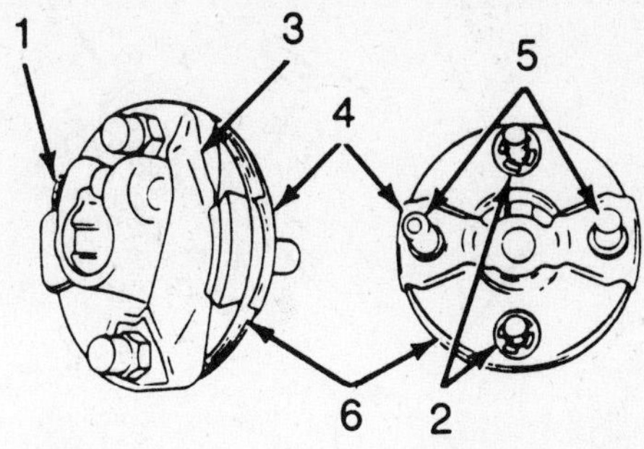

1. Bolt
2. Nuts and washers
3. Capturing strap
4. Reinforcement
5. Alignment pins
6. Wafer

Flexible coupling

8. Remove the screws securing the two halves of the floor pan cover, then remove the screws securing the halves and seal to the floor pan and remove the covers.
9. Move the front seat as far back as possible to provide maximum clearance.
10. Remove the two column bracket-to-instrument panel nuts and carefully remove from vehicle. Additional help should be obtained to guide the lower shift levers through the firewall opening.

Mandatory Preliminary Instructions

1. Assemble the lower dash cover and upper dash cover to the seal with fasteners that are part of the seal.
2. Attach bracket to jacket and tighten four bolts to specified torque.

Mandatory Installation Sequence

1. Position column in body and position flange to rag joint and install lock washers and nuts (May be tightened to specified torque at this time). Coupling on manual steering must be installed prior to column installation.
2. Loosely assemble (2) capsules nuts at the instrument panel bracket.
3. Position lower clamp and tighten attaching nuts to specified torque.
4. Tighten two nuts at capsules to specified torque.
5. Install seal and covers to dash.
6. Install attaching screws and tighten to specified torque.
7. Tighten two nuts at capsules to specified torque if not already done.
8. Remove plastic spacers from flexible coupling pins.
9. Install transmission indicator cable on column automatics.
10. Install the instrument panel trim cover.
11. Connect the transmission control linkage at the shift tube levers.
12. Install the steering wheel as outlined previously in this section.
13. Connect the battery ground cable.

Mandatory System Requirements

1. Pot joint operating angle must be 1½° ± 4°.
2. Flexible coupling must not be distorted greater than ± 0.06 in. (1.5mm) due to pot joint bottoming, in either direction.

C and K Series

1. Disconnect the battery ground cable.
2. Remove the steering wheel.
3. Disconnect the transmission linkage at the column levers.
4. Matchmark the pot joint and steering shaft. Remove the pot joint bolt from the steering shaft.
5. Remove the steering column shrouds.
6. Remove the nuts, bolts and stering column support bracket.
7. Remove the column-to-floor plate bolts.

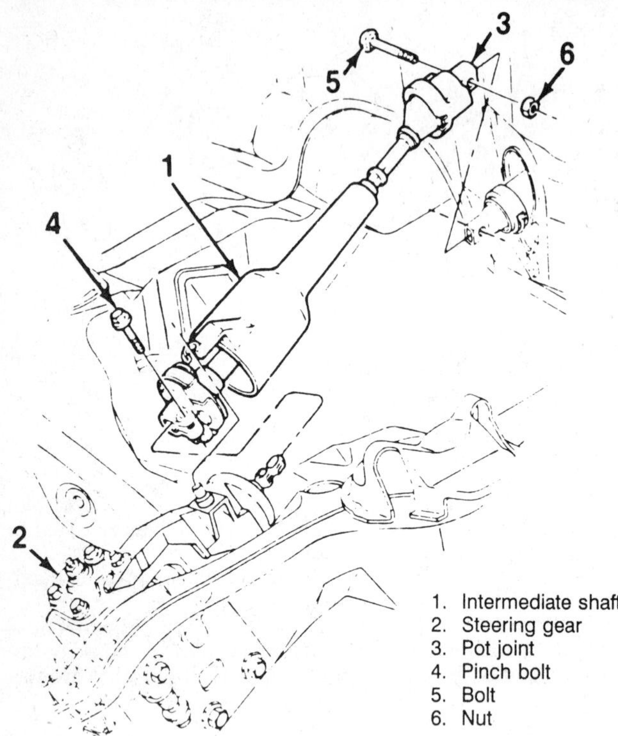

C/K series intermediate shaft installation

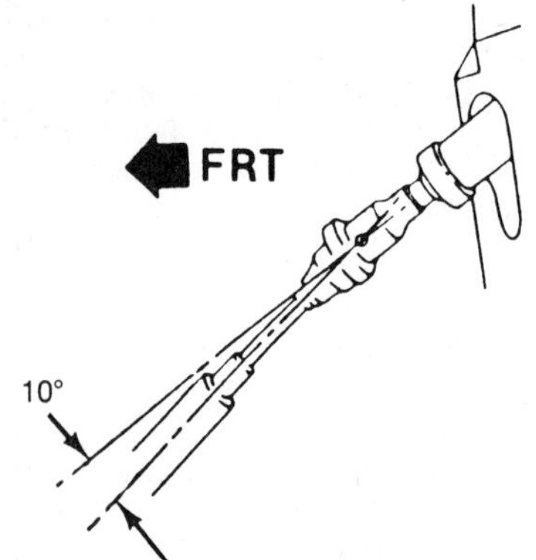

C/K series pot joint angle

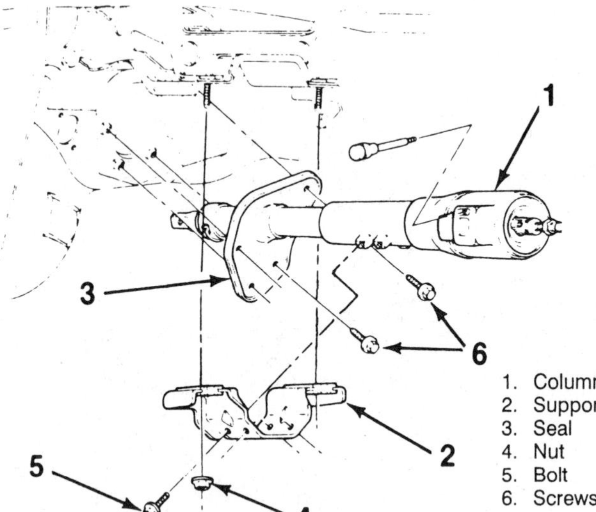

C/K series steering column installation

8. Disconnect the neutral start switch and back-up light switch wiring.

9. Lift out the column, rotating it as necessary for clearance.

To install:

10. Install the column, rotating it as necessary for clearance.

11. Install the nuts, bolts and stering column support bracket. Make them finger-tight, for now.

12. Guide the steering shaft into the pot joint, aligning the matchmarks. Install the pot joint bolt, passing through the cutout in the shaft. Torque the bolt to 22 ft. lbs.

NOTE: The pot joint angle must not exceed 12½°.

13. Install the column-to-floor plate bolts. Torque the bolts to 22 ft. lbs.

14. Connect the neutral start switch and back-up light switch wiring.

15. Install the steering column shrouds.

16. Connect the transmission linkage at the column levers.

17. Install the steering wheel.

18. Connect the battery ground cable.

DISASSEMBLY – STANDARD COLUMN

1. Remove the four dash panel bracket-to-column screws and lay the bracket in a safe place to prevent damage to the mounting capsules.

2. Place the column in a vise using both weld nuts of either Set A or B or shown in Figure. The vise jaws must clamp onto the sides of the weld nuts indicated by arrows shown on Set B.

WARNING: Do not place the column in a vise by clamping onto one weld nut of both sets A and B or by clamping onto the sides not indicated by arrows, since damage to the column could result.

3. Remove the Directional Signal Switch, Lock Cylinder, and Ignition Switch as outlined previously in this section.

4. Column Shift Models – Drive out the upper shift lever pivot pin and remove the shift lever.

5. Remove the upper bearing thrust washer. Remove the four screws attaching the turn signal and ignition lock housing to the jacket and remove the housing assembly.

6. Remove the thrust cap from the lower side of the housing.

7. Lift the ignition switch actuating rod and rack assembly, the rack preload spring and the shaft lock bolt and spring assembly out of the housing.

8. Remove the shift lever detent plate (shift gate).

9. Remove the ignition switch actuator sector through the lock cylinder hole by pushing firmly on the block tooth of the sector with a blunt punch or screwdriver.

10. Remove the gearshift lever housing and shroud from the jacket assembly (transmission control lock tube housing and shroud on floor shift models).

11. Remove the shift lever spring from the gearshift lever housing (lock tube spring on floor shift models).

12. Pull the steering shaft from lower end of the jacket assembly.

13. Remove the two screws holding the back-up switch or neutral safety switch to the column and remove the switch.

14. Remove the lower bearing retainer clip.

15. Automatic and Floorshift Columns – Remove the lower bearing retainer, bearing adapter assembly, shift tube thrust

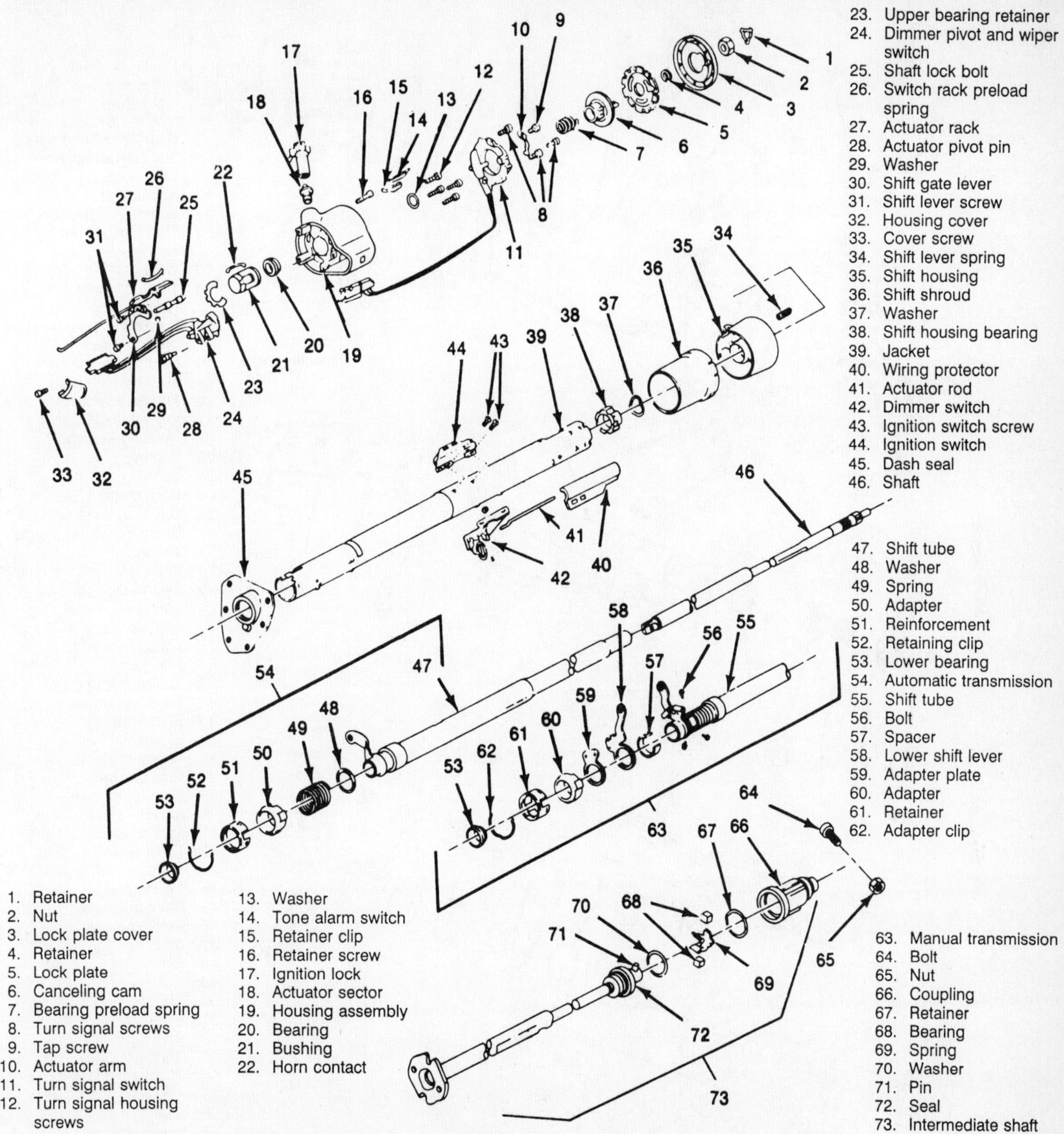

Standard steering column for R/V series with column shift

spring and washer. The lower bearing may be removed from the adapter by light pressure on the bearing outer race. Slide out the shift tube assembly.

ASSEMBLY – STANDARD COLUMNS

NOTE: Apply a thin coat of lithium soap grease to all friction surfaces.

1. Install the sector into the turn signal and lock cylinder housing. Install the sector in the lock cylinder hole over the sector shaft with the tang end to the outside of the hole. Press the sector over the shaft with a blunt tool.
2. Install the shift lever detent plate onto the housing.
3. Insert the rack preload spring into the housing from the bottom side. The long section should be toward the hand wheel and hook onto the edge of the housing.
4. Assemble the locking bolt onto the crossover arm on the rack and insert the rack and lock bolt assembly into the housing from the bottom with the teeth up (toward hand wheel) and toward the centerline of the column. Align the 1st tooth on the

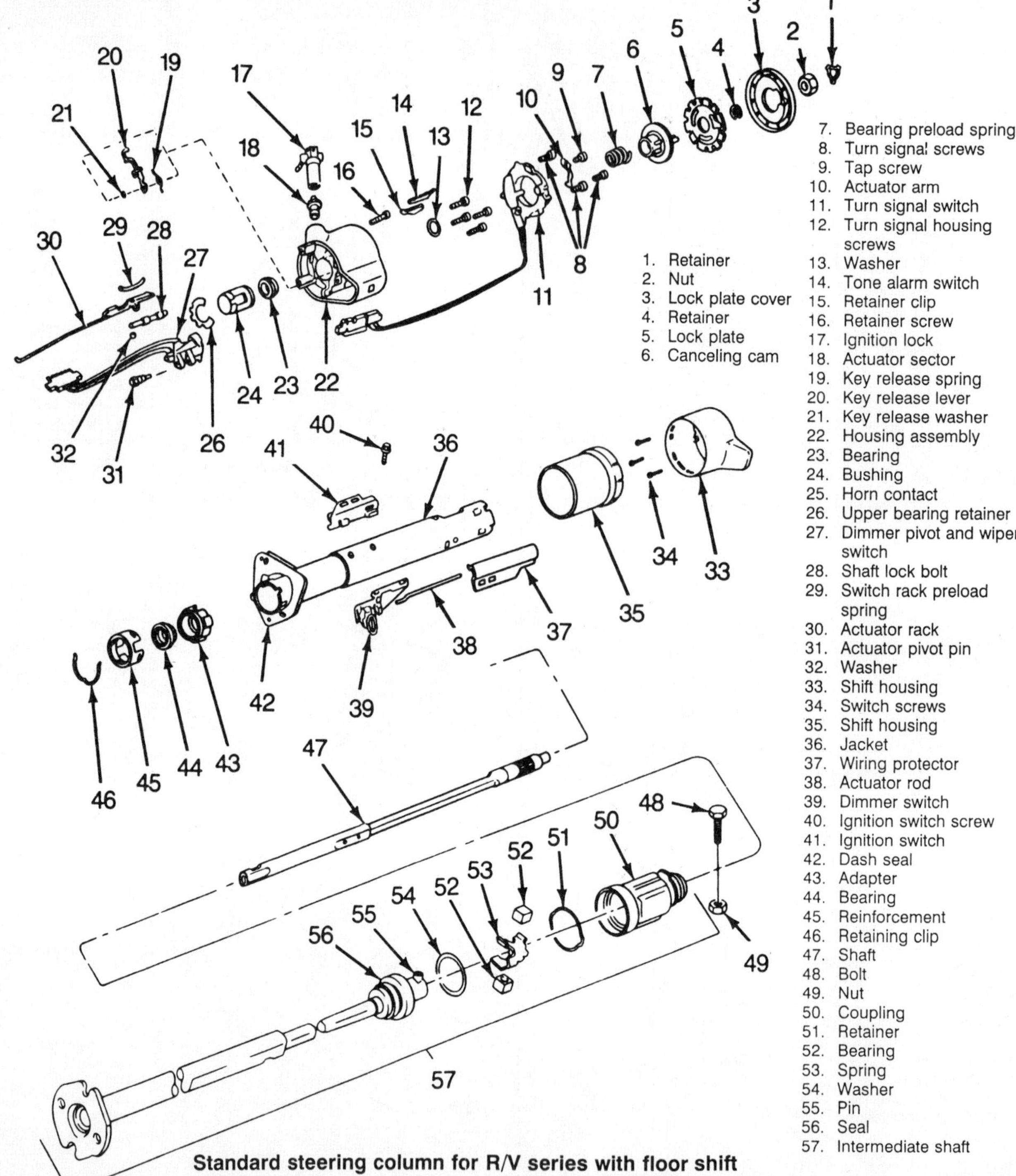

Standard steering column for R/V series with floor shift

sector with the 1st tooth on the rack; if aligned properly, the block teeth will line up when the rack assembly is pushed all the way in.

5. Install the thrust cup on the bottom hub of the housing.

6. Install the gearshift housing lower bearing. Insert the bearing from the very end of the jacket. Aligning the indentations in the bearing with the projections on the jacket. If the bearing is not installed correctly, it will not rest on all of the stops provided.

7. Install the shift lever spring into the gearshift lever (or lock tube) housing. Install the housing and shroud assemblies onto the upper end of the mast jacket. Rotate the housing to be sure it is seated in the bearing.

8. With the shift lever housing in place, install the turn signal and lock cylinder housing onto the jacket. The gearshift housing should be in **Park** position and the rack pulled downward. Be sure the turn signal housing is seated on the jacket and drive the four screws.

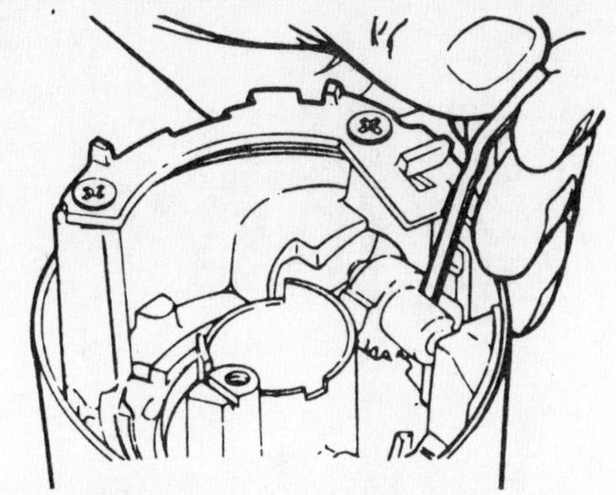
Rack preload spring installation – R/V series

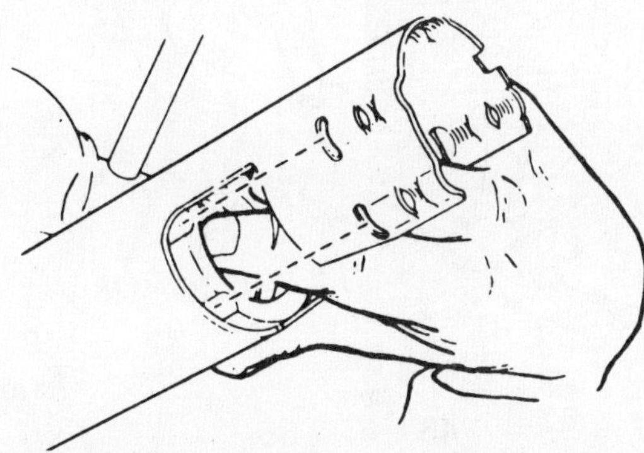
Shift housing lower bearing installation – R/V series

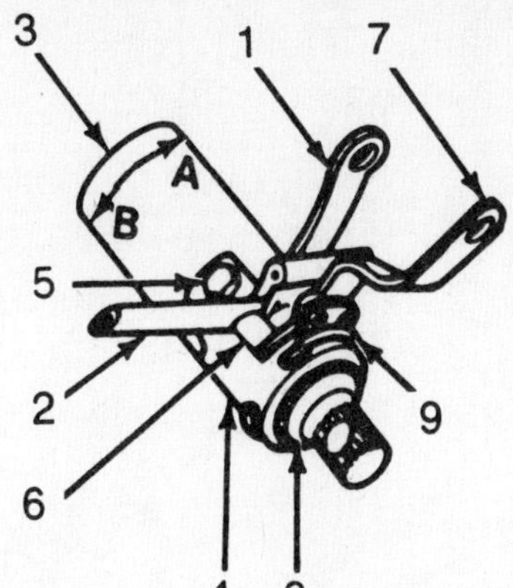

Lower bearing adjustment – R/V series

9. Press the lower bearing into the adapter assembly.
10. Insert the shift tube assembly into the lower end of the jacket and rotate until the upper shift tube key slides into the housing keyway.
11. Automatic and Floor Shift Columns – Assemble the spring and lower bearing and adapter assembly into the bottom of the jacket. Holding the adapter in place, install the lower bearing reinforcement and retainer clip. Be sure the clip snaps into the jacket and reinforcement slots.
12. Install the neutral safety or back-up switch as outlined in Section 7 of this manual.
13. Slide the steering shaft into the column and install the upper bearing thrust washer.
14. Install the turn signal switch, lock cylinder assembly and ignition switch as previously outlined in this section.
15. Install the shift lever and shift lever pivot pin.
16. Remove the column from the vise.
17. Install the dash bracket to the column; torque the screws to specifications.

DISASSEMBLY – TILT COLUMNS

Special tools J-21854-1, and J-23072, or their equivalents, are necessary for this procedure.

1. Remove the four screws retaining the dash mounting bracket to the column and set the bracket aside to protect the breakaway capsules.
2. Mount the column in a vise using both weld nuts of either Set A or B. The vise jaws must clamp onto the sides of the weld nuts indicated by arrows shown on Set B.

WARNING: Do not place the column in a vise by clamping onto only one weld nut, by clamping onto one weld nut of both Sets A and B or by clamping onto the sides not indicated by arrows, since damage to the column could result.

3. Remove the directional signal switch, lock cylinder and ignition switch as outlined previously in this section.
4. Remove the tilt release lever. Drive out the shift lever pivot pin and remove the shift lever from the housing.
5. Remove the three turn signal housing screws and remove the housing.
6. Install the tilt release lever and place the column in the full up position. Remove the tilt lever spring retainer using a #3 phillips screwdriver that just fits into the slot opening. Insert the phillips screwdriver in the slot, press in approximately $^{3}/_{16}$ in. (5mm), turn approximately ⅛ turn counterclockwise until the ears align the the grooves in the housing and remove the retainer, spring and guide.
7. Remove the pot joint to steering shaft clamp bolt and remove the intermediate shaft and pot joint assembly. Push the upper steering shaft in sufficiently to remove the steering shaft upper bearing inner race and seat. Pry off the lower bearing retainer clip and remove the bearing reinforcement, bearing and bearing adapter assembly from the lower end of the mast jacket.
8. Remove the upper bearing housing pivot pins using Tool J-21854-1.
9. Install the tilt release lever and disengage the lock shoes. Remove the bearing housing by pulling upward to extend the rack full down, and then moving the housing to the left to disengage the ignition switch rack from the actuator rod.
10. Remove the steering shaft assembly from the upper end of the column.
11. Disassemble the steering shaft by removing the centering spheres and the anti-lash spring.
12. Remove the transmission indicator wire, if so equipped.
13. Remove the four steering shaft bearing housing support to gearshift housing screws and remove the bearing housing support. Remove the ignition switch actuator rod.
14. Remove the shift tube retaining rings with a screwdriver and then remove the thrust washer.
15. Install Tool J-23072 into the lock plate, making sure that the tool screws have good thread engagement in the lock plate, then turning the center screw clockwise, force the shift tube from the housing. Remove the shift tube (transmission control lock tube on floor shift models) from the lower end of the mast jacket. Remove Tool J-23072.

WARNING: When removing the shift tube, be sure to guide the lower end through the slotted opening in the mast jacket. If the tube is allowed to interfere with the jacket in any way, damage to the tube and jacket could result.

16. Remove the bearing housing support lock plate by sliding it out of the jacket notches, tipping it down toward the housing

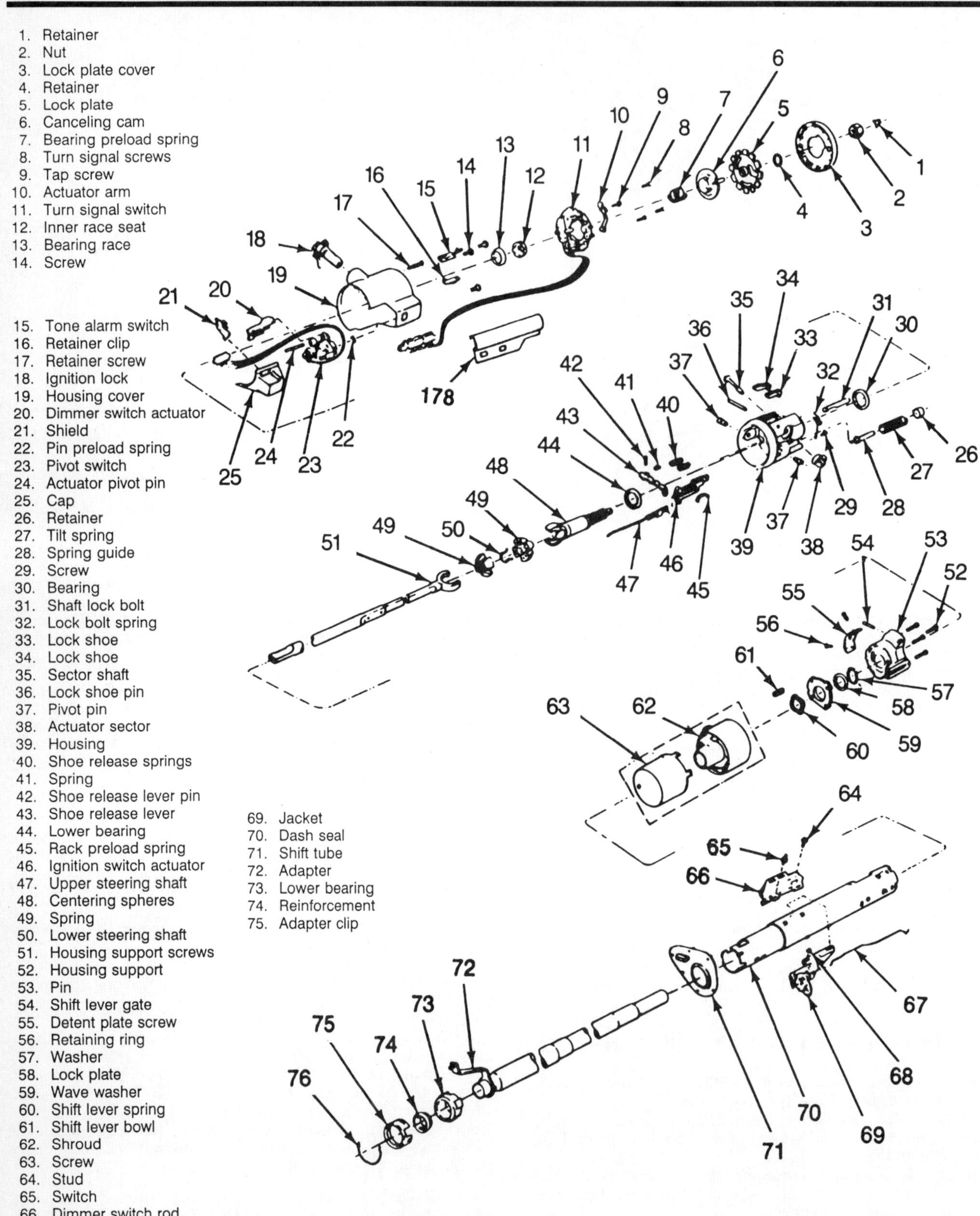
1. Retainer
2. Nut
3. Lock plate cover
4. Retainer
5. Lock plate
6. Canceling cam
7. Bearing preload spring
8. Turn signal screws
9. Tap screw
10. Actuator arm
11. Turn signal switch
12. Inner race seat
13. Bearing race
14. Screw
15. Tone alarm switch
16. Retainer clip
17. Retainer screw
18. Ignition lock
19. Housing cover
20. Dimmer switch actuator
21. Shield
22. Pin preload spring
23. Pivot switch
24. Actuator pivot pin
25. Cap
26. Retainer
27. Tilt spring
28. Spring guide
29. Screw
30. Bearing
31. Shaft lock bolt
32. Lock bolt spring
33. Lock shoe
34. Lock shoe
35. Sector shaft
36. Lock shoe pin
37. Pivot pin
38. Actuator sector
39. Housing
40. Shoe release springs
41. Spring
42. Shoe release lever pin
43. Shoe release lever
44. Lower bearing
45. Rack preload spring
46. Ignition switch actuator
47. Upper steering shaft
48. Centering spheres
49. Spring
50. Lower steering shaft
51. Housing support screws
52. Housing support
53. Pin
54. Shift lever gate
55. Detent plate screw
56. Retaining ring
57. Washer
58. Lock plate
59. Wave washer
60. Shift lever spring
61. Shift lever bowl
62. Shroud
63. Screw
64. Stud
65. Switch
66. Dimmer switch rod
67. Nut
68. Dimmer switch
69. Jacket
70. Dash seal
71. Shift tube
72. Adapter
73. Lower bearing
74. Reinforcement
75. Adapter clip

Tilt column – R/V series with column shift

1. Retainer
2. Nut
3. Lock plate cover
4. Retainer
5. Lock plate
6. Canceling cam
7. Bearing preload spring
8. Turn signal screws
9. Tap screw
10. Actuator arm
11. Turn signal switch
12. Inner race seat
13. Bearing race
14. Screw
15. Tone alarm switch
16. Retainer clip
17. Retainer screw
18. Ignition lock
19. Housing cover
20. Dimmer switch actuator
21. Shield
22. Pin preload spring
23. Pivot switch
24. Actuator pivot pin
25. Cap
26. Retainer
27. Tilt spring
28. Spring guide
29. Screw
30. Bearing
31. Shaft lock bolt
32. Lock bolt spring
33. Lock shoe
34. Lock shoe
35. Sector shaft
36. Lock shoe pin
37. Pivot pin
38. Actuator sector
39. Housing
40. Shoe release springs
41. Spring
42. Shoe release lever pin
43. Shoe release lever
44. Lower bearing
45. Rack preload spring
46. Actuator rack
47. Ignition switch actuator
48. Upper steering shaft
49. Centering spheres
50. Spring
51. Lower steering shaft
52. Housing support screws
53. Housing support
54. Pin
55. Shift lever gate
56. Detent plate screw
57. Lock plate
58. Screw
59. Stud
60. Switch
61. Dimmer switch rod
62. Nut
63. Dimmer switch
64. Jacket
65. Key release lever
66. Key release spring
67. Shroud
68. Lower bearing
69. Retainer
70. Screws

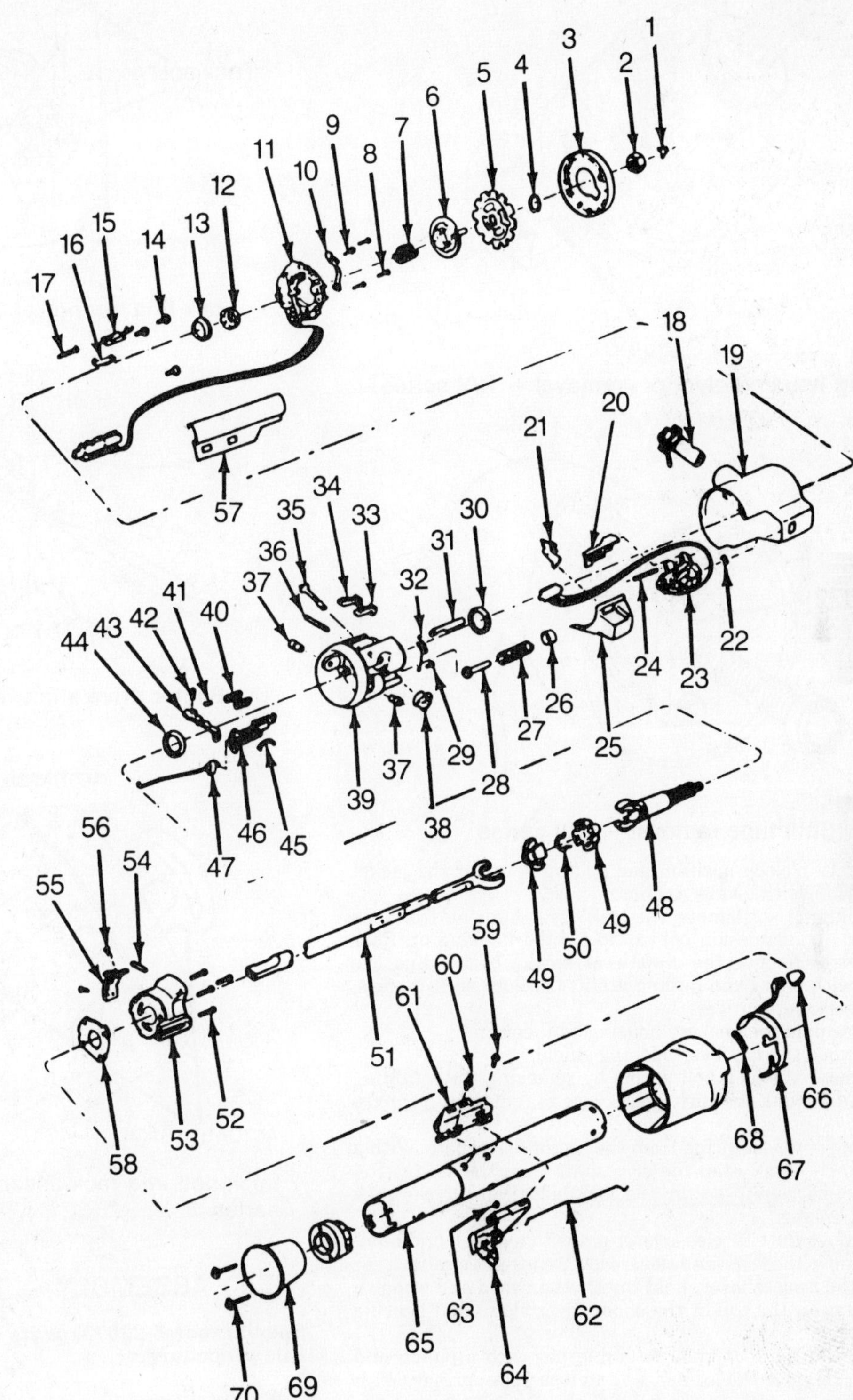

Tilt column — R/V series with floor shift

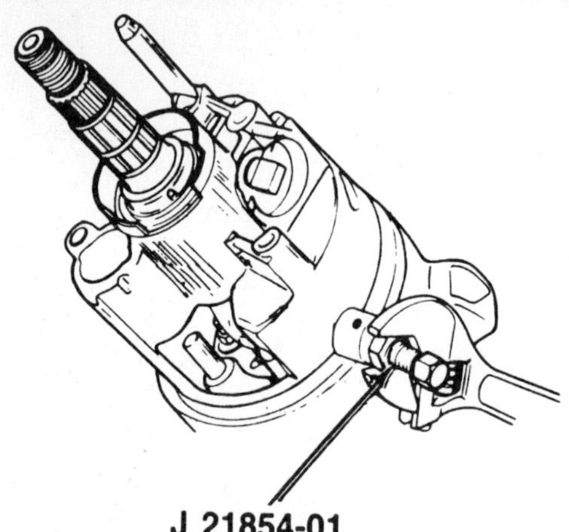

Bearing housing pivot pin removal – R/V series

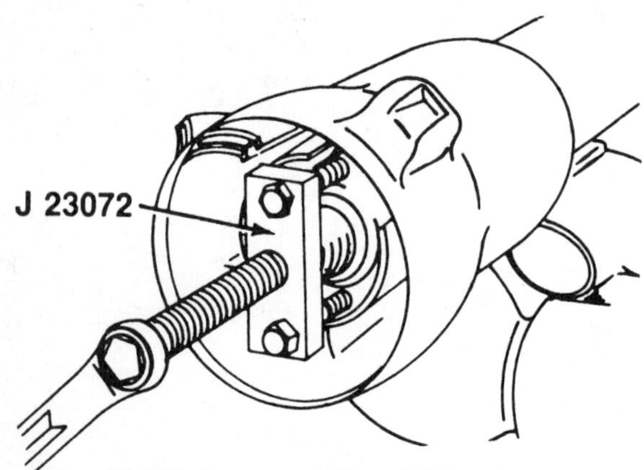

Shift tube removal – R/V series

hub at the 12 o'clock position and sliding it under the jacket opening. Remove the wave washer.

17. All columns – Remove the shift lever housing from the mast jacket (transmission control lock tube housing on floor shift models). Remove the shift lever spring by winding the spring up with pliers and pulling it out. On floor shift models, remove the spring plunger.

18. Disassemble the bearing housing as follows:

a. Remove the tilt lever opening shield.

b. Remove the lock bolt spring by removing the retaining screw and moving the spring clockwise to remove it from the bolt.

c. Remove the snapring from the sector driveshaft. With a small punch, lightly tap the driveshaft from the sector. Remove the driveshaft, sector and lock bolt. Remove the rack and rack spring.

d. Remove the tilt release lever pin with a punch and hammer. Remove the lever and release lever spring. To relieve the load on the release lever, hold the shoes inward and wedge a block between the top of the shoes (over slots) and bearing housing.

e. Remove the lock shoe retaining pin with a punch and hammer. Remove the lock shoes and lock shoe springs. With the tilt lever opening on the left side and shoes facing up, the four slot shoe is on the left.

f. Remove the bearings from the bearing housing only if they are to be replaced. Remove the separator and balls from the bearings. Place the housing on work bench and with a pointed punch against the back surface of the race, carefully hammer the race out of the housing until a bearing puller an be used. Repeat for the other race.

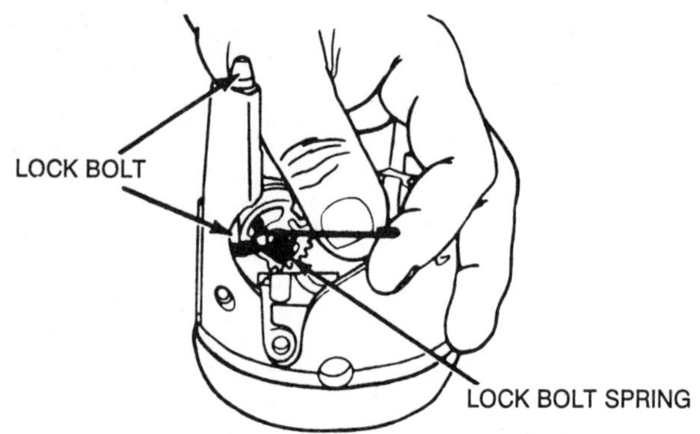

Lock bolt spring replacement – R/V series

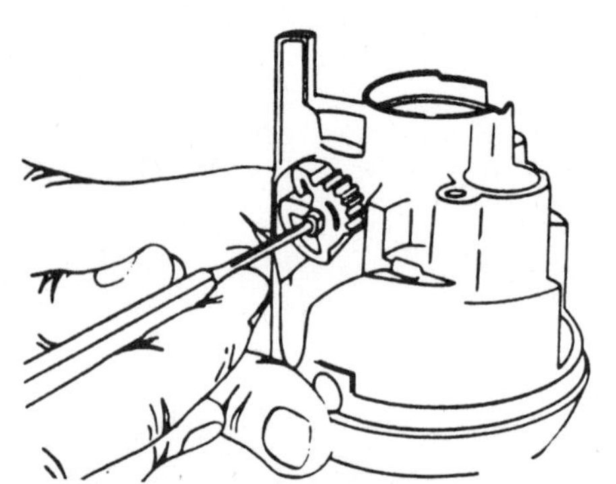
Sector drive shaft removal – R/V series

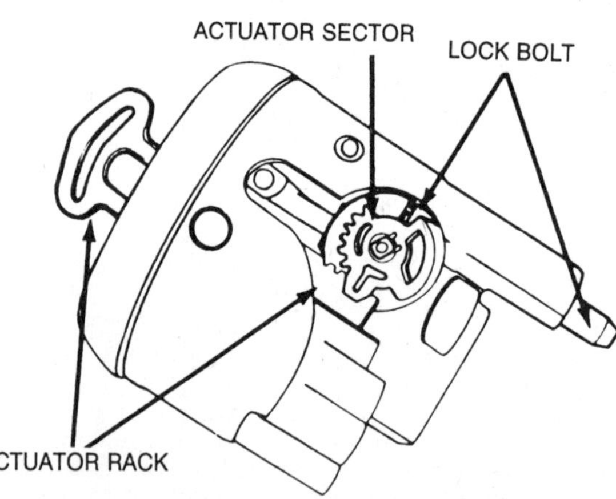

Lock bolt and rack assembly installation – R/V series

ASSEMBLY – TILT COLUMNS

Special tool J-23073, or its equivalent, is necessary for this procedure.

NOTE: Apply a thin coat of lithium grease to all friction surfaces.

1. If the bearing housing was disassembled, repeat the following steps:

a. Press the bearings into the housing, if removed, using a suitable size socket. Be careful not to damage the housing or bearing during installation.

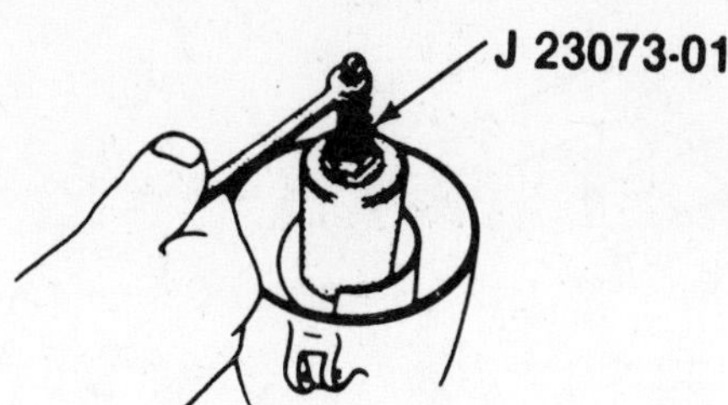

Shift tube installation – R/V series

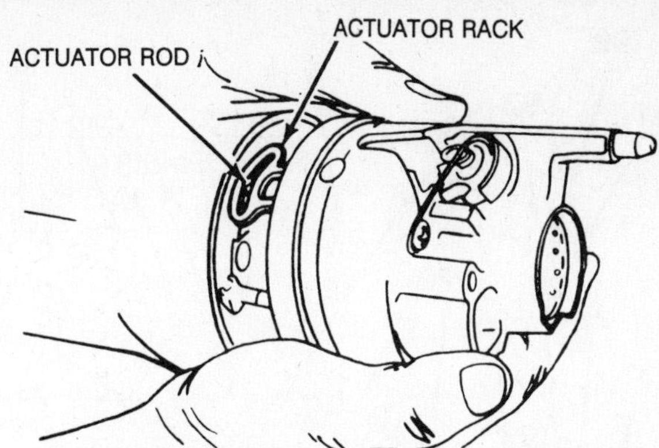

Bearing housing installation – R/V series

b. Install the lock shoe springs, lock shoes and shoe pin in the housing. Use an approximate 0.180 in. (4.5mm) rod to line up the shoes for pin installation.

c. Install the shoe release lever, spring and pin. To relieve the load on the release lever, hold the shoes inward and wedge a block between the top of the shoes (over slots) and bearing housing.

d. Install the sector driveshaft into the housing. Lightly tap the sector onto the shaft far enough to install the snapring. Install the snapring.

e. Install the lock bolt and engage it with the sector cam surface. Then install the rack and spring. The block tooth on the rack should engage the block tooth on the sector. Install the external tilt release lever.

f. Install the lock bolt spring and retaining screw. Tighten the screw to 35 inch lbs.

2. Install the shift lever spring into the housing by winding it up with pliers and pushing it into the housing. On floor shift models, install the plunger, slide the gearshift lever housing onto the mast jacket.

3. Install the bearing support lock plate wave washer.

4. Install the bearing support lock plate. Work it into the notches in the jacket by tipping it toward the housing hub at the 12 o'clock position and sliding it under the jacket opening. Slide the lock plate into the notches in the jacket.

5. Carefully install the shift tube into the lower end of the mast jacket. Align keyway in the tube with the key in the shift lever housing. Install the wobble plate end of Tool J-23073 into the upper end of the shift tube far enough to reach the enlarged portion of the tube. Then install the adapter over the end of the tool, seating it against the lock plate. Place the nut on the threaded end of the tool and pull the shift tube into the housing. Remove Tool J-23073.

WARNING: Do not push or tap on the end of the shift tube. Be sure that the shift tube lever is aligned with the slotted opening at the lower end of the mast jacket or damage to the shift tube and mast jacket could result.

6. Install the bearing support thrust washer and retaining ring by pulling the shift lever housing up far enough to compress the wave washer.

7. Install the bearing support by aligning the **V** in the support with the **V** in the jacket. Insert the screws through the support and into the lock plate and torque to 60 inch lbs.

8. Align the lower bearing adapter with the notches in the jacket and push the adapter into the lower end of the mast jacket. Install lower bearing, bearing reinforcement and retaining clip, being sure that the clip is aligned with the slots in the reinforcement, jacket and adapter.

9. Install the centering spheres and anti-lash spring in the upper shaft. Install the lower shaft from the same side of the spheres that the spring ends protrude.

10. Install the steering shaft assembly into the shift tube from the upper end. Carefully guide the shaft through the shift tube and bearing.

11. Install the ignition switch actuator rod through the shift lever housing and insert in the slot in the bearing support. Extend the rack downward from the bearing housing.

12. Assemble the bearing housing over the steering shaft and engage the rack over the end of the actuator rod.

13. With the external release lever installed, hold the lock shoes in the disengaged position and assemble the bearing housing over the steering shaft until the pivot pin holes line up.

14. Install the pivot pins.

15. Place the bearing housing in the full up position and install the tilt lever spring guide, spring and spring retainer. With a suitable screwdriver, push the retainer in and turn clockwise to engage in the housing.

16. Install the upper bearing inner race and race seat.

17. Install the tilt lever opening shield.

18. Remove the tilt release lever, install the turn signal housing and torque the three retaining screws to 45 inch lbs.

19. Install the tilt release lever and shift lever. Drive the shift lever pin in.

20. Install the lock cylinder, turn signal switch and ignition switch as outlined previously in this section.

21. Align the groove across the upper end of the pot joint with the flat on the steering shaft. Assemble the intermediate shaft assembly to the upper shaft. Install the clamp and bolt and torque the nut to specifications.

WARNING: The clamp bolt must pass through the shaft undercut, or damage may occur to the components.

22. Install the neutral safety switch or back-up switch as outlined in this Section.

23. Install the four dash panel bracket to column screws and torque to specifications.

NOTE: Be sure that the slotted openings in the bracket (for the mounting capsules) face the upper end of the steering column.

Flexible Coupling

REPLACEMENT

R and V Series

1. Remove the coupling-to-flange bolts and washers.
2. Remove the clamp bolt.
3. Remove the steering gear-to-frame bolts. Lower the gear just far enough to remove the coupling.
4. Remove the coupling from the steering gear wormshaft. You may have to tap it off with a plastic mallet.

To install:

5. Align the flat on the wormshaft with the flat in the coupling and install the coupling on the steering gear wormshaft

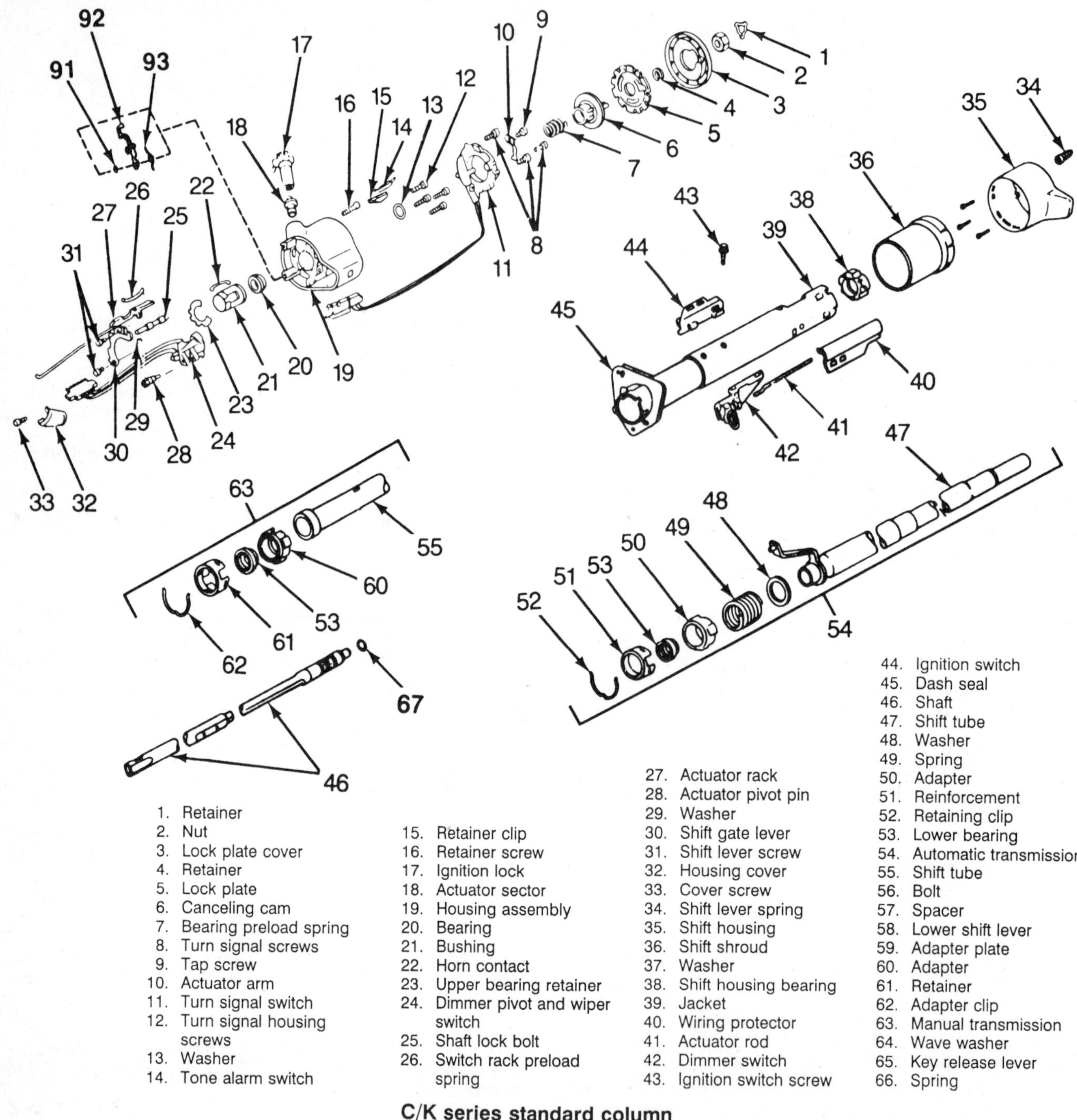

C/K series standard column

until the coupling bottoms against the reinforcement on the wormshaft. You may have to tap it on with a plastic mallet.

6. Raise the gear into position, guiding the flexible coupling bolts into their holes in the steering shaft flange. Install the steering gear-to-frame bolts. Torque the bolts to 65 ft. lbs.

7. Install the clamp bolt. Make sure it passes through the cutout. Torque the olt to 31 ft. lbs.

8. Install the coupling-to-flange bolts and washers. Torque them to 20 ft. lbs. The coupling-to-flange relationship must be within ¼–¾ in. (6–19mm) from flat.

CAUTION

All suspension and steering fasteners are important attaching parts in that they could affect the performance of vital components and systems, and/or could result in major repair expense. They must be replaced with one of the same part number or with an equivalent part if replacement becomes necessary. Do not use a replacement part of lesser quality or substitute design. Torque values must be used as specified during reassembly to assure proper retention of these parts. Observe all nut and bolt torque specifications.

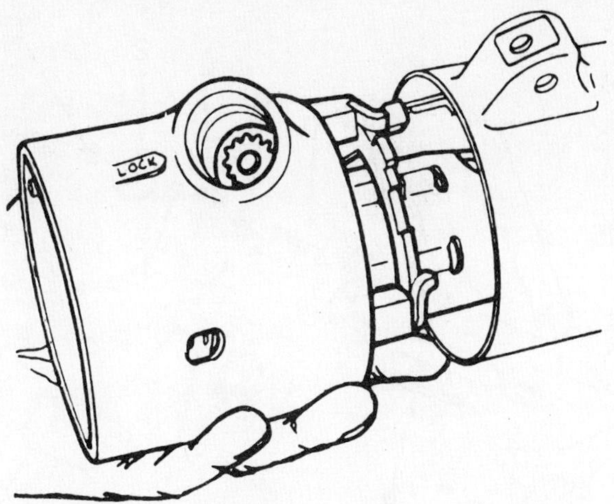

Removing the turn signal housing – C/K series

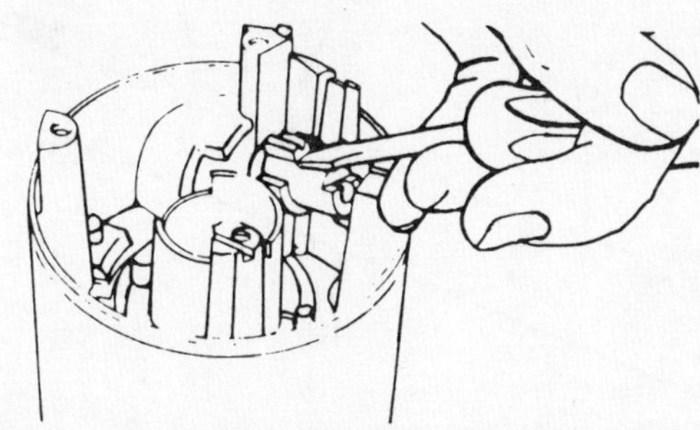
Removing the ignition switch actuator sector – C/K series

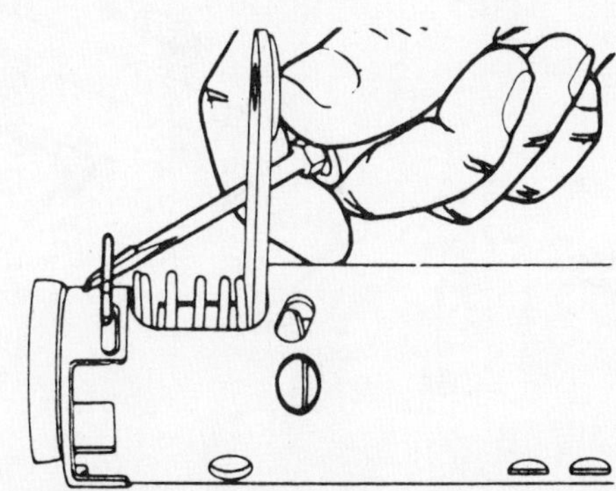
Removing the lower bearing retainer – C/K series

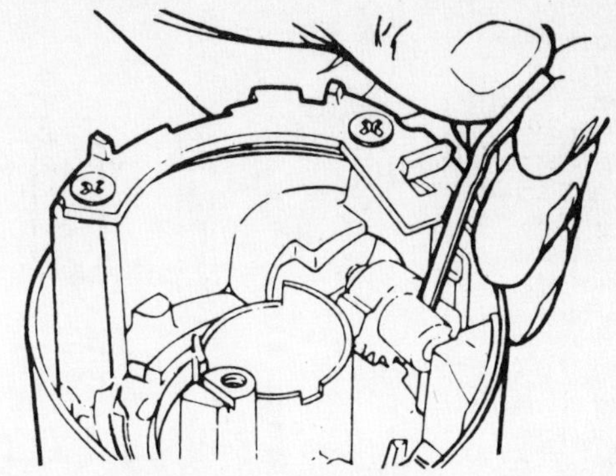
Installing the rack preload spring – C/K series

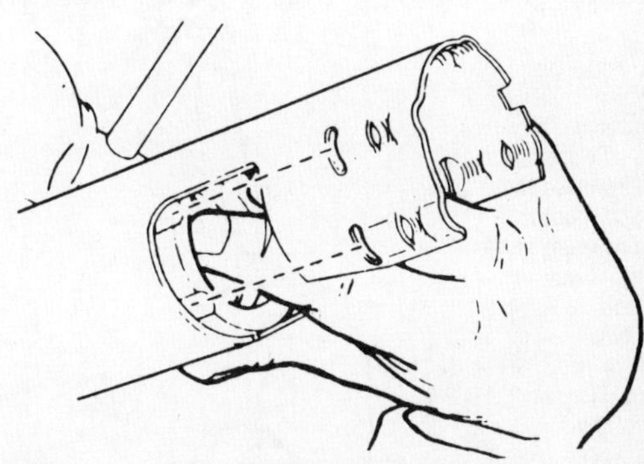
Installing the shift housing lower bearing – C/K series

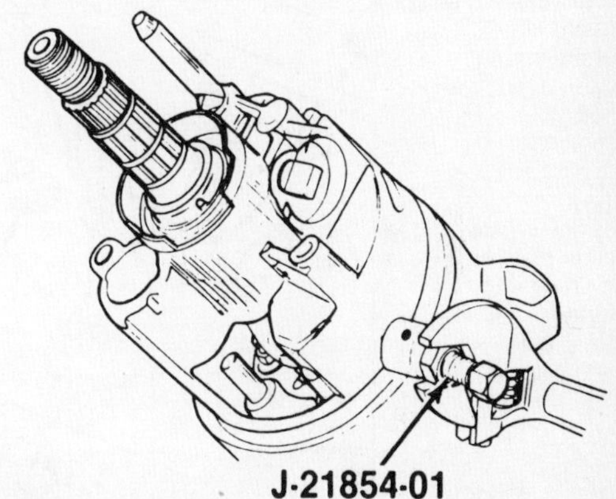

Removing the bearing housing pivot rings – C/K series

Intermediate Shaft

REMOVAL AND INSTALLATION

C and K Series

1. Set the front wheels in the straight-ahead position.
2. Matchmark the relationships of the pot joint-to-steering shaft and the flexible coupling-to-wormshaft.
3. Remove the pinch bolt from each end opf the shaft.
4. Slide the shaft up on the stering shaft to clear the wormshaft. If you can't slide it far enough, remove the steering gear-to-frame bolts and lower the gear.
5. Installation is the reverse of removal. Torque the gear-to-frame bolts to 55 ft. lbs.; the pinch bolts to 22 ft. lbs.

CAUTION

All suspension and steering fasteners are important attaching parts in that they could affect the performance of vital components and systems, and/or could result in major repair expense. They must be replaced with one of the same part number or with an equivalent part if replacement becomes necessary. Do not use a replacement part of lesser quality or substitute design. Torque values must be used as specified during reassembly to assure proper retention of these parts. Observe all nut and bolt torque specifications.

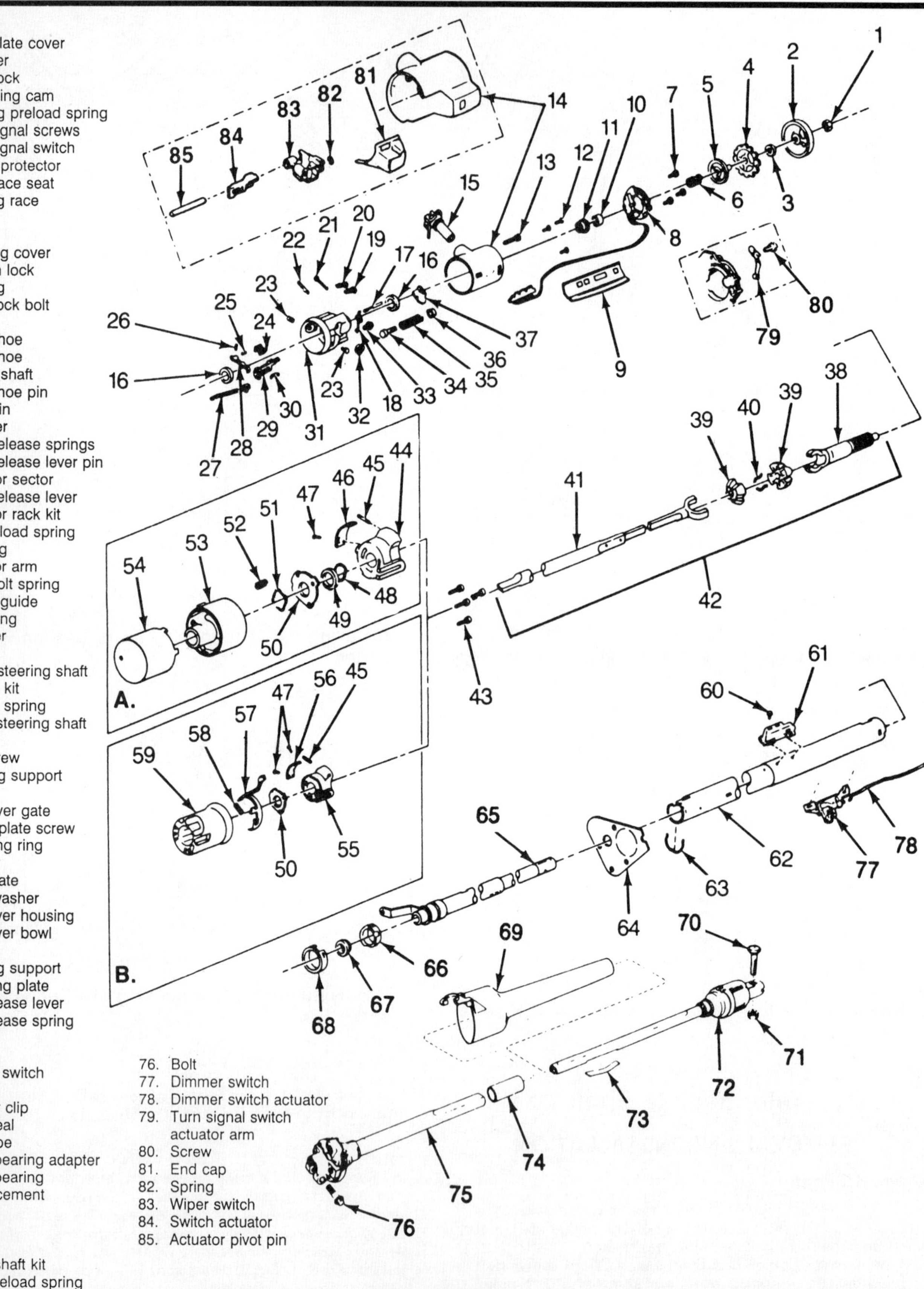

1. Nut
2. Lock plate cover
3. Retainer
4. Shaft lock
5. Canceling cam
6. Bearing preload spring
7. Turn signal screws
8. Turn signal switch
9. Wiring protector
10. Inner race seat
11. Bearing race
12. Screw
13. Screw
14. Housing cover
15. Ignition lock
16. Bearing
17. Shaft lock bolt
18. Spring
19. Lock shoe
20. Lock shoe
21. Sector shaft
22. Lock shoe pin
23. Pivot pin
24. Retainer
25. Shoe release springs
26. Shoe release lever pin
27. Actuator sector
28. Shoe release lever
29. Actuator rack kit
30. Pin preload spring
31. Housing
32. Actuator arm
33. Lock bolt spring
34. Spring guide
35. Tilt spring
36. Retainer
37. Shield
38. Upper steering shaft
39. Sphere kit
40. Sphere spring
41. Lower steering shaft
42. Shaft
43. Tap screw
44. Housing support
45. Pin
46. Shift lever gate
47. Detent plate screw
48. Retaining ring
49. Washer
50. Lock plate
51. Wave washer
52. Shift lever housing
53. Shift lever bowl
54. Shroud
55. Housing support
56. Retaining plate
57. Key release lever
58. Key release spring
59. Shroud
60. Screw
61. Ignition switch
62. Jacket
63. Adapter clip
64. Dash seal
65. Shift tube
66. Lower bearing adapter
67. Lower bearing
68. Reinforcement
69. Shield
70. Bolt
71. Nut
72. Upper shaft kit
73. Rack preload spring
74. Seal
75. Lower shaft kit
76. Bolt
77. Dimmer switch
78. Dimmer switch actuator
79. Turn signal switch actuator arm
80. Screw
81. End cap
82. Spring
83. Wiper switch
84. Switch actuator
85. Actuator pivot pin

C/K series tilt column

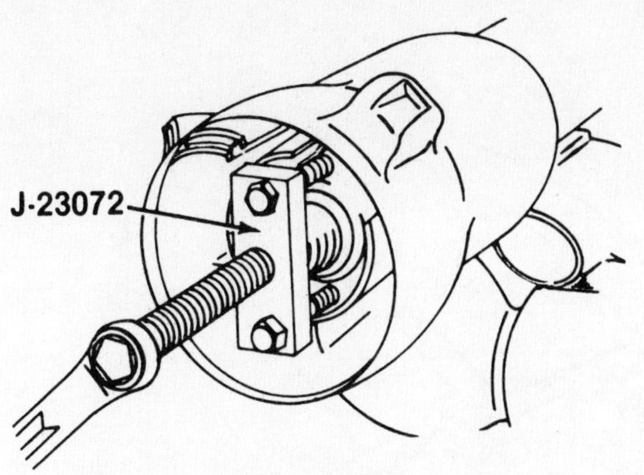

Removing the shift tube – C/K series

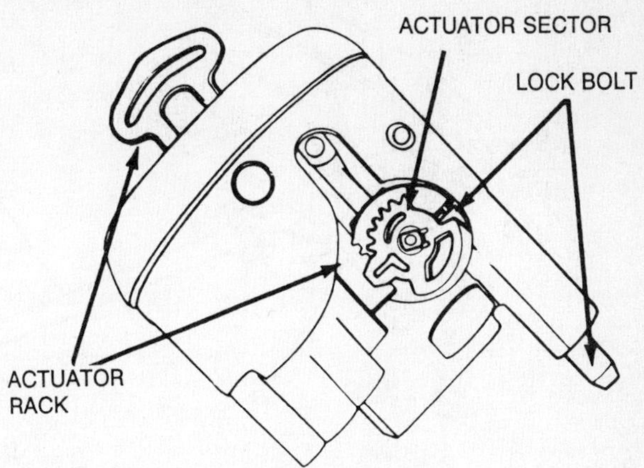

Installing the lock bolt and rack – C/K series

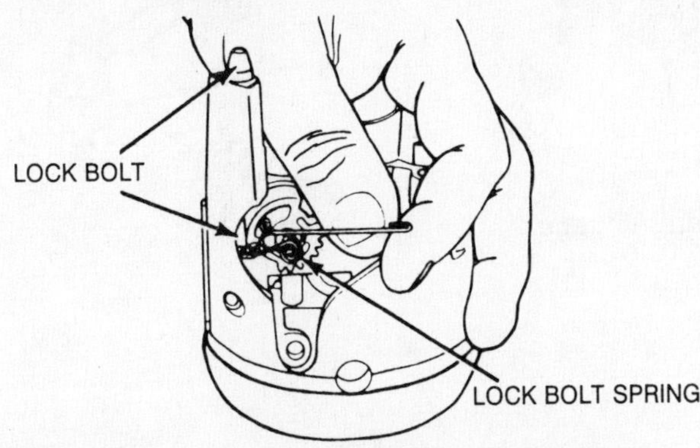

Replacing the lock bolt spring – C/K series

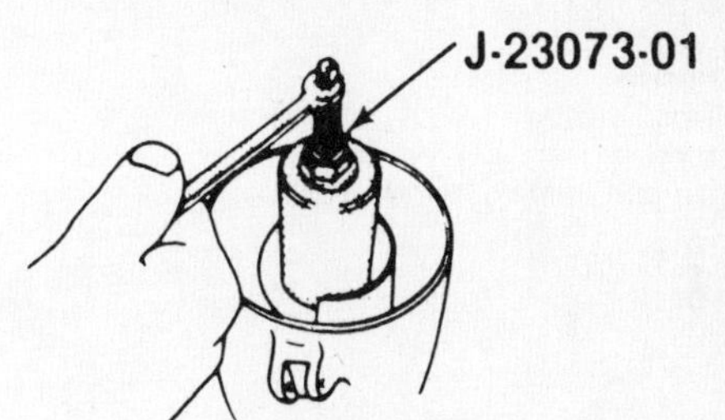

Installing the shift tube – C/K series

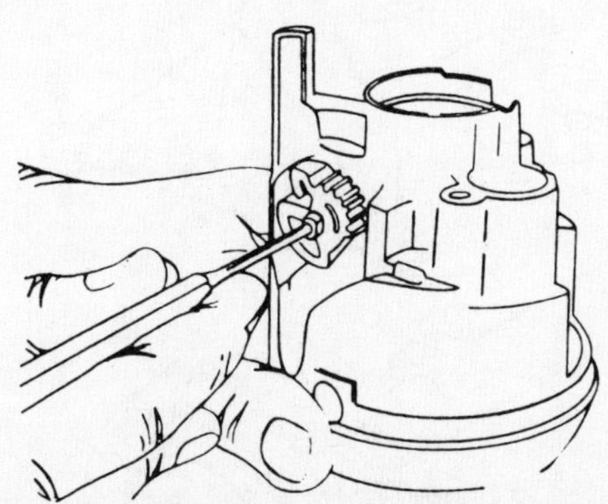
Removing the sector drive shaft – C/K series

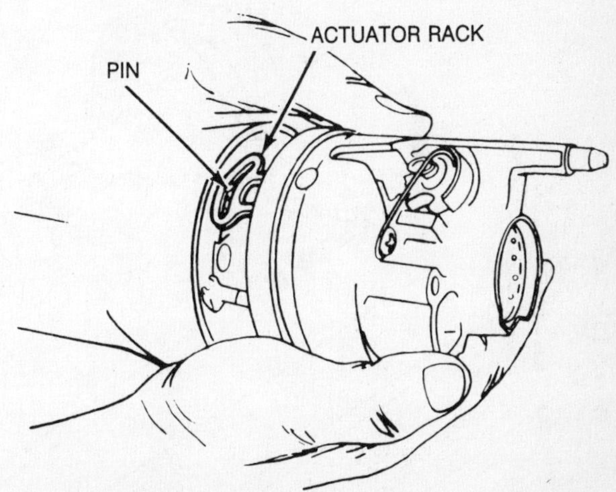

Installing the bearing housing – C/K series

Pitman Arm
REMOVAL AND INSTALLATION

R and V Series

1. Raise and support the front end on jackstands.
2. Remove nut from pitman arm ball stud.
3. Remove pitman arm or relay rod from ball stud by tapping on side of rod or arm (in which the stud mounts) with a hammer while using a heavy hammer or similar tool as a backing. Pull on linkage to remove from stud.
4. Remove pitman arm nut from pitman shaft or clamp bolt from pitman arm, and mark relation of arm position to shaft.
5. Remove pitman arm, using a large puller.

To install:

6. Install pitman arm on pitman shaft, lining up the marks made upon removal.

1. Idler arm
2. Relay rod
3. Tie rod
4. Knuckle
5. Pitman arm
6. Steering gear
7. Idler arm frame support

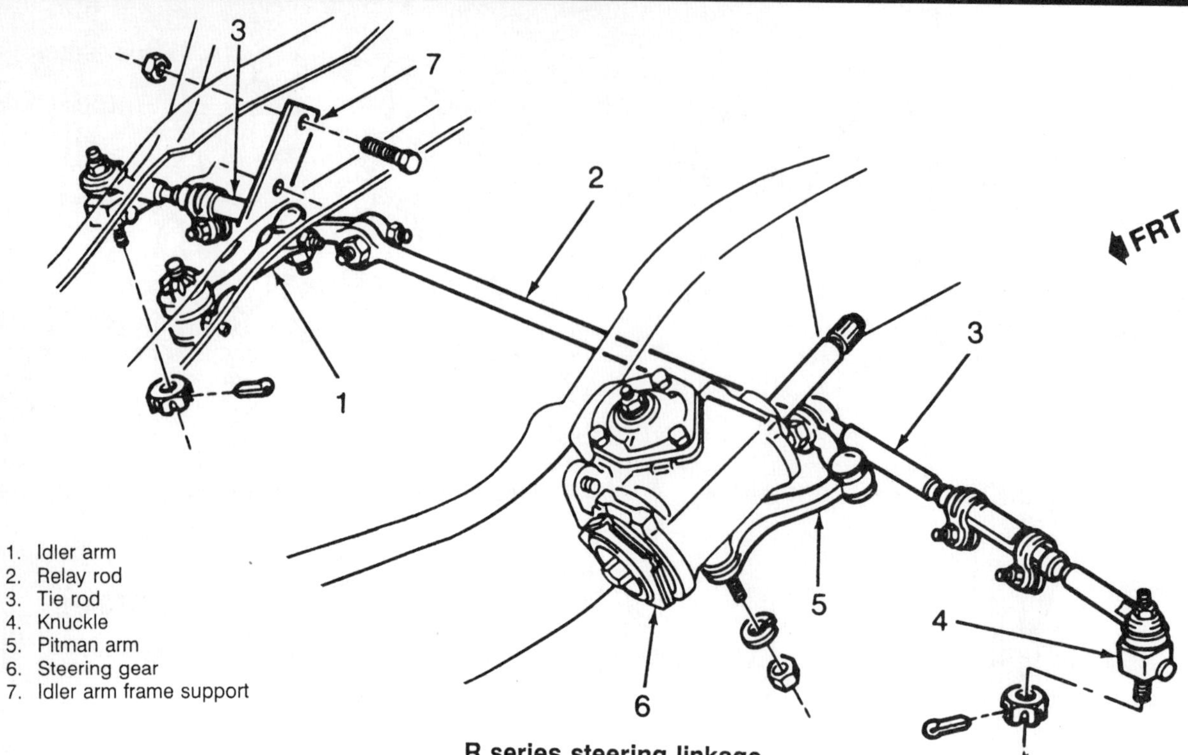

R series steering linkage

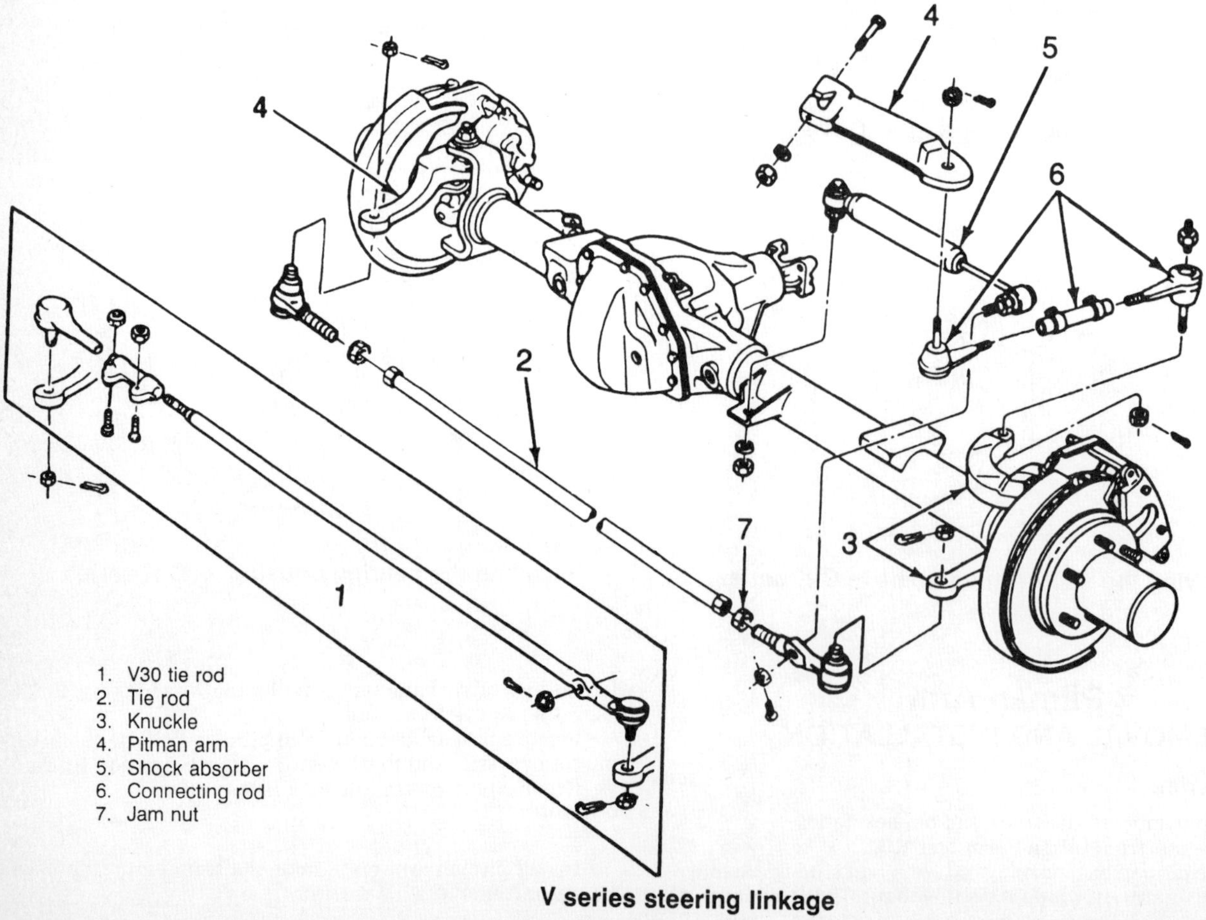

1. V30 tie rod
2. Tie rod
3. Knuckle
4. Pitman arm
5. Shock absorber
6. Connecting rod
7. Jam nut

V series steering linkage

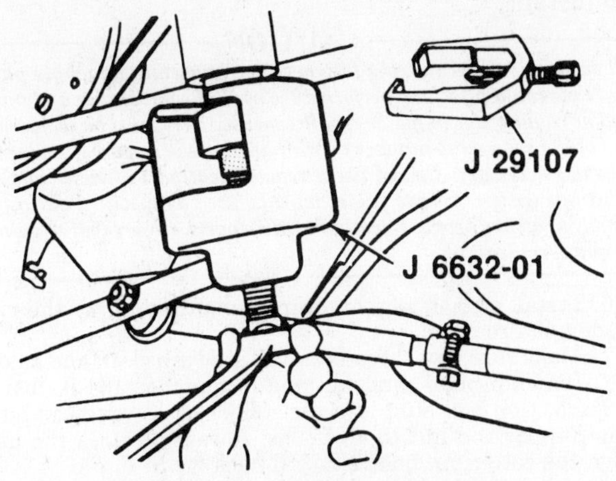

Removing the pitman arm

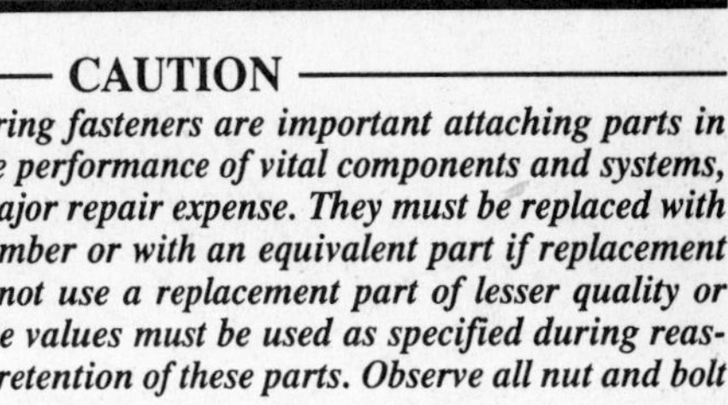

CAUTION

All suspension and steering fasteners are important attaching parts in that they could affect the performance of vital components and systems, and/or could result in major repair expense. They must be replaced with one of the same part number or with an equivalent part if replacement becomes necessary. Do not use a replacement part of lesser quality or substitute design. Torque values must be used as specified during reassembly to assure proper retention of these parts. Observe all nut and bolt torque specifications.

NOTE: If a clamp type pitman arm is used, spread the pitman arm just enough, with a wedge, to slip arm onto pitman shaft. Do not spread pitman arm more than required to slip over pitman shaft with hand pressure. Do not hammer or damage to steering gear may result. Be sure to install the hardened steel washer before installing the nut.

7. Make sure that threads on ball studs and in ball stud nuts are clean and smooth. If threads are not clean and smooth, ball studs may turn in sockets when attempting to tighten nut. Check condition of ball stud seals; replace if necessary.

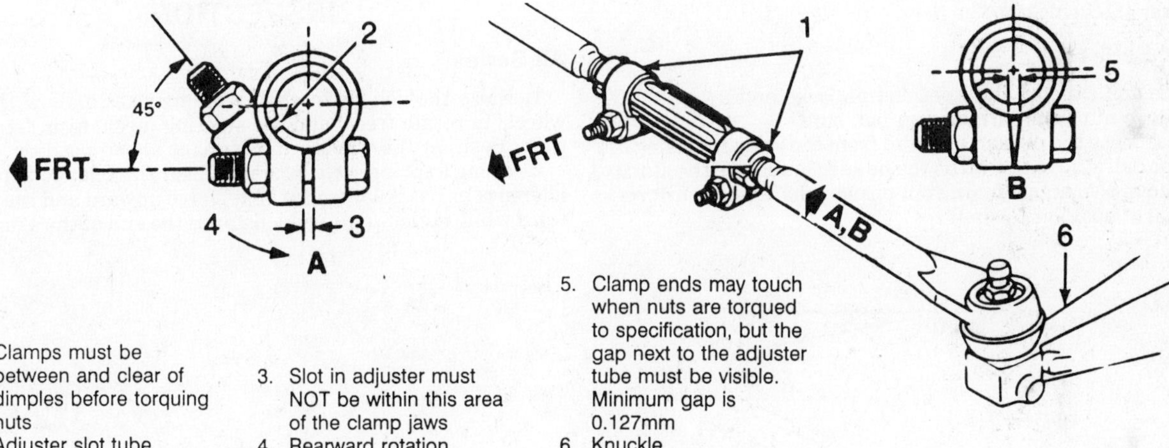

1. Clamps must be between and clear of dimples before torquing nuts
2. Adjuster slot tube
3. Slot in adjuster must NOT be within this area of the clamp jaws
4. Rearward rotation
5. Clamp ends may touch when nuts are torqued to specification, but the gap next to the adjuster tube must be visible. Minimum gap is 0.127mm
6. Knuckle

Tie rod clamp and adjuster tube positioning – R series

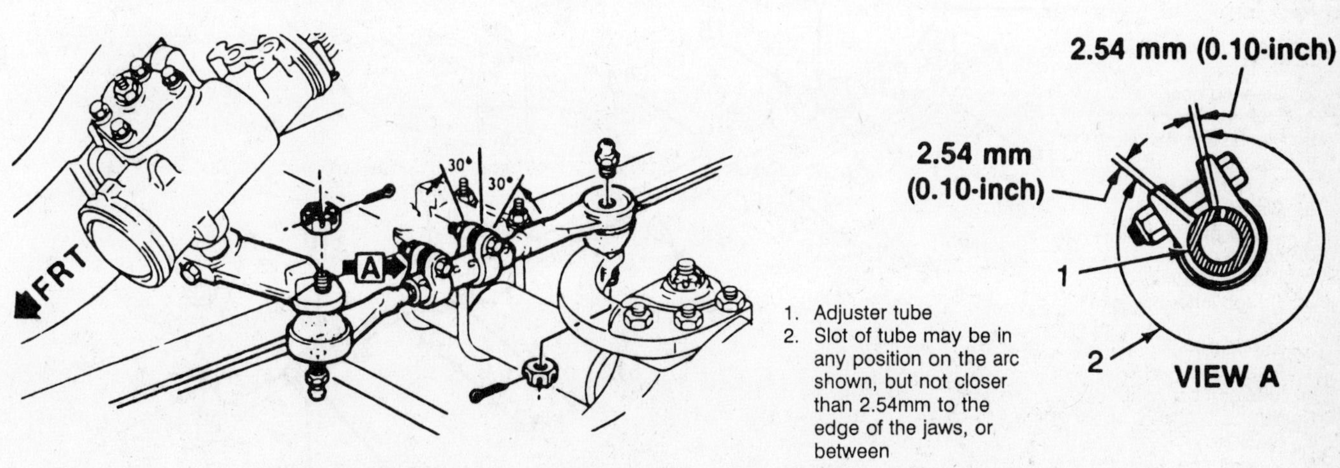

1. Adjuster tube
2. Slot of tube may be in any position on the arc shown, but not closer than 2.54mm to the edge of the jaws, or between

Connecting rod clamp and adjuster tube positioning – V series

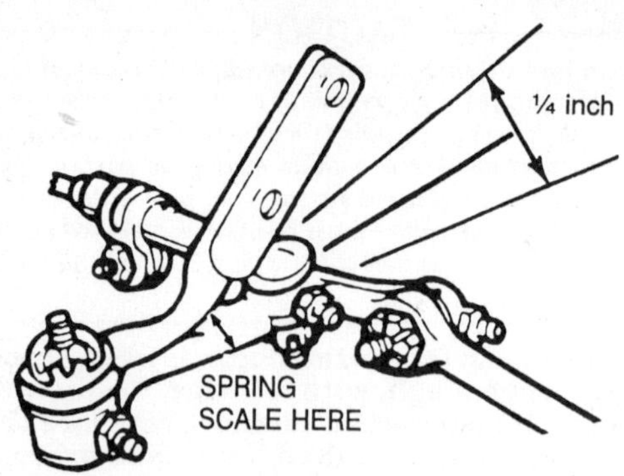

Idler movement check – C series

8. Install pitman shaft nut or pitman arm clamp bolt and torque to 184 ft. lbs. on R Series; 125 ft. lbs. on V Series.

9. Position ball stud onto pitman arm or relay rod. Use a ⅝ in.–18 free spinning nut to seat the tapers, as shown. Torque the pitman arm-to-relay rod nut to 66 ft. lbs. Always advance the nut to align the cotter pin hole. NEVER back it off!

10. Lubricate ball studs.

11. Lower the vehicle to the floor.

C and K Series

1. Raise and support the front end on jackstands.

2. Remove nut from pitman arm ball stud.

3. Break loose the pitman ball stud from the relay rod using a screw-type ball stud tool. Pull on the linkage to remove the stud.

4. Remove pitman arm nut from pitman shaft, and mark relation of arm position to shaft.

5. Remove pitman arm using a puller.

To install:

CAUTION

All suspension and steering fasteners are important attaching parts in that they could affect the performance of vital components and systems, and/or could result in major repair expense. They must be replaced with one of the same part number or with an equivalent part if replacement becomes necessary. Do not use a replacement part of lesser quality or substitute design. Torque values must be used as specified during reassembly to assure proper retention of these parts. Observe all nut and bolt torque specifications.

6. Install pitman arm on pitman shaft, lining up the marks made upon removal.

7. Make sure that threads on ball stud are clean and smooth.

8. Install pitman shaft nut and torque it to 184 ft. lbs.

9. Position ball stud into the relay rod. Torque the pitman arm-to-relay rod nut to 40 ft. lbs. Always advance the nut to align the cotter pin hole. NEVER back it off!

10. Lubricate the ball stud.

11. Lower the vehicle to the floor.

Idler Arm

INSPECTION

All Series

1. Raise the vehicle in such a manner as to allow the front wheels to rotate freely and the steering mechanism freedom to turn. Position the wheels in a straight ahead position.

2. Using a spring scale located as near the relay rod end of the idler arm as possible, exert a 25 lb. force upward and then downward while noticing the total distance the end of the arm moves.

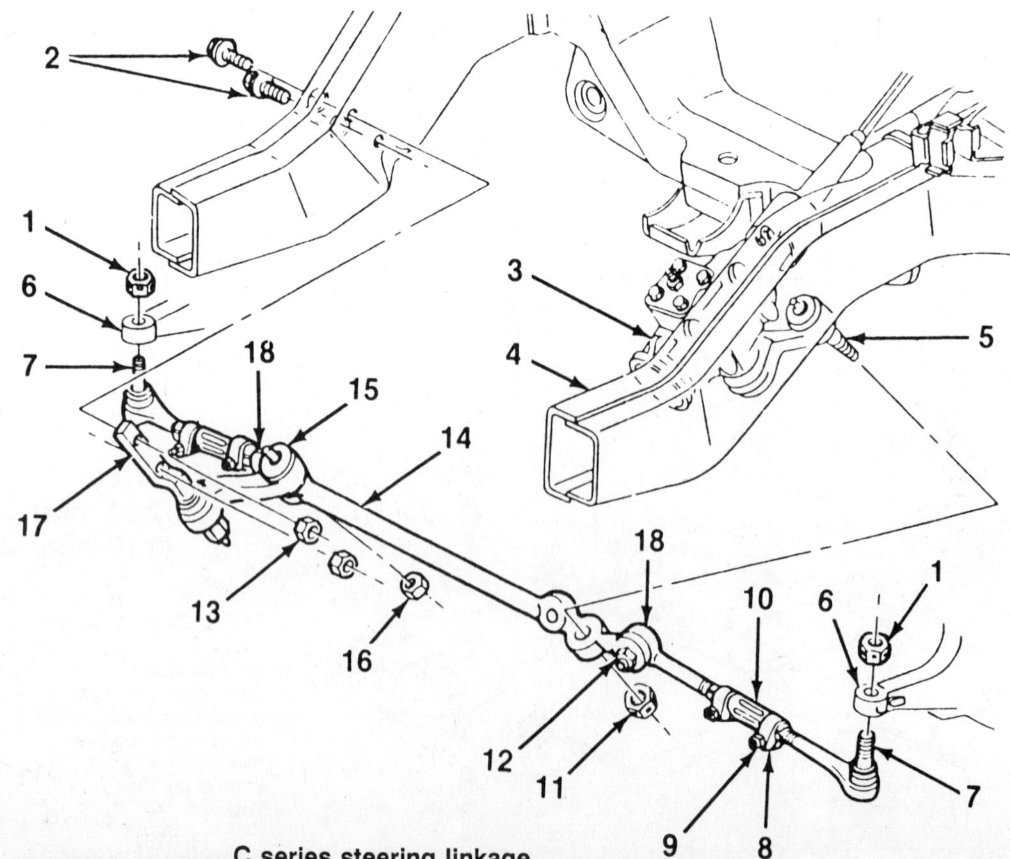

1. Tie rod outer ball nut
2. Bolts
3. Steering gear
4. Frame
5. Pitman arm ball stud
6. Knuckle
7. Tie rod ball stud
8. Clamp
9. Clamp nut
10. Adjuster tube
11. Pitman arm nut
12. Tie rod inner ball joint nut
13. Nut
14. Relay rod
15. Idler arm ball joint
16. Nut
17. Bracket
18. Tie rod inner ball joint

C series steering linkage

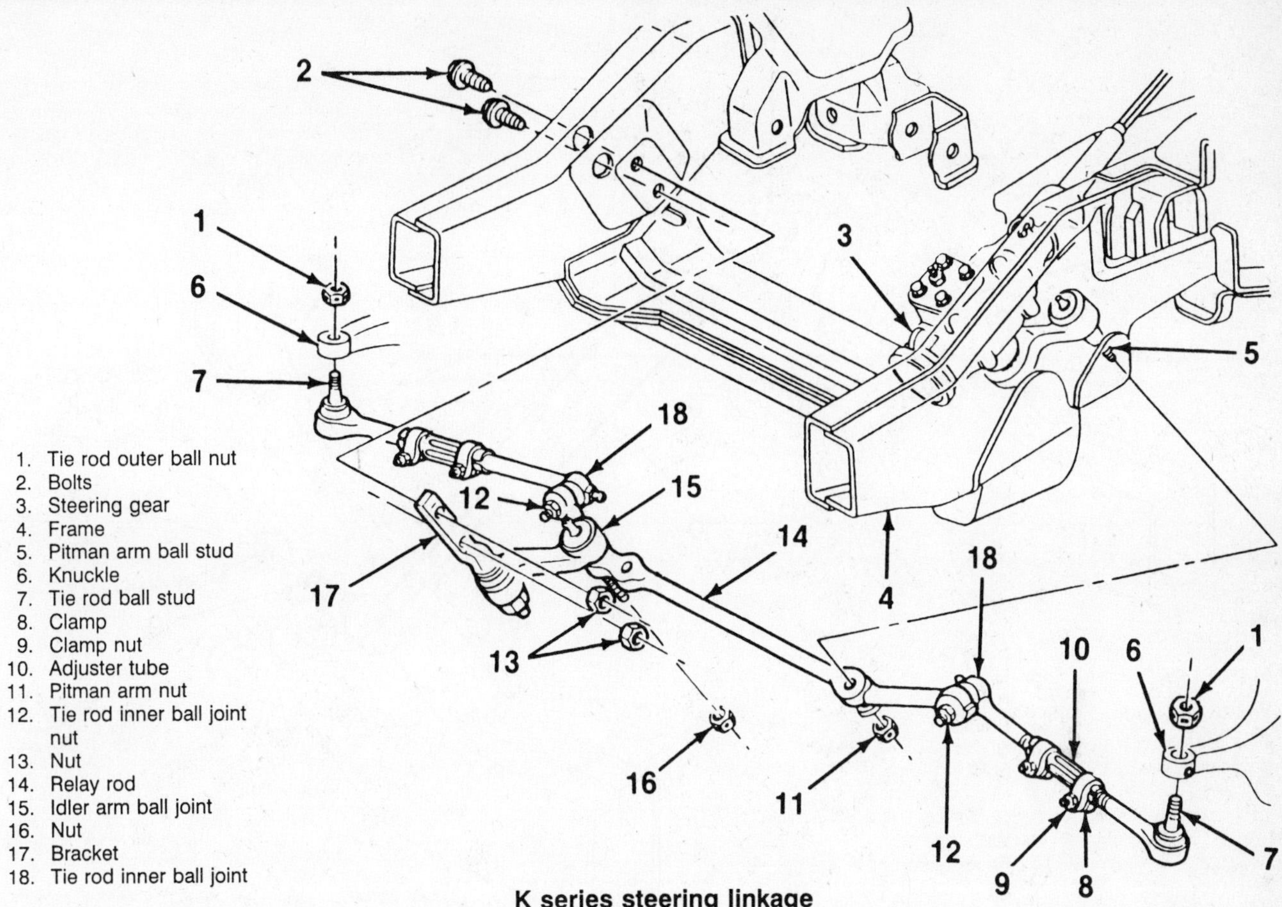

K series steering linkage

This distance should not exceed ± $^1/_{16}$ in. (1.6mm) for a total acceptable movement of $^1/_8$ in. (3mm). It is necessary to ensure that the correct load is applied to the arm since it will move more when higher loads are applied. It is also necessary that a scale or ruler be rested against the frame and used to determine the amount of movement since observers tend to over-estimate the actual movement when a scale is not used. The idler arm should always be replaced if it fails this test.

NOTE: Jerking the right front wheel and tire assembly back and forth, thus causing an up and down movement in the idler arm is not an acceptable method of checking since there is no control on the amount of force being applied.

Caution should be used in assuming shimmy complaints are caused by loose idler arms. Before suspecting suspension or steering components, technicians should eliminate shimmy excitation factors, such as dynamic imbalance, run-out or force variation of wheel and tire assemblies and road surface irregularities.

REMOVAL AND INSTALLATION

R and V Series

1. Raise and support the front end on jackstands.
2. Remove the nut from ball stud at the relay rod.
3. Using a screw-type ball joint tool, separate the ball stud from the relay rod.
4. Remove the idler arm to frame bolts and remove the idler arm assembly.

To install:

CAUTION

All suspension and steering fasteners are important attaching parts in that they could affect the performance of vital components and systems, and/or could result in major repair expense. They must be replaced with one of the same part number or with an equivalent part if replacement becomes necessary. Do not use a replacement part of lesser quality or substitute design. Torque values must be used as specified during reassembly to assure proper retention of these parts. Observe all nut and bolt torque specifications.

5. Position the idler arm on the frame and install the mounting bolts. Torque the bolts to 30 ft. lbs.
6. Make sure that the threads on the ball stud and in the ball stud nut are clean and smooth. If threads are not clean and smooth, ball stud may turn in the socket when attempting to tighten nut. Check condition of ball stud seal; replace if necessary.
7. Install the idler arm ball stud in the relay rod, making certain the seal is positioned properly. Use a $^5/_8$ in.–18 free-spinning nut to seat the tapers, as shown. Torque the nut to 66 ft. lbs. Always advance the nut to align the cotter pin hole. NEVER back it off!
8. Lower the vehicle to the floor.

C and K Series

1. Raise and support the front end on jackstands.
2. Remove the idler arm bracket-to-frame bolts and nuts.
3. Remove the idler arm ball stud nut. Discard the nut.

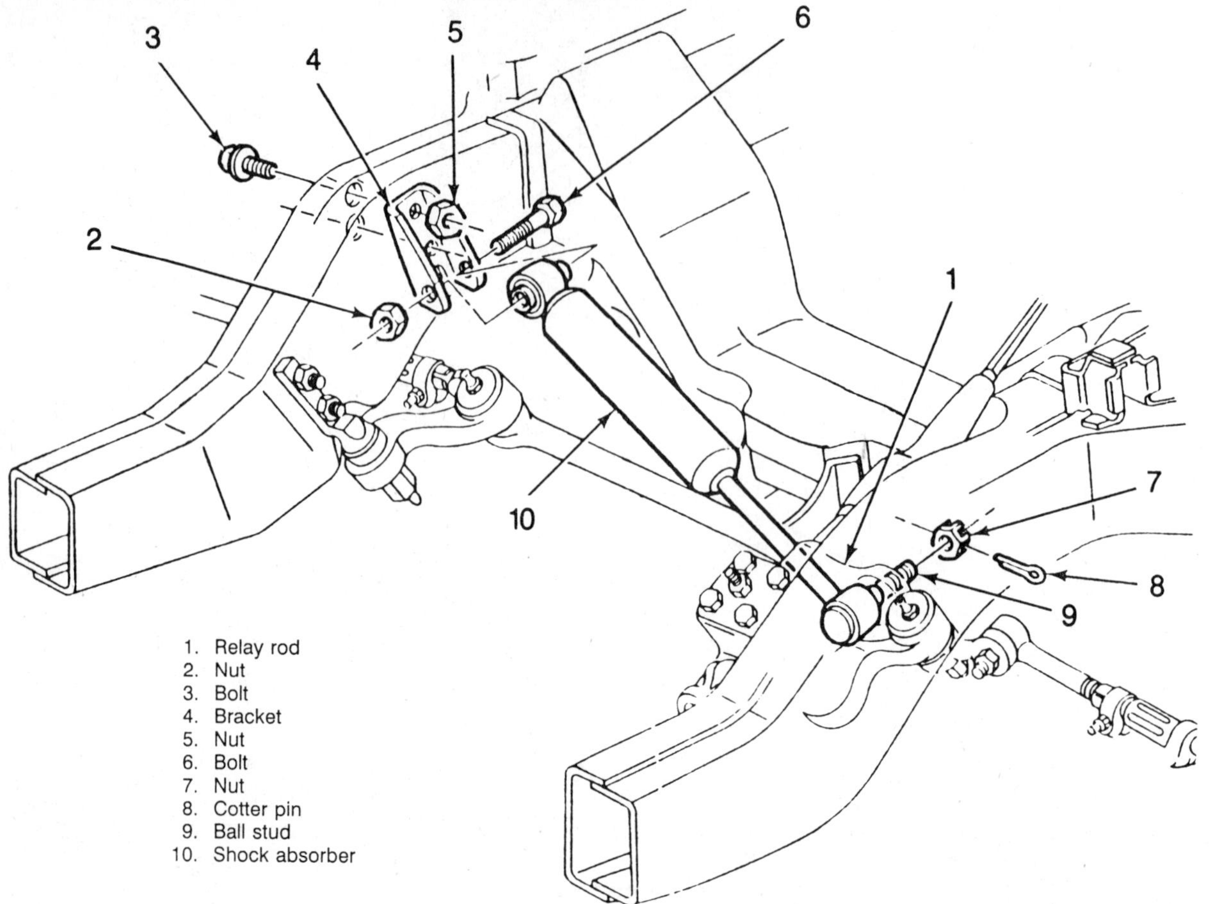

C series steering shock absorber

4. Using a screw-type ball joint tool, separate the idler arm from the relay rod.
5. Installation is the reverse of removal. Make sure the ball stud is positioned squarely in the relay rod before tightening the nut. Tighten the frame-to-bracket bolts to 78 ft. lbs.; the new ball stud nut to 40 ft. lbs.

CAUTION

All suspension and steering fasteners are important attaching parts in that they could affect the performance of vital components and systems, and/or could result in major repair expense. They must be replaced with one of the same part number or with an equivalent part if replacement becomes necessary. Do not use a replacement part of lesser quality or substitute design. Torque values must be used as specified during reassembly to assure proper retention of these parts. Observe all nut and bolt torque specifications.

6. Have the alignment checked and adjusted as necessary.

Relay Rod (Center Link)

REMOVAL AND INSTALLATION

R and V Series

1. Raise and support the vehicle with jackstands.
2. Remove the inner ends of the tie rods from the relay rod.
3. Remove the nuts from the pitman and idler arm ball studs at the relay rod.
4. Using a screw-type ball joint tool, separate the relay rod from the pitman and idler arms.
5. Remove the relay rod from the vehicle.

To install:

CAUTION

All suspension and steering fasteners are important attaching parts in that they could affect the performance of vital components and systems, and/or could result in major repair expense. They must be replaced with one of the same part number or with an equivalent part if replacement becomes necessary. Do not use a replacement part of lesser quality or substitute design. Torque values must be used as specified during reassembly to assure proper retention of these parts. Observe all nut and bolt torque specifications.

6. Make sure that threads on the ball studs and in the ball stud nuts are clean and smooth. If the threads are not clean and smooth, ball studs may turn in sockets when attempting to tighten nut. Check condition of ball stud seals; replace if necessary.
7. Connect the relay rod to the idler arm and pitman arm ball studs, making certain the seals are in place. Use a free-spinning nut to seat the tapers, as shown. Torque the nuts to 66 ft. lbs. Always advance the nut to align the cotter pin hole. NEVER back it off!
8. Install the tie rods to the center link as previously described under Tie Rod Installation. Lubricate the tie rod ends.
9. Lower the vehicle to the floor.
10. Have the alignment checked.

C and K Series

1. Raise and support the vehicle with jackstands.
2. Disconnect the steering shock absorber from the relay rod.

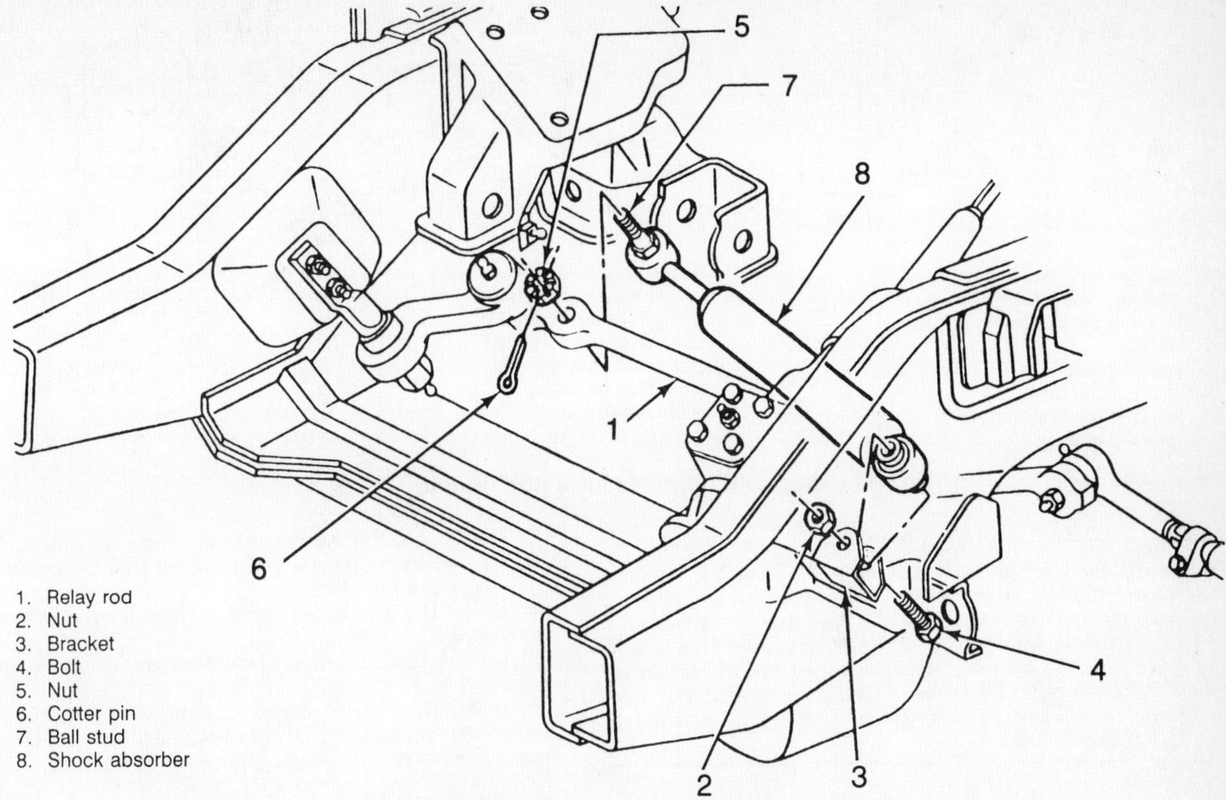

K series steering shock absorber

3. Remove the nut and disconnect the inner tie rod ball joint from the relay rod using a screw-type ball joint tool. Discard the nut.
4. Remove the nuts from the pitman and idler arm ball studs at the relay rod. Discard the nuts.
5. Using a screw-type ball joint tool, disconnect the relay rod from the pitman and idler arm.
6. Remove the relay rod from the vehicle.

To install:

CAUTION

All suspension and steering fasteners are important attaching parts in that they could affect the performance of vital components and systems, and/or could result in major repair expense. They must be replaced with one of the same part number or with an equivalent part if replacement becomes necessary. Do not use a replacement part of lesser quality or substitute design. Torque values must be used as specified during reassembly to assure proper retention of these parts. Observe all nut and bolt torque specifications.

7. Make sure that threads on the ball studs and in the ball stud nuts are clean and smooth. If the threads are not clean and smooth, ball studs may turn in sockets when attempting to tighten nut. Check condition of ball stud seals; replace if necessary.
8. Connect the relay rod to the idler arm and pitman arm ball studs, making certain the seals are in place. Use a free-spinning nut to seat the tapers, as shown. Torque the new nuts to 40 ft. lbs.
9. Install the tie rod to the center link. Torque the new nut to 40 ft. lbs.
10. Install the shock absorber. Torque the frame end nut to 30 ft. lbs.; the relay rod end nut to 46 ft. lbs. Always advance the nut to align the cotter pin hole. NEVER back it off!
11. Lower the vehicle to the floor.
12. Have the alignment checked.

Steering Linkage Shock Absorber

REMOVAL AND INSTALLATION

R and V Series

1. Remove the cotter pins and nuts and remove the unit.
2. Installation is the reverse of removal. Torque the tie rod end nut to 46 ft. lbs.; the frame end nut to 81 ft. lbs. Always advance the nut to align the cotter pin hole. NEVER back it off!

CAUTION

All suspension and steering fasteners are important attaching parts in that they could affect the performance of vital components and systems, and/or could result in major repair expense. They must be replaced with one of the same part number or with an equivalent part if replacement becomes necessary. Do not use a replacement part of lesser quality or substitute design. Torque values must be used as specified during reassembly to assure proper retention of these parts. Observe all nut and bolt torque specifications.

C and K Series

1. Raise and support the front end on jackstands.
2. Remove the frame end nut and bolt.
3. Remove the cotter pin and nut from the relay rod end. It may be necessary to separate the shock from the relay rod with a screw-type ball joint tool.
4. Installation is the reverse of removal. Torque the frame end nut and bolt to 30 ft. lbs.; the relay rod end nut to 46 ft. lbs. Always advance the nut to align the cotter pin hole. NEVER back it off! A maximum torque of 59 ft. lbs. is permissable to align the hole.

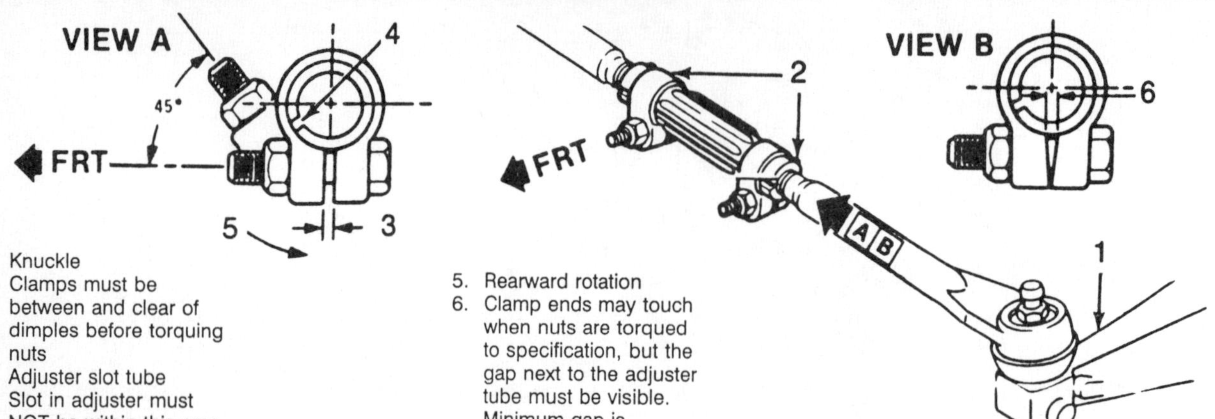
VIEW A
4
45°
FRT
5
3
FRT
2
VIEW B
6
A B
1
1. Knuckle
2. Clamps must be between and clear of dimples before torquing nuts
3. Adjuster slot tube
4. Slot in adjuster must NOT be within this area of the clamp jaws
5. Rearward rotation
6. Clamp ends may touch when nuts are torqued to specification, but the gap next to the adjuster tube must be visible. Minimum gap is 0.127mm

Tie rod clamp and adjuster tube positioning – C/K series

CAUTION

All suspension and steering fasteners are important attaching parts in that they could affect the performance of vital components and systems, and/or could result in major repair expense. They must be replaced with one of the same part number or with an equivalent part if replacement becomes necessary. Do not use a replacement part of lesser quality or substitute design. Torque values must be used as specified during reassembly to assure proper retention of these parts. Observe all nut and bolt torque specifications.

Tie Rod Ends

REMOVAL AND INSTALLATION

R Series

1. Loosen the tie rod adjuster sleeve clamp nuts.
2. Remove the tie rod end stud cotter pin and nut.
3. Use a screw-type tie rod removal tool to loosen the stud.
4. Remove the inner stud in the same way.
5. Unscrew the tie rod end from the threaded sleeve. The threads may be left or right hand threads. Count the number of turns required to remove it.
6. To install, grease the threads and turn the new tie rod end in as many turns as were needed to remove it. This will give approximately correct toe-in. Tighten the clamp bolts to 14 ft. lbs.

CAUTION

All suspension and steering fasteners are important attaching parts in that they could affect the performance of vital components and systems, and/or could result in major repair expense. They must be replaced with one of the same part number or with an equivalent part if replacement becomes necessary. Do not use a replacement part of lesser quality or substitute design. Torque values must be used as specified during reassembly to assure proper retention of these parts. Observe all nut and bolt torque specifications.

7. Tighten the stud nuts to 45 ft. lbs. and install new cotter pins. You may tighten the nut to align the cotter pin, but don't loosen it.
8. Adjust the toe-in.

Tie Rod

REMOVAL AND INSTALLATION

V Series

1. Remove the cotter pins and nuts from the tie rod assembly.
2. Disconnect the steering shock absorber from the tie rod.
3. Use a screw-type tie rod removal tool to loosen the ball studs from the knuckles.
4. Count the number of exposed threads on each tie rod end and record it.
5. Loosen the tie rod end lock nuts and unscrew the tie rod ends.
6. Installation is the reverse of removal. When installing the tie rod ends, turn them in until the same number of threads previously visible are achieved. Tighten the locknuts.

CAUTION

All suspension and steering fasteners are important attaching parts in that they could affect the performance of vital components and systems, and/or could result in major repair expense. They must be replaced with one of the same part number or with an equivalent part if replacement becomes necessary. Do not use a replacement part of lesser quality or substitute design. Torque values must be used as specified during reassembly to assure proper retention of these parts. Observe all nut and bolt torque specifications.

7. Install the tie rod assembly in the knuckles and tighten the castellated nuts to 40 ft. lbs. Always advance the nut to align the cotter pin hole. NEVER back it off!
8. Tighten the tie rod end locknuts to 175 ft. lbs.

C and K Series

1. Raise and support the front end on jackstands.
2. Remove the nut from the knucle end ball stud. Discard the nut.
3. Using a screw-type ball joint tool, separate the tie rod ball stud from the knuckle.
4. Remove the nut from the relay rod end ball stud.
5. Using a screw-type ball joint tool, separate the tie rod ball stud from the relay rod.
6. Clean the threaded parts of the tie rod ends thoroughly and count the exact number of threads exposed on each tie rod end. Measure the overall length of the tie rod assembly.
7. Loosen the clamp nuts, spread the clamps and unscrew each tie rod end.

To install:

8. Coat the threaded parts of the new tie rod ends with chassis grease. Screw the tie rod ends into the sleeve until the exact number of threads is exposed on each tie rod end. Check the overall length of the new assembly. Adjust as necessary. Don't tighten the clamp nuts yet.

CAUTION

All suspension and steering fasteners are important attaching parts in that they could affect the performance of vital components and systems, and/or could result in major repair expense. They must be replaced with one of the same part number or with an equivalent part if replacement becomes necessary. Do not use a replacement part of lesser quality or substitute design. Torque values must be used as specified during reassembly to assure proper retention of these parts. Observe all nut and bolt torque specifications.

9. Position the tie rod assembly in the relay rod and install a new nut on the ball stud. Torque the nut to 40 ft. lbs.
10. Position the other tie rod end in the knuckle. Install the new nut and torque it to 40 ft. lbs.
11. Before tightening the clamp nuts:
    a. Each clamp must be positioned between the locating dimples at each end of the adjuster.
    b. The clamps must be positioned with the nut facing forward and within 45° of horizontal.
    c. The split in the sleeve must be position at a point just above the clamp nut.
12. Tighten the clamp nuts to 14 ft. lbs. When the clamp nuts are tightened, the clamp ends may touch, but the split in the clamp, at the adjuster sleeve, must never be less than 0.127mm (0.005 in.).

Connecting Rod

REMOVAL AND INSTALLATION

V Series

1. Remove the cotter pins and nuts from each end of the connecting rod.
2. Using a screw type remover tool, break loose the connecting rod from the pitman arm and steering knuckle.
3. If the connecting rod ends are being replaced, note the length of the complete assembly and record it. Also note the respective directions of the ends when installed.
4. Loosen the clamp bolts and unscrew the ends. If the bolts are rusted, replace them.
5. Installation is the reverse of removal. Torque the clamp bolts to 40 ft. lbs.; the ball stud nuts to 89 ft. lbs. Always advance the nut to align the cotter pin hole. NEVER back it off!

CAUTION

All suspension and steering fasteners are important attaching parts in that they could affect the performance of vital components and systems, and/or could result in major repair expense. They must be replaced with one of the same part number or with an equivalent part if replacement becomes necessary. Do not use a replacement part of lesser quality or substitute design. Torque values must be used as specified during reassembly to assure proper retention of these parts. Observe all nut and bolt torque specifications.

Manual Steering Gear 1988 C and K Series Only

ADJUSTMENT

Before any steering gear adjustments are made, it is recommended that the front end of the truck be raised and a thorough inspection be made for stiffness or lost motion in the steering gear, steering linkage and front suspension. Worn or damaged parts should be replaced, since a satisfactory adjustment of the steering gear cannot be obtained if bent or badly worn parts exist.

It is also very important that the steering gear be properly aligned in the truck. Misalignment of the gear places a stress on the steering worm shaft, therefore a proper adjustment is impossible. To align the steering gear, loosen the steering gear-to-frame mounting bolts to permit the gear to align itself. Check the steering gear to frame mounting seat. If there is a gap at any of the mounting bolts, proper alignment may be obtained by placing shims where excessive gap appears. Tighten the steering gear-to-frame bolts. Alignment of the gear in the truck is very important and should be done carefully so that a satisfactory, trouble-free gear adjustment may be obtained.

The steering gear is of the recirculating ball nut type. The ball nut, mounted on the worm gear, is driven by means of steel balls which circulate in helical grooves in both the worm and nut. Ball return guides attached to the nut serve to recirculate the two sets of balls in the grooves. As the steering wheel is turned to the right, the ball nut moves upward. When the wheel is turned to the left, the ball nut moves downward.

Before doing the adjustment procedures given below, ensure that the steering problem is not caused by faulty suspension components, bad front end alignment, etc. Then, proceed with the following adjustments.

Bearing Drag

1. Disconnect the pitman arm from the gear.
2. Disconnect the battery ground cable.
3. Remove the horn cap.
4. Turn the steering wheel gently to the left stop, then back ½ turn.
5. Position an inch-pound torque wrench on the steering wheel nut and rotate it through a 90° arc. Note the torque. Proper torque is 5–8 inch lbs.
6. If the torque is incorrect, loosen the adjuster plug locknut and back off the plug ¼ turn, then tighten the plug to give the proper torque.
7. Hold the plug and tighten the adjuster plug locknut to 85 ft. lbs.

Overcenter Preload

1. Turn the steering wheel lock-to-lock counting the total number of turns. Turn the wheel back ½ the total number of turns to center it.
2. Turn the lash (sector shaft) adjuster screw clockwise to remove all lash between the ball nut and sector teeth. Tighten the locknut to 25 ft. lbs.
3. Using a torque wrench on the steering wheel nut, observe the highest reading while the gear is turned through the center position. It should be 4–10 inch lbs.
4. If necessary repeat adjust the preload with the adjuster screw. Tighten the locknut to 22 ft. lbs.

REMOVAL AND INSTALLATION

1. Raise and support the front end on jackstands.
2. Set the front wheels in the straight-ahead position.
3. Disconnect the flexible coupling shield.
4. Remove the attaching nut and remove the adapter.
5. Remove the flexible coupling pinch bolt.
6. Mark the relationship of the pitman arm to the pitman shaft.
7. Remove the pitman shaft nut and then remove the pitman arm from the pitman shaft, using a puller.
8. Remove the steering gear to frame bolts and remove the gear assembly.

To install:

9. Place the steering gear in position, guiding the wormshaft into the flexible coupling.
10. Install the steering gear to frame bolts and torque to 100 ft. lbs.

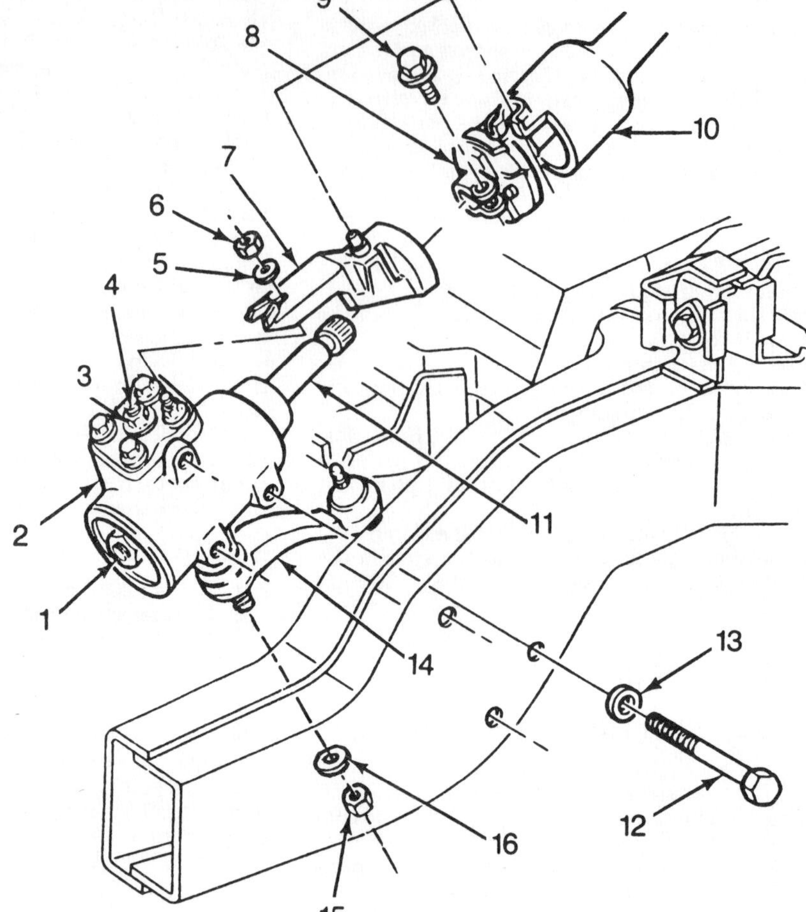

Manual steering gear – C/K series

CAUTION

All suspension and steering fasteners are important attaching parts in that they could affect the performance of vital components and systems, and/or could result in major repair expense. They must be replaced with one of the same part number or with an equivalent part if replacement becomes necessary. Do not use a replacement part of lesser quality or substitute design. Torque values must be used as specified during reassembly to assure proper retention of these parts. Observe all nut and bolt torque specifications.

11. Install the flexible coupling pinch bolt. The bolt must pass through the cutout in the wormshaft. Torque the pinch bolt to 22 ft. lbs.
12. Install the adapter on the gear box. Torque the nut to 5 inch lbs.
13. Connect the flexible coupling shield.
14. Install the pitman arm onto the pitman shaft, lining up the marks made at removal. Install the pitman shaft nut and torque it to 185 ft. lbs.

PITMAN SHAFT SEAL REPLACEMENT

It is possible to replace the seal without removing the gear box from the truck.

1. Raise and support the front end on jackstands.
2. Remove the pitman arm from the steering shaft.
3. Rotate the steering wheel lock-to-lock, counting the exact number of turns and return the wheel exactly ½ that many to center the gear box. The flat on the wormshaft should be at the 12 o'clock position.
4. Remove the side cover bolts.
5. Remove the pitman shaft/side cover assembly from the gear box.

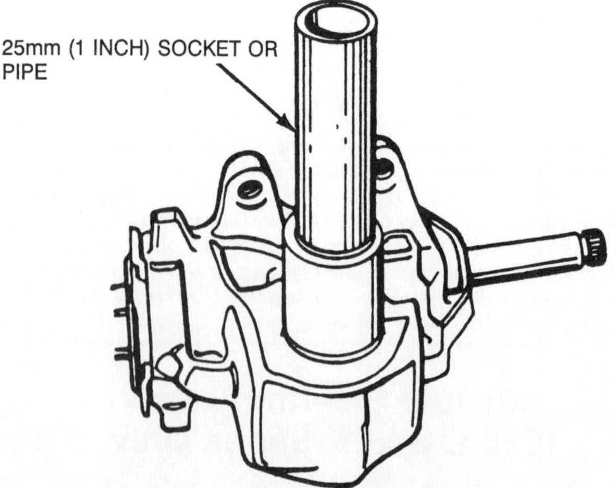

Pitman shaft seal replacement

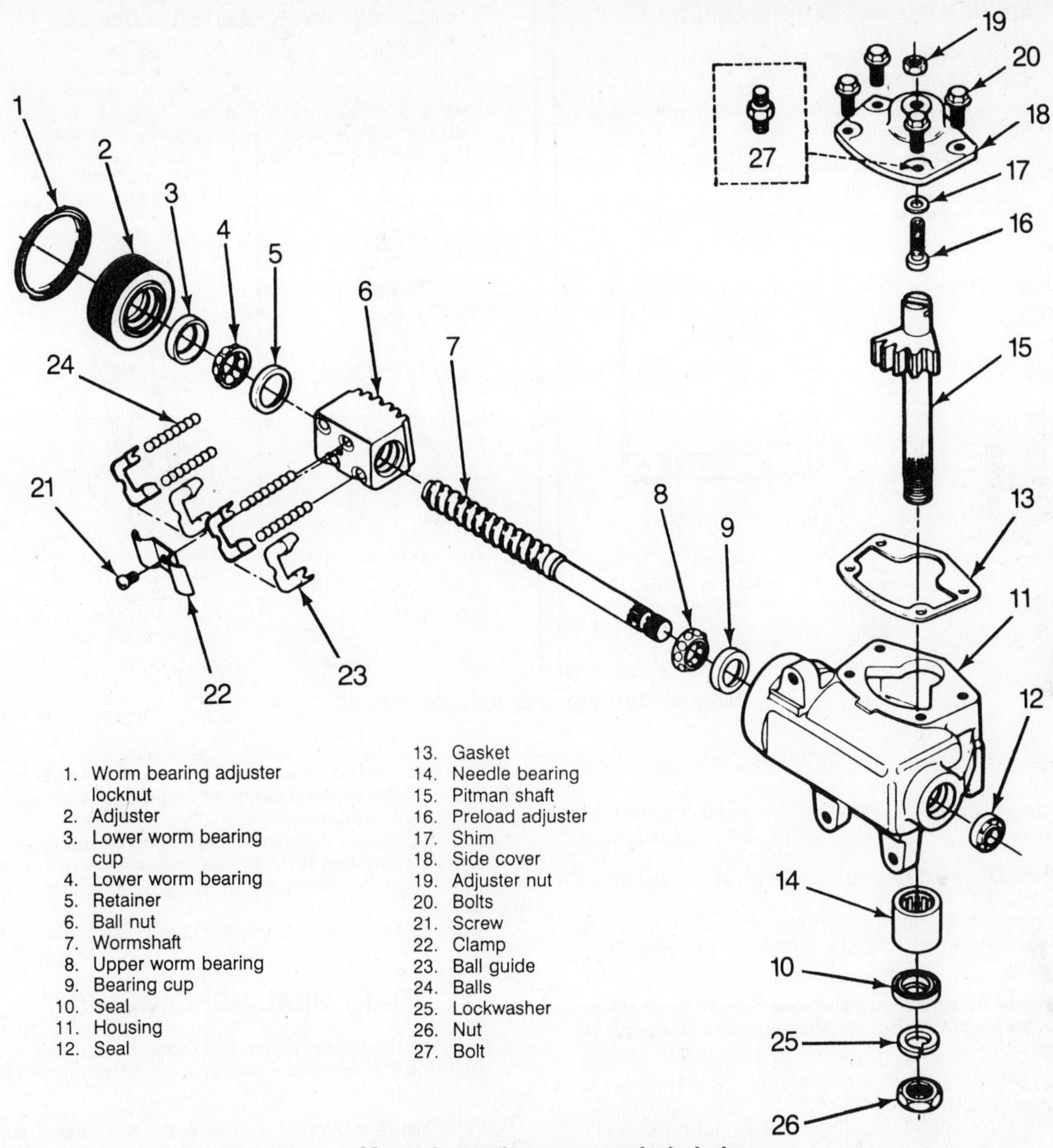

Manual steering gear exploded view

6. Using a small prybar, pry out the seal from the gear box. Be careful to avoid damage to the seal bore.

7. Remove the adjusting screw locknut, remove the pitman shaft from the side cover and turn the adjusting screw fully counterclockwise.

To install:

CAUTION

All suspension and steering fasteners are important attaching parts in that they could affect the performance of vital components and systems, and/or could result in major repair expense. They must be replaced with one of the same part number or with an equivalent part if replacement becomes necessary. Do not use a replacement part of lesser quality or substitute design. Torque values must be used as specified during reassembly to assure proper retention of these parts. Observe all nut and bolt torque specifications.

8. Coat the new seal with steering gear lubricant.

9. Position the seal in its bore and tap it into place using a 1 in. pipe or socket.

10. Place the pitman shaft in the gear box so that the center tooth of the pitman sgaft sector enters the center tooth space of the ball nut.

11. Fill the gear housing with steering gear lubricant.

12. Place a new gasket on the housing and install the side cover onto the adjuster screw. Reach through the threaded hole in the side cover and turn the adjuster screw with a screwdriver, counterclockwise, until it bottoms and turns back in ¼ turn.

13. Install the side cover bolts. Torque them to 33 ft. lbs.

14. Install the locknut and perform the gear adjustment sequence outlined above.

15. Tighten the locknut to 22 ft. lbs.

16. Install the pitman arm.

DISASSEMBLY

1. Place the steering gear in a vise, clamping onto one of the

ADJUST WORM BEARING PRELOAD

1 Tighten worm bearing adjuster until it bottoms then loosen one-quarter turn

2 Carefully turn the wormshaft all the way to end of travel then turn back one-half turn

3 Tighten adjuster plug until torque wrench reads 0.6 to 1.0 N m (5 to 8 in. lbs.)

4. Tighten locknut using punch against edge of slot.

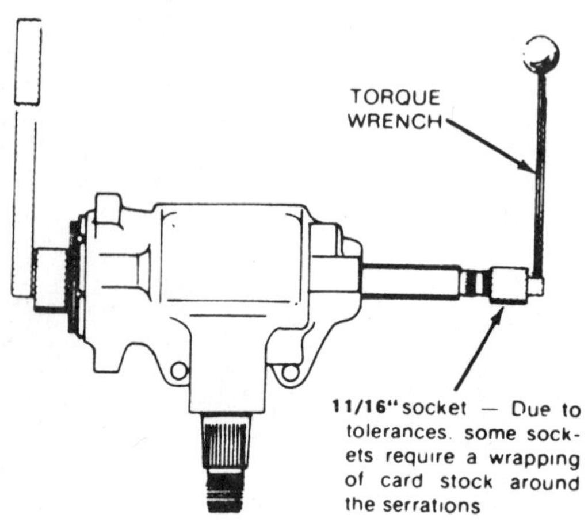
TORQUE
WRENCH
11/16" socket — Due to tolerances, some sockets require a wrapping of card stock around the serrations

ADJUST "OVER CENTER" PRELOAD

A Back off preload adjuster until it stops, then turn it in one full turn

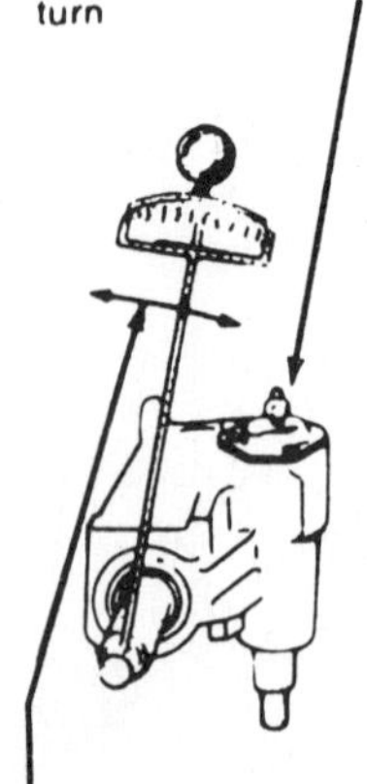

With gear at center of travel, check torque to turn stub shaft (reading #1)

B Turn adjuster in until torque to turn stub shaft is 0.5 to 1.2 N m (4 to 10 in. lbs.) more than reading #1

Torque adjuster lock nut to 34 N m (25 ft lbs.) Prevent adjuster screw from turning while torqueing lock nut

Manual steering gear adjustments

mounting tabs. The wormshaft should be in a horizontal position.

2. Rotate the wormshaft from stop to stop and count the total number of turns. Turn back exactly halfway, placing the gear on center.

3. Remove the three self locking bolts which attach the sector cover to the housing.

4. Using a plastic hammer, tap lightly on the end of the sector shaft and lift the sector cover and sector shaft assembly from the gear housing.

NOTE: It may be necessary to turn the wormshaft by hand until the sector will pass through the opening in the housing.

5. Remove the locknut from the adjuster plug and remove the adjuster plug assembly.

6. Pull the wormshaft and ball nut an assembly from the housing.

NOTE: Damage may be done to the ends of the ball guides if the ball nut is allowed to rotate to the end of the worm.

7. Remove the worm shaft upper bearing from inside the gear housing.

8. Pry the wormshaft lower bearing retainer from the adjuster plug housing and remove the bearing.

9. Remove the locknut from the lash adjuster screw in the sector cover. Turn the lash adjuster screw clockwise and remove it from the sector cover. Slide the adjuster screw and shim out of the slot in the end of the sector shaft.

10. Pry out and discard both the sector shaft and wormshaft seals.

INSPECTION

1. Wash all parts in cleaning solvent and blow dry with an air hose.

2. Use a magnifying glass and inspect the bearings and bearing caps for signs of indentation, or chipping. Replace any parts that show signs of damage.

3. Check the fit of the sector shaft in the bushings in the sector cover and housing. If these bushings are worn, a new sector cover and bushing assembly or housing bushing should be installed.

4. Check steering gear wormshaft assembly for being bent or damaged.

SHAFT SEAL REPLACEMENT

1. Remove the old seal from the pump body.

2. Install the new seal by pressing the outer diameter of the seal with a suitable size socket.

NOTE: Make sure the socket is large enough to avoid damaging the external lip of the seal.

SECTOR SHAFT BUSHING REPLACEMENT

1. Place the steering gear housing in an arbor press.

2. Press the sector shaft bushing from the housing.

NOTE: Service bushings are bored to size and require no further reaming.

SECTOR COVER BUSHING REPLACEMENT

The sector cover bushing is not serviced separately. The entire sector cover assembly including the bushing must be replaced as a unit.

BALL NUT SERVICE

If there is any indication of binding or tightness when the ball

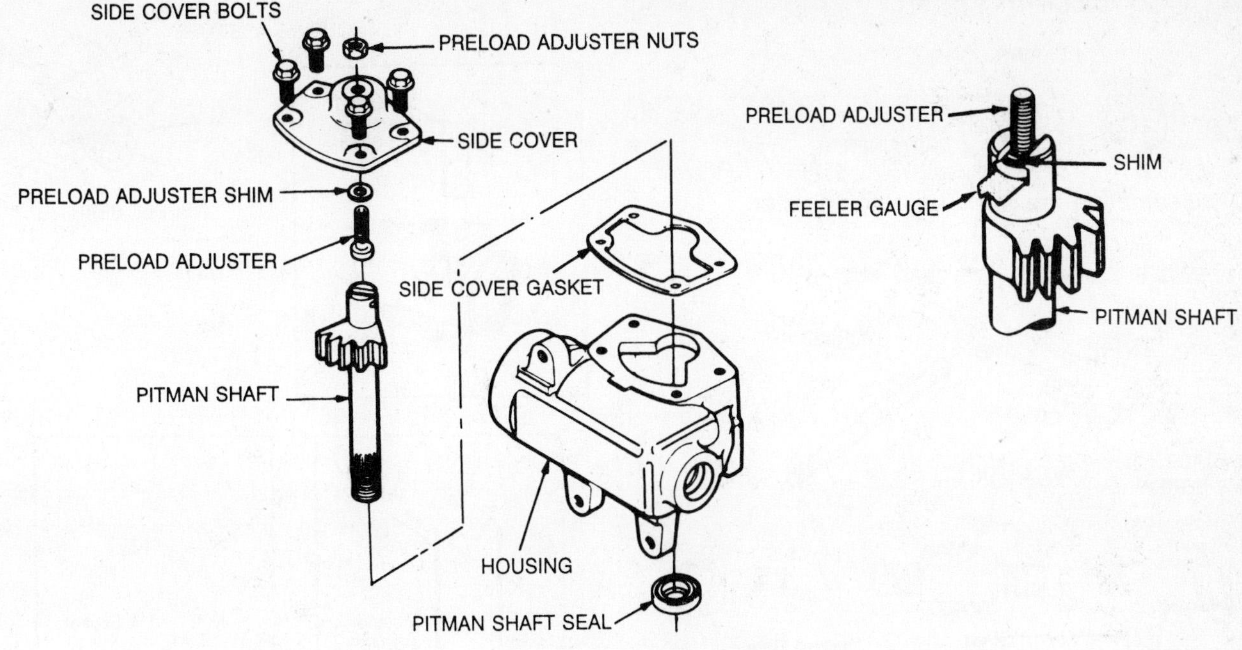

Side cover installation

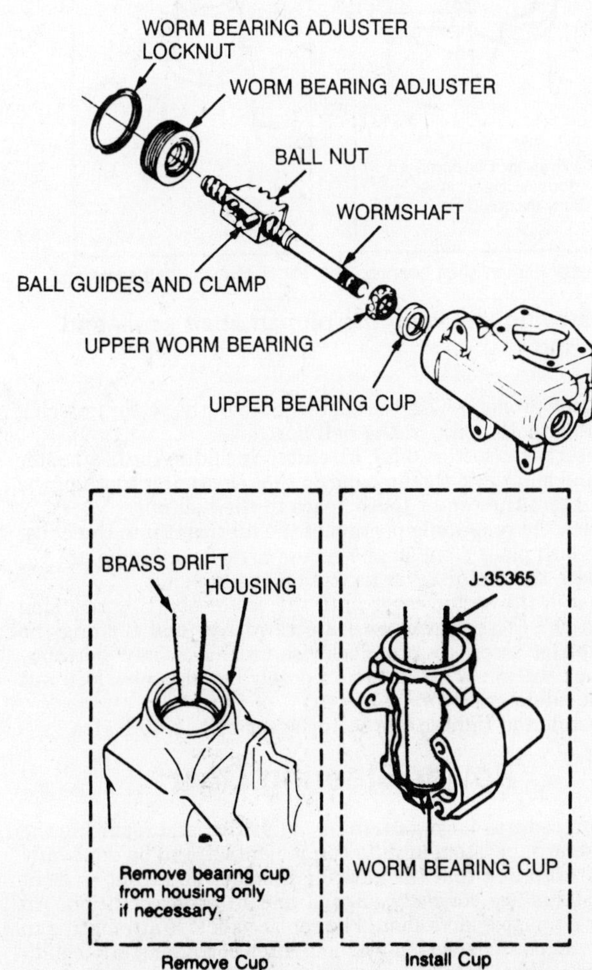

Removing/installing wormshaft and ball nut

nut is rotated on the worm the unit should be disassembled, cleaned and inspected as follows:

Ball Nut Disassembly

1. Remove the screws and clamp retaining the ball guides in the ball nut. Pull the guides out of the ball nut.
2. Turn the ball nut upside down and rotate the wormshaft back and forth until all the balls have dropped out of the ball nut. The ball nut can now be pulled endwise off the worm.
3. Wash all parts in solvent and dry them with air. Use a magnifying glass and inspect the worm and nut grooves and the surface of all balls for signs of indentation. Check all ball guides for damage at the ends. Replace any damaged parts.

Ball Nut Assembly

1. Slip the ball nut over the worm with the ball guide holes up and the shallow end of the ball nut teeth to the left from the steering wheel position. Sight through the ball guide to align the grooves in the worm.
2. Place two ball guide halves together and insert them in the upper circuit in the ball nut. Place the two remaining guides together and insert them in the lower circuit.
3. Count out 25 balls and place them in a suitable container. This is the proper number of balls for one circuit.
4. Load the 25 balls into one of the guide holes while turning the wormshaft gradually away from that hole.
5. Fill the remaining ball circuit in the same manner.
6. Assemble the ball guide clamp to the ball nut and tighten the screws to 18–24 inch lbs.
7. Check the assembly by rotating the ball nut on the worm to see that it moves freely.

NOTE: Do not rotate the ball nut to the end of the worm threads as this may damage the ball guides.

ASSEMBLY

1. Coat the threads of the adjuster plug, sector cover bolts and lash adjuster with a non-drying oil resistant sealing compound.

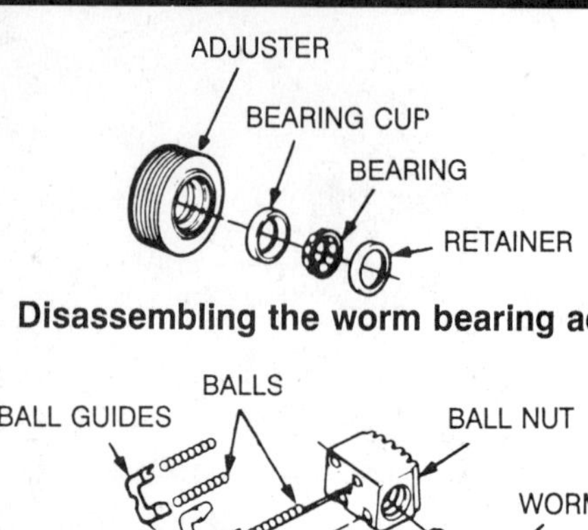

Disassembling the worm bearing adjuster

Disassembling wormshaft and ball nut

NOTE: Do not apply compound to the female threads. Use extreme care when applying compound to the bearing adjuster so that it does not come in contact with the wormshaft bearing.

2. Place the steering gear housing in a vise with the wormshaft bore horizontal and the sector cover opening up.
3. Make sure that all seals, bushings and bearing cups are installed in the gear housing and that the ball nut is installed on the wormshaft.
4. Slip the wormshaft upper bearing assembly over the wormshaft and insert the wormshaft and ball nut assembly into the housing, feeding the end of the shaft through the upper ball bearing cup and seal.
5. Place the wormshaft lower bearing assembly in the adjuster plug bearing cup and press the stamped retainer into place with a suitable size socket.
6. Install the adjuster plug and locknut into the lower end of the housing while carefully guiding the end of the wormshaft into the bearing until nearly all end play has been removed from the wormshaft.
7. Position the lash adjuster including the shim in the slotted end of the sector shaft.

NOTE: End clearance should not be greater than 0.002 in. (0.051mm). If the end clearance is greater than 0.002 in. (0.051mm), a shim package is available with thicknesses of 0.063 in. (1.6mm), 0.065 in. (1.65mm), 0.067 in. (1.70mm), 0.069 (1.75mm).

8. Lubricate the steering gear with 11 oz. (312g) of steering gear grease. Rotate the wormshaft until the ball nut is at the other end of its travel and then pack as much new lubricant into the housing as possible without losing out the sector shaft opening. Rotate the wormshaft until the ball nut is at the other end of its travel and pack as much lubricant into the opposite end as possible.
9. Rotate the wormshaft until the ball nut is in the center of travel. This is to make sure that the sector shaft and ball nut will engage properly with the center tooth of the sector entering the center tooth space in the ball nut.

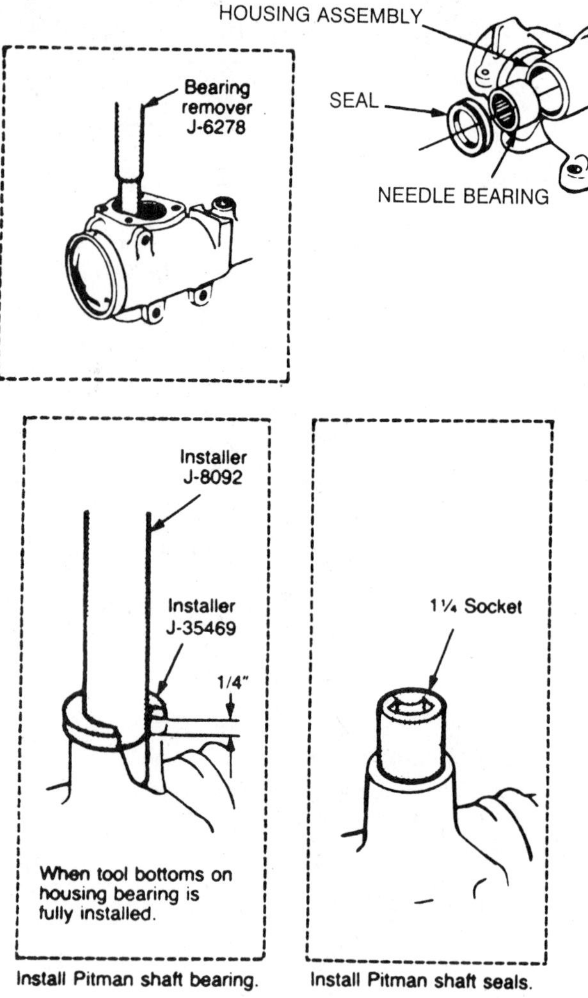

Removing/installing the pitman shaft seals and bearing

10. Insert the sector shaft assembly including lash adjuster screw and shim into the housing so that the center tooth of the sector enters the center tooth space in the ball nut.
11. Pack the remaining portion of the lubricant into the housing and also place some in the sector cover bushing hole.
12. Place the sector cover gasket on the housing.
13. Install the sector cover onto the sector shaft by reaching through the sector cover with a screwdriver and turning the lash adjuster screw counterclockwise until the screw bottoms, then back the screw off ½ turn. Loosely install a new lock nut onto the adjuster screw.
14. Install and tighten the sector cover bolt to 30 ft. lbs.

Power Steering Gear

The procedures for maintaining, adjusting, and repairing the power steering system and its components are to be done only after determining that the steering linkages and front suspension systems are correctly aligned and in good condition. All worn or damaged parts should be replaced before attempting to service the power steering system. After correcting any condition that could affect the power steering, do the preliminary test of the steering system components.

PRELIMINARY TESTS

Proper lubrication of the steering linkage and the front suspension components is very important for the proper operation of the steering systems of trucks equipped with power steering. Most all power steering systems use the same lubricant in the steering gear box as in the power steering pump reservoir, and the fluid level is maintained at the pump reservoir.

With power cylinder assist power steering, the steering gear is of the standard mechanical type and the lubricating oil is self contained within the gear box and the level is maintained by the removal of a filler plug on the gear box housing. The control valve assembly is mounted on the gear box and is lubricated by power steering oil from the power steering pump reservoir, where the level is maintained.

REMOVAL AND INSTALLATION

R and V Series

1. Raise and support the front end on jackstands.
2. Set the front wheels in the straight ahead position.
3. Disconnect the battery ground cable.
4. Place a drain pan under the gear and disconnect the fluid lines. Cap the openings.
5. Remove the flexible coupling pinch bolt.
6. Mark the relationship of the pitman arm to the pitman shaft.
7. Remove the pitman shaft nut and then remove the pitman arm from the pitman shaft, using a puller.
8. Remove the steering gear to frame bolts and remove the gear assembly.

To install:

CAUTION

All suspension and steering fasteners are important attaching parts in that they could affect the performance of vital components and systems, and/or could result in major repair expense. They must be replaced with one of the same part number or with an equivalent part if replacement becomes necessary. Do not use a replacement part of lesser quality or substitute design. Torque values must be used as specified during reassembly to assure proper retention of these parts. Observe all nut and bolt torque specifications.

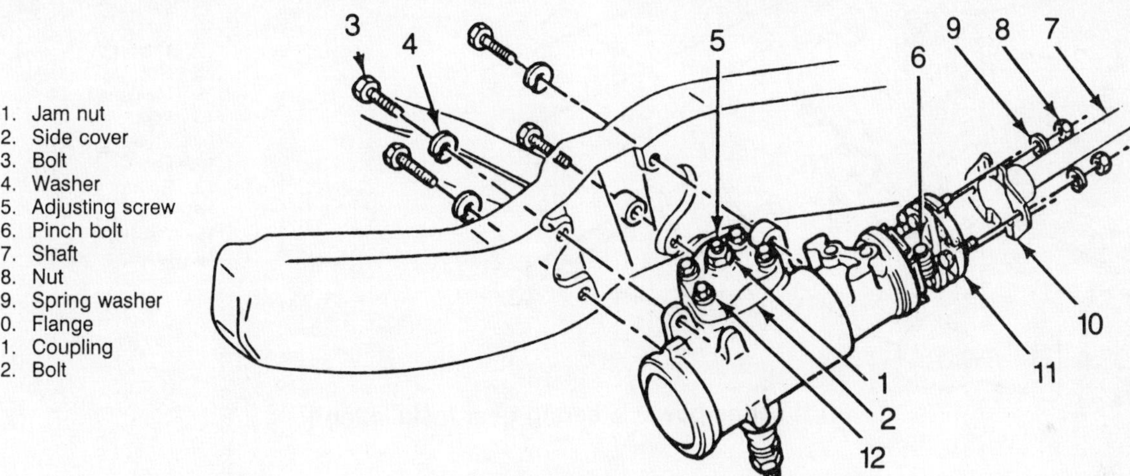

R series steering gear installation

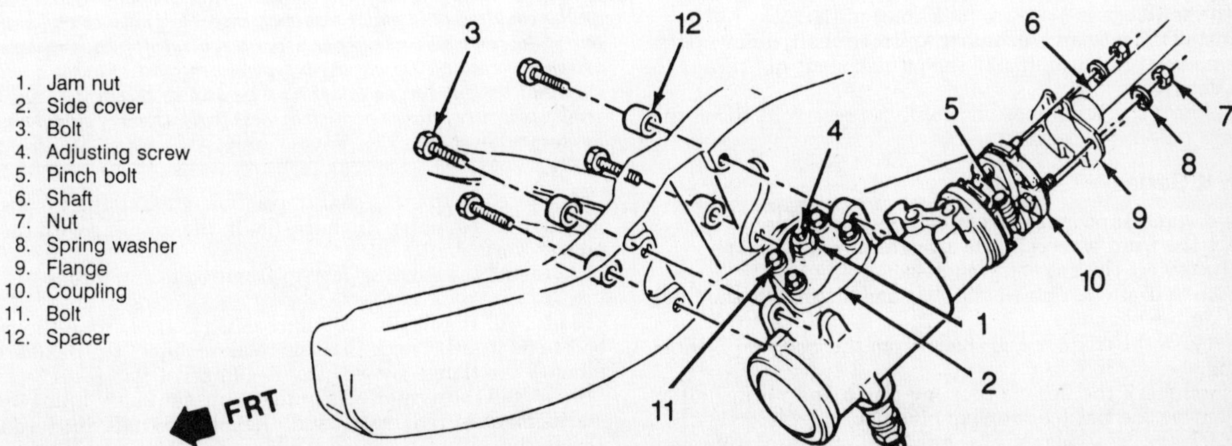

V series steering gear installation

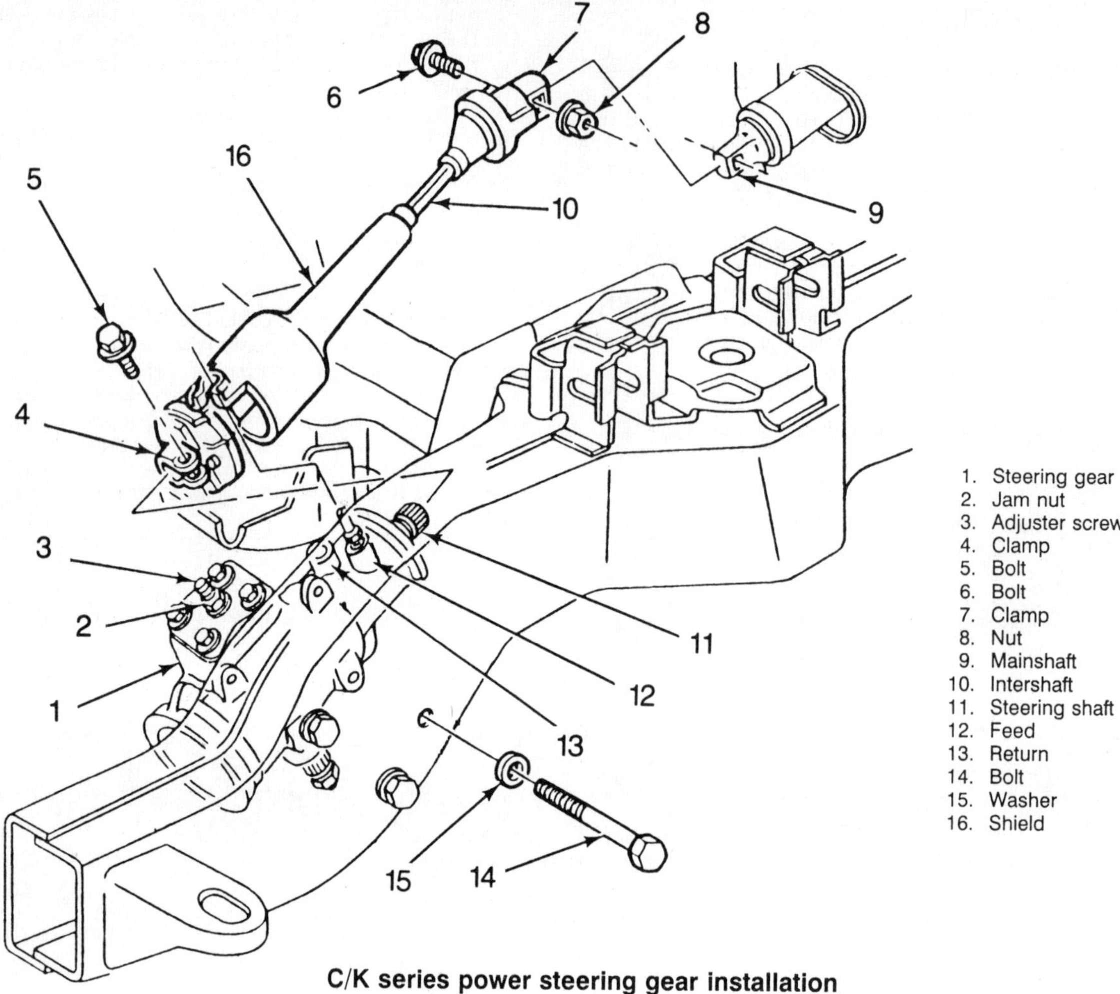

C/K series power steering gear installation

9. Place the steering gear in position, guiding the wormshaft into flexible coupling. Align the flat in the coupling with the flat on the wormshaft.
10. Install the steering gear to frame bolts and torque to 66 ft. lbs.
11. Install the flexible coupling pinch bolt. Torque the pinch bolt to 30 ft. lbs. Check that the relationship of the flexible coupling to the flange is 1/4–3/4 in. (6–19mm) of flat.
12. Install the pitman arm onto the pitman shaft, lining up the marks made at removal. Install the pitman shaft nut torque to 185 ft. lbs.
13. Connect the fluid lines and refill the reservoir. Bleed the system.

C and K Series

1. Raise and support the front end on jackstands.
2. Set the front wheels in the straight ahead position.
3. Disconnect the battery ground cable.
4. Place a drain pan under the gear and disconnect the fluid lines. Cap the openings.
5. Remove the adapter and shield from the gear and flexible coupling.
6. Matchmark the flexible coupling clamp and wormshaft.
7. Remove the flexible coupling pinch bolt.
8. Mark the relationship of the pitman arm to the pitman shaft.
9. Remove the pitman shaft nut and then remove the pitman arm from the pitman shaft, using a puller.
10. Remove the steering gear to frame bolts and remove the gear assembly.

To install:

CAUTION

All suspension and steering fasteners are important attaching parts in that they could affect the performance of vital components and systems, and/or could result in major repair expense. They must be replaced with one of the same part number or with an equivalent part if replacement becomes necessary. Do not use a replacement part of lesser quality or substitute design. Torque values must be used as specified during reassembly to assure proper retention of these parts. Observe all nut and bolt torque specifications.

11. Place the steering gear in position, guiding the wormshaft into flexible coupling. Align the flat in the coupling with the flat on the wormshaft.
12. Install the steering gear-to-frame bolts and torque to 69 ft. lbs.
13. Install the flexible coupling pinch bolt. Torque the pinch bolt to 30 ft. lbs. Check that the relationship of the flexible coupling to the flange is 1/4–3/4 in. (6–19mm) of flat.
14. Install the pitman arm onto the pitman shaft, lining up the marks made at removal. Install the pitman shaft nut torque to 185 ft. lbs.
15. Install the adapter and shield.
16. Connect the fluid lines and refill the reservoir. Bleed the system.

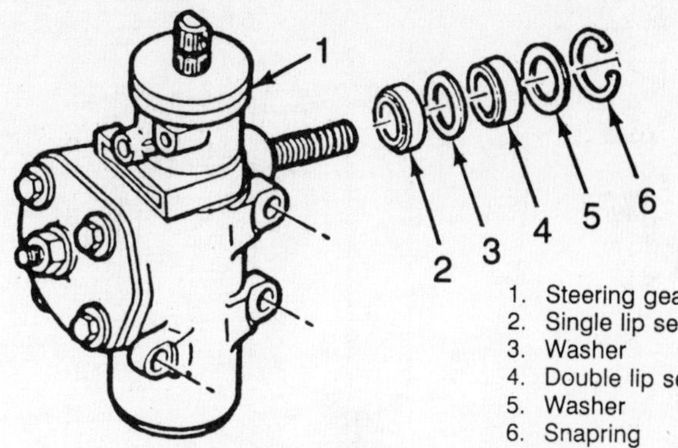

Pitman shaft seal – 1st design

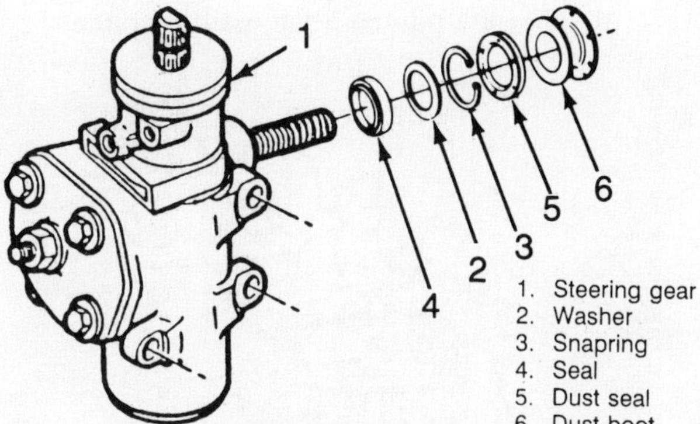

Pitman shaft seal – 2nd design

PITMAN SHAFT SEAL REPLACEMENT

It is possible to replace the seal with the gear box in the truck.

First Design

1. Remove the pitman arm as described above.
2. Place a drain pan under the gear and disconnect the fluid lines. Cap all openings.
3. Using internal snapring pliers, remove the snapring from the shaft.
4. Start the engine and turn the steering wheel to the full left position, holding it there for about 2 seconds at a time until the pitman shaft seals and washers are forced out of the housing. Turn the engine of
5. Remove the seals and washers from the shaft.

To install:

6. Check the seal bore for burrs and remove any that are found.
7. Clean the seal bore area thoroughly.
8. Coat the new seals with power steering fluid.
9. Cover the pitman shaft with a layer of plastic tape to protect the seals.
10. Install the single lip seal and washer using a seal driver such as J–6219. Install it just far enough to allow installation of the other parts. DON'T LET IT BOTTOM ON THE END OF THE COUNTERBORE!
11. Install the double lip seal and washer with the tool.
12. Install the snapring.
13. Install the pitman arm.
14. Connect the fluid lines.
15. Refill and bleed the system.

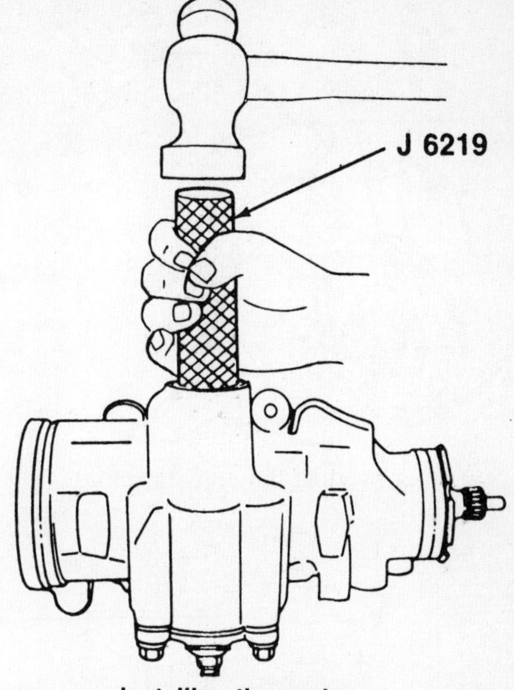

Installing the seals

Second Design

1. Raise and support the front end on jackstands.
2. Remove the pitman arm as described above.
3. Remove the dust boot from the pitman shaft.
4. Remove the dust seal.
5. Remove the internal snapring.
6. Place a drain pan under the gear box.
7. Start the engine and turn the steering wheel from stop-to-stop, bouncing the steering wheel off of the stops, until the seal is forced from the gear box. Shut off the engine.
8. Remove the washer and seal from the shaft.

To install:

9. Thoroughly clean the seal bore and remove any burrs.
10. Cover the pitman shaft with a layer of plastic tape to protect the seal.
11. Coat the new seal with power steering fluid.
12. Install the seal and washer using a seal driver such as J–6219. The seal should be driven in just far enough to install the snapring.
13. Turn the steering wheel from stop-to-stop, counting the total number of turns. Return the wheel ½ that many turns to center the gear shaft.
14. Install the dust seal and boot.
15. Install the pitman arm.
16. Refill and bleed the system.

ADJUSTMENTS

For proper adjustment, remove the gear from the truck, drain all the fluid from the gear and place the gear in a vise.

It is important that the adjustments be made in the order given.

Worm Bearing Preload

R AND V SERIES

1. Remove the adjuster plug locknut.
2. Turn the adjuster plug in clockwise until firmly bottomed. Then, tighten it to 20 ft. lbs.

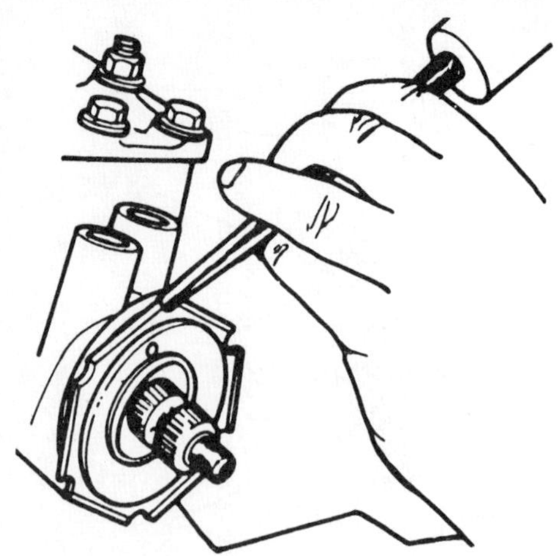
Loosening the adjuster plug

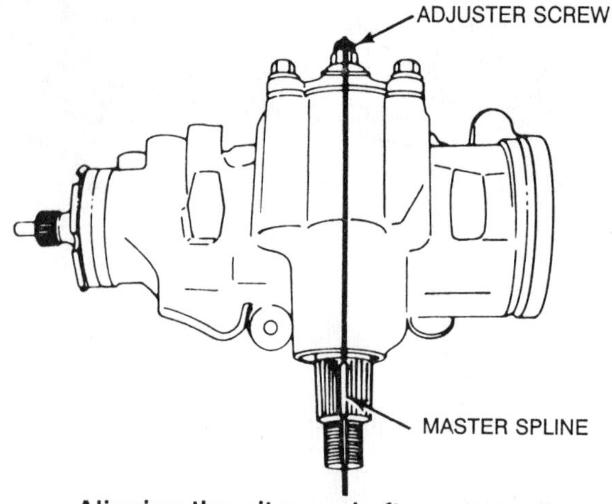

Aligning the pitman shaft master spline

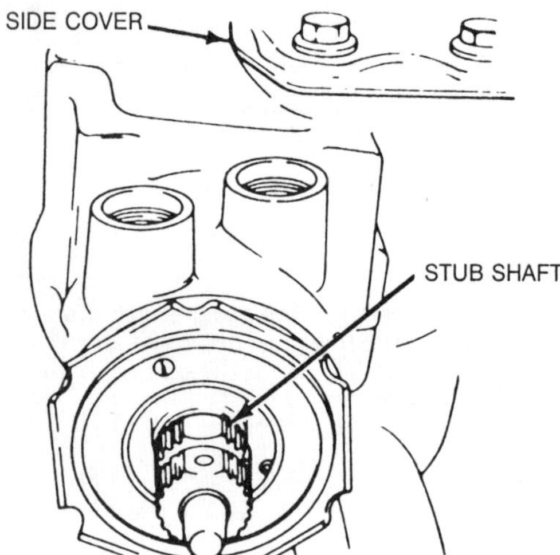

Aligning the stub shaft

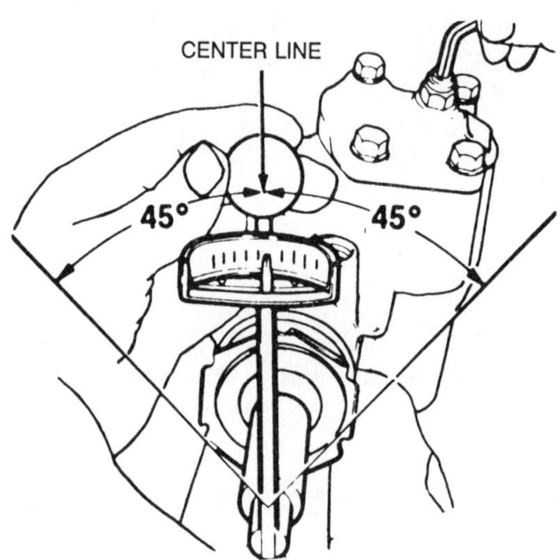

Checking over-center rotational torque

3. Place an index mark on the gear housing in line with one of the holes in the adjuster plug.
4. Measure counterclockwise from the mark about 1/4 inch and make another mark on the housing.
5. Rotate the adjuster plug counterclockwise until the hole is aligned with the second mark.
6. Install the locknut. Hold the plug and tighten the locknut to 81 ft. lbs.
7. Place an inch pound torque wrench and 12-point deep socket on the stub shaft and measure the stub shaft rotating torque, starting with the torque wrench handle in a vertical position to a point 1/4 turn to either side. Note your reading. The proper torque should be 4–10 inch lbs. If the reading is incorrect, whether your adjustment was done incorrectly or there is gear damage.

C AND K SERIES

1. Remove the adjuster plug locknut.
2. Turn the adjuster plug in clockwise until firmly bottomed. Then, tighten it to 20 ft. lbs.
3. Place an index mark on the gear housing in line with one of the holes in the adjuster plug.
4. Measure counterclockwise from the mark about 1/2 inch and make another mark on the housing.
5. Rotate the adjuster plug counterclockwise until the hole is aligned with the second mark.
6. Install the locknut. Hold the plug and tighten the locknut to 32 ft. lbs.

Overcenter Preload

R and V Series

1. Loosen the locknut and turn the pitman shaft adjuster screw counterclockwise until it is all the way out. Then, turn it in 1/2 turn.
2. Rotate the stub shaft from stop to stop, counting the total number of turns, then turn it back 1/2 that number to center the gear.
3. Place an inch-pound torque wrench in a vertical position on the stub shaft and measure the torque necessary to rotate the shaft to a point 45° to either side of center. Record the highest reading.

On gears with less than 400 miles, the reading should be 6–10 inch lbs. higher than the worm bearing preload torque previously recorded, but not to exceed 18 inch lbs..

On gears with more than 400 miles, the reading should be 4–5 inch lbs. higher, but not to exceed 14 inch lbs.

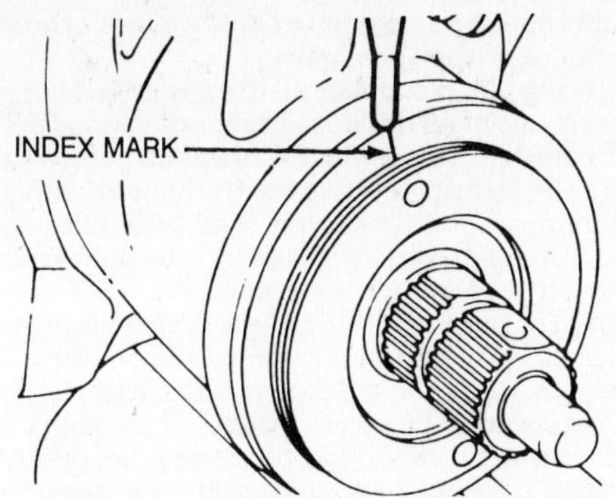

Marking housing even with adjuster plug

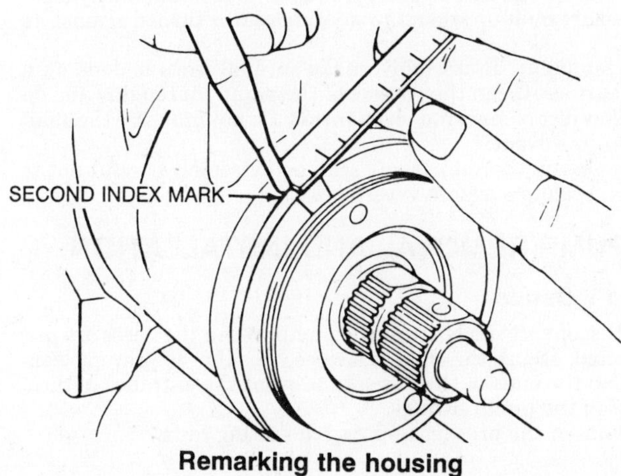

Remarking the housing

4. If necessary, adjust the reading by turning the adjuster screw.
5. When the adjustment is made, hold the screw and tighten the locknut to 35 ft. lbs.
6. Install the gear.

C and K Series

1. Rotate the stub shaft from stop to stop, counting the total number of turns, then turn it back ½ that number to center the gear.
2. Loosen the locknut and turn the pitman shaft adjuster screw counterclockwise until it is all the way out. Then, turn it in 1 full turn.
3. Place an inch-pound torque wrench in a vertical position on the stub shaft and measure the torque necessary to rotate the shaft to a point 45° to either side of center. Record the highest reading.
4. Turn the adjuster plug in until the torque required to rotate the shaft is 6–10 inch lbs. higher than the previously recorded torque.
5. When the adjustment is made, hold the screw and tighten the locknut to 32 ft. lbs.

Power Steering Pump

AIR BLEEDING

Air bubbles in the power steering system must be removed from the fluid. Be sure the reservoir is filled to the proper level and the fluid is warmed up to operating temperature. Then, turn the steering wheel through its full travel three or four times until all the air bubbles are removed. Do not hold the steering wheel against its stops. Recheck the fluid level.

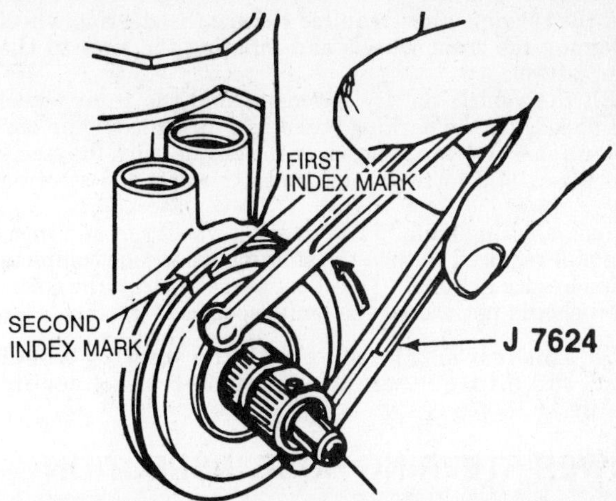

Aligning the adjuster plug with the second mark

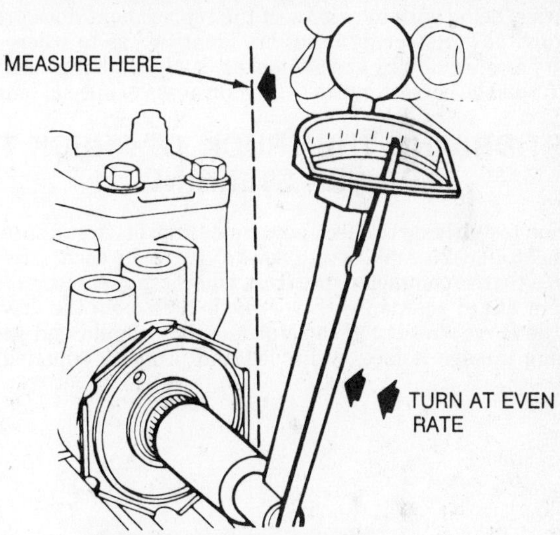

Checking rotational torque

FLUID LEVEL CHECK

1. Run the engine until the fluid is at the normal operating temperature. Then, turn the steering wheel through its full travel three or four times, and shut off the engine.
2. Check the fluid level in the steering reservoir. If the fluid level is low, add enough fluid to raise the level to the Full mark on the dipstick or filler tube.

PUMP BELT CHECK

Inspect the pump belt for cracks, glazing, or worn places. Using a belt tension gauge, check the belt tension for the proper range of adjustment. The amount of tension varies with the make of truck and the condition of the belt. New belts (those belts used less than 15 minutes) require a higher figure. The belt deflection method of adjustment may be used only if a belt tension gauge is not available. The belt should be adjusted for a deflection of ¼–⅜ in. (6–9mm).

Check all possible leakage points (hoses, power steering pump, or steering gear) for loss of fluid. Turn engine on and rotate the steering wheel from stop to stop several times. Tighten all loose fittings and replace any defective lines or valve seats.

Check the turning effort required to turn the steering wheel after aligning the front wheels and inflating the tires to the proper pressure.

1. With the vehicle on dry pavement and the front wheel straight ahead, set the parking brake and turn the engine on.
2. After a short warmup period for the engine, turn the steering wheel back and forth several times to warm the steering fluid.
3. Attach a spring scale to the steering wheel rim and measure the pull required to turn the steering wheel one complete revolution in each direction. The effort needed to turn the steering wheel should not exceed the limits specified.

NOTE: This test may be done with the steering wheel removed and a torque wrench applied on the steering wheel nut.

POWER STEERING HOSE INSPECTION

Inspect both the input and output hoses of the power steering pump for worn spots, cracks, or signs of leakage. Replace hose if defective, being sure to reconnect the replacement hose properly. Many power steering hoses are identified as to where they are to be connected by special means, such as fittings that will only fit on the correct pump fitting, or hoses of special lengths.

TEST DRIVING THE TRUCK TO CHECK THE POWER STEERING

When test driving to check power steering, drive at a speed between 15 and 20 mph. Make several turns in each direction. When a turn is completed, the front wheels should return to the straight ahead position with very little help from the driver.

If the front wheels fail to return as they should and yet the steering linkage is free, well oiled and properly adjusted, the trouble is probably due to misalignment of the power cylinder or improper adjustment of the spool valve.

The power steering pump supplies all the power assist used in power steering systems of all designs. There are various designs of pumps used by the truck manufacturers but all pumps supply power to operate the steering systems with the least effort. All power steering pumps have a reservoir tank built onto the oil pump. These pumps are driven by belt turned by pulleys on the engine, normally on the front of the crankshaft.

During operation of the engine at idle speed, there is provision for the power steering pump to supply more fluid pressure. During driving speeds or when the truck is moving straight ahead, less pressure is needed and the excess is relieved through a pressure relief and flow control valve. The pressure relief part of the valve is inside the flow control and is basically the same for all pumps. The flow control valve regulates, or controls, the constant flow of fluid from the pump as it varies with the demands of the steering gear. The pressure relief valve limits the hydraulic pressure built up when the steering gear is turned against its stops.

During pump disassembly, make sure all work is done on a clean surface. Clean the outside of the pump thoroughly and do not allow dirt of any kind to get inside. Do not immerse the shaft oil seal in solvent.

If replacing the rotor shaft seal, be extremely careful not to scratch sealing surfaces with tools.

PUMP REMOVAL AND INSTALLATION

R and V Series

1. Disconnect the hoses at the pump. When the hoses are disconnected, secure the ends in a raised position to prevent leakage. Cap the ends of the hoses to prevent the entrance of dirt.
2. Cap the pump fittings.
3. Loosen the bracket-to-pump mounting nuts.

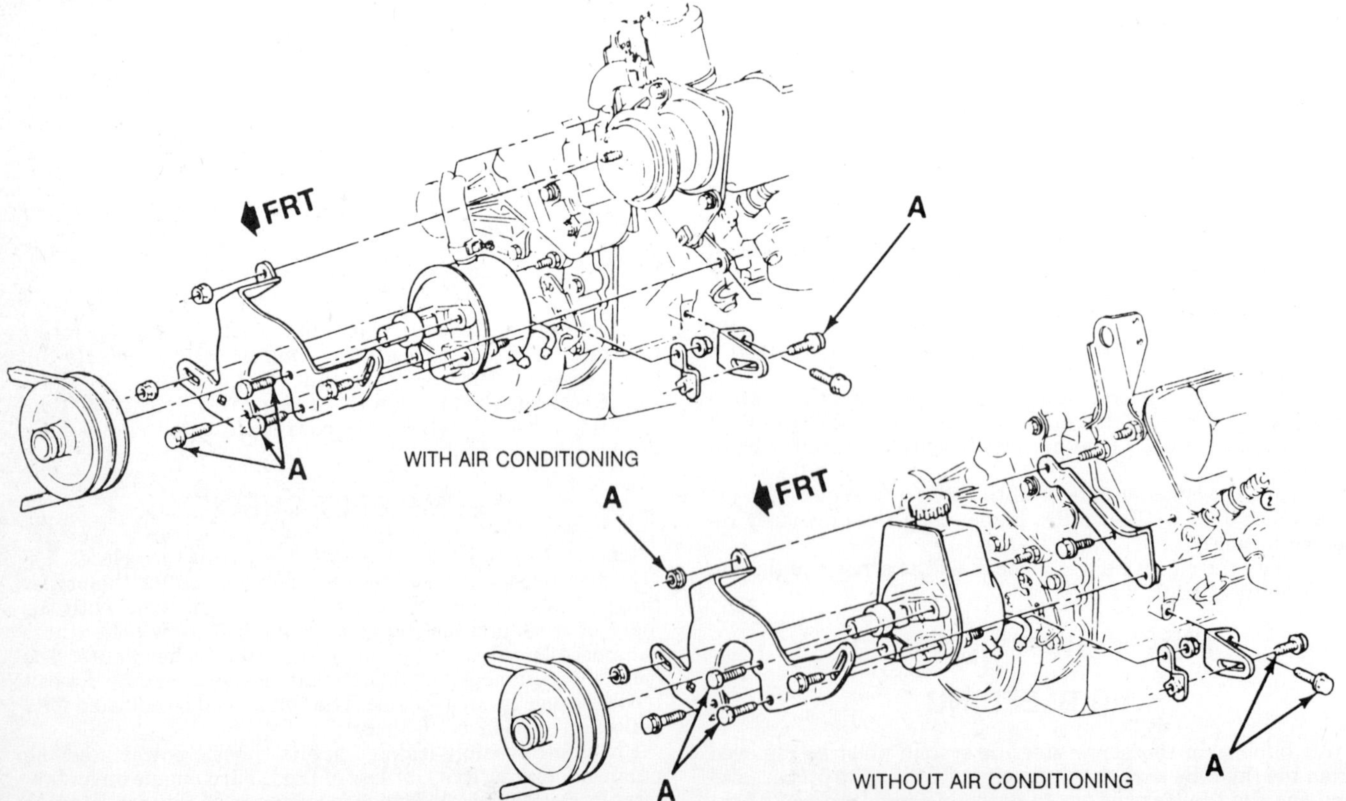

Power steering pump installation for R/V series with the 8-6.2L

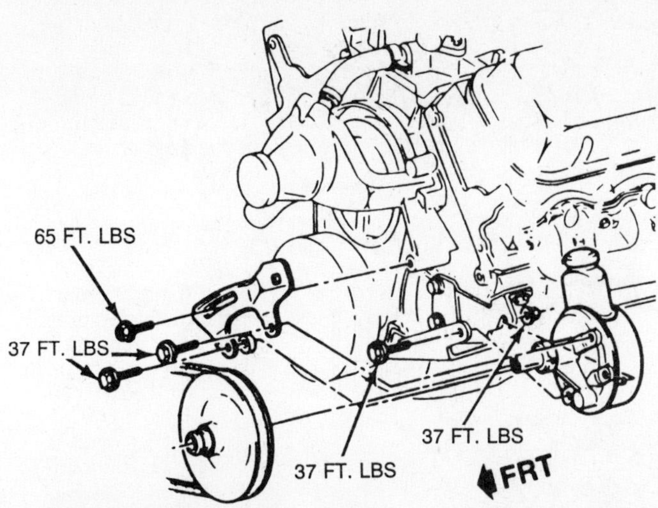

Power steering pump installation for R/V 20/2500 series with the 8-7.4L

4. Remove the pump drive belt.
5. Remove the bracket-to-pump bolts and remove the pump from the truck.
6. If a new pump is being installed, remove the pulley with a pulley puller such as J–25034–B. Install the pulley on the new pump with a forcing screw and washer.
6. Installation is the reverse of removal. Tighten all bolts and nuts securely. Fill the reservoir and bleed the pump by turning the pulley counterclockwise (as viewed from the front) until bubbles stop forming. Bleed the system as outlined following.

C and K Series

1. Disconnect the hoses at the pump. When the hoses are disconnected, secure the ends in a raised position to prevent leakage. Cap the ends of the hoses to prevent the entrance of dirt.
2. Cap the pump fittings.
3. Loosen the belt tensioner.
4. Remove the pump drive belt.
5. Remove the pulley with a pulley puller such as J–29785–A.
6. Remove the following fasteners:
   - 6–4.3L, 8–5.0L, 8–5.7L engines: front mounting bolts
   - 8–7.4L engine: rear brace
   - 8–6.2L diesel: front brace and rear mounting nuts
7. Lift out the pump.

To install:

8. Position the pump and install the braces and fasteners.
9. Observe the following torques:
   - 6–4.3L, 8–5.0L, 8–5.7L engines, front mounting bolts: 37 ft. lbs.
   - 8–7.4L engine, rear brace nut: 61 ft. lbs.; rear brace bolt: 24 ft. lbs.; mounting bolts: 37 ft. lbs.
   - 8–6.2L diesel, front brace: 30 ft. lbs.; rear mounting nuts: 17 ft. lbs.
10. Install the pulley with J–25033–B.
11. Remove the pump drive belt.
12. Install the hoses.
13. Fill and bleed the system.

BLEEDING THE HYDRAULIC SYSTEM

1. Fill the reservoir to the proper level and let the fluid remain undisturbed for at least 2 minutes.
2. Start the engine and run it for only about 2 seconds.
3. Add fluid as necessary.

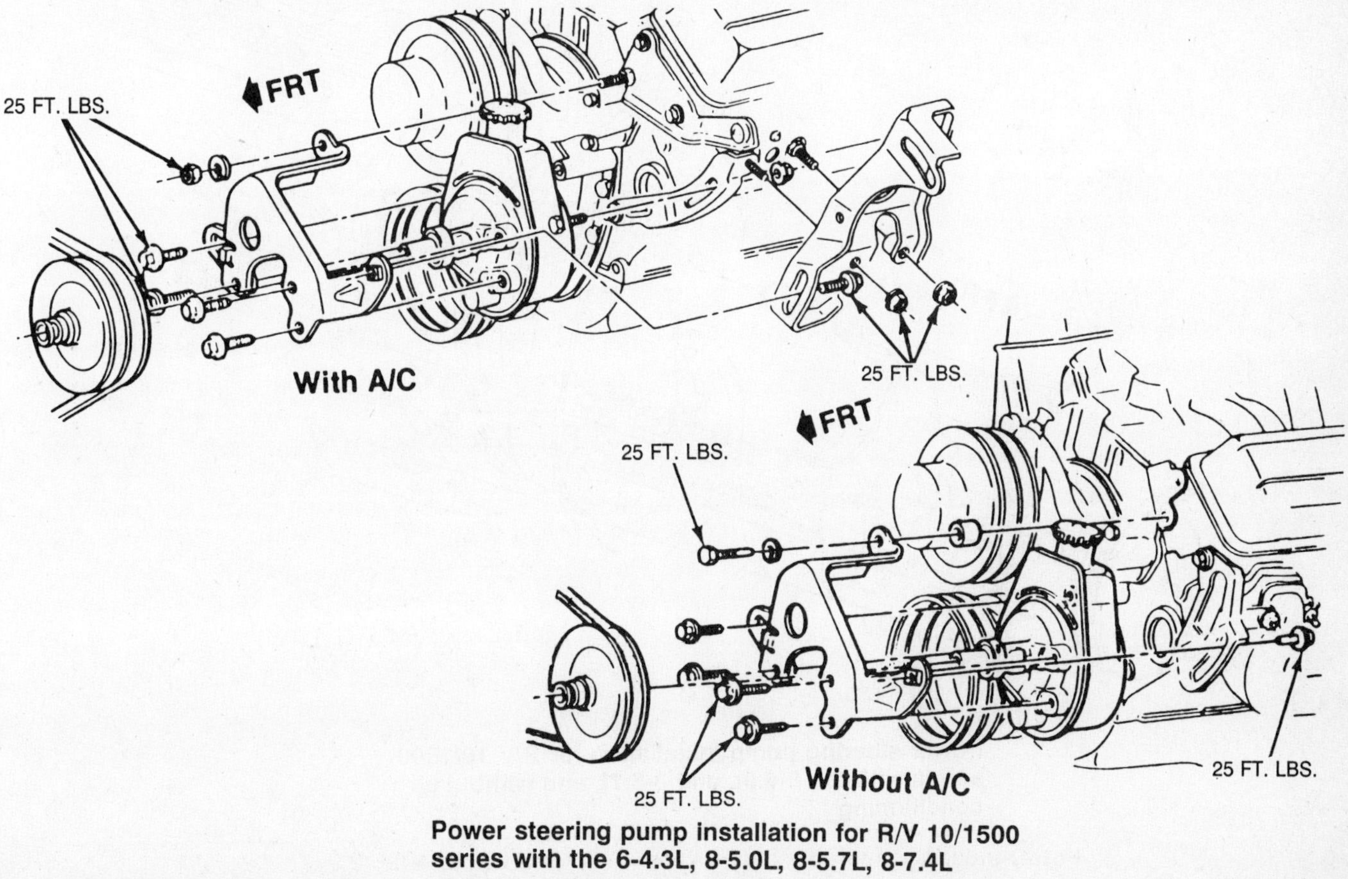

Power steering pump installation for R/V 10/1500 series with the 6-4.3L, 8-5.0L, 8-5.7L, 8-7.4L

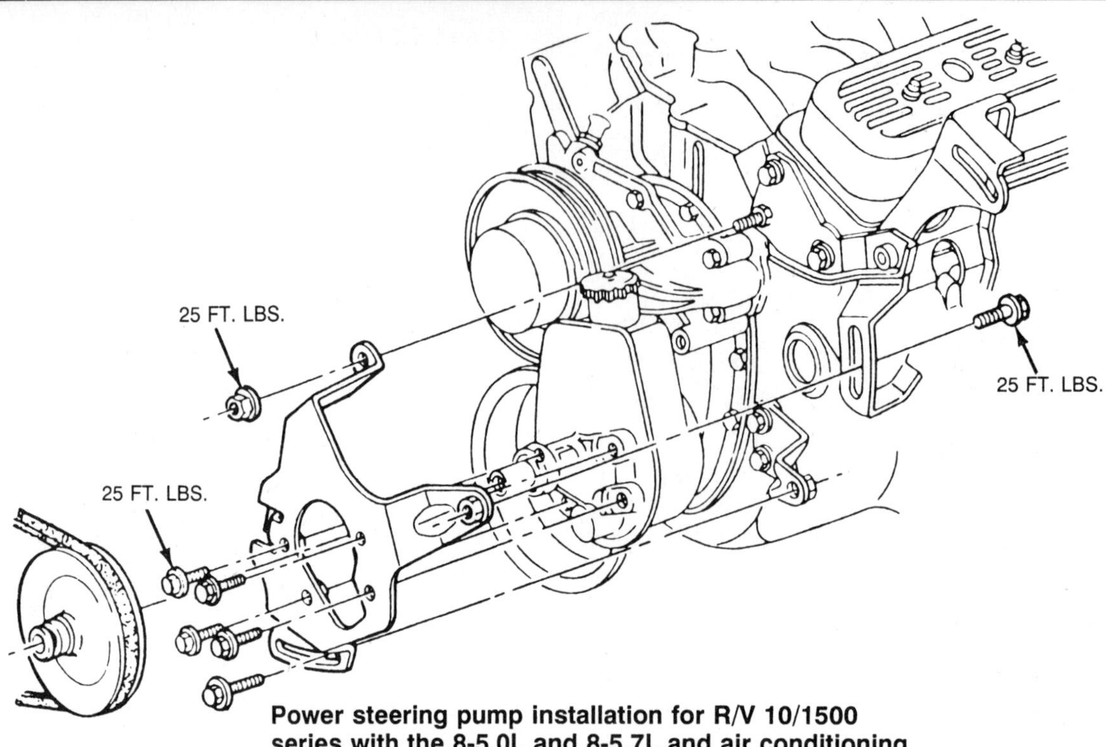

Power steering pump installation for R/V 10/1500 series with the 8-5.0L and 8-5.7L and air conditioning

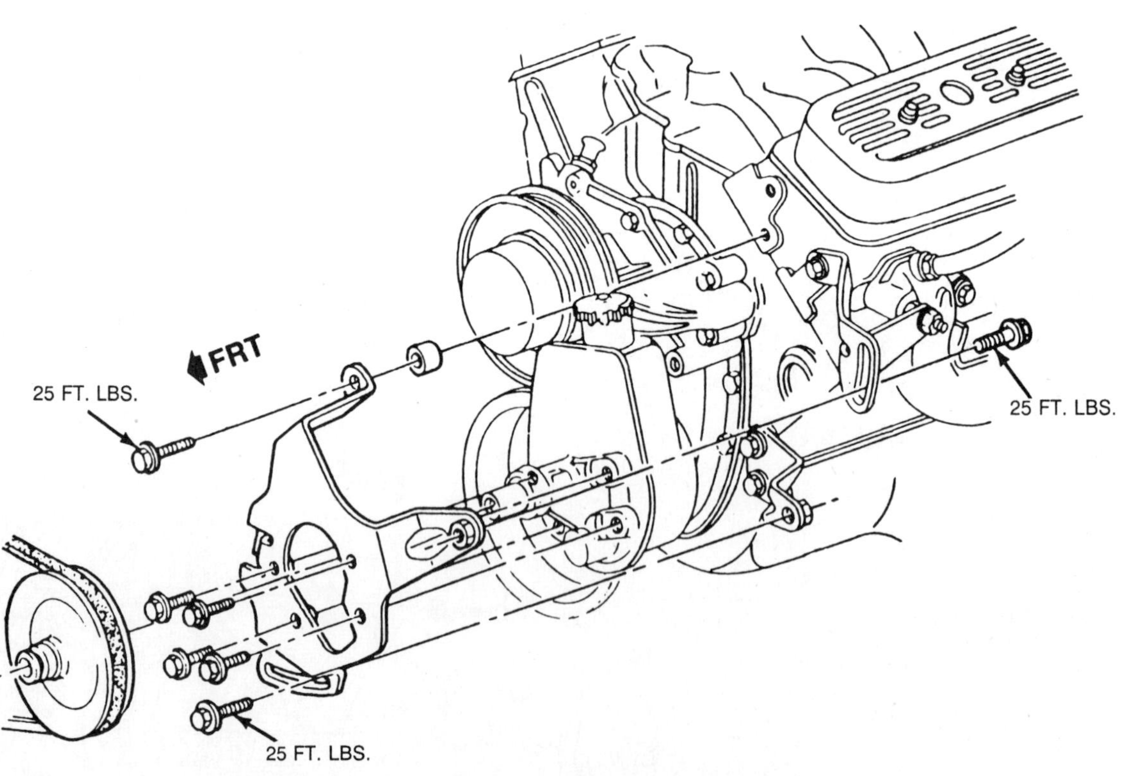

Power steering pump installation for R/V 10/1500 series with the 8-5.0L and 8-5.7L and without air conditioning

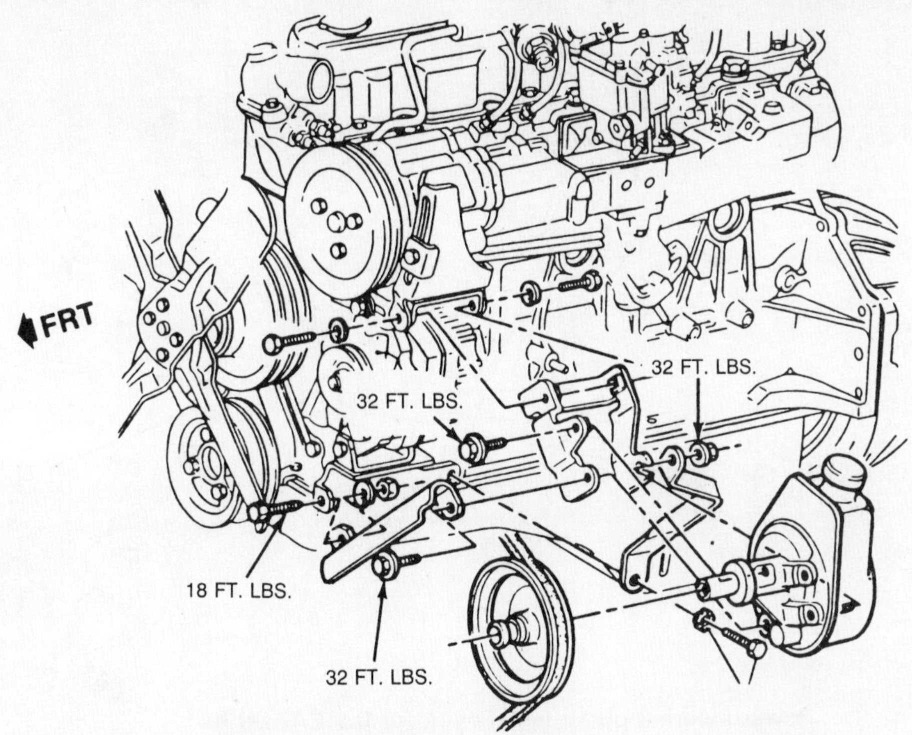

Power steering pump installation for R/V 20/2500 series with the 6-4.8L

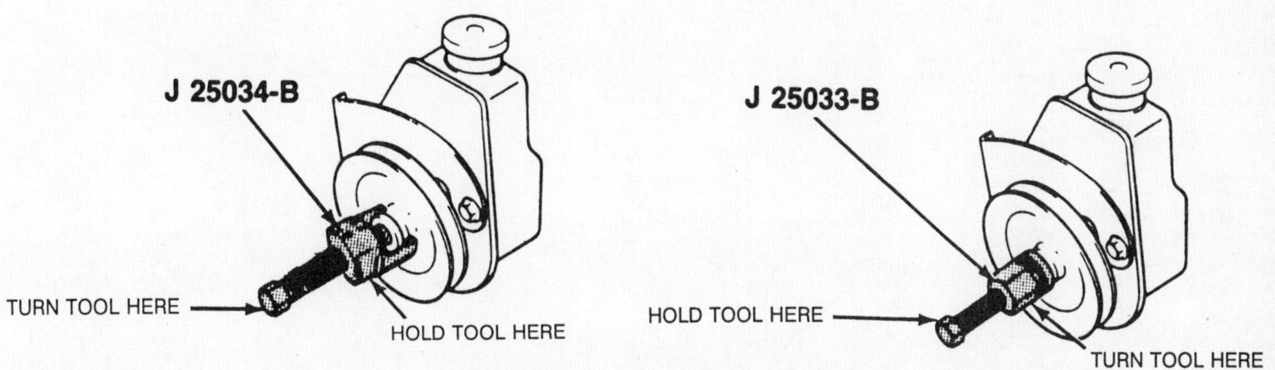

Removing and installing the pulley

4. Repeat Steps 1–3 until the level remains constant.
5. Raise the front of the vehicle so that the front wheels are off the ground. Set the parking brake and block both rear wheels front and rear. Manual transmissions should be in Neutral; automatic transmissions should be in Park.
6. Start the engine and run it at approximately 1500 rpm.
7. Turn the wheels (off the ground) to the right and left, lightly contacting the stops.
8. Add fluid as necessary.
9. Lower the vehicle and turn the wheels right and left on the ground.
10. Check the level and refill as necessary.
11. If the fluid is extremely foamy, let the truck stand for a few minutes with the engine off and repeat the procedure. Check the belt tension and check for a bent or loose pulley. The pulley should not wobble with the engine running.
12. Check that no hoses are contacting any parts of the truck, particularly sheet metal.
13. Check the oil level and refill as necessary. This step and the next are very important. When willing, follow Steps 1–10 above
14. Check for air in the fluid. Aerated fluid appears milky. If air is present, repeat the above operation. If it is obvious that the pump will not respond to bleeding after several attempts, a pressure test may be required.

The procedures for maintaining, adjusting, and repairing the power steering systems and components discussed in this chapter are to be done only after determining that the steering linkages and front suspension systems are correctly aligned and in good condition. All worn or damaged parts should be replaced before attempting to service the power steering system. After correcting any condition that could affect the power steering, do the preliminary tests of the steering system components.

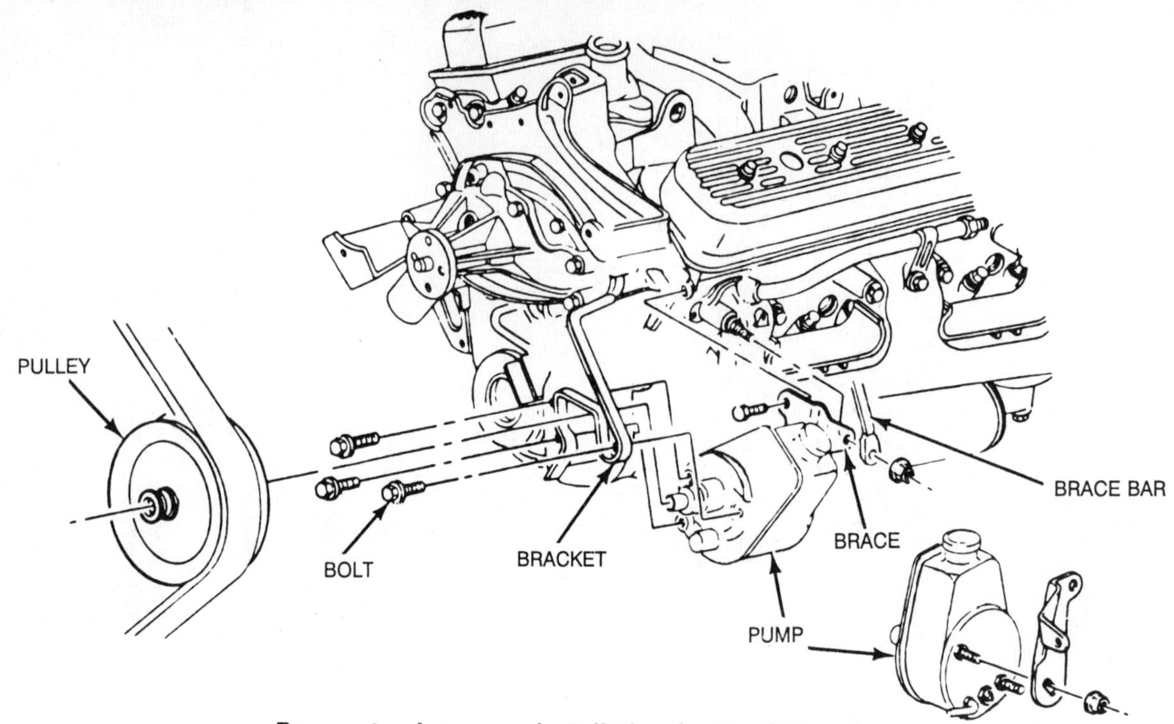

Power steering pump installation for the C/K series with the 6-4.3L, 8-5.0L and 8-5.7L

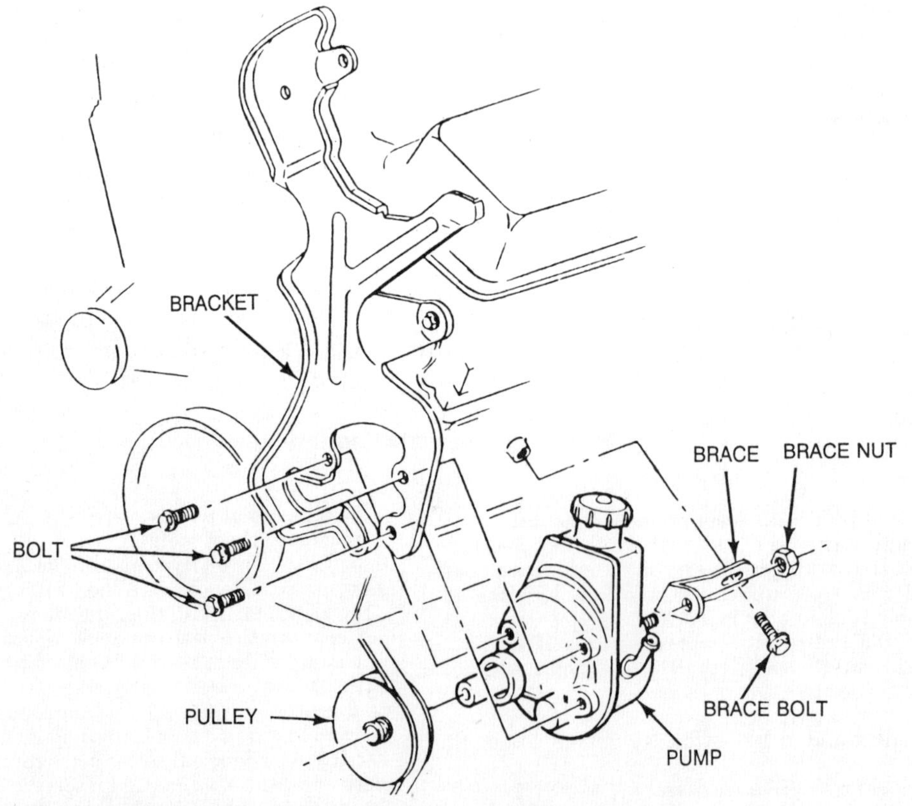

Power steering pump installation for the C/K 10/20 series with the 8-7.4L

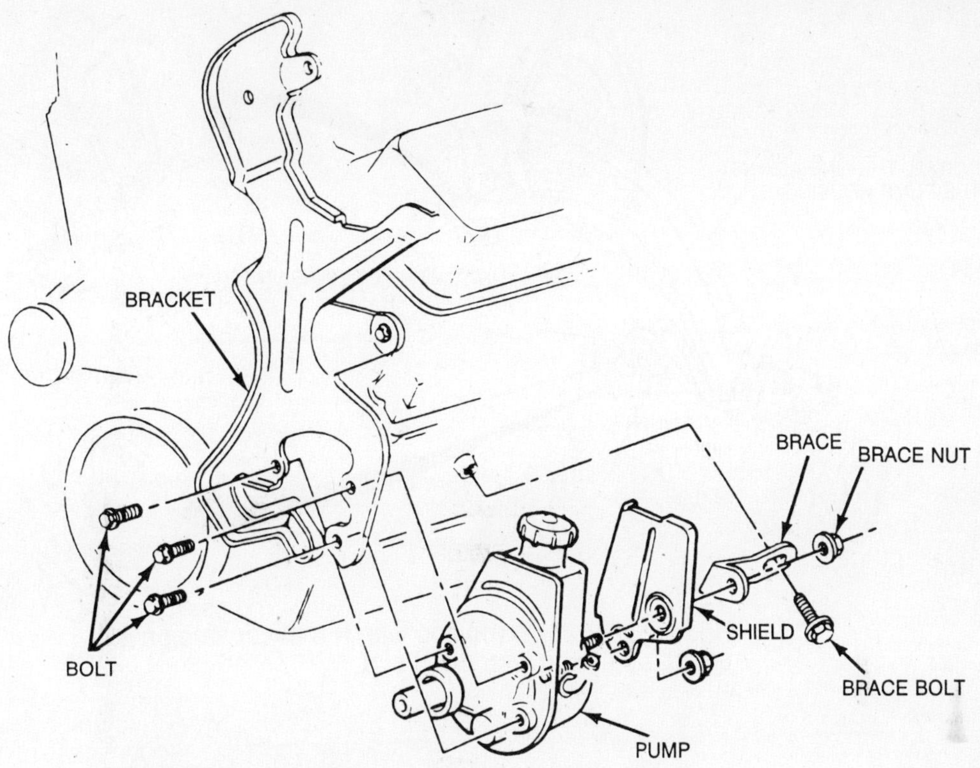

Power steering pump installation for the C/K 30 series with the 8-7.4L

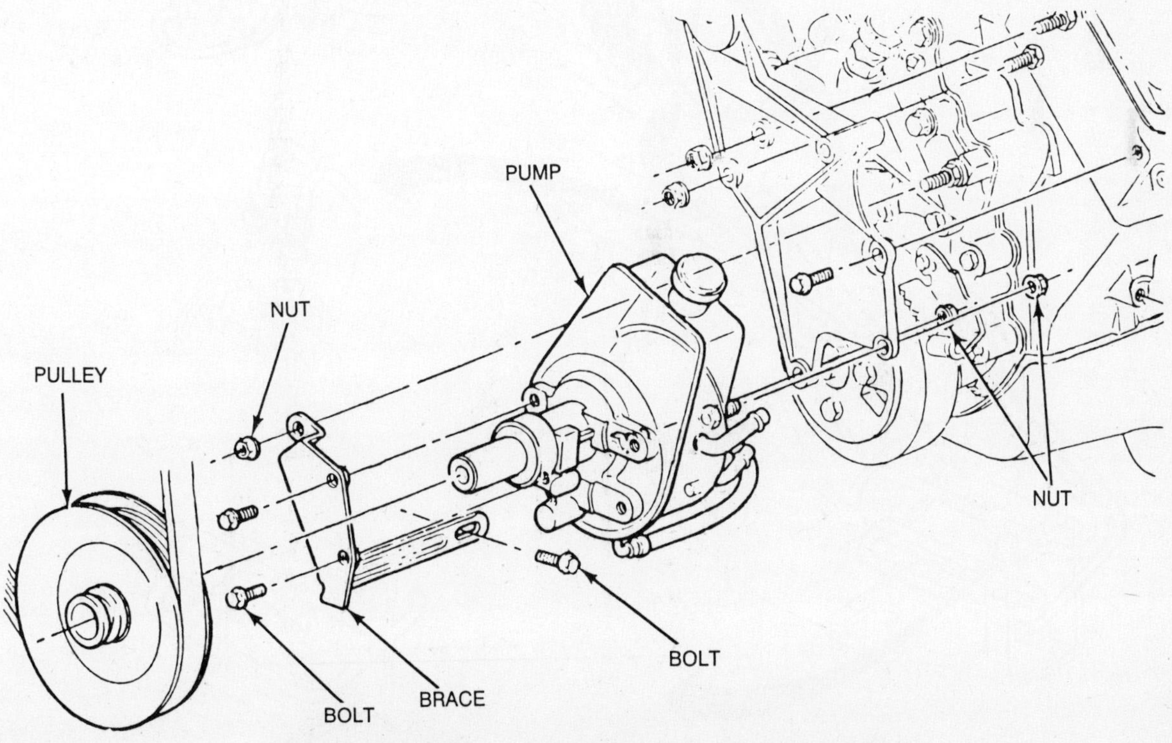

Power steering pump installation for the C/K series with the 8-6.2L

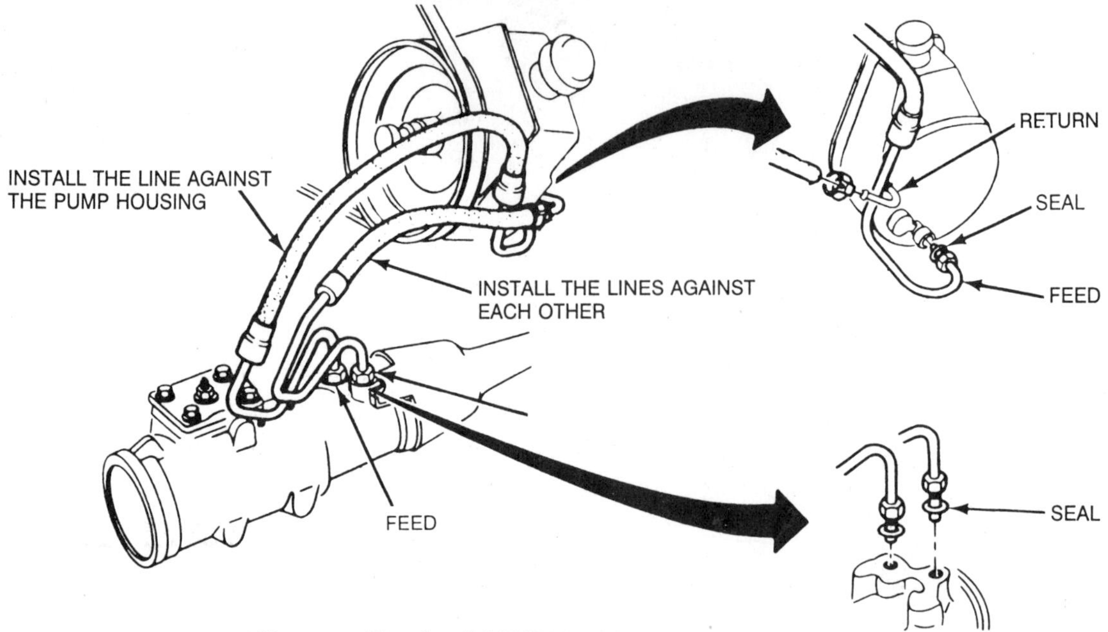

Hose routing for C100/200 with the 6-4.3L, 8-5.0L and 8-5.7L and K100 with the 8-5.7L

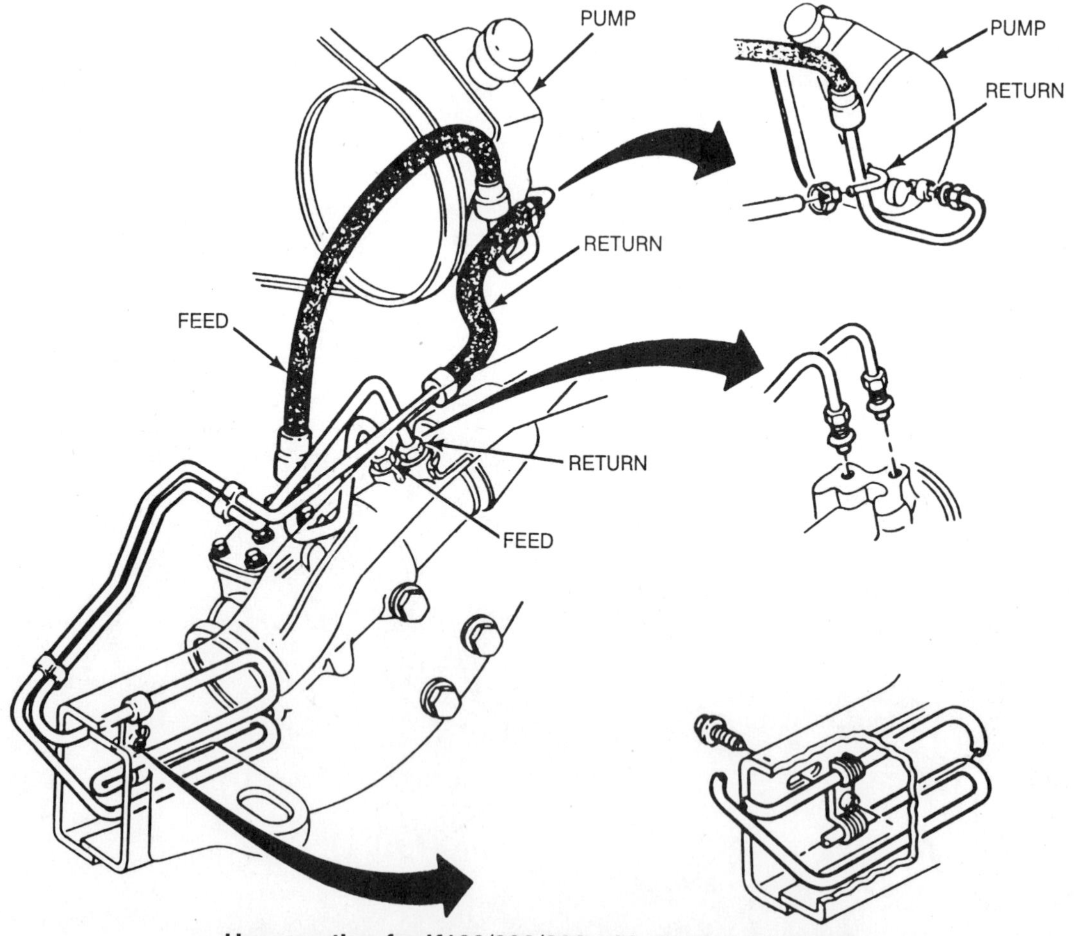

Hose routing for K100/200/300 with the 6-4.3L, 8-5.0L and 8-5.7L and 8-7.4L

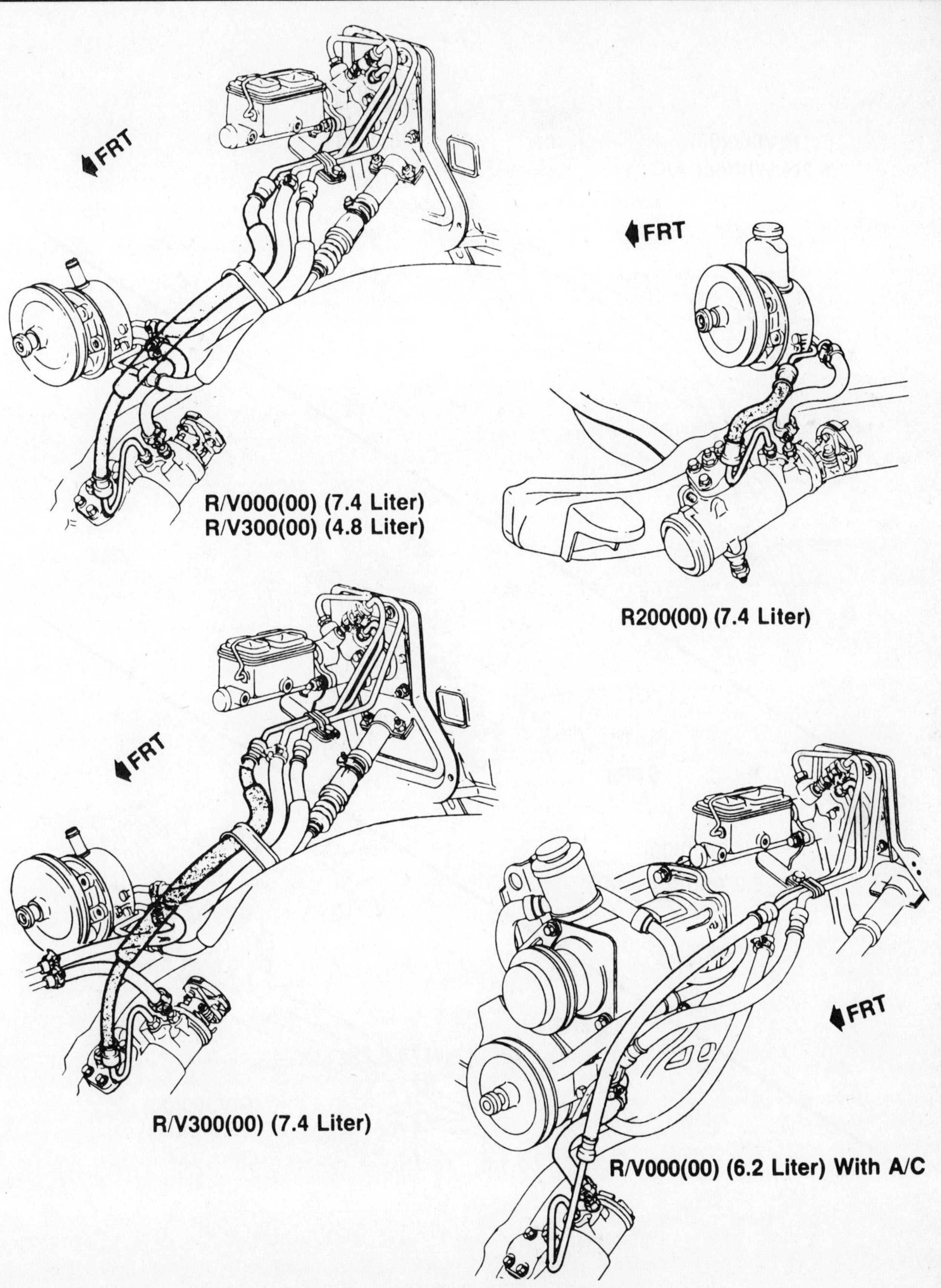

Power steering hose routing for R/V series

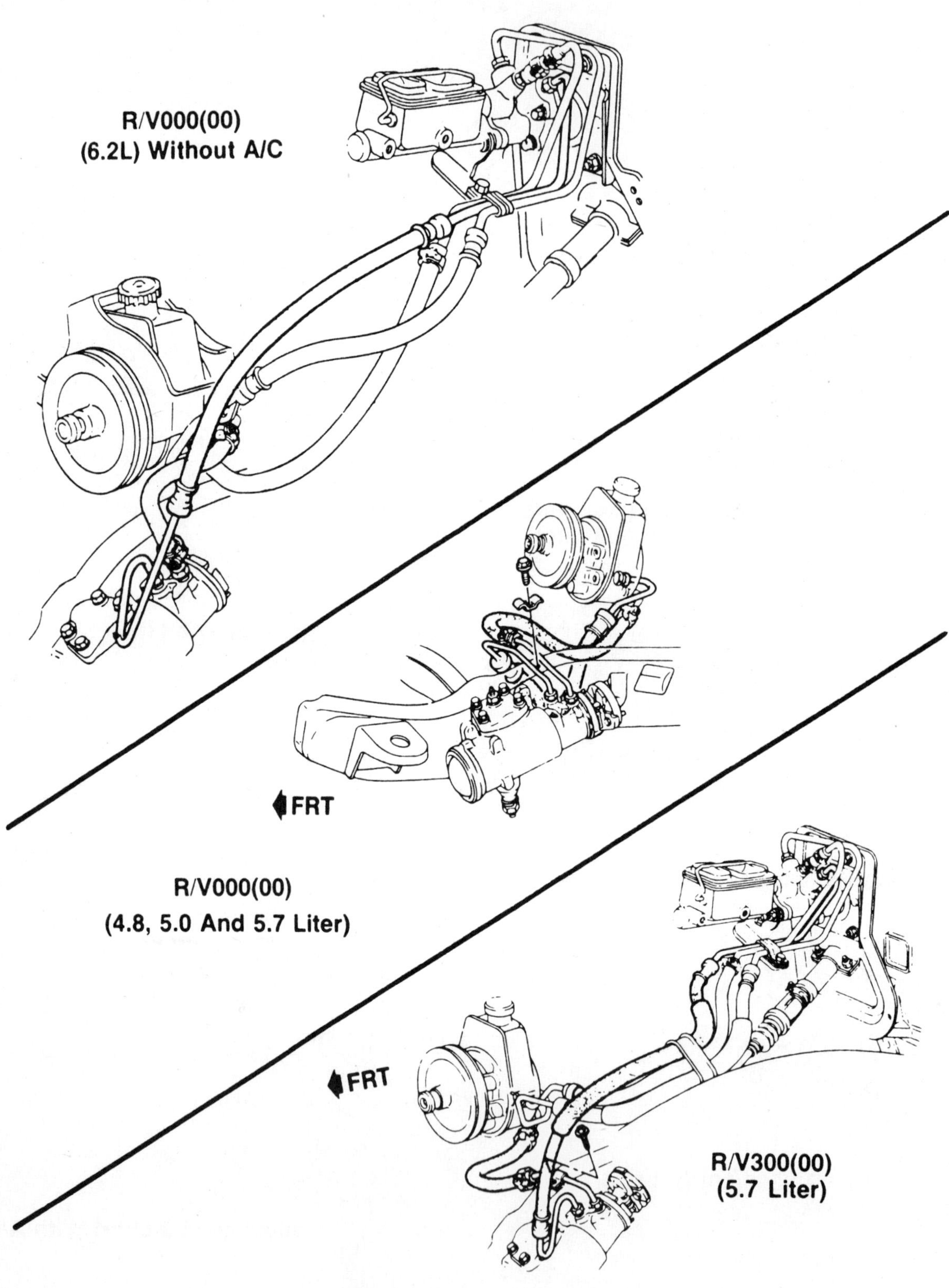

Power steering hose routing for R/V series

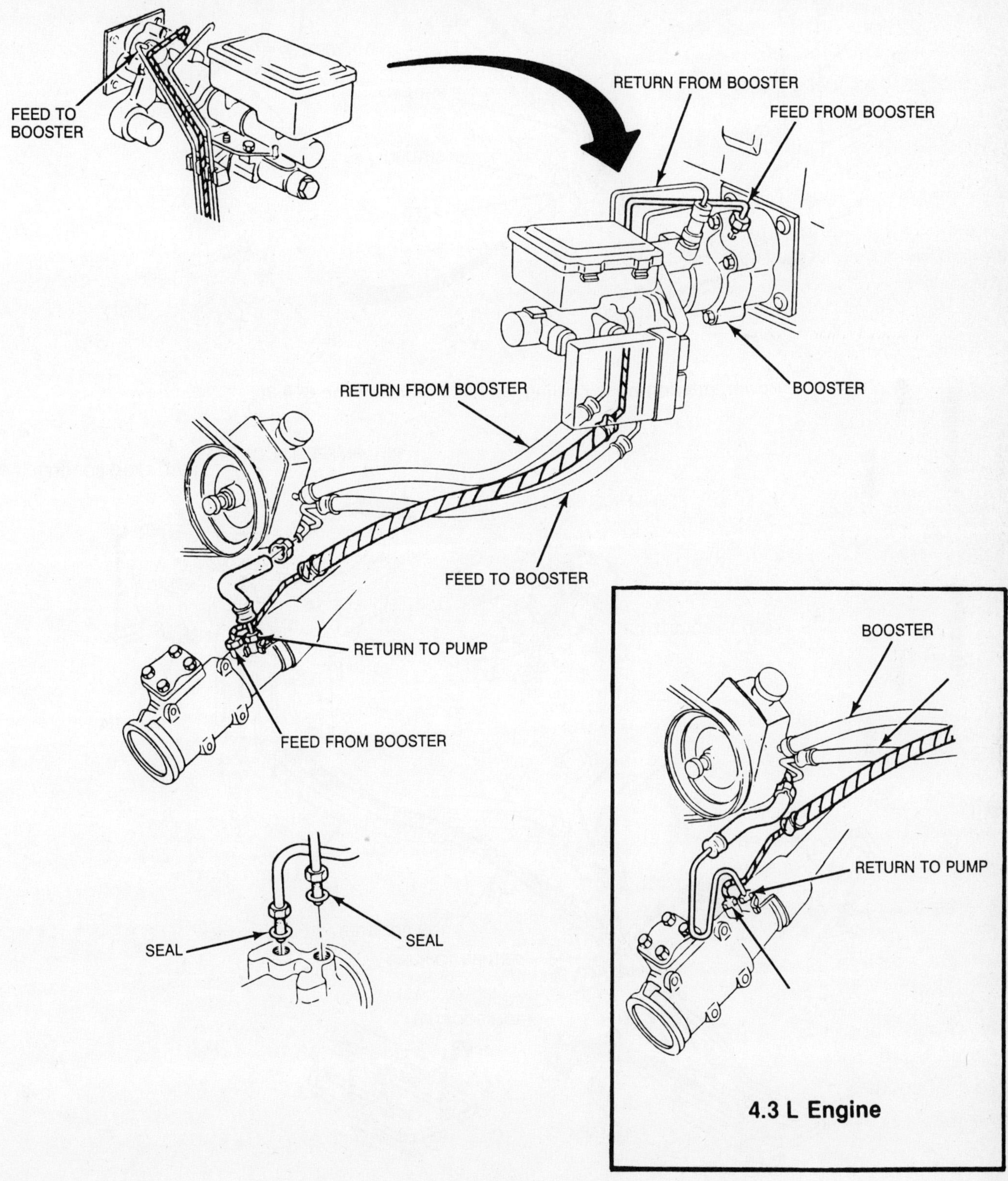

Hose routing for CK200 with the 8-5.7L and CK300 with the 8-5.7L and 8-7.4L and heavy duty chassis

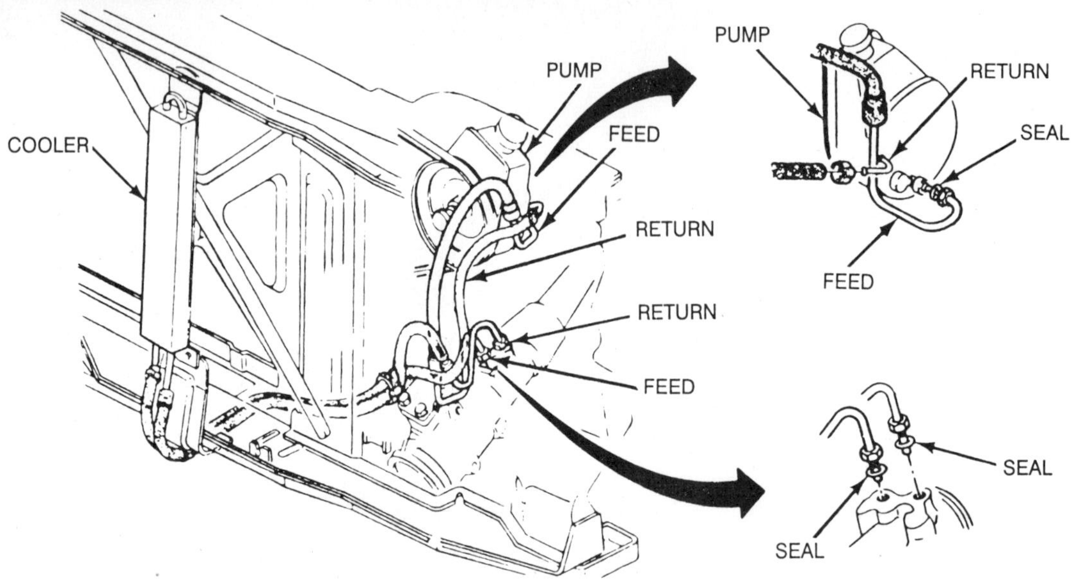

Power steering hose routing for K100/200 with the 6- 4.3L

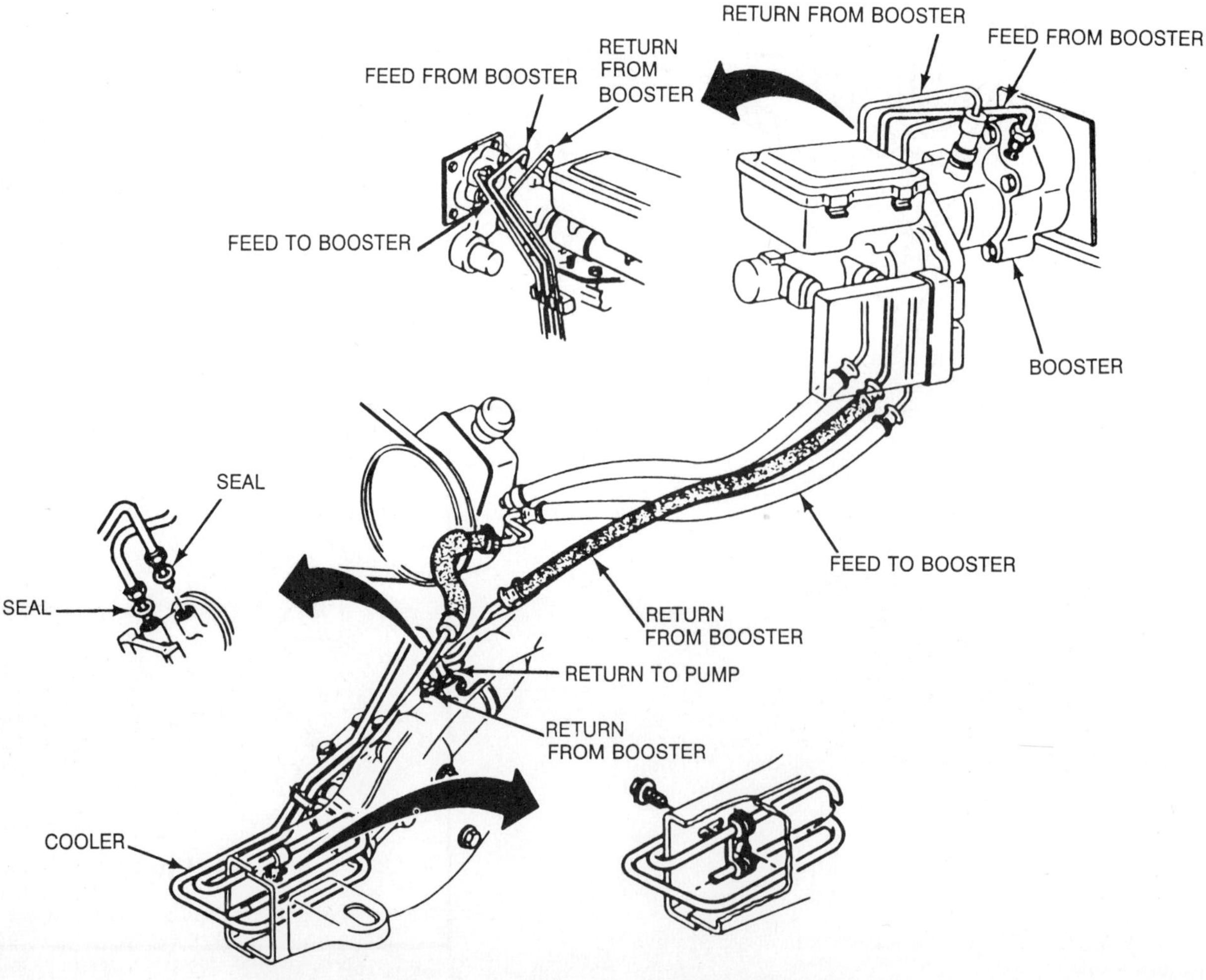

Power steering hose routing for C/K200/300 with the 8-5.7L and 8-7.4L

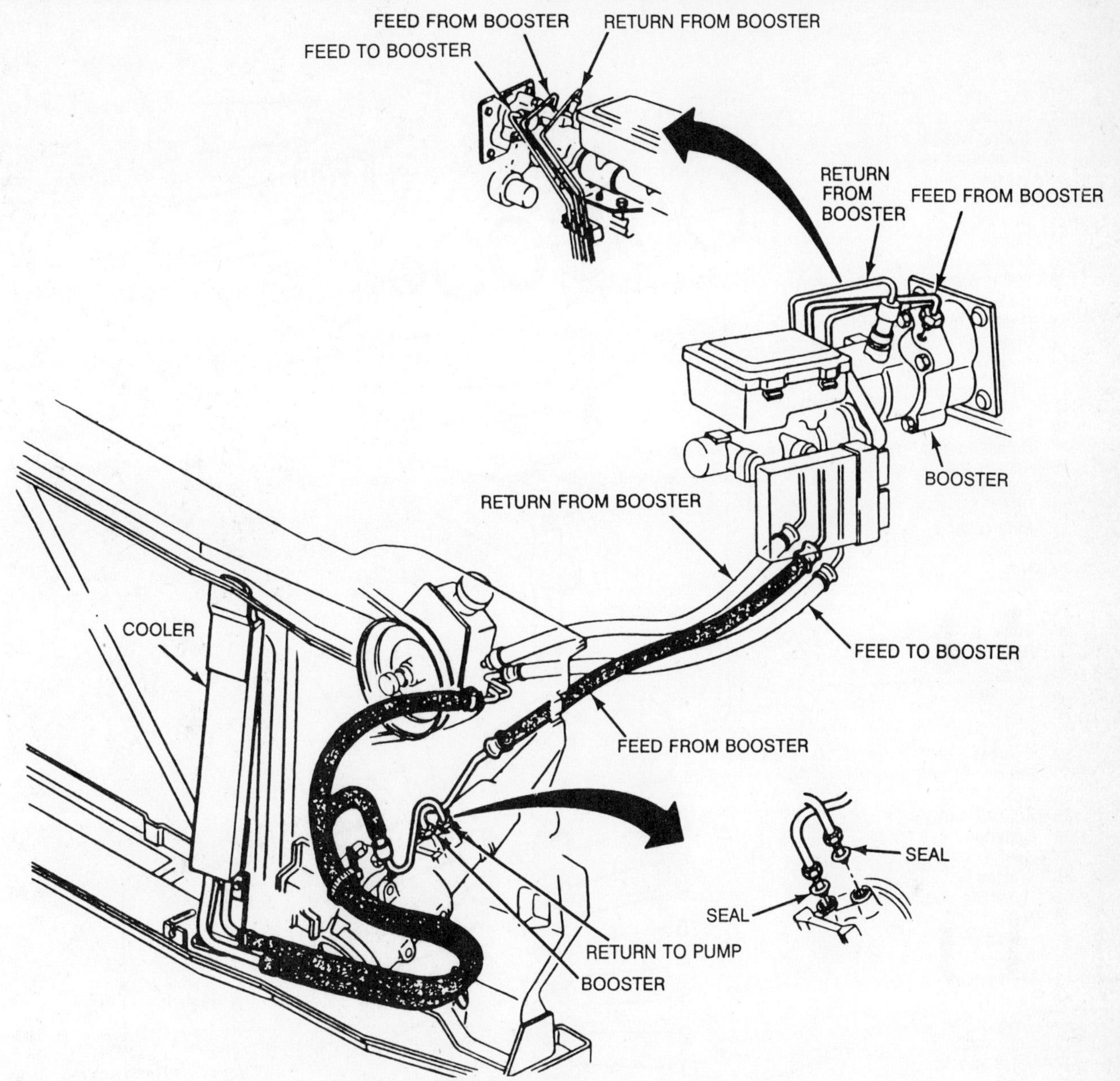

Power steering hose routing for C/K100/200 with the 8-6.2L

PUMP OVERHAUL

The vane type power steering pump is used in Saginaw steering systems. Centrifugal force moves a number of vanes outward against the pump ring, causing a pumping action of the fluid to the control valve.

Disassembly

1. Clean the outside of the pump in a non-toxic solvent before disassembling.
2. Mount the pump in a vise, being careful not to squeeze the front hub too tight.
3. Remove the union and seal.
4. Remove the reservoir retaining studs and separate the reservoir from the housing.
5. Remove the mounting bolt and union O-rings.
6. Remove the filter and filter cage; discard the element.
7. Remove the end plate retaining ring by compressing the retaining ring and then prying it out with a removal tool. The retaining ring may be compressed by inserting a small punch in the ⅛ in. (3mm) diameter hole in the housing and pushing in until the ring clears the groove.
8. Remove the end plate. The end plate is spring loaded and should rise above the housing level. If it is stuck inside the housing, a slight rocking or gentle tapping should free the plate.
9. Remove the shaft woodruff key and tap the end of the shaft gently to free the pressure plate, pump ring, rotor assembly, and thrust plate. Remove these parts as one unit.
10. Remove the end plate O-ring. Separate the pressure plate, pump ring, rotor assembly, and thrust plate.

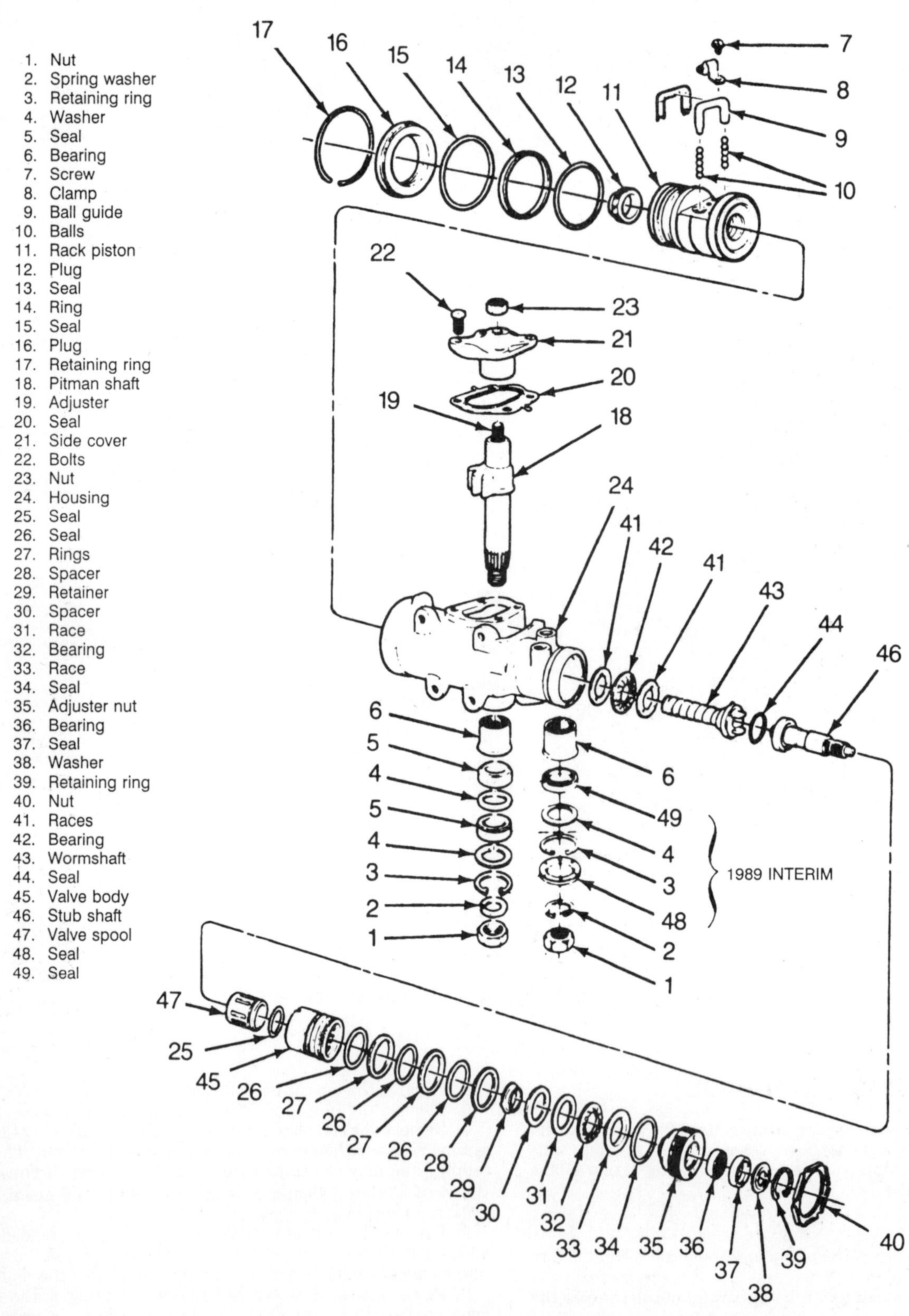
1. Nut
2. Spring washer
3. Retaining ring
4. Washer
5. Seal
6. Bearing
7. Screw
8. Clamp
9. Ball guide
10. Balls
11. Rack piston
12. Plug
13. Seal
14. Ring
15. Seal
16. Plug
17. Retaining ring
18. Pitman shaft
19. Adjuster
20. Seal
21. Side cover
22. Bolts
23. Nut
24. Housing
25. Seal
26. Seal
27. Rings
28. Spacer
29. Retainer
30. Spacer
31. Race
32. Bearing
33. Race
34. Seal
35. Adjuster nut
36. Bearing
37. Seal
38. Washer
39. Retaining ring
40. Nut
41. Races
42. Bearing
43. Wormshaft
44. Seal
45. Valve body
46. Stub shaft
47. Valve spool
48. Seal
49. Seal
1989 INTERIM

R/V series power steering gear exploded view

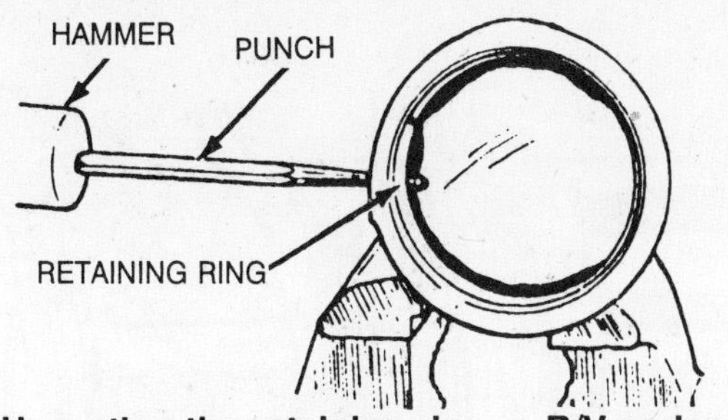

Unseating the retaining ring – R/V series

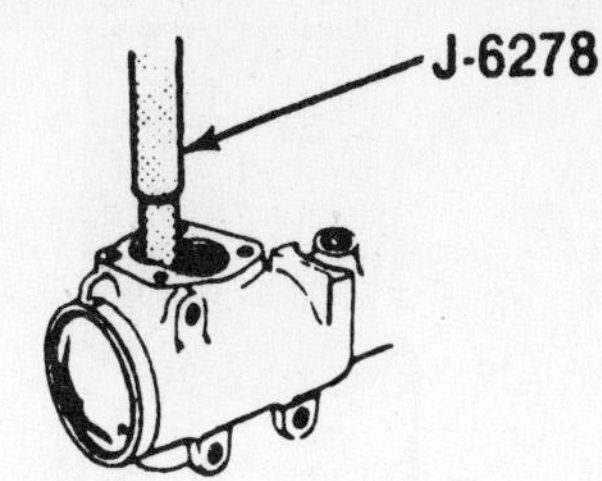

Removing the pitman shaft bearing – R/V series

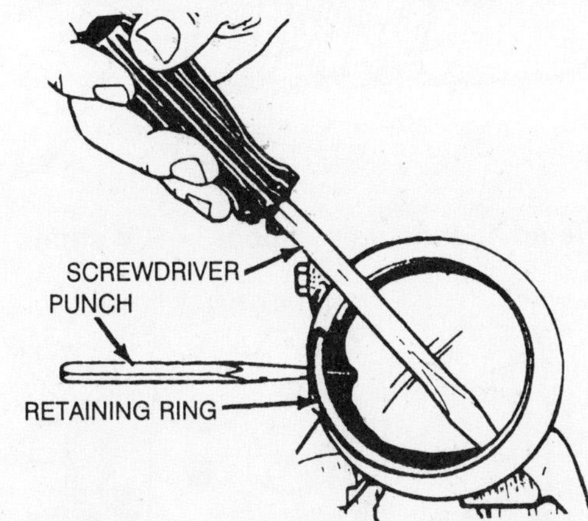

Removing the retaining ring – R/V series

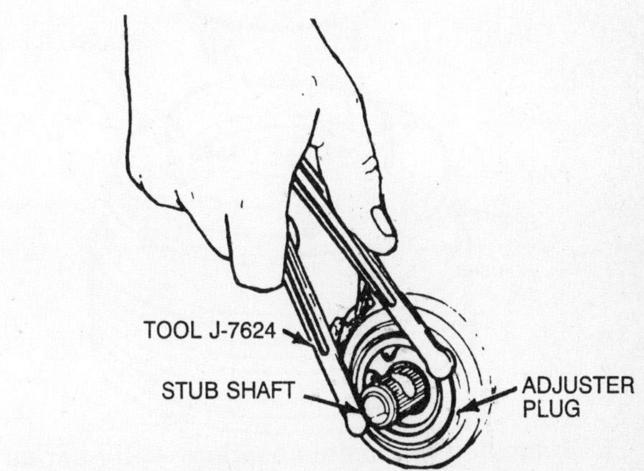

Removing the adjusting plug – R/V series

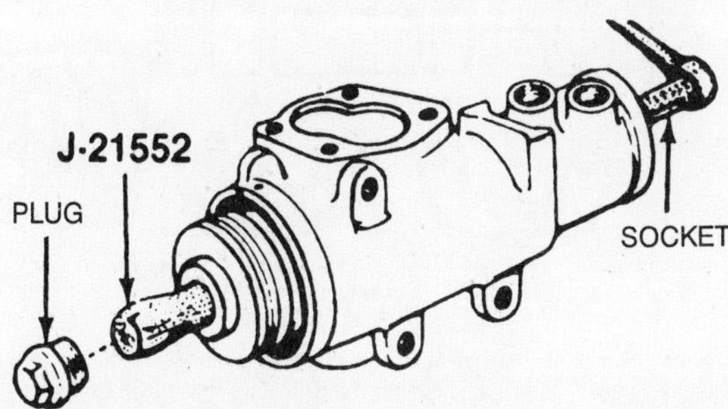

Removing the plug and piston rack – R/V series

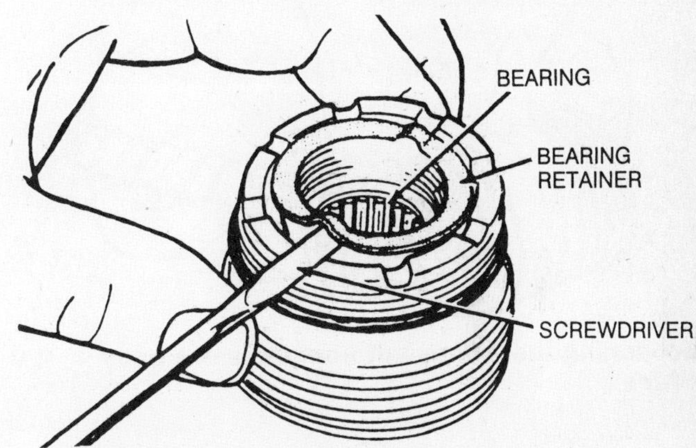

Removing the bearing retainer – R/V series

11. Clean all metal parts in a non-toxic solvent and inspect them as given below:

a. Check the flow control valve for free movement in the housing bore. If the valve is sticking, see if there is dirt or a rough spot in the bore.

b. Check the cap screw in the end of the flow control valve for looseness. Tighten if necessary being careful not to damage the machined surfaces.

c. Inspect the pressure plate and the pump plate surfaces for flatness and check that there are no cracks or scores in the parts. Do not mistake the normal wear marks for scoring.

d. Check the vanes in the rotor assembly for free movement and that they were installed with the radiused edge toward the pump ring.

e. If the flow control valve plunger is defective, install a new part. The valve is factory calibrated and supplied as a unit.

f. Check the driveshaft for worn splines, breaks, bushing material pick-up, etc.

g. Replace all rubber seals and O-rings removed from the pump.

h. Check the reservoir, studs, casting, etc. for burrs and other defects that would impair operation.

Assembly

1. Install a new shaft seal in the housing and insert the shaft at the hub end of housing, splined end entering mounting face side.
2. Install the thrust plate on the dowel pins with the ported side facing the rear of the pump housing.
3. Install the rotor on the pump shaft over the splined end. Be sure the rotor moves freely on the splines. Countersunk side must be toward the shaft.
4. Install the shaft retaining ring. Install the pump ring on the dowel pins with the rotation arrow toward the rear of the pump housing. Rotation is clockwise as seen from the pulley.
5. Install the vanes in the rotor slots with the radius edge towards the outside.

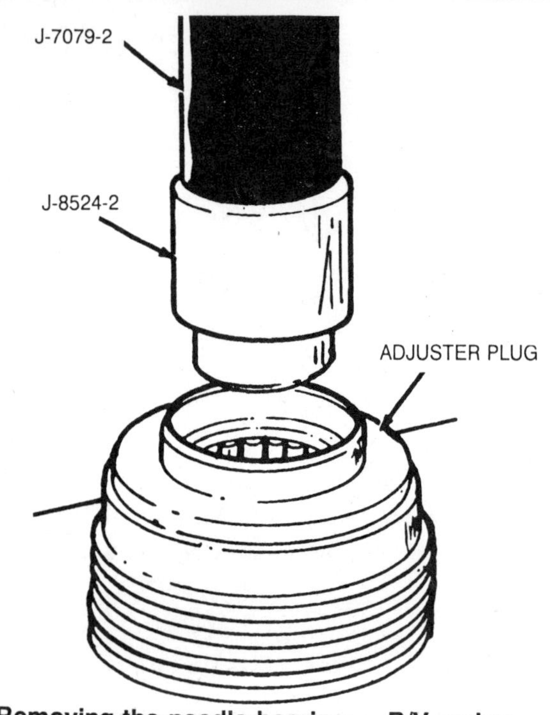

Removing the needle bearing – R/V series

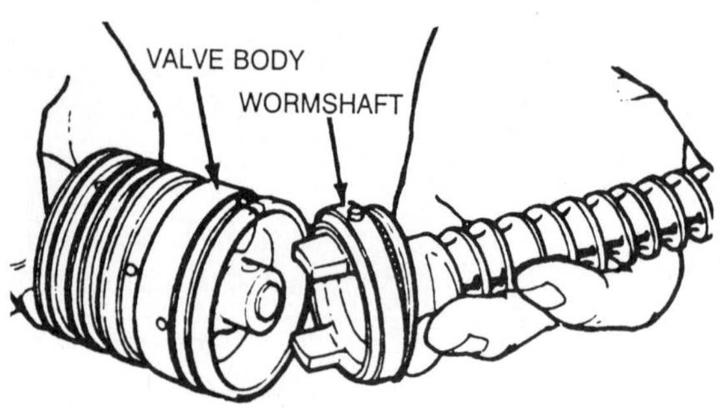

Separating the wormshaft from the valve body – R/V series

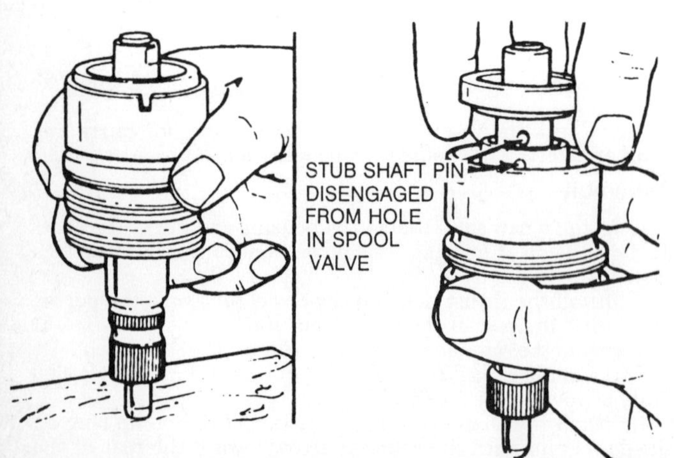

Removing the stub shaft – R/V series

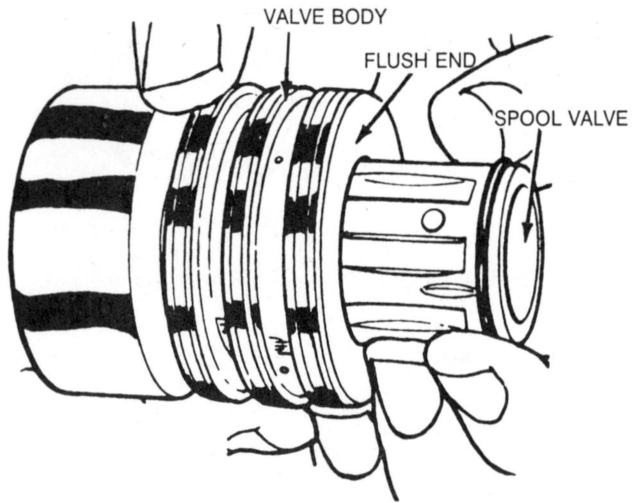

Removing the valve spool – R/V series

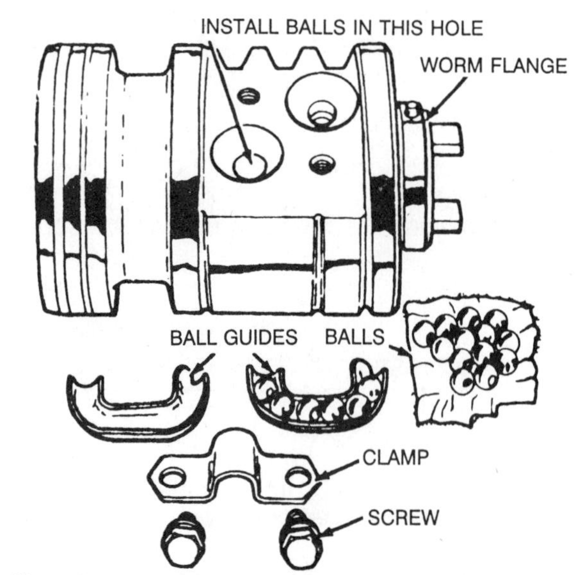

Installing the balls in the piston rack – R/V series

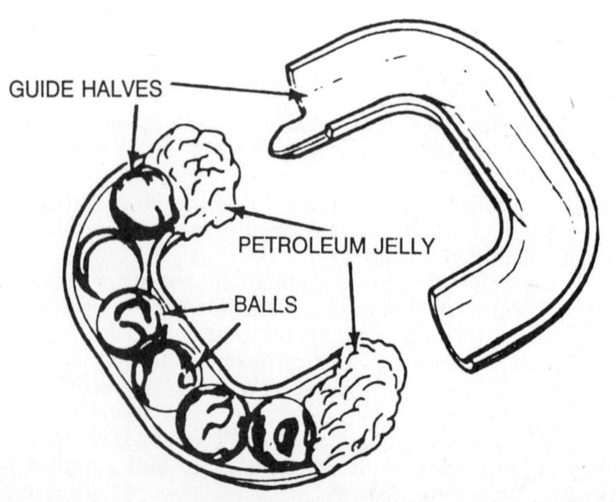

Retaining the balls in the ball guide – R/V series

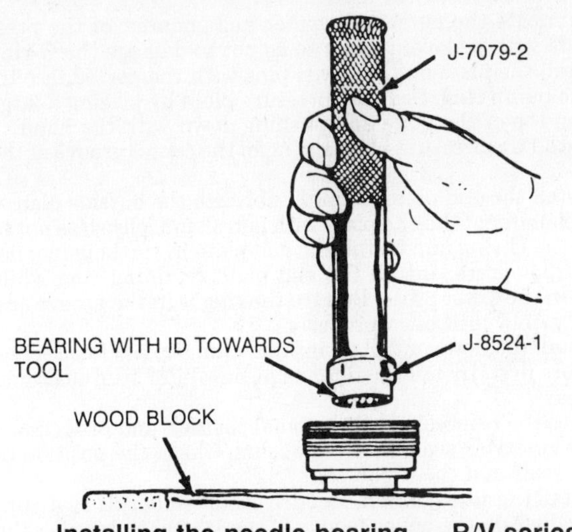

Installing the needle bearing – R/V series

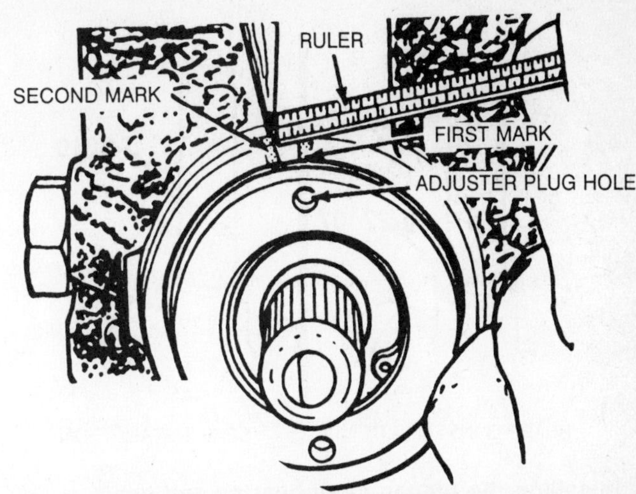

Remarking the housing – R/V series

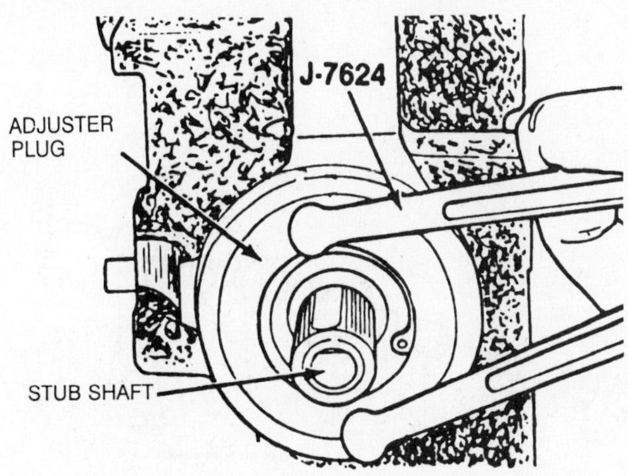

Bottoming the adjuster plug – R/V series

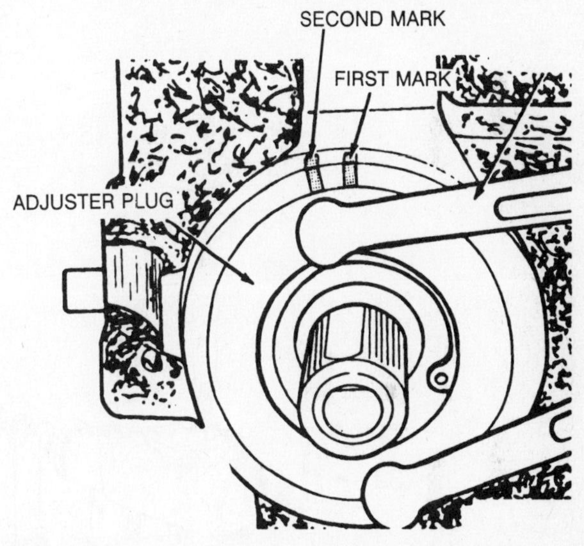

Aligning the adjuster hole with the second mark – R/V series

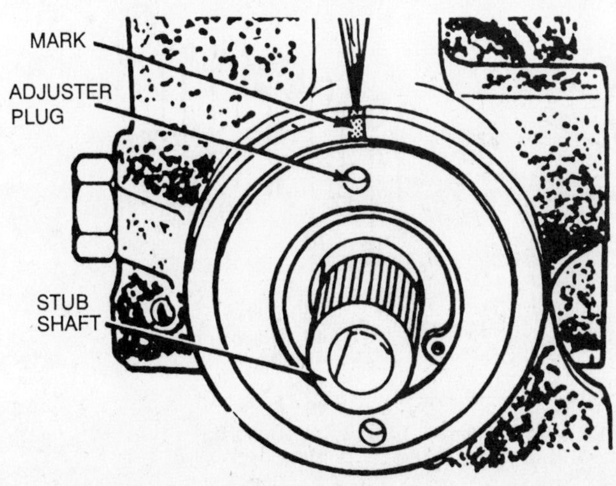

Marking the housing – R/V series

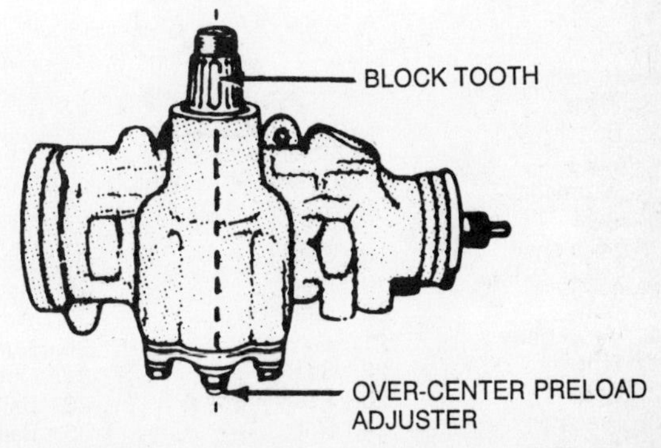

Pitman shaft over-center sector adjustment – R/V series

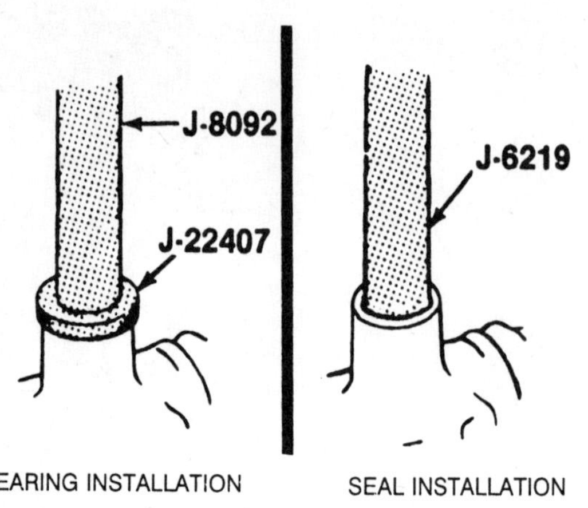

Installing the pitman shaft bearing and seals – R/V series

6. Lubricate the outside diameter and chamfer of the pressure plate with petroleum jelly so as not to damage the O-ring and install the plate on the dowel pins with the ported face toward the pump ring. Seat the pressure plate by placing a large socket on top of the plate and pushing down with the hand.

7. Install the pressure plate spring in the center groove of the plate.

8. Install the end plate O-ring. Lubricate the outside diameter and chamfer of the end plate with petroleum jelly so as not to damage the O-ring and install the end plate in the housing, using an arbor press. Install the end plate retaining ring while pump is in the arbor press. Be sure the ring is in the groove and the ring gap is positioned properly.

9. Install the flow control spring and plunger, hex head screw end in bore first. Install the filter cage, new filter stud seals and union seal.

10. Place the reservoir in the normal position and press down until the reservoir seats on the housing. Check the position of the stud seals and the union seal.

11. Install the studs, union, and driveshaft woodruff key. Support the shaft on the opposite side of the key when tapping the key into place.

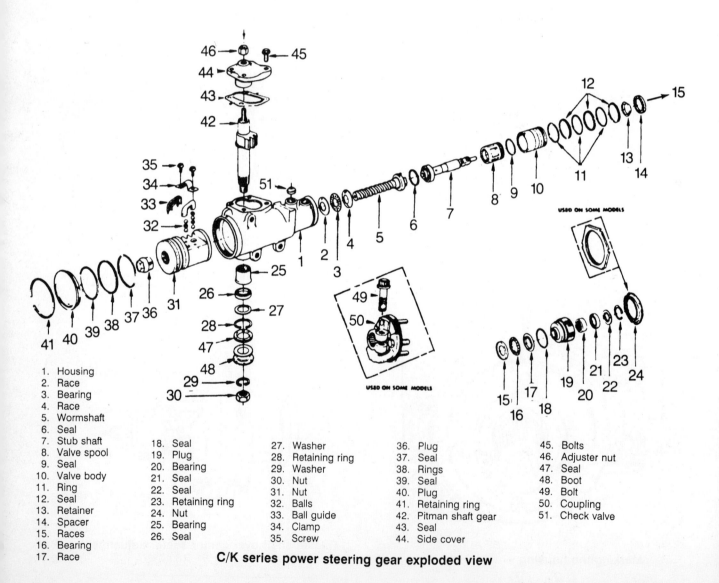

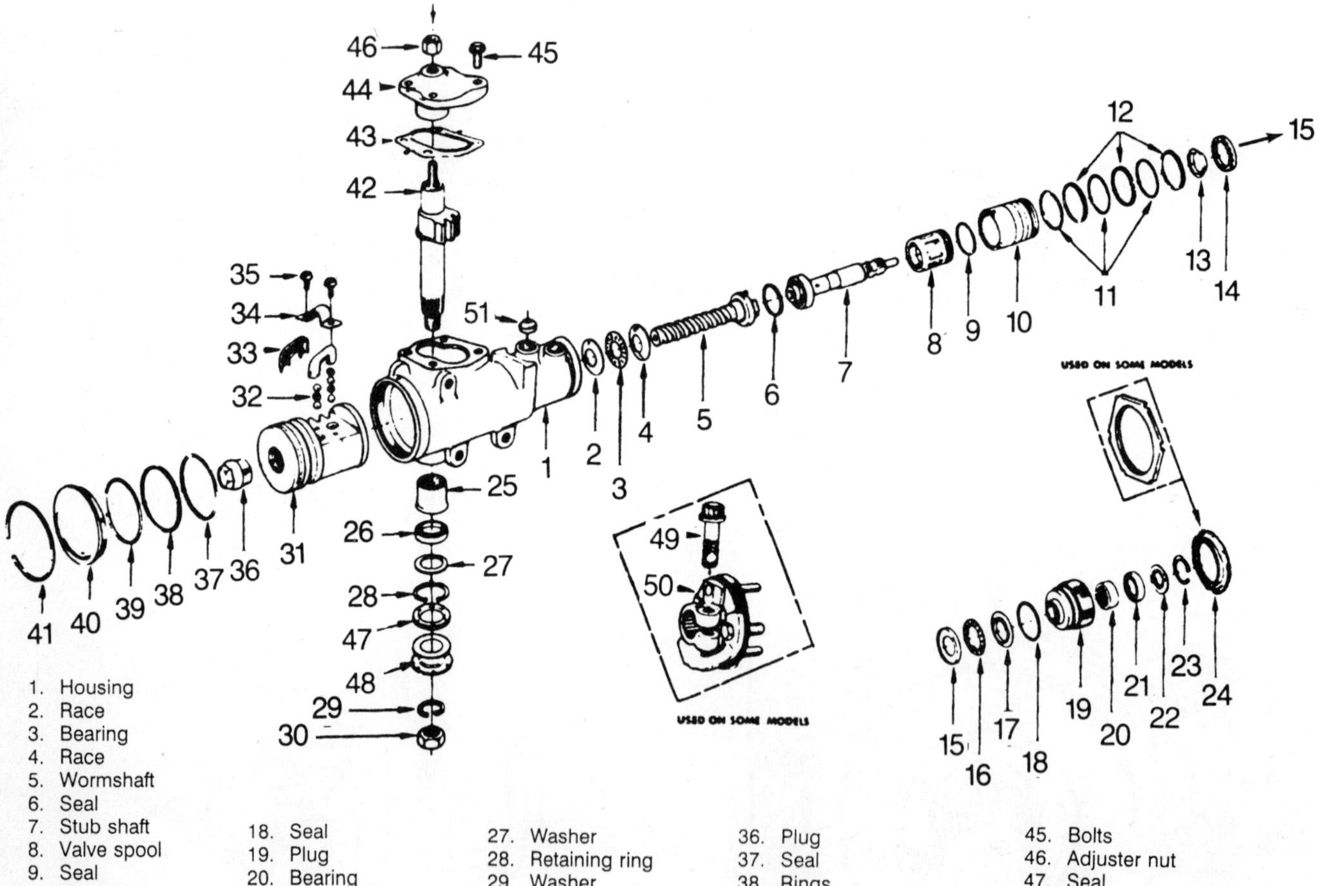

1. Housing
2. Race
3. Bearing
4. Race
5. Wormshaft
6. Seal
7. Stub shaft
8. Valve spool
9. Seal
10. Valve body
11. Ring
12. Seal
13. Retainer
14. Spacer
15. Races
16. Bearing
17. Race
18. Seal
19. Plug
20. Bearing
21. Seal
22. Seal
23. Retaining ring
24. Nut
25. Bearing
26. Seal
27. Washer
28. Retaining ring
29. Washer
30. Nut
31. Nut
32. Balls
33. Ball guide
34. Clamp
35. Screw
36. Plug
37. Seal
38. Rings
39. Seal
40. Plug
41. Retaining ring
42. Pitman shaft gear
43. Seal
44. Side cover
45. Bolts
46. Adjuster nut
47. Seal
48. Boot
49. Bolt
50. Coupling
51. Check valve

C/K series power steering gear exploded view

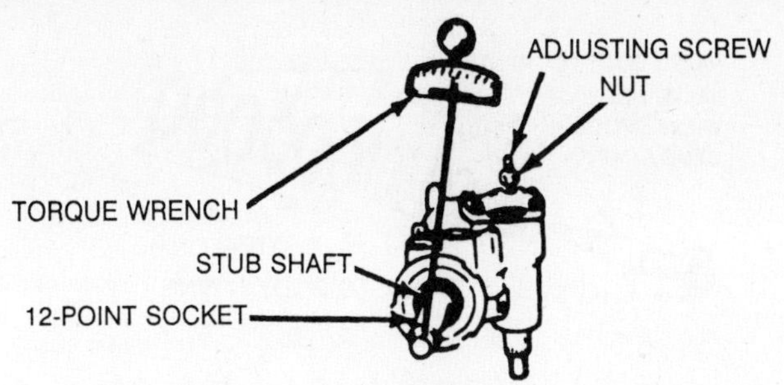

Aligning the over-center preload – R/V series

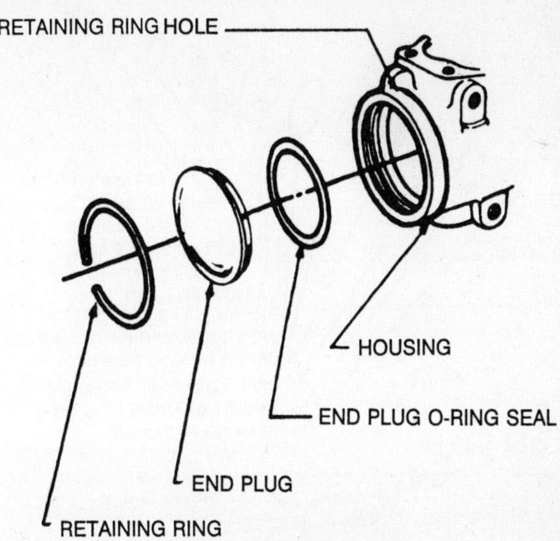

Removing/installing housing end – C/K series

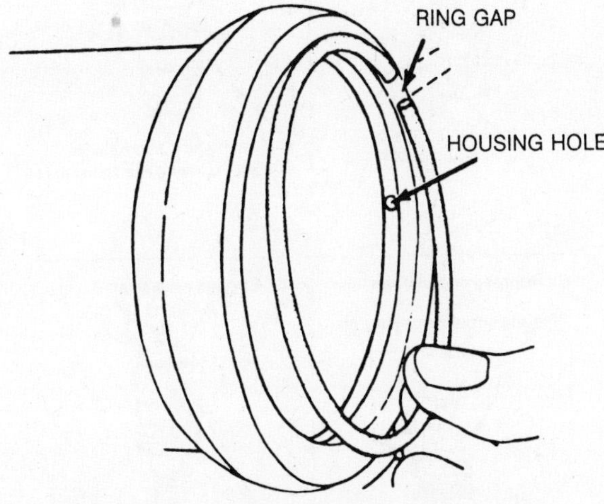

Installing the retaining ring – R/V series

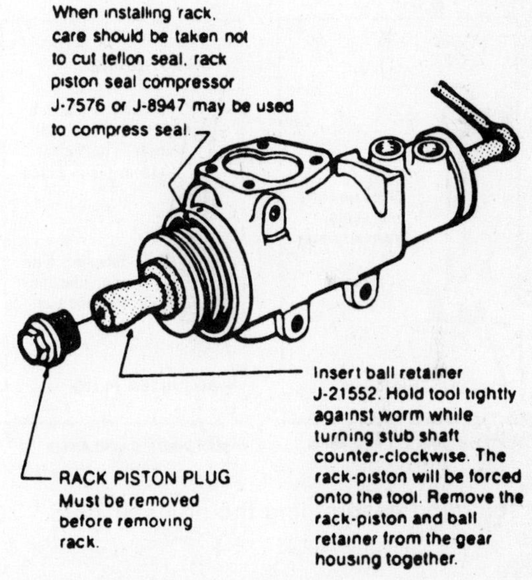

Removing/installing rack piston – C/K series

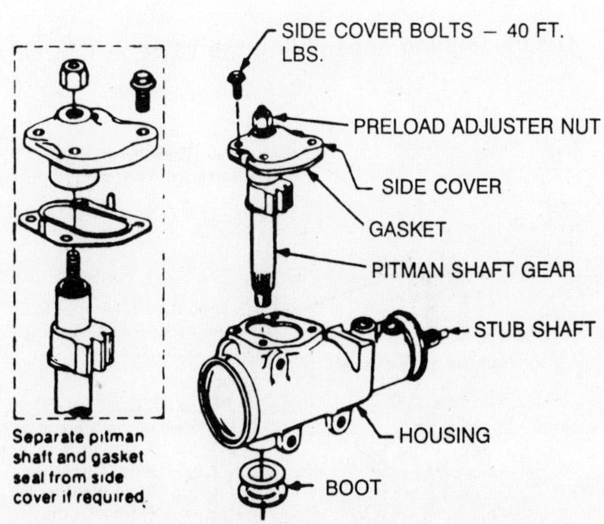

Removing/installing pitman shaft and side cover – C/K series

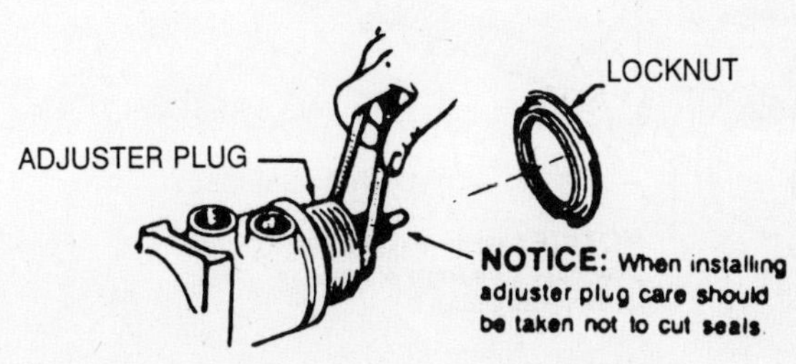

Removing/installing the adjuster plug – C/K series

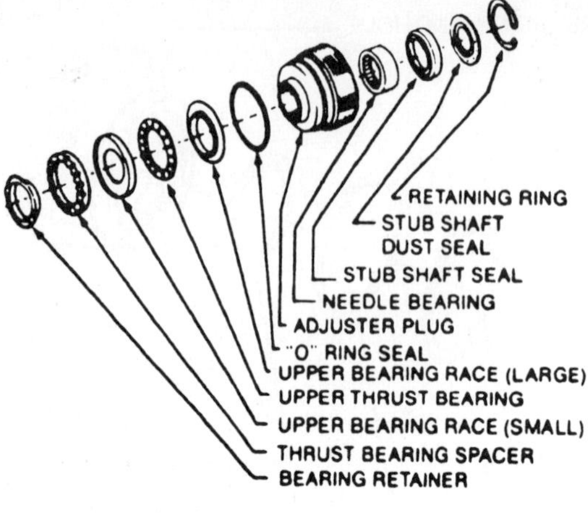

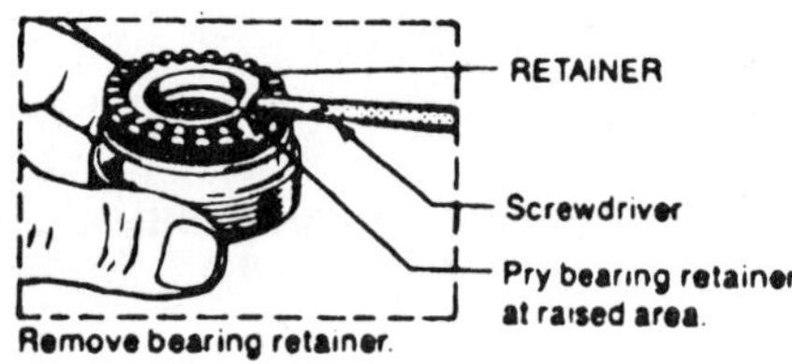

Remove bearing retainer.

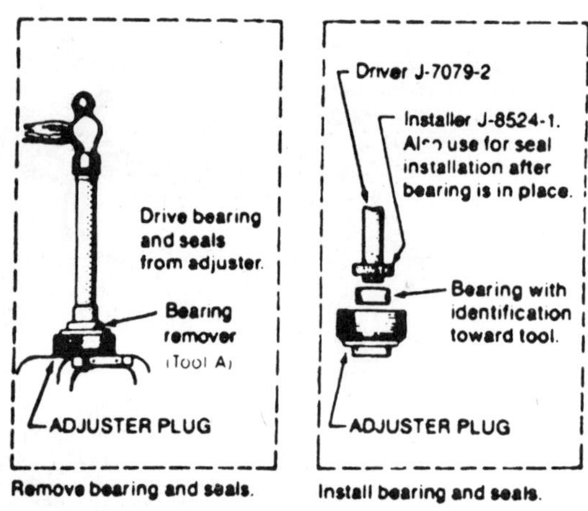

Remove bearing and seals. Install bearing and seals.

Disassembling/assembling the adjuster plug – C/K series

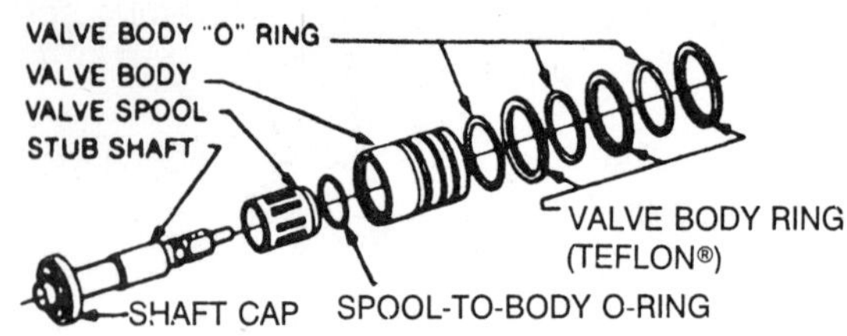

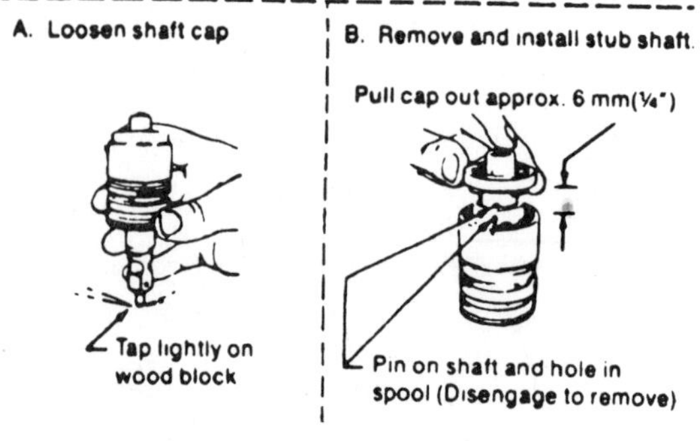

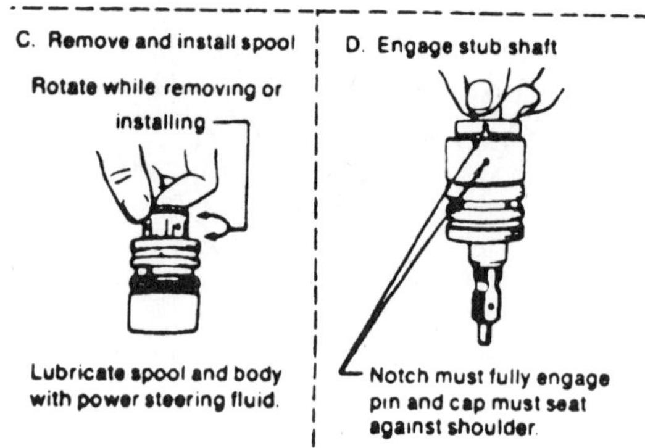

Disassembling/assembling the valve – C/K series

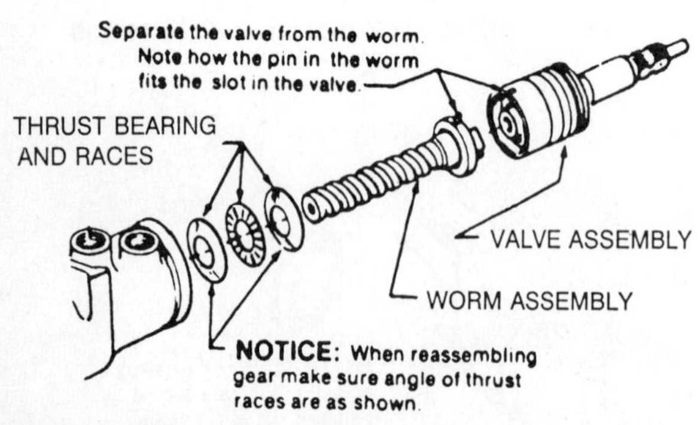

Removing/installing the bearing, worm and valve – C/K series

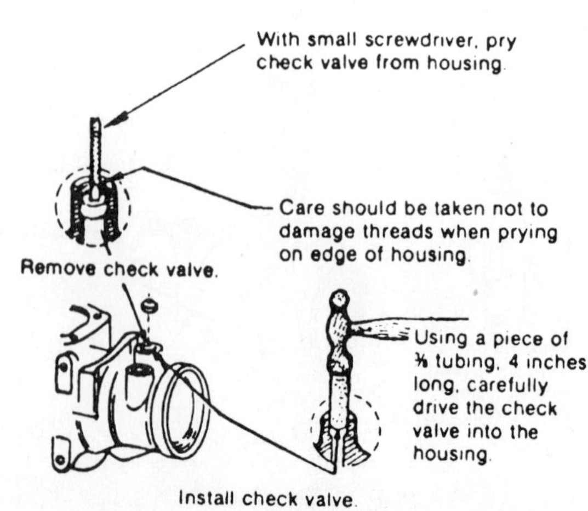

With small screwdriver, pry check valve from housing.
Care should be taken not to damage threads when prying on edge of housing.
Remove check valve.
Using a piece of ⅜ tubing, 4 inches long, carefully drive the check valve into the housing.

Install check valve.

Removing/installing the check valve – C/K series

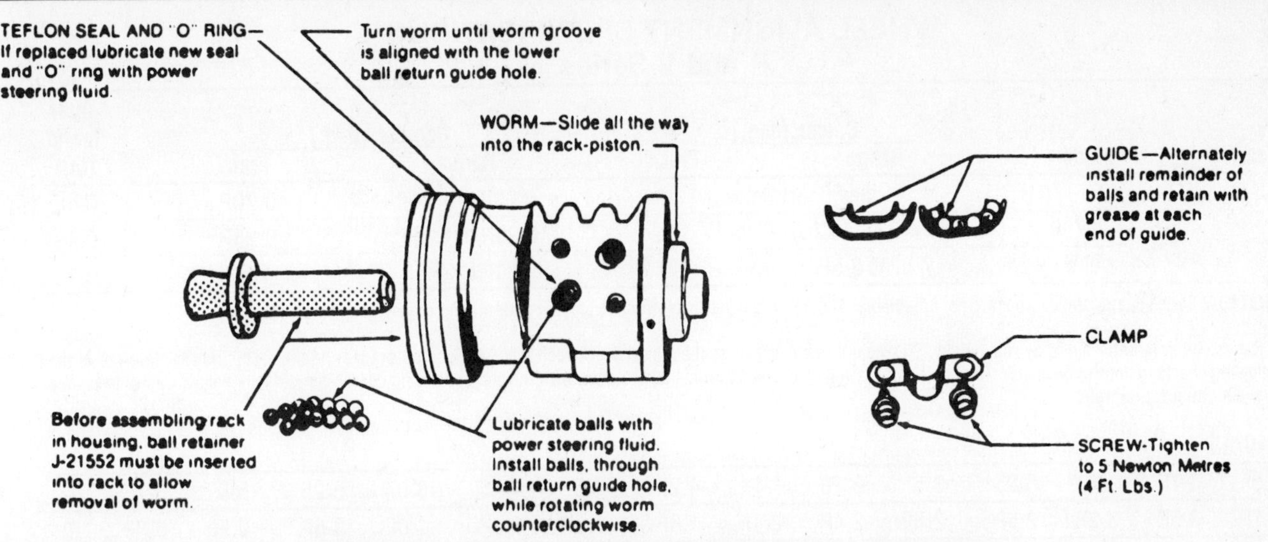

TEFLON SEAL AND "O" RING—If replaced lubricate new seal and "O" ring with power steering fluid.
Turn worm until worm groove is aligned with the lower ball return guide hole.
WORM—Slide all the way into the rack-piston.
GUIDE—Alternately install remainder of balls and retain with grease at each end of guide.

Before assembling rack in housing, ball retainer J-21552 must be inserted into rack to allow removal of worm.
Lubricate balls with power steering fluid. Install balls, through ball return guide hole, while rotating worm counterclockwise.
SCREW-Tighten to 5 Newton Metres (4 Ft. Lbs.)

Disassembling/assembling the rack piston — C/K series

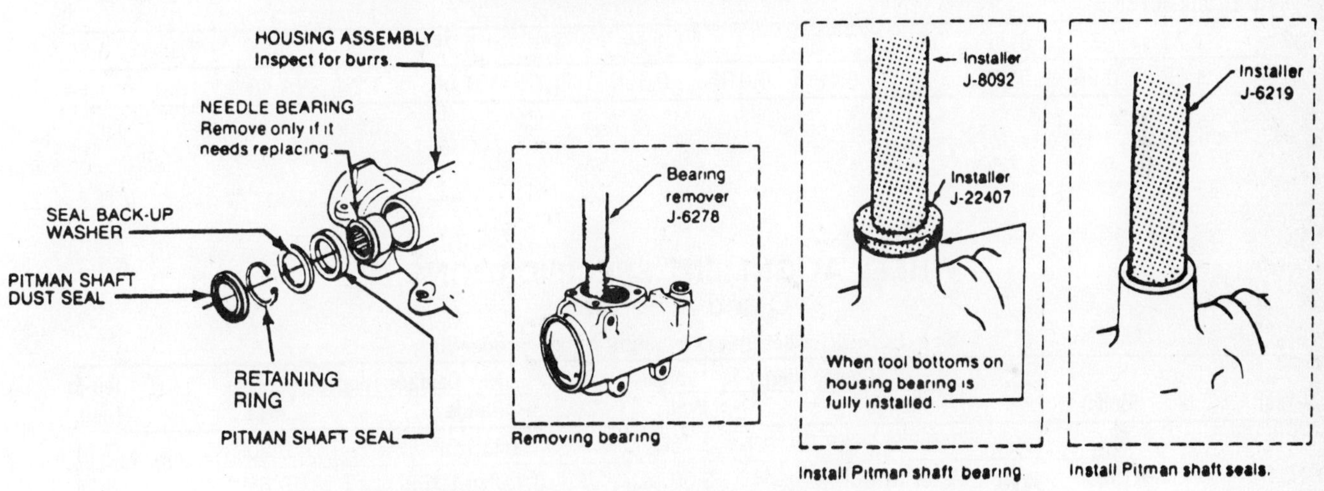

HOUSING ASSEMBLY Inspect for burrs.
NEEDLE BEARING Remove only if it needs replacing.
SEAL BACK-UP WASHER

Bearing remover J-6278

Installer J-8092
Installer J-22407
When tool bottoms on housing bearing is fully installed.

Installer J-6219

Removing/installing the pitman seals and bearing — C/K series

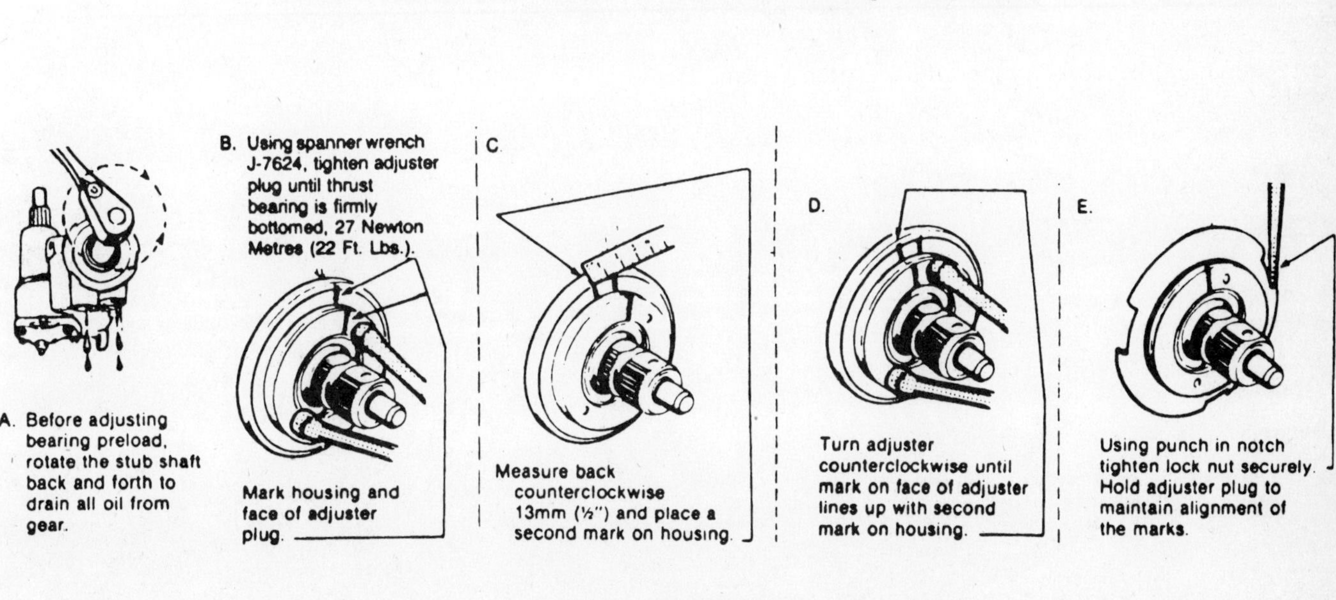

A. Before adjusting bearing preload, rotate the stub shaft back and forth to drain all oil from gear.
B. Using spanner wrench J-7624, tighten adjuster plug until thrust bearing is firmly bottomed, 27 Newton Metres (22 Ft. Lbs.).
Mark housing and face of adjuster plug.
C.
Measure back counterclockwise 13mm (½") and place a second mark on housing.
D.
Turn adjuster counterclockwise until mark on face of adjuster lines up with second mark on housing.
E.
Using punch in notch tighten lock nut securely. Hold adjuster plug to maintain alignment of the marks.

Adjusting the thrust bearing preload — C/K series

WHEEL ALIGNMENT SPECIFICATIONS
R and V Series

Year	Model	Caster (deg.) Range	Caster (deg.) Pref.	Camber (deg.) Range	Camber (deg.) Pref.	Total Toe-in (in.)
All	R10	See Chart Below		0.20P to 1.20P	0.70P	0.18
	R20/30	See Chart Below		0.25N to 0.75P	0.25P	0.18
	All V	7.5P to 8.5P	8P	1P to 2P	1.5P	0.12

NOTE: V Series caster and camber are not adjustable. The figure given is for reference only, in determining damaged components.

R Series caster is determined by ride height. Ride height is measured as the distance between the bumper stop bracket on the axle, and the frame. Use the following charts to determine caster. The ride height in inches is given reading left-to-right with the corresponding caster immediately below. Caster tolerance is plus or minus 1 degree.

R10/15

2.5	2.75	3	3.25	3.5	3.75	4	4.25	4.5	4.75	5.0	5.25	5.5	5.75	6.0
3.7P	3.5P	3.2P	2.9P	2.6P	2.4P	2.1P	1.8P	1.5P	1.3P	1.0P	0.8P	0.5P	0.3P	0

R20/25 and 30/35

2.5	2.75	3	3.25	3.5	3.75	4	4.25	4.5	4.75	5.0	5.25	5.5	5.75
1.5P	1.2P	0.9P	0.6P	0.3P	0.1P	0.01N	0.15N	0.7N	1.0N	1.2N	1.4N	1.6N	1.8N

WHEEL ALIGNMENT SPECIFICATIONS
C and K Series

See the text for setting ride height before proceeding

Year	Model	Caster (deg.) Range	Caster (deg.) Pref.	Camber (deg.) Range	Camber (deg.) Pref.	Toe-in (deg.)
All	All C	2.75P to 4.75P	3.75P	0 to 1.0P	0.50P	0.24
	K15/25	2.0P to 4.0P	3.0P	0.15P to 1.15P	0.65P	0.24
	K35	2.0P to 4.0P	3.0P	0 to 1.0P	0.50P	0.24

Brakes

QUICK REFERENCE INDEX

GENERAL INDEX

BRAKE SYSTEMS

Operation

All Chevrolet and GMC trucks are equipped with a split hydraulic braking system. The system is designed with separate systems for the front and rear brakes using a dual master cylinder with separate reservoirs. If a hydraulic component should fail in either the front or the rear system, the truck can still be stopped with reasonable control.

Trucks are equipped with disc brakes at the front and self-adjusting drum brakes at the rear. The drum brakes are of the duo-servo anchor pin self-adjusting type, while the front disc brakes are single piston sliding caliper types.

Rear Wheel Anti-Lock Brake System C and K Series

NOTE: Service on components peculiar to the ABS system will be found at the end of this Section

Essentially, this system controls the lock-up of the rear wheels during braking by electronically monitoring wheel rotational speed and vehicle momentum. The actual regulation process is directly controlled by regulating the brake hydraulic pressure at the rear wheel brakes.

Main system operating components are:

- A control valve, made up of a dump valve which releases pressure into an accumulator and an isolation valve which maintains rear brake pressure. The control valve is located near the combination valve master cylinder.
- An Electronic Control Unit (ECU), which controls the control valve. The ECU is located next to the master cylinder and is operated by signals received from the speed sensor located in the transmission, and the brake light switch. If the tire size and/or axle ratio are changed, the speed sensor must be changed.

The ABS system is wired into the existing brake warning light on the dash.

Brake Adjustments

DRUM BRAKES

These brakes are equipped with self-adjusters and no manual adjustment is necessary, except when brake linings are replaced.

DISC BRAKES

These brakes are inherently self-adjusting and no adjustment is ever necessary or possible.

Brake Pedal

CHECKING PEDAL TRAVEL

The stop light switch provides for an automatic adjustment for the brake pedal when it is returned to its stop. With pedal in fully released position, the stop light switch plunger should be fully depressed against the pedal shank. Adjust the switch by moving in or out as necessary.

R and V Series

Periodically check the pedal travel. With the engine off and the brakes cold, pump the pedal at least 3 times to expell all vacuum from the power brake booster. Use a yardstick to measure the distance between the lower edge of the steering wheel rim to

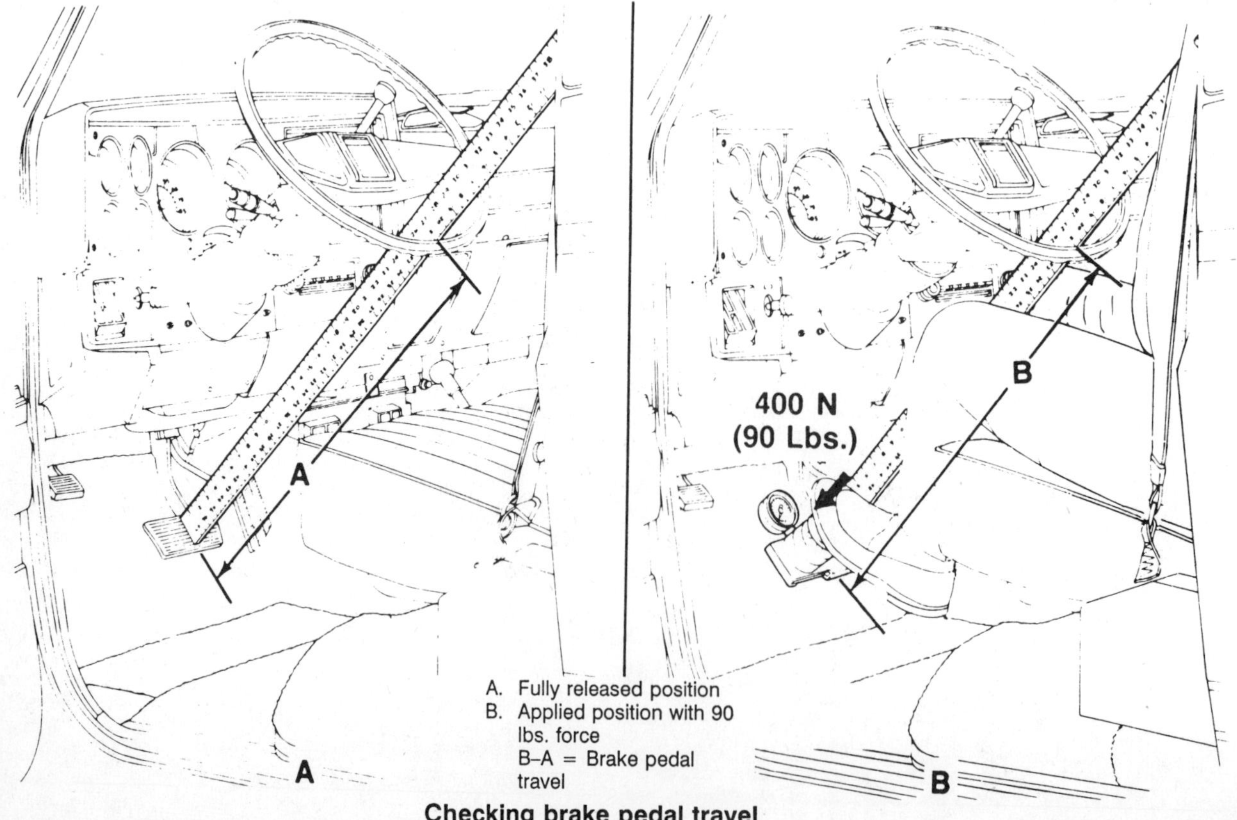

Checking brake pedal travel

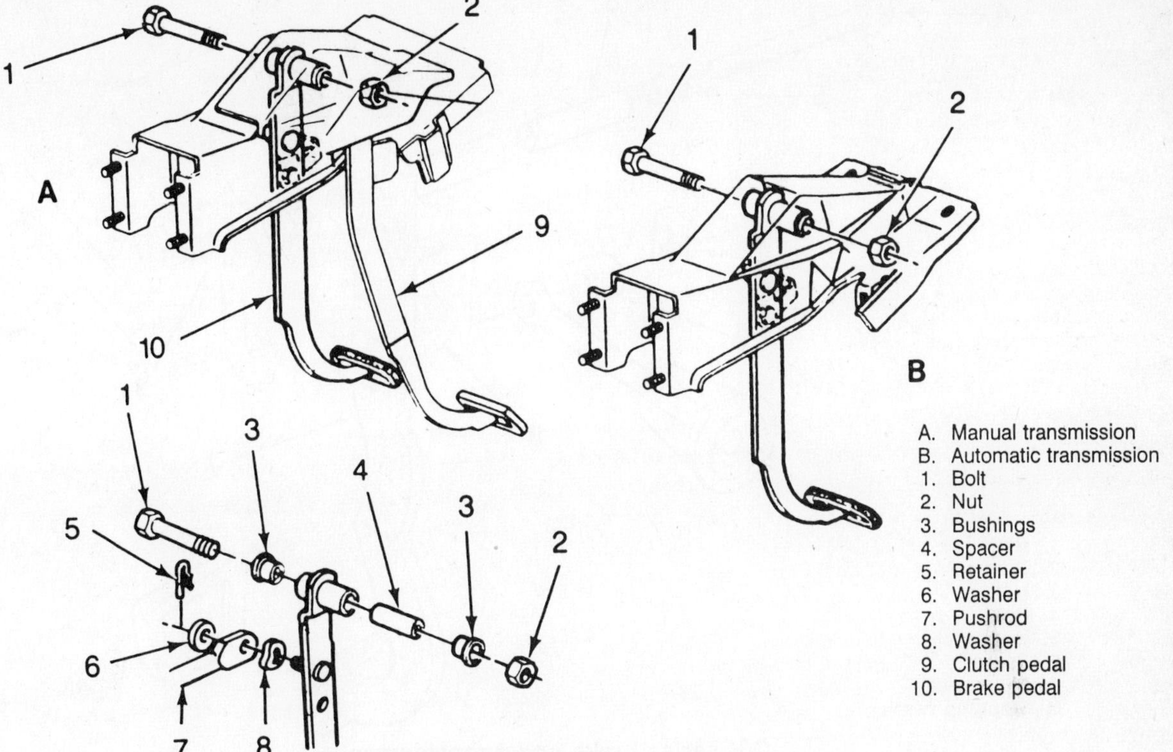

R/V series brake pedal components

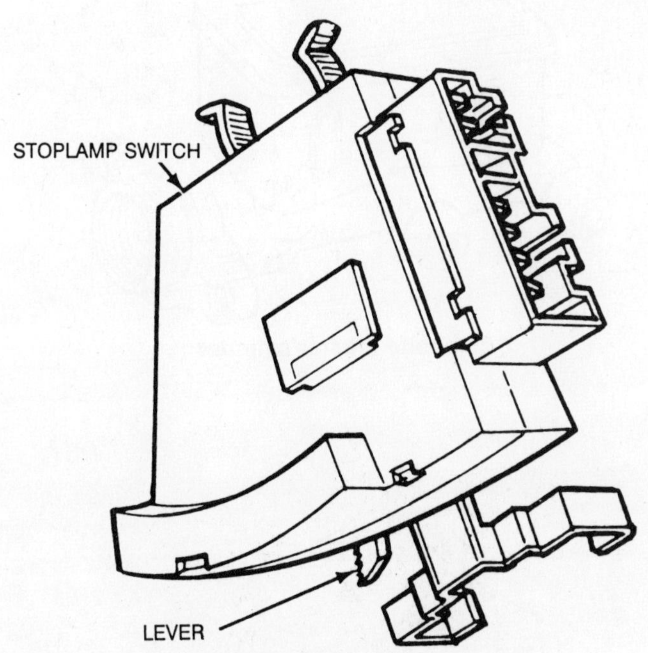

C/K series brake light switch

the top of the pedal. Then measure the distance while holding the pedal in the fully depressed position – about 90 lbs. of force. Calculate the difference bewteen the 2 readings. The distance should be 115mm for trucks with manual brakes; 90mm for trucks with power brakes.

C and K Series

Periodically check the pedal travel. With the engine off and the brakes cold, pump the pedal at least 3 times to expell all vacuum from the power brake booster. Use a yardstick to measure the distance that the pedal can be depressed from the fully released position to the fully applied position – about 90 lbs. of force.

The distance should be 140mm for trucks with manual brakes; 140mm for trucks with vacuum type power brakes; 113mm for trucks with anti-lock brakes.

REMOVAL AND INSTALLATION

R and V Series

1. Remove the retaining pin and washer, and disconnect the pushrod from the pedal arm.
2. Disconnect the return spring at the pedal arm.
3. Remove the brake pedal pivot bolt and nut and remove the pedal.

NOTE: On trucks with manual transmission, as you pull out the pivot bolt, slide a rod in behind it to hold the clutch pedal in place.

4. Installation is the reverse of removal. Tighten the pivot bolt nut to 25 ft. lbs.

C and K Series

1. Unplug the connector from the brake light switch.
2. Remove the retainer and bushing and slide the pedal pushrod off its stud.
3. Remove the pedal pivot bolt and nut, along with the spacer and bushings. Remove the pedal.
4. Installation is the reverse of removal. Tighten the bolt to 35 ft. lbs.

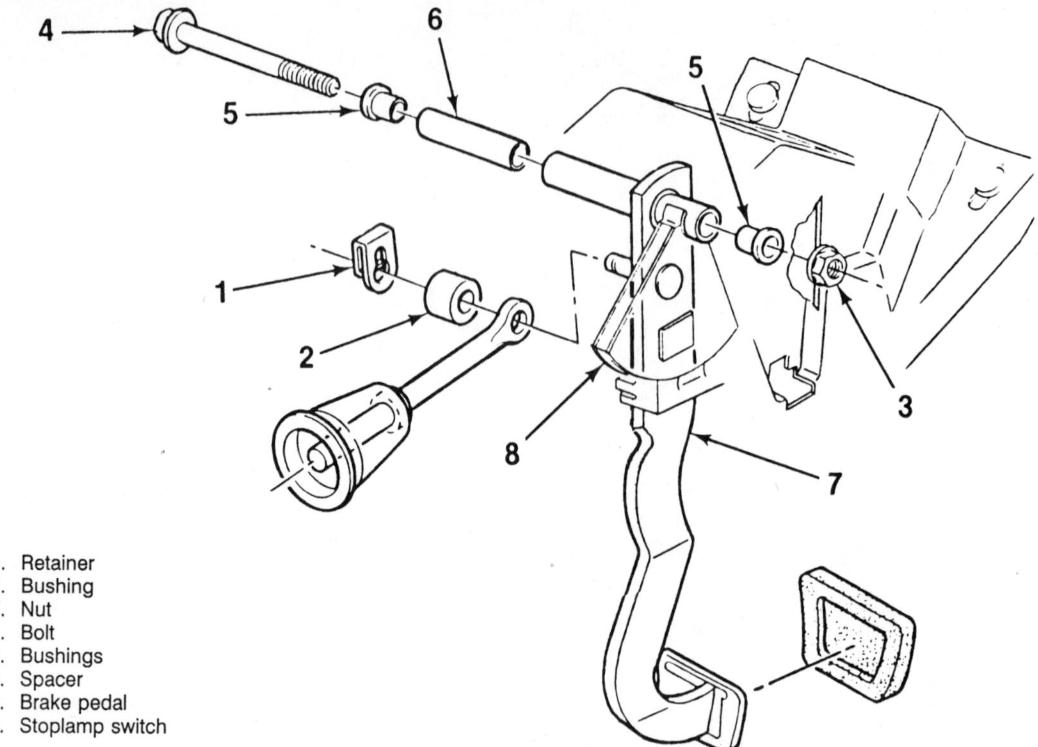

C/K series brake pedal replacement

Brake Light Switch

ADJUSTMENT

R and V Series

The design of the switch and valve mounting provides for automatic adjustment when the brake pedal is manually returned to its mechanical stop as follows:

1. With brake pedal depressed, press the switch in until it firmly seats on the clip. Note that audible clicks can be heard as threaded portion of switch is pushed through the clip.
2. Pull brake pedal fully against pedal stop, until audible click sounds can no longer be heard.
3. Release brake pedal, then repeat Step 2 to assure that no audible click sounds remain.

Electrical contact should be made when the brake pedal is depressed 1.0–1.24 in. (25–31mm) from its fully released position.

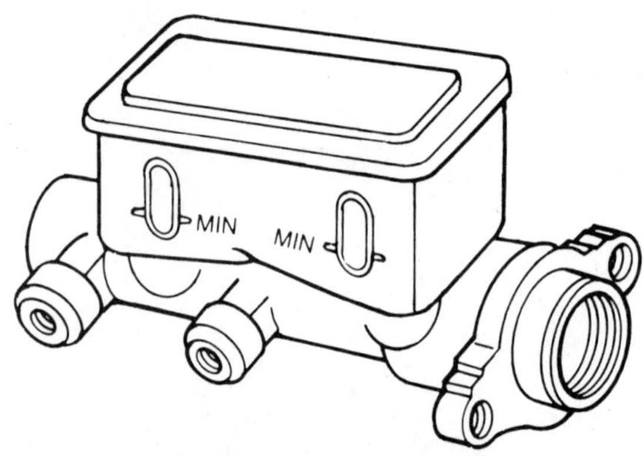

Composite master cylinder

C and K Series

1. Depress the brake pedal fully and hold it.
2. Pull the lever, on the bottom of the switch, back to its stop.
3. Release the pedal.

REMOVAL AND INSTALLATION

1. Remove the clip (R and V Series) or unclip the switch (C and K Series) and unplug the electrical connector from the brake light switch.
2. Installation is the reverse of removal.

Master Cylinder

REMOVAL AND INSTALLATION

WARNING: Clean any master cylinder parts in alcohol or brake fluid. Never use mineral based cleaning sol-

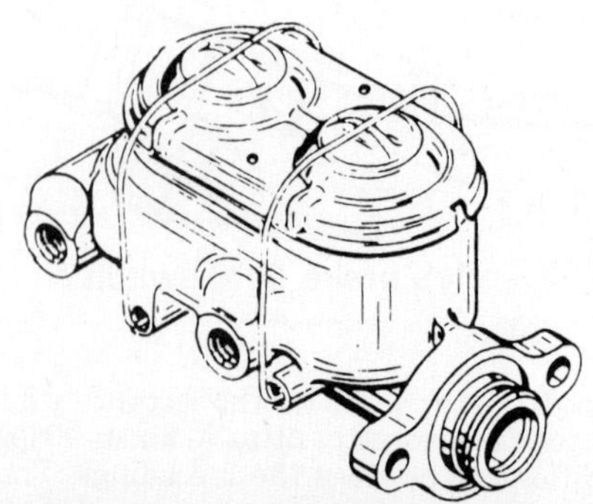

Cast iron master cylinder

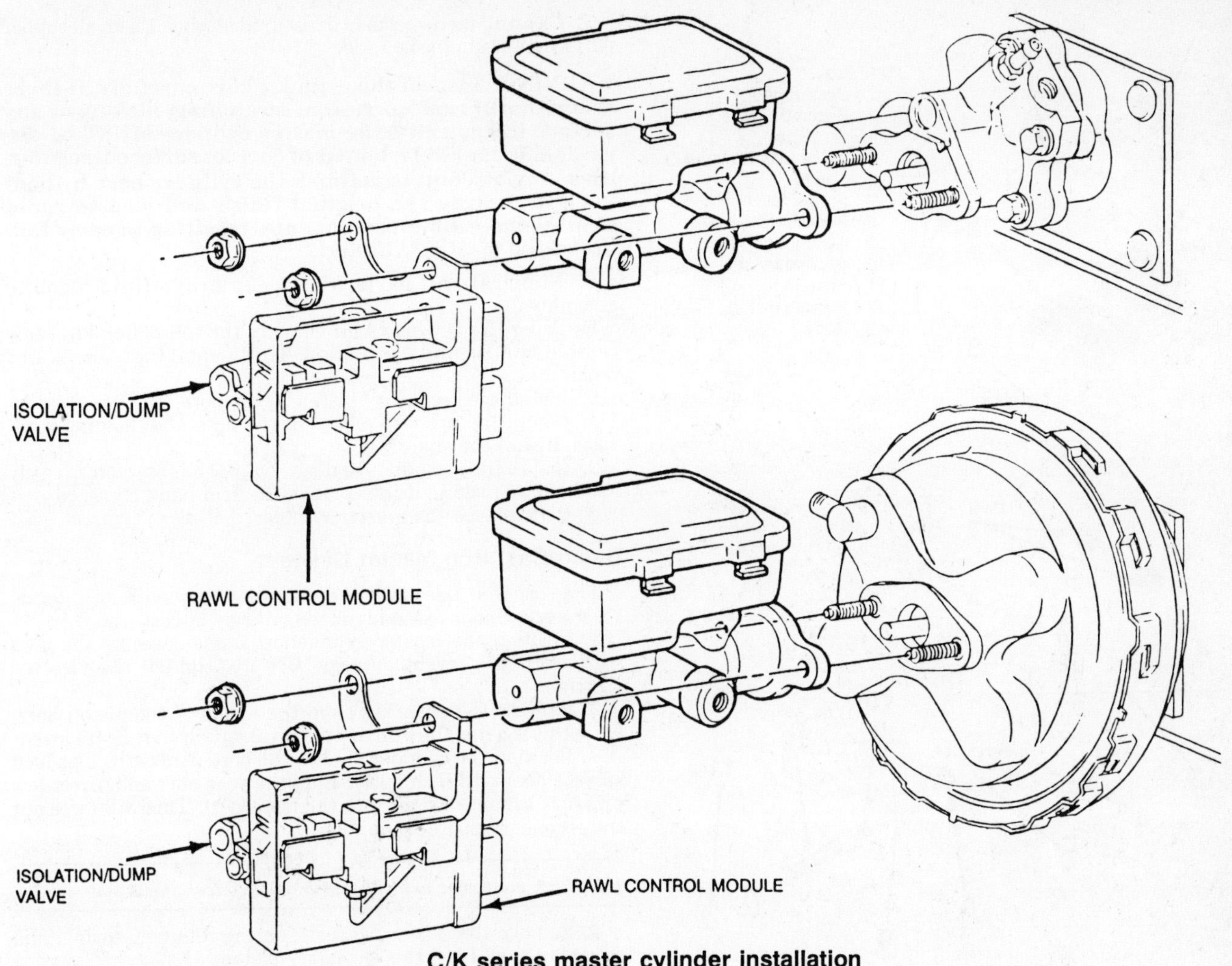

C/K series master cylinder installation

vents such as gasoline, kerosene, carbon tetrachloride, acetone, or paint thinner as these will destroy rubber parts.

Do not allow brake fluid to spill on the vehicle's finish, it will remove the paint. Flush the area with water.

1. Using a clean cloth, wipe the master cylinder and its lines to remove excess dirt and then place cloths under the unit to absorb spilled fluid.
2. Remove the hydraulic lines from the master cylinder and plug the outlets to prevent the entrance of foreign material. On trucks with ABS, disconnect the lines at the isolation/dump valve.
3. Remove the master cylinder attaching bolts or, on trucks with ABS, the attaching bolts from the isolation/dump valve, and remove the master cylinder from the brake booster, or, on trucks with manual brakes, the firewall.

CAUTION

On trucks with ABS, never let brake fluid or your skin touch the ECU electrical connections! Also, never let the isolation/dump valve hang by its wiring!

To install:

5. Position the master cylinder or, on trucks with ABS the master cylinder and isolation/dump valve, on the booster or firewall. Torque the nuts to 20 ft. lbs.
6. Connect the brake lines and fill the master cylinder reservoirs to the proper levels.
7. Bleed the brakes master cylinder, then the complete system.

OVERHAUL

NOTE: It is much easier to purchase a rebuilt master cylinder than to try to rebuild yours, yourself.

Composite Bodied Master Cylinders

These units are identified by a cylinder body with a separate reservoir mounted on top of the cylinder.

1. Remove the cover and drain all the fluid from the reservoir.
2. Clamp the cylinder in a vise on its mounting flange.
3. Using a small prybar, pry off the reservoir and remove the grommets.
4. Remove the snapring and pull out the primary piston assembly.
5. Position the cylinder so that the bore is towards a padded surface about an inch away. Plug the rear port and direct low pressure compressed air into the front port. This will force out the secondary piston assembly.

CAUTION

The piston may come out with considerable force! Shield your eyes!

6. Remove the seals, spring retainer and spring from the secondary piston.

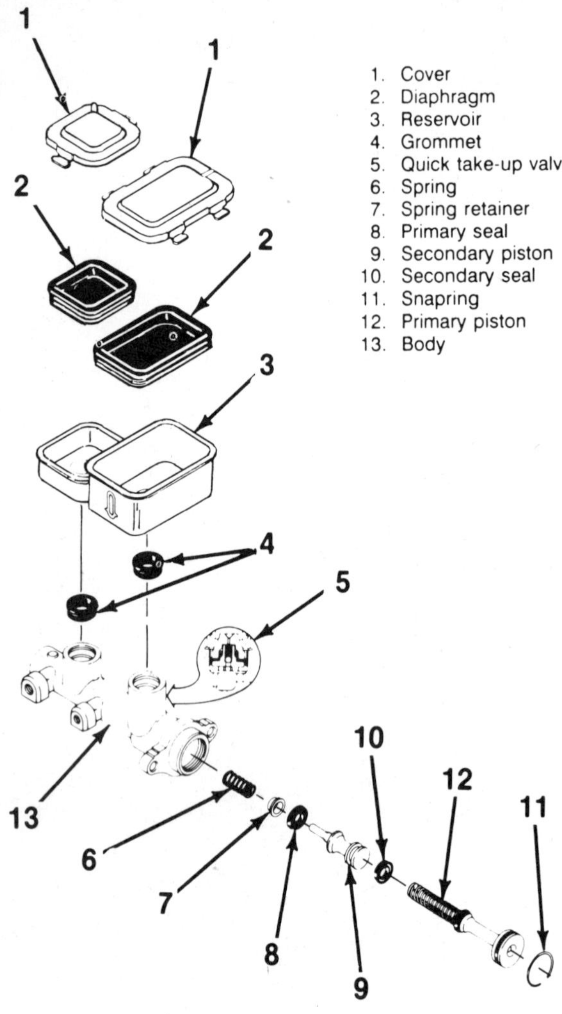

Composite master cylinder exploded view

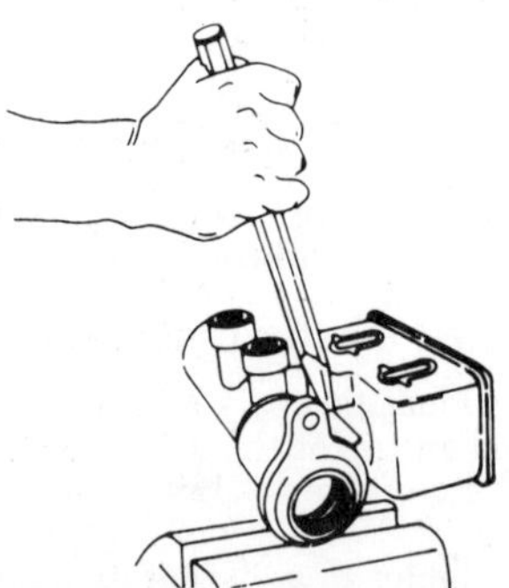

Removing the reservoir

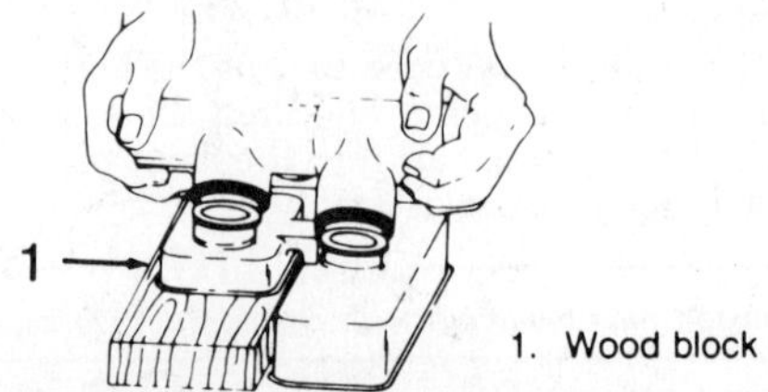

Installing the reservoir

7. Clean all metal parts in denatured alcohol. Clean all rubber parts with clean brake fluid.

WARNING: Inspect the cylinder bore carefully. If there is any sign of rust, corrosion, scratching, nicking or any surface irregularity, the master cylinder MUST be discarded. It cannot be honed to correct surface irregularities. Any attempt to refinish the cylinder bore by honing will destroy the original finish and lead to rapid wear of the rubber components, resulting in early failure of the master cylinder!

8. Lubricate all parts with clean brake fluid prior to assembly.
9. Using the new parts provided in the rebuilding kit, reassemble the secondary piston. The primary piston is not repairable.
10. Install the secondary piston in the bore.
11. Install the primary piston in the bore and, holding it inward, install the snapring.
12. Install the grommets and reservoir. The reservoir is easily installed by rocking it into place with firm hand pressure.
13. Bench-bleed the master cylinder.

Delco Cast Iron Master Cylinder

The cast iron Deco unit is a one-piece body with an integral reservoir/cylinder assembly made entirely of cast iron.

1. Position the master cylinder in a vise covering the jaws with cloth to prevent damage. (Do not tighten the vise too tightly).
2. Remove the snapring from the inside of the piston bore. Once this is done, the primary piston assembly may be removed.
3. Position the cylinder so that the bore is towards a padded surface about an inch away. Plug the rear port and direct low pressure compressed air into the front port. This will force out the secondary piston assembly.

CAUTION

The piston may come out with considerable force! Shield your eyes!

4. Remove the secondary seals, spring retainer, spring, and secondary seal from the secondary piston.
5. Remove the tube seats, if necessary, by threading a self-tapping screw into each seat any pulling the seat out with locking pliers.
6. Clean all metal parts in denatured alcohol. Clean all rubber parts with clean brake fluid.

WARNING: Inspect the cylinder bore carefully. If there is any sign of rust, corrosion, scratching, nicking or any surface irregularity, the master cylinder MUST be discarded. It cannot be honed to correct surface irregularities. Any attempt to refinish the cylinder bore by honing will destroy the original finish and lead to rapid wear of the rubber components, resulting in early failure of the master cylinder!

7. Lubricate all parts with clean brake fluid prior to assembly.
8. Using the new parts provided in the rebuilding kit, reassemble the secondary piston. The primary piston is not repairable.
9. Install the secondary piston in the bore.
10. Install the primary piston in the bore and, holding it inward, install the snapring.
11. Install new tube seats, seating them using a nut the same size as a brake line nut.
12. Bench-bleed the master cylinder.

Bendix Master Cylinder

This unit is identified by the separate reservoir secured to the

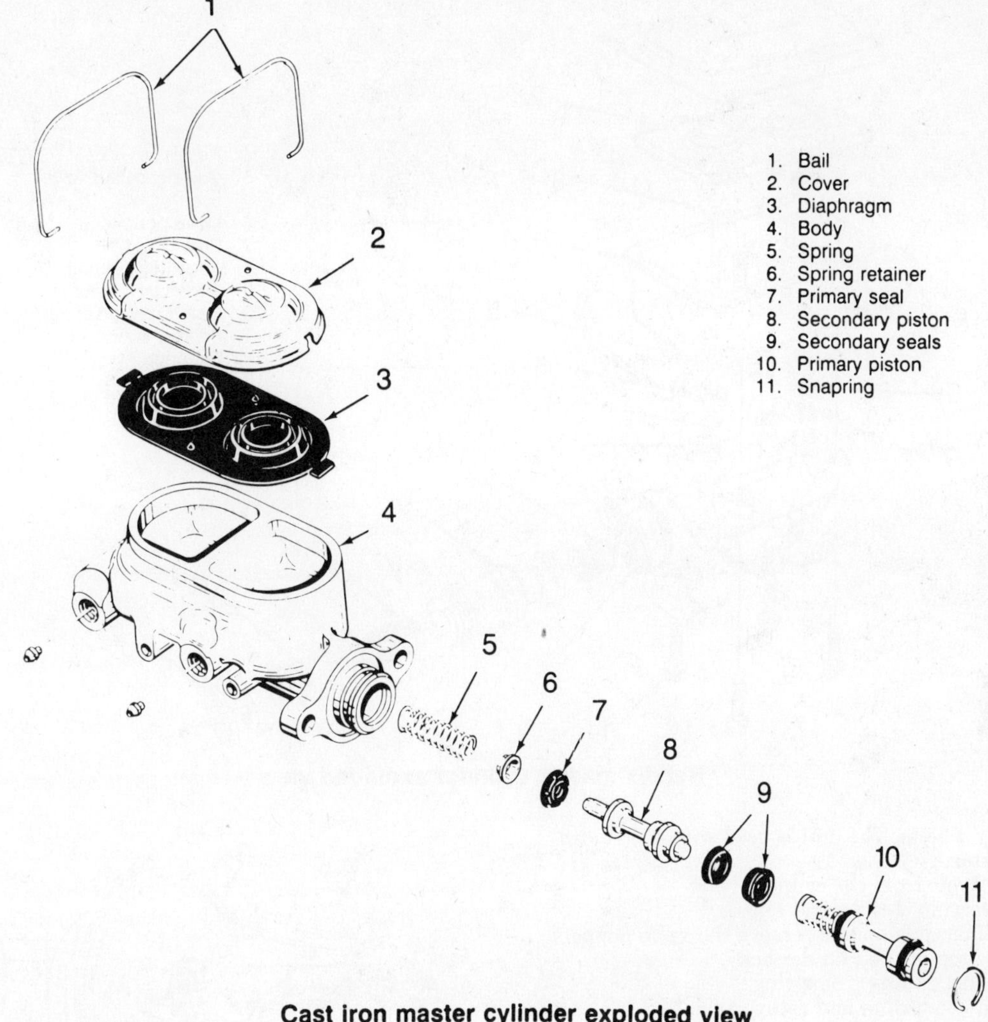

Cast iron master cylinder exploded view

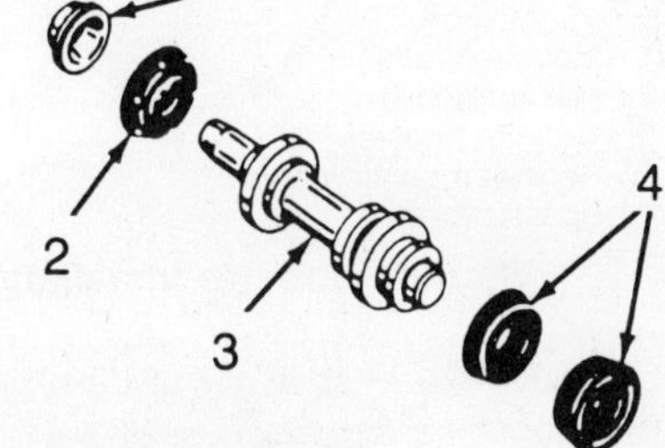

Secondary piston

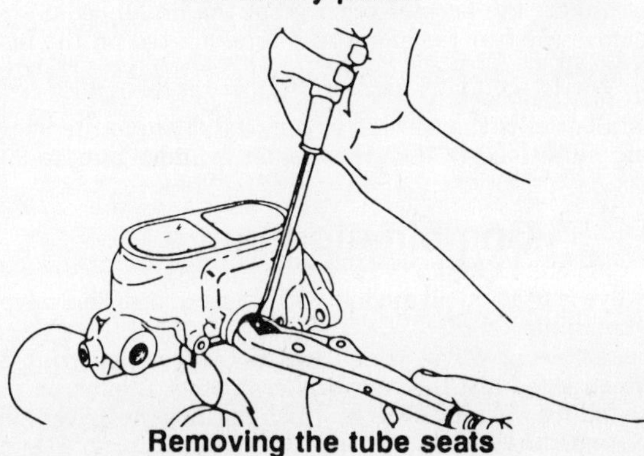

Removing the tube seats

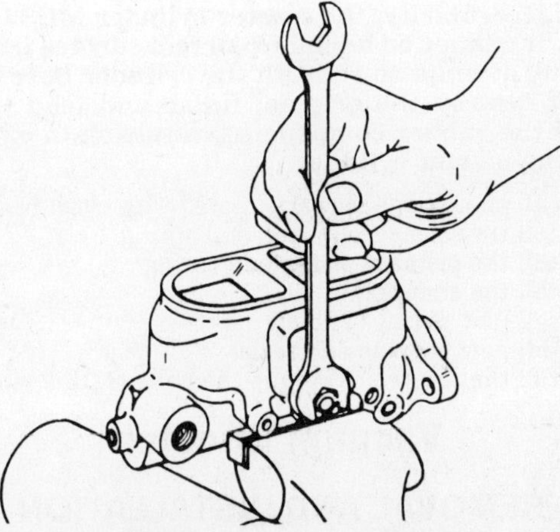

Installing the tube seats

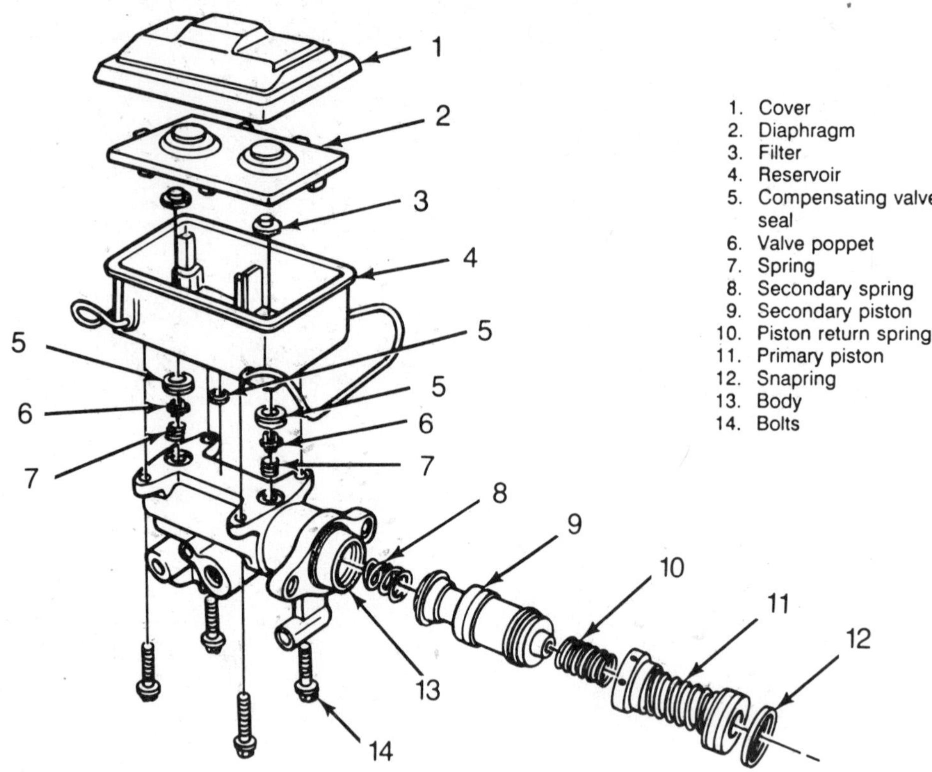

Bendix master cylinder exploded view

top of the cylinder by 4 bolts. The unit is used with the Hydro-boost hydraulic booster.

1. Unbolt the reservoir from the cylinder body.
2. Remove the reservoir O-rings and seals.
3. Depress the primary piston and remove the valve poppets and springs from the top of the cylinder body.
4. Remove the piston retaining snapring.
5. Remove the primary piston and return spring.
6. Plug the front port, aim the cylinder at a close, padded surface (about an inch away) and apply low pressure compressed air to the rear port. This will force out the secondary piston. Remove the spring, also.
7. Clean all metal parts thoroughly with denatured alcohol and discard all rubber parts.

WARNING: Inspect the cylinder bore carefully. If there is any sign of rust, corrosion, scratching, nicking or any surface irregularity, the master cylinder MUST be discarded. It cannot be honed to correct surface irregularities. Any attempt to refinish the cylinder bore by honing will destroy the original finish and lead to rapid wear of the rubber components, resulting in early failure of the master cylinder!

8. Install all new rubber parts coated with clean brake fluid.
9. Install the secondary piston and spring.
10. Install the primary piston and spring.
11. Install the snapring.
12. Install new O-rings and springs.
13. Install new poppets and seals.
14. Install the reservoir. Torque the bolts to 13 ft. lbs.

Vacuum Booster

REMOVAL AND INSTALLATION

1. Unbolt the master cylinder from the booster and pull it off the studs, CAREFULLY! It is not necessary to disconnect the brake lines.

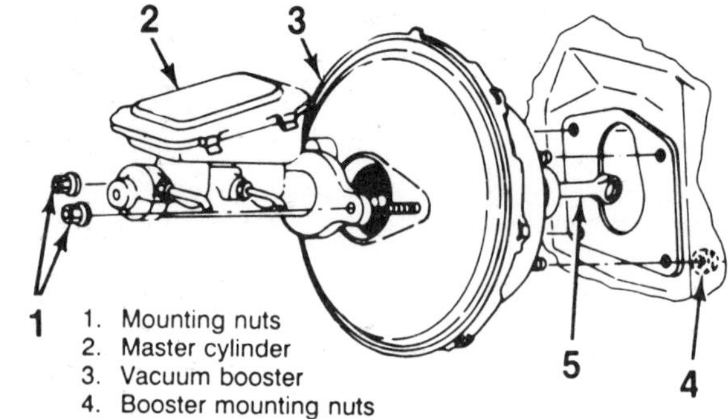

Vacuum booster installation

2. Disconnect the vacuum hose from the check valve.
3. Disconnect the booster pushrod at the brake pedal.
4. Remove the booster mounting nuts, located on the inside of the firewall.
5. Lift off the booster.
6. Installation is the reverse of removal. Torque the booster mounting nuts to 20 ft. lbs.; the master cylinder nuts to 20 ft. lbs.

Combination Valve

This valve is used on all models with disc brakes. The valve itself is a combination of:

1. The metering valve, which will not allow the front disc brakes to engage until the rear brakes contact the drum.
2. The failure warning switch, which notifies the driver if one of the systems has a leak.

3. The proportioner which limits rear brake pressure and delays rear wheel skid.

CENTERING THE SWITCH

Whenever work on the brake system is done it is possible that the brake warning light will come on and refuse to go off when the work is finished. In this event, the switch must be centered.

1. Raise and support the truck.
2. Attach a bleeder hose to the rear brake bleed screw and immerse the other end of the hose in a jar of clean brake fluid.
3. Be sure that the master cylinder is full.
4. When bleeding the brakes, the pin in the end of the metering portion of the combination valve must be held in the open position (with the tool described in the brake bleeding section installed under the pin mounting bolt). Be sure to tighten the bolt after removing the tool.
5. Turn the ignition key ON. Open the bleed screw while an assistant applies heavy pressure on the brake pedal. The warning lamp should light. Close the bleed screw before the helper releases the pedal.
6. To reset the switch, apply heavy pressure to the pedal. This will apply hydraulic pressure to the switch which will recenter it.
7. Repeat Step 5 for the front bleed screw.
8. Turn the ignition OFF and lower the truck.

NOTE: If the warning lamp does not light during Step 5, the switch is defective and must be replaced.

VALVE REPLACEMENT

R and V Series

1. Disconnect the hydraulic lines and plug to prevent dirt from entering the system.
2. Disconnect the warning switch harness.
3. Remove the retaining bolts and remove the valve.
4. Install in reverse of removal and bleed the brake system.

C Series with Manual Brakes

1. Disconnect the brake lines at the valve. Plug or cap the lines and ports.
2. Unplug the switch wiring connector.
3. Remove the valve-to-bracket bolts.
4. Installation is the reverse of removal. Tighten the bolts to 20 ft. lbs. Bleed the system.

C and K Series with Power Brakes

1. Disconnect the brake lines at the switch. Plug or cap the lines and ports.
2. Unplug the warning switch wiring connector.
3. Remove the anit-lock brake system control module from the bracket. See the procedure later in this section.

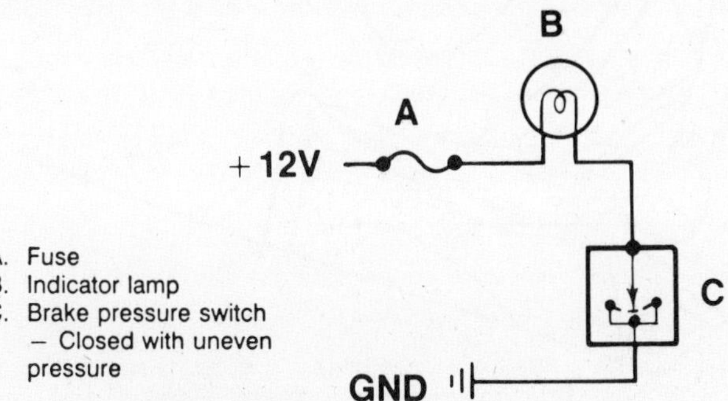

Brake pressure warning circuit

4. Remove the bolts attaching the ABS isolation/dump valve to the bracket. See the procedure later in this section.
5. Remove the nuts that attach the master cylinder and bracket to the booster.
6. Remove the bracket and combination valve assembly.

To install:

7. Position the bracket/valve assembly and install the master cylinder-to-booster nuts. Torque the nuts to 20 ft. lbs.
8. Install the ABS isloation/dump valve nuts. Torque them to 20 ft. lbs.
9. Install the ABS control module.
10. Connect the wiring.
11. Connect the hydraulic lines.
12. Bleed the system.

Height Sensing Proportioning Valve R and V 30 Series

This valve distributes braking pressure evenly from front-to-rear depending on either a light or heavy load condition.

CAUTION

Adjustment of the valve is determined by the distance between the axle and frame. The addition of such aftermarket items as air shocks, lift kits and addition spring leaves will render the valve inoperable, resulting in unsatisfactory brake performance, accident and injury!

REMOVAL AND INSTALLATION

NOTE: Special gauging tools are required for this job.

1. Raise and support the rear end on jackstands under the frame, allowing the axle to hang freely.
2. Clean the exterior of the valve.
3. Disconnect the brake lines at the valve. Cap the lines.
4. Remove the valve shaft-to-lever nut.
5. Remove the valve-to-bracket bolts.

To install:

6. Position the valve on the bracket and tighten the bolts securely.
7. Adjust the valve as described below.
8. Connect the lever to the valve shaft and torque the nut to 89 inch lbs.
9. Connect the brake lines.
10. Bleed the brakes.

ADJUSTMENT

If front wheel lock-up at moderate brake pressure is experienced with the vehicle at or near maximum GVWR, or, whenever the valve is replaced, the valve must be adjusted.

NOTE: Special gauging tools are required for this job.

1. Raise and support the rear end on jackstands under the frame, allowing the axle to hang freely.
2. Remove the shaft-to-lever nut and disconnect the lever from the shaft.
3. Obtain the proper gauge:

- R and V with Extra Capacity Rear Spring option: part number 14061394; color green; code A
- R Series without Extra Capacity Rear Spring option, and with either the 6–4.3L or 8–5.7L engine: part number 14061395; color black; code B.
- V Series without Extra Capacity Rear Spring option and with the diesel engine or the 8–5.7L engine: part number 14061396; color blue; code C.
- R and V Series with VD1 tire option: part number 15592484; color red; code D.
- V Series, except above: part number 15548904; color yellow; code E.

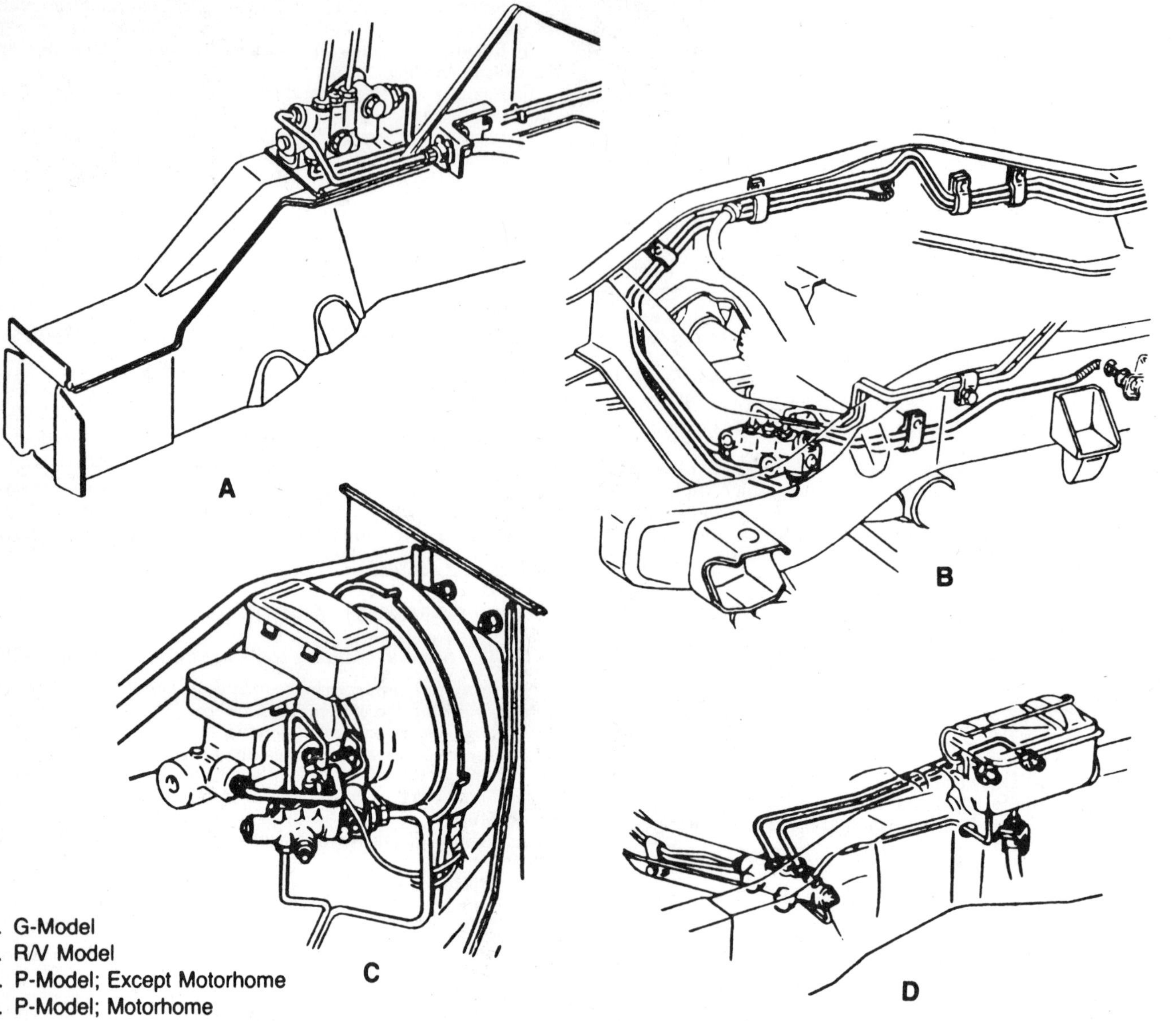

A

B

C

D

A. G-Model
B. R/V Model
C. P-Model; Except Motorhome
D. P-Model; Motorhome

R/V series combination valve location

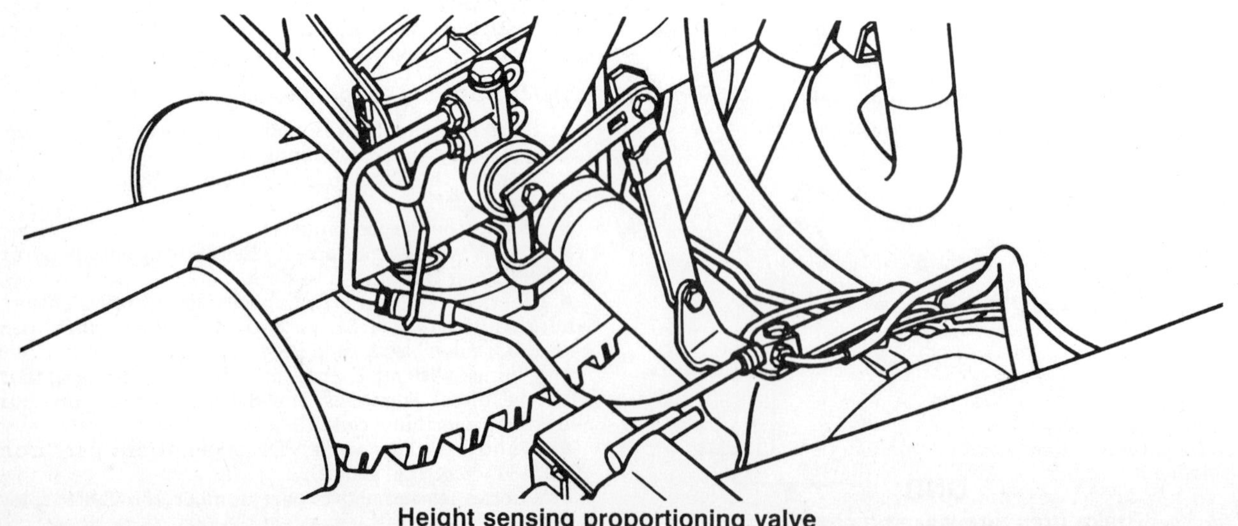

Height sensing proportioning valve

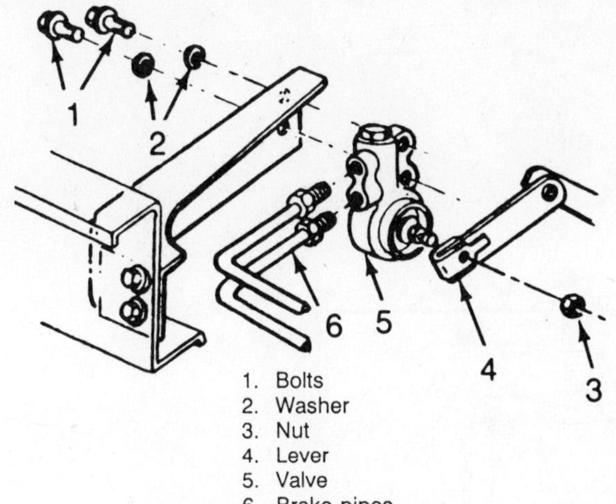

Proportioning valve installation

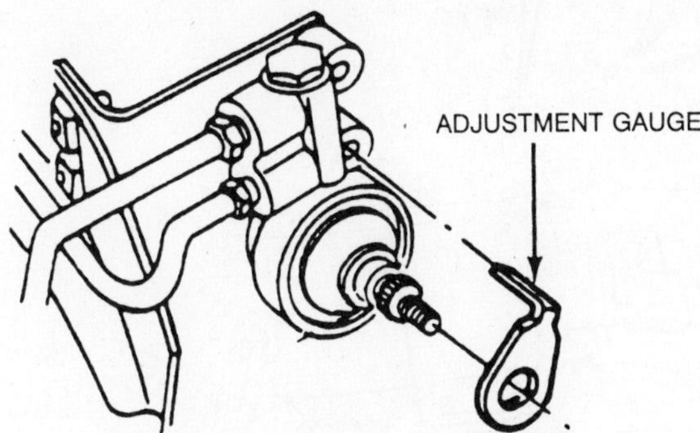

Installing the adjustment gauge

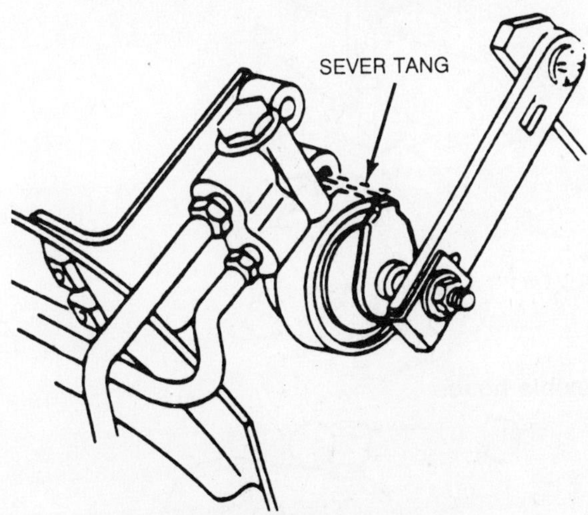

Severing the adjustment tang

4. Rotate the valve shaft to permit installation of the gauge. The center hole of the gauge must seat on the D-shape of the valve shaft. The gauge tang must seat in the valve mounting hole.
5. Install the lever on the shaft. Don't force it into position.
6. Install the nut on the shaft and tighten it to 89 inch lbs.
7. Break off or cut the tang on the gauge.
8. Road test the truck. The gauge will stay in place.

Brake Hoses

REPLACEMENT

1. Clean the connection thoroughly before opening it.
2. Unscrew the connection at the steel pipe or junction block and/or remove the bolt at the caliper. Discard any copper washers.
3. Remove any retaining clips and/or brackets securing the hose to the frame or control arm.
4. Cap all openings.
5. Installation is the reverse of removal. Always use new copper washers. The hose should not be twisted or in contact with any suspension component. Observe the following torques:
   - Brake hose-to-caliper bolt: 32 ft. lbs.
   - Front brake hose-to-frame nut: 58 inch lbs.
   - Front brake hose bracket bolt: 12 ft. lbs.
   - Rear brake hose-to-rear axle junction block: 12 inch lbs.

Brake Pipes

REMOVAL AND INSTALLATION

CAUTION

When replacing a steel brake pipe, always use steel tubing of the same pressure rating and corrosion resistance. The replacement pipe must be of the same diameter.

Copper tubing must never be used as a replacement for steel brake pipes!

Brake pipes running parallel must be separated by at least ¼ in. (6mm) along their common run.

1. Clean the pipe fittings and disconnect the pipe at each end. Where necessary, always use a back-up wrench. Cap all openings.
2. Cut the new pipe to length, adding ⅛ inch for each flare.
3. Always double-flare the pipe ends. Single flaring cannot withstand the pressure.
4. Always use a tubing bender when bending the pipe.
5. All brake pipe nuts should be torqued to 12 ft. lbs.

Hydro-Boost

Diesel engined trucks and some 30/3500 series trucks and motor home chassis are equipped with the Bendix Hydro-boost system. This power brake booster obtains hydraulic pressure from the power steering pump, rather than vacuum pressure from the intake manifold as in most gasoline engine brake booster systems.

HYDRO-BOOST SYSTEM CHECKS

1. A defective Hydro-Boost cannot cause any of the following conditions:
   a. Noisy brakes
   b. Fading pedal
   c. Pulling brakes.

   If any of these occur, check elsewhere in the brake system.
2. Check the fluid level in the master cylinder. It should be within ¼ in. (6mm) of the top. If is isn't add only DOT-3 or DOT-4 brake fluid until the correct level is reached.
3. Check the fluid level in the power steering pump. The engine should be at normal running temperature and stopped. The level should register on the pump dipstick. Add power steering fluid to bring the reservoir level up to the correct level. Low fluid level will result in both poor steering and stopping ability.

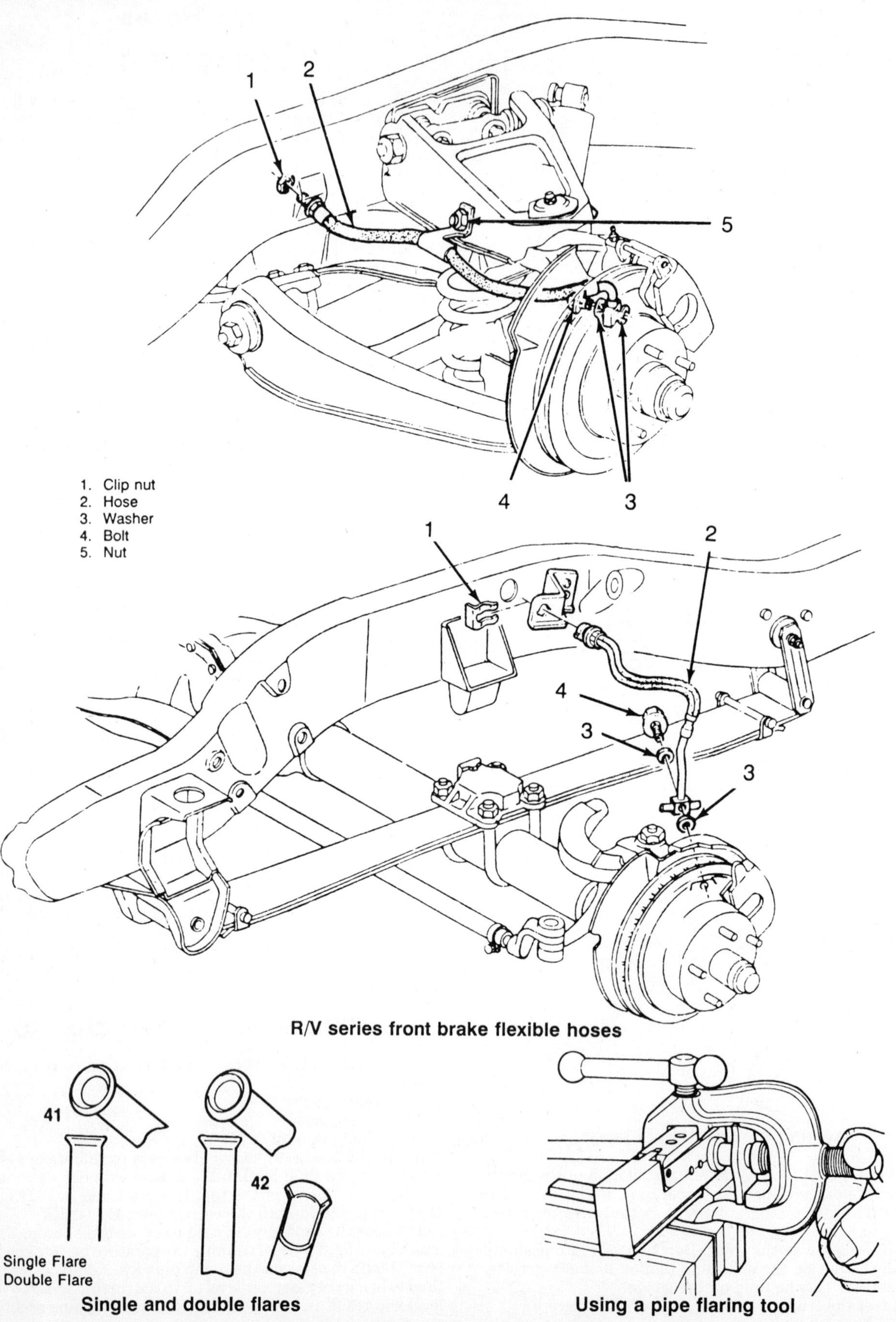

R/V series front brake flexible hoses

Single and double flares

Using a pipe flaring tool

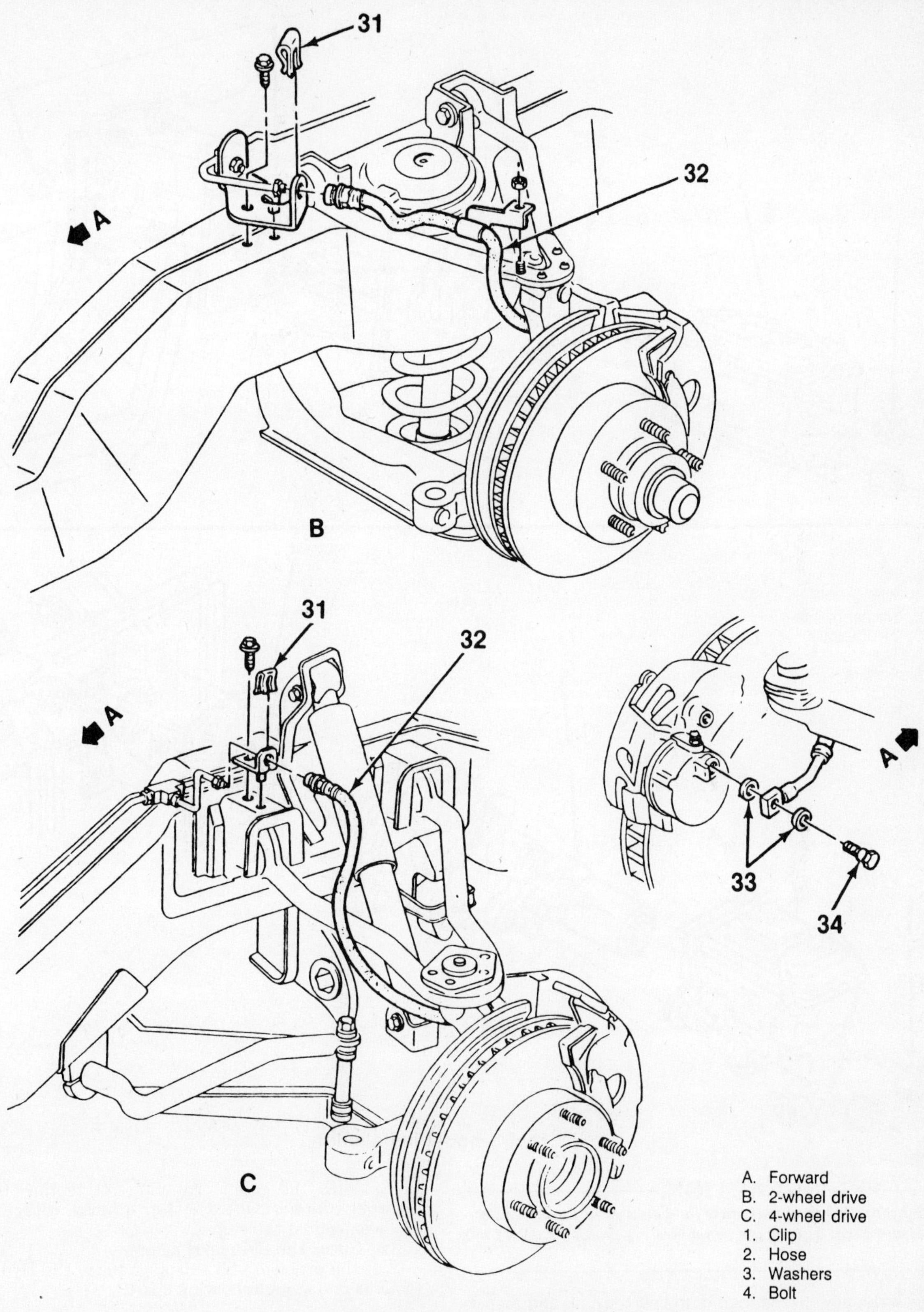

C/K series front brake flexible hoses

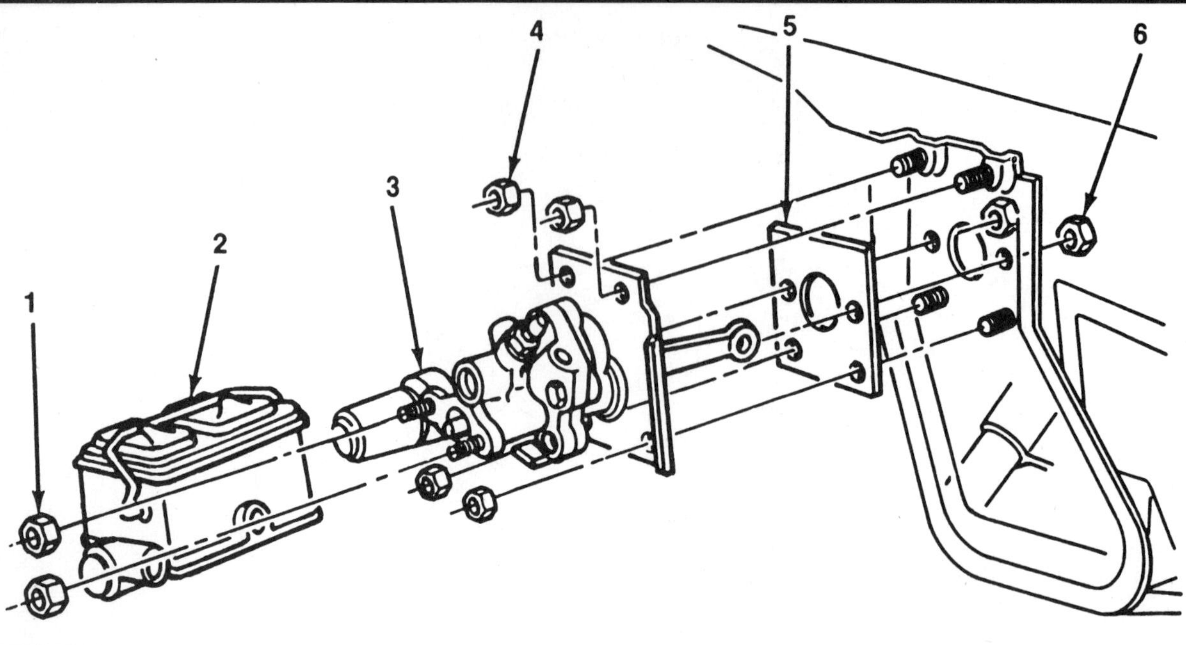

1. Nut
2. Master cylinder
3. Hydro-boost
4. Nut
5. Gasket
6. Nut

Hydro-boost installation

CAUTION

The brake hydraulic system uses brake fluid only, while the power steering and Hydro-Boost systems use power steering fluid only. Don't mix the two!

4. Check the power steering pump belt tension, and inspect all the power steering/Hydro-Boost hoses for kinks or leaks.
5. Check and adjust the engine idle speed, as necessary.
6. Check the power steering pump fluid for bubbles. If air bubbles are present in the fluid, bleed the system:
   a. Fill the power steering pump reservoir to specifications with the engine at normal operating temperature.
   b. With the engine running, rotate the steering wheel through its normal travel 3 or 4 times, without holding the wheel against the stops.
   c. Check the fluid level again.
7. If the problem still exists, go on to the Hydro-Boost test sections and troubleshooting chart.

HYDRO-BOOST TESTS

Functional Test

1. Check the brake system for leaks or low fluid level. Correct as necessary.

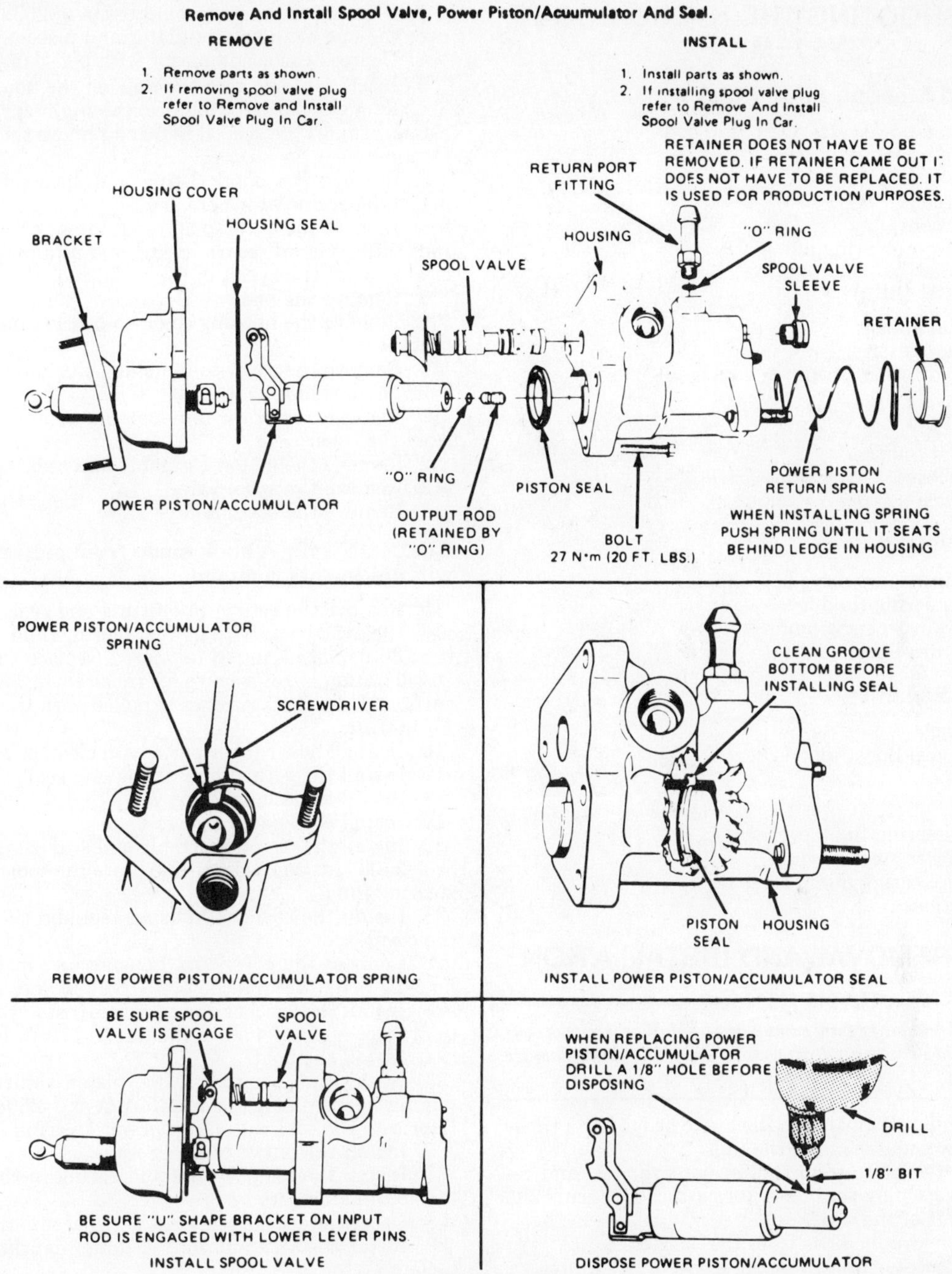

Remove And Install Spool Valve, Power Piston/Acuumulator And Seal.

REMOVE

1. Remove parts as shown.
2. If removing spool valve plug refer to Remove and Install Spool Valve Plug In Car.

INSTALL

1. Install parts as shown.
2. If installing spool valve plug refer to Remove And Install Spool Valve Plug In Car.

RETAINER DOES NOT HAVE TO BE REMOVED. IF RETAINER CAME OUT IT DOES NOT HAVE TO BE REPLACED. IT IS USED FOR PRODUCTION PURPOSES.

RETURN PORT FITTING
HOUSING COVER
HOUSING SEAL
BRACKET
HOUSING
"O" RING
SPOOL VALVE
SPOOL VALVE SLEEVE
RETAINER
"O" RING
POWER PISTON/ACCUMULATOR
OUTPUT ROD (RETAINED BY "O" RING)
PISTON SEAL
BOLT 27 N·m (20 FT. LBS.)
POWER PISTON RETURN SPRING
WHEN INSTALLING SPRING PUSH SPRING UNTIL IT SEATS BEHIND LEDGE IN HOUSING

POWER PISTON/ACCUMULATOR SPRING
SCREWDRIVER
REMOVE POWER PISTON/ACCUMULATOR SPRING

CLEAN GROOVE BOTTOM BEFORE INSTALLING SEAL
PISTON SEAL
HOUSING
INSTALL POWER PISTON/ACCUMULATOR SEAL

BE SURE SPOOL VALVE IS ENGAGE
SPOOL VALVE
BE SURE "U" SHAPE BRACKET ON INPUT ROD IS ENGAGED WITH LOWER LEVER PINS
INSTALL SPOOL VALVE

WHEN REPLACING POWER PISTON/ACCUMULATOR DRILL A 1/8" HOLE BEFORE DISPOSING
DRILL
1/8" BIT
DISPOSE POWER PISTON/ACCUMULATOR

Hydro-boost overhaul

2. Place the transmission in Neutral and stop the engine. Apply the brakes 4 or 5 times to empty the accumulator.

3. Keep the pedal depressed with moderate (25–40 lbs.) pressure and start the engine.

4. The brake pedal should fall slightly and then push back up against your foot. If no movement is felt, the Hydro-Boost system is not working.

Accumulator Leak Test

1. Run the engine at normal idle. Turn the steering wheel against one of the stops; hold it there for no longer than 5 seconds. Center the steering wheel and stop the engine.

2. Keep applying the brakes until a hard pedal is obtained. There should be a minimum of 1 power assisted brake application when pedal pressure of 20–25 lbs. is applied.

3. Start the engine and allow it to idle. Rotate the steering wheel against the stop. Listen for a light hissing sound; this is the accumulator being charged. Center the steering wheel and stop the engine.

4. Wait one hour and apply the brakes without starting the engine. As in step 2, there should be at least 1 stop with power assist. If not, the accumulator is defective and must be replaced.

TROUBLESHOOTING THE HYDRO-BOOST SYSTEM

High Pedal and Steering Effort (Idle)

1. Loosen/broken power steering pump belt
2. Low power steering fluid level
3. Leaking hoses or fittings
4. Low idle speed
5. Hose restriction
6. Defective power steering pump

High Pedal Effort (Idle)

1. Binding pedal/linkage
2. Fluid contamination
3. Defective Hydro-Boost unit

Poor Pedal Return

1. Binding pedal linkage
2. Restricted booster return line
3. Internal return system restriction

Pedal Chatter/Pulsation

1. Power steering pump drive belt slipping
2. Low power steering fluid level
3. Defective power steering pump
4. Defective Hydro-Boost unit

Brakes Overly Sensitive

1. Binding linkage
2. Defective Hydro-Boost unit

Noise

1. Low power steering fluid level
2. Air in the power steering fluid
3. Loose power steering pump drive belt
4. Hose restrictions

BOOSTER REMOVAL AND INSTALLATION

CAUTION

Power steering fluid and brake fluid cannot be mixed. If brake seals contact the steering fluid or steering seals contact the brake fluid, damage will result!

1. Turn the engine off and pump the brake pedal 4 or 5 times to deplete the accumulator inside the unit.
2. Remove the two nuts from the master cylinder, and remove the cylinder keeping the brake lines attached. Secure the master cylinder out of the way.
3. Remove the hydraulic lines from the booster.
4. Remove the booster unit from the firewall.
5. To install, reverse the removal procedure. Torque the nuts to booster mounting nuts to 20 ft. lbs.; the master cylinder mounting nuts to 20 ft. lbs. Bleed the Hydro-Boost system.

OVERHAUL

The following special tools, or their equivalents, are necessary for this procedure: J–26889, and J–24551–A or J–25083.

CAUTION

The Hydro-Boost accumulator contains compressed gas. Always use the proper tools and follow the procedures exactly to avoid personal injury. Do not apply heat to the accumulator. Do not attempt to repair an inoperative accumulator; always replace it with a new accumulator. Dispose of an inoperative accumulator by drilling a $^1/_{16}$ inch diameter hole through the end of the accumulator can opposite the O-ring.

1. Place accumulator compressor J–26889, or equivalent, over the end of the accumulator and place a nut on the stud.
2. Depress the accumulator with a C-clamp.
3. Insert a punch into the hole on the housing.
4. Remove the accumulator retaining snapring, release the C-clamp, remove the special tool and remove the accumulator and O-ring.
5. Remove the plug, O-ring and spring from the housing above the accumlator bore.
6. Remove the outlet pushrod retainer and remove the pushrod, baffle, piston return spring and retaining washer.
7. Saw off the eyelet of the pedal rod.
8. Remove the boot.
9. Remove the housing cover-to-bracket nut and remove the bracket.
10. Remove the cover-to-housing bolts and separate the cover from the housing.
11. Remove the cover-to-housing seal and the pushrod seal from the cover.
12. Remove the piston assembly and seal.
13. Remove the spool valve.
14. Remove the accumulator valve.

CHILTON TIP: A hook made from picture hanging wire will aid in this removal.

15. Remove the return line fitting and seal.
16. Clean all parts with power steering fluid. If the spool valve is at all damaged, pitted or scored, replace the entire booster. Discoloration is not a cause for replacement. Discard all rubber parts and use the new ones supplied with the rebuilding kit.

To install:

16. Coat all new rubber parts with clean power steering fluid.
17. Install the return line fitting and seal.
18. Install the accumulator valve.
19. Install the spool valve.
20. Install the piston assembly and seal using tool J–24551–A or J–25083, or equivalent. Lubricate the tool with clean power steering fluid.
21. Install the cover-to-housing seal and the pushrod seal in the cover.
22. Connect the cover and housing and install the cover-to-housing bolts. Torque the bolts to 22 ft. lbs.
23. Install the bracket on the cover. Install the housing cover-to-bracket nut and torque the nut to 110 ft. lbs.
24. Install the boot.
25. Install the pushrod, baffle, piston return spring and retaining washer using tool J–24551–A or J–25083, or equivalent. Lubricate the tool with clean power steering fluid.
26. Install the outlet pushrod retainer.
27. Install the plug, O-ring and spring in the housing above the accumlator bore.
28. Using the special tool, install the accumulator and O–ring.
29. Install the accumulator retaining snapring and release the C-clamp.
30. Using the pedal rod repair kit, install a jam nut on the pedal rod and adjust the new eyelet to give a pedal travel distance of 3.5 in. (89mm). Adjust this distance as follows:
    a. Using a yardstick, measure the distance from the top of the pedal pad to the lower edge of the steering wheel rim.
    b. Depress the pedal as hard as you can. If you have a pedal effort gauge, that's 90 lbs. of force.
    c. With the pedal depressed, remeasure the distance. The difference between the two readings is the pedal travel.

Bleeding the Brakes

Without Hydro-Boost or ABS

The brake system must be bled when any brake line is disconnected or there is air in the system.

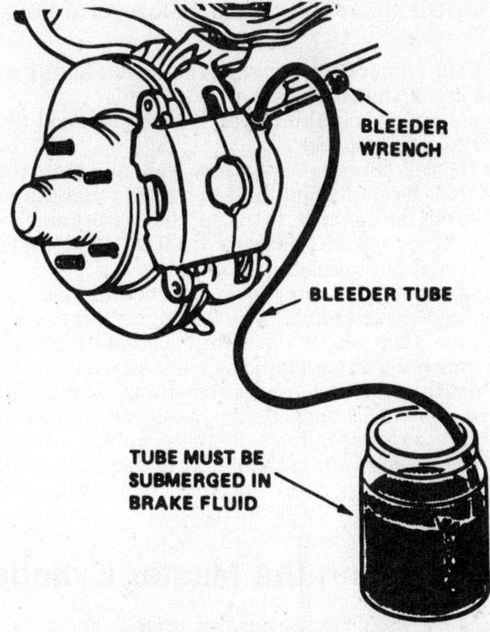

Brake bleeding equipment

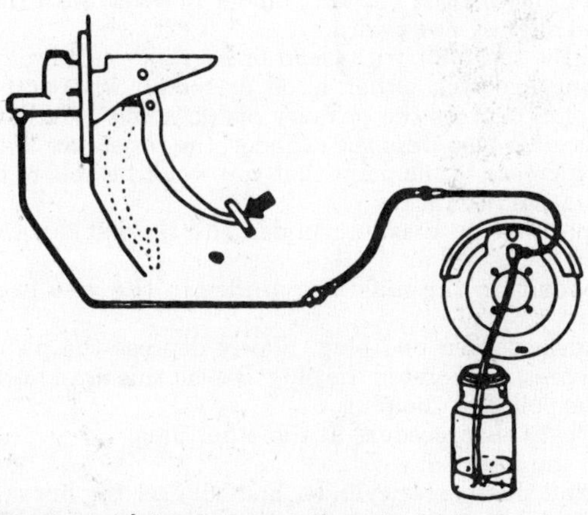

Have an assistant pump, then hold in the brake pedal, while you bleed each wheel

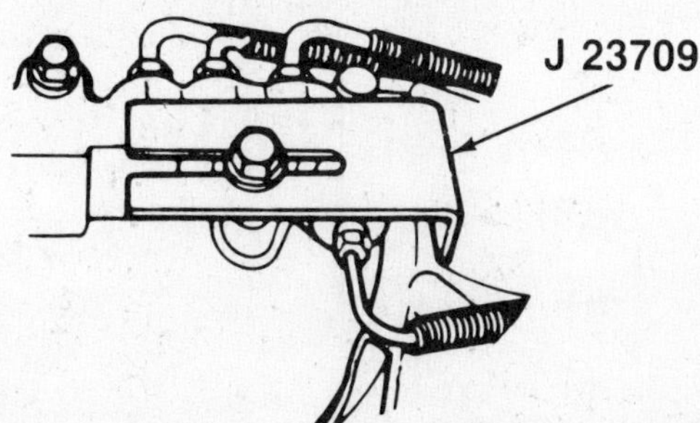

Using the combination valve depressor on the R/V series

NOTE: Never bleed a wheel cylinder when a drum is removed.

1. Clean the master cylinder of excess dirt and remove the cylinder cover and the diaphragm.
2. Fill the master cylinder to the proper level. Check the fluid level periodically during the bleeding process, and replenish it as necessary. Do not allow the master cylinder to run dry, or you will have to start over.

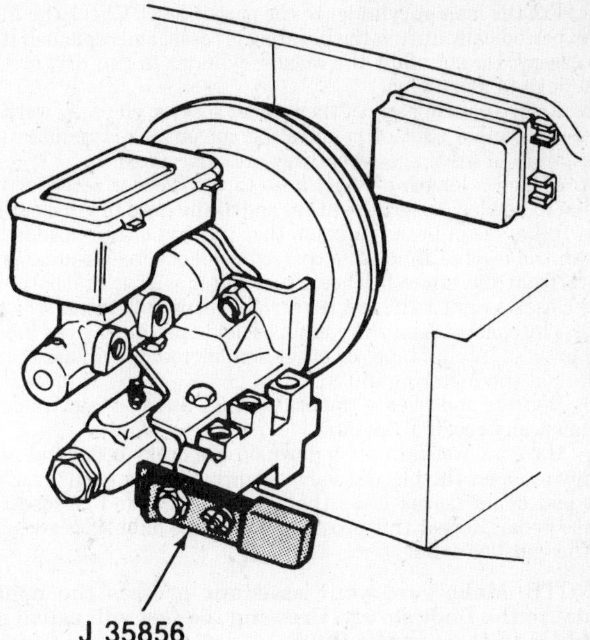

Using the combination valve depressor on the C/K series

3. Before opening any of the bleeder screws, you may want to give each one a shot of penetrating solvent. This reduces the possibility of breakage when they are unscrewed.
4. Attach a length of vinyl hose to the bleeder screw of the brake to be bled. Insert the other end of the hose into a clear jar half full of clean brake fluid, so that the end of the hose is beneath the level of fluid. The correct sequence for bleeding is to work from the brake farthest from the master cylinder to the one closest; right rear, left rear, right front, left front.
5. The combination valve must be held open during the bleeding process. A clip, tape, or other similar tool (or an assistant) will hold the metering pin in.
6. Depress and release the brake pedal three or four times to exhaust any residual vacuum.
7. Have an assistant push down on the brake pedal and hold it down. Open the bleeder valve slightly. As the pedal reaches the end of its travel, close the bleeder screw and release the brake pedal. Repeat this process until no air bubbles are visible in the expelled fluid.

NOTE: Make sure your assistant presses the brake pedal to the floor slowly. Pressing too fast will cause air bubbles to form in the fluid.

8. Repeat this procedure at each of the brakes. Remember to check the master cylinder level occasionally. Use only fresh fluid to refill the master cylinder, not the stuff bled from the system.
9. When the bleeding process is complete, refill the master cylinder, install its cover and diaphragm, and discard the fluid bled from the brake system.

With ABS

The brake system must be bled when any brake line is disconnected or there is air in the system.

NOTE: Never bleed a wheel cylinder when a drum is removed.

1. Clean the master cylinder of excess dirt and remove the cylinder cover and the diaphragm.

2. Fill the master cylinder to the proper level. Check the fluid level periodically during the bleeding process, and replenish it as necessary. Do not allow the master cylinder to run dry, or you will have to start over.

3. Before opening any of the bleeder screws, you may want to give each one a shot of penetrating solvent. This reduces the possibility of breakage when they are unscrewed.

4. Attach a length of vinyl hose to the bleeder screw of the brake to be bled. Insert the other end of the hose into a clear jar half full of clean brake fluid, so that the end of the hose is beneath the level of fluid. The correct sequence for bleeding is to work from the brake farthest from the master cylinder to the one closest; right rear, left rear, right front, left front.

5. The combination valve must be held open during the bleeding process. A clip, tape, or other similar tool (or an assistant) will hold the metering pin in.

6. Depress and release the brake pedal three or four times to exhaust any residual vacuum.

7. Have an assistant push down on the brake pedal and hold it down. Open the bleeder valve slightly. As the pedal reaches the end of its travel, close the bleeder screw and release the brake pedal. Repeat this process until no air bubbles are visible in the expelled fluid.

NOTE: Make sure your assistant presses the brake pedal to the floor slowly. Pressing too fast will cause air bubbles to form in the fluid.

8. Repeat this procedure at each of the brakes. Remember to check the master cylinder level occasionally. Use only fresh fluid to refill the master cylinder, not the stuff bled from the system.

9. When the bleeding process is complete, refill the master cylinder, install its cover and diaphragm, and discard the fluid bled from the brake system.

10. Refill the jar with clean brake fluid and attach the bleed hose to the bleed valve on the Isolation/Dump valve.

11. Have your assistant slowly depress the brake pedal and hold it. Loosen the bleed valve and expell the air. Tighten the valve and slowly release the pedal.

12. Wait 15 seconds and repeat this procedure. Repeat bleeding the Isolation/Dump valve until all the air is expelled.

Hydro-boost System Bleeding

The system should be bled whenever the booster is removed and installed.

1. Fill the power steering pump until the fluid level is at the base of the pump reservoir neck. Disconnect the battery lead from the distributor.

NOTE: Remove the electrical lead to the fuel solenoid terminal on the injection pump before cranking the engine.

2. Jack up the front of the car, turn the wheels all the way to the left, and crank the engine for a few seconds.

3. Check steering pump fluid level. If necessary, add fluid to the Add mark on the dipstick.

4. Lower the car, connect the battery lead, and start the engine. Check fluid level and add fluid to the Add mark is necessary. With the engine running, turn the wheels from side to side to bleed air from the system. Make sure that the fluid level stays above the internal pump casting.

5. The Hydro-Boost system should now be fully bled. If the fluid is foaming after bleeding, stop the engine, let the system set for one hour, then repeat the second part of Step 4.

The preceding procedures should be effective in removing the excess air from the system, however sometimes air may still remain trapped. When this happens the booster may make a gulping noise when the brake is applied. Lightly pumping the brake pedal with the engine running should cause this noise to disappear. After the noise stops, check the pump fluid level and add as necessary.

Bench Bleeding the Master Cylinder

This procedure should be performed prior to installing the master cylinder.

1. Plug the outlet ports to prevent pressurized fluid from escaping and mount the master cylinder in a vise with the front end tilted slightly downward.

2. Fill the reservoir with clean brake fluid.

3. Using a dowel, either wood or metal, with a rounded, smooth end, depress the primary piston about 1 inch, several times. As air is bled from the cylinder, the resistance at the piston will increase to the point that you won't be able to depress the piston the full inch.

4. Reposition the master cylinder with the end slight up. Repeat Step 3.

5. Reposition the master cylinder in the vise in a level position.

6. Slightly loosen one plug. Slowly depress the piston and hold it depressed. Tighten the plug. Repeat this until no air, just fluid, is expelled at the plug.

7. Repeat this procedure at the other plug.

8. Fill the reservoir.

9. Install the master cylinder and connect the lines. Repeat Steps 6 and 7 at each line.

10. Once the master cylinder is bled and installed, bleed the entire system.

FRONT DISC BRAKES

Two different caliper designs are used. A Delco disc brake system is used on all models except R and V 30 Series and 3500 motorhome chassis. These trucks use a Bendix system.

Brake Pads

INSPECTION

Support the front suspension on jackstands and remove the wheels. Look in at the ends of the caliper to check the lining thickness of the outer pad. Look through the inspection hole in the top of the caliper to check the thickness of the inner pad. Minimum acceptable pad thickness is $^1/_{32}$ in. (0.8mm) from the rivet heads on original equipment riveted linings and ½ in. (13mm) lining thickness on bonded linings.

NOTE: These manufacturer's specifications may not agree with your state inspection law.

All original equipment pads are the riveted type; unless you want to remove the pads to measure the actual thickness from the rivet heads, you will have to make the limit for visual inspection $^1/_{16}$ in. (1.6mm) or more. The same applies if you don't know what kind of lining you have. Original equipment pads and GM replacement pads have an integral wear sensor. This is a spring steel tab on the rear edge of the inner pad which produces a squeal by rubbing against the rotor to warn that the pads have reached their wear limit. They do not squeal when the brakes are applied.

The squeal will eventually stop if worn pads aren't replaced. Should this happen, replace the pads immediately to prevent expensive rotor (disc) damage.

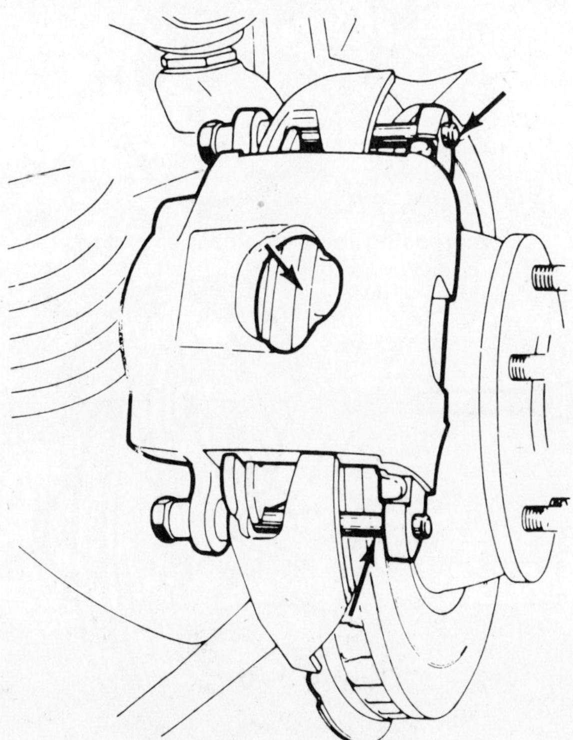

Lining inspection points

REPLACEMENT

Delco System

1. Remove the cover on the master cylinder and siphon out ⅔ of the fluid. This step prevents spilling fluid when the piston is pushed back.
2. Raise and support the front end on jackstands.
3. Remove the wheels.
4. Push the brake piston back into its bore using a C-clamp to pull the caliper outward.
5. Remove the two bolts which hold the caliper and then lift the caliper off the disc.

CAUTION

Do not let the caliper assembly hang by the brake hose.

6. Remove the inboard and outboard shoe.

NOTE: If the pads are to be reinstalled, mark them inside and outside.

7. Remove the pad support spring from the piston.

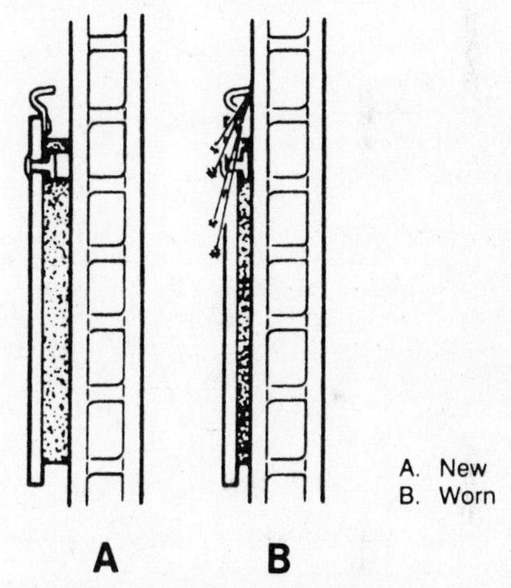

Brake pad wear indicators

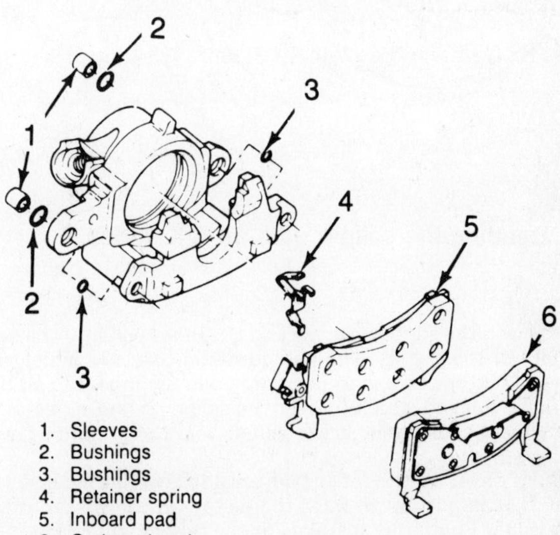

Delco brake pads

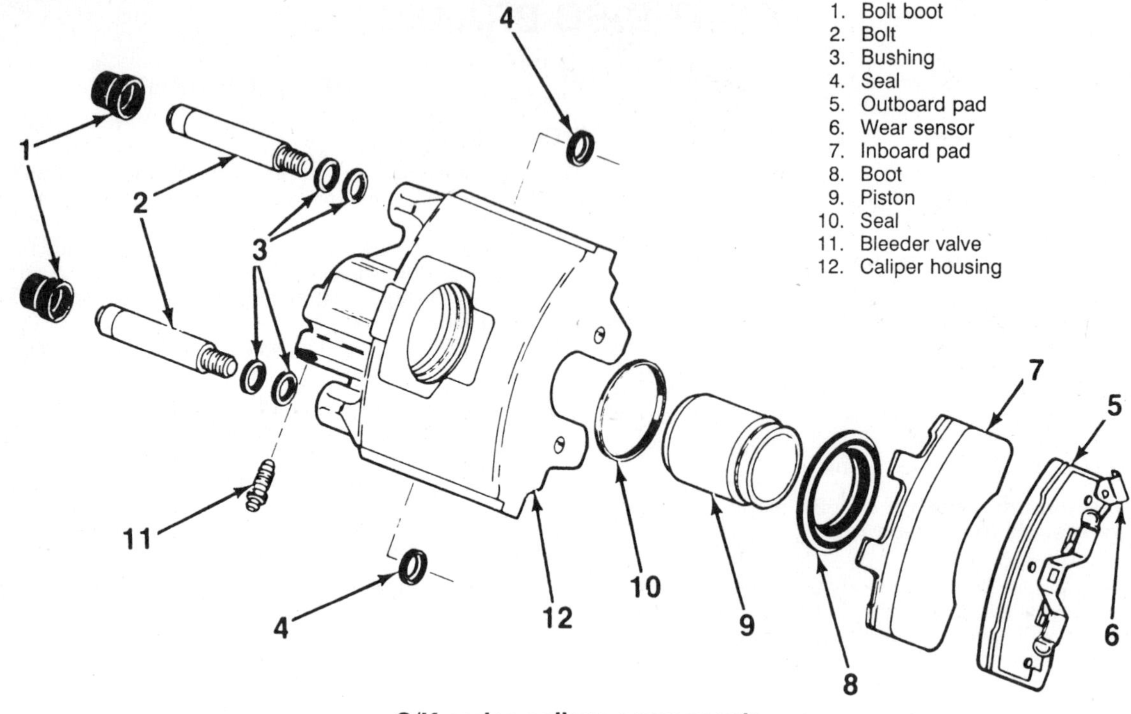

C/K series caliper components

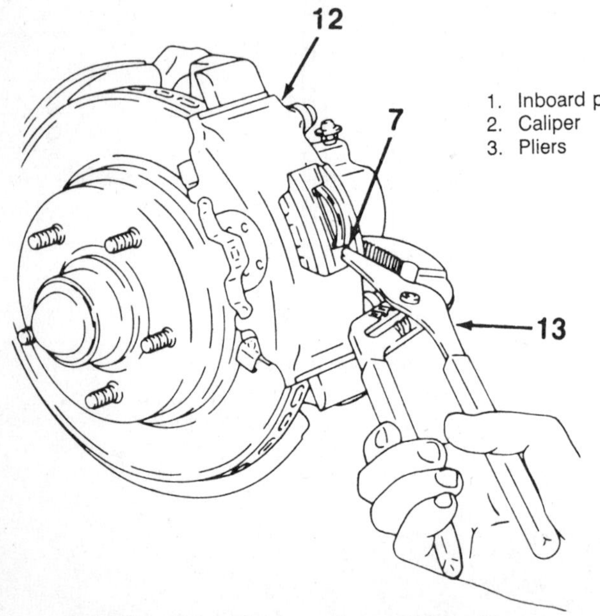

Bending the caliper ears on C/K series

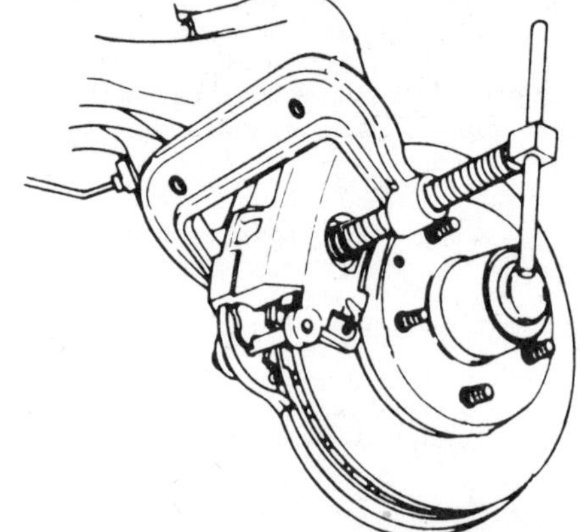

Compressing the Delco caliper piston

To install:

8. Position the support spring and the inner pad into the center cavity of the piston. The outboard pad has ears which are bent over to keep the pad in position while the inboard pad has ears on the top end which fit over the caliper retaining bolts. A spring which is inside the brake piston hold the bottom edge of the inboard pad.

9. Push down on the inner pad until it lays flat against the caliper. It is important to push the piston all the way into the caliper if new linings are installed or the caliper will not fit over the rotor.

10. Position the outboard pad with the ears of the pad over the

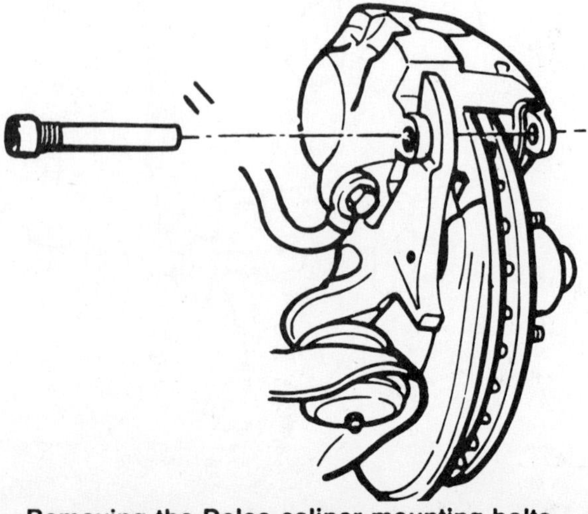

Removing the Delco caliper mounting bolts

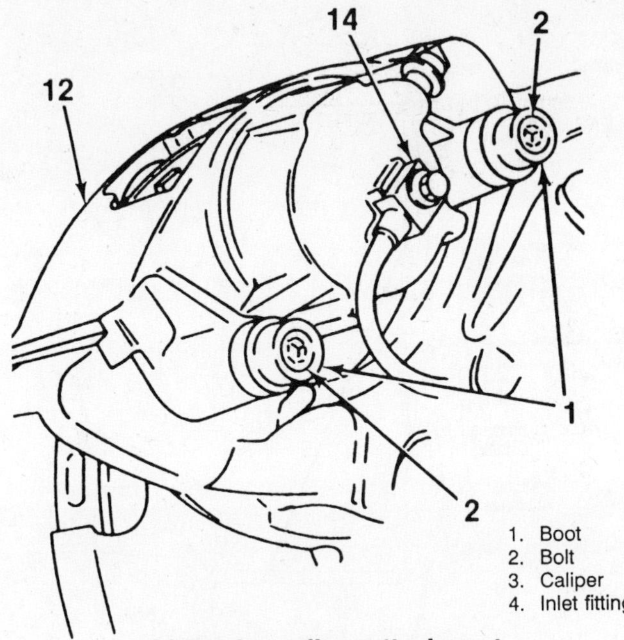

C/K series caliper attachment

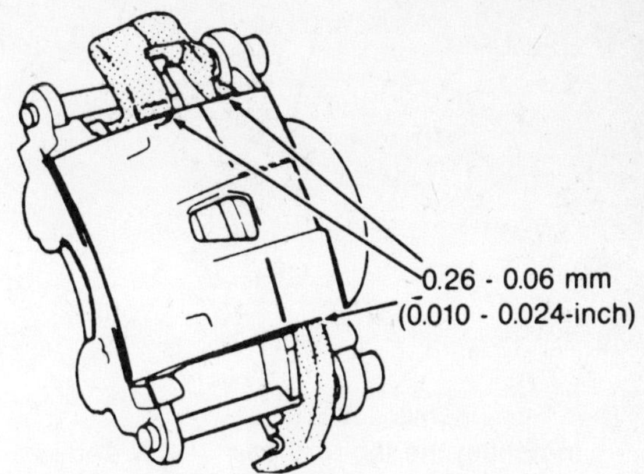

R/V series caliper-to-knuckle clearances

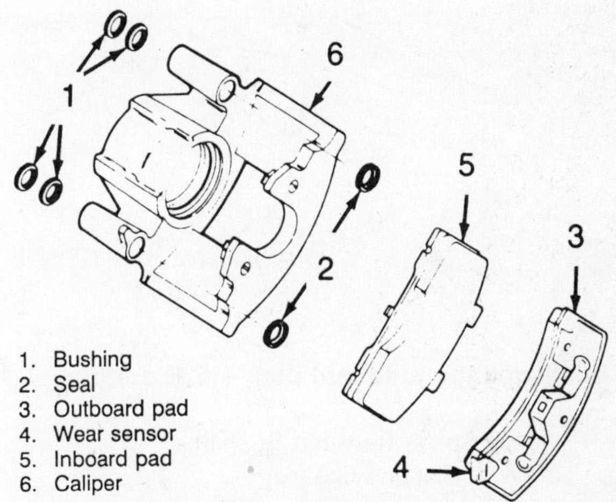

C/K series pad assembly

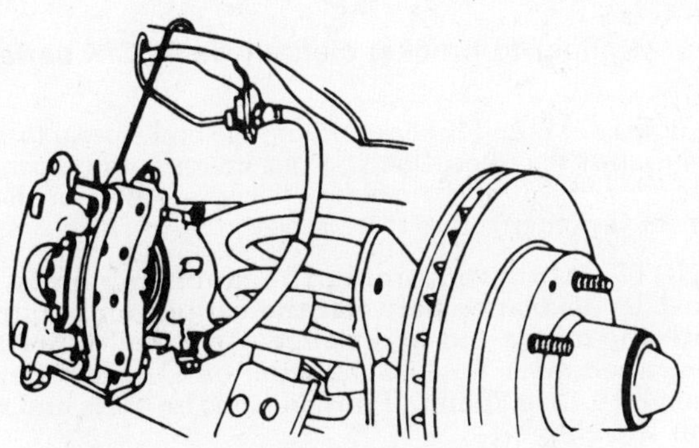

Suspend the caliper out of the way

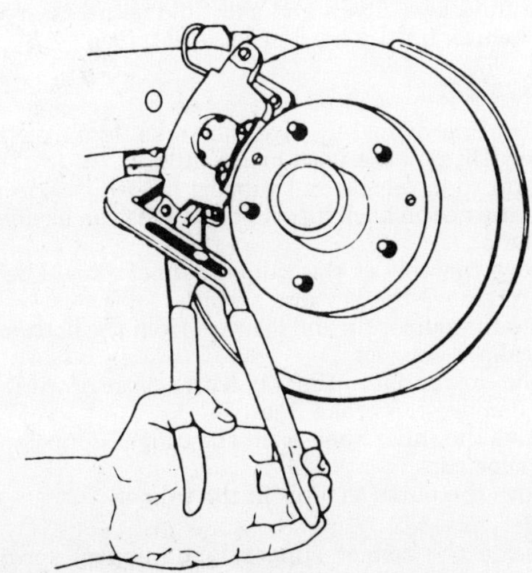

Compressing the Delco brake pad ears

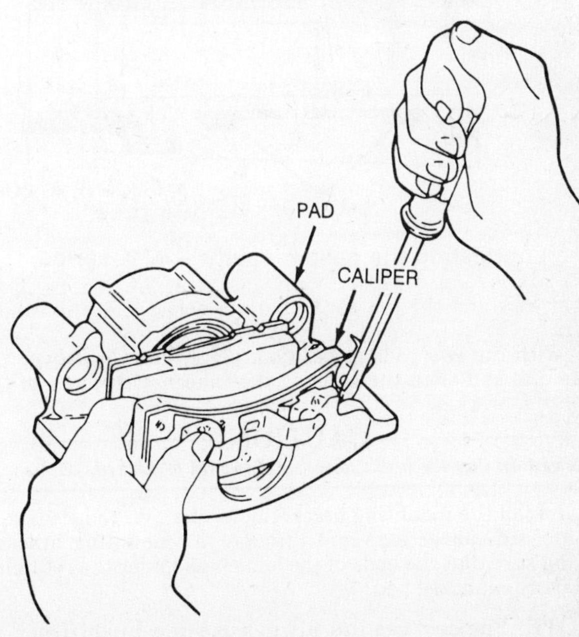

Removing the outboard shoe and lining

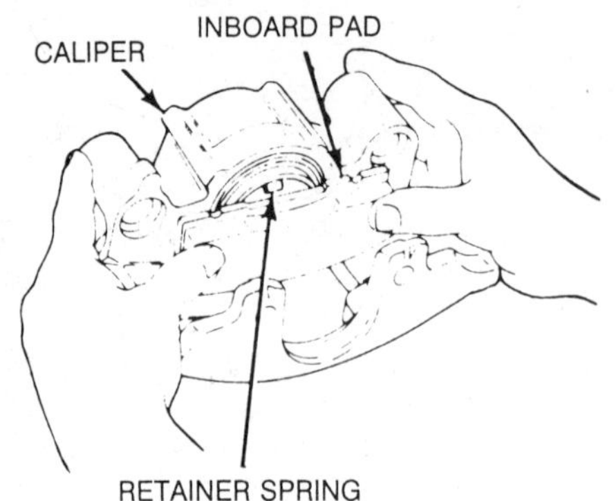

Installing the inboard pad – C/K series

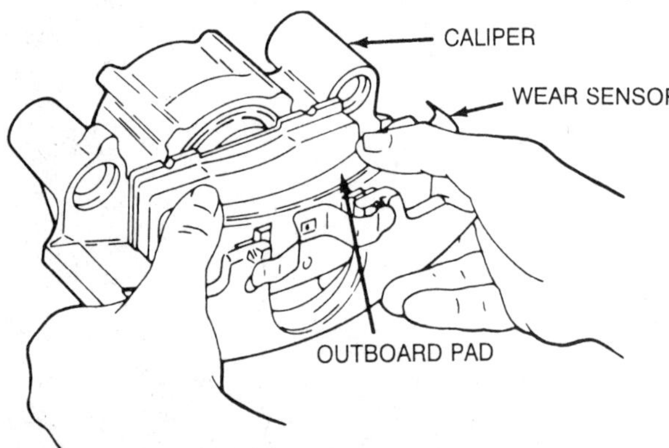

Installing the outboard pad – C/K series

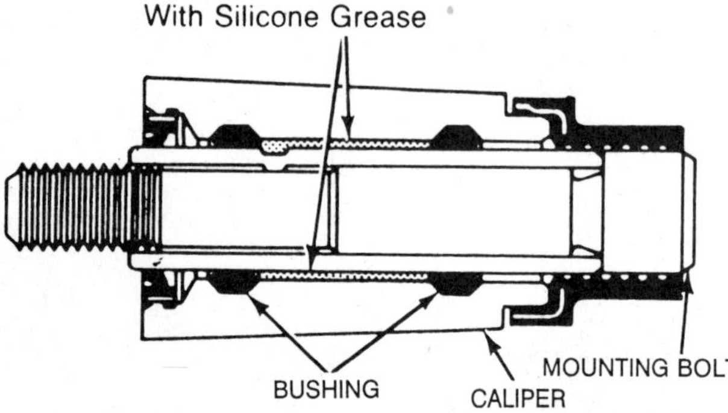

Lubricating the caliper cavity – C/K series

caliper ears and the tab at the bottom engaged in the caliper cutout.

11. With the two pads in position, place the caliper over the brake disc and align the holes in the caliper with those of the mounting bracket.

CAUTION

Make certain that the brake hose is not twisted or kinked.

12. Install the mounting bracket bolts through the sleeves in the inboard caliper ears and through the mounting bracket, making sure that the ends of the bolts pass under the retaining ears on the inboard pad.

NOTE: For best results, always use new bushings, bolt sleeves and bolt boot.

13. Tighten the mounting bolts to 35 ft. lbs for R and V Series; 28 ft. lbs. for C and K Series. Pump the brake pedal to seat the pad against the rotor. Don't do this unless both calipers are in place. Use a pair of channel lock pliers to bend over the upper ears of the outer pad so it isn't loose.

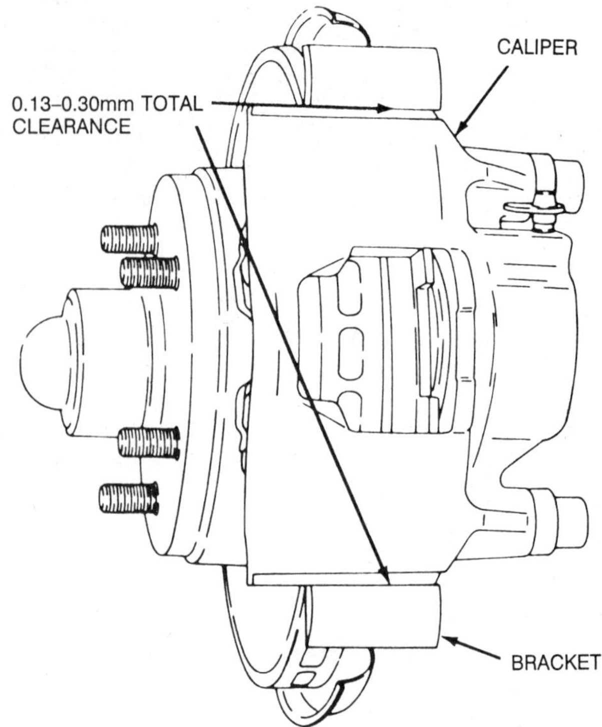

Caliper-to-bracket clearances – C/K series

NOTE: After tightening the mounting bolts, there must be clearance between the caliper and knuckle at both the upper and lower edge. On R and V Series, the clearance must be 0.06–0.26mm; on C and K Series, it must be 0.13–0.30mm. If not, loosen the bolts and reposition the claiper.

14. Install the front wheel and lower the truck.
15. Add fluid to the master cylinder reservoirs so that they are ¼ in. (6mm) from the top.
16. Test the brake pedal by pumping it to obtain a hard pedal. Check the fluid level again and add fluid as necessary. Do not move the vehicle until a hard pedal is obtained.

Bendix System

1. Remove approximately ⅓ of the brake fluid from the master cylinder. Discard the used brake fluid.
2. Jack up your vehicle and support it with jackstands.
3. Push the piston back into its bore. This can be done by suing a C-clamp.
4. Remove the bolt at the caliper support key. Use a brass drift pin to remove the key and spring.
5. Rotate the caliper up and forward from the bottom and lift it off the caliper support.
6. Tie the caliper out of the way with a piece of wire. Be careful not to damage the brake line.
7. Remove the inner shoe from the caliper support. Discard the inner shoe clip.
8. Remove the outer shoe from the caliper.

To install:

9. Lubricate the caliper support and support spring, with silicone.
10. Install a NEW inboard shoe clip on the shoe.

11. Install the lower end of the inboard shoe into the groove provided in the support. Slide the upper end of the shoe into position. Be sure the clip remains in position.
10. Position the outboard shoe in the caliper with the ears at the top of the shoe over the caliper ears and the tab at the bottom of the shoe engaged in the caliper cutout. If assembly is difficult, a C-clamp may be used. Be careful not to mar the lining.

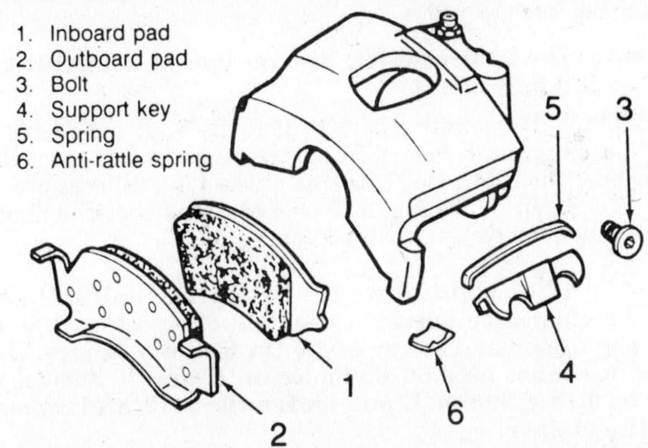

Bendix caliper brake pads and related parts

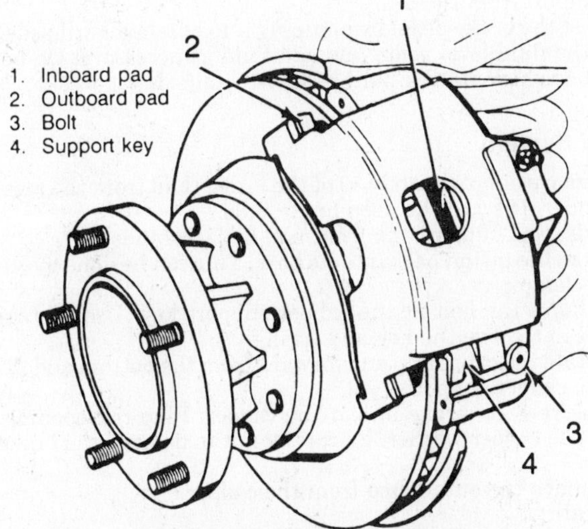

Bendix disc brake assembly

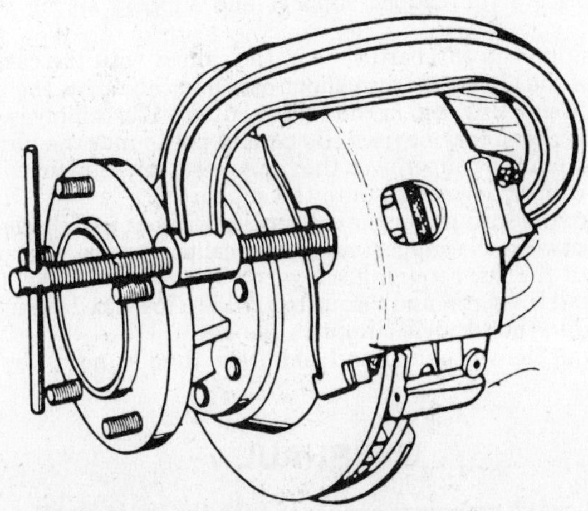
Compressing the Bendix caliper piston

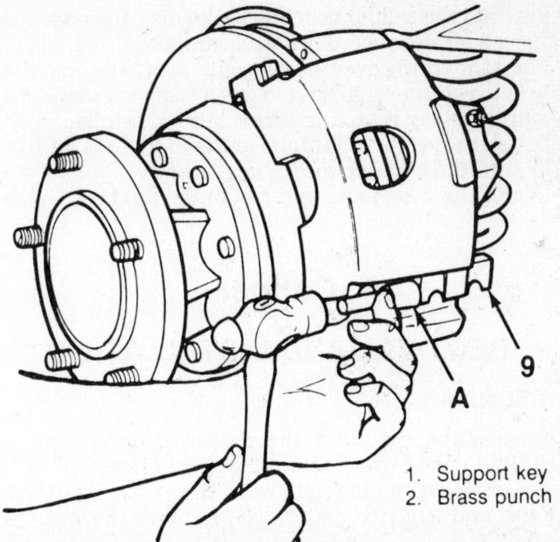

Removing the Bendix caliper support key

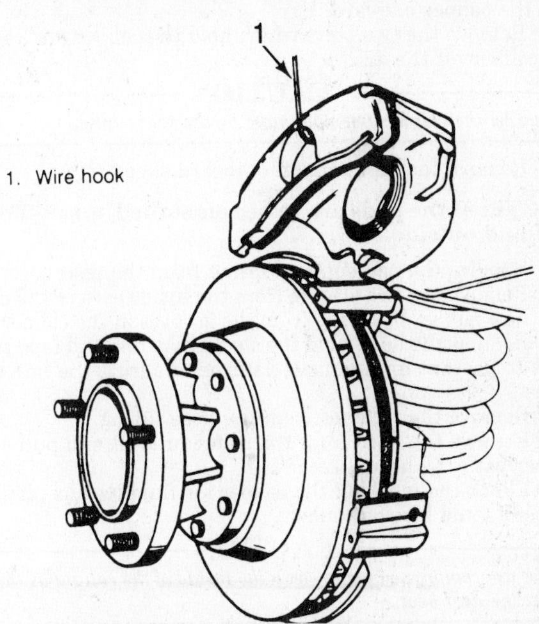

Suspending the Bendix caliper

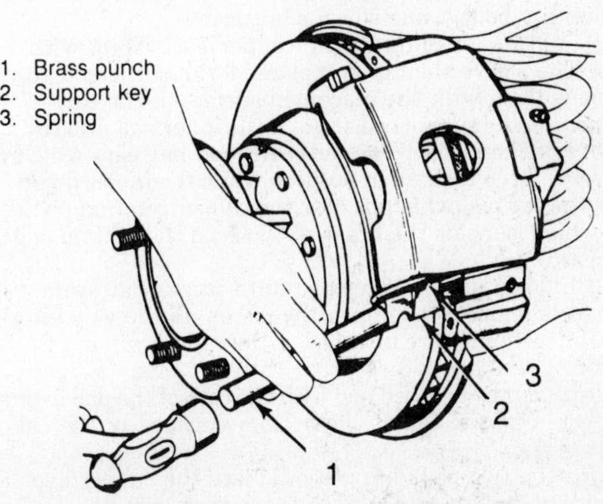

Installing the Bendix caliper support key

11. Position the caliper over the brake disc, top edge first. Rotate the caliper downward onto the support.
12. Place the spring over the caliper support key, install the assembly between the support and lower caliper groove. Tap into place until the key retaining screw can be installed.
13. Install the screw and torque to 12–18 ft. lbs. The boss must fit fully into the circular cutout in the key.
14. Install the wheel and and add brake fluid as necessary.

Caliper

REMOVAL AND INSTALLATION

Delco System

1. Remove the cover on the master cylinder and siphon enough fluid out of the reservoirs to bring the level to ⅓ full. This step prevents spilling fluid when the piston is pushed back.
2. Raise and support the vehicle. Remove the front wheels and tires.
3. Push the brake piston back into its bore using a C-clamp to pull the caliper outward.
4. Remove the two bolts which hold the caliper and then lift the caliper off the disc.

CAUTION

Do not let the caliper assembly hang by the brake hose.

5. Remove the inboard and outboard shoe.

NOTE: If the pads are to be reinstalled, mark them inside and outside.

6. Remove the pad support spring from the piston.
7. Remove the two sleeves from the inside ears of the caliper and the 4 rubber bushings from the grooves in the caliper ears.
8. Remove the hose from the steel brake line and tape the fittings to prevent foreign material from entering the line or the hoses.
9. Remove the retainer from the hose fitting.
10. Remove the hose from the frame bracket and pull off the caliper with the hose attached.
11. Check the inside of the caliper for fluid leakage; if so, the caliper should be overhauled.

CAUTION

Do not use compressed air to clean the inside of the caliper as this may unseat the dust boot.

12. Connect the brake line to start re-installaiton. Lubricate the sleeves, rubber bushings, bushing grooves, and the end of the mounting bolts using silicone lubricant.
13. Install new bushing in the caliper ears along with new sleeves. The sleeve should be replaced so that the end toward the shoe is flush with the machined surface of the ear.
14. Position the support spring and the inner pad into the center cavity of the piston. The outboard pad has ears which are bent over to keep the pad in position while the inboard pad has ears on the top end which fit over the caliper retaining bolts. A spring which is inside the brake piston hold the bottom edge of the inboard pad.
15. Push down on the inner pad until it lays flat against the caliper. It is important to push the piston all the way into the caliper if new linings are installed or the caliper will not fit over the rotor.
16. Position the outboard pad with the ears of the pad over the caliper ears and the tab at the bottom engaged in the caliper cutout.
17. With the two pads in position, place the caliper over the brake disc and align the holes in the caliper with those of the mounting bracket.

CAUTION

Make certain that the brake hose is not twisted or kinked.

18. Fill the cavity between the bolt bushings with silicone grease. Install the mounting bracket bolts through the sleeves in the inboard caliper ears and through the mounting bracket, making sure that the ends of the bolts pass under the retaining ears on the inboard pad.

NOTE: For best results, always use new bushings, sleeves and bolt boots.

19. Tighten the mounting bolts to 35 ft. lbs. on R and V Series; 28 ft. lbs. on C and K Series. Pump the brake pedal to seat the pad against the rotor. Don't do this unless both calipers are in place. Use a pair of channel lock pliers to bend over the upper ears of the outer pad so it isn't loose.

NOTE: After tightening the mounting bolts, there must be clearance between the caliper and knuckle at both the upper and lower edge. On R and V Series, the clearance must be 0.06–0.26mm; on C and K Series, it must be 0.13–0.30mm. If not, loosen the bolts and reposition the claiper.

20. Install the front wheel and lower the truck.
21. Add fluid to the master cylinder reservoirs so that they are ¼ in. (6mm) from the top.
22. Test the brake pedal by pumping it to obtain a hard pedal. Check the fluid level again and add fluid as necessary. Do not move the vehicle until a hard pedal is obtained.

Bendix System

1. Remove approximately ⅓ of the brake fluid from the master cylinder. Discard the used brake fluid.
2. Raise and support the front end on jackstands.
3. Push the piston back into its bore. This can be done by suing a C-clamp.
4. Remove the bolt at the caliper support key. Use a brass drift pin to remove the key and spring.
5. Rotate the caliper up and forward from the bottom and lift it off the caliper support.
6. Unscrew the brake line at the caliper. Plug the opening. Discard the copper washer. Be careful not to damage the brake line.
7. Remove the outer shoe from the caliper.

To install:

8. Using a new copper washer, connect the brake line at the caliper. Torque the connector to 32 ft. lbs.
9. Lubricate the caliper support and support spring with silicone.
10. Position the outboard shoe in the caliper with the ears at the top of the shoe over the caliper ears and the tab at the bottom of the shoe engaged in the caliper cutout. If assembly is difficult, a C-clamp may be used. Be careful not to mar the lining.
11. Position the caliper over the brake disc, top edge first. Rotate the caliper downward onto the support.
12. Place the spring over the caliper support key, install the assembly between the support and lower caliper groove. Tap into place until the key retaining screw can be installed.
13. Install the screw and torque to 12–18 ft. lbs. The boss must fit fully into the circular cutout in the key.
14. Install the wheel and and add brake fluid as necessary.

OVERHAUL

The following procedure applies to both the Delco and Bendix types of calipers.

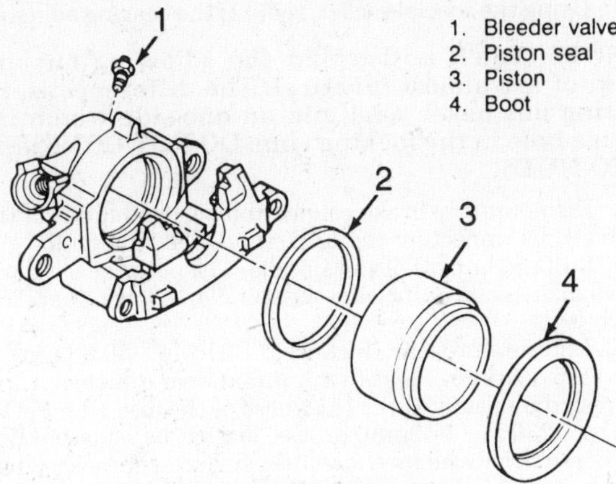

Delco caliper components

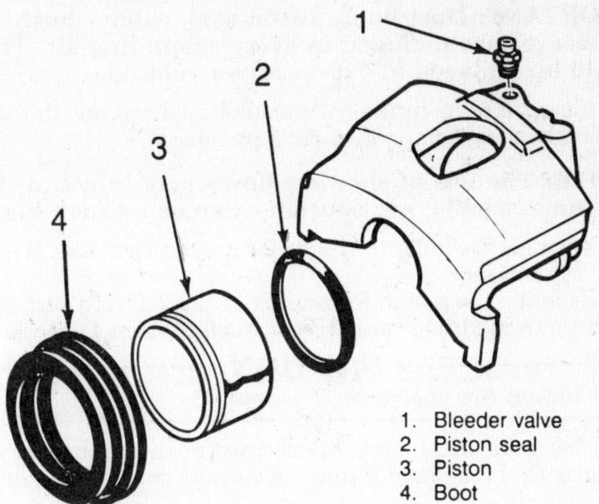

Bendix caliper components

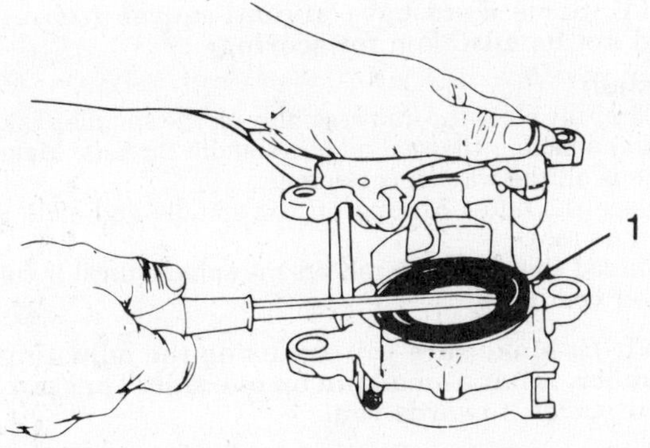

Removing the Delco piston boot

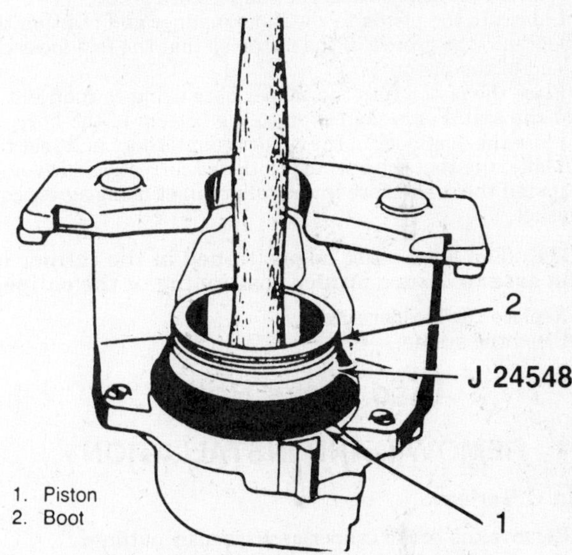

Installing the Bendix caliper piston

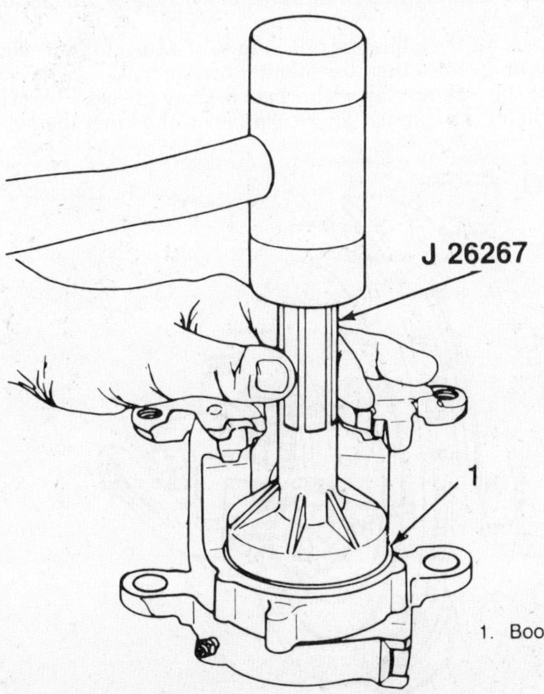

Installing the Delco piston boot

CAUTION

Use only denatured alcohol to clean metal parts and brake fluid to clean rubber parts. Never use any mineral based cleaning solvents such as gasoline or kerosene as these solvents will deteriorate rubber parts.

1. Remove the caliper, clean it and place it on a clean and level work surface.
2. Remove the brake hose from the caliper and discard the copper gasket. Check the brake hose for cracks or deterioration. Replace the hose as necessary.
3. Drain the brake fluid from the caliper.
4. Pad the interior of the caliper with cloth and then apply compressed air to the caliper inlet hose.

CAUTION

Do not place your hands or fingers in front of the piston in an attempt to catch it! Use just enough air pressure to ease the piston out of the bore.

5. Remove the piston dust boot by prying it out with a screwdriver. Use caution when performing this procedure.
6. Remove the piston seal from the caliper piston bore using a small piece of wood or plastic. DO NOT use any type of metal tool for this procedure.
7. Remove the bleeder valve from the caliper.

IMPORTANT: Dust boot, piston seal, rubber bushings, and sleeves are included in every rebuilding kit. These should be replaced at every caliper rebuild.

8. Clean all parts in the recommended solvent and dry them completely using compressed air if possible.

NOTE: The use of shop air hoses may inject oil film into the assembly; use caution when using such hoses.

9. Examine the mounting bolts for rust or corrosion. Replace them as necessary.
10. Examine the piston for scoring, nicks, or worn plating. If any of these conditions are present, replace them as necessary.

CAUTION

Do not use any type of abrasive on the piston!

11. Check the piston bore. Small defects can be removed with crocus cloth. If the bore cannot be cleaned in this manner, replace the caliper.
12. Lubricate the piston bore and the new piston seal with brake fluid. Place the seal in the caliper bore groove.
13. Lubricate the piston in the same manner and position the new boot into the groove in the piston so that the fold faces the open end of the piston.
14. Place the piston into the caliper bore using caution not to unseat the seal. Force the piston to the bottom of the bore.
15. Place the dust boot in the caliper counterbore and seat the boot. Make sure that the boot in positioned correctly and evenly.
16. Install the brake hose in the caliper inlet using a new copper gasket.

NOTE: The hose must be positioned in the caliper locating gate to assure proper positioning of the caliper.

17. Replace the bleeder screw.
18. Bleed the system.

Disc Brake Rotor

REMOVAL AND INSTALLATION

R and C Series

1. Remove the brake caliper as previously outlined.
2. Remove the outer wheel bearing. (Refer to Section 1 for the proper procedure).
3. Remove the rotor from the spindle.
4. Reverse procedure to install. Adjust the bearings. See Section 1.

V Series

NOTE: Before starting:
a. You'll need a special wheel bearing nut socket for your ½ inch drive ratchet. These sockets are available through auto parts stores and catalogs. You can't do this job properly without it!
b. You'll need a ½ inch drive torque wrench.
c. Have a clean container, like a shoe box, for the parts as you remove them.
d. Have PLENTY of paper towels handy.

1. Raise and support the front end on jackstands.
2. Remove the wheels.
3. Remove the hubs. See the procedures above.
4. Wipe the inside of the hub to remove as much grease as possible.
5. Using your bearing nut socket, remove the locknut from the spindle.
6. With the locknut off you'll be able to see the locking ring on the adjusting nut. Remove the locking ring. A tool such as a dental pick will make this easier.
7. Using the special socket, remove the bearing adjusting nut.

NOTE: You'll notice that the adjusting nut and the locknut are almost identical. The difference is, the adjusting nut has a small pin on one side which indexes with a hole in the locking ring. DO NOT CONFUSE THE TWO NUTS!

8. Dismount the brake caliper and suspend it out of the way, without disconnecting the brake line. See Section 9.
9. Pull the hub off of the spindle. The outer bearing will tend to fall out as soon as it clears the spindle, so have a hand ready to catch it.

The minimum wear thickness, 1.215 in. (30.86mm), is cast into each disc hub. This is a minimum wear dimension and not a refinish dimension. If the thickness of the disc after refinishing will be 1.230 in. (31.2mm) or less, it must be replaced. Refinishing is required whenever the disc surface shows scoring or severe rust scale. Scoring not deeper than 0.015 in. (0.38mm) in depth can be corrected by refinishing.

NOTE: Some discs have an anti-squeal groove. This should not be mistaken for scoring.

To install:

10. Carefully place the hub assembly on the spindle. Take care to avoid damaging the seal on the spindle threads. Make sure the hub is all the way on the spindle.
11. Place the outer bearing on the spindle and slide it into place in its race.
12. Thread the adjusting nut on the spindle until it contacts the outer bearing.

WARNING: Make sure you are using the adjusting nut. Remember, it has a small pin on one side. That pin must face outwards, towards you!

13. Using the special socket and the torque wrench:
    a. Tighten the adjusting nut to 50 ft. lbs. while rotating the hub.
    b. Back off the adjusting nut until it is loose.
    c. While rotating the hub, tighten the adjusting nut to 35 ft. lbs. for automatic locking hubs or 50 ft. lbs. for manual locking hubs.
    d. Back off the adjusting nut ¼ to ⅜ of a turn for automatic hubs or ⅙ to ¼ turn for manual hubs.
14. Coat the locking ring with wheel bearing grease. Place the locking rin on the spindle. There is a tab on the inner diameter

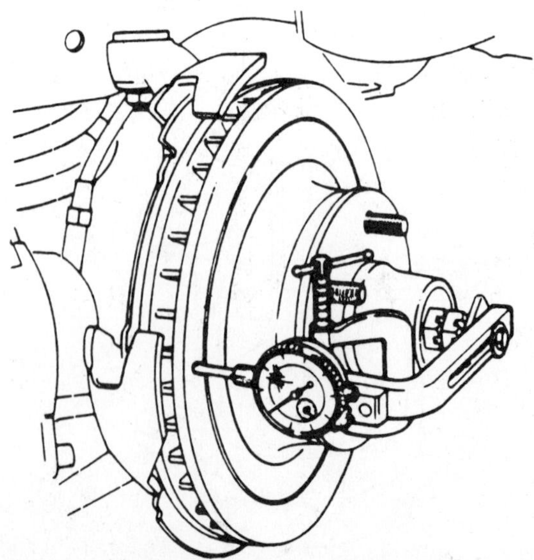

Checking rotor lateral runout

of the ring which must fit in the slot on the top of the spindle. Slide the locking ring in until it contacts the adjusting nut. The pin on the adjusting nut must enter one of the holes in the locking ring. You can tell that the locking ring is seated properly when you see the grease on the ring get pushed out of one of the holes by the pin, *and* the ring does not rock from side-to-side when you press on either side with your finger.

If the locking ring and pin don't index, take note of how far off they are, pull the ring off the spindle and turn the nut, either by hand or with the socket, just enough for a goo fit. Try the locking ring again.

15. When the locking ring engages the adjusting nut pin properly, your bearing adjustment is set. Thread the locknut onto the spindle until it contacts the locking ring.

16. Tighten the locknut to *at least* 160 ft. lbs. This locknut ensures that the locking ring and adjusting nut don't move. Overtightening the locknut has no effect on the bearing adjustment.

17. Install the locking hub.
18. Install the caliper.
19. Install the wheel.

K Series

LEFT SIDE

1. Raise and support the front end on jackstands.
2. Remove the wheel.
3. Remove the skid plate.
4. Remove the left stabilizer bar clamp.
5. Remove the left stabilizer bar bolt, spacer and bushings at the lower control arm.
6. Disconnect the left inner tie rod end from the steering relay rod.
7. Remove the hub nut and washer.
8. Using a puller, force the outer end of the axle shaft out of the hub. Remove hub/rotor.

To install:

9. Position the shaft in the hub and install the washer and hub nut. Insert a drift in the rotor vanes and tighten the hub nut to 175 ft. lbs.
10. Remove the drift.
11. Connect the left inner tie rod end at the steering relay rod. Torque the nut to 35 ft. lbs.
12. Install the left stabilizer bar bolt, spacer and bushings at the lower control arm. Torque the bolt to 24 ft. lbs.
13. Install the left stabilizer bar clamp. Torque the bolts to 12 ft. lbs.
14. Install the skid plate.

RIGHT SIDE

1. Raise and support the front end on jackstands.
2. Remove the wheel.
3. Remove the skid plate.
4. Remove the right stabilizer bar clamp.
5. Remove the right stabilizer bar bolt, spacer and bushings at the lower control arm.
6. Disconnect the right inner tie rod end from the steering relay rod.
7. Remove the hub nut and washer. Insert a long drift or dowel through the vanes in the brake rotor to hold the rotor while loosening the nut.
8. Using a puller, force the outer end of the axle shaft out of the hub. Remove the hub/rotor.

To install:

9. Position the shaft in the hub and install the washer and hub nut. Leave the drift in the rotor vanes and tighten the hub nut to 175 ft. lbs.
10. Connect the right inner tie rod end at the steering relay rod. Torque the nut to 35 ft. lbs.
11. Install the right stabilizer bar bolt, spacer and bushings at the lower control arm. Torque the bolt to 12 ft. lbs.
12. Install the right stabilizer bar clamp. Torque the bolts to 24 ft. lbs.
13. Install the skid plate.

DRUM BRAKES

Drum

REMOVAL AND INSTALLATION

Semi-Floating Axles

1. Raise and support the rear end on jackstands.
2. Remove the wheel.
3. Pull the drum from the brake assembly. If the brake drums have been scored from worn linings, the brake adjuster must be backed off so that the brake shoes will retract from the drum. The adjuster can be backed off by inserting a brake adjusting tool through the access hole provided. In some cases the access hole is provided in the brake drum. A metal cover plate is over the hole. This may be removed by using a hammer and chisel.
4. To install, reverse the removal procedure.

Full Floating Axles

To remove the drums from full floating rear axles, use the Axle Shaft Removal and Installation procedure in Section 7. Full floating rear axles can readily be identified by the bearing housing protruding through the center of the wheel.

NOTE: Make sure all metal particles are removed from the brake drum before reassembly.

INSPECTION

Lining

Remove the drum and inspect the lining thickness on both brake shoes. A front brake lining should be replaced if it is less than $\frac{1}{8}$ in. (3mm) thick at the lowest point on the brake shoe. The wear limit for rear brake linings is $\frac{1}{16}$ in. (1.6mm).

NOTE: Brake shoes should always be replaced in axle sets. The wear specifications given may disagree with your state inspection rules.

Drum

When the drum is removed, it should be inspected for cracks, scores, or other imperfections. These must be corrected before the drum is replaced.

CAUTION

If the drum is found to be cracked, replace it. Do not attempt to service a cracked drum.

Minor drum score marks can be removed with fine emery cloth. Heavy score marks must be removed by turning the drum. This is removing metal from the entire inner surface of the drum on a lathe in order to level the surface. Automotive machine shops and some large parts stores are equipped to perform this operation.

If the drum is not scored, it should be polished with fine emery cloth before replacement. If the drum is resurfaced, it should not be enlarged more than 0.060 in. (1.524mm).

NOTE: Your state inspection law may disagree with this specification.

It is advisable, while the drums are off, to check them for out-of-round. An inside micrometer is necessary for an exact measurement, therefore unless this tool is available, the drums should be taken to a machine shop to be checked. Any drum which is more than 0.006 in. (0.1524mm) out-of-round will result in an inaccurate brake adjustment and other problems, and should be refinished or replaced.

NOTE: Make all measurements at right angles to each other and at the open and closed edges of the drum machined surface.

Brake Shoes

REMOVAL AND INSTALLATION

All R and V Series
C and K Series with Full Floating Axle

CAUTION

Brake shoes contain asbestos, which has been determined to be a cancer causing agent. Never clean the brake surfaces with compressed air! Avoid inhaling any dust from any brake surface! When cleaning brake surfaces, use a commercially available brake cleaning fluid.

1. Jack up and securely support the vehicle.
2. Loosen the parking brake equalizer enough to remove all tension on the brake cable.
3. Remove the brake drums.

WARNING: The brake pedal must not be depressed while the drums are removed!

4. Using a brake tool, remove the shoe springs. You can do this with ordinary tools, buy it isn't easy.
5. Remove the self-adjuster actuator spring.

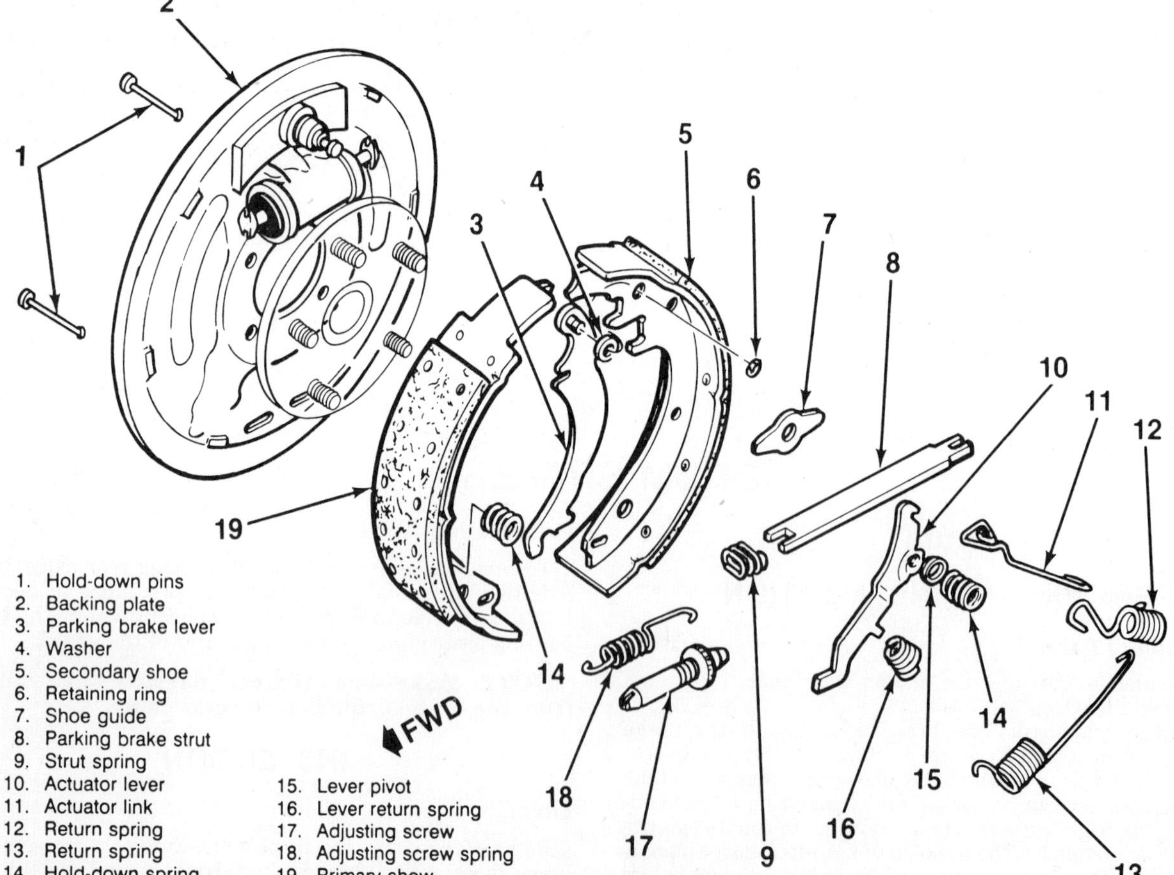

Drum brake components

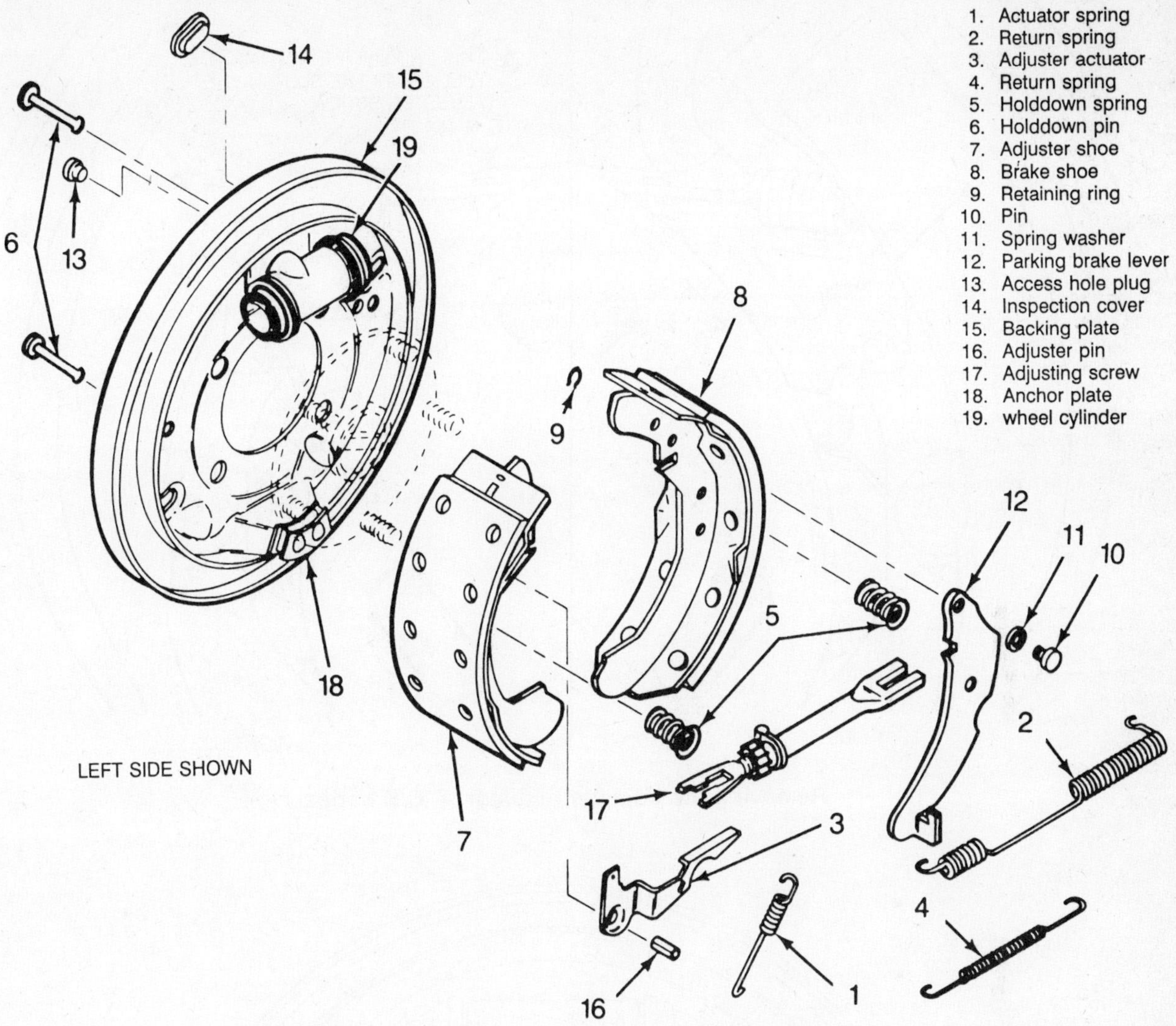

1. Actuator spring
2. Return spring
3. Adjuster actuator
4. Return spring
5. Holddown spring
6. Holddown pin
7. Adjuster shoe
8. Brake shoe
9. Retaining ring
10. Pin
11. Spring washer
12. Parking brake lever
13. Access hole plug
14. Inspection cover
15. Backing plate
16. Adjuster pin
17. Adjusting screw
18. Anchor plate
19. wheel cylinder
LEFT SIDE SHOWN

C/K series rear brakes components — semi-floating axles

LEFT SIDE SHOWN
BACKING PLATE
SCREWDRIVER

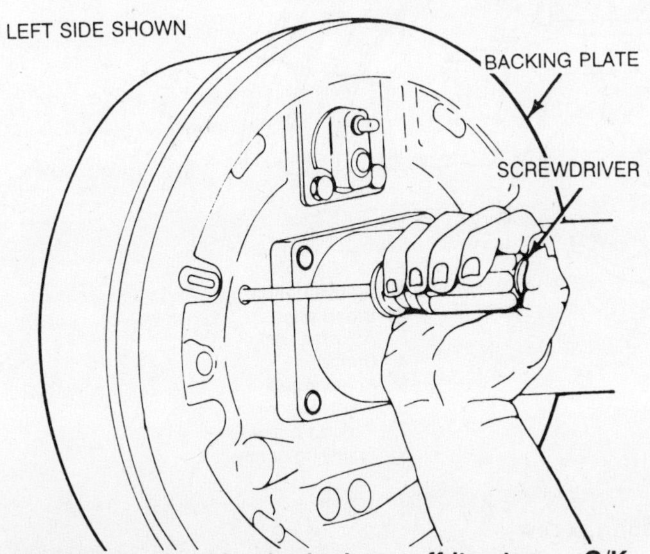

Pushing the parking brake lever off its stop — C/K series

6. Remove the link from the secondary shoe by pulling it from the anchor pin.

7. Remove the holddown pins. These are the brackets which run though the backing plate. They can be removed with a pair of pliers. Reach around the rear of the backing plate and hold the back of the pin. Turn the top of the pin retainer 45° with the plier. This will align the elongated tang with the slot in the retainer. Be careful, as the pin is spring loaded and may fly off when released. Use the same procedure for the other pin assembly.

8. Remove the adjuster actuator assembly.

NOTE: Since the actuator, pivot, and override spring are considered an assembly it is not recommended that they be disassembled.

9. Remove the shoes from the backing plate. Make sure that you have a secure grip on the assembly as the bottom spring will still exert pressure on the shoes. Slowly let the tops of the shoes come together and the tension will decrease and the adjuster and spring may be removed.

NOTE: If the linings are to be reused, mark them for identification.

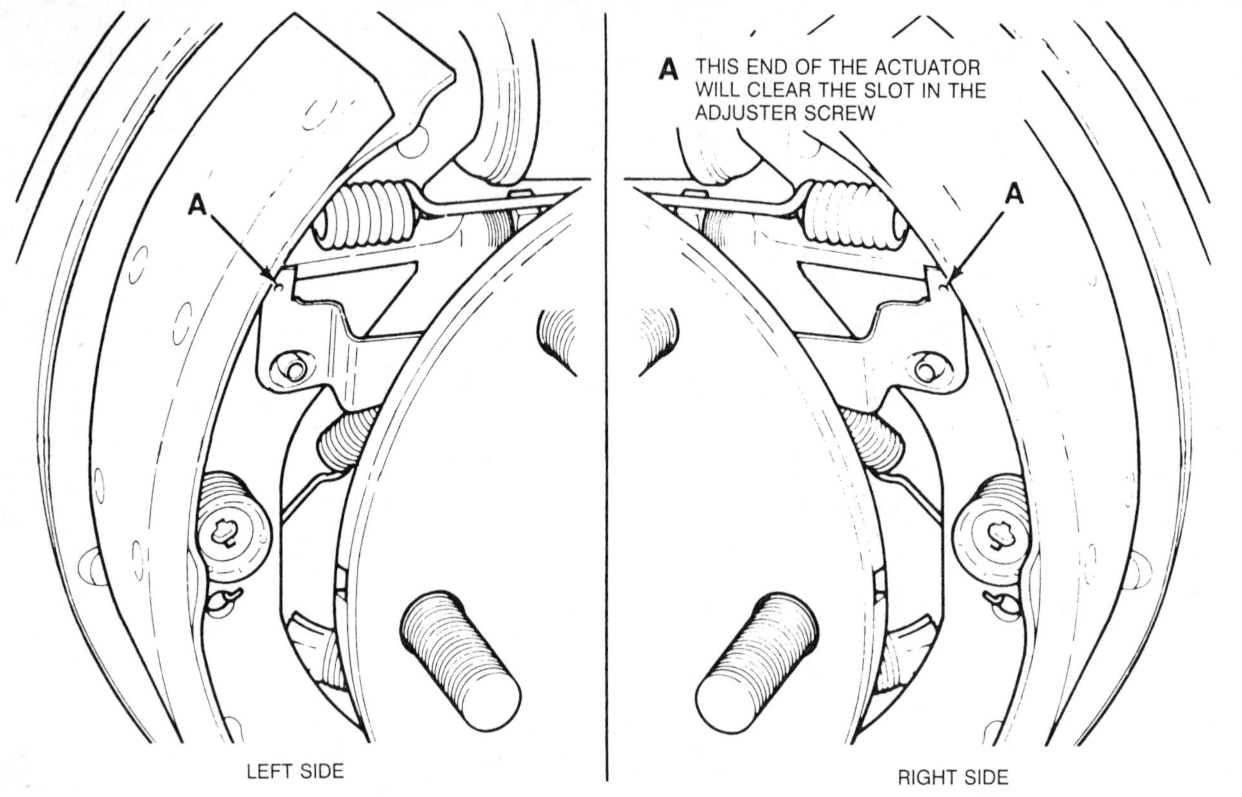

Removing the adjuster actuator – C/K series

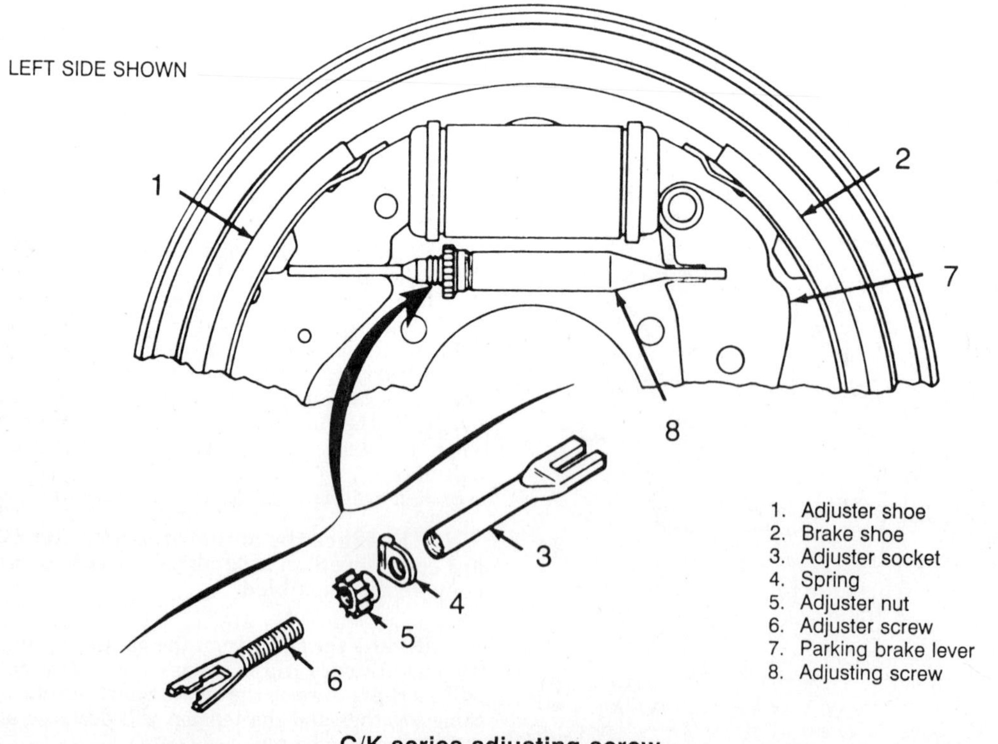

C/K series adjusting screw

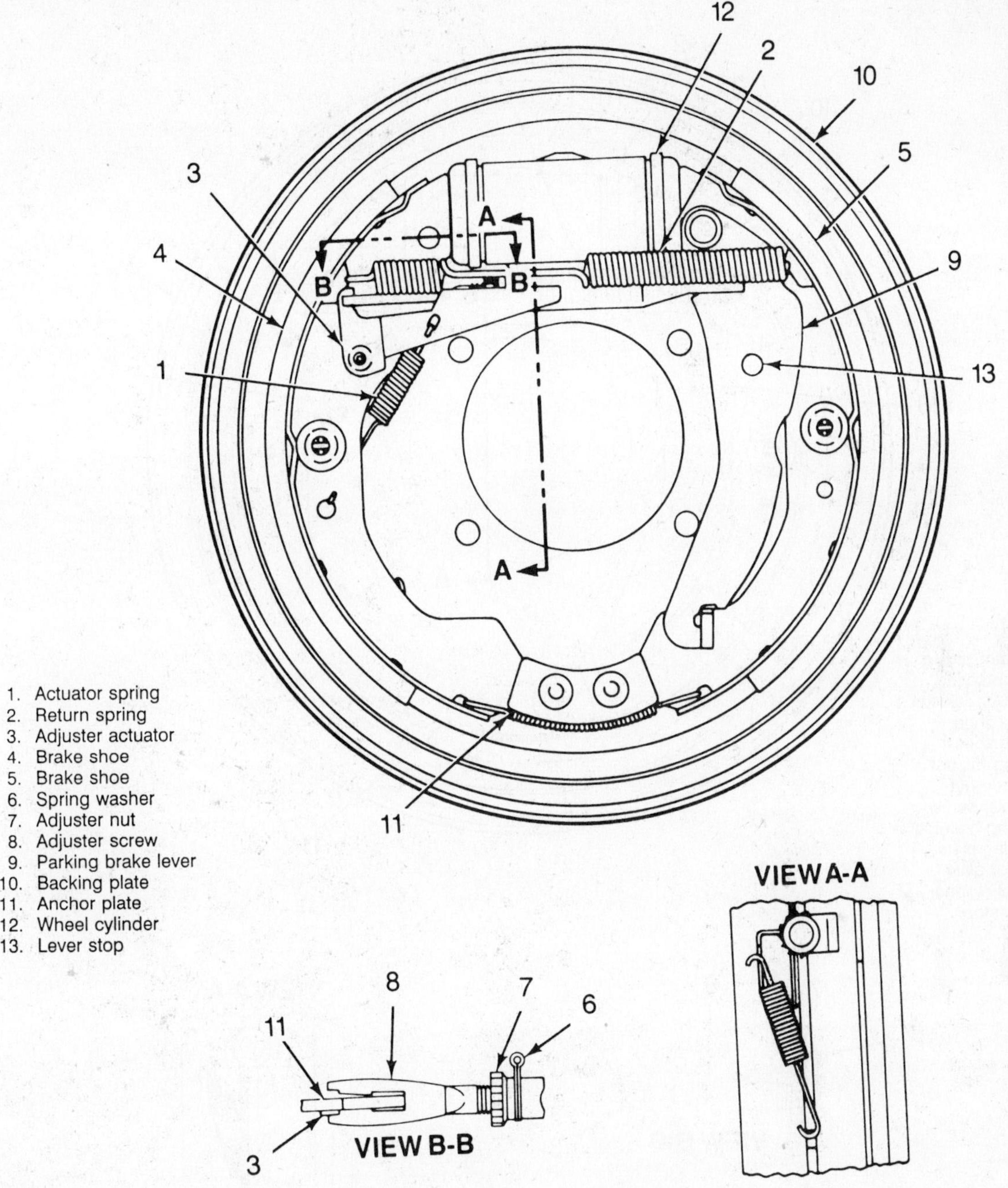

C/K series left side assembled

10. Remove the rear parking brake lever from the secondary shoe. Using a pair of plier, pull back on the spring which surrounds the cable. At the same time, remove the cable from the notch in the shoe bracket. Make sure that the spring does not snap back or injury may result.

11. Use a brake cleaning fluid to remove dirt from the brake drum. Check the drums for scoring and cracks. Have the drums checked for out-of-round and service the drums as necessary.

12. Check the wheel cylinders by carefully pulling the lower edges of the wheel cylinder boots away from the cylinders. If there is excessive leakage, the inside of the cylinder will be moist with fluid. If there is any leakage at all, a cylinder overhaul is in order. DO NOT delay, as a brake failure could result.

NOTE: A small amount of fluid will be present to act as a lubricant for the wheel cylinder pistons.

13. Check the flange plate, which is located around the axle, for leakage of differential lubricant. This condition cannot be overlooked as the lubricant will be absorbed into the brake linings and brake failure will result. Replace the seals as necessary. See Section 7 for details.

NOTE: If new linings are being installed, check them against the old units for length and type.

14. Check the new linings for imperfections.

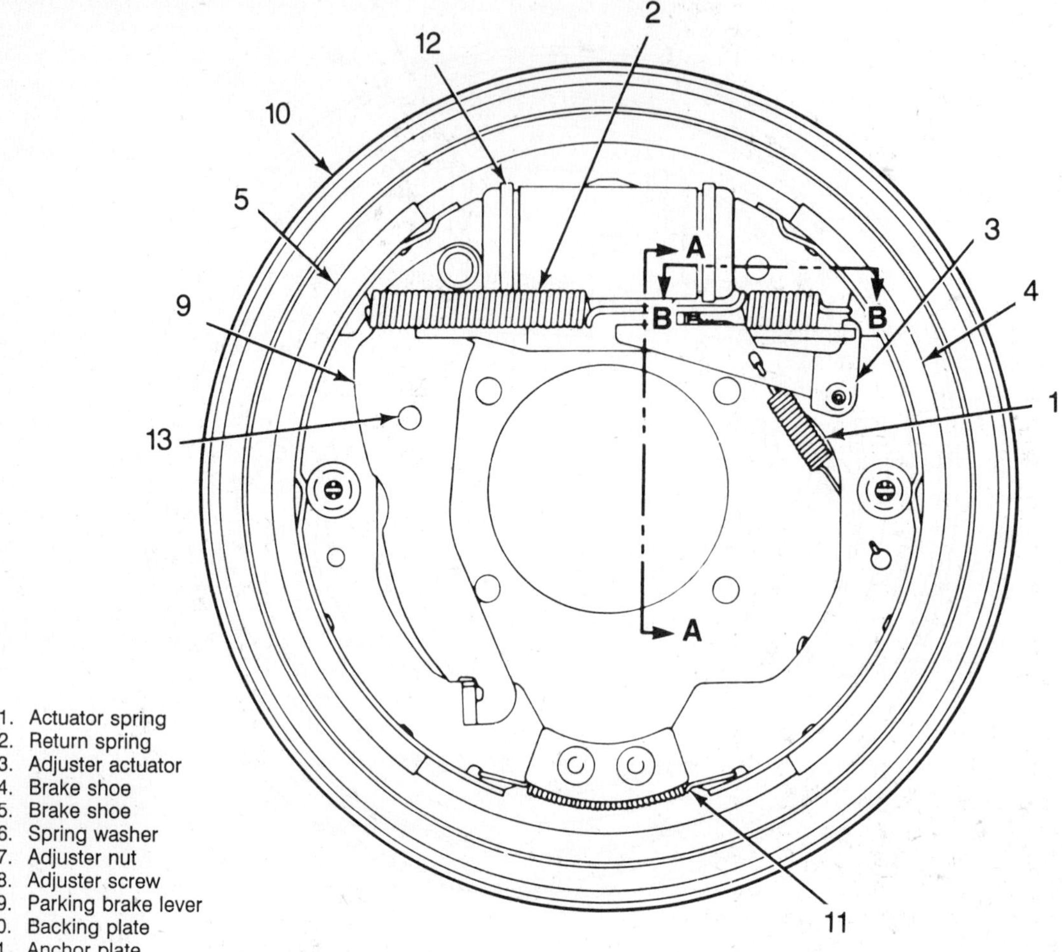

1. Actuator spring
2. Return spring
3. Adjuster actuator
4. Brake shoe
5. Brake shoe
6. Spring washer
7. Adjuster nut
8. Adjuster screw
9. Parking brake lever
10. Backing plate
11. Anchor plate
12. Wheel cylinder
13. Lever stop

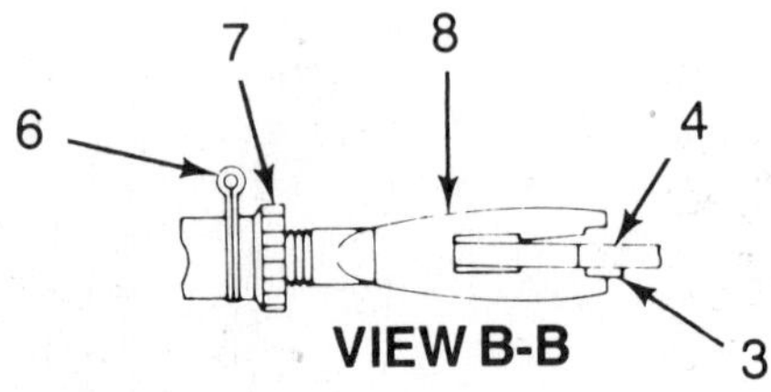

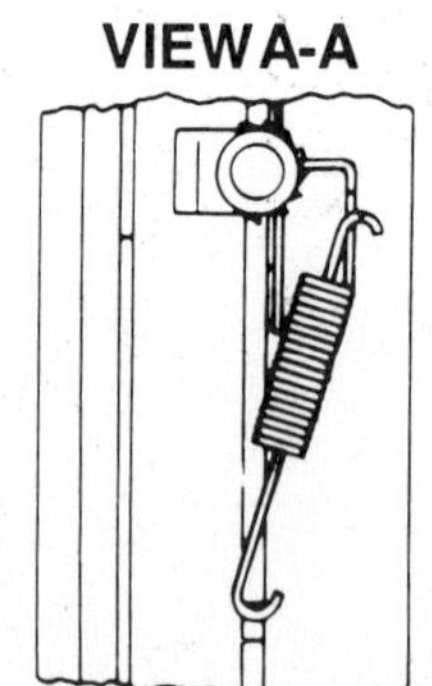

C/K series right side assembled

CAUTION

It is important to keep your hands free of dirt and grease when handling the brake shoes. Foreign matter will be absorbed into the linings and result in unpredictable braking.

15. Lightly lubricate the parking brake and cable and the end of the parking brake lever where it enters the shoe. Use high temperature, waterproof, grease or special brake lube.

16. Install the parking brake lever into the secondary shoe with the attaching bolt, spring washer, lockwasher, and nut. It is important that the lever move freely before the shoe is attached. Move the assembly and check for proper action.

17. Lubricate the adjusting screw and make sure that it works freely. Sometimes the adjusting screw will not move due to lack of lubricant or dirt contamination and the brakes will not adjust. In this case, the adjuster should be disassembled, thoroughly cleaned, and lubricated before installation.

18. Connect the brake shoe spring to the bottom portion of both shoes. Make certain that the brake linings are installed in the correct manner, the primary and secondary shoe in the cor-

rect position. If you are not sure remove the other brake drum and check it.

19. Install the adjusting mechanism below the spring and separate the top of the shoes.

Make the following checks before installation:

a. Be certain that the right hand thread adjusting screw is on the left hand side of the vehicle and the left hand screw is on the right hand side of the vehicle.

b. Make sure that the star adjuster is aligned with the adjusting hole.

c. The adjuster should be installed with the starwheel nearest the secondary shoe and the tension spring away from the adjusting mechanism;

d. If the original linings are being reused, put them back in their original locations.

20. Install the parking brake cable.

21. Position the primary shoe (the shoe with the short lining) first. Secure it with the holddown pin and with its spring by pushing the pin through the back of the backing plate and, while holding it with one hand, install the spring and the retainer using a pair of needlenose pliers. Install the adjuster actuator assembly.

22. Install the parking brake strut and the strut spring by pulling back the spring with pliers and engaging the end of the cable onto the brake strut and then releasing the spring.

23. Place the small metal guide plate over the anchor pin and position the self-adjuster wire cable eye.

CAUTION

The wire should not be positioned with the conventional brake installation tool or damage will result. It should be positioned on the actuator assembly first and then placed over the anchor pin stud by hand with the adjuster assembly in full downward position.

24. Install the actuator return spring. DO NOT pry the actuator lever to install the return spring. Position it using the end of a screwdriver or another suitable tool.

NOTE: If the return springs are bent or in any way distorted, they should be replaced.

25. Using the brake installation tool, place the brake return springs in position. Install the primary spring first over the anchor pin and then place the spring from the secondary show over the wire link end.

26. Pull the brake shoes away from the backing plate and apply a thin coat of high temperature, waterproof, grease or special brake lube in the brake shoe contact points.

CAUTION

Only a small amount is necessary. Keep the lubricant away from the brake linings.

27. Once the complete assembly has been installed, check the operation of the self-adjusting mechanism by moving the actuating lever by hand.

28. Adjust the brakes.

a. Turn the star adjuster until the drum slides over the brakes shoes with only a slight drag. Remove the drum:

b. Turn the adjuster back 1¼ turns.

c. Install the drum and wheel and lower the vehicle.

CAUTION

Avoid overtightening the lug nuts to prevent damage to the brake drum. Alloy wheels can also be cracked by overtightening. Use of a torque wrench is highly recommended.

d. If the adjusting hole in the drum has been punched out, make certain that the insert has been removed from the inside of the drum. Install a rubber hole cover to keep dirt out of the brake assembly. Also, be sure that the drums are installed in the same position as they were when removed, with the locating tang in line with the locating hole in the axle shaft flange.

e. Make the final adjustment by backing the vehicle and pumping the brakes until the self-adjusting mechanisms adjust to the proper level and the brake pedal reaches satisfactory height.

29. Adjust the parking brake. Details are given later.

C and K Series with Semi-floating Axle

CAUTION

Brake shoes contain asbestos, which has been determined to be a cancer causing agent. Never clean the brake surfaces with compressed air! Avoid inhaling any dust from any brake surface! When cleaning brake surfaces, use a commercially available brake cleaning fluid.

1. Jack up and securely support the vehicle.
2. Loosen the parking brake equalizer enough to remove all tension on the brake cable.
3. Remove the brake drums. If difficulty is till encountered, remove the access hole plug in the backing plate and insert a metal rod to push the parking brake lever off its stop.

WARNING: The brake pedal must not be depressed while the drums are removed!

4. Raise the lever arm of the actuator until the upper end is clear of the slot in the adjuster screw. Slide the actuator off the adjuster pin.
5. Disconnect the actuator from the brake shoe.
6. Remove the holddown pins. These are the brackets which run though the backing plate. They can be removed with a pair of pliers. Reach around the rear of the backing plate and hold the back of the pin. Turn the top of the pin retainer 45° with the plier. This will align the elongated tang with the slot in the retainer. Be careful, as the pin is spring loaded and may fly off when released. Use the same procedure for the other pin assembly.
7. Pull the lower ends of the shoes apart and lift the lower return spring over the anchor plate. Remove the spring from the shoes.
8. Lift the shoes and upper return spring along with the adjusting screw, from the backing plate. Some spreading of the shoes is necessary to clear the wheel cylinder and axle flange. Remove the upper spring.
9. Remove the retaining ring, pin, spring washer and parking brake lever.

NOTE: If the linings are to be reused, mark them for identification.

10. Use a brake cleaning fluid to remove dirt from the brake drum. Check the drums for scoring and cracks. Have the drums checked for out-of-round and service the drums as necessary.
11. Check the wheel cylinders by carefully pulling the lower edges of the wheel cylinder boots away from the cylinders. If there is excessive leakage, the inside of the cylinder will be moist with fluid. If there is any leakage at all, a cylinder overhaul is in order. DO NOT delay, as a brake failure could result.

NOTE: A small amount of fluid will be present to act as a lubricant for the wheel cylinder pistons.

12. Check the flange plate, which is located around the axle, for leakage of differential lubricant. This condition cannot be overlooked as the lubricant will be absorbed into the brake linings and brake failure will result. Replace the seals as necessary. See Section 7 for details.

NOTE: If new linings are being installed, check them against the old units for length and type.

13. Check the new linings for imperfections.

CAUTION

It is important to keep your hands free of dirt and grease when handling the brake shoes. Foreign matter will be absorbed into the linings and result in unpredictable braking.

14. Install the parking brake lever assembly The concave side of the washer should be against the shoe.
15. Install the adjuster pin in the shoe so that the pin projects 6.8–7.0mm from the side of the shoe where the actuator is installed.
16. Apply an approved brake lubricant grease to the threads of the adjuster screw, socket and socket face.
17. Make certain that the brake linings are positioned correctly and connect the upper spring. If you are not sure of which shoe goes where, remove the other brake drum and check it.
18. Install the adjusting mechanism between the shoes. Make the following checks before installation:
    a. Be certain that the adjusting screw assembly engages the adjuster shoe and parking brake lever.
    b. Make sure that the spring clip is positioned towars the backing plate.
    c. The linings are in the correct positions. The shoe with the parking brake lever is the rear shoe.
19. Coat the shoe mounting pads on the backing plate with a thin coat of lithium grease.
20. Position the assembly on the backing plate, engaging the upper shoe ends with the wheel cylinder pushrods.
21. Hook the lower return spring into the shoe ends and spread the shoes, guiding the lower spring over the anchor plate. Don't over-stretch the spring; you'll ruin it. The spring can't be stretched, sfaely, more than 4¼ in. (108mm).
22. Install the hold-down spring assemblies.
23. Place the adjuster actuator over the end of the adjusting pin so its top leg engages the notch in the adjuster screw.
24. Install the actuator spring. Make sure that the free end of the actuator engage the notch of the adjuster nut. Don't over-stretch the spring. Its maximum stretch is 3¼ in. (83mm).
25. Connect the parking brake cable to the lever. Adjust the parking brake:
    a. Measure the brake drum inside diameter.
    b. Turn the adjuster nut until the brake shoe maximum diameter is 0.01–0.02 in. (0.25–50mm) less than the brake drum diameter.
    c. Make sure that the stops on the parking brake levers are against the dge of the brake shoe web. If the cable is holding the stops off the edge, loosen the adjustment.
    d. Tighten the cable at the adjuster nut until the lever stops begin to move off the shoe webs.
    e. Loosen the adjustment nut until the lever stops are *just* touching the shoe webs. There should be no more than 0.5mm clearance between the stops and the webs.
26. Install the drums and wheels.
27. Pump the brake pedal 30–35 times with normal force. Pause about 1 second between each stroke.
28. Depress the parking brake pedal 6 clicks. The wheels should be locked.
29. Release the parking brake. The wheels should rotate freely.

Wheel Cylinders

REMOVAL AND INSTALLATION

All Series

1. Raise and support the axle.
2. Remove the wheel and tire.
3. Back off the brake adjustment if necessary and remove the drum.

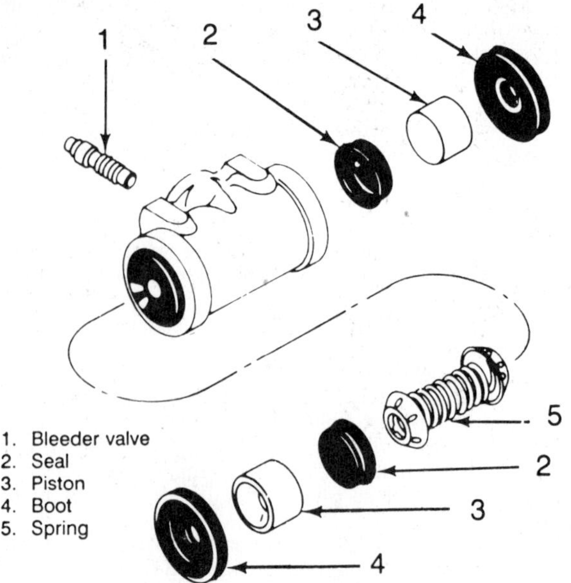

Wheel cylinder exploded view

4. Disconnect and plug the brake line.
5. Remove the brake shoes as described above.
6. Remove the bolts securing the wheel cylinder to the backing plate.
7. Disengage the wheel cylinder pushrods from the brake shoes and remove the wheel cylinder.
8. Installation is the reverse of removal. Torque the mounting bolts to 15 ft. lbs. Bleed the system.

OVERHAUL

Overhaul kits for wheel cylinders are readily available. However, you may decide that the small, additional cost of purchasing new wheel cylinders is worth the aggravation of rebuilding your old ones.

When rebuidling and installing wheel cylinders, avoid getting any contaminants into the system. Always install clean, new high quality brake fluid. If dirty or improper fluid has been used, it will be necessary to drain the entire system, flush the system with proper brake fluid, replace all rubber components, refill, and bleed the system.

1. Remove the rubber boots from the cylinder ends with pliers. Discard the boots.
2. Remove and discard the pistons and cups.
3. Wash the cylinder and metal parts in denatured alcohol or clean brake fluid.

CAUTION

Never use a mineral based solvent such as gasoline, kerosene, or paint thinner for cleaning purposes. These solvents will swell rubber components and quickly deteriorate them.

4. Allow the parts to air dry or use compressed air. Do not use rags for cleaning since lint will remain in the cylinder bore.
5. Inspect the piston and replace it if it shows scratches.
6. Lubricate the cylinder bore and counterbore with clean brake fluid.
7. Install the rubber cups (flat side out) and then the pistons (flat side in).
8. Insert new boots into the counterbores by hand. Do not lubricate the boots.

Brake Backing Plate

REMOVAL AND INSTALLATION

All Series

1. Remove the brake shoes and wheel cylinder as previously outlined.
2. Remove the axles as outlined in Section 7.
3. Remove the attaching bolts and pull off the backing plate.
4. Install all parts as outlined and torque the backing plate retaining bolts to:

- Models with 8½ in. (216mm) ring gear, semi-floating axle: 35 ft. lbs.
- All other models: 105 ft. lbs.

PARKING BRAKE

ADJUSTMENT

The rear brakes serve a dual purpose. They are used as service brakes and as parking brakes. To obtain proper adjustment of the parking brake, the service brakes must first be properly adjusted as outlined earlier.

1. Apply the parking brake 4 clicks from the fully released position.
2. Raise and support the vehicle.
3. Loosen the locknut at the equalizer.
4. Tighten or loosen the adjusting nut until a moderate drag is felt when the rear wheels are rotated forward.
5. Tighten the locknut.
6. Release the parking brake and rotate the rear wheels. No drag should be felt. If even a light drag is felt, readjust the parking brake.
7. Lower the vehicle.

NOTE: If a new parking brake cable is being installed, pre-stretch it by applying the parking brake hard about three times before making adjustments.

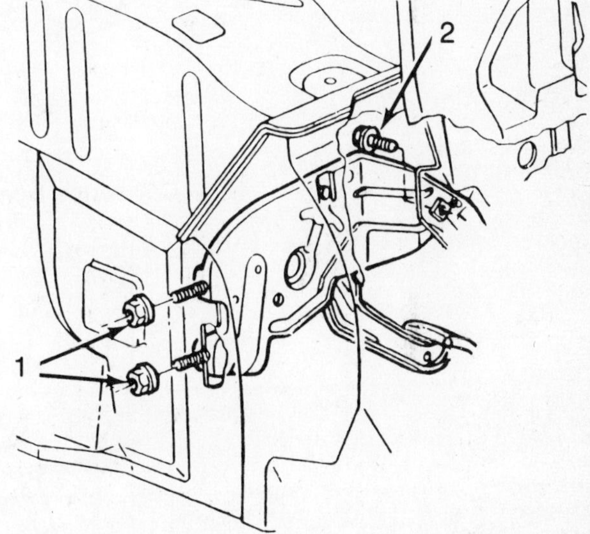

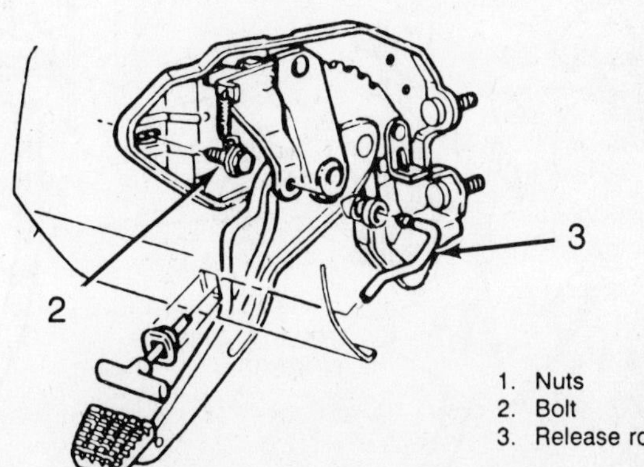

R/V series parking brake pedal

Parking Brake Cables

FRONT CABLE REPLACEMENT

1. Raise vehicle on hoist.
2. Remove adjusting nut from equalizer.
3. Remove retainer clip from rear portion of front cable at frame and from lever arm.
4. Disconnect front brake cable from parking brake pedal or lever assemblies. Remove front brake cable. On some models, it may assist installation of new cable if a heavy cord is tied to other end of cable in order to guide new cable through proper routing.
5. Install cable by reversing removal procedure.
6. Adjust parking brake.

CENTER CABLE REPLACEMENT

1. Raise vehicle on hoist.
2. Remove adjusting nut from equalizer.
3. Unhook connector at each end and disengage hooks and guides.

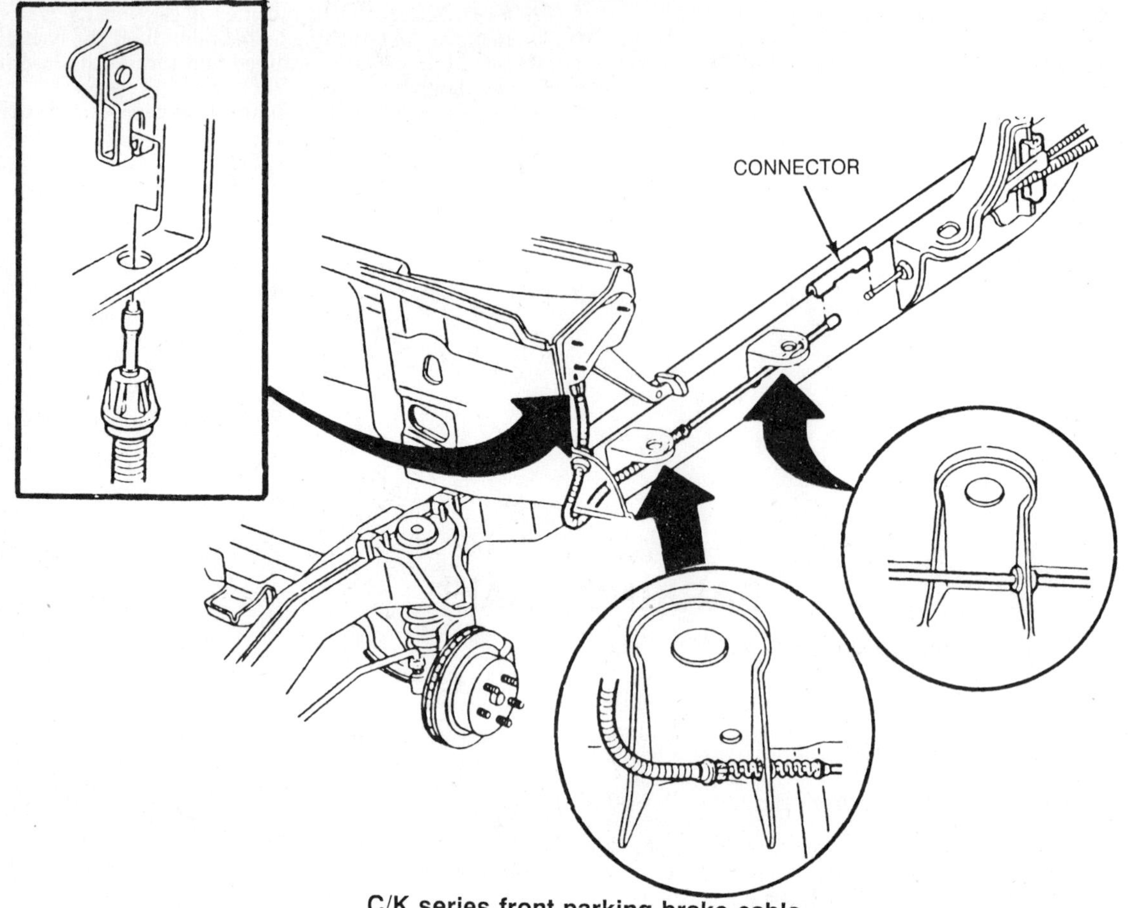

C/K series front parking brake cable

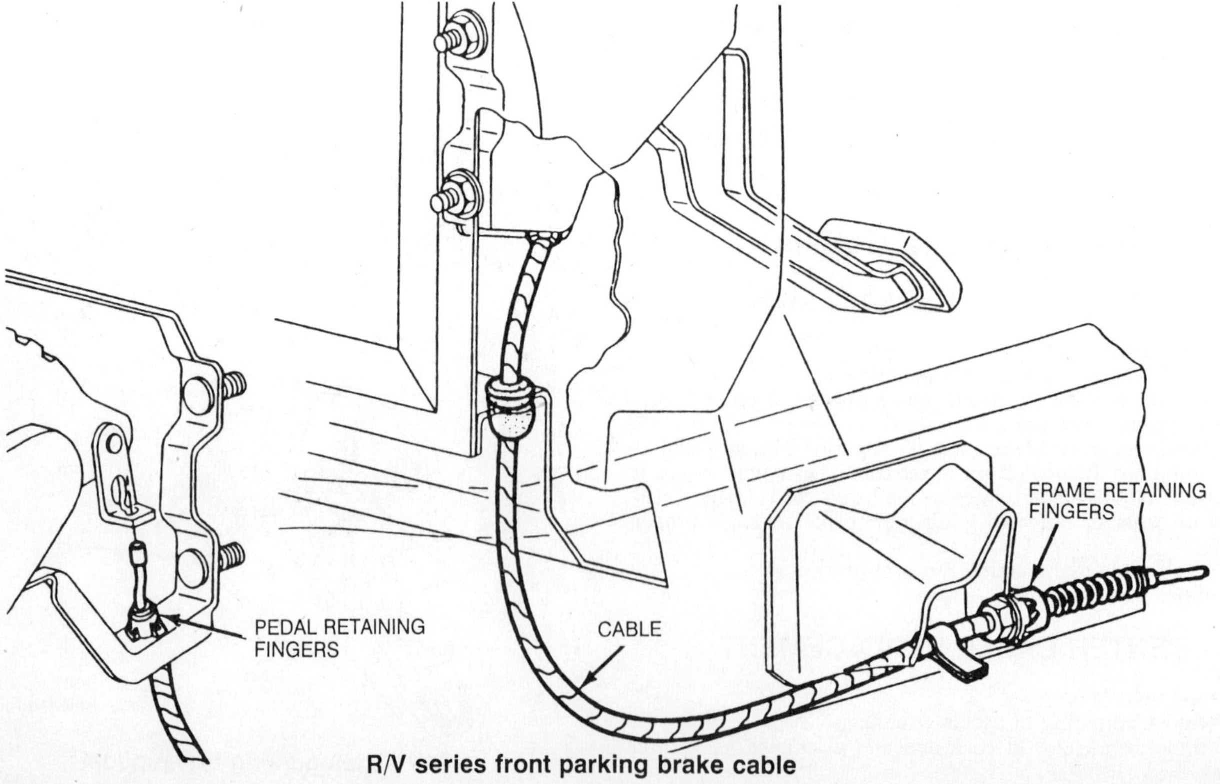

R/V series front parking brake cable

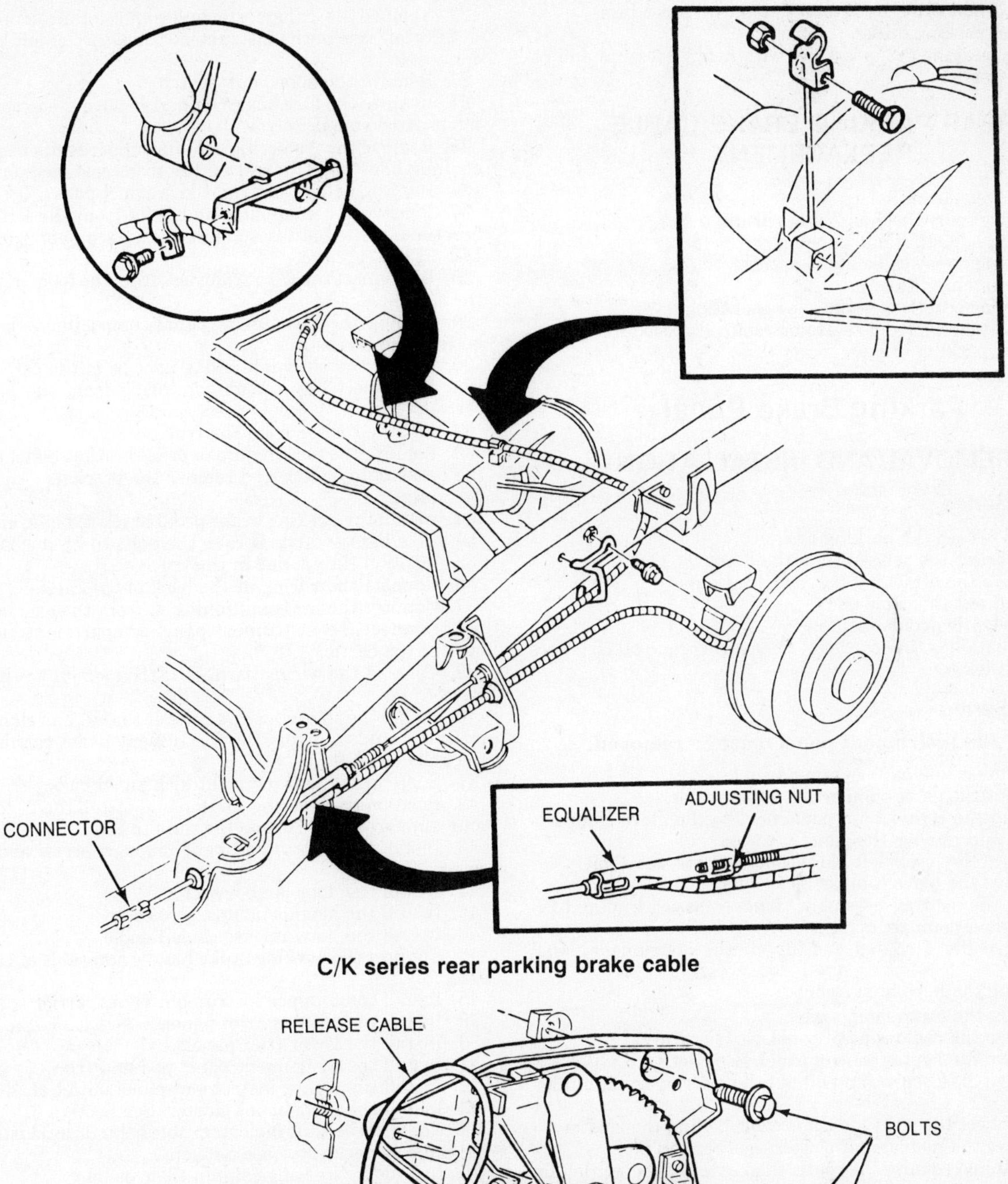

EQUALIZER
ADJUSTING NUT
CONNECTOR

C/K series rear parking brake cable

RELEASE CABLE
BOLTS
HANDLE

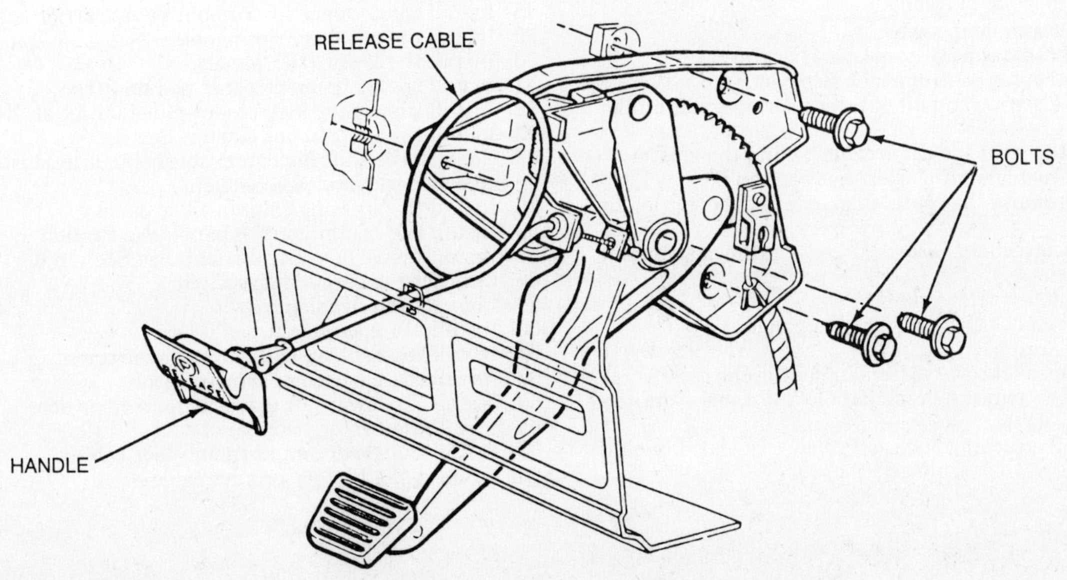

C/K series parking brake pedal components

4. Install new cable by reversing removal procedure.
5. Adjust parking brake.
6. Apply parking brake 3 times with heavy pressure and repeat adjustment.

REAR PARKING BRAKE CABLE REPLACEMENT

1. Raise vehicle on hoist.
2. Remove rear wheel and brake drum.
3. Loosen adjusting nut at equalizer.
4. Disengage rear cable at connector.
5. Bend retainer fingers.
6. Disengage cable at brake shoe operating lever.
7. Install new cable by reversing removal procedure.
8. Adjust parking brake.

Parking Brake Pedal

REMOVAL AND INSTALLATION

R and V Series

1. Fully release the parking brake.
2. Disconnect the relase rod at the lever.
3. Remove the attaching bolt and stud nuts.
4. Disconnect the cable end.
5. Lift out the pedal assembly.
6. Installation is the reverse of removal. Torque all fasteners to 100 inch lbs.

C and K Series

NOTE: The instrument panel must be removed.

1. Disconnect the battery ground cable.
2. Pry out the glove compartment door cable.
3. Lift up the center trim panel next to the glove compartment door and remove the panel.
4. Remove the lower left glove compartment door bolt.
5. Remove the glove compartment door.
6. Open the ashtray assembly, remove the ashtray and remove the glove compartment.
7. Remove the 4 screws and lift off the instrument panel bezel.
8. Unplug the headlamp switch.
9. Unplug the cargo lamp switch.
10. Remove the radio control panel. See Section 6.
11. Remove the heater control panel. See Section 6.
12. Remove the 2 screws and lift out the steering column filler panel.
13. Disconnect the shift indicator cable behind the cluster.
14. Remove the instrument cluster. See Section 6.
15. Unbolt and remove the center instrument panel outlet air duct.
16. Remove the attaching bolts and remove the instrument panel pod and trim.
17. Remove the lower trim panels.
18. Pry up and remove the speaker trim panels.
19. Remove the 5 upper instrument panel carrier screws: 1 from under each speaker cover; 3 from under the defroster vent.
20. Disconnect the parking brake handle and cable from the ratchet assembly.
21. Remove the 2 attaching bolts and remove the hood release cable handle.
22. Remove the 2 diagnostic link connector attaching bolts under the left side of the instrument panel carrier and remove the connector.
23. Remove the door jamb switch.
24. Remove the fuse box cover and remove the exposed instrument panel support screw.
25. Remove the 2 steering column support nuts and lower the column, allowing it to rest on the front seat cushion.
26. Pry off the left and right kick panel pads.
27. Remove the snap clips and bolts from the left and right bracket-mounted studs support the instrument panel carrier. Lift off the carrier.
28. Disconnect the wiring harness from the loom at the back of the carrier.
29. Unplug the instrument panel compartment lamp at the back of the carrier.
30. Unbolt the air conditioning duct from the carrier.
31. Disconnect any remaining wiring from the back of the carrier.
32. Lift the carrier from the truck.
33. Remove the parking brake pedal bracket bolts, disconnect the brake light switch and remove the bracket.

To install:

34. Install the parking brake pedal bracket, bolts, and connect the brake light switch. Torque the bolts to 18 ft. lbs.
35. Position the carrier in the truck.
36. Connect the wiring at the back of the carrier.
37. Connect the air conditioning at from the carrier.
38. Connect the instrument panel compartment lamp at the back of the carrier.
39. Connect the wiring harness at the loom at the back of the carrier.
40. Install the snap clips and bolts at the left and right bracket-mounted studs support the instrument panel carrier. Torque the bolts to 20 ft. lbs.
41. Snap on the left and right kick panel pads.
42. Position the steering column and install the 2 steering column support nuts. Torque the nuts to 20 ft. lbs.
43. Install the instrument panel support screw and fuse box cover.
44. Install the door jamb switch.
45. Install the diagnostic link connector.
46. Install the hood release cable handle.
47. Connect the parking brake handle and cable at the ratchet assembly.
48. Install the 5 upper instrument panel carrier screws.
49. Install the speaker trim panels.
50. Install the lower trim panels.
51. Install the instrument panel pod and trim.
52. Install the center instrument panel outlet air duct.
53. Install the instrument cluster. See Section 6.
54. Connect the shift indicator cable behind the cluster. Adjust the cable as necessary. See Section 7.
55. Install the steering column filler panel.
56. Install the heater control panel. See Section 6.
57. Install the radio control panel. See Section 6.
58. Connect the cargo lamp switch.
59. Connect the headlamp switch.
60. Install the instrument panel bezel.
61. Install the ashtray and glove compartment.
62. Install the glove compartment door.
63. Install the lower left glove compartment door bolt.
64. Install the center trim panel.
65. Install the glove compartment door cable.
66. Connect the battery ground cable.

ABS SYSTEM SERVICE

Electronic Control Unit

REPLACEMENT

The ECU is located next to the master cylinder.

1. Disconnect the wiring connecto.
2. Pry on the tab at the rear of the ECU and pull it forward to remove it.
3. Installation is the reverse of removal.

CAUTION

Never let brake fluid come in contact with the electrical connection and pins, nor should your skin touch them! Damage to the ECU will result.

Isolation/Dump Valve

REPLACEMENT

The valve is located next to the master cylinder.

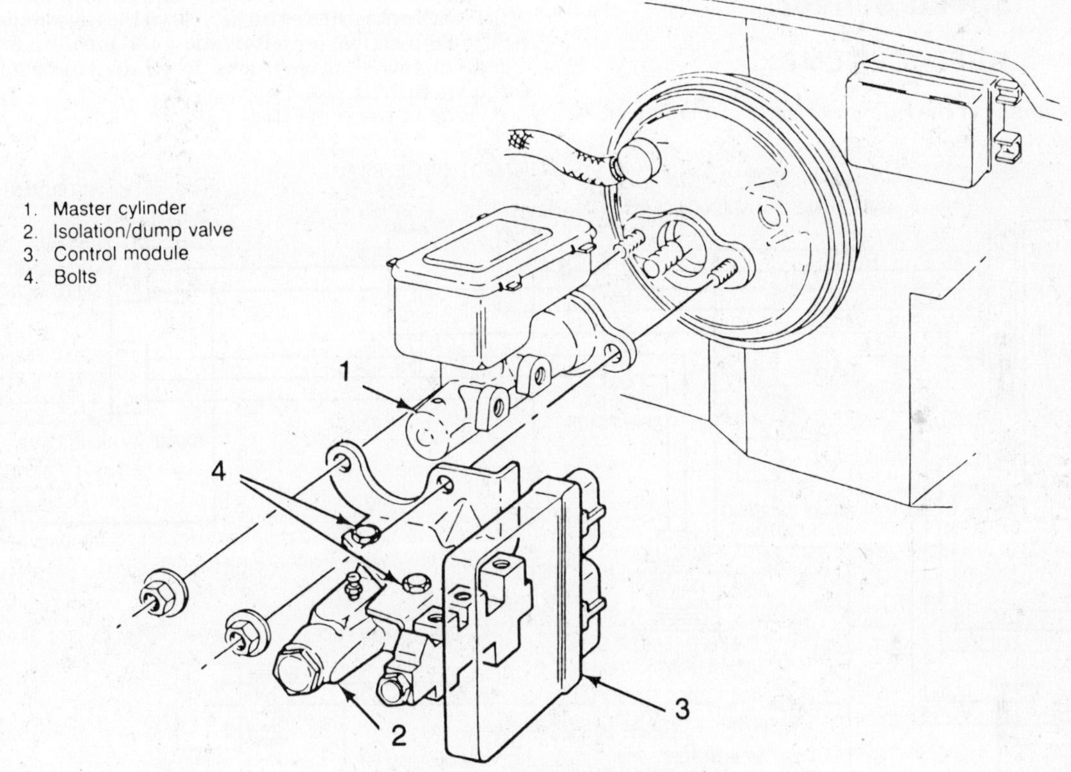

ECU and isolation/dump valve

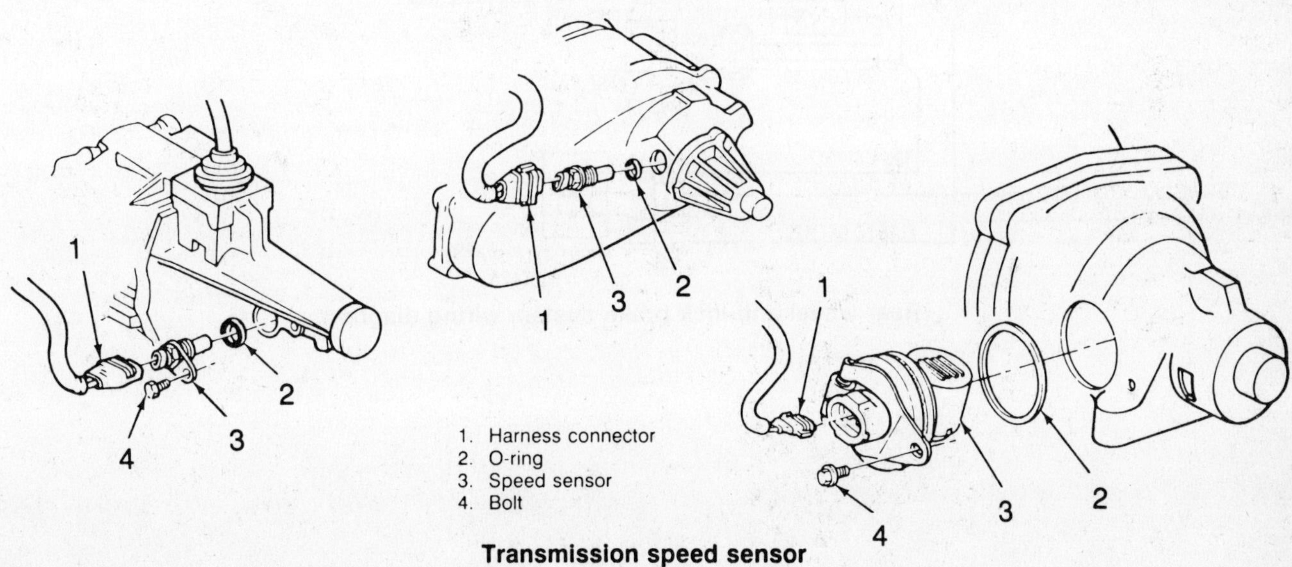

Transmission speed sensor

1. Disconenct the brake lines at the valve. Cap the openings.
2. Remove the attaching nuts from the valve.
3. Disconnect the bottom electrical connector at the ECU.

CAUTION

Never let brake fluid come in contact with the electrical connection and pins, nor should your skin touch them! Damage to the ECU will result.

4. Remove the valve.
5. Installation is the reverse of removal. Torque the mounting nuts to 21 ft. lbs. Torque the brake lines to 18 ft. lbs. Bleed the system.

Speed Sensor

REPLACEMENT

The sensor is located at the left rear of the transmission on 2-wheel drive trucks, or the left rear of the transfer case on 4-wheel drive trucks.

Before replacing a suspected defective sensor, check its resistance with an ohmmeter. Resistance should be 900–2000Ω.

1. Unplug the wiring connector.

2a. On 2-wheel drive trucks, remove the attaching bolt and pull the sensor from the transmission.

2b. On 4-wheel drive trucks, unscrew the sensor from the transfer case.

NOTE: Some fluid may spill from the transmission.

3. Remove and discard the O-ring.

To install:

4. Install a new O-ring coated with clean transmission fluid.

5a. On 2-wheel drive trucks, install the sensor and torque the bolt to 96 inch lbs. for automatics; 108 inch lbs. for manuals.

5b. On 4-wheel drive trucks, screw the sensor into place and torque it to 32 ft. lbs.

6. Plug in the connector.

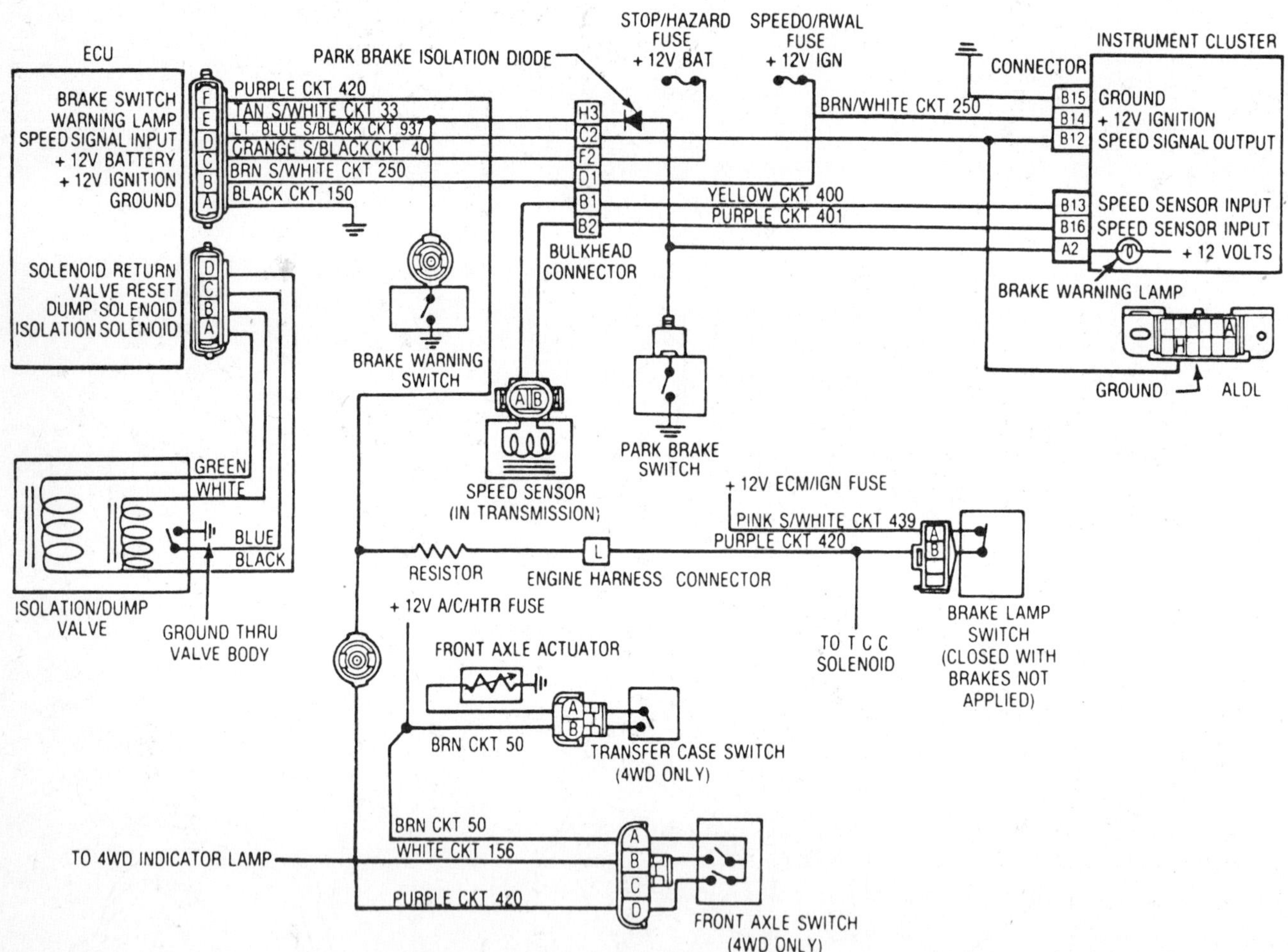

Rear wheel anti-lock brake system wiring diagram

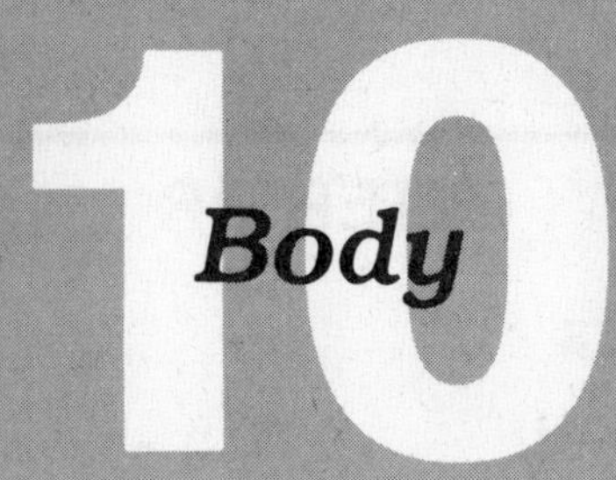

10 Body

QUICK REFERENCE INDEX

GENERAL INDEX

EXTERIOR

Front or Rear Side Doors

REMOVAL AND INSTALLATION

R and V Series

NOTE: If the door being removed is to be reinstalled, matchmark the hinge position.

1. If the door is to be replaced with a new one, remove the trim panels weathersheets and all molding.
2. If the door is to be replaced with a new one, remove the glass, locks and latches.
3. If equipped with a wiring harness, remove the trim panl and disconnect the harness. Guide the wiring out of the door.
4. Support the door and remove the hinge-to-body attaching bolts. Lift the door from the truck.
5. Installation is the reverse of removal.
6. Perform the alignment procedures indicated below.

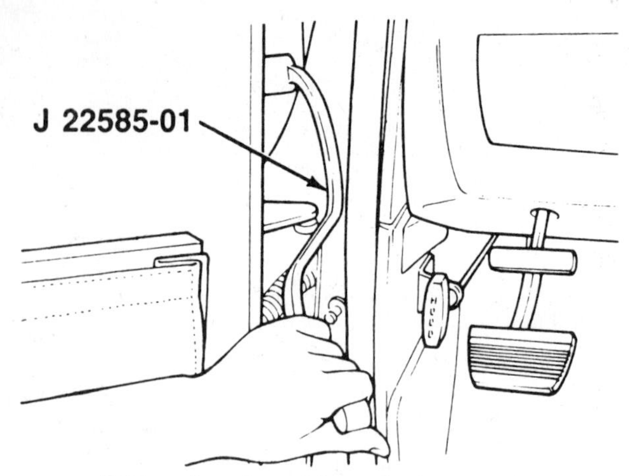

R/V series door hinge bolt wrench

ALIGNMENT

NOTE: The holes for the hinges are oversized to provide for latitude in alignment. Align the door hinges first, then the striker.

Hinges

1. If a door is being installed, first mount the door and tighten the hinge bolts lightly.

NOTE: If the door has not been removed, determine which hinge bolts must be loosed to effect alignment.

2. Loosen the necessary bolts just enough to allow the door to be moved with a padded prybar.
3. Move the door in small movements and check the fit after each movement.

NOTE: Be sure that there is no binding or interference with adjacent panels.

4. Keep repeating this procedure until the door is properly aligned.
   - Door edge-to-rocker panel: 6mm ± 2mm
   - Door edge-to-roof panel: 5mm ± 2mm
   - Door edge-to-rear pillar: 5mm ± 2mm
   - Door edge-to-front pillar: 2mm ± 1½mm
5. Tighten all the bolts.

NOTE: Shims may be either fabricated or purchased to install behind the hinges as an aid in alignment.

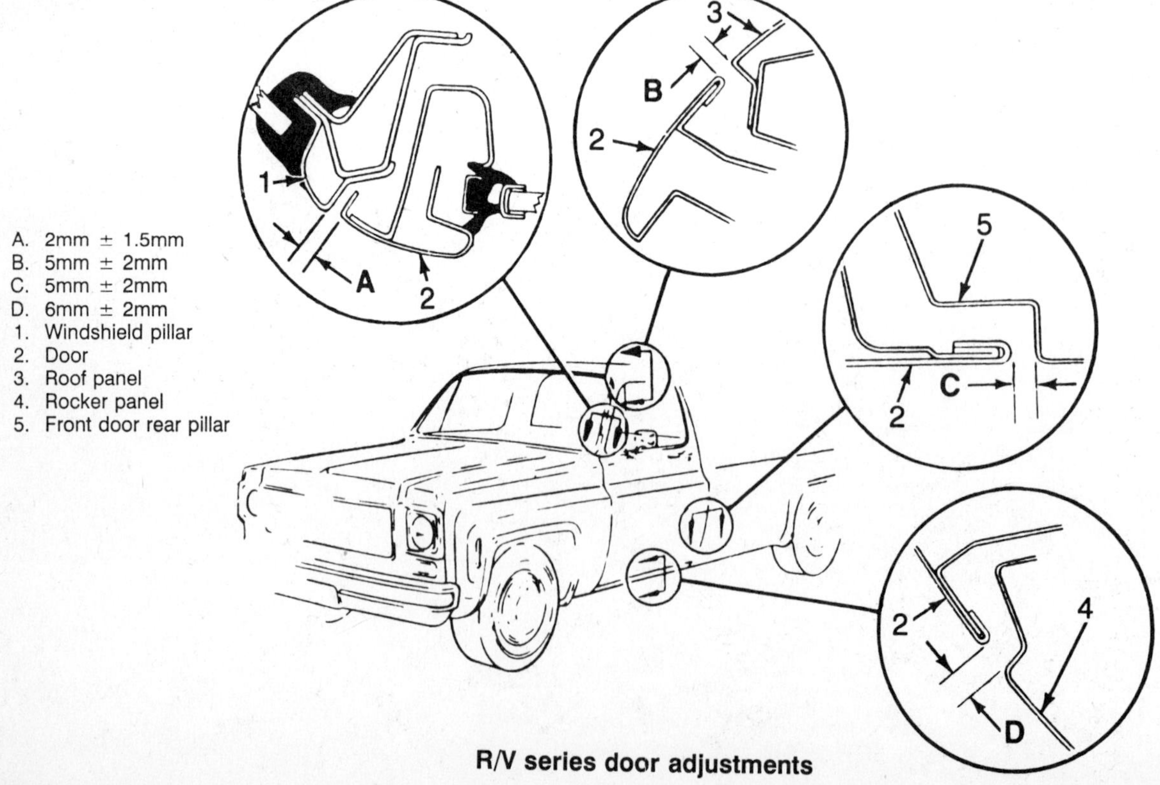

R/V series door adjustments

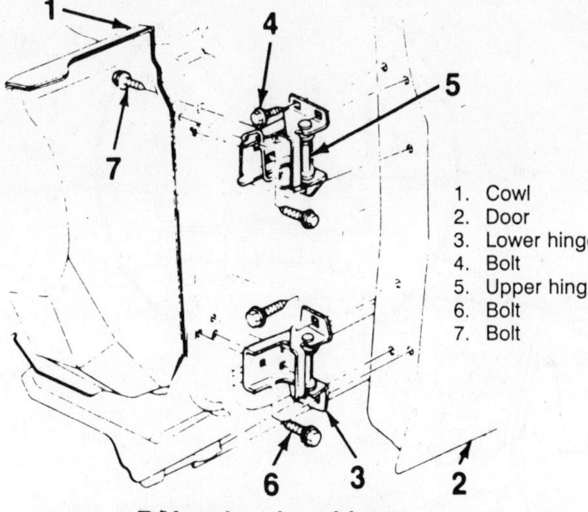

R/V series door hinge

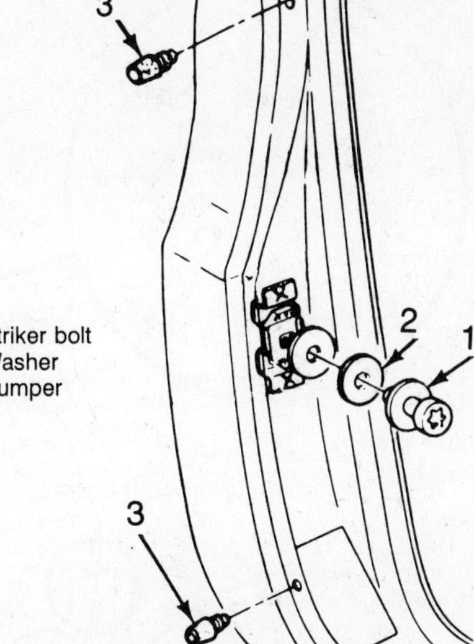

R/V series door striker

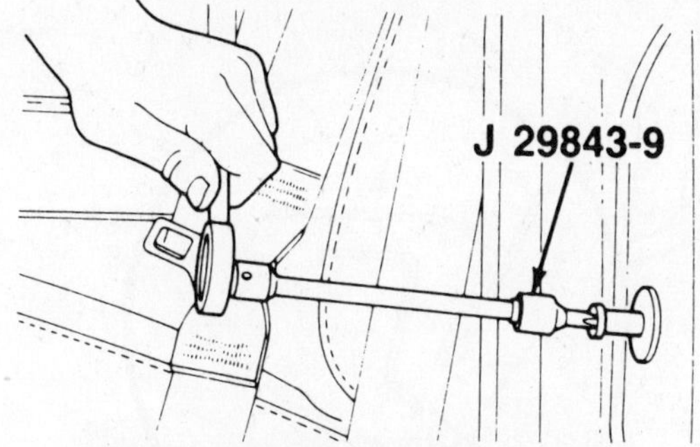

R/V series striker bolt removal

Striker Plate

NOTE: The striker is attached to the pillar using oversized holes, providing latitude in movement. Striker plate bolt torque is 46 ft. lbs.

Striker adjustment is made by loosening the bolts and moving the striker plate in the desired direction or adding or deleting the shims behind the plate, or both.

The striker is properly adjusted when the locking latch enters the striker without rubbing and the door closed fully and solidly, with no play when closed.

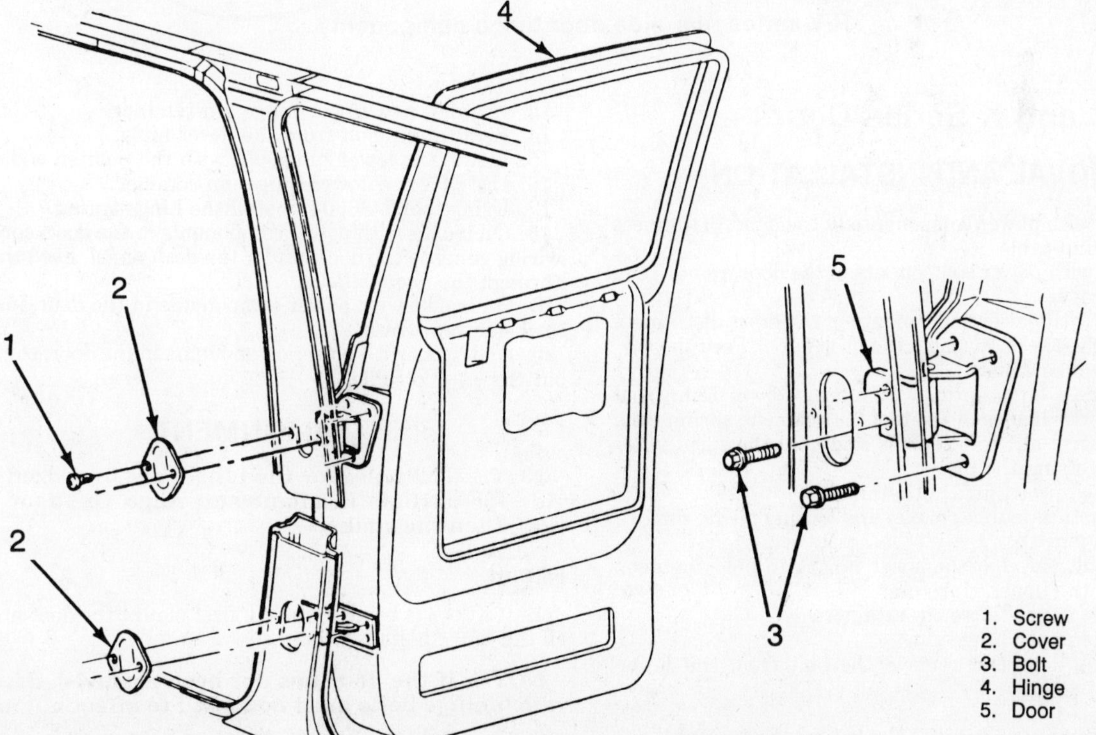

R/V series rear side door adjustments

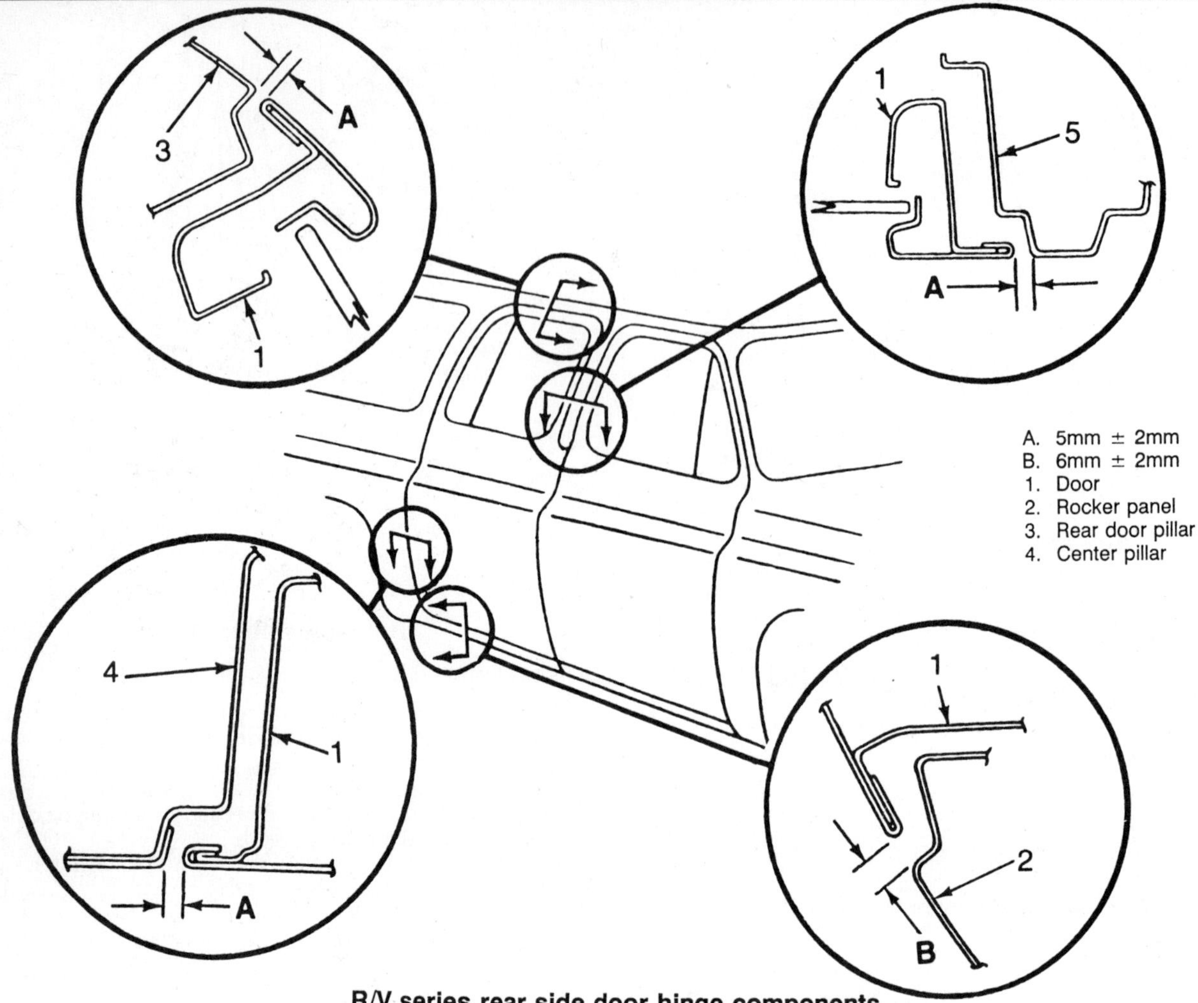

R/V series rear side door hinge components

C and K Series Doors

REMOVAL AND INSTALLATION

1. On trucks with power components in the door, disconnect the battery ground cable.
2. On trucks with power components in the door, remove the cowl side vent cover.
3. On trucks with power components in the door, disconnect the wiring going to the door, under the dash panel. Feed the wiring through the door pillar.
4. Cover the door hinge spring with a heavy towel. Using tool J-36604, insert the blades of the tool between the spring coils and turn the barrel nut to compress and hold the spring. Remove the spring using the tool.
5. Remove the lower hinge pin retainer.
6. Using a plastic or rubber mallet and locking pliers, remove the lower hinge pin.
7. Install a bolt through the lower hinges to hold the door while removing the upper hinge pin.
8. Remove the upper hinge pin retainer.
9. Remove the upper hinge pin.
10. Support the door and remove the bolt from the lower hinge.

To install:

11. Position the door and install the bolt in the lower hinge.
12. Install the upper hinge pin. with the pointed end up.
13. Install a new upper hinge pin retainer.
14. Remove the bolt from the lower hinges.
15. Install the lower hinge pin with the pointed end down.
16. Install a new lower hinge pin retainer.
17. Using tool J-36604, install the hinge spring.
18. On trucks with power components in the door, connect the wiring going to the door, under the dash panel. Feed the wiring through the door pillar.
19. On trucks with power components in the door, install the cowl side vent cover.
20. On trucks with power components in the door, connect the battery ground cable.

ALIGNMENT

NOTE: The holes for the hinges are oversized to provide for latitude in alignment. Align the door hinges first, then the striker.

Hinges

1. If a door is being installed, first mount the door and tighten the hinge bolts lightly.

NOTE: If the door has not been removed, determine which hinge bolts must be loosed to effect alignment.

2. Loosen the necessary bolts just enough to allow the door to be moved with a padded prybar.

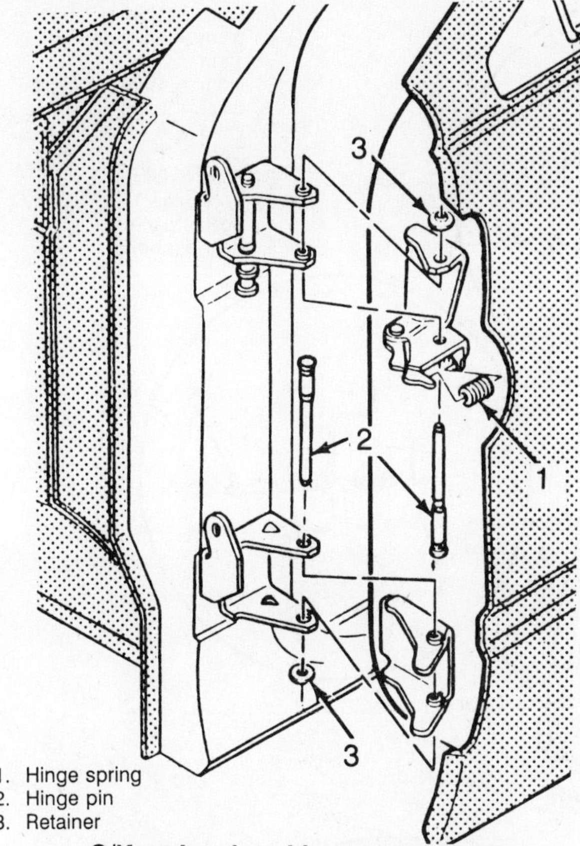

1. Hinge spring
2. Hinge pin
3. Retainer

C/K series door hinge components

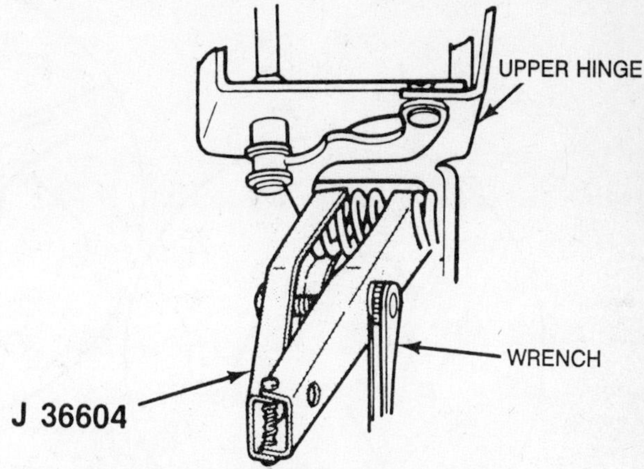

C/K series hinge spring removal

3. Move the door in small movements and check the fit after each movement.

NOTE: Be sure that there is no binding or interference with adjacent panels.

4. Keep repeating this procedure until the door is properly aligned.

- Door edge-to-rocker panel: 6mm + 2mm; − 1mm
- Door edge-to-roof panel: 6mm + 2mm; − 0mm
- Door edge-to-rear pillar: 4mm ± 1mm
- Door edge-to-front pillar: 7mm ± 0mm
- Door front edge-to-fender: 5mm ± 1mm

5. Tighten all the bolts to 26 ft. lbs.

NOTE: Shims may be either fabricated or purchased to install behind the hinges as an aid in alignment.

Striker Plate

NOTE: The striker is attached to the pillar using oversized holes, providing latitude in movement. Striker plate bolt torque is 46 ft. lbs.

Striker adjustment is made by loosening the bolts and moving the striker plate in the desired direction or adding or deleting the shims behind the plate, or both.

The striker is properly adjusted when the locking latch enters the striker without rubbing and the door closed fully and solidly, with no play when closed.

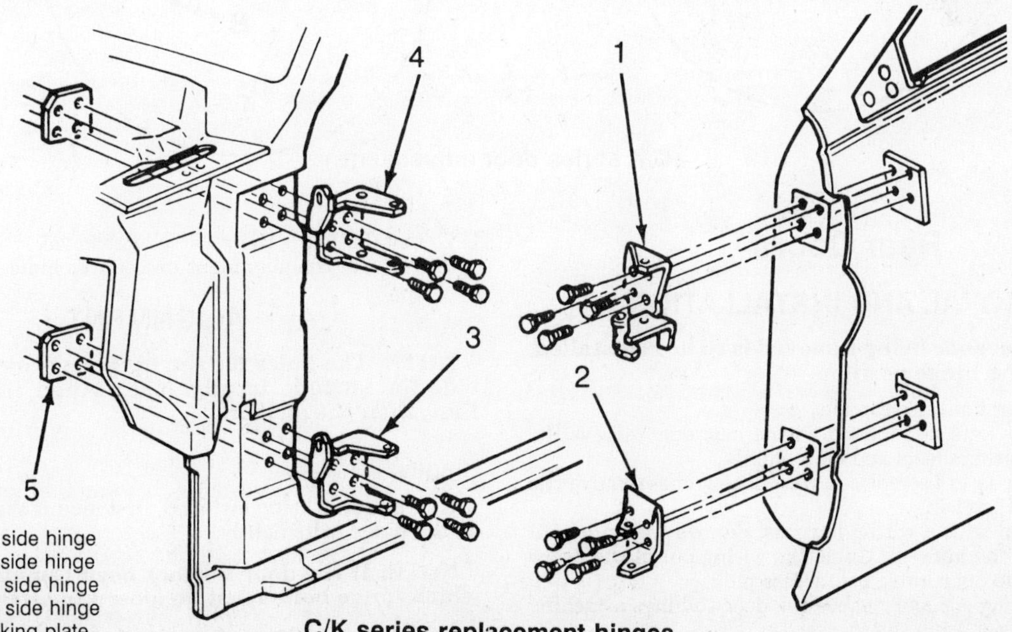

1. Upper door side hinge
2. Lower door side hinge
3. Lower body side hinge
4. Upper body side hinge
5. Tapped backing plate

C/K series replacement hinges

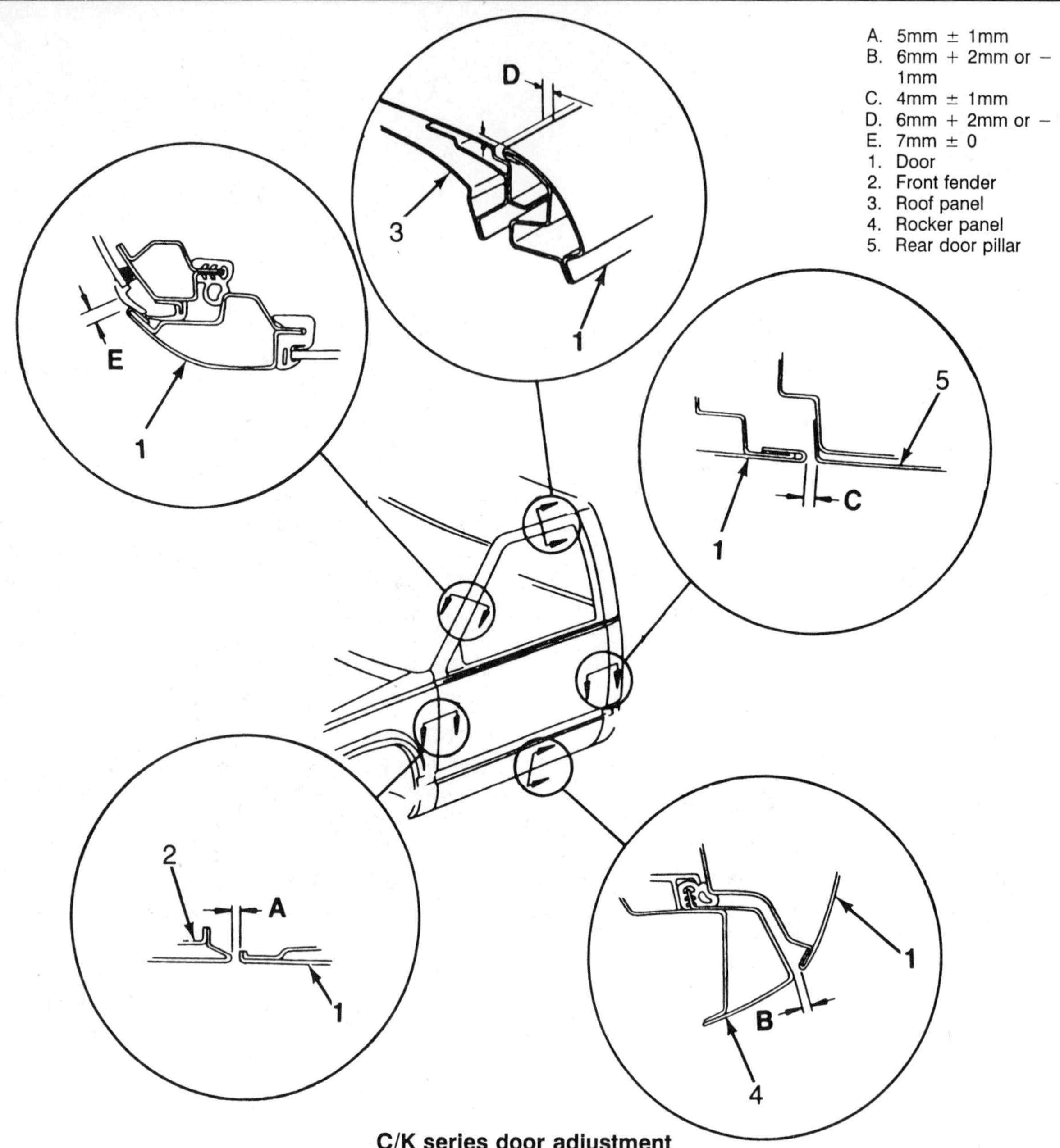

C/K series door adjustment

Rear Doors

REMOVAL AND INSTALLATION

NOTE: If the door being removed is to be reinstalled, matchmark the hinge position.

1. Remove the limiter strap pin.
2. If the door is to be replaced with a new one, remove the trim panels weathersheets and all molding.
3. If the door is to be replaced with a new one, remove the glass, locks and latches.
4. If equipped with a wiring harness, remove the trim panl and disconnect the harness. Guide the wiring out of the door.
5. Remove the door hinge bolt access plug.
6. Support the door and remove the door-to-hinge attaching bolts. Lift the door from the truck.
7. Installation is the reverse of removal.
8. Perform the alignment procedures indicated below.

ALIGNMENT

NOTE: The holes for the hinges are oversized to provide for latitude in alignment. Align the door hinges first, then the striker.

Hinges

1. If a door is being installed, first mount the door and tighten the hinge bolts lightly.

NOTE: If the door has not been removed, determine which hinge bolts must be loosed to effect alignment.

2. Loosen the necessary bolts just enough to allow the door to

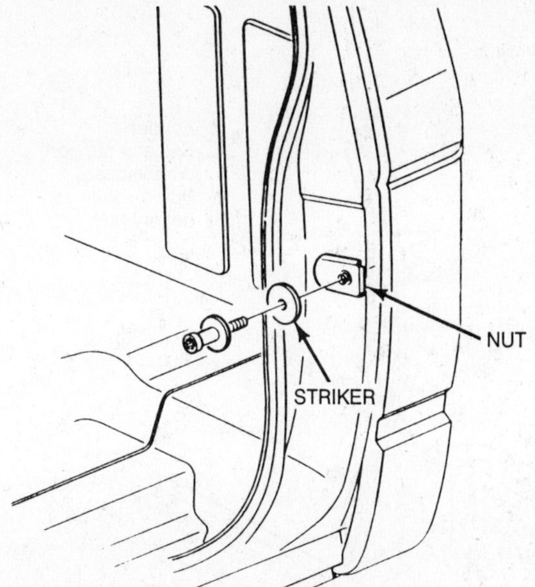

C/K series door striker components

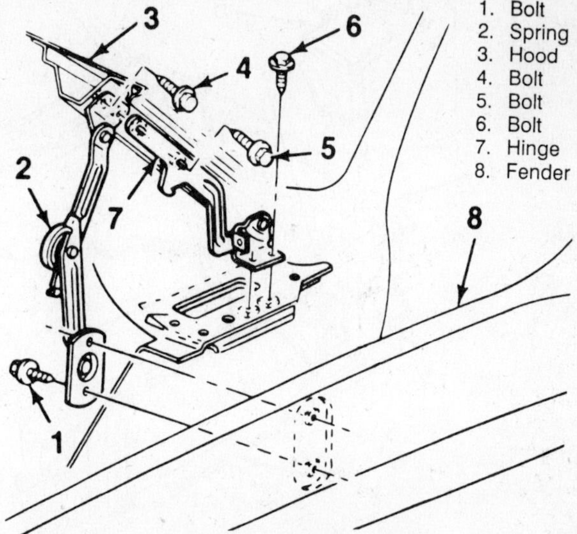

R/V series hood hinge

be moved with a padded prybar.

3. Move the door in small movements and check the fit after each movement.

NOTE: Be sure that there is no binding or interference with adjacent panels.

4. Keep repeating this procedure until the door is properly aligned.

- Door panel lower edge-to-platform panel: 7mm ± 2mm
- Door outer panel-to-platform panel (closed): 14mm ± 1.5mm
- Door edge-to-roof panel: 5mm ± 2mm
- Door edge-to-pillar: 5mm ± 2mm
- Door edge-to-door edge (closed): 5mm ± 2mm

5. Tighten all the bolts.

NOTE: Shims may be either fabricated or purchased to install behind the hinges as an aid in alignment.

Striker Plate

NOTE: The striker is attached to the pillar using oversized holes, providing latitude in movement. Striker plate bolt torque is 46 ft. lbs.

Striker adjustment is made by loosening the bolts and moving the striker plate in the desired direction or adding or deleting the shims behind the plate, or both.

The striker is properly adjusted when the locking latch enters the striker without rubbing and the door closed fully and solidly, with no play when closed.

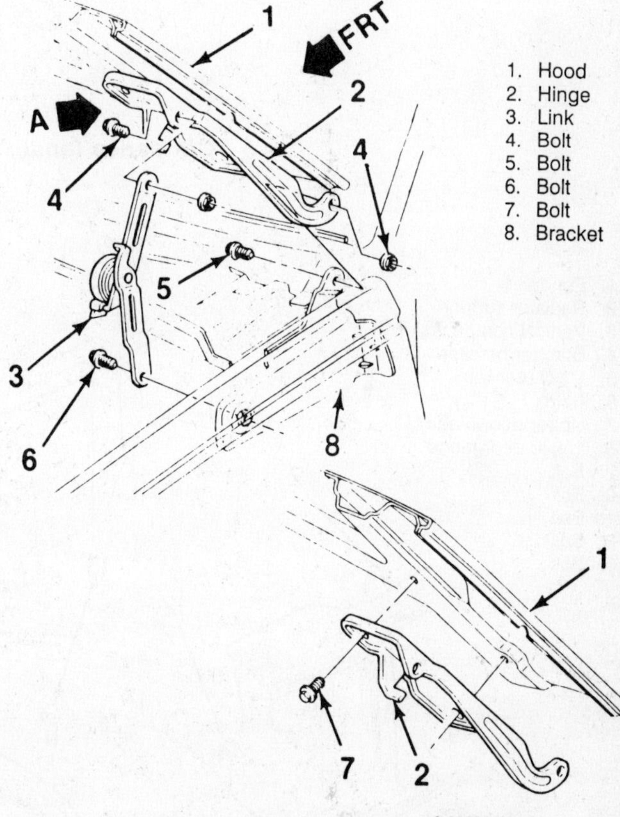

C/K series hood hinge

Hood

REMOVAL AND INSTALLATION

NOTE: You are going to need an assistant for this job.

R and V Series

1. Open the hood and trace the outline of the hinges on the hood.
2. While an assistant holds the hood, remove the hinge-to-hood bolts and lift the hood off.
3. Installation is the reverse of removal. Torque the bolts to 18 ft. lbs.
4. Adjust hood alignment, if necessary.

C and K Series

1. Open the hood and trace the outline of the hinges on the hood.

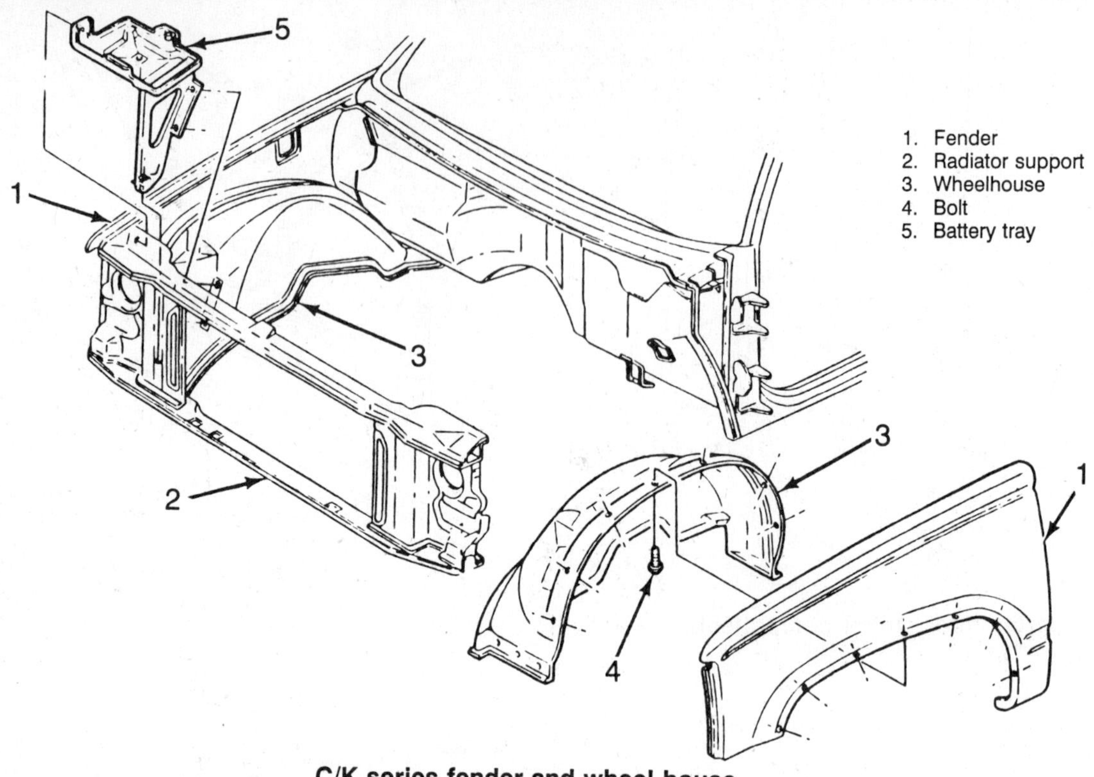

C/K series fender and wheel house

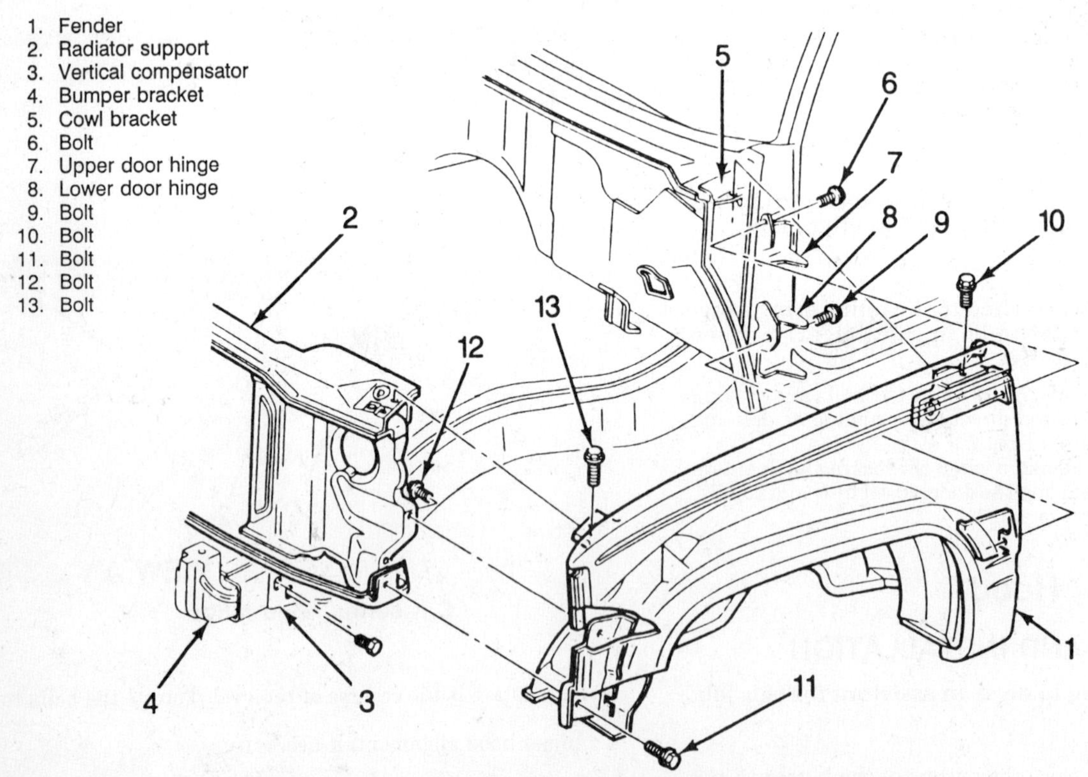

Front fender removal – C/K series

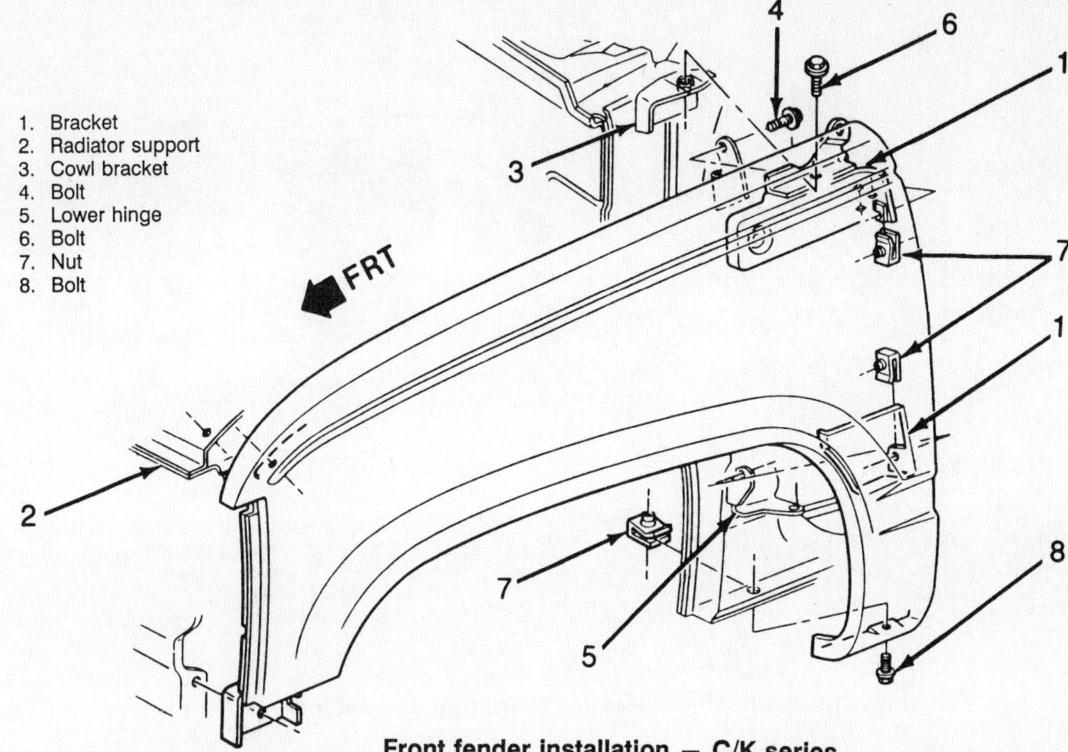

Front fender installation – C/K series

2. Remove the hood seals from the hinges.
3. While an assistant holds the hood, remove the hinge-to-link bolts and lower the hood.
4. Remove the outboard section of the cowl vent grille.
5. Remove the hinge-to-fender bracket bolts.
6. Lift off the hood.
7. Installation is the reverse of removal. Torque the bolts to 18 ft. lbs.
8. Adjust hood alignment, if necessary.

ALIGNMENT

1. Hood alignment can be adjusted front-to-rear or side-to-side by loosening the hood-to-hinge or hinge-to-body bolts.
2. The front edge of the hood can be adjusted for closing height by adding or deleting shims under the hinges.
3. The rear edge of the hood can be adjusted for closing height by raising or lowering the hood bumpers.

Front Fenders

REMOVAL AND INSTALLATION

C and K Series

1. Remove the hood link from the fender.
2. Remove the hinge-to-fender bolts.
3. Remove the hood.
4. Remove the antenna assembly.
5. Remove the air cleaner hose from the fender.
6. Remove the battery and tray.
7. Remove the forward air inlet duct assembly from the fender.
8. Disconnect all wiring at their clips on the fender.
9. Remove the trouble light.
10. Remove the fender-to-wheelwell bolts.
11. Remove the 3 fender-to-radiator support bolts.
12. Remove the lower fender-to-cab bolt.
13. Open the door and remove the fender-to-door hinges bolts.
14. Lift off the fender.

To install:

15. Position the fender.
16. Install the fender-to-door hinges bolts. Torque them to 18 ft. lbs.
17. Install the lower fender-to-cab bolt. Torque it to 18 ft. lbs.
18. Install the 3 fender-to-radiator support bolts. Torque them to 18 ft. lbs.
19. Install the fender-to-wheelwell bolts. Torque them to 18 ft. lbs.
20. Install the trouble light.
21. Connect all wiring at their clips on the fender.
22. Install the forward air inlet duct assembly.
23. Install the battery and tray.
24. Install the air cleaner hose.
25. Install the antenna assembly.
26. Install the hood.
27. Install the hinge-to-fender bolts. Torque them to 18 ft. lbs.
28. Install the hood link.

R and V Series

1. Remove the hood.
2. Remove the headlamp bezel.
3. Remove the headlamp.
4. Remove the grille molding nuts.
5. Remove the upper and lower molding clip nuts.
6. Remove the grille molding.
7. Remove the lower radiator grille-to-fender bolts.
8. Remove the cowl vent grille.
9. Remove hood spring assemblies.
10. Remove the fender-to-radiator support bolts.
11. Remove the wheelwell panel-to-splash shield bolts.

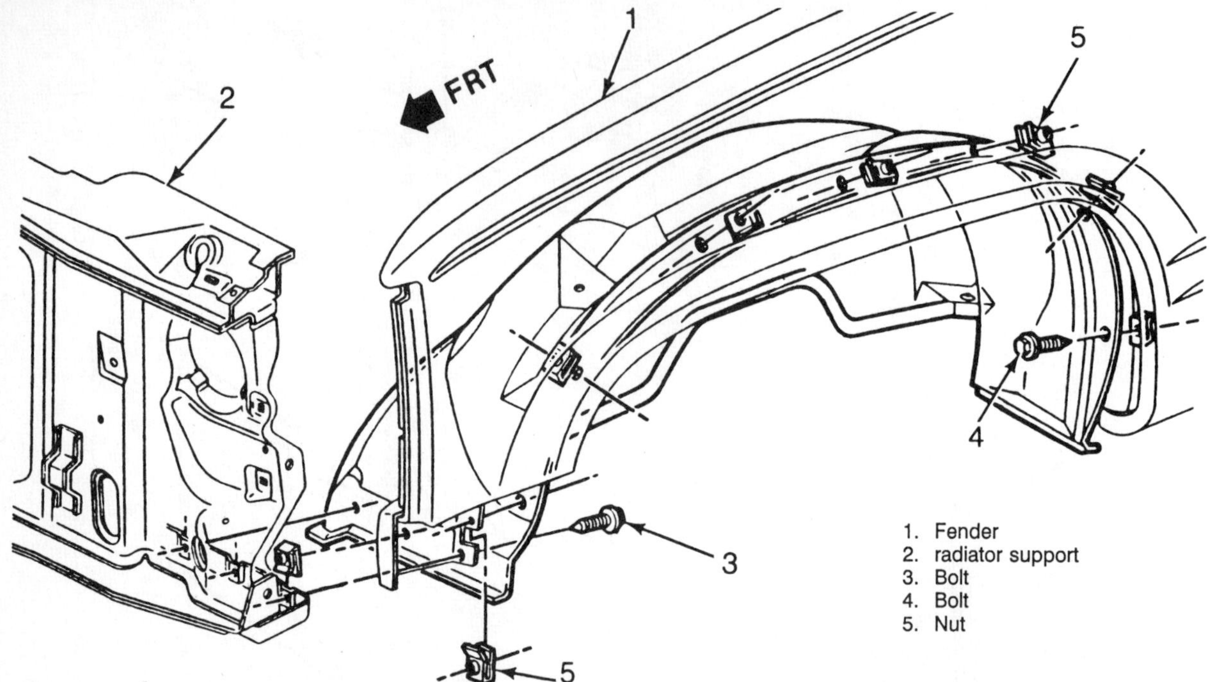

C/K series front wheelhouse-to-radiator support attachment

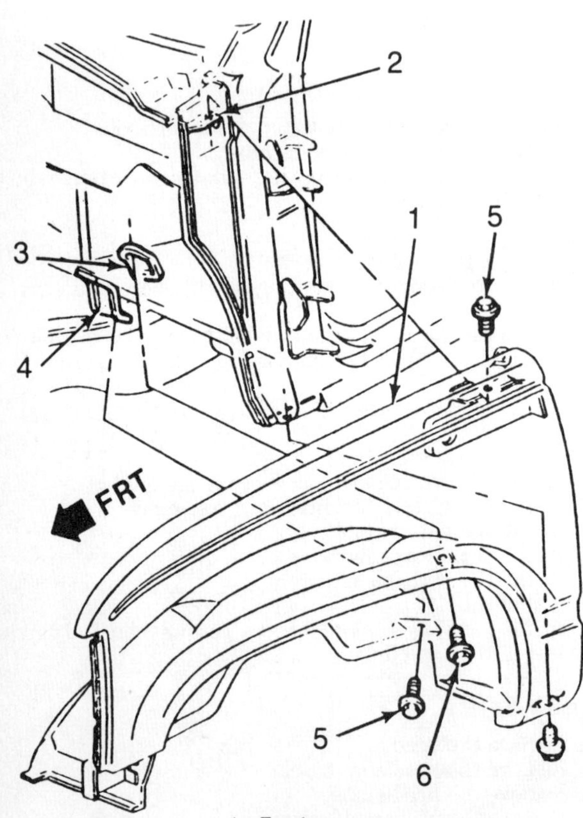

C/K series front wheelhouse-to-cowl attachment

12. Carefull pry out the splash shield retainers and remove the shields.
13. Remove the wheelwell panel-to-fender bolts.
14. Remove the lower door pillar-to-fender bolt and any shims.
15. Open the door and remove the fender-to-cowl bolt and any shims.
16. Remove the upper fender-to-door pillar bolt and any shims.
17. Lift the fender from the truck.

To install:

18. Position the fender on the truck.
19. Install the upper fender-to-door pillar bolt and any shims. Make the bolt finger tight for now.

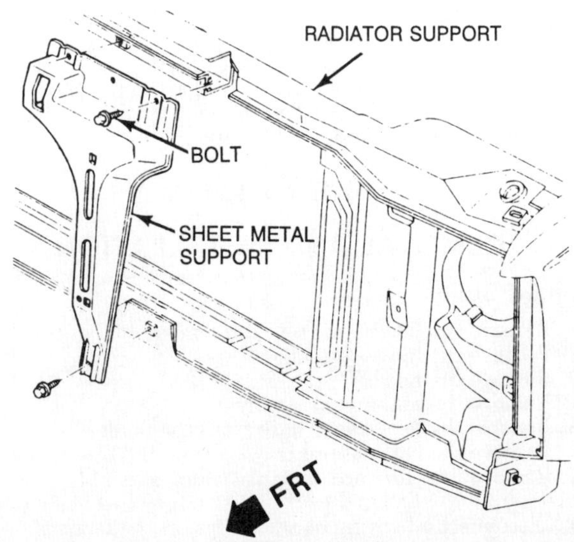

C/K series front sheet metal support

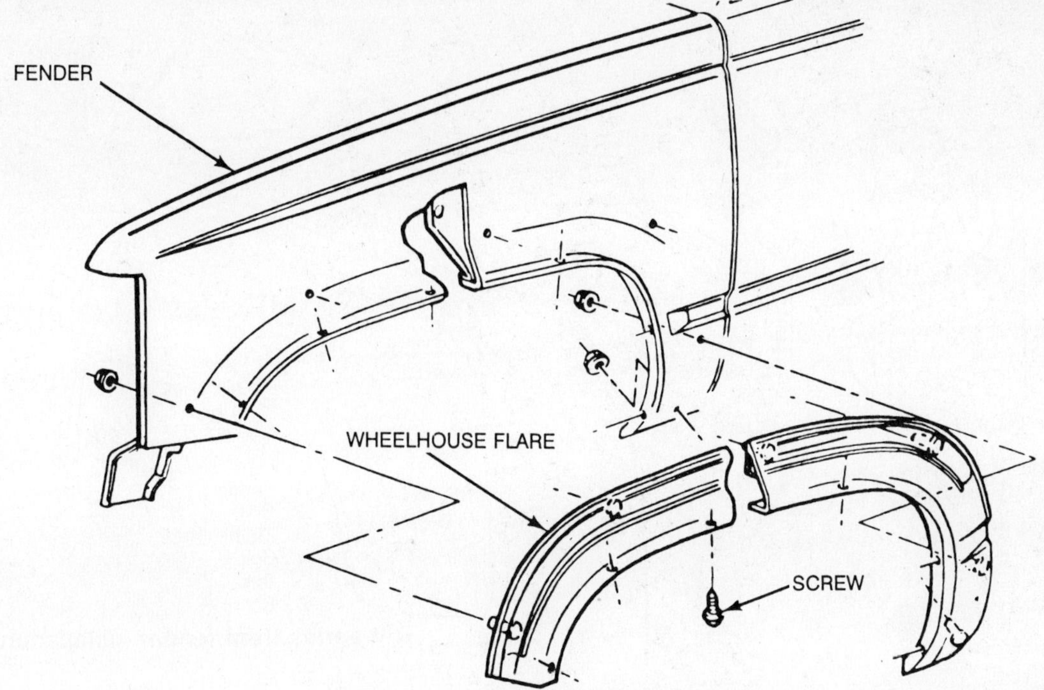

C/K series front fender wheelhouse

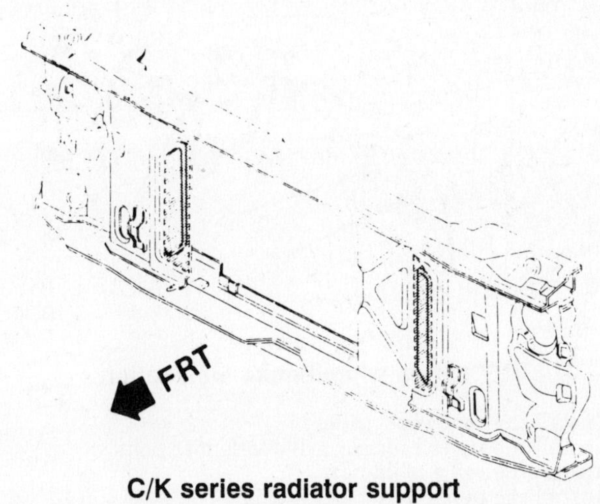

C/K series radiator support

20. Install the fender-to-cowl bolt and any shims. Make the bolt finger-tight for now.
21. Install the lower door pillar-to-fender bolt and any shims. Make the bolt finger-tight for now.
22. Install the fender-to-radiator support bolts. Tighten the bolts to 13 ft. lbs.
23. Install the wheelwell panel-to-fender bolts. Tighten the bolts to 13 ft. lbs.
24. Tighten the lower door pillar-to-fender bolt to 31 ft. lbs.
25. Install the splash shield. Tighten the wheelwell panel-to-splash shield bolts to 13 ft. lbs.
26. Tighten the fender-to-cowl bolt and upper fender-to-door pillar bolt to 31 ft. lbs.
27. Install hood spring assemblies. Torque the bolts to 20 ft. lbs.

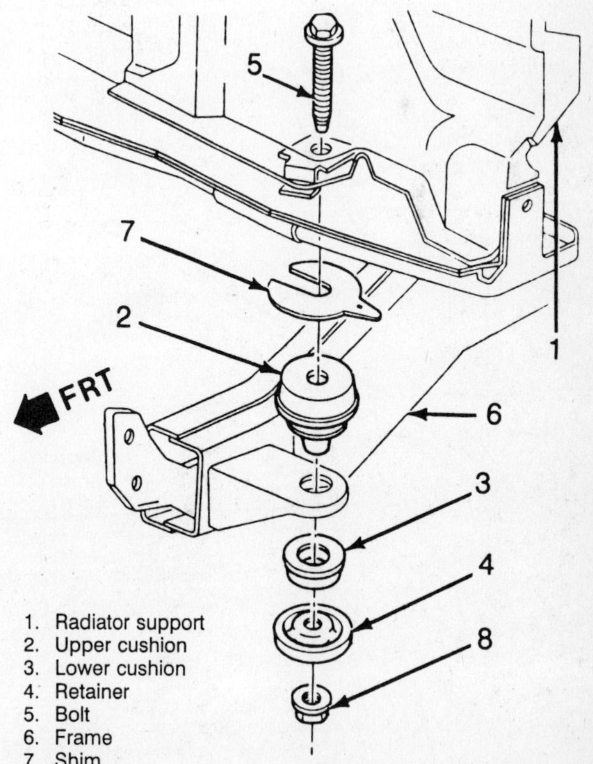

C/K series fender-to-radiator support attachment

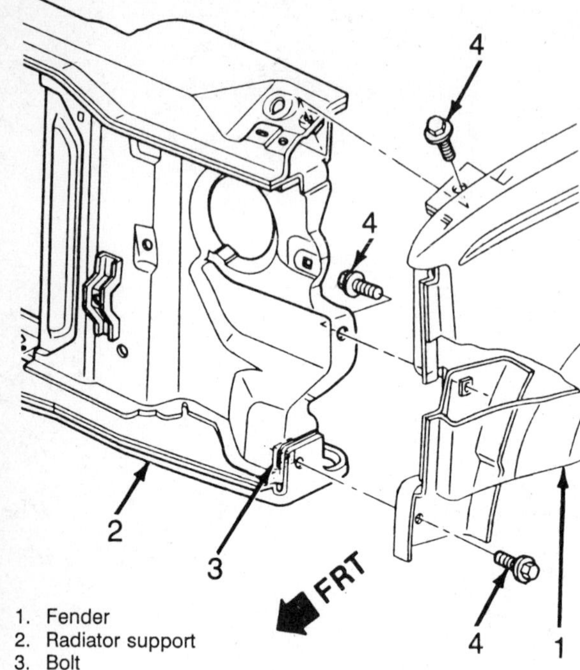

C/K series radiator support installation

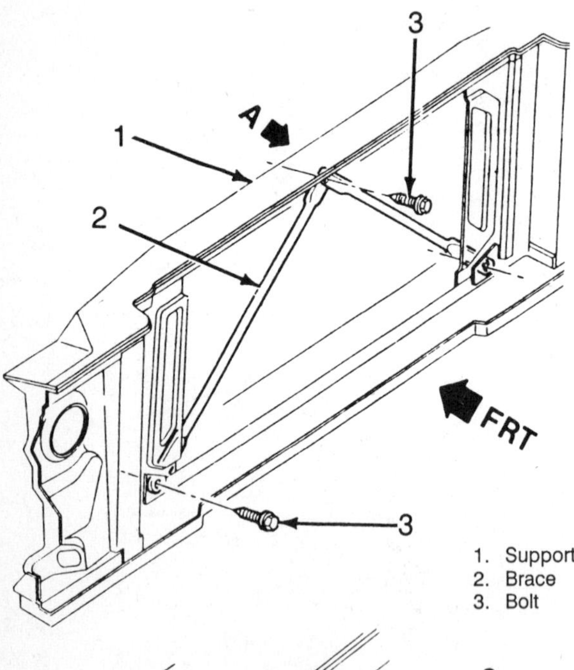

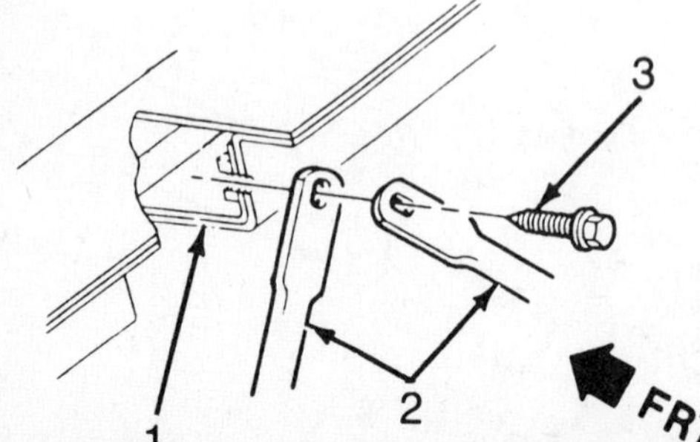

C/K series radiator support brace

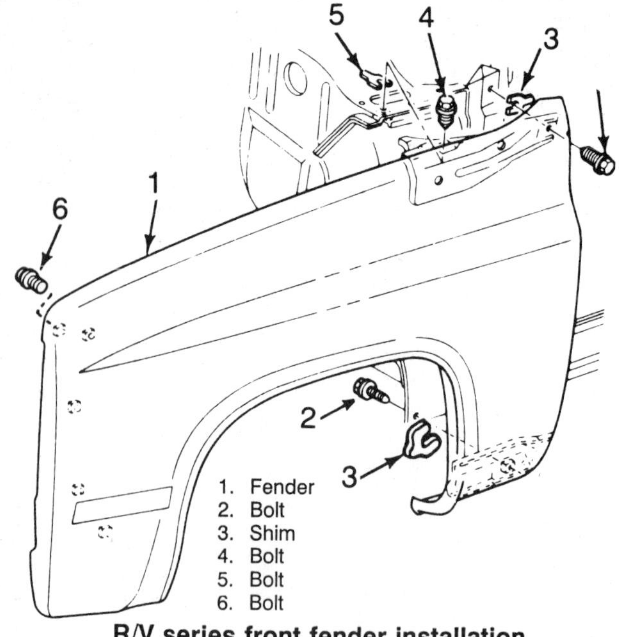

R/V series front fender installation

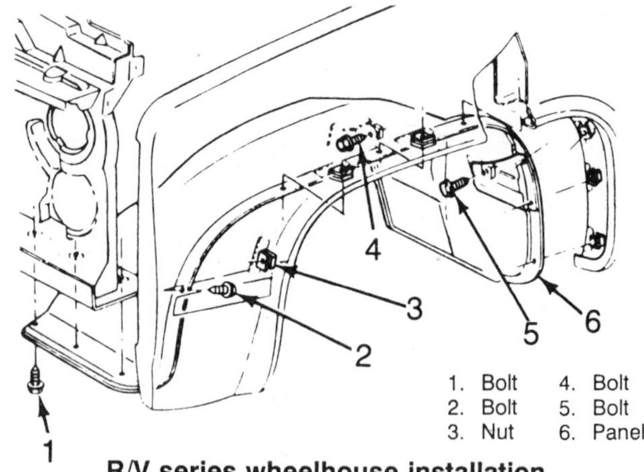

R/V series wheelhouse installation

28. Install the cowl vent grille.
29. Install the lower radiator grille-to-fender bolts.
30. Install the grille molding.
31. Install the upper and lower molding clip nuts.
32. Install the grille molding nuts.
33. Install the headlamp.
34. Install the headlamp bezel.
35. Install the hood.

Step Side Rear Fenders

REMOVAL AND INSTALLATION

C and K Series

1. Remove the step pads.
2. Remove the fender-to-brace bolts.
3. Remove the brace-to-support bolts.
4. Remove the fender-to-support screws.
5. Remove the tail light side panel screws.
6. Remove the fender-to-bracket screws.
7. Remove the fender-to-side panel screws.
8. Lift off the fender.

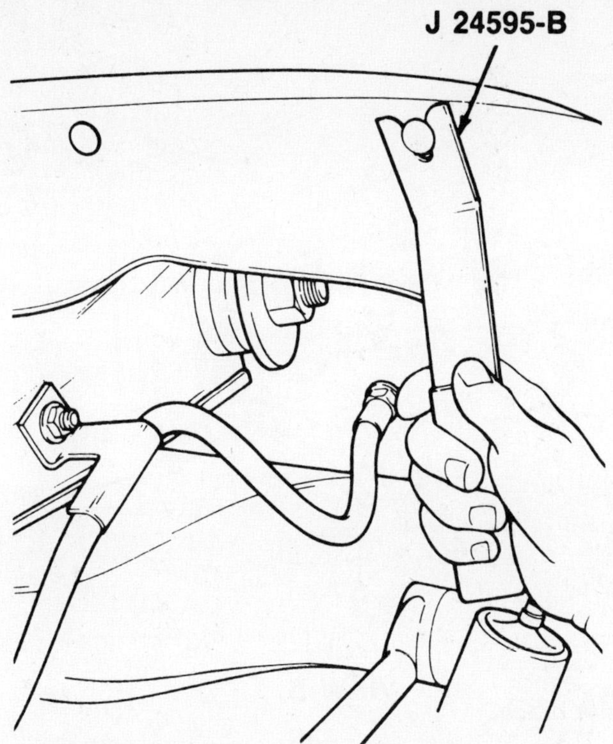

Removing shield retainers — R/V series

9. Installation is the reverse of removal. Torque all fasteners to 18 ft. lbs.

Dual Wheel Fenders

REMOVAL AND INSTALLATION

C and K Series

1. Disconnect the side marker wiring.
2. Remove the fender-to-brace bolts.
3. Remove the fender-to-side panel screws.
4. Lift off the fender.
5. Installation is the reverse of removal. Torque all fasteners to 18 ft. lbs.

R and V Series

1. Disconnect the lamp wiring.
2. Remove the fender-to-brace bolts.
3. Remove the fender-to-side panel nuts and bolts.
4. Remove the fender support bracket.
5. Lift off the fender.
6. Installation is the reverse of removal. Torque all fasteners to 13 ft. lbs.

Pickup Box

REMOVAL AND INSTALLATION

C and K Series

1. Disconnect the rear lighting wires.

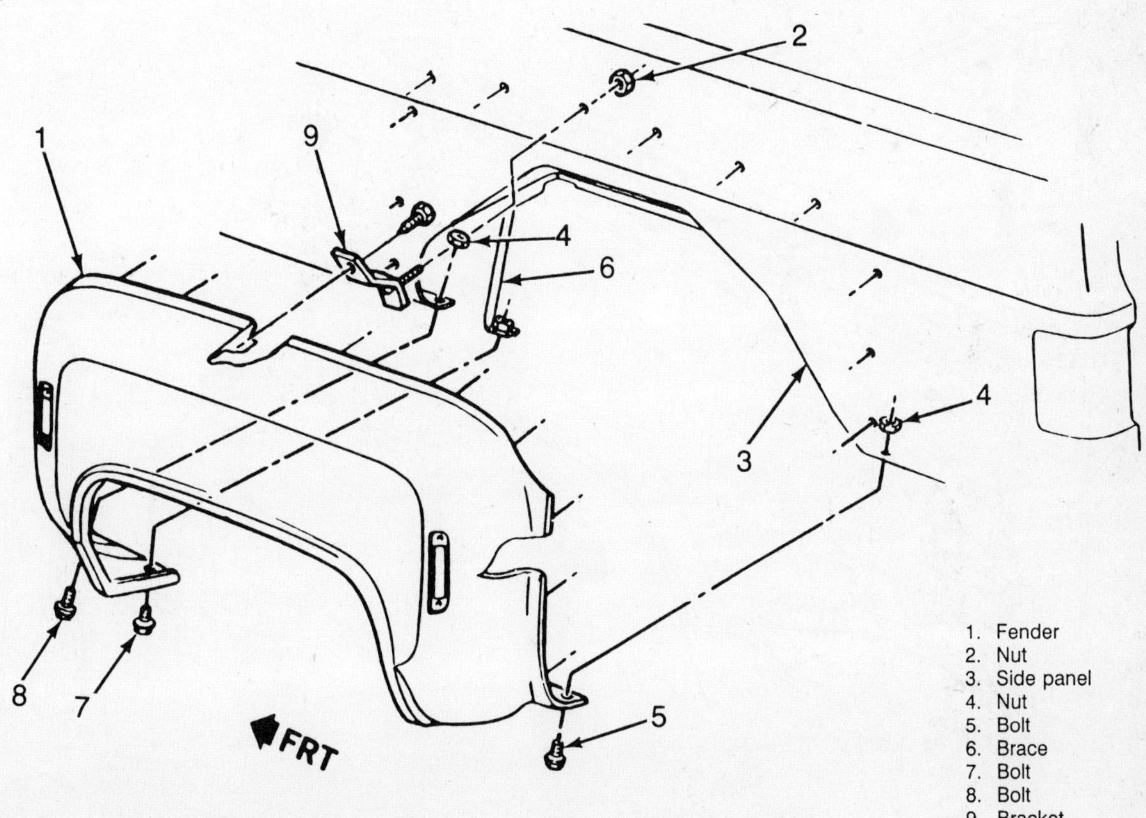

R/V series dual wheel rear fender installation

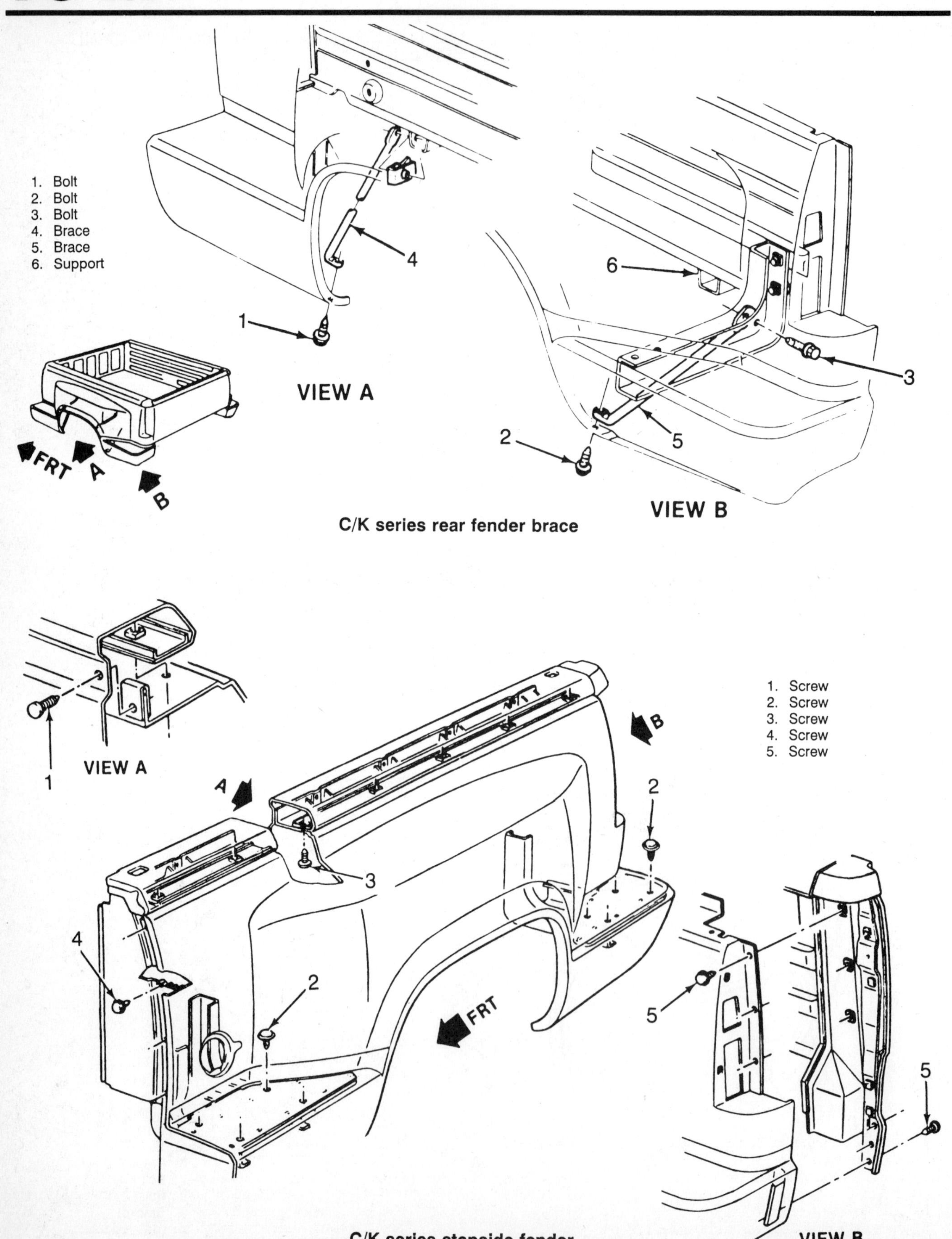

C/K series rear fender brace

C/K series stepside fender

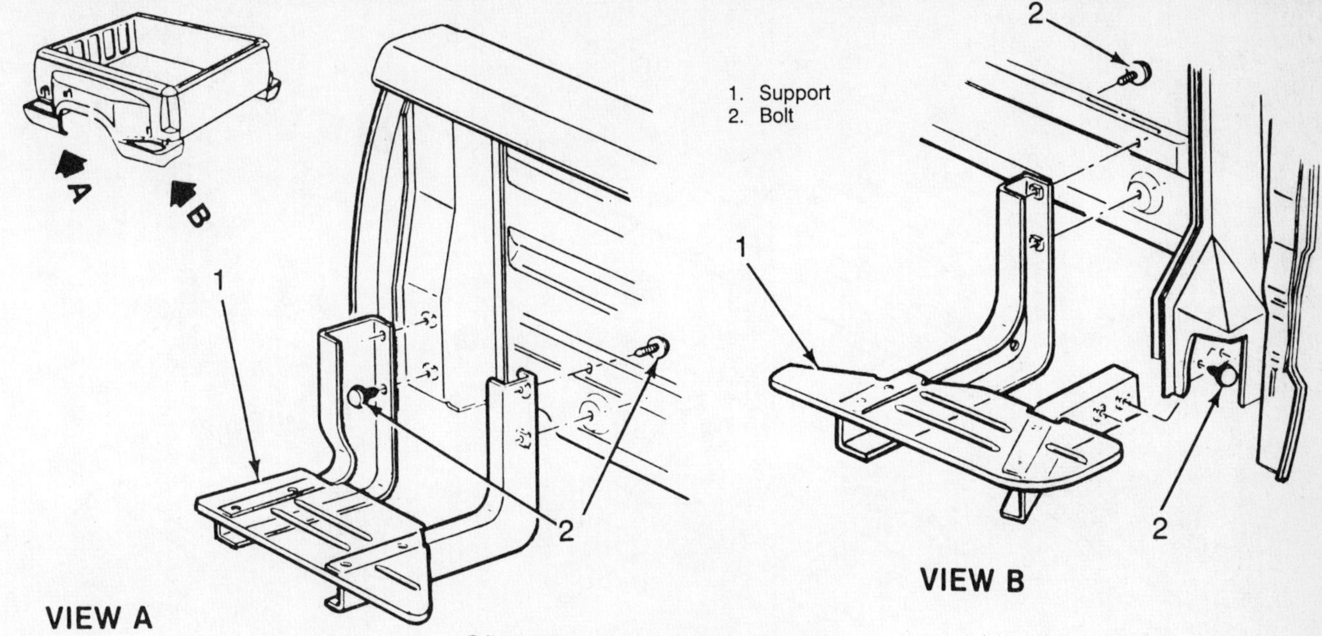

C/K series rear fender supports

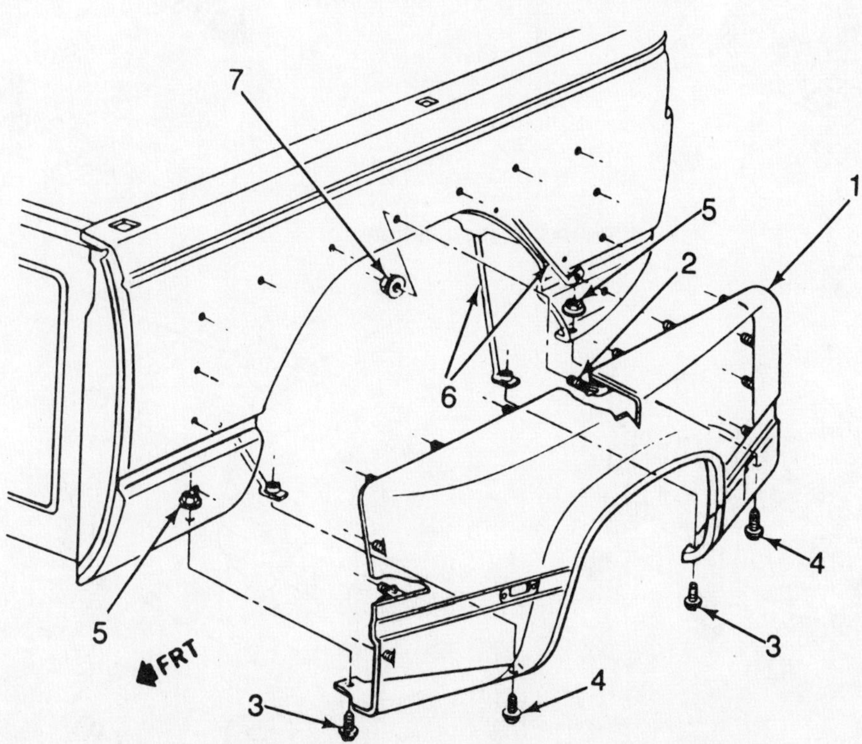

C/K series dual rear wheel fender installation

2. Open the gas cap cover and remove the filler neck-to-side panel screws.
3. From under the truck, remove the 8 bolts securing the box to the frame rails.
4. Remove the bolts securing the front of the box to the frame rail brackets.
5. Lift the box from the frame.
6. Installation is the reverse of removal. Torque the box bolts to 52 ft. lbs.

Cab Mount Bushings

REPLACEMENT

1. Raise the side of the truck to be worked on, with a floor jack.
2. Place jackstands under the cab on that side.
3. Remove the bolt, bushing retainer and lower bushing.

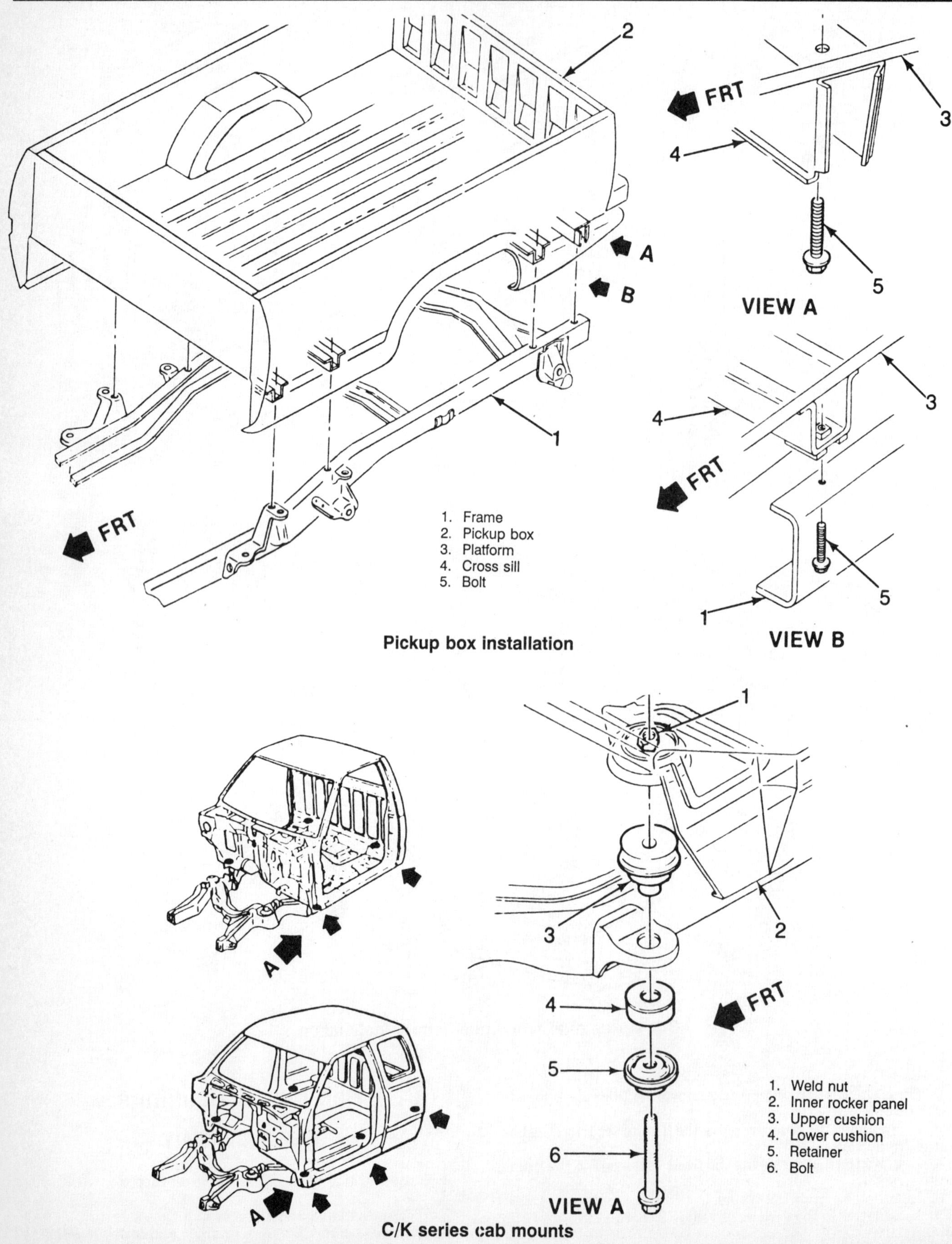

Pickup box installation

C/K series cab mounts

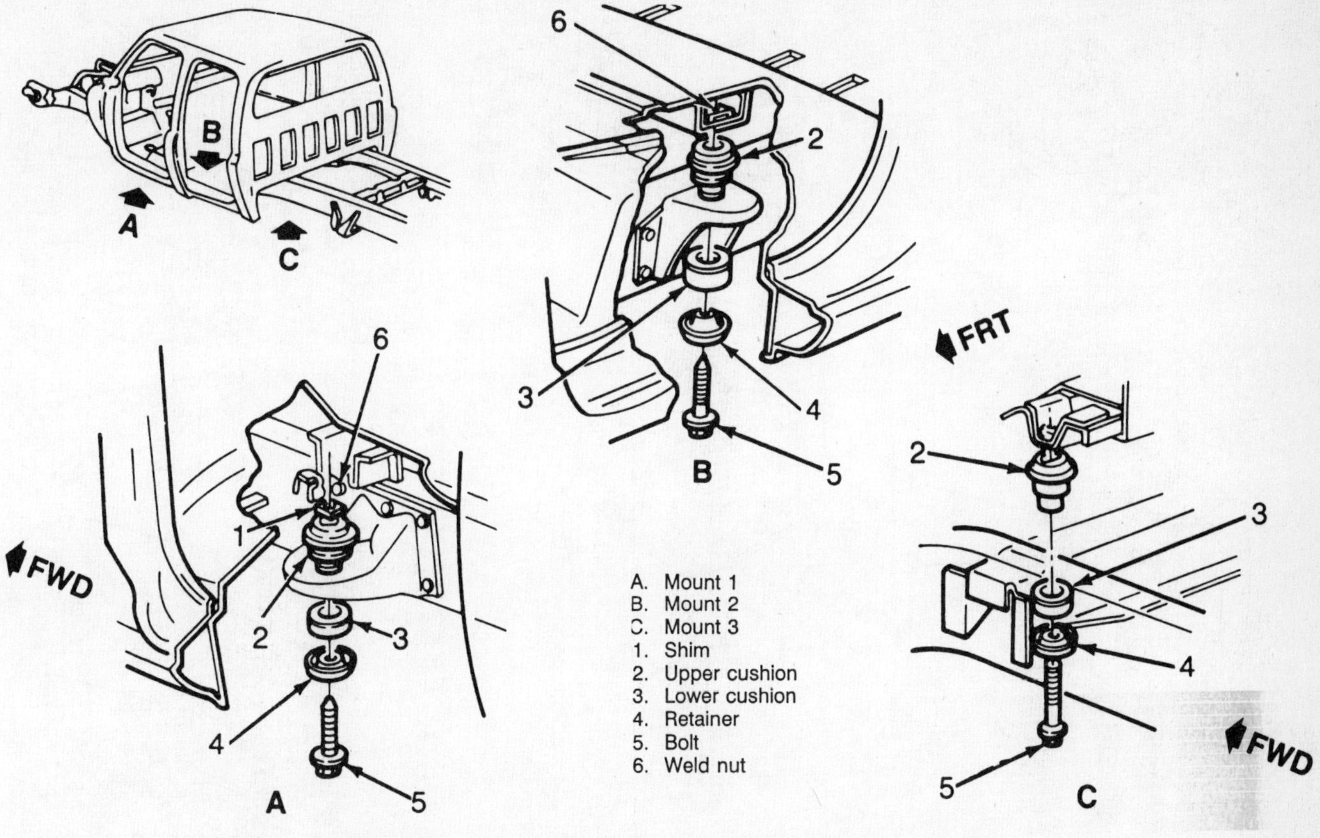

A
B
C
FRT
FWD
FWD
A. Mount 1
B. Mount 2
C. Mount 3
1. Shim
2. Upper cushion
3. Lower cushion
4. Retainer
5. Bolt
6. Weld nut

Cab mounts for the R/V series with Bonus or Crew cab

A
B
FWD
FWD
1. Shim
2. Upper cushion
3. Lower cushion
4. Bolt
5. Bolt
6. Weld nut

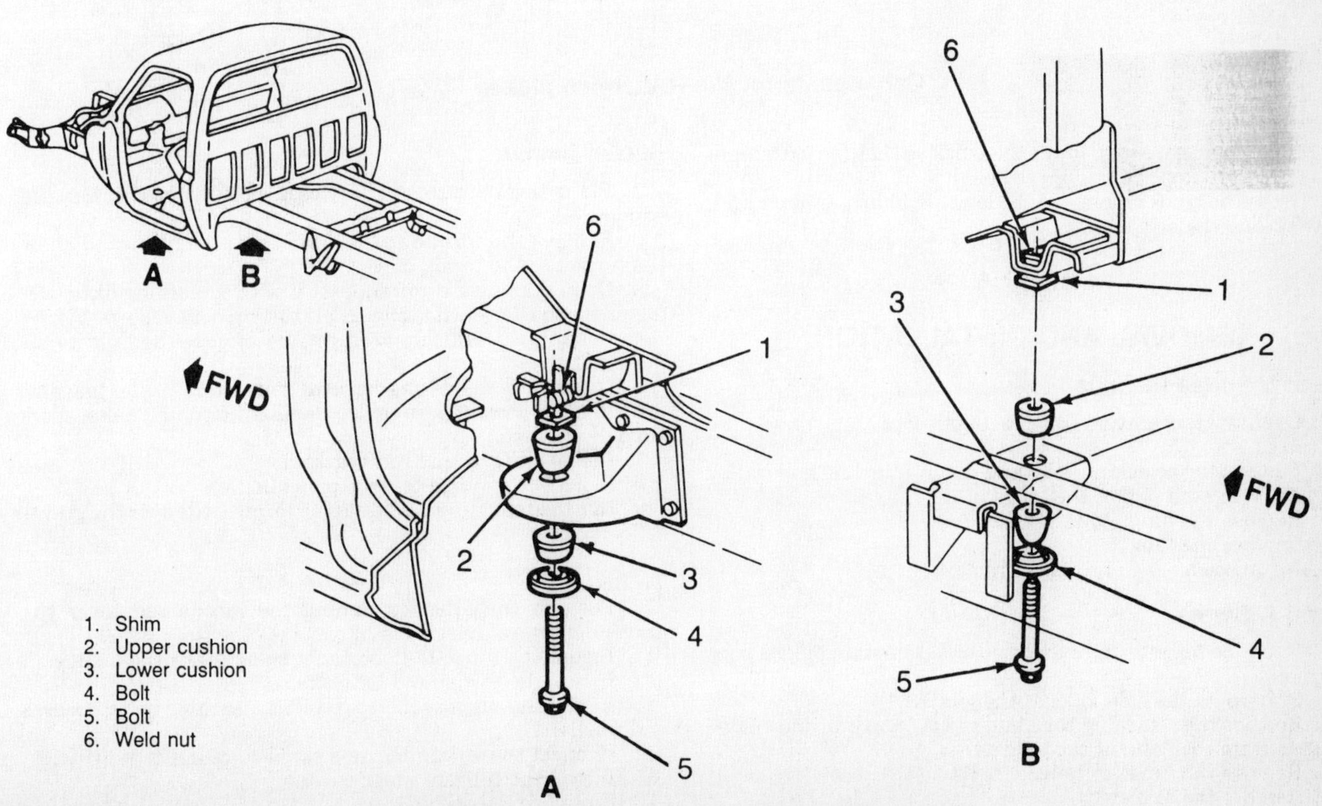

Cab mounts for the R/V series with Regular Cab

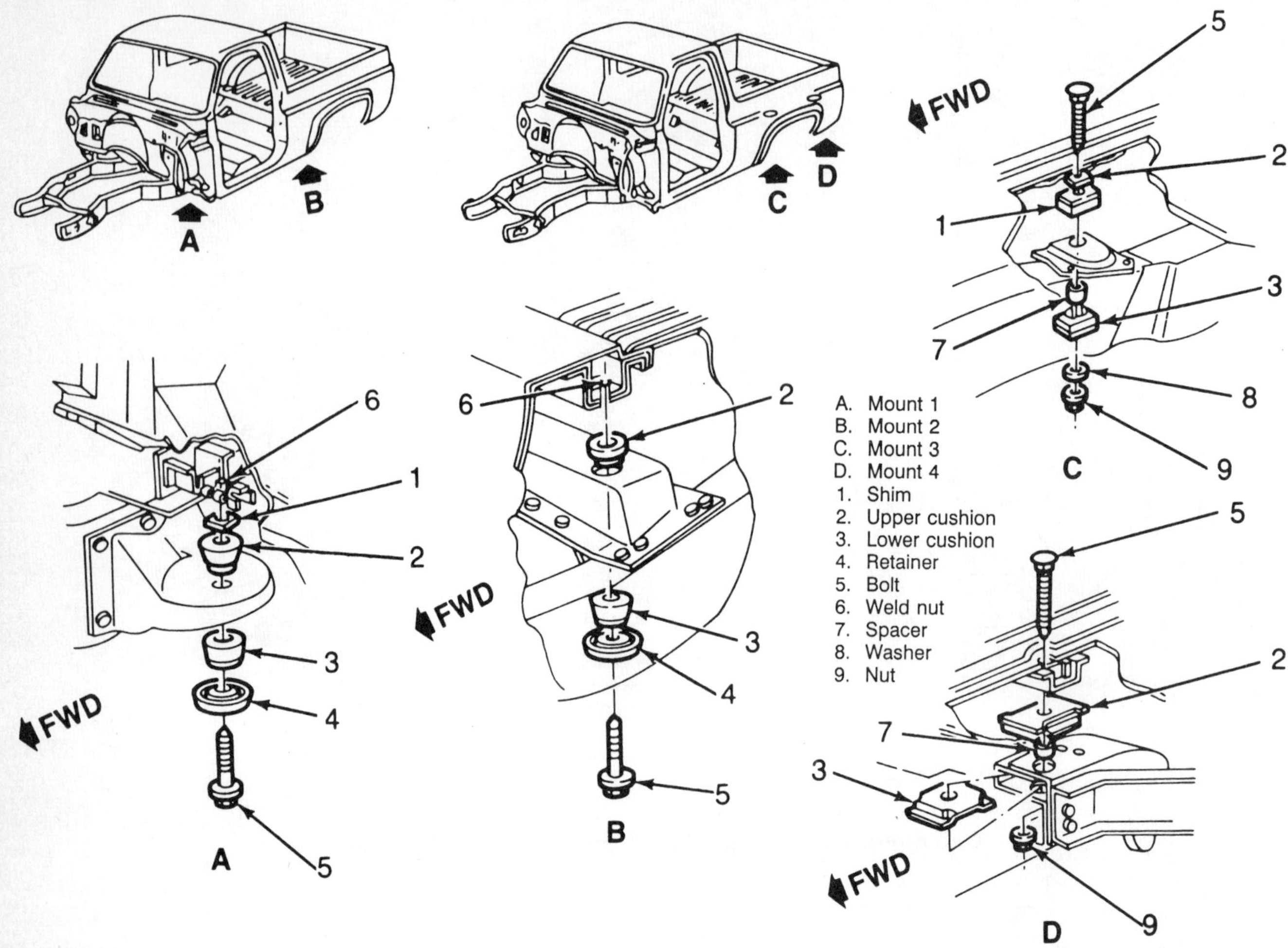

Cab mounts for the R/V series pickup

4. Slowly and carefully, lower the truck so that the jackstand raises the cab. Replace the upper bushing.
5. Raise the truck and install the lower bushing, retainer and bolt. Torque the bolt to 55 ft. lbs.

Tailgate

REMOVAL AND INSTALLATION

R and V Series Pickups

1. Open the tailgate and support it with something like a picnic table.
2. Remove the attaching bolts and remove the link and striker plate from each end of the tailgate.
3. Remove the hinge-to-tailgate bolts.
4. Remove the tailgate.
5. Installation is the reverse of removal.

C and K Series

1. Open the tailgate and support it with something like a picnic table.
2. Pull up on the side links at the joints.
3. Remove the attaching bolts and remove the link and striker plate from each end of the tailgate.
4. Remove the hinge-to-tailgate bolts.
5. Remove the tailgate.
6. Installation is the reverse of removal.

Blazer/Jimmy

1. Place the tailgate in the closed position and lower the window.
2. Remove the torque rod-to-frame stud and nut and allow the torque rod to swing down.
3. Open the tailgate and support it with something like a picnic table, so there is no tension on the support cables.
4. Remove the attaching screws and remove the tailgate inner cover.
5. Disconnect the wiring harness connectors in the tailgate.
6. Remove the support cables-to-pillar attaching bolts, spacers and washers.
7. Remove the torque rod brackets.
8. Remove the hinge-to-floor panel bolts.
9. Lift the tailgate off, guiding the torque rods over the gravel deflectors.

To install:

10. Position the tailgate, guiding the torque rods over the gravel deflectors. Insert the hinges into the floor panel slots.
11. Install the hinge-to-floor panel bolts. Make them snug.
12. Install the torque rod brackets.
13. Install the support cables-to-pillar attaching bolts, spacers and washers.
14. Connect the wiring harness connectors in the tailgate.
15. Install the tailgate inner cover.
16. Close the tailgate.
17. Install the torque rod-to-frame stud and nut.

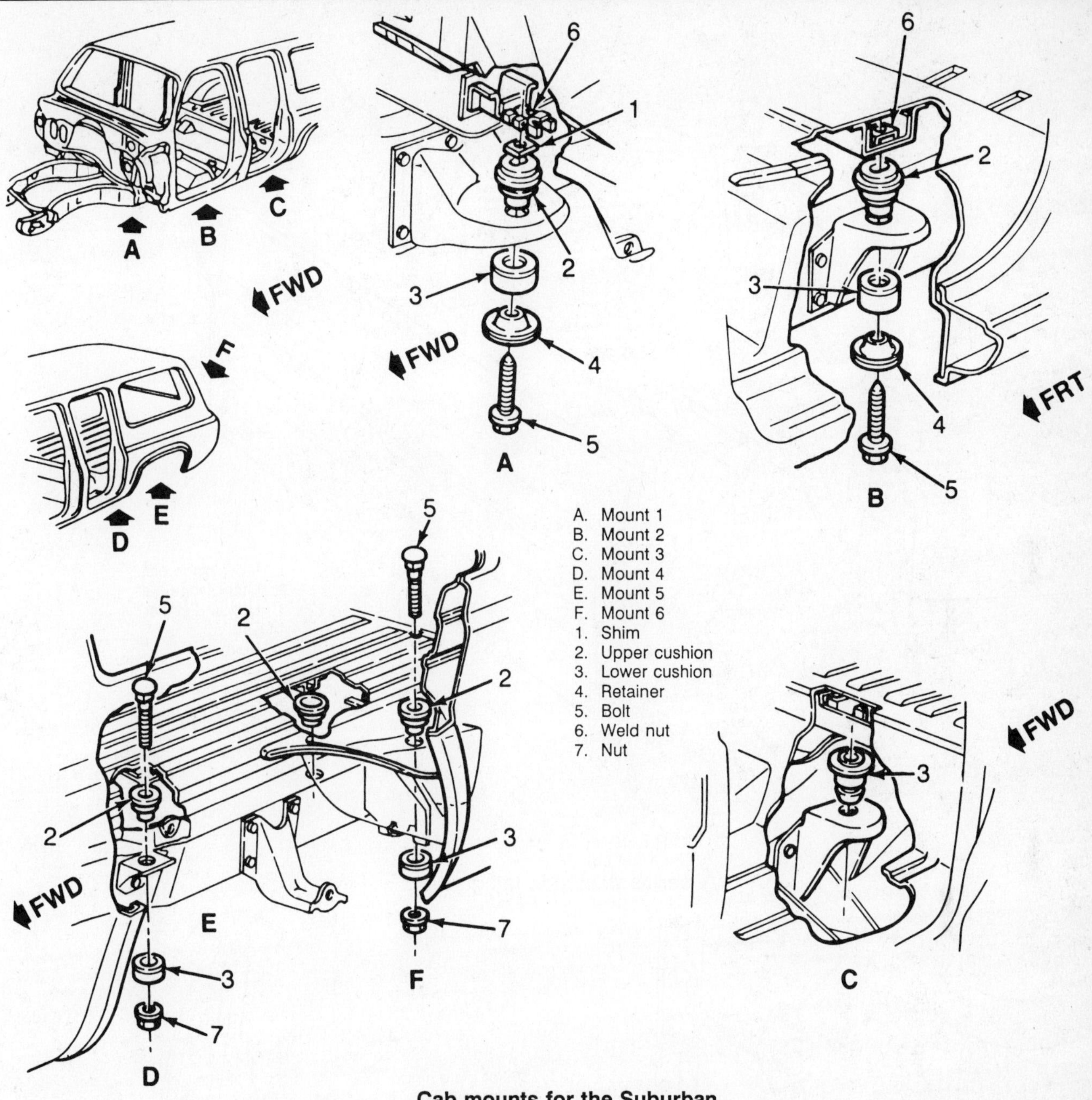

Cab mounts for the Suburban

18. Align the tailgate in the opening and tighten the hinge bolts securely.

Suburban

1. Open the tailgate and support it with something like a picnic table, so there is no tension on the support cables.
2. Unbolt the torque rod bracket.
3. Remove the attaching screws and remove the tailgate inner cover.
4. Disconnect the wiring harness connectors in the tailgate.
5. Remove the hinge access cover and seal.
6. Lift the tailgate to the almost-closed position, hold it there, and remove the hinge-to-tailgate bolts.
7. Lower the tailgate and support it so there is no tension on the cables and remove the support cables-to-pillars attaching bolts and washers.
8. Lift the tailgate off, along with the torque rod.

To install:

9. Position the tailgate, along with the torque rods, in the opening, aligning the hinges.
10. Install the support cables-to-pillar attaching bolts, spacers and washers.
11. Install the hinge-to-floor panel bolts. Tighten them securely.
12. Install the hinge cover and seal.
13. Connect the wiring harness connectors in the tailgate.

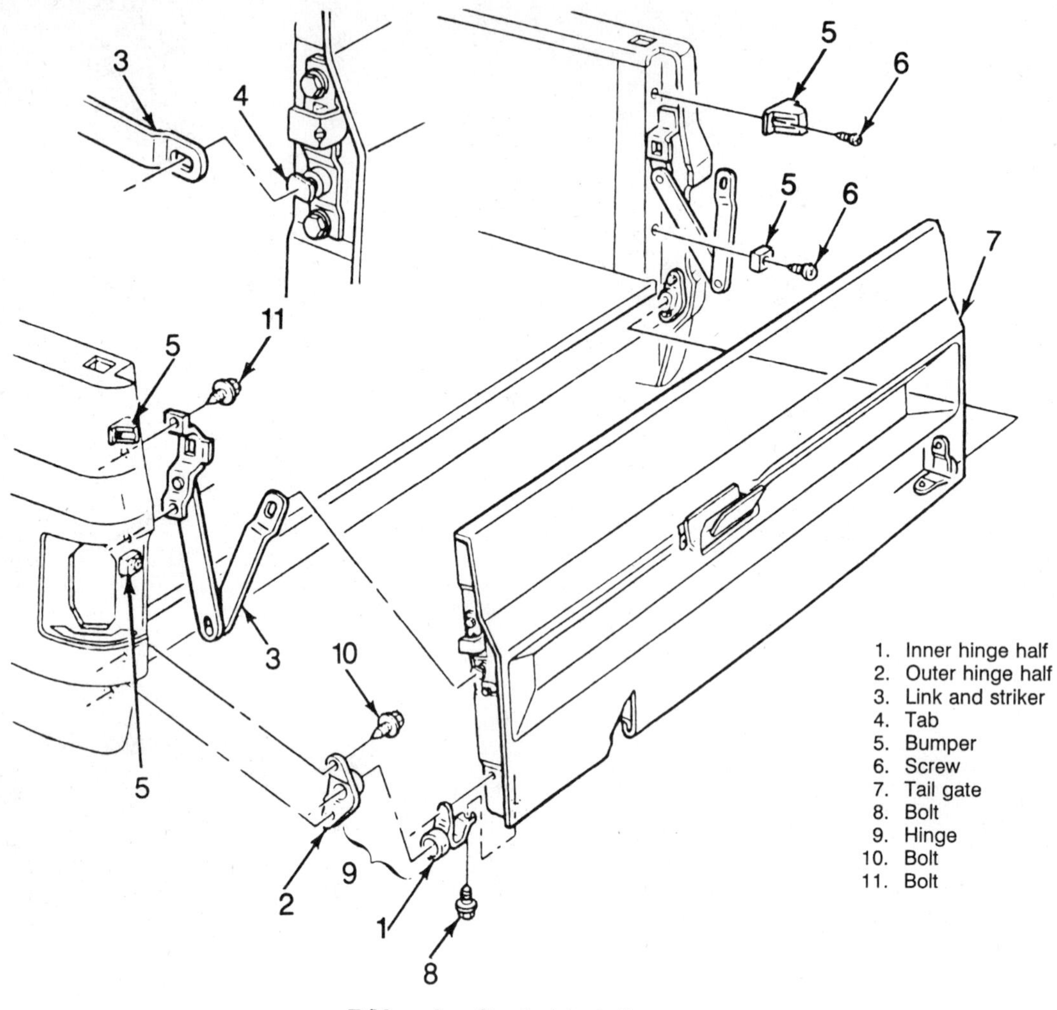

R/V series fleet side tail gate

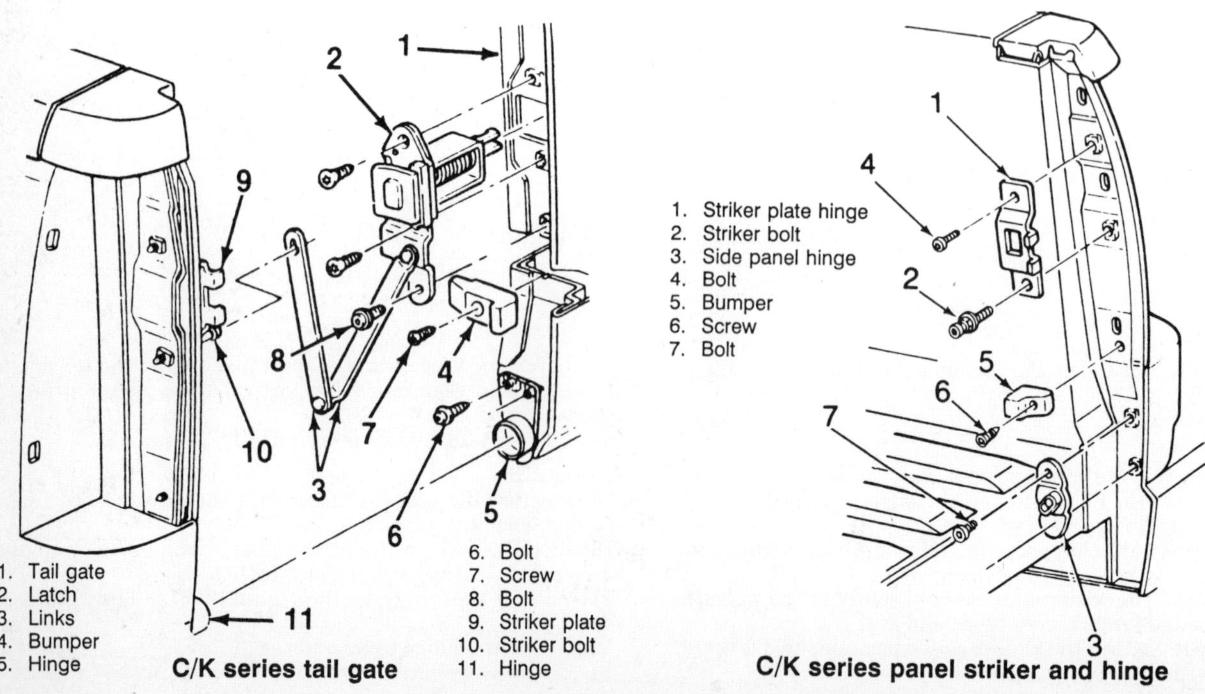

C/K series tail gate

C/K series panel striker and hinge

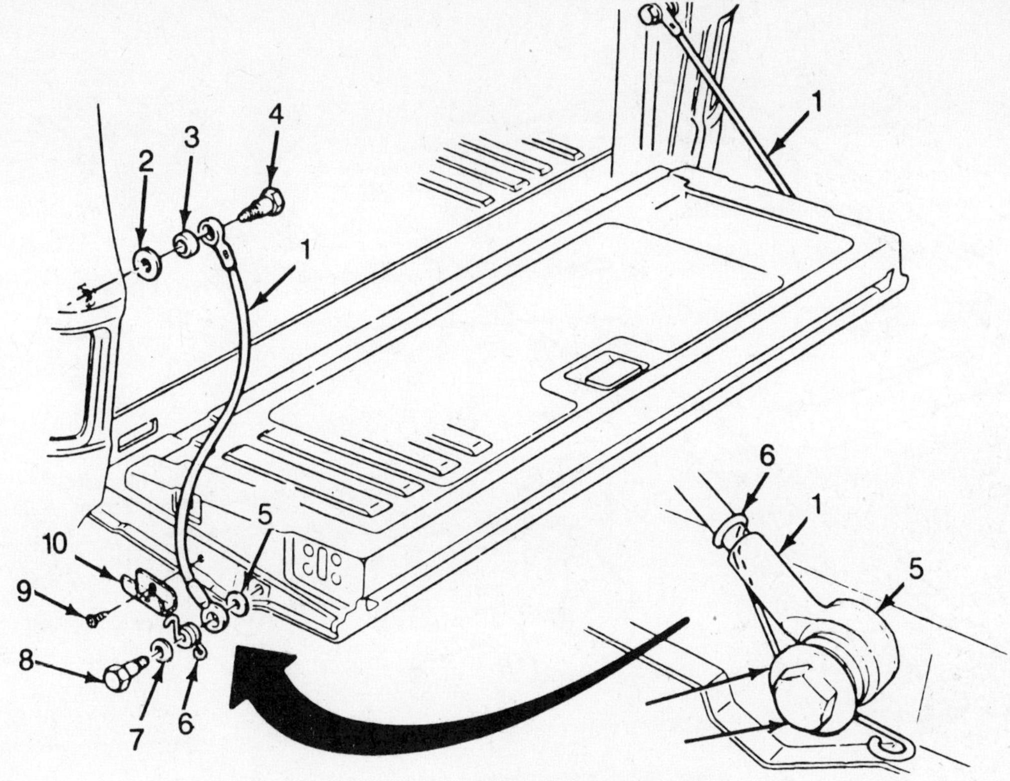

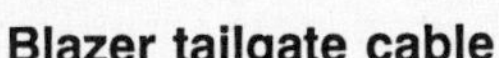
Blazer tailgate cable

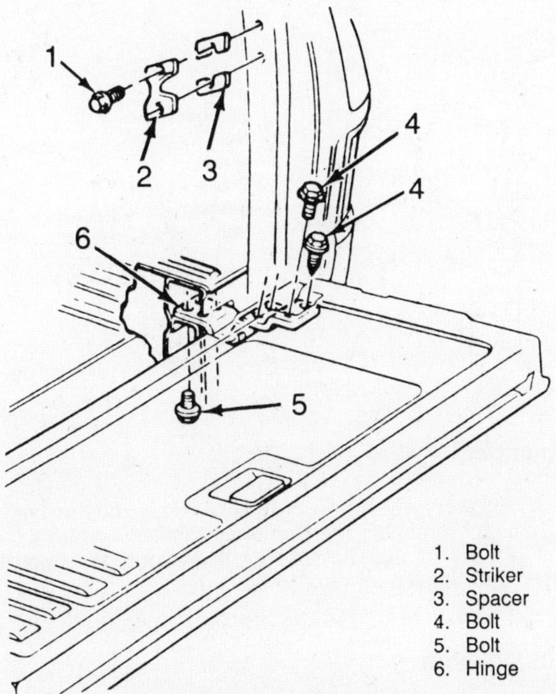

Blazer tailgate hinge

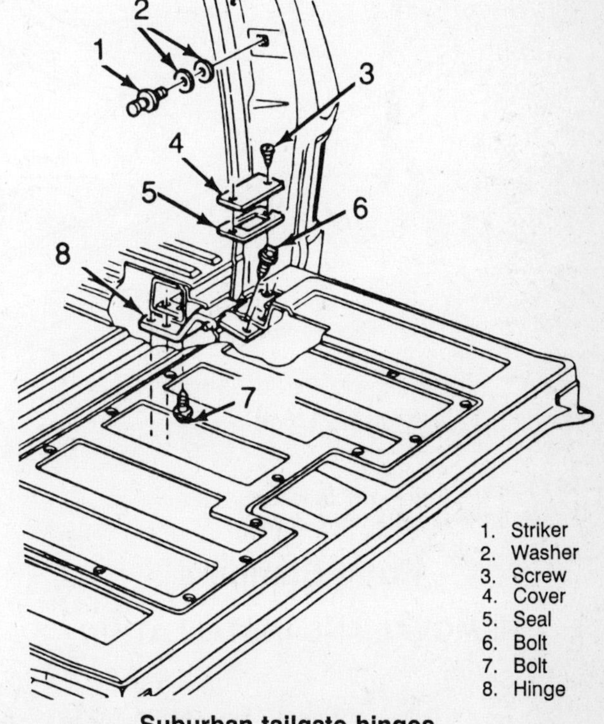

Suburban tailgate hinges

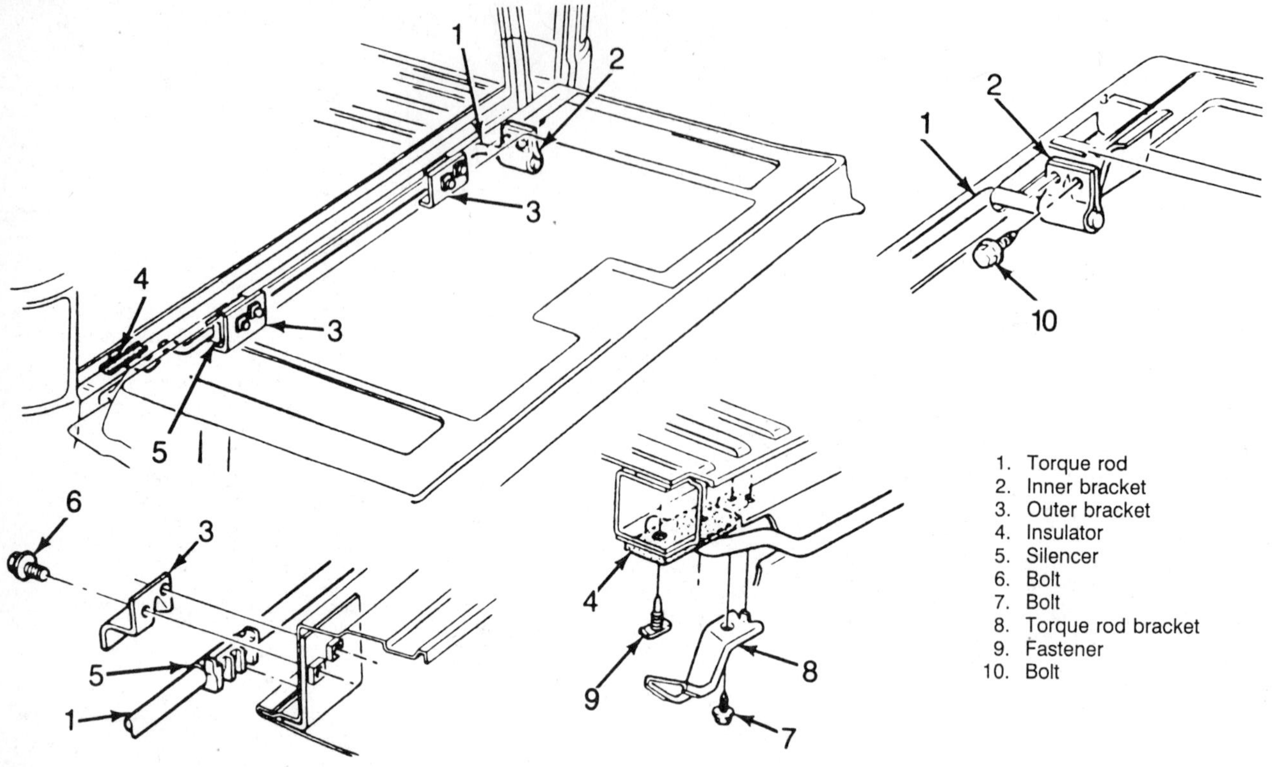

1. Torque rod
2. Inner bracket
3. Outer bracket
4. Insulator
5. Silencer
6. Bolt
7. Bolt
8. Torque rod bracket
9. Fastener
10. Bolt

Suburban tailgate torque rod

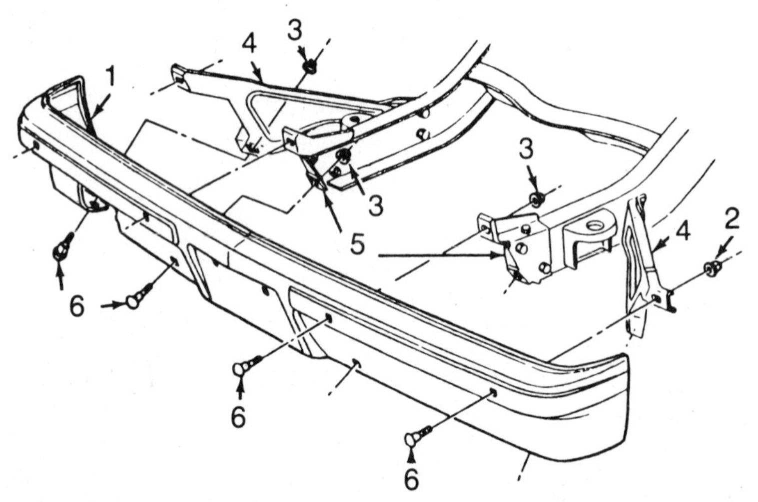

1. Bumper bar
2. Nut
3. Nut
4. Brace
5. Bracket
6. Bolt

R/V series front bumper

14. Install the torque rod brackets.
15. Install the tailgate inner cover.

Front Bumpers

REMOVAL AND INSTALLATION

R and V Series

1. Remove the bolts securing the bumper face bar to the left and right bumper brackets.
2. Remove the bolts securing the bumper face bar to the left and right bumper braces and remove the bumper from the vehicle.
3. If necessary, the brackets and braces may be removed from the frame by removing the retaining bolts.
4. For ease of installation use something to support the bumper and tighten all nuts to 66 ft. lbs.

C and K Series

1. Remove the bumper-to-brace bolts.
2. Remove the bumper-to-bracket bolts.
3. Remove the bumper.
4. Installation is the reverse of removal. Torque all bolts to 74 ft. lbs.

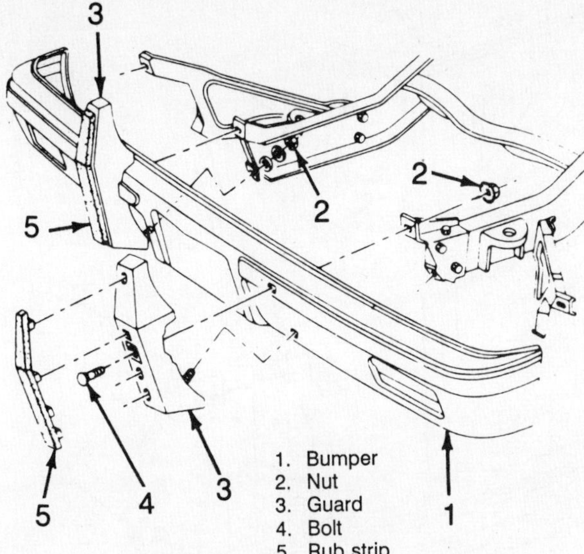

R/V series front bumper guards

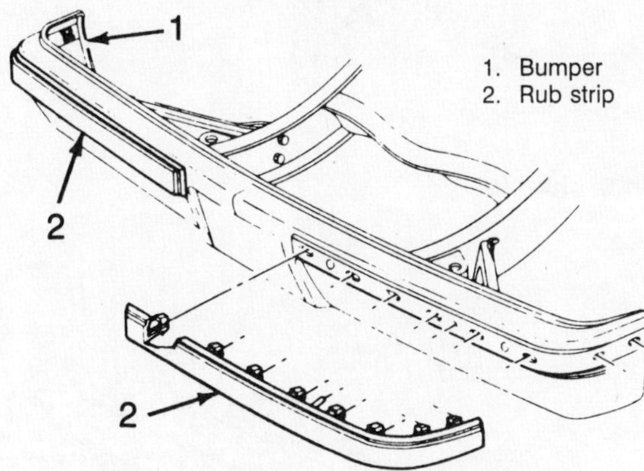

R/V series front bumper rub strip

Rear Bumpers

REMOVAL AND INSTALLATION

Blazer/Jimmy and Suburban Regular Cab, Bonus Cab and Crew Cab

1. Remove the bolts securing the bumper face bar to the left and right bumper braces. Disconnect the license lamp wiring.
2. Remove the bolts securing the bumper face bar to the left and right bumper brackets and remove the bumper from the vehicle.
3. If necessary, the brackets, braces and rear stone shield may be removed from the frame by removing the retaining bolts.
4. For ease of installation use something to support the bumper. Tighten the bracket and brace nuts to 70 ft. lbs. Connect the license lamp wiring.

All R and V Series with Rear Step Bumper

1. Remove the bracket-to-bumper nuts and bolts.
2. Remove the brace-to-bumper nuts, spring washers, washers and bolts.
3. Lift the bumper from the truck.
4. Installation is the reverse of removal. Tighten all nuts to 52 ft. lbs.

C and K Series

1. Remove the bracket-to-bumper nuts and bolts.
2. Remove the brace-to-bumper nuts, washers and bolts.
3. Lift the bumper from the truck.
4. Installation is the reverse of removal. Tighten all bolts to 65 ft. lbs.

Weight Distribution Tow Hitch

REMOVAL AND INSTALLATION

NOTE: This procedure applies only to factory-installed hitches.

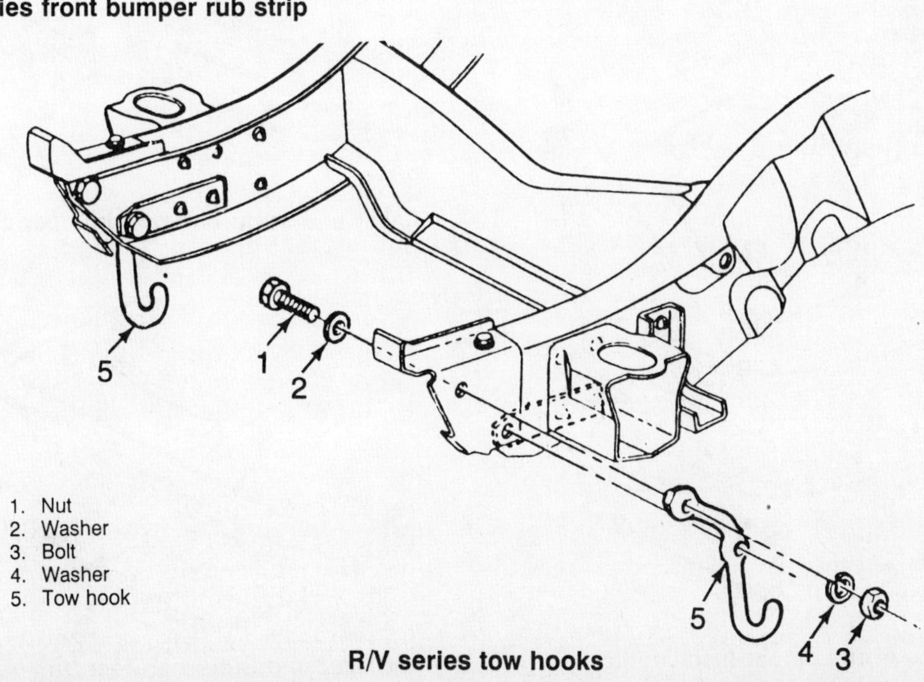

R/V series tow hooks

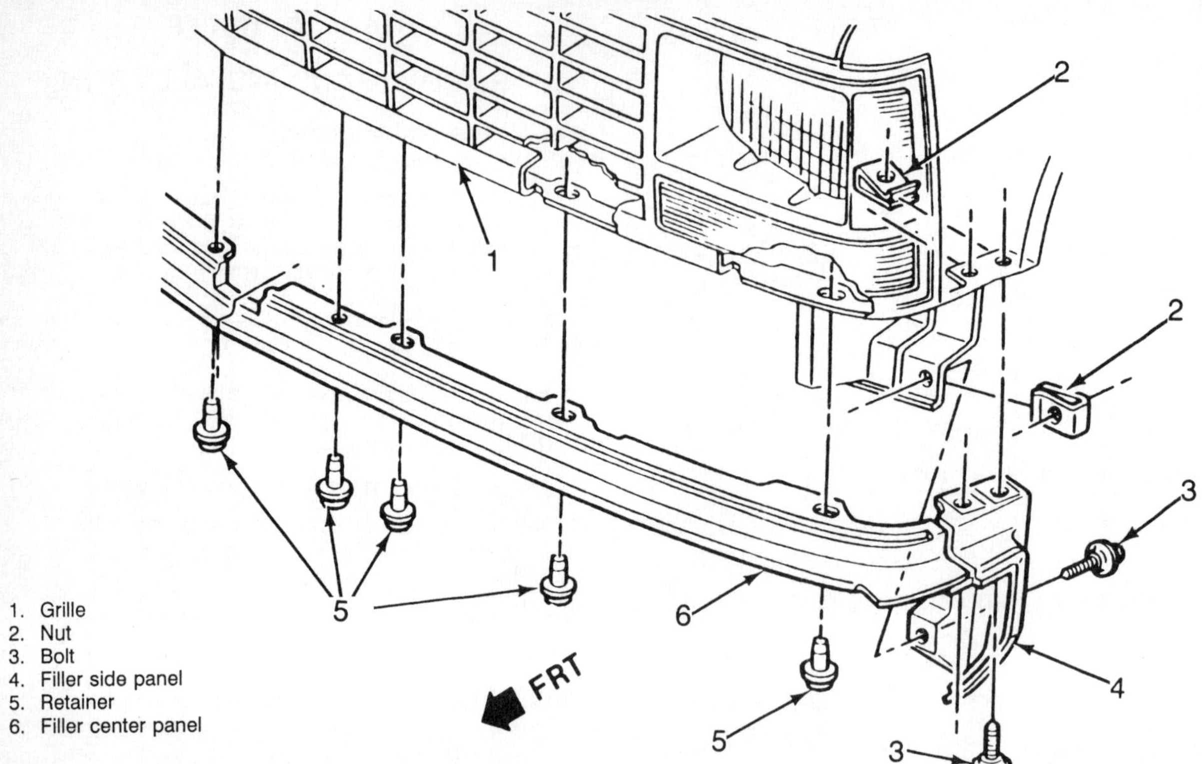

C/K series front bumper filler panels

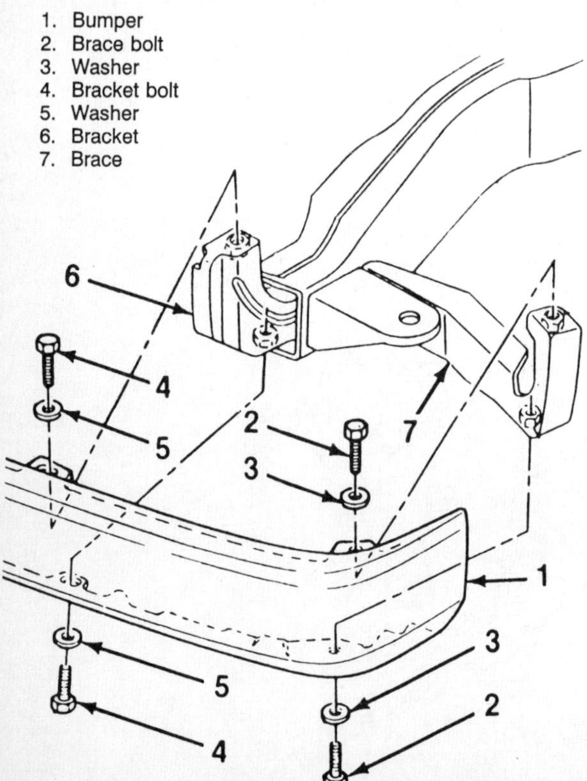

C/K series front bumper installation

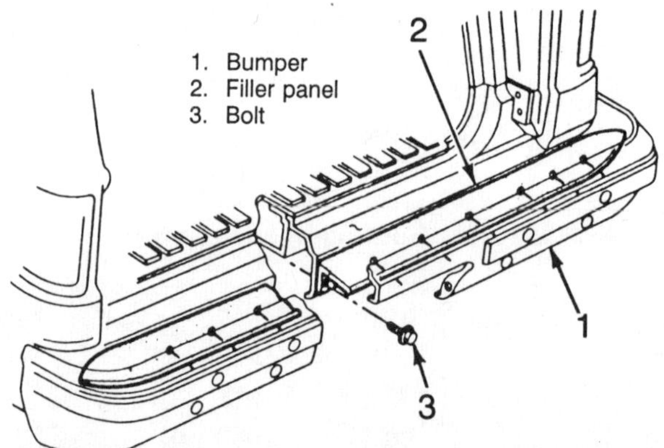

Blazer and Suburban rear bumper center filler strip

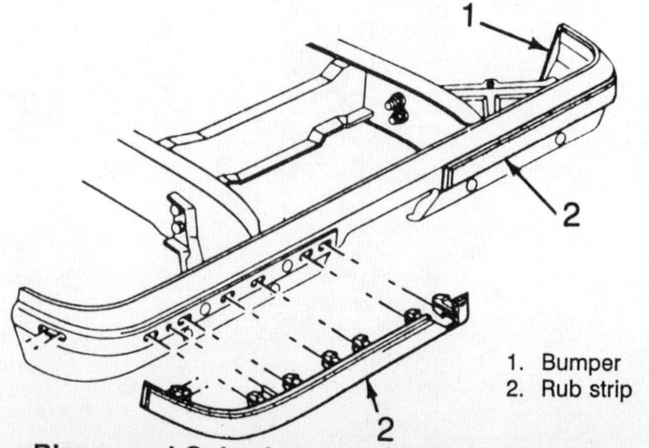

Blazer and Suburban rear bumper rub strip

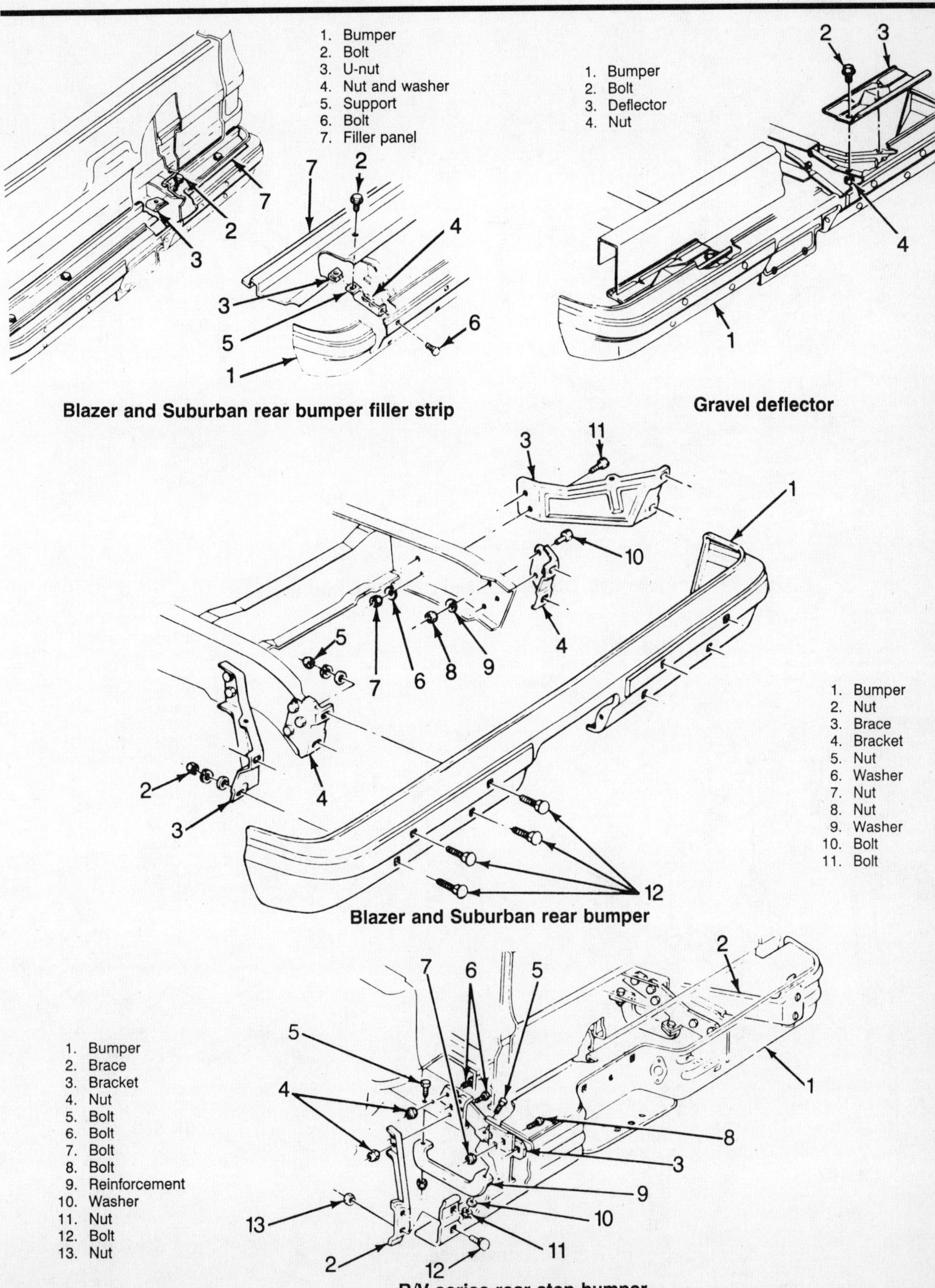

Blazer and Suburban rear bumper filler strip

Gravel deflector

Blazer and Suburban rear bumper

R/V series rear step bumper

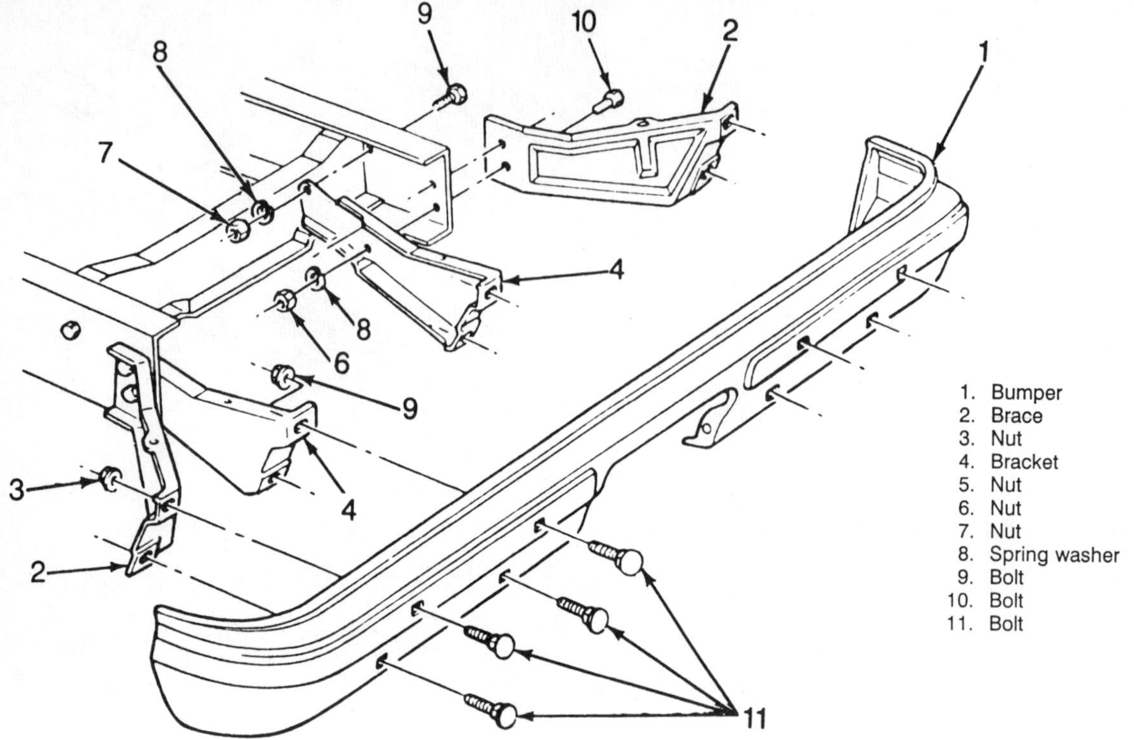

R/V series regular cab, Bonus cab and Crew Cab rear bumper

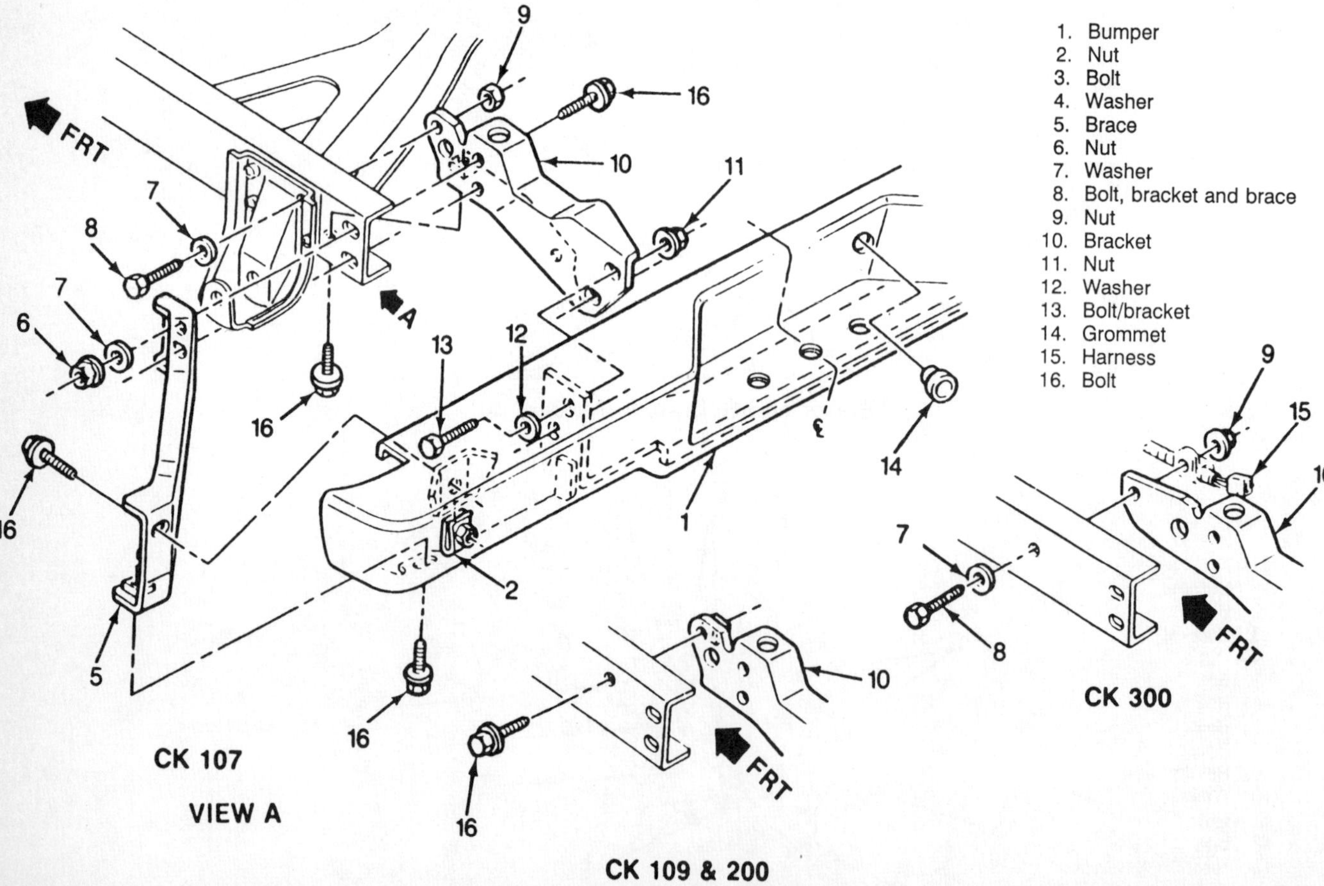

1. Bumper
2. Nut
3. Bolt
4. Washer
5. Brace
6. Nut
7. Washer
8. Bolt, bracket and brace
9. Nut
10. Bracket
11. Nut
12. Washer
13. Bolt/bracket
14. Grommet
15. Harness
16. Bolt

FRT

VIEW A

CK 107

CK 300

CK 109 & 200

C/K series rear bumper

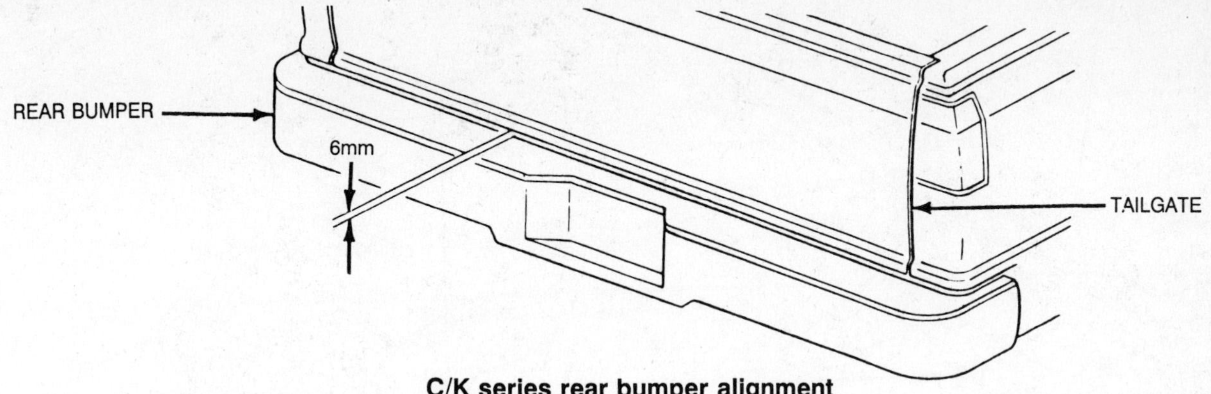

C/K series rear bumper alignment

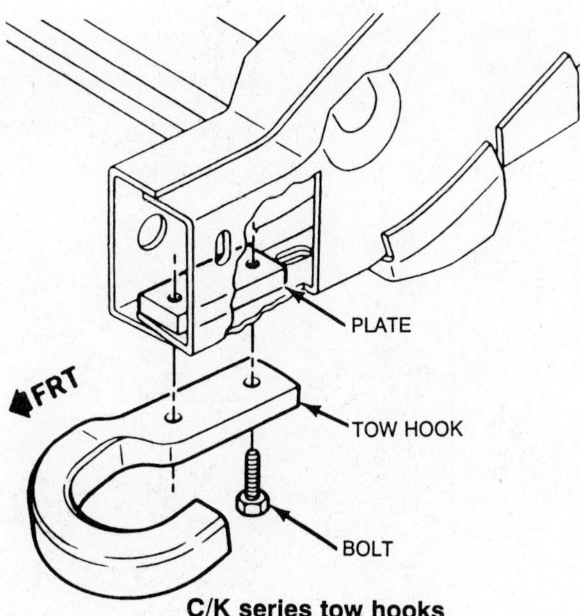

C/K series tow hooks

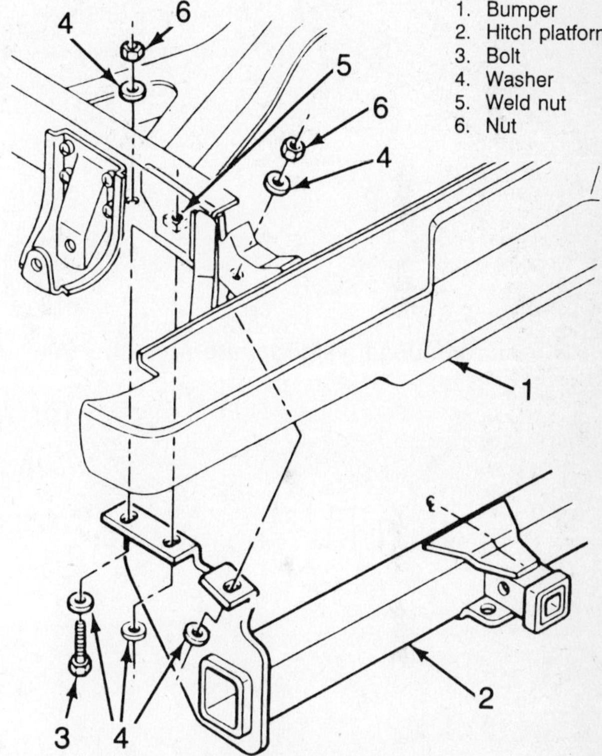

C/K series weight distribution hitch

C and K Series

1. Support the hitch and remove the bolts, washers and nuts securing the hitch to the frame rails.
2. Installation is the reverse of removal. Torque all bolts to 70 ft. lbs.

Suburban

1. Support the hitch and remove the bolts, washers and nuts securing the hitch to the frame rails.
2. Installation is the reverse of removal. Torque the rear bolts to 70 ft. lbs.; the front nuts to 52 ft. lbs.

Blazer/Jimmy

1. Support the hitch and remove the bolts, washers and nuts securing the hitch to the frame rails.
2. Installation is the reverse of removal. Torque the rear bolts to 54 ft. lbs.; the front bolts to 51 ft. lbs.

Dead Weight Tow Hitch

REMOVAL AND INSTALLATION

NOTE: This procedure applies only to factory-installed hitches.

Blazer/Jimmy and Suburban

1. Remove the bracket assembly nuts and bolts from the frame.
2. Remove the support nuts and bolts from the bumper.
3. Remove the hitch.
4. Remove the chain bracket nut and bolt.
5. Remove the chain bracket.
6. Remove the support and and bar assembly.

To install:

7. Install the bracket on the frame. Torque the bracket-to-frame nuts to 52 ft. lbs.
8. Assemble the bar, support and chain bracket. Install the nut and bolt loosely.
9. Mount the assembly on the bumper.
10. Torque the bar-to-bracket bolt to 70 ft. lbs.; the bar-to-support nut to 52 ft. lbs.; the support-to-bumper nuts to 24 ft. lbs.

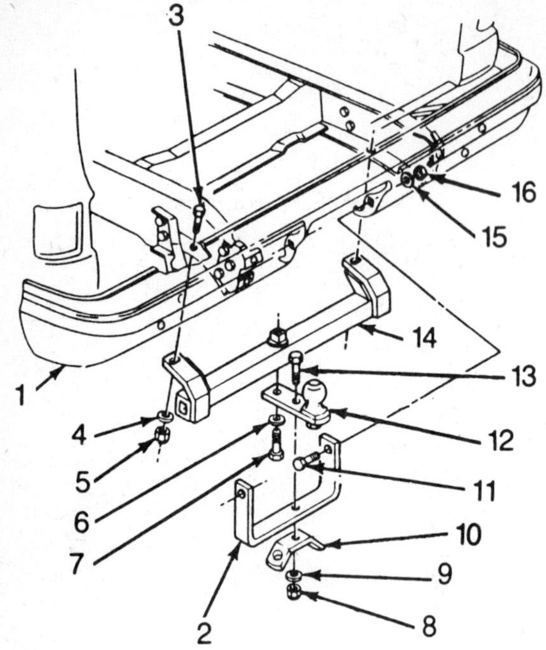

1. Bumper
2. Support
3. Bolt
4. Washer
5. Nut
6. Washer
7. Bolt
8. Nut
9. Washer
10. Chain bracket
11. Bolt
12. Bar
13. Bolt
14. Bracket
15. Washer
16. Nut

Suburban dead weight platform hitch

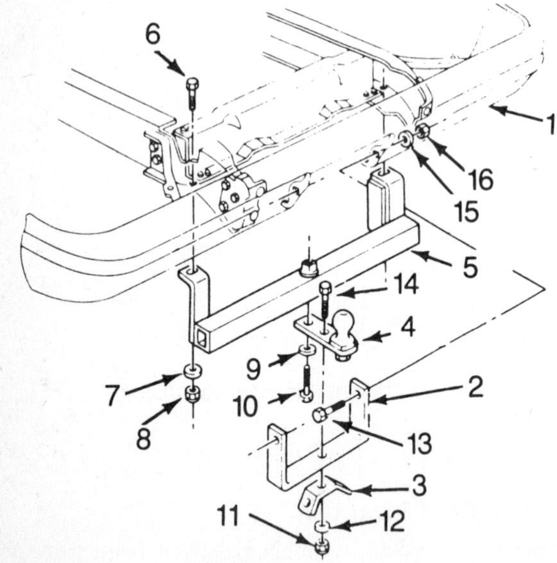

1. Bumper
2. Support
3. Chain bracket
4. Bar
5. Bracket
6. Bolt
7. Washer
8. Nut
9. Washer
10. Bolt
11. Nut
12. Washer
13. Bolt
14. Bolt
15. Washer
16. Nut

Blazer dead weight platform hitch

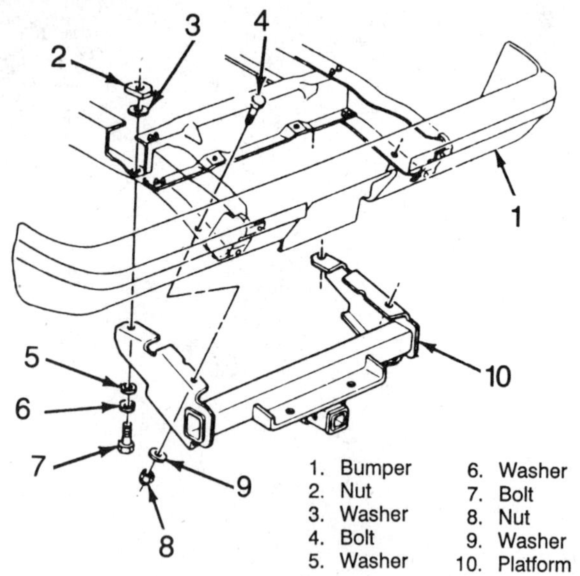

1. Bumper
2. Nut
3. Washer
4. Bolt
5. Washer
6. Washer
7. Bolt
8. Nut
9. Washer
10. Platform

Suburban weight distribution hitch

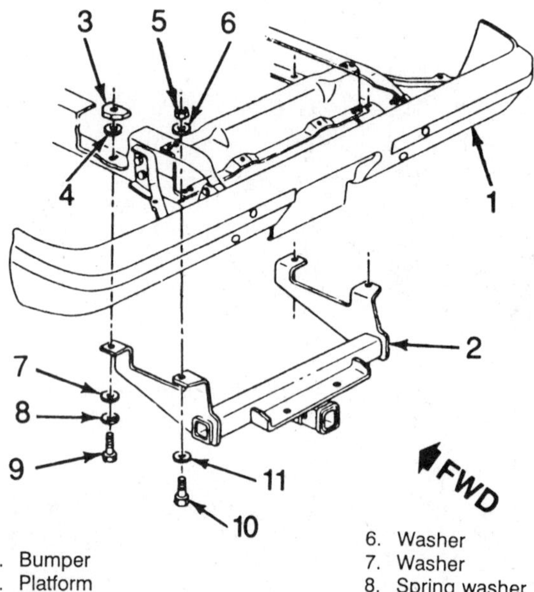

1. Bumper
2. Platform
3. Nut
4. Washer
5. Nut
6. Washer
7. Washer
8. Spring washer
9. Bolt
10. Bolt
11. Washer

Blazer weight distribution platform hitch

Grille and Molding

REMOVAL AND INSTALLATION

R and V Series

1. Remove the lower radiator grille-to-grille bolts.
2. Remove the radiator support-to-grille bolts.
3. Slide the bottom of the grille out and lower the grille from the truck.
4. Remove the headlight bezels.
5. Remove the headlights.
6. Remove the nuts securing the molding to the fender, radiator support and lower grille panel.
7. Remove the molding.
8. Remove the molding clips.
9. Remove the lower radiator grille-to-fender bolts.
10. Remove the lower radiator grille-to-sheet metal support bolts.
11. Remove the lower radiator grille.

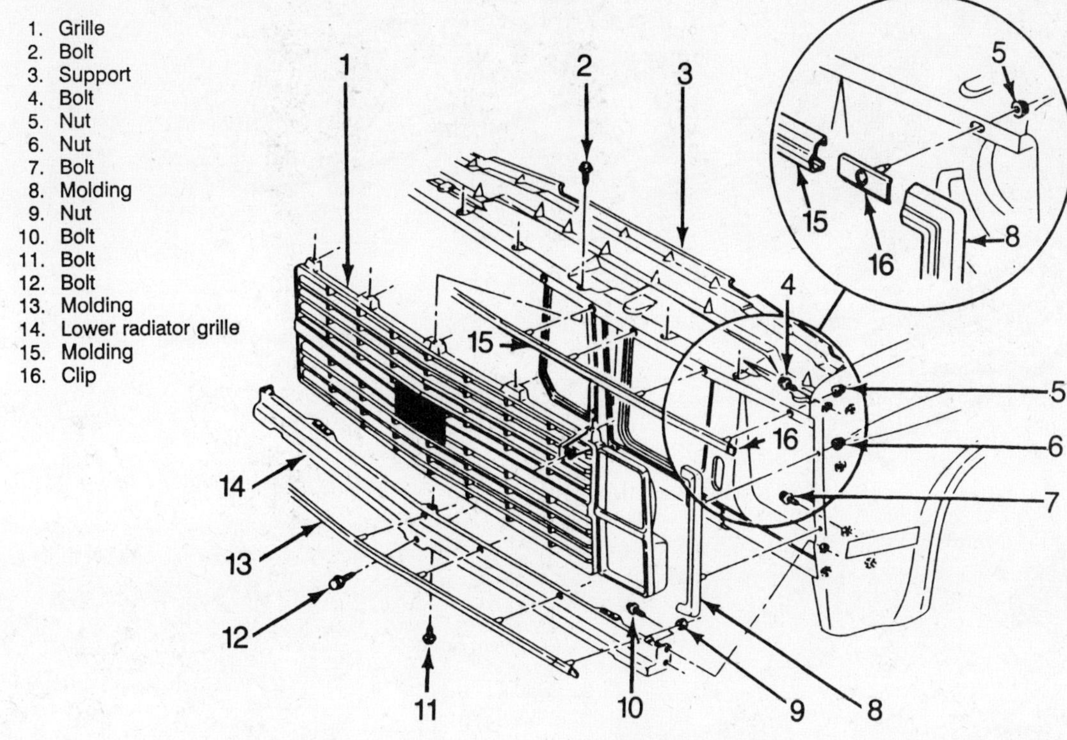

R/V series grille

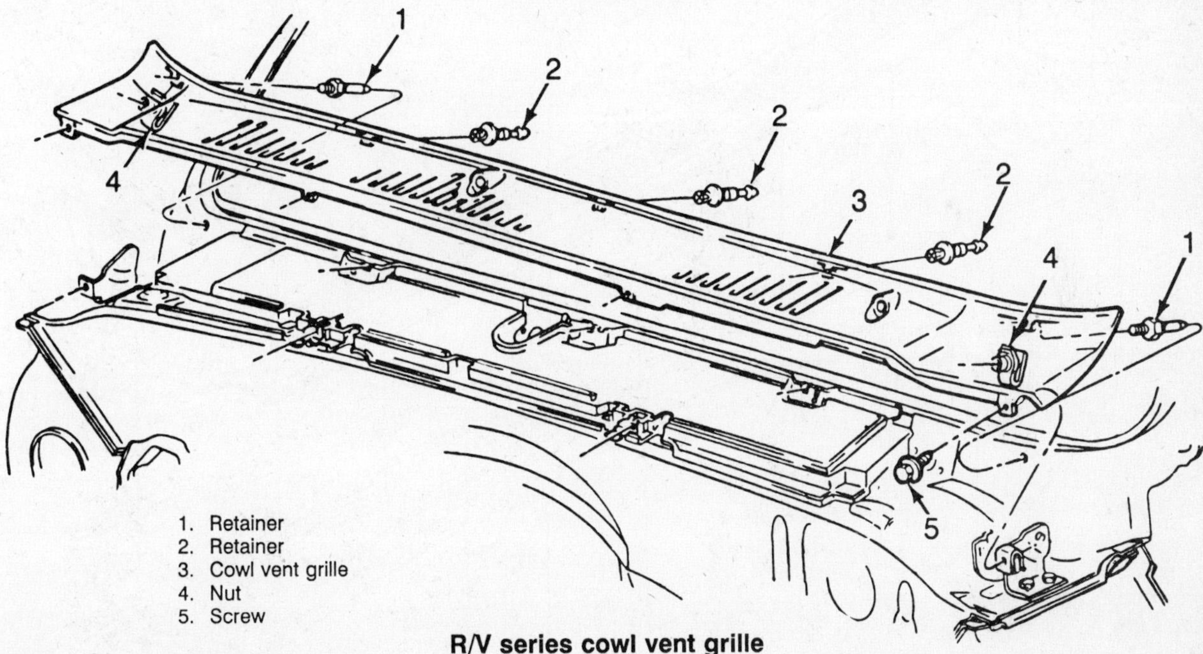

R/V series cowl vent grille

To install:

12. Position the lower radiator grille on the truck.
13. Install the lower radiator grille-to-sheet metal support bolts.
14. Install the lower radiator grille-to-fender bolts.
15. Install the upper molding on the radiator support with clips and nuts. Make the nuts finger-tight.
16. Install the lower molding. on the radiator support with clips and nuts. Make the nuts finger-tight.
17. Install the right and left moldings on the fenders.

NOTE: The moldings must butt against the upper and lower moldings and are clipped to them.

18. Tighten the nuts securing the moldings.
19. Install the headlights.
20. Install the headlight bezels.
21. Insert the top of the grille into the underside of the radiator support, then, slide the bottom of the grille into place.
22. Install the radiator support-to-grille bolts.
23. Install the lower radiator grille-to-grille bolts.

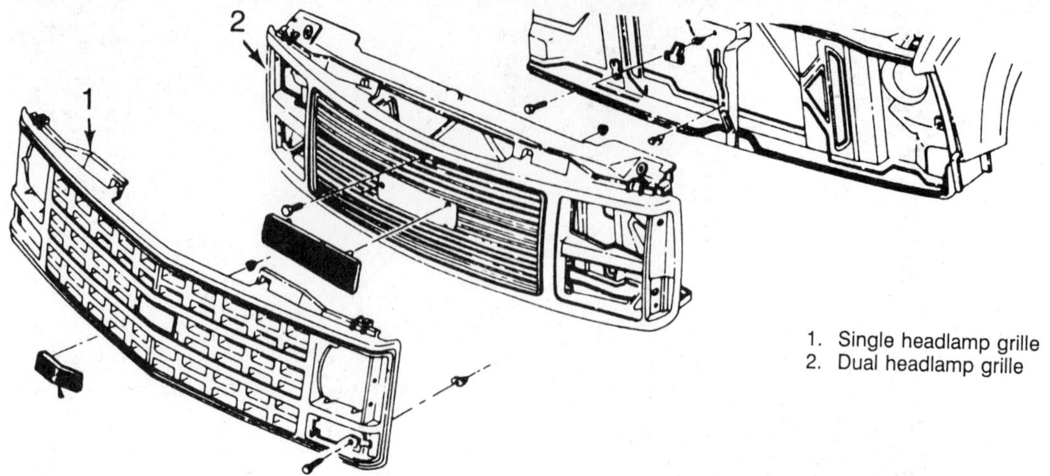

C/K series radiator grille

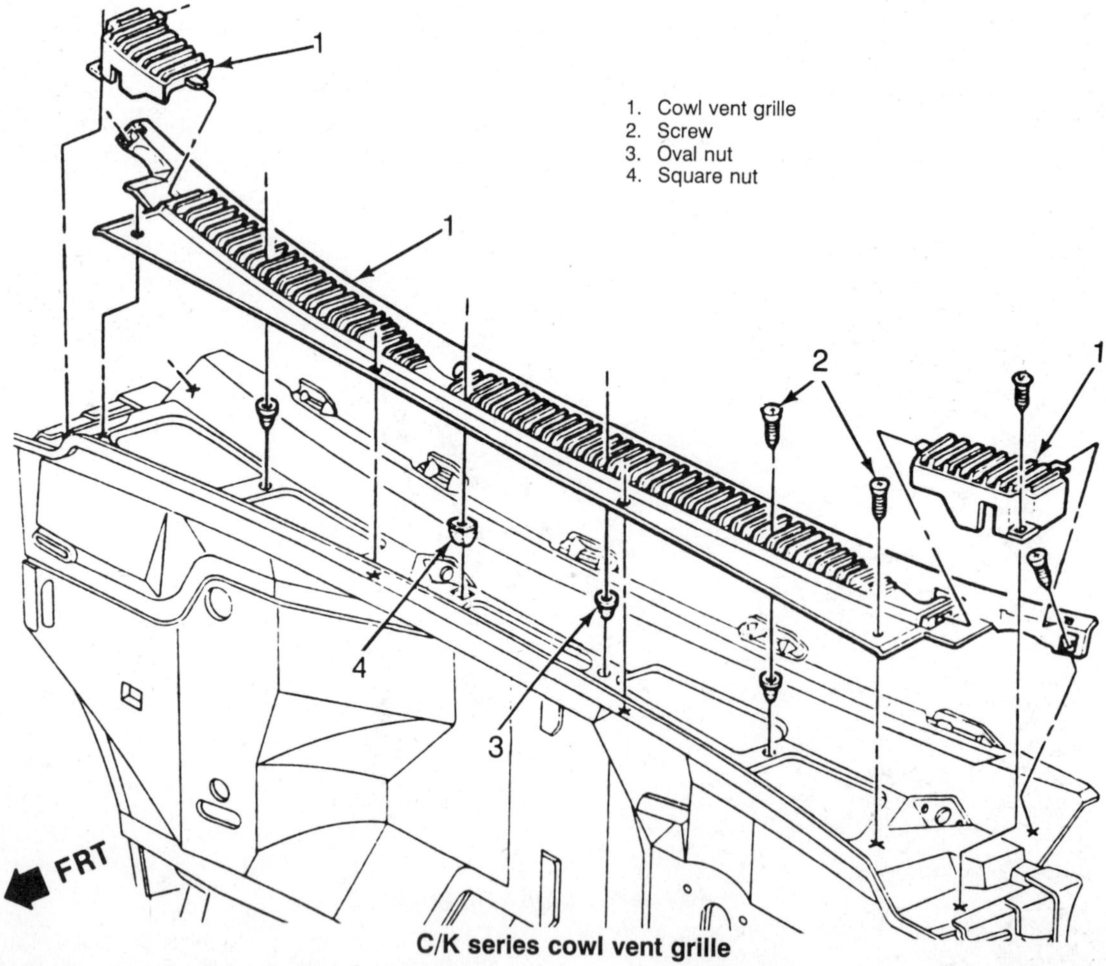

1. Cowl vent grille
2. Screw
3. Oval nut
4. Square nut

C/K series cowl vent grille

C and K Series

1. Remove the parking lamps and side marker lamps. See Section 6.
2. Remove the 2 grille-to-latch support bolts.
3. Remove the 1 grille bracket-to-latch support bolt.
4. Remove the 6 grille-to-radiator support bolts.
5. Lift the grille and filler panels from the truck.
6. Installation is the reverse of removal.

Outside Rear View Mirror

REMOVAL AND INSTALLATION

Standard Type

1. Remove the mirror to bracket screw and remove the mirror from the door.

2. Remove the bracket to door bolts and remove the bracket and gasket from the vehicle.
3. Installation is the reverse of removal.

Below Eyeline Type

1. Remove the mirror cover screw and lift the cover and pivot the mirror towards the window.
2. Remove the mirror to door bolts and remove the mirror and seal from the door.
3. To install, position the mirror and seal to the door and install the retaining bolts.
4. Pivot the mirror away from the window, and lower the mirror cover.
5. Installation is the reverse of removal.

West Coast Type

1. Remove the mirror bracket to door bracket nuts, bolts and bushings.
2. Remove the mirror bracket from the vehicle.
3. Remove the door bracket nuts and bolts and remove the bracket from the door.
4. Installation is the reverse of removal.

Antenna

REMOVAL AND INSTALLATION

Fender Mounted Type

1. Use two separate wrenches to prevent the cable assembly from turning and and remove the mast nut.
2. Remove the rod and mast assembly.
3. Remove the bezel.
4. Remove the screws from the body and cable assembly.
5. Remove the insulator.
6. Installation is the reverse of removal.

Windshield Type

On these models the antenna is part of the windshield. Replace the cable as follows:

1. Disconnect the battery ground cable.
2. Unsnap the antenna cable from the windshield.
3. Remove the bracket to dash panel screws.
4. Disconnect the cable at the rear of the radio receiver and remove the cable assembly.

Blazer/Jimmy Roof

REMOVAL AND INSTALLATION

1. Lower the rear window.
2. Remove the roof inner edge trim panels.
3. Remove the roof-to-body attaching bolts.
4. Using an assistant, break loose the roof from the insulating strips. Carefully lift the roof from the truck.

CAUTION

It is very heavy and awkward! Be careful to avoid flexing the roof or letting it crash into anything!

5. Without flexing the top, carefully place it on two 2×4 pieces of lumber.
6. Installation is the reverse of removal. Replace any damaged insulation.

INTERIOR

Door Trim Panels

REMOVAL AND INSTALLATION

R and V Series Front Side Door

1. Remove the window handle by depressing the door panel and removing the retaining clip.
2. Remove the door lock knob.
3. Remove the arm rest.
4. Snap off the trim covers and remove the screws retaining the assist strap, if so equipped.
5. Remove the 4 screws securing the lower edge of trim panel.
6. Remove the screw at the door handle cover plate and the screw located under the arm rest pad.
7. Remove the trim panel by carefully prying out at the trim retainers located around the perimeter of the panel.

To install:

NOTE: Before installing the door trim assembly, check that all trim retainers are securely installed to the assembly and are not damaged.

8. Pull the door inside handle inward, then position trim assembly to inner panel, inserting door handle through handle hole in panel.
9. Position rim assembly to door inner panel so trim retainers are aligned with attaching holes in panel and tap retainers into holes with a clean rubber mallet.
10. Install previously removed items.

R and V Series Rear Side Door

1. Remove the window handle by depressing the door panel and removing the retaining clip.
2. Remove the door lock knob.
3. Remove the arm rest.
4. Snap off the trim covers and remove the screws retaining the assist strap, if so equipped.
5. Remove the 3 screws securing the lower edge of trim panel.
6. Remove the screw at the door handle cover plate and the screw located under the arm rest pad.
7. Remove the trim panel by carefully prying out at the trim retainers located around the perimeter of the panel.

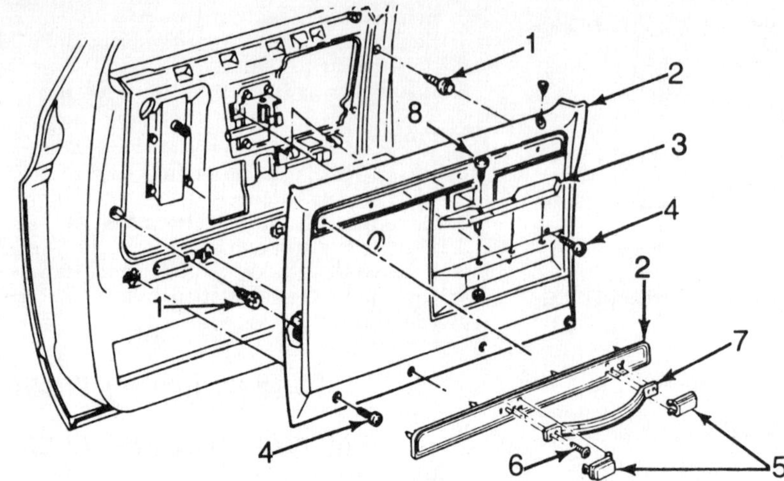

R/V series front door trim panel

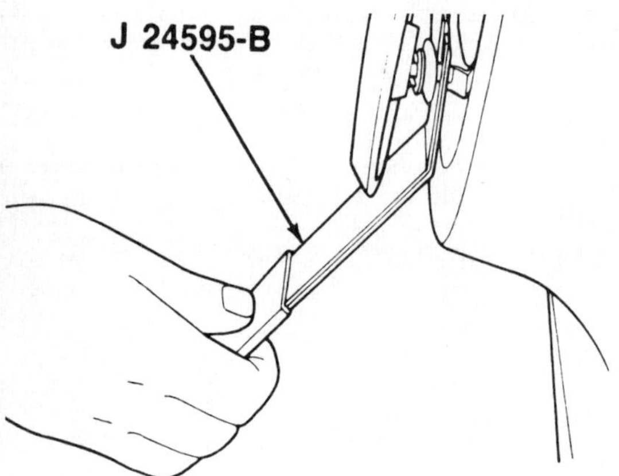

R/V series door trim clip remover

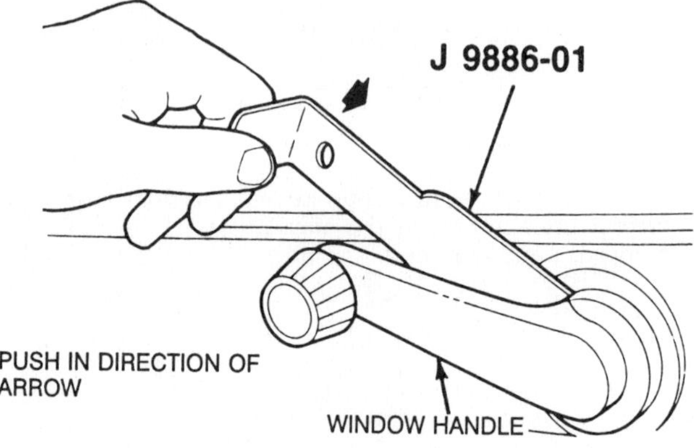

R/V series handle clip remover

To install:

NOTE: Before installing the door trim assembly, check that all trim retainers are securely installed to the assembly and are not damaged.

8. Pull the door inside handle inward, then position trim assembly to inner panel, inserting door handle through handle hole in panel.
9. Position rim assembly to door inner panel so trim retainers are aligned with attaching holes in panel and tap retainers into holes with a clean rubber mallet.
10. Install previously removed items.

C and K Series

1. Remove the window handle by depressing the door panel and removing the retaining clip.
2. Remove the door lock knob.
3. Remove the arm rest.
4. Snap off the trim covers and remove the screws retaining the assist strap, if so equipped.
5. Remove the electrical switch panel, if so equipped.
6. Remove the trim panel by carefully prying out at the trim retainers located around the perimeter of the panel.

To install:

NOTE: Before installing the door trim assembly, check that all trim retainers are securely installed to the assembly and are not damaged.

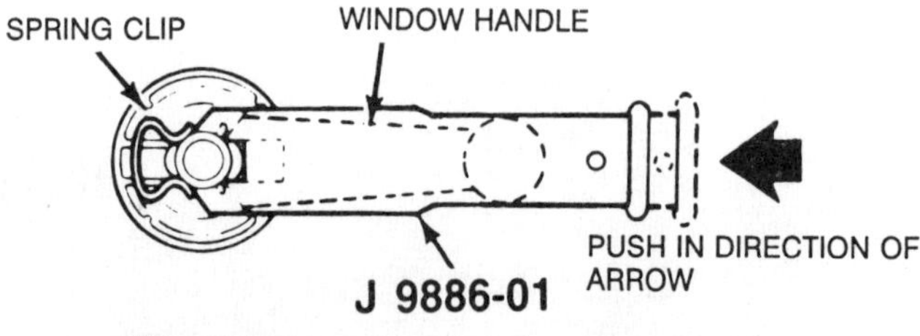

Rear view of the handle clip remover

7. Pull the door inside handle inward, then position trim assembly to inner panel, inserting door handle through handle hole in panel.
8. Position rim assembly to door inner panel so trim retainers are aligned with attaching holes in panel and tap retainers into holes with a clean rubber mallet.
9. Install previously removed items.

Suburban Rear Doors

1. Remove the lower trim molding screws and lift off the molding.
2. Disconnect the limiter strap from the door.
3. Remove the trim panel-to-door screws and remove the panel.
4. Installation is the reverse of removal.

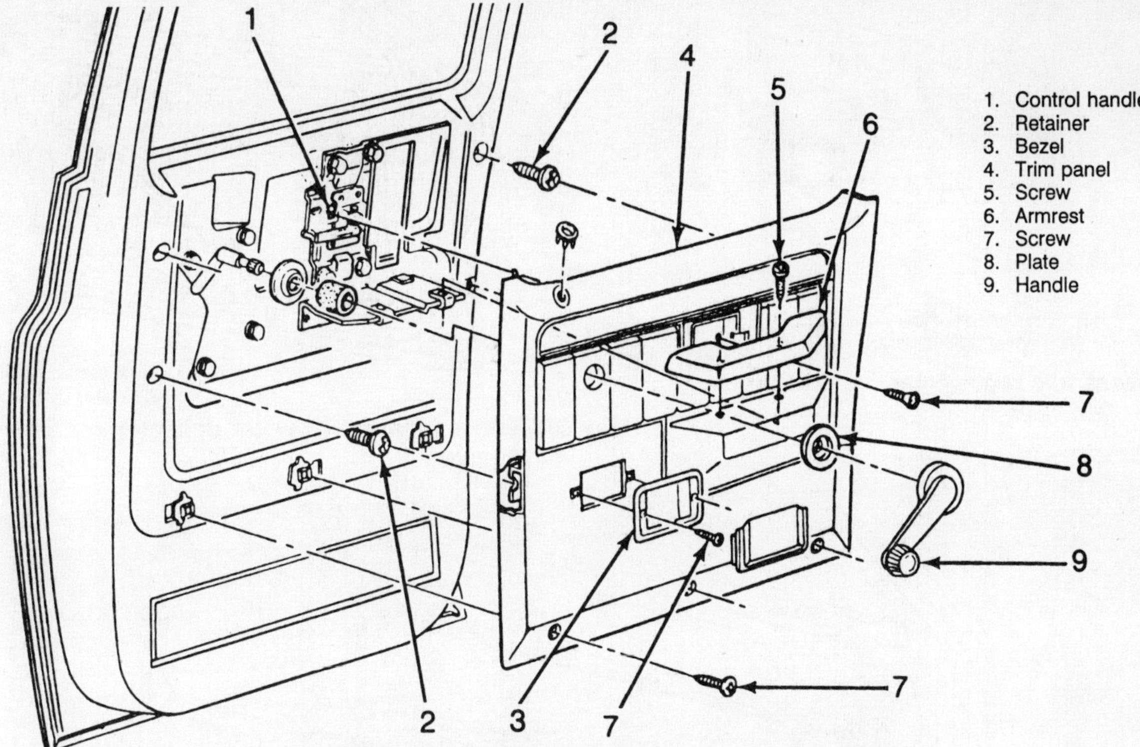

R/V series rear side door trim panel components

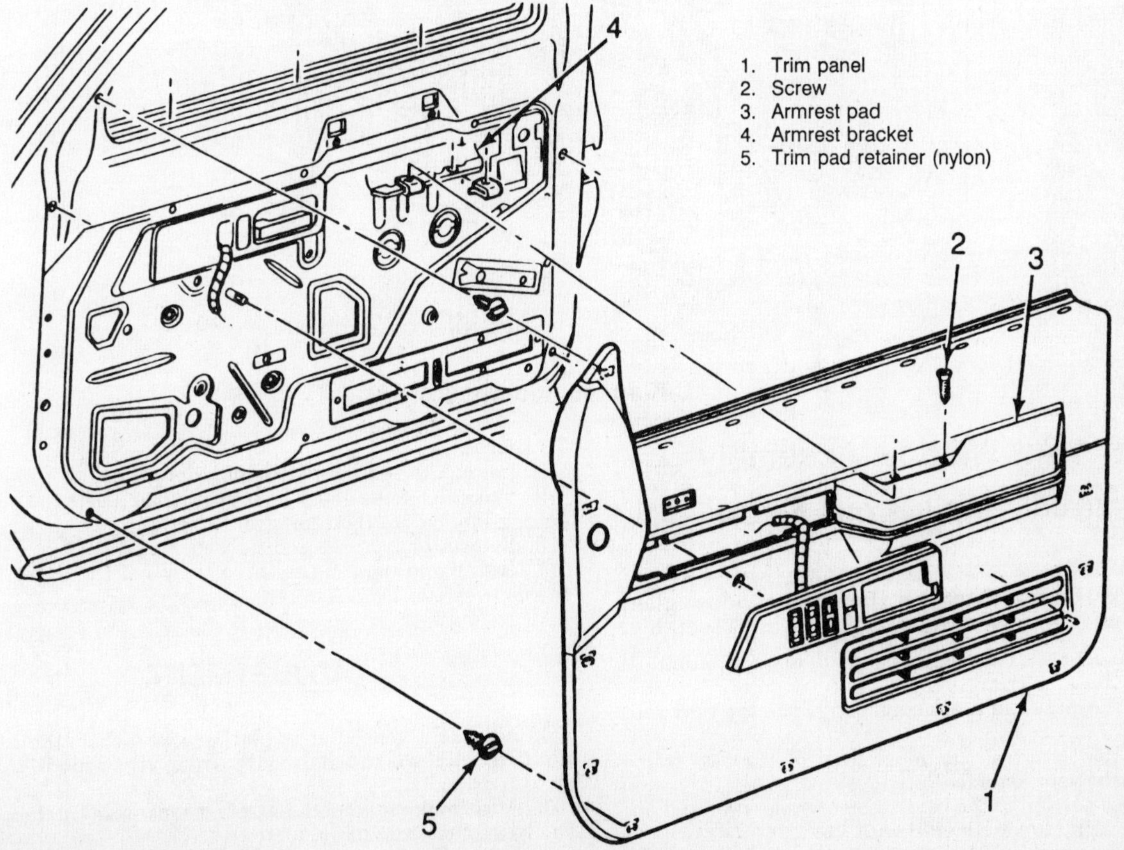

C/K series door trim panel

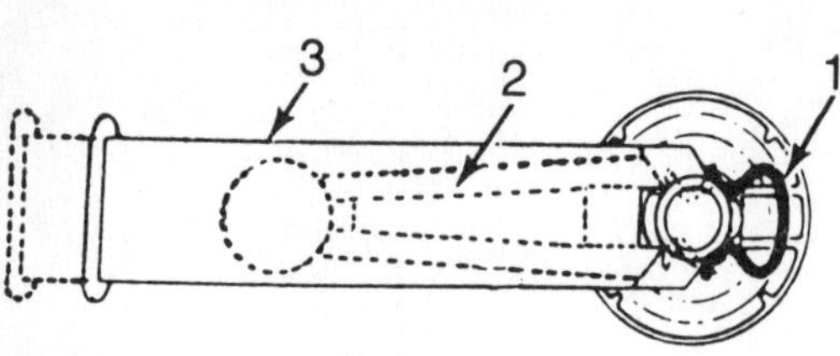

Window handle replacement — C/K series

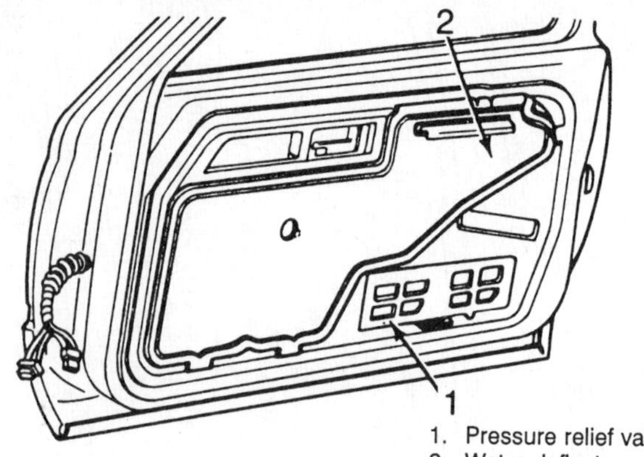

C/K series inner panel water deflector and pressure relief valve

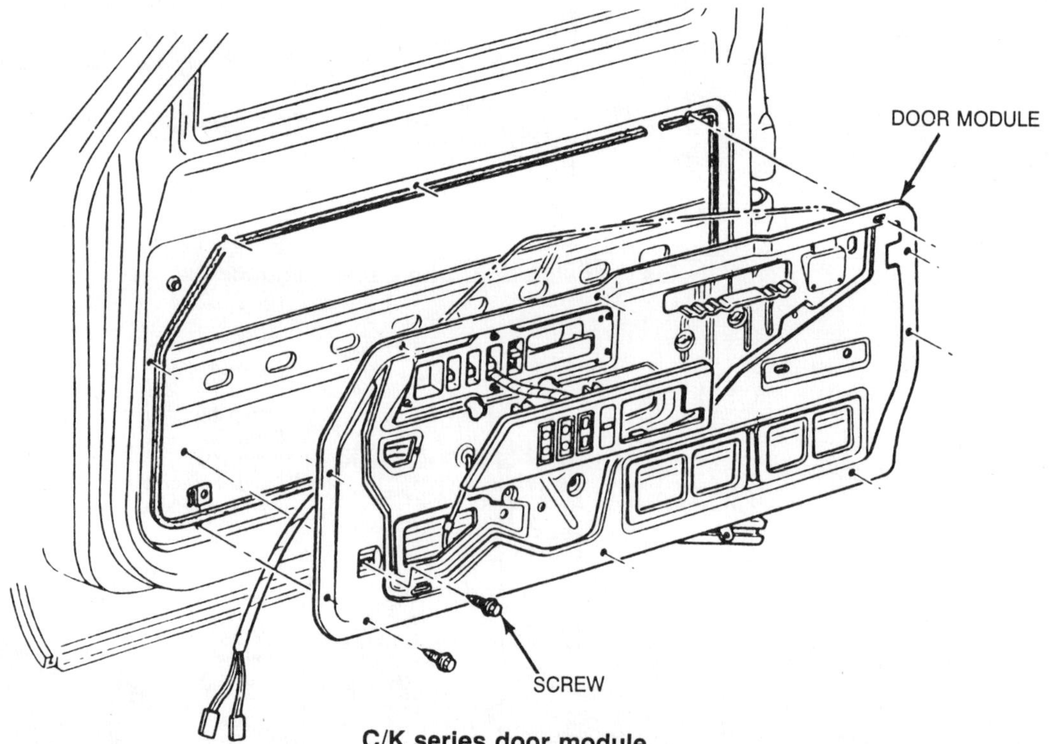

C/K series door module

Door Vent Window Assembly

REMOVAL AND INSTALLATION

R and V Series

NOTE: The channel between the door window glass and door vent is removed as part of the vent assembly.

1. Place the door window glass in the full down position.
2. Remove the door trim panel.
3. Remove the glass run channel molding from the vent window area.
4. Remove the screws at the upper front of the door frame which secure the vent assembly.
5. Pull upper portion of the vent assembly rearward and upward while rotating it counterclockwise.
7. Turn vent assembly 90° and carefully remove by guiding it up and out.

To install:

8. Lower the ventilator assembly into the door frame.
9. Make sure the rubber lip is positioned inside the inner and outer panel before tightening the screws.
10. Reinstall all screws and tighten.
11. Install and tighten the three screws at the upper front of the door.

ADJUSTMENT

1. Adjust the ventilator by placing a wrench on the adjusting nut through the access hole and turning vent window to the desired tension.
2. After making adjustment bend tabs over the hex nut on the base of the assembly.
3. Install arm rest screws and trim panel.
4. Install window regulator handle.

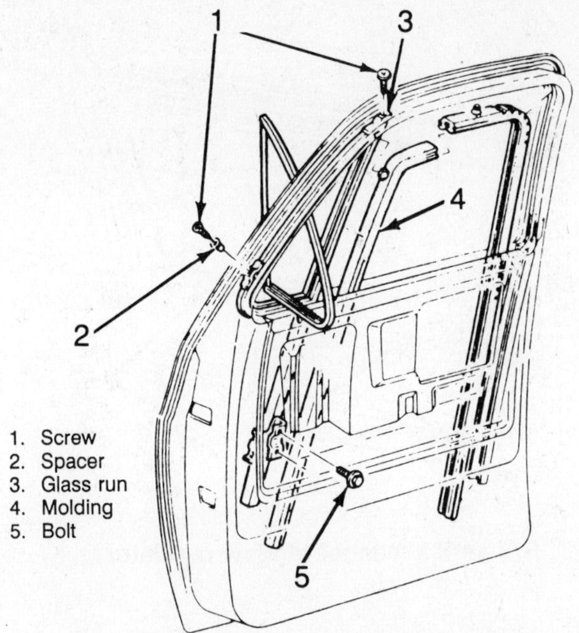

Door vent window run channel components

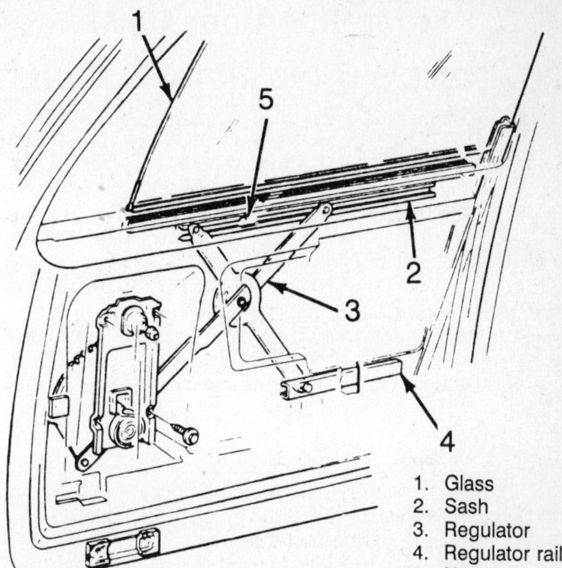

R/V series front door window and related components

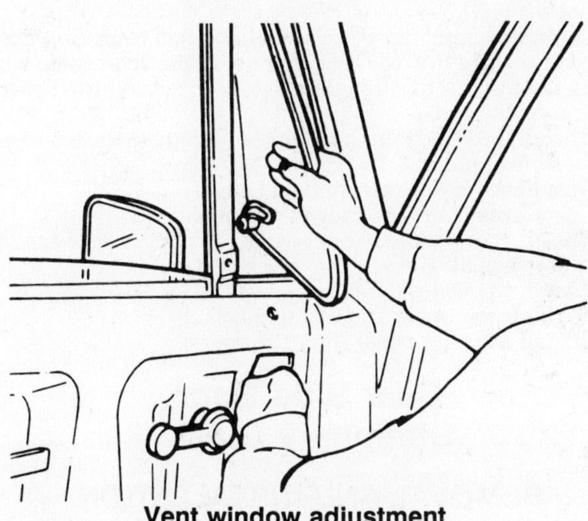
Vent window adjustment

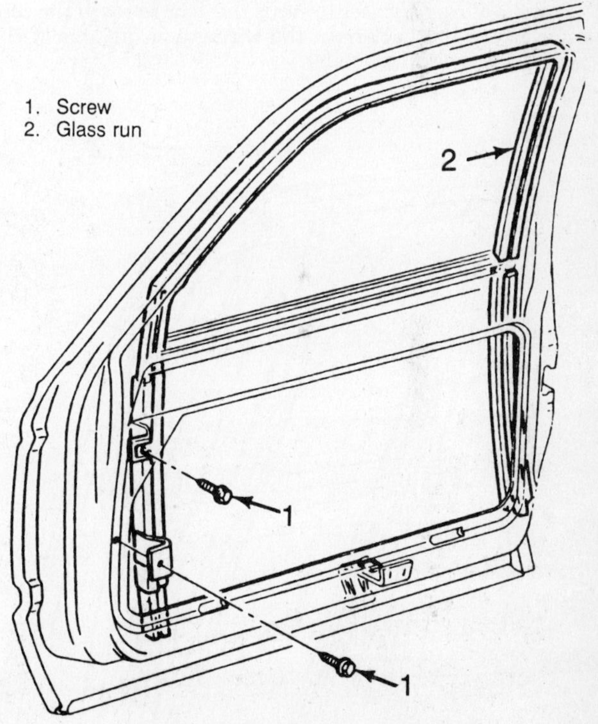

C/K series glass run channel

VENT WINDOW GLASS REPLACEMENT

1. Using an oil can, squirt Prepsol® or an equivalent on the glass filler all around the glass channel or frame to soften the old seal. When the seal is softened, remove the glass from the channel.
2. Thoroughly clean the inside of the glass channel with sandpaper, removing all rust etc.
3. Using new glass channel filler, cut the piece to be installed two inches longer than necessary for the channel.
4. Place this piece of filler (sandstoned side of filler away from glass) evenly over the edge of the glass which will fit in the channel.

The extra filler extending beyond the rear edge of the glass should be pinched together to hold it in place during glass installation.

5. Brush the inside of the channel with ordinary engine oil. This will enable the glass and filler to slide freely into the channel.
6. Push the glass with the filler around it into the channel until it is firmly seated.
7. After the glass is firmly in place, the oil softens the filler, causing it to swell, thereby making a water tight seal.
8. Trim off all excess filler material around the channel.

NOTE: Glass should be installed so that the rear edge is parallel to the division post.

9. Allow full cure before water testing.

Front Side Door Glass

REMOVAL AND INSTALLATION

R and V Series

1. Lower the door glass completely.
2. Remove the trim panel from the door.
3. Remove the vent window assembly as previously outlined.
4. Slide the glass forward until the front roller is in line with the notch in the sash channel.
5. Push window forward and tilt the front portion of window up until rear roller is disengaged.
6. Put window assembly in normal position (level) and raise straight up and out.
7. Installation is the reverse of removal.

C and K Series

1. Lower the door glass completely.
2. Remove the trim panel from the door.
3. Remove the water deflector by peeling it back.
4. Remove the module panel screws.
5. Remove the door lock rods from the module and tape them to the door.
6. Remove the lower run channel bolt.
7. Loosen the upper run channel bolt.
8. Move the run channel away from the glass.
9. Pull the wiring harness towards the door to reach the connector. Remove the boot from the wiring and disconnect the harness at the door hinge pillar.

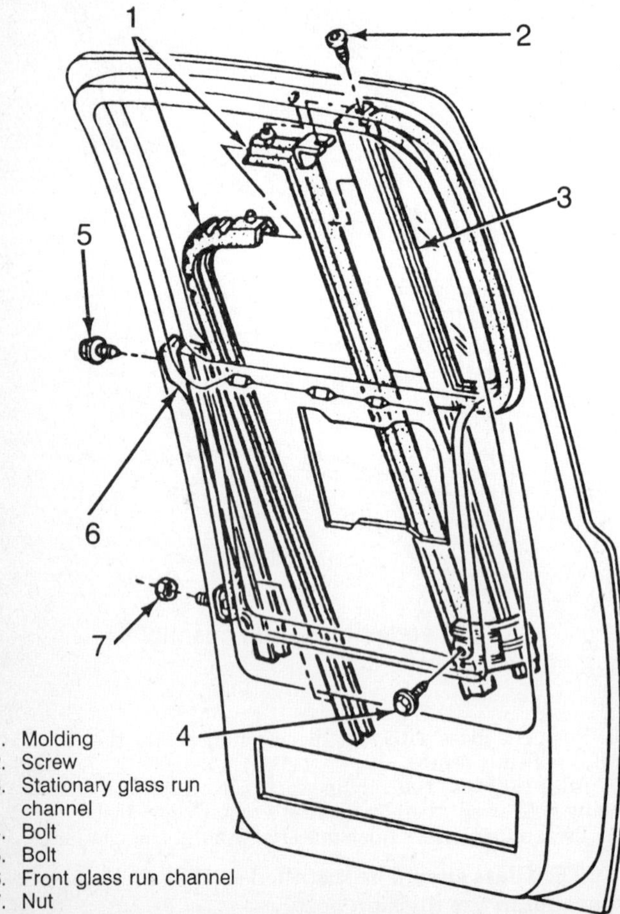

R/V series stationary glass and related components

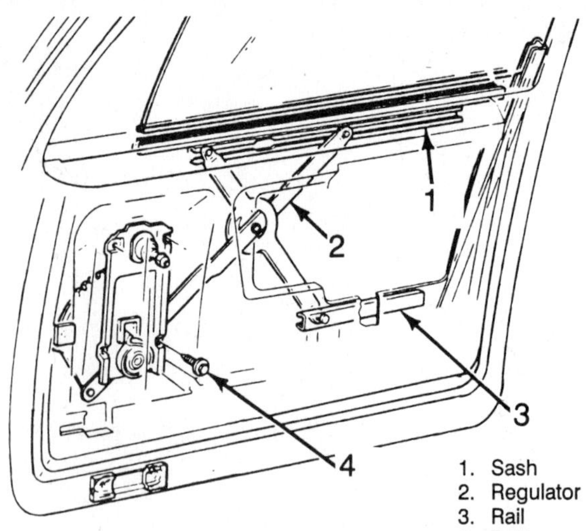

R/V series manual window regulator

10. Remove the module and window assembly from the door frame by tilting it and lowering it from the door.
11. Fold back the tab on the channel and slide the glass out.

To install:

13. Slide the glass into the channel and fold over the tab.
14. Fit the glass into the rear channel in the door, then, while pulling the channel towards the glass, fit the glass into the front run channel.
15. Install the boot from the wiring and connect the harness at the door hinge pillar.
16. Install the lower run channel bolt.
17. Install the door lock rods at the module.
18. Install the module panel screws, starting at the top left, then the top right.
19. Install the water deflector.
20. Tighten the upper run channel bolt.
21. Install the trim panel from the door.

Rear Side Door Stationary Glass

REMOVAL AND INSTALLATION

R and V Series

1. Place the window in the fully lowered position.
2. Remove the door trim panel.
3. Pull out the glass run channel molding.
4. Remove the door panel-to-run channel bolt.
5. Remove the door frame-to-run channel screw.
6. Pull the stationary glass/run channel assembly from the door, by pulling the top of the channel rearwards away from the door frame while rotating it out of the door.
7. Installation is the reverse of removal.

NOTE: The door frame-to-run channel screw must pass through the run channel molding slot.

Rear Side Door Window Glass

REMOVAL AND INSTALLATION

R and V Series

1. Lower the door glass completely.

2. Remove the trim panel from the door.
3. Remove the stationary window assembly as previously outlined.
4. Slide the glass rearward until the rear roller is in line with the notch in the sash channel. Disengage the roller from the channel.
5. Push window rearward and tilt it up until front roller is disengaged.
6. Put window assembly in normal position (level) and raise straight up and out.
7. Installation is the reverse of removal.

Front Side Door Manual Window Regulator

REMOVAL AND INSTALLATION

R and V Series

1. Place the window in the full up position and hold it there with heavy tape.
2. Remove the door trim panel.
3. Remove the regulator attaching bolts.
4. Slide the regulator rearward to disengage the rear roller from the sash channel.
5. Disengage the lower roller from the regulator rail.
6. Disengage the forward roller from the sash channel at the notch.
7. Fold the regulator down and remove it.
8. Installation is the reverse of removal.

C and K Series

1. Remove the door trim panel.
2. Remove the water deflector by peeling it back.
3. Disconnect the door lock linkage.
4. Loosen the upper run channel bolt.
5. Move the run channel away from the glass.
6. Remove the window assembly from the door frame by tilting it and lowering it from the door.
7. Fold back the tab on the channel and slide the glass out.
8. Drill out the regulator assembly rivets.
9. Remove the regulator.

To install:

10. Install the regulator. Use bolts and nuts to replace the rivets.
11. Disconnect the door lock linkage.
12. Install the water deflector by peeling it back.
13. Slide the glass into the channel and fold over the tab.
14. Fit the glass into the rear channel in the door, then, while pulling the channel towards the glass, fit the glass into the front run channel.
15. Install the lower run channel bolt.
16. Install the door lock linkage.
17. Install the door trim panel.

Rear Side Door Manual Window Regulator

REMOVAL AND INSTALLATION

R and V Series

1. Remove the door trim panel.
2. Remove the window glass as described above.
3. Remove the regulator attaching bolts.
4. Fold the regulator down and remove it.
5. Installation is the reverse of removal.

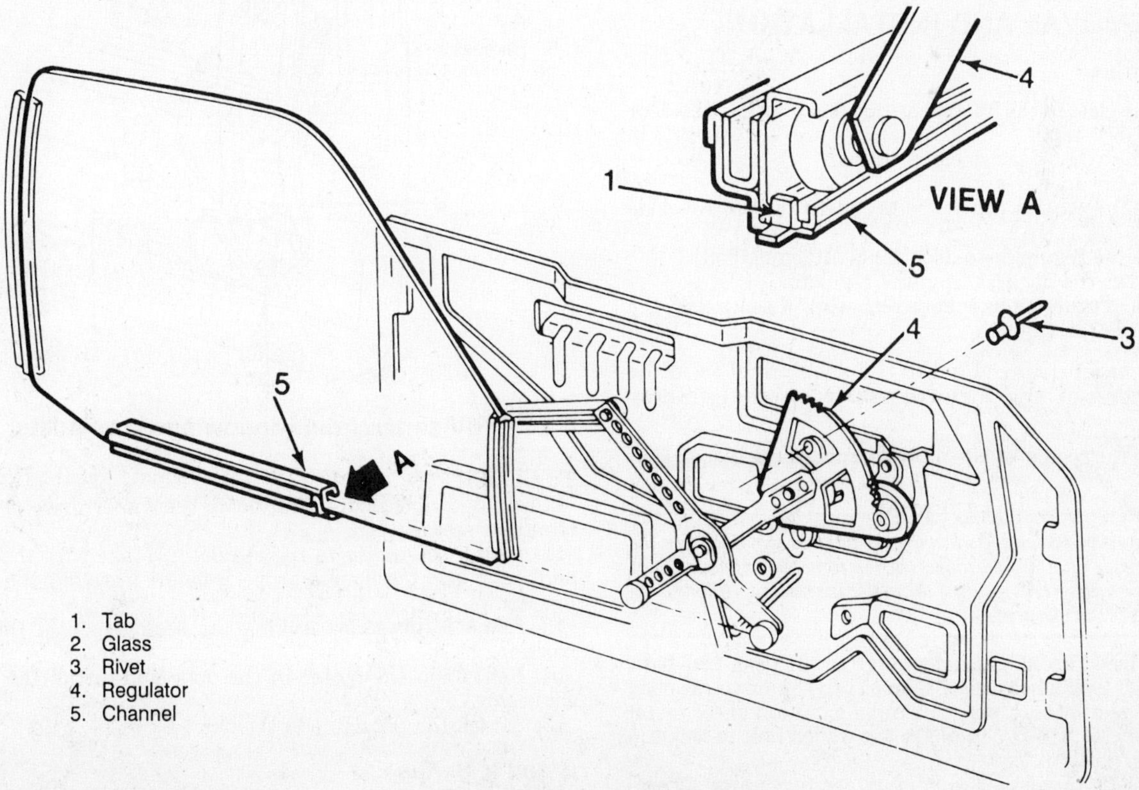

C/K series window regulator

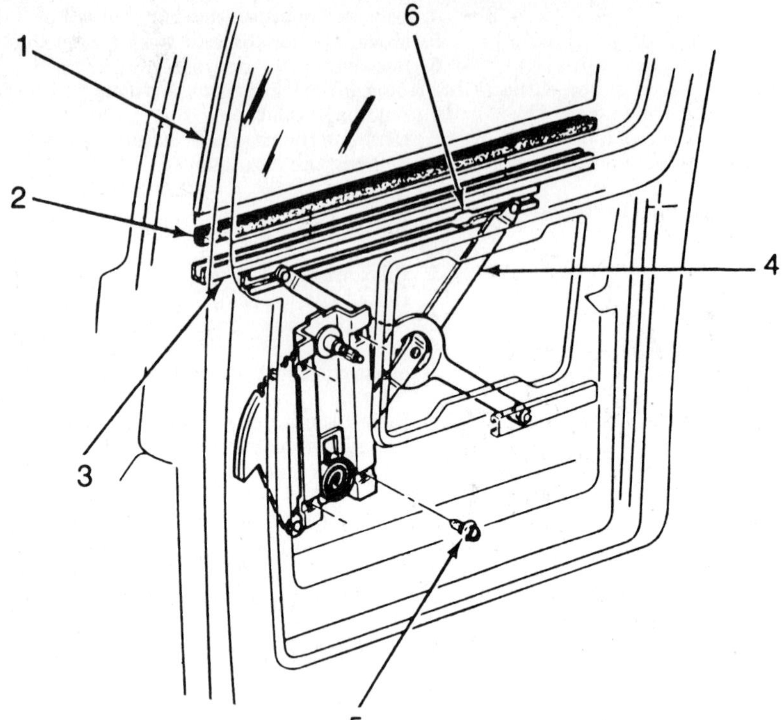

R/V series rear side window components

Front Side Door Power Window Regulator and Motor

REMOVAL AND INSTALLATION

R and V Series

1. Raise the glass to the full up position and tape it to the door frame with fabric tape.
2. Disconnect the negative battery cable.
3. Remove the door trim panel.
4. Remove the window control bolts and lay the control aside for access.
5. Remove the regulator-to-door panel attaching bolts.
6. Disconnect the harness from the regulator.
7. Slide the regulator assembly rearward, disengaging the rollers from the sash panel.

NOTE: A notch is provided in the sash panel to allow disengagement of the forward roller on the window regulator.

8. Remove the regulator assembly through the access hole in the door.

CAUTION

The next step must be performed when the regulator is removed from the door. The regulator lift arms are under tension from the counterbalance spring and can cause serious injury if the motor is removed without locking the sector gear in position.

9. Drill a hole through the regulator sector gear and back plate. DO NOT drill a hole closer than ½ in. (13mm) to the edge of the sector gear or back plate. Install a pan head sheet metal tapping screw (No. 10–12 × ¾ in.) in the drilled hole to lock the sector gear in position.
10. Remove the motor-to-regulator attaching screws and remove the motor from the regulator.

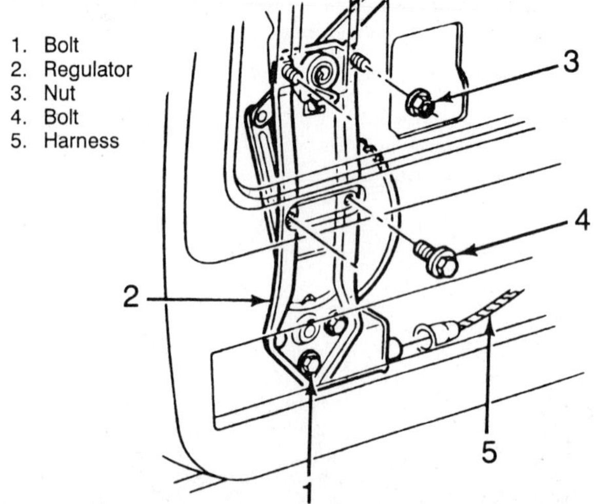

R/V series front window power regulator

To install:

11. Prior to installation, lubricate the motor drive gear and regulator sector teeth.
12. Install the motor to the regulator. Make sure the motor and sector gear teeth mesh properly before installing the retaining screws.
13. Remove the screw locking the sector gear in the fixed position.
14. Reposition the motor in the door and install the wiring connector.
15. Attach the regulator to the door.

C and K Series

1. Disconnect the battery ground cable.

2. Remove the door trim panel.
3. Remove the water deflector by peeling it back.
4. Disconnect the door lock rods at the module.
5. Loosen the upper run channel bolt.
6. Move the run channel away from the glass.
7. Pull the wiring harness towards the door to reach the connector. Remove the boot from the wiring and disconnect the harness at the door hinge pillar.
8. Remove the module and window assembly from the door frame by tilting it and lowering it from the door.
9. Fold back the tab on the channel and slide the glass out.
10. On trucks with power components, drill out the rivets from the inner handle housing.
11. Drill out the regulator assembly rivets.
12. Remove the regulator/motor assembly.

CAUTION

The next step must be performed when the regulator is removed from the door. The regulator lift arms are under tension from the counterbalance spring and can cause serious injury if the motor is removed without locking the sector gear in position.

13. Install a pan head sheet metal tapping screw through the sector gear and backiong plate in the hole provided, to lock the sector gear in position.
14. Drill out the motor-to-regulator attaching rivets and remove the motor from the regulator.

To install:

15. Prior to installation, lubricate the motor drive gear and regulator sector teeth.
16. Install the motor to the regulator. Make sure the motor and sector gear teeth mesh properly before installing the replacement attaching bolts and nuts.
17. Remove the screw locking the sector gear in the fixed position.
18. Reposition the motor/regulator in the door and install the wiring connector.
19. Attach the regulator to the door.
20. Slide the glass out into the channel and fold over the tab.

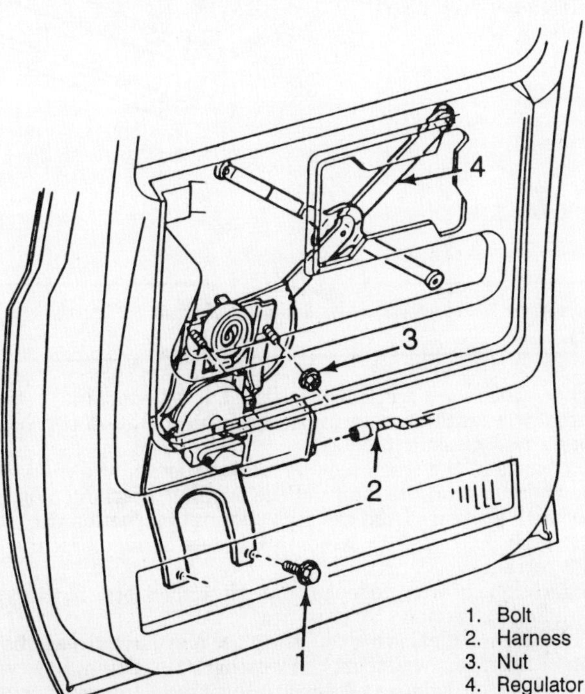

R/V series rear side window power regulator

21. Fit the glass into the rear channel in the door, then, while pulling the channel towards the glass, fit the glass into the front run channel.
22. Install the boot from the wiring and connect the harness at the door hinge pillar.
23. Install the lower run channel bolt.
24. Install the door lock rods at the module.
25. Install the module panel screws, starting at the top left, then the top right.
26. Install the water deflector.
27. Tighten the upper run channel bolt.
28. Install the trim panel on the door.

Rear Side Door Power Window Regulator and Motor

REMOVAL AND INSTALLATION

R and V Series

1. Disconnect the negative battery cable.
2. Remove the door trim panel.
3. Remove the window glass as described above.
4. Remove the regulator-to-door panel attaching bolts.
5. Disconnect the harness from the regulator.
6. Remove the regulator assembly through the access hole in the door.

CAUTION

The next step must be performed when the regulator is removed from the door. The regulator lift arms are under tension from the counterbalance spring and can cause serious injury if the motor is removed without locking the sector gear in position.

7. Drill a hole through the regulator sector gear and back plate. DO NOT drill a hole closer than ½ in. (13mm) to the edge of the sector gear or back plate. Install a pan head sheet metal tapping screw (No. 10–12 × ¾ in.) in the drilled hole to lock the sector gear in position.
8. Remove the motor-to-regulator attaching screws and remove the motor from the regulator.

To install:

9. Prior to installation, lubricate the motor drive gear and regulator sector teeth.
10. Install the motor to the regulator. Make sure the motor and sector gear teeth mesh properly before installing the retaining screws.
11. Remove the screw locking the sector gear in the fixed position.
12. Reposition the motor in the door and install the wiring connector.
13. Attach the regulator to the door.
14. The remainder of installation is the reverse of removal.

Rear Door Stationary Glass, or Rear Cab Window Glass

REMOVAL AND INSTALLATION

R and V Series

1. On rear cab windows with a defogger grid, unclip the connectors.
2. Remove the interior trim moldings from around the window. On the rear doors, it may be necessary to drill out the weatherstripping rivets. Use a ¼ inch bit.
3. Break loose the seal between the weatherstripping and the body panels.
4. Have someone outside push inward on the glass while you catch it.

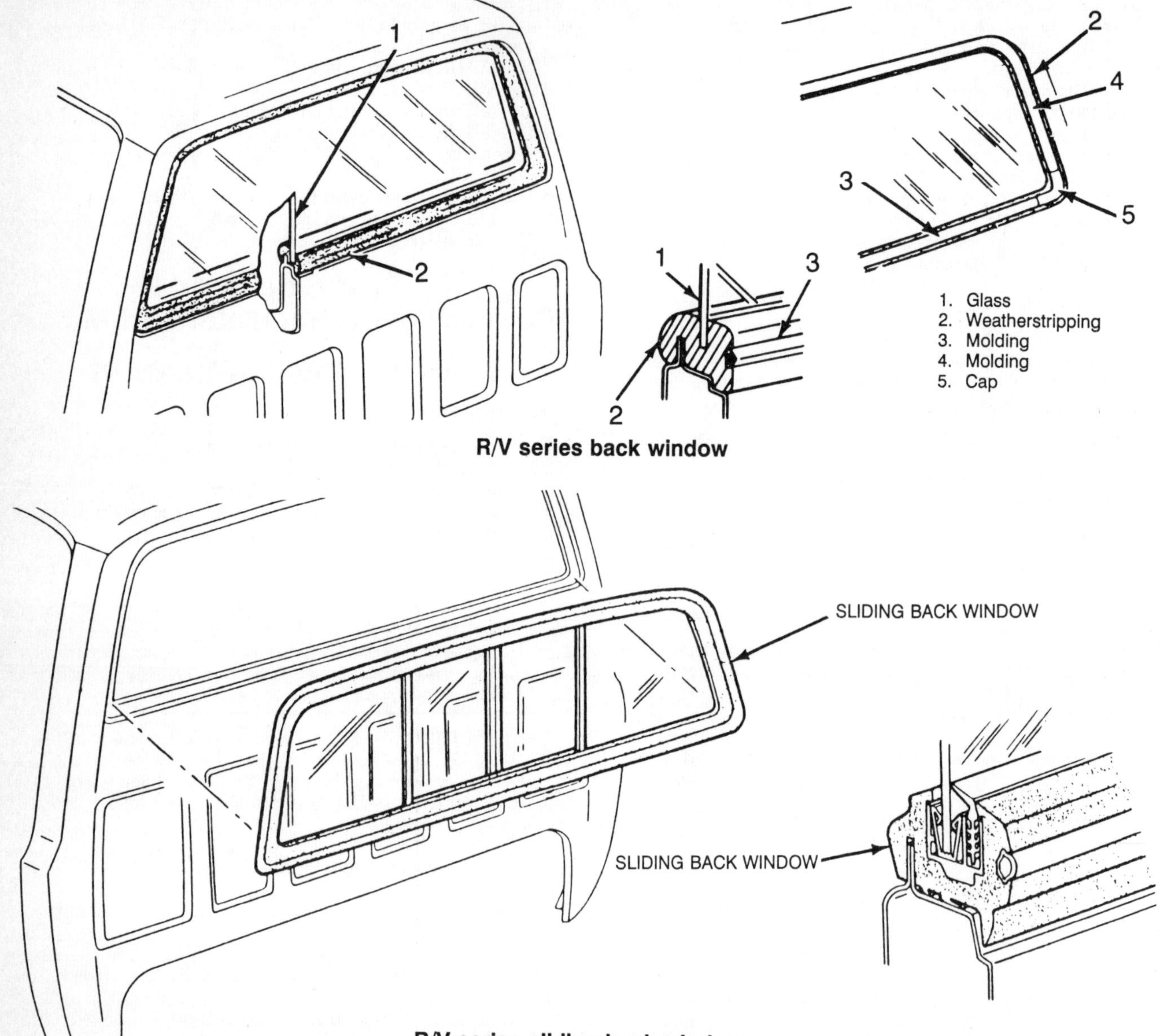

R/V series back window

R/V series sliding back window

5. Clean all old sealer from the glass and weatherstripping.

6. Fill the glass channel in the weatherstripping with a $^3/_{16}$ in. (5mm) bead of sealer.

7. Fit the glass in the weatherstripping and place a ¼ in. (6mm) diameter cord in the frame cavity around the outside diameter of the weatherstripping. Allow the ends of the cord to hang down the outside of the glass from the top center.

8. Place the glass and weatherstripping in the vehicle opening. Pull on the cord ends to pull the lip of the weatherstripping over the body panel.

9. Install the trim molding. If the trim was held by rivets, replace them with $^3/_{16}$ in. blind rivets and a rivet gun.

C and K Series Windshield

NOTE: Bonded windshields require special tools and special removal procedures to be removed without being broken. For this reason we recommend that you refer all removal and installation to a qualified technician.

CAUTION

Always wear heavy gloves when handling glass to reduce the risk of injury.

When replacing a cracked windshield, it is important that the cause of the crack be determined and the condition corrected, before a new glass is installed.

The cause of the crack may be an obstruction or a high spot somewhere around the flange of the opening; cracking may not occur until pressure from the high spot or obstruction becomes particularly high due to winds, extremes of temperature, or rough terrain.

Suggestions of what to look for are described later in this section under inspection.

When a windshield is broken, the glass may have already have fallen or been removed from the weatherstrip. Often, however, it is necessary to remove a cracked or otherwise imperfect windshield that is still intact. In this case, it is a good practise to crisscross the glass with strips of masking tape before removing

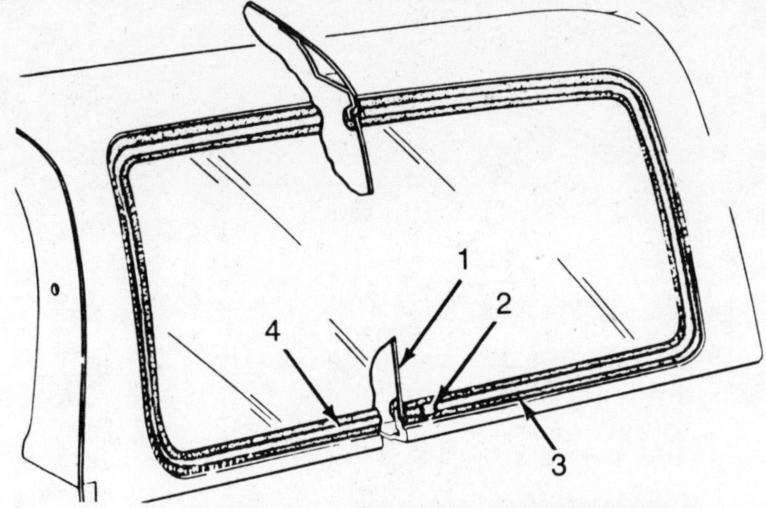

R/V series body side window

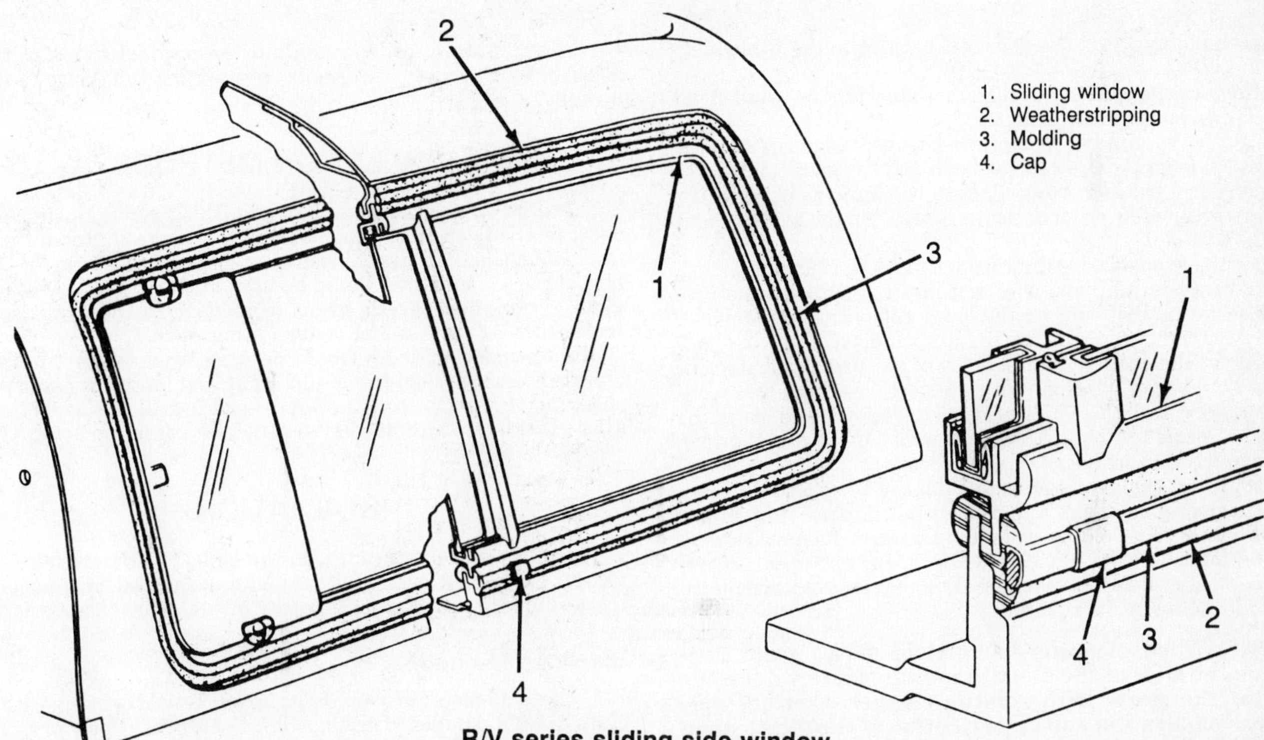

R/V series sliding side window

the it; this will help hold the glass together and minimize the risk of injury.

If a crack extends to the edge of the glass, mark the point where the crack meets the weather strip. (Use a piece of chalk and mark the point on the cab, next to the weatherstrip.) Later, when examining the flange of the opening for a cause of the crack start at the point marked.

The higher the temperature of the work area, the more pliable the weather strip will be. The more pliable the weather strip, the more easily the windshield can be removed.

Before removing the glass, cover the instrument panel, and the surrounding sheet metal with protective covering and remove the wiper arms.

There are two methods of windshield removal, depending on the method of windshield replacement chosen. When using the short method of installation, it is important to cut the glass from the urethane adhesive as close to the glass as possible. This is due to the fact that the urethane adhesive will be used to provide a base for the replacement windshield.

When using the extended method of windshield replacement, all the urethane adhesive must be removed from the pinchweld flange so, the process of cutting the window from the adhesive is less critical.

Special tool J–24402–A, Glass Sealant Remover Knife, and J–24709–01 Urethane Glass Sealant Remove, or their equivalents are required to perform this procedure.

REMOVAL

1. Place the protective covering around the area where the glass will be removed.
2. Remove the windshield wiper arms, antenna mast, and the

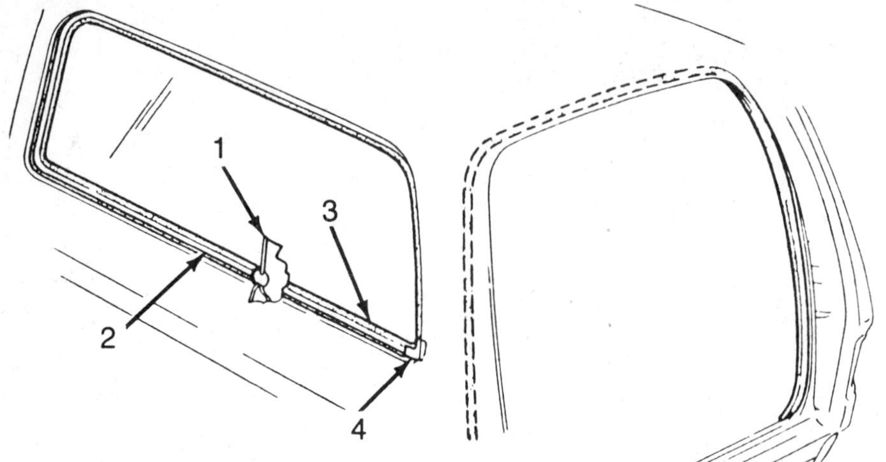

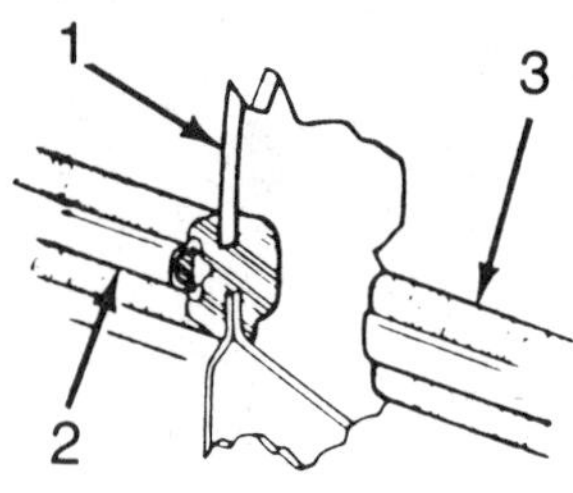

Suburban rear stationary window

interior moldings. Pull the door seal back from the windshield area.

3. Remove the cowl vent grille, rear view mirror, windshield stop screws and speaker grilles.

4a. If the windshield is broken: Using J-24402-A cut the windshield from the urethane adhesive. If the short method of glass replacement is to be used, keep the knife as close to the glass as possible in order to leave a base for the replacement glass.

4b. If the windshield is unbroken: Cut a 6 ft. (183mm) length of 0.02 in. (0.5mm) piano wire and insert it through the urethane sealer at any point on the lower edge of the windshield. Wrap each end of the wire around a wood dowel to act as handles. Spray the entire circumference of the urethane adhesive with a liquid soap solution. With a helper, saw back and forth with the wire until the windshield is cut free of the adhesive. Be careful to avoid contacting the glass with the wire. If the soap solution dries, spray ahead of your cut.

5. With the help of an assistant, remove the glass.

6. If the original glass is to be reinstalled, place it on a protected bench or a holding or holding fixture. Remove any remaining adhesive with a razor blade or a sharp scraper. Any remaining traces of adhesive material can be removed with denatured alcohol or lacquer thinner.

NOTE: When cleaning windshield glass, avoid contacting the edge of the plastic laminate material (on the edge of the glass) with volatile cleaner. Contact may cause discoloration and deterioration of the plastic laminate. Do not use a petroleum based solvent such as gasoline or kerosene. The presence of oil will prevent the adhesion of new material.

INSPECTION

An inspection of the windshield opening, the weather strip, and the glass may reveal the cause of a broken windshield. This can help prevent future breakage. If there is no apparent cause of breakage, the weatherstrip should be removed from the flange of the opening and the flange inspected. Look for high weld or solder spots, hardened spot welds sealer, or any other obstruction or irregularity in the flange. Check the weatherstrip for irregularities or obstructions in it.

Check the windshield to be installed to make sure that it does not have any chipped edges. Chipped edges can be ground off, restoring a smooth edge to the glass, and minimizing concentrations of pressure that cause breakage. Remove no more than necessary, in an effort to maintain the original shape of the glass and the proper clearance between it and the flange of the opening.

INSTALLATION METHODS

There are two methods used for windshield replacement. The short method described previously in the removal procedure is used when the urethane adhesive can be used as a base for the new glass. This method would be used in the case of a cracked glass, if, no other service needs to be done to the windshield frame such as sheet metal or repainting work.

The extended method should be used when work must be done to the windshield frame such as straightening or repairing sheet metal or repainting the windshield frame. In this method all of the urethane adhesive must be removed from the pinchweld flange.

INSTALLATION

To replace a urethane adhered windshield, GM adhesive service kit No. 1052420 contains the materials needed, and must be used to insure the original integrity of the windshield design.

Extended Method

1. Clean all metal surrounding the windshield opening with a clean alcohol dampened cloth. Allow the alcohol to air dry.

2. Apply the pinchweld primer found in the service kit to the pinchweld area. Do not let any of the primer touch any of the exposed paint because damage to the finish may occur. Allow thirty minutes for the primer to dry.

3. Follow the steps listed under Short Method for the remainder of the procedure.

Short Method

1. Thoroughly clean the edge of the glass to which the adhesive material will be applied with a clean alcohol dampened cloth. Allow the alcohol to dry.

2. Apply the clear glass primer in the kit to the inner edge of the windshield from the edge of the glass inward ¾ in. (19mm). Apply the primer around the entire perimeter of the glass. Allow the primer to cure for thirty minutes.

3. Apply the blackout primer to the glass in the same area as the clear primer. Allow the blackout primer to dry to the touch.

4. Apply a bead of urethane, 1mm high, over the primer.

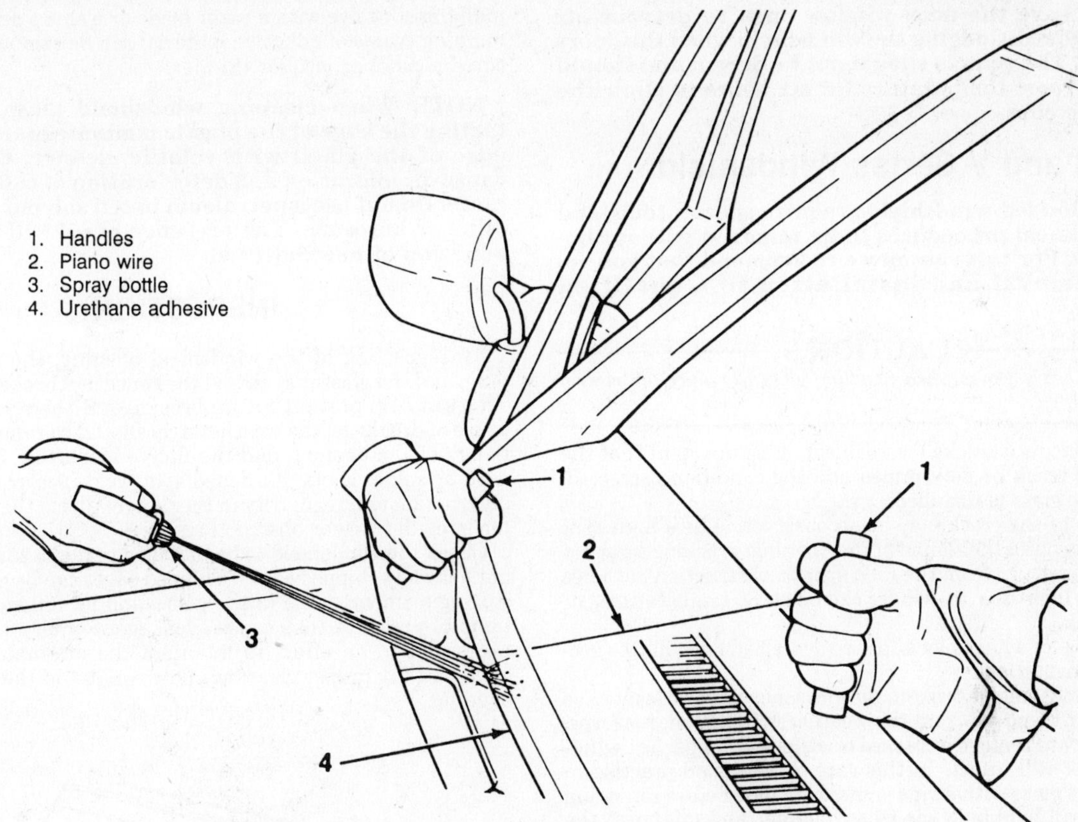

Cutting the C/K series windshield from the frame

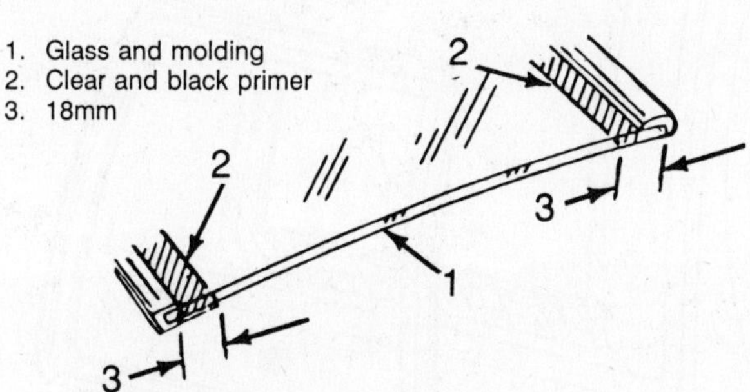

C/K series windshield primer locations

5. Drill or punch a hole in the center of each tab at the bottom of the windshield.

6. With the aid of a helper, lift the glass into the opening. Align the groove in each upper, outer edge of the windshield molding with the door edge.

7. Install the windhsield stop screws.

8. Cut the tip of the adhesive cartridge approximately $^{3}/_{16}$ in. (5mm) from the end of the tip.

9. Apply a smooth continuous bead of adhesive into the gap between the glass edge and the sheet metal. Use a flat bladed tool to paddle the material into position if necessary. Be sure that the adhesive contacts the entire edge of the glass, and extends to fill the gap between the glass and the primer sheet metal (extended method) or solidified urethane base (short method).

10. Spray a mist of water onto the urethane. Water will assist in the curing process.

11. Install the wiper arms.

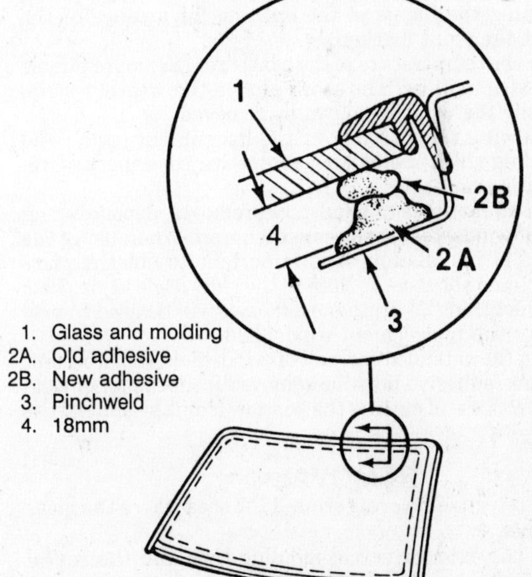

C/K series windshield urethane adhesive locations

12. Install the interior garnish moldings.

13. Install the rear view mirror.

14. Install the speaker grilles, cowl vent grille and antenna mast.

NOTE: Leave the door window open to prevent air pressure from dislodging the windshield when the doors are closed. The vehicle should not be driven and should remain at room temperature for six hours to allow the adhesive to cure.

R and V Series Windshield

NOTE: Bonded windshields require special tools and special removal procedures to be removed without being broken. For this reason we recommend that you refer all removal and installation to a qualified technician.

CAUTION

Always wear heavy gloves when handling glass to reduce the risk of injury.

When replacing a cracked windshield, it is important that the cause of the crack be determined and the condition corrected, before a new glass is installed.

The cause of the crack may be an obstruction or a high spot somewhere around the flange of the opening; cracking may not occur until pressure from the high spot or obstruction becomes particularly high due to winds, extremes of temperature, or rough terrain.

Suggestions of what to look for are described later in this section under inspection.

When a windshield is broken, the glass may have already have fallen or been removed from the weatherstrip. Often, however, it is necessary to remove a cracked or otherwise imperfect windshield that is still intact. In this case, it is a good practise to crisscross the glass with strips of masking tape before removing the it; this will help hold the glass together and minimize the risk of injury.

If a crack extends to the edge of the glass, mark the point where the crack meets the weather strip. (Use a piece of chalk and mark the point on the cab, next to the weatherstrip.) Later, when examining the flange of the opening for a cause of the crack start at the point marked.

The higher the temperature of the work area, the more pliable the weather strip will be. The more pliable the weather strip, the more easily the windshield can be removed.

Before removing the glass, cover the instrument panel, and the surrounding sheet metal with protective covering and remove the wiper arms.

There are two methods of windshield removal, depending on the method of windshield replacement chosen. When using the short method of installation, it is important to cut the glass from the urethane adhesive as close to the glass as possible. This is due to the fact that the urethane adhesive will be used to provide a base for the replacement windshield.

When using the extended method of windshield replacement, all the urethane adhesive must be removed from the pinchweld flange so, the process of cutting the window from the adhesive is less critical.

REMOVAL

1. Place a protective covering around the area where the glass will be removed.
2. Remove the exterior reveal molding caps and the reveal moldings.
3. With the help of an assistant inside the truck, apply firm pressure to the edge of the glass while forcing the weatherstripping from the flange with a flat, wood spatula, or similar tool. Remove the glass.
4. Remove the excess urethane and remaining weatherstripping from the pinchweld flange.
5. Thoroughly clean the pinchweld with a clean, dry cloth.
6. If the original glass is to be reinstalled, place it on a protected bench or a holding or holding fixture. Remove any remaining adhesive with a razor blade or a sharp scraper. Any remaining traces of adhesive material can be removed with denatured alcohol or lacquer thinner.

NOTE: When cleaning windshield glass, avoid contacting the edge of the plastic laminate material (on the edge of the glass) with volatile cleaner. Contact may cause discoloration and deterioration of the plastic laminate. Do not use a petroleum based solvent such as gasoline or kerosene. The presence of oil will prevent the adhesion of new material.

INSPECTION

An inspection of the windshield opening, the weatherstripping, and the glass may reveal the cause of a broken windshield. This can help prevent future breakage. If there is no apparent cause of breakage, the weatherstrip should be removed from the flange of the opening and the flange inspected. Look for high weld or solder spots, hardened spot welds sealer, or any other obstruction or irregularity in the flange. Check the weatherstrip for irregularities or obstructions in it.

Check the windshield to be installed to make sure that it does not have any chipped edges. Chipped edges can be ground off, restoring a smooth edge to the glass, and minimizing concentrations of pressure that cause breakage. Remove no more than necessary, in an effort to maintain the original shape of the glass and the proper clearance between it and the flange of the opening.

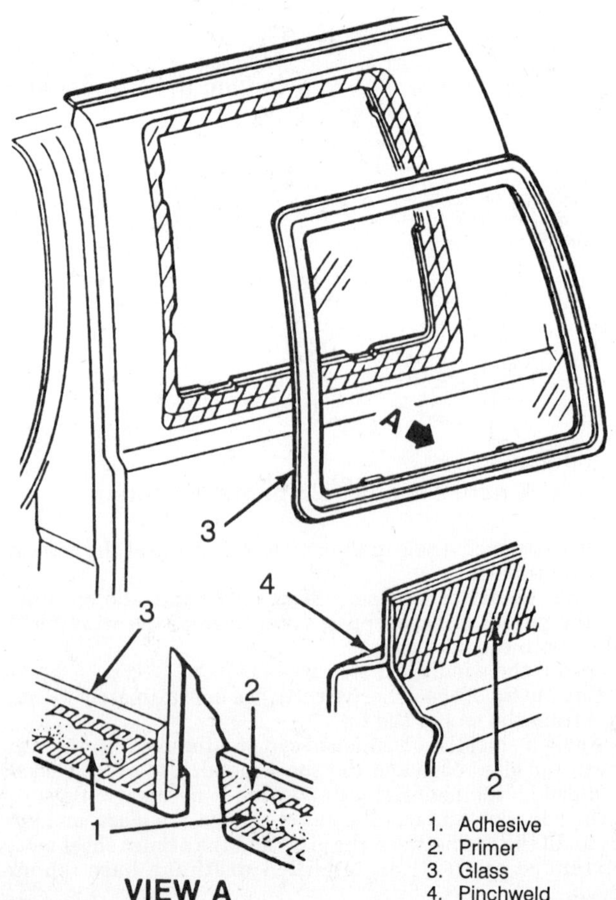

C/K series extended cab stationary side glass primer and adhesive locations

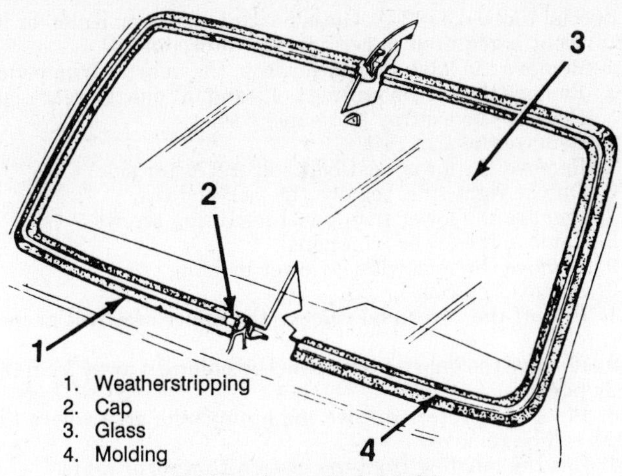

1. Weatherstripping
2. Cap
3. Glass
4. Molding

R/V series windshield

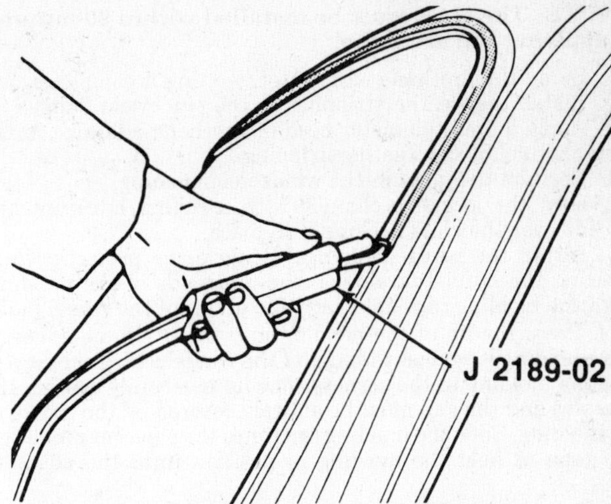

R/V series windshield molding installation

Check the fit of the new windshield, before trying to install it. The glass and flange should overlap by 5mm. If the windshield is too big, you'll have to grind the edge of the glass or or rework the metal edge of the flange.

If the overlap is too small, you can build up the flange by brazing a length of ⅛ in. (3mm) wire to the edge of the flange. Usually, it is sufficient to build up the flange on one side and halfway around one corner. Taper the ends of the wire.

INSTALLATION KIT

To replace a urethane adhered windshield, GM adhesive service kit No. 9636067 contains some of the materials needed, and must be used to insure the original integrity of the windshield design. Materials in this kit include:

1. One tube of adhesive material.
2. One dispensing nozzle.
3. Steel music wire.
4. Rubber cleaner.
5. Rubber Primer.
6. Pinchweld primer.
7. Blackout primer.
8. Filler strip (for use on windshield installations for vehicles equipped with embedded windshield antenna).
9. Primer applicators.

Other materials are required for windshield installation which are not included in the service kit.

These include:

1. GM rubber lubricant No. 1051717.
2. Alcohol for cleaning the edge of the glass.
3. Adhesive dispensing gun J-24811 or its equivalent.
4. A commercial type razor knife.
5. Two rubber support spacers.

INSTALLATION

1. Clean all metal surrounding the windshield opening with a clean alcohol dampened cloth. Allow the alcohol to air dry.
2. Apply the pinchweld primer found in the service kit to the pinchweld area. Do not let any of the primer touch any of the exposed paint because damage to the finish may occur. Allow 30 minutes for the primer to dry.
3. Apply rubber cleaner to both channels of the weatherstripping. Wait 5 minutes and wipe thr channels dry with a clean cloth.
4. Apply rubber primer to both channels of the weatherstripping. Allow the primer to cure for 30 minutes.
5. Thoroughly clean the edge of the glass to which the adhesive material will be applied with a clean alcohol dampened cloth. Allow the alcohol to dry.
6. Apply blackout primer to the inside edge of the glass. Start 10mm from the edge and work the primer towards the edge. Allow the primer to dry.
7. Apply a 6mm diameter bead of urethane adhesive to the center of the pinchweld flange and completely around the windshield opening.

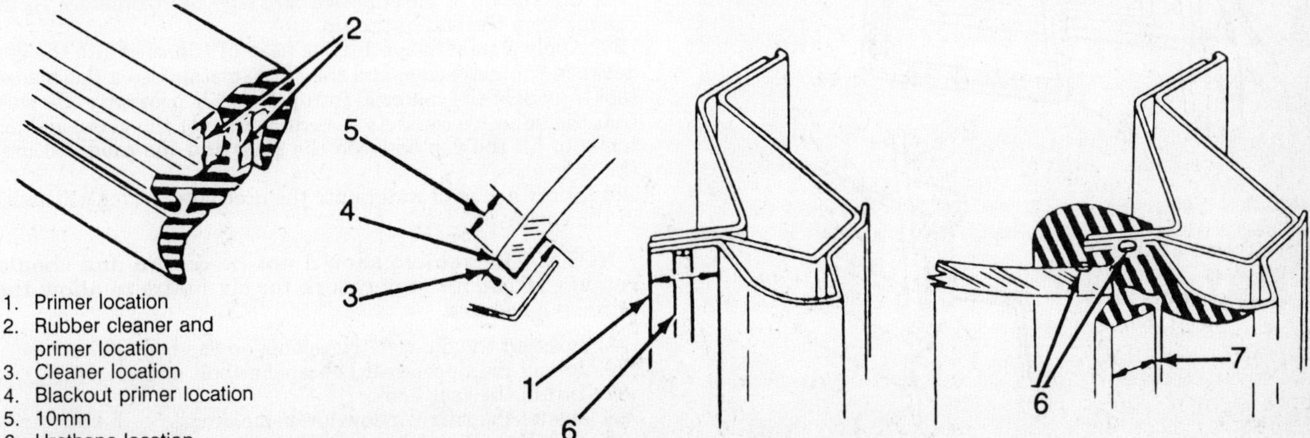

1. Primer location
2. Rubber cleaner and primer location
3. Cleaner location
4. Blackout primer location
5. 10mm
6. Urethane location
7. Rubber lubricant location

R/V series windshield primer and adhesive locations

NOTE: The glass must be installed within 20 minutes of applying the urethane!

8. Spray the urethane with water, wetting it completely.
9. Install the weatherstripping on the pinchweld flange.
10. Apply a 5mm diameter bead of urethane adhesive in the glass channel of the weatherstripping.
11. Position the glass in the windshield opening.
12. Coat the lockstrip channel with a rubber lubricant and work it over the glass, locking it in place.
13. Install the reveal moldings. Remove the protective tape covering the butyl adhesive on the underside of the molding. Push the molding caps onto each end of one of the reveal moldings. Press the lip of the molding into the urethane adhesive while holding it against the edge of the windshield. Take care to seat the molding in the corners. The lip must fully contact the adhesive and the gap must be entirely covered by the crown of the molding. Slide the molding caps onto the adjacent moldings. Use tape to hold the molding in position until the adhesive cures.

NOTE: The vehicle should not be driven and should remain at room temperature for six hours to allow the adhesive to cure.

Stationary Body Side Window C and K Series Extended Cab

REPLACEMENT

NOTE: Bonded windows require special tools and special removal procedures to be removed without being broken. For this reason we recommend that you refer all removal and installation to a qualified technician.

CAUTION

Always wear heavy gloves when handling glass to reduce the risk of injury.

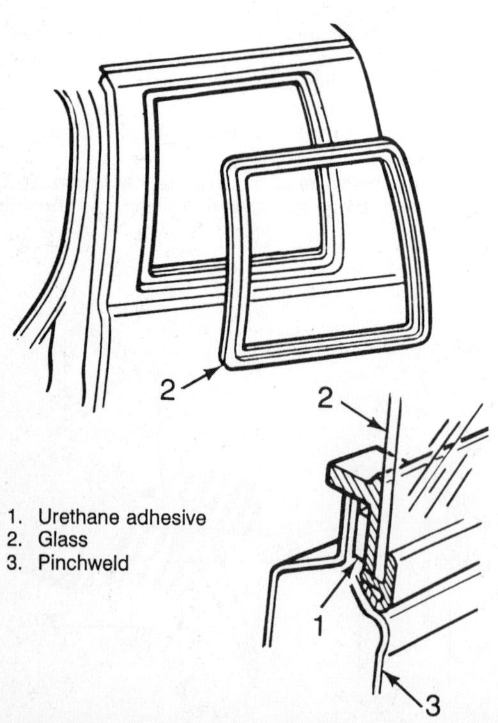

C/K series extended cab stationary side glass

Special tool J-24402-A, Glass Sealant Remover Knife, or its equivalent is required to perform this procedure.

1. Remove the latch trim cover from the quarter trim panel.
2. Remove the seat mounting bolts and lift out the rear seat.
3. Remove the ashtray and panel pocket.
4. Remove the arm rest.
5. Remove the lower seat belt bolt (retractor side).
6. On the right side, remove the jack and tray.
7. Remove the lower trim panel mounting screws.
8. Remove the lower trim panel.
9. Remove the rear window lower molding.
10. Remove the coat hook.
11. Pry off the cover and remove the upper seat belt anchor bolt.
12. Remove the quarter trim panel by pulling it away from the body pillar.
13. Place the protective covering around the area where the glass will be removed.
14. Cut the molding from the glass with a razor knife.
15. Using J-24402-A cut the windshield from the urethane adhesive. Keep the knife as close to the glass as possible in order to leave a base for the replacement glass.
16. Wipe away an loose adhesive.

To install:

17. If the original glass is to be reinstalled, place it on a protected bench or a holding or holding fixture. Remove any remaining adhesive with a razor blade or a sharp scraper. Any remaining traces of adhesive material can be removed with denatured alcohol or lacquer thinner.

NOTE: When cleaning windshield glass, avoid contacting the edge of the plastic laminate material (on the edge of the glass) with volatile cleaner. Contact may cause discoloration and deterioration of the plastic laminate. Do not use a petroleum based solvent such as gasoline or kerosene. The presence of oil will prevent the adhesion of new material.

To replace the glass, GM adhesive service kit No. 1052420 contains the materials needed.

18. Thoroughly clean the edge of the glass to which the adhesive material will be applied with a clean alcohol dampened cloth. Allow the alcohol to dry.
19. Apply the clear glass primer in the kit to the inner edge of the windshield from the edge of the glass inward ¾ in. (19mm). Apply the primer around the entire perimeter of the glass. Allow the primer to cure for thirty minutes.
20. Apply the blackout primer to the glass in the same area as the clear primer. Allow the blackout primer to dry to the touch.
21. Lift the glass into the opening. Center the glass in the opening, on top of the support molding.
22. Cut the tip of the adhesive cartridge approximately $^{3}/_{16}$ in. (5mm) from the end of the tip.
23. Apply a smooth continuous bead of adhesive into the gap between the glass edge and the sheet metal. Use a flat bladed tool to paddle the material into position if necessary. Be sure that the adhesive contacts the entire edge of the glass, and extends to fill the gap between the glass and the solidified urethane base.
24. Spray a mist of water onto the urethane. Water will assist in the curing process.

NOTE: The vehicle should not be driven and should remain at room temperature for six hours to allow the adhesive to cure.

25. Position the quarter trim panel on the body pillar.
26. Install the upper seat belt anchor bolt and cover.
27. Install the coat hook.
28. Install the rear window lower molding.
29. Install the lower trim panel.
30. Install the lower trim panel mounting screws.
31. On the right side, install the jack and tray.

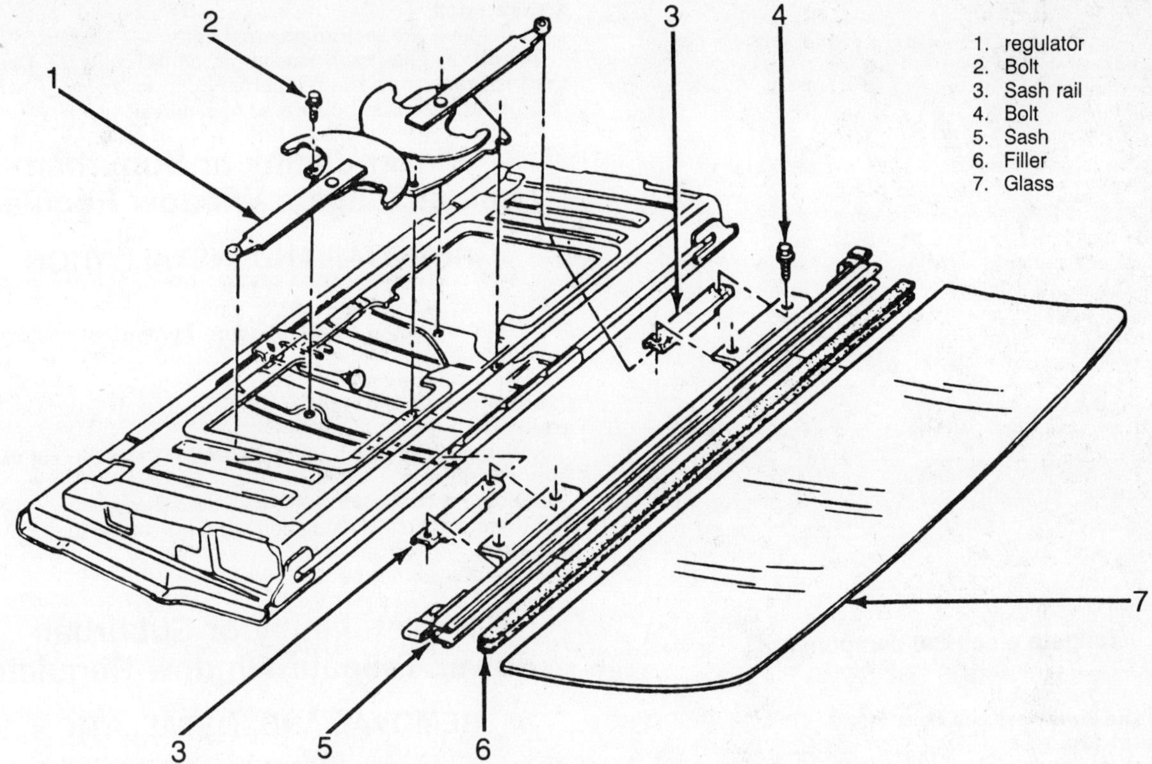

Blazer tailgate window and related components

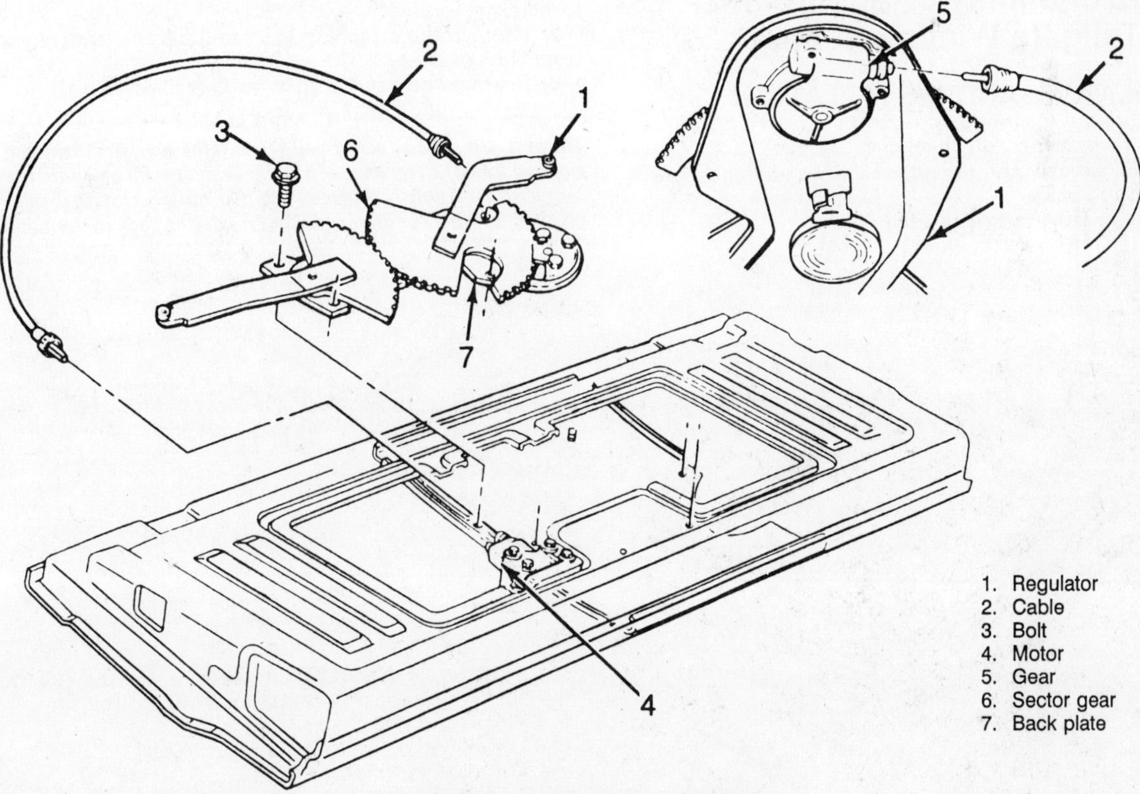

Tailgate power window regulator

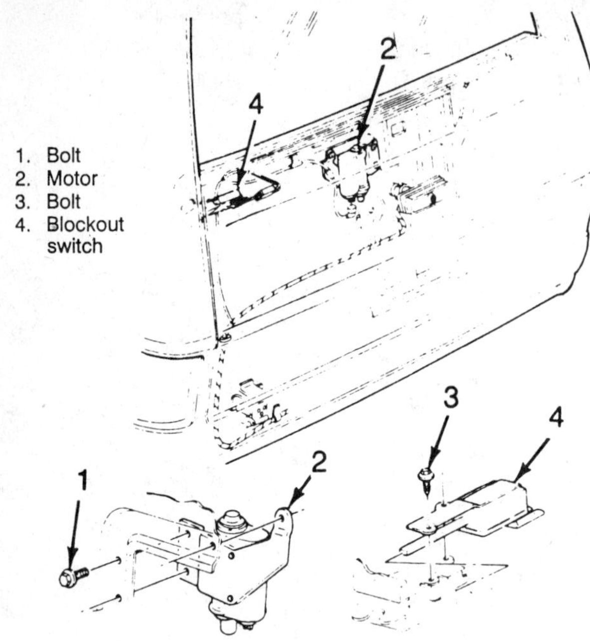

Tailgate electrical components

32. Install the lower seat belt bolt.
33. Install the arm rest.
34. Install the ashtray and panel pocket.
35. Install the seat.
36. Install the latch trim cover.

Blazer/Jimmy or Suburban Tailgate Window Glass

REMOVAL AND INSTALLATION

1. Remove the window run channel caps.
2. Lower the window and pry out the inner and outer glass seals. They clip in place.
3. Remove the tailgate cover plate.
4. Raise the window so that the window sash channel bolts are accessible.
5. Remove the sash-to-channel bolts.
6. Pull the glass/sash assembly from the tailgate. Disconnect the sash rails from the regulator.
7. Installation is the reverse of removal.

Blazer/Jimmy or Suburban Manual Tailgate Window Regulator

REMOVAL AND INSTALLATION

1. Remove the tailgate cover plate.
2. Disconnect the tailgate handle control rod from the handle.
3. Remove the handle.
4. Disconnect the right and left latch rods from the control assembly.
5. Remove the attaching bolts and lift the control assembly from the tailgate.
6. Remove the window glass as described above.
7. Remove the attaching bolts and lift the regulator from the tailgate.
8. Installation is the reverse of removal.

Blazer/Jimmy or Suburban Power Tailgate Window Regulator

REMOVAL AND INSTALLATION

1. Remove the tailgate cover plate.
2. Disconnect the tailgate handle control rod from the handle.
3. Remove the handle.
4. Disconnect the right and left latch rods from the control assembly.
5. Remove the attaching bolts and lift the control assembly from the tailgate.
6. Remove the window glass as described above.

CAUTION

The next step must be performed before if the gearbox is removed or disengaged from the regulator arms. The regulator lift arms are under tension from the counterbalance spring and can cause serious injury if the gearbox is removed without locking the sector gear in position.

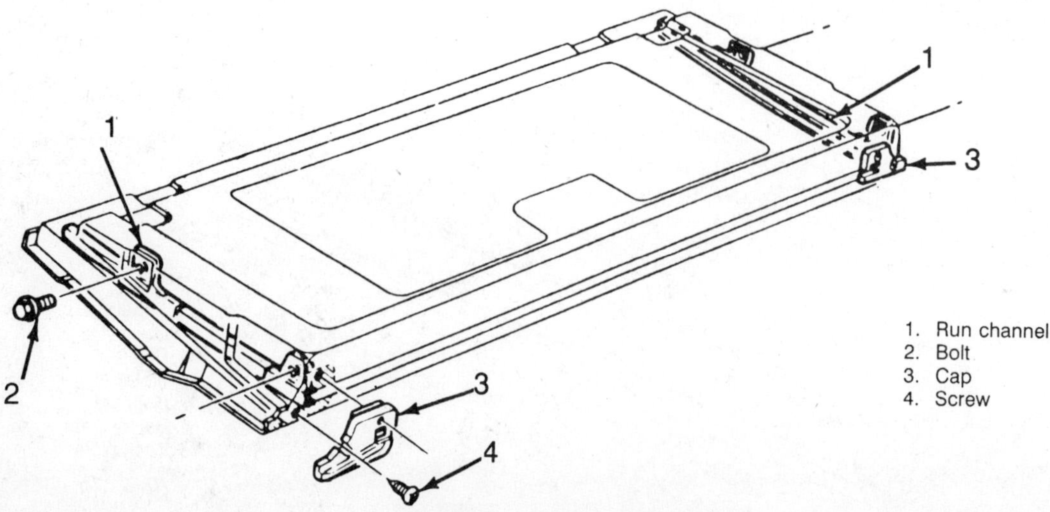

Blazer tailgate run channel

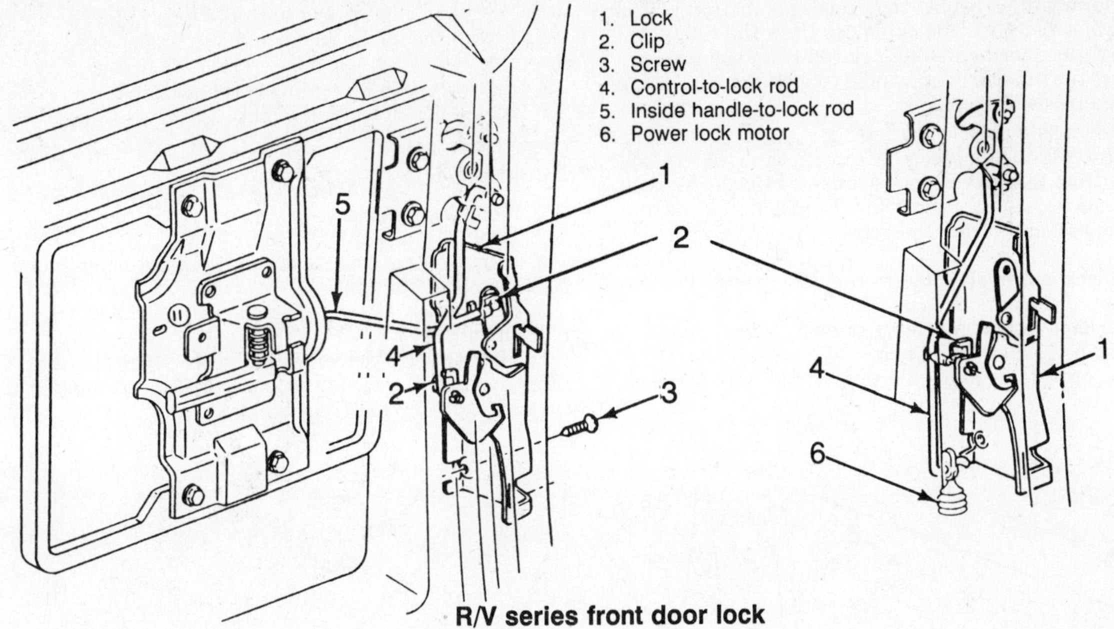

R/V series front door lock

7. Drill a ⅛ in. hole through the regulator sector gear and back plate. Install a pan head sheet metal tapping screw in the drilled hole to lock the sector gear in position.
8. Disconnect the drive cable at the regulator.
9. Remove the attaching bolts and lift the regulator from the tailgate.
10. Unbolt the gear assembly from the regulator.

To install:

11. Assemble the gearbox and regulator.
12. Install the regulator in the tailgate.
13. Connect the drive cable at the regulator.
14. Remove the head sheet metal tapping screw used to lock the sector gear in position.
15. Install the window glass as described above.
16. Install the control assembly in the tailgate.
17. Connect the right and left latch rods at the control assembly.
18. Install the handle.
19. Connect the tailgate handle control rod at the handle.
20. Install the tailgate cover plate.

Blazer/Jimmy or Suburban Tailgate Window Motor and Blockout Switch

REMOVAL AND INSTALLATION

1. Remove the tailgate cover plate.
2. Disconnect the wiring harness at the motor and switch.
3. Disconnect the cable from the motor.
4. Remove the attaching bolts and lift out the motor.
5. Remove the attaching screws, disconnect the latch rods and remove the latch, containing the blockout switch.
6. Installation is the reverse of removal.

Door Lock Cylinder

REMOVAL AND INSTALLATION

NOTE: A key code is stamped on the lock cylinder to aid in replacing lost keys.

1. Raise the widow.
2. Remove the door trim panel.
3. Slide the lock cylinder retaining clip off of the cylinder.
4. Remove the lock cylinder from the door.
5. Installation is the reverse of removal.

Door Lock Assembly

REMOVAL AND INSTALLATION

R and V Series

1. Raise the window completely.
2. Remove the door trim panel.

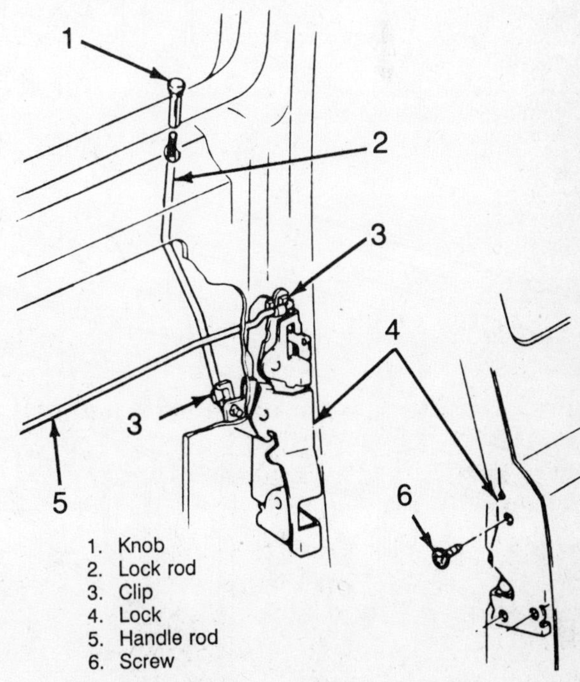

R/V series rear side door lock

3. Using a suitable flat bladed tool, push on the top of the door lock rod clips and pivot the clip away from the rod.
4. Disconnect the door handle to lock rod from the lock.
5. Disconnect the outside door handle to lock rod clip, using the same procedure as in step 3.
6. Remove the inside door lock knob.
7. Remove the door to lock assembly screws, then tilt the lock assembly away from the outside lock cylinder. Pull the lock assembly downward to make clearance for the inside lock rod and remove the lock assembly from the door.

To install:

8. Align the lock rod to the hole in the door panel. Tilt the lock assembly onto the outside lock cylinder.
9. Install the door to lock assembly screws.
10. Install the inside door lock knob.
11. Install the outside door handle to lock rod onto the lock assembly.
12. Pivot the clip up and onto the lock rod.
13. Install the inside door handle to the lock rod onto the lock assembly.
14. Pivot the clip up and onto the lock rod.
15. Install the door trim panel.

C and K Series

1. Door trim panel.
2. Peel off the water deflector.
3. Remove the door module attaching screws and tilt the module out at the top.
4. Disconnect the outside handle lock rod from the lock mechanism.
5. Using a screwdriver, reach between the glass and door and press down on the top of the lock cylinder assembly to disengage the lock cylinder rod from the cylinder.

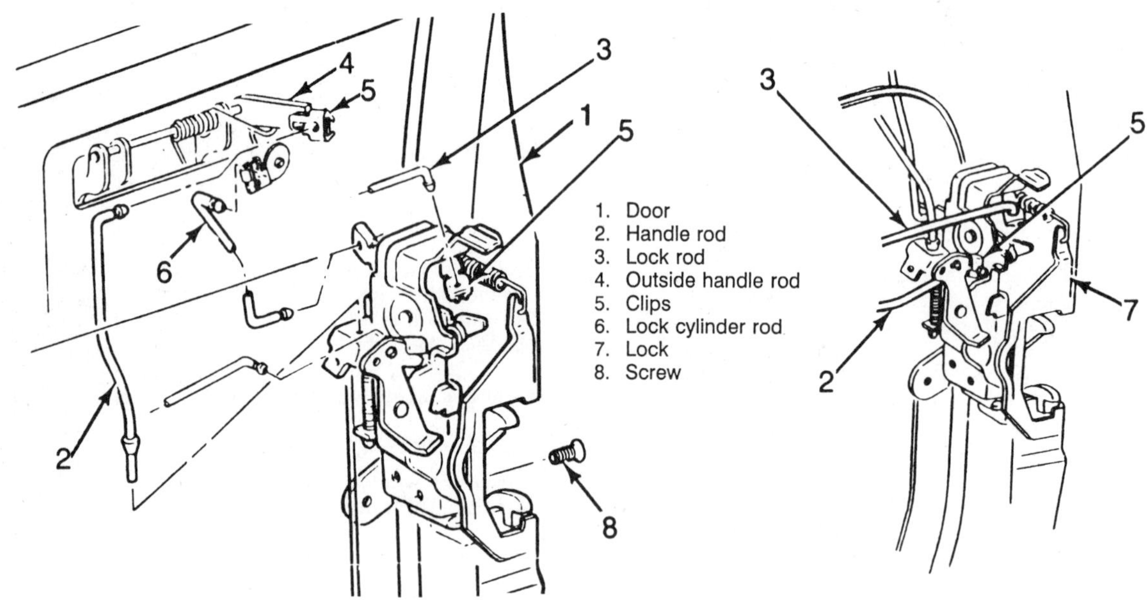

C/K series door lock

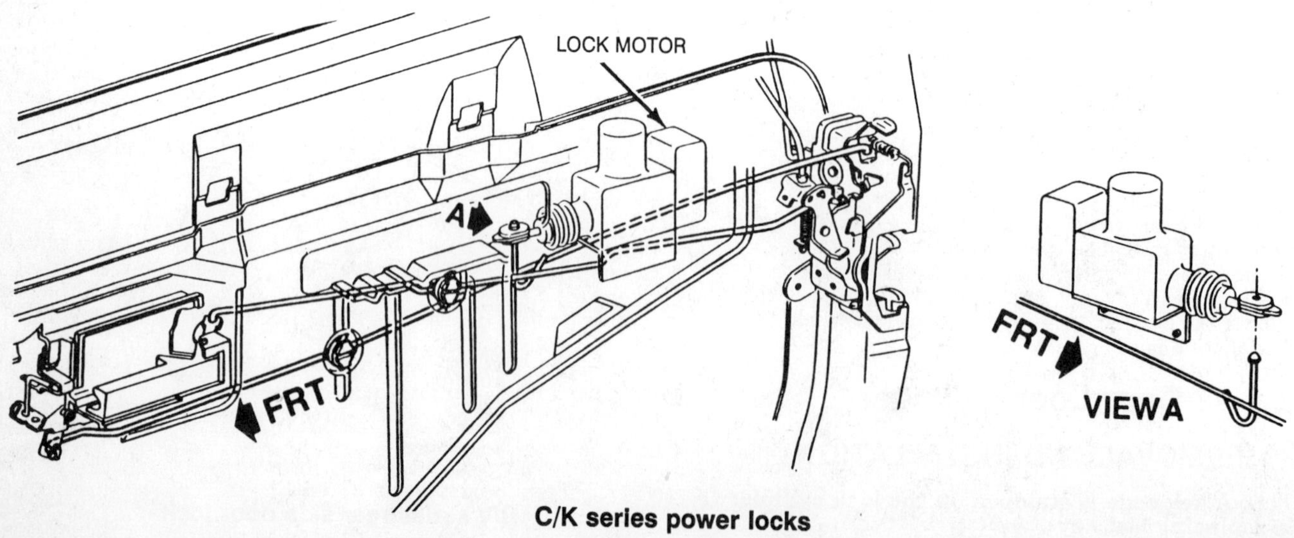

C/K series power locks

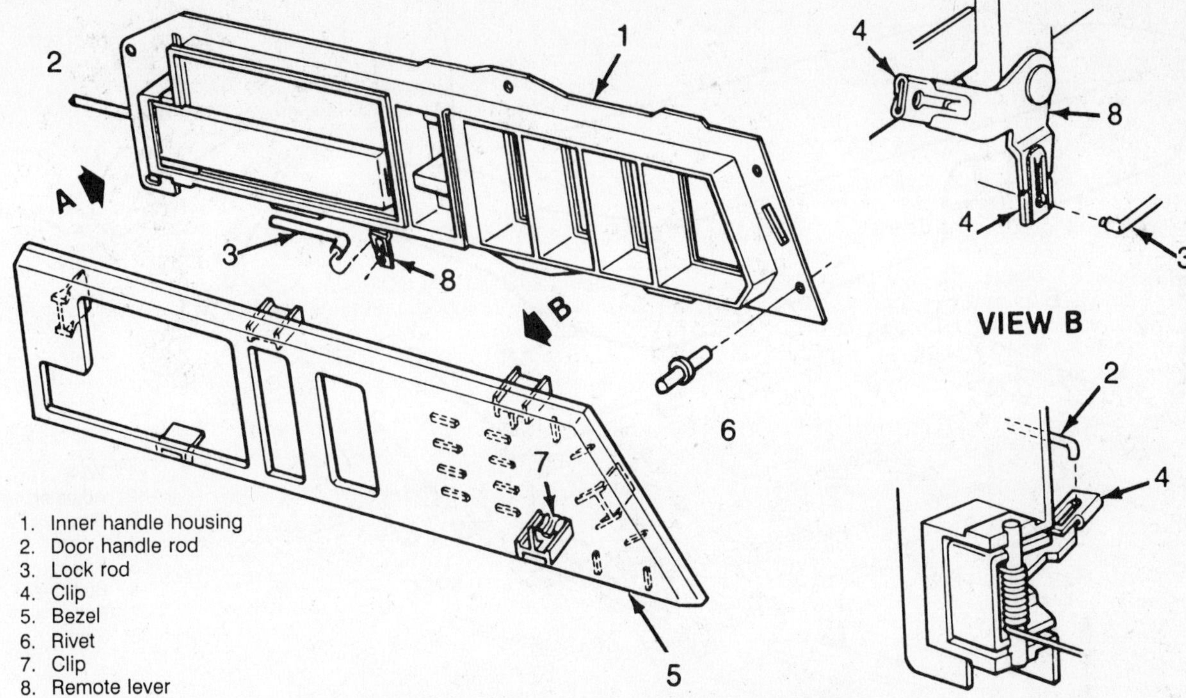

C/K series door inner handle components

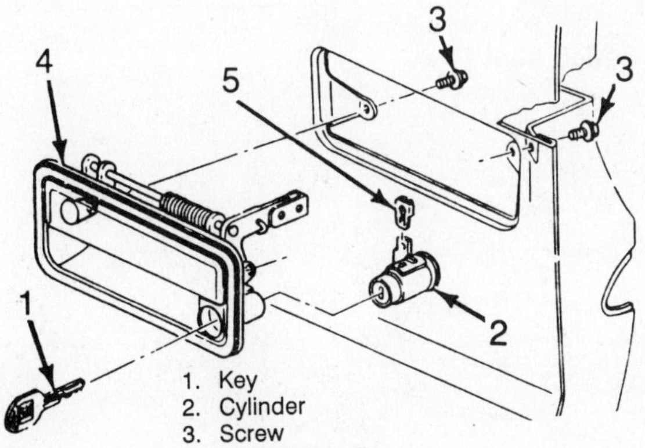

1. Key
2. Cylinder
3. Screw
4. Outside handle
5. Clip

C/K series door lock cylinder and outside handle

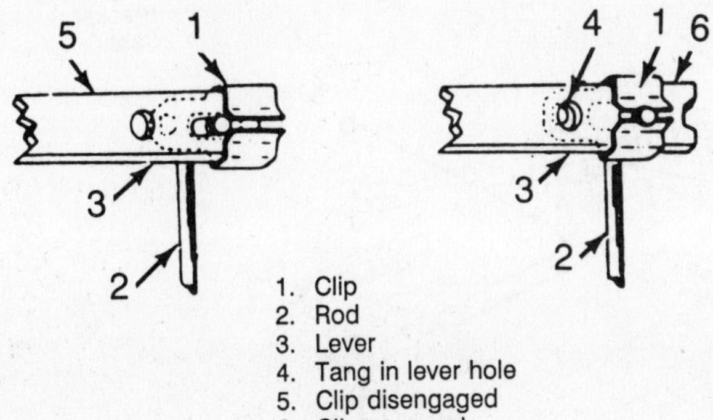

C/K series door clips

6. Remove the lock mechanism attaching screws and remove the mechanism.
7. Installation is the reverse of removal.

Door Module

REMOVAL AND INSTALLATION

C and K Series

1. Disconnect the battery ground cable.
2. Remove the door trim panel.
3. Remove the water deflector by peeling it back.
4. Lower the window all the way.
5. Remove the module attaching screws.
6. Disconnect the door lock rods at the module and tape them to the door.
7. Pull the wiring harness towards the door to reach the connector. Remove the boot from the wiring and disconnect the harness at the door hinge pillar. Push the harness into the door.
8. Loosen the upper run channel bolt.
9. Move the run channel away from the glass.
10. Remove the module and window assembly from the door frame by tilting it and lowering it from the door.

To install:

11. Fit the glass into the rear channel in the door, then, while pulling the channel towards the glass, fit the glass into the front run channel.
12. Install the boot on the wiring and connect the harness at the door hinge pillar.
13. Install the lower run channel bolt.
14. Install the door lock rods at the module.
15. Install the module panel screws, starting at the top left, then the top right.
16. Install the water deflector.
17. Tighten the upper run channel bolt.
18. Install the trim panel on the door.

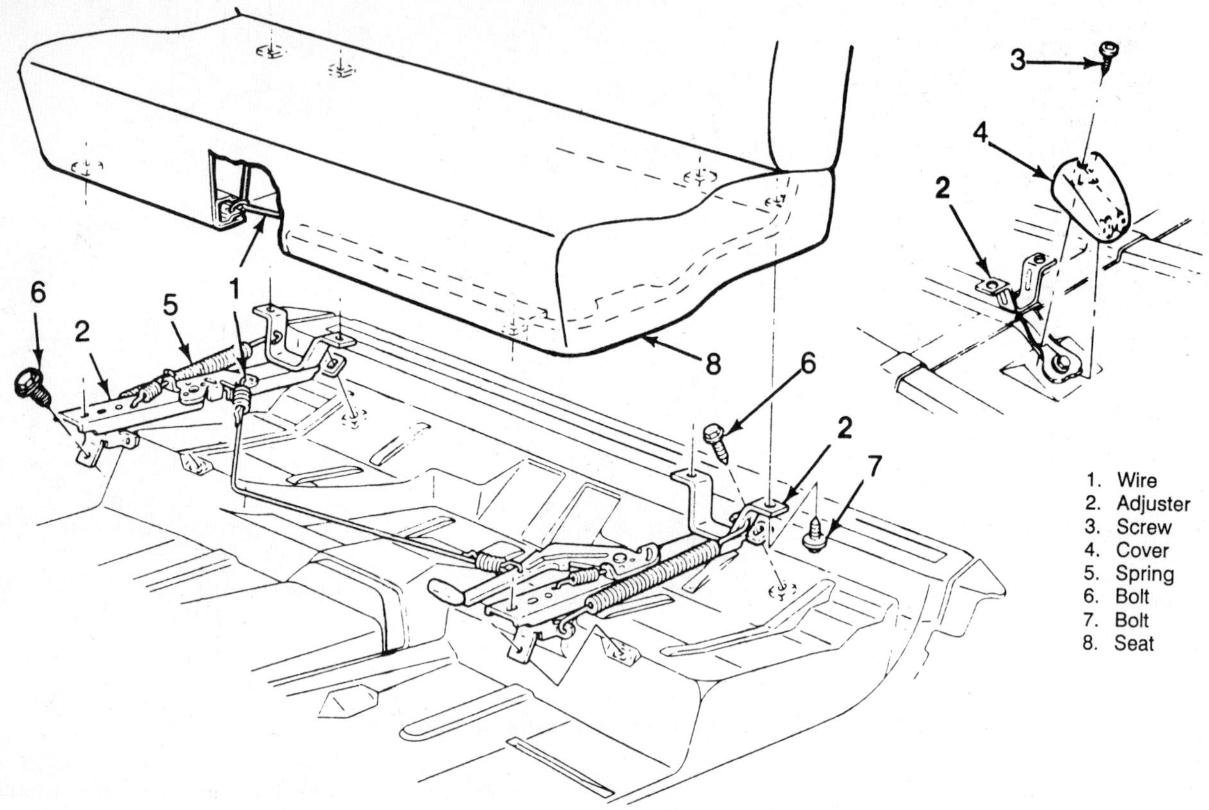

R/V series front bench seat

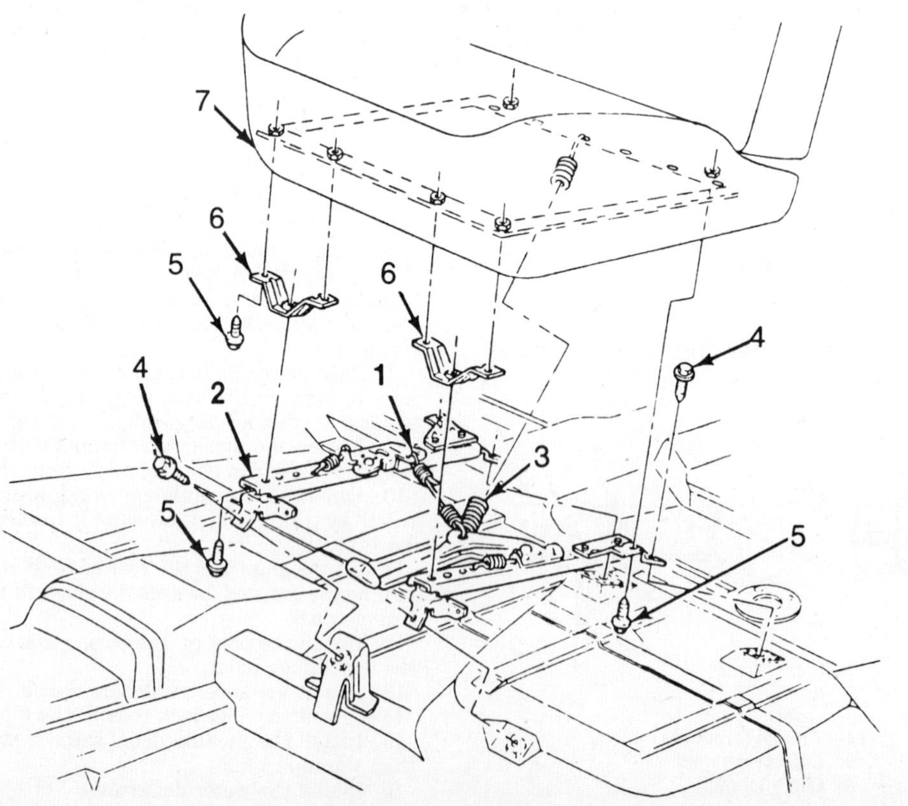

R/V series bucket seat

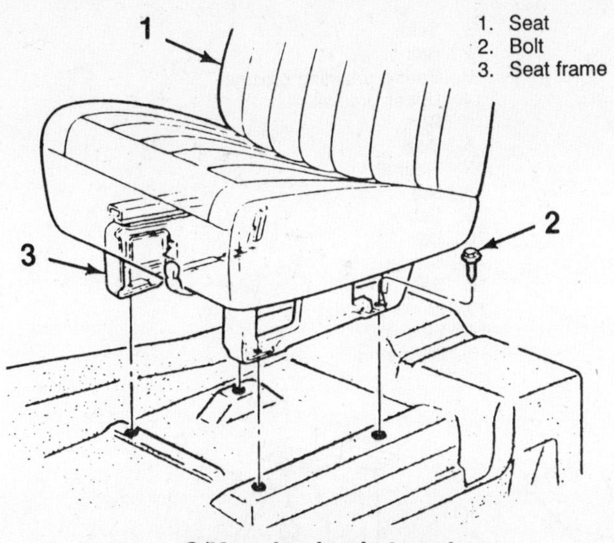

C/K series bucket seat

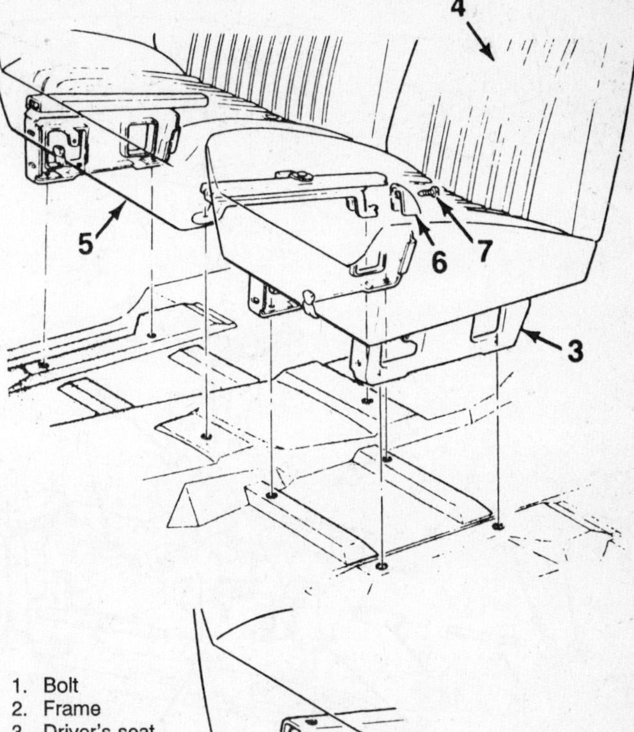

C/K series split front bench seat

Inside Rear View Mirror

REPLACEMENT

1. Remove the screw retaining the mirror to its glass mounted bracket.
2. Install the mirror to the bracket and tighten as necessary.

Front Seats

REMOVAL AND INSTALLATION

R and V Series
Except Blazer/Jimmy Passenger's Bucket Seat

1. Remove the bolt covers, if so equipped.
2. Remove the seat adjuster to floor panel bolts.

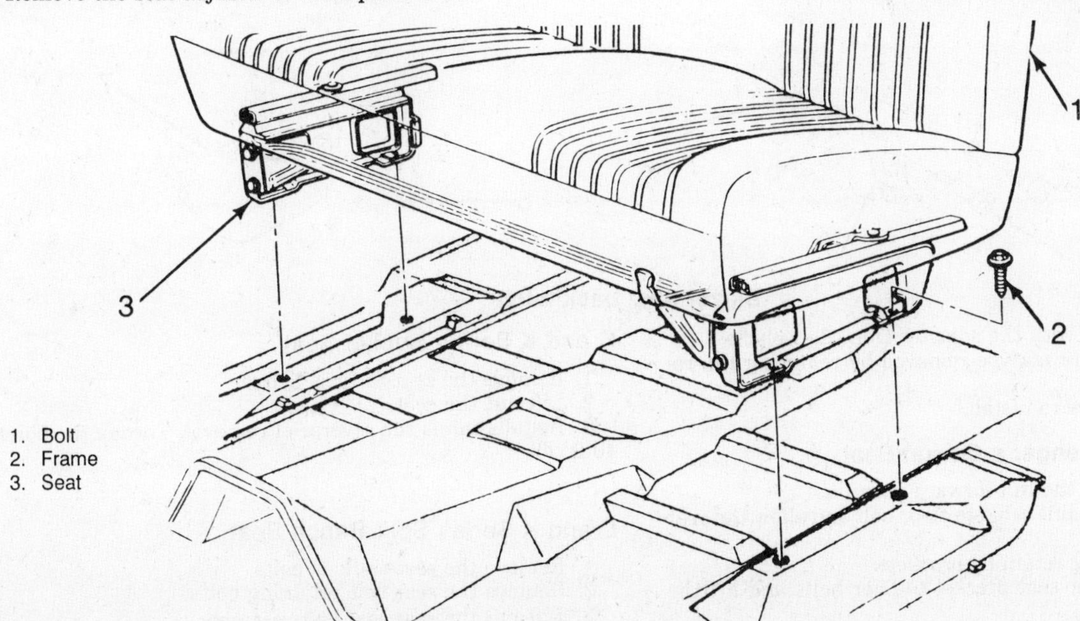

C/K series front bench seat installation

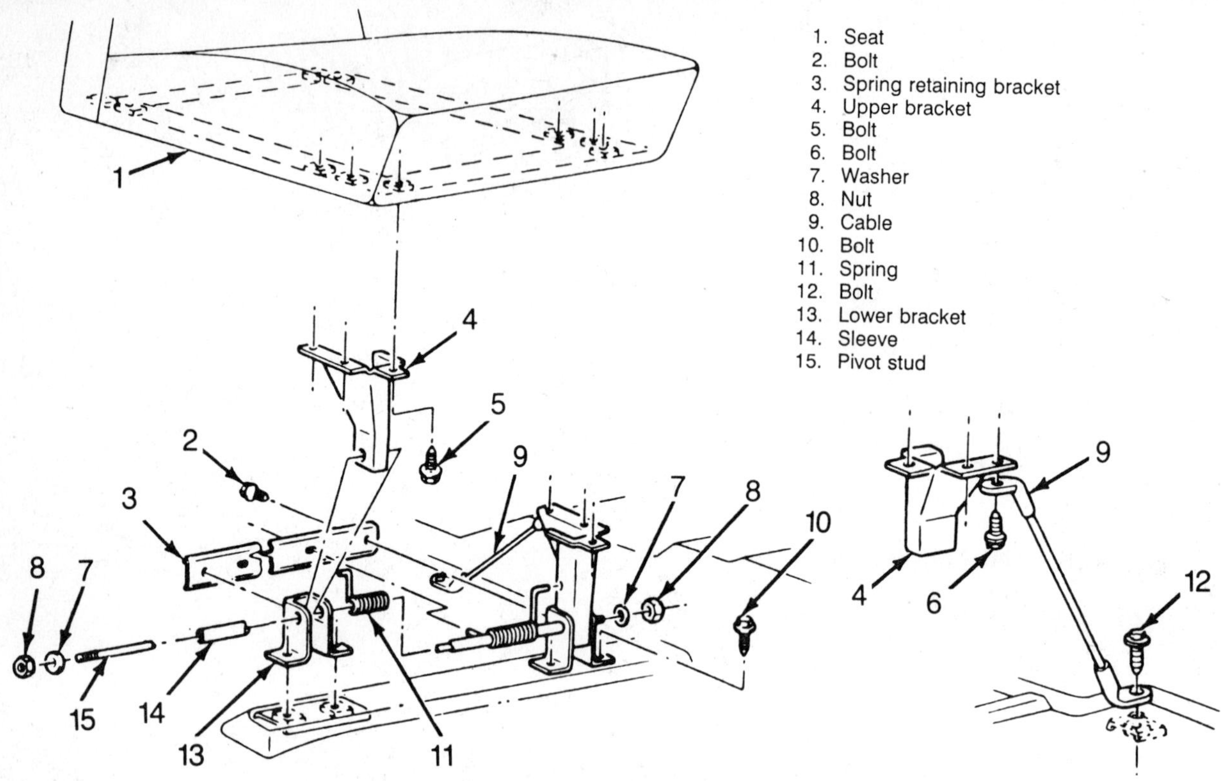

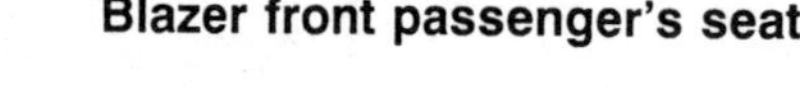
Blazer front passenger's seat

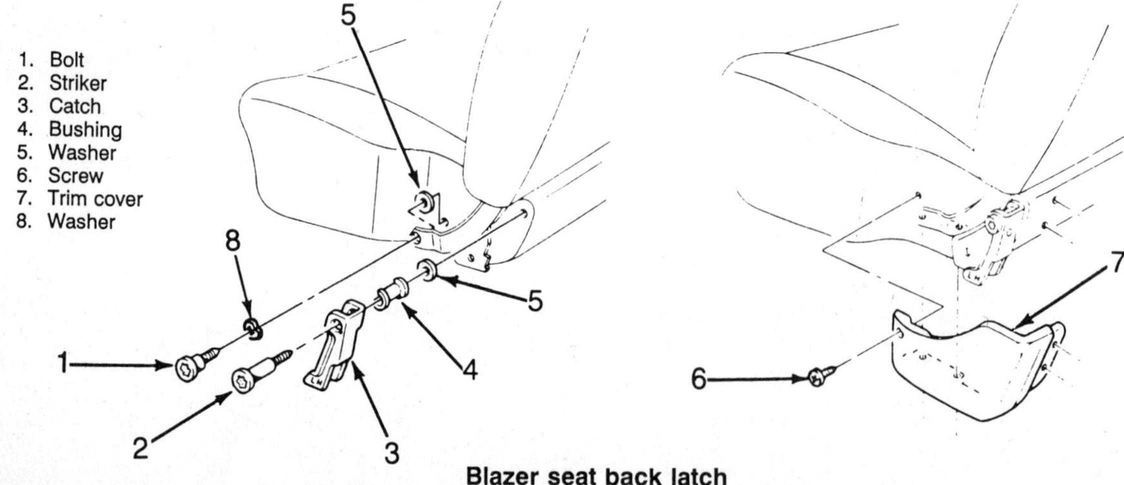

Blazer seat back latch

3. Remove the seat with the adjuster from the vehicle.
4. The seat adjusters may be removed by removing the retaining bolts.
5. Reverse the above to install.

Blazer/Jimmy Passenger's Bucket Seat

1. Place the seat in the full forward position.
2. Remove the restraint cable-to-floor bolt and allow the seat to tip forward.
3. Unbolt the spring retaining brackets.
4. Remove the lower seat bracket-to-floor bolts and lift the seat from the truck.
5. Installation is the reverse of removal. Torque the bolts to 40 ft. lbs.

C and K Series Bucket Seat

1. Remove the seat-to-floor bolts.
2. Lift out the seat.
3. Installation is the reverse of removal. Torque the bolts to 40 ft. lbs.

C and K Series Split Bench Seat

1. Remove the seat-to-floor bolts.
2. Remove the seat belt retaining bolts.
3. Lift out the seat/seat belt assembly.
4. Installation is the reverse of removal. Torque the seat and belt bolts to 40 ft. lbs.

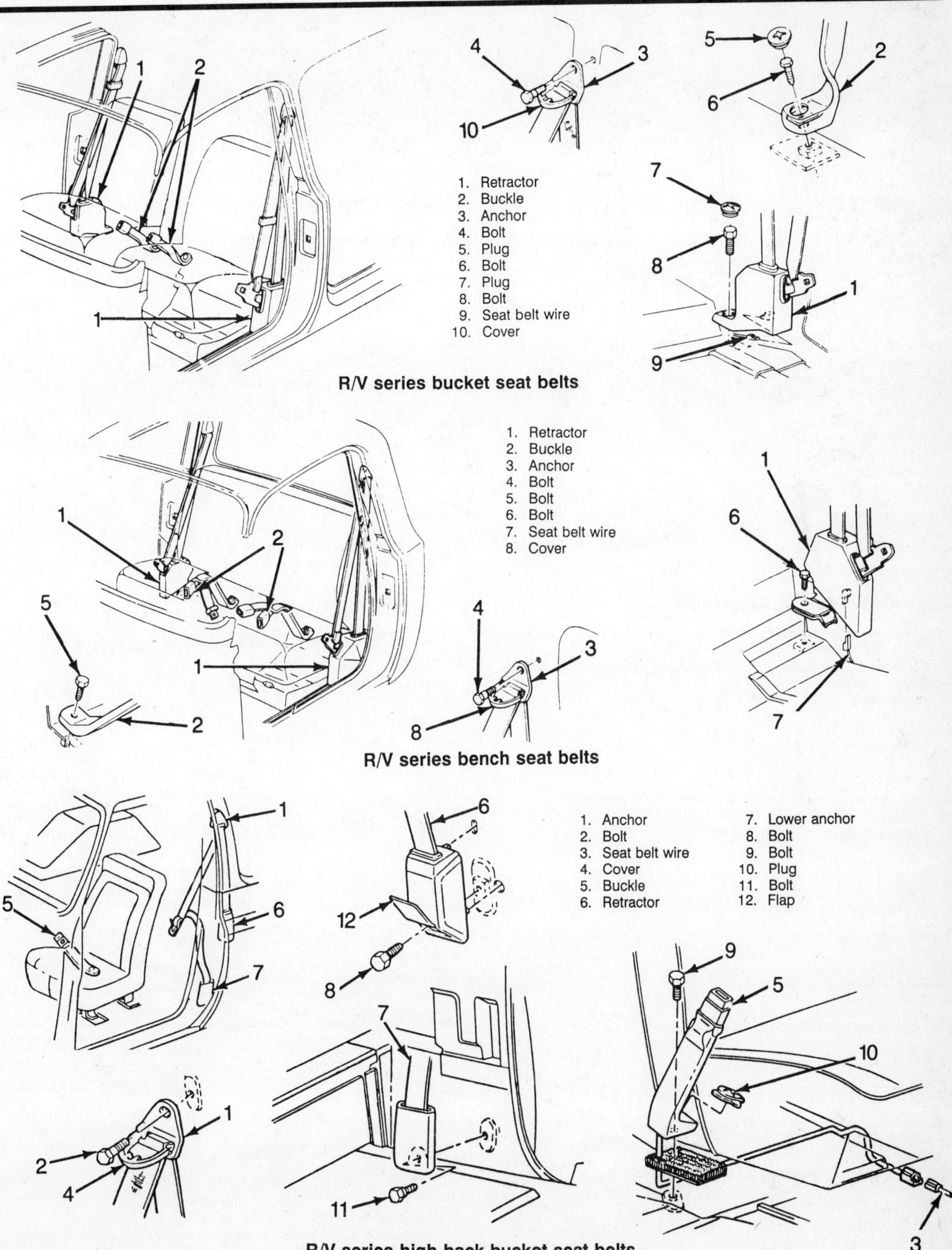

R/V series bucket seat belts

R/V series bench seat belts

R/V series high back bucket seat belts

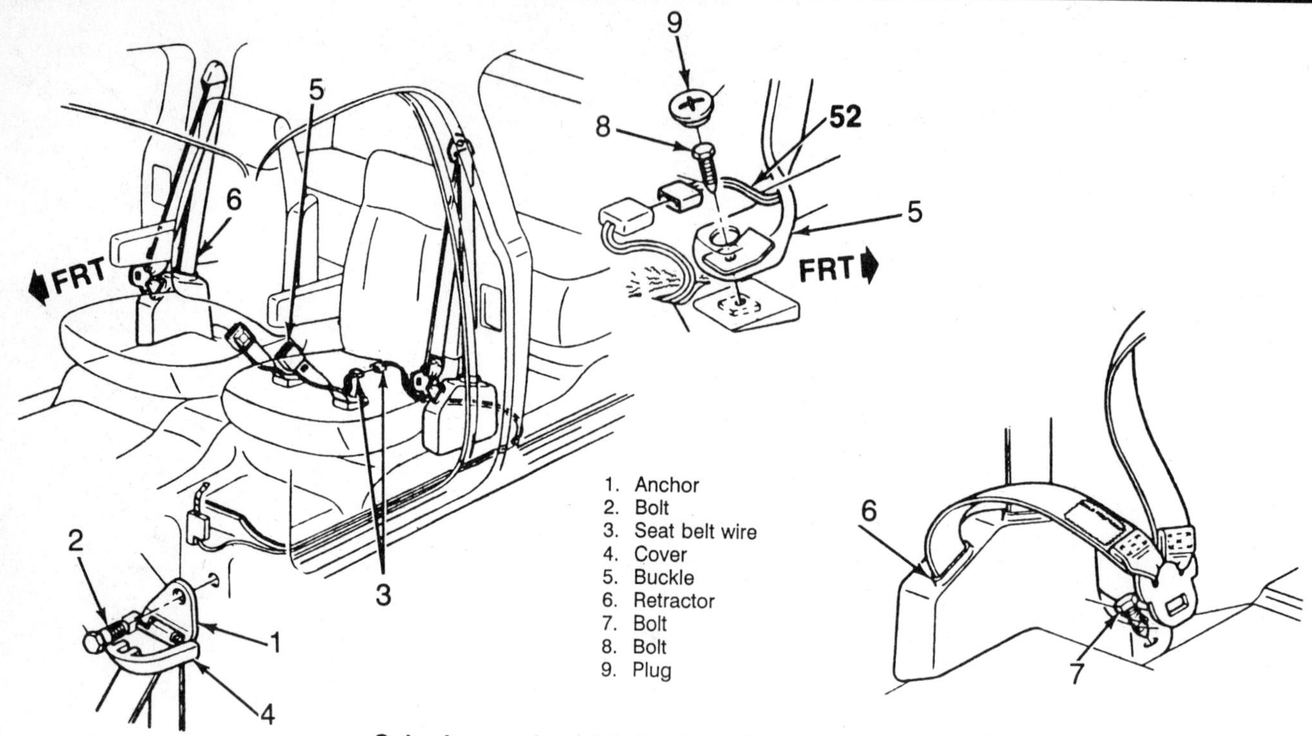

Suburban series high back bucket seat belts

C and K Series Solid Bench Seat

1. Remove the seat-to-floor bolts.
2. Lift out the seat.
3. Installation is the reverse of removal. Torque the bolts to 40 ft. lbs.

Suburban Center Seat

REMOVAL AND INSTALLATION

Seatback

1. Fold the seatback forward.

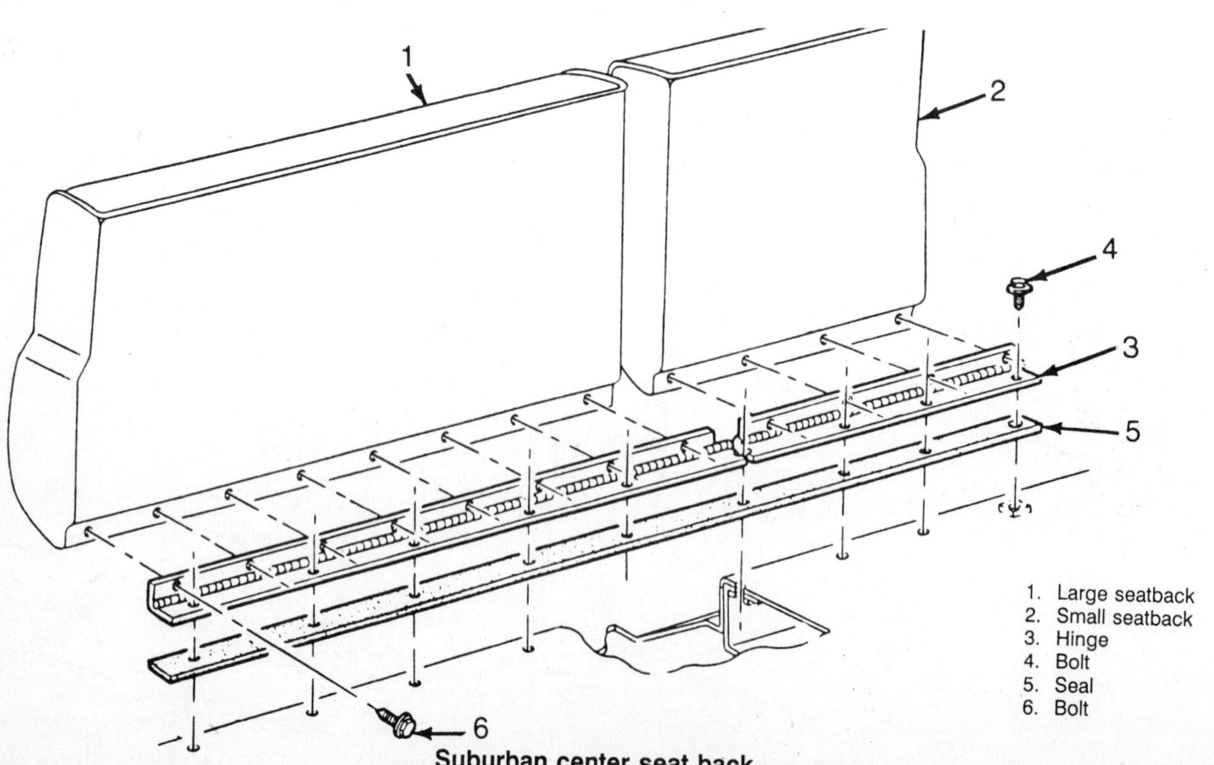

Suburban center seat back

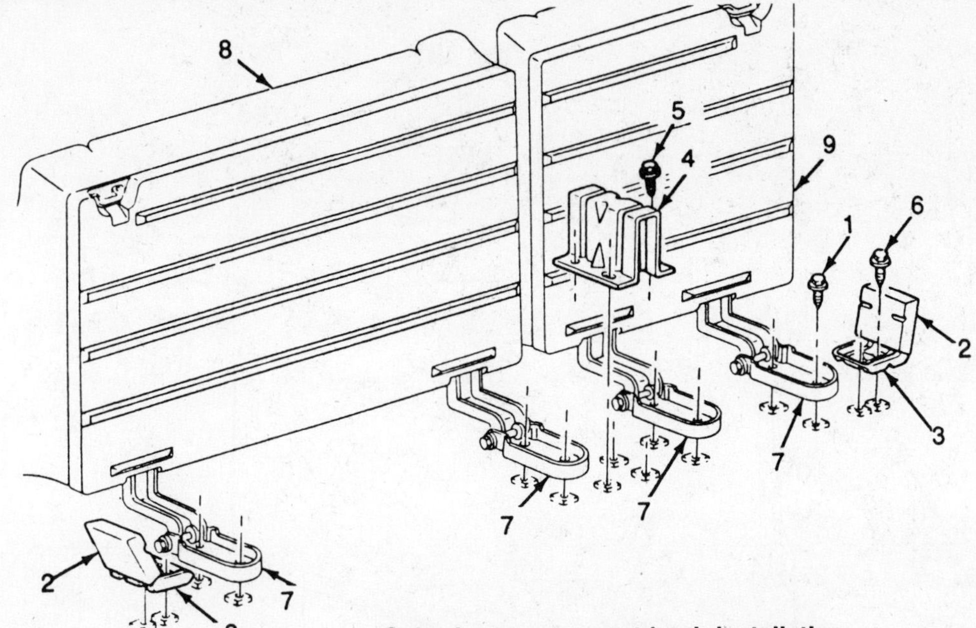

8
5
4
9
6
1
2
3
7
7
7
7
2
3
7
1. Bolt
2. Cover
3. Bracket
4. Stop
5. Bolt
6. Bolt
7. Bracket
8. Large seat
9. Small seat

Suburban center seat back installation

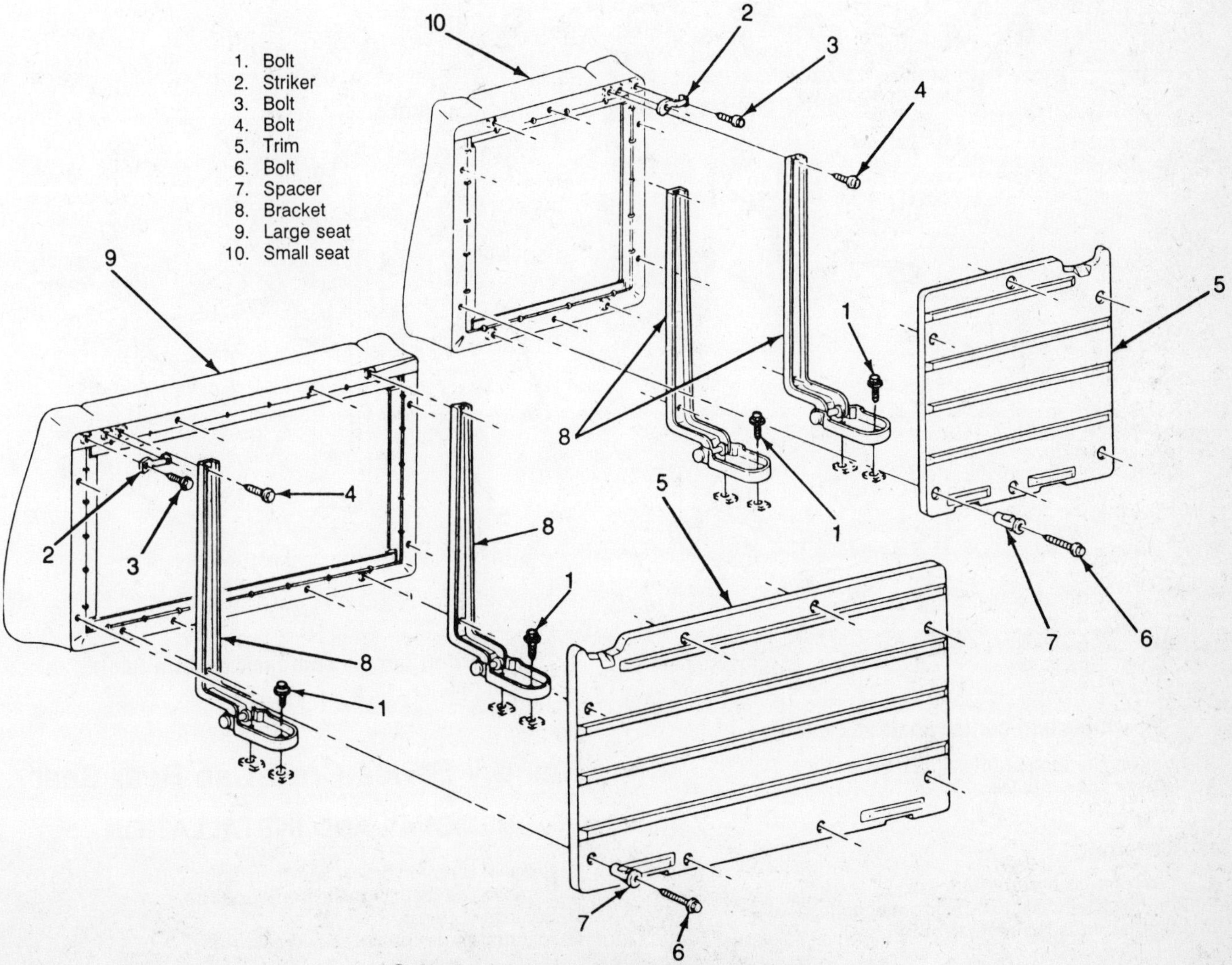

1. Bolt
2. Striker
3. Bolt
4. Bolt
5. Trim
6. Bolt
7. Spacer
8. Bracket
9. Large seat
10. Small seat
10
2
3
4
9
5
1
8
1
5
2
3
4
8
1
8
1
7
6
7
6

Suburban center seat bottom brackets

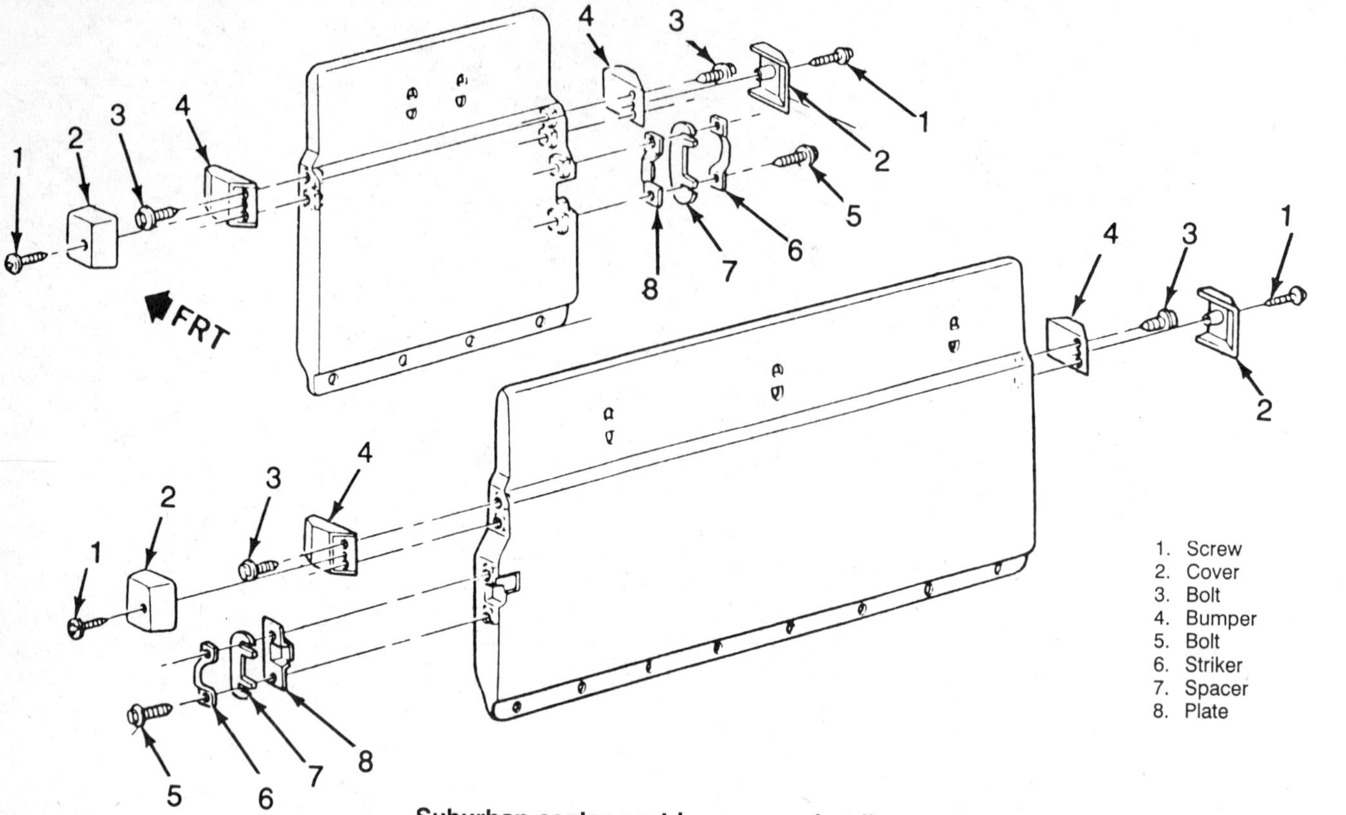

1. Screw
2. Cover
3. Bolt
4. Bumper
5. Bolt
6. Striker
7. Spacer
8. Plate

Suburban center seat bumper and striker

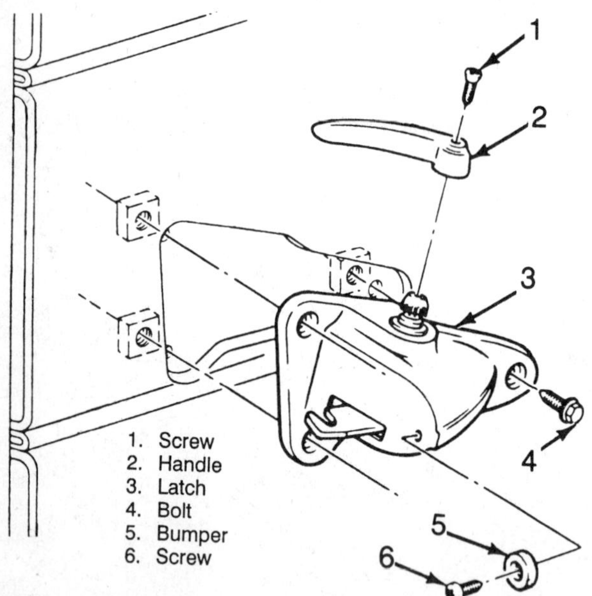

Suburban center seatback latch

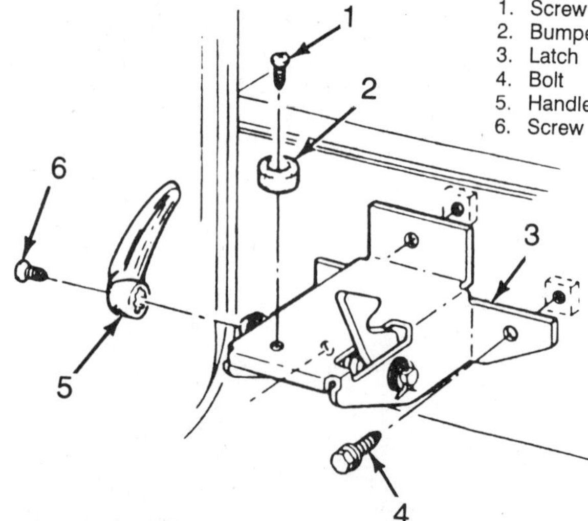

Suburban center seatback bottom latch

2. Remove the hinge-to-floor panel bolts.
3. Remove the seatback.
4. Installation is the reverse of removal.

Seat Bottom

1. Fold the seat bottom forward.
2. Remove the bracket-to-floor panel bolts.
3. Installation is the reverse of removal.

R and V Series Crew Cab Rear Seat

REMOVAL AND INSTALLATION

1. Remove the rear bracket-to-floor bolts.
2. Remove the front bracket-to-floor bolts.
3. Remove the seat.
4. Installation is the reverse of removal.

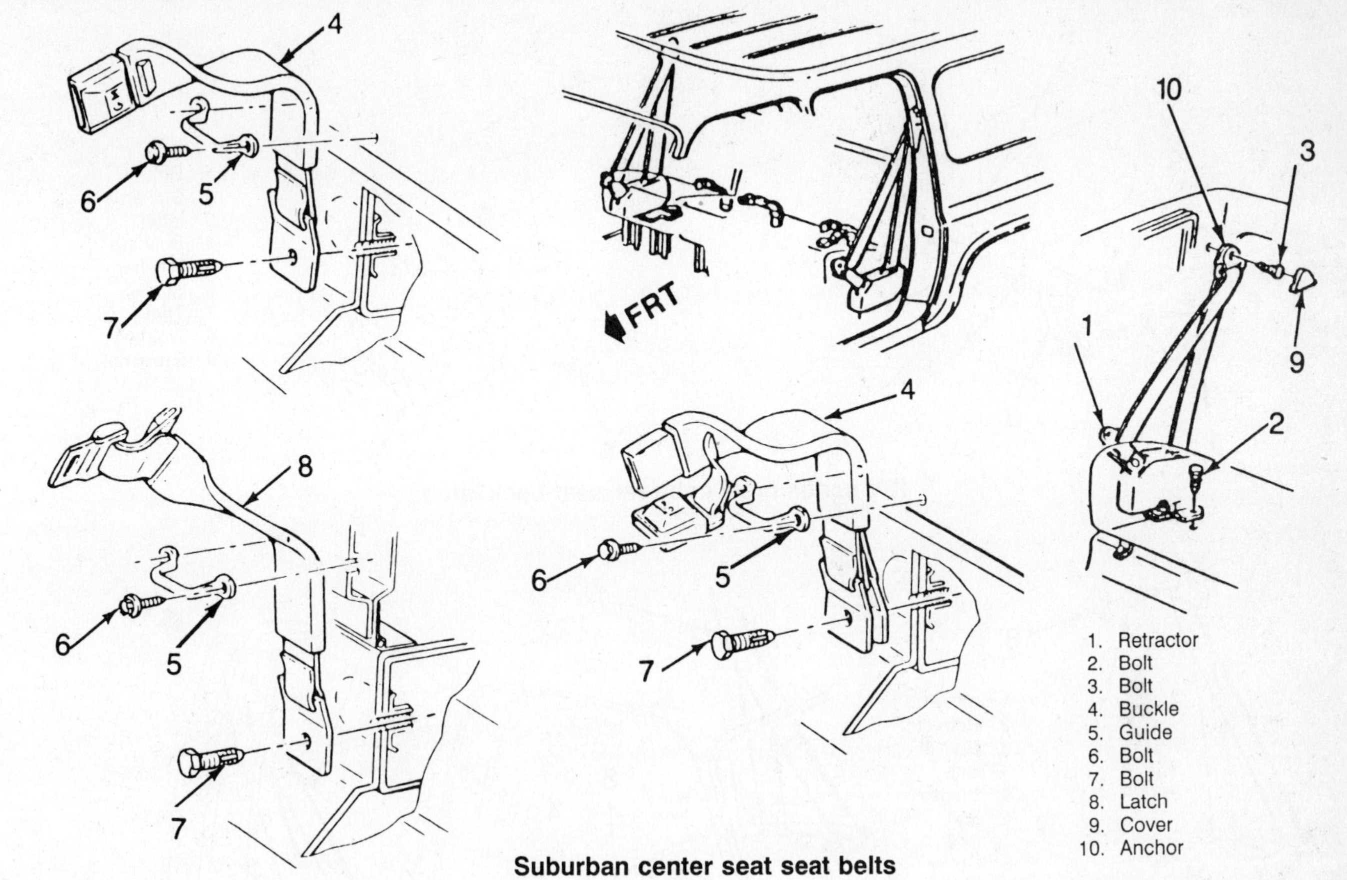

4
10
3
6
5
FRT
7
1
9
2
8
4
6
5
6
5
7
7
1. Retractor
2. Bolt
3. Bolt
4. Buckle
5. Guide
6. Bolt
7. Bolt
8. Latch
9. Cover
10. Anchor

Suburban center seat seat belts

1
2
1. Bolt
2. Rear bracket
3. Bolt
4. Front bracket
5. Bolt
3
4
5
3

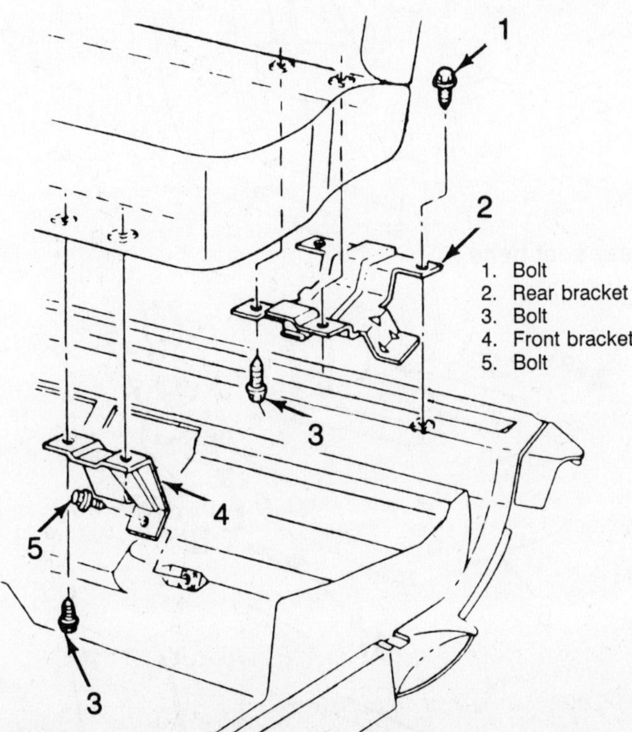

R/V series crew cab rear seats

C and K Series Extended Cab Rear Seat

REMOVAL AND INSTALLATION

1. Remove the seat retaining bolts.
2. Lift out the seat.
3. Installation is the reverse of removal. Torque the bolts to 12 ft. lbs.

Blazer/Jimmy Rear Seat

REMOVAL AND INSTALLATION

1. Fold the seat forward.
2. Remove the hinge-to-floor bolts and spring washers.
3. Lift the seat from the truck.
4. Installation is the reverse of removal.

Suburban Rear Seat

REMOVAL AND INSTALLATION

1. Unlatch the seat and pull it towards the rear of the truck.
2. Installation is the reverse of removal. After latching the seat. Push and pull on it to make sure it's latched.

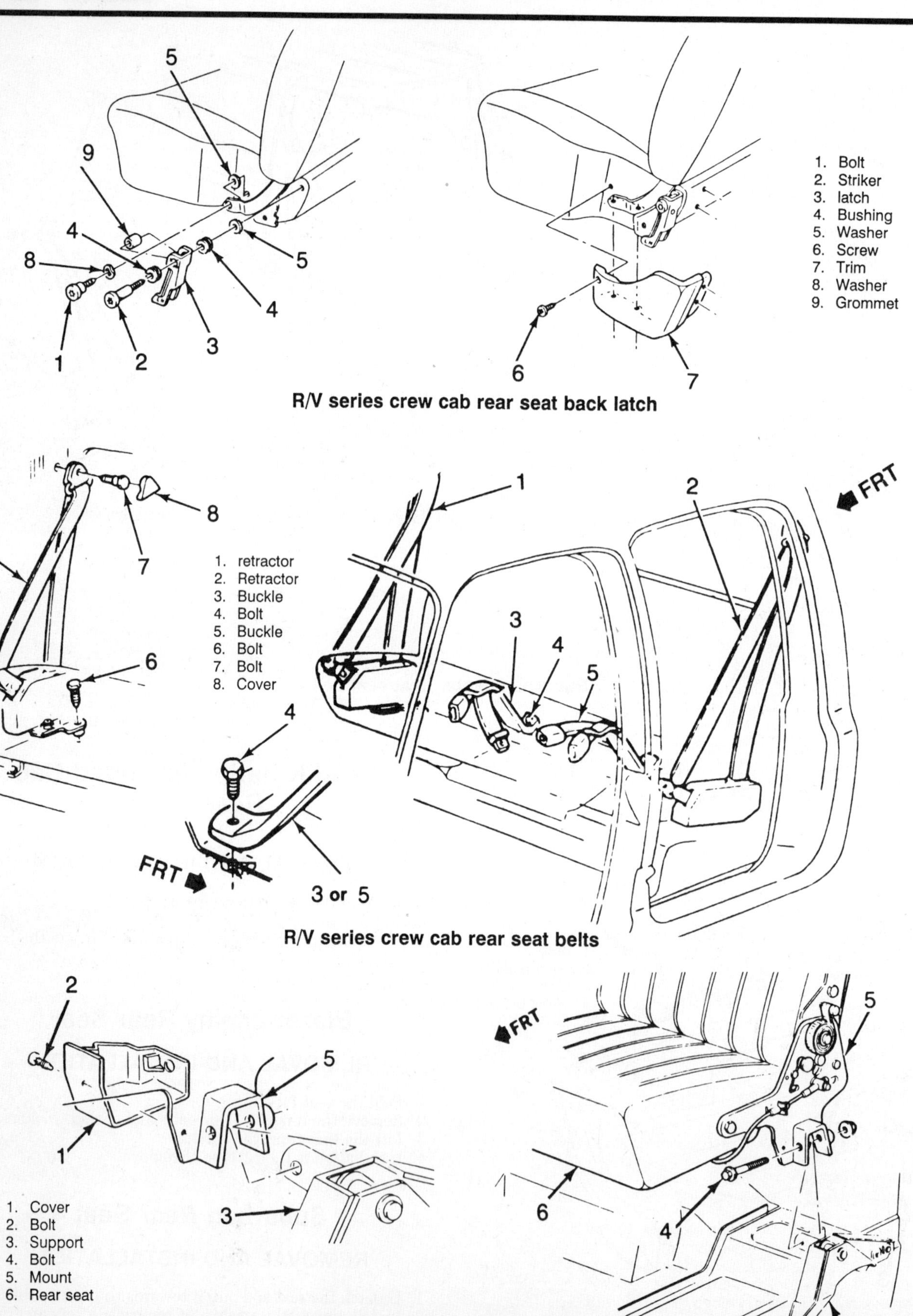

R/V series crew cab rear seat back latch

R/V series crew cab rear seat belts

C/K series extended cab rear seats

1. Weld nuts
2. Bolt
3. Support

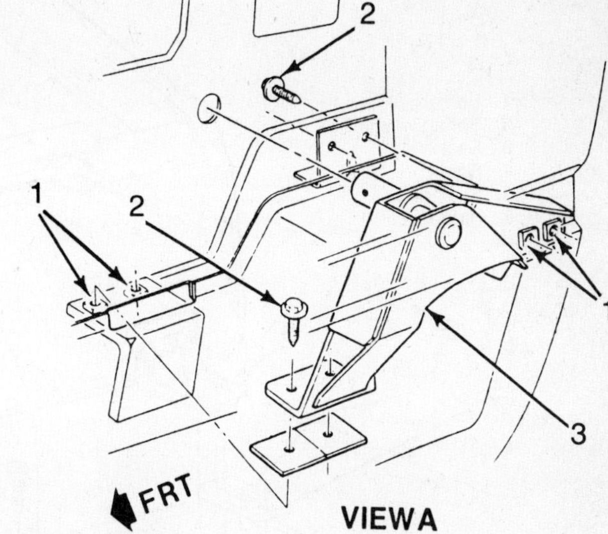

C/K series rear seat support

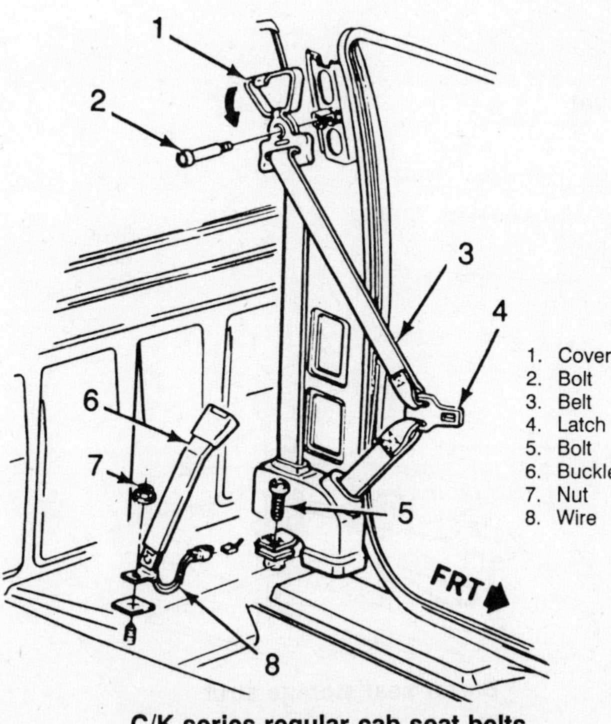

1. Cover
2. Bolt
3. Belt
4. Latch
5. Bolt
6. Buckle
7. Nut
8. Wire

C/K series regular cab seat belts

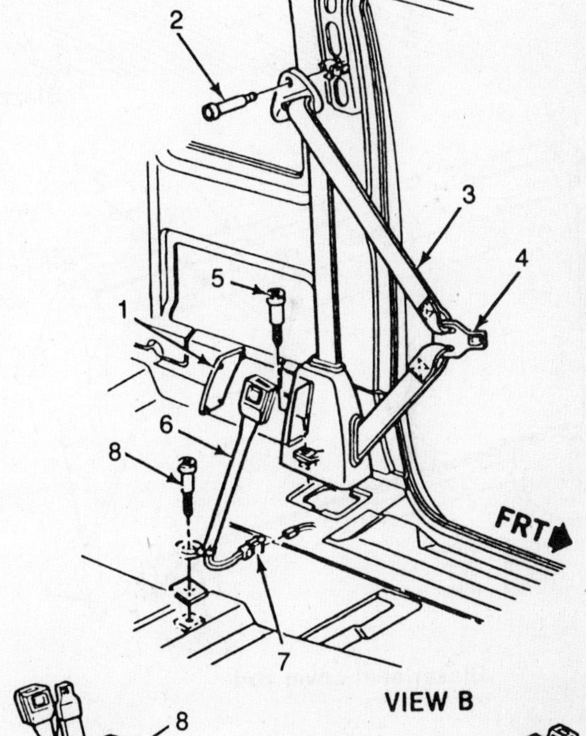

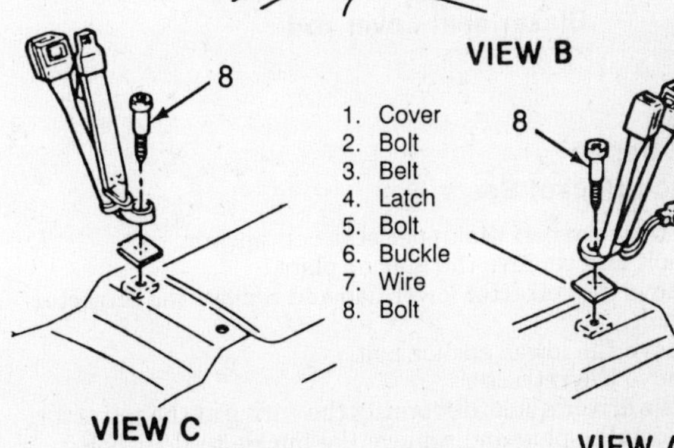

1. Cover
2. Bolt
3. Belt
4. Latch
5. Bolt
6. Buckle
7. Wire
8. Bolt

C/K series extended cab split front seat belt

Seat Belts

REMOVAL AND INSTALLATION

All R and V Series Front Except High Back Bucket Seats

1. Pry the cover off the upper seat belt anchor.
2. Unbolt and remove the anchor plate.
3. Remove the plug and remove the retractor-to-floor bolt.
4. On the driver's side, disconnect the wiring at the retractor.
5. Remove the plug and remove the buckle-to-floor bolt.
6. Installation is the reverse of removal. Torque all bolts to 37 ft. lbs.

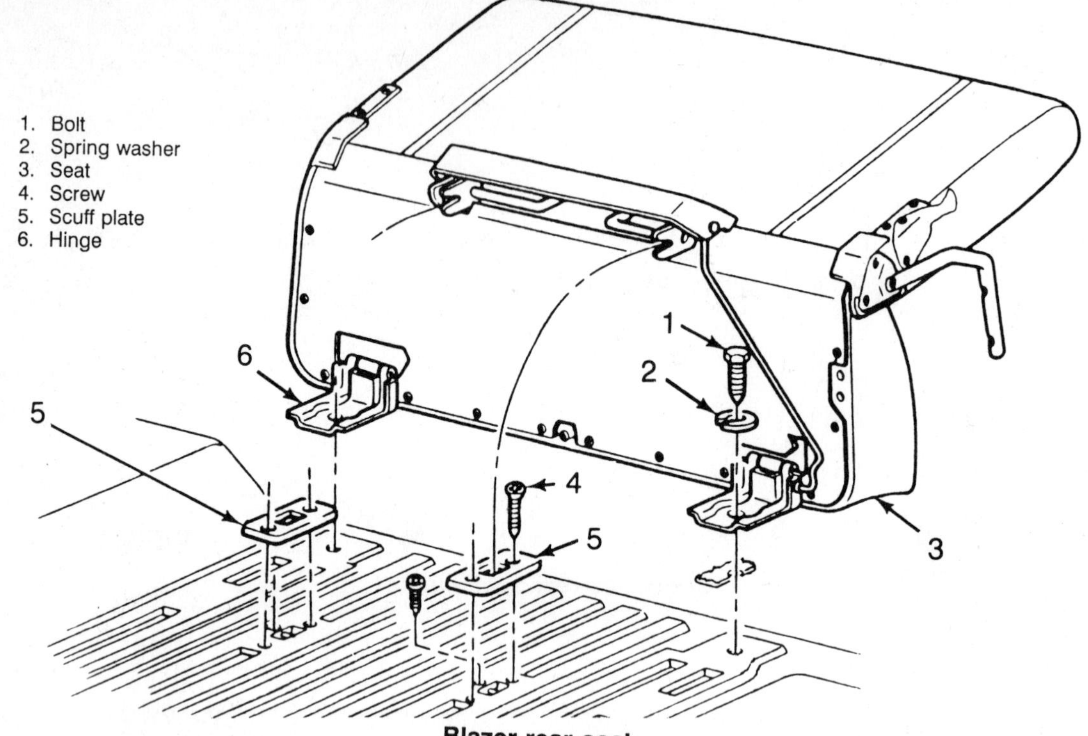

Blazer rear seat

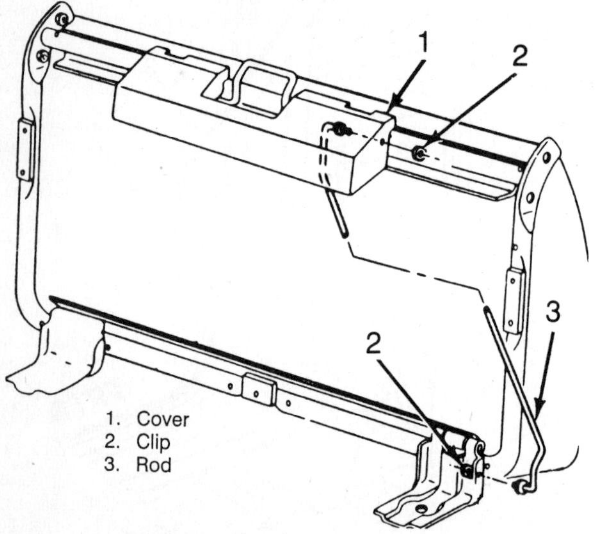

Blazer seat cover rod

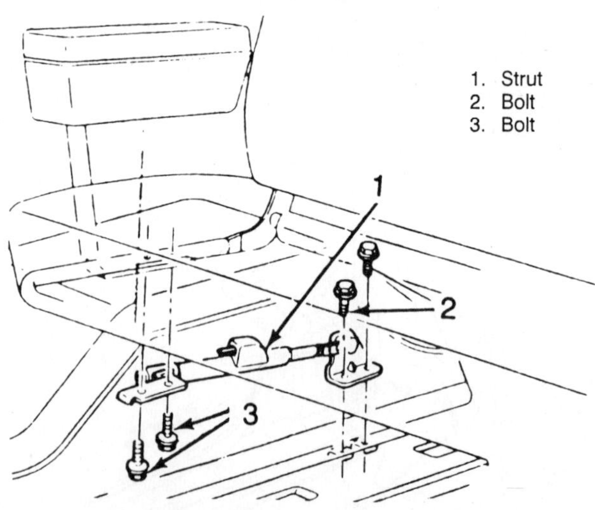

Blazer seat storage strut

R and V Series

High Back Bucket Seats

1. Pry the cover off the upper seat belt anchor.
2. Unbolt and remove the anchor plate.
3. Remove the retractor lower flap and remove the retractor-to-pillar bolt.
4. Remove the lower anchor bolt.
5. Remove the retractor.
6. On the driver's side, disconnect the wiring at the retractor.
7. Remove the plug and remove the buckle-to-floor bolt.
8. Installation is the reverse of removal. Torque all bolts to 37 ft. lbs.

C and K Series

1. Pry the cover off the upper seat belt anchor.
2. Unbolt and remove the anchor plate.
3. Remove the retractor attaching bolts.
4. Unbolt the buckle assemblies from the floor panel.
5. On the driver's side, disconnect the wiring at the retractor.
6. Installation is the reverse of removal. On Regular Cabs, torque the buckle-to-floor panel stud nut to 32 ft. lbs. Torque all nuts and bolts to 40 ft. lbs.

Suburban Center Seat

1. Fold the seat bottoms forward.

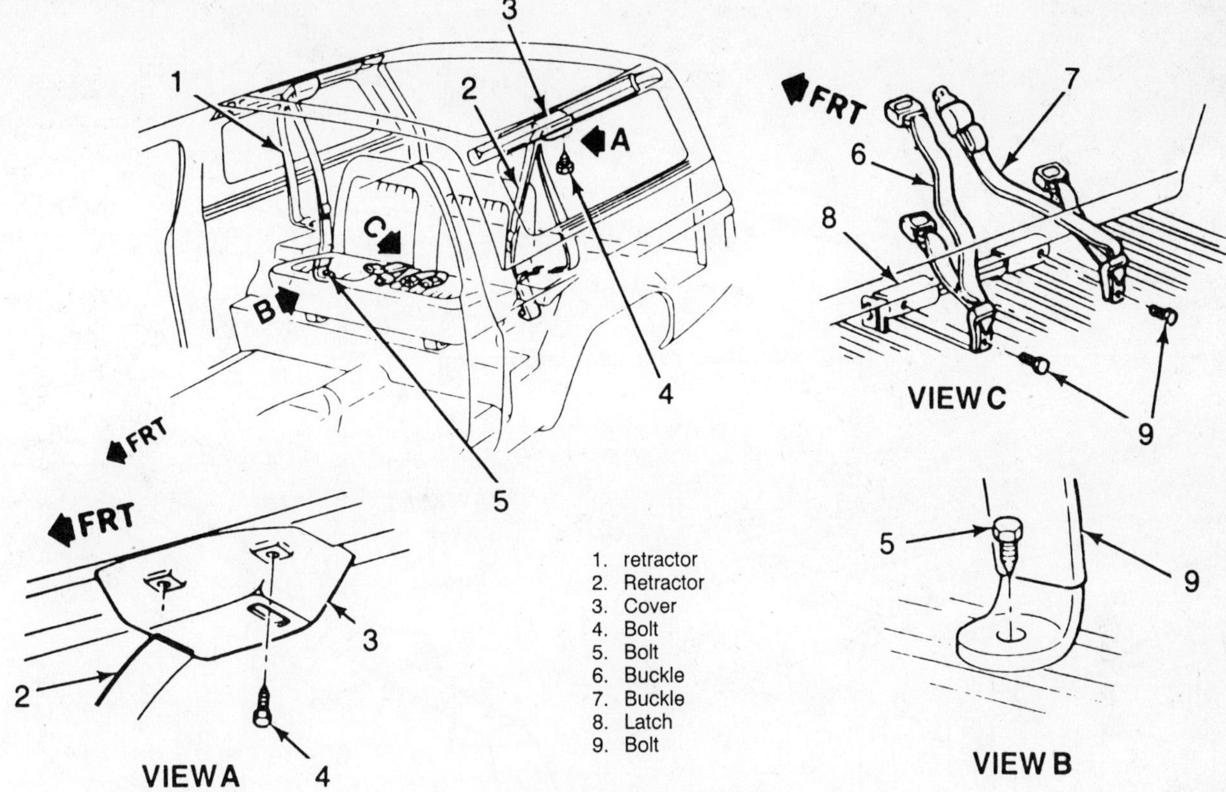

Blazer rear seat belts

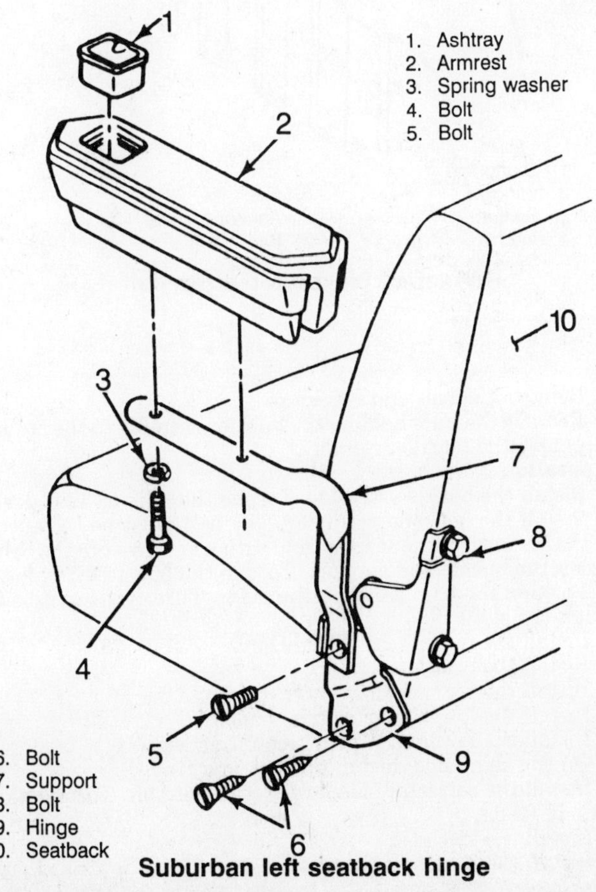

Suburban left seatback hinge

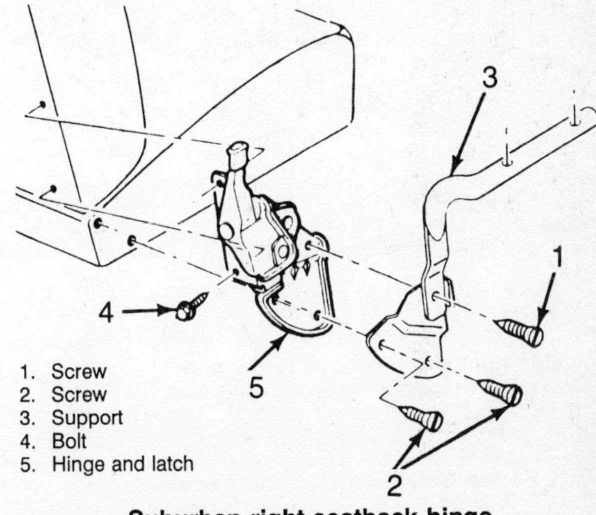

Suburban right seatback hinge

2. Take note of the belt positions.
3. Pry the cover off the upper seat belt anchor.
4. Remove the anchor bolt.
5. Remove the retractor.
6. Remove the guide assemblies.
7. Remove the buckle and latch plate assemblies.
8. Installation is the reverse of removal. Torque all bolts to 37 ft. lbs.

R and V Series Crew Cab Rear Seats

1. Pry the cover off the upper seat belt anchor.

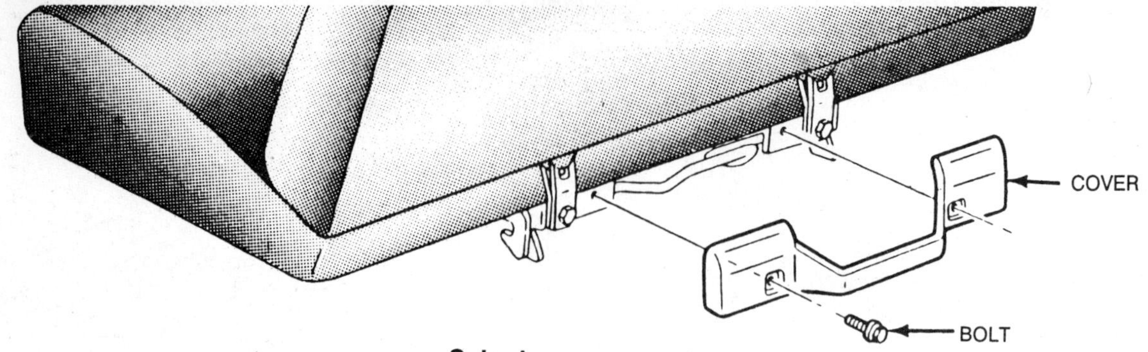

Suburban rear seat latch cover

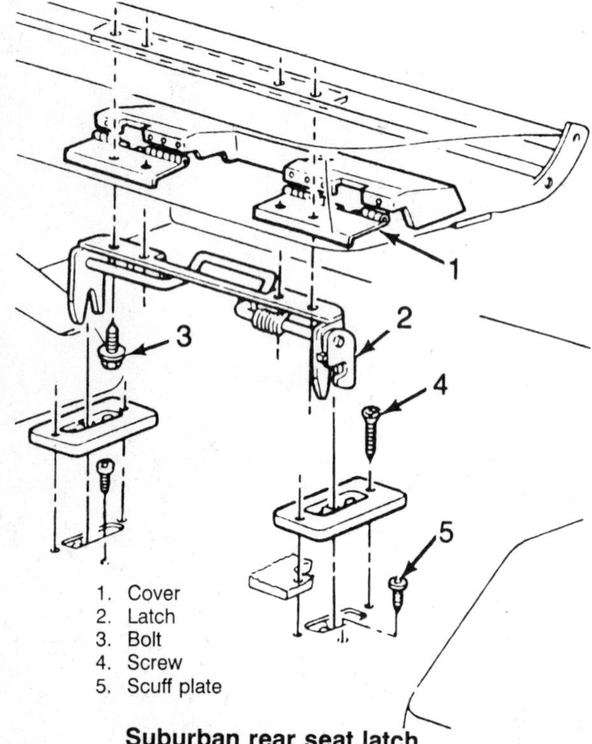

Suburban rear seat latch

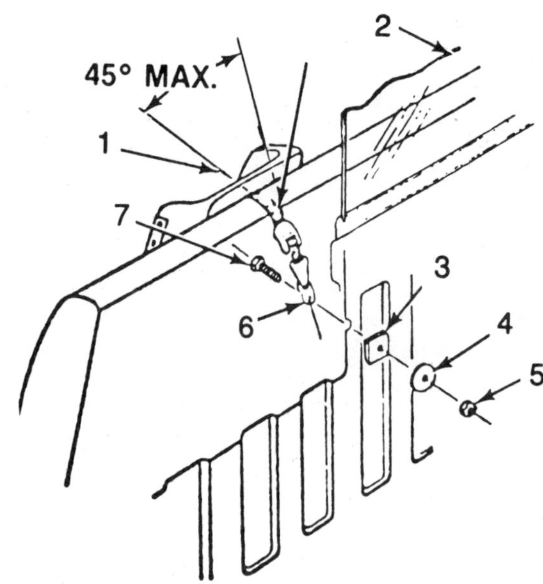

R/V series pickup top strap belt

2. Remove the retractor-to-cab panel bolts.
3. Remove the retractor-to-floor panel bolts.
4. Installation is the reverse of removal. Torque all bolts to 40 ft. lbs.

C and K Series Extended Cab Rear Seats

1. Remove the rear seat.
2. Remove the buckle from the rear seat support.
3. Remove the ashtray and panel pocket.
4. Remove the arm rest.
5. Remove the retractor side, lower seat belt bolt.
6. On the right side, remove the jack and tray.
7. Remove the lower trim panel mounting screws.
8. Remove the lower quarter trim panel.
9. Remove the rear window lower molding.
10. Remove the coat hook.
11. Remove the upper seat belt anchor bolt.
12. Pull the trim panel away from the pillar. Thread the seat belt through the slot.
13. Remove the retractor-to-body bolt.
14. Remove the belt and retractor.
15. Remove the nuts holding the buckle assembly to the studs and remove the buckle assembly.

To install:

16. Install the buckle assembly. Torque the nuts to 32 ft. lbs.
17. Install the belt and retractor. The belt must be installed with the buckle facing outwards and with a half twist in the belt between the buckle and support. Torque the bolt to 40 ft. lbs.
18. Position the trim panel on the pillar. Thread the seat belt through the slot.
19. Install the upper seat belt anchor.
20. Install the coat hook.
21. Install the rear window lower molding.
22. Install the lower quarter trim panel.
23. Install the lower trim panel mounting screws.
24. On the right side, install the jack and tray.
25. Install the retractor side, lower seat belt bolt. Torque the bolt to 40 ft. lbs.
26. Install the arm rest.
27. Install the ashtray and panel pocket.

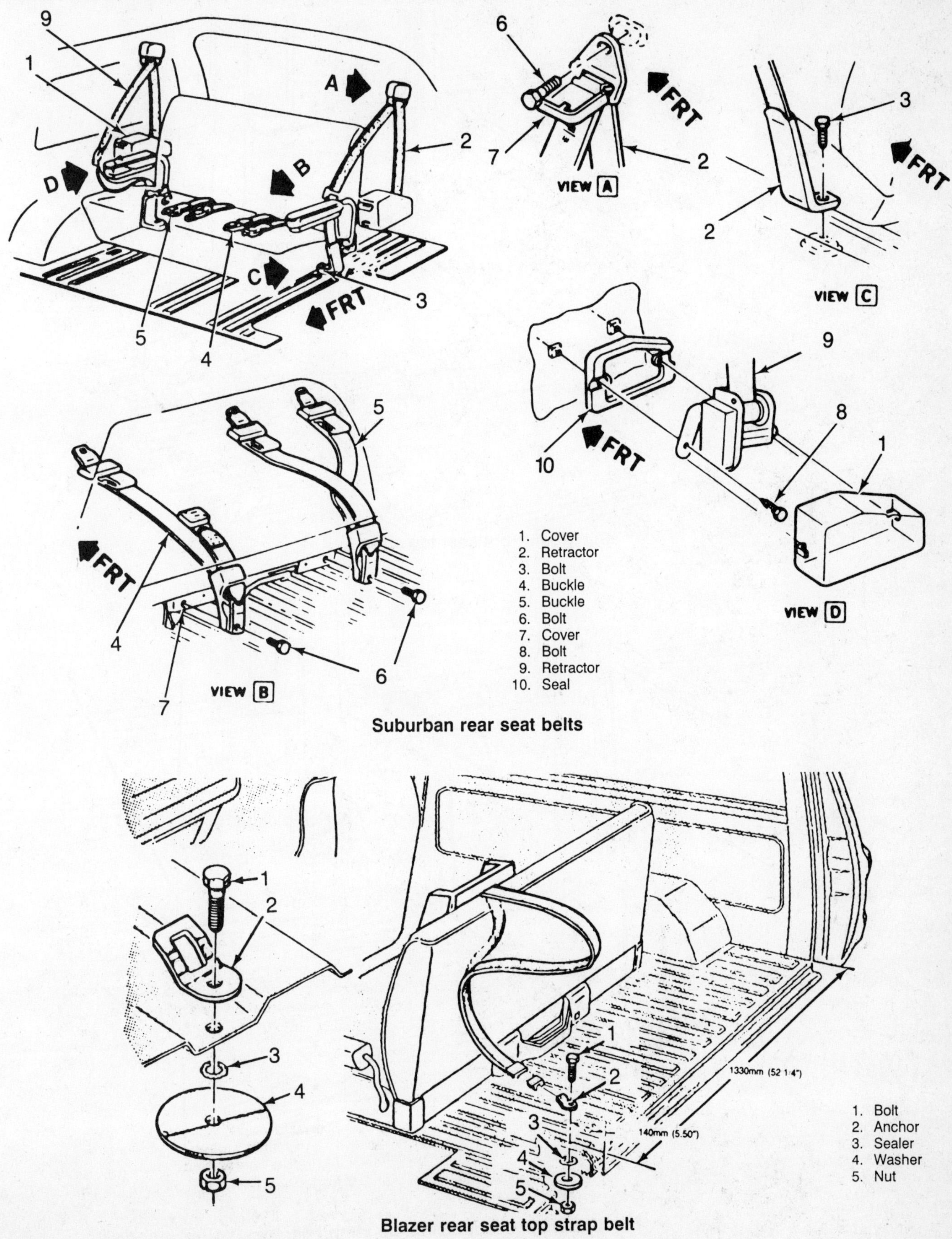

Suburban rear seat belts

Blazer rear seat top strap belt

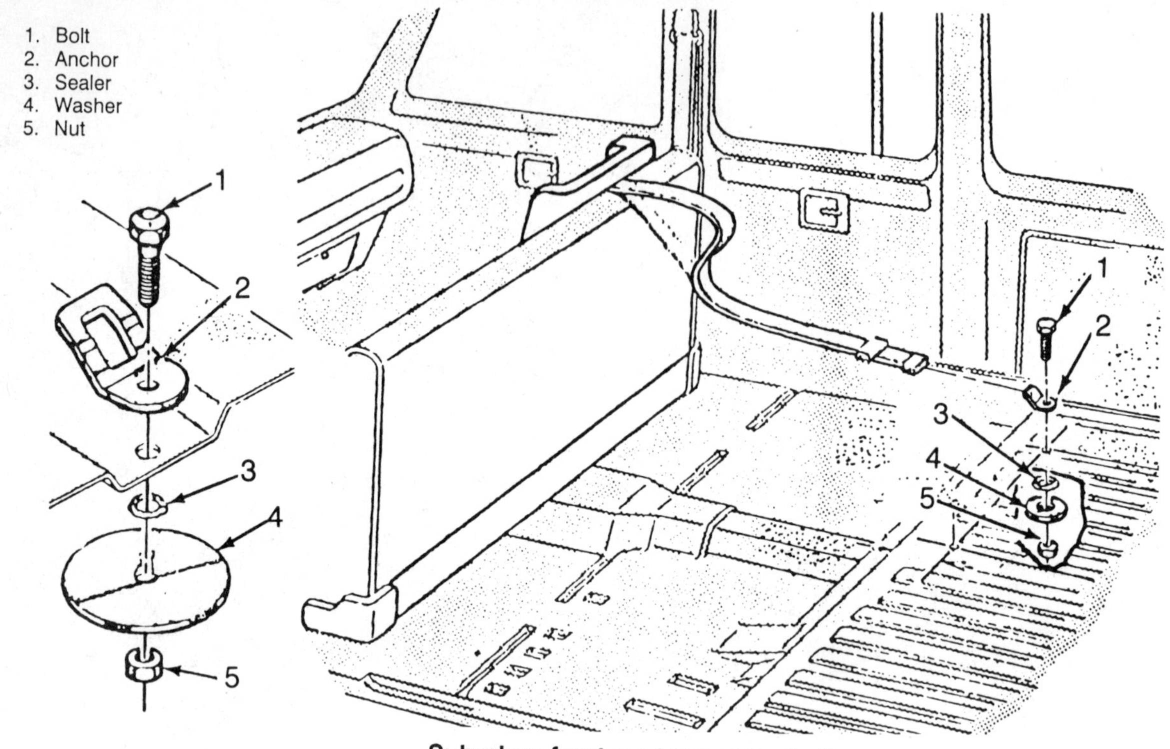

Suburban front seat top strap belt

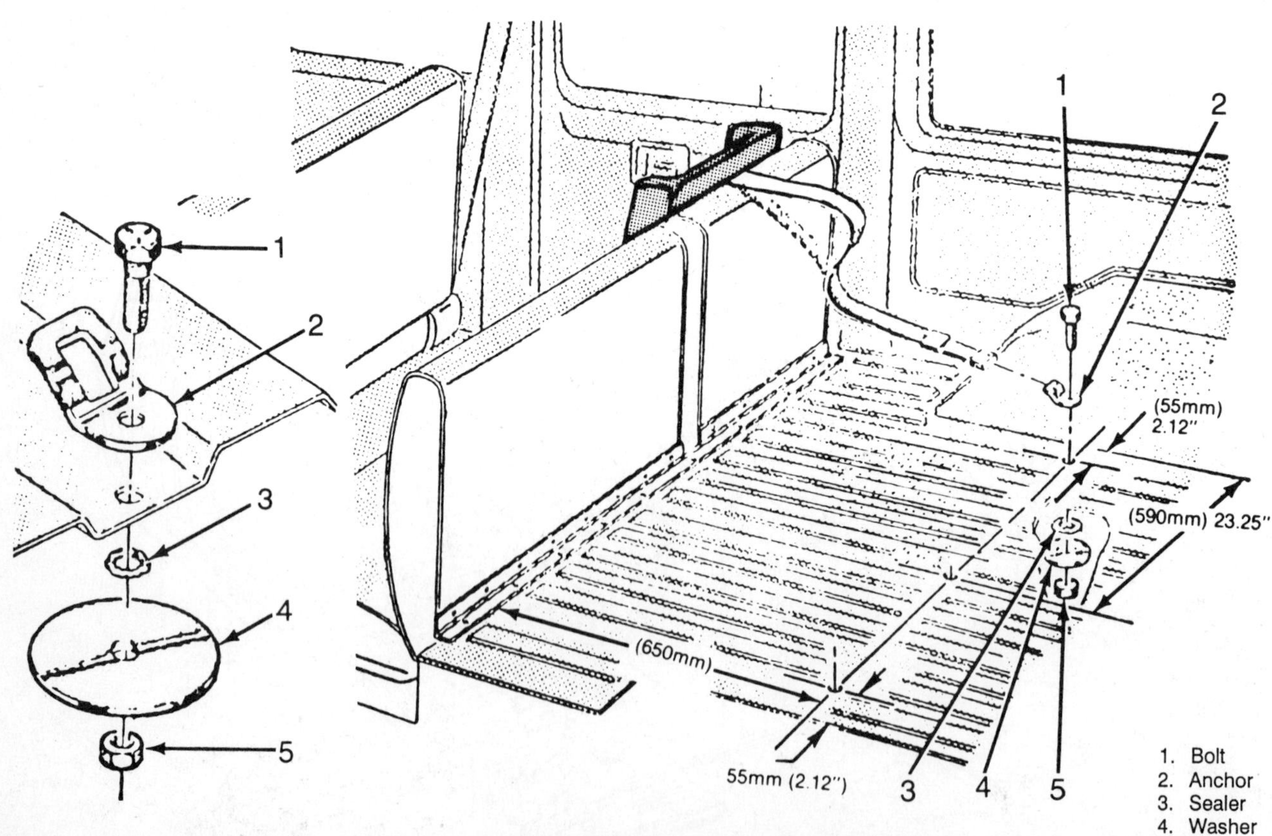

Suburban second seat top strap belt

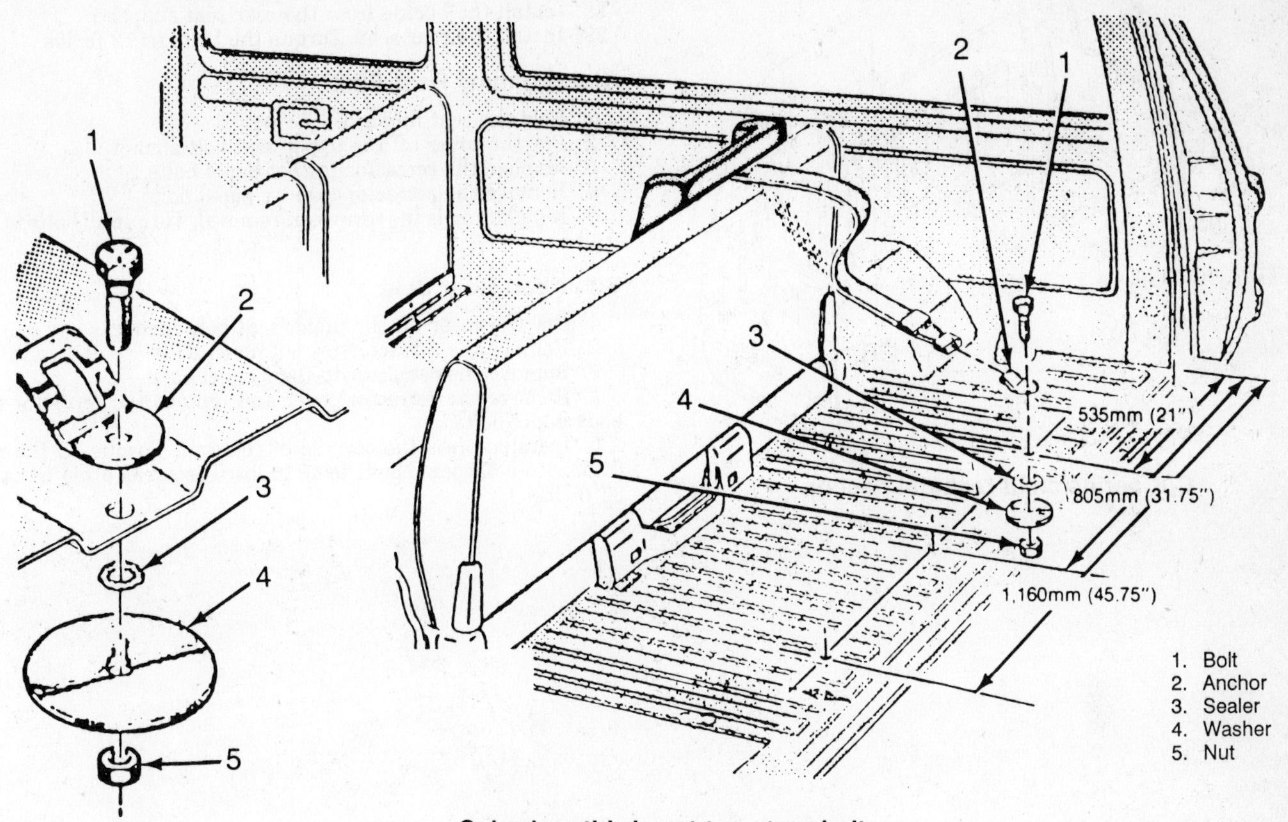

Suburban third seat top strap belt

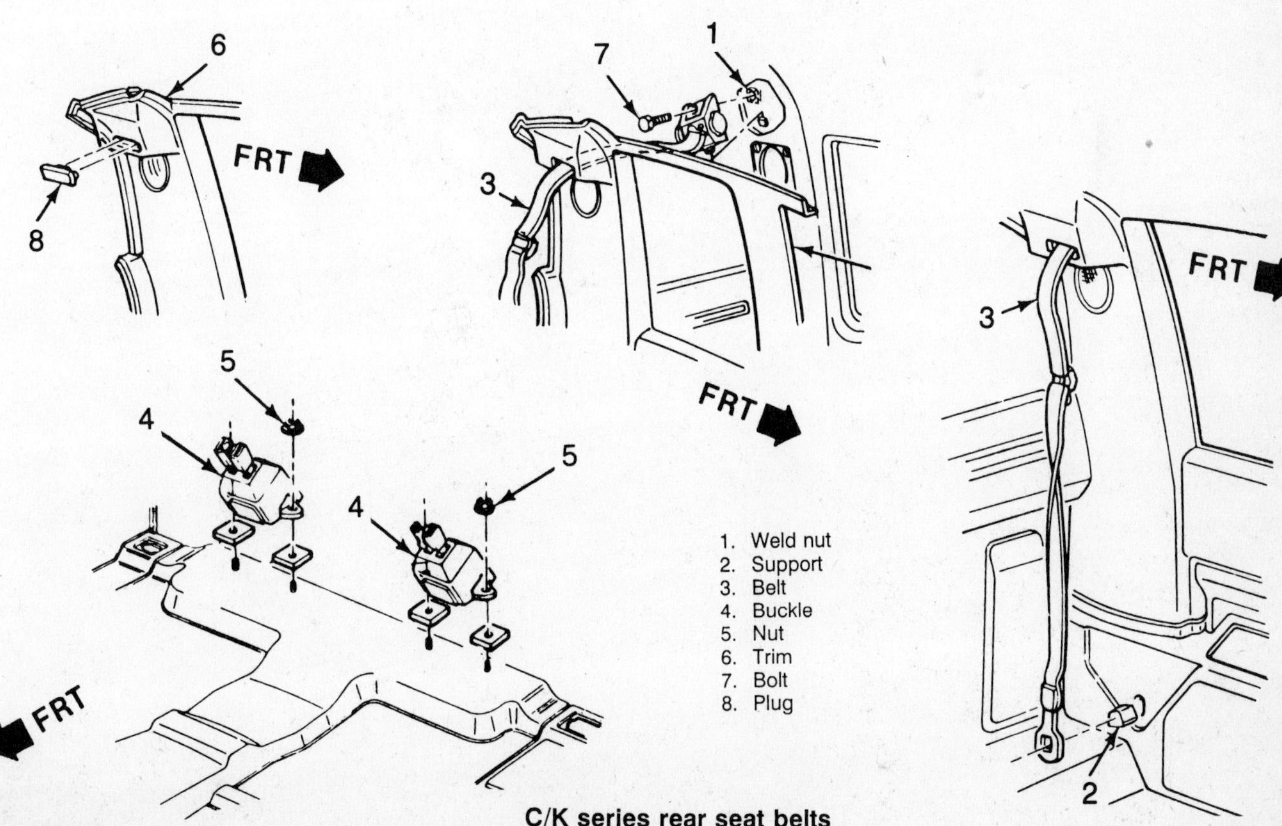

C/K series rear seat belts

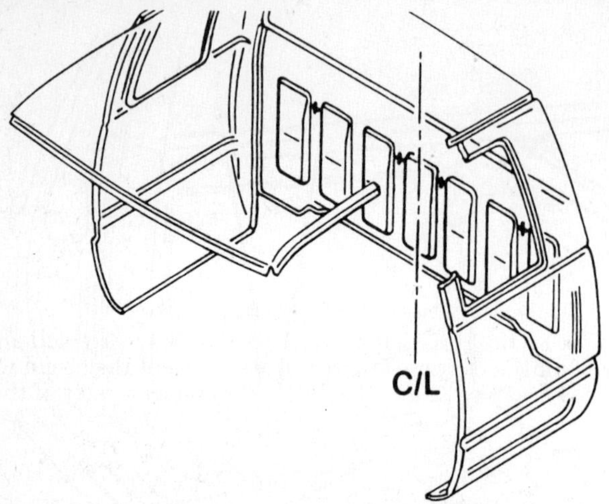

C/K series child restraint anchor

28. Install the buckle from the rear seat support.
29. Install the rear seat. Torque the bolts to 12 ft. lbs.

Blazer/Jimmy Rear Seat

1. Fold the seat forward.
2. Pry the cover off the upper seat belt anchor.
3. Remove the retractor-to-roof panel bolts.
4. Remove the retractor-to-floor panel bolts.
5. Installation is the reverse of removal. Torque all bolts to 38 ft. lbs.

Suburban Rear Seat

1. Pry the cover off the upper seat belt anchor.
2. Remove the retractor-to-roof panel bolts.
3. Remove the retractor-to-floor panel bolts.
4. Remove the retractor cover and remove the retractor-to-body panel bolts.
5. Installation is the reverse of removal. Torque all the retractor-to-body panel bolts to 49 ft. lbs. Torque all other bolts to 37 ft. lbs.

Glossary

AIR/FUEL RATIO: The ratio of air to gasoline by weight in the fuel mixture drawn into the engine.

AIR INJECTION: One method of reducing harmful exhaust emissions by injecting air into each of the exhaust ports of an engine. The fresh air entering the hot exhaust manifold causes any remaining fuel to be burned before it can exit the tailpipe.

ALTERNATOR: A device used for converting mechanical energy into electrical energy.

AMMETER: An instrument, calibrated in amperes, used to measure the flow of an electrical current in a circuit. Ammeters are always connected in series with the circuit being tested.

AMPERE: The rate of flow of electrical current present when one volt of electrical pressure is applied against one ohm of electrical resistance.

ANALOG COMPUTER: Any microprocessor that uses similar (analogous) electrical signals to make its calculations.

ARMATURE: A laminated, soft iron core wrapped by a wire that converts electrical energy to mechanical energy as in a motor or relay. When rotated in a magnetic field, it changes mechanical energy into electrical energy as in a generator.

ATMOSPHERIC PRESSURE: The pressure on the Earth's surface caused by the weight of the air in the atmosphere. At sea level, this pressure is 14.7 psi at 32°F (101 kPa at 0°C).

ATOMIZATION: The breaking down of a liquid into a fine mist that can be suspended in air.

AXIAL PLAY: Movement parallel to a shaft or bearing bore.

BACKFIRE: The sudden combustion of gases in the intake or exhaust system that results in a loud explosion.

BACKLASH: The clearance or play between two parts, such as meshed gears.

BACKPRESSURE: Restrictions in the exhaust system that slow the exit of exhaust gases from the combustion chamber.

BAKELITE: A heat resistant, plastic insulator material commonly used in printed circuit boards and transistorized components.

BALL BEARING: A bearing made up of hardened inner and outer races between which hardened steel balls roll.

BALLAST RESISTOR: A resistor in the primary ignition circuit that lowers voltage after the engine is started to reduce wear on ignition components.

BEARING: A friction reducing, supportive device usually located between a stationary part and a moving part.

BIMETAL TEMPERATURE SENSOR: Any sensor or switch made of two dissimilar types of metal that bend when heated or cooled due to the different expansion rates of the alloys. These types of sensors usually function as an on/off switch.

BLOWBY: Combustion gases, composed of water vapor and unburned fuel, that leak past the piston rings into the crankcase during normal engine operation. These gases are removed by the PCV system to prevent the buildup of harmful acids in the crankcase.

BRAKE PAD: A brake shoe and lining assembly used with disc brakes.

BRAKE SHOE: The backing for the brake lining. The term is, however, usually applied to the assembly of the brake backing and lining.

BUSHING: A liner, usually removable, for a bearing; an anti-friction liner used in place of a bearing.

BYPASS: System used to bypass ballast resistor during engine cranking to increase voltage supplied to the coil.

CALIPER: A hydraulically activated device in a disc brake system, which is mounted straddling the brake rotor (disc). The caliper contains at least one piston and two brake pads. Hydraulic pressure on the piston(s) forces the pads against the rotor.

CAMSHAFT: A shaft in the engine on which are the lobes (cams) which operate the valves. The camshaft is driven by the crankshaft, via a belt, chain or gears, at one half the crankshaft speed.

CAPACITOR: A device which stores an electrical charge.

CARBON MONOXIDE (CO): A colorless, odorless gas given off as a normal byproduct of combustion. It is poisonous and extremely dangerous in confined areas, building up slowly to toxic levels without warning if adequate ventilation is not available.

CARBURETOR: A device, usually mounted on the intake manifold of an engine, which mixes the air and fuel in the proper proportion to allow even combustion.

CATALYTIC CONVERTER: A device installed in the exhaust system, like a muffler, that converts harmful byproducts of combustion into carbon dioxide and water vapor by means of a heat-producing chemical reaction.

CENTRIFUGAL ADVANCE: A mechanical method of advancing the spark timing by using flyweights in the distributor that react to centrifugal force generated by the distributor shaft rotation.

CHECK VALVE: Any one-way valve installed to permit the flow of air, fuel or vacuum in one direction only.

GLOSSARY

CHOKE: A device, usually a moveable valve, placed in the intake path of a carburetor to restrict the flow of air.

CIRCUIT: Any unbroken path through which an electrical current can flow. Also used to describe fuel flow in some instances.

CIRCUIT BREAKER: A switch which protects an electrical circuit from overload by opening the circuit when the current flow exceeds a predetermined level. Some circuit breakers must be reset manually, while most reset automatically

COIL (IGNITION): A transformer in the ignition circuit which steps up the voltage provided to the spark plugs.

COMBINATION MANIFOLD: An assembly which includes both the intake and exhaust manifolds in one casting.

COMBINATION VALVE: A device used in some fuel systems that routes fuel vapors to a charcoal storage canister instead of venting them into the atmosphere. The valve relieves fuel tank pressure and allows fresh air into the tank as the fuel level drops to prevent a vapor lock situation.

COMPRESSION RATIO: The comparison of the total volume of the cylinder and combustion chamber with the piston at BDC and the piston at TDC.

CONDENSER: 1. An electrical device which acts to store an electrical charge, preventing voltage surges.
2. A radiator-like device in the air conditioning system in which refrigerant gas condenses into a liquid, giving off heat.

CONDUCTOR: Any material through which an electrical current can be transmitted easily.

CONTINUITY: Continuous or complete circuit. Can be checked with an ohmmeter.

COUNTERSHAFT: An intermediate shaft which is rotated by a mainshaft and transmits, in turn, that rotation to a working part.

CRANKCASE: The lower part of an engine in which the crankshaft and related parts operate.

CRANKSHAFT: The main driving shaft of an engine which receives reciprocating motion from the pistons and converts it to rotary motion.

CYLINDER: In an engine, the round hole in the engine block in which the piston(s) ride.

CYLINDER BLOCK: The main structural member of an engine in which is found the cylinders, crankshaft and other principal parts.

CYLINDER HEAD: The detachable portion of the engine, fastened, usually, to the top of the cylinder block, containing all or most of the combustion chambers. On overhead valve engines, it contains the valves and their operating parts. On overhead cam engines, it contains the camshaft as well.

DEAD CENTER: The extreme top or bottom of the piston stroke.

DETONATION: An unwanted explosion of the air/fuel mixture in the combustion chamber caused by excess heat and compression, advanced timing, or an overly lean mixture. Also referred to as "ping".

DIAPHRAGM: A thin, flexible wall separating two cavities, such as in a vacuum advance unit.

DIESELING: A condition in which hot spots in the combustion chamber cause the engine to run on after the key is turned off.

DIFFERENTIAL: A geared assembly which allows the transmission of motion between drive axles, giving one axle the ability to turn faster than the other.

DIODE: An electrical device that will allow current to flow in one direction only.

DISC BRAKE: A hydraulic braking assembly consisting of a brake disc, or rotor, mounted on an axle, and a caliper assembly containing, usually two brake pads which are activated by hydraulic pressure. The pads are forced against the sides of the disc, creating friction which slows the vehicle.

DISTRIBUTOR: A mechanically driven device on an engine which is responsible for electrically firing the spark plug at a predetermined point of the piston stroke.

DOWEL PIN: A pin, inserted in mating holes in two different parts allowing those parts to maintain a fixed relationship.

DRUM BRAKE: A braking system which consists of two brake shoes and one or two wheel cylinders, mounted on a fixed backing plate, and a brake drum, mounted on an axle, which revolves around the assembly. Hydraulic action applied to the wheel cylinders forces the shoes outward against the drum, creating friction, slowing the vehicle.

DWELL: The rate, measured in degrees of shaft rotation, at which an electrical circuit cycles on and off.

ELECTRONIC CONTROL UNIT (ECU): Ignition module, module, amplifier or igniter. See Module for definition.

ELECTRONIC IGNITION: A system in which the timing and firing of the spark plugs is controlled by an electronic control unit, usually called a module. These systems have no points or condenser.

ENDPLAY: The measured amount of axial movement in a shaft.

ENGINE: A device that converts heat into mechanical energy.

EXHAUST MANIFOLD: A set of cast passages or pipes which conduct exhaust gases from the engine.

FEELER GAUGE: A blade, usually metal, of precisely predetermined thickness, used to measure the clearance between two parts. These blades usually are available in sets of assorted thicknesses.

F-Head: An engine configuration in which the intake valves are in the cylinder head, while the camshaft and exhaust valves are located in the cylinder block. The camshaft operates the intake valves via lifters and pushrods, while it operates the exhaust valves directly.

FIRING ORDER: The order in which combustion occurs in the cylinders of an engine. Also the order in which spark is distributed to the plugs by the distributor.

FLATHEAD: An engine configuration in which the camshaft and all the valves are located in the cylinder block.

FLOODING: The presence of too much fuel in the intake manifold and combustion chamber which prevents the air/fuel mixture from firing, thereby causing a no-start situation.

FLYWHEEL: A disc shaped part bolted to the rear end of the crankshaft. Around the outer perimeter is affixed the ring gear. The starter drive engages the ring gear, turning the flywheel, which rotates the crankshaft, imparting the initial starting motion to the engine.

FOOT POUND (ft.lb. or sometimes, ft. lbs.): The amount of energy or work needed to raise an item weighing one pound, a distance of one foot.

FUSE: A protective device in a circuit which prevents circuit overload by breaking the circuit when a specific amperage is present. The device is constructed around a strip or wire of a lower amperage rating than the circuit it is designed to protect. When an amperage higher than that stamped on the fuse is present in the circuit, the strip or wire melts, opening the circuit.

GEAR RATIO: The ratio between the number of teeth on meshing gears.

GENERATOR: A device which converts mechanical energy into electrical energy.

HEAT RANGE: The measure of a spark plug's ability to dissipate heat from its firing end. The higher the heat range, the hotter the plug fires.

HUB: The center part of a wheel or gear.

HYDROCARBON (HC): Any chemical compound made up of hydrogen and carbon. A major pollutant formed by the engine as a byproduct of combustion.

HYDROMETER: An instrument used to measure the specific gravity of a solution.

INCH POUND (in.lb. or sometimes, in. lbs.): One twelfth of a foot pound.

INDUCTION: A means of transferring electrical energy in the form of a magnetic field. Principle used in the ignition coil to increase voltage.

INJECTION PUMP: A device, usually mechanically operated, which meters and delivers fuel under pressure to the fuel injector.

INJECTOR: A device which receives metered fuel under relatively low pressure and is activated to inject the fuel into the engine under relatively high pressure at a predetermined time.

INPUT SHAFT: The shaft to which torque is applied, usually carrying the driving gear or gears.

INTAKE MANIFOLD: A casting of passages or pipes used to conduct air or a fuel/air mixture to the cylinders.

JOURNAL: The bearing surface within which a shaft operates.

KEY: A small block usually fitted in a notch between a shaft and a hub to prevent slippage of the two parts.

MANIFOLD: A casting of passages or set of pipes which connect the cylinders to an inlet or outlet source.

MANIFOLD VACUUM: Low pressure in an engine intake manifold formed just below the throttle plates. Manifold vacuum is highest at idle and drops under acceleration.

MASTER CYLINDER: The primary fluid pressurizing device in a hydraulic system. In automotive use, it is found in brake and hydraulic clutch systems and is pedal activated, either directly or, in a power brake system, through the power booster.

MODULE: Electronic control unit, amplifier or igniter of solid state or integrated design which controls the current flow in the ignition primary circuit based on input from the pick-up coil. When the module opens the primary circuit, the high secondary voltage is induced in the coil.

NEEDLE BEARING: A bearing which consists of a number (usually a large number) of long, thin rollers.

OHM: (Ω) The unit used to measure the resistance of conductor to electrical flow. One ohm is the amount of resistance that limits current flow to one ampere in a circuit with one volt of pressure.

OHMMETER: An instrument used for measuring the resistance, in ohms, in an electrical circuit.

OUTPUT SHAFT: The shaft which transmits torque from a device, such as a transmission.

OVERDRIVE: A gear assembly which produces more shaft revolutions than that transmitted to it.

OVERHEAD CAMSHAFT (OHC): An engine configuration in which the camshaft is mounted on top of the cylinder head and operates the valve either directly or by means of rocker arms.

OVERHEAD VALVE (OHV): An engine configuration in which all of the valves are located in the cylinder head and the camshaft is located in the cylinder block. The camshaft operates the valves via lifters and pushrods.

OXIDES OF NITROGEN (NOx): Chemical compounds of nitrogen produced as a byproduct of combustion. They combine with hydrocarbons to produce smog.

OXYGEN SENSOR: Used with the feedback system to sense the presence of oxygen in the exhaust gas and signal the computer which can reference the voltage signal to an air/fuel ratio.

PINION: The smaller of two meshing gears.

PISTON RING: An open ended ring which fits into a groove on the outer diameter of the piston. Its chief function is to form a seal between the piston and cylinder wall. Most automotive pistons have three rings: two for compression sealing; one for oil sealing.

PRELOAD: A predetermined load placed on a bearing during assembly or by adjustment.

PRIMARY CIRCUIT: Is the low voltage side of the ignition system which consists of the ignition switch, ballast resistor or resistance wire, bypass, coil, electronic control unit and pick-up coil as well as the connecting wires and harnesses.

PRESS FIT: The mating of two parts under pressure, due to the inner diameter of one being smaller than the outer diameter of the other, or vice versa; an interference fit.

GLOSSARY

RACE: The surface on the inner or outer ring of a bearing on which the balls, needles or rollers move.

REGULATOR: A device which maintains the amperage and/or voltage levels of a circuit at predetermined values.

RELAY: A switch which automatically opens and/or closes a circuit.

RESISTANCE: The opposition to the flow of current through a circuit or electrical device, and is measured in ohms. Resistance is equal to the voltage divided by the amperage.

RESISTOR: A device, usually made of wire, which offers a preset amount of resistance in an electrical circuit.

RING GEAR: The name given to a ring-shaped gear attached to a differential case, or affixed to a flywheel or as part a planetary gear set.

ROLLER BEARING: A bearing made up of hardened inner and outer races between which hardened steel rollers move.

ROTOR: 1. The disc-shaped part of a disc brake assembly, upon which the brake pads bear; also called, brake disc.
2. The device mounted atop the distributor shaft, which passes current to the distributor cap tower contacts.

SECONDARY CIRCUIT: The high voltage side of the ignition system, usually above 20,000 volts. The secondary includes the ignition coil, coil wire, distributor cap and rotor, spark plug wires and spark plugs.

SENDING UNIT: A mechanical, electrical, hydraulic or electromagnetic device which transmits information to a gauge.

SENSOR: Any device designed to measure engine operating conditions or ambient pressures and temperatures. Usually electronic in nature and designed to send a voltage signal to an on-board computer, some sensors may operate as a simple on/off switch or they may provide a variable voltage signal (like a potentiometer) as conditions or measured parameters change.

SHIM: Spacers of precise, predetermined thickness used between parts to establish a proper working relationship.

SLAVE CYLINDER: In automotive use, a device in the hydraulic clutch system which is activated by hydraulic force, disengaging the clutch.

SOLENOID: A coil used to produce a magnetic field, the effect of which is produce work.

SPARK PLUG: A device screwed into the combustion chamber of a spark ignition engine. The basic construction is a conductive core inside of a ceramic insulator, mounted in an outer conductive base. An electrical charge from the spark plug wire travels along the conductive core and jumps a preset air gap to a grounding point or points at the end of the conductive base. The resultant spark ignites the fuel/air mixture in the combustion chamber.

SPLINES: Ridges machined or cast onto the outer diameter of a shaft or inner diameter of a bore to enable parts to mate without rotation.

TACHOMETER: A device used to measure the rotary speed of an engine, shaft, gear, etc., usually in rotations per minute.

THERMOSTAT: A valve, located in the cooling system of an engine, which is closed when cold and opens gradually in response to engine heating, controlling the temperature of the coolant and rate of coolant flow.

TOP DEAD CENTER (TDC): The point at which the piston reaches the top of its travel on the compression stroke.

TORQUE: The twisting force applied to an object.

TORQUE CONVERTER: A turbine used to transmit power from a driving member to a driven member via hydraulic action, providing changes in drive ratio and torque. In automotive use, it links the driveplate at the rear of the engine to the automatic transmission.

TRANSDUCER: A device used to change a force into an electrical signal.

TRANSISTOR: A semi-conductor component which can be actuated by a small voltage to perform an electrical switching function.

TUNE-UP: A regular maintenance function, usually associated with the replacement and adjustment of parts and components in the electrical and fuel systems of a vehicle for the purpose of attaining optimum performance.

TURBOCHARGER: An exhaust driven pump which compresses intake air and forces it into the combustion chambers at higher than atmospheric pressures. The increased air pressure allows more fuel to be burned and results in increased horsepower being produced.

VACUUM ADVANCE: A device which advances the ignition timing in response to increased engine vacuum.

VACUUM GAUGE: An instrument used to measure the presence of vacuum in a chamber.

VALVE: A device which control the pressure, direction of flow or rate of flow of a liquid or gas.

VALVE CLEARANCE: The measured gap between the end of the valve stem and the rocker arm, cam lobe or follower that activates the valve.

VISCOSITY: The rating of a liquid's internal resistance to flow.

VOLTMETER: An instrument used for measuring electrical force in units called volts. Voltmeters are always connected parallel with the circuit being tested.

WHEEL CYLINDER: Found in the automotive drum brake assembly, it is a device, actuated by hydraulic pressure, which, through internal pistons, pushes the brake shoes outward against the drums.